CRITICAL THEORY SINCE PLATO

Revised Edition

EDITED BY

Hazard Adams

University of Washington

HEINLE & HEINLE

THOMSON LEARNING

Australia • Canada • Mexico • Singapore • Spain
United Kingdom • United States

HEINLE & HEINLE

THOMSON LEARNING

Acquisitions Editor: *Stephen T. Jordan*
Production Editor: *Socorro P. Gonzales*
Production Manager: *Mary Kay Yearin*
Designer: *Lori J. McThomas*

Permissions Editor: *Eleanor Garner*
Compositor: *GTS Graphics*
Printer: *R.R. Donnelley (Crawfordsville)*

For more information about our products,
contact us at:
Thompson Learning Academic Resource Center
1–800–423–0563

For permission to use material from this text,
contact us by:
Phone: 1–800–730–2214 **Fax:** 1–800–730–2215
Web: http://www.thomsonrights.com

Library of Congress Catalog Number: 91–752533
ISBN: 0–15–516143–1

Asia
Thomson Learning
60 Albert Street, #15–01
Albert Complex
Singapore 189969

Australia
Nelson Thomson Learning
102 Dodds Street
South Melbourne, Victoria 3205
Australia

Canada
Nelson Thomson Learning
1120 Birchmount Road
Toronto, Ontario M1K 5G4
Canada

Europe/Middle East/Africa
Thomson Learning
Berkshire House
168–173 High Holborn
London WC1 V7AA
United Kingdom

Latin America
Thomson Learning
Seneca, 53
Colonia Polanco
11560 Mexico D.F.
Mexico

Spain
Paraninfo Thomson Learning
Calle/Magallanes, 25
28015 Madrid, Spain

Preface

This revised edition maintains the plan of the first edition published in 1971: a general introduction, chronological arrangement of the texts, headnotes and brief bibliographical information, editorial footnotes, and index. The aim is to present a single volume that will provide material for a reasonably thorough course of readings in the history of critical theory in Western culture. As in the first edition I have arbitrarily excluded works of practical critical analysis and chosen not to organize any of the material by alleged schools, movements, or types of critical theories. Such rubrics have a way of expressing transient interests, particularly with respect to recent work, and discouraging recognition of other significance that particular essays may have. The anthology, thus, invites the reader to view at the outset each selection as the expression of an individual voice with something important and, in many cases, representative to say. The term "critical theory" is used here not in the sense employed by the Frankfurt social critics but to include speculative writing about the nature of literature and the problems of critical discourse about it. A few selections are included because they are discourses on language presenting arguments that have had strong indirect influence on critical thought.

This volume spans more than two thousand years of Western culture. Courses of study limited to objects of so-called Western discourse have recently come under attack, and there is no question that the relationship of the Western tradition to other cultures is being rethought. In time, the history of critical theory will include discourses from the past unknown or insufficiently familiar to present-day Western scholars of the subject. Other traditions will become better known to the West, and there will be comparative studies. It is almost certain, however, that these traditions will be seen as separate up to and including most of the twentieth century, when communication among various parts of the globe increased astonishingly. Even when these traditions become better known through translations, historical studies, and specialized collections, I suspect that the Western tradition of critical theory will maintain its great importance, especially with respect to the influence it exerts on scholars worldwide.

The latter half of the twentieth century has been a period of profoundly important developments, and it will come as no surprise to the reader that major changes in this edition have to do with selections written since about 1910. We are still in the process of trying to understand the history of critical theory in this period. It is a subject that has always had very fuzzy edges. In recent decades it has been more and more difficult to decide how to encompass it. *Critical Theory Since 1965,* edited by myself and Leroy Searle (Tallahassee: Florida State University Press, 1986) augments the present volume with additional selections.

I remain in the debt of many people who contributed in one way or another to completion of the first edition: the late Howard S. Babb, Theodore Brunner, the late Peter Colaclides, Mary Gazlay, Judd Hubert, Ronald Kotrc, Murray Krieger, and Paul Schimmelpfennig. I am, of course, indebted to many historians and anthologists of criticism who have preceded me. I should also like to thank particularly, among many who have influenced the selections here, Ernst Behler, Robert L. Montgomery, Leroy Searle, Steven Shaviro and Evan Watkins.

HAZARD ADAMS

Contents

Introduction

I

The recent activity in literary theory, to say nothing of theoretical discourse in other fields related to it, has been so enormous that to attempt to encompass a representative selection in one volume, as well as examples of historical significance since Plato, may seem foolish indeed. Furthermore, critical schools and fashions are born, flourish, and decline much more rapidly now than in any past era, so that it has become increasingly more difficult to assess the lasting value of much that is written, let alone read it all. From time to time a cry has gone up that all critical theory before a certain date is now mercifully obsolete, that one may safely ignore it. It is a cry that has always proved to express the illusions of naive exuberance or insufficient skepticism. Even though a case can be made that the history of critical theory is one of cyclical error, the history is important to know about if only because of this. But there are other reasons. The story of critical theory is a part of that intellectual and cultural history by which we come to know a certain dimension of ourselves. It is valuable to observe shifts in theoretical interest and to grasp the forces at play in them. Also, there are past critics who are so good at what they do that there is a special kind of pleasure and education in reading them. In the end, historical learning in any area of human endeavor generates a sense of connections and discontinuities across space and time, exercises the intellect, and brings, in individual cases, unique rewards.

II

In the first edition I commended to readers a discussion of orientations of critical theories set forth in M. H. Abrams' *The Mirror and the Lamp* (1953). It has proved helpful to many, and I comment on it again here, following it with a discussion of my own fourfold division of the history of critical theory into phases. Abrams' division is also fourfold. Some trace of each type of theory he mentions is present in any age, but he sees each orientation as dominant in some era. The four and the order of their dominance are as follows: mimetic theories, pragmatic theories, expressive theories, and objective theories.

Mimetic theories, or those that privilege the relation of the literary work to the world and usually define literature in terms of imitation (*mimesis*), seem to be as old as criticism itself. Fundamentally, in their most extreme forms mimetic theories judge a work on the accuracy or the verisimilitude of its presentation of an external reality. They held sway until our knowledge of external reality began persistently to be questioned. Some of these theories tend to value a sort of "photographic" reproduction; others are content with "truth to life"; still others, fixed to some form of Platonism, see poetic truth in terms of its allegorical representation of ideas. There is little doubt that mimesis was the dominant critical term from Plato well into the Renaissance, though during that long stretch of time it underwent several shifts of meaning and was employed ingeniously by many critics against Plato and even against the notion of copying.

When pragmatic theories began to appear—those that emphasize the reader's relation to the work—they did so for a while without diminishing the importance of mimesis. Both Plato and Aristotle took significant account of reader and audience. Early rhetorically orientated theorists like the so-called Longinus emphasized poetic effect, and the idea that poetry delighted and taught was a classical invention commonly expressed all the way from Horace to Sir Philip Sidney. There had always been in the Middle Ages and well into the eighteenth century a strongly moralistic, didactic criticism. In the eighteenth century, didactic criticism shared power with the new aesthetics and the concept of affect. Alexander Baumgarten established the term "aesthetic" at mid-century, and thereafter theories of aesthetic pleasure abounded, culminating in the *Critique of Judgment* (1790) of Immanuel Kant.

More radical locations of the poetic work in the reader occurred in the nineteenth century with the extreme subjectivism of Walter Pater and Anatole France, and recent decades have seen a resurgence of interest in readers from the pedagogical emphasis of Louise Rosenblatt through psychological theories to Stanley Fish's notion of reader communities as establishing standards of meaning.

The expressivist orientation that came with romanticism in the late eighteenth century and has never entirely left us had few precursors up until the time of Jean-Jacques Rousseau. Very little attention had been paid to authorial individuality as something to be conveyed by a literary work. Indeed, there was hardly, if any, interest in the idea that writers had personalities to express. Biographies had been written, but seldom of poets. When Izaak Walton wrote his brief life of John Donne (1640) he did not mention Donne's poetry but concentrated on his life and career in the church. Wordsworth's notion, offered in 1800, that a poem was the inner made outer was revolutionary and helped set in motion an emphasis on the poet in the poem still powerful today in spite of the efforts of objectivist theorists, such as T. S. Eliot, to eradicate it. Early in the twentieth century, Eliot insisted that the poet's effort should be to flee personality and that criticism should concentrate on the poem apart from its author.

Objectivist theories, the fourth of Abrams' orientations, arose principally from aesthetic speculations derived from Kant that tended to treat art objects as in some ways autonomous. In England and America they were also strongly supported by a neoclassical reaction against romanticism. The attitude of people like Eliot and T. E. Hulme was passed on to a younger generation of poets and critics. Objectivist judgment concentrated on the poetic object as a unique system of internal relations. One early version of this view is represented by the phrase "poetry for poetic's sake," used as the title of a well-known essay by A. C. Bradley. The objectivist emphasis developed further along two independent lines, one that of the Russian Formalists (see Shklovsky and Eichenbaum) and the other that of the American New Critics (see Ransom, Blackmur, Brooks, Wimsatt, and Beardsley), who attacked any determination of meaning in a work by recourse either to authorial intention or to a reader's response.

But objectivist theories came under severe attack from a variety of quarters for attempting to isolate the poem from life and particularly from politics. The assault began early with Leon Trotsky's critique of the Russian Formalists and complaints by the so-called New Humanists and the academic literary historians against the New Critics. A resurgence of interest in romanticism, led by Northrup Frye, brought another kind of critique. Since that time a variety of theories, almost all anti-objectivist, have arisen, and the present situation has been aptly described as a cacophony of voices.

Abrams' classification is finally less valuable for its attachment of its types to certain eras than for its use as a simple taxonomy of critical orientations either dominant or latent in most theories.

III

A complimentary way to grasp the long history with which we are concerned is to notice the relations of literary theory to philosophical emphases in different eras. If we recognize the radical simplification implicit in any such effort, we can divide the history of philosophy and of literary theory into four major phases of general emphasis. The first three phases I shall name the ontological, the epistemological, and the linguistic. The first and by far the longest phase, the ontological, addressed the question of the nature of Being and existence. Plato's location of Being in the eternal ideas or forms led to his characterization of poetry as a twice removed copy of Being. Aristotle's shifting of Being and redefinition of ideas and forms also redefined imitation. It is no surprise that this emphasis raised over and over again the question of the status of literary fictions. The questions of Being and verisimilitude dominated philosophy and critical theory through the Middle Ages and well into the Renaissance.

Then, however, the emphasis shifted to what had come to be regarded as a prior question. One no longer began with the problem of Being but instead with that of knowing. The two classic expressions of the epistomological problem are those of René Descartes and John Locke in the seventeenth century. Descartes' rationalism thought out the problem beginning with the human subject's own indubitable knowledge—"I think, therefore I am." Descartes then proceeded to deduce further knowledge. Locke's empiricism divided experience into secondary (subjective) and primary (objective) qualities, privileging all that was primary, that is, all that was ascertainable as real through measurement. Knowledge became identical with the results of scientific method. The epistemological age threatened to separate poetry from reality in a new way, or rather reserved the real world for science and tended to drive poetry into subjectivity. A variety of movements tacitly or explicitly accepted poetic subjectivity, either to exploit it by identifying poetry with the expression of irrational, personal, often isolated experience or to overcome it to some extent by at least a partial recapture of objectivity, either of taste (David Hume), of morality (John Dennis, Samuel Johnson), or, later, of scientific method itself (Emile Zola). At the same time, the epistemological phase focused much attention on the mind, giving sanction to an interest in subjectivity. But the mind could also be objectified and studied systematically, or at least so it began to be hoped, and poetry once again found itself embattled. The epistemological phase greatly enlivened critical discourse, rescuing it from a vocabulary of mimesis that had fairly well exhausted itself; but until poetry could find a theory that would overcome its relegation to subjectivity, it would suffer denigration of its value.

The rise of aesthetics was one such attempt, particularly Kant's efforts to establish what he oxymoronically called "subjective universality" in aesthetic response. But, as is so often the case, the problem was not so much solved as shelved in favor of another one: As the ontological question led to the epistemological one, so the epistemological question led to the linguistic one. To ask about Being led inevitably to ask about how and what we can know. But other questions came to seem prior to this one. Can what we call knowing occur apart from language, to what extent does language inform us, and to what extent are we enclosed within it? For a very long time, with some important exceptions, philosophers considered language as a way of expressing and communicating prior experiences and ideas, which it translated into or represented in words. But as the epistemological phase developed it seemed that the matter was much more complicated, that language, not merely perception, played a constitutive role in the way reality appeared to us. The idea of language as imitating or representing some prior entity now had to vie with the idea that language made these entities or at least established the limits within which entities existed for us.

The querying of language had begun at least as early as Plato's *Cratylus,* but the great surge of interest occurred in the seventeenth and eighteenth centuries and has never died out, though it has taken a variety of forms: historical (including search for origins), philological, semantic, and semiotic, roughly in that order. John Locke found it necessary in 1690 to devote a part of his *Essay Concerning Human Understanding* to language, though he clung to a traditionalist view, for the most part. Giovanni Battista Vico in *The New Science* (1725), ahead of his time, proposed a radical new way of considering language that related its source and fundamental nature to what he called "poetic logic." The origin of language became a popular topic on which many, including Rousseau, wrote; but eventually the approach died out as it became clear that the origin of language was as mysterious as the origin of humanity. Indeed, the two things came often to be thought of as a twinbirth, man being characterized as a linguistic creature. Views of this sort, set forth by Wilhelm von Humboldt early in the nineteenth century, have been echoed in various ideological contexts by a variety of twentieth-century philosophers and writers, including Walter Benjamin, Ernst Cassirer, Martin Heidegger, and Kenneth Burke.

It has always been recognized, of course, that poetry is composed of language. From the earliest times poets have been obsessed with language as the medium of their art. The elaborate development of the discipline of rhetoric in the ancient world attests to an interest in the ways language can be employed to specific effects. The Renaissance produced numerous treatises on linguistic devices, especially tropes and prosody. But the new linguistic age saw language as fundamental to human nature, not just as a human tool. The more recent excursion into language theory known as semiotics or the theory of signs is, however, less interested in these anthropological matters than in analyzing language as if it has its own life or is itself a system. The source of this interest is mainly structuralist linguistics, grounded in the work of Ferdinand de Saussure, the terminology of which has flooded later twentieth-century theory in America by way of Europe, where structuralist linguistics displayed a relation to Russian Formalism. In England and America it met another movement that in its own way had emphasized language. I. A. Richards' semantically oriented views led to his characterization of a poem not as an imitation or expression but simply a "piece of language," and his student William Empson studied poems as texts in which linguistic ambiguities abounded. T. S. Eliot emphasized the objectivity of the poem as a linguistic artifact, although Eliot did not foresee the lengths to which later theorists would take his notions. Richards and Eliot strongly influenced the American New Criticism, sponsored principally by John Crowe Ransom and carried out in theory and practice by such critics as Cleanth Brooks, R. P. Blackmur, Allen Tate, Robert Penn Warren, W. K. Wimsatt, and Monroe C. Beardsley. The New Critics knew virtually nothing of European criticism and linguistics until the arrival in this country of René Wellek, and even then his views took on their coloring. The terminology of the New Criticism remained derived, when it was philosophical, from Kant, semantics, and the English critics known to it, mainly Coleridge.

Until sometime in the mid-nineteen sixties the New Criticism's academic followers dominated literary study as it was professed in American and to some extent in English universities. The first major and most articulate response to the New Criticism was the work of Northrop Frye in his *Anatomy of Criticism* (1957), perhaps the most impressive single work of criticism of the century, certainly the wittiest, and the most ambitious effort in a long time to provide a general theory that would encompass most past literary thought. Frye provided his own phasal history of criticism, absorbed the New Criticism into one phase, and offered a paradox that identified criticism with both science and art, suggesting prophetically that the venerable distinction between science and art had to be rethought. Frye's work had some affinities with structuralism, but without its terminology and with links to the English tradition of criticism. Mainly, however, it was grounded in Frye's vision of William Blake's theory of art.

When structuralism first came to America, principally through Saussure, Roland Barthes, and the anthropology of Claude Lévi-Strauss, it had a very short life in its pure form, for in 1966 at a conference at the Johns Hopkins University Jacques Derrida delivered his now notorious paper "Structure, Sign and Play in the Discourse of the Human Sciences." Thus was born Deconstruction, a critique of the structuralist position as grounded in Saussure's linguistics and Lévi-Strauss's anthropology. Derrida pointed to inconsistencies in structuralism by showing that structuralist theory claimed a possible origin or center of meaning even as its position led logically to the rejection of such a notion. A new deconstructive terminology flooded critical theory.

By this time, rather than the world containing language, language seemed to contain the world. Edward W. Said, desiring to restore the primacy of the world, characterized such theorizing as "wall-to-wall language." Roland Barthes had carried the principle of linguistic structure into a variety of areas, so that aspects of the world— myth, fashion, sport, etc.—all copied the structure of language. It seemed that if there was anything left of mimesis, its direction had been entirely reversed. The world as we can know it copied the structure of language.

Structuralism dissolved substance into sets of pure relations. Rather than things, structuralism was concerned with the relations that things brought into existence. Thus it was the relational space or the "difference" between things, that became important, not things. The model was Saussurean language as a system of differences, each linguistic unit definable in terms of its difference from all the other units in the system. Derrida's argument was that such systems could have no center or grounding point, or first word, that meaning never came to rest in any origin. The search for meaning was involved in an infinite regress, and interpretation as it had traditionally been understood and practiced was a philosophically impossible activity. Rigorously pursued, it produced unresolvable contradictions or *aporias.*

Deconstruction evolved, against Derrida's deliberate resistance to method, a critical technique that threatened to dominate the American academy as had the New Criticism, though it was much less popular in Derrida's France. Certainly one way to consider deconstruction is to think of it as the culmination in theory of the linguistic age. In spite of continued interest in language, recent movements have sought to free themselves from what has been called the "prison house of language." Though it may be too early to try to name the age that follows on the age of linguistics, it is certainly an age of political and cultural critique.

IV

Reservations about the New Criticism, when it replaced the old philologists, historicists, and Marxists as dominant in the academy, had been mainly political, accusing it either of reactionary views or of isolation from life in a new form of aestheticism. This accusation has also been made against Deconstruction, though Derrida himself could certainly not be identified as a political reactionary or a conservative. Quite the contrary. Still, Deconstruction's emphasis on the final elusiveness of centers or grounds and its theory of difference is anathema to any explicitly ideological or materialistically grounded position. Nevertheless, it has left its mark, if only to make confrontation of the complexity of language a necessity in any theory.

Deconstruction has not, however, been the only linguistically based theory, or in many people's eyes even the dominant one. The work of Ludwig Wittgenstein and his influence on a generation of British and American academic philosophers who came to engage almost exclusively in language analysis has also had its effect. But Wittgenstein's early work found no place for poetry, and his followers tended to think of poetry as a sort of aberration of language rather than its Viconian source. The later Wittgenstein, who treated language in terms of what it can accomplish rather than in terms of questions of signification in the *Philosophical Investigations* (1958), produced speculation far more interesting to critics and by no means yet exhausted by them.

V

It is worthwhile to mention and briefly characterize some of the movements that now argue for space in any study of recent critical theory. They are all locatable with respect to the matter of political and cultural critique, and they all grow out of the political and social ferment of the late sixties and the dominant interests of a generation now assuming power in the academic world, where most criticism and almost all critical theory is now written.

A Marxist-derived social criticism has been present for over a century now. Marxist historical thought is important in the writings of many recent critics, as for example Raymond Williams. Though often not as doctrinaire as the Marxist critics of the nineteen thirties, such writing is strongly committed to a particular version of history, and it reads literature as embodied by class conflict. The loosely ordered congeries of studies known as the New Historicism often retains Marxist historical notions, but it is usually more directly under the influence of the analysis of cultural institutions made by Michel Foucault beginning in the nineteen sixties. Foucault also wrote on language, but he eschewed the prison-house notion of it, favoring a theory in which "power" is prior to language. The trace of structuralism in his work is the notion of "relations" of power as the dominating force in societies. New Historicism, strongly secular, concentrates on specific historical instances and frequently seems written from some political position expressing a sort of utopian desire.

Political vision is expressed in the critique of colonialism, represented here by the work of Chinua Achebe and Edward W. Said, which often proceeds by revealing colonialist and racist attitudes in canonical literary texts or, on a larger scale, engages whole cultural myths, as in Said's influential *Orientalism* (1978). In these works, criticism is always seen as a political act in the service of some moral principle, and little interest is shown in what earlier generations called aesthetic matters and on which a good amount of their criticism concentrated.

Perhaps the most successful of these political movements has been feminism, which has produced enough variety of theoretical positions to fill a number of anthologies of its own. Feminism has recovered and revered the writings of many women excluded from the so-called literary canon and raised many voices against the canon's sexual (and racial) exclusiveness. It has shown how male writing has excluded the female perspective and even actively opposed or disdained women and so-called female values. It has created a form of textual analysis sensitive to gender differences. In some of its more adventurous and debatable efforts it has made use of feminist psychological theories and has even offered a notion of female language that looks sometimes quite a lot like what earlier male and female modernist writers had called experimental.

All of these developments are grounded either on a certain set of moral principles or on a theory of power (or both) and are activist in the desire to change society.

It may seem surprising at first that many varieties of reader-oriented criticism have definite connections to these power-oriented forms of theory. Reader-oriented criticism is varied in its intellectual sources. One version of it is psychoanalytical and empirical, as in the work of Norman O. Holland; another is pedagogically inspired and pragmatic (Louise Rosenblatt). But if reader-oriented theory is not to return to the radical subjectivity of Pater and France, to some form of subjective universality, as in Kant, or to a phenomenological fictionalizing of the reader, as in Wolfgang Iser, there must be recourse to the notion of a community of readers that tacitly sets standards. This is the position to which Stanley Fish came. When one takes Fish's step, one comes to ask what power establishes the community's criteria, and we return to the arena of political and cultural critique.

In these movements the question of language is less stridently asked, but it does not go away. The influence of analytic language philosophy is present in Fish's approach; feminism has had a troubled relation to Deconstruction; and so on. Language cannot go away. Nor do world, reader, and poet, nor, for that matter, imitation (now metamorphosed by linguistic skepticism into "representation") or the problem of Being. The *status* of questions about them changes.

But is there a thing called a literary text after all, or are all texts, to some degree at least, literary? And if so, what meaning can "literary" or "literature" retain? The Viconian identification of the literary with tropes eventually led to the discovery of the significant role of tropes in virtually all writing. Thus Hayden White showed in *Metahistory* (1973) that historians could be characterized by the kinds of tropes they employed (though one might claim that the tropes employed *them*). Often critical forays found a substantial fiction-making in biographical, philosophical, and even scientific writing, indeed in criticism itself. Some critics, like Geoffrey Hartman, went so far as to identify criticism with literature, and others (Edward W. Said) argued for the "equality" of critical and literary discourses, claiming that criticism should not be regarded as "secondary." Indeed, it has long been difficult to know where to draw the line. Plato and Dryden wrote dialogues that appear in this book. Horace, Boileau, and Pope wrote poems that are present here. Critical theory turns up in a variety of recognized literary forms. Part of the tendency to identify criticism and literature was grounded in analogical thinking with a political perspective. Why should literature be "privileged," like a colonialist, over criticism? The problem remained, however, to convince poets and most people outside of academia of this, and to ask whether the difference inevitably meant privilege and inequality, both being concerns of critics of colonialism, racism, and sexism.

One of the interesting aspects of the recent history of criticism has been the fate of evaluation. Most people think of criticism as the reviewing of books, an activity of making presumably informed judgments; but theoretical critics since the time of Kant up to the quite recent past gradually abandoned judgment in favor of interpretation and structural analysis. The first phase of this withdrawal was into defenses of poetry, rather than judgments of particular works, against the domination of science. The defenses persisted through the New Critics but then tended to be abandoned. Now it is more likely to be criticism or theory that is defended, as in Murray Krieger's "An Apology for Poetics" (1981). In *Anatomy of Criticism,* Frye considered genuine literary judgment tacit; when it was explicit the criteria turned out to be derived from another discipline—politics, history, psychology, ideology, moral philosophy, etc. The recent return to evaluation seems to bear Frye out, since whether it is tacit or explicit it is usually grounded in some vision of political morality, and works are now frequently judged for political "correctness" with respect to questions of race, class, and gender. Recent criticism has investigated racism in Joseph Conrad (Chinua Achebe), colonialism in E. M. Forster, class in Yeats, and sexist bias in Western literature generally. Since matters of race, class, and gender can be found in almost all texts in some form, the critics of the age of political and cultural critique are not likely to want to discriminate finely among genres or kinds of literary techniques. In hardly any present-day criticism is a term like "beauty" employed except as representative of a suspect discourse, an irrelevant formalism.

By contrast to earlier ages, today's theoretical criticism is written almost exclusively by people holding academic positions, and few of these are themselves poets, novelists, or dramatists. This development has many causes and some results that have changed the scene rather drastically. Only one of the latter I shall mention here. It is the tendency among recent academic critics to spend far less time discussing what at least used to be called "literary" texts and more time debating each other's theories. In earlier ages, poets like Dante, Sidney, and Wordsworth wrote erudite defenses of their own poetic practices that were of general theoretical interest. Many of the earliest New Critics were poets or novelists, and it is no surprise that programs in creative writing developed along with the New Criticism, which was in some important respects strongly oriented to a writerly perspective. Today's theorist may be more interested in, and read more, psychoanalytic or political writing and even publish more about philosophical or anthropological discourses, than literature in the traditional sense.

It has been, to borrow Said's phrase, an age of "wall-to-wall" theory in whatever it is that literary study has become. In an essay called "Mixed Genres" (1980) Clifford Gertz, an anthropologist, discussed this situation as ubiquitous in the "human sciences." The risks of superficiality and perhaps ideological dogmatism are greater, but there is also a new vision that stretches from discipline to discipline. Some think it may signal a new Renaissance.

Plato

c. 427 — c. 347 B.C.

Student of Socrates and founder of the Academy in Athens, Plato is the first major figure in the history of Western philosophy. His political and moral philosophy dominate what he says about literature. He locates reality in what he calls "ideas," or "forms," rather than in the world of "appearances" that we experience through the senses. He regards objects we perceive through the senses as merely copies of the ideas. Our rational powers acquaint us with the ideas and with truth. The poet, restricted to imitating the realm of appearances, makes only copies of copies, and his creation is thus twice removed from reality. Furthermore, he is probably possessed by a madness and not in control of himself when he writes. Since the poet's activity leads men away from truth, Plato considers him dangerous to society. With some misgivings (since he greatly admired fine poetry), Plato found that he must banish the poet from the republic or limit him by strict censorship to songs offering innocuous praise of the state.

In *Ion*, Plato's Socrates converses with the accomplished rhapsode Ion, a professional reciter of epic poetry. He seeks to demolish Ion's claim that as a rhapsode he is an expert critic of Homer's work by asking him whether he is an expert on everything mentioned in Homer and forcing him to admit that he is not. Socrates will not allow Ion to argue that he is an expert on the poem itself as an object or an indivisible whole; for Socrates, it is merely a collection of copies of copies of the ideas, or forms, that it mentions. Socrates treats the poem only in terms of its subject matter or content; he simply ignores its existence as a formal structure. This emphasis leads us to consider Plato the founder of the moralistic and didactic criticism that tends to separate form and content, to emphasize content, and to erect external moral standards. It is perhaps ironic that he should be thought so, for in *Republic* and *Laws* he argues that poetry is morally dangerous. Later Platonists, including Plotinus, maintained a similar theory of ideas but defended poetry as an avenue to a grasp of intellectual beauty. Others found in Plato's own tendency to mythmaking in his dialogues the establishment of an allegorical tradition in which many works were interpreted as repositories of Platonic ideas. A defense of this mode of interpretation is made in the essay by Henry Reynolds. Even a criticism that defines poetry as antirational and without content, such as found in the works of some Romantic critics, might be considered Platonic, for Plato objected to poetry on the grounds of its irrationality.

The influence of Plato on subsequent theorists has been immense. Generally, critics who have been concerned with the moral and didactic content of literature have been considered in some sense Platonic. Among twentieth-century New Critics, such as Ransom, this term is not one of approbation, since to them it suggests separation of form and content and little interest in the ontological status of the poem.

Plato's dialogue on language, *Cratylus*, is of particular interest to contemporary criticism with its strong concern with linguistic matters, for it raises the question of the relation of words to things and to each other.

There are numerous translations of Plato's works. A good standard one is that by Benjamin Jowett, *The Dialogues of Plato,* 4th ed. (4 vols., 1953). All standard histories of philosophy, aesthetics, and criticism devote space to Plato. Helpful general studies are G. M. A. Grube, *Plato's Thought* (1935), and F. M. Cornford, *Plato's Cosmology* (1937). On Plato as a literary theorist consult J. W. H. Atkins, *Literary Criticism in Antiquity*, Vol. I (1934); Katharine Gilbert, "The Relation of the Moral to the Aesthetic Standard in Plato," *Philosophical Review*, XLIII (1934), 279–94; A. H. Gilbert, "Did Plato Banish the Poets or the Critics?" *Studies in Philology*, XXXVI (1939), 1–19; Craig La Drière, "The Problem of Plato's *Ion,*" *Journal of Aesthetics and Art Criticism,* X (1951), 26–34; Rupert C. Lodge, *Plato's Theory of Art* (1953); G. M. A. Grube, *The Greek and Roman Critics* (1965), 46–65; and Julius A. Elias, *Plato's Defence of Poetry* (1984).

Ion

Persons of the Dialogue

Socrates

Ion

Socrates   Welcome, Ion. Are you from your native city of Ephesus?

Ion   No, Socrates; but from Epidaurus, where I attended the festival of Aesculapius.[1]

Socrates   Indeed! Do the Epidaurians have a contest of rhapsodes in his honor?

Ion   O yes; and of other kinds of music.

Socrates   And were you one of the competitors—and did you succeed?

Ion   I—we—obtained the first prize of all, Socrates.

Socrates   Well done; now we must win another victory, at the Panathenaea.

Ion   It shall be so, please heaven.

Socrates   I have often envied the profession of a rhapsode, Ion; for it is a part of your art to wear fine clothes and to look as beautiful as you can, while at the same time you are obliged to be continually in the company of many good poets, and especially of Homer,[2] who is the best and most divine of them, and to understand his mind, and not merely learn his words by rote; all this is a thing greatly to

be envied. I am sure that no man can become a good rhapsode who does not understand the meaning of the poet. For the rhapsode ought to interpret the mind of the poet to his hearers, but how can he interpret him well unless he knows what he means? All this is much to be envied, I repeat.

Ion   Very true, Socrates; interpretation has certainly been the most laborious part of my art; and I believe myself able to speak about Homer better than any man; and that neither Metrodorus of Lampsacus, nor Stesimbrotus of Thasos, nor Glaucon, nor anyone else who ever was, had as good ideas about Homer as I have, or as many.

Socrates   I am glad to hear you say so, Ion; I see that you will not refuse to acquaint me with them.

Ion   Certainly, Socrates; and you really ought to hear how exquisitely I display the beauties of Homer. I think that the Homeridae[3] should give me a golden crown.[4]

Socrates   I shall take an opportunity of hearing your embellishments of him at some other time. But just now I should like to ask you a question: Does your art extend to Hesiod and Archilochus, or to Homer only?

Ion   To Homer only; he is in himself quite enough.

Socrates   Are there any things about which Homer and Hesiod agree?

Ion   Yes; in my opinion there are a good many.

Socrates   And can you interpret what Homer says about these matters better than what Hesiod says?

Ion   I can interpret them equally well, Socrates, where they agree.

Socrates   But what about matters in which they do not agree? For example, about divination of which both Homer and Hesiod have something to say—

Ion   Very true.

ION. Plato's *Ion* was composed about 390 B.C. The text is from Benjamin Jowett, tr., *The Dialogues of Plato*, 4th ed. (Oxford, Eng.: Clarendon Press, 1953), and is reprinted by permission of the Clarendon Press.

[1]God of healing, worshiped in Greece under the name Asclepius.

[2]The works attributed to Homer were probably written between 1200 and 800 B.C. "To be continually in the company of" means here "to read the works of frequently."

[3]Poets who composed in the style of Homer.

[4][Jowett's editors] Or, "I think I have well deserved the golden crown given me by the Homeridae."

Socrates Would you or a good prophet be a better interpreter of what these two poets say about divination, not only when they agree, but when they disagree?

Ion A prophet.

Socrates And if you were a prophet, and could interpret them where they agree, would you not know how to interpret them also where they disagree?

Ion Clearly.

Socrates But how did you come to have this skill about Homer only, and not about Hesiod or the other poets? Does not Homer speak of the same themes which all other poets handle? Is not war his great argument? And does he not speak of human society and of intercourse of men, good and bad, skilled and unskilled, and of the gods conversing with one another and with mankind, and about what happens in heaven and in the world below, and the generations of gods and heroes? Are not these the themes of which Homer sings?

Ion Very true, Socrates.

Socrates And do not the other poets sing of the same?

Ion Yes, Socrates; but not in the same way as Homer.

Socrates What, in a worse way?

Ion Yes, in a far worse.

Socrates And Homer in a better way?

Ion He is incomparably better.

Socrates And yet surely, my dear friend Ion, where many people are discussing numbers, and one speaks better than the rest, there is somebody who can judge which of them is the good speaker?

Ion Yes.

Socrates And he who judges of the good will be the same as he who judges of the bad speakers?

Ion The same.

Socrates One who knows the science of arithmetic?

Ion Yes.

Socrates Or again, if many persons are discussing the wholesomeness of food, and one speaks better than the rest, will he who recognizes the better speaker be a different person from him who recognizes the worse, or the same?

Ion Clearly the same.

Socrates And who is he, and what is his name?

Ion The physician.

Socrates And speaking generally, in all discussions in which the subject is the same and many men are speaking, will not he who knows the good know the bad speaker also? For obviously if he does not know the bad, neither will he know the good, when the same topic is being discussed.

Ion True.

Socrates We find, in fact, that the same person is skillful in both?

Ion Yes.

Socrates And you say that Homer and the other poets, such as Hesiod and Archilochus, speak of the same things, although not in the same way; but the one speaks well and the other not so well?

Ion Yes; and I am right in saying so.

Socrates And if you know the good speaker, you ought also to know the inferior speakers to be inferior?

Ion It would seem so.

Socrates Then, my dear friend, can I be mistaken in saying that Ion is equally skilled in Homer and in other poets, since he himself acknowledges that the same person will be a good judge of all those who speak of the same things; and that almost all poets do speak of the same things?

Ion Why then, Socrates, do I lose attention and have absolutely no ideas of the least value and practically fall asleep when anyone speaks of any other poet; but when Homer is mentioned, I wake up at once and am all attention and have plenty to say?

Socrates The reason, my friend, is not hard to guess. No one can fail to see that you speak of Homer without any art or knowledge. If you were able to speak of him by rules of art, you would have been able to speak of all other poets; for poetry is a whole.

Ion Yes.

Socrates And when anyone acquires any other art as a whole, the same may be said of them. Would you like me to explain my meaning, Ion?

Ion Yes, indeed, Socrates; I very much wish that you would: for I love to hear you wise men talk.

Socrates O that we were wise, Ion, and that you could truly call us so; but you rhapsodes and actors, and the poets whose verses you sing, are wise; whereas I am a common man, who only speaks the truth. For consider what a very commonplace and trivial thing is this which I have said—a thing which any man might say: that when a man has acquired a knowledge of a whole art, the inquiry into good and bad is one and the same. Let us consider this matter; is not the art of painting a whole?

Ion Yes.

Socrates And there are and have been many painters good and bad?

Ion Yes.

Socrates And did you ever know anyone who was skillful in pointing out the excellences and defects of Polygnotus the son of Aglaophon, but incapable of criticizing other painters; and when the work of any other painter was produced, went to sleep and was at a loss, and had no ideas; but when he had to give his opinion about Polygnotus, or whoever the painter might be, and about him only, woke up and was attentive and had plenty to say?

Ion   No indeed, I have never known such a person.

Socrates   Or take sculpture—did you ever know of anyone who was skillful in expounding the merits of Daedalus the son of Metion, or of Epeius the son of Panopeus, or of Theodorus the Samian, or of any individual sculptor; but when the works of sculptors in general were produced, was at a loss and went to sleep and had nothing to say?

Ion   No indeed; no more than the other.

Socrates   And if I am not mistaken, you never met with anyone among flute-players or harp-players or singers to the harp or rhapsodes who was able to discourse of Olympus or Thamyras or Orpheus, or Phemius the rhapsode of Ithaca, but was at a loss when he came to speak of Ion of Ephesus, and had no notion of his merits or defects?

Ion   I cannot deny what you say, Socrates. Nevertheless I am conscious in my own self, and the world agrees with me, that I do speak better and have more to say about Homer than any other man; but I do not speak equally well about others. After all, there must be some reason for this; what is it?

Socrates   I see the reason, Ion; and I will proceed to explain to you what I imagine it to be. The gift which you possess of speaking excellently about Homer is not an art, but, as I was just saying, an inspiration; there is a divinity moving you, like that contained in the stone which Euripides calls a magnet, but which is commonly known as the stone of Heraclea. This stone not only attracts iron rings, but also imparts to them a similar power of attracting other rings; and sometimes you may see a number of pieces of iron and rings suspended from one another so as to form quite a long chain: and all of them derive their power of suspension from the original stone. In like manner the Muse first of all inspires men herself; and from these inspired persons a chain of other persons is suspended, who take the inspiration. For all good poets, epic as well as lyric, compose their beautiful poems not by art, but because they are inspired and possessed. And as the Korybantian revelers[5] when they dance are not in their right mind, so the lyric poets are not in their right mind when they are composing their beautiful strains: but when falling under the power of music and meter they are inspired and possessed; like Bacchic maidens who draw milk and honey from the rivers when they are under the influence of Dionysus[6] but not when they are in their right mind. And the soul of the lyric poet does the same, as they themselves say; for they tell us that they bring songs from honeyed fountains, culling them out of the gardens and dells of the Muses; they, like the bees, winging their way from flower to flower. And this is true. For the poet is a light and winged and holy thing, and there is no invention in him until he has been inspired and is out of his senses, and reason is no longer in him: no man, while he retains that faculty, has the oracular gift of poetry.[7]

Many are the noble words in which poets speak concerning the actions of men; but like yourself when speaking about Homer, they do not speak of them by any rules of art: they are simply inspired to utter that to which the Muse impels them, and that only; and when inspired, one of them will make dithyrambs,[8] another hymns of praise, another choral strains, another epic or iambic verses, but not one of them is of any account in the other kinds. For not by art does the poet sing, but by power divine; had he learned by rules of art, he would have known how to speak not of one theme only, but of all; and therefore God takes away reason from poets, and uses them as his ministers, as he also uses the pronouncers of oracles and holy prophets, in order that we who hear them may know them to be speaking not of themselves, who utter these priceless words while bereft of reason, but that God himself is the speaker, and that through them he is addressing us. And Tynnichus the Chalcidian affords a striking instance of what I am saying: he wrote no poem that anyone would care to remember but the famous paean which is in everyone's mouth, one of the finest lyric poems ever written, simply an invention of the Muses, as he himself says. For in this way God would seem to demonstrate to us and not to allow us to doubt that these beautiful poems are not human, nor the work of man, but divine and the work of God; and that the poets are only the interpreters of the gods by whom they are severally possessed. Was not this the lesson which God intended to teach when by the mouth of the worst of poets he sang the best of songs? Am I not right, Ion?

Ion   Yes, indeed, Socrates, I feel that you are; for your words touch my soul, and I am persuaded that in these works the good poets, under divine inspiration, interpret to us the voice of the gods.

---

[5]The Korybantes were mystic divinities often associated with the mother-goddesses Rhea and Demeter and worshiped in enthusiastic festivals.

[6]Greek god of wine and natural passions, called Bacchus by the Romans. He is often contrasted with Apollo, who is associated with intellect and rationality. The terms *Apollonian* and *Dionysiac* are employed by Nietzsche in *The Birth of Tragedy* (pp. 629–34) to describe two major forces in Greek tragedy.

[7]This passage is profitably compared to Keats's letter to Benjamin Bailey (pp. 493–94), which is less extreme but in some ways similar in attitude.

[8]Dionysiac choric hymns.

Socrates   And you rhapsodists are the interpreters of the poets?

Ion   There again you are right.

Socrates   Then you are the interpreters of interpreters?

Ion   Precisely.

Socrates   I wish you would frankly tell me, Ion, what I am going to ask of you: When you produce the greatest effect upon the audience in the recitation of some striking passage, such as the apparition of Odysseus leaping forth on the floor, recognized by the suitors and shaking out his arrows at his feet, or the description of Achilles springing upon Hector, or the sorrows of Andromache, Hecuba, or Priam—are you in your right mind? Are you not carried out of yourself, and does not your soul in an ecstasy seem to be among the persons or places of which you are speaking, whether they are in Ithaca or in Troy or whatever may be the scene of the poem?

Ion   That proof strikes home to me, Socrates. For I must frankly confess that at the tale of pity my eyes are filled with tears, and when I speak of horrors, my hair stands on end and my heart throbs.

Socrates   Well, Ion, and what are we to say of a man who at a sacrifice or festival, when he is dressed in an embroidered robe, and has golden crowns upon his head, of which nobody has robbed him, appears weeping or panic-stricken in the presence of more than twenty thousand friendly faces, when there is no one despoiling or wronging him—is he in his right mind or is he not?

Ion   No indeed, Socrates, I must say that, strictly speaking, he is not in his right mind.

Socrates   And are you aware that you produce similar effects on most of the spectators?

Ion   Only too well; for I look down upon them from the stage, and behold the various emotions of pity, wonder, sternness, stamped upon their countenances when I am speaking: and I am obliged to give my very best attention to them; for if I make them cry I myself shall laugh, and if I make them laugh I myself shall cry, when the time of payment arrives.

Socrates   Do you know that the spectator is the last of the rings which, as I am saying, receive the power of the original magnet from one another? The rhapsode like yourself and the actor are intermediate links, and the poet himself is the first of them. Through all these God sways the souls of men in any direction which he pleases, causing each link to communicate the power to the next. Thus there is a vast chain of dancers and masters and undermasters of choruses, who are suspended, as if from the stone, at the side of the rings which hang down from the Muse. And every poet has some Muse from whom he is suspended, and by whom he is said to be possessed, which is nearly the same thing; for he is taken hold of. And from these first rings, which are the poets, depend others, some deriving their inspiration from Orpheus, others from Musaeus; but the greater number are possessed and held by Homer. Of whom, Ion, you are one, and are possessed by Homer; and when anyone repeats the words of another poet you go to sleep, and know not what to say; but when anyone recites a strain of Homer you wake up in a moment, and your soul leaps within you, and you have plenty to say; for not by art or knowledge about Homer do you say what you say, but by divine inspiration and by possession; just as the Korybantian revelers too have a quick perception of that strain only which is appropriated to the god by whom they are possessed, and have plenty of dances and words for that, but take no heed of any other. And you, Ion, when the name of Homer is mentioned have plenty to say, and have nothing to say of others. You ask, "Why is this?" The answer is that your skill in the praise of Homer comes not from art but from divine inspiration.

Ion   That is good, Socrates; and yet I doubt whether you will ever have eloquence enough to persuade me that I praise Homer only when I am mad and possessed; and if you could hear me speak of him I am sure you would never think this to be the case.

Socrates   I should like very much to hear you, but not until you have answered a question which I have to ask. On what part of Homer do you speak well?—not surely about every part?

Ion   There is no part, Socrates, about which I do not speak well: of that I can assure you.

Socrates   Surely not about things in Homer of which you have no knowledge?

Ion   And what is there in Homer of which I have no knowledge?

Socrates   Why, does not Homer speak in many passages about arts? For example, about driving; if I can only remember the lines I will repeat them.

Ion   I remember, and will repeat them.

Socrates   Tell me then, what Nestor says to Antilochus, his son, where he bids him be careful of the turn at the horse race in honor of Patroclus.

Ion   "Bend gently," he says, "in the polished chariot to the left of them, and urge the horse on the right hand with whip and voice; and slacken the rein. And when you are at the goal, let the left horse draw near, so that the nave of the well-wrought wheel may appear to graze the extremity; but have a care not to touch the stone."[9]

---

[9] *Iliad*, XXIII. 335.

Socrates   Enough. Now, Ion, will the charioteer or the physician be the better judge of the propriety of these lines?

Ion   The charioteer, clearly.

Socrates   And will the reason be that this is his art, or will there be any other reason?

Ion   No, that will be the reason.

Socrates   And every art is appointed by God to have knowledge of a certain work; for that which we know by the art of the pilot we shall not succeed in knowing also by the art of medicine?

Ion   Certainly not.

Socrates   Nor shall we know by the art of the carpenter that which we know by the art of medicine?

Ion   Certainly not.

Socrates   And this is true of all the arts—that which we know with one art we shall not know with the other? But let me ask a prior question: You admit that there are differences of arts?

Ion   Yes.

Socrates   You would argue, as I should, that if there are two kinds of knowledge, dealing with different things, these can be called different arts?

Ion   Yes.

Socrates   Yes, surely; for if the object of knowledge were the same, there would be no meaning in saying that the arts were different—since they both gave the same knowledge. For example, I know that here are five fingers, and you know the same. And if I were to ask whether I and you became acquainted with this fact by the help of the same art of arithmetic, you would acknowledge that we did?

Ion   Yes.

Socrates   Tell me, then, what I was intending to ask you—whether in your opinion this holds universally? If two arts are the same, must not they necessarily have the same objects? And if one differs from another, must it not be because the object is different?

Ion   That is my opinion, Socrates.

Socrates   Then he who has no knowledge of a particular art will have no right judgment of the precepts and practice of that art?

Ion   Very true.

Socrates   Then which will be the better judge of the lines which you were reciting from Homer, you or the charioteer?

Ion   The charioteer.

Socrates   Why, yes, because you are a rhapsode and not a charioteer.

Ion   Yes.

Socrates   And the art of the rhapsode is different from that of the charioteer?

Ion   Yes.

Socrates   And if a different knowledge, then a knowledge of different matters?

Ion   True.

Socrates   You know the passage in which Hecamede, the concubine of Nestor, is described as giving to the wounded Machaon a posset, as he says, "made with Pramnian wine; and she grated cheese of goat's milk with a grater of bronze, and at his side placed an onion which gives a relish to drink."[10] Now would you say that the art of the rhapsode or the art of medicine was better able to judge of the propriety of these lines?

Ion   The art of medicine.

Socrates   And when Homer says, "And she descended into the deep like a leaden plummet, which, set in the horn of ox that ranges the fields, rushes along carrying death among the ravenous fishes,"[11] will the art of the fisherman or of the rhapsode be better able to judge what these lines mean, and whether they are accurate or not?

Ion   Clearly, Socrates, the art of the fisherman.

Socrates   Come now, suppose that you were to say to me: "Since you, Socrates, are able to assign different passages in Homer to their corresponding arts, I wish that you would tell me what are the passages of which the excellence ought to be judged by the prophet and prophetic art"; and you will see how readily and truly I shall answer you. For there are many such passages, particularly in the *Odyssey;* as, for example, the passage in which Theoclymenus the prophet of the house of Melampus says to the suitors:

Wretched men! what is happening to you? Your heads and your faces and your limbs underneath are shrouded in night; and the voice of lamentation bursts forth, and your cheeks are wet with tears. And the vestibule is full, and the court is full, of ghosts descending into the darkness of Erebus, and the sun has perished out of heaven, and an evil mist is spread abroad.[12]

And there are many such passages in the *Iliad* also; as for example in the description of the battle near the rampart, where he says:

As they were eager to pass the ditch, there came to them an omen: a soaring eagle, skirting the people

---

[10] *Iliad*, XI. 639–40.
[11] *Iliad*, XXIV. 80.
[12] *Odyssey*, XX. 351.

on his left, bore a huge blood-red dragon in his talons, still living and panting; nor had he yet resigned the strife, for he bent back and smote the bird which carried him on the breast by the neck, and he in pain let him fall from him to the ground into the midst of the multitude. And the eagle, with a cry, was borne afar on the wings of the wind.[13]

These are the sort of things which I should say that the prophet ought to consider and determine.

Ion   And you are quite right, Socrates, in saying so.

Socrates   Yes, Ion, and you are right also. And as I have selected from the *Iliad* and *Odyssey* for you passages which describe the office of the prophet and the physician and the fisherman, do you, who know Homer so much better than I do, Ion, select for me passages which relate to the rhapsode and the rhapsode's art, and which the rhapsode ought to examine and judge of better than other men.

Ion   All passages, I should say, Socrates.

Socrates   Not all, Ion, surely. Have you already forgotten what you were saying? A rhapsode ought to have a better memory.

Ion   Why, what am I forgetting?

Socrates   Do you not remember that you declared the art of the rhapsode to be different from the art of the charioteer?

Ion   Yes, I remember.

Socrates   And you admitted that being different they would know different objects?

Ion   Yes.

Socrates   Then upon your own showing the rhapsode, and the art of the rhapsode, will not know everything?

Ion   I should exclude such things as you mention, Socrates.

Socrates   You mean to say that you would exclude pretty much the subjects of the other arts. As he does not know all of them, which of them will he know?

Ion   He will know what a man and what a woman ought to say, and what a freeman and what a slave ought to say, and what a ruler and what a subject.

Socrates   Do you mean that a rhapsode will know better than the pilot what the ruler of a sea-tossed vessel ought to say?

Ion   No; the pilot will know best.

Socrates   Or will the rhapsode know better than the physician what the ruler of a sick man ought to say?

Ion   Again, no.

Socrates   But he will know what a slave ought to say?

Ion   Yes.

Socrates   Suppose the slave to be a cowherd; the rhapsode will know better than the cowherd what he ought to say in order to soothe infuriated cows?

Ion   No, he will not.

Socrates   But he will know what a spinning-woman ought to say about the working of wool?

Ion   No.

Socrates   At any rate he will know what a general ought to say when exhorting his soldiers?

Ion   Yes, that is the sort of thing which the rhapsode will be sure to know.

Socrates   What! Is the art of the rhapsode the art of the general?

Ion   I am sure that I should know what a general ought to say.

Socrates   Why, yes, Ion, because you may possibly have the knowledge of a general as well as that of a rhapsode; and you might also have a knowledge of horsemanship as well as of the lyre, and then you would know when horses were well or ill managed. But suppose I were to ask you: By the help of which art, Ion, do you know whether horses are well managed, by your skill as a horseman or as a performer on the lyre—what would you answer?

Ion   I should reply, by my skill as a horseman.

Socrates   And if you judged of performers on the lyre, you would admit that you judged of them as a performer on the lyre, and not as a horseman?

Ion   Yes.

Socrates   And in judging of the general's art, do you judge as a general, or as a good rhapsode?

Ion   To me there appears to be no difference between them.

Socrates   What do you mean? Do you mean to say that the art of the rhapsode and of the general is the same?

Ion   Yes, one and the same.

Socrates   Then he who is a good rhapsode is also a good general?

Ion   Certainly, Socrates.

Socrates   And he who is a good general is also a good rhapsode?

Ion   No; I do not agree to that.

Socrates   But you do agree that he who is a good rhapsode is also a good general.

Ion   Certainly.

Socrates   And you are the best of Hellenic rhapsodes?

Ion   Far the best, Socrates.

Socrates   And are you also the best general, Ion?

---

[13]*Iliad*, XII. 200.

Ion   To be sure, Socrates; and Homer was my master.

Socrates   But then, Ion, why in the name of goodness do you, who are the best of generals as well as the best of rhapsodes in all Hellas, go about reciting rhapsodies when you might be a general? Do you think that the Hellenes are in grave need of a rhapsode with his golden crown, and have no need at all of a general?

Ion   Why, Socrates, the reason is that my countrymen, the Ephesians, are the servants and soldiers of Athens, and do not need a general; and that you and Sparta are not likely to appoint me, for you think that you have enough generals of your own.

Socrates   My good Ion, did you never hear of Apollodorus of Cyzicus?

Ion   Who may he be?

Socrates   One who, though a foreigner, has often been chosen their general by the Athenians: and there is Phanosthenes of Andros, and Heraclides of Clazomenae, whom they have also appointed to the command of their armies and to other offices, although aliens, after they had shown their merit. And will they not choose Ion the Ephesian to be their general, and honor him, if they deem him qualified? Were not the Ephesians originally Athenians, and Ephesus is no mean city? But, indeed, Ion, if you are correct in saying that by art and knowledge you are able to praise Homer, you do not deal fairly with me, and after all your professions of knowing many glorious things about Homer, and promises that you would exhibit them, you only deceive me, and so far from exhibiting the art of which you are a master, will not, even after my repeated entreaties, explain to me the nature of it. You literally assume as many forms as Proteus,[14] twisting and turning up and down, until at last you slip away from me in the disguise of a general, in order that you may escape exhibiting your Homeric lore. And if you have art, then, as I was saying, in falsifying your promise that you would exhibit Homer, you are not dealing fairly with me. But if, as I believe, you have no art, but speak all these beautiful words about Homer unconsciously under his inspiring influence, then I acquit you of dishonesty, and shall only say that you are inspired. Which do you prefer to be thought, dishonest or inspired?

Ion   There is a great difference, Socrates, between the two alternatives; and inspiration is by far the nobler.

Socrates   Then, Ion, I shall assume the nobler alternative; and attribute to you in your praises of Homer inspiration, and not art.

---

[14]Greek sea god who could change his shape at will.

Republic

From

Book II

Persons of the Dialogue

Socrates
Adeimantus

Come then, and let us pass a leisure hour in storytelling, and our story shall be the education of our heroes.

By all means.

And what shall be their education? It would be hard, I think, to find a better than the traditional system, which has two divisions, gymnastic for the body, and music[1] for the soul.

True.

Presumably we shall begin education with music, before gymnastic can begin.

By all means.

And when you speak of music, do you include literature or not?

I do.

And literature may be either true or false?[2]

Yes.

Both have a part to play in education. But we must begin with the false?

I do not understand your meaning, he said.

You know, I said, that we begin by telling children stories which, though not wholly destitute of truth, are in the main fictitious; and these stories are told them when they are not of an age for gymnastics.

Very true.

That was my meaning when I said that we must teach music before gymnastics.

REPUBLIC.   Plato's *Republic* was composed about 373 B.C. The text is from Benjamin Jowett, tr., *The Dialogues of Plato*, 4th ed. (Oxford, Eng.: Clarendon Press, 1953), and is reprinted by permission of the Clarendon Press.

[1][Jowett's editors] This term, as is evident from the context, here includes literature.

[2]This discussion dealing with the truth or falsity of poetry and a similar discussion in Plato's *Sophist* begin a tradition in criticism. Defenders of poetry have developed various arguments explaining why it is "true," from Plotinus' treatment of art and spiritual beauty (see *On the Intellectual Beauty*, pp. 100–06), through Sidney's assumption of poetry's allegorical truth (see *An Apology for Poetry*, pp. 143–62), to Mazzoni's distinction, borrowed directly from *Sophist*, between icastic and fantastic imitation (see *On the Defense of the* Comedy *of Dante*, p. 164), and finally to theories that suggest that poetry is a special mode of knowledge.

Quite right, he said.

You know also that the beginning is the most important part of any work, especially in the case of a young and tender thing; for that is the time at which the character is being formed and the desired impression is more readily taken.

Quite true.

And shall we just carelessly allow children to hear any casual tales which may be devised by casual persons, and to receive into their minds ideas for the most part the very opposite of those which we shall wish them to have when they are grown up?

We cannot.

Then the first thing will be to establish a censorship of the writers of fiction, and let the censors receive any tale of fiction which is good, and reject the bad; and we will persuade mothers and nurses to tell their children the authorized ones only. Let them fashion the mind with such tales, even more fondly than they mold the body with their hands; but most of those which are now in use must be discarded.

Of what tales are you speaking? he said.

You may find a model of the lesser in the greater, I said; for they must both be of the same type, and the same spirit ought to be found in both of them.

Very likely, he replied; but I do not as yet know what you would term the greater.

Those, I said, which are narrated by Homer and Hesiod, and the rest of the poets, who have ever been the great storytellers of mankind.

But which stories do you mean, he said; and what fault do you find with them?

A fault which is fundamental and most serious, I said; the fault of saying what is false, and doing so for no good purpose.

But when is this fault committed?

Whenever an erroneous representation is made of the nature of gods and heroes—as when a painter paints a picture not having the shadow of a likeness to his subject.

Yes, he said, that sort of thing is certainly very blamable; but what are the stories which you mean?

First of all, I said, there was that greatest of all falsehoods on great subjects, which the misguided poet told about Ouranos—I mean what Hesiod says that Ouranos did, and how Kronos retaliated on him.[3] The doings of Kronos, and the sufferings which in turn his son inflicted upon him, even if they were true, ought certainly not to be lightly told to young and thoughtless persons; if possible, they had better be buried in silence. But if there is an absolute necessity for

their mention, a chosen few might hear them in a mystery;[4] and they should sacrifice not a common [Eleusinian] pig, but some huge and unprocurable victim, so that the number of the hearers may be very few indeed.

Why, yes, said he, those stories are extremely objectionable.

Yes, Adeimantus, they are stories not to be repeated in our state; the young man should not be told that in committing the worst of crimes he is far from doing anything outrageous; and that even if he chastises in savage fashion his father when he does wrong, he will only be following the example of the first and greatest among the gods.[5]

I entirely agree with you, he said; in my opinion those stories are quite unfit to be repeated.

Neither, if we mean our future guardians to regard the habit of lightly quarreling among themselves as of all things the basest, should any word be said to them of the wars in heaven, and of the plots and fightings of the gods against one another, for they are not true. No, we shall never mention the battles of the giants, or let them be embroidered on garments; and we shall be silent about the innumerable other quarrels of gods and heroes with their friends and relatives. If we intend to persuade them that quarreling is unholy, and that never up to this time has there been any hatred between citizens, then the stories which old men and old women tell them as children should be in this strain; and when they grow up, the poets also should be obliged to compose for them in a similar spirit. But the narrative of Hephaestus binding Hera his mother,[6] or how on another occasion his father sent him flying for taking her part when she was being beaten,[7] and all the battles of the gods in Homer—these tales must not be admitted into our state, whether they are supposed to have an allegorical meaning or not. For a young person cannot judge what is allegorical and what is literal; anything that he receives into his mind at that age is likely to become indelible and unalterable; and therefore it is most important that the tales which the young first hear should be models of virtuous thoughts.

There you are right, he replied; but if anyone asks where are such models to be found and of what tales are you speaking—how shall we answer him?

I said to him, You and I, Adeimantus, at this moment are not poets, but founders of a state: now the founders of a

---

[3]Ouranos (Uranus) confined his children, whom he hated, in Tartarus. He was castrated and dethroned by the Titan Kronos, who later lost the throne to Zeus (Hesiod, *Theogony*, 154, 459).

[4]Religious rite.

[5]"The first and greatest among the gods" refers to Zeus.

[6]Kept ignorant of his parentage, Hephaestus, son of Zeus and Hera, trapped Hera in a chair until she told him who his parents were.

[7]When Hephaestus took Hera's part in an argument with Zeus, Zeus hurled him from Olympus down to the island of Lemnos. Some writers attributed his lameness to this fall.

state ought to know the general forms in which poets should cast their tales, and the limits which must be observed by them, but to make the tales is not their business.

Very true, he said; but what are these forms of theology which you mean?

Something of this kind, I replied: God is always to be represented as he truly is, whatever be the sort of poetry, epic, lyric or tragic, in which the representation is given.

Right.

And is he not truly good? And must he not be represented as such?

Certainly.

And no good thing is hurtful?

No, indeed.

And that which is not hurtful hurts not?

Certainly not.

And that which hurts not does no evil?

No.

And can that which does no evil be a cause of evil?

Impossible.

And the good is advantageous?

Yes.

And therefore the cause of well-being?

Yes.

It follows therefore that the good is not the cause of all things, but of those which are as they should be; and it is not to be blamed for evil.

Assuredly.

Then God, if he be good, is not the author of all things, as the many assert, but he is the cause of a few things only, and not of most things that occur to men. For few are the goods of human life, and many are the evils, and the good is to be attributed to God alone; of the evils the causes are to be sought elsewhere, and not in him.

That appears to me to be most true, he said.

Then we must not listen to Homer or to any other poet who is guilty of the folly of saying that "two casks lie at the threshold of Zeus, full of lots, one of good, the other of evil lots"; and that he to whom Zeus gives a mixture of the two "sometimes meets with evil fortune, at other times with good"; but that he to whom is given the cup of unmingled ill, "him wild hunger drives o'er the beauteous earth." And again—"Zeus, who is the dispenser of good and evil to us."[8] And if anyone asserts that the violation of oaths and treaties, which was really the work of Pandarus,[9] was brought about by Athena and Zeus, or that the strife and competition be-

tween the gods was instigated by Themis and Zeus, he shall not have our approval; neither will we allow our young men to hear the words of Aeschylus, that "God plants guilt among men when he desires utterly to destroy a house." And if a poet writes of the sufferings of Niobe—the subject of the tragedy in which these iambic verses occur—or of the house of Pelops, or of the Trojan War or on any similar theme, either we must not permit him to say that these are the works of God, or if they are of God, he must devise some explanation of them such as we are seeking: he must say that God did what was just and right, and they were the better for being punished. But that those who are punished are miserable, and that God is the author of their misery—the poet is not to be permitted to say; though he may say that the wicked were miserable because they required to be punished, and were benefited by receiving punishment from God; but that God being good is the author of evil to anyone is to be denied. We shall insist that it is not said or sung or heard in verse or prose by anyone whether old or young in any well-ordered commonwealth. Such a fiction would be impious, disastrous to us, and inconsistent with itself.

I agree with you, he replied, and am ready to give my assent to the law.

Let this then be one of our rules and principles concerning the gods, to which our poets and reciters will be expected to conform—that God is not the author of all things, but of good only.

That will do, he said.

And what do you think of a second principle? Do you think that God is a magician, and of a nature to appear insidiously now in one shape, and now in another—sometimes really changing and passing into many forms, sometimes deceiving us with the semblance of such transformations; or is he one and the same immutably fixed in his own proper image?

I cannot answer you, he said, without more thought.

Well, I said; but if we suppose a change in anything, that change must be effected either by the thing itself, or by some other thing?

Most certainly.

And things which are at their best are also least liable to be altered or discomposed; for example, when healthiest and strongest, the human frame is least liable to be affected by meats and drinks and fatigue, and the plant which is in the fullest vigor also suffers least from winds or the heat of the sun or any similar causes.

Of course.

And will not the bravest and wisest soul be least confused or deranged by any external influence?

True.

[8]*Iliad*, XXIV. 527 *ff.*
[9]*Iliad*, II. 69.

And the same principle, as I should suppose, applies to all composite things—furniture, houses, garments: when good and well made, they are least altered by time and circumstances.

Very true.

Then everything which is good, whether made by art or nature, or both, is least liable to suffer change from without?

True.

But surely God and the things of God are in every way perfect?

Of course they are.

Then he can least of all be compelled by external influence to take many shapes?

Certainly.

But may he not change and transform himself?

Clearly, he said, that must be the case if he is changed at all.

And will he then change himself for the better and fairer, or for the worse and more unsightly?

If he change at all he can only change for the worse, for we cannot suppose him to be deficient either in virtue or beauty.

Very true, Adeimantus; but then, would anyone, whether God or man, in your opinion deliberately make himself worse in any respect?

Impossible.

Then it is impossible that God should ever be willing to change; being, as is supposed, the fairest and best that is conceivable, every one of the gods remains absolutely and forever in his own form.

That necessarily follows, he said, in my judgment.

Then, I said, my dear friend, let none of the poets tell us that "the gods, taking the disguise of strangers from other lands, walk up and down cities in all sorts of forms";[10] and let no one slander Proteus and Thetis,[11] neither let anyone, either in tragedy or in any other kind of poetry, introduce Hera disguised in the likeness of a priestess asking an alms "for the life-giving daughters of Inachus the river of Argos"—let us have none of that repertoire of falsehoods. Neither must we have mothers under the influence of the poets scaring their children with a bad version of these myths—telling how certain gods, as they say, "go about by night in the likeness of so many strangers and in divers forms"; but let them take heed lest they make cowards of their children, and at the same time speak blasphemy against the gods.

Heaven forbid, he said.

But although the gods are themselves unchangeable, still by witchcraft and deception they may make us think that they appear in various forms?

Perhaps, he replied.

Well, but can you imagine that a god would deign to be false of speech, or false in deed by putting forth a phantom of himself?

I cannot say, he replied.

Do you not know, I said, that true falsehood, if such an expression may be allowed, is hated of all gods and men?

What do you mean? he said.

I mean that no one willingly deceives with that which is the truest and highest part of himself, and about the truest and highest matters; there, above all, he is most afraid of embracing falsehood.

Still, he said, I do not comprehend you.

The reason is, I replied, that you attribute some profound meaning to my words; but I am only saying that deceiving, or being deceived or uninformed, about realities in his very soul, and in that part to have and embrace falsehood, is what every man will least tolerate. Indeed, it is in such circumstances that falsehood is most detested.

By far the most.

Consequently as I was just now remarking, this ignorance in the soul of him who is deceived may be called true falsehood; for the lie in words is only a kind of imitation and shadowy image of a previous affection[12] of the soul, not pure unadulterated falsehood. Am I not right?

Perfectly right.

True falsehood is hated not only by the gods, but also by men?

Yes.

What should be said of the lie in words? When, and in what relationship, may it be useful and not repugnant to us? Presumably in relation to enemies, or again, when those whom we call our friends in a fit of madness or illusion are going to do some harm, then it is useful and is a sort of medicine or preventive; also in the tales of mythology, of which we were just now speaking—because we do not know the truth about ancient times, we make falsehood as much like truth as we can, and so turn it to account.

Very true, he said.

But for which of these reasons might God find falsehood useful? Can we suppose that he is ignorant of antiquity, and therefore has recourse to invention?

That would be ridiculous, he said.

---

[10]*Odyssey*, XVII. 485.
[11]Thetis is the wife of Peleus, by whom she became the mother of Achilles. Like Proteus, a marine deity, she could change shape.

---

[12]A state of being.

Then the lying poet has no place in our idea of God?

I should say not.

Or perhaps he may tell a lie because he is afraid of enemies?

That is inconceivable.

But he may have friends who are senseless or mad?

But no mad or senseless person can be a friend of God.

Then no motive can be imagined why God should lie?

None whatever.

Then the superhuman and divine is absolutely incapable of falsehood?

Yes.

Then is God perfectly simple and true both in word and deed; he changes not, and does not deceive others, waking or dreaming, either by phantasms or by sign or by word.

Your thoughts, he said, are the reflection of my own.

You agree with me then, I said, that this is the second type or form in which men should write and speak about divine things. The gods are not magicians who transform themselves, neither do they deceive mankind in word or deed.

I grant that.

Then, although we are admirers of Homer, we shall not admire the lying dream which Zeus sends to Agamemnon; neither will we praise the verses of Aeschylus in which Thetis says that Apollo at her nuptials

was celebrating in song her fair progeny, whose days were to be long and to know no sickness. And when he had spoken of my lot as in all things blessed of heaven, he raised a note of triumph and cheered my soul. And I thought that the word of Phoebus,[13] being divine and full of prophecy, would not fail. And now he himself who uttered the strain, he who was present at the banquet, and who said this—he it is who has slain my son.[14]

These are the kind of sentiments about the gods which will arouse our anger; and he who utters them shall be refused a chorus; neither shall we allow teachers to make use of them in the instruction of the young, meaning, as we do, that our guardians, as far as men can be, should be god-fearing and godlike.

I entirely agree, he said, in these principles, and would lay them down as laws.

---

[13]Apollo as sun god.
[14][Jowett] From a lost play.

From

Book III

Persons of the Dialogue

Socrates
Adeimantus
Glaucon

Then as far as the gods are concerned, I said, such tales are to be told, and such others are not to be told to our disciples from their youth upwards, if we mean them to honor the gods and their parents, and to value friendship with one another.

Yes; and I think that our principles are right, he said.

But if they are to be courageous, must they not learn other lessons besides these, and lessons of such a kind as will take away the fear of death? Can any man be courageous who has the fear of death in him?

Certainly not, he said.

And can he be fearless of death, or will he choose death in battle rather than defeat and slavery, who believes the world below to be real and terrible?

Impossible.

Then we must assume a control over the narrators of this class of tales as well as over the others, and beg them not simply to revile, but rather to commend the world below, intimating to them that their descriptions are untrue, and will do harm to our future warriors.

That will be our duty, he said.

Then, I said, we shall have to obliterate many obnoxious passages, beginning with the verses, "I would rather be a serf on the land of a poor and portionless man than rule over all the dead who have come to naught."[15] We must also expunge the verse, which tells us how Pluto feared "lest the mansions grim and squalid which the gods abhor should be seen both of mortals and immortals."[16] And again: "O heavens! verily in the house of Hades there is soul and ghostly form, but no mind at all in them!"[17] Again of Tiresias: "[To him even after death did Persephone grant mind,] that he alone should be wise; but the other souls are flitting shades."[18] Again: "The soul flying from the limbs had gone to Hades, lamenting her fate, leaving manhood and youth."[19]

---

[15]*Odyssey*, XI. 489.
[16]*Iliad*, XX. 64.
[17]*Iliad*, XXIII. 103.
[18]*Odyssey*, X. 495.
[19]*Iliad*, XVI. 856.

Again: "And the soul, with shrilling cry, passed like smoke beneath the earth."[20] And, "As bats in hollow of mystic cavern, whenever any of them has dropped out of the string and falls from the rock, fly shrilling and cling to one another, so did they with shrilling cry hold together as they moved."[21] And we must beg Homer and the other poets not to be angry if we strike out these and similar passages, not because they are unpoetical, or unattractive to the popular ear, but because the greater the poetical charm of them, the less are they meet for the ears of boys and men who are meant to be free, and who should fear slavery more than death.

Undoubtedly.

Also we shall have to reject all the terrible and appalling names which describe the world below— Cocytus and Styx, ghosts under the earth, and sapless shades, and any similar words of which the very mention causes a shudder to pass through the inmost soul of him who hears them. I do not say that these horrible stories may not have a use of some kind; but there is a danger that our guardians[22] may be rendered too excitable and effeminate by them.

There is a real danger, he said.

Then we must have no more of them.

True.

Our poets must sing in another and a nobler strain.

Clearly.

And shall we proceed to get rid of the weepings and wailings of famous men?

They will go with the rest.

But shall we be right in getting rid of them? Reflect: our principle is that the good man will not consider death terrible to any other good man who is his comrade.

Yes; that is our principle.

And therefore he will not sorrow for his departed friend as though he had suffered anything terrible?

He will not.

Another thing which we should say of him is that he is the most sufficient for himself and his own happiness, and therefore is least in need of other men.

True, he said.

And for this reason the loss of a son or brother, or any deprivation of fortune, is to him of all men least terrible.

Assuredly.

And therefore he will be least likely to lament, and will bear with the greatest equanimity any misfortune of this sort which may befall him.

Yes, he will feel such a misfortune far less than another.

Then we shall be right in getting rid of the lamentations of famous men, and making them over to women (and not even to women who are good for anything), or to men of a baser sort, that those who are being educated by us to be the defenders of their country may scorn to do the like.

That will be very right.

Then we will once more entreat Homer and the other poets not to depict Achilles,[23] who is the son of a goddess, first lying on his side, then on his back, and then on his face; then starting up and sailing[24] in a frenzy along the shores of the barren sea; now taking the sooty ashes in both his hands[25] and pouring them over his head, or weeping and wailing in the various modes which Homer has delineated. Nor should he describe Priam the kinsman of the gods as praying and beseeching, "rolling in the dirt, calling each man loudly by his name."[26] Still more earnestly will we beg of him at all events not to introduce the gods lamenting and saying, "Alas! my misery! Alas! that I bore the bravest to my sorrow."[27] But if he must introduce the gods, at any rate let him not dare so completely to misrepresent the greatest of the gods, as to make him say—"O heavens! with my eyes verily I behold a dear friend of mine chased round and round the city, and my heart is sorrowful."[28] Or again: "Woe is me that I am fated to have Sarpedon, dearest of men to me, subdued at the hands of Patroclus the son of Menoetius."[29] For if, my dear Adeimantus, our young men seriously listen to such unworthy representations of the gods, instead of laughing at them as they ought, hardly will any of them deem that he himself, being but a man, can be dishonored by similar actions; neither will he rebuke any inclination which may arise in his mind to say and do the like. And instead of having any shame or endurance, he will be always whining and lamenting on slight occasions.

Yes, he said, that is most true.

Yes, I replied; but that surely is what ought not to be, as the argument has just proved to us; and by that proof we must abide until it is disproved by a better.

It ought not to be.

Neither ought our guardians to be given to laughter. For a fit of laughter which has been indulged to excess almost always demands a violent reaction.

---

[20]*Iliad*, XXIII. 100.
[21]*Odyssey*, XXIV. 6.
[22]Those who will be educated to become guardians of the society.

[23]*Iliad*, XXIV. 10.
[24][Jowett's editors] Perhaps in a metaphorical sense "reeling." Plato has slightly altered the text of Homer.
[25]*Iliad*, XVIII. 23.
[26]*Iliad*, XXII. 414.
[27]*Iliad*, XVIII. 54.
[28]*Iliad*, XXII. 168.
[29]*Iliad*, XVI. 433.

So I believe.

Then persons of worth, even if only mortal men, must not be represented as overcome by laughter, and still less must such a representation of the gods be allowed.

Still less of the gods, as you say, he replied.

Then we shall not suffer such an expression to be used about the gods as that of Homer when he describes how "inextinguishable laughter arose among the blessed gods, when they saw Hephaestus bustling about the mansion."[30] On your views, we must not admit them.

On my views, if you like to father them on me;[31] that we must not admit them is certain.

Again, truth should be highly valued; if we were right in saying that falsehood is useless to the gods, and useful only as a medicine to men, then the use of such medicines should be restricted to physicians; private individuals have no business with them.

Clearly not, he said.

Then if anyone at all is to have the privilege of lying, the rulers of the state should be the persons; and they, in their dealings either with enemies or with their own citizens, may be allowed to lie for the public good. But nobody else should meddle with anything of the kind; and although the rulers have this privilege, for a private man to lie to them in return is to be deemed a more heinous fault than for the patient or the pupil of a gymnasium not to speak the truth about his own bodily illnesses to the physician or to the trainer, or for a sailor not to tell the captain what is happening about the ship and the rest of the crew, and how things are going with himself or his fellow sailors.

Most true, he said.

If, then, the ruler catches in a lie anybody beside himself in the state, "any of the craftsmen, whether he be priest or physician or carpenter,"[32] he will punish him for introducing a practice which is equally subversive and destructive of ship or state.

Most certainly, he said, if our talk about the state is ever translated into action.[33]

In the next place our youth must be temperate?

Certainly.

Are not the chief elements of temperance, speaking generally, obedience to commanders and command of oneself in the pleasures of eating and drinking, and of sexual relations?

True.

Then we shall approve such language as that of Diomede in Homer, "Friend, sit still and obey my word,"[34] and the verses which follow, "The Greeks marched breathing prowess,[35]/ . . . in silent awe of their leaders,"[36] and other sentiments of the same kind.

We shall.

What of this line, "O heavy with wine, who hast the eyes of a dog and the heart of a stag,"[37] and of the words which follow? Would you say that these, or any similar impertinences which private individuals are supposed to address to their rulers, whether in verse or prose, are well or ill spoken?

They are ill spoken.

They may very possibly afford some amusement, but they do not conduce to temperance. And therefore they are likely to do harm to our young men—you would agree with me there?

Yes.

And then, again, to make the wisest of men say that nothing in his opinion is more glorious than "when the tables are full of bread and meat, and the cupbearer carries round wine which he draws from the bowl and pours into the cups";[38] is it fit or conducive to self-control for a young man to hear such words? Or the verse "The saddest of fates is to die and meet destiny from hunger"?[39] What would you say again to the tale of Zeus, who, while other gods and men were asleep and he the only person awake, lay devising plans, but forgot them all in a moment through his lust, and was so completely overcome at the sight of Hera that he would not even go into the hut, but wanted to lie with her on the ground, declaring that he had never been in such a state of rapture before, even when they first used to meet one another "without the knowledge of their parents";[40] or that other tale of how Hephaestus, because of similar goings-on, cast a chain around Ares and Aphrodite?[41]

Indeed, he said, I am strongly of opinion that they ought not to hear that sort of thing.

But any instances of endurance of various ills by famous men which are recounted or represented in drama, these they ought to see and hear; as, for example, what is said in the verses "He smote his breast, and thus reproached his heart,/Endure, my heart; far worse hast thou endured!"[42]

---

[30]*Iliad*, I. 599. The gods ridiculed his lameness.
[31]"To father them on me" means here "to call me the author of them."
[32]*Odyssey*, XVII. 383.
[33][Jowett] Or, "if his words are accompanied by actions."

[34]*Iliad*, IV. 412.
[35]*Iliad*, III. 3.
[36]*Iliad*, IV. 431.
[37]*Iliad*, I. 225.
[38]*Odyssey*, IX. 8.
[39]*Odyssey*, XII. 342.
[40]*Iliad*, XIV. 294.
[41]*Odyssey*, VIII. 266.
[42]*Odyssey*, XX. 17–18.

Certainly, he said.

In the next place, we must not let them be receivers of bribes or lovers of money.

Certainly not.

Neither must we sing to them of "gifts persuading gods, and persuading reverend kings."[43] Neither is Phoenix, the tutor of Achilles, to be approved or deemed to have given his pupil good counsel when he told him that if the Greeks offered him gifts he should assist them;[44] but that without a gift he should not lay aside his anger. Neither will we believe or acknowledge Achilles himself to have been such a lover of money that he took Agamemnon's gifts, or that when he had received payment he restored the dead body of Hector, but that without payment he was unwilling to do so.[45]

Undoubtedly, he said, these are not sentiments which can be approved.

Loving Homer as I do, I hardly like to say that to attribute these feelings to Achilles, or to accept such a narrative from others, is downright impiety. As little can I believe the narrative of his insolence to Apollo, where he says, "Thou hast wronged me, O far-darter,[46] most abominable of deities./ Verily I would be even with thee, if I had only the power";[47] or his insubordination to the river god,[48] on whose divinity he is ready to lay hands; or his offering to the dead Patroclus of his own hair,[49] which had been previously dedicated to the other river-god Spercheius, and that he actually performed this vow; or that he dragged Hector round the tomb of Patroclus,[50] and slaughtered the captives at the pyre;[51] all this we shall declare to be untrue, and shall not allow our citizens to be persuaded that he, the wise Cheiron's pupil, the son of a goddess and of Peleus who was the most modest of men and third in descent from Zeus, was so confused within as to be afflicted with two seemingly inconsistent diseases, meanness, not untainted by avarice, and overweening contempt of gods and men.

You are quite right, he replied.

And let us equally refuse to believe, or allow to be repeated, the tale of Theseus son of Poseidon, and Pirithous son of Zeus, going forth as they did to perpetrate a horrid rape,[52] or of any other hero or son of a god daring to do such impious and dreadful things as they falsely ascribe to them in our day: and let us further compel the poets to declare either that these acts were not done by them, or that they were not the sons of gods—both in the same breath they shall not be permitted to affirm. We will not have them trying to persuade our youth that the gods are the authors of evil, and that heroes are no better than men—sentiments which, as we were saying, are neither pious nor true, for we have already proved that evil cannot come from the gods.

Assuredly not.

And further they are likely to have a bad effect on those who hear them; for everybody will begin to excuse his own vices when he is convinced that similar wickednesses are always being perpetrated by "the kindred of the gods, near descendants of Zeus, who worship him their ancestor at his altar, aloft in air on the peak of Ida," and who have "the blood of deities yet flowing in their veins."[53]

And therefore let us put an end to such tales, lest they engender laxity of morals among the young.

By all means, he replied.

But now that we are determining what classes of tales are or are not to be told, let us see whether any have been omitted by us. The manner in which gods and demigods and heroes and the world below should be treated has been already laid down.

Very true.

And it remains for us to decide what to say about men?

Clearly so.

But we are not in a condition to answer this question at present, my friend.

Why not?

Because, if I am not mistaken, we shall have to say that, about men, poets and storytellers are guilty of making the gravest misstatements when they tell us that wicked men are often happy and the good miserable; and that injustice is profitable when undetected, but that justice is a man's own loss and another's gain—these things we shall forbid them to utter, and command them to sing and describe the opposite.

To be sure we shall, he replied.

But if you admit that I am right in this, then I shall maintain that you have implied the principle for which we have been all along contending.

I grant the truth of your inference.

That such things are or are not to be said about men is a question which we cannot determine until we have discovered what justice is, and how naturally advantageous to the possessor, whether he seem to be just or not.

[43][Jowett] Quoted by Suidas as attributed to Hesiod.
[44]*Iliad*, IX. 515.
[45]*Iliad*, XXIV. 175.
[46]"Far-darter" refers to Apollo's skill as an archer.
[47]*Iliad*, XXII. 15.
[48]*Iliad*, XXI. 130, 233 *ff*.
[49]*Iliad*, XXIII. 151.
[50]*Iliad*, XXII. 395.
[51]*Iliad*, XXIII. 175
[52]Pirithous aided Theseus in carrying off Helen, then a child, to Aphidnae. Theseus then aided Pirithous in an attempt to carry off Persephone from the underworld.

[53][Jowett] From the *Niobe* of Aeschylus.

Most true, he said.

Enough of the subjects of poetry: let us now speak of the style; and when this has been considered, both matter and manner will have been completely treated.

I do not understand what you mean, said Adeimantus.

Then I must make you understand; and perhaps I may be more intelligible if I put the matter in this way. You are aware, I suppose, that all mythology and poetry is a narration of events, either past, present, or to come?

Certainly, he replied.

And narration may be either simple narration, or imitation, or a union of the two?[54]

That again, he said, I do not quite understand.

I fear that I must be an absurdly vague teacher. Like a bad speaker, therefore, I will not take the whole of the subject, but will break a piece off in illustration of my meaning. You know the first lines of the *Iliad*, in which the poet says that Chryses prayed Agamemnon to release his daughter, and that Agamemnon flew into a passion with him; whereupon Chryses, failing of his object, invoked the anger of the god against the Achaeans. Now as far as these lines, "And he prayed all the Greeks, but especially the two sons of Atreus, the chiefs of the people,"[55] the poet is speaking in his own person; he never even tries to distract us by assuming another character. But in what follows he takes the person of Chryses, and then he does all that he can to make us believe that the speaker is not Homer, but the aged priest himself. And in this double form he has cast the entire narrative of the events which occurred at Troy and in Ithaca and throughout the *Odyssey*.

Yes.

And a narrative it remains both in the speeches which the poet recites from time to time and in the intermediate passages?

Quite true.

But when the poet speaks in the person of another, may we not say that he assimilates his style to that of the person who, as he informs you, is going to speak?

Certainly we may.

And this assimilation of himself to another, either by the use of voice or gesture, is the imitation of the person whose character he assumes?

Of course.

Then in this case the narrative of the poet, whether Homer or another, may be said to proceed by way of imitation?

Very true.

Or, if the poet were at no time to disguise himself, then again the imitation would be dropped, and his poetry become simple narration. However, in order that you may not have to repeat that you do not understand, I will show how the change might be effected. If Homer had said, "The priest came, having his daughter's ransom in his hands, supplicating the Achaeans, and above all the kings"; and then if, instead of speaking in the person of Chryses, he had continued in his own person, the words would have been, not imitation, but simple narration. The passage would have run as follows (I am no poet, and therefore I drop the meter), "The priest came and prayed the gods on behalf of the Greeks that they might capture Troy and return safely home, but begged that they would give him back his daughter, and take the ransom which he brought, and respect the god. Thus he spoke, and the other Greeks revered the priest and assented. But Agamemnon was wroth, and bade him depart and not come again, lest the staff and chaplets[56] of the god should be of no avail to him, and told him that before his daughter should be released, she should grow old with him in Argos. And then he told him to go away and not to provoke him, if he intended to get home unscathed. And the old man went away in fear and silence, and, when he had left the camp, he called upon Apollo by his many names, reminding him of everything which he had done pleasing to him, whether in building his temples or in offering sacrifice, and praying that his good deeds might be returned to him and that the Achaeans might expiate his tears by the arrows of the god"—and so on. In this way the whole becomes simple narrative.

I understand, he said.

And you must realize that an opposite case occurs, when the poet's comments are omitted and the passages of dialogue only are left.

That also, he said, I understand; you mean, for example, as in tragedy.

You have conceived my meaning perfectly; and I think I can now make clear what you failed to apprehend before, that some poetry and mythology are wholly imitative (and, as you say, I mean tragedy and comedy); there is likewise the opposite style, in which the poet is the only speaker—of this the dithyramb affords the best example; and the combination of both is found in epic, and in several other styles of poetry. Do I take you with me?

Yes, he said; I see now what you meant.

I will ask you to remember also what I began by saying, that we had done with the subject and might proceed to the style.

Yes, I remember.

[54]Here Plato employs *imitation* not in the sense in which Socrates and Ion discuss copies of the Platonic ideas but to distinguish narrative techniques.
[55]*Iliad*, I. 15–16.

[56]Wreaths or garlands for the head.

In saying this, I intended to imply that we must come to an understanding about the mimetic art— whether the poets, in narrating their stories, are to be allowed by us to imitate, and if so, whether in whole or in part, and if the latter, in what parts; or should all imitation be prohibited?

You mean, I suspect, to ask whether tragedy and comedy shall be admitted into our state?

Perhaps, I said; but there may be more than this in question: I really do not know as yet, but whither the argument may blow, thither we go.

And go we will, he said.

Then, Adeimantus, let me ask you to consider whether our guardians should or should not be fond of imitation; or rather, has not this question been decided by the rule already laid down that one man can only do one thing well, and not many; and that one who grasps at many will altogether fail of gaining much reputation in any?

Certainly.

And this is equally true of imitation; no one man can imitate many things as well as he would imitate a single one?

He cannot.

Then the same person will hardly be able to play a serious part in life, and at the same time to be an imitator and imitate many other parts as well; for even when two species of imitation are nearly allied, the same persons cannot succeed in both, as, for example, the writers of tragedy and comedy—did you not just now call them imitations?

Yes, I did; and you are right in thinking that the same persons cannot succeed in both.

Any more than they can be rhapsodists and actors at once?

True.

Neither do comic and tragic writers employ the same actors; yet all these things are imitations.

They are so.

And human nature, Adeimantus, appears to have been coined into yet smaller pieces, and to be as incapable of imitating many things well, as of performing well the actions of which the imitations are copies.

Quite true, he replied.

If then we adhere to our original notion and bear in mind that our guardians, released from every other business, are to dedicate themselves wholly to the maintenance of the freedom of the state, making this their craft and engaging in no work which does not bear on this end, then they ought not to practice or even imitate anything else; if they imitate at all, they should imitate from youth upward only those characters which are suitable to their profession—the courageous, temperate, holy, free, and the like; but they should not depict or be skillful at imitating any kind of illiberality or baseness, lest the fruit of imitation should be reality. Did you

never observe how imitations, beginning in early youth and continuing far into life, at length grow into habits and become a second nature, affecting body, voice, and mind?

Yes, certainly, he said.

Then, I said, we will not allow those for whom we profess a care and of whom we say that they ought to be good men, to imitate a woman, whether young or old, quarreling with her husband, or striving and vaunting against the gods in conceit of her happiness, or when she is in affliction, or sorrow, or weeping; and certainly not one who is in sickness, love, or labor.

Very right, he said.

Neither must they represent slaves, male or female, performing the offices of slaves?

They must not.

And surely not bad men, whether cowards or any others, who do the reverse of what we have just been prescribing, who scold or mock or revile one another in drink or out of drink, or who in any other manner sin against themselves and their neighbors in word or deed, as the manner of such is. Neither should they be trained to imitate the action or speech of madmen; they must be able to recognize madness and vice in man or woman, but none of these things is to be practiced or imitated.

Very true, he replied.

Neither may they imitate smiths or other artificers, or oarsmen, or boatswains, or the like?

How can they, he said, when they are not allowed to apply their minds to the callings of any of these?

Nor may they imitate the neighing of horses, the bellowing of bulls, the murmur of rivers and roll of the ocean, thunder, and all that sort of thing?

Nay, he said, if madness be forbidden, neither may they copy the behavior of madmen.

You mean, I said, if I understand you aright, that there is one sort of narrative style which is likely to be employed by an upright and good man when he has anything to say, and another sort, very unlike it, which will be preferred by a man of an opposite character and education.

And which are these two sorts? he asked.

As for the man of orderly life, I answered, when the time comes to describe some saying or action of another good man—I think he will be willing to personate him, and will not be ashamed of this sort of imitation: he will be most ready to play the part of the good man when he is acting firmly and wisely; less often and in a less degree when he is overtaken by illness or love or drink, or has met with any other disaster. But when he comes to a character which is unworthy of him, he will not seriously assume the likeness of his inferior, and will do so, if at all, for a moment only when he is performing some good action; at other times he will be ashamed, both because he is not trained in imitation of such characters, and because he disdains to fashion and frame himself after the baser models; he feels the employment of such an art, unless in jest, to be beneath him.

So I should expect, he replied.

Then he will adopt a mode of narration such as we have illustrated out of Homer, that is to say, his style will be both imitative and narrative; but there will be, in a long story, only a small proportion of the former. Do you agree?

Certainly, he said; that is the model which such a speaker must necessarily take.

But there is another sort of character who will narrate anything, and, the worse he is, the more unscrupulous he will be; nothing will be too bad for him: and he will be ready to imitate anything, in right good earnest, and before a large company. As I was just now saying, he will attempt to represent the roll of thunder, the noise of wind and hail, or the creaking of wheels, and pulleys, and the various sounds of flutes, pipes, trumpets, and all sorts of instruments: he will bark like a dog, bleat like a sheep, or crow like a cock; his entire art will consist in imitation of voice and gesture, or will be but slightly blended with narration.

That, he said, will be his mode of speaking.

These, then, are the two kinds of style I had in mind.

Yes.

And you would agree with me in saying that one of them is simple and has but slight changes; and that if an author expresses this style in fitting harmony and rhythm, he will find himself, if he does his work well, keeping pretty much within the limits of a single harmony (for the changes are not great), and in like manner he will make a similar choice of rhythm?

That is quite true, he said.

Whereas the other requires all sorts of harmonies and all sorts of rhythms if the music and the style are to correspond, because the style has all sorts of changes.

That is also perfectly true, he replied.

And do not the two styles, or the mixture of the two, comprehend all poetry and every form of expression in words? No one can say anything except in one or other of them or in both together.

They include all, he said.

And shall we receive into our state all the three styles, or one only of the two unmixed styles? Or would you include the mixed?

I should prefer only to admit the pure imitator of virtue.

Yes, I said, Adeimantus; and yet the mixed style is also charming: and indeed the opposite style to that chosen by you is by far the most popular with children and their attendants, and with the masses.

I do not deny it.

But I suppose you would argue that such a style is unsuitable to our state, in which human nature is not twofold or manifold, for one man plays one part only?

Yes; quite unsuitable.

And this is the reason why in our state, and in our state only, we shall find a shoemaker to be a shoemaker and not a pilot also, and a husbandman to be a husbandman and not a dicast[57] also, and a soldier a soldier and not a trader also, and the same throughout?

True, he said.

And therefore when any one of these pantomimic gentlemen, who are so clever that they can imitate anything, comes to us and makes a proposal to exhibit himself and his poetry, we will fall down and worship him as a sacred, marvelous, and delightful being; but we must also inform him that in our state such as he are not permitted to exist; the law will not allow them. And so when we have anointed him with myrrh, and set a garland of wool upon his head, we shall send him away to another city. For we mean to employ for our souls' health the rougher and severer poet or storyteller, who will imitate the style of the virtuous only, and will follow those models which we prescribed at first when we began the education of our soldiers.

We certainly will, he said, if we have the power.

Then now, my friend, I said, that part of music or literary education which relates to the story or myth may be considered to be finished; for the matter and manner have both been discussed.

I think so too, he said.

Next in order will follow melody and song.

That is obvious.

Everyone now would be able to discover what we ought to say about them, if we are to be consistent with ourselves.

I fear, said Glaucon, laughing, that the word *everyone* hardly includes me, for I cannot at the moment say what they should be, though I have a suspicion.

At any rate you are aware that a song or ode has three parts—the words, the melody, and the rhythm.

Yes, he said; so much as that I know.

And as for the words, there will surely be no difference between words which are and which are not set to music; both will conform to the same laws, and these have been already determined by us?

Yes.

And the melody and rhythm will be in conformity with the words?

---

[57] Juror.

Certainly.

We were saying, when we spoke of the subject matter, that we had no need of lamentation and strains of sorrow?

True.

And which are the harmonies expressive of sorrow? You are musical, and can tell me.

The harmonies which you mean are the mixed or tenor Lydian, and the full-toned or bass Lydians, and suchlike.

These then, I said, must be banished; even to women who have a character to maintain they are of no use, and much less to men.

Certainly.

In the next place, drunkenness and softness and indolence are utterly unbecoming the character of our guardians.

Utterly unbecoming.

And which are the soft and convivial harmonies?

The Ionian, he replied, and some of the Lydian which are termed relaxed.

Well, and are these of any use for warlike men?

Quite the reverse, he replied; and if so the Dorian and the Phrygian are the only ones which you have left.

I answered: Of the harmonies I know nothing, but would have you leave me one which can render the note or accent which a brave man utters in warlike action and in stern resolve; and when his cause is failing, and he is going to wounds or death or is overtaken by disaster in some other form, at every such crisis he meets the blows of fortune with firm step and a determination to endure; and an opposite kind for times of peace and freedom of action, when there is no pressure of necessity, and he is seeking to persuade God by prayer, or man by instruction and admonition, or when on the other hand he is expressing his willingness to yield to the persuasion or entreaty or admonition of others. And when in this manner he has attained his end, I would have the music show him not carried away by his success, but acting moderately and wisely in all circumstances, and acquiescing in the event. These two harmonies I ask you to leave; the strain of necessity and the strain of freedom, the strain of the unfortunate and the strain of the fortunate, the strain of courage, and the strain of temperance; these, I say, leave.

And these, he replied, are the Dorian and Phrygian harmonies of which I was just now speaking.

Then, I said, if these and these only are to be used in our songs and melodies, we shall not want multiplicity of strings or a panharmonic scale?

I suppose not.

Then we shall not maintain the artificers of lyres with three corners and complex scales, or the makers of any other many-stringed, curiously harmonized instruments?

Certainly not.

But what do you say to flute-makers and flute-players? Would you admit them into our state when you reflect that in this composite use of harmony the flute is worse than any stringed instrument; even the panharmonic music is only an imitation of the flute?

Clearly not.

There remain then only the lyre and the harp for use in the city, and the shepherds in the country may have some kind of pipe.

That is surely the conclusion to be drawn from the argument.

The preferring of Apollo and his instruments to Marsyas and his instruments is not at all strange, I said.[58]

Not at all, he replied.

And so, by the dog of Egypt, we have been unconsciously purging the state, which not long ago we termed luxurious.

And we have done wisely, he replied.

Then let us now finish the purgation, I said. Next in order to harmonies, rhythms will naturally follow, and they should be subject to the same rules, for we ought not to seek out complex systems of meter, and a variety of feet, but rather to discover what rhythms are the expressions of a courageous and harmonious life; and when we have found them, we shall adapt the foot and the melody to words having a like spirit, not the words to the foot and melody. To say what these rhythms are will be your duty—you must teach me them, as you have already taught me the harmonies.

But, indeed, he replied, I cannot tell you. I know from observation that there are some three principles of rhythm out of which metrical systems are framed, just as in sounds there are four notes[59] out of which all the harmonies are composed. But of what sort of lives they are severally the imitations I am unable to say.

Then, I said, we must take Damon[60] into our counsels; and he will tell us what rhythms are expressive of meanness, or insolence, or fury, or other unworthiness, and what are to be reserved for the expression of opposite feelings. And I think that I have an indistinct recollection of his mentioning a complex Cretic rhythm; also a dactylic or heroic, and he arranged them in some manner which I do not quite understand, making the rhythms equal in the rise and fall of the foot, long and short alternating; and, unless I am mistaken, he spoke of an iambic as well as of a trochaic rhythm, and

---

[58]In a contest with Apollo, which Marsyas lost, Marsyas played the flute, Apollo the lyre.

[59][Jowett] I.e., the four notes of the tetrachord.

[60]A celebrated musician and sophist.

assigned to them short and long quantities.[61] Also in some cases he appeared to praise or censure the movement of the foot quite as much as the rhythm; or perhaps a combination of the two; for I am not certain what he meant. These matters, however, as I was saying, had better be referred to Damon himself, for the analysis of the subject would be difficult, you know?

Rather so, I should say.

But it does not require much analysis to see that grace or the absence of grace accompanies good or bad rhythm.

None at all.

And also that good and bad rhythm naturally assimilate to a good and bad style; and that harmony and discord in like manner follow style; for our principle is that rhythm and harmony are regulated by the words, and not the words by them.

Just so, he said, they should follow the words.

And will not the words and the character of the style depend on the temper of the soul?

Yes.

And everything else on the style?

Yes.

Then beauty of style and harmony and grace and good rhythm depend on simplicity—I mean the true simplicity of a rightly and nobly ordered mind and character, not that other simplicity which is only a euphemism for folly?[62]

Very true, he replied.

And if our youth are to do their work in life, must they not make these graces and harmonies their perpetual aim?

They must.

And surely the art of the painter and every other creative and constructive art are full of them—weaving, embroidery, architecture, and every kind of manufacture; also nature, animal and vegetable—in all of them there is grace or the absence of grace. And ugliness and discord and inharmonious motion are nearly allied to ill words and ill nature, as grace and harmony are the twin sisters of goodness and self-restraint and bear their likeness.

That is quite true, he said.

But shall our superintendence go no further, and are the poets only to be required by us to express the image of the good in their works, on pain, if they do anything else, of expulsion from our state? Or is the same control to be extended to other artists, and are they also to be prohibited from exhibiting the opposite forms of vice and intemperance and meanness and deformity in sculpture and building and the other creative arts; and is he who cannot conform to this rule of ours to be prevented from practicing his art in our state, lest the taste of our citizens be corrupted by him? We would not have our guardians grow up amid images of moral deformity, as in some noxious pasture, and there browse and feed upon many a baneful herb and flower day by day, little by little, until they silently gather a festering mass of corruption in their own soul. Let us rather search for artists who are gifted to discern the true nature of the beautiful and graceful; then will our youth dwell in a land of health, amid fair sights and sounds, and receive the good in everything; and beauty, the effluence of fair works, shall flow into the eye and ear, like a health-giving breeze from a purer region, and insensibly draw the soul from earliest years into likeness and sympathy with the beauty of reason.

There can be no nobler training than that, he replied.

And therefore, I said, Glaucon, musical training is a more potent instrument than any other, because rhythm and harmony find their way into the inward places of the soul, on which they mightily fasten, imparting grace, and making the soul of him who is rightly educated graceful, or of him who is ill educated ungraceful; and also because he who has received this true education of the inner being will most shrewdly perceive omissions or faults in art and nature, and with a true taste, while he praises and rejoices over and receives into his soul the good, and becomes noble and good, he will justly blame and hate the bad, now in the days of his youth, even before he is able to know the reason why; and when reason comes he will recognize and salute the friend with whom his education has made him long familiar.

Yes, he said, I quite agree with you in thinking that it is for such reasons that they should be trained in music.

Just as in learning to read, I said, we were satisfied when we knew the letters of the alphabet, few as they are, in all their recurring combinations; not slighting them as unimportant whether they occupy a space large or small, but everywhere eager to make them out, because we knew we should not be perfect in the art of reading until we could do so:

True—

And as we recognize the reflection of letters in water, or in a mirror, only when we know the letters themselves, the same art and study giving us the knowledge of both:

Exactly—

---

[61][Jowett] Socrates expresses himself carelessly in accordance with his assumed ignorance of the details of the subject. In the first part of the sentence he appears to be speaking of paeonic rhythms, which are in the ratio of 3/2; in the second part, of dactylic and anapestic rhythms, which are in the ratio of 1/1; in the last clause, of iambic and trochaic rhythms, which are in the ratio of 1/2 or 2/1.

[62]Plato's conception of beauty is abstract. It is an "idea," and it has obvious affinities to mathematical proportion. Thus Plato assumes a principle of beauty exterior to a work, to which, one might conclude, the work should conform. The work does not generate its own principles of beauty. Beauty is equated with the good and with the one; lowly imitations, with the many. Lowly imitations copy copies of the single or *one* idea from which the copies are ultimately derived. This single idea is the good. The matter of beauty as harmony and proportion is discussed in *Laws*.

Even so, as I maintain, neither we nor the guardians, whom we say that we have to educate, can ever become musical until we and they know the essential forms of temperance, courage, liberality, magnanimity, and their kindred, as well as the contrary forms, in all their combinations, and can recognize them and their images wherever they are found, not slighting them either in small things or great, but believing them all to be within the sphere of one art and study.

Most assuredly.

And when nobility of soul is observed in harmonious union with beauty of form, and both are cast from the same mold, that will be the fairest of sights to him who has an eye to see it?

The fairest indeed.

From

Book X

Persons of the Dialogue

Socrates
Glaucon

Of the many excellences which I perceive in the order of our state, there is none which upon reflection pleases me better than the rule about poetry.

To what do you refer?

To our refusal to admit the imitative kind of poetry, for it certainly ought not to be received; as I see far more clearly now that the parts of the soul have been distinguished.

What do you mean?

Speaking in confidence, for you will not denounce me to the tragedians and the rest of the imitative tribe, all poetical imitations are ruinous to the understanding of the hearers, unless as an antidote they possess the knowledge of the true nature of the originals.

Explain the purport of your remark.

Well, I will tell you, although I have always from my earliest youth had an awe and love of Homer which even now makes the words falter on my lips, for he seems to be the great captain and teacher of the whole of that noble tragic company; but a man is not to be reverenced more than the truth, and therefore I will speak out.

Very good, he said.

Listen to me then, or rather, answer me.

Put your question.

Can you give me a general definition of imitation? For I really do not myself understand what it professes to be.

A likely thing, then, that I should know.

There would be nothing strange in that, for the duller eye may often see a thing sooner than the keener.

Very true, he said; but in your presence, even if I had any faint notion, I could not muster courage to utter it. Will you inquire yourself?

Well then, shall we begin the inquiry at this point, following our usual method: Whenever a number of individuals have a common name, we assume that there is one corresponding idea or form[63]— do you understand me?

I do.

Let us take, for our present purpose, any instance of such a group; there are beds and tables in the world—many of each, are there not?

Yes.

But there are only two ideas or forms of such furniture—one the idea of a bed, the other of a table.

True.

And the maker of either of them makes a bed or he makes a table for our use, in accordance with the idea—that is our way of speaking in this and similar instances—but no artificer makes the idea itself: how could he?

Impossible.

And there is another artificer—I should like to know what you would say of him.

Who is he?

One who is the maker of all the works of all other workmen.

What an extraordinary man!

Wait a little, and there will be more reason for your saying so. For this is the craftsman who is able to make not only furniture of every kind, but all that grows out of the earth, and all living creatures, himself included; and besides these he can make earth and sky and the gods, and all the things which are in heaven or in the realm of Hades under the earth.

He must be a wizard and no mistake.

Oh! You are incredulous, are you? Do you mean that there is no such maker or creator, or that in one sense there might be a maker of all these things but in another not? Do you see that there is a way in which you could make them all yourself?

And what way is this? he asked.

An easy way enough; or rather, there are many ways in which the feat might be quickly and easily accomplished, none quicker than that of turning a mirror round and round—you would soon enough make the sun and the heavens, and the earth and yourself, and other animals and plants,

---

[63][Jowett's editors] Or (probably better): "we have been accustomed to assume that there is one single idea corresponding to each group of particulars; and to these we give the same name (as we give the idea)."

and furniture and all the other things of which we were just now speaking, in the mirror.

Yes, he said; but they would be appearances only.

Very good, I said, you are coming to the point now. And the painter too is, as I conceive, just such another—a creator of appearances, is he not?

Of course.

But then I suppose you will say that what he creates is untrue. And yet there is a sense in which the painter also creates a bed? Is there not?

Yes, he said, but here again, an appearance only.

And what of the maker of the bed? Were you not saying that he too makes, not the idea which according to our view is the real object denoted by the word *bed,* but only a particular bed?

Yes, I did.

Then if he does not make a real object he cannot make what *is,* but only some semblance of existence; and if anyone were to say that the work of the maker of the bed, or of any other workman, has real existence, he could hardly be supposed to be speaking the truth.

Not, at least, he replied, in the view of those who make a business of these discussions.

No wonder, then, that his work too is an indistinct expression of truth.

No wonder.

Suppose now that by the light of the examples just offered we inquire who this imitator is?

If you please.

Well then, here we find three beds: one existing in nature, which is made by God, as I think that we may say—for no one else can be the maker?

No one, I think.

There is another which is the work of the carpenter?

Yes.

And the work of the painter is a third?

Yes.

Beds, then, are of three kinds, and there are three artists who superintend them: God, the maker of the bed, and the painter?

Yes, there are three of them.

God, whether from choice or from necessity, made one bed in nature and one only: two or more such beds neither ever have been nor ever will be made by God.

Why is that?

Because even if he had made but two, a third would still appear behind them of which they again both possessed the form, and that would be the real bed and not the two others.

Very true, he said.

God knew this, I suppose, and he desired to be the real maker of a real bed, not a kind of maker of a kind of bed, and therefore he created a bed which is essentially and by nature one only.

So it seems.

Shall we, then, speak of him as the natural author or maker of the bed?

Yes, he replied; inasmuch as by the natural process of creation he is the author of this and of all other things.

And what shall we say of the carpenter—is not he also the maker of a bed?

Yes.

But would you call the painter an artificer and maker?

Certainly not.

Yet if he is not the maker, what is he in relation to the bed?

I think, he said, that we may fairly designate him as the imitator of that which the others make.

Good, I said; then you call him whose product is third in the descent from nature, an imitator?

Certainly, he said.

And so if the tragic poet is an imitator, he too is thrice removed from the king and from the truth; and so are all other imitators.

That appears to be so.

Then about the imitator we are agreed. And what about the painter?—Do you think he tries to imitate in each case that which originally exists in nature, or only the creations of artificers?

The latter.

As they are or as they appear? You have still to determine this.

What do you mean?

I mean to ask whether a bed really becomes different when it is seen from different points of view, obliquely or directly or from any other point of view? Or does it simply appear different, without being really so? And the same of all things.

Yes, he said, the difference is only apparent.

Now let me ask you another question: Which is the art of painting designed to be—an imitation of things as they are, or as they appear—of appearance or of reality?

Of appearance, he said.

Then the imitator is a long way off the truth, and can reproduce all things because he lightly touches on a small part of them, and that part an image. For example: A painter will paint a cobbler, carpenter, or any other artisan, though he knows nothing of their arts; and, if he is a good painter, he may deceive children or simple persons when he shows them his picture of a carpenter from a distance, and they will fancy that they are looking at a real carpenter.

Certainly.

And surely, my friend, this is how we should regard all

such claims: whenever anyone informs us that he has found a man who knows all the arts, and all things else that anybody knows, and every single thing with a higher degree of accuracy than any other man—whoever tells us this, I think that we can only retort that he is a simple creature who seems to have been deceived by some wizard or imitator whom he met, and whom he thought all-knowing, because he himself was unable to analyze the nature of knowledge and ignorance and imitation.

Most true.

And next, I said, we have to consider tragedy and its leader, Homer; for we hear some persons saying that these poets know all the arts; and all things human; where virtue and vice are concerned, and indeed all divine things too; because the good poet cannot compose well unless he knows his subject, and he who has not this knowledge can never be a poet. We ought to consider whether here also there may not be a similar illusion. Perhaps they may have come across imitators and been deceived by them; they may not have remembered when they saw their works that these were thrice removed from the truth, and could easily be made without any knowledge of the truth, because they are appearances only and not realities? Or, after all, they may be in the right, and good poets do really know the things about which they seem to the many to speak so well?

The question, he said, should by all means be considered.

Now do you suppose that if a person were able to make the original as well as the image, he would seriously devote himself to the image-making branch? Would he allow imitation to be the ruling principle of his life, as if he had nothing higher in him?

I should say not.

But the real artist, who had real knowledge of those things which he chose also to imitate, would be interested in realities and not in imitations; and would desire to leave as memorials of himself works many and fair; and, instead of being the author of encomiums, he would prefer to be the theme of them.

Yes, he said, that would be to him a source of much greater honor and profit.

Now let us refrain, I said, from calling Homer or any other poet to account regarding those arts to which his poems incidentally refer: we will not ask them, in case any poet has been a doctor and not a mere imitator of medical parlance, to show what patients have been restored to health by a poet, ancient or modern, as they were by Asclepius; or what disciples in medicine a poet has left behind him, like the Asclepiads. Nor shall we press the same question upon them about the other arts. But we have a right to know respecting warfare, strategy, the administration of states and the education

of man, which are the chiefest and noblest subjects of his poems, and we may fairly ask him about them. "Friend Homer," then we say to him, "if you are only in the second remove from truth in what you say of virtue, and not in the third—not an image-maker, that is, by our definition, an imitator—and if you are able to discern what pursuits make men better or worse in private or public life, tell us what state was ever better governed by your help? The good order of Lacedaemon is due to Lycurgus, and many other cities great and small have been similarly benefited by others; but who says that you have been a good legislator to them and have done them any good? Italy and Sicily boast of Charondas, and there is Solon who is renowned among us; but what city has anything to say about you?" Is there any city which he might name?

I think not, said Glaucon; not even the Homerids themselves pretend that he was a legislator.

Well, but is there any war on record which was carried on successfully owing to his leadership or counsel?

There is not.

Or is there anything comparable to those clever improvements in the arts, or in other operations, which are said to have been due to men of practical genius such as Thales the Milesian or Anacharsis the Scythian?

There is absolutely nothing of the kind.

But, if Homer never did any public service, was he privately a guide or teacher of any? Had he in his lifetime friends who loved to associate with him, and who handed down to posterity a Homeric way of life, such as was established by Pythagoras who was especially beloved for this reason and whose followers are to this day conspicuous among others by what they term the Pythagorean way of life?

Nothing of the kind is recorded of him. For surely, Socrates, Creophylus, the companion of Homer, that child of flesh, whose name always makes us laugh, might be more justly ridiculed for his want of breeding, if what is said is true, that Homer was greatly neglected by him in his own day when he was alive?

Yes, I replied, that is the tradition. But can you imagine, Glaucon, that if Homer had really been able to educate and improve mankind—if he had been capable of knowledge and not been a mere imitator—can you imagine, I say, that he would not have attracted many followers, and been honored and loved by them? Protagoras of Abdera, and Prodicus of Ceos, and a host of others, have only to whisper to their contemporaries: "You will never be able to manage either your own house or your own state until you appoint us to be your ministers of education"—and this ingenious device of theirs has such an effect in making men love them that their companions all but carry them about on their shoulders. And is it conceivable that the contemporaries of Homer, or again of Hesiod, would have allowed either of them to go about as rhapsodists, if they had really been able to help mankind forward in virtue? Would they not have been as unwilling to part with them as with gold, and have compelled them to stay at home with them? Or, if the master would not stay, then the disciples would have followed him about everywhere, until they had got education enough?

Yes, Socrates, that, I think, is quite true.

Then must we not infer that all these poetical individuals, beginning with Homer, are only imitators, who copy images of virtue and the other themes of their poetry, but have no contact with the truth? The poet is like a painter who, as we have already observed, will make a likeness of a cobbler though he understands nothing of cobbling; and his picture is good enough for those who know no more than he does, and judge only by colors and figures.

Quite so.

In like manner the poet with his words and phrases[64] may be said to lay on the colors of the several arts, himself understanding their nature only enough to imitate them; and other people, who are as ignorant as he is, and judge only from his words, imagine that if he speaks of cobbling, or of military tactics, or of anything else, in meter and harmony and rhythm, he speaks very well—such is the sweet influence which melody and rhythm by nature have. For I am sure that you know what a poor appearance the works of poets make when stripped of the colors which art puts upon them, and recited in simple prose. You have seen some examples?

Yes, he said.

They are like faces which were never really beautiful, but only blooming, seen when the bloom of youth has passed away from them?

Exactly.

Come now, and observe this point: The imitator or maker of the image knows nothing, we have said, of true existence; he knows appearances only. Am I not right?

Yes.

Then let us have a clear understanding, and not be satisfied with half an explanation.

Proceed.

Of the painter we say that he will paint reins, and he will paint a bit?

Yes.

And the worker in leather and brass will make them?

Certainly.

But does the painter know the right form of the bit and reins? Nay, hardly even the workers in brass and leather who

make them; only the horseman who knows how to use them—he knows their right form.

Most true.

And may we not say the same of all things?

What?

That there are three arts which are concerned with all things: one which uses, another which makes, a third which imitates them?

Yes.

And the excellence and beauty and rightness of every structure, animate or inanimate, and of every action of man, is relative solely to the use for which nature or the artist has intended them.

True.

Then beyond doubt it is the user who has the greatest experience of them, and he must report to the maker the good or bad qualities which develop themselves in use; for example, the flute-player will tell the flute-maker which of his flutes is satisfactory to the performer;[65] he will tell him how he ought to make them, and the other will attend to his instructions?

Of course.

So the one pronounces with knowledge about the goodness and badness of flutes, while the other, confiding in him, will make them accordingly?

True.

The instrument is the same, but about the excellence or badness of it the maker will possess a correct belief, since he associates with one who knows, and is compelled to hear what he has to say; whereas the user will have knowledge?

True.

But will the imitator have either? Will he know from use whether or no that which he paints is correct or beautiful? Or will he have right opinion from being compelled to associate with another who knows and gives him instructions about what he should paint?

Neither.

Then an imitator will no more have true opinion than he will have knowledge about the goodness or badness of his models?

I suppose not.

The imitative poet will be in a brilliant state of intelligence about the theme of his poetry?

Nay, very much the reverse.

And still he will go on imitating without knowing what makes a thing good or bad, and may be expected therefore

---

[65][Jowett's editors] Or, to avoid the repetition of ὑπηρετεῖν in a different sense: "will make a report to the flute-maker, *who assists him in his playing*, about the flutes."

to imitate only that which appears to be good to the ignorant multitude?

Just so.

Thus far then we are pretty well agreed that the imitator has no knowledge worth mentioning of what he imitates. Imitation is only a kind of play or sport, and the tragic poets, whether they write in iambic or in heroic[66] verse, are imitators in the highest degree?

Very true.

And now tell me, I conjure you—this imitation is concerned with an object which is thrice removed from the truth?

Certainly.

And what kind of faculty in man is that to which imitation makes its special appeal?

What do you mean?

I will explain: The same body does not appear equal to our sight when seen near and when seen at a distance?

True.

And the same objects appear straight when looked at out of the water, and crooked when in the water; and the concave becomes convex, owing to the illusion about colors to which the sight is liable. Thus every sort of confusion is revealed within us; and this is that weakness of the human mind on which the art of painting in light and shadow, the art of conjuring, and many other ingenious devices impose, having an effect upon us like magic.

True.

And the arts of measuring and numbering and weighing come to the rescue of the human understanding—there is the beauty of them—with the result that the apparent greater or less, or more or heavier, no longer have the mastery over us, but give way before the power of calculation and measuring and weighing?

Most true.

And this, surely, must be the work of the calculating and rational principle in the soul?

To be sure.

And often when this principle measures and certifies that some things are equal, or that some are greater or less than others, it is, at the same time, contradicted by the appearance which the objects present?

True.

But did we not say that such a contradiction is impossible—the same faculty cannot have contrary opinions at the same time about the same thing?

We did; and rightly.

Then that part of the soul which has an opinion contrary to measure can hardly be the same with that which has an opinion in accordance with measure?

True.

And the part of the soul which trusts to measure and calculation is likely to be the better one?

Certainly.

And therefore that which is opposed to this is probably an inferior principle in our nature?

No doubt.

This was the conclusion at which I was seeking to arrive when I said that painting or drawing, and imitation in general, are engaged upon productions which are far removed from truth, and are also the companions and friends and associates of a principle within us which is equally removed from reason, and that they have no true or healthy aim.

Exactly.

The imitative art is an inferior who from intercourse with an inferior has inferior offspring.

Very true.

And is this confined to the sight only, or does it extend to the hearing also, relating in fact to what we term poetry?

Probably the same would be true of poetry.

Do not rely, I said, on a probability derived from the analogy of painting; but let us once more go directly to that faculty of the mind with which imitative poetry has converse, and see whether it is good or bad.

By all means.

We may state the question thus: Imitation imitates the actions of men, whether voluntary or involuntary, on which, as they imagine, a good or bad result has ensued, and they rejoice or sorrow accordingly. Is there anything more?

No, there is nothing else.

But in all this variety of circumstances is the man at unity with himself—or rather, as in the instance of sight there was confusion and opposition in his opinions about the same things, so here also is there not strife and inconsistency in his life? Though I need hardly raise the question again, for I remember that all this has been already admitted; and the soul has been acknowledged by us to be full of these and ten thousand similar oppositions occurring at the same moment?

And we were right, he said.

Yes, I said, thus far we were right; but there was an omission which must now be supplied.

What was the omission?

Were we not saying that a good man, who has the misfortune to lose his son or anything else which is most dear to him, will bear the loss with more equanimity than another?

Yes, indeed.

---

[66]Dactylic hexameter.

But will he have no sorrow, or shall we say that although he cannot help sorrowing, he will moderate his sorrow?

The latter, he said, is the truer statement.

Tell me: will he be more likely to struggle and hold out against his sorrow when he is seen by his equals, or when he is alone in a deserted place?

The fact of being seen will make a great difference, he said.

When he is by himself he will not mind saying many things which he would be ashamed of anyone hearing, and also doing many things which he would not care to be seen doing?

True.

And doubtless it is the law and reason in him which bids him resist; while it is the affliction itself which is urging him to indulge his sorrow?

True.

But when a man is drawn in two opposite directions, to and from the same object, this, as we affirm, necessarily implies two distinct principles in him?

Certainly.

One of them is ready to follow the guidance of the law?

How do you mean?

The law would say that to be patient under calamity is best, and that we should not give way to impatience, as the good and evil in such things are not clear, and nothing is gained by impatience; also, because no human thing is of serious importance, and grief stands in the way of that which at the moment is most required.

What is most required? he asked.

That we should take counsel about what has happened, and when the dice have been thrown, according to their fall, order our affairs in the way which reason deems best; not, like children who have had a fall, keeping hold of the part struck and wasting time in setting up a howl, but always accustoming the soul forthwith to apply a remedy, raising up that which is sickly and fallen, banishing the cry of sorrow by the healing art.

Yes, he said, that is the true way of meeting the attacks of fortune.

Well then, I said, the higher principle is ready to follow this suggestion of reason?

Clearly.

But the other principle, which inclines us to recollection of our troubles and to lamentation, and can never have enough of them, we may call irrational, useless, and cowardly?

Indeed, we may.

Now does not the principle which is thus inclined to complaint, furnish a great variety of materials for imitation?

Whereas the wise and calm temperament, being always nearly equable, is not easy to imitate or to appreciate when imitated, especially at a public festival when a promiscuous crowd is assembled in a theater. For the feeling represented is one to which they are strangers.

Certainly.

Then the imitative poet who aims at being popular is not by nature made, nor is his art intended, to please or to affect the rational principle in the soul; but he will appeal rather to the lachrymose and fitful temper, which is easily imitated?

Clearly.

And now we may fairly take him and place him by the side of the painter, for he is like him in two ways: first, inasmuch as his creations have an inferior degree of truth—in this, I say, he is like him; and he is also like him in being the associate of an inferior part of the soul; and this is enough to show that we shall be right in refusing to admit him into a state which is to be well ordered, because he awakens and nourishes this part of the soul, and by strengthening it impairs the reason. As in a city when the evil are permitted to wield power and the finer men are put out of the way, so in the soul of each man, as we shall maintain, the imitative poet implants an evil constitution, for he indulges the irrational nature which has no discernment of greater and less, but thinks the same thing at one time great and at another small—he is an imitator of images and is very far removed from the truth.

Exactly.

But we have not yet brought forward the heaviest count in our accusation—the power which poetry has of harming even the good (and there are very few who are not harmed), is surely an awful thing?

Yes, certainly, if the effect is what you say.

Hear and judge: The best of us, as I conceive, when we listen to a passage of Homer or one of the tragedians, in which he represents some hero who is drawling out his sorrows in a long oration, or singing, and smiting his breast—the best of us, you know, delight in giving way to sympathy, and are in raptures at the excellence of the poet who stirs our feelings most.

Yes, of course I know.

But when any sorrow of our own happens to us, then you may observe that we pride ourselves on the opposite quality—we would fain be quiet and patient; this is considered the manly part, and the other which delighted us in the recitation is now deemed to be the part of a woman.

Very true, he said.

Now can we be right in praising and admiring another who is doing that which any one of us would abominate and be ashamed of in his own person?

No, he said, that is certainly not reasonable.

Nay, I said, quite reasonable from one point of view.

What point of view?

If you consider, I said, that when in misfortune we feel a natural hunger and desire to relieve our sorrow by weeping and lamentation, and that this very feeling which is starved and suppressed in our own calamities is satisfied and delighted by the poets—the better nature in each of us, not having been sufficiently trained by reason or habit, allows the sympathetic element to break loose because the sorrow is another's; and the spectator fancies that there can be no disgrace to himself in praising and pitying anyone who while professing to be a brave man, gives way to untimely lamentation; he thinks that the pleasure is a gain, and is far from wishing to lose it by rejection of the whole poem. Few persons ever reflect, as I should imagine, that the contagion must pass from others to themselves. For the pity which has been nourished and strengthened in the misfortunes of others is with difficulty repressed in our own.

How very true!

And does not the same hold also of the ridiculous? There are jests which you would be ashamed to make yourself, and yet on the comic stage, or indeed in private, when you hear them, you are greatly amused by them, and are not at all disgusted at their unseemliness—the case of pity is repeated—there is a principle in human nature which is disposed to raise a laugh, and this, which you once restrained by reason because you were afraid of being thought a buffoon, is now let out again; and having stimulated the risible faculty at the theater, you are betrayed unconsciously to yourself into playing the comic poet at home.

Quite true, he said.

And the same may be said of lust and anger and all the other affections, of desire and pain and pleasure, which are held to be inseparable from every action—in all of them poetry has a like effect; it feeds and waters the passions instead of drying them up; she lets them rule, although they ought to be controlled if mankind are ever to increase in happiness and virtue.

I cannot deny it.

Therefore, Glaucon, I said, whenever you meet with any of the eulogists of Homer declaring that he has been the educator of Hellas, and that he is profitable for education and for the ordering of human things, and that you should take him up again and again and get to know him and regulate your whole life according to him, we may love and honor those who say these things—they are excellent people, as far as their lights extend; and we are ready to acknowledge that Homer is the greatest of poets and first of tragedy writers; but we must remain firm in our conviction that hymns to the gods and praises of famous men are the only poetry which

ought to be admitted into our state. For if you go beyond this and allow the honeyed Muse to enter, either in epic or lyric verse, not law and the reason of mankind, which by common consent have ever been deemed best,[67] but pleasure and pain will be the rulers in our state.

That is most true, he said.

And now since we have reverted to the subject of poetry, let this our defense serve to show the reasonableness of our former judgment in sending away out of our state an art having the tendencies which we have described; for reason constrained us. But that she may not impute to us any harshness or want of politeness, let us tell her that there is an ancient quarrel between philosophy and poetry; of which there are many proofs, such as the saying of "the yelping hound howling at her lord," or of one "mighty in the vain talk of fools," and "the mob of sages circumventing Zeus," and the "subtle thinkers who are beggars after all";[68] and there are innumerable other signs of ancient enmity between them. Notwithstanding this, let us assure the poetry which aims at pleasure, and the art of imitation, that if she will only prove her title to exist in a well-ordered state we shall be delighted to receive her—we are very conscious of her charms; but it would not be right on that account to betray the truth. I dare say, Glaucon, that you are as much charmed by her as I am, especially when she appears in Homer?

Yes, indeed, I am greatly charmed.

Shall I propose, then, that she be allowed to return from exile, but upon this condition only—that she make a defense of herself in some lyrical or other meter?

Certainly.

And we may further grant to those of her defenders who are lovers of poetry and yet not poets the permission to speak in prose on her behalf: let them show not only that she is pleasant but also useful to states and to human life, and we will listen in a kindly spirit; for we shall surely be the gainers if this can be proved, that there is a use in poetry as well as a delight?

Certainly, he said, we shall be the gainers.

If her defense fails, then, my dear friend, like other persons who are enamored of something, but put a restraint upon themselves when they think their desires are opposed to their interests, so too must we after the manner of lovers give her up, though not without a struggle. We too are inspired by that love of such poetry which the education of noble states has implanted in us, and therefore we shall be glad if she appears at her best and truest; but so long as she

---

[67][Jowett's editors] Or, "law and principle which the community in every case has pronounced to be the best."

[68][Jowett's editors] Reading and sense uncertain. The origin of all these quotations is unknown.

is unable to make good her defense, this argument of ours shall be a charm to us, which we will repeat to ourselves while we listen to her strains; that we may not fall away into the childish love of her which captivates the many. At all events we are well aware[69] that poetry, such as we have described, is not to be regarded seriously as attaining to the truth; and he who listens to her, fearing for the safety of the city which is within him, should be on his guard against her seductions and make our words his law.

Yes, he said, I quite agree with you.

Yes, I said, my dear Glaucon, for great is the issue at stake, greater than appears, whether a man is to be good or bad. And what will anyone be profited if under the influence of honor or money or power, aye, or under the excitement of poetry, he neglect justice and virtue?

Yes, he said; I have been convinced by the argument, as I believe that anyone else would have been.

From

Cratylus

Persons of the Dialogue

Hermogenes
Socrates
Cratylus

[Hermogenes has been querying Socrates about the meanings and derivations of words.]

Hermogenes   Well, then, let me ask about the greatest and noblest, such as ἀλήθεια (truth) and ψεῦδος (falsehood) and ὄν (being), not forgetting to inquire why the word ὄνομα (name), which is the theme of our discussion, has this name of ὄνομα.

Socrates   You know the word μαίεσθαι (to seek)?

Hermogenes   Yes—meaning the same as ϛητεῖν (to inquire).

Socrates   The word ὄνομα seems to be a compressed sentence, signifying ὄν οὗ ϛήτημα (being for which

there is a search), as is still more obvious in ὀνομαστόν (notable), which states in so many words that real existence is that for which there is a seeking (ὄν οὗ μάσμα); ἀλήθεια is also an agglomeration of θεία ἄλη (divine wandering), implying the divine motion of existence. ψεῦδος (falsehood) is the opposite of motion; here is another ill name given by the legislator to stagnation and forced inaction, which he compares to sleep (εὕδειν), but the original meaning of the word is disguised by the addition of ψ. Ὄν and οὐσία are ἰόν with an ι broken off; this agrees with the true principle, for being (ὄν) is also moving (ἰόν), and the same may be said of not-being, which is likewise called not-going (οὐκίον or οὐκι ὄν = οὐκ ἰόν).

Hermogenes   You have hammered away at them manfully, but suppose that some were to say to you, What is the word ἰόν, and what are ῥέον and δοῦν? Show me their fitness.

Socrates   You mean to say, how should I answer him?

Hermogenes   Yes.

Socrates   One way of giving the appearance of an answer has been already suggested.

Hermogenes   What way?

Socrates   To say that names which we do not understand are of foreign origin, and this is very likely the right answer, and something of this kind may be true of them, but also the original forms of words may have been lost in the lapse of ages; names have been so twisted in all manner of ways that I should not be surprised if the old language when compared with that now in use would appear to us to be a barbarous tongue.

Hermogenes   Very likely.

Socrates   Yes, very likely. But still the inquiry demands our earnest attention and we must not flinch. For we should remember that if a person goes on analyzing names into words,[1] and inquiring also into the elements out of which the words are formed, and keeps on always repeating this process, he who has to answer him must at last give up the inquiry in despair.

Hermogenes   Very true.

Socrates   And at what point ought he to lose heart and give up the inquiry? Must he not stop when he comes to the names which are the elements of all other names and sentences? For these cannot be supposed to be made up of other names. The word ἀγαθόν (good), for example, is, as we were saying, a compound of ἀγαοτός (admirable) and θοός (swift). And probably θοός is made up of other ele-

---

[69][Jowett] Or, if we accept Madvig's ingenious but unnecessary emendation ἀσόμεθα, "At all events we will sing, that," etc.

CRATYLUS.   Plato's *Cratylus* is thought to have been composed shortly before *Republic*, which is usually dated circa 373 B.C. The text is from Benjamin Jowett, tr., *The Dialogues of Plato*, 3rd edition (Oxford: Clarendon Press, 1892; 1st edition, 1871).

---

[1]By this Socrates means the original words.

ments, and these again of others. But if we take a word which is incapable of further resolution, then we shall be right in saying that we have at last reached a primary element, which need not be resolved any further.

Hermogenes   I believe you to be in the right.

Socrates   And suppose the names about which you are now asking should turn out to be primary elements. Must not their truth or law be examined according to some new method?

Hermogenes   Very likely.

Socrates   Quite so, Hermogenes. All that has preceded would lead to this conclusion. And if, as I think, the conclusion is true, then I shall again say to you, come and help me, that I may not fall into some absurdity in stating the principle of primary names.

Hermogenes   Let me hear, and I will do my best to assist you.

Socrates   I think that you will acknowledge with me that one principle is applicable to all names, primary as well as secondary—when they are regarded simply as names, there is no difference in them.

Hermogenes   Certainly not.

Socrates   All the names that we have been explaining were intended to indicate the nature of things.

Hermogenes   Of course.

Socrates   And that this is true of the primary quite as much as of the secondary names is implied in their being names.

Hermogenes   Surely.

Socrates   But the secondary, as I conceive, derive their significance from the primary.

Hermogenes   That is evident.

Socrates   Very good, but then how do the primary names which precede analysis show the natures of things, as far as they can be shown, which they must do, if they are to be real names? And here I will ask you a question. Suppose that we had no voice or tongue, and wanted to communicate with one another. Should we not, like the deaf and dumb, make signs with the hands and head and the rest of the body?

Hermogenes   There would be no choice, Socrates.

Socrates   We should imitate the nature of the thing; the elevation of our hands to heaven would mean lightness and upwardness; heaviness and downwardness would be expressed by letting them drop to the ground; if we were describing the running of a horse, or any other animal, we should make our bodies and their gestures as like as we could to them.

Hermogenes   I do not see that we could do anything else.

Socrates   We could not, for by bodily imitation only can the body ever express anything.

Hermogenes   Very true.

Socrates   And when we want to express ourselves, either with the voice, or tongue, or mouth, the expression is simply their imitation of that which we want to express?

Hermogenes   It must be so, I think.

Socrates   Then a name is a vocal imitation of that which the vocal imitator names or imitates?

Hermogenes   I think so.

Socrates   Nay, my friend, I am disposed to think that we have not reached the truth as yet.

Hermogenes   Why not?

Socrates   Because if we have we shall be obliged to admit that the people who imitate sheep, or cocks, or other animals, name that which they imitate.

Hermogenes   Quite true.

Socrates   Then could I have been right in what I was saying?

Hermogenes   In my opinion, no. But I wish that you would tell me, Socrates, what sort of an imitation is a name?

Socrates   In the first place, I should reply, not a musical imitation, although that is also vocal, nor, again, an imitation of what music imitates; these, in my judgment, would not be naming. Let me put the matter as follows. All objects have sound and figure, and many have color?

Hermogenes   Certainly.

Socrates   But the art of naming appears not to be concerned with imitations of this kind. The arts which have to do with them are music and drawing?

Hermogenes   True.

Socrates   Again, is there not an essence of each thing, just as there is a color, or sound? And is there not an essence of color and sound as well as of anything else which may be said to have an essence?

Hermogenes   I should think so.

Socrates   Well, and if anyone could express the essence of each thing in letters and syllables, would he not express the nature of each thing?

Hermogenes   Quite so.

Socrates   The musician and the painter were the two names which you gave to the two other imitators. What will this imitator be called?

Hermogenes   I imagine, Socrates, that he must be the namer, or name giver, of whom we are in search.

Socrates   If this is true, then I think that we are in a condition to consider the names ῥοή (stream), ἰέναι (to go), σχέσις (retention), about which you were asking, and we may see whether the namer has grasped the nature of them in letters and syllables in such a manner as to imitate the essence or not.

Hermogenes   Very good.

Socrates   But are these the only primary names, or are there others?

Hermogenes   There must be others.

Socrates   So I should expect. But how shall we further analyze them, and where does the imitator begin? Imitation of the essence is made by syllables and letters. Ought we not, therefore, first to separate the letters, just as those who are beginning rhythm first distinguish the powers of elementary and then of compound sounds, and when they have done so, but not before, proceed to the consideration of rhythms?

Hermogenes   Yes.

Socrates   Must we not begin in the same way with letters—first separating the vowels, and then the consonants and mutes, into classes, according to the received distinctions of the learned, also the semivowels, which are neither vowels nor yet mutes, and distinguishing into classes the vowels themselves? And when we have perfected the classification of things, we shall give their names, and see whether, as in the case of letters, there are any classes to which they may be all referred, and hence we shall see their natures, and see, too, whether they have in them classes as there are in the letters. And when we have well considered all this, we shall know how to apply them to what they resemble, whether one letter is used to denote one thing, or whether there is to be an admixture of several of them, just as, in painting, the painter who wants to depict anything sometimes uses purple only, or any other color, and sometimes mixes up several colors, as his method is when he has to paint flesh color or anything of that kind—he uses his colors as his figures appear to require them. And so, too, we shall apply letters to the expression of objects, either single letters when required, or several letters, and so we shall form syllables, as they are called, and from syllables make nouns and verbs, and thus, at last, from the combinations of nouns and verbs arrive at language, large and fair and whole. And as the painter made a figure, even so shall we make speech by the art of the namer or the rhetorician, or by some other art. Not that I am literally speaking of ourselves, but I was carried away—meaning to say that this was the way in which not we, but the ancients formed language, and what they put together we must take to pieces in like manner, if we are to attain a scientific view of the whole subject. And we must see whether the primary, and also whether the secondary elements are rightly given or not, for if they are not, the composition of them, my dear Hermogenes, will be a sorry piece of work, and in the wrong direction.

Hermogenes   That, Socrates, I can quite believe.

Socrates   Well, but do you suppose that you will be able to analyse them in this way? for I am certain that I should not.

Hermogenes   Much less am I likely to be able.

Socrates   Shall we leave them, then? or shall we seek to discover, if we can, something about them, according to the measure of our ability, saying by way of preface, as I said before of the Gods, that of the the truth about them we know nothing, and do but entertain human notions of them. And in this present inquiry, let us say to ourselves, before we proceed, that the higher method is the one which we or others who would analyse language to any good purpose must follow; but under the circumstances, as men say, we must do as well as we can. What do you think?

Hermogenes   I very much approve.

Socrates   That objects should be imitated in letters and syllables, and so find expression, may appear ridiculous, Hermogenes, but it cannot be avoided—there is no better principle to which we can look for the truth of first names. Deprived of this, we must have recourse to divine help, like the tragic poets, who in any perplexity have their Gods waiting in the air; and must get out of our difficulty in like fashion, by saying that 'the Gods gave the first names, and therefore they are right.' This will be the best contrivance, or perhaps that other notion may be even better still, of deriving them from some barbarous people, for the barbarians are older than we are; or we may say that antiquity has cast a veil over them, which is the same sort of excuse as the last; for all these are not reasons but only ingenious excuses for having no reasons concerning the truth of words. And yet any sort of ignorance of first or primitive names involves an ignorance of secondary words; for they can only be explained by the primary. Clearly then the professor of languages should be able to give a very lucid explanation of first names, or let him be assured he will only talk nonsense about the rest. Do you not suppose this to be true?

Hermogenes   Certainly, Socrates.

Socrates   My first notions of original names are truly wild and ridiculous, though I have no objection to impart them to you if you desire, and I hope that you will communicate to me in return anything better which you may have.

Hermogenes   Fear not; I will do my best.

Socrates   In the first place, the letter ρ appears to me to be the general instrument expressing all motion (κίνησις). But I have not yet explained the meaning of this latter word, which is just ἴεσις (going); for the letter η was not in use among the ancients, who only employed ε; and the root is κίειν, which is a foreign form, the same as ἰέναι. And the old word κίνησις will be correctly given as ἴεσις in corresponding modern letters. Assuming this foreign root κίειν, and allowing for the change of the η and the insertion of the ν, we have κίνησις, which should have been κιείνησις or εἶσις; and στάσις is the negative of ἰένα (or εἶσις), and has been improved into στάστς. Now the letter ῥ, as I was saying, appeared to the imposer of names an excellent instrument for the expression of motion; and he frequently uses the letter for this purpose: for example, in the actual words ῥεῖν and ῥοὴ he represents motion by ῥ; also in the words τρόμος (trembling), τραχὺς (rugged); and again, in words such as κρούειν (strike), θραύειν (crush), ἐρείκειν (bruise), θρύπτειν (break), κερματίξειν (crumble), ῥυμβεῖν (whirl): of all these sorts of movements he generally finds an expression in the letter R, because, as I imagine, he had observed that the tongue was most agitated and least at rest in the pronunciation of this letter, which he therefore used in order to express motion, just as by the letter ι he expresses the subtle elements which pass through all things. This is why he uses the letter ι as imitative of motion, ἰέναι, ἴεσθαι. And there is another class of letters, φ, ψ, σ and ξ, of which the pronunciation is accompanied by great expenditure of breath; these are used in the imitation of such notions as ψυχρὸν (shivering), ξέον (seething), σείεσθαι (to be shaken), σεισμὸς (shock), and are always introduced by the giver of names when he wants to imitate what is φυσῶδες (windy). He seems to have thought that the closing and pressure of the tongue in the utterance of δ and τ was expressive of binding and rest in a place: he further observed the liquid movement of λ, in the pronunciation of which the tongue slips, and in this he found the expression of smoothness, as in λεῖος (level), and in the word ὀλτσκάνειν (to slip) itself, λιπαρὸν (sleek), in the word κολλῶδες (gluey), and the like: the heavier sound of γ detained the slipping tongue, and the union of the two gave the notion of a glutinous clammy nature, as in γλίσχρος, γλυκὺς, γλοιῶδες. The ν he observed to be sounded from within, and therefore to have a notion of inwardness; hence he introduced the sound in ἔνδον and ἐντός: α he assigned to the expression of size, and η of length, because they are great letters: ο was the sign of roundness, and therefore there is plenty of ο mixed up in the word γογγύλον (round). Thus did the legislator, reducing all things into letters and syllables, and impressing on them names and signs, and out of them by imitation compounding other signs. That is my view, Hermogenes, of the truth of names; but I should like to hear what Cratylus has more to say.

Hermogenes   But, Socrates, as I was telling you before, Cratylus mystifies me; he says that there is a fitness of names, but he never explains what is this fitness, so that I cannot tell whether his obscurity is intended or not. Tell me now, Cratylus, here in the presence of Socrates, do you agree in what Socrates has been saying about names, or have you something better of your own? and if you have, tell me what you view is, and then you will either learn of Socrates, or Socrates and I will learn of you.

Cratylus   Well, but surely, Hermogenes, you do not suppose that you can learn, or I explain, any subject of importance all in a moment—at any rate, not such a subject as language, which is, perhaps, the very greatest of all.

Hermogenes   No, indeed, but, as Hesiod says, and I agree with him, 'to add little to little'[2] is worth while. And, therefore, if you think that you can add anything at all, however small, to our knowledge, take a little trouble and oblige Socrates, and me too, who certainly have a claim upon you.

Socrates   I am by no means positive, Cratylus, in the view which Hermogenes and myself have worked out, and therefore do not hesitate to say what you think, which if it be better than my own view I shall gladly accept. And I should not be at all surprised to find that you have found some better notion. For you have evidently reflected on these matters and have had teachers, and if you have really a better theory of the truth of names, you may count me in the number of disciples.

Cratylus   You are right, Socrates, in saying that I have made a study of these matters, and I might possibly convert you into a disciple. But I fear that the opposite is more probable, and I already find myself moved to say to you what Achilles in the 'Prayers' says to Ajax,

> Illustrious Ajax, son of Telamon, lord of the
> people,
> You appear to have spoken in all things much to
> my mind.[3]

And you, Socrates, appear to me to be an oracle, and to give answers much to my mind, whether you are inspired by Euthyphro, or whether some Muse may have long been an inhabitant of your breast, unconsciously to yourself.

Socrates   Excellent Cratylus, I have long been wondering at my own wisdom. I cannot trust myself. And I think that I ought to stop and ask myself, What am I saying? For there is nothing worse than self-deception—when the deceiver is always at home and always with you—it is quite terrible, and therefore I ought often to retrace my steps and endeavor to 'look fore and aft,'[4] in the words of the aforesaid Homer. And now let me see, where are we? Have we not been saying that the correct name indicates the nature of the thing? Has this proposition been sufficiently proved?

Cratylus   Yes, Socrates, what you say, as I am disposed to think, is quite true.

---

[2][Jowett] *Works and Days*, 9.359.
[3][Jowett] *Iliad*, 9.644 sq.
[4][Jowett] *Iliad*, 1.343, 3.109.

Socrates   Names, then, are given in order to instruct?

Cratylus   Certainly.

Socrates   And naming is an art, and has artificers?

Cratylus   Yes.

Socrates   And who are they?

Cratylus   The legislators, of whom you spoke at first.[5]

Socrates   And does this art grow up among men like other arts? Let me explain what I mean. Of painters, some are better and some worse?

Cratylus   Yes.

Socrates   The better painters execute their works, I mean their figures, better, and the worse execute them worse. And of builders also, the better sort build fairer houses, and the worse build them worse.

Cratylus   True.

Socrates   And among legislators, there are some who do their work better and some worse?

Cratylus   No, there I do not agree with you.

Socrates   Then you do not think that some laws are better and others worse?

Cratylus   No, indeed.

Socrates   Or that one name is better than another?

Cratylus   Certainly not.

Socrates   Then all names are rightly imposed?

Cratylus   Yes, if they are names at all.

Socrates   Well, what do you say to the name of our friend Hermogenes, which was mentioned before—assuming that he has nothing of the nature of Hermes in him, shall we say that this is a wrong name, or not his name at all?[6]

Cratylus   I should reply that Hermogenes is not his name at all, but only appears to be his, and is really the name of somebody else, who has the nature which corresponds to it.

Socrates   And if a man were to call him Hermogenes, would he not be even speaking falsely? For there may be a doubt whether you can call him Hermogenes, if he is not.

Cratylus   What do you mean?

Socrates   Are you maintaining that falsehood is impossible? For if this is your meaning I should answer that there have been plenty of liars in all ages.

Cratylus   Why, Socrates, how can a man say that which is not—say something and yet say nothing? For is not falsehood saying the thing which is not?

Socrates   Your argument, friend, is too subtle for a man of my age. But I should like to know whether you are one of those philosophers who think that falsehood may be spoken but not said?

Cratylus   Neither spoken nor said.

Socrates   Nor uttered nor addressed? For example, if a person, saluting you in a foreign country, were to take your hand and say, Hail, Athenian stranger, Hermogenes, son of Smicrion—these words, whether spoken, said, uttered, or addressed, would have no application to you but only to our friend Hermogenes, or perhaps to nobody at all?

Cratylus   In my opinion, Socrates, the speaker would only be talking nonsense.

Socrates   Well, but that will be quite enough for me, if you will tell me whether the nonsense would be true or false, or partly true and partly false, which is all that I want to know.

Cratylus   I should say that he would be putting himself in motion to no purpose, and that his words would be an unmeaning sound like the noise of hammering at a brazen pot.

Socrates   But let us see, Cratylus, whether we cannot find a meeting point, for you would admit that the name is not the same with the thing named?

Cratylus   I should.

Socrates   And would you further acknowledge that the name is an imitation of the thing?

Cratylus   Certainly.

Socrates   And you would say that pictures are also imitations of things, but in another way?

Cratylus   Yes.

Socrates   I believe you may be right, but I do not rightly understand you. Please to say, then, whether both sorts of imitation—I mean both pictures or words—are not equally attributable and applicable to the things of which they are the imitation.

Cratylus   They are.

Socrates   First look at the matter thus. You may attribute the likeness of the man to the man, and of the woman to the woman, and so on?

Cratylus   Certainly.

Socrates   And conversely you may attribute the likeness of the man to the woman, and of the woman to the man?

Cratylus   Very true.

Socrates   And are both modes of assigning them right, or only the first?

---

[5]Early in the dialogue Socrates and Hermogenes have agreed that the legislator is the giver of names. Shelley uses the term "legislator" in this sense in his *Defense of Poetry*. See pp. 517 and pp. 529.

[6]Early in the dialogue there has been a discussion of what we call proper names.

Cratylus   Only the first.

Socrates   That is to say, the mode of assignment which attributes to each that which belongs to it and is like it?

Cratylus   That is my view.

Socrates   Now then, as I am desirous that we being friends should have a good understanding about the argument, let me state my view to you. The first mode of assignment, whether applied to figures or to names, I call right, and when applied to names only, true as well as right, and the other mode of giving and assigning the name which is unlike, I call wrong, and in the case of names, false as well as wrong.

Cratylus   That may be true, Socrates, in the case of pictures; they may be wrongly assigned. But not in the case of names—they must be always right.

Socrates   Why, what is the difference? May I not go to a man and say to him, This is your picture, showing him his own likeness, or perhaps the likeness of a woman, and when I say show, I mean bring before the sense of sight.

Cratylus   Certainly.

Socrates   And may I not go to him again, and say, This is your name? For the name, like the picture, is an imitation. May I not say to him, This is your name? And may I not then bring to his sense of hearing the imitation of himself, when I say, This is a man, or of a female of the human species, when I say, This is a woman, as the case may be? Is not all that quite possible?

Cratylus   I would fain agree with you, Socrates, and therefore I say, granted.

Socrates   That is very good of you, if I am right, which need hardly be disputed at present. But if I can assign names as well as pictures to objects, the right assignment of them we may call truth, and the wrong assignment of them falsehood. Now if there be such a wrong assignment of names, there may also be a wrong or inappropriate assignment of verbs, and if of names and verbs then of the sentences, which are made up of them. What do you say, Cratylus?

Cratylus   I agree, and think that what you say is very true.

Socrates   And further, primitive nouns may be compared to pictures, and in pictures you may either give all the appropriate colors and figures, or you may not give them all—some may be wanting—or there may be too many or too much of them—may there not?

Cratylus   Very true.

Socrates   And he who gives all gives a perfect picture or figure, and he who takes away or adds also gives a picture or figure, but not a good one.

Cratylus   Yes.

Socrates   In like manner, he who by syllables and letters imitates the nature of things, if he gives all that is appropriate will produce a good image, or in other words a name, but if he subtracts or perhaps adds a little, he will make an image but not a good one; whence I infer that some names are well and others ill made.

Cratylus   That is true.

Socrates   Then the artist of names may be sometimes good, or he may be bad?

Cratylus   Yes.

Socrates   And this artist of names is called the legislator?

Cratylus   Yes.

Socrates   Then like other artists the legislator may be good or he may be bad; it must surely be so if our former admissions hold good.

Cratylus   Very true, Socrates, but the case of language, you see, is different. For when by the help of grammar we assign the letters α or β, or any other letters, to a certain name, then, if we add, or subtract, or misplace a letter, the name which is written is not only written wrongly, but not written at all, and in any of these cases becomes other than a name.

Socrates   But I doubt whether your view is altogether correct, Cratylus.

Cratylus   How so?

Socrates   I believe that what you say may be true about numbers, which must be just what they are, or not be at all. For example, the number ten at once becomes other than ten if a unit be added or subtracted, and so of any other number, but this does not apply to that which is qualitative or to anything which is represented under an image. I should say rather that the image, if expressing in every point the entire reality, would no longer be an image. Let us suppose the existence of two objects. One of them shall be Cratylus, and the other the image of Cratylus, and we will suppose, further, that some god makes not only a representation such as a painter would make of your outward form and color, but also creates an inward organization like yours, having the same warmth and softness, and into this infuses motion, and soul, and mind, such as you have, and in a word copies all your qualities, and places them by you in another form. Would you say that this was Cratylus and the image of Cratylus, or that there were two Cratyluses?

Cratylus   I should say that there were two Cratyluses.

Socrates   Then you see, my friend, that we must find some other principle of truth in images, and also in names, and not insist that an image is no longer an image when something is added or subtracted. Do you not perceive that images are very far from having qualities which are the exact counterpart of the realities which they represent?

Cratylus   Yes, I see.

Socrates   But then how ridiculous would be the effect of names on things, if they were exactly the same with them! For they would be the doubles of them, and no one would be able to determine which were the names and which were the realities.

Cratylus   Quite true.

Socrates   Then fear not, but have the courage to admit that one name may be correctly and another incorrectly given, and do not insist that the name shall be exactly the same with the thing, but allow the occasional substitution of a wrong letter, and if of a letter also of a noun in a sentence, and if of a noun in a sentence also of a sentence which is not appropriate to the matter, and acknowledge that the thing may be named, and described, so long as the general character of the thing which you are describing is retained. And this, as you will remember, was remarked by Hermogenes and myself in the particular instance of the names of the letters.

Cratylus   Yes, I remember.

Socrates   Good, and when the general character is preserved, even if some of the proper letters are wanting, still the thing is signified—well, if all the letters are given, not well, when only a few of them are given. I think that we had better admit this, lest we be punished like travelers in Aegina who wander about the street late at night, and likewise told by truth herself that we have arrived too late. Or if not, you must find out some new notion of correctness of names, and no longer maintain that a name is the expression of a thing in letters or syllables, for if you say both, you will be inconsistent with yourself.

Cratylus   I quite acknowledge, Socrates, what you say to be very reasonable.

Socrates   Then as we are agreed thus far, let us ask ourselves whether a name rightly imposed ought not to have the proper letters.

Cratylus   Yes.

Socrates   And the proper letters are those which are like the things?

Cratylus   Yes.

Socrates   Enough then of names which are rightly given. And in names which are incorrectly given, the greater part may be supposed to be made up of proper and similar letters, or there would be no likeness, but there will be likewise a part which is improper and spoils the beauty and formation of the word. You would admit that?

Cratylus   There would be no use, Socrates, in my quarreling with you, since I cannot be satisfied that a name which is incorrectly given is a name at all.

Socrates   Do you admit a name to be the representation of a thing?

Cratylus   Yes, I do.

Socrates   But do you not allow that some nouns are primitive, and some derived?

Cratylus   Yes, I do.

Socrates   Then if you admit that primitive or first nouns are representations of things, is there any better way of framing representations than by assimilating them to the objects as much as you can? Or do you prefer the notion of Hermogenes and of many others, who say that names are conventional, and have a meaning to those who have agreed about them, and who have previous knowledge of the things intended by them, and that convention is the only principle? And whether you abide by our present convention, or make a new and opposite one, according to which you call small great and great small—that, they would say, makes no difference, if you are only agreed. Which of these two notions do you prefer?

Cratylus   Representation by likeness, Socrates, is infinitely better than representation by any chance sign.

Socrates   Very good, but if the name is to be like the thing, the letters out of which the first names are composed must also be like things. Returning to the image of the picture, I would ask how anyone could ever compose a picture which would be like anything at all, if there were not pigments in nature which resembled the things imitated, and out of which the picture is composed.

Cratylus   Impossible.

Socrates   No more could names ever resemble any actually existing thing, unless the original elements of which they are compounded bore some degree of resemblance to the objects of which the names are the imitation. And the original elements are letters?

Cratylus   Yes.

Socrates   Let me now invite you to consider what Hermogenes and I were saying about sounds. Do you agree with me that the letter ρ is expressive of rapidity, motion, and hardness? Were we right or wrong in saying so?

Cratylus   I should say that you were right.

Socrates   And that λ was expressive of smoothness, and softness, and the like?

Cratylus   There again you were right.

Socrates   And yet, as you are aware, that which is called by us σκληρότης, is by the Eretrians called σκληρότηρ.

Cratylus   Very true.

Socrates   But are the letters ρ and σ equivalents, and is there the same significance to them in the termination ρ, which there is to us in σ, or is there no significance to one of us?

Cratylus   Nay, surely there is a significance to both of us.

Socrates   In so far as they are like, or in so far as they are unlike?

Cratylus   In so far as they are like.

Socrates   Are they altogether alike?

Cratylus   Yes, for the purpose of expressing motion.

Socrates   And what do you say of the insertion of the λ? For that is expressive not of hardness but of softness.

Cratylus   Why, perhaps the letter λ is wrongly inserted, Socrates, and should be altered into ρ, as you were saying to Hermogenes, and in my opinion rightly, when you spoke of adding and subtracting letters upon occasion.

Socrates   Good, but still the word is intelligible to both of us. When I say σκληρός (hard), you know what I mean.

Cratylus   Yes, my dear friend, and the explanation of that is custom.

Socrates   And what is custom but convention? When I utter a sound which I understand, and you know that I understand the meaning of the sound—this is what you are saying?

Cratylus   Yes.

Socrates   And if when I speak you know my meaning, there is an indication given by me to you?

Cratylus   Yes.

Socrates   This indication of my meaning may proceed from unlike as well as from like, for example, in the λ of σκληρότης. But if this is true, then you have made a convention with yourself, and the correctness of a name turns out to be convention, since letters which are unlike are indicative equally with those which are like, if they are sanctioned by custom and convention. And even supposing that you distinguish custom from convention ever so much, still you must say that the signification of words is given by custom and not by likeness, for custom may indicate by the unlike as well as by the like. But as we are agreed thus far, Cratylus, for I shall assume that your silence gives consent, then custom and convention must be supposed to contribute to the indication of our thoughts. For suppose we take the instance of number. How can you ever imagine, my good friend, that you will find names resembling every individual number, unless you allow that which you term convention and agreement to have authority in determining the correctness of names? I quite agree with you that words should as far as

possible resemble things, but I fear that this dragging in of resemblance, as Hermogenes says, is a shabby thing, which has to be supplemented by the mechanical aid of convention with a view to correctness. For I believe that if we could always, or almost always, use likenesses, which are perfectly appropriate, this would be the most perfect state of language, as the opposite is the most imperfect. But let me ask you, what is the force of names, and what is the use of them?

Cratylus   The use of names, Socrates, as I should imagine, is to inform. The simple truth is that he who knows names knows also the things which are expressed by them.

Socrates   I suppose you mean to say, Cratylus, that as the name is, so also is the thing, and that he who knows the one will also know the other, because they are similar, and all similars fall under the same art or science, and therefore you would say that he who knows names will also know things.

Cratylus   That is precisely what I mean.

Socrates   But let us consider what is the nature of this information about things which, according to you, is given us by names. Is it the best sort of information? Or is there any other? What do you say?

Cratylus   I believe that to be both the only and the best sort of information about them—there can be no other.

Socrates   But do you believe that in the discovery of them he who discovers the names discovers also the things, or is this only the method of instruction, and is there some other method of inquiry and discovery?

Cratylus   I certainly believe that the methods of inquiry and discovery are of the same nature as instruction.

Socrates   Well, but do you not see, Cratylus, that he who follows names in the search after things, and analyzes their meaning, is in great danger of being deceived?

Cratylus   How so?

Socrates   Why clearly he who first gave names gave them according to his conception of the things which they signified—did he not?

Cratylus   True.

Socrates   And if his conception was erroneous, and he gave names according to his conception, in what position shall we who are his followers find ourselves? Shall we not be deceived by him?

Cratylus   But, Socrates, am I not right in thinking that he must surely have known, or else, as I was saying, his names would not be names at all? And you have a clear proof that he has not missed the truth, and the proof is—that he is perfectly consistent. Did you ever observe in speaking that all the words which you utter have a common character and purpose?

Socrates   But that, friend Cratylus, is no answer. For if he did begin in error, he may have forced the remainder into agreement with the original error and with himself; there would be nothing strange in this, any more than in geometric diagrams, which have often a slight and invisible flaw in the first part of the process, and are consistently mistaken in the long deductions which follow. And this is the reason why every man should expend his chief thought and attention on the consideration of his first principles—are they or are they not rightly laid down? And when he has duly sifted them, all the rest will follow. Now I should be astonished to find that names are really consistent. And here let us revert to our former discussion. Were we not saying that all things are in motion and progress and flux, and that this idea of motion is expressed by names? Do you not conceive that to be the meaning of them?

Cratylus   Yes, that is assuredly their meaning, and the true meaning.

Socrates   Let us revert to ἐπιστήμη (knowledge), and observe how ambiguous this word is, seeming rather to signify stopping the soul at things than going round with them, and therefore we should leave the beginning as at present, and not reject the ε, but make an insertion of an ι instead of an ε (not πιστήμη, but ἐπιιστήμη). Take another example. Βέβαιον (sure) is clearly the expression of station and position, and not of motion. Again, the word ἱστορία (inquiry) bears upon the face of it the stopping (ἱστάναι) of the stream, and the word πιστόν (faithful) certainly indicates cessation of motion; then, again, μνήμη (memory), as anyone may see, expresses rest in the soul, and not motion. Moreover, words such as ἁμαρτία and συμφορά, which have a bad sense, viewed in the light of their etymologies will be the same as σύνεσις and ἐπιστήμη and other words which have a good sense (cf. ὁμαρτεῖν, συνιέναι, ἐπεσθαι, συμφέρεσθαι). And much the same may be said of ἀμαθία and ἀκολασία, for ἀμαθία (ignorance) may be explained as ἡ ἅμα θεῷ ἰόντος πορεία (the progress of one who goes with God), and ἀκολασία (unrestraint) as ἡ ἀκολουθία τοῖς πράγμασιν (movement in company with things). Thus the names which in these instances we find to have the worst sense will turn out to be framed on the same principle as those which have the best. And anyone I believe who would take the trouble might find many other examples in which the giver of names indicates, not that things are in motion or progress, but that they are at rest, which is the opposite of motion.

Cratylus   Yes, Socrates, but observe, the greater number express motion.

Socrates   What of that, Cratylus? Are we to count them like votes? And is correctness of names the voice of the majority? Are we to say of whichever sort there are most, those are the true ones?

Cratylus   No, that is not reasonable.

Socrates   Certainly not. But let us have done with this question and proceed to another, about which I should like to know whether you think with me. Were we not lately acknowledging that the first givers of names in states, both Hellenic and barbarous, were the legislators, and that the art which gave names was the art of the legislator?

Cratylus   Quite true.

Socrates   Tell me, then, did the first legislators, who were the givers of the first names, know or not know the things which they named?

Cratylus   They must have known, Socrates.

Socrates   Why, yes, friend Cratylus, they could hardly have been ignorant.

Cratylus   I should say not.

Socrates   Let us return to the point from which we digressed. You were saying, if you remember, that he who gave names must have known the things which he named. Are you still of that opinion?

Cratylus   I am.

Socrates   And would you say that the giver of the first names had also a knowledge of the things he named?

Cratylus   I should.

Socrates   But how could he have learned or discovered things from names if the primitive names were not yet given? For, if we are correct in our view, the only way of learning and discovering things is either to discover names for ourselves or to learn them from others.

Cratylus   I think that there is a good deal in what you say, Socrates.

Socrates   But if things are only to be known through names, how can we suppose that the givers of names had knowledge, or were legislators, before there were names at all, and therefore before they could have known them?

Cratylus   I believe, Socrates, the true account of the matter to be that a power more than human gave things their first names, and that the names which are thus given are necessarily their true names.

Socrates   Then how came the giver of the names, if he was an inspired being or god, to contradict himself? For were we not saying just now that he made some names expressive of rest and others of motion? Were we mistaken?

Cratylus   But I suppose one of the two not to be names at all.

Socrates   And which, then, did he make, my good friend—those which are expressive of rest, or those which are expressive of motion? This is a point which, as I said before, cannot be determined by counting them.

Cratylus   No, not in that way, Socrates.

Socrates   But if this is a battle of names, some of them asserting that they are like the truth, others contending that *they* are, how or by what criterion are we to decide between them? For there are no other names to which appeal can be made, but obviously recourse must be had to another standard which, without employing names, will make clear which of the two are right, and this must be a standard which shows the truth of things.

Cratylus   I agree.

Socrates   But if that is true, Cratylus, then I suppose that things may be known without names?

Cratylus   Clearly.

Socrates   But how would you expect to know them? What other way can there be of knowing them, except the true and natural way, through their affinities, when they are akin to each other, and through themselves? For that which is other and different from them must signify something other and different from them.

Cratylus   What you are saying is, I think, true.

Socrates   Well, but reflect. Have we not several times acknowledged that names rightly given are the likenesses and images of the things which they name?

Cratylus   Yes.

Socrates   Let us suppose that to any extent you please you can learn things through the medium of names, and suppose also that you can learn them from the things themselves. Which is likely to be the nobler and clearer way—to learn of the image, whether the image and the truth of which the image is the expression have been rightly conceived, or to learn of the truth whether the truth and the image of it have been duly executed?

Cratylus   I should say that we must learn of the truth.

Socrates   How real existence is to be studied or discovered is, I suspect, beyond you and me. But we may admit so much, that the knowledge of things is not to be derived from names. No, they must be studied and investigated in themselves.

Cratylus   Clearly, Socrates.

Socrates   There is another point. I should not like us to be imposed upon by the appearance of such a multitude of names, all tending in the same direction. I myself do not deny that the givers of names did really give them under the idea that all things were in motion and flux, which was their sincere but, I think, mistaken opinion. And having fallen into a kind of whirlpool themselves, they are carried round, and want to drag us in after them. There is a matter, master Cratylus, about which I often dream, and should like to ask your opinion. Tell me whether there is or is not any

absolute beauty or good, or any other absolute existence.

Cratylus   Certainly, Socrates, I think so.

Socrates   Then let us seek the true beauty, not asking whether a face is fair, or anything of that sort, for all such things appear to be in a flux, but let us ask whether the true beauty is not always beautiful.

Cratylus   Certainly.

Socrates   And can we rightly speak of a beauty which is always passing away, and is first this and then that? Must not the same thing be born and retire and vanish while the word is in our mouths?

Cratylus   Undoubtedly.

Socrates   Then how can that be a real thing which is never in the same state? For obviously things which are the same cannot change while they remain the same, and if they are always the same and in the same state, and never depart from their original form, they can never change or be moved.

Cratylus   Certainly they cannot.

Socrates   Nor yet can they be known by anyone, for at the moment that the observer approaches, then they become other and of another nature, so that you cannot get any further in knowing their nature or state, for you cannot know that which has no state.

Cratylus   True.

Socrates   Nor can we reasonably say, Cratylus, that there is knowledge at all, if everything is in a state of transition and there is nothing abiding. For knowledge too cannot continue to be knowledge unless continuing always to abide and exist. But if the very nature of knowledge changes, at the time when the change occurs there will be no knowledge, and if the transition is always going on, there will always be no knowledge, and, according to this view, there will be no one to know and nothing to be known. But if that which knows and that which is known exist ever, and the beautiful and the good and every other thing also exist, then I do not think that they can resemble a process or flux, as we were just now supposing. Whether there is this eternal nature in things, or whether the truth is what Heraclitus and his followers and many others say, is a question hard to determine, and no man of sense will like to put himself or the education of his mind in the power of names. Neither will he so far trust names or the givers of names as to be confident in any knowledge which condemns himself and other existences to an unhealthy state of unreality; he will not believe that all things leak like a pot, or imagine that the world is a man who has a running at the nose. This may be true, Cratylus, but is also very likely to be untrue, and therefore I would not have you be too easily persuaded of it. Reflect well and like a man, and do not easily accept such a doctrine, for you are young and of an age to learn. And when you have found the truth, come and tell me.

Cratylus   I will do as you say, though I can assure you, Socrates, that I have been considering the matter already, and the result of a great deal of trouble and consideration is that I incline to Heraclitus.

Socrates   Then, another day, my friend, when you come back, you shall give me a lesson, but at present, go into the country, as you are intending, and Hermogenes shall set you on your way.

Cratylus   Very good, Socrates. I hope, however, that you will continue to think about these things yourself.

Aristotle

384 — 322 B.C.

The first extant treatise on poetry in the Western world was written by Aristotle, a student of Plato. Though Aristotle's *Rhetoric* and *Metaphysics* contain important remarks bearing on literature, his *Poetics*, fragmentary as it is and probably passed to us through the hands of a student, stands as his major contribution to literary theory. Its influence has been tremendous, even though it was lost for some centuries before its reappearance in the Renaissance. Commentaries on the *Poetics* abound from that time, perhaps the most important of them being Castelvetro's.

Aristotle approaches literature as if he were a classical biologist. He intends to classify and categorize kinds of literature systematically, and he begins with tragic drama, though in passing he has some remarks to make about epic. The treatise breaks off before he comes to comedy, but by that time our sense of his method is already established. He is the first critic to attempt a systematic discussion of genres.

It appears that Aristotle means to answer Plato's criticism of the poet as a mere imitator of appearances. He disagrees with Plato about where to locate reality. He does not believe that the world of appearances is merely an ephemeral copy of the changeless ideas; he believes that change is a fundamental process of nature, which he regards as a creative force with a direction. Reality, for Aristotle, is the process by which a form manifests itself through the concrete and by which the concrete takes on meaning working in accordance with ordered principles. The poet's imitation is an analogue of this process; he takes a form from nature and reshapes it in a different matter or medium. This medium, which the form does not inhabit in nature, is the source of each work's inward principle of order and consequently of its independence from slavish copying. The poet is thus an imitator *and* a creator. It is through his peculiar sort of imitation that the poet discovers the ultimate form of actions. The operating principle of order in literature Aristotle identifies with plot. The poet makes the meaning of events by making their structure, and he does this in a medium, which is words. Art is thus a sort of improvement on nature in that the poet has brought to completion what nature, operating with different principles of order, is still endeavoring to complete.

These Aristotelian ideas have influenced criticism from the Renaissance even to our own day. Renaissance critics often sought to find a middle ground between Plato and Aristotle, but the Platonic location of reality in the ideas inevitably intervened. Then neoclassical critics, following Castelvetro, extended to extremes what appeared in Aristotle to be prescriptions (see particularly Corneille on the unities). Other followers of Aristotle have tended to emphasize either his theory of imitation or his analytic procedures in describing structure. Aristotle's attention to the poem as an object capable of discussion in terms of its formal nature is probably his greatest contribution to critical theory, though his definition of tragedy as a catharsis of pity and fear has been much discussed among those critics interested in the relation of the poem to the reader.

A complete translation of Aristotle's works is that by J. A. Smith and W. D. Ross (II vols., 1908–31). Translations of *Poetics* abound: one should consult Ingram Bywater, *Aristotle on the Art of Poetry* (1909); G. F. Else, *Aristotle's* Poetics: *The Argument* (1957); and Leon Golden, *Aristotle's* Poetics: *A Translation and Commentary for Students of Literature* (1968). Commentaries accompany these translations. That by O. B. Hardison, which accompanies Golden's translation, is of particular value to the student. See also F. L. Lucas, *Tragedy in Relation to Aristotle's* Poetics (1928); Richard McKeon, "Literary Criticism and the Concept of Imitation in Antiquity," R. S. Crane, ed., *Critics and Criticism* (1952), 147–75; W. D. Ross, *Aristotle, A Complete Exposition of His Work and Thought,* 5th ed. (1953); Humphrey House, *Aristotle's* Poetics (1956); H. D. Goldstein, "Mimesis and Catharsis Reexamined," *Journal of Aesthetics and Art Criticism,* XXIV (1966), 567–77; Teddy Brunius, *Imagination and Katharsis* (1966); Richard Janko, *Aristotle on Comedy* (1984); and Stephen Halliwell, *Aristotle's* Poetics (1986).

POETICS

I

I propose to treat of poetry in itself and of its various kinds, noting the essential quality of each; to inquire into the structure of the plot as requisite to a good poem; into the number and nature of the parts of which a poem is composed; and similarly into whatever else falls within the same inquiry. Following, then, the order of nature, let us begin with the principles which come first.

2. Epic poetry and tragedy, comedy also and dithyrambic poetry,[1] and the music of the flute and of the lyre in most of their forms, are all in their general conception modes of imitation. 3. They differ, however, from one another in three respects—the medium, the objects, the manner or mode of imitation, being in each case distinct.

4. For as there are persons who, by conscious art or mere habit, imitate and represent various objects through the medium of color and form, or again by the voice; so in the arts above mentioned, taken as a whole, the imitation is produced by rhythm, language, or "harmony," either singly or combined.

Thus in the music of the flute and of the lyre, "harmony" and rhythm alone are employed; also in other arts, such as that of the shepherd's pipe, which are essentially similar to these. 5. In dancing, rhythm alone is used without "harmony"; for even dancing imitates character, emotion, and action, by rhythmical movement.

6. There is another art which imitates by means of language alone, and that either in prose or verse—which verse, again, may either combine different meters or consist of but one kind—but this has hitherto been without a name. 7. For there is no common term we could apply to the mimes of Sophron and Xenarchus and the Socratic dialogues on the one hand; and, on the other, to poetic imitations in iambic, elegiac, or any similar meter. People do, indeed, add the word *maker* or *poet* to the name of the meter, and speak of elegiac poets, or epic (that is, hexameter) poets, as if it were not the imitation that makes the poet, but the verse that entitles them all indiscriminately to the name. 8. Even when a treatise on medicine or natural science is brought out in verse, the name of poet is by custom given to the author; and yet Homer and Empedocles have nothing in common but the meter, so that it would be right to call the one poet, the other physicist rather than poet.[2] 9. On the same principle, even if a writer in his poetic imitation were to combine all meters, as Chaeremon[3] did in his *Centaur,* which is a medley composed of meters of all kinds, we should bring

---

POETICS.   Aristotle's *Poetics* was composed about 330 B.C. The text is from S. H. Butcher, tr., *Aristotle's Theory of Poetry and Fine Art,* 4th ed. (New York: Dover Publications, Inc., 1955). Reprinted through permission of the publisher. Passages sometimes considered additions by copyists are enclosed in brackets. The symbols < > enclose conjectural supplements to the text, and the double asterisk indicates a lacuna in the text.

[1] Early Greek lyric poetry originating in songs sung at festivals of Dionysus.

[2] This matter of the importance of verse as a definitive element in the poem is discussed by a number of later critics including Scaliger.

[3] All but fragments of the plays of this fourth-century B.C. Athenian tragic poet have been lost. Of the other works Aristotle discusses in *Poetics,* all but the *Odyssey* and the *Iliad* written between the sixth and the fourth centuries B.C., many have been completely lost: the plays of Cleophon and Hegemon, the poems of Timotheus and Philoxenus about the Cyclops, the burlesque poem *Margites* originally attributed to Homer, the plays of Agathon, Sophocles' *Lynceus,* Astydamas' *Alcmaeon,* Telegonus' *Wounded Odysseus,* and the plays of Carcinus, Dicaeogenes, and Polyidus the Sophist.

him too under the general term poet. So much then for these distinctions.

10. There are, again, some arts which employ all the means above mentioned—namely, rhythm, tune and meter. Such are dithyrambic and nomic poetry,[4] and also tragedy and comedy; but between them the difference is, that in the first two cases these means are all employed in combination, in the latter, now one means is employed, now another.

Such, then, are the differences of the arts with respect to the medium of imitation.

II

Since the objects of imitation are men in action, and these men must be either of a higher or a lower type (for moral character mainly answers to these divisions, goodness and badness being the distinguishing marks of moral differences), it follows that we must represent men either as better than in real life, or as worse, or as they are. It is the same in painting. Polygnotus depicted men as nobler than they are, Pauson as less noble, Dionysius drew them true to life.

2. Now it is evident that each of the modes of imitation above mentioned will exhibit these differences, and become a distinct kind in imitating objects that are thus distinct. 3. Such diversities may be found even in dancing, flute-playing, and lyre playing. So again in language, whether prose or verse unaccompanied by music. Homer, for example, makes men better than they are; Cleophon as they are; Hegemon the Thasian, the inventor of parodies, and Nicochares, the author of the *Deiliad* worse than they are. 4. The same thing holds good of dithyrambs and nomes; here too one may portray different types, as Timotheus and Philoxenus differed in representing their Cyclopes. The same distinction marks off tragedy from comedy; for comedy aims at representing men as worse, tragedy as better than in actual life.

III

There is still a third difference—the manner in which each of these objects may be imitated. For the medium being the same, and the objects the same, the poet may imitate by narration—in which case he can either take another personality as Homer does, or speak in his own person, unchanged[5]—or he may present all his characters as living and moving before us.

2. These, then, as we said at the beginning, are the three differences which distinguish artistic imitation— the medium, the objects and the manner. So that from one point of view, Sophocles[6] is an imitator of the same kind as Homer— for both imitate higher types of character; from another point of view, of the same kind as Aristophanes—for both imitate persons acting and doing. 3. Hence, some say, the name of "drama" is given to such poems, as representing action. For the same reason the Dorians claim the invention both of tragedy and comedy. The claim to comedy is put forward by the Megarians—not only by those of Greece proper, who allege that it originated under their democracy, but also by the Megarians of Sicily, for the poet Epicharmus, who is much earlier than Chionides and Magnes, belonged to that country. Tragedy too is claimed by certain Dorians of the Peloponnese. In each case they appeal to the evidence of language. The outlying villages, they say, are by them called κῶμαι, by the Athenians δῆμοι: and they assume that comedians were so named not from κωμάζειν, "to revel," but because they wandered from village to village (κατὰ κώμας), being excluded contemptuously from the city. They add also that the Dorian word for "doing" is δρᾶν, and the Athenian, πράττειν.

4. This may suffice as to the number and nature of the various modes of imitation.

IV

Poetry in general seems to have sprung from two causes, each of them lying deep in our nature. 2. First, the instinct of imitation is implanted in man from childhood, one difference between him and other animals being that he is the most imitative of living creatures, and through imitation he learns his earliest lessons; and no less universal is the pleasure felt in things imitated. 3. We have evidence of this in the facts of experience. Objects which in themselves we view with pain, we delight to contemplate when reproduced with minute fidelity: such as the forms of the most ignoble animals and of dead bodies. 4. The cause of this again is, that to learn gives the liveliest pleasure, not only to philosophers but to men in general; whose capacity, however, of learning is more limited. 5. Thus the reason why men enjoy seeing a likeness is, that in contemplating it they find themselves learning or inferring, and saying perhaps, "Ah, that is he." For if you happen not to have seen the original, the pleasure will be due

---

[4]A type of Greek poetry written to be sung and accompanied by flute or lyre, usually addressed to Apollo.

[5]This distinction is made by Plato in *Republic* (see p. 26).

[6]The tragedies of Sophocles (496?–406 B.C.), author of the Oedipus trilogy, figure strongly as models in *Poetics*.

not to the imitation as such, but to the execution, the coloring, or some such other cause.

6. Imitation, then, is one instinct of our nature. Next, there is the instinct for "harmony" and rhythm, meters being manifestly sections of rhythm. Persons, therefore, starting with this natural gift developed by degrees their special aptitudes, till their rude improvisations gave birth to poetry.

7. Poetry now diverged in two directions, according to the individual character of the writers. The graver spirits imitated noble actions, and the actions of good men. The more trivial sort imitated the actions of meaner persons, at first composing satires, as the former did hymns to the gods and the praises of famous men. 8. A poem of the satirical kind cannot indeed be put down to any author earlier than Homer; though many such writers probably there were. But from Homer onward, instances can be cited—his own *Margites*, for example, and other similar compositions. The appropriate meter was also here introduced; hence the measure is still called the iambic or lampooning measure, being that in which people lampooned one another. 9. Thus the older poets were distinguished as writers of heroic or of lampooning verse.

As, in the serious style, Homer is preeminent among poets, for he alone combined dramatic form with excellence of imitation, so he too first laid down the main lines of comedy, by dramatizing the ludicrous instead of writing personal satire. His *Margites* bears the same relation to comedy that the *Iliad* and *Odyssey* do to tragedy. 10. But when tragedy and comedy came to light, the two classes of poets still followed their natural bent: the lampooners became writers of comedy, and the epic poets were succeeded by tragedians, since the drama was a larger and higher form of art.

11. Whether tragedy has as yet perfected its proper types or not; and whether it is to be judged in itself, or in relation also to the audience—this raises another question. 12. Be that as it may, tragedy—as also comedy—was at first mere improvisation. The one originated with the authors of the dithyramb, the other with those of the phallic songs, which are still in use in many of our cities. Tragedy advanced by slow degrees; each new element that showed itself was in turn developed. Having passed through many changes, it found its natural form, and there it stopped.

13. Aeschylus first introduced a second actor; he diminished the importance of the chorus, and assigned the leading part to the dialogue. Sophocles raised the number of actors to three, and added scene-painting. 14. Moreover, it was not till late that the short plot was discarded for one of greater compass, and the grotesque diction of the earlier sa-

tyric form[7] for the stately manner of tragedy. The iambic measure then replaced the trochaic tetrameter, which was originally employed when the poetry was of the satyric order, and had greater affinities with dancing. Once dialogue had come in, nature herself discovered the appropriate measure. For the iambic is, of all measures, the most colloquial: we see it in the fact that conversational speech runs into iambic form more frequently than into any other kind of verse; rarely into hexameters, and only when we drop the colloquial intonation. 15. The additions to the number of "episodes" or acts, and the other accessories of which tradition tells, must be taken as already described; for to discuss them in detail would, doubtless, be a large undertaking.

V

Comedy is, as we have said, an imitation of characters of a lower type—not, however, in the full sense of the word *bad,* the ludicrous being merely a subdivision of the ugly. It consists in some defect or ugliness which is not painful or destructive. To take an obvious example, the comic mask is ugly and distorted, but does not imply pain.

2. The successive changes through which tragedy passed, and the authors of these changes, are well known, whereas comedy has had no history, because it was not at first treated seriously. It was late before the Archon[8] granted a comic chorus to a poet; the performers were till then voluntary. Comedy had already taken definite shape when comic poets, distinctively so called, are heard of. 3. Who introduced masks, or prologues, or increased the number of actors—these and other similar details remain unknown. As for the plot, it came originally from Sicily; but of Athenian writers Crates was the first who, abandoning the "iambic" or lampooning form, generalized his themes and plots.

4. Epic poetry agrees with tragedy insofar as it is an imitation in verse of characters of a higher type. They differ, in that epic poetry admits but one kind of meter, and is narrative in form. They differ, again, in their length: for tragedy endeavors, as far as possible, to confine itself to a single revolution of the sun, or but slightly to exceed this limit; whereas the epic action has no limits of time.[9] This, then, is

---

[7]Plays of Dorian invention, usually burlesques of mythological characters or events. Satyrs formed the chorus.

[8]One of the nine Athenian magistrates.

[9]Neoclassical theorists hardened this observation into a rule, the "unity of time."

a second point of difference; though at first the same free-dom was admitted in tragedy as in epic poetry.

5. Of their constituent parts some are common to both, some peculiar to tragedy. Whoever, therefore, knows what is good or bad tragedy, knows also about epic poetry. All the elements of an epic poem are found in tragedy, but the elements of a tragedy are not all found in the epic poem.

VI

Of the poetry which imitates in hexameter verse, and of comedy, we will speak hereafter.[10] Let us now discuss tragedy, resuming its formal definition, as resulting from what has been already said.

2. Tragedy, then, is an imitation of an action that is serious, complete, and of a certain magnitude; in language embellished with each kind of artistic ornament, the several kinds being found in separate parts of the play; in the form of action, not of narrative; through pity and fear effecting the proper purgation of these emotions. 3. By *language embellished,* I mean language into which rhythm, "harmony," and song enter. By the *several kinds in separate parts,* I mean, that some parts are rendered through the medium of verse alone, others again with the aid of song.

4. Now as tragic imitation implies persons acting, it necessarily follows, in the first place, that spectacular equipment[11] will be a part of tragedy. Next, song and diction, for these are the medium of imitation. By *diction* I mean the mere metrical arrangement of the words: as for *song,* it is a term whose sense everyone understands.

5. Again, tragedy is the imitation of an action; and an action implies personal agents, who necessarily possess certain distinctive qualities both of character and thought; for it is by these that we qualify actions themselves, and these—thought and character—are the two natural causes from which actions spring, and on actions again all success or failure depends. 6. Hence, the plot is the imitation of the action—for by *plot* I here mean the arrangement of the incidents. By character I mean that in virtue of which we ascribe certain qualities to the agents. Thought is required wherever a statement is proved, or, it may be, a general truth enunciated. 7. Every tragedy, therefore, must have six parts, which parts determine its quality—namely, plot, character, diction,

thought, spectacle, song. Two of the parts constitute the medium of imitation, one the manner, and three the objects of imitation. And these complete the list. 8. These elements have been employed, we may say, by the poets to a man; in fact, every play contains spectacular elements as well as character, plot, diction, song, and thought.

9. But most important of all is the structure of the incidents. For tragedy is an imitation, not of men, but of an action and of life, and life consists in action, and its end is a mode of action, not a quality. 10. Now character determines men's qualities, but it is by their actions that they are happy or the reverse. Dramatic action, therefore, is not with a view to the representation of character; character comes in as subsidiary to the actions. Hence the incidents and the plot are the end of a tragedy; and the end is the chief thing of all. 11. Again, without action there cannot be a tragedy; there may be without character. The tragedies of most of our modern poets fail in the rendering of character; and of poets in general this is often true. It is the same in painting; and here lies the difference between Zeuxis and Polygnotus. Polygnotus delineates character well: the style of Zeuxis is devoid of ethical quality. 12. Again, if you string together a set of speeches expressive of character, and well finished in point of diction and thought, you will not produce the essential tragic effect nearly so well as with a play which, however deficient in these respects, yet has a plot and artistically constructed incidents. 13. Besides which, the most powerful elements of emotional interest in tragedy—*peripeteia* or reversal of the situation, and recognition scenes—are parts of the plot. 14. A further proof is, that novices in the art attain to finish of diction and precision of portraiture before they can construct the plot. It is the same with almost all the early poets.

The plot, then, is the first principle, and, as it were, the soul of a tragedy: character holds the second place. 15. A similar fact is seen in painting. The most beautiful colors, laid on confusedly, will not give as much pleasure as the chalk outline of a portrait. Thus tragedy is the imitation of an action, and of the agents mainly with a view to the action.

16. Third in order is thought—that is, the faculty of saying what is possible and pertinent in given circumstances. In the case of oratory, this is the function of the political art and of the art of rhetoric: and so indeed the older poets make their characters speak the language of civic life; the poets of our time, the language of the rhetoricians.

17. Character is that which reveals moral purpose, showing what kind of things a man chooses or avoids. Speeches, therefore, which do not make this manifest, or in which the speaker does not choose or avoid anything

---

[10]This part of *Poetics* is lost. For an attempt to construct an Aristotelian theory of comedy, see Lane Cooper, *An Aristotelian Theory of Comedy* (1922).

[11]By "spectacular equipment" Aristotle means the stage-setting and the various machinery of the theater that produce what is seen.

whatever, are not expressive of character. Thought, on the other hand, is found where something is proved to be or not to be, or a general maxim is enunciated.

18. Fourth among the elements enumerated comes diction; by which I mean, as has been already said, the expression of the meaning in words; and its essence is the same both in verse and prose.

19. Of the remaining elements song holds the chief place among the embellishments.

The spectacle has, indeed, an emotional attraction of its own, but, of all the parts, it is the least artistic, and connected least with the art of poetry. For the power of tragedy, we may be sure, is felt even apart from representation and actors. Besides, the production of spectacular effects depends more on the art of the stage machinist than on that of the poet.

VII

These principles being established, let us now discuss the proper structure of the plot, since this is the first and most important thing in tragedy.

2. Now, according to our definition, tragedy is an imitation of an action that is complete, and whole, and of a certain magnitude; for there may be a whole that is wanting in magnitude. 3. A whole is that which has a beginning, a middle, and an end. A beginning is that which does not itself follow anything by causal necessity, but after which something naturally is or comes to be. An end, on the contrary, is that which itself naturally follows some other thing, either by necessity, or as a rule, but has nothing following it. A middle is that which follows something as some other thing follows it. A well constructed plot, therefore, must neither begin nor end at haphazard, but conform to these principles.

4. Again, a beautiful object, whether it be a picture of a living organism or any whole composed of parts, must not only have an orderly arrangement of parts, but must also be of a certain magnitude; for beauty depends on magnitude and order. Hence an exceedingly small picture cannot be beautiful; for the view of it is confused, the object being seen in an almost imperceptible moment of time. Nor, again, can one of vast size be beautiful; for as the eye cannot take it all in at once, the unity and sense of the whole is lost for the spectator; as for instance if there were one a thousand miles long. 5. As, therefore, in the case of animate bodies and organisms a certain magnitude is necessary, and a magnitude which may be easily embraced in one view; so in the plot, a certain

length is necessary, and a length which can be easily embraced by the memory.[12] 6. The limit of length in relation to dramatic competition and sensuous presentment, is no part of artistic theory. For had it been the rule for a hundred tragedies to compete together, the performance would have been regulated by the water-clock—as indeed we are told was formerly done. 7. But the limit as fixed by the nature of the drama itself is this: the greater the length, the more beautiful will the piece be by reason of its size, provided that the whole be perspicuous. And to define the matter roughly, we may say that the proper magnitude is comprised within such limits, that the sequence of events, according to the law of probability or necessity, will admit of a change from bad fortune to good, or from good fortune to bad.

VIII

Unity of plot does not, as some persons think, consist in the unity of the hero. For infinitely various are the incidents in one man's life, which cannot be reduced to unity; and so, too, there are many actions of one man out of which we cannot make one action.[13] 2. Hence the error, as it appears, of all poets who have composed a Heracleid, a Theseid, or other poems of the kind. They imagine that as Heracles was one man, the story of Heracles must also be a unity. 3. But Homer, as in all else he is of surpassing merit, here too—whether from art or natural genius—seems to have happily discerned the truth. In composing the *Odyssey* he did not include all the adventures of Odysseus—such as his wound on Parnassus, or his feigned madness at the mustering of the host—incidents between which there was no necessary or probable connection: but he made the *Odyssey,* and likewise the *Iliad,* to center round an action that in our sense of the word is one. 4. As therefore, in the other imitative arts, the imitation is one when the object imitated is one, so the plot, being an imitation of an action, must imitate one action and that a whole, the structural union of the parts being such that, if any one of them is displaced or removed, the whole will be disjointed and disturbed. For a thing whose presence or absence makes no visible difference, is not an organic part of the whole.

---

[12]Theories of the beautiful and sublime in the eighteenth and early nineteenth centuries (Addison, Burke, Kant, Schopenhauer) may be considered with Aristotle's conception of magnitude in mind.

[13]Romantic theories emphasizing organicism and expressivism seem often to imply that the unity of the hero's life provides the unity of the poem.

IX

It is, moreover, evident from what has been said, that it is not the function of the poet to relate what has happened, but what may happen—what is possible according to the law of probability or necessity. 2. The poet and the historian differ not by writing in verse or in prose. The work of Herodotus might be put into verse, and it would still be a species of history, with meter no less than without it. The true difference is that one relates what has happened, the other what may happen. 3. Poetry, therefore, is a more philosophical and a higher thing than history: for poetry tends to express the universal, history the particular.[14] 4. By the universal I mean how a person of a certain type will on occasion speak or act, according to the law of probability or necessity; and it is this universality at which poetry aims in the names she attaches to the personages. The particular is—for example—what Alcibiades did or suffered. 5. In comedy this is already apparent: for here the poet first constructs the plot on the lines of probability, and then inserts characteristic names—unlike the lampooners who write about particular individuals. 6. But tragedians still keep to real names, the reason being that what is possible is credible: what has not happened we do not at once feel sure to be possible: but what has happened is manifestly possible: otherwise it would not have happened. 7. Still there are some tragedies in which there are only one or two well-known names, the rest being fictitious. In others, none are well known—as in Agathon's *Antheus,* where incidents and names alike are fictitious, and yet they give none the less pleasure. 8. We must not, therefore, at all costs keep to the received[15] legends, which are the usual subjects of tragedy. Indeed, it would be absurd to attempt it; for even subjects that are known are known only to a few, and yet give pleasure to all. 9. It clearly follows that the poet or "maker" should be the maker of plots rather than of verses; since he is a poet because he imitates, and what he imitates are actions. And even if he chances to take a historical subject, he is none the less a poet; for there is no reason why some events that have actually happened should not conform to the law of the probable and possible, and in virtue of that quality in them he is their poet or maker.

10. Of all plots and actions the episodic are the worst. I call a plot "episodic" in which the episodes or acts succeed one another without probable or necessary sequence. Bad poets compose such pieces by their own fault, good poets, to please the players; for, as they write show pieces for competition, they stretch the plot beyond its capacity, and are often forced to break the natural continuity.

11. But again, tragedy is an imitation not only of a complete action, but of events inspiring fear or pity. Such an effect is best produced when the events come on us by surprise; and the effect is heightened when, at the same time, they follow as cause and effect. 12. The tragic wonder will then be greater than if they happened of themselves or by accident; for even coincidences are most striking when they have an air of design. We may instance the statue of Mitys at Argos, which fell upon his murderer while he was a spectator at a festival, and killed him. Such events seem not to be due to mere chance. Plots, therefore, constructed on these principles are necessarily the best.

X

Plots are either simple or complex, for the actions in real life, of which the plots are an imitation, obviously show a similar distinction. 2. An action which is one and continuous in the sense above defined, I call simple, when the change of fortune takes place without reversal of the situation and without recognition.

A complex action is one in which the change is accompanied by such reversal, or by recognition, or by both. 3. These last should arise from the internal structure of the plot, so that what follows should be the necessary or probable result of the preceding action. It makes all the difference whether any given event is a case of *propter hoc* or *post hoc.*[16]

XI

Reversal of the situation is a change by which the action veers round to its opposite, subject always to our rule of probability or necessity. Thus in the *Oedipus,* the messenger comes to cheer Oedipus and free him from his alarms about his mother, but by revealing who he is, he produces the opposite effect. Again in the *Lynceus,* Lynceus is being led away to his death, and Danaus goes with him, meaning to

---

[14]The matter of universals and particulars becomes of special importance in the eighteenth century and later, when the distinction is made between art, which expresses the particular, and science, which expresses the general. See Cassirer, *Art,* pp. 928–30.

[15]Traditionally accepted.

[16]"Because of this" or "after this."

slay him; but the outcome of the action is, that Danaus is killed and Lynceus saved.

2. Recognition, as the name indicates, is a change from ignorance to knowledge, producing love or hate between the persons destined by the poet for good or bad fortune. The best form of recognition is coincident with a reversal of the situation, as in the *Oedipus*. 3. There are indeed other forms. Even inanimate things of the most trivial kind may sometimes be objects of recognition. Again, we may recognize or discover whether a person has done a thing or not. But the recognition which is most intimately connected with the plot and action is, as we have said, the recognition of persons. 4. This recognition, combined with reversal, will produce either pity or fear; and actions producing these effects are those which, by our definition, tragedy represents. Moreover, it is upon such situations that the issues of good or bad fortune will depend. 5. Recognition, then, being between persons, it may happen that one person only is recognized by the other—when the latter is already known—or it may be necessary that the recognition should be on both sides. Thus Iphigenia is revealed to Orestes by the sending of the letter; but another act of recognition is required to make Orestes known to Iphigenia.

6. Two parts, then, of the plot—reversal of the situation and recognition—turn upon surprises. A third part is the scene of suffering. The scene of suffering is a destructive or painful action, such as death on the stage, bodily agony, wounds, and the like.

XII

[The parts of tragedy which must be treated as elements of the whole, have been already mentioned. We now come to the quantitative parts—the separate parts into which tragedy is divided—namely, prologue, episode, exode, choric song; this last being divided into parode and stasimon. These are common to all plays: peculiar to some are the songs of actors from the stage and the commoi.

2. The prologue is that entire part of a tragedy which precedes the parode of the chorus. The episode is that entire part of a tragedy which is between complete choric songs. The exode is that entire part of a tragedy which has no choric song after it. Of the choric part the parode is the first undivided utterance of the chorus: the stasimon is a choric ode without anapests or trochaic tetrameters: the commos is a joint lamentation of chorus and actors. 3. The parts of tragedy which must be treated as elements of the whole have been already mentioned. The quantitative parts—the separate parts into which it is divided—are here enumerated.]

XIII

As the sequel to what has already been said, we must proceed to consider what the poet should aim at, and what he should avoid, in constructing his plots; and by what means the specific effect of tragedy will be produced.

2. A perfect tragedy should, as we have seen, be arranged not on the simple but on the complex plan. It should, moreover, imitate actions which excite pity and fear, this being the distinctive mark of tragic imitation. It follows plainly, in the first place, that the change of fortune presented must not be the spectacle of a virtuous man brought from prosperity to adversity: for this moves neither pity nor fear; it merely shocks us. Nor, again, that of a bad man passing from adversity to prosperity: for nothing can be more alien to the spirit of tragedy; it possesses no single tragic quality; it neither satisfies the moral sense, nor calls forth pity or fear.[17] Nor, again, should the downfall of the utter villain be exhibited. A plot of this kind would, doubtless, satisfy the moral sense, but it would inspire neither pity nor fear; for pity is aroused by unmerited misfortune, fear by the misfortune of a man like ourselves. Such an event, therefore, will be neither pitiful nor terrible. 3. There remains, then, the character between these two extremes—that of a man who is not eminently good and just, yet whose misfortune is brought about not by vice or depravity, but by some error or frailty. He must be one who is highly renowned and prosperous—a personage like Oedipus, Thyestes, or other illustrious men of such families.

4. A well-constructed plot should, therefore, be single in its issue, rather than double as some maintain. The change of fortune should be not from bad to good, but, reversely, from good to bad. It should come about as the result not of vice, but of some great error or frailty, in a character either such as we have described, or better rather than worse. 5. The practice of the stage bears out our view. At first the poets recounted any legend that came in their way. Now, the best tragedies are founded on the story of a few houses—on the fortunes of Alcmaeon, Oedipus, Orestes, Meleager, Thyestes, Telephus, and those others who have done or suffered something terrible. A tragedy, then, to be perfect according to the rules of art should be of this construction. 6. Hence they are in error who censure Euripides just because he follows this principle in his plays, many of which

---

[17]Later arguments, beginning with Horace (see *Art of Poetry*, p. 72), that poetry delights and teaches, are related to this statement but seem increasingly rigid in respect to what may be thought truly didactic or delightful.

end unhappily. It is, as we have said, the right ending. The best proof is that on the stage and in dramatic competition, such plays, if well worked out, are the most tragic in effect; and Euripides, faulty though he may be in the general management of his subject, yet is felt to be the most tragic of the poets.

7. In the second rank comes the kind of tragedy which some place first. Like the *Odyssey,* it has a double thread of plot, and also an opposite catastrophe for the good and for the bad. It is accounted the best because of the weakness of the spectators; for the poet is guided in what he writes by the wishes of his audience. 8. The pleasure, however, thence derived is not the true tragic pleasure. It is proper rather to comedy, where those who, in the piece, are the deadliest enemies—like Orestes and Aegisthus—quit the stage as friends at the close, and no one slays or is slain.

XIV

Fear and pity may be aroused by spectacular means; but they may also result from the inner structure of the piece, which is the better way, and indicates a superior poet. For the plot ought to be so constructed that, even without the aid of the eye, he who hears the tale told will thrill with horror and melt to pity at what takes place. This is the impression we should receive from hearing the story of the *Oedipus.* 2. But to produce this effect by the mere spectacle is a less artistic method, and dependent on extraneous aids. Those who employ spectacular means to create a sense not of the terrible but only of the monstrous, are strangers to the purpose of tragedy; for we must not demand of tragedy any and every kind of pleasure, but only that which is proper to it. 3. And since the pleasure which the poet should afford is that which comes from pity and fear through imitation, it is evident that this quality must be impressed upon the incidents.

Let us then determine what are the circumstances which strike us as terrible or pitiful.

4. Actions capable of this effect must happen between persons who are either friends or enemies or indifferent to one another. If an enemy kills an enemy, there is nothing to excite pity either in the act or the intention—except so far as the suffering in itself is pitiful. So again with indifferent persons. But when the tragic incident occurs between those who are near or dear to one another—if, for example, a brother kills, or intends to kill, a brother, a son his father, a mother her son, a son his mother, or any other deed of the kind is done—these are the situations to be looked for by the poet. 5. He may not indeed destroy the framework of the received legends—the fact, for instance, that Clytemnestra was slain

by Orestes and Eriphyle by Alcmaeon—but he ought to show invention of his own, and skillfully handle the traditional material. Let us explain more clearly what is meant by skillful handling.

6. The action may be done consciously and with knowledge of the persons, in the manner of the older poets. It is thus too that Euripides makes Medea slay her children. Or, again, the deed of horror may be done, but done in ignorance, and the tie of kinship or friendship be discovered afterwards. The *Oedipus* of Sophocles is an example. Here, indeed, the incident is outside the drama proper; but cases occur where it falls within the action of the play: one may cite the *Alcmaeon* of Astydamas, or Telegonus in the *Wounded Odysseus.* 7. Again, there is a third case— < to be about to act with knowledge of the persons and then not to act. The fourth case is > when someone is about to do an irreparable deed through ignorance, and makes the discovery before it is done. These are the only possible ways. For the deed must either be done or not done—and that wittingly or unwittingly. But of all these ways, to be about to act knowing the persons, and then not to act, is the worst. It is shocking without being tragic, for no disaster follows. It is, therefore, never, or very rarely, found in poetry. One instance, however, is in the *Antigone,* where Haemon threatens to kill Creon. 8. The next and better way is that the deed should be perpetrated. Still better, that it should be perpetrated in ignorance, and the discovery made afterwards. There is then nothing to shock us, while the discovery produces a startling effect. 9. The last case is the best, as when in the *Cresphontes* Merope is about to slay her son, but, recognizing who he is, spares his life. So in the *Iphigenia,* the sister recognizes the brother just in time. Again in the *Helle,* the son recognizes the mother when on the point of giving her up. This, then, is why a few families only, as has been already observed, furnish the subjects of tragedy. It was not art, but happy chance, that led poets to look for such situations and so impress the tragic quality upon their plots. They are compelled, therefore, to have recourse to those houses whose history contains moving incidents like these.

Enough has now been said concerning the structure of the incidents, and the proper constitution of the plot.

XV

In respect of character there are four things to be aimed at. First, and most important, it must be good. Now any speech or action that manifests moral purpose of any kind will be expressive of character: the character will be good if the purpose is good. This rule is relative to each class. Even a woman may be good, and also a slave; though the woman may be said to be an inferior being, and the slave quite worthless. 2. The second thing to aim at is propriety. There is a type of manly valor; but valor in a woman, or unscrupulous cleverness, is inappropriate. 3. Thirdly, character must be true to life: for this is a distinct thing from goodness and propriety, as here described. 4. The fourth point is consistency: for though the subject of the imitation, who suggested the type, be inconsistent, still he must be consistently inconsistent. 5. As an example of motiveless degradation of character, we have Menelaus in the *Orestes:* of character indecorous and inappropriate, the lament of Odysseus in the *Scylla,* and the speech of Melanippe: of inconsistency, the *Iphigenia at Aulis*—for Iphigenia the suppliant in no way resembles her later self.

6. As in the structure of the plot, so too in the portraiture of character, the poet should always aim either at the necessary or the probable. Thus a person of a given character should speak or act in a given way, by the rule either of necessity or of probability; just as this event should follow that by necessary or probable sequence. 7. It is therefore evident that the unraveling of the plot, no less than the complication, must arise out of the plot itself, it must not be brought about by the *deus ex machina*—as in the *Medea,* or in the return of the Greeks in the *Iliad*. The *deus ex machina* should be employed only for events external to the drama—for antecedent or subsequent events, which lie beyond the range of human knowledge, and which require to be reported or foretold; for to the gods we ascribe the power of seeing all things. Within the action there must be nothing irrational. If the irrational cannot be excluded, it should be outside the scope of the tragedy. Such is the irrational element in the *Oedipus* of Sophocles.

8. Again, since tragedy is an imitation of persons who are above the common level, the example of good portrait-painters should be followed. They, while reproducing the distinctive form of the original, make a likeness which is true to life and yet more beautiful. So too the poet, in representing men who are irascible or indolent, or have other defects of character, should preserve the type and yet ennoble it. In this way Achilles is portrayed by Agathon and Homer.

9. These then are rules the poet should observe. Nor should he neglect those appeals to the senses, which, though not among the essentials, are the concomitants of poetry; for here too there is much room for error. But of this enough has been said in our published treatises.

XVI

What recognition is has been already explained. We will now enumerate its kinds.

First, the least artistic form, which, from poverty of wit, is most commonly employed—recognition by signs. 2. Of these some are congenital—such as "the spear which the earthborn race bear on their bodies," or the stars introduced by Carcinus in his *Thyestes*. Others are acquired after birth; and of these some are bodily marks, as scars; some external tokens, as necklaces, or the little ark in the *Tyro* by which the discovery is effected. 3. Even these admit of more or less skillful treatment. Thus in the recognition of Odysseus by his scar, the discovery is made in one way by the nurse, in another by the swineherds. The use of tokens for the express purpose of proof—and, indeed, any formal proof with or without tokens—is a less artistic mode of recognition. A better kind is that which comes about by a turn of incident, as in the bath scene in the *Odyssey*.

4. Next come the recognitions invented at will by the poet, and on that account wanting in art. For example, Orestes in the *Iphigenia* reveals the fact that he is Orestes. She, indeed, makes herself known by the letter; but he, by speaking himself and saying what the poet, not what the plot requires. This, therefore, is nearly allied to the fault above mentioned—for Orestes might as well have brought tokens with him. Another similar instance is the "voice of the shuttle" in the *Tereus* of Sophocles.

5. The third kind depends on memory when the sight of some object awakens a feeling: as in the *Cyprians* of Dicaeogenes, where the hero breaks into tears on seeing the picture; or again in the "Lay of Alcinous," where Odysseus, hearing the minstrel play the lyre, recalls the past and weeps; and hence the recognition.

6. The fourth kind is by process of reasoning. Thus in the *Choëphori*—"Someone resembling me has come: no one resembles me but Orestes: therefore Orestes has come." Such too is the discovery made by Iphigenia in the play of Polyidus the Sophist. It was a natural reflection for Orestes to make, "So I too must die at the altar like my sister." So, again, in the *Tydeus* of Theodectes, the father says, "I came to find my son, and I lose my own life." So too in the *Phineidae:* the women, on seeing the place, inferred their fate—"Here we are doomed to die, for here we were cast forth." 7. Again, there is a composite kind of recognition involving false inference on the part of one of the characters, as in the *Odysseus Disguised as a Messenger*. A said < that no one else was able to bend the bow; . . . hence B (the disguised Odysseus) imagined that A would > recognize the bow which, in fact, he had not seen; and to bring about a recognition by this means—the expectation that A would recognize the bow—is false inference.

8. But, of all recognitions, the best is that which arises from the incidents themselves, where the startling discovery is made by natural means. Such is that in the *Oedipus* of

Sophocles, and in the *Iphigenia;* for it was natural that Iphigenia should wish to dispatch a letter. These recognitions alone dispense with the artificial aid of tokens or amulets. Next come the recognitions by process of reasoning.

XVII

In constructing the plot and working it out with the proper diction, the poet should place the scene, as far as possible, before his eyes. In this way, seeing everything with the utmost vividness, as if he were a spectator of the action, he will discover what is in keeping with it, and be most unlikely to overlook inconsistencies. The need of such a rule is shown by the fault found in Carcinus. Amphiaraus was on his way from the temple. This fact escaped the observation of one who did not see the situation. On the stage, however, the piece failed, the audience being offended at the oversight.

2. Again, the poet should work out his play, to the best of his power, with appropriate gestures; for those who feel emotion are most convincing through natural sympathy with the characters they represent; and one who is agitated storms, one who is angry rages, with the most lifelike reality. Hence poetry implies either a happy gift of nature or a strain of madness. In the one case a man can take the mold of any character; in the other, he is lifted out of his proper self.

3. As for the story, whether the poet takes it ready-made or constructs it for himself, he should first sketch its general outline, and then fill in the episodes and amplify in detail. The general plan may be illustrated by the *Iphigenia.* A young girl is sacrificed; she disappears mysteriously from the eyes of those who sacrificed her; she is transported to another country where the custom is to offer up all strangers to the goddess. To this ministry she is appointed. Some time later her own brother chances to arrive. The fact that the oracle for some reason ordered him to go there, is outside the general plan of the play. The purpose, again, of his coming is outside the action proper. However, he comes, he is seized, and, when on the point of being sacrificed, reveals who he is. The mode of recognition may be either that of Euripides or of Polyidus, in whose play he exclaims very naturally— "So it was not my sister only, but I too, who was doomed to be sacrificed"; and by that remark he is saved.

4. After this, the names being once given, it remains to fill in the episodes. We must see that they are relevant to the action. In the case of Orestes, for example, there is the madness which led to his capture, and his deliverance by means of the purificatory rite. 5. In the drama, the episodes are short, but it is these that give extension to epic poetry. Thus the story of the *Odyssey* can be stated briefly. A certain man is absent from home for many years; he is jealously watched by Poseidon, and left desolate. Meanwhile his home is in a wretched plight—suitors are wasting his substance and plotting against his son. At length, tempest-tossed, he himself arrives; he makes certain persons acquainted with him; he attacks the suitors with his own hand, and is himself preserved while he destroys them. This is the essence of the plot; the rest is episode.

XVIII

Every tragedy falls into two parts—complication and unraveling or dénouement. Incidents extraneous to the action are frequently combined with a portion of the action proper, to form the complication; the rest is the unraveling. By the complication I mean all that extends from the beginning of the action to the part which marks the turning-point to good or bad fortune. The unraveling is that which extends from the beginning of the change to the end. Thus, in the *Lynceus* of Theodectes, the complication consists of the incidents presupposed in the drama, the seizure of the child, and then again * * < The unraveling > extends from the accusation of murder to the end.

2. There are four kinds of tragedy, the complex, depending entirely on reversal of the situation and recognition; the pathetic (where the motive is passion) —such as the tragedies on Ajax and Ixion; the ethical (where the motives are ethical)—such as the *Phthiotides* and the *Peleus.* The fourth kind is the simple. < We here exclude the purely spectacular element >, exemplified by the *Phorcides,* the *Prometheus,* and scenes laid in Hades. 3. The poet should endeavor, if possible, to combine all poetic elements; or failing that, the greatest number and those the most important; the more so, in face of the caviling criticism of the day. For whereas there have hitherto been good poets, each in his own branch, the critics now expect one man to surpass all others in their several lines of excellence.

In speaking of a tragedy as the same or different, the best test to take is the plot. Identity exists where the complication and unraveling are the same. Many poets tie the knot well, but unravel it ill. Both arts, however, should always be mastered.

4. Again, the poet should remember what has been often said, and not make an epic structure into a tragedy—by an epic structure I mean one with a multiplicity of plots—as if, for instance, you were to make a tragedy out of the entire story of the *Iliad.* In the epic poem, owing to its length, each part assumes its proper magnitude. In the drama the result is far from answering to the poet's expectation. 5. The proof is that the poets who have dramatized the whole story of the fall of Troy, instead of selecting portions like Euripides; or

who have taken the whole tale of Niobe, and not a part of her story, like Aeschylus, either fail utterly or meet with poor success on the stage. Even Agathon has been known to fail from this one defect. In his reversals of the situation, however, he shows a marvelous skill in the effort to hit the popular taste—to produce a tragic effect that satisfies the moral sense. 6. This effect is produced when the clever rogue, like Sisyphus, is outwitted, or the brave villain defeated. Such an event is probable in Agathon's sense of the word: "it is probable," he says, "that many things should happen contrary to probability."

7. The chorus too should be regarded as one of the actors; it should be an integral part of the whole, and share in the action, in the manner not of Euripides but of Sophocles. As for the later poets, their choral songs pertain as little to the subject of the piece as to that of any other tragedy. They are, therefore, sung as mere interludes—a practice first begun by Agathon. Yet what difference is there between introducing such choral interludes, and transferring a speech, or even a whole act, from one play to another?

XIX

It remains to speak of diction and thought, the other parts of tragedy having been already discussed. Concerning thought, we may assume what is said in the rhetoric, to which inquiry the subject more strictly belongs. 2. Under thought is included every effect which has to be produced by speech, the subdivisions being—proof and refutation; the excitation of the feelings, such as pity, fear, anger, and the like; the suggestion of importance or its opposite. 3. Now, it is evident that the dramatic incidents must be treated from the same points of view as the dramatic speeches, when the object is to evoke the sense of pity, fear, importance, or probability. The only difference is, that the incidents should speak for themselves without verbal exposition; while the effects aimed at in speech should be produced by the speaker, and as a result of the speech. For what were the business of a speaker, if the thought were revealed quite apart from what he says?

4. Next, as regards diction. One branch of the inquiry treats of the modes of utterance. But this province of knowledge belongs to the art of delivery and to the masters of that science. It includes, for instance—what is a command, a prayer, a statement, a threat, a question, an answer, and so forth. 5. To know or not to know these things involves no serious censure upon the poet's art. For who can admit the fault imputed to Homer by Protagoras—that in the words, "Sing, goddess, of the wrath," he gives a command under the idea that he utters a prayer? For to tell someone to do a thing or not to do it is, he says, a command. We may, therefore, pass this over as an inquiry that belongs to another art, not to poetry.

XX

[Language in general includes the following parts: letter, syllable, connecting word, noun, verb, inflection or case, sentence or phrase.

2. A letter is an indivisible sound, yet not every such sound, but only one which can form part of a group of sounds. For even brutes utter indivisible sounds, none of which I call a letter. 3. The sound I mean may be either a vowel, a semivowel, or a mute. A vowel is that which without impact of tongue or lip has an audible sound. A semivowel, that which with such impact has an audible sound, as *s* and *r*. A mute, that which with such impact has by itself no sound, but joined to a vowel sound becomes audible, as *g* and *d*. 4. These are distinguished according to the form assumed by the mouth and the place where they are produced; according as they are aspirated or smooth, long or short; as they are acute, grave, or of an intermediate tone; which inquiry belongs in detail to the writers in meter.

5. A syllable is a nonsignificant sound, composed of a mute and a vowel: for *gr* without *a* is a syllable, as also with *a—gra*. But the investigation of these differences belongs also to metrical science.

6. A connecting word is a nonsignificant sound, which neither causes nor hinders the union of many sounds into one significant sound; it may be placed at either end or in the middle of a sentence. Or, a nonsignificant sound, which out of several sounds, each of them significant, is capable of forming one significant sound—as ἀμφί, περί, and the like. 7. Or, a nonsignificant sound, which marks the beginning, end, or division of a sentence; such, however, that it cannot correctly stand by itself at the beginning of a sentence—as μέν, ἤτοι, δέ.

8. A noun is a composite significant sound, not marking time, of which no part is in itself significant: for in double or compound words we do not employ the separate parts as if each were in itself significant. Thus in Theodorus, *god-given,* the δῶρον or "gift" is not in itself significant.

9. A verb is a composite significant sound, marking time, in which, as in the noun, no part is in itself significant. For *man* or *white* does not express the idea of *when;* but *he walks* or *he has walked* does connote time, present or past.

10. Inflection belongs both to the noun and verb, and expresses either the relation *of, to,* or the like; or that of number, whether one or many, as *man* or *men;* or the modes or tones in actual delivery, e.g. a question or a command. *Did he go?* and *go* are verbal inflections of this kind.

11. A sentence or phrase is a composite significant sound, some at least of whose parts are in themselves significant; for not every such group of words consists of verbs and nouns—"the definition of man," for example—but it may dispense even with the verb. Still it will always have some significant part, as *in walking*, or *Cleon son of Cleon*. A sentence or phrase may form a unity in two ways—either as signifying one thing, or as consisting of several parts linked together. Thus the *Iliad* is one by the linking together of parts, the definition of man by the unity of the thing signified.]

XXI

Words are of two kinds, simple and double. By simple I mean those composed of nonsignificant elements, such as γῆ. By double or compound, those composed either of a significant and nonsignificant element (though within the whole word no element is significant), or of elements that are both significant. A word may likewise be triple, quadruple, or multiple in form, like so many Massilian expressions, e.g. *Hermo-caico-xanthus* < who prayed to Father Zeus. >

2. Every word is either current, or strange, or metaphorical, or ornamental, or newly coined, or lengthened, or contracted, or altered.

3. By a current or proper word I mean one which is in general use among a people; by a strange word, one which is in use in another country. Plainly, therefore, the same word may be at once strange and current, but not in relation to the same people. The word οἴγυνον, "lance," is to the Cyprians a current term but to us a strange one.

4. Metaphor is the application of an alien name by transference either from genus to species, or from species to genus, or from species to species, or by analogy, that is, proportion. 5. Thus from genus to species, as: "There lies my ship"; for lying at anchor is a species of lying. From species to genus, as: "Verily ten thousand noble deeds hath Odysseus wrought"; for ten thousand is a species of large number, and is here used for a large number generally. From species to species, as: "With blade of bronze drew away the life," and "Cleft the water with the vessel of unyielding bronze." Here ἀρύσαι, "to draw away," is used for ταμεῖν, "to cleave," and ταμεῖν again for ἀρύσαι—each being a species of taking away. 6. Analogy or proportion is when the second term is to the first as the fourth to the third. We may then use the fourth for the second, or the second for the fourth. Sometimes too we qualify the metaphor by adding the term to which the proper word is relative. Thus the cup is to Dionysus as the shield to Ares. The cup may, therefore, be called "the shield of Dionysus," and the shield, "the cup

of Ares." Or, again, as old age is to life, so is evening to day. Evening may therefore be called "the old age of the day," and old age, "the evening of life," or, in the phrases of Empedocles, "life's setting sun." 7. For some of the terms of the proportion there is at times no word in existence; still the metaphor may be used. For instance, to scatter seed is called sowing: but the action of the sun in scattering his rays is nameless. Still this process bears to the sun the same relation as sowing to the seed. Hence the expression of the poet "sowing the god-created light." 8. There is another way in which this kind of metaphor may be employed. We may apply an alien term, and then deny of that term one of its proper attributes; as if we were to call the shield, not "the cup of Ares," but "the wineless cup."

< An ornamental word . . . >

9. A newly coined word is one which has never been even in local use, but is adopted by the poet himself. Some such words there appear to be: as ἐρνύγες, "sprouters," for κέρατα, "horns," and ἀρητήρ, "supplicator," for ἱερεύς, "priest."

10. A word is lengthened when its own vowel is exchanged for a longer one, or when a syllable is inserted. A word is contracted when some part of it is removed. Instances of lengthening are—πόληος for πόλεως, and Πηληιάδεω for Πηλείδου: of contraction—κρῖ, δῶ and ὄψ as in μία γίνεται ἀμφοτέρων ὄψ.

11. An altered word is one in which part of the ordinary form is left unchanged, and part is recast; as in δεξιτερὸν κατὰ μαζόν, δεξιτερόν is for δεξιόν.

12. [Nouns in themselves are either masculine, feminine, or neuter. Masculine are such as end in ν, ρ, ς, or in some letter compounded with ς—these being two, ψ and ξ. Feminine, such as end in vowels that are always long, namely η and ω, and—of vowels that admit of lengthening—those in α. Thus the number of letters in which nouns masculine and feminine end is the same; for ψ and ξ are equivalent to endings in ς. No noun ends in a mute or vowel short by nature. Three only end in ι—μέλι, κόμμι, πέπερι: five end in υ. Neuter nouns end in these two latter vowels; also in ν and ς.]

XXII

The perfection of style is to be clear without being mean. The clearest style is that which uses only current or proper words; at the same time it is mean—witness the poetry of Cleophon and of Sthenelus. That diction, on the other hand, is lofty and raised above the commonplace which employs unusual words. By unusual, I mean strange (or rare) words, metaphorical, lengthened—anything, in short, that differs from the normal idiom. 2. Yet a style wholly composed of such words is either a riddle or a jargon; a riddle, if it consists of metaphors; a jargon, if it consists of strange (or rare) words. For the essence of a riddle is to express true facts under impossible combinations. Now this cannot be done by any arrangement of ordinary words, but by the use of metaphor it can. Such is the riddle—"A man I saw who on another man had glued the bronze by aid of fire," and others of the same kind. A diction that is made up of strange (or rare) terms is a jargon. 3. A certain infusion, therefore, of these elements is necessary to style; for the strange (or rare) word, the metaphorical, the ornamental, and the other kinds above mentioned, will raise it above the commonplace and mean, while the use of proper words will make it perspicuous. 4. But nothing contributes more to produce a clearness of diction that is remote from commonness than the lengthening, contraction, and alteration of words. For by deviating in exceptional cases from the normal idiom, the language will gain distinction; while, at the same time, the partial conformity with usage will give perspicuity. 5. The critics, therefore, are in error who censure these licenses of speech, and hold the author up to ridicule. Thus Eucleides, the elder, declared that it would be an easy matter to be a poet if you might lengthen syllables at will. He caricatured the practice in the very form of his diction, as in the verse: Ἐπιχάρην εἶδον Μαραθῶνάδε βαδίζοντα,[18] or, οὐκ ἄν γ' ἐράμενος τὸν ἐκείνου ἐλλέβορον.[19] 6. To employ such license at all obtrusively is, no doubt, grotesque; but in any mode of poetic diction there must be moderation. Even metaphors, strange (or rare) words, or any similar forms of speech, would produce the like effect if used without propriety, and with the express purpose of being ludicrous. 7. How great a difference is made by the appropriate use of lengthening, may be seen in epic poetry by the insertion of ordinary forms in the verse. So, again, if we take a strange (or rare) word, a metaphor, or any similar mode of expression, and replace it by the current or proper term, the truth of our observation will be manifest. For example Aeschylus and Euripides each composed the same iambic line. But the alteration of a single word by Euripides, who employed the rare term instead of the ordinary one, makes one verse appear beautiful and the other trivial. Aeschylus in his *Philoctetes* says: φαγέδαινα <δ'> ἥ μου σάρκας ἐσθίει ποδός.[20] Euripides substitutes θοινᾶται "feasts on" for ἐσθίει "feeds on." Again, in the line, νῦν δέ μ' ἐὼν ὀλίγος τε καὶ οὐτιδανὸς καὶ ἀεικής,[21] the difference will be felt if we substitute the common words,

νῦν δέ μ' ἐὼν μικρός τε καὶ ἀσθενικὸς καὶ ἀειδής.[22] Or, if for the line, δίφρον ἀεικέλιον καταθεὶς ὀλίγην τε τράπεζαν,[23] we read, δίφρον μοχθηρὸν καταθεὶς μικράν τε τράπεζαν.[24] Or, for ἠιόνες βοόωσιν, ἠιόνες κράζουσιν.[25]

8. Again, Ariphrades ridiculed the tragedians for using phrases which no one would employ in ordinary speech: for example, δωμάτων ἄπο instead of ἀπὸ δωμάτων, σέθεν, ἐγὼ δέ νιν, Ἀχιλλέως πέρι instead of περὶ Ἀχιλλέως,[26] and the like. It is precisely because such phrases are not part of the current idiom that they give distinction to the style. This, however, he failed to see.

9. It is a great matter to observe propriety in these several modes of expression as also in compound words, strange (or rare) words, and so forth. But the greatest thing by far is to have a command of metaphor. This alone cannot be imparted by another; it is the mark of genius, for to make good metaphors implies an eye for resemblances.

10. Of the various kinds of words, the compound are best adapted to dithyrambs, rare words to heroic poetry, metaphors to iambic. In heroic poetry, indeed, all these varieties are serviceable. But in iambic verse, which reproduces, as far as may be, familiar speech, the most appropriate words are those which are found even in prose. These are—the current or proper, the metaphorical, the ornamental.

Concerning tragedy and imitation by means of action this may suffice.

XXIII

As to that poetic imitation which is narrative in form and employs a single meter, the plot manifestly ought, as in a tragedy, to be constructed on dramatic principles. It should have for its subject a single action, whole and complete, with a beginning, a middle, and an end. It will thus resemble a living organism in all its unity, and produce the pleasure proper to it. It will differ in structure from historical compositions, which of necessity present not a single action, but a single period, and all that happened within that period to one person or to many, little connected together as the events may be. 2. For as the sea-fight at Salamis and the battle with the Carthaginians in Sicily took place at the same time, but did not tend to any one result, so in the sequence of events, one thing sometimes follows another, and yet no single re-

---

[18]"I saw Epichares walking toward Marathon."
[19]"I might not be wanting his hellebore."
[20]"The cancer that feeds on my foot's flesh."
[21]"But now one, being meager and of no valor and unimportant."

[22]"But now one, being small and puny and unsightly."
[23]"Having set forth a lowly seat and a mean table."
[24]"Having set forth a poor seat and a small table."
[25]"The shores howl, the shores squall."
[26]The anastrophic use of prepositions, that is, the inversion of customary word order, is uncommon and never occurs in prose.

sult is thereby produced. Such is the practice, we may say, of most poets. 3. Here again, then, as has been already observed, the transcendent excellence of Homer is manifest. He never attempts to make the whole war of Troy the subject of his poem, though that war had a beginning and an end. It would have been too vast a theme, and not easily embraced in a single view. If, again, he had kept it within moderate limits, it must have been overcomplicated by the variety of the incidents. As it is, he detaches a single portion, and admits as episodes many events from the general story of the war—such as the catalogue of the ships and others—thus diversifying the poem. All other poets take a single hero, a single period, or an action single indeed, but with a multiplicity of parts. Thus did the author of the *Cypria* and of the *Little Iliad*. 4. For this reason the *Iliad* and the *Odyssey* each furnish the subject of one tragedy, or, at most, of two; while the *Cypria* supplies materials for many, and the *Little Iliad* for eight—the *Award of the Arms*, the *Philoctetes*, the *Neoptolemus*, the *Eurypylus*, the *Mendicant Odysseus*, the *Laconian Women*, the *Fall of Ilium*, the *Departure of the Fleet*.

XXIV

Again, epic poetry must have as many kinds as tragedy: it must be simple, or complex, or "ethical," or "pathetic." The parts also, with the exception of song and spectacle, are the same; for it requires reversals of the situation, recognitions, and scenes of suffering. 2. Moreover, the thoughts and the diction must be artistic. In all these respects Homer is our earliest and sufficient model. Indeed each of his poems has a twofold character. The *Iliad* is at once simple and "pathetic," and the *Odyssey* complex (for recognition scenes run through it), and at the same time "ethical." Moreover, in diction and thought they are supreme.

3. Epic poetry differs from tragedy in the scale on which it is constructed, and in its meter. As regards scale or length, we have already laid down an adequate limit: the beginning and the end must be capable of being brought within a single view. This condition will be satisfied by poems on a smaller scale than the old epics, and answering in length to the group of tragedies presented at a single sitting.

4. Epic poetry has, however, a great—a special—capacity for enlarging its dimensions, and we can see the reason. In tragedy we cannot imitate several lines of actions carried on at one and the same time; we must confine ourselves to the action on the stage and the part taken by the players. But in epic poetry, owing to the narrative form, many events simultaneously transacted can be presented; and these, if relevant to the subject, add mass and dignity to the poem. The epic has here an advantage, and one that conduces to grandeur of effect, to diverting the mind of the hearer, and relieving the story with varying episodes. For sameness of incident soon produces satiety, and makes tragedies fail on the stage.

5. As for the meter, the heroic measure[27] has proved its fitness by the test of experience. If a narrative poem in any other meter or in many meters were now composed, it would be found incongruous. For of all measures the heroic is the stateliest and the most massive; and hence it most readily admits rare words and metaphors, which is another point in which the narrative form of imitation stands alone. On the other hand, the iambic and the trochaic tetrameter are stirring measures, the latter being akin to dancing, the former expressive of action. 6. Still more absurd would it be to mix together different meters, as was done by Chaeremon. Hence no one has ever composed a poem on a great scale in any other than heroic verse. Nature herself, as we have said, teaches the choice of the proper measure.

7. Homer, admirable in all respects, has the special merit of being the only poet who rightly appreciates the part he should take himself. The poet should speak as little as possible in his own person, for it is not this that makes him an imitator. Other poets appear themselves upon the scene throughout, and imitate but little and rarely. Homer, after a few prefatory words, at once brings in a man, or woman, or other personage; none of them wanting in characteristic qualities, but each with a character of his own.

8. The element of the wonderful is required in tragedy. The irrational, on which the wonderful depends for its chief effects, has wider scope in epic poetry, because there the person acting is not seen. Thus, the pursuit of Hector would be ludicrous if placed upon the stage—the Greeks standing still and not joining in the pursuit, and Achilles waving them back. But in the epic poem the absurdity passes unnoticed. Now the wonderful is pleasing: as may be inferred from the fact that everyone tells a story with some addition of his own, knowing that his hearers like it. 9. It is Homer who has chiefly taught other poets the art of telling lies skillfully.[28] The secret of it lies in a fallacy. For, assuming that if one thing is or becomes, a second is or becomes, men imagine that, if the second is, the first likewise is or becomes. But this is a false inference. Hence, where the first thing is untrue, it is quite unnecessary, provided the second be true, to add that the first is or has become. For the mind, knowing the second to be true, falsely infers the truth of the first. There is an example of this in the bath scene of the *Odyssey*.

---

[27]Dactylic hexameter.

[28]See Sidney, *An Apology for Poetry,* p. 155, and Wilde, *The Decay of Lying,* pp. 658–70.

10. Accordingly, the poet should prefer probable impossibilities to improbable possibilities.[29] The tragic plot must not be composed of irrational parts. Everything irrational should, if possible, be excluded; or, at all events, it should lie outside the action of the play (as, in the *Oedipus,* the hero's ignorance as to the manner of Laius' death); not within the drama—as in the *Electra,* the messenger's account of the Pythian games; or, as in the *Mysians,* the man who comes from Tegea to Mysia and is still speechless. The plea that otherwise the plot would have been ruined, is ridiculous; such a plot should not in the first instance be constructed. But once the irrational has been introduced and an air of likelihood imparted to it, we must accept it in spite of the absurdity. Take even the irrational incidents in the *Odyssey,* where Odysseus is left upon the shore of Ithaca. How intolerable even these might have been would be apparent if an inferior poet were to treat the subject. As it is, the absurdity is veiled by the poetic charm with which the poet invests it.

11. The diction should be elaborated in the pauses of the action, where there is no expression of character or thought. For, conversely, character and thought are merely obscured by a diction that is over-brilliant.

XXV

With respect to critical difficulties and their solutions, the number and nature of the sources from which they may be drawn may be thus exhibited.

The poet being an imitator, like a painter or any other artist, must of necessity imitate one of three objects—things as they were or are, things as they are said or thought to be, or things as they ought to be. 2. The vehicle of expression is language—either current terms or, it may be, rare words or metaphors. There are also many modifications of language, which we concede to the poets. 3. Add to this, that the standard of correctness is not the same in poetry and politics, any more than in poetry and any other art. Within the art of poetry itself there are two kinds of faults—those which touch its essence, and those which are accidental. 4. If a poet has chosen to imitate something, < but has imitated it incorrectly > through want of capacity, the error is inherent in the poetry. But if the failure is due to a wrong choice—if he has represented a horse as throwing out both his off legs at once,

or introduced technical inaccuracies in medicine, for example, or in any other art—the error is not essential to the poetry. These are the points of view from which we should consider and answer the objections raised by the critics.[30]

5. First as to matters which concern the poet's own art. If he describes the impossible, he is guilty of an error; but the error may be justified, if the end of the art be thereby attained (the end being that already mentioned)—if, that is, the effect of this or any other part of the poem is thus rendered more striking. A case in point is the pursuit of Hector. If, however, the end might have been as well, or better, attained without violating the special rules of the poetic art, the error is not justified: for every kind of error should, if possible, be avoided.

Again, does the error touch the essentials of the poetic art, or some accident of it? For example, not to know that a hind has no horns is a less serious matter than to paint it inartistically.

6. Further, if it be objected that the description is not true to fact, the poet may perhaps reply, "But the objects are as they ought to be": just as Sophocles said that he drew men as they ought to be; Euripides, as they are. 7. In this way the objection may be met. If however, the representation be of neither kind, the poet may answer, "This is how men say the thing is." This applies to tales about the gods. It may well be that these stories are not higher than fact nor yet true to fact: they are, very possibly, what Xenophanes says of them.[31] But anyhow, "this is what is said." Again, a description may be no better than the fact: "still, it was the fact"; as in the passage about the arms: "Upright upon their butt-ends stood the spears." This was the custom then, as it now is among the Illyrians.

8. Again, in examining whether what has been said or done by someone is poetically right or not, we must not look merely to the particular act or saying, and ask whether it is poetically good or bad. We must also consider by whom it is said or done, to whom, when, by what means, or for what end; whether, for instance, it be to secure a greater good, or avert a greater evil.

9. Other difficulties may be resolved by due regard to the usage of language. We may note a rare word, as in οὐρῆας μὲν πρῶτον, where the poet perhaps employs οὐρῆας not in the sense of mules, but of sentinels. So, again, of Dolon: "ill-favored indeed he was to look upon." It is not meant that his body was ill-shaped, but that his face was

---

[29]On this point one may contrast Aristotle's system, which emphasizes the medium and the poetic whole, with Plato's, which emphasizes naive imitation. See Mazzoni on icastic and fantastic imitation in *On the Defense of the Comedy of Dante,* p. 166.

[30]This section (XXV. 1–4) appears to be a direct response to Plato's theory of imitation.

[31]Xenophanes, philosopher and poet of the sixth century B.C., said that stories about the gods at least reflected men's opinions about the gods.

ugly; for the Cretans used the word εὐειδές, "well-fa-vored," to denote a fair face. Again, ζωρότερον δὲ κέραιε, "mix the drink livelier," does not mean "mix it stronger" as for hard drinkers, but "mix it quicker."

10. Sometimes an expression is metaphorical, as "Now all gods and men were sleeping through the night," while at the same time the poet says: "Often indeed as he turned his gaze to the Trojan plain, he marveled at the sound of flutes and pipes." *All* is here used metaphorically for *many,* all being a species of many. So in the verse, "alone she hath no part . . . ," οἴη, "alone," is metaphorical; for the best known may be called the only one.

11. Again, the solution may depend upon accent or breathing. Thus Hippias of Thasos solved the difficulties in the line, δίδομεν (διδόμεν) δέ οἱ, and τὸ μὲν οὖ (οὐ) καταπύθεται ὄμβρῳ.

12. Or again, the question may be solved by punctua-tion, as in Empedocles, "Of a sudden things became mortal that before had learnt to be immortal, and things unmixed before mixed."

13. Or again, by ambiguity of meaning, as in παρῴχη-κεν δὲ πλέω νύξ, where the word πλέω is ambiguous.

14. Or by the usage of language. Thus any mixed drink is called οἶνος, "wine." Hence Ganymede is said "to pour the wine to Zeus," though the gods do not drink wine. So too workers in iron are called χαλκέας, or workers in bronze. This, however, may also be taken as a metaphor.

15. Again, when a word seems to involve some incon-sistency of meaning, we should consider how many senses it may bear in the particular passage. 16. For example: "there was stayed the spear of bronze"—we should ask in how many ways we may take "being checked there." The true mode of interpretation is the precise opposite of what Glau-con mentions. Critics, he says, jump at certain groundless conclusions; they pass adverse judgment and then proceed to reason on it; and, assuming that the poet has said whatever they happen to think, find fault if a thing is inconsistent with their own fancy. The question about Icarius has been treated in this fashion. The critics imagine he was a Lacedaemonian. They think it strange, therefore, that Telemachus should not have met him when he went to Lacedaemon. But the Ce-phallenian story may perhaps be the true one. They allege that Odysseus took a wife from among themselves, and that her father was Icadius not Icarius. It is merely a mistake, then, that gives plausibility to the objection.

17. In general, the impossible must be justified by ref-erence to artistic requirements, or to the higher reality, or to received opinion. With respect to the requirements of art, a probable impossibility is to be preferred to a thing improba-ble and yet possible. Again, it may be impossible that there should be men such as Zeuxis painted. "Yes," we say, "but the impossible is the higher thing; for the ideal type must surpass the reality." To justify the irrational, we appeal to what is commonly said to be. In addition to which, we urge that the irrational sometimes does not violate reason; just as "it is probable that a thing may happen contrary to probability."

18. Things that sound contradictory should be exam-ined by the same rules as in dialectical refutation—whether the same thing is meant, in the same relation, and in the same sense. We should therefore solve the question by reference to what the poet says himself or to what is tacitly assumed by a person of intelligence.

19. The element of the irrational, and, similarly, de-pravity of character, are justly censured when there is no inner necessity for introducing them. Such is the irrational element in the introduction of Aegeus of Euripides, and the badness of Menelaus in the *Orestes.*

20. Thus, there are five sources from which critical ob-jections are drawn. Things are censured either as impossible, or irrational, or morally hurtful, or contradictory, or contrary to artistic correctness. The answers should be sought under the twelve heads above mentioned.

XXVI

The question may be raised whether the epic or tragic mode of imitation is the higher. If the more refined art is the higher, and the more refined in every case is that which appeals to the better sort of audience, the art which imitates anything and everything is manifestly most unrefined.[32] The audience is supposed to be too dull to comprehend unless something of their own is thrown in by the performers, who therefore indulge in restless movements. Bad flute-players twist and twirl, if they have to represent "the quoit-throw," or hustle the coryphaeus when they perform the "Scylla." 2. Trag-edy, it is said, has this same defect. We may compare the opinion that the older actors entertained of their successors. Mynniscus used to call Callippides "ape" on account of the extravagance of his action, and the same view was held of Pindarus. Tragic art, then, as a whole, stands to epic in the same relation as the younger to the elder actors. So we are told that epic poetry is addressed to a cultivated audience,

---

[32]Aristotle here introduces the whole problem of judgment by way of affect and the problem of taste—problems that he indirectly touched on earlier in *Poetics* (p. 53) when he mentioned purgation (catharsis). See Hume, *Of the Standard of Taste,* pp. 307–15.

who do not need gesture; tragedy, to an inferior public. 3. Being then unrefined, it is evidently the lower of the two.

Now, in the first place, this censure attaches not to the poetic but to the histrionic art; for gesticulation may be equally overdone in epic recitation, as by Sosistratus, or in lyrical competition, as by Mnasitheus the Opuntian. Next, all action is not to be condemned—any more than all dancing—but only that of bad performers. Such was the fault found in Callippides, as also in others of our own day, who are censured for representing degraded women. Again, tragedy like epic poetry produces its effect even without action; it reveals its power by mere reading. If, then, in all other respects it is superior, this fault, we say, is not inherent in it.

4. And superior it is, because it has all the epic elements—it may even use the epic meter—with the music and spectacular effects as important accessories; and these produce the most vivid of pleasures. Further, it has vividness of impression in reading as well as in representation. 5. Moreover, the art attains its end within narrower limits; for the concentrated effect is more pleasurable than one which is spread over a long time and so diluted. What, for example, would be the effect of the *Oedipus* of Sophocles, if it were cast into a form as long as the *Iliad?* 6. Once more, the epic imitation has less unity; as is shown by this, that any epic poem will furnish subjects for several tragedies. Thus if the story adopted by the poet has a strict unity, it must either be concisely told and appear truncated; or, if it conform to the epic canon of length, it must seem weak and watery. < Such length implies some loss of unity, > if, I mean, the poem is constructed out of several actions, like the *Iliad* and the *Odyssey,* which have many such parts, each with a certain magnitude of its own. Yet these poems are as perfect as possible in structure; each is, in the highest degree attainable, an imitation of a single action.

7. If then, tragedy is superior to epic poetry in all these respects, and, moreover, fulfills its specific function better as an art—for each art ought to produce, not any chance pleasure, but the pleasure proper to it, as already stated—it plainly follows that tragedy is the higher art, as attaining its end more perfectly.

8. Thus much may suffice concerning tragic and epic poetry in general; their several kinds and parts, with the number of each and their differences; the causes that make a poem good or bad; the objections of the critics and the answers to these objections.

Horace

65–8 B.C.

The verse letter of Horace (Quintus Horatius Flaccus) to the Piso family does not stand out as particularly profound beside the theoretical work of Aristotle or the moral philosophy of Plato. Horace is, perhaps, a little too enamored of ancient Greek literary practice, and he is clearly more interested in the practical question of how the poet may delight and instruct an intelligent reader than he is in defining what a poem is or what literature is. Nevertheless, in his own urbane way Horace comments on widely divergent problems of literary composition and offers useful advice to the prospective writer. To the student of the history of criticism, his work is of interest because a number of its catch phrases have had considerable influence particularly in the neoclassical movements in France and England.

"It is an old question," he remarks, "whether a praiseworthy poem be the creation of nature or art." Horace's version of imitation recognizes the importance of copying nature but emphasizes imitation of the methods of other authors. This emphasis is echoed by neoclassical writers like Boileau and Pope, and it is heard in a modern version in Eliot and in Frye, both of whom are deeply concerned with the continuity of literary tradition. The idea that the poem is like a picture, attributed to Horace through interpretation of the phrase *ut pictura poesis*, is not original with him but apparently traceable back to Simonides, a Greek poet of the fifth century B.C. It has been yanked from its context in Horace by most commentators and left devoid of qualifications. Horace says that poetry is like painting in that some works will be more effective viewed up close, others farther off. He uses this analogy to emphasize the variety of poetry rather than to limit it to the effects of painting in words. Though Horace does see similarities between the poem and painting and tends to think of the poem in spatial figures, he can hardly be held responsible for the tendency of later critics of neoclassical persuasion to extend the analogy. One may compare Lessing's discussion of the differences between poetry and the plastic arts in *Laocoön* to the tenets of those who, thinking they follow Horace, emphasize the similarities.

Horace emphasizes decorum, by which he means the rightness of each part to the whole. He is not, however, an organicist believing that internal order or organic unity is the only value. Though he thinks that the poet may invent if his invention is in harmony with itself, there are definite limits beyond which good taste should not carry an author. Later neoclassical critics occasionally turned his suggestions and comments into rigid law. We value him most for his sense of restraint and his view of the artist as a craftsman. His concept of decorum—important to Boileau and Pope—leads to a concern with the relation of the poem to the reader.

A useful standard edition is the Loeb Classics *Satires, Epistles and Ars Poetica,* edited by H. R. Fairclough (1936). See Grant Showerman, *Horace and His Influence*

(1922); A. Y. Campbell, *Horace: A New Interpretation* (1924); J. W. H. Atkins, *Literary Criticism in Antiquity*, Vol. II (1934); P. F. Saintonge and others, *Horace: Three Phases of His Influence* (1936); L. P. Wilkinson, *Horace and His Lyric Poetry* (1945); Edouard Fraenkel, *Horace* (1957); C. O. Brink, *Horace on Poetry* (1963); G. M. A. Grube, *The Greek and Roman Critics* (1965); and G. C. Fiske, *Lucilius and Horace: A Study of the Classical Theory of Imitation* (1966). On *ut pictura poesis* see W. G. Howard, *"Ut Pictura Poesis,"* PMLA, XXIV (1909), 46–123; Cicely Davies, *"Ut Pictura Poesis," Modern Language Review,* XXX (1935), 159–69; and Kenneth J. Reckford, *Horace* (1969).

Art of Poetry

[*Unity and simplicity of form.*] If a painter should decide to join the neck of a horse to a human head, and to lay many-colored feathers upon limbs taken from here or there, so that what is a comely woman above ended as a dark, grotesque fish below, could you, my friends, if you were allowed to see it, keep from laughing? Believe me, dear Pisos,[1] a book may be like just such a picture if it portray idle imaginings shaped like the dreams of a sick man, so that neither head nor foot can be properly ascribed to any one shape. You may say, "Painters and Poets have always had an equal privilege of daring to do anything they wish." This is true; as poets, we claim this licence for ourselves, and grant it to others. But we do not carry it so far as to allow that savage animals should be united with tame, serpents with birds, lambs with tigers.

Works with solemn beginnings, which start with great promises, often have one or two purple patches tacked on, in order to catch the eye. For example, there may be a description of Diana's grove and altar, and of "the moving stream that winds through the fair fields," or the River Rhine, or a description of a rainbow. This is not the place for such things. Perhaps you can sketch a cypress tree. But what has that to do with the matter if you have been commissioned to portray a sailor struggling in despair to escape from a shipwreck? A wine-jar may be intended at the start; why, then, from the potter's wheel, does it end up as a pitcher? In short, whatever your work may be, let it at least have simplicity and unity.

Among us poets, most—O father and sons worthy of you—are deceived by a superficial idea of the correct thing to do. I try to be brief, and only end by being obscure. Attempting to be smooth, one simply ends up lacking vigor and fire. Another, in striving for the sublime, may fall into bombast; while still another, by being too cautious and afraid of the storm, creeps along the ground. If one has a single subject, and then tries too eagerly to vary it by any means possible, one is then like a painter who puts a dolphin into a forest, or a wild boar on top of the ocean-waves. Avoiding a fault [in this case attempting to avoid monotony], one may fall into a worse one unless there be real artistic skill.

The humblest craftsman over near the Aemilian school[2] will model fingernails and imitate waving hair in bronze; but the total work will be unhappy because he does not know how to represent it as a unified whole. I should no more wish to be like him, if I desired to compose something, than to be praised for my dark hair and eyes and yet go through life with my nose turned awry. You who write, take a subject equal to your powers, and consider at length how much your shoulders can bear. Neither proper words nor lucid order will be lacking to the writer who chooses a subject within his powers. The excellence and charm of the arrangement, I believe, consists in the ability to say only what needs to be said at the time, deferring or omitting many points for the moment. The author of the long-promised poem must accept and reject as he proceeds. (Ll. 1–45.)

[*Words.*] In addition to using taste and care in arranging words, you will express yourself most effectively if you give novelty to a familiar word by means of a skilful setting. If you have to use new terms for out-of-the-way things, you then have a chance to coin words unheard of by the Cethegi,[3] who wear loincloths [and are thus too old-fashioned to wear tunics]; and you will be allowed the licence of doing this if

---

ART OF POETRY.   Horace's *Art of Poetry,* sometimes called the *Epistle to the Pisos,* was composed about 20 B.C. The text is from Walter Jackson Bate, ed., *Criticism: The Major Texts* (New York: Harcourt Brace Jovanovich, Inc., 1970) and translated by the editor. Reprinted by permission of the publisher.
[1][Bate] Horace's *Art of Poetry* is in the form of an epistle addressed to the father and two sons of the Piso family.

---

[2][Bate] A school for gladiators; the shops of the bronzeworkers were located here.
[3]Orators.

you do it moderately. New and lately coined words will also be accepted if they are drawn from the Greek fountain; but the spring must be tapped sparingly. Why should a Roman refuse this privilege to Virgil and Varius when it was allowed to Caecilius and Plautus? Why should I be grudged the liberty of adding a few words when Cato and Ennius have enriched our native language and brought forth new terms for things?[4] It has always been and always will be allowed to issue words bearing the stamp of the present day.

As the forest changes its leaves at the decline of the year, so, among words, the oldest die; and like all things young, the new ones grow and flourish. We, and all that belongs to us, are destined for death. And this is so whether we build a harbor, channeling the sea into the shelter of the land in order to protect our fleets from the north winds—a kingly work indeed; or whether a marsh, long a waste and passable only by boats, is drained and tilled in order to feed neighboring cities; or whether a river that formerly destroyed crops has been diverted into a better channel. All mortal things shall perish; still less shall the currency and charm of words always endure. Many words that have lapsed in use will be reborn, and many now in high repute will die, if custom wills it, within whose power lie the judgment, rule, and standard of speech. (Ll. 46–72.)

[*Meter.*] Homer has shown in what meter [dactylic hexameter] the deeds of kings and captains and the sorrows of war may be written. Verses of unequal lengths, paired in couplets,[5] were used for elegies, and later for the sentiments felt when prayers were granted. But it is unknown and still disputed who the writer was who first used these elegiac verses. Anger armed Archilochus[6] with his own verse form, the *iambic*. Both Comedy and Tragedy have adopted this meter as best fitted for dialogue, able to drown out the noise of the audience, and suitable for action. (Ll. 73–82.)

[*Appropriateness of style.*] The Muse has granted to the lyre the task of celebrating gods and the children of gods, the champion in boxing, the victorious horse in a race, the desire of lovers, and the carefree pleasure in wine. If I am unable to understand and retain these clear-cut distinctions and poetic genres, why should I be considered a poet? Why, through false shame, should I prefer to be ignorant rather than to know? A subject for Comedy refuses to be written in verse suitable for Tragedy. In a similar way, the banquet of Thyestes could not be related in lines suitable to ordinary life and hence appropriate for Comedy. Let each style keep the place to which it belongs. Yet these are times when even Comedy elevates its style, and an angry Chremes raves with swelling voice. Also, in Tragedy, Telephus and Peleus[7] often give vent to their sorrow in the language of prose when, in poverty and exile, they discard their bombast and *sesquipedalian* words [words a foot and a half long] in order to touch the heart of the spectator with their grief. (Ll. 83–98.)

[*Dramatic characters must be convincing: the poet must identify himself with them, and also must portray them with probability and consistency, and thus maintain decorum.*] It is not enough for poems to be beautiful; they must be affecting, and must lead the heart of the hearer as they will. As people's faces smile on those who smile, in a similar way they sympathize with those who weep. If you wish me to weep, you must first feel grief yourself. Only then, O Telephus or Peleus, will your misfortunes affect me. If your words are not appropriate, I shall laugh or go to sleep. Sad words are appropriate to a sorrowful face, furious words are fitting to the angry, gay jests to the merry, serious words to the solemn. For Nature first forms us within to meet all the changes of fortune. She causes us to rejoice or impels us to anger, or burdens us down to the ground with a heavy grief. Afterwards, with the tongue as her interpreter, she expresses the emotions of the heart. If the words of a speaker seem inappropriate to his situation, the Romans, both the aristocracy and the populace, will simply laugh. It will make a great difference whether it is a god who is speaking or a hero, a ripe old man or a youth still in his flower, a wealthy woman or a bustling nurse, a traveling merchant or the tiller of a fertile farm, a Colchian or an Assyrian, one raised in Thebes or in Argos.

Either follow tradition or else make what you invent be consistent. If, in writing, you wish to bring in the famous Achilles, let him be restless, irascible, unyielding, and fierce. Let him refuse to allow any laws to apply to himself; let him place his trust in his sword. Let your Medea be fierce and firm, your Ino sorrowful, your Ixion faithless, your Io a wan-

---

[4][Bate] Lucius Varius Rufus (*c.* 74–14 B.C.), friend of Virgil and Horace, was author of the tragedy *Thyestes*. Of the earlier writers, mentioned by Horace as coining words, Caecilius Statius (died *c.* 168 B.C.), was a Roman comic poet; and his friend Ennius was noted as a tragic and narrative poet who tried to adapt the Latin language to the Homeric hexameter, and to refine literature and the language according to Greek example. M. Portius Cato (234–149 B.C.), or "Cato the Elder" was the first important Latin prose writer. The plays of Plautus (*c.* 250–184 B.C.), the Roman comic dramatist, were closely modeled after Greek originals.

[5][Bate] The "elegiac" couplet consisted of a hexameter followed by a pentameter, the shorter second line giving the couplet a melancholy and falling rhythm.

[6][Bate] A remarkable Greek satirist (seventh century B.C.), famous for his bitter and effective realism.

[7][Bate] Chremes was a comic character in Terence. Peleus was the father of Achilles, and Telephus, the son-in-law of Priam, was wounded and later cured by Achilles.

derer, your Orestes despondent.[8] If you try something not yet attempted in the theater, and boldly create a new character, have him remain to the close the sort of person he was when he first appeared, and keep him consistent.[9] It is hard to treat a commonly known subject in an original way. It is better to dramatize the *Iliad* into acts than to offer a subject unknown and unsung. In publicly known matters, you will be able to achieve originality if you do not translate word for word, nor jump into a narrow imitative groove, from which both fear and the rules followed in the given work prevent your escape. (Ll. 99–135.)

[*The building up of interest.*] Nor should you begin as the Cyclic writer of old began: "I shall sing the fortune of Priam, and the noble war." What will this boaster produce worthy of this mouthing? Mountains will labor, and bring forth a mere mouse. How much more fitting for a writer not to make such an inept claim: "Muse, tell me of the man who, after Troy fell, saw the cities and manners of many people."[10] He does not intend to give you smoke after the first flash, but rather light after the smoke, so that he will set forth in time some notable and striking tales: Antiphates, Scylla, Charybdis, the Cyclops. Nor does he start the tale of Diomed's return with the story of Meleager's death, nor begin the Trojan war by telling of the twin eggs.[11] Instead, he always hastens to the climax, and plunges the listener into the middle of things as though they were already known. He leaves out what he is afraid he cannot make more illustrious with his touch, and he invents, mixing fiction with truth, in such a way that the beginning, middle, and end are all appropriate with each other. (Ll. 136–152.)

[*Types of character and other rules of decorum.*] Hear what I, and the people with me, expect. If you want an appreciative listener who waits till the close, staying until the singing attendant cries out, "Applaud!"—you must mark the characteristics of each period of life and present what is fitting to the various natures and ages. The boy who has just

learned to speak and walk loves to play with his friends, flies into anger, and forgets it quickly, changing every hour. The beardless stripling, now free from his tutor, delights in horses, dogs, and in the grassy, sunlit field. He is soft as wax in being influenced by evil; he is rude to advisers, slow to provide sensibly for himself, wasteful with money, high-spirited, passionate, but quick to change in his desires. With different interests, the maturer mind of the man seeks wealth and friendship. He serves ambition, and is afraid of doing whatever he might later wish undone. Many evils plague the old man, whether he seeks wealth and then like a miser abstains from using it, or because he is without spirit or courage in all his affairs, slow, greedy for a longer life, petulant, obstinate, or the sort of person who glorifies his own boyhood days and damns the present youth. Old age brings many blessings; it also takes many away. Lest the role of old age be assigned to a youth, or that of grown manhood to a child, we should always emphasize the characteristics appropriate to each age.

Events are either acted out on the stage or else they are narrated. Now the mind is much less stirred by hearing things described than it is by actually seeing them, with one's own eyes, as a spectator. On the other hand, you must not show on the stage itself the kind of thing that should have taken place behind the scenes. In fact, many things must be kept from sight for an actor to tell about later. For example, Medea should not butcher her children in plain view of the audience, nor the wicked Atreus cook human flesh in public.[12] Nor, of course, should Procne be transformed into a bird, nor Cadmus into a serpent. Whatever you try to show me openly in this way simply leaves me unbelieving and rather disgusted.

Let your play, if it is to continue to have appeal and be produced, have five acts, no more nor less. And do not have a god—a *deus ex machina*—intervene unless there is a knot worthy of having such a deliverer to untie it![13] Nor should there be a fourth actor trying to speak.[14] (Ll. 153–192.)

[*The Chorus.*] The Chorus ought to maintain the part and function of an actor with vigor, and not sing anything between the acts that does not advance the action or fit into the plot. It should take the side of the good, give them friendly advice, control the angry, and show affection to

---

[8][Bate] Because of her husband's desertion of her, Medea (the subject of the tragedy by Euripedes) killed her children in order to make her husband suffer. Ino lost one of her children because she angered the goddess Hera. Ixion, who slew his father-in-law after inviting him to a feast, was shunned by men, rescued by Zeus, proved faithless to him, was then banished to Hades, and as punishment was tied to a perpetually revolving wheel. Io, the mistress of Zeus, was transformed into a heifer, was pursued by jealous Hera, Zeus's wife, and forced to wander. Orestes, son of Agamemnon, avenged his mother's killing of his father by slaying her and her consort.

[9]Compare the more sophisticated advice of Aristotle (see *Poetics*, XV. 4, p. 58) that if a character is inconsistent he should be consistently inconsistent.

[10][Bate] The opening of the *Odyssey*.

[11][Bate] Meleager, an uncle of Diomed, died before Diomed was born. The twin eggs were the offspring of Leda and Zeus, who assumed the form of a swan when with Leda. From one of the eggs came Helen, and thus ultimately the Trojan War.

---

[12][[Bate] Atreus, king of Mycenae, killed the two sons of his brother Thyestes, and placed their flesh before their father at a banquet. Procne, the sister of Philomela, was according to the Latin version of the legend, changed into a swallow. Another ancient legend tells the story of Cadmus, king of Illyria, and his wife Harmonia, who were changed into serpents and carried to the Elysian fields.

[13]See Aristotle, *Poetics*, IX, 13, p. 155.

[14][Bate] Compare Aristotle, *Poetics*, IV, 13, p. 52.

those who are afraid to do evil. It should praise moderation in eating, healthful justice and laws, and peace, with the gates of cities lying open. It should respect secrets, and it should implore the gods to remove good fortune from the arrogant and bring it back to the miserable. (Ll. 193–200.)

[*The use of music.*] At one time, the flute, not decked out in brass as it is now, rivaling the trumpet, but slight, simple, and with few stops, was used to set the tone and accompany the Chorus. With its sound, it filled the benches, which were not yet too crowded, and where—when people gathered—there were few enough so that they could be easily counted, and those were thrifty, virtuous, and honest. But later on, nations that were victorious in war began to widen their boundaries, and longer walls were built around their cities. On feast-days, people were able to give themselves up freely to drinking in the daytime; and then greater licence was given to music and rhythm. For what taste could one expect to find in an ignorant crowd, free from its daily toil, in the peasant mixed with the city-dweller, the low-born with the nobles? Therefore, the flute-player added movement and decoration to his earlier art. He now began to strut across the stage, trailing a robe. New sounds were added to the restrained music of the lyre. A hurried style brought with it a new sort of language; and wise, prophetic sayings were also brought forth to sound like the oracles of Delphi. (Ll. 201–219.)

[*Satyric drama.*[15]] The poet who first competed in tragic verse for the prize of a wretched goat soon began to bring on to the stage naked, rustic satyrs. Without losing dignity, he introduced coarse jests; for only by the lure and charm of novelty could he hold the sort of spectator who, after the Bacchic rites, was completely drunk and wild. In amusing the audience with the laughter and jests of your satyrs, however, and in passing from grave to gay, it is more fitting to do it in such a way that no god or hero whom you are bringing on the stage, and whom we have been accustomed to see in royal gold and purple, should be allowed to sink down into the low talk of dingy taverns, or, in trying to raise himself, simply clutch at clouds and emptiness. Tragedy scorns any temptation to babble light verses, as a matron who is asked to dance on festal days takes her place among the impudent satyrs with modest shame. If I were writing Satyric plays, O Pisos, I should not, for my part, wish to use only ordinary, unadorned language, I should not wish to get so far away from the language of Tragedy that no one could tell who is speaking—whether it is Davus, or bold Pythias, who cheated Simo out of a talent, or whether it is Silenus,[16] who guards and serves his divine charge.

For me, the ideal of poetic style is to mould familiar material with such skill that anyone might hope to achieve the same feat. And yet so firmly would the material be ordered and interconnected (and such is the beauty that one may draw out in that way from the familiar) that he would work and sweat in vain to rival it. Therefore, to my mind, when these rustic fauns are introduced on the stage, they should not act as though they had dwelt in the streets and the forum, languishing with adolescent love-verses, or cracking obscene and embarrassing jokes. The knights, and people of any standing or estate, do not enjoy and wish to offer a crown to everything that pleases the sort of people who buy popcorn and candy.[17] (Ll. 220–250.)

[*Rhythms and verse-forms.*] A short syllable followed by a long one is called an "iambus." This is a rapid foot. Hence the term "trimeter" was given to straight iambic lines that had as many as six beats.[18] Not long ago, however, since it is a tolerant and accommodating form of meter, it admitted the weighty spondee [two long stresses], in order to allow the line to move with more stately slowness, but still with the provision that the iambic always retain its place at least in the second and fourth feet of the line. In what some like to call the "noble" trimeters of Accius, the iambic foot rarely appears; and also in the pompous lines with which Ennius blessed the stage one sees either hasty or careless work, or else sheer ignorance of the art of poetry. Not all critics can notice faulty meter. Therefore our Roman poets have been granted an indulgence quite undeserved. Is that any excuse for me to run wild and write without restraint? Or, supposing that my faults will be noticed by everyone, should I consider myself safe just because I keep within the limits of whatever is pardoned? I may perhaps escape blame by doing that, but I shall have deserved no praise. As for yourselves, thumb through and study the Greek masterpieces by day and night. But, you will say, our forefathers admired the wit and meter of Plautus! Yes, they admired both with tolerance, not to say stupidity, if you and I are any judges of the difference between coarse and urbane language, or have

---

[15][Bate] Horace supposed that the term "tragedy" (that is "goat-song") arose because the dramas had once been written for the prize of a goat. Actually, the participants were originally dressed in goat skins; hence the origin of the word. Satyric dramas (not to be confused with *satiric*) mark a survival of this custom. Greek tragedies were performed in trilogies; and at their conclusion, as a fourth drama, was presented a *satyric* play, partly serious and partly jesting, in which the chorus consisted of satyrs clothed in goat skins.

[16][Bate] Not to be confused with Damon and Pythias. Davus, a male slave, and Pythius, a female, who deceived her master, Simo, are typical comic characters in Terence; whereas Silenus, the teacher of Bacchus and the merry and wise father of the satyrs, was a philosopher.

[17][Bate] That is, the Roman equivalent, roasted peas and chestnuts.

[18][Bate] Because it was sufficiently rapid for two feet to make one metrical unit, a six-foot iambic line would nevertheless be called a "trimeter."

any ability to detect true rhythm by the ear and the finger. (Ll. 251–274.)

[*Origin and early development of the drama.*] Thespis[19] is said to have been the man who discovered Tragedy—a type of poetry hitherto unknown—and to have carried his plays around on wagons to be sung and acted by players whose faces had been smeared with wine-lees. Later on, Aeschylus, who invented the use of the mask and the tragic robe, had his players act on a stage built of small planks, and taught them to talk in lofty words and move in a stately manner with buskined feet. Then came the Old Comedy, popular with everyone. But its free manner degenerated into an excess of violence that deserved to be restrained. It yielded to regulation, and the Chorus, with its ability to do harm now removed, simply sank into silence, to its own shame. Our own poets have left no style unattempted. Nor is it least to their credit that they have been courageous enough to leave the footsteps of the Greeks and celebrate the deeds of their own nation, whether in Comedy or Tragedy. Rome would be as eminent in literature as it is in valor and arms if its poets, one and all, did not find a laborious use of the file [20] so exasperating. O descendants of Numa Pompilius, condemn a poem that time and labor have not corrected and refined tenfold, down to the very fingernail. (Ll. 275–294.)

[*The importance of urbanity and serious craftsmanship.*] Just because Democritus believes that sheer native genius is better than wretched art, and excludes sane poets from Helicon,[21] a good number do not cut their fingernails and beards. They live in solitude and stay away from the baths, since anyone can acquire the distinction and name of a poet if he never entrusts to Licinus, the barber, a head that three Anticyras[22] could not remedy! I suppose I am quite a fool, then, to go and purge myself of bile when the spring comes. Otherwise no one could write better poems! But then, the game would hardly be worth it. So what I shall try to do, therefore, is to serve as a whetstone which, though it cannot itself do any cutting, is able to sharpen steel. Though I myself write nothing worth while, I shall at least teach the duty and office of the poet, instruct him where to get his materials, show what moulds and develops him, what is fitting to him and what is not, where the good can lead him and where the wrong. (Ll. 295–308.)

[*Wisdom and intellectual insight the first requisite of the poet.*] In all good writing the source and fountain is wisdom. The Socratic writings can offer you the material; and when the subject is grasped, the words will come easily. He who has learned what he owes his nation and his friends, what love is due to a parent, brother, and guest, what the duty of a senator or a judge, what the role of a general sent to war, will know how to give the appropriate nature to each character. I should counsel one who has learned the art of imitation to turn to life and real manners as his model, and draw from there a living language. Sometimes a play, interspersed with commonplaces and having an appropriate characterization, even though lacking in beauty, power, and art, still gives delight to the people and entertains them more than do verses without matter or mere trifling songs.

To the Greeks, who desired only glory, the Muse gave genius and greatness of style. Our Roman youth, however, learn how to divide the *as*[23] into a hundred parts. "Let the son of Albinus answer: if you take from five-twelfths an ounce, how much is left? You ought to know by now!" A third of an *as*." "Splendid! *You'll* be able to look after *yourself!* And if you add an ounce, how much is that?" "One half an *as*." When this interest in commercial gain has stained the soul, how can we expect to have poems worthy of being preserved in cedar oil and kept in cypress cases? (Ll. 309–332.)

[*The end of poetry.*] The aim of the poet is to inform or delight, or to combine together, in what he says, both pleasure and applicability to life.[24] In instructing, be brief in what you say in order that your readers may grasp it quickly and retain it faithfully. Superfluous words simply spill out when the mind is already full. Fiction invented in order to please should remain close to reality. Your play must not demand that the audience believe anything you take a whim to portray. You cannot have a living child snatched from the belly of Lamia[25] after she has devoured him. The elders of Rome censure poetry that lacks instruction; the young aristocrats, on the other hand, scorn austere poetry. He who combines the useful and the pleasing wins out by both instructing and delighting the reader. That is the sort of book that will make money for the publisher, cross the seas, and extend the fame of the author. (Ll. 333–347.)

[*The difference between isolated faults and habitual blundering.*] There are faults, however, that we can willingly forgive. For the string does not always give out the sound that the mind and hand wished. When you desire a flat, it often gives you a sharp. The arrow, too, does not always hit its mark. When the beauties in a poem predominate, I shall not make an issue of a few blemishes that have resulted from

---

[19][Bate] The Greek poet (sixth century B.C.) who first introduced an actor to reply to the Chorus.

[20][Bate] The metaphor is drawn from sculpture, the file being used to give a completely smooth finish.

[21][Bate] A mountain sacred to the Muses, where the fountain Hippocrene flowed.

[22][Bate] Anticyra was a town famous for producting hellebore, a drug useful in killing lice and other insects.

[23][Bate] A Roman unit of money which is divisible into twelve "ounces."

[24]A statement that is much repeated by Renaissance and later critics.

[25][Bate] A witch, in Greek nursery lore, who ate children.

carelessness or human frailty. How shall we sum up the matter, then? As a copyist deserves to be condemned if, after being constantly warned, he keeps on making the same mistake, and as a musician is laughed at if he always falters on the same note, in a similar way I regard the poet that blunders constantly as being like Choerilus,[26] whose two or three good lines cause surprised laughter. I am also irritated whenever the great Homer nods. But then, when a work is long, sleep inevitably creeps over it. Poetry is like painting. One work will please you more if you stand close to it; the other strikes more if you stand farther away.[27] One shows more to advantage when seen in the shadow; another, unafraid of the sharp view of the critic, ought to be viewed in the light. One will please only once; the other, though looked at ten times, will continue to please. (Ll. 347–365.)

[*Prudent awareness of one's own limitations.*] You, elder youth of the Piso family, though your judgment has profited from your father's training and though you are sensible in your own right, take this to heart and remember it: only in certain things can mediocrity be tolerated or forgiven. A lawyer, pleading an ordinary suit, may fall short of the eloquent Messalla, and know less than Aulus Cascellius, but he is still respected. But neither gods, men, nor booksellers, tolerate a mediocre poet. At a pleasant banquet, poor music, cheap perfume, and poppy seeds mixed with Sardinian honey, are offensive; the banquet could have done very well without them. And in a similar way, a poem, born and created in order to give the soul delight, if once it falls short of the highest excellence, sinks to the lowest level. If a person cannot play a game, he refrains from trying to handle the weapons used in the Campus Martius; and if he is unfamiliar with the ball, quoit, or hoop, he remains apart lest, with perfectly good reason, the nearby crowd laugh at him. On the other hand, a person will dare to write poetry without knowing how to do it. "Why not?" he thinks. He is a free man, well born, perhaps with a knight's income, and has a good character. But *you*, I am sure, will do or say nothing stupid; you have enough judgment and good sense not to do so. Still, if you ever do write anything, show it first to Maecius the critic, or to your father, or to me. Then put your manuscript back in the closet, and keep it for nine years. One can always destroy what one has not yet published; but a word that is published can never be canceled. (Ll. 366–389.)

[*The traditional power of poetry in influencing man.*] While men still dwelt in the wood, Orpheus, the priest and interpreter of the gods drew them away from slaughtering each other and from foul living. Hence the legend that he tamed tigers and fierce lions. Hence also the story that Amphion, founder of Thebes, moved stones by the sound of his lyre, and led them to go wherever he wished by his supplicating magic. In olden times, this was regarded as wisdom: to mark a line between the public and private rights, the differences between sacred and secular, to prohibit promiscuous living, assign rights to the married, build towns, and engrave laws on wooden tablets. Thus honor and fame came to poets and their verses, as if they were divine. Afterwards, Homer became renowned; and Tyrtaeus[28] with his songs inspired men's hearts to perform warlike deeds. Oracles were delivered in verse, and the conduct of life was taught in them. The favor of kings was solicited in Pierian[29] strains, and festal dramas celebrated the conclusion of great labors. Therefore you do not need to feel ashamed for the Muse, skilled at the lyre, and for Apollo, the god of poetry. (Ll. 390–407.)

[*The importance to the poet of informed labor and rational restraint.*] It is asked whether a praiseworthy poem is the product of Nature or of conscious Art. For my own part, I do not see the value of study without native ability, nor of genius without training: so completely does each depend on the other and blend with it. The athlete who wishes to reach the longed-for goal has striven and borne much in boyhood, has endured heat and cold, and kept away from women and wine. The flute-player at the Pythian games has learned his lessons and submitted to a teacher. Today people think it enough to say: "I fashion wonderful poems. The devil take the hindmost [as though poetry were a game]. It's not right for me to be left behind, and admit I do not know what I have never really learned."

Like a crier who collects a crowd to buy his wares, a poet, if rich in land or investments, bids his flatterers come to the call of gain. Though he can serve a costly banquet, go surety for a man who is bankrupt, or rescue someone snared in the grim suit-at-law, I should be surprised if, with all his good fortune, he can distinguish between a false and true friend. When you give someone a present, do not then ask him, when he is filled with joy because of your gift, to listen to your verses. For he will simply exclaim: "Beautiful!

---

[26][Bate] A minor epic poet (fourth century B.C.) who accompanied Alexander the Great on his campaigns. Alexander, who said that he would rather have been the Thersites of Homer than the Achilles of Choerilus, offered him a piece of gold for every good verse he wrote, and apparently did not deplete his treasury in doing so.

[27]This is the famous *ut pictura poesis* passage, much referred to and remarked on for centuries, and usually taken much more literally (rather than analogically) than Horace intends here. The sentence in the original Latin reads: *Ut pictura poesis: erit quae, si propius stes, te capeat magis, et quaedam, si longius abstes.* The analogy held until the early nineteenth century when it came to be displaced by the notion that all art aspires to the condition of music.

[28][Bate] A Greek schoolmaster who composed war songs that were popular with the Spartans.

[29][Bate] Pieria was the birthplace of the Muses.

good! perfect!'' He will change color, drop tears from his friendly eyes, leap up, and stamp the ground. Just as the hired mourners at a funeral lament and do more than those who really grieve, so the insincere admirer seems to be more moved than a true one. We are told that kings, when they wish to see whether a man is worthy of their friendship, test him by getting him drunk. In a similar way, if you write poems, do not be taken in by the spirit of the fox. If you read anything to Quintilius,[30] however, he would say ''Correct this or that, please.'' If after trying it vainly two or three times, you said you could not do better, he would have you cut out the offending lines and take them back to the anvil. If you chose simply to defend the passage rather than improve it, he would waste no more words or effort. And you might then love yourself and your work all alone, without rivals. A good, sensible critic will censure weak lines and condemn harsh ones. He will draw a line through those that are awkward, and will cut off pretentious decorations. He will force you to clarify obscure passages; he will point out doubtful meanings, and mark what ought to be changed. He will prove to be another Aristarchus.[31] He will not say:

---

[30][Bate] A famous Homeric scholar of Alexandria (second century B.C.).

[31][Bate] A Greek critic of Alexandria (c. 220–143 B.C.), supposed author of more than eight hundred commentaries, editor of the major Greek poets and tragedians, particularly Homer, and famous in antiquity as the prototype of the severely alert and demanding critic.

''Why should I disagree with my friend about trifles?'' For it is trifles of this sort that get the friend into trouble when he has been laughed at and unfavorably received.

As people avoid someone afflicted with the itch, with jaundice, the fits, or insanity, so sensible men stay clear of a mad poet. Children tease him and rash fools follow him. Spewing out verses, he wanders off, with his head held high, like a fowler with his eyes on the blackbirds; and if he falls into a well or ditch, he may call out, ''Help, fellow citizens!''—but no one cares to help him. If anyone did wish to aid him by letting down a rope, I should say: ''How do you know he didn't throw himself down on purpose, and doesn't want to be saved?'' And I should tell him how the Sicilian poet, Empedocles, met his end: wishing to be thought an immortal god, he deliberately leapt into the burning crater of Aetna. You must allow poets to have the right and ability to destroy themselves. Saving a man against his will is as bad as murder. He is not doing this for the first time. And if he is pulled out now, he will not become like other people and get over this desire for a famous death. Nor is it clear why he writes verses. Perhaps he defiled the family grave, or disturbed a consecrated spot. He is mad, at any rate; and like a bear that has been strong enough to break the bars of its cage, he frightens away both the learned and the ignorant by reciting his verses. If he catches a victim, he clings to him and reads him to death, like a leech that will not leave the skin until it is filled with blood. (Ll. 408–476.)

Longinus

First Century A.D.

Rather than declaring poetic inspiration a dangerous divine madness, as did Plato, Longinus inquires how it is best employed. His treatment of the sublime is an effort to balance and blend inspiration and rhetorical mastery. Thus, though he writes in the tradition of classical rhetoricians, devoting much space to a discussion of various rhetorical devices, he is not interested merely in persuasion and does not view tropes as merely supporting argument. Further, he emphasizes not only the learning of rhetorical devices but also the imitation and emulation of great writers because they had great souls. He postulates that there is something more to writing than can be conventionally learned. Skill in invention and ordering of the parts of a whole are important, but sublimity "flashing forth at the right moment scatters everything before it like a thunderbolt." Still, these transporting moments depend on the whole. It is not simply a matter of giving way to any stray inspiration and writing "naturally," for nature is herself ordered, and unordered sublimity is ineffective. There is also a pompous, false sublimity: "evil are the swellings, both in the body and in diction."

Though Longinus seems to be demonstrating that sublimity cannot really be defined, he proceeds to mention five elements that help create elevated language. The first of these is a quality of the author rather than of the poem: the sublime author must have the "power of forming great conceptions" (elevation of mind). Sublimity is the "echo of a great soul." The second quality he describes simply as "vehement and inspired passion." Whether this is a characteristic of the author or of the poem or of both he does not make clear. The final three can be considered features of the poem: the due formation of figures of speech, noble diction, and dignified and elevated composition. He advises the imitation and emulation of the spirit of great writers, values truth and reality over the fabulous, and argues that grandeur with some faults is preferable to moderate success because of the importance of "sheer elevation of spirit" in the former. The dissertation breaks off shortly after he has indicated that the decline of democratic government has probably been a reason for the decline in sublimity among writers.

The idea of the sublime became fashionable in the eighteenth century partly as a result of Longinus' essay. Interest in the term went hand in hand with interest in the effect of objects on the mind. Addison, Burke, Kant, and Schopenhauer each defined the sublime in his own way, but they had in common an interest in the audience. Longinus' treatment of the subject, infused as it is with a consideration of tropes, refers sublimity to the work itself and to the author.

The translation by W. R. Roberts (1899) may be supplemented by the Loeb Classics translation of W. H. Fyfe (1927). See J. W. H. Atkins, *Literary Criticism in Antiquity* (1934); T. R. Henn, *Longinus and English Criticism* (1934); S. H. Monk,

The Sublime: A Study of Critical Theories in Eighteenth-Century England (1935); Jules Brody, *Boileau and Longinus* (1957); G. M. A. Grube, *The Greek and Roman Critics* (1965); and Demetrio St. Marin, *Bibliography of the Essay on the Sublime* (1965).

On the Sublime

I

You will remember, my dear Postumius Terentianus, that when we examined together the treatise of Caecilius on the sublime, we found that it fell below the dignity of the whole subject, while it failed signally to grasp the essential points, and conveyed to its readers but little of that practical help which it should be a writer's principal aim to give. In every systematic treatise two things are required. The first is a statement of the subject; the other, which although second in order ranks higher in importance, is an indication of the methods by which we may attain our end. Now Caecilius seeks to show the nature of the sublime by countless instances as though our ignorance demanded it, but the consideration of the means whereby we may succeed in raising our own capacities to a certain pitch of elevation he has, strangely enough, omitted as unnecessary. 2. However, it may be that the man ought not so much to be blamed for his shortcomings as praised for his happy thought and his enthusiasm. But since you have urged me, in my turn, to write a brief essay on the sublime for your special gratification, let us consider whether the views I have formed contain anything which will be of use to public men. You will yourself, my friend, in accordance with your nature and with what is fitting, join me in appraising each detail with the utmost regard for truth; for he answered well who, when asked in what qualities we resemble the gods, declared that we do so in benevolence and truth. 3. As I am writing to you, my good friend, who are well versed in literary studies, I feel almost absolved from the necessity of premising at any length that sublimity is a certain distinction and excellence in expression, and that it is from no other source than this that the greatest poets and writers have derived their eminence and gained an immortality of renown. 4. The effect of elevated language upon an audience is not persuasion but transport. At every time and in every way imposing speech, with the spell it throws over us, prevails over that which aims at persuasion and gratification. Our persuasions we can usually control, but the influences of the sublime bring power and irresistible might to bear, and reign supreme over every hearer. Similarly, we see skill in invention, and due order and arrangement of matter, emerging as the hard-won result not of one thing nor of two, but of the whole texture of the composition, whereas sublimity flashing forth at the right moment scatters everything before it like a thunderbolt, and at once displays the power of the orator in all its plenitude. But enough; for these reflections, and others like them, you can, I know well, my dear Terentianus, yourself suggest from your own experience.

II

First of all, we must raise the question whether there is such a thing as an art of the sublime or lofty. Some hold that those are entirely in error who would bring such matters under the precepts of art. A lofty tone, says one, is innate, and does not come by teaching; nature is the only art that can compass it. Works of nature are, they think, made worse and altogether feebler when wizened by the rules of art. 2. But I maintain that this will be found to be otherwise if it be observed that, while nature as a rule is free and independent in matters of passion and elevation, yet is she wont not to act at random and utterly without system. Further, nature is the original and vital underlying principle in all cases, but system can define limits and fitting seasons, and can also contribute the safest rules for use and practice. Moreover, the expression of the sublime is more exposed to danger when it goes its own way without the guidance of knowledge—when it is suffered to be unstable and unballasted—when it is left at the mercy of mere momentum and ignorant audacity. It is true that it often needs the spur, but it is also true that it often needs the curb. 3. Demosthenes expresses the view, with regard to human life in general, that good fortune is the greatest of blessings, while good counsel, which occupies the second place, is

---

ON THE SUBLIME. The author and date of composition of *On the Sublime*, sometimes called *On Great Writing*, are unknown. We call the author Longinus because the work was long, but mistakenly, attributed to Cassius Longinus, a Greek philosopher of the the third century A.D. Conjecture places composition in the first century A.D. The oldest known manuscript is that of the tenth century, and it is incomplete. It was first published in 1554 by the Italian critic Robortelli. The text is from W. R. Roberts, tr., *Longinus on the Sublime* (Cambridge, Eng.: Cambridge University Press, 1899). Ellipses indicate lost passages. The sources of Longinus' quotations from other works are identified as fully as possible in the footnotes. Some quotations cannot be traced to a work or even linked with an author.

hardly inferior in importance, since its absence contributes inevitably to the ruin of the former. This we may apply to diction, nature occupying the position of good fortune, art that of good counsel. Most important of all, we must remember that the very fact that there are some elements of expression which are in the hands of nature alone, can be learnt from no other source than art. If, I say, the critic of those who desire to learn were to turn these matters over in his mind, he would no longer, it seems to me, regard the discussion of the subject as superfluous or useless. . . .

III

Quell they the oven's far-flung splendor-glow!
Ha, let me but one hearth-abider mark—
One flame-wreath torrentlike I'll whirl on high;
I'll burn the roof, to cinders shrivel it!—
Nay, now my chant is not of noble strain.[1]

Such things are not tragic but pseudotragic—"flame-wreaths," and "belching to the sky," and Boreas represented as a "flute-player," and all the rest of it. They are turbid in expression and confused in imagery rather than the product of intensity, and each one of them, if examined in the light of day, sinks little by little from the terrible into the contemptible. But since even in tragedy, which is in its very nature stately and prone to bombast, tasteless tumidity is unpardonable, still less, I presume, will it harmonize with the narration of fact. 2. And this is the ground on which the phrases of Gorgias of Leontini are ridiculed when he describes Xerxes as the "Zeus of the Persians" and vultures as "living tombs." So is it with some of the expressions of Callisthenes which are not sublime but high-flown, and still more with those of Cleitarchus, for the man is frivolous and blows, as Sophocles has it, "on pigmy hautboys: mouthpiece have they none." Other examples will be found in Amphicrates and Hegesias and Matris, for often when these writers seem to themselves to be inspired they are in no true frenzy but are simply trifling. 3. Altogether, tumidity seems particularly hard to avoid. The explanation is that all who aim at elevation are so anxious to escape the reproach of being weak and dry that they are carried, as by some strange law of nature, into the opposite extreme. They put their trust in the maxim that "failure in a great attempt is at least a noble error."

---

[1] From the lost play *Oreithyia* by Aeschylus.

4. But evil are the swellings, both in the body and in diction, which are inflated and unreal, and threaten us with the reverse of our aim; for nothing, say they, is drier than a man who has the dropsy. While tumidity desires to transcend the limits of the sublime, the defect which is termed puerility is the direct antithesis of elevation, for it is utterly low and mean and in real truth the most ignoble vice of style. What, then, is this puerility? Clearly, a pedant's thoughts, which begin in learned trifling and end in frigidity. Men slip into this kind of error because, while they aim at the uncommon and elaborate and most of all at the attractive, they drift unawares into the tawdry and affected. 5. A third, and closely allied, kind of defect in matters of passion is that which Theodorus used to call "parenthyrsus." By this is meant unseasonable and empty passion, where no passion is required, or immoderate, where moderation is needed. For men are often carried away, as if by intoxication, into displays of emotion which are not caused by the nature of the subject, but are purely personal and wearisome. In consequence they seem to hearers who are in no wise affected to act in an ungainly way. And no wonder; for they are beside themselves, while their hearers are not. But the question of the passions we reserve for separate treatment.

IV

Of the second fault of which we have spoken—frigidity—Timaeus supplies many examples. Timaeus was a writer of considerable general ability, who occasionally showed that he was not incapable of elevation of style. He was learned and ingenious, but very prone to criticize the faults of others while blind to his own. Through his passion for continually starting novel notions, he often fell into the merest childishness. 2. I will set down one or two examples only of his manner, since the greater number have been already appropriated by Caecilius. In the course of a eulogy on Alexander the Great, he describes him as "the man who gained possession of the whole of Asia in fewer years than it took Isocrates to write his *Panegyric* urging war against the Persians." Strange indeed is the comparison of the man of Macedon with the rhetorician. How plain it is, Timaeus, that the Lacedaemonians, thus judged, were far inferior to Isocrates in prowess, for they spent thirty years in the conquest of Messene, whereas he composed his *Panegyric* in ten. 3. Consider again the way in which he speaks of the Athenians who were captured in Sicily. "They were punished because they had acted impiously towards Hermes and mutilated his images, and the infliction of punishment was chiefly due to Hermocrates the son of Hermon, who was descended, in the paternal line, from the outraged god." I am surprised, beloved Terentianus, that he does not write with regard to the despot Dionysius that "Dion and Heracleides deprived him of his sovereignty because he had acted impiously towards Zeus and Heracles." 4. But why speak of Timaeus when even those heroes of literature, Xenophon and Plato, though trained in the school of Socrates, nevertheless sometimes forget themselves for the sake of such paltry pleasantries? Xenophon writes in the *Polity of the Lacedaemonians:* "You would find it harder to hear their voice than that of busts of marble, harder to deflect their gaze than that of statues of bronze; you would deem them more modest than the very maidens in their eyes."[2]

It was worthy of an Amphicrates and not of a Xenophon to call the pupils of our eyes "modest maidens." Good heavens, how strange it is that the pupils of the whole company should be believed to be modest notwithstanding the common saying that the shamelessness of individuals is indicated by nothing so much as the eyes! "Thou sot, that hast the eyes of a dog," as Homer has it.[3] 5. Timaeus, however, has not left even this piece of frigidity to Xenophon, but clutches it as though it were hid treasure. At all events, after saying of Agathocles that he abducted his cousin, who had been given in marriage to another man, from the midst of the nuptial rites, he asks, "Who could have done this had he not had wantons, in place of maidens, in his eyes?" 6. Yes, and Plato (usually so divine) when he means simply *tablets* says, "They shall write and preserve *cypress* memorials in the temples."[4]

And again, "As touching walls, Megillus, I should hold with Sparta that they be suffered to lie asleep in the earth and not summoned to arise."[5] 7. The expression of Herodotus to the effect that beautiful women are "eye-smarts" is not much better.[6] This, however, may be condoned in some degree since those who use this particular phrase in his narrative are barbarians and in their cups, but not even in the mouths of such characters is it well that an author should suffer, in the judgment of posterity, from an unseemly exhibition of triviality.

V

All these ugly and parasitical growths arise in literature from a single cause, that pursuit of novelty in the expression of

[2]III. 5.
[3]*Iliad*, I. 225.
[4]*Laws*, V. 741.
[5]*Laws*, VI. 778.
[6]*History,*V. 18.

ideas which may be regarded as the fashionable craze of the day. Our defects usually spring, for the most part, from the same sources as our good points. Hence, while beauties of expression and touches of sublimity, and charming elegances withal, are favorable to effective composition, yet these very things are the elements and foundation, not only of success, but also of the contrary. Something of the kind is true also of variations and hyperboles and the use of the plural number, and we shall show subsequently the dangers to which these seem severally to be exposed. It is necessary now to seek and to suggest means by which we may avoid the defects which attend the steps of the sublime.

VI

The best means would be, my friend, to gain, first of all, clear knowledge and appreciation of the true sublime. The enterprise is, however, an arduous one. For the judgment of style is the last and crowning fruit of long experience. Nonetheless, if I must speak in the way of precept, it is not impossible perhaps to acquire discrimination in these matters by attention to some such hints as those which follow.

VII

You must know, my dear friend, that it is with the sublime as in the common life of man. In life nothing can be considered great which it is held great to despise. For instance, riches, honors, distinctions, sovereignties, and all other things which possess in abundance the external trappings of the stage, will not seem, to a man of sense, to be supreme blessings, since the very contempt of them is reckoned good in no small degree, and in any case those who could have them, but are high-souled enough to disdain them, are more admired than those who have them. So also in the case of sublimity in poems and prose writings, we must consider whether some supposed examples have not simply the appearance of elevation with many idle accretions, so that when analyzed they are found to be mere vanity—objects which a noble nature will rather despise than admire. 2. For, as if instinctively, our soul is uplifted by the true sublime; it takes a proud flight, and is filled with joy and vaunting, as though it had itself produced what it has heard. 3. When, therefore, a thing is heard repeatedly by a man of intelligence, who is well-versed in literature, and its effect is not to dispose the soul to high thoughts, and it does not leave in the mind more food for reflection than the words seem to convey, but falls, if examined carefully through and through, into disesteem, it cannot rank as true sublimity because it does not survive a first hearing. For that is really great which bears a repeated examination, and which it is difficult or rather impossible to withstand, and the memory of which is strong and hard to efface. 4. In general, consider those examples of sublimity to be fine and genuine which please all and always. For when men of different pursuits, lives, ambitions, ages, languages, hold identical views on one and the same subject, then that verdict which results, so to speak, from a concert of discordant elements makes our faith in the object of admiration strong and unassailable.

VIII

There are, it may be said, five principal sources of elevated language. Beneath these five varieties there lies, as though it were a common foundation, the gift of discourse, which is indispensable. First and most important is the power of forming great conceptions, as we have elsewhere explained in our remarks on Xenophon. Secondly, there is vehement and inspired passion. These two components of the sublime are for the most part innate. Those which remain are partly the product of art. The due formation of figures deals with two sorts of figures, first those of thought and secondly those of expression. Next there is noble diction, which in turn comprises choice of words, and use of metaphors, and elaboration of language. The fifth cause of elevation—one which is the fitting conclusion of all that have preceded it—is dignified and elevated composition. Come now, let us consider what is involved in each of these varieties, with this one remark by way of preface, that Caecilius has omitted some of the five divisions, for example, that of passion. 2. Surely he is quite mistaken if he does so on the ground that these two, sublimity and passion, are a unity, and if it seems to him that they are by nature one and inseparable. For some passions are found which are far removed from sublimity and are of a low order, such as pity, grief and fear; and on the other hand there are many examples of the sublime which are independent of passion, such as the daring words of Homer with regard to the Aloadae, to take one out of numberless instances, "Yea, Ossa in fury they strove to upheave on Olympus on high, / With forest-clad Pelion above, that thence they might step to the sky."[7] And so of the words which follow

with still greater force: "Ay, and the deed had they done."[8] 3. Among the orators, too, eulogies and ceremonial and occasional addresses contain on every side examples of dignity and elevation, but are for the most part void of passion. This is the reason why passionate speakers are the worst eulogists, and why, on the other hand, those who are apt in encomium are the least passionate. 4. If, on the other hand, Caecilius thought that passion never contributes at all to sublimity, and if it was for this reason that he did not deem it worthy of mention, he is altogether deluded. I would affirm with confidence that there is no tone so lofty as that of genuine passion, in its right place, when it bursts out in a wild gust of mad enthusiasm and as it were fills the speaker's words with frenzy.

IX

Now the first of the conditions mentioned, namely elevation of mind, holds the foremost rank among them all. We must, therefore, in this case also, although we have to do rather with an endowment than with an acquirement, nurture our souls (as far as that is possible) to thoughts sublime, and make them always pregnant, so to say, with noble inspiration. 2. In what way, you may ask, is this to be done? Elsewhere I have written as follows: "Sublimity is the echo of a great soul." Hence also a bare idea, by itself and without a spoken word, sometimes excites admiration just because of the greatness of soul implied. Thus the silence of Ajax in the underworld is great and more sublime than words.[9] 3. First, then, it is absolutely necessary to indicate the source of this elevation, namely, that the truly eloquent must be free from low and ignoble thoughts. For it is not possible that men with mean and servile ideas and aims prevailing throughout their lives should produce anything that is admirable and worthy of immortality. Great accents we expect to fall from the lips of those whose thoughts are deep and grave. 4. Thus it is that stately speech comes naturally to the proudest spirits. You will remember the answer of Alexander to Parmenio when he said "For my part I had been well content." . . .

. . . the distance from earth to heaven; and this might well be considered the measure of Homer no less than of strife. 5. How unlike to this the expression which is used of sorrow by Hesiod, if indeed the *Shield* is to be attributed to Hesiod: "Rheum from her nostrils was trickling."[10] The

---

[7]*Odyssey,* XI. 315–16.

[8]*Odyssey,* XI. 317.
[9]*Odyssey,* XI. 543.
[10]*Shield of Hercules,* 267, attributed by some to Hesiod.

image he has suggested is not terrible but rather loathsome. Contrast the way in which Homer magnifies the higher powers:

And far as a man with his eyes through the sea line haze may
    discern,
On a cliff as he sitteth and gazeth away o'er the wine-dark
    deep,
So far at a bound do the loud-neighing steeds of the deathless
    leap.[11]

He makes the vastness of the world the measure of their leap. The sublimity is so overpowering as naturally to prompt the exclamation that if the divine steeds were to leap thus twice in succession they would pass beyond the confines of the world. 6. How transcendent also are the images in the Battle of the Gods:

Far round wide heaven and Olympus echoed his clarion of
    thunder;
And Hades, king of the realm of shadows, quaked
    thereunder.
And he sprang from his throne, and he cried aloud in the
    dread of his heart
Lest o'er him earth-shaker Poseidon should cleave the
    ground apart,
And revealed to immortals and mortals should stand those
    awful abodes,
Those mansions ghastly and grim, abhorred of the very
    gods.[12]

You see, my friend, how the earth is torn from its foundations, Tartarus itself is laid bare, the whole world is upturned and parted asunder, and all things together—heaven and hell, things mortal and things immortal—share in the conflict and the perils of that battle! 7. But although these things are awe-inspiring, yet from another point of view, if they be not taken allegorically, they are altogether impious, and violate our sense of what is fitting. Homer seems to me, in his legends of wounds suffered by the gods, and of their feuds, reprisals, tears, bonds, and all their manifold passions, to have made, as far as lay within his power, gods of the men concerned in the Siege of Troy, and men of the gods. But

whereas we mortals have death as the destined haven of our ills if our lot is miserable, he portrays the gods as immortal not only in nature but also in misfortune. 8. Much superior to the passages respecting the Battle of the Gods are those which represent the divine nature as it really is—pure and great and undefiled; for example, what is said of Poseidon in a passage fully treated by many before ourselves:

Her far-stretching ridges, her forest-trees, quaked in
    dismay,
And her peaks, and the Trojans' towns, and the ships of
    Achaia's array,
Beneath his immortal feet, as onward Poseidon strode.
Then over the surges he drave: leapt sporting before the god
Sea-beasts that uprose all around from the depths, for their
    king they knew,
And for rapture the sea was disparted, and onward the car-
    steeds flew.[13]

9. Similarly, the legislator of the Jews, no ordinary man, having formed and expressed a worthy conception of the might of the Godhead, writes at the very beginning of his laws, "God said,"—what? "Let there be light, and there was light; let there be land, and there was land."[14] 10. Perhaps I shall not seem tedious, my friend, if I bring forward one passage more from Homer—this time with regard to the concerns of *men*—in order to show that he is wont himself to enter into the sublime actions of his heroes. In his poem the battle of the Greeks is suddenly veiled by mist and baffling night. Then Ajax, at his wits' end, cries:

Zeus, Father, yet save thou Achaia's sons from beneath the
    gloom
And make clear day, and vouchsafe unto us with our eyes to
    see!
So it be but in light, destroy us![15]

That is the true attitude of an Ajax. He does not pray for life, for such a petition would have ill beseemed a hero. But since in the hopeless darkness he can turn his valor to no noble end, he chafes at his slackness in the fray and craves the boon of immediate light, resolved to find a death worthy of his

---

[11]*Iliad*, V. 770–72.
[12]*Iliad*, XX. 61–65; XXI. 388.

[13]*Iliad*, XIII. 18, 19, 27–29; XX. 60.
[14]Genesis 1:3.
[15]*Iliad*, XVII. 645–47.

bravery, even though Zeus should fight in the ranks against him. 11. In truth, Homer in these cases shares the full inspiration of the combat, and it is neither more nor less than true of the poet himself that

Mad rageth he as Ares the shaker of spears, or as mad flames leap
Wild-wasting from hill unto hill in the folds of a forest deep,
And the foam-froth fringeth his lips.[16]

He shows, however, in the *Odyssey* (and this further observation deserves attention on many grounds) that, when a great genius is declining, the special token of old age is the love of marvelous tales. 12. It is clear from many indications that the *Odyssey* was his second subject. A special proof is the fact that he introduces in that poem remnants of the adventures before Ilium as episodes, so to say, of the Trojan War. And indeed, he there renders a tribute of mourning and lamentation to his heroes as though he were carrying out a long-cherished purpose. In fact, the *Odyssey* is simply an epilogue to the *Iliad:*

There lieth Ajax the warrior wight, Achilles is there,
There is Patroclus, whose words had weight as a god he
    were;
There lieth mine own dear son.[17]

13. It is for the same reason, I suppose, that he has made the whole structure of the *Iliad,* which was written at the height of his inspiration, full of action and conflict, while the *Odyssey* for the most part consists of narrative, as is characteristic of old age. Accordingly, in the *Odyssey* Homer may be likened to a sinking sun, whose grandeur remains without its intensity. He does not in the *Odyssey* maintain so high a pitch as in those poems of Ilium. His sublimities are not evenly sustained and free from the liability to sink; there is not the same profusion of accumulated passions, nor the supple and oratorical style, packed with images drawn from real life. You seem to see henceforth the ebb and flow of greatness, and a fancy roving in the fabulous and incredible, as though the ocean were withdrawing into itself and were being laid bare within its own confines. 14. In saying this I have not forgotten the tempests in the *Odyssey* and the story of the Cyclops and the like. If I speak of old age, it is nevertheless

the old age of Homer. The fabulous element, however, prevails throughout this poem over the real. The object of this digression has been, as I said, to show how easily great natures in their decline are sometimes diverted into absurdity, as in the incident of the wine-skin and of the men who were fed like swine by Circe ("whining porkers," as Zoilus called them), and of Zeus like a nestling nurtured by the doves, and of the hero who was without food for ten days upon the wreck, and of the incredible tale of the slaying of the suitors.[18] For what else can we term these things than veritable dreams of Zeus? 15. These observations with regard to the *Odyssey* should be made for another reason—in order that you may know that the genius of great poets and prose-writers, as their passion declines, finds its final expression in the delineation of character. For such are the details which Homer gives, with an eye to characterization, of life in the home of Odysseus; they form as it were a comedy of manners.

X

Let us next consider whether we can point to anything further that contributes to sublimity of style. Now, there inhere in all things by nature certain constituents which are part and parcel of their substance. It must needs be, therefore, that we shall find one source of the sublime in the systematic selection of the most important elements, and the power of forming, by their mutual combination, what may be called one body. The former process attracts the hearer by the choice of the ideas, the latter by the aggregation of those chosen. For instance, Sappho everywhere chooses the emotions that attend delirious passion from its accompaniments in actual life. Wherein does she demonstrate her supreme excellence? In the skill with which she selects and binds together the most striking and vehement circumstances of passion:

2. Peer of gods he seemeth to me, the blissful
    Man who sits and gazes at thee before him,
        Close beside thee sits, and in silence hears thee Silverly
            speaking,

    Laughing love's low laughter. Oh this, this only
    Stirs the troubled heart in my breast to tremble!
    For should I but see thee a little moment,
        Straight is my voice hushed;

---

[16]*Iliad*, XV. 605–07.
[17]*Odyssey*, III. 109–11.

[18]*Odyssey*, IX. 182; X. 17, 237; XII. 62, 447; XXII. 79.

Yea, my tongue is broken, and through and through me
'Neath the flesh impalpable fire runs tingling;
Nothing see mine eyes, and a noise of roaring Waves in
    my ear sounds;

Sweat runs down in rivers, a tremor seizes
All my limbs, and paler than grass in autumn,
Caught by pains of menacing death, I falter, Lost in the
    love-trance.

3. Are you not amazed how at one instant she summons, as
though they were all alien from herself and dispersed, soul,
body, ears, tongue, eyes, color? Uniting contradictions, she
is, at one and the same time, hot and cold, in her senses and
out of her mind, for she is either terrified or at the point of
death. The effect desired is that not one passion only should
be seen in her, but a concourse of the passions. All such
things occur in the case of lovers, but it is, as I said, the
selection of the most striking of them and their combination
into a single whole that has produced the singular excellence
of the passage. In the same way Homer, when describing
tempests, picks out the most appalling circumstances. 4. The
author of the *Arimaspeia* thinks to inspire awe in the following way:

A marvel exceeding great is this withal to my soul—
Men dwell on the water afar from the land, where deep seas
    roll.
Wretches are they, for they reap but a harvest of travail and
    pain,
Their eyes on the stars ever dwell, while their hearts abide in
    the main.
Often, I ween, to the gods are their hands upraised on high,
And with hearts in misery heavenward-lifted in prayer do
    they cry.[19]

It is clear, I imagine, to everybody that there is more
elegance than terror in these words. 5. But what says Homer?
Let one instance be quoted from among many:

And he burst on them like as a wave swift-rushing beneath
    black clouds,
Heaved huge by the winds, bursts down on a ship, and the
    wild foam shrouds
From the stem to the stern her hull, and the storm-blast's
    terrible breath
Roars in the sail, and the heart of the shipmen shuddereth

In fear, for that scantly upborne are they now
    from the clutches of death.[20]

6. Aratus has attempted to convert this same expression to
his own use: "And a slender plank averteth their death."
Only, he has made it trivial and neat instead of terrible. Furthermore, he has put bounds to the danger by saying "A
plank keeps off death." After all, it *does* keep it off. Homer,
however, does not for one moment set a limit to the terror of
the scene, but draws a vivid picture of men continually in
peril of their lives, and often within an ace of perishing with
each successive wave. Moreover, he has in the words ὑπὲκ
θανάτοιο, forced into union, by a kind of unnatural compulsion, prepositions not usually compounded. He has thus tortured his line into the similitude of the impending calamity,
and by the constriction of the verse has excellently figured
the disaster, and almost stamped upon the expression the
very form and pressure of the danger, ὑπὲκ θανάτοιο φέρον-
ται. 7. This is true also of Archilochus in his account of the
shipwreck, and of Demosthenes in the passage which begins
"It was evening," where he describes the bringing of the
news.[21] The salient points they selected, one might say, according to merit and massed them together, inserting in the
midst nothing frivolous, mean, or trivial. For these faults mar
the effect of the whole, just as though they introduced chinks
or fissures into stately and co-ordered edifices, whose walls
are compacted by their reciprocal adjustment.

XI

An allied excellence to those already set forth is that which
is termed *amplification*. This figure is employed when the
narrative or the course of a forensic argument admits, from
section to section, of many starting points and many pauses,
and elevated expressions follow, one after the other, in an
unbroken succession and in an ascending order. 2. And this
may be effected either by way of the rhetorical treatment of
commonplaces, or by way of intensification (whether events
or arguments are to be strongly presented), or by the orderly
arrangement of facts or of passions; indeed, there are innumerable kinds of amplification. Only, the orator must in
every case remember that none of these methods by itself,
apart from sublimity, forms a complete whole, unless indeed
where pity is to be excited or an opponent to be disparaged.
In all other cases of amplification, if you take away the sub-

---

[19]Once, but no longer, attributed to Aristeas, a Greek poet of the eighth or
    ninth century B.C.

[20]*Iliad*, XV. 624–28.
[21]*On the Crown*, 169.

lime, you will remove as it were the soul from the body. For the vigor of the amplification at once loses its intensity and its substance when not resting on a firm basis of the sublime. 3. Clearness, however, demands that we should define concisely how our present precepts differ from the point under consideration a moment ago, namely the marking-out of the most striking conceptions and the unification of them; and wherein, generally, the sublime differs from amplification.

XII

Now the definition given by the writers on rhetoric does not satisfy me. Amplification is, say they, discourse which invests the subject with grandeur. This definition, however, would surely apply in equal measure to sublimity and passion and figurative language, since they too invest the discourse with a certain degree of grandeur. The point of distinction between them seems to me to be that sublimity consists in elevation, while amplification embraces a multitude of details. Consequently, sublimity is often comprised in a single thought, while amplification is universally associated with a certain magnitude and abundance. 2. Amplification (to sum the matter up in a general way) is an aggregation of all the constituent parts and topics of a subject, lending strength to the argument by dwelling upon it, and differing herein from proof that, while the latter demonstrates the matter under investigation. . . .

With his vast riches Plato swells, like some sea, into a greatness which expands on every side. 3. Wherefore it is, I suppose, that the orator in his utterance shows, as one who appeals more to the passions, all the glow of a fiery spirit. Plato, on the other hand, firm-planted in his pride and magnificent stateliness, cannot indeed be accused of coldness, but he has not the same vehemence. 4. And it is in these same respects, my dear friend Terentianus, that it seems to me (supposing always that we Greeks are allowed to have an opinion upon the point) that Cicero differs from Demosthenes in elevated passages. For the latter is characterized by sublimity which is for the most part rugged, Cicero by profusion. Our orator,[22] owing to the fact that in his vehemence—aye, and in his speed, power and intensity—he can as it were consume by fire and carry away all before him, may be compared to a thunderbolt or flash of lightning. Cicero, on the other hand, it seems to me, after the manner of a widespread conflagration, rolls on with all-devouring flames, having within him an ample and biding store of fire, distributed now at this point now at that, and fed by an un-

ceasing succession. 5. This, however, you[23] will be better able to decide; but the great opportunity of Demosthenes' highpitched elevation comes where intense utterance and vehement passion are in question, and in passages in which the audience is to be utterly enthralled. The profusion of Cicero is in place where the hearer must be flooded with words, for it is appropriate to the treatment of commonplaces, and to perorations for the most part and digressions, and to all descriptive and declamatory passages, and to writings on history and natural science, and to many other departments of literature.

XIII

To return from my digression. Although Plato thus flows on with noiseless stream, he is none the less elevated. You know this because you have read the *Republic* and are familiar with his manner. "Those," says he,

> who are destitute of wisdom and goodness and are ever present at carousals and the like are carried on the downward path, it seems, and wander thus throughout their life. They never look upwards to the truth, nor do they lift their heads, nor enjoy any pure and lasting pleasure, but like cattle they have their eyes ever cast downwards and bent upon the ground and upon their feeding-places, and they graze and grow fat and breed, and through their insatiate desire of these delights they kick and butt with horns and hoofs of iron and kill one another in their greed.[24]

2. This writer shows us, if only we were willing to pay him heed, that another way (beyond anything we have mentioned) leads to the sublime. And what, and what manner of way, may that be? It is the imitation and emulation of previous great poets and writers. And let this, my dear friend, be an aim to which we steadfastly apply ourselves. For many men are carried away by the spirit of others as if inspired, just as it is related of the Pythian priestess when she approaches the tripod, where there is a rift in the ground which (they say) exhales divine vapor. By heavenly power thus communicated she is impregnated and straightway delivers oracles in virtue of the afflatus.[25] Similarly from the great

---

[22]Demosthenes.

[23][Roberts] You Romans.

[24]IX. 586.

[25]Inspiration. Longinus advises a different way of imitating great writers from the way Horace suggests. One seeks to be possessed by their spirit and genius, not merely to copy their techniques. Longinus considers valuable the inspired state that Plato attacked.

natures of the men of old there are borne in upon the souls of those who emulate them (as from sacred caves) what we may describe as effluences, so that even those who seem little likely to be possessed are thereby inspired and succumb to the spell of the others' greatness. 3. Was Herodotus alone a devoted imitator of Homer? No, Stesichorus even before his time, and Archilochus, and above all Plato, who from the great Homeric source drew to himself innumerable tributary streams. And perhaps we should have found it necessary to prove this, point by point, had not Ammonius and his followers selected and recorded the particulars. 4. This proceeding is not plagiarism; it is like taking an impression from beautiful forms or figures or other works of art. And it seems to me that there would not have been so fine a bloom of perfection on Plato's philosophical doctrines, and that he would not in many cases have found his way to poetical subject matter and modes of expression, unless he had with all his heart and mind struggled with Homer for the primacy, entering the lists like a young champion matched against the man whom all admire, and showing perhaps too much love of contention and breaking a lance with him as it were, but deriving some profit from the contest none the less. For, as Hesiod says, "This strife is good for mortals."[26] And in truth that struggle for the crown of glory is noble and best deserves the victory in which even to be worsted by one's predecessors brings no discredit.

XIV

Accordingly it is well that we ourselves also, when elaborating anything which requires lofty expression and elevated conception, should shape some idea in our minds as to how perchance Homer would have said this very thing, or how it would have been raised to the sublime by Plato or Demosthenes or by the historian Thucydides. For those personages, presenting themselves to us and inflaming our ardor and as it were illumining our path, will carry our minds in a mysterious way to the high standards of sublimity which are imaged within us. 2. Still more effectual will it be to suggest this question to our thoughts: What sort of hearing would Homer, had he been present, or Demosthenes have given to this or that when said by me, or how would they have been affected by the other? For the ordeal is indeed a severe one, if we presuppose such a tribunal and theater for our own utterances, and imagine that we are undergoing a scrutiny of our writings before these great heroes, acting as judges and witnesses.

3. A greater incentive still will be supplied if you add the question, in what spirit will each succeeding age listen to me who have written thus? But if one shrinks from the very thought of uttering aught that may transcend the term of his own life and time, the conceptions of his mind must necessarily be incomplete, blind, and as it were untimely born, since they are by no means brought to the perfection needed to ensure a futurity of fame.

XV

Images, moreover, contribute greatly, my young friend, to dignity, elevation, and power as a pleader. In this sense some call them mental representations. In a general way the name of *image* or *imagination* is applied to every idea of the mind, in whatever form it presents itself, which gives birth to speech. But at the present day the word is predominantly used in cases where, carried away by enthusiasm and passion, you think you see what you describe, and you place it before the eyes of your hearers.

2. Further, you will be aware of the fact that an image has one purpose with the orators and another with the poets, and that the design of the poetical image is enthrallment, of the rhetorical—vivid description. Both, however, seek to stir the passions and the emotions.

> Mother!—'beseech thee, hark not thou on me
> Yon maidens gory-eyed and snaky-haired!
> Lo there!—lo there!—they are nigh—they leap
>   on me![27]

And: "Ah! she will slay me! whither can I fly?"[28]

In these scenes the poet himself saw Furies, and the image in his mind he almost compelled his audience also to behold. 3. Now, Euripides is most assiduous in giving the utmost tragic effect to these two emotions—fits of love and madness. Herein he succeeds more, perhaps, than in any other respect, although he is daring enough to invade all the other regions of the imagination. Notwithstanding that he is by nature anything but elevated, he forces his own genius, in many passages, to tragic heights, and everywhere in the matter of sublimity it is true of him (to adopt Homer's words) that "the tail of him scourgeth his ribs and his flanks to left and to right,/And he lasheth himself into frenzy, and spurreth him on to the fight."[29]

---

[26]*Works and Days,* 24.

[27]Euripides, *Orestes,* 255–57.
[28]Euripides, *Iphigenia in Tauris,* 291.
[29]*Iliad,* XX. 170–71.

4. When the Sun hands the reins to Phaethon, he says

> "Thou, driving, trespass not on Libya's sky,
> Whose heat, by dews untempered, else shall split
> Thy car asunder."

And after that,

> "Speed onward toward the Pleiads seven thy course."
> Thus far the boy heard; then he snatched the reins:
> He lashed the flanks of that wing-wafted team;
> Loosed rein; and they through folds of cloudland soared.
> Hard after on a fiery star his sire
> Rode, counseling his son—"Ho! thither drive!
> Hither thy car turn—hither!"

Would you not say that the soul of the writer enters the chariot at the same moment as Phaethon and shares in his dangers and in the rapid flight of his steeds? For it could never have conceived such a picture had it not been borne in no less swift career on that journey through the heavens. The same is true of the words which Euripides attributes to his Cassandra: "O chariot-loving Trojans." 5. Aeschylus, too, ventures on images of a most heroic stamp. An example will be found in his *Seven Against Thebes,* where he says

> For seven heroes, squadron-captains fierce,
> Over a black-rimmed shield have slain a bull,
> And, dipping in the bull's blood each his hand,
> By Ares and Enyo, and by Panic
> Lover of blood, have sworn.[30]

In mutual fealty they devoted themselves by that joint oath to a relentless doom. Sometimes, however, he introduces ideas that are rough-hewn and uncouth and harsh; and Euripides, when stirred by the spirit of emulation, comes perilously near the same fault, even in spite of his own natural bent. 6. Thus in Aeschylus the palace of Lycurgus at the coming of Dionysus is strangely represented as possessed: "A frenzy thrills the hall; the roofs are bacchant/With ecstasy:" an idea which Euripides has echoed, in other words, it is true, and with some abatement of its crudity, where he says: "The whole mount shared their bacchic ecstasy."[31] 7. Magnificent are the images which Sophocles has conceived of the death of Oedipus, who makes ready his burial amid the portents of the sky.[32] Magnificent, too, is the passage where the Greeks are on the point of sailing away and Achilles appears above his tomb to those who are putting out to sea—a scene which I doubt whether anyone has depicted more vividly than Simonides. But it is impossible to cite all the examples that present themselves. 8. It is no doubt true that those which are found in the poets contain, as I said, a tendency to exaggeration in the way of the fabulous and that they transcend in every way the credible, but in oratorical imagery the best feature is always its reality and truth. Whenever the form of a speech is poetical and fabulous and breaks into every kind of impossibility, such digressions have a strange and alien air. For example, the clever orators forsooth of our day, like the tragedians, see Furies, and—fine fellows that they are—cannot even understand that Orestes when he cries "Unhand me!—of mine Haunting Fiends thou art—/ Dost grip my waist to hurl me into hell!"[33] has these fancies because he is mad. 9. What, then, can oratorical imagery effect? Well, it is able in many ways to infuse vehemence and passion into spoken words, while more particularly when it is combined with the argumentative passages it not only persuades the hearer but actually makes him its slave. Here is an example. "Why, if at this very moment," says Demosthenes,

> a loud cry were to be heard in front of the courts,
> and we were told that the prison-house lies open
> and the prisoners are in full flight, no one, whether
> he be old or young, is so heedless as not to lend
> aid to the utmost of his power; aye, and if anyone
> came forward and said that yonder stands the man
> who let them go, the offender would be promptly
> put to death without a hearing.[34]

10. In the same way, too, Hyperides on being accused, after he had proposed the liberation of the slaves subsequently to the great defeat, said "This proposal was framed, not by the orator, but by the battle of Chaeroneia." The speaker has here at one and the same time followed a train of reasoning and indulged a flight of imagination. He has, therefore, passed the bounds of mere persuasion by the boldness of his conception. 11. By a sort of natural law in all such matters we always attend to whatever possesses superior force; whence it is that we are drawn away from demonstration pure and simple to any startling image within whose dazzling brilliancy the argument lies concealed. And it is not unreasonable that we should be affected in this way, for when two things are brought together, the more powerful

---

[30]42–46.
[31]*Bacchae,* 726.
[32]*Oedipus at Colonus,* 1586.
[33]Euripides, *Orestes,* 264.
[34]*Against Timocrates,* 208.

always attracts to itself the virtue of the weaker. 12. It will be enough to have said thus much with regard to examples of the sublime in thought, when produced by greatness of soul, imitation, or imagery.

XVI

Here, however, in due order comes the place assigned to figures; for they, if handled in the proper manner, will contribute, as I have said, in no mean degree to sublimity. But since to treat thoroughly of them all at the present moment would be a great, or rather an endless task, we will now, with the object of proving our proposition, run over a few only of those which produce elevation of diction. 2. Demosthenes is bringing forward a reasoned vindication of his public policy. What was the natural way of treating the subject? It was this. "You were not wrong, you who engaged in the struggle for the freedom of Greece. You have domestic warrant for it. For the warriors of Marathon did no wrong, nor they of Salamis, nor they of Plataea."[35] When, however, as though suddenly inspired by heaven and as it were frenzied by the god of prophecy, he utters his famous oath by the champions of Greece ("assuredly ye did no wrong; I swear it by those who at Marathon stood in the forefront of the danger"), in the public view by this one figure of adjuration, which I here term apostrophe, he deifies his ancestors. He brings home the thought that we ought to swear by those who have thus nobly died as we swear by gods, and he fills the mind of the judges with the high spirit of those who there bore the brunt of the danger, and he has transformed the natural course of the argument into transcendent sublimity and passion and that secure belief which rests upon strange and prodigious oaths. He instills into the minds of his hearers the conviction—which acts as a medicine and an antidote—that they should, uplifted by these eulogies, feel no less proud of the fight against Philip than of the triumph at Marathon and Salamis. By all these means he carries his hearers clean away with him through the employment of a single figure. 3. It is said, indeed, that the germ of the oath is found in Eupolis: "For, by the fight I won at Marathon, / No one shall vex my soul and rue it not." But it is not sublime to swear by a person in any chance way; the sublimity depends upon the place and the manner and the circumstances and the motive. Now in the passage of Eupolis there is nothing but the mere oath, addressed to the Athenians when still prosperous and in no need of comfort. Furthermore, the poet in his oath has not made divinities of the men in order so to create in his hearers a worthy conception of their valor, but he has wandered away from those who stood in the forefront of the danger to an inanimate thing—the fight. In Demosthenes the oath is framed for vanquished men, with the intention that Chaeroneia should no longer appear a failure to the Athenians. He gives them at one and the same time, as I remarked, a demonstration that they have done no wrong, an example, the sure evidence of oaths, a eulogy, an exhortation. 4. And since the orator was likely to be confronted with the objection, "You are speaking of the *defeat* which has attended your administration, and yet you swear by *victories,*" in what follows he consequently measures even individual words, and chooses them unerringly, showing that even in the revels of the imagination sobriety is required. "Those," he says, "who stood in the forefront of the danger at Marathon, and those who fought by sea at Salamis and Artemisium, and those who stood in the ranks at Plataea." Nowhere does he use the word *conquered,* but at every turn he has evaded any indication of the result, since it was fortunate and the opposite of what happened at Chaeroneia. So he at once rushes forward and carries his hearer off his feet. "All of whom," says he, "were accorded a public burial by the state, Aeschines, and not *the successful only.*"

XVII

I ought not, my dear friend, to omit at this point an observation of my own, which shall be most concisely stated. It is that, by a sort of natural law, figures bring support to the sublime, and on their part derive support in turn from it in a wonderful degree. Where and how, I will explain. The cunning use of figures is peculiarly subject to suspicion, and produces an impression of ambush, plot, fallacy. This is so when the plea is addressed to a judge with absolute powers, and particularly to despots, kings, and leaders in positions of superiority. Such a one at once feels resentment if, like a foolish boy, he is tricked by the paltry figures of the oratorical craftsman. Construing the fallacy into a personal affront, sometimes he becomes quite wild with rage, or if he controls his anger, steels himself utterly against persuasive words. Wherefore a figure is at its best when the very fact that it is a figure escapes attention. 2. Accordingly, sublimity and passion form an antidote and a wonderful help against the mistrust which attends upon the use of figures. The art which craftily employs them lies hid and escapes all future suspicion, when once it has been associated with beauty and sublimity. A sufficient proof is the passage already adduced, "By the men of Marathon I swear." By what means has the

---

[35]*On the Crown,* 208.

orator here concealed the figure? Clearly, by the very excess of light. For just as all dim lights are extinguished in the blaze of the sun, so do the artifices of rhetoric fade from view when bathed in the pervading splendor of sublimity. 3. Something like this happens also in the art of painting. For although light and shade, as depicted in colors, lie side by side upon the same surface, light nevertheless meets the vision first, and not only stands out, but also seems far nearer. So also with the manifestations of passion and the sublime in literature. They lie nearer to our minds through a sort of natural kinship and through their own radiance, and always strike our attention before the figures, whose art they throw into the shade and as it were keep in concealment.

XVIII

But what are we next to say of questions and interrogations? Is it not precisely by the visualizing qualities of these figures that Demosthenes strives to make his speeches far more effective and impressive? "Pray tell me—tell me, you sir—do you wish to go about and inquire of one another, is there any news? Why, what greater news could there be than this, that a Macedonian is subduing Greece? Is Philip dead? No; but he is ill. Dead or ill, what difference to you? Should anything happen to him, you will speedily create another Philip."[36] Again he says, "Let us sail against Macedonia. Where shall we find a landing-place? someone asks. The war itself will discover the weak places in Philip's position."[37] All this, if stated plainly and directly, would have been altogether weaker. As it is, the excitement, and the rapid play of question and answer, and the plan of meeting his own objections as though they were urged by another, have by the help of the figure made the language used not only more elevated but also more convincing. 2. For an exhibition of passion has a greater effect when it seems not to be studied by the speaker himself but to be inspired by the occasion; and questions asked and answered by oneself simulate a natural outburst of passion. For just as those who are interrogated by others experience a sudden excitement and answer the inquiry incisively and with the utmost candor, so the figure of question and answer leads the hearer to suppose that each deliberate thought is struck out and uttered on the spur of the moment, and thus beguiles his reason. We may further quote that passage of Herodotus which is regarded as one of the most elevated: "if thus. . ."

XIX

The words issue forth without connecting links and are poured out as it were, almost outstripping the speaker himself. "Locking their shields," says Xenophon, "they thrust fought slew fell."[38] 2. And so with the words of Eurylochus: "We passed, as thou badst, Odysseus, midst twilight of oak-trees round./ There amidst of the forest-glens a beautiful palace we found."[39] For the lines detached from one another, but nonetheless hurried along, produce the impression of an agitation which interposes obstacles and at the same time adds impetuosity. This result Homer has produced by the omission of conjunctions.

XX

A powerful effect usually attends the union of figures for a common object, when two or three mingle together as it were in partnership, and contribute a fund of strength, persuasiveness, beauty. Thus, in the speech against Meidias, examples will be found of asyndeton, interwoven with instances of anaphora and diatyposis.[40] "For the smiter can do many things (some of which the sufferer cannot even describe to another) by attitude, by look, by voice."[41] 2. Then, in order that the narrative may not, as it advances, continue in the same groove (for continuance betokens tranquility, while passion—the transport and commotion of the soul—sets order at defiance), straightway he hurries off to other asyndeta and repetitions. "By attitude, by look, by voice, when he acts with insolence, when he acts like an enemy, when he smites with his fists, when he smites you like a slave." By these words the orator produces the same effect as the assailant—he strikes the mind of the judges by the swift succession of blow on blow. 3. Starting from this point again, as suddenly as a gust of wind, he makes another attack. "When smitten with blows of fists," he says, "when smitten upon the cheek. These things stir the blood, these drive men beyond themselves, when unused to insult. No one can, in describing them, convey a notion of the indignity they imply." So he maintains throughout, though with continual variation, the essential character of the repetitions and asyndeta. In this way, with him, order is disorderly, and on the other hand disorder contains a certain element of order.

---

[36]*Philippics*, I. 10.
[37]*Philippics*, I. 44.

---

[38]*Hellenica*, IV. 3, 19.
[39]*Odyssey*, X. 251–52.
[40]Asyndeton is the omission of the conjunction connecting clauses in a sentence; anaphora, the repetition of a word or phrase at the beginning of successive clauses; and diatyposis, vivid description.
[41]Demosthenes, *Against Meidias*, 72.

XXI

Come now, add, if you please, in these cases connecting particles after the fashion of the followers of Isocrates. Furthermore, this fact too must not be overlooked that the smiter may do many things, first by attitude, then by look, then again by the mere voice. You will feel, if you transcribe the passage in this orderly fashion, that the rugged impetuosity of passion, once you make it smooth and equable by adding the copulatives, falls pointless and immediately loses all its fire. 2. Just as the binding of the limbs of runners deprives them of their power of rapid motion, so also passion, when shackled by connecting links and other appendages, chafes at the restriction, for it loses the freedom of its advance and its rapid emission as though from an engine of war.

XXII

Hyperbata, or inversions, must be placed under the same category. They are departures in the order of expressions or ideas from the natural sequence; and they bear, it may be said, the very stamp and impress of vehement emotion. Just as those who are really moved by anger, or fear, or indignation, or jealousy, or any other emotion (for the passions are many and countless, and none can give their number), at times turn aside, and when they have taken one thing as their subject often leap to another, foisting in the midst some irrelevant matter, and then again wheel round to their original theme, and driven by their vehemence, as by a veering wind, now this way now that with rapid changes, transform their expressions, their thoughts, the order suggested by a natural sequence, into numberless variations of every kind; so also among the best writers it is by means of hyperbaton that imitation approaches the effects of nature. For art is perfect when it seems to be nature, and nature hits the mark when she contains art hidden within her. We may illustrate by the words of Dionysius of Phocaea in Herodotus. "Our fortunes lie on a razor's edge, men of Ionia; for freedom or for bondage, and that the bondage of runaway slaves. Now, therefore, if you choose to submit to hardships, you will have toil for the moment, but you will be able to overcome your foes."[42]

2. Here the natural order would have been: "Men of Ionia, now is the time for you to meet hardships; for our fortunes lie on a razor's edge." But the speaker postpones the words "men of Ionia." He starts at once with the danger of the situation, as though in such imminent peril he had no

time at all to address his hearers. Moreover, he inverts the order of ideas. For instead of saying that they ought to endure hardships, which is the real object of his exhortation, he first assigns the reason because of which they ought to endure hardships, in the words "our fortunes lie on a razor's edge." The result is that what he says seems not to be premeditated but to be prompted by the necessities of the moment. 3. In a still higher degree Thucydides is most bold and skillful in disjoining from one another by means of transpositions things that are by nature intimately united and indivisible. Demosthenes is not so masterful as Thucydides, but of all writers he most abounds in this kind of figure, and through his use of hyperbata makes a great impression of vehemence, yes, and of unpremeditated speech, and moreover draws his hearers with him into all the perils of his long inversions. 4. For he will often leave in suspense the thought which he has begun to express, and meanwhile he will heap, into a position seemingly alien and unnatural, one thing upon another parenthetically and from any external source whatsoever, throwing his hearer into alarm lest the whole structure of his words should fall to pieces, and compelling him in anxious sympathy to share the peril of the speaker; and then unexpectedly, after a long interval, he adds the long-awaited conclusion at the right place, namely the end, and produces a far greater effect by this very use, so bold and hazardous, of hyperbaton. Examples may be spared because of their abundance.

XXIII

The figures which are termed polyptota—accumulations, and variations, and climaxes—are excellent weapons of public oratory, as you are aware, and contribute to elegance and to every form of sublimity and passion. Again, how greatly do changes of cases, tenses, persons, numbers, genders, diversify and enliven exposition. 2. Where the use of numbers is concerned, I would point out that style is not adorned only or chiefly by those words which are, as far as their forms go, in the singular but in meaning are, when examined, found to be plural: as in the lines "A countless crowd forthright/Far-ranged along the beaches were clamoring 'Thunny in sight!' " The fact is more worthy of observation that in certain cases the use of the plural (for the singular) falls on the ear with still more imposing effect and impresses us by the very sense of multitude which the number conveys.

3. Such are the words of Oedipus in Sophocles:

> O nuptials, nuptials,
> Ye gendered me, and, having gendered, brought
> To light the selfsame seed, and so revealed

Sires, brothers, sons, in one—all kindred blood!—
Brides, mothers, wives, in one!—yea, whatso deeds
Most shameful among humankind are done.[43]

The whole enumeration can be summed up in a single proper name—on the one side Oedipus, on the other Jocasta. Nonetheless, the expansion of the number into the plural helps to pluralize the misfortunes as well. There is a similar instance of multiplication in the line: "Forth Hectors and Sarpedons marching came," and in that passage of Plato concerning the Athenians which we have quoted elsewhere. 4. "For no Pelopes, nor Cadmi, nor Aegypti and Danai, nor the rest of the crowd of born foreigners dwell with us, but ours is the land of pure Greeks, free from foreign admixture," etc.[44] For naturally a theme seems more imposing to the ear when proper names are thus added, one upon the other, in troops. But this must only be done in cases in which the subject admits of amplification or redundancy or exaggeration or passion—one or more of these—since we all know that a richly caparisoned style is extremely pretentious.

XXIV

Further (to take the converse case) particulars which are combined from the plural into the singular are sometimes most elevated in appearance. "Thereafter," says Demosthenes, "all Peloponnesus was at variance."[45] "And when Phrynichus had brought out a play entitled *The Capture of Miletus,* the whole theater burst into tears,"[46] For the compression of the number from multiplicity into unity gives more fully the feeling of a single body. 2. In both cases the explanation of the elegance of expression is, I think, the same. Where the words are singular, to make them plural is the mark of unlooked-for passion; and where they are plural, the rounding of a number of things into a fine-sounding singular is surprising owing to the converse change.

XXV

If you introduce things which are past as present and now taking place, you will make your story no longer a narration but an actuality. Xenophon furnishes an illustration. "A man," says he, "has fallen under Cyrus' horse, and being trampled strikes the horse with his sword in the belly. He rears and unseats Cyrus, who falls."[47] This construction is specially characteristic of Thucydides.

XXVI

In like manner the interchange of persons produces a vivid impression, and often makes the hearer feel that he is moving in the midst of perils: "Thou hadst said that with toil unspent, and all unwasted of limb, / They closed in the grapple of war, so fiercely they rushed to the fray;"[48] and the line of Aratus: "Never in that month launch thou forth amid lashing seas."[49] 2. So also Herodotus: "From the city of Elephantine thou shalt sail upwards, and then shalt come to a level plain; and after crossing this tract, thou shalt embark upon another vessel and sail for two days, and then shalt thou come to a great city whose name is Meroe."[50] Do you observe, my friend, how he leads you in imagination through the region and makes you *see* what you hear? All such cases of direct personal address place the hearer on the very scene of action. 3. So it is when you seem to be speaking, not to all and sundry, but to a single individual: "But Tydeides—thou wouldst not have known him, for whom that hero fought."[51] You will make your hearer more excited and more attentive, and full of active participation, if you keep him on the alert by words addressed to himself.

XXVII

There is further the case in which a writer, when relating something about a person, suddenly breaks off and converts himself into that selfsame person. This species of figure is a kind of outburst of passion:

Then with a far-ringing shout to the Trojans Hector cried,
Bidding them rush on the ships, bidding leave the spoils
    blood-dyed—
And whomso I mark from the galleys aloof on the farther
    side,
I will surely devise his death.[52]

[43]*Oedipus the King,* 1403–08.
[44]*Menexinus,* 245.
[45]*On the Crown,* 18.
[46]Herodotus, *History,* VI. 21.
[47]*Cyropaedia,* VII. i. 37.
[48]*Iliad,* XV. 697–98.
[49]*Phenomena,* 287.
[50]*History,* II. 29.
[51]*Iliad,* V. 85.
[52]*Iliad,* XV. 346–49.

The poet assigns the task of narration, as is fit, to himself, but the abrupt threat he suddenly, with no note of warning, attributes to the angered chief. It would have been frigid had he inserted the words, "Hector said so and so." As it is, the swift transition of the narrative has outstripped the swift transitions of the narrator. 2. Accordingly this figure should be used by preference when a sharp crisis does not suffer the writer to tarry, but constrains him to pass at once from one person to another. An example will be found in Hecataeus: "Ceyx treated the matter gravely, and straightway bade the descendants of Heracles depart; for I am not able to succor you. In order, therefore, that ye may not perish yourselves and injure me, get you gone to some other country." 3. Demosthenes in dealing with Aristogeiton has, somewhat differently, employed this variation of person to betoken the quick play of emotion. "And will none of you," he asks, "be found to be stirred by loathing or even by anger at the violent deeds of this vile and shameless fellow, who—you whose license of speech, most abandoned of men, is not confined by barriers nor by doors, which might perchance be opened!"[53] With the sense thus incomplete, he suddenly breaks off and in his anger almost tears asunder a single expression into two persons—"he who, O thou most abandoned!" Thus, although he has turned aside his address and seems to have left Aristogeiton, yet through passion he directs it upon him with far greater force. 4. Similarly with the words of Penelope:

Herald, with what behest art thou come from the suitor-
    band?
To give to the maids of Odysseus the godlike their command
To forsake their labors, and yonder for them the banquet to
    lay?
I would that of all their wooing this were the latest day,
That this were the end of your banquets, your uttermost
    reveling-hour,
Ye that assemble together and all our substance devour,
The wise Telemachus' store, as though ye never had heard,
In the days overpast of your childhood, your fathers' praising
    word,
How good Odysseus was.[54]

XXVIII

As to whether or no periphrasis[55] contributes to the sublime, no one, I think, will hesitate. For just as in music the so-called accompaniments bring out the charm of the melody, so also periphrasis often harmonizes with the normal expression and adds greatly to its beauty, especially if it has a quality which is not inflated and dissonant but pleasantly tempered. 2. Plato will furnish an instance in proof at the opening of his funeral oration. "In truth they have gained from us their rightful tribute, in the enjoyment of which they proceed along their destined path, escorted by their country publicly, and privately each by his kinsmen."[56] Death he calls "their destined path," and the tribute of accustomed rites he calls "being escorted publicly by their fatherland." Is it in a slight degree only that he has magnified the conception by the use of these words? Has he not rather, starting with unadorned diction, made it musical, and shed over it like a harmony the melodious rhythm which comes from periphrasis? 3. And Xenophon says, "You regard toil as the guide to a joyous life. You have garnered in your souls the goodliest of all possessions and the fittest for warriors. For you rejoice in praise more than in all else."[57] In using, instead of "you are willing to toil," the words "you deem toil the guide to a joyous life," and in expanding the rest of the sentence in like manner, he has annexed to his eulogy a lofty idea. 4. And so with that inimitable phrase of Herodotus: "The goddess afflicted with an unsexing malady those Scythians who had pillaged the temple."[58]

XXIX

A hazardous business, however, eminently hazardous, is periphrasis, unless it be handled with discrimination; otherwise it speedily falls flat, with its odor of empty talk and its swelling amplitude. This is the reason why Plato (who is always strong in figurative language, and at times unseasonably so) is taunted because in his *Laws* he says that "neither gold nor silver treasure should be allowed to establish itself and abide in the city."[59] The critic says that, if he had been forbidding the possession of cattle, he would obviously have spoken of ovine and bovine treasure.

2. But our parenthetical disquisition with regard to the use of figures as bearing upon the sublime has run to sufficient length, my dear Terentianus; for all these things lend additional passion and animation to style, and passion is as intimately allied with sublimity as sketches of character with entertainment.

---

[53]*Against Aristogeiton,* I. 27.
[54]*Odyssey,* IV. 681–89.
[55]Circumlocution.

[56]*Menexinus,* 236.
[57]*Cyropaedia,* I. v. 12.
[58]*History,* I. 105.
[59]VII. 801.

XXX

Since, however, it is the case that, in discourse, thought and diction are for the most part developed one through the other, come let us proceed to consider any branches of the subject of diction which have so far been neglected. Now it is, no doubt, superfluous to dilate to those who know it well upon the fact that the choice of proper and striking words wonderfully attracts and enthralls the hearer, and that such a choice is the leading ambition of all orators and writers, since it is the direct agency which ensures the presence in writings, as upon the fairest statues, of the perfection of grandeur, beauty, mellowness, dignity, force, power, and any other high qualities there may be, and breathes into dead things a kind of living voice. All this it is, I say, needless to mention, for beautiful words are in very truth the peculiar light of thought. 2. It may, however, be pointed out that stately language is not to be used everywhere, since to invest petty affairs with great and high-sounding names would seem just like putting a full-sized tragic mask upon an infant boy. But in poetry and . . .

XXXI

. . . full of vigor and racy; and so is Anacreon's line, "That Thracian mare no longer do I heed. " In this way, too, that original expression of Theopompus merits praise. Owing to the correspondence between word and thing it seems to me to be highly expressive; and yet Caecilius for some unexplained reason finds fault with it. "Philip," says Theopompus, "had a genius for *stomaching* things." Now a homely expression of this kind is sometimes much more telling than elegant language, for it is understood at once since it is drawn from common life, and the fact that it is familiar makes it only the more convincing. So the words *stomaching things* are used most strikingly of a man who, for the sake of attaining his own ends, patiently and with cheerfulness endures things shameful and vile. 2. So with the words of Herodotus. "Cleomenes," he says, "went mad, and with a small sword cut the flesh of his own body into strips, until he slew himself by making mincemeat of his entire person."[60] And, "Pythes fought on shipboard, until he was utterly hacked to pieces."[61] These phrases graze the very edge of vulgarity, but they are saved from vulgarity by their expressiveness.

XXXII

Further, with regard to the number of metaphors to be employed, Caecilius seems to assent to the view of those who lay it down that not more than two, or at the most three, should be ranged together in the same passage. Demosthenes is, in fact, the standard in this as in other matters. The proper time for using metaphors is when the passions roll like a torrent and sweep a multitude of them down their resistless flood. 2. "Men," says he,

> who are vile flatterers, who have maimed their own fatherlands each one of them, who have toasted away their liberty first to Philip and now to Alexander, who measure happiness by their belly and their lowest desires, and who have overthrown that liberty and that freedom from despotic mastery which to the Greeks of an earlier time were the rules and standards of good.[62]

Here the orator's wrath against the traitors throws a veil over the number of the tropes. 3. In the same spirit, Aristotle and Theophrastus point out that the following phrases serve to soften bold metaphors—*as if,* and *as it were,* and *if one may so say,* and *if one may venture such an expression;* for the qualifying words mitigate, they say, the audacity of expression. 4. I accept that view, but still for number and boldness of metaphors I maintain, as I said in dealing with figures, that strong and timely passion and noble sublimity are the appropriate palliatives. For it is the nature of the passions, in their vehement rush, to sweep and thrust everything before them, or rather to demand hazardous turns as altogether indispensable. They do not allow the hearer leisure to criticize the number of the metaphors because he is carried away by the fervor of the speaker. 5. Moreover, in the treatment of commonplaces and in descriptions there is nothing so impressive as a number of tropes following close one upon the other. It is by this means that in Xenophon the anatomy of the human tabernacle is magnificently depicted, and still more divinely in Plato. Plato says that its head is a citadel; in the midst, between the head and the breast, is built the neck like some isthmus. The vertebrae, he says, are fixed beneath like pivots. Pleasure is a bait which tempts men to ill, the tongue the test of taste; the heart is the knot of the veins and the wellspring of the blood that courses round impetuously, and it is stationed in the guard-house of the body. The passages by which the blood races this way and that he names

---

[60]*History,* VI. 75
[61]*History,* VII. 181.

[62]*On the Crown,* 296.

alleys. He says that the gods, contriving succor for the beating of the heart (which takes place when dangers are expected, and when wrath excites it, since it then reaches a fiery heat), have implanted the lungs, which are soft and bloodless and have pores within, to serve as a buffer, in order that the heart may, when its inward wrath boils over, beat against a yielding substance and so escape injury. The seat of the desires he compared to the women's apartments in a house, that of anger to the men's. The spleen he called the napkin of the inward parts, whence it is filled with secretions and grows to a great and festering bulk. After this, the gods canopied the whole with flesh, putting forward the flesh as a defense against injuries from without, as though it were a hair-cushion. The blood he called the fodder of the flesh. "In order to promote nutrition," he continues, "they irrigated the body, cutting conduits as in gardens, in order that, with the body forming a set of tiny channels, the streams of the veins might flow as from a never-failing source." When the end comes, he says that the cables of the soul are loosed like those of a ship, and she is allowed to go free.[63] 6. Examples of a similar nature are to be found in a never-ending series. But those indicated are enough to show that figurative language possesses great natural power, and that metaphors contribute to the sublime; and at the same time that it is impassioned and descriptive passages which rejoice in them to the greatest extent. 7. It is obvious, however, even though I do not dwell upon it, that the use of tropes, like all other beauties of expression, is apt to lead to excess. On this score Plato himself is much criticized, since he is often carried away by a sort of frenzy of words into strong and harsh metaphors and into inflated allegory. "For it is not readily observed," he says, "that a city ought to be mixed like a bowl, in which the mad wine seethes when it has been poured in, though when chastened by another god who is sober, falling thus into noble company, it makes a good and temperate drink."[64] For to call water "a sober god," and mixing "chastening," is—the critics say—the language of a poet, and one who is in truth far from sober. 8. Fastening upon such defects, however, Caecilius ventured, in his writings in praise of Lysias, to make the assertion that Lysias was altogether superior to Plato. In so doing he gave way to two blind impulses of passion. Loving Lysias better even than himself, he nevertheless hates Plato more perfectly than he loves Lysias. In fact, he is carried away by the spirit of contention, and even his premises are not, as he thought, admitted. For he prefers the orator as faultless and immaculate to Plato as one who has often made mistakes. But the truth is not of this nature, nor anything like it.

XXXIII

Come, now, let us take some writer who is really immaculate and beyond reproach. Is it not worthwhile, on this very point, to raise the general question whether we ought to give the preference, in poems and prose writings, to grandeur with some attendant faults, or to success which is moderate but altogether sound and free from error? Aye, and further, whether a greater number of excellences, or excellences higher in quality, would in literature rightly bear away the palm? For these are inquiries appropriate to a treatise on the sublime, and they imperatively demand a settlement. 2. For my part, I am well aware that lofty genius is far removed from flawlessness; for invariable accuracy incurs the risk of pettiness, and in the sublime, as in great fortunes, there must be something which is overlooked. It may be necessarily the case that low and average natures remain as a rule free from failing and in greater safety because they never run a risk or seek to scale the heights, while great endowments prove insecure because of their very greatness. 3. In the second place, I am not ignorant that it naturally happens that the worse side of human character is always the more easily recognized, and that the memory of errors remains indelible, while that of excellences quickly dies away. 4. I have myself noted not a few errors on the part of Homer and other writers of the greatest distinction, and the slips they have made afford me anything but pleasure. Still I do not term them willful errors, but rather oversights of a random and casual kind, due to neglect and introduced with all the heedlessness of genius. Consequently I do not waver in my view that excellences higher in quality, even if not sustained throughout, should always on a comparison be voted the first place, because of their sheer elevation of spirit if for no other reason. Granted that Apollonius in his *Argonautica* shows himself a poet who does not trip, and that in his pastorals Theocritus is, except in a few externals, most happy, would you not, for all that, choose to be Homer rather than Apollonius? 5. Again: Does Eratosthenes in the *Ergione* (a little poem which is altogether free from flaw) show himself a greater poet than Archilochus with the rich and disorderly abundance which follows in his train and with that outburst of the divine spirit within him which it is difficult to bring under the rules of law? Once more: In lyric poetry would you prefer to be Bacchylides rather than Pindar? And in tragedy to be Ion of Chios rather than—Sophocles? It is true that Bacchylides

---

[63]Plato, *Timaeus*, 65–85.
[64]*Laws*, VI. 773.

and Ion are faultless and entirely elegant writers of the polished school, while Pindar and Sophocles, although at times they burn everything before them as it were in their swift career, are often extinguished unaccountably and fail most lamentably. But would anyone in his senses regard all the compositions of Ion put together as an equivalent for the single play of the *Oedipus?*

XXXIV

If successful writing were to be estimated by number of merits and not by the true criterion, thus judged Hyperides would be altogether superior to Demosthenes. For he has a greater variety of accents than Demosthenes and a greater number of excellences, and like the pentathlete he falls just below the top in every branch. In all the contests he has to resign the first place to his rivals, while he maintains that place as against all ordinary persons. 2. Now Hyperides not only imitates all the strong points of Demosthenes with the exception of his composition, but he has embraced in a singular degree the excellences and graces of Lysias as well. For he talks with simplicity, where it is required, and does not adopt like Demosthenes one unvarying tone in all his utterances. He possesses the gift of characterization in a sweet and pleasant form and with a touch of piquancy. There are innumerable signs of wit in him—the most polished raillery, high-bred ease, supple skill in the contests of irony, jests not tasteless or rude after the well-known Attic manner but naturally suggested by the subject, clever ridicule, much comic power, biting satire with well-directed fun, and what may be termed an inimitable charm investing the whole. He is excellently fitted by nature to excite pity; in narrating a fable he is facile, and with his pliant spirit he is also most easily turned towards a digression (as for instance in his rather poetical presentation of the story of Leto), while he has treated his funeral oration in the epideictic[65] vein with probably unequalled success. 3. Demosthenes, on the other hand, is not an apt delineator of character, he is not facile, he is anything but pliant or epideictic, he is comparatively lacking in the entire list of excellences just given. Where he forces himself to be jocular and pleasant, he does not excite laughter but rather becomes the subject of it, and when he wishes to approach the region of charm, he is all the farther removed from it. If he had attempted to write the short speech about

Phryne or about Athenogenes, he would have all the more commended Hyperides to our regard. 4. The good points of the latter, however, many though they be, are wanting in elevation; they are the staid utterances of a sober-hearted man and leave the hearer unmoved, no one feeling terror when he reads Hyperides. But Demosthenes draws—as from a store—excellences allied to the highest sublimity and perfected to the utmost, the tone of lofty speech, living passions, copiousness, readiness, speed (where it is legitimate), and that power and vehemence of his which forbid approach. Having, I say, absorbed bodily within himself these mighty gifts which we may deem heaven-sent (for it would not be right to term them human), he thus with the noble qualities which are his own routs all comers even where the qualities he does not possess are concerned, and overpowers with thunder and with lightning the orators of every age. One could sooner face with unflinching eyes a descending thunderbolt than meet with steady gaze his bursts of passion in their swift succession.

XXXV

But in the case of Plato and Lysias there is, as I said, a further point of difference. For not only in the degree of his excellences, but also in their number, Lysias is much inferior to Plato; and at the same time he surpasses him in his faults still more than he falls below him in his excellences. 2. What fact, then, was before the eyes of those superhuman writers who, aiming at everything that was highest in composition, contemned an all-pervading accuracy? This besides many other things, that Nature has appointed us men to be no base or ignoble animals; but when she ushers us into life and into the vast universe as into some great assembly, to be as it were spectators of the mighty whole and the keenest aspirants for honor, forthwith she implants in our souls the unconquerable love of whatever is elevated and more divine than we. 3. Wherefore not even the entire universe suffices for the thought and contemplation within the reach of the human mind, but our imaginations often pass beyond the bounds of space, and if we survey our life on every side and see how much more it everywhere abounds in what is striking, and great, and beautiful, we shall soon discern the purpose of our birth. 4. This is why, by a sort of natural impulse, we admire not the small streams, useful and pellucid though they be, but the Nile, the Danube or the Rhine, and still more the ocean. Nor do we view the tiny flame of our own kindling (guarded in lasting purity as its light ever is) with greater awe than the celestial fires though they are often shrouded in

---

[65]Declamatory, either encomium or invective.

darkness; nor do we deem it a greater marvel than the craters of Etna, whose eruptions throw up stones from its depths and great masses of rock, and at times pour forth rivers of that pure and unmixed subterranean fire. 5. In all such matters we may say that what is useful or necessary men regard as commonplace, while they reserve their admiration for that which is astounding.

XXXVI

Now as regards the manifestations of the sublime in literature, in which grandeur is never, as it sometimes is in nature, found apart from utility and advantage, it is fitting to observe at once that, though writers of this magnitude are far removed from faultlessness, they nonetheless all rise above what is mortal; that all other qualities prove their possessors to be men, but sublimity raises them near the majesty of God; and that, while immunity from errors relieves from censure, it is grandeur that excites admiration. 2. What need to add thereto that each of these supreme authors often redeems all his failures by a single sublime and happy touch, and (most important of all) that if one were to pick out and mass together the blunders of Homer, Demosthenes, Plato, and all the rest of the greatest writers, they would be found to be a very small part, nay an infinitesimal fraction, of the triumphs which those heroes achieve on every hand? This is the reason why the judgment of all posterity—a verdict which envy itself cannot convict of perversity—has brought and offered those meeds of victory which up to this day it guards intact and seems likely still to preserve, "long as earth's waters shall flow, and her tall trees burgeon and bloom." 3. In reply, however, to the writer who maintains that the faulty *Colossus* is not superior to the *Spearman* of Polycleitus, it is obvious to remark among many other things that in art the utmost exactitude is admired, grandeur in the works of nature; and that it is by nature that man is a being gifted with speech. In statues likeness to man is the quality required; in discourse we demand, as I said, that which transcends the human. 4. Nevertheless—and the counsel about to be given reverts to the beginning of our memoir—since freedom from failings is for the most part the successful result of art, and excellence (though it may be unevenly sustained) the result of sublimity, the employment of art is in every way a fitting aid to nature; for it is the conjunction of the two which tends to ensure perfection.

Such are the decisions to which we have felt bound to come with regard to the questions proposed; but let every man cherish the view which pleases him best.

XXXVII

Closely related to metaphors (for we must return to our point) are comparisons and similes, differing only in this respect. . . .

XXXVIII

. . . such hyperboles as: "unless you carry your brains trodden down in your heels."[66] It is necessary, therefore, to know where to fix the limit in each case; for an occasional overshooting of the mark ruins the hyperbole, and such expressions, when strained too much, lose their tension, and sometimes swing round and produce the contrary effect. 2. Isocrates, for example, fell into unaccountable puerility owing to the ambition which made him desire to describe everything with a touch of amplification. The theme of his *Panegyric* is that Athens surpasses Lacedaemon in benefits conferred upon Greece, and yet at the very outset of his speech he uses these words: "Further, language has such capacity that it is possible thereby to debase things lofty and invest things small with grandeur, and to express old things in a new way, and to discourse in ancient fashion about what has newly happened.[67] "Do you then, Isocrates," it may be asked, "mean in that way to interchange the facts of Lacedaemonian and Athenian history?" For in his eulogy of language he has, we may say, published to his hearers a preamble warning them to distrust himself. 3. Perhaps, then, as we said in dealing with figures generally, those hyperboles are best in which the very fact that they are hyperboles escapes attention. This happens when, through stress of strong emotion, they are uttered in connection with some great crisis, as is done by Thucydides in the case of those who perished in Sicily. "The Syracusans," he says, "came down to the water's edge and began the slaughter of those chiefly who were in the river, and the water at once became polluted, but none the less it was swallowed although muddy and mixed with blood, and to most it was still worth fighting for."[68] That a draught of blood and mud should still be worth fighting for, is rendered credible by the intensity of the emotion at a great crisis. 4. So with the passage in which Herodotus tells of those who fell at Thermopylae. "On this spot,"

---

[66]*On Halonesus,* 45, attributed by some to Demosthenes.
[67]8.
[68]*History of the Peloponnesian War,* VII. 84.

he says, "the barbarians buried them as they defended themselves with daggers—those of them who had daggers still left—and with hands and mouths."[69] Here you may be inclined to protest against the expressions "fight with their very mouths" against men in armor, and "being buried" with darts. At the same time the narrative carries conviction; for the event does not seem to be introduced for the sake of the hyperbole, but the hyperbole to spring naturally from the event. 5. For (as I never cease to say) the deeds and passions which verge on transport are a sufficient lenitive and remedy for every audacity of speech. This is the reason why the quips of comedy, although they may be carried to the extreme of absurdity, are plausible because they are so amusing. For instance, "Smaller his field was than a Spartan letter." For mirth, too, is an emotion, an emotion which has its root in pleasure. 6. Hyperboles are employed in describing things small as well as great, since exaggeration is the common element in both cases. And, in a sense, ridicule is an amplification of the paltriness of things.

XXXIX

The fifth of those elements contributing to the sublime which we mentioned, my excellent friend, at the beginning, still remains to be dealt with, namely the arrangement of the words in a certain order. In regard to this, having already in two treatises sufficiently stated such results as our inquiry could compass, we will add, for the purpose of our present undertaking, only what is absolutely essential, namely the fact that harmonious arrangement is not only a natural source of persuasion and pleasure among men but also a wonderful instrument of lofty utterance and of passion. 2. For does not the flute instill certain emotions into its hearers and as it were make them beside themselves and full of frenzy, and supplying a rhythmical movement constrain the listener to move rhythmically in accordance therewith and to conform himself to the melody, although he may be utterly ignorant of music? Yes, and the tones of the harp, although in themselves they signify nothing at all, often cast a wonderful spell, as you know, over an audience by means of the variations of sounds, by their pulsation against one another, and by their mingling in concert. 3. And yet these are mere semblances and spurious copies of persuasion, not (as I have said) genuine activities of human nature. Are we not, then,

to hold that composition (being a harmony of that language which is implanted by nature in man and which appeals not to the hearing only but to the soul itself), since it calls forth manifold shapes of words, thoughts, deeds, beauty, melody, all of them born at our birth and growing with our growth, and since by means of the blending and variation of its own tones it seeks to introduce into the minds of those who are present the emotion which affects the speaker and since it always brings the audience to share in it and by the building of phrase upon phrase raises a sublime and harmonious structure: are we not, I say, to hold that harmony by these selfsame means allures us and invariably disposes us to stateliness and dignity and elevation and every emotion which it contains within itself, gaining absolute mastery over our minds? But it is folly to dispute concerning matters which are generally admitted, since experience is proof sufficient. 4. An example of a conception which is usually thought sublime and is really admirable is that which Demosthenes associates with the decree: "This decree caused the danger which then beset the city to pass by just-as a cloud."[70] But it owes its happy sound no less to the harmony than to the thought itself. For the thought is expressed throughout in dactylic rhythms, and these are most noble and productive of sublimity; and therefore it is that they constitute the heroic, the finest meter that we know. For if you derange the words of the sentence and transpose them in whatever way you will, as for example "This decree just-as a cloud caused the danger of the time to pass by"; nay, if you cut off a single syllable only and say "caused to pass by as a cloud," you will perceive to what an extent harmony is in unison with sublimity. For the very words "just-as a cloud" begin with a long rhythm, which consists of four metrical beats; but if one syllable is cut off and we read "as a cloud," we immediately maim the sublimity by the abbreviation. Conversely, if you elongate the word and write "caused to pass by just-as-if a cloud," it means the same thing, but no longer falls with the same effect upon the ear, inasmuch as the abrupt grandeur of the passage loses its energy and tension through the lengthening of the concluding syllables.

XL

Among the chief causes of the sublime in speech, as in the structure of the human body, is the collocation of members,

---

[69]*History,* VII. 225.

[70]*On the Crown,* 188.

a single one of which if severed from another possesses in itself nothing remarkable, but all united together make a full and perfect organism. So the constituents of grandeur, when separated from one another, carry with them sublimity in distraction this way and that, but when formed into a body by association and when further encircled in a chain of harmony they become sonorous by their very rotundity; and in periods sublimity is, as it were, a contribution made by a multitude. 2. We have, however, sufficiently shown that many writers and poets who possess no natural sublimity and are perhaps even wanting in elevation have nevertheless, although employing for the most part common and popular words with no striking associations of their own, by merely joining and fitting these together, secured dignity and distinction and the appearance of freedom from meanness. Instances will be furnished by Philistus among many others, by Aristophanes in certain passages, by Euripides in most. 3. In the last-mentioned author, Heracles, after the scene in which he slays his children, uses the words: "Full-fraught am I with woes—no space for more."[71] The expression is a most ordinary one, but it has gained elevation through the aptness of the structure of the line. If you shape the sentence in a different way, you will see this plainly, the fact being that Euripides is a poet in virtue of his power of composition rather than of his invention. 4. In the passage which describes Dirce torn away by the bull:

> Whitherso'er he turned
> Swift wheeling round, he haled and hurled withal
> Dame, rock, oak, intershifted ceaselessly.

the conception itself is a fine one, but it has been rendered more forcible by the fact that the harmony is not hurried or carried as it were on rollers, but the words act as buttresses for one another and find support in the pauses, and issue finally in a well-grounded sublimity.

XLI

There is nothing in the sphere of the sublime, that is so lowering as broken and agitated movement of language, such as is characteristic of pyrrhics and trochees and dichorees,[72] which fall altogether to the level of dance music. For all overrhythmical writing is at once felt to be affected and finical and wholly lacking in passion owing to the monotony of its superficial polish. 2. And the worst of it all is that, just as petty lays draw their hearer away from the point and compel his attention to themselves, so also overrhythmical style does not communicate the feeling of the words but simply the feeling of the rhythm. Sometimes, indeed, the listeners knowing beforehand the due terminations stamp their feet in time with the speaker, and as in a dance give the right step in anticipation. 3. In like manner those words are destitute of sublimity which lie too close together, and are cut up into short and tiny syllables, and are held together as if with wooden bolts by sheer inequality and ruggedness.

XLII

Further, excessive concision of expression tends to lower the sublime, since grandeur is marred when the thought is brought into too narrow a compass. Let this be understood not of proper compression, but of what is absolutely petty and cut into segments. For concision curtails the sense, but brevity goes straight to the mark. It is plain that, vice versa, prolixities are frigid, for so is everything that resorts to unseasonable length.

XLIII

Triviality of expression is also apt to disfigure sublimity. In Herodotus, for example, the tempest is described with marvelous effect in all its details, but the passage surely contains some words below the dignity of the subject. The following may serve as an instance—"when the sea seethed."[73] The word *seethed* detracts greatly from the sublimity because it is an ill-sounding one. Further, "the wind," he says, "grew fagged," and those who clung to the spars met "an unpleasant end."[74] The expression *grew fagged* is lacking in dignity, being vulgar; and the word *unpleasant* is inappropriate to so great a disaster. 2. Similarly, when Theopompus had dressed out in marvelous fashion the descent of the Persian king upon Egypt, he spoilt the whole by some petty words.

> For which of the cities (he says) or which of the
> tribes in Asia did not send envoys to the Great

---

[71]*Heracles*, 1245.
[72]A pyrrhic is a metrical foot consisting of two short syllables; a trochee, a foot consisting of one long syllable followed by one short syllable. A dichoree consists of two trochees treated as a unit.

---

[73]*History*, VII. 188.
[74]*History*, VII. 191; VIII. 13.

King? Which of the products of the earth or of the achievements of art was not, in all its beauty or preciousness, brought as an offering to his presence? Consider the multitude of costly coverlets and mantles, in purple or white or embroidery; the multitude of pavilions of gold furnished with all things useful; the multitude, too, of tapestries and costly couches. Further, gold and silver plate richly wrought, and goblets and mixing bowls, some of which you might have seen set with precious stones, and others finished with care and at great price. In addition to all this, countless myriads of Greek and barbaric weapons, and beasts of burden beyond all reckoning and victims fattened for slaughter, and many bushels of condiments, and many bags and sacks and sheets of papyrus and all other useful things, and an equal number of pieces of salted flesh from all manner of victims, so that the piles of them were so great that those who were approaching from a distance took them to be hills and eminences confronting them.

3. He runs off from the more elevated to the more lowly, whereas he should, on the contrary, have risen higher and higher. With his wonderful description of the whole outfit he mixes bags and condiments and sacks, and conveys the impression of a confectioner's shop! For just as if, in the case of those very adornments, between the golden vessels and the jeweled mixing bowls and the silver plate and the pavilions of pure gold and the goblets, a man were to bring and set in the midst paltry bags and sacks, the proceeding would have been offensive to the eye, so do such words when introduced out of season constitute deformities and as it were blots on the diction.

4. He might have described the scene in broad outline just as he says that hills blocked their way, and with regard to the preparations generally have spoken of "wagons and camels and the multitude of beasts of burden carrying everything that ministers to the luxury and enjoyment of the table," or have used some such expression as "piles of all manner of grain and things which conduce preeminently to good cookery and comfort of body," or if he must necessarily put it in so uncompromising a way, he might have said that "all the dainties of cooks and caterers were there." 5. In lofty passages we ought not to descend to sordid and contemptible language unless constrained by some overpowering necessity, but it is fitting that we should use words worthy of the subject and imitate nature, the artificer of man, for she has not placed in full view our grosser parts or the means of purging our frame, but has hidden them away as far as was possible, and as Xenophon says has put their channels

in the remotest background, so as not to sully the beauty of the entire creature. 6. But enough; there is no need to enumerate, one by one, the things which produce triviality. For since we have previously indicated those qualities which render style noble and lofty, it is evident that their opposites will for the most part make it low and base.

XLIV

It remains however (as I will not hesitate to add, in recognition of your love of knowledge) to clear up, my dear Terentianus, a question which a certain philosopher has recently mooted. "I wonder," he says, "as no doubt do many others, how it happens that in our time there are men who have the gift of persuasion to the utmost extent, and are well fitted for public life, and are keen and ready, and particularly rich in all the charms of language, yet there no longer arise really lofty and transcendent natures unless quite exceptionally. So great and worldwide a dearth of high utterance attends our age." 2. "Can it be," he continued, "that we are to accept the trite explanation that democracy is the kind nursing-mother of genius, and that literary power may be said to share its rise and fall with democracy and democracy alone? For freedom, it is said, has power to feed the imaginations of the lofty-minded and to inspire hope, and where it prevails there spreads abroad the eagerness of mutual rivalry and the emulous pursuit of the foremost place. 3. Moreover, owing to the prizes which are open to all under popular government, the mental excellences of the orator are continually exercised and sharpened, and as it were rubbed bright, and shine forth (as it is natural they should) with all the freedom which inspires the doings of the state. Today," he went on, "we seem in our boyhood to learn the lessons of a righteous servitude, being all but enswathed in its customs and observances, when our thoughts are yet young and tender, and never tasting the fairest and most productive source of eloquence (by which," he added, "I mean freedom), so that we emerge in no other guise than that of sublime flatterers." 4. This is the reason, he maintained, why no slave ever becomes an orator, although all other faculties may belong to menials. In the slave there immediately burst out signs of fettered liberty of speech, of the dungeon as it were, of a man habituated to buffetings. 5. "For the day of slavery," as Homer has it, "takes away half our manhood."[75] "Just as," he proceeded, "the cages (if what I hear is true) in which are kept the pygmies, commonly called *nani,* not only hinder the

---

[75] *Odyssey,* XVII. 322.

growth of the creatures confined within them, but actually attenuate them through the bonds which beset their bodies, so one has aptly termed all servitude (though it be most righteous) the cage of the soul and a public prison-house." 6. I answered him thus: "It is easy, my good sir, and characteristic of human nature, to find fault with the age in which one lives. But consider whether it may not be true that it is not the world's peace that ruins great natures, but far rather this war illimitable which holds our desires in its grasp, aye, and further still those passions which occupy as with troops our present age and utterly harry and plunder it. For the love of money, (a disease from which we all now suffer sorely) and the love of pleasure make us their thralls, or rather, as one may say, drown us body and soul in the depths, the love of riches being a malady which makes men petty, and the love of pleasure one which makes them most ignoble. 7. On reflection I cannot discover how it is possible for us, if we value boundless wealth so highly, or (to speak more truly) deify it, to avoid allowing the entrance into our souls of the evils which are inseparable from it. For vast and unchecked wealth is accompanied, in close conjunction and step for step, as they say, by extravagance, and as soon as the former opens the gates of cities and houses, the latter immediately enters and abides. And when time has passed the pair build nests in the lives of men, as the wise say, and quickly give themselves to the rearing of offspring, and breed ostentation, and vanity, and luxury, no spurious progeny of theirs, but only too legitimate. If these children of wealth are permitted to come to maturity, straightway they beget in the soul inexorable masters—insolence, and lawlessness, and shamelessness. 8. This must necessarily happen, and men will no longer lift up their eyes or have any further regard for fame, but the ruin of such lives will gradually reach its complete consummation and sublimities of soul fade and wither away

and become contemptible, when men are lost in admiration of their own mortal parts and omit to exalt that which is immortal. 9. For a man who has once accepted a bribe for a judicial decision cannot be an unbiased and upright judge of what is just and honorable (since to the man who is venal his own interests must seem honorable and just), and the same is true where the entire life of each of us is ordered by bribes, and huntings after the death of others, and the laying of ambushes for legacies, while gain from any and every source we purchase—each one of us—at the price of life itself, being the slaves of pleasure. In an age which is ravaged by plagues so sore, is it possible for us to imagine that there is still left an unbiased and incorruptible judge of works that are great and likely to reach posterity, or is it not rather the case that all are influenced in their decisions by the passion for gain? 10. Nay, it is perhaps better for men like ourselves to be ruled than to be free, since our appetites, if let loose without restraint upon our neighbors like beasts from a cage, would set the world on fire with deeds of evil. 11. Summing up, I maintained that among the banes of the natures which our age produces must be reckoned that half-heartedness in which the life of all of us with few exceptions is passed, for we do not labor or exert ourselves except for the sake of praise and pleasure, never for those solid benefits which are a worthy object of our own efforts and the respect of others. 12. But "'tis best to leave these riddles unresolved,"[76] and to proceed to what next presents itself, namely the subject of the passions, about which I previously undertook to write in a separate treatise. These form, as it seems to me, a material part of discourse generally and of the sublime itself. . . .

---

[76]Euripides, *Electra*, 379.

Plotinus

204–270

The neo-Platonic philosopher Plotinus, curiously enough, challenges Plato's theory that art imitates nature and is thus twice removed from the ideas, or reality. Plotinus gives art a higher position in his system. He does not disparage art because of its relation to the visible world, which is an emanation from the ultimately unknowable "One." The One expresses itself in a triad, the Good, the Intellect and its knowledge, and the All-Soul. Everything emanates from the One and strives to return to it. Beauty, as Plotinus laboriously defines it, is central to his system, since the more beautiful a thing is, the closer it is to the One. Sheer symmetry is not necessarily, as in earlier Greek aesthetics, a sign of beauty.

Although Plotinus never discusses literary art, his general remarks in *On the Intellectual Beauty,* the Eighth Tractate of the Fifth Ennead, can be brought to bear on literary matters. The beauty of the artist's creation lies not in any physical object that it copies or matter that it shapes, but in what the artist imposes on his materials. In the imposition, the artist turns his materials into something other than what they were, makes them into a new form; this attainment comes from within the artist, who is capable of adding where nature is lacking. Plotinus implies that there is a struggle between the artist and his materials, and that in the successful work of art the materials are partly subdued. When this occurs, the form in the artist's mind, which is derived from intellect and ultimately from the One, is given some visible expression. "Phidias wrought the *Zeus* upon no model among things of sense but by apprehending what form Zeus must take if he chose to become manifest to sight."

In contrast to Plato, Plotinus considers the artist a creator of vehicles of valuable, though imperfect, spiritual insight. Plotinus' artist does not work by rational principles; he does not, as Plato would have had him, lead us to the ideas through the use of reason. Rather, he tries to express in an artistic medium some insight into the One. The Platonism of expressivist critics of the Romantic movement was strongly influenced by Plotinean attitudes. The theories of Shelley and Keats, for example, recall Plotinus' remark that "the artist himself goes back, after all, to that wisdom in nature which is embodied in himself; and this is not a wisdom built up of theorems but one totality, not a wisdom consisting of manifold detail coordinated into a unity but rather a unity working out into detail." This emphasis on the mind and the activity of the author and the distinction between true artistic wisdom and discursive knowledge is a distant precursor of Romantic theories of the imagination developed by Coleridge and his contemporaries.

A standard translation is that by Stephen MacKenna, *The Enneads,* revised by B. S. Page (1956). For commentary see W. R. Inge, *The Philosophy of Plotinus* (1918); P. V. Pistorius, *Plotinus and Neoplatonism* (1952); Eugénie de Keyser, *La signification* de l'art dans les Ennéades de Plotin (1955); Emile Bréhier, *The Philosophy of Plotinus* (1958); John Bussanich, *The One and Its Relation to Intellect in Plotinus* (1967); and Gerard O'Daly, *Plotinus' Philosophy of the Self* (1973).

On the Intellectual Beauty

It is a principle with us that one who has attained to the vision of the intellectual cosmos and grasped the beauty of the authentic intellect will be able also to come to understand the father and transcendent of that divine being. It concerns us, then, to try to see and say, for ourselves and as far as such matters may be told, how the beauty of the divine intellect and of the intellectual cosmos may be revealed to contemplation.

Let us go to the realm of magnitudes—suppose two blocks of stone lying side by side: one is unpatterned, quite untouched by art; the other has been minutely wrought by the craftsman's hands into some statue of god or man, a Grace or a Muse, or if a human being, not a portrait but a creation in which the sculptor's art has concentrated all loveliness.

Now it must be seen that the stone thus brought under the artist's hand to the beauty of form is beautiful not as stone—for so the crude block would be as pleasant—but in virtue of the form or idea introduced by the art. This form is not in the material; it is in the designer before ever it enters the stone; and the artificer holds it not by his equipment of eyes and hands but by his participation in his art. The beauty, therefore, exists in a far higher state in the art; for it does not come over integrally into the work; that original beauty is not transferred; what comes over is a derivative and a minor: and even that shows itself upon the statue not integrally and with entire realization of intention but only in so far as it has subdued the resistance of the material.

Art, then, creating in the image of its own nature and content, and working by the idea or reason-principle of the beautiful object it is to produce, must itself be beautiful in a far higher and purer degree since it is the seat and source of that beauty, indwelling in the art, which must naturally be more complete than any comeliness of the external. In the degree in which the beauty is diffused by entering into matter, it is so much the weaker than that concentrated in unity; everything that reaches outwards is the less for it, strength less strong, heat less hot, every power less potent, and so beauty less beautiful.

Then again every prime cause must be, within itself, more powerful than its effect can be: the musical does not derive from an unmusical source but from music; and so the art exhibited in the material work derives from an art yet higher.[1]

Still the arts are not to be slighted on the ground that they create by imitation of natural objects; for, to begin with, these natural objects are themselves imitations; then, we must recognize that they give no bare reproduction of the thing seen but go back to the reason-principles from which nature itself derives, and, furthermore, that much of their work is all their own; they are holders of beauty and add where nature is lacking.[2] Thus Phidias wrought the *Zeus* upon no model among things of sense but by apprehending what form Zeus must take if he chose to become manifest to sight.[3]

2. But let us leave the arts and consider those works produced by nature and admitted to be naturally beautiful which the creations of art are charged with imitating, all reasoning life and unreasoning things alike, but especially the consummate among them, where the molder and maker has subdued the material and given the form he desired. Now what is the beauty here? It has nothing to do with the blood or the menstrual process: either there is also a color and form apart from all this or there is nothing unless sheer ugliness or (at best) a bare recipient, as it were the mere matter of beauty.

Whence shone forth the beauty of Helen, battle-sought; or of all those women like in loveliness to Aphrodite; or of Aphrodite herself; or of any human being that has been perfect in beauty; or of any of these gods manifest to sight, or unseen but carrying what would be beauty if we saw?

ON THE INTELLECTUAL BEAUTY. Plotinus wrote *The Enneads,* of which this selection is a part, in about 260. They were edited and published between 300 and 305 by Porphyry, Greek scholar, philosopher, and student of religions. The text is from Stephen MacKenna, tr., *The Enneads,* revised by B. S. Page (London: Faber & Faber, 1956), and is reprinted by permission of Faber & Faber Ltd.

[1]As "beauty" moves out from the One through the artist to the materials he shapes, it becomes weaker.
[2]Here Plotinus seems to answer Plato directly.
[3]The statue called the *Olympian Zeus,* known only from descriptions by ancient writers, was among the most famous works of Phidias, Greek sculptor of the fifth century B.C.

In all these is it not the idea, something of that realm but communicated to the produced from within the producer, just as in works of art, we held, it is communicated from the arts to their creations? Now we can surely not believe that, while the made thing and the idea thus impressed upon matter are beautiful, yet the idea not so alloyed but resting still with the creator—the idea primal, immaterial, firmly a unity—is not beauty.

If material extension were in itself the ground of beauty, then the creating principle, being without extension, could not be beautiful: but beauty cannot be made to depend upon magnitude since, whether in a large object or a small, the one idea equally moves and forms the mind by its inherent power. A further indication is that as long as the object remains outside us we know nothing of it; it affects us by entry; but only as an idea can it enter through the eyes which are not of scope to take an extended mass: we are, no doubt, simultaneously possessed of the magnitude which, however, we take in not as mass but by an elaboration upon the presented form.

Then again the principle producing the beauty must be, itself, ugly, neutral, or beautiful: ugly, it could not produce the opposite; neutral, why should its product be the one rather than the other? The nature, then, which creates things so lovely must be itself of a far earlier[4] beauty; we, undisciplined in discernment of the inward, knowing nothing of it, run after the outer, never understanding that it is the inner which stirs us,[5] we are in the case of one who sees his own reflection but not realizing whence it comes goes in pursuit of it.

But that the thing we are pursuing is something different and that the beauty is not in the concrete object is manifest from the beauty there is in matters of study, in conduct and custom; briefly, in soul or mind. And it is precisely here that the greater beauty lies, perceived whenever you look to the wisdom in a man and delight in it, not wasting attention on the face, which may be hideous, but passing all appearance by catching only at the inner comeliness, the truly personal; if you are still unmoved and cannot acknowledge beauty under such conditions, then looking to your own inner being you will find no beauty to delight you and it will be futile in that state to seek the greater vision, for you will be questing it through the ugly and impure.

This is why such matters are not spoken of to everyone; you, if you are conscious of beauty within, remember.

3. Thus there is in the nature-principle itself an ideal archetype of the beauty that is found in material forms and,

of that archetype again, the still more beautiful archetype in soul, source of that in nature. In the proficient soul this is brighter and of more advanced loveliness: adorning the soul and bringing to it a light from that greater light which is beauty primally, its immediate presence sets the soul reflecting upon the quality of this prior, the archetype which has no such entries, and is present nowhere but remains in itself alone, and thus is not even to be called a reason-principle but is the creative source of the very first reason-principle which is the beauty to which soul serves as matter.[6]

This prior, then, is the intellectual-principle,[7] the veritable, abiding and not fluctuant since not taking intellectual quality from outside itself. By what image, thus, can we represent it? We have nowhere to go but to what is less. Only from itself can we take an image of it; that is, there can be no representation of it, except in the sense that we represent gold by some portion of gold—purified, either actually or mentally, if it be impure—insisting at the same time that this is not the total thing gold, but merely the particular gold of a particular parcel. In the same way we learn in this matter from the purified intellect in ourselves or, if you like, from the gods and the glory of the intellect in them.

For assuredly all the gods are august and beautiful in a beauty beyond our speech. And what makes them so? Intellect; and especially intellect operating within them (the divine sun and stars) to visibility. It is not through the loveliness of their corporeal forms: even those that have body are not gods by that beauty; it is in virtue of intellect that they, too, are gods, and as gods beautiful. They do not veer between wisdom and folly: in the immunity of intellect unmoving and pure, they are wise always, all-knowing, taking cognizance not of the human but of their own being and of all that lies within the contemplation of intellect. Those of them whose dwelling is in the heavens are ever in this meditation—what task prevents them?—and from afar they look, too, into that further heaven by a lifting of the head. The gods belonging to that higher heaven itself, they whose station is upon it and in it, see and know in virtue of their omnipresence to it. For all There[8] is heaven; earth is heaven, and sea heaven; and animal and plant and man; all is the heavenly content of that heaven: and the gods in it, despising neither men nor anything else that is there where all is of the heavenly order, traverse all that country and all space in peace.

---

[4]Not temporally but spiritually prior or closer to the One.
[5]"Inner" refers to that which is closer to the One and is "in" man; "outer," to that which is beyond man, in matter.

---

[6]The movement from soul to nature-principle to matter is an outward movement away from the One toward greater diversity but less "reality." For Plotinus the artist's struggle with matter is an effort to restore it to greater unity with the One by investing it with form.
[7]One of the triad composing the One.
[8]See Yeats's poem *There*, where Yeats adopts something similar to Plotinus' conception.

4. To "live at ease" is There; and to these divine beings verity is mother and nurse, existence and sustenance; all that is not of process but of authentic being they see, and themselves in all: for all is transparent, nothing dark, nothing resistant; every being is lucid to every other, in breadth and depth; light runs through light. And each of them contains all within itself, and at the same time sees all in every other, so that everywhere there is all, and all is all and each all, and infinite the glory. Each of them is great; the small is great; the sun, There, is all the stars; and every star, again, is all the stars and sun. While some one manner of being is dominant in each, all are mirrored in every other.

Movement There is pure (as self-caused), for the moving principle is not a separate thing to complicate it as it speeds.

So, too, repose is not troubled, for there is no admixture of the unstable; and the beauty is all beauty since it is not resident in what is not beautiful. Each There walks upon no alien soil; its place is its essential self; and, as each moves, so to speak, towards what is above, it is attended by the very ground from which it starts: there is no distinguishing between the being and the place; all is intellect, the principle and the ground on which it stands, alike. Thus we might think that our visible sky (the ground or place of the stars), lit as it is, produces the light which reaches us from it, though of course this is really produced by the stars (as it were, by the principles of light alone, not also by the ground as the analogy would require).

In our realm[9] all is part rising from part and nothing can be more than partial; but There each being is an eternal product of a whole and is at once a whole and an individual manifesting as part but, to the keen vision There, known for the whole it is.

The myth of Lynceus seeing into the very deeps of the earth tells us of those eyes in the divine. No weariness overtakes this vision which yet brings no such satiety as would call for its ending; for there never was a void to be filled so that, with the fullness and the attainment of purpose, the sense of sufficiency be induced: nor is there any such incongruity within the divine that one being There could be repulsive to another: and of course all There are unchangeable. This absence of satisfaction means only a satisfaction leading to no distaste for that which produces it; to see is to look the more, since for them to continue in the contemplation of an infinite self and of infinite objects is but to acquiesce in the bidding of their nature.

Life, pure, is never a burden; how then could there be weariness There where the living is most noble? That very life is wisdom, not a wisdom built up by reasonings but complete from the beginning, suffering no lack which could set it inquiring, a wisdom primal, unborrowed, not something added to the being, but its very essence. No wisdom, thus, is greater; this is the authentic knowing, assessor to the divine intellect as projected into manifestation simultaneously with it; thus, in the symbolic saying, justice is assessor to Zeus.

(Perfect wisdom:) for all the principles of this order, dwelling There, are as it were visible images projected from themselves, so that all becomes an object of contemplation to contemplators immeasurably blessed. The greatness and power of the wisdom There we may know from this, that it embraces all the real beings, and has made all and all follow it, and yet that it is itself those beings, which sprang into being with it, so that all is one and the essence There is wisdom. If we have failed to understand, it is that we have thought of knowledge as a mass of theorems and an accumulation of propositions, though that is false even for our sciences of the sense-realm. But in case this should be questioned, we may leave our own sciences for the present, and deal with the knowing in the supreme at which Plato glances where he speaks of "that knowledge which is not a stranger in something strange to it"—though in what sense, he leaves us to examine and declare, if we boast ourselves worthy of the discussion. This is probably our best starting point.

5. All that comes to be, work of nature or of craft, some wisdom has made: everywhere a wisdom presides at a making.

No doubt the wisdom of the artist may be the guide of the work; it is sufficient explanation of the wisdom exhibited in the arts; but the artist himself goes back, after all, to that wisdom in nature which is embodied in himself; and this is not a wisdom built up of theorems but one totality, not a wisdom consisting of manifold detail coordinated into a unity but rather a unity working out into detail.

Now, if we could think of this as the primal wisdom, we need look no further, since, at that, we have discovered a principle, which is neither a derivative nor a "stranger in something strange to it." But if we are told that, while this reason-principle is in nature, yet nature itself is its source, we ask how nature came to possess it; and, if nature derived it from some other source, we ask what that other source may be; if, on the contrary, the principle is self-sprung, we need look no further: but if (as we assume) we are referred to the intellectual-principle we must make clear whether the intellectual-principle engendered the wisdom: if we learn that it did, we ask whence: if from itself, then inevitably it is itself wisdom.

The true wisdom, then (found to be identical with the intellectual-principle), is real being; and real being is wisdom; it is wisdom that gives value to real being; and being

---

[9]The realm of matter and of sense perception.

is real in virtue of its origin in wisdom. It follows that all forms of existence not possessing wisdom are, indeed, beings in right of the wisdom which went to their forming, but, as not in themselves possessing it, are not real beings.

We cannot, therefore, think that the divine beings of that sphere, or the other supremely blessed There, need look to our apparatus of science: all of that realm (the very beings themselves), all is noble image, such images as we may conceive to lie within the soul of the wise—but There not as inscription but as authentic existence. The ancients had this in mind when they declared the ideas (forms) to be beings, essentials.

6. Similarly, as it seems to me, the wise of Egypt—whether in precise knowledge or by a prompting of nature—indicated the truth where, in their effort towards philosophical statement, they left aside the writing forms that take in the detail of words and sentences—those characters that represent sounds and convey the propositions of reasoning—and drew pictures instead, engraving in the temple-inscriptions a separate image for every separate item: thus they exhibited the absence of discursiveness in the intellectual realm.

For each manifestation of knowledge and wisdom is a distinct image, an object in itself, an immediate unity, not an aggregate of discursive reasoning and detailed willing. Later from this wisdom in unity there appears, in another form of being, an image, already less compact, which announces the original in terms of discourse and unravels the causes by which things are such that the wonder rises how a generated world can be so excellent.[10]

For, one who knows must declare his wonder that this wisdom, while not itself containing the causes by which being exists and takes such excellence, yet imparts them to the entities produced according to its canons. This excellence, whose necessity is scarcely or not at all manifest to search, exists, if we could but find it out, before all searching and reasoning.

What I say may be considered in one chief thing, and thence applied to all the particular entities:

7. Consider the universe: we are agreed that its existence and its nature come to it from beyond itself; are we, now, to imagine that its maker first thought it out in detail—the earth, and its necessary situation in the middle; water and, again, its position as lying upon the earth; all the other elements and objects up to the sky in due place and order; living beings with their appropriate forms as we know them, their inner organs and their outer limbs—and that having

thus appointed every item beforehand, he then set about the execution?

Such designing was not even possible; how could the plan for a universe come to one that had never looked outward? Nor could he work on material gathered from elsewhere as our craftsmen do, using hands and tools; feet and hands are of the later order.

One way, only, remains: all things must exist in something else; of that prior—since there is no obstacle, all being continuous within the realm of reality—there has suddenly appeared a sign, an image, whether given forth directly or through the ministry of soul or of some phase of soul matters nothing for the moment: thus the entire aggregate of existence springs from the divine world, in greater beauty There because There unmingled but mingled here.

From the beginning to end all is gripped by the forms of the intellectual realm: matter itself is held by the ideas of the elements and to these ideas are added other ideas and others again, so that it is hard to work down to crude matter beneath all that sheathing of idea. Indeed since matter itself is, in its degree, an idea—the lowest—all this universe is idea and there is nothing that is not idea as the archetype was. And all is made silently, since nothing had part in the making but being and idea—a further reason why creation went without toil. The exemplar was the idea of an all and so an all must come into being.

Thus nothing stood in the way of the idea, and even now it dominates, despite all the clash of things: the creation is not hindered on its way even now; it stands firm in virtue of being all. To me, moreover, it seems that if we ourselves were archetypes, ideas, veritable being, and the idea with which we construct here were our veritable essence, then our creative power, too, would toillessly effect its purpose: as man now stands, he does not produce in his work a true image of himself: become man, he has ceased to be the all; ceasing to be man—we read—"he soars aloft and administers the cosmos entire"; restored to the all he is maker of the all.

But—to our immediate purpose—it is possible to give a reason why the earth is set in the midst and why it is round and why the ecliptic runs precisely as it does, but, looking to the creating principle, we cannot say that because this was the way therefore things were so planned: we can say only that because the exemplar is what it is, therefore the things of this world are good; the causing principle, we might put it, reached the conclusion before all formal reasoning and not from any premises, not by sequence or plan but before either, since all of that order is later, all reason, demonstration, persuasion.

Since there is a source, all the created must spring from it and in accordance with it; and we are rightly told not to go

---

[10]See Wheelwright's distinction between modes of discourse and his concept of iconic signification in *The Logical and the Translogical,* pp. 1022–31.

seeking the causes impelling a source to produce, especially when this is the perfect sufficient source and identical with the term: a source which is source and term must be the all-unity, complete in itself.

8. This then is beauty primally: it is entire and omnipresent as an entirety; and therefore in none of its parts or members lacking in beauty; beautiful thus beyond denial. Certainly it cannot be anything (be, for example, beauty) without being wholly that thing; it can be nothing which it is to possess partially or in which it utterly fails (and therefore it must entirely be beauty entire).

If this principle were not beautiful, what other could be? Its prior does not deign to be beautiful; that which is the first to manifest itself—form and object of vision to the intellect—cannot but be lovely to see. It is to indicate this that Plato, drawing on something well within our observation, represents the Creator as approving the work he has achieved: the intention is to make us feel the lovable beauty of the archetype and of the divine idea; for to admire a representation is to admire the original upon which it was made.

It is not surprising if we fail to recognize what is passing within us: lovers, and those in general that admire beauty here, do not stay to reflect that it is to be traced, as of course it must be, to the beauty There. That the admiration of the Demiurge[11] is to be referred to the ideal exemplar is deliberately made evident by the rest of the passage: "He admired; and determined to bring the work into still closer likeness with the exemplar": he makes us feel the magnificent beauty of the exemplar by telling us that the beauty sprung from this world is, itself, a copy of that.

And indeed if the divine did not exist, the transcendently beautiful, in a beauty beyond all thought, what could be lovelier than the things we see? Certainly no reproach can rightly be brought against this world save only that it is not that.

9. Let us, then, make a mental picture of our universe: each member shall remain what it is, distinctly apart; yet all is to form, as far as possible, a complete unity so that whatever comes into view, say the outer orb of the heavens, shall bring immediately with it the vision, on the one plane, of the sun and of all the stars with earth and sea and all living things as if exhibited upon a transparent globe.

Bring this vision actually before your sight, so that there shall be in your mind the gleaming representation of a sphere, a picture holding all the things of the universe moving or in repose or (as in reality) some at rest, some in motion. Keep this sphere before you, and from it imagine another, a sphere stripped of magnitude and of spatial differences; cast out your inborn sense of matter, taking care not merely to attenuate it: call on God, maker of the sphere whose image you now hold, and pray him to enter. And may he come bringing his own universe with all the gods that dwell in it—he who is the one God and all the gods, where each is all, blending into a unity, distinct in powers but all one god in virtue of that one divine power of many facets.

More truly, this is the one God who is all the gods; for, in the coming to be of all those, this, the one, has suffered no diminishing. He and all have one existence, while each again is distinct. It is distinction by state without interval: there is no outward form to set one here and another there and to prevent any from being an entire identity; yet there is no sharing of parts from one to another. Nor is each of those divine wholes a power in fragment, a power totaling to the sum of the measurable segments: the divine is one all-power, reaching out to infinity, powerful to infinity: and so great is God that his very members are infinites. What place can be named to which he does not reach?

Great, too, is this firmament of ours and all the powers constellated within it, but it would be greater still, unspeakably, but that there is inbound in it something of the petty power of body; no doubt the powers of fire and other bodily substances might themselves be thought very great, but in fact, it is through their failure in the true power that we see them burning, destroying, wearing things away, and slaving towards the production of life; they destroy because they are themselves in process of destruction, and they produce because they belong to the realm of the produced.

The power in that other world has merely being and beauty of being. Beauty without being could not be, nor being voided of beauty: abandoned of beauty, being loses something of its essence. Being is desirable because it is identical with beauty; and beauty is loved because it is being. How then can we debate which is the cause of the other, where the nature is one? The very figment of being needs some imposed image of beauty to make it passable,[12] and even to ensure its existence; it exists to the degree in which it has taken some share in the beauty of idea; and the more deeply it has drawn on this, the less imperfect it is, precisely because the nature which is essentially the beautiful has entered into it the more intimately.

10. This is why Zeus, although the oldest of the gods and their sovereign, advances first (in the Phaedrus myth) towards that vision, followed by gods and demigods and such souls as are of strength to see. That being appears before them from some unseen place and rising loftily over them pours its light upon all things, so that all gleams in its

---

[11]Creator.

[12]Acceptable.

radiance; it upholds some beings, and they see; the lower are dazzled and turn away, unfit to gaze upon that sun, the trouble falling the more heavily on those most remote.

Of those looking upon that being and its content, and able to see, all take something but not all the same vision always: intently gazing, one sees the fount and principle of justice, another is filled with the sight of moral wisdom, the original of that quality as found, sometimes at least, among men, copied by them in their degree from the divine virtue which, covering all the expanse, so to speak, of the intellectual realm is seen, last attainment of all, by those who have known already many splendid visions.

The gods see, each singly and all as one. So, too, the souls; they see all There in right of being sprung, themselves, of that universe and therefore including all from beginning to end and having their existence There if only by that phase which belongs inherently to the divine, though often too they are There entire, those of them that have not incurred separation.

This vision Zeus takes and it is for such of us, also, as share his love and appropriate our part in the beauty There, the final object of all seeing, the entire beauty upon all things; for all There sheds radiance, and floods those that have found their way thither so that they too become beautiful; thus it will often happen that men climbing heights where the soil has taken a yellow glow will themselves appear so, borrowing color from the place on which they move. The color flowering on that other height we speak of is beauty; or rather all There is light and beauty, through and through, for the beauty is no mere bloom upon the surface.

To those that do not see entire, the immediate impression is alone taken into account; but those drunken with this wine, filled with the nectar, all their soul penetrated by this beauty, cannot remain mere gazers: no longer is there a spectator outside gazing on an outside spectacle; the clear-eyed hold the vision within themselves, though, for the most part, they have no idea that it is within but look towards it as to something beyond them and see it as an object of vision caught by a direction of the will.

All that one sees as a spectacle is still external; one must bring the vision within and see no longer in that mode of separation but as we know ourselves; thus a man filled with a god—possessed by Apollo or by one of the Muses—need no longer look outside for his vision of the divine being; it is but finding the strength to see divinity within.

11. Similarly anyone, unable to see himself, but possessed by that god, has but to bring that divine-within before his consciousness and at once he sees an image of himself, himself lifted to a better beauty: now let him ignore that image, lovely though it is, and sink into a perfect self-identity, no such separation remaining; at once he forms a multiple unity with the god silently present; in the degree of his power and will, the two become one; should he turn back to the former duality, still he is pure and remains very near to the god; he has but to look again and the same presence is there.

This conversion brings gain: at the first stage, that of separation, a man is aware of self; but retreating inwards, he becomes possessor of all; he puts sense away behind him in dread of the separated life and becomes one in the divine; if he plans to see in separation, he sets himself outside.

The novice must hold himself constantly under some image of the divine being and seek in the light of a clear conception; knowing thus, in a deep conviction, whither he is going—into what a sublimity he penetrates—he must give himself forthwith to the inner and, radiant with the divine intellections (with which he is now one), be no longer the seer, but, as that place has made him, the seen.

Still, we will be told, one cannot be in beauty and yet fail to see it. The very contrary: to see the divine as something external is to be outside of it; to become it is to be most truly in beauty: since sight deals with the external, there can here be no vision unless in the sense of identification with the object.

And this identification amounts to a self-knowing, a self-consciousness, guarded by the fear of losing the self in the desire of a too wide awareness.

It must be remembered that sensations of the ugly and evil impress us more violently than those of what is agreeable and yet leave less knowledge as the residue of the shock: sickness makes the rougher mark, but health, tranquilly present, explains itself better; it takes the first place, it is the natural thing, it belongs to our being; illness is alien, unnatural, and thus makes itself felt by its very incongruity, while the other conditions are native and we take no notice. Such being our nature, we are most completely aware of ourselves when we are most completely identified with the object of our knowledge.

This is why in that other sphere, when we are deepest in that knowledge by intellection, we are aware of none; we are expecting some impression on sense, which has nothing to report since it has seen nothing and never could in that order see anything. The unbelieving element is sense; it is the other, the intellectual-principle, that sees; and if this too doubted, it could not even credit its own existence, for it can never stand away and with bodily eyes apprehend itself as a visible object.

12. We have told how this vision is to be procured, whether by the mode of separation or in identity: now, seen either way, what does it give to report?

The vision has been of God in travail of a beautiful offspring, God engendering a universe within himself in a painless labor and—rejoiced in what he has brought into being, proud of his children—keeping all closely by him, for the pleasure he has in his radiance and in theirs.

Of this offspring—all beautiful, but most beautiful those that have remained within—only one has become manifest without; from him (Zeus, sovereign over the visible universe), the youngest born, we may gather, as from some image, the greatness of the Father and of the brothers that remain within the Father's house.

Still the manifested God cannot think that he has come forth in vain from the Father; for through him another universe has arisen, beautiful as the image of beauty, and it could not be lawful that beauty and being should fail of a beautiful image.

This second cosmos at every point copies the archetype: it has life and being in copy, and has beauty as springing from that diviner world. In its character of image it holds, too, that divine perpetuity without which it would only at times be truly representative and sometimes fail like a construction of art; for every image whose existence lies in the nature of things must stand during the entire existence of the archetype.

Hence it is false to put an end to the visible sphere as long as the intellectual endures, or to found it upon a decision taken by its maker at some given moment.

That teaching shirks the penetration of such a making as is here involved: it fails to see that as long as the supreme is radiant there can be no failing of its sequel but, that existing, all exists. And—since the necessity of conveying our meaning compels such terms—the supreme has existed forever and forever will exist.

13. The god fettered (as in the Kronos myth[13]) to an unchanging identity leaves the ordering of this universe to his son (to Zeus), for it could not be in his character to neglect his rule within the divine sphere, and, as though sated with the authentic-beauty, seek a lordship too recent and too poor for his might. Ignoring this lower world, Kronos (intellectual-principle) claims for himself his own father (Ouranos, the absolute, or one) with all the upward-tending between them: and he counts all that tends to the inferior, beginning from his son (Zeus, the all-soul), as ranking beneath him. Thus he holds a mid-position determined on the one side by the differentiation implied in the severance from the very highest and, on the other, by that which keeps him apart from the link between himself and the lower: he stands between a greater father and an inferior son. But since that father is too lofty to be thought of under the name of beauty, the second god remains the primally beautiful.

Soul also has beauty, but is less beautiful than intellect as being its image and therefore, though beautiful in nature, taking increase of beauty by looking to that original. Since then the all-soul—to use the more familiar term—since Aphrodite herself is so beautiful, what name can we give to that other? If soul is so lovely in its own right, of what quality must that prior be? And since its being is derived, what must that power be from which the soul takes the double beauty, the borrowed and the inherent?

We ourselves possess beauty when we are true to our own being; our ugliness is in going over to another order; our self-knowledge, that is to say, is our beauty; in self-ignorance we are ugly.

Thus beauty is of the divine and comes thence only.

Do these considerations suffice to a clear understanding of the intellectual sphere or must we make yet another attempt by another road?

---

[13]Kronos was the Titan who ruled before he was unseated by Zeus.

Saint Augustine

354–430

On Christian Doctrine brings Augustine to the attention of modern semioticians and literary theorists. His attention to the sign is not new with him, but he formulated a theory of it that gave it particular importance in the tradition of Christian interpretation of Scripture and paved the way for later elaborate theories of allegory, such as those we see in Saint Thomas Aquinas and Dante. For Augustine, signs are "things used to signify something" and words are things the whole use of which is signification. But if all signs are things, all things are not signs. Here he seems to resist any elaborate construction of a complete theory of "correspondences" such as is found in later mystics and in critics like Baudelaire, where all of nature is a language. A sign is important because it points to something else, and that something else is ultimately for Augustine the Trinity of Father, Son, and Holy Ghost. The value of the sign, therefore, is not in itself as pleasurable but rather in its use in the movement of signification toward God. Signs cannot embody God, however, because God is ineffable. Augustine does not have a theory of the miraculous symbol. When he speaks of enjoyment it is not the enjoyment of the aesthetic surface of the sign, but of its ultimate signified. This view leads to concepts of allegory in medieval criticism in which the surface hides, but then yields, a depth of intellectual beauty. Thus Augustine anticipates also quite recent valorizations of allegory over symbolism.

Augustine's treatment of a passage from the Song of Solomon in the selection below has been much cited. In it he reads the passage allegorically and admits failure to understand fully why the passage's figurative language gives him more pleasure than a nonfigurative expression of the same idea would. He does tentatively venture that what is discovered with difficulty gives pleasure, and this notion is repeated even into Renaissance criticism. The distinction that Augustine draws previous to this discussion between the natural and the conventional sign leads in later language theory to the same distinction and to the theory of the arbitrary nature of the linguistic sign.

Saint Augustine's works (in Latin) are collected in *Opera omnia* (1836–1838). For commentary see H. J. Marrou, *Saint Augustin et la fin de la culture antique* (1938); Étienne Gilson, *Introduction à l'étude de saint Augustin* (1939); R. W. Battenhouse et al., *A Companion to the Study of St. Augustine* (1955); Peter Brown, *Augustine of Hippo: A Biography* (1967); Robert A. Markus, ed., *Augustine: A Collection of Critical Essays* (contains B. D. Jackson's "The Theory of Signs in St. Augustine's *De doctrina Christiana*") (1972); Robert E. Meagher, *An Introduction to St. Augustine* (1978); Robert J. O'Connell, *Art and Christian Intelligence in St. Augustine* (1978); and Henry Chadwick, *Augustine* (1986).

From

On Christian Doctrine

Book One

I

1. There are two things necessary to the treatment of the Scriptures: a way of discovering those things which are to be understood, and a way of teaching what we have learned. We shall speak first of discovery and second of teaching. This is a great and arduous work, and since it is difficult to sustain, I fear some temerity in undertaking it. It would be thus indeed if I relied on myself alone, but now while the hope of completing such a work lies in Him from whom I have received much concerning these things in thought, it is not to be feared that He will cease giving me more when I have begun to use what He has already given me. Everything which does not decrease on being given away is not properly owned when it is owned and not given. For He says, "He that hath, to him shall be given."[1] Therefore He will give to those that have, that is, to those benevolently using that which they have received He will increase and heap up what He gives. There were at one time five loaves and at another time seven before they began to be given to the needy;[2] and when this began to be done, baskets and hampers were filled, although thousands of men were fed. Just as the loaves increased when they were broken, the Lord has granted those things necessary to the beginning of this work, and when they begin to be given out they will be multiplied by His inspiration, so that in this task of mine I shall not only suffer no poverty of ideas but shall rejoice in wonderful abundance.

II

2. All doctrine concerns either things or signs, but things are learned by signs. Strictly speaking, I have here called a "thing" that which is not used to signify something else, like wood, stone, cattle, and so on; but not that wood concerning which we read that Moses cast it into bitter wa-

ters that their bitterness might be dispelled,[3] nor that stone which Jacob placed at his head,[4] nor that beast which Abraham sacrificed in place of his son.[5] For these are things in such a way that they are also signs of other things.[6] There are other signs whose whole use is in signifying, like words. For no one uses words except for the purpose of signifying something. From this may be understood what we call "signs"; they are things used to signify something. Thus every sign is also a thing, for that which is not a thing is nothing at all; but not every thing is also a sign. And thus in this distinction between things and signs, when we speak of things, we shall so speak that, although some of them may be used to signify something else, this fact shall not disturb the arrangement we have made to speak of things as such first and of signs later. We should bear in mind that now we are to consider what things are, not what they signify beyond themselves.

III

3. Some things are to be enjoyed, others to be used, and there are others which are to be enjoyed and used. Those things which are to be enjoyed make us blessed. Those things which are to be used help and, as it were, sustain us as we move toward blessedness in order that we may gain and cling to those things which make us blessed. If we who enjoy and use things, being placed in the midst of things of both kinds, wish to enjoy those things which should be used, our course will be impeded and sometimes deflected, so that we are retarded in obtaining those things which are to be enjoyed, or even prevented altogether, shackled by an inferior love.

IV

4. To enjoy something is to cling to it with love for its own sake. To use something, however, is to employ it in obtaining that which you love, provided that it is worthy of love. For an illicit use should be called rather a waste or an abuse. Suppose we were wanderers who could not live in blessedness except at home, miserable in our wandering and desiring to end it and to return to our native country. We would need vehicles for land and sea which could be used to help us to reach our homeland, which is to be enjoyed. But if the amenities of the journey and the motion of the vehicles

ON CHRISTIAN DOCTRINE. Augustine's *On Christian Doctrine* was begun in about 396 and completed in 426. Reprinted by permission of Macmillan Publishing Company. The text is from D. W. Robertson, Jr., tr., *On Christian Doctrine.* Copyright © 1985 by Macmillan Publishing Company. Copyright © 1958.
[1][Robertson] Matt. 13. 12.
[2][Robertson] Matt. 14. 17; 15. 34.

[3][Robertson] Exod. 15. 25.
[4][Robertson] Gen. 28. 11.
[5][Robertson] Gen. 22. 13.
[6][Robertson] According to St. Augustine, the "wood" is a sign of the cross. The "stone" and the "beast" represent the human nature of Christ.

itself delighted us, and we were led to enjoy those things which we should use, we should not wish to end our journey quickly, and, entangled in a perverse sweetness, we should be alienated from our country, whose sweetness would make us blessed. Thus in this mortal life, wandering from God,[7] if we wish to return to our native country where we can be blessed we should use this world and not enjoy it, so that the "invisible things" of God "being understood by the things that are made"[8] may be seen, that is, so that by means of corporal and temporal things we may comprehend the eternal and spiritual.

V

5. The things which are to be enjoyed are the Father, the Son, and the Holy Spirit, a single Trinity, a certain supreme thing common to all who enjoy it, if, indeed, it is a thing and not rather the cause of all things, or both a thing and a cause. It is not easy to find a name proper to such excellence, unless it is better to say that this Trinity is one God and that "of him, and by him, and in him are all things."[9] Thus there are the Father, the Son, and the Holy Spirit, and each is God, and at the same time all are one God; and each of them is a full substance, and at the same time all are one substance. The Father is neither the Son nor the Holy Spirit; the Son is neither the Father nor the Holy Spirit; the Holy Spirit is neither the Father nor the Son. But the Father is the Father uniquely; the Son is the Son uniquely; and the Holy Spirit is the Holy Spirit uniquely. All three have the same eternity, the same immutability, the same majesty, and the same power. In the Father is unity, in the Son equality, and in the Holy Spirit a concord of unity and equality; and these three qualities are all one because of the Father, all equal because of the Son, and all united because of the Holy Spirit.

VI

6. Have we spoken or announced anything worthy of God? Rather I feel that I have done nothing but wish to speak: if I have spoken, I have not said what I wished to say. Whence do I know this, except because God is ineffable? If what I said were ineffable, it would not be said. And for this reason God should not be said to be ineffable, for when this is said something is said. And a contradiction in terms is created, since if that is ineffable which cannot be spoken, then that is not ineffable which can be called ineffable. This

contradiction is to be passed over in silence rather than resolved verbally. For God, although nothing worthy may be spoken of Him, has accepted the tribute of the human voice and wished us to take joy in praising Him with our words. In this way he is called *Deus*. Although He is not recognized in the noise of these two syllables, all those who know the Latin language, when this sound reaches their ears, are moved to think of a certain most excellent immortal nature.

XXXV

39. The sum of all we have said since we began to speak of things thus comes to this: it is to be understood that the plenitude and the end of the Law and of all the sacred Scriptures is the love of a Being which is to be enjoyed and of a being that can share that enjoyment with us, since there is no need for a precept that anyone should love himself. That we might know this and have the means to implement it, the whole temporal dispensation was made by divine Providence for our salvation. We should use it, not with an abiding but with a transitory love and delight like that in a road or in vehicles or in other instruments, or, if it may be expressed more accurately, so that we love those things by which we are carried along for the sake of that toward which we are carried.

XXXVI

40. Whoever, therefore, thinks that he understands the divine Scriptures or any part of them so that it does not build the double love of God and of our neighbor does not understand it at all. Whoever finds a lesson there useful to the building of charity, even though he has not said what the author may be shown to have intended in that place, has not been deceived, nor is he lying in any way. Lying involves the will to speak falsely; thus we find many who wish to lie, but no one who wishes to be deceived. Since a man lies knowingly but suffers deception unwittingly, it is obvious that in a given instance a man who is deceived is better than a man who lies, because it is better to suffer iniquity than to perform it. Everyone who lies commits iniquity, and if anyone thinks a lie may sometimes be useful, he must think that iniquity is sometimes useful also. But no one who lies keeps faith concerning that about which he lies. For he wishes that the person to whom he lies should have that faith in him which he does not himself keep when he lies. But every violator of faith is iniquitous. Either iniquity is sometimes useful, which is impossible, or a lie is always useless.

41. But anyone who understands in the Scriptures something other than that intended by them is deceived, al-

---

[7][Robertson] Cf. 2 Cor. 5. 6 (Vulg.).
[8][Robertson] Rom. 1. 20.
[9][Robertson] Rom. 11. 36.

though they do not lie. However, as I began to explain, if he is deceived in an interpretation which builds up charity, which is the end of the commandments, he is deceived in the same way as a man who leaves a road by mistake but passes through a field to the same place toward which the road itself leads. But he is to be corrected and shown that it is more useful not to leave the road, lest the habit of deviating force him to take a crossroad or a perverse way.

XXXVII

In asserting rashly that which the author before him did not intend, he may find many other passages which he cannot reconcile with his interpretation. If he acknowledges these to be true and certain, his first interpretation cannot be true, and under these conditions it happens, I know not why, that, loving his own interpretation, he begins to become angrier with the Scriptures than he is with himself. And if he thirsts persistently for the error, he will be overcome by it. "For we walk by faith and not by sight,"[10] and faith will stagger if the authority of the Divine Scriptures wavers. Indeed, if faith staggers, charity itself languishes. And if anyone should fall from faith, it follows that he falls also from charity, for a man cannot love that which he does not believe to exist. On the other hand, a man who both believes and loves, by doing well and by obeying the rules of good customs, may bring it about that he may hope to arrive at that which he loves. Thus there are these three things for which all knowledge and prophecy struggle: faith, hope, and charity.

XXXVIII

42. But the vision we shall see will replace faith, and that blessedness to which we are to come will replace hope; and when these things are falling away, charity will be increased even more. If we love in faith what we have not seen, how much more will we love it when we begin to see it? And if we love in hope what we have not attained, how much more will we love it when we have attained it? Between temporal and eternal things there is this difference: a temporal thing is loved more before we have it, and it begins to grow worthless when we gain it, for it does not satisfy the soul, whose true and certain rest is eternity; but the eternal is more ardently loved when it is acquired than when it is merely desired. It is possible for no one desiring it to expect it to be more valuable than it actually is so that he may find it less worthy than he expected it to be. However highly anyone

approaching it may value it, he will find it more valuable when he attains it.

XXXIX

43. Thus a man supported by faith, hope, and charity, with an unshaken hold upon them, does not need the Scriptures except for the instruction of others. And many live by these three things in solitude without books. Whence in these persons I think the saying is already exemplified, "whether prophecies shall be made void, or tongues shall cease, or knowledge shall be destroyed."[11] In them, as if by instruments of faith, hope, and charity, such an erudition has been erected that, holding fast to that which is perfect, they do not seek that which is only partially so[12]—perfect, that is, in so far as perfection is possible in this life. For in comparison with the life to come, the life of no just and holy man is perfect here. Hence "there remain," he says, "faith, hope, and charity, these three: but the greatest of these is charity."[13] And when anyone shall reach the eternal, two of these having fallen away, charity will remain more certain and more vigorous.

XL

44. Therefore, when anyone knows the end of the commandments to be charity "from a pure heart, and a good conscience, and an unfeigned faith,"[14] and has related all of his understanding of the Divine Scriptures to these three, he may approach the treatment of these books with security. For when he says "charity" he adds "from a pure heart," so that nothing else would be loved except that which should be loved. And he joins with this "a good conscience" for the sake of hope, for he in whom there is the smallest taint of bad conscience despairs of attaining that which he believes in and loves. Third, he says "an unfeigned faith." If our faith involves no lie, then we do not love that which is not to be loved, and living justly, we hope for that which will in no way deceive our hope.

With this I have said as much as I wished to say concerning faith at the present time, since in other books either by others or by myself much has already been said. Then may this be the limit to this book. In the remainder we shall discuss signs, in so far as God has granted us ability.

---

[10][Robertson] 2 Cor. 5. 7.

[11][Robertson] 1 Cor. 13. 8.
[12][Robertson] 1 Cor. 13. 10.
[13][Robertson] 1 Cor. 13. 13.
[14][Robertson] 1 Tim. 1. 5.

Book Two

I

1. Just as I began, when I was writing about things, by warning that no one should consider them except as they are, without reference to what they signify beyond themselves, now when I am discussing signs I wish it understood that no one should consider them for what they are but rather for their value as signs which signify something else. A sign is a thing which causes us to think of something beyond the impression the thing itself makes upon the senses. Thus if we see a track, we think of the animal that made the track; if we see smoke, we know that there is a fire which causes it; if we hear the voice of a living being, we attend to the emotion it expresses; and when a trumpet sounds, a soldier should know whether it is necessary to advance or to retreat, or whether the battle demands some other response.

2. Among signs, some are natural and others are conventional. Those are natural which, without any desire or intention of signifying, make us aware of something beyond themselves, like smoke which signifies fire. It does this without any will to signify, for even when smoke appears alone, observation and memory of experience with things bring a recognition of an underlying fire. The track of a passing animal belongs to this class, and the face of one who is wrathful or sad signifies his emotion even when he does not wish to show that he is wrathful or sad, just as other emotions are signified by the expression even when we do not deliberately set out to show them. But it is not proposed here to discuss signs of this type. Since the class formed a division of my subject, I could not disregard it completely, and this notice of it will suffice.

II

3. Conventional signs are those which living creatures show to one another for the purpose of conveying, in so far as they are able, the motion of their spirits or something which they have sensed or understood. Nor is there any other reason for signifying, or for giving signs, except for bringing forth and transferring to another mind the action of the mind in the person who makes the sign. We propose to consider and to discuss this class of signs in so far as men are concerned with it, for even signs given by God and contained in the Holy Scriptures are of this type also, since they were presented to us by the men who wrote them. Animals also have signs which they use among themselves, by means of which they indicate their appetites. For a cock who finds food makes a sign with his voice to the hen so that she runs to him. And the dove calls his mate with a cry or is called by her in turn, and there are many similar examples which may be adduced. Whether these signs, or the expression or cry of a man in pain, express the motion of the spirit without intention of signifying or are truly shown as signs is not in question here and does not pertain to our discussion, and we remove this division of the subject from this work as superfluous.

III

4. Among the signs by means of which men express their meanings to one another, some pertain to the sense of sight, more to the sense of hearing, and very few to the other senses. For when we nod, we give a sign only to the sight of the person whom we wish by that sign to make a participant in our will. Some signify many things through the motions of their hands, and actors give signs to those who understand with the motions of all their members as if narrating things to their eyes. And banners and military standards visibly indicate the will of the captains. And all of these things are like so many visible words. More signs, as I have said, pertain to the ears, and most of these consist of words. But the trumpet, the flute, and the harp make sounds which are not only pleasing but also significant, although as compared with the number of verbal signs the number of signs of this kind are few. For words have come to be predominant among men for signifying whatever the mind conceives if they wish to communicate it to anyone. However, Our Lord gave a sign with the odor of the ointment with which His feet were anointed;[15] and the taste of the sacrament of His body and blood signified what He wished;[16] and when the woman was healed by touching the hem of His garment,[17] something was signified. Nevertheless, a multitude of innumerable signs by means of which men express their thoughts is made up of words. And I could express the meaning of all signs of the type here touched upon in words, but I would not be able at all to make the meanings of words clear by these signs.

IV

5. But because vibrations in the air soon pass away and remain no longer than they sound, signs of words have been constructed by means of letters. Thus words are shown to the

---

[15][Robertson] John 12. 3–8. For the "odor of the ointment," see 3. 12. 18.
[16][Robertson] Matt. 26. 28; Luke 22. 19–20.
[17][Robertson] Matt. 9. 20–22.

eyes, not in themselves but through certain signs which stand for them. These signs could not be common to all peoples because of the sin of human dissension which arises when one people seizes the leadership for itself. A sign of this pride is that tower erected in the heavens where impious men deserved that not only their minds but also their voices should be dissonant.[18]

V

6. Thus it happened that even the Sacred Scripture, by which so many maladies of the human will are cured, was set forth in one language, but so that it could be spread conveniently through all the world it was scattered far and wide in the various languages of translators that it might be known for the salvation of peoples who desired to find in it nothing more than the thoughts and desires of those who wrote it and through these the will of God, according to which we believe those writers spoke.

VI

7. But many and varied obscurities and ambiguities deceive those who read casually, understanding one thing instead of another; indeed, in certain places they do not find anything to interpret erroneously, so obscurely are certain sayings covered with a most dense mist. I do not doubt that this situation was provided by God to conquer pride by work and to combat disdain in our minds, to which those things which are easily discovered seem frequently to become worthless. For example, it may be said that there are holy and perfect men with whose lives and customs as an exemplar the Church of Christ is able to destroy all sorts of superstitions in those who come to it and to incorporate them into itself, men of good faith, true servants of God, who, putting aside the burden of the world, come to the holy laver of baptism and, ascending thence, conceive through the Holy Spirit and produce the fruit of a twofold love of God and their neighbor. But why is it, I ask, that if anyone says this he delights his hearers less than if he had said the same thing in expounding that place in the Canticle of Canticles where it is said of the Church, as she is being praised as a beautiful woman, "Thy teeth are as flocks of sheep, that are shorn, which come up from the washing, all with twins, and there is none barren among them"?[19] Does one learn anything else besides that which he learns when he hears the same thought

expressed in plain words without this similitude? Nevertheless, in a strange way, I contemplate the saints more pleasantly when I envisage them as the teeth of the Church cutting off men from their errors and transferring them to her body after their hardness has been softened as if by being bitten and chewed. I recognize them most pleasantly as shorn sheep having put aside the burdens of the world like so much fleece, and as ascending from the washing, which is baptism, all to create twins, which are the two precepts of love, and I see no one of them sterile of this holy fruit.

8. But why it seems sweeter to me than if no such similitude were offered in the divine books, since the thing perceived is the same, is difficult to say and is a problem for another discussion. For the present, however, no one doubts that things are perceived more readily through similitudes and that what is sought with difficulty is discovered with more pleasure. Those who do not find what they seek directly stated labor in hunger; those who do not seek because they have what they wish at once frequently become indolent in disdain. In either of these situations indifference is an evil. Thus the Holy Spirit has magnificently and wholesomely modulated the Holy Scriptures so that the more open places present themselves to hunger and the more obscure places may deter a disdainful attitude. Hardly anything may be found in these obscure places which is not found plainly said elsewhere.

VIII

12. But let us turn our attention to the third step which I have decided to treat as the Lord may direct my discourse. He will be the most expert investigator of the Holy Scriptures who has first read all of them and has some knowledge of them, at least through reading them if not through understanding them. That is, he should read those that are said to be canonical. For he may read the others more securely when he has been instructed in the truth of the faith so that they may not preoccupy a weak mind nor, deceiving it with vain lies and fantasies, prejudice it with something contrary to sane understanding. In the matter of canonical Scriptures he should follow the authority of the greater number of catholic Churches, among which are those which have deserved to have apostolic seats and to receive epistles. He will observe this rule concerning canonical Scriptures, that he will prefer those accepted by all catholic Churches to those which some do not accept; among those which are not accepted by all, he should prefer those which are accepted by the largest number of important Churches to those held by a few minor Churches of less authority. If he discovers that some are maintained by the larger number of Churches, others by the

---

[18][Robertson] Cf. Gen. 11. 1–9.
[19][Robertson] Cf. Cant. (Song of Sol.) 4. 2.

Churches of weightiest authority, although this condition is not likely, he should hold them to be of equal value.

IX

14. In all of these books those fearing God and made meek in piety seek the will of God. And the first rule of this undertaking and labor is, as we have said, to know these books even if they are not understood, at least to read them or to memorize them, or to make them not altogether unfamiliar to us. Then those things which are put openly in them either as precepts for living or as rules for believing are to be studied more diligently and more intelligently, for the more one learns about these things the more capable of understanding he becomes. Among those things which are said openly in Scripture are to be found all those teachings which involve faith, the mores of living, and that hope and charity which we have discussed in the previous book. Then, having become familiar with the language of the Divine Scriptures, we should turn to those obscure things which must be opened up and explained so that we may take examples from those things that are manifest to illuminate those things which are obscure, bringing principles which are certain to bear on our doubts concerning those things which are uncer-

tain. In this undertaking memory is of great value, for if it fails rules will not be of any use.

X

15. There are two reasons why things written are not understood: they are obscured either by unknown or by ambiguous signs. For signs are either literal or figurative. They are called literal when they are used to designate those things on account of which they were instituted; thus we say *bos* [ox] when we mean an animal of a herd because all men using the Latin language call it by that name just as we do. Figurative signs occur when that thing which we designate by a literal sign is used to signify something else; thus we say "ox" and by that syllable understand the animal which is ordinarily designated by that word, but again by that animal we understand an evangelist, as is signified in the Scripture, according to the interpretation of the Apostle, when it says, "Thou shalt not muzzle the ox that treadeth out the corn."[20]

---

[20][Robertson] Deut. 25. 4. For the apostolic interpretation see 1 Cor. 9. 9; 1 Tim. 5. 18.

Manlius Severinus Boethius

480–524

Boethius' great learning is reflected in his *Consolation of Philosophy*. At one time he set out to translate all of both Plato and Aristotle into Latin, and he hoped eventually to produce a philosophy that transcended their differences. Basically, however, he was more influenced by Plato. The selection below, from near the beginning of Book I, suggests that Boethius had accepted Plato's idea that there is an ancient quarrel between philosophy and poetry and that poetry is dangerous because it feeds the passions. But Boethius also had religious reasons for suspicion of the Muses. One was simply that the Muses were pagan and another was that the arts catered to sensuous and earthly interests. In the medieval Christian ascetic view, the arts were considered trivial by comparison to theological pursuits. Boethius follows the Church fathers generally in his suspicion of art. This is not to say, however, that medieval Christianity put an end to theoretical developments. Rather, theoretical interest expressed itself in allegorical interpretation of Scripture, the methods of which came to be applied to secular works.

Boethius also wrote dissertations on music and arithmetic in which one finds traditional classical emphases on harmony and abstract formal order. Here again the roots of Boethius' aesthetic are Platonic and, through Augustine's *De Musica,* Pythagorean.

A useful abridged version of the *Consolation* is the edition by J. J. Buchanan (1957). See also H. M. Barrett, *Boethius, Some Aspects of His Times and Work* (1940); Margaret Gibson (ed.), *Boethius: His Life, Thought, and Influence* (1981); Henry Chadwick, *Boethius: The Consolations of Music, Logic, Theology, and Philosophy* (1981); Edmund Reiss, *Boethius* (1982); and Seth Lerer, *Boethius and Dialogue* (1985).

The Consolation of Philosophy

From

Book I

Prose I: Philosophy Approaches Boethius: The Form of Her Appearance Is Allegorical

While I was pondering thus in silence and using my pen to set down my tearful complaint, there appeared to me standing overhead a woman whose countenance was full of majesty, whose gleaming eyes surpassed in power of insight those of ordinary mortals, whose color was full of life, and whose strength was still intact though she was so full of years that by no means would it be believed that she was of our times. One could but doubt her varying stature, for at one moment she repressed it to the common measure of man, at another she seemed to touch with her crown the very heavens; and when she raised her head higher it pierced even the sky and baffled the sight of those who would look upon it. Her clothes were wrought of the finest thread by subtle workmanship into an indissoluble material. These she had woven with her own hands, as I learned afterwards from her own disclosure. Their color was somewhat dimmed by the dullness of long neglect, as happens likewise in the case of smoke-grimed death masks. On the border below was woven the symbol Π, on that above was to be read a Θ.[1] And between the two letters there could be seen degrees by which, as by the rungs of a ladder, ascent might be made from the lower principle to the higher. Yet the hands of certain rough men had torn this garment and had snatched such pieces as they could therefrom. In her right hand she carried books; in her left she brandished a scepter.

When she saw that the Muses of poetry were present by my couch giving words to my lamenting, she was stirred a while; her eyes flashed fiercely as she said: "Who has suffered these seducing mummers[2] to approach this sick man? Never have they nursed his sorrowings with any remedies, but rather fostered them with poisonous sweets. These are they who stifle the fruit-bearing harvest of reason with the barren briars of the passions; they do not free the minds of men from disease but accustom them thereto. I would think it less grievous if your allurements drew away from me some common man like those of the vulgar herd, seeing that in such a one my labors would be harmed not at all. But this man has been nurtured in the lore of Eleatics and Academics.[3] Away with you, sirens, seductive even to perdition, and leave him to my Muses to be cared for and healed!"

Thus rebuked, that band cast a saddened glance upon the ground, confessing their shame in blushes, and passed forth dismally over the threshold.

THE CONSOLATION OF PHILOSOPHY. Boethius wrote *Consolatione Philosophiae* about 523. The text is from *The Consolation of Philosophy,* edited and abridged by J. J. Buchanan (New York: Frederick Ungar, 1957), pp. 1–3. Reprinted by permission of the publisher. Buchanan's text is based on the W. V. Cooper translation, but revised.

[1] [Buchanan] Π and Θ are the first letters of the Greek words denoting practical and theoretical, the two divisions of philosophy.

[2] That is, actors, players, in a derogatory sense. The drama was opposed by Augustine and the Church generally. Here Boethius suggests that the Muses represent false copying and the making of dangerous delusions.

[3] Two schools of Greek philosophy. The Eleatics were followers of Xenophanes of Colophon, a sixth-century B.C. philosopher who lived in Elea. The Academic school of philosophy was founded by Plato, who taught for forty years at the grove called Academy outside Athens.

Saint Thomas Aquinas

1225–1274

Attitudes toward the interpretation of Holy Scripture that developed early in the Christian era are represented in the selection below from the *Summa Theologica*. Allegorical interpretation of Homer can be found as early as the sixth century B.C. and was still being practiced in the third century A.D. by Porphyry. Neo-Platonic allegorizing can be found throughout the history of literary criticism up to our own day. Christian hermeneutics probably began with the adoption of the methods of Philo Judaeus, a philosopher of the first century A.D., by the churchmen Origen, Clement, Jerome, Augustine, and Gregory. The fourfold interpretive system Aquinas uses was probably first worked out in the fifth century A.D. It is a reflection of the fundamental idea that the world itself is a symbol subject to interpretation as the work of God. This principle was adopted without its theological overtones by the nineteenth-century French symbolists, such as Baudelaire, whose sonnet *Correspondences* no doubt owes more to the pagan saying that things below copy things above.

Aquinas believes the system is applicable only to Scripture. However, Dante extends the principles of interpretation to secular writing in his letter to Can Grande della Scala. Aquinas argues that spiritual truths are properly and naturally taught by figures taken from corporeal things and, contrary to Boethius, that for these truths to be veiled is not harmful dissimulation but the cause of beneficial exercise for the mind. His twofold system of interpretation, involving the historical, or literal, level of meaning and the spiritual level, is really fourfold, like Dante's, for the spiritual is divided into three parts—allegorical, moral, and anagogical. There is plenty of evidence that the Thomistic system has been imposed arbitrarily on literary works, but it did open up the possibility of discovering multiple meanings in poems. This interest in the relationship between signs or symbols and what they signify or denote arose again in the Romantic period in discussions of symbolism, particularly in the work of Coleridge and Carlyle, and in the twentieth century. In Frye's theory of symbols, the terms *literal, allegorical,* and *anagogic* reappear with new, though related, meanings.

The standard translation of *Summa Theologica* is by the Dominican Fathers (1927). See also *The Basic Writings of Saint Thomas Aquinas,* edited by A. C. Pegis (2 vols., 1945). For commentary consult Leonard Callahan, *A Theory of Esthetic According to the Principles of St. Thomas Aquinas* (1927); Thomas Gilby, *Poetic Experience* (1934, 1967); John Duffy, *A Philosophy of Poetry Based on Thomistic Principles* (1945); and T. F. Torrance, "Scientific Hermeneutics According to St. Thomas Aquinas," *Journal of Biblical Studies,* new series XIII (1962), 259–89. The 1929 work of Etienne Gilson, *The Philosophy of St. Thomas Aquinas* has now been translated, as has Umberto Eco's *The Aesthetics of Thomas Aquinas* (1970).

From

The Nature and Domain of Sacred Doctrine

In Ten Articles

To place our purpose within definite limits, we must first investigate the nature and domain of sacred doctrine. Concerning this there are ten points of inquiry: (1) Whether sacred doctrine is necessary? (2) Whether it is a science?[1] (3) Whether it is one or many? (4) Whether it is speculative or practical? (5) How it is compared with other sciences? (6) Whether it is a wisdom? (7) Whether God is its subject matter? (8) Whether it is argumentative? (9) Whether it rightly employs metaphors and similes? (10) Whether the sacred Scripture of this doctrine may be expounded in different senses?

Ninth Article
Whether
Holy Scripture
Should Use
Metaphors?

We proceed thus to the ninth article:

Objection 1. It seems that Holy Scripture should not use metaphors. For that which is proper to the lowest science seems not to befit this science, which holds the highest place of all. But to proceed by the aid of various similitudes and figures is proper to poetic, the least of all the sciences. Therefore it is not fitting that this science should make use of such similitudes.

Objection 2. Further, this doctrine seems to be intended to make truth clear. Hence a reward is held out to those who manifest it. "They that explain me shall have life everlasting" (Ecclesiasticus 24:31). But by such similitudes truth is obscured. Therefore to put forward divine truths

under the likeness of corporeal things does not befit this doctrine.

Objection 3. Further, the higher creatures are, the nearer they approach to the divine likeness. If therefore any creature be taken to represent God, this representation ought chiefly to be taken from the higher creatures, and not from the lower; yet this is often found in the Scriptures.

On the contrary, it is written (Osee 11:10): "I have multiplied visions, and I have used similitudes by the ministry of the prophets." But to put forward anything by means of similitudes is to use metaphors. Therefore sacred doctrine may use metaphors.

I answer that, it is befitting Holy Scripture to put forward divine and spiritual truths by means of comparisons with material things. For God provides for everything according to the capacity of its nature. Now it is natural to man to attain to intellectual truths through sensible things, because all our knowledge originates from sense. Hence in Holy Scripture spiritual truths are fittingly taught under the likeness of material things. That is what Dionysius says: "We cannot be enlightened by the divine rays except they be hidden within the covering of many sacred veils."[2] It is also befitting Holy Scripture, which is proposed to all without distinction of persons—"To the wise and to the unwise I am a debtor" (Romans 1:14)—that spiritual truths be expounded by means of figures taken from corporeal things, in order that thereby even the simple who are unable by themselves to grasp intellectual things may be able to understand it.

Reply to Objection 1. Poetry makes use of metaphors to produce a representation, for it is natural to man to be pleased with representations. But sacred doctrine makes use of metaphors as both necessary and useful.

Reply to Objection 2. The ray of divine revelation is not extinguished by the sensible imagery wherewith it is veiled, as Dionysius says;[3] and its truth so far remains that it does not allow the minds of those to whom the revelation has been made, to rest in the likenesses, but raises them to the knowledge of intelligible truths; and through those to whom the revelation has been made others also may receive instruction in these matters. Hence those things that are taught metaphorically in one part of Scripture, in other parts

---

THE NATURE AND DOMAIN OF SACRED DOCTRINE. The *Summa Theologica*, of which this selection is a part, was written from 1256 to 1272. The text is from *Introduction to Saint Thomas Aquinas*, edited by Anton Pegis. Reprinted by permission of Modern Library, a division of Random House, Inc. According to Pegis the correct title of the work is *Summa* or *Summa Theologiae*. It may be interpreted to mean the highest or ultimate theology.
[1]"Science" here means a true branch of learning proceeding by rational principles.

[2]*Of the Celestial Hierarchy*, I. 2. *Of the Celestial Hierarchy* is one of a number of theological writings of unknown origin that had great influence on medieval thought. Scholars are now certain that these works, long attributed to Dionysius Areopagiticus, an Athenian convert to Christianity in the first century A.D., were written in the fourth or fifth century A.D. The author is traditionally called pseudo-Dionysius or the pseudo-Areopagite.
[3]*Of the Celestial Hierarchy*, I. 2.

are taught more openly. The very hiding of truth in figures is useful for the exercise of thoughtful minds, and as a defense against the ridicule of the unbelievers, according to the words, "Give not that which is holy to dogs" (Matthew 7:6).

Reply to Objection 3. As Dionysius says,[4] it is more fitting that divine truths should be expounded under the figure of less noble than of nobler bodies; and this for three reasons. First, because thereby men's minds are the better freed from error. For then it is clear that these things are not literal descriptions of divine truths, which might have been open to doubt had they been expressed under the figure of nobler bodies, especially in the case of those who could think of nothing nobler than bodies. Second, because this is more befitting the knowledge of God that we have in this life. For what he is not is clearer to us than what he is. Therefore similitudes drawn from things farthest away from God form within us a truer estimate that God is above whatsoever we may say or think of him. Third, because thereby divine truths are the better hidden from the unworthy.

Tenth Article
Whether
In Holy Scripture
A Word May Have
Several Senses?

We proceed thus to the tenth article:

Objection 1. It seems that in Holy Scripture a word cannot have several senses, historical or literal, allegorical, tropological or moral, and anagogical.[5] For many different senses in one text produce confusion and deception and destroy all force of argument. Hence no argument, but only fallacies, can be deduced from a multiplicity of propositions. But Holy Scripture ought to be able to state the truth without any fallacy. Therefore in it there cannot be several senses to a word.

Objection 2. Further, Augustine says that "the Old Testament has a fourfold division: according to history, etiology, analogy, and allegory."[6] Now these four seem altogether different from the four divisions mentioned in the first objection. Therefore it does not seem fitting to explain the same word of Holy Scripture according to the four different senses mentioned above.

Objection 3. Further, besides these senses, there is the parabolical, which is not one of these four.

On the contrary, Gregory says: "Holy Spirit by the manner of its speech transcends every science, because in one and the same sentence, while it describes a fact, it reveals a mystery."[7]

I answer that, the author of Holy Scripture is God, in whose power it is to signify his meaning, not by words only (as man also can do) but also by things themselves. So, whereas in every other science things are signified by words, this science has the property that the things signified by the words have themselves also a signification. Therefore that first signification whereby words signify things belongs to the first sense, the historical or literal. That signification whereby things signified by words have themselves also a signification is called the spiritual sense, which is based on the literal, and presupposes it. Now this spiritual sense has a threefold division. For as the Apostle says (Hebrews 10:1) the Old Law is a figure of the New Law, and Dionysius says "the New Law itself is a figure of future glory."[8] Again, in the New Law, whatever our Head has done is a type of what we ought to do. Therefore, so far as the things of the Old Law signify the things of the New Law, there is the allegorical sense; so far as the things done in Christ, or so far as the things which signify Christ, are signs of what we ought to do, there is the moral sense. But so far as they signify what relates to eternal glory, there is the anagogical sense. Since the literal sense is that which the author intends, and since the author of Holy Scripture is God, who by one act comprehends all things by his intellect, it is not unfitting, as Augustine says,[9] if, even according to the literal sense, one word in Holy Scripture should have several senses.

Reply to Objection 1. The multiplicity of these senses does not produce equivocation or any other kind of multiplicity, seeing that these senses are not multiplied because one word signifies several things, but because the things signified by the words can be themselves signs of other things. Thus in Holy Scripture no confusion results, for all the senses are founded on one—the literal—from which alone can any argument be drawn, and not from those intended allegorically, as Augustine says.[10] Nevertheless, nothing of Holy Scripture perishes because of this, since nothing necessary to faith is contained under the spiritual sense which is not elsewhere put forward clearly by the Scripture in its literal sense.

---

[4]*Of the Celestial Hierarchy*, II. 2.
[5]These are the four levels upon which interpretation is made. See also Dante, *The Banquet* and his letter to Can Grande della Scala, pp. 121–22.
[6]*Of the Value of Belief*, III.

[7]*Precepts (Moralia)*, XX. 1.
[8]*Of Ecclesiastical Hierarchy*, V. 2. This idea is the basis of a typological reading of the Bible.
[9]*Confessions*, XII. 31.
[10]*Letters*, XCIII. 8.

Reply to Objection 2. These three—history, etiology, analogy—are grouped under the literal sense. For it is called history, as Augustine expounds,[11] whenever anything is simply related; it is called etiology when its cause is assigned, as when our Lord gave the reason why Moses allowed the putting away of wives—namely, because of the hardness of men's hearts (Matthew 19:8); it is called analogy whenever the truth of one text of Scripture is shown not to contradict the truth of another. Of these four, allegory alone stands for the three spiritual senses. Thus Hugh of St. Victor includes the anagogical under the allegorical sense, laying down three senses only—the historical, the allegorical, and the tropological.[12]

Reply to Objection 3. The parabolical sense is contained in the literal, for by words things are signified properly and figuratively. Nor is the figure itself, but that which is figured, the literal sense. When Scripture speaks of God's arm, the literal sense is not that God has such a member, but only what is signified by this member, namely, operative power. Hence it is plain that nothing false can ever underlie the literal sense of Holy Scripture.

---

[11]*Of the Value of Belief,* 3.

[12]See *Of the Sacraments,* I. 4, and *Of Scriptures and Sacred Writers,* 3.

Dante Alighieri

1265–1321

Dante's invocation of the fourfold scheme of interpretation in *The Banquet* and in the letter to Can Grande follows that of Aquinas and his early Christian predecessors. These statements have been of particular interest to students of *The Divine Comedy*. It is possible, however, that Dante has led his readers somewhat astray, for it is difficult to discover all the levels of meaning working in quite so explicit a way as his remarks suggest. (As Helmut Hatzfield has suggested, it is also possible that Dante is not the author of the letter.) In any case we see in the letter Aquinas' principles applied to secular writing. For Dante and others the allegorical mode was not merely a matter of artistic cleverness; it was part and parcel of their way of thinking about the world, which was itself considered full of symbolic meaning—like a work of art, we might say today. Then the simile would have been reversed: the work of art is symbolic, like the world.

Dante's definition of his great work as a "comedy" seems to reflect a rather simplified approach to genres in light of Aristotle's detailed definition of tragedy, but it does serve to broaden the scope of the term and free it from narrow association with the amusing or farcical.

A good translation of *The Banquet* is that by W. W. Jackson, *Dante's* Convivio (1909). A translation of the letter to Can Grande appears in C. S. Latham, *A Translation of Dante's Eleven Letters* (1891). Important critical works include H. F. Dunbar, *Symbolism in Medieval Thought* (1929); C. S. Singleton, *Dante Studies 1, Commedia, Elements of Structure* (1954); P. J. Toynbee, *Dante Alighieri, His Life and Works* (1965); and three studies by Erich Auerbach, "Typological Symbolism in Medieval Literature," *Yale French Studies,* IX (1952), *Mimesis* (1953), *Dante, Poet of the Secular World* (1961); Robert Hollander, *Allegory in Dante's Commedia* (1969); Guiseppe Mazzotta, *Dante, Poet of the Desert: History and Allegory in the* Divine Comedy (1979).

From

The Banquet

I say that, as is affirmed in the first chapter, it is meet for this exposition to be both literal and allegorical.[1] And to make this intelligible, it should be known that writings can be understood and ought to be expounded chiefly in four senses. The first is called literal, and this is that sense which does not go beyond the strict limits of the letter; the second is called allegorical, and this is disguised under the cloak of such stories, and is a truth hidden under a beautiful fiction. Thus Ovid says that Orpheus with his lyre made beasts tame, and trees and stones move towards himself; that is to say that the wise man by the instrument of his voice makes cruel hearts grow mild and humble, and those who have not the life of science and of art move to his will, while they who have no rational life are as it were like stones. And wherefore

---

THE BANQUET. *Il Convivio* was written sometime between 1304 and 1308. The text is from W. W. Jackson, tr., *Dante's Convivio* (Oxford, Eng.: Clarendon Press, 1909).
[1]Compare Aquinas, *The Nature and Domain of Sacred Doctrine*, pp. 117–19.

this disguise was invented by the wise will be shown in the last tractate but one. Theologians indeed do not apprehend this sense in the same fashion as poets; but, inasmuch as my intention is to follow here the custom of poets, I will take the allegorical sense after the manner which poets use.

The third sense is called moral; and this sense is that for which teachers ought as they go through writings intently to watch for their own profit and that of their hearers; as in the Gospel when Christ ascended the Mount to be transfigured, we may be watchful of his taking with himself the three Apostles out of the twelve; whereby morally it may be understood that for the most secret affairs we ought to have few companions.

The fourth sense is called anagogic, that is, above the senses; and this occurs when a writing is spiritually expounded which even in the literal sense by the things signified likewise gives intimation of higher matters belonging to the eternal glory; as can be seen in that song of the prophet which says that, when the people of Israel went up out of Egypt, Judea was made holy and free. And although it be plain that this is true according to the letter, that which is spiritually understood is not less true, namely, that when the soul issues forth from sin she is made holy and free as mistress of herself.

From

Letter to Can Grande Della Scala

6. Therefore it we desire to furnish some introduction to a part of any work, it behooves us to furnish some knowledge of the whole of which it is a part. Wherefore I too, desiring to furnish something by way of introduction to the above-named portion of the *Comedy*,[1] have thought that something concerning the whole work should be premised, that the approach to the part should be the easier and more complete. There are six things then which must be inquired into at the beginning of any work of instruction; to wit, the subject, agent, form, and end, the title of the work, and the branch of philosophy it concerns. And there are three of these wherein this part which I purposed to design for you

differs from the whole; to wit, subject, form, and title; whereas in the others it differs not, as is plain on inspection. And so, an inquiry concerning these three must be instituted specially with reference to the work as a whole; and when this has been done the way will be sufficiently clear to the introduction of the part. After that we shall examine the other three, not only with reference to the whole but also with reference to that special part which I am offering to you.

7. To elucidate, then, what we have to say, be it known that the sense of this work is not simple, but on the contrary it may be called polysemous, that is to say, "of more senses than one"; for it is one sense which we get through the letter, and another which we get through the thing the letter signifies; and the first is called literal, but the second allegorical or mystic. And this mode of treatment, for its better manifestation, may be considered in this verse: "When Israel came out of Egypt, and the house of Jacob from a people of strange speech, Judea became his sanctification, Israel his power."[2] For if we inspect the letter alone the departure of the children of Israel from Egypt in the time of Moses is presented to us; if the allegory, our redemption wrought by Christ; if the moral sense, the conversion of the soul from the grief and misery of sin to the state of grace is presented to us; if the anagogical, the departure of the holy soul from the slavery of this corruption to the liberty of eternal glory is presented to us. And although these mystic senses have each their special denominations, they may all in general be called allegorical, since they differ from the literal and historical; for *allegory* is derived from *alleon,* in Greek, which means the same as the Latin *alienum* or *diversum.*

8. When we understand this we see clearly that the subject round which the alternative senses play must be twofold. And we must therefore consider the subject of this work as literally understood, and then its subject as allegorically intended. The subject of the whole work, then, taken in the literal sense only, is "the state of souls after death," without qualification, for the whole progress of the work hinges on it and about it. Whereas if the work be taken allegorically the subject is "man, as by good or ill deserts, in the exercise of the freedom of his choice, he becomes liable to rewarding or punishing justice."

9. Now the form is twofold, the form of the treatise and the form of the treatment. The form of the treatise is threefold, according to its threefold division. The first division is that by which the whole work is divided into three cantiche; the second that whereby each cantica is divided into cantos; the third, that whereby each canto is divided into lines. The form or method of treatment is poetic, fictive, descriptive, digressive, transumptive; and likewise proceeding by defi-

---

LETTER TO CAN GRANDE DELLA SCALA. This letter to a friend and patron of Dante's who lived in Verona was written about 1318. Some doubt has been cast on Dante's authorship (see Helmut Hatzfield; "Modern Literary Scholarship as Reflected in Dante Criticism," *Comparative Literature,* III [1951], 296), but it is still popularly attributed to him. The text is from P. H. Wicksteed, tr., *Translations of the Later Works of Dante* (London: J. M. Dent & Sons, 1904). Reprinted by permission of the publisher.

[1]Dante is referring to Part III of *The Divine Comedy,* "Paradise," which he dedicated to Can Grande.

[2]Psalms 114:1–2.

nition, division, proof, refutation, and setting forth of examples.

10. The title of the work is, "Here beginneth the *Comedy* of Dante Alighieri, a Florentine by birth, not by character." To understand which, be it known that *comedy* is derived from *comus,* "a village," and *oda,* which is, "song"; whence comedy is, as it were, "rustic song." So comedy is a certain kind of poetic narration differing from all others. It differs, then, from tragedy in its content, in that tragedy begins admirably and tranquilly, whereas its end or exit is foul and terrible; and it derives its name from *tragus,* which is a "goat" and *oda,* as though to say "goat-song," that is fetid like a goat, as appears from Seneca in his tragedies; whereas comedy introduces some harsh complication, but brings its matter to a prosperous end, as appears from Terence, in his comedies. And hence certain writers, on introducing themselves, have made it their practice to give the salutation: "I wish you a tragic beginning and a comic end." They likewise differ in their mode of speech, tragedy being exalted and sublime, comedy lax and humble, as Horace has it in his *Poetica,* where he gives comedians leave sometimes to speak like tragedians and conversely:

> *Interdum tamen et vocem comaedia tollit,*
> *Iratusque Chremes tumido delitigat ore;*
> *Et tragicus plerumque dolet sermone pedestri.*[3]

And hence it is evident that the title of the present work is "the *Comedy.*" For if we have respect to its content, at the beginning it is horrible and fetid, for it is hell; and in the end it is prosperous, desirable, and gracious, for it is paradise. If we have respect to the method of speech the method is lax and humble, for it is the vernacular speech in which very women communicate. There are also other kinds of poetic narration, as the bucolic song, elegy, satire, and the utterance of prayer, as may also be seen from Horace in his *Poetica.* But concerning them naught need at present be said.

11. There can be no difficulty in assigning the subject of the part I am offering you; for if the subject of the whole, taken literally, is "the state of souls after death," not limited but taken without qualification, it is clear that in this part that same state is the subject, but with a limitation, to wit, "the state of blessed souls after death"; and if the subject of the whole work taken allegorically is "man as by good or ill deserts, in the exercise of the freedom of his choice, he becomes liable to rewarding or punishing justice," it is manifest that the subject in this part is contracted to "man as by good deserts, he becomes liable to rewarding justice."

12. And in like manner the form of the part is clear from the form assigned to the whole; for if the form of the treatise as a whole is threefold, in this part it is twofold only, namely, division of the cantiche and of the cantos. The first division cannot be a part of its special form, since it is itself a part under that first division.

13. The title of the work is also clear, for if the title of the whole work is "Here beginneth the *Comedy,*" and so forth as set out above, the title of this part will be "Here beginneth the third cantica of Dante's *Comedy,* which is entitled Paradise."

14. Having investigated the three things in which the part differs from the whole, we must examine the other three, in which there is no variation from the whole. The agent, then, of the whole and of the part is the man already named, who is seen throughout to be such.

15. The end of the whole and of the part may be manifold, to wit, the proximate and the ultimate, but dropping all subtle investigation, we may say briefly that the end of the whole and of the part is to remove those living in this life from the state of misery and lead them to the state of felicity.

---

[3]"But yet sometimes comedy raises its tone and a Chremes in his wrath declaims his wrongs in mouthing phrase; and in the same way Telephus and Peleus, so tragical generally, in their pain take to the language of prose." *Art of Poetry,* p. 69.

Giovanni Boccaccio

1313–1375

The interpretive methods suggested by Aquinas for divine texts and by Dante for secular ones were certainly in Boccaccio's mind when he wrote about the differences between poetry and theology, which he avers lie in subject matter more than in method. Poetry makes fictions, whereas theology always tells the truth. Boccaccio defends poetry, however, against those who say that because it lies it is therefore fundamentally immoral. Holding that poetry is allegorical and truthful at hidden levels, though untruthful on the surface, he defends the use of allegory in the same way as Aquinas: meaning acquired by toil should ultimately be of more pleasure and better retained. He also indicates that the truth of poetry often comes in the form of a generalization about life or manners expressed in a fiction. Jesus himself uttered parables of this sort. When their subject is the same, poetry and theology are nearly the same.

Boccaccio defends the pagan poets, insisting that they clothe many physical and moral truths in their inventions. His arguments tend to summarize assumptions underlying the whole hermeneutic tradition even from pre-Christian times, when Homer and Hesiod were subjected to allegorical interpretation. Boccaccio, like medieval theorists and Renaissance critics as late as Sidney, insisted that a hidden moral meaning redeemed poetry's "lies." It took longer for critics to arrive at the idea that there is something that poetry uniquely does, that *truth* in the sense of rationality is perhaps not quite the right word for it. Only with a renewed interest in symbolism and theories of language among twentieth-century critics was there an effort to define the poem's mode of knowledge or truth in terms that avoided rationality on the one hand and mysticism and irrationality on the other.

C. G. Osgood's *Boccaccio on Poetry* (1930, 1956) contains with commentary and introduction the Preface and Books XIV and XV of the *Genealogy of the Gentile Gods*. See also J. R. Smith, *The Earliest Lives of Dante* (1901, 1963); T. C. Chubb, *The Life of Giovanni Boccaccio* (1930); Vittore Branca, *Boccaccio: The Man and His Works* (1976); and Thomas G. Bergin, *Boccaccio* (1981).

Life of Dante

From

Chapter IX

Digression Concerning Poetry

If we apply our minds, and examine it by reason, I think we can easily discover that the ancient poets have followed, so far as is possible for the human mind, the steps of the Holy Spirit, which, as we see in Holy Scripture, revealed to future generations its highest secrets by the mouths of many, making them utter under a veil that which in due time it intended to make known openly through works. Therefore, if we closely examine their writings, we shall see that poets described beneath the mask of certain fictions (to the end that the imitator might not appear different from the thing imitated) that which had been, or which was in their day, or that which they presumed or desired would happen in the future.

Wherefore, although the two forms of writing do not have the same end in view, but only a like method of treatment—whereto my mind is chiefly directed at present—the same praise may be given to both in the words of Gregory,[1] who said of the sacred Scripture what may also be said of poetry, namely, that in the same account it discloses the text and its underlying mystery. Thus at the same moment by the one it disciplines the wise, and by the other it strengthens the foolish. It possesses openly that by virtue of which it may nourish little children, and preserves in secret that whereby it holds rapt in admiration the minds of sublime thinkers. Thus it is like a river, if I may use the figure, wherein the little lamb may wade, and the great elephant freely swim. But let us proceed to the verification of these statements.

Chapter X

On the Difference Between Poetry and Theology

Holy Scripture—which we call theology—sometimes under the form of history, again in the meaning of a vision, now by the signification of a lament, and in many other ways, designs to reveal to us the high mystery of the incarnation of the Divine Word, his life, the circumstances of his death, his victorious resurrection and wonderful ascension, and his other acts, so that, being thus taught, we may attain to that glory which he by his death and resurrection opened to us, after it had been long closed through the sin of the first man. In like manner do poets in their works—which we term poetry—sometimes under fictions of various gods, again by the transformation of men into imaginary forms, and at times by gentle persuasion, reveal to us the causes of things, the effects of virtues and of vices, what we ought to flee and what follow; in order that we may attain by virtuous action the end that they, although they did not rightly know the true God, believed to be our supreme salvation.

Thus the Holy Spirit wished to show by the green bush, wherein Moses saw God like unto a burning flame,[2] the virginity of her that above every other creature is pure, who was to be the habitation and retreat of the Lord of Nature, and yet was not to be contaminated by her conception, nor by the birth of the Word of the Father. In the vision seen by Nebuchadnezzar[3] of the statue of many metals, demolished by a stone which, in turn, was changed into a mountain, the Holy Spirit would declare that all past ages were to be overthrown by the doctrine of Christ, who was and is a living rock, and that the Christian religion, born of this rock, was to become a thing immovable and ever-enduring like the mountains. By the lamentations of Jeremiah it would proclaim the future destruction of Jerusalem.

In like manner our poets, in feigning that Saturn had many children, of whom he devoured all save four, desired to make us perceive merely that Saturn is time, wherein everything is brought forth, and which, even as it produces, also destroys all things and brings them to naught. The four children undevoured by him are first, Jupiter, that is, the element of fire; secondly, Juno, spouse and sister of Jupiter, in other words the air, by means of which fire works its effects here below; thirdly, Neptune, god of the sea, or the element of water; the fourth and last is Pluto, god of hell, that is, the earth, which is lower than any other element.

Similarly, our poets feign that Hercules was transformed from a man into a god, and Lycaon into a wolf. They

---

LIFE OF DANTE. *Vita di Dante* was written in 1364 and first published in 1477. The text is from J. R. Smith, tr., *The Earliest Lives of Dante* (New York: Holt, Rinehart and Winston, 1901).
[1](540?–604), pope from 590 to 604, author of numerous theological works.

---

[2]Genesis 3:2.
[3]Daniel 2:31–35. In this paragraph Boccaccio performs a typological reading of the Bible, in which the New Testament is prefigured in the Old. See Aquinas, *The Nature and Domain of Sacred Doctrine*, p. 118.

wished to point the moral that by virtuous action, like that of Hercules, man becomes a god by participation in heaven, and that by acting viciously with Lycaon, albeit one seem a man, of a truth he can be said to be that beast which everyone knows through an effect most similar to his defect; even as Lycaon, by reason of his greed and avarice, is represented as changed into a wolf, since these are the characteristics of a wolf. Likewise our poets imagine the beauty of the Elysian Fields, by which I understand the sweetness of paradise; and the obscurity of Dis,[4] which I take to mean the bitterness of hell. This they did that we, attracted by the pleasure of the one and terrified by the suffering of the other, might pursue the virtues that will lead us to Elysium, and flee the vices that would cause us to be ferried over to Dis.

I omit the illumination of these things by more detailed illustration, for—although I should wish to make them as clear as is possible and fitting, since they would be most pleasing and would strengthen my argument—I doubt not that I should be carried much farther than the main subject requires, and further than that I do not wish to go.

Certainly enough has been said to make us understand that theology and poetry agree in their method of treatment. But in their subject matter I say they are not only most diverse, but are even to some extent opposed to each other. For the subject of sacred theology is divine truth, while that of ancient poetry is the men and gods of the pagans. They are opposed, in that theology presupposes nothing unless it be true, while poetry puts forth certain things as true that are surely false, misleading, and contrary to the Christian religion. But certain lackwits rise up against the poets, saying that they have composed evil and indecent fables not consonant with the truth, and that they ought to show their ability and teach their doctrines to mortals in other form than that of fictions; and for this reason I wish to proceed a little further in the present reasoning.

Let these persons, then, consider the visions of Daniel, Isaiah, Ezekiel, and others of the Old Testament, which, described by the divine pen, are revealed by him for whom there is neither beginning nor end. Let them in the New Testament also consider the visions of the Evangelist, which are full of wonderful truth for those who understand them. And if no poetic fable is found that is so far from truth or probability as, in many places on the surface, these appear to be, let it be conceded, on the other hand, that poets alone have written fables that are not likely to give either pleasure or profit. I might proceed without replying to the censure which they pass on poets because they have made known their teachings in fables or under the guise of fables, for I know that while in this they foolishly blame the poets, they incautiously fall into censuring that Spirit who is no less than the Way, the Truth, and the Life. Yet, notwithstanding, I have in mind to satisfy them somewhat.

It is manifest that everything acquired by labor has more sweetness than that which comes without effort. The obvious truth, since it is quickly and easily seized, delights us and passes into the memory. But in order that, acquired by toil, it should be more pleasing and for that reason the better retained, the poets concealed it under many things that are not, apparently, in accord therewith.[5] They chose fables rather than any other disguise, because the beauties thereof attract those whom neither philosophic demonstrations nor persuasions are able to draw. What shall we say, then, of poets? Shall we hold that they were madmen, as these present lackwits, not knowing whereof they speak, deem them? Certainly they were not. They were rather in their acts men of profound understanding, which is hidden in the fruit, and of an excellent and highly wrought eloquence, which is evident in the bark and leaves. But let us return to the place where we left off.

I say that theology and poetry can be considered as almost one and the same thing when their subject is the same. Indeed I go further, and assert that theology is simply the poetry of God. What is it but poetic fiction to say in one place of Scripture that Christ is a lion and in another a lamb, now that he is a serpent and now a dragon, and in still another place that he is a rock? And he is called by many other names, to repeat all of which would take too long. What else signify the words of the Savior in the Gospel, if not a teaching different from the outward sense, which manner of speaking we term, using a more common word, allegory. It is clear, then, that not only is poetry theology, but also that theology is poetry. And truly if my words, in so great a matter, merit little credence, I shall not be disturbed; at least let Aristotle, a most worthy authority on all great questions, be believed, who affirmed that he found the poets were the first theologians.[6] Let this suffice for this part, and let us turn to show why poets alone among learned men have been granted the honor of the laurel crown.

---

[4]Roman god of the underworld.

[5]An argument employed by Aquinas.
[6]*Metaphysics*, III. 4.

Genealogy of the Gentile Gods

From

Book XIV

VII. The Definition of Poetry, Its Origin, and Function[1]

This poetry, which ignorant triflers cast aside, is a sort of fervid and exquisite invention, with fervid expression, in speech or writing, of that which the mind has invented. It proceeds from the bosom of God, and few, I find, are the souls in whom this gift is born; indeed so wonderful a gift it is that true poets have always been the rarest of men. This fervor of poesy is sublime in its effects: it impels the soul to a longing for utterance; it brings forth strange and unheard-of creations of the mind;[2] it arranges these meditations in a fixed order, adorns the whole composition with unusual interweaving of words and thoughts; and thus it veils truth in a fair and fitting garment of fiction.[3] Further, if in any case the invention so requires, it can arm kings, marshal them for war, launch whole fleets from their docks, nay, counterfeit sky, land, sea, adorn young maidens with flowery garlands, portray human character in its various phases, awake the idle, stimulate the dull, restrain the rash, subdue the criminal, and distinguish excellent men with their proper need of praise: these, and many other such, are the effects of poetry. Yet if any man who has received the gift of poetic fervor shall imperfectly fulfill its function here described, he is not, in my opinion, a laudable poet. For, however deeply the poetic impulse stirs the mind to which it is granted, it very rarely accomplishes anything commendable if the instru-

ments by which its concepts are to be wrought out are wanting—I mean, for example, the precepts of grammar and rhetoric, an abundant knowledge of which is opportune. I grant that many a man already writes his mother tongue admirably, and indeed has performed each of the various duties of poetry as such; yet over and above this, it is necessary to know at least the principles of the other liberal arts, both moral and natural, to possess a strong and abundant vocabulary, to behold the monuments and relics of the ancients, to have in one's memory the histories of the nations, and to be familiar with the geography of various lands, of seas, rivers, and mountains.

Furthermore, places of retirement, the lovely handiwork of nature herself, are favorable to poetry, as well as peace of mind and desire for worldly glory; the ardent period of life also has very often been of great advantage. If these conditions fail, the power of creative genius frequently grows dull and sluggish.

Now since nothing proceeds from this poetic fervor, which sharpens and illumines the powers of the mind, except what is wrought out by art, poetry is generally called an art. Indeed the word *poetry* has not the origin that many carelessly suppose, namely *poio, pois,* which is but Latin *fingo, fingis;* rather it is derived from a very ancient Greek word *poetes,*[4] which means in Latin exquisite discourse (*exquisita locutio*). For the first men who, thus inspired, began to employ an exquisite style of speech, such, for example, as song in an age hitherto unpolished, to render this unheard-of discourse sonorous to their hearers, let it fall in measured periods; and lest by its brevity it fail to please, or, on the other hand, become prolix and tedious, they applied to it the standard of fixed rules, and restrained it within a definite number of feet and syllables. Now the product of this studied method of speech they no longer called by the more general term poesy, but poem. Thus as I said above, the name of the art, as well as its artificial product, is derived from its effect.

Now though I allege that this science of poetry has ever streamed forth from the bosom of God upon souls while even yet in their tenderest years, these enlightened cavilers will perhaps say that they cannot trust my words. To any fair-minded man the fact is valid enough from its constant recurrence. But for these dullards I must cite witnesses to it. If, then, they will read what Cicero, a philosopher rather than a poet, says in his oration delivered before the senate in behalf of Aulus Licinius Archias, perhaps they will come more eas-

---

GENEALOGY OF THE GENTILE GODS. *De Genealogiis* was written about 1366. The text is from Charles G. Osgood, tr., *Boccaccio on Poetry,* copyright © 1930, by Princeton University Press, 1956 by The Liberal Arts Press, Inc. Reprinted by permission of The Liberal Arts Press Division of The Bobbs-Merrill Company, Inc.

[1][Osgood] Perhaps the most significant chapter; it embodies most of Boccaccio's ideas about poetry: definition, etymology, elements and conditions of creation, effects and function, and the superiority of poetry to mere rhetoric. In setting these down, Boccaccio has consulted his own experience as a poet as well as traditional criticism, especially as recorded in Petrarch, Dante, Isidore, Macrobius, Augustine, and Cicero.

[2]This idea may go back to Plato's idea of the poet's "possession" and to his concept of "fantastic" imitation in *Sophist*. Note its presence in Sidney, *An Apology for Poetry,* p. 145. Sidney probably got it from the sixteenth-century Italian critic Minturno.

[3]This suggests an allegorical meaning as the "truth" of the poem.

[4][Osgood] Boccaccio's limitations in Greek have allowed him to follow Isidore of Seville (*Etymology,* VIII. vii. 2, *De poeta*)—bad etymology and all— in this whole passage, as did writers before him who knew no Greek. . . .

ily to believe me. He says: "And yet we have it on the high-est and most learned authority, that while other arts are mat-ters of science and formula and technique, poetry depends solely upon an inborn faculty, is evoked by a purely mental activity, and is infused with a strange supernal inspiration."

But not to protract this argument, it is now sufficiently clear to reverent men, that poetry is a practical art, springing from God's bosom and deriving its name from its effect, and that is has to do with many high and noble matters that con-stantly occupy even those who deny its existence. If my op-ponents ask when and in what circumstances, the answer is plain: the poets would declare with their own lips under whose help and guidance they compose their inventions when, for example, they raise flights of symbolic steps to heaven, or make thick-branching trees spring aloft to the very stars, or go winding about mountains to their summits. Haply, to disparage this art of poetry now unrecognized by them, these men will say that it is rhetoric which the poets employ. Indeed, I will not deny it in part, for rhetoric has also its own inventions. Yet, in truth, among the disguises of fiction rhetoric has no part, for whatever is composed as under a veil, and thus exquisitely wrought, is poetry and po-etry alone.[5]

IX. It Is Rather Useful than Damnable to Compose Stories

These fine cattle bellow still further to the effect that poets are tale-mongers, or, to use the lower and more hateful term which they sometimes employ in their resentment—liars. No doubt the ignorant will regard such an imputation as partic-ularly objectionable. But I scorn it. The foul language of some men cannot infect the glorious name of the illustrious. Yet I grieve to see these revilers in a purple rage let them-selves loose upon the innocent. If I conceded that poets deal in stories, in that they are composers of fiction, I think I hereby incur no further disgrace than a philosopher would in drawing up a syllogism. For if I show the nature of a fable or story, its various kinds, and which kinds these "liars" em-ploy, I do not think the composers of fiction will appear guilty of so monstrous a crime as these gentlemen maintain. First of all, the word *fable* (*fabula*) has an honorable origin in the verb *for, faris,* hence "conversation" (*confabulatio*), which means only "talking together" (*collocutio*). This is clearly shown by Luke in his gospel, where he is speaking of the two disciples who went to the village of Emmaus after

the Passion. He says: "And they talked together of all these things which had happened. And it came to pass, that, while they communed together, and reasoned, Jesus himself drew near, and went with them."[6]

Hence, if it is a sin to compose stories, it is a sin to converse, which only the veriest fool would admit. For na-ture has not granted us the power of speech unless for pur-poses of conversation, and the exchange of ideas.

But, they may object, nature meant this gift for a useful purpose, not for idle nonsense; and fiction is just that—idle nonsense. True enough, if the poet had intended to compose a mere tale. But I have time and time again proved that the meaning of fiction is far from superficial. Wherefore, some writers have framed this definition of fiction (*fabula*): Fic-tion is a form of discourse, which, under guise of invention, illustrates or proves an idea; and, as its superficial aspect is removed, the meaning of the author is clear. If, then, sense is revealed from under the veil of fiction, the composition of fiction is not idle nonsense. Of fiction I distinguish four kinds. The first superficially lacks all appearance of truth; for example, when brutes or inanimate things converse. Aesop, an ancient Greek, grave and venerable, was past master in this form; and though it is a common and popular form both in city and country, yet Aristotle, chief of the Peripatetics,[7] and a man of divine intellect, did not scorn to use it in his books. The second kind at times superficially mingles fiction with truth, as when we tell of the daughters of Minyas at their spinning, who, when they spurned the orgies of Bacchus, were turned to bats; or the mates of the sailor Acestes, who for contriving the rape of the boy Bacchus, were turned to fish.[8] This form has been employed from the beginning by the most ancient poets, whose object it has been to clothe in fiction divine and human matters alike; they who have fol-lowed the sublimer inventions of the poets have improved upon them; while some of the comic writers have perverted them, caring more for the approval of a licentious public than for honesty. The third kind is more like history than fiction, and famous poets have employed it in a variety of ways. For however much the heroic poets seem to be writing history—as Virgil in his description of Aeneas tossed by the storm, or Homer in his account of Ulysses bound to the mast to escape the lure of the Sirens' song—yet their hidden meaning is far other than appears on the surface. The better of the comic poets, Terence and Plautus, for example, have also employed this form, but they intend naught other than the literal mean-ing of their lines. Yet by their art they portray varieties of

---

[5]Although allegory alone does not distinguish poetry from rhetoric, Boccac-cio obviously considers it important.

[6]Luke 24:14–15.
[7]Disciples of Aristotle, who walked about while he was teaching.
[8]Myths recorded in Ovid, *Metamorphoses*, III. 582–686; IV. 31–415.

human nature and conversation, incidentally teaching the reader and putting him on his guard. If the events they describe have not actually taken place, yet since they are common, they could have occurred, or might at some time.[9] My opponents need not be so squeamish—Christ, who is God, used this sort of fiction again and again in his parables!

The fourth kind contains no truth at all, either superficial or hidden, since it consists only of old wives' tales.

Now, if my eminent opponents condemn the first kind of fiction, then they must include the account in Holy Writ describing the conference of the trees of the forest on choosing a king.[10] If the second, then nearly the whole sacred body of the Old Testament will be rejected. God forbid, since the writings of the Old Testament and the writings of the poets seem as it were to keep step with each other, and that too in respect to the method of their composition. For where history is lacking, neither one concerns itself with the superficial possibility, but what the poet calls fable or fiction our theologians have named figure. The truth of this may be seen by fairer judges than my opponents, if they will but weigh in a true scale the outward literary semblance of the visions of Isaiah, Ezekiel, Daniel, and other sacred writers on the one hand, with the outward literary semblance of the fiction of poets on the other. If they find any real discrepancy in their methods, either of implication or exposition, I will accept their condemnation. If they condemn the third form of fiction, it is the same as condemning the form which our Savior Jesus Christ, the Son of God, often used when he was in the flesh, though Holy Writ does not call it *poetry,* but *parable;* some call it *exemplum,* because it is used as such.

I count as naught their condemnation of the fourth form of fiction, since it proceeds from no consistent principle, nor is fortified by the reinforcement of any of the arts, nor carried logically to a conclusion. Fiction of this kind has nothing in common with the works of the poets, though I imagine these objectors think poetry differs from it in no respect.

I now ask whether they are going to call the Holy Spirit, or Christ, the very God, liars, who both in the same Godhead have uttered fictions. I hardly think so, if they are wise. I might show them, your Majesty,[11] if there were time, that difference of names constitutes no objection where methods agree. But they may see for themselves. Fiction, which they scorn because of its mere name, has been the means, as we often read, of quelling minds aroused to a mad rage, and subduing them to their pristine gentleness. Thus, when the Roman plebs seceded from the senate, they were called back from the sacred mount to the city by Menenius Agrippa, a man of great influence, all by means of a story. By fiction, too, the strength and spirits of great men worn out in the strain of serious crises, have been restored. This appears, not by ancient instance alone, but constantly. One knows of princes who have been deeply engaged in important matters, but after the noble and happy disposal of their affairs of state, obey, as it were, the warning of nature, and revive their spent forces by calling about them such men as will renew their weary minds with diverting stories and conversation. Fiction has, in some cases, sufficed to lift the oppressive weight of adversity and furnish consolation, as appears in Lucius Apuleius; he tells how the highborn maiden Charis, while bewailing her unhappy condition as captive among thieves, was in some degree restored through hearing from an old woman the charming story of Psyche.[12] Through fiction, it is well known, the mind that is slipping into inactivity is recalled to a state of better and more vigorous fruition. Not to mention minor instances, such as my own, I once heard Giacopo Sanseverino, Count of Tricarico and Chiarmonti, say that he had heard his father tell of Robert, son of King Charles—himself in after time the famous King of Jerusalem and Sicily—how as a boy he was so dull that it took the utmost skill and patience of his master to teach him the mere elements of letters. When all his friends were nearly in despair of his doing anything, his master, by the most subtle skill, as it were, lured his mind with the fables of Aesop into so grand a passion for study and knowledge, that in a brief time he not only learned the liberal arts familiar to Italy, but entered with wonderful keenness of mind into the very inner mysteries of sacred philosophy. In short, he made of himself a king whose superior in learning men have not seen since Solomon.

Such then is the power of fiction that it pleases the unlearned by its external appearance, and exercises the minds of the learned with its hidden truth; and thus both are edified and delighted[13] with one and the same perusal. Then let not these disparagers raise their heads to vent their spleen in scornful words, and spew their ignorance upon poets! If they have any sense at all, let them look to their own speciousness before they try to dim the splendor of others with the cloud of their maledictions. Let them see, I pray, how pernicious are their jeers, fit to rouse the laughter only of girls. When they have made themselves clean, let them purify the tales of others, mindful of Christ's commandment to the accusers

---

[9]Reminiscent of Aristotle's idea of plausibility. See *Poetics,* IX. 4, p. 55.
[10]Judges 9:8–15.
[11]The *Genealogy* is dedicated to Hugo IV, king of Cyprus from 1324 to 1358, even though Hugo had died before it was finished.

[12]*The Golden Ass,* IV. 21.
[13]See Horace, *Art of Poetry,* above, p. 73.

of the woman taken in adultery, that he who was without sin should cast the first stone.

XIII. Poets Are Not Liars

These enemies of poetry further utter the taunt that poets are liars. This position they try to maintain by the hackneyed objection that poets write lies in their narratives, to wit, that a human being was turned into a stone—a statement in every aspect contrary to the truth. They urge besides that poets lie in asserting that there are many gods, though it is established in all certainty that there is but One—the True and Omnipotent.[14] They add that the greatest Latin poet, Virgil, told the more or less untrue story of Dido,[15] and allege other like instances. I fancy they think their point is already won, and so indeed it would be, were there no one to repel their boorish vociferations with the truth. Yet further discussion seems hardly necessary for I supposed that I had already answered this objection above,[16] where at sufficient length I defined a story, its kinds, what sorts the poets employ, and wherefore.

But if the matter is to be resumed, I insist that, whatever those fellows think, poets are not liars. I had supposed that a lie was a certain very close counterfeit of the truth which served to destroy the true and substitute the false. Augustine mentions eight kinds of lies,[17] of which some are, to be sure, graver than others, yet none, if we employ them consciously, free from sin and the mark of infamy that denotes a liar. If the enemies of poetry will consider fairly the meaning of this definition, they will become aware that their charge of falsehood is without force, since poetic fiction has nothing in common with any variety of falsehood, for it is not a poet's purpose to deceive anybody with his inventions; furthermore, poetic fiction differs from a lie in that in most instances it bears not only no close resemblance to the literal truth, but no resemblance at all; on the contrary, it is quite out of harmony and agreement with the literal truth.

Yet there is one kind of fiction very like the truth, which as I said, is more like history than fiction, and which by most ancient agreement of all peoples has been free from taint of falsehood. This is so in virtue of their consent from of old that anyone who could might use it as an illustration in which the literal truth is not required, nor its opposite forbidden. And if one considers the function of the poet already described, clearly poets are not constrained by this bond to employ literal truth on the surface of their inventions; besides, if the privilege of ranging through every sort of fiction be denied them, their office will altogether resolve itself into naught.

Again: if all my preceding argument should deserve reprobation—and I hardly think it possible—yet this fact remains irrefutable, that no one can in the proper discharge of his duty incur by that act the taint of infamy. If the judge, for example, lawfully visits capital punishment upon malefactors, it is not called homicide. Neither is a soldier who wastes the enemy's fields called a robber. Though a lawyer gives his client advice not wholly just, yet if he breaks not the bounds of the law he does not deserve to be called a falsifier. So also a poet, however he may sacrifice the literal truth in invention, does not incur the ignominy of a liar, since he discharges his very proper function not to deceive, but only by way of invention.

Yet if they will insist that whatever is not literally true, is, however uttered, a lie, I accept it for purposes of argument; if not, I will spend no more energy in demolishing this objection of theirs. Rather I will ask them to tell me what name should be applied to those parts of the Revelation of John the Evangelist—expressed with amazing majesty of inner sense, though often at first glance quite contrary to the truth—in which he has veiled the great mysteries of God. And what will they call John himself? What too will they call the other writers who have employed the same style to the same end? I certainly should not dare answer for them "lies" and "liars," even if I might. Yet I know well they will say what I myself in part am about to say—should anyone ask me—that John and the other prophets were men of absolute truthfulness, a point already conceded. My opponents will add that their writings are not fiction but rather figures, to use the correct term, and their authors are figurative writers. O silly subterfuge! As if I were likely to believe that two things to all appearances exactly alike should gain the power of different effects by mere change or difference of name.

But not to dispute the point, I grant they are figures. Then, let me ask, does the truth which they express lie on their surface? If they wish me to think it does, what else is it but a lie thus to veil the eyes of my understanding, as they also veil the truth beneath? Well then, if these sacred writers must be called liars, though not held such, since indeed they are none, no more are poets to be considered liars who lean with their whole weight upon mere invention.

Yet without question poets do say in their works that there are many gods, when there is but One. But they should not therefore be charged with falsehood, since they neither believe nor assert it as a fact, but only as a myth or fiction, according to their wont. Who is witless enough to suppose that a man deeply versed in philosophy hasn't any more

---

[14][Osgood] The oft-repeated argument of early apologists, particularly Tertullian, Arnobius, Lactantis, and Augustine.

[15]See Augustine, *Confessions*, I. 13. He makes a criticism of spending time reading poetic fictions, which he considers a waste.

[16]In Chapter 9.

[17]*On Lying*, 14.

sense than to accept polytheism? As sensible men we must easily admit that the learned have been most devoted investigators of the truth, and have gone as far as the human mind can explore; thus they know beyond any shadow of doubt that there is but one God. As for poets, their own works clearly show that they have attained to such knowledge. Read Virgil and you will find the prayer: "If any vows, Almighty Jove, can bend Thy will"[18]—an epithet which you will never see applied to another god. The multitude of other gods they looked upon not as gods, but as members or functions of the Divinity; such was Plato's opinion, and we call him a theologian. But to these functions they gave a name in conformity with deity because of their veneration for the particular function in each instance.

But I do not expect these disturbers to hold their peace here. They will cry out the louder that poets have written many lies about this one true God—whom, as I have just said, they recognize—and on that count deserve to be called liars. Of course I do not doubt that pagan poets had an imperfect sense of the true God, and so sometimes wrote of him what was not altogether true—a lie, as their accusers call it. But for all that I think they should hardly be called liars. There are two kinds of liars: first, those who knowingly and willfully lie, whether to injure another person or not, or even to help him. These should not be called merely liars, but, more appropriately, "willful deceivers." The second class are those who have told a falsehood without knowing it. Among these last a further discussion is in order. For in some cases ignorance is neither to be excused nor endured. For example, the law forbids any man privately to hold a citizen prisoner. John Doe has detained Richard Roe, his debtor, and pleads exemption from fine through ignorance of the law; but since such ignorance of the law seems stupid and negligent, it can constitute no defense. Likewise a Christian who is of age should find no protection in ignorance of the articles of faith. On the other hand there are those whose ignorance is excusable, such as boys ignorant of philosophy or a mountaineer ignorant of navigation, or a man congenitally blind who does not know his letters. Such are the pagan poets who, with all their knowledge of the liberal arts, poetry, and philosophy, could not know the truth of Christianity; for that light of the eternal truth which lighteth every man that cometh into the world had not yet shone forth upon the nations. Not yet had these servants gone throughout all the earth bidding every man to the supper of the Lamb. To the Israelites alone had this gift been granted of knowing the true God aright, and truly worshiping him. But they never invited anyone to share the great feast with them, nor admitted any of the Gentiles at their doors. And if pagan poets wrote not the whole truth concerning the true God, though they thought they did, such ignorance is an acceptable excuse and they ought not to be called liars.

But my opponents will say, that whatever ignorance occasioned the lie, he who told it, is nonetheless a liar. True; but I repeat, they who sinned in pardonable ignorance are not to be damned by the same token as the offenders whose ignorance was crass and negligent; for the law, both in its equity and its austerity, holds them excused, wherefore, they incur not the brand of a lie.

If these disparagers still insist in spite of everything that poets are liars, I accuse the philosophers, Aristotle, Plato, and Socrates of sharing their guilt. Now, I expect, these expert critics will again lift their voices to heaven and cry to the sound of harp and cithera that this objection of theirs has suffered no harm. Fools! Though one small shield be shattered, the whole front does not waver. Let them not exult, but remember how often they have now been belabored and beaten back.

Their objection to Virgil—that no wise man would ever consent to tell the story of Dido—is utterly false. With his profound knowledge of such lore, he was well aware that Dido had really been a woman of exceptionally high character, who would rather die by her own hand than subdue the vow of chastity fixed deep in her heart to a second marriage. But that he might attain the proper effect of his work under the artifice of a poetic disguise, he composed a story in many respects like that of this historic Dido, according to the privilege of poets established by ancient custom. Possibly someone more worthy of a reply than my opponents—perhaps even thou, O Prince—may ask to what purpose this was necessary for Virgil. By way of fitting answer let me then say that his motive was fourfold.

First, that in the same style which he had adopted for the *Aeneid* he might follow the practice of earlier poets, particularly Homer, whom he imitated in this work. For poets are not like historians, who begin their account at some convenient beginning and describe events in the unbroken order of their occurrence to the end. Such, we observe, was Lucan's method, wherefore many think of him rather as a metrical historian than a poet.[19] But poets, by a far nobler device, begin their proposed narrative in the midst of the events, or sometimes even near the end; and thus they find excuse for telling preceding events which seem to have been omitted.

---

[18]*Aeneid*, II. 689.

[19]This point about Lucan, a Roman epic poet of the first century A.D. is later made by Scaliger.

Thus Homer, in the *Odyssey*, begins, as it were, near the end of Ulysses's wanderings and shows him wrecked upon the Phaeacian shore, then has him tell King Alcinous everything that had happened to him hitherto since he left Troy. Virgil chose the same method in describing Aeneas as a fugitive from the shore of Troy after the city was razed. He found no place so appropriate on which to land him before he reached Italy as the coast of Africa; for at any nearer point he had been sailing continuously among his enemies the Greeks. But since the shore of Africa was at that time still the home of rude and barbarous rustics, he desired to bring his hero to somebody worthy of regard who might receive him and urge him to tell of his own fate and that of the Trojans. Such a one above all he found in Dido, who, to be sure, is supposed to have dwelt there not then, but many generations later, yet Dido he presents as already living, and makes her the hostess of Aeneas; and we read how at her command he told the story of his own troubles and those of his friends.

Virgil's second purpose,[20] concealed within the poetic veil, was to show with what passions human frailty is infested, and the strength with which a steady man subdues them. Having illustrated some of these, he wished particularly to demonstrate the reasons why we are carried away into wanton behavior by the passion of concupiscence; so he introduces Dido, a woman of distinguished family, young, fair, rich, exemplary, famous for her purity, ruler of her city and people, of conspicuous wisdom and eloquence, and, lastly, a widow, and thus from former experience in love, the more easily disposed to that passion. Now all these qualifications are likely to excite the mind of a highborn man, particularly an exile and castaway thrown destitute upon an unknown shore. So he represents in Dido the attracting power of the passion of love, prepared for every opportunity, and in Aeneas one who is readily disposed in that way and at length overcome. But after showing the enticements of lust, he points the way of return to virtue by bringing in Mercury, messenger of the gods, to rebuke Aeneas, and call him back from such indulgence to deeds of glory. By Mercury, Virgil means either remorse, or the reproof of some outspoken friend, either of which rouses us from slumber in the mire of turpitude, and calls us back into the fair and even path to glory. Then we burst the bonds of unholy delight, and, armed with new fortitude, we unfalteringly spurn all seductive flattery, and tears, prayers, and such, and abandon them as naught.

Virgil's third purpose is to extol, through his praise of Aeneas, the *gens Julia* in honor of Octavius; this he does by showing him resolutely and scornfully setting his heel upon the wanton and impure promptings of the flesh and the delights of women.

It is Virgil's fourth purpose to exalt the glory of the name of Rome. This he accomplishes through Dido's execrations at her death; for they imply the wars between Carthage and Rome, and prefigure the triumphs which the Romans gained thereby—a sufficient glorification of the city's name.

Thus it appears that Virgil is not a liar, whatever the unthinking suppose; nor are the others liars who compose in the same manner.

XVII. That Poets Are Merely Apes of the Philosophers

A few of the enemies of poetry who would outdo the rest in their attack say that poets are but apes of the philosophers. I cannot make sure whether such eructation comes from a wish to raise a general laugh, like their cheap jokes among silly girls, or whether it rises from real conviction, or from a mere low and idle desire to ridicule. If the first, then the wise should suffer it to pass, though with some feeling of indignation. For they often see eminent men bantered by the ignorant, who at many a street corner appear disguised as filleted asses, or hogs in their trappings, or in fringed and variegated skins of different beasts; and thus disguised freely utter, with less impropriety, any ribald lampoons they can make up. But if this charge against poets comes from conviction or from desire to ridicule, it is, in either case, both stupid and vicious. The apes' natural and invariable habit (as I remember saying elsewhere) is to imitate as far as they can everything they see, even to the actions of men. Whence these men speciously infer that poets, being imitators, are therefore apes of the philosophers: now this is not so absurd, even if it were true; for philosophers have been for the most part honorable men, and inventors of noble arts. But the ignorant deceive themselves. If they but understood the works of the poets, they would see that, far from being apes, they should be reckoned of the very number of the philosophers, since they never veil with their inventions anything which is not wholly consonant with philosophy as judged by the opinions of the ancients. And then, too, the pure imitator never sets foot outside his model's track—a fact not observed in poets. For though their destination is the same as that of the philosophers, they do not arrive by the same road. The philosopher, everyone knows, by a process of syllogizing, dis-

---

[20]Virgil's "second purpose" seems to correspond to the allegorical and moral levels described by Aquinas and Dante. See Aquinas, *The Nature and Domain of Sacred Doctrine*, pp. 117–19, and Dante, *The Banquet*, p. 120–21. Boccaccio's explanation follows that of Fulgentius, a Latin grammarian of the sixth century A.D., who described the *Aeneid* as a picture of human life.

proves what he considers false, and in like manner proves his theory, and does all this as obviously as he can. The poet conceives his thought by contemplation, and, wholly without the help of syllogism, veils it as subtly and skillfully as he can under the outward semblance of his invention. The philosopher as a rule employs an unadorned prose style, with something of scorn for literary embellishment. The poet writes in meter, with an artist's most scrupulous care, and in a style distinguished by exquisite charm. It is, furthermore, a philosopher's business to dispute in the lecture room, but a poet's to sing in solitude. With such discrepancy between them, the poet cannot prove to be "the ape of the philosopher." If they called them apes of nature, the epithet might be less irritating, since the poet tries with all his powers to set forth in noble verse the effects, either of nature herself, or of her eternal and unalterable operation. If my opponents care to consider it, they will perceive the forms, habits, discourse, and actions of all animate things, the courses of heaven and the stars, the shattering force of the winds, the roar and crackling of flames, the thunder of the waves, high mountains and shady groves, and rivers in their courses—all these will they find so vividly set forth that the very objects will seem actually present in the tiny letters of the written poem. In this sense, I admit, the poets are apes, and I hold it a task full of honor to attempt with art what nature performs in the fullness of her power. So much upon this point. It would be better for such critics if they would use their best efforts to make us all become apes of Christ, rather than jeer at the labors of poets, which they do not understand. Sometimes people who try to scratch another's itching back feel someone's bloody nails in their own skin—and not so pleasantly either!

From

Book XV

VIII. The Pagan Poets of Mythology Are Theologians

There are certain pietists who, in reading my words, will be moved by holy zeal to charge me with injury to the most sacrosanct Christian religion; for I allege that the pagan poets are theologians—a distinction which Christians grant only to those instructed in sacred literature. These critics I hold in high respect; and I thank them in anticipation for such criticism, for I feel that it implies their concern for my welfare. But the carelessness of their remarks shows clearly the narrow limitations of their reading. If they had read widely, they could not have overlooked that very well-

known work on the *City of God,* they might have seen how, in the sixth book, Augustine cites the opinion of the learned Varro, who held that theology is threefold in its divisions—mythical, physical, and civil.[21] It is called mythical, from the Greek *mythicon,* "a myth," and in this kind, as I have already said, is adapted to the use of the comic stage. But this form of literature is reprobate among better poets on account of its obscenity. Physical theology is, as etymology shows, natural and moral, and being commonly thought a very useful thing, it enjoys much esteem. Civil or political theology, sometimes called the theology of state worship, relates to the commonwealth, but through the foul abominations of its ancient ritual, it was repudiated by them of the true faith and the right worship of God. Now of these three, physical theology is found in the great poets since they clothe many a physical and moral truth in their inventions, including within their scope not only the deeds of great men, but matters relating to their gods. And particularly, as they first composed hymns of praise to the gods, and, as I have said, in a poetic guise, presented their great powers and acts, they won the name of theologians even among the primitive pagans. Indeed Aristotle[22] himself avers that they were the first to ponder theology; and though they got their name from no knowledge or lore of the true God, yet at the advent of true theologians they could not lose it, so great was the natural force of the word derived from the theory of any divinity whatsoever. Aware, I suppose, that the title "theologian" once fairly won, cannot be lost, the present-day theologians call themselves professors of sacred theology to distinguish themselves from theologians of mythological cast or any other. Such distinction admits no possible exception as implying an injury to the name of Christianity. Do we not speak of all mortals who have bodies and rational souls as men? Some may be Gentiles, some Israelites, some Agarenes, some Christians, and some so depraved as to deserve the name of gross beasts, not men. Yet we do not wrong our Savior by calling them men, though with his Godhead he is

---

[21][Osgood] *City of God,* VI. 5: "Now what are we to say of this proposition of his [Varro's] namely, that there are three kinds of theology, that is, of the account which is given of the gods; and of these, the one is called mythical, the other physical, and the third civil? Did the Latin usage permit, we should call the kind which he has placed first in order 'fabular' (*fabulare*), but let us call it 'fabulous' (*fabulosum*), for 'mythical' is derived from the Greek μῦθος, a fable; but that the second should be called 'natural,' the usage of speech now admits; the third he himself has designated in Latin calling it 'civil.' Then he says, 'they call that kind "mythical" which the poets chiefly use; "physical" that which the philosophers use; "civil" that which the people use.'" Augustine condemns the first and third forthwith. For the second, embodying as it does profound if erroneous doctrine about nature and God, he has more respect (VII. 5 *ff.*). On this Boccaccio leans, though one suspects his citation of Augustine as a flourish for effect upon his opponents.

[22]*Metaphysics,* II. iv. 12.

known to have been literally human. No more is there any harm in speaking of the old poets as theologians. Of course, if any one were to call them sacred, the veriest fool would detect the falsehood.

On the other hand there are times, as in this book, when the theology of the ancients will be seen to exhibit what is right and honorable, though in most such cases it should be considered rather physiology or ethology than theology, according as the myths embody the truth concerning physical nature or human. But the old theology can sometimes be employed in the service of catholic truth, if the fashioner of the myths should choose. I have observed this in the case of more than one orthodox poet in whose investiture of fiction the sacred teachings were clothed. Nor let my pious critics be offended to hear the poets sometimes called even sacred theologians. In like manner sacred theologians turn physical when occasion demands; if in no other way, at least they prove themselves physical theologians as well as sacred when they express truth by the fable of the trees choosing a king.

Lodovico Castelvetro

1505–1571

In his commentary on Aristotle's *Poetics,* particularly on Chapter XXIV, Castelvetro establishes the unities of time and place as rules of the drama. For this he is popularly known. In his treatment of the unity of time he makes demands more rigid than Aristotle's—demands later endorsed by many neoclassical critics. In this, as in his view that poetry should serve to keep the common people happy, he displays a curious literal-minded utilitarianism.

It is true that at times Castelvetro's rationalism hardens Aristotle's remarks into rigid precepts. It is also true, however, that Castelvetro gets around to making some subtle comments not only on Aristotle but on Plato as well. He is not alone among Renaissance Italians in his prolixity and in what would be, if his style were not so complicated, a leisurely approach to major issues. Castelvetro contributes a rather confusing chapter to the history of the distinction between poetry and history. At first disregarding the possibility, later taken up by Mazzoni, that poetry may be fantastic, Castelvetro limits the poet to inventing his plots and not taking them from history. Then he qualifies that distinction to the point of contradiction in a much subtler discussion of historical tragedies, in which he makes a great deal of the genius of the poet who is able to employ historical events and personages.

Perhaps the most charming and finally the most telling of Castelvetro's illustrations is his story of Michelangelo restoring the beard to a statue of a river god. In relating this story, Castelvetro's emphasis on the importance of the relationship among the parts of a work comes closer to a truly Aristotelian attitude toward the structure of a work of art than do his more rigid discussions of verisimilitude and the unities.

No full translation of Castelvetro's commentary on Aristotle's *Poetics* is available, though an edition was published in Italian in 1978. The reader may consult A. H. Gilbert's *Literary Criticism: Plato to Dryden* (1962) for a selection. See H. B. Charlton, *Castelvetro's Theory of Poetry* (1913), and R. C. Melzi, *Castelvetro's Annotations to the "Inferno"* (1966). The major histories of this period of Italian criticism are Joel E. Spingarn, *A History of Literary Criticism in the Renaissance* (1899); Baxter Hathaway, *The Age of Criticism* (1962); and Bernard Weinberg, *A History of Literary Criticism in the Italian Renaissance* (1961) in two volumes.

From

The *Poetics* of Aristotle Translated and Explained

I

[28] . . . Aristotle writes that the sciences and the arts and history are not subjects of poetry. But I, who do not in the least have an opinion different from Aristotle's and think he is entirely correct, believe I can explain the reasons which have led me to hold the same views; which if not altogether identical with Aristotle's, are perhaps not very different. . . . Poetry is a likeness of or resemblance to history. And, since history is divided into two main parts, that is, subject matter and words, so poetry is divided into two main parts which are likewise subject matter and words. But history and poetry differ in these two parts in that history does not have a subject matter provided by the talent of the historian; rather it is prepared for him by the course of worldly events or by the manifest or hidden will of God. The words are provided by the historian, but they are the sort used in reasoning. The subject matter of poetry is discovered and imagined by the talent of the poet, and its words are not the sort used in reasoning, because men are not accustomed to reason in verse. But the words of poetry are composed in measured verse by the working of the poet's genius.

Now the subject matter of poetry ought to be similar to that of history and resemble it, but it should not be identical, because if it were it would no longer be similar or resembling and if it were not similar or resembling, the poet would not have exerted himself at all and would not have shown the sharpness of his talent in discovering it and hence would not deserve praise. And especially he would not deserve that praise by which he is thought to be more divine than human; for he knows how to manage a tale, imagined by himself about things which have never happened, so as to make it no less delightful and no less verisimilar than what occurs through the course of worldly events or the infinite providence of God, either manifest or hidden. Therefore when the poet takes his subject matter from history, that is, from events which have happened, he takes no pains, nor is it clear that he is either a good or a bad poet, that is, that he does or

does not know how to discover things like the truth, and he cannot be praised for making resemblances and thus he is criticized [29] and considered to have little judgment because he has not recognized this. Or else he is thought to possess an evil and deceptive nature if with the covering and colors of poetic language he has tried to dupe his readers or listeners into believing that there is poetic material beneath his words and hence to gain false commendation for it. Logically, therefore, Lucan, Silius Italicus, and Girolamo Fracastoro in his *Joseph* are to be removed from the company of poets and deprived of the glorious title of poetry because in their writings they have treated material already dealt with by historians, and when it has not already been dealt with by historians, it is sufficient that it has already happened and was not thought up by these writers.[1]

From this also it can be understood that the arts and sciences cannot be the subject matter of poetry and cannot with approval be included in poems, because the arts and sciences, having already been considered and understood by reasons which are necessary and verisimilar and by the long experience of philosophers and artists, are in the same position as history and things which have already occurred. The poet who merely embellishes with poetic language the subjects already established and written by others, and about which it can be said that history has already been composed, has no place here in the sense that he can boast of being a poet. Therefore it is not astonishing if those versifiers, Empedocles, Lucretius, Nicander, Serenus, Girolamo Fracastoro in his *Syphilis,* Aratus, Manilius, Giovanni Pontano in his *Urania,* and Virgil in his *Georgics,* are not accepted into the company of poets, for even if they themselves have been the first to discover some science or art, not deriving them from another philosopher or artist, and have revealed their discoveries in verse, they should not thereby be called poets.[2] For if they have discovered some science or art by speculation, they have still discovered something already in existence and bound to continue to exist in the nature of things, something with which that science is concerned or according to which that art is constituted. They will have discharged the office of a good philosopher or a good artist, but not of a good poet, which is by observation to make resemblances of the truth about what happens to men through fortune, and by resemblances to provide delight to the audience, leaving the discovery of the truth derived from natural or accidental things to the philosopher or to the artists who

---

THE *Poetics* OF ARISTOTLE. Castelvetro's commentary *Poetica d'Aristotele vulgarizzata et sposta* was published in 1570 and revised in 1576. The text printed here was translated especially for this book by R. L. Montgomery. Chapter numbers are those of Aristotle's *Poetics.* Bracketed numbers refer to the pages of Castelvetro's edition of 1576.

---

[1]Scaliger makes a similar remark on Lucan.
[2]Aristotle raises the question of whether Empedocles, a writer of the fifth century B.C., was a poet. See *Poetics,* I. 8, p. 50. The poets to whom Castelvetro refers wrote discourses on various subjects in verse.

have their own ways of delighting or entertaining which are quite distant from that of the poet.

In addition to this, the subject matter of the arts and sciences, for another reason more evident to common sense, cannot be the subject matter of poetry, inasmuch as poetry has been found solely to delight and recreate; and I say to delight and recreate the minds of the vulgar multitude and common people. They do not understand the reasons, distinctions, or arguments subtle and remote from the practice of common men which philosophers use in investigating the truth of things and artists in practicing their skills. It is not fitting that a listener, when another speaks to him, should be annoyed or displeased, for we are naturally uncommonly irritated when another [30] speaks to us in a way which we cannot understand. Therefore if we concede that the subject matter of the arts and sciences is the subject matter of poetry, we will also concede that either poetry was not discovered to delight or that it was not meant for the common people, but so that it might instruct and that for the sake of those sophisticated in letters and dissertation. This will be acknowledged to be false by what we shall prove as we proceed.

Now because poetry has been found, as I say, to delight and recreate the common people, it ought to have as its subject matter those things which can be understood by the common people and which, when they are understood, make them happy. These are things which happen daily, which are talked about by the people, and which resemble news of the world and history. And for this reason, I affirm, with respect to the subject matter, that poetry is a likeness of or resemblance to history. The subject matter, because it resembles history, not only makes its inventor glorious and makes and constitutes him a poet, but also delights more than an account of things that have really happened . . . . To which may be added versification, by which the poet speaks marvelously and delightfully . . . for example, by being able without unseemliness to raise his voice on the stage so that the people may listen in complete comfort. . . . Because, then, the subject matter of the arts and sciences is not understood by the people, not only should it be avoided and shunned as the universal subject of a poem, but also we must guard against using any part of the arts and sciences in any place in the poem. In this respect Lucan and Dante in his *Comedy* have especially and unnecessarily erred when they reveal the time of year and the time of day and night by astrology. Neither Homer nor Virgil in the *Aeneid* ever fell into this error. Therefore I cannot but be somewhat amazed at Quintilian who supposes that no one ignorant of the art of astrology or unskilled in philosophy can be a good reader of poetry.[3] . . .

IV

[65] Aristotle did not hold the opinion that poetry was a special gift of the gods, yielded to one man rather than to another, as is the gift of prophecy and similar privileges which do not derive from nature and are not common to all. Doubtless he means, even though he does not state it openly, to challenge the opinion which some have attributed to Plato that poetry is infused in men by divine frenzy. This opinion must have had its origin in the ignorance of the common people, and it flourished and gained favor through the vainglory of poets for this reason and in this way. Anything which someone else does is highly regarded and admired by those who lack the ability to do it themselves, and because men commonly measure the bodily strength and the skill of others by their own, they consider a miracle and a special gift of God what they cannot obtain by their own natural powers and see that others have obtained. Therefore the first poets were reputed by the ignorant to be filled with the divine spirit and assisted by God. They admired excessively the invention of the fable in the poets' compositions, and also the continuation of many verses by which the fable was revealed, and they were especially admiring when they saw the divine response of Apollo given in such verses, for they thought that through these the gods spoke. Therefore they could not understand that it was possible that the poet could invent a fable so like the truth and so delightful, and after he invented it, they could not see how he could lay it out in verse and in verse so well chosen that such things could not be made by other than human means. . . . This popular belief, though false, was pleasing to poets because it afforded them great praise and they were considered dear to the gods. Therefore they nourished the belief with their consent, and making it seem that things were as they said, they began at the opening of their works to invoke the aid of the Muses [66] and of Apollo, the god who rules over poetry, and to pretend that they uttered their poems through the mouths of those gods. . . . It is therefore mistaken to attribute to Plato his opinion about the frenzy induced in the poet by the gods, for, as I have said, its origin is in the agreement of poets cultivating their own interest. When Plato mentions it in his books, he is undoubtedly joking, as it is usually his habit to do in similar situations. Thus in the *Phaedrus,* when he says the lover is possessed by madness and wants to prove that not everyone possessed by madness is necessarily in the grasp of an evil spirit, he suggests that it is a benevolent madness which possesses the prophetic women at Delphos and the priests at Dodona, and the Sybil, and other diviners,

---

[3]*Institutes,* I. 4.

and poets. But he is not really proving that poets are possessed by any divine madness; rather he is adducing a similar case by an example such as was commonly believed.[4] . . . And he writes jokingly in the *Apology* of Socrates when he says that poets do not understand what they write in their poems when moved by divine madness.[5] This is plain enough, for if he were speaking seriously and believed that poems derived from divine inspiration, why did he exclude them from his republic? . . .

[68] The imitation natural to men is one thing; that required of poetry is another. For the imitation of others which is natural to men and which is in them from childhood, by which they first acquire knowledge, by which all men are disposed more than animals, and as a result of which they are made glad, is nothing other than following the example of others and doing as they do without knowing the reason why. But the imitation required of poetry not only does not follow the examples set by another, nor does it do what others do without knowing the reason why they do so, but it also does something quite different from what is available and proposes instead, so to speak, an example for which it is necessary that the poet know very well the reasons why he does what he does. And he must take time to think and to discern, insofar as he can with certainty, that the imitation required of poetry does not consist, and ought not to consist, in what may be called literal copying, but does consist, or ought to, in what may be called the struggle of the poet and the disposition of fortune or the course of worldly affairs, in finding an accident in human behavior delightful [69] to hear and marvelous. . . .

VI

[116] Because it seemed to Plato that tragedy by the example of tragic characters could injure citizens and debase good customs in them, making them vile, cowardly, and sentimental, he did not wish tragedy to be represented in his republic, for he believed that if the people heard and saw men thought to be valorous doing and saying things which sentimental people do and say, then the frightened and the vile would console themselves and pardon weakness of spirit in themselves, as well as fear and pusillanimity, seeing that they had companions among the great, such as kings. And following

such examples they would let themselves improperly be moved by such passion.[6] But Aristotle, so that men [117] would not believe, on the authority of Plato, that he himself, writing about the method of tragedy, had contrived to present it as an art harmful to the citizenry and apt to contaminate their morals, affirmed that tragedy functioned in precisely the opposite way. That is, by its example and by its frequent representation it brings spectators from baseness to magnanimity, from anxiety to security, and from sentimentality to severity, habituating them by repeated usage of things worthy of pity, fear, and baseness to be neither sentimental, nor fearful, nor base; for tragedy by means of the aforesaid passions, terror and pity, purges and expels those same passions from the hearts of men. Now to make clearly understood what Aristotle perhaps wanted to say but uttered darkly and scarcely hinted at, either because, as is often said, his remarks in this book are brief notes for use in a larger work, or because he did not wish openly to censure the opinion of his master Plato, whom he held in some reverence, it is necessary to realize that just as pure wine of a certain quantity, which has had no drop of water mixed in it, has more vigor and spirit than the same amount of wine of equal quality mixed with a large proportion of water, for although it is greater in quantity than the former, by the addition of so much water it becomes watery and loses all its previous vigor and spirit; so the love of fathers for their children is much greater and more fervent and they care for them better when there are few, that is three or two or one, than they would for many, that is a hundred or a thousand or more. Likewise men's pity and fear directed towards a few pitiful and fearful cases are more vigorous and move them more powerfully than if they are scattered among a greater number of events worthy of pity and fear. Therefore tragedy which represents to us similar actions and makes us see and hear them more often than we would see and hear them without it is the cause of pity and terror being diminished in us because we have to divide the effect of these passions among so many diverse actions. We see the proof of this most appreciably during epidemics, for at the beginning when three or four people begin to die we find ourselves moved by pity and fear, but then when we see hundreds and thousands die, the feeling of pity and fear ceases in us. We know this also by the experience of dangerous skirmishes in which new soldiers are at first terrified by the booming of the guns and arquebuses[7] and experience the greatest pity for the dead and wounded, but after they have been in many battles they stand fast and see before their eyes companions wounded and dead

---

[4]See Plato, *Ion,* pp. 13–16. Castelvetro's argument is not powerful enough to reason away Socrates' words, which definitely attribute poetry and other forms of prophetic utterance and ecstatic behavior to divine inspiration.

[5]Plato, *Apology,* 22. Socrates does appear to exaggerate in this passage, for he is illustrating the point that his wisdom, though superior to that of poets and soothsayers, is nevertheless worthless.

[6]See Plato, *Republic,* pp. 18–22.

---

[7]An early portable gun.

without feeling much pity. Perhaps these reasons, although they are quite powerful, are not so important that because of them the law forbidding tragedy ought to be annulled, since they are directed elsewhere [118] toward the target Plato aimed at in his prohibition. And so that the way things are may be clear it must be understood that there are persons who undergo the most fearful and pitiful experiences, such as those previously mentioned. These persons are of two sorts, the strong and the timid, and similarly the actions are of two sorts, the rare and the frequent, and both have diverse effects according to the diverse ways in which they occur. Therefore if the persons who suffer are strong and patient, the example of their suffering and patience affects the souls of others and expels fear and pity, but if those persons are timid and weak, their example increases terror and pity in the spectators and confirms them in their fearfulness and weakness. . . . Similarly if fearful and pitiful actions are rare they move men to terror and pity more, but if they occur frequently they are less moving and because of their frequency they can purge terror and pity from the hearts of mortal men. This occurs for two reasons: one is that when we witness the occurrence of many misfortunes which do not involve us, little by little we feel more secure and convince ourselves that God, who has watched over us many times in the past, will also protect us in the future; the other is that those misfortunes which happen frequently and to many people, do not seem so fearful and as a result do not seem so pitiful, although we may be sure that they will touch us since we see that so many others have not been spared. . . . Plato, then, when he forbids tragedy as inducing fear and pity, forbids it because of the example of respected persons who exhibit weakness of soul in adversity, is harmful to the people.[8] If this is so, it is so because in tragedy as Plato understood it the same type of character is always introduced. . . .

[140] If the plot is the end of tragedy, and hence of any kind of poem (for the plot occupies the same place in any kind of poem as it does in tragedy), then it is final and not accessory to the morals of the characters but on the contrary their morals are accessory to the plot. Then their morals do not occupy the final place and are accessory to the plot, and it follows that many authors of great renown in letters among the ancients and moderns, among them Julius Caesar della Scala, or Scaliger, have gravely erred in supposing that the intention of good poets, such as Homer and Virgil in their most famous works, the *Iliad,* the *Odyssey,* and the *Aeneid,* is to depict and exhibit to the world, let us say, a commander in the most excellent manner possible, or a brave leader or a wise man, and their natures, and similar nonsense. If this is

true, the moral qualities of characters would not be used by poets to support the action, as Aristotle says; on the contrary, the action would be used to exhibit moral qualities. Otherwise, if this material were primary and not accessory, it could not be poetic subject matter, being naturally the subject of philosophy, treated by many philosophers and especially by Aristotle and Theophrastus.[9] Therefore, good poets such as Homer and Virgil in their most famous works, and others like them, have tried to compose a proper fable, according to which the characters and moral qualities are suited, and thus more appealing, in other words marvelous and verisimilar. . . .

VIII

[178] Aristotle . . . stubbornly demands that the action which comprises the plot should be one and concern one character only, and if there are other actions that they support each other. He adduces no reason or proof for this except the example of the tragic poets and Homer who have adhered to the single action of a single character in composing the fable. But [179] it can be easily seen that in tragedy and comedy the fable has a single action, or two when by one depending on the other they can be thought single, and it has most often a single character rather than one family, not because the fable is unsuited to more than one action, but because the length of time of twelve hours at most and restrictions of place in which the action is represented do not permit a multitude of actions, or even the actions of one family, nor for that matter the whole of one action, if it is somewhat long. And this is the principal and necessary reason why the fable of tragedy and of comedy ought to be one, that is containing the single action of one character, or two thought of as one because of their dependence on each other. This motive of limited time and place could not work so as to restrict Homer to a single action of a single character in the epic, which can narrate not just a single action, but more, and longer, and occurring in diverse lands.

IX

[188] In the plot of tragedy and epic there necessarily occur events which have been reported to have taken place in the

---

[8]See *Republic,* p. 19.

[9]See Aristotle's *Nichomachean Ethics* and Theophrastus' *Characters,* both influential in neoclassical literary characterization. At this point one might well weigh Sidney's discussion of "the speaking picture of poesy" against Castelvetro's priorities. In his *Apology for Poetry* Sidney remarks: "let but Sophocles bring you Ajax on a stage, killing and whipping sheep and oxen, thinking them the army of Greeks, with their chieftains Agamemnon and Menelaus, and tell me if you have not a more familiar insight into anger than finding in the schoolmen his genus and difference" (p. 148).

life of a particular man, and which are known in a summary way, as, for example, Orestes, accompanied by his friend Pylades and aided by him and by his sister Electra, murdering his mother Clytemnestra. But no one knows particularly or exactly the ways and means he took to accomplish the murder. Now the reason is clear, and so abundantly clear, that it can be demonstrated, for it is proper that the plot of tragedy and epic should accept things which have actually happened and which are common to it and to historical truth. For the plot of these two kinds of poetry should include action not simply human but also magnificent and regal. And if it ought to include regal events, it follows that it includes action that has actually occurred and is certain, and is the action of a king who has existed and is known to have existed, since we are unable to imagine a king who has not existed nor attribute any action to him. And insofar as he existed and is known to have existed, we cannot attribute to him actions which have not occurred. It would be as if we were to say that before the Roman republic was established there was a king of the Romans named Julius and then say that he lay with his daughter, or as if we were to say that Julius Caesar the permanent dictator of the Romans murdered his wife Calpurnia when he discovered her in adultery; for it is not true that any king of the Romans was so named or so committed any such incestuous act, and it is equally untrue that Julius Caesar discovered his wife in adultery and murdered her. Because kings are known through fame and through history, as well as their notable actions, to introduce new names of kings and to attribute to them new actions is to contradict history and fame and to sin against open truth. This is a much greater sin in the composition of the plot than to sin in verisimilitude. Therefore the plots of all tragedies and all epics are and ought to be composed of events which can be called historical, although for several reasons Aristotle had a different view. . . . [189] But the abovementioned events ought not to be manifested by history or fame except summarily and in a general way, so that the poet can perform his task and show his skill in discovering the ways and particular means by which these incidents have had their fulfillment. For if these ways and particular means by which these incidents were brought to completion were made clear in other ways, we would not have material suitable for the plot, nor would it be pertinent to the poet, but to the historians. Neither with all this should we allow the opinion that it is easier to compose the plot of a tragedy or an epic than that of a comedy, just because in the plots of those poems the poets does not invent everything on his own, as he does in comedy. . . .

Now to fill in the plot of comedy the poet by his skill finds universal and particular incidents. And because they are completely invented by him, neither events which have occurred nor history has any part. He also supplies names for the characters as it pleases him and can do so without inconvenience and he ought reasonably to do so. He can construct the incident he has chosen in all its parts and accordingly it should deal with a private person about whom, along with the incidents that have happened to him, there is no knowledge, and they will not be passed on to the memory of those in the future either by history or fame. Therefore, someone who makes up new and entire incidents involving private persons and gives them names as it pleases him, cannot be contradicted by history or fame as having reported falsehoods. And if he wishes rational men to think him a poet, that is, an inventor, he ought to invent everything, because, since the private subject matter makes it easy for him, he can invent it. But no one ought to believe that the inventor of the comic plot has license to invent new cities he has imagined, or rivers, or mountains, or kingdoms or customs or laws, or to alter the course of nature, making it snow in summer or putting the harvest in winter, and so on. For it is fitting to follow history and truth, if in constructing his plot he happens to require such things, just as in the same way it is fitting for the poet making a tragic or epic plot. . . . Therefore the possibility that things have happened, which is the subject of poetry and the actuality of what has happened, which is the subject of history, distinguish the former from the latter, and this is the essential difference between the two, and not what some have asserted, that is, that history is distinguished from poetry by its prose and poetry from history by its verse.[10] . . .

[213] It appears that if things which have happened cannot constitute poetry and do not contribute to the constitution of a poem, they ought to contribute to the distinction and diminution of poetry when they are mingled with things which might possibly happen in the future and with things invented by the poet, if we compare actual events with those which might happen in the future mixed with what [214] can really happen in the future. That is, it would seem that the plot of tragedy and epic, when made up of actions which have occurred, and retaining true names (as we have shown plots ought to be formed) would make its author less a poet than the author of a comedy or of the plot of a tragedy in which all the events and names are invented, as is the case with the tragedy of Agathon called *The Flowers*. For if the plot entirely made up of events which have occurred does not allow him to be a poet at all, then the plot made up in part of events which have occurred would to that extent deny him his role as poet and so he would be less a poet than he who is totally the poet because his plot is made up of events entirely invented or events which could happen in the future.

---

[10]This discussion can be profitably compared to Scaliger's in *Poetics*.

Nonetheless it is my judgment that the maker of the tragic and epic taken from history and with real names should not be considered a lesser poet than the maker of a plot in which every event and every name is imaginary. Perhaps instead he ought to be considered greater. For events which have occurred, with which the first sort of poet is concerned in making the plot of epic and tragedy, are not so many nor are they spread out in such a way that they relieve him of the effort of invention, for everyone can imagine similar things without great subtlety of wit. We may suppose something that every man can easily imagine, such as the story in broad outline of a son who murders his mother who has murdered her husband and hounded her son out of the kingdom so she may enjoy her lover. But the difficulty is in finding the means for the son to achieve this murder in a marvelous fashion such as has not occurred previously. This difficulty is greater than that of inventing the general line of plot and the particular ways and means by which it draws to a conclusion, since the general line of the plot invented by the poet is not so fixed or stable that it cannot be altered or changed, if it turns out to be appropriate or if he is unable to make his characters clever or dull or endowed with other qualities, as he judges it to be best according to the ways which occurred to him initially of making a fine plot. Whoever takes his plot from events which have occurred cannot do this, since he is held within certain limits from which he is not allowed to escape.

And to show by one example what this difference is, I say that not many years ago during excavations in Rome there was found a marble statue of a large, fine river god whose beard was broken and sparse, and by means of that portion which remained on the chin it was evident that the entire beard, according to proportion, would reach to the navel, even though the point of the beard was seen to rest high on the chest without reaching any further. Everyone marveled at this, and no one was able to imagine what that beard was like when it was intact. Only Michelangelo Buonarroti, a sculptor of most rare skill who was present, stood still for a while, and realizing how things stood, said, "Bring me some clay." It was brought and he formed that part of the beard which was lacking of such a size that it matched [215] the proportions of the rest. And fastening it on he drew it down to the navel. Then tying it up with one knot he showed clearly that the point of the beard he had formed struck the high point of the chest at the same place as the broken beard. Therefore to the great admiration of all those present he showed how the missing beard was made and how it was knotted. And there was no one there who did not judge that Michelangelo for subtlety of wit in having restored that missing beard so remarkably was to be preferred before any other artist in having made an entire beard suitable to his

judgment without regard to any of the remaining pieces of the original beard.

XIII

[275] Now whether it is true or false that tragedy can have no other subject matter than what is fearful or pitiable, I will not at the moment discuss. But it does seem that this has not been proven by Aristotle in the things he has said so far, although he does assume that they are proven. But since he has set out to contradict Plato, who said that tragedy is injurious to the people's good morals, he does not wish to approve a kind of tragedy other than that which according to him is advantageous in providing the people with good morals and by means of fear and pity purges those same passions, driving them out of the souls of the people in the manner we have mentioned above. And he is so intent on this matter that he does not avoid contradicting himself and the things he has said previously. Therefore if poetry is established primarily for delight and not for profit, as he has shown, in speaking of the origin of poetry in general, why does he say that in tragedy, which is a kind of poetry, utility is what is principally sought for? Why is not delight principally sought without regard to utility? Either he ought to ignore utility or at least he should not give it so much attention that he rejects all other kinds of tragedy which lack it. He should restrict himself to one single kind of utility, that which effects only the purgation of fear and pity. And even so, if utility is to be considered, other kinds of tragedy can be presented, as for example that which deals with the change of good men from misery to happiness, or of evil men from happiness to misery, so that the people, convinced by the examples proposed, may confirm themselves in the holy belief that God [276] looks after the world and the special providence of his own, defending them and confounding his and their enemies. . . .

XIV

The delight proper to tragedy is that which derives from fear and pity proceeding from the change from happiness to misery due to the error of a person of middling virtue. But someone may ask what sort of delight it is which derives from watching a good man undeservedly forced from happiness to misery, since that ought not rationally to give delight but displeasure. Now I have no doubt that Aristotle meant by the word *pleasure* the purgation and expulsion of fear and pity from the human soul by means of the operation of the same passions, in the fashion which I have already explained above at length. Thus purgation and expulsion, if they proceed as he affirms from those same passions, can quite properly be called *hedone* [ἡδονή], that is, pleasure or delight, and strictly speaking it ought to be called utility, for it is health of mind gotten through bitter medicine. Therefore pleasure derived from pity and fear, which is truly pleasure, is that which we have previously called oblique pleasure. And it occurs when, feeling pain from the misery which comes unjustly to another, we recognize that we are good, since injustice displeases us. This recognition is the greatest pleasure for us, by reason of the natural love which we have for ourselves. And added to this pleasure is another which is not in the least trivial, that is, when we see tribulations beyond reason which have come upon others and which might possibly come upon us or upon others like us, we realize tacitly and unconsciously that we are subject to the same fortune and that we cannot trust in the tranquil course of worldly things. This delight is much greater than if another, acting as a teacher and openly presenting the subject, instructs us in the same lesson. For the experience of events which have happened impresses doctrine more in our minds than the mere voice of the teacher, and we rejoice more in the little which we learn for ourselves than in the greater amount which we learn from others, since we cannot learn from others if we do not confess ourselves to be ignorant of what we learn and obliged to them for what we learn from them. And perhaps the wise man was thinking of such things when he said that it is better to go to the house of mourning than to the house of banqueting.[11]

XVII

[374] It has been concluded that he who knows how to transform himself into an impassioned person is also skilled at representing such a character, that is, he knows without art how to say and do those things which are suited to someone in a state of passion. And not everyone is apt for this, but only those endowed with a good wit, and an impassioned person can be represented not only by this means but also by another, which is to consider carefully what people in a state of passion say and do in such circumstances. This method is not for everyone, but only for the gifted man. It follows,

then, that poetry is conceived and practiced by the gifted man and not the madman, as some have said, for the madman is not able to assume various passions, nor is he a careful observer of what impassioned men say and do. But we should be aware of what seems to me to be an error in the text, since the words ἢ μανικοῦ ("or of the madman") should be written οὐ μανικοῦ ("not of the madman"). . . . It is not surprising that *not* should be made *or* by those who have already swallowed that opinion about poetic furor, which was foisted upon minds of men as we have explained above, and which the arguments of Aristotle have refuted. It is true that the reading *or of the madman* can be retained without wandering much from the idea expressed above if we read *or of the madman* as *rather than of the madman.* . . . That is, Aristotle says that poetry is usually the work of the gifted man rather than of the madman, but because *than* put in the place of *rather than* seems to be more appropriate to verse than to prose, we stand on what we said at first.

XXIV

[533] Now to understand fully what is being discussed, it must be remembered that Aristotle said before that there were two dimensions to tragedy, one accessible to the senses and external and measurable by the clock; the other accessible to the intellect and internal and measurable by the mind and which comprises the movement from misery to happiness or from happiness to misery. The duration which is accessible to the senses and is measured by the clock, cannot last more than one revolution of the sun over the earth for the reasons mentioned above; this duration, which has nothing to do with art according to Aristotle, nevertheless is shaped by and receives its measure from the time of the intellectual dimension, for the two cannot be diverse in time measurement. For, as we said above, as much length of time is to be taken in representing in tragedy an action moving from misery to happiness or from happiness to misery as would elapse in the actual or imagined occurrence of the action.[12]

---

[11]Ecclesiastes 7:4: "The heart of the wise is in the house of mourning; but the heart of fools is in the house of mirth."

[12]This passage is representative of a number of commentaries insisting on the so-called unity of time. See particularly Corneille, *Of the Three Unities,* pp. 206–12.

Sir Philip Sidney

1554–1586

Though not a very original theorist, Sidney is interesting because he provides a fairly clear and extensive picture of Renaissance critical attitudes. His sources are Plato, Aristotle, Horace, Castelvetro, and perhaps Scaliger. *An Apology for Poetry* answers an attack made on poetry by the Puritan Stephen Gosson in his *School of Abuse*. Sidney faces the following traditional complaints: first, that poetry is a waste of time, an argument that goes back at least to Tertullian; second, that it is the "mother of lies," a view implicit in Plato and Augustine and of particular force in the Puritan ethic; third, that it is the "nurse of abuse" and teaches sinful things; and finally, that Plato, an important and wise authority, banished the poets from his republic. Against these arguments he avers that in early societies poetry was the main source of education; that it exercised a moral influence on the culture; and that the poet was revered by all. Picking up the famous phrase from Horace, Sidney argues that the poet still teaches and delights principally by means of allegory, but that he goes beyond nature to offer visions of better things: "Nature never set forth the earth in so rich tapestry as divers poets have done—neither with pleasant rivers, fruitful trees, sweet-smelling flowers, nor whatsoever else may make the too much loved earth more lovely. Her world is brazen, the poets only deliver a golden." This passage seems very rich in its sources. It suggests perhaps the Aristotelian idea that the poet brings to completion that which nature is always in the process of trying to complete. But it also has a neo-Platonic ring to it, reversing in a Plotinian way Plato's attack on the poet as copier and suggesting the vision of a higher level of reality in particular images.

Sidney seems to be repeating Scaliger when he remarks that "only the poet, disdaining to be tied to any such subjection, lifted up with the vigor of his own invention, doth grow in effect another nature . . . ." The passage has interested modern readers, for it seems to anticipate a Romantic concept of the creative imagination. That idea, however, is based on an epistemology unknown to Sidney and his contemporaries. Rather, he is probably elaborating on remarks made by Scaliger in connection with a contrast between poetry and history. Scaliger's description, like Sidney's, is neo-Platonic in its idea that the poet improves on appearances. Sidney's remark that the poet does not lie because he never affirms also sounds modern, suggesting, for example, Richards' "pseudostatements," but Sidney does not have a modern theory of language.

The *Defense* has been edited by A. S. Cook (1890); the *Apology* by E. S. Shuckburgh (1891) and J. C. Collins (1907). See also J. E. Spingarn, *Literary Criticism in the Renaissance* (1899); Gregory Smith, *Elizabethan Critical Essays,* Vol. I (1904); M. W. Wallace, *The Life of Sir Philip Sidney* (1915); K. O. Myrick, *Sir Philip Sidney as a Literary Craftsman* (1935); Forrest Robinson, *The Shape of Things Known: Sid-*

ney's Apology and Its Philosophical Tradition (1972); Andrew D. Weiner, *Sir Philip Sidney and the Poetics of Protestantism* (1978); and John Webster, (ed.) *William Temple's Analysis of Sir Philip Sidney's* Apology for Poetry (1984).

An Apology
for Poetry

When the right virtuous Edward Wotton and I were at the Emperor's Court together, we gave ourselves to learn horsemanship of John Pietro Pugliano, one that with great commendation had the place of an esquire in his stable. And he, according to the fertileness of the Italian wit, did not only afford us the demonstration of his practice, but sought to enrich our minds with the contemplations there which he thought most precious. But with none I remember mine ears were at any time more loaden, than when (either angered with slow payment, or moved with our learnerlike admiration) he exercised his speech in the praise of his faculty. He said soldiers were the noblest estate of mankind, and horsemen the noblest of soldiers. He said they were the masters of war and ornaments of peace; speedy goers and strong abiders; triumphers both in camps and courts. Nay, to so unbelieved a point he proceeded, as that no earthly thing bred such wonder to a prince as to be a good horseman. Skill of government was but a *pedenteria*[1] in comparison. Then would he add certain praises, by telling what a peerless beast a horse was, the only serviceable courtier without flattery, the beast of most beauty, faithfulness, courage, and such more, that, if I had not been a piece of a logician before I came to him, I think he would have persuaded me to have wished myself a horse. But thus much at least with his no few words he drove into me, that self-love is better than any gilding to make that seem gorgeous wherein ourselves are parties. Wherein, if Pugliano's strong affection and weak arguments will not satisfy you, I will give you a nearer example of myself, who (I know not by what mischance) in these my not old years and idlest times having slipped into the title of a poet, am provoked to say something unto you in the defense of that my unelected vocation, which if I handle with more good will than good reasons, bear with me, since the scholar is to be pardoned that followeth the steps of his mas-

---

AN APOLOGY FOR POETRY. The essay was written in 1583 and published in two versions in 1595, the *Defence of Poesie* and the *Apologie for Poetrie*. The text is based on the second version.

[1]"Pedantry," or pointless learning.

ter. And yet I must say that, as I have just cause to make a pitiful defense of poor Poetry, which from almost the highest estimation of learning is fallen to be the laughingstock of children, so have I need to bring some more available proofs, since the former is by no man barred of his deserved credit, the silly latter hath had even the names of philosophers used to the defacing of it, with great danger of civil war among the Muses.

And first, truly, to all them that professing learning inveigh against poetry may justly be objected, that they go very near to ungratefulness, to seek to deface that which, in the noblest nations and languages that are known, hath been the first light-giver to ignorance, and first nurse, whose milk by little and little enabled them to feed afterwards of tougher knowledges. And will they now play the hedgehog that, being received into the den, drove out his host, or rather the vipers, that with their birth kill their parents? Let learned Greece in any of her manifold sciences be able to show me one book before Musaeus, Homer, and Hesiod, all three nothing else but poets. Nay, let any history be brought that can say any writers were there before them, if they were not men of the same skill, as Orpheus, Linus, and some other are named, who, having been the first of that country that made pens deliverers of their knowledge to their posterity, may justly challenge to be called their fathers in learning, for not only in time they had this priority (although in itself antiquity be venerable) but went before them, as causes to draw with their charming sweetness the wild untamed wits to an admiration of knowledge, so, as Amphion was said to move stones with his poetry to build Thebes, and Orpheus to be listened to by beasts—indeed stony and beastly people. So among the Romans were Livius Andronicus, and Ennius. So in the Italian language the first that made it aspire to be a treasurehouse of science were the poets Dante, Boccaccio, and Petrarch. So in our English were Gower and Chaucer.

After whom, encouraged and delighted with their excellent foregoing, others have followed, to beautify our mother tongue, as well in the same kind as in other arts. This did so notably show itself, that the philosophers of Greece durst not a long time appear to the world but under the masks of poets. So Thales, Empedocles, and Parmenides sang their natural philosophy in verses; so did Pythagoras and Phocylides their moral counsels; so did Tyrtaeus in war matters, and Solon in matters of policy:[2] or rather, they, being poets, did exercise their delightful vein in those points of highest knowledge, which before them lay hid to the world. For that wise Solon was directly a poet it is manifest, having written in verse the notable fable of the Atlantic Island, which was continued by Plato.

And truly, even Plato, whosoever well considereth shall find that in the body of his work, though the inside and strength were philosophy, the skin as it were and beauty depended most of poetry: for all standeth upon dialogues, wherein he feigneth many honest burgesses of Athens to speak of such matters, that, if they had been set on the rack, they would never have confessed them, besides his poetical describing the circumstances of their meetings, as the well ordering of a banquet, the delicacy of a walk, with interlacing mere tales, as Gyges' Ring,[3] and others, which who knoweth not to be flowers of poetry did never walk into Apollo's garden.

And even historiographers (although their lips sound of things done, and verity be written in their foreheads) have been glad to borrow both fashion and perchance weight of poets. So Herodotus entitled his history by the name of the nine Muses; and both he and all the rest that followed him either stole or usurped of poetry their passionate describing of passions, the many particularities of battles, which no man could affirm, or, if that be denied me, long orations put in the mouths of great kings and captains, which it is certain they never pronounced. So that, truly, neither philosopher nor historiographer could at the first have entered into the gates of popular judgments, if they had not taken a great passport of poetry, which in all nations at this day, were learning flourisheth not, is plain to be seen, in all which they have some feeling of poetry. In Turkey, besides their lawgiving divines, they have no other writers but poets. In our neighbor country Ireland, where truly learning goeth very bare, yet are their poets held in a devout reverence. Even among the most barbarous and simple Indians where no writing is, yet have they their poets, who make and sing songs, which they call *areytos,* both of their ancestors' deeds and praises of their gods—a sufficient probability that, if ever learning come among them, it must be by having their hard dull wits softened and sharpened with the sweet delights of poetry. For until they find a pleasure in the exercises of the mind, great promises of much knowledge will little persuade

them that know not the fruits of knowledge. In Wales, the true remnant of the ancient Britons, as there are good authorities to show the long time they had poets, which they called bards, so through all the conquests of Romans, Saxons, Danes, and Normans, some of whom did seek to ruin all memory of learning from among them, yet do their poets, even to this day, last; so as it is not more notable in soon beginning than in long continuing. But since the authors of most of our sciences were the Romans, and before them the Greeks, let us a little stand upon their authorities, but even so far as to see what names they have given unto this now scorned skill.

Among the Romans a poet was called *vates,* which is as much as a diviner, foreseer, or prophet, as by his conjoined words *vaticinium* and *vaticinari* is manifest: so heavenly a title did that excellent people bestow upon this heart-ravishing knowledge. And so far were they carried into the admiration thereof, that they thought in the chanceable hitting upon any such verses great foretokens of their following fortunes were placed. Whereupon grew the word of *sortes Virgilianae,* when, by sudden opening Virgil's book, they lighted upon any verse of his making: whereof the histories of the emperors' lives are full, as of Albinus, the governor of our island, who in his childhood met with this verse, *"Arma amens capio nec sat rationis in armis";*[4] and in his age performed it: which, although it were a very vain and godless superstition, as also it was to think that spirits were commanded by such verses—whereupon this word charms, derived of *carmina,* ''cometh''—so yet serveth it to show the great reverence those wits were held in. And altogether not without ground, since both the Oracles of Delphos and Sibylla's prophecies were wholly delivered in verses. For that same exquisite observing of number and measure in words, and that high flying liberty of conceit proper to the poet, did seem to have some divine force in it.

And may not I presume a little further, to show the reasonableness of this word *vates,* and say that the holy David's Psalms are a divine poem? If I do, I shall not do it without the testimony of great learned men, both ancient and modern. But even the name Psalms will speak for me, which, being interpreted, is nothing but ''songs''; then that it is fully written in meter, as all learned Hebricians agree, although the rules be not yet fully found; lastly and principally, his handling his prophecy, which is merely poetical. For what else is the awaking his musical instruments, the often and

---

[2]Sidney tends to blur traditional distinctions between poetry and other kinds of writing.

[3]In *Republic,* II, Plato tells of the descent of Gyges, a shepherd boy, into a chasm in which he finds a ring that can render him invisible.

---

[4]''Insane, I take arms, nor is there reason for arms.'' *Aeneid,* II. 314.

free changing of persons, his notable *prosopopeias*,[5] when he maketh you, as it were, see God coming in his majesty, his telling of the beasts' joyfulness, and hills' leaping, but a heavenly poesy, wherein almost he showeth himself a passionate lover of that unspeakable and everlasting beauty to be seen by the eyes of the mind, only cleared by faith? But truly now having named him, I fear me I seem to profane that holy name, applying it to poetry, which is among us thrown down to so ridiculous an estimation. But they that with quiet judgments will look a little deeper into it, shall find the end and working of it such, as, being rightly applied, deserveth not to be scourged out of the church of God.

But now, let us see how the Greeks named it, and how they deemed of it. The Greeks called him "a poet," which name hath, as the most excellent, gone through other languages. It cometh of this word *poiein,* which is "to make": wherein, I know not whether by luck or wisdom, we Englishmen have met with the Greeks in calling him a *maker:* which name, how high and incomparable a title it is, I had rather were known by marking the scope of other sciences than by my partial allegation.

There is no art delivered to mankind that hath not the works of nature for his principal object, without which they could not consist, and on which they so depend, as they become actors and players, as it were, of what nature will have set forth. So doth the astronomer look upon the stars, and, by that he seeth, setteth down what order nature hath taken therein. So do the geometrician and arithmetician in their diverse sorts of quantities. So doth the musician in times tell you which by nature agree, which not. The natural philosopher thereon hath his name, and the moral philosopher standeth upon the natural virtues, vices, and passions of man; and "follow nature" (saith he) "therein, and thou shalt not err." The lawyer saith what men have determined; the historian what men have done. The grammarian speaketh only of the rules of speech; and the rhetorician and logician, considering what in nature will soonest prove and persuade, thereon give artificial rules, which still are compassed within the circle of a question according to the proposed matter. The physician weigheth the nature of a man's body, and the nature of things helpful or hurtful unto it. And the metaphysic, though it be in the second and abstract notions, and therefore be counted supernatural, yet doth he indeed build upon the depth of nature. Only the poet, disdaining to be tied to any such subjection, lifted up with the vigor of his own invention, doth grow in effect another nature, in making things

either better than nature bringeth forth, or, quite anew, forms such as never were in nature, as the Heroes, Demigods, Cyclopes, Chimeras, Furies, and such like: so as he goeth hand in hand with nature, not enclosed within the narrow warrant of her gifts, but freely ranging only within the zodiac of his own wit.[6]

Nature never set forth the earth in so rich tapestry as divers poets have done—neither with pleasant rivers, fruitful trees, sweet-smelling flowers, nor whatsoever else may make the too much loved earth more lovely. Her world is brazen, the poets only deliver a golden. But let those things alone, and go to man—for whom as the other things are, so it seemeth in him her uttermost cunning is employed—and know whether she have brought forth so true a lover as Theagenes, so constant a friend as Pylades, so valiant a man as Orlando, so right a prince as Xenophon's Cyrus, so excellent a man every way as Virgil's Aeneas. Neither let this be jestingly conceived, because the works of the one be essential, the other in imitation or fiction; for any understanding knoweth the skill of the artificer standeth in that idea or foreconceit of the work, and not in the work itself. And that the poet hath that idea is manifest, by delivering them forth in such excellency as he hath imagined them. Which delivering forth also is not wholly imaginative, as we are wont to say by them that build castles in the air: but so far substantially it worketh, not only to make a Cyrus, which had been but a particular excellency, as nature might have done, but to bestow a Cyrus upon the world, to make many Cyruses, if they will learn aright why and how that maker made him.

Neither let it be deemed too saucy a comparison to balance the highest point of man's wit with the efficacy of nature; but rather give right honor to the heavenly Maker of that maker, who, having made man to his own likeness, set him beyond and over all the works of that second nature: which in nothing he showeth so much as in poetry, when with the force of a divine breath he bringeth things forth far surpassing her doings, with no small argument to the incredulous of that first accursed fall of Adam, since our erected wit maketh us know what perfection is, and yet our infected will keepeth us from reaching unto it. But these arguments will by few be understood, and by fewer granted. Thus much (I hope) will be given me, that the Greeks with some probability of reason gave him the name above all names of learning. Now let us go to a more ordinary opening of him, that the truth may be more palpable: and so I hope, though we

---

[5]"Personification."

[6]This paragraph is perhaps the most famous in the *Apology*. Compare to Scaliger, *Poetics.*

get not so unmatched a praise as the etymology of his names will grant, yet his very description, which no man will deny, shall not justly be barred from a principal commendation.

Poesy therefore is an art of imitation, for so Aristotle[7] termeth it in his word *mimesis,* that is to say, a representing, counterfeiting, or figuring forth—to speak metaphorically, a speaking picture; with this end, to teach and delight.[8] Of this have been three several kinds. The chief, both in antiquity and excellency, were they that did imitate the inconceivable excellencies of God. Such were David in his Psalms; Solomon in his Song of Songs, in his Ecclesiastes, and Proverbs; Moses and Deborah in their Hymns; and the writer of Job, which, beside other, the learned Emanuel Tremellius and Franciscus Junius do entitle the poetical part of the Scripture. Against these none will speak that hath the Holy Ghost in due holy reverence.

In this kind, though in a full wrong divinity, were Orpheus, Amphion, Homer in his *Hymns,* and many other, both Greeks and Romans, and this poesy must be used by whosoever will follow St. James's counsel in singing psalms when they are merry, and I know is used with the fruit of comfort by some, when, in sorrowful pangs of their death-bringing sins, they find the sonsolation of the never-leaving goodness.

The second kind is of them that deal with matters, philosophical: either moral, as Tyrtaeus, Phocylides, and Cato; or natural, as Lucretius and Virgil's *Georgics;* or astronomical, as Manilius and Pontanus; or historical, as Lucan;[9] which who mislike, the fault is in their judgments quite out of taste, and not in the sweet food of sweetly uttered knowledge. But because this second sort is wrapped within the fold of the proposed subject, and takes not the course of his own invention, whether they properly be poets or no let grammarians dispute; and go to the third, indeed right poets, of whom chiefly this question ariseth, betwixt whom and these second is such a kind of difference as betwixt the meaner sort of painters, who counterfeit only such faces as are set before them, and the more excellent, who, having no law but wit, bestow that in colors upon you which is fittest for the eye to see, as the constant though lamenting look of Lucretia, when she punished in herself another's fault.

Wherein he painteth not Lucretia whom he never saw, but painteth the outward beauty of such a virtue. For these third be they which most properly do imitate to teach and delight, and to imitate borrow nothing of what is, hath been,

or shall be; but range, only reined with learned discretion, into the divine consideration of what may be, and should be.[10] These be they that, as the first and most noble sort may justly be termed *vates,* so these are waited on in the excellentest languages and best understandings, with the foredescribed name of poets; for these indeed do merely make to imitate, and imitate both to delight and teach, and delight to move men to take that goodness in hand, which without delight they would fly as from a stranger, and teach, to make them know that goodness whereunto they are moved: which being the noblest scope to which ever any learning was directed, yet want there not idle tongues to bark at them. These be subdivided into sundry more special denominations. The most notable be the heroic, lyric, tragic, comic, satiric, iambic, elegiac, pastoral, and certain others, some of these being termed according to the matter they deal with, some by the sorts of verses they liked best to write in; for indeed the greatest part of poets have appareled their poetical inventions in that numbrous kind of writing which is called verse—indeed but appareled, verse being but an ornament and no cause to poetry, since there have been many most excellent poets that never versified, and now swarm many versifiers that need never answer to the name of poets. For Xenophon, who did imitate so excellently as to give us *effigiem iusti imperii,* "the portraiture of a just empire," under name of Cyrus (as Cicero saith of him), made therein an absolute heroical poem.

So did Heliodorus in his sugared invention of that picture of love in *Theagenes and Chariclea;* and yet both these writ in prose: which I speak to show that it is not rhyming and versing that maketh a poet—no more than a long gown maketh an advocate, who though he pleaded in armor should be an advocate and no soldier.[11] But it is that feigning notable images of virtues, vices, or what else, with that delightful teaching, which must be the right describing note to know a poet by, although indeed the senate of poets hath chosen verse as their fittest raiment, meaning, as in matter they passed all in all, so in manner to go beyond them—not speaking (table talk fashion or like men in a dream) words as they chanceably fall from the mouth, but peising[12] each syllable of each word by just proportion according to the dignity of the subject.

Now therefore it shall not be amiss first to weigh this latter sort of poetry by his works, and then by his parts, and, if in neither of these anatomies he be condemnable, I hope

---

[7]See *Poetics,* I. 2, p. 50.

[8]See Horace, *Art of Poetry,* pp. 73 and n. 27.

[9]Castelvetro excludes some of these men from the ranks of poets. See *The Poetics of Aristotle,* p. 135. Scaliger admits Lucan.

[10]See Aristotle, *Poetics,* IX. 2, p. 55.

[11]Sidney follows the Aristotelian idea here. Compare Aristotle, *Poetics,* IX. 2, p. 55.

[12]Giving weight to.

we shall obtain a more favorable sentence. This purifying of wit, this enriching of memory, enabling of judgment, and enlarging of conceit, which commonly we call learning, under what name soever it come forth, or to what immediate end soever it be directed, the final end is to lead and draw us to as high a perfection as our degenerate souls, made worse by their clayey lodgings, can be capable of. This, according to the inclination of the man, bred many formed impressions. For some that thought this felicity principally to be gotten by knowledge and no knowledge to be so high and heavenly as acquaintance with the stars, gave themselves to astronomy; others, persuading themselves to be demigods if they knew the causes of things, became natural and supernatural philosophers; some an admirable delight drew to music; and some the certainty of demonstration to the mathematics. But all, one and other, having this scope—to know, and by knowledge to lift up the mind from the dungeon of the body to the enjoying his own divine essence. But when by the balance of experience it was found that the astronomer looking to the stars might fall into a ditch, that the inquiring philosopher might be blind in himself, and the mathematician might draw forth a straight line with a crooked heart, then, lo, did proof, the overruler of opinions, make manifest that all these are but serving sciences, which, as they have each a private end in themselves, so yet are they all directed to the highest end of the mistress-knowledge, by the Greeks called *architectonike,* which stands (as I think) in the knowledge of a man's self, in the ethic and politic consideration, with the end of well doing and not of well knowing only—even as the saddler's next end is to make a good saddle, but his farther end to serve a nobler faculty, which is horsemanship; so the horseman's to soldiery, and the soldier not only to have the skill, but to perform the practice of a soldier. So that, the ending end of all earthly learning being virtuous action, those skills, that most serve to bring forth that, have a most just title to be princes over all the rest. Wherein we can show the poet's nobleness, by setting him before his other competitors, among whom as principal challengers step forth the moral philosophers, whom, me thinketh, I see coming towards me with a sullen gravity, as though they could not abide vice by daylight, rudely clothed for to witness outwardly their contempt of outward things, with books in their hands against glory, whereto they set their names, sophistically speaking against subtlety, and angry with any man in whom they see the foul fault of anger. These men casting largesse as they go of definitions, divisions, and distinctions, with a scornful interrogative do soberly ask whether it be possible to find any path so ready to lead a man to virtue as that which teacheth what virtue is—and teacheth it not only by delivering forth his very being, his causes, and effects, but also by making known his enemy, vice (which must be destroyed), and his cumbersome servant, passion (which must be mastered), by showing the generalities that containeth it, and the specialities that are derived from it; lastly, by plain setting down, how it extendeth itself out of the limits of a man's own little world to the government of families, and maintaining of public societies.

The historian scarcely giveth leisure to the moralist to say so much, but that he, laden with old mouse-eaten records, authorizing himself (for the most part) upon other histories, whose greatest authorities are built upon the notable foundation of hearsay; having much ado to accord differing writers and to pick truth out of partiality; better acquainted with a thousand years ago than with the present age, and yet better knowing how this world goeth than how his own wit runneth; curious for antiquities and inquisitive of novelties; a wonder to young folks and a tyrant in table talk, denieth, in a great chafe, that any man for teaching of virtue, and virtuous actions, is comparable to him. "I am *'lux vitae, temporum magistra, vita memoriae, nuntia vetustatis,'* " &c.[13]

The philosopher (saith he)

teacheth a disputative virtue, but I do an active. His virtue is excellent in the dangerless Academy of Plato, but mine showeth forth her honorable face in the battles of Marathon, Pharsalia, Poitiers, and Agincourt. He teacheth virtue by certain abstract considerations, but I only bid you follow the footing of them that have gone before you. Old-aged experience goeth beyond the fine-witted philosopher, but I give the experience of many ages. Lastly, if he make the song book, I put the learner's hand to the lute; and if he be the guide, I am the light.

Then would he allege you innumerable examples, conferring story by story, how much the wisest senators and princes have been directed by the credit of history, as Brutus, Alphonsus of Aragon, and who not, if need be? At length the long line of their disputation maketh a point in this, that the one giveth the precept, and the other the example.

Now, whom shall we find (since the question standeth for the highest form in the school of learning) to be moderator? Truly, as me seemeth, the poet; and if not a moderator, even the man that ought to carry the title from them both, and much more from all other serving sciences. Therefore

---

[13]"The light of life, the master of the times, the life of memory, the messenger of antiquity." Cicero, *On Oratory,* II. ix. 36.

compare we the poet with the historian, and with the moral philosopher; and, if he go beyond them both, no other human skill can match him. For as for the Divine, with all reverence it is ever to be excepted, not only for having his scope as far beyond any of these as eternity exceedeth a moment, but even for passing each of these in themselves.

And for the lawyer, though Jus be the daughter of justice, and justice the chief of virtues, yet because he seeketh to make men good rather *formidine poenae* than *virtutis amore*,[14] or, to say righter, doth not endeavor to make men good, but that their evil hurt not others, having no care, so he be a good citizen, how bad a man he be: therefore, as our wickedness maketh him necessary, and necessity maketh him honorable, so is he not in the deepest truth to stand in rank with these who all endeavor to take naughtiness away, and plant goodness even in the secretest cabinet of our souls. And these four are all that any way deal in that consideration of men's manners, which being the supreme knowledge, they that best breed it deserve the best commendation.

The philosopher therefore and the historian are they which would win the goal, the one by precept, the other by example. But both, not having both, do both halt. For the philosopher, setting down with thorny argument the bare rule, is so hard of utterance, and so misty to be conceived, that one that hath no other guide but him shall wade in him till he be old before he shall find sufficient cause to be honest. For his knowledge standeth so upon the abstract and general, that happy is that man who may understand him, and more happy that can apply what he doth understand.

On the other side, the historian, wanting the precept, is so tied, not to what should be but to what is, to the particular truth of things and not to the general reason of things, that his example draweth no necessary consequence, and therefore a less fruitful doctrine.

Now doth the peerless poet perform both: for whatsoever the philosopher saith should be done, he giveth a perfect picture of it in someone by whom he presupposeth it was done; so as he coupleth the general notion with the particular example. A perfect picture I say, for he yieldeth to the powers of the mind an image of that whereof the philosopher bestoweth but a wordish description: which doth neither strike, pierce, nor possess the sight of the soul so much as that other doth.[15]

---

[14]"Through fear of punishment" rather than through "love of virtue."

[15]Sidney's placing poetry midway between the precept of philosophy and the example of history leads to allegorical readings of poems and gives a new meaning to the idea of the poem as a "speaking picture." The original comparison to philosophy and history is Aristotle's. See *Poetics*, I. 7–8, and IX. 1–4, pp. 50 and 55.

For as in outward things, to a man that had never seen an elephant or a rhinoceros, who should tell him most exquisitely all their shapes, color, bigness, and particular marks, or of a gorgeous palace the architecture, with declaring the full beauties might well make the hearer able to repeat, as it were by rote, all he had heard, yet should never satisfy his inward conceits with being witness to itself of a true lively knowledge: but the same man, as soon as he might see those beasts well painted, or the house well in model, should straightways grow, without need of any description, to a judicial comprehending of them: so no doubt the philosopher with his learned definition—be it of virtue, vices, matters of public policy or private government—replenisheth the memory with many infallible grounds of wisdom, which, notwithstanding, lie dark before the imaginative and judging power, if they be not illuminated or figured forth by the speaking picture of poesy.

Tully taketh much pains, and many times not without poetical helps, to make us know the force love of our country hath in us. Let us but hear old Anchises speaking in the midst of Troy's flames, or see Ulysses in the fullness of all Calypso's delights bewail his absence from barren and beggarly Ithaca. Anger, the Stoics say, was a short madness: let but Sophocles bring you Ajax on a stage, killing and whipping sheep and oxen, thinking them the army of Greeks, with their chieftains Agamemnon and Menelaus, and tell me if you have not a more familiar insight into anger than finding in the schoolmen his genus and difference. See whether wisdom and temperance in Ulysses and Diomedes, valor in Achilles, friendship in Nisus and Euryalus, even to an ignorant man carry not an apparent shining, and, contrarily, the remorse of conscience in Oedipus, the soon repenting pride of Agamemnon, the self-devouring cruelty in his father Atreus, the violence of ambition in the two Theban brothers, the sour-sweetness of revenge in Medea, and, to fall lower, the Terentian Gnatho and our Chaucer's Pandar so expressed that we now use their names to signify their trades; and finally, all virtues, vices, and passions so in their own natural seats laid to the view, that we seem not to hear of them, but clearly to see through them. But even in the most excellent determination of goodness, what philosopher's counsel can so readily direct a prince, as the feigned Cyrus in Xenophon; or a virtuous man in all fortunes, as Aeneas in Virgil; or a whole commonwealth, as the way of Sir Thomas More's *Utopia?* I say the way, because where Sir Thomas More erred, it was the fault of the man and not of the poet, for that way of patterning a commonwealth was most absolute, though he perchance hath not so absolutely performed it. For the question is, whether the feigned image of poesy or the regular instruction of philosophy hath the more force in teaching: wherein if the philosophers have more rightly showed themselves philosophers than the poets have attained to the high top of their profession, as in truth, *"mediocribus esse poetis, / Non dii, non homines, non concessere columnae"*; [16] it is, I say again, not the fault of the art, but that by few men that art can be accomplished.

Certainly, even our Saviour Christ could as well have given the moral commonplaces of uncharitableness and humbleness as the divine narration of Dives and Lazarus; or of disobedience and mercy, as that heavenly discourse of the lost child and the gracious father; but that his through-searching wisdom knew the estate of Dives burning in hell, and of Lazarus being in Abraham's bosom, would more constantly (as it were) inhabit both the memory and judgment. Truly, for myself, meseems I see before my eyes the lost child's disdainful prodigality, turned to envy a swine's dinner: which by the learned divines are thought not historical acts, but instructing parables. For conclusion, I say the philosopher teacheth, but he teacheth obscurely, so as the learned only can understand him; that is to say, he teacheth them that are already taught. But the poet is the food for the tenderest stomachs, the poet is indeed the right popular philosopher, whereof Aesop's tales give good proof: whose pretty allegories, stealing under the formal tales of beasts, make many, more beastly than beasts, begin to hear the sound of virtue from these dumb speakers.

But now may it be alleged that, if this imagining of matters be so fit for the imagination, then must the historian needs surpass, who bringeth you images of true matters, such as indeed were done, and not such as fantastically or falsely may be suggested to have been done. Truly, Aristotle himself, in his discourse of poesy, plainly determineth this question, saying that poetry is *philosophoteron* and *spoudaioteron,* that is to say, it is more philosophical and more studiously serious than history. His reason is, because poesy dealeth with *katholou,* that is to say, with the universal consideration, and the history with *kathekaston,* the particular: "now," saith he, "the universal weighs what is fit to be said or done, either in likelihood or necessity (which the poesy considereth in his imposed names), and the particular only marks whether Alcibiades did, or suffered, this or that." [17] Thus far Aristotle: which reason of his (as all his) is most full of reason. For indeed, if the question were whether it were better to have a particular act truly or falsely set down, there is no doubt which is to be chosen, no more than whether you had rather have Vespasian's picture right as he

was, or at the painter's pleasure nothing resembling. But if the question be for your own use and learning, whether it be better to have it set down as it should be, or as it was, then certainly is more doctrinable the feigned Cyrus in Xenophon than the true Cyrus in Justin, and the feigned Aeneas in Virgil than the right Aeneas in Dares Phrygius.

As to a lady that desired to fashion her countenance to the best grace, a painter should more benefit her to portrait a most sweet face, writing Canidia upon it, than to paint Canidia as she was, who, Horace sweareth, was foul and ill favored.

If the poet do his part aright, he will show you in Tantalus, Atreus, and such like, nothing that is not to be shunned; in Cyrus, Aeneas, Ulysses, each thing to be followed; where the historian, bound to tell things as things were, cannot be liberal (without he will be poetical) of a perfect pattern, but, as in Alexander or Scipio himself, show doings, some to be liked, some to be misliked. And then how will you discern what to follow but by your own discretion, which you had without reading Quintus Curtius? And whereas a man may say, though in universal consideration of doctrine the poet prevaileth, yet that the history, in his saying such a thing was done, doth warrant a man more in that he shall follow.

The answer is manifest: that if he stand upon that *was*— as if he should argue, because it rained yesterday, therefore it should rain today—then indeed it hath some advantage to a gross conceit; but if he know an example only informs a conjectured likelihood, and so go by reason, the poet doth so far exceed him, as he is to frame his example to that which is most reasonable, be it in warlike, politic, or private matters; where the historian in his bare *was* hath many times that which we call fortune to overrule the best wisdom. Many times he must tell events whereof he can yield no cause: or, if he do, it must be poetical. For that a feigned example hath as much force to teach as a true example (for as for to move, it is clear, since the feigned may be tuned to the highest key of passion), let us take one example wherein a poet and a historian do concur.

Herodotus and Justin do both testify that Zopyrus, King Darius's faithful servant, seeing his master long resisted by the rebellious Babylonians, feigned himself in extreme disgrace of his king: for verifying of which, he caused his own nose and ears to be cut off, and so flying to the Babylonians, was received, and for his known valor so far credited, that he did find means to deliver them over to Darius. Much like matter doth Livy record of Tarquinius and his son. Xenophon excellently feigneth such another stratagem performed by Abradates in Cyrus's behalf. Now would I fain know, if occasion be presented unto you to serve your prince by such

---

[16] "To poets to be second-rate is a privilege which neither men nor gods nor bookstalls ever allowed." Horace, *Art of Poetry,* p. 73.

[17] Aristotle, *Poetics,* IX. 2–4, p. 55.

an honest dissimulation, why you do not as well learn it of Xenophon's fiction as of the other's verity—and truly so much the better, as you shall save your nose by the bargain; for Abradates did not counterfeit so far. So then the best of the historian is subject to the poet; for whatsoever action, or faction, whatsoever counsel, policy, or war stratagem the historian is bound to recite, that may the poet (if he list) with his imitation make his own, beautifying it both for further teaching, and more delighting, as it pleaseth him, having all, from Dante's heaven to his hell, under the authority of his pen. Which if I be asked what poets have done so, as I might well name some, yet say I, and say again, I speak of the art, and not of the artificer.

Now, to that which commonly is attributed to the praise of histories, in respect of the notable learning is gotten by marking the success, as though therein a man should see virtue exalted and vice punished—truly that commendation is peculiar to poetry, and far off from history. For indeed poetry ever setteth virtue so out in her best colors, making Fortune her well-waiting handmaid, that one must needs be enamored of her. Well may you see Ulysses in a storm, and in other hard plights; but they are but exercises of patience and magnanimity, to make them shine the more in the near-following prosperity. And of the contrary part, if evil men come to the stage, they ever go out (as the tragedy writer answered to one that misliked the show of such persons) so manacled as they little animate folks to follow them. But the historian, being captived to the truth of a foolish world, is many times a terror from well doing, and an encouragement to unbridled wickedness.

For see we not valiant Miltiades rot in his fetters: the just Phocion and the accomplished Socrates put to death like traitors; the cruel Severus live prosperously; the excellent Severus miserably murdered; Sylla and Marius dying in their beds; Pompey and Cicero slain then when they would have thought exile a happiness?

See we not virtuous Cato driven to kill himself, and rebel Caesar so advanced that his name yet, after 1,600 years, lasteth in the highest honor? And mark but even Caesar's own words of the forenamed Sylla (who in that only did honestly, to put down his dishonest tyranny). *Literas nescivit,*[18] as if want of learning caused him to do well. He meant it not by poetry, which, not content with earthly plagues, deviseth new punishments in hell for tyrants, nor yet by philosophy, which teacheth *Occidendos esse;*[19] but no doubt by skill in history, for that indeed can afford your Cypselus, Periander, Phalaris, Dionysius, and I know not how many more

of the same kennel, that speed well enough in their abominable injustice or usurpation. I conclude, therefore, that he excelleth history, not only in furnishing the mind with knowledge, but in setting it forward to that which deserveth to be called and accounted good: which setting forward, and moving to well doing, indeed setteth the laurel crown upon the poet as victorious, not only of the historian, but over the philosopher, howsoever in teaching it may be questionable.

For suppose it be granted (that which I suppose with great reason may be denied) that the philosopher, in respect of his methodical proceeding, doth teach more perfectly than the poet, yet do I think that no man is so much *philophilosophos* as to compare the philosopher, in moving, with the poet.

And that moving is of a higher degree than teaching, it may by this appear, that it is well-nigh the cause and the effect of teaching. For who will be taught, if he be not moved with desire to be taught, and what so much good doth that teaching bring forth (I speak still of moral doctrine) as that it moveth one to do that which it doth teach? For, as Aristotle saith, it is not *gnosis* but *praxis*[20] must be the fruit. And how *praxis* cannot be, without being moved to practice, it is no hard matter to consider.

The philosopher showeth you the way, he informeth you of the particularities, as well of the tediousness of the way, as of the pleasant lodging you shall have when your journey is ended, as of the many by-turnings that may divert you from your way. But this is to no man but to him that will read him, and read him with attentive studious painfulness; which constant desire whosoever hath in him, hath already passed half the hardness of the way, and therefore is beholding to the philosopher but for the other half. Nay truly, learned men have learnedly thought that where once reason hath so much overmastered passion as that the mind hath a free desire to do well, the inward light each mind hath in itself is as good as a philosopher's book; seeing in nature we know it is well to do well, and what is well and what is evil, although not in the words of art which philosophers bestow upon us. For out of natural conceit the philosophers drew it; but to be moved to do that which we know, or to be moved with desire to know, *Hoc opus, hic labor est.*[21]

Now therein of all sciences (I speak still of human, and according to the humane conceits) is our poet the monarch. For he doth not only show the way, but giveth so sweet a prospect into the way, as will entice any man to enter into it. Nay, he doth, as if your journey should lie through a fair vineyard, at the first give you a cluster of grapes, that, full of

---

[18]"He was ignorant of literature."
[19]"They are to be put to death."

[20]Not "knowledge" but "action."
[21]"This the work, this the labor." *Aeneid,* VI. 129.

that taste, you may long to pass further. He beginneth not with obscure definitions, which must blur the margent[22] with interpretations, and load the memory with doubtfulness; but he cometh to you with words set in delightful proportion, either accompanied with, or prepared for, the well-enchanting skill of music; and with a tale forsooth he cometh unto you, with a tale which holdeth children from play, and old men from the chimney corner. And, pretending no more, doth intend the winning of the mind from wickedness to virtue: even as the child is often brought to take most wholesome things by hiding them in such other as have a pleasant taste: which, if one should begin to tell them the nature of aloes or rhubarb they should receive, would sooner take their physic at their ears than at their mouth. So is it in men (most of which are childish in the best things, till they be cradled in their graves): glad they will be to hear the tales of Hercules, Achilles, Cyrus, and Aeneas; and, hearing them, must needs hear the right description of wisdom, valor, and justice; which, if they had been barely, that is to say philosophically, set out, they would swear they be brought to school again.

That imitation whereof poetry is, hath the most conveniency to nature of all other, insomuch that, as Aristotle saith, those things which in themselves are horrible, as cruel battles, unnatural monsters, are made in poetical imitation delightful. Truly, I have known men, that even with reading *Amadis de Gaule* (which God knoweth wanteth much of a perfect poesy) have found their hearts moved to the exercise of courtesy, liberality, and especially courage.

Who readeth Aeneas carrying old Anchises on his back, that wisheth not it were his fortune to perform so excellent an act? Whom do not the words of Turnus move, the tale of Turnus having planted his image in the imagination?—*"Fugientem haec terra videbit? / Usque adeone mori miserum est?"*[23] Where the philosophers, as they scorn to delight, so must they be content little to move, saving wrangling whether virtue be the chief or the only good, whether the contemplative or the active life do excel: which Plato and Boethius well knew, and therefore made Mistress Philosophy very often borrow the masking raiment of Poesy. For even those hardhearted evil men who think virtue a school name, and know no other good but *indulgere genio*,[24] and therefore despise the austere admonitions of the philosopher, and feel not the inward reason they stand upon, yet will be content to be delighted—which is all the good fellow poet seemeth to promise—and so steal to see the form of good-

ness, which seen they cannot but love ere themselves be aware, as if they took a medicine of cherries. Infinite proofs of the strange effects of this poetical invention might be alleged; only two shall serve, which are so often remembered as I think all men know them.

The one of Menenius Agrippa, who, when the whole people of Rome had resolutely divided themselves from the Senate, with apparent show of utter ruin, though he were (for that time) an excellent orator, came not among them upon trust of figurative speeches or cunning insinuations, and much less with farfetched maxims of philosophy, which (especially if they were Platonic) they must have learned geometry before they could well have conceived; but forsooth he behaves himself like a homely and familiar poet. He telleth them a tale, that there was a time when all the parts of the body made a mutinous conspiracy against the belly, which they thought devoured the fruits of each other's labor: they concluded they would let so unprofitable a spender starve. In the end, to be short (for the tale is notorious, and as notorious that it was a tale), with punishing the belly they plagued themselves. This applied by him wrought such effect in the people, as I never read that ever words brought forth but then so sudden and so good an alteration; for upon reasonable conditions a perfect reconcilement ensued. The other is of Nathan the Prophet, who, when the holy David had so far forsaken God as to confirm adultery with murder, when he was to do the tenderest office of a friend, in laying his own shame before his eyes, sent by God to call again so chosen a servant, how doth he it but by telling of a man whose beloved lamb was ungratefully taken from his bosom?—the application most divinely true, but the discourse itself feigned. Which made David (I speak of the second and instrumental cause) as in a glass to see his own filthiness, as that heavenly Psalm of Mercy well testifieth.

By these, therefore, examples and reasons, I think it may be manifest that the poet, with that same hand of delight, doth draw the mind more effectually than any other art doth: and so a conclusion not unfitly ensueth, that, as virtue is the most excellent resting place for all worldly learning to make his end of, so poetry, being the most familiar to teach it, and most princely to move towards it, in the most excellent work is the most excellent workman. But I am content not only to decipher him by his works (although works in commendation or dispraise must ever hold an high authority), but more narrowly will examine his parts: so that, as in a man, though all together may carry a presence full of majesty and beauty, perchance in some one defectious piece we may find a blemish. Now in his parts, kinds, or species (as you list to term them), it is to be noted that some poesies have coupled together two or three kinds, as tragical and comical, whereupon is risen the tragicomical. Some, in the

---

[22]In Sidney's day, the margins of the page were often used for notes.
[23]"Will this land see [Turnus] in flight? Is it so miserable to die?" *Aeneid*, XII. 645–46.
[24]"To indulge one's nature."

like manner, have mingled prose and verse, as Sannazzaro and Boethius. Some have mingled matters heroical and pastoral. But that cometh all to one in this question, for, if severed they be good, the conjunction cannot be hurtful. Therefore, perchance forgetting some, and leaving some as needless to be remembered, it shall not be amiss in a word to cite the special kinds, to see what faults may be found in the right use of them.

Is it then the pastoral poem which is misliked? For perchance where the hedge is lowest they will soonest leap over. Is the poor pipe disdained, which sometime out of Melibaeus' mouth can show the misery of people under hard lords or ravening soldiers, and again, by Tityrus, what blessedness is derived to them that lie lowest from the goodness of them that sit highest; sometimes, under the pretty tales of wolves and sheep, can include the whole considerations of wrongdoing and patience; sometimes show that contention for trifles can get but a trifling victory; where perchance a man may see that even Alexander and Darius, when they strave who should be cock of this world's dunghill, the benefit they got was that the afterlivers may say, *"Haec memini et victum frustra contendere Thirsin: / Ex illo Coridon, Coridon es tempore nobis"?*[25]

Or is it the lamenting elegiac, which in a kind heart would move rather pity than blame, who bewails with the great philosopher Heraclitus the weakness of mankind and the wretchedness of the world; who surely is to be praised, either for compassionate accompanying just causes of lamentation, or for rightly pointing out how weak be the passions of woefulness? Is it the bitter but wholesome iambic, which rubs the galled mind, in making shame the trumpet of villainy with bold and open crying out against naughtiness? Or the satiric, who *"omne vafer vitium ridenti tangit amico";*[26] who sportingly never leaveth until he make a man laugh at folly, and, at length ashamed, to laugh at himself, which he cannot avoid, without avoiding the folly; who, while *"circum praecordia ludit,"*[27] giveth us to feel how many headaches a passionate life bringeth us to; how, when all is done, *"est Ulubris animus si nos non deficit aequus?"*[28]

No, perchance it is the comic, whom naughty playmakers and stage-keepers have justly made odious. To the argument of abuse I will answer after. Only thus much now is to be said, that the comedy is an imitation of the common errors of our life, which he representeth in the most ridiculous and scornful sort that may be, so as it is impossible that any beholder can be content to be such a one.

Now, as in geometry the oblique must be known as well as the right, and in arithmetic the odd as well as the even, so in the actions of our life who seeth not the filthiness of evil wanteth a great foil to perceive the beauty of virtue. This doth the comedy handle so in our private and domestical matters, as with hearing it we get as it were an experience, what is to be looked for of a niggardly Demea, of a crafty Davus, of a flattering Gnatho, of a vainglorious Thraso; and not only to know what effects are to be expected, but to know who be such, by the signifying badge given them by the comedian. And little reason hath any man to say that men learn evil by seeing it so set out; since, as I said before, there is no man living but, by the force truth hath in nature, no sooner seeth these men play their parts, but wisheth them in *pistrinum;*[29] although perchance the sack of his own faults lie so behind his back that he seeth not himself dance the same measure; whereto yet nothing can more open his eyes than to find his own actions contemptibly set forth. So that the right use of comedy will (I think) by nobody be blamed, and much less of the high and excellent tragedy, that openeth the greatest wounds, and showeth forth the ulcers that are covered with tissue; that maketh kings fear to be tyrants, and tyrants manifest their tyrannical humors; that, with stirring the affects of admiration and commiseration, teacheth the uncertainty of this world, and upon how weak foundations gilden roofs are builded; that maketh us know, *"Qui sceptra saevus duro imperio regit, / Timet timentes, metus in auctorem redit."*[30]

But how much it can move, Plutarch yieldeth a notable testimony of the abominable tyrant Alexander Phaeraeus, from whose eyes a tragedy, well made and represented, drew abundance of tears, who, without all pity, had murdered infinite numbers, and some of his own blood, so as he, that was not ashamed to make matters for tragedies, yet could not resist the sweet violence of a tragedy.

And if it wrought no further good in him, it was that he, in despite of himself, withdrew himself from hearkening to that which might mollify his hardened heart. But it is not the tragedy they do mislike; for it were too absurd to cast out so excellent a representation of whatsoever is most worthy to be learned. Is it the lyric that most displeaseth, who with his turned lyre, and well-accorded voice, giveth praise, the reward of virtue, to virtuous acts, who gives moral precepts,

---

[25]"I remember those things, and that Thyrsus, conquered, strove in vain." Virgil, *Eclogue,* VII. 69–70.

[26]"The rogue touches every vice, while he makes his friend laugh." Persius, *Satires,* I. 116–17.

[27]"He plays about the heart."

[28]"Is happiness to be found in Ulubra if balance does not fail us?" Horace, *Epistles,* I. xi. 30

[29]A mill in which slaves were put to work as punishment.

[30]"The savage tyrant who wields his scepter with a heavy hand fears the timid, and fear returns to its author." Seneca, *Oedipus,* 705–06.

and natural problems, who sometimes raiseth up his voice to the height of the heavens, in singing the lauds of the immortal God? Certainly, I must confess my own barbarousness, I never heard the old song of Percy and Douglas[31] that I found not my heart moved more than with a trumpet; and yet is it sung but by some blind crowder, with no rougher voice than rude style; which, being so evil appareled in the dust and cobwebs of that uncivil age, what would it work, trimmed in the gorgeous eloquence of Pindar? In Hungary I have seen it the manner at all feasts, and other such meetings, to have songs of their ancestors' valor; which that right soldierlike nation think the chiefest kindlers of brave courage. The incomparable Lacedaemonians did not only carry that kind of music ever with them to the field, but even at home, as such songs were made, so were they all content to be the singers of them, when the lusty men were to tell what they did, the old men what they had done, and the young men what they would do. And where a man may say that Pindar many times praiseth highly victories of small moment, matters rather of sport than virtue; as it may be answered, it was the fault of the poet, and not of the poetry, so indeed the chief fault was in the time and custom of the Greeks, who set those toys at so high a price that Philip of Macedon reckoned a horse race won at Olympus among his three fearful felicities. But as the inimitable Pindar often did, so is that kind most capable and most fit to awake the thoughts from the sleep of idleness, to embrace honorable enterprises.

There rests the heroical, whose very name (I think) should daunt all backbiters; for by what conceit can a tongue be directed to speak evil of that which draweth with it no less champions than Achilles, Cyrus, Aeneas, Turnus, Tydeus, and Rinaldo? Who doth not only teach and move to a truth, but teacheth and moveth to the most high and excellent truth; who maketh magnanimity and justice shine throughout all misty fearfulness and foggy desires; who, if the saying of Plato and Tully[32] be true, that who could see virtue would be wonderfully ravished with the love of her beauty—this man sets her out to make her more lovely in her holiday apparel, to the eye of any that will deign not to disdain until they understand. But if anything be already said in the defense of sweet Poetry, all concurreth to the maintaining the heroical, which is not only a kind, but the best and most accomplished kind of poetry.[33] For as the image of each action stirreth and instructeth the mind, so the lofty image of such worthies most inflameth the mind with desire to be worthy, and in-

forms with counsel how to be worthy. Only let Aeneas be worn in the tablet of your memory, how he governeth himself in the ruin of his country, in the preserving his old father, and carrying away his religious ceremonies, in obeying the god's commandment to leave Dido, though not only all passionate kindness, but even the human consideration of virtuous gratefulness, would have craved other of him; how in storms, how in sports, how in war, how in peace, how a fugitive, how victorious, how besieged, how besieging, how to strangers, how to allies, how to enemies, how to his own; lastly, how in his inward self, and how in his outward government, and I think, in a mind not prejudiced with a prejudicating humor, he will be found in excellency fruitful, yea, even as Horace saith, *"melius Chrysippo et Crantore."*[34]

But truly I imagine it falleth out with these poetwhippers, as with some good women, who often are sick, but in faith they cannot tell where. So the name of poetry is odious to them, but neither his cause nor effects, neither the sum that contains him nor the particularities descending from him, give any fast handle to their carping dispraise.

Since then poetry is of all human learning the most ancient and of most fatherly antiquity, as from whence other learnings have taken their beginnings; since it is so universal that no learned nation doth despise it, nor no barbarous nation is without it; since both Roman and Greek gave divine names unto it, the one of *prophesying,* the other of *making,* and that indeed that name of *making* is fit for him, considering that whereas other arts retain themselves within their subject, and receive, as it were, their being from it, the poet only bringeth his own stuff, and doth not learn a conceit out of a matter, but maketh matter for a conceit; since neither his description nor his end containeth any evil, the thing described cannot be evil; since his effects be so good as to teach goodness and to delight the learners; since therein (namely in moral doctrine, the chief of all knowledges) he doth not only far pass the historian, but, for instructing, is well-nigh comparable to the philosopher, and, for moving, leaves him behind him; since the Holy Scripture (wherein there is no uncleanness) hath whole parts in it poetical, and that even our Saviour Christ vouchsafed to use the flowers of it; since all his kinds are not only in their united forms but in their severed dissections fully commendable; I think (and think I think rightly) the laurel crown appointed for triumphing captains doth worthily (of all other learnings) honor the poet's triumph. But because we have ears as well as tongues, and that the lightest reasons that may be will seem to weigh greatly, if nothing be put in the counterbalance, let us hear,

---

[31]The ballad *Chevy Chase,* one of the oldest ballads in English.
[32]Cicero.
[33]Here Sidney expresses a Renaissance attitude that is contrary to Aristotle, who favored tragedy over epic.

---

[34]"Better than Chrysippus and Crantor." *Epistles,* I. ii. 4.

and, as well as we can, ponder, what objections may be made against this art, which may be worthy either of yielding or answering.

First, truly I note not only in these *mysomousoi,* "poet-haters," but in all that kind of people who seek a praise by dispraising others, that they do prodigally spend a great many wandering words in quips and scoffs, carping and taunting at each thing, which, by stirring the spleen, may stay the brain from a thorough beholding the worthiness of the subject.

Those kind of objections, as they are full of very idle easiness, since there is nothing of so sacred a majesty but that an itching tongue may rub itself upon it, so deserve they no other answer, but, instead of laughing at the jest, to laugh at the jester. We know a playing wit can praise the discretion of an ass, the comfortableness of being in debt, and the jolly commodity of being sick of the plague. So of the contrary side, if we will turn Ovid's verse, *"Ut lateat virtus proximitate mali,"* that "good lie hid in nearness of the evil," Agrippa will be as merry in showing the vanity of science as Erasmus was in commending of folly.[35] Neither shall any man or matter escape some touch of these smiling railers. But for Erasmus and Agrippa, they had another foundation than the superficial part would promise. Marry, these other pleasant faultfinders, who will correct the verb before they understand the noun, and confute others' knowledge before they confirm their own, I would have them only remember that scoffing cometh not of wisdom; so as the best title in true English they get with their merriments is to be called good fools, for so have our grave forefathers ever termed that humorous kind of jesters. But that which giveth greatest scope to their scorning humors is rhyming and versing. It is already said (and, as I think, truly said) it is not rhyming and versing that maketh poesy. One may be a poet without versing, and a versifier without poetry. But yet presuppose it were inseparable (as indeed it seemeth Scaliger judgeth) truly it were an inseparable commendation.[36] For if *oratio* next to *ratio,* "speech" next to "reason," be the greatest gift bestowed upon mortality, that cannot be praiseless which doth most polish that blessing of speech; which considers each word, not only (as a man may say) by his forcible quality, but by his best measured quantity, carrying even in themselves a harmony (without, perchance, number, measure, order, proportion be in our time grown odious). But lay aside

the just praise it hath, by being the only fit speech for music (music, I say, the most divine striker of the senses), thus much is undoubtedly true, that if reading be foolish without remembering, memory being the only treasurer of knowledge, those words which are fittest for memory are likewise most convenient for knowledge.

Now, that verse far exceedeth prose in the knitting up of the memory, the reason is manifest—the words (besides their delight, which hath a great affinity to memory) being so set as one word cannot be lost but the whole work fails; which accuseth itself, calleth the remembrance back to itself, and so most strongly confirmeth it. Besides, one word so, as it were, begetting another, as, be it in rhyme or measured verse, by the former a man shall have a near guess to the follower: lastly, even they that have taught the art of memory have showed nothing so apt for it as a certain room divided into many places well and thoroughly known. Now, that hath the verse in effect perfectly, every word having his natural seat, which seat must needs make the words remembered. But what needeth more in a thing so known to all men? Who is it that ever was a scholar that doth not carry away some verses of Virgil, Horace, or Cato, which in his youth he learned, and even to his old age serve him for hourly lessons? But the fitness it hath for memory is notably proved by all delivery of arts: wherein for the most part, from grammar to logic, mathematic, physic, and the rest, the rules chiefly necessary to be borne away are compiled in verses. So that, verse being in itself sweet and orderly, and being best for memory, the only handle of knowledge, it must be in jest that any man can speak against it. Now then go we to the most important imputations laid to the poor poets. For aught I can yet learn, they are these. First, that there being many other more fruitful knowledges, a man might better spend his time in them than in this. Secondly, that it is the mother of lies. Thirdly, that it is the nurse of abuse, infecting us with many pestilent desires, with a siren's sweetness drawing the mind to the serpent's tale of sinful fancy—and herein, especially, comedies give the largest field to ear (as Chaucer saith)—how both in other nations and in ours, before poets did soften us, we were full of courage, given to martial exercises, the pillars of manlike liberty, and not lulled asleep in shady idleness with poets' pastimes. And lastly, and chiefly, they cry out with an open mouth, as if they outshot Robin Hood, that Plato banished them out of his commonwealth.[37] Truly, this is much, if there be much truth in it. First, to the first, that a man might better spend his time is a reason indeed: but it doth (as they say) but *petere*

[35]Sidney is referring to a treatise entitled *On the Uncertainty and Vanity of the Sciences and Art* by Henry Cornelius Agrippa (1486–1535), a German physician and astrologer, and to the famous satire *The Praise of Folly* by Desiderius Erasmus (1466?–1536), a Dutch humanist.
[36]See Scaliger's identification of poetry with verse, in *Poetics.*

[37]See *Republic,* pp. 22–23.

principium:[38] for if it be, as I affirm, that no learning is so good as that which teacheth and moveth to virtue, and that none can both teach and move thereto so much as poetry, then is the conclusion manifest that ink and paper cannot be to a more profitable purpose employed. And certainly, though a man should grant their first assumption, it should follow (methinks) very unwillingly, that good is not good because better is better. But I still and utterly deny that there is sprung out of earth a more fruitful knowledge. To the second therefore, that they should be the principal liars, I answer paradoxically, but truly, I think truly, that of all writers under the sun the poet is the least liar and, though he would, as a poet can scarcely be a liar. The astronomer, with his cousin the geometrician, can hardly escape, when they take upon them to measure the height of the stars.

How often, think you, do the physicians lie, when they aver things good for sicknesses, which afterwards send Charon a great number of souls drowned in a potion before they come to his ferry? And no less of the rest, which take upon them to affirm. Now, for the poet, he nothing affirms, and therefore never lieth. For, as I take it, to lie is to affirm that to be true which is false; so as the other artists, and especially the historian, affirming many things, can, in the cloudy knowledge of mankind, hardly escape from many lies. But the poet (as I said before) never affirmeth.[39] The poet never maketh any circles about your imagination, to conjure you to believe for true what he writes. He citeth not authorities of other histories, but even for his entry calleth the sweet Muses to inspire into him a good invention; in truth, no laboring to tell you what is, or is not, but what should or should not be. And therefore, though he recount things not true, yet because he telleth them not for true, he lieth not—without we will say that Nathan lied in his speech, before alleged, to David; which as a wicked man durst scarce say, so think I none so simple would say that Aesop lied in the tales of his beasts: for who thinks that Aesop writ it for actually true were well worthy to have his name chronicled among the beasts he writeth of.

What child is there that, coming to a play, and seeing *Thebes* written in great letters upon an old door, doth believe that it is Thebes? If then a man can arrive, at that child's age, to know that the poets' persons and doings are but pictures what should be, and not stories what have been, they will never give the lie to things not affirmatively but allegorically and figuratively written. And therefore, as in history, looking for truth, they go away full fraught with falsehood, so in poesy, looking for fiction, they shall use the narration but as an imaginative ground plot of a profitable invention.

But hereto is replied, that the poets give names to men they write of, which argueth a conceit of an actual truth, and so, not being true, proves a falsehood. And doth the lawyer lie then, when under the names of John a Stile and John a Noakes he puts his case? But that is easily answered. Their naming of men is but to make their picture the more lively, and not to build any history; painting men, they cannot leave men nameless. We see we cannot play at chess but that we must give names to our chessmen; and yet, methinks, he were a very partial champion of truth that would say we lied for giving a piece of wood the reverend title of a bishop. The poet nameth Cyrus or Aeneas no other way than to show what men of their fames, fortunes, and estates should do.

Their third is, how much it abuseth men's wit, training it to wanton sinfulness and lustful love: for indeed that is the principal, if not the only, abuse I can hear alleged. They say the comedies rather teach than reprehend amorous conceits. They say the lyric is larded with passionate sonnets, the elegiac weeps the want of his mistress, and that even to the heroical Cupid hath ambitiously climbed. Alas, Love, I would thou couldst as well defend thyself as thou canst offend others. I would those on whom thou dost attend could either put thee away, or yield good reason why they keep thee. But grant love of beauty to be a beastly fault (although it be very hard, since only man, and no beast, hath that gift to discern beauty); grant that lovely name of Love to deserve all hateful reproaches (although even some of my masters the philosophers spent a good deal of their lamp-oil in setting forth the excellency of it); grant, I say, whatsoever they will have granted; that not only love, but lust, but vanity, but (if they list) scurrility, possesseth many leaves of the poets' books: yet think I, when this is granted, they will find their sentence may with good manners put the last words foremost, and not say that poetry abuseth man's wit, but that man's wit abuseth poetry.

For I will not deny but that man's wit may make poesy, which should be *eikastike,* which some learned have defined, "figuring forth good things," to be *phantastike,* which doth, contrariwise, infect the fancy with unworthy objects,[40] as the painter, that should give to the eye either some excellent perspective, or some fine picture, fit for building or fortification, or containing in it some notable example, as Abraham sacrificing his son Isaac, Judith killing Holofernes, David fight-

---

[38]"Beg the question."
[39]Compare Wilde, *The Decay of Lying,* pp. 658–70.

[40]This distinction originates in Plato's *Sophist.* It is taken up by Mazzoni. See *On the Defense of the* Comedy *of Dante,* p. 166. Sidney puts a rather moralistic meaning on the terms in comparison to Mazzoni.

ing with Goliath, may leave those, and please an ill-pleased eye with wanton shows of better hidden matters. But what, shall the abuse of a thing make the right use odious? Nay truly, though I yield that poesy may not only be abused, but that being abused, by the reason of his sweet charming force, it can do more hurt than any other army of words, yet shall it be so far from concluding that the abuse should give reproach to the abused, that contrariwise it is a good reason, that whatsoever, being abused, doth most harm, being rightly used (and upon the right use each thing conceiveth his title), doth most good.

Do we not see the skill of physic (the best rampire to our often-assaulted bodies), being abused, teach poison, the most violent destroyer? Doth not knowledge of law, whose end is to even and right all things, being abused, grow the crooked fosterer of horrible injuries? Doth not (to go to the highest) God's word abused breed heresy, and his name abused become blasphemy? Truly, a needle cannot do much hurt, and as truly (with leave of ladies be it spoken) it cannot do much good. With a sword thou mayest kill thy father, and with a sword thou mayest defend thy prince and country. So that, as in their calling poets the fathers of lies they say nothing, so in this their argument of abuse they prove the commendation.

They allege herewith, that before poets began to be in price our nation hath set their heart's delight upon action, and not upon imagination, rather doing things worthy to be written, than writing things fit to be done. What that beforetime was, I think scarcely Sphinx can tell, since no memory is so ancient that hath the precedence of poetry. And certain it is that, in our plainest homeliness, yet never was the Albion nation without poetry. Marry, this argument, though it be leveled against poetry, yet is it indeed a chain-shot against all learning, or bookishness, as they commonly term it. Of such mind were certain Goths, of whom it is written that, having in the spoil of a famous city taken a fair library, one hangman, belike, fit to execute the fruits of their wits, who had murdered a great number of bodies, would have set fire to it. "No," said another very gravely, "take heed what you do, for while they are busy about these toys, we shall with more leisure conquer their countries."

This indeed is the ordinary doctrine of ignorance, and many words sometimes I have heard spent in it: but because this reason is generally against all learning, as well as poetry, or rather, all learning but poetry; because it were too large a digression to handle, or at least too superfluous (since it is manifest that all government of action is to be gotten by knowledge, and knowledge best by gathering many knowledges, which is reading), I only, with Horace, to him that is

of that opinion, *"iubeo stultum esse libenter"*;[41] for as for poetry itself, it is the freest from this objection. For poetry is the companion of the camps.

I dare undertake, Orlando Furioso, or honest King Arthur, will never displease a soldier: but the quiddity of *ens* and *prima materia* [42] will hardly agree with a corselet. And therefore, as I said in the beginning, even Turks and Tartars are delighted with poets. Homer, a Greek, flourished before Greece flourished. And if to a slight conjecture a conjecture may be opposed, truly it may seem, that, as by him their learned men took almost their first light of knowledge, so their active men received their first motions of courage. Only Alexander's example may serve, who by Plutarch is accounted of such virtue, that fortune was not his guide but his footstool; whose acts speak for him, though Plutarch did not—indeed the Phoenix of warlike princes. This Alexander left his schoolmaster, living Aristotle, behind him, but took dead Homer with him. He put the philosopher Callisthenes to death for his seeming philosophical, indeed mutinous, stubbornness, but the chief thing he ever was heard to wish for was that Homer had been alive. He well found he received more bravery of mind by the pattern of Achilles than by hearing the definition of fortitude: and therefore, if Cato misliked Fulvius for carrying Ennius with him to the field, it may be answered that, if Cato misliked it, the noble Fulvius liked it, or else he had not done it: for it was not the excellent Cato Uticensis (whose authority I would much more have reverenced), but it was the former, in truth a bitter punisher of faults, but else a man that had never well sacrificed to the Graces. He misliked and cried out upon all Greek learning, and yet, being eighty years old, began to learn it, belike fearing that Pluto understood not Latin. Indeed, the Roman laws allowed no person to be carried to the wars but he that was in the soldier's roll, and therefore, though Cato misliked his unmustered person, he misliked not his work. And if he had, Scipio Nasica, judged by common consent the best Roman, loved him. Both the other Scipio brothers, who had by their virtues no less surnames than of Asia and Afric, so loved him that they caused his body to be buried in their sepulcher. So as Cato's authority being but against his person, and that answered with so far greater than himself, is herein of no validity. But now indeed my burden is great; now Plato's name is laid upon me, whom, I must confess, of all philosophers I have ever esteemed most worthy of reverence, and with great reason, since of all philosophers he is the most poetical. Yet

---

[41] "I bid him be as foolish as he wishes." *Satires,* I. i. 63.
[42] The essential quality of "being" and "prime matter."

if he will defile the fountain out of which his flowing streams have proceeded, let us boldly examine with what reasons he did it. First truly, a man might maliciously object that Plato, being a philosopher, was a natural enemy of poets. For indeed, after the philosophers had picked out of the sweet mysteries of poetry the right discerning true points of knowledge, they forthwith, putting it in method, and making a school art of that which the poets did only teach by a divine delightfulness, beginning to spurn at their guides, like ungrateful 'prentices, were not content to set up shops for themselves, but sought by all means to discredit their masters; which by the force of delight being barred them, the less they could overthrow them, the more they hated them. For indeed, they found for Homer seven cities strove who should have him for their citizen; where many cities banished philosophers as not fit members to live among them. For only repeating certain of Euripides' verses, many Athenians had their lives saved of the Syracusians, when the Athenians themselves thought many philosophers unworthy to live.

Certain poets, as Simonides and Pindarus, had so prevailed with Hiero the First, that of a tyrant they made him a just king; where Plato could do so little with Dionysius, that he himself of a philosopher was made a slave. But who should do thus, I confess, should requite the objections made against poets with like cavillation against philosophers; as likewise one should do that should bid one read *Phaedrus* or *Symposium* in Plato, or the discourse of love in Plutarch, and see whether any poet do authorize abominable filthiness, as they do. Again, a man might ask out of what commonwealth Plato did banish them. In sooth, thence where he himself alloweth community of women. So as belike this banishment grew not for effeminate wantonness, since little should poetical sonnets be hurtful when a man might have what woman he listed. But I honor philosophical instructions, and bless the wits which bred them: so as they be not abused, which is likewise stretched to poetry.

St. Paul himself, who yet, for the credit of poets, allegeth twice two poets, and one of them by the name of a prophet, setteth a watchword upon philosophy—indeed upon the abuse. So doth Plato upon the abuse, not upon poetry. Plato found fault that the poets of his time filled the world with wrong opinions of the gods, making light tales of that unspotted essence, and therefore would not have the youth depraved with such opinions. Herein may much be said; let this suffice: the poets did not induce such opinions, but did imitate those opinions already induced. For all the Greek stories can well testify that the very religion of that time stood upon many and many-fashioned gods, not taught so by the poets, but followed according to their nature of imitation. Who list may read in Plutarch the discourses of Isis and Osiris, of the cause why oracles ceased, of the divine providence, and see whether the theology of that nation stood not upon such dreams which the poets indeed superstitiously observed, and truly (since they had not the light of Christ) did much better in it than the philosophers, who, shaking off superstition, brought in atheism. Plato therefore (whose authority I had much rather justly construe than unjustly resist) meant not in general of poets, in those words of which Julius Scaliger saith, *"Qua authoritate barbari quidam atque hispidi abuti velint ad poetas e republica exigendos";*[43] but only meant to drive out those wrong opinions of Deity (whereof now, without further law, Christianity hath taken away all the hurtful belief), perchance (as he thought) nourished by the then esteemed poets. And a man need go no further than to Plato himself to know his meaning: who, in his dialogue called *Ion,* giveth high and rightly divine commendation to poetry. So as Plato, banishing the abuse, not the thing, not banishing it, but giving due honor unto it, shall be our patron and not our adversary. For indeed I had much rather (since truly I may do it) show their mistaking of Plato (under whose lion's skin they would make an asslike braying against poesy) than go about to overthrow his authority; whom, the wiser a man is, the more just cause he shall find to have in admiration; especially since he attributeth unto poesy more than myself do, namely, to be a very inspiring of a divine force, far above man's wit, as in the afore-named dialogue is apparent.[44]

Of the other side, who would show the honors have been by the best sort of judgments granted them, a whole sea of examples would present themselves: Alexanders, Caesars, Scipios, all favorers of poets; Laelius, called the Roman Socrates, himself a poet, so as part of *Heautontimorumenos*[45] in Terence was supposed to be made by him, and even the Greek Socrates, whom Apollo confirmed to be the only wise man, is said to have spent part of his old time in putting Aesop's fables into verses. And therefore, full evil should it become his scholar Plato to put such words in his master's mouth against poets. But what need more? Aristotle writes the *Art of Poesy:* and why, if it should not be written? Plutarch teacheth the use to be gathered of them, and how, if they should not be read? And who reads Plutarch's either history or philosophy, shall find he trimmeth both their gar-

---

[43]"Which authority some crude and insensible men would construe to the exclusion of poets from the republic." Scaliger *Poetics.*
[44]Sidney distorts Plato's position in *Ion* (see pp. 13–14) and tries to turn it to the poet's advantage.
[45]*The Self-Tormentor.*

ments with guards of poesy. But I list not to defend poesy with the help of her underling historiography. Let it suffice that it is a fit soil for praise to dwell upon; and what dispraise may set upon it, is either easily overcome, or transformed into just commendation. So that, since the excellencies of it may be so easily and so justly confirmed, and the low-creeping objections so soon trodden down; it not being an art of lies, but of true doctrine; not of effeminateness, but of notable stirring of courage; not of abusing man's wit, but of strengthening man's wit; not banished, but honored by Plato; let us rather plant more laurels for to engarland our poets' heads (which honor of being laureate, as besides them only triumphant captains wear, is a sufficient authority to show the price they ought to be had in) than suffer the ill-favoring breath of such wrong-speakers once to blow upon the clear springs of poesy.

But since I have run so long a career in this matter, me-thinks, before I give my pen a full stop, it shall be but a little more lost time to inquire why England (the mother of excellent minds) should be grown so hard a stepmother to poets, who certainly in wit ought to pass all other, since all only proceedeth from their wit, being indeed makers of themselves, not takers of others. How can I but exclaim, *"Musa, mihi causas memora, quo numine laeso!"*[46] Sweet Poesy, that hath anciently had kings, emperors, senators, great captains, such as, besides a thousand others, David, Adrian, Sophocles, Germanicus, not only to favor poets, but to be poets; and of our nearer times can present for her patrons a Robert, king of Sicily, the great King Francis of France, King James of Scotland; such cardinals as Bembus and Bibbiena: such famous preachers and teachers as Beza and Melancthon; so learned philosophers as Fracastorius and Scaliger; so great orators as Pontanus and Muretus; so piercing wits as George Buchanan; so grave counselors as, besides many, but before all, that Hospital of France, than whom (I think) that realm never brought forth a more accomplished judgment, more firmly builded upon virtue—I say these, with numbers of others, not only to read others' poesies, but to poetize for others' reading—that poesy, thus embraced in all other places, should only find in our time a hard welcome in England, I think the very earth lamenteth it, and therefore decketh our soil with fewer laurels than it was accustomed. For heretofore poets have in England also flourished, and, which is to be noted, even in those times when the trumpet of Mars did sound loudest. And now that an overfaint quietness should seem to strew the house for poets, they are almost in as good reputation as the mountebanks at Venice. Truly even

that, as of the one side it giveth great praise to poesy, which like Venus (but to better purpose) hath rather be troubled in the net with Mars than enjoy the homely quiet of Vulcan; so serves it for a piece of a reason why they are less grateful to idle England, which now can scarce endure the pain of a pen. Upon this necessarily followeth, that base men with servile wits undertake it, who think it enough if they can be rewarded of the printer. And so as Epaminondas is said, with the honor of his virtue, to have made an office, by his exercising it, which before was contemptible, to become highly respected, so these, no more but setting their names to it, by their own disgracefulness disgrace the most graceful poesy. For now, as if all the Muses were got with child, to bring forth bastard poets, without any commission they do post over the banks of Helicon, till they make the readers more weary than post-horses, while, in the meantime, they, *"queis meliore luto finxit praecordia Titan,"*[47] are better content to suppress the outflowing of their wit, than, by publishing them, to be accounted knights of the same order. But I that, before ever I durst aspire unto the dignity, am admitted into the company of the paper-blurrers, do find the very true cause of our wanting estimation is want of desert, taking upon us to be poets in despite of Pallas. Now, wherein we want desert were a thankworthy labor to express: but if I knew, I should have mended myself. But I, as I never desired the title, so have I neglected the means to come by it. Only, overmastered by some thoughts, I yielded an inky tribute unto them. Marry, they that delight in poesy itself should seek to know what they do, and how they do, and, especially, look themselves in an unflattering glass of reason, if they be inclinable unto it. For poesy must not be drawn by the ears; it must be gently led, or rather it must lead; which was partly the cause that made the ancient-learned affirm it was a divine gift, and no human skill; since all other knowledges lie ready for any that hath strength of wit; a poet no industry can make, if his own genius be not carried unto it; and therefore is it an old proverb, *Orator fit, poeta nascitur.*[48] Yet confess I always that as the fertilest ground must be manured, so must the highest-flying wit have a Daedalus to guide him. That Daedalus, they say, both in this and in other, hath three wings to bear itself up into the air of due commendation: that is, art, imitation, and exercise. But these, neither artificial rules nor imitative patterns, we much cumber ourselves withal. Exercise indeed we do, but that very fore-backwardly: for where we should exercise to know, we exercise as having known: and so is our brain delivered of much mat-

---

[46]"Muse, relate to me how her divinity was injured!" *Aeneid,* I. 8.

[47]"The hearts of whom Titan has formed of finer clay." Juvenal, *Satires,* XIV. 35.

[48]"The orator is made, the poet born."

ter which never was begotten by knowledge. For, there being two principal parts—matter to be expressed by words and words to express the matter—in neither we use art or imitation rightly. Our matter is *quodlibet*[49] indeed, though wrongly performing Ovid's verse, *"Quicquid conabar dicere, versus erat":*[50] never marshaling it into an assured rank, that almost the readers cannot tell where to find themselves.

Chaucer, undoubtedly, did excellently in his *Troilus and Cressida;* of whom, truly, I know not whether to marvel more, either that he in that misty time could see so clearly, or that we in this clear age walk so stumblingly after him. Yet had he great wants, fit to be forgiven in so reverent antiquity. I account the *Mirror of Magistrates* meetly furnished of beautiful parts, and in the Earl of Surrey's *Lyrics* many things tasting of a noble birth, and worthy of a noble mind. The *Shepherd's Calendar* hath much poetry in his eclogues, indeed worthy the reading, if I be not deceived. That same framing of his style to an old rustic language I dare not allow, since neither Theocritus in Greek, Virgil in Latin, nor Sannazzaro in Italian did affect it. Besides these, do I not remember to have seen but few (to speak boldly) printed, that have poetical sinews in them: for proof whereof, let but most of the verses be put in prose, and then ask the meaning; and it will be found that one verse did but beget another, without ordering at the first what should be at the last; which becomes a confused mass of words, with a tingling sound of rhyme, barely accompanied with reason.

Our tragedies and comedies (not without cause cried out against), observing rules neither of honest civility nor of skillful poetry, excepting *Gorboduc* (again, I say, of those that I have seen), which notwithstanding, as it is full of stately speeches and wellsounding phrases, climbing to the height of Seneca's style, and as full of notable morality, which it doth most delightfully teach, and so obtain the very end of poesy, yet in truth it is very defectious in the circumstances, which grieveth me, because it might not remain as an exact model of all tragedies. For it is faulty both in place and time, the two necessary companions of all corporal actions. For where the stage should always represent but one place, and the uttermost time presupposed in it should be, both by Aristotle's precept and common reason, but one day, there is both many days, and many places, inartificially imagined.[51] But if it be so in *Gorboduc,* how much more in all the rest, where you shall have Asia of the one side, and Africa of the other, and so many other underkingdoms, that

the player, when he cometh in, must ever begin with telling where he is, or else the tale will not be conceived? Now ye shall have three ladies walk to gather flowers and then we must believe the stage to be a garden. By and by we hear news of shipwreck in the same place, and then we are to blame if we accept it not for a rock.

Upon the back of that comes out a hideous monster, with fire and smoke, and then the miserable beholders are bound to take it for a cave. While in the meantime two armies fly in, represented with four swords and bucklers, and then what hard heart will not receive it for a pitched field? Now, of time they are much more liberal, for ordinary it is that two young princes fall in love. After many traverses, she is got with child, delivered of a fair boy; he is lost, groweth a man, falls in love, and is ready to get another child; and all this in two hours' space: which, how absurd it is in sense, even sense may imagine, and art hath taught, and all ancient examples justified, and, at this day, the ordinary players in Italy will not err in. Yet will some bring in an example of *Eunuchus* in Terence,[52] that containeth matter of two days, yet far short of twenty years. True it is, and so was it to be played in two days, and so fitted to the time it set forth. And though Plautus hath in one place done amiss, let us hit with him, and not miss with him. But they will say, How then shall we set forth a story, which containeth both many places and many times? And do they not know that a tragedy is tied to the laws of poesy, and not of history; not bound to follow the story, but, having liberty, either to feign a quite new matter, or to frame the history to the most tragical conveniency? Again, many things may be told which cannot be showed, if they know the difference betwixt reporting and representing. As, for example, I may speak (though I am here) of Peru, and in speech digress from that to the description of Calicut; but in action I cannot represent it without Pacolet's horse. And so was the manner the ancients took, by some nuncius[53] to recount things done in former time or other place. Lastly, if they will represent an history, they must not (as Horace saith) begin *ab ovo,*[54] but they must come to the principal point of that one action which they will represent. By example this will be best expressed. I have a story of young Polydorus, delivered for safety's sake, with great riches, by his father Priam to Polymnestor, king of Thrace, in the Trojan war time. He, after some years, hearing the overthrow of Priam, for to make the treasure his own, murdereth the child. The body of the child is taken up by Hecuba. She, the same day, findeth a slight to be revenged most cruelly of the tyrant.

---

[49]A subtle theological question proposed as an exercise for argument.
[50]"Whatever I tried to say, it was verse." *Tristia,* IV. x. 26.
[51]Here Sidney follows Castelvetro and others in ascribing unity of time to Aristotle. See Castelvetro, *The Poetics of Aristotle,* p. 141.

[52]Sidney's mistake. He should refer to *The Self-Tormentor* of Terence.
[53]Messenger.
[54]"From the egg." See *Art of Poetry,* p. 70.

Where now would one of our tragedy writers begin, but with the delivery of the child? Then should he sail over into Thrace, and so spend I know not how many years, and travel numbers of places. But where doth Euripides? Even with the finding of the body, leaving the rest to be told by the spirit of Polydorus. This need no further to be enlarged; the dullest wit may conceive it. But besides these gross absurdities, how all their plays be neither right tragedies, nor right comedies, mingling kings and clowns, not because the matter so carrieth it, but thrust in clowns by head and shoulders, to play a part in majestical matters, with neither decency nor discretion, so as neither the admiration and commiseration, nor the right sportfulness, is by their mongrel tragicomedy obtained. I know Apuleius did somewhat so, but that is a thing recounted with space of time, not represented in one moment: and I know the ancients have one or two examples of tragicomedies, as Plautus hath *Amphitrio.* But, if we mark them well, we shall find, that they never, or very daintily, match hornpipes and funerals. So falleth it out that, having indeed no right comedy, in that comical part of our tragedy we have nothing but scurrility, unworthy of any chaste ears, or some extreme show of doltishness, indeed fit to lift up a loud laughter, and nothing else: where the whole tract of a comedy should be full of delight, as the tragedy should be still maintained in a well-raised admiration. But our comedians think there is no delight without laughter; which is very wrong, for though laughter may come with delight, yet cometh it not of delight, as though delight should be the cause of laughter; but well may one thing breed both together. Nay, rather in themselves they have, as it were, a kind of contrariety: for delight we scarcely do but in things that have a conveniency to ourselves or to the general nature: laughter almost ever cometh of things most disproportioned to ourselves and nature. Delight hath a joy in it, either permanent or present. Laughter hath only a scornful tickling.

For example, we are ravished with delight to see a fair woman, and yet are far from being moved to laughter. We laugh at deformed creatures, wherein certainly we cannot delight. We delight in good chances, we laugh at mischances; we delight to hear the happiness of our friends, or country, at which he were worthy to be laughed at that would laugh. We shall, contrarily, laugh sometimes to find a matter quite mistaken and go down the hill against the bias, in the mouth of some such men, as for the respect of them one shall be heartily sorry, yet he cannot choose but laugh; and so is rather pained than delighted with laughter. Yet deny I not but that they may go well together. For as in Alexander's picture well set out we delight without laughter, and in twenty mad antics we laugh without delight, so in Hercules, painted with his great beard and furious countenance, in woman's attire,

spinning at Omphale's commandment, is breedeeth both delight and laughter. For the representing of so strange a power in love procureth delight: and the scornfulness of the action stirreth laughter. But I speak to this purpose, that all the end of the comical part be not upon such scornful matters as stirreth laughter only, but, mixed with it, that delightful teaching which is the end of poesy. And the great fault even in that point of laughter, and forbidden plainly by Aristotle,[55] is that they stir laughter in sinful things, which are rather execrable than ridiculous; or in miserable, which are rather to be pitied than scorned. For what is it to make folks gape at a wretched beggar, or a beggarly clown; or, against the law of hospitality, to jest at strangers, because they speak not English so well as we do? What do we learn, since it is certain *"Nil habet infelix paupertas durius in se, / Quam quod ridiculos homines facit"?*[56] But rather a busy loving courtier, a heartless threatening Thraso, a self-wise-seeming schoolmaster, an awry-transformed traveler—these if we saw walk in stage names, which we play naturally, therein were delightful laughter, and teaching delightfulness: as in the other, the tragedies of Buchanan do justly bring forth a divine admiration. But I have lavished out too many words of this play matter. I do it because, as they are excelling parts of poesy, so is there none so much used in England, and none can be more pitifully abused; which, like an unmannerly daughter showing a bad education, causeth her mother poesy's honesty to be called in question. Other sorts of poetry almost have we none, but that lyrical kind of songs and sonnets: which, Lord, if he gave us so good minds, how well it might be employed, and with how heavenly fruit, both private and public, in singing the praises of the immortal beauty, the immortal goodness of that God who giveth us hands to write and wits to conceive; of which we might well want words, but never matter; of which we could turn our eyes to nothing, but we should ever have new budding occasions. But truly many of such writings as come under the banner of unresistible love, if I were a mistress, would never persuade me they were in love; so coldly they apply fiery speeches, as men that had rather read lovers' writings, and so caught up certain swelling phrases (which hang together like a man which once told me the wind was at northwest, and by south, because he would be sure to name winds enough), than that in truth they feel those passions, which easily (as I think) may be betrayed by that same forcibleness or *energia* (as the Greeks call it) of the writer. But let this be a sufficient though

---

[55]See *Poetics,* V. 1, p. 52. Sidney distorts Aristotle here.
[56]"Unhappy poverty has nothing worse in itself than that it makes men ridiculous." Juvenal, *Satires,* II. 152–53.

short note, that we miss the right use of the material point of poesy.

Now, for the outside of it, which is words, or (as I may term it) diction, it is even well worse. So is that honey-flowing matron eloquence appareled, or rather disguised, in a courtesanlike painted affectation: one time with so far-fetched words, they may seem monsters, but must seem strangers, to any poor Englishman; another time, with coursing of a letter, as if they were bound to follow the method of a dictionary; another time, with figures and flowers, extremely winter-starved. But I would this fault were only peculiar to versifiers, and had not as large possession among prose-printers, and (which is to be marveled) among many scholars, and (which is to be pitied) among some preachers. Truly I could wish, if at least I might be so bold to wish in a thing beyond the reach of my capacity, the diligent imitators of Tully and Demosthenes (most worthy to be imitated) did not so much keep Nizolian paper books of their figures and phrases, as by attentive translation (as it were) devour them whole, and make them wholly theirs. For now they cast sugar and spice upon every dish that is served to the table, like those Indians, not content to wear earrings at the fit and natural place of the ears, but they will thrust jewels through their nose and lips, because they will be sure to be fine.

Tully, when he was to drive out Catiline, as it were with a thunderbolt of eloquence, often used that figure of repetition, *"Vivit. Vivit? Imo in Senatum venit,"* &c.[57] Indeed, inflamed with a well-grounded rage, he would have his words (as it were) double out of his mouth, and so do that artificially which we see men do in choler naturally. And we, having noted the grace of those words, hale them in sometime to a familiar epistle, when it were too much choler to be choleric. Now for similitudes in certain printed discourses, I think all herberists, all stories of beasts, fowls, and fishes are rifled up, that they come in multitudes to wait upon any of our conceits; which certainly is as absurd a surfeit to the ears as is possible: for the force of a similitude not being to prove anything to a contrary disputer, but only to explain to a willing hearer; when that is done, the rest is a most tedious prattling, rather overswaying the memory from the purpose whereto they were applied, than any whit informing the judgment, already either satisfied, or by similitudes not to be satisfied. For my part, I do not doubt, when Antonius and Crassus, the great forefathers of Cicero in eloquence, the one (as Cicero testifieth of them) pretended not to know art, the other not to set by it, because with a plain sensibleness they might win credit of popular ears; which credit is the nearest

step to persuasion; which persuasion is the chief mark of oratory—I do not doubt (I say) that but they used these knacks very sparingly; which, who doth generally use, any man may see doth dance to his own music; and so be noted by the audience more careful to speak curiously than to speak truly.

Undoubtedly (at least to my opinion undoubtedly) I have found in divers small-learned courtiers a more sound style than in some professors of learning: of which I can guess no other cause, but that the courtier, following that which by practice he findeth fittest to nature, therein (though he know it not) doth according to art, though not by art: where the other, using art to show art, and not to hide art (as in these cases he should do), flieth from nature, and indeed abuseth art.

But what? Methinks I deserve to be pounded for straying from poetry to oratory: but both have such an affinity in this wordish consideration, that I think this digression will make my meaning receive the fuller understanding—which is not to take upon me to teach poets how they should do, but only, finding myself sick among the rest, to show some one or two spots of the common infection grown among the most part of writers: that, acknowledging ourselves somewhat awry, we may bend to the right use both of matter and manner; whereto our language giveth us great occasion, being indeed capable of any excellent exercising of it. I know some will say it is a mingled language. And why not so much the better, taking the best of both the other? Another will say it wanteth grammar. Nay truly, it hath that praise, that it wanteth grammar: for grammar it might have, but it needs it not; being so easy of itself, and so void of those cumbersome differences of cases, genders, moods, and tenses, which I think was a piece of the Tower of Babylon's curse, that a man should be put to school to learn his mother tongue. But for the uttering sweetly and properly the conceits of the mind, which is the end of speech, that hath it equally with any other tongue in the world: and is particularly happy in compositions of two or three words together, near the Greek, far beyond the Latin: which is one of the greatest beauties can be in a language.

Now, of versifying there are two sorts, the one ancient, the other modern: the ancient marked the quantity of each syllable, and according to that framed his verse; the modern observing only number (with some regard of the accent), the chief life of it standeth in that like sounding of the words, which we call rhyme. Whether of these be the most excellent, would bear many speeches. The ancient (no doubt) more fit for music, both words and tune observing quantity, and more fit lively to express divers passions, by the low and lofty sound of the well-weighed syllable. The latter likewise, with his rhyme, striketh a certain music to the ear: and, in

---

[57] "He lives. He lives? He even comes into the Senate."

fine, since it doth delight, though by another way, it obtains the same purpose: there being in either sweetness, and wanting in neither majesty. Truly the English, before any other vulgar language I know, is fit for both sorts: for, for the ancient, the Italian is so full of vowels that it must ever be cumbered with elisions; the Dutch so, of the other side, with consonants, that they cannot yield the sweet sliding fit for a verse; the French, in his whole language, hath not one word that hath his accent in the last syllable saving two, called *antepenultima;* and little more hath the Spanish: and, therefore, very gracelessly may they use dactyls. The English is subject to none of these defects.

Now, for the rhyme, though we do not observe quantity, yet we observe the accent very precisely: which other languages either cannot do, or will not do so absolutely. That *caesura,* or breathing place in the midst of the verse, neither Italian nor Spanish have, the French, and we, never almost fail of. Lastly, even the very rhyme itself the Italian cannot put in the last syllable, by the French named the "masculine rhyme," but still in the next to the last, which the French call the "female," or the next before that, which the Italians term *sdrucciola.* The example of the former is *buono:suono,* of the *sdrucciola, femina: semina.* The French, of the other side, hath both the male, as *bon:son,* and the female, as *plaise:taise,* but the *sdrucciola* he hath not: where the English hath all three, as *due:true, father:rather, motion:potion,* with much more which might be said, but that I find already the triflingness of this discourse is much too much enlarged. So that since the ever-praiseworthy poesy is full of virtue-breeding delightfulness, and void of no gift that ought to be in the noble name of learning; since the blames laid against it are either false or feeble; since the cause why it is not esteemed in England is the fault of poet-apes, not poets; since, lastly, our tongue is most fit to honor poesy, and to be honored by poesy; I conjure you all that have had the evil luck to read this ink-wasting toy of mine, even in the name of the nine Muses, no more to scorn the sacred mysteries of poesy, no more to laugh at the name of *poets,* as though they were next inheritors to fools, no more to jest at the reverent title of a *rhymer;* but to believe, with Aristotle, that they were the ancient treasurers of the Grecians' divinity; to believe, with Bembus,[58] that they were first bringers-in of all civility; to believe, with Scaliger, that no philosopher's precepts can sooner make you an honest man than the reading of Virgil; to believe, with Clauserus, the translator of Cornutus, that it pleased the heavenly Deity, by Hesiod and Homer, under the veil of fables, to give us all knowledge, logic, rhetoric, philosophy, natural and moral, and *Quid non?;*[59] to believe, with me, that there are many mysteries contained in poetry, which of purpose were written darkly, least by profane wits it should be abused; to believe, with Landino, that they are so beloved of the gods that whatsoever they write proceeds of a divine fury; lastly, to believe themselves, when they tell you they will make you immortal by their verses.

Thus doing, your name shall flourish in the printers' shops; thus doing, you shall be of kin to many a poetical preface; thus doing, you shall be most fair, most rich, most wise, most all; you shall dwell upon superlatives. Thus doing, though you be *"libertino patre natus,"* you shall suddenly grow *"Herculea proles,"* *"si quid mea carmina possunt."*[60] Thus doing, your soul shall be placed with Dante's Beatrix, or Virgil's Anchises. But if (fie of such a but) you be born so near the dull-making cataract of Nilus that you cannot hear the planetlike music of poetry, if you have so earth-creeping a mind that it cannot lift itself up to look to the sky of poetry, or rather, by a certain rustical disdain, will become such a mome as to be a momus of poetry; then, though I will not wish unto you the ass's ears of Midas, nor to be driven by a poet's verses (as Bubonax was) to hang himself, nor to be rhymed to death, as is said to be done in Ireland; yet thus much curse I must send you, in the behalf of all poets, that while you live, you live in love, and never get favor for lacking skill of a sonnet, and, when you die, your memory die from the earth for want of an epitaph.

---

[58]Pietro Bembo (1470–1547), Italian critic.

[59]"What not?"

[60]Thus doing, though you be "the son of a freed man," you shall suddenly grow "Herculean offsprings," "if my poems can accomplish anything." Phrases from Horace, Ovid, and Virgil, respectively.

Jacopo Mazzoni

1548–1598

Because he was fundamentally a philosopher, Mazzoni was attracted in his two defenses of Dante to numerous theoretical issues: the differences between Plato and Aristotle, the credible impossible and the incredible possible, and truth and falsehood in poetry.

According to Mazzoni, poetry admits of three definitions, depending on one's point of view. Thus from one perspective poetry is simply imitation, the making of an "idol," with "no other end in its artifice than to represent and resemble." Mazzoni argues that "imitative" arts are those that "have objects which have no other existence or use except by reason of imitation or in imitation." Mazzoni also defines poetry in terms of its result in the reader, namely delight. Finally, he recognizes that from the point of view of the "civil faculty," or the principles for understanding the proper organizations and functions of human society, the poem delights usefully. In his plurality of definitions, he attempts to preserve his belief in the intrinsic uniqueness of poetry while yet recognizing its "use."

Much of Mazzoni's discussion centers on whether poetry expresses "truth." He turns to Plato's distinction in the *Sophist* between icastic and fantastic imitation, indicates that both kinds of imitation are acceptable in poems, and adopts Aristotle's preference for the "credible impossible," or fantastic imitation, over the "incredible possible," arguing all the while for the freedom of the work from canons of naive realism.

Imitation and *idol* are the key terms in Mazzoni. The poet "imitates," and he makes an "idol." Of major importance to his view is the idea that the idol is particular, credible, and verisimilar, but not necessarily true. Indeed, that it may be false makes no final difference. What is important is the illusion that has been created. "The verisimilitude which is sought by the poets," he says, "is of such a nature that it is feigned by poets according to their own will." Mazzoni draws a distinction, then, between poetry and history, poetry and science; thus he seems to anticipate modern efforts to distinguish poetic from other uses of language.

Mazzoni's work has never been translated in full. A. H. Gilbert, *Literary Criticism: Plato to Dryden* (1962) provides a selection, and Robert L. Montgomery (1983) has translated the introduction and summary of the *Defense* with a general introduction. See Baxter Hathaway, *The Age of Criticism* (1962) and *Marvels and Commonplaces* (1968); and Murray Krieger, "Jacopo Mazzoni, Depository of Diverse Critical Traditions or Source of a New One," in R. P. Armato and J. M. Spalik, eds., *Medieval Epic to the "Epic Theater" of Brecht* (1968).

On the Defense of the *Comedy* of Dante

From

Introduction and Summary

[5] It is the common view of the philosophic schools that the arts and sciences have come to be distinct and different by means of individual and particular objects and subjects. . . . Some have supposed . . . that the objects of the arts and sciences differ according to differences among things insofar as they are things. And from this they are constrained to admit two very extraordinary conclusions. The first is that metaphysics is a total science, that which considers, so to speak, universal being, and that the other arts and sciences are a part of it, because each one of these is a part of universal being. The other conclusion is that each particular art and science must have something for a subject which could not be the subject of another art or science. . . . Both these conclusions are false. . . . Following the Peripatetics,[1] I say, as they believe, that the arts and sciences derive their true and real distinctiveness from their objects, not insofar as they are things but insofar as they are knowable things, supposing that things can be said to be capable of being devised. . . . In the same way, the division of the objects of the senses is not apprehended through a classification of their qualities as such but [6] by a classification of sensible things insofar as they are sensible. . . . By means of this discourse we can establish two firm conclusions. The first is that metaphysics is not a total science . . . that is, it does not totally comprehend other sciences as its parts. But we can say that it is a special science distinct from all others by virtue of having an object quite different, in its mode of being known, from the objects of the other sciences. A nice corollary derives from this first conclusion, which is that the definition of poetics given by Mirandola and his followers—that poetics is that part of philosophy which deals with human actions insofar as they are imitable in verse, number, and harmony—is false and perhaps ridiculous. The second conclusion is that since the division of knowable things (and not of things) separates the sciences, it necessarily follows that the same things can be treated in diverse sciences under diverse modes of knowledge and consideration. . . . Therefore, just as the sciences are differentiated by their objects, not insofar as they are things but insofar as they are knowable, so the arts, of whatever sort they may be, are classified not by their objects insofar as they are things, but by their objects insofar as they are (I cannot say it otherwise if I wish to speak accurately) capable of being devised.

And because of this subject I find no doctrine more copious or sound than [7] that taught by Plato in the tenth book of the *Republic*,[2] therefore following his lead I say that there are three types of object and that they have three types of artifice, which as a result constitute three species of art. . . . They are "idea," "work," and "idol." The idea is the object of the ruling, or we might say governing arts. The work is the object of the fabricating arts. And the idol is the object of the imitative arts. Therefore the modes of the objects of the arts insofar as they are capable of being treated by artifice are three: the observable, the fabricable, the imitable. The arts which only contemplate things pertinent to some object are the ruling arts, and they are founded in the idea. Such is the art of horsemanship when it deals with the bridle. For the art of horsemanship does not consist in making the bridle but is concerned solely with the idea of how it must work and then prescribes to the rider the rules by which he must hold the bridle so as to guide the horse. The art which makes the bridle (which was first conceived by the ruling art) is that which has the work as object. So it is bridlemaking which fashions the work of the bridle, and that is all it does. The imitative arts are so named because they deal with the object only insofar as it is imitable; hence Plato said that they have the idol as object, which means a simulacrum or image of some other thing. Since, therefore, the same thing can be treated by different sciences under different modes of the knowable, then also the same thing can be submitted to different arts by different modes of artifice. And we have a clear example in the bridle which belongs to the art of horsemanship when considered in its idea, to the art of bridlemaking when made as a work, and to painting when imitated as an idol.

But there may be doubt as to the importance of distinguishing the imitative arts from the others. For it would seem that the fabricating arts also deserve the name of imitation, since each one imitates with its work the model of the idea conceived by the ruling art. As, for example, the art of bridlemaking conforms to the idea conceived by horsemanship. . . . I reply (as I said before) that the distinction between

---

ON THE DEFENSE OF THE *Comedy* OF DANTE. *Della defesa della* Commedia *di Dante* was first published in 1587. It may be that the work was actually written by Tuccio del Corno from notes supplied by Mazzoni. It was preceded by the shorter *Discorso in difeso della* Commedia *del divino poeta Dante,* published in 1572. The text printed here was translated especially for this book by R. L. Montgomery. Bracketed numbers refer to the pages of the 1688 edition.
[1] Followers of Aristotle.

[2] See pp. 31–38.

arts derives from their objects insofar as they are variously capable of being devised. Now the artifice of the work consists not only in representing the idea of the ruling art, [8] but also serves other ends. And so we can say that bridle-making forms the bridle in accordance with the idea conceived by horsemanship, but yet this bridle is not made in order to represent the similitude of the idea, but rather so that it can be used in the various ways of managing horses. Hence we see that the artifice of the fabricating arts takes its direction from another art whose sole aim is to represent and resemble; therefore I say that the fabricating arts cannot be called imitative. But those arts which have the idol as object, have an object with no other end in its artifice than to represent and resemble; hence they are justly called imitative. And just as philosophy has called the logical faculty rational, not because it uses reason—for in this sense all the arts and faculties are rational—but because it has an object which takes all its being from reason and in reason; so I say that the imitative arts are so named not because they use imitation—for in this sense all the arts are more or less some kind of imitation—but because they have objects which have no other existence or use except by reason of imitation or in imitation. This I believe is what Plato wished to show in the second book of the *Laws* where he said, "The rightness of an imitation consists in this, as we said, that it is made of such a nature and size that the imitation expresses the nature and size of the object itself."³ . . .

In this way, therefore, the idol is the object of the imitative arts. . . . [9] The idol . . . is an image and similitude of some other thing, and it can come into being, as Plato has taught us in the *Sophist* and in the sixth book of the *Republic,* either with or without our agency. And that which comes into being without human agency has its origin either in material things or in spiritual. Those which originate in material things are understood to be in that portion of visible being which Plato in the sixth book of the *Republic* calls obscure. And so that everyone may understand what I mean it must be remembered that Plato divides existing things into two species: one he called intelligible; the other, visible. And again he wished to subdivide both species into two parts, the clear and the obscure. Now he calls that portion of visible things clear which includes plants, animals, the heavens, the elements, and all complex and simple things. But about the obscure portion of the visible he has reasoned as follows: "A portion of the visible kind contains images, for I call images first shadows, then simulacra, which appear in water

and in solid bodies as denseness, lightness, etc."⁴ . . . I believe idols are of this species. . . .

[12] Now coming to our proposition I say that when I earlier concluded that idols are the objects of the imitative arts, I did not refer to the sort of idols which originate without human artifice . . . but to those which do originate by our artifice, which are born only in our imagination and our intellect by means of our choice and will, as idols in painting, sculpture, and similar things. I conclude, then, that this species of idol is that which is a suitable object of human imitation and that when Aristotle says in the first chapter of the *Poetics* that all the species of poetry are imitation, he means that imitation which has for its object idols which derive totally from human artifice.⁵ . . . But it appears that the words of Suidas are contrary to this proposition; he believes that idols which derive from human artifice are not suitable objects for the imitative arts, but that idols joined to a different thing, which he calls similitudes, are. Here are his words: "Idols are effigies of things which do not subsist, such as Tritons, Sphinxes, Centaurs. But similitudes are the images of things which do subsist, such as beasts and men."⁶ According to this statement of Suidas, we have two sorts of imitation. One represents the true, as a painter does when he depicts with colors the effigy of a man who is known; and the other represents the caprice of the imitator, as the painter when he depicts according to the whim of his imagination; and we see at the same time that the idol is the object of this second sort of imitation and that the similitude is the object of the first. Therefore it is not true that the idol which derives from human artifice is a suitable object for every imitation.

I reply that that view of Suidas about idols is too restricted and also contrary to that held by other writers. . . . [13] In addition, Plato in the *Sophist* has left a statement that there are two species of imitation, one of which he calls icastic, representing things which are truly found to exist, or at least have been found to exist; the other he calls fantastic, of which we have examples in paintings which are made according to the caprice of the artist. And moreover he himself says in the tenth book of the *Republic* that the idol is the

---

³*Laws,* II. 668. Jowett translates this passage: "And the truth of an imitation consists, as we were saying, in rendering the thing imitated according to quantity and quality."

⁴Plato, *Republic,* VI. 509–10. See also *Sophist,* 253–36.
⁵Mazzoni expands his concept of the idol in Book III, the main body of his *Defense:* "[564] I say therefore that anyone who with words expounds some true concept in a certain fashion creates idols by means of his speaking, since each concept is a similitude and image of the thing to which it corresponds, and likewise names appear, according to Plato and also Aristotle, to be like idols and imitations of things. In this way not only history, but also natural philosophy and every one of the other arts which teaches something or deals with truth, makes quasi-idols with its languages and imitates things with concepts and names."
⁶Suidas is the supposed compiler of the *Suda Lexicon* (c. 1000), a combined dictionary and encyclopedia gathered from a wide variety of sources.

object of every imitation.[7] Therefore, the idol is also common to fantastic imitation. . . . Now I add that under this sort of imitative art, or under this imitation, poetry ought to be placed, as a species under its genus. . . .

[15] As for Aristotle, I believe that he establishes poetic imitation as an analogous genus which contains within itself four species. The first and most important is the dramatic-fantastic, which is imitation because it necessarily contains within itself two sorts of idol and image. One is that of the person represented [i.e., the actor]. The other is the false but verisimilar image which the actor represents, since he does not represent the literally true but the verisimilar; he therefore represents the idol or simulacrum of the true. The second species is dramatic-icastic imitation, which always necessarily contains the idol of a real person. The third species is narrative-fantastic imitation, which doubtless always includes the idol and simulacrum of the true, and may also have another feature, always found in narrative-icastic imitation, which we will consider now. The fourth and last species is narrative-icastic poetry which contains those idols and images consisting in particularization.[8] . . . I add that even if Aristotle has indeed called all four species of poetry imitation, nevertheless when he compares dramatic and narrative imitation, he considers dramatic more worthy of the name of imitation, to the extent that he sometimes calls narrative the otiose part of the poem and not imitation; but this must always be understood to hold in [the context of] comparison with dramatic poetry, and not absolutely. . . .

Now coming to Plato I say that he also has in some places denied that narrative poetry is imitation. . . . [16] Yet he also has maintained that narrative poetry is not imitation when compared with dramatic representation, but one ought not to conclude from this that speaking absolutely he believes that poetic narration is not imitation. And moreover I say that he himself in the *Sophist* has said that narrative is imitation.[9] . . .

As for narrative-icastic poetry, I say that the poet is also obliged to imitate, which he does rightly if he sets out to describe anything in a most particular manner. Therefore in this fashion also idols and images are made suitable to narrative. . . . [20] I conclude therefore that poetic narration is also the icastic form of idols and images and is consequently imitation by means of particularization. . . . [22] I believe it is likely that when Plato differentiated narrative poetry from imitation, he meant that compared to dramatic representation it did not merit the name of imitation. . . . But we ought not, because of that, assert that speaking absolutely poetic narration is not in some fashion imitative, also according to the concept of Plato. It can therefore be understood as a firm and fixed conclusion that the genus of poetry is imitation and so consequently all species of poetry make idols and images in the way already mentioned. And because the rightness of imitation [23] . . . consists in the precise representation of things, it then follows that a fundamental error in poetics would be to represent by distortion or dissimilarity. . . . For this reason it seems that Plato in the second book of the *Republic* thinks that Homer erred fundamentally in his imitation by representing many most ugly vices of the gods and heroes when he ought to have done just the opposite by representing with proper imitation the divine and heroic natures.[10] . . . It is also a fact that Proclus has justified the distortions through which poets ascribe many vices to the gods on the grounds that they were writing allegories.[11] . . .

[35] We can now discuss the subject and material proper to poetry. In the opinion of many they are falsehood and lies, but that when these are verisimilar they are an adequate subject for poetry. And they let themselves be persuaded to believe this because they think that the true poet is he who derives his poem from his own invention, adding that whoever [36] takes his subject from somewhere other than his own invention does not deserve the name of a true poet. They also believe that this was Aristotle's view when he called Empedocles more a natural philosopher than a poet because he sought to expound the truth of natural things in verse, rather than to expound his own invention.[12] . . . It also seems that Plato supported this view in the *Phaedo* when he said, "He who hopes to be a poet ought not only to put together words, but also to compose."[13] Plutarch, in the little

---

[7]See Plato, *Sophist,* 235–36; and *Republic,* p. 36. The drift of Mazzoni's understanding of the difference between icastic and fantastic imagery may be gathered from the following remarks in Book III of his *Defense:* "[580] it can probably be said that fantastic and icastic imitation are determined by the true and the false, not insofar as they are in themselves true and false, but insofar as they are considered true and false in the mind of the poet. . . . That poet who creates his own invention as a consequence produces it by the living power of his own imagination, even if by chance it conforms to what has happened in history. And thus not only, according to his belief, does he have the false as an object, but also its form and structure are in his imagination. It thus seems reasonable that these suit the title of fantastic imitator."

[8]Mazzoni argues in Book III that "narration" has a special virtue in addition to those it shares with rhetoric: "[974] And that virtue is particularity, through which the poet should extend and display the parts of his concept because in this way he will be apt to imitate and make resemblances of everything he may have occasion to discuss."

[9]Plato does not say this directly; rather he suggests that all image-making is imitation. See *Sophist,* 265.

[10]See *Republic,* p. 20.

[11]Mazzoni expands on this traditional idea in portions of Book III, "[807–08] each time poets have sought to follow the marvelous on the literal level they have uttered incredible things. . . . The license has sometimes been conceded to poets to feign the impossible in the literal sense while following the credible in the allegorical sense." These propositions are liberally illustrated with examples from classical literature and commentaries, chiefly Homer and Proclus.

[12]See *Poetics,* I. 8, p. 50.

[13]50.

book where he asks whether the Athenians have acquired greater glory through arms or letters, writes as follows:

> They say also that one of the friends of Menander said to him, "The feasts of Bacchus are approaching; have you not made a comedy?" And Menander replied, "I have made a comedy, for I have discovered the fable and given it its order. All that remains is to add the verse." For poets believe the fable to be more essential than the words. Corinna said to Pindar when he was still young and boldly using his eloquence, that he was ignorant of poetics because he put no fables in his writings, which is the proper work of a poet.

And Plutarch adds, "It is certain also that Plato himself wrote that the occupation of poetry is the composition of fables."[14]

On the basis of all these authorities and many others, one could easily fall in with the view of those who say that poetry has no other subject but the fabulous and false, though joined to the verisimilar, since according to the rule of Aristotle, verisimilitude is required in the fables of poets. Nevertheless I say that this opinion is not correct for many reasons, some of which I shall select as they come to mind. . . . Consider first that the false verisimilar occurs in some other arts which are different from poetry, as in rhetoric. . . . [37] And in this respect I recall having read a very fine dialogue by Signor Camillo Paleotti . . . in which he . . . shows . . . that the false verisimilar is greatly abused by the corrupt world in that it is a nearly universal subject of the arts, sciences, and education. Therefore it cannot be concluded that it is a fit and adequate subject of the poet's art. For if this were the true subject of poetry, it would mean that poetry could not in any way be capable of truth, and yet Plato writes, and Aristotle confirms, and reason convinces us, that quite the contrary is so. Therefore Plato in the *Republic* and the *Laws,* having approved that kind of poetry that deals with the gods in accordance with the truth, showed that as a consequence the truth is not alien to poetry.[15] Likewise Aristotle has confirmed this conclusion in three places in the *Poetics.*[16] . . . In all three places, and especially in the last, we see plainly that Aristotle concedes that poetry sometimes has the true for its subject, and we see that because of all that has been said above, the idols of icastic imitation are, according to Aristotle, poetic idols.

But besides the authority of Plato and Aristotle, there is also reason which proves that the poet sometimes speaks the truth, for in narrating the wandering of certain heroes, he often could not help but describe the location of cities. When the poet adheres to geographical truth, it must be [38] said that either he forfeits the name of poet for the time being (which is completely ridiculous) or we must confess that sometimes the true can be a poetic subject. And we have already shown that idols and images can be made from true things, both narratively and dramatically. According to all these considerations we ought to affirm two conclusions as true. The first is that the false is not always necessarily the subject of poetry. The second is that, since the subject of poetry is sometimes the true and sometimes the false, it is therefore necessary to establish a poetic subject that in itself can be sometimes true and sometimes false.[17]

Therefore it seems that we ought to reject that point of view which seemed to prove that poetic subjects are always false. . . .

Now if we remove the false and accept the true in its place, we do not thereby destroy poetry, since we have already said that it can tolerate the true. The same can be said of the possible, because if in poetry we put the impossible in its place, it does not by this become either improved or deficient. But if the credible is removed and the incredible put in its place, the nature of poetry is totally destroyed. And on the other hand whoever takes the credible and totally removes the possible, nevertheless has a poetic subject, as Ar-

---

[14]"Were the Athenians More Famous in War or in Wisdom?" *Moralia* (Loeb edition, Vol. IV, p. 507).

[15]See *Republic,* pp. 37–38. Mazzoni is reading Plato in his own way. In this passage cited Plato asserts that only poetry containing acceptable doctrine belongs in the state, and in the passage from the *Republic* he says flatly that poetry, "is not to be regarded seriously as attaining to the truth."

[16]See *Poetics,* IX. 1–4, and XXV. 1 and 5–8, pp. 55 and 64.

[17]For Mazzoni this involves the purpose for which idols and images are used. In Book III he argues to this point: "[564–65] But yet I say that the language of history and the arts and sciences does not use poetic imitation, and that the poet who treats either of history or of the arts or sciences will use poetic imitation, which we have above called similitudinousness (*similitudinaria*). According to the understanding of those who ought to know . . . the idol is that which has no other use in itself but to represent and resemble. And because the concepts of philosophy are not true and perfect idols (since they are not made solely to represent but to instruct and to disclose the truth of things), therefore we can say that history, and whatever else teaches things that are true, even if by means of its concepts it forms idols, does not form them insofar as they are idols, that is, it does not form them for the sole purpose of representing and resembling something else. Rather it moves to another mode and another cause of the object, that is, to recount the truth of what has happened or to teach some doctrine. But the imitator fabricates the perfect idol, that is, the idol insofar as it is an idol, which means . . . the idol insofar as it represents and resembles something else. So we can conclude that the historian and the poet who has history for the subject of his poem are different in that the historian will recount things in order to leave behind a memory of the truth, but the poet will write to imitate and leave behind a simulacrum, insofar as it is a simulacrum, of the truth. And the poet will be constrained to write with greater diligence than the historian and to ornament his writing with many poetic lights and colors so that the simulacrum which he wishes to form may be better seen and understood by everyone who reads his poem."

istotle has clearly testified: "For in what belongs to poetry the credible impossible is preferable to the incredible and possible."[18] [39] Therefore it should be said that among all the subjects for poetry there is none more proper than the credible, and all the more because by its nature the credible contains both the true and false, since many times not only the true but also the false is credible.[19] . . . And therefore I think that the credible is a subject correlative to belief, that is, to persuasion or faith. And belief, generally speaking, is an aspect of conclusions, as are opinion and knowledge. But knowledge derives from necessary causes, which cannot be said of opinion or of faith, which have contingent causes. Therefore it is plain that all the difficulty lies in knowing how to recognize the difference between opinion and belief. . . .

[40] First I say that persuasion concentrates on the particular as its instrument and means for proving its conclusions. And therefore it makes use of enthymemes and examples, both of which are lacking in universal propositions. . . . The means of proving conclusions are particulars, and they are ordinarily drawn from sensible objects. . . . And please note that I am speaking of belief and faith which originate in human arguments and not those founded in divine revelation. Hence we see that persuasion and belief concern the particular. But opinion always concerns the universal. This refers to the way of proving a conclusion rather than to the conclusion itself, for I am quite well aware that opinion [41] can be about the conclusion of some particular emotion which is involved in some particular subject. But still I say that the means by which one attempts to prove a conclusion are universal. . . . Persuasion derives from those things which can move not just the intellect but also the appetite. This is to say that persuasion, deriving from particular and sensible means, therefore derives from things which can also move the appetite; but opinion, deriving from universal types, therefore derives from things which do not have the power to move the appetite. . . . In infinite questions, in which natural things are treated in a persuasive way, there is produced in the human mind conviction alone without any stirring of the appetite. But whenever moral matters are involved in the same infinite questions and are primarily under the jurisdiction of good and bad, one cannot convince the human intellect without some stirring of the appetite, as the following example illustrates: As to whether one ought to choose a beautiful or an ugly wife, it is clear that many things could be said on both sides of the question which would have the power to stir the appetite, even if by its nature the question is infinite.[20] Therefore, when Cicero says that infinite questions have as their end a conviction which must be chosen, he means that in all infinite questions treated in a persuasive manner there is always this end. But he does not absolutely deny that sometimes in infinite questions stirring of the soul has a place. With these considerations in mind, it can be concluded that the second difference, that between opinion and persuasion, is that persuasion can be derived from things which have the power to move the appetite. I say "can be derived" because it is not always so, as is seen in infinite questions about natural things which are treated in a persuasive way [42] that is with sensible and particular means. But opinion derives from things which cannot ever stir the appetite, for they are universals. Therefore the credible is the object of the kind of persuasion I have just now discussed.

And because we have already concluded, with the authority of Aristotle, that the credible is the subject of the poet's art, it seems that from what has been said we can establish three conclusions. The first is that because the poet always deals with the credible, he ought as a consequence to treat everything in a way consistent with credibility, that is, he ought always necessarily to use individual and sensible means to represent the things about which he writes, whatever they may be. And when he treats things pertinent to contemplative doctrine, he ought to make every effort to represent them with idols and sensible simulacra, which Empedocles did not do.[21] He was therefore said to be a physicist more often than a poet. But in this respect Dante is certainly magnificent, as I will show more fully in the fifth book. For now we can be content with this single example in which, speaking of the holy and ineffable Trinity, he writes:

> In the profound and clear being of the exalted light there appeared to me three turning wheels of three colors and a single extent. And the one seemed reflected from the other, as rainbow from rainbow, and the third seemed a flame breathing equally from the one and from the other.[22]

And for this reason it happens that the poet frequently uses comparison and long, distinct parables. And whoever

---

[18]*Poetics*, XXIV. 10, p. 64.
[19]See n. II, above.
[20]Mazzoni is referring to Cicero's dialogue *Of the Classification of Rhetoric* (Loeb edition, p. 357): "Questions . . . are of two kinds; one kind is limited by its referring to *particular (finitum)* occasions and persons, and this I call a cause, and the other is *unlimited (infinitum)*, that is, marked by no persons or occasions, and this I designate a thesis." In this treatise Cicero generally assigns finite questions a role in moving the feelings and infinite questions the task of persuading the judgment in more general matters.
[21]See Aristotle, *Poetics*, I. 8, p. 50.
[22]*The Divine Comedy*, "Paradise," XXXIII. 115–20.

asks why the poet is at least obligated to use this mode of the credible in his narrative must be satisfied with the following answer: the poet must speak to the people, among whom are many vulgar and ill-educated men, and therefore if he should present knowledge in a fashion [43] suited to the sciences, they would not understand him. For this reason he treats things in a credible fashion, that is, he teaches them by means of comparisons and similitudes taken from sensible things. And the people, who know that truth resides in sensible things as they are treated by the poet, easily believe that the same is true of intelligible things.

From this we can conclude that the poet is not forbidden to deal with things pertinent to the sciences and to the speculative intellect if he deals with them in credible manner, fashioning poetic idols and images, as Dante with most marvelous and noble art has presented the whole of intellectual being and the intelligible world itself to the eyes of everyone by means of idols and most beautiful images. I recall that in the *Phaedrus* Plato, exalting his own invention, wrote thus: "But none of the poets has ever treated or ever will treat the place above the heavens as it should be treated."[23] But if he had seen the third canticle of Dante, he would doubtless have acknowledged the inferiority of his own invention and given the palm to Dante, and therefore to the poets for knowing how to make idols and images appropriate to bringing the people to understand the quality of the supercelestial world. . . .

The second conclusion is that since the poet's subject is the credible, he ought therefore to place the credible in opposition to the true, the false, the possible, and the impossible; that is to say, he ought to rely more on the credible than on any of the others mentioned. Hence if by chance two things should be available to him, one false but credible and the other true but incredible (or at least scarcely credible), then the poet ought entirely to leave the true aside and follow the credible.

The third and last conclusion, which is almost a corollary to the two preceding, is that poetry, by relying more on the credible than on the true, ought to be classified under the rational faculty, which the ancients called sophistic. And to entirely understand this truth, which, if I am not mistaken, has up to now remained obscure, it must be known that the poetic art can be regarded as two modes: according as it concerns the laws of the poetic idol or according as it makes and forms the idol.

I say that the first mode ought to be called poetic and the second "poetry." According to the first mode, poetic is

an art which governs the idol and uses it and is part of the civil faculty,[24] as we will show presently.

According to the second mode the poetic art is that which forms and fabricates the idol and is a species of the rational faculty; and, as I have said, it is to be classified under sophistic, since it disregards the truth. But I recognize that I have offended the poets by giving their art, which until now has been considered divine, the title of sophistic, which is considered ugly and infamous. Therefore to console them some, I wish to pause a bit over the art of the sophists and at the same time show where it possesses good and where evil views. . . . [45] Sophistic was that which treated all things rhetorically, that is credibly, and which certainly argued somewhat boastfully about its propositions and chose feigned subjects, such as Orestes or Alcmaeon, imitating them both together and representing them by means of idols. That this representation by idols and images was proper to the sophistic art is clearly shown by Plato in the *Sophist*[25] where he uses the term εἰδωλοποιητίκην, or fabricator of images, as that which represents what appears to be true. This is also confirmed by Alexander Aphrodisias in his commentary on the *Elenches* of Aristotle. Philostratus . . . wishing to prove that Prodicus of Ceos was also a sophist shows that he made a book in which he dealt with one thing pertinent to moral philosophy by means of idols and images, that is, the appetites for virtue and vice which in the young man struggle for supremacy.

> And for this reason Prodicus of Ceos wrote a pleasant speech in which virtue and vice appeared to Hercules in feminine form. Vice was adorned and variously colored and Virtue was as chance found her. They made obvious offers to the young Hercules. Vice offered ease and softness and Virtue hardship and fatigue.[26]

It seems to me then that it is reasonable to say that poetry should be classified under the ancient form of sophistic, since it also treats things credibly and speaks with such audacity that it claims by means of the Muse and Apollo to know all things. Certainly Hesiod as a poet has the lofty arrogance [46] to suggest that in an instant he learned all things past, present, and future; for this reason I am delighted with the opinion of a very learned commentator on the *Poetics* who believes that it is entirely inappropriate for the poet to

---

[23]247.

[24]Rational principles for understanding the proper organization and functions of human society.
[25]236, 239.
[26]Philostratus, *Lives of the Sophists,* 481 (Loeb edition, p. 9).

use words or ways of speaking in any fashion that might cast doubt on the things he says. For since he professes credibility above all, he ought to recount everything with great assurance and boldness. For this reason as well the poet deserves the name of sophist. But even more he deserves it because he is a maker of idols and images. . . .

Philostratus also says that the old sophists spoke freely of the gods and heroes, a subject firmly considered proper to poets. Therefore by this also we can conclude that poetry is a species of old sophistic. But to understand perfectly everything pertinent to this subject it is necessary to know all the other kinds of sophistic and then to see which are appropriate to poetry and which are not. . . . Old sophistic was not essentially different from the second sophistic, except that the old used fictitious names and the second used real names. Hence it can be said that icastic poetry is a species of the second sophistic and fantastic poetry a species of old sophistic. Now I believe that everyone is capable of understanding that Philostratus thought that the sophistic art set aside the true to concern itself with the credible and that he thought it worthy [47] and noble, not vile and infamous, as Boethius preferred to label it, and perhaps also Plato and Aristotle. But in order to reconcile those authors who censure and those who praise sophistic, it must be understood that sophistic was assumed to deviate in some way from the rules of genuine philosophy. Now genuine philosophy is accustomed to direct the intellect by means of truth and the will by means of the good. Therefore sophistic, which is totally the opposite of genuine philosophy, is accustomed to mislead the intellect by means of the false and the will by means of evil. This was the sort of sophistic censured by Plato, Aristotle, and all their followers, and it appears that Plato sought to include the poetry of Homer in this species of sophistic, as that which misled the intellect by representing falsehoods about the gods and heroes and which misled the will by the variety of its imitation and by stirring up our passions immoderately. . . . And therefore it can be said that any other poetry similar to Homer's may be classified under the sophistic censured by that philosopher. . . .

Therefore one species of sophistic censured by the philosophers is that which misleads the intellect by the false and the will by injustice. Likewise under that sophistic they classify that sort of poetry which produces the same disorders and which does not truly deserve the name of poetry since it does not form its idols in conformity with the laws of poetry for governing and using idols.

The other species of sophistic is that which Philostratus called the old sophistic and which, though it does offer feigned things to the intellect, does not mislead the will, but wholly and in every way tries to make it conform to what is just. And this species of sophistic was not censured by the ancients. And if it should seem to anyone that it deserved blame for misleading the intellect by some falsehood, I say it must be understood that the ancient philosophers [48] (in this respect they were out of step with the truth of sacred theology) praised this distortion in certain instances when it was directed to an honest end. So Plato allowed his magistrates to lie to his citizens for the purpose of some public good. I leave out the fact that this kind of sophistic almost always contained some truth under the surface of first appearances. Now I say that fantastic poetry regulated by proper rules is part of the old sophistic, since it also submits feigned things to our intellect to control the appetite and many times contains the truth of many noble concepts under the surface of the fiction.

The third species of sophistic is what Philostratus called the second sophistic which does not propose feigned names or business, but true names and real events, upon which it discourses according to the laws of justice. . . . And this species is also called sophistic because even though it dealt with truth for the sake of justice, it nevertheless dealt with it in a credible way; hence it sometimes departed from truth when it recognized that falsehood was a more credible or a more effective instrument in persuading. . . . In my judgment icastic poetry ought to be classified under this third species of sophistic, for it represents true actions and people, though always in a credible way.

Therefore according to everything I have said about sophistic I believe that everyone can understand [49] fundamentals of the view that poetry is a rational faculty and that among the rational faculties it ought not to be classified with that which seeks to teach the truth and which opposes the truth to all other things, but under that which exerts its full force to seek out credible appearances and which opposes them to the truth. . . .

I conclude then with assurance that poetry is a sophistic art: because of imitation, which is its proper genus; because of the credible, which is its subject; and because of delight, which is its end. Also, because it is under that genus, because it has that subject, and because it concentrates on that end, poetry is many times forced to find a place for the false. . . . [50] And therefore the credible is the subject of poetry. But because it is also the subject of rhetoric, it is still necessary to see in what mode the credible can become suitable to poetry and in what mode suitable to rhetoric, since we do not wish to fall into the error of those who prefer the verisimilar and false. I say, then, that the credible, insofar as it is marvelous, is the subject of poetry, because the poet must not only utter credible things but also marvelous things. Thus, when he can do so credibly, he falsifies human and natural history and passes on to impossibilities.[27] . . . If there were presented to the poet two things equally credible, but one more marvelous than the other, even though it were false, but not impossible, that is what the poet ought to choose, rejecting the other.

But perhaps there is some doubt that the credible and marvelous can be found together with the true. And perhaps it can be thought that it was poorly expressed above, that poetry is sometimes capable of truth. I reply that there are some truths which are sometimes more marvelous than the false, not only in the natural world . . . but also in human history. . . . On this topic there remains only to deal with those [51] authorities who seem to prove that the false, insofar as it is verisimilar, is the subject of poetry. I say then in the first place that it is true that Aristotle remarked that Empedocles was more a physicist than a poet.[28] And this was confirmed by Plutarch in his book on listening to poetry in these words: "We do not know of any poetry without fables and fictions. For the verses of Empedocles and Parmenides, the *Theriaca* of Nicander, and the sayings of Theognis are more often treatises which to avoid the baseness of prose took on the grandeur and rhythm of poetry as vehicles."[29] Now as for Aristotle, there are two ways of responding. The first is that he did say that Empedocles was more a physicist than a poet, but he did not say absolutely that Empedocles was not a poet, and thus, in affirming that he was more physicist than poet, he was in some way a poet, since, as the grammarians say, the comparative supports the positive.

The second way of responding to Aristotle is that it can be said . . . that Empedocles did not deserve the name of poet, not because he dealt with truth (for it has already been shown that poetry is capable of the truth) but because he dealt scientifically with things pertaining to the sciences, where he would be obliged, were he a poet, to treat them credibly, that is by making idols and images and joining to them a way of instructing the sensitive powers more often than the intellect. As for Plutarch, I say that he speaks either

of the true and perfect poet who (as I have said) ought sooner to be placed under fantastic rather than icastic imitation; or, truly, what is apparently opposite to the views of Aristotle and Plato, that is that poetry has nothing at all to do with the truth. . . . To the text of Aristotle, in which he writes that the history of Herodotus spread out in verse would always be history and thus unworthy of the name of poetry, we reply that it is true: but it does not follow that history cannot in some way be a poem when it represents the marvelous as credible by means of idols and particularized images. But when it narrates in a way suited to history without making idols and images, even if displayed in verse, it always remains history. . . . [52] Also the true can be improved by narrating it in conformity with the credible and by making idols and images of it. And for this reason I believe that icastic poetry, which takes its truth from history, can nevertheless on that account make many things its own by rendering that history in exact particulars.

As for the authority of Plato in the *Phaedo,* I say that he has written of fantastic poetry which always has a fabulous subject or creates a fictitious one or falsifies true history.[30] And therefore he says that the poet merits his name more for inventing his fable than for inventing his verses. Or it could be said that he finds a fable at the heart of each invention which is suited to poems and calls it a fable because thereby these subjects are more like the false and fabulous. But it ought to be said because of this that Plato does not believe that the true can be a poetic subject since in many other places he says quite the contrary. . . .

Summing up then what has been said above about the subject of poetry: it ought to be credible and at the same time marvelous; and linking this subject to the form which has already been made manifest, we can now say that poetry is an imitation made with harmony, rhythm, and verse joined to or accompanied by the credible and marvelous. . . .

To discover a cause peculiar to poetry with some assurance, I believe that there is no more certain way than to consider what that art is that reveals the use of poetry, because this, if I am not mistaken, will show us the origin and end of poetry. Hence I believe that the civil faculty is that which shows not only the use of poetry, but next considers the standards and rules of the poetic idol. I am drawn to this view by the following consideration, namely, that all natural forces [53] and arts which derive from human reason are usually directed towards contrary objects, as for example medicine, which not only deals with health and health-giving potions

---

[27]Mazzoni explores this point at some length in Book III: "[584] The true and perfect poet, then, prefers that sort of fable which has, among others, three conditions: novelty, credibility, and the marvelous. And if we wish to consider seriously these three conditions, we will discover that the fable in fantastic poetry is always the impossible credible, because the fantastic poet always presents the audience of his poem with an action which either has not taken place or has not taken place in the fashion imitated by the poet. Now what is above all impossible is an event which either has not taken place or has not taken place in the way revealed by the poet, since it would be impossible that past events would occur in a manner other than that in which they did occur. In any case, the clever poet unfolds his actions so as to make them credible to the people who listen to him."

[28]See *Poetics,* I. 8, p. 55.

[29]"How a Young Man Ought to Study Poetry," *Moralia* (Loeb edition, Vol. I, pp. 83–85).

[30]Mazzoni may be referring to *Phaedrus,* 229–30 or 265, though in neither place does Plato make precisely these assertions.

but also with sickness and deadly potions. And so we can say that the legal profession also is one which comprehends not only justice but also injustice.

Now given these considerations, I say that the civil faculty professes to understand not only the propriety of human actions but also the propriety of the cessation of these actions, which is opposite to the first propriety, as deprivation is to habit. But because someone might suspect that the habits of our intellect and of human arts are concerned only with positive contrariety, and not the negative, I therefore suggest that the positive and the negative are always the concern of the same art. As, for example, the natural philosopher not only considers the contrariety of motion insofar as it is positive, that is, the contrariety which is found in motion according to which it moves either upwards or downwards; but also he considers the negative contrariety which is implied in motion, and is its cessation, that is, stasis. Also zoology deals not only with the contrariety of difference which makes different species, but also with negative contrarieties, such as life and death. . . . But the cessation of activity . . . ought to dispose and prepare men so that they are more apt and eager for renewed activity. Therefore the same faculty [54] will provide the law of activity and of its cessation. And please note that I do not take cessation as total negation but as cessation of important and difficult activities. And so in the above meaning of cessation we include activities of pleasure and amusement which we engage in for recreation and entertainment. Thus it can be said that the contrariety either of activity or of cessation is not just negative . . . but also positive. It is negative insofar as cessation means an absence of important activity. It is positive insofar as the cessation of important activity contains some pleasant activity apt to restore the spirits tired out by some more serious business. . . .

Thus it seems to me that it can be firmly stated that, since this contrariety of cessation and activity is both negative and positive, it ought to be considered as part of one art and by one faculty. But the civil faculty is that which is concerned with the propriety of activity; therefore it ought also to be concerned with the propriety of cessation. In this are contained, as I have said, all activities done for amusement, that is, everything which gives pleasure. Therefore consideration of the legitimacy of pleasures will no doubt be pertinent in some way to the civil faculty and to moral philosophy. But of all the pleasures there is none more worthy, more noble, or more primary than that given by the works of poets. Therefore the civil faculty should take care to consider the norm and legitimacy of the pleasure of poetry first before all others. Now the fact that poetry was thought a pleasure by the ancients is shown . . . by the authority of Virgil, Horace, Timocles the comic poet, Plato in the tenth book of the *Republic,* and in the fifth book of the *Laws,* and Eusebius of Caesarea in the twelfth book of his *Evangelical Preparations.* . . .

All these considerations, it seems to me, make it reasonable to say that the civil faculty ought to be divided into two main parts, one of which deals with the principles of activity and has been given the general name of politics, or civil affairs. The other deals with the principles of cessation, or the law of recreation, and has been called poetics. And for this reason I believe that the *Poetics* is the ninth book of the *Politics,* and this belief of mine seems to me all the more reasonable because Aristotle in the eighth book of the *Politics* already begins to discuss music and the first principles of poetry so that step by step he may come to discuss the management of the civil faculty. So I can say that the first seven books of the *Politics* deal with the civil faculty in action and the last two (so to speak) deal with the civil faculty at rest, which we have just named poetics.

And therefore poetic is part of the civil faculty and is that which prescribes the norms, the rules, and the laws of the poetic idol for poetry. So that one may say that poetic deals with the concept of the idol, and poetry makes the idol. Hence in its genus poetic is the art governing and using the idol made by poets. . . . And poetry in its genus is the fabricating art of the idol which then is used by poetics and the civil faculty. Therefore we can add the efficient cause to what was written above relative to the definition of poetry and say: Poetry is an imitation made with harmony, number, and verses accompanied by and joined with credible or marvelous things which have been discovered by the civil faculty. . . .

[56] I say then that many people would find it most unusual (and with good reason) if one should ask writers whether delight or utility were the end of poetry. For if it is true that poetry is an imitative art, and that each imitative art has the idol as its object, and that idol . . . is of value only through representing and resembling, then it appears to me that one must say that poetry has no other aim than to represent and resemble. Therefore it is not reasonable to inquire whether the aim of poetry is to be useful or delightful. I suggest that if the aim of poetry were to be useful or delightful, it would not be an imitative art. . . .

[58] Now it ought to be known that, as Aristotle has said in the tenth book of the *Ethics,* [59] delight is an accident belonging to some activities, and among others it is no doubt quite natural to imitation, since it appears to be joined to imitation in such a way that no kind of imitation can be found that does not also give delight and pleasure.[31] . . . Since, then imitation is always allied to delight, it has there-

---

[31]See *Nichomachean Ethics,* X. iv.

fore happened that those who have wished to devise entertainments and amusements have created some sort of imitation. . . . We can cite the game of primero in which is represented the image of an ochlocracy, that is, the kind of republic in which the common people are more powerful than the nobles. For as in this sort of republic the nobles are weak and the common people are strong, so in the game the noblest cards, commonly called court cards, are the least valuable and of smaller worth than the other cards which because of their ignobility the common people have come to call *cartaccie* ["waste paper"]. Now since in this game imitation can be considered for its own sake and in this case has no other purpose than to represent the image of an ochlocracy, and since entertainments and amusements can be considered in such a way that we recognize no other ends for them than delight and pleasure; so I say that poetry can likewise be thought of as an imitative art, and as amusement and entertainment. [60] In the first instance it has as its aim the precision of the idol, that is, that things be imitated properly. But in the second instance it concentrates on the aims of delight and pleasure which are joined to good and perfect imitation. I conclude, therefore, that poetry as an imitative art has the precision of the idol for its aim, but as a thing to be used for amusement and recreation and to effect some cessation of more serious and strict business, it proposes delight as its aim, which derives from suitable imitation. Now this delight which poetry effects can be considered in two modes, that is, either for itself alone, free and without laws; or insofar as it is subordinate to and regulated by the civil faculty. In the first mode is the aim of that sort of poetry which was gathered under sophistic and is worthy of blame since it is such that it disorders the appetite with immoderate pleasure and makes it in every way rebellious to reason and also causes damage and harm to virtuous living.

This is the sort of poetry which Plato drove out of his republic. . . .

If, then, we [61] are to reason about the aim of this sort of poetry, we can certainly say that as an imitative art it should have the precision of the idol as its aim, but that as amusement it has only pleasure as its aim. But if this delight is considered insofar as it is regulated and given its quality by the civil faculty, it is necessary to say that it should be directed towards the useful. Consequently that kind of poetry which was classified under praiseworthy sophistic (this is, the sort which regulates the appetite and subordinates it to reason) would be considered as amusement qualified by the civil faculty and would have the useful for its end. . . .

[64] Now without any doubt I believe that, as regards the aim of poetry, this is true: that perfect poetry considers delight for the purpose of utility. . . . I say then that true poetry is amusement and receives its quality from the civil faculty and insofar as it is amusement it has delight for its aim. But insofar as it receives its quality from and, so to speak, is given its character by moral philosophy, it places delight first and gives us profit afterwards. . . .

[69] But now to come to the end of this definition, I think that it would be well to assemble in a brief epilogue everything mentioned above concerning the final cause of poetry. I say therefore that since the tongue is always an instrument of the concupiscible power and has gratification as its aim, but that nevertheless when it is considered as an instrument of the irascible power, its end is the defense of the animal soul, and that when it is considered as an instrument of the rational power, its aim is speech; so in the same way poetry is always an imitative art, and as such its end is always to represent the images of things directly. But nevertheless considered as recreation deriving its quality from the civil faculty, its aim is delight, but directed towards utility. From this premise it seems to me that we can conclude that poetry will admit of three definitions, according as it is thought of in three ways: as imitation, as pure enjoyment, or as enjoyment deriving its quality from the civil faculty.

In the first mode perhaps it can be defined thus: Poetry is an imitative art made with verses, number, and harmony accompanied with or joined to the credible marvelous and devised by the human intellect for the suitable representation of the images of things.

In the second mode perhaps this second definition will serve: Poetry is an imitative recreation made with verses, number, and harmony accompanied by or joined with the credible marvelous and devised by the human intellect for delight. . . .

[70] The third mode perhaps admits of this last definition: Poetry is an imitative recreation made with verses, number, and harmony accompanied by or joined to the credible marvelous and devised by the civil faculty to delight the people usefully. . . .

From these three definitions follow necessarily four corollaries. The first is that poetry understood in the first mode is not regulated or governed by the civil faculty. The second corollary is that only poetry understood in the third mode is that which is regulated and governed by moral philosophy and the civil faculty. The [71] third corollary is that poetic, which considers the idol belonging to the first mode and at the same time considers the idol of the second mode, ought not in any way to be called a part of moral philosophy. The fourth and last corollary is that only the poetic which deals with the idol of the third mode of poetry is that which is worthy to be named part of the civil faculty, according to the rules of which each good poet ought to fashion his poem, as indeed Dante has done better than all the others. . . .

From

Book I

[278] I say, then, that the fantasy is the power of the soul common to dreams and to poetic verisimilitude. But because my opponents do not doubt of what I too believe, that the fantasy is the power upon which the dream is founded (which Aristotle said many times and which has been repeated more often by his followers), it is therefore well to explain that poetic verisimilitude is also based on the same power. The verisimilitude which is sought by the poets is of such a nature that it is feigned by poets according to their own will. Therefore it is necessary that it should be fashioned by that power which has the virtue of forming concepts in accordance with the will. Now this power cannot in any way be intellectual, for the intellectual power is necessary in producing concepts in accordance with the nature of objects. Hence the subtle [279] Scotus in many places in his *Sentences* says that the intellect is a capacity more natural than free. Therefore it is necessary that the power fitted to generate verisimilar concepts dependent upon the will be the power of the phantasy, called by the Latins *imaginative*. And all that we have said was stated first by Aristotle in the second book of *De Anima:*

> It is in our power to imagine not only things which can be, but also those which cannot, such as men with three heads and three bodies, as Geryon in the fables is supposed to have been, and as men with wings, like Zetes and Calais the sons of Boreas, and the Centaurs and Scylla and Charybdis. For in whatever way a painter may depict an animal of any form, so it is possible to create it in the mind. In addition when we think that some formidable and fearful calamity may occur, we immediately dismiss our courage and our whole body trembles, we shake, and we grow pale. . . . But when we build these things in our mind (as when we imagine terrifying earthquakes and the fierce aspects of wild beasts), we are not affected at all, no consternation follows, and just as paintings do not affect us, neither do visions nor those figments which we willfully gather together. From this we can distinguish imagination from opinion and apprehension.[32]

Therefore if I am not mistaken we can clearly see that the fantasy is the proper power of the poetic fable, since it alone is capable of those fictions which we ourselves are able to create. [280] From this it follows necessarily that poetry is composed of feigned and imagined things, because it is based in the fantasy.

---

[32]This quotation is not from Aristotle, whose remarks on the imagination are more cursory, but from the commentary of Themistius, philosopher and rhetorician of the fourth century A.D.

Torquato Tasso

1544–1595

Among the greatest of the poets of the Renaissance, Tasso is also well known for his critical writings, especially the discourse in which he defended his own epic practice. The best known of his epics is *Jerusalem Delivered* (completed 1575, published 1581), on the subject of the First Crusade. The *Discorsi del Poema Eroica* was written after *Jerusalem Delivered* was completed and before it was revised and extended into the poem *Jerusalem Conquered.* Tasso was well aware of the major critical issues of his time and the pressures to which poet and critic had to respond. As Cavalchini and Samuel point out in their introduction to their translation of the *Discorsi,* "Tasso took them all into account, reconciling society's demand that poetry should entertain, the Church's demand that poetry should encourage the faith, the humanist's veneration for antiquity, the modernist's self-applause—and managed not to degrade poetry into entertainment, confuse it with propaganda (in the original sense of that term), disparage ancients, medievals, or moderns; he even managed not to be anti-Aristotelian or anti-Platonic."

Indeed, in Book One, Tasso follows an Aristotelian procedure in producing a definition of epic that is somewhat in parallel and contrast to Aristotle's definition of tragedy, though it is not stated completely in any one place, but is accumulated as he goes along. The aim of Book One is to set forth a definition as the basis for a general theory of epic. Thus Tasso begins by asking what the *idea* of a heroic poem is by raising the question of poetry in general. Aristotelian imitation is invoked as a common property of all poetry, and poetry's purpose is defined as "to help men by the example of human deeds" and to provide "pleasure directed toward usefulness," usefulness having human virtue as its end.

Tasso places the epic under poetic imitation, employing "imitation" in the broader sense to include narration, while still contrasting it with tragedy with respect to mode of imitation. Rather than purgation, which is the end Aristotle gave to tragedy, epic moves its reader to wonder, though it is not the only genre that does so. It is an "imitation of a nobler action, great and perfect, narrated in the loftiest verse, with the purpose of moving the mind to wonder and thus being useful." At the conclusion of the sixth and last book of the *Discorsi,* Tasso offers a contrast between epic and tragedy that shows wonder to be at the service of human improvement: ". . . if there are two ways of improving us through example, one inciting us to good works by showing the reward of excellence and an almost divine worth, the other frightening us from evil with penalties, the first is the way of epic, the second that of tragedy, which for this reason is less useful and gives less delight."

The standard edition of Tasso's *Discourses* is *Discorsi dell' Arte Poetica e del Poema Eroica,* edited by Luigi Poma (1964). See Bernard Weinberg, *A History of Literary Criticism in the Italian Renaissance* (1961).

From

Discourses on the Heroic Poem

Book One

To begin with then, I say that in all things one must consider the end, as Aristotle declares in his *Topics*. But the end, being single, cannot be found in many particulars. Still, by considering the good in various particular goodnesses, we form the idea of the good, just as Zeuxis formed the idea of the beautiful when he wished to paint Helen in Croton.[1] And this is perhaps the difference between the ideas of natural things in the divine mind and those of artificial things which the human intellect figures to itself: with one the universal exists before, and with the other after the things themselves. The idea of an artistic product is formed after consideration of many things, among which that one is best which most closely approximates to the idea. And since I have to show the idea of the most excellent kind of poem, the heroic, I must not offer only one poem, even the most beautiful, as example, but, collecting the beauties and perfections of many, I must explain how the most perfect and most beautiful can be fashioned.

But first we must find out what the heroic poem is, or rather what its genre is, and then examine the idea, since from the idea, as Aristotle says, again in the *Topics,* one knows if the definition is right. Although in some things this principle does not in fact work well, in the matter of which we are speaking we may certainly consider idea and definition together. Furthermore, if—the arguments being so many—we ought to look at the exemplar, let us turn to the idea itself, since the idea is the true exemplar. Indeed, we may use the complete definition in place of rule and example, as Alexander of Aphrodisias teaches when expounding that same passage in Aristotle. Let us therefore study first what a poem is, or poetry in general, and then we will find the definition of this species—I mean the heroic or epic poem, as it may be called.

Poetry has many species: one is the epic; the others are tragedy, comedy, and songs accompanied by the cithara, bagpipes, reedpipes, or other pastoral instruments. They are all alike in that they imitate. We may therefore affirm that poetry is nothing other than imitation. But painting, sculpture, and other similar arts also imitate; and hence the necessity of clarifying the differences that separate poetry from the other imitative arts. Clearly they do not differ because of the subjects imitated, since the same subject—the Trojan war or the wanderings of Ulysses—may be taken by painter and poet; it is not then a difference in the actions imitated that makes the arts different, but rather that one uses colours and the other words, either with or without meter.

Poetry then is an imitation in verse. But imitation of what? Of human and divine actions, the Stoics said. It follows that those who do not sing human or divine actions are not poets. Thus Homer was not a poet when he described the war between the frogs and the mice,[2] nor Virgil when he described the customs, laws, and wars of the bees.[3] On the other hand, he who describes divine actions is a poet. Thus Empedocles was a poet when he taught how Love and Discord corrupt this perceptible world and generate the intelligible one; and Plato too when he had Timaeus narrate how God the father, calling together the other lesser gods, created the world[4]—or if he was not a complete poet, because he did not use verse, at least he deserves the name by virtue of what he imitated. But if this is so, then, since all the acts of nature are governed by divine providence, whoever describes them would be a poet. Nor do I think epic poets would have excluded from their number Homer, Empedocles, Parmenides, Oppian, or others who borrowed true poets' verse like a cart, as Plutarch says.[5] Perhaps they would have excluded Lucretius, since he denies their ancient notion of πρόνοια, and makes the creation of the world not a divine act but the work of chance. Such acts are not, in Aristotle's opinion, appropriate for poetry. Someone, however, may ask why only divine and human actions are appropriate and not the actions of the elements and other natural forces.

If all actions can be imitated, then the kinds of action being many, the kinds of poem must also be many; and since in this equivocal genre [of action], as Simplicius says in [his commentary on] the *Categories* [of Aristotle], the first species is contemplation, which is the action of the intellect, acts of contemplation can also be imitated by poets. Some indeed contend that the subject of Dante's poem is a contemplation because that voyage of his to Hell and Purgatory has no meaning other than the speculations of his mind.[6] Others pre-

DISCOURSES ON THE HEROIC POEM. *Discorsi Del Poema Eroica* was first published in Naples in 1594. This selection is reprinted from *Discourses on the Heroic Poem* by Torquato Tasso translated by Mariella Cavalchini and Irene Samuel (1973). © Oxford University Press. Reprinted by permission of Oxford University Press.
[1][All footnotes except for local references are by the translators.] Cicero tells the story in *De Inventione* 2. I. 1–3.

[2]*Batromyomachia.*
[3]The Fourth Georgic.
[4]*Timaeus* 41A ff.
[5]*How to Read the Poets* 16.
[6]Notably the position of Jacopo Mazzoni in his *Difesa della Commedia di Dante* (Cesena, 1587).

fer to call his subject a dream, like the *Trionfi* of Petrarch and the *Amorosa Visione* of Boccaccio. But those who hold this view oppose his subject, even more than Plato opposes imitation itself on the ground that the idea has the first degree of truth, the natural form or thing itself the second degree, and the imitation or image the third.[7] For the imitator who represents not a true action but a dream would be still more imperfect—giving the image of an action still further removed from the truth. Plato's doctrine permits no other conclusion, although Synesius wrote that fables originate in dreams and that a dream may perfectly well be the end, as it is the beginning of a fable.

Now Aristotle, although he maintains that Empedocles is more physicist than poet, does not conclude that he is not a poet at all. And if he is in some sort a poet, the actions of the elements do constitute a subject for poetry, though at the lowest level. Therefore Lucretius and Pontano are poets too, and others who have written in verse about nature. If this definition is correct, poetry ought not to be defined as the imitation of human and divine actions, since that would exclude imitation of the elements and other natural phenomena, and imitations of animals, and thus exclude the work not only of Empedocles, Lucretius, and Oppian but even some of Homer's.

For another thing, it seems to me that no divine action is imitated as such, since, so far as it is divine, it cannot be imitated by any of the means proper to poetry. Still Aristotle writes in the first book of his *Politics* that many represent the lives, appearances, and features of the gods in the semblance of man; and Isocrates said that the poetry of Homer and the first tragedies were worth marvelling at because, having considered the nature of the human mind, they used both forms in an unusual way, he handling the wars and battles of the demigods in fictions, they presenting their fables directly to the eyes.[8] And Marcus Tullius Cicero said that Homer approximated the human to the divine, *mallem divina ad nos,*[9] meaning that he described the gods as men and human passions as divine, because to speak and to consult are human acts, as getting angry and feeling pity are human passions. Athanasius too—to add a religious writer to so many pagan ones—in his book *Contra Gentiles*[10] stated that the gentiles'

god is a mixture of the reasonable and the unreasonable, since his form joins the human and the bestial—as for example the Egyptians' Dog-headed Anubis—and that they even attributed to their gods deeds almost bestial. Hence, if the painter when he portrays Jupiter and Mars, Isis and Osiris, paints nothing but a human or animal form, since he cannot imitate divinity, so too the poet is an imitator not of divine forms and deeds, but mainly or properly of human ones. The difference between the imitator of divine and human things is thus as great as that between ideas proper and what we call images and likenesses. Among ideas too, as Aristotle observes in the first book of his *Metaphysics* (and his commentator Alexander agrees), there is this, or a comparable, difference between the rational and the irrational. It is no wonder, then, if images are similarly formed. But going back to Homer, I say that if he imitates the gods under the almost opposite guise of human forms, deeds, and passions, we may assert that he is an imitator of human actions and of those of the gods in so far as they are human. So too, in his battle of the frogs and mice, he transfers to animals words, feelings, and habits which are proper to men. I would therefore conclude that poetry is nothing but an imitation of human actions, which are properly imitable, and that all others are imitated not in themselves but by accident, and not as principal but as accessory. In this manner it is also possible to imitate the actions not only of animals, such as the battle of the unicorn and the elephant, or of the swan and the eagle, but also of nature, as sea storms, pestilence, floods, fire, earthquakes, and the like.

Furthermore, since, as we have said, every definition should look to the best, in defining poetry we have to set before ourselves an excellent purpose. But the best purpose is to help men by the example of human deeds, since the example of animals cannot be equally useful and that of divine actions is not suited to us. Poetry, therefore, should be directed to this purpose. Poetry, then, is an imitation of human actions, fashioned to teach us how to live. And since every action is performed with some reflection and choice, poetry will deal with moral habit and with thought, which the Greeks called διάνοια.[11] And although such imitation affords immense pleasure, one cannot say that the purposes are two, one being pleasure, the other utility, as Horace seems to have suggested in the line,

Poets aim either to benefit, or to amuse,[12]

---

[7]See Plato, pp. 18–19.

[8]See Isocrates, *To Nicocles* 48–9. The passage presents a number of difficulties. We follow Poma's reading *usarono* (for *usiamo* in the text of 1594—see Poma, p. 300, note to 65, 26), and translate *falsamente* 'in fictions' to approximate Tasso's words both to the passage in Isocrates and to his own meaning.

[9]'The divine rather to us.' Cicero, *Tusculan Disputations* I. 26. 65. Cicero in fact writes *divina mallem ad nos,* and Tasso slightly blurs the point of the passage: 'Homer . . . attributed human feelings to the gods: I had *rather* he had attributed *divine feelings* to us.'

[10]I. 9. 20B ff.

[11]From Aristotle's *Poetics* VI, 16. See p. 53. Tasso uses *costume* (usually in the plural *costumi*) to translate ἦθος and *sentenzia* (elsewhere *sentenza,* the equivalent of Latin *sententia*) to translate διάνοια.

[12]Aut prodesse volunt aut delectare poetae. (*Ars Poetica* 333.)

for one single art cannot have two purposes, one independent of the other. Either it should set aside the benefit of warning and advising, as Isocrates holds, and in accordance with the example of Homer and the tragic poets turn the whole force of its words entirely to delight; or, if it wishes to be useful, it should direct its pleasure to this end. It may be that pleasure directed to usefulness is the end of poetry. That is why we read in Isocrates's second oration[13] that the ancient poets left instructions for life, as a result of which men became better, and in the *Panathenaicus* that poetry deters us from many crimes. That is why no other training is more suitable for the young. Its usefulness, however, is rather to be judged by the art which is the architect of the others: the statesman is the one who ought to consider what poetry and what delight to forbid so that pleasure, which should be like the honey smeared on a cup when one gives medicine to a child, may not affect us like deadly poison or keep our minds idle. The poet then is to set as his purpose not delight—the opinion incidentally of Eratosthenes, which Strabo picked up, defending Homer against accusations—but usefulness, because poetry, as that author, following the view of the ancients, held, is a first philosophy which instructs us from our early years in moral habits and the principles of life. Indeed his followers held that only the poet is wise.

We should at least grant that the end of poetry is not just any enjoyment but only that which is coupled with virtue, since it is utterly unworthy of a good poet to give the pleasure of reading about base and dishonest deeds, but proper to give the pleasure of learning together with virtue. Hence perhaps the purpose of pleasure (as Fracastoro held in his *Dialogue on Poetry*)[14] is not to be scorned; on the contrary, to aim at pleasure is nobler than to aim at profit, since enjoyment is sought for itself, and other things for its sake. In this respect it is like happiness, which is man's goal as citizen; indeed nothing can be found more like happiness. Besides, it favours virtue since it exalts human nature, as we read in Athenaeus; wherefore those who love enjoyment usually become generous and magnificent. But the useful is not sought for itself but for something else; this is why it is a less noble purpose than pleasure and has less resemblance to the final purpose. Then if the poet as such has this aim, he will not wander far from the mark to which he should address his thoughts as an archer points his arrows. But as a citizen, or at least in so far as his art is subordinate to the queen of the arts, he seeks the sort of profit that is virtuous rather than useful.

Of the two ends, therefore, that the poet sets himself, one pertains to his art, the other to the higher art. But in regarding his own end, he must be careful that he does not through excess fall into the very opposite, for virtuous delights are contrary to vicious ones. They merit no praise at all, therefore, who have described amorous embraces in the fashion of Ariosto depicting Ruggiero with Alcina, or Ricciardetto with Fiordispina. And perhaps Trissino too might better have kept silent about many things when he virtually sets before our eyes the amorous pleasure that the emperor Justinian took in his wife. But he meant to imitate Homer, who feigns that Juno and Jupiter on the summit of Mount Ida were covered by a cloud, an invention that [Bernardo] Tasso charmingly carries over in his *Amadigi*,[15] when he describes the embrace of Mirinda and Alidoro, as though to hint that the rest must be hidden under a cloud of silence. Virgil is decidedly modest about the love-making of Aeneas and Dido, and only briefly mentions what followed the rain sent by Juno:

'To the same cave came Dido and the Trojan chief, etc.'[16]

Thus, as we have said, poetry is an imitation of human actions with the purpose of being useful by pleasing, and the poet is an imitator who could, as many have, use his art to delight without profiting. If he avoids that, he is a good poet, and in this perhaps like the orator, who is judged, as Aristotle held,[17] not only for his skill but for his will, and unlike the dialectician, who is esteemed not for his disposition but for his talent. Occasionally a definition defines not the thing simply, but the thing in its perfection, as Aristotle himself says in the *Topics*. To this type belongs the definition of the orator as the man who knows everything worthy of belief on any matter whatever, and overlooks nothing—he is indeed the faultless orator. Perhaps this definition is what moved Strabo, the first to say that the poet's virtue accompanies that of the man, and that no one can be a good poet who is not a good man.[18] Later Quintilian was inspired to define the orator as a good man trained in speaking, disregarding the words of Aristotle, which call him not a good man, but a good orator.[19] I doubt, however, that this definition of Quin-

---

[13]*To Nicocles* 43.
[14]Girolamo Fracastoro, *Naugerius, sive De Poetrica Dialogus,* tr. Ruth Kelso (Urbana, Illinois, 1924), especially pp. 66–71, where Navagero explains the great utility of poetry.
[15]Canto 34.
[16]Speluncam Dido dux et Troianus eandem deveniunt, etc. (*Aeneid* 4. 165–6.)
[17]*Rhetoric* 1, 2, 1356ᵃ.
[18]The *locus classicus* on the poet as a good man appears in Strabo's *Geography* 1. 25.
[19]Tasso may have in mind Quintilian, *Institutes of Oratory* 2. 15. 33–5 and Aristotle, *Rhetoric* 2. 1. 3–7.

tilian's deserved the reproach of Cavalcanti, since the perfectly equipped orator could not really be defined otherwise. To be sure, goodness is no part of his skill, but a perfection of his moral nature. But if any objection is to be made, that of Alexander of Aphrodisias is applicable: this kind of definition defines not the whole but the part. And perhaps Quintilian did not mean to apply his definition to all, but only to the perfect orator. Similarly, in the definition of the poet, whoever says that the poet is both a good man and a good imitator of human actions and moral habits, whose purpose is profit with delight, may not be giving a definition that fits all poets; but he does define the most excellent.

Well then, if the poet is an imitator of human actions and habits, poetry will be an imitation of the same things; and if he is a good imitator, his poetry will be good. Some, however, have maintained that the poet is not to regard the goodness of things so much as their beauty. Among them is Navagero, in Fracastoro, where he proves that the poet's aim is to consider the idea of the beautiful,[20] and almost contradicts the view of Aristotle in his *Ethics* that the idea is not practically useful at all. But whatever Aristotle held on that point, and however his Greek commentator explained it, I certainly cannot object to the poet's concentrating on the idea of beauty. Still, if the ideas to which the orator is accustomed to direct his gaze are several, as Hermogenes liked to think, I don't know why the poet must consider only that of beauty, and not the other six as well. But apparently Navagero thought that the form of beauty contains all the others or that the beautiful appears in all of them, in as much as the beautiful is inherent in clarity, grandeur, swiftness, passion, gravity, and truth. And if I am not mistaken, Navagero wanted clarity to be not only clear, but at once clear and beautiful; and so with all the other forms. But since this issue belongs particularly to diction, I shall deal with it when I come to discuss the art of using words.

Now, the opinion of Maximus of Tyre does not seem to me contemptible, that philosophy and poetry are two in name but of a single substance, as light is in respect to the sun. He defines poetry as a philosophy ancient in time, metrical in sound, fictitious in subject. But philosophy, according to him, is a youthful poetry, looser in rhythm, and more open in its arguments. Now my view is that the manner of considering things differentiates one from the other: poetry considers them in as much as they are beautiful, and philosophy in as much as they are good, as the same author elsewhere notes, saying that Homer had to do two things, one pertaining to philosophy, the other to poetry, that there he

regarded virtue, here the image of the fable.[21] Poetry then seeks and yearns for beauty and strives to reveal it in two ways: one narration, the other representation, both of which are contained under imitation as their genus. But sometimes it is named from one particular manner of imitation. Those therefore who have defined poetry as a narration of a memorable and possible human action have offered a definition applicable not to all kinds of poetry but only to the epic poem, or the heroic, if we prefer that name; they have excluded tragedy and comedy, unless the term narration involves an ambiguity which they might have cleared up better with the help of Aristotle's authority, as I have occasionally done, and others too more perfectly. We shall say then that narrating is proper to the epic, the name used for those who write of the deeds of heroes, as by Cicero, for example, and Eustathius, the commentator on Homer. And a further difference between epic poetry and tragedy, besides the mode, arises from the difference in the means or instruments employed to imitate; for tragedy, in order to purge the soul, uses rhythm and harmony in addition to verse. Epic and tragedy differ then in two ways: in the means they use to imitate and in their mode of imitating. They agree in one element, the things imitated, since tragedy too, as Aristotle says in the *Problems,* represents the actions of heroes. But from comedy the heroic poem differs in every way since it differs also in the things and persons imitated. Let us put aside tragedy and comedy, as well as the kind of narrative which resembles comedy as the *Iliad* resembles tragedy in that it imitates base things as Homer did in the *Margites,* in imitation of which perhaps our poet created Margut.[22] My chief intention is not to discuss these and other species.

I say that the heroic poem is an imitation of an action noble, great, and perfect, narrated in the loftiest verse, with the aim of giving profit through delight, so that the delight may get us to read more willingly and thus not lose the profit. But all poetry, of course, profits by delighting: tragedy profits by delighting, and so too comedy. Now the end of each ought to be peculiar to it: as the art of making bridles has one aim and that of making halberds another, although both are subordinate to the art of war and directed to the single goal it sets, in the same way tragedy should have one

---

[20]Cf. *Naugerius,* tr. Kelso, p. 69.

[21]The first reference to Maximus of Tyre is to *Dissertationes* 29, end of 169, where poetry as compared to philosophy is said to be 'tempore vetustior, harmonia metrica, argumento fabulosa'. The second reference is apparently to 16. 95B, where philosophy is compared in this respect with painting, but at the end of the passage Homer is said to have done two things in his books, 'quorum alterum ad poësin pertinet, et fabulae speciem habet: alterum ad Philosophiam, et virtutem commendat, veritatem docet'.

[22]Tasso writes *nostri poeti* implying that Margut also appears in works other than Pulci's *Morgante.*

end, comedy another, the epic poem another still—or another effect since the form of each thing is distinguished by its proper effect. Now the effect of tragedy is to purge the soul by terror and compassion, and that of comedy is to move laughter at base things (as Maggi declares in his separate study *De Ridiculis*). From this effect comedy derives its usefulness, since as we laugh at the baseness we see in others, we grow ashamed to commit similar baseness. The epic poem ought therefore to afford its own delight with its own effect—which is perhaps to move wonder, an effect that seems far from peculiar to it, since tragedy too moves wonder, as the words of Isocrates that I have already cited suggest: 'That is why Homer's poetry and those who first conceived of tragic plays are worthy of admiration.'[23] Still we may argue that if wonder arises from novelty, Homer's poetry might seem wonderful, but not tragedy, which dealt many years later with the same subjects, long familiar to everyone throughout Greece—unless perhaps it was the new mode of handling that made what was worn by time and use seem marvellous, as it no longer did in later tragedians. Still many statements in Aristotle's *Poetics* imply that tragedy should move wonder, and particularly this:

> since tragedy represents not only a complete action but also incidents that cause fear and pity, and this happens most of all when the incidents are unexpected and yet one is a consequence of the other. For in that way the incidents will cause more amazement than if they happened mechanically and accidentally, etc.[24]

Moreover, marvellous events make horror and pity easier to induce. And comedy too moves wonder, baseness alone without wonder being insufficient to make us laugh at things that seem ugly: when the wonder or novelty stops, laughter too stops. All the same, to move wonder fits no kind of poetry so much as epic: so Aristotle[25] teaches, and Homer himself in Hector's flight; for the wonder that almost stuns us as we see one man alone dismaying an entire army with his threats and gestures would be inappropriate to tragedy, yet makes the epic poem marvellous. Nor would the death of Hector or others be appropriate on stage; these, as Philostratus tells in the *Life of Apollonius,* were forbidden by Aeschylus, who indeed won the name 'father of tragedy' because he largely mitigated its crudity. Nor would the metamorphosis

of Cadmus into a serpent, which Ovid quite properly narrated, be appropriate to the stage, nor that of Arethusa, or the nymphs transformed into ships[26] in Virgil, or Proteus into the many shapes described in the *Georgics* and earlier in the *Odyssey,* nor that in the circle of thieves of which Dante boasts: 'Let Ovid be silent about Cadmus and Arethusa; for if in his lines he turns him into a serpent and her into a fountain, I do not grudge it to him.'[27] So too with the metamorphosis in Boccaccio of Fileno[28] into a spring, or in Boiardo of the sorcerer into various shapes,[29] or of Ariosto's Astolfo into myrtle.[30] And so too with many other transformations that we read of with wonder in many other poets, ancient and modern. We gladly read in epic about many wonders that might be unsuitable on stage, both because they are proper to epic and because the reader allows many liberties which the spectator forbids. The use of machines is seldom therefore praised in tragedy, while in the epic gods and angels frequently descend from heaven and participate in human actions, giving counsel and help, as Apollo and Minerva do in the *Iliad* and *Odyssey* of Homer and in the *Ercole* of Giraldi, Venus in Virgil's *Aeneid* and in Bolognetti, and many other gods in these and other poems. So too the angel Michael descends in *Orlando Furioso*[31] and the angel Palladio and Nettunio in the *Italia Liberata.*[32] Thus all these poems seem conceived and brought to a conclusion virtually by providence itself, to which tragedy grants scarcely any role since there it would also cause indignation, which Aristotle did not allow.[33] Giraldi and others, therefore, should not have introduced Nemesis on the stage. Moreover, other kinds of poem move wonder in order to move laughter or compassion or some other emotion. But the epic poet has no other purpose, moves compassion in order to move wonder, and in fact moves it much more powerfully and more often. We shall then say that the epic poem is an imitation of a noble action, great and perfect, narrated in the loftiest verse, with the purpose of moving the mind to wonder and thus being useful.

The epic poem, like any other thing that is a whole, has its components. Its qualitative components are doubtless four: [First is] the fable, which Aristotle defines as the imi-

---

[23]Tasso gives the passage from *To Nicocles* 48–9 in Italian.
[24]*Poetics* IX, 11–12. See p. 55.
[25]*Poetics* XXIV, 8. See p. 63.

---

[26]Tasso miswrites *delle ninfe converse in navi* (of the nymphs transformed into ships) for the transformation of the ships into nymphs in *Aeneid* 9. 80–122.
[27]   Taccia di Cadmo e d'Aretusa Ovidio;
    ché se quello in serpente e questa in fonte
    converte poetando, io non l'invidio.
    (*Inferno* 25. 97–9.)
[28]In *Filocolo.*
[29]*Orlando Furioso* 6. 26–53.
[30]Cantos 5 ff.
[31]Malagigi in *Orlando Innamorato.*
[32]Canto 14.
[33]*Poetics* XV, 7.

tation of the action and for its sake of those who perform the action—this part he calls the first principle and soul of the poem. The second is the moral habit of the persons introduced in the fable. The third is thought. The last is diction.[34] But the number of quantitative parts is more doubtful, although they can perhaps be divided into another four thus: in the first part, which corresponds to the prologue of tragedy, the poet proposes, narrates, declares the present state of things, and supplies information about the past, as Homer does in his poems, particularly the *Odyssey;* in the second part, things become disturbed; in the third they begin to unravel; in the fourth they reach their end, their completion, so to speak. And if we wish to use their proper names, they can be called the introduction, the perturbation, the reversal, and the conclusion. Among these I have not counted the episode, although this part is proper to both tragic and epic poems, more in fact to epic, since there its place is not fixed, as the quantitative parts must be. One might also take the quantitative parts as only three: the beginning, the middle, and the end, as Aristotle calls them in defining the whole. But this division is more appropriate to poems whose fable is not involved but simple. The parts of the fable are three. [First is] the reversal, which the Greeks called peripeteia, a change from good to bad fortune or from bad to good; in the heroic poem it is a double change, because some characters pass from prosperity to adversity and others the reverse. Still it ought always to be a change for the better because the happier ending is more suitable to this kind of poem. Pulci, therefore, does not merit much praise for ending with the death of Orlando and other paladins.[35] The second part of the fable is recognition, a passing from ignorance to knowledge of persons once known and later forgotten, whether simple, as that of Ulysses, or mutual, as between Iphigenia and Orestes; and this passage should cause either happiness or misery. The third part is *pathos,* that is a grievous perturbation full of anxieties, such as deaths and wounds and lamentations and complaints, which can move pity; and this part can be seen at the end of the *Iliad.*

Now, having ascertained the nature of this noblest kind of poem and its parts, we may proceed to consider with what art they may be composed, and then judge the definition of the idea. We shall also give some attention to the material, because artificial forms involve consideration of their material. And by the material of poetry I do not mean letters, syllables, words, as Scaliger did, since these may be the materials of both speech and verse; the material of poetry to my

mind is properly defined as the subject which it undertakes to treat. As Porphyry says, in all things a certain something is usually present that corresponds proportionally to matter and form; and this is not properly the end, as Scaliger thought, because the matter is never the end, nor are the material and the final cause the same. Rather, the formal and final causes usually go together; as the Latins say, they coincide. The end, therefore, is the form given by the skill of the poet, who, by adding, diminishing, and varying, disposes the matter and gives another aspect to the action and things he deals with.

Here I would make a fresh start in my treatment of the poet's art if I were not faced with an objection Castelvetro makes against Aristotle: that he ought not to have dealt with the poetic before the historic art, since just as history precedes poetry and truth verisimilitude, so the art of setting down the true should be given first, and then that of adorning the verisimilar—which might not be necessary after the first. Such an opinion strikes me as based on two fundamental concepts, one altogether false: that history precedes poetry. For poets are the most ancient of all writers, and historians began to write centuries later; for which reason we ought not to call that art first whose matter was born later. Moreover, if the historian's art allows a place to rhythm, ornament, and figures of speech, who does not know that these were virtually lent to the writer by the poet? Neither the orator nor others who write prose have therefore anything that is not, so to speak, usurped. But if Castelvetro or others should reply that history, although perhaps second in time, comes first in nature in as much as it sets down the true, which precedes its semblance, I would answer that the poet considers the verisimilar only as it is universal, and therefore it was correct to give precedence to the art of writing on the universal. Nor need we argue whether the universal exists before or after particular things; as Aristotle said more than once, it is enough that it is better known. Aristotle did not give instructions for writing history, perhaps because he thought it a simpler matter. If it belongs to the orator, rhetorical precepts are enough; and if it has some things of its own, as Demetrius Phalereus[36] implies (assigning one kind of sentence structure to the historian, another to the orator), this is not enough to justify a distinct and separate art. The same skill can be employed on the true and the verisimilar. In fact when Aristotle says that poetry deals rather with the universal, he implies the function of history, which is to narrate the particular. But this is not imitating, since imitation is by its nature linked not with truth, but with verisimilitude. Historians, then,

[34]*Poetics* VI, 7–18.
[35]*Morgante* 27. 149–53.

[36]*On Style* 1. 19–21.

ought not to imitate; and if the speeches they include are not without imitation, it is usually because the historian does not narrate what was said in the senate or the army, but what is likely to have been said. Indeed the kind of oration appropriate to the historian is the indirect rather than the direct, as Trogus Pompeius thought. In many speeches in the Greek historians Herodotus and Xenophon, and others later, one sees almost a poetic imitation, where the historian, not content with his own territory, seems to trespass on the confines of poetry. But these things, if I may, I shall examine in the proper place, putting on one side of the scale the judgement of Polybius, who both wrote history and taught how it should be written, and of Dionysius of Halicarnassus, who wrote a commentary on Thucydides, and on the other the authority of Thucydides himself and the other two historians named above, as well as Livy and Sallust, the most highly esteemed Latin historians, who, if I am right, imitated the Greeks. This imitation, however, is not the kind we are discussing, nor the kind Fracastoro meant,[37] which is unsuitable to the historian. Thus, given the diversity of writers and their views, it will not seem superfluous to deal with the historian's art. But now I propose to write of the things I have begun.

---

[37]See Fracastoro, *Naugerius,* tr. Kelso, pp. 56 ff.

Sir Francis Bacon

1561–1626

Champion of the empirical method, Bacon makes an interesting distinction between history and poetry that reflects new and elaborate divisions of experience into subjective and objective realms: Poesy "doth raise and erect the mind, by submitting the shows of things to the desires of the mind, whereas reason doth buckle and bow the mind unto the nature of things." This definition has a neo-Platonic ring. Bacon would seem to agree with Sidney that poetry presents a better world than the real one we live in, since it can express our desires as well as our experience, to which history is properly tied. Further, because it submits to the desires of the mind, poetry is involved with morality or a vision of the good.

Bacon does not think of all poetry as hiding an allegorical meaning, but he believes that some of it does, and he distinguishes "poesy parabolical" from other, more straightforward kinds. He recognizes that many stories ingeniously interpreted as parables were probably not originally intended as such, and we sense in him a considerable impatience with poetic allegory, for which he was criticized by Henry Reynolds.

A standard edition is that by James Spedding, R. L. Ellis, and D. D. Heath, eds., (3 vols., 1870). See also C. D. Broad, *The Philosophy of Francis Bacon* (1926); M. W. Bundy, "Bacon's True Opinion of Poetry," *Studies in Philology,* XXXII (1930), 244–64; L. C. Knights, "Bacon and the Seventeenth-Century Dissociation of Sensibility," *Scrutiny,* XI (1943), 268–85; Karl R. Wallace, *Francis Bacon on Communication and Rhetoric* (1943); F. H. Anderson, *The Philosophy of Francis Bacon* (1948); D. G. James, *The Dream of Learning* (1951); and J. L. Harrison, "Bacon's View of Rhetoric, Poetry, and the Imagination," *Huntington Library Quarterly,* XX (1957), 107–26.

From

The Advancement of Learning

Poesy is a part of learning in measure of words for the most part restrained, but in all other points extremely licensed, and doth truly refer to the imagination, which, being not tied to the laws of matter, may at pleasure join that which nature hath severed, and sever that which nature hath joined, and so make unlawful matches and divorces of things: "*Pictoribus atque poetis,* etc."[1] It is taken in two senses in respect of words or matter. In the first sense it is but a character of style, and belongeth to arts of speech, and is not pertinent for the present. In the latter, it is, as hath been said, one of the principal portions of learning, and is nothing else but feigned history, which may be styled as well in prose as in verse.

The use of this feigned history hath been to give some shadow of satisfaction to the mind of man in those points wherein the nature of things doth deny it, the world being in proportion inferior to the soul; by reason whereof there is agreeable to the spirit of man a more ample greatness, a more exact goodness, and a more absolute variety than can be found in the nature of things. Therefore, because the acts or events of true history have not that magnitude which satisfieth the mind of man, poesy feigneth acts and events greater and more heroical; because true history propoundeth the successes and issues of actions not so agreeable to the merits of

---

THE ADVANCEMENT OF LEARNING. *The Advancement of Learning* was first published in 1605. The text is based on the 1605 edition.
[1]"To painters and poets." Horace, *Art of Poetry,* p. 68. Horace's remark warns against unnatural violations of nature.

virtue and vice, therefore poesy feigns them more just in retribution and more according to revealed providence; because true history representeth actions and events more ordinary and less interchanged, therefore poesy endueth them with more rareness and more unexpected and alternative variations: so as it appeareth that poesy serveth and confereth to magnanimity, morality, and to delectation. And therefore it was ever thought to have some participation of divineness, because it doth raise and erect the mind, by submitting the shows of things to the desires of the mind, whereas reason doth buckle and bow the mind unto the nature of things. And we see that by these insinuations and congruities with man's nature and pleasure, joined also with the agreement and consort it hath with music, it hath had access and estimation in rude times and barbarous regions, where other learning stood excluded.

The division of poesy which is aptest in the propriety thereof (besides those divisions which are common unto it with history, as feigned chronicles, feigned lives, and the appendices of history, as feigned epistles, feigned orations, and the rest) is into poesy narrative, representative, and allusive. The narrative is a mere imitation of history with the excesses before remembered, choosing for subject commonly wars and love, rarely state, and sometimes pleasure or mirth. Representative is as a visible history, and is an image of actions as if they were present, as history is of actions in nature as they are, that is past; allusive, or parabolical, is a narration applied only to express some special purpose or conceit: which latter kind of parabolical wisdom was much more in use in the ancient times, as by the fables of Aesop, and the brief sentences of the seven,[2] and the use of hieroglyphics may appear. And the cause was for that it was then of necessity to express any point of reason which was more sharp or subtle than the vulgar in that manner, because men in those times wanted both variety of examples and subtlety of conceit: and as hieroglyphics were before letters, so parables were before arguments: and nevertheless now and at all times they do retain much life and vigor, because reason cannot be so sensible, nor examples so fit.

But there remaineth yet another use of poesy parabolical opposite to that which we last mentioned; for that tendeth to demonstrate and illustrate that which is taught or delivered, and this other to retire and obscure it: that is, when the secrets and mysteries of religion, policy, or philosophy, are involved in fables or parables. Of this in divine poesy we see the use is authorized. In heathen poesy we see the exposition

of fables doth fall out sometimes with great felicity, as in the fable that the giants being overthrown in their way against the gods, the earth their mother in revenge thereof brought forth fame:

> *Illam terra parens ira irritata deorem,*
> *Extremam, ut perhibent, Caeo Enceladoque sororem*
> *Progenuit:*[3]

expounded that when princes and monarchs have suppressed actual and open rebels, then the malignity of people, which is the mother of rebellion, doth bring forth libels and slanders, and taxations of the states, which is of the same kind with rebellion, but more feminine: so in the fable that the rest of the gods having conspired to bind Jupiter, Pallas called Briareus with his hundred hands to his aid, expounded that monarchies need not fear any curbing of their absoluteness by mighty subjects, as long as by wisdom they keep the hearts of the people, who will be sure to come in on their side: so in the fable that Achilles was brought up under Chyron the centaur, who was part a man and part a beast, expounded ingenuously, but corruptly, by Machiavelli that it belongeth to the education and discipline of princes to know as well how to play the part of the lion in violence and the fox in guile, as of the man in virtue and justice. Nevertheless in many the like encounters, I do rather think that the fable was first and the exposition devised than that the moral was first and thereupon the fable framed. For I find it was an ancient vanity in Chrysippus that troubled himself with great contention to fasten the assertions of the Stoics upon the fictions of the ancient poets: but yet that all the fables and fictions of the poets were but pleasure and not figure, I interpose no opinion. Surely of those poets which are now extant, even Homer himself (notwithstanding he was made a kind of scripture by the later schools of the Grecians) yet I should without any difficulty pronounce, that his fables had no such inwardness in his own meaning: but what they might have, upon a more original tradition, is not easy to affirm, for he was not the inventor of many of them. In this third part of learning which is poesy, I can report no deficience. For being as a plant that cometh of the lust of the earth, without a formal seed, it hath sprung up and spread abroad, more than any other kind: but to ascribe unto it that which is due for the expressing of affections, passions, corruptions and customs, we are beholding to poets more than to the philosophers' works, and for wit and eloquence not much less than to orators' harangues.

---

[2]There were different lists of the seven so-called wise men of Greece. They usually included Thales, Solon, Bias, Pittacus, Periander, Chilon, and Cleabolus.

[3]"Angered by the Gods, Mother Earth, it is said, gave birth to the last one, sister to Caeus and Enceladus." *Aeneid,* IV. 178.

Henry Reynolds

fl. 1627–1632

Mythomystes by Henry Reynolds, a little-known writer, begins as one of those many polemics that defend the ancient writers against the moderns. In this respect it is most notable for the spirit of its invective. Of the less talented among the moderns Reynolds remarks,

> The rack will not be able to make the most advised among twenty of them confess, to have farther inquired, or attended to more, in the best of their authors they have chosen to read and study, than merely his style, phrase, and manner of expression; or scarce suffered themselves to look beyond the dimension of their own brain, for any better counsel or instruction elsewhere.

It is through Reynolds' praise of the wisdom of the ancients and his attack on the shallowness of the moderns that his essay becomes a defense (and a very single-minded one, indeed) of neo-Platonic and occult allegorizations of myth and literature. This mode of interpretation, not unusual in Reynolds' time, was revived in the Romantic age by Thomas Taylor and has been applied by twentieth-century critics to the writings of Blake, Yeats, and others.

Allegorical interpretations of Homer date back to the sixth century B.C. Neo-Platonic readings were common in the early Christian period, the most famous perhaps being Porphyry's interpretation of the cave of the nymphs passage from the *Odyssey*. Reynolds supposes the existence of a tradition of hidden wisdom, perpetuated mainly by poets. The interpreter seeks the "senses and meanings of fables taken out and separated from their husks and involvements." Reynolds is critical of those moderns who learn only "style, phrase, and manner of expression" from the ancients. He consistently separates content from formal concerns and clearly is most interested in the hidden content of ancient works—"secreter mysteries, and abstrusities of most high divinity, hidden and concealed under the bark and rude cover of the words." The work of the moderns who are ignorant of these mysteries remains trivial for him.

Toward the end of his essay Reynolds criticizes Bacon for offering learned interpretations of ancient fables on the one hand and doubting on the other that they really contain arcane wisdom. All in all, Reynolds believes, the ancients excelled the moderns because they studied wisdom; indeed they held it in such great respect that they concealed it by allegory from vulgar minds. Like Sidney, Reynolds defends poetry because of its allegorical content, but Sidney sees other aspects of literary art that are apparently beyond the more single-minded Reynolds.

The essay was originally published with an appendix offering the reasons for Plato's banishment of poets from the republic and the story of Narcissus "briefly mythologized."

Very little is known about Reynolds. The contemporary poet Michael Drayton dedicated a poem to him in 1627, and it was probably about this time that Reynolds translated Tasso's *Aminta* and wrote, in addition to *Mythomystes,* a book of tales imitated from Anguillara's *Ovid.* Little has been written about Reynolds. See J. E. Spingarn, *Critical Essays of the Seventeenth Century* (1907) I, xx–xxii, and A. M. Cinquemani, "Henry Reynolds' *Mythomystes* and the Continuity of Ancient Modes of Allegoresis in Seventeenth-Century England," *PMLA,* LXXXV (1970), 1040–49.

Mythomystes

To the candid and ingenuous reader: Look not, generous reader (for such I write to) for more in the few following leaves, than a plain and simple verity; unadorned at all with elocution, or rhetorical phrase; glosses fitter perhaps to be set upon silken and thin paradoxical semblances, than appertaining to the care of who desires to lay down a naked and unmasked truth. Nor expect here an encomium or praise of any such thing as the world ordinarily takes poesy for; that same thing being (as I conceive) a superficial mere outside of sense, or gay bark only (without the body) of reason; witness so many excellent wits that have taken so much pains in these times to defend her; which sure they would not have done, if what is generally received nowadays for poesy, were not merely a faculty, or occupation of so little consequence, as by the lovers thereof rather to be (in their own favor) excused, than for any good in the thing itself, to be commended. Nor must thou here expect thy solution, if thy curiosity invite thee to a satisfaction in any the underaccidents, but in merely the essential form, of true poesy: such I call the accidents or appendixes thereto, as conduce somewhat to the matter, and end, nothing to the real form and essence thereof. And these accidents (as I call them) our commenders and defenders of poesy have chiefly, and indeed sufficiently insisted, and dilated upon; and are first, those flowers (as they are called) of rhetoric, consisting of their anaphoras, epistrophes, metaphors, metonymys, synecdoches and those their other potent tropes and figures; helps (if at all of use to furnish out expressions with) much properer sure, and more fitly belonging to poesy than oratory; yet such helps, as if nature have not beforehand in his birth, given a poet, all such

forced art will come behind as lame to the business, and deficient, as the best-taught country Morris dancer with all his bells and napkins, will ill deserve to be in an Inn of Court at Christmas, termed the thing they call a fine reveler. The other accidents of poesy, and that are the greater part of the appurtenances thereof, in the account of our poets of these times, are also here utterly unmentioned; such as are, what sort of poem may admit the blank verse, what requires exact rhyme; where the strong line (as they call it), where the gentle, sorts best; what subject must have the verse of so many feet, what of other; where the masculine rhyme, where the feminine, and where the three-syllabled (which the Italians call their *rhyme sdrucciole*) are to be used. These (I say) and the like adjuncts of poesy, (elsewhere amply discoursed of by many curious wits), are not here mentioned. Only what I conceived fit to speak (and with what brevity I could) of the ancient poets in general, and of the form and real essence of true poesy, considered merely in its own worth and validity, without extrinsic and suppeditative[1] ornament at all, together with the parallel of their foil (our modern poets and poesies), I have (to the end to redeem in some part, and vindicate that excellent art from the injury it suffers in the world's general misprision and misconstruction thereof) here touched, and but touched; the rather to awake some abler understanding than my own, to the pursuit (if they please) of a theme (I conceive) well worthy a greater industry, and happier leisures than I myself possess.

I have thought upon the times we live in; and am forced to affirm the world is decrepit, and out of its age and doting estate, subject to all the imperfections that are inseparable from that wrack and maim of nature, that the young behold with horror, and the sufferers thereof lie under with murmur and languishment. Even the general soul of this great creature, whereof every one of ours is a several piece, seems bedridden, as upon her deathbed, and near the time of her dissolution to a second better estate, and being: the years of her

---

MYTHOMYSTES. *Mythomystes* was probably published in 1632. It is subtitled "Wherein a short survey is taken of the nature and value of true poesy and depth of the ancients above our modern poets." The text is based on the 1632(?) edition and J. E. Spingarn's edition of 1907. Latin phrases and quotations that are not immediately translated in the text by Reynolds are translated in the footnotes.

---

[1]Supporting, or useful.

strength are past; and she is now nothing but disease for the soul's health is no other than merely the knowledge of the truth of things. Which health, the world's youth enjoyed; and hath now exchanged for it, all the diseases of all errors, heresies, and different sects and schisms of opinions and understandings in all matter of arts, sciences, and learnings whatsoever. To help on these diseases to incurability, what age hath ever been so fruitful of liberty in all kinds, and of all permission and allowance for this reason of ours, to run wildly all her own hurtfullest ways without bridle, bound, or limit at all? For instance; what books have we of whatever knowledge, or in what mysteries soever, wisely by our ancients (for avoiding of this present malady the world is now fallen into) couched, and carefully enfolded, but must be by every illiterate person without exception, deflowered and broken open, or broken in pieces, because beyond his skill to unlock them? Or what law have we that provides for the restraint of these myriads of hotheaded wranglers, and ignorant writers and teachers, which, out of the bare privilege of perhaps but puny graduate in some university, will venture upon all, even the most removed and most abstruse knowledges, as perfect understanders and expounders of them, upon the single warrant of their own brain; or inventors of better themselves, than all antiquity could deliver down to them; out of the treasonous mint of their own imaginations? What havoc, what mischief to all learnings, and how great a multiplicity of poisonous errors and heresies must not of necessity hence ensue, and overspread the face of all truths whatsoever?

Among these heresies (to omit those in matter of divinity, or the right form of worshiping God, which the doctors of his church are fitter to make the subjects of their tongues and pens, than I, a layman, and all unworthy the task), among, I say, these (if I may so call them) heresies, or ridiculous absurdities in matter of humane letters, and their professors in these times, I find none so gross, nor indeed any so great scandal, or maim to humane learning, as in the almost general abuse, and violence offered to the excellent art of poesy; first, by those learned (as they think themselves) of our days, who call themselves poets; and next, by such as out of their ignorance, heed not how much they profane that high and sacred title in calling them so.

From the number of these first mentioned (for, for the last, I will not mention them; nor yet say as a grave father, and holy one too, of certain obstinate heretics said, *"Decipiantur in nomine diaboli";*[2] but charitably wish their reformation, and cure of their blindness) from the multitude (I

say) of the common rhymers in these our modern times, and modern tongues, I will exempt some few, as of a better rank and condition than the rest. And first to begin with Spain. I will say it may justly boast to have afforded (but many ages since) excellent poets, as Seneca, the tragedian, Lucan, and Martial the epigrammatist, with others; and in these latter times, as diverse in prose, some good theologians also in rhyme, but for other poesies in their (now spoken) tongue, of any great name (not to extol their trifling, though extolled *Celestina,* nor the second part of their *Diana de Montemayor,* better much than the first; and these but poetic prosers neither), I cannot say it affords many, if any at all: the inclination of that people being to spend much more with, and more happily in those prose romances they abound in, such as their *Lazarillo, Don Quixote, Guzman,* and those kind of cuentos[3] of their picaros, and gitanillas,[4] than in rhyme. The French likewise, more than for a Ronsard, or Desportes, but chiefly their Salluste (who may pass among the best of our moderns), I can say little of. Italy hath in all times, as in all abilities of the mind besides, been much fertiler than either of these, in poets. Among who (to omit a Petrarch, who though he was an excellent rhymer in his own tongue, and for his Latin *Africa* justly deserved the laurel that was given him; yet was a much excellenter philosopher in prose; and with him, a Bembo, Dante, Ang[elo], Politian[i], Caporali, Pietro Aretino, Sannazaro, Guarini, and divers others, men of rare fancy all) I must prefer chiefly three; as the grave and learned Tasso, in his *Sette giorni,* (a divine work) and his *Gerusalemme liberata,* so far as an excellent pile of merely moral philosophy may deserve. Then, Ariosto, for the artful woof of his ingenious, though unmeaning fables; the best, perhaps, have in that kind been sung since Ovid. And lastly, that smooth-writ *Adonis* of Marino, full of various conception, and diversity of learning. The Dutch I cannot mention, being a stranger to their minds, and manners; therefore I will return home to my countrymen, and mother tongue: And here, exempt from the rest, a Chaucer, for some of his poems; chiefly his *Troilus and Cressida.* Then the generous and ingenious Sidney, for his smooth and artful *Arcadia* (and who I could wish had chosen rather to have left us of his pen, an encomiastic poem in honor, than prose-apology in defense, of his favorite, the excellent art of poesy). Next, I must approve the learned Spenser, in the rest of his poems, no less than his *Faerie Queene,* an extract body of the ethic doctrine: though some good judgments have wished (and perhaps not without cause) that he had therein been a little freer of his

---

[2]"Let them be deceived in the name of the devil."

[3]Short stories.
[4]Rogues and gypsies.

fiction, and not so close-riveted to his moral; no less than many do to Daniel's *Civil Wars,* that it were (though otherwise a commendable work) yet somewhat more than a true chronicle history in rhyme; who, in other less labored things, may have indeed more happily (however, always clearly and smoothly) written. We have among us a late-writ *Polyolbion* also, and an *Agincourt,* wherein I will only blame their honest author's ill fate, in not having laid him out some happier clime, to have given honor and life to, in some happier language. After these (besides some late dead) there are others now living, dramatic and lyric writers, that I must deservedly commend for those parts of fancy and imagination they possess; and should much more, could we see them somewhat more, force those gifts, and liberal graces of nature, to the end she gave them; and therewith, work and constantly tire upon solid knowledges; the which having from the rich founts of our reverend ancients, drawn with unwearied, and wholesomely employed industries; they might in no less pleasing and profitable fictions than they have done (the very fittest conduit pipes) derive down to us the understanding of things even farthest removed from us, and most worthy our speculation, and knowledge. But alas, such children of obedience, I must take leave to say, the most of our ordinary pretenders to poesy nowadays, are to their own, and the diseased times' ill habits, as the rack will not be able to make the most advised among twenty of them confess, to have farther inquired, or attended to more, in the best of their authors they have chosen to read and study, than merely his style, phrase, and manner of expression; or scarce suffered themselves to look beyond the dimension of their own brain, for any better counsel or instruction elsewhere. What can we expect then of the poems they write? Or what can a man methinks liken them more fitly to, than to Ixion's issue?[5] For he that with merely a natural vein (and a little vanity of nature, which I can be content to allow a poet) writes without other grounds of solid learning, than the best of these ungrounded rhymers understand or aim at, what does he more than embrace assembled clouds with Ixion, and beget only monsters? This might yet be borne with, did not these people as confidently usurp to themselves the title of scholars, and learned men, as if they possessed the knowledges of all the magi, the wise East did ever breed; when, let me demand but a reason for security of my judgment in allowing them for such, they straight give me to know they understand the Greek, and Latin; and in conclusion, I discover, the complete crown of all their ambition is but to be styled by others a good Latinist or Grecian, and then they style themselves good scholars. So would I too, had I not beforehand been taught to say: *"Non quia Graeca scias, vel calles verba Latina, doctus es aut sapiens, sed quia vera vides";*[6] and besides, happened to know a late travailing Odcombian[7] among us; that became (I know not for what mortaller sin than his variety of language) the common scorn, and contempt of all the abusive wits of the time; yet possessed both those languages in great perfection; as his eloquent orations in both tongues (and uttered upon his own head without prompting) have ever sufficiently testified. Now, finding this to be the greater part of the scholarship these our poets endeavor to have, and which many of them also have; I find with all, they sit down as satisfied, as if their unfurnished breasts contained each one that learning and wisdom of an Orpheus, Virgil, Hesiod, Pindarus, and Homer all together. When as, what have they else but the bark and clothing merely wherein their high and profound doctrines lay? Never looking farther into those their golden fictions for any higher sense, or anything diviner in them enfolded and hid from the vulgar, but lulled with the marvelous expression and artful contexture of their fables—*"tanquam parvi pueri"* (as one says) *"per brumam ad ignem sessitantes, aniles nugas fabellasque de poetis imbibunt, com interim de utiliore sanctioreque sententia minime sunt solliciti."*[8]

I have stayed longer, and rubbed harder methinks than needs, upon the sore of our nowaday poets. Let me leave them, and look back to the never enough honored ancients; and set them before our eyes, who no less deservedly wore the name of prophets, and privy counselors of the gods (to use their own phrase, or sons of the gods, as Plato calls them) than poets. To the end we may, if in this declining state of the world we cannot rectify our oblique one, by their perfect and straight line, yet endeavor it: and in the meantime give the awful reverence due to them, for the many regions of distance between their knowledges and ours. And this that we may the better do, let us parallel them with the poets (if I may so call them) of our times, in three things only, and so carry along together their straight and our crooked line; for our better knowledge of them, and reformation of ourselves. In the first place then, let us take a survey of their natural inclination and propensity to the acquisition of the knowledge of truth, by what is delivered to us of them; as also, of

---

[5]Centaurus, the first centaur, was born of the union of Ixion with a cloud-image of Hera. Zeus substituted the cloud for Hera in order to thwart Ixion's planned seduction of her.

[6]"You are learned and wise not because you know Greek and Latin, but because you [can] see the truth."

[7]Thomas Coryate (1577?–1617), English traveler born at Odcombe and author of *Coryate's Crudities,* an account of his travels on foot.

[8]"Just as small boys who sit by the fire on a cold winter's day, taking in old women's trifles and tales about the poets, while at the same time showing no concern whatsoever about more useful and sacred matters."

their willing neglect, and aversion from all worldly business and cogitations that might be hindrances in the way to their desired end.

1. It is in humane experience found, as well as by all writers determined, that the powerfullest of all the affects of the mind is love, and therefore the divine Plato says, it is justly called *roma;* which among the Greeks, is force, potency, or vehemence. Of this love there be two kinds; celestial or intellectual; or else carnal or vulgar. Of both these kinds Solomon hath spoken excellently; of the vulgar, in his proverbs as a moral, and in his *Ecclesiastes* as a natural philosopher; and divinelike of the divine and intellectual love in his canticle; for which it is called among all the rest of the Holy Scripture *Canticum canticorum,* as the most sacred and divine. The object of this celestial or intellectual love (for the other, or vulgar love it concerns me not to mention) is the excellency of the beauty of supernal and intellectual things: to the contemplation whereof, rational and wise spirits are forcibly raised and lifted aloft; yea, lifted oftentimes so far (says Plato) above mortality, as even— *"in Deum transeunt,"*[9] and so full fraught with the delight and abundance of the pleasure they feel in those their elevations, raptures, and mental alienations (wherein the soul remains for a time quite separated as it were from the body) do not only sing with the ingenious Ovid: *"Est Deus in nobis, agitante calescimus illo,"*[10] but in an ecstatic manner, and to use Plato's phrase— *"divino afflatu concitati,"*[11] cry out with the entranced Zoroaster—"Ope thine eyes, ope them wide; raise and lift them aloft."[12] And of this, the excellent Prince Jo[sephus] Picus-Mirandula (in a discourse of his upon the doctrine of Plato) gives the reason; saying:

Such, whose understanding (being by philosophical study refined and illuminated) knows this sensible beauty to be but the image of another more pure and excellent, leaving the love of this, desire to see the other; and persevering in this elevation of the mind, arrive at last to that celestial love; which although it lives in the understanding of the soul of every man, yet they only (says he) make use of it, and they are but few, who separating themselves wholly from the care of the body, seem thence oftentimes ecstatic, and as it were quite rav-

ished and exalted above the earth and all earthly amusements.

And farther, in another place of that treatise, adds that many with the fervent love of the beauty and excellence of intellectual things, have been so raised above all earthly considerations, as they have lost the use of their corporal eyes. "Homer," (says he) "with seeing the ghost of Achilles, which inspired him with that poetic fury, that who with understanding reads, shall find to contain in it all intellectual contemplation, was thereby deprived" (or feigned to be deprived) "of his corporal eyesight," as one that seeing all things above, could not attend to the heeding of trivial and meaner things below. And such rapture of the spirit, is expressed (says he)

in the fable of Tiresias that Callimachus sings; who for having seen Pallas naked (which signifies no other than that ideal beauty, whence proceeds all sincere wisdom, and not clothed or covered with corporal matter) became suddenly blind, and was by the same Pallas made a prophet; so as that which blinded his corporal eyes, opened to him the eyes of his understanding; by which he saw not only all things past, but also all that were to come.

Lo, these, and such spirits as these the learned Picus speaks of, such were those of those ancient fathers of all learning, and Tiresias-like prophets, as poets: such their neglect of the body, and business of the world! Such their blindness to all things of trivial and inferior condition; and such lastly were those ecstatic elevations; or that truly divinus furor of theirs, which Plato speaking of says it is—"a thing so sacred, as— *non sine maximo favore Dei comparari queat";* cannot be attained to without the wonderful favor of God.[13] And which self thing themselves meant in their fable of that beautiful Ganymede they sing of (which interpreted, is the contemplation of the soul, or the rational part of man), so dear to the God of gods and men, as that he raiseth it up to heaven, there to pour out to him (as they make him his cupbearer) the sovereign nectar of sapience and wisdom, the liquor he is only best pleased and delighted with. These were those fathers (as I lately called them) and founts of knowledge and learning; or nurses of wisdom, from whose pregnant breasts the whole world hath sucked the best part of all the humane knowledge it hath; and from whose wise and excellent fables (as one of our late mythologians truly notes):

---

[9]Reynolds is probably referring to remarks in *Ion:* "They transcend unto God" (p. 14).
[10]"God is within us, [and] we become inflamed with him stimulating us." *Fasti,* VI. 5.
[11]Probably *Ion:* "Roused by divine inspiration" (p. 14).
[12]The quotations here are from Pico, *Comments,* III. 4. Giovanni Pico della Mirandola (1463–94) was an Italian humanist scholar.

---

[13]*Ion,* p. 14.

all those were after them called philosophers took their grounds and first *initia philosophandi;* adding, that their philosophy was no other than merely—*fabularum sensa ab involucris exuuiisque fabularum explicata*—the senses and meanings of fables taken out and separated from their husks and involvements. With whom the excellent Jo[sephus] Picus (or rather Phoenix as wise men have named him) consenting, says in his *Apologia* (speaking of the poesies of Zoroaster and Orpheus)—*"Orpheus apud Graecos ferme intiger; Zoroaster apud eos mancus, apud Caldaeos absolutior legitur.*[14] *Ambo"* (says he) *"priscae Sapientiae patres et authores."* Both of them fathers and authors of the ancient wisdom. With these also the most authentic Iamblicus, the Caldean, who writes—Pythagoras had—*Orphicam Theologiam tanquam exemplar, ad quam ipse suam effingeret formaretque philosophiam";* the theology of Orpheus as his copy and pattern, by which he formed and fashioned his philosophy.[15] I will add a word more of the before cited Picus; who thus far farther of Orpheus in particular says—*"Secreta de numeris doctrina, et quicquid magnum sublimeque habuit Graeca philosophia, ab Orphei institutis ut a primo fonte manavit,"* the mystical doctrine of numbers, and whatever the Greek philosophy had in it great and high, flowed all from the institutions of Orpheus, as from their first fount.[16] And of the rest of his rank and fraternity, those *"Sapientiae patres, ac duces"*[17] (as Plato calls those old excellent poets), I will conclude in general, with the testimony of first, the now-mentioned Plato; who says likewise elsewhere *"Nihil aliud sunt quam deorum interpretes";* they are no other than the interpreters of the gods. And in another place that—their *"praeclara poemata non hominum sunt inventa, sed caelestia munera."* Their excellent poems are not the inventions of men, but gifts and graces of heaven.[18] And lastly with Farra the learned Alexandrian, who, speaking likewise of the old poets, says—"Their fables are all full of most high mysteries; and have in them that splendor that is shed into the fancy and intellect, ravished, and inflamed with divine fury." And in the same treatise makes this particular mention of some of them—"and in those times flourished Linus, Orpheus, Musaeus, Homer, Hesiod, and all the other most famous of that truly golden age."[19]

Now to apply this short view we have taken of these ancient poets; whither there appears aught in any our stu-dents, or writers of our times, be they poets or philosophers (I put them together, as who are, or should be both professors of but one, and the same learning, though by the one received and delivered in the apparel of verse, the other of prose) that may in any degree of coherence suffer a parallel with either the inclinations or abilities of such as these before mentioned, I wish we could see cause to grant, but rather, that there is in them (for aught appears) no such inclination to the love or search of any great or high truths (for the truth's sake, merely) nor the like neglect of the world and blindness to the vanities thereof, in respect of it, nor lastly, any fruits from them, favoring of the like industry, or bearing any shadow scarce of similitude with that of theirs, we may positively affirm; as a truth no less obvious to every man's eye, than the lamentable cause and occasion thereof is to every man's understanding; which is the mean account, or rather contempt and scorn that in these days, all ungaining sciences, and that conduce not immediately to worldly profit, or popular eminence, are held in the poet especially.

> *Qual vaghezza di lauro, qual di mirto?*
> *Povera, e nuda vai filosofia,*
> *Dice la turba al vil guadagno intesa.*[20]

Whence it is, that much time spent in solid countemplative studies is held vain and unnecessary; and these slight flashes of ungrounded fancy, (ingenious nothings, and mere embroideries upon cobwebs) that the world swarms with (like sophisticate alchemy gold that will not abide the first touch, yet glitters more in the eye than the sad weightier true gold), are only labored for and attended to; because they take best, and most please the corrupt taste and false appetite of the sordid and barbarous times we live in. And yet to speak a truth, I cannot herein blame the diseased world so much, as I do the infelicity of that sacred art of poesy; which like the sovereign prescriptions of a Galen or Hippocrates, ordered and dispensed by illiterate empirics or dogleeches, must needs (as the best physics ill handled) prove but so much variety of poison instead of cure. And such are the mountebank rhymers of the time, and so faulty, that have so much abused their profession, and the world; and stuck so general a scandal upon that excellent physic of the mind; with the poison of their meretricious flatteries, and base servile fawning at the heels of worldly wealth and greatness, as makes it abhorred of all men; and most, of those that are of most understanding. For indeed what can be more contemptible, or

---

[14]"Among the Greeks Orpheus is virtually complete; Zoroaster is incomplete among them; among the Chaldeans more fully collected." From Pico's *Oration on the Dignity of Man,* part of which appears in the *Apology.*

[15]*Apology.*

[16]*Apology.*

[17]"Fathers and leaders of wisdom."

[18]*Ion,* p. 14, and *Phaedrus.*

[19]Alessandro Farra, *Settenario.*

[20]"What is the enticement of laurel, what of myrtle? / Poor and nude, you go, philosophy, / Says the mob, with base rewards concerned." Petrarch, *La gola e'l sonno e'oziose piume.*

breed a greater indignation in wise and understanding minds, than to see the study of wisdom made not only a mercenary, but vicious occupation. And that same—*"pudicam Palladem"* (as a wise author from the like resentment aptly says) *"deorum munere inter homines divers antem eiici, explodi exibilavi; non habere qui amet, qui faveat, nisi ipsa quasi prostans, et praefloratae virginitatis accepta mercedula, maleparatum aes in amatoris arculam referat."*[21]

2. The second great disparity, that I find between those ancient fathers of learning, and our modern writers, is in the price and estimation they held their knowledges in. Which appears in the care they took to conceal them from the unworthy vulgar; and which doth no less commend their wisdom, than conclude (by their contrary course) our moderns, empty, and barren of anything rare and precious in them; who in all probability would not prostitute all they know to the rape and spoil of every illiterate reader, were they not conscious to themselves their treasure deserves not many locks to guard it under. But that I may not conclude upon a —*non concessum,*[22] for I remember I have heard it affirmed (and by some too that the time calls scholars), that the ancients certainly spoke their meanings as plain as they could, and were the honester men for doing so; and there may be more birds besides, of the same feather with these; therefore I will in charity speak a word or two for these people's instruction; and in the mean between the whining Heraclitus and overrigid Democritus (as much as in me lies) *comiter erranti monstrare viam.*[23]

Let such then as are to learn whither to conceal their knowledges, was the intent and studied purpose of the ancient poets all, and most of the ancient philosophers also, let such I say, know, that, when in the world's youth and capabler estate, those old, wise Egyptian priests began to search out the mysteries of nature (which was at first the whole world's only divinity), they devised, to the end to retain among themselves what they had found (lest it should be abused and vilified by being delivered to the vulgar), certain marks, and characters of things, under which all the precepts of their wisdom were contained; which marks they called hieroglyphics or sacred engravings. And more than thus, they delivered little: or whatever it was, yet always *dissimulanter,*[24] and in enigmas and mystical riddles, as their follow-

ings disciples also did. And this proviso of theirs, those images of Sphinx they placed before all their temples did insinuate; and which they set for admonitions, that high and mystical matters should by riddles and enigmatical knots be kept inviolate from the profane multitude. I will give instance of one or two of them. The authentic testimony late cited (to other purpose) by me of Orpheus, and his learning, (viz. that he was one of the *"priscae sapientiae patres,"* and that the *"secreta de numeris doctrina"* and whatever the Greek philosophy had in it—*"magnum et sublime,"* did from his institutions, *"ut a primo fonte manare,"*[25] hath these words immediately following—*"Sed qui erat veterum mos philosophorum, ita Orpheus suorum dogmatum mysteria fabularum intexit involucris, et poetico velamento dissimulavit; ut si quis legat illos hymnos nihil subesse credat praeter fabellas nugasque meracissimas"*—but as it was the manner of the ancient philosophers, so Orpheus within the folds and involvements of fables, hid the mysteries of his doctrine; and dissembled them under a poetic mask; so as who reads those hymns of his, will not believe anything to be included under them, but mere tales and trifles.[26] Homer likewise, by the same mouth positively averred to have included in his two poems of *Iliads* and *Odysseys*—all intellectual contemplation; and which are called the sun and moon of the earth, for the light they bear (as one well notes) before all learning (and of which Democritus speaking—as Farra the Alxandrian observes—says "it was impossible but Homer, to have composed so wonderful works, must have been endued with a divine and inspired nature; who under a curious, and pleasing veil of fable, hath taught the world how great and excellent the beauty of true wisdom is."[27] No less than Ang[elus] Politianus who says, *"Omnia in his, et ab his sunt omnia."*[28]); yet what appears (I say) in these works of Homer the mere, or ignorant reader, at all of doctrine or document, or more, than two fictious impossible tales, or lies of many men that never were, and thousands of deeds that never were done? Nor less cautious than these, were most of the ancient philosophers also. The divine Plato writing to a friend of his *"de supremis substantius—per aenigmata"* (says he) *"dicendum est: nesi epistola forte ad aliorum pervenerit manus, quae tibi scribimus, ab alius intelligantur"*— we must write in enigmas and riddles; lest if it come to other hands; what we write to thee, be understood by others. Aristotle of those his books, wherein he treats of supernatural

---

[21] "I have thrown out, booted out, hissed out chaste Pallas, who was sojourning among men as a gift from the gods; in order for her not to have anyone who would love her or who would lie close to her unless she, like a prostitute would stash away, in her money box, her ill-gotten gain, the price of her deflowered virginity." Pico, *Apology.*
[22] "Nonconcession."
[23] "Obligingly pointed out the way to the wanderer."
[24] "Slyly" or "in a misleading fashion."

[25] "Fathers of ancient wisdom" . . . "secret of doctrine of numbers" . . . "great and sublime" . . . "flow forth as from a fountainhead." Pico, *Apology.*
[26] Pico, *Apology.*
[27] *Settenario.*
[28] "All things are in this and from this." *Sylvae.*

things, says (as Aulus Gellius testifies) that—they were—"*editi, et non editi*"; as much as to say, mystically or enigmatically written; adding farther—*cognobiles iis tantum erunt qui nos audiunt*"—they shall be only known to our hearers or disciples.[29] And this closeness Pythagoras also having learned of those his masters, and taught it his disciples, he was made the master of silence. And who, as all the doctrines he delivered were (after the manner of the Hebrews, Egyptians, and most ancient poets) laid down in enigmatical and figurative notions, so one among other of his is this—"Give not readily thy right hand to everyone," by which precept (says the profound Iamblicus) that great master advertiseth that we ought not to communicate to unworthy minds, and not yet practiced in the understanding of occult doctrines, those mysterious instructions that are only to be opened (says he) and taught to sacred and sublime wits, and such as have been a long time exercised and versed in them.

Now, from this means that the first ancients used, of delivering their knowledges thus among themselves by word of mouth; and by successive reception from them down to after ages, that art of mystical writing by numbers, wherein they couched under a fabulous attire, those their verbal instructions, was after, called *scientia cabalae,* or the science of reception: *cabala* among the Hebrews signifying no other than the Latin *receptio:* a learning by the ancients held in high estimation and reverence and not without great reason; for if God (as the excellent Jo[sephus] Picus rehearses)—"*nihil casu, sed omnia per suam sapientiam ut in pondere et mensura, ita in numero disposuit*"; did nothing by chance, but through his wisdom disposed all things as in weight and measure, so likewise in number;[30] (and which taught the ingenious Salluste to say, that,

> Sacred harmony
> And law of number did accompany
> Th' almighty most, when first his ordinance
> Appointed earth to rest, and heaven to dance).[31]

Well might Plato consequently affirm that—"among all liberal arts, and contemplative sciences, the chiefest and most divine was the—*scientia numerandi,*" and who likewise questioning why man was the wisest of animals, answers himself again (as Aristotle in his *Problems* observes)—"*quia numerare novit*"—because he could number no less than Avenzoar the Babylonian, whose frequent word by Al-

bumazar's report (as Picus-Mirandula notes) was—"*eum omnia nosse qui noverat numerare*"—that he knows all things that knows numbers.[32] But howsoever an art thus highly cried up by the ancients; yet a learning (I say) now more than half lost; or at least by such as possess any limb of it, rather talked of, than taught. Rabanus a great doctor of the Christian church only excepted, who hath writ a particular book—*de Numerorum virtutibus,* by diverse others, as Ambrose, Nazianzen, Origin, Augustine, and many more (as the learned Jo[sephus] Picus at large in his *Apology* shows) reverently mentioned, but never published in their writings. And I am fully of opinion (which till I find reason to recant, I will not be ashamed to own) that the ignorance of this art, and the world's maim in the want, or not understanding of it, is insinuated in the poet's generally sung fable of Orpheus: whom they feign to have recovered his Eurydice from hell, with his music; that is truth and equity, from darkness of barbarism and ignorance, with his profound and excellent doctrines; but, that in the thick, caliginous way to the upper earth, she was lost again; and remains lost to us, that read and understand him not, for want, merely for the knowledge of that art of numbers that should unlock and explain his mystical meanings to us.

This learning of the Egyptians (thus concealed by them, as I have showed) being transferred from them to the Greeks; was by them from hand to hand delivered still in fabulous riddles among them; and thence down to the Latins. Of which beads, the ingenious Ovid has made a curious and excellent chain; though perhaps he understood not their depth; as our wisest naturalists doubt not to affirm, his other countrymen Lucretius, and that more learned scholar (I mean imitator) of Hesiod, the singular Virgil, did; and which are the sinews and marrow, no less than stars and ornaments of his incomparable poems: and still by them, as by their masters before them, preserved with equal care, from the mischief of divulgation, or profanation: a vice by the ancients in general, no less than by Moses particularly, in the delivering of the law (according to the opinions of the most learned, both Christian divines, and Jewish rabines) with singular caution provided against and avoided. "Write," (said the Angel to Esdras) "all these things that thou hast seen, in a book, and hide them, and teach them only to the wise of the people, whose hearts thou knowest may comprehend and keep these secrets."[33] And since I late mentioned that great secretary of God, Moses, to whose sacred pen as we cannot attribute too much, so, that we may give the greater reverence to him, and consequently the greater credit to the authority of those an-

[29]*Attican Nights,* XX. 5.
[30]*Apology.*
[31]Guillaume de Salluste, sieur Du Bartas, *Divine Weeks and Works.*

[32]*Apology.*
[33]II Esdras 12: 37.

cient followers and imitators of his, or (that I may righter say, and not unreverently) those joint runners with him in the same example of closeness, and care to conceal, I will speak a word or two of him. And upon the warrant of greater understandings than my own, aver that it is the firm opinion of all ancient writers, which (as an indubitable troth) they do all with one mouth confirm, that the full and entire knowledge of all wisdom both divine and humane, is included in the five books of the Mosaic law—*"dissimulata autem, et occultata"* (as the excellent Jo[sephus] Picus in his learned exposition upon him says) *"in literis ipsis, quibus dictiones legis contextae sunt"*—but hidden and disguised even in the letters themselves that form the precepts of the law.[34] And the same Picus, in another discourse of his upon the books of Moses more at large to the same purpose says—*"Scribunt non modo celebres Hebraeorum doctores"* (whom afterwards he names, as)

> *Rabi Eliazar, Rabi Moysis de Egypto, Rabi Simeon Ben Lagis, Rabi Ismahel, Rabi Iodam, et Rabi Nachinan; sed ex nostris quoque Esdras, Hilarius, et Origines, Mosem non legem modo, quam quinque exaratam libris posteris reliquit, sed secretiorem quoque, et veram legis enarrationem in monte divinitus accepisse. Praeceptum autem ei a Deo, ut legem quicem populo publicaret, legis autem interpretationem nec traderet literis nec invulgaret, sed ipse Jesu Nave tantum; tum ille, alliis deinceps sacerdotum primoribus, magna silentii religione revelaret*

—the most renowed and authentic not only among the Hebrew doctors, as Rabbi Eliazar, Rabbi Moses of Egypt, Rabbi Symeon, etc. but among ours also, Esdras, Hillary, and Origin, do write that Moses received from God upon the mount not the law only, which he hath left in five books exactly delivered to posterity, but the more hidden also, and true explanation of the law: but with all, was warned and commanded by God, that as he should publish the law to the people, so the interpretation thereof, he should neither commit to letters nor divulge; but he to Joshua only and Joshua to the other succeeding primaries among the priests; and that, under a great religion of secrecy; and concludes—

> *Et merito quidem; nam satis erat vulgaribus, et per simplicem historiam nunc Dei potentiam, nunc in improbos iram, in bonos clementiam, in omnes justitiam agnoscere, et per divina salutariaque*

praecepta, ad bene beateque vivendum et cultum relligionis institui; at misteria secretiora, et sub cortice legis rudique verborum praetextu latitantia altissimae divinitatis arcana plebi palam facere, quid erat aliud quam dare sanctum canibus, et inter spargere margaritas

—and not without great reason; for it was enough for the multitude to be by merely the simple story, taught and made to know, now the power of God, now his wrath against the wicked, clemency towards the good, and justice to all; and by divine and wholesome precepts instructed in the ways of religion, and holy life. But those secreter mysteries, and abstrusities of most high divinity, hidden and concealed under the bark and rude cover of the words, to have divulged and laid these open to the vulgar; what had it been other than to give holy things to dogs, and cast pearls among swine?[35] So he. And this little that I have here rehearsed (for in a thing so known to all that are knowers, methinks I have said rather too much than otherwise) shall serve for instance of Moses his mystical manner of writing. Which I have the rather done for instruction of some ignorant, though stiff opposers of this truth, that I have lately met with; but chiefly in justification of those other wise ancients of his, and succeeding times, poets, and philosophers, that were no less careful than Moses was, not to give—*"sanctum canibus,"* (as before said) nor *"inter porcos spargere margaritas."*

Now to go about to examine whither it appears our moderns (poets especially, for I will exempt diverse late prose writers), have any the like closeness as before mentioned; were a work sure as vain and unnecessary, as it is a truth firm and unquestionable, that they possess the knowledge of no such mysteries as deserve the use of any art at all for their concealing.

3. The last, and greatest disparity, and wherein above all others, the grossest defect and maim appears, in our moderns (and especially poets) in respect of the ancients; is their general ignorance, even throughout all of them, in any the mysteries and hidden properties of nature; which was an unconcerning inquisition it appears not in their writings they have at all troubled their heads with. Poets I said especially (and indeed only) for we have many prose men excellent natural philosophers in these late times; and that observe strictly that closeness of their wise masters the reverend ancients; so as nowadays our philosophers are all our poets, or what our poets should be; and our poesies grown to be little better than fardels of such small ware as those merchants the French call

---

[34]*Heptaplus.*

[35]*Apology.*

peddlers, carry up and down to sell; whistles, painted rattles, and suchlike Bartholomew-babies;[36] for what other are our common uninstructing fabulous rhymes, than amusements for fools and children? But our rhymes (say they) are full of moral doctrine; be it so. But why not delivered then in plain prose, and as openly to every man's understanding, as it deserves to be taught, and commonly known by everyone? The ancients (say they) were authors of fables, which they sang in measured numbers, as we in imitation of them do. True: but sure enough their meanings were of more high nature, and more difficult to be found out, than any book of manners we shall readily meet withal, affords; else they had not writ them so obscurely, or we should find them out more easily, and make some use of them: whereas not understanding nor seeking to understand them, we make none at all. We live in a mist, blind and benighted; and since our first father's disobedience poisoned himself and his posterity, man is become the imperfectest and most deficient animal of all the field: for then he lost that instinct that the beast retains; though with him the beast, and with it the whole vegetable and general terrene nature also suffered, and still groans under the loss of their first purity, occasioned by his fall. What concerns him now so nearly as to attend to the cultivating or refining, and thereby advancing of his rational part, to the purchase and regaining of his first lost felicity? And what means to conduce to this purchase, can there be, but the knowledge first, and love next (for none can love but what he first knows) of his Maker, for whose love and service he was only made? And how can this blind, lame, and utterly imperfect man, with so great a load to boot of original and actual offense upon his back, hope to approach this supreme altitude, and immensity, which *"in quella inaccessibil luce, / Quasi in alta caligine s'asconde"*[37] (as an excellent poetess describes the inscrutable being of God), but by two means only: the one, by laying his burden on him that on his cross bore the burden of all our defects, and interpositions between us and the hope of the vision of his blessed essence face to face hereafter; and the other, by careful search of him here in this life (according to St. Paul's instruction), in his works; who tells us—"those invisible things of God are clearly seen, being understood by the things that are made";[38] or by the works of his blessed hands? So as, between these two main and only means of acquiring here the knowledge, and hereafter the vision of him wherein all our present and future

happiness consists, what middle place (to descend to my former discourse) can these men's moral philosophy (trow we) challenge? Which in its first master's and teacher's time, before there was any better divinity known, might well enough pass for a coarse kind of divinity; but however, such as one, as (with the leaves of our poets) needs no fiction to clothe or conceal it in. And therefore utterly unfit to be the subject of poems: since it contains in it but the obvious restraints or impulsions of the humane sense and will, to or from what it only beforehand (without extrinsic force or law) feels and knows it ought to shun, or embrace. The other two more removed and harder lessons do certainly more in the affair both of soul and body, concern us. And these (if we be wise enough to love ourselves so well), we must seek and take from the hands of their fittest teachers. As, in the first, we need go no farther (though learned and wise writers have made mention, and to high purpose, of a *theologia philosophica,* as they call some of the doctrines of the ancient poets) than to the doctors, and doctrines of that church that God died to plant, and which shall live till the world's death. And for instruction in our next necessary lesson, to wit, the mysteries of nature, we must, if we will follow Plato's advice—"inquire of those" (and by them be directed) "who lived nearest to the time of the gods"; meaning the old wise ethnics: among whom, the best masters were certainly most, if not all of them, poets; and from whose fires (as I have formerly touched) the greatest part of all humane knowledges have taken their first light. Among these, I say, and not elsewhere (excepting the sacred Old Law only) must we search for the knowledge of the wise, and hidden ways and workings of our great God's handmaid, Nature. But alas who finds, or who seeks nowadays to find them? Nay (what is more strange) there want not of these learned of our times, that will not be entreated to admit those excellent masters of knowledge to mean (if they allow them any meaning) scarce other at all, than merely moral doctrine.

I have known Latin and Greek interpreters of them in these times; men otherwise of much art, and such as able to render their author's phrase to the height of their good, in our worse language; yet ask the most, as I have some of them, and I fear they will answer, as one (and the best) of our Greek translators[39] hath ingenuously confessed to me, that for more than matter of morality, he hath discovered little in his author's meanings. Yet my old good friend as well as I wish him, (and very well I wish him for those parts of fancy, industry, and meritorious ability that are in him) must pardon

---

[36]Dolls sold at Bartholomew Fair, a fair held in London on St. Bartholomew's Day (August 24) from 1133 to 1855.
[37]"In that inaccessible light, / As in an exalted fog, it hides." Vittoria Colonna, *Rhyme of the Three Gentlewomen.*
[38]Romans I:20.

---

[39]George Chapman (1559?–1634), English poet, playwright, and translator of Homer.

me that I affirm, it is not truer that there ever was such a thing as a Musaeus, or Hesiod, or Homer, whom he has taught to speak excellent English; than it is, that the least part of the doctrine (or their wisest expositors abuse me, and other ignorants with me) that they meant to lay down in those their wise, though impossible fables, was matter of manners, but chiefly nature: no less than in the rest of those few before, and many after them, whom all antiquity has cried up for excellent poets, and called their works perfect poems.

For proof of which truth; we will first mention two or three of the best of them; and to omit the multiplicity of less authentic testimonies, that all authors are full of, allege only the before cited Mirandula, who speaking of that —*"Magia naturalis,"* or natural wisdom, or as he defines it—*"exacta et absoluta cognitio omnium rerum naturalium"*—the exact and absolute knowledge of all natural things (which the ancients were masters of) says, that in that art (among some others he mentions) *"Praestitit Homerus,"* Homer excelled; and who—*"ut omnes alias sapientias, ita hanc quoque; sub sui Ulyxis erroribus dissimulavit"*—as all other knowledges, so hath hiddenly laid down this also in his *Ulysses* his travels.[40] As likewise of Orpheus—*"Nihil efficacius hymnis Orphei in naturali magia, si debita musica, animi intentio, et coeterae circumstantiae quas nôrunt sapientes fuerint adhibitae":* There is nothing of greater efficacy than the hymns of Orpheus in natural magic, if the fitting music, intention of the mind, and other circumstances which are known to the wise, be considered and applied.[41] And again—"that they are of no less power in natural magic," or to the understanding thereof, "than the psalms of David are in the Cabal," or to understand the cabalistic science by. And lastly, Zoroaster; who that he was a possessor likewise of that—*"absoluta cognitio rerum naturalium"* before mentioned, no less than of that theological philosophy his expounders find in him, may appear by that doctrine of his (in particular) of the—*"scala a Tartaro ad primum ignem,"*[42] which the learned Jo[sephus] Picus interprets—*"Seriem naturarum universi a non gradu materiae, ad eum qui est super omnem gradum graduate protensum"*—the series or concatenation of the universal natures, from a no degree (as he speaks) of matter, to him that is above or beyond all degree graduately extended;[43] no less than by that attribute (in general) given him by all the learned of all ages; viz: that he was one of the greatest (as first) of natural magicians, or masters of the absolute knowledge of all nature.

To omit (as I said) the testimonies of an infinity of other authors in confirmation of the before-affirmed troth; who knows not, that most, if not all of those fables in all the rest of the ancients, of their gods and goddesses especially, with the affinities, intercourses, and commerces between themselves, and with others (of which, as Homer, that Greek oracle is abundantly full, so the rest, as a Hesiod, Linus the Master, and Musaeus the scholar of Orpheus, and, as we have said, Zoroaster, and Orpheus himself, and all those most ancient, if we may believe their best expounders and relaters of most we have of them, made the main grounds and subjects of their writings); who knows not (I say) that most, if not all, of those their fables of this kind, and which have of all learned, in all ages, been chiefly termed poetic, and fittest matter for poesy; have never been by any wise expounder made to mean other than merely the generation of the elements, with their virtues, and changes; the courses of the stars, with their powers, and influences; and all the most important secrets of nature, hanging necessarily upon the knowledge of these; which could not suffer so simple a relation as the ethic doctrine requires; because by the vulgarity of those, much mischief must in all reason ensue; being (also) of those tenderer things, that are soonest profaned and vilified by their cheapness; and this, cannot for the general benefit of mankind be among the plainest of lessons too commonly known and openly divulged to everybody.

I will not deny but the ancients mingled much doctrine of morality (yea, high divinity also) with their natural philosophy; as the late mentioned Zoroaster first; who hath divinely sung of the essence and attributes of God and was (as the learned Farra avouches)—"the first author of that religious philosophy, or philosophical religion, that was after followed and amplified by Mercurius Trismegistus, Orpheus, Aglaophemus, Pythagoras, Eudoxus, Socrates, Plato, etc."[44] And Orpheus next; who, as he writ particular books; of astrology, first (as Lucian tells us) of any man; as also of diseases and their cures; of the natures and qualities of the elements; of the force of love or agreement in natural things; and many more that we read of, besides his hymns which are perhaps the greatest part of what now remains of him here among us: so his expounders likewise find in him that *theologia philosophica* as they call it, which they give to Zoroaster. Witness Pausanias, who reports—*"Orpheus multa humanae politicaeque vitae utilia invenit: et universam theologiam primus aperuit, et nefariorum facinorum expiationes excogitavit, etc."*[45] But let us hear how himself sings;

---

[40]*Apology.*
[41]*Conclusions.*
[42]"A ladder from Tartarus to the first fire."
[43]*Conclusions.*

[44]*Settenario.*
[45]"Orpheus came upon many things useful to human and political life, and he was the first to reveal the universal theology and thought out expiations for nefarious deeds." *Boetia.*

and which is by Eusebius Pamphilus, in his honor rehearsed.

> O you that virtue follow, to my sense
> Bend your attentive minds: Profane ones hence.
> And thou Musaeus, who alone the shine
> Highly contemplat'st of the forms divine,
> Learn my notes; which with th' inward eye
>   behold,
> And untouched in thy sacred bosom hold.
> Incline thee by my safe-advising verse
> To the high author of this universe.
> One only, all immortal, such is he;
> Whose being I discover thus to thee;
> This alone-perfect, this eternal king
> Raised above all, created ev'rything,
> And all things governs, with the Spirit alone
> (Not otherwise) to be beheld, or known.
> From him no ill springs; there's no god but he.
> Think now, and look about thee prudently;
> And better to discover him, lo I
> His tracts and footsteps upon earth, and high
> Strong hand behold, but cannot him descry;
> Who (to an unimaginable height
> Raised) in dark clouds conceals him from my
>   sight.
> Only a Chaldean saw him;[46] and the grace
> Hath now aloft to view him face to face.
> His sacred right hand grasps the ocean; and
> Touched with it, the proud mountains trembling
>   stand
> Ev'n from the deep roots to their utmost height:
> Nor feels at all th' immenseness of their weight,
> He, who above the heav'n doth dwell, yet guides
> And governs all that under heav'n abides,
> O'er all, through all doth his vast power extend;
> Of th' universe beginning, midds, and end.[47]

And as these two divine authors in particular, so likewise among the rest of the ancient poets in general, I will grant they have in their poesies (as I have said) mingled much morality with their ethic doctrine. As in their Hercules, Theseus, Ulysses, Aeneas, and other their heroes they have given example of all virtues; and punished all vices; as pride and ambition, in their giants and Titans, etc. Contempt of the gods, in their Niobe, Arachne, Cassiope, Medusa, Amphion, Mar-

syas, the Mineides, etc., murder, lust, covetise, and the rest, in their Lycaon, Ixion, Sisyphus, Midas, Tantalus, Titius, etc. Yet questionless infinite many more of their fables than these (though even these and the rest of this kind want not among our best mythologians their physic, as well as ethic meanings), as all those of their gods and goddesses, with their powers and dignities, and all passage of affinity and commerce between themselves; and between them and others, were (as I have said before) made to mean mere matter of nature; and in no possibility of sense to be wrested to the doctrine of manners, unless a man will (withal) be so inhumane as to allow all those riots, rapes, murders, adulteries, incests, and those *nefaria* and *nefanda,* unnaturally seeming vices that they tell of them, to be (literally or morally taken) fit examples of manners, or wholesome instructions for the lives of men to be leveled and directed by.

Whereas, on the contrary side (that I may instance some of them) who can make that rape of Proserpine, whom her mother Ceres (that under the species of corn might include as well the whole genus of the vegetable nature) sought so long for in the earth, to mean other, than the putrefaction, and succeeding generation of the seeds we commit to Pluto, or the earth? Whom they make the god of wealth, calling him also *Dis-quasi dives*[48] (the same in Latin that Pluto is in Greek) rich, or wealthy, because all things have their original from the earth, and return to the earth again. Or what can Jupiter's blasting of his beloved Semele, after his having deflowered her, and the wrapping of his son he got on her (Bacchus, or wine) in his thigh after his production, mean other than the necessity of the air's heat to his birth, in the generation; and (after a violent pressure and delaceration of his mother the grape) the like close imprisoning of him also, in a fit vessel, till he gain his full maturity, and come to be fit aliment?

After these two particular scandalous fables, and which I will call but inferior speculations, yet necessary documents, because, of the natures of corn, and wine, the *sustentacula vitae;*[49] to omit the adultery of Mars and Venus, by which the chemists will have meant the inseparability of those two metals that carry their names; witness that exuberance of Venus—or copper which we call vitriol, that is seldom or never found without some mixture more or less of Mars or iron in it; as her husband Vulcan, or material fire finds and shows the practitioners in chemistry. And with this, other also of the like obvious kind of truths in nature; as Hebe's stumbling and falling with the nectar bowl in her hand, and thereby discovering her hidden parts to the gods, as she

---

[46][Reynolds] Meaning sure Moses, who the holy writ says—saw God face to face, unless with Eusebius, we will have him mean the patriarch Abraham.
[47]*Evangelical Preparation.*

[48]Dis is the Roman god of the underworld. The Latin word *dives* means rich.
[49]"Mainstay of life."

served them at their board; meaning the nakedness of the trees and plants in autumn, when all their leaves are fallen from them by the downfall or departure of the spring, which their Hebe, or goddess of youth as the ancients called her (because the spring renews and makes young all things) means. And with these, the incest of Mirrha with her father; meaning the myrrh-tree, which the sun (father of plants) inflames, and making overtures in it, there flows thence that odorous Sabaean gum we call myrrh (meant by her child Adonis, which interpreted is sweet, pleasant, or delightful). To omit (I say) these, and the like trivialer (though true) observations in nature; and that carry also so foul a face to the eye; I would ask who can make those fights and contentions that the wise Homer feigns between his gods and goddesses to mean other than the natural contrariety of the elements: and especially of the fire and water; which as they are tempered and reconciled by the air, so Juno (which signifies the airy region) reconciles, and accords the warring gods. And next, what in general those frequent, and no less scandalous brawls between Jupiter and (his wife and sister) Juno, can be made to mean other, than those meteors occasioned by the upper and lower region of the air's differing temperatures: or what all those his unlawful loves, his compressing so many dryads, naiads, and nereiads (wood nymphs, and water nymphs) and the rest, can mean other than merely the fire's power upon the earth, and waters; (a study of a higher nature and vaster extent than the first alleged) and which Jupiter's incest with his sister Ceres likewise means; and is the same with the tale of the contention of Phaeton which is Incendium, with the son of Isis which is Terra.

A theme too infinite to pursue; and no less a fault here, than (perhaps) a folly at all to mention: for (besides the being a subject utterly unfit to suffer a mixture with a discourse of so light a nature as this of mine, where a slight touch at the general mistake and abuse of poesy in our times, was only intended) suppose a man should (whereas I have here laid down the fair sense of but two or three of the foulest of them) be at the pains of running through all the fables of the ancients, and out of them show the reader, and lead him by the fingers as it were (who yet can discover nothing but matter of manners in them) to the speculation of the entire secret of our great god of nature, in his miraculous fabric of this world (which, their god Pan, or the universal simple bodies, and seeds of all nature, gotten by Mercury of the divine will, by which all things came to be created means;) and (beginning with Moses) show him how the spirit of God first moving upon the waters (a mystery perhaps by few of our duller moderns understood, though a Thales Milesius, or Heraclitus the Ephesian, two heathens, could instruct them) they feign him under the name of Jupiter, by compressing Latona (meaning the shades or darkness of the first chaos) to have begot on her, Apollo and Diana, which is the sun and moon, when he said—*"fiat lux, et lux fuit,"*[50] and carry him along from this beginning to the end and complete knowledge of all nature (which as Moses darkly, they no less darkly delivered); suppose (I say) a man should take this task upon him, I would fain know who they are that would be perhaps, at least, that were, fit readers nowadays of such a treatise? Because what one of a million of our scholars or writers among us, understands, or cares to be made understand scarce the lowest and trivialest of nature's ways? Much less seeks to draw (by wisely observing her higher and more hidden workings) any profitabler use or benefit from them, for their own, or the public good, than perhaps to make an almanac, or a diving boat to take butts or crabs under water with; or else some Dutch waterbellows, by rarefying water into a compressed air to blow the fire withal?

When as if they could, but from that poor step, learn the way to get a little higher up the right scale of nature, and really indeed accord, and make a firm peace and agreement between all the discordant elements; and (as the fable of Cupid's wrestle with Pan, and overcoming him, teaches them the beginning of all nature's productions are love and strife) endeavor to irritate also, and force this Pan, or simple matter of things to his fit procreative ability, by an industrious and wise strife and colluctation with him; then they might perhaps do somewhat in philosophy not unworth the talking of. No less than our common practitioners in physic might better deserve their names than most of them do (for to be a physician, what is it but to be a general naturalist, not mere transcriber and applier of particular book recipes?); if they would but practice, by that rule and base of nature the world was built upon, to make likewise and establish that equality and concord between those warring elements (which are the complexions) in man's body, that one exceed not another in their qualities: Or if they could but give better instance of their acquaintance with the ways of philosophy, than in burdening and oppressing nature, rather than otherwise, as most of them do, with their crude vegetable and mineral physics, for not understanding the necessity (or though they did, yet not the art) of exalting and bettering their natures, by correcting or removing their inbred imperfections, with that fit preparation that nature teaches them.

The hidden workings of which wise mistress, could we fully in all her ways comprehend, how much would it clear, and how infinitely ennoble our blind and groveling conditions, by exalting our understandings to the sight (as I have

---

[50]"Let there be light and there was light."

before touched) of God, or—"those invisible things of God" (to use St. Paul's words once again) "which are clearly seen, being understood by the things that are made";[51] and thence instructing us, not saucily to leap, but by the links of that golden chain of Homer, that reaches from the foot of Jupiter's throne to the earth, more knowingly, and consequently more humbly climb up to him, who ought to be indeed the only end and period of all our knowledge, and understanding; the which in us though but a small faint beam of that our great blessed sun, yet is that breath of life that he breathed into us, to draw us thereby (*"fecisti nos Domine propter te";*[52] says the holy St. Augustine) nearer to him, than all irrational animals of his making; as a no less tenderly loving Father, than immense and omnipotent Creator.

To whom as we cannot give too much love and reverence; so neither can we with too wary hands approach his sacred mysteries in Holy Writ. Howbeit I must (to return home to my former discourse) in honor and just praise of the before-mentioned wise ancients (and with the premised befitting caution) not doubt to say, that as his instructions in the Holy Scripture, and especially in the Old Law, must of necessity reach as far father than the bare historical truth (though not in the same manner) as extends the difference in ourselves between nature alone, and nature and grace united; so likewise, that one, and a great portion of the doctrine of that part of Holy Writ, the wise ethnics undoubtedly possessed in all perfection; to wit, the knowledge of all nature's most high and hidden ways and workings: and though far short in the safer part of wisdom, of their more enlightened successors, yet was the bare light (or rather fire) of nature in them, enough to draw them as high as reason could help flesh and blood to reach heaven with. Nay, which is more, were it not wide of my purpose (though it contradicts it not) to consider them other than mere children of nature, I might perhaps gain favor of some of our weaker persuaders in their spiritual cures (if to flank and strengthen the divine letter with profaner authorities, be in this backward and incredulous age, not irrequisite) by paralleling in the historical part I mean chiefly, and as it lies, the sacred letter and ethnic poesies together to a large extension: and beginning with Moses, show them, all those—*dii majorum gentium*[53] from Saturn to Deucalion's deluge, were but names for Adam, Cain, Lamech and the rest of their successors to Noah's flood: nor that their Rhea (or Terra, mother of all the gods) and Venus, could be other than Moses his Eva and Noema. What other can Hesiod's Pandora—the first and beautifullest of all women, by whom all evils were dispersed and spread

upon the earth, mean than Moses his Eve? What can Homer's Ate, whom he calls the first daughter of Jupiter, and a woman pernicious and harmful to all us mortals; and in another place tells how the wisest of men was cozened and deceived by his wife; what can he, I say, mean in these women but Eve? What was the poet's Bacchus but his Noah, or Noachus, first corrupted to Boachus, and after, by removing a letter, to Bacchus; who (as Moses tells us of Noah) was the first likewise in their account, that planted the vine, and taught men the use of wines soon after the universal deluge? What can be plainer than that by their Janus they meant Noah also, whom they give two faces to, for having seen both the old and new world; and which, his name (in Hebrew, Jain, or wine) likewise confirms; Noah being (as we late alleged Moses for witness) the first inventor of the use of wines? What could they mean by their Golden Age, when—

> *Nulli subigebant arva coloni;*
>
> . . .
>
> *Ipsaque tellus*
> *Omnia liberius, nullo poscente ferebat;*[54]

but the state of man before his sin? And consequently by their Iron Age, but the world's infelicity, and miseries that succeeded his fall? When—

> *Luctus, et ultrices posuere cubillia curae;*
> *Pallentesque habitant morbi, tristisque senectus,*
> *Et metus, et majesuada fames, et turpis egestas.*[55]

Lastly, (for I have too much already exceeded my commission) what can *Adonis horti*[56] among the poets mean other than Moses his Eden, or terrestrial Paradise? The Hebrew *Eden* being *Voluptas* or *Delitiae,* whence the Greek ἡδονή (or pleasure) seems necessarily derived: the Chaldeans and Persians (so I am told) called it *Pardeis,* the Greeks, παράδεισος, the Latins altered the Greek name to *Paradisus;* which as Eden, is (as, Aulus Gellius defines it) *"Locus amaenissimus, et voluptatis plenissimus";*[57] the which self thing the ancient both poets and philosophers certainly meant by their —*horti Hesperidum*[58] likewise.

---

[51]*Confessions.*

[52]"Lord, you created us for yourself."

[53]"Gods of the greater nations."

[54]"No farmers subdued the land, and the earth produced more freely with no one begging." Virgil, *Georgics,* I. 125, 127–28.

[55]"Mourning and vengeful cares have made their bed; there live pale disease and sorrowful old age and fear and evil creating hunger and foul poverty." *Aeneid,* VI. 274–76.

[56]"Gardens of Adonis."

[57]"A most charming place, and one filled to the brim with pleasure." *Attican Nights.*

[58]"Gardens of the Hesperides."

Now though we reverence Moses more (as we ought to do) than these his condisciples, because inspired so far above them with the immediate spirit of Almighty God; yet ought we nevertheless to reverence them, and the wisdom of their fables, however not understood by everybody: his condisciples I call them, because they read both under their Egyptian teachers one lesson; and were (as Moses himself says) expert in the learning of the Egyptians: yea, many of them (and poets all) were (to speak fitlier) the teachers of that learning themselves, and masters therein no less than Moses. How can we then indeed attribute too much to their knowledges, though delivered out of wise consideration in riddles and fictious tales?

But alas (with shame enough may we speak it) so far are we nowadays from giving the due to them they deserve, as those their learned and excellent fables seem rather read to be abused, then studied in these times; and even by people too that are, or would be accounted profound men.

What child of learning or lover of truth could abide to see great pretenders to learning among us, that doubt, and obstinately too, whether the precious treasure of that wisdom of the ancients, so carefully by them left sealed up to the use of their true heirs (the wise and worthy of their posterity) be any more indeed than a legacy of mere old wives' tales to poison the world with. If we will call this but ignorance, let us go farther; and suppose that a man[59] (nor unlearned one neither) shall have taken pains in four or five fables of the ancients to unfold and deliver us much doctrine and high meanings in them, which he calls their wisdom; and yet the same man in another treatise of his, shall say of those ancient fables—"I think they were first made, and their expositions devised afterward": and a little after—"Of Homer himself, notwithstanding he was made a kind of scripture by the latter schools of the Grecians, yet I should without any difficulty pronounce his fables had in his own meaning no such inwardness, etc." What shall we make of such willing contradictions, when a man to vent a few fancies of his own, shall tell us first, they are the wisdom of the ancients; and next,

that those ancient fables were but mere fables, and without wisdom or meaning, till their expositors gave them a meaning; and then, scornfully and contemptuously (as if all poetry were but play-vanity) shut up that discourse of his of poetry, with—"It is not good to stay too long in the theater."

But let me not stick too long neither in this mire; nor seem oversensible of wrong to what can suffer none; for— "*Veritas*" (says the Holy Writ) "*magna est, et praevalebit*":[60] and such are (nor less great and prevailing than truth itself) those before-mentioned arcana of our wise ancients; which no barbarism I know can efface; nor all the damps and thick fogs by dull and dirty ignorance breathed on them, darken at all, or hide from the quick eye of select and happier understandings; who know full well, the ripest fruits of knowledge grow ever highest; while the lowerhanging boughs (for everyone's grip) are either barren, or their fruit too sour to be worth the gathering. And among such may they ever rest, safe wrapped up in their husks, and involvements: and let our writers write (if it can be no better) and rhymers rhyme still after their accustomed and most accepted manner, and still captivate and ravish their like hearers. Though in my own inclination, I could with much juster alacrity, than in person of the Roman poet, with his—"*Vilia miretur vulgus,*"[61] or Roman orator, with his—"*Similes habent sua labra lactucas*"[62] (while he laughed to see a greedy ass at his suitable thistles), wish we might each one, according to the measure of his illumination, and by the direction of God's two great books, that of his law first, and that of the creature next, (wherein, to use the excellent Jo[sephus] Picus his phrase—"*leguntur magnalia Dei*"—the wonderful things of God are read)[63] run on together in a safe and firm rod of truth: to the end that vindicating some part of our lost heritage and beatitude here, we may thence (an advantage the holy Maximus Tyrius says the more happy spirits have over others) arrive the less aliens and strangers in the land of our eternal heritage, and beatitude hereafter.

---

[59]Francis Bacon, *On the Wisdom of the Ancients*. See Bacon's *Advancement of Learning*, pp. 183–84, to which Reynolds later refers.

[60]"Truth is great and will prevail."
[61]"Let the rabble admire worthless things." Ovid, *Amores.*
[62]"Like lips, like lettuce" or "like has met its like." Jerome, *Epistles.*
[63]*Conclusions.*

Thomas Hobbes

1588–1679

In his characteristically analytic fashion, the philosopher Hobbes begins his *Answer to Davenant's Preface to* Gondibert with a conventional review of the major genres of literature and then proceeds to some remarks about whether or not the poet can properly exceed the possibility of nature in his inventions. Hobbes, in deciding that the poet cannot do so, seems to limit the poet's activity to a sort of "realism." The poet must rely on his own "experience and knowledge of nature," particularly human nature. There is nothing in Hobbes of recourse to Platonic ideas or visionary grandeur; he is a rationalist and materialist. In his general orientation he resembles Bacon. His insistence on the realistic and the probable seems less dogged when we come to understand that he is really attacking outrageous incongruities in fiction and is mostly concerned with consistency and decorum in all aspects of the work of art.

A standard edition of Hobbes is William Molesworth, ed., *English Works* (16 vols., 1839–45). See C. M. Dowlin, *Davenant's* Gondibert, *Its Preface and Hobbes' Answer: A Study in Neo-classicism* (1934); C. D. Thorpe, *The Aesthetic Theory of Thomas Hobbes* (1940); Martin Kallich, "The Association of Ideas and Critical Theory: Hobbes, Locke, and Addison," *English Literary History,* XII (1945), 290–315; Tom Sorell, *Hobbes* (1986); and G. A. J. Rogers and Alan Ryan, *Perspectives on Thomas Hobbes* (1986).

Answer to Davenant's Preface to *Gondibert*

Sir,

If to commend your poem I should only say, in general terms, that in the choice of your argument, the disposition of the parts, the maintenance of the characters of your persons, the dignity and vigor of your expression, you have performed all the parts of various experience, ready memory, clear judgment, swift and well-governed fancy, though it were enough for the truth, it were too little for the weight and credit of my testimony. For I lie open to two exceptions, one of an incompetent, the other of a corrupted witness. Incompetent, because I am not a poet; and corrupted with the honor done me by your preface. The former obliges me to say something, by the way, of the nature and differences of poesy.

As philosophers have divided the universe, their subject, into three regions, celestial, aerial, and terrestrial, so the poets (whose work it is, by imitating human life in delightful and measured lines, to avert men from vice and incline them to virtuous and honorable actions) have lodged themselves in the three regions of mankind, court, city, and country, correspondent in some proportion to those three regions of the world. For there is in princes and men of conspicuous power, anciently called heroes, a luster and influence upon the rest of men resembling that of the heavens, and an insincereness, inconstancy, and troublesome humor of those that dwell in populous cities, like the mobility, blustering, and impurity of the air; and a plainness, and though dull, yet a nutritive faculty in rural people, that endures a comparison with the earth they labor.

ANSWER TO DAVENANT'S PREFACE TO *Gondibert*. Hobbes's *Answer* was published in 1650. The text is based on the edition of 1651. Sir William Davenant (1606–68) published Books I and II and part of Book III of his epic poem *Gondibert* in 1650. The work was never finished.

From hence have proceeded three sorts of poesy, heroic, scommatic,[1] and pastoral. Every one of these is distinguished again in the manner of representation, which sometimes is narrative, wherein the poet himself relateth, and sometimes dramatic, as when the persons are every one adorned and brought upon the theater to speak and act their own parts. There is therefore neither more nor less than six sorts of poesy. For the heroic poem narrative, such as is yours, is called an epic poem. The heroic poem dramatic is tragedy. The scommatic narrative is satire, dramatic is comedy. The pastoral narrative is called simply pastoral, anciently bucolic; the same dramatic, pastoral comedy. The figure therefore of an epic poem and of a tragedy ought to be the same, for they differ no more but in that they are pronounced by one or many persons. Which I insert to justify the figure of yours, consisting of five books divided into songs, or cantos, as five acts divided into scenes has ever been the approved figure of a tragedy.

They that take for poesy whatsoever is writ in verse will think this division imperfect, and call in sonnets, epigrams, eclogues, and the like pieces, which are but essays and parts of an entire poem, and reckon Empedocles and Lucretius (natural philosophers) for poets, and the moral precepts of Phocylides, Theognis, and the quatrains of Pybrach and the history of Lucan, and others of that kind amongst poems, bestowing on such writers for honor the name of poets rather than of historians or philosophers.[2] But the subject of a poem is the manners of men, not natural causes; manners presented, not dictated; and manners feigned, as the name of poesy imports, not found in men. They that give entrance to fictions writ in prose err not so much, but they err: for prose requireth delightfulness, not only of fiction, but of style, in which, if prose contend with verse, it is with disadvantage and, as it were, on foot against the strength and wings of Pegasus.

For verse amongst the Greeks was appropriated anciently to the service of their gods, and was the holy style, the style of the oracles, the style of the laws, and the style of men that publicly recommended to their gods the vows and thanks of the people, which was done in their holy songs called hymns, and the composers of them were called prophets and priests before the name of poet was known. When afterwards the majesty of that style was observed, the poets chose it as best becoming their high invention. And for the antiquity of verse, it is greater than the antiquity of letters. For it is certain Cadmus[3] was the first that from Phoenicia, a country that neighboreth Judea, brought the use of letters into Greece. But the service of the gods and the laws, which by measured sounds were easily committed to the memory, had been long time in use before the arrival of Cadmus there.

There is, besides the grace of style, another cause why the ancient poets chose to write in measured language, which is this. Their poems were made at first with intention to have them sung, as well epic as dramatic—which custom hath been long time laid aside, but began to be revived, in part, of late years in Italy—and could not be made commensurable to the voice or instruments in prose, the ways and motions whereof are so uncertain and undistinguished, like the way and motion of a ship in the sea, as not only to discompose the best composers, but also to disappoint sometimes the most attentive reader and put him to hunt counter for the sense. It was therefore necessary for poets in those times to write in verse.

The verse which the Greeks and Latins, considering the nature of their own languages, found by experience most grave, and for an epic poem most decent, was their hexameter, a verse limited not only in the length of the line, but also in the quantity of the syllables. Instead of which we use the line of ten syllables, recompensing the neglect of their quantity with the diligence of rhyme. And this measure is so proper for a heroic poem as without some loss of gravity and dignity it was never changed. A longer is not far from ill prose, and a shorter is a kind of whisking, you know, like the unlacing rather than the singing of a Muse. In an epigram or a sonnet a man may vary his measures, and seek glory from a needless difficulty, as he that contrived verses into the forms of an organ, a hatchet, an egg, an altar, and a pair of wings; but in so great and noble a work as is an epic poem, for a man to obstruct his own way with unprofitable difficulties is great imprudence. So likewise to choose a needless and difficult correspondence of rhyme is but a difficult toy, and forces a man sometimes for the stopping of a chink to say somewhat he did never think; I cannot therefore but very much approve your stanza, wherein the syllables in every verse are ten, and the rhyme alternate.

For the choice of your subject, you have sufficiently justified yourself in your preface. But because I have observed in Virgil, that the honor done to Aeneas and his companions has so bright a reflection upon Augustus Caesar and other great Romans of that time as a man may suspect him not constantly possessed with the noble spirit of those his heroes, and believe you are not acquainted with any great man of the race of Gondibert, I add to your justification the purity of your purpose, in having no other motive of your labor but to adorn virtue and procure her lovers, than which there cannot be a worthier design, and more becoming noble poesy.

---

[1]Satirical.

[2]Hobbes sides with Aristotle, *Poetics*, I. 8–10 (p. 50), in declaring that verse is not necessarily a sign of a poem.

[3]In legend a Phoenician prince who founded Thebes and later reigned as its king.

In that you make so small account of the example of almost all the approved poets, ancient and modern, who thought fit in the beginning and sometimes also in the progress of their poems, to invoke a Muse or some other deity that should dictate to them or assist them in their writings, they that take not the laws of art from any reason of their own but from the fashion of precedent times will perhaps accuse your singularity. For my part, I neither subscribe to their accusation, nor yet condemn that heathen custom otherwise than as accessory to their false religion. For their poets were their divines, had the name of prophets, exercised amongst the people a kind of spiritual authority, would be thought to speak by a divine spirit, have their works which they writ in verse (the divine style) pass for the word of God and not of man, and to be hearkened to with reverence. Do not our divines (excepting the style) do the same, and by us that are of the same religion cannot justly be reprehended for it? Besides, in the use of the spiritual calling of divines, there is danger sometimes to be feared from want of skill, such as is reported of unskillful conjurers, that mistaking the rites and ceremonious points of their art, call up such spirits as they cannot at their pleasure allay again, by whom storms are raised that overthrow buildings and are the cause of miserable wrecks at sea. Unskillful divines do oftentimes the like: for when they call unseasonably for zeal there appears a spirit of cruelty; and by the like error, instead of truth they raise discord; instead of wisdom, fraud; instead of reformation, tumult; and controversy instead of religion. Whereas in the heathen poets, at least in those whose works have lasted to the time we are in, there are none of those indiscretions to be found that tended to subversion or disturbance of the commonwealths wherein they lived. But why a Christian should think it an ornament to his poem, either to profane the true God or invoke a false one, I can imagine no cause but a reasonless imitation of custom, of a foolish custom, by which a man, enabled to speak wisely from the principles of nature and his own meditation, loves rather to be thought to speak by inspiration, like a bagpipe.

Time and education begets experience; experience begets memory; memory begets Judgment and Fancy: Judgment begets the strength and structure, and Fancy begets the ornaments of a poem. The ancients therefore fabled not absurdly in making memory the mother of the Muses. For memory is the world (though not really, yet so as in a looking glass) in which the Judgment, the severer sister, busieth herself in a grave and rigid examination of all the parts of nature, and in registering by letters their order, causes, uses, differences, and resemblances; whereby the Fancy, when any work of art is to be performed, finds her materials at hand and prepared for use, and needs no more than a swift motion over them, that what she wants, and is there to be had, may not lie too long unespied. So that when she seemeth to fly from one Indies to the other, and from heaven to earth, and to penetrate into the hardest matter and obscurest places, into the future and into herself, and all this in a point of time, the voyage is not very great, her self being all she seeks; and her wonderful celerity consisteth not so much in motion as in copious imagery discreetly ordered and perfectly registered in the memory, which most men under the name of philosophy have a glimpse of, and is pretended to by many that, grossly mistaking her, embrace contention in her place. But so far forth as the fancy of man has traced the ways of true philosophy, so far it hath produced very marvelous effects to the benefit of mankind. All that is beautiful or defensible in building, or marvelous in engines and instruments of motion, whatsoever commodity men receive from the observations of the heavens, from the description of the earth, from the account of time, from walking on the seas, and whatsoever distinguisheth the civility of Europe from the barbarity of the American savages, is the workmanship of Fancy but guided by the precepts of true philosophy. But where these precepts fail, as they have hitherto failed in the doctrine of moral virtue, there the architect, Fancy, must take the philosophers part upon herself. He therefore that undertakes a heroic poem, which is to exhibit a venerable and amiable image of heroic virtue, must not only be the poet, to place and connect, but also the philosopher, to furnish and square his matter, that is, to make both body and soul, color and shadow of his poem out of his own store: which how well you have performed I am now considering.

Observing how few the persons be you introduce in the beginning, and how in the course of the actions of these (the number increasing) after several confluences they run all at last into the two principal streams of your poem, Gondibert and Oswald, methinks the fable is not much unlike the theater. For so, from several and far distant sources, do the lesser brooks of Lombardy, flowing into one another, fall all at last into two main rivers, the Po and the Adice. It hath the same resemblance also with a man's veins, which, proceeding from different parts, after the like concourse insert themselves at last into the two principal veins of the body. But when I considered that also the actions of men, which singly are inconsiderable, after many conjunctures grow at last either into one great protecting power or into two destroying factions, I could not but approve the structure of your poem, which ought to be no other than such as an imitation of human life requireth.

In the streams themselves I find nothing but settled valor, clean honor, calm counsel, learned diversion, and pure love, save only a torrent or two of ambition, which, though a fault, has somewhat heroic in it, and therefore must have place in a heroic poem. To show the reader in what place he shall find every excellent picture of virtue you have drawn is too long. And to show him one is to prejudice the rest; yet I cannot forbear to point him to the description of love in the person of Birtha, in the seventh canto of the second book. There has nothing been said of that subject neither by the ancient nor modern poets comparable to it. Poets are painters: I would fain see another painter draw so true, perfect, and natural a love to the life, and make use of nothing but pure lines, without the help of any the least uncomely shadow, as you have done. But let it be read as a piece by itself, for in the most equal height of the whole the eminence of parts is lost.

There are some that are not pleased with fiction, unless it be bold, not only to exceed the work, but also the possibility of nature: they would have impenetrable armors, enchanted castles, invulnerable bodies, iron men, flying horses, and a thousand other such things, which are easily feigned by them that dare. Against such I defend you (without assenting to those that condemn either Homer or Virgil) by dissenting only from those that think the beauty of a poem consisteth in the exorbitancy of the fiction. For as truth is the bound of historical, so the resemblance of truth is the utmost limit of poetical liberty. In old time amongst the heathen such strange fictions and metamorphoses were not so remote from the articles of their faith as they are now from ours, and therefore were not so unpleasant. Beyond the actual works of nature a poet may now go; but beyond the conceived possibility of nature, never. I can allow a geographer to make in the sea a fish or a ship which by the scale of his map would be two or three hundred miles long, and think it done for ornament, because it is done without the precincts of his undertaking; but when he paints an elephant so, I presently apprehend it as ignorance, and a plain confession of *terra incognita.*

As the description of great men and great actions is the constant design of a poet, so the descriptions of worthy circumstances are necessary accessions to a poem, and being well performed are the jewels and most precious ornaments of poesy. Such in Virgil are the funeral games of Anchises, the duel of Aeneas and Turnus, etc.; and such in yours are The Hunting, The Bataile,[4] The City Mourning, The Funeral, The House of Astragon, The Library, and The Temple, equal to his, or those of Homer whom he imitated.

There remains now no more to be considered but the expression, in which consisteth the countenance and color of a beautiful Muse, and is given her by the poet out of his own provision, or is borrowed from others. That which he hath of his own is nothing but experience and knowledge of nature, and specially human nature, and is the true and natural color. But that which is taken out of books (the ordinary boxes of counterfeit complexion) shows well or ill, as it hath more or less resemblance with the natural, and are not to be used without examination unadvisedly. For in him that professes the imitation of nature, as all poets do, what greater fault can there be than to betray an ignorance of nature in his poem—especially having a liberty allowed him, if he meet with anything he cannot master, to leave it out?

That which giveth a poem the truth and natural color consisteth in two things, which are, to know well, that is, to have images of nature in the memory distinct and clear, and to know much. A sign of the first is perspicuity, property, and decency, which delight all sorts of men, either by instructing the ignorant or soothing the learned in their knowledge. A sign of the latter is novelty of expression, and pleaseth by excitation of the mind; for novelty causeth admiration, and admiration curiosity, which is a delightful appetite of knowledge.

There be so many words in use at this day in the English tongue, that though of *magnifique* sound, yet (like the windy blisters of a troubled water) have no sense at all, and so many others that lose their meaning by being ill coupled, that it is a hard matter to avoid them; for having been obtruded upon youth in the schools by such as make it, I think, their business there (as 'tis expressed by the best poet) "with terms to charm the weak and pose the wise,"[5] they grow up with them, and, gaining reputation with the ignorant, are not easily shaken off.

To this palpable darkness I may also add the ambitious obscurity of expressing more than is perfectly conceived, or perfect conception in fewer words than it requires. Which expressions, though they have had the honor to be called strong lines, are indeed no better than riddles, and, not only to the reader but also after a little time to the writer himself, dark and troublesome.

To the property of expression I refer that clearness of memory by which a poet, when he hath once introduced any person whatsoever speaking in his poem, maintaineth in him to the end the same character he gave him in the beginning. The variation whereof is a change of pace that argues the poet tired.

Of the indecencies of a heroic poem the most remarkable are those that show disproportion either between the persons and their actions, or between the manners of the poet and the poem. Of the first kind is the uncomeliness of representing in great persons the inhuman vice of cruelty or the sordid vice of lust and drunkenness. To such parts as those

---

[4]Battle.

[5]*Gondibert,* I. 5.

the ancient approved poets thought it fit to suborn, not the persons of men, but of monsters and beastly giants, such as Polyphemus, Cacus, and the centaurs. For it is supposed a Muse, when she is invoked to sing a song of that nature, should maidenly advise the poet to set such persons to sing their own vices upon the stage, for it is not so unseemly in a tragedy. Of the same kind it is to represent scurrility or any action or language that moveth much laughter. The delight of an epic poem consisteth not in mirth, but admiration. Mirth and laughter is proper to comedy and satire. Great persons that have their minds employed on great designs have not leisure enough to laugh, and are pleased with the contemplation of their own power and virtues, so as they need not the infirmities and vices of other men to recommend themselves to their own favor by comparison, as all men do when they laugh. Of the second kind, where the disproportion is between the poet and the persons of his poem, one is in the dialect of the inferior sort of people, which is always different from the language of the court. Another is to derive the illustration of anything from such metaphors or comparisons as cannot come into men's thoughts but by mean conversation and experience of humble or evil arts, which the person of an epic poem cannot be thought acquainted with.

From knowing much, proceedeth the admirable variety and novelty of metaphors and similitudes, which are not possible to be lighted on in the compass of a narrow knowledge. And the want whereof compelleth a writer to expressions that are either defaced by time or sullied with vulgar or long use. For the phrases of poesy, as the airs of music, with often hearing become insipid, the reader having no more sense of their force than our flesh is sensible of the bones that sustain it. As the sense we have of bodies consisteth in change and variety of impression, so also does the sense of language in the variety and changeable use of words. I mean not in the affectation of words newly brought home from travail, but in new and withal significant translation to our purposes of those that be already received, and in farfetched but withal apt, instructive, and comely similitudes.

Having thus, I hope, avoided the first exception against the incompetency of my judgment, I am but little moved with the second, which is of being bribed by the honor you have done me by attributing in your preface somewhat to my judgment. For I have used your judgment no less in many things of mine, which coming to light will thereby appear the better. And so you have your bribe again.

Having thus made way for the admission of my testimony, I give it briefly thus: I never yet saw poem that had so much shape of art, health or morality, and vigor and beauty of expression as this of yours. And but for the clamor of the multitude, that hide their envy of the present under a reverence of antiquity, I should say further that it would last as long as either the *Aeneid* or *Iliad,* but for one disadvantage; and the disadvantage is this: The languages of the Greeks and Romans, by their colonies and conquests, have put off flesh and blood, and are becoming immutable, which none of the modern tongues are like to be. I honor antiquity, but that which is commonly called old time is young time. The glory of antiquity is due, not to the dead, but to the aged.

And now, while I think on it, give me leave with a short discord to sweeten the harmony of the approaching close. I have nothing to object against your poem, but dissent only from something in your preface sounding to the prejudice of age. 'Tis commonly said that old age is a return to childhood: which methinks you insist on so long, as if you desired it should be believed. That's the note I mean to shake a little. That saying, meant only of the weakness of body, was wrested to the weakness of mind by froward children, weary of the controlment of their parents, masters, and other admonitors. Secondly, the dotage and childishness they ascribe to age is never the effect of time, but sometimes of the excesses of youth, and not a returning to, but a continual stay with, childhood. For they that, wanting the curiosity of furnishing their memories with the rarities of nature in their youth, and pass their time in making provision only for their ease and sensual delight, are children still at what years soever, as they that coming into a populous city, never going out of their inn, are strangers still, how long soever they have been there. Thirdly, there is no reason for any man to think himself wiser today than yesterday, which does not equally convince he shall be wiser tomorrow than today.

Fourthly, you will be forced to change your opinion hereafter when you are old; and in the meantime you discredit all I have said before in your commendation, because I am old already. But no more of this.

I believe, sir, you have seen a curious kind of perspective, where he that looks through a short hollow pipe upon a picture containing divers figures sees none of those that are there painted, but some one person made up of their parts, conveyed to the eye by the artificial cutting of a glass. I find in my imagination an effect not unlike it from your poem. The virtues you distribute there amongst so many noble persons represent in the reading the image but of one man's virtue to my fancy, which is your own, and that so deeply imprinted as to stay forever there, and govern all the rest of my thoughts and affections in the way of honoring and serving you to the utmost of my power, that am, sir.

Your most humble and obedient servant,

THOMAS HOBBES
Paris, January 10, 1650

Pierre Corneille

1606–1684

In France and England during the seventeenth and early eighteenth centuries there was a tendency to read Aristotle as a prescriptive rather than descriptive critic. There was considerable discussion of the so-called unities of action, time, and place, derived rather unfairly from his *Poetics,* and critics varied considerably in the rigidity with which they prescribed these unities. Though Corneille is often alleged to have been rigidly prescriptive, careful reading of his third discourse, *Of the Three Unities,* reveals the practical attitude of a working playwright. At the end of the discourse, for example, he indicates that he discovers his own adherence to the unity of place, rigidly defined, in only three of his plays; and he says that he will be indulgent with those other dramatists who "may succeed on the stage through some appearance of regularity." He suggests that it is easy for critics to be severe, but let them write a few plays and they might "slacken the rules." Corneille is thus not as committed to exterior canons of judgment as the earlier commentator on the unities, Castelvetro; nor does he approach the dogmatism of such English critics as Dennis and Thomas Rymer. Indeed, he has an attitude similar to that of another working playwright, Dryden, whom he influenced.

Corneille tries to refer rules of dramatic art to common sense and to the situation of the audience as well as to Aristotle. He is quite aware that Aristotle insisted only on the unity of action and recognized that the ancients sometimes observed the unity of time. He knows that Aristotle said nothing of the unity of place, but believes that something like unity of place follows logically from unity of time and unity of action. It must be remembered that Corneille was naturally thinking of how to make effective the sort of play he was used to. In respect to such plays the "rules" may be more suitable than we are now willing to admit.

Translations of the major plays are available in Lacy Lockert, tr., *Chief Plays of Corneille* (1957). An important critical study is Benedetto Croce, *Ariosto, Shakespeare, and Corneille* (1920). For an understanding of Corneille's role as a critic, see Pierre Legouis, "Corneille and Dryden as Dramatic Critics," *Seventeenth-Century Essays Presented to Sir Herbert Grierson* (1938), 269–78; Robert Mantero, *Corneille critique et son temps: Ogier, Mairet, Scudéry* (1964); Gordon Pocock, *Corneille and Racine: Problems of Tragic Form* (1973); Mitchell Greenberg, *Corneille, Classicism, and the Ruses of Symmetry* (1986); and A. Donald Sellstrom, *Corneille, Tasso, and Modern Poetics* (1986).

Of the Three Unities of Action, Time, and Place

The two preceding discourses and the critical examination of the plays which my first two volumes contain have furnished me so many opportunities to explain my thoughts on these matters that there would be little left for me to say if I absolutely forbade myself to repeat.

I hold then, as I have already said, that in comedy, unity of action consists in the unity of plot or the obstacle to the plans of the principal actors, and in tragedy in the unity of peril, whether the hero falls victim to it or escapes. It is not that I claim that several perils cannot be allowed in the latter or several plots or obstacles in the former, provided that one passes necessarily from one to the other; for then escape from the first peril does not make the action complete since the escape leads to another danger; and the resolution of one plot does not put the actors at rest since they are confounded afresh in another. My memory does not furnish me any ancient examples of this multiplicity of perils linked each to each without the destruction of the unity of action; but I have noted independent double action as a defect in *Horace* and in *Théodore,* for it is not necessary that the first kill his sister upon gaining his victory nor that the other give herself up to martyrdom after having escaped prostitution; and if the death of Polyxène and that of Astyanax in Seneca's *Trojan Women* do not produce the same irregularity I am very much mistaken.[1]

In the second place, the term *unity of action* does not mean that tragedy should show only one action on the stage. The one which the poet chooses for his subject must have a beginning, a middle, and an end; and not only are these three parts separate actions which find their conclusion in the principal one, but, moreover, each of them may contain several others with the same subordination. There must be only one complete action, which leaves the mind of the spectator serene; but that action can become complete only through several others which are less perfect and which, by serving as preparation, keep the spectator in a pleasant suspense. This is what must be contrived at the end of each act in order to give continuity to the action. It is not necessary that we know exactly what the actors are doing in the intervals which separate the acts, nor even that they contribute to the action when they do not appear on the stage; but it is necessary that each act leave us in the expectation of something which is to take place in the following one.

If you asked me what Cléopâtre is doing in *Rodogune* between the time when she leaves her two sons in the second act until she rejoins Antiochus in the fourth, I should be unable to tell you, and I do not feel obliged to account for her; but the end of this second act prepares us to see an amicable effort by the two brothers to rule and to hide Rodogune from the venomous hatred of their mother. The effect of this is seen in the third act, whose ending prepares us again to see another effort by Antiochus to win back these two enemies one after the other and for what Séleucus does in the fourth, which compels that unnatural mother[2] to resolve upon what she tries to accomplish in the fifth, whose outcome we await with suspense.

In *Le Menteur* the actors presumably make use of the whole interval between the third and fourth acts to sleep; their rest, however, does not impede the continuity of the action between those two acts because the third does not contain a complete event. Dorante ends it with his plan to seek ways to win back the trust of Lucrèce, and at the very beginning of the next he appears so as to be able to talk to one of her servants and to her, should she show herself.

When I say that it is not necessary to account for what the actors do when they are not onstage, I do not mean that it is not sometimes very useful to give such an accounting, but only that one is not forced to do it, and that one ought to take the trouble to do so only when what happens behind the scenes is necessary for the understanding of what is to take place before the spectators. Thus I say nothing of what Cléopâtre did between the second and the fourth acts, because during all that time she can have done nothing important as regards the principal action which I am preparing for; but I point out in the very first lines of the fifth act that she has used the interval between these latter two for the killing of Séleucus, because that death is part of the action. This is what leads me to state that the poet is not required to show all the particular actions which bring about the principal one; he must choose to show those which are the most advantageous, whether by the beauty of the spectacle or by the brilliance or violence of the passions they produce, or by some other attraction which is connected with them, and to hide the others behind the scenes while informing the spectator of

---

OF THE THREE UNITIES. Corneille's *Of the Three Unities* was published in 1660. The text, translated by Donald Schier, is from Scott Elledge and Donald Schier, eds., *The Continental Model: Selected French Critical Essays of the Seventeenth Century.* Copyright © 1960, University of Minnesota Press, Minneapolis. Reprinted by permission of the publisher.

[1]*Horace* and *Théodore* are two plays by Corneille. In this discourse, he repeatedly turns to his own work for examples, comparing and contrasting his plays with those of classical dramatists, such as Seneca, Sophocles, Terence, and Euripides.

---

[2]Cléopâtre.

them by a narration or by some other artistic device; above all, he must remember that they must all be so closely connected that the last are produced by the preceding and that all have their source in the protasis which ought to conclude the first act. This rule, which I have established in my first discourse, although it is new and contrary to the usage of the ancients, is founded on two passages of Aristotle. Here is the first of them: "There is a great difference," he says, "between events which succeed each other and those which occur because of others."[3] The Moors come into the *Cid* after the death of the Count and not because of the death of the Count; and the fisherman comes into *Don Sanche* after Charles is suspected of being the Prince of Aragon and not because he is suspected of it; thus both are to be criticized. The second passage is even more specific and says precisely "that everything that happens in tragedy must arise necessarily or probably from what has gone before."[4]

The linking of the scenes which unites all the individual actions of each act and of which I have spoken in criticizing *La Suivante* is a great beauty in a poem and one which serves to shape continuity of action through continuity of presentation; but, in the end, it is only a beauty and not a rule. The ancients did not always abide by it although most of their acts have but two or three scenes. This made things much simpler for them than for us, who often put as many as nine or ten scenes into each act. I shall cite only two examples of the scorn with which they treated this principle: one is from Sophocles, in *Ajax,* whose monologue before he kills himself has no connection with the preceding scene; the other is from the third act of Terence's *The Eunuch,* where Antipho's soliloquy has no connection with Chremes and Pythias, who leave the stage when he enters. The scholars of our century, who have taken the ancients for models in the tragedies they have left us, have even more neglected that linking than did the ancients, and one need only glance at the plays of Buchanan, Grotius, and Heinsius, of which I spoke in the discussion of *Polyeucte,* to agree on that point. We have so far accustomed our audiences to this careful linking of scenes that they cannot now witness a detached scene without considering it a defect; the eye and even the ear are outraged by it even before the mind has been able to reflect upon it. The fourth act of *Cinna* falls below the others through this flaw; and what formerly was not a rule has become one now through the assiduousness of our practice.

I have spoken of three sorts of linkings in the discussion of *La Suivante:* I have shown myself averse to those of

sound, indulgent to those of sight, favorable to those of presence and speech; but in these latter I have confused two things which ought to be separated. Links of presence and speech both have, no doubt, all the excellence imaginable; but there are links of speech without presence and of presence without speech which do not reach the same level of excellence. An actor who speaks to another from a hiding place without showing himself forms a link of speech without presence which is always effective; but that rarely happens. A man who remains onstage merely to hear what will be said by those whom he sees making their entrance forms a link of presence without speech; this is often clumsy and falls into mere pretense, being contrived more to accede to this new convention which is becoming a precept than for any need dictated by the plot of the play. Thus, in the third act of *Pompée*, Achorée, after having informed Charmion of the reception Caesar gave to the king when he presented to him the head of that hero, remains on the stage where he sees the two of them come together merely to hear what they will say and report it to Cléopâtre. Ammon does the same thing in the fourth act of *Andromède* for the benefit of Phinée, who retires when he sees the king and all his court arriving. Characters who become mute connect rather badly scenes in which they play little part and in which they count for nothing. It is another matter when they hide in order to find out some important secret from those who are speaking and who think they are not overheard, for then the interest which they have in what is being said, added to a reasonable curiosity to find out what they cannot learn in any other way, gives them an important part in the action despite their silence; but in these two examples Ammon and Achorée lend so cold a presence to the scenes they overhear that, to be perfectly frank, whatever feigned reason I give them to serve as pretext for their action, they remain there only to connect the scenes with those that precede, so easily can both plays dispense with what they do.

Although the action of the dramatic poem must have its unity, one must consider both its parts: the complication and the resolution. "The complication is composed," according to Aristotle,

in part of what has happened offstage before the beginning of the action which is there described, and in part from what happens onstage; the rest belongs to the resolution. The change of fortune forms the separation of these two parts. Everything which precedes it is in the first part, and this change, with what follows it, concerns the other.[5]

---

[3] *Poetics*, X. 3, p. 55.
[4] *Poetics*, X. 3, p. 55.

[5] *Poetics*, XVIII. 1, p. 59.

The complication depends entirely upon the choice and industrious imagination of the poet and no rule can be given for it, except that in it he ought to order all things according to probability or necessity, a point which I have discussed in the second discourse; to this I add one piece of advice, which is that he involve himself as little as possible with things which have happened before the action he is presenting. Such narrations are annoying, usually because they are not expected, and they disturb the mind of the spectator, who is obliged to burden his memory with what has happened ten or twelve years before in order to understand what he is about to see; but narrations which describe things which happened and take place behind the scenes once the action has started always produce a better effect because they are awaited with some curiosity and are a part of the action which is being shown. One of the reasons why so many illustrious critics favor *Cinna* above anything else I have done is that it contains no narration of the past, the one Cinna makes in describing his plot to Emilie being rather an ornament which tickles the mind of the spectators than a necessary marshaling of the details they must know and impress upon their memories for the understanding of what is to come. Emilie informs them adequately in the first two scenes that he is conspiring against Augustus in her favor, and if Cinna merely told her that the plotters are ready for the following day he would advance the action just as much as by the hundred lines he uses to tell both what he said to them and the way in which they received his words. There are plots which begin at the very birth of the hero like that of *Héraclius,* but these great efforts of the imagination demand an extraordinary attention of the spectator and often keep him from taking a real pleasure in the first performance, so much do they weary him.

In the resolution I find two things to avoid: the mere change of intention and the machine.[6] Not much skill is required to finish a poem when he who has served as the obstacle to the plans of the principal actors for four acts desists in the fifth without being constrained to do so by any remarkable event; I have spoken of this in the first discourse and I shall add nothing to that here. The machine requires no more skill when it is used only to bring down a god who straightens everything out when the actors are unable to do so. It is thus that Apollo functions in the *Orestes:*[7] this prince and his friend Pylades, accused by Tyndarus and Menelaus of the death of Clytemnestra and condemned after prosecution by them, seize Helen and Hermione; they kill, or think they kill the first, and threaten to do so the same with the other if the sentence pronounced against them is not revoked. To smooth out these difficulties Euripides seeks nothing subtler than to bring Apollo down from heaven, and he, by absolute authority, orders that Orestes marry Hermione and Pylades Electra; and lest the death of Helen prove an obstacle to this, it being improbable that Hermione would marry Orestes since he had just killed her mother, Apollo informs them that she is not dead, that he has protected her from their blows and carried her off to heaven at the moment when they thought they were killing her. This use of the machine is entirely irrelevant, being founded in no way on the rest of the play, and makes a faulty resolution. But I find a little too harsh the opinion of Aristotle, who puts on the same level the chariot Medea uses to flee from Corinth after the vengeance she has taken on Creon. It seems to me there is a sufficient basis for this in the fact that she has been made a magician and that actions of hers as far surpassing natural forces as that one have been mentioned in the play. After what she did for Jason at Colchis and after she had made his father Aeson young again following his return, and after she had attached invisible fire to the gift she gave to Creusa, the flying chariot is not improbable and the poem has no need of other preparation for that extraordinary effect. Seneca gives it preparation by this line which Medea speaks to her nurse: *"Tuum quoque ipsa ipsa corpus hinc mecum aveham;"*[8] and I by this one which she speaks to Aegeus: "I shall follow you tomorrow by a new road." Thus the condemnation of Euripides, who took no precautions, may be just and yet not fall on Seneca or on me; and I have no need to contradict Aristotle in order to justify myself on this point.

From the action I turn to the acts, each of which ought to contain a portion of it, but not so equal a portion that more is not reserved for the last than for the others and less given to the first than to the others. Indeed, in the first act one may do no more than depict the moral nature of the characters and mark off how far they have got in the story which is to be presented. Aristotle does not prescribe the number of the acts; Horace limits it to five;[9] and although he prohibits having fewer, the Spaniards are obstinate enough to stop at three and the Italians often do the same thing. The Greeks used to separate the acts by the chanting of the chorus, and since I think it reasonable to believe that in some of their poems they made it chant more than four times, I should not want to say they never exceeded five. This way of distinguishing the acts was less handy than ours, for either they paid attention to what the chorus was chanting or they did not; if they did, the mind of the spectators was too tense and had no time

---

[6]*Deus ex machina.* See Aristotle, *Poetics,* XV. 7, p. 58.
[7]By Euripides.

[8]"You, too, poor corpse, I bear away with me." Seneca, *Medea.*
[9]*Art of Poetry,* p. 70.

in which to rest; if they did not, attention was too much dissipated by the length of the chant, and when a new act began, an effort of memory was needed to recall to the imagination what had been witnessed and at what point the action had been interrupted. Our orchestra presents neither of these two inconveniences; the mind of the spectator relaxes while the music is playing and even reflects on what he has seen, to praise it or to find fault with it depending on whether he has been pleased or displeased; and the short time the orchestra is allowed to play leaves his impressions so fresh that when the actors return he does not need to make an effort to recall and resume his attention.

The number of scenes in each act has never been prescribed by rule, but since the whole act must have a certain number of lines which make its length proportionate to that of the others, one may include in it more or fewer scenes depending on whether they are long or short to fill up the time which the whole act is to consume. One ought, if possible, to account for the entrance and exit of each actor; I consider this rule indispensable, especially for the exit, and think there is nothing so clumsy as an actor who leaves the stage merely because he has no more lines to speak.

I should not be so rigorous for the entrances. The audience expects the actor, and although the setting represents the room or the study of whoever is speaking, yet he cannot make his appearance there unless he comes out from behind the tapestry, and it is not always easy to give a reason for what he has just done in town before returning home, since sometimes it is even probable that he has not gone out at all. I have never seen anybody take offense at seeing Emilie begin *Cinna* without saying why she has come to her room; she is presumed to be there before the play begins, and it is only stage necessity which makes her appear from behind the scenes to come there. Thus I should willingly dispense from the rigors of the rule the first scene of each act but not the others, because once an actor is on the stage anyone who enters must have a reason to speak to him or, at least, must profit from the opportunity to do so when it offers. Above all, when an actor enters twice in one act, in comedy or in tragedy, he must either lead one to expect that he will soon return when he leaves the first time, like Horace in the second act and Julie in the third act of *Horace,* or explain on returning why he has come back so soon.

Aristotle wishes the well-made tragedy to be beautiful and capable of pleasing without the aid of actors and quite aside from performance.[10] So that the reader may more easily experience that pleasure, his mind, like that of the spectator, must not be hindered, because the effort he is obliged to

make to conceive and to imagine the play for himself lessens the satisfaction which he will get from it. Therefore, I should be of the opinion that the poet ought to take great care to indicate in the margin the less important actions which do not merit being included in the lines, and which might even mar the dignity of the verse if the author lowered himself to express them. The actor easily fills this need on the stage, but in a book one would often be reduced to guessing and sometimes one might even guess wrong, unless one were informed in this way of these little things. I admit that this is not the practice of the ancients; but you must also allow me that because they did not do it they have left us many obscurities in their poems which only masters of dramatic art can explain; even so, I am not sure they succeed as often as they think they do. If we forced ourselves to follow the method of the ancients completely, we should make no distinction between acts and scenes because the Greeks did not. This failure on their part is often the reason that I do not know how many acts there are in their plays, nor whether at the end of an act the player withdraws so as to allow the chorus to chant, or whether he remains onstage without any action while the chorus is chanting, because neither they nor their interpreters have deigned to give us a word of indication in the margin.

We have another special reason for not neglecting that helpful little device as they did: this is that printing puts our plays in the hands of actors who tour the provinces and whom we can thus inform of what they ought to do, for they would do some very odd things if we did not help them by these notes. They would find themselves in great difficulty at the fifth act of plays that end happily, where we bring together all the actors on the stage (a thing which the ancients did not do); they would often say to one what is meant for another, especially when the same actor must speak to three or four people one after the other. When there is a whispered command to make, like Cléopâtre's to Laonice which sends her to seek poison, an aside would be necessary to express this in verse if we were to do without the marginal indications, and that seems to me much more intolerable than the notes, which give us the real and only way, following the opinion of Aristotle, of making the tragedy as beautiful in the reading as in performance, by making it easy for the reader to imagine what the stage presents to the view of the spectators.

The rule of the unity of time is founded on this statement of Aristotle "that the tragedy ought to enclose the duration of its action in one journey of the sun or try not to go much beyond it."[11] These words gave rise to a famous dispute

---

[10]*Poetics,* XXVI, 2, p. 65.

[11]*Poetics,* V. 4, p. 52.

as to whether they ought to be understood as meaning a nat-ural day of twenty-four hours or an artificial day of twelve; each of the two opinions has important partisans, and, for myself, I find that there are subjects so difficult to limit to such a short time that not only should I grant the twenty-four full hours but I should make use of the license which the philosopher gives to exceed them a little and should push the total without scruple as far as thirty. There is a legal maxim which says that we should broaden the mercies and narrow the rigors of the law, *odia restringenda, favores ampliandi;* and I find that an author is hampered enough by this con-straint which forced some of the ancients to the very edge of the impossible. Euripides, in *The Suppliants,* makes Theseus leave Athens with an army, fight a battle beneath the walls of Thebes, which was ten or twelve leagues away, and return victorious in the following act; and between his departure and the arrival of the messenger who comes to tell the story of his victory, the chorus has only thirty-six lines to speak. That makes good use of such a short time. Aeschylus makes Agamemnon come back from Troy with even greater speed. He had agreed with Clytemnestra, his wife, that as soon as the city was taken he would inform her by signal fires built on the intervening mountains, of which the second would be lighted as soon as the first was seen, the third at the sight of the second, and so on; by this means she was to learn the great news the same night. However, scarcely had she learned it from the signal fires when Agamemnon arrives, whose ship, although battered by a storm, if memory serves, must have traveled as fast as the eye could see the lights. The *Cid* and *Pompée,* where the action is a little precipitate, are far from taking so much license; and if they force ordinary probability in some way, at least they do not go as far as such impossibilities.

Many argue against this rule, which they call tyranni-cal, and they would be right if it were founded only on the authority of Aristotle; but what should make it acceptable is the fact that common sense supports it. The dramatic poem is an imitation, or rather a portrait of human actions, and it is beyond doubt that portraits gain in excellence in proportion as they resemble the original more closely. A performance lasts two hours and would resemble reality perfectly if the action it presented required no more for its actual occur-rence. Let us then not settle on twelve or twenty-four hours, but let us compress the action of the poem into the shortest possible period, so that the performance may more close-ly resemble reality and thus be more nearly perfect. Let us give, if that is possible, to the one no more than the two hours which the other fills. I do not think that *Rodogune* re-quires much more, and perhaps two hours would be enough for *Cinna.* If we cannot confine the action within the two hours, let us take four, six, or ten, but let us not go much

beyond twenty-four for fear of falling into lawlessness and of so far reducing the scale of the portrait that it no longer has its proportionate dimensions and is nothing but imper-fection.

Most of all, I should like to leave the matter of duration to the imagination of the spectators and never make definite the time the action requires unless the subject needs this pre-cision, but especially not when probability is a little forced, as in the *Cid,* because precision serves only to make the crowded action obvious to the spectator. Even when no vio-lence is done to a poem by the necessity of obeying this rule, why must one state at the beginning that the sun is rising, that it is noon at the third act, and that the sun is setting at the end of the last act? This is only an obtrusive affectation; it is enough to establish the possibility of the thing in the time one gives to it and that one be able to determine the time easily if one wishes to pay attention to it, but without being compelled to concern oneself with the matter. Even in those actions which take no longer than the performance it would be clumsy to point out that a half hour has elapsed between the beginning of one act and the beginning of the next.

I repeat what I have said elsewhere, that when we take a longer time, as, for instance, ten hours, I should prefer that the eight extra be used up in the time between the acts and that each act should have as its share only as much time as performance requires, especially when all scenes are closely linked together. I think, however, that the fifth act, by special privilege, has the right to accelerate time so that the part of the action which it presents may use up more time than is necessary for performance. The reason for this is that the spectator is by then impatient to see the end, and when the outcome depends on actors who are offstage, all the dialogue given to those who are onstage awaiting news of the others drags and action seems to halt. There is no doubt that from the point where Phocas exits in the fifth act of *Héraclius* until Amyntas enters to relate the manner of his death, more time is needed for what happens offstage than for the speak-ing of the lines in which Héraclius, Martian, and Pulchérie complain of their misfortune. Prusias and Flaminius, in the fifth act of *Nicomède,* do not have the time they would need to meet at sea, take counsel with each other, and return to the defense of the queen; and the Cid has not enough time to fight a duel with Don Sanche during the conversations of the Infanta with Léonor and of Chimène with Elvire. I was aware of this and yet have had no scruples about this accel-eration of which, perhaps, one might find several examples among the ancients, but the laziness of which I have spoken will force me to rest content with this one, which is from the *Andria* of Terence. Simo slips his son Pamphilus into the house of Glycerium in order to get the old man, Crito, to come out and to clear up with him the question of the birth of his mistress, who happens to be the daughter of Chremes. Pamphilus enters the house, speaks to Crito, asks him for the favor and returns with him; and during this exit, this request, and this reentry, Simo and Chremes, who remain onstage, speak only one line each, which could not possibly give Pamphilus more than time enough to ask where Crito is, certainly not enough to talk with him and to explain to him the reasons for which he should reveal what he knows about the birth of the unknown girl.

When the conclusion of the action depends on actors who have not left the stage and about whom no one is awaiting news, as in *Cinna* and *Rodogune,* the fifth act has no need of this privilege because then all the action takes place in plain sight, as does not happen when part of it occurs offstage after the beginning of the act. The other acts do not merit the same freedom. If there is not time enough to bring back an actor who had made his exit, or to indicate what he has done since that exit, the accounting can be postponed to the following act; and the music, which separates the two acts, may use up as much time as is necessary; but in the fifth act no postponement is possible: attention is exhausted and the end must come quickly.

I cannot forget that although we must reduce the whole tragic action to one day, we can nevertheless make known by a narration or in some other more artful way what the hero of the tragedy has been doing for several years, because there are plays in which the crux of the plot lies in an obscurity of birth which must be brought to light, as in *Oedipus.* I shall not say again that the less one burdens oneself with past actions, the more favorable the spectator will be, because of the lesser degree of trouble he is given when everything takes place in the present and no demands are made on his memory except for what he has seen; but I cannot forget that the choice of a day both illustrious and long-awaited is a great ornament to a poem. The opportunity for this does not always present itself, and in all that I have written until now you will find only four of that kind: the day in *Horace* when two nations are to decide the question of supremacy of empire by a battle; and the ones in *Rodogune, Andromède,* and *Don Sanche.* In *Rodogune* it is a day chosen by two sovereigns for the signature of a treaty of peace between the hostile crowns, for a complete reconciliation of the two rival governments through a marriage, and for the elucidation of a more than twenty-year-old secret concerning the right of succession of one of the twin princes on which the fate of the kingdom depends, as does the outcome of both their loves. The days in *Andromède* and *Don Sanche* are not of lesser importance, but, as I have just said, such opportunities do not often present themselves, and in the rest of my works I have been able to choose days remarkable only for what

chance makes happen on them and not by the use to which public arrangements destined them long ago.

As for the unity of place, I find no rule concerning it in either Aristotle or Horace. This is what leads many people to believe that this rule was established only as a consequence of the unity of one day, and leads them to imagine that one can stretch the unity of place to cover the points to which a man may go and return in twenty-four hours. This opinion is a little too free, and if one made an actor travel posthaste, the two sides of the theater might represent Paris and Rouen. I could wish, so that the spectator is not at all disturbed, that what is performed before him in two hours might actually be able to take place in two hours, and that what he is shown in a stage setting which does not change might be limited to a room or a hall depending on a choice made beforehand; but often that is so awkward, if not impossible, that one must necessarily find some way to enlarge the place as also the time of the action. I have shown exact unity of place in *Horace, Polyeucte,* and *Pompée,* but for that it was necessary to present either only one woman, as in *Polyeucte;* or to arrange that the two who are presented are such clsoe friends and have such closely related interests that they can be always together, as in *Horace;* or that they may react as in *Pompée* where the stress of natural curiosity drives Cléopâtre from her apartments in the second act and Cornélie in the fifth; and both enter the great hall of the king's palace in anticipation of the news they are expecting. The same thing is not true of *Rodogune:* Cléopâtre and she have interests which are too divergent to permit them to express their most secret thoughts in the same place. I might say of that play what I have said of *Cinna,* where, in general, everything happens in Rome and, in particular, half of the action takes place in the quarters of Auguste and half of it in Emilie's apartments. Following that arrangement, the first act of this tragedy would be laid in Rodogune's antechamber, the second, in Cléopâtre's apartments, the third, in Rodogune's; but if the fourth act can begin in Rodogune's apartments it cannot finish there, and what Cléopâtre says to her two sons one after the other would be badly out of place there. The fifth act needs a throne room where a great crowd can be gathered. The same problem is found in *Héraclius.* The first act could very well take place in Phocas's quarters, the second, in Léontine's apartments; but if the third begins in Pulchérie's rooms it cannot end there, and it is outside the bounds of probability that Phocas should discuss the death of her brother in Pulchérie's apartments.

The ancients, who made their kings speak in a public square, easily kept a rigorous unity of place in their tragedies. Sophocles, however, did not observe it in his *Ajax,* when the hero leaves the stage to find a lonely place in which to kill himself and does so in full view of the people; this easily leads to the conclusion that the place where he kills himself is not the one he has been seen to leave, since he left it only to choose another.

We do not take the same liberty of drawing kings and princesses from their apartments, and since often the difference and the opposition on the part of those who are lodged in the same palace do not allow them to take others into their confidence or to disclose their secrets in the same room, we must seek some other compromise about unity of place if we want to keep it intact in our poems; otherwise we should have to decide against many plays which we see succeeding brilliantly.

I hold, then, that we ought to seek exact unity as much as possible, but as this unity does not suit every kind of subject, I should be very willing to concede that a whole city has unity of place. Not that I should want the stage to represent the whole city, that would be somewhat too large, but only two or three particular places enclosed within its walls. Thus the scene of *Cinna* does not leave Rome, passing from the apartments of Auguste to the house of Emilie. *Le Menteur* takes place in the Tuileries and in the Place Royale at Paris, and *La Suite* shows us the prison and Mélisse's house at Lyons. The *Cid* increases even more the number of particular places without leaving Seville; and since the close linking of scenes is not observed in that play, the stage in the first act is supposed to represent Chimène's house, the Infante's apartments in the king's palace, and the public square; the second adds to these the king's chamber. No doubt there is some excess in this freedom. In order to rectify in some way this multiplication of places when it is inevitable, I should wish two things done: first, that the scene should never change in a given act but only between the acts, as is done in the first three acts of *Cinna;* the other, that these two places should not need different stage settings and that neither of the two should ever be named, but only the general place which includes them both, as Paris, Rome, Lyons, Constantinople, and so forth. This would help to deceive the spectator, who, seeing nothing that would indicate the difference in the places, would not notice the change, unless it was maliciously and critically pointed out, a thing which few are capable of doing, most spectators being warmly intent upon the action which they see on the stage. The pleasure they take in it is the reason why they do not seek out its imperfections lest they lose their taste for it; and they admit such an imperfection only when forced, when it is too obvious, as in *Le Menteur* and *La Suite,* where the different settings force them to recognize the multiplicity of places in spite of themselves.

But since people of opposing interests cannot with verisimilitude unfold their secrets in the same place, and since they are sometimes introduced into the same act through the linking of scenes which the unity of place necessarily produces, one must find some means to make it compatible with the contradiction which rigorous probability finds in it, and consider how to preserve the fourth act of *Rodogune* and the third of *Héraclius,* in both of which I have already pointed out the contradiction which lies in having enemies speak in the same place. Jurists allow legal fictions, and I should like, following their example, to introduce theatrical fictions by which one could establish a theatrical place which would not be Cléopâtre's chamber nor Rodogune's, in the play of that name, nor that of Phocas, of Léontine or of Pulchérie in *Héraclius,* but a room contiguous to all these other apartments, to which I should attribute these two privileges: first, that each of those who speaks in it is presumed to enjoy the same secrecy there as if he were in his own room; and second, that whereas in the usual arrangement it is sometimes proper for those who are onstage to go off, in order to speak privately with others in their rooms, these latter might meet the former onstage without shocking convention, so as to preserve both the unity of place and the linking of scenes. Thus Rodogune, in the first act, encounters Laonice, whom she must send for so as to speak with her; and, in the fourth act, Cléopâtre encounters Antiochus on the very spot where he has just moved Rodogune to pity, even though in utter verisimilitude the prince ought to seek out his mother in her own room since she hates the princess too much to speak to him in Rodogune's, which following the first scene, would be the locus of the whole act, if one did not introduce that compromise which I have mentioned into the rigorous unity of place.

Many of my plays will be at fault in the unity of place if this compromise is not accepted, for I shall abide by it always in the future when I am not able to satisfy the ultimate rigor of the rule. I have been able to reduce only three plays, *Horace, Polyeucte,* and *Pompée,* to the requirements of the rule. If I am too indulgent with myself as far as the others are concerned, I shall be even more so for those which may succeed on the stage through some appearance of regularity. It is easy for critics to be severe; but if they were to give ten or a dozen plays to the public, they might perhaps slacken the rules more than I do, as soon as they have recognized through experience what constraint their precision brings about and how many beautiful things it banishes from our stage. However that may be, these are my opinions, or if you prefer, my heresies concerning the principal points of the dramatic art, and I do not know how better to make the ancient rules agree with modern pleasures. I do not doubt that one might easily find better ways of doing that, and I shall be ready to accept them when they have been put into practice as successfully as, by common consent, mine have been.

John Dryden

1631–1700

Although it cannot be described as a theoretical work, Dryden's *Essay of Dramatic Poesy* provides perhaps the fullest single account of issues and attitudes in neoclassical criticism. And it is particularly important because it belies one popular view of neoclassical criticism, namely, that it was wholly dogmatic and a slave to its own arbitrary decrees. Dryden is not imprisoned by rules and is able to see many sides of the issues he raises. At the center of his essay lies the classical idea of decorum enunciated by Horace, but decorum is never for Dryden merely obeisance to the prevailing fashion.

The essay, strongly influenced by Corneille and Ben Jonson, is written in the form of a dialogue among four gentlemen: Eugenius, Crites, Lisideius, and Neander. The last, Neander, seems to speak for Dryden himself. First they consider whether the ancients or the moderns wrote better, a quarrel of some popularity later satirized by Jonathan Swift. This question turns into a discussion of the so-called unities of time, place, and action, what they are, and whether they must be observed. Discussion then moves to a relative judgment of the French and English playwrights and whether the traditional genres of tragedy and comedy ought properly to be mixed in a single work, as the English had done. There is finally a consideration of the propriety of writing plays in rhymed verse.

Eugenius argues that the moderns excel the ancients, having profited from the rules that the ancient writers laid down; he remarks in passing that the ancients did not themselves observe the unity of place. Crites, defending the ancients, points out that they invented the principles of dramatic art enunciated by Aristotle and Horace, who established the unities adopted by the French; he observes that the greatest English modern, Ben Jonson, followed the ancients. Crites, who is opposed to rhyme in plays, argues that though the moderns excel in science, the ancient age was the true age of poetry. Lisideius, who defines a play as "a just and lively image of human nature, representing its passions and humors, and the changes of fortune to which it is subject for the delight and instruction of mankind," defends the French playwrights and attacks the English tendency to mix genres. Neander, who has the last word, adopts a position favoring the moderns, respectful of the ancients, critical of too rigid insistence on dramatic laws, and willing to accept rhyme in its proper place.

In Lisideius' definition, which is provisionally accepted by the other three, there are two fundamental theoretical points: drama is an imitation, and its aim is to delight and teach. The essay becomes deeply involved with the problem of imitation when it considers how closely the dramatist must adhere to the unities of time, place, and action. If imitation means that the play must create a direct illusion of "real" life, then the unities must be strictly observed; but if it does not, then the question is perhaps what formal integrity, independent of a sort of naive realism, the playwright ought to be seeking. The principle of decorum in Dryden is associated finally with an idea of formal integrity.

In 1668 Dryden also wrote a "Defense" of his essay, devoted mainly to advocating the use of rhyme. In the course of this essay, he remarks: "Delight is the chief, if not the only, end of poetry: instruction can be admitted but in the second place, for poesy only instructs as it delights." A slippery statement, it nevertheless places Dryden on the side of delight in an old argument.

Dryden's critical works are available in a number of editions. That by W. P. Ker, *Essays by John Dryden* (2 vols., 1900), though still useful, has largely been superseded by George Watson's *John Dryden: Of Dramatic Poesy and Other Critical Essays* (2 vols., 1962). Commentary on Dryden includes A. M. Ellis, "Horace's Influence on Dryden," *Philological Quarterly,* IV (1925), 39–60; L. I. Bredvold, *The Intellectual Milieu of John Dryden* (1934); Hoyt Trowbridge, "The Place of Rules in Dryden's Criticism," *Modern Philology,* XLIV (1946–47), 84–96; F. L. Huntley, *On Dryden's Essay of Dramatic Poesy* (1951); Phillip Harth, *Contexts of Dryden's Thought* (1968); H. James Jensen, *A Glossary of John Dryden's Critical Terms* (1969); Robert D. Hume, *Dryden's Criticism* (1970); and Edward Pechter, *Dryden's Classical Theory of Literature* (1975).

An Essay of Dramatic Poesy

It was that memorable day,[1] in the first summer of the late war, when our navy engaged the Dutch; a day wherein the two most mighty and best appointed fleets which any age had ever seen, disputed the command of the greater half of the globe, the commerce of nations, and the riches of the universe. While these vast floating bodies, on either side, moved against each other in parallel lines, and our countrymen, under the happy conduct of his Royal Highness, went breaking, by little and little, into the line of the enemies; the noise of the cannon from both navies reached our ears about the city, so that all men being alarmed with it, and in a dreadful suspense of the event which we knew was then deciding, everyone went following the sound as his fancy led him; and leaving the town almost empty, some took towards the park, some cross the river, others down it; all seeking the noise in the depth of silence.

Among the rest, it was the fortune of Eugenius, Crites, Lisideius, and Neander,[2] to be in company together; three of them persons whom their wit and quality have made known to all the town; and whom I have chose to hide under these borrowed names, that they may not suffer by so ill a relation as I am going to make of their discourse.

Taking then a barge which a servant of Lisideius has provided for them, they made haste to shoot the bridge, and left behind them that great fall of waters which hindered them from hearing what they desired: after which, having disengaged themselves from many vessels which rode at anchor in the Thames, and almost blocked up the passage towards Greenwich, they ordered the watermen to let fall their oars more gently; and then, everyone favoring his own curiosity with a strict silence, it was not long ere they perceived the air break about them like the noise of distant thunder, or of swallows in a chimney: those little undulations of sound, though almost vanishing before they reached them, yet still seeming to retain somewhat of their first horror, which they had betwixt the fleets. After they had attentively listened till

---

AN ESSAY OF DRAMATIC POESY. The essay was first published in 1668. A revised edition was published in 1684. The text is based on the 1668 edition. Dryden often slightly misquotes the Roman writers to whom he refers.
[1] June 3, 1665.

[2] The characters have sometimes been identified as follows: Eugenius: Charles Sackville (1638–1707); Crites: Sir Robert Howard (1626–98), Dryden's brother-in-law, a poet and playwright; Lisideius: Sir Charles Sedley (c. 1639–1701), a playwright; Neander: Dryden.

such time as the sound by little and little went from them, Eugenius, lifting up his head, and taking notice of it, was the first who congratulated to the rest that happy omen of our nation's victory: adding, "We had but this to desire in confirmation of it, that we might hear no more of that noise, which was now leaving the English coast." When the rest had concurred in the same opinion, Crites, a person of a sharp judgment, and somewhat too delicate a taste in wit, which the world have mistaken in him for ill-nature, said, smiling to us, that if the concernment of this battle had not been so exceeding great, he could scarce have wished the victory at the price he knew he must pay for it, in being subject to the reading and hearing of so many ill verses as he was sure would be made upon it. Adding, that no argument could 'scape some of those eternal rhymers, who watch a battle with more diligence than the ravens and birds of prey; and the worst of them surest to be first in upon the quarry: while the better able either out of modesty writ not at all, or set that due value upon their poems, as to let them be often called for and long expected! "There are some of those impertinent people you speak of," answered Lisideius, "who to my knowledge are already so provided, either way, that they can produce not only a panegyric upon the victory, but, if need be, a funeral elegy on the Duke; and after they have crowned his valor with many laurels, at last deplore the odds under which he fell, concluding that his courage deserved a better destiny." All the company smiled at the conceit of Lisideius; but Crites, more eager than before, began to make particular exceptions against some writers, and said, the public magistrate ought to send betimes to forbid them; and that it concerned the peace and quiet of all honest people, that ill poets should be as well silenced as seditious preachers. "In my opinion," replied Eugenius, "you pursue your point too far; for as to my own particular, I am so great a lover of poesy, that I could wish them all rewarded, who attempt but to do well; at least, I would not have them worse used than Sylla the Dictator did one of their brethren heretofore: *'Quem in concione vidimus,'* says Tully, *'cum ei libellum malus poeta de populo subjecisset, quod epigramma in eum fecisset tantummodo alternis versibus longiusculis, statim ex iis rebus quas tunc vendebat jubere ei praemium tribui, sub ea conditione ne quid postea scriberet.'"*[3] "I could wish with all my heart," replied Crites, "that many whom we

know were as bountifully thanked upon the same condition—that they would never trouble us again. For amongst others, I have a mortal apprehension of two poets, whom this victory with the help of both her wings, will never be able to escape." "'Tis easy to guess whom you intend," said Lisideius; "and without naming them, I ask you, if one of them does not perpetually pay us with clenches[4] upon words, and a certain clownish kind of raillery? If now and then he does not offer at a catachresis or Clevelandism,[5] wresting and torturing a word into another meaning: in fine, if he be not one of those whom the French could call *un mauvais bouffon;*[6] one that is so much a well-willer to the satire, that he spares no man; and though he cannot strike a blow to hurt any, yet ought to be punished for the malice of the action, as our witches are justly hanged, because they think themselves so; and suffer deservedly for believing they did mischief, because they meant it." "You have described him," said Crites, "so exactly, that I am afraid to come after you with my other extremity of poetry. He is one of those who, having had some advantage of education and converse, knows better than the other what a poet should be, but puts it into practice more unluckily than any man; his style and matter are everywhere alike: he is the most calm, peaceable writer you ever read: he never disquiets your passions with the least concernment, but still leaves you in as even a temper as he found you; he is a very leveler in poetry: he creeps along with ten little words in every line, and helps out his numbers with *for to,* and *unto* and all the pretty expletives he can find, till he drags them to the end of another line; while the sense is left tired halfway behind it: he doubly starves all his verses, first for want of thought, and then of expression; his poetry neither has wit in it, nor seems to have it; like him in Martial: *'Pauper videri Cinna vult, et est pauper.'*[7]

"He affects plainness, to cover his want of imagination: when he writes the serious way, the highest flight of his fancy is some miserable antithesis, or seeming contradiction; and in the comic he is still reaching at some thin conceit, the ghost of a jest, and that too flies before him, never to be caught; these swallows which we see before us on the Thames are the just resemblance of his wit: you may observe how near the water they stoop, how many proffers they make to dip, and yet how seldom they touch it; and when they do,

---

[3]We note that in an assembly once, when a bad poet handed up from the crowd a small book in which he had composed an epigram about him, only in somewhat long alternating verse, he at once ordered that he be given a reward from among those things that he was selling, on condition that he never again write anything." Cicero, *In Defense of Archius,* X. 25.

[4]Plays on words, puns.

[5]Catachresis is the incorrect use of words, usually an outlandish metaphor or Clevelandism, which refers to John Cleveland, English satiric metaphysical poet (1613–58).

[6]"A sorry jester."

[7]Cinna wishes to appear poor, and is poor." *Epigrams,* VIII. 19.

'tis but the surface: they skim over it but to catch a gnat, and then mount into the air and leave it.''

"Well, gentlemen," said Eugenius, "you may speak your pleasure of these authors; but though I and some few more about the town may give you a peaceable hearing, yet assure yourselves, there are multitudes who would think you malicious and them injured: especially him whom you first described; he is the very withers of the city: they have bought more editions of his works than would serve to lay under all their pies at the Lord Mayor's Christmas. When his famous poem first came out in the year 1660, I have seen them reading it in the midst of 'change time; nay so vehement they were at it, that they lost their bargain by the candles' ends; but what will you say, if he has been received amongst the great ones? I can assure you he is, this day, the envy of a great person who is lord in the art of quibbling; and who does not take it well, that any man should intrude so far into his province." "All I would wish," replied Crites, "is that they who love his writings, may still admire him, and his fellow poet: *'Qui Bavium non odit, &c.,'*[8] is curse sufficient." "And farther," added Lisideius, "I believe there is no man who writes well, but would think himself very hardly dealt with, if their admirers should praise anything of his: *'Nam quos contemnimus, eorum quoque laudes contemnimus.'"*[9] "There are so few who write well in this age," says Crites, "that methinks any praises should be welcome; they neither rise to the dignity of the last age, nor to any of the ancients: and we may cry out of the writers of this time, with more reason than Petronius of his, *'Pace vestra liceat dixisse, primi omnium eloquentiam perdidistis':*[10] you have debauched the true old poetry so far, that nature, which is the soul of it, is not in any of your writings."

"If your quarrel," said Eugenius, "to those who now write, be grounded only on your reverence to antiquity, there is no man more ready to adore those great Greeks and Romans than I am: but on the other side, I cannot think so contemptibly of the age I live in, or so dishonorably of my own country, as not to judge we equal the ancients in most kinds of poesy, and in some surpass them; neither know I any reason why I may not be zealous for the reputation of our age, as we find the ancients themselves in reference to those who lived before them. For you hear your Horace saying, *'Indignor quidquam reprehendi, non quia crasse / Compositum, illepidève putetur, sed quia nuper.'*[11] And after: *'Si meliora*

dies, ut vina, poemata reddit, / Scire velim, pretium chartis quotus arroget annus?'*[12]

"But I see I am engaging in a wide dispute, where the arguments are not like to reach close on either side; for poesy is of so large an extent, and so many both of the ancients and moderns have done well in all kinds of it, that in citing one against the other, we shall take up more time this evening than each man's occasions will allow him: therefore I would ask Crites to what part of poesy he would confine his arguments, and whether he would defend the general cause of the ancients against the moderns, or oppose any age of the moderns against this of ours?"

Crites, a little while considering upon this demand, told Eugenius he approved his propositions, and if he pleased, he would limit their dispute to dramatic poesy; in which he thought it not difficult to prove, either that the ancients were superior to the moderns, or the last age to this of ours.

Eugenius was somewhat surprised, when he heard Crites make choice of that subject. "For ought I see," said he, "I have undertaken a harder province than I imagined; for though I never judged the plays of the Greek or Roman poets comparable to ours, yet, on the other side, those we now see acted come short of many which were written in the last age: but my comfort is, if we are o'ercome, it will be only by our own countrymen: and if we yield to them in this one part of poesy, we more surpass them in all the other: for in the epic or lyric way, it will be hard for them to show us one such amongst them, as we have many now living, or who lately were so: they can produce nothing so courtly writ, or which expresses so much the conversation of a gentleman, as Sir John Suckling; nothing so even, sweet, and flowing, as Mr. Waller; nothing so majestic, so correct, as Sir John Denham; nothing so elevated, so copious, and full of spirit, as Mr. Cowley; as for the Italian, French, and Spanish plays, I can make it evident, that those who now write surpass them; and that the drama is wholly ours."

All of them were thus far of Eugenius his opinion, that the sweetness of English verse was never understood or practiced by our fathers; even Crites himself did not much oppose it: and every one was willing to acknowledge how much our poesy is improved by the happiness of some writers yet living; who first taught us to mold our thoughts into easy and significant words; to retrench the superfluities of expression, and to make our rhyme so properly a part of the verse, that is should never mislead the sense, but itself be led and governed by it.

---

[8]"Who does not hate Bavius . . . ." Virgil, *Eclogues*, III. 90.

[9]"For we despise the praises of those we despise."

[10]"By your leave, let me say you were first to destroy eloquence for all." *Satyricon*, 2.

[11]"I am offended when something is criticized, not because it is badly composed, or thought to lack charm, but because it is recent." *Epistles*, II. i. 76.

[12]"If time causes poems to improve like wine, how many years, I would like to know, will it take?" *Epistles*, II. i. 34.

Eugenius was going to continue this discourse, when Lisideius told him it was necessary, before they proceeded further, to take a standing measure of their controversy; for how was it possible to be decided who writ the best plays, before we know what a play should be? But, this once agreed on by both parties, each might have recourse to it, either to prove his own advantages, or to discover the failings of his adversary.

He had no sooner said this, but all desired the favor of him to give the definition of a play; and they were the more importunate, because neither Aristotle, nor Horace, nor any other, who writ of that subject, had ever done it.

Lisideius, after some modest denials, at last confessed he had a rude notion of it; indeed, rather a description than a definition; but which served to guide him in his private thoughts, when he was to make a judgment of what others writ: that he conceived a play ought to be, *a just and lively image of human nature, representing its passions and humors, and the changes of fortune to which it is subject, for the delight and instruction of mankind.*

This definition, though Crites raised a logical objection against it; that it was only *a genere et fine,*[13] and so not altogether perfect; was yet well received by the rest: and after they had given order to the watermen to turn their barge, and row softly, that they might take the cool of the evening in their return, Crites, being desired by the company to begin, spoke on behalf of the ancients, in this manner:

"If confidence presage a victory, Eugenius, in his own opinion, has already triumphed over the ancients: nothing seems more easy to him, than to overcome those whom it is our greatest praise to have imitated well; for we do not only build upon their foundation, but by their models. Dramatic poesy had time enough, reckoning from Thespis (who first invented it) to Aristophanes, to be born, to grow up, and to flourish in maturity. It has been observed of arts and sciences, that in one and the same century they have arrived to a great perfection; and no wonder, since every age has a kind of universal genius, which inclines those that live in it to some particular studies: the work then being pushed on by many hands, must of necessity go forward.

"Is it not evident, in these last hundred years (when the study of philosophy[14] has been the business of all the virtuosi in Christendom), that almost a new nature has been revealed to us? That more errors of the school have been detected, more useful experiments in philosophy have been made, more noble secrets in optics, medicine, anatomy, astronomy, discovered, than in all those credulous and doting ages from

Aristotle to us? So true is it, that nothing spreads more fast than science, when rightly and generally cultivated.

"Add to this, the more than common emulation that was in those times of writing well; which though it be found in all ages and all persons that pretend to the same reputation, yet poesy, being then in more esteem than now it is, had greater honors decreed to the professors of it, and consequently the rivalship was more high between them; they had judges ordained to decide their merit, and prizes to reward it; and historians have been diligent to record of Aeschylus, Euripides, Sophocles, Lycophron, and the rest of them, both who they were that vanquished in these wars of the theater, and how often they were crowned: while the Asian kings and Grecian commonwealths scarce afforded them a nobler subject than the unmanly luxuries of a debauched court, or giddy intrigues of a factious city. *'Alit aemulatio ingenia,'* says Paterculus, *'et nunc invidia, nunc admiratio incitationem accendit':* emulation is the spur of wit; and sometimes envy, sometimes admiration, quickens our endeavors.[15]

"But now, since the rewards of honor are taken away, that virtuous emulation is turned into direct malice; yet so slothful, that it contents itself to condemn and cry down others, without attempting to do better: 'tis a reputation too unprofitable, to take the necessary pains for it; yet, wishing they had it is incitement enough to hinder others from it. And this, in short, Eugenius, is the reason why you have now so few good poets, and so many severe judges. Certainly, to imitate the ancients well, much labor and long study is required; which pains, I have already shown, our poets would want encouragement to take, if yet they had ability to go through with it. Those ancients have been faithful imitators and wise observers of that nature which is so torn and ill represented in our plays; they have handed down to us a perfect resemblance of her; which we, like ill copiers, neglecting to look on, have rendered monstrous, and disfigured. But, that you may know how much you are indebted to those your masters, and be ashamed to have so ill requited them, I must remember you, that all the rules by which we practice the drama at this day (either such as relate to the justness and symmetry of the plot, or the episodical ornaments, such as descriptions, narrations, and other beauties, which are not essential to the play) were delivered to us from the observations which Aristotle made, of those poets, which either lived before him, or were his contemporaries: we have added nothing of our own, except we have the confidence to say our wit is better; of which none boast in this our age, but such as understand not theirs. Of that book which Aristotle

---

[13]"By genre and purpose."
[14]The term is used in the larger sense to denote all branches of learning.

[15]*History of Rome,* I. 17.

has left us, περί τῆς Ποιητικῆς ,[16] Horace his *Art of Poetry* is an excellent comment, and, I believe, restores to us that second book of his concerning comedy, which is wanting in him.

"Out of these two have been extracted the famous rules, which the French call *des trois unités,*[17] or, the three unities, which ought to be observed in every regular play; namely, of time, place, and action.

"The unity of time they comprehend in twenty-four hours, the compass of a natural day, or as near as it can be contrived; and the reason of it is obvious to everyone—that the time of the feigned action, or fable of the play, should be proportioned as near as can be to the duration of that time in which it is represented: since therefore, all plays are acted on the theater in a space of time much within the compass of twenty-four hours, that play is to be thought the nearest imitation of nature, whose plot or action is confined within that time; and, by the same rule which concludes this general proportion of time, it follows, that all the parts of it are to be equally subdivided; as namely, that one act take not up the supposed time of half a day, which is out of proportion to the rest; since the other four are then to be straitened within the compass of the remaining half: for it is unnatural that one act, which being spoke or written is not longer than the rest, should be supposed longer by the audience; 'tis therefore the poet's duty, to take care that no act should be imagined to exceed the time in which it is represented on the stage; and that the intervals and inequalities of time be supposed to fall out between the acts.

"This rule of time, how well it has been observed by the ancients, most of their plays will witness; you see them in their tragedies (wherein to follow this rule, is certainly most difficult) from the very beginning of their plays, falling close into that part of the story which they intend for the action or principal object of it, leaving the former part to be delivered by narration: so that they set the audience, as it were, at the post where the race is to be concluded; and, saving them the tedious expectation of seeing the poet set out and ride the beginning of the course, you behold him not till he is in sight of the goal, and just upon you.

"For the second unity, which is that of place, the ancients meant by it, that the scene ought to be continued through the play, in the same place where it was laid in the beginning: for the stage on which it is represented being but one and the same place, it is unnatural to conceive it many; and those far distant from one another. I will not deny but,

by the variation of painted scenes, the fancy, which in these cases will contribute to its own deceit, may sometimes imagine it several places, with some appearance of probability; yet it still carries the greater likelihood of truth, if those places be supposed so near each other, as in the same town or city; which may all be comprehended under the larger domination of one place; for a greater distance will bear no proportion to the shortness of time which is allotted in the acting, to pass from one of them to another; for the observation of this, next to the ancients, the French are to be most commended. They tie themselves so strictly to the unity of place, that you never see in any of their plays, a scene changed in the middle of an act: if the act begins in a garden, a street, or chamber, 'tis ended in the same place; and that you may know it to be the same, the stage is so supplied with persons, that it is never empty all the time: he that enters the second, has business with him who was on before; and before the second quits the stage, a third appears who has business with him. This Corneille calls *'la liaison des scènes,'* the continuity or joining of the scenes; and 'tis a good mark of a well-contrived play, when all the persons are known to each other, and every one of them has some affairs with all the rest.

"As for the third unity, which is that of action, the ancients meant no other by it than what the logicians do by their *finis,* the end or scope of any action; that which is the first in intention, and last in execution: now the poet is to aim at one great and complete action, to the carrying on of which all things in his play, even the very obstacles, are to be subservient; and the reason of this is as evident as any of the former.

"For two actions, equally labored and driven on by the writer, would destroy the unity of the poem; it would be no longer one play, but two: not but that there may be many actions in a play, as Ben Jonson has observed in his *Discoveries;*[18] but they must be all subservient to the great one, which our language happily expresses in the name of *underplots:* such as in Terence's *Eunuch* is the difference and reconcilement of Thais and Phaedria, which is not the chief business of the play, but promotes the marriage of Chaerea

---

[16]*Poetics.*
[17]See Corneille, *Of the Three Unities,* pp. 206–12; and Castelvetro, *The Poetics of Aristotle,* p. 138.

---

[18]"Now that it should be one and entire: one is considerable two ways; either as it is only separate, and by itself; or as being composed of many parts, it begins to be one as those parts grow or are wrought together. That it should be one the first way alone, and by itself, no man that hath tasted letters ever would say, especially having required before a just magnitude, and equal proportion of the parts themselves. Neither of which can possibly be if the action be single and separate, not composed of parts, which laid together in themselves, with an equal and fitting proportion, tend to the same end; which thing out of antiquity itself hath deceived many, and more this day it doth deceive." *Discoveries,* IV.

and Chremes's sister, principally intended by the poet. There ought to be but one action, says Corneille, that is, one complete action which leaves the mind of the audience in a full repose; but this cannot be brought to pass but by many other imperfect actions, which conduce to it, and hold the audience in a delightful suspense of what will be.

"If by these rules (to omit many other drawn from the precepts and practice of the ancients) we should judge our modern plays, 'tis probable that few of them would endure the trial: that which should be the business of a day, takes up in some of them an age; instead of one action, they are the epitomes of a man's life; and for one spot of ground (which the stage should represent) we are sometimes in more countries than the map can show us.

"But if we will allow the ancients to have contrived well, we must acknowledge them to have writ better; questionless we are deprived of a great stock of wit in the loss of Menander among the Greek poets, and of Caecilius, Afranius, and Varius, among the Romans; we may guess at Menander's excellency by the plays of Terence, who translated some of his; and yet wanted so much of him, that he was called by C. Caesar the half-Menander; and of Varius, by the testimonies of Horace, Martial, and Velleius Paterculus. 'Tis probable that these, could they be recovered, would decide the controversy; but so long as Aristophanes in the old comedy, and Plautus in the new are extant, while the tragedies of Euripides, Sophocles, and Seneca, are to be had, I can never see one of those plays which are now written, but it increases my admiration of the ancients. And yet I must acknowledge farther, that to admire them as we ought, we should understand them better than we do. Doubtless many things appear flat to us, whose wit depended on some custom or story, which never came to our knowledge; or perhaps on some criticism in their language, which being so long dead, and only remaining in their books, 'tis not possible they should make us know it perfectly. To read Macrobius, explaining the propriety and elegancy of many words in Virgil, which I had before passed over without consideration, as common things, is enough to assure me that I ought to think the same of Terence; and that in the purity of his style (which Tully so much valued that he ever carried his works about him) there is yet left in him great room for admiration, if I knew but where to place it. In the meantime I must desire you to take notice, that the greatest man of the last age (Ben Jonson) was willing to give place to them in all things: he was not only a professed imitator of Horace, but a learned plagiary of all the others; you track him everywhere in their snow: if Horace, Lucan, Petronius Arbiter, Seneca, and Juvenal, had their own from him, there are few serious thoughts which are new in him: you will pardon me, therefore, if I presume he loved their fashion, when he wore their clothes. But since I have otherwise a great veneration for him, and you, Eugenius, prefer him above all other poets, I will use no farther argument to you than his example: I will produce Father Ben to you, dressed in all the ornaments and colors of the ancients; you will need no other guide to our party, if you follow him; and whether you consider the bad plays of our age, or regard the good ones of the last, both the best and worst of the modern poets will equally instruct you to esteem the ancients."

Crites had no sooner left speaking, but Eugenius, who had waited with some impatience for it, thus began:

"I have observed in your speech, that the former part of it is convincing as to what the moderns have profited by the rules of the ancients; but in the latter you are careful to conceal how much they have excelled them; we own all the helps we have from them, and want neither veneration nor gratitude while we acknowledge that to overcome them we must make use of the advantages we have received from them: but to these assistances we have joined our own industry; for, had we sat down with a dull imitation of them, we might then have lost somewhat of the old perfection, but never acquired any that was new. We draw not therefore after their lines, but those of nature; and having the life before us, besides the experience of all they knew, it is no wonder if we hit some airs and features which they have missed. I deny not what you urge of arts and sciences, that they have flourished in some ages more than others; but your instance in philosophy makes for me: for if natural causes be more known now than in the time of Aristotle, because more studied, it follows that poesy and other arts may, with the same pains, arrive still nearer to perfection; and, that granted, it will rest for you to prove that they wrought more perfect images of human life than we; which seeing in your discourse you have avoided to make good, it shall now be my task to show you some part of their defects, and some few excellencies of the moderns. And I think there is none among us can imagine I do it enviously, or with purpose to detract from them; for what interest of fame or profit can the living lose by the reputation of the dead? On the other side, it is a great truth which Velleius Paterculus affirms: '*Audita visis libentius laudamus; et praesentia invidia, praeterita admiratione prosequimur; et his nos obrui, illis instrui credimus*':[19] that praise or censure is certainly the most sincere, which unbribed posterity shall give us.

"Be pleased then in the first place to take notice, that the Greek poesy, which Crites has affirmed to have arrived

---

[19] "We praise more gladly things heard than seen; and we accompany envy for the present with admiration for the past: and we believe we are oppressed by the former, instructed by the latter." *History of Rome*, II. 92.

to perfection in the reign of the old comedy, was so far from it, that the distinction of it into acts was not known to them; or if it were, it is yet so darkly delivered to us that we cannot make it out.

"All we know of it is, from the singing of their chorus; and that too is so uncertain, that in some of their plays we have reason to conjecture they sung more than five times. Aristotle indeed divides the integral parts of a play into four. First, the protasis, or entrance, which gives light only to the characters of the persons, and proceeds very little into any part of the action. Secondly, the epitasis, or working up of the plot; where the play grows warmer, the design or action of it is drawing on, and you see something promising that it will come to pass. Thirdly, the catastasis, or counterturn, which destroys that expectation, embroils the action in new difficulties, and leaves you far distant from that hope in which it found you; as you may have observed in a violent stream resisted by a narrow passage—it runs round to an eddy, and carries back the waters with more swiftness than it brought them on. Lastly, the catastrophe, which the Grecians called λύσις, the French *le dénouement,* and we the discovery or unraveling of the plot: there you see all things settling again upon their first foundations; and, the obstacles which hindered the design or action of the play once removed, it ends with that resemblance of truth and nature, that the audience are satisfied with the conduct of it. Thus this great man delivered to us the image of a play; and I must confess it is so lively, that from thence much light has been derived to the forming it more perfectly into acts and scenes: but what poet first limited to five the number of the acts, I know not; only we see it so firmly established in the time of Horace, that he gives it for a rule in comedy; *'Neu brevior quinto, neu sit productior actu.'*[20] So that you see the Grecians cannot be said to have consummated this art; writing rather by entrances, than by acts, and having rather a general indigested notion of a play, than knowing how and where to bestow the particular graces of it.

"But since the Spaniards at this day allow but three acts, which they call *jornadas,* to a play, and the Italians in many of theirs follow them, when I condemn the ancients, I declare it is not altogether because they have not five acts to every play, but because they have not confined themselves to one certain number: it is building a house without a model; and when they succeeded in such undertakings, they ought to have sacrificed to Fortune, not to the Muses.

"Next, for the plot, which Aristotle called τὸ μῦθος, and often τῶν πραγμάτων σύνθεσις,[21] and from him the Romans *fabula,* it has already been judiciously observed by a late writer, that in their tragedies it was only some tale derived from Thebes or Troy, or at least something that happened in those two ages; which was worn so threadbare by the pens of all the epic poets, and even by tradition itself of the talkative Greeklings, (as Ben Jonson calls them,) that before it came upon the stage, it was already known to all the audience: and the people, so soon as ever they heard the name of Oedipus, knew as well as the poet, that he had killed his father by a mistake, and committed incest with his mother, before the play; that they were now to hear of a great plague, an oracle, and the ghost of Laius: so that they sat with a yawning kind of expectation, till he was to come with his eyes pulled out, and speak a hundred or two of verses in a tragic tone, in complaint of his misfortunes. But one Oedipus, Hercules, or Medea, had been tolerable: poor people, they 'scaped not so good cheap; they had still the *chapon bouillé*[22] set before them till their appetites were cloyed with the same dish, and, the novelty being gone, the pleasure vanished; so that one main end of dramatic poesy in its definition, which was to cause delight, was of consequence destroyed.

"In their comedies, the Romans generally borrowed their plots from the Greek poets; and theirs was commonly a little girl stolen or wandered from her parents, brought back unknown to the same city, there got with child by some lewd young fellow, who, by the help of his servant, cheats his father; and when her time comes, to cry *'Juno Lucina, fer opem,'*[23] one or other sees a little box or cabinet which was carried away with her, and so discovers her to her friends, if some god do not prevent it, by coming down in a machine, and take the thanks of it to himself.

"By the plot you may guess much of the characters of the persons. An old father, who would willingly, before he dies, see his son well married; his debauched son, kind in his nature to his wench, but miserably in want of money; a servant or slave, who has so much wit to strike in with him, and help to dupe his father; a braggadocio captain, a parasite, and a lady of pleasure.

"As for the poor honest maid, whom all the story is built upon, and who ought to be one of the principal actors in the play, she is commonly a mute in it: she has the breed-

---

[20] "Let it be neither shorter nor longer than five acts." *Art of Poetry,* p. 70.

[21] "The putting together of the actions."
[22] "Boiled capon," or "tasty dish."
[23] "Juno, goddess of births, help."

ing of the old Elizabeth way, for maids to be seen and not to be heard; and it is enough you know she is willing to be married, when the fifth act requires it.

"These are plots built after the Italian mode of houses; you see through them all at once: the characters are indeed the imitations of nature, but so narrow, as if they had imitated only an eye or an hand, and did not dare to venture on the lines of a face, or the proportion of a body.

"But in how strait a compass soever they have bounded their plots and characters, we will pass it by, if they have regularly pursued them, and perfectly observed those three unities of time, place, and action; the knowledge of which you say is derived to us from them. But in the first place give me leave to tell you, that the unity of place, however it might be practiced by them, was never any of their rules: we neither find it in Aristotle, Horace, or any who have written of it, till in our age the French poets first made it a precept of the stage. The unity of time, even Terence himself (who was the best and most regular of them) has neglected: his *Heauton-timorumenos,* or *Self-Punisher,* takes up visibly two days; therefore, says Scaliger, the two first acts concluding the first day were acted overnight; the three last on the ensuing day; and Euripides, in tying himself to one day, has committed an absurdity never to be forgiven him; for in one of his tragedies he has made Theseus go from Athens to Thebes, which was about forty English miles, under the walls of it to give battle, and appear victorious in the next act; and yet, from the time of his departure to the return of the nuntius, who gives the relation of his victory, Aethra and the chorus have but thirty-six verses; that is not for every mile a verse.

"The like error is as evident in Terence his *Eunuch,* when Laches, the old man, enters in a mistake the house of Thais; where, betwixt his exit and the entrance of Pythias, who comes to give an ample relation of the garboils he has raised within, Parmeno, who was left upon the stage, has not above five lines to speak. *'C'est bien employer un temps si court,'*[24] says the French poet, who furnished me with one of the observations: and almost all their tragedies will afford us examples of the like nature.

" 'Tis true, they have kept the continuity, or, as you called it, *'liaison des scènes,'* somewhat better: two do not perpetually come in together, talk, and go out together; and other two succeed them, and do the same throughout the act, which the English call by the name of single scenes; but the reason is, because they have seldom above two or three

scenes, properly so-called, in every act; for it is to be accounted a new scene, not every time the stage is empty; but every person who enters, though to others, makes it so; because he introduces a new business. Now the plots of their plays being narrow, and the persons few, one of their acts was written in a less compass than one of our well-wrought scenes; and yet they are often deficient even in this. To go no further than Terence; you find in the *Eunuch* Antipho entering single in the midst of the third act, after Cremes and Pythias were gone off; in the same play you have likewise Dorias beginning the fourth act alone; and after she had made a relation of what was done at the soldier's entertainment (which by the way was very inartificial, because she was presumed to speak directly to the audience, and to acquaint them with what was necessary to be known, but yet should have been so contrived by the poet as to have been told by persons of the drama to one another, and so by them to have come to the knowledge of the people), she quits the stage, and Phaedria enters next, alone likewise: he also gives you an account of himself, and of his returning from the country, in monologue; to which unnatural way of narration Terence is subject in all his plays. In his *Adelphi,* or *Brothers,* Syrus and Demea enter after the scene was broken by the departure of Sostrata, Geta, and Canthara; and indeed you can scarce look into any of his comedies, where you will not presently discover the same interruption.

"But as they have failed both in laying of their plots, and managing of them, swerving from the rules of their own art by misrepresenting nature to us, in which they have ill satisfied one intention of a play, which was delight; so in the instructive part they have erred worse: instead of punishing vice and rewarding virtue, they have often shown a prosperous wickedness, and an unhappy piety: they have set before us a bloody image of revenge in Medea, and given her dragons to convey her safe from punishment; a Priam and Astyanax murdered, and Cassandra ravished, and the lust and murder ending in the victory of him who acted them: in short, there is no indecorum in any of our modern plays, which if I would excuse, I could not shadow with some authority from the ancients.

"And one farther note of them let me leave you: tragedies and comedies were not writ then as they are now, promiscuously, by the same person; but he who found his genius bending to the one, never attempted the other way. This is so plain, that I need not instance to you, that Aristophanes, Plautus, Terence, never any of them writ a tragedy; Aeschylus, Euripides, Sophocles, and Seneca, never meddled with comedy: the sock and buskin were not worn by the same poet. Having then so much care to excel in one kind, very

---

[24] "It is well to employ a time so short." Corneille, *Of the Three Unities,* pp. 209–10.

little is to be pardoned them, if they miscarried in it; and this would lead me to the consideration of their wit, had not Crites given me sufficient warning not to be too bold in my judgment of it; because, the languages being dead, and many of the customs and little accidents on which it depended lost to us, we are not competent judges of it. But though I grant that here and there we may miss the application of a proverb or a custom, yet a thing well said will be wit in all languages; and though it may lose something in the translation, yet to him who reads it in the original, 'tis still the same: he has an idea of its excellency, though it cannot pass from his mind into any other expression or words than those in which he finds it. When Phaedria, in the *Eunuch,* had a command from his mistress to be absent two days, and, encouraging himself to go through with it, said, *'Tandem ego non illa caream, si sit opus, vel totum triduum?'*[25]—Parmeno, to mock the softness of his master, lifting up his hands and eyes, cries out, as it were in admiration, *'Hui! universum triduum!'*[26] the elegancy of which *'universum,'* though it cannot be rendered in our language, yet leaves an impression on our souls: but this happens seldom in him; in Plautus oftener, who is infinitely too bold in his metaphors and coining words, out of which many times his wit is nothing; which questionless was one reason why Horace falls upon him so severely in those verses:

> *Sed proavi nostri Plautinos et numeros et*
> *Laudavere sales, nimium patienter utrumque,*
> *Ne dicam stolidè.*[27]

For Horace himself was cautious to obtrude a new word on his readers, and makes custom and common use the best measure of receiving it into our writings:

> *Multa renascentur quae nunc cecidere, cadentque*
> *Quae nunc sunt in honore vocabula, si volet usus,*
> *Quem penes arbitrium est, et jus, et norma loquendi.*[28]

"The not observing this rule is that which the world has blamed in our satirist, Cleveland: to express a thing hard and unnaturally, is his new way of elocution. 'Tis true, no poet but may sometimes use a catachresis: Virgil does it—*'Mis-*

taque ridenti colocasia fundei acantho'[29]—in his eclogue of *Pollio;* and in his seventh *Aeneid.*

> *mirantur et undae,*
> *Miratur nemus insuetum fulgentia longe*
> *Scuta virum fluvio pictasque innare carinas.*[30]

And Ovid once so modestly, that he asks leave to do it: *'quem, si verbo audacia detur, / Haud metuam summi dixisse palatia caeli':*[31] calling the court of Jupiter by the name of Augustus his palace; though in another place he is more bold, where he says, *'et longas visent Capitolia pompas.'*[32] But to do this always, and never be able to write a line without it, though it may be admired by some few pedants, will not pass upon those who know that wit is best conveyed to us in the most easy language; and is most to be admired when a great thought comes dressed in words so commonly received, that it is understood by the meanest apprehensions, as the best meat is the most easily digested: but we cannot read a verse of Cleveland's without making a face at it, as if every word were a pill to swallow: he gives us many times a hard nut to break our teeth, without a kernel for our pains. So that there is this difference betwixt his *Satires* and Doctor Donne's; that the one gives us deep thoughts in common language, though rough cadence; the other gives as common thoughts in abstruse words: 'tis true, in some places his wit is independent of his words, as in that of the *Rebel Scot:* 'Had Cain been Scot, God would have changed his doom; / Not forced him wander, but confined him home.'[33]

" *'Si sic omnia dixisset!'*[34] This is wit in all languages: 'tis like Mercury, never to be lost or killed: and so that other—'For beauty, like white powder, makes no noise, / And yet the silent hypocrite destroys.'[35] You see, the last line is highly metaphorical, but it is so soft and gentle, that it does not shock us as we read it.

"But, to return from whence I have digressed, to the considerations of the ancients' writing, and their wit; of which by this time you will grant us in some measure to be fit judges. Though I see many excellent thoughts in Seneca, yet he of them who had a genius most proper for the stage,

[25]"Shall I not do without her, if it is necessary, even for three whole days?" Terence, *Eunuch,* II. i.

[26]"Alas! three whole days." Terence, *Eunuch,* II. i. 18.

[27]"But our ancestors lauded both the meters and wit of Plautus, admiring each tolerantly, I shall not say stupidly." *Art of Poetry,* p. 71.

[28]"Many words will revive that are now out of use, and many which are now esteemed will die out, if custom wills it, in whose power is the decision, both the law and the norms of speech." *Art of Poetry,* pp. 68–69.

[29]"And the colocasia will bloom, mingled with the laughing acanthus." *Eclogues,* IV. 20.

[30]"The woods and waters wonder at the gleam of shields, and painted ships, that stem the stream." *Aeneid,* VIII. 91. (Dryden's translation.)

[31]"If verbal license is granted, I shall not at all fear to call it the palace of the sky." *Metamorphoses,* I. 175.

[32]"And the Capitol sees long processions." *Metamorphoses,* I. 561.

[33]John Cleveland, *Rebel Scot,* 63–64.

[34]"If only he had said it all this way." Juvenal, *Satires,* X. 123.

[35]Cleveland, *Rupertismus,* 39–40.

was Ovid; he had a way of writing so fit to stir up a pleasing admiration and concernment, which are the objects of a tragedy, and to show the various movements of a soul combating betwixt two different passions, that, had he lived in our age, or in his own could have writ with our advantages, no man but must have yielded to him; and therefore I am confident the *Medea* is none of his: for, though I esteem it for the gravity and sententiousness of it, which he himself concludes to be suitable to a tragedy—'*Omne genus scripti gravitate tragaedia vincit*'[36]—yet it moves not my soul enough to judge that he, who in the epic way wrote things so near the drama as the story of Myrrha, of Caunus and Biblis, and the rest, should stir up no more concernment where he most endeavored it. The masterpiece of Seneca I hold to be that scene in the *Troades,* where Ulysses is seeking for Astyanax to kill him; there you see the tenderness of a mother so represented in Andromache, that it raises compassion to a high degree in the reader, and bears the nearest resemblance of anything in their tragedies to the excellent scenes of passion in Shakespeare, or in Fletcher: for love scenes, you will find few among them; their tragic poets dealt not with that soft passion, but with lust, cruelty, revenge, ambition, and those bloody actions they produced; which were more capable of raising horror than compassion in an audience: leaving love untouched, whose gentleness would have tempered them, which is the most frequent of all the passions, and which being the private concernment of every person, is soothed by viewing its own image in a public entertainment.

"Among their comedies, we find a scene or two of tenderness, and that where you would least expect it, in Plautus; but to speak generally, their lovers say little, when they see each other, but '*anima mea, vita mea:* ζωή καὶ ψυχή, '[37] as the women in Juvenal's time used to cry out in the fury of their kindness: then indeed to speak sense were an offense. Any sudden gust of passion (as an ecstasy of love in an unexpected meeting) cannot better be expressed than in a word and a sigh, breaking one another. Nature is dumb on such occasions; and to make her speak, would be to represent her unlike herself. But there are a thousand other concernments of lovers, as jealousies, complaints, contrivances, and the like, where not to open their minds at large to each other, were to be wanting to their own love, and to the expectation of the audience; who watch the movements of their minds, as much as the changes of their fortunes. For the imaging of the first is properly the work of a poet; the latter he borrows of the historian."

Eugenius was proceeding in that part of his discourse, when Crites interrupted him. "I see," said he, "Eugenius and I are never like to have this question decided betwixt us; for he maintains the moderns have acquired a new perfection in writing; I can only grant they have altered the mode of it. Homer described his heroes men of great appetites, lovers of beef broiled upon the coals, and good fellows; contrary to the practice of the French romances, whose heroes neither eat, nor drink, nor sleep, for love. Virgil makes Aeneas a bold avower of his own virtues: '*Sum pius Aeneas, fama super aethera notus*';[38] which in the civility of our poets is the character of a fanfaron or Hector: for with us the knight takes occasion to walk out, or sleep, to avoid the vanity of telling his own story, which the trusty squire is ever to perform for him. So in their love scenes, of which Eugenius spoke last, the ancients were more hearty, we more talkative: they writ love as it was then the mode to make it; and I will grant thus much to Eugenius, that perhaps one of their poets, had he lived in our age, '*si foret hoc nostrum fato delapsus in aevum*'[39] (as Horace says of Lucilius), he had altered many things; not that they were not as natural before, but that he might accommodate himself to the age he lived in. Yet in the meantime, we are not to conclude anything rashly against those great men, but preserve to them the dignity of masters, and give that honor to their memories, '*quos Libitina sacravit,*'[40] part of which we expect may be paid to us in future times."

This moderation of Crites, as it was pleasing to all the company, so it put an end to that dispute; which Eugenius, who seemed to have the better of the argument, would urge no farther: but Lisideius, after he had acknowledged himself of Eugenius his opinion concerning the ancients, yet told him, he had forborne, till his discourse were ended, to ask him why he preferred the English plays above those of other nations? and whether we ought not to submit our stage to the exactness of our next neighbors?

"Though," said Eugenius, "I am at all times ready to defend the honor of my country against the French, and to maintain, we are as well able to vanquish them with our pens, as our ancestors have been with their swords; yet, if you please," added he, looking upon Neander, "I will commit this cause to my friend's management; his opinion of our plays is the same with mine: and besides, there is no reason, that Crites and I, who have now left the stage, should reenter so suddenly upon it; which is against the laws of comedy."

---

[36]"Tragedy excels all other kinds of writing in gravity." *Tristia,* II. 381.
[37]"My soul, my life."

[38]"I am the pious Aeneas, famed above the heavens." *Aeneid,* I. 378.
[39]"If dropped by fate into our age." Horace, *Satires,* I. x. 68.
[40]"Which Libitina has made sacred." Horace, *Epistles,* II. i. 49.

"If the question had been stated," replied Lisideius, "who had writ best, the French or English, forty years ago, I should have been of your opinion, and adjudged the honor to our own nation; but since that time," said he, turning towards Neander, "we have been so long together bad Englishmen, that we had not leisure to be good poets. Beaumont, Fletcher, and Jonson (who were only capable of bringing us to that degree of perfection which we have) were just then leaving the world; as if (in an age of so much horror) wit, and those milder studies of humanity, had no farther business among us. But the Muses, who ever follow peace, went to plant in another country: it was then that the great Cardinal of Richelieu began to take them into his protection; and that, by his encouragement, Corneille, and some other Frenchmen, reformed their theater, which before was as much below ours, as it now surpasses it and the rest of Europe. But because Crites in his discourse for the ancients has prevented me, by touching upon many rules of the stage which the moderns have borrowed from them, I shall only, in short, demand of you, whether you are not convinced that of all nations the French have best observed them? In the unity of time you find them so scrupulous, that it yet remains a dispute among their poets, whether the artificial day of twelve hours, more or less, be not meant by Aristotle, rather than the natural one of twenty-four; and consequently, whether all plays ought not to be reduced into that compass. This I can testify, that in all their dramas writ within these last twenty years and upwards, I have not observed any that have extended the time to thirty hours: in the unity of place they are full as scrupulous; for many of their critics limit it to that very spot of ground where the play is supposed to begin; none of them exceed the compass of the same town or city. The unity of action in all plays is yet more conspicuous; for they do not burden them with underplots, as the English do: which is the reason why many scenes of our tragicomedies carry on a design that is nothing of kin to the main plot; and that we see two distinct webs in a play, like those in ill-wrought stuffs; and two actions, that is, two plays, carried on together, to the confounding of the audience; who, before they are warm in their concernments for one part, are diverted to another; and by that means espouse the interest of neither. From hence likewise it arises, that the one half of our actors are not known to the other. They keep their distances, as if they were Montagues and Capulets, and seldom begin an acquaintance till the last scene of the fifth act, when they are all to meet upon the stage. There is no theater in the world has anything so absurd as the English tragicomedy; 'tis a drama of our own invention, and the fashion of it is enough to proclaim it so; here a course of mirth, there another of sadness and passion, a third of honor, and fourth a

duel: thus, in two hours and a half, we run through all the fits of Bedlam. The French affords you as much variety on the same day, but they do it not so unseasonably, or *mal à propos,* as we: our poets present you the play and the farce together; and our stages still retain somewhat of the original civility of the *Red Bull: 'Atque ursum et pugiles media inter carmina poscunt.'*[41] The end of tragedies or serious plays, says Aristotle, is to beget admiration, compassion, or concernment; but are not mirth and compassion things incompatible? and is it not evident that the poet must of necessity destroy the former by intermingling of the latter? That is, he must ruin the sole end and object of his tragedy, to introduce somewhat that is forced in, and is not of the body of it. Would you not think that physician mad, who, having prescribed a purge, should immediately order you to take restringents upon it?

"But to leave our plays, and return to theirs. I have noted one great advantage they have had in the plotting of their tragedies; that is, they are always grounded upon some known history: according to that of Horace, *'Ex noto fictum carmen sequar';*[42] and in that they have so imitated the ancients, that they have surpassed them. For the ancients, as was observed before, took for the foundation of their plays some poetical fiction, such as under that consideration could move but little concernment in the audience, because they already knew the event of it. But the French goes farther: *'Atque ita mentitur, sic veris falsa remiscet, / Primo ne medium, medio ne discrepet imum.'*[43] He so interweaves truth with probable fiction, that he puts a pleasing fallacy upon us; mends the intrigues of fate, and dispenses with the severity of history, to reward that virtue which has been rendered to us there unfortunate. Sometimes the story has left the success so doubtful, that the writer is free, by the privilege of a poet, to take that which of two or more relations will best suit with his design: as for example, the death of Cyrus, whom Justin and some others report to have perished in the Scythian war, but Xenophon affirms to have died in his bed of extreme old age. Nay more, when the event is past dispute, even then we are willing to be deceived, and the poet, if he contrives it with appearance of truth, has all the audience of his party; at least during the time his play is acting: so naturally we are kind to virtue, when our own interest is not in question, that we take it up as the general concernment of mankind. On the other side, if you consider the historical

---

[41]"In the middle of plays, they demand a bear and boxers." Horace, *Epistles,* II. i. 185.

[42]"From known stories I shall make a poem." *Art of Poetry,* p. 71.

[43]"He so lies, so mingles the false with the true, that one cannot distinguish beginning, middle, and end." Horace, *Art of Poetry,* pp. 69–70.

plays of Shakespeare, they are rather so many chronicles of kings, or the business many times of thirty or forty years, cramped into a representation of two hours and a half; which is not to imitate or paint nature, but rather to draw her in miniature, to take her in little; to look upon her through the wrong end of a perspective, and receive her images not only much less, but infinitely more imperfect than the life: this, instead of making a play delightful, renders it ridiculous: '*Quodcunque ostendis mihi sic, incredulus odi.*'[44] For the spirit of man cannot be satisfied but with truth, or at least verisimility; and a poem is to contain, if not τὰ ἔτυμα, yet ἐτύμοισιν ὁμοῖα,[45] as one of the Greek poets has expressed it.

"Another thing in which the French differ from us and from the Spaniards, is, that they do not embarrass, or cumber themselves with too much plot; they only represent so much of a story as will constitute one whole and great action sufficient for a play; we, who undertake more, do but multiply adventures; which, not being produced from one another, as effects from causes, but barely following, constitute many actions in the drama, and consequently make it many plays.

"But by pursuing close one argument, which is not cloyed with many turns, the French have gained more liberty for verse, in which they write; they have leisure to dwell on a subject which deserves it; and to represent the passions (which we have acknowledged to be the poet's work), without being hurried from one thing to another, as we are in the plays of Calderon, which we have seen lately upon our theaters, under the name of Spanish plots. I have taken notice but of one tragedy of ours, whose plot has the uniformity and unity of design in it, which I have commended in the French; and that is *Rollo,* or rather, under the name of Rollo, the story of Bassianus and Geta in Herodian: there indeed the plot is neither large nor intricate, but just enough to fill the minds of the audience, not to cloy them. Besides, you see it founded upon the truth of history, only the time of the action is not reduceable to the strictness of the rules; and you see in some places a little farce mingled, which is below the dignity of the other parts; and in this all our poets are extremely peccant: even Ben Jonson himself, in *Sejanus* and *Catiline,* has given us this oleo[46] of a play, this unnatural mixture of comedy and tragedy; which to me sounds just as ridiculously as the history of David with the merry humors of Goliath. In *Sejanus* you may take notice of the scene betwixt Livia and the physician, which is a pleasant satire upon the artificial

helps of beauty: in *Catiline* you may see the parliament of women; the little envies of them to one another; and all that passes betwixt Curio and Fulvia: scenes admirable in their kind, but of an ill mingle with the rest.

"But I return again to the French writers, who, as I have said, do not burden themselves too much with plot, which has been reproached to them by an ingenious person of our nation as a fault; for, he says, they commonly make but one person considerable in a play; they dwell on him, and his concernments, while the rest of the persons are only subservient to set him off. If he intends this by it, that there is one person in the play who is of greater dignity than the rest, he must tax, not only theirs, but those of the ancients, and which he would be loath to do, the best of ours; for it is impossible but that one person must be more conspicuous in it than any other, and consequently the greatest share in the action must devolve on him. We see it so in the management of all affairs; even in the most equal aristocracy, the balance cannot be so justly poised, but someone will be superior to the rest, either in parts, fortune, interest, or the consideration of some glorious exploit; which will reduce the greatest part of business into his hands.

"But, if he would have us to imagine, that in exalting one character the rest of them are neglected, and that all of them have not some share or other in the action of the play, I desire him to produce any of Corneille's tragedies, wherein every person, like so many servants in a well-governed family, has not some employment, and who is not necessary to the carrying on of the plot, or at least to your understanding it.

"There are indeed some protatic persons[47] in the ancients, whom they make use of in their plays, either to hear or give the relation: but the French avoid this with great address, making their narrations only to or by such, who are some way interested in the main design. And now I am speaking of relations, I cannot take a fitter opportunity to add this in favor of the French, that they often use them with better judgment and more *à propos* than the English do. Not that I commend narrations in general—but there are two sorts of them. One, of those things which are antecedent to the play, and are related to make the conduct of it more clear to us. But 'tis a fault to choose such subjects for the stage as will force us on that rock, because we see they are seldom listened to by the audience, and that is many times the ruin of the play; for, being once let pass without attention, the audience can never recover themselves to understand the plot: and indeed it is somewhat unreasonable that they

---

[44]"Whatever you thus show me I find incredible and odious." Horace, *Art of Poetry,* p. 70.

[45]"True things" yet "things like the truth." Hesiod, *Theogony,* 27.

[46]Hotchpotch or medley.

---

[47]Characters appearing only in the introductory part of the play.

should be put to so much trouble, as that, to comprehend what passes in their sight, they must have recourse to what was done, perhaps, ten or twenty years ago.

"But there is another sort of relations, that is, of things happening in the action of the play, and supposed to be done behind the scenes; and this is many times both convenient and beautiful; for by it the French avoid the tumult which we are subject to in England, by representing duels, battles, and the like: which renders our stage too like the theaters where they fight prizes. For what is more ridiculous than to represent an army with a drum and five men behind it; all which the hero of the other side is to drive in before him; or to see a duel fought, and one slain with two or three thrusts of the foils, which we know are so blunted, that we might give a man an hour to kill another in good earnest with them.

"I have observed that in all our tragedies, the audience cannot forbear laughing when the actors are to die; it is the most comic part of the whole play. All passions may be lively represented on the stage, if to the well-writing of them the actor supplies a good commanded voice, and limbs that move easily; and without stiffness; but there are many actions which can never be imitated to a just height: dying especially is a thing which none but a Roman gladiator could naturally perform on the stage, when he did not imitate or represent, but naturally do it; and therefore it is better to omit the representation of it.

"The words of a good writer, which describe it lively, will make a deeper impression of belief in us than all the actor can persuade us to, when he seems to fall dead before us; as a poet in the description of a beautiful garden, or a meadow, will please our imagination more than the place itself can please our sight. When we see death represented, we are convinced it is but fiction; but when we hear it related, our eyes, the strongest witnesses, are wanting, which might have undeceived us; and we are willing to favor the sleight, when the poet does not too grossly impose on us. They therefore who imagine these relations would make no concernment in the audience, are deceived, by confounding them with the other, which are of things antecedent to the play: those are made often in cold blood, as I may say, to the audience; but these are armed with our concernments, which were before awakened in the play. What the philosophers say of motion, that, when it is once begun, it continues of itself, and will do so to eternity, without some stop put to it, is clearly true on this occasion: the soul, being already moved with the characters and fortunes of those imaginary persons, continues going of its own accord; and we are no more weary to hear what becomes of them when they are not on the stage, than we are to listen to the news of an absent mistress. But it is objected, that if one part of the play may be related, then

why not all? I answer, some parts of the action are more fit to be represented, some to be related. Corneille says judiciously, that the poet is not obliged to expose to view all particular actions which conduce to the principal: he ought to select such of them to be seen, which will appear with the greatest beauty, either by the magnificence of the show, or the vehemence of passions which they produce, or some other charm which they have in them; and let the rest arrive to the audience by narration. 'Tis a great mistake in us to believe the French present no part of the action on the stage; every alteration or crossing of a design, every new-sprung passion, and turn of it, is a part of the action, and much the noblest, except we conceive nothing to be action till they come to blows; as if the painting of the hero's mind were not more properly the poet's work than the strength of his body. Nor does this anything contradict the opinion of Horace, where he tells us, *'Segnius irritant animos demissa per aurem, / Quam quae sunt oculis subjecta fidelibus.'* For he says immediately after,

> *Non tamen intus*
> *Digna geri promes in scenam; multaque tolles*
> *Ex oculis, quae mox narret facundia praesens.*

Among which many he recounts some: *'Nec pueros coram populo Medea trucidet, / Aut in avem Progne mutetur, Cadmus in anguem'; &c.*[48] That is, those actions which by reason of their cruelty will cause aversion in us, or by reason of their impossibility, unbelief, ought either wholly to be avoided by a poet, or only delivered by narration. To which we may have leave to add such as to avoid tumult (as was before hinted), or to reduce the plot into a more reasonable compass of time, or for defect of beauty in them, are rather to be related than presented to the eye. Examples of all these kinds are frequent, not only among all the ancients, but in the best received of our English poets. We find Ben Jonson using them in his *Magnetic Lady,* where one comes out from dinner, and relates the quarrels and disorders of it, to save the undecent appearance of them on the stage, and to abbreviate the story; and this in express imitation of Terence, who had done the same before him in his *Eunuch,* where Pythias makes the like relation of what had happened within at the soldier's entertainment. The relations likewise of Sejanus's death, and the

---

[48]"What we hear through the ears stirs the mind less forcefully than what are placed before trustworthy eyes." . . . "Do not bring on the stage that which should be done off of it; keep many things from sight and presently narrate them with eloquence." . . . "Do not let Medea kill her children before the audience, nor change Procne into a bird, Cadmus into a snake." *Art of Poetry,* p. 70.

prodigies before it, are remarkable; the one of which was hid from sight, to avoid the horror and tumult of the representation; the other, to shun the introducing of things impossible to be believed. In that excellent play, *The King and No King,* Fletcher goes yet farther; for the whole unraveling of the plot is done by narration in the fifth act, after the manner of the ancients; and it moves great concernment in the audience, though it be only a relation of what was done many years before the play. I could multiply other instances, but these are sufficient to prove that there is no error in choosing a subject which requires this sort of narrations; in the ill-managing of them, there may.

"But I find I have been too long in this discourse, since the French have many other excellencies not common to us; as that you never see any of their plays end with a conversion, or simple change of will, which is the ordinary way which our poets use to end theirs. It shows little art in the conclusion of a dramatic poem, when they who have hindered the felicity during the four acts, desist from it in the fifth, without some powerful cause to take them off; and though I deny not but such reasons may be found, yet it is a path that is cautiously to be trod, and the poet is to be sure he convinces the audience that the motive is strong enough. As for example, the conversion of the usurer in *The Scornful Lady,* seems to me a little forced; for, being a usurer, which implies a lover of money to the highest degree of covetousness (and such the poet has represented him), the account he gives for the sudden change is, that he has been duped by the wild young fellow; which in reason might render him more wary another time, and make him punish himself with harder fare and coarser clothes, to get it up again: but that he should look on it as a judgment, and so repent, we may expect to hear of in a sermon, but I should never endure it in a play.

"I pass by this; neither will I insist on the care they take, that no person after his first entrance shall ever appear, but the business which brings him upon the stage shall be evident; which, if observed, must needs render all the events in the play more natural; for there you see the probability of every accident, in the cause that produced it; and that which appears chance in the play, will seem so reasonable to you, that you will there find it almost necessary: so that in the exits of the actors you have a clear account of their purpose and design in the next entrance (though, if the scene be well wrought, the event will commonly deceive you), for there is nothing so absurd, says Corneille, as for an actor to leave the stage, only because he has no more to say.[49]

"I should now speak of the beauty of their rhyme, and the just reason I have to prefer that way of writing in tragedies before ours in blank verse; but because it is partly received by us, and therefore not altogether peculiar to them, I will say no more of it in relation to their plays. For our own, I doubt not but it will exceedingly beautify them; and I can see but one reason why it should not generally obtain, that is, because our poets write so ill in it. This indeed may prove a more prevailing argument than all others which are used to destroy it, and therefore I am only troubled when great and judicious poets, and those who are acknowledged such, have writ or spoke against it: as for others, they are to be answered by that one sentence of an ancient author: '*Sed ut primo ad consequendos eos quos priores ducimus, accendimur, ita ubi aut praeteriri, aut aequari eos posse desperavimus, studium cum spe senescit: quod, scilicet, assequi non potest, sequi desinit . . . praeteritoque eo in quo eminere non possumus, aliquid in quo nitamur, conquirimus.*' "[50]

Lisideius concluded in this manner; and Neander, after a little pause, thus answered him:

"I shall grant Lisideius, without much dispute, a great part of what he has urged against us; for I acknowledge that the French contrive their plots more regularly, and observe the laws of comedy, and decorum of the stage (to speak generally), with more exactness than the English. Farther, I deny not but he has taxed us justly in some irregularities of ours, which he has mentioned; yet, after all, I am of opinion that neither our faults nor their virtues are considerable enough to place them above us.

"For the lively imitation of nature being in the definition of a play, those which best fulfill that law ought to be esteemed superior to the others. 'Tis true, those beauties of the French poesy are such as will raise perfection higher where it is, but are not sufficient to give it where it is not: they are indeed the beauties of a statue, but not of a man, because not animated with the soul of poesy, which is imitation of humor and passions: and this Lisideius himself, or any other, however biased to their party, cannot but acknowledge, if he will either compare the humors of our comedies, or the characters of our serious plays, with theirs. He that will look upon theirs which have been written till these last ten years, or thereabouts, will find it a hard matter to pick out two or three passable humors amongst them. Corneille himself, their archpoet, what has he produced except *The*

---

[49]*Of the Three Unities,* p. 209.

[50]But as we are inspired at first to follow those whom we consider leaders, so when we despair of the possibility of excelling or equaling them, our enthusiasm declines with our hope; for, of course, what it is not able to attain it ceases to follow . . . that being past in which we are not able to excel, we seek something else for which to strive." Paterculus, *History of Rome,* I. 17.

Liar, and you know how it was cried up in France; but when it came upon the English stage, though well translated, and that part of Dorant acted to so much advantage by Mr. Hart as I am confident it never received in its own country, the most favorable to it would not put it in competition with many of Fletcher's or Ben Jonson's. In the rest of Corneille's comedies you have little humor; he tells you himself, his way is, first to show two lovers in good intelligence with each other; in the working up of the play to embroil them by some mistake, and in the latter end to clear it, and reconcile them.

"But of late years Molière, the younger Corneille, Quinault, and some others, have been imitating afar off the quick turns and graces of the English stage. They have mixed their serious plays with mirth, like our tragicomedies, since the death of Cardinal Richelieu; which Lisideius and many others not observing, have commended that in them for a virtue which they themselves no longer practice. Most of their new plays are, like some of ours, derived from the Spanish novels. There is scarce one of them without a veil, and a trusty Diego,[51] who drolls much after the rate of the *Adventures.* But their humors, if I may grace them with that name, are so thin sown, that never above one of them comes up in any play. I dare take upon me to find more variety of them in some one play of Ben Jonson's, than in all theirs together; as he who has seen *The Alchemist, The Silent Woman,* or *Bartholomew Fair,* cannot but acknowledge with me.

"I grant the French have performed what was possible on the groundwork of the Spanish plays; what was pleasant before, they have made regular: but there is not above one good play to be writ on all those plots; they are too much alike to please often; which we need not the experience of our own stage to justify. As for their new way of mingling mirth with serious plot, I do not, with Lisideius, condemn the thing, though I cannot approve their manner of doing it. He tells us, we cannot so speedily recollect ourselves after a scene of great passion and concernment, as to pass to another of mirth and humor, and to enjoy it with any relish: but why should he imagine the soul of man more heavy than his senses? Does not the eye pass from an unpleasant object to a pleasant in a much shorter time than is required to this? And does not the unpleasantness of the first commend the beauty of the latter? The old rule of logic might have convinced him, that contraries, when placed near, set off each other. A continued gravity keeps the spirit too much bent; we must refresh it sometimes, as we bait in a journey, that we may go on with greater ease. A scene of mirth, mixed with tragedy,

has the same effect upon us which our music has betwixt the acts; and that we find a relief to us from the best plots and language of the stage, if the discourses have been long. I must therefore have stronger arguments, ere I am convinced that compassion and mirth in the same subject destroy each other; and in the meantime cannot but conclude, to the honor of our nation, that we have invented, increased, and perfected a more pleasant way of writing for the stage, than was ever known to the ancients or moderns of any nation, which is tragicomedy.

"And this leads me to wonder why Lisideius and many others should cry up the barrenness of the French plots, above the variety and copiousness of the English. Their plots are single; they carry on one design, which is pushed forward by all the actors, every scene in the play contributing and moving towards it. Our plays, besides the main design, have underplots or by-concernments, of less considerable persons and intrigues, which are carried on with the motion of the main plot: just as they say the orb of the fixed stars, and those of the planets, though they have motions of their own, are whirled about by the motion of the *primum mobile,* in which they are contained. That similitude expresses much of the English stage; for if contrary motions may be found in nature to agree; if a planet can go east and west at the same time, one way by virtue of his own motion, the other by the force of the first mover, it will not be difficult to imagine how the underplot, which is only different, not contrary to the great design, may naturally be conducted along with it.

"Eugenius has already shown us, from the confession of the French poets, that the unity of action is sufficiently preserved, if all the imperfect actions of the play are conducing to the main design; but when those petty intrigues of a play are so ill ordered, that they have no coherence with the other, I must grant that Lisideius has reason to tax that want of due connection; for coordination in a play is as dangerous and unnatural as in a state. In the meantime he must acknowledge, our variety, if well ordered, will afford a greater pleasure to the audience.

"As for his other argument, that by pursuing one single theme they gain an advantage to express and work up the passions, I wish any example he could bring from them would make it good; for I confess their verses are to me the coldest I have ever read. Neither, indeed, is it possible for them, in the way they take, so to express passion, as that the effects of it should appear in the concernment of an audience, their speeches being so many declamations, which tire us with the length; so that instead of persuading us to grieve for their imaginary heroes, we are concerned for our own trouble, as we are in the tedious visits of bad company; we are in pain till they are gone. When the French stage came to

---

[51] A comic servant in *The Adventures of Five Hours* (1663) by Samuel Tuke, adapted from a play attributed to Calderon.

be reformed by Cardinal Richelieu, those long harangues were introduced, to comply with the gravity of a churchman. Look upon the *Cinna* and the *Pompey;* they are not so properly to be called plays, as long discourses of reasons of state; and *Polyeucte* in matters of religion is as solemn as the long stops upon our organs. Since that time it is grown into a custom, and their actors speak by the hourglass, as our parsons do; nay, they account it the grace of their parts, and think themselves disparaged by the poet, if they may not twice or thrice in a play entertain the audience with a speech of an hundred or two hundred lines. I deny not but this may suit well enough with the French; for as we, who are a more sullen people, come to be diverted at our plays, so they, who are of an airy and gay temper, come thither to make themselves more serious: and this I conceive to be one reason why comedy is more pleasing to us, and tragedies to them. But to speak generally: it cannot be denied that short speeches and replies are more apt to move the passions and beget concernment in us, than the other; for it is unnatural for anyone in a gust of passion to speak long together, or for another in the same condition to suffer him, without interruption. Grief and passion are like floods raised in little brooks by a sudden rain; they are quickly up; and if the concernment be poured unexpectedly in upon us, it overflows us: but a long sober shower gives them leisure to run out as they came in, without troubling the ordinary current. As for comedy, repartee is one of its chiefest graces; the greatest pleasure of the audience is a chase of wit, kept up on both sides, and swiftly managed. And this our forefathers, if not we, have had in Fletcher's plays, to a much higher degree of perfection than the French poets can arrive at.

"There is another part of Lisideius his discourse, in which he has rather excused our neighbors, than commended them; that is, for aiming only to make one person considerable in their plays. 'Tis very true what he has urged, that one character in all plays, even without the poet's care, will have advantage of all the others; and that the design of the whole drama will chiefly depend on it. But this hinders not that there may be more shining characters in the play: many persons of a second magnitude, nay, some so very near, so almost equal to the first, that greatness may be opposed to greatness, and all the persons be made considerable, not only by their quality, but their action. 'Tis evident that the more the persons are, the greater will be the variety of the plot. If then the parts are managed so regularly, that the beauty of the whole be kept entire, and that the variety become not a perplexed and confused mass of accidents, you will find it infinitely pleasing to be led in a labyrinth of design, where you see some of your way before you, yet discern not the end till you arrive at it. And that all this is practicable, I can produce for examples many of our English plays: as *The Maid's Tragedy, The Alchemist, The Silent Woman:* I was going to have named *The Fox,* but that the unity of design seems not exactly observed in it; for there appear two actions in the play; the first naturally ending with the fourth act; the second forced from it in the fifth: which yet is the less to be condemned in him, because the disguise of Volpone, though it suited not with his character as a crafty or covetous person, agreed well enough with that of a voluptuary; and by it the poet gained the end he aimed at, the punishment of vice, and the reward of virtue, which that disguise produced. So that to judge equally of it, it was an excellent fifth act, but not so naturally proceeding from the former.

"But to leave this, and pass to the latter part of Lisideius his discourse, which concerns relations: I must acknowledge with him, that the French have reason when they hide that part of the action which would occasion too much tumult on the stage, and choose rather to have it made known by narration to the audience. Farther, I think it very convenient, for the reasons he has given, that all incredible actions were removed; but, whether custom has so insinuated itself into our countrymen, or nature has so formed them to fierceness, I know not; but they will scarcely suffer combats and other objects of horror to be taken from them. And indeed, the indecency of tumults is all which can be objected against fighting: for why may not our imagination as well suffer itself to be deluded with the probability of it, as with any other thing in the play? For my part, I can with as great ease persuade myself that the blows which are struck, are given in good earnest, as I can, that they who strike them are kings or princes, or those persons which they represent. For objects of incredibility, I would be satisfied from Lisideius, whether we have any so removed from all appearance of truth, as are those of Corneille's *Andromède;* a play which has been frequented the most of any he has writ. If the Perseus, or the son of an heathen god, the Pegasus, and the monster, were not capable to choke a strong belief, let him blame any representation of ours hereafter. Those indeed were objects of delight; yet the reason is the same as to the probability: for he makes it not a ballet or masque, but a play, which is to resemble truth. But for death, that it ought not to be represented, I have, besides the arguments alleged by Lisideius, the authority of Ben Jonson, who has forborne it in his tragedies; for both the death of Sejanus and Catiline are related: though in the latter I cannot but observe one irregularity of that great poet; he has removed the scene in the same act from Rome to Catiline's army, and from thence again to Rome; and besides, has allowed a very inconsiderable time, after Catiline's speech, for the striking of the battle, and the return of Petreius, who is to relate the event of it to the senate: which I should not animadvert on him, who was otherwise a painful observer of τὸ πρέπον, or the *decorum* of the stage, if he had not used extreme severity in his judgment on the incomparable Shakespeare for the same fault.—To conclude on this subject of relations; if we are to be blamed for showing too much of the action, the French are as faulty for discovering too little of it: a mean betwixt both should be observed by every judicious writer, so as the audience may neither be left unsatisfied by not seeing what is beautiful or shocked by beholding what is either incredible or undecent.

"I hope I have already proved in this discourse, that though we are not altogether so punctual as the French, in observing the laws of comedy, yet our errors are so few, and little, and those things wherein we excel them so considerable, that we ought of right to be preferred before them. But what will Lisideius say, if they themselves acknowledge they are too strictly tied up by those laws, for breaking which he has blamed the English? I will allege Corneille's words, as I find them in the end of his discourse of the three unities: *'Il est facile aux spéculatifs d'être sévères,' &c.;* 'tis easy for speculative persons to judge severely; but if they would produce to public view ten or twelve pieces of this nature, they would perhaps give more latitude to the rules than I have done, when, by experience, they had known how much we are bound up and constrained by them, and how many beauties of the stage they banished from it.[52] To illustrate a little what he has said: by their servile observations of the unities of time and place, and integrity of scenes, they have brought on themselves that dearth of plot, and narrowness of imagination, which may be observed in all their plays. How many beautiful accidents might naturally happen in two or three days, which cannot arrive with any probability in the compass of twenty-four hours? There is time to be allowed also for maturity of design, which, amongst great and prudent persons, such as are often represented in tragedy, cannot, with any likelihood of truth, be brought to pass at so short a warning. Farther; by tying themselves strictly to the unity of place, and unbroken scenes, they are forced many times to omit some beauties which cannot be shown where the act began; but might, if the scene were interrupted, and the stage cleared for the persons to enter in another place; and therefore the French poets are often forced upon absurdities; for if the act begins in a chamber, all the persons in the play must have some business or other to come thither, or else they are not to be shown that act; and sometimes their characters are very unfitting to appear there. As, suppose it were the king's bedchamber; yet the meanest man in the tragedy must come

and dispatch his business there, rather than in the lobby or courtyard (which is fitter for him), for fear the stage should be cleared, and the scenes broken. Many times they fall by it in a greater inconvenience; for they keep their scenes unbroken, and yet change the place; as in one of their newest plays, where the act begins in the street. There a gentleman is to meet his friend; he sees him with his man, coming out from his father's house; they talk together, and the first goes out: the second, who is a lover, has made an appointment with his mistress; she appears at the window, and then we are to imagine the scene lies under it. This gentleman is called away, and leaves his servant with his mistress; presently her father is heard from within; the young lady is afraid the servingman should be discovered, and thrusts him in through a door, which is supposed to be her closet. After this, the father enters to the daughter, and now the scene is in a house; for he is seeking from one room to another for this poor Philipin, or French Diego, who is heard from within drolling and breaking many a miserable conceit upon his sad condition. In this ridiculous manner the play goes on, the stage being never empty all the while: so that the street, the window, the houses, and the closet, are made to walk about, and the persons to stand still. Now what, I beseech you, is more easy than to write a regular French play, or more difficult than write an irregular English one, like those of Fletcher, or of Shakespeare?

"If they content themselves, as Corneille did, with some flat design, which, like an ill riddle, is found out ere it be half proposed, such plots we can make every way regular, as easily as they; but whene'er they endeavor to rise to any quick turns and counterturns of plot, as some of them have attempted, since Corneille's plays have been less in vogue, you see they write as irregularly as we, though they cover it more speciously. Hence the reason is perspicuous, why no French plays, when translated, have, or ever can succeed on the English stage. For, if you consider the plots, our own are fuller of variety; if the writing, ours are more quick and fuller of spirit; and therefore 'tis a strange mistake in those who decry the way of writing plays in verse, as if the English therein imitated the French. We have borrowed nothing from them; our plots are weaved in English looms: we endeavor therein to follow the variety and greatness of characters which are derived to us from Shakespeare and Fletcher; the copiousness and well-knitting of the intrigues we have from Jonson; and for the verse itself we have English precedents of elder date than any of Corneille's plays. Not to name our old comedies before Shakespeare, which were all writ in verse of six feet, or Alexandrines, such as the French now use, I can show in Shakespeare, many scenes of rhyme together, and the like in Ben Jonson's tragedies: in *Catiline*

---

[52]p. 212.

and *Sejanus* sometimes thirty or forty lines, I mean besides the chorus, or the monologues; which, by the way, showed Ben no enemy to this way of writing, especially if you look upon his *Sad Shepherd,* which goes sometimes on rhyme, sometimes on blank verse, like a horse who eases himself on trot and amble. You find him likewise commending Fletcher's pastoral of *The Faithful Shepherdess,* which is for the most part rhyme, though not refined to that purity to which it hath since been brought. And these examples are enough to clear us from a servile imitation of the French.

"But to return from whence I have digressed: I dare boldly affirm these two things of the English drama; first, that we have many plays of ours as regular as any of theirs, and which, besides, have more variety of plot and characters; and secondly, that in most of the irregular plays of Shakespeare or Fletcher (for Ben Jonson's are for the most part regular) there is a more masculine fancy and greater spirit in the writing, than there is in any of the French. I could produce, even in Shakespeare's and Fletcher's works, some plays which are almost exactly formed; as *The Merry Wives of Windsor,* and *The Scornful Lady:* but because (generally speaking) Shakespeare, who writ first, did not perfectly observe the laws of comedy, and Fletcher, who came nearer to perfection, yet through carelessness made many faults; I will take the pattern of a perfect play from Ben Jonson, who was a careful and learned observer of the dramatic laws, and from all his comedies I shall select *The Silent Woman;* of which I will make a short examen, according to those rules which the French observe."

As Neander was beginning to examine *The Silent Woman,* Eugenius, looking earnestly upon him; "I beseech you, Neander," said he, "gratify the company, and me in particular, so far, as before you speak of the play, to give us a character of the author; and tell us frankly your opinion, whether you do not think all writers, both French and English, ought to give place to him."

"I fear," replied Neander, "that in obeying your commands I shall draw a little envy on myself. Besides, in performing them, it will be first necessary to speak somewhat of Shakespeare and Fletcher, his rivals in poesy; and one of them, in my opinion, at least his equal, perhaps his superior.

"To begin, then, with Shakespeare. He was the man who of all modern, and perhaps ancient poets, had the largest and most comprehensive soul. All the images of nature were still present to him, and he drew them, not laboriously, but luckily; when he describes anything, you more than see it, you feel it too. Those who accuse him to have wanted learning, give him the greater commendation: he was naturally learned; he needed not the spectacles of books to read nature; he looked inwards, and found her there. I cannot say he is

everywhere alike; were he so, I should do him injury to compare him with the greatest of mankind. He is many times flat, insipid; his comic wit degenerating into clenches, his serious swelling into bombast. But he is always great, when some great occasion is presented to him; no man can say he ever had a fit subject for his wit, and did not then raise himself as high above the rest of poets, *'Quantum lenta solent inter viburna cupressi.'* [53] The consideration of this made Mr. Hales of Eton say, that there was no subject of which any poet ever writ, but he would produce it much better treated of in Shakespeare; and however others are now generally preferred before him, yet the age wherein he lived, which had contempories with him Fletcher and Jonson, never equaled them to him in their esteem: and in the last king's court, when Ben's reputation was at highest, Sir John Suckling, and with him the greater part of the courtiers, set our Shakespeare far above him.

"Beaumont and Fletcher, of whom I am next to speak, had, with the advantage of Shakespeare's wit, which was their precedent, great natural gifts, improved by study: Beaumont especially being so accurate a judge of plays, that Ben Jonson, while he lived, submitted all his writings to his censure, and, 'tis thought, used his judgment in correcting, if not contriving, all his plots. What value he had for him, appears by the verses he writ to him; and therefore I need speak no farther of it. The first play that brought Fletcher and him in esteem was their *Philaster:* for before that, they had written two or three very unsuccessfully, as the like is reported of Ben Jonson, before he writ *Every Man in His Humor.* Their plots were generally more regular than Shakespeare's, especially those which were made before Beaumont's death; and they understood and imitated the conversation of gentlemen much better; whose wild debaucheries, and quickness of wit in repartees, no poet can ever paint as they have done. Humor, which Ben Jonson derived from particular persons, they made it not their business to describe: they represented all the passions very lively, but above all, love. I am apt to believe the English language in them arrived to its highest perfection: what words have since been taken in, are rather superfluous than ornamental. Their plays are now the most pleasant and frequent entertainments of the stage; two of theirs being acted through the year for one of Shakespeare's or Jonson's: the reason is, because there is a certain gaiety in their comedies, and pathos in their more serious plays, which suits generally with all men's humors. Shakespeare's language is likewise a little obsolete, and Ben Jonson's wit comes short of theirs.

---

[53] "As cypresses usually do among supple trees." Virgil, *Eclogues,* I. 25.

"As for Jonson, to whose character I am now arrived, if we look upon him while he was himself (for his last plays were but his dotages), I think him the most learned and judicious writer which any theater ever had. He was a most severe judge of himself, as well as others. One cannot say he wanted wit, but rather that he was frugal of it. In his works you find little to retrench or alter. Wit, and language, and humor also in some measure, we had before him; but something of art was wanting to the drama, till he came. He managed his strength to more advantage than any who preceded him. You seldom find him making love in any of his scenes, or endeavoring to move the passions; his genius was too sullen and saturnine to do it gracefully, especially when he knew he came after those who had performed both to such a height. Humor was his proper sphere; and in that he delighted most to represent mechanic people. He was deeply conversant in the ancients, both Greek and Latin, and he borrowed boldly from them: there is scarce a poet or historian among the Roman authors of those times whom he has not translated in *Sejanus* and *Catiline*. But he had done his robberies so openly, that one may see he fears not to be taxed by any law. He invades authors like a monarch; and what would be theft in other poets, is only victory in him. With the spoils of these writers he so represents old Rome to us, in its rites, ceremonies, and customs, that if one of their poets had written either of his tragedies, we had seen less of it than in him. If there was any fault in his language, 'twas that he weaved it too closely and laboriously, in his serious plays: perhaps too, he did a little too much romanize our tongue, leaving the words which he translated almost as much Latin as he found them: wherein, though he learnedly followed the idiom of their language, he did not enough comply with the idiom of ours. If I would compare him with Shakespeare, I must acknowledge him the more correct poet, but Shakespeare the greater wit. Shakespeare was the Homer, or father of our dramatic poets; Jonson was the Virgil, the pattern of elaborate writing; I admire him, but I love Shakespeare. To conclude of him; as he has given us the most correct plays, so in the precepts which he has laid down in his *Discoveries,* we have as many and profitable rules for perfecting the stage, as any wherewith the French can furnish us.

"Having thus spoken of the author, I proceed to the examination of his comedy, *The Silent Woman.*"

Examen of The Silent Woman

"To begin first with the length of the action; it is so far from exceeding the compass of a natural day, that it takes not up an artificial one. 'Tis all included in the limits of three hours and an half, which is no more than is required for the presentment on the stage. A beauty perhaps not much observed;

if it had, we should not have looked on the Spanish translation of *Five Hours* with so much wonder. The scene of it is laid in London; the latitude of place is almost as little as you can imagine; for it lies all within the compass of two houses, and after the first act, in one. The continuity of scenes is observed more than in any of our plays, except his own *Fox* and *Alchemist*. They are not broken above twice or thrice at most in the whole comedy; and in the two best of Corneille's plays, the *Cid* and *Cinna,* they are interrupted once apiece. The action of the play is entirely one; the end or aim of which is the settling Morose's estate on Dauphine. The intrigue of it is the greatest and most noble of any pure unmixed comedy in any language; you see in it many persons of various characters and humors, and all delightful: as first, Morose, or an old man, to whom all noise but his own talking is offensive. Some who would be thought critics, say this humor of his is forced: but to remove that objection, we may consider him first to be naturally of a delicate hearing, as many are, to whom all sharp sounds are unpleasant; and secondly, we may attribute much of it to the peevishness of his age, or the wayward authority of an old man in his own house, where he may make himself obeyed; and this the poet seems to allude to in his name Morose. Besides this, I am assured from divers persons, that Ben Jonson was actually acquainted with such a man, one altogether as ridiculous as he is here represented. Others say, it is not enough to find one man of such an humor; it must be common to more, and the more common the more natural. To prove this, they instance in the best of comical characters, Falstaff: there are many men resembling him; old, fat, merry, cowardly, drunken, amorous, vain, and lying. But to convince these people, I need but tell them, that humor is the ridiculous extravagance of conversation, wherein one man differs from all others. If then it be common, or communicated to many, how differs it from other men's? Or what indeed causes it to be ridiculous so much as the singularity of it? As for Falstaff, he is not properly one humor, but a miscellany of humors or images, drawn from so many several men: that wherein he is singular is his wit, or those things he says *praeter expectatum,* unexpected by the audience; his quick evasions, when you imagine him surprised, which, as they are extremely diverting of themselves, so receive a great addition from his person; for the very sight of such an unwieldy old debauched fellow is a comedy alone. And here, having a place so proper for it, I cannot but enlarge somewhat upon this subject of humor into which I am fallen. The ancients had little of it in their comedies; for the τὸ γελοῖον [54] of the old comedy, of which Aristophanes was chief, was not so much to imitate a man, as

---

[54] "Ridiculous."

to make the people laugh at some odd conceit, which had commonly somewhat of unnatural or obscene in it. Thus, when you see Socrates brought upon the stage, you are not to imagine him made ridiculous by the imitation of his actions, but rather by making him perform something very unlike himself; something so childish and absurd, as by comparing it with the gravity of the true Socrates, makes a ridiculous object for the spectators. In their new comedy which succeeded, the poets sought indeed to express the ἦθος,[55] as in their tragedies the πάθος[56] of mankind. But this ἦθος contained only the general characters of men and manners; as old men, lovers, servingmen, courtesans, parasites, and such other persons as we see in their comedies; all which they made alike: that is, one old man or father, one lover, one courtesan, so like another, as if the first of them had begot the rest of every sort: *'Ex homine hunc natum dicas.'*[57] The same custom they observed likewise in their tragedies. As for the French, though they have the word *humeur* among them, yet they have small use of it in their comedies or farces; they being but ill imitations of the *ridiculum,* or that which stirred up laughter in the old comedy. But among the English 'tis otherwise: where by humor is meant some extravagant habit, passion, or affection, particular (as I said before) to some one person, by the oddness of which, he is immediately distinguished from the rest of men; which being lively and naturally represented, most frequently begets that malicious pleasure in the audience which is testified by laughter; as all things which are deviations from common customs are ever the aptest to produce it: though by the way this laughter is only accidental, as the person represented is fantastic or bizarre; but pleasure is essential to it, as the imitation of what is natural. The description of these humors, drawn from the knowledge and observation of particular persons, was the peculiar genius and talent of Ben Jonson; to whose play I now return.

"Besides Morose, there are at least nine or ten different characters and humors in *The Silent Woman;* all which persons have several concernments of their own, yet are all used by the poet, to the conducting of the main design to perfection. I shall not waste time in commending the writing of this play; but I will give you my opinion, that there is more wit and acuteness of fancy in it than in any of Ben Jonson's. Besides, that he has here described the conversation of gentlemen in the persons of True-Wit, and his friends, with more gaiety, air, and freedom, than in the rest of his comedies. For the contrivance of the plot, 'tis extreme elaborate, and yet withal easy; for the λύσις, or untying of it, 'tis so admirable, that when it is done, no one of the audience would think the poet would have missed it; and yet it was concealed so much before the last scene, that any other way would sooner have entered into your thoughts. But I dare not take upon me to commend the fabric of it, because it is altogether so full of art, that I must unravel every scene in it to commend it as I ought. And this excellent contrivance is still the more to be admired, because 'tis comedy, where the persons are only of common rank, and their business private, not elevated by passions or high concernments, as in serious plays. Here everyone is a proper judge of all he sees, nothing is represented but that with which he daily converses: so that by consequence all faults lie open to discovery, and few are pardonable. 'Tis this which Horace has judiciously observed:

> *Creditur, ex medio quia res arcessit, habere*
> *Sudoris minimum; sed habet comedia tanto*
> *Plus oneris, quanto veniae minus.*[58]

But our poet who was not ignorant of these difficulties, had prevailed himself of all advantages; as he who designs a large leap takes his rise from the highest ground. One of these advantages is that which Corneille has laid down as the greatest which can arrive to any poem, and which he himself could never compass above thrice in all his plays; viz. the making choice of some signal and long-expected day, whereon the action of the play is to depend. This day was that designed by Dauphine for the settling of his uncle's estate upon him; which to compass, he contrives to marry him. That the marriage had been plotted by him long beforehand, is made evident by what he tells True-Wit in the second act, that in one moment he had destroyed what he had been raising many months.

"There is another artifice of the poet, which I cannot here omit, because by the frequent practice of it in his comedies he has left it to us almost as a rule; that is, when he has any character or humor wherein he would show a *coup de maître,* or his highest skill, he recommends it to your observation by a pleasant description of it before the person first appears. Thus, in *Bartholomew Fair* he gives you the pictures of Numps and Cokes, and in this those of Daw, Lafoole, Morose, and the collegiate ladies; all which you hear described before you see them. So that before they come upon the stage, you have a longing expectation of them, which prepares you to receive them favorably; and when they are there, even from their first appearance you are so

---

[55] "Ethos," or character.
[56] "Pathos," or suffering.
[57] "You would say this one was born from that man." Terence, *Eunuch,* III. ii. 7.

[58] "It is thought that because it draws its materials from common life comedy requires the least pains, but it is as much more difficult as it has less indulgence." *Epistles,* II. 1.

far acquainted with them, that nothing of their humor is lost to you.

"I will observe yet one thing further of this admirable plot; the business of it rises in every act. The second is greater than the first; the third than the second; and so forward to the fifth. There too you see, till the very last scene, new difficulties arising to obstruct the action of the play; and when the audience is brought into despair that the business can naturally be effected, then, and not before, the discovery is made. But that the poet might entertain you with more variety all this while, he reserves some new characters to show you, which he opens not till the second and third act. In the second Morose, Daw, the Barber, and Otter; in the third the collegiate ladies: all which he moves afterwards in by-walks, or underplots, as diversions to the main design, lest it should grow tedious, though they are still naturally joined with it, and somewhere or other subservient to it. Thus, like a skillful chess-player, by little and little he draws out his men, and makes his pawns of use to his greater persons.

"If this comedy and some others of his were translated into French prose (which would now be no wonder to them, since Molière has lately given them plays out of verse, which have not displeased them), I believe the controversy would soon be decided betwixt the two nations, even making them the judges. But we need not call our heroes to our aid; be it spoken to the honor of the English, our nation can never want in any age such who are able to dispute the empire of wit with any people in the universe. And though the fury of a civil war, and power for twenty years together abandoned to a barbarous race of men, enemies of all good learning, had buried the Muses under the ruins of monarchy; yet, with the restoration of our happiness, we see revived poesy lifting up its head, and already shaking off the rubbish which lay so heavy on it. We have seen since his Majesty's return, many dramatic poems which yield not to those of any foreign nation, and which deserve all laurels but the English. I will set aside flattery and envy: it cannot be denied but we have had some little blemish either in the plot or writing of all those plays which have been made within these seven years (and perhaps there is no nation in the world so quick to discern them, or so difficult to pardon them, as ours): yet if we can persuade ourselves to use the candor of that poet, who, though the most severe of critics, has left us this caution by which to moderate our censures—*'ubi plura nitent in carmine, non ego paucis / Offendar maculis'*[59]—if, in consid-

eration of their many and great beauties, we can wink at some slight and little imperfections, if we, I say, can be thus equal to ourselves, I ask no favor from the French. And if I do not venture upon any particular judgment of our late plays, 'tis out of the consideration which an ancient writer gives me: *'vivorum, ut magna admiratio, ita censura difficilis':* [60] betwixt the extremes of admiration and malice, 'tis hard to judge uprightly of the living. Only I think it may be permitted me to say, that as it is no lessening to us to yield to some plays, and those not many, of our own nation in the last age, so can it be no addition to pronounce of our present poets, that they have far surpassed all the ancients, and the modern writers of other countries."

This, my Lord, was the substance of what was then spoke on that occasion; and Lisideius, I think, was going to reply, when he was prevented thus by Crites: "I am confident," said he, "that the most material things that can be said have been already urged on either side; if they have not, I must beg of Lisideius that he will defer his answer till another time: for I confess I have a joint quarrel to you both, because you have concluded, without any reason given for it, that rhyme is proper for the stage. I will not dispute how ancient it hath been among us to write this way; perhaps our ancestors knew no better till Shakespeare's time. I will grant it was not altogether left by him, and that Fletcher and Ben Jonson used it frequently in their pastorals, and sometimes in other plays. Farther, I will not argue whether we received it originally from our own countrymen, or from the French; for that is an inquiry of as little benefit, as theirs who, in the midst of the great plague, were not so solicitous to provide against it, as to know whether we had it from the malignity of our own air, or by transportation from Holland. I have therefore only to affirm, that it is not allowable in serious plays; for comedies, I find you already concluding with me. To prove this, I might satisfy myself to tell you, how much in vain it is for you to strive against the stream of the people's inclination; the greatest part of which are prepossessed so much with those excellent plays of Shakespeare, Fletcher, and Ben Jonson, which have been written out of rhyme, that except you could bring them such as were written better in it, and those too by persons of equal reputation with them, it will be impossible for you to gain your cause with them, who will still be judges. This it is to which, in fine, all your reasons must submit. The unanimous consent of an audience is so powerful, that even Julius Caesar (as Macrobius reports of him), when he was perpetual dictator, was not able to bal-

---

[59]"Where many things shine out in a poem, I shall not be offended at little faults." Horace, *Art of Poetry,* pp. 72–73.

[60]"As admiration of the living is great, so censure is difficult." Paterculus, *History of Rome,* II. 36.

ance it on the other side. But when Laberius, a Roman knight, at his request contended in the mime with another poet, he was forced to cry out, *'Etiam favente me victus es, Laberi.'*[61] But I will not on this occasion take the advantage of the greater number, but only urge such reasons against rhyme, as I find in the writings of those who have argued for the other way. First then, I am of opinion, that rhyme is unnatural in a play, because dialogue there is presented as the effect of sudden thought: for a play is the imitation of nature; and since no man without premeditation speaks in rhyme, neither ought he to do it on the stage. This hinders not but the fancy may be there elevated to an higher pitch of thought than it is in ordinary discourse; for there is a probability that men of excellent and quick parts may speak noble things extempore: but those thoughts are never fettered with the numbers or sound of verse without study, and therefore it cannot be but unnatural to present the most free way of speaking in that which is the most constrained. For this reason, says Aristotle, 'tis best to write tragedy in that kind of verse which is the least such, or which is nearest prose: and this amongst the ancients was the iambic, and with us is blank verse, or the measure of verse kept exactly without rhyme.[62] These numbers therefore are fittest for a play; the others for a paper of verses, or a poem; blank verse being as much below them, as rhyme is improper for the drama. And if it be objected that neither are blank verses made extempore, yet, as nearest nature, they are still to be preferred. But there are two particular exceptions, which many besides myself have had to verse; by which it will appear yet more plainly how improper it is in plays. And the first of them is grounded on that very reason for which some have commended rhyme; they say, the quickness of repartees in argumentative scenes receives an ornament from verse. Now what is more unreasonable than to imagine that a man should not only light upon the wit, but the rhyme too, upon the sudden? This nicking of him who spoke before both in sound and measure, is so great a happiness, that you must at least suppose the persons of your play to be born poets: *'Arcades omnes, et cantare pares, et respondere parati':*[63] they must have arrived to the degree of *'quicquid conabar dicere'*[64]—to make verses almost whether they will or no. If they are anything below this, it will look rather like the design of two, than the answer of one: it will appear that your actors hold intelligence together;

that they perform their tricks like fortune-tellers, by confederacy. The hand of art will be too visible in it, against that maxim of all professions, *'Ars est celare artem,'* that it is the greatest perfection of art to keep itself undiscovered. Nor will it serve you to object, that however you manage it, 'tis still known to be a play; and, consequently, the dialogue of two persons understood to be the labor of one poet. For a play is still an imitation of nature; we know we are to be deceived, and we desire to be so; but no man ever was deceived but with a probability of truth; for who will suffer a gross lie to be fastened on him? Thus we sufficiently understand, that the scenes which represent cities and countries to us are not really such, but only painted on boards and canvas; but shall that excuse the ill painture or designment of them? Nay, rather ought they not to be labored with so much the more diligence and exactness, to help the imagination? Since the mind of man does naturally tend to, and seek after truth; and therefore the nearer anything comes to the imitation of it, the more it pleases.

"Thus, you see, your rhyme is uncapable of expressing the greatest thoughts naturally, and the lowest it cannot with any grace: for what is more unbefitting the majesty of verse, than to call a servant, or bid a door be shut in rhyme? And yet this miserable necessity you are forced upon. But verse, you say, circumscribes a quick and luxuriant fancy, which would extend itself too far on every subject, did not the labor which is required to well-turned and polished rhyme, set bounds to it. Yet this argument, if granted, would only prove that we may write better in verse, but not more naturally. Neither is it able to evince that; for he who wants judgment to confine his fancy in blank verse, may want it as much in rhyme; and he who has it will avoid errors in both kinds. Latin verse was as great a confinement to the imagination of those poets, as rhyme to ours; and yet you had Ovid saying too much on every subject. *'Nescivit,'* says Seneca, *'quod bene cessit relinquere':*[65] of which he gives you one famous instance in his description of the deluge: *'Omnia pontus erat, deerant quoque litora ponto';* now all was sea, nor had that sea a shore.[66] Thus Ovid's fancy was not limited by verse, and Virgil needed not verse to have bounded his.

"In our own language we see Ben Jonson confining himself to what ought to be said, even in the liberty of blank verse; and yet Corneille, the most judicious of the French poets, is still varying the same sense a hundred ways, and dwelling eternally on the same subject, though confined by

---

[61]Even with my favor you are defeated, Laberius." Macrobius, *Saturnalia,* II. 7.

[62]*Poetics,* IV. 14, p. 52.

[63]"All the Arcadians, prepared both to sing together and to respond." Virgil, *Eclogues,* VII. 4.

[64]"To say whatever I attempted." Ovid, *Tristia,* IV. x. 25.

---

[65]"He did not know how to end when he should have." Ovid, quoted in Seneca, *Controversies,* IX. 5.

[66]Ovid, *Metamorphoses,* I. 292.

rhyme. Some other exceptions I have to verse; but being these I have named are for the most part already public, I conceive it reasonable they should first be answered.''

"It concerns me less than any," said Neander (seeing he had ended), "to reply to this discourse; because when I should have proved that verse may be natural in plays, yet I should always be ready to confess, that those which I have written in this kind come short of that perfection which is required. Yet since you are pleased I should undertake this province, I will do it, though with all imaginable respect and deference, both to that person from whom you have borrowed your strongest arguments, and to whose judgment, when I have said all, I finally submit. But before I proceed to answer your objections, I must first remember you, that I exclude all comedy from my defense; and next that I deny not but blank verse may be also used; and content myself only to assert, that in serious plays where the subject and characters are great, and the plot unmixed with mirth, which might allay or divert these concernments which are produced, rhyme is there as natural and more effectual than blank verse.

"And now having laid down this as a foundation, to begin with Crites, I must crave leave to tell him, that some of his arguments against rhyme reach no farther than, from the faults or defects of ill rhyme, to conclude against the use of it in general. May not I conclude against blank verse by the same reason? If the words of some poets who write in it, are either ill chosen, or ill placed, which makes not only rhyme, but all kind of verse in any language unnatural, shall I, for their vicious affectation, condemn those excellent lines of Fletcher, which are written in that kind? Is there any thing in rhyme more constrained than this line in blank verse, *I heaven invoke, and strong resistance make?* where you see both the clauses are placed unnaturally, that is, contrary to the common way of speaking, and that without the excuse of a rhyme to cause it: yet you would think me very ridiculous, if I should accuse the stubbornness of blank verse for this, and not rather the stiffness of the poet. Therefore, Crites, you must either prove that words, though well chosen, and duly placed, yet render not rhyme natural in itself; or that, however natural and easy the rhyme may be, yet it is not proper for a play. If you insist on the former part, I would ask you, what other conditions are required to make rhyme natural in itself, besides an election of apt words, and a right disposing of them? For the due choice of your words expresses your sense naturally, and the due placing them adapts the rhyme to it. If you object that one verse may be made for the sake of another, though both the words and rhyme be apt, I answer, it cannot possibly so fall out; for either there is a dependence of sense betwixt the first line and the second, or

there is none; if there be that connection, then in the natural position of the words the latter line must of necessity flow from the former; if there be no dependence, yet still the due ordering of words makes the last line as natural in itself as the other: so that the necessity of a rhyme never forces any but bad or lazy writers to say what they would not otherwise. 'Tis true, there is both care and art required to write in verse. A good poet never concludes upon the first line, till he has sought out such a rhyme as may fit the sense, already prepared to heighten the second: many times the close of the sense falls into the middle of the next verse, or farther off, and he may often prevail himself of the same advantages in English which Virgil had in Latin; he may break off in the hemistich,[67] and begin another line. Indeed, the not observing these two last things, makes plays which are writ in verse so tedious: for though, most commonly, the sense is to be confined to the couplet, yet nothing that does *perpetuo tenore fluere,* run in the same channel, can please always. 'Tis like the murmuring of a stream, which not varying in the fall, causes at first attention, at last drowsiness. Variety of cadences is the best rule; the greatest help to the actors, and refreshment to the audience.

"If then verse may be made natural in itself, how becomes it improper to a play? You say the stage is the representation of nature, and no man in ordinary conversation speaks in rhyme. But you foresaw when you said this, that it might be answered—neither does any man speak in blank verse, or in measure without rhyme. Therefore you concluded, that which is nearest nature is still to be preferred. But you took no notice that rhyme might be made as natural as blank verse, by the well placing of the words, &c. All the difference between them, when they are both correct, is, the sound in one, which the other wants; and if so, the sweetness of it, and all the advantage from it, which are handled in the preface to *The Rival Ladies,* will yet stand good. As for that place of Aristotle, where he says, plays should be writ in that kind of verse which is nearest prose, it makes little for you; blank verse being properly but measured prose. Now measure alone, in any modern language, does not constitute verse; those of the ancients in Greek and Latin consisted in quantity of words, and a determinate number of feet. But when, by the inundation of the Goths and Vandals into Italy, new languages were brought in, and barbarously mingled with the Latin, of which the Italian, Spanish, French, and ours (made out of them and the Teutonic) are dialects, a new way of poesy was practiced; new, I say, in those countries, for in all probability it was that of the conquerors in their

---

[67]Half a line of verse.

own nations. This new way consisted in measure or number of feet, and rhyme; the sweetness of rhyme, and observation of accent, supplying the place of quantity in words, which could neither exactly be observed by those barbarians, who knew not the rules of it, neither was it suitable to their tongues, as it had been to the Greek and Latin. No man is tied in modern poesy to observe any farther rule in the feet of his verse, but that they be dissyllables; whether spondee, trochee, or iambic, it matters not; only he is obliged to rhyme. Neither do the Spanish, French, Italian, or Germans, acknowledge at all, or very rarely, any such kind of poesy as blank verse amongst them. Therefore, at most 'tis but a poetic prose, a *sermo pedestris;* and as such, most fit for comedies, where I acknowledge rhyme to be improper. Farther; as to that quotation of Aristotle, our couplet verses may be rendered as near prose as blank verse itself, by using those advantages I lately named, as breaks in a hemistich, or running the sense into another line, thereby making art and order appear as loose and free as nature: or not tying ourselves to couplets strictly, we may use the benefit of the Pindaric way practiced in *The Siege of Rhodes;* where the numbers vary, and the rhyme is disposed carelessly, and far from often chiming. Neither is that other advantage of the ancients to be despised, of changing the kind of verse when they please, with the change of the scene, or some new entrance; for they confine not themselves always to iambics, but extend their liberty to all lyric numbers, and sometimes even to hexameter. But I need not go so far to prove that rhyme, as it succeeds to all other offices of Greek and Latin verse, so especially to this of plays, since the custom of all nations at this day confirms it, all the French, Italian, and Spanish tragedies are generally writ in it; and sure the universal consent of the most civilized parts of the world ought in this, as it doth in other customs, to include the rest.

"But perhaps you may tell me, I have proposed such a way to make rhyme natural, and consequently proper to plays, as is unpracticable; and that I shall scarce find six or eight lines together in any play, where the words are so placed and chosen as is required to make it natural. I answer, no poet need constrain himself at all times to it. It is enough he makes it his general rule; for I deny not but sometimes there may be a greatness in placing the words otherwise; and sometimes they may sound better, sometimes also the variety itself is excuse enough. But if, for the most part, the words be placed as they are in the negligence of prose, it is sufficient to denominate the way practicable; for we esteem that to be such, which in the trial oftener succeeds than misses. And thus far you may find the practice made good in many plays: where you do not, remember still, that if you cannot find six natural rhymes together, it will be as hard for you to produce as many lines in blank verse, even among the greatest of our poets, against which I cannot make some reasonable exception.

"And this, Sir, calls to my remembrance the beginning of your discourse, where you told us we should never find the audience favorable to this kind of writing, till we could produce as good plays in rhyme, as Ben Jonson, Fletcher, and Shakespeare, had writ out of it. But it is to raise envy to the living, to compare them with the dead. They are honored, and almost adored by us, as they deserve; neither do I know any so presumptuous of themselves as to contend with them. Yet give me leave to say thus much, without injury to their ashes; that not only we shall never equal them, but they could never equal themselves, were they to rise and write again. We acknowledge them our fathers in wit; but they have ruined their estates themselves before they came to their children's hands. There is scarce a humor, a character, or any kind of plot, which they have not blown upon. All comes sullied or wasted to us: and were they to entertain this age, they could not make so plenteous treatments out of such decayed fortunes. This therefore will be a good argument to us, either not to write at all, or to attempt some other way. There is no bays to be expected in their walks: *'tentanda via est, qua me quoque possum tollere humo.'*[68]

"This way of writing in verse they have only left free to us; our age is arrived to a perfection in it, which they never knew; and which (if we may guess by what of theirs we have seen in verse, as *The Faithful Shepherdess,* and *Sad Shepherd*) 'tis probable they never could have reached. For the genius of every age is different; and though ours excel in this, I deny not but that to imitate nature in that perfection which they did in prose, is a greater commendation than to write in verse exactly. As for what you have added, that the people are not generally inclined to like this way; if it were true, it would be no wonder, that betwixt the shaking off an old habit, and the introducing of a new, there should be difficulty. Do we not see them stick to Hopkins' and Sternhold's psalms, and forsake those of David, I mean Sandys his translation of them? If by the people you understand the multitude, the οἱ πολλοί, 'tis no matter what they think; they are sometimes in the right, sometimes in the wrong: their judgment is a mere lottery. *'Est ubi plebs rectè putat, est ubi peccat.'*[69] Horace says it of the vulgar, judging poesy. But if you mean the mixed audience of the populace and the noblesse, I dare confidently affirm that a great part of the latter sort are already favorable to verse; and that no serious plays

---

[68]"I must find a way by which I can raise myself from the earth." Virgil, *Georgics,* III. 8–9.
[69]"Sometimes the people are right, sometimes not." Horace, *Epistles,* II. 63.

written since the king's return have been more kindly received by them, than *The Siege of Rhodes,* the *Mustapha, The Indian Queen,* and *Indian Emperor.*[70]

"But I come now to the inference of your first argument. You said the dialogue of plays is presented as the effect of sudden thought, but no man speaks suddenly, or extempore, in rhyme; and you inferred from thence, that rhyme, which you acknowledge to be proper to epic poesy, cannot equally be proper to dramatic, unless we could suppose all men born so much more than poets, that verses should be made in them, not by them.

"It has been formerly urged by you, and confessed by me, that since no man spoke any kind of verse extempore, that which was nearest nature was to be preferred. I answer you, therefore, by distinguishing betwixt what is nearest to the nature of comedy, which is the imitation of common persons and ordinary speaking, and what is nearest the nature of a serious play: this last is indeed the representation of nature, but 'tis nature wrought up to an higher pitch. The plot, the characters, the wit, the passions, the descriptions, are all exalted above the level of common converse, as high as the imagination of the poet can carry them, with proportion to verisimility. Tragedy, we know, is wont to imagine to us the minds and fortunes of noble persons, and to portray these exactly; heroic rhyme is nearest nature, as being the noblest kind of modern verse. *'Indignatur enim privatis et prope socco / Dignis carminibus narrari coena Thyestae,'*[71] says Horace: and in another place, *'Effutire leves indigna tragaedia versus.'*[72] Blank verse is acknowledged to be too low for a poem, nay more, for a paper of verses; but if too low for an ordinary sonnet, how much more for tragedy, which is by Aristotle, in the dispute betwixt the epic poesy and the dramatic, for many reasons he there alleges, ranked above it?

"But setting this defense aside, your argument is almost as strong against the use of rhyme in poems as in plays; for the epic way is everywhere interlaced with dialogue, or discoursive scenes; and therefore you must either grant rhyme to be improper there, which is contrary to your assertion, or admit it into plays by the same title which you have given it to poems. For though tragedy be justly preferred above the other, yet there is a great affinity between them, as may easily be discovered in that definition of a play which Lisideius gave us. The genus of them is the same, a just and lively image of human nature, in its actions, passions, and traverses of fortune: so is the end, namely, for the delight and benefit of mankind. The characters and persons are still the same, viz. the greatest of both sorts; only the manner of acquainting us with those actions, passions, and fortunes, is different. Tragedy performs it viva voce, or by action, in dialogue; wherein it excels the epic poem, which does it chiefly by narration, and therefore is not so lively an image of human nature. However, the agreement betwixt them is such, that if rhyme be proper for one, it must be for the other. Verse, 'tis true, is not the effect of sudden thought; but this hinders not that sudden thought may be represented in verse, since those thoughts are such as must be higher than nature can raise them without premeditation, especially to a continuance of them, even out of verse; and consequently you cannot imagine them to have been sudden either in the poet or in the actors. A play, as I have said, to be like nature, is to be set above it; as statues which are placed on high are made greater than the life, that they may descend to the sight in their just proportion.

"Perhaps I have insisted too long on this objection; but the clearing of it will make my stay shorter on the rest. You tell us, Crites, that rhyme appears most unnatural in repartees, or short replies: when he who answers, it being presumed he knew not what the other would say, yet makes up that part of the verse which was left incomplete, and supplies both the sound and measure of it. This, you say, looks rather like the confederacy of two, than the answer of one.

"This, I confess, is an objection which is in everyone's mouth, who loves not rhyme: but suppose, I beseech you, the repartee were made only in blank verse, might not part of the same argument be turned against you? For the measure is as often supplied there, as it is in rhyme; the latter half of the hemistich as commonly made up, or a second line subjoined as a reply to the former; which any one leaf in Jonson's plays will sufficiently clear to you. You will often find in the Greek tragedians, and in Seneca, that when a scene grows up into the warmth of repartees, which is the close fighting of it, the latter part of the trimeter is supplied by him who answers; and yet it was never observed as a fault in them by any of the ancient or modern critics. The case is the same in our verse, as it was in theirs; rhyme to us being in lieu of quantity to them. But if no latitude is to be allowed a poet, you take from him not only his license of *'quidlibet audendi,'*[73] but you tie him up in a straiter compass than you would a philosopher. This is indeed *'Musas colere severiores.'*[74] You would have him follow nature, but he must follow her on foot: you have dismounted him from his Pegasus. But you tell us, this sup-

---

[70]*The Indian Queen* and *Indian Emperor* were written by Dryden, the former in collaboration with Robert Howard.

[71]"It is improper for the banquet of Thyestes to be told in familiar verses and comic style." Horace, *Art of Poetry,* p. 69.

[72]"It is improper for tragedy to babble forth light verses." *Art of Poetry,* p. 71.

[73]"Trying anything." Horace, *Art of Poetry,* p. 68.

[74]"To worship the severer Muses." Martial, *Epigrams,* IX. 12.

plying the last half of a verse, or adjoining a whole second to the former, looks more like the design of two, than the answer of one. Supposing we acknowledge it: how comes this confederacy to be more displeasing to you, than in a dance which is well contrived? You see there the united design of many persons to make up one figure: after they have separated themselves in many petty divisions, they rejoin one by one into a gross: the confederacy is plain amongst them, for chance could never produce any thing so beautiful; and yet there is nothing in it that shocks your sight. I acknowledge the hand of art appears in repartee, as of necessity it must in all kinds of verse. But there is also the quick and poignant brevity of it (which is an high imitation of nature in those sudden gusts of passion) to mingle with it; and this, joined with the cadency and sweetness of the rhyme, leaves nothing in the soul of the hearer to desire. 'Tis an art which appears; but it appears only like the shadowings of painture, which being to cause the rounding of it, cannot be absent; but while that is considered, they are lost: so while we attend to the other beauties of the matter, the care and labor of the rhyme is carried from us, or at least drowned in its own sweetness, as bees are sometimes buried in their honey. When a poet has found the repartee, the last perfection he can add to it, is to put it into verse. However good the thought may be, however apt the words in which 'tis couched, yet he finds himself at a little unrest, while rhyme is wanting: he cannot leave it till that comes naturally, and then is at ease, and sits down contented.

"From replies, which are the most elevated thoughts of verse, you pass to the most mean ones, those which are common with the lowest of household conversation. In these, you say, the majesty of verse suffers. You instance in the calling of a servant, or commanding a door to be shut, in rhyme. This, Crites, is a good observation of yours, but no argument: for it proves no more but that such thoughts should be waived, as often as may be, by the address of the poet. But suppose they are necessary in the places where he uses them, yet there is no need to put them into rhyme. He may place them in the beginning of a verse, and break it off, as unfit, when so debased, for any other use; or granting the worst, that they require more room than the hemistich will allow, yet still there is a choice to be made of the best words, and least vulgar (provided they be apt) to express such thoughts. Many have blamed rhyme in general, for this fault, when the poet with a little care might have redressed it. But they do it with no more justice, than if English poesy should be made ridiculous for the sake of the water poet's[75] rhymes. Our language is noble, full, and significant; and I know not why he

who is master of it may not clothe ordinary things in it as decently as the Latin, if he use the same diligence in his choice of words. *'Delectus verborum origo est eloquentiae.'*[76] It was the saying of Julius Caesar, one so curious in his, that none of them can be changed but for a worse. One would think, *unlock the door,* was a thing as vulgar as could be spoken; and yet Seneca could make it sound high and lofty in his Latin: *'Reserate clusos regii postes laris';* set wide the palace gates.[77]

"But I turn from this exception, both because it happens not above twice or thrice in any play that those vulgar thoughts are used; and then too, were there no other apology to be made, yet the necessity of them, which is alike in all kind of writing, may excuse them. Besides that the great eagerness and precipitation with which they are spoken makes us rather mind the substance than the dress; that for which they are spoken, rather than what is spoke. For they are always the effect of some hasty concernment, and something of consequence depends on them.

"Thus, Crites, I have endeavored to answer your objections; it remains only that I should vindicate an argument for verse, which you have gone about to overthrow. It had formerly been said, that the easiness of blank verse renders the poet too luxuriant, but that the labor of rhyme bounds and circumscribes an overfruitful fancy; the sense there being commonly confined to the couplet, and the words so ordered that the rhyme naturally follows them, not they the rhyme. To this you answered, that it was no argument to the question in hand; for the dispute was not which way a man may write best, but which is most proper for the subject on which he writes.

"First, give me leave, sir, to remember you, that the argument against which you raised this objection, was only secondary: it was built on this hypothesis, that to write in verse was proper for serious plays. Which supposition being granted (as it was briefly made out in that discourse, by showing how verse might be made natural), it asserted, that this way of writing was a help to the poet's judgment, by putting bounds to a wild overflowing fancy. I think, therefore, it will not be hard for me to make good what it was to prove. But you add, that were this let pass, yet he who wants judgment in the liberty of his fancy, may as well show the defect of it when he is confined to verse; for he who has judgment will avoid errors, and he who has it not, will commit them in all kinds of writing.

"This argument, as you have taken it from a most acute person, so I confess it carries much weight in it: but by using

---

[75]John Taylor (1580–1653), poet and Thames River boatman.

[76]"Choice of words is the origin of eloquence." Cicero, *Brutus,* LXXII. 253.
[77]*Phaedra,* 871.

the word *judgment* here indefinitely, you seem to have put a fallacy upon us. I grant, he who has judgment, that is, so profound, so strong, so infallible a judgment, that he needs no helps to keep it always poised and upright, will commit no faults either in rhyme or out of it. And on the other extreme, he who has a judgment so weak and crazed that no helps can correct or amend it, shall write scurvily out of rhyme, and worse in it. But the first of these judgments is nowhere to be found, and the latter is not fit to write at all. To speak therefore of judgment as it is in the best poets; they who have the greatest proportion of it, want other helps than from it, within. As for example, you would be loath to say, that he who was endued with a sound judgment had no need of history, geography, or moral philosophy, to write correctly. Judgment is indeed the master workman in a play; but he requires many subordinate hands, many tools to his assistance. And verse I affirm to be one of these; 'tis a rule and line by which he keeps his building compact and even, which otherwise lawless imagination would raise either irregularly or loosely. At least, if the poet commits errors with this help, he would make greater and more without it: 'tis, in short, a slow and painful, but the surest kind of working. Ovid, whom you accuse for luxuriancy in verse, had perhaps been farther guilty of it, had he writ in prose. And for your instance of Ben Jonson, who, you say, writ exactly without the help of rhyme; you are to remember, 'tis only an aid to a luxuriant fancy, which his was not: as he did not want imagination, so none ever said he had much to spare. Neither was verse then refined so much to be an help to that age, as it is to ours. Thus then the second thoughts being usually the best, as receiving the maturest digestion from judgment, and the last and most mature product of those thoughts being artful and labored verse it may well be inferred, that verse is a great help to a luxuriant fancy; and this is what that argument which you opposed was to evince."

Neander was pursuing this discourse so eagerly, that Eugenius had called to him twice or thrice, ere he took notice that the barge stood still, and that they were at the foot of Somerset Stairs, where they had appointed it to land. The company were all sorry to separate so soon, though a great part of the evening was already spent; and stood awhile looking back on the water, which the moonbeams played upon, and made it appear like floating quicksilver: at last they went up through a crowd of French people, who were merrily dancing in the open air, and nothing concerned for the noise of guns which had alarmed the town that afternoon. Walking thence together to the piazza, they parted there; Eugenius and Lisideius to some pleasant appointment they had made, and Crites and Neander to their several lodgings.

Nicolas Boileau-Despréaux

1636–1711

Boileau's poem *The Art of Poetry* is best read as a sort of codification of French neoclassicism as it was practiced by the great French writers, particularly Corneille and Racine. By no means original, it follows in a tradition that includes the critical work of Malherbe and Chapelain. In attitude it has much in common with the critical writings of Boileau's contemporary René Rapin. The classical sources are, of course, Aristotle and Horace. Boileau's influence was strong in England: Dryden translated *The Art of Poetry*, substituting more or less appropriate English names for those of the French writers mentioned, and Pope's *Essay on Criticism* is in its debt.

No one has accused Boileau, despite his influence, of an excess of theoretical subtlety. In a defense of him against romantic attacks, Irving Babbitt remarked, "Boileau was simply a wit and man of the world, not especially logical or imaginative or profound, but with an admirable integrity of character and an extraordinarily keen and correct sensibility."

Boileau's classicism is urbane and lacks the dogmatism that characterized so much of the critical writing of his contemporaries, who took remarks by Aristotle and Horace and hardened them into rules, such as those of the three unities preached by Corneille. It was a popular opinion that in order to imitate nature one should imitate the classical writers, and Boileau agrees. But he is not all rationalism and no feeling. He cautions restraint but believes with Racine that the secret the artist must know is how "to please and to touch." The writer should fly neither too high nor too low; a meadow brook is more pleasing than a torrent. Such remarks appealed, no doubt, to the anti-Romantic classicists of the early twentieth century, particularly Hulme, who accused the Romantic poets of flying off into the "circumambient gas."

Boileau argues that expression follows thought and that before writing one should learn to think. "Let language always be sacred to you," he warns. (Such remarks provide a contrast to post-Romantic theorizing, such as that by Croce, which generally identifies intuition with expression and sees language as a means of creating thought.) If Boileau tends to split form and content in some of his remarks, he is nevertheless interested in their relationship. Rhyme and sense must agree, he insists, and superfluous decoration is always bad.

A useful collection is Ernest Dilworth, ed., *Boileau: Selected Criticism* (1965). See also A. F. B. Clark, *Boileau and the French Classical Critics in England (1660–1830)* (1925); Jules Brody, *Boileau and Longinus* (1956); Julian Eugene White, *Nicolas Boileau* (1968); and Gordon Pocock, *Boileau and the Nature of Neo-Classicism* (1980).

The Art of Poetry

Canto I

It is in vain that a rash author attempts the Parnassian heights of the art of verse: if he is conscious of no occult heavenly influence, if the star he was born under has not made him a poet, he will remain imprisoned always in the narrowness of his powers. Apollo will be deaf to him, and Pegasus will balk.

O you then, who, burning with a perilous zeal, follow the thorny path of wit, take care you do not waste away over fruitless verses or mistake a love of rhyming for genius. Beware the lure of a vainglorious pleasure, and consider at length the character of your mind and your capacity.

Nature, fertile in excellent minds, has a way of dividing talents among authors. This one can picture, in verse, an amorous flame; this other, with an amusing stroke, can point up an epigram. Malherbe is able to extol the exploits of a hero; Racan to sing of Phyllis, of shepherds, and of woods. But it often happens that a mind through self-flattery and self-love is ignorant of itself, and misunderstands its own genius. Thus a certain man[1] whom once we saw, with Faret, blackening the walls of a pub with his rhymes,[2] goes off singing with insolence as well as impropriety of the triumphal flight of the Hebrew people, and, pursuing Moses through the desert, gets himself drowned with Pharaoh in the sea.

Whether your subject matter is sublime or amusing, be sure that good sense and rhyme always agree. There is no real opposition between them, for rhyme is a slave, whose duty it is to obey. If from the outset you accustom your mind to take pains in searching for the right rhyme, you will learn to find it with ease. Rhyme bends willingly to the yoke of reason, and, far from obstructing, serves and adorns it. But neglect rhyme and she rebels, and if she is to be recaptured, sense must run after her. Love reason, then; let all that you write borrow both its luster and its worth from her alone.

The majority, carried away by a witless fury of composition, go far off the track of reason in search of their thought; they feel that they would demean themselves, in those monstrous verses of theirs, if they were to think what somebody else was equally capable of thinking. Let us avoid these excesses: let us leave it to the Italians to be madly dazzled with all these false diamonds. Everything ought to move in the direction of good sense, but the way is slippery and hard to keep to. Swerve from it ever so little and you are finished. It often happens that there is only one road for reason to take.

You will sometimes see an author who is too full of his subject, and who will not stop until he has exhausted it. If he comes upon a palace he depicts its façade for me; after that he walks me from terrace to terrace: here a flight of steps presents itself to our view, over there runs a gallery; that balcony there is enclosed with a golden balustrade. He counts the circles and ovals on the ceilings: "Naught but festoons they are, and astragals."[3] I jump forty pages to get to the end, and barely make my escape through the garden. Flee the sterile plenty of these authors, and do not burden yourself with a single useless detail. Every superfluous word is insipid and offensive; the surfeited mind instantly rejects it. The man who doesn't know when to stop never learned how to write.

Fear of one evil often leads us into a worse. Wishing to strengthen a feeble line, you make it rough; trying not to be wordy, I become obscure; rather than overdress his Muse, a writer may leave her nakedness too much exposed; another, from fear of being low, gets lost in the clouds.

If you wish to deserve the regard of the public, constantly vary your style when writing. Too even a style, one that is always uniform, is brilliant in vain: the brightness will put us to sleep. Those authors are seldom read who, born to bore us, seem always to be droning psalms on a single note.

Happy the poet whose voice can nimbly pass from the solemn to the dulcet, from the amusing to the stern! His book, beloved of heaven, and cherished by readers, is often surrounded by purchasers at Barbin's.

Whatever you write, avoid the low: the commonest of styles is capable of a nobility of its own. In defiance of good sense, brazen burlesque deluded people at first, pleasing them by its novelty. One no longer found anything in verse but vulgar puns; Parnassus talked the language of the markets; poetic license was no longer bridled; Apollo was travestied into a Tabarin.[4] That plague infected the provinces, and went from learned man and bourgeois all the way to princes. The poorest joker had his devoted public; everybody—even d'Assouci[5]—found readers. But at last the court

---

THE ART OF POETRY. Boileau's *L'Art poétique,* composed over a period of five years, was first published in 1674. The text is from Ernest Dilworth, tr., *Nicolas Boileau-Despréaux: Selected Criticism.* Copyright © 1965 by The Bobbs-Merrill Company, Inc. Reprinted by permission of the publishers.
[1]Marc Antoine de Gérard Saint-Amant (1594–1661), author of the poem *Moïse sauvé.*
[2]Boileau is alluding here to Martial's epigram (XII. lxi) about a drunken poet who scribbled on a latrine wall.

[3][Dilworth] Scudéry, in *Alaric,* III, takes nearly three hundred verses to describe an enchanted palace. "Verse of Scudéry," says Boileau. "Astragals" are "crowns" in the original.
[4][Dilworth] Antoine Girard (1584–1626), king of charlatans and prototype of the buffoon in French literature of the seventeenth century. . . .
[5][Boileau] A pitiful author, who wrote *Ovide en belle humeur.*

saw this style for what it was, disdained the careless extravagance of such verses, learned to distinguish the simple from the flat and the clownish, and left it to the provincials to admire *Typhon*.[6] Never allow this style to sully your work. Let us imitate the elegant playfulness of Marot, and leave burlesque to the clowns of the Pont Neuf.[7]

But neither should you follow the example of Brébeuf, and, even in a *Pharsalia,* pile the river banks with "A hundred plaintive mountains of the dead and dying."[8] Take more care with your style. Be simple but with artistry; be great without pride, agreeable without artificiality.

Offer nothing to the reader but what may give him pleasure. Keep a critical ear for cadences: be sure that always in your verses the sense, interrupting the flow of words, suspends the half-line and marks the caesura. Take care that a vowel is not in such haste to be on its way that it is rammed on the road by another one. There is such a thing as a happy choice of harmonious words. Avoid the detestable competition of unpleasant sounds: the meatiest verse, the noblest thought, is unable to please the mind when the ear hurts.

In the early days of French poetry, caprice was the only lawmaker. Rhyme, at the end of an unmetrical assemblage of words, took the place of ornament, of numbers, and of cadence. Villon was the first, in those uncivilized centuries, who was able to put in order the confused art of our old romance writers.[9] Soon afterwards Marot caused ballades to flourish, made triolets, rhymed mascarades, yoked rondeaus to regular refrains, and showed us entirely new roads to rhyming. Ronsard, who followed him, regulating everything according to another method, threw it all into confusion, made an art of poetry to suit himself, and yet for a long time had a happy lot. But in the next age his Muse, that spoke Greek and Latin in the French language, saw, by a grotesque change, the pedantic splendor fall away from her lofty words. This proud poet, fallen from such a height, made Desportes and Bertaut more cautious.

At last came Malherbe, who made French appreciate for the first time a fine cadence in verse, who taught them the power of a word set in the right place, and brought the Muse under the rules. Redeemed by this wise writer, our tongue no longer shocked the refined ear with roughness. Stanzas learned how to come gracefully to a close, and one verse no longer had the audacity to run on into another. All acknowledged his laws, and this faithful guide of the authors of his time serves as a model still. Follow in his footsteps, then; cherish his purity, and imitate the clarity of his felicitous style. If the sense of your verses is slow in making itself clear, my mind at once begins to relax its hold, and, promptly detaching itself from your futile discourse, refuses to follow an author who is always having to be sought out.

There are certain minds whose darksome thoughts are always cumbered with a thick cloud; the light of reason cannot pierce it. Before writing, then, learn how to think. Expression follows thought, and will be as clear or obscure as the thought was in the first place. What is clearly understood is clearly expressed, and the words to say it come easily.

Above all, let language be always sacred to you, even in the extremest moments of poetic rage. Your melodious sound is thrown away on me if the word is unsuitable or the phrase clumsily turned. My mind is not open to a pompous barbarism or to the proud solecism of a bombastic verse. In a word, without reverence for language the most godlike of authors remains, no matter what he does, a wretched writer.

Work in a leisurely way, whatever orders urge you on,[10] and don't pride yourself on excessive speed. So rapid a style, one that rhymes on the run, is less a sign of overflowing imagination than it is of little judgment. I like a brook that winds slowly over its soft sands in a meadow full of flowers, better than a torrent in flood that, with tempestuous current, rolls, full of gravel, over muddy ground. Make haste slowly; and, without losing heart, put your work back on the anvil twenty times. Polish it ceaselessly, and polish it again; add sometimes, blot out often.

It is no use for a scattering of good things to sparkle every so often in a work that swarms with faults. Everything there should be in place; the beginning, the end, should correspond with the middle; the pieces, selected and fitted together with a delicate artistry, should form no more than a single whole of various parts; never should the discourse wander too far from the subject in search of some brilliant phrase.

Do you fear for your verses the experience of public censure? Be a severe critic of yourself. Ignorance is always ready to admire itself.

Make friends who will be quick to criticize you. May they be the sincere confidants of your writings and the zealous adversaries of all your faults. In their presence lay aside the arrogance of an author. But know how to tell a friend from a flatterer, the sort that seems to be praising you but

---

[6] *Typhon ou la Gigantomachie: poème burlesque* by Paul Scarron (1610–60).

[7] [Boileau] Quacks and marionette showmen have long been in the habit of stationing themselves on the Pont Neuf.

[8] [Dilworth] From Book VII of the translation of Lucan's *Pharsalia* (1658) by Georges de Brébeuf (1617–61). He had written a burlesque of Lucan in 1656, and one of the seventh book of the *Aeneid* in 1651.

[9] [Boileau] Most of our oldest French romances, such as the *Roman de la rose* and several others, are written in a verse that is undisciplined and confused.

[10] [Boileau] Scudéry always used to say, as an excuse for working so fast, that he had orders to finish the job.

actually is mocking and deceiving you. Be pleased at advice rather than at praise.

A flatterer immediately sets to work exclaiming with admiration; every verse he hears enraptures him. Everything is charming, divine; not a word pains him. He pounds on the floor with joy, he weeps with tenderness; he piles up gorgeous panegyric all over you. Truth does not have anything like so impetuous an air.

A wise friend, always rigorous, inflexible, never gives you any peace where your faults are concerned. Your careless passages he finds quite unpardonable; badly arranged verses he sends home again; he curbs the ambitious swelling of words; here he finds that the meaning offends, and farther on it's the phrasing; "Your construction seems to grow a bit obscure." "This term is equivocal; you must clear it up." That is how a true friend talks to you. But many an author is so unreasonable as to suppose that he has an interest in preserving every one of his lines as it is, and from the first takes over the privilege of the offended party.

"The phrasing of this line," you will say, "is inelegant."

"Ah, sir," he unhesitatingly replies, "for this line I beg your indulgence!"

"This word seems flat; I would leave it out."

"But that's my finest passage!"

"This expression does not satisfy me."

"But everyone admires it!"

And so he is steadfast in unsaying nothing. If a word in his work seems to have hurt you, that is good reason for not taking it out. Yet, to hear him, he dearly loves criticism, and you exercise despotic power over his verses. But all this fine talk with which he has just flattered you is nothing but a trap to hold you while he recites them. He leaves you, shortly; and, pleased with his Muse, goes looking for some conceited ass to take advantage of—for he often finds one.

If our age is fertile in foolish authors, it is no less so in foolish admirers, and you will find them not only in town and country, but in the trains of dukes and princes. The most insipid work has always found zealous partisans at court; and—to bring this to an end at last with a touch of satire— "a fool always finds a worse fool to admire him."

Canto II

As a country lass, on the most splendid of holidays, does not load her head with rubies, or mingle with gold the flash of diamonds, but plucks in a neighboring field the finest of ornaments; so, pleasing in its air but modest in its style, should an elegant idyl shine forth. Its manner is unostentatious, simple, and artless, free of the pride of presumption. In its gentleness it should caress, tickle, arouse, never daunting the ear with grand words.

But often a rhymer working in this style will, frustrated, angrily throw down the flute and the oboe, and, in the mad inflation of his mood, burst into the middle of his eclogue with a trumpet. Pan, fleeing the sound, hides in the reeds, and in fear the nymphs retire beneath the surface of the streams.

On the other hand there is the low writer who makes his shepherds talk like ordinary villagers. His dull and boorish verses, stripped of what is attractive, are always falling on their face and groveling deplorably. It's as if Ronsard had come back to play his Gothic idyls on his rustic pipes, and, without regard for how it sounds, turn Lycidas into Pierrot, and Phyllis into Toinon.

It is not easy to find the way between these two extremes. To do so, follow Theocritus and Virgil: keep with you those delicate writings, dictated by the Graces; turn their pages day and night. Only their learned verses can teach you an author's art of coming down to earth without vulgarity; how to sing of Flora, fields, of Pomona, orchards; how to stir two shepherds into flute combat, sing the sweet lure of love, change Narcissus into a flower, cover Daphne with bark; and the art by which sometimes the eclogue still makes countryside and woods worthy of a consul. Such are the power and the grace of Virgil's poem.[11]

In a higher strain, yet not a bold one, the plaintive elegy, dressed in mourning and with disheveled hair, laments over a grave; or it may paint the joy and grief of lovers, may flatter, threaten, provoke or appease a mistress. Yet if these blessed caprices are to be well expressed, it is not enough to be a poet; one must be a lover.

I hate those empty and affected authors who tell me about their fires, always ice-cold; who suffer artful torments and, unmovedly mad, for the sake of rhyming set themselves up as lovers paralyzed with bashfulness. Their sweetest raptures are but empty phrases; all they know how to do is load themselves with chains, praise God for their martyrdom, adore their prison, and start a quarrel between reason and sensibility. It was not in this ridiculous vein that in old times Love dictated the verses in which Tibullus sighed, and, moving the tender Ovid to sweet song, passed on to us the charming lessons in his art. In elegy only the heart must speak.

The ode, more brilliant and no less vigorous, in its ambitious flight rising to heaven, holds poetical converse with the gods. It opens the barrier to the athletes in Pisa, hymns a

---

[11]Boileau has here quoted freely from *Eclogues,* IV. 3.

dusty conqueror at the end of his course, leads bloodstained Achilles to the banks of Simoïs, or makes the Schelde bow beneath the yoke of Louis. Sometimes like a bee the ode sets out with ardor to despoil the riverbank of flowers: paints feasting, dance, and laughter, boasts of a kiss plucked from the lips of Iris, softly resisting, and by sweet caprice refusing sometimes to give in order to be ravished of it. The impetuous style of the ode often moves at random; a fine disorder here is an effect of art.

Away with those timid rhymers whose phlegmatic imagination, even at its warmest, keeps to a didactic regularity; those meager historians who, in celebrating the explosive progress of a hero, follow the order of time. They don't dare even for a moment to lose sight of anything: in order to capture Dôle we must first preside at the surrender of Lille, and with a preciseness like Mézeray's,[12] we must already have knocked down the ramparts of Courtrai. Toward them Apollo was always a niggard of his fire.

It is said, by the way, that this whimsical deity, wishing once to drive French rhymers to distraction, invented the rigorous laws of the sonnet. He decreed that in two quatrains with lines all of one length, only two rhymes should strike the ear; and that six lines should follow, skillfully divided by their sense into two tercets. License he banished from this form of poem. He himself meted out its harmony and its rhythm; forbade a weak verse ever to enter it, or a word once admitted to dare show itself again. He dowered it, though, with a supreme beauty: a faultness sonnet is worth a long poem. But in vain do a thousand authors hope to arrive at one; that lucky phoenix is still to be found. In Gombauld, Maynard, and Malleville, hardly can one admire one or two in a thousand; the rest, as little read as those of Pelletier, have got from Sercy's to the grocer's in a single jump.[13] No matter what one has to say within the prescribed limits of the sonnet, there is always either too much or too little room.

The epigram, more free in its more narrow limits, is often just a witty remark ornamented with two rhyming words. Formerly unknown to our writers, conceits came into our verse from Italy. The crowd, dazzled by their false charms, ran avidly after this new attraction. Encouraged in their impudence by public favor, conceits in torrents inundated Parnassus. First off the madrigal became involved with them; the proud sonnet itself was smitten with them; tragedy

made them the delight of its life; the elegy bedecked its mournful caprices with them. A hero on the stage took care to costume himself in them, and no lover dared breathe a sigh any more that was not ingenious. All the pastoral swains, in their new complaints, were noticed to be even more faithful to conceits than to their fair ones. Every word always had two different faces, not only in verse but in prose. The lawyer in court made his style bristle with conceits; the preacher sowed the Gospel with them.

Outraged reason at last awoke and drove them out of serious discourse for good; but though declaring them disreputable in all such writing, out of mercy allowed them to appear in the epigram—so long as the wit, brilliant in relevance, turned on the thought and not on the words. And so on all sides the disorders came to an end. Yet some sorry comedians remained at court, insipid wags, pitiful buffoons, superannuated adherents of vulgar wordplay. This is not to say that no poet of any discrimination will play on a word in passing, or ever distort a meaning to good effect; but avoid any ridiculous excess of this kind, and don't always be putting a frivolous point on the tail of a foolish epigram.

Every kind of poem shines with its own beauty. There is an artlessness about the rondeau, Gallic by birth; the ballade, thrall to its old maxims, often owes all its luster to the freaks of rhyme; the madrigal, both simpler and more noble, breathes sweetness, tenderness, and love.

The desire to show itself, and not to slander, armed truth with the verse of satire. Lucilius was the first who boldly held the mirror up to the vices of the Romans. He avenged humble virtue against haughty wealth, and the honest man on foot against the rascal in a litter.

Horace mixed with this harshness his sprightliness of mind. One could no longer with impunity be either a fop or a fool; and woe to the man deserving of censure whose name could be slipped into a line without spoiling the meter!

Persius tried to put more meaning than words into his obscure but concentrated and forcible verses.

Juvenal, brought up in the clamor of school, drove his biting hyperbole beyond measure. His works, full as they are of horrid facts, sparkle with sublime beauties. Whether upon the arrival of a note from Capri he shatters the adored statue of Sejanus; whether he makes the senators run to the council as pale sycophants of a suspicious tyrant; or whether, going to an extreme of Latin luxury, he sells Messalina to the porters of Rome, his fiery works are equally brilliant.

Régnier, the ingenious disciple of these masters, in fact our only satirist who was formed on their model, has, in spite of his old-fashioned style, some fresh virtues in him. If only his discourse did not frighten away the chaste reader by being redolent of certain places frequented by the author, and

---

[12][Dilworth] François Eudes de Mézeray (1610–83), historiographer of the king and permanent secretary of the Academy. The reference is apparently to his *Chronological Compendium of the History of France*. Boileau is not speaking of historical accuracy, but of overparticularity.

[13][Dilworth] Sercy was palace bookseller. Americans may need to be reminded that in certain times and places paper has not been thrown away.

if only the boldness of his cynical lines did not often alarm the modest ear!

The Latin writer uses words that are an affront to decency. But the French reader wishes to be respected; he is outraged by the license of the least impurity of meaning, should it go undraped in chaste language. In satire give me a spirit of candor; deliver us from a shameless man who preaches a sense of shame.

Borrowing the habit this kind of poem has of making witticisms, the Frenchman, born mischievous, invented the vaudeville,[14] that pleasant indiscretion which passes singing from mouth to mouth, and grows as it goes along. In these verses French freedom displays itself: that child of pleasure chooses to be born in mirth. But, dangerous jester, see that you do not make God the subject of some dreadful piece of foolery: all these games that are started by atheism lead the joker sadly to the gallows at last.[15] Even in songs, good sense and art are necessary. Yet wine and luck have been known sometimes to inspire a thick-witted Muse, and, in the absence of genius, furnish Linière with a couplet. But take care that you don't get puffed up with foolish pride over some meaningless piece of luck that caused you to go on rhyming. It often happens that having just finished some ditty or other, the proud author immediately assumes the right to believe himself a poet. He will not sleep again till he has done a sonnet. Every morning he makes fair copies of six impromptus. In fact it's a miracle if, in his unpredictable transports, printing his ridiculous reveries, he doesn't have himself put in the front all crowned with laurels, engraved by the hand of Nanteuil.

Canto III

There is no serpent, no odious monster that, when imitated by art, cannot delight the eye; the artifice of a delicate brush turns the most frightful object into a pleasing one. Thus, to charm us, weeping tragedy told us of the agonies of blood-stained Oedipus, put into words the terror of Orestes the parricide; and then, to divert us, drew our tears.

You then who, seized with an ardent love for the theater, contend for the prize in noble verse: if you wish to put on works to which all Paris in a crowd will give its approbation, works that are always more beautiful the more they are seen, and that people still call for after twenty years have passed, then in every speech let passion seek out the heart and stir in being stirred. If the pleasing rage of a fine burst of oratory often fails to fill our soul with a beguiling pity or a gratifying terror, you parade your learned scenes in vain; your cold ratiocination can only chill a spectator already sluggish at applause, who, pardonably fatigued with the futile efforts of your rhetoric, either falls asleep or grows censorious. The secret is from the beginning to please and to touch:[16] find out ways to catch and hold me.

Let the action be planned from the very first verses to smooth my way painlessly into the subject. I am not impressed by a character who, in his slowness at expressing himself, is quite unable to tell me what he wants in the first place, and who, unskillfully disentangling a difficult plot, turns my diversion into hard labor. I would rather have him give his name with an "I am Orestes," or "Agamemnon," than set about benumbing the ears with a confused accumulation of marvels, and say nothing to the mind. It is never too soon to make the subject clear.

Let the place where the events occur be fixed, as well as clearly designated. Beyond the Pyrenees a rhymer may without peril make one day on the stage represent years; often enough the hero of one of those barbarous plays is a child in the first act and a graybeard in the last. But we, whom reason binds to its rules, prefer that the action be artfully managed—that a single thing done, in one place, in one day, hold that crowded theater to the end.

Never offer the spectator anything incredible; truth, however, may sometimes be improbable. The absurdly marvelous has no attractions for me; the mind is not affected by what it does not believe. What ought not to be seen should be narrated to us. The eyes in seeing would get a better grasp of it, but there are things that judicious art must withdraw from the eyes and offer to the ear.

Let the complications, ever increasing from scene to scene, be cleared up expeditiously once they have reached their height. The mind is never more vividly impressed than when, having been closely involved in a plot, it finds the sudden revelation of a secret changing everything, and giving an unforeseen aspect to the whole.

At its birth formless and coarse, tragedy at first consisted of nothing but a simple chorus in which the performers strove, by dancing and by singing the praises of the god of grapes, to assure themselves of a rich vintage. Wine and joy roused their spirits; the most accomplished of the singers received a he-goat as his prize.

---

[14][Dilworth] In the sense of a satiric song.
[15][Dilworth] A young poet named Petit had in 1665 been hanged and burned for a careless impiety or two.

---

[16][Dilworth] "The chief rule is to please and to touch." Racine, Preface to *Bérénice* (1670).

Thespis, besmeared with wine-lees, was the first to lead this mad happy rout through the towns, and to certain passers-by with a new spectacle put on by a cartful of ill-adorned actors.

Aeschylus put characters into the chorus, covered the faces with a more seemly mask, and set the actor, wearing a sock,[17] on the boards of a raised stage. Finally Sophocles, giving free play to his genius, increased the dignity of tragedy, made it more harmonious, interested the chorus in all the action, polished any roughness of expression, and brought the form, in Greece, to those divine heights that Latin weakness never attained to.

Since the theater was abhorred by our pious ancestors, it was for a long time in France an unknown pleasure. A band of rude pilgrims, it is said, gave the first public performance in Paris, and, foolishly zealous in their artlessness, played the parts of the saints, the Virgin, and God himself out of piety. In the end, with increase of knowledge the devout imprudence of these proceedings was recognized. These unofficial preachers were driven out; we saw the rebirth of Hector, Andromache, Ilium—only the actors laid aside the antique mask, and the place of chorus and its music was taken by the violin.

Love, fertile in tender sentiments, took possession of the theater, before long, as it had of the novel. The surest way to the heart is through a sensitive portrayal of that passion. Very well, then, paint your amorous heroes; but don't make insipid shepherds out of them: take care to draw Achilles as a different sort of lover from Thyrsis and Philène;[18] don't turn a Cyrus into an Artamène;[19] and see that love, often striven against out of compunction, appears as a weakness and not a virtue.

Preserve your heroes from the pettiness of the heroes of romance; yet give the great-hearts a few weaknesses. Achilles would be unsatisfactory if he were less hasty and hot-headed; I like to see him shed tears when he is wronged. In these little faults of character the mind takes pleasure in recognizing nature itself. Let him be drawn in your writings after this model: let Agamemnon be proud, arrogant, selfish; give Aeneas an austere reverence for his gods. Keep up the individual character of everyone. Study the customs of centuries and of countries. Different climates tend to make for different humors.

Be careful, then, not to do as is done in *Clélie*,[20] to give a French air and a French spirit to ancient Italy, and, painting our own portrait under Roman names, to make Cato a gallant and Brutus a beau. Everything is easily excusable in a novel by the frivolity of the form; fiction need do no more than amuse us for the moment. Too much severity in that moment would be unseasonable. But the stage demands exactness of judgment; strict decorum needs to be maintained there.

Are you inventing a new character? See that in everything he does he is in accord with himself, and that to the very end he is the same man as he was in the beginning.

An egotistical writer tends unconsciously to make his heroes resemble himself. In a Gascon author, the hero will be all Gascon in temperament; Calprenède and Juba[21] speak in the same strain.

Nature is more various and more wise. Each passion speaks a different language: anger is arrogant, and demands haughty words; dejection expresses itself in less lordly terms.

Do not bring the distressed Hecuba on to lament bombastically before a Troy in flames; nor, without good reason, tell us in what horrid lands "through seven mouths the Euxine receives the Tanaïs."[22] All these pompous piles of verbal trifling come from a declaimer with an appetite for words. In affliction a man must bend low. To draw tears from me, you must first weep yourself. Those big words, then, that are stuffed into the mouth of a character do not come from a heart touched by his misery.

Our theater, so fertile in caviling critics, is a perilous field to come forth in. An author makes no easy conquests there, where there are always mouths ready to hiss him. Everyone is privileged to call him an ass and an ignoramus; it's a right they buy with their ticket. To please, he must turn himself inside out a hundred ways; sometimes he has to lift his head high, sometimes abase himself; he must always everywhere be producing noble sentiments; he must be easy, solid, pleasant, profound; he must incessantly stir us with surprising touches; he must dash from marvel to marvel; and everything he says must be easy to remember and so keep his work in our heads for a long time afterwards.

This is the way tragedy acts, works, and unfolds itself.

In an even grander strain, the epic carries on its vast narrative of long-continued action. Fable is its support; it lives by the marvelous. There everything is put to work for

---

[17][Dilworth] *Cothurne* (buskin) would have fitted into the line, but the error remains.

[18][Dilworth] Thyrsis: see the first idyl of Theocritus and the seventh eclogue of Virgil. For this apparently un-Carthaginian Philaenus, see Molières' *Pastorale comique*.

[19][Dilworth] Fictional name for Cyrus, in Mlle. de Scudéry's *Le grand Cyrus* (1656).

[20]A novel by Mlle. de Scudéry.

[21]Juba is a character in the novel *Cléopâtre* by La Calprenède (1614–63).

[22][Dilworth] See the opening speech, given by Hecuba, in Seneca's *Troades*. The Tanaïs is the Don.

our enchantment. Everything takes on a body, a soul, a mind, a face. Every virtue becomes a god. Minerva is prudence, Venus beauty. There thunder is not caused by vapor, but by Jupiter, armed to terrify mankind. A terrible storm at sea is Neptune, in anger, mastering the waves. Echo is no longer a noise resounding in the air but a nymph in tears, complaining of Narcissus. And so the poet, in the midst of this throng of noble fictions, revels in a thousand devices, decorates, elevates, embellishes, ennobles all things, and finds flowers continually blossoming at his hand. For Aeneas and his ships, driven off course by the wind, to be carried by a storm to the shores of Africa is only a commonplace adventure, a hardly surprising stroke of fortune. But for Juno, constant in her hatred, to pursue over the seas the survivors of Ilium; for Aeolus to drive them from Italy for her sake by opening the Aeolian prisons of the mutinous winds; for Neptune, rising in anger over the sea, by means of a single word to calm the waves, make peace in the air above them, and wrench the ships free from Syrtis—this is what strikes us with wonder, impresses us, holds our attention.

Without all these ornaments verse grows languid; poetry dies, or feebly crawls along; and the poet is no more than a timid orator, no more than the dull teller of an empty tale.

It is likewise useless for our misguided authors to banish these long-accepted ornaments for their verse, and to try to make God, the saints, and the prophets do the work of those gods who were born of the brains of poets; to surround the reader with hellfire in every line, and offer him nothing but Ashtoreth, Beelzebub, and Lucifer. The terrible mysteries of the Christian faith cannot be brightened up by means of machinery. The Gospel affords the soul only penance on the one hand and condign torment on the other, and the ill-advised mixture of your own attempts at the marvelous gives even Gospel truth the air of fable. And after all, what a scene to present us with: the devil, in his desire to humble your hero, always raging against heaven, and often showing himself a match for God!

Tasso, it will be said, did it successfully. I do not wish to put him on trial just now, but whatever our century proclaims in his praise, his book would not have shed luster on Italy if his sage and endlessly oratorical hero had done no more than bring Satan to his senses at the end, and if Rinaldo, Argante, and Tancred and his mistress, had not relieved the dreariness of the subject.

Not that, on a Christian subject, I approve of a madly idolatrous and pagan author. But in a profane and smiling work, not to dare to use the device of fable; to drive the Tritons from their empire of the waters; to rob Pan of his flute and the Fates of their shears; to prevent Charon from ferrying monarch as well as shepherd in his fatal bark—this is to be

ridiculously ruled by an unnecessary scruple, and to attempt to please readers without giving them pleasure. It won't be long before we are forbidden to picture Prudence, to blindfold Themis and give her a pair of scales, to call before our eyes War with his brazen front, or Time who flees, hourglass in hand—and Allegory is, with mistaken zeal, driven out of all writing as a kind of idolatry. Let the zealots congratulate themselves on their pious error, but as for us, let us banish an idle fear and, fabulous Christians that we are, keep our fancy from making of the God of truth a God of lies.

Fable offers the mind a thousand delights. All its felicitous names seem born for verse: Ulysses, Agamemnon, Orestes, Idomeneus, Helen, Menelaus, Paris, Hector, Aeneas. What a project the ignorant poet has made for himself who, with all the choice of heroes, lights on Childebrand![23] The harsh or bizarre sound of a single name may burlesque or barbarize a whole poem.

Do you want your work to please for a long time and not grow wearisome? Choose a hero, then, likely to interest me—a hero splendid in his valor, magnificent in his virtues. Let everything about him, even his faults, be of heroic proportions; let his wondrous exploits be worthy of our attention: let him be of the breed of Caesar, Alexander, or Louis, not that of Polynices and his perfidious brother. One grows tired of the deeds of a commonplace conqueror.

Do not offer us a subject too full of incident. The wrath of Achilles alone, skillfully managed, abundantly satisfies what is required for an entire *Iliad.* Abundance in excess of need is likely to impoverish the whole.

In narration be quick and concise, in description opulent and stately. The latter is the place for displaying the beauties of diction. In this kind of writing, never present us with any low circumstances; do not imitate that fool[24] who, in describing the sea, and, between its parted waves the Hebrews, rescued from the yoke of their unjust masters, puts the fish at the windows to watch them pass by; and describes the little child who runs ahead, hops, and runs back, joyously offering his mother a pebble he holds in his hand. That fixes our attention on matters that are too unprofitable. Make your work of a proper size.

Let your beginning be simple and unaffected. Don't start off mounted on Pegasus and shouting in a thunderous voice, "I sing the conqueror of the conquerors of the earth."[25] What will the author produce after all this clamor?

---

[23][Dilworth] Hero of epic poem *The Saracens Driven from France,* by the Sieur de Sainte-Garde. Childebrand was a brother of Charles Martel. Not everyone in Boileau's time found the name absurdly, repulsively Gothic.

[24]Saint-Amant in his *Moïse sauvé.*

[25]From Scudéry's *Alaric.*

The mountain in labor brings forth a mouse. O how much better I like that skillful author who, without making any such exalted promises, tells me at the start, in an easy, sweet, simple, harmonious strain, "I sing of battles, and that pious man who, led from Phrygian shores to Ausonia, was the first to set foot in the Lavinian countryside." His Muse does not announce her arrival by setting the place ablaze. And to give us much, she promises us but little. You will see her, shortly, lavish of wonders, uttering oracles concerning the destiny of the Romans, painting the dark torrents of Styx and Acheron, and the Caesars already wandering in Elysium.

Enliven your work with a world of verbal figures. Let everything in it make an agreeable picture. It is quite possible to be at the same time both impressive and pleasant, and I hate a tedious and heavy sublimity. I prefer Ariosto, with his comic fables, to those cold and melancholy authors who, in their somberness, would think themselves dishonored if ever the Graces were to smooth the wrinkles from their brow.

One might say that, in order to please, Homer, taught by nature, had stolen away the girdle of Venus.[26] His book is a rich treasury of delight; everything he has touched has turned to gold. In his hands everything takes on a new grace. He never wearies us; every page is our diversion. A happy warmth animates his writing. He never loses himself in digressions. He follows no methodical plan, but his subject develops, of itself, both clearly and coherently. Without special preparative measures, everything is yet smoothly prepared for. Each line, each word, runs toward the outcome. Cherish his writings, then, with a sincere love. To know how to enjoy them is to have profited from them already. .

An excellent poem, one in which all goes forward in connected fashion, is not the sort of work to be produced by sudden impulse. It takes time and pains, and such careful craftsmanship as is never the 'prentice work of a schoolboy. But often some unskillful poet among us, in being warmed sometimes with poetic fire, inflating his chimerical fancy with futile pride, takes the heroic trumpet boldly in hand. His unruly Muse, in vagrant verses, never gets off the ground except by leaps and bounds; and his imagination, destitute of common sense and learning, faints at each step for want of nourishment. But the public, prompt to scorn him, tries in vain to disabuse him of his delusion of merit; he himself applauds his meager genius, and he with his own hands offers himself the incense that others deny him. Compared with him, Virgil has no invention; Homer knows nothing about high poetry. If his century rebels against that judg-

ment, he at once appeals to posterity. But until such time as good sense returns to us and triumphantly brings his works once more into the light of day—until then the piles of them in a dark corner of the bookshop will put up a pitiful resistance against worms and dust. Let us allow them to fight it out together in peace and quiet, and pursue our own subject without losing ourselves in bypaths.

The success of tragedy in ancient Athens was responsible for the birth of comedy. In it the Greek, born a mocker, discharged in humorous play the venom of his natural malice. Wisdom, wit, virtue were prey to insolent outbursts of farcical merriment. One saw a poet approved by the public grow rich by ridiculing merit, and Socrates, by his means, in a chorus of clouds, attract the catcalls of a vile rabble. In the end a stop was put to such license. The civil authority sought the aid of the law, and poets became better behaved in being forbidden to name names and faces. The stage lost its old fury. Comedy learned to laugh without ill-feeling, learned how to instruct and reprove without bile or venom, and gave, in the verses of Menander, an innocent pleasure. Artfully portrayed in this new mirror, one was pleased with one's reflection, or else was sure one wasn't there at all. Many a miser was the first to laugh at the faithful picture of a miser modeled on himself; and a thousand coxcombs, finely drawn, failed to recognize their own portraits.

Let nature, then, be your sole study, you who aspire to honors in comic writing. Whoever knows mankind well, and has the penetration of mind to have seen into the depths of so many hidden hearts; whoever intimately knows what a prodigal is, and a miser, an upright man, a conceited ass, a jealous man, an eccentric—he will be able to exhibit them successfully on the stage, and make them live, move, and speak for us. Make your pictures of them always natural, and painted in the most lively colors. Nature, fertile in individual character, appears in every soul marked with different traits. A gesture betrays her, the slightest little thing reveals her, but not everyone has the eyes to see her.

Time, which changes all things, changes our humors too. Every age has its pleasures, its attitude of mind, and its customs.

A young man, full of fiery impulse, is easy prey to vice; he is egotistical in his reasoning, volatile in his desires, stubborn under correction, and mad in his pleasures.

A man's next age, a riper one, has a wiser air about it. Now he pushes into the company of powerful people; he intrigues, takes care of himself, prepares to hold his own against the blows of fate, and eyes the far future in the present.

Peevish old age, an incessant accumulator, watches over the treasures it piles up, though not for itself; pursues

---

[26][Dilworth] The reference is to *Iliad*, XIV, in which Hera borrows that girdle in order to waken the interest of Zeus.

all its aims at a slow, a frozen pace; deplores the present and boasts of the past; and, incapable of pleasures in which the young are intemperate, condemns in them the sweetness of life that age refuses him.

Do not make your characters talk indiscriminately, an old man like a young one, or a young one like an old.

Study the court, be familiar with the town, for both are rich in models. If Molière had done so, he might perhaps have come away with the prize in the art he practiced; if he had been less the friend of the populace and had not so often distorted the countenances in those most skillful paintings of his; if he had not taken leave of refinement and charm for the sake of farce, and shamelessly joined Tabarin to Terence. In the ridiculous sack enveloping Scapin[27] I do not recognize the author of the *Misanthrope*.[28]

Comedy, the enemy of signs and tears, bars the tragic from its verses, but it is not its business to go into the marketplace and charm the crowds with vulgarities and dirty jokes. The figures of comedy should do their trifling nobly; its well-tied knot should untie easily. Be sure that the action, guided by reason, never gets lost on an empty stage; that the mild and lowly style of comedy raises itself up at just the proper moments. Let it be full of witty sayings, and full of passions handled with delicacy, and let the scenes always be joined one to the other.

Guard against joking at the cost of good sense. Never deviate from nature. Consider the way a father in Terence sets about rebuking a son for his imprudence in love; the way in which that lover lends an ear to his lessons, and then runs off to his mistress to forget all that nonsense. It is not a portrait, not an image or likeness; it's a real lover, a real son, a real father.

For the stage I like an agreeable writer who does not dishonor himself in the eyes of the spectator, but pleases by appealing to reason, and never offends against it. But as for the sham comedian with his dirty double meanings, who has nothing but indecency to divert me with, let him, if he will be so good, go mount a trestle-stage and amuse the lackeys of the Pont Neuf with his tasteless nonsense and his masquerades.

Canto IV

Once upon a time there lived in Florence a doctor who was a learned braggart, they say, and a celebrated assassin. For a long time he was the sole cause of public misery: here you have the orphaned son asking him to give him back a father; there, a brother mourning a brother poisoned. One man dies empty of blood, another full of senna.[29] At the sight of this doctor a cold turns into pleurisy, and with his help an aching head is soon delirious. Finally he leaves town, universally detested. The one friend of his who has remained alive takes him into his house—a superb structure. This man is a wealthy priest, mad about architecture. From the outset, our doctor sounds as if he had been born into that art; he talks about buildings like a Mansard. He condemns the façade of a new salon that is building, points out another place for the dark entrance-hall, sanctions turning the staircase the other way round. His friend takes it all in and calls for his mason. The mason comes, listens, approves, and mends his ways. Finally (to cut these wonders short) our assassin renounces his inhuman art, taking leave of the suspect science of Galen, turns himself from a bad doctor into a good architect, henceforth with rule and square in hand.

His example may stand for us as an excellent precept. Rather be a mason, if you have talent for it, rather be a respected workman in a necessary art, than a common writer and vulgar poet. In every other art there are different degrees, and one can with honor occupy the second rank; but in the perilous art of verse and prose, there are no degrees between the mediocre and the worthless. To call a man a frigid writer is to call him a detestable one. Boyer is as bad as Pinchêne, so far as the reader is concerned. Rampale and Ménardière are hardly any more often read nowadays than Magnon, du Souhait, Corbin, and La Morlière. A fool at least makes us laugh, and may cheer us up, but a frigid writer can only bore us. I prefer Bergerac, with his burlesque audacity, to those verses in which Motin, growing cold, freezes his reader.

Don't get drunk on the flattering praise you will sometimes receive from a crowd of frivolous admirers in those literary retreats where applause is so easy. A piece of writing that holds up under being read aloud may not, in print and in broad daylight, be able to endure the gaze of a penetrating eye. The tragic fate of a hundred authors is well known; and Gombauld, once so highly praised, stays in the shop unsold.

Be assiduous in seeking advice; listen to everybody: the opinion of a fool is sometimes important. No matter what verses Apollo inspires you with, don't dash off right away to read them to everybody. Take care not to be like that impetuous rhymer who greets everyone he knows with a melodious recital of his empty verses, and pursues with them people who merely pass by him in the street. The holiest of temples,

---

[27][Dilworth] Actually enveloping Géronte, but this is figuratively, enveloping the play. The plot, but not the sack, of the *Fourberies de Scapin* comes from Terence's *Phormio*.

[28]Molière.

[29]A purgative.

of which angels are in awe, is not safe from the incursions of his Muse.[30]

As I said before, be glad of censure, and, bowing to reason, correct your work without grumbling. But do not submit as soon as any fool reproves you.

Often, in his pride, a subtle ignoramus will with unjust antipathy condemn an entire play, even the noble daring of its finest verses. There is no use refuting his worthless judgments, for he is quite complacent about them; and his feeble intelligence, debilitated and deprived of light, thinks that nothing escapes it. His advice is to be feared; if you follow it you may drown while trying to avoid a reef.

Choose a solid and salutary critic, whom reason leads and knowledge lights the way for; one whose unerring pencil goes right toward the spot that one feels is weak and would prefer to conceal from oneself. He alone will clear up your foolish doubts, relieve your trembling spirit of its scruples. It is he who will tell you by what happy transport a vigorous mind, too much constrained by art, sometimes escapes from prescribed rules, having learned from art itself how to leap their bounds. But this perfect critic is rarely found. One man who excels at writing verses is stupid at judging it; another, whose verses have distinguished him, never himself distinguished Virgil from Lucan.[31]

Authors, lend an ear to my precepts. Would you have men value your rich inventions? Let your Muse, fertile in learned lessons, everywhere attach the amusing to the solid and useful. A wise reader shuns a trivial amusement; he prefers to turn his diversion to his profit.

Let your mind and morals, as reflected in your works, offer none but a worthy image of you. I cannot think well of those dangerous authors who, in verse, infamously desert from the ranks of honor, and, betraying virtue on paper, make vice attractive to the eyes of their readers.

I am not, however, one of those dismal souls who for the sake of literary purity would banish love altogether, deprive the stage of so precious an ornament, and give both Rodrigue and Chimène the name of poisoners.[32] The least virtuous love, when chastely expressed, arouses in us not the slightest shameful impulse. Dido wails and displays her charms to me in vain; I condemn her offense while sharing her tears.

The virtuous author of innocent verse may tickle the senses but does not corrupt the heart. His fire lights no criminal flame. Cherish virtue, then; nourish your soul with it. Meanness of heart will always make itself felt in a man's verses, no matter how full of noble vigor his mind may be.

Above all do not fall into that contemptible jealousy which is the malign madness of vulgar minds. A sublime writer cannot be infected with it; it's a vice that pursues mediocrity. That dark rival of bright merit cabals incessantly against him among the great, and, unable to stand as high, seeks to take him down. Let us not descend to such cowardly intrigue; let us not advance to honor by dishonorable scheming.

Do not let writing be your continual employment. Cultivate your friends, be a man to be counted on. It is a small thing to be pleasant or charming in a book; one also ought to know how to talk, and how to live.

Work for the sake of fame; sordid gain ought never to be the object of a distinguished writer. I know that a noble mind may, without disgrace and without offense, draw a legitimate tribute from his work. But I cannot put up with these renowned authors who, sated with glory and famished for money,[33] hire their Apollo out to a bookseller, and turn a divine art into a mercenary trade.

In the days before reason, unfolding itself through the voice, had instructed the human race, had taught it laws, all men followed in the ways of rude nature and, dispersed in the woods, precipitated themselves on their prey. Force stood in the place of law and equity; murder was practiced with impunity. But at last the tuneful art of expressing oneself in words softened the harshness of savage custom, brought together the scattered human beings in the forest, enclosed cities within walls and ramparts, frightened insolence with the sight of torture, and put helpless innocence under the protection of law.

They say that this order was the fruit of the first poetry ever. And thus those tales familiar everywhere: that at the strains with which Orpheus brimmed the mountains of Thrace, mollified tigers stripped themselves of their audacity; that stones moved to the chords played by Amphion, and raised themselves in order into Theban walls. These were miracles produced by harmony while it was being born. Since then, Heaven has made oracles speak in verse; Apollo breathed his rage in verse from the lips of a priest shaken with divine frenzy. Soon Homer, by bringing to life the heroes of old days, stimulated the hearts of men to new great exploits. Hesiod, in his turn, came to hasten, by useful lessons, the harvest of too sluggish fields. The wisdom of a

[30][Dilworth] Charles Dupérier (d. 1692) recited *his* verses to Boileau all during Mass. He was well known for his Latin poems.
[31]This distinction between Lucan and other writers goes back to Scaliger.
[32]Characters in Corneille's *Le Cid.* Boileau refers to Scudéry's attack upon the play in his *Observations,* part of a controversy about the play.

[33][Dilworth] According to Brossette, Boileau congratulated Corneille on the success of his tragedies and the glory they had brought him: "Yes," said Corneille, "I've had a bellyful of glory, and I'm famished for money."

thousand works was introduced to mortals with the aid of verse, and everywhere her precepts, which are conquerors of minds, being first brought in by the ear, entered into hearts. For so many blessed good deeds the revered Muses were given due homage in Greece; and their art, attracting the worship of mortals, saw altars raised to its glory in a hundred places. But in the end, poverty brought on meanness, and Parnassus forgot its original nobility; a vile appetite for gain, infecting the minds of writers, soiled all writing with gross fictions, and, giving birth to a thousand frivolous works, everywhere engaged in the buying and selling of thoughts and words.

Do not sully yourself with so low a vice. If gold alone is invincibly attractive to you avoid those charming regions that are watered by Permessus;[34] its banks are not the place where wealth resides; to the most learned authors, as to the greatest warriors, Apollo promises only a name and some laurels. "But wait a moment," says someone. "A poor and hungry Muse can't live on fame. An author who, pursued by importunate need, hears at evening the cry of his empty entrails, has little taste for a sweet promenade on Helicon. When Horace sees maenads, he has drunk his fill;[35] free from the cares of a Colletet, he can dine without waiting for the success of a sonnet."

True, and yet our own Parnassus is seldom so shockingly disgraced. What have we to fear in this century, when the arts bask in the beams of a favorable star, when the wise foresight of an enlightened prince sees to it that poverty shall be unknown to merit?

Muses, tell your nurslings how to sing his glory. His name is better for them than all your lessons. May Corneille, for his sake once more afire, be again the Corneille of *The Cid* and of *Horace.* May Racine, bringing forth new miracles, draw the pictures of all his heroes after his model. May Benserade delight all the salons with his name as warbled by the fair. May Segrais in eclogues charm the woods with that name. May the point of epigram grow finer for his sake. But what happy author will, in another *Aeneid,* lead this Alcides to the banks of the trembling Rhine? What learned lyre will make the rocks and the woods march, once more, to the sound of his exploits: will sing of Batavia dismayed in the storm, drowning herself to escape out of shipwreck; will list the battalions buried under Maestricht in those terrible attacks watched keenly by the sun?

But while I speak, new glory calls you to follow this swift conqueror into the Alps. Already Dôle and Salins have bowed beneath the yoke; Besançon on its rock still smokes from the thunderbolt. Where are all those great warriors whose fatal confederations were supposed to throw up so many barriers against this flood? Have they some idea still of arresting it while they flee, proud of the shameful distinction of having known how to evade it? How many walls pulled down! How many towns taken by force! What harvests of glory piled up along the way!

To sing them, authors, you will have to put more fuel on your fires. This is not a subject for common exertions.

As for myself, brought up on satire as I have been, I dare not handle, as yet, the trumpet and the lyre. But you will see me in this glorious field, encouraging you at least with my voice and with my eyes, offering you these lessons which my Muse, still young, brought home to Parnassus from her dealings with Horace; you will find me supporting your fervor, rousing your spirits, and showing you, far off, the garland and the prize. Yet pardon me if, full of this lofty zeal, and as a faithful observer of all the remarkable stages you have passed, sometimes I separate the true gold from the false, and attack the faults of unpolished writers—a rather tedious censor, though often a necessary one, better at blaming others than at doing well himself.

---

[34]A brook sacred to Apollo.

[35][Dilworth] Here Boileau translates Juvenal [*Satires*], VII. 59, as above, in the references to Orpheus, Amphion, and Homer, he has imitated Horace, *Art of Poetry* [p. 73].

John Locke

1632–1704

One of the most influential of English philosophers, Locke is best known for his epistemological and political views. As an epistemologist, he was an associationist who saw knowledge as beginning with simple sense perceptions (single ideas) and combining these into complex abstract ideas. He founded an empiricism based on a hard and fast distinction between the primary qualities of experience, those things that are measurable, and secondary qualities (color, smell, sound, taste, etc.), which he held to be produced as the result of the impact of the primary qualities on the passively perceiving subject. Thus Locke invented a version of the opposition between the object and the subject. Unlike the subject invented by rationalists like René Descartes, this subject is born with no innate ideas; it is a *tabula rasa,* or blank tablet, upon which natural experience writes. As a political philosopher, Locke heavily influenced the writers of the American documents of independence, holding for the equality of all human beings, a "social contract" governed by the natural law of equality, and a government operating by checks and balances.

Of his two major works, both published in 1690, *Two Treatises on Civil Government* and *An Essay Concerning Human Understanding,* the latter has a significant bearing on literary theory. In it, Locke does not speak of literature, in which he seems to have had little interest, but he does set forth as the subject of Book Three a theory of words. For Locke, words are signs of ideas, always based on experience, that precede them. Their relation to these ideas is purely arbitrary, though after repeated use they seem natural. Except for proper names, words are general and do not refer to specific objects. Rather, they signify abstract ideas built up from combinations of simple ones. These ideas are the "nominal" essences of genera and species, there being no "real" essences hidden and unknown to us. After a discussion of the "imperfection" of words and the sources of misunderstanding to which the use of language is prone, Locke remarks of the difficulties we encounter in the interpretation of ancient authors. Though they may use the same words, the ideas these words may denote can differ widely. Locke's giving the priority to ideas over words leads him in his chapter on the abuse of words to inveigh against figurative language, or tropes, "which insinuate wrong ideas, move the passions, and thereby mislead the judgment." For Locke, rhetoric is the instrument of error and deceit.

The attack on rhetoric is, of course, not new with Locke, for Plato raised similar complaints against the Sophists and invented a distrust of poetry that persisted into Locke's time and after. Both regard mathematics as the only really trustworthy language. Locke locates truth in the empirically derived ideas; Plato houses truth in a realm of pure mathematical forms.

The treatment of rhetoric since the eighteenth century has gradually turned Locke's views inside out. Words came to be seen as having a constitutive role in making ideas. The reversal culminates in recent theories like Paul de Man's, where all language is inescapably rhetorical, and in deconstruction generally, where the signified is not a prior idea but merely other words, which in turn signify other words in an infinite verbal chain where meaning (as pure idea or fixed referent) is infinitely deferred.

Locke's *Philosophical Works* were edited in 1901 by J. A. St. John. See Kenneth MacLean, *John Locke and English Literature of the Eighteenth Century* (1936); Ernest L. Tuveson, *Imagination as a Means of Grace: Locke and the Aesthetics of Romanticism* (1960); John W. Yolton, *Locke and the Compass of Human Understanding* (1970); Herman Perret, *Idéologie et sémiologie chez Locke et Condillac* (1975); I. C. Tipton, ed., *Locke on Human Understanding* (1984); and John W. Yolton, *Locke: An Introduction* (1985).

From

An Essay Concerning Human Understanding

Book Three

Chapter II

Of the Signification of Words

Sect. 1. *Words are sensible signs necessary for communication.*—Man, though he has great variety of thoughts, and such from which others, as well as himself, might receive profit and delight; yet they are all within his own breast, invisible and hidden from others, nor can of themselves be made to appear. The comfort and advantage of society not being to be had without communication of thoughts, it was necessary that man should find out some external sensible signs, whereby those invisible ideas which his thoughts are made up of, might be made known to others. For this purpose nothing was so fit, either for plenty or quickness, as those articulate sounds, which, with so much ease and variety, he found himself able to make. Thus we may conceive how words which were by nature so well adapted to that purpose, come to be made use of by men, as the signs of their ideas; not by any natural connexion that there is between particular articulate sounds, and certain ideas, for then there would be but one language among all men: but by a voluntary imposition, whereby such a word is made arbitrarily the mark of such an idea. The use then of words is to be sensible marks of ideas; and the ideas they stand for are their proper and immediate signification.

Sect. 2. *Words are the sensible signs of his ideas who uses them.*—The use men have of these marks being either to record their own thoughts for the assistance of their own memory, or, as it were, to bring out their ideas, and lay them before the view of others; words in their primary or immediate signification stand for nothing but the ideas in the mind of him that uses them, how imperfectly soever or carelessly those ideas are collected from the things which they are supposed to represent. When a man speaks to another, it is that he may be understood; and the end of speech is, that those sounds, as marks, may make known his ideas to the hearer. That then which words are the marks of, are the ideas of the speaker: nor can any one apply them as marks immediately to any thing else but the ideas that he himself hath. For this would be to make them signs of his own conceptions, and yet apply them to other ideas; which would be to make them signs, and not signs of his ideas at the same time; and so, in effect, to have no signification at all. Words being voluntary signs, they cannot be voluntary signs imposed by him on things he knows not. That would be to make them signs of nothing, sounds without signification. A man cannot make his words the signs either of qualities in things, or of conceptions in the mind of another, whereof he has none in his own. Until he has some ideas of his own, he cannot suppose them to correspond with the conceptions of another man; nor can he use any signs for them; for thus they would be the signs of he knows not what, which is, in truth, to be the signs of nothing. But when he represents to himself other men's ideas by some of his own, if he consent to give them the same names that other men do, it is still to his own ideas; to ideas that he has, and not to ideas that he has not.

Sect. 3. This is so necessary in the use of language, that in this respect the knowing and the ignorant, the learned and unlearned, use the words they speak (with any meaning) all

---

AN ESSAY CONCERNING HUMAN UNDERSTANDING. *An Essay Concerning Human Understanding* was first published in London in 1690.

alike. They, in every man's mouth, stand for the ideas he has, and which he would express by them. A child having taken notice of nothing in the metal he hears called gold, but the bright shining yellow colour, he applies the word gold only to his own idea of that colour, and nothing else; and therefore calls the same colour in a peacock's tail, gold. Another, that hath better observed, adds to shining yellow great weight; and then the sound gold, when he uses it, stands for a complex idea of a shining yellow, and very weighty substance. Another adds to those qualities, fusibility: and then the word gold signifies to him a body, bright, yellow, fusible, and very heavy. Another adds malleability. Each of these uses equally the word gold, when they have occasion to express the idea which they have applied it to; but it is evident, that each can apply it only to his own idea; nor can he make it stand as a sign of such a complex idea as he has not.

Sect. 4. *Words often secretly referred, first, to the ideas in other men's minds.*—But though words, as they are used by men, can properly and immediately signify nothing but the ideas that are in the mind of the speaker; yet they in their thoughts give them a secret reference to two other things.

First, They suppose their words to be marks of the ideas in the minds also of other men, with whom they communicate: for else they should talk in vain, and could not be understood, if the sounds they applied to one idea were such as by the hearer were applied to another; which is to speak two languages. But in this, men stand not usually to examine whether the idea they and those they discourse with have in their minds be the same: but think it enough that they use the word, as they imagine, in the common acceptation of that language; in which they suppose that the idea they make it a sign of is precisely the same, to which the understanding men of that country apply that name.

Sect. 5. *Secondly, to the reality of things.*—Secondly, Because men would not be thought to talk barely of their own imaginations, but of things as really they are; therefore they often suppose their words to stand also for the reality of things. But this relating more particularly to substances, and their names, as perhaps the former does to simple ideas and modes, we shall speak of these two different ways of applying words more at large, when we come to treat of the names of mixed modes and substances in particular: though give me leave here to say, that it is a perverting the use of words, and brings unavoidable obscurity and confusion into their signification, whenever we make them stand for any thing but those ideas we have in our own minds.

Sect. 6. *Words by use readily excite ideas.*—Concerning words, also, it is farther to be considered: first, that they being immediately the signs of men's ideas; and by that means the instruments whereby men communicate their con-

ceptions, and express to one another those thoughts and imaginations they have within their own breasts; there comes by constant use to be such a connexion between certain sounds and the ideas they stand for, that the names heard almost as readily excite certain ideas, as if the objects themselves, which are apt to produce them, did actually affect the senses. Which is manifestly so in all obvious sensible qualities, and in all substances that frequently and familiarly occur to us.

Sect. 7. *Words often used without signification.*—Secondly, That though the proper and immediate signification of words are ideas in the mind of the speaker, yet because by familiar use from our cradles we come to learn certain articulate sounds very perfectly, and have them readily on our tongues, and always at hand in our memories, but yet are not always careful to examine or settle their significations perfectly; it often happens that men, even when they would apply themselves to an attentive consideration, do set their thoughts more on words than things. Nay, because words are many of them learned before the ideas are known for which they stand; therefore some, not only children, but men, speak several words no otherwise than parrots do, only because they have learned them, and have been accustomed to those sounds. But so far as words are of use and signification, so far is there a constant connexion between the sound and the idea, and a designation that the one stands for the other; without which application of them, they are nothing but so much insignificant noise.

Sect. 8. *Their signification perfectly arbitrary.*—Words, by long and familiar use, as has been said, come to excite in men certain ideas so constantly and readily, that they are apt to suppose a natural connexion between them. But that they signify only men's peculiar ideas, and that by a perfect arbitrary imposition, is evident, in that they often fail to excite in others (even that use the same language) the same ideas we take them to be the signs of; and every man has so inviolable a liberty to make words stand for what ideas he pleases, that no one hath the power to make others have the same ideas in their minds that he has, when they use the same words that he does. And therefore the great Augustus himself, in the possession of that power which ruled the world, acknowledged he could not make a new Latin word; which was as much as to say, that he could not arbitrarily appoint what idea any sound should be a sign of in the mouths and common language of his subjects. It is true, common use, by a tacit consent, appropriates certain sounds to certain ideas in all languages, which so far limits the signification of that sound, that unless a man applies it to the same idea, he does not speak properly: and let me add, that unless a man's words excite the same ideas in the hearer which he makes them stand for in speaking, he does not speak intelligibly. But whatever be the consequence of any man's using of words differently, either from their general meaning, or the particular sense of the person to whom he addresses them, this is certain their signification, in his use of them, is limited to his ideas, and they can be signs of nothing else.

Chapter III

Of General Terms

Sect. 1. *The greatest part of words general.*—All things that exist being particulars, it may perhaps be thought reasonable that words, which ought to be conformed to things, should be so too; I mean in their signification: but yet we find the quite contrary. The far greatest part of words, that make all languages, are general terms; which has not been the effect of neglect or chance, but of reason and necessity.

Sect. 2. *For every particular thing to have a name is impossible.*—First, It is impossible that every particular thing should have a distinct peculiar name. For the signification and use of words, depending on that connexion which the mind makes between its ideas, and the sounds it uses as signs of them, it is necessary, in the application of names to things, that the mind should have distinct ideas of the things, and retain also the particular name that belongs to every one, with its peculiar appropriation to that idea. But it is beyond the power of human capacity to frame and retain distinct ideas of all the particular things we meet with; every bird and beast men saw, every tree and plant that affected the senses could not find a place in the most capacious understanding. If it be looked on as an instance of a prodigious memory, that some generals have been able to call every soldier in their army by his proper name, we may easily find a reason why men have never attempted to give names to each sheep in their flock, or crow that flies over their head; much less to call every leaf of plants, or grain of sand that came in their way, by a peculiar name.

Sect. 3. *And useless.*—Secondly, If it were possible, it would yet be useless; because it would not serve to the chief end of language. Men would in vain heap up names of particular things that would not serve them to communicate their thoughts. Men learn names, and use them in talk with others, only that they may be understood; which is then only done, when by use or consent the sound I make by the organs of speech excites in another man's mind, who hears it, the idea I apply it to in mine, when I speak it. This cannot be done by names applied to particular things, whereof I alone having the ideas in my mind, the names of them could not

be significant or intelligible to another who was not acquainted with all those very particular things which had fallen under my notice.

Sect. 4. Thirdly, But yet granting this also feasible (which I think is not), yet a distinct name for every particular thing would not be of any great use for the improvement of knowledge; which, though founded in particular things, enlarges itself by general views; to which things reduced, into sorts under general names, are properly subservient. These, with the names belonging to them, come within some compass, and do not multiply every moment, beyond what either the mind can contain, or use requires: and therefore, in these, men have for the most part stopped; but yet not so as to hinder themselves from distinguishing particular things by appropriated names where convenience demands it. And therefore in their own species, which they have most to do with, and wherein they have often occasion to mention particular persons, they make use of proper names; and their distinct individuals have distinct denominations.

Sect. 5. *What things have proper names.*—Besides persons, countries also, cities, rivers, mountains, and other the like distinctions of place, have usually found peculiar names, and that for the same reason; they being such as men have often an occasion to mark particularly, and, as it were, set before others in their discourses with them. And I doubt not, but if we had reason to mention particular horses, as often as we have to mention particular men we should have proper names for the one as familiar as for the other; and Bucephalus would be a word as much in use as Alexander. And therefore we see that, among jockies, horses have their proper names to be known and distinguished by as commonly as their servants; because, among them, there is often occasion to mention this or that particular horse, when he is out of sight.

Sect. 6. *How general words are made.*—The next thing to be considered is, how general words come to be made. For since all things that exist are only particulars, how come we by general terms, or where find we those general natures they are supposed to stand for? Words become general, by being made the signs of general ideas; and ideas become general, by separating from them the circumstances of time, and place, and any other ideas, that may determine them to this or that particular existence. By this way of abstraction, they are made capable of representing more individuals than one; each of which having in it a conformity to that abstract idea, is (as we call it) of that sort.

Sect. 7. But to deduce this a little more distinctly, it will not perhaps be amiss to trace our notions and names from their beginning, and observe by what degrees we proceed, and by what steps we enlarge our ideas from our first infancy. There is nothing more evident, than that the ideas of the persons children converse with (to instance in them alone) are like the persons themselves, only particular. The ideas of the nurse and the mother are well framed in their minds; and, like pictures of them there, represent only those individuals. The names they first gave to them are confined to these individuals; and the names of nurse and mamma the child uses, determine themselves to those persons. Afterwards, when time and a larger acquaintance have made them observe, that there are a great many other things in the world, that in some common agreements of shape, and several other qualities, resemble their father and mother, and those persons they have been used to, they frame an idea, which they find those many particulars do partake in; and to that they give, with others, the name man for example. And thus they come to have a general name, and a general idea. Wherein they make nothing new, but only leave out the complex idea they had of Peter and James, Mary and Jane, that which is peculiar to each, and retain only what is common to them all.

Sect. 8. By the same way that they come by the general name and idea of man, they easily advance to more general names and notions. For observing that several things that differ from their idea of man, and cannot therefore be comprehended under that name, have yet certain qualities, wherein they agree with man, by retaining only those qualities, and uniting them into one idea, they have again another and more general idea; to which having given a name, they make a term of a more comprehensive extension: which new idea is made, not by any new addition, but only, as before, by leaving out the shape, and some other properties signified by the name man, and retaining only a body, with life, sense, and spontaneous motion, comprehended under the name animal.

Sect. 9. *General natures are nothing but abstract ideas.*—That this is the way whereby men first formed general ideas, and general names to them, I think, is so evident, that there needs no other proof of it, but the considering of a man's self, or others, and the ordinary proceedings of their minds in knowledge: and he that thinks general natures or notions are any thing else but such abstract and partial ideas of more complex ones, taken at first from particular existences, will, I fear, be at a loss where to find them. For let any one reflect, and then tell me, wherein does his idea of man differ from that of Peter and Paul; or his idea of horse from that of Bucephalus, but in the leaving out something that is peculiar to each individual, and retaining so much of those particular complex ideas of several particular existences as they are found to agree in? Of the complex ideas signified by the names man and horse leaving out but those particulars wherein they differ, and retaining only those wherein they agree, and of those making a new distinct com-

plex idea, and giving the name animal to it; one has a more general term, that comprehends with man several other creatures. Leave out of the idea of animal, sense and spontaneous motion; and the remaining complex idea, made up of the remaining simple ones of body, life and nourishment, becomes a more general one, under the more comprehensive term *vivens.* And not to dwell longer upon this particular, so evident in itself, by the same way the mind proceeds to body, substance, and at last to being, thing, and such universal terms, which stand for any of our ideas whatsoever. To conclude, this whole mystery of *genera* and *species,* which make such a noise in the schools, and are with justice so little regarded out of them, is nothing else but abstract ideas, more or less comprehensive, with names annexed to them. In all which this is constant and unvariable, that every more general term stands for such an idea, as is but a part of any of those contained under it.

Sect. 10. *Why the genus is ordinarily made use of in definitions.*—This may show us the reason why, in the defining of words, which is nothing but declaring their significations, we make use of the genus, or next general word that comprehends it. Which is not out of necessity, but only to save the labour of enumerating the several simple ideas, which the next general word or genus stands for; or, perhaps, sometimes the shame of not being able to do it. But though defining by *genus* and *differentia* (I crave leave to use these terms of art, though originally Latin, since they most properly suit those notions they are applied to) I say, though defining by the *genus* be the shortest way, yet I think it may be doubted whether it be the best. This I am sure, it is not the only, and so not absolutely necessary. For definition being nothing but making another understand by words what idea the term defined stands for, a definition is best made by enumerating those simple ideas that are combined in the signification of the term defined; and if instead of such an enumeration men have accustomed themselves to use the next general term, it has not been out of necessity, or for greater clearness, but for quickness and despatch sake. For, I think, that to one who desired to know what idea the word man stood for, it should be said, that man was a solid extended substance, having life, sense, spontaneous motion, and the faculty of reasoning; I doubt not but the meaning of the term man would be as well understood, and the idea it stands for be at least as clearly made known, as when it is defined to be a rational animal: which, by the several definitions of animal, *vivens,* and *corpus,* resolves itself into those enumerated ideas. I have, in explaining the term man, followed here the ordinary definition of the schools: which though, perhaps, not the most exact, yet serves well enough to my present purpose. And one may, in this instance, see what gave occasion to the rule, that a definition must consist of *genus* and *differentia;* and it suffices to show us the little necessity there is of such a rule, or advantage in the strict observing of it. For definitions, as has been said, being only the explaining of one word by several others, so that the meaning or idea it stands for may be certainly known; languages are not always so made according to the rules of logic, that every term can have its signification exactly and clearly expressed by two others. Experience sufficiently satisfies us to the contrary; or else those who have made this rule have done ill, that they have given us so few definitions conformable to it. But of definitions, more in the next chapter.

Sect. 11. *General and universal are creatures of the understanding.*—To return to general words, it is plain by what has been said, that general and universal belong not to the real existence of things; but are the inventions and creatures of the understanding, made by it, for its own use, and concern only signs, whether words or ideas. Words are general, as has been said, when used for signs of general ideas, and so are applicable indifferently to many particular things: and ideas are general, when they are set up as the representatives of many particular things; but universality belongs not to things themselves which are all of them particular in their existence; even those words and ideas which in their signification are general. When therefore we quit particulars, the generals that rest are only creatures, of our own making; their general nature being nothing but the capacity they are put into by the understanding, of signifying or representing many particulars. For the signification they have is nothing but a relation, that by the mind of man is added to them.

Sect. 12. *Abstract ideas are the essences of the genera and species.*—The next thing therefore to be considered is, what kind of signification it is that general words have. For, as it is evident that they do not signify barely one particular thing; for then they would not be general terms, but proper names; so on the other side it is as evident, they do not signify a plurality; for man and men would then signify the same, and the distinction of numbers (as the grammarians call them) would be superfluous and useless. That then which general words signify is a sort of things; and each of them does that by being a sign of an abstract idea in the mind, to which idea, as things existing are found to agree, so they come to be ranked under that name; or, which is all one, be of that sort. Whereby, it is evident that the essences of the sorts, or (if the Latin word pleases better) species of things, are nothing else but these abstract ideas. For the having the essence of any species being that which makes any thing to be of that species, and the conformity to the idea to which the name is annexed being that which gives a right to

that name; the having the essence, and the having that conformity, must needs be the same thing; since to be of any species, and to have a right to the name of that species, is all one. As, for example, to be a man, or of the species man, and to have a right to the name man, is the same thing. Again, to be a man or of the species man, and have the essence of a man, is the same thing. Now since nothing can be a man, or have a right to the name man, but what has a conformity to the abstract idea the name man stands for; nor any thing be a man, or have a right to the species man, but what has the essence of that species: it follows that the abstract idea for which the name stands, and the essence of the species is one and the same. From whence it is easy to observe, that the essences of the sorts of things, and consequently the sorting of this, is the workmanship of the understanding, that abstracts and makes those general ideas.

Sect. 13. *They are the workmanship of the understanding, but have their foundation in the similitude of things.*—I would not here be thought to forget, much less to deny, that nature in the production of things makes several of them alike; there is nothing more obvious, especially in the races of animals and all things propagated by seed. But yet, I think, we may say the sorting of them under names is the workmanship of the understanding, taking occasion from the similitude it observes among them to make abstract general ideas, and set them up in the mind, with names annexed to them, as patterns or forms (for in that sense the word form has a very proper signification), to which as particular things existing are found to agree, so they come to be of that species, have that denomination, or are put into that *classis.* For when we say, this is a man, that a horse; this justice, that cruelty; this a watch, that a jack; what do we else but rank things under different specific names, as agreeing to those abstract ideas, of which we have made those names the signs? And what are the essences of those species, set out and marked by names, but those abstract ideas in the mind; which are, as it were, the bonds between particular things that exist, and the names they are to be ranked under? And when general names have any connexion with particular beings, these abstract ideas are the medium that unites them; so that the essences of species, as distinguished and denominated by us, neither are, nor can be any thing, but those precise abstract ideas we have in our minds. And therefore the supposed real essences of substances, if different from our abstract ideas, cannot be the essences of the species we rank things into. For two species may be one as rationally as two different essences be the essence of one species: and I demand what are the alterations may, or may not, be in a horse or lead, without making either of them to be of another species? In determining the species of things by our abstract ideas, this is easy to resolve: but if any one will regulate himself herein by supposed real essences, he will, I suppose, be at a loss; and he will never be able to know when any thing precisely ceases to be of the species of a horse or lead.

Sect. 14. *Each distinct abstract idea is a distinct essence.*—Nor will any one wonder that I say these essences, or abstract ideas (which are the measures of name, and the boundaries of species), are the workmanship of the understanding, who considers, that at least the complex ones are often, in several men, different collections of simple ideas; and therefore that is covetousness to one man, which is not so to another. Nay, even in substances, where their abstract ideas seem to be taken from the things themselves, they are not constantly the same; no, not in that species which is most familiar to us, and with which we have the most intimate acquaintance; it having been more than once doubted, whether the fœtus born of a woman were a man; even so far, as that it hath been debated, whether it were, or were not to be nourished and baptized; which could not be, if the abstract idea or essence, to which the name man belonged, were of nature's making, and were not the uncertain and various collection of simple ideas, which the understanding puts together, and then abstracting it, affixed a name to it. So that in truth every distinct abstract idea is a distinct essence: and the names that stand for such distinct ideas are the names of things essentially different. Thus a circle is as essentially different from an oval, as a sheep from a goat; and rain is as essentially different from snow, as water from earth; the abstract idea which is the essence of one being impossible to be communicated to the other. And thus any two abstract ideas, that in any part vary one from another, with two distinct names annexed to them, constitute two distinct sorts, or, if you please, species, as essentially different, as any two of the most remote or opposite in the world.

Sect. 15. *Real and nominal essences.*—But since the essences of things are thought by some (and not without reason) to be wholly unknown, it may not be amiss to consider the several significations of the word essence.

First, essence may be taken for the being of any thing, whereby it is what it is. And thus the real internal, but generally, in substances, unknown constitution of things, whereon their discoverable qualities depend, may be called their essence. This is the proper original signification of the word, as is evident from the formation of it; *essentia,* in its primary notation, signifying properly being. And in this sense it is still used, when we speak of the essence of particular things, without giving them any name.

Secondly, the learning and disputes of the schools having been much busied about genus and species, the word essence has almost lost its primary signification; and instead of the real constitution of things, has been almost wholly applied to the artificial constitution of genus and species. It is true, there is ordinarily supposed a real constitution of the sorts of things; and it is past doubt, there must be some real constitution, on which any collection of simple ideas coexisting must depend. But it being evident that things are ranked under names into sorts or species, only as they agree to certain abstract ideas to which we have annexed those names, the essence of each genus or sort comes to be nothing but that abstract idea, which the general or sortal (if I may have leave so to call it from sort, as I do general from genus) name stands for. And this we shall find to be that which the word essence imports in its most familiar use. These two sorts of essences, I suppose, may not unfitly be termed, the one the real, the other the nominal essence.

Sect. 16. *Constant connexion between the name and nominal essence.*—Between the nominal essence and the name there is so near a connexion, that the name of any sort of things cannot be attributed to any particular being but what has this essence, whereby it answers that abstract idea, whereof that name is the sign.

Sect. 17. *Supposition, that species are distinguished by their real essences, useless.*—Concerning the real essences of corporeal substances (to mention these only), there are, if I mistake not, two opinions. The one is of those who, using the word essence for they know not what, suppose a certain number of those essences, according to which all natural things are made, and wherein they do exactly every one of them partake, and so become of this or that species. The other and more rational opinion is, of those who look on all natural things to have a real, but unknown constitution of their insensible parts; from which flow those sensible qualities which serve us to distinguish them one from another, according as we have occasion to rank them into sorts under common denominations. The former of these opinions, which supposes these essences as a certain number of forms or moulds, wherein all natural things that exist are cast and do equally partake, has, I imagine, very much perplexed the knowledge of natural things. The frequent productions of monsters, in all the species of animals, and of changelings and other strange issues of human birth, carry with them difficulties not possible to consist with this hypothesis: since it is as impossible that two things, partaking exactly of the same real essence, should have different properties, as that two figures partaking of the same real essence of a circle should have different properties. But were there no other reason against it, yet the supposition of essences that cannot be known, and the making of them nevertheless to be that which distinguishes the species of things, is so wholly useless and unserviceable to any part of our knowledge, that that alone were sufficient to make us lay it by, and content ourselves with such essences of the sorts or species of things, as come within the reach of our knowledge; which, when seriously considered, will be found, as I have said, to be nothing else but those abstract complex ideas to which we have annexed distinct general names.

Sect. 18. *Real and nominal essence the same in simple ideas and modes, different in substances.*—Essences being thus distinguished into nominal and real, we may farther observe, that in the species of simple ideas and modes, they are always the same, but in substances, always quite different. Thus a figure, including a space between three lines, is the real as well as nominal essence of a triangle; it being not only the abstract idea to which the general name is annexed, but the very *essentia* or being of the thing itself, that foundation from which all its properties flow, and to which they are all inseparably annexed. But it is far otherwise concerning that parcel of matter which makes the ring on my finger, wherein these two essences are apparently different. For it is the real constitution of its insensible parts, on which depend all those properties of colour, weight, fusibility, fixedness, &c. which are to be found in it, which constitution we know not, and so having no particular idea of, have no name that is the sign of it. But yet it is its colour, weight, fusibility, fixedness, &c. which makes it to be gold, or gives it a right to that name, which is therefore its nominal essence; since nothing can be called gold, but what has a conformity of qualities to that abstract complex idea to which that name is annexed. But this distinction of essences belonging particularly to substances, we shall, when we come to consider their names, have an occasion to treat of more fully.

Sect. 19. *Essences ingenerable and incorruptible.*— That such abstract ideas, with names to them, as we have been speaking of, are essences, may farther appear by what we are told concerning essences, viz. that they are all ingenerable and incorruptible: which cannot be true of the real constitutions of things, which begin and perish with them. All things that exist, besides their author, are all liable to change; especially those things we are acquainted with, and have ranked into bands under distinct names or ensigns. Thus that which was grass to-day is to-morrow the flesh of a sheep, and within a few days after becomes part of a man: in all which, and the like changes, it is evident their real essence, *i. e.* that constitution, whereon the properties of these several things depended, is destroyed, and perishes with them. But essences being taken for ideas, established in the mind, with names annexed to them, they are supposed to remain steadily the same, whatever mutations the particular substances are liable to. For whatever becomes of Alexander

and Bucephalus, the ideas to which man and horse are annexed are supposed nevertheless to remain the same; and so the essences of those species are preserved whole and undestroyed, whatever changes happen to any or all of the individuals of those species. By this means, the essence of a species rests safe and entire, without the existence of so much as one individual of that kind. For were there now no circle existing any where in the world (as perhaps that figure exists not any where exactly marked out), yet the idea annexed to that name would not cease to be what it is; nor cease to be as a pattern to determine which of the particular figures we meet with have or have not a right to the name circle, and so to show which of them, by having that essence, was of that species. And though there neither were nor had been in nature such a beast as an unicorn, or such a fish as a mermaid; yet supposing those names to stand for complex abstract ideas, that contained no inconsistency in them, the essence of a mermaid is as intelligible as that of a man; and the idea of an unicorn as certain, steady, and permanent as that of a horse. From what has been said, it is evident, that the doctrine of the immutability of essences proves them to be only abstract ideas; and is founded on the relation established between them and certain sounds as signs of them; and will always be true as long as the same name can have the same signification.

Sect. 20. *Recapitulation.*—To conclude, this is that which in short I would say, viz. that all the great business of *genera* and species, and their essences, amounts to no more but this, that men making abstract ideas, and settling them in their minds with names annexed to them, do thereby enable themselves to consider things, and discourse of them, as it were in bundles, for the easier and readier improvement and communication of their knowledge; which would advance but slowly, were their words and thoughts confined only to particulars.

Chapter IX

Of the Imperfection of Words

Sect. 1. *Words are used for recording and communicating our thoughts.*—From what has been said in the foregoing chapters, it is easy to perceive what imperfection there is in language, and how the very nature of words makes it almost unavoidable for many of them to be doubtful and uncertain in their significations. To examine the perfection or imperfection of words it is necessary first to consider their use and end: for as they are more or less fitted to attain that, so are they more or less perfect. We have, in the former part of this discourse, often upon occasion mentioned a double use of words.

First, one for the recording of our own thoughts.

Secondly, the other for the communicating of our thoughts to others.

Sect. 2. *Any words will serve for recording.*—As to the first of these, for the recording our own thoughts for the help of our own memories, whereby, as it were, we talk to ourselves, any words will serve the turn. For since sounds are voluntary and indifferent signs of any ideas, a man may use what words he pleases, to signify his own ideas to himself; and there will be no imperfection in them, if he constantly use the same sign for the same idea, for then he cannot fail of having his meaning understood, wherein consists the right use and perfection of language.

Sect. 3. *Communication by words civil or philosophical.*—As to communication of words, that too has a double use.

I. Civil.

II. Philosophical.

First, by their civil use, I mean such a communication of thoughts and ideas by words, as may serve for the upholding common conversation and commerce, about the ordinary affairs and conveniences of civil life, in the societies of men one among another.

Secondly, by the philosophical use of words, I mean such a use of them as may serve to convey the precise notions of things, and to express, in general propositions, certain and undoubted truths, which the mind may rest upon, and be satisfied with, in its search after true knowledge. These two uses are very distinct, and a great deal less exactness will serve in the one than in the other, as we shall see in what follows.

Sect. 4. *The imperfection of words in the doubtfulness of their signification.*—The chief end of language in communication being to be understood, words serve not well for that end, neither in civil nor philosophical discourse, when any word does not excite in the hearer the same idea which it stands for in the mind of the speaker. Now since sounds have no natural connexion with our ideas, but have all their signification from the arbitrary imposition of men, the doubtfulness and uncertainty of their signification, which is the imperfection we here are speaking of, has its cause more in the ideas they stand for, than in any incapacity there is in one sound more than in another, to signify any idea: for in that regard they are all equally perfect.

That then which makes doubtfulness and uncertainty in the signification of some more than other words, is the difference of ideas they stand for.

Sect. 5. *Causes of their imperfection.*—Words having naturally no signification, the idea which each stands for must be learned and retained by those who would exchange thoughts, and hold intelligible discourse with others in any language. But this is hardest to be done where,

First, the ideas they stand for are very complex, and made up of a great number of ideas put together.

Secondly, where the ideas they stand for have no certain connexion in nature; and so no settled standard, any where in nature existing, to rectify and adjust them by.

Thirdly, when the signification of the word is referred to a standard, which standard is not easy to be known.

Fourthly, where the signification of the word, and the real essence of the thing, are not exactly the same.

These are difficulties that attend the signification of several words that are intelligible. Those which are not intelligible at all, such as names standing for any simple ideas, which another has not organs or faculties to attain,—as the names of colours to a blind man, or sounds to a deaf man,—need not here be mentioned.

In all these cases we shall find an imperfection in words, which I shall more at large explain, in their particular application to our several sorts of ideas; for if we examine them, we shall find that the names of mixed modes are most liable to doubtfulness and imperfection, for the two first of these reasons; and the names of substances chiefly for the two latter.

Sect. 6. *The names of mixed modes doubtful.*—First, the names of mixed modes are many of them liable to great uncertainty and obscurity in their signification.

First, because the ideas they stand for are so complex.—I. Because of that great composition these complex ideas are often made up of. To make words serviceable to the end of communication, it is necessary (as has been said) that they excite in the hearer exactly the same idea they stand for in the mind of the speaker. Without this, men fill one another's heads with noise and sounds; but convey not thereby their thoughts, and lay not before one another their ideas, which is the end of discourse and language. But when a word stands for a very complex idea that is compounded and decompounded, it is not easy for men to form and retain that idea so exactly as to make the name in common use stand for the same precise idea, without any the least variation. Hence it comes to pass, that men's names of very compound ideas, such as for the most part are moral words, have seldom, in two different men, the same precise signification; since one man's complex idea seldom agrees with another's, and often differs from his own, from that which be had yesterday, or will have to-morrow.

Sect. 7. *Secondly, because they have no standards.*—
II. Because the names of mixed modes, for the most part, want standards in nature, whereby men may rectify and adjust their significations; therefore they are very various and doubtful. They are assemblages of ideas put together at the pleasure of the mind, pursuing its own ends of discourse, and suited to its own notions; whereby it designs not to copy any thing really existing, but to denominate and rank things, as they come to agree with those archetypes or forms it has made. He that first brought the word sham, or wheedle, or banter, in use, put together, as he thought fit, those ideas he made it stand for; and as it is with any new names of modes, that are now brought into any language, so it was with the old ones, when they were first made use of. Names therefore that stand for collections of ideas which the mind makes at pleasure, must needs be of doubtful signification, when such collections are nowhere to be found constantly united in nature, nor any patterns to be shown whereby men may adjust them. What the word murder, or sacrilege, &c. signifies, can never be known from things themselves: there be many of the parts of those complex ideas which are not visible in the action itself; the intention of the mind, or the relation of holy things, which make a part of murder or sacrilege, have no necessary connexion with the outward and visible action of him that commits either: and the pulling the trigger of the gun, with which the murder is committed, and is all the action that perhaps is visible, has no natural connexion with those other ideas that make up the complex one, named murder. They have their union and combination only from the understanding, which unites them under one name: but uniting them without any rule or pattern, it cannot be but that the signification of the name that stands for such voluntary collections should be often various in the minds of different men, who have scarce any standing rule to regulate themselves and their notions by, in such arbitrary ideas.

Sect. 8. *Propriety not a sufficient remedy.*—It is true, common use, that is the rule of propriety, may be supposed here to afford some aid, to settle the signification of language; and it cannot be denied but that in some measure it does. Common use regulates the meaning of words pretty well for common conversation; but nobody having an authority to establish the precise signification of words, nor determine to what ideas any one shall annex them, common use is not sufficient to adjust them to philosophical discourses; there being scarce any name of any very complex idea (to say nothing of others) which in common use has not a great latitude, and which, keeping within the bounds of propriety, may not be made the sign of far different ideas.

Besides, the rule and measure of propriety itself being nowhere established, it is often matter of dispute whether this or that way of using a word be propriety of speech or no. From all which it is evident, that the names of such kind of very complex ideas are naturally liable to this imperfection, to be of doubtful and uncertain signification; and even in men that have a mind to understand one another, do not always stand for the same idea in speaker and hearer. Though the names glory and gratitude be the same in every man's mouth through a whole country, yet the complex collective idea, which every one thinks on, or intends by that name, is apparently very different in men using the same language.

Sect. 9. *The way of learning these names contributes also to their doubtfulness.*—The way also wherein the names of mixed modes are ordinarily learned, does not a little contribute to the doubtfulness of their signification. For if we will observe how children learn languages, we shall find that to make them understand what the names of simple ideas, or substances, stand for, people ordinarily show them the thing whereof they would have them have the idea; and then repeat to them the name that stands for it, as white, sweet, milk, sugar, cat, dog. But as for mixed modes, especially the most material of them, moral words, the sounds are usually learned first; and then to know what complex ideas they stand for, they are either beholden to the explication of others, or (which happens for the most part) are left to their own observation and industry; which being little laid out in the search of the true and precise meaning of names, these moral words are in most men's mouths little more than bare sounds; or when they have any, it is for the most part but a very loose and undetermined, and consequently obscure and confused signification. And even those themselves, who have with more attention settled their notions, do yet hardly avoid the inconvenience, to have them stand for complex ideas, different from those which other, even intelligent and studious men, make them the signs of. Where shall one find any, either controversial debate, or familiar discourse, concerning honour, faith, grace, religion, church, &c. wherein it is not easy to observe the different notions men have of them? which is nothing but this, that they are not agreed in the signification of those words, nor have in their minds the same complex ideas which they make them stand for: and so all the contests that follow thereupon are only about the meaning of a sound. And hence we see, that in the interpretation of laws, whether divine or human, there is no end; comments beget comments, and explications make new matter for explications; and of limiting, distinguishing, varying the signification of these moral words, there is no end. These ideas of men's making are, by men still having the same power, multiplied *in infinitum*. Many a man who was pretty well satisfied of the meaning of a text of scripture, or clause in the code, at first reading, has by consulting commentators quite lost the sense of it, and by those elucidations given rise or increase to his doubts, and drawn obscurity upon the place. I say not this, that I think commentaries needless; but to show how uncertain the names of mixed modes naturally are, even in the mouths of those who had both the intention and the faculty of speaking as clearly as language was capable to express their thoughts.

Sect. 10. *Hence unavoidable obscurity in ancient authors.*—What obscurity this has unavoidably brought upon the writings of men, who have lived in remote ages and in different countries, it will be needless to take notice; since the numerous volumes of learned men, employing their thoughts that way, are proofs more than enough to show what attention, study, sagacity, and reasoning are required, to find out the true meaning of ancient authors. But there being no writings we have any great concernment to be very solicitous about the meaning of, but those that contain either truths we are required to believe, or laws we are to obey, and draw inconveniences on us when we mistake or transgress; we may be less anxious about the sense of other authors, who writing but their own opinions, we are under no greater necessity to know them, than they to know ours. Our good or evil depending not on their decrees, we may safely be ignorant of their notions: and therefore, in the reading of them, if they do not use their words with a due clearness and perspicuity, we may lay them aside, and, without any injury done them, resolve thus with ourselves:

"Si non vis intelligi, debes negligi."

Sect. 11. *Names of substances of doubtful signification.*—If the signification of the names of mixed modes are uncertain, because there be no real standards existing in nature to which those ideas are referred, and by which they may be adjusted, the names of substances are of a doubtful signification, for a contrary reason, viz. because the ideas they stand for are supposed conformable to the reality of things, and are referred to standards made by nature. In our ideas of substances, we have not the liberty, as in mixed modes, to frame what combinations we think fit, to be the characteristical notes to rank and denominate things by. In these we must follow nature, suit our complex ideas to real existences, and regulate the signification of their names by the things themselves, if we will have our names to be the signs of them, and stand for them. Here, it is true, we have patterns to follow, but patterns that will make the signification of their names very uncertain; for names must be of a very unsteady and various meaning, if the ideas they stand for be referred to

standards without us, that either cannot be known at all, or can be known but imperfectly and uncertainly.

Sect. 12. *Names of substances referred, first, to real essences that cannot be known.*—The names of substances have, as has been shown, a double reference in their ordinary use.

First, sometimes they are made to stand for, and so their signification is supposed to agree to, the real constitution of things, from which all their properties flow, and in which they all centre. But this real constitution, (or as it is apt to be called) essence, being utterly unknown to us, any sound that is put to stand for it must be very uncertain in its application; and it will be impossible to know what things are, or ought to be, called a horse, or anatomy, when those words are put for real essences that we have no ideas of at all. And therefore, in this supposition, the names of substances being referred to standards that cannot be known, their significations can never be adjusted and established by those standards.

Sect. 13. *Secondly, to coexisting qualities, which are known but imperfectly.*—The simple ideas that are found to coexist in substances being that which their names immediately signify, these, as united in the several sorts of things, are the proper standards to which their names are referred, and by which their significations may be best rectified. But neither will these archetypes so well serve this purpose, as to leave these names without very various and uncertain significations: because these simple ideas that coexist, and are united in the same subject, being very numerous, and having all an equal right to go into the complex specific idea, which the specific name is to stand for; men, though they propose to themselves the very same subject to consider, yet frame very different ideas about it; and so the name they use for it unavoidably comes to have, in several men, very different significations. The simple qualities which make up the complex ideas, being most of them powers, in relation to changes, which they are apt to make in, or receive from other bodies, are almost infinite. He that shall but observe what a great variety of alterations any one of the baser metals is apt to receive from the different application only of fire; and how much a greater number of changes any of them will receive in the hands of a chemist, by the application of other bodies; will not think it strange that I count the properties of any sort of bodies not easy to be collected, and completely known by the ways of inquiry, which our faculties are capable of. They being therefore at least so many that no man can know the precise and definite number, they are differently discovered by different men, according to their various skill, attention, and ways of handling; who therefore cannot choose but have different ideas of the same substance, and therefore make the signification of its common name very various and uncertain. For the complex ideas of substances being made up of such simple ones as are supposed to co-exist in nature, every one has a right to put into his complex ideas those qualities he has found to be united together. For though in the substance of gold one satisfied himself with colour and weight, yet another thinks solubility in aq. regia as necessary to be joined with that colour in his idea of gold as any one does its fusibility; solubility in aq. regia being a quality as constantly joined with its colour and weight, as fusibility, or any other; others put into it ductility or fixed-ness, &c. as they have been taught by tradition or experience. Who of all these has established the right signification of the word gold? or who shall be the judge to determine? Each has its standard in nature, which he appeals to; and with reason thinks he has the same right to put into his complex idea, signified by the word gold, those qualities which upon trial he has found united, as another, who has not so well exam-ined, has to leave them out; or a third, who has made other trials, has to put in others. For the union in nature of these qualities being the true ground of their union in one complex idea, who can say one of them has more reason to be put in, or left out, than another? From hence it will always unavoid-ably follow, that the complex ideas of substances, in men using the same name for them, will be very various; and so the significations of those names very uncertain.

Sect. 14. *Thirdly, to coexisting qualities which are known but imperfectly.*—Besides, there is scarce any partic-ular thing existing, which, in some of its simple ideas, does not communicate with a greater, and in others a less number of particular beings: who shall determine, in this case, which are those that are to make up the precise collection that is to be signified by the specific name; or can, with any just au-thority, prescribe which obvious or common qualities are to be left out; or which more secret, or more particular are to be put into the signification of the name of any substance? All which together seldom or never fail to produce that various and doubtful signification in the names of substances, which causes such uncertainty, disputes, or mistakes, when we come to a philosophical use of them.

Sect. 15. *With this imperfection, they may serve for civil, but not well for philosophical use.*—It is true, as to civil and common conversation, the general names of substances, regulated in their ordinary signification by some obvious qualities, (as by the shape and figure in things of known sem-inal propagation, and in other substances, for the most part, by colour, joined with some other sensible qualities) do well enough to design the things men would be understood to speak of; and so they usually conceive well enough the sub-stances meant by the word gold, or apple, to distinguish the one from the other. But in philosophical inquiries and de-

bates, where general truths are to be established, and conse-quences drawn from positions laid down—there the precise signification of the names of substances will be found, not only not to be well established, but also very hard to be so. For example, he that shall make malleableness, or a certain degree of fixedness, a part of his complex idea of gold, may make propositions concerning gold, and draw consequences from them, that will truly and clearly follow from gold, taken in such a signification; but yet such as another man can never be forced to admit, nor be convinced of their truth, who makes not malleableness, or the same degree of fixedness, part of that complex idea, that the name gold, in his use of it, stands for.

Sect. 16. *Instance liquor.*—This is a natural, and al-most unavoidable imperfection in almost all the names of substances, in all languages whatsoever, which men will eas-ily find, when once passing from confused or loose notions, they come to more strict and close inquiries: for then they will be convinced how doubtful and obscure those words are in their signification, which in ordinary use appeared very clear and determined. I was once in a meeting of very learned and ingenious physicians, where by chance there arose a question, whether any liquor passed through the filaments of the nerves. The debate having been managed a good while, by variety of arguments on both sides, I (who had been used to suspect that the greatest parts of disputes were more about the signification of words than a real difference in the con-ception of things) desired, that before they went any farther on in this dispute, they would first examine, and establish among them, what the word liquor signified. They at first were a little surprised at the proposal; and had they been per-sons less ingenious, they might perhaps have taken it for a very frivolous or extravagant one; since there was no one there that thought not himself to understand very perfectly what the word liquor stood for; which I think, too, none of the most perplexed names of substances. However, they were pleased to comply with my motion; and, upon examination, found that the signification of that word was not so settled and certain as they had all imagined, but that each of them made it a sign of a different complex idea. This made them believe that the main of their dispute was about the signifi-cation of the term; and that they differed very little in their opinions concerning some fluid and subtle matter passing through the conduits of the nerves, though it was not so easy to agree whether it was to be called liquor or no—a thing which, when considered, they thought it not worth the con-tending about.

Sect. 17. *Instance Gold.*—How much this is the case in the greatest part of disputes that men are engaged so hotly in, I shall perhaps have an occasion in another place to take notice. Let us only here consider a little more exactly the fore-mentioned instance of the word gold, and we shall see how hard it is precisely to determine its signification. I think all agree to make it stand for a body of a certain yellow shining colour; which being the idea to which children have annexed that name, the shining yellow part of a peacock's tail is properly to them gold. Others finding fusibility, joined with that yellow colour in certain parcels of matter, make of that combination a complex idea, to which they give the name gold, to denote a sort of substances; and so exclude from being gold all such yellow shining bodies as by fire will be reduced to ashes; and admit to be of that species, or to be comprehended under that name gold, only such substances, as having that shining yellow colour, will by fire be reduced to fusion, and not to ashes. Another, by the same reason, adds the weight; which being a quality as straightly joined with that colour as its fusibility, he thinks has the same reason to be joined in its idea, and to be signified by its name; and therefore the other made up of body, of such a colour and fusibility, to be imperfect; and so on of all the rest: wherein no one can show a reason why some of the inseparable qualities, that are always united in nature, should be put into the nominal essence, and others left out; or why the word gold, signifying that sort of body the ring on his finger is made of, should determine that sort, rather by its colour, weight, and fusibility, than by its colour, weight and solubility in aq. regia: since the dissolving of it by that liquor is as inseparable from it as the fusion by fire; and they are both of them nothing but the relation which that substance has to two other bodies, which have a power to operate differently upon it. For by what right is it that fusibility comes to be a part of the essence signified by the word gold, and solubility but a property of it; or why is its colour part of the essence, and its malleableness but a property? That which I mean is this: that these being all but properties depending on its real constitution, and nothing but powers, either active or passive, in reference to other bodies; no one has authority to determine the signification of the word gold (as referred to such a body existing in nature) more to one collection of ideas to be found in that body than to another: whereby the signification of that name must unavoidably be very uncertain; since, as has been said, several people observe several properties in the same substance; and, I think, I may say nobody at all. And therefore we have but very imperfect descriptions of things, and words have very uncertain significations.

Sect. 18. *The names of simple ideas the least doubtful.*—From what has been said, it is easy to observe what has been before remarked, viz. That the names of simple ideas are, of all others, the least liable to mistakes, and that for these reasons. First, because the ideas they stand for, being

each but one single perception, are much easier got, and more clearly retained, than the more complex ones; and therefore are not liable to the uncertainty which usually attends those compounded ones of substances and mixed modes, in which the precise number of simple ideas, that make them up, are not easily agreed, and so readily kept in the mind: and secondly, because they are never referred to any other essence, but barely that perception they immediately signify; which reference is that which renders the signification of the names of substances naturally so perplexed, and gives occasion to so many disputes. Men that do not perversely use their words, or on purpose set themselves to cavil, seldom mistake, in any language which they are acquainted with, the use and signification of the names of simple ideas: white and sweet, yellow and bitter, carry a very obvious meaning with them, which every one precisely comprehends, or easily perceives he is ignorant of, and seeks to be informed. But what precise collection of simple ideas modesty or frugality stand for in another's use, is not so certainly known. And however we are apt to think we well enough know what is meant by gold or iron; yet the precise complex idea others make them the signs of, is not so certain; and I believe it is very seldom that, in speaker and hearer, they stand for exactly the same collection: which must needs produce mistakes and disputes, when they are made use of in discourses, wherein men have to do with universal propositions, and would settle in their minds universal truths, and consider the consequences that follow from them.

Sect. 19. *And next to them, simple modes.*—By the same rule, the names of simple modes are, next to those of simple ideas, least liable to doubt and uncertainty, especially those of figure and number, of which men have so clear and distinct ideas. Who ever, that had a mind to understand them, mistook the ordinary meaning of seven, or a triangle? And in general the least compounded ideas in every kind have the least dubious names.

Sect. 20. *The most doubtful are the names of very compounded mixed modes and substances.*—Mixed modes, therefore, that are made up but of a few and obvious simple ideas, have usually names of no very uncertain signification; but the same names of mixed modes, which comprehend a great number of simple ideas, are commonly of a very doubtful and undetermined meaning, as has been shown. The names of substances, being annexed to ideas that are neither the real essences nor exact representations of the patterns they are referred to, are liable yet to greater imperfection and uncertainty, especially when we come to a philosophical use of them.

Sect. 21. *Why this imperfection charged upon words.*—The great disorder that happens in our names of substances, proceeding for the most part from our want of knowledge, and inability to penetrate into their real constitutions, it may probably be wondered, why I charge this as an imperfection rather upon our words than understandings. This exception has so much appearance of justice, that I think myself obliged to give a reason why I have followed this method. I must confess, then, that when I first began this discourse of the understanding, and a good while after, I had not the least thought that any consideration of words was at all necessary to it. But when, having passed over the original and composition of our ideas, I began to examine the extent and certainty of our knowledge, I found it had so near a connexion with words, that, unless their force and manner of signification were first well observed, there could be very little said clearly and pertinently concerning knowledge; which being conversant about truth, had constantly to do with propositions; and though it terminated in things, yet it was for the most part so much by the intervention of words, that they seemed scarce separable from our general knowledge. At least, they interpose themselves so much between our understandings and the truth, which it would contemplate and apprehend, that, like the medium through which visible objects pass, their obscurity and disorder do not seldom cast a mist before our eyes, and impose upon our understandings. If we consider, in the fallacies men put upon themselves as well as others, and the mistakes in men's disputes and notions, how great a part is owing to words, and their uncertain or mistaken significations—we shall have reason to think this no small obstacle in the way to knowledge; which, I conclude, we are the more carefully to be warned of, because it has been so far from being taken notice of as an inconvenience, that the arts of improving it have been made the business of men's study, and obtained the reputation of learning and subtility, as we shall see in the following chapter. But I am apt to imagine, that were the imperfections of language, as the instruments of knowledge, more thoroughly weighed, a great many of the controversies that make such a noise in the world, would of themselves cease; and the way to knowledge, and perhaps peace, too, lie a great deal opener than it does.

Sect. 22. *This should teach us moderation, in imposing our own sense of old authors.*—Sure I am, that the signification of words, in all languages, depending very much on the thoughts, notions, and ideas of him that uses them, must unavoidably be of great uncertainty to men of the same language and country. This is so evident in the Greek authors, that he that shall peruse their writings, will find in almost every one of them a distinct language, though the same words. But when to this natural difficulty in every country there shall be added different countries and remote ages, wherein the speakers and writers had very different notions, tempers, customs, ornaments, and figures of speech, &c. every one of which influenced the signification of their words then, though to us now they are lost and unknown; it would become us to be charitable one to another in our interpretations or misunderstanding of those ancient writings; which, though of great concernment to be understood, are liable to the unavoidable difficulties of speech, which (if we except the names of simple ideas, and some very obvious things) is not capable, without a constant defining the terms, of conveying the sense and intention of the speaker, without any manner of doubt and uncertainty to the hearer. And in discourses of religion, law, and morality, as they are matters of the highest concernment, so there will be the greatest difficulty.

Sect. 23. The volumes of interpreters and commentators on the old and new Testaments are but too manifest proofs of this. Though every thing said in the text be infallibly true, yet the reader may be, nay cannot choose but be, very fallible in the understanding of it. Nor is to be wondered, that the will of God, when clothed in words, should be liable to that doubt and uncertainty which unavoidably attends that sort of conveyance; when even his Son, whilst clothed in flesh, was subject to all the frailties and inconveniences of human nature, sin excepted: and we ought to magnify his goodness, that he hath spread before all the world such legible characters of his works and providence, and given all mankind so sufficient a light of reason, that they to whom this written word never came, could not (whenever they set themselves to search) either doubt of the being of a God, or of the obedience due to him. Since then the precepts of natural religion are plain, and very intelligible to all mankind, and seldom come to be controverted; and other revealed truths, which are conveyed to us by books and languages, are liable to the common and natural obscurities and difficulties incident to words; methinks it would become us to be more careful and diligent in observing the former, and less magisterial, positive, and imperious in imposing our own sense and interpretations of the latter.

Chapter X

Of the Abuse of Words

Sect. 23. To conclude this consideration of the imperfection, and the abuse of language; the ends of language in our discourse with others, being chiefly these three: First, to make known one man's thoughts or ideas to another. Secondly, to do it with as much ease and quickness, as is possible; and thirdly, thereby to convey the knowledge of things. Language is either abused, or deficient, when it fails in any of these three.

First, words fail in the first of these ends, and lay not open one man's ideas to another's view. First, when men have names in their mouths without any determined ideas in their minds, whereof they are the signs: or secondly, when they apply the common received names of any language to ideas, to which the common use of that language does not apply them: or thirdly, when they apply them very unsteadily, making them stand now for one, and by and by for another idea.

Sect. 24. Secondly, men fail of conveying their thoughts, with all the quickness and ease that may be, when they have complex ideas, without having distinct names for them. This is sometimes the fault of language itself, which has not in it a sound yet applied to such a signification: and sometimes the fault of the man, who has not yet learned the name for that idea he would show another.

Sect. 25. Thirdly, there is no knowledge of things conveyed by man's words, when their ideas agree not to the reality of things. Though it be a defect, that has its original in our ideas, which are not so conformable to the nature of things, as attention, study, and application might make them: Yet it fails not to extend itself to our words too, when we use them as signs of real beings, which never yet had any reality or existence.

Sect. 26. First, he that hath words of any language, without distinct ideas in his mind, to which he applies them, does, so far as he uses them in discourse, only make a noise without any sense or signification; and how learned soever he may seem by the use of hard words, or learned terms, is not much more advanced thereby in knowledge, than he would be in learning, who had nothing in his study but the bare titles of books, without possessing the contents of them. For all such words however put into discourse, according to the right construction of grammatical rules, or the harmony of well turned periods, do yet amount to nothing but bare sounds, and nothing else.

Sect. 27. Secondly, he that has complex ideas, without particular names for them, would be in no better case than a bookseller, who had in his warehouse volumes that lay there unbound, and without titles; which he could therefore make known to others only by showing the loose sheets, and communicating them only by tale. This man is hindered in his discourse for want of words to communicate his complex ideas, which he is therefore forced to make known by an enumeration of the simple ones that compose them; and so is fain often to use twenty words to express what another man signifies in one.

Sect. 28. Thirdly, he that puts not constantly the same sign for the same idea, but uses the same words sometimes in one, and sometimes in another signification, ought to pass in the schools and conversation for as fair a man as he does in the market and exchange, who sells several things under the same name.

Sect. 29. Fourthly, he that applies the words of any language to ideas different from those to which the common use of that country applies them, however his own understanding may be filled with truth and light, will not by such words be able to convey much of it to others, without defining his terms. For however the sounds are such as are familiarly known, and easily enter the ears of those who are accustomed to them; yet standing for other ideas than those they usually are annexed to, and are wont to excite in the mind or the hearers, they cannot make known the thoughts of him who thus uses them.

Sect. 30. Fifthly, he that imagined to himself substances such as never have been, and filled his head with ideas which have not any correspondence with the real nature of things, to which yet he gives settled and defined names, may fill his discourse, and perhaps another man's head, with the fantastical imaginations of his own brain, but will be very far from advancing thereby one jot in real and true knowledge.

Sect. 31. He that hath names without ideas, wants meaning in his words, and speaks only empty sounds. He that hath complex ideas without names for them, wants liberty and despatch in his expressions, and is necessitated to use periphrases. He that uses his words loosely and unsteadily, will either be not minded, or not understood. He that applies his names to ideas different from their common use, wants propriety in his language, and speaks gibberish. And he that hath the ideas of substances disagreeing with the real existence of things, so far wants the materials of true knowledge in his understanding, and hath instead thereof chimeras.

Sect. 32. *How in substances.*—In our notions concerning substances, we are liable to all the former inconveniences: v. g. 1. He that uses the word tarantula, without having any imagination or idea what it stands for, pronounces a good word; but so long means nothing at all by it. 2. He that in a new discovered country shall see several sorts of animals and vegetables, unknown to him before, may have as true ideas of them as of a horse or a stag; but can speak of them only by a description, till he shall either take the names the natives call them by, or give them names himself. 3. He that uses the word body sometimes for pure extension, and sometimes for extension and solidity together, will talk very fallaciously. 4. He that gives the name horse to that idea which common usage calls mule, talks improperly, and will not be understood. 5. He that thinks the name centaur stands for some real being, imposes on himself, and mistakes words for things.

Sect. 33. *How in modes and relations.*—In modes and relations generally we are liable only to the four first of these inconveniences; viz. 1. I may have in my memory the names of modes, as gratitude or charity, and yet not have any precise ideas annexed in my thoughts to those names. 2. I may have ideas, and not know the names that belong to them; v. g. I may have the idea of a man's drinking till his colour and humour be altered, till his tongue trips, and his eyes look red, and his feet fail him; and yet not know that it is to be called drunkenness. 3. I may have the ideas of virtues or vices, and names also, but apply them amiss: v. g. when I apply the name frugality to that idea which others call and signify by this sound, covetousness. 4. I may use any of those names with inconstancy. 5. But, in modes and relations I cannot have ideas disagreeing to the existence of things: for modes being complex ideas made by the mind at pleasure; and relation being but by way of considering or comparing two things together, and so also an idea of my own making; these ideas can scarce be found to disagree with any thing existing, since they are not in the mind as the copies of things regularly made by nature, nor as properties inseparably flowing from the internal constitution or essence of any substance; but as it were patterns lodged in my memory, with names annexed to them, to denominate actions and relations by, as they come to exist. But the mistake is commonly in my giving a wrong name to my conceptions; and so using words in a different sense from other people, I am not understood, but am thought to have wrong ideas of them, when I give wrong names to them. Only if I put in my ideas of mixed modes or relations any inconsistent ideas together, I fill my head also with chimeras; since such ideas, if well examined, cannot so much exist in the mind, much less any real being ever be denominated from them.

Sect. 34. *Figurative speech also an abuse of language.*—Sixthly, since wit and fancy find easier entertainment in the world than dry truth and real knowledge, figurative speeches and allusion in language will hardly be admitted as an imperfection or abuse of it. I confess, in discourses where we seek rather pleasure and delight than information and improvement, such ornaments as are borrowed from them can scarce pass for faults. But yet if we would speak of things as they are, we must allow that all the art of rhetoric, besides order and clearness, all the artificial and figurative application of words eloquence hath invented, are for nothing else but to insinuate wrong ideas, move the passions, and thereby mislead the judgment, and so indeed are perfect cheats; and, therefore, however laudable or allowable oratory may render them in harangues and popular addresses, they are certainly, in all discourses that pretend to inform or instruct, wholly to be avoided; and where truth and knowledge are concerned, cannot but be thought a great fault, either of the language or person that makes use of them. What, and how various they are, will be superfluous here to take notice; the books of rhetoric which abound in the world will instruct those who want to be informed: only I can not but observe how little the preservation and improvement of truth and knowledge is the care and concern of mankind; since the arts of fallacy are endowed and preferred. It is evident how much men love to deceive and be deceived, since rhetoric, that powerful instrument of error and deceit, has its established professors, is publicly taught, and has always been had in great reputation: and, I doubt not, but it will be thought great boldness, if not brutality in me, to have said thus much against it. Eloquence, like the fair sex, has too prevailing beauties in it to suffer itself ever to be spoken against. And it is in vain to find fault with those arts of deceiving wherein men find pleasure to be deceived.

John Dennis

1657–1734

Dennis' *Advancement and Reformation of Modern Poetry* reveals the influence of Longinus' treatise on the sublime. Boileau had translated and written on Longinus and Dryden had been interested in him. Dennis, however, was the first English critic to develop a theory of the sublime, particularly with respect to feelings of sublimity in the reader. His theory of poetry is based on poetry's emotive power and, as such, marks an interesting departure from most neoclassical criticism, even though his basic methodology and stubborn insistence on rules are typically neoclassical.

A cantankerous personality, Dennis embroiled himself in the old argument concerning the merits of the ancients and the moderns. Though he wishes to show that the moderns should be able to equal the ancients, nevertheless the ancients come off better for having had superior subject matter. Poetry, as Dennis defines it, is distinguished by the presence of a single quality, passion. The highest passion is produced by a religious subject. Later chapters of his essay endeavor to show that the ancients achieved poetic heights when their religion flowered and there was thus religious ground for poetic enthusiasm. Dennis concludes:

> And thus I have endeavored to show in the former part of this book, that the principal reason why the ancient poets excelled the moderns in the greatness of poetry was because they incorporated poetry with religion; and in the second part that the moderns, by joining the Christian religion with poetry, will have the advantage of the ancients, that is, that they will have the assistance of a religion that is more agreeable to the design of poetry than the Grecian religion.

In Dennis' view the moderns have apparently not exploited their opportunity.

The standard edition is E. N. Hooker, *The Critical Works of John Dennis* (2 vols., 1939–43). Volume II contains an indispensable biographical and critical introduction. See also H. G. Paul, *John Dennis: His Life and Criticism* (1911). There is a discussion of Dennis' criticism in S. H. Monk, *The Sublime: A Study of Critical Theories in XVIII-Century England* (1935), and in J. W. H. Atkins, *English Literary Criticism: 17th and 18th Centuries* (1952); Joan C. Grace, *Tragic Theory in the Critical Works of Thomas Rymer, John Dennis, and John Dryden* (1975); and Avon Jack Murphy, *John Dennis* (1984).

The Advancement and Reformation of Modern Poetry

Chapter IV

That the Ancient Poets Derived Their Greatness from the Nature of Their Subjects

If the ancient poets excelled the moderns in the greatness of poetry, that is, in epic poetry, in tragedy, and in the greater ode, they must necessarily derive their preeminence from the subjects of which they treated, since it has been plainly made to appear that they could not derive it from any external or internal advantage. And it follows, that the subjects which were handled by the ancients must be different from those which have been treated of by the moderns. And if the poems which have been written by the ancients of the forementioned kinds were very much greater than those which have been produced by the moderns, why then it follows that the subjects were very different. But here the favorers of the moderns assert that the advantage which is to be drawn from the subject is purely on the side of the moderns. For who, for example, will compare the achievements of Achilles and Aeneas, the event of which was only the reducing two pitiful paltry burgs with the glorious actions of some of our modern captains? But then the partisans of the ancients reply that there is a difference between one subject and another, which their adversaries seem not to have thought of. For, say they, human subjects can never differ so much among themselves as sacred subjects differ from human, for the difference between the two last is as great as that between God and man, which we know is infinite. Now, say they, sacred subjects are infinitely more susceptible of the greatness of poetry than profane ones can be. And the subjects of the ancients in the forementioned poems were sacred. Now that we may engage the lovers of the ancients in their turns by supporting their just pretensions, let us endeavor to show in the following chapters that sacred poems must be greater than profane ones can be, supposing equality of genius and equal art in the writers, and that the poems of the ancients in the forementioned kinds were sacred. But in order to the doing that, we must declare what poetry is and what is its chief excellence.

Chapter V

That Passion Is the Chief Thing in Poetry and That All Passion Is Either Ordinary Passion or Enthusiasm

But, before we proceed, let us define poetry; which is the first time that a definition has been given of that noble art; for neither ancient nor modern critics have defined poetry in general.[1]

Poetry, then, is an imitation of nature by a pathetic and numerous[2] speech. Let us explain it.

As poetry is an art, it must be an imitation of nature. That the instrument with which it makes its imitation is speech need not be disputed. That that speech must be musical no one can doubt: for numbers distinguish the parts of poetic diction from the periods of prose. Now numbers are nothing but articulate sounds, and their pauses measured by their proper proportions of time. And the periods of prosaic diction are articulate sounds, and their pauses unmeasured by such proportions. That the speech by which poetry makes its imitation must be pathetic is evident, for passion is still more necessary to it than harmony. For harmony only distinguishes its instrument from that of prose, but passion distinguishes its very nature and character. For therefore poetry is poetry, because it is more passionate and sensual than prose. A discourse that is written in very good numbers, if it wants passion, can be but measured prose. But a discourse that is everywhere extremely pathetic, and consequently everywhere bold and figurative, is certainly poetry without numbers.

Passion, then, is the characteristical mark of poetry, and consequently must be everywhere. For wherever a discourse is not pathetic, there it is prosaic. As passion in a poem must be everywhere, so harmony is usually diffused throughout it. But passion answers the two ends of poetry better than harmony can do, and upon that account is preferable to it: for first it pleases more, which is evident: for passion can please without harmony, but harmony tires without passion. And in tragedy and in epic poetry a man may instruct without harmony, but never without passion: for the one instructs by admiration, and the other by compassion and terror. And as

---

MODERN POETRY. Dennis' *Advancement and Reformation of Modern Poetry* was first published in 1701. The text is based on the second printing of the essay in Dennis' *Miscellaneous Tracts* (1727).

---

[1]This is not true, of course, though poetry may not have been defined successfully.

[2]By "numerous" Dennis means rhythmic or musical. It is curious that he proceeds to deny his own definition by allowing the existence of a "poetry without numbers."

for the greater ode, if it wants passion, it becomes hateful and intolerable, and its sentences grow contemptible.

Passion is the characteristical mark of poetry, and therefore it must be everywhere; for without passion there can be no poetry, no more than there can be painting. And though the poet and the painter describe action, they must describe it with passion. Let anyone who beholds a piece of painting, where the figures are shown in action, conclude that if the figures are without passion the painting is contemptible. There must be passion everywhere in poetry and painting, and the more passion there is, the better the poetry and the painting unless the passion is too much for the subject;[3] and the painter and the poet arrive at the height of their art when they describe a great deal of action with a great deal of passion. It is plain, then, from what has been said, that passion in poetry must be everywhere, for where there is no passion there can be no poetry, but that which we commonly call passion cannot be everywhere in any poem. There must be passion, then, that must be distinct from ordinary passion, and that must be enthusiasm. I call that *ordinary passion,* whose cause is clearly comprehended by him who feels it, whether it be admiration, terror, or joy; and I call the very same passions *enthusiasms,* where their cause is not clearly comprehended by him who feels them. And these enthusiastic passions are sometimes simple, and sometimes complicated, of all which we shall show examples lower. And thus I have shown that the chief thing in poetry is passion; but here the reader is desired to observe, that by *poetry* we mean poetry in general, and the body of poetry; for the form or soul of particular poems, that is allowed by all to be a fable. But passion is the chief thing in the body of poetry, as spirit is in the human body.[4] For without spirit the body languishes, and the soul is impotent: now everything that they call spirit or genius in poetry, in short everything that pleases, and consequently moves in the poetic diction, is passion, whether it be ordinary or enthusiastic.

And thus we have shown what the chief excellence in the body of poetry is, which we have proved to be passion. Let us now proceed to the proofs of what we propounded, that sacred subjects are more susceptible of passion than profane ones, and that the subjects of the ancients were sacred in their greater poetry—I mean either sacred in their own natures, or by their manner of handling them.

Chapter VI

That Passion Is More to Be Derived from a Sacred Subject Than from a Profane One

We have proved that passion is the chief thing in poetry, and that spirit or genius, and in short everything that moves, is passion. Now if the chief thing in poetry be passion, why, then, the chief thing in great poetry must be great passion. We have shown, too, that passion in poetry is of two sorts, ordinary passion or enthusiasm. Let us now proceed to convince the reader that a sacred poem is more susceptible of passion than a profane one can be; which to effect, let us show two things, that a sacred subject is as susceptible of ordinary passions as a profane one can be, and more susceptible of the enthusiastic.

The first is evident from experience: for the poetry among the ancients which shall be hereafter proved to be sacred, had in it greater ordinary passions than their human poetry either had or could possibly have.

'Tis now our business to show that religious subjects are capable of supplying us with more frequent and stronger enthusiasms than the profane. And in order to the clearing this, let us inquire what poetical enthusiasm is. Poetical enthusiasm is a passion guided by judgment, those cause is not comprehended by us. That it is a passion is plain, because it moves. That the cause is not comprehended is self-evident. That it ought to be guided by judgment is indubitable. For otherwise it would be madness, and not poetical passion. But now let us inquire what the cause of poetical enthusiasm is, that has been hitherto not comprehended by us. That enthusiasm moves, is plain to sense; why, then, it moved the writer: but if it moved the writer, it moved him while he was thinking. Now what can move a man while he is thinking but the thoughts that are in his mind?[5] In short, enthusiasm as well as ordinary passions must proceed from the thoughts, as the passions of all reasonable creatures must certainly do: but the reason why we know not the causes of enthusiastic as well as of ordinary passions, is because we are not so used to them, and because they proceed from thoughts, that latently and unobserved by us carry passion along with them. Here it would be no hard matter to prove that most of our thoughts are naturally attended with some sort and some degree of passion. And 'tis the expression of this passion which

---

[3]This remark suggests the twentieth-century concept of sentimentality in I. A. Richards and others.
[4]Dennis recalls Longinus' idea of the sublime in this passage.

[5]Dennis' essay here exemplifies a turning toward interest in the psychology of the reader.

gives us so much pleasure, both in conversation and in human authors. For I appeal to any man who is not altogether a philosopher, whether he is not most pleased with conversation and books that are spirited. Now how can this spirit please him, but because it moves him, or what can move him but passion? We never speak for so much as a minute together without different inflections of voice. Now anyone will find upon reflection that these variations and those inflections mark our different passions. But all this passes unregarded by us, by reason of long use, and the incredible celerity of our thoughts, whose motion is so swift that it is even to ourselves imperceptible; unless we come to reflect, and everyone will not be at the trouble of that. Now these passions, when they grow strong, I call enthusiastic motions, and the stronger they are the greater the enthusiasm must be. If anyone asks what sort of passions these are, that thus unknown to us flow from these thoughts, to him I answer that the same sort of passions flow from the thoughts that would do from the things of which those thoughts are ideas. As for example, if the thing we think of is great, why, then, admiration attends the idea of it; and if it is very great, amazement. If the thing is pleasing and delightful, why then joy and gaiety flow from the idea of it; if it is sad, melancholy; if it is mischievous and powerful, then the imagination of it is attended with terror; and if 'tis both great and likely to do hurt and powerful, why then the thought of it is at once accompanied with wonder, terror, and astonishment. Add to all this that the mind producing these thoughts conceives by reflection a certain pride and joy and admiration, as at the conscious view of its own excellence.

Now he who strictly examines the enthusiasm that is to be met with in the greater poetry will find that it is nothing but the forementioned passions, either simple or complicated, proceeding from the thoughts from which they naturally flow, as being the thoughts or images of things that carry those passions along with them, as we shall show by examples in the following chapter.

But these passions that attend upon our thoughts are seldom so strong as they are in those kind of thoughts which we call images. For they, being the very lively pictures of the things which they represent, set them, as it were, before our very eyes. But images are never so admirably drawn as when they are drawn in motion; especially if the motion is violent. For the mind can never imagine violent motion without being in a violent agitation itself; and the imagination being fired with that agitation sets the very things before our eyes, and consequently makes us have the same passions that we should have from the things themselves. For the warmer the imagination is, the more present the things are to us of which we draw the images; and, therefore, when once the imagination is so inflamed as to get the better of the understanding, there is no difference between the images and the things themselves; as we see, for example, in fears and madmen.

Thus have we shown that enthusiasm flows from the thoughts, and consequently from the subject from which the thoughts proceed. For, as the spirit in poetry is to be proportioned to the thought—for otherwise it does not naturally flow from it, and consequently is not guided by judgment—so the thought is to be proportioned to the subject. Now no subject is so capable of supplying us with thoughts that necessarily produce these great and strong enthusiasms as a religious subject: for all which is great in religion is most exalted and amazing, all that is joyful is transporting, all that is sad is dismal, and all that is terrible is astonishing.

Alexander Pope

1688–1744

Thoroughly neoclassical in its premises, the *Essay on Criticism* follows in the tradition of Horace and Boileau. Pope's approach differs from that of the two previous poets, however, in that his advice is mainly for critics and secondarily for poets. Nevertheless he must establish the principles of sound artistic practice. The basic rule of art for Pope is to "follow nature." Nature he sees in an Aristotelian way as a process. This fundamental form of reality is the proper object of imitation. As for rules, they are but "nature methodized"; the form of nature is nature's own self-made restraint. But the poet can transgress the rules if the basic aim of poetry is achieved. In these remarks Pope comes near to expressing an idea of the sublime. Clearly the poet must have a strong sense of literary tradition in order to make intelligent judgments, and the critic must have it too. Pope, in lines that have since become famous, notes Virgil's discovery that to imitate Homer is also to imitate nature.

Most important, the critic should avoid pride; he should try to sense and share the spirit in which his author wrote. Pope goes beyond this precept to remind critics that the author cannot accomplish more than he intends. This argument raises problems that have been of interest to the modern critical mind: the question of the usefulness of knowing a poet's intention, which is disputed by Wimsatt and Beardsley, and the relationship between intuition and expression, which Croce discusses in his *Aesthetic*.

Certainly what Pope recommends to the critic is superior to the varieties of critical narrowness that he draws up for censure: blind invocation of rules, judgment on a part in isolation from the whole, total emphasis on conceits, imagery, or prosody. He is equally critical of slavery to fashion and to personal whim, and he insists on the critic's having the qualities of honesty, modesty, and courage. The critics whom he selects for his admiration indicate his stance: Aristotle, Horace, Dionysius of Halicarnassus, Petronius Arbiter, Quintilian, Longinus, Erasmus, Vida (who wrote an "Art of Poetry"), and finally Boileau. The Earl of Roscommon, a Restoration writer who translated Horace, and William Walsh, a minor poet and friend of Pope's, are also praised. It is clear that at age twenty-one the prodigious Pope takes up, with this poem, defense of the classical tradition.

The standard edition of Pope is the Twickenham edition of the *Works,* edited by John Butt (6 vols., 1939–67). See also Joseph Warton, *An Essay on the Genius and Writings of Pope* (2 vols., 1756, 1782); Austin Warren, *Pope as Critic and Humanist* (1929); E. N. Hooker, "Pope on Wit: The *Essay on Criticism,*" *Hudson Review,* II (1950), 84–100; William Empson, " 'Wit' in the *Essay on Criticism,*" *Hudson Review,* II (1950), 559–77; Arthur Fenner, Jr., "The Unity of Pope's *Essay on Criticism,*" *Philological Quarterly,* XXXIX (1960), 435–56; Bertrand A. Goldgar, ed., *Literary Criticism of Alexander Pope* (1965); and Maynard Mack, *Alexander Pope: A Life* (1985).

An Essay on Criticism

—Si quid novisti rectius istis,
Candidus imperti; si non, his utere mecum.[1]
                                        HORACE

Part I

'Tis hard to say, if greater want of skill
Appear in writing or in judging ill;
But, of the two, less dang'rous is th' offense
To tire our patience, then mislead our sense:
Some few in that, but numbers err in this,
Ten censure wrong for one who writes amiss;
A fool might once himself alone expose;
Now one in verse makes many more in prose.
　　'Tis with our judgments as our watches, none
Go just alike, yet each believes his own.　　　　　　10
In poets as true genius is but rare,
True taste as seldom is the critic's share;
Both must alike from heav'n derive their light,
These born to judge, as well as those to write.
Let such teach others who themselves excel,
And censure freely, who have written well.
Authors are partial to their wit,[2] 'tis true,
But are not critics to their judgment too?
　　Yet, if we look more closely, we shall find
Most have the seeds of judgment in their mind.　　20
Nature affords at least a glimm'ring light;
The lines, though touched but faintly, are drawn right:
But as the slightest sketch, if justly traced
Is by ill-coloring but the more disgraced,
So by false learning is good sense defaced:
Some are bewildered in the maze of schools,[3]
And some made coxcombs nature meant but fools:
In search of wit,[4] these lose their common sense,
And then turn critics in their own defense:
Each burns alike, who can, or cannot write,　　　　30
Or with a rival's, or a eunuch's spite.
All fools have still[5] an itching to deride,
And fain would be upon the laughing side.

If Maevius[6] scribble in Apollo's spite,
There are who judge still worse than he can write.
　　Some have at first for wits,[7] then poets passed,
Turned critics next, and proved plain fools at last.
Some neither can for wits nor critics pass,
As heavy mules are neither horse nor ass.
Those half-learned witlings, num'rous in our isle,　　40
As half-formed insects on the banks of Nile;[8]
Unfinished things, one knows not what to call,
Their generation's so equivocal;
To tell[9] them would a hundred tongues require,
Or one vain wit's, that might a hundred tire.
　　But you who seek to give and merit fame,
And justly bear a critic's noble name,
Be sure yourself and your own reach to know,
How far your genius, taste, and learning go;
Launch not beyond your depth, but be discreet,　　50
And mark that point where sense and dullness meet.
　　Nature to all things fixed the limits fit,
And wisely curbed proud man's pretending wit.
As on the land while here the ocean gains,
In other parts it leaves wide sandy plains;
Thus in the soul while memory prevails,
The solid pow'r of understanding fails;
Where beams of warm imagination play,
The memory's soft figures melt away.
One science only will one genius fit;　　　　　　60
So vast is art, so narrow human wit:
Not only bounded to peculiar arts,
But oft' in those confined to single parts.
Like kings we lose the conquest gained before,
By vain ambition still to make them more:
Each might his sev'ral province well command,
Would all but stoop to what they understand.
　　First follow nature, and your judgment frame
By her just standard, which is still[10] the same:
Unerring nature! still divinely bright,　　　　　70
One clear, unchanged, and universal light,
Life, force, and beauty, must to all impart,
At once the source, and end, and test of art.
Art from that fund each just supply provides;
Works without show, and without pomp presides:[11]
In some fair body thus th' informing soul

AN ESSAY ON CRITICISM. Pope's *Essay on Criticism* was first published in
1711. It may have been composed as early as 1707.
[1] "If you know of any maxims superior to these, let me know of them; if not,
　make use of these as I do." *Epistles,* I. vi.
[2] The genius of their own writing.
[3] Schools of criticism.
[4] Genius, intellect.
[5] Always.

[6] Poet contemporary with Horace.
[7] Geniuses.
[8] It was thought, though not with any certainty, that insects were formed by
　the sun on the Nile's banks.
[9] Count.
[10] Always.
[11] See Horace, *Art of Poetry,* p. 69.

With spirits feeds, with vigor fills the whole;
Each motion guides, and ev'ry nerve sustains,
Itself unseen, but in th' effects remains.
Some, to whom heav'n in wit has been profuse,   80
Want as much more, to turn it to its use;
For wit and judgment often are at strife,
Though meant each other's aid, like man and wife.
'Tis more to guide, than spur the Muse's steed;
Restrain his fury, then provoke his speed:
The winged courser, like a gen'rous horse,
Shows most true mettle when you check his course.
   Those rules of old discovered, not devised,
Are nature still, but nature methodized:
Nature, like liberty, is but restrained   90
By the same laws which first herself ordained.
   Hear how learned Greece her useful rules indites,
When to repress, and when indulge our flights:
High on Parnassus' top her sons she showed,
And pointed out those arduous paths they trod;
Held from afar, aloft, th' immortal prize,
And urged the rest by equal steps to rise.
Just precepts thus from great examples giv'n,
She drew from them what they derived from heav'n;
The gen'rous critic fanned the poet's fire,   100
And taught the world with reason to admire.
Then criticism the Muse's handmaid proved,
To dress her charms, and make her more beloved:
But following wits from that intention strayed;
Who could not win the mistress, wooed the maid;
Against the poets their own arms they turned,
Sure to hate most the men from whom they learned.
So modern 'pothecaries, taught the art
By doctors' bills[12] to play the doctor's part,
Bold in the practice of mistaken rules,   110
Prescribe, apply, and call their masters fools.
Some on the leaves of ancient authors prey;
Nor time nor moths e'er spoiled so much as they:
Some dryly plain, without invention's aid,
Write dull receipts how poems may be made;
These leave the sense, their learning to display,
And those explain the meaning quite away.
   You then whose judgment the right course would steer,
Know well each ancient's proper character;
His fable,[13] subject, scope[14] in ev'ry page;   120
Religion, country, genius of his age:

Without all these at once before your eyes,
Cavil you may, but never criticize.
Be Homer's works your study and delight,
Read them by day, and meditate by night;
   Thence form your judgment, thence your maxims bring,
And trace the Muses upward to their spring.
Still with itself compared, his text peruse;
And let your comment be the Mantuan Muse.[15]
   When first young Maro[16] in his boundless mind
A work t' outlast immortal Rome designed,   130
Perhaps he seemed above the critic's law,
And but from nature's fountain scorned to draw:
But when t' examine every part he came,
Nature and Homer were, he found, the same.
Convinced, amazed, he checks the bold design,
And rules as strict his labored work confine
As if the Stagyrite[17] o'erlooked each line.
Learn hence for ancient rules a just esteem;
To copy nature is to copy them.   140
   Some beauties yet no precept can declare,[18]
For there's a happiness as well as care.
Music resembles poetry; in each
Are nameless graces which no methods teach,
And which a master hand alone can reach.
If, where the rules not far enough extend,
(Since rules were made but to promote their end)
Some lucky license answer to the full
Th' intent proposed, that license is a rule.
Thus Pegasus, a nearer way to take,   150
May boldly deviate from the common track.
Great wits sometimes may gloriously offend,
And rise to faults true critics dare not mend;
From vulgar bounds with brave disorder part,
And snatch a grace beyond the reach of art,
Which, without passing through the judgment, gains
The heart, and all its end at once attains.
In prospects thus some objects please our eyes,
Which out of nature's common order rise,
The shapeless rock, or hanging precipice.   160
But though the ancients thus their rules invade,
(As kings dispense with laws themselves have made)
Moderns, beware! or if you must offend
Against the precept, ne'er transgress its end;
Let it be seldom, and compelled by need;
And have, at least, their precedent to plead;

---

[12]Prescriptions.
[13]Plot.
[14]Aim.

[15]Virgil, born at Mantua.
[16]Virgil.
[17]Aristotle, born at Stagyra.
[18]Explain.

The critic else proceeds without remorse,
Seizes your fame, and puts his laws in force.
    I know there are, to whose presumptuous thoughts
Those freer beauties, ev'n in them, seem faults.   170
Some figures monstrous and misshaped appear,
Considered singly, or beheld too near,
Which, but proportioned to their light,[19] or place,
Due distance reconciles to form and grace.
A prudent chief not always must display
His pow'rs in equal ranks, and fair array,
But with th' occasion and the place comply,
Conceal his force, nay, seem sometimes to fly.
Those oft' are stratagems which errors seem,
Nor is it Homer nods but we that dream.[20]   180
    Still green with bays each ancient altar stands,
Above the reach of sacrilegious hands;
Secure from flames, from envy's fiercer rage,
Destructive war, and all-involving age.
See, from each clime, the learned their incense bring;
Hear, in all tongues consenting paeans ring!
In praise so just let ev'ry voice be joined,
And fill the gen'ral chorus of mankind.
Hail, bards triumphant! Born in happier days;
Immortal heirs of universal praise!   190
Whose honors with increase of ages grow,
As streams roll down, enlarging as they flow;
Nations unborn your mighty names shall sound,
And worlds applaud, that must not yet be found!
O may some spark of your celestial fire,
The last, the meanest of your sons inspire
(That on weak wings, from far, pursues your flights;
Glows while he reads, but trembles as he writes)
To teach vain wits[21] a science little known,
T' admire superior sense, and doubt their own!   200

Part II

Of all the causes which conspire to blind
Man's erring judgment, and misguide the mind,
What the weak head with strongest bias rules,
Is pride, the never-failing vice of fools.
Whatever nature has in worth denied,
She gives in large recruits of needful pride;
For as in bodies, thus in souls, we find
What wants in blood and spirits, swelled with wind:
Pride, where wit fails, steps in to our defense,
And fills up all the mighty void of sense: 210
If once right reason drives that cloud away,
Truth breaks upon us with resistless day.
Trust not yourself; but, your defects to know,
Make use of ev'ry friend—and ev'ry foe.
    A little learning is a dang'rous thing;
Drink deep, or taste not the Pierian spring:[22]
There shallow draughts intoxicate the brain,
And drinking largely sobers us again.
Fired at first sight with what the Muse imparts,
In fearless youth we tempt the heights of arts,   220
While from the bounded level of our mind,
Short views we take, nor see the lengths behind;
But more advanced, behold with strange surprise,
New distant scenes of endless science rise!
So pleased at first the tow'ring Alps we try,
Mount o'er the vales, and seem to tread the sky,
Th' eternal snows appear already past,
And the first clouds and mountains seem the last:
But those attained, we tremble to survey
The growing labors of the lengthened way;   230
Th' increasing prospect tires our wand'ring eyes,
Hills peep o'er hills, and Alps on Alps arise!
    A perfect judge will read each work of wit
With the same spirit that its author writ;
Survey the whole, nor seek slight faults to find
Where nature moves, and rapture warms the mind;
Nor lose for that malignant dull delight,
The gen'rous pleasure to be charmed with wit.
But in such lays as neither ebb nor flow,
Correctly cold, and regularly low,   240
That, shunning faults, one quiet tenor keep,
We cannot blame indeed—but we may sleep.
In wit, as nature, what affects our hearts
Is not th' exactness of peculiar parts;
'Tis not a lip, or eye, we beauty call,
But the joint force and full result of all.
Thus when we view some well-proportioned dome,
(The world's just wonder,[23] and ev'n thine, O Rome![24])
No single parts unequally surprise,
All comes united to th' admiring eyes;   250
No monstrous height, or breadth, or length, appear;

---

[19]Pope here refers to the famous *ut pictura poesis* passage in Horace's *Art of Poetry*, p. 73, where Horace remarks that some paintings are better viewed close up, some far away. Transposed to a discussion of literature, "light" means something like "context."

[20]The allusion to Horace continues. Horace remarks that Homer's art occasionally fails. Pope suggests that it is the readers, not Homer, who "nod."

[21]Writers.

---

[22]Pieria is by legend the birthplace of the Muses.

[23]The sky.

[24]The dome of St. Peter's.

The whole at once is bold, and regular.
     Whoever thinks a faultless piece to see,
Thinks what ne'er was, nor is, nor e'er shall be.
In ev'ry work regard the writer's end,
Since none can compass more than they intend;
And if the means be just, the conduct true,
Applause, in spite of trivial faults, is due.
As men of breeding, sometimes men of wit,
T' avoid great errors, must the less commit;   260
Neglect the rules each verbal critic[25] lays,
For not to know some trifles is a praise.
Most critics, fond of some subservient art,
Still make the whole depend upon a part:
They talk of principles, but notions prize,
And all to one loved folly sacrifice.
     Once on a time, La Mancha's knight,[26] they say,
A certain bard encount'ring on the way,
Discoursed in terms as just, with looks as sage,
As e'er could Dennis,[27] of the Grecian stage;   270
Concluding all were desp'rate sots and fools,
Who durst depart from Aristotle's rules.
Our author, happy in a judge so nice,
Produced his play, and begged the knight's advice;
Made him observe the subject, and the plot,
The manners, passions, unities;[28] what not?
All which, exact to rule, were brought about,
Were but a combat in the lists left out.
     "What! leave the combat out?" exclaims the knight.
"Yes, or we must renounce the Stagyrite."   280
"Not so, by heav'n!" (he answers in a rage)
"Knights, squires, and steeds, must enter on the stage."
"So vast a throng, the stage can ne'er contain."
"Then build a new, or act it in a plain."
     Thus critics of less judgment than caprice,
Curious,[29] not knowing, not exact[30] but nice,[31]
Form short ideas, and offend in arts
(As most in manners) by a love to parts.
     Some to conceit alone their taste confine,
And glitt'ring thoughts struck out at ev'ry line;   290
Pleased with a work where nothing's just or fit;
One glaring chaos and wild heap of wit.

Poets, like painters, thus unskilled to trace
The naked nature, and the living grace,
With golds and jewels cover ev'ry part,
And hide with ornaments their want of art.
True wit[32] is nature to advantage dressed;
What oft' was thought, but ne'er so well expressed;
Something, whose truth convinced at sight we find,
That gives us back the image of our mind.   300
As shades more sweetly recommend the light,
So modest plainness set off sprightly wit:
For works may have more wit than does them good,
As bodies perish through excess of blood.
     Others for language all their care express,
And value books, as women men, for dress:
Their praise is still—the style is excellent;
The sense, they humbly take upon content.[33]
Words are like leaves, and where they most abound,
Much fruit of sense beneath is rarely found.   310
False eloquence, like the prismatic glass,
Its gaudy colors spreads on ev'ry place;
The face of nature we no more survey,
All glares alike, without distinction gay;
But true expression, like th' unchanging sun,
Clears and improves whate'er it shines upon,
It gilds all objects, but it alters none.
Expression is the dress of thought, and still[34]
Appears more decent,[35] as more suitable:
A vile conceit in pompous words expressed   320
Is like a clown in regal purple dressed:
For diff'rent styles with diff'rent subjects sort,
As several garbs with country, town, and court.
Some by old words to fame have made pretense,
Ancients in praise, mere moderns in their sense;
Such labored nothings, in so strange a style,
Amaze th' unlearned, and make the learned smile.
Unlucky, as Fungoso[36] in the play,
These sparks with awkward vanity display
What the fine gentleman wore yesterday;   330
And but so mimic ancient wits at best,
As apes our grandsires, in their doublets dressed.
In words, as fashions, the same rule will hold;
Alike fantastic, if too new, or old:
Be not the first by whom the new are tried,
Nor yet the last to lay the old aside.

---

[25] A critic concerned with the finer points of language.
[26] Don Quixote.
[27] See Dennis, *Modern Poetry*, p. 269.
[28] See Castelvetro, *The* Poetics *of Aristotle*, pp. 140–41 and Corneille, *Of the Three Unities*, pp. 205–12, both of whom discuss the unities of time and place.
[29] Fastidious.
[30] Sound.
[31] Punctilious.

---

[32] The quality of genius in literature.
[33] On faith.
[34] Always.
[35] Attractive.
[36] A character in Ben Jonson's *Every Man Out of His Humor* (1599).

But most by numbers judge a poet's song,
And smooth or rough, with them, is right or wrong:
In the bright Muse, though thousand charms conspire,
Her voice is all these tuneful fools admire;   340
Who haunt Parnassus but to please their ear,
Not mend their minds; as some to church repair
Not for the doctrine, but the music there.
These equal syllables alone require,
Though oft' the ear the open vowels tire;
While expletives their feeble aid do join,
And ten low[37] words oft' creep in one dull line:
While they ring round the same unvaried chimes,
With sure returns of still expected rhymes;
Where'er you find "the cooling western breeze,"   350
In the next line, it "whispers through the trees":
If crystal streams "with pleasing murmurs creep,"
The reader's threatened (not in vain) with "sleep":
Then, at the last and only couplet, fraught
With some unmeaning thing they call a thought,
A needless Alexandrine[38] ends the song,
That, like a wounded snake, drags its slow length along.
Leave such to tune their own dull rhymes, and know
What's roundly smooth, or languishingly slow;
And praise the easy vigor of a line   360
Where Denham's strength, and Waller's sweetness join.
True ease in writing comes from art, not chance,
As those move easiest who have learned to dance.
'Tis not enough no harshness gives offense;
The sound must seem an echo to the sense.
Soft is the strain when zephyr gently blows,
And the smooth stream in smoother numbers flows;
But when loud surges lash the sounding shore,
The hoarse, rough verse should like the torrent roar:
When Ajax strives some rock's vast weight to throw,
The line too labors, and the words move slow: 370
Not so when swift Camilla[39] scours the plain,
Flies o'er th' unbending corn, and skims along the main.
Hear how Timotheus'[40] varied lays surprise,
And bid alternate passions fall and rise,
While at each change, the son of Libyan Jove[41]
Now burns with glory, and then melts with love;
Now his fierce eyes with sparkling fury glow,
Now sighs steal out, and tears begin to flow:
Persians and Greeks like turns of nature[42] found,   380

And the world's victor stood subdued by sound!
The pow'r of music all our hearts allow,
And what Timotheus was, is Dryden now.
    Avoid extremes, and shun the fault of such
Who still are pleased too little or too much.
At ev'ry trifle scorn to take offense,
That always shews great pride, or little sense:
Those heads, as stomachs, are not sure the best
Which nauseate all, and nothing can digest.
Yet let not each gay turn thy rapture move;   390
For fools admire, but men of sense approve:
As things seem large which we through mists descry,
Dullness is ever apt to magnify.
    Some foreign writers, some our own despise;
The ancients only, or the moderns prize.
Thus wit, like faith, by each man is applied
To one small sect, and all are damned beside.
Meanly they seek the blessing to confine,
And force that sun but on a part to shine,
Which not alone the southern wit sublimes,[43]   400
But ripens spirits in cold northern climes;
Which, from the first has shone on ages past,
Enlights the present, and shall warm the last;
Though each may feel increases and decays,
And see now clearer and now darker days;
Regard not then if wit be old or new,
But blame the false, and value still[44] the true.
    Some ne'er advance a judgment of their own
But catch the spreading notion of the town;
They reason and conclude by precedent,   410
And own stale nonsense which they ne'er invent
Some judge of authors' names, not works, and then
Nor praise nor blame the writings, but the men
Of all this servile herd, the worst is he
That in proud dullness joins with quality;[45]
A constant critic at the great man's board,
To fetch and carry nonsense for my lord.
What woeful stuff this madrigal would be,
In some starved hackney sonneteer, or me!
But let a lord once own the happy lines,   420
How the wit brightens! How the style refines!
Before his sacred name flies ev'ry fault,
And each exalted stanza teems with thought!
    The vulgar thus through imitation err,
As oft the learned by being singular;
So much they scorn the crowd, that if the throng

---

[37]Commonplace.
[38]A line of iambic hexameter.
[39]An Amazon in *Aeneid*.
[40]The court musician of Alexander the Great.
[41]"The son of Libyan Jove" refers to Alexander the Great.
[42]"Like turns of nature" means "similar changes of feeling."

---

[43]Elevates.
[44]Always.
[45]People of high rank.

By chance go right, they purposely go wrong:
So schismatics[46] the plain believers quit,
And are but damned for having too much wit.
Some praise at morning what they blame at night,
But always think the last opinion right.   430
A Muse by these is like a mistress used,
This hour she's idolized, the next abused;
While their weak heads, like towns unfortified,
'Twixt sense and nonsense daily change their side.
Ask them the cause; they're wiser still they say;
And still tomorrow's wiser than today.
We think our fathers fools, so wise we grow;
Our wiser sons, no doubt, will think us so.
Once school-divines[47] this zealous isle o'erspread;   440
Who knew most sentences, was deepest read:
Faith, gospel, all, seemed made to be disputed,
And none had sense enough to be confuted.
Scotists and Thomists,[48] now in peace remain,
Amidst their kindred cobwebs in Duck Lane.[49]
If faith itself has diff'rent dresses worn,
What wonder modes in wit should take their turn?
Oft' leaving what is natural and fit,
The current folly proves[50] the ready wit;
And authors think their reputation safe,   450
Which lives as long as fools are pleased to laugh.
    Some, valuing those of their own side or mind,
Still make themselves the measure of mankind:
Fondly[51] we think we honor merit then,
When we but praise ourselves in other men.
Parties in wit attend on those of state,
And public faction doubles private hate.
Pride, malice, folly, against Dryden rose,
In various shapes of parsons, critics, beaus;
But sense survived when merry jests were past;   460
For rising merit will buoy up at last.
Might he return, and bless once more our eyes,
New Blackmores and new Milbourns must arise.
Nay, should great Homer lift his awful head,
Zoilus[52] again would start up from the dead.
Envy will merit, as its shade, pursue;
But like a shadow, proves the substance true:
For envied wit, like Sol eclipsed, makes known
Th' opposing body's grossness, not its own.

---

[46]Members of a religious faction.
[47]Theologians.
[48]Followers of the medieval philosopher Duns Scotus and Thomas Aquinas.
[49]A London street where used books were sold.
[50]Offers an opportunity to.
[51]Foolishly.
[52]A severe critic of Homer.

When first that sun too pow'rful beams displays,   470
It draws up vapors which obscure its rays;
But ev'n those clouds at last adorn its way,
Reflect new glories, and augment the day.
    Be thou the first true merit to befriend;
His praise is lost, who stays till all commend.
Short is the date, alas! of modern rhymes,
And 'tis but just to let them live betimes.
No longer now that golden age appears,
When patriarch wits survived a thousand years;
Now length of fame (our second life) is lost,   480
And bare threescore is all ev'n that can boast;
Our sons their fathers' failing language see,
And such as Chaucer is, shall Dryden be.
So when the faithful pencil has designed
Some bright idea of the master's mind,
Where a new world leaps out at his command,
And ready nature waits upon his hand;
When the ripe colors soften and unite,
And sweetly melt into just shade and light;
When mellowing years their full perfection give,   490
And each bold figure just begins to live,
The treach'rous colors the fair art betray,
And all the bright creation fades away!
    Unhappy wit, like most mistaken things,
Atones not for that envy which it brings;
In youth alone its empty praise we boast,
But soon the short-lived vanity is lost;
Like some fair flow'r the early spring supplies,
That gaily blooms, but ev'n in blooming dies.
What is this wit, which must our cares employ?   500
The owner's wife, that other men enjoy;
Then most our trouble still when most admired,
And still the more we give, the more required;
Whose fame with pains we guard, but lose with ease,
Sure some to vex, but never all to please;
'Tis what the vicious fear, the virtuous shun,
By fools 'tis hated, and by knaves undone!
    If wit so much from ign'rance undergo,
Ah, let not learning too commence its foe!
Of old, those met rewards who could excel,   510
And such were praised who but endeavored well:
Though triumphs were to gen'rals only due,
Crowns were reserved to grace the soldiers too.
Now, they who reach Parnassus' lofty crown,
Employ their pains to spurn some others down
And while self-love each jealous writer rules,
Contending wits become the sport of fools;
But still the worst with most regret commend,
For each ill author is as bad a friend.
To what base ends, and by what abject ways,   520

Are mortals urged through sacred[53] lust of praise!
Ah, ne'er so dire a thirst of glory boast,
Nor in the critic let the man be lost.
Good nature and good sense must ever join;
To err is human, to forgive, divine.
    But if in noble minds some dregs remain
Not yet purged off, of spleen and sour disdain,
Discharge that rage on more provoking crimes,
Nor fear a dearth in these flagitious times.
No pardon vile obscenity should find,   530
Though wit and art conspire to move your mind;
But dullness with obscenity must prove
As shameful sure as impotence in love.
In the fat age of pleasure, wealth, and ease,
Sprung the rank weed, and thrived with large increase:
When love was all an easy monarch's[54] care;
Seldom at council, never in a war,
Jilts[55] ruled the state, and statesmen farces writ;
Nay, wits had pensions, and young lords had wit;
The fair sat panting at a courtier's play,   540
And not a mask[56] went unimproved away;
The modest fan was lifted up no more,
And virgins smiled at what they blushed before.
The foll'wing license of a foreign reign[57]
Did all the dregs of bold Socinus[58] drain;
Then unbelieving priests reformed the nation,
And taught more pleasant methods of salvation;
Where heaven's free subjects might their rights dispute,
Lest God himself should seem too absolute:
Pulpits their sacred satire learned to spare,   550
And vice admired[59] to find a flatt'rer there!
Encouraged thus, wit's Titans braved the skies,
And the press groaned with licensed blasphemies.
These monsters, critics! with your darts engage,
Here point your thunder, and exhaust your rage!
Yet shun their fault, who, scandalously nice,
Will needs mistake an author into vice:
All seems infected that th' infected spy,
As all looks yellow to the jaundiced eye.

Part III

Learn then what morals critics ought to show,   560
For 'tis but half a judge's task, to know.

---

[53]Accursed.
[54]Charles II.
[55]Mistresses.
[56]A woman wearing a mask, a fashion of the day.
[57]William III came from the Netherlands.
[58]Faustus Socinus (1539–1604), heretical theologian.
[59]Marveled.

'Tis not enough, taste, judgment, learning, join;
In all you speak, let truth and candor shine,
That not alone what to your sense is due
All may allow, but seek your friendship too.
    Be silent always when you doubt your sense,
And speak, though sure, with seeming diffidence:
Some positive, persisting fops we know,
Who, if once wrong, will needs be always so;
But you with pleasure own your errors past,   570
And make each day a critique on the last.
    'Tis not enough your counsel still be true;
Blunt truths more mischief than nice falsehoods do;
Men must be taught as if you taught them not,
And things unknown proposed as things forgot.
Without good breeding truth is disapproved;
That only makes superior sense beloved.
    Be niggards of advice on no pretense,
For the worst avarice is that of sense.
With mean complaisance ne'er betray your trust,   580
Nor be so civil as to prove unjust.
Fear not the anger of the wise to raise;
Those best can bear reproof, who merit praise.
    'Twere well might critics still this freedom take,
But Appius[60] reddens at each word you speak,
And stares, tremendous, with a threat'ning eye,
Like some fierce tyrant in old tapestry.
Fear most to tax an honorable fool,
Whose right it is uncensured, to be dull:
Such, without wit, are poets when they please,   590
As without learning they can take degrees.[61]
Leave dang'rous truths to unsuccessful satires,
And flattery to fulsome dedicators,
Whom, when they praise, the world believes no more,
Than when they promise to give scribbling o'er.
'Tis best sometimes your censure to restrain,
And charitably let the dull be vain;
Your silence there is better than your spite,
For who can rail so long as they can write?
Still humming on, their drowsy course they keep,
And lashed so long, like tops, are lashed asleep.   600
False steps but help them to renew the race,
As, after stumbling, jades will mend their pace.
What crowds of these, impenitently bold,
In sounds and jingling syllables grown old.
Still run on poets in a raging vein,
Ev'n to the dregs and squeezing of the brain,
Strain out the last dull droppings of their sense,
And rhyme with all the rage of impotence.

---

[60]John Dennis.
[61]A reference to the privileges given nobles at the universities.

Such shameless bards we have; and yet, 'tis true,
There are as mad, abandoned critics too.   611
The bookful blockhead, ignorantly read,
With loads of learnèd lumber in his head,
With his own tongue still edifies his ears,
And always list'ning to himself appears:
All books he reads, and all he reads assails,
From Dryden's *Fables* down to Durfey's *Tales*.
With him most authors steal their works, or buy;
Garth did not write his own *Dispensary*.
Name a new play, and he's the poet's friend,   620
Nay, showed his faults—but when would poets mend?
No place so sacred from such fops is barred,
Nor is Paul's church more safe than Paul's churchyard:[62]
Nay, fly to altars, there they'll talk you dead;
For fools rush in where angels fear to tread.
Distrustful sense with modest caution speaks,
It still looks home, and short excursions makes;
But rattling nonsense in full volleys breaks,
And never shocked, and never turned aside,
Bursts out, resistless, with a thund'ring tide.   630
  But where's the man, who counsel can bestow,
Still pleased to teach, and yet not proud to know?
Unbiased, or by favor, or by spite,
Not dully prepossessed, nor blindly right;
Though learned, well-bred; and though well-bred, sincere;
Modestly bold, and humanly severe;
Who to a friend his faults can freely show,
And gladly praise the merit of a foe?
Blessed with a taste exact, yet unconfined;
A knowledge both of books and humankind;   640
Gen'rous converse; a soul exempt from pride;
And love to praise, with reason on his side?
  Such once were critics; such the happy few
Athens and Rome in better ages knew.
The mighty Stagyrite first left the shore,
Spread all his sails, and durst the deeps explore;
He steered securely, and discovered far,
Led by the light of the Maeonian star.[63]
Poets, a race long unconfined and free,
Still fond and proud of savage liberty,   650
Received his[64] laws, and stood convinced 'twas fit,
Who conquered nature, should preside o'er wit.
  Horace still charms with graceful negligence,
And without method talks us into sense;
Will, like a friend, familiarly convey
The truest notions in the easiest way.

He, who supreme in judgment, as in wit,
Might boldly censure, as he boldly writ,
Yet judged with coolness, though he sung with fire;
His precepts teach but what his works inspire.   660
Our critics take a contrary extreme,
They judge with fury, but they write with phlegm:
Nor suffers Horace more in wrong translations
By wits, than critics in as wrong quotations.
  See Dionysius Homer's thoughts refine,
And call new beauties forth from ev'ry line!
  Fancy and art in gay Petronius please,
The scholar's learning, with the courtier's ease.
  In grave Quintilian's copious work, we find
The justest rules, and clearest method joined.   670
Thus useful arms in magazines we place,
All ranged in order, and disposed with grace;
But less to please the eye, than arm the hand,
Still fit for use, and ready at command.
  Thee, bold Longinus! All the Nine inspire,
And bless their critic with a poet's fire:
An ardent judge, who, zealous in his trust,
With warmth gives sentence, yet is always just;
Whose own example strengthens all his laws;
And is himself that great sublime he draws.   680
  Thus long succeeding critics justly reigned,
License repressed, and useful laws ordained.
Learning and Rome alike in empire grew,
And arts still followed where her eagles flew;
From the same foes, at last, both felt their doom,
And the same age saw learning fall, and Rome.
With tyranny, then superstition joined,
As that the body, this enslaved the mind;
Much was believed, but little understood,
And to be dull was construed to be good;   690
A second deluge learning thus o'er-run,
And the monks finished what the Goths begun.
  At length Erasmus, that great injured name,
(The glory of the priesthood, and the shame!)
Stemmed the wild torrent of a barb'rous age,
And drove those holy vandals off the stage.
  But see! Each Muse, in Leo's[65] golden days;
Starts from her trance, and trims her withered bays;
Rome's ancient genius, o'er its ruins spread,
Shakes off the dust, and rears his rev'rend head.   700
Then sculpture and her sister arts revive;
Stones leaped to form, and rocks began to live;
With sweeter notes each rising temple rung;
A Raphael painted, and a Vida sung.

---

[62]Place of booksellers.
[63]Homer.
[64]Aristotle's.

[65]Leo X (1475–1521), pope from 1513 to 1521.

Immortal Vida: on whose honored brow
The poet's bays and critic's ivy grow:
Cremona now shall ever boast thy name,
As next in place to Mantua, next in fame!
　　　But soon by impious arms from Latium[66] chased,
Their ancient bounds the banished Muses passed:　　　710
Thence arts o'er all the northern world advance,
But critic learning flourished most in France;
The rules a nation, born to serve, obeys;
And Boileau still in right of Horace sways.
But we, brave Britons, foreign laws, despised,
And kept unconquered, and uncivilized;
Fierce for the liberties of wit, and bold,
We still defied the Romans, as of old.
Yet some there were, among the sounder few
Of those who less presumed, and better knew,　　　720
Who durst assert the juster ancient cause,
And here restored wit's fundamental laws.
Such was the Muse, whose rules and practice tell
"Nature's chief masterpiece is writing well."[67]

Such was Roscommon, not more learned than good,
With manners gen'rous as his noble blood;
To him the wit of Greece and Rome was known,
And ev'ry author's merit, but his own.
Such late was Walsh—the Muse's judge and friend,
Who justly knew to blame or to commend;　　　730
To failings mild, but zealous for desert;
The clearest head, and the sincerest heart.
Thus humble praise, lamented shade! Receive;
This praise at least a grateful Muse may give:
The Muse, whose early voice you taught to sing,
Prescribed her heights, and pruned[68] her tender wing,
(Her guide now lost) no more attempts to rise,
But in low numbers[69] short excursions tries;
Content, if hence th' unlearned their wants may view,
The learned reflect on what before they knew:　　　740
Careless of censure, nor too fond of fame;
Still pleased to praise, yet not afraid to blame;
Averse alike to flatter, or offend;
Not free from faults, nor yet too vain to mend.

---

[66]Italy.
[67]John Sheffield, *Essay on Poetry.*

[68]Preened.
[69]Verses.

Joseph Addison

1672–1719

In his essays on the pleasures of the imagination Addison is concerned with the effect of the work on the reader and thus deals with questions that in the eighteenth century came to be classified under the term *aesthetics*. The matter he treats is subsequently considered by Burke, Hume, and Kant. Addison goes beyond those critics who merely indicate that literature delights and teaches to discuss what he calls the "primary" and "secondary" pleasures of the imagination. Though he uses terms employed earlier by Locke (and later, but differently, by Coleridge), his meanings for them are his own: the primary pleasures are those resulting from our immediate experience of objects; the secondary pleasures arise from our experience of *ideas* of such objects when the objects are not actually present to perception but are represented to us. Pleasures of the imagination are not as "refined" as those of the understanding, since the imagination does not inquire into causes, but they are more obvious and easier to acquire.

Addison does not proceed in his thinking quite to an idea of an "aesthetic emotion" or "aesthetic distance," as do Kant and later theorists; but he does point out that it is possible for something disagreeable in life to be presented agreeably in description. His explanation of this is not, however, very convincing: he thinks that we are pleased in the face of a disagreeable, terrifying, or pitiful representation because we are not ultimately affected by it. We are happy with our good fortune.

Like a number of critics before him, Addison believes that art improves on nature and direct experience. Adopting Locke's concept of the association of ideas, he argues that the imagination compares ideas previously derived from direct experience with ideas derived from art. Those from nature often suffer by comparison. He admits that he cannot really explain why we should derive so much pleasure from these comparisons or from the act of comparison implicit in mimicry. He concludes with a passage reminiscent of Sidney's remark that the poet goes beyond nature to deliver a golden world. It is clear that though Addison cannot answer many of the questions he raises, nevertheless those questions are important ones. They became the concern of theorists for at least one hundred years.

The definitive edition of *The Spectator* is that by D. F. Bond (5 vols., 1965). G. A. Aitken has edited both *The Spectator* (8 vols., 1898) and *The Tatler* (4 vols., 1898–99). For commentary on Addison see C. D. Thorpe, "Addison and Hutcheson on the Imagination," *English Literary History,* II (1935), 215–34; Martin Kallich, "The Association of Ideas: Hobbes, Locke, and Addison," *English Literary History,* XII (1945), 290–315; C. D. Thorpe, "Addison's Contribution to Criticism," *The Seventeenth Century: Studies by R. F. Jones and others* (1951); L. A. Eliosoff, *The Cultural Milieu of Addison's Literary Criticism* (1963); E. and D. Bloom, eds., *Addison and Steele: The Critical Heritage* (1980); and Robert M. Otten, *Joseph Addison* (1982).

On the Pleasures of the Imagination

The Spectator

Number 411

June 21, 1712

*Avia Pieridum peragro loca, nullius ante
Trita solo; juvat integros accedere fonteis;
Atque haurire:*[1]

LUCRETIUS

Our sight is the most perfect and most delightful of all our senses. It fills the mind with the largest variety of ideas, converses with its objects at the greatest distance, and continues the longest in action without being tired or satiated with its proper enjoyments. The sense of feeling can indeed give us a notion of extension, shape, and all other ideas that enter at the eye, except colors; but at the same time it is very much straitened and confined in its operations, to the number, bulk, and distance of its particular objects. Our sight seems designed to supply all these defects, and may be considered as a more delicate and diffusive kind of touch, that spreads itself over an infinite multitude of bodies, comprehends the largest figures, and brings into our reach some of the most remote parts of the universe.

It is this sense which furnishes the imagination with its ideas; so that by the pleasures of the imagination or fancy (which I shall use promiscuously) I here mean such as arise from visible objects, either when we have them actually in our view, or when we call up their ideas into our minds by paintings, statues, descriptions, or any the like occasion. We cannot indeed have a single image in the fancy that did not make its first entrance through the sight; but we have the power of retaining, altering and compounding those images, which we have once received, into all the varieties of picture and vision that are most agreeable to the imagination; for by this faculty a man in a dungeon is capable of entertaining himself with scenes and landskips more beautiful than any that can be found in the whole compass of nature.

There are few words in the English language which are employed in a more loose and uncircumscribed sense than those of the *fancy* and the *imagination*. I therefore thought it necessary to fix and determine the notion of these two words, as I intend to make use of them in the thread of my following speculations, that the reader may conceive rightly what is the subject which I proceed upon. I must therefore desire to remember, that by the pleasures of the imagination, I mean only such pleasures as arise originally from sight, and that I divide these pleasures into two kinds: my design being first of all to discourse of those primary pleasures of the imagination, which entirely proceed from such objects as are before our eyes; and in the next place to speak of those secondary pleasures of the imagination which flow from the ideas of visible objects, when the objects are not actually before the eye, but are called up into our memories, or formed into agreeable visions of things that are either absent or fictitious.[2]

The pleasures of the imagination, taken in their full extent, are not so gross as those of sense, nor so refined as those of the understanding. The last are, indeed, more preferable, because they are founded on some new knowledge or improvement in the mind of man; yet it must be confessed, that those of the imagination are as great and as transporting as the other. A beautiful prospect delights the soul, as much as a demonstration; and a description in Homer has charmed more readers than a chapter in Aristotle. Besides the pleasures of the imagination have this advantage, above those of the understanding, that they are more obvious, and more easy to be acquired. It is but opening the eye, and the scene enters. The colors paint themselves on the fancy, with very little attention of thought or application of mind in the beholder. We are struck, we know not how, with the symmetry of anything we see, and immediately assent to the beauty of an object, without inquiring into the particular causes and occasions of it.

A man of a polite imagination is let into a great many pleasures, that the vulgar are not capable of receiving. He can converse with a picture, and find an agreeable companion in a statue. He meets with a secret refreshment in a description, and often feels a greater satisfaction in the prospect of fields and meadows, than another does in the possession. It gives him, indeed, a kind of property in everything he sees, and makes the most rude uncultivated parts of nature administer to his pleasures: so that he looks upon the world, as it were, in another light, and discovers in it a multitude of charms, that conceal themselves from the generality of mankind.

There are, indeed, but very few who know how to be idle and innocent, or have a relish of any pleasures that are

---

ON THE PLEASURES OF THE IMAGINATION. These three essays on the pleasures of the imagination appeared in three issues of *The Spectator* published in June, 1712.

[1]"I travel through the untrodden places of the Muses, where no one has gone before; it is a delight to approach fresh springs, and to drink." *On the Nature of Things*, I. 926–28.

[2]Addison's use of *primary* and *secondary* loosely recalls John Locke's use of the terms to mean objective and subjective qualities of experience. However, the distinction Addison makes is not the one Locke makes.

not criminal; every diversion they take is at the expense of some one virtue or another, and their very first step out of business is into vice or folly. A man should endeavor, therefore, to make the sphere of his innocent pleasures as wide as possible, that he may retire into them with safety, and find in them such a satisfaction as a wise man would not blush to take. Of this nature are those of the imagination, which do not require such a bent of thought as is necessary to our more serious employments, nor at the same time, suffer the mind to sink into that negligence and remissness, which are apt to accompany our more sensual delights, but, like a gentle exercise to the faculties, awaken them from sloth and idleness, without putting them upon any labor or difficulty.

We might here add, that the pleasures of the fancy are more conducive to health, than those of the understanding, which are worked out by dint of thinking, and attended with too violent a labor of the brain. Delightful scenes, whether in nature, painting, or poetry, have a kindly influence on the body, as well as the mind, and not only serve to clear and brighten the imagination, but are able to disperse grief and melancholy, and to set the animal spirits in pleasing and agreeable motions. For this reason Sir Francis Bacon, in his essay upon health, has not thought it improper to prescribe to his reader a poem or a prospect, where he particularly dissuades him from knotty and subtle disquisitions, and advises him to pursue studies that fill the mind with splendid and illustrious objects, as histories, fables, and contemplations of nature.

I have in this paper, by way of introduction, settled the notion of those pleasures of the imagination which are the subject of my present undertaking, and endeavored, by several considerations, to recommend to my reader the pursuit of those pleasures. I shall, in my next paper, examine the several sources from whence these pleasures are derived.

The Spectator

Number 416

June 27, 1712

Quatenus hoc simile est oculis, quod mente videmus.[3]
LUCRETIUS

I at first divided the pleasures of the imagination, into such as arise from objects that are actually before our eyes, or that once entered in at our eyes, and are afterwards called up into the mind, either barely by its own operations, or on occasion of something without us, as statues or descriptions. We have already considered the first division, and shall therefore enter on the other, which, for distinction sake, I have called the secondary pleasures of the imagination. When I say the ideas we receive from statues, descriptions, or such like occasions, are the same that were once actually in our view, it must not be understood that we had once seen the very place, action, or person which are carved or described. It is sufficient, that we have seen places, persons, or actions in general, which bear a resemblance, or at least some remote analogy with what we find represented. Since it is in the power of the imagination, when it is once stocked with particular ideas, to enlarge, compound, and vary them at her own pleasure.[4]

Among the different kinds of representation, statuary is the most natural, and shews us something *likest* the object that is represented. To make use of a common instance, let one who is born blind take an image in his hands, and trace out with his fingers the different furrows and impressions of the chisel, and he will easily conceive how the shape of a man, or beast, may be represented by it; but should he draw his hand over a picture, where all is smooth and uniform, he would never be able to imagine how the several prominencies and depressions of a human body could be shewn on a plain piece of canvas, that has in it no unevenness or irregularity. Description runs yet further from the things it represents than painting; for a picture bears a real resemblance to its original, which letters and syllables are wholly void of Colors speak all languages, but words are understood only by such a people or nation. For this reason, though men's necessities quickly put them on finding out speech, writing is probably of a later invention than painting; particularly we are told, that in America when the Spaniards first arrived there, expresses were sent to the Emperor of Mexico in paint, and the news of his country delineated by the strokes of a pencil, which was a more natural way than that of writing, though at the same time much more imperfect, because it is impossible to draw the little connections of speech, or to give the picture of a conjunction or an adverb. It would be yet more strange to represent visible objects by sounds that have no ideas annexed to them, and to make something like description in music. Yet it is certain, there may be confused, imperfect notions of this nature raised in the imagination by an artificial composition of notes; and we find that great masters in the art are able, sometimes to set their hearers in the heat and hurry of a battle, to overcast their minds with melancholy scenes and apprehensions of deaths and funer-

---

[3] "How similar is what we see with our minds to what we see with our eyes." Slightly misquoted from *On the Nature of Things,* IV. 750–51.

[4] Here Addison refers to the common Lockean notion of the association of ideas.

als, or to lull them into pleasing dreams of groves and Elysiums.

In all these instances, this secondary pleasure of the imagination proceeds from that action of the mind, which compares the ideas arising from the original objects, with the ideas we receive from the statue, picture, description, or sound that represents them. It is impossible for us to give the necessary reason, why this operation of the mind is attended with so much pleasure, as I have before observed on the same occasion; but we find a great variety of entertainments derived from this single principle: for it is this that not only gives us a relish of statuary, painting and description, but makes us delight in all the actions and arts of mimicry. It is this that makes the several kinds of wit pleasant, which consists, as I have formerly shewn, in the affinity of ideas: And we may add, it is this also that raises the little satisfaction we sometimes find in the different sorts of false wit; whether it consist in the affinity of letters, as an anagram, acrostic; or of syllables, as in doggerel rhymes, echoes; or of words, as in puns, quibbles; or of a whole sentence or poem, to wings, and altars. The final cause, probably, of annexing pleasure to this operation of the mind, was to quicken and encourage us in our searches after truth, since the distinguishing one thing from another, and the right discerning betwixt our ideas, depends wholly upon our comparing them together, and observing the congruity or disagreement that appears among the several works of nature.

But I shall here confine myself to those pleasures of the imagination, which proceed from ideas raised by *words,* because most of the observations that agree with descriptions are equally applicable to painting and statuary.

Words, when well chosen, have so great a force in them, that a description often gives us more lively ideas than the sight of things themselves. The reader finds a scene drawn in stronger colors, and painted more to the life in his imagination, by the help of words, than by an actual survey of the scene which they describe. In this case the poet seems to get the better of nature; he takes, indeed, the landskip after her, but gives it more vigorous touches, heightens its beauty, and so enlivens the whole piece, that the images which flow from the objects themselves appear weak and faint, in comparison of those that come from the expressions. The reason, probably, may be, because in the survey of any object, we have only so much of it painted on the imagination, as comes in at the eye; but in its description, the poet gives us as free a view of it as he pleases, and discovers to us several parts, that either we did not attend to, or that lay out of our sight when we first beheld it. As we look on any object, our idea of it is, perhaps, made up of two or three simple ideas; but when the poet represents it, he may either give us a more

complex idea of it, or only raise in us such ideas as are most apt to affect the imagination.

It may be here worth our while to examine, how it comes to pass that several readers, who are all acquainted with the same language, and know the meaning of the words they read, should nevertheless have a different relish of the same descriptions. We find one transported with a passage, which another runs over with coldness and indifference, or finding the representation extremely natural, where another can perceive nothing of likeness and conformity. This different taste must proceed either from the perfection of imagination in one more than in another, or from the different ideas that several readers affix to the same words. For, to have a true relish, and form a right judgment of a description, a man should be born with a good imagination, and must have well weighed the force and energy that lie in the several words of a language, so as to be able to distinguish which are most significant and expressive of their proper ideas, and what additional strength and beauty they are capable of receiving from conjunction with others. The fancy must be warm, to retain the print of those images it hath received from outward objects; and the judgment discerning, to know what expressions are most proper to clothe and adorn them to the best advantage. A man who is deficient in either of these respects, though he may receive the general notion of a description, can never see distinctly all its particular beauties: as a person with a weak sight may have the confused prospect of a place that lies before him, without entering into its several parts, or discerning the variety of its colors in their full glory and perfection.

The Spectator

Number 418

June 30, 1712

. . . Ferat et rubus asper amomum.[5]
VIRGIL

The pleasures of these secondary views of the imagination, are of a wider and more universal nature than those it has when joined with sight; for not only what is great, strange or beautiful, but anything that is disagreeable when looked upon, pleases us in an apt description. Here, therefore, we must inquire after a new principle of pleasure, which is noth-

---

[5]"Rough bramble bears balsam." *Eclogues,* VI. 3–4.

ing else but the action of the mind, which *compares* the ideas that arise from words, with the ideas that arise from the objects themselves; and why this operation of the mind is attended with so much pleasure, we have before considered. For this reason therefore, the description of a dunghill is pleasing to the imagination, if the image be represented to our minds by suitable expressions; though, perhaps, this may be more properly called the pleasure of the understanding than of the fancy, because we are not so much delighted with the image that is contained in the description, as with the aptness of the description to excite the image.

But if the description of what is little, common or deformed, be acceptable to the imagination, the description of what is great, surprising or beautiful, is much more so; because here we are not only delighted with *comparing* the representation with the original, but are highly pleased with the original itself. Most readers, I believe, are more charmed with Milton's description of paradise, than of hell; they are both, perhaps, equally perfect in their kind, but in the one the brimstone and sulphur are not so refreshing to the imagination, as the beds of flowers and the wilderness of sweets in the other.

There is yet another circumstance which recommends a description more than all the rest, and that is, if it represents to us such objects as are apt to raise a secret ferment in the mind of the reader, and to work, with violence, upon his passions. For, in this case, we are at once warmed and enlightened, so that the pleasure becomes more universal, and is several ways qualified to entertain us. Thus, in painting, it is pleasant to look on the picture of any face, where the resemblance is hit, but the pleasure increases, if it be the picture of a face that is beautiful, and is still greater if the beauty be softened with an air of melancholy or sorrow. The two leading passions which the more serious parts of poetry endeavor to stir up in us, are terror and pity. And here, by the way, one would wonder how it comes to pass, that such passions as are very unpleasant at all other times, are very agreeable when excited by proper descriptions. It is not strange, that we should take delight in such passages as are apt to produce hope, joy, admiration, love, or the like emotions in us, because they never rise in the mind without an inward pleasure which attends them. But how comes it to pass, that we should take delight in being terrified or dejected by a description, when we find so much uneasiness in the fear or grief which we receive from any other occasion?

If we consider, therefore, the nature of this pleasure, we shall find that it does not arise so properly from the description of what is terrible, as from the reflection we make on ourselves at the time of reading it. When we look on such hideous objects, we are not a little pleased to think we are in no danger of them. We consider them at the same time, as dreadful and harmless; so that the more frightful appearance they make, the greater is the pleasure we receive from the sense of our own safety. In short, we look upon the terrors of a description with the same curiosity and satisfaction that we survey a dead monster.

> *Informe cadaver*
> *Protrahitur, nequeunt expleri corda tuendo*
> *Terribiles oculos: vultum, villosaque setis*
> *Pectora semiferi, atque extinctos faucibus ignes.*[6]
> VIRGIL

It is for the same reason that we are delighted with the reflecting upon dangers that are past, or in looking on a precipice at a distance, which would fill us with a different kind of horror, if we saw it hanging over our heads.

In the like manner, when we read of torments, wounds, deaths, and the like dismal accidents, our pleasure does not flow so properly from the grief which such melancholy descriptions give us, as from the secret comparison which we make between ourselves and the person who suffers. Such representations teach us to set a just value upon our own condition, and make us prize our good fortune, which exempts us from the like calamities. This is, however, such a kind of pleasure as we are not capable of receiving, when we see a person actually lying under the tortures that we meet with in a description; because, in this case, the object presses too close upon our senses, and bears so hard upon us, that it does not give us time or leisure to reflect on ourselves. Our thoughts are so intent upon the miseries of the sufferer, that we cannot turn them upon our own happiness. Whereas, on the contrary, we consider the misfortunes we read in history or poetry, either as past, or as fictitious, so that the reflection upon ourselves rises in us insensibly, and overbears the sorrow we conceive for the sufferings of the afflicted.

But because the mind of man requires something more perfect in matter, than what it finds there, and can never meet with any sight in nature which sufficiently answers its highest ideas of pleasantness; or, in other words, because the imagination can fancy to itself things more great, strange, or beautiful, than the eye ever saw, and is still sensible of some defect in what it has seen; on this account it is the part of a poet to humor the imagination in its own notions, by mending and perfecting nature where he describes a reality, and

---

[6] "The hideous cadaver is dragged along; their hearts cannot be satisfied gazing on the terrible eyes, the countenance, and the shaggy hair of the chest of the half-wild creature and the extinct fire from his throat." *Aeneid,* VIII. 264.

by adding greater beauties than are put together in nature, where he describes a fiction.[7]

He is not obliged to attend her in the slow advances which she makes from one season to another, or to observe her conduct in the successive production of plants and flowers. He may draw into his description all the beauties of the spring and autumn, and make the whole year contribute something to render it the more agreeable. His rose trees, woodbines and jessamines may flower together, and his beds be covered at the same time with lilies, violets, and amaranths. His soil is not restrained to any particular set of plants, but is proper either for oaks or myrtles, and adapts itself to the products of every climate. Oranges may grow wild in it; myrrh may be met with in every hedge, and if he thinks it proper to have a grove of spices, he can quickly command sun enough to raise it. If all this will not furnish out an agreeable scene, he can make several new species of flowers, with richer scents and higher colors than any that grow in the gardens of nature. His consorts of birds may be as full and harmonious, and his woods as thick and gloomy as he pleases. He is at no more expense in the long vista, than a short one, and can as easily throw his cascades from a precipice of half a mile high, as from one of twenty yards. He has his choice of the winds, and can turn the course of his rivers in all the variety of meanders, that are most delightful to the reader's imagination. In a word, he has the modeling of nature in his own hands, and may give her what charms he pleases, provided he does not reform her too much, and run into absurdities, by endeavoring to excel.

---

[7]For Addison, then, the poet's aim in improving on nature is not the neo-Platonic one of bringing man nearer to "reality"; his aim is rather to provide pleasure.

Giambattista Vico

1668–1744

Vico, in *The New Science,* offered a retort to prevailing rationalistic theories of human development, including the development of language. He conceived of a heroic age in which men constructed myths, symbols, and rituals that served as the basis for the slow growth of the human consciousness of history and reality. This "poetic wisdom" led to abstract thought, but not without an eventual loss of spirit and imaginative life. Vico's method of studying anything was to speculate on its origins.

In defining poetry Vico treats its origins in the primitive imagination: the first men "gave the things they wondered at substantial being after their own ideas." He offers a concept of "sympathetic nature" that anticipates Romantic criticism, the work of modern anthropologists, and a number of critics who have employed the terms *myth* and *ritual.* He gives a new twist to Aristotle's rationalistic conception of the "credible impossibility"; he sees it characteristically in its historical origins as the result of primitive wonder and imaginative power. He values Homer and ancient poets very highly as the creators of culture. The philosophers, who followed them, he holds, built up systems of abstract thought from the poets' imaginative creations. Thus Vico is one of the earliest theorists to base the importance of art on the principle that abstract thought emerges from iconic expression or mythical thinking. As a consequence Vico reverses the usual rationalistic definitions of the poetic tropes as special kinds of deviation from rational linguistic procedures. He sees them as both temporally and logically prior to abstract thought; they are "necessary modes of expression." In taking this position he anticipates remarks by Blake in *The Marriage of Heaven and Hell* and parts of Cassirer's analysis of mythical thinking as a "symbolic form."

As an interpreter of ancient myths Vico differs from Platonists like Porphyry, Henry Reynolds, and Thomas Taylor. He considers myths to be "true narrations," or imaginative representations of historical events and movements, rather than allegories of mystical or philosophical concepts.

The New Science *of Giambattista Vico,* translated by T. G. Bergin and M. H. Fisch (1968), is a revised translation of the third edition. Bergin and Fisch have also translated *Autobiography of Giambattista Vico* (1944). For commentary see Benedetto Croce, *The Philosophy of Giambattista Vico* (1913); H. P. Adams, *The Life and Writings of Giambattista Vico* (1935); and A. A. Grimaldi, *The Universal Humanity of Giambattista Vico* (1958); G. Tagliacozzo and H. White eds., *Giambattista Vico: An International Symposium* (1969); Leon Pompa, *Vico: A Study of the New Science* (1975); Isaiah Berlin, *Vico and Herder* (1976); Donald Philip Verene, *Vico's Science of Imagination* (1981); and Gino Bedani, *Vico Revisited* (1989), and *New Vico Studies* (1981).

From

The New Science

Premising such reflections on the vain opinion of their own antiquity held by these gentile nations and above all by the Egyptians,[1] we should begin our study of gentile learning [*tutto lo scibile gentilesco*] by scientifically ascertaining this important starting point—where and when that learning had its first beginnings in the world—and by adducing human reasons thereby in support of Christian faith [*tutto il credibile cristiano*], which takes its start from the fact that the first people of the world were the Hebrews, whose prince was Adam, created by the true God at the time of the creation of the world. It follows that the first science to be learned should be mythology or the interpretation of fables; for, as we shall see, all the histories of the gentiles have their beginnings in fables, which were the first histories of the gentile nations. By such a method the beginnings of the sciences as well as of the nations are to be discovered, for they sprang from the nations and from no other source. It will be shown throughout this work that they had their beginnings in the public needs or utilities of the peoples and that they were later perfected as acute individuals applied their reflection to them. This is the proper starting point for universal history, which all scholars say is defective in its beginnings.

* * *

We have said above in the Axioms that all the histories of the gentile nations have had fabulous beginnings, that among the Greeks (who have given us all we know of gentile antiquity) the first sages were the theological poets, and that the nature of everything born or made betrays the crudeness of its origin. It is thus and not otherwise that we must conceive the origins of poetic wisdom. And as for the great and sovereign esteem in which it has been handed down to us, this has its origin in the two conceits, that of nations and that of scholars, and it springs even more from the latter than from the former. For just as Manetho, the Egyptian high priest, translated all the fabulous history of Egypt into a sub-

lime natural theology, so the Greek philosophers translated theirs into philosophy.[2] And they did so not merely for the reason that the histories as they had come down to both alike were most unseemingly, but for the following five reasons as well.

The first was reverence for religion, for the gentile nations were everywhere founded by fables on religion. The second was the grand effect thence derived, namely this civil world, so wisely ordered that it could only be the effect of a superhuman wisdom. The third was the occasions which, as we shall see, these fables, assisted by the veneration of religion and the credit of such great wisdom, gave the philosophers for instituting research and for meditating lofty things in philosophy. The fourth was the ease with which they were thus enabled, as we shall also show farther on, to explain their sublime philosophical meditations by means of the expressions happily left them by the poets. The fifth and last, which is the sum of them all, is the confirmation of their own meditations which the philosophers derived from the authority of religion and the wisdom of the poets. Of these five reasons, the first two and the last contain the praises of the divine wisdom which ordained this world of nations, and the witness the philosophers bore to it even in their errors. The third and fourth are deceptions permitted by divine providence, that thence there might arise philosophers to understand and recognize it for what it truly is, an attribute of the true God.

Throughout this book it will be shown that as much as the poets had first sensed in the way of vulgar wisdom, the philosophers later understood in the way of esoteric wisdom; so that the former may be said to have been the sense and the latter the intellect of the human race. What Aristotle said of the individual man is therefore true of the race in general: *"Nihil est in intellectu quin prius fuerit in sensu."*[3] That is, the human mind does not understand anything of which it has had no previous impression (which our modern metaphysicians call *occasion*) from the senses. Now the mind uses the intellect when, from something it senses, it gathers something which does not fall under the senses; and this proper meaning of the Latin verb *intelligere*.

Now, before discussing poetic wisdom, it is necessary for us to see what wisdom in general is. Wisdom is the faculty which commands all the disciplines by which we acquire all the sciences and arts that make up humanity. Plato defines wisdom as "the perfecter of man."[4] Man, in his

---

THE NEW SCIENCE. Vico's *Principii d'una scienza nuova* was first published in 1725. The text is from Thomas Goddard Bergin and Harold Fisch, trs., *The New Science of Giambattista Vico: unabridged translation of the Third Edition (1744)* with the addition of "Practice of the New Science." Copyright © by Cornell University. Used by permission of Cornell University Press.
[1]Vico argues that the Egyptians were not as ancient a nation as supposed, that the human mind "is often led to believe that the things it does not know are vastly greater than in fact they are."

[2]See Blake, *The Marriage of Heaven and Hell*, p. 401.
[3]*On the Soul*, 432.
[4]*Alcibiades*, I. 124.

proper being as man, consists of mind and spirit, or, if we prefer, of intellect and will. It is the function of wisdom to fulfill both these parts in man, the second by way of the first, to the end that by a mind illuminated by knowledge of the highest institutions, the spirit may be led to choose the best. The highest institutions in this universe are those turned toward and conversant with God; the best are those which look to the good of all mankind. The former are called divine institutions, the latter human. True wisdom, then, should teach the knowledge of divine institutions in order to conduct human institutions to the highest good. We believe that this was the plan upon which Marcus Terentius Varro, who earned the title "most learned of the Romans," erected his great work, [*The Antiquities*] *Of Divine and Human Institutions,* of which the injustice of time has unhappily bereft us. We shall treat of these institutions in the present book so far as the weakness of our education and the meagerness of our erudition permit.

Wisdom among the gentiles began with the Muse, defined by Homer in a golden passage of the *Odyssey* as "knowledge of good and evil,"[5] and later called divination. It was on the natural prohibition of this practice, as something naturally denied to man, that God founded the true religion of the Hebrews, from which our Christian religion arose. The Muse must thus have been properly at first the science of divining by auspices, and this was the vulgar wisdom of all nations, of which we shall have more to say presently. It consisted in contemplating God under the attributer of his providence, so that from *divinari* his essence came to be called divinity. We shall see presently that the theological poets, who certainly founded the humanity of Greece, were versed in this wisdom, and this explains why the Latins called the judicial astrologers "professors of wisdom." Wisdom was later attributed to men renowned for useful counsels given to mankind, as in the case of the Seven Sages of Greece. The attribution was then extended to men who for the good of peoples and nations wisely ordered and governed commonwealths. Still later the word *wisdom* came to mean knowledge of natural divine things; that is, metaphysics, called for that reason divine science, which, seeking knowledge of man's mind in God, and recognizing God as the source of all truth, must recognize him as the regulator of all good. So that metaphysics must essentially work for the good of the human race, whose preservation depends on the universal belief in a provident divinity. It is perhaps for having demonstrated this providence that Plato deserved to be called divine; and that which denies to God this great attrib-

ute must be called stupidity rather than wisdom. Finally among the Hebrews, and thence among us Christians, wisdom was called the science of eternal things revealed by God; a science which, among the Tuscans, considered as knowledge of the true good and true evil, perhaps owed to that fact the first name they gave it, "science in divinity."

We must therefore distinguish more truly than Varro did the three kinds of theology. First, poetic theology, that of the theological poets, which was the civil theology of all the gentile nations. Second, natural theology, that of the metaphysicians. Third, our Christian theology, a mixture of civil and natural with the loftiest revealed theology; all three united in the contemplation of divine providence. (Our third kind takes the place of Varro's poetic theology, which among the gentiles was the same as civil theology, though he distinguished it from both civil and natural theology because, sharing the vulgar common error that the fables contained high mysteries of sublime philosophy, he believed it to be a mixture of the two.) Divine providence has so conducted human institutions that, starting from the poetic theology which regulated them by certain sensible signs believed to be divine counsels sent to man by the gods, and by means of the natural theology which demonstrates providence by eternal reasons which do not fall under the senses, the nations were disposed to receive revealed theology in virtue of a supernatural faith, superior not only to the senses but to human reason itself.

But because metaphysics is the sublime science which distributes their determinate subject matters to all the so-called subaltern sciences; and because the wisdom of the ancients was that of the theological poets, who without doubt were the first sages of the gentile world; and because the origins of all things must by nature have been crude: for all these reasons we must trace beginnings of poetic wisdom to a crude metaphysics. From this, as from a trunk, there branch out from one limb logic, morals, economics, and politics, all poetic; and from another, physics, the mother of cosmography and astronomy, the latter of which gives their certainty to its two daughters, chronology and geography—all likewise poetic. We shall show clearly and distinctly how the founders of gentile humanity by means of their natural theology (or metaphysics) imagined the gods; how by means of their logic they invented languages; by morals, created heroes; by economics, founded families, and by politics, cities; by their physics, established the beginnings of things as all divine; by the particular physics of man, in a certain sense created themselves; by their cosmography, fashioned for themselves a universe entirely of gods; by astronomy, carried the planets and constellations from earth to heaven; by chronology, gave a beginning to [measured] times; and how

---

[5]XIII. 63.

by geography the Greeks, for example, described the [whole] world within their own Greece.

Thus our science comes to be at once a history of the ideas, the customs, and the deeds of mankind. From these three we shall derive the principles of the history of human nature, which we shall show to be the principles of universal history, which principles it seems hitherto to have lacked.

* * *

From these first men, stupid, insensate, and horrible beasts, all the philosophers and philologians should have begun their investigations of the wisdom of the ancient gentiles; that is, from the giants in the proper sense in which we have just taken them. (Father Boulduc in his *De ecclesia ante Legem* says the scriptural names of the giants signify "pious, venerable and illustrious men"; but this can be understood only of the noble giants who by divination founded the gentile religions and gave the giants its name.) And they should have begun with metaphysics, which seeks its proof not in the external world but within the modifications of the mind of him who meditates it. For since this world of nations has certainly been made by men, it is within these modifications that its principles should have been sought. And human nature, so far as it is like that of animals, carries with it this property, that the senses are its sole way of knowing things.

Hence poetic wisdom, the first wisdom of the gentile world, must have begun with a metaphysic not rational and abstract like that of learned men now, but felt and imagined as that of these first men must have been, who, without power of ratiocination, were all robust sense and vigorous imagination. This metaphysics was their poetry, a faculty born with them (for they were furnished by nature with these senses and imaginations); born of their ignorance of causes, for ignorance, the mother of wonder, made everything wonderful to men who were ignorant of everything. Their poetry was at first divine, because, as we saw in the passage from Lactantius,[6] they imagined the causes of the things they felt and wondered at to be gods. (This is now confirmed by the American Indians, who call gods all the things that surpass their small understanding. We may add the ancient Germans dwelling about the Arctic Ocean, of whom Tacitus tells that they spoke of hearing the sun pass at night from west to east through the sea, and affirmed that they saw the gods. These very rude and simple nations help us to a much better under-

standing of the founders of the gentile world with whom we are now concerned.) At the same time they gave the things they wondered at substantial being after their own ideas, just as children do, whom we see take inanimate things in their hands and play with them and talk to them as though they were living persons.

In such fashion the first men of the gentile nations, children of nascent mankind, created things according to their own ideas. But this creation was infinitely different from that of God. For God, in his purest intelligence, knows things, and, by knowing them, creates them; but they, in their robust ignorance, did it by virtue of a wholly corporeal imagination. And because it was quite corporeal, they did it with marvelous sublimity; a sublimity such and so great that it excessively perturbed the very persons who by imagining did the creating, for which they were called *poets,* which is Greek for *creators.* Now this is the threefold labor of great poetry: (1) to invent sublime fables suited to the popular understanding, (2) to perturb to excess, with a view to the end proposed: (3) to teach the vulgar to act virtuously, as the poets have taught themselves; as will presently be shown. Of this nature of human institutions it remained an eternal property, expressed in a noble phrase of Tacitus, that frightened men vainly "no sooner imagine than they believe" (*fingunt simul creduntque*).

Of such natures must have been the first founders of gentile humanity when at last the sky fearfully rolled with thunder and flashed with lightning, as could not but follow from the bursting upon the air for the first time of an impression so violent. As we have postulated, this occurred a hundred years after the flood in Mesopotamia and two hundred years after it throughout the rest of the world; for it took that much time to reduce the earth to such a state that, dry of the moisture of the universal flood, it could send up dry exhalations or matter igniting in the air to produce lightning. Thereupon a few giants, who must have been the most robust, and who were dispersed through the forest on the mountain heights where the strongest beasts have their dens, were frightened and astonished by the great effect whose cause they did not know, and raised their eyes and became aware of the sky. And because in such a case the nature of the human mind leads it to attribute its own nature to the effect, and because in that state their nature was that of men all robust bodily strength, who expressed their very violent passions by shouting and grumbling, they pictured the sky to themselves as a great animated body, which in that aspect they called Jove, the first god of the so-called greater gentes,[7]

---

[6][Vico] That is a golden passage in Lactantius Fermianus [*Divine Institutions, I.* 15] where he considers the origins of idolatry, saying: "Rude men at first called [them, i.e., the king and his family] gods either for their wonderful excellence (wonderful it seemed to men still rude and simple), or, as commonly happens, in admiration of present power, or on account of the benefits by which they had been brought to humanity."

[7]"Nations," by which Vico means a race or group having a common origin, a common language, or common institutions.

who meant to tell them something by the hiss of his bolts and the clap of his thunder. And thus they began to exercise that natural curiosity which is the daughter of ignorance and the mother of knowledge, and which, opening the mind of man, gives birth to wonder. This characteristic still persists in the vulgar, who, when they see a comet or sundog or some other extraordinary thing in nature, and particularly in the countenance of the sky, at once turn curious and anxiously inquire what it means. When they wonder at the prodigious effects of the magnet on iron, even in this age of minds enlightened and instructed by philosophy, they come out with this: that the magnet has an occult sympathy for the iron; and they make of all nature a vast animate body which feels passions and effects.

But the nature of our civilized minds is so detached from the senses, even in the vulgar, by abstractions corresponding to all the abstract terms our languages abound in, and so refined by the art of writing, and as it were spiritualized by the use of numbers, because even the vulgar know how to count and reckon, that it is naturally beyond our power to form the vast image of this mistress called Sympathetic Nature. Men shape the phrase with their lips but have nothing in their minds; for what they have in mind is falsehood, which is nothing; and their imagination no longer avails to form a vast false image. It is equally beyond our power to enter into the vast imagination of those first men, whose minds were not in the least abstract, refined, or spiritualized, because they were entirely immersed in the senses, buffeted by the passions, buried in the body. That is why we said above that we can scarcely understand, still less imagine, how those first men thought who founded gentile humanity.

In this fashion the first theological poets created the first divine fable, the greatest they ever created: that of Jove, king and father of men and gods, in the act of hurling the lightning bolt; an image so popular, disturbing, and instructive that its creators themselves believed in it, and feared, revered, and worshiped it in frightful religions. And by that trait of the human mind noticed by Tacitus whatever these men saw, imagined, or even made or did themselves they believed to be Jove; and to all of the universe that came within their scope, and to all its parts, they gave the being of animate substance. This is the civil history of the expression "All things are full of Jove" (*Iovis omnia plena*)[8] by which Plato later understood the ether which penetrates and fills everything.[9] But for the theological poets Jove was no higher than the mountain peaks. The first men, who spoke by signs,

naturally believed that lightning bolts and thunderclaps were signs made to them by Jove; whence from *nuo,* "to make a sign," came *numen,* "the divine will," by an idea more than sublime and worthy to express the divine majesty. They believed that Jove commanded by signs, that such signs were real words, and that nature was the language of Jove. The science of this language the gentiles universally believed to be divination, which by the Greeks was called theology, meaning the science of the language of the gods. Thus Jove acquired the fearful kingdom of the lightning and became the king of men and gods; and he acquired the two titles, that of best (*optimus*) in the sense of strongest (*fortissimus*) (as by a reverse process *fortis* meant in early Latin what *bonus* did in late), and that of greatest (*maximus*) from his vast body, the sky itself. From the first great benefit he conferred on mankind by not destroying it with his bolts, he received the title *Soter,* or savior. (This is the first of three principles we have taken for our science.) And for having put an end to the feral wandering of these few giants, so that they became the princes of the gentes, he received the epithet *Stator,* stayer or establisher. The Latin philologians explain this epithet too narrowly from Jove, invoked by Romulus, having stopped the Romans in their flight from the battle with the Sabines.

Thus the many Joves the philologians wonder at are so many physical histories preserved for us by the fables, which prove the universality of the flood. For every gentile nation had its Jove, and the Egyptians had the conceit to say that their Jove Ammon was the most ancient of them all.

Thus in accordance with what has been said about the principles of the poetic characters, Jove was born naturally in poetry as a divine character or imaginative universal, to which everything having to do with the auspices was referred by all the ancient gentile nations, which must therefore all have been poetic by nature. Their poetic wisdom began with this poetic metaphysics, which contemplated God by the attribute of his providence; and they were called theological poets, or sages who understood the language of the gods expressed in the auspices of Jove; and were properly called divine in the sense of diviners, from *divinari,* "to divine or predict." Their science was called Muse, defined by Homer as the knowledge of good and evil; that is, divination, on the prohibition of which God ordained his true religion for Adam. Because they were versed in this mystic theology, the Greek poets, who explained the divine mysteries of the auspices and oracles, were called *mystae,* which Horace learnedly renders "interpreters of the gods."[10] Every gentile nation had its own sibyl versed in this science, and

---

[8]Virgil, *Eclogues,* III. 60.
[9]*Cratylus,* 412.
[10]*Art of Poetry,* p. 73.

we find mention of twelve of them. Sibyls and oracles are the most ancient institutions of the gentile world.

All the things here discussed agree with that golden passage of Eusebius [i.e., Lactantius] on the origins of idolatry: that the first people, simple and rough, invented the gods "from terror of present power." Thus it was fear which created gods in the world; not fear awakened in men by other men, but fear awakened in men by themselves. Along with this origin of idolatry is demonstrated likewise the origin of divination, which was brought into the world at the same birth. The origins of these two were followed by that of the sacrifices made to procure or rightly understand the auspices.

That such was the origin of poetry is finally confirmed by this eternal property of it: that its proper material is the credible impossibility.[11] It is impossible that bodies should be minds, yet it was believed that the thundering sky was Jove. And nothing is dearer to poets than singing the marvels wrought by sorceresses by means of incantations. All this is to be explained by a hidden sense the nations have of the omnipotence of God. From this sense springs another by which all peoples are naturally led to do infinite honors to divinity. In this manner the poets founded religions among the gentiles.

All that has been so far said here upsets all the theories of the origin of poetry from Plato and Aristotle down to Patrizzi,[12] Scaliger, and Castelvetro. For it has been shown that it was deficiency of human reasoning power that gave rise to poetry so sublime that the philosophies which came afterward, the arts of poetry and of criticism, have produced none equal or better and have even prevented its production. Hence it is Homer's privilege to be, of all the sublime, that is, the heroic poets, the first in the order of merit as well as in that of age. This discovery of the origins of poetry does away with the opinion of the matchless wisdom of the ancients, so ardently sought after from Plato to Bacon's *De sapientia veterum*.[13] For the wisdom of the ancients was the vulgar wisdom of the lawgivers who founded the human race, not the esoteric wisdom of great and rare philosophers. Whence it will be found, as it has been in the case of Jove, that all the mystic meanings of lofty philosophy attributed by the learned to the Greek fables and the Egyptian hieroglyphics are as impertinent as the historical meanings they both must have had are natural.

* * *

That which is metaphysics insofar as it contemplates things in all the forms of their being, is logic insofar as it considers things in all the forms by which they may be signified. Accordingly, as poetry has been considered by us above as a poetic metaphysics in which the theological poets imagined bodies to be for the most part divine substances, so now that same poetry is considered as poetic logic, by which it signifies them.

Logic comes from *logos,* whose first and proper meaning was *fabula,* "fable," carried over into Italian as *favella,* "speech." In Greek the fable was also called *mythos,* "myth," whence comes the Latin *mutus,* "mute." For speech was born in mute times as mental [or sign] language, which Strabo in a golden passage says existed before vocal or articulate [language]; whence *logos* means both "word" and "idea." It was fitting that the matter should be so ordered by divine providence in religious times, for it is an eternal property of religions that they attach more importance to meditation than to speech. Thus the first language in the first mute times of the nations must have begun with signs, whether gestures or physical objects, which had natural relations to the ideas [to be expressed]. For this reason *logos,* or "word," meant also "deed" to the Hebrews and "thing" to the Greeks, as Thomas Gataker observes in his *De instrumenti stylo.*[14] Similarly, *mythos* came to be defined for us as *vera narratio,* or "true speech," the natural speech which first Plato and then Iamblichus said had been spoken in the world at one time. But this was mere conjecture on their part, and Plato's effort to recover this speech in the *Cratylus* was therefore vain, and he was criticized for it by Aristotle and Galen. For that first language, spoken by the theological poets, was not a language in accord with the nature of things it dealt with (as must have been the sacred language invented by Adam, to whom God granted divine onomathesia, the giving of names to things according to the nature of each), but was a fantastic speech making use of physical substances endowed with life and most of them imagined to be divine.

This is the way in which the theological poets apprehended Jove, Cybele or Berecynthia, and Neptune, for example, and, at first mutely pointing, explained them as substances of the sky, the earth, and the sea, which they imagined to be animate divinities and were therefore true to their senses in believing them to be gods. By means of these three divinities, in accordance with what we have said above

---

[11]See Aristotle, *Poetics,* XXIV. 10, p. 64, and Mazzoni, *On the Defense of the Comedy of Dante,* p. 170.
[12]Francesco Patrizzi (1529–97), philosopher, poet, and critic.
[13]*The Wisdom of the Ancients* (1609).

---

[14]A dissertation on the style of the New Testament written by Thomas Gataker (1574–1654), English divine and critic.

concerning poetic characters, they explained everything appertaining to the sky, the earth, and the sea. And similarly by means of the other divinities they signified the other kinds of things appertaining to each, denoting all flowers, for instance, by Flora, and all fruits by Pomona. We nowadays reverse this practice in respect of spiritual things, such as the faculties of the human mind, the passions, virtues, vices, sciences, and arts; for the most part the ideas we form of them are so many feminine personifications, to which we refer all the causes, properties, and effects that severally appertain to them. For when we wish to give utterance to our understanding of spiritual things, we must seek aid from our imagination to explain them and, like painters, form human images of them. But these theological poets, unable to make use of the understanding, did the opposite and more sublime thing: they attributed senses and passions, as we saw not long since, to bodies, and to bodies as vast as sky, sea, and earth. Later, as these vast imaginations shrank and the power of abstraction grew, the personifications were reduced to diminutive signs. Metonymy drew a cloak of learning over the prevailing ignorance of these origins of human institutions, which have remained buried until now. Jove becomes so small and light that he is flown about by an eagle. Neptune rides the waves in a fragile chariot. And Cybele rides seated on a lion.[15]

Thus the mythologies, as their name indicates, must have been the proper languages of the fables; the fables being imaginative class concepts, as we have shown, the mythologies must have been the allegories corresponding to them. Allegory is defined as *diversiloquium* insofar as, by identity not of proportion but (to speak scholastically) of predicability, allegories signify the diverse species or the diverse individuals comprised under these genera. So that they must have a univocal signification connoting a quality common to all their species and individuals (as Achilles connotes an idea of valor common to all strong men, or Ulysses an idea of prudence common to all wise men); such that these allegories must be the etymologies of the poetic languages, which would make their origins all univocal, whereas those of the vulgar languages are more often analogical. We also have the definition of the word *etymology* itself as meaning *veriloquium,* just as fable was defined as *vera narratio.*

All the first tropes are corollaries of this poetic logic. The most luminous and therefore the most necessary and frequent is metaphor. It is most praised when it gives sense and passion to insensate things, in accordance with the metaphysics above discussed, by which the first poets attributed

to bodies the being of animate substances, with capacities measured by their own, namely sense and passion, and in this way made fables of them. Thus every metaphor so formed is a fable in brief. This gives a basis for judging the time when metaphors made their appearance in the languages. All the metaphors conveyed by likenesses taken from bodies to signify the operations of abstract minds must date from times when philosophies were taking shape. The proof of this is that in every language the terms needed for the refined arts and recondite sciences are of rustic origin.

It is noteworthy that in all languages the greater part of the expressions relating to inanimate things are formed by metaphor from the human body and from the human senses and passions. Thus, head for top or beginning; the brow and shoulders of a hill; the eyes of needles and of potatoes; mouth for any opening; the lip of a cup or pitcher; the teeth of a rake, a saw, a comb; the beard of wheat; the tongue of a shoe; the gorge of a river; a neck of land; an arm of the sea; the hands of a clock; heart for center (the Latins used *umbilicus,* navel, in this sense); the belly of a sail; foot for end or bottom; the flesh of fruits; a vein of rock or mineral; the blood of grapes for wine; the bowels of the earth.[16] Heaven or the sea smiles; the wind whistles; the waves murmur; a body groans under a great weight. The farmers of Latium used to say fields were thirsty, bore fruit, were swollen with grain; and our rustics speak of plants making love, vines going mad, resinous trees weeping. Innumerable other examples could be collected from all languages. All of which is a consequence of our axiom that man in his ignorance makes himself the rule of the universe, for in the examples cited he has made of himself an entire world. So that, as rational metaphysics teaches that man becomes all things by understanding them (*homo intelligendo fit omnia*), this imaginative metaphysics shows that man becomes all things by *not* understanding them (*homo non intelligendo fit omnia*); and perhaps the latter proposition is truer than the former, for when man understands he extends his mind and takes in the things, but when he does not understand he makes the things out of himself and becomes them by transforming himself into them.

In such a logic, sprung from such a metaphysics, the first poets had to give names to things from the most particular and the most sensible ideas. Such ideas are the sources, respectively, of synecdoche and metonymy. Metonymy of agent for act resulted from the fact that names for agents

---

[15]See Blake, *The Marriage of Heaven and Hell,* p. 401.

[16][Bergin and Fisch] Several of Vico's examples for which there are no common English parallels are here omitted, and substitutions are made for several others.

were commoner than names for acts. Metonymy of subject for form and accident was due to inability to abstract forms and qualities from subjects. Certainly metonymy of cause for effect produced in each case a little fable, in which the cause was imagined as a woman clothed with her effects: ugly Poverty, sad Old Age, pale Death.

Synecdoche developed into metaphor as particulars were elevated into universals or parts united with the other parts together with which they make up their wholes. Thus the term *mortals* was originally and properly applied only to men, as the only beings whose mortality there was any occasion to notice. The use of *head* for man or person, so frequent in vulgar Latin, was due to the fact that in the forests only the head of a man could be seen from a distance. The word *man* itself is abstract, comprehending as in a philosophic genius the body and all its parts, the mind and all its faculties, the spirit and all its dispositions. In the same way, *tignum* and *culmen,* "log" and "top," came to be used with entire propriety when thatching was the practice for rafter and thatch; and later, with the adornment of cities, they signified all the materials and trim of a building. Again, *tectum,* "roof," came to mean a whole house because in the first times a covering sufficed for a house. Similarly, *puppis,* "poop," for a ship, because it was the highest part and therefore the first to be seen by those on shore; as in the returned barbarian times a ship was called a sail. Similarly, *mucro,* "point," for sword, because the latter is an abstract word and as in a genus comprehends pummel, hilt, edge, and point; and it was the point they felt which aroused their fear. Similarly, the material for the formed whole, as *iron* for sword, because they did not know how to abstract the form from the material. That bit of synecdoche and metonymy, *Tertia messis erat* ("It was the third harvest"), was doubtless born of a natural necessity, for it took more than a thousand years for the astronomical term *year* to rise among the nations; and even now the Florentine peasantry say, "We have reaped so many times," when they mean "so many years." And that knot of two synecdoches and a metonymy, *Post aliquot, mea regna videns, mirabor, aristas?* ("After a few harvests shall I wonder at seeing my kingdoms?"),[17] betrays only too well the poverty of expression of the first rustic times, in which the phrase "so many ears of wheat"—even more particular than harvests—was used for "so many years." And because of the excessive poverty of the expression, the grammarians have assumed an excess of art behind it.

Irony certainly could not have begun until the period of reflection, because it is fashioned of falsehood by dint of a reflection which wears the mask of truth. Here emerges a great principle of human institutions, confirming the origin of poetry disclosed in this work: that since the first men of the gentile world had the simplicity of children, who are truthful by nature, the first fables could not feign anything false; they must therefore have been, as they have been defined above, true narrations.

From all this it follows that all the tropes (and they are all reducible to the four types above discussed), which have hitherto been considered ingenious inventions of writers, were necessary modes of expression of all the first poetic nations, and had originally their full native propriety. But these expressions of the first nations later became figurative when, with the further development of the human mind, words were invented which signified abstract forms or genera comprising their species or relating parts with their wholes. And here begins the overthrow of two common errors of the grammarians: that prose speech is proper speech, and poetic speech improper; and that prose speech came first and afterward speech in verse.

Poetic monsters and metamorphoses arose from a necessity of this first humane nature, its inability to abstract forms or properties from subjects. By their logic they had to put subjects together in order to put their forms together, or to destroy a subject in order to separate its primary form from the contrary form which had been imposed upon it. Such a putting together of ideas created the poetic monsters. In Roman law, as Antoine Favre observes in his *Iurisprudentiae papinianeae scientia,*[18] children born of prostitutes are called monsters because they have the nature of men together with the bestial characteristic of having been born of vagabond or uncertain unions. And it was as being monsters of this sort, we shall find, that children born of noble women without benefit of solemn nuptials were commanded by the Law of the Twelve Tables to be thrown into the Tiber.

The distinguishing of ideas produced metamorphoses. Among other examples preserved by ancient jurisprudence is the heroic Latin phrase *fundum fieri,* "to become ground of," used in place of *auctorem fieri,* to become author of, to authorize, to ratify; the explanation being that, as the ground supports the farm or soil and that which is sown, planted, or built thereon, so the ratifier supports an act which without his ratification would fail; and he does this by quitting the

---

[17]Virgil, *Eclogues,* I. 69.

[18]Antoine Favre, late sixteenth-century lawyer and writer.

form of a being moving at will, which he is, and taking on the contrary form of a stable thing.

*   *   *

The philosophers and philologians should all have begun to treat of the origins of languages and letters from the following principles. (1) That the first men of the gentile world conceived ideas of things by imaginative characters of animate and mute substances. (2) That they expressed themselves by means of gestures or physical objects which had natural relations with the ideas; for example, three ears of grain, or acting as if swinging a scythe three times, to signify three years. (3) That they thus expressed themselves by a language with natural significations. (Plato and Iamblichus said such a language had once been spoken in the world; it must have been the most ancient language of Atlantis, which scholars would have us believe expressed ideas by the nature of the things, that is, by their natural properties.) It is because the philosophers and philologians have treated separately these two things which are naturally conjoined [—the origins of languages and letters—] that the inquiry into the origins of letters has proved so difficult for them—as difficult as that into the origins of languages, with which they have been either not at all or very little concerned.

Edmund Burke

1729–1797

Burke's premises in his *Philosophical Inquiry into the Origin of Our Ideas of the Sublime and Beautiful,* like Addison's in his essays on the pleasures of the imagination, are those of the empirical tradition of John Locke. He assumes that all our knowledge comes via sense experience and that we combine the simple ideas of sense into more complex ones. For Burke, the "imagination" or "a sort of creative power" (what Coleridge later calls the "fancy") operates in two ways: by "representing at pleasure the images of things in the order and manner in which they were received by the senses" and by "combining those images in a new manner, and according to a different order." Thus the imagination can never produce anything "absolutely new"; it can at the most combine and reorder basic sense perceptions.

Burke's acknowledgment that we take pleasure in resemblances shows his concern with the problem of imitation. He is wary of Plato's criticism of the artist as a servile copier and suggests that the painter's failure to please the shoemaker in his representation of a shoe "was no impeachment to the taste of the painter; it only showed some want of knowledge in the art of making shoes." In raising this issue, Burke is concerned primarily with the problem of "taste" and whether there is a single standard, a logic of taste. He admits that the painter and the shoemaker differ in knowledge but insists that they share something too: "the pleasure arising from a natural object, so far as each perceives it justly imitated; the satisfaction in seeing an agreeable figure; the sympathy proceeding from a striking and affecting incident." Indeed, these matters of taste are more common to men than the results of reason, though there are differences in the degree to which men possess sensibility. Burke also believes that taste improves as judgment improves through increased knowledge, attention, and exercise. He finds taste and judgment intertwined in all human activity.

The body of Burke's treatise is concerned with the ideas of the sublime and beautiful. Here he is clearly in the debt of Longinus, but his fundamental orientation is different. Longinus writes of ways of achieving sublimity in a literary work. Burke proceeds from the subjective aesthetic experience of the reader to a discussion of what causes a response that may be described as sublime:

> Whatever is fitted in any sort to excite the ideas of pain, and danger, that is to say, whatever is in any sort terrible, or is conversant about terrible objects, or operates in a manner analogous to terror, is a source of the sublime; that is, it is productive of the strongest emotion which the mind is capable of feeling.

The standard edition of *A Philosophical Inquiry into the Origin of Our Ideas of the Sublime and Beautiful* is that edited with a long introduction by J. T. Boulton (1958). The six-volume edition of the *Works* edited by William Willis (1936) may also be consulted. Criticism includes T. M. Moore, *The Background of Burke's Theory of the*

Sublime (1938); S. H. Monk, *The Sublime* (1938); Dixon Wecter, "Burke's Theory Concerning Words, Images, and Emotions," *PMLA*, LV (1940), 167–81; W. J. Hipple, Jr., *The Beautiful, the Sublime, and the Picturesque in Eighteenth-Century British Aesthetic Theory* (1957); Gerald Chapman, *Edmund Burke: The Practical Imagination* (1967); George W. Fasel, *Edmund Burke* (1983); and Stanley Ayling, *Edmund Burke: His Life and Opinions* (1988).

From

A Philosophical Inquiry Into the Origin of Our Ideas of the Sublime and Beautiful

Introduction
Of Taste

On a superficial view we may seem to differ very widely from each other in our reasonings, and no less in our pleasures: but, notwithstanding this difference, which I think to be rather apparent than real, it is probable that the standard both of reason and taste is the same in all human creatures. For if there were not some principles of judgment as well as of sentiment common to all mankind, no hold could possibly be taken either on their reason or their passions, sufficient to maintain the ordinary correspondence of life. It appears indeed to be generally acknowledged, that with regard to truth and falsehood there is something fixed. We find people in their disputes continually appealing to certain tests and standards, which are allowed on all sides, and are supposed to be established in our common nature. But there is not the same obvious concurrence in any uniform or settled principles which relate to taste. It is even commonly supposed that this delicate and aerial faculty, which seems too volatile to endure even the chains of a definition, cannot be properly tried by any test, nor regulated by any standard. There is so continual a call for the exercise of the reasoning faculty; and it is so much strengthened by perpetual contention, that certain maxims of right reason seem to be tacitly settled amongst the most ignorant. The learned have improved on this rude science, and reduced those maxims into a system. If taste has not been so happily cultivated, it was not that the subject was

barren, but that the laborers were few or negligent; for to say the truth, there are not the same interesting motives to impel us to fix the one, which urge us to ascertain the other. And, after all, if men differ in their opinions concerning such matters, their difference is not attended with the same important consequences; else I make no doubt but that the logic of taste, if I may be allowed the expression, might very possibly be as well digested, and we might come to discuss matters of this nature with as much certainty, as those which seem more immediately within the province of mere reason. And, indeed, it is very necessary, at the entrance into such an inquiry as our present, to make this point as clear as possible; for if taste has no fixed principles, if the imagination is not affected according to some invariable and certain laws, our labor is likely to be employed to very little purpose; as it must be judged a useless, if not an absurd undertaking, to lay down rules for caprice, and to set up for a legislator of whims and fancies.

The term *taste,* like all other figurative terms, is not extremely accurate; the thing which we understand by it is far from a simple and determinate idea in the minds of most men, and it is therefore liable to uncertainty and confusion. I have no great opinion of a definition, the celebrated remedy for the cure of this disorder. For, when we define, we seem in danger of circumscribing nature within the bounds of our own notions, which we often take up by hazard or embrace on trust, or form out of a limited and partial consideration of the object before us, instead of extending our ideas to take in all that nature comprehends, according to her manner of combining. We are limited in our inquiry by the strict laws to which we have submitted at our setting out. *"Circa vilem patulumque morabimur orbem, / Unde pudor proferre pedem vetat aut operis lex."*[1]

A definition may be very exact, and yet go but a very little way towards informing us of the nature of the thing defined; but let the virtue of a definition be what it will, in the order of things, it seems rather to follow than to precede our inquiry, of which it ought to be considered as the result.

THE SUBLIME AND BEAUTIFUL. *A Philosophical Inquiry into the Origin of Our Ideas of the Sublime and Beautiful* was first published in 1757; a revised edition appeared in 1759. The text is based on the 1759 edition.

[1] "We shall linger with the low and open world, from which modesty and the law of work prevent our feet from moving." Horace, *Art of Poetry* (p. 70), but misquoted.

It must be acknowledged that the methods of disquisition and teaching may be sometimes different, and on very good reason undoubtedly; but, for my part, I am convinced that the method of teaching which approaches most nearly to the method of investigation is incomparably the best; since, not content with serving up a few barren and lifeless truths, it leads to the stock on which they grew; it tends to set the reader himself in the track of invention, and to direct him into those paths in which the author has made his own discoveries, if he should be so happy as to have made any that are valuable.

But to cut off all pretense for caviling, I mean by the word *taste,* no more than that faculty or those faculties of the mind, which are affected with, or which form a judgment of, the works of imagination and the elegant arts. This is, I think, the most general idea of that word, and what is the least connected with any particular theory. And my point in this inquiry is, to find whether there are any principles, on which the imagination is affected, so common to all, so grounded and certain, as to supply the means of reasoning satisfactorily about them. And such principles of taste I fancy there are; however paradoxical it may seem to those, who on a superficial view imagine that there is so great a diversity of tastes, both in kind and degree, that nothing can be more indeterminate.

All the natural powers in man, which I know, that are conversant about external objects, are the senses; the imagination; and the judgment. And first with regard to the senses. We do and we must suppose, that as the conformation of their organs are nearly or altogether the same in all men, so the manner of perceiving external objects is in all men the same, or with little difference. We are satisfied that what appears to be light to one eye, appears light to another; that what seems sweet to one palate, is sweet to another; that what is dark and bitter to this man, is likewise dark and bitter to that; and we conclude in the same manner of great and little, hard and soft, hot and cold, rough and smooth; and indeed of all the natural qualities and affections of bodies. If we suffer ourselves to imagine, that their senses present to different men different images of things, this skeptical proceeding will make every sort of reasoning on every subject vain and frivolous, even that skeptical reasoning itself which had persuaded us to entertain a doubt concerning the agreement of our perceptions. But as there will be little doubt that bodies present similar images to the whole species, it must necessarily be allowed, that the pleasures and the pains which every object excites in one man, it must raise in all mankind, whilst it operates naturally, simply, and by its proper powers only; for if we deny this, we must imagine that the same cause, operating in the same manner, and on subjects of the same kind, will produce different effects; which would be highly absurd. Let us first consider this point in the sense of taste, and the rather as the faculty in question has taken its name from that sense. All men are agreed to call vinegar sour, honey sweet, and aloes bitter; and as they are all agreed in finding these qualities in those objects, they do not in the least differ concerning their effects with regard to pleasure and pain. They all concur in calling sweetness pleasant, and sourness and bitterness unpleasant. Here there is no diversity in their sentiments; and that there is not, appears fully from the consent of all men in the metaphors which are taken from the sense of taste. A sour temper, bitter expressions, bitter curses, a bitter fate, are terms well and strongly understood by all. And we are altogether as well understood when we say, a sweet disposition, a sweet person, a sweet condition and the like. It is confessed, that custom and some other causes have made many deviations from the natural pleasures or pains which belong to these several tastes; but then the power of distinguishing between the natural and the acquired relish remains to the very last. A man frequently comes to prefer the taste of tobacco to that of sugar, and the flavor of vinegar to that of milk; but this makes no confusion in tastes, whilst he is sensible that the tobacco and vinegar are not sweet, and whilst he knows that habit alone has reconciled his palate to these alien pleasures. Even with such a person we may speak, and with sufficient precision, concerning tastes. But should any man be found who declares, that to him tobacco has a taste like sugar, and that he cannot distinguish between milk and vinegar; or that tobacco and vinegar are sweet, milk bitter, and sugar sour; we immediately conclude that the organs of this man are out of order, and that his palate is utterly vitiated. We are as far from conferring with such a person upon tastes, as from reasoning concerning the relations of quantity with one who should deny that all the parts together were equal to the whole. We do not call a man of this kind wrong in his notions, but absolutely mad. Exceptions of this sort, in either way, do not at all impeach our general rule, nor make us conclude that men have various principles concerning the relations of quantity or the taste of things. So that when it is said, taste cannot be disputed, it can only mean, that no one can strictly answer what pleasure or pain some particular man may find from the taste of some particular thing. This indeed cannot be disputed; but we may dispute, and with sufficient clearness too, concerning the things which are naturally pleasing or disagreeable to the sense. But when we talk of any peculiar or acquired relish, then we must know the habits, the prejudices, or the distempers of this particular man, and we must draw our conclusion from those.

This agreement of mankind is not confined to the taste solely. The principle of pleasure derived from sight is the same in all. Light is more pleasing than darkness. Summer, when the earth is clad in green, when the heavens are serene and bright, is more agreeable than winter, when everything makes a different appearance. I never remember that anything beautiful, whether a man, a beast, a bird, or a plant, was ever shown, though it were to a hundred people, that they did not all immediately agree that it was beautiful, though some might have thought that it fell short of their expectation, or that other things were still finer. I believe no man thinks a goose to be more beautiful than a swan, or imagines that what they call a Friesland hen excels a peacock. It must be observed too, that the pleasures of the sight are not near so complicated, and confused, and altered by unnatural habits and associations, as the pleasures of the taste are; because the pleasures of the sight more commonly acquiesce in themselves; and are not so often altered by considerations which are independent of the sight itself. But things do not spontaneously present themselves to the palate as they do to the sight; they are generally applied to it, either as food or as medicine; and from the qualities which they possess for nutritive or medicinal purposes they often form the palate by degrees, and by force of these associations. Thus opium is pleasing to Turks, on account of the agreeable delirium it produces. Tobacco is the delight of Dutchmen, as it diffuses a torpor and pleasing stupefaction. Fermented spirits please our common people, because they banish care, and all consideration of future or present evils. All of these, together with tea and coffee, and some other things, have passed from the apothecary's shop to our tables, and were taken for health long before they were thought of for pleasure. The effect of the drug has made us use it frequently; and frequent use, combined with the agreeable effect, has made the taste itself at last agreeable. But this does not in the least perplex our reasoning; because we distinguish to the last the acquired from the natural relish. In describing the taste of an unknown fruit, you would scarcely say that it had a sweet and pleasant flavor like tobacco, opium, or garlic, although you spoke to those who were in the constant use of these drugs, and had great pleasure in them. There is in all men a sufficient remembrance of the original natural causes of pleasure, to enable them to bring all things offered to their senses to that standard, and to regulate their feelings and opinions by it. Suppose one who had so vitiated his palate as to take more pleasure in the taste of opium than in that of butter or honey, to be presented with a bolus of squills; there is hardly any doubt but that he would prefer the butter or honey to this nauseous morsel, or to any other bitter drug to which he had not been accustomed; which proves that his palate was naturally like that of other men in all things, that it is still like the palate of other men in many things, and only vitiated in some particular points. For in judging of any new thing, even of a taste similar to that which he had been formed by habit to like, he finds his palate affected in the natural manner, and on the common principles. Thus the pleasure of all the senses, of the sight, and even of the taste, that most ambiguous of the senses, is the same in all, high and low, learned and unlearned.

Besides the ideas, with their annexed pains and pleasures, which are presented by the sense; the mind of man possesses a sort of creative power of its own; either in representing at pleasure the images of things in the order and manner in which they were received by the senses, or in combining those images in a new manner, and according to a different order. This power is called imagination;[2] and to this belongs whatever is called wit, fancy, invention, and the like. But it must be observed, that this power of the imagination is incapable of producing anything absolutely new; it can only vary the disposition of those ideas which it has received from the senses. Now the imagination is the most extensive province of pleasure and pain, as it is the region of our fears and our hopes, and of all our passions that are connected with them; and whatever is calculated to affect the imagination with these commanding ideas, by force of any original natural impression, must have the same power pretty equally over all men. For since the imagination is only the representation of the senses, it can only be pleased or displeased with the images, from the same principle on which the sense is pleased or displeased with the realities; and consequently there must be just as close an agreement in the imaginations as in the senses of men. A little attention will convince us that this must of necessity be the case.

But in the imagination, besides the pain or pleasure arising from the properties of the natural object, a pleasure is perceived from the resemblance which the imitation has to the original: the imagination, I conceive, can have no pleasure but what results from one or other of these causes. And these causes operate pretty uniformly upon all men, because they operate by principles in nature, and which are not derived from any particular habits or advantages. Mr. Locke very justly and finely observes of wit, that it is chiefly conversant in tracing resemblances; he remarks, at the same time, that the business of judgment is rather in finding differences.[3] It may perhaps appear, on this supposition, that there is no material distinction between the wit and the judgment, as they both seem to result from different operations of the same faculty of comparing. But in reality, whether they are or are not dependent on the same power of the mind, they differ so very materially in many respects, that a perfect

---

[2] Compare Coleridge's definition in *Biographia Literaria*, p. 478.
[3] John Locke, *An Essay Concerning Human Understanding*, II. xi. 2.

union of wit and judgment is one of the rarest things in the world. When two distinct objects are unlike to each other, it is only what we expect; things are in their common way; and therefore they make no impression on the imagination: but when two distinct objects have a resemblance, we are struck, we attend to them, and we are pleased. The mind of man has naturally a far greater alacrity and satisfaction in tracing resemblances than in searching for differences: because by making resemblances we produce new images; we unite, we create, we enlarge our stock; but in making distinctions we offer no food at all to the imagination; the task itself is more severe and irksome, and what pleasure we derive from it is something of a negative and indirect nature. A piece of news is told me in the morning; this, merely as a piece of news, as a fact added to my stock, gives me some pleasure. In the evening I find there was nothing in it. What do I gain by this, but the dissatisfaction to find that I had been imposed upon? Hence it is that men are much more naturally inclined to belief than to incredulity. And it is upon this principle, that the most ignorant and barbarous nations have frequently excelled in similitudes, comparisons, metaphors, and allegories, who have been weak and backward in distinguishing and sorting their ideas. And it is for a reason of this kind, that Homer and the oriental writers, though very fond of similitudes, and though they often strike out such as are truly admirable, seldom take care to have them exact; that is, they are taken with the general resemblance, they paint it strongly, and they take no notice of the difference which may be found between the things compared.

Now as the pleasure of resemblance is that which principally flatters the imagination, all men are nearly equal in this point, as far as their knowledge of the things represented or compared extends. The principle of this knowledge is very much accidental, as it depends upon experience and observation, and not on the strength or weakness of any natural faculty; and it is from this difference in knowledge, that what we commonly, though with no great exactness, call a difference in taste proceeds. A man to whom sculpture is new, sees a barber's block, or some ordinary piece of statuary; he is immediately struck and pleased, because he sees something like a human figure; and, entirely taken up with this likeness, he does not at all attend to its defects. No person, I believe, at the first time of seeing a piece of imitation ever did. Some time after, we suppose that this novice lights upon a more artificial work of the same nature; he now begins to look with contempt on what he admired at first; not that he admired it even then for its unlikeness to a man, but for that general though inaccurate resemblance which it bore to the human figure. What he admired at different times in these so different figures, is strictly the same; and though his knowl-

edge is improved, his taste is not altered. Hitherto his mistake was from a want of knowledge in art, and this arose from his inexperience; but he may be still deficient from a want of knowledge in nature. For it is possible that the man in question may stop here, and that the masterpiece of a great hand may please him no more than the middling performance of a vulgar artist; and this not for want of better or higher relish, but because all men do not observe with sufficient accuracy on the human figure to enable them to judge properly of an imitation of it. And that the critical taste does not depend upon a superior principle in men, but upon superior knowledge, may appear from several instances. The story of the ancient painter and the shoemaker is very well known. The shoemaker set the painter right with regard to some mistakes he had made in the shoe of one of his figures, which the painter, who had not made such accurate observations on shoes, and was content with a general resemblance, had never observed. But this was no impeachment to the taste of the painter; it only showed some want of knowledge in the art of making shoes.[4] Let us imagine, that an anatomist had come into the painter's working room. His piece is in general well done, the figure in question in a good attitude, and the parts well adjusted to their various movements; yet the anatomist, critical in his art, may observe the swell of some muscle not quite just in the peculiar action of the figure. Here the anatomist observes what the painter had not observed; and he passes by what the shoemaker had remarked. But a want of the last critical knowledge in anatomy no more reflected on the natural good taste of the painter, or of any common observer of his piece, than the want of an exact knowledge in the formation of a shoe. A fine piece of a decollated head of St. John the Baptist was shown to a Turkish emperor: he praised many things, but he observed one defect: he observed that the skin did not shrink from the wounded part of the neck. The sultan on this occasion, though his observation was very just, discovered no more natural taste than the painter who executed this piece, or than a thousand European connoisseurs, who probably would have made the same observation. His Turkish majesty had indeed been well acquainted with that terrible spectacle, which the others could only have represented in their imagination. On the subject of their dislike there is a difference between all these people, arising from the different kinds and degrees of their knowledge; but there is something in common to the painter, the shoemaker, the anatomist, and the Turkish emperor, the pleasure arising from a natural object,

---

[4]Pliny, *Natural History,* XXV. 84–85. Burke uses the story here as a criticism of the argument Plato raises against poetry.

so far as each perceives it justly imitated; the satisfaction in seeing an agreeable figure; the sympathy proceeding from a striking and affecting incident. So far as taste is natural, it is nearly common to all.

In poetry, and other pieces of imagination, the same parity may be observed. It is true, that one man is charmed with *Don Belianis,*[5] and reads Virgil coldly; whilst another is transported with the *Aeneid,* and leaves *Don Belianis* to children. These two men seem to have a taste very different from each other; but in fact they differ very little. In both these pieces, which inspire such opposite sentiments, a tale exciting admiration is told; both are full action, both are passionate; in both are voyages, battles, triumphs, and continual changes of fortune. The admirer of *Don Belianis* perhaps does not understand the refined language of the *Aeneid,* who, if it was degraded into the style of the *Pilgrim's Progress,* might feel it in all its energy, on the same principle which made him an admirer of *Don Belianis.*

In his favorite author he is not shocked with the continual breaches of probability, the confusion of times, the offenses against manners, the trampling upon geography; for he knows nothing of geography and chronology, and he has never examined the grounds of probability. He perhaps reads of a shipwreck on the coast of Bohemia; wholly taken up with so interesting an event, and only solicitous for the fate of his hero, he is not in the least troubled at this extravagant blunder. For why should he be shocked at a shipwreck on the coast of Bohemia, who does not know but that Bohemia may be an island in the Atlantic Ocean? And after all, what reflection is this on the natural good taste of the person here supposed?

So far then as taste belongs to the imagination, its principle is the same in all men; there is no difference in the manner of their being affected, nor in the causes of the affection; but in the degree there is a difference, which arises from two causes principally; either from a greater degree of natural sensibility, or from a closer and longer attention to the object. To illustrate this by the procedure of the senses, in which the same difference is found, let us suppose a very smooth marble table to be set before two men; they both perceive it to be smooth, and they are both pleased with it because of this quality. So far they agree. But suppose another, and after that another table, the latter still smoother than the former, to be set before them. It is now very probable that these men, who are so agreed upon what is smooth, and in the pleasure from thence, will disagree when they come to

settle which table has the advantage in point of polish. Here is indeed the great difference between tastes, when men come to compare the excess or diminution of things which are judged by degree and not by measure. Nor is it easy, when such a difference arises, to settle the point, if the excess or diminution be not glaring. If we differ in opinion about two quantities, we can recourse to a common measure, which may decide the question with the utmost exactness; and this, I take it, is what gives mathematical knowledge a greater certainty than any other. But in things whose excess is not judged by greater or smaller, as smoothness and roughness, hardness and softness, darkness and light, the shades of colors, all these are very easily distinguished when the difference is any way considerable, but not when it is minute, for want of some common measures, which perhaps may never come to be discovered. In these nice cases, supposing the acuteness of the sense equal, the greater attention and habit in such things will have the advantage. In the question about the tables, the marble-polisher will unquestionably determine the most accurately. But notwithstanding this want of a common measure for settling many disputes relative to the senses, and their representative the imagination, we find that the principles are the same in all, and that there is no disagreement until we come to examine into the preeminence or difference of things, which brings us within the province of the judgment.

So long as we are conversant with the sensible qualities of things, hardly any more than the imagination seems concerned; little more also than the imagination seems concerned when the passions are represented, because by the force of natural sympathy they are felt in all men without any recourse to reasoning, and their justness recognized in every breast. Love, grief, fear, anger, joy, all these passions have, in their turns, affected every mind; and they do not affect it in an arbitrary or casual manner, but upon certain, natural, and uniform principles. But as many of the works of imagination are not confined to the representation of sensible objects, nor to efforts upon the passions, but extend themselves to the manners, the characters, the actions, and designs of men, their relations, their virtues and vices, they come within the province of the judgment, which is improved by attention, and by the habit of reasoning. All these make a very considerable part of what are considered as the objects of taste; and Horace sends us to the schools of philosophy and the world for our instruction in them.[6] Whatever certainty is to be acquired in morality and the science of life; just the same degree of certainty have we in what relates to them in

---

[5]*The Famous and Delectable History of Don Belianis of Greece* (1673), an anonymous chapbook.

[6]*Art of Poetry,* p. 72.

works of imitation. Indeed it is for the most part in our skill in manners, and in the observances of time and place, and of decency in general, which is only to be learned in those schools to which Horace recommends us, that what is called taste, by way of distinction, consists: and which is in reality no other than a more refined judgment. On the whole, it appears to me, that what is called taste, in its most general acceptation, is not a simple idea, but is partly made up of a perception of the primary pleasures of sense, of the secondary pleasures of the imagination, and of the conclusions of the reasoning faculty, concerning the various relations of these, and concerning the human passions, manners, and actions. All this is requisite to form taste, and the groundwork of all these is the same in the human mind; for as the senses are the great originals of all our ideas, and consequently of all our pleasures, if they are not uncertain and arbitrary, the whole groundwork of taste is common to all, and therefore there is a sufficient foundation for a conclusive reasoning on these matters.

Whilst we consider taste merely according to its nature and species, we shall find its principles entirely uniform; but the degree in which these principles prevail, in the several individuals of mankind, is altogether as different as the principles themselves are similar. For sensibility and judgment, which are the qualities that compose what we commonly call a *taste,* vary exceedingly in various people. From a defect in the former of these qualities arises a want of taste; a weakness in the latter constitutes a wrong or a bad one. There are some men formed with feelings so blunt, with tempers so cold and phlegmatic, that they can hardly be said to be awake during the whole course of their lives. Upon such persons the most striking objects make but a faint and obscure impression. There are others so continually in the agitation of gross and merely sensual pleasures, or so occupied in the low drudgery of avarice, or so heated in the chase of honors and distinction, that their minds, which had been used continually to the storms of these violent and tempestuous passions, can hardly be put in motion by the delicate and refined play of the imagination. These men, though from a different cause, become as stupid and insensible as the former; but whenever either of these happen to be struck with any natural elegance or greatness, or with these qualities in any work of art, they are moved upon the same principle.

The cause of a wrong taste is a defect of judgment. And this may arise from a natural weakness of understanding (in whatever the strength of that faculty may consist), or, which is much more commonly the case, it may arise from a want of a proper and well-directed exercise, which alone can make it strong and ready. Besides, that ignorance, inattention, prej-

udice, rashness, levity, obstinacy, in short, all those passions, and all those vices, which pervert the judgment in other matters, prejudice it no less in this its more refined and elegant province. These causes produce different opinions upon everything which is an object of the understanding, without inducing us to suppose that there are no settled principles of reason. And indeed, on the whole, one may observe, that there is rather less difference upon matters of taste among mankind, than upon most of those which depend upon the naked reason; and that men are far better agreed on the excellence of a description in Virgil, than on the truth or falsehood of a theory of Aristotle.

A rectitude of judgment in the arts, which may be called a good taste, does in a great measure depend upon sensibility; because if the mind has no bent to the pleasures of the imagination, it will never apply itself sufficiently to works of that species to acquire a competent knowledge of them. But though a degree of sensibility is requisite to form a good judgment, yet a good judgment does not necessarily arise from a quick sensibility to pleasure; it frequently happens that a very poor judge, merely by force of a greater complexional sensibility, is more affected by a very poor piece, than the best judge by the most perfect; for as everything new, extraordinary, grand, or passionate, is well calculated to affect such a person, and that the faults do not affect him, his pleasure is more pure and unmixed; and as it is merely a pleasure of the imagination, it is much higher than any which is derived from a rectitude of judgment; the judgment is for the greater part employed in throwing stumbling blocks in the way of the imagination, in dissipating the scenes of its enchantment, and in tying us down to the disagreeable yoke of our reason: for almost the only pleasure that men have in judging better than others, consists in a sort of conscious pride and superiority, which arises from thinking rightly; but then this is an indirect pleasure, a pleasure which does not immediately result from the object which is under contemplation. In the morning of our days, when the senses are unworn and tender, when the whole man is awake in every part, and the gloss of novelty fresh upon all the objects that surround us, how lively at that time are our sensations, but how false and inaccurate the judgments we form of things! I despair of ever receiving the same degree of pleasure from the most excellent performances of genius, which I felt at that age from pieces which my present judgment regards as trifling and contemptible. Every trivial cause of pleasure is apt to affect the man of too sanguine a complexion: his appetite is too keen to suffer his taste to be delicate; and he is in all respects what Ovid says of himself in love, *"Molle meum levibus cor est violabile telis, / Et semper causa est, cur ego semper amem."*[7] One of this character can never be a refined judge; never what the comic poet calls *"elegans formarum spectator."*[8] The excellence and force of a composition must always be imperfectly estimated from its effect on the minds of any, except we know the temper and character of those minds. The most powerful effects of poetry and music have been displayed, and perhaps are still displayed, where these arts are but in a very low and imperfect state. The rude hearer is affected by the principles which operate in these arts even in their rudest condition; and he is not skillful enough to perceive the defects. But as the arts advance toward their perfection, the science of criticism advances with equal pace, and the pleasure of judges is frequently interrupted by the faults which are discovered in the most finished compositions.

Before I leave this subject, I cannot help taking notice of an opinion which many persons entertain, as if the taste were a separate faculty of the mind, and distinct from the judgment and imagination; a species of instinct, by which we are struck naturally, and at first glance, without any previous reasoning, with the excellences or the defects of a composition. So far as the imagination and the passions are concerned, I believe it true, that the reason is little consulted; but where disposition, where decorum, where congruity are concerned, in short, wherever the best taste differs from the worst, I am convinced that the understanding operates, and nothing else; and its operation is in reality far from being always sudden, or, when it is sudden, it is often far from being right. Men of the best taste by consideration come frequently to change these early and precipitate judgments, which the mind, from its aversion to neutrality and doubt loves to form on the spot. It is known that the taste (whatever it is) is improved exactly as we improve our judgment, by extending our knowledge, by a steady attention to our object, and by frequent exercise. They who have not taken these methods, if their taste decides quickly, it is always uncertainly; and their quickness is owing to their presumption and rashness, and not to any sudden irradiation, that in a moment dispels all darkness from their minds. But they who have cultivated that species of knowledge which makes the object of taste, by degrees and habitually attain not only a soundness but a readiness of judgment, as men do by the same methods on all other occasions. At first they are obliged to spell, but at last they read with ease and with celerity; but this celerity of its operations is no proof that the taste is a distinct faculty. Nobody, I believe, has attended the course

of a discussion which turned upon matters within the sphere of mere naked reason, but must have observed the extreme readiness with which the whole process of the argument is carried on, the grounds discovered, the objections raised and answered, and the conclusions drawn from premises, with a quickness altogether as great as the taste can be supposed to work with; and yet where nothing but plain reason either is or can be suspected to operate. To multiply principles for every different appearance is useless, and unphilosophical too in a high degree.

This matter might be pursued much farther; but it is not the extent of the subject which must prescribe our bounds, for what subject does not branch out to infinity? It is the nature of our particular scheme, and the single point of view in which we consider it, which ought to put a stop to our reseachers.

Section VII

Of the Sublime

Whatever is fitted in any sort to excite the ideas of pain, and danger, that is to say, whatever is in any sort terrible, or is conversant about terrible objects, or operates in a manner analogous to terror, is a source of the sublime; that is, it is productive of the strongest emotion which the mind is capable of feeling. I say the strongest emotion, because I am satisfied the ideas of pain are much more powerful than those which enter on the part of pleasure. Without all doubt, the torments which we may be made to suffer, are much greater in their effect on the body and mind, than any pleasures which the most learned voluptuary could suggest, or than the liveliest imagination, and the most sound and exquisitely sensible body could enjoy. Nay I am in great doubt, whether any man could be found who would earn a life of the most perfect satisfaction, at the price of ending it in the torments, which justice inflicted in a few hours on the late unfortunate regicide in France.[9] But as pain is stronger in its operation than pleasure, so death is in general a much more affecting idea than pain; because there are very few pains, however exquisite, which are not preferred to death; nay, what generally makes pain itself, if I may say so, more painful, is, that it is considered as an emissary of this king of terrors. When danger or pain press too nearly, they are incapable of giving

---

[7]"My soft heart is vulnerable to light darts, and there is always a reason why I am always in love." *Heroides,* XV. 79–80, but misquoted.
[8]"A refined observer of forms." Terence, *Eunuch,* 566.

[9]Robert Damiens (1714–57), who attempted to murder Louis XV and was tortured to death.

any delight, and are simply terrible; but at certain distances, and with certain modifications, they may be, and they are delightful, as we every day experience. The cause of this I shall endeavor to investigate hereafter.

Section X
Of Beauty

The passion which belongs to generation, merely as such, is lust only; this is evident in brutes, whose passions are more unmixed, and which pursue their purposes more directly than ours. The only distinction they observe with regard to their mates, is that of sex. It is true, that they stick severally to their own species in preference to all others. But this preference, I imagine, does not arise from any sense of beauty which they find in their species, as Mr. Addison supposes,[10] but from a law of some other kind to which they are subject; and this we may fairly conclude, from their apparent want of choice amongst those objects to which the barriers of their species have confined them. But man, who is a creature adapted to a greater variety and intricacy of relation, connects with the general passion, the idea of some social qualities, which direct and heighten the appetite which he has in common with all other animals; and as he is not designed like them to live at large, it is fit that he should have something to create a preference, and fix his choice; and this in general should be some sensible quality; as no other can so quickly, so powerfully, or so surely produce its effect. The object therefore of this mixed passion which we call love, is the beauty of the sex. Men are carried to the sex in general, as it is the sex, and by the common law of nature; but they are attached to particulars by personal beauty. I call beauty a social quality; for where women and men, and not only they, but when other animals give us a sense of joy and pleasure in beholding them (and there are many that do so), they inspire us with sentiments of tenderness and affection towards their persons; we like to have them near us, and we enter willingly into a kind of relation with them, unless we should have strong reasons to the contrary. But to what end, in many cases, this was designed, I am unable to discover; for I see no greater reason for a connection between man and several animals who are attired in so engaging a manner, than between him and some others who entirely want this attraction, or possess it in a far weaker degree. But it is probable, that providence did not make even this distinction, but with a view to some great end, though we cannot perceive distinctly what it is, as his wisdom is not our wisdom, nor our ways his ways.

Section XXVII
The Sublime and Beautiful Compared

On closing this general view of beauty, it naturally occurs, that we should compare it with the sublime; and in this comparison there appears a remarkable contrast. For sublime objects are vast in their dimensions, beautiful ones comparatively small; beauty should be smooth, and polished; the great, rugged and negligent; beauty should shun the right line, yet deviate from it insensibly; the great in many cases loves the right line, and when it deviates, it often makes a strong deviation; beauty should not be obscure; the great ought to be dark and gloomy; beauty should be light and delicate; the great ought to be solid, and even massive. They are indeed ideas of a very different nature, one being founded on pain, the other on pleasure; and however they may vary afterwards from the direct nature of their causes, yet these causes keep up an eternal distinction between them, a distinction never to be forgotten by any whose business it is to affect the passions. In the infinite variety of natural combinations we must expect to find the qualities of things the most remote imaginable from each other united in the same object. We must expect also to find combinations of the same kind in the works of art. But when we consider the power of an object upon our passions, we must know that when anything is intended to affect the mind by the force of some predominant property, the affection produced is like to be the more uniform and perfect, if all the other properties or qualities of the object be of the same nature, and tending to the same design as the principal; "If black, and white blend, soften, and unite, / A thousand ways, are there no black and white?"[11] If the qualities of the sublime and beautiful are sometimes united, does this prove, that they are the same, does it prove, that they are any way allied, does it prove even that they are not opposite and contradictory? Black and white may soften, may blend, but they are not therefore the same. Nor when they are so softened and blended with each other, or with different colors, is the power of black as black, or of white as white, so strong as when each stands uniform and distinguished.

---

[10]In *The Spectator*, Number 413.

[11]Alexander Pope, *An Essay on Man*, II. 213–14, but misquoted.

David Hume

1711–1776

Hume's literary essays continue the emphasis on the psychology of reader and audience that we find in Addison and Burke. Rigidly empirical, Hume called in question most of the assumptions of classical rationalist philosophy. Although fully cognizant of the immense difficulties of arriving at a standard of taste, his essay *Of the Standard of Taste* is very critical of total subjective relativism. There are principles of art based on the experience of what has pleased, not on what is true or false. In order to discover these principles the critic must have recourse to the "common sentiments of human nature." But there are countless variables; a reader's sentiments are affected by time, place, and situation. Therefore, Hume seems to propose a certain state of mind as the source of the standard of taste. It is not then a matter of calling for a majority vote. In order for a reader's vote to count, so to speak, he must exhibit "a perfect serenity of mind, a recollection of thought, a due attention to the object" a "delicacy of imagination," and lack of prejudice, freedom from slavish love of current or local fashion. Furthermore, to exercise judgment in this state of mind requires practice. Hasty judgments are likely to be wrong or at least superficial.

After making it seem virtually impossible ever to discover a person of adequate delicacy in the proper state of mind and thus an adequate standard, Hume points out that indeed it seems in practice more possible than we would suppose. Terence and Virgil have stood the test of time, while philosophers and their theories have been subject to endless disputes. Thus man seems more capable of consistent exercise of taste than of reason.

Useful texts are *The Essays, Moral, Political, and Literary,* edited by T. H. Green and T. H. Grose (4 vols., 1874–75), and *Essential Works of David Hume,* edited by Ralph Cohen (1965). See also J. F. Doering, "Hume and the Theory of Tragedy," *PMLA* LI (1937), 1130–44; N. K. Smith, *The Philosophy of David Hume* (1941); Martin Kallich, "The Associationist Criticism of Francis Hutcheson and David Hume," *Studies in Philology,* XLIII (1946), 644–67; Teddy Brunius, *David Hume on Criticism* (1952); E. C. Mossner, *The Life of David Hume* (1954); A. J. Ayer, *Hume* (1980); and John Mullan, *Sentiment and Sociability: The Language of Feeling in the Eighteenth Century* (1988).

Of the Standard of Taste

The great variety of taste, as well as of opinion, which prevails in the world, is too obvious not to have fallen under everyone's observation. Men of the most confined knowledge are able to remark a difference of taste in the narrow circle of their acquaintance, even where the persons have been educated under the same government, and have early imbibed the same prejudices. But those, who can enlarge their view to contemplate distant nations and remote ages, are still more surprised at the great inconsistence and contrariety. We are apt to call barbarous whatever departs widely from our own taste and apprehension: but soon find the epithet of reproach retorted on us. And the highest arrogance and self-conceit is at last startled, on observing an equal assurance on all sides, and scruples, amidst such a contest of sentiment, to pronounce positively in its own favor.

As this variety of taste is obvious to the most careless inquirer; so will it be found, on examination, to be still greater in reality than in appearance. The sentiments of men often differ with regard to beauty and deformity of all kinds, even while their general discourse is the same. There are certain terms in every language, which import blame, and others praise; and all men, who use the same tongue, must agree in their application of them. Every voice is united in applauding elegance, propriety, simplicity, spirit in writing; and in blaming fustian, affectation, coldness, and a false brilliancy: but when critics come to particulars, this seeming unanimity vanishes; and it is found, that they had affixed a very different meaning to their expressions. In all matters of opinion and science, the case is opposite: The difference among men is there oftener found to lie in generals than in particulars; and to be less in reality than in appearance. An explanation of the terms commonly ends the controversy; and the disputants are surprised to find, that they had been quarreling, while at bottom they agreed in their judgment.

Those who found morality on sentiment, more than on reason, are inclined to comprehend ethics under the former observation, and to maintain, that, in all questions, which regard conduct and manners, the difference among men is really greater than at first sight it appears. It is indeed obvious that writers of all nations and all ages concur in applauding justice, humanity, magnanimity, prudence, veracity; and in blaming the opposite qualities. Even poets and other authors, whose compositions are chiefly calculated to please the imagination, are yet found, from Homer down to Fénelon,[1] to inculcate the same moral precepts, and to bestow their applause and blame on the same virtues and vices. This great unanimity is usually ascribed to the influence of plain reason; which, in all these cases, maintains similar sentiments in all men, and prevents those controversies, to which the abstract sciences are so much exposed. So far as the unanimity is real, this account may be admitted as satisfactory: but we must also allow that some part of the seeming harmony in morals may be accounted for from the very nature of language. The word *virtue,* with its equivalent in every tongue, implies praise; as that of *vice* does blame: And no one, without the most obvious and grossest impropriety, could affix reproach to a term, which in general acceptation is understood in a good sense; or bestow applause, where the idiom requires disapprobation. Homer's general precepts, where he delivers any such, will never be controverted; but it is obvious, that, when he draws particular pictures of manners, and represents heroism in Achilles and prudence in Ulysses, he intermixes a much greater degree of ferocity in the former, and of cunning and fraud in the latter, than Fénelon would admit of. The sage Ulysses in the Greek poet seems to delight in lies and fictions, and often employs them without any necessity or even advantage: But his more scrupulous son, in the French epic writer, exposes himself to the most imminent perils, rather than depart from the most exact line of truth and veracity.

The admirers and followers of the Alcoran[2] insist on the excellent moral precepts interspersed throughout that wild and absurd performance. But it is to be supposed, that the Arabic words, which correspond to the English, equity, justice, temperance, meekness, charity, were such as, from the constant use of that tongue, must always be taken in a good sense; and it would have argued the greatest ignorance, not of morals, but of language, to have mentioned them with any epithets, besides those of applause and approbation. But would we know, whether the pretended prophet had really attained a just sentiment of morals? Let us attend to his narration; and we shall soon find, that he bestows praise on such instances of treachery, inhumanity, cruelty, revenge, bigotry, as are utterly incompatible with civilized society. No steady rule of right seems there to be attained to; and every action is blamed or praised, so far only as it is beneficial or hurtful to the true believers.

The merit of delivering true general precepts in ethics is indeed very small. Whoever recommends any moral vir-

---

OF THE STANDARD OF TASTE. *Of the Standard of Taste* was first published as part of Hume's *Four Dissertations* in 1757.

[1]François Fénelon (1651–1715), French churchman and writer.
[2]The Koran, sacred book of Moslems.

tues, really does no more than is implied in the terms themselves. That people, who invented the word *charity,* and used it in a good sense, inculcated more clearly and much more efficaciously, the precept, ''be charitable,'' than any pretended legislator or prophet, who should insert such a maxim in his writings. Of all expressions, those, which, together with their other meaning, imply a degree either of blame or approbation, are the least liable to be perverted or mistaken.

It is natural for us to seek a standard of taste; a rule by which the various sentiments of men may be reconciled; at least, a decision afforded, confirming one sentiment, and condemning another.

There is a species of philosophy, which cuts off all hopes of success in such an attempt, and represents the impossibility of ever attaining any standard of taste. The difference, it is said, is very wide between judgment and sentiment. All sentiment is right; because sentiment has a reference to nothing beyond itself, and is always real, wherever a man is conscious of it. But all determinations of the understanding are not right; because they have a reference to something beyond themselves, to wit, real matter of fact; and are not always conformable to that standard. Among a thousand different opinions which different men may entertain of the same subject, there is one, and but one, that is just and true; and the only difficulty is to fix and ascertain it. On the contrary, a thousand different sentiments, excited by the same object, are all right: because no sentiment represents what is really in the object. It only marks a certain conformity or relation between the object and the organs or faculties of the mind; and if that conformity did not really exist, the sentiment could never possibly have being. Beauty is no quality in things themselves: it exists merely in the mind which contemplates them; and each mind perceives a different beauty. One person may even perceive deformity, where another is sensible of beauty; and every individual ought to acquiesce in his own sentiment, without pretending to regulate those of others. To seek the real beauty, or real deformity, is as fruitless an inquiry, as to pretend to ascertain the real sweet or real bitter. According to the disposition of the organs, the same object may be both sweet and bitter; and the proverb has justly determined it to be fruitless to dispute concerning tastes. It is very natural, and even quite necessary, to extend this axiom to mental, as well as bodily taste; and thus common sense, which is so often at variance with philosophy, especially with the skeptical kind, is found, in one instance at least, to agree to pronouncing the same decision.

But though this axiom, by passing into a proverb, seems to have attained the sanction of common sense; there is certainly a species of common sense which opposes it, at least serves to modify and restrain it. Whoever would assert an equality of genius and elegance between Ogilby[3] and Milton, or Bunyan and Addison, would be thought to defend no less an extravagance, than if he had maintained a molehill to be as high as Tenerife,[4] or a pond as extensive as the ocean. Though there may be found persons, who give the preference to the former authors, no one pays attention to such a taste; and we pronounce without scruple the sentiment of these pretended critics to be absurd and ridiculous. The principle of the natural equality of tastes is then totally forgot, and while we admit it on some occasions, where the objects seem near an equality, it appears an extravagant paradox, or rather a palpable absurdity, where objects so disproportioned are compared together.

It is evident that none of the rules of composition are fixed by reasoning *a priori,* or can be esteemed abstract conclusions of the understanding, from comparing those habitudes and relations of ideas, which are eternal and immutable. Their foundation is the same with that of all the practical sciences, experience; nor are they anything but general observations, concerning what has been universally found to please in all countries and in all ages. Many of the beauties of poetry and even of eloquence are founded on falsehood and fiction, on hyperboles, metaphors, and an abuse or perversion of terms from their natural meaning. To check the sallies of the imagination, and to reduce every expression to geometrical truth and exactness, would be the most contrary to the laws of criticism; because it would produce a work, which, by universal experience, has been found the most insipid and disagreeable. But though poetry can never submit to exact truth, it must be confined by rules of art, discovered to the author either by genius or observation. If some negligent or irregular writers have pleased, they have not pleased by their transgressions of rule or order, but in spite of these transgressions: They have possessed other beauties, which were conformable to just criticism; and the force of these beauties has been able to overpower censure, and give the mind a satisfaction superior to the disgust arising from the blemishes. Ariosto[5] pleases; but not by his monstrous and improbable fictions, by his bizarre mixture of the serious and comic styles, by the want of coherence in his stories, or by the continual interruptions of his narration. He charms by the force and clearness of his expression, by the readiness and variety of his inventions, and by his natural pictures of the passions, especially those of the gay and amorous kind: And however his faults may diminish our satisfaction, they are

---

[3]John Ogilby (1600–56), poet, translator, and printer.
[4]A mountain in the Canary Islands.
[5]Lodovico Ariosto (1474–1533), Italian poet, author of *Orlando Furioso.*

not able entirely to destroy it. Did our pleasure really arise from those parts of his poem, which we denominate faults, this would be no objection to criticism in general: It would only be an objection to those particular rules of criticism, which would establish such circumstances to be faults, and would represent them as universally blamable. If they are found to please, they cannot be faults; let the pleasure, which they produce, be ever so unexpected and unaccountable.

But though all the general rules of art are founded only on experience and on the observation of the common sentiments of human nature, we must not imagine, that, on every occasion, the feelings of men will be conformable to these rules. Those finer emotions of the mind are of a very tender and delicate nature, and require the concurrence of many favorable circumstances to make them play with facility and exactness, according to their general and established principles. The least exterior hindrance to such small springs, or the least internal disorder, disturbs their motion, and confounds the operation of the whole machine. When we would make an experiment of this nature, and would try the force of any beauty or deformity, we must choose with care a proper time and place, and bring the fancy to a suitable situation and disposition. A perfect serenity of mind, a recollection of thought, a due attention to the object; if any of these circumstances be wanting, our experiment will be fallacious, and we shall be unable to judge of the catholic and universal beauty. The relation, which nature has placed between the form and the sentiment, will at least be more obscure; and it will require greater accuracy to trace and discern it. We shall be able to ascertain its influence not so much from the operation of each particular beauty, as from the durable admiration, which attends those works, that have survived all the caprices of mode and fashion, all the mistakes of ignorance and envy.

The same Homer, who pleased at Athens and Rome two thousand years ago, is still admired at Paris and at London. All the changes of climate, government, religion, and language, have not been able to obscure his glory. Authority or prejudice may give a temporary vogue to a bad poet or orator; but his reputation will never be durable or general. When his compositions are examined by posterity or by foreigners, the enchantment is dissipated, and his faults appear in their true colors. On the contrary, a real genius, the longer his works endure, and the more wide they are spread, the more sincere is the admiration which he meets with. Envy and jealousy have too much place in a narrow circle; and even familiar acquaintance with his person may diminish the applause due to his performances: but when these obstructions are removed, the beauties, which are naturally fitted to excite agreeable sentiments, immediately display their energy; and while the world endures, they maintain their authority over the minds of men.

It appears than, that, amidst all the variety and caprice of taste, there are certain general principles of approbation or blame, whose influence a careful eye may trace in all operations of the mind. Some particular forms or qualities, from the original structures of the internal fabric, are calculated to please, and others displease; and if they fail of their effect in any particular instance, it is from some apparent defect or imperfection in the organ. A man in a fever would not insist on his palate as able to decide concerning flavors; nor would one, affected with the jaundice, pretend to give a verdict with regard to colors. In each creature, there is a sound and defective state; and the former alone can be supposed to afford us a true standard of taste and sentiment. If, in the sound state of the organ, there be an entire or a considerable uniformity of sentiment among men, we may thence derive an idea of the perfect beauty; in like manner as the appearance of objects in daylight, to the eye of a man in health, is denominated their true and real color, even while color is allowed to be merely a phantasm of the senses.

Many and frequent are the defects in the internal organs which prevent or weaken the influence of those general principles, on which depends our sentiment of beauty or deformity. Though some objects, by the structure of the mind, be naturally calculated to give pleasure, it is not to be expected, that in every individual the pleasure will be equally felt. Particular incidents and situations occur, which either throw a false light on the objects, or hinder the true from conveying to the imagination the proper sentiment and perception.

One obvious cause, why many feel not the proper sentiment of beauty, is the want of that delicacy of imagination, which is requisite to convey a sensibility of those finer emotions. This delicacy everyone pretends to: everyone talks of it; and would reduce every kind of taste or sentiment to its standard. But as our intention in this essay is to mingle some light of the understanding with the feeling of sentiment, it will be proper to give a more accurate definition of delicacy, than has hitherto been attempted. And not to draw our philosophy from too profound a source, we shall have recourse to a noted story in *Don Quixote*.

"It is with good reason," says Sancho to the squire with the great nose, "that I pretend to have a judgment in wine: this is a quality hereditary in our family. Two of my kinsmen were once called to give their opinion of a hogshead, which was supposed to be excellent, being old and of a good vintage. One of them tastes it; considers it; and after mature reflection pronounces the wine to be good, were it not for a small taste of leather, which he perceived in it. The other, after using the same precautions, gives also his verdict in favor of the wine; but with the reserve of a taste of iron, which he could easily distinguish. You cannot imagine how much they were both ridiculed for their judgment. But who laughed in the end? On emptying the hogshead, there was found at the bottom, an old key with a leathern thong tied to it.''

The great resemblance between mental and bodily taste will easily teach us to apply this story. Though it be certain that beauty and deformity, more than sweet and bitter, are not qualities in objects, but belong entirely to the sentiment, internal or external; it must be allowed, that there are certain qualities in objects, which are fitted by nature to produce those particular feelings. Now as these qualities may be found in a small degree, or may be mixed and confounded with each other, it often happens, that the taste is not affected with such minute qualities, or is not able to distinguish all the particular flavors, amidst the disorder, in which they are presented. Where the organs are so fine, as to allow nothing to escape them; and at the same time so exact as to perceive every ingredient in the composition: this we call delicacy of taste, where we employ these terms in the literal or metaphorical sense. Here then the general rules of beauty are of use; being drawn from established models, and from the observation of what pleases or displeases, when presented singly and in a high degree: and if the same qualities, in a continued composition and in a smaller degree, affect not the organs with a sensible delight or uneasiness, we exclude the person from all pretensions to this delicacy. To produce these general rules or avowed patterns of composition is like finding the key with the leathern thong; which justified the verdict of Sancho's kinsmen, and confounded those pretended judges who had condemned them. Though the hogshead had never been emptied, the taste of the one was still equally delicate, and that of the other equally dull and languid: but it would have been more difficult to have proved the superiority of the former, to the conviction of every bystander. In like manner, though the beauties of writing had never been methodized, or reduced to general principles; though no excellent models had ever been acknowledged; the different degrees of taste would still have subsisted, and the judgment of one man been preferable to that of another; but it would not have been so easy to silence the bad critic, who might always insist upon his particular sentiment, and refuse to submit to his antagonist. But when we show him an avowed principle of art; when we illustrate this principle by examples, whose operation, from his own particular taste, he acknowledges to be conformable to the principle; when we prove, that the same principle may be applied to the present case, where he did not perceive or feel its influence: he must conclude, upon the whole, that the fault lies in himself, and that he wants the delicacy, which is requisite to make him sensible of every beauty and every blemish, in any composition or discourse.

It is acknowledged to be the perfection of every sense or faculty, to perceive with exactness its most minute objects, and allow nothing to escape its notice and observation. The smaller the objects are, which become sensible to the eye, the finer is that organ, and the more elaborate its make and composition. A good palate is not tried by strong flavors; but by a mixture of small ingredients, where we are still sensible of each part, notwithstanding its minuteness and its confusion with the rest. In like manner, a quick and acute perception of beauty and deformity must be the perfection of our mental taste; nor can a man be satisfied with himself while he suspects, that any excellence or blemish in a discourse has passed him unobserved. In this case, the perfection of the man, and the perfection of the sense or feeling, are found to be united. A very delicate palate, on many occasions, may be a great inconvenience both to a man himself and to his friends: but a delicate taste of wit or beauty must always be a desirable quality; because it is the source of all the finest and most innocent enjoyments, of which human nature is susceptible. In this decision the sentiments of all mankind are agreed. Wherever you can ascertain a delicacy of taste, it is sure to meet with approbation; and the best way of ascertaining it is to appeal to those models and principles, which have been established by the uniform consent and experience of nations and ages.

But though there be naturally a wide difference in point of delicacy between one person and another, nothing tends further to increase and improve this talent, than practice in a particular art, and the frequent survey or contemplation of a particular species of beauty. When objects of any kind are first presented to the eye or imagination, the sentiment, which attends them, is obscure and confused; and the mind is, in a great measure, incapable of pronouncing concerning their merits or defects. The taste cannot perceive the several excellences of the performance; much less distinguish the particular character of each excellency, and ascertain its quality and degree. If it pronounce the whole in general to be beautiful or deformed, it is the utmost that can be expected; and even this judgment, a person, so unpracticed, will be apt to deliver with great hesitation and reserve. But allow him to acquire experience in those objects, his feeling becomes more exact and nice: he not only perceives the beauties and defects of each part, but marks the distinguishing species of each quality, and assigns it suitable praise or blame. A clear and distinct sentiment attends him through the whole survey of the objects; and he discerns that very degree and kind of approbation or displeasure, which each part is naturally fitted to produce. The mist dissipates, which seemed formerly to hang over the object: the organ acquires greater perfection in its operations; and can pronounce, without danger of mistake, concerning the merits of every performance. In a word, the same address and dexterity, which practice gives to the execution of any work, is also acquired by the same means, in the judging of it.

So advantageous is practice to the discernment of beauty, that, before we can give judgment on any work of importance, it will even be requisite, that that very individual performance be more than once perused by us, and be surveyed in different lights with attention and deliberation. There is a flutter or hurry of thought which attends the first perusal of any piece, and which confounds the genuine sentiment of beauty. The relation of the parts is not discerned: the true characters of style are little distinguished: the several perfections and defects seem wrapped up in a species of confusion, and present themselves indistinctly to the imagination. Not to mention, that there is a species of beauty, which, as it is florid and superficial, pleases at first; but being found incompatible with a just expression either of reason or passion, soon palls upon the taste, and is then rejected with disdain, at least rated at much lower value.

It is impossible to continue in the practice of contemplating any order of beauty, without being frequently obliged to form comparisons between the several species and degrees of excellence, and estimating their proportion to each other. A man, who has had no opportunity of comparing the different kinds of beauty, is indeed totally unqualified to pronounce an opinion with regard to any object presented to him. By comparison alone we fix the epithets of praise or blame, and learn how to assign the due degree of each. The coarsest daubing contains a certain luster of colors and exactness of imitation, which are so far beauties, and would affect the mind of a peasant or Indian with the highest admiration. The most vulgar ballads are not entirely destitute of harmony or nature; and none but a person, familiarized to superior beauties, would pronounce their numbers harsh, or narration uninteresting. A great inferiority of beauty gives pain to a person conversant in the highest excellence of the kind, and is for that reason pronounced a deformity: as the most finished object, with which we are acquainted, is naturally supposed to have reached the pinnacle of perfection, and to be entitled to the highest applause. One accustomed to see, and examine, and weigh the several performances, admired in different ages and nations, can only rate the merits of a work exhibited to his view, and assign its proper rank among the productions of genius.

But to enable a critic the more fully to execute this undertaking, he must preserve his mind free from all prejudice, and allow nothing to enter into his consideration, but the very object which is submitted to his examination. We may observe, that every work of art, in order to produce its due effect on the mind, must be surveyed in a certain point of view, and cannot be fully relished by persons, whose situation, real or imaginary, is not conformable to that which is required by the performance. An orator addresses himself to a particular audience, and must have a regard to their particular genius, interest, opinions, passions, and prejudices; otherwise he hopes in vain to govern their resolutions, and inflame their affections. Should they even have entertained some prepossessions against him, however unreasonable, he must not overlook this disadvantage; but, before he enters upon the subject, must endeavor to conciliate their affection, and acquire their good graces. A critic of a different age or nation, who should peruse this discourse, must have all these circumstances in his eye, and must place himself in the same situation as the audience, in order to form a true judgment of the oration. In like manner, when any work is addressed to the public, though I should have a friendship or enmity with the author, I must depart from this situation; and considering myself as a man in general, forget, if possible, my individual being and my peculiar circumstances. A person influenced by prejudice, complies not with this condition; but obstinately maintains his natural position, without placing himself in that point of view, which the performance supposes. If the work be addressed to persons of a different age or nation, he makes no allowance for their peculiar views and prejudices; but, full of the manners of his own age and country, rashly condemns what seemed admirable in the eyes of those for whom alone the discourse was calculated. If the work be executed for the public, he never sufficiently enlarges his comprehension, or forgets his interest as a friend or enemy, as a rival or commentator. By this means, his sentiments are perverted; nor have the same beauties and blemishes the same influence upon him, as if he had imposed a proper violence on his imagination, and had forgotten himself for a moment. So far his taste evidently departs from the true standard; and of consequence loses all credit and authority.

It is well known, that in all questions, submitted to the understanding, prejudice is destructive of sound judgment, and perverts all operations of the intellectual faculties: it is no less contrary to good taste; nor has it less influence to corrupt our sentiment of beauty. It belongs to good sense to check its influence in both cases; and in this respect, as well as in many others, reason, if not an essential part of taste, is at least requisite to the operations of this latter faculty. In all the nobler productions of genius, there is a mutual relation and correspondence of parts; nor can either the beauties or blemishes be perceived by him, whose thought is not capacious enough to comprehend all those parts, and compare them with each other, in order to perceive the consistence and uniformity of the whole. Every work of art has also a certain end or purpose, for which it is calculated; and is to be deemed more or less perfect, as it is more or less fitted to attain this end. The object of eloquence is to persuade, of history to instruct, of poetry to please by means of the passions and the imagination. These ends we must carry constantly in our view, when we peruse any performance; and we must be able to judge how far the means employed are adapted to their respective purposes. Besides every kind of composition, even the most poetical, is nothing but a chain of propositions and reasonings; not always, indeed, the justest and most exact, but still plausible and specious, however disguised by the coloring of the imagination. The persons introduced in tragedy and epic poetry, must be represented as reasoning, and thinking, and concluding, and acting, suitably to their character and circumstances; and without judgment, as well as taste and invention, a poet can never hope to succeed in so delicate an undertaking. Not to mention, that the same excellence of faculties which contributes to the improvement of reason, the same clearness of conception, the same exactness of distinction, the same vivacity of apprehension, are essential to the operations of true taste, and are its infallible concomitants. It seldom, or never happens, that a man of sense, who has experience in any art, cannot judge of its beauty; and it is no less rare to meet with a man who has a just taste without a sound understanding.

Thus, though the principles of taste be universal, and, nearly, if not entirely the same in all men; yet few are qualified to give judgment on any work of art, or establish their own sentiment as the standard of beauty. The organs of internal sensation are seldom so perfect as to allow the general principles their full play, and produce a feeling correspondent to those principles. They either labor under some defect, or are vitiated by some disorder; and by that means, excite a sentiment, which may be pronounced erroneous. When the critic has no delicacy, he judges without any distinction, and is only affected by the grosser and more palpable qualities of the object: the finer touches pass unnoticed and disregarded. Where he is not aided by practice, his verdict is attended with confusion and hesitation. Where no comparison has been employed, the most frivolous beauties, such as rather merit the name of defects, are the objects of his admiration. Where he lies under the influence of prejudice, all his natural sentiments are perverted. Where good sense is wanting, he is not qualified to discern the beauties of design and reasoning, which are the highest and most excellent. Under some or other of these imperfections, the generality of men labor; and

hence a true judge in the finer arts is observed, even during the most polished ages, to be so rare a character: strong sense, united to delicate sentiment, improved by practice, perfected by comparison, and cleared of all prejudice, can alone entitle critics to this valuable character; and the joint verdict of such, wherever they are to be found, is the true standard of taste and beauty.

But where are such critics to be found? By what marks are they to be known? How distinguish them from pretenders? These questions are embarrassing; and seem to throw us back into the same uncertainty, from which, during the course of this essay, we have endeavored to extricate ourselves.

But if we consider the matter aright, these are questions of fact, not of sentiment. Whether any particular person be endowed with good sense and a delicate imagination, free from prejudice, may often be the subject of dispute, and be liable to great discussion and inquiry: But that such a character is valuable and estimable will be agreed in by all mankind. Where these doubts occur, men can do no more than in other disputable questions, which are submitted to the understanding: they must produce the best arguments, that their invention suggests to them; they must acknowledge a true and decisive standard to exist somewhere, to wit, real existence and matter of fact; and they must have indulgence to such as differ from them in their appeals to this standard. It is sufficient for our present purpose, if we have proved, that the taste of all individuals is not upon an equal footing, and that some men in general, however difficult to be particularly pitched upon, will be acknowledged by universal sentiment to have a preference above others.

But in reality the difficulty of finding, even in particulars, the standard of taste, is not so great as it is represented. Though in speculation, we may readily avow a certain criterion in science and deny it in sentiment, the matter is found in practice to be much more hard to ascertain in the former case than in the latter. Theories of abstract philosophy, systems of profound theology, have prevailed during one age: in a successive period, these have been universally exploded: their absurdity has been detected: other theories and systems have supplied their place, which again gave place to their successors: and nothing has been experienced more liable to the revolutions of chance and fashion than these pretended decisions of science. The case is not the same with beauties of eloquence and poetry. Just expressions of passion and nature are sure, after a little time, to gain public applause, which they maintain forever. Aristotle, and Plato, and Epicurus, and Descartes, may successively yield to each other: but Terence and Virgil maintain a universal, undisputed empire over the minds of men. The abstract philosophy of

Cicero has lost its credit: the vehemence of his oratory is still the object of our admiration.

Though men of delicate taste be rare, they are easily to be distinguished in society, by the soundness of their understanding and the superiority of their faculties above the rest of mankind. The ascendant, which they acquire, gives a prevalence to that lively approbation, with which they receive any productions of genius, and renders it generally predominant. Many men, when left to themselves, have but a faint and dubious perception of beauty, who yet are capable of relishing any fine stroke, which is pointed out to them. Every convert to the admiration of the real poet or orator is the cause of some new conversion. And though prejudices may prevail for a time, they never unite in celebrating any rival to the true genius, but yield at last to the force of nature and just sentiment. Thus, though a civilized nation may easily be mistaken in the choice of their admired philosopher, they never have been found long to err, in their affection for a favorite epic or tragic author.

But notwithstanding all our endeavors to fix a standard of taste, and reconcile the discordant apprehensions of men, there still remain two sources of variation, which are not sufficient indeed to confound all the boundaries of beauty and deformity, but will often serve to produce a difference in the degrees of our approbation or blame. The one is the different humors of particular men; the other, the particular manners and opinions of our age and country. The general principles of taste are uniform in human nature: where men vary in their judgments, some defect or perversion in the faculties may commonly be remarked; proceeding either from prejudice, from want of practice, or want of delicacy; and there is just reason for approving one taste, and condemning another. But where there is such a diversity in the internal frame or external situation as is entirely blameless on both sides, and leaves no room to give one the preference above the other; in that case a certain degree of diversity in judgment is unavoidable, and we seek in vain for a standard, by which we can reconcile the contrary sentiments.

A young man, whose passions are warm, will be more sensibly touched with amorous and tender images, than a man more advanced in years, who takes pleasure in wise, philosophical reflections concerning the conduct of life and moderation of the passions. At twenty, Ovid may be the favorite author; Horace at forty; and perhaps Tacitus at fifty. Vainly would we, in such cases, endeavor to enter into the sentiments of others, and divest ourselves of those propensities, which are natural to us. We choose our favorite author as we do our friend, from a conformity of humor and disposition. Mirth or passion, sentiment or reflection; whichever of these most predominates in our temper, it gives us a peculiar sympathy with the writer who resembles us.

One person is more pleased with the sublime; another with the tender; a third with raillery. One has a strong sensibility to blemishes, and is extremely studious of correctness: another has a more lively feeling of beauties, and pardons twenty absurdities and defects for one elevated or pathetic stroke. The ear of this man is entirely turned toward conciseness and energy; that man is delighted with a copious, rich, and harmonious expression. Simplicity is affected by one; ornament by another. Comedy, tragedy, satire, odes, have each its partisans, who prefer that particular species of writing to all others. It is plainly an error in a critic, to confine his approbation to one species or style of writing, and condemn all the rest. But it is almost impossible not to feel a predilection for that which suits our particular turn and disposition. Such preferences are innocent and unavoidable, and can never reasonably be the object of dispute, because there is no standard, by which they can be decided.

For a like reason, we are more pleased, in the course of our reading, with pictures and characters, that resemble objects which are found in our own age or country, than with those which describe a different set of customs. It is not without some effort, that we reconcile ourselves to the simplicity of ancient manners, and behold princesses carrying water from the spring, and kings and heroes dressing their own victuals. We may allow in general, that the representation of such manners is no fault in the author, nor deformity in the piece; but we are not so sensibly touched with them. For this reason, comedy is not easily transferred from one age or nation to another. A Frenchman or Englishman is not pleased with the *Andria* of Terence, or *Clitia* of Machiavel; where the fine lady, upon whom all the play turns, never once appears to the spectators, but is always kept behind the scenes, suitably to the reserved humor of the ancient Greeks and modern Italians. A man of learning and reflection can make allowance for these peculiarities of manners; but a common audience can never divest themselves so far of their usual ideas and sentiments, as to relish pictures which in no wise resemble them.

But here there occurs a reflection, which may, perhaps, be useful in examining the celebrated controversy concerning ancient and modern learning; where we often find the one side excusing any seeming absurdity in the ancients from the manners of the age, and the other refusing to admit this excuse, or at least, admitting it only as an apology for the author, not for the performance. In my opinion, the proper boundaries in this subject have seldom been fixed between the contending parties. Where any innocent peculiarities of manners are represented, such as those above mentioned, they ought certainly to be admitted; and a man, who is shocked with them, gives an evident proof of false delicacy and refinement. The poet's monument more durable than brass must fall to the ground like common brick or clay, were men to make no allowance for the continual revolutions of manners and customs, and would admit of nothing but what was suitable to the prevailing fashion. Must we throw aside the pictures of our ancestors, because of their ruffs and farthingales? But where the ideas of morality and decency alter from one age to another, and where vicious manners are described, without being marked with the proper characters of blame and disapprobation; this must be allowed to disfigure the poem, and to be a real deformity. I cannot, nor is it proper I should, enter into such sentiments; and however I may excuse the poet, on account of the manners of his age, I never can relish the composition. The want of humanity and of decency, so conspicuous in the characters drawn by several of the ancient poets, even sometimes by Homer and the Greek tragedians, diminishes considerably the merit of their noble performances, and gives modern authors an advantage over them. We are not interested in the fortunes and sentiments of such rough heroes: we are displeased to find the limits of vice and virtue so much confounded: and whatever indulgence we may give to the writer on account of his prejudices, we cannot prevail on ourselves to enter into his sentiments, or bear an affection to characters, which we plainly discover to be blamable.

The case is not the same with moral principles, as with speculative opinions of any kind. These are in continual flux and revolution. The son embraces a different system from the father. Nay, there scarcely is any man, who can boast of great constance and uniformity in this particular. Whatever speculative errors may be found in the polite writings of any age or country, they detract but little from the value of those compositions. There needs but a certain turn of thought or imagination to make us enter into all the opinions, which then prevailed, and relish the sentiments or conclusions derived from them. But a very violent effort is requisite to change our judgment of manners, and excite sentiments of approbation or blame, love or hatred, different from those to which the mind from long custom has been familiarized. And where a man is confident of the rectitude of that moral standard, by which he judges, he is justly jealous of it, and will not pervert the sentiments of his heart for a moment, in complaisance to any writer whatsoever.

Of all speculative errors, those, which regard religion, are the most excusable in compositions of genius; nor is it ever permitted to judge of the civility or wisdom of any people, or even of single persons, by the grossness of refinement of their theological principles. The same good sense, that directs men in the ordinary occurrences of life, is not harkened to in religious matters, which are supposed to be placed altogether above the cognizance of human reason. On this account, all the absurdities of the pagan system of theology must be overlooked by every critic, who would pretend to form a just notion of ancient poetry; and our posterity, in their turn, must have the same indulgence to their forefathers. No religious principles can ever be imputed as a fault to any poet, while they remain merely principles, and take no such strong possession of his heart, as to lay him under the imputation of bigotry or superstition. Where that happens, they confound the sentiments of morality, and alter the natural boundaries of vice and virtue. They are therefore eternal blemishes, according to the principle above mentioned; nor are the prejudices and false opinions of the age sufficient to justify them.

It is essential to the Roman Catholic religion to inspire a violent hatred of every other worship, and to represent all pagans, Mahometans, and heretics as the objects of divine wrath and vengeance. Such sentiments, though they are in reality very blamable, are considered as virtues by the zealots of that communion, and are represented in their tragedies and epic poems as a kind of divine heroism. This bigotry has disfigured two very fine tragedies of the French theater, *Polyeucte* and *Athalie;*[6] where an intemperate zeal for particular modes of worship is set off with all the pomp imaginable, and forms the predominant character of the heroes. "What is this," says the sublime Joad to Josabet, finding her in discourse with Mathan, the priest of Baal, "does the daughter of David speak to this traitor? Are you not afraid, lest the earth should open and pour forth flames to devour you both? Or lest these holy walls should fall and crush you together? What is his purpose? Why comes that enemy of God hither to poison the air, which we breathe, with his horrid presence?" Such sentiments are received with great applause on the theater of Paris; but at London the spectators would be full as much pleased to hear Achilles tell Agamemnon, that he was a dog in his forehead, and a deer in his heart, or Jupiter threaten Juno with a sound drubbing, if she will not be quiet.

Religious principles are also a blemish in any polite composition, when they rise up to superstition, and intrude themselves into every sentiment, however remote from any connection with religion. It is no excuse for the poet, that the customs of his country had burthened life with so many religious ceremonies and observances, that no part of it was exempt from that yoke. It must forever be ridiculous in Petrarch to compare his mistress Laura, to Jesus Christ. Nor is it less ridiculous in that agreeable libertine, Boccace,[7] very seriously to give thanks to God Almighty and the ladies, for their assistance in defending him against his enemies.

---

[6]*Athalie,* by Racine (1691); *Polyeucte,* by Corneille (1643).
[7]Boccaccio.

Samuel Johnson

1709–1784

Johnson is among the last neoclassical critics; he fares less well as a consistent theorist than as a practical critic of penetrating insights, absolute honesty, and common sense. The selections below reveal some of his fundamental assumptions. Two of the most important are his grounding of critical judgment on morality and his idea that poets should concern themselves with representing general nature rather than particular experience. Both of these premises raise interesting problems from the point of view of later critics, such as the Romantics, who generally judged moralistic criticism as narrow and insisted that the poet expresses particular experience. Yet later critics could not succeed in dismissing Johnson, for even if this theory seemed to them inadequate, they had to acknowledge the common sense of his many insights into particular works.

Johnson's realistic attitude resists the "wild strain of imagination" that led to pastoral conventions and the machinery of giants, knights, and imaginary castles. He shows respect for the more realistic temper of his contemporaries. Yet this interest is secondary to his moral concerns. The more realistic writer runs a greater moral risk than concocters of unlikely romances, since the latter's tales are so improbable as not to be believed in the first place. Contemporaries, Johnson observed, because they come closer to truth, must also come closer to the right in what they present. It is obviously difficult to resolve in a single criticism the desire for realism with an insistence that wickedness either not be represented at all or get its just deserts.

The question of whether poets represent general nature or particular experience is one that has intrigued critics for a long time. Johnson's preference for general nature was endorsed by Joshua Reynolds, attacked by Blake, and then worried by a number of Romantic critics. The key passage in Imlac's discourse on poetry in *Rasselas* is the remark: "The business of a poet . . . is to examine, not the individual, but the species; to remark general properties and large appearances: he does not number the streaks of the tulip. . . ." When Johnson mentions the "species" he seems not to be discussing some Platonic universal idea but a generalization from sense experience. The nature Johnson's poet imitates is what may be abstracted from numerous particular experiences and found to be common to all the objects of a class. Thus the neoclassical concept of the object of art shifts from Platonic universals to the generalized abstraction. In his attack on this point of view Blake asks where except "in the mind of a fool" such generalizations exist.

Johnson's Preface to *Shakespeare* expresses the fundamental notions mentioned above and also deals with a number of other matters. Commenting on the argument over the ancients and moderns, he observes that time is finally the best critical test of a work. His discussion of the unities of action, time, and place is perhaps the ultimate word on the subject and is typical of Johnson's appeal to common sense in dealing with a critical issue.

Sir John Hawkins' fifteen-volume edition of Johnson's works (1787–89), long the standard collection, has been followed by the Yale edition, edited by A. T. Hazen and others (1958ff). Standard editions of Johnson's critical works include *Lives of the English Poets,* edited by G. B. Hill (1905), and *Johnson on Shakespeare,* edited by Sir Walter Raleigh (1908). The following commentaries are useful: W. R. Keast, "The Theoretical Foundations of Johnson's Criticism," R. S. Crane, ed., *Critics and Criticism* (1952); J. H. Hagstrum, *Samuel Johnson's Literary Criticism* (1952); Allen Tate, "Johnson on the Metaphysical Poets," *The Forlorn Demon* (1953), 112–30; W. J. Bate, *The Achievement of Samuel Johnson* (1955); Martin Kallich, "Samuel Johnson's Principles of Criticism and Imlac's 'Dissertation upon Poetry,' " *Journal of Aesthetics and Art Criticism,* XXV (1966), 71–82; James Boulton, ed., *Johnson: The Critical Heritage* (1971); Leopold Damrosch, *The Uses of Johnson's Criticism* (1976); Joel Westheimer, *Imitation* (1984); and Nicholas Hudson, *Samuel Johnson and Eighteenth Century Thought* (1988).

On Fiction

The Rambler

Number 4

Saturday, March 31, 1750

Simul et jucunda et idonea dicere Vitae.[1]
HORACE

And join both profit and delight in one.
CREECH

The works of fiction, with which the present generation seems more particularly delighted, are such as exhibit life in its true state, diversified only by accidents that daily happen in the world, and influenced by passions and qualities which are really to be found in conversing with mankind.

This kind of writing may be termed not improperly the comedy of romance, and is to be conducted nearly by the rules of cosmic poetry. Its province is to bring about natural events by easy means, and to keep up curiosity without the help of wonder: it is therefore precluded from the machines and expedients of the heroic romance, and can neither em-

ploy giants to snatch away a lady from the nuptial rites, nor knights to bring her back from captivity; it can neither bewilder its personages in deserts, nor lodge them in imaginary castles.

I remember a remark made by Scaliger upon Pontanus,[2] that all his writings are filled with the same images; and that if you take from him his lilies and his roses, his satyrs and his dryads, he will have nothing left that can be called poetry. In like manner, almost all the fictions of the last age will vanish, if you deprive them of a hermit and a wood, a battle and a shipwreck.

Why this wild strain of imagination found reception so long, in polite and learned ages, it is not easy to conceive; but we cannot wonder that, while readers could be procured, the authors were willing to continue it: for when a man had by practice gained some fluency of language, he had no further care than to retire to his closet, let loose his invention, and heat his mind with incredibilities; a book was thus produced without fear of criticism, without the toil of study, without knowledge of nature, or acquaintance with life.

The task of our present writers is very different; it requires, together with that learning which is to be gained from books, that experience which can never be attained by solitary diligence, but must arise from general converse, and accurate observation of the living world. Their performances have, as Horace expresses it, *"plus oneris quantum veniae minus,"* little indulgence, and therefore more difficulty.[3] They are engaged in portraits of which everyone knows the original, and can detect any deviation from exactness of

---

ON FICTION. Johnson's essay on fiction first appeared in *The Rambler,* Number 4, Saturday, March 31, 1750.
[1] "To speak of life both agreeably and appropriately." *Art of Poetry,* p. 72.

[2] *Poetics,* V. 4.
[3] *Epistles,* II. i. 170.

resemblance. Other writings are safe, except from the malice of learning, but these are in danger from every common reader; as the slipper ill executed was censured by a shoemaker who happened to stop in his way at the Venus of Apelles.[4]

But the fear of not being approved as just copiers of human manners, is not the most important concern that an author of this sort ought to have before him. These books are written chiefly to the young, the ignorant, and the idle, to whom they serve as lectures of conduct, and introductions into life. They are the entertainment of minds unfurnished with ideas, and therefore easily susceptible of impressions; not fixed by principles, and therefore easily following the current of fancy; not informed by experience, and consequently open to every false suggestion and partial account.

That the highest degree of reverence should be paid to youth, and that nothing indecent should be suffered to approach their eyes or ears are precepts extorted by sense and virtue from an ancient writer, by no means eminent for chastity of thought.[5] The same kind, though not the same degree of caution, is required to everything which is laid before them, to secure them from unjust prejudices, perverse opinions, and incongruous combinations of images.

In the romances formerly written, every transaction and sentiment was so remote from all that passes among men, that the reader was in very little danger of making any applications to himself; the virtues and crimes were equally beyond his sphere of activity; and he amused himself with heroes and with traitors, deliverers and persecutors, as with beings of another species, whose actions were regulated upon motives of their own, and who had neither faults nor excellencies in common with himself.

But when an adventurer is leveled with the rest of the world, and acts in such scenes of the universal drama, as may be the lot of any other man; young spectators fix their eyes upon him with closer attention, and hope by observing his behavior and success to regulate their own practices, when they shall be engaged in the like part.

For this reason these familiar histories may perhaps be made of greater use than the solemnities of professed morality, and convey the knowledge of vice and virtue with more efficacy than axioms and definitions. But if the power of example is so great, as to take possession of the memory by a kind of violence, and produce effects almost without the intervention of the will, care ought to be taken that, when the choice is unrestrained, the best examples only should be exhibited; and that which is likely to operate so strongly, should not be mischievous or uncertain in its effects.

The chief advantage which these fictions have over real life is, that their authors are at liberty, though not to invent, yet to select objects, and to cull from the mass of mankind, those individuals upon which the attention ought most to be employed; as a diamond, though it cannot be made, may be polished by art, and placed in such a situation, as to display that luster which before was buried among common stones.

It is justly considered as the greatest excellency of art, to imitate nature; but it is necessary to distinguish those parts of nature, which are most proper for imitation: greater care is still required in representing life, which is so often discolored by passion, or deformed by wickedness. If the world be promiscuously described, I cannot see of what use it can be to read the account; or why it may not be as safe to turn the eye immediately upon mankind, as upon a mirror which shows all that presents itself without discrimination.

It is therefore not a sufficient vindication of a character, that it is drawn as it appears, for many characters ought never to be drawn; nor of a narrative, that the train of events is agreeable to observation and experience, for that observation which is called knowledge of the world, will be found much more frequently to make men cunning than good. The purpose of these writings is surely not only to show mankind, but to provide that they may be seen hereafter with less hazard; to teach the means of avoiding the snares which are laid by treachery for innocence, without infusing any wish for that superiority with which the betrayer flatters his vanity; to give the power of counteracting fraud, without the temptation to practice it; to initiate youth by mock encounters in the art of necessary defense, and to increase prudence without impairing virtue.

Many writers, for the sake of following nature, so mingle good and bad qualities in their principal personages, that they are both equally conspicuous; and as we accompany them through their adventures with delight, and are led by degrees to interest ourselves in their favor, we lose the abhorrence of their faults, because they do not hinder our pleasure, or, perhaps, regard them with some kindness for being united with so much merit.

There have been men indeed splendidly wicked, whose endowments threw a brightness on their crimes, and whom scarce any villainy made perfectly detestable, because they never could be wholly divested of their excellencies; but such have been in all ages the great corrupters of the world, and their resemblance ought no more to be preserved, than the art of murdering without pain.

Some have advanced, without due attention to the consequences of this notion, that certain virtues have their cor-

---

[4]See Burke, *The Sublime and Beautiful*, p. 302. The story is from Pliny, *Natural History*, XXXV. 84–85.
[5]Juvenal, *Satires*, XIV.

respondent faults; and therefore that to exhibit either apart is to deviate from probability. Thus men are observed by Swift to be "grateful in the same degree as they are resentful." This principle, with others of the same kind, supposes man to act from a brute impulse, and pursue a certain degree of inclination, without any choice of the object; for, otherwise, though it should be allowed that gratitude and resentment arise from the same constitution of the passions, it follows not that they will be equally indulged when reason is consulted; yet unless that consequence be admitted, this sagacious maxim becomes an empty sound, without any relation to practice or to life.

Nor it is evident, that even the first motions to these effects are always in the same proportion. For pride, which produces quickness of resentment, will obstruct gratitude, by unwillingness to admit that inferiority which obligation implies; and it is very unlikely, that he who cannot think he receives a favor will acknowledge or repay it.

It is of the utmost importance to mankind, that positions of this tendency should be laid open and confuted; for while men consider good and evil as springing from the same root, they will spare the one for the sake of the other, and in judging, if not of others at least of themselves, will be apt to estimate their virtues by their vices. To this fatal error all those will contribute, who confound the colors of right and wrong, and instead of helping to settle their boundaries, mix them with so much art, that no common mind is able to disunite them.

In narratives, where historical veracity has no place, I cannot discover why there should not be exhibited the most perfect idea of virtue; of virtue not angelical nor above probability, for what we cannot credit we shall never imitate, but the highest and purest that humanity can reach, which, exercised in such trials as the various revolutions of things shall bring upon it, may, by conquering some calamities, and enduring others, teach us what we may hope, and what we can perform. Vice, for vice is necessary to be shewn, should always disgust; nor should the graces of gaiety, or the dignity of courage, be so united with it, as to reconcile it to the mind. Wherever it appears, it should raise hatred by the malignity of its practices, and contempt by the meanness of its stratagems; for while it is supported by either parts or spirit, it will be seldom heartily abhorred. The Roman tyrant was content to be hated, if he was but feared; and there are thousands of the readers of romances willing to be thought wicked, if they may be allowed to be wits. It is therefore to be steadily inculcated, that virtue is the highest proof of understanding, and the only solid basis of greatness; and that vice is the natural consequence of narrow thoughts, that it begins in mistake, and ends in ignominy.

From

Rasselas

Chapter X

Imlac's History Continued. A Dissertation Upon Poetry

"Wherever I went, I found that poetry was considered as the highest learning, and regarded with a veneration somewhat approaching to that which man would pay to the angelic nature. And it yet fills me with wonder, that, in almost all countries, the most ancient poets are considered as the best: whether it be that every other kind of knowledge is an acquisition gradually attained, and poetry is a gift conferred at once; or that the first poetry of every nation surprised them as a novelty, and retained the credit by consent which it received by accident at first: or whether, as the province of poetry is to describe nature and passion, which are always the same, the first writers took possession of the most striking objects for description, and the most probable occurrences for fiction, and left nothing to those that followed them, but transcription of the same events, new combinations of the same images. Whatever be the reason, it is commonly observed that the early writers are in possession of nature, and their followers of art: that the first excel in strength and invention, and the latter in elegance and refinement.

"I was desirous to add my name to this illustrious fraternity. I read all the poets of Persia and Arabia, and was able to repeat by memory the volumes that are suspended in the mosque of Mecca. But I soon found that no man was ever great by imitation. My desire of excellence impelled me to transfer my attention to nature and to life. Nature was to be my subject, and men to be my auditors: I could never describe what I had not seen: I could not hope to move those with delight or terror, whose interests and opinions I did not understand.

"Being now resolved to be a poet, I saw everything with a new purpose; my sphere of attention was suddenly magnified: no kind of knowledge was to be overlooked. I ranged mountains and deserts for images and resemblances, and pictured upon my mind every tree of the forest and

---

RASSELAS. Johnson's tale *The History of Rasselas, Prince of Abyssinia,* was first published in 1759.

flower of the valley. I observed with equal care the crags of the rock and the pinnacles of the palace. Sometimes I wandered along the mazes of the rivulet, and sometimes watched the changes of the summer clouds. To a poet nothing can be useless. Whatever is beautiful, and whatever is dreadful, must be familiar to his imagination: he must be conversant with all that is awfully vast or elegantly little. The plants of the garden, the animals of the wood, the minerals of the earth, and meteors of the sky, must all concur to store his mind with inexhaustible variety: for every idea is useful for the enforcement or decoration of moral or religious truth; and he, who knows most, will have most power of diversifying his scenes, and of gratifying his reader with remote allusions and unexpected instruction.

"All the appearances of nature I was therefore careful to study, and every country which I have surveyed has contributed something to my poetical powers."

"In so wide a survey," said the prince, "you must surely have left much unobserved. I have lived, till now, within the circuit of these mountains, and yet cannot walk abroad without the sight of something which I had never beheld before, or never heeded."

"The business of a poet," said Imlac, "is to examine, not the individual, but the species; to remark general properties and large appearances: he does not number the streaks of the tulip, or describe the different shades in the verdure of the forest. He is to exhibit in his portraits of nature such prominent and striking features, as recall the original to every mind; and must neglect the minuter discriminations, which one may have remarked, and another have neglected, for those characteristics which are alike obvious to vigilance and carelessness.

"But the knowledge of nature is only half the task of a poet; he must be acquainted likewise with all the modes of life. His character requires that he estimate the happiness and misery of every condition; observe the power of all the passions in all their combinations, and trace the changes of the human mind as they are modified by various institutions and accidental influences of climate or custom, from the sprightliness of infancy to the despondence of decrepitude. He must divest himself of the prejudices of his age or country; he must consider right and wrong in their abstracted and invariable state; he must disregard present laws and opinions, and rise to general and transcendental truths, which will always be the same: he must therefore content himself with the slow progress of his name; contemn the applause of his own time, and commit his claims to the justice of posterity. He must write as the interpreter of nature, and the legislator of mankind, and consider himself as presiding over the thoughts and manners of future generations; as a being superior to time and place.

"His labor is not yet at an end: he must know many languages and many sciences; and, that his style may be worthy of his thoughts, must, by incessant practice, familiarize to himself every delicacy of speech and grace of harmony."

From

Preface to *Shakespeare*

That praises are without reason lavished on the dead, and that the honors due only to excellence are paid to antiquity, is a complaint likely to be always continued by those, who, being able to add nothing to truth, hope for eminence from the heresies of paradox; or those, who, being forced by disappointment upon consolatory expedients, are willing to hope from posterity what the present age refuses, and flatter themselves that the regard which is yet denied by envy, will be at last bestowed by time.

Antiquity, like every other quality that attracts the notice of mankind, has undoubtedly votaries that reverence it, not from reason, but from prejudice. Some seem to admire indiscriminately whatever has been long preserved, without considering that time has sometimes cooperated with chance; all perhaps are more willing to honor past than present excellence; and the mind contemplates genius through the shades of age, as the eye surveys the sun through artificial opacity. The great contention of criticism is to find the faults of the moderns, and the beauties of the ancients. While an author is yet living we estimate his powers by his worst performance, and when he is dead, we rate them by his best.

To works, however, of which the excellence is not absolute and definite, but gradual and comparative; to works not raised upon principles demonstrative and scientific, but appealing wholly to observation and experience, no other test can be applied than length of duration and continuance of esteem. What mankind have long possessed they have often examined and compared; and if they persist to value the possession, it is because frequent comparisons have confirmed opinion in its favor. As among the works of nature no man can properly call a river deep, or a mountain high, without the knowledge of many mountains, and many rivers; so in the productions of genius, nothing can be styled excellent till it has been compared with other works of the same kind. Demonstration immediately displays its power, and has

---

PREFACE TO *Shakespeare*. Johnson's Preface to *Shakespeare* was first published in 1765 in his eight-volume edition of Shakespeare's plays. The text printed here comprises the first part of the essay.

nothing to hope or fear from the flux of years; but works tentative and experimental must be estimated by their proportion to the general and collective ability of man, as it is discovered in a long succession of endeavors. Of the first building that was raised, it might be with certainty determined that it was round or square; but whether it was spacious or lofty must have been referred to time. The Pythagorean scale of numbers was at once discovered to be perfect; but the poems of Homer we yet know not to transcend the common limits of human intelligence, but by remarking, that nation after nation, and century after century, has been able to do little more than transpose his incidents, new-name his characters, and paraphrase his sentiments.

The reverence due to writings that have long subsisted arise therefore not from any credulous confidence in the superior wisdom of past ages, or gloomy persuasion of the degeneracy of mankind, but is the consequence of acknowledged and indubitable positions, that what has been longest known has been most considered, and what is most considered is best understood.

The poet, of whose works I have undertaken the revision, may now begin to assume the dignity of an ancient, and claim the privilege of established fame and prescriptive veneration. He has long outlived his century, the term commonly fixed as the test of literary merit. Whatever advantages he might once derive from personal allusions, local customs, or temporary opinions, have for many years been lost; and every topic of merriment, or motive of sorrow, which the modes of artificial life afforded him, now only obscure the scenes which they once illuminated. The effects of favor and competition are at an end; the tradition of his friendships and his enmities has perished; his works support no opinion with arguments, nor supply any faction with invectives; they can neither indulge vanity nor gratify malignity; but are read without any other reason than the desire of pleasure, and are therefore praised only as pleasure is obtained; yet, thus unassisted by interest or passion, they have passed through variations of taste and changes of manners, and, as they devolved from one generation to another, have received new honors at every transmission.

But because human judgment, though it be gradually gaining upon certainty, never becomes infallible; and approbation, though long continued, may yet be only the approbation of prejudice or fashion; it is proper to inquire, by what peculiarities of excellence Shakespeare has gained and kept the favor of his countrymen.

Nothing can please many, and please long, but just representations of general nature. Particular manners, can be known to few, and therefore few only can judge how nearly they are copied. The irregular combinations of fanciful invention may delight awhile, by that novelty of which the common satiety of life sends us all in quest; but the pleasures of sudden wonder are soon exhausted, and the mind can only repose on the stability of truth.

Shakespeare is above all writers, at least above all modern writers, the poet of nature; the poet that holds up to his readers a faithful mirror of manners and of life. His characters are not modified by the customs of particular places, unpracticed by the rest of the world; by the peculiarities of studies or professions, which can operate but upon small numbers; or by the accidents of transient fashions or temporary opinions: they are the genuine progeny of common humanity, such as the world will always supply, and observation will always find. His persons act and speak by the influence of those general passions and principles by which all minds are agitated, and the whole system of life is continued in motion. In the writings of other poets a character is too often an individual; in those of Shakespeare it is commonly a species.

It is from this wide extension of design that so much instruction is derived. It is this which fills the plays of Shakespeare with practical axioms and domestic wisdom. It was said of Euripides, that every verse was a precept; and it may be said of Shakespeare, that from his works may be collected a system of civil and economical prudence. Yet his real power is not shewn in the splendor of particular passages, but by the progress of his fable, and the tenor of his dialogue; and he that tries to recommend him by select quotations, will succeed like the pedant in Hierocles, who, when he offered his house to sale, carried a brick in his pocket as a specimen.

It will not easily be imagined how much Shakespeare excels in accommodating his sentiments to real life, but by comparing him with other authors. It was observed of the ancient schools of declamation, that the more diligently they were frequented, the more was the student disqualified for the world, because he found nothing there which he should ever meet in any other place. The same remark may be applied to every stage but that of Shakespeare. The theater, when it is under any other direction, is peopled by such characters as were never seen, conversing in a language which was never heard, upon topics which will never rise in the commerce of mankind. But the dialogue of this author is often so evidently determined by the incident which produces it, and is pursued with so much ease and simplicity, that it seems scarcely to claim the merit of fiction, but to have been gleaned by diligent selection out of common conversation, and common occurrences.

Upon every other stage the universal agent is love, by whose power all good and evil is distributed, and every action quickened or retarded. To bring a lover, a lady and a rival into the fable; to entangle them in contradictory obligations, perplex them with oppositions of interest, and harass them with violence of desires inconsistent with each other; to make them meet in rapture and part in agony; to fill their mouths with hyperbolical joy and outrageous sorrow; to distress them as nothing human ever was delivered; is the business of a modern dramatist. For this probability is violated, life is misrepresented, and language is depraved. But love is only one of many passions; and as it has no great influence upon the sum of life, it has little operation in the dramas of a poet, who caught his ideas from the living world, and exhibited only what he saw before him. He knew, that any other passion, as it was regular or exorbitant, was a cause of happiness or calamity.

Characters thus ample and general were not easily discriminated and preserved, yet perhaps no poet ever kept his personages more distinct from each other. I will not say with Pope,[1] that every speech may be assigned to the proper speaker, because many speeches there are which have nothing characteristical; but perhaps, though some may be equally adapted to every person, it will be difficult to find any that can be properly transferred from the present possessor to another claimant. The choice is right, when there is reason for choice.

Other dramatists can only gain attention by hyperbolical or aggravated characters, by fabulous and unexampled excellence or depravity, as the writers of barbarous romances invigorated the reader by a giant and a dwarf; and he that should form his expectations of human affairs from the play, or from the tale, would be equally deceived. Shakespeare has no heroes; his scenes are occupied only by men, who act and speak as the reader thinks that he should himself have spoken or acted on the same occasion: Even where the agency is supernatural the dialogue is level with life. Other writers disguise the most natural passions and most frequent incidents; so that he who contemplates them in the book will not know them in the world: Shakespeare approximates the remote, and familiarizes the wonderful; the event which he represents will not happen, but if it were possible, its effects would probably be such as he has assigned; and it may be said, that he has not only shewn human nature as it acts in real exigencies, but as it would be found in trials, to which it cannot be exposed.

This therefore is the praise of Shakespeare, that his drama is the mirror of life; that he who has 'mazed his imagination, in following the phantoms which other writers raise up before him, may here be cured of his delirious ecstasies, by reading human sentiments in human language, by scenes from which a hermit may estimate the transactions of the world, and a confessor predict the progress of the passions.

His adherence to general nature has exposed him to the censure of critics, who form their judgments upon narrow principles. Dennis and Rymer think his Romans not sufficiently Roman; and Voltaire censures his kings as not completely royal. Dennis is offended, that Menenius, a senator of Rome, should play the buffoon;[2] and Voltaire perhaps thinks decency violated when the Danish usurper is represented as a drunkard. But Shakespeare always makes nature predominate over accident; and if he preserves the essential character, is not very careful of distinctions superinduced and adventitious. His story requires Romans or kings, but he thinks only on men. He knew that Rome, like every other city, had men of all dispositions; and wanting a buffoon, he went into the senate house for that which the senate house would certainly have afforded him. He was inclined to shew a usurper and a murderer not only odious but despicable, he therefore added drunkenness to his other qualities, knowing that kings love wine like other men, and that wine exerts its natural power upon kings. These are the petty cavils of petty minds; a poet overlooks the casual distinction of country and condition, as a painter, satisfied with the figure, neglects the drapery.

The censure which he has incurred by mixing comic and tragic scenes, as it extends to all his works, deserves more consideration. Let the fact be first stated, and then examined.

Shakespeare's plays are not in the rigorous and critical sense either tragedies or comedies, but compositions of a distinct kind; exhibiting the real state of sublunary nature, which partakes of good and evil, joy and sorrow, mingled with endless variety of proportion and innumerable modes of combination: and expressing the course of the world, in which the loss of one is the gain of another; in which, at the same time, the reveler is hasting to his wine, and the mourner burying his friend; in which the malignity of one is sometimes defeated by the frolic of another; and many mischiefs and many benefits are done and hindered without design.

Out of this chaos of mingled purposes and casualties the ancient poets, according to the laws which custom had prescribed, selected, some the crimes of men, and some their absurdities; some the momentous vicissitudes of life, and some the lighter occurrences; some the terrors of distress, and some the gaieties of prosperity. Thus rose the two modes of imitation, known by the names of tragedy and comedy, compositions intended to promote different ends by contrary means, and considered as so little allied, that I do not recollect among the Greeks or Romans a single writer who attempted both.

---

[1] In his Preface to *Shakespeare*.

[2] In his *Essay on the Genius and Writings of Shakespeare*.

Shakespeare has united the powers of exciting laughter and sorrow not only in one mind, but in one composition. Almost all his plays are divided between serious and ludicrous characters, and, in the successive evolutions of the design, sometimes produce seriousness and sorrow, and sometimes levity and laughter.

That this is a practice contrary to the rules of criticism will be readily allowed; but there is always an appeal open from criticism to nature. The end of writing is to instruct; the end of poetry is to instruct by pleasing. That the mingled drama may convey all the instruction of tragedy or comedy cannot be denied, because it includes both in its alterations of exhibition and approaches nearer than either to the appearance of life, by shewing how great machinations and slender designs may promote or obviate one another, and the high and the low cooperate in the general system by unavoidable concatenation.

It is objected, that by this change of scenes the passions are interrupted in their progression, and that the principal event, being not advanced by a due gradation of preparatory incidents, wants at last the power to move, which constitutes the perfection of dramatic poetry. This reasoning is so specious, that it is received as true even by those who in daily experience feel it to be false. The interchanges of mingled scenes seldom fail to produce the intended vicissitudes of passion. Fiction cannot move so much, but that the attention may be easily transferred; and though it must be allowed that pleasing melancholy be sometimes interrupted by unwelcome levity, yet let it be considered likewise, that melancholy is often not pleasing, and that the disturbance of one man may be the relief of another; that different auditors have different habitudes; and that, upon the whole, all pleasure consists in variety.

The players, who in their edition divided our author's works into comedies, histories, and tragedies, seem not to have distinguished the three kinds by any very exact or definite ideas.

An action which ended happily to the principal persons, however serious or distressful through its intermediate incidents, in their opinion, constituted a comedy. This idea of a comedy continued long amongst us; and plays were written, which, by changing the catastrophe, were tragedies today, and comedies tomorrow.

Tragedy was not in those times a poem of more general dignity or elevation than comedy; it required only a calamitous conclusion, with which the common criticism of that age was satisfied, whatever lighter pleasure it afforded in its progress.

History was a series of actions, with no other than chronological succession, independent on each other, and without any tendency to introduce or regulate the conclu-

sion. It is not always very nicely distinguished from tragedy. There is not much nearer approach to unity of action in the tragedy of *Antony and Cleopatra,* than in the history of *Richard the Second.* But a history might be continued through many plays; as it had no plan, it had no limits.

Through all these denominations of the drama, Shakespeare's mode of composition is the same; an interchange of seriousness and merriment, by which the mind is softened at one time, and exhilarated at another. But whatever be his purpose, whether to gladden or depress, or to conduct the story, without vehemence or emotion, through tracts of easy and familiar dialogue, he never fails to attain his purpose; as he commands us, we laugh or mourn, or sit silent with quiet expectation, in tranquility without indifference.

When Shakespeare's plan is understood, most of the criticisms of Rymer and Voltaire vanish away. The play of *Hamlet* is opened, without impropriety, by two sentinels; Iago bellows at Brabantio's window, without injury to the scheme of the play, though in terms which a modern audience would not easily endure; the character of Polonius is seasonable and useful; and the gravediggers themselves may be heard with applause.

Shakespeare engaged in dramatic poetry with the world open before him; the rules of the ancients were yet known to few; but public judgment was unformed; he had no example of such fame as might force him upon imitation, nor critics of such authority as might restrain his extravagance: He therefore indulged his natural disposition, and his disposition, as Rymer has remarked, led him to comedy. In tragedy he often writes, with great appearance of toil and study, what is written at last with little felicity; but in his comic scenes, he seems to produce without labor what no labor can improve. In tragedy he is always struggling after some occasion to be comic; but in comedy he seems to repose, or to luxuriate, as in a mode of thinking congenial to his nature. In his tragic scenes there is always something wanting, but his comedy often surpasses expectation or desire. His comedy pleases by the thoughts and the language, and his tragedy for the greater part by incident and action. His tragedy seems to be skill, his comedy to be instinct.

The force of his comic scenes has suffered little diminution from the changes made by a century and a half, in manners or in words. As his personages act upon principles arising from genuine passion, very little modified by particular forms, their pleasures and vexations are communicable to all times and to all places; they are natural, and therefore durable; the adventitious peculiarities of personal habits, are only superficial dies, bright and pleasing for a little while, yet soon fading to a dim tint, without any remains of former luster; but the discriminations of true passion are the colors of nature; they pervade the whole mass, and can only perish

with the body that exhibits them. The accidental compositions of heterogeneous modes are dissolved by the chance
which combined them; but the uniform simplicity of primitive qualities neither admits increase, nor suffers decay. The
sand heap by one flood is scattered by another, but the rock
always continues in its place. The stream of time, which is
continually washing the dissoluble fabrics of other poets,
passes without injury by the adamant of Shakespeare.

If there be, what I believe there is, in every nation, a
style which never becomes obsolete, a certain mode of phraseology so consonant and congenial to the analogy and principles of its respective language as to remain settled and unaltered; this style is probably to be sought in the common
intercourse of life, among those who speak only be understood, without ambition of elegance. The polite are always
catching modish innovations, and the learned depart from
established forms of speech, in hope of finding or making
better; those who wish for distinction forsake the vulgar,
when the vulgar is right; but there is a conversation above
grossness and below refinement, where propriety resides,
and where this poet seems to have gathered his comic dialogue. He is therefore more agreeable to the ears of the present age than any other author equally remote, and among his
other excellencies deserves to be studied as one of the original masters of our language.

These observations are to be considered not as unexcep-
tionably constant, but as containing general and predominant
truth. Shakespeare's familiar dialogue is affirmed to be
smooth and clear, yet not wholly without ruggedness or difficulty; as a country may be eminently fruitful, though it has
spots unfit for cultivation: His characters are praised as natural, though their sentiments are sometimes forced, and their
actions improbable; as the earth upon the whole is spherical,
though its surface is varied with protuberances and cavities.

Shakespeare with his excellencies has likewise faults,
and faults sufficient to obscure and overwhelm any other
merit. I shall shew them in the proportion in which they appear to me, without envious malignity or superstitious veneration. No question can be more innocently discussed than
a dead poet's pretensions to renown; and little regard is due
to that bigotry which sets candor higher than truth.

His first defect is that to which may be imputed most of
the evil in books or in men. He sacrifices virtue to convenience, and is so much more careful to please than to instruct, that he seems to write without any moral purpose.
From his writings indeed a system of social duty may be
selected, for he that thinks reasonably must think morally;
but his precepts and axioms drop casually from him; he
makes no just distribution of good or evil, nor is always careful to shew in the virtuous a disapprobation of the wicked;

he carries his persons indifferently through right and wrong,
and at the close dismisses them without further care, and
leaves their examples to operate by chance. This fault the
barbarity of his age cannot extenuate; for it is always a writer's duty to make the world better, and justice is a virtue
independent on time or place.

The plots are often so loosely formed, that a very slight
consideration may improve them, and so carelessly pursued,
that he seems not always fully to comprehend his own design. He omits opportunities of instructing or delighting
which the train of his story seems to force upon him, and
apparently rejects those exhibitions which would be more
affecting, for the sake of those which are more easy.

It may be observed, that in many of his plays the latter
part is evidently neglected. When he found himself near the
end of his work, and, in view of his reward, he shortened the
labor to snatch the profit. He therefore remits his efforts
where he should most vigorously exert them, and his catastrophe is improbably produced or imperfectly represented.

He had no regard to distinction of time or place, but
gives to one age or nation, without scruple, the customs, institutions, and opinions of another, at the expense not only
of likelihood, but of possibility. These faults Pope has endeavored, with more zeal than judgment, to transfer to his
imagined interpolators. We need not wonder to find Hector
quoting Aristotle, when we see the loves of Theseus and
Hippolyta combined with the gothic mythology of fairies.
Shakespeare, indeed, was not the only violator of chronology, for in the same age Sidney, who wanted not the advantages of learning, has, in his, *Arcadia,* confounded the
pastoral with the feudal times the days of innocence, quiet
and security, with those of turbulence, violence, and
adventure.

In his comic scenes he is seldom very successful, when
he engages his characters in reciprocations of smartness and
contests of sarcasm; their jests are commonly gross, and
their pleasantry licentious; neither his gentlemen nor his ladies have much delicacy, nor are sufficiently distinguished
from his clowns by any appearance of refined manners.
Whether he represented the real conversation of his time is
not easy to determine; the reign of Elizabeth is commonly
supposed to have been a time of stateliness, formality and
reserve; yet perhaps the relaxations of that severity were not
very elegant. There must, however, have been always some
modes of gaiety preferable to others, and a writer ought to
choose the best.

In tragedy his performance seems constantly to be
worse, as his labor is more. The effusions of passion which
exigence forces out are for the most part striking and energetic; but whenever he solicits his invention, or strains his

faculties, the offspring of his throes is tumor, meanness, tediousness, and obscurity.

In narration he affects a disproportionate pomp of diction, and a wearisome train of circumlocution, and tells the incident imperfectly in many words, which might have been more plainly delivered in few. Narration in dramatic poetry is naturally tedious, as it is inactive, and obstructs the progress of the action; it should therefore always be rapid, and enlivened by frequent interruption. Shakespeare found it an encumbrance, and instead of lightening it by brevity, endeavored to recommend it by dignity and splendor.

His declamations or set speeches are commonly cold and weak, for his power was the power of nature; when he endeavored, like other tragic writers, to catch opportunities of amplification, and instead of inquiring what the occasion demanded, to show how much his stores of knowledge could supply, he seldom escapes without the pity or resentment of his reader.

It is incident to him to be now and then entangled with an unwieldly sentiment, which he cannot well express, and will not reject; he struggles with it awhile, and if it continues stubborn, comprises it in words such as occur, and leaves it to be disentangled and evolved by those who have more leisure to bestow upon it.

Not that always where the language is intricate the thought is subtle, or the image always great where the line is bulky; the equality of words to things is very often neglected, and trivial sentiments and vulgar ideas disappoint the attention, to which they are recommended by sonorous epithets and swelling figures.

But the admirers of this great poet have never less reason to indulge their hopes of supreme excellence, than when he seems fully resolved to sink them in dejection, and mollify them with tender emotions by the fall of greatness, the danger of innocence, or the crosses of love. He is not long soft and pathetic without some idle conceit, or contemptible equivocation. He no sooner begins to move, than he counteracts himself; and terror and pity, as they are rising in the mind, are checked and blasted by sudden frigidity.

A quibble is to Shakespeare, what luminous vapors are to the traveler; he follows it at all adventures; it is sure to lead him out of his way, and sure to engulf him in the mire. It has some malignant power over his mind, and its fascinations are irresistible. Whatever be the dignity or profundity of his disquisition, whether he be enlarging knowledge or exalting affection, whether he be amusing attention with incidents, or enchaining it in suspense, let but a quibble spring up before him, and he leaves his work unfinished. A quibble is the golden apple for which he will always turn aside from his career, or stoop from his elevation. A quibble, poor and

barren as it is, gave him such delight, that he was content to purchase it, by the sacrifice of reason, propriety and truth. A quibble was to him the fatal Cleopatra for which he lost the world, and was content to lose it.

It will be thought strange, that, in enumerating the defects of this writer, I have not yet mentioned his neglect of the unities; his violation of those laws which have been instituted and established by the joint authority of poets and critics.

For his other deviations from the art of writing I resign him to critical justice, without making any other demand in his favor, than that which must be indulged to all human excellence: that his virtues be rated with his failings: but, from the censure which this irregularity may bring upon him, I shall, with due reverence to that learning which I must oppose, adventure to try how I can defend him.

His histories, being neither tragedies nor comedies, are not subject to any of their laws; nothing more is necessary to all the praise which they expect, than that the changes of action be so prepared as to be understood, that the incidents be various and affecting, and the characters consistent, natural, and distinct. No other unity is intended, and therefore none is to be sought.

In his other works he has well enough preserved the unity of action. He has not, indeed, an intrigue regularly perplexed and regularly unraveled: he does not endeavor to hide his design only to discover it, for this is seldom the order of real events, and Shakespeare is the poet of nature: But his plan has commonly what Aristotle requires, a beginning, a middle, and an end;[3] one event is concatenated with another, and the conclusion follows by easy consequence. There are perhaps some incidents that might be spared, as in other poets there is much talk that only fills up time upon the stage; but the general system makes gradual advances, and the end of the play is the end of expectation.

To the unities of time and place he has shewn no regard; and perhaps a nearer view of the principles on which they stand will diminish their value, and withdraw from them the veneration which, from the time of Corneille,[4] they have very generally received, by discovering that they have given more trouble to the poet, than pleasure to the auditor.

The necessity of observing the unities of time and place arises from the supposed necessity of making the drama credible. The critics hold it impossible, that an action of months or years can be possibly believed to pass in three hours; or that the spectator can suppose himself to sit in the

---

[3]See *Poetics,* VII. 3, p. 54
[4]See *Of the Three Unities,* pp. 205–12.

theater, while ambassadors go and return between distant kings, while armies are levied and towns besieged, while an exile wanders and returns, or till he whom they saw courting his mistress, shall lament the untimely fall of his son. The mind revolts from evident falsehood, and fiction loses its force when it departs from the resemblance of reality.

From the narrow limitation of time necessarily arises the contraction of place. The spectator, who knows that he saw the first act at Alexandria, cannot suppose that he sees the next at Rome, at a distance to which not the dragons of Medea could, in so short a time, have transported him; he knows with certainty that he has not changed his place, and he knows that place cannot change itself; that what was a house cannot become a plain; that what was Thebes can never be Persepolis.

Such is the triumphant language with which a critic exults over the misery of an irregular poet, and exults commonly without resistance or reply. It is time therefore to tell him by the authority of Shakespeare, that he assumes, as an unquestionable principle, a position, which, while his breath is forming it into words, his understanding pronounces to be false. It is false, that any representation is mistaken for reality; that any dramatic fable in its materiality was ever credible, or, for a single moment, was ever credited.

The objection arising from the impossibility of passing the first hour at Alexandria, and the next at Rome, supposes, that when the play opens, the spectator really imagines himself at Alexandria, and believes that his walk to the theater has been a voyage to Egypt, and that he lives in the days of Antony and Cleopatra. Surely he that imagines this may imagine more. He that can take the stage at one time for the palace of the Ptolemies, may take it in half an hour for the promontory of Actium. Delusion, if delusion be admitted, has no certain limitation; if the spectator can be once persuaded, that his old acquaintance are Alexander and Caesar, that a room illuminated with candles is the plain of Pharsalia, or the bank of Granicus, he is in a state of elevation above the reach of reason, or of truth, and from the heights of empyrean poetry, may despise the circumscriptions of terrestrial nature. There is no reason why a mind thus wandering in ecstasy should count the clock, or why an hour should not be a century in that calenture of the brains that can make the stage a field.

The truth is, that the spectators are always in their senses, and know, from the first act to the last, that the stage is only a stage, and that the players are only players. They came to hear a certain number of lines recited with just gesture and elegant modulation. The lines relate to some action, and an action must be in some place; but the different actions that complete a story may be in places very remote from each other; and where is the absurdity of allowing that space to represent first Athens, and then Sicily, which was always known to be neither Sicily nor Athens, but a modern theater?

By supposition, as place is introduced, time may be extended; the time required by the fable elapses for the most part between the acts; for, of so much of the action as is represented, the real and poetical duration is the same. If, in the first act, preparations for war against Mithridates are represented to be made in Rome, the event of the war may, without absurdity, be represented, in the catastrophe, as happening in Pontus; we know that there is neither war, nor preparation for war; we know that we are neither in Rome nor Pontus; that neither Mithridates nor Lucullus are before us. The drama exhibits successive imitations of successive actions; and why may not the second imitation represent an action that happened years after the first, if it be so connected with it, that nothing but time can be supposed to intervene? Time is, of all modes of existence, most obsequious to the imagination; a lapse of years is as easily conceived as a passage of hours. In contemplation we easily contract the time of real actions, and therefore willingly permit it to be contracted when we only see their imitation.

It will be asked, how the drama moves, if it is not credited. It is credited with all the credit due to a drama. It is credited, whenever it moves, as a just picture of a real original; as representing to the auditor what he would himself feel, if he were to do or suffer what is there feigned to be suffered or to be done. The reflection that strikes the heart is not, that the evils before us are real evils, but that they are evils to which we ourselves may be exposed. If there be any fallacy, it is not that we fancy the players, but that we fancy ourselves unhappy for a moment; but we rather lament the possibility than suppose the presence of misery, as a mother weeps over her babe, when she remembers that death may take it from her. The delight of tragedy proceeds from our consciousness of fiction; if we thought murders and treasons real, they would please no more.

Imitations produce pain or pleasure, not because they are mistaken for realities, but because they bring realities to mind. When the imagination is recreated by a painted landscape, the trees are not supposed capable to give us shade, or the fountains coolness; but we consider how we should be pleased with such fountains playing beside us, and such woods waving over us. We are agitated in reading the history of Henry the Fifth, yet no man takes his book for the field of Agincourt. A dramatic exhibition is a book recited with concomitants that increase or diminish its effect. Familiar comedy is often more powerful in the theater, than in the page; imperial tragedy is always less. The humor of Petruchio may be heightened by grimace; but what voice or what gesture can hope to add dignity or force to the soliloquy of Cato?

A play read, affects the mind like a play acted. It is

therefore evident, that the action is not supposed to be real; and it follows, that between the acts a longer or shorter time may be allowed to pass, and that no more account of space or duration is to be taken by the auditor of a drama, than by the reader of a narrative, before whom may pass in an hour the life of a hero, or the revolutions of an empire.

Whether Shakespeare knew the unities, and rejected them by design, or deviated from them by happy ignorance, it is, I think, impossible to decide, and useless to inquire. We may reasonably suppose, that, when he rose to notice, he did not want the counsels and admonitions of scholars and critics, and that he at last deliberately persisted in a practice, which he might have begun by chance. As nothing is essential to the fable, but unity of action, and as the unities of time and place arise evidently from false assumptions, and, by circumscribing the extent of the drama, lessen its variety, I cannot think it much to be lamented, that they were not known by him, or not observed: nor, if such another poet could arise, should I very vehemently reproach him, that his first act passed at Venice, and his next in Cyprus. Such violations of rules merely positive, become the comprehensive genius of Shakespeare, and such censures are suitable to the minute and slender criticism of Voltaire:

Non usque adeo permiscuit imis
Longus summa dies, ut non, si voce Metelli
Serventur leges, malint a Caesare tolli.[5]

---

[5] "A long time has not so confused the highest and lowest that the laws made by Metellus may not wish to be overthrown by Caesar." Lucan, *Pharsalia*, III. 138–40.

Yet when I speak thus slightly of dramatic rules, I cannot but recollect how much wit and learning may be produced against me; before such authorities I am afraid to stand, not that I think the present question one of those that are to be decided by mere authority, but because it is to be suspected, that these precepts have not been so easily received but for better reasons than I have yet been able to find. The result of my inquiries, in which it would be ludicrous to boast of impartiality, is, that the unities of time and place are not essential to a just drama, that though they may sometimes conduce to pleasure, they are always to be sacrificed to the nobler beauties of variety and instruction; and that a play, written with nice observation of critical rules, is to be contemplated as an elaborate curiosity, as the product of superfluous and ostentatious art, by which is shewn, rather what is possible, than what is necessary.

He that, without diminution of any other excellence, shall preserve all the unities unbroken, deserves the like applause with the architect, who shall display all the orders of architecture in a citadel, without any deduction from its strength; but the principal beauty of a citadel is to exclude the enemy; and the greatest graces of a play, are to copy nature and instruct life.

Perhaps what I have here not dogmatically but deliberately written, may recall the principles of the drama to a new examination. I am almost frightened at my own temerity; and when I estimate the fame and the strength of those that maintain the contrary opinion, am ready to sink down in reverential silence; as Aeneas withdrew from the defense of Troy, when he saw Neptune shaking the wall, and Juno heading the besiegers.

Edward Young

1683–1765

Two critical tendencies that flowered in the Romantic period are foreshadowed in Young's *Conjectures on Original Composition.* First, primary interest turned from the relationship between the work and the reader to that between the author and his work. Second, emphasis shifted from discussion of rules and conventions of literary state-ment to interest in originality and innate "genius." One notes this tendency in Young's treatment of *imitation,* by which he means only the imitation of other authors, mainly the ancients. He is bold enough to depart from Pope's argument that Virgil discovered the imitation of Homer and of nature to be the same. For Young the proper object of imitation is not an ancient author's work but his "spirit" and his "taste." It is a dis-tinction that is difficult to sustain, since the only avenue to understanding an ancient author's spirit or taste usually lies in his works; but clearly Young's aim is to change the main preoccupations of criticism as it had been practiced by the neoclassicists, and to emphasize the uniqueness of personal genius and the element of poetry that is "beyond prose reason." He does not try to distinguish poetry from prose by an analysis of their language or languages; he does not have a theory of language adequate to the task. Rather he proceeds to discuss elements that are alleged to be characteristic of the author himself.

Quite naturally, Young finds himself embroiled in the old controversy of the ancients versus the moderns. Although Young argues that the ancients excelled the moderns, he does not believe that they necessarily must. Slavish adherence to the ways of the ancients has suppressed innate genius and diminished the modern capacity for greatness. But genius can appear at any time. This is not to say that one should be ignorant of the classics. They are part of one's education.

Young turns to metaphors of organicism and natural growth for his description of original composition and thus presages the proliferation of these metaphors in the work of Romantic critics: "The mind of a man of genius is a fertile and pleasant field . . . . An original may be said to be of a vegetable nature; it rises spontaneously from the vital root of genius; it grows, it is not made."

The *Poetical Works* of Young were edited in two volumes by John Mitford (1844). *Conjectures on Original Composition in a Letter to the Author of* Sir Charles Grandi-son has been edited by E. J. Morley (1918). See also H. C. Shelley, *The Life and Letters of Edward Young* (1914); Isabel St. John Bliss, *Edward Young* (1969); and Joel Weinsheimer, *Imitation* (1984).

From

Conjectures on Original Composition

In a Letter to the Author of

Sir Charles Grandison

Dear Sir,

We confess the follies of youth without a blush; not so, those of age. However, keep me a little in countenance, by considering, that age wants amusements more, though it can justify them less, than the preceding periods of life. How you may relish the pastime here sent you, I know not. It is miscellaneous in its nature, somewhat licentious in its conduct; and, perhaps, not overimportant in its end. However, I have endeavored to make some amends, by digressing into subjects more important, and more suitable to my season of life. A serious thought standing single among many of a lighter nature, will sometimes strike the careless wanderer after amusement only, with useful awe: as monumental marbles scattered in a wide pleasure-garden (and such there are) will call to recollection those who would never have sought it in a churchyard-walk of mournful yews.

To one such monument I may conduct you, in which is a hidden luster, like the sepulchral lamps of old; but not like those will this be extinguished, but shine the brighter for being produced, after so long concealment, into open day.

You remember that your worthy patron, and our common friend, put some questions on the serious drama, at the same time when he desired our sentiments on original, and on moral composition.[1] Though I despair of breaking through the frozen obstructions of age, and care's incumbent cloud, into that flow of thought, and brightness of expression, which subjects so polite require; yet will I hazard some conjectures on them.

I begin with original composition; and the more willingly, as it seems an original subject to me, who have seen nothing hitherto written on it: but, first, a few thoughts on composition in general. Some are of opinion, that its growth, at present, is too luxuriant; and that the press is overcharged.

Overcharged, I think, it could never be, if none were admitted, but such as brought their imprimatur from sound understanding, and the public good. Wit, indeed, however brilliant, should not be permitted to gaze self-enamored on its useless charms, in that fountain of fame (if so I may call the press), if beauty is all that it has to boast; but, like the first Brutus,[2] it should sacrifice its most darling offspring to the sacred interests of virtue, and real service of mankind.

This restriction allowed, the more composition the better. To men of letters, and leisure, it is not only a noble amusement, but a sweet refuge; it improves their parts, and promotes their peace: It opens a back door out of the bustle of this busy, and idle world, into a delicious garden of moral and intellectual fruits and flowers; the key of which is denied to the rest of mankind. When stung with idle anxieties, or teased with fruitless impertinence, or yawning over insipid diversions, then we perceive the blessing of a lettered recess. With what a gust do we retire to our disinterested, and immortal friends in our closet, and find our minds, when applied to some favorite theme, as naturally, and as easily quieted, and refreshed, as a peevish child (and peevish children are we all till we fall asleep) when laid to the breast? Our happiness no longer lives on charity; nor bids fair for a fall, by leaning on that most precarious, and thorny pillow, another's pleasure, for our repose. How independent of the world is he, who can daily find new acquaintance, that at once entertain, and improve him, in the little world, the minute but fruitful creation, of his own mind?

These advantages composition affords us, whether we write ourselves, or in more humble amusement peruse the works of others. While we bustle through the thronged walks of public life, it gives us a respite, at least, from care; a pleasing pause of refreshing recollection. If the country is our choice, or fate, there it rescues us from sloth and sensuality, which, like obscene vermin, are apt gradually to creep unperceived into the delightful bowers of our retirement, and to poison all its sweets. Conscious guilt robs the rose of its scent, the lily of its luster; and makes an Eden a deflowered, and dismal scene.

Moreover, if we consider life's endless evils, what can be more prudent, than to provide for consolation under them? A consolation under them the wisest of men have found in the pleasures of the pen. Witness, among many more, Thucydides, Xenophon, Tully, Ovid, Seneca, Pliny the younger, who says *"In uxoris infirmitate, et amicorum periculo, aut morte turbatus, ad studia, unicum doloris levamen-*

CONJECTURES ON ORIGINAL COMPOSITION. *Conjectures on Original Composition* was first published in 1759. The author of the novel *Sir Charles Grandison* (1753) is Young's friend Samuel Richardson, who suggested the essay to Young and helped him revise it before publication.
[1]The "patron" and "friend" is Richardson.

---

[2]Lucius Junius Brutus (sixth–fifth century B.C.), the first consul, is said to have put his two sons to death for their participation in a conspiracy.

tum, confugio."[3] And why not add to these their modern equals, Chaucer, Raleigh, Bacon, Milton, Clarendon, under the same shield, unwounded by misfortune, and nobly smiling in distress?

Composition was a cordial to these under the frowns of fortune; but evils there are, which her smiles cannot prevent, or cure. Among these are the languors of old age. If those are held honorable, who in a hand benumbed by time have grasped the just sword in defense of their country; shall they be less esteemed, whose unsteady pen vibrates to the last in the cause of religion, of virtue, of learning? Both these are happy in this, that by fixing their attention on objects most important, they escape numberless little anxieties, and that *tedium vitae*[4] which often hangs so heavy on its evening hours. May not this insinuate some apology for my spilling ink, and spoiling paper, so late in life?

But there are, who write with vigor, and success, to the world's delight, and their own renown. These are the glorious fruits where genius prevails. The mind of a man of genius is a fertile and pleasant field, pleasant as Elysium, and fertile as Tempe; it enjoys a perpetual spring. Of that spring, originals are the fairest flowers: imitations are of quicker growth, but fainter bloom. Imitations are of two kinds; one of nature, one of authors: the first we call originals, and confine the term imitation to the second. I shall not enter into the curious inquiry of what is, or is not, strictly speaking, original, content with what all must allow, that some compositions are more so than others; and the more they are so, I say, the better. Originals are, and ought to be, great favorites, for they are great benefactors; they extend the republic of letters, and add a new province to its dominion: imitators only give us a sort of duplicates of what we had, possibly much better, before; increasing the mere drug of books, while all that makes them valuable, knowledge and genius, are at a stand. The pen of an original writer, like Armida's wand, out of a barren waste calls a blooming spring: out of that blooming spring an imitator is a transplanter of laurels, which sometimes die on removal, always languish in a foreign soil.

But suppose an imitator to be most excellent (and such there are), yet still he but nobly builds on another's foundation; his debt is, at least, equal to his glory; which therefore, on the balance, cannot be very great. On the contrary, an original, though but indifferent (its originality being set aside), yet has something to boast; it is something to say with

him in Horace, *"Meo sum pauper in aere";*[5] and to share ambition with no less than Caesar, who declared he had rather be the first in a village, than the second at Rome.

Still farther: an imitator shares his crown, if he has one, with the chosen object of his imitation; an original enjoys an undivided applause. An original may be said to be of a vegetable nature; it rises spontaneously from the vital root of genius;[6] it grows, it is not made: imitations are often a sort of manufacture wrought up by those mechanics, art, and labor, out of preexistent materials not their own.

Again: we read imitation with somewhat of his languor, who listens to a twice-told tale: our spirits rouse at an original; that is a perfect stranger, and all throng to learn what news from a foreign land: And though it comes, like an Indian prince, adorned with feathers only, having little of weight; yet of our attention it will rob the more solid, if not equally new: Thus every telescope is lifted at a new-discovered star; it makes a hundred astronomers in a moment, and denies equal notice to the sun. But if an original, by being as excellent, as new, adds admiration to surprise, then are we at the writer's mercy; on the strong wing of his imagination, we are snatched from Britain to Italy, from climate to climate, from pleasure to pleasure; we have no home, no thought, of our own; till the magician drops his pen: and then falling down into ourselves, we awake to flat realities, lamenting the change, like the beggar who dreamt himself a prince.

It is with thoughts, as it is with words; and with both, as with men; they may grow old, and die. Words tarnished, by passing through the mouths of the vulgar, are laid aside as inelegant, and obsolete. So thoughts, when become too common, should lose their currency; and we should send new metal to the mint, that is, new meaning to the press. The division of tongues at Babel did not more effectually debar men from making themselves a name (as the Scripture speaks) than the too great concurrence, or union of tongues will do forever. We may as well grow good by another's virtue, or fat by another's food, as famous by another's thought. The world will pay its debt of praise but once; and instead of applauding, explode a second demand, as a cheat.

If it is said, that most of the Latin classics, and all the Greek, except perhaps, Homer, Pindar, and Anacreon, are in the number of imitators, yet receive our highest applause; our answer is, that they though not real, are accidental originals; the works they imitated, few excepted, are lost: they,

---

[3] "With my wife ill, and my friends in danger, and troubled by death, I flee to studies, the single comfort for sorrow." Pliny, *Epistles,* VIII. 19.
[4] "Tedium of life."

[5] "I am poor in my property," that is, poor but not in debt. *Epistles,* II. ii. 12.
[6] Note here the appearance of organic metaphors for the imagination. See M. H. Abrams, *The Mirror and the Lamp: Romantic Theory and the Critical Tradition* (1953), especially 201 *ff.* for their use in Romantic literature.

on their father's decease, enter as lawful heirs, on their estates in fame: the fathers of our copyists are still in possession; and secured in it, in spite of Goths, and flames by the perpetuating power of the press. Very late must a modern imitator's fame arrive, if it waits for their decease.

An original enters early on reputation: fame, fond of new glories, sounds her trumpet in triumph at its birth; and yet how few are awakened by it into the noble ambition of like attempts? Ambition is sometimes no vice in life; it is always a virtue in composition. High in the towering Alps is the fountain of the Po; high in fame, and in antiquity, is the fountain of an imitator's undertaking; but the river, and the imitation, humbly creep along the vale. So few are our originals, that, if all other books were to be burnt, the lettered world would resemble some metropolis in flames where a few incombustible buildings, a fortress, temple, or tower, lift their heads, in melancholy grandeur, amid the mighty ruin. Compared with this conflagration, old Omar lighted up but a small bonfire, when he heated the baths of the barbarians, for eight months together, with the famed Alexandrian library's inestimable spoils, that no profane book might obstruct the triumphant progress of his holy Alcoran[7] round the globe.

But why are originals so few? Not because the writer's harvest is over, the great reapers of antiquity having left nothing to be gleaned after them; nor because the human mind's teeming time is past, or because it is incapable of putting forth unprecedented births; but because illustrious examples engross, prejudice, and intimidate. They engross our attention, and so prevent a due inspection of ourselves; they prejudice our judgment in favor of their abilities, and so lessen the sense of our own; and they intimidate us with the splendor of their renown, and thus under diffidence bury our strength. Nature's impossibilities, and those of diffidence lie wide asunder.

Let it not be suspected, that I would weakly insinuate anything in favor of the moderns, as compared with ancient authors: no, I am lamenting their great inferiority. But I think it is no necessary inferiority; that it is not from divine destination, but from some cause far beneath the moon: I think that human souls, through all periods, are equal; that due care, and exertion, would set us nearer our immortal predecessors than we are at present; and he who questions and confutes this, will show abilities not a little tending toward a proof of that equality, which he denies.

After all, the first ancients had no merit in being originals: they could not be imitators. Modern writers have a choice to make; and therefore have a merit in their power.

They may soar in the regions of liberty, or move in the soft fetters of easy imitation; and imitation has as many plausible reasons to urge, as pleasure has to offer to Hercules. Hercules made the choice of a hero, and so became immortal.

Yet let not assertors of classic excellence imagine, that I deny the tribute it so well deserves. He that admires not ancient authors, betrays a secret he would conceal, and tells the world, that he does not understand them. Let us be as far from neglecting, as from copying, their admirable compositions; sacred be their rights, and inviolable their fame. Let our understanding feed on theirs; they afford the noblest nourishment; but let them nourish, not annihilate, our own. When we read, let our imagination kindle at their charms; when we write, let our judgment shut them out of our thoughts; treat even Homer himself as his royal admirer was treated by the cynic; bid him stand aside, nor shade our composition from the beams of our own genius; for nothing original can rise, nothing immortal, can ripen, in any other sun.

Must we then, you say, not imitate ancient authors? Imitate them, by all means; but imitate aright. He that imitates the divine *Iliad,* does not imitate Homer; but he who takes the same method, which Homer took, for arriving at a capacity of accomplishing a work so great. Tread in his steps to the sole fountain of immortality; drink where he drank, at the true Helicon, that is, at the breast of nature: imitate; but imitate not the composition, but the man. For may not this paradox pass into a maxim? viz. "The less we copy the renowned ancients, we shall resemble them the more."

But possibly you may reply, that you must either imitate Homer, or depart from nature.[8] Not so: for suppose you was to change place, in time, with Homer; then, if you write naturally, you might as well charge Homer with an imitation of you. Can you be said to imitate Homer for writing so, as you would have written, if Homer had never been? As far as a regard to nature, and sound sense, will permit a departure from your great predecessors; so far, ambitiously, depart from them; the farther from them in similitude, the nearer are you to them in excellence; you rise by it into an original; become a noble collateral, not a humble descendant from them. Let us build our compositions with the spirit, and in the taste, of the ancients; but not with their materials: thus will they resemble the structures of Pericles at Athens, which Plutarch commends for having had an air of antiquity as soon as they were built. All eminence, and distinction, lies out of the beaten road; excursion, and deviation, are

---

[7] The Koran, sacred book of Moslems.

[8] Young refers here to Pope's remark in his *Essay on Criticism,* 135 (see p. 275) that Virgil discovered the imitation of nature and of Homer to be the same.

necessary to find it; and the more remote your path from the highway, the more reputable; if, like poor Gulliver (of whom anon) you fall not into a ditch, in your way to glory.

What glory to come near, what glory to reach, what glory (presumptuous thought!) to surpass, our predecessors? And is that then in nature absolutely impossible? Or is it not, rather, contrary to nature to fail in it? Nature herself sets the ladder, all wanting is our ambition to climb. For by the bounty of nature we are as strong as our predecessors; and by the favor of time (which is but another round in nature's scale) we stand on higher ground. As to the first, were they more than men? Or are we less? Are not our minds cast in the same mold with those before the flood? The flood affected matter; mind escaped. As to the second; though we are moderns, the world is an ancient; more ancient far, than when they, whom we most admire, filled it with their fame. Have we not their beauties, as stars, to guide; their defects, as rocks, to be shunned; the judgment of ages on both, as a chart to conduct, and a sure helm to steer us in our passage to greater perfection than theirs? And shall we be stopped in our rival pretensions to fame by this just reproof? *"Stat contra, dicitque tibi tua pagina, fur es."*[9] It is by a sort of noble contagion, from a general familiarity with their writings, and not by any particular sordid theft, that we can be the better for those who went before us. Hope we, from plagiarism, any dominion in literature; as that of Rome arose from a nest of thieves?

Rome was a powerful ally to many states; ancient authors are our powerful allies; but we must take heed, that they do not succor, till they enslave, after the manner of Rome. Too formidable an idea of their superiority, like a specter, would fright us out of a proper use of our wits; and dwarf our understanding, by making a giant of theirs. Too great awe for them lays genius under restraint, and denies it that free scope, that full elbowroom, which is requisite for striking its most masterly strokes. Genius is a masterworkman, learning is but an instrument; and an instrument, though most valuable, yet not always indispensable. Heaven will not admit of a partner in the accomplishment of some favorite spirits; but rejecting all human means, assumes the whole glory to itself. Have not some, though not famed for erudition, so written, as almost to persuade us, that they shone brighter, and soared higher, for escaping the boasted aid of that proud ally?

Nor is it strange; for what, for the most part, mean we by genius, but the power of accomplishing great things without the means generally reputed necessary to that end? A genius differs from a good understanding, as a magician from a good architect; that raises his structure by means invisible; this by the skillful use of common tools. Hence genius has ever been supposed to partake of something divine. *Nemo unquam vir magnus fuit, sine aliquo afflatu divino.*[10]

Learning, destitute of this superior aid, is fond, and proud, of what has cost it much pains; is a great lover of rules, and boaster of famed examples: as beauties less perfect, who owe half their charms to cautious art, learning inveighs against natural unstudied graces, and small harmless inaccuracies, and sets rigid bounds to that liberty, to which genius often owes its supreme glory; but the no-genius its frequent ruin. For unprescribed beauties, and unexampled excellence, which are characteristics of genius, lie without the pale of learning's authorities, and laws; which pale, genius must leap to come at them: but by that leap, if genius is wanting, we break our necks; we lose that little credit, which possibly we might have enjoyed before. For rules, like crutches, are a needful aid to the lame, though an impediment to the strong. A Homer casts them away; and, like his Achilles, *"Jura negat sibi nata, nihil non arrogat,"*[11] by native force of mind. There is something in poetry beyond prose-reason; there are mysteries in it not to be explained, but admired; which render mere prose-men infidels to their divinity. And here pardon a second paradox; viz. "Genius often then deserves most to be praised, when it is most sure to be condemned; that is, when its excellence, from mounting high, to weak eyes is quite out of sight."

If I might speak farther of learning, and genius, I would compare genius to virtue, and learning to riches. As riches are most wanted where there is least virtue; so learning where there is least genius. As virtue without much riches can give happiness, so genius without much learning can give renown. As it is said in Terence, *"Pecuniam negligere interdum maximum est lucrum";*[12] so to neglect of learning, genius sometimes owes its greater glory. Genius, therefore, leaves but the second place, among men of letters, to the learned. It is their merit, and ambition, to fling light on the works of genius, and point out its charms. We most justly reverence their informing radius for that favor; but we must much more admire the radiant stars pointed out by them.

A star of the first magnitude among the moderns was Shakespeare; among the ancients, Pindar; who (as Vossius tells us) boasted of his no-learning, calling himself the eagle,

---

9"Your page stands against you and says to you that you are a thief." Martial, *Epigrams,* I. lv. 12.

10"No one was ever a great man without some divine inspiration."
11"He says that the laws are not created for him, and he claims everything [for himself]." Horace, *Art of Poetry,* p. 69.
12"To neglect money is sometimes the greatest gain." *Adelphi,* 215–16.

for his flight above it. And such genii as these may, indeed, have much reliance on their own native powers. For genius may be compared to the natural strength of the body; learning to the super induced accouterments of arms: if the first is equal to the proposed exploit, the latter rather encumbers, than assists; rather retards, than promotes, the victory. *"Sacer nobis inest Deus,"*[13] says Seneca. With regard to the moral world, conscience, with regard to the intellectual, genius, is that god within. Genius can set us right in composition, without the rules of the learned; as conscience sets us right in life, without the laws of the land; this, singly, can make us good, as men: that, singly, as writers, can, sometimes, make us great.

I say, sometimes, because there is a genius, which stands in need of learning to make it shine. Of genius there are two species, an earlier, and a later; or call them infantine, and adult. An adult genius comes out of nature's hand, as Pallas out of Jove's head, at full growth, and mature: Shakespeare's genius was of this kind; on the contrary, Swift stumbled at the threshold, and set out for distinction on feeble knees: his was an infantine genius; a genius, which, like other infants, must be nursed, and educated, or it will come to naught: Learning is its nurse, and tutor; but this nurse may overlay with an indigested load, which smothers common sense; and this tutor may mislead, with pedantic prejudice, which vitiates the best understanding: as too great admirers of the fathers of the church have sometimes set up their authority against the true sense of Scripture; so too great admirers of the classical fathers have sometimes set up their authority, or example, against reason. *"Neve minor, neu sit quinto productior actu fabula."*[14] So says Horace, so says ancient example. But reason has not subscribed. I know but one book that can justify our implicit acquiescence in it: and (by the way) on that book a noble disdain of undue deference to prior opinion has lately cast, and is still casting, a new and inestimable light.

But, superstition for our predecessors set aside, the classics are forever our rightful and revered masters in composition; and our understandings bow before them: but when? When a master is wanted; which, sometimes, as I have shown, is not the case. Some are pupils of nature only, nor go farther to school: from such we reap often a double advantage; they not only rival the reputation of the great ancient authors, but also reduce the number of mean ones among the moderns. For when they enter on subjects which have been in former hands, such is their superiority, that, like a tenth wave, they overwhelm, and bury in oblivion all that went before: and thus not only enrich and adorn, but remove a load, and lessen the labor, of the lettered world.

"But," you say, "since originals can arise from genius only, and since genius is so very rare, it is scarce worthwhile to labor a point so much, from which we can reasonably expect so little." To show that genius is not so very rare as you imagine, I shall point out strong instances of it, in a far distant quarter from that mentioned above. The minds of the schoolmen were almost as much cloistered as their bodies; they had but little learning, and few books; yet may the most learned be struck with some astonishment at their so singular natural sagacity, and most exquisite edge of thought. Who would expect to find Pindar and Scotus, Shakespeare and Aquinas, of the same party? Both equally shew an original, unindebted, energy; the *vigor igneus,* and *caelestis origo,*[15] burns in both; and leaves us in doubt whether genius is more evident in the sublime flights and beauteous flowers of poetry, or in the profound penetrations, and marvelously keen and minute distinctions, called the thorns of the schools. There might have been more able consuls called from the plow, than ever arrived at that honor: Many a genius, probably, there has been, which could neither write, nor read. So that genius, that supreme luster of literature, is less rare than you conceive.

By the praise of genius we detract not from learning; we detract not from the value of gold, by saying that diamond has greater still. He who disregards learning, shows that he wants its aid; and he that overvalues it, shows that its aid has done him harm. Overvalued indeed it cannot be, if genius, as to composition, is valued more. Learning we thank, genius we revere; that gives us pleasure, this gives us rapture; that informs, this inspires; and is itself inspired; for genius is from heaven, learning from man: this sets us above the low, and illiterate; that, above the learned, and polite. Learning is borrowed knowledge; genius is knowledge innate, and quite our own. Therefore, as Bacon observes, it may take a nobler name, and be called wisdom;[16] in which sense of wisdom, some are born wise.

But here a caution is necessary against the most fatal of errors in those automaths, those self-taught philosophers of our age, who set up genius, and often, mere fancied genius, not only above human learning, but divine truth. I have called genius wisdom; but let it be remembered, that in the most renowned ages of the most refined heathen wisdom (and theirs is not Christian) "the world by wisdom knew not

---

[13]"Sacred is the god dwelling in us."
[14]"The play should be neither shorter nor longer than five acts." Horace, *Art of Poetry,* p. 70.

[15]"Glowing energy" and "heavenly origin."
[16]*The Advancement of Learning.*

God, and it pleased God by the foolishness of preaching to save those that believed."[17] In the fairyland of fancy, genius may wander wild; there it has a creative power, and may reign arbitrarily over its own empire of chimeras. The wide field of nature also lies open before it, where it may range unconfined, make what discoveries it can, and sport with its infinite objects uncontrolled, as far as visible nature extends, painting them as wantonly as it will: but what painter of the most unbounded and exalted genius can give us the true portrait of a seraph? He can give us only what by his own or others' eyes, has been seen; though that indeed infinitely compounded, raised, burlesqued, dishonored, or adorned: in like manner, who can give us divine truth unrevealed? Much less should any presume to set aside divine truth when revealed, as incongruous to their own sagacities—is this too serious for my subject? I shall be more so before I close.

Having put in a caveat against the most fatal of errors, from the too great indulgence of genius, return we now to that too great suppression of it, which is detrimental to composition; and endeavor to rescue the writer, as well as the man. I have said, that some are born wise; but they, like those that are born rich, by neglecting the cultivation and produce of their own possessions, and by running in debt, may be beggared at last; and lose their reputations, as younger brothers' estates, not by being born with less abilities than the rich heir, but at too late an hour.

Many a great man has been lost to himself, and the public, purely because great ones were born before him. Hermias, in his collections on Homer's blindness, says, that Homer requesting the gods to grant him a sight of Achilles, that hero rose, but in armor so bright, that it struck Homer blind with the blaze. Let not the blaze of even Homer's Muse darken us to the discernment of our own powers; which may possibly set us above the rank of imitators; who, though most excellent, and even immortal (as some of them are) yet still but *dii minorum gentium,*[18] nor can expect the largest share of incense, the greatest profusion of praise, on their secondary altars.

But farther still: a spirit of imitation hath many ill effects; I shall confine myself to three. First, it deprives the liberal and politer arts of an advantage which the mechanic enjoy: In these, men are ever endeavoring to go beyond their predecessors; in the former, to follow them. And since copies surpass not their originals, as streams rise not higher than their spring, rarely so high; hence, while arts mechanic are in perpetual progress, and increase, the liberal are in retro-

gradation, and decay. These resemble pyramids, are broad at bottom, but lessen exceedingly as they rise; those resemble rivers which, from a small fountainhead, are spreading ever wider and wider, as they run. Hence it is evident, that different portions of understanding are not (as some imagine) allotted to different periods of time; for we see, in the same period, understanding rising in one set of artists, and declining in another. Therefore nature stands absolved, and our inferiority in composition must be charged on ourselves.

Nay, so far are we from complying with a necessity, which nature lays us under, that, secondly, by a spirit of imitation we counteract nature, and thwart her design. She brings us into the world all originals: no two faces, no two minds, are just alike; but all bear nature's evident mark of separation on them. Born originals, how comes it to pass that we die copies? That meddling ape imitation, as soon as we come to years of indiscretion (so let me speak), snatches the pen, and blots out nature's mark of separation, cancels her kind intention, destroys all mental individuality; the lettered world no longer consists of singulars, it is a medley, a mass; and a hundred books, at bottom, are but one. Why are monkeys such masters of mimicry? Why receive they such a talent at imitation? Is it not as the Spartan slaves received a license for ebriety;[19] that their betters might be ashamed of it?

The third fault to be found with a spirit of imitation is, that with great incongruity it makes us poor, and proud: makes us think little, and write much; gives us huge folios, which are little better than more reputable cushions to promote our repose. Have not some sevenfold volumes put us in mind of Ovid's sevenfold channels of the Nile at the conflagration? *"Ostia septem / Pulverulenta vacant septem sine flumine valles."*[20] Such leaden labors are like Lycurgus's iron money, which was so much less in value than in bulk, that it required barns for strongboxes, and a yoke to draw five hundred pounds.[21]

But notwithstanding these disadvantages of imitation, imitation must be the lot (and often an honorable lot it is) of most writers. If there is a famine of invention in the land, like Joseph's brethren, we must travel far for food; we must visit the remote, and rich, ancients; but an inventive genius may safely stay at home; that, like the widow's cruse,[22] is divinely replenished from within; and affords us a miracu-

---

[17]I Corinthians 1:21.
[18]"Gods of lesser classes."

[19]Drunkenness.
[20]"Its seven mouths dusty and empty, seven valleys without streams." *Metamorphoses,* II. 255–56.
[21]According to false tradition, Lycurgus, the Spartan lawgiver (ninth century B.C.?), abolished gold and silver currency and substituted iron.
[22]I Kings 17:16.

lous delight. Whether our own genius be such, or not, we diligently should inquire; that we may not go abegging with gold in our purse. For there is a mine in man, which must be deeply dug ere we can conjecture its contents. Another often sees that in us, which we see not ourselves; and may there not be that in us which is unseen by both? That there may, chance often discovers, either by a luckily chosen theme, or a mighty premium, or an absolute necessity of exertion, or a noble stroke of emulation from another's glory; as that on Thucydides from hearing Herodotus repeat part of his history at the Olympic games: had there been no Herodotus, there might have been no Thucydides, and the world's admiration might have begun at Livy for excellence in that province of the pen. Demosthenes had the same stimulation on hearing Callistratus; or Tully[23] might have been the first of consummate renown at the bar.

Quite clear of the dispute concerning ancient and modern learning, we speak not of performance, but powers. The modern powers are equal to those before them; modern performance in general is deplorably short. How great are the names just mentioned? Yet who will dare affirm, that as great may not rise up in some future, or even in the present age? Reasons there are why talents may not appear, none why they may not exist, as much in one period as another. An evocation of vegetable fruits depends on rain, air, and sun; an evocation of the fruits of genius no less depends on externals. What a marvelous crop bore it in Greece, and Rome? And what a marvelous sunshine did it there enjoy? What encouragement from the nature of their governments, and the spirit of their people? Virgil and Horace owed their divine talents to heaven; their immortal works, to men; thank Maecenas and Augustus for them. Had it not been for these, the genius of those poets had lain buried in their ashes. Athens expended on her theater, painting, sculpture, and architecture, a tax levied for the support of a war. Caesar dropped his papers when Tully spoke; and Philip trembled at the voice of Demosthenes: and has there arisen but one Tully, one Demosthenes, in so long a course of years? The powerful eloquence of them both in one stream, should never bear me down into the melancholy persuasion, that several have not been born, though they have not emerged. The sun as much exists in a cloudy day, as in a clear; it is outward, accidental circumstances that with regard to genius either in nation, or age, *"Collectas fugat nubes, solemque reducit."*[24] As great, perhaps, greater than those mentioned (presumptuous as it may sound) may, possibly, arise; for who hath fathomed the

mind of man? Its bounds are as unknown, as those of the creation; since the birth of which, perhaps, not one has so far exerted, as not to leave his possibilities beyond his attainments, his powers beyond his exploits. Forming our judgments altogether by what has been done, without knowing, or at all inquiring, what possibly might have been done, we naturally enough fall into too mean an opinion of the human mind. If a sketch of the divine *Iliad* before Homer wrote, had been given to mankind, by some superior being, or otherwise, its execution would, probably, have appeared beyond the power of man. Now, to surpass it, we think impossible. As the first of these opinions would evidently have been a mistake, why may not the second be so too? Both are founded on the same bottom; on our ignorance of the possible dimensions of the mind of man.

Nor are we only ignorant of the dimensions of the human mind in general, but even of our own. That a man may be scarce less ignorant of his own powers, than an oyster of its pearl, or a rock of its diamond; that he may possess dormant, unsuspected abilities, till awakened by loud calls, or stung up by striking emergencies, is evident from the sudden eruption of some men, out of perfect obscurity, into public admiration, on the strong impulse of some animating occasion; not more to the world's great surprise, than their own. Few authors of distinction but have experienced something of this nature, at the first beamings of their yet unsuspected genius on their hitherto dark composition: the writer starts at it, as at a lucid meteor in the night; is much surprised; can scarce believe it true. During his happy confusion, it may be said to him, as to Eve at the lake, "What there thou seest, fair creature, is thyself."[25] Genius, in this view, is like a dear friend in our company under disguise; who, while we are lamenting his absence, drops his mask, striking us, at once, with equal surprise and joy. This sensation, which I speak of in a writer, might favor, and so promote, the fable of poetic inspiration: a poet of a strong imagination, and stronger vanity, on feeling it, might naturally enough realize the world's mere compliment, and think himself truly inspired. Which is not improbable; for enthusiasts of all kinds do no less.

Since it is plain that men may be strangers to their own abilities; and by thinking meanly of them without just cause, may possibly lose a name, perhaps a name immortal; I would find some means to prevent these evils. Whatever promotes virtue, promotes something more, and carries its good influence beyond the moral man: to prevent these evils, I borrow two golden rules from ethics, which are no less golden in

---

[23]Cicero.
[24]"Drives away the gathered clouds, and brings back the sun." *Aeneid,* I. 143.

[25]*Paradise Lost,* IV. 468.

composition, than in life. 1. Know thyself; 2dly, Reverence thyself: I design to repay ethics in a future letter, by two rules from rhetoric for its service.

1st. Know thyself. Of ourselves it may be said, as Martial says of a bad neighbor, *"Nil tam prope, proculque nobis."*[26] Therefore dive deep into thy bosom; learn the depth, extent, bias, and full forte of thy mind; contract full intimacy with the stranger within thee; excite and cherish every spark of intellectual light and heat, however smothered under former negligence, or scattered through the dull, dark mass of common thoughts; and collecting them into a body, let thy genius rise (if a genius thou hast) as the sun from chaos; and if I should then say, like an Indian, worship it, (though too bold) yet should I say little more than my second rule enjoins, (viz.) reverence thyself.

That is, let not great examples, or authorities, browbeat thy reason into too great a diffidence of thyself: thyself so reverence, as to prefer the native growth of thy own mind to the richest import from abroad; such borrowed riches make us poor. The man who thus reverences himself, will soon find the world's reverence to follow his own. His works will stand distinguished; his the sole property of them; which property alone can confer the noble title of an author; that is, of one who (to speak accurately) thinks, and composes; while other invaders of the press, how voluminous, and learned soever, (with due respect be it spoken) only read, and write.

This is the difference between those two luminaries in literature, the well-accomplished scholar, and the divinely-inspired enthusiast; the first is, as the bright morning star; the second, as the rising sun. The writer who neglects those two rules above will never stand alone; he makes one of a group, and thinks in wretched unanimity with the throng: incumbered with the notions of others, and impoverished by their abundance, he conceives not the least embryo of new thought; opens not the least vista through the gloom of ordinary writers, into the bright walks of rare imagination, and singular design; while the true genius is crossing all public roads into fresh untrodden ground; he, up to the knees in antiquity, is treading the sacred footsteps of great examples, with the blind veneration of a bigot saluting the papal toe; comfortably hoping full absolution for the sins of his own understanding, from the powerful charm of touching his idol's infallibility.

Such meanness of mind, such prostration of our own powers, proceeds from too great admiration of others. Admiration has, generally, a degree of two very bad ingredients in it; of ignorance, and of fear; and does mischief in composition, and in life. Proud as the world is, there is more superiority in it given, than assumed: and its grandees of all kinds owe more of their elevation to the littleness of others' minds, than to the greatness of their own. Were not prostrate spirits their voluntary pedestals, the figure they make among mankind would not stand so high. Imitators and translators are somewhat of the pedestal kind, and sometimes rather raise their original's reputation, by showing him to be by them inimitable, than their own. Homer has been translated into most languages; Aelian tells us, that the Indians, (hopeful tutors!) have taught him to speak their tongue. What expect we from them? Not Homer's Achilles, but something, which, like Patroclus, assumes his name, and, at its peril, appears in his stead; nor expect we Homer's Ulysses, gloriously bursting out of his cloud into royal grandeur, but an Ulysses under disguise, and a beggar to the last. Such is that inimitable father of poetry, and oracle of all the wise, whom Lycurgus transcribed; and for an annual public recital of whose works Solon enacted a law; that it is much to be feared, that his so numerous translations are but as the published testimonials of so many nations, and ages, that this author so divine is untranslated still.

But here, *"Cynthius aurem / Vellit,"*[27] and demands justice for his favorite, and ours. Great things he has done; but he might have done greater. What a fall is it from Homer's numbers, free as air, lofty and harmonious as the spheres, into childish shackles, and tinkling sounds! But, in his fall, he is still great—

> Nor appears
> Less than archangel ruined, and the excess
> Of glory obscured.[28]

Had Milton never wrote, Pope had been less to blame: But when in Milton's genius, Homer, as it were, personally rose to forbid Britons doing him that ignoble wrong; it is less pardonable, by that effeminate decoration, to put Achilles in petticoats a second time: how much nobler had it been, if his numbers had rolled on in full flow, through the various modulations of masculine melody, into those grandeurs of solemn sound, which are indispensably demanded by the native dignity of heroic song? How much nobler, if he had resisted the temptation of that gothic demon, which modern poesy tasting, became mortal? O how unlike the deathless, divine harmony of three great names (how justly joined), of Milton,

---

[26]"Nothing so near, yet so far from us." *Epigrams,* I. lxxxvi. 10.

[27]"Apollo plucks my ear," Virgil, *Eclogues,* VI. 3–4.
[28]*Paradise Lost,* I. 592–94.

Greece, and Rome? His verse, but for this little speck of mortality, in its extreme parts, as his hero had in his heel; like him, had been invulnerable, and immortal. But, unfortunately, that was undipped in Helicon; as this, in Styx. Harmony as well as eloquence is essential to poesy; and a murder of his music is putting half Homer to death. *Blank* is a term of diminution; what we mean by blank verse, is, verse unfallen, uncursed; verse reclaimed, reinthroned in the true language of the gods; who never thundered nor suffered their Homer to thunder, in rhyme; and therefore, I beg you, my friend, to crown it with some nobler term; nor let the greatness of the thing lie under the defamation of such a name.

But supposing Pope's *Iliad* to have been perfect in its kind; yet it is a translation still; which differs as much from an original, as the moon from the sun. "—*Phoeben alieno*

jusserat igne / Impleri, solemque suo."[29] But as nothing is more easy than to write originally wrong; originals are not here recommended, but under the strong guard of my first rule—know thyself. Lucian, who was an original, neglected not this rule, if we may judge by his reply to one who took some freedom with him. He was at first, an apprentice to a statuary; and when he was reflected on as such, by being called Prometheus, he replied, "I am indeed the inventor of new work, the model of which I owe to none; and, if I do not execute it well, I deserve to be torn by twelve vultures, instead of one."

---

[29] "He had ordered Phoebe to shine with another's light, the sun with its own." Claudian, *Against Rufinus*, I. 9–10.

Gotthold Ephraim Lessing

1729–1781

In his important work on Greek art, published in 1755, Johann Winckelmann analyzed the famous statue of Laocoön and his children struggling with two serpents. Winckelmann was interested in the representation of Laocoön's attitude and wondered specifically why his mouth was not open to express his agony. He concluded that Greek ideals of restraint forbade it. This discussion served as the impetus for Lessing's *Laocoön.* Lessing claims that to have the mouth open would be indecorous; further, the moment caught in the sculpture is that before the cry.

Lessing goes on to formulate fundamental differences between sculpture and painting and poetry. In his view sculpture and painting have no temporal dimension, whereas poetry can present actions in time: sculpture and painting "can imitate actions, but only by way of indication, and through the means of bodies." Poetry can paint bodies, "but only by way of indication, and through the means of actions." Thus in poetry there is a considerable "frugality in the description of bodily objects."

There had been a long tradition of criticism tending to blur the differences between the various media of art. The idea of the poem as a "speaking picture" extended back to the earliest Greek artists and was given force by readers of Horace's phrase *"ut pictura poesis"* (as in painting, so in poetry). The movement gained strength from Romantic tendencies to locate art in the artist's inspiration and feelings. Thus all the arts, including music, could be considered emanations of a common "meaning." Lessing, then, did not succeed in making his distinctions reign supreme, though he did influence numerous later critics, including Schiller in his *On Naive and Sentimental Poetry,* to draw a distinction between spatial and temporal arts.

Lessing's analysis implies that art is fundamentally mimetic. Modern art raises new questions about the relation of temporal activity to static representation. Nevertheless, Lessing's argument, though probably too rigid, does emphasize the fact that each medium has particular limitations and possibilities.

Numerous translations of *Laocoön* exist; the most useful are by E. C. Beasley (1853), Ellen Frothingham (1873), Sir Robert Phillimore (1874), Albert Hamann (1892), L. E. Upcott (1895), and E. A. McCormick (1962). *Selected Prose Works,* translated by E. C. Beasley and Helen Zimmern (1879), contains selections from Lessing's *Hamburg Dramaturgy* (1767–68). See also W. G. Howard, "Burke Among the Forerunners of Lessing," *PMLA,* XXII (1907), 608–32; Irving Babbitt, *The New Laocoön* (1910); J. G. Robertson, *Lessing's Dramatic Theory* (1939); F. O. Nolte, *Lessing's* Laocoön (1940); Max Kommeril, *Lessing und Aristoteles* (1940); Peter Heller, *Dialectics and Nihilism* (1966); and V. A. Rudowski, "Action as the Essence of Poetry: A Revaluation of Lessing's Argument," *PMLA,* LXXXII (1967), 333–41.

From

Laocoön

Chapter XVI

But I will try to consider the matter upon first principles. I reason in this way. If it be true that painting, in its imitations, makes use of entirely different means and signs from those which poetry employs; the former employing figures and colors in space, the latter articulate sounds in time—if, incontestably, signs must have a proper relation to the thing signified, then coexistent signs can only express objects which are coexistent, or the parts of which coexist, but signs which are successive can only express objects which are in succession, or the parts of which succeed one another in time. Objects which coexist, or the parts of which coexist, are termed bodies. It follows that bodies, with their visible properties, are the proper objects of painting. Objects which succeed, or the parts of which succeed to each other, are called generally actions. It follows that actions are the proper object of poetry.

But all bodies do not exist only in space, but also in time. They have continued duration, and in every moment of their duration may assume a different appearance and stand in a different relation. Each of these momentary appearances and relations is the effect of a preceding, and the cause of a subsequent action, and so presents to us, as it were, a center of action. It follows that painting can imitate actions, but only by way of indication, and through the means of bodies.

On the other hand, actions cannot subsist by themselves, but must be dependent on certain beings. Insofar, now, as these beings are bodies, or may be regarded as such, poetry also paints bodies, but only by way of indication, and through the means of actions.

Painting, with regard to compositions in which the objects are coexistent, can only avail itself of one moment of action, and must therefore choose that which is the most pregnant, and by which what has gone before and what is to follow will be most intelligible.

And even thus poetry, in her progressive imitations, can only make use of one single property of bodies, and must therefore choose that one which conveys to us the most sensible idea of the form of the body, from that point of view for which it employs it.

From this is derived the rule of the unity of picturesque epithets, and of frugality in the description of bodily objects.

I should put little confidence in this dry chain of argument did I not find it fully confirmed by the practice of Homer, or rather, I should say, if the practice of Homer had not introduced me to it. Upon these principles only the great manner of the Greek can be defined and explained, and the sentence which it deserves be passed on the directly opposite manner of so many modern poets who wish to rival the painter in a performance in which they must necessarily be surpassed by him. I find that Homer paints nothing but progressive actions, and paints all bodies and individual things only on account of their relation to these actions, and generally with a single trait. What wonder is it, then, that the painter, where Homer has painted, finds little or nothing for himself to do, and that his harvest is only to be gathered where history brings together a multitude of beautiful bodies, in beautiful attitudes, within a space favorable to art, while the poet himself may paint as little as he pleases these bodies, these attitudes, and this space? Let anyone go through the whole series of paintings, piece by piece, which Caylus[1] has taken from him, and he will find a confirmation of this remark.

Here I leave the Count, who would make the color-grinding stone of the painter the touchstone of the poet, in order that I may throw a greater light upon the manner of Homer.

I say that Homer usually makes use of one trait. A ship is to him at one time a dark ship, at another a hollow ship, at another a swift ship, at the most a well-rowed black ship. He goes no farther in the painting of a ship but the navigation, the departure, the arrival of the ship; out of these he makes a detailed picture, a picture out of which the painter must make five or six separate pictures if he wishes to place it entirely upon his canvas.

If particular circumstances compel Homer to fix our attention for a longer time upon one individual corporeal object, he nevertheless produces no picture which the painter can imitate with his pencil; but he knows how to use numberless expedients of art, so as to place this single object in a successive series of moments, and for the last of which the painter is obliged to wait, in order that he may show us completely formed that object, the gradual formation of which we have seen in the poet. For example, when Homer wishes to show us the chariot of Juno, he makes Hebe put together

---

LAOCOÖN. Lessing's *Laokoön* was first published in 1766. The text is from the translation by Sir Robert Phillimore (1874).

[1]Anne Claude, Comte de Caylus, *Tableaux tirés de l'*Iliade, *de l'*Odysée *de* Homère *et de l'*Enéide *de Virgile* (1754–58).

every piece of it before our eyes. We see the spokes and the axletrees, and the driving-seat, the pole, the traces, and the straps, not brought together as a whole, but as they are separately put together by the hands of Hebe. Upon the wheels alone the poet lavishes more than one trait, and he shows us the eight brazen spokes, the golden fellies, the tires of bronze, the silver naves—each individual separate thing. One might almost say, that because there were more wheels than one, therefore he was obliged to spend much more time on their description than the putting on of each particular part would in reality have required.

> Ἥβη δ᾽ ἀμφ᾽ ὀχέεσσι θοῶς βάλε καμπύλα κύκλα,
> Χάλκεα, ὀκτάκνημα, σιδηρέῳ ἄξονι ἀμφίς.
> Τῶν ἤτοι χρυσέη ἴτυς ἄφθιτος, αὐτὰρ ὕπερθεν
> Χάλκε᾽ ἐπίσσωτρα, προσαρηρότα, θαῦμα ἰδέσθαι.
> Πλῆμναι δ᾽ ἀργύρου εἰσὶ περίδρομοι ἀμφοτέρωθεν.
> Δίφρος δὲ χρυσέοισι καὶ ἀργυρέοισιν ἱμᾶσιν
> Ἐντέταται. δοιαὶ δὲ περίδρομοι ἄντυγές εἰσιν.
> Τοῦ δ᾽ ἐξ ἀργύρεος ῥυμὸς πέλεν. αὐτὰρ ἐπ᾽ ἄκρῳ
> Δῆσε χρύσειον καλὸν ζυγόν, ἐν δὲ λέπαδνα
> Κάλ᾽ ἔβαλε χρύσει᾽. . . .[2]

Does Homer wish to show us how Agamemnon was clad? Then the king must put on his whole clothing piece by piece before our eyes—the soft undergarment, the great mantle, the beautiful sandals, the sword—and then he is ready, and grasps the scepter. We see the raiment in which the poet paints the act of his being clothed; another would have painted the clothes in detail down to the smallest fringe, and we shall have seen nothing of the action of putting on the raiment.

> Μαλακὸν δ᾽ ἔνδυνε χιτῶνα,
> Καλὸν, νηγάνεον. περὶ δὲ μέγα βάλλετο φᾶρος.
> Ποσσὶ δ᾽ ὑπὸ λιπαροῖσιν ἐδήσατο καλὰ πέδιλα.
> Ἀμφὶ δ᾽ ἄρ᾽ ὤμοισιν βάλετο ξίφος ἀργυρόηλον,
> Εἵλετο δὲ σκῆπτρον πατρώϊον, ἄφθιτον αἰεί.[3]

And as to that scepter which here is only described as ancestral and immortal, as in another place one like it is described only as χρυσείοις ἥλοισι πεπαρμένον, garnished with golden bosses, when I say we are to have a more complete and more accurate picture of this mighty scepter, what is it that Homer does? Does he paint for us, besides the golden bosses, the wood of which it is made, and the carved head? Yes, it would have been so in a description of heraldic art, in order that in future time it might be possible to make one exactly like it. And I am certain that many a modern poet would have given such an heraldic description, with the simple and honest notion that he himself was really painting because a painter could imitate him. But did Homer trouble himself with considering how far he should leave the painter behind him? Instead of a description he gives us the history of the scepter: first we see it as worked by Vulcan; next it glitters in the hand of Jupiter; then it proclaims the dignity of Mercury; then it becomes the commander staff of the warrior Pelops; and then it is the pastoral staff of the peaceful Atreus.

> Σκῆπτρον ἔχων, τὸ μὲν Ἥφαιστος κάμε τεύχων,
> Ἥφαιστος μὲν δῶκε Διῒ Κρονίωνι ἄνακτι.
> Αὐτὰρ ἄρα Ζεὺς δῶκε διακτόρῳ Ἀργειφόντῃ.
> Ἑρμείας δὲ ἄναξ δῶκεν Πέλοπι πληξίππῳ.
> Αὐτὰρ ὁ αὖτε Πέλοψ δῶκ᾽ Ἀτρέϊ, ποιμένι λαῶν.
> Ἀτρεὺς δὲ θνήσκων ἔλιπεν πολύαρνι Θυέστῃ.
> Αὐτὰρ ὁ αὖτε Θυέστ᾽ Ἀγαμέμνονι λεῖπε φορῆναι.
> Πολλῇσιν νήσοισι καὶ Ἄργεϊ παντὶ ἀνάσσειν.[4]

And thus, at last, I am better acquainted with this scepter than if a painter had placed it before my eyes, or a second Vulcan delivered it into my hand. I should not be surprised to find that one of the ancient expositors of Homer had admired this passage, as containing the most perfect allegory of the origin, the progress, the establishment, and finally of the hereditary character of kingly authority among men. I should smile, indeed, if I were to read that Vulcan, who wrought the scepter, represented fire, that thing which is most indispensable to the support of man, that relief of our necessities which had induced the first mortals to subject themselves to the rule of a single person; that the first king was a son of Time (Ζεὺς Κρονίων), a venerable old man,

---

[2]"Her golden-bridled steeds / Then Saturn's daughter brought abroad; and Hebe, she proceeds, / T' address her chariot instantly; she gives it—either wheel / Beamed with eight spokes of sounding brass; the axletree was steel, / The fell'ffs incorruptible gold, their upper bands of brass, / Their matter most unvalued, their work of wondrous grace. / The naves in which the spokes were driven, were all with silver bound; / The chariot's seat, two hoops of gold and silver strengthened round; / Edged with a gold and silver fringe; the beam that looked before, / Was massy silver; on whose top, geres all of gold it wore, / And golden poitrils." *Iliad*, 722–31 (Chapman's translation.)

[3]"The dream gone, his voice still murmured / About the king's ears: who sat up, put on him in his bed / His silken inner weed; fair, new, and then in haste arose; / Cast on his ample mantle, tied to his soft feet fair shoes; / His silver-hilted sword he hung about his shoulders, took / His father's scepter never stained; which then abroad he shook." *Iliad*, 42–46 (Chapman's translation).

[4]"Then stood divine Atrides up, and in his hand compressed / His scepter, th' elaborate work of fiery Mulciber: / Who gave it to Saturnian Jove; Jove to his messenger; / His messenger, Argicides, to Pelops, skilled in horse; / Pelops to Atreus, chief of men: he dying, gave it course / To prince Thyestes, rich in herds; Thyestes to the hand / Of Agamemnon rendered it, and with it the command / Of many isles, and Argos all." *Iliad*, 101–08 (Chapman's translation).

who wished to share his power with an eloquent clever man, with a Mercury (διακτόρῳ Ἀργειφόντῃ), or entirely to give it up to him; that the wise orator, at a time when the young state was threatened by foreign foes, had delivered up his supreme authority to the bravest warrior (Πέλοπι πληξίππῳ); that the brave warrior, after he had subdued the enemy and secured the state, had found means to transfer it to his son, who, as a peace-loving ruler, as a beneficent pastor of his people, had made them acquainted with good living and abundance (ποιμὴν λαῶν), whereby he had paved the way after his death for the wealthiest of his relations (πολύαρνι Θυέστῃ): so that what hitherto confidence had bestowed and merit had considered rather as a burthen than a dignity, should now be obtained by presents and bribes, and secured forever to the family, like any other acquired property. I should smile, but I should notwithstanding be confirmed in my esteem for the poet to whom so much could be attributed.

But this lies out of my path, and I consider the history of the scepter merely as an artifice to induce us to contemplate for a while an individual thing without introducing us to a frigid description of its separate parts. Also, when Achilles swears by his scepter to avenge the contumely with which Agamemnon has treated him, Homer gives us the history of this scepter. We see it green and flourishing on the mountain, the steel severs it from the trunk, strips off its leaves and bark, and makes it a fitting instrument to signify, in the hands of the judges of the people, their divine dignity.

> Καὶ μὰ τόδε σκῆπτρον, τὸ μὲν οὔποτε φύλλα καὶ ὄζους
> Φύσει, ἐπειδὴ πρῶτα τομὴν ἐν ὄρεσσι λέλοιπεν,
> Οὐδ' ἀναθηλήσει. περὶ γάρ ῥά ἑ χαλκὸς ἔλεψεν
> Φύλλα τε καὶ φλοιόν. νῦν αὖτέ μιν υἷες Ἀχαιῶν
> Ἐν παλάμῃς φορέυσι δικασπόλοι, οἵ τε θέμιστας
> Πρὸς Διὸς εἰρύαται.⁵

It was not so much the object of Homer to paint two scepters of different materials and forms, as to make a clear and plain representation to us of the difference of power of which these scepters were the emblems. The former, a work by Vulcan; the latter cut on the mountain by an unknown hand: the former, the ancient possession of a noble house; the latter destined for the strongest hand: the former in the

hand of a monarch stretched over many islands and over the whole of Argos; the latter borne by one chosen out of the midst of the Greeks, to whom, with others, the administration of the laws was confided. This was really the distance at which Agamemnon and Achilles stood from each other; a distance which Achilles himself, in spite of all his blind wrath, could not do otherwise than confess.

But not only on those occasions when Homer combines with his descriptions of this kind ulterior objects, but also when he only desires to show us the picture, he will disperse, as it were, the picture in a kind of history of the object, in order that the different parts of it, which in nature we see combined together, may in his picture as naturally seem to follow upon each other, and to keep true step with the flow of his narrative. For example, he wishes to paint for us the bow of Pandarus: a bow of horn, of such-and-such a length, well-polished, and tipped at both ends with beaten gold. What does he do? Does he give us a dry enumeration of all its properties, one after the other? No such thing: that would be to give an account of a bow, to enumerate its qualities; but not to paint one. He begins with the chase of the wild goat, out of whose horns the bow is made. Pandarus had lain in wait for him in the rocks, and had slain him: the horns were of extraordinary size, and on that account he destined them for a bow. They are brought to the workshop; the artist unites, polishes, decorates them. And so, as I have said, we see the gradual formation by the poet of that which we can only see in a completed form in the work of the painter.

> Τόξον ἐΰξοον, ἰξάλου αἰγὸς
> Ἀγρίου, ὅν ῥά ποτ' αὐτός, ὑπὸ στρένοιο τυχήσας,
> Πέτρης ἐκβαίνοντα δεδεγμένος ἐν προδοκῇσιν,
> Βεβλήκει πρὸς στῆθος. ὁ δ' ὕπτιος ἔμπεσε πέτρῃ.
> Τοῦ κέρα ἐκ κεφαλῆς ἐκκαιδεκάδωρα πεφύκει.
> Καὶ τὰ μὲν ἀσκήσας κεραοξόος ἤραρε τέκτων,
> Πᾶν δ' εὖ λειήνας, χρυσέην ἐπέθηκε κορώνην.⁶

I should never have done if I were to transcribe all the instances of this kind. They will occur in multitudes to him who really knows his Homer.

---

⁵"Yet I vow, and by a great oath swear, / Even by this scepter, that as this never again shall bear / Green leaves or branches, nor increase with any growth his size; / Nor did since first it left the hills, and had his faculties / And ornaments bereft with iron; which now to other end / Judges of Greece bear, and their laws, received from Jove, defend." *Iliad,* 234–39 (Chapman's translation).

⁶"Who instantly drew forth a bow most admirably made / Of th' antler of a jumping goat, bred in a steep upland, / Which archerlike (as long before he took his hidden stand / The doomed one skipping from a rock) into the breast he smote, / And headlong felled him from his cliff. The forehead of the goat / Held out a wondrous goodly palm, that sixteen branches brought, / Of all of which (joined) an useful bow a skillful bowyer wrought, / Which piked and polished both the ends he hid with horns of gold." *Iliad,* 105–11 (Chapman's translation).

Sir Joshua Reynolds

1723–1792

Although Reynolds' *Discourses* concern painting, they are of particular value to the student of literary theory because they express so clearly a number of principles implicit in eighteenth-century attitudes toward art in general, including literature. In *Discourse III* Reynolds argues that the artist seeks to represent not "singular forms, local customs, particularities, and details," but the "central form" of the object. This "central form" sometimes appears to Reynolds as a sort of Platonic idea, but usually it is, as in Johnson's remark about the streaks of the tulip, a generalization from the particularities of sense data, or, as Reynolds puts it, "the abstract of the various individual forms belonging to that class." Art receives its perfection from its approximation to an ideal beauty. The young artist becomes skilled by observing, selecting, digesting, methodizing, and comparing observations.

Reynolds was influenced by the tradition of English empirical philosophy and the association of ideas, and argues from the assumption that we build up complex ideas by comparing and combining simple perceptions of sense into new wholes. His argument defending the generalized abstraction in art comes under attack in Blake's marginalia to the *Discourses,* where Blake defends the work of art as a minute particularity. The trend from Romanticism to modernism follows Blake's line rather than Reynolds', though the line becomes tangled in controversy at times. One problem the controversy raises is whether there is ultimately a logic of art that allows a particularity or a concretion in some way to *be* a universal without metamorphosing into a generalization and thus losing its claim to being immediately real.

The *Discourses* were written and delivered over a number of years, and one can see the change in emphasis by reading consecutively the three reprinted here. *Discourse VII,* though more flexible than *Discourse III* in its treatment of imitation, reflects the attitudes of British empiricists, particularly those of Burke in his *Inquiry. Discourse XIII* departs from a rigidly rationalistic attitude toward creativity and taste, proposing a concept of intuition and adopting a more flexible attitude toward imitation.

Editions of the *Discourses* include those of E. G. Johnson (1891), Roger Fry (1905), Louis Dimier (1909), R. R. Wark (1959), and H. W. Beechey, in the two-volume collection of Reynolds' *Literary Works* (1835). F. W. Hilles, *The Literary Career of Sir Joshua Reynolds* (1936), is an indispensable commentary, with a bibliography of Reynolds' writings. See also Scott Elledge, "The Background and Development in English Criticism of the Theories of Generality and Particularity," *PMLA,* LXII (1947), 147–82; and Ellis Waterhouse, *Reynolds* (1973).

From

Discourses on Art

Discourse III

Gentlemen,

It is not easy to speak with propriety to so many students of different ages and different degrees of advancement. The mind requires nourishment adapted to its growth; and what may have promoted our earlier efforts might retard us in our nearer approaches to perfection.

The first endeavors of a young painter, as I have remarked in a former discourse, must be employed in the attainment of mechanical dexterity, and confined to the mere imitation of the object before him. Those who have advanced beyond the rudiments, may, perhaps, find advantage in reflecting on the advice which I have likewise given them, when I recommended the diligent study of the works of our great predecessors; but I at the same time endeavored to guard them against an implicit submission to the authority of any one master however excellent: or by a strict imitation of his manner, precluding themselves from the abundance and variety of nature. I will now add that nature herself is not to be too closely copied. There are excellencies in the art of painting beyond what is commonly called the imitation of nature: and these excellencies I wish to point out. The students who, having passed through the initiatory exercises, are more advanced in the art, and who, sure of their hand, have leisure to exert their understanding, must now be told, that a mere copier of nature can never produce anything great; can never raise and enlarge the conceptions, or warm the heart of the spectator.

The wish of the genuine painter must be more extensive: instead of endeavoring to amuse mankind with the minute neatness of his imitations, he must endeavor to improve them by the grandeur of his ideas; instead of seeking praise by deceiving the superficial sense of the spectator, he must strive for fame by captivating the imagination.

The principle now laid down, that the perfection of this art does not consist in mere imitation, is far from being new

---

DISCOURSES ON ART. Under the sponsorship of George III, a number of English painters organized the Royal Academy in 1768. A charter member and the Academy's first president, Reynolds delivered the first of his fifteen discourses on art at the official opening of the Academy in 1769. The third discourse was delivered in 1770, the seventh in 1776, and the thirteenth in 1786. The discourses were first published together in 1797 in the edition edited by Edmond Malone, though all had been published individually before then. The text is based on Malone's third edition (1801).

or singular. It is, indeed, supported by the general opinion of the enlightened part of mankind. The poets, orators, and rhetoricians of antiquity are continually enforcing this position: that all the arts receive their perfection from an ideal beauty, superior to what is to be found in individual nature. They are ever referring to the practice of the painters and sculptors of their times, particularly Phidias (the favorite artist of antiquity), to illustrate their assertions. As if they could not sufficiently express their admiration of his genius by what they knew, they have recourse to poetical enthusiasm. They call it inspiration; a gift from heaven. The artist is supposed to have ascended the celestial regions, to furnish his mind with this perfect idea of beauty. "He," says Proclus,

> who takes for his model such forms as nature produces, and confines himself to an exact imitation of them, will never attain to what is perfectly beautiful. For the works of nature are full of disproportion, and fall very short of the true standard of beauty. So that Phidias, when he formed his Jupiter, did not copy any object ever presented to his sight; but contemplated only that image which he had conceived in his mind from Homer's description.[1]

And thus Cicero, speaking of the same Phidias: "Neither did this artist," says he,

> when he carved the image of Jupiter or Minerva, set before him any one human figure, as a pattern, which he was to copy; but having a more perfect idea of beauty fixed in his mind, this he steadily contemplated, and to the imitation of this all his skill and labor were directed.[2]

The moderns are not less convinced than the ancients of this superior power existing in the art; nor less sensible of its effects. Every language has adopted terms expressive of this excellence. The *gusto grande* of the Italians, the *beau idéal* of the French, and the *great style,* and *taste* among the English, are but different appellations of the same thing. It is this intellectual dignity, they say, that ennobles the painter's art; that lays the line between him and the mere mechanic; and produces those great effects in an instant, which eloquence and poetry, by slow and repeated efforts, are scarcely able to attain.

---

[1]*On Plato's* Timaeus, II.
[2]*On Oratory,* II. 9.

Such is the warmth with which both the ancients and moderns speak of this divine principle of the art; but, as I have formerly observed, enthusiastic admiration seldom promotes knowledge. Though a student by such praise may have his attention roused, and a desire excited of running in this great career, yet it is possible that what has been said to excite, may only serve to deter him. He examines his own mind, and perceives there nothing of that divine inspiration with which, he is told, so many others have been favored. He never traveled to heaven to gather new ideas; and he finds himself possessed of no other qualifications than what mere common observation and a plain understanding can confer. Thus he becomes gloomy amidst the splendor of figurative declamation, and thinks it hopeless to pursue an object which he supposes out of reach of human industry.

But on this, as upon many other occasions, we ought to distinguish how much is to be given to enthusiasm, and how much to reason. We ought to allow for, and we ought to commend, that strength of vivid expression which is necessary to convey, in its full force, the highest sense of the most complete effect of art; taking care at the same time, not to lose in terms of vague admiration, that solidity and truth of principle, upon which alone we can reason, and may be enabled to practice.

It is not easy to define in which this great style consists; nor to describe, by words, the proper means of acquiring it, if the mind of the student should be at all capable of such an acquisition. Could we teach taste or genius by rules, they would be no longer taste and genius. But though there neither are, nor can be, any precise invariable rules for the exercise, or the acquisition, of these great qualities, yet we may truly say that they always operate in proportion to our attention in observing the works of nature, to our skill in selecting, and to our care in digesting, methodizing, and comparing our observations. There are many beauties in our art that seem, at first, to lie without the reach of precept, and yet may easily be reduced to practical principles. Experience is all in all; but it is not everyone who profits by experience; and most people err, not so much from want of capacity to find their object, as from not knowing what object to pursue. This great ideal perfection and beauty are not to be sought in the heavens, but upon the earth. They are about us, and upon every side of us. But the power of discovering what is deformed in nature, or in other words, what is particular and uncommon, can be acquired only by experience; and the whole beauty and grandeur of the arts consists, in my opinion, in being able to get above all singular forms, local customs, particularities, and details of every kind.

All the objects which are exhibited to our view by nature, upon close examination will be found to have their blemishes and defects. The most beautiful forms have something about them like weakness, minuteness, or imperfection. But it is not every eye that perceives these blemishes. It must be an eye long used to the contemplation and comparison of these forms; and which, by a long habit of observing what any set of objects of the same kind have in common, has acquired the power of discerning what each wants in particular. This long laborious comparison should be the first study of the painter who aims at the greatest style. By this means, he acquires a just idea of beautiful forms; he corrects nature by herself, her imperfect state by her more perfect. His eye being enabled to distinguish the accidental deficiencies, excrescences, and deformities of things, from their general figures, he makes out an abstract idea of their forms more perfect than any one original; and, what may seem a paradox, he learns to design naturally by drawing his figures unlike to any one object. This idea of the perfect state of nature, which the artist calls the ideal beauty, is the great leading principle, by which works of genius are conducted. By this Phidias acquired his fame. He wrought upon a sober principle, what has so much excited the enthusiasm of the world; and by this method you, who have courage to tread the same path, may acquire equal reputation.

This is the idea which has acquired, and which seems to have a right to, the epithet of *divine;* as it may be said to preside, like a supreme judge, over all the productions of nature; appearing to be possessed of the will and intention of the Creator, as far as they regard the external form of living beings. When a man once possesses this idea in its perfection, there is no danger but that he will be sufficiently warmed by it himself, and be able to warm and ravish everyone else.

Thus it is from a reiterated experience, and a close comparison of the objects in nature, that an artist becomes possessed of the idea of that central form, if I may so express it, from which every deviation is deformity. But the investigation of this form, I grant, is painful, and I know but of one method of shortening the road; this is, by a careful study of the works of the ancient sculptors; who, being indefatigable in the school of nature, have left models of that perfect form behind them, which an artist would prefer as supremely beautiful, who had spent his whole life in that single contemplation. But if industry carried them thus far, may not you also hope for the same reward from the same labor? We have the same school opened to us that was opened to them; for nature denies her instructions to none who desire to become her pupils.

This laborious investigation, I am aware, must appear superfluous to those who think everything is to be done by felicity, and the powers of native genius. Even the great

Bacon treats with ridicule the idea of confining proportion to rules, or of producing beauty by selection. "A man cannot tell," says he, "whether Apelles or Albert Dürer were the more trifler: whereof the one would make a personage by geometrical proportions; the other, by taking the best parts out of divers faces, to make one excellent . . . The painter," he adds, "must do it by a kind of felicity . . . and not by rule."[3]

It is not safe to question any opinion of so great a writer, and so profound a thinker, as undoubtedly Bacon was. But he studies brevity to excess; and therefore his meaning is sometimes doubtful. If he means that beauty has nothing to do with rule, he is mistaken. There is a rule, obtained out of general nature, to contradict which is to fall into deformity. Whenever anything is done beyond this rule, it is in virtue of some other rule which is followed along with it, but which does not contradict it. Everything which is wrought with certainty is wrought upon some principle. If it is not, it cannot be repeated. If by felicity is meant anything of chance or hazard, or something born with a man, and not earned, I cannot agree with this great philosopher. Every object which pleases must give us pleasure upon some certain principles; but as the objects of pleasure are almost infinite, so their principles vary without end, and every man finds them out, not by felicity or successful hazard, but by care and sagacity.

To the principle I have laid down, that the idea of beauty in each species of beings is an invariable one, it may be objected that in every particular species there are various central forms, which are separate and distinct from each other, and yet are undeniably beautiful; that in the human figure, for instance, the beauty of *Hercules* is one, of the *Gladiator* another, of the *Apollo* another; which makes so many different ideas of beauty.[4]

It is true, indeed, that these figures are each perfect in their kind, though of different characters and proportions; but still none of them is the representation of an individual, but of a class. And as there is one general form, which, as I have said, belongs to the human kind at large, so in each of these classes there is one common idea and central form, which is the abstract of the various individual forms belonging to that class. Thus, though the forms of childhood and age differ exceedingly, there is a common form in childhood, and a common form in age, which is the more perfect as it is more remote from all peculiarities. But I must add further,

that though the most perfect forms of each of the general divisions of the human figure are ideal, and superior to any individual form of that class; yet the highest perfection of the human figure is not to be found in any one of them. It is not in the *Hercules,* nor in the *Gladiator,* nor in the *Apollo;* but in that form which is taken from all, and which partakes equally of the activity of the *Gladiator,* of the delicacy of the *Apollo,* and of the muscular strength of the *Hercules.* For perfect beauty in any species must combine all the characters which are beautiful in that species. It cannot consist in any one to the exclusion of the rest: no one, therefore, must be predominant, that no one may be deficient.

The knowledge of these different characters, and the power of separating and distinguishing them, are undoubtedly necessary to the painter, who is to vary his compositions with figures of various forms and proportions, though he is never to lose sight of the general idea of perfection in each kind.

There is, likewise, a kind of symmetry, or proportion, which may properly be said to belong to deformity. A figure lean or corpulent, tall or short, though deviating from beauty, may still have a certain union of the various parts, which may contribute to make them on the whole not unpleasing.

When the artist has by diligent attention acquired a clear and distinct idea of beauty and symmetry; when he has reduced the variety of nature to the abstract idea; his next task will be to become acquainted with the genuine habits of nature, as distinguished from those of fashion. For in the same manner, and on the same principles, as he has acquired the knowledge of the real forms of nature, distinct from accidental deformity, he must endeavor to separate simple chaste nature from those adventitious, those affected and forced airs or actions with which she is loaded by modern education.

Perhaps I cannot better explain what I mean, than by reminding you of what was taught us by the professor of anatomy, in respect to the natural position and movement of the feet. He observed, that the fashion of turning them outwards was contrary to the intent of nature, as might be seen from the structure of the bones, and from the weakness that proceeded from that manner of standing. To this we may add the erect position of the head, the projection of the chest, the walking with straight knees, and many such actions, which we know to be merely the result of fashion, and what nature never warranted, as we are sure that we have been taught them when children.

I have mentioned but a few of those instances, in which vanity or caprice have contrived to distort and disfigure the human form: your own recollection will add to these a thousand more of ill-understood methods, which have been

---

[3][Malone] *Essays,* p. 252, edited 1625.
[4]Reynolds is referring to three famous sculptures: the *Farnese Hercules,* the *Borghese Warrior,* and the *Apollo Belvedere.*

practiced to disguise nature among our dancing-masters, hair-dressers, and tailors, in their various schools of deformity.[5]

However the mechanic and ornamental arts may sacrifice to fashion, she must be entirely excluded from the art of painting; the painter must never mistake this capricious changeling for the genuine offspring of nature; he must divest himself of all prejudices in favor of his age or country; he must disregard all local and temporary ornaments, and look only on those general habits which are everywhere and always the same, he addresses his works to the people of every country and every age, he calls upon posterity to be his spectators, and says with Zeuxis, *"in aeternitatem pingo."*[6]

The neglect of separating modern fashions from the habits of nature leads to that ridiculous style which has been practiced by some painters, who have given to Grecian heroes the airs and graces practiced in the court of Louis the Fourteenth; an absurdity almost as great as it would have been to have dressed them after the fashion of that court.

To avoid this error, however, and to retain the true simplicity of nature, is a task more difficult than at first sight it may appear. The prejudices in favor of the fashions and customs that we have been used to, and which are justly called a second nature, make it too often difficult to distinguish that which is natural, from that which is the result of education; they frequently even give a predilection in favor of the artificial mode; and almost everyone is apt to be guided by those local prejudices, who has not chastised his mind and regulated the instability of his affections by the eternal invariable idea of nature.

Here then, as before, we must have recourse to the ancients as instructors. It is from a careful study of their works that you will be enabled to attain to the real simplicity of nature; they will suggest many observations which would probably escape you, if your study were confined to nature alone. And, indeed, I cannot help suspecting that in this instance the ancients had an easier task than the moderns. They had, probably, little or nothing to unlearn, as their manners were nearly approaching to this desirable simplicity; while the modern artist, before he can see the truth of things, is obliged to remove a veil, with which the fashion of the times has thought proper to cover her.

Having gone thus far in our investigation of the great style in painting; if we now should suppose that the artist has found the true idea of beauty, which enables him to give his works a correct and perfect design; if we should suppose also, that he has acquired a knowledge of the unadulterated habits of nature, which gives him simplicity; the rest of his task is, perhaps, less than is generally imagined. Beauty and simplicity have so great a share in the composition of a great style, that he who has acquired them has little else to learn. It must not, indeed, be forgotten, that there is a nobleness of conception, which goes beyond anything in the mere exhibition even of perfect form; there is an art of animating and dignifying the figures with intellectual grandeur, of impressing the appearance of philosophic wisdom or heroic virtue. This can only be acquired by him that enlarges the sphere of his understanding by a variety of knowledge, and warms his imagination with the best productions of ancient and modern poetry.

A hand thus exercised, and a mind thus instructed, will bring the art to a higher degree of excellence than, perhaps, it has hitherto attained in this country. Such a student will disdain the humbler walks of painting, which, however profitable, can never assure him a permanent reputation. He will leave the meaner artist servilely to suppose that those are the best pictures, which are most likely to deceive the spectator. He will permit the lower painter, like the florist or collector of shells to exhibit the minute discriminations, which distinguish one object of the same species from another; while he, like the philosopher, will consider nature in the abstract, and represent in every one of his figures the character of its species.

If deceiving the eye were the only business of the art, there is no doubt, but the minute painter would be more apt to succeed: but it is not the eye, it is the mind, which the painter of genius desires to address; nor will he waste a moment upon those smaller objects, which only serve to catch the sense, to divide the attention, and to counteract his great design of speaking to the heart.

This is the ambition which I wish to excite in your minds; and the object I have had in my view, throughout this discourse, is that one great idea, which gives to painting its true dignity, which entitles it to the name of a liberal art, and ranks it as a sister of poetry.

It may possibly have happened to many young students, whose application was sufficient to overcome all difficulties, and whose minds were capable of embracing the most extensive views, that they have, by a wrong direction originally given, spent their lives in the meaner walks of painting, without ever knowing there was a nobler to pursue. Albert Dürer, as Vasari has justly remarked, would, probably, have been one of the first painters of his age (and he lived in an era of great artists), had he been initiated into those great principles of the art, which were so well understood and practiced by

---

[5][Malone] "Those" says Quintilian, "who are taken with the outward show of things, think that there is more beauty in persons who are trimmed, curled, and painted, than uncorrupt nature can give; as if beauty were merely the effect of the corruption of manners."

[6]"I paint for eternity."

his contemporaries in Italy. But unluckily having never seen or heard of any other manner, he, without doubt, considered his own as perfect.

As for the various departments of painting, which do not presume to make such high pretensions, they are many. None of them are without their merit, though none enter into competition with this universal presiding idea of the art. The painters who have applied themselves more particularly to low and vulgar characters, and who express with precision the various shades of passion, as they are exhibited by vulgar minds (such as we see in the works of Hogarth), deserve great praise; but as their genius has been employed on low and confined subjects, the praise which we give must be as limited as its object. The merrymaking or quarreling of the boors of Teniers; the same sort of productions of Brouwer, or Ostade, are excellent in their kind; and the excellence and its praise will be in proportion as, in those limited subjects and peculiar forms, they introduce more or less of the expression of those passions as they appear in general and more enlarged nature. This principle may be applied to the battlepieces of Bourgognone, the French gallantries of Watteau, and even beyond the exhibition of animal life, to the landscapes of Claude Lorraine, and the seaviews of Vandervelde. All these painters have, in general, the same right, in different degrees, to the name of a painter, which a satirist, an epigrammatist, a sonneteer, a writer of pastorals, or descriptive poetry, has to that of a poet.

In the same rank, and perhaps of not so great merit, is the cold painter of portraits. But this correct and just imitation of his object has its merits. Even the painter of still life, whose highest ambition is to give a minute representation of every part of those low objects which he sets before him, deserves the praise in proportion to his attainment; because no part of this excellent art, so much the ornament of polished life, is destitute of value and use. These, however, are by no means the views to which the mind of the student ought to be primarily directed. Having begun by aiming at better things, if from particular inclination, or from the taste of the time and place he lives in, or from necessity, or from failure in the highest attempts, he is obliged to descend lower, he will bring into the lower sphere or art a grandeur of composition and character that will raise and ennoble his works far above their natural rank.

A man is not weak, though he may not be able to wield the club of Hercules; nor does a man always practice that which he esteems the best; but does that which he can best do. In moderate attempts, there are many walks open to the artist. But as the idea of beauty is of necessity but one, so there can be but one great mode of painting, the leading principle of which I have endeavored to explain.

I should be sorry, if what is here recommended, should be at all understood to countenance a careless or indetermined manner of painting. For though the painter is to overlook the accidental discriminations of nature, he is to exhibit distinctly, and with precision, the general forms of things. A firm and determined outline is one of the characteristics of the great style in painting; and let me add, that he who possesses the knowledge of the exact form which every part of nature ought to have, will be fond of expressing that knowledge with correctness and precision in all his works.

To conclude; I have endeavored to reduce the idea of beauty to general principles; and I had the pleasure to observe that the professor of painting proceeded in the same method, when he showed you that the artifice of contrast was founded but on one principle. I am convinced that this is the only means of advancing science; of clearing the mind from a confused heap of contradictory observations, that do but perplex and puzzle the student when he compares them, or misguide him if he gives himself up to their authority: bringing them under one general head, can alone give rest and satisfaction to an inquisitive mind.

Discourse VII

Gentlemen,

It has been my uniform endeavor, since I first addressed you from this place, to impress you strongly with one ruling idea. I wished you to be persuaded, that success in your art depends almost entirely on your own industry; but the industry which I principally recommended, is not the industry of the hands, but of the mind.

As our art is not a divine gift, so neither is it a mechanical trade. Its foundations are laid in solid science: and practice, though essential to perfection, can never attain that to which it aims, unless it works under the direction of principle.

Some writers upon art carry this point too far, and suppose that such a body of universal and profound learning is requisite, that the very enumeration of its kinds is enough to frighten a beginner. Vitruvius, after going through the many accomplishments of nature, and the many acquirements of learning, necessary to an architect, proceeds with great gravity to assert, that he ought to be well skilled in the civil law; that he may not be cheated in the title of the ground he builds on. But without such exaggeration, we may go so far as to assert, that a painter stands in need of more knowledge than is to be picked off his palette, or collected by looking on his model, whether it be in life or in picture. He can never be a great artist, who is grossly illiterate.

Every man whose business is description, ought to be tolerably conversant with the poets, in some language or other; that he may imbibe a poetical spirit, and enlarge his stock of ideas. He ought to acquire a habit of comparing and digesting his notions. He ought not to be wholly unacquainted with that part of philosophy which gives an insight into human nature, and relates to the manners, characters, passions, and affections. He ought to know something concerning the mind, as well as a great deal concerning the body of man. For this purpose, it is not necessary that he should go into such a compass of reading, as must, by distracting his attention, disqualify him for the practical part of his profession, and makes him sink the performer in the critic. Reading, if it can be made the favorite recreation of his leisure hours, will improve and enlarge his mind, without retarding his actual industry. What such partial and desultory reading cannot afford, may be supplied by the conversation of learned and ingenious men, which is the best of all substitutes for those who have not the means or opportunities of deep study. There are many such men in this age; and they will be pleased with communicating their ideas to artists, when they see them curious and docile, if they are treated with that respect and deference which is so justly their due. Into such society, young artists, if they make it the point of their ambition, will by degrees be admitted. There, without formal teaching, they will insensibly come to feel and reason like those they live with, and find a rational and systematic taste imperceptibly formed in their minds, which they will know how to reduce to a standard, by applying general truth to their own purposes, better perhaps than those to whom they owed the original sentiment.

Of these studies, and this conversation, the desired and legitimate offspring is a power of distinguishing right from wrong; which power applied to works of art, is denominated *taste*. Let me then, without further introduction, enter upon an examination, whether taste be so far beyond our reach, as to be unattainable by care; or be so very vague and capricious, that no care ought to be employed about it.

It has been the fate of arts to be enveloped in mysterious and incomprehensible language, as if it was thought necessary that even the terms should correspond to the idea entertained of the instability and uncertainty of the rules which they expressed.

To speak of genius and taste, as in any way connected with reason or common sense, would be, in the opinion of some towering talkers, to speak like a man who possessed neither; who had never felt that enthusiasm, or, to use their own inflated language, was never warmed by that Promethean fire, which animates the canvas and vivifies the marble.

If, in order to be intelligible, I appear to degrade art by bringing her down from her visionary situation in the clouds, it is only to give her a more solid mansion upon the earth. It is necessary that at some time or other we should see things as they really are, and not impose on ourselves by that false magnitude with which objects appear when viewed indistinctly as through a mist.

We will allow a poet to express his meaning, when his meaning is not well known to himself, with a certain degree of obscurity, as it is one source of the sublime. But when, in plain prose, we gravely talk of courting the Muse in shady bowers; waiting the call and inspiration of Genius, finding out where he inhabits, and where he is to be invoked with the greatest success; of attending to times and seasons when the imagination shoots with the greatest vigor, whether at the summer solstice or the vernal equinox; sagaciously observing how much the wild freedom and liberty of imagination is cramped by attention to established rules; and how this same imagination begins to grow dim in advanced age, smothered and deadened by too much judgment; when we talk such language, or entertain such sentiments as these, we generally rest contented with mere words, or at best entertain notions not only groundless, but pernicious.

If all this means, what it is very possible was originally intended only to be meant, that in order to cultivate an art, a man secludes himself from the commerce of the world, and retires into the country at particular seasons; or that at one time of the year his body is in better health, and consequently his mind fitter for the business of hard thinking than at another time; or that the mind may be fatigued and grow confused by long and unremitted application; this I can understand. I can likewise believe, that a man eminent when young for possessing poetical imagination, may, from having taken another road, so neglect its cultivation, as to shew less of its powers in his latter life. But I am persuaded, that scarce a poet is to be found from Homer down to Dryden, who preserved a sound mind in a sound body, and continued practicing his profession to the very last, whose latter works are not as replete with the fire of imagination, as those which were produced in his more youthful days.

To understand literally these metaphors or ideas expressed in poetical language, seems to be equally absurd as to conclude, that because painters sometimes represent poets writing from the dictates of a little winged boy or genius, that this same genius did really inform him in a whisper what he was to write; and that he is himself but a mere machine, unconscious of the operations of his own mind.

Opinions generally received and floating in the world, whether true or false, we naturally adopt and make our own; they may be considered as a kind of inheritance to which we succeed and are tenants for life, and which we leave to our posterity very nearly in the condition in which we received it; it not being much in any one man's power either to impair or improve it. The greatest part of these opinions, like current coin in its circulation, we are used to take without weighing or examining; but by this inevitable inattention many adulterated pieces are received, which, when we seriously estimate our wealth, we must throw away. So the collector of popular opinions, when he embodies his knowledge, and forms a system, must separate those which are true from those which are only plausible. But it becomes more peculiarly a duty to the professors of art not to let any opinions relating to *that* art pass unexamined. The caution and circumspection required in such examination we shall presently have an opportunity of explaining.

Genius and taste, in their common acceptation, appear to be very nearly related; the difference lies only in this, that genius has superadded to it a habit of power of execution: or we may say, that taste, when this power is added, changes its name, and is called genius. They both, in the popular opinion, pretend to an entire exemption from the restraint of rules. It is supposed that their powers are intuitive; that under the name of genius great works are produced, and under the name of taste an exact judgment is given, without our knowing why, and without our being under the least obligation to reason, precept, or experience.

One can scarce state these opinions without exposing their absurdity; yet they are constantly in the mouths of men, and particularly of artists. They who have thought seriously on this subject, do not carry the point so far; yet I am persuaded, that even among those few who may be called thinkers, the prevalent opinion allows less than it ought to the powers of reason; and considers the principles of taste, which give all their authority to the rules of art, as more fluctuating, and as having less solid foundations, than we shall find, upon examination, they really have.

The common saying, that "tastes are not to be disputed," owes its influence, and its general reception, to the same error which leads us to imagine this faculty of too high an original to submit to the authority of an earthly tribunal. It likewise corresponds with the notions of those who consider it as a mere phantom of the imagination, so devoid of substance as to elude all criticism.

We often appear to differ in sentiments from each other, merely from the inaccuracy of terms, as we are not obliged to speak always with critical exactness. Something of this too may arise from want of words in the language in which we speak, to express the more nice discriminations which a deep investigation discovers. A great deal however of this difference vanishes, when each opinion is tolerably explained and understood by constancy and precision in the use of terms.

We apply the term *taste* to that act of the mind by which we like or dislike, whatever be the subject. Our judgment upon an airy nothing, a fancy which has no foundation, is called by the same name which we give to our determination concerning those truths which refer to the most general and most unalterable principles of human nature; to the works which are only to be produced by the greatest efforts of the human understanding. However inconvenient this may be, we are obliged to take words as we find them; all we can do is to distinguish the things to which they are applied.

We may let pass those things which are at once subjects of taste and sense, and which having as much certainty as the senses themselves, give no occasion to inquiry or dispute. The natural appetite or taste of the human mind is for truth; whether that truth results from the real agreement or equality of original ideas among themselves; from the agreement of the representation of any object with the thing represented; or from the correspondence of the several parts of any arrangement with each other. It is the very same taste which relishes a demonstration in geometry, that is pleased with the resemblance of a picture to an original, and touched with the harmony of music.

All these have unalterable and fixed foundations in nature, and are therefore equally investigated by reason, and known by study; some with more, some with less clearness, but all exactly in the same way. A picture that is unlike, is false. Disproportionate ordonnance of parts is not right; because it cannot be true, until it ceases to be a contradiction to assert, that the parts have no relation to the whole. Coloring is true when it is naturally adapted to the eye, from brightness, from softness, from harmony, from resemblance; because these agree with their object, nature, and therefore are true; as true as mathematical demonstration; but known to be true only to those who study these things.

But beside real, there is also apparent truth, or opinion, or prejudice. With regard to real truth, when it is known, the taste which conforms to it, is, and must be, uniform. With regard to the second sort of truth, which may be called truth upon sufferance, or truth by courtesy, it is not fixed, but variable. However, whilst these opinions and prejudices, on which it is founded, continue, they operate as truth; and the art whose office it is to please the mind, as well as instruct it, must direct itself according to opinion, or it will not attain its end.

In proportion as these prejudices are known to be generally diffused, or long received, the taste which conforms to them approaches nearer to certainty, and to a sort of resemblance to real science, even where opinions are found to be no better than prejudices. And since they deserve, on account of their duration and extent, to be considered as really true, they become capable of no small degree of stability and determination by their permanent and uniform nature.

As these prejudices become more narrow, more local, more transitory, this secondary taste becomes more and more fantastical; recedes from real science; is less to be approved by reason, and less followed in practice; though in no case perhaps to be wholly neglected, where it does not stand, as it sometimes does, in direct defiance of the most respectable opinions received amongst mankind.

Having laid down these positions, I shall proceed with less method, because less will serve, to explain and apply them.

We will take it for granted, that reason is something invariable and fixed in the nature of things; and without endeavoring to go back to an account of first principles, which forever will elude our search, we will conclude, that whatever goes under the name of taste, which we can fairly bring under the dominion of reason, must be considered as equally exempt from change. If therefore, in the course of this inquiry, we can shew that there are rules for the conduct of the artist which are fixed and invariable, it follows of course, that the art of the connoisseur, or, in other words, taste, has likewise invariable principles.

Of the judgment which we make on the works of art, and the preference that we give to one class of art over another, if a reason be demanded, the question is perhaps evaded by answering, I judge from my taste; but it does not follow that a better answer cannot be given, though, for common gazers, this may be sufficient. Every man is not obliged to investigate the causes of his approbation or dislike.

The arts would lie open forever to caprice and casualty, if those who are to judge of their excellencies had no settled principles by which they are to regulate their decisions, and the merit or defect of performances were to be determined by unguided fancy. And indeed we may venture to assert, that whatever speculative knowledge is necessary to the artist, is equally and indispensably necessary to the connoisseur.

The first idea that occurs in the consideration of what is fixed in art, or in taste, is that presiding principle of which I have so frequently spoken in former discourses—the general idea of nature. The beginning, the middle, and the end of everything that is valuable in taste, is comprised in the knowledge of what is truly nature; for whatever notions are not conformable to those of nature, or universal opinion, must be considered as more or less capricious.

My notion of nature comprehends not only the forms which nature produces, but also the nature and internal fabric and organization, as I may call it, of the human mind and imagination. The terms *beauty,* or *nature,* which are general ideas, are but different modes of expressing the same thing, whether we apply these terms to statues, poetry, or picture. Deformity is not nature, but an accidental deviation from her accustomed practice. This general idea therefore ought to be called *nature,* and nothing else, correctly speaking, has a right to that name. But we are so far from speaking, in common conversation, with any such accuracy, that, on the contrary, when we criticize Rembrandt and other Dutch painters, who introduced into their historical pictures exact representations of individual objects with all their imperfections, we say—though it is not in a good taste, yet it is nature.

This misapplication of terms must be very often perplexing to the young student. Is not art, he may say, an imitation of nature? Must he not therefore who imitates her with the greatest fidelity, be the best artist? By this mode of reasoning Rembrandt has a higher place than Raphael. But a very little reflection will serve to shew us that these particularities cannot be nature: for how can that be the nature of man, in which no two individuals are the same?

It plainly appears, that as a work is conducted under the influence of general ideas, or partial, it is principally to be considered as the effect of a good or a bad taste.

As beauty therefore does not consist in taking what lies immediately before you, so neither, in our pursuit of taste, are those opinions which we first received and adopted, the best choice, or the most natural to the mind and imagination. In the infancy of our knowledge we seize with greediness the good that is within our reach; it is by after-consideration, and in consequence of discipline, that we refuse the present for a greater good at a distance. The nobility or elevation of all arts, like the excellency of virtue itself, consists in adopting this enlarged and comprehensive idea; and all criticism built upon the more confined view of what is natural, may properly be called shallow criticism, rather than false: its defect is, that the truth is not sufficiently extensive.

It has sometimes happened, that some of the greatest men in our art have been betrayed into errors by this confined mode of reasoning. Poussin, who, upon the whole, may be produced as an artist strictly attentive to the most enlarged and extensive ideas of nature, from not having settled principles on this point, has in one instance at least, I think, deserted truth for prejudice. He is said to have vindicated the conduct of Julio Romano for his inattention to the masses of light and shade, or grouping the figures in *The Battle of Constantine,* as if designedly neglected, the better to correspond with the hurry and confusion of a battle. Poussin's own conduct in many of his pictures, makes us more easily give credit to this report. That it was too much his own practice, *The Sacrifice to Silenus,* and *The Triumph of Bacchus and Ariadne,* may be produced as instances; but this principle is still more apparent, and may be said to be even more ostentatiously displayed in his *Perseus* and *Medusa's Head*.

This is undoubtedly a subject of great bustle and tumult, and that the first effect of the picture may correspond to the subject, every principle of composition is violated; there is no principal figure, no principal light, no groups; everything is dispersed, and in such a state of confusion that the eye finds no repose anywhere. In consequence of the forbidding appearance, I remember turning from it with disgust, and should not have looked a second time, if I had not been called back to a closer inspection. I then indeed found, what we may expect always to find in the works of Poussin, correct drawing, forcible expression, and just character; in short all the excellencies which so much distinguish the works of this learned painter.

This conduct of Poussin I hold to be entirely improper to imitate. A picture should please at first sight, and appear to invite the spectator's attention: if on the contrary the general effect offends the eye, a second view is not always sought, whatever more substantial and intrinsic merit it may possess.

Perhaps no apology ought to be received for offenses committed against the vehicle (whether it be the organ of seeing, or of hearing,) by which our pleasures are conveyed to the mind. We must take care that the eye be not perplexed and distracted by a confusion of equal parts, or equal lights, or offended by an unharmonious mixture of colors, as we should guard against offending the ear by unharmonious sounds. We may venture to be more confident of the truth of this observation, since we find that Shakespeare, on a parallel occasion, has made Hamlet recommend to the players a precept of the same kind—never to offend the ear by harsh sounds: "In the very torrent, tempest, and whirlwind of your passion," says he, "you must acquire and beget a temperance that may give it smoothness." And yet, at the same time, he very justly observes, "The end of playing, both at the first, and now, was and is, to hold, as 'twere, the mirror up to nature."[7] No one can deny, that violent passions will naturally emit harsh and disagreeable tones: yet this great poet and critic thought that this imitation of nature would cost too much, if purchased at the expense of disagreeable sensations, or, as he expresses it of "splitting the ear." The poet and actor, as well as the painter of genius who is well acquainted with all the variety and sources of pleasure in the mind and imagination, has little regard or attention to common nature, or creeping after common sense. By overleaping those narrow bounds, he more effectually seizes the whole mind, and more powerfully accomplishes his purpose. This success is ignorantly imagined to proceed from inattention to all rules, and a defiance of reason and judgment; whereas it is in truth acting according to the best rules and the justest reason.

He who thinks nature, in the narrow sense of the word, is alone to be followed, will produce but a scanty entertainment for the imagination: everything is to be done with which it is natural for the mind to be pleased, whether it proceeds from simplicity or variety, uniformity or irregularity; whether the scenes are familiar or exotic; rude and wild, or enriched and cultivated; for it is natural for the mind to be pleased with all these in their turn. In short, whatever pleases has in it what is analogous to the mind, and is therefore, in the highest and best sense of the word, natural.

It is the sense of nature or truth which ought more particularly to be cultivated by the professors of art; and it may be observed, that many wise and learned men, who have accustomed their minds to admit nothing for truth but what can be proved by mathematical demonstration, have seldom any relish for those arts which address themselves to the fancy, the rectitude and truth of which is known by another kind of proof: and we may add, that the acquisition of this knowledge requires as much circumspection and sagacity, as is necessary to attain those truths which are more capable of demonstration. Reason must ultimately determine our choice on every occasion; but this reason may still be exerted ineffectually by applying to taste principles which, though right as far as they go, yet do not reach the object. No man, for instance, can deny, that it seems at first view very reasonable, that a statue which is to carry down to posterity the resemblance of an individual, should be dressed in the fashion of the times, in the dress which he himself wore: this would certainly be true, if the dress were part of the man; but after a time, the dress is only an amusement for an antiquarian; and if it obstructs the general design of the piece, it is to be disregarded by the artist. Common sense must here give way to a higher sense. In the naked form, and in the disposition of the drapery, the difference between one artist and another is principally seen. But if he is compelled to exhibit the modern dress, the naked form is entirely hid, and the drapery is already disposed by the skill of the tailor. Were a Phidias to obey such absurd commands, he would please no more than an ordinary sculptor, since, in the inferior parts of every art, the learned and the ignorant are nearly upon a level.

These were probably among the reasons that induced the sculptor of that wonderful figure of Laocoön[8] to exhibit

---

[7] *Hamlet*, III. ii. 6–8, 22–24.

[8] An important Hellenistic sculpture that depicts the Trojan priest of Apollo, Laocoön, and his two sons being attacked by two great serpents. Lessing also uses this sculpture as a central example in his essay *Laocoön* (though not in the selection reprinted above).

him naked, notwithstanding he was surprised in the act of sacrificing to Apollo, and consequently ought to have been shewn in his sacerdotal habits, if those greater reasons had not preponderated. Art is not yet in so high estimation with us, as to obtain so great a sacrifice as the ancients made, especially the Grecians; who suffered themselves to be represented naked, whether they were generals, lawgivers, or kings.

Under this head of balancing and choosing the greater reason, or of two evils taking the least, we may consider the conduct of Rubens in the Luxembourg gallery, where he has mixed allegorical figures with representations of real personages, which must be acknowledged to be a fault; yet, if the artist considered himself as engaged to furnish this gallery with a rich, various, and splendid ornament, this could not be done, at least in an equal degree, without peopling the air and water with these allegorical figures: he therefore accomplished all that he purposed. In this case all lesser considerations, which tend to obstruct the great end of the work, must yield and give way.

The variety which portraits and modern dresses, mixed with allegorical figures, produce, is not to be slightly given up upon a punctilio of reason, when that reason deprives the art in a manner of its very existence. It must always be remembered that the business of a great painter, is to produce a great picture, he must therefore take especial care not to be cajoled by specious arguments out of his materials.

What has been so often said to the disadvantage of allegorical poetry—that it is tedious, and uninteresting—cannot with the same propriety be applied to painting, where the interest is of a different kind. If allegorical painting produces a greater variety of ideal beauty, a richer, a more various and delightful composition, and gives to the artist a greater opportunity of exhibiting his skill, all the interest he wishes for is accomplished: such a picture not only attracts, but fixes the attention.

If it be objected that Rubens judged ill at first in thinking it necessary to make his work so very ornamental, this puts the question upon new ground. It was his peculiar style; he could paint in no other; and he was selected for that work, probably, because it was his style. Nobody will dispute but some of the best of the Roman or Bolognian schools would have produced a more learned and more noble work.

This leads us to another important province of taste, that of weighing the value of the different classes of the art, and of estimating them accordingly.

All arts have means within them of applying themselves with success both to the intellectual and sensitive part of our natures. It cannot be disputed, supposing both these means put in practice with equal abilities, to which we ought to give the preference; to him who represents the heroic arts and more dignified passions of man, or to him who, by the help of meretricious ornaments, however elegant and graceful, captivates the sensuality, as it may be called, of our taste. Thus the Roman and Bolognian schools are reasonably preferred to the Venetian, Flemish, or Dutch schools, as they address themselves to our best and noblest faculties.

Well-turned periods in eloquence, or harmony of numbers in poetry, which are in those arts what coloring is in painting, however highly we may esteem them, can never be considered as of equal importance with the art of unfolding truths that are useful to mankind, and which make us better or wiser. Nor can those works which remind us of the poverty and meanness of our nature, be considered as of equal rank with what excites ideas of grandeur, or raises and dignifies humanity; or, in the words of a late poet, which makes the beholder "learn to venerate himself as man."[9]

It is reason and good sense therefore which ranks and estimates every art, and every part of that art, according to its importance, from the painter of animated, down to inanimated nature. We will not allow a man, who shall prefer the inferior style, to say it is his taste; taste here has nothing, or at least ought to have nothing to do with the question. He wants not taste, but sense, and soundness of judgment.

Indeed perfection in an inferior style may be reasonably preferred to mediocrity in the highest walks of art. A landskip of Claude Lorrain may be preferred to a history by Luca Giordano; but hence appears the necessity of the connoisseur's knowing in what consists the excellency of each class, in order to judge how near it approaches to perfection.

Even in works of the same kind, as in history-painting, which is composed of various parts, excellence of an inferior species, carried to a very high degree, will make a work very valuable, and in some measure compensate for the absence of the higher kinds of merit. It is the duty of the connoisseur to know and esteem, as much as it may deserve, every part of painting: he will not then think even Bassano unworthy of his notice; who, though totally devoid of expression, sense, grace, or elegance, may be esteemed on account of his admirable taste of colors, which, in his best works, are little inferior to those of Titian.

Since I have mentioned Bassano, we must do him likewise the justice to acknowledge, that though he did not aspire to the dignity of expressing the characters and passions of men, yet, with respect to facility and truth in his manner of touching animals of all kinds, and giving them what painters call "their character," few have ever excelled him.

---

[9]Oliver Goldsmith, *The Traveler,* 334.

To Bassano we may add Paul Veronese and Tintoret, for their entire inattention to what is justly thought the most essential part of our art, the expression of the passions. Notwithstanding these glaring deficiencies, we justly esteem their works; but it must be remembered, that they do not please from those defects, but from their great excellencies of another kind, and in spite of such transgressions. These excellencies too, as far as they go, are founded in the truth of general nature; they tell the truth, though not the whole truth.

By these considerations, which can never be too frequently impressed, may be obviated two errors which I observed to have been, formerly at least, the most prevalent, and to be most injurious to artists; that of thinking taste and genius to have nothing to do with reason, and that of taking particular living objects for nature.

I shall now say something on that part of taste, which, as I have hinted to you before, does not belong so much to the external form of things, but is addressed to the mind, and depends on its original frame, or, to use the expression, the organization of the soul; I mean the imagination and the passions. The principles of these are as invariable as the former, and are to be known and reasoned upon in the same manner, by an appeal to common sense deciding upon the common feelings of mankind. This sense, and these feelings appear to me of equal authority, and equally conclusive. Now this appeal implies a general uniformity and agreement in the minds of men. It would be else an idle and vain endeavor to establish rules of art; it would be pursuing a phantom to attempt to move affections with which we were entirely unacquainted. We have no reason to suspect there is a greater difference between our minds than between our forms; of which, though there are no two alike, yet there is a general similitude that goes through the whole race of mankind; and those who have cultivated their taste can distinguish what is beautiful or deformed, or, in other words, what agrees with or deviates from the general idea of nature, in one case, as well as in the other.

The internal fabric of our minds, as well as the external form of our bodies, being nearly uniform; it seems then to follow of course, that as the imagination is incapable of producing anything originally of itself, and can only vary and combine those ideas with which it is furnished by means of the senses, there will be necessarily an agreement in the imaginations as in the senses of men.[10] There being this agreement, it follows, that in all cases, in our lightest amusements, as well as in our most serious actions and engagements of life, we must regulate our affections of every kind

by that of others. The well-disciplined mind acknowledges this authority, and submits its own opinion to the public voice. It is from knowing what are the general feelings and passions of mankind, that we acquire a true idea of what imagination is; though it appears as if we had nothing to do but to consult our own particular sensations, and these were sufficient to ensure us from all error and mistake.

A knowledge of the disposition and character of the human mind can be acquired only by experience: a great deal will be learned, I admit, by a habit of examining what passes in our bosoms, what are our own motives of action, and of what kind of sentiments we are conscious on any occasion. We may suppose an uniformity, and conclude that the same effect will be produced by the same cause in the minds of others. This examination will contribute to suggest to us matters of inquiry; but we can never be sure that our own sensations are true and right, till they are confirmed by more extensive observation. One man opposing another determines nothing; but a general union of minds, like a general combination of the forces of all mankind, makes a strength that is irresistible. In fact, as he who does not know himself does not know others, so it may be said with equal truth, that he who does not know others, knows himself but very imperfectly.

A man who thinks he is guarding himself against prejudices by resisting the authority of others, leaves open every avenue to singularity, vanity, self-conceit, obstinacy, and many other vices, all tending to warp the judgment, and prevent the natural operation of his faculties. This submission to others is a deference which we owe, and indeed are forced involuntarily to pay. In fact, we never are satisfied with our opinions, whatever we may pretend, till they are ratified and confirmed by the suffrages of the rest of mankind. We dispute and wrangle forever; we endeavor to get men to come to us, when we do not go to them.

He therefore who is acquainted with the works which have pleased different ages and different countries, and has formed his opinion on them, has more materials, and more means of knowing what is analogous to the mind of man, than he who is conversant only with the works of his own age or country. What has pleased, and continues to please, is likely to please again: hence are derived the rules of art, and on this immovable foundation they must ever stand.

This search and study of the history of the mind ought not to be confined to one art only. It is by the analogy that one art bears to another, that many things are ascertained, which either were but faintly seen, or, perhaps, would not have been discovered at all, if the inventor had not received the first hints from the practices of a sister art on a similar occasion. The frequent allusions which every man who treats

---

[10]See Burke, *The Sublime and Beautiful*, p. 301

of any art is obliged to make to others in order to illustrate and confirm his principles, sufficiently shew their near connection and inseparable relation.

All arts having the same general end, which is to please; and addressing themselves to the same faculties through the medium of the senses; it follows that their rules and principles must have as great affinity as the different materials and the different organs or vehicles by which they pass to the mind, will permit them to retain.

We may therefore conclude, that the real substance, as it may be called, of what goes under the name of taste, is fixed and established in the nature of things; that there are certain and regular causes by which the imagination and passions of men are affected; and that the knowledge of these causes is acquired by a laborious and diligent investigation of nature, and by the same slow progress as wisdom or knowledge of every kind, however instantaneous its operations may appear, when thus acquired.

It has been often observed, that the good and virtuous man alone can acquire this true or just relish even of works of art. This opinion will not appear entirely without foundation, when we consider that the same habit of mind which is acquired by our search after truth in the more serious duties of life, is only transferred to the pursuit of lighter amusements. The same disposition, the same desire to find something steady, substantial, and durable, on which the mind can lean as it were, and rest with safety, actuates us in both cases. The subject only is changed. We pursue the same method in our search after the idea of beauty and perfection in each; of virtue, by looking forwards beyond ourselves to society, and to the whole; of arts, by extending our views in the same manner to all ages and all times.

Every art, like our own, has in its composition fluctuating as well as fixed principles. It is an attentive inquiry into their difference that will enable us to determine how far we are influenced by custom and habit, and what is fixed in the nature of things.

To distinguish how much has solid foundation, we may have recourse to the same proof by which some hold that wit ought to be tried; whether it preserves itself when translated. That wit is false, which can subsist only in one language; and that picture which pleases only one age or one nation, owes its reception to some local or accidental association of ideas.

We may apply this to every custom and habit of life. Thus the general principles of urbanity, politeness, or civility, have been ever the same in all nations; but the mode in which they are dressed, is continually varying. The general idea of shewing respect is by making yourself less; but the manner, whether by bowing the body, kneeling, prostration,

pulling off the upper part of our dress, or taking away the lower,[11] is a matter of custom.

Thus in regard to ornaments, it would be unjust to conclude that because they were at first arbitrarily contrived, they are therefore undeserving of our attention; on the contrary, he who neglects the cultivation of those ornaments, acts contrary to nature and reason. As life would be imperfect without its highest ornaments, the arts, so these arts themselves would be imperfect without their ornaments. Though we by no means ought to rank these with positive and substantial beauties, yet it must be allowed that a knowledge of both is essentially requisite towards forming a complete, whole, and perfect taste. It is in reality from the ornaments that arts receive their peculiar character and complexion; we may add, that in them we find the characteristical mark of a national taste; as by throwing up a feather in the air, we know which way the wind blows, better than by a more heavy matter.

The striking distinction between the works of the Roman, Bolognian, and Venetian schools, consists more in that general effect which is produced by colors, than in the more profound excellencies of the art; at least it is from thence that each is distinguished and known at first sight. Thus it is the ornaments, rather than the proportions of architecture, which at the first glance distinguish the different orders from each other; the Doric is known by its triglyphs, the Ionic by its volutes, and the Corinthian by its acanthus.

What distinguishes oratory from a cold narration, is a more liberal, though chaste, use of those ornaments which go under the name of figurative and metaphorical expressions; and poetry distinguishes itself from oratory by words and expressions still more ardent and glowing. What separates and distinguishes poetry, is more particularly the ornament of verse: it is this which gives it its character, and is an essential without which it cannot exist. Custom has appropriated different meter to different kinds of composition, in which the world is not perfectly agreed. In England the dispute is not yet settled, which is to be preferred, rhyme or blank verse. But however we disagree about what these metrical ornaments shall be, that some meter is essentially necessary, is universally acknowledged.

In poetry or eloquence, to determine how far figurative or metaphorical language may proceed, and when it begins to be affectation or beside the truth, must be determined by taste; though this taste, we must never forget, is regulated

---

[11][Malone] "Put off thy shoes from off thy feet; for the place whereon thou standest is holy ground." Exodus 3:5.

and formed by the presiding feelings of mankind, by those works which have approved themselves to all times and all persons. Thus, though eloquence has undoubtedly an essential and intrinsic excellence, and immovable principles common to all languages, founded in the nature of our passions and affections; yet it has its ornaments and modes of address, which are merely arbitrary. What is approved in the eastern nations as grand and majestic, would be considered by the Greeks and Romans as turgid and inflated; and they, in return, would be thought by the Orientals to express themselves in a cold and insipid manner.

We may add likewise to the credit of ornaments, that it is by their means that art itself accomplishes its purpose. Fresnoy calls coloring, which is one of the chief ornaments of painting, *"lena sororis,"*[12] that which procures lovers and admirers to the more valuable excellencies of the art.

It appears to be the same right turn of mind which enables a man to acquire the truth, or the idea of what is right, in the ornaments, as in the more stable principles of art. It has still the same center of perfection, though it is the center of a smaller circle.

To illustrate this by the fashion of dress, in which there is allowed to be a good or bad taste. The component parts of dress are continually changing from great to little, from short to long; but the general form still remains: it is still the same general dress which is comparatively fixed, though on a very slender foundation; but it is on this which fashion must rest. He who invents with the most success, or dresses in the best taste, would probably, from the same sagacity employed to greater purposes, have discovered equal skill, or have formed the same correct taste, in the highest labors of art.

I have mentioned taste in dress, which is certainly one of the lowest subjects to which this word is applied; yet, as I have before observed, there is a right even here, however narrow its foundation respecting the fashion of any particular nation. But we have still more slender means of determining, to which of the different customs of different ages or countries we ought to give the preference, since they seem to be all equally removed from nature. If a European, when he has cut off his beard, and put false hair on his head, or bound up his own hair in regular hard knots, as unlike nature as he can possibly make it; and after having rendered them immovable by the help of the fat of hogs, has covered the whole with flour, laid on by a machine with the utmost regularity; if, when thus attired he issues forth, and meets a Cherokee Indian, who has bestowed as much time at his toilet, and laid

on with equal care and attention his yellow and red ocher on particular parts of his forehead or cheeks; as he judges most becoming; whoever of these two despises the other for his attention to the fashion of his country, whichever first feels himself provoked to laugh, is the barbarian.

All these fashions are very innocent; neither worth disquisition, nor any endeavor to alter them; as the change would, in all probability, be equally distant from nature. The only circumstances against which indignation may reasonably be moved, is where the operation is painful or destructive of health, such as some of the practices at Otaheite,[13] and the strait lacing of the English ladies; of the last of which practices, how destructive it must be to health and long life, the professor of anatomy took an opportunity of proving a few days since in this Academy.

It is in dress as in things of greater consequence. Fashions originate from those only who have the high and powerful advantages of rank, birth and fortune. Many of the ornaments of art, those at least for which no reason can be given, are transmitted to us, are adopted, and acquire their consequence from the company in which we have been used to see them. As Greece and Rome are the fountains from whence have flowed all kinds of excellence, to that veneration which they have a right to claim for the pleasure and knowledge which they have afforded us, we voluntarily add our approbation of every ornament and every custom that belonged to them, even to the fashion of their dress. For it may be observed that, not satisfied with them in their own place, we make no difficulty of dressing statues of modern heroes or senators in the fashion of the Roman armor or peaceful robe; we go so far as hardly to bear a statue in any other drapery.

The figures of the great men of those nations have come down to us in sculpture. In sculpture remain almost all the excellent specimens of ancient art. We have so far associated personal dignity to the persons thus represented, and the truth of art to their manner of representation, that it is not in our power any longer to separate them. This is not so in painting; because having no excellent ancient portraits, that connection was never formed. Indeed we could no more venture to paint a general officer in a Roman military habit, than we could make a statue in the present uniform. But since we have no ancient portraits, to shew how ready we are to adopt those kind of prejudices, we make the best authority among the moderns serve the same purpose. The great variety of excellent portraits with which Van Dyck has enriched this

---

[12]"Gentle sisters."

[13]Tahiti.

nation, we are not content to admire for their real excellence, but extend our approbation even to the dress which happened to be the fashion of that age. We all very well remember how common it was a few years ago for portraits to be drawn in this fantastic dress, and this custom is not yet entirely laid aside. By this means it must be acknowledged very ordinary pictures acquired something of the air and effect of the works of Van Dyck, and appeared therefore at first sight to be better pictures than they really were; they appeared so, however, to those only who had the means of making this association; and when made, it was irresistible. But this association is nature, and refers to that secondary truth that comes from conformity to general prejudice and opinion; it is therefore not merely fantastical. Besides the prejudice which we have in favor of ancient dresses, there may be likewise other reasons for the effect which they produce; among which we may justly rank the simplicity of them, consisting of little more than one single piece of drapery, without those whimsical capricious forms by which all other dresses are embarrassed.

Thus, though it is from the prejudices we have in favor of the ancients, who have taught us architecture, that we have adopted likewise their ornaments; and though we are satisfied that neither nature nor reason are the foundation of those beauties which we imagine we see in that art, yet if anyone, persuaded of this truth, should therefore invent new orders of equal beauty, which we will suppose to be possible, they would not please; nor ought he to complain, since the old has that great advantage of having custom and prejudice on its side. In this case we leave what has every prejudice in its favor, to take that which will have no advantage over what we have left, but novelty; which soon destroys itself, and at any rate is but a weak antagonist against custom.

Ancient ornaments, having the right of possession, ought not to be removed, unless to make room for that which not only has higher pretensions, but such pretensions as will balance the evil and confusion which innovation always brings with it.

To this we may add, that even the durability of the materials will often contribute to give a superiority to one object over another. Ornaments in buildings, with which taste is principally concerned, are composed of materials which last longer than those of which dress is composed; the former therefore make higher pretensions to our favor and prejudice.

Some attention is surely due to what we can no more get rid of than we can go out of ourselves. We are creatures of prejudice; we neither can nor ought to eradicate it; we must only regulate it by reason; which kind of regulation is indeed little more than obliging the lesser, the local and temporary prejudices, to give way to those which are more durable and lasting.

He therefore who in his practice of portrait-painting wishes to dignify his subject, which we will suppose to be a lady, will not paint her in the modern dress, the familiarity of which alone is sufficient to destroy all dignity. He takes care that his work shall correspond to those ideas and that imagination which he knows will regulate the judgment of others; and therefore dresses his figure something with the general air of the antique for the sake of dignity, and preserves something of the modern for the sake of likeness. By this conduct his works correspond with those prejudices which we have in favor of what we continually see; and the relish of the antique simplicity corresponds with what we may call the more learned and scientific prejudice.

There was a statue made not long since of Voltaire, which the sculptor, not having that respect for the prejudices of mankind which he ought to have had, made entirely naked, and as meager and emaciated as the original is said to be. The consequence was what might have been expected; it remained in the sculptor's shop, though it was intended as a public ornament and a public honor to Voltaire, for it was procured at the expense of his contemporary wits and admirers.

Whoever would reform a nation, supposing a bad taste to prevail in it, will not accomplish his purpose by going directly against the stream of their prejudices. Men's minds must be prepared to receive what is new to them. Reformation is a work of time. A national taste, however, wrong it may be, cannot be totally changed at once; we must yield a little to the prepossession which has taken hold on the mind, and we may then bring people to adopt what would offend them, if endeavored to be introduced by violence. When Battista Franco was employed, in conjunction with Titian, Paul Veronese and Tintoret, to adorn the library of St. Mark, his work, Vasari says, gave less satisfaction than any of the others: the dry manner of the Roman school was very ill calculated to please eyes that had been accustomed to the luxuriancy, splendor, and richness of Venetian coloring. Had the Romans been the judges of this work, probably the determination would have been just contrary; for in the more noble parts of the art, Battista Franco was perhaps not inferior to any of his rivals.

Gentlemen,

It has been the main scope and principal end of this discourse to demonstrate the reality of a standard in taste, as well as in corporeal beauty; that a false or depraved taste is a thing as well known, as easily discovered, as anything that is deformed, misshapen, or wrong, in our form or outward make; and that this knowledge is derived from the uniformity of sentiments among mankind, from whence proceeds the knowledge of what are the general habits of nature; the result of which is an idea of perfect beauty.

If what has been advanced be true, that beside this beauty or truth, which is formed on the uniform, eternal and immutable laws of nature, and which of necessity can be but one; that beside this one immutable verity there are likewise what we have called apparent or secondary truths, proceeding from local and temporary prejudices, fancies, fashions, or accidental connection of ideas; if it appears that these last have still their foundation, however slender, in the original fabric of our minds; it follows that all these truths or beauties deserve and require the attention of the artist, in proportion to their stability or duration, or as their influence is more or less extensive. And let me add, that as they ought not to pass their just bounds, so neither do they, in a well-regulated taste, at all prevent or weaken the influence of those general principles, which alone can give to art its true and permanent dignity.

To form this just taste is undoubtedly in your own power; but it is to reason and philosophy that you must have recourse; from them you must borrow the balance by which is to be weighed and estimated the value of every pretension that intrudes itself on your notice.

The general objection which is made to the introduction of philosophy into the regions of taste, is, that it checks and restrains the flights of the imagination, and gives that timidity which an overcarefulness not to err or act contrary to reason is likely to produce. It is not so. Fear is neither reason nor philosophy. The true spirit of philosophy, by giving knowledge, gives a manly confidence, and substitutes rational firmness in the place of vain presumption. A man of real taste is always a man of judgment in other respects; and those inventions which either disdain or shrink from reason, are generally, I fear, more like the dreams of a distempered brain than the exalted enthusiasm of a sound and true genius. In the midst of the highest flights of fancy or imagination, reason ought to preside from first to last, though I admit her more powerful operation is upon reflection.

Let me add, that some of the greatest names of antiquity, and those who have most distinguished themselves in works in genius and imagination, were equally eminent for their critical skill. Plato, Aristotle, Cicero, and Horace; and among the moderns, Boileau, Corneille, Pope, and Dryden, are at least instances of genius not being destroyed by attention or subjection to rules and science. I should hope therefore, that the natural consequence of what has been said, would be, to excite in you a desire of knowing the principles and conduct of the great masters of our art, and respect and veneration for them when known.

Discourse XIII

Gentlemen,

To discover beauties, or to point out faults, in the works of celebrated masters, and to compare the conduct of one artist with another, is certainly no mean or inconsiderable part of criticism; but this is still no more than to know the art through the artist. This test of investigation must have two capital defects; it must be narrow, and it must be uncertain. To enlarge the boundaries of the art of painting, as well as to fix its principles, it will be necessary, that, that art, and those principles should be considered in their correspondence with the principles of the other arts, which like this, address themselves primarily and principally to the imagination. When those connected and kindred principles are brought together to be compared, another comparison will grow out of this; that is, the comparison of them all with those of human nature, from whence arts derive the materials upon which they are to produce their effects.

When this comparison of art with art, and of all arts with the nature of man, is once made with success, our guiding lines are as well ascertained and established, as they can be in matters of this description.

This, as it is the highest style of criticism, is at the same time the soundest; for it refers to the eternal and immutable nature of things.

You are not to imagine that I mean to open to you at large, or to recommend to your research, the whole of this vast field of science. It is certainly much above my faculties to reach it; and though it may not be above yours, to comprehend it fully, if it were fully and properly brought before you, yet perhaps the most perfect criticism requires habits of speculation and abstraction, not very consistent with the employment which ought to occupy, and the habits of mind which ought to prevail in a practical artist. I only point out to you these things, that when you do criticize (as all who work on a plan, will criticize more or less), your criticism may be built on the foundation of true principles; and that though you may not always travel a great way, the way that you do travel may be the right road.

I observe, as a fundamental ground, common to all the arts with which we have any concern in this discourse, that they address themselves only to two faculties of the mind, its imagination and its sensibility.

All theories which attempt to direct or control the art, upon any principles falsely called rational, which we form to ourselves upon a supposition of what ought in reason to be the end or means of art, independent of the known first effect produced by objects on the imagination, must be false and delusive. For though it may appear bold to say it, the imagination is here the residence of truth. If the imagination be affected, the conclusion is fairly drawn; if it be not affected, the reasoning is erroneous, because the end is not obtained; the effect itself being the test, and the only test, of the truth and efficacy of the means.

There is in the commerce of life, as in art, a sagacity which is far from being contradictory to right reason, and is superior to any occasional exercise of that faculty, which supersedes it; and does not wait for the slow progress of deduction, but goes at once, by what appears a kind of intuition, to the conclusion. A man endowed with this faculty, feels and acknowledges the truth, though it is not always in his power, perhaps, to give a reason for it; because he cannot recollect and bring before him all the materials that gave birth to his opinion; for very many and very intricate considerations may unite to form the principle, even of small and minute parts, involved in, or dependent on, a great system of things: though these in process of time are forgotten, the right impression still remains fixed in his mind.

This impression is the result of the accumulated experience of our whole life, and has been collected, we do not always know how, or when. But this mass of collective observation, however acquired, ought to prevail over that reason, which however powerfully exerted on any particular occasion, will probably comprehend but a partial view of the subject; and our conduct in life as well as in the arts, is, or ought to be, generally governed by this habitual reason: it is our happiness that we are enabled to draw out on such funds. If we were obliged to enter into a theoretical deliberation on every occasion, before we act, life would be at a stand, and art would be impracticable.

It appears to me therefore, that our first thoughts, that is, the effect which any thing produces on our minds on its first appearance, is never to be forgotten; and it demands for that reason, because it is the first, to be laid up with care. If this be not done, the artist may happen to impose on himself by partial reasoning; by a cold consideration of those animated thoughts which proceed, not perhaps from caprice or rashness (as he may afterwards conceit) but from the fullness of his mind, enriched with the copious stores of all the various inventions which he had ever seen, or had ever passed in his mind. These ideas are infused into his design, without any conscious effort; but if he be not on his guard, he may reconsider and correct them, till the whole matter is reduced to a commonplace invention.

This is sometimes the effect of what I mean to caution you against; that is to say, an unfounded distrust of the imagination and feeling, in favor of narrow, partial, confined, argumentative theories; and of principles that seem to apply to the design in hand; without considering those general impressions on the fancy in which real principles of sound reason, and of much more weight and importance, are involved, and, as it were, lie hid, under the appearance of a sort of vulgar sentiment.

Reason, without doubt, must ultimately determine everything; at this minute it is required to inform us when that very reason is to give way to feeling.

Though I have often spoke of that mean conception of our art which confines it to mere imitation, I must add, that it may be narrowed to such a mere matter of experiment, as to exclude from it the application of science, which alone gives dignity and compass to any art. But to find proper foundations for science is neither to narrow or to vulgarize it; and this is sufficiently exemplified in the success of experimental philosophy. It is the false system of reasoning, grounded on a partial view of things, against which I would most earnestly guard you. And I do it the rather, because those narrow theories, so coincident with the poorest and most miserable practice, and which are adopted to give it countenance, have not had their origin in the poorest minds, but in the mistakes, or possibly in the mistaken interpretations, of great and commanding authorities. We are not therefore in this case misled by feeling, but by false speculation.

When such a man as Plato speaks of painting as only an imitative art, and that our pleasure proceeds from observing and acknowledging the truth of the imitation, I think he misleads us by a partial theory.[14] It is in this poor, partial, and so far, false, view of the art, that Cardinal Bembo has chosen to distinguish even Raphael himself, whom our enthusiasm honors with the name of divine. The same sentiment is adopted by Pope in his epitaph on Sir Godfrey Kneller; and he turns the panegyric solely on imitation, as it is a sort of deception.

I shall not think my time misemployed, if by any means I may contribute to confirm your opinion of what ought to be the object of your pursuit; because, though the best critics must always have exploded this strange idea, yet I know that there is a disposition towards a perpetual recurrence to it, on account of its simplicity and superficial plausibility. For this reason I shall beg leave to lay before you a few thoughts on

---

[14]See *Republic*, pp. 31–33.

this subject; to throw out some hints that may lead your minds to an opinion (which I take to be the truth), that painting is not only to be considered as an imitation, operating by deception, but that it is, and ought to be, in many points of view, and strictly speaking, no imitation at all of external nature. Perhaps it ought to be as far removed from the vulgar idea of imitation, as the refined civilized state in which we live, is removed from a gross state of nature; and those who have not cultivated their imaginations, which the majority of mankind certainly have not, may be said, in regard to arts, to continue in this state of nature. Such men will always prefer imitation to that excellence which is addressed to another faculty that they do not possess; but these are not the persons to whom a painter is to look, any more than a judge of morals and manners ought to refer controverted points upon those subjects to the opinions of people taken from the banks of the Ohio, or from New Holland.

It is the lowest style only of arts, whether of painting, poetry, or music, that may be said, in the vulgar sense, to be naturally pleasing. The higher efforts of those arts, we know by experience, do not affect minds wholly uncultivated. This refined taste is the consequence of education and habit; we are born only with a capacity of entertaining this refinement, as we are born with a disposition to receive and obey all the rules and regulations of society; and so far it may be said to be natural to us, and no further.

What has been said, may shew the artist how necessary it is, when he looks about him for the advice and criticism of his friends, to make some distinction of the character, taste, experience, and observation in this art, of those, from whom it is received. An ignorant uneducated man may, like Apelles' critic, be a competent judge of the truth of the representation of a sandal;[15] or to go somewhat higher, like Molière's old woman, may decide upon what is nature, in regard to comic humor; but a critic in the higher style of art, ought to possess the same refined taste, which directed the artist in his work.

To illustrate this principle by a comparison with other arts, I shall now produce some instances to shew, that they, as well as our own art, renounce the narrow idea of nature, and the narrow theories derived from that mistaken principle, and apply to that reason only which informs us not what imitation is, a natural representation of a given object, but what it is natural for the imagination to be delighted with. And perhaps there is no better way of acquiring this knowl-

edge, than by this kind of analogy: each art will corroborate and mutually reflect the truth on the other. Such a kind of juxtaposition may likewise have this use, that whilst the artist is amusing himself in the contemplation of other arts, he may habitually transfer the principles of those arts to that which he professes; which ought to be always present to his mind, and to which everything is to be referred.

So far is art from being derived from, or having any immediate intercourse with, particular nature as its model, that there are many arts that set out with a professed deviation from it.

This is certainly not so exactly true in regard to painting and sculpture. Our elements are laid in gross common nature, an exact imitation of what is before us: but when we advance to the higher state, we consider this power of imitation, though first in the order of acquisition, as by no means in the scale of perfection.

Poetry addresses itself to the same faculties and the same dispositions as painting, though by different means. The object of both is to accommodate itself to all the natural propensities and inclinations of the mind. The very existence of poetry depends on the license it assumes of deviating from actual nature, in order to gratify natural propensities by other means, which are found by experience full as capable of affording such gratification. It sets out with a language in the highest degree artificial, a construction of measured words, such as never is, nor ever was used by man. Let this measure be what it may, whether hexameter or any other meter used in Latin or Greek—or rhyme, or blank verse varied with pauses and accents, in modern languages—they are all equally removed from nature, and equally a violation of common speech. When this artificial mode has been established as the vehicle of sentiment, there is another principle in the human mind, to which the work must be referred, which still renders it more artificial, carries it still further from common nature, and deviates only to render it more perfect. That principle is the sense of congruity, coherence, and consistency, which is a real existing principle in man; and it must be gratified. Therefore having once adopted a style and a measure not found in common discourse, it is required that the sentiments also should be in the same proportion elevated above common nature, from the necessity of there being an agreement of the parts among themselves, that one uniform whole may be produced.

To correspond therefore with this general system of deviation from nature, the manner in which poetry is offered to the ear, the tone in which it is recited, should be as far removed from the tone of conversation, as the words of which that poetry is composed. This naturally suggests the idea of

---

[15]See Burke, *The Sublime and Beautiful,* pp. 302–03, and Johnson, *On Fiction,* p. 318.

modulating the voice by art, which I suppose may be considered as accomplished to the highest degree of excellence in the recitative of the Italian opera; as we may conjecture it was in the chorus that attended the ancient drama. And though the most violent passions, the highest distress, even death itself, are expressed in singing or recitative, I would not admit as sound criticism the condemnation of such exhibitions on account of their being unnatural.

If it is natural for our senses, and our imaginations, to be delighted with singing, with instrumental music, with poetry, and with graceful action, taken separately; (none of them being in the vulgar sense natural, even in that separate state; it is conformable to experience, and therefore agreeable to reason as connected with and referred to experience, that we should also be delighted with this union of music, poetry, and graceful action, joined to every circumstance of pomp and magnificence calculated to strike the senses of the spectator. Shall reason stand in the way, and tell us we ought not to like what we know we do like, and prevent us from feeling the full effect of this complicated exertion of art? This is what I would understand by poets and painters being allowed to dare everything; for what can be more daring, than accomplishing the purpose and end of art, by a complication of means, none of which have their archetypes in actual nature?

So far therefore is servile imitation from being necessary, that whatever is familiar, or in any way reminds us of what we see and hear every day, perhaps does not belong to the higher provinces of art, either in poetry or painting. The mind is to be transported, as Shakespeare expresses it, "beyond the ignorant present," to ages past. Another and a higher order of beings is supposed; and to those beings everything which is introduced into the work must correspond. Of this conduct, under these circumstances, the Roman and Florentine schools afford sufficient examples. Their style by this means is raised and elevated above all others, and by the same means the compass of art itself is enlarged.

We often see grave and great subjects attempted by artists of another school; who, though excellent in the lower class of art, proceeding on the principles which regulate that class, and not recollecting, or not knowing, that they were to address themselves to another faculty of the mind, have become perfectly ridiculous.

The picture which I have at present in my thoughts is a sacrifice of Iphigenia, painted by Jan Steen, a painter of whom I have formerly had occasion to speak with the highest approbation; and even in this picture, the subject of which is by no means adapted to his genius, there is nature and expression; but it is such expression, and the countenances are so familiar, and consequently so vulgar, and the whole accompanied with such finery of silks and velvet, that one would be almost tempted to doubt, whether the artist did not purposely intend to burlesque his subject.

Instances of the same kind we frequently see in poetry. Parts of Hobbes's translation of Homer are remembered and repeated merely for the familiarity and meanness of their phraseology, so ill corresponding with the ideas which ought to have been expressed, and, as I conceive, with the style of the original.

We may proceed in the same manner through the comparatively inferior branches of art. There are in works of that class, the same distinction of a higher and a lower style; and they take their rank and degree in proportion as the artist departs more, or less, from common nature, and makes it an object of his attention to strike the imagination of the spectator by ways belonging specially to art—unobserved and untaught out of the school of its practice.

If our judgments are to be directed by narrow, vulgar, untaught or rather ill-taught reason, we must prefer a portrait by Denner or any other high finisher, to those of Titian or Van Dyck; and a landskip of Vanderhyde to those of Titian or Rubens; for they are certainly more exact representations of nature.

If we suppose a view of nature represented with all the truth of the camera obscura,[16] and the same scene represented by a great artist, how little and mean will the one appear in comparison of the other, where no superiority is supposed from the choice of the subject. The scene shall be the same, the difference only will be in the manner in which it is presented to the eye. With what additional superiority then will the same artist appear when he has the power of selecting his materials, as well as elevating his style? Like Nicolas Poussin, he transports us to the environs of ancient Rome, with all the objects which a literary education makes so precious and interesting to man: or, like Sebastian Bourdon, he leads us to the dark antiquity of the pyramids of Egypt; or, like Claude Lorrain, he conducts us to the tranquillity of Arcadian scenes and fairyland.

Like the history-painter, a painter of landskips in this style and with this conduct, sends the imagination back into antiquity; and, like the poet, he makes the elements sympathize with his subject: whether the clouds roll in volumes like those of Titian or Salvator Rosa, or, like those of Claude, are gilded with the setting sun; whether the mountains have sudden and bold projections, or are gently sloped; whether

---

[16]An optical apparatus that projects images on an opposite surface. Its principal use today is for making enlarged or reduced copies of maps and drawings.

the branches of his trees shoot out abruptly in right angles from their trunks, or follow each other with only a gentle inclination. All these circumstances contribute to the general character of the work, whether it be of the elegant, or of the more sublime kind. If we add to this the powerful materials of lightness and darkness, over which the artist has complete dominion, to vary and dispose them as he pleases; to diminish, or increase them as will best suit his purpose, and correspond to the general idea of his work: a landskip thus conducted, under the influence of a poetical mind, will have the same superiority over the more ordinary and common views, as Milton's *Allegro* and *Penseroso* have over a cold prosaic narration or description; and such a picture would make a more forcible impression on the mind than the real scenes, were they presented before us.

If we look abroad to other arts, we may observe the same distinction, the same division into two classes, each of them acting under the influence of two different principles, in which the one follows nature, the other varies it, and sometimes departs from it.

The theater, which is said "to hold the mirror up to nature,"[17] comprehends both those ideas. The lower kind of comedy, or farce, like the inferior style of painting, the more naturally it is represented, the better; but the higher appears to me to aim no more at imitation, so far as it belongs to anything like deception, or to expect that the spectators should think that the events there represented are really passing before them, than Raphael in his cartoons, or Poussin in his sacraments, expected it to be believed, even for a moment, that what they exhibited were real figures.

For want of this distinction, the world is filled with false criticism. Raphael is praised for naturalness and deception, which he certainly has not accomplished, and as certainly never intended; and our late great actor, Garrick, has been as ignorantly praised by his friend Fielding; who doubtless imagined he had hit upon an ingenious device, by introducing in one of his novels (otherwise a work of the highest merit), an ignorant man, mistaking Garrick's representation of a scene in Hamlet, for reality. A very little reflection will convince us, that there is no one circumstance in the whole scene that is of the nature of deception. The merit and excellence of Shakespeare and of Garrick, when they were engaged in such scenes, is of a different and much higher kind. But what adds to the falsity of this intended compliment, is, that the best stage representation appears even more unnatural to a person of such a character, who is supposed never to have seen a play before, than it does to those who have had

a habit of allowing for those necessary deviations from nature which the art requires.[18]

In theatric representation, great allowances must always be made for the place in which the exhibition is represented; for the surrounding company, the lighted candles, the scenes visibly shifted in your sight; and the language of blank verse, so different from common English; which merely as English must appear surprising in the mouths of Hamlet, and all the court and natives of Denmark. These allowances are made; but their being made puts an end to all manner of deception: and further; we know that the more low, illiterate, and vulgar any person is, the less he will be disposed to make these allowances, and of course to be deceived by any imitation; the things in which the trespass against nature and common probability is made in favor of the theater, being quite within the sphere of such uninformed men.

Though I have no intention of entering into all the circumstances of unnaturalness in theatrical representations, I must observe, that even the expression of violent passion, is not always the most excellent in proportion as it is the most natural: so great terror and such disagreeable sensations may be communicated to the audience, that the balance may be destroyed by which pleasure is preserved, and holds its predominancy in the mind: violent distortion of action, harsh screamings of the voice, however great the occasion, or however natural on such occasion, are therefore not admissible in the theatric art. Many of these allowed deviations from nature arise from the necessity which there is, that everything should be raised and enlarged beyond its natural state; that the full effect may come home to the spectator, which otherwise would be lost in the comparatively extensive space of the theater. Hence the deliberate and stately step, the studied grace of action, which seems to enlarge the dimensions of the actor, and alone to fill the stage. All this unnaturalness, though right and proper in its place, would appear affected and ridiculous in a private room; *quid enim deformius, quam scenam in vitam transferre?*[19]

And here I must observe, and I believe it may be considered as a general rule, that no art can be engrafted with success on another art. For though they all profess the same origin, and to proceed from the same stock, yet each has its own peculiar modes both of imitating nature, and of deviating from it, each for the accomplishment of its own particular purpose. These deviations, more especially, will not bear transplantation to another soil.

---

[17]*Hamlet*, III. ii. 24.

[18]See Johnson, Preface to *Shakespeare*, p. 325.
[19]"For what is more disgraceful than transferring what belongs on the stage into life?"

If a painter should endeavor to copy the theatrical pomp and parade of dress and attitude, instead of that simplicity, which is not a greater beauty in life, than it is in painting, we should condemn such pictures as painted in the meanest style.

So also gardening, as far as gardening is an art, or entitled to that appellation, is a deviation from nature; for if the true taste consists, as many hold, in banishing every appearance of art, or any traces of the footsteps of man, it would then be no longer a garden. Even though we define it, "Nature to advantage dressed,"[20] and in some sense it is such, and much more beautiful and commodious for the recreation of man; it is however, when so dressed, no longer a subject for the pencil of a landskip-painter, as all landskip-painters know, who love to have recourse to nature herself, and to dress her according to the principles of their own art; which are far different from those of gardening, even when conducted according to the most approved principles, and such as a landskip-painter himself would adopt in the disposition of his own grounds, for his own private satisfaction.

I have brought together as many instances as appear necessary, to make out the several points which I wished to suggest to your consideration in this discourse; that your own thoughts may lead you further in the use that may be made of the analogy of the arts, and of the restraint which a full understanding of the diversity of many of their principles ought to impose on the employment of that analogy.

The great end of all those arts is, to make an impression on the imagination and the feeling. The imitation of nature frequently does this. Sometimes it fails, and something else succeeds. I think therefore the true test of all the arts, is not solely whether the production is a true copy of nature, but whether it answers the end of art, which is to produce a pleasing effect upon the mind.

It remains only to speak a few words of architecture, which does not come under the denomination of an imitative art. It applies itself, like music (and I believe we may add poetry) directly to the imagination, without the intervention of any kind of imitation.

There is in architecture, as in painting, an inferior branch of art, in which the imagination appears to have no concern. It does not however acquire the name of a polite and liberal art, from its usefulness, or administering to our wants or necessities, but from some higher principle: we are sure that in the hands of a man of genius it is capable of inspiring sentiment, and of filling the mind with great and sublime ideas.

It may be worth the attention of artists, to consider what materials are in their hands, that may contribute to this end; and whether this art has it not in its power to address itself to the imagination with effect, by more ways than are generally employed by architects.

To pass over the effect produced by that general symmetry and proportion, by which the eye is delighted, as the ear is with music, architecture certainly possesses many principles in common with poetry and painting. Among those which may be reckoned as the first, is, that of affecting the imagination by means of association of ideas. Thus, for instance, as we have naturally a veneration for antiquity, whatever building brings to our remembrance ancient customs and manners, such as the castles of the barons of ancient chivalry, is sure to give this delight. Hence it is that "towers and battlements"[21] are so often selected by the painter and the poet, to make a part of the composition of their ideal landskip; and it is from hence in a great degree, that in the buildings of Vanbrugh, who was a poet as well as an architect, there is a greater display of imagination, than we shall find perhaps in any other; and this is the ground of the effect which we feel in many of his works, notwithstanding the faults with which many of them are justly charged. For this purpose, Vanbrugh appears to have had recourse to some principles of the Gothic architecture; which, not so ancient as the Grecian, is more so to our imagination, with which the artist is more concerned than with absolute truth.

The barbaric splendor of those Asiatic buildings, which are now publishing by a member of this Academy, may possibly, in the same manner, furnish an architect, not with models to copy, but with hints of composition and general effect, which would not otherwise have occurred.

It is, I know, a delicate and hazardous thing (and as such I have already pointed it out), to carry the principles of one art to another, or even to reconcile in one object the various modes of the same art, when they proceed on different principles. The sound rules of the Grecian architecture are not to be lightly sacrificed. A deviation from them, or even an addition to them, is like a deviation or addition to, or from, the rules of other arts, fit only for a great master, who is thoroughly conversant in the nature of man, as well as all combinations in his own art.

It may not be amiss for the architect to take advantage sometimes of that to which I am sure the painter ought always to have his eyes open, I mean the use of accidents; to follow when they lead, and to improve them, rather than al-

---

[20]See Pope, *An Essay on Criticism,* 297, p. 277.

[21][Malone] "Towers and battlements it sees / Bosm'd high in tufted trees." Milton, *L'Allegro* [77].

ways to trust to a regular plan. It often happens that additions have been made to houses, at various times, for use or pleasure. As such buildings depart from regularity, they now and then acquire something of scenery by this accident, which I should think might not unsuccessfully be adopted by an architect, in an original plan, if it does not too much interfere with convenience. Variety and intricacy is a beauty and excellence in every other of the arts which address the imagination; and why not in architecture?

The forms and turnings of the streets of London, and other old towns, are produced by accident, without any original plan or design; but they are not always the less pleasant to the walker or spectator, on that account. On the contrary, if the city had been built on the regular plan of Sir Christopher Wren, the effect might have been, as we know it is in some new parts of the town, rather unpleasing; the uniformity might have produced weariness, and a slight degree of disgust.

I can pretend to no skill in the detail of architecture. I judge now of the art, merely as a painter. When I speak of Vanbrugh, I mean to speak of him in the language of our art. To speak then of Vanbrugh in the language of a painter, he had originality of invention, he understood light and shadow, and had great skill in composition. To support his principal object, he produced his second and third groups or masses; he perfectly understood in his art what is the most difficult in ours, the conduct of the background, by which the design and invention is set off to the greatest advantage. What the background is in painting, in architecture is the real ground on which the building is erected; and no architect took greater care than he that his work should not appear crude and hard: that is, it did not abruptly start out of the ground without expectation or preparation.

This is a tribute, which a painter owes to an architect who composed like a painter; and was defrauded of the due reward of his merit by the wits of his time, who did not understand the principles of composition in poetry better than he; and who knew little, or nothing, of what he understood perfectly, the general ruling principles of architecture and painting. His fate was that of the great Perrault; both were the objects of the petulant sarcasms of factious men of letters; and both have left some of the fairest ornaments which to this day decorate their several countries; the façade of the Louvre, Blenheim, and castle Howard.

Upon the whole, it seems to me, that the object and intention of all the arts is to supply the natural imperfection of things, and often to gratify the mind by realizing and embodying what never existed but in the imagination.

It is allowed on all hands, that facts, and events, however they may bind the historian, have no dominion over the poet or the painter. With us, history is made to bend and conform to this great idea of art. And why? Because these arts, in their highest province, are not addressed to the gross senses, but to the desires of the mind, to that spark of divinity which we have within, impatient of being circumscribed and pent up by the world which is about us. Just so much as our art has of this, just so much of dignity, I had almost said of divinity, it exhibits; and those of our artists who possessed this mark of distinction in the highest degree, acquired from thence the glorious appellation of divine.

Denis Diderot

1713–1784

Diderot was one of the great figures of the Enlightenment. Famous principally for the enormously influential Encyclopedia of twenty-eight volumes, published under his editorship in collaboration with Jean d'Alembert, he was also the author of philosophical works, satires, novels, and plays. Diderot's essay *Paradoxe sur le comédien,* written in the form of a dialogue, ruptures the usual theoretical compact between poet, actor, work, and audience which declares that what the poet experiences and writes about and the actor acts is authentically felt and that this is what, conveyed to an audience, moves it. In a dialogue that in manner and to a considerable degree in thought anticipates Oscar Wilde's attack on the truth of imitation, Diderot attacks the notion of sentiment as sincerely conveyed by an actor. Diderot insists, contrary, incidentally, to statements in earlier works he had written, that the actor must have in himself an "unmoved disinterested onlooker" in order to move an audience. To play from the heart is to be subject to waves of feeling and to risk the destruction of unity. To imitate nature is not to *be* natural. It must be the audience that feels, not the actor, who must sedulously imitate feeling. Thus imitation is clearly identified with artifice: "What, then is truth for stage purposes? It is the conforming of action, diction, face, voice, movement, and gesture, to an ideal type invented by the poet, and frequently enhanced by the player."

Although Diderot does not dwell long on the poet's role, he does make clear that poetic composition begins when sensibility is dulled. He is advocating a sort of psychical distance that Keats later characterized as "negative capability" and even Wordsworth, the champion of feeling, kept a place for in his notion that poetic emotion is an "emotion recollected in tranquillity." Clearly Diderot is attacking the sort of emotional excess that can occur in a cult of sensibility. At the same time he opposes those notions of the "falsity" of acting common in puritanical opposition to the theater by insisting on the integrity of artistry, even though the picture he draws of the typical actor is hardly very flattering.

William Archer's answer to Diderot, written in 1888, is published with Diderot's essay in the book from which this selection is reprinted. See among recent work on Diderot, David Funt, *Diderot and the Esthetics of the Enlightenment* (1968); Lester G. Crocker, *Diderot's Chaotic Order* (1974); Otis Fellows, *Diderot* (1977); Merle L. Perkins, *Diderot and the Time-Space Continuum* (1982); Geoffrey Bremner, *Order and Chance: The Pattern of Diderot's Thought* (1983); Peter France, *Diderot* (1983); Jay Caplan, *Framed Narratives: Diderot's Genealogy of the Beholder* (1985); James Creech, *Diderot: Thresholds of Representation* (1986); and Derek F. Connon, *Innovation and Renewal: A Study of the Theatrical Works of Diderot* (1989).

From

The Paradox of Acting

It is Nature who bestows personal gifts—appearance, voice, judgment, tact. It is the study of the great models, the knowledge of the human heart, the habit of society, earnest work, experience, close acquaintance with the boards, which perfect Nature's gifts. The actor who is merely a mimic can count upon being always tolerable; his playing will call neither for praise nor for blame.

The Second   Or else for nothing but blame.

The First   Granted. The actor who goes by Nature alone is often detestable, sometimes excellent. But in whatever line, beware of a level mediocrity. No matter how harshly a beginner is treated, one may easily foretell his future success. It is only the incapables who are stifled by cries of 'Off! off!'[1] How should Nature without Art make a great actor when nothing happens on the stage exactly as it happens in nature, and when dramatic poems are all composed after a fixed system of principles? And how can a part be played in the same way by two different actors when, even with the clearest, the most precise, the most forceful of writers, words are no more, and never can be more, than symbols, indicating a thought, a feeling, or an idea; symbols which need action, gesture, intonation, expression, and a whole context of circumstance, to give them their full significance? When you have heard these words—

'Que fait là votre main?'
'Je tâte votre habit, l'étoffe en est moelleuse'
['Your hand—what does it there?'
'It feels your robe; 'tis soft and pleasant to the touch']

what do you know of their meaning? Nothing. Weigh well what follows, and remember how often and how easily it happens that two speakers may use the same words to express entirely different thoughts and matters. The instance I am going to cite is a very singular one; it is the very work of your friend that we have been discussing. Ask a French actor what he thinks of it; he will tell you that every word of it is true. Ask an English actor, and he will swear that, *'By God, there's not a sentence to change!* It is the very gospel of the stage!' However, since there is nothing in common between the way of writing comedy and tragedy in England, and the way of writing stage poems in France; since, according to Garrick[2] himself, an actor who will play you a scene of Shakespeare to perfection is ignorant of the first principles of declamation needed for Racine; since, entwined by Racine's musical lines as if by so many serpents whose folds compress his head, his feet, his hands, his legs, and his arms, he would, in attempting these lines, lose all liberty of action; it follows obviously that the French and the English actors, entirely at one as to the soundness of our author's principles, are yet at variance, and that the technical terms of the stage are so broad and so vague that men of judgment, and of diametrically opposite views, yet find in them the light of conviction. Now hold closer than ever to your maxim, *'Avoid explanation if what you want is a mutual understanding.'*[3]

The Second   You think that in every work, and especially in this, there are two distinct meanings, both expressed in the same terms, one understood in London, the other in Paris?

The First   Yes; and that these terms express so clearly the two meanings that your friend himself has fallen into a trap. In associating the names of English with those of French actors, applying to both the same precepts, giving to both the same praise and the same reproofs, he has doubtless imagined that what he said of the one set was equally true of the other.

The Second   According to this, never before was author so wrong-headed.

The First   I am sorry to admit that this is so, since he uses the same words to express one thing at the Crossroads of Bussy and another thing at Drury Lane. Of course I may be wrong. But the important point on which your author and I are entirely at variance concerns the qualities above all necessary to a great actor. In my view he must have a deal of judgment. He must have in himself an unmoved and disinterested onlooker. He must have, consequently, penetration and no sensibility; the art of mimicking everything, or, which comes to the same thing, the same aptitude for every sort of character and part.

The Second   No sensibility?

The First   None. I have not yet arranged my ideas logically, and you must let me tell them to you as they come to me, with the same want of order that marks your friend's book. If the actor were full, really full, of feeling, how could

---

THE PARADOX OF ACTING. *Paradoxe sur le Comédien* was written in the 1770s and revised in 1778. It was not published until 1830. Excerpts from *The Paradox of Acting* by Denis Diderot. Copyright © 1957 by Hill and Wang, Inc. Reprinted by permission of Hill and Wang, a division of Farrar, Straus and Giroux, Inc.
[1][Pollock] Cf. Lord Beaconsfield's 'You *shall* hear me one day,' at the end of his first unsuccessful and derided speech in the House of Commons.

[2]David Garrick (1717–1779), English actor.
[3][Pollock] This was a favourite aphorism of Grimm, to whom the first sketch of the *Paradoxe* was addressed *à propos* of *Garrick, ou les Acteurs Anglais.* It is given in vol. viii. of M. Assézat's edition. (Paris: Garnier frères.)

he play the same part twice running with the same spirit and success? Full of fire at the first performance, he would be worn out and cold as marble at the third. But take it that he is an attentive mimic and thoughtful disciple of Nature, then the first time he comes on the stage as Augustus, Cinna, Orosmanes, Agamemnon, or Mahomet, faithful copying of himself and the effects he has arrived at, and constantly observing human nature, will so prevail that his acting, far from losing in force, will gather strength with the new observations he will make from time to time. He will increase or moderate his effects, and you will be more and more pleased with him. If he is himself while he is playing, how is he to stop being himself? If he wants to stop being himself, how is he to catch just the point where he is to stay his hand?

What confirms me in this view is the unequal acting of players who play from the heart. From them you must expect no unity. Their playing is alternately strong and feeble, fiery and cold, dull and sublime. To-morrow they will miss the point they have excelled in to-day; and to make up for it will excel in some passage where last time they failed.[4] On the other hand, the actor who plays from thought, from study of human nature, from constant imitation of some ideal type, from imagination, from memory, will be one and the same at all performances, will be always at his best mark; he has considered, combined, learnt and arranged the whole thing in his head; his diction is neither monotonous nor dissonant. His passion has a definite course—it has bursts, and it has reactions; it has a beginning, a middle, and an end. The accents are the same, the positions are the same, the movements are the same; if there is any difference between two performances, the latter is generally the better. He will be invariable; a looking-glass, as it were, ready to reflect realities, and to reflect them ever with the same precision, the same strength, and the same truth. Like the poet he will dip for ever into the inexhaustible treasure-house of Nature, instead of coming very soon to an end of his own poor resources.

What acting was ever more perfect than Clairon's?[5] Think over this, study it; and you will find that at the sixth performance of a given part she has every detail of her acting by heart, just as much as every word of her part. Doubtless she has imagined a type, and to conform to this type has been her first thought; doubtless she has chosen for her purpose the highest, the greatest, the most perfect type her imagination could compass. This type, however, which she has borrowed from history, or created as who should create some vast spectre in her own mind, is not herself. Were it indeed bounded by her own dimensions, how paltry, how feeble would be her playing! When, by dint of hard work, she has got as near as she can to this idea, the thing is done; to preserve the same nearness is a mere matter of memory and practice. If you were with her while she studied her part how many times you would cry out, *That is right!* and how many times she would answer, *You are wrong!*

Just so a friend of Le Quesnoy's[6] once cried, catching him by the arm, 'Stop! you will make it worse by bettering it—you will spoil the whole thing!, 'What I have done,' replied the artist, panting with exertion, 'you have seen; what I have got hold of and what I mean to carry out to the very end you cannot see.'

I have no doubt that Clairon goes through just the same struggles as Le Quesnoy in her first attempts at a part; but once the struggle is over, once she has reached the height she has given to her spectre, she has herself well in hand, she repeats her efforts without emotion. As it will happen in dreams, her head touches the clouds, her hands stretch to grasp the horizon on both sides; she is the informing soul of a huge figure, which is her outward casing, and in which her efforts have enclosed her. As she lies careless and still on a sofa with folded arms and closed eyes she can, following her memory's dream, hear herself, see herself, judge herself, and judge also the effects she will produce. In such a vision she has a double personality; that of the little Clairon and of the great Agrippina.

The Second   According to you the likest thing to an actor, whether on the boards or at his private studies, is a group of children who play at ghosts in a graveyard at dead of night, armed with a white sheet on the end of a broomstick, and fending forth from its shelter hollow groans to frighten wayfarers.

The First   Just so, indeed. Now with Dumesnil[7] it is a different matter: she is not like Clairon. She comes on

---

[4][Pollock] This was, according to good authority, the case with Talma in his earlier days; and was certainly so with M. Mounet Sully in his earlier days. Both actors learnt by experience the unwisdom of relying upon inspiration alone.

[5][Pollock] Mlle. Clairon was born in Condé in 1723, and received her first impulse to go on the stage from seeing Mlle. Dangeville taking a dancing lesson in a room of which the windows were opposite to those of the attic in which Clairon's ill-natured mother had locked her up. She made her first pearance with the Italian company at the age of thirteen; then made a great success in comedy parts in the provinces; and at the age of eighteen came back to Paris. Here she appeared first at the Opera; then, in September 1743, at the Français, where she took every one by surprise by choosing to play Phèdre, and playing it with complete success. For twenty years from this time onwards she remained queen of the French stage. She left the stage in 1788 and died in 1803.

[6][Pollock] This is a mistake of Diderot's. The person referred to is Duquesnoy the Belgian sculptor.

[7][Pollock] Mlle. Dumesnil was born in 1713—not, as M. de Manne says in his *La Troupe de Voltaire,* in 1711. She came to Paris from the provinces in 1737, and made her first appearance at the Français in the same year as Clytemnestra in *Iphigénie en Aulide.* She was admitted the following year, left the stage in 1776, and died in year XI. of the Republic.

the stage without knowing what she is going to say; half the time she does not know what she is saying: but she has one sublime moment. And pray, why should the actor be different from the poet, the painter, the orator, the musician? It is not in the stress of the first burst that characteristic traits come out; it is in moments of stillness and self-command; in moments entirely unexpected. Who can tell whence these traits have their being? They are a sort of inspiration. They come when the man of genius is hovering between nature and his sketch of it, and keeping a watchful eye on both. The beauty of inspiration, the chance hits of which his work is full, and of which the sudden appearance startles himself, have an importance, a success, a sureness very different from that belonging to the first fling. Cool reflection must bring the fury of enthusiasm to its bearings.

The extravagant creature who loses his self-control has no hold on us; this is gained by the man who is self-controlled. The great poets, especially the great dramatic poets, keep a keen watch on what is going on, both in the physical and the moral world.

The Second   The two are the same.

The First   They dart on everything which strikes their imagination; they make, as it were, a collection of such things. And from these collections, made all unconsciously, issue the grandest achievements of their work.

Your fiery, extravagant, sensitive fellow, is for ever on the boards; he acts the play, but he gets nothing out of it. It is in him that the man of genius finds his model. Great poets, great actors, and, I may add, all great copyists of Nature, in whatever art, beings gifted with fine imagination, with broad judgment, with exquisite tact, with a sure touch of taste, are the least sensitive of all creatures. They are too apt for too many things, too busy with observing, considering, and reproducing, to have their inmost hearts affected with any liveliness. To me such an one always has his portfolio spread before him and his pencil in his fingers.

It is we who feel; it is they who watch, study, and give us the result.[8] And then . . . well, why should I not say it? Sensibility is by no means the distinguishing mark of a great genius. He will have, let us say, an abstract love of justice, but he will not be moved to temper it with mercy. It is the head, not the heart, which works in and for him. Let some unforeseen opportunity arise, the man of sensibility will lose it; he will never be a great king, a great minister, a great commander, a great advocate, a great physician. Fill the front of a theatre with tearful creatures, but I will none of them on the boards. Think of women, again. They are miles beyond

us in sensibility; there is no sort of comparison between their passion and ours. But as much as we are below them in action, so much are they below us in imitation. If a man who is really manly drops a tear, it touches us more nearly than a storm of weeping from a woman. In the great play, the play of the world, the play to which I am constantly recurring, the stage is held by the fiery souls, and the pit is filled with men of genius. The actors are in other words madmen; the spectators, whose business it is to paint their madness, are sages. And it is they who discern with a ready eye the absurdity of the motley crowd, who reproduce it for you, and who make you laugh both at the unhappy models who have bored you to death and at yourself. It is they who watch you, and who give you the mirth-moving picture of the tiresome wretch and of your own anguish in his clutches.[9]

You may prove this to demonstration, and a great actor will decline to acknowledge it; it is his own secret. A middling actor or a novice is sure to contradict you flatly; and of some others it may be said that they believe they feel, just as it has been said of some pious people that they believe they believe; and that without faith in the one case and without sensibility in the other there is no health.

This is all very well, you may reply; but what of these touching and sorrowful accents that are drawn from the very depth of a mother's heart and that shake her whole being? Are these not the result of true feeling? are these not the very inspiration of despair? Most certainly not. The proof is that they are all planned; that they are part of a system of declamation; that, raised or lowered by the twentieth part of a quarter of a tone, they would ring false; that they are in subjection to a law of unity; that, as in harmony, they are arranged in chords and in discords; that laborious study is needed to give them completeness; that they are the elements necessary to the solving of a given problem; that, to hit the right mark once, they have been practised a hundred times; and that, despite all this practice, they are yet found wanting. Look you, before he cries '*Zaïre vous pleurez,*' or '*Vous y serez ma fille,*' the actor has listened over and over again to his own voice. At the very moment when he touches your heart he is listening to his own voice; his talent depends not, as you think, upon feeling, but upon rendering so exactly the outward signs of feeling, that you fall into the trap. He has rehearsed to himself every note of his passion. He has learnt before a mirror every particle of his depair. He knows exactly when he must produce his handkerchief and shed tears; and you will see him weep at the word, at the syllable, he has chosen, not a second sooner or later. The broken voice, the half-uttered words, the stifled or prolonged notes of agony,

---

[8][Pollock] This was so with Goethe, to take an instance; and not improbably so with Shakespeare.

[9][Pollock] Cf. *inter alia* Horace, *Satires,* Book I., Sat. IX.; and *Les Fâcheux.*

the trembling limbs, the faintings, the bursts of fury—all this is pure mimicry, lessons carefully learned, the grimacing of sorrow, the magnificent aping which the actor remembers long after his first study of it, of which he was perfectly conscious when he first put it before the public, and which leaves him, luckily for the poet, the spectator, and himself, a full freedom of mind. Like other gymnastics, it taxes only his bodily strength. He puts off the sock or the buskin; his voice is gone; he is tired; he changes his dress, or he goes to bed; and he feels neither trouble, nor sorrow, nor depression, nor weariness of soul. All these emotions he has given to you. The actor is tired, you are unhappy; he has had exertion without feeling, you feeling without exertion. Were it otherwise the player's lot would be the most wretched on earth: but he is not the person he represents; he plays it, and plays it so well that you think he is the person; the deception is all on your side; he knows well enough that he is not the person.

For diverse modes of feeling arranged in concert to obtain the greatest effect, scored orchestrally, played *piano* and played *forte,* harmonised to make an individual effect—all that to me is food for laughter. I hold to my point, and I tell you this: 'Extreme sensibility makes middling actors; middling sensibility makes the ruck of bad actors; in complete absence of sensibility is the possibility of a sublime actor.' The player's tears come from his brain, the sensitive being's from his heart; the sensitive being's soul gives unmeasured trouble to his brain; the player's brain gives sometimes a touch of trouble to his soul: he weeps as might weep an unbelieving priest preaching of the Passion; as a seducer might weep at the feet of a woman whom he does not love, but on whom he would impose; like a beggar in the street or at the door of a church—a beggar who substitutes insult for vain appeal; or like a courtesan who has no heart, and who abandons herself in your arms.

Have you ever thought on the difference between the tears raised by a tragedy of real life and those raised by a touching narrative? You hear a fine piece of recitation; by little and little your thoughts are involved, your heart is touched, and your tears flow. With the tragedy of real life the thing, the feeling and the effect, are all one; your heart is reached at once, you utter a cry, your head swims, and the tears flow. These tears come of a sudden, the others by degrees. And here is the superiority of a true effect of nature over a well-planned scene. It does at one stroke what the scene leads up to by degrees, but it is far more difficult to reproduce its effect; one incident ill given would shatter it. Accents are more easily mimicked than actions, but actions go straighter to the mark. This is the basis of a canon to which I believe there is not exception. If you would avoid coldness you must complete your effect by action and not by talk.

So, then, have you no objection to make? Ah! I see! You give a recitation in a drawing-room; your feelings are stirred; your voice fails you; you burst into tears. You have, as you say, felt, and felt deeply. Quite so; but had you made up your mind to that? Not at all. Yet you were carried away, you surprised and touched your hearers, you made a great hit. All this is true enough. But now transfer your easy tone, your simple expression, your every-day bearing, to the stage, and, I assure you, you will be paltry and weak. You may cry to your heart's content, and the audience will only laugh. It will be the tragedy outside a booth at a fair.[10] Do you suppose that the dialogue of Corneille, of Racine, of Voltaire, or, let me add, of Shakespeare, can be given with your ordinary voice and with your fireside tone? No; not a bit more than you would tell a fireside story with the open-mouthed emphasis fit for the boards.

The Second   Perhaps Racine and Corneille, great names as they are, did nothing of account.

The First   Oh, blasphemy! Who could dare to say it? Who to endorse it? The merest word Corneille wrote cannot be given in everyday tone.

But, to go back, it must have happened to you a hundred times that at the end of your recitation, in the very midst of the agitation and emotion you have caused in your drawingroom audience, a fresh guest has entered, and wanted to hear your again. You find it impossible, you are weary to the soul. Sensibility, fire, tears, all have left you. Why does not the actor feel the same exhaustion? Because there is a world of difference between the interests excited by a flattering tale and by your fellow-man's misfortune. Are you Cinna? Have you ever been Cleopatra, Merope, Agrippina? Are these same personages on the stage ever historical personages? Not at all. They are the vain images of poetry. No, nor even that. They are the phantoms fashioned from this or that poet's special fantasy. They are well enough on the stage, these hippogriffs, so to call them, with their actions, their bearing, their intonations. They would make but a sorry figure in history; they would raise laughter in society. People would whisper to each other, 'Is this fellow mad? Where in the world does this Don Quixote come from? Who is the inventor of all this stuff? In what world do people talk like this?'

The Second   And why are they not intolerable on the stage?

---

[10][Pollock] *'Ce ne sera pas une tragédie, ce sera une parade tragique que vous jouerez.'* [It will be not a tragedy that you enact, but samples of a tragicomedy.]

Parade tragique is the brief sketch of a tale of horror given by strolling players outside their booth by way of tempting spectators to the fuller performance to be given inside.

The First   Because there is such a thing as stage convention. As old a writer as Æschylus laid this down as a formula—it is a protocol three thousand years old.

The Second   And will this protocol go on much longer?

The First   That I cannot tell you. All I know is that one gets further away from it as one gets nearer to one's own time and country. Find me a situation closer to that of Agamemnon in the first scene of *Iphigenia* than that of *Henri IV.:* when, beset by fears only too well founded, he said to those around him, 'They will kill me; there is nothing surer; they will kill me!' Suppose that great man, that superb and hapless monarch, troubled in the night-watches with this deadly presentiment, got up and knocked at the door of Sully, his minister and friend—is there, think you, a poet foolish enough to make Henri say—

'Oui, c'est Henri, s'est ton roi qui t'éveille;
Viens, reconnais la voix qui frappe ton oreille?'
(Ay, it is Agamemnon [Henri], 'tis thy King
That wakes thee; his the voice that strikes thine ear.)

Or to make Sully reply—

'C'est vous-même, seigneur? Quel important besoin
Vous a faît devancer l'aurore de si loin?
A peine un faible jour vous éclaire et me guide,
Vos yeux seuls et les miens sont ouverts . . . '[11]
[Is't thou indeed, my lord? What grave concern
Has made thee leave thy couch before the dawn?
A feeble light scarce lets me see thy face,
No eyes but ours are open yet in Aulis. . . .]

The Second   Perhaps Agamemnon really talked like that.

The First   No more than Henri IV. did. Homer talks like that; Racine talks like that; poetry talks like that; and this pompous language can only be used by unfamiliar personages, spoken from poetical lips, with a poetical tone. Reflect a little as to what, in the language of the theatre, is *being true*. It is showing things as they are in nature? Certainly not. Were it so the true would be the commonplace. What, then,

is truth for stage purposes? It is the conforming of action, diction, face, voice, movement, and gesture, to an ideal type invented by the poet, and frequently enhanced by the player. That is the strange part of it. This type not only influences the tone, it alerts the actor's very walk and bearing. And hence it is that the player in private and the player on the boards are two personages, so different that one can scarce recognise the player in private. The first time I saw Mlle. Clairon in her own house I exclaimed, by a natural impulse, 'Ah, mademoiselle, I thought you were at least a head taller!'

An unhappy, a really unhappy woman, may weep and fail to touch you; worse than that, some trivial disfigurement in her may incline you to laughter; the accent which is apt to her is to your ears dissonant and vexatious; a movement which is habitual to her makes her grief show ignobly and sulkily to you; almost all the violent passions lend themselves to grimaces which a tasteless artist will copy but too faithfully, and which a great actor will avoid. In the very whirlwind of passion we would have a man preserve his manly dignity. And what is the effect of this heroic effort? To give relief and temperance to sorrow. We would have this heroine fall with a becoming grace, that hero die like a gladiator of old in the midst of the arena to the applause of the circus, with a noble grace, with a fine and picturesque attitude. And who will execute this design of ours? The athlete who is mastered by pain, shattered by his own sensibility, or the athlete who is trained, who has self-control, who, as he breathes his last sigh, remembers the lessons of the gymnasium? Neither the gladiator of old nor the great actor dies as people die in their beds; it is for them to show us another sort of death, a death to move us; and the critical spectator will feel that the bare truth, the unadorned fact, would seem despicable and out of harmony with the poetry of the rest.

Not, mark you, that Nature unadorned has not her moments of sublimity; but I fancy that if there is any one sure to give and preserve their sublimity it is the man who can feel it with his passion and his genius, and reproduce it with complete self-possession.

I will not, however, deny that there is a kind of acquired or factitious sensibility; but if you would like to know what I think about it, I hold it to be nearly as dangerous as natural sensibility. By little and little it leads the actor into mannerism and monotony. It is an element opposed to the variety of a great actor's functions. He must often strip it from him; and it is only a head of iron which can make such a self-abnegation. Besides, it is far better for the ease and success of his study, for the catholicity of his talent and the perfection of his playing, that there should be no need of this strange parting of self from self. Its extreme difficulty, confining each actor to one single line, leads perforce to a numerous company, where every part is ill played; unless, in-

---

[11][Pollock] There were believers in poets quite foolish enough for this long after Diderot's time. It was precisely because this sort of diction was dropped for a more natural one in *Hernani* that the play, from its first scene, raised such a storm among the classicists—as he who will may read in the pages of Théophile Gautier. The lines quoted are from the speeches of Agamemnon and Arcas in the opening of Racine's *Iphigénie,* the name Henri being substituted for Agamemnon. The English version is from *The Dramatic Works of Jean Racine: A Metrical English Version,* by Robert Bruce Boswell (London: George Bell and Sons, 1901).

deed, the natural order of things is reversed, and the pieces are made for the actors. To my thinking the actors, on the contrary, ought to be made for the pieces.[12]

The Second   But if a crowd of people collected in the street by some catastrophe begin of a sudden, and each in his own way, and without any concert, to exhibit a natural sensibility, they will give you a magnificent show, and display you a thousand types, valuable for sculpture, music, and poetry.

The First   True enough. But will this show compare with one which is the result of a pre-arranged plan, with the harmony which the artist will put into it when he transfers it from the public way to his stage or canvas? If you say it will, then I shall make you this answer: What is this boasted magic of art if it only consists in spoiling what both nature and chance have done better than art? Do you deny that one can improve on nature? Have you never, by way of praising a woman, said she is as lovely as one of Raphael's Madonnas? Have you never cried, on seeing a fine landscape, 'It's as good as a description in a novel?' Again, you are talking to me of a reality. I am talking to you of an imitation. You are talking to me of a passing moment in Nature. I am talking to you of a work of Art, planned and composed—a work which is built up by degrees, and which lasts. Take now each of these actors; change the scene in the street as you do on the boards, and show me your personages left successively to themselves, two by two or three by three. Leave them to their own swing; make them full masters of their actions; and you will see what a monstrous discord will result. You will get over this by making them rehearse together. Quite so. And then good-bye to their natural sensibility; and so much the better.

A play is like any well-managed association, in which each individual sacrifices himself for the general good and effect. And who will best take the measure of the sacrifice? The enthusiast or the fanatic? Certainly not. In society, the man of judgment; on the stage, the actor whose wits are always about him. Your scene in the street has the same relation to a scene on the stage that a band of savages has to a company of civilised men.

Now is the time to talk to you of the disastrous influence which a middling associate has on a first-rate player. This player's conception is admirable; but he has to give up his ideal type in order to come down to the level of the poor wretch who is playing with him. Then he says farewell to his

study and his taste. As happens with talks in the street or at the fireside, the principal speaker lowers his tone to that of his companion. Or if you would like another illustration, take that of whist, where you lose a deal of your own skill if you cannot rely on your partner. More than this, Clairon will tell you, if you ask her, that Le Kain[13] would maliciously make her play badly or inadequately, and that she would avenge herself by getting him hissed. What, then, are two players who mutually support each other? Two personages whose types are, in due proportion, either equal, or else in them the subordination demanded by the circumstances, as laid down by the poet, is observed. But for this there would be an excess, either of strength or of weakness; and such a want of harmony as this is avoided more frequently by the strong descending to the weak than by its raising the weak to its own level. And pray, do you know the reason of the numberless rehearsals that go on? They are to strike the balance between the different talents of the actors, so as to establish a general unity in the playing. When the vanity of an individual interferes with this balance the result is to injure the effect and to spoil your enjoyment; for it is seldom that the excellence of one actor can atone for the mediocrity, which it brings into relief, of his companions. I have known a great actor suffer from his temperament in this way. The stupid public said he was extravagant, instead of discerning that his associate was inadequate.

Come, you are a poet; you have a piece for the stage; and I leave you to choose between actors with the soundest judgments and the coolest heads and actors of sensibility. But before you make up your mind let me ask you one question. What is the time of life for a great actor? The age when one is full of fire, when the blood boils in the veins, when the slightest check troubles one to the soul, when the wit blazes at the veriest spark? I fancy not. The man whom Nature stamps an actor does not reach his topmost height until he has had a long experience, until the fury of the passions is subdued, until the head is cool and the heart under control. The best wine is harsh and crude in its fermenting. It is by long lying in the cask that it grows generous. Cicero, Seneca, and Plutarch, I take to represent the three ages of composition in men. Cicero is often but a blaze of straw, pretty to

---

[12][Pollock] Note by the publishers of the small popular edition in Paris:—'Our modern authors have ended in always writing their pieces for this or that actor. Hence the short life which their productions will have.' The practice, I may add, is, unfortunately, by no means unknown in England.

[13][Pollock] Le Kain made his first appearance at the Français in September 1750, as Titus in Voltaire's *Brutus*. His success was gained in spite of natural disadvantages in voice and personal appearance. He owed much to Clairon, but more to unceasing study and application. What helped him in the first instance to please critical taste was that, like Garrick, he was the first to venture on varying the conventional sing-song of declamation. Later he and Clairon reformed the stage costume. Much of interest will be found about him in the lately published pamphlet, *Talma on the Actor's Art*. He was great as a tragedian; good as a comedian. He died in February 1778.

look at; Seneca a fire of vine-branches, hurtful to look at; but when I stir old Plutarch's ashes I come upon the great coals of a fire that gives me a gentle warmth.

. . .

Is it at the moment when you have just lost your friend or your adored one that you set to work at a poem on your loss? No! ill for him who at such a moment takes pleasure in his talent. It is when the storm of sorrow is over, when the extreme of sensibility is dulled, when the event is far behind us, when the soul is calm, that one remembers one's eclipsed happiness, that one is capable of appreciating one's loss, that memory and imagination unite, one to retrace the other to accentuate, the delights of a past time: then it is that one regains self-possession and expression. One writes of one's falling tears, but they do not fall while one is hunting a strong epithet that always escapes one; one writes of one's falling tears, but they do not fall while one is employed in polishing one's verse; or if the tears do flow the pen drops from the hand: one falls to feeling, and one ceases writing.

Again, it is with intense pleasure as with intense pain—both are dumb. A tender-hearted and sensitive man sees again a friend he has missed during a long absence; the friend makes an unexpected reappearance, and the other's heart is touched; he rushes to him, he embraces him, he would speak, but cannot; he stammers and trips over his words; he says he knows not what, he does not hear the answer: if he could see that the delight is not mutual, how hurt he would be! Judge, this picture being true, how untrue are the stage meetings, where both friends are so full of intelligence and self-control. What could I not say to you of the insipid and eloquent disputes as to who is to die, or rather who is not to die, but that this text, on which I should enlarge for ever, would take us far from our subject? Enough has been said for men of true and fine taste; what I could add would teach nothing to the rest. Now, who is come to the rescue of these absurdities so common on the stage? The actor? and what actor?

The circumstances in which sensibility is as hurtful in society as on the stage are a thousand to one. Take two lovers, both of whom have their declaration to make. Who will come out of it best? Not I, I promise you. I remember that I approached the beloved object with fear and trembling; my heart beat, my ideas grew confused, my voice failed me, I mangled all I said; I cried *yes* for *no;* I made a thousand blunders; I was illimitably inept; I was absurd from top to toe, and the more I saw it, the more absurd I became. Meanwhile, under my very eyes, a gay rival, light-hearted and agreeable, master of himself, pleased with himself, losing no opportunity for the finest flattery, made himself entertaining

and agreeable, enjoyed himself; he implored the touch of a hand which was at once given him, he sometimes caught it without asking leave, he kissed it once and again. I the while, alone in a corner, avoiding a sight which irritated me, stifling in my sighs, cracking my fingers with grasping my wrists, plunged in melancholy, covered with a cold sweat, I could neither show nor conceal my vexation. People say of love that it robs witty men of their wit, and gives it to those who had none before: in other words, makes some people sensitive and stupid, others cold and adventurous.

The man of sensibility obeys the impulse of Nature, and gives nothing more or less than the cry of his very heart; the moment he moderates or strengthens this cry he is no longer himself, he is an actor.

The great actor watches appearances; the man of sensibility is his model; he thinks over him, and discovers by after-reflection what it will be best to add or cut away. And so from mere argument he goes to action.

. . .

Is there such a thing as artificial sensibility? Consider, sensibility, whether acquired or inborn, is not in place in all characters. What, then, is the quality acquired which makes an actor great in *l'Avare, le Joueur, le Flatteur, le Grondeur, le Médecin malgré lui* (the least sensitive or moral personage yet devised by a poet), *le Bourgeois Gentilhomme, la Malade Imaginaire, la Cœur Imaginaire*—in Nero, in Mithridates, in Atreus, in Phocas, in Sertorius, and in a host of other characters, tragic and comic, where sensibility is diametrically opposed to the spirit of the part? It is the faculty of knowing and imitating all natures. Believe me, we need not multiply causes when one cause accounts for all appearances.

Sometimes the poet feels more deeply than the actor; sometimes, and perhaps oftener, the actor's conception is stronger than the poet's; and there is nothing truer than Voltaire's exclamation, when he heard Clairon in a piece of his, *'Did I really write that?'* Does Clairon know more about it than Voltaire? Anyhow, at that moment the ideal type in the speaking of the part went well beyond the poet's ideal type in the writing of it. But this ideal type was not Clairon. Where, then, lay her talent? In imagining a mighty shape, and in copying it with genius. She imitated the movement, the action, the gesture, the whole embodiment of a being far greater than herself. She had learnt that Æschines, repeating a speech of Demosthenes, could never reproduce 'the roar of the brute.' He said to his disciples, 'If this touches you, or nearly, what would have been the effect *si audivissetis bestiam mugientem* [had you heard the roaring beast]?' The poet had engendered the monster, Clairon made it roar.

It would be a strange abuse of language to give the name of sensibility to this faculty of reproducing all natures, even ferocious natures. Sensibility, according to the only acceptation yet given of the term, is, as it seems to me, that disposition which accompanies organic weakness, which follows on easy affection of the diaphragm, on vivacity of imagination, on delicacy of nerves, which inclines one to being compassionate, to being horrified, to admiration, to fear, to being upset, to tears, to faintings, to rescues, to flights, to exclamations, to loss of self-control, to being contemptuous, disdainful, to having no clear notion of what is true, good, and fine, to being unjust, to going mad. Multiply souls of sensibility, and you will multiply in the same proportion good and bad actions of every kind, extravagant praise and extravagant blame.

. . .

The Second   A great actor's soul is formed of the subtle element with which a certain philosopher filled space, an element neither cold nor hot, heavy nor light, which affects no definite shape, and, capable of assuming all, keeps none.

The First   A great actor is neither a pianoforte, nor a harp, nor a spinnet, nor a violin, nor a violoncello; he has no key peculiar to him; he takes the key and the tone fit for his part of the score, and he can take up any. I put a high value on the talent of a great actor; he is a rare being—as rare as, and perhaps greater than, a poet.

He who in society makes it his object, and unluckily has the skill, to please every one, is nothing, has nothing that belongs to him, nothing to distinguish him, to delight some and weary others. He is always talking, and always talking well; he is an adulator by profession, he is a great courtier, he is a great actor.

The Second   A great courtier, accustomed since he first drew breath to play the part of a most ingenious puppet,[14] takes every kind of shape at the pull of the string in his master's hands.

The First   A great actor is also a most ingenious puppet, and his strings are held by the poet, who at each line indicates the true form he must take.

The Second   So then a courtier, an actor, who can take only one form, however beautiful, however attractive it may be, are a couple of wretched pasteboard figures?

The First   I have no thought of calumniating a profession I like and esteem—I mean, the actor's. I should be in despair if a misunderstanding of my observations cast a shade of contempt on men of a rare talent and a true usefulness, on the scourges of absurdity and vice, on the most eloquent preachers of honesty and virtue, on the rod which the man of genius wields to chastise knaves and fools. But look around you, and you will see that people of never-failing gaiety have neither great faults nor great merits; that as a rule people who lay themselves out to be agreeable are frivolous people, without any sound principle; and that those who, like certain persons who mix in our society, have no character, excel in playing all.

Has not the actor a father, a mother, a wife, children, brothers, sisters, acquaintances, friends, a mistress? If he were endowed with that exquisite sensibility which people regard as the thing principally needed for his profession, harassed and struck like us with an infinity of troubles in quick succession, which sometimes wither and sometimes tear our hearts, how many days would he have left to devote to our amusement? Mighty few. The Groom of the Chambers would vainly interpose his sovereignty, the actor's state would often make him answer, 'My lord, I cannot laugh today,' or, 'It is over cares other than Agamemnon's that I would weep.' It is not known, however, that the troubles of life, common to actors as to us, and far more opposed to the free exercise of their calling, often interrupt them.

In society, unless they are buffoons, I find them polished, caustic, and cold; proud, light of behavior, spendthrifts, self-interested; struck rather by our absurdities than touched by our misfortunes; masters of themselves at the spectacle of an untoward incident or the recital of a pathetic story; isolated, vagabonds, at the command of the great; little conduct, no friends, scarce any of those holy and tender ties which associate us in the pains and pleasures of another, who in turn shares our own. I have often seen an actor laugh off the stage; I do not remember to have ever seen one weep. What do they, then, with this sensibility that they arrogate and that people grant them? Do they leave it on the stage at their exit, to take it up again at their next entrance?

What makes them slip on the sock or the buskin? Want of education, poverty, a libertine spirit. The stage is a resource, never a choice. Never did actor become so from love of virtue, from desire to be useful in the world, or to serve his country of family; never from any of the honourable motives which might incline a right mind, a feeling heart, a sensitive soul, to so fine a profession.

I myself, in my young days, hesitated between the Sorbonne and the stage. In the bitterest depth of winter I used to go and recite aloud parts in Molière and in Corneille in the solitary alleys of the Luxembourg. What was my project? To gain applause? Perhaps. To mix on intimate terms with ac-

---

14[Pollock] *Pantin*. A figure cut out in card, with strings attached to it. I have used the word puppet to avoid roundabout expression.

tresses whom I found charming, and who I knew were not straitlaced? Certainly. I know not what I would not have done to please Gaussin, who was then making her first appearance, and was beauty itself; or Dangeville,[15] who on the stage was so full of charm.

It has been said that actors have no character, because in playing all characters they lose that which Nature gave them, and they become false just as the doctor, the surgeon, and the butcher, become hardened. I fancy that here cause is confounded with effect, and that they are fit to pay all characters because they have none.

. . .

'My friend, there are three types—Nature's man, the poet's man, the actor's man. Nature's is less great than the poet's, the poet's less great than the great actor's, which is the most exalted of all. This last climbs on the shoulders of the one before him and shuts himself up inside a great basket-work figure of which he is the soul. He moves this figure so as to terrify even the poet, who no longer recognises himself; and he terrifies us, as you have very well put it, just as children frighten each other by tucking up their little skirts and putting them over their heads, shaking themselves about, and imitating as best they can the croaking lugubrious accents of the spectre that they counterfeit. Have you not seen engravings of children's sports?[16] Have you not observed an urchin coming forward under a hideous old man's mask, which hides him from head to foot? Behind this mask he laughs at his little companions, who fly in terror before him. This urchin is the true symbol of the actor; his comrades are the symbol of the audience. If the actor has but middling sensibility, and if that is his ony merit, will you not call him a middling man? Take care, for this is another trap I am laying for you. And if he is endowed with extreme sensibility what will come of it?—What will come of it? That he will either play no more, or play ludicrously ill; yes, ludicrously; and to prove it you can see the same thing in me when you like. If I have a recital of some pathos to give, a strange trouble arises in my heart and head; my tongue trips, my voice changes, my ideas wander, my speech hangs fire. I babble; I perceive it; tears course down my checks; I am silent. But with this I make an effect—in private life; on the stage I should be hooted.

Why?

Because people come not to see tears, but to hear speeches that draw tears; because this truth of nature is out of tune with the truth of convention. Let me explain myself: I mean that neither the dramatic system, nor the action, nor the poet's speeches, would fit themselves to my stifled, broken, sobbing declamation. You see that it is not allowable to imitate Nature, even at her best, or Truth too closely; there are limits within which we must restrict ourselves.

---

[15][Pollock] Mlle. Dangeville was born in Paris in 1714. Daughter of a ballet-master and an actress, she made her first appearance at the Français at the age of seven and a half. Her official first appearance was made in 1730, as Lisette in Destouches's *Médisant*. She was admitted two months afterwards, remained on the stage till 1763, and died in 1796. The editor of the *Mémoires Secrets*, echoing public opinion, wrote of her: 'You alone, inimitable Dangeville, never grow old. So fresh, so novel are you, that each time we see you we take to be the first time. Nature has showered her gifts on you, as though Art had refused to endow you; and Art has hastened to enrich you with her perfection as though Nature had granted you nought.' Her first appearances were so successful that it was said of her at the time that she began where great actresses left off.

---

[16][Pollock] For special instances of such plates M. Assézat refers us to *Les Jeux des Anciens,* by M. Becq de Fouquières (in 8vo. Reinwald, 1869).

Immanuel Kant

1724–1804

Kant's aesthetic theory in the *Critique of Judgment* has its foundation in the epistemological position he expounded in the *Critique of Pure Reason.* There he proposed the existence of the "manifold of sensation," the raw data collected and organized by the mind through the creative power of the sensibility. The sensibility abstracts from the manifold, formulating the world intellectually according to space and time, the a priori forms of consciousness. Kant postulates that we can never know directly "things in themselves"; we cast all our perceptions into the forms of space and time, which are the spectacles we all wear but can never remove. At a higher level, further removed from direct sensation, the power of the understanding comes into play and schematizes our sensible experience according to "categories"—unity, plurality, totality, substance, causation, and so on. These categories govern our conceptual thought. Just as we cannot experience anything without putting on the spectacles of space and time, so we cannot think without casting our thoughts into the categories.

Kant opposes aesthetic judgments to teleological judgments. Teleological judgments consider objects and their purposes and thus have to do with concepts and the categories. Aesthetic judgments, however, do not consider the object with respect to an outer purpose. There are two kinds of aesthetic judgments, those of the beautiful and those of the sublime. Neither aesthetic judgment can be called objective or logical. Both are subjective. Feelings of pleasure and pain are distinguished from aesthetic judgments, for the former are subjective and individual, while the latter, though subjective, are universal and "disinterested."

Kant argues that in order to find an object beautiful we need not have a concept of how it is to be used or what it ought to be. Indeed, to make that kind of judgment is to refer the object to some preconceived notion and thus to make a logical rather than an aesthetic judgment. Each aesthetic judgment is singular: we can declare a rose beautiful, but to say that roses are beautiful is to make a logical judgment based on a generalization. An object judged aesthetically cannot be judged in terms of an external purpose, for if it were, it would be judged logically by how well it succeeds in its purpose or conforms to some external standard. Kant speaks paradoxically of the aesthetic object as having "purposiveness without purpose" or having "internal" purposiveness. The canon of accuracy implied by the Platonic idea of imitation is thus irrelevant to aesthetic judgment. All neoclassical external canons of beauty are likewise of no value, for they posit an external standard or purpose.

In Kant's theorizing we can observe a shift from interest in the reader's subjectivity and his response to art toward concern with the internality of the work itself. With no exterior purpose admitted and no exterior ideal of beauty allowed, the work must generate its own standard, its own internal purpose. Even though Kant ultimately refers all experience of art back to the reader, he concedes that we must talk about the work itself, pretending that what we say about it is independent of ourselves.

The sublime differs from the beautiful, for the beautiful implies form and boundary, while the sublime implies the boundless, that which is "absolutely great." To our imaginations the sublime object is formless and beyond cognition. We take pleasure in sublime experiences even as we recognize fear, because we see in the experience that we possess a faculty of mind that surpasses sense and imagination. The sublime does not lead to disinterested contemplation, as does the beautiful, but to deep feeling. Even so, Kant makes a strong effort to establish its purposelessness.

The direct influence of the *Critique of Judgment* is vast. Coleridge's distinction between the beautiful and the agreeable in his *Principles of Genial Criticism* is drawn straight from it. There are close affinities between Kant's theories and Schiller's idea of art as "play." Valéry's distinction between language as walking and language as dancing translates Kant's paradox of purposiveness without a purpose into new terms. The list of influences could be expanded almost endlessly.

The influence of Kant's epistemology in the *Critique of Pure Reason* is as important to literary theory as the influence of the *Critique of Judgment*. The principle of symbolic forms in Cassirer and other theorists of the twentieth century is neo-Kantian. Much of the so-called New Criticism in America—that of Ransom, Tate, and Vivas, for example—requires a neo-Kantian theory of knowledge in order to support its claims for poetry.

Among the most useful translations of Kant's works are *Critique of Judgment,* translated by J. H. Bernard, 2nd ed., rev. (1931); *Prolegomena to Any Future Metaphysic,* translated by Paul Carus (1902); *Critique of Pure Reason,* translated by N. K. Smith, rev. ed. (1933); *Critique of Practical Reason,* translated by L. W. Beck (1949); and *Observations on the Feelings of the Beautiful and Sublime,* translated by J. T. Goldthwaite (1960). Among the great number of studies of Kant the most useful include N. K. Smith, *A Commentary to Kant's* Critique of Pure Reason, 2nd ed., rev. (1929); René Wellek, *Immanuel Kant in England* (1931); H. N. Lee, "Kant's Theory of Aesthetics," *Philosophical Review,* XL (1931), 537–48; Israel Knox, *The Aesthetic Theories of Kant, Hegel, and Schopenhauer* (1936); H. W. Cassirer, *Commentary on Kant's* Critique of Judgment (1938); Karl Jaspers, *Kant* (1962); R. L. Zimmerman, "Kant: The Aesthetic Judgment," *Journal of Aesthetics and Art Criticism,* XXI (1963), 333–44; R. P. Wolff, ed., *Kant, A Collection of Critical Essays* (1967); Lucien Goldmann, *Kant* (1971); Francis X. Coleman, *The Harmony of Reason* (1974); Donald W. Crawford, *Kant's Aesthetic Theory* (1974); Eva Schaper, *Studies in Kant's Aesthetics* (1979); Paul Guyer, *Kant and the Claims of Taste*; and Ted Cohen and Paul Guyer, eds., *Essays in Kant's Aesthetics* (1982).

From

Critique of Judgment

First Book

Analytic
of the Beautiful

First Moment

Of the Judgment of Taste,[1] *According to Quality*

I. The Judgment of Taste Is Aesthetical

In order to distinguish whether anything is beautiful or not, we refer the representation, not by the understanding to the object for cognition, but by the imagination (perhaps in conjunction with the understanding) to the subject and its feeling of pleasure or pain. The judgment of taste is therefore not a judgment of cognition, and is consequently not logical but aesthetical, by which we understand that whose determining ground can be *no other than subjective*. Every reference of representations, even that of sensations, may be objective (and then it signifies the real [element] of an empirical representation), save only the reference to the feeling of pleasure and pain, by which nothing in the object is signified, but through which there is a feeling in the subject as it is affected by the representation.

To apprehend a regular, purposive building by means of one's cognitive faculty (whether in a clear or a confused way of representation) is something quite different from being conscious of this representation as connected with the sensation of satisfaction. Here the representation is altogether referred to the subject and to its feeling of life, under the name of the feeling of pleasure or pain. This establishes a quite separate faculty of distinction and of judgment, adding

nothing to cognition, but only comparing the given representation in the subject with the whole faculty of representations, of which the mind is conscious in the feeling of its state. Given representations in a judgment can be empirical (consequently, aesthetical); but the judgment which is formed by means of them is logical, provided they are referred in the judgment to the object. Conversely, if the given representations are rational, but are referred in a judgment simply to the subject (to its feeling), the judgment is so far always aesthetical.

II. The Satisfaction Which Determines the Judgment of Taste Is Disinterested

The satisfaction which we combine with the representation of the existence of an object is called "interest." Such satisfaction always has reference to the faculty of desire, either as its determining ground or as necessarily connected with its determining ground. Now when the question is if a thing is beautiful, we do not want to know whether anything depends or can depend on the existence of the thing, either for myself or for anyone else, but how we judge it by mere observation (intuition or reflection). If anyone asks me if I find that palace beautiful which I see before me, I may answer: I do not like things of that kind which are made merely to be stared at. Or I can answer like that Iroquois sachem, who was pleased in Paris by nothing more than by the cook shops. Or again, after the manner of Rousseau, I may rebuke the vanity of the great who waste the sweat of the people on such superfluous things. In fine, I could easily convince myself that if I found myself on an uninhabited island without the hope of ever again coming among men, and could conjure up just such a splendid building by my mere wish, I should not even give myself the trouble if I had a sufficiently comfortable hut. This may all be admitted and approved, but we are not now talking of this. We wish only to know if this mere representation of the object is accompanied in me with satisfaction, however indifferent I may be as regards the existence of the object of this representation. We easily see that, in saying it is *beautiful* and in showing that I have taste, I am concerned, not with that in which I depend on the existence of the object, but with that which I make out of this representation in myself. Everyone must admit that a judgment about beauty, in which the least interest mingles, is very partial and is not a pure judgment of taste. We must not be in the least prejudiced in favor of the existence of the things, but be quite indifferent in this respect, in order to play the judge in things of taste.

CRITIQUE OF JUDGMENT. Kant's *Kritik der Urteilschaft* was first published in 1790. The text is from the second edition, revised, of the translation by J. H. Bernard (1931). Reprinted by permission of the Hafner Publishing Company, Inc.

[1][Kant] The definition of "taste" which is laid down here is that it is the faculty of judging of the beautiful. But the analysis of judgments of taste must show what is required in order to call an object beautiful. The moments to which this judgment has regard in its reflection I have sought in accordance with the guidance of the logical functions of judgment (for in a judgment of taste a reference to the understanding is always involved). I have considered the moment of quality first because the aesthetical judgment upon the beautiful first pays attention to it.

We cannot, however, better elucidate this proposition, which is of capital importance, than by contrasting the pure disinterested[2] satisfaction in judgments of taste with that which is bound up with an interest, especially if we can at the same time be certain that there are no other kinds of interest than those which are to be now specified.

IV. The Satisfaction in the Good Is Bound Up with Interest

Whatever by means of reason pleases through the mere concept is *good.* That which pleases only as a means we call *good for something* (the useful), but that which pleases for itself is *good in itself.* In both there is always involved the concept of a purpose, and consequently the relation of reason to the (at least possible) volition, and thus a satisfaction in the *presence* of an object or an action, i.e. some kind of interest.

In order to find anything good, I must always know what sort of a thing the object ought to be, i.e. I must have a concept of it. But there is no need of this to find a thing beautiful. Flowers, free delineations, outlines intertwined with one another without design and called conventional foliage, have no meaning, depend on no definite concept, and yet they please. The satisfaction in the beautiful must depend on the reflection upon an object, leading to any concept (however indefinite), and it is thus distinguished from the pleasant, which rests entirely upon sensation.

. . .

V. Comparison of the Three Specifically Different Kinds of Satisfaction

The pleasant and the good have both a reference to the faculty of desire, and they bring with them, the former a satisfaction pathologically conditioned (by impulses, stimuli), the latter a pure practical satisfaction which is determined not merely by the representation of the object but also by the represented connection of the subject with the existence of the object. It is not merely the object that pleases, but also its

existence. On the other hand, the judgment of taste is merely *contemplative;* i.e., it is a judgment which, indifferent as regards the existence of an object, compares its character with the feeling of pleasure and pain. But this contemplation itself is not directed to concepts; for the judgment of taste is not a cognitive judgment (either theoretical or practical), and thus is not *based* on concepts, nor has its concepts as its *purpose.*

The pleasant, the beautiful, and the good designate then three different relations of representations to the feeling of pleasure and pain, in reference to which we distinguish from one another objects or methods of representing them. And the expressions corresponding to each, by which we mark our complacency in them, are not the same. That which *gratifies* a man is called *pleasant;* that which merely *pleases* him is *beautiful;* that which is *esteemed* or *approved* by him, i.e. that to which he accords an objective worth, is *good.* Pleasantness concerns irrational animals also, but beauty only concerns men, i.e. animal, but still rational, beings—not merely qua rational (e.g. spirits), but qua animal also—and the good concerns every rational being in general. This is a proposition which can only be completely established and explained in the sequel. We may say that, of all these three kinds of satisfaction, that of taste in the beautiful is alone a disinterested and *free* satisfaction; for no interest, either of sense or of reason, here forces our assent. Hence we may say of satisfaction that it is related in the three aforesaid cases to *inclination,* to *favor,* or to *respect.* Now *favor* is the only free satisfaction. An object of inclination and one that is proposed to our desire by a law of reason leave us no freedom in forming for ourselves anywhere an object of pleasure. All interest presupposes or generates a want, and, as the determining ground of assent, it leaves the judgment about the object no longer free.

As regards the interest of inclination in the case of the pleasant, everyone says that hunger is the best sauce, and everything that is eatable is relished by people with a healthy appetite; and thus a satisfaction of this sort shows no choice directed by taste. It is only when the want is appeased that we can distinguish which of many men has or has not taste. In the same way there may be manners (conduct) without virtue, politeness without good will, decorum without modesty, etc. For where the moral law speaks there is no longer, objectively, a free choice as regards what is to be done; and to display taste in its fulfillment (or in judging of another's fulfillment of it) is something quite different from manifesting the moral attitude of thought. For this involves a command and generates a want, while moral taste only plays with the objects of satisfaction, without attaching itself to one of them.

[2][Kant] A judgment upon an object of satisfaction may be quite *disinterested,* but yet very *interesting,* i.e. not based upon an interest, but bringing an interest with it; of this kind are all pure moral judgments. Judgments of taste, however, do not in themselves establish any interest. Only in society is it *interesting* to have taste; the reason of this will be shown in the sequel.

Explanation of the Beautiful Resulting from the First Moment

Taste is the faculty of judging of an object or a method of representing it by an *entirely disinterested* satisfaction or dissatisfaction. The object of such satisfaction is called *beautiful.*[3]

Second Moment

of the Judgment of Taste, According to Quantity

VI. The Beautiful Is That Which Apart from Concepts Is Represented as the Object of a Universal Satisfaction

This explanation of the beautiful can be derived from the preceding explanation of it as the object of an entirely disinterested satisfaction. For the fact of which everyone is conscious, that the satisfaction is for him quite disinterested, implies in his judgment a ground of satisfaction for all men. For since it does not rest on any inclination of the subject (nor upon any other premeditated interest), but since the person who judges feels himself quite *free* as regards the satisfaction which he attaches to the object, he cannot find the ground of this satisfaction in any private conditions connected with his own subject, and hence it must be regarded as grounded on what he can presuppose in every other person. Consequently he must believe that he has reason for attributing a similar satisfaction to everyone. He will therefore speak of the beautiful as if beauty were a characteristic of the object and the judgment logical (constituting a cognition of the object by means of concepts of it), although it is only aesthetical and involves merely a reference of the representation of the object to the subject. For it has this similarity to a logical judgment that we can presuppose its validity for all men. But this universality cannot arise from concepts; for from concepts there is no transition to the feeling of pleasure or pain (except in pure practical laws, which bring an interest with them such as is not bound up with the pure judgment of taste). Consequently the judgment of taste, accompanied

with the consciousness of separation from all interest, must claim validity for every man, without this universality depending on objects. That is, there must be bound up with it a title to subjective universality.

VII. Comparison of the Beautiful with the Pleasant and the Good by Means of the Above Characteristic

As regards the pleasant, everyone is content that his judgment, which he bases upon private feeling and by which he says of an object that it pleases him, should be limited merely to his own person. Thus he is quite contented that if he says, "Canary wine is pleasant," another man may correct his expression and remind him that he ought to say, "It is pleasant *to me.*" And this is the case not only as regards the taste of the tongue, the palate, and the throat, but for whatever is pleasant to anyone's eyes and ears. To one, violet color is soft and lovely; to another, it is washed-out and dead. One man likes the tone of wind instruments, another that of strings. To strive here with the design of reproving as incorrect another man's judgment which is different from our own, as if the judgments were logically opposed, would be folly. As regards the pleasant, therefore, the fundamental proposition is valid: *everyone has his own taste* (the taste of sense).

The case is quite different with the beautiful. It would (on the contrary) be laughable if a man who imagined anything to his own taste thought to justify himself by saying: "This object (the house we see, the coat that person wears, the concert we hear, the poem submitted to our judgment) is beautiful *for me.*" For he must not call it *beautiful* if it merely pleases him. Many things may have for him charm and pleasantness—no one troubles himself at that—but if he gives out anything as beautiful, he supposes in others the same satisfaction; he judges not merely for himself, but for everyone, and speaks of beauty as if it were a property of things. Hence he says "the *thing* is beautiful"; and he does not count on the agreement of others with this his judgment of satisfaction, because he has found this agreement several times before, but he *demands* it of them. He blames them if they judge otherwise and he denies them taste, which he nevertheless requires from them. Here, then, we cannot say that each man has his own particular taste. For this would be as much as to say that there is no taste whatever, i.e. no aesthetical judgment which can make a rightful claim upon everyone's assent.

At the same time we find as regards the pleasant that there is an agreement among men in their judgments upon it in regard to which we deny taste to some and attribute it to others, by this not meaning one of our organic senses, but a

[3][Bernard] Ueberweg points out (*History of Philosophy,* Vol. II, p. 528, English translation) that Mendelssohn had already called attention to the disinterestedness of our satisfaction in the beautiful. "It appears," says Mendelssohn, "to be a particular mark of the beautiful, that it is contemplated with quiet satisfaction, that it pleases, even though it be not in our possession, and even though we be never so far removed from the desire to put it to our use." But, of course, as Ueberweg remarks, Kant's conception of disinterestedness extends far beyond the idea of merely not desiring to possess the object.

faculty of judging in respect of the pleasant generally. Thus we say of a man who knows how to entertain his guests with pleasures (of enjoyment for all the senses), so that they are all pleased, "he has taste." But here the universality is only taken comparatively; and there emerge rules which are only *general* (like all empirical ones), and not *universal,* which latter the judgment of taste upon the beautiful undertakes or lays claim to. It is a judgment in reference to sociability, so far as this rests on empirical rules. In respect of the good it is true that judgments make rightful claim to validity for everyone; but the good is represented only *by means of a concept* as the object of a universal satisfaction, which is the case neither with the pleasant nor with the beautiful.

VIII. The Universality of the Satisfaction Is Represented in a Judgment of Taste Only as Subjective

· · ·

In respect of logical quantity, all judgments of taste are *singular* judgments. For because I must refer the object immediately to my feeling of pleasure and pain, and that not by means of concepts, they cannot have the quantity of objective generally valid judgments. Nevertheless, if the singular representation of the object of the judgment of taste, in accordance with the conditions determining the latter, were transformed by comparison into a concept, a logically universal judgment could result therefrom. E.g., I describe by a judgment of taste the rose that I see as beautiful. But the judgment which results from the comparison of several singular judgments, "Roses in general are beautiful," is no longer described simply as aesthetical, but as a logical judgment based on an aesthetical one. Again the judgment, "The rose is pleasant" (to use) is, although aesthetical and singular, not a judgment of taste but of sense. It is distinguished from the former by the fact that the judgment of taste carries with it an *aesthetic quantity* of universality, i.e. of validity for everyone, which cannot be found in a judgment about the pleasant. It is only judgments about the good which, although they also determine satisfaction in an object, have logical and not merely aesthetical universality, for they are valid of the object as cognitive of it, and thus are valid for everyone.

If we judge objects merely according to concepts, then all representation of beauty is lost. Thus there can be no rule according to which anyone is to be forced to recognize anything as beautiful. We cannot press upon others by the aid of any reasons or fundamental propositions our judgment that a coat, a house, or a flower is beautiful. People wish to submit the object to their own eyes, as if the satisfaction in it depended on sensation; and yet, if we then call the object beautiful, we believe that we speak with a universal voice, and we claim the assent of everyone, although on the contrary all private sensation can only decide for the observer himself and his satisfaction.

We may see now that in the judgment of taste nothing is postulated but such a *universal voice,* in respect of the satisfaction without the intervention of concepts, and thus the *possibility* of an aesthetical judgment that can, at the same time, be regarded as valid for everyone. The judgment of taste itself does not *postulate* the agreement of everyone (for that can only be done by a logically universal judgment because it can adduce reasons); it only *imputes* this agreement to everyone, as a case of the rule in respect of which it expects, not confirmation by concepts, but assent from others. The universal voice is, therefore, only an idea (we do not yet inquire upon what it rests). It may be uncertain whether or not the man who believes that he is laying down a judgment of taste is, as a matter of fact, judging in conformity with that idea; but that he refers his judgment thereto, and consequently that it is intended to be a judgment of taste, he announces by the expression "beauty." He can be quite certain of this for himself by the mere consciousness of the separating off everything belonging to the pleasant and the good from the satisfaction which is left; and this is all for which he promises himself the agreement of everyone—a claim which would be justifiable under these conditions, provided only he did not often make mistakes, and thus lay down an erroneous judgment of taste.

IX. Investigation of the Question Whether in the Judgment of Taste the Feeling of Pleasure Precedes or Follows the Judging of the Object

· · ·

If the given representation which occasions the judgment of taste were a concept uniting understanding and imagination in the judging of the object, into a cognition of the object, the consciousness of this relation would be intellectual (as in the objective schematism of the judgment of which the *Critique*[4] treats). But then the judgment would not be laid down in reference to pleasure and pain, and consequently would not be a judgment of taste. But the judgment of taste, independently of concepts, determines the object in respect of satisfaction and of the predicate of beauty. Therefore that subjective unity of relation can only make itself known by means of sensation. The excitement of both faculties

---

[4][Bernard] *Critique of Pure Reason,* "Analytic," Book II, Chapter 1.

(imagination and understanding) to indeterminate but yet, through the stimulus of the given sensation, harmonious activity, viz. that which belongs to cognition in general, is the sensation whose universal communicability is postulated by the judgment of taste. An objective relation can only be thought, but yet, so far as it is subjective according to its conditions, can be felt in its effect on the mind; and, of a relation based on no concept (like the relation of the representative powers to a cognitive faculty in general), no other consciousness is possible than that through the sensation of the effect, which consists in the more lively play of both mental powers (the imagination and the understanding) when animated by mutual agreement. A representation which, as individual and apart from comparison with others, yet has an agreement with the conditions of universality which it is the business of the understanding to supply, brings the cognitive faculties into that proportionate accord which we require for all cognition, and so regard as holding for everyone who is determined to judge by means of understanding and sense in combination (i.e. for every man).

Explanation of the Beautiful Resulting from the Second Moment

The *beautiful* is that which pleases universally without requiring a concept.

Third Moment

of Judgments of Taste, According to the Relation of the Purposes Which Are Brought Into Consideration in Them

. . .

XI. The Judgment of Taste Has Nothing at Its Basis but the Form of the Purposiveness of an Object (or of Its Mode of Representation)

Every purpose, if it be regarded as a ground of satisfaction, always carries with it an interest—as the determining ground of the judgment—about the object of pleasure. Therefore no subjective purpose can lie at the basis of the judgment of taste. But also the judgment of taste can be determined by no representation of an objective purpose, i.e. of the possibility of the object itself in accordance with principles of purposive combination, and consequently by no concept of the good, because it is an aesthetical and not a cognitive judgment. It

therefore has to do with no *concept* of the character and internal or external possibility of the object by means of this or that cause, but merely with the relation of the representative powers to one another, so far as they are determined by a representation.

Now this relation in the determination of an object as beautiful is bound up with the feeling of pleasure, which is declared by the judgment of taste to be valid for everyone; hence a pleasantness merely accompanying the representation can as little contain the determining ground of the judgment as the representation of the perfection of the object and the concept of the good can. Therefore it can be nothing else than the subjective purposiveness in the representation of an object without any purpose (either objective or subjective), and thus it is the mere form of purposiveness in the representation by which an object is *given* to us, so far as we are conscious of it, which constitutes the satisfaction that we without a concept judge to be universally communicable; and, consequently, this is the determining ground of the judgment of taste.

. . .

XIII. The Pure Judgment of Taste Is Independent of Charm and Emotion

Every interest spoils the judgment of taste and takes from its impartiality, especially if the purposiveness is not, as with the interest of reason, placed before the feeling of pleasure but grounded on it. This last always happens in an aesthetical judgment upon anything, so far as it gratifies or grieves us. Hence judgments so affected can lay no claim at all to a universally valid satisfaction, or at least so much the less claim, in proportion as there are sensations of this sort among the determining grounds of taste. That taste is always barbaric which needs a mixture of *charms* and *emotions* in order that there may be satisfaction, and still more so if it make these the measure of its assent.

Nevertheless charms are often not only taken account of in the case of beauty (which properly speaking ought merely to be concerned with form) as contributory to the aesthetical universal satisfaction, but they are passed off as in themselves beauties; and thus the matter of satisfaction is substituted for the form. This misconception, however, which like so many others, has something true at its basis, may be removed by a careful determination of these concepts.

A judgment of taste on which charm and emotion have no influence (although they may be bound up with the satisfaction in the beautiful)—which therefore has as its determining ground merely the purposiveness of the form—is a *pure judgment of taste.*

XIV. Elucidation by Means of Examples

Aesthetical judgments can be divided just like theoretical (logical) judgments into empirical and pure. The first assert pleasantness or unpleasantness; the second assert the beauty of an object or of the manner of representing it. The former are judgments of sense (material aesthetical judgments); the latter as formal are alone strictly judgments of taste.

A judgment of taste is therefore pure only so far as no merely empirical satisfaction is mingled with its determining ground. But this always happens if charm or emotion have any share in the judgment by which anything is to be described as beautiful.

Now here many objections present themselves which, fallaciously, put forward charm not merely as a necessary ingredient of beauty, but as alone sufficient to justify a thing's being called beautiful. A mere color, e.g. the green of a grass plot, a mere tone (as distinguished from sound and noise), like that of a violin, are by most people described as beautiful in themselves, although both seem to have at their basis merely the matter of representations, viz. simply sensation, and therefore only deserve to be called pleasant. But we must at the same time remark that the sensations of colors and of tone have a right to be regarded as beautiful only in so far as they are *pure.* This is a determination which concerns their form and is the only element of these representations which admits with certainty of universal communicability; for we cannot assume that the quality of sensations is the same in all subjects, and we can hardly say that the pleasantness of one color or the tone of one musical instrument is judged preferable to that of another in the same way by everyone.

If we assume with Euler that colors are isochronous vibrations (*pulsus*) of the ether, as sounds are of the air in a state of disturbance, and—what is the most important—that the mind not only perceives by sense the effect of these in exciting the organ, but also perceives by reflection the regular play of impressions (and thus the form of the combination of different representations)—which I very much doubt—then colors and tone cannot be reckoned as mere sensations, but as the formal determination of the unity of a manifold of sensations, and thus as beauties.

But "pure" in a simple mode of sensation means that its uniformity is troubled and interrupted by no foreign sensation, and it belongs merely to the form; because here we can abstract from the quality of that mode of sensation (abstract from the colors and tone, if any, which it represents).

Hence all simple colors, so far as they are pure, are regarded as beautiful; composite colors have not this advantage because, as they are not simple, we have no standard for judging whether they should be called pure or not.

But as regards the beauty attributed to the object on account of its form, to suppose it to be capable of augmentation through the charm of the object is a common error and one very prejudicial to genuine, uncorrupted, well-founded taste. We can doubtless add these charms to beauty, in order to interest the mind by the representation of the object, apart from the bare satisfaction received, and thus they may serve as a recommendation of taste and its cultivation, especially when it is yet crude and unexercised. But they actually do injury to the judgment of taste if they draw attention to themselves as the grounds for judging of beauty. So far are they from adding to beauty that they must only be admitted by indulgence as aliens, and provided always that they do not disturb the beautiful form in cases when taste is yet weak and unexercised.

In painting, sculpture, and in all the formative arts—in architecture and horticulture, so far as they are beautiful arts—the *delineation* is the essential thing; and here it is not what gratifies in sensation but what pleases by means of its form that is fundamental for taste. The colors which light up the sketch belong to the charm; they may indeed enliven the object for sensation, but they cannot make it worthy of contemplation and beautiful. In most cases they are rather limited by the requirements of the beautiful form, and even where charm is permissible it is ennobled solely by this.

Every form of the objects of sense (both of external sense and also mediately of internal) is either *figure* or *play.* In the latter case it is either play of figures (in space, viz. pantomime and dancing) or the mere play of sensations (in time). The *charm* of colors or of the pleasant tones of an instrument may be added, but the *delineation* in the first case and the composition in the second constitute the proper object of the pure judgment of taste. To say that the purity of colors and of tones, or their variety and contrast, seem to add to beauty does not mean that they supply a homogeneous addition to our satisfaction in the form because they are pleasant in themselves; but they do so because they make the form more exactly, definitely, and completely, intuitible, and besides, by their charm excite the representation, while they awaken and fix our attention on the object itself.

Even what we call "ornaments" [*parerga*], i.e. those things which do not belong to the complete representation of the object internally as elements, but only externally as complements, and which augment the satisfaction of taste, do so only by their form; as, for example, the frames of pictures or the draperies of statues or the colonnades of palaces. But if the ornament does not itself consist in beautiful form, and if it is used as a golden frame is used, merely to recommend the painting by its *charm,* it is then called *finery* and injures genuine beauty.

Emotion, that is, a sensation in which pleasantness is produced by means of a momentary checking and a consequent more powerful outflow of the vital force, does not belong at all to beauty. But sublimity [with which the feeling of emotion is bound up] requires a different standard of judgment from that which is at the foundation of taste; and thus a pure judgment of taste has for its determining ground neither charm nor emotion—in a word, no sensation as the material of aesthetical judgment.

XV. The Judgment of Taste Is Quite Independent of the Concept of Perfection

Objective purposiveness can only be cognized by means of the reference of the manifold to a definite purpose, and therefore only through a concept. From this alone it is plain that the beautiful, the judging of which has at its basis a merely formal purposiveness, i.e. a purposiveness without purpose, is quite independent of the concept of the good, because the latter presupposes an objective purposiveness, i.e. the reference of the object to a definite purpose.

Objective purposiveness is either external, i.e. the *utility,* or internal, i.e. the *perfection* of the object. That the satisfaction in an object, on account of which we call it beautiful, cannot rest on the representation of its utility is sufficiently obvious from the two preceding sections; because in that case it would not be an immediate satisfaction in the object, which is the essential condition of a judgment about beauty. But objective internal purposiveness, i.e. perfection, comes nearer to the predicate of beauty; and it has been regarded by celebrated philosophers[5] as the same as beauty, with the proviso, *if it is thought in a confused way.* It is of the greatest importance in a critique of taste to decide whether beauty can thus actually be resolved into the concept of perfection.

To judge of objective purposiveness we always need, not only the concept of a purpose, but (if that purposiveness is not to be external utility but internal) the concept of an internal purpose which shall contain the ground of the internal possibility of the object. Now as a purpose in general is that whose *concept* can be regarded as the ground of the pos-

sibility of the object itself; so, in order to represent objective purposiveness in a thing, the concept of *what sort of thing it is to be* must come first. The agreement of the manifold in it with this concept (which furnishes the rule for combining the manifold) is the *qualitative perfection* of the thing. Quite different from this is *quantitative* perfection, the completeness of a thing after its kind, which is a mere concept of magnitude (of totality).[6] In this *what the thing ought to be* is conceived as already determined, and it is only asked if it has *all* its requisites. The formal element in the representation of a thing, i.e. the agreement of the manifold with a unity (it being undetermined what this ought to be), gives to cognition no objective purposiveness whatever. For since abstraction is made of this unity as *purpose* (what the thing ought to be), nothing remains but the subjective purposeness of the representations in the mind of the intuiting subject. And this, although it furnishes a certain purposiveness of the representative state of the subject, and so a facility of apprehending a given form by the imagination, yet furnishes no perfection of an object, since the object is not here conceived by means of the concept of a purpose. For example, if in a forest I come across a plot of sward around which trees stand in a circle and do not then represent to myself a purpose, viz. that it is intended to serve for country dances, not the least concept of perfection is furnished by the mere form. But to represent to oneself a formal *objective* purposiveness without purpose, i.e. the mere form of a *perfection* (without any matter and without the *concept* of that with which it is accordant, even if it were merely the idea of conformity to law in general), is a veritable contradiction.

Now the judgment of taste is an aesthetical judgment, i.e. such as rests on subjective grounds, the determining ground of which cannot be a concept, and consequently cannot be the concept of a definite purpose. Therefore by means of beauty, regarded as a formal subjective purposiveness, there is in no way thought a perfection of the object, as a purposiveness alleged to be formal but which is yet objective. And thus to distinguish between the concepts of the beautiful and the good as if they were only different in logical form, the first being a confused, the second a clear concept of perfection, but identical in content and origin, is quite fallacious. For then there would be no *specific* difference be-

---

[5][Bernard] Kant probably refers here to Baumgarten (1714–62), who was the first writer to give the name of aesthetics to the philosophy of taste. He defined beauty as "perfection apprehended through the senses." Kant is said to have used as a textbook at lectures a work by Meier, a pupil of Baumgarten's, on this subject.

[6][Bernard] Cf. Preface to the *Metaphysical Elements of Ethics,* p. v: "The word *perfection* is liable to many misconceptions. It is sometimes understood as a concept belonging to transcendental philosophy; viz. the concept of the *totality* of the manifold, which, taken together, constitutes a thing; sometimes, again, it is understood as belonging to teleology, so that it signifies the agreement of the characteristics of a thing with a *purpose.* Perfection in the former sense might be called *quantitative* (material), in the latter *qualitative* (formal), perfection."

tween them, but a judgment of taste would be as much a cognitive judgment as the judgment by which a thing is described as good; just as when the ordinary man says that fraud is unjust he bases his judgment on confused grounds, while the philosopher bases it on clear grounds, but both on identical principles of reason. I have already, however, said that an aesthetical judgment is unique of its kind and gives absolutely no cognition (not even a confused cognition) of the object; this is only supplied by a logical judgment. On the contrary, it simply refers the representation, by which an object is given, to the subject, and brings to our notice no characteristic of the object, but only the purposive form in the determination of the representative powers which are occupying themselves therewith. The judgment is called aesthetical just because its determining ground is not a concept, but the feeling (of internal sense) of that harmony in the play of the mental powers, so far as it can be felt in sensation. On the other hand, if we wish to call confused concepts and the objective judgment based on them aesthetical, we will have an understanding judging sensibly or a sense representing its objects by means of concepts both of which are contradictory. The faculty of concepts, be they confused or clear, is the understanding; and although understanding has to do with the judgment of taste as an aesthetical judgment (as it has with all judgments), yet it has to do with it, not as a faculty by which an object is cognized, but as the faculty which determines the judgment and its representation (without any concept) in accordance with its relation to the subject and the subject's internal feeling, in so far as this judgment may be possible in accordance with a universal rule.

XVI. The Judgment of Taste, by Which an Object Is Declared to Be Beautiful Under the Condition of a Definite Concept, Is Not Pure

There are two kinds of beauty: free beauty (*pulchritudo vaga*), or merely dependent beauty (*pulchritudo adhaerens*). The first presupposes no concept of what the object ought to be; the second does presuppose such a concept and the perfection of the object in accordance therewith. The first is called the (self-subsistent) beauty of this or that thing; the second, as dependent upon a concept (conditioned beauty), is ascribed to objects which come under the concept of a particular purpose.

Flowers are free natural beauties. Hardly anyone but a botanist knows what sort of a thing a flower ought to be; and even he, though recognizing in the flower the reproductive organ of the plant, pays no regard to this natural purpose if he is passing judgment on the flower by taste. There is, then, at the basis of this judgment no perfection of any kind, no

internal purposiveness, to which the collection of the manifold is referred. Many birds (such as the parrot, the hummingbird, the bird of paradise) and many sea shells are beauties, in themselves, which do not belong to any object determined in respect of its purpose by concepts, but please freely and in themselves. So also delineations *à la grecque,* foliage for borders or wall papers, mean nothing in themselves; they represent nothing—no object under a definite concept—and are free beauties. We can refer to the same class what are called in music fantasies (i.e. pieces without any theme), and in fact all music without words.

In the judging of a free beauty (according to the mere form), the judgment of taste is pure. There is presupposed no concept of any purpose which the manifold of the given object is to serve, and which therefore is to be represented in it. By such a concept the freedom of the imagination which disports itself in the contemplation of the figure would be only limited.

But human beauty (i.e. of a man, a woman, or a child), the beauty of a horse, or a building (be it church, palace, arsenal, or summer house), presupposes a concept of the purpose which determines what the thing is to be, and consequently a concept of its perfection; it is therefore adherent beauty. Now as the combination of the pleasant (in sensation) with beauty, which properly is only concerned with form, is a hindrance to the purity of the judgment of taste, so also is its purity injured by the combination with beauty of the good (viz. that manifold which is good for the thing itself in accordance with its purpose).

We could add much to a building which would immediately please the eye if only it were not to be a church. We could adorn a figure with all kinds of spirals and light but regular lines, as the New Zealanders do with their tattooing, if only it were not the figure of a human being. And again this could have much finer features and a more pleasing and gentle cast of countenance provided it were not intended to represent a man, much less a warrior.

Now the satisfaction in the manifold of a thing in reference to the internal purpose which determines its possibility is a satisfaction grounded on a concept; but the satisfaction in beauty is such as presupposes no concept, but is immediately bound up with the representation through which the object is given (not through which it is thought). If now the judgment of taste in respect of the beauty of a thing is made dependent on the purpose in its manifold, like a judgment of reason, and thus limited, it is no longer a free and pure judgment of taste.

It is true that taste gains by this combination of aesthetical with intellectual satisfaction, inasmuch as it becomes fixed; and though it is not universal, yet in respect to certain purposively determined objects it becomes possible to prescribe rules for it. These, however, are not rules of taste, but merely rules for the unification of taste with reason, i.e. of the beautiful with the good, by which the former becomes available as an instrument of design in respect of the latter. Thus the tone of mind which is self-maintaining and of subjective universal validity is subordinated to the way of thinking which can be maintained only by painful resolve, but is of objective universal validity. Properly speaking, however, perfection gains nothing by beauty, or beauty by perfection; but when we compare the representation by which an object is given to us with the object (as regards what it ought to be) by means of a concept, we cannot avoid considering along with it the sensation in the subject. And thus when both states of mind are in harmony our *whole faculty* of representative power gains.

A judgment of taste, then, in respect of an object with a definite internal purpose, can only be pure if either the person judging has no concept of this purpose or else abstracts from it in his judgment. Such a person, although forming an accurate judgment of taste in judging of the object as free beauty, would yet by another who considers the beauty in it only as a dependent attribute (who looks to the purpose of the object) be blamed and accused of false taste, although both are right in their own way—the one in reference to what he has before his eyes, the other in reference to what he has in his thought. By means of this distinction we can settle many disputes about beauty between judges of taste, by showing that the one is speaking of free, the other of dependent, beauty—that the first is making a pure, the second an applied, judgment of taste.

XVII. Of the Ideal of Beauty

There can be no objective rule of taste which shall determine by means of concepts what is beautiful. For every judgment from this source is aesthetical; i.e. the feeling of the subject, and not a concept of the object, is its determining ground. To seek for a principle of taste which shall furnish, by means of definite concepts, a universal criterion of the beautiful is fruitless trouble, because what is sought is impossible and self-contradictory. The universal communicability of sensation (satisfaction or dissatisfaction) without the aid of a concept—the agreement, as far as is possible, of all times and peoples as regards this feeling in the representation of certain objects—this is the empirical criterion, although weak and hardly sufficing for probability, of the derivation of a taste, thus confirmed by examples, from the deep-lying general grounds of agreement in judging of the forms under which objects are given.

Hence we consider some products of taste as *exemplary*. Not that taste can be acquired by imitating others, for it must

be an original faculty. He who imitates a model shows no doubt, in so far as he attains to it, skill; but only shows taste in so far as he can judge of this model itself.[7] It follows from hence that the highest model, the archetype of taste, is a mere idea, which everyone must produce in himself and according to which he must judge every object of taste, every example of judgment by taste, and even the taste of everyone. *Idea* properly means a rational concept, and *ideal* the representation of an individual being, regarded as adequate to an idea.[8] Hence that archetype of taste, which certainly rests on the indeterminate idea that reason has of a maximum, but which cannot be represented by concepts but only in an individual presentation, is better called the ideal of the beautiful. Although we are not in possession of this, we yet strive to produce it in ourselves. But it can only be an ideal of the imagination, because it rests on a presentation and not on concepts, and the imagination is the faculty of presentation. How do we arrive at such an ideal of beauty? A priori, or empirically? Moreover, what species of the beautiful is susceptible of an ideal?

First, it is well to remark that the beauty for which an ideal is to be sought cannot be *vague* beauty, but is *fixed* by a concept of objective purposiveness; and thus it cannot appertain to the object of a quite pure judgment of taste, but to that of a judgment of taste which is in part intellectual. That is, in whatever grounds of judgment an ideal is to be found, an idea of reason in accordance with definite concepts must lie at its basis, which determines a priori the purpose on which the internal possibility of the object rests. An ideal of beautiful flowers, of a beautiful piece of furniture, of a beautiful view, is inconceivable. But neither can an ideal be represented of a beauty dependent on definite purposes, e.g. of a beautiful dwelling house, a beautiful tree, a beautiful garden, etc.; presumably because their purpose is not sufficiently determined and fixed by the concept, and thus the purposiveness is nearly as free as in the case of *vague* beauty. The only being which has the purpose of its existence in itself is *man,* who can determine his purposes by reason; or, where he must receive them from external perception, yet can compare them with essential and universal purposes and can judge this their accordance aesthetically. This *man* is,

---

[7][Kant] Models of taste as regards the arts of speech must be composed in a dead and learned language. The first in order that they may not suffer that change which inevitably comes over living languages, in which noble expressions become flat, common ones antiquated, and newly created ones have only a short circulation. The second because learned languages have a grammar which is subject to no wanton change of fashion, but the rules of which are preserved unchanged.

[8][Bernard] This distinction between an *idea* and an *ideal,* as also the further contrast between ideals of the reason and ideals of the imagination, had already been given by Kant in the *Critique of Pure Reason,* "Dialectic," Book II, Chapter 3, Section 1.

then, alone of all objects in the world, susceptible of an ideal of *beauty,* as it is only *humanity* in his person, as an intelligence, that is susceptible of the ideal of *perfection.*

But there are here two elements. *First,* there is the aesthetical *normal idea,* which is an individual intuition (of the imagination), representing the standard of our judgment upon man as a thing belonging to a particular animal species. *Secondly,* there is the *rational idea* which makes the purposes of humanity, so far as they cannot be sensibly represented the principle for judging of a figure through which, as their phenomenal effect, those purposes are revealed. The normal idea of the figure of an animal of a particular race must take its elements from experience. But the greatest purposiveness in the construction of the figure that would be available for the universal standard of aesthetical judgment upon each individual of this species—the image which is as it were designedly at the basis of nature's technique, to which only the whole race and not any isolated individual is adequate—this lies merely in the idea of the judging subject. And this, with its proportions as an aesthetical idea, can be completely presented *in concreto* in a model. In order to make intelligible in some measure (for who can extract her whole secret from nature?) how this comes to pass, we shall attempt a psychological explanation.

We must remark that, in a way quite incomprehensible by us, the imagination cannot only recall on occasion the signs for concepts long past, but can also reproduce the image of the figure of the object out of an unspeakable number of objects of different kinds or even of the same kind. Further, if the mind is concerned with comparisons, the imagination can, in all probability, actually, though unconsciously, let one image glide into another; and thus, by the concurrence of several of the same kind, come by an average, which serves as the common measure of all. Everyone has seen a thousand full-grown men. Now if you wish to judge of their normal size, estimating it by means of comparison, the imagination (as I think) allows a great number of images (perhaps the whole thousand) to fall on one another. If I am allowed to apply here the analogy of optical presentation, it is in the space where most of them are combined and inside the contour, where the place is illuminated with the most vivid colors, that the *average size* is cognizable, which, both in height and breadth, is equally far removed from the extreme bounds of the greatest and smallest stature. And this is the stature of a beautiful man. (We could arrive at the same thing mechanically by adding together all thousand magnitudes, heights, breadths, and thicknesses, and dividing the sum by a thousand. But the imagination does this by means of a dynamical effect, which arises from the various impressions of such figures on the organ of internal sense.) If now, in a similar way, for this average man we

seek the average head, for this head the average nose, etc., such figure is at the basis of the normal idea in the country where the comparison is instituted. Thus necessarily under these empirical conditions a Negro must have a different normal idea of the beauty of the human figure from a white man, a Chinaman a different normal idea from a European, etc. And the same is the case with the model of a beautiful horse or dog (of a certain breed). This *normal idea* is not derived from proportions gotten from experience [and regarded] *as definite rules,* but in accordance with it rules for judging become in the first instance possible. It is the image for the whole race, which floats among all the variously different intuitions of individuals, which nature takes as archetype in her productions of the same species, but which appears not to be fully reached in an individual case. It is by no means the whole *archetype of beauty* in the race, but only the form constituting the indispensable condition of all beauty, and thus merely *correctness* in the mental presentation of the race. It is, like the celebrated *Doryphorus* of Polycletus,[9] the *rule* (Myron's *Cow*[10] might also be used thus for its kind). It can therefore contain nothing specifically characteristic, for otherwise it would not be the *normal idea* for the race. Its presentation pleases, not by its beauty, but merely because it contradicts no condition, under which alone a thing of this kind can be beautiful. The presentation is merely correct.[11]

We must yet distinguish the *normal idea* of the beautiful from the *ideal,* which latter, on grounds already alleged, we can only expect in the *human* figure. In this the ideal consists in the expression of the *moral,* without which the object would not please universally and thus positively (not merely negatively in an accurate presentation). The visible expression of moral ideas that rule men inwardly can indeed only be gotten from experience; but to make its connection with all which our reason unites with the morally good in the idea of the highest purposiveness—goodness of heart, pu-

---

9[Bernard] Polycletus of Argos flourished about 430 B.C. His statue of the *Spearbearer* (*Doryphorus*) afterward became known as the *Canon,* because in it the artist was supposed to have embodied a perfect representation of the ideal of the human figure.

10[Bernard] This was a celebrated statue executed by Myron, a Greek sculptor, contemporary with Polycletus.

11[Kant] It will be found that a perfectly regular countenance, such as a painter might wish to have for a model, ordinarily tells us nothing because it contains nothing characteristic, and therefore rather expresses the idea of the race than the specific traits of a person. The exaggeration of a characteristic of this kind, i.e. such as does violence to the normal idea (the purposiveness of the race), is called *caricature.* Experience also shows that these quite regular countenances commonly indicate internally only a mediocre man, presumably (if it may be assumed that external nature expresses the proportions of internal) because, if no mental disposition exceeds that proportion which is requisite in order to constitute a man free from faults, nothing can be expected of what is called *genius,* in which nature seems to depart from the ordinary relations of the mental powers on behalf of some special one.

rity, strength, peace, etc.—visible as it were in bodily mani-festation (as the effect of that which is internal) requires a union of pure ideas of reason with great imaginative power even in him who wishes to judge of it, still more in him who wishes to present it. The correctness of such an ideal of beauty is shown by its permitting no sensible charm to min-gle with the satisfaction in the object, and yet allowing us to take a great interest therein. This shows that a judgment in accordance with such a standard can never be purely aes-thetical, and that a judgment in accordance with an ideal of beauty is not a mere judgment of taste.

Explanation of the Beautiful Derived from This Third Moment

Beauty is the form of the *purposiveness* of an object, so far as this is perceived in it *without any representation of a purpose.*[12]

Second Book

Analytic of the Sublime

XXIII. Transition from the Faculty Which Judges of the Beautiful to That Which Judges of the Sublime

The beautiful and the sublime agree in this that both please in themselves. Further, neither presupposes a judgment of sense nor a judgment logically determined, but a judgment of reflection. Consequently the satisfaction belonging to them does not depend on a sensation, as in the case of the pleasant, nor on a definite concept, as in the case of the good; but it is nevertheless referred to concepts, although indeter-minate ones. And so the satisfaction is connected with the mere presentation of the object or with the faculty of pre-sentation, so that in the case of a given intuition this faculty or the imagination is considered as in agreement with the *faculty of concepts* of understanding or reason, regarded as promoting these latter. Hence both kinds of judgments are *singular,* and yet announce themselves as universally valid

for every subject; although they lay claim merely to the feel-ing of pleasure, and not to any cognition of the object.

But there are also remarkable differences between the two. The beautiful in nature is connected with the form of the object, which consists in having definite boundaries. The sublime, on the other hand, is to be found in a formless ob-ject, so far as in it or by occasion of it *boundlessness* is rep-resented, and yet its totality is also present to thought. Thus the beautiful seems to be regarded as the presentation of an indefinite concept of understanding, the sublime as that of a like concept of reason. There the satisfaction in the one case is bound up with the representation of *quality,* in the other with that of *quantity.* And the latter satisfaction is quite dif-ferent in kind from the former, for this [the beautiful] directly brings with it a feeling of the furtherance of life, and thus is compatible with charms and with the play of the imagina-tion. But the other the feeling of the sublime is a pleasure that arises only indirectly; viz. it is produced by the feeling of a momentary checking of the vital powers and a conse-quent stronger outflow of them, so that it seems to be re-garded as emotion—not play, but earnest in the exercise of the imagination. Hence it is incompatible with physical charm; and as the mind is not merely attracted by the object but is ever being alternately repelled, the satisfaction in the sublime does not so much involve the positive pleasure as admiration or respect, which rather deserves to be called negative pleasure.

But the inner and most important distinction between the sublime and beautiful is, certainly, as follows. (Here, as we are entitled to do, we only bring under consideration in the first instance the sublime in natural objects, for the sub-lime of art is always limited by the conditions of agreement with nature.) Natural beauty (which is independent) brings with it a purposiveness in its form by which the object seems to be, as it were, preadapted to our judgment, and thus con-stitutes in itself an object of satisfaction. On the other hand, that which excites in us, without any reasoning about it, but in the mere apprehension of it, the feeling of the sublime may appear, as regards its form, to violate purpose in respect of the judgment, to be unsuited to our presentative faculty, and as it were to do violence to the imagination; and yet it is judged to be only the more sublime.

Now we may see from this that, in general, we express ourselves incorrectly if we call any *object of nature* sublime, although we can quite correctly call many objects of nature beautiful. For how can that be marked by an expression of approval which is apprehended in itself as being a violation of purpose? All that we can say is that the object is fit for the presentation of a sublimity which can be found in the mind, for no sensible form can contain the sublime properly so-called. This concerns only ideas of the reason which, al-

---

[12][Kant] It might be objected to this explanation that there are things in which we see a purposive form without cognizing any purpose in them, like the stone implements often gotten from old sepulchral tumuli with a hole in them, as if for a handle. These, although they plainly indicate by their shape a purposiveness of which we do not know the purpose, are nevertheless not described as beautiful. But if we regard a thing as a work of art, that is enough to make us admit that its shape has reference to some design and definite purpose. And hence there is no immediate satisfaction in the con-templation of it. On the other hand a flower, e.g. a tulip, is regarded as beau-tiful, because in perceiving it we find a certain purposiveness which, in our judgment, is referred to no purpose at all.

though no adequate presentation is possible for them, by this inadequateness that admits of sensible presentation are aroused and summoned into the mind. Thus the wide ocean, disturbed by the storm, cannot be called sublime. Its aspect is horrible; and the mind must be already filled with manifold ideas if it is to be determined by such an intuition to a feeling itself sublime, as it is incited to abandon sensibility and to busy itself with ideas that involve higher purposiveness.

Independent natural beauty discovers to us a technique of nature which represents it as a system in accordance with laws, the principle of which we do not find in the whole of our faculty of understanding. That principle is the principle of purposiveness, in respect of the use of our judgment in regard to phenomena, which requires that these must not be judged as merely belonging to nature in its purposeless mechanism, but also as belonging to something analogous to art. It therefore actually extends, not indeed our cognition of natural objects, but our concept of nature, which is now not regarded as mere mechanism but as art. This leads to profound investigations as to the possibility of such a form. But in what we are accustomed to call sublime there is nothing at all that leads to particular objective principles and forms of nature corresponding to them; so far from it that, for the most part, nature excites the ideas of the sublime in its chaos or in its wildest and most irregular disorder and desolation, provided size and might are perceived. Hence, we see that the concept of the sublime is not nearly so important or rich in consequences as the concept of the beautiful; and that, in general, it displays nothing purposive in nature itself, but only in that possible use of our intuitions of it by which there is produced in us a feeling of a purposiveness quite independent of nature. We must seek a ground external to ourselves for the beautiful of nature, but seek it for the sublime merely in ourselves and in our attitude of thought, which introduces sublimity into the representation of nature. This is a very needful preliminary remark, which quite separates the ideas of the sublime from that of a purposiveness of *nature* and makes the theory of the sublime a mere appendix to the aesthetical judging of that purposiveness, because by means of it no particular form is represented in nature, but there is only developed a purposive use which the imagination makes of its representation.

XXIV. Of the Divisions of an Investigation into the Feeling of the Sublime

. . .

But the analysis of the sublime involves a division not needed in the case of the beautiful, viz. a division into the *mathematically* and the *dynamically sublime.*

For the feeling of the sublime brings with it as its characteristic feature a *movement* of the mind bound up with the judging of the object, while in the case of the beautiful taste presupposes and maintains the mind in *restful* contemplation. Now this movement ought to be judged as subjectively purposive (because the sublime pleases us), and thus it is referred through the imagination either to the *faculty of cognition* or *of desire.* In either reference the purposiveness of the given representation ought to be judged only in respect of this *faculty* (without purpose or interest), but in the first case it is ascribed to the object as a *mathematical* determination of the imagination, in the second as *dynamical.* And hence we have this twofold way of representing the sublime.

A. Of the Mathematically Sublime

XXV. Explanation of the Term Sublime

We call that *sublime* which is *absolutely great.* But to be great and to be a great something are quite different concepts (*magnitudo* and *quantitas*). In like manner to say simply (*simpliciter*) that anything is *great* is quite different from saying that it is *absolutely great* (*absolute, non comparative magnum*). The latter is *what is great beyond all comparison.* What now is meant by the expression that anything is great or small or of medium size? It is not a pure concept of understanding that is thus signified; still less is it an intuition of sense; and just as little is it a concept of reason, because it brings with it no principle of cognition. It must therefore be a concept of judgment or derived from one, and a subjective purposiveness of the representation in reference to the judgment must lie at its basis. That anything is a magnitude (*quantum*) may be cognized from the thing itself, without any comparison of it with other things, viz. if there is a multiplicity of the homogeneous constituting one thing. But to cognize *how great* it is always requires some other magnitude as a measure. But because the judging of magnitude depends, not merely on multiplicity (number), but also on the magnitude of the unit (the measure), and since, to judge of the magnitude of this latter again requires another as measure with which it may be compared, we see that the determination of the magnitude of phenomena can supply no absolute concept whatever of magnitude, but only a comparative one.

If now I say simply that anything is great, it appears that I have no comparison in view, at least none with an objective measure, because it is thus not determined at all how great the object is. But although the standard of comparison is merely subjective, yet the judgment nonetheless claims universal assent; "this man is beautiful" and "he is tall" are judgments, not limited merely to the judging subject, but, like theoretical judgments, demanding the assent of everyone.

In a judgment by which anything is designated simply as great, it is not merely meant that the object has a magnitude, but that this magnitude is superior to that of many other objects of the same kind, without, however, any exact determination of this superiority. Thus there is always at the basis of our judgment a standard which we assume as the same for everyone; this, however, is not available for any logical (mathematically definite) judging of magnitude, but only for aesthetical judging of the same, because it is a merely subjective standard lying at the basis of the reflective judgment upon magnitude. It may be empirical, as, e.g., the average size of the men known to us, of animals of a certain kind, trees, houses, mountains, etc. Or it may be a standard given a priori which, through the defects of the judging subject, is limited by the subjective conditions of presentation *in concreto*, as, e.g., in the practical sphere, the greatness of a certain virtue or of the public liberty and justice in a country, or, in the theoretical sphere, the greatness of the accuracy or the inaccuracy of an observation or measurement that has been made, etc.

Here it is remarkable that, although we have no interest whatever in an object—i.e. its existence is indifferent to us—yet its mere size, even if it is considered as formless, may bring a satisfaction with it that is universally communicable and that consequently involves the consciousness of a subjective purposiveness in the use of our cognitive faculty. This is not indeed a satisfaction in the object (because it may be formless), as in the case of the beautiful, in which the reflective judgment finds itself purposively determined in reference to cognition in general, but a satisfaction in the extension of the imagination by itself.

If (under the above limitation) we say simply of an object "it is great," this is no mathematically definite judgment, but a mere judgment of reflection upon the representation of it, which is subjectively purposive for a certain use of our cognitive powers in the estimation of magnitude; and we always then bind up with the representation a kind of respect, as also a kind of contempt, for what we simply call "small." Further, the judging of things as great or small extends to everything, even to all their characteristics; thus we describe beauty as great or small. The reason of this is to be sought in the fact that whatever we present in intuition according to the precept of the judgment (and thus represent aesthetically) is always a phenomenon, and thus a quantum.

But if we call anything, not only great, but absolutely great in every point of view (great beyond all comparison), i.e. sublime, we soon see that it is not permissible to seek for an adequate standard of this outside itself, but merely in it-

self. It is a magnitude which is like itself alone. It follows hence that the sublime is not to be sought in the things of nature, but only in our ideas; but in which of them it lies must be reserved for the "Deduction."

The foregoing explanation can be thus expressed: *the sublime is that in comparison with which everything else is small.* Here we easily see that nothing can be given in nature, however great it is judged by us to be, which could not, if considered in another relation, be reduced to the infinitely small; and conversely there is nothing so small which does not admit of extension by our imagination to the greatness of a world if compared with still smaller standards. Telescopes have furnished us with abundant material for making the first remark, microscopes for the second. Nothing, therefore, which can be an object of the senses is, considered on this basis, to be called sublime. But because there is in our imagination a striving toward infinite progress and in our reason a claim for absolute totality, regarded as a real idea, therefore this very inadequateness for that idea in our faculty for estimating the magnitude of things of sense excites in us the feeling of a supersensible faculty. And it is not the object of sense, but the use which the judgment naturally makes of certain objects on behalf of this latter feeling that is absolutely great, and in comparison every other use is small. Consequently it is the state of mind produced by a certain representation with which the reflective judgment is occupied, and not the object, that is to be called sublime.

We can therefore append to the preceding formulas explaining the sublime this other: *the sublime is that, the mere ability to think which shows a faculty of the mind surpassing every standard of sense.*

XXVI. Of That Estimation of the Magnitude of Natural Things Which Is Requisite for the Idea of the Sublime

. . .

Nature is . . . sublime in those of its phenomena whose intuition brings with it the idea of its infinity. This last can only come by the inadequacy of the greatest effort of our imagination to estimate the magnitude of an object. But now, in mathematical estimation of magnitude, the imagination is equal to providing a sufficient measure for every object, because the numerical concepts of the understanding, by means of progression, can make any measure adequate to any given magnitude. Therefore it must be the *aesthetical* estimation of magnitude in which the effort toward comprehension surpasses the power of the imagination. Here it is felt that we can comprehend in a whole of intuition the progressive apprehension, and at the same time we perceive the inadequacy of this faculty, unbounded in its progress, for grasping and using any fundamental measure available for the estimation of magnitude with the easiest application of the understanding. Now the proper unchangeable fundamental measure of nature is its absolute whole, which, regarding nature as a phenomenon, would be infinity comprehended. But since this fundamental measure is a self-contradictory concept (on account of the impossibility of the absolute totality of an endless progress), that magnitude of a natural object on which the imagination fruitlessly spends its whole faculty of comprehension must carry our concept of nature to a supersensible substrate (which lies at its basis and also at the basis of our faculty of thought). As this, however, is great beyond all standards of sense, it makes us judge as *sublime*, not so much the object, as our own state of mind in the estimation of it.

Therefore, just as the aesthetical judgment in judging the beautiful refers the imagination in its free play to the *understanding,* in order to harmonize it with the *concepts* of the latter in general (without any determination of them), so does the same faculty, when judging a thing as sublime, refer itself to the *reason,* in order that it may subjectively be in accordance with its *ideas* (no matter what they are)—i.e. that it may produce a state of mind conformable to them and compatible with that brought about by the influence of definite (practical) ideas upon feeling.

We hence see also that true sublimity must be sought only in the mind of the subject judging, not in the natural object the judgment upon which occasions this state. Who would call sublime, e.g., shapeless mountain masses piled in wild disorder upon one another with their pyramids of ice, or the gloomy, raging sea? But the mind feels itself raised in its own judgment if, while contemplating them without any reference to their form, and abandoning itself to the imagination and to the reason—which, although placed in combination with the imagination without any definite purpose, merely extends it—it yet finds the whole power of the imagination inadequate to its ideas.

Examples of the mathematically sublime of nature in mere intuition are all the cases in which we are given, not so much a larger numerical concept, as a large unit for the measure of the imagination (for shortening the numerical series). A tree, the height of which we estimate with reference to the height of a man, at all events gives a standard for a mountain; if this were a mile high, it would serve as unit for the number expressive of the earth's diameter, so that the latter might be made intuitible. The earth's diameter would supply a unit for the known planetary system; this again for the Milky Way; and the immeasurable number of Milky Way

systems called nebulae, which presumably constitute a system of the same kind among themselves, lets us expect no bounds here. Now the sublime in the aesthetical judging of an immeasurable whole like this lies, not so much in the greatness of the number of units, as in the fact that in our progress we ever arrive at yet greater units. To this the systematic division of the universe contributes, which represents every magnitude in nature as small in its turn, and represents our imagination with its entire freedom from bounds, and with it nature, as a mere nothing in comparison with the ideas of reason if it is sought to furnish a presentation which shall be adequate to them.

XXVII. Of the Quality of the Satisfaction in Our Judgments upon the Sublime

The feeling of our incapacity to attain to an idea *which is a law for us* is *respect.* Now the idea of the comprehension of every phenomenon that can be given us in the intuition of a whole is an idea prescribed to us by a law of reason, which recognizes no other measure, definite, valid for everyone, and invariable, than the absolute whole. But our imagination, even in its greatest efforts, in respect of that comprehension which we expect from it of a given object in a whole of intuition (and thus with reference to the presentation of the idea of reason) exhibits its own limits and inadequacy, although at the same time it shows that its destination is to make itself adequate to this idea regarded as a law. Therefore the feeling of the sublime in nature is respect for our own destination, which, by a certain subreption, we attribute to an object of nature (conversion of respect for the idea of humanity in our own subject into respect for the object). This makes intuitively evident the superiority of the rational determination of our cognitive faculties to the greatest faculty of our sensibility.

The feeling of the sublime is therefore a feeling of pain arising from the want of accordance between the aesthetical estimation of magnitude formed by the imagination and the estimation of the same formed by reason. There is at the same time a pleasure thus excited, arising from the correspondence with rational ideas of this very judgment of the inadequacy of our greatest faculty of sense, insofar as it is a law for us to strive after these ideas. In fact it is for us a law (of reason) and belongs to our destination to estimate as small, in comparison with ideas of reason, everything which nature, regarded as an object of sense, contains that is great for us; and that which arouses in us the feeling of this supersensible destination agrees with that law. Now the greatest effort of the imagination in the presentation of the unit for the estimation of magnitude indicates a reference to something *absolutely great,* and consequently a reference to the law of reason, which bids us take this alone as our highest measure of magnitude. Therefore the inner perception of the inadequacy of all sensible standards for rational estimation of magnitude indicates a correspondence with rational laws; it involves a pain, which arouses in us the feeling of our supersensible destination, according to which it is purposive and therefore pleasurable to find every standard of sensibility inadequate to the ideas of understanding.

The mind feels itself *moved* in the representation of the sublime in nature, while in aesthetical judgments about the beautiful it is in *restful* contemplation. This movement may (especially in its beginnings) be compared to a vibration, i.e. to a quickly alternating attraction toward, and repulsion from, the same object. The transcendent (toward which the imagination is impelled in its apprehension of intuition) is for the imagination like an abyss in which it fears to lose itself; but for the rational idea of the supersensible it is not transcendent, but in conformity with law to bring about such an effort of the imagination, and consequently here there is the same amount of attraction as there was of repulsion for the mere sensibility. But the judgment itself always remains in this case only aesthetical, because, without having any determinate concept of the object at its basis, it merely represents the subjective play of the mental powers (imagination and reason) as harmonious through their very contrast. For just as imagination and *understanding,* in judging of the beautiful, generate a subjective purposiveness of the mental powers by means of their harmony, so [in this case] imagination and *reason* do so by means of their conflict. That is, they bring about a feeling that we possess pure self-subsistent reason, or a faculty for the estimation of magnitude, whose superiority can be made intuitively evident only by the inadequacy of that faculty imagination which is itself unbounded in the presentation of magnitudes (of sensible objects).

. . .

B. Of the Dynamically Sublime in Nature

XXVIII. Of Nature Regarded as Might

Might is that which is superior to great hindrances. It is called *dominion* if it is superior to the resistance of that which itself possesses might. Nature, considered in an aesthetical judgment as might that has no dominion over us, is *dynamically sublime.*

If nature is to be judged by us as dynamically sublime, it must be represented as exciting fear (although it is not true conversely that every object which excites fear is regarded in our aesthetical judgment as sublime). For in aesthetical judgments (without the aid of concepts) superiority to hindrances can only be judged according to the greatness of the resistance. Now that which we are driven to resist is an evil and, if we do not find our faculties a match for it, is an object of fear. Hence nature can be regarded by the aesthetical judgment as might, and consequently as dynamically sublime, only so far as it is considered an object of fear.

But we can regard an object as *fearful* without being afraid *of* it, viz. if we judge of it in such a way that we merely *think* a case in which we would wish to resist it and yet in which all resistance would be altogether vain. Thus the virtuous man fears God without being afraid of him, because to wish to resist him and his commandments he thinks is a case that he need not apprehend. But in every such case that he thinks as not impossible, he cognizes him as fearful.

He who fears can form no judgment about the sublime in nature, just as he who is seduced by inclination and appetite can form no judgment about the beautiful. The former flies from the sight of an object which inspires him with awe, and it is impossible to find satisfaction in a terror that is seriously felt. Hence the pleasurableness arising from the cessation of an uneasiness is *a state of joy.* But this, on account of the deliverance from danger which is involved, is a state of joy when conjoined with the resolve that we shall no more be exposed to the danger; we cannot willingly look back upon our sensations of danger, much less seek the occasion for them again.

Bold, overhanging, and, as it were, threatening rocks; clouds piled up in the sky, moving with lightning flashes and thunder peals; volcanoes in all their violence of destruction; hurricanes with their track of devastation; the boundless ocean in a state of tumult; the lofty waterfall of a mighty river, and such like—these exhibit our faculty of resistance as insignificantly small in comparison with their might. But the sight of them is the more attractive, the more fearful it is, provided only that we are in security; and we willingly call these objects sublime, because they raise the energies of the soul above their accustomed height and discover in us a faculty of resistance of a quite different kind, which gives us courage to measure ourselves against the apparent almightiness of nature.

Now, in the immensity of nature and in the insufficiency of our faculties to take in a standard proportionate to the aesthetical estimation of the magnitude of its *realm,* we find our own limitation, although at the same time in our rational faculty we find a different, nonsensuous standard, which has that infinity itself under it as a unity, in comparison with which everything in nature is small, and thus in our mind we find a superiority to nature even in its immensity. And so also the irresistibility of its might, while making us recognize our own physical impotence, considered as beings of nature, discloses to us a faculty of judging independently of and a superiority over nature, on which is based a kind of self-preservation entirely different from that which can be attacked and brought into danger by external nature. Thus humanity in our person remains unhumiliated, though the individual might have to submit to this dominion. In this way nature is not judged to be sublime in our aesthetical judgments in so far as it excites fear, but because it calls up that power in us (which is not nature) of regarding as small the things about which we are solicitous (goods, health, and life), and of regarding its might (to which we are no doubt subjected in respect of these things) as nevertheless without any dominion over us and our personality to which we must bow where our highest fundamental propositions, and their assertion or abandonment, are concerned. Therefore nature is here called sublime merely because it elevates the imagination to a presentation of those cases in which the mind can make felt the proper sublimity of its destination, in comparison with nature itself.

. . .

Sublimity . . . does not reside in anything of nature, but only in our mind, insofar as we can become conscious that we are superior to nature within, and therefore also to nature without us (so far as it influences us). Everything that excites this feeling in us, e.g. the *might* of nature which calls forth our forces, is called then (although improperly) sublime. Only by supposing this idea in ourselves and in reference to it are we capable of attaining to the idea of the sublimity of that Being which produces respect in us, not merely by the might that it displays in nature, but rather by means of the faculty which resides in us of judging it fearlessly and of regarding our destination as sublime in respect of it.

XLIX. Of the Faculties of the Mind That Constitute Genius

We say of certain products of which we expect that they should at least in part appear as beautiful art, they are without *spirit*,[13] although we find nothing to blame in them on the score of taste. A poem may be very neat and elegant, but

---

[13][Bernard] In English we would rather say "without soul," but I prefer to translate *Geist* consistently by "spirit," to avoid the confusion of it with *Seele.*

without spirit. A history may be exact and well arranged, but without spirit. A festal discourse may be solid and at the same time elaborate, but without spirit. Conversation is often not devoid of entertainment, but it is without spirit; even of a woman we say that she is pretty, an agreeable talker, and courteous, but without spirit. What then do we mean by *spirit?*

Spirit, in an aesthetical sense, is the name given to the animating principle of the mind. But that by means of which this principle animates the soul, the material which it applies to that purpose, is what puts the mental powers purposively into swing, i.e. into such a play as maintains itself and strengthens the mental powers in their exercise.

Now I maintain that this principle is no other than the faculty of presenting *aesthetical ideas.* And by an *aesthetical idea* I understand that representation of the imagination which occasions much thought, without however any definite thought, i.e. any *concept,* being capable of being adequate to it; it consequently cannot be completely compassed and made intelligible by language. We easily see that it is the counterpart (pendant) of a *rational idea,* which conversely is a concept to which no *intuition* (or representation of the imagination) can be adequate.

The imagination (as a productive faculty of cognition) is very powerful in creating another nature, as it were, out of the material that actual nature gives it. We entertain ourselves with it when experience becomes too commonplace, and by it we remold experience, always indeed in accordance with analogical laws, but yet also in accordance with principles which occupy a higher place in reason (laws, too, which are just as natural to us as those by which understanding comprehends empirical nature). Thus we feel our freedom from the law of association (which attaches to the empirical employment of imagination), so that the material supplied to us by nature in accordance with this law can be worked up into something different which surpasses nature.

Such representations of the imagination we may call *ideas,* partly because they at least strive after something which lies beyond the bounds of experience and so seek to approximate to a presentation of concepts of reason (intellectual ideas), thus giving to the latter the appearance of objective reality, but especially because no concept can be fully adequate to them as internal intuitions. The poet ventures to realize to sense, rational ideas of invisible beings, the kingdom of the blessed, hell, eternity, creation, etc.; or even if he deals with things of which there are examples in experience—e.g. death, envy and all vices, also love, fame, and the like—he tries, by means of imagination, which emulates the play of reason in its quest after a maximum, to go beyond the limits of experience and to present them to sense with a completeness of which there is no example in nature. This is properly speaking the art of the poet, in which the faculty of aesthetical ideas can manifest itself in its entire strength. But this faculty, considered in itself, is properly only a talent (of the imagination).

If now we place under a concept a representation of the imagination belonging to its presentation, but which occasions in itself more thought than can ever be comprehended in a definite concept and which consequently aesthetically enlarges the concept itself in an unbounded fashion, the imagination is here creative, and it brings the faculty of intellectual ideas (the reason) into movement; i.e. by a representation more thought (which indeed belongs to the concept of the object) is occasioned than can in it be grasped or made clear.

Those forms which do not constitute the presentation of a given concept itself but only, as approximate representations of the imagination, express the consequences bound up with it and its relationship to other concepts, are called (aesthetical) *attributes* of an object whose concept as a rational idea cannot be adequately presented. Thus Jupiter's eagle with the lightning in its claws is an attribute of the mighty king of heaven, as the peacock is of his magnificent queen. They do not, like *logical attributes,* represent what lies in our concepts of the sublimity and majesty of creation, but something different, which gives occasion to the imagination to spread itself over a number of kindred representations that arouse more thought than can be expressed in a concept determined by words. They furnish an *aesthetical idea,* which for that rational idea takes the place of logical presentation; and thus, as their proper office, they enliven the mind by opening out to it the prospect into an illimitable field of kindred representations. But beautiful art does this not only in the case of painting or sculpture (in which the term "attribute" is commonly employed); poetry and rhetoric also get the spirit that animates their works simply from the aesthetical attributes of the object, which accompany the logical and stimulate the imagination, so that it thinks more by their aid, although in an undeveloped way, than could be comprehended in a concept and therefore in a definite form of words. For the sake of brevity, I must limit myself to a few examples only.

When the great King in one of his poems expresses himself as follows:

Oui, finissons sans trouble et mourons sans regrets,
En laissant l'univers comblé de nos bienfaits.
Ainsi l'astre du jour au bout de sa carrière,
Répand sur l'horizon une douce lumière;

Et les derniers rayons qu'il darde dans les airs,
Sont les derniers soupirs qu'il donne à l'univers;[14]

he quickens his rational idea of a cosmopolitan disposition at the end of life by an attribute which the imagination (in remembering all the pleasures of a beautiful summer day that are recalled at its close by a serene evening) associates with that representation, and which excites a number of sensations and secondary representations for which no expression is found. On the other hand, an intellectual concept may serve conversely as an attribute for a representation of sense, and so can quicken this latter by means of the idea of the supersensible, but only by the aesthetical element, that subjectively attaches to the concept of the latter, being here employed. Thus, for example, a certain poet says, in his description of a beautiful morning: "The sun arose / As calm from virtue springs." The consciousness of virtue, if we substitute it in our thoughts for a virtuous man, diffuses in the mind a multitude of sublime and restful feelings, and a boundless prospect of a joyful future, to which no expression that is measured by a definite concept completely attains.[15]

In a word, the aesthetical idea is a representation of the imagination associated with a given concept, which is bound up with such a multiplicity of partial representations in its free employment that for it no expression marking a definite concept can be found; and such a representation, therefore, adds to a concept much ineffable thought, the feeling of which quickens the cognitive faculties, and with language, which is the mere letter, binds up spirit also.

·   ·   ·

LIII. *Comparison of the Respective Aesthetical Worth of the Beautiful Arts*

Of all the arts *poetry* (which owes its origin almost entirely to genius and will least be guided by precept or example)

---

[14]"Yes, let us end without disorder and die without regrets, / Leaving the universe filled with our blessings. / Thus the daystar at the end of its course, / Sheds on the horizon a gentle light; / And the last rays that it beams into the air, / Are the last sighs that it gives to the universe." [Bernard] Barni quotes these lines as occurring in one of Frederick the Great's French poems: "Epître au maréchal Keith, sur les vaines terreurs de la mort et les frayeurs d'une autre vie"; but I have not been able to verify his reference. Kant here translates them into German.

[15][Kant] Perhaps nothing more sublime was ever said and no sublimer thought ever expressed than the famous inscription on the Temple of Isis (Mother Nature): "I am all that is and that was and that shall be, and no mortal hath lifted my veil." Segner availed himself of this idea in a *suggestive* vignette prefixed to his *Natural Philosophy,* in order to inspire beforehand the pupil whom he was about to lead into that temple with a holy awe, which should dispose his mind to serious attention.

maintains the first rank. It expands the mind by setting the imagination at liberty and by offering, within the limits of a given concept, amid the unbounded variety of possible forms accordant therewith, that which unites the presentment of this concept with a wealth of thought to which no verbal expression is completely adequate, and so rising aesthetically to ideas. It strengthens the mind by making it feel its faculty—free, spontaneous, and independent of natural determination—of considering and judging nature as a phenomenon in accordance with aspects which it does not present in experience either for sense or understanding, and therefore of using it on behalf of, and as a sort of schema for, the supersensible. It plays with illusion, which it produces at pleasure, but without deceiving by it; for it declares its exercise to be mere play, which however can be purposively used by the understanding. Rhetoric, insofar as this means the art of persuasion, i.e. of deceiving by a beautiful show (*ars oratoria*), and not mere elegance of speech (eloquence and style), is a dialectic which borrows from poetry only so much as is needful to win minds to the side of the orator before they have formed a judgment and to deprive them of their freedom; it cannot therefore be recommended either for the law courts or for the pulpit. For if we are dealing with civil law, with the rights of individual persons, or with lasting instruction and determination of people's minds to an accurate knowledge and a conscientious observance of their duty, it is unworthy of so important a business to allow a trace of any luxuriance of wit and imagination to appear, and still less any trace of the art of talking people over and of captivating them for the advantage of any chance person. For although this art may sometimes be directed to legitimate and praiseworthy designs, it becomes objectionable when in this way maxims and dispositions are spoiled in a subjective point of view, though the action may objectively be lawful. It is not enough to do what is right; we should practice it solely on the ground that it is right. Again, the mere concept of this species of matters of human concern, when clear and combined with a lively presentation of it in examples, without any offense against the rules of euphony of speech or propriety of expression, has by itself for ideas of reason (which collectively constitute eloquence) sufficient influence upon human minds; so that it is not needful to add the machinery of persuasion, which, since it can be used equally well to beautify or to hide vice and error, cannot quite lull the secret suspicion that one is being artfully overreached. In poetry everything proceeds with honesty and candor. It declares itself to be a mere entertaining play of the imagination, which wishes to proceed as regards form in harmony with the laws of the understanding; and it does not desire to steal upon and ensnare the understanding by the aid of sensible presentation.[16]

---

[16][Kant] I must admit that a beautiful poem has always given me a pure gratification, while the reading of the best discourse, whether of a Roman orator or of a modern parliamentary speaker or of a preacher, has always been mingled with an unpleasant feeling of disapprobation of a treacherous art which means to move men in important matters like machines to a judgment that must lose all weight for them on quiet reflection. Readiness and accuracy in speaking (which taken together constitute rhetoric) belong to beautiful art, but the art of the orator (*ars oratoria*), the art of availing oneself of the weaknesses of men for one's own designs (whether these be well meant or even actually good does not matter), is worthy of no *respect*. Again, this art only reached its highest point, both at Athens and at Rome, at a time when the state was hastening to its ruin and true patriotic sentiment had disappeared. The man who, along with a clear insight into things, has in his power a wealth of pure speech, and who with a fruitful imagination capable of presenting his ideas unites a lively sympathy with what is truly good, is the *vir bonus dicendi peritus,* the orator without art but of great impressiveness, as Cicero has it, though he may not always remain true to this ideal.

Mary Wollstonecraft

1759–1797

From

A Vindication of the Rights of Woman

Mary Wollstonecraft's *A Vindication of the Rights of Woman* (1792) well deserves its rank as the first great feminist work. It is her most famous work, but not her first—or last. She had already published fiction when in 1790 she answered Edmund Burke's *Reflections on the Revolution in France* with her *A Vindication of the Rights of Man* before Thomas Paine wrote his *Rights of Man* (1791–1792). Having associated with Dissenters who supported the French Revolution, she was outraged at Burke's attack and in turn opposed British identification of security of property with liberty, arguing for the break up of large estates and going on to propose numerous reforms, both economic and social. The book made her well known.

In *A Vindication of the Rights of Woman* she went beyond her Dissenter friends, whose views remained strictly patriarchal. Written in about six weeks, the book was insufficiently revised but nevertheless achieves an effective tone. In general, the fundamental principles enunciated are that the mind does not know sex and that, as Claire Tomalin has remarked ". . . society is wasting its assets if it retains women in the role of convenient domestic slaves and alluring mistresses, denies them economic independence and encourages them to be docile and attentive to their looks to the exclusion of all else."

Chapter Six, below, of the *Vindication* follows a long chapter that discusses a number of writers' attitudes toward female character and education. Wollstonecraft accepts the common theory of the association of ideas set forth in David Hartley's *Observations of Man* (1749) and employed by David Hume in his *Enquiry Concerning Human Understanding.* Her emphasis on the importance of impressions leads her in Chapter Thirteen, Part Two, to attack the sentimental novels of her time for their pernicious influences on women's intellectual development.

Mary Wollstonecraft's works include *Thoughts on the Education of Daughters* (1787); *Original Stories* (1788); *A Vindication of the Rights of Man* (1790); *A Vindication of the Rights of Woman* (1792); *A Historical and Moral View of the Origin and Progress of the French Revolution* (1794); *Letters Written during a Short Residence in Sweden, Norway and Denmark* (1796); and *Posthumous Works* (ed. Godwin, 1798).

A VINDICATION OF THE RIGHTS OF WOMAN. Wollstonecraft's *Vindication* was first published in London in 1792. It was followed in the same year by the second edition, which is the basis for the text reprinted here.

See Emma Rauschenbusch-Clough, *A Study of Mary Wollstonecraft and the Rights of Woman* (1898); Virginia Woolf, "Mary Wollstonecraft," *The Second Common Reader* (1932); Margaret George, *One Woman's Situation* (1970); Eleanor Flexner, *Mary Wollstonecraft* (1972); and Claire Tomalin, *The Life and Death of Mary Wollstonecraft* (1974).

Chapter VI

The Effect Which an Early Association of Ideas Has upon the Character

Educated in the enervating style recommended by the writers on whom I have been animadverting; and not having a chance, from their subordinate state in society, to recover their lost ground, is it surprising that women everywhere appear a defect in nature? Is it surprising, when we consider what a determinate effect an early association of ideas has on the character, that they neglect their understandings, and turn all their attention to their persons?

The great advantages which naturally result from storing the mind with knowledge, are obvious from the following considerations. The association of our ideas is either habitual or instantaneous; and the latter mode seems rather to depend on the original temperature of the mind than on the will. When the ideas, and matters of fact, are once taken in, they lie by for use, till some fortuitous circumstance makes the information dart into the mind with illustrative force, that has been received at very different periods of our lives. Like the lightning's flash are many recollections; one idea assimilating and explaining another, with astonishing rapidity. I do not now allude to that quick perception of truth, which is so intuitive that it baffles research, and makes us at a loss to determine whether it is reminiscence or ratiocination, lost sight of in its celerity, that opens the dark cloud. Over those instantaneous associations we have little power; for when the mind is once enlarged by excursive flights, or profound reflection, the raw materials will, in some degree, arrange themselves. The understanding, it is true, may keep us from going out of drawing when we group our thoughts, or transcribe from the imagination the warm sketches of fancy; but the animal spirits, the individual character, give the colouring. Over this subtle electric fluid,[1] how little power do we

possess, and over it how little power can reason obtain! These fine intractable spirits appear to be the essence of genius, and beaming in its eagle eye, produce in the most eminent degree the happy energy of associating thoughts that surprise, delight, and instruct. These are the glowing minds that concentrate pictures for their fellow-creatures; forcing them to view with interest the objects reflected from the impassioned imagination, which they passed over in nature.

I must be allowed to explain myself. The generality of people cannot see or feel poetically, they want fancy, and therefore fly from solitude in search of sensible objects; but when an author lends them his eyes they can see as he saw, and be amused by images they could not select, though lying before them.

Education thus only supplies the man of genius with knowledge to give variety and contrast to his associations; but there is an habitual association of ideas, that grows 'with our growth,'[2] which has a great effect on the moral character of mankind; and by which a turn is given to the mind that commonly remains throughout life. So ductile is the understanding, and yet so stubborn, that the associations which depend on adventitious circumstances, during the period that the body takes to arrive at maturity, can seldom be disentangled by reason. One idea calls up another, its old associate, and memory, faithful to the first impressions, particularly when the intellectual powers are not employed to cool our sensations, retraces them with mechanical exactness.

This habitual slavery, to first impressions, has a more baneful effect on the female than the male character, because business and other dry employments of the understanding, tend to deaden the feelings and break associations that do violence to reason. But females, who are made women of when they are mere children, and brought back to childhood when they ought to leave the go-cart forever, have not sufficient strength of mind to efface the superinductions of art that have smothered nature.

Every thing that they see or hear serves to fix impressions, call forth emotions, and associate ideas, that give a sexual character to the mind. False notions of beauty and delicacy stop the growth of their limbs and produce a sickly soreness, rather than delicacy of organs; and thus weakened

---

[1][Wollstonecraft] "I have sometimes, when inclined to laugh at materialists, asked whether, as the most powerful effects in nature are apparently produced by fluids, the magnetic, &c. the passions might not be fine volatile fluids that embraced humanity, keeping the more refractory elementary parts together—or whether they were simply a liquid fire that pervaded the more sluggish materials, giving them life and heat?" [Reference is to the views of Newton and the Associationists who posited a pervasive fluid that carried vibrations to the perceiver.]

[2]Alexander Pope, *Essay on Man* II. 136.

by being employed in unfolding instead of examining the first associations, forced on them by every surrounding object, how can they attain the vigour necessary to enable them to throw off their factitious character?—where find strength to recur to reason and rise superiour to a system of oppression, that blasts the fair promises of spring? This cruel association of ideas, which every thing conspires to twist into all their habits of thinking, or, to speak with more precision, of feeling, receives new force when they begin to act a little for themselves; for they then perceive that it is only through their address to excite emotions in men, that pleasure and power are to be obtained. Besides, the books professedly written for their instruction, which make the first impression on their minds, all inculcate the same opinions. Educated then in worse than Egyptian bondage, it is unreasonable, as well as cruel, to upbraid them with faults that can scarcely be avoided, unless a degree of native vigour be supposed, that falls to the lot of very few amongst mankind.

For instance, the severest sarcasms have been levelled against the sex, and they have been ridiculed for repeating 'a set of phrases learnt by rote,'[3] when nothing could be more natural, considering the education they receive, and that their 'highest praise is to obey, unargued'[4]—the will of man. If they be not allowed to have reason sufficient to govern their own conduct—why, all they learn—must be learned by rote! And when all their ingenuity is called forth to adjust their dress, 'a passion for a scarlet coat,'[5] is so natural, that it never surprised me; and, allowing Pope's summary of their character to be just, 'that every woman is at heart a rake,'[6] why should they be bitterly censured for seeking a congenial mind, and preferring a rake to a man of sense?

Rakes know how to work on their sensibility, whilst the modest merit of reasonable men has, of course, less effect on their feelings, and they cannot reach the heart by the way of the understanding, because they have few sentiments in common.

It seems a little absurd to expect women to be more reasonable than men in their *likings,* and still to deny them the uncontrouled use of reason. When do men *fall-in-love* with sense? When do they, with their superior powers and advantages, turn from the person to the mind? And how can they then expect women, who are only taught to observe behaviour, and acquire manners rather than morals, to despise what they have been all their lives labouring to attain? Where

are they suddenly to find judgment enough to weigh patiently the sense of an awkward virtuous man, when his manners, of which they are made critical judges, are rebuffing, and his conversation cold and dull, because it does not consist of pretty repartees, or well turned compliments? In order to admire or esteem any thing for a continuance, we must, at least, have our curiosity excited by knowing, in some degree, what we admire; for we are unable to estimate the value of qualities and virtues above our comprehension. Such a respect, when it is felt, may be very sublime; and the confused consciousness of humility may render the dependent creature an interesting object, in some points of view; but human love must have grosser ingredients; and the person very naturally will come in for its share—and, an ample share it mostly has!

Love is, in a great degree, an arbitrary passion, and will reign, like some other stalking mischiefs, by its own authority, without deigning to reason; and it may also be easily distinguished from esteem, the foundation of friendship, because it is often excited by evanescent beauties and graces, though, to give an energy to the sentiment, something more solid must deepen their impression and set the imagination to work, to make the most fair—the first good.

Common passions are excited by common qualities.— Men look for beauty and the simper of good-humoured docility: women are captivated by easy manners; a gentleman-like man seldom fails to please them, and their thirsty ears eagerly drink the insinuating nothings of politeness, whilst they turn from the unintelligible sounds of the charmer— reason, charm he never so wisely. With respect to superficial accomplishments, the rake certainly has the advantage; and of these females can form an opinion, for it is their own ground. Rendered gay and giddy by the whole tenor of their lives, the very aspect of wisdom, or the severe graces of virtue, must have a lugubrious appearance to them; and produce a kind of restraint from which they and love, sportive child, naturally revolt. Without taste, excepting of the lighter kind, for taste is the offspring of judgment, how can they discover that true beauty and grace must arise from the play of the mind? and how can they be expected to relish in a lover what they do not, or very imperfectly, possess themselves? The sympathy that unites hearts, and invites to confidence, in them is so very faint, that it cannot take fire, and thus mount to passion. No, I repeat it, the love cherished by such minds, must have grosser fewel!

The inference is obvious; till women are led to exercise their understandings, they should not be satirized for their attachment to rakes; or even for being rakes at heart, when it appears to be the inevitable consequence of their education. They who live to please—must find their enjoyments, their

---

[3] Jonathan Swift, "The Furniture of a Woman's Mind."
[4] John Milton, *Paradise Lost* IV. 636–638.
[5] Swift, *op. cit.*
[6] Pope, *Moral Essays* II. 215–216.

happiness, in pleasure! It is a trite, yet true remark, that we never do any thing well, unless we love it for its own sake.

Supposing, however, for a moment, that women were, in some future revolution of time, to become, what I sincerely wish them to be, even love would acquire more serious dignity, and be purified in its own fires; and virtue giving true delicacy to their affections, they would turn with disgust from a rake. Reasoning then, as well as feeling, the only province of woman, at present, they might easily guard against exterior graces, and quickly learn to despise the sensibility that had been excited and hackneyed in the ways of women, whose trade was vice; and allurements, wanton airs. They would recollect that the flame, one must use appropriated expressions, which they wished to light up, had been exhausted by lust, and that the sated appetite, losing all relish for pure and simple pleasures, could only be roused by licentious arts or variety. What satisfaction could a woman of delicacy promise herself in a union with such a man, when the very artlessness of her affection might appear insipid? Thus does Dryden describe the situation,

> ———'Where love is duty, on the female side,
> 'On theirs mere sensual gust, and sought with
>   surly pride.'[7]

But one grand truth women have yet to learn, though much it imports them to act accordingly. In the choice of a husband, they should not be led astray by the qualities of a lover—for a lover the husband, even supposing him to be wise and virtuous, cannot long remain.

Were women more rationally educated, could they take a more comprehensive view of things, they would be contented to love but once in their lives; and after marriage calmly let passion subside into friendship—into that tender intimacy, which is the best refuge from care; yet is built on such pure, still affections, that idle jealousies would not be allowed to disturb the discharge of the sober duties of life, or to engross the thoughts that ought to be otherwise employed. This is a state in which many men live; but few, very few women. And the difference may easily be accounted for, without recurring to a sexual character. Men, for whom we are told women were made, have too much occupied the thoughts of women; and this association has so entangled love with all their motives of action; and, to harp a little on an old string, having been solely employed either to prepare themselves to excite love, or actually putting their lessons in

practice, they cannot live without love. But, when a sense of duty, or fear of shame, obliges them to restrain this pampered desire of pleasing beyond certain lengths, too far for delicacy, it is true, though far from criminality, they obstinately determine to love, I speak of the passion, their husbands to the end of the chapter—and then acting the part which they foolishly exacted from their lovers, they become abject woers, and fond slaves.

Men of wit and fancy are often rakes; and fancy is the food of love. Such men will inspire passion. Half the sex, in its present infantine state, would pine for a Lovelace;[8] a man so witty, so graceful, and so valiant; and can they *deserve* blame for acting according to principles so constantly inculcated? They want a lover, and protector; and behold him kneeling before them—bravery prostrate to beauty! The virtues of a husband are thus thrown by love into the background, and gay hopes, or lively emotions, banish reflection till the day of reckoning comes; and come it surely will, to turn the sprightly lover into a surly suspicious tyrant, who contemptuously insults the very weakness he fostered. Or, supposing the rake reformed, he cannot quickly get rid of old habits. When a man of abilities is first carried away by his passions, it is necessary that sentiment and taste varnish the enormities of vice, and give a zest to brutal indulgences; but when the gloss of novelty is worn off, and pleasure palls upon the sense, lasciviousness becomes barefaced, and enjoyment only the desperate effort of weakness flying from reflection as from a legion of devils. Oh! virtue, thou art not an empty name! All that life can give—thou givest!

If much comfort cannot be expected from the friendship of a reformed rake of superiour abilities, what is the consequence when he lacketh sense, as well as principles? Verily misery, in its most hideous shape. When the habits of weak people are consolidated by time, a reformation is barely possible; and actually makes the beings miserable who have not sufficient mind to be amused by innocent pleasure; like the tradesman who retires from the hurry of business, nature presents to them only a universal blank; and the restless thoughts prey on the damped spirits.[9] Their reformation, as well as his retirement, actually makes them wretched because it deprives them of all employment, by quenching the hopes and fears that set in motion their sluggish minds.

---

[7]John Dryden, *Palamon and Arcite* III. 231–232.

[8]Character in Samuel Richardson's *Clarissa*.

[9][Wollstonecraft] I have frequently seen this exemplified in women whose beauty could no longer be repaired. They have retired from the noisy scenes of dissipation; but, unless they become methodists, the solitude of the select society of their family connections of acquaintance, has presented only a fearful void; consequently, nervous complaints, and all the vapourish train of idleness, rendered them quite as useless, and far more unhappy, than when they joined the giddy throng.

If such be the force of habit; if such be the bondage of folly, how carefully ought we to guard the mind from storing up vicious associations; and equally careful should we be to cultivate the understanding, to save the poor wight from the weak dependent state of even harmless ignorance. For it is the right use of reason alone which makes us independent of every thing—excepting the unclouded Reason—'Whose service is perfect freedom.'

Chapter XIII

Some Instances of the Folly Which the Ignorance of Women Generates; with Concluding Reflections on the Moral Improvement That a Revolution in Female Manners Might Naturally Be Expected to Produce

There are many follies, in some degree, peculiar to women: sins against reason of commission as well as of omission; but all flowing from ignorance or prejudice, I shall only point out such as appear to be particularly injurious to their moral character. And in animadverting on them, I wish especially to prove, that the weakness of mind and body, which men have endeavoured, impelled by various motives, to perpetuate, prevents their discharging the peculiar duty of their sex: for when weakness of body will not permit them to suckle their children, and weakness of mind makes them spoil their tempers—is woman in a natural state?

. . .

Section II

Another instance of that feminine weakness of character, often produced by a confined education, is a romantic twist of the mind, which has been very properly termed *sentimental.*

Women subjected by ignorance to their sensations, and only taught to look for happiness in love, refine on sensual feelings, and adopt metaphysical notions respecting that passion, which lead them shamefully to neglect the duties of life, and frequently in the midst of these sublime refinements they plump into actual vice.

These are the women who are amused by the reveries of the stupid novelists, who, knowing little of human nature, work up stale tales, and describe meretricious scenes, all retailed in a sentimental jargon, which equally tend to corrupt the taste, and draw the heart aside from its daily duties. I do not mention the understanding, because never having been

exercised, its slumbering energies rest inactive, like the lurking particles of fire which are supposed universally to pervade matter.

Females, in fact, denied all political privileges, and not allowed, as married women, excepting in criminal cases, a civil existence, have their attention naturally drawn from the interest of the whole community to that of the minute parts, though the private duty of any member of society must be very imperfectly performed when not connected with the general good. The mighty business of female life is to please, and restrained from entering into more important concerns by political and civil oppression, sentiments become events, and reflection deepens what it should, and would have effaced, if the understanding had been allowed to take a wider range.

But, confined to trifling employments, they naturally imbibe opinions which the only kind of reading calculated to interest an innocent frivolous mind, inspires. Unable to grasp any thing great, is it surprising that they find the reading of history a very dry task, and disquisitions addressed to the understanding intolerably tedious, and almost unintelligible? Thus are they necessarily dependent on the novelist for amusement. Yet, when I exclaim against novels, I mean when contrasted with those works which exercise the understanding and regulate the imagination.—For any kind of reading I think better than leaving a blank still a blank, because the mind must receive a degree of enlargement and obtain a little strength by a slight exertion of its thinking powers; besides, even the productions that are only addressed to the imagination, raise the reader a little above the gross gratification of appetites, to which the mind has not given a shade of delicacy.

This observation is the result of experience; for I have known several notable women, and one in particular, who was a very good woman—as good as such a narrow mind would allow her to be, who took care that her daughters (three in number) should never see a novel. As she was a woman of fortune and fashion, they had various masters to attend them, and a sort of menial governess to watch their footsteps. From their masters they learned how tables, chairs, &c. were called in French and Italian; but as the few books thrown in their way were far above their capacities, or devotional, they neither acquired ideas nor sentiments, and passed their time, when not compelled to repeat *words,* in dressing, quarrelling with each other, or conversing with their maids by stealth, till they were brought into company as marriageable.

Their mother, a widow, was busy in the mean time in keeping up her connections, as she termed a numerous acquaintance, lest her girls should want a proper introduction into the great world. And these young ladies, with minds vulgar in every sense of the word, and spoiled tempers, entered life puffed up with notions of their own consequence, and looking down with contempt on those who could not vie with them in dress and parade.

With respect to love, nature, or their nurses, had taken care to teach them the physical meaning of the word; and, as they had few topics of conversation, and fewer refinements of sentiment, they expressed their gross wishes not in very delicate phrases, when they spoke freely, talking of matrimony.

Could these girls have been injured by the perusal of novels? I almost forgot a shade in the character of one of them; she affected a simplicity bordering on folly, and with a simper would utter the most immodest remarks and questions, the full meaning of which she had learned whilst secluded from the world, and afraid to speak in her mother's presence, who governed with a high hand: they were all educated, as she prided herself, in a most exemplary manner; and read their chapters and psalms before breakfast, never touching a silly novel.

This is only one instance; but I recollect many other women who, not led by degrees to proper studies, and not permitted to choose for themselves, have indeed been overgrown children; or have obtained, by mixing in the world, a little of what is termed common sense: that is, a distinct manner of seeing common occurrences, as they stand detached: but what deserves the name of intellect, the power of gaining general or abstract ideas, or even intermediate ones, was out of the question. Their minds were quiescent, and when they were not roused by sensible objects and employments of that kind, they were low-spirited, would cry, or go to sleep.

When, therefore, I advise my sex not to read such flimsy works, it is to induce them to read something superiour; for I coincide in opinion with a sagacious man, who, having a daughter and niece under his care, pursued a very different plan with each.

The niece, who had considerable abilities, had, before she was left to his guardianship, been indulged in desultory reading. Her he endeavoured to lead, and did lead to history and moral essays; but his daughter, whom a fond weak mother had indulged, and who consequently was averse to every thing like application, he allowed to read novels: and used to justify his conduct by saying that if she ever attained a relish for reading them, he should have some foundation to work upon; and that erroneous opinions were better than none at all.

In fact the female mind has been so totally neglected, that knowledge was only to be acquired from this muddy source, till from reading novels some women of superiour talents learned to despise them.

The best method, I believe, that can be adopted to correct a fondness for novels is to ridicule them: not indiscriminately, for then it would have little effect; but, if a judicious person, with some turn for humour, would read several to a young girl, and point out both by tones, and apt comparisons with pathetic incidents and heroic characters in history, how foolishly and ridiculously they caricatured human nature, just opinions might be substituted instead of romantic sentiments.

In one respect, however, the majority of both sexes resemble, and equally shew a want of taste and modesty. Ignorant women, forced to be chaste to preserve their reputation, allow their imagination to revel in the unnatural and meretricious scenes sketched by the novel writers of the day, slighting as insipid the sober dignity and matron graces of history,[10] whilst men carry the same vitiated taste into life, and fly for amusement to the wanton, from the unsophisticated charms of virtue, and the grave respectability of sense.

Besides, the reading of novels makes women, and particularly ladies of fashion, very fond of using strong expressions and superlatives in conversation; and, though the dissipated artificial life which they lead prevents their cherishing any strong legitimate passion, the language of passion in affected tones slips for ever from their glib tongues, and every trifle produces those phosphoric bursts which only mimick in the dark the flame of passion.

---

[10][Wollstonecraft] I am not alluding to that superiority of mind which leads to the creation of ideal beauty, when he, surveyed with a penetrating eye, appears a tragi-comedy, in which little can be seen to satisfy the heart without the help of fancy.

William Blake

1757–1827

Although Blake's recent influence, partly via the criticism of Frye, has been considerable, his poetry and his other writings were virtually unknown in his day. He anticipated the interests of a number of Romantic critics who did not know of his work. In *The Marriage of Heaven and Hell* there is a highly condensed myth of the dissociation of reason and imagination similar to Schiller's in his *Letters on the Aesthetic Education of Man,* though Blake pushes the disaster farther back in time. In his discussion of his painting of Chaucer's Canterbury pilgrims there is the germ of a theory of archetypes that anticipates Schelling's remarks on particulars and universals in his essay *On the Relation of the Plastic Arts to Nature.* This interest, which is closely tied to an interest in myth, is developed in a description of a lost painting, *The Ancient Britons.* The artist's proper attention to "minute particulars" is the foundation of his critical annotations to Reynolds' *Discourses.* Blake's distinction between "vision" and "allegory" (in another place "allegory addressed to the intellectual powers" as against that addressed to the "corporeal understanding") arises from his attack on generalized abstractions as the aim of art and is roughly allied to Romantic comparisons of symbolism and allegory. Most of Blake's criticism is immediately concerned with painting, but it is not inaccurate to apply it generally to literature. His own longer poems, *The Four Zoas, Milton,* and *Jerusalem,* carry into practice, indeed include a vision of, the artistic activity he advocates in his prose.

Blake raises numerous other issues connected to those already mentioned. He anticipates to some extent Croce's argument that intuition and expression are the same and goes even further toward the idea that the creative act is unified: "Invention depends altogether upon execution and organization." He objects strenuously to the empiricist notion in Burke and Reynolds that we create only by recombining the simple elements of sense data into new arrangements. This sort of activity he attributes scornfully to the "daughters of memory." He believes that the imagination is truly creative and that man does not come into the world a *tabula rasa.* For him, the opinions of Burke and Reynolds lead to allegory addressed to the "corporeal understanding," the generalized abstractions that disregard "minute discrimination": "What is general nature? Is there such a thing? What is general knowledge? Is there such a thing? Strictly speaking, all knowledge is particular." Blake's idea of universality proceeds from identifying microcosm with macrocosm, a sophistication of what Cassirer later called "mythical thinking."

There are two standard texts of Blake: *The Poetry and Prose of William Blake,* edited by D. V. Erdman and Harold Bloom (1965), and *The Complete Writings of William Blake,* edited by Geoffrey Keynes (1966). The biography by Alexander Gilchrist, *The Life of William Blake* (1863, rev. 1880), is best consulted in the Everyman's Library edition. Important critical writing on Blake includes Northrop Frye,

Fearful Symmetry (1947) and "Blake's Treatment of the Archetype," *English Institute Essays* (1950); D. V. Erdman, *Blake: Prophet Against Empire* (1954); P. F. Fisher, *The Valley of Vision* (1961); Hazard Adams, *William Blake: A Reading of the Shorter Poems* (1963); Harold Bloom, *Blake's Apocalypse* (1963); W. J. T. Mitchell, *Blake's Composite Art;* Morris Eaves, *Blake's Theory of Art* (1982); Nelson Hilton, *Literal Imagination: Blake's Vision of Words;* Robert N. Essick, *William Blake and the Language of Adam* (1989): and Hazard Adams, ed., *Essays on William Blake* (1991).

From

The Marriage of Heaven and Hell

The ancient poets animated all sensible objects with gods or geniuses, calling them by the names and adorning them with the properties of woods, rivers, mountains, lakes, cities, nations, and whatever their enlarged and numerous senses could perceive.

And particularly they studied the genius of each city and country, placing it under its mental deity,

Till a system was formed, which some took advantage of, and enslaved the vulgar by attempting to realize or abstract the mental deities from their objects: thus began priesthood;

Choosing forms of worship from poetic tales.[1]

And at length they pronounced that the gods had ordered such things.

Thus men forgot that all deities reside in the human breast.

From

Letter to Thomas Butts

Allegory addressed to the intellectual powers, while it is altogether hidden from the corporeal understanding, is my def-

inition of the most sublime poetry; it is also somewhat in the same manner defined by Plato.

From

Annotations to Reynolds' *Discourses*

Malone's Account of Reynolds' Life and Writings

Page III

[Blake] Invention depends altogether upon execution or organization; as that is right or wrong so is the invention perfect or imperfect. Whoever is set to undermine the execution of art is set to destroy art. Michelangelo's art depends on Michelangelo's execution altogether.

Page XVI

[Reynolds] I proceeded to copy some of those excellent works. I viewed them again and again. . . . In a short time a new taste and new perceptions began to dawn on me. . . . The truth is, that if these works had really been what I expected, they would have contained beauties superficial and alluring, but by no means such as would have entitled them to the great reputation which they have so long and so justly obtained.

THE MARRIAGE OF HEAVEN AND HELL. Blake engraved *The Marriage of Heaven and Hell* some time between 1790 and 1793. This excerpt is from plate 11. The text is from *The Poetry and Prose of William Blake,* copyright © 1965 by David V. Erdman and Harold Bloom, by permission of Doubleday & Company, Inc.; compared with Geoffrey Keynes, ed., *The Complete Writings of William Blake* (1966), by permission of Oxford University Press.

[1]Compare Schiller, *Letters on the Aesthetic Education of Man,* pp. 416–27.

LETTER TO THOMAS BUTTS. Blake's letter to Thomas Butts, from which this sentence is taken, was written on July 6, 1803. The text is from Geoffrey Keynes, ed., *The Letters of William Blake* (1956). Reprinted by permission of Rupert Hart-Davis Ltd.

ANNOTATIONS TO REYNOLDS' *Discourses*. Around 1808, in a copy of Volume I of *The Works of Sir Joshua Reynolds,* 2nd ed. (3 vols., 1798), edited by Edmond Malone, Blake annotated Malone's introduction and the first eight discourses. The complete texts of *Discourse III* and *Discourse VII* appear on pp. 403–408. The text is from *The Poetry and Prose of William Blake,* copyright © 1965 by David V. Erdman and Harold Bloom, by permission of Doubleday & Company, Inc.; compared with Geoffrey Keynes, ed., *The Complete Writings of William Blake* (1966), by permission of The Nonesuch Press Ltd. and Geoffrey Keynes.

All this concession is to prove that genius is acquired, as follows in the next page.

Page XVII

I am now clearly of opinion, that a relish for the higher excellencies of art is an acquired taste, which no man ever possessed without long cultivation, and great labor . . . we are often ashamed of our apparent dullness; as if it were to be expected that our minds, like tinder, should instantly catch fire from the divine spark of Raphael's genius.

A mock.

. . . but let it be always remembered, that the exlence of his style is not on the surface, but lies deep; and at the first view is seen but mistily.

A mock.

It is the florid style, which strikes at once, and captivates the eye for a time. . . .

A lie: The florid style, such as the Venetian and the Flemish, never struck me at once nor at all.
The style that strikes the eye is the true style, but a fool's eye is not to be a criterion.

Page XIX

How incapable of producing anything of their own, those are, who have spent most of their time in making finished copies, is an observation well known to all who are conversant with our art.

Finished? What does he mean? Niggling without the correct and definite outline? If he means that copying correctly is a hindrance, he is a liar, for that is the only school to the language of art.

Page XCVIII

But this disposition to abstractions, to generalizing and classification, is the great glory of the human mind.

To generalize is to be an idiot. To particularize is the alone distinction of merit. General knowledges are those knowledges that idiots possess.

Discourse I
Page 14

But young men have not only this frivolous ambition of being thought masters of execution, inciting them on one hand, but also their natural sloth tempting them on the other.

Execution is the chariot of genius.

Discourse II
Page 32

How incapable those are of producing anything of their own, who have spent much of their time in making finished copies, is well known to all who are conversant with our art.

This is most false, for no one can ever design till he has learned the language of art by making many finished copies both of nature and art and of whatever comes in his way from earliest childhood. The difference between a bad artist and a good one is: the bad artist seems to copy a great deal. The good one really does copy a great deal.

Page 33

The great use in copying, if it be at all useful, should seem to be in learning to color; yet even coloring will never be perfectly attained by servilely copying the model before you.

Contemptible: Servile copying is the great merit of copying.

Page 34

Following these rules, and using these precautions, when you have clearly and distinctly learned in what good coloring consists, you cannot do better than have recourse to nature herself, who is always at hand, and in comparison of whose true splendor the best colored pictures are but faint and feeble.

Nonsense: Every eye sees differently. As the eye, such the object.

Page 35

Instead of copying the touches of those great masters, copy only their conceptions. . . . Labor to invent on their general principles and way of thinking. . . . how a Michelangelo or Raphael would have treated this subject.

General principles again: Unless you consult particulars you cannot even know or see Michelangelo or Raphael or anything else.

But as mere enthusiasm will carry you but a little way. . . .

Mere enthusiasm is the all in all! Bacon's philosophy has ruined England. Bacon is only Epicurus over again.[1]

Page 37

Few have been taught to any purpose who have not been their own teachers.

True.

Page 40

A facility of drawing, like that of playing upon a musical instrument, cannot be acquired but by an infinite number of acts.

True.

Page 41

I would particularly recommend that after your return from the Academy . . . you would endeavor to draw the figure by memory.

Good advice.

But while I mention the port-crayon as the student's constant companion, he must still remember that the pencil is the instrument by which he must hope to obtain eminence.

Nonsense!

Page 42

The Venetian and Flemish schools, which owe much of their fame to coloring. . . .

—because they could not draw.

Page 43

Those of Titian, Paul Veronese, Tintoret, and the Bassans are in general slight and undetermined. Their sketches on paper are as rude as their pictures are excellent in regard to harmony of coloring. Correggio and Baroccio have left few, if any, finished drawings behind them. And in the Flemish school, Rubens and Van Dyck made their drawings for the most part in color or in chiaroscuro.

All the pictures said to be by these men are the labored fabrications of journey-work. They could not draw.

Page 48

The well-grounded painter . . . is contented that all shall be as great as himself, who have undergone the same fatigue. . . .

The man who asserts that there is no such thing as softness in art, and that everything in art is definite and determinate, has not been told this by practice, but by inspiration and vision, because vision is determinate and perfect, and he copies that without fatigue, everything being definite and determinate. Softness is produced alone by comparative strength and weakness in the marking out of the forms. I say these principles could never be found out by the study of nature without con- or innate science.

Discourse III

Page 50

A work of genius is a work "not to be obtained by the invocation of memory and her siren daughters, but by devout prayer to that eternal spirit, who can enrich with all utterance and knowledge and sends out his seraphim with the hallowed fire of his altar to touch and purify the lips of whom he pleases."[2]

MILTON

[1]See Bacon, *The Advancement of Learning,* pp. 183–84.

[2]*Reason in Church Government.*

The following discourse is particularly interesting to block-heads, as it endeavors to prove that there is no such thing as inspiration and that any man of a plain understanding may by thieving from others become a Michelangelo.

Page 52

The wish of the genuine painter must be more extensive: instead of endeavoring to amuse mankind with the minute neatness of his imitations, he must endeavor to improve them by the grandeur of his ideas.

Without minute neatness of execution the sublime cannot exist! Grandeur of ideas is founded on precision of ideas.

Page 54

The moderns are not less convinced than the ancients of this superior power existing in the art; nor less sensible of its effects.

I wish that this was true.

Page 55

Such is the warmth with which both the ancients and moderns speak of this divine principle of the art;

And such is the coldness with which Reynolds speaks! And such is his enmity.

. . . enthusiastic admiration seldom promotes knowledge.

Enthusiastic admiration is the first principle of knowledge and its last. Now he begins to degrade, to deny and to mock.

. . . He examines his own mind, and perceives there nothing of that divine inspiration, with which, he is told, so many others have been favored.

The man who on examining his own mind finds nothing of inspiration ought not dare to be an artist; he is a fool and a cunning knave suited to the purposes of evil demons.

Page 56

He never traveled to heaven to gather new ideas;

and he finds himself possessed of no other qualifications than what mere common observation and a plain understanding can confer.

The man who never in his mind and thoughts traveled to heaven is no artist.

Artists who are above a plain understanding are mocked and destroyed by this president of fools.

But on this, as upon many other occasions, we ought to distinguish how much is to be given to enthusiasm, and how much to reason . . . taking care . . . not to lose . . . that solidity and truth of principle, upon which alone we can reason, and may be enabled to practice.

It is evident that Reynolds wished none but fools to be in the arts and in order to this, he calls all others vague enthusiasts or madmen.

What has reasoning to do with the art of painting?

Page 57

. . . most people err, not so much from want of capacity to find their object, as from not knowing what object to pursue.

The man who does not know what object to pursue is an idiot.

This great ideal perfection and beauty are not to be sought in the heavens, but upon the earth.

A lie!

They are about us, and upon every side of us.

A lie!

But the power of discovering what is deformed in nature, or in other words, what is particular and uncommon, can be acquired only by experience;

A lie!

Page 58

. . . and the whole beauty of the art consists, in my opinion, in being able to get above all singular forms, local customs, particularities, and details of every kind.

A folly! Singular and particular detail is the foundation of the sublime.

> All the objects which are exhibited to our view by nature, upon close examination will be found to have their blemishes and defects. The most beautiful forms have something about them like weakness, minuteness, or imperfection.

Minuteness is their whole beauty.

> This idea of the perfect state of nature, which the artist calls the ideal beauty, is the great leading principle by which works of genius are conducted.

Knowledge of ideal beauty is not to be acquired. It is born with us. Innate ideas are in every man, born with him; they are truly himself. The man who says that we have no innate ideas must be a fool and knave, having no conscience or innate science.

Page 60

> Thus it is from a reiterated experience and a close comparison of the objects in nature, that an artist becomes possessed of the idea of that central form . . . from which every deviation is deformity.

One central form composed of all other forms being granted, it does not therefore follow that all other forms are deformity.

All forms are perfect in the poet's mind, but these are not abstracted nor compounded from nature, but are from imagination.

Page 61

> Even the great Bacon treats with ridicule the idea of confusing proportion to rules, or of producing beauty by selection.

The great Bacon he is called—I call him the little Bacon—says that everything must be done by experiment; his first principle is unbelief, and yet here he says that art must be produced without such method. He is like Sir Joshua, full of self-contradiction and knavery.

> There is a rule, obtained out of general nature, to contradict which is to fall into deformity.

What is general nature? Is there such a thing? What is general knowledge? Is there such a thing? Strictly speaking, all knowledge is particular.

Page 62

> To the principle I have laid down, that the idea of beauty in each species of beings is an invariable one, it may be objected, that in every particular species there are various central forms, which are separate and distinct from each other, and yet are each undeniably beautiful.

Here he loses sight of a central form and gets into many central forms.

Page 63

> It is true, indeed, that these figures are each perfect in their kind, though of different characters and proportions; but still none of them is the representation of an individual, but of a class.

Every class is individual.

> Thus, though the forms of childhood and age differ exceedingly, there is a common form in childhood, and a common form in age, which is the more perfect, as it is more remote from all peculiarities.

There is no end to the follies of this man. Childhood and age are equally belonging to every class.

> . . . though the most perfect forms of each of the general divisions of the human figure are ideal and superior to any individual form of that class, yet the highest perfection of the human figure is not to be found in any one of them. It is not in the *Hercules*, nor in the *Gladiator*, nor in the *Apollo*. . . .

Here he comes again to his central form.

Page 64

> There is, likewise, a kind of symmetry, or proportion, which may properly be said to belong to deformity. A figure lean or corpulent, tall or short, though deviating from beauty, may still have a certain union of the various parts.

The symmetry of deformity is a pretty foolery. Can any man who thinks talk so? Leanness or fatness is not deformity, but

Reynolds thought character itself extravagance and deformity. Age and youth are not classes, but properties of each class; so are leanness and fatness.

Page 65

When the artist has by diligent attention acquired a clear and distinct idea of beauty and symmetry; when he has reduced the variety of nature to the abstract idea. . . .

What folly!

Page 67

. . . [the painter] must divest himself of all prejudices in favor of his age or country; he must disregard all local and temporary ornaments, and look only on those general habits, which are everywhere and always the same.

Generalizing in everything, the man would soon be a fool, but a cunning fool.

Page 71

Albert Dürer, as Vasari has justly remarked, would, probably, have been one of the first painters of his age . . . had he been initiated into those great principles of the art, which were so well understood and practiced by his contemporaries in Italy.

What does this mean, "would have been one of the first painters of his age"? Albert Dürer is, not would have been. Besides, let them look at Gothic figures and Gothic buildings and not talk of Dark Ages or of any age. Ages are all equal. But genius is always above the age.

Page 74

I should be sorry, if what is here recommended, should be at all understood to countenance a careless or indetermined manner of painting. For though the painter is to overlook the accidental discriminations of nature, he is to exhibit distinctly, and with precision, the general forms of things.

Here he is for determinate and yet for indeterminate. Distinct general form cannot exist. Distinctness is particular, not general.

Page 75

A firm and determined outline is one of the characteristics of the great style in painting; and let me add, that he who possesses the knowledge of the exact form which every part of nature ought to have, will be fond of expressing that knowledge with correctness and precision in all his works.

A noble sentence!
Here is a sentence, which overthrows all his book.

To conclude; I have endeavored to reduce the idea of beauty to general principles. . . .

. . . Bacon's philosophy makes both statesmen and artists fools and knaves.

Discourse IV

Page 78

The two following discourses are particularly calculated for the setting ignorant and vulgar artists as models of execution in art. Let him who will, follow such advice. I will not. I know that the man's execution is as his conception and no better.

Page 79

The value and rank of every art is in proportion to the mental labor employed in it, or the mental pleasure produced by it.

Why does he not always allow this?

Page 80

I have formerly observed that perfect form is produced by leaving out particularities, and retaining only general ideas. . . .

General ideas again!

Invention in painting does not imply the invention of the subject; for that is commonly supplied by the poet or historian.

All but names of persons and places is invention both in poetry and painting.

Page 82

. . . the usual and most dangerous error is on the side of minuteness, and therefore I think caution most necessary where most have failed.

Here is nonsense.

Page 83

The general idea constitutes real excellence. All smaller things, however perfect in their way, are to be sacrificed without mercy to the greater.

Sacrifice the parts, what becomes of the whole?

Even in portraits, the grace, and, we may add, the likeness, consists more in taking the general air, than in observing the exact similitude of every feature.

How ignorant!

Page 86

A painter of portraits retains the individual likeness; a painter of history shows the man by showing his actions.

If he does not show the man as well as the action, he is a poor artist.

Page 106

A history painter paints man in general; a portrait painter, a particular man, and consequently a defective model.

A history painter paints the hero, and not man in general, but most minutely in particular.

Page III

The errors of genius . . . are pardonable, and none even of the more exalted painters are wholly free of them. . . .

Genius has no error; it is ignorance that is error.

Pages 117–18

If you mean to preserve the most perfect beauty in its most perfect state, you cannot express the passions, all of which produce distortion and deformity, more or less, in the most beautiful faces.

What nonsense!
   Passion and expression is beauty itself. The face that is incapable of passion and expression is deformity itself. Let it be painted and patched and praised and advertised forever, it will only be admired by fools.[3]

Page 119

We can easily, like the ancients, suppose a Jupiter to be possessed of all those powers and perfections which the subordinate deities were endowed with separately. Yet, when they employed their art to represent him, they confined his character to majesty alone.

False: the ancients were chiefly attentive to complicated and minute discrimination of character; it is the whole of art.

Page 120

[Pliny wrongfully] observes . . . in a statue . . . three different characters.

Reynolds cannot bear expression.

Discourse VI

Page 154

We may venture to say, that as art shall advance. . . .

If art was progressive we should have had Michelangelos and Raphaels to succeed and to improve upon each other. But it is not so. Genius dies with its possessor and comes not again till another is born with it.[4]

---

[3]Compare Schelling, *On the Relation of the Plastic Arts to Nature*, pp. 457–67.
[4]The attack on art as progressive is shared by most critics after Blake. It is part of an attempt to distinguish art from science, which builds on past accumulation of information. In Blake and the Romantics it begins with the close identification of the unique individual artist with his work.

Page 155

It must of necessity be, that even works of genius, like every other effect, as they must have their cause, must likewise have their rules.

Identities or things are neither cause nor effect. They are eternal.

Page 157

. . . our minds should be habituated to the contemplation of excellence; and that, far from being contented to make such habits the discipline of our youth only, we should to the last moment of our lives, continue a settled intercourse with all the true examples of grandeur. Their inventions are not only the food of our infancy, but the substance which supplies the fullest maturity of our vigor.

Reynolds thinks that man learns all that he knows. I say on the contrary that man brings all that he has or can have into the world with him. Man is born like a garden ready planted and sown. This world is too poor to produce one seed.

Page 180

Men who although thus bound down by the almost invincible powers of early habits, have still exerted extraordinary abilities within their narrow and confined circle; and have, from the natural vigor of their mind, given a very interesting expression and force and energy to their works.

He who can be bound down is no genius. Genius cannot be bound; it may be rendered indignant and outrageous. "Oppression makes the wise man mad" (Solomon).

Discourse VII

Page 188

The purpose of the following discourse is to prove that taste and genius are not of heavenly origin and that all who have supposed that they are so are to be considered as weakheaded fanatics.

The obligations Reynolds has laid on bad artists of all classes will at all times make them his admirers, but most especially for this discourse, in which it is proved that the stupid are born with faculties equal to other men, only they have not cultivated them because they thought it not worth the trouble.

Page 194

We will allow a poet to express his meaning, when his meaning is not well known to himself, with a certain degree of obscurity, as it is one source of the sublime.

Obscurity is neither the source of the sublime nor of anything else.

But when, in plain prose, we gravely talk of courting the muse in shady bowers; waiting the call and inspiration of Genius . . . sagaciously observing how much the wild freedom and liberty of imagination is cramped by attention to established rules . . . we generally rest contented with mere words, or at best entertain notions not only groundless but pernicious.

The ancients and the wisest of the moderns were of the opinion that Reynolds condemns and laughs at.

Page 195

. . . scarce a poet is to be found . . . who preserved a sound mind in a sound body, and continued practicing his profession to the very last, whose latter works are not as replete with the fire of imagination, as those which were produced in his more youthful days.

As replete, but not more replete.

To understand literally these metaphors or ideas expressed in poetical language, seems to be equally absurd as to conclude . . .

The ancients did not mean to impose when they affirmed their belief in vision and revelation. Plato was in earnest: Milton was in earnest. They believed that God did visit man really and truly and not as Reynolds pretends.

Page 196

. . . that because painters sometimes represent poets writing from the dictates of a little winged boy or genius, that this same genius really did inform him in a whisper what he was to write; and that he is himself but a mere machine, unconscious of the operations of his own mind.

How very anxious Reynolds is to disprove and condemn spiritual perception!

Page 197

It is supposed that their poems are intuitive, that under the name of genius great works are produced, and under the name of taste an exact judgment given, without our knowing why, and without our being under the least obligation to reason, precept, or experience.

Who ever said this?

One can scarcely state these opinions without exposing their absurdity. . . .

He states absurdities in company with truths and calls both absurd.

Page 198

. . . I am persuaded, that even among those few who may be called thinkers, the prevalent opinion allows less than it ought to the powers of reason. . . .

The artifice of the Epicurean philosophers is to call all other opinions unsolid and unsubstantial than those which are derived from earth.

We often appear to differ in sentiments from each other, merely from the inaccuracy of terms.

It is not in terms that Reynolds and I disagree. Two contrary opinions can never by any language be made alike. I say, taste and genius are not teachable or acquirable, but are born with us. Reynolds says the contrary.

Page 199

. . . we are obliged to take words as we find them; all we can do is to distinguish the things to which they are applied.

This is false; the fault is not in words, but in things. Locke's opinions of words and their fallaciousness are artful opinions and fallacious also.

Page 200

It is the very same taste which relishes a demonstration in geometry, that is pleased with the resemblance of a picture to an original, and touched with the harmony of music.

Demonstration, similitude and harmony are objects of reasoning. Invention, identity and melody are objects of intuition.

Page 201

Coloring is true when it is naturally adapted to the eye, from brightness, from softness, from harmony, from resemblance; because these agree with their object, nature, and therefore are true; as true as mathematical demonstration. . . .

God forbid that truth should be confined to mathematical demonstration!

But beside real, there is also apparent truth, or opinion, or prejudice. With regard to real truth, when it is known, the taste which conforms to it, is, and must be, uniform.

He who does not know truth at sight is unworthy of her notice.

In proportion as these prejudices are known to be generally diffused, or long received, the taste which conforms to them approaches nearer to certainty, and to a sort of resemblance to real science, even where opinions are found to be no better than prejudices.

Here is a great deal to do to prove that all truth is prejudice, for all that is valuable in knowledge is superior to demonstrative science, such as is weighed or measured.

Page 202

As these prejudices become more narrow, more local, more transitory, this secondary taste becomes more and more fantastical. . . .

And so he thinks he has proved that genius and inspiration are all a hum.

> Having laid down these positions, I shall proceed with less method. . . .

He calls the above proceeding with method!

> We will take it for granted, that reason is something invariable and fixed in the nature of things. . . .

Reason, or a ratio of all we have known, is not the same it shall be when we know more; he therefore takes a falsehood for granted to set out with.

Page 203

> . . . we will conclude, that whatever goes under the name of taste, which we can fairly bring under the dominion of reason, must be considered as equally exempt from change.

Now this is supreme fooling.

> The arts would lie open forever to caprice and casualty, if those who are to judge of their excellencies had no settled principles by which they are to regulate their decisions. . . .

He may as well say that if man does not lay down settled principles, the sun will not rise in the morning.

Page 204

> My notion of nature comprehends not only the forms which nature produces, but also the nature and internal fabric and organization, as I may call it, of the human mind and imagination.

Here is a plain confession that he thinks mind and imagination not to be above the mortal and perishing nature. Such is the end of Epicurean or Newtonian philosophy; it is atheism.

Page 208

> This [Poussin's painting of Perseus with Medusa's head] is undoubtedly a subject of great bustle and tumult, and that the first effect of the picture may correspond to the subject, every principle of composition is violated; there is no principal figure, no principal light, no groups . . . . I remember turning from it with disgust. . . .

Reynolds's eye could not bear characteristic coloring or light and shade.

> This conduct of Poussin I hold to be entirely improper to imitate. A picture should please at first sight. . . .

Please whom? Some men cannot see a picture except in a dark corner.

Page 209

> No one can deny, that violent passions will naturally emit harsh and disagreeable tones. . . .

Violent passions emit the real, good and perfect tones.

Page 214

> If it be objected that Rubens judged ill at first in thinking it necessary to make his work so very ornamental, this puts the question upon new ground.

Here it is called ornamental that the Roman and Bolognian schools may be insinuated not to be ornamental.

Page 215

> Nobody will dispute but some of the best of the Roman or Bolognian schools would have produced a more learned and more noble work.

Learned and noble is ornamental.

> This leads us to another important province of taste, that of weighing the value of the different classes of the art, and of estimating them accordingly.

A fool's balance is no criterion because, though it goes down on the heaviest side, we ought to look what he puts into it.

Page 232

If a European, when he has cut off his beard, and put false hair on his head, or bound up his own natural hair in regular hard knots, as unlike nature as he can possible make it . . . meets a Cherokee Indian, who has . . . laid on with equal care and attention his yellow and red ocher on particular parts of his forehead and cheeks . . . whoever of these two despises the other for this attention to the fashion of his country, whichever first feels himself provoked to laugh, is the barbarian.

Excellent!

Page 242

In the midst of the highest flights of fancy or imagination, reason ought to preside from first to last. . . .

If this is true, it is a devilish foolish thing to be an artist.

Discourse VIII

Page 244

Burke's *Treatise on the Sublime and Beautiful*[5] is founded on the opinions of Newton and Locke; on this treatise Reynolds has grounded many of his assertions in all his discourses. I read Burke's treatise when very young; at the same time I read Locke on human understanding and Bacon's *Advancement of Learning,*[6] on every one of these books I wrote my opinions, and on looking them over find that my notes on Reynolds in this book are exactly similar. I felt the same contempt and abhorrence then that I do now. They mock inspiration and vision. Inspiration and vision was then, and now is, and I hope will always remain, my element, my eternal dwelling place; how can I then hear it condemned without returning scorn for scorn?

---

[5]See pp. 299–306. Blake attacks particularly Burke's principle of the association of ideas.
[6]See pp. 183–84.

A Descriptive Catalogue

From

The Canterbury Pilgrims

The characters of Chaucer's pilgrims are the characters which compose all ages and nations: as one age falls, another rises, different to mortal sight, but to immortals only the same; for we see the same characters repeated again and again, in animals, vegetables, minerals, and in men; nothing new occurs in identical existence; accident ever varies, substance can never suffer change nor decay.

Of Chaucer's characters, as described in his *Canterbury Tales,* some of the names or titles are altered by time, but the characters themselves forever remain unaltered, and consequently they are the physiognomies or lineaments of universal human life, beyond which nature never steps. Names alter; things never alter. I have known multitudes of those who would have been monks in the age of monkery, who in this deistical age are deists. As Newton numbered the stars, and as Linneus numbered the plants, so Chaucer numbered the classes of men.

The Ancient Britons

In the last battle of King Arthur, only three Britons escaped; these were the Strongest Man, the Beautifullest Man and the Ugliest Man: these three marched through the field unsubdued, as gods, and the sun of Britain set, but shall arise again with tenfold splendor when Arthur shall awake from sleep, and resume his dominion over earth and ocean.

The three general classes of men, who are represented by the most beautiful, the most strong, and the most ugly, could not be represented by any historical facts but those of our own country, the ancient Britons, without violating costume. The Britons (say historians) were naked civilized men, learned, studious, abstruse in thought and contemplation; naked, simple, plain in their acts and manners; wiser than

---

A DESCRIPTIVE CATALOGUE. Blake's *Descriptive Catalogue* was printed for an exhibition of sixteen of his paintings in London in 1809. The text is from *The Poetry and Prose of William Blake,* copyright © 1965 by David V. Erdman and Harold Bloom, by permission of Doubleday & Company, Inc.; compared with Geoffrey Keynes, ed., *The Complete Writings of William Blake* (1966), by permission of The Nonesuch Press Ltd. and Geoffrey Keynes.

after-ages. They were overwhelmed by brutal arms, all but a small remnant; Strength, Beauty, and Ugliness escaped the wreck, and remain forever unsubdued, age after age.

The British antiquities are now in the artist's hands; all his visionary contemplations, relating to his own country and its ancient glory, when it was, as it again shall be, the source of learning and inspiration. Arthur was a name for the constellation Arcturus, or Boötes, the keeper of the North Pole. And all the fables of Arthur and his Round Table; of the warlike naked Britons; of Merlin; of Arthur's conquest of the whole world; of his death, or sleep, and promise to return again; of the Druid monuments or temples; of the pavement of Watling Street; of London stone; of the caverns in Cornwall, Wales, Derbyshire, and Scotland; of the giants of Ireland and Britain; of the elemental beings called by us the general name of fairies; and of these three who escaped, namely Beauty, Strength, and Ugliness. Mr. B.[1] has in his hands poems of the highest antiquity: Adam was a Druid, and Noah; also Abraham was called to succeed the Druidical age, which began to turn allegoric and mental signification into corporeal command, whereby human sacrifice would have depopulated the earth. All these things are written in Eden. The artist is an inhabitant of that happy country; and if everything goes on as it has begun, the world of vegetation and generation may expect to be opened again to heaven, through Eden, as it was in the beginning.

The Strong Man represents the human sublime. The Beautiful Man represents the human pathetic, which was in the wars of Eden divided into male and female. The Ugly Man represents the human reason. They were originally one man, who was fourfold; he was self-divided, and his real humanity slain on the stems of generation, and the form of the fourth was like the Son of God. How he became divided is a subject of great sublimity and pathos. The artist has written it under inspiration, and will, if God please, publish it; it is voluminous, and contains the ancient history of Britain, and the world of Satan and of Adam.

In the meantime he has painted this picture, which supposes that in the reign of that British prince, who lived in the fifth century, there were remains of those naked heroes in the Welsh mountains; they are there now, Gray saw them in the person of his bard on Snowdon;[2] there they dwell in naked simplicity; happy is he who can see and converse with them above the shadows of generation and death. The giant Albion, was patriarch of the Atlantic; he is the Atlas of the Greeks, one of those the Greeks called Titans. The stories of Arthur are the acts of Albion applied to a prince of the fifth century, who conquered Europe, and held the empire of the world in the dark age, which the Romans never again recovered. In this picture, believing with Milton the ancient British history, Mr. B. has done as all the ancients did, and as all the moderns who were worthy of fame, given the historical fact in its poetical vigor so as it always happens, and not in that dull way that some historians pretend, who, being weakly organized themselves, cannot see either miracle or prodigy; all is to them a dull round of probabilities and possibilities; but the history of all times and places is nothing else but improbabilities; what we should say was impossible if we did not see it always before our eyes.

The antiquities of every nation under heaven, is no less sacred than that of the Jews. They are the same thing, as Jacob Bryant and all antiquaries have proved. How other antiquities came to be neglected and disbelieved, while those of the Jews are collected and arranged, is an inquiry worthy both of the antiquarian and the divine. All had originally one language, and one religion: this was the religion of Jesus, the everlasting Gospel. Antiquity preaches the Gospel of Jesus. The reasoning historian, turner and twister of causes and consequences, such as Hume, Gibbon, and Voltaire, cannot with all their artifice turn or twist one fact or disarrange self-evident action and reality. Reasons and opinions concerning acts are not history. Acts themselves alone are history, and these are neither the exclusive property of Hume, Gibbon, nor Voltaire, Echard, Rapin, Plutarch, nor Herodotus. Tell me the acts, O historian, and leave me to reason upon them as I please; away with your reasoning and your rubbish! All that is not action is not worth reading. Tell me the what; I do not want you to tell me the why, and the how; I can find that out myself, as well as you can, and I will not be fooled by you into opinions, that you please to impose, to disbelieve what you think improbable or impossible. His opinions, who does not see spiritual agency, is not worth any man's reading; he who rejects a fact because it is improbable, must reject all history and retain doubts only.

It has been said to the artist, "take the *Apollo* for the model of your Beautiful Man, and the *Hercules* for your Strong Man, and the *Dancing Fawn* for your Ugly Man." Now he comes to his trial. He knows that what he does is not inferior to the grandest antiques. Superior they cannot be, for human power cannot go beyond either what he does, or what they have done; it is the gift of God, it is inspiration and vision. He had resolved to emulate those precious remains of antiquity; he has done so and the result you behold; his ideas of strength and beauty have not been greatly different. Poetry as it exists now on earth, in the various remains of ancient

---

[1]Blake is probably referring to himself and his own prophetic poems, which he claimed were "dictated" to him.

[2]A reference to Gray's poem *The Bard,* for which Blake did a painting described in this catalogue.

authors, music as it exists in old tunes or melodies, painting and sculpture as it exists in the remains of antiquity and in the works of more modern genius, is inspiration, and cannot be surpassed; it is perfect and eternal. Milton, Shakespeare, Michelangelo, Raphael, the finest specimens of ancient sculpture and painting and architecture, Gothic, Grecian, Hindu and Egyptian, are the extent of the human mind. The human mind cannot go beyond the gift of God, the Holy Ghost. To suppose that art can go beyond the finest specimens of art that are now in the world, is not knowing what art is; it is being blind to the gifts of the spirit.

It will be necessary for the painter to say something concerning his ideas of beauty, strength, and ugliness.

The beauty that is annexed and appended to folly, is a lamentable accident and error of the mortal and perishing life; it does but seldom happen; but with this unnatural mixture the sublime artist can have nothing to do; it is fit for the burlesque. The beauty proper for sublime art is lineaments, or forms and features that are capable of being the receptacles of intellect; accordingly the painter has given in his beautiful man, his own idea of intellectual beauty. The face and limbs that deviates or alters least, from infancy to old age, is the face and limbs of greatest beauty and perfection.

The ugly, likewise, when accompanied and annexed to imbecility and disease, is a subject for burlesque and not for historical grandeur; the artist has imagined his ugly man, one approaching to the beast in features and form, his forehead small, without frontals; his jaws large; his nose high on the ridge, and narrow; his chest, and the stamina of his make, comparatively little, and his joints and his extremities large; his eyes, with scarce any whites, narrow and cunning, and everything tending toward what is truly ugly, the incapability of intellect.

The artist has considered his strong man as a receptacle of wisdom, a sublime energizer; his features and limbs do not spindle out into length without strength, nor are they too large and unwieldy for his brain and bosom. Strength consists in accumulation of power to the principal seat, and from thence a regular gradation and subordination; strength is compactness, not extent nor bulk.

The Strong Man acts from conscious superiority, and marches on in fearless dependence on the divine decrees, raging with the inspiration of a prophetic mind. The Beautiful Man acts from duty and anxious solicitude for the fates of those for whom he combats. The Ugly Man acts from love of carnage, and delight in the savage barbarities of war, rushing with sportive precipitation into the very teeth of the affrighted enemy.

The Roman soldiers rolled together in a heap before them: "Like the rolling thing before the whirlwind''; each show a different character, and a different expression of fear, or revenge, or envy, or blank horror, or amazement, or devout wonder and unresisting awe.

The dead and the dying Britons, naked, mingled with armed Romans, strew the field beneath. Among these the last of the bards who were capable of attending warlike deeds is seen falling, outstretched among the dead and the dying, singing to his harp in the pains of death.

Distant among the mountains are Druid temples, similar to Stonehenge. The sun sets behind the mountains, bloody with the day of battle.

The flush of health in flesh exposed to the open air, nourished by the spirits of forests and floods in that ancient happy period, which history has recorded, cannot be like the sickly daubs of Titian or Rubens. Where will the copier of nature, as it now is, find a civilized man, who has been accustomed to go naked? Imagination only can furnish us with coloring appropriate, such as is found in the frescoes of Raphael and Michelangelo: the disposition of forms always directs coloring in works of true art. As to a modern man, stripped from his load of clothing, he is like a dead corpse. Hence Rubens, Titian, Correggio and all of that class, are like leather and chalk; their men are like leather, and their women like chalk, for the disposition of their forms will not admit of grand coloring; in Mr. B.'s Britons the blood is seen to circulate in their limbs: he defies competition in coloring.

From

A Vision of the Last Judgment

The Last Judgment will be when all those are cast away who trouble religion with questions concerning good and evil or eating of the tree of those knowledges or reasonings which hinder the vision of God, turning all into a consuming fire. When imagination, art and science and all intellectual gifts, all the gifts of the Holy Ghost, are looked upon as of no use and only contention remains to man, then the Last Judgment begins, and its vision is seen by the imaginative eye of everyone according to the situation he holds.

A VISION OF THE LAST JUDGMENT. Blake's description of his painting *The Last Judgment*, now lost, was written in a manuscript notebook, known as the Rossetti Manuscript, in 1810. The text is from *The Poetry and Prose of William Blake*, copyright © 1965 by David V. Erdman and Harold Bloom, by permission of Doubleday & Company, Inc.; compared with Geoffrey Keynes, ed., *The Complete Writings of William Blake* (1966), by permission of The Nonsuch Press Ltd. and Geoffrey Keynes.

The Last Judgment is not fable or allegory, but vision. Fable or allegory are a totally distinct and inferior kind of poetry. Vision or imagination is a representation of what eternally exists, really and unchangeably. Fable or allegory is formed by the daughters of memory. Imagination is surrounded by the daughters of inspiration, who in the aggregate are called Jerusalem. Fable is allegory, but what critics call the fable is vision itself. The Hebrew Bible and the Gospel of Jesus are not allegory, but eternal vision or imagination of all that exists. Note here that fable or allegory is seldom without some vision. *Pilgrim's Progress* is full of it, the Greek poets the same; but allegory and vision ought to be known as two distinct things, and so called for the sake of eternal life.[1] Plato has made Socrates say that poets and prophets do not know or understand what they write or utter; this is a most pernicious falsehood. If they do not, pray, is an inferior kind to be called knowing? Plato confutes himself.

The Last Judgment is one of these stupendous visions. I have represented it as I saw it; to different people it appears differently as everything else does; for though on earth things seem permanent, they are less permanent than a shadow, as we all know too well.

The nature of visionary fancy, or imagination, is very little known, and the eternal nature and permanence of its ever-existent images is considered as less permanent than the things of vegetative and generative nature; yet the oak dies as well as the lettuce, but its eternal image and individuality never dies, but renews by its seed; just so the imaginative image returns by the seed of contemplative thought; the writings of the prophets illustrate these conceptions of the visionary fancy by their various sublime and divine images as seen in the worlds of vision.

---

[1]Compare this definition to that in the letter to Thomas Butts, p. 401.

On Homer's Poetry

Every poem must necessarily be a perfect unity, but why Homer's is peculiarly so, I cannot tell; he has told the story of Bellerophon and omitted the Judgment of Paris, which is not only a part, but a principal part, of Homer's subject.

But when a work has unity, it is as much in a part as in the whole; the torso is as much a unity as the *Laocoön*.

As unity is the cloak of folly, so goodness is the cloak of knavery. Those who will have unity exclusively in Homer come out with a moral like a sting in the tail. Aristotle says characters are either good or bad;[1] now goodness or badness has nothing to do with character: an apple tree, a pear tree, a horse, a lion, are characters, but a good apple tree or a bad is an apple tree still; a horse is not more a lion for being a bad horse: that is its character: its goodness or badness is another consideration.

It is the same with the moral of a whole poem as with the moral goodness of its parts. Unity and morality are secondary considerations, and belong to philosophy and not to poetry, to exception and not to rule, to accident and not to substance; the ancients called it eating of the tree of good and evil.

The Classics! It is the classics, and not Goths nor monks, that desolate Europe with wars.

ON HOMER'S POETRY. The plate from which *On Homer's Poetry* was printed was etched in about 1820. The text is from *The Poetry and Prose of William Blake,* copyright © 1965 by David V. Erdman and Harold Bloom, by permission of Doubleday & Company, Inc.; compared with Geoffrey Keynes, ed., *The Writings of William Blake* (1966), by permission of the Nonesuch Press Ltd. and Geoffrey Keynes.
[1]This is not exactly what Aristotle said (see *Poetics,* II. 1, p. 51).

Friedrich von Schiller

1759–1805

Schiller proposes early in his *Letters on the Aesthetic Education of Man* his own form of what has come to be called, in Eliot's phrase, the "dissociation of sensibility." Eliot locates the bifurcation of man's sensibility into sense and intellect some time in the seventeenth century. Schiller places it much earlier. Civilization itself brought about a division in man; the intuitive and the speculative understanding withdrew from each other in defensive hostility; imagination and abstraction stood opposed. The division was fully established by the rise of the state and man's subservience to it.

Schiller's aesthetic speculations express the belief that there is a means by which man can regain his freedom from division, and that the means is art, taken in a very broad sense. Schiller is thus interested in determining the nature of art by explaining its value, indeed its use. But he would eschew the word *use,* for it implies utilitarian concerns. He is a Kantian, but he goes beyond Kant to formulate his own dialectic. Man possesses two fundamental drives, the sensuous drive (*Stofftrieb*) and the formal drive (*Formtrieb*). The former is characterized by the domination of change: "Man in this state is nothing but a unit of quantity, an occupied moment of time." He is dominated by sensation. The formal drive, on the other hand, annuls time and change "in its quest for the abstract, eternal, and absolute." From it emerge laws.

These drives demand reconciliation or transcendence in a higher drive, which Schiller calls the play-drive (*Spieltrieb*) and which he associates with art. In play it should be possible for man to "combine the greatest fullness of existence with the highest autonomy and freedom." Play in Schiller is nothing trivial. It is the expression of man's fullest nature in aesthetic experience, the healing of division. Schiller describes it much as Kant describes aesthetic "disinterest" and "purposiveness without a purpose." In play the mind is free and self-contained, dominated neither by "sense" nor by "form." By associating the experiencing of art with freedom Schiller makes huge claims for its cultural value: "Man is more than a match for any of nature's terrors once he knows how to give it form and convert it into an object of his contemplation."

Schiller's most famous theoretical work in addition to the *Letters* is the essay *On Naive and Sentimental Poetry,* in which he speculates on the differences between early and later, more sophisticated poetry in Western culture. The essay represents a concern with the problem of art's relation to the state of the culture at a given time. Schiller sought to defend the reflective or "sentimental" poetry of his age in terms of the new cultural situation.

Schiller's criticism and writings on aesthetics are in *The Works of Schiller,* edited by N. H. Dole (1902). *Letters on the Aesthetic Education of Man* have also been translated by Reginald Snell (1954) and by E. M. Wilkinson and L. A. Willoughby (1967). Commentaries include Victor Basch, *La Poétique de Schiller* (1911); E. C. Welm, *The Philosophy of Schiller in Its Historical Relations* (1912); Frederic Ewen, *The Prestige of Schiller in England 1788–1859* (1932); George Lukács, "Schillers Theorie der modernen Literatur," *Goethe und seine Zeit* (1947); Wilham Witte, *Schiller* (1949); Eva Schaper, "Friedrich Schiller: Adventures of a Kantian," *British Journal of Aesthetics,* IV (1964), 348–62; Emil Staiger, *Friedrich Schiller* (1967); Ronald Duncan Miller, *Schiller and the Ideal of Freedom* (1970); John Simons, *Friedrich Schiller* (1981); Leonard P. Wassell, *The Philosophical Background of Friedrich Schiller's Aesthetics of Living Form* (1982); and Philip J. Kain, *Schiller, Hegel, and Marx* (1982).

Letters on the Aesthetic Education of Man

From

Sixth Letter

Closer attention to the character of our age will . . . reveal an astonishing contrast between contemporary forms of humanity and earlier ones, especially the Greek. The reputation for culture and refinement, on which we otherwise rightly pride ourselves *vis-à-vis* humanity in its merely natural state, can avail us nothing against the natural humanity of the Greeks. For they were wedded to all the delights of art and all the dignity of wisdom, without however, like us, falling a prey to their seduction. The Greeks put us to shame not only by a simplicity to which our age is a stranger; they are at the same time our rivals, indeed often our models, in those very excellences with which we are wont to console ourselves for the unnaturalness of our manners. In fullness of form no less than of content, at once philosophic and creative, sensitive and energetic, the Greeks combined the first youth of imagination with the manhood of reason in a glorious manifestation of humanity.

At that first fair awakening of the powers of the mind, sense and intellect did not as yet rule over strictly separate domains; for no dissension had as yet provoked them into hostile partition and mutual demarcation of their frontiers. Poetry had not as yet coquetted with wit, nor speculation prostituted itself to sophistry. Both of them could, when need arose, exchange functions, since each in its own fashion paid honor to truth. However high the mind might soar, it always drew matter lovingly along with it; and however fine and

sharp the distinctions it might make, it never proceeded to mutilate. It did indeed divide human nature into its several aspects, and project these in magnified form into the divinities of its glorious pantheon; but not by tearing it to pieces; rather by combining its aspects in different proportions, for in no single one of their deities was humanity in its entirety ever lacking. How different with us moderns! With us too the image of the human species is projected in magnified form into separate individuals—but as fragments, not in different combinations, with the result that one has to go the rounds from one individual to another in order to be able to piece together a complete image of the species. With us, one might almost be tempted to assert, the various faculties appear as separate in practice as they are distinguished by the psychologist in theory, and we see not merely individuals, but whole classes of men, developing but one part of their potentialities, while of the rest, as in stunted growths, only vestigial traces remain.

I do not underrate the advantages which the human race today, considered as a whole and weighed in the balance of intellect, can boast in the face of what is best in the ancient world. But it has to take up the challenge in serried ranks, and let whole measure itself against whole. What individual modern could sally forth and engage, man against man, with an individual Athenian for the prize of humanity?

Whence this disadvantage among individuals when the species as a whole is at such an advantage? Why was the individual Greek qualified to be the representative of his age, and why can no single modern venture as much? Because it was from all-unifying nature that the former, and from the all-dividing intellect that the latter, received their respective forms.

It was civilization itself which inflicted this wound upon modern man. Once the increase of empirical knowledge, and more exact modes of thought, made sharper divisions between the sciences inevitable, and once the increasingly complex machinery of state necessitated a more rigorous separation of ranks and occupations, then the inner unity of human nature was severed too, and a disastrous conflict set its harmonious powers at variance. The intuitive and the speculative understanding now withdrew in hostility to

LETTERS ON THE AESTHETIC EDUCATION OF MAN. Schiller's *Briefe über die ästhetische Erziehung des Menschen* were first published in 1795. The text is from *On the Aesthetic Education of Man, in a Series of Letters,* edited and translated by E. M. Wilkinson and L. A. Willoughby (Oxford, Eng.: The Clarendon Press, 1967), and is reprinted by permission of the publishers.

take up positions in their respective fields, whose frontiers they now began to guard with jealous mistrust; and with this confining of our activity to a particular sphere we have given ourselves a master within, who not infrequently ends by suppressing the rest of our potentialities. While in the one a riotous imagination ravages the hard-won fruits of the intellect, in another the spirit of abstraction stifles the fire at which the heart should have warmed itself and the imagination been kindled.

This disorganization, which was first started within man by civilization and learning, was made complete and universal by the new spirit of government. It was scarcely to be expected that the simple organization of the early republics should have survived the simplicity of early manners and conditions; but instead of rising to a higher form of organic existence it degenerated into a crude and clumsy mechanism. That polypoid character of the Greek states, in which every individual enjoyed an independent existence but could, when need arose, grow into the whole organism, now made way for an ingenious clockwork, in which, out of the piecing together of innumerable but lifeless parts, a mechanical kind of collective life ensued. State and church, laws and customs, were now torn asunder; enjoyment was divorced from labor, the means from the end, the effort from the reward. Everlastingly chained to a single little fragment of the whole, man himself develops into nothing but a fragment; everlastingly in his ear the monotonous sound of the wheel that he turns, he never develops the harmony of his being, and instead of putting the stamp of humanity upon his own nature, he becomes nothing more than the imprint of his occupation or of his specialized knowledge. But even that meager, fragmentary participation, by which individual members of the state are still linked to the whole, does not depend upon forms which they spontaneously prescribe for themselves (for how could one entrust to their freedom of action a mechanism so intricate and so fearful of light and enlightenment?); it is dictated to them with meticulous exactitude by means of a formulary which inhibits all freedom of thought. The dead letter takes the place of living understanding, and a good memory is a safer guide than imagination and feeling.

Twelfth Letter

Towards the accomplishment of this twofold task—of giving reality to the necessity within, and subjecting to the law of necessity of reality without—we are impelled by two opposing forces which, since they drive us to the realization of their object, may aptly be termed drives. The first of these, which I will call the sensuous drive, proceeds from the physical existence of man, or his sensuous nature. Its business is

to set him within the limits of time, and to turn him into matter—not to provide him with matter, since that, of course, would presuppose a free activity of the person capable of receiving such matter, and distinguishing it from the self as from that which persists. By matter in this context we understand nothing more than change, or reality which occupies time. Consequently this drive demands that there shall be change, that time shall have a content. This state, which is nothing but time occupied by content, is called sensation, and it is through this alone that physical existence makes itself known.

Since everything that exists in time exists as a succession, the very fact of something existing at all means that everything else is excluded. When we strike a note on an instrument, only this single note, of all those it is capable of emitting, is actually realized; when man is sensible of the present, the whole infinitude of his possible determinations is confined to this single mode of his being. Wherever, therefore, this drive functions exclusively, we inevitably find the highest degree of limitation. Man in this state is nothing but a unit of quantity, an occupied moment of time—or rather, he is not at all, for his personality is suspended as long as he is ruled by sensation, and swept along by the flux of time.[1]

The domain of this drive embraces the whole extent of man's finite being. And since form is never made manifest except in some material, nor the absolute except through the medium of limitation, it is indeed to this sensuous drive that the whole of man's phenomenal existence is ultimately tied. But although it is this drive alone which awakens and develops the potentialities of man, it is also this drive alone which makes their complete fulfillment impossible. With indestructible chains it binds the ever-soaring spirit to the world of sense, and summons abstraction from its most unfettered excursions into the infinite back to the limitations of the present. Thought may indeed escape it for the moment, and a firm will triumphantly resist its demands; but suppressed nature soon resumes her rights, and presses for reality of existence, for some content to our knowing and some purpose for our doing.

---

[1] [Schiller] For this condition of self-loss under the dominion of feeling linguistic usage has the very appropriate expression: to be beside oneself, i.e., to be outside of one's own self. Although this turn of phrase is only used when sensation is intensified into passion, and the condition becomes more marked by being prolonged, it can nevertheless be said that everyone is beside himself as long as he does nothing but feel. To return from this condition to self-possession is termed, equally aptly: to be oneself again, i.e., to return into one's own self, to restore one's person. Of someone who has fainted, by contrast, we do not say that he is beside himself, but that he is away from himself, i.e., he has been rapt away from his self, whereas in the former case he is merely not in his self. Consequently, someone who has come out of a faint has merely come to himself, which state is perfectly compatible with being beside oneself.

The second of the two drives, which we may call the formal drive, proceeds from the absolute existence of man, or from his rational nature, and is intent on giving him the freedom to bring harmony into the diversity of his manifestations, and to affirm his person among all his changes of condition. Since this person, being an absolute and indivisible unity, can never be at variance with itself, since we are to all eternity we ourselves, that drive which insists on affirming the personality can never demand anything but that which is binding upon it to all eternity; hence it decides forever as it decides for this moment, and commands for this moment what it commands forever. Consequently it embraces the whole sequence of time, which is as much as to say: it annuls time and annuls change. It wants the real to be necessary and eternal, and the eternal and the necessary to be real. In other words, it insists on truth and on the right.

If the first drive only furnishes cases, this second one gives laws—laws for every judgment, where it is a question of knowledge, laws for every will, where it is a question of action. Whether it is a case of knowing an object, i.e., of attributing objective validity to a condition of our subject, or of acting upon knowledge, i.e., of making an objective principle the determining motive of our condition—in both cases we wrest this our condition from the jurisdiction of time, and endow it with reality for all men and all times, that is with universality and necessity. Feeling can only say: this is true for this individual and at this moment, and another moment, another individual can come along and revoke assertions made thus under the impact of momentary sensation. But once thought pronounces: that is, it decides forever and aye, and the validity of its verdict is guaranteed by the personality itself, which defies all change. Inclination can only say: this is good for you as an individual and for your present need; but your individuality and your present need will be swept away by change, and what you now so ardently desire will one day become the object of your aversion. But once the moral feeling says: this shall be, it decides forever and aye— once you confess truth because it is truth, and practice justice because it is justice, then you have made an individual case into a law for all cases, and treated one moment of your life as if it were eternity.

Where, then, the formal drive holds sway, and the pure object acts within us, we experience the greatest enlargement of being: all limitations disappear, and from the mere unit of quantity to which the poverty of his senses reduced him, man has raised himself to a unity of ideas embracing the whole realm of phenomena. During this operation we are no longer in time; time, with its whole never-ending succession, is in us. We are no longer individuals; we are species. The judgment of all minds is expressed through our own, the choice of all hearts is represented by our action.

Thirteenth Letter

At first sight nothing could seem more diametrically opposed than the tendencies of these two drives, the one pressing for change, the other for changelessness. And yet it is these two drives which, between them, exhaust our concept of humanity, and make a third fundamental drive which might possibly reconcile the two a completely unthinkable concept. How, then, are we to restore the unity of human nature which seems to be utterly destroyed by this primary and radical opposition?

It is true that their tendencies do indeed conflict with each other, but—and this is the point to note—not in the same objectives, and things which never make contact cannot collide. The sensuous drive does indeed demand change; but it does not demand the extension of this to the person and its domain, does not demand a change of principles. The formal drive insists on unity and persistence—but it does not require the condition to be stabilized as well as the person, does not require identity of sensation. The two are, therefore, not by nature opposed; and if they nevertheless seem to be so, it is because they have become opposed through a wanton transgression of nature, through mistaking their nature and function, and confusing their spheres of operation.[2] To watch over these, and secure for each of these two drives its proper frontiers, is the task of culture, which is, therefore, in duty

---

[2][Schiller] Once you postulate a primary, and therefore necessary, antagonism between these two drives, there is, of course, no other means of maintaining unity in man than by unconditionally subordinating the sensuous drive to the rational. From this, however, only uniformity can result, never harmony, and man goes on forever being divided. Subordination there must, of course, be; but it must be reciprocal. For even though it is true that limitation can never be the source of the absolute, and hence freedom never be dependent upon time, it is no less certain that the absolute can of itself never be the source of limitation, or a condition in time be dependent upon freedom. Both principles are, therefore, at once subordinated to each other and coordinated with each other, that is to say, they stand in reciprocal relation to one another: without form no matter, and without matter no form. (This concept of reciprocal action, and its fundamental importance, is admirably set forth in Fichte's *Fundaments of the Theory of Knowledge,* Leipzig, 1794.) How things stand with the person in the realm of ideas we frankly do not know; but that it can never become manifest in the realm of time without taking on matter, of that we are certain. In this realm, therefore, matter will have some say, and not merely in a role subordinate to form, but also coordinate with it and independently of it. Necessary as it may be, therefore, that feeling should have no say in the realm of reason, it is no less necessary that reason should not presume to have a say in the realm of feeling. Just by assigning to each of them its own sphere, we are by that very fact excluding the one from it, and setting bounds to each, bounds which can only be transgressed at the risk of detriment to both.

In the transcendental method of philosophizing, where everything depends on clearing form of content, and obtaining necessity in its pure state, free of all admixture with the contingent, one easily falls into thinking of material things as nothing but an obstacle, and of imagining that our sensuous nature, just because it happens to be a hindrance in this operation, must of necessity be in conflict with reason. Such a way of thinking is, it is true, wholly alien to the spirit of the Kantian system, but it may very well be found in the letter of it.

bound to do justice to both drives equally: not simply to maintain the rational against the sensuous, but the sensuous against the rational too. Hence its business is twofold: first, to preserve the life of sense against the encroachments of freedom; and second, to secure the personality against the forces of sensation. The former it achieves by developing our capacity for feeling, the latter by developing our capacity for reason.

Since the world is extension in time, i.e., change, the perfection of that faculty which connects man with the world will have to consist in maximum changeability and maximum extensity. Since the person is persistence within change, the perfection of that faculty which is to oppose change will have to be maximum autonomy and maximum intensity. The more facets his receptivity develops, the more labile it is, and the more surface it presents to phenomena, so much more world does man apprehend, and all the more potentialities does he develop in himself. The more power and depth the personality achieves, and the more freedom reason attains, so much more world does man comprehend, and all the more form does he create outside of himself. His education will therefore consist, firstly, in procuring for the receptive faculty the most manifold contacts with the world, and, within the purview of feeling, intensifying passivity to the utmost; secondly, in securing for the determining faculty the highest degree of independence from the receptive, and, within the purview of reason, intensifying activity to the utmost. Where both these aptitudes are conjoined, man will combine the greatest fullness of existence with the highest autonomy and freedom, and instead of losing himself to the world, will rather draw the latter into himself in all its infinitude of phenomena, and subject it to the unity of his reason.

But man can turn these relations upside down, and thus miss his destiny in two different ways. He can transfer the intensity required by the active function to the passive, let his sensuous drive encroach upon the formal, and make the receptive faculty do the work of the determining one. Or he can assign to the active function that extensity which is proper to the passive, let the formal drive encroach upon the sensuous, and substitute the determining faculty for the receptive one. In the first case he will never be himself; in the second he will never be anything else; and for that very reason, therefore, he will in both cases be neither the one nor the other, consequently—a nonentity.[3]

For if the sensuous drive becomes the determining one, that is to say, if the senses assume the role of legislator and the world suppresses the person, then the world ceases to be an object precisely to the extent that it becomes a force. From the moment that man is merely a content of time, he ceases to exist, and has in consequence no content either.

---

when the functions of thought and will encroach upon those of intuition and feeling.

One of the chief reasons why our natural sciences make such slow progress is obviously the universal, and almost uncontrollable, propensity to teleological judgments, in which, once they are used constitutively, the determining faculty is substituted for the receptive. However strong and however varied the impact made upon our organs by nature, all her manifold variety is then entirely lost upon us, because we are seeking nothing in her but what we have put into her; because, instead of letting her come in upon us, we are thrusting ourselves out upon her with all the impatient anticipations of our reason. If, then, in the course of centuries, it should happen that a man tries to approach her with his sense-organs untroubled, innocent and wide open, and, thanks to this, should chance upon a multitude of phenomena which we, with our tendency to prejudge the issue, have overlooked, then we are mightily astonished that so many eyes in such broad daylight should have noticed nothing. This premature hankering after harmony before we have even got together the individual sounds which are to go to its making, this violent usurping of authority by ratiocination in a field where its right to give orders is by no means unconditional, is the reason why so many thinking minds fail to have any fruitful effect upon the advancement of science; and it would be difficult to say which has done more harm to the progress of knowledge: a sense-faculty unamenable to form, or a reasoning faculty which will not stay for a content.

It would be no less difficult to determine which does more to impede the practice of brotherly love: the violence of our passions, which disturbs it, or the rigidity of our principles, which chills it—the egotism of our senses or the egotism of our reason. If we are to become compassionate, helpful, effective human beings, feeling and character must unite, even as wide-open senses must combine with vigor of intellect if we are to acquire experience. How can we, however laudable our precepts, how can we be just, kindly, and human towards others, if we lack the power of receiving into ourselves, faithfully and truly, natures unlike ours, of feeling our way into the situation of others, of making other people's feelings our own? But in the education we receive, no less than in that we give ourselves, this power gets repressed in exactly the measure that we seek to break the force of passions, and strengthen character by means of principles. Since it costs effort to remain true to one's principles when feeling is easily stirred, we take the easier way out and try to make character secure by blunting feeling; for it is, of course, infinitely easier to have peace and quiet from an adversary you have disarmed than to master a spirited and active foe. And this, for the most part, is the cooperation that is meant when people speak of forming character; and that, even in the best sense of the word, where it implies the cultivation of the inner, and not merely of the outer, man. A man so formed will, without doubt, be immune from the danger of being crude nature or of appearing as such; but he will at the same time be armored by principle against all natural feeling, and be equally inaccessible to the claims of humanity from without as he is to those of humanity from within.

It is a most pernicious abuse of the ideal of perfection, to apply it in all its rigor, either in our judgments of other people, or in those cases where we have to act on their behalf. The former leads to sentimental idealism; the latter to hardness and coldness of heart. We certainly make our duty to society uncommonly easy for ourselves by mentally substituting for the actual man who claims our help the ideal man who could in all probability help himself. Severity with oneself combined with leniency towards others is a sign of the truly excellent character. But mostly the man who is lenient to others will also be lenient with himself; and he who is severe with himself will be the same with others. To be lenient to oneself and severe towards others is the most contemptible character of all.

---

[3][Schiller] The pernicious effect, upon both thought and action, of an undue surrender to our sensual nature will be evident to all. Not quite so evident, although just as common, and no less important, is the nefarious influence exerted upon our knowledge and upon our conduct by a preponderance of rationality. Permit me therefore to recall, from the great number of relevant instances, just two which may serve to throw light upon the damage caused

With his personality his condition, too, is annulled, because these two concepts are reciprocally related—because change demands a principle of permanence, and finite reality an infinite reality. If, on the other hand, the formal drive becomes receptive, that is to say, if thought forestalls feeling and the person supplants the world, then the person ceases to be autonomous force and subject precisely to the extent that it forces its way into the place of the object—because, in order to become manifest, the principle of permanence requires change, and absolute reality has need of limitation. From the moment that man is only form, he ceases to have a form; the annulling of his condition, consequently, involves that of his person too. In a single word, only inasmuch as he is autonomous, is there reality outside him and is he receptive to it; and only inasmuch as he is receptive, is there reality within him and is he a thinking force.

Both drives, therefore, need to have limits set to them and, inasmuch as they can be thought of as energies, need to be relaxed; the sense-drive so that it does not encroach upon the domain of law, the formal drive so that it does not encroach on that of feeling. But the relaxing of the sense-drive must in no wise be the result of physical impotence or blunted feeling, which never merits anything but contempt. It must be an act of free choice, an activity of the person which, by its intensity, moderates that of the senses and, by mastering impressions, robs them of their depth only in order to give them increased surface. It is character which must set bounds to temperament, for it is only to profit the mind that sense may go short. In the same way the relaxing of the formal drive must not be the result of spiritual impotence or flabbiness of thought or will; for this would only degrade man. It must, if it is to be at all praiseworthy, spring from abundance of feeling and sensation. Sense herself must, with triumphant power, remain mistress of her own domain, and resist the violence which the mind, by its usurping tactics, would fain inflict upon her. In a single word: Personality must keep the sensuous drive within its proper bounds, and receptivity, or nature, must do the same with the formal drive.

Fourteenth Letter

We have now been led to the notion of a reciprocal action between the two drives, reciprocal action of such a kind that the activity of the one both gives rise to, and sets limits to, the activity of the other, and in which each in itself achieves its highest manifestation precisely by reason of the other being active.

Such reciprocal relation between the two drives is, admittedly, but a task enjoined upon us by reason, a problem which man is only capable of solving completely in the perfect consummation of his existence. It is, in the most precise sense of the word, the idea of his human nature, hence something infinite, to which in the course of time he can approximate ever more closely, but without ever being able to reach it. "He is not to strive for form at the cost of reality, nor for reality at the cost of form; rather is he to seek absolute being by means of a determinate being, and a determinate being by means of infinite being. He is to set up a world over against himself because he is person, and he is to be person because a world stands over against him. He is to feel because he is conscious of himself, and be conscious of himself because he feels."—That he does actually conform to this idea, that he is consequently, in the fullest sense of the word, a human being, is never brought home to him as long as he satisfies only one of these two drives to the exclusion of the other, or only satisfies them one after the other. For as long as he only feels, his person, or his absolute existence, remains a mystery to him; and as long as he only thinks, his existence in time, or his condition, does likewise. Should there, however, be cases in which he were to have this twofold experience simultaneously, in which he were to be at once conscious of his freedom and sensible of his existence, were, at one and the same time, to feel himself matter and come to know himself as mind, then he would in such cases, and in such cases only, have a complete intuition of his human nature, and the object which afforded him this vision would become for him a symbol of his accomplished destiny and, in consequence (since that is only to be attained in the totality of time), serve him as a manifestation of the infinite.

Assuming that cases of this sort could actually occur in experience, they would awaken in him a new drive which, precisely because the other two drives cooperate within it, would be opposed to each of them considered separately and could justifiably count as a new drive. The sense-drive demands that there shall be change and that time shall have a content; the form-drive demands that time shall be annulled and that there shall be no change. That drive, therefore, in which both the others work in concert (permit me for the time being, until I have justified the term, to call it the play-drive), the play-drive, therefore, would be directed towards annulling time within time, reconciling becoming with absolute being and change with identity.

The sense-drive wants to be determined, wants to receive its object; the form-drive wants itself to determine, wants to bring forth its object. The play-drive, therefore, will endeavor so to receive as if it had itself brought forth, and so to bring forth as the intuitive sense aspires to receive.

The sense-drive excludes from its subject all autonomy and freedom; the form-drive excludes from its subject all dependence, all passivity. Exclusion of freedom, however, implies physical necessity, exclusion of passivity moral necessity. Both drives, therefore, exert constraint upon the psyche; the former through the laws of nature, the latter through the laws of reason. The play-drive, in consequence, as the one in which both the others act in concert, will exert upon the psyche at once a moral and a physical constraint; it will, therefore, since it annuls all contingency, annul all constraint too, and set man free both physically and morally. When we embrace with passion someone who deserves our contempt, we are painfully aware of the compulsion of nature. When we feel hostile towards another who compels our esteem, we are painfully aware of the compulsion of reason. But once he has at the same time engaged our affection and won our esteem, then both the compulsion of feeling and the compulsion of reason disappear and we begin to love him, i.e., we begin to play with both our affection and our esteem.

Since, moreover, the sense-drive exerts a physical, the form-drive a moral constraint, the first will leave our formal, the second our material disposition at the mercy of the contingent; that is to say, it is a matter of chance whether our happiness will coincide with our perfection or our perfection with our happiness. The play-drive, in consequence, in which both work in concert, will make our formal as well as our material disposition, our perfection as well as our happiness, contingent. It will therefore, just because it makes both contingent and because with all constraint all contingency too disappears, abolish contingency in both, and, as a result, introduce form into matter and reality into form. To the extent that it deprives feelings and passions of their dynamic power, it will bring them into harmony with the ideas of reason; and to the extent that it deprives the laws of reason of their moral compulsion, it will reconcile them with the interests of the senses.

Fifteenth Letter

I am drawing ever nearer the goal towards which I have been leading you by a not exactly encouraging path. If you will consent to follow me a few steps further along it, horizons all the wider will unfold and a pleasing prospect perhaps requite you for the labor of the journey.

The object of the sense-drive, expressed in a general concept, we call life, in the widest sense of this term: a concept designating all material being and all that is immediately present to the senses. The object of the form-drive, expressed in a general concept, we call form, both in the figurative and in the literal sense of this word: a concept which includes all the formal qualities of things and all the relations of these to our thinking faculties. The object of the play-drive, represented in a general schema, may therefore

be called living form: a concept serving to designate all the aesthetic qualities of phenomena and, in a word, what in the widest sense of the term we call beauty.

According to this explanation, if such it be, the term beauty is neither extended to cover the whole realm of living things nor is it merely confined to this realm. A block of marble, though it is and remains lifeless, can nevertheless, thanks to the architect or the sculptor, become living form; and a human being, though he may live and have form, is far from being on that account a living form. In order to be so, his form would have to be life, and his life form. As long as we merely think about his form, it is lifeless, a mere abstraction; as long as we merely feel his life, it is formless, a mere impression. Only when his form lives in our feeling and his life takes on form in our understanding, does he become living form; and this will always be the case whenever we adjudge him beautiful.

But because we know how to specify the elements which when combined produce beauty, this does not mean that its genesis has as yet in any way been explained; for that would require us to understand the actual manner of their combining, and this, like all reciprocal action between finite and infinite, remains forever inaccessible to our probing. Reason, on transcendental grounds, makes the following demand: Let there be a bond of union between the form-drive and the material drive; that is to say, let there be a play-drive, since only the union of reality with form, contingency with necessity, passivity with freedom, makes the concept of human nature complete. Reason must make this demand because it is reason—because it is its nature to insist on perfection and on the abolition of all limitation, and because any exclusive activity on the part of either the one drive or the other leaves human nature incomplete and gives rise to some limitation within it. Consequently, as soon as reason utters the pronouncement: Let humanity exist, it has by that very pronouncement also promulgated the law: Let there be beauty. Experience can provide an answer to the question whether there is such a thing as beauty, and we shall know the answer once experience has taught us whether there is such a thing as humanity. But how there can be beauty, and how humanity is possible, neither reason nor experience can tell us.

Man, as we know, is neither exclusively matter nor exclusively mind. Beauty, as the consummation of his humanity, can therefore be neither exclusively life nor exclusively form. Not mere life, as acute observers, adhering too closely to the testimony of experience, have maintained, and to which the taste of our age would fain degrade it; not mere form, as it has been adjudged by philosophers whose speculations led them too far away from experience, or by artists who, philosophizing on beauty, let themselves be too exclusively guided by the needs of their craft.[4] It is the object common to both drives, that is to say, the object of the play-drive. This term is fully justified by linguistic usage, which is wont to designate as *play* everything which is neither subjectively nor objectively contingent, and yet imposes no kind of constraint either from within or from without. Since, in contemplation of the beautiful, the psyche finds itself in a happy medium between the realm of law and the sphere of physical exigency, it is, precisely because it is divided between the two, removed from the constraint of the one as of the other. The material drive, like the formal drive, is wholly earnest in its demands; for, in the sphere of knowledge, the former is concerned with the reality, the latter with the necessity of things; while in the sphere of action, the first is directed towards the preservation of life, the second towards the maintenance of dignity: both, therefore, towards truth and towards perfection. But life becomes of less consequence once human dignity enters in, and duty ceases to be a constraint once inclination exerts its pull; similarly our psyche accepts the reality of things, or material truth, with greater freedom and serenity once this latter encounters formal truth, or the law of necessity, and no longer feels constrained by abstraction once this can be accompanied by the immediacy of intuition. In a word: By entering into association with ideas all reality loses its earnestness because it then becomes of small account; and by coinciding with feeling necessity divests itself of its earnestness because it then becomes of light weight.

But, you may long have been tempted to object, is beauty not degraded by being made to consist of mere play and reduced to the level of those frivolous things which have always borne this name? Does it not belie the rational concept as well as the dignity of beauty—which is, after all, here being considered as an instrument of culture—if we limit it to mere play? And does it not belie the empirical concept of play—a concept which is, after all, entirely compatible with the exclusion of all taste—if we limit it merely to beauty?

But how can we speak of mere play, when we know that it is precisely play and play alone, which of all man's states and conditions is the one which makes him whole and unfolds both sides of his nature at once? What you, according to your idea of the matter, call limitation, I, according to

mine—which I have justified by proof—call expansion. I, therefore, would prefer to put it exactly the opposite way round and say: the agreeable, the good, the perfect, with these man is merely in earnest; but with beauty he plays. True, we must not think here of the various forms of play which are in vogue in actual life, and are usually directed to very material objects. But then in actual life we should also seek in vain for the kind of beauty with which we are here concerned. The beauty we find in actual existence is precisely what the play-drive we find in actual existence deserves; but with the ideal of beauty that is set up by reason, an ideal of the play-drive, too, is enjoined upon man, which he must keep before his eyes in all his forms of play.

We shall not go far wrong when trying to discover a man's ideal of beauty if we inquire how he satisfies his play-drive. If at the Olympic Games the peoples of Greece delighted in the bloodless combats of strength, speed, and agility, and in the nobler rivalry of talents, and if the Roman people regaled themselves with the death throes of a vanquished gladiator or of his Libyan opponent, we can, from this single trait, understand why we have to seek the ideal forms of a Venus, a Juno, an Apollo, not in Rome, but in Greece.[5] Reason, however, declares: The beautiful is to be neither mere life, nor mere form, but living form, i.e., beauty; for it imposes upon man the double law of absolute formality and absolute reality. Consequently reason also makes the pronouncement: With beauty man shall only play, and it is with beauty only that he shall play.

For, to mince matters no longer, man only plays when he is in the fullest sense of the word a human being, and he is only fully a human being when he plays. This proposition, which at the moment may sound like a paradox, will take on both weight and depth of meaning once we have got as far as applying it to the twofold earnestness of duty and of destiny. It will, I promise you, prove capable of bearing the whole edifice of the art of the beautiful, and of the still more difficult art of living. But it is, after all, only in philosophy that the proposition is unexpected; it was long ago alive and operative in the art and in the feeling of the Greeks, the most distinguished exponents of both; only they transferred to Olympus what was meant to be realized on earth. Guided by the truth of that same proposition, they banished from the

---

[4][Schiller] Burke, in his *Philosophical Inquiry into the Origin of Our Ideas of the Sublime and the Beautiful* [pp. 299–306], makes beauty into mere life. As far as I know, every adherent of dogmatic philosophy, who has ever confessed his belief on this subject, makes it into mere form: among artists, Raphael Mengs, in his *Reflections on Taste in Painting*, not to speak of others. In this, as in everything else, critical philosophy has opened up the way whereby empiricism can be led back to principles, and speculation back to experience.

[5][Schiller] If (to confine ourselves to the modern world) we compare horse racing in London, bullfights in Madrid, *spectacles* in the Paris of former days, the gondola races in Venice, animal baiting in Vienna, and the gay attractive life of the Corso in Rome, it will not be difficult to determine the different nuances of taste among these different peoples. However, there is far less uniformity among the amusements of the common people in these different countries than there is among those of the refined classes in those same countries, a fact which it is easy to account for.

brow of the blessed gods all the earnestness and effort which furrow the cheeks of mortals, no less than the empty pleasures which preserve the smoothness of a vacuous face; freed those ever-contented beings from the bonds inseparable from every purpose, every duty, every care, and made idleness and indifferency the enviable portion of divinity—merely a more human name for the freest, most sublime state of being. Both the material constraint of natural laws and the spiritual constraint of moral laws were resolved in their higher concept of necessity, which embraced both worlds at once; and it was only out of the perfect union of those two necessities that for them true freedom could proceed. Inspired by this spirit, the Greeks effaced from the features of their ideal physiognomy, together with inclination, every trace of volition too; or rather they made both indiscernible, for they knew how to fuse them in the most intimate union. It is not grace, nor is it yet dignity, which speaks to us from the superb countenance of a Juno Ludovisi; it is neither the one nor the other because it is both at once. While the woman-god demands our veneration, the godlike woman kindles our love; but even as we abandon ourselves in ecstasy to her heavenly grace, her celestial self-sufficiency makes us recoil in terror. The whole figure reposes and dwells in itself, a creation completely self-contained, and, as if existing beyond space, neither yielding nor resisting; here is no force to contend with force, no frailty where temporality might break in. Irresistibly moved and drawn by those former qualities, kept at a distance by these latter, we find ourselves at one and the same time in a state of utter repose and supreme agitation, and there results that wondrous stirring of the heart for which mind has no concept nor speech any name.

Twenty-First Letter

There is, as I observed at the beginning of the last letter, a twofold condition of determinability and a twofold condition of determination. I can now clarify this statement.

The psyche may be said to be determinable simply because it is not determined at all; but it is also determinable inasmuch as it is determined in a way which does not exclude anything, i.e., when the determination it undergoes is of a kind which does not involve limitation. The former is mere indetermination (it is without limits, because it is without reality); the latter is aesthetic determinability (it has no limits, because it embraces all reality).

And the psyche may be said to be determined inasmuch as it is limited at all; but it is also determined inasmuch as it limits itself, by virtue of its own absolute power. It finds it-

self in the first of these two states whenever it feels; in the second, whenever it thinks. What thought is in respect of determination, therefore, the aesthetic disposition is in respect of determinability; the former is limitation by virtue of the infinite force within it, the latter is negation by virtue of the infinite abundance within it. Even as sensation and thought have one single point of contact—viz., that in both states the psyche is determined, and man is something, either individual or person, to the exclusion of all else—but in all other respects are poles apart: so, in like manner, aesthetic determinability has one single point of contact with mere indetermination—viz., that both exclude any determinate mode of existence—while in all other respects they are to each other as nothing is to everything, hence, utterly and entirely different. If, therefore, the latter—indetermination through sheer absence of determination—was thought of as an empty infinity, then aesthetic freedom of determination, which is its counterpart in reality, must be regarded as an infinity filled with content: an idea which accords completely with the results of the foregoing inquiry.

In the aesthetic state, then, man is naught, if we are thinking of any particular result rather than of the totality of his powers, and considering the absence in him of any specific determination. Hence we must allow that those people are entirely right who declare beauty, and the mood it induces in us, to be completely indifferent and unfruitful as regards either knowledge or character. They are entirely right; for beauty produces no particular result whatsoever, neither for the understanding nor for the will. It accomplishes no particular purpose, neither intellectual nor moral; it discovers no individual truth, helps us to perform no individual duty and is, in short, as unfitted to provide a firm basis for character as to enlighten the understanding. By means of aesthetic culture, therefore, the personal worth of a man, or his dignity, inasmuch as this can depend solely upon himself, remains completely indeterminate; and nothing more is achieved by it than that he is henceforth enabled by the grace of nature to make of himself what he will—that the freedom to be what he ought to be is completely restored to him.

But precisely thereby something infinite is achieved. For as soon as we recall that it was precisely of this freedom that he was deprived by the one-sided constraint of nature in the field of sensation and by the exclusive authority of reason in the realm of thought, then we are bound to consider the power which is restored to him in the aesthetic mode as the highest of all bounties, as the gift of humanity itself. True, he possesses this humanity *in potentia* before every determinate condition into which he can conceivably enter. But he loses it in practice with every determinate condition into which he does enter. And if he is to pass into a condition of an opposite nature, this humanity must be restored to him each time anew through the life of the aesthetic.[6]

It is, then, not just poetic license but philosophical truth when we call beauty our second creatress. For although it only offers us the possibility of becoming human beings, and for the rest leaves it to our own free will to decide how far we wish to make this a reality, it does in this resemble our first creatress, nature, which likewise conferred upon us nothing more than the power of becoming human, leaving the use and practice of that power to our own free will and decision.

Twenty-Second Letter

If, then, in one respect the aesthetic mode of the psyche is to be regarded as naught—once, that is, we have an eye to particular and definite effects—it is in another respect to be looked upon as a state of supreme reality, once we have due regard to the absence of all limitation and to the sum total of the powers which are conjointly active within it. One cannot, then, say that those people are wrong either who declare the aesthetic state to be the most fruitful of all in respect of knowledge and morality. They are entirely right; for a disposition of the psyche which contains within it the whole of human nature, must necessarily contain within it *in potentia* every individual manifestation of it too; and a disposition of the psyche which removes all limitations from the totality of human nature must necessarily remove them from every individual manifestation of it as well. Precisely on this account, because it takes under its protection no single one of man's faculties to the exclusion of the others, it favors each and all of them without distinction; and it favors no single one more than another for the simple reason that it is the ground of possibility of them all. Every other way of exercising its functions endows the psyche with some special aptitude—but only at the cost of some special limitation; the aesthetic alone leads to the absence of all limitation. Every

other state into which we can enter refers us back to a preceding one, and requires for its termination a subsequent one; the aesthetic alone is a whole in itself, since it comprises within itself all the conditions of both its origin and its continuance. Here alone do we feel reft out of time, and our human nature expresses itself with a purity and integrity, as though it had as yet suffered no impairment through the intervention of external forces.

That which flatters our senses in immediate sensation exposes our susceptible and labile psyche to every impression—but only by rendering us proportionately less fitted for exertion. That which tenses our intellectual powers and invites them to form abstract concepts, strengthens our mind for every sort of resistance—but only by hardening it and depriving us of sensibility in proportion as it fosters greater independence of action. Precisely because of this, the one no less than the other must lead to exhaustion, since material cannot for long dispense with shaping power, nor power with material to be shaped. If, by contrast, we have surrendered to the enjoyment of genuine beauty, we are at such a moment master in equal degree of our passive and of our active powers, and we shall with equal ease turn to seriousness or to play, to repose or to movement, to compliance or to resistance, to the discussions of abstract thought or to the direct contemplation of phenomena.

This lofty equanimity and freedom of the spirit, combined with power and vigor, is the mood in which a genuine work of art should release us, and there is no more certain touchstone of true aesthetic excellence. If, after enjoyment of this kind, we find ourselves disposed to prefer some one particular mode of feeling or action, but unfitted or disinclined for another, this may serve as infallible proof that we have not had a purely aesthetic experience—whether the cause lies in the object or in our own response or, as is almost always the case, in both at once.

Since in actuality no purely aesthetic effect is ever to be met with (for man can never escape his dependence upon conditioning forces), the excellence of a work of art can never consist in anything more than a high approximation to that ideal of aesthetic purity; and whatever the degree of freedom to which it may have been sublimated, we shall still leave it in a particular mood and with some definite bias. The more general the mood and the less limited the bias produced in us by any particular art, or by any particular product of the same, then the nobler that art and the more excellent that product will be. One can test this by considering works from different arts and different works from the same art. We leave a beautiful piece of music with our feeling excited, a beautiful poem with our imagination quickened, a beautiful sculpture or building with our understanding awakened. But

---

[6][Schiller] Admittedly the rapidity with which certain types pass from sensation to thought or decision scarcely—if indeed at all—allows them to become aware of the aesthetic mode through which they must in that time necessarily pass. Such natures cannot for any length of time tolerate the state of indetermination, but press impatiently for some result which in the state of aesthetic limitlessness they cannot find. In others, by contrast, who find enjoyment more in the feeling of total capacity than in any single action, the aesthetic state tends to spread itself over a much wider area. Much as the former dread emptiness, just as little are the latter capable of tolerating limitation. I need scarcely say that the former are born for detail and subordinate occupations, the latter, provided they combine this capacity with a sense of reality, destined for wholeness and for great roles.

should anyone invite us, immediately after a sublime musical experience, to abstract thought; or employ us, immediately after a sublime poetic experience, in some routine business of everyday life; or try, immediately after the contemplation of beautiful paintings or sculptures, to inflame our imagination or surprise our feeling—he would certainly be choosing the wrong moment. The reason for this is that even the most ethereal music has, by virtue of its material, an even greater affinity with the senses than true aesthetic freedom really allows; that even the most successful poem partakes more of the arbitrary and casual play of the imagination, as the medium through which it works, than the inner lawfulness of the truly beautiful really permits; that even the most excellent sculpture—the most excellent, perhaps, most of all—does, by virtue of its conceptual precision, border upon the austerity of science. Nevertheless, the greater the degree of excellence attained by a work in any of these three arts, the more these particular affinities will disappear; and it is an inevitable and natural consequence of their approach to perfection that the various arts, without any displacement of their objective frontiers, tend to become ever more like each other in their effect upon the psyche. Music, at its most sublime, must become sheer form and affect us with the serene power of antiquity. The plastic arts, at their most perfect, must become music and move us by the immediacy of their sensuous presence. Poetry, when most fully developed, must grip us powerfully as music does, but at the same time, like the plastic arts, surround us with serene clarity. This, precisely, is the mark of perfect style in each and every art: that it is able to remove the specific limitations of the art in question without thereby destroying its specific qualities, and through a wise use of its individual peculiarities, is able to confer upon it a more general character.[7]

And it is not just the limitations inherent in the specific character of a particular art that the artist must seek to overcome through his handling of it; it is also the limitations inherent in the particular subject matter he is treating. In a truly successful work of art the contents should effect nothing, the form everything; for only through the form is the whole man affected, through the subject matter, by contrast, only one or other of his functions. Subject matter, then, however sublime and all-embracing it may be, always has a limiting effect upon the spirit, and it is only from form that true aesthetic freedom can be looked for. Herein, then, resides the real secret of the master in any art: that he can make his form consume his material; and the more pretentious, the more seductive this material is in itself, the more it seeks to impose itself upon us, the more highhandedly it thrusts itself forward with effects of its own, or the more the beholder is inclined to get directly involved with it, then the more triumphant the art which forces it back and asserts its own kind of dominion over him. The psyche of the listener or spectator must remain completely free and inviolate; it must go forth from the magic circle of the artist pure and perfect as it came from the hands of the Creator. The most frivolous theme must be so treated that it leaves us ready to proceed directly from it to some matter of the utmost import; the most serious material must be so treated that we remain capable of exchanging it forthwith for the lightest play. Arts which affect the passions, such as tragedy, do not invalidate this: in the first place, they are not entirely free arts since they are enlisted in the service of a particular aim (that of pathos); and in the second, no true connoisseur of art will deny that works even of this class are the more perfect, the more they respect the freedom of the spirit even amid the most violent storms of passion. There does indeed exist a fine art of passion; but a fine passionate art is a contradiction in terms; for the unfailing effect of beauty is freedom from passion. No less self-contradictory is the notion of a fine art which teaches (didactic) or improves (moral); for nothing is more at variance with the concept of beauty than the notion of giving the psyche any definite bias.[8]

But it is by no means always a proof of formlessness in the work of art itself if it makes its effect solely through its contents; this may just as often be evidence of a lack of form in him who judges it. If he is either too tensed or too relaxed, if he is used to apprehending either exclusively with the intellect or exclusively with the senses, he will, even in the case of the most successfully realized whole, attend only to the parts, and in the presence of the most beauteous form respond only to the matter. Receptive only to the raw material, he has first to destroy the aesthetic organization of a work before he can take pleasure in it, and laboriously scratch away until he has uncovered all those individual details which the master, with infinite skill, had caused to disappear in the harmony of the whole. The interest he takes in it is quite simply either a moral or a material interest; but what precisely it ought to be, namely aesthetic, that it certainly is not. Such readers will enjoy a serious and moving poem as though it were a sermon, a naive or humorous one

---

[7]Here Schiller recognizes the differences among the arts (see Lessing, *Laocoön*, pp. 339–41), but finds those differences transcended in the effect on the audience.

[8]Schiller's aesthetic is concerned with the reader, as is Kant's, but it seeks to overcome the traditional Horatian assumption that the effect of art (if it is on this basis that we are to define art) is properly discussed in terms of its ability to delight and to teach.

as though it were an intoxicating drink. And if they were sufficiently lacking in taste to demand edification of a tragedy or an epic—and were it about the Messiah himself—they will certainly not fail to take exception to a poem in the manner of Anacreon or Catullus.

From

Twenty-Fifth Letter

From being a slave of nature, which he remains as long as he merely feels it, man becomes its lawgiver from the moment he begins to think it. That which hitherto merely dominated him as force, now stands before his eyes as object. Whatsoever is object for him has no power over him; for in order to be object at all, it must be subjected to the power that is his. To the extent that he imparts form to matter, and for precisely as long as he imparts it, he is immune to its effects; for spirit cannot be injured by anything except that which robs it of its freedom, and man gives evidence of his freedom precisely by giving form to that which is formless. Only where sheer mass, ponderous and inchoate, holds sway, its murky contours shifting within uncertain boundaries, can fear find its seat; man is more than a match for any of nature's terrors once he knows how to give it form and convert it into an object of his contemplation. Once he begins to assert his independence in the face of nature as phenomenon, then he also asserts his dignity *vis-à-vis* nature as force, and with noble freedom rises in revolt against his ancient gods. Now they cast off those ghastly masks which were the anguish of his childhood and surprise him with his own image by revealing themselves as projections of his own mind. The monstrous divinity of the Oriental, which rules the world with the blind strength of a beast of prey, shrinks in the imagination of the Greeks into the friendly contours of a human being. The empire of the Titans falls, and infinite force is tamed by infinite form.

But whilst I was merely seeking a way out from the material world and a transition to the world of spirit, my imagination has run away with me and carried me into the very heart of this latter. Beauty, which is what we were out to seek, already lies behind us; we have o'erleapt it completely in passing from mere life directly to pure form and the pure object. But a sudden leap of this kind is contrary to human nature, and in order to keep step with this latter we shall have to turn back once more to the world of sense.

Beauty is, admittedly, the work of free contemplation, and with it we do indeed enter upon the world of ideas—but, it should be emphasized, without therefore leaving behind the world of sense, as is the case when we proceed to knowledge of truth. Truth is the pure product of abstracting from everything which is material and contingent; it is object, pure and unadulterated, in which none of the limitations of the subject may persist, pure autonomous activity without any admixture of passivity. True, even from the highest abstractions, there is a way back to sense; for thought affects our inner life of feeling, and the perception of logical and moral unity passes over into a feeling of sensuous congruence. But when we take such delight in intellectual knowledge, we distinguish very exactly between our perception and our feeling, and look upon the latter as something incidental, which could well be absent without the knowledge therefore ceasing to be knowledge or truth being any the less true. But it would be a vain undertaking to try to clear our perception of beauty of these connections with feeling—which is why it will not do to think of the one as the effect of the other, but is imperative to consider each as being, at the same time and reciprocally, both effect and cause. In the pleasure we take in knowledge we distinguish without difficulty the transition from activity to passivity, and are clearly aware that the first is over when the latter begins. In the delight we take in beauty, by contrast, no such succession of activity and passivity can be discerned; reflection is here so completely interfused with feeling that we imagine that the form is directly apprehended by sense. Beauty, then, is indeed an object for us, because reflection is the condition of our having any sensation of it; but it is at the same time a state of the perceiving subject, because feeling is a condition of our having any perception of it. Thus beauty is indeed form, because we contemplate it; but it is at the same time life, because we feel it. In a word: it is at once a state of our being and an activity we perform.

And just because it is both these things at once, beauty provides us with triumphant proof that passivity by no means excludes activity, nor matter form, nor limitation infinity—that, in consequence, the moral freedom of man is by no means abrogated through his inevitable dependence upon physical things. Beauty is proof of this and, I must add, she alone can furnish such proof. For since in the enjoyment of truth, or logical unity, feeling is not inevitably and of necessity one with thought, but merely follows incidentally upon it, truth can only offer us proof that sensuousness can follow upon rationality, or vice versa; but not that both exist together, nor that they reciprocally work upon each other, nor that they are absolutely and of necessity to be united. On the contrary, from the fact that feeling is excluded as long as we are thinking, and thinking excluded as long as we are feeling, the incompatibility of our two natures would have to be inferred; and, indeed, analytical philosophers are unable to adduce any better proof that pure reason can in practice be realized in human kind than that this is in fact enjoined upon them. But since in the enjoyment of beauty, or aesthetic unity, an actual union and interchange between matter and form, passivity and activity, momentarily takes place, the compatibility of our two natures, the practicability of the infinite being realized in the finite, hence the possibility of sublimest humanity, is thereby actually proven.

We need, then, no longer feel at a loss for a way which might lead us from our dependence upon sense towards moral freedom, since beauty offers us an instance of the latter being perfectly compatible with the former, an instance of man not needing to flee matter in order to manifest himself as spirit. But if he is already free while still in association with sense, as the fact of beauty teaches, and if freedom is something absolute and supra-sensual, as the very notion of freedom necessarily implies, then there can no longer be any question of how he is to succeed in raising himself from the limited to the absolute, or of how, in his thinking and willing, he is to offer resistance to the life of sense, since this has already happened in beauty. There can, in a single word, no longer be any question of how he is to pass from beauty to truth, since this latter is potentially contained in the former, but only a question of how he is to clear a way for himself from common reality to aesthetic reality, from mere life-serving feelings to feelings of beauty.

Friedrich Schlegel

1772–1829

Friedrich Schlegel was perhaps the leading theorist of German romanticism. Together with his brother August Wilhelm, he edited the important periodical *Athenaeum* from 1798 to 1800. In the *Athenaeum* the brothers, with Friedrich Schleiermacher and the poet Novalis (Friedrich von Hardenberg), published a series of fragments, the most important of which were written by Friedrich Schlegel. These, which ranged widely over a variety of thoughts—literary, moral, philosophical, and political—, were preceded by the *Lyceum Fragments,* written entirely by Friedrich. These fragments appeared in the *Lyceum der schönen Kunste* (1797) and were widely regarded as the initial expression of romanticism. A selection appears here under the title *Critical Fragments.* Although the fragments take up many matters, including questions about classicism, perhaps the most important is the attention given to the concepts of wit and irony. The former term is elevated to great heights, for wit is clearly identified with genius and inventive power; yet this can be seen only by a reading of several fragments with their cumulative effect.

Irony is perhaps more important, though always involved dialectically with wit. The section of the essay "On Incomprehensibility" reprinted here is really a commentary or enlargement on two *Lyceum Fragments,* number 48 and 108, which are quoted in full in the essay. It is irony that "opposes" wit, always, when successful, intruding a skeptical perspective, in which the writer overcomes the finite limits of his own creativity. Thus the skeptical aspect of irony is actually seen as enabling an advance to a higher level, which, however, reveals human limitation in that the object of knowledge or intellectual desire remains infinite and unattainable. Thus irony can be characterized as both a "divine breath" (42) and a "transcendental buffonery," rising above its own art, virtue, or genius, even as it remains on earth.

Schlegel's critical writings are collected in six volumes by Ernst Behler and Hans Eichner in Friedrich Schlegel, *Kritische Schriften und Fragmente* (1988). Ernst Behler, ed., *Friedrich Schlegel in Zelbstzeugnissen und Bilddocumenten* (1966) documents and discusses Schlegel's life. See Hans Eichner, *Friedrich Schlegel* (1970) for biography, also his *Charakteristiken und Kritiken I (1796–1801)* (1967) for a study of Schlegel's critical theory. See also Benno von Wiese, *Friedrich Schlegel* (1927) and, Hans Eichner, "Friedrich Schlegel's Theory of Romantic Poetry," *PMLA* 71 (1956), 1018–1041; Victor Lange, "Friedrich Schlegel's Literary Criticism," *Comparative Literature* 7, Fall 1955, 289–305; René Wellek, *A History of Modern Criticism, 1750–1950* II (1955); and Ernst Behler and Roman Struc, eds. and trans., *Dialogue on Poetry and Literary Aphorisms* (1968).

From

Critical Fragments (Lyceum Fragments)

7. My essay on the study of Greek poetry is a mannered prose hymn to the objective quality in poetry. The worst thing about it, it seems to me, is the complete lack of necessary irony; and the best, the confident assumption that poetry is infinitely valuable—as if that were a settled thing.

8. A good preface must be at once the square root and the square of its book.

9. Wit is absolute social feeling, or fragmentary genius.

12. One of two things is usually lacking in the so-called Philosophy of Art: either philosophy or art.

14. In poetry too every whole can be a part and every part really a whole.

18. Novels have a habit of concluding in the same way that the Lord's Prayer begins: with the kingdom of heaven on earth.

20. A classical text must never be entirely comprehensible. But those who are cultivated and who cultivate themselves must always want to learn more from it.

21. Just as a child is only a thing which wants to become a human being, so a poem is only a product of nature which wants to become a work of art.

23. Every good poem must be wholly intentional and wholly instinctive. That is how it becomes ideal.

25. The two main principles of the so-called historical criticism are the Postulate of Vulgarity and the Axiom of the Average. The Postulate of Vulgarity: everything great, good, and beautiful is improbable because it is extraordinary and, at the very least, suspicious. The Axiom of the Average: as we and our surroundings are, so must it have been always and everywhere, because that, after all, is so very natural.

26. Novels are the Socratic dialogues of our time. And this free form has become the refuge of common sense in its flight from pedantry.

27. The critic is a reader who ruminates. Therefore he ought to have more than one stomach.

28. Feeling (for a particular art, science, person, etc.) is divided spirit, is self-restriction: hence a result of self-creation and self-destruction.

CRITICAL FRAGMENTS. The *Critical Fragments* first appeared in the *Lyceum* in 1797. They are reprinted from Peter Firchow, ed., *Friedrich Schlegel's Lucinde and the Fragments,* Minneapolis: University of Minnesota Press, 1971. Reprinted by permission of the publisher.

30. In modern tragedy, fate is sometimes replaced by God the Father, more often by the devil himself. How is it that this hasn't yet inspired some scholar to formulate a theory of the diabolic genre?

36. Whoever hasn't yet arrived at the clear realization that there might be a greatness existing entirely outside his own sphere and for which he might have absolutely no feeling; whoever hasn't at least felt obscure intimations concerning the approximate location of this greatness in the geography of the human spirit: that person either has no genius in his own sphere, or else he hasn't been educated yet to the niveau of the classic.

37. In order to write well about something, one shouldn't be interested in it any longer. To express an idea with due circumspection, one must have relegated it wholly to one's past; one must no longer be preoccupied with it. As long as the artist is in the process of discovery and inspiration, he is in a state which, as far as communication is concerned, is at the very least intolerant. He wants to blurt out everything, which is a fault of young geniuses or a legitimate prejudice of old bunglers. And so he fails to recognize the value and the dignity of self-restriction, which is after all, for the artist as well as the man, the first and the last, the most necessary and the highest duty. Most necessary because wherever one does not restrict oneself, one is restricted by the world; and that makes one a slave. The highest because one can only restrict oneself at those points and places where one possesses infinite power, self-creation, and self-destruction. Even a friendly conversation which cannot be broken off at any moment, completely arbitrarily, has something intolerant about it. But a writer who can and does talk himself out, who keeps nothing back for himself, and likes to tell everything he knows, is to be pitied. There are only three mistakes to guard against. First: What appears to be unlimited free will, and consequently seems and should seem to be irrational or supra-rational, nonetheless must still at bottom be simply necessary and rational; otherwise the whim becomes willful, becomes intolerant, and self-restriction turns into self-destruction. Second: Don't be in too much of a hurry for self-restriction, but first give rein to self-creation, invention, and inspiration, until you're ready. Third: Don't exaggerate self-restriction.

40. In the sense in which it has been defined and used in Germany, aesthetic is a word which notoriously reveals an equally perfect ignorance of the thing and of the language. Why is it still used?

48. Irony is the form of paradox. Paradox is everything simultaneously good and great.

51. To use wit as an instrument for revenge is as shameful as using art as a means for titillating the senses.

52. Instead of description, one occasionally gets in poems a rubric announcing that here something or other should really have been described, but the artist was prevented from doing so and most humbly begs to be excused.

53. In respect to their unity, most modern poems are allegories (mysteries, moralities) or novellas (adventures, intrigues), or a mixture or dilution of these.

54. There are writers who drink the absolute like water; and books in which even the dogs refer to the infinite.

55. A really free and cultivated person ought to be able to attune himself at will to being philosophical or philological, critical or poetical, historical or rhetorical, ancient or modern: quite arbitrarily, just as one tunes an instrument, at any time and to any degree.

56. Wit is logical sociability.

57. If some mystical art lovers who think of every criticism as a dissection and every dissection as a destruction of pleasure were to think logically, then ''wow'' would be the best criticism of the greatest work of art. To be sure, there are critiques which say nothing more, but only take much longer to say it.

58. Just as mankind prefers a great to a just action, so too the artist wants to ennoble and instruct.

59. Chamfort's pet idea that wit is a substitute for an impossible happiness—a small percentage, as it were, of the unpaid debt on the greatest good for which a bankrupt nature must settle—is not much better than Shaftesbury's[1] idea that wit is the touchstone of truth, or the more vulgar prejudice that moral ennoblement is the highest end of the fine arts. Wit is its own end, like virtue, like love and art. This brilliant man felt, so it seems, the infinite value of wit, and since French philosophy is inadequate for an understanding of this, he sought instinctively to join what was best in him to what is first and best in that philosophy. And as a maxim, the thought that the wise man must confront fate always *en état d'épigramme* is beautiful and truly cynical.

60. All the classical poetical genres have now become ridiculous in their rigid purity.

61. Strictly understood, the concept of a scientific poem is quite as absurd as that of a poetical science.

62. We already have so many theories about poetical genres. Why have we no concept of poetical genre? Perhaps then we would have to make do with a single theory of poetical genres.

63. Not art and works of art make the artist, but feeling and inspiration and impulse.

64. There should be a new *Laokoön*[2] to determine the limits of music and philosophy. For a proper appreciation of a number of literary works we still need a theory of grammatical music.

65. Poetry is republican speech: a speech which is its own law and end unto itself, and in which all the parts are free citizens and have the right to vote.

67. In England, wit is at least a profession if not an art. There everything becomes craftsmanlike, and in that island even the *roués* are pedants. So too their *wits:* they introduce an absolute willfulness—whose illusion gives to wit its romantic and piquant quality—into reality and so manage to live wittily. Hence their talent for folly. They die for their principles.

70. People who write books and imagine that their readers are the public and that they must educate it soon arrive at the point not only of despising their so-called public but of hating it. Which leads absolutely nowhere.

73. What is lost in average, good, or even first-rate translations is precisely the best part.

78. Many of the very best novels are compendia, encyclopedias of the whole spiritual life of a brilliant individual. Works which have this quality, even if they are cast in a completely different mold—like *Nathan*[3]—thereby take on a novelistic hue. And every human being who is cultivated and who cultivates himself contains a novel within himself. But it isn't necessary for him to express it and write it out.

80. I'm disappointed in not finding in Kant's family tree of basic concepts the category ''almost,'' a category that has surely accomplished, and spoiled, as much in the world and in literature as any other. In the mind of natural skeptics it colors all other concepts and perceptions.

84. From what the moderns aim at, we learn what poetry should become; from what the ancients have done, what it has to be.

85. Every honest author writes for nobody or everybody. Whoever writes for some particular group does not deserve to be read.

86. The function of criticism, people say, is to educate one's readers! Whoever wants to be educated, let him educate himself. This is rude: but it can't be helped.

89. Isn't it unnecessary to write more than one novel, unless the artist has become a new man? It's obvious that frequently all the novels of a particular author belong together and in a sense make up only one novel.

90. Wit is an explosion of confined spirit.

91. The ancients are not the Jews, Christians, or En-

[1][Firchow] Anthony Ashley Cooper, Third Earl of Shaftesbury (1671–1713). English moral philosopher and one of the shaping spirits of the eighteenth century.

[2]*Laocoön* by Gotthold Ephraim Lessing (1766), see pp. 339–41.
[3]Lessing's play *Nathan der Weise* (1779).

glish of poetry. They are not an arbitrarily chosen artistic people of God; nor do they have the only true saving aesthetic faith; nor do they have a monopoly on poetry.

93. In the ancients we see the perfected letter of all poetry; in the moderns we see its growing spirit.

96. A good riddle should be witty; otherwise nothing remains once the answer has been found. And there's a charm in having a witty idea which is enigmatic to the point of needing to be solved: only its meaning should be immediately and completely clear as soon as it's been hit upon.

98. The following are universally valid and fundamental laws of written communication: (1) one should have something to communicate; (2) one should have somebody to whom one wants to communicate it; (3) one should really be able to communicate it and share it with somebody, not simply express oneself. Otherwise it would be wiser to keep silent.

99. Whoever isn't completely new himself judges the new as if it were old; and the old seems ever new until one grows old oneself.

100. The poetry of one writer is termed philosophical, of another philological, of a third, rhetorical, etc. But what then is poetical poetry?

103. Many works that are praised for the beauty of their coherence have less unity than a motley heap of ideas simply animated by the ghost of a spirit and aiming at a single purpose. What really holds the latter together is that free and equal fellowship in which, so the wise men assure us, the citizens of the perfect state will live at some future date; it's that unqualifiedly sociable spirit which, as the beau monde maintains, is now to be found only in what is so strangely and almost childishly called the great world. On the other hand, many a work of art whose coherence is never questioned is, as the artist knows quite well himself, not a complete work but a fragment, or one or more fragments, a mass, a plan. But so powerful is the instinct for unity in mankind that the author himself will often bring something to a kind of completion which simply can't be made a whole or a unit; often quite imaginatively and yet completely unnaturally. The worst thing about it is that whatever is draped about the solid, really existent fragments in the attempt to mug up a semblance of unity consists largely of dyed rags. And if these are touched up cleverly and deceptively, and tastefully displayed, then that's all the worse. For then he deceives even the exceptional reader at first, who has a deep feeling for what little real goodness and beauty is still to be found here and there in life and letters. That reader is then forced to make a critical judgment to get at the right perception of it! And no matter how quickly the dissociation takes place, still the first fresh impression is lost.

107. The ancients are masters of poetical abstraction; the moderns are better at poetical speculation.

108. Socratic irony is the only involuntary and yet completely deliberate dissimulation. It is equally impossible to feign it or divulge it. To a person who hasn't got it, it will remain a riddle even after it is openly confessed. It is meant to deceive no one except those who consider it a deception and who either take pleasure in the delightful roguery of making fools of the whole world or else become angry when they get an inkling they themselves might be included. In this sort of irony, everything should be playful and serious, guilelessly open and deeply hidden. It originates in the union of *savoir vivre* and scientific spirit, in the conjunction of a perfectly instinctive and a perfectly conscious philosophy. It contains and arouses a feeling of indissoluble antagonism between the absolute and the relative, between the impossibility and the necessity of complete communication. It is the freest of all licenses, for by its means one transcends oneself; and yet it is also the most lawful, for it is absolutely necessary. It is a very good sign when the harmonious bores are at a loss about how they should react to this continuous self-parody, when they fluctuate endlessly between belief and disbelief until they get dizzy and take what is meant as a joke seriously and what is meant seriously as a joke. For Lessing irony is instinct; for Hemsterhuis[4] it is classical study; for Hülsen[5] it arises out of the philosophy of philosophy and surpasses these others by far.

109. Gentle wit, or wit without a barb, is a privilege of poetry which prose can't encroach upon: for only by means of the sharpest focus on a single point can the individual idea gain a kind of wholeness.

112. The analytic writer observes the reader as he is; and accordingly he makes his calculations and sets up his machines in order to make the proper impression on him. The synthetic writer constructs and creates a reader as he should be; he doesn't imagine him calm and dead, but alive and critical. He allows whatever he has created to take shape gradually before the reader's eyes, or else he tempts him to discover it himself. He doesn't try to make any particular impression on him, but enters with him into the sacred relationship of deepest symphilosophy or sympoetry.

115. The whole history of modern poetry is a running commentary on the following brief philosophical text: all art should become science and all science art; poetry and philosophy should be made one.

---

[4]Francois Hemsterhuis (1721–1790), Dutch philosopher.
[5][Firchow] August Ludwig Hülsen (1765–1810), German philosopher and educator, friend of Fichte and the Schlegel brothers.

117. Poetry can only be criticized by way of poetry. A critical judgment of an artistic production has no civil rights in the realm of art if it isn't itself a work of art, either in its substance, as a representation of a necessary impression in the state of becoming, or in the beauty of its form and open tone, like that of the old Roman satires.

118. Isn't everything that is capable of becoming shop-worn already twisted or trite to begin with?

121. The simplest and most immediate questions, like Should we criticize Shakespeare's works as art or as nature? and Are epic and tragedy essentially different or not? and Should art deceive or merely seem to do so? are all questions that can't be answered without the deepest consideration and the most erudite history of art.

123. It is thoughtless and immodest presumption to want to learn something about art from philosophy. There are many who start out that way as if they hope to find something new there, since philosophy, after all, can't and shouldn't be able to do more than order the given artistic experiences and the existing artistic principles into a science, and raise the appreciation of art, extend it with the help of a thoroughly learned history of art, and create here as well that logical mood which unites absolute tolerance with absolute rigor.

From

Athenaeum Fragments

12. It has been said of many monarchs that they would have been admirable citizens; only as kings were they failures. Can we say the same of the Bible? Is it also just an admirable everyday book whose only fault is that it should have become the Bible?

68. The only true lover of art is the man who can renounce some of his wishes entirely whenever he finds others completely fulfilled, who can rigorously evaluate even what he loves most, who will, if necessary, submit to explanations, and has a sense for the history of art.

71. People always talk about how an analysis of the beauty of a work of art supposedly disturbs the pleasure of

the art lover. Well, the real lover just won't let himself be disturbed!

116. Romantic poetry is a progressive, universal poetry. Its aim isn't merely to reunite all the separate species of poetry and put poetry in touch with philosophy and rhetoric. It tries to and should mix and fuse poetry and prose, inspiration and criticism, the poetry of art and the poetry of nature; and make poetry lively and sociable, and life and society poetical; poeticize wit and fill and saturate the forms of art with every kind of good, solid matter for instruction, and animate them with the pulsations of humor. It embraces everything that is purely poetic, from the greatest systems of art, containing within themselves still further systems, to the sigh, the kiss that the poetizing child breathes forth in artless song. It can so lose itself in what it describes that one might believe it exists only to characterize poetical individuals of all sorts; and yet there still is no form so fit for expressing the entire spirit of an author: so that many artists who started out to write only a novel ended up by providing us with a portrait of themselves. It alone can become, like the epic, a mirror of the whole circumambient world, an image of the age. And it can also—more than any other form—hover at the midpoint between the portrayed and the portrayer, free of all real and ideal self-interest, on the wings of poetic reflection, and can raise that reflection again and again to a higher power, can multiply it in an endless succession of mirrors. It is capable of the highest and most variegated refinement, not only from within outwards, but also from without inwards; capable in that it organizes—for everything that seeks a wholeness in its effects—the parts along similar lines, so that it opens up a perspective upon an infinitely increasing classicism. Romantic poetry is in the arts what wit is in philosophy, and what society and sociability, friendship and love are in life. Other kinds of poetry are finished and are now capable of being fully analyzed. The romantic kind of poetry is still in the state of becoming; that, in fact, is its real essence: that it should forever be becoming and never be perfected. It can be exhausted by no theory and only a divinatory criticism would dare try to characterize its ideal. It alone is infinite, just as it alone is free; and it recognizes as its first commandment that the will of the poet can tolerate no law above itself. The romantic kind of poetry is the only one that is more than a kind, that is, as it were, poetry itself: for in a certain sense all poetry is or should be romantic.

121. An idea is a concept perfected to the point of irony, an absolute synthesis of absolute antitheses, the continual self-creating interchange of two conflicting thoughts. An ideal is at once idea and fact. If ideals don't have as much individuality for the thinker as the gods of antiquity do for the artist, then any concern with ideas is no more than a bor-

ATHENAEUM FRAGMENTS. The *Athanaeum Fragments* first appeared in the *Athenaeum* from 1798 to 1800. They are reprinted from Peter Firchow, tr., *Friedrich Schlegel's* Lucinde *and the Fragments,* Minneapolis: University of Minnesota Press, 1971. Reprinted by permission.

ing and laborious game of dice with hollow phrases, or, in the manner of the Chinese bonzes, a brooding contemplation of one's own nose. Nothing is more wretched and contempt-ible than this sentimental speculation without any object. But one shouldn't call this mysticism, since this beautiful old word is so very useful and indispensable for absolute philos-ophy, from whose perspective the spirit regards everything as a mystery and a wonder, while from other points of view it would appear theoretically and practically normal. Specu-lation *en detail* is as rare as abstraction *en gros,* and yet it is these that beget the whole substance of scientific wit, these that are the principles of higher criticism, the highest rungs of spiritual cultivation. The great practical abstraction is what makes the ancients—among whom this was an in-stinct—actually ancients. In vain did individuals express the ideal of their species completely, if the species themselves, strictly and sharply isolated, weren't freely surrendered, as it were, to their originality. But to transport oneself arbitrarily now into this, now into that sphere, as if into another world, not merely with one's reason and imagination, but with one's whole soul; to freely relinquish first one and then another part of one's being, and confine oneself entirely to a third; to seek and find now in this, now in that individual the be-all and end-all of existence, and intentionally forget everyone else: of this only a mind is capable that contains within itself simultaneously a plurality of minds and a whole system of persons, and in whose inner being the universe which, as they say, should germinate in every monad, has grown to fullness and maturity.

123. Isn't poetry the noblest and worthiest of the arts for this, among other reasons: that in it alone drama becomes possible?

139. From the romantic point of view, even the vaga-ries of poetry have their value as raw materials and prelimi-naries for universality, even when they're eccentric and mon-strous, provided they have some saving grace, provided they are original.

252. A real aesthetic theory of poetry would begin with the absolute antithesis of the eternally unbridgeable gulf be-tween art and raw beauty. It would describe their struggle and conclude with the perfect harmony of artistic and natural poetry. This is to be found only among the ancients and would in itself constitute nothing but a more elevated history of the spirit of classical poetry. But a philosophy of poetry as such would begin with the independence of beauty, with the proposition that beauty is and should be distinct from truth and morality, and that it has the same rights as these: some-thing that—for those who are able to understand it at all—follows from the proposition I = I. It would waver between the union and the division of philosophy and poetry, between

poetry and practice, poetry as such and the genres and kinds of poetry; and it would conclude with their complete union. Its beginning would provide the principles of pure poetics; its middle the theory of the particular, characteristically modern types of poetry: the didactic, the musical, the rhetor-ical in a higher sense, etc. The keystone would be a philoso-phy of the novel, the rough outlines of which are contained in Plato's political theory. Of course, to the ephemeral, unen-thusiastic dilettantes, who are ignorant of the best poets of all types, this kind of poetics would seem very much like a book of trigonometry to a child who just wants to draw pic-tures. Only a man who knows or possesses a subject can make use of the philosophy of that subject; only he will be able to understand what that philosophy means and what it's attempting to do. But philosophy can't inoculate someone with experience and sense, or pull them out of a hat—and it shouldn't want to do so. To those who knew it already, phi-losophy of course brings nothing new; but only through it does it become knowledge and thereby assume a new form.

255. The more poetry becomes science, the more it also becomes art. If poetry is to become art, if the artist is to have a thorough understanding and knowledge of his ends and means, his difficulties and his subjects, then the poet will have to philosophize about his art. If he is to be more than a mere contriver and artisan, if he is to be an expert in his field and understand his fellow citizens in the kingdom of art, then he will have to become a philologist as well.

256. The basic error of sophistic aesthetics is to con-sider beauty merely as something given, as a psychological phenomenon. Of course, beauty isn't simply the empty thought of something that should be created, but at the same time the thing itself, one of the human spirit's original ways of acting: not simply a necessary fiction, but also a fact, that is, an eternally transcendental one.

304. Philosophy too is the result of two conflicting forces—of poetry and practice. Where these interpenetrate completely and fuse into one, there philosophy comes into being; and when philosophy disintegrates, it becomes my-thology or else returns to life. The wisdom of the Greeks was created out of poetry and law. The most sublime philosophy, some few surmise, may once again turn to poetry; and it is in fact a common occurrence that ordinary people only begin to philosophize according to their own lights after they've stopped living. It seems to me that Schelling's real vocation is to describe better this chemical process of philosophizing, to isolate, wherever possible, its dynamic laws and to sepa-rate philosophy—which always must organize and disorgan-ize itself anew—into its living, fundamental forces, and trace these back to their origins. On the other hand, his polemics, particularly his literary critique of philosophy, seem to me to

represent a false tendency; and his gift for universality is probably still not sufficiently developed to be able to discover in the philosophy of physics what it seeks.

305. Intention taken to the point of irony and accompanied by the arbitrary illusion of its self-destruction is quite as naive as instinct taken to the point of irony. Just as the naive plays with the contradictions between theory and practice, so the grotesque plays with the wonderful permutations of form and matter, loves the illusion of the random and the strange and, as it were, coquettes with infinite arbitrariness. Humor deals with being and nonbeing, and its true essence is reflection. Hence its closeness to the elegy and to everything transcendental; and hence its arrogance and its bent for the mysticism of wit. Just as genius is necessary to naiveté, so too an earnest, pure beauty is a requisite of humor. Most of all humor likes to hover about the gently and clearly flowing rhapsodies of philosophy or poetry, and abhors cumbersome masses and disconnected parts.

324. All genres are good, says Voltaire, except the one that's boring. But what is the boring genre? It may be bigger than all the rest, and many paths may lead to it. But the shortest probably is when a work itself is unsure of its own proper genre. Did Voltaire never follow this path?

325. Just as Simonides[1] called poetry a talking picture, and painting a mute poem, so might one say that history is philosophy in the state of becoming, and philosophy completed history. But Apollo, who neither speaks nor keeps silent but intimates, no longer is worshipped; and wherever a Muse shows herself, people immediately want to carry her off to be cross-examined. How perversely even Lessing treats this clever Greek's beautiful insight, who perhaps had no opportunity to think of "descriptive poetry,"[2] and who would have considered it quite unnecessary to remember that poetry is spiritual music also, since it would never have occurred to him that the two arts could be separated.

365. Mathematics is, as it were, sensual logic. It relates to philosophy as the material arts, music and sculpture, relate to poetry.

372. In the works of the greatest poets there often breathes the spirit of a different art. Might not this be the case with painters too? Doesn't Michelangelo in a certain sense paint like a sculptor, Raphael like an architect, Correggio like a musician? And surely they aren't for this reason lesser painters than Titian, who was only a painter.

434. Should poetry simply be divided up? Or should it remain one and indivisible? Or fluctuate between division and union? Most of the ways of conceiving a poetical world are still as primitive and childish as the old pre-Copernican ideas of astronomy. The usual classifications of poetry are mere dead pedantry designed for people with limited vision. Whatever somebody is capable of producing, or whatever happens to be in fashion, is the stationary earth at the center of all things. But in the universe of poetry nothing stands still, everything is developing and changing and moving harmoniously; and even the comets obey invariable laws of motion. But until the course of these heavenly bodies can be calculated and their return predicted, the true world system of poetry won't have been discovered.

450. Rousseau's polemic against poetry is really only a bad imitation of Plato. Plato is more against poets than he is against poetry; he thought of philosophy as the most daring dithyramb and the most monodic music. Epicurus is the real enemy of art, for he wants to root out imagination and retain sense only. Spinoza might be viewed as the enemy of poetry in quite a different way: because he demonstrates how far one can get with philosophy and morality unaided by poetry, and because it is very much in the spirit of his system not to isolate poetry.

451. Universality is the successive satiation of all forms and substances. Universality can attain harmony only through the conjunction of poetry and philosophy; and even the greatest, most universal works of isolated poetry and philosophy seem to lack this final synthesis. They come to a stop, still imperfect but close to the goal of harmony. The life of the Universal Spirit is an unbroken chain of inner revolutions; all individuals—that is, all original and eternal ones—live in him. He is a genuine polytheist and bears within himself all Olympus.

From

On Incomprehensibility

In order to facilitate a survey of the whole system of irony, we would like to mention here a few of the choicest kinds. The first and most distinguished of all is coarse irony. It is to be found in the real nature of things and is one of the most widespread of substances; it is properly at home in the his-

---

[1]Greek poet, fifth century B.C.
[2][Firchow] English in the original.

ON INCOMPREHENSIBILITY. "On Incomprehensibility" was first published in the *Athenaeum* in 1800. It is reprinted here in part from Peter Firchow, tr., *Friedrich Schlegel's* Lucinde *and the Fragments,* Minneapolis: University of Minnesota Press, 1971. Reprinted by permission.

tory of mankind. Next there is fine or delicate irony; then extra-fine. Scaramouche employs the last type when he seems to be talking amicably and earnestly with someone when really he is only waiting for the chance to give him— while preserving the social amenities—a kick in the behind. This kind of irony is also to be found in poets, as well as straightforward irony, a type that flourishes most purely and originally in old gardens where wonderfully lovely grottoes lure the sensitive friend of nature into their cool wombs only to be-splash him plentifully from all sides with water and thereby wipe him clean of delicacy. Further, dramatic irony; that is, when an author has written three acts, then unexpectedly turns into another man and now has to write the last two acts. Double irony, when two lines of irony run parallel side-by-side without disturbing each other: one for the gallery, the other for the boxes, though a few little sparks may also manage to get behind the scenes. Finally, there is the irony of irony. Generally speaking, the most fundamental irony of irony probably is that even it becomes tiresome if we are always being confronted with it. But what we want this irony to mean in the first place is something that happens in more ways than one. For example, if one speaks of irony without using it, as I have just done; if one speaks of irony ironically without in the process being aware of having fallen into a far more noticeable irony; if one can't disentangle oneself from irony anymore, as seems to be happening in this essay on incomprehensibility; if irony turns into a mannerism and becomes, as it were, ironical about the author; if one has prom-

ised to be ironical for some useless book without first having checked one's supply and then having to produce it against one's will, like an actor full of aches and pains; and if irony runs wild and can't be controlled any longer.

What gods will rescue us from all these ironies? The only solution is to find an irony that might be able to swallow up all these big and little ironies and leave no trace of them at all. I must confess that at precisely this moment I feel that mine has a real urge to do just that. But even this would only be a short-term solution. I fear that if I understand correctly what destiny seems to be hinting at, then soon there will arise a new generation of little ironies: for truly the stars augur the fantastic. And even if it should happen that everything were to be peaceful for a long period of time, one still would not be able to put any faith in this seeming calm. Irony is something one simply cannot play games with. It can have incredibly long-lasting aftereffects. I have a suspicion that some of the most conscious artists of earlier times are still carrying on ironically, hundreds of years after their deaths, with their most faithful followers and admirers. Shakespeare has so infinitely many depths, subterfuges, and intentions. Shouldn't he also, then, have had the intention of concealing insidious traps in his works to catch the cleverest artists of posterity, to deceive them and make them believe before they realize what they're doing that they are somewhat like Shakespeare themselves? Surely, he must be in this respect as in so many others much more full of intentions than people usually think.

William Wordsworth

1770–1850

Wordsworth's Preface to the second edition of *Lyrical Ballads,* a major expression of the spirit of English Romanticism, shifts emphasis from the relationship between poem and reader to that between poet and poem. This is not to say that Wordsworth abandons concern for his reader. He is deeply interested in speaking to the reader, in the moral effect of his work. He considers the poet a teacher not of concepts but of immediate intuitions of nature. Nevertheless he defines the poem primarily in terms of its author's creative activity. He approaches the idea of a poem by first discussing the idea of a poet: "a man speaking to men: a man, it is true, endowed with more lively sensibility, more enthusiasm and tenderness, who has a greater knowledge of human nature, and a more comprehensive soul, than are supposed to be common among mankind." He goes on to describe the poet as one who is able to be affected more than others by imagining things not immediately present to his perceptions.

Wordsworth then describes the poem as the result of these powers and activities. It is a "spontaneous overflow of powerful feelings; it takes its origin from emotion recollected in tranquility." Both parts of this statement are important, the second qualifying the first: Wordsworth makes clear that the poem does not simply rush forth; memory and contemplation come into play in its composition. Nevertheless, emphasis in the definition is on the dominance of feeling over intellect.

This dominance is asserted also in Wordsworth's description of the poem's aim: in a poem the "feeling therein developed gives importance to the action and situation, and not the action and situation to the feeling." In the Preface we are able to observe most clearly the flowering of an attitude that seems to have gone beyond the Aristotelian concept of the poem as an imitation of an action. No longer is the poem's end the shaping of an action. It is rather expression of an emotion by means of such shaping. This attitude, apparent in germinal form during the eighteenth century in the work of Young and in the surge of interest in Longinus, distinguishes between feeling, which unifies, and the analytic powers, which dissect and break up experience. Feeling becomes the real basis of imagination, which is the power to grasp nature in its totality and to order one's experience.

The Preface is well known for the theory of poetic diction that Wordsworth offers in it. He attacks the popular style of his time as employing a "gaudy and inane phraseology" that veils nature rather than reveals its spirit. This argument is partly an outgrowth of Wordsworth's own preference for rural over urban life. In his view, simple, concrete language expresses a close relationship to "the permanent forms of nature," which he associates with rural speech and rural life. The hackneyed verbal conventions of eighteenth-century poetry he associates with urban artificiality. Coleridge criticized this theory effectively, though not totally fairly, in his *Biographia Literaria.*

The literary criticism of Wordsworth has been collected by N. C. Smith (1905). Also useful is M. L. Peacock, Jr., *Critical Opinions of William Wordsworth* (1950). The standard edition of the *Poetical Works* is that of Ernest de Selincourt and Helen Darbishire (4 vols., 1941–47). See also G. McL. Harper, *William Wordsworth: His Life, Works, and Influence* (2 vols., 1916); M. L. Barstow, *Wordsworth's Theory of Poetic Diction* (1917); Arthur Beatty, *William Wordsworth: His Doctrine and Art in Their Historical Relations* (1922); D. G. James, *Scepticism and Poetry* (1937); C. D. Thorpe, "The Imagination: Coleridge versus Wordsworth," *Philological Quarterly,* XVIII (1939), 1–18; R. D. Havens, *The Mind of a Poet* (1941); John Jones, *The Egotistical Sublime: A History of Wordsworth's Imagination* (1954); E. D. Hirsch, Jr., *Wordsworth and Schelling* (1960); G. H. Hartman, *Wordsworth's Poetry, 1787–1814* (1964); W. J. B. Owen, *Wordsworth as Critic* (1969); James A. W. Heffernan, *Wordsworth's Theory of Poetry* (1969); Geoffrey Durrant, *Wordsworth and the Great System* (1970); Albert O. Wlecke, *Wordsworth and the Sublime* (1973); Frances Ferguson, *Wordsworth: Language as Counter-Spirit* (1977); and Theresa M. Kelley, *Wordsworth's Revisionary Aesthetics* (1988).

Preface to the Second Edition of *Lyrical Ballads*

The first volume of these poems has already been submitted to general perusal. It was published, as an experiment, which, I hoped, might be of some use to ascertain how far, by fitting to metrical arrangement a selection of the real language of men in a state of vivid sensation, that sort of pleasure and that quantity of pleasure may be imparted, which a poet may rationally endeavor to impart.

I had formed no very inaccurate estimate of the probable effect of those poems: I flattered myself that they who should be pleased with them would read them with more than common pleasure: and, on the other hand, I was well aware, that by those who should dislike them they would be read with more than common dislike. The result has differed from my expectation in this only, that a greater number have been pleased than I ventured to hope I should please.

Several of my friends are anxious for the success of these poems, from a belief that, if the views with which they are composed were indeed realized, a class of poetry would be produced, well adapted to interest mankind permanently, and not unimportant in the quality, and in the multiplicity of

its moral relations: and on this account they have advised me to prefix a systematic defense of the theory upon which the poems were written. But I was unwilling to undertake the task, knowing that on this occasion the reader would look coldly upon my arguments, since I might be suspected of having been principally influenced by the selfish and foolish hope of *reasoning* him into an approbation of these particular poems: and I was still more unwilling to undertake the task, because, adequately to display the opinions, and fully to enforce the arguments, would require a space wholly disproportionate to a preface. For, to treat the subject with the clearness and coherence of which it is susceptible, it would be necessary to give a full account of the present state of the public taste in this country, and to determine how far this taste is healthy or depraved; which, again, could not be determined without pointing out in what manner language and the human mind act and react on each other, and without retracing the revolutions, not of literature alone, but likewise of society itself. I have therefore altogether declined to enter regularly upon this defense; yet I am sensible that there would be something like impropriety in abruptly obtruding upon the public, without a few words of introduction, poems so materially different from those upon which general approbation is at present bestowed.

It is supposed, that by the act of writing in verse an author makes a formal engagement that he will gratify certain known habits of association; that he not only thus apprises the reader that certain classes of ideas and expressions will be found in his book, but that others will be carefully

PREFACE TO THE SECOND EDITION OF *Lyrical Ballads.* The second edition of *Lyrical Ballads* was published in 1800. Wordsworth subsequently revised the Preface, and the final version appeared in the edition of his poems published in 1849–50. The text follows that version.

excluded. This exponent or symbol held forth by metrical language must in different eras of literature have excited very different expectations: for example, in the age of Catullus, Terence, and Lucretius, and that of Statius or Claudian; and in our own country, in the age of Shakespeare and Beaumont and Fletcher, and that of Donne and Cowley, or Dryden, or Pope. I will not take upon me to determine the exact import of the promise which, by the act of writing in verse, an author in the present day makes to his reader: but it will undoubtedly appear to many persons that I have not fulfilled the terms of an engagement thus voluntarily contracted. They who have been accustomed to the gaudiness and inane phraseology of many modern writers, if they persist in reading this book to its conclusion, will, no doubt, frequently have to struggle with feelings of strangeness and awkwardness: they will look round for poetry, and will be induced to inquire by what species of courtesy these attempts can be permitted to assume that title. I hope therefore the reader will not censure me for attempting to state what I have proposed to myself to perform; and also (as far as the limits of a preface will permit) to explain some of the chief reasons which have determined me in the choice of my purpose: that at least he may be spared any unpleasant feeling of disappointment, and that I myself may be protected from one of the most dishonorable accusations which can be brought against an author; namely, that of an indolence which prevents him from endeavoring to ascertain what is his duty, or, when his duty is ascertained, prevents him from performing it.

The principal object, then, proposed in these poems was to choose incidents and situations from common life, and to relate or describe them, throughout, as far as was possible, in a selection of language really used by men, and, at the same time, to throw over them a certain coloring of imagination, whereby ordinary things should be presented to the mind in an unusual aspect; and further, and above all, to make these incidents and situations interesting by tracing in them, truly though not ostentatiously, the primary laws of our nature: chiefly, as far as regards the manner in which we associate ideas in a state of excitement. Humble and rustic life was generally chosen, because, in that condition, the essential passions of the heart find a better soil in which they can attain their maturity, are less under restraint, and speak a plainer and more emphatic language; because in that condition of life our elementary feelings coexist in a state of greater simplicity, and, consequently, may be more accurately contemplated, and more forcibly communicated; because the manners of rural life germinate from those elementary feelings, and, from the necessary character of rural occupations, are more easily comprehended, and are more durable; and, lastly, because in that condition the passions of men are incorporated with the beautiful and permanent forms of nature. The language, too, of these men has been adopted (purified indeed from what appears to be its real defects, from all lasting and rational causes of dislike or disgust) because such men hourly communicate with the best objects from which the best part of language is originally derived; and because, from their rank in society and the sameness and narrow circle of their intercourse, being less under the influence of social vanity, they convey their feelings and notions in simple and unelaborated expressions. Accordingly, such a language, arising out of repeated experience and regular feelings, is a more permanent, and a far more philosophical language than that which is frequently substituted for it by poets, who think that they are conferring honor upon themselves and their art, in proportion as they separate themselves from the sympathies of men, and indulge in arbitrary and capricious habits of expression, in order to furnish food for fickle tastes, and fickle appetites, of their own creation.[1]

I cannot, however, be insensible to the present outcry against the triviality and meanness, both of thought and language, which some of my contemporaries have occasionally introduced into their metrical compositions; and I acknowledge that this defect, where it exists, is more dishonorable to the writer's own character than false refinement or arbitrary innovation, though I should contend at the same time it is far less pernicious in the sum of its consequences. From such verses the poems in these volumes will be found distinguished at least by one mark of difference, that each of them has a worthy *purpose*. Not that I always began to write with a distinct purpose formally conceived; but habits of meditation have, I trust, so prompted and regulated my feelings, that my descriptions of such objects as strongly excite those feelings will be found to carry along with them a *purpose*. If this opinion be erroneous, I can have little right to the name of a poet. For all good poetry is the spontaneous overflow of powerful feelings: and though this be true, poems to which any value can be attached were never produced on any variety of subjects but by a man who, being possessed of more than usual organic sensibility, had also thought long and deeply. For our continued influxes of feeling are modified and directed by our thoughts, which are indeed the representatives of all our past feelings; and, as by contemplating the relation of these general representatives to each other, we

---

[1][Wordsworth] It is worthwhile here to observe that the affecting parts of Chaucer are almost always expressed in language pure and universally intelligible even to this day.

discover what is really important to men, so, by the repetition and continence of this act, our feelings will be connected with important subjects, till at length, if we be originally possessed of much sensibility, such habits of mind will be produced that, by obeying blindly and mechanically the impulses of those habits, we shall describe objects, and utter sentiments, of such a nature, and in such connection with each other, that the understanding of the reader must necessarily be in some degree enlightened, and his affections strengthened and purified.

It has been said that each of these poems has a purpose. Another circumstance must be mentioned which distinguishes these poems from the popular poetry of the day; it is this, that the feeling therein developed gives importance to the action and situation, and not the action and situation to the feeling.

A sense of false modesty shall not prevent me from asserting that the reader's attention is pointed to this mark of distinction, far less for the sake of these particular poems than from the general importance of the subject. The subject is indeed important! For the human mind is capable of being excited without the application of gross and violent stimulants; and he must have a very faint perception of its beauty and dignity who does know know this, and who does not further know that one being is elevated above another in proportion as he possesses this capability. It has therefore appeared to me that to endeavor to produce or enlarge this capability is one of the best services in which, at any period, a writer can be engaged; but this service, excellent at all times, is especially so at the present day. For a multitude of causes, unknown to former times, are now acting with a combined force to blunt the discriminating powers of the mind, and, unfitting it for all voluntary exertion, to reduce it to a state of almost savage torpor. The most effective of these causes are the great national events which are daily taking place,[2] and the increasing accumulation of men in cities, where the uniformity of their occupations produces a craving for extraordinary incident, which the rapid communication of intelligence hourly gratifies. To this tendency of life and manners the literature and theatrical exhibitions of the country have conformed themselves. The invaluable works of our elder writers, I had almost said the works of Shakespeare and Milton, are driven into neglect by frantic novels,[3] sickly and stupid German tragedies, and deluges of idle and extravagant stories in verse.—When I think upon this degrading thirst after outrageous stimulation, I am almost ashamed to have

[2]Among these, the war with France.
[3]Wordsworth refers to the popular "gothic novels" of the time.

spoken of the feeble endeavor made in these volumes to counteract it; and, reflecting upon the magnitude of the general evil, I should be oppressed with no dishonorable melancholy, had I not a deep impression of certain inherent and indestructible qualities of the human mind, and likewise of certain powers in the great and permanent objects that act upon it, which are equally inherent and indestructible; and were there not added to this impression a belief that the time is approaching when the evil will be systematically opposed, by men of greater powers, and with far more distinguished success.

Having dwelt thus long on the subjects and aim of these poems, I shall request the reader's permission to apprise him of a few circumstances relating to their *style,* in order, among other reasons, that he may not censure me for not having performed what I never attempted. The reader will find that personifications of abstract ideas rarely occur in these volumes, and are utterly rejected, as an ordinary device to elevate the style, and raise it above prose. My purpose was to imitate, and, as far as possible, to adopt the very language of men; and assuredly such personifications do not make any natural or regular part of that language. They are, indeed, a figure of speech occasionally prompted by passion, and I have made use of them as such; but have endeavored utterly to reject them as a mechanical device of style, or as a family language which writers in meter seem to lay claim to by prescription. I have wished to keep the reader in the company of flesh and blood, persuaded that by so doing I shall interest him. Others who pursue a different track will interest him likewise; I do not interfere with their claim, but wish to prefer a claim of my own. There will also be found in these volumes little of what is usually called poetic diction; as much pains has been taken to avoid it as is ordinarily taken to produce it; this has been done for the reason already alleged, to bring my language near to the language of men; and further, because the pleasure which I have proposed to myself to impart is of a kind very different from that which is supposed by many persons to be the proper object of poetry. Without being culpably particular, I do not know how to give my reader a more exact notion of the style in which it was my wish and intention to write, than by informing him that I have at all times endeavored to look steadily at my subject; consequently there is, I hope, in these poems little falsehood of description, and my ideas are expressed in language fitted to their respective importance. Something must have been gained by this practice, as it is friendly to one property of all good poetry, namely, good sense: but it has necessarily cut me off from a large portion of phrases and figures of speech which from father to son have long been regarded as the common inheritance of poets. I have also thought it expedient to restrict myself still further, having abstained from the use of many expressions, in themselves proper and beautiful, but which have been foolishly repeated by bad poets, till such feelings of disgust are connected with them as it is scarcely possible by any art of association to overpower.

If in a poem there should be found a series of lines, or even a single line, in which the language, though naturally arranged, and according to the strict laws of meter, does not differ from that of prose, there is a numerous class of critics, who, when they stumble upon these prosaisms, as they call them, imagine that they have made a notable discovery, and exult over the poet as over a man ignorant of his own profession. Now these men would establish a canon of criticism which the reader will conclude he must utterly reject, if he wishes to be pleased with these volumes. And it would be a most easy task to prove to him that not only the language of a large portion of every good poem, even of the most elevated character, must necessarily, except with reference to the meter, in no respect differ from that of good prose, but likewise that some of the most interesting parts of the best poems will be found to be strictly the language of prose when prose is well written. The truth of this assertion might be demonstrated by innumerable passages from almost all the poetical writings, even of Milton himself. To illustrate the subject in a general manner, I will here adduce a short composition of Gray, who was at the head of those who, by their reasonings, have attempted to widen the space of separation betwixt prose and metrical composition, and was more than any other man curiously elaborate in the structure of his own poetic diction.

> In vain to me the smiling mornings shine,
> And reddening Phoebus lifts his golden fire:
> The birds in vain their amorous descant join,
> Or cheerful fields resume their green attire.
> These ears, alas! for other notes repine;
> *A different object do these eyes require;*
> *My lonely anguish melts no heart but mine;*
> *And in my breast the imperfect joys expire;*
> Yet morning smiles the busy race to cheer,
> And new-born pleasure brings to happier men;
> The fields to all their wonted tribute bear;
> To warm their little loves the birds complain.
> *I fruitless mourn to him that cannot hear,*
> *And weep the more because I weep in vain.*[4]

It will easily be perceived, that the only part of this sonnet which is of any value is the lines printed in italics; it is

---

[4]*Sonnet on the Death of Mr. Richard West.*

equally obvious that, except in the rhyme, and in the use of the single word *fruitless* for fruitlessly, which is so far a defect, the language of these lines does in no respect differ from that of prose.

By the foregoing quotation it has been shown that the language of prose may yet be well adapted to poetry; and it was previously asserted that a large portion of the language of every good poem can in no respect differ from that of good prose. We will go further. It may be safely affirmed that there neither is, nor can be, any *essential* difference between the language of prose and metrical composition. We are fond of tracing the resemblance between poetry and painting, and, accordingly, we call them sisters: but where shall we find bonds of connection sufficiently strict to typify the affinity betwixt metrical and prose composition? They both speak by and to the same organs; the bodies in which both of them are clothed may be said to be of the same substance, their affections are kindred, and almost identical, not necessarily differing even in degree; poetry[5] sheds no tears "such as angels weep," but natural and human tears; she can boast of no celestial ichor that distinguishes her vital juices from those of prose; the same human blood circulates through the veins of them both.

If it be affirmed that rhyme and metrical arrangement of themselves constitute a distinction which overturns what has just been said on the strict affinity of metrical language with that of prose, and paves the way for other artificial distinctions which the mind voluntarily admits, I answer that the language of such poetry as is here recommended is, as far as is possible, a selection of the language really spoken by men; that this selection, wherever it is made with true taste and feeling, will of itself form a distinction far greater than would at first be imagined, and will entirely separate the composition from the vulgarity and meanness of ordinary life; and, if meter be superadded thereto, I believe that a dissimilitude will be produced altogether sufficient for the gratification of a rational mind. What other distinction would we have? Whence is it to come? And where is it to exist? Not, surely, where the poet speaks through the mouths of his characters: it cannot be necessary here, either for elevation of style, or any of its supposed ornaments: for, if the poet's subject be judiciously chosen, it will naturally, and upon fit occasion, lead him to passions the language of which, if se-

---

[5][Wordsworth] I here use the word *poetry* (though against my own judgment) as opposed to the word *prose*, and synonymous with metrical composition. But much confusion has been introduced into criticism by this contradiction of poetry and prose, instead of the more philosophical one of poetry and matter of fact, or science. The only strict antithesis to prose is meter; nor is this, in truth, a strict antithesis, because lines and passages of meter so naturally occur in writing prose, that it would be scarcely possible to avoid them, even were it desirable.

lected truly and judiciously, must necessarily be dignified and variegated, and alive with metaphors and figures. I forbear to speak of an incongruity which would shock the intelligent reader, should the poet interweave any foreign splendor of his own with that which the passion naturally suggests: it is sufficient to say that such addition is unnecessary. And surely it is more probable that those passages which with propriety abound with metaphors and figures will have their due effect, if, upon other occasions where the passions are of a milder character, the style also be subdued and temperate.

But as the pleasure which I hope to give by the poems now presented to the reader must depend entirely on just notions upon this subject, and as it is in itself of high importance to our taste and moral feelings, I cannot content myself with these detached remarks. And if, in what I am about to say, it shall appear to some that my labor is unnecessary, and that I am like a man fighting a battle without enemies, such persons may be reminded that, whatever be the language outwardly holden by men, a practical faith in the opinions which I am wishing to establish is almost unknown. If my conclusions are admitted, and carried as far as they must be carried if admitted at all, our judgments concerning the works of the greatest poets both ancient and modern will be far different from what they are at present, both when we praise, and when we censure; and our moral feelings influencing and influenced by these judgments will, I believe, be corrected and purified.

Taking up the subject, then, upon general grounds, let me ask, what is meant by the word *poet?* What is a poet? To whom does he address himself? And what language is to be expected from him?—He is a man speaking to men: a man, it is true, endowed with more lively sensibility, more enthusiasm and tenderness, who has a greater knowledge of human nature, and a more comprehensive soul, than are supposed to be common among mankind; a man pleased with his own passions and volitions, and who rejoices more than other men in the spirit of life that is in him; delighting to contemplate similar volitions and passions as manifested in the goings-on of the universe, and habitually impelled to create them where he does not find them. To these qualities he has added a disposition to be affected more than other men by absent things as if they were present; an ability of conjuring up in himself passions which are indeed far from being the same as those produced by real events, yet (especially in those parts of the general sympathy which are pleasing and delightful) do more nearly resemble the passions produced by real events than anything which, from the motions of their own minds merely, other men are accustomed to feel in themselves—whence, and from practice, he has acquired a greater readiness and power in expressing what he thinks and feels, and especially those thoughts and feelings which, by his own choice, or from the structure of his own mind, arise in him without immediate external excitement.

But whatever portion of this faculty we may suppose even the greatest poet to possess, there cannot be a doubt that the language which it will suggest to him must often, in liveliness and truth, fall short of that which is uttered by men in real life under the actual pressure of those passions, certain shadows of which the poet thus produces, or feels to be produced, in himself.

However exalted a notion we would wish to cherish of the character of a poet, it is obvious that while he describes and imitates passions, his employment is in some degree mechanical, compared with the freedom and power of real and substantial action and suffering. So that it will be the wish of the poet to bring his feelings near to those of the persons whose feelings he describes,—nay, for short spaces of time, perhaps, to let himself slip into an entire delusion, and even confound and identify his own feelings with theirs; modifying only the language which is thus suggested to him by a consideration that he describes for a particular purpose, that of giving pleasure. Here, then, he will apply the principle of selection which has been already insisted upon. He will depend upon this for removing what would otherwise be painful or disgusting in the passion; he will feel that there is no necessity to trick out or to elevate nature; and, the more industriously he applies this principle, the deeper will be his faith that no words which *his* fancy or imagination can suggest will be to be compared with those which are the emanations of reality and truth.

But it may be said by those who do not object to the general spirit of these remarks, that, as it is impossible for the poet to produce upon all occasions language as exquisitely fitted for the passion as that which the real passion itself suggests, it is proper that he should consider himself as in the situation of a translator, who does not scruple to substitute excellencies of another kind for those which are unattainable by him, and endeavors occasionally to surpass his original, in order to make some amends for the general inferiority to which he feels that he must submit. But this would be to encourage idleness and unmanly despair. Further, it is the language of men who speak of what they do not understand; who talk of poetry as of a matter of amusement and idle pleasure; who will converse with us as gravely about a *taste* for poetry, as they express it, as if it were a thing as indifferent as a taste for rope dancing, or Frontiniac or Sherry. Aristotle, I have been told, has said that poetry is the most philosophic of all writing:[6] it is so: its object is truth,

------

[6]Aristotle (*Poetics,* IX. 2–5, p. 55) says that poetry is more philosophical than history, by which he means that poetry is more universal.

not individual and local, but general, and operative; not standing upon external testimony, but carried alive into the heart by passion; truth which is its own testimony, which gives competence and confidence to the tribunal to which it appeals, and receives them from the same tribunal. Poetry is the image of man and nature. The obstacles which stand in the way of the fidelity of the biographer and historian, and of their consequent utility, are incalculably greater than those which are to be encountered by the poet who comprehends the dignity of his art. The poet writes under one restriction only, namely, the necessity of giving immediate pleasure to a human being possessed of that information which may be expected from him, not as a lawyer, a physician, a mariner, an astronomer, or a natural philosopher, but as a man. Except this one restriction, there is no object standing between the poet and the image of things; between this, and the biographer and historian, there are a thousand.

Nor let this necessity of producing immediate pleasure be considered as a degradation of the poet's art. It is far otherwise. It is an acknowledgment of the beauty of the universe, an acknowledgment the more sincere, because not formal, but indirect; it is a task light and easy to him who looks at the world in the spirit of love: further, it is a homage paid to the native and naked dignity of man, to the grand elementary principle of pleasure, by which he knows, and feels, and lives, and moves. We have no sympathy but what is propagated by pleasure: I would not be misunderstood; but wherever we sympathize with pain, it will be found that the sympathy is produced and carried on by subtle combinations with pleasure. We have no knowledge, that is, no general principles drawn from the contemplation of particular facts, but what has been built up by pleasure, and exists in us by pleasure alone. The man of science, the chemist and mathematician, whatever difficulties and disgusts they may have had to struggle with, know and feel this. However painful may be the objects with which the anatomist's knowledge is connected, he feels that his knowledge is pleasure; and where he has no pleasure he has no knowledge. What then does the poet? He considers man and the objects that surround him as acting and reacting upon each other, so as to produce an infinite complexity of pain and pleasure; he considers man in his own nature and in his ordinary life as contemplating this with a certain quantity of immediate knowledge, with certain convictions, intuitions, and deductions, which from habit acquire the quality of intuitions; he considers him as looking upon this complex scene of ideas and sensations, and finding everywhere objects that immediately excite in him sympathies which, from the necessities of his nature, are accompanied by an overbalance of enjoyment.

To this knowledge which all men carry about with them, and to these sympathies in which, without any other

discipline than that of our daily life, we are fitted to take delight, the poet principally directs his attention. He considers man and nature as essentially adapted to each other, and the mind of man as naturally the mirror of the fairest and most interesting properties of nature. And thus the poet, prompted by this feeling of pleasure, which accompanies him through the whole course of his studies, converses with general nature, with affections akin to those which, through labor and length of time, the man of science has raised up in himself, by conversing with those particular parts of nature which are the objects of his studies. The knowledge both of the poet and the man of science is pleasure; but the knowledge of the one cleaves to us as a necessary part of our existence, our natural and unalienable inheritance; the other is a personal and individual acquisition, slow to come to us, and by no habitual and direct sympathy connecting us with our fellow beings. The man of science seeks truth as a remote and unknown benefactor; he cherishes and loves it in his solitude: the poet, singing a song in which all human beings join with him, rejoices in the presence of truth as our visible friend and hourly companion. Poetry is the breath and finer spirit of all knowledge; it is the impassioned expression which is in the countenance of all science. Emphatically may it be said of the poet, as Shakespeare hath said of man, "that he looks before and after." He is the rock of defense for human nature; an upholder and preserver, carrying everywhere with him relationship and love. In spite of difference of soil and climate, of language and manners, of laws and customs: in spite of things silently gone out of mind, and things violently destroyed; the poet binds together by passion and knowledge the vast empire of human society, as it is spread over the whole earth, and over all time. The objects of the poet's thoughts are everywhere; though the eyes and senses of man are, it is true, his favorite guides, yet he will follow wheresoever he can find an atmosphere of sensation in which to move his wings. Poetry is the first and last of all knowledge—it is as immortal as the heart of man. If the labors of men of science should ever create any material revolution, direct or indirect, in our condition, and in the impressions which we habitually receive, the poet will sleep then no more than at present; he will be ready to follow the steps of the man of science, not only in those general indirect effects, but he will be at his side, carrying sensation into the midst of the objects of the science itself. The remotest discoveries of the chemist, the botanist, or mineralogist, will be as proper objects of the poet's art as any upon which it can be employed, if the time should ever come when these things shall be familiar to us, and the relations under which they are contemplated by the followers of these respective sciences shall be manifestly and palpably material to us as enjoying and suffering beings. If the time should ever come when what is now called science, thus familiarized to men, shall be ready to put on, as it were, a form of flesh and blood, the poet will lend his divine spirit to aid the transfiguration, and will welcome the being thus produced, as a dear and genuine inmate of the household of man.—It is not, then, to be supposed that anyone who holds that sublime notion of poetry which I have attempted to convey, will break in upon the sanctity and truth of his pictures by transitory and accidental ornaments, and endeavor to excite admiration of himself by arts the necessity of which must manifestly depend upon the assumed meanness of his subject.

What has been thus far said applies to poetry in general, but especially to those parts of composition where the poet speaks through the mouths of his characters; and upon this point it appears to authorize the conclusion that there are few persons of good sense who would not allow that the dramatic parts of composition are defective, in proportion as they deviate from the real language of nature, and are colored by a diction of the poet's own, either peculiar to him as an individual poet or belonging simply to poets in general; to a body of men who, from the circumstance of their compositions being in meter, it is expected will employ a particular language.

It is not, then, in the dramatic parts of composition that we look for this distinction of language; but still it may be proper and necessary where the poet speaks to us in his own person and character. To this I answer by referring the reader to the description before given of a poet. Among the qualities there enumerated as principally conducing to form a poet, is implied nothing differing in kind from other men, but only in degree. The sum of what was said is, that the poet is chiefly distinguished from other men by a greater promptness to think and feel without immediate external excitement, and a greater power in expressing such thoughts and feelings as are produced in him in that manner. But these passions and thoughts and feelings are the general passions and thoughts and feelings of men. And with what are they connected? Undoubtedly with our moral sentiments and animal sensations, and with the causes which excite these; with the operations of the elements, and the appearances of the visible universe; with storm and sunshine, with the revolutions of the seasons, with cold and heat, with loss of friends and kindred, with injuries and resentments, gratitude and hope, with fear and sorrow. These, and the like, are the sensations and objects which the poet describes, as they are the sensations of other men, and the objects which interest them. The poet thinks and feels in the spirit of human passions. How, then, can his language differ in any material degree from that of all other men who feel vividly and see clearly? It might be *proved* that it is impossible. But supposing that this were not the case, the poet might then be allowed to use

a peculiar language when expressing his feelings for his own gratification, or that of men like himself. But poets do not write for poets alone, but for men. Unless, therefore, we are advocates for that admiration which subsists upon ignorance, and that pleasure which arises from hearing what we do not understand, the poet must descend from this supposed height; and, in order to excite rational sympathy, he must express himself as other men express themselves. To this it may be added that while he is only selecting from the real language of men, or, which amounts to the same thing, composing accurately in the spirit of such selection, he is treading upon safe ground, and we know what we are to expect from him. Our feelings are the same with respect to meter; for, as it may be proper to remind the reader, the distinction of meter is regular and uniform, and not, like that which is produced by what is usually called *poetic diction,* arbitrary, and subject to infinite caprices upon which no calculation whatever can be made. In the one case, the reader is utterly at the mercy of the poet, respecting what imagery or diction he may choose to connect with the passion; whereas in the other, the meter obeys certain laws, to which the poet and reader both willingly submit because they are certain, and because no interference is made by them with the passion, but such as the concurring testimony of ages has shown to heighten and improve the pleasure which coexists with it.

It will now be proper to answer an obvious question, namely, why, professing these opinions, have I written in verse? To this, in addition to such answer as is included in what has been already said, I reply, in the first place, because, however I may have restricted myself, there is still left open to me what confessedly constitutes the most valuable object of all writing, whether in prose or verse—the great and universal passions of men, the most general and interesting of their occupations, and the entire world of nature before me—to supply endless combinations of forms and imagery. Now, supposing for a moment that whatever is interesting in these objects may be as vividly described in prose, why should I be condemned for attempting to superadd to such description the charm which, by the consent of all nations, is acknowledged to exist in metrical language? To this, by such as are yet unconvinced, it may be answered that a very small part of the pleasure given by poetry depends upon the meter, and that it is injudicious to write in meter, unless it be accompanied with the other artificial distinctions of style with which meter is usually accompanied, and that, by such deviation, more will be lost from the shock which will thereby be given to the reader's associations than will be counterbalanced by any pleasure which he can derive from the general power of numbers. In answer to those who still contend for the necessity of accompanying meter with certain appropriate colors of style in order to the accomplishment of its appropriate end, and who also, in my opinion, greatly underrate the power of meter in itself, it might, perhaps, as far as relates to these volumes, have been almost sufficient to observe that poems are extant, written upon more humble subjects, and in a still more naked and simple style, which have continued to give pleasure from generation to generation. Now if nakedness and simplicity be a defect, the fact here mentioned affords a strong presumption that poems somewhat less naked and simple are capable of affording pleasure at the present day; and what I wished *chiefly* to attempt, at present, was to justify myself for having written under the impression of this belief.

But various causes might be pointed out why, when the style is manly, and the subject of some importance, words metrically arranged will long continue to impart such a pleasure to mankind as he who proves the extent of that pleasure will be desirous to impart. The end of poetry is to produce excitement in coexistence with an overbalance of pleasure; but, by the supposition, excitement is an unusual and irregular state of the mind; ideas and feelings do not, in that state, succeed each other in accustomed order. If the words, however, by which this excitement is produced be in themselves powerful, or the images and feelings have an undue proportion of pain connected with them, there is some danger that the excitement may be carried beyond its proper bounds. Now the copresence of something regular, something to which the mind has been accustomed in various moods and in a less excited state, cannot but have great efficacy in tempering and restraining the passion by an intertexture of ordinary feeling, and of feeling not strictly and necessarily connected with the passion. This is unquestionably true; and hence, though the opinion will at first appear paradoxical, from the tendency of meter to divest language, in a certain degree, of its reality, and thus to throw a sort of half-consciousness of unsubstantial existence over the whole composition, there can be little doubt but that more pathetic situations and sentiments, that is, those which have a greater proportion of pain connected with them, may be endured in metrical composition, especially in rhyme, than in prose. The meter of the old ballads is very artless, yet they contain many passages which would illustrate this opinion; and, I hope, if the following poems be attentively perused, similar instances will be found in them. This opinion may be further illustrated by appealing to the reader's own experience of the reluctance with which he comes to the reperusal of the distressful parts of *Clarissa Harlowe,* or *The Gamester,* while Shakespeare's writings, in the most pathetic scenes, never act upon us, as pathetic, beyond the bounds of pleasure—an effect which, in a much greater degree than might at first be imagined, is to be ascribed to small but continual and regular

impulses of pleasurable surprise from the metrical arrangement.—On the other hand (what it must be allowed will much more frequently happen) if the poet's words should be incommensurate with the passion, and inadequate to raise the reader to a height of desirable excitement, then (unless the poet's choice of his meter has been grossly injudicious) in the feelings of pleasure which the reader has been accustomed to connect with meter in general, and in the feeling, whether cheerful or melancholy, which he has been accustomed to connect with that particular movement of meter, there will be found something which will greatly contribute to impart passion to the words, and to effect the complex end which the poet proposes to himself.

If I had undertaken a *systematic* defense of the theory here maintained, it would have been my duty to develop the various causes upon which the pleasure received from metrical language depends. Among the chief of these causes is to be reckoned a principle which must be well known to those who have made any of the arts the object of accurate reflection; namely, the pleasure which the mind derives from the perception of similitude in dissimilitude. This principle is the great spring of the activity of our minds, and their chief feeder. From this principle the direction of the sexual appetite, and all the passions connected with it, take their origin: it is the life of our ordinary conversation; and upon the accuracy with which similitude are perceived, depend our taste and our moral feelings. It would not be a useless employment to apply this principle to the consideration of meter, and to show that meter is hence enabled to afford much pleasure, and to point out in what manner that pleasure is produced. But my limits will not permit me to enter upon this subject, and I must content myself with a general summary.

I have said that poetry is the spontaneous overflow of powerful feelings; it takes its origin from emotion recollected in tranquility: the emotion is contemplated till, by a species of reaction, the tranquility gradually disappears, and an emotion, kindred to that which was before the subject of contemplation, is gradually produced, and does itself actually exist in the mind. In this mood successful composition generally begins, and in a mood similar to this it is carried on; but the emotion, of whatever kind, and in whatever degree, from various causes, is qualified by various pleasures, so that in describing any passions whatsoever, which are voluntarily described, the mind will, upon the whole, be in a state of enjoyment. If nature be thus cautious to preserve in a state of enjoyment a being so employed, the poet ought to profit by the lesson held forth to him, and ought especially to take care that, whatever passions he communicates to his reader, those passions, if his reader's mind be sound and vigorous, should always be accompanied with an overbalance of pleasure. Now the music of harmonious metrical language, the sense of difficulty overcome, and the blind association of pleasure which has been previously received from works of rhyme or meter of the same or similar construction, an indistinct perception perpetually renewed of language closely resembling that of real life, and yet, in the circumstance of meter, differing from it so widely—all these imperceptibly make up a complex feeling of delight, which is of the most important use in tempering the painful feeling always found intermingled with powerful descriptions of the deeper passions. This effect is always produced in pathetic and impassioned poetry; while in lighter compositions the ease and gracefulness with which the poet manages his numbers are themselves confessedly a principal source of the gratification of the reader. All that it is *necessary* to say, however, upon this subject, may be effected by affirming, what few persons will deny, that of two descriptions, either of passions, manners, or characters each of them equally well executed, the one in prose and the other in verse, the verse will be read a hundred times where the prose is read once.

Having thus explained a few of my reasons for writing in verse, and why I have chosen subjects from common life, and endeavored to bring my language near to the real language of men, if I have been too minute in pleading my own cause, I have at the same time been treating a subject of general interest; and for this reason a few words shall be added with reference solely to these particular poems, and to some defects which will probably be found in them. I am sensible that my associations must have sometimes been particular instead of general, and that, consequently, giving to things a false importance, I may have sometimes written upon unworthy subjects; but I am less apprehensive on this account, than that my language may frequently have suffered from those arbitrary connections of feelings and ideas with particular words and phrases, from which no man can altogether protect himself. Hence I have no doubt that, in some instances, feelings, even of the ludicrous, may be given to my readers by expressions which appeared to me tender and pathetic. Such faulty expressions, were I convinced they were faulty at present, and that they must necessarily continue to be so, I would willingly take all reasonable pains to correct. But it is dangerous to make these alterations on the simple authority of a few individuals, or even of certain classes of men; for where the understanding of an author is not convinced, or his feelings altered, this cannot be done without great injury to himself: for his own feelings are his stay and support; and, if he set them aside in one instance, he may be induced to repeat this act till his mind shall lose all confidence in itself, and become utterly debilitated. To this it may

be added that the critic ought never to forget that he is himself exposed to the same errors as the poet, and perhaps in a much greater degree: for there can be no presumption in saying of most readers that it is not probable they will be so well acquainted with the various stages of meaning through which words have passed, or with the fickleness or stability of the relations of particular ideas to each other; and, above all, since they are so much less interested in the subject, they may decide lightly and carelessly.

Long as the reader has been detained, I hope he will permit me to caution him against a mode of false criticism which has been applied to poetry, in which the language closely resembles that of life and nature. Such verses have been triumphed over in parodies, of which Dr. Johnson's stanza is a fair specimen:

> I put my hat upon my head
> And walked into the Strand,
> And there I met another man
> Whose hat was in his hand.

Immediately under these lines let us place one of the most justly admired stanzas of the *Babes in the Woods.*[7]

> These pretty babes with hand in hand
> Went wandering up and down;
> But never more they saw the man
> Approaching from the town.

In both these stanzas the words, and the order of the words in no respect differ from the most unimpassioned conversation. There are words in both, for example, *the Strand* and *the town,* connected with none but the most familiar ideas; yet the one stanza we admit as admirable, and the other as a fair example of the superlatively contemptible. Whence arises this difference? Not from the meter, not from the language, not from the order of the words; but the *matter* expressed in Dr. Johnson's stanza is contemptible. The proper method of treating trivial and simple verses to which Dr. Johnson's stanza would be a fair parallelism, is not to say, this is a bad kind of poetry, or, this is not poetry; but, this wants sense; it is neither interesting in itself, nor can *lead* to anything interesting; the images neither originate in that sane state of feeling which arises out of thought, nor can excite thought or feeling in the reader. This is the only sensible manner of dealing with such verses. Why trouble yourself about the species till you have previously decided upon

---

[7]An anonymous ballad.

the genus? Why take pains to prove that an ape is not a Newton, when it is self-evident that he is not a man?

One request I must make of my reader, which is, that in judging these poems he would decide by his own feelings genuinely, and not by reflection upon what will probably be the judgment of others. How common is it to hear a person say, I myself do not object to this style of composition, or this or that expression, but to such and such classes of people it will appear mean or ludicrous! This mode of criticism, so destructive of all sound unadulterated judgment, is almost universal: let the reader then abide, independently, by his own feelings, and, if he finds himself affected, let him not suffer such conjectures to interfere with his pleasure.

If an author, by any single composition, has impressed us with respect for his talents, it is useful to consider this as affording a presumption that on other occasions, where we have been displeased, he nevertheless may not have written ill or absurdly; and further, to give him so much credit for this one composition as may induce us to review what has displeased us with more care than we should otherwise have bestowed upon it. This is not only an act of justice, but, in our decisions upon poetry especially, may conduce in a high degree to the improvement of our own taste; for an *accurate* taste in poetry, and in all the other arts, as Sir Joshua Reynolds has observed, is an *acquired* talent, which can only be produced by thought and a long-continued intercourse with the best models of composition.[8] This is mentioned, not with so ridiculous a purpose as to prevent the most inexperienced reader from judging for himself (I have already said that I wish him to judge for himself), but merely to temper the rashness of decision, and to suggest that, if poetry be a subject on which much time has not been bestowed, the judgment may be erroneous; and that, in many cases, it necessarily will be so.

Nothing would, I know, have so effectually contributed to further the end which I have in view, as to have shown of what kind the pleasure is, and how that pleasure is produced, which is confessedly produced by metrical composition essentially different from that which I have here endeavored to recommend: for the reader will say that he has been pleased by such composition; and what more can be done for him? The power of any art is limited; and he will suspect that, if it be proposed to furnish him with new friends, that can be only upon condition of his abandoning his old friends. Besides, as I have said, the reader is himself conscious of the pleasure which he has received from such composition, composition to which he has peculiarly attached the endearing name of poetry; and all men feel an habitual gratitude, and something of an honorable bigotry, for the objects which have long continued to please them: we not only wish to be pleased, but to be pleased in that particular way in which we have been accustomed to be pleased. There is in these feelings enough to resist a host of arguments; and I should be the less able to combat them successfully, as I am willing to allow that, in order entirely to enjoy the poetry which I am recommending, it would be necessary to give up much of what is ordinarily enjoyed. But, would my limits have permitted me to point out how this pleasure is produced, many obstacles might have been removed, and the reader assisted in perceiving that the powers of language are not so limited as he may suppose; and that it is possible for poetry to give other enjoyments, of a purer, more lasting, and more exquisite nature. This part of the subject has not been altogether neglected, but it has not been so much my present aim to prove that the interest excited by some other kinds of poetry is less vivid, and less worthy of the nobler powers of the mind, as to offer reasons for presuming that, if my purpose were fulfilled, a species of poetry would be produced which is genuine poetry, in its nature well adapted to interest mankind permanently, and likewise important in the multiplicity and quality of its moral relations.

From what has been said, and from a perusal of the poems, the reader will be able clearly to perceive the object which I had in view: he will determine how far it has been attained; and, what is a much more important question, whether it will be worth attaining: and upon the decision of these two questions will rest my claim to the approbation of the public.

---

[8] See *Discourse VII*, pp. 408–11.

Germaine Necker de Staël

1766–1817

Madame de Staël, as she is usually called, was unquestionably one of the most remarkable women of her time. Daughter of the French statesman Jacques Necker, whose dismissal as director of finances by Louis XVI led to the fall of the Bastille, she was involved in politics through her affairs with famous men, her spirited opposition to Napoleon (which earned her banishment from Paris), and her own writings. It is not surprising, therefore, that her writings on literature often convey a strong concern with social relations, nationality, and the situation of women, the last of which in various ages she comments on here and there in *Literature Considered in Its Relation to Social Institutions.* The essay begins with a consideration of the Ancient Greeks and proceeds to modern times. A child of the Enlightenment, de Staël saw the relation of literature and society as one of mutual influence under the presumption of "the slow but continual march of the human mind in philosophy and its rapid but interrupted progress in the arts." She wrote quite consciously from the point of view of a certain political order, which was republican and devoted to liberty and equality among both people and nations. The new political order would be the result of a halting progress from feudalism through absolutism to representative government. A new art appropriate to a new political order was inevitable; new literary values would arise: "In a monarchy, people hold up to ridicule those manners that do not conform to received practices. In a republic, the subject of the shafts of ridicule ought to be the human failings that harm the general welfare." But progress is never smooth and never without its retrograde movements. In her time, she saw the French Revolution produce violence, tyranny, and eventually Napoleon, whom she wrote about critically in *Considerations on the Principal Events of the French Revolution* (1816). She remembers first meeting him: ". . . when I was somewhat recovered from the confusion of admiration, a very strong sense of fear followed." Nevertheless, it was she who years later, after he had exiled her, warned him of a plot on his life.

Perhaps because she was suspicious of what happened to the political movements that reached their goals, she seemed to align herself in the realm of literature with neither romanticism nor classicism, though she was one of those to popularize these terms. Rather she sought a position that would ensure human progress, drawing on the best of both movements.

For Madame de Staël's writings translated into English see Vivian Folkenflik, ed., *An Extraordinary Woman: Selected Writings of Germaine de Staël* (1987). See also Wayne Andrews, *Germaine: A Portrait of Madame de Staël* (1963); Helen B. Posgate, *Madame de Staël* (1968); and Robert de Luppé, *Les Idées litteraires de Madame de Staël et l'héritage des lumières* (1969).

From

Literature Considered in Its Relation to Social Institutions

Part Two. The Present State of Enlightenment in France and Its Future Progress
Chapter I. General View of Part Two

I have followed the history of the human mind from Homer to 1789. In my national pride, I considered the period of the French Revolution as a new era for the intellectual world. Perhaps it is only a dreadful event! Perhaps the influence of old customs will not allow this event to bring forth either a productive institution or a philosophical result for a long time. In any case, since this second part contains some general ideas on the progress of the human mind, it may be useful to develop these notions even if they should be applicable only to another country or another age.

I believe it always worth while to consider what must be the character of the literature of a great nation, an enlightened nation, where liberty and political equality are established, and where customs are consistent with its institutions. There is only one nation in the world to which some of these reflections are already appropriate: the Americans. They do not yet have a well-developed literature, but when their civil officials are called upon to appeal to public opinion in any way, they are eminently talented in stirring all the emotions by the expression of simple truths and honest sentiments—which is already to understand the most useful secrets of style.

These observations, applied to France, cannot be divorced from the results already produced by the Revolution; and these results, it must be admitted, are detrimental to manners, letters, and philosophy. In the course of this work I have shown how the mingling of Northern and Southern peoples led to barbarism for a time, though it eventually resulted in very great progress for learning and civilization. The introduction of a new class into the government of France had to produce a similar effect. This Revolution may in the long run enlighten a greater mass of men but for sev-

eral years the vulgarity of language, manners, and opinion must cause taste and reason to retrogress in many respects. It is in the very nature of revolution to arrest the progress of enlightenment for some years and then to give it a new impetus. We must first examine the two principal obstacles to the development of the mind: the loss of refinement of manners and of that emulation that the rewards of public opinion can stimulate. When I have presented the various ideas pertinent to this matter, I shall consider to what extent literature and philosophy are perfectible if we overcome the mistakes of revolution without renouncing with them the truths that give thinking Europe an interest in the foundation of a free and just republic.

Chapter II. Taste, Refinement of Manners, and Their Literary and Political Influence

For some time, people in France believed that it was necessary to make a revolution in literature too, and to grant the widest latitude to the rules of taste in every *genre*. Nothing would be more contrary to the progress of literature, to that advancement that so effectively promotes the spread of philosophic learning, and consequently to the maintenance of liberty. Nothing could be more fatal to the improvement of morals, one of the chief goals at which republican institutions ought to aim. The exaggerated refinements of some communities in the Old Regime no doubt have no relation to the true principles of taste, which always conform to reason. But we can banish some conventional rules without upsetting the boundaries that mark the path of genius and preserve decency and dignity in both speech and writing.

The French nation was too civilized in some respects; its institutions and social customs took the place of natural feelings.

Vanity alone absorbed almost every class. Men lived only to produce an effect around them, to obtain a conventional superiority over their immediate rivals in order to stir up the envy that they themselves would experience in their turn. From individual to individual and class to class, long-suffering vanity was never at rest except upon the throne. In every other status, from the highest to the lowest, men spent their lives comparing themselves with their equals or superiors.

By being extended too far, this despotism of public opinion could ultimately injure true talent. The rules of good manners and taste became daily more refined and further removed from the mark of nature. There was freedom of man-

LITERATURE IN ITS RELATION TO SOCIAL INSTITUTIONS. *De la Litterature considerée dans ses rapports avec les institutions sociales* was first published in 1800. The selection here is reprinted from *Politics, Literature, and National Character,* translated and edited by Morroe Berger (Doubleday & Co., 1964). Reprinted by permission of the estate of Morroe Berger.

ners without abandonment of awareness of difference. Good manners graded people instead of uniting them.

Yet people wanted to establish a sort of equality, the sort that on the surface placed all minds and personalities on the same level, an equality that burdened distinguished men and relieved jealous mediocrity. The art of avoiding the dangers of the mind was the sole use of the mind.

After having refined taste, the tyranny of ridicule, which was especially characteristic of the last years of the Old Regime, ended by using force; and literature could have been affected. To lend greater nobility to writings and greater vigor to persons, taste should not be surrendered to the elegant and mannered customs of aristocratic communities, however noteworthy they may be for their perfection of charm. Their despotism would bring about serious disadvantages for liberty, political equality, and even higher literature. Yet, on the other hand, how much would not bad taste, pushed to the point of vulgarity, hinder literary glory, morality, liberty, and everything good and lofty in the relations among men?

Since the Revolution, a revolting vulgarity of manners has often been attached to the exercise of the least authority. The defects of power are contagious. In France especially it seems that power influences not only deeds and speech but almost the inner thoughts of the sycophants who surround powerful men.

Bad taste, such as has prevailed for several years of the Revolutionary period, is not only detrimental to the relations between society and literature but also strikes at morality. People make so bold as to joke about their own baseness and vices, to acknowledge them shamelessly, and to flout those timid souls who still shrink from this degrading levity.

People are rather generally convinced that the republican spirit calls for a change in the character of literature. I consider this notion correct but in a different sense from that given it. The republican spirit calls for more rigor in good taste, which is inseparable from good manners. It also undoubtedly permits literature to convey a more forceful kind of beauty, a more philosophical and more moving portrait of the great events of life. Montesquieu, Rousseau, and Condillac belonged in advance to this republican spirit. They began the desirable revolution in the character of French works: this revolution must be completed. Since a republic necessarily brings forth stronger emotions, the art of portrayal must grow as its subjects grow. But by an odd contrast, it is largely the licentious and the shallow *genre* that has sought to take advantage of the liberty that literature was believed to have acquired.

The precepts of taste as they apply to republican literature are more simple but no less rigorous than those adopted by the writers of the age of Louis XIV.[1] Under the monarchy, convention was sometimes substituted for reason and propriety for true feelings. But since in a republic taste should consist only in perfect understanding of all true and enduring relations, to lack the elements of taste is to be unaware of the real nature of things.

Under the monarchy, it was often necessary to disguise bold condemnation, to veil a new opinion under the form of received prejudices. The taste that had to be brought to these various appearances required an unusually delicate *finesse*. But the guise of truth, in a free country, is in harmony with truth itself. Expression and feeling ought to spring from the same source.

Formerly, people combined nobility of manners with an almost habitual practice of jesting. This combination presupposes a perfection of taste and refinement, a sense of one's superiority, power, and status which education for equality does not develop. This elegance, grand and trivial at the same time, probably does not suit republican manners; it is too distinctively characteristic of the practices of great wealth and high status. Intellect is more democratic; it waxes at random among all men independent enough to have some leisure. It is intellect, therefore, that we must encourage above all in literature, by devoting ourselves less to subjects that depend exclusively upon formal elegance.

Politeness is the tie society has established between strangers. Certain qualities attach us to family, friends, and the unfortunate. But in all those relations that have not yet assumed the character of a duty, civility of manners anticipates sympathy, moderates firm beliefs, and maintains for every one the place in the world that his merit ought to bring him. It marks the degree of respect to which each person has raised himself; in this sense, it distributes the rewards that are the goal of life's labors.

Women and great men, love and glory, are the only ideas and feelings that can find a strong echo in the mind. But how shall a pure and proud model of woman be found in a country where social relations are not guarded by the most rigorous propriety? Where shall we find standards of virtue when women themselves—those independent judges of life's struggles—have permitted their noble instinct for lofty sentiments to wither? A woman loses her charm not merely by the indelicate speech she may indulge in but also by what she hears, by what others may dare to say in her presence. In the bosom of her family, modesty and simplicity suffice to maintain the respect a woman ought to demand. But in the social world, more is necessary: the elegance of

---

[1] Reigned 1643–1715.

her speech and the loftiness of her manners form part of her dignity and can alone command respect.

Under the monarchy, the spirit of chivalry, the ceremony of rank, the magnificence of wealth—everything that strikes the imagination—compensated in some respects for the lack of true merit. But in a republic women no longer count for anything if they do not inspire respect everywhere by their natural nobility. As soon as an illusion is banished, a reality must be substituted. As soon as an ancient prejudice is destroyed, a new virtue is needed. So a republic, far from having to afford greater liberty in customary social relations, must protect itself much more scrupulously against all kinds of lapses from propriety; for all distinctions in it are based only on personal qualities. If a reputation is in the slightest injured it is no longer possible, as in a monarchy, for a man to improve his position by his rank, birth, or any privilege extraneous to his own merit.

It is essential in France to establish ties that can reconcile opposing groups, and civility is an effective means to achieve this goal. It would unite all enlightened men, who would constitute a court of opinion which would dispense blame or praise with some justice.

This court would also exert an influence upon literature. Writers would know where to rediscover national taste and intellect, and would labor to portray and enlarge it.

Civility alone can soften the asperities of the partisan spirit. It permits mutual toleration long before affection, and intercourse long before agreement. And so our profound aversion for those we did not know is gradually weakened by conversation, consideration, and solicitude, which kindles sympathy and leads us ultimately to find fellow men among those we formerly regarded as enemies.

Chapter III. Emulation

I certainly cannot deny that for several years the condition of France has been much more adverse to the development of talent and the mind than most periods of history.

It would appear, on first glance, that civil disturbances, by overturning the old social ranks, must afford natural ability the exercise and development of all its powers. That was undoubtedly the case in the beginning. But at the end of a short time the rebels conceived a hatred for enlightenment at least equal to what the old defenders of prejudices felt.

If revolutionary movements extend beyond the goal they sought to achieve, power falls into the hands of increasingly ignorant classes of society.

To encourage men of letters is to place them under whatever power rewards them. To do so is to consider literary genius apart from the world of society and political interests, to treat it like the talent for music or painting or any art outside of intellect itself, that is to say, the whole of man.

It is only in free states that the genius for action and the genius for reflection can be united. In the Old Regime it was desirable that literary talent should almost always imply the absence of political talent.

In absolute monarchies people want a kind of mystery to suffuse the qualities suited to government so that an influential and barren mediocrity may push aside a superior intellect.

Great talent is no doubt necessary in order to govern well. But it was only in order to brush aside talent that people tried to argue that the reflection that creates the profound philosopher, the great writer, and the eloquent orator has no connection with the rules that should guide the leaders of nations. Chancellor Bacon, Temple the *chevalier,* L'Hôpital,[2] etc., were philosophers, literary men, yet proved themselves to be leading statesmen.

For the happiness of mankind, the great men charged with its destiny must have a certain number of very different qualities in almost equal degrees. A single type of superiority is not enough to win over the various forms of opinion and worth, nor does it, if I may put it so, adequately personify the conception we like to develop of a man of renown.

But, it may be said, what ought to be feared above all in a republic is enthusiasm for one man.

Nothing is less philosophical—that is to say, nothing would lead less to happiness—than the jealous narrow-mindedness that would deprive nations of their place in history by equalizing the reputations of men. Every effort should be made to spread general education. But along with this great concern for the promotion of knowledge we must allow the goal of individual glory. A republic must give much more scope to this motive of emulation than any other form of government, for it grows richer with the manifold labors emulation inspires. Only a small number of men succeed, but all may aspire. And if fame crowns only success, the effort itself often has some hidden use.

The guiding principle of a republic in which political equality is sacred ought to be the establishment of the most pronounced distinctions among men in accordance with their talents and qualities.

Conquerors fear the soldiers who have helped them conquer their empire, priests fear the very fanaticism on which all their power depends, and the ambitious mistrust

---

[2]Francis Bacon (see p. 183). [Berger] Sir William Temple (1628–99), and Michel de L'Hôpital (1505–73).

their own devices—but enlightened men who reach the highest rank in the state do not cease to love and to disseminate knowledge. Reason has nothing to fear from reason, and philosophic minds base their strength upon their peers.

Chapter IV. Women Who Cultivate Literature

The place of women in society is still uncertain in many respects. The desire to please stirs them to action but reason counsels them to remain obscure, and everything in their success as well as their failure is arbitrary. In the present state of things, they are for the most part in neither the world of nature nor of society. What succeeds for some ruins others. Their virtues sometimes injure them and their defects aid them. They are now everything, now nothing.

It would certainly be much better, in general, if women devoted themselves solely to the domestic virtues. But men's judgment of them is strange: they more readily forgive women failure in their obligations than when they attract attention by their distinguished talents. They tolerate degradation of feeling in women if it is accompanied by mediocrity of intellect, while they cannot forgive genuine superiority in a woman of the most perfect integrity.

I shall develop the various causes of this oddity. I shall begin by examining the fate of women who cultivate literature in monarchies and in republics. I shall try to describe the principal differences these two political conditions must create in the destiny of women who aspire to literary fame, and I shall then consider in a general way the degree of happiness renown can promise them.

In monarchies they have to fear ridicule, in republics hate.

It is in the nature of things that in a monarchy, where sensitivity to the proprieties is so refined, every unusual action, every motion to depart from one's proper place, must at first appear ridiculous.

Men can always conceal their vanity and their desire for approval under the guise or the reality of greater and nobler emotions. But when women write, the public, generally assuming that the primary motive is the desire to show their cleverness, only reluctantly bestows its approval. It senses that they cannot do without approval, and this gives rise to the temptation to withhold it.

Some of these disadvantages cannot be found in republics, especially in one whose goal is the promotion of knowledge. It would perhaps be natural that, in such a state, literature properly so called would become the assignment of women and that men would devote themselves solely to higher philosophy.

The education of women has in all free countries been in accordance with the nature of the country's constitution. In Sparta they were conditioned to the practices of war. In Rome austere and patriotic qualities were required of them. If the principal drive in the French Republic is to be emulation in knowledge and philosophy, it would be reasonable to encourage women to cultivate their minds so that men could converse with them upon ideas that would hold their interest.

Yet since the Revolution men have thought it politically and morally useful to reduce women to the most absurd mediocrity. They have addressed women only in wretched language as devoid of refinement as of wit. Women have had no incentive to develop their minds: manners have thus not improved.

As soon as a woman is marked as a distinguished person, the public in general is prejudiced against her. The common people never judge except according to certain universal rules to which they can cling without risk. Men of intellect, astonished to meet rivals among women, can judge them with neither the generosity of an adversary nor the indulgence of a protector. In this new conflict they follow neither the rules of honor nor of kindness.

If, as a crowning misfortune, a woman acquired a noteworthy fame in the midst of political discord, her influence would be considered unlimited even if she exercised none at all. She would be blamed for all the acts of her friends, and would be detested for everything she loved. People would first attack this defenseless object before taking on those whom they might still fear.

In this description I have spoken only of the injustice of men toward distinguished women. But is not that of women themselves also to be feared? Do they not secretly stir up the malevolence of men? Do they ever join a famous woman in order to help her, to defend her, to support her unsteady footsteps?

That is still not all. Opinion seems to release man from all obligations toward a woman whose superior intellect is acknowledged. Toward her, he may be ungrateful, false, and wicked—opinion will not avenge her. *Is she not an unusual woman?* Say no more.

Chapter V. Works of Imagination

It is easy to indicate the defects that good taste always prohibits in literature, but it is not so easy to point the road the imagination should follow in the future in order to produce new impressions. The Revolution has necessarily destroyed the basis of certain literary techniques. Let us begin by examining these methods, and we shall be led naturally to some notions about the new resources that can still be discovered.

Imaginative works act upon us in two ways, by presenting us clever pictures that give rise to levity, or by stirring our emotions. These emotions spring from relations inherent in human nature. Levity is often only the result of the various and sometimes arbitrary relations created by men in society. Though levity depends in several respects upon circumstances of the moment, the soul's emotions have an enduring foundation that scarcely changes with political events.

The more we simplify institutions, the more we obliterate the distinctions from which the philosophic mind can draw striking contrasts. Voltaire's works serve best to show how a rational political order deprives levity of its material. Voltaire ceaselessly contrasted what ought to have been with what was, pedantry in form with frivolity in essence, the austerity of religious doctrines with the loose habits of those who taught them, the ignorance of great men with their power.

The Americans would hardly sense the merit of a comic situation that alluded to institutions entirely foreign to their form of government. They might listen to such things because of their connections with Europe, but their writers would never think of exerting themselves upon such a subject. Every jest that strikes at civil and political institutions contrary to natural reason loses its effect when it attains its goal, the reform of the social order.

When society advances along the path of reason, discouragement especially must be avoided. But jests, after having been useful in destroying the power of prejudices, can then work only upon the power of true feelings, attacking the basis of moral life that must support individuals and mankind.

Clever works undoubtedly have a different kind of levity than the one that depends almost entirely upon jests concerning the social order or human destiny. This is the precise and subtle observation of passions and dispositions. The genius of Molière is the most sublime example of this superior talent. Voltaire was not able to produce any dramatic effect in this *genre,* however sharp his habitual turn of mind. So it remains for us to discover what subjects of comedy can best succeed in a free state.

There are two very distinct kinds of ridicule among men, that which depends upon nature itself, and that which changes as society changes. Absurdities of the latter type must be far less numerous in countries where political equality prevails, for there social relations come closer to natural relations and the properties are in greater accord with reason. One could have been a man of great merit under the Old Regime and yet be made to look ridiculous by an absolute ignorance of the ways of society. The true decencies, in a free state, can be offended only by real defects of mind or character.

Under the monarchy, it was often necessary to know how to reconcile dignity with material interest, the appearance of courage with the private plan of flattery, the air of indifference with the persistence of concern for personal interest, the reality of bondage with the affectation of independence. The necessity to overcome so many difficulties could easily make anyone who did not know the art of evading them look ridiculous. In a republic, more simplicity in manners and attitudes provide authors with many fewer comic scenes.

Among Molière's plays there are some based solely upon established prejudices, such as *Le Bourgeois Gentilhomme, George Dandin,* etc., but there are also some, such as *L'Avare, Le Tartuffe,* etc., which portray men of all countries and all times; and these would suit a free government, if not in every detail then at least as a whole.

The comedy that attacks human failings is more striking but also more bitter than the one that recalls ordinary absurdities or odd practices. We experience a feeling mixed with pathos in the most comic scenes of *Le Tartuffe* because they recall the malice that is natural to mankind. But when the jests attack the failings that derive from certain prejudices—or the prejudices themselves—the hope we retain of correcting them suffuses a milder levity over the impression caused by the ridicule. In a government based upon reason there can be neither talent nor cause for this kind of mild levity, so creative minds must turn rather toward higher comedy, the most philosophical of all works of the imagination, which presupposes the most profound study of the human heart. A republic can stimulate a new emulation in this domain.

In a monarchy, people like to hold up to ridicule those manners that do not conform to received practices. In a republic, the subject of the shafts of ridicule ought to be the human failings that harm the general welfare. I shall mention one noteworthy example of the new subjects comedy can deal with and the new goal it ought to set for itself.

In *Le Misanthrope,* it is Philinte who is rational and Alceste at whom we laugh. A modern author,[3] developing these two personalities in a continuation of their lives, has shown Alceste to be generous and loyal in friendship, and Philinte privately greedy and tyrannically self-centered. I believe that

---

[3][Berger] Fabre d'Eglantine, in *Le Philinte de Molière* (1790), cited by Paul van Tieghem, ed. of *De la Littérature,* Vol. II, p. 348, n. 1.

in his play the author has taken the point of view that comedy must offer from now on. The negative failings, so to speak, those arising from the want of certain qualities, ought now to be attacked in the drama. It is necessary to draw attention to certain forms behind which so many men withdraw in order to be themselves at peace or to be false with decency. The republican spirit requires positive virtues, public virtues.

One may well ask: What will provide contrast and variety, and how will vivid impressions originate? Some rather unexpected ones must emerge from this new *genre*. The immoral behavior of men toward women, for example, has been continually presented on the stage deliberately to ridicule the deceived women. The trust women may have in the feelings they inspire can be, with reason, the subject of ridicule. But the author's talent would be greater, and the subject treated more noble, if ridicule were directed rather toward the deceiver, if the oppressor were attacked and not the victim. It is easy to attack what is wrong in itself, but it would be more to the point to coat immorality with a veneer of folly—and it can be done.

Men who would impose their vices and depravities as so many more charms, whose pretension to ingenuity is such that they would practically boast even to you of having cleverly betrayed you if they did not anticipate that you might one day realize it, these men who would conceal their incapacity by their wickedness, flattering themselves no one will ever discover that an intellect so forcefully opposed to universal morality may be so weak in its political notions, these personalities so indifferent to the opinion of decent men but so afraid before powerful men, these false purveyors of vice, these scoffers at noble principles, these mockers of sensitive souls—it is they who must be subjected to the ridicule they devise for others, who must be exposed as wretched beings, and abandoned to children's jeers.

Tragedy concerns unchanging feelings; and since it portrays grief, the source of its effects is inexhaustible. It is nevertheless altered, as are all products of the human mind, by social institutions and the customs that rest upon them.

The themes of the ancients and their imitators produce fewer effects in a republic than in a monarchy. Distinctions of rank make the pains of reverses of fate more poignant, and place a huge gap between misfortune and the throne, which the mind cannot bridge without a shudder.

The ancients often exiled and destroyed royalty, but in our day it is merely analyzed, and nothing could be more damaging to dramatic effect. The splendor of power, the respect it inspires, the pity felt for those who lose it when they are believed to be entitled to it—all these feelings act upon the mind independent of the author's ability, and their vigor would be greatly reduced in the political order I am assuming. Man merely as man has suffered too much to be capable of a special emotional response to the misfortune of those in high places or to conditions peculiar to only a few people.

We must, however, avoid transforming tragedy into tragi-comedy,[4] and to do so we must understand the difference between these two *genres*. This difference does not lie entirely in the social position of the characters but in the nobility and depth of the emotions the author portrays.

The events of private life are adequate for a tragi-comedy, whereas for an event to become a theme for tragedy it must generally involve the concerns of whole nations. Nevertheless, tragic nobility must be sought in the loftiness of ideas and in the depth of feelings rather than in recollections of historical allusions.

The philosophical bent that provides generalizations, and the system of political equality, must give our tragedies a new character. This is no reason to reject historical themes, but great men must be portrayed as having feelings that arouse the sympathy of all people, and humble deeds must be exalted through nobility of character. We must elevate character instead of perfecting notions of conventionality.

Conventionality on the stage is inseparable from aristocracy of social rank in government; the one cannot be sustained without the other. The dramatic art, deprived of all of these artificial resources, can grow only through philosophy and sensibility. And in this sense it has no limits, for grief is one of the most powerful means of development for the human mind.

Life slips by, so to speak, unnoticed by contented people. But when the soul is in travail, reflection is exerted to seek some hope or to find some cause of regret, to probe the past or divine the future. In tranquillity and happiness, this faculty of observation is directed almost entirely toward external objects, but in misfortune we exercise it only upon our own impressions.

Philosophy covers all the arts of the imagination as well as works of reason. In this age, men are interested only in human emotions. Externals are clear and decided; only moral existence, in its hidden workings, is still an object of surprise and can alone produce a strong impression.

Poetry of the imagination will no longer make progress in France. Philosophical ideas and strong emotions will be put into verse, but in our age the human mind has reached a point that no longer allows either illusions or the enthusiasm that creates scenes and fables calculated to stun the mind.

---

[4][Berger] The French word *drame* referred to a mixture of tragedy and comedy in which there were characters of high and low station and the ending was happy though the action was fundamentally serious or tragic.

A weariness of life, when it does not lead to despair but allows complete detachment, together with the love of renown, can inspire great beauty of feeling. Everything is contemplated from a certain height, everything appears in strong colors. Among the ancients, the more readily was one's imagination delighted, the better poet one was. In our day, the imagination must be as disenchanted with hope as with reason. It is only thus that the philosophical imagination can produce great results.

In order to succeed in works of the imagination, we must perhaps offer a lenient moral code where there are strict morals, but where morals are corrupt an austere moral code must be steadfastly presented. This general maxim is especially applicable to our age.

Friedrich Wilhelm von Schelling

1775–1854

Schelling rejected Kant's idea that "things in themselves" are unknowable. Instead he posited a subject and object that are joined in aesthetic activity. This joining is a creative act. Further, Schelling saw man's creativity as analogous to the unconscious creativity of nature. This view influenced Coleridge's definition of the primary imagination in *Biographia Literaria:* "The living power and prime agent of all human perception, and a repetition in the finite mind of the eternal act of creation in the infinite *I am.*" Coleridge, however, seems to give consciousness to the "infinite *I am,*" while Schelling's "nature" seems to work unconsciously.

In *On the Relation of the Plastic Arts to Nature,* Schelling makes some interesting comments on those whose epistemology posits a dead, objective nature. He observes that although they consider that objective, natural world dead, they still think of art as copying it, holding to a theory of naive realism. The truth is that a less doggedly realistic art, freed of the idea of servile imitation, is more likely to achieve truth. There is no lifeless nature ("the unknowing cannot be known"); nature strives for shape, just as man tries to shape nature in art. In artistic activity the mind seeks to join subject and object, finite and infinite, soul and nature. It is never clear in Schelling's work whether or not the whole value of art is in the imaginative act that goes to produce it. Is the experiencing of a work of art also the experiencing of the joining of subject and object? Is it actually the joining of subject and object? Or is it only the acknowledgment that such an act has been accomplished by the artist? Or is it the observation of the *representation* of such an act? It appears that for Schelling a work of art must be considered as very closely related to its author, as the direct *expression* of his experience. Perhaps the real work of art is not what we, as observers, have before us but the *activity* of its making. If this is so, what precisely is the value of the object before us? We shall not find answers to these questions in Schelling, but his discourse raises them.

Schelling also took up the problem of universals and particulars. How can the particularity of art express universality? Johnson and Reynolds treated this problem by identifying universality and generality. Their approach was unacceptable to Romantic theorists, for it adopts a mode of scientific procedure—generalization from sense data—that Romantics generally considered antithetical to art. The Romantics invented a distinction between symbolism and allegory that reduced allegory to personified generalization and described the symbol as containing universality, by paradox, in its particularity. Schelling argues along these lines in his *Philosophy of Art.* In *On the Relation of the Plastic Arts to Nature* he holds that the particular gains universality through its self-identity and the resistance of its form to the universe; the artist does not try to exhibit "the empty shell or limitation of the individual . . . but, more than this, its vital idea. . . . he makes the individual a world in itself, a class, an eternal prototype." Schelling is here reminiscent of Blake describing his painting of the Canterbury pilgrims, remarking that all classes are individual, and tending to "see the world in a grain of sand."

Schelling's most specific treatment of literature comes in the *Philosophy of Art,* where he reveals himself to be one of the Romantic critics most interested in the relationships of poetry and mythology. It is in mythology that we discover the union of the particular and the universal; indeed, myth is indifferent to the distinction. Here presumably we find reconstituted the unified mental spirit that Schiller, in his *Letters on the Aesthetic Education of Man,* declared to be lost after the time of the ancient Greeks. It is Greek mythology with which Schelling is mainly concerned, although he recognizes Christian and other mythologies and foresees the growth of new mythologies, even individual ones. In the selection below, Schelling's belief in the close relationship of myth and art is reflected in the remark, "Sculpture, even if no mythology had preceded it, would of itself have come upon gods, and have invented such if it found none." This particular interpretation of the relationship of art and myth is developed in various ways by many later critics, including Wheelwright and Frye.

Schelling is infuriatingly vague at times, and he is considered rather a sentimentalizer of Kantian ideas. Nevertheless, he had a large influence. Much of Coleridge's *Biographia Literaria* is sheer Schelling, and Schelling's ideas can be detected behind those of numerous critics for a century after he had expressed them.

Another translation of this essay appears in Herbert Read's *The True Voice of Feeling* (1953). The *Sämtliche Werke,* edited by K. F. A. Schelling in 14 volumes, appeared from 1856–1861. Schelling's works translated into English include *Of Human Freedom* (tr. 1936); *On University Studies* (tr. 1966); *System of Transcendental Idealism* (tr. 1978); *Bruno, or On the Natural and the Divine Principle in Things* (tr. 1984); and *Philosophy of Art* (1989). See Jean Gibilin, *L'Esthétique de Schelling d'après la philosophie de l'art* (1934); E. L. Fackenheim, "Schelling's Philosophy of the Literary Arts," *Philosophical Quarterly,* IV (1954), 310–326; H. M. Schueller, "Schelling's Theory of the Metaphysics of Music," *Journal of Aesthetics and Art Criticism,* XV (1957), 461–76; E. D. Hirsch, Jr., *Wordsworth and Schelling* (1960); Robert F. Brown, *The Later Philosophy of Schelling* (1977); Joseph L. Esposito, *Schelling's Idealism and Philosophy of Nature* (1977); Alan White, *Schelling: An Introduction to the System of Freedom* (1983); and Werner Marx, *The Philosophy of F. W. J. Schelling* (1984); and Hegel's *The Difference Between Fichte's and Schelling's System of Philosophy* was translated in 1977.

From

On the Relation of the Plastic Arts to Nature

Plastic art, according to the most ancient expression, is silent poetry.[1] The inventor of this definition no doubt meant thereby that the former, like the latter, is to express spiritual thoughts—conceptions whose source is the soul; only not by speech, but, like silent nature, by shape, by form, by corporeal, independent works.

Plastic art, therefore, evidently stands as a uniting link between the soul and nature, and can be apprehended only in the living center of both. Indeed, since plastic art has its relation to the soul in common with every other art, and particularly with poetry, that by which it is connected with nature, and, like nature, a productive force, remains as its sole peculiarity; so that to this alone can a theory relate which shall be satisfactory to the understanding, and helpful and profitable to art itself.

We hope, therefore, in considering plastic art in relation to its true prototype and original source, nature, to be able to contribute something new to its theory—to give some additional exactness or clearness to the conceptions of it; but, above all, to set forth the coherence of the whole structure of art in the light of a higher necessity.

But has not science[2] always recognized this relation? Has not indeed every theory of modern times taken its departure from this very position, that art should be the imitator of nature? Such has indeed been the case. But what should this broad general proposition profit the artist, when the notion of nature is of such various interpretation, and when there are almost as many differing views of it as there are various modes of life? Thus, to one, nature is nothing more than the lifeless aggregate of an indeterminable crowd of objects, or the space in which, as in a vessel, he imagines things placed; to another, only the soil from which he draws his nourishment and support; to the inspired seeker alone, the holy, ever-creative original energy of the world, which generates and busily evolves all things out of itself.

The proposition would indeed have a high significance, if it taught art to emulate this creative force; but the sense in which it was meant can scarcely be doubtful to one acquainted with the universal condition of science at the time when it was first brought forward. Singular enough that the very persons who denied all life to nature should set it up for imitation in art! To them might be applied the words of a profound writer: "Your lying philosophy has put nature out of the way; and why do you call upon us to imitate her? Is it that you may renew the pleasure by perpetrating the same violence on the disciples of nature?"[3]

Nature was to them not merely a dumb, but an altogether lifeless image, in whose inmost being even no living word dwelt; a hollow scaffolding of forms, of which as hollow an image was to be transferred to the canvas, or hewn out of stone.

This was the proper doctrine of those more ancient and savage nations, who, as they saw in nature nothing divine, fetched idols out of her; whilst, to the susceptive Greeks, who everywhere felt the presence of a vitally efficient principle, genuine gods arose out of nature.

But is, then, the disciple of nature to copy everything in nature without distinction?—and, of everything, every part? Only beautiful objects should be represented; and, even in these, only the beautiful and perfect.

Thus is the proposition further determined, but, at the same time, this asserted, that, in nature, the perfect is mingled with the imperfect, the beautiful with the unbeautiful. Now, how should he who stands in no other relation to nature than that of servile imitation, distinguish the one from the other? It is the way of imitators to appropriate the faults of their model sooner and easier than its excellences, since the former offer handles and tokens more easily grasped; and thus we see that imitators of nature in this sense have imitated oftener, and even more affectionately, the ugly than the beautiful.

If we regard in things, not their principle, but the empty abstract form, neither will they say anything to our soul; our own heart, our own spirit we must put to it, that they answer us.

But what is the perfection of a thing? Nothing else than the creative life in it, its power to exist. Never, therefore, will he, who fancies that nature is altogether dead, be successful in that profound process (analogous to the chemical) whence proceeds, purified as by fire, the pure gold of beauty and truth.

ON THE RELATION OF THE PLASTIC ARTS TO NATURE. Schelling's *Über das Verhältnis der bildenden Künste zu der Natur* was originally delivered as a lecture in 1807. The text is from an abbreviated version translated by J. E. Cabot, *The German Classics* (New York: German Publication Society, 1913).
[1] This is the converse of the *ut pictura poesis* concept derived from Horace (*Art of Poetry*, p. 73). It reflects the remark attributed by Plutarch to Simonides that painting is mute poetry and that poetry is a speaking picture.
[2] *Science* is employed here in the old, broader sense of systematic philosophical knowledge.

[3] [Cabot] J. G. Hamann, *Hellenistische Briefe,* I. 189.

Nor was there any change in the main view of the relation of art to nature, even when the unsatisfactoriness of the principle began to be more generally felt; no change, even by the new views and new knowledge so nobly established by Johann Winckelmann.[4] He indeed restored to the soul its full efficiency in art, and raised it from its unworthy dependence into the realm of spiritual freedom. Powerfully moved by the beauty of form in the works of antiquity, he taught that the production of ideal nature, of nature elevated above the actual, together with the expression of spiritual conceptions, is the highest aim of art.

But if we examine in what sense this surpassing of the actual by art has been understood by the most, it turns out that, with this view also, the notion of nature as mere product, of things as a lifeless result, still continued; and the idea of a living creative nature was in no wise awakened by it. Thus these ideal forms also could be animated by no positive insight into their nature; and if the forms of the actual were dead for the dead beholder, these were not less so. Were no independent production of the actual possible, neither would there be of the ideal. The object of the imitation was changed; the imitation remained. In the place of nature were substituted the sublime works of antiquity, whose outward forms the pupils busied themselves in imitating, but without the spirit that fills them. These forms, however, are as unapproachable, nay, more so, than the works of nature, and leave us yet colder if we bring not to them the spiritual eye to penetrate through the veil and feel the stirring energy within.

On the other hand, artists, since that time, have indeed received a certain ideal impetus, and notions of a beauty superior to matter; but these notions were like fair words, to which the deeds do not correspond. While the previous method in art produced bodies without soul, this view taught only the secret of the soul, but not that of the body. The theory had, as usual, passed with one hasty stride to the opposite extreme; but the vital mean it had not yet found.

Who can say that Winckelmann had not penetrated into the highest beauty? But with him it appeared in its dissevered elements only: on the one side as beauty in idea, and flowing out from the soul; on the other, as beauty of forms.

But what is the efficient link that connects the two? Or by what power is the soul created together with the body, at once and as if with one breath? If this lies not within the power of art, as of nature, then it can create nothing whatever. This vital connecting link, Winckelmann did not determine; he did not teach how, from the idea, forms can be pro-

duced. Thus art went over to that method which we would call the retrograde, since it strives from the form to come at the essence. But not thus is the unlimited reached; it is not attainable by mere enhancement of the limited. Hence, such works as have had their beginning in form, with all elaborateness on that side, show, in token of their origin, an incurable want at the very point where we expect the consummate, the essential, the final. The miracle by which the limited should be raised to the unlimited, the human become divine, is wanting; the magic circle is drawn, but the spirit that it should enclose, appears not, being disobedient to the call of him who thought a creation possible through mere form.

. . .

Nature meets us everywhere, at first with reserve, and in form more or less severe. She is like that quiet and serious beauty, that excites not attention by noisy advertisement, nor attracts the vulgar gaze.

How can we, as it were, spiritually melt this apparently rigid form, so that the pure energy of things may flow together with the force of our spirit and both become one united mold? We must transcend form, in order to gain it again as intelligible, living, and truly felt. Consider the most beautiful forms; what remains behind after you have abstracted from them the creative principle within? Nothing but mere unessential qualities, such as extension and the relations of space. Does the fact that one portion of matter exists near another, and distinct from it, contribute anything to its inner essence? Or does it not rather contribute nothing? Evidently the latter. It is not mere contiguous existence, but the manner of it, that makes form; and this can be determined only by a positive force, which is even opposed to separateness, and subordinates the manifoldness of the parts to the unity of one idea—from the force that works in the crystal to the force which, comparable to a gentle magnetic current, gives to the particles of matter in human form that position and arrangement among themselves, through which the idea, the essential unity and beauty, can become visible.

Not only, however, as active principle, but as spirit and effective science, must the essence appear to us in the form, in order that we may truly apprehend it. For all unity must be spiritual in nature and origin; and what is the aim of all investigation of nature but to find science therein? For that wherein there is no understanding cannot be the object of understanding; the unknowing cannot be known. The science by which nature works is not, however, like human science, connected with reflection upon itself; in it, the conception is not separate from the act, nor the design from the execution. Therefore, rude matter strives, as it were, blindly, after regular shape, and unknowingly assumes pure stereo-

---

[4](1717–68), German archeologist and scholar of classic art. In 1755 he published his famous work on Greek art (which was the immediate occasion of Lessing's *Laocoön*, pp. 339–41).

metric forms, which belong, nevertheless, to the realm of ideas, and are something spiritual in the material.

The sublimest arithmetic and geometry are innate in the stars, and unconsciously displayed by them in their motions. More distinctly, but still beyond their grasp, the living cognition appears in animals; and thus we see them, though wandering about without reflection, bring about innumerable results far more excellent than themselves: the bird that, intoxicated with music, transcends itself in soullike tones; the little artistic creature, that, without practice or instruction, accomplishes light works of architecture; but all directed by an overpowering spirit, that lightens in them already with single flashes of knowledge, but as yet appears nowhere as the full sun, as in man.

This formative science in nature and art is the link that connects idea and form, body and soul. Before everything stands an eternal idea, formed in the infinite understanding; but by what means does this idea pass into actuality and embodiment? Only through the creative science that is as necessarily connected with the infinite understanding, as in the artist the principle that seizes the idea of unsensuous beauty is linked with that which sets it forth to the senses.

If that artist be called happy and praiseworthy before all to whom the gods have granted this creative spirit, then that work of art will appear excellent which shows to us, as in outline, this unadulterated energy of creation and activity of nature.

It was long ago perceived that, in art, not everything is performed with consciousness; that, with the conscious activity, an unconscious action must combine; and that it is of the perfect unity and mutual interpenetration of the two that the highest in art is born.

Works that want this seal of unconscious science are recognized by the evident absence of life self-supported and independent of the producer; as, on the contrary, where this acts, art imparts to its work, together with the utmost clearness to the understanding, that unfathomable reality wherein it resembles a work of nature.

It has often been attempted to make clear the position of the artist in regard to nature, by saying that art, in order to be such, must first withdraw itself from nature, and return to it only in the final perfection. The true sense of this saying, it seems to us, can be no other than this—that in all things in nature, the living idea shows itself only blindly active; were it so also in the artist, he would be in nothing distinct from nature. But, should he attempt consciously to subordinate himself altogether to the actual, and render with servile fidelity the already existing, he would produce larvae, but no works of art. He must therefore withdraw himself from the product, from the creature, but only in order to raise himself

to the creative energy, spiritually seizing the same. Thus he ascends into the realm of pure ideas; he forsakes the creature, to regain it with thousandfold interest, and in this sense certainly to return to nature. This spirit of nature working at the core of things, and speaking through form and shape as by symbols only, the artist must certainly follow with emulation; and only so far as he seizes this with genial imitation has he himself produced anything genuine.[5] For works produced by aggregation, even of forms beautiful in themselves, would still be destitute of all beauty, since that, through which the work on the whole is truly beautiful, cannot be mere form. It is above form—it is essence, the universal, the look and expression of the indwelling spirit of nature.

Now it can scarcely be doubtful what is to be thought of the so-called idealizing of nature in art, so universally demanded. This demand seems to arise from a way of thinking, according to which not truth, beauty, goodness, but the contrary of all these, is the actual. Were the actual indeed opposed to truth and beauty, it would be necessary for the artist, not to elevate or idealize it, but to get rid of and destroy it, in order to create something true and beautiful. But how should it be possible for anything to be actual except the true; and what is beauty, if not full, complete being?

What higher aim, therefore, could art have, than to represent that which in nature actually *is?* Or how should it undertake to excel so-called actual nature, since it must always fall short of it?

For does art impart to its works actual, sensuous life? This statue breathes not, is stirred by no pulsation, warmed by no blood.

But both the pretended excelling and the apparent falling short show themselves as the consequences of one and the same principle, as soon as we place the aim of art in the exhibiting of that which truly is.

Only on the surface have its works the appearance of life; in nature, life seems to reach deeper, and to be wedded entirely with matter. But does not the continual mutation of matter and the universal lot of final dissolution teach us the unessential character of this union, and that it is no intimate fusion? Art, accordingly, in the merely superficial animation of its works, but represents nothingness as nonexisting.

How comes it that, to every tolerably cultivated taste, imitations of the so-called actual, even though carried to deception, appear in the last degree untrue—nay, produce the impression of specters; whilst a work in which the idea is

---

[5]On symbols compare Coleridge, *The Statesman's Manual,* p. 476, and Carlyle, *Symbols,* pp. 546–49. Schelling's statement suggests that the literary work is symbolic in the way that nature is symbolic. This is the sense in which art imitates nature.

predominant strikes us with the full force of truth, conveying us then only to the genuinely actual world? Whence comes it, if not from the more or less obscure feeling which tells us that the idea alone is the living principle in things, but all else unessential and vain shadow?

On the same ground may be explained all the opposite cases which are brought up as instances of the surpassing of nature by art. In arresting the rapid course of human years; in uniting the energy of developed manhood with the soft charm of early youth; or exhibiting a mother of grown-up sons and daughters in the full possession of vigorous beauty—what does art except to annul what is unessential, time?

If, according to the remark of a discerning critic, every growth in nature has but an instant of truly complete beauty, we may also say that it has, too, only an instant of full existence. In this instant it is what it is in all eternity; besides this, it has only a coming into and a passing out of existence. Art, in representing the thing at that instant, removes it out of time, and sets it forth in its pure being, in the eternity of its life.

After everything positive and essential had once been abstracted from form, it necessarily appeared restrictive, and, as it were, hostile, to the essence; and the same theory that had reproduced the false and powerless ideal, necessarily tended to the formless in art. Form would indeed be a limitation of the essence if it existed independent of it. But if it exists with and by means of the essence, how could this feel itself limited by that which it has itself created? Violence would indeed be done it by a form forced upon it, but never by one proceeding from itself. In this, on the contrary, it must rest contented, and feel its own existence to be perfect and complete.

Determinateness of form is in nature never a negation, but ever an affirmation. Commonly, indeed, the shape of a body seems a confinement; but could we behold the creative energy it would reveal itself as the measure that this energy imposes upon itself, and in which it shows itself a truly intelligent force; for in everything is the power of self-rule allowed to be an excellence, and one of the highest.

In like manner most persons consider the particular in a negative manner—i.e., as that which is not the whole or all. Yet no particular exists by means of its limitation, but through the indwelling force with which it maintains itself as a particular whole, in distinction from the universe.

This force of particularity, and thus also of individuality, showing itself as vital character, the negative conception of it is necessarily followed by an unsatisfying and false view of the characteristic in art. Lifeless and of intolerable hardness would be the art that should aim to exhibit the empty shell or limitation of the individual. Certainly we desire to see not merely the individual, but, more than this, its vital idea. But if the artist has seized the inward creative spirit and essence of the idea, and sets this forth, he makes the individual a world in itself, a class, an eternal prototype;[6] and he who has grasped the essential character needs not to fear hardness and severity, for these are the conditions of life. Nature, that in her completeness appears as the utmost benignity, we see, in each particular, aiming even primarily and principally at severity, seclusion and reserve. As the whole creation is the work of the utmost externization and renunciation [*Entäusserung*], so the artist must first deny himself and descend into the particular, without shunning isolation, nor the pain, the anguish of form.

Nature, from her first works, is throughout characteristic; the energy of fire, the splendor of light, she shuts up in hard stone, the tender soul of melody in severe metal; even on the threshold of life, and already meditating organic shape, she sinks back overpowered by the might of form, into petrifaction.

The life of the plant consists in still receptivity, but in what exact and severe outline is this passive life enclosed! In the animal kingdom the strife between life and form seems first properly to begin; her first works nature hides in hard shells, and, where these are laid aside, the animated world attaches itself again through its constructive impulse to the realm of crystallization. Finally she comes forward more boldly and freely, and vital, important characteristics show themselves, being the same through whole classes. Art, however, cannot begin so far down as nature. Though beauty is spread everywhere, yet there are various grades in the appearance and unfolding of the essence, and thus of beauty. But art demands a certain fullness, and desires not to strike a single note or tone, nor even a detached accord, but at once the full symphony of beauty.

Art, therefore, prefers to grasp immediately at the highest and most developed, the human form. For since as in all other creatures only single fulgurations, in man alone full entire being appears without abatement, art is not only permitted but required to see the sum of nature in man alone. But precisely on this account—that she here assembles all in one point—nature repeats her whole multiformity, and pursues again in a narrower compass the same course that she had gone through in her wide circuit.

Here, therefore, arises the demand upon the artist first to be true and faithful in detail, in order to come forth complete and beautiful in the whole. Here he must wrestle with

---

[6]See Blake, *A Descriptive Catalogue*, p. 411.

the creative spirit of nature (which in the human world also deals out character and stamp in endless variety), not in weak and effeminate, but stout and courageous conflict.

Persevering exercise in the study of that by virtue of which the characteristic in things is a positive principle, must preserve him from emptiness, weakness, inward inanity, before he can venture to aim, by ever higher combination and final melting together of manifold forms, to reach the extremest beauty in works uniting the highest simplicity with infinite meaning.

Only through the perfection of form can form be made to disappear; and this is certainly the final aim of art in the characteristic. But as the apparent harmony that is even more easily reached by the empty and frivolous than by others, is yet inwardly vain; so in art the quickly attained harmony of the exterior, without inward fullness. And if it is the part of theory and instruction to oppose the spiritless copying of beautiful forms, especially must they oppose the tendency toward an effeminate characterless art, which gives itself, indeed, higher names, but therewith only seeks to hide its incapacity to fulfill the fundamental conditions.

That lofty beauty in which the fullness of form causes form itself to disappear, was adopted by the modern theory of art, after Winckelmann, not only as the highest, but as the only standard. But as the deep foundation upon which it rests was overlooked, it resulted that a negative conception was formed even of that which is the sum of all affirmation.

Winckelmann compares beauty with water drawn from the bosom of the spring, which, the less taste it has, the wholesomer it is esteemed. It is true that the highest beauty is characterless, but so we say of the universe that it has no determinate dimension, neither length, breadth nor depth, since it has all in equal infinity; or that the art of creative nature is formless, because she herself is subjected to no form.

In this and in no other sense can we say that Grecian art in its highest development rises into the characterless; but it did not aim immediately at this. It was from the bonds of nature that it struggled upward to divine freedom. From no lightly scattered seed, but only from a deeply enfolded kernel, could this heroic growth spring up. Only mighty emotions, only a deep stirring of the fancy through the impression of all-enlivening, all-commanding energies of nature, could stamp upon art that invincible vigor with which from the rigid, secluded earnestness of earlier productions up to the period of works overflowing with sensuous grace, it ever remained faithful to truth, and produced the highest spiritual reality which it is given to mortals to behold.

In like manner, as their tragedy commences with the grandest characteristicness in morals, so the beginning of their plastic art was the earnestness of nature, and the stern goddess of Athens its first and only Muse.

This epoch is marked by that style which Winckelmann describes as the still harsh and severe, from which the next or lofty style was able to develop itself by the mere enhancement of the characteristic into the sublime and the simple.

For in the statues of the most perfect or divine natures not only all the complexity of form of which human nature is capable had to be united, but moreover the union must be such as may be conceived to exist in the system of the universe itself—the lower forms, or those relating to inferior attributes, being comprehended under higher, and all at last under one supreme form, in which they indeed extinguish one another as separately existing, but still continue in essence and efficiency.

Thus, though we cannot call this high and self-sufficing beauty characteristic, so far as herewith is connected the notion of limitation or conditionality in the manifestation, yet still the characteristic continues efficient, though indistinguishable, within; as in the crystal, although transparent, the texture nevertheless remains; each characteristic element has its weight, however slight, and helps to bring about the sublime equipoise of beauty.

The outer side or basis of all beauty is beauty of form. But as form cannot exist without essence, wherever form is, there also is character, whether in visible presence or only perceptible in its effects. Characteristic beauty, therefore, is beauty in the root, from which alone beauty can arise as the fruit. Essence may, indeed, outgrow form, but even then the characteristic remains as the still efficient groundwork of the beautiful.

That most excellent critic,[7] to whom the gods have given sway over nature as well as art, compares the characteristic in its relation to beauty, with the skeleton in its relation to the living form. Were we to interpret this striking simile in our sense, we should say that the skeleton, in nature, is not, as in our thought, detached from the living whole; that the firm and the yielding, the determining and the determined, mutually presuppose each other, and can exist only together; thus that the vitally characteristic is already the whole form, the result of the action and reaction of bone and flesh, of active and passive. And although art, like nature, in its higher developments, thrusts inward the previously visible skeleton, yet the latter can never be opposed to shape and beauty, since it has always a determining share in the production of the one as well as of the other.

---

[7][Cabot] Goethe, *Werke* (1840), XXX. 352.

But whether that high and independent beauty should be the only standard in art, as it is the highest, seems to depend on the degree of fullness and extent that belongs to the particular art.

Nature, in her wide circumference, ever exhibits the higher with the lower; creating in man the godlike, she elaborates in all her other productions only its material and foundation, which must exist in order that in contrast with it the essence as such may appear. And even in the higher world of man the great mass serves again as the basis upon which the godlike that is preserved pure in the few, manifests itself in legislation, government, and the establishment of religion. So that wherever art works with more of the complexity of nature, it may and must display, together with the highest measure of beauty, also its groundwork and raw material, as it were, in distinct appropriate forms.

Here first prominently unfolds itself the difference in nature of the forms of art.

Plastic art, in the more exact sense of the term, disdains to give space outwardly to the object, but bears it within itself. This, however, narrows its field; it is compelled, indeed, to display the beauty of the universe almost in a single point. It must therefore aim immediately at the highest, and can attain complexity only separately and in the strictest exclusion of all conflicting elements. By isolating the purely animal in human nature it succeeds in forming inferior creations too, harmonious and even beautiful, as we are taught by the beauty of numerous fauns preserved from antiquity; yea, it can, parodying itself like the merry spirit of nature, reverse its own ideal, and, for instance, in the extravagance of the Silenic figures,[8] by light and sportive treatment appear freed again from the pressure of matter.

But in all cases it is compelled strictly to isolate the work, in order to make it self-consistent and a world in itself; since for this form of art there is no higher unity, in which the dissonance of particulars should be melted into harmony.

Painting, on the contrary, in the very extent of its sphere, can better measure itself with the universe, and create with epic profusion. In an *Iliad* there is room even for a Thersites;[9] and what does not find a place in the great epic of nature and history!

Here the particular scarcely counts anything by itself; the universe takes its place, and that, which by itself would not be beautiful, becomes so in the harmony of the whole. If in an extensive painting, uniting forms by the allotted space, by light, by shade, by reflection, the highest measure of beauty were everywhere employed, the result would be the most unnatural monotony; for, as Winckelmann says, the highest idea of beauty is everywhere one and the same, and scarcely admits of variation. The detail would be preferred to the whole, where, as in every case in which the whole is formed by multiplicity, the detail must be subordinate to it.

In such a work, therefore, a gradation of beauty must be observed, by which alone the full beauty concentrated in the focus becomes visible; and from an exaggeration of particulars proceeds an equipoise of the whole. Here, then, the limited and characteristic finds its place; and theory at least should direct the painter, not so much to the narrow space in which the entire beauty is concentrically collected, as to the characteristic complexity of nature, through which alone he can impart to an extensive work the full measure of living significance.

Thus thought, among the founders of modern art, the noble Leonardo; thus Raphael, the master of high beauty, who shunned not to exhibit it in smaller measure, rather than to appear monotonous, lifeless, and unreal—though he understood not only how to produce it, but also how to break up uniformity by variety of expression.

For, although character can show itself also in rest and equilibrium of form, it is only in action that it becomes truly alive.

By character we understand a unity of several forces, operating constantly to produce among them a certain equipoise and determinate proportion, to which, if undisturbed, a like equipoise in the symmetry of the forms corresponds. But if this vital unity is to display itself in act and operation, this can only be when the forces, excited by some cause to rebellion, forsake their equilibrium. Everyone sees that this is the case in the passions.

Here we are met by the well-known maxim of the theorists, which demands that passion should be moderated as far as possible, in its actual outburst, that beauty of form may not be injured. But we think this maxim should rather be reversed, and read thus—that passion should be moderated by beauty itself. For it is much to be feared that this desired moderation too may be taken in a negative sense—whereas, what is really requisite is to oppose to passion a positive force. For as virtue consists, not in the absence of passions but in the mastery of the spirit over them, so beauty is preserved, not by their removal or abatement, but by the mastery of beauty over them.

The forces of passion must actually show themselves—it must be seen that they are prepared to rise in mutiny, but are kept down by the power of character, and break against the forms of firmly founded beauty, as the waves of a stream that just fills, but cannot overflow its banks. Otherwise, this

---

[8] Woodland, satyrlike spirits, named after Silenus, a forest god and foster father of Dionysus.
[9] The loud and carping character in the *Iliad*.

striving after moderation would resemble only the method of those shallow moralists, who, the more readily to dispose of man, prefer to mutilate his nature; and who have so entirely removed every positive element from actions that the people gloat over the spectacle of great crimes, in order to refresh themselves at last with the view of something positive.

In nature and art the essence strives first after actualization, or exhibition of itself in the particular. Thus in each the utmost severity is manifested at the commencement; for without bound, the boundless could not appear; without severity, gentleness could not exist; and if unity is to be perceptible, it can only be through particularity, detachment, and opposition. In the beginning, therefore, the creative spirit shows itself entirely lost in the form, inaccessibly shut up, and even in its grandeur still harsh. But the more it succeeds in uniting its entire fullness in one product, the more it gradually relaxes from its severity; and where it has fully developed the form, so as to rest contented and self-collected in it, it seems to become cheerful and begins to move in gentle lines. This is the period of its fairest maturity and blossom, in which the pure vessel has arrived at perfection; the spirit of nature becomes free from its bonds, and feels its relationship to the soul. By a gentle morning blush stealing over the whole form, the coming soul announces itself; it is not yet present, but everything prepares for its reception by the delicate play of gentle movements; the rigid outlines melt and temper themselves into flexibility; a lovely essence, neither sensuous nor spiritual, but which cannot be grasped, diffuses itself over the form, and entwines itself with every outline, every vibration of the frame.

This essence, not to be seized, as we have already remarked, but yet perceptible to all, is what the language of the Greeks designed by the name *charis,* ours as *grace.*

Wherever, in a fully developed form, grace appears, the work is complete on the side of nature; nothing more is wanting; all demands are satisfied. Here, already, soul and body are in complete harmony; body is form, grace is soul, although not soul in itself, but the soul of form, or the soul of nature.

Art may linger, and remain stationary at this point; for already, on one side at least, its whole task is finished. The pure image of beauty arrested at this point is the goddess of love.

But the beauty of the soul in itself, joined to sensuous grace, is the highest apotheosis of nature.

The spirit of nature is only in appearance opposed to the soul; essentially, it is the instrument of its revelation; it brings about indeed the antagonism that exists in all things, but only that the one essence may come forth, as the utmost benignity, and the reconciliation of all the forces.

All other creatures are driven by the mere force of nature, and through it maintain their individuality; in man alone, as the central point, arises the soul, without which the world would be like the natural universe without the sun.

The soul in man, therefore, is not the principle of individuality, but that whereby he raises himself above all egoism, whereby he becomes capable of self-sacrifice, of disinterested love, and (which is the highest) of the contemplation and knowledge of the essence of things, and thus of art.

In him it is no longer concerned about matter nor has it immediate concern with it, but with the spirit only as the life of things. Even while appearing in the body, it is yet free from the body, the consciousness of which hovers in the soul in the most beauteous shapes only as a light, undisturbing dream. It is no quality, no faculty, nor anything special of the sort; it knows not, but is science; it is not good, but goodness; it is not beautiful, as body even may be, but beauty itself.

In the first instance, it is true, in a work of art, the soul of the artist is seen as invention in the detail, and in the total result as the unity that hovers over the work in serene stillness. But the soul must be visible in objective representation, as the primeval energy of thought, in portraitures of human beings, altogether filled by an idea, by a noble contemplation; or as indwelling, essential goodness.

Each of these finds its distinct expression even in the completest repose, but a more living one where the soul can reveal itself in activity and antagonism; and since it is by the passions mainly that the peace of life is interrupted, it is the generally received opinion that the beauty of the soul shows itself especially in its quiet supremacy amid the storm of the passions.

But here an important distinction is to be made. For the soul must not be called upon to moderate those passions which are only an outbreak of the lower spirits of nature, nor can it be displayed in antithesis with these; for where calm considerateness is still in contention with them, the soul has not yet appeared; they must be moderated by unassisted nature in man, by the might of the spirit. But there are cases of a higher sort, in which not a single force alone, but the intelligent spirit itself breaks down all barriers—cases, indeed, where even the soul is subjected by the bond that connects it with sensuous existence, to pain, which should be foreign to its divine nature; where man feels himself hard fought and attacked in the root of his existence, not by mere powers of nature, but by moral forces; where innocent error hurries him into crime, and thus into misery; where deep-felt injustice excites to rebellion the holiest feelings of humanity.

This is the case in all situations, truly, and, in a high sense, tragic, such as the tragedy of the ancients brings before our eyes. Where blindly passionate forces are aroused, the collected spirit is present as the guardian of beauty; but if the spirit itself be carried away, as by an irresistible might, what power shall watch over and protect sacred beauty? Or, if even the soul participate in the struggle, how shall it save itself from pain and from desecration?

Arbitrarily to restrain the power of pain, of feeling in revolt, would be to sin against the very meaning and aim of art, and would betray a want of feeling and soul in the artist himself.

Already therein, that beauty, based on grand and firmly established forms, has become character, art has provided the means of displaying without injury to symmetry the whole intensity of feeling. For where beauty rests on mighty forms, as upon immovable pillars, even a slight change in its relations, scarcely touching the form, causes us to infer the great force that was necessary in order to provide it. Still more does grace sanctify pain. It is the essential nature of grace that it does not know itself; but not being willfully acquired, it also cannot be willfully lost. When intolerable anguish, when even madness, sent by avenging gods, takes away consciousness and reason, grace stands as a protecting demon by the suffering person, and prevents it from manifesting anything unseemly, anything discordant to humanity, but sees to it that, if the person falls, it falls at least a pure and unspotted victim.

Although not yet the soul itself, but its forebodings only, grace accomplishes by natural means what the soul does by a divine power, in transforming pain, torpor, even death itself, into beauty.

Yet grace, which thus maintained itself in the extremest adversity, would be dead, without its transfiguration by the soul. But what expression can belong to the soul in this situation? It delivers itself from pain, and comes forth conquering, not conquered, by relinquishing its connection with sensuous existence.

It is for the natural spirit to exert its energies for the preservation of sensuous existence; the soul enters not into this contest, but its presence moderates even the storms of painfully struggling life. Outward force can take away only outward goods, but not reach the soul; it can tear asunder a temporal bond, not dissolve the eternal one of a truly divine love. Not hard and unfeeling, nor giving up love itself, on the contrary the soul displays in pain this love alone, as the sentiment that outlasts sensuous existence, and thus raises itself above the ruins of outward life or fortune in divine glory.

It is this expression of the soul that the creator of the *Niobe* has presented to us. All the means by which art tempers even the terrible, are here made use of. Mightiness of form, sensuous grace, nay, even the nature of the subject matter itself, soften the expression, through this, that pain, transcending all expression, annihilates itself, and beauty, which it seemed impossible to preserve from destruction when alive, is protected from injury by the commencing torpor.

But what would it all be without the soul, and how does this manifest itself?

We see on the countenance of the mother, not grief alone for the already prostrated flower of her children; not alone deadly anxiety for the preservation of those yet remaining, and of the youngest daughter, who has fled for safety to her bosom; nor resentment against the cruel deities; least of all, as is pretended, cool defiance—all these we see, indeed, but not these alone; for, through grief, anxiety, and resentment streams, like a divine light, eternal love, as that which alone remains; and in this is preserved the mother, as one who was not, but now *is* a mother, and who remains united with the beloved ones by an eternal bond.

Everyone acknowledges that greatness, purity, and goodness of soul have also their sensuous expressions. But how is this conceivable, unless the principle that acts in matter be itself cognate and similar to soul?

For the representation of the soul there are again gradations in art, according as it is joined with the merely characteristic, or in visible union with the charming and graceful.

Who perceives not already, in the tragedies of Aeschylus, the presence of that lofty morality which is predominant in the works of Sophocles? But in the former it is enveloped in a bitter rind, and passes less into the whole work, since the bond of sensuous grace is still wanting. But out of this severity, and the still rude charms of earlier art, could proceed the grace of Sophocles, and with it the complete fusion of the two elements, which leaves us doubtful whether it is more moral or sensuous grace that enchants us in the works of this poet.

The same is true of the plastic productions of the early and severe style, in comparison with the gentleness of the later.

If grace, besides being the transfiguration of the spirit of nature, is also the medium of connection between moral goodness and sensuous appearance, it is evident how art must tend from all points toward it as its center. This beauty, which results from the perfect interpenetration of moral goodness and sensuous grace, seizes and enchants us when we meet it, with the force of a miracle. For, whilst the spirit of nature shows itself everywhere else independent of the soul, and, indeed, in a measure opposed to it, here, it seems, as if by voluntary accord, and the inward fire of divine love, to melt into union with it; the remembrance of the fundamental unity of the essence of nature and the essence of the soul comes over the beholder with sudden clearness—the conviction that all antagonism is only apparent, that love is the bond of all things, and pure goodness the foundation and substance of the whole creation.

Here art, as it were, transcends itself, and again becomes means only. On this summit sensuous grace becomes in turn only the husk and body of a higher life; what was before a whole is treated as a part, and the highest relation of art and nature is reached in this—that it makes nature the medium of manifesting the soul which it contains.

But though in this blossoming of art, as in the blossoming of the vegetable kingdom, all the previous stages are repeated, yet, on the other hand, we may see in what various directions art can proceed from this center. Especially does the difference in nature of the two forms of plastic art here show itself most strongly. For sculpture, representing its ideas by corporeal things, seems to reach its highest point in the complete equilibrium of soul and matter—if it give a preponderance to the latter it sinks below its own idea—but it seems altogether impossible for it to elevate the soul at the expense of matter, since it must thereby transcend itself. The perfect sculptor indeed, as Winckelmann remarks apropos of the *Belvedere Apollo,* will use no more material than is needful to accomplish his spiritual purpose; but also, on the other hand, he will put into the soul no more energy than is at the same time expressed in the material; for precisely upon this, fully to embody the spiritual, depends his art. Sculpture, therefore, can reach its true summit only in the representation of those natures in whose constitution it is implied that they actually embody all that is contained in their idea or soul; thus only in divine natures. So that sculpture, even if no mythology had preceded it, would of itself have come upon gods, and have invented such if it found none.

Moreover as the spirit, on this lower platform, has again the same relation to matter that we have ascribed to the soul (being the principle of activity and motion, as matter is that of rest and inaction), the law that regulates expression and passion must be a fundamental principle of its nature.

But this law must be applicable not only to the lower passions, but also equally to those higher and godlike passions, if it is permitted so to call them, by which the soul is affected in rapture, in devotion, in adoration. Hence, since from these passions the gods alone are exempt, sculpture is inclined from this side also to the imaging of divine natures.

The nature of painting, however, seems to differ entirely from that of sculpture. For the former represents objects, not like the latter, by corporeal things, but by light and color, through a medium therefore itself incorporeal and in a measure spiritual. Painting, moreover, gives out its productions nowise as the things themselves, but expressly as pictures. From its very nature therefore it does not lay as much stress on the material as sculpture, and seems indeed for this reason, while exalting the material above the spirit, to degrade itself more than sculpture in a like case; on the other hand to be so much more justified in giving a clear preponderance to the soul.

Where it aims at the highest it will indeed ennoble the passions by character, or moderate them by grace, or manifest in them the power of the soul: but on the other hand it is precisely those higher passions, depending on the relationship of the soul with a supreme being, that are entirely suited to the nature of painting. Indeed, while sculpture maintains an exact balance between the force whereby a thing exists outwardly and acts in nature and that by virtue of which it lives inwardly and as soul, and excludes mere suffering even from matter, painting may soften in favor of the soul the characteristicness of the force and activity in matter, and transform it into resignation and endurance, making it apparent that man becomes more generally susceptible to the inspirations of the soul, and to higher influences in general.

This diametrical difference explains of itself not only the necessary predominance of sculpture in the ancient, and of painting in the modern world (since in the former the tone of mind was thoroughly plastic, whereas the latter makes even the soul the passive instrument of higher revelations); but this also is evident—that it is not enough to strive after the plastic in form and manner of representation, but that it is requisite, before all, to think and to feel plastically, that is, antiquely.

And as the deviation of sculpture into the picturesque is destructive to art, so the narrowing down of painting to the conditions and forms belonging to sculpture is an arbitrarily imposed limitation. For while sculpture, like gravitation, acts toward one point, it is permitted to painting, as to light, to fill all space with its creative energy.

This unlimited universality of painting is demonstrated by history itself, and by the examples of the greatest masters, who, without injury to the essential character of their art, have developed to perfection each particular stage by itself, so that we can find also in the history of art the same sequence that may be pointed out in its nature—not indeed in exact order of time, but yet substantially. For thus is represented in Michelangelo the oldest and mightiest epoch of liberated art, that in which it displays its yet uncontrolled strength in gigantic progeny; as in the fables of the symbolic foreworld, the earth, after the embrace of Uranus, brought forth at first Titans and heaven-storming giants before the mild reign of the serene gods began.

Thus the painting of the Last Judgment, with which, as the sum of his art, that giant spirit filled the Sistine Chapel, seems to remind us more of the first ages of the earth and its products, than of its last. Attracted toward the most hidden abysses of organic, particularly of the human form, he shuns not the terrible; nay, he seeks it purposely, and startles it from its repose in the dark workshops of nature. Want of delicacy, grace, pleasingness, he balances by the extremest energy; and if he excites horror by his representations, it is the terror that, according to fable, the ancient god Pan spreads around him when he suddenly appears in the assemblies of men.

It is the method of nature to produce the extraordinary by isolation and the exclusion of opposed qualities. Thus, it was necessary that, in Michelangelo, earnestness and the deep significant energy of nature should prevail, rather than a sense of the grace and sensibility that belong to the soul, in order to display the extreme of pure plastic force in the painting of modern times.

After the earlier violence and the vehement impulse of birth is assuaged, the spirit of nature is transfigured into soul, and grace is born. This point art reached, after Leonardo da Vinci, in Correggio, in whose works the sensuous soul is the active principle of beauty.

. . .

As the modern fable of Psyche closes the circle of the old mythology; so painting, by giving a preponderance to the soul, attained a new, though not a higher step of art.

This Guido Reni strove after, and became the proper painter of the soul. Such seems to us to be the necessary interpretation of his whole endeavor, often uncertain, and, in many of his works, losing itself in the vague.

This is shown, as, perhaps, in few of his other pictures, in the masterpiece that is offered to the admiration of all in the great collection of our king.

In the figure of the heavenward ascending Virgin, all harshness and sternness are effaced, even to the last trace; and, indeed, does not painting itself seem in it to soar upward, transfigured on its own pinions, as the liberated Psyche delivered from the severity of form?

Here nothing outward remains, with separate natural force; everything expresses receptivity and still endurance, even the perishable flesh, the character of which the Italian language designates by the term *morbidezza,* altogether unlike that with which Raphael invests the descending Queen of Heaven, as she appears to the adoring pope and a saint.

Though the remark be well founded, that the original of Guido's female heads is the *Niobe* of antiquity, yet the ground of this similarity is surely no mere intentional imitation; perhaps a like aim led to like means.

As the *Florentine Niobe* is an extreme in sculpture, and the representation in it of the soul, so this well-known picture is an extreme in painting, which here ventures to lay aside even the requisite of shade and the obscure, and to work almost with pure light.

Even though it might be permitted to painting, from its peculiar nature, to give a distinct preponderance to the soul, yet theory and instruction will do best constantly to aim at that original center, whence alone art may be produced ever anew; whereas, at the stage last mentioned, it must necessarily stand still, or degenerate into cramped mannerism. For even that higher passion is opposed to the idea of having reached the acme of energy, whose image and reflex art is called upon to display.

A right intelligence will ever enjoy seeing a creature worthily, and, as far as possible, also individually, represented; yea, Deity itself would look down with pleasure on a being that, gifted with a pure soul, should stoutly assert the dignity of its nature outwardly also, and by its sensually efficient existence.

We have seen how the work of art, springing up out of the depths of nature, begins with determinateness and limitation, unfolds its inward plenitude and infinity, is finally transfigured in grace, and at last attains to soul. But we can conceive only in detail what, in the creative act of mature art, is but one operation. No theory and no rules can give this spiritual, creative power. It is the pure gift of nature, which here, for the second time, makes a close; for, having fully actualized herself, she invests the creature with her creative energy. But as, in the grand progress of art, these different stages appeared successively, until, at the highest, all joined in one; so also, in particulars, sound culture can spring up only where it has unfolded itself regularly from the germ and root to the blossom.

The requirement that art, like everything living, should commence from the first rudiments, and, to renew its youth, constantly return to them, may seem a hard doctrine to an age that has so often been assured that it has only to take from works of art already in existence the most consummate beauty, and thus, as at a step to reach the final goal. Have we not already the excellent, the perfect? How then should we return to the rudimentary and unformed?

Had the great founders of modern art thought thus, we should never have seen their miracles. Before them also stood the creations of the ancients, round statues and works in relief, which they might have transferred immediately to their canvas. But such an appropriation of a beauty not self-won, and therefore unintelligible, would not satisfy an artistic instinct that aimed throughout at the fundamental, and from which the beautiful was again to create itself with free original energy. They were not afraid, therefore, to appear simple, artless, dry, beside those exalted ancients; nor to cherish art for a long time in the undistinguished bud, until the period of grace had arrived.

Whence comes it that we still look upon these works of the older masters, from Giotto to the teacher of Raphael, with a sort of reverence, indeed with a certain predilection, if not that the faithfulness of their endeavor, and the grand earnestness of their serene voluntary limitation, compel our respect and admiration.

The same relation that they held to the ancients, the present generation holds to them. Their time and ours are joined by no living transmission, no link of continuous, organic growth; we must reproduce art in the way they did, but with energy of our own, in order to be like them.[10]

Even that Indian summer of art, at the end of the sixteenth and the beginning of the seventeenth centuries, could call forth only a few new blossoms on the old stem, but no productive germs, still less plant a new tree of art. But to set aside the works of perfected art, and to seek out its scanty and simple beginnings, as some have desired, would be a new and perhaps greater mistake; it would be no real return to the fundamental; simplicity would be affectation, and grow into hypocritical show.

But what prospect does the present time offer for an art springing from a vigorous germ, and growing up from the root? For it is in a great measure dependent on the character of its time; and who would promise the approbation of the present time to such earnest beginnings, when art, on the one hand, scarcely obtains equal consideration with other instruments of prodigal luxury, and, on the other, artists and amateurs, with entire want of ability to grasp nature, praise and demand the ideal?

Art springs only from that powerful striving of the inmost powers of the heart and the spirit, which we call inspiration. Everything that from difficult or small beginnings has grown up to great power and height, owes its growth to inspiration. Thus spring empires and states, thus arts and sciences. But it is not the power of the individual that accomplishes this, but the spirit alone, that diffuses itself over all. For art especially is independent on the tone of the public mind, as the more delicate plants on atmosphere and weather; it needs a general enthusiasm for sublimity and beauty, like that which, in the time of the Medici, as a warm breath of spring, called forth at once and together all those great spirits.

* * *

It is only when the public life is actuated by the same forces through whose energy art is elevated, that the latter can derive any advantage from it; for art cannot, without giving up the nobility of its nature, aim at anything outward.

Art and science can move only on their own axes; the artist, like every spiritual laborer, can follow only the law that God and nature have written in his heart. None can help him—he must help himself; nor can he be outwardly rewarded, since anything that he should produce for the sake of aught out of itself, would thereby become a nullity; hence, too, no one can direct him, nor prescribe the path he is to tread. Is he to be pitied if he has to contend against his time, he is deserving of contempt if he truckle to it. But how should it be even possible for him to do this? Without great general enthusiasm there are only sects—no public opinion; not an established taste, not the great ideas of a whole people, but the voices of a few arbitrarily appointed judges, determine as to merit; and art, which in its elevation is self-sufficing, courts favor, and serves where it should rule.

To different ages are given different inspirations. Can we expect none for this age, since the new world now forming itself, as it exists in part already outwardly, in part inwardly and in the hearts of men, can no longer be measured by any standard of previous opinion, and since everything, on the contrary, loudly demands higher standards and an entire renovation?

Should not the sense to which nature and history have more livingly unfolded themselves, restore to art also its great arguments? The attempt to draw sparks from the ashes of the past, and fan them again into universal flame, is a vain endeavor. Only a revolution in the ideas themselves is able to raise art from its exhaustion; only new knowledge, new faith, can inspire it for the work by which it can display, in a renewed life, a splendor like the past.

An art in all respects the same as that of foregoing centuries, will never return; for nature never repeats herself. Such a Raphael will never be again, but another, who shall have reached in an equally original manner the summit of art. Only let the fundamental conditions be fulfilled, and renewed art will show, like that which preceded it, in its first works, its aim and intent. In the production of the distinctly characteristic, if it proceed from a fresh original energy, grace is already present, even though hidden, and in both the advent of the soul already determined. Works produced in this manner, even in their rudimentary imperfection, are necessary and eternal.

---

[10]Compare Young, *Conjectures on Original Composition*, p. 331.

Samuel Taylor Coleridge

1772–1834

The great breadth of Coleridge's interests and the fact that his theoretical remarks are scattered through numerous works make a representative selection difficult. The selections below illustrate two major influences on Coleridge's thought, Kant and Schelling. *On the Principles of Genial Criticism* displays the influence of Kant's *Critique of Judgment* in its attempt to distinguish the "beautiful" from the "agreeable" on the one hand and from the "good" on the other. Coleridge's discussion recalls Kant's treatment of the beautiful and his idea of purposiveness without a purpose. Schelling's influence appears in the *Biographia Literaria,* where whole passages are actually translations, with occasional interpolations, from the *System of Transcendental Idealism.* Indeed, the selection below from Chapter XII is nearly all Schelling. Though some commentators on Coleridge have found the chapter unimportant, it is a statement of fundamental epistemological ideas on which Coleridge's critical theory rests. It is intimately connected with his famous definitions of imagination and fancy in Chapter XIII.

For purposes of introduction, it is perhaps possible to isolate three of Coleridge's interests. The first is his concern with universality and particularity. In a work of art the universal dwells *in* the particular; the particular does not simply stand *for* the universal. In making this argument he displays the influence of Plotinus and of a number of theologians. His definition of the beautiful as "multeity in unity" is an expression of this stance. The second is his location of the mediation between universal and particular in what he calls the symbol. He distinguishes it, as do several Romantic theorists, from allegory. The symbol joins things held apart in discursive thought. It is the vehicle of the beautiful, in that the beautiful joins multeity and unity. The third is his interest in the psychology of creation, which leads him to consider the work of art in terms of the artist's activity. Following his Schellingean epistemology, he sees the artist joining subject and object in an act analogous to God's creative act. Thus man reconciles himself with nature. Art becomes for Coleridge a special mode of knowing. In a letter written in 1802 he remarked, "A poet's heart and intellect should be combined, intimately combined and unified, with the great appearances in nature—and not merely held in solution and loose mixture with them, in the shape of formal similes."

Coleridge is perhaps the major English exponent of organicism as a metaphor in the theory of art. He opposes organic form to the mechanical form resulting from the operation of fancy. The work of art must grow organically from within itself. Its principles of order are finally internal and not imposed from without. We see this principle expressed in his remarks about Shakespeare: "No work of true genius dares want its appropriate form." Attacking those neoclassicists who saw Shakespeare as an untutored, wild, and irregular genius, Coleridge argues for an organic conception of artistic order.

The influence of Coleridge is as varied as it is immense. Few modern critics have not found something of his to use. He is more than simply a link with the Germans from whom he borrowed (indeed stole) so much. Sensitive to almost all the major critical problems, he says something somewhere about each of them.

Many volumes of the new edition of Coleridge's works edited by Kathleen Coburn have appeared. Consult also the complete works edited by W. G. T. Shedd (7 vols., 1889). See also J. H. Muirhead, *Coleridge as Philosopher* (1930); René Wellek, *Immanuel Kant in England* (1931); Gordon McKenzie, *Organic Unity in Coleridge* (1939); Herbert Read, *Coleridge as Critic* (1948); James V. Baker, *The Sacred River: Coleridge's Theory of Imagination* (1957); J. Appleyard, *Coleridge's Philosophy of Literature* (1965); Walter Jackson Bate, *Coleridge* (1968); R. L. Brett, *Fancy and Imagination* (1969); Gian N. G. Orsini, *Coleridge and German Idealism* (1969); James R. Jackson, *Method and Imagination in Coleridge's Criticism* (1969); Owen Barfield, *What Coleridge Thought* (1971); Jerome Christensen, *Coleridge's Blessed Machine of Language* (1981); Timothy Corrigan, *Coleridge, Language and Criticism* (1982); Paul Hamilton, *Coleridge's Poetics* (1983); James C. McKusick, *Coleridge's Philosophy of Language* (1986); A. C. Goodson, *Verbal Imagination* (1988); and Nigel Leask, *The Politics of Imagination in Coleridge's Thought* (1988).

Shakespeare's Judgment Equal to His Genius

Thus, then, Shakespeare appears, from his *Venus and Adonis* and *Rape of Lucrece* alone, apart from all his great works, to have possessed all the conditions of the true poet.[1] Let me now proceed to destroy, as far as may be in my power, the popular notion that he was a great dramatist by mere instinct, that he grew immortal in his own despite, and sank below men of second- or third-rate power when he attempted aught beside the drama—even as bees construct their cells and manufacture their honey to admirable perfection; but would in vain attempt to build a nest. Now this mode of reconciling a compelled sense of inferiority with a feeling of pride began in a few pedants, who, having read that Sophocles was the great model of tragedy, and Aristotle the infallible dictator of its rules, and finding that the *Lear, Hamlet, Othello,* and other masterpieces were neither in imitation of Sophocles

nor in obedience to Aristotle—and, not having (with one or two exceptions) the courage to affirm, that the delight which their country received from generation to generation, in defiance of the alterations of circumstances and habits, was wholly groundless—took upon them, as a happy medium and refuge, to talk of Shakespeare as a sort of beautiful *lusus naturae,*[2] a delightful monster, wild, indeed, and without taste or judgment, but like the inspired idiots so much venerated in the East, uttering, amid the strangest follies, the sublimest truths. In nine places out of ten in which I find his awful name mentioned, it is with some epithet of "wild," "irregular," "pure child of nature," etc. If all this be true, we must submit to it; though to a thinking mind it cannot but be painful to find any excellence, merely human, thrown out of all human analogy, and thereby leaving us neither rules for imitation, nor motives to imitate; but, if false, it is a dangerous falsehood; for it affords a refuge to secret self-conceit, enables a vain man at once to escape his reader's indignation by general swollen panegyrics, and merely by his *ipse dixit*[3] to treat as contemptible what he has not intellect enough to comprehend, or soul to feel, without assigning any reason, or referring his opinion to any demonstrative principle; thus leaving Shakespeare as a sort of grand lama, adored

---

SHAKESPEARE'S JUDGMENT EQUAL TO HIS GENIUS. Coleridge's lecture *Shakespeare's Judgment Equal to His Genius* was first published in 1836 but may have been delivered as early as 1808.
[1] In an earlier lecture, *Shakespeare as a Poet Generally,* Coleridge had discussed *Venus and Adonis* and *The Rape of Lucrece.*

[2] "Sport of nature."
[3] "The master has said it."

indeed, and his very excrements prized as relics, but with no authority or real influence. I grieve that every late voluminous edition of his works would enable me to substantiate the present charge with a variety of facts, one-tenth of which would of themselves exhaust the time allotted to me. Every critic, who has or has not made a collection of black letter books—in itself a useful and respectable amusement—puts on the seven-league boots of self-opinion, and strides at once from an illustrator into a supreme judge, and blind and deaf, fills his three-ounce phial at the waters of Niagara; and determines positively the greatness of the cataract to be neither more nor less than his three-ounce phial has been able to receive.

I think this a very serious subject. It is my earnest desire—my passionate endeavor—to enforce at various times and by various arguments and instances the close and reciprocal connection of just taste with pure morality. Without that acquaintance with the heart of man, or that docility and childlike gladness to be made acquainted with it, which those only can have, who dare look at their own hearts—and that with a steadiness which religion only has the power of reconciling with sincere humility; without this, and the modesty produced by it, I am deeply convinced that no man, however wide his erudition, however patient his antiquarian researches, can possibly understand, or be worthy of understanding, the writings of Shakespeare.

Assuredly, that criticism of Shakespeare will alone be genial which is reverential. The Englishman, who without reverence, a proud and affectionate reverence, can utter the name of William Shakespeare, stands disqualified for the office of critic. He wants one at least of the very senses, the language of which he is to employ, and will discourse, at best, but as a blind man, while the whole harmonious creation of light and shade with all its subtle interchange of deepening and dissolving colors rises in silence to the silent fiat of the uprising Apollo. However inferior in ability I may be to some who have followed me, I own I am proud that I was the first in time who publicly demonstrated to the full extent of the position, that the supposed irregularity and extravagancies of Shakespeare were the mere dreams of a pedantry that arraigned the eagle because it had not the dimensions of the swan. In all the successive courses of lectures delivered by me, since my first attempt at the Royal Institution, it has been, and it still remains, my object, to prove that in all points from the most important to the most minute, the judgment of Shakespeare is commensurate with his genius, nay, that his genius reveals itself in his judgment, as in its most exalted form. And the more gladly do I recur to this subject from the clear conviction, that to judge aright, and with distinct consciousness of the grounds of our judgment, concerning the works of Shakespeare, implies the power and the means of judging rightly of all other works of intellect, those of abstract science alone excepted.

It is a painful truth that not only individuals, but even whole nations, are ofttimes so enslaved to the habits of their education and immediate circumstances, as not to judge disinterestedly even on those subjects, the very pleasure arising from which consists in its disinterestedness, namely, on subjects of taste and polite literature. Instead of deciding concerning their own modes and customs by any rule of reason, nothing appears rational, becoming, or beautiful to them, but what coincides with the peculiarities of their education. In this narrow circle, individuals may attain to exquisite discrimination, as the French critics have done in their own literature; but a true critic can no more be such without placing himself on some central point, from which he may command the whole, that is, some general rule, which, founded in reason, or the faculties common to all men, must therefore apply to each, than an astronomer can explain the movements of the solar system without taking his stand in the sun. And let me remark, that this will not tend to produce despotism, but, on the contrary, true tolerance, in the critic. He will, indeed, require, as the spirit and substance of a work, something true in human nature itself, and independent of all circumstances; but in the mode of applying it, he will estimate genius and judgment according to the felicity with which the imperishable soul of intellect shall have adapted itself to the age, the place, and the existing manners. The error he will expose lies in reversing this, and holding up the mere circumstances as perpetual, to the utter neglect of the power which can alone animate them. For art cannot exist without, or apart from, nature; and what has man of his own to give to his fellowman, but his own thoughts and feelings, and his observations so far as they are modified by his own thoughts or feelings?

Let me, then, once more submit this question to minds emancipated alike from national, or party, or sectarian prejudice. Are the plays of Shakespeare works of rude uncultivated genius, in which the splendor of the parts compensates, if aught can compensate, for the barbarous shapelessness and irregularity of the whole? Or is the form equally admirable with the matter, and the judgment of the great poet not less deserving our wonder than his genius? Or, again, to repeat the question in other words: Is Shakespeare a great dramatic poet on account only of those beauties and excellencies which he possesses in common with the ancients, but with diminished claims to our love and honor to the full extent of his differences from them? Or are these very differences additional proofs of poetic wisdom, at once results and symbols of living power as contrasted with lifeless mechanism—

of free and rival originality as contradistinguished from servile imitation, or, more accurately, a blind copying of effects, instead of a true imitation of the essential principles? Imagine not that I am about to oppose genius to rules. No! The comparative value of these rules is the very cause to be tried. The spirit of poetry, like all other living powers, must of necessity circumscribe itself by rules, were it only to unite power with beauty. It must embody in order to reveal itself; but a living body is of necessity an organized one; and what is organization but the connection of parts in and for a whole, so that each part is at once end and means? This is the discovery of criticism; it is a necessity of the human mind; and all nations have felt and obeyed it, in the invention of meter, and measured sounds, as the vehicle and *involucrum*[4] of poetry, itself a fellow-growth from the same life, even as the bark is to the tree!

No work of true genius dares want its appropriate form, neither indeed is there any danger of this. As it must not, so genius cannot, be lawless: for it is even this that constitutes it genius—the power of acting creatively under laws of its own origination. How then comes it that not only single *Zoili*,[5] but whole nations have combined in unhesitating condemnation of our great dramatist, as a sort of African nature, rich in beautiful monsters, as a wild heath where islands of fertility look the greener from the surrounding waste, where the loveliest plants now shine out among unsightly weeds, and now are choked by their parasitic growth, so intertwined that we cannot disentangle the weed without snapping the flower? In this statement I have had no reference to the vulgar abuse of Voltaire, save as far as his charges are coincident with the decisions of Shakespeare's own commentators and (so they would tell you) almost idolatrous admirers. The true ground of the mistake lies in the confounding mechanical regularity with organic form. The form is mechanic, when on any given material we impress a predetermined form, not necessarily arising out of the properties of the material; as when to a mass of wet clay we give whatever shape we wish it to retain when hardened. The organic form, on the other hand, is innate; it shapes, as it develops, itself from within, and the fullness of its development is one and the same with the perfection of its outward form. Such as the life is, such is the form. Nature, the prime genial artist, inexhaustible in diverse powers, is equally inexhaustible in forms, each exterior is the physiognomy of the being within its true image reflected and thrown out from the concave mirror: and even such is the appropriate excellence of her chosen poet, of our own Shakespeare, himself a nature humanized, a genial understanding, directing self-consciously a power and an implicit wisdom deeper even than our consciousness.

I greatly dislike beauties and selections in general; but as proof positive of his unrivaled excellence, I should like to try Shakespeare by this criterion. Make out your amplest catalogue of all the human faculties, as reason or the moral law, the will, the feeling of the coincidence of the two (a feeling *sui generis et demonstratio demonstrationum*[6]) called the conscience, the understanding, or prudence, wit, fancy, imagination, judgment, and then of the objects on which these are to be employed, as the beauties, the terrors, and the seeming caprices of nature, the capabilities, that is, the actual and the ideal, of the human mind, conceived as an individual or as a social being, as in innocence or in guilt, in a play-paradise or in a war field of temptation; and then compare with Shakespeare under each of these heads all or any of the writers in prose and verse that have ever lived! Who, that is competent to judge, doubts the result? And ask your own hearts, ask your own commonsense to conceive the possibility of this man being—I say not, the drunken savage of that wretched sciolist, whom Frenchmen, to their shame, have honored before their elder and better worthies—but the anomalous, the wild, the irregular, genius of our daily criticism! What! Are we to have miracles in sport?—Or, I speak reverently, does God choose idiots by whom to convey divine truths to man?

On the Principles of Genial Criticism

From

Essay Third

I proceed to my promised and more amusing task, that of establishing, illustrating, and exemplifying the distinct powers of the different modes of pleasure excited by the works of nature or of human genius with their exponent and appropriable terms. . . .

---

[4]"Clothing."

[5]Zoilus was a critic of Homer.

[6]"Of its own kind (unique) and self-demonstrative."

ON THE PRINCIPLES OF GENIAL CRITICISM. *On the Principles of Genial Criticism Concerning the Fine Arts* was first published in 1814 in a Bristol periodical.

Agreeable

We use this word in two senses; in the first for whatever agrees with our nature, for that which is congruous with the primary constitution of our senses. Thus green is naturally agreeable to the eye. In this sense the word expresses, at least involves, a preestablished harmony between the organs and their appointed objects. In the second sense, we convey by the word *agreeable,* that the thing has by force of habit (thence called a second nature) been made to agree with us; or that it has become agreeable to us by its recalling to our minds some one or more things that were dear and pleasing to us; or lastly, on account of some after pleasure or advantage, of which it has been the constant cause or occasion. Thus by force of custom men *make* the taste of tobacco,[1] which was at first hateful to the palate, agreeable to them; thus too, as our Shakespeare observes, "Things base and vile, holding no quality, / Love can transpose to form and dignity—"[2] the crutch that had supported a revered parent, after the first anguish of regret, becomes agreeable to the affectionate child; and I once knew a very sensible and accomplished Dutch gentleman, who, spite of his own sense of the ludicrous nature of the feeling, was more delighted by the first grand concert of frogs he heard in this country, than he had been by Catalina singing in the compositions of Cimarosa. The last clause needs no illustrations, as it comprises all the objects that are agreeable to us, only because they are the means by which we gratify our smell, touch, palate, and mere bodily feeling.

Beautiful

The beautiful, contemplated in its essentials, that is, in *kind* and not in *degree,* is that in which the *many,* still seen as many, becomes one. Take a familiar instance, one of a thousand. The frost on a windowpane has by accident crystallized into a striking resemblance of a tree or a seaweed. With what pleasure we trace the parts, and their relations to each other, and to the whole! Here is the stalk or trunk, and here the branches or sprays—sometimes even the buds or flowers. Nor will our pleasure be less, should the caprice of the crystallization represent some object disagreeable to us, provided only we can see or fancy the component parts each in relation to each, and all forming a whole. A lady would see an admirably painted tiger with pleasure, and at once pronounce it beautiful—nay, an owl, a frog, or a toad, who would have shrieked or shuddered at the sight of the things themselves. So far is the beautiful from depending wholly on association, that it is frequently produced by the mere removal of associations.[3] Many a sincere convert to the beauty of various insects, as of the dragonfly, the fangless snake, &c., has natural history made, by exploding the terror or aversion that had been connected with them.

The most general definition of beauty, therefore, is—that I may fulfill my threat of plaguing my readers with hard words—multeity in unity. Now it will be always found, that whatever is the definition of the *kind,* independent of degree, becomes likewise the definition of the highest degree of that kind. An old coach wheel lies in the coachmaker's yard, disfigured with tar and dirt (I purposely take the most trivial instances)—if I turn away my attention from these, and regard the *figure* abstractly, "still," I might say to my companion, "there is beauty in that wheel, and you yourself would not only admit, but would feel it, had you never seen a wheel before. See how the rays proceed from the center to the circumferences, and how many different images are distinctly comprehended at one glance, as forming one whole, and each part in some harmonious relation to each and to all." But imagine the polished golden wheel of the chariot of the sun, as the poets have described it: then the figure, and the real thing so figured, exactly coincide. There is nothing heterogeneous, nothing to abstract from: by its perfect smoothness and circularity in width, each part is (if I may borrow a metaphor from a sister sense) as perfect a melody, as the whole is a complete harmony. This, we should say, is beautiful throughout. Of all "the many," which I actually see, each and all are really reconciled into unity: while the effulgence from the whole coincides with, and seems to represent, the effluence of delight from my own mind in the intuition of it.

It seems evident then, first, that beauty is harmony, and subsists only in composition, and secondly, that the first species of the agreeable can alone be a component part of the beautiful, that namely which is naturally consonant with our senses by the preestablished harmony between nature and the human mind; and thirdly, that even of this species, those objects only can be admitted (according to rule the first) which belong to the eye and ear, because they alone are susceptible of distinction of parts. Should an Englishman gazing on a mass of cloud rich with the rays of the rising sun exclaim, even without distinction of, or reference to its form,

---

[1] Compare Burke, *The Sublime and Beautiful,* p. 301.
[2] *Midsummer Night's Dream,* I. i. 232–33. But Coleridge substitutes *quality* for *quantity.*

---

[3] Here Coleridge nearly suggests what comes to be called psychical distance.

or its relation to other objects, "How beautiful!" I should have no quarrel with him. First, because by the law of association there is in all visual beholdings at least an indistinct subsumption of form and relation; and, secondly, because even in the coincidence between the sight and the object there is an approximation to the reduction of the many into one. But who, that heard a Frenchman call the flavor of a leg of mutton a beautiful taste would not immediately recognize him for a Frenchman, even though there should be neither grimace or characteristic nasal twang? The result, then, of the whole is that the shapely (i.e. *formosus*) joined with the naturally agreeable, constitutes what, speaking accurately, we mean by the word *beautiful* (i.e. *pulcher*).

But we are conscious of faculties far superior to the highest impressions of sense; we have life and free will.—What then will be the result, when the beautiful, arising from regular form, is so modified by the perception of life and spontaneous action, as that the latter only shall be the object of our conscious *perception,* while the former merely acts, and yet does effectively act, on our feelings? With pride and pleasure I reply by referring my reader to the group in Mr. Allston's[4] grand picture of the *Dead Man Reviving from the Touch of the Bones of the Prophet Elisha,* beginning with the slave at the head of the reviving body, then proceeding to the daughter clasping her swooning mother; to the mother, the wife of the reviving man; then to the soldier behind who supports her; to the two figures eagerly conversing: and lastly, to the exquisitely graceful girl who is bending downward, and whose hand nearly touches the thumb of the slave! You will find, what you had not suspected, that you have here before you a circular group. But by what variety of life, motion, and passion is all the stiffness, that would result from an obvious regular figure swallowed up, and the figure of the group as much concealed by the action and passion, as the skeleton, which gives the form of the human body, is hidden by the flesh and its endless outlines!

In Raphael's admirable *Galatea* (the print of which is doubtless familiar to most of my readers) the circle is perceived at first sight; but with what multiplicity of rays and chords within the area of the circular group, with what elevations and depressions of the circumference, with what an endless variety and sportive wildness in the component figure, and in the junctions of the figures, is the balance, the perfect reconciliation, effected between these two conflicting principles of the free life, and of the confining form! How

entirely is the stiffness that would have resulted from the obvious regularity of the latter, *fused* and (if I may hazard so bold a metaphor) almost *volatilized* by the interpenetration and electrical flashes of the former.

But I shall recur to this consummate work for more specific illustrations hereafter: and have indeed in some measure offended already against the laws of method, by anticipating materials which rather belong to a more advanced stage of the disquisition. It is time to recapitulate, as briefly as possible, the arguments already advanced, and having summed up the result, to leave behind me this, the only portion of these essays, which, as far as the subject itself is concerned, will demand any *effort* of attention from a reflecting and intelligent reader. And let me be permitted to remind him, that the distinctions, which it is my object to prove and elucidate, have not merely a foundation in nature and the noblest faculties of the human mind, but are likewise the very groundwork, nay, an indispensable condition, of all *rational* inquiry concerning the arts. For it is self-evident, that whatever may be judged of differently by different persons, in the very same degree of moral and intellectual cultivation, extolled by one and condemned by another, without any error being assignable to either, can never be an object of general principles: and vice versa, that whatever can be brought to the test of general principles presupposes a distinct origin from these pleasures and tastes, which, for the wisest purposes, are made to depend on local and transitory fashions, accidental associations, and the peculiarities of individual temperament: to all which the philosopher, equally with the well-bred man of the world, applies the old adage, *de gustibus non est disputandum.*[5] Be it, however, observed that *de gustibus* is by no means the same as *de gustu,* nor will it escape the scholar's recollection, that taste, in its metaphorical use, was first adopted by the Romans, and unknown to the less luxurious Greeks, who designed this faculty, sometimes by the word αἴσθησις, and sometimes by φιλοκαλία—ἀνδρῶν τῶν καο' ἡμᾶς φιλοκαλώτατος γεγονώς—i.e. "endowed by nature with the most exquisite taste of any man of our age," says Porphyry of his friend, Castricius. Still, this metaphor, borrowed from the pregustatores of the old Roman banquets, is singularly happy and appropriate. In the palate, the perception of the object and its qualities is involved in the *sensation,* in the mental taste it is involved in the *sense.* We have a *sensation* of sweetness, in a healthy palate, from honey; a *sense* of beauty, in an uncorrupted taste, from the view of the rising or setting sun.

---

[4]Washington Allston (1779–1843), American painter and a friend of Coleridge's. Coleridge wrote the three essays in *On the Principles of Genial Criticism* in order to draw attention to an exhibit of Allston's works.

---

[5]"There is no disputing tastes."

Recapitulation

Principle the First

That which has become, or which has been *made* agreeable to us, from causes not contained in its own nature, or in its original conformity to the human organs and faculties; that which is not pleasing for its own sake, but by connection or association with some other thing, separate or separable from it, is neither beautiful, nor capable of being a component part of beauty: though it may greatly increase the sum of our pleasure, when it does not interfere with the beauty of the object, nay, even when it detracts from it. A moss rose, with a sprig of myrtle and jasmine, is not more *beautiful* from having been plucked from the garden, or presented to us by the hand of the woman we love, but is abundantly more delightful. The total pleasure received from one of Mr. Bird's finest pictures may, without any impeachment of our taste, be the greater from his having introduced into it the portrait of one of our friends, or from our pride in him as our townsman, or from our knowledge of his personal qualities; but the amiable artist would rightly consider it a coarse compliment, were it affirmed, that the *beauty* of the piece, or its merit as a work of genius, was the more perfect on this account. I am conscious that I look with a stronger and more pleasurable emotion at Mr. Allston's large landscape, in the spirit of Swiss scenery, from its having been the occasion of my first acquaintance with him in Rome. This may or may not be a compliment to *him;* but the true compliment to the picture was made by a lady of high rank and cultivated taste, who declared, in my hearing, that she never stood before that landscape without seeming to feel the breeze blow out of it upon her. But the most striking instance is afforded by the portrait of a departed or absent friend or parent; which is endeared to us, and more delightful, from some awkward position of the limbs, which had defied the contrivances of art to render it picturesque, but which was the characteristic habit of the original.

Principle the Second

That which is naturally agreeable and consonant to human nature, so that the exceptions may be attributed to disease or defect; that, the pleasure from which is contained in the immediate impression; cannot, indeed, with strict propriety, be called beautiful, exclusive of its relations, but one among the component parts of beauty, in whatever instance it is susceptible of existing as a part of whole. This, of course, excludes the mere objects of the taste, smell, and feeling, though the sensation from these, especially from the latter when organized into touch, may secretly, and without our consciousness, enrich and vivify the perceptions and images of the eye and ear; which alone are true organs of sense, their sensations in a healthy or uninjured state being too faint to be noticed by the mind. We may, indeed, in common conversation, call purple a beautiful color, or the tone of a single note on an excellent pianoforte a beautiful tone; but if we were questioned, we should agree that a rich or delightful color; a rich, or sweet, or clear tone; would have been more appropriate—and this with less hesitation in the latter instance than in the former, because the single tone is more manifestly of the nature of a *sensation,* while color is the medium which seems to blend sensation and perception, so as to hide, as it were, the former in the latter; the direct opposite of which takes place in the lower senses of feeling, smell, and taste. (In strictness, there is even in these an ascending scale. The smell is less sensual and more sentient than mere feeling, the taste than the smell, and the eye than the ear: but between the ear and the taste exists the chasm or break, which divides the beautiful and the elements of beauty from the merely agreeable.) When I reflect on the manner in which smoothness, richness of sound, &c., enter into the formation of the beautiful, I am induced to suspect that they act negatively rather than positively. Something there must be to realize the form, something in and by which the *forma informans*[6] reveals itself: and these, less than any that could be substituted, and in the least possible degree, distract the attention, in the least possible degree obscure the idea, of which they (composed into outline and surface) are the symbol. An illustrative hint may be taken from a pure crystal, as compared with an opaque, semiopaque or clouded mass, on the one hand, and with a perfectly transparent body, such as the air, on the other. The crystal is lost in the light, which yet it contains, embodies, and gives a shape to; but which passes shapeless through the air, and, in the ruder body, is either quenched or dissipated.

Principle the Third

The safest definition, then, of beauty, as well as the oldest, is that of Pythagoras: the reduction of many to one—or, as finely expressed by the sublime discipline of Ammonius,[7] τὸ ἄμερες ὄν, ἐν πολλοῖξ φανταζόμενον, of which the following may be offered as both paraphrase and corollary. *The*

---

[6]"Shaping form."
[7]The "sublime disciple" is Plotinus.

sense of beauty subsists in simultaneous intuition of the relation of parts, each to each, and of all to a whole: exciting an immediate and absolute complacency, without intervenence, therefore, of any interest, sensual or intellectual. The beautiful is thus at once distinguished both from the agreeable, which is beneath it, and from the good, which is above it: for both these have an interest necessarily attached to them: both act on the will, and excite a desire for the actual existence of the image or idea contemplated: while the sense of beauty rests gratified in the mere contemplation or intuition, regardless whether it be a fictitious Apollo, or a real Antinous.

The Mystics meant the same, when they define beauty as the subjection of matter to spirit so as to be transformed into a symbol, in and through which the spirit reveals itself; and declare *that* the *most* beautiful, where the most obstacles to a full manifestation have been most perfectly overcome.

. . .

Scholium

We have sufficiently distinguished the beautiful from the agreeable, by the sure criterion, that, when we find an object agreeable, the *sensation* of pleasure always precedes the judgment, and is its determining cause. We *find* it agreeable. But when we declare an object beautiful, the contemplation or intuition of its beauty precedes the *feeling* of complacency, in order of nature at least: nay, in great depression of spirits may even exist without sensibly producing it.

> A grief without a pang, void, dark, and drear!
> A stifled, drowsy, unimpassioned grief,
> That finds no natural outlet, no relief
> In word, or sigh, or tear!
> O dearest lady! in this heartless mood,
> To other thoughts by yon sweet throstle
> wooed!
> All this long eve, so balmy and serene,
> Have I been gazing at the western sky.[8]

Now the least reflection convinces us that our sensations, whether of pleasure or of pain, are the incommunicable parts of our nature; such as can be reduced to no universal rule; and in which therefore we have no right to expect that others should agree with us, or to blame them for disagreement. That the Greenlander prefers train oil to olive oil, and even to wine, we explain at once by our knowledge of the climate

and productions to which he has been habituated. Were the man as enlightened as Plato, his palate would still find that most agreeable to which it had been most accustomed. But when the Iroquois sachem, after having been led to the most perfect specimens of architecture in Paris, said that he saw nothing so beautiful as the cook's shops,[9] we attribute this without hesitation to savagery of intellect, and infer with certainty that the sense of the beautiful was either altogether dormant in his mind, or at best very imperfect. The beautiful, therefore, not originating in the sensations, must belong to the intellect: and therefore we *declare* an object beautiful, and feel an inward right to *expect* that others should coincide with us. But we feel no right to *demand* it: and this leads us to that, which hitherto we have barely touched upon, and which we shall now attempt to illustrate more fully, namely, to the distinction of the beautiful from the good.

Let us suppose Milton in company with some stern and prejudiced Puritan, contemplating the front of York Cathedral, and at length expressing his admiration of its beauty. We will suppose it too at that time of his life, when his religious opinions, feelings, and prejudices most nearly coincided with those of the rigid antiprelatists. P.: Beauty; I am sure, it is not the beauty of holiness. M.: True; but yet it is beautiful. P.: It delights not me. What is it good for? Is it of any use but to be stared at? M.: Perhaps not! But still it is beautiful. P.: But call to mind the pride and wanton vanity of those cruel shavelings, that wasted the labor and substance of so many thousand poor creatures in the erection of this haughty pile. M.: I do. But still it is very beautiful. P.: Think how many score of places of worship, incomparably better suited both for prayer and preaching, and how many faithful ministers might have been maintained, to the blessing of tens of thousands, to them and their children's children, with the treasures lavished on this worthless mass of stone and cement. M.: Too true! But nevertheless it is *very* beautiful. P.: And it is not merely useless; but it feeds the pride of the prelates, and keeps alive the popish and carnal spirit among the people. M.: Even so! And I presume not to question the wisdom, nor detract from the pious zeal, of the first reformers of Scotland, who for these reasons destroyed so many fabrics, scarce inferior in beauty to this now before our eyes. But I did not call it *good,* nor have I told thee, brother! that if this were leveled with the ground, and existed only in the works of the modeler or engraver, that I should desire to reconstruct it. The good consists in the congruity of a thing with the laws of the reason and the nature of the will, and in its fitness to determine the latter to actualize the former: and

---

[8]Part of stanza 2 of Coleridge's *Dejection: An Ode.*

[9]Kant used the same example in his *Critique of Judgment,* p. 376.

it is always discursive.[10] The beautiful arises from the perceived harmony of an object, whether sight or sound, with the inborn and constitutive rules of the judgment and imagination: and it is always intuitive. As light to the eye, even such is beauty to the mind, which cannot but have complacency in whatever is perceived as preconfigured to its living faculties. Hence the Greeks called a beautiful object καλόν quasi καλοῦν, i.e. *calling on* the soul, which receives instantly, and welcomes it as something connatural.

From
The Statesman's Manual

It is among the miseries of the present age that it recognizes no *medium* between literal and metaphorical. Faith is either to be buried in the dead letter, or its name and honors usurped by a counterfeit product of the mechanical understanding, which in the blindness of self-complacency confounds symbols with allegories. Now an allegory is but a translation of abstract notions into a picture language, which is itself nothing but an abstraction from objects of the senses; the principal being more worthless even than its phantom proxy, both alike unsubstantial, and the former shapeless to boot. On the other hand a symbol . . . is characterized by a translucence of the special in the individual, or of the general in the special, or of the universal in the general; above all by the translucence of the eternal through and in the temporal. It always partakes of the reality which it renders intelligible; and while it enunciates the whole, abides itself as a living part in that unity of which it is the representative.

Biographia Literaria

From

Chapter XII

All knowledge rests on the coincidence of an object with a subject. (My readers have been warned in a former chapter

---

[10]Coleridge here identifies the good with conceptualization, as did Kant.
THE STATESMAN'S MANUAL. *The Statesman's Manual* first appeared in 1816.
BIOGRAPHIA LITERARIA. *Biographia Literaria* was written in 1815 and first published two years later.

that, for their convenience as well as the writer's, the term *subject* is used by me in its scholastic sense as equivalent to mind or sentient being, and as the necessary correlative of object or *quicquid objicitur menti*.[1]) For we can *know* that only which is true: and the truth is universally placed in the coincidence of the thought with the thing, of the representation with the object represented.

Now the sum of all that is merely objective we will henceforth call *nature,* confining the term to its passive and material sense, as comprising all the phenomena by which its existence is made known to us. On the other hand the sum of all that is subjective, we may comprehend in the name of the *self* or *intelligence.* Both conceptions are in necessary antithesis. Intelligence is conceived of as exclusively representative, nature as exclusively represented; the one as conscious the other as without consciousness. Now in all acts of positive knowledge there is required a reciprocal concurrence of both, namely of the conscious being, and of that which is in itself unconscious. Our problem is to explain this concurrence, its possibility and its necessity.

During the act of knowledge itself, the objective and subjective are so instantly united, that we cannot determine to which of the two the priority belongs. There is here no first, and no second; both are coinstantaneous and one. While I am attempting to explain this intimate coalition, I must suppose it dissolved. I must necessarily set out from the one, to which therefore I give hypothetical antecedence, in order to arrive at the other. But as there are but two factors or elements in the problem, subject and object, and as it is left indeterminate from which of them I should commence, there are two cases equally possible.

I. Either the Objective Is Taken as the First, and Then We Have to Account for the Supervention of the Subjective, Which Coalesces With it

The notion of the subjective is not contained in the notion of the objective. On the contrary they mutually exclude each other. The subjective therefore must supervene to the objective. The conception of nature does not apparently involve the co-presence of an intelligence making an ideal duplicate of it, i.e. representing it. This desk for instance would (according to our natural notions) be, though there should exist no sentient being to look at it. This then is the problem of natural philosophy. It assumes the objective or unconscious nature as the first, and has therefore to explain how intelli-

---

[1]"Whatever is placed before (posed for) the mind."

gence can supervene to it, or how itself can grow into intelligence. If it should appear, that all enlightened naturalists, without having distinctly proposed the problem to themselves, have yet constantly moved in the line of its solution, it must afford a strong presumption that the problem itself is founded in nature. For if all knowledge has as it were two poles reciprocally required and presupposed, all sciences must proceed from the one or the other, and must tend toward the opposite as far as the equatorial point in which both are reconciled and become identical. The necessary tendence therefore of all natural philosophy is from nature to intelligence; and this, and no other, is the true ground and occasion of the instinctive striving to introduce theory into our views of natural phenomena. The highest perfection of natural philosophy would consist in the perfect spiritualization of all the laws of nature into laws of intuition and intellect. The phenomena (*the material*) must wholly disappear, and the laws alone (*the formal*) must remain. Thence it comes, that in nature itself the more the principle of law breaks forth, the more does the *husk* drop off, the phenomena themselves become more spiritual and at length cease altogether in our consciousness. The optical phenomena are but a geometry, the lines of which are drawn by light, and the materiality of this light itself has already become matter of doubt. In the appearances of magnetism all trace of matter is lost, and of the phenomena of gravitation, which not a few among the most illustrious Newtonians have declared no otherwise comprehensible than as an immediate spiritual influence, there remains nothing but its law, the execution of which on a vast scale is the mechanism of the heavenly motions.[2] The theory of natural philosophy would then be completed, when all nature was demonstrated to be identical in essence with that, which in its highest known power exists in man as intelligence and self-consciousness; when the heavens and the earth shall declare not only the power of their Maker, but the glory and the presence of their God, even as he appeared to the great prophet during the vision of the mount in the skirts of his divinity.

This may suffice to show, that even natural science, which commences with the material phenomenon as the reality and substance of things existing, does yet by the necessity of theorizing unconsciously, and as it were instinctively, end in nature as an intelligence; and by this tendency the science of nature becomes finally natural philosophy, the one of the two poles of fundamental science.

II. Or the Subjective Is Taken as the First, and the Problem Then Is, How There Supervenes to It a Coincident Objective

In the pursuit of these sciences, our success in each depends on an austere and faithful adherence to its own principles with a careful separation and exclusion of those, which appertain to the opposite science. As the natural philosopher, who directs his views to the objective, avoids above all things the intermixture of the subjective in his knowledge, as for instance, arbitrary suppositions or rather suffictions, occult qualities, spiritual agents, and the substitution of final for efficient causes; so on the other hand, the transcendental or intelligential philosopher is equally anxious to preclude all interpolation of the objective into the subjective principles of his science, as for instance the assumption of impresses or configurations in the brain, correspondent to miniature pictures on the retina painted by rays of light from supposed originals, which are not the immediate and real objects of vision, but deductions from it for the purposes of explanation. This purification of the mind is effected by an absolute and scientific skepticism, to which the mind voluntarily determines itself for the specific purpose of future certainty. Descartes who (in his meditations) himself first, at least of the moderns, gave a beautiful example of this voluntary doubt, this self-determined indetermination, happily expresses its utter difference from the skepticism of vanity or irreligion: *"Nec tamen in eo scepticos imitabar, qui dubitant tantum ut dubitent, et praeter incertitudinem ipsam nihil quaerunt. Nam contra totus in eo eram ut aliquid certi reperirem."*[3] Nor is it less distinct in its motives and final aim, than in its proper objects, which are not as in ordinary skepticism the prejudices of education and circumstance, but those original and innate prejudices which nature herself has planted in all men, and which to all but the philosopher are the first principles of knowledge, and the final test of truth.

Now these essential prejudices are all reducible to the one fundamental presumption, that there exist things without us. As this on the one hand originates, neither in grounds nor arguments, and yet on the other hand remains proof against all attempts to remove it by grounds or arguments (*"naturam*

---

[2]Up to this point in the selection Coleridge has been translating from and adding to a passage in Schelling's *System of Transcendental Idealism.*

[3]"But I did not, in this matter, imitate those skeptics who raise doubt merely for the sake of raising doubt, and who seek nothing but uncertainty itself. For, by contrast, I devoted myself wholly to find something which might be certain." *Discourse on Method,* Lecture III.

furca expellas tamen usque redibit"[4]); on the one hand lays claim to immediate certainty as a position at once indemonstrable and irresistible, and yet on the other hand, inasmuch as it refers to something essentially different from ourselves, nay even in opposition to ourselves, leaves it inconceivable how it could possibly become a part of our immediate consciousness (in other words how that, which *ex hypothesi* is and continues to be extrinsic and alien to our being, should become a modification of our being); the philosopher therefore compels himself to treat this faith as nothing more than a prejudice, innate indeed and connatural, but still a prejudice.

The other position, which not only claims but necessitates the admission of its immediate certainty, equally for the scientific reason of the philosopher as for the common sense of mankind at large, namely, *I am,* cannot so properly be entitled a prejudice. It is groundless indeed; but then in the very idea it precludes all ground, and separated from the immediate consciousness loses its whole sense and import. It is groundless; but only because it is itself the ground of all other certainty. Now the apparent contradiction, that the former position, namely, the existence of things without us, which from its nature cannot be immediately certain, should be received as blindly and as independently of all grounds as the existence of our own being, the transcendental philosopher can solve only by the supposition, that the former is unconsciously involved in the latter; that it is not only coherent but identical, and one and the same thing with our own immediate self-consciousness. To demonstrate this identity is the office and object of his philosophy.

If it be said, that this is idealism, let it be remembered that it is only so far idealism, as it is at the same time, and on that very account, the truest and most binding realism. For wherein does the realism of mankind properly consist? In the assertion that there exists a something without them, what, or how, or where they know not, which occasions the objects of their perception? Oh no! This is neither connatural nor universal. It is what a few have taught and learned in the schools, and which the many repeat without asking themselves concerning their own meaning. The realism common to all mankind is far elder and lies infinitely deeper than this hypothetical explanation of the origin of our perceptions, an explanation skimmed from the mere surface of mechanical philosophy. It is the table itself, which the man of common sense believes himself to see, not the phantom of a table, from which he may argumentatively deduce the reality of a table, which he does not see. If to destroy the reality of all, that we actually behold, be idealism, what can be more egregiously so, than the system of modern metaphysics, which banishes us to a land of shadows, surrounds us with apparitions, and distinguishes truth from illusion only by the majority of those who dream the same dream? "*I* asserted that the world was mad," exclaimed poor Lee, "and the world said, that I was mad, and confound them, they outvoted me."

It is to the true and original realism, that I would direct the attention. This believes and requires neither more nor less, than the object which it beholds or presents to itself, is the real and very object. In this sense, however much we may strive against it, we are all collectively born idealists, and therefore and only therefore are we at the same time realists. But of this the philosophers of the schools know nothing, or despise the faith as the prejudice of the ignorant vulgar, because they live and move in a crowd of phrases and notions from which human nature has long ago vanished. Oh, ye that reverence yourselves, and walk humbly with the divinity in your own hearts, ye are worthy of a better philosophy! Let the dead bury the dead, but do you preserve your human nature, the depth of which was never yet fathomed by a philosophy made up of notions and mere logical entities.

From

Chapter XIII

The imagination then, I consider either as primary, or secondary. The primary imagination I hold to be the living power and prime agent of all human perception, and as a repetition in the finite mind of the eternal act of creation in the infinite *I am.* The secondary imagination I consider as an echo of the former, coexisting with the conscious will, yet still as identical with the primary in the *kind* of its agency, and differing only in *degree,* and in the *mode* of its operation. It dissolves, diffuses, dissipates, in order to recreate; or where this process is rendered impossible, yet still at all events it struggles to idealize and to unify. It is essentially *vital,* even as all objects (*as* objects) are essentially fixed and dead.

Fancy, on the contrary, has no other counters to play with, but fixities and definites. The fancy is indeed no other than a mode of memory emancipated from the order of time and space; while it is blended with, and modified by that empirical phenomenon of the will, which we express by the word *choice.* But equally with the ordinary memory the fancy must receive all its materials ready made from the law of association.

---

[4]"If you drive out nature with a pitchfork, she will soon find a way back." Horace, *Epistles,* X. 24.

From

Chapter XIV

. . . in order to render myself intelligible I must . . . in as few words as possible, explain my ideas, first, of a POEM; and secondly, of POETRY itself, in *kind,* and in *essence.*[1]

The office of philosophical *disquisition* consists in just *distinction;* while it is the privilege of the philosopher to preserve himself constantly aware, that distinction is not division. In order to obtain adequate notions of any truth, we must intellectually separate its distinguishable parts; and this is the technical *process* of philosophy. But having so done, we must then restore them in our conceptions to the unity, in which they actually co-exist; and this is the *result* of philosophy. A poem contains the same elements as a prose composition; the difference therefore must consist in a different combination of them, in consequence of a different object proposed. According to the difference of the object will be the difference of the combination. It is possible, that the object may be merely to facilitate the recollection of any given facts or observations by artificial arrangement; and the composition will be a poem, merely because it is distinguished from prose by metre, or by rhyme, or by both conjointly. In this, the lowest sense, a man might attribute the name of a poem to the well known enumeration of the days in the several months;

Thirty days hath September,
April, June, and November, &c.

and others of the same class and purpose. And as a particular pleasure is found in anticipating the recurrence of sounds and quantities, all compositions that have this charm superadded, whatever be their contents, *may* be entitled poems.

So much for the superficial *form.* A difference of object and contents supplies an additional ground of distinction. The immediate purpose may be the communication of truths; either of truth absolute and demonstrable, as in works of science; or of facts experienced and recorded, as in history. Pleasure, and that of the highest and most permanent kind, may *result* from the *attainment* of the end; but it is not itself the immediate end. In other works the communication of

pleasure may be the immediate purpose; and though truth, either moral or intellectual, ought to be the *ultimate* end, yet this will distinguish the character of the author, not the class to which the work belongs. Blest indeed is that state of society, in which the immediate purpose would be baffled by the perversion of the proper ultimate end; in which no charm of diction or imagery could exempt the Bathyllus even of an Anacreon, or the Alexis of Virgil,[2] from disgust and aversion!

But the communication of pleasure may be the immediate object of a work not metrically composed; and that object may have been in a high degree attained, as in novels and romances. Would then the mere superaddition of metre, with or without rhyme, entitle *these* to the name of poems? The answer is, that nothing can permanently please, which does not contain in itself the reason why it is so, and not otherwise. If metre be superadded, all other parts must be made consonant with it. They must be such, as to justify the perpetual and distinct attention to each part, which an exact correspondent recurrence of accent and sound are calculated to excite. The final definition then, so deduced, may be thus worded. A poem is that species of composition, which is opposed to works of science, by proposing for its *immediate* object pleasure, not truth; and from all other species (having *this* object in common with it) it is discriminated by proposing to itself such delight from the *whole,* as is compatible with a distinct gratification from each component *part.*

Controversy is not seldom excited in consequence of the disputants attaching each a different meaning to the same word; and in few instances has this been more striking, than in disputes concerning the present subject. If a man chooses to call every composition a poem, which is rhyme, or measure, or both, I must leave his opinion uncontroverted. The distinction is at least competent to characterize the writer's intention. If it were subjoined, that the whole is likewise entertaining or affecting, as a tale, or as a series of interesting reflections, I of course admit this as another fit ingredient of a poem, and an additional merit. But if the definition sought for be that of a *legitimate* poem, I answer, it must be one, the parts of which mutually support and explain each other; all in their proportion harmonizing with, and supporting the purpose and known influences of metrical arrangement. The philosophic critics of all ages coincide with the ultimate judgement of all countries, in equally denying the praises of

---

[1] Coleridge has been discussing his differences with the argument of Wordsworth's preface to the second edition of *Lyrical Ballads* (1800). See pp. 436–446.

[2] Bathyllus of Samos, loved by Anacreon. See Ode 29. Alexis: see Virgil's *Eclogue* 2.

a just poem, on the one hand, to a series of striking lines or distichs, each of which absorbing the whole attention of the reader to itself disjoins it from its context, and makes it a separate whole, instead of an harmonizing part; and on the other hand, to an unsustained composition, from which the reader collects rapidly the general result unattracted by the component parts. The reader should be carried forward, not merely or chiefly by the mechanical impulse of curiosity, or by a restless desire to arrive at the final solution; but by the pleasureable activity of mind excited by the attractions of the journey itself. Like the motion of a serpent, which the Egyptians made the emblem of intellectual power; or like the path of sound through the air; at every step he pauses and half recedes, and from the retrogressive movement collects the force which again carries him onward. *Precipitandus est liber* spiritus, says Petronius Arbiter most happily. The epithet, *liber,* here balances the preceding verb; and it is not easy to conceive more meaning condensed in fewer words.

But if this should be admitted as a satisfactory character of a poem, we have still to seek for a definition of poetry. The writings of PLATO, and Bishop TAYLOR, and the *Theoria Sacra* of BURNET,[3] furnish undeniable proofs that poetry of the highest kind may exist without metre, and even without the contradistinguishing objects of a poem. The first chapter of Isaiah (indeed a very large proportion of the whole book) is poetry in the most emphatic sense; yet it would be not less irrational than strange to assert, that pleasure, and not truth, was the immediate object of the prophet. In short, whatever *specific* import we attach to the word poetry, there will be found involved in it, as a necessary consequence, that a poem of any length neither can be, or ought to be, all poetry. Yet if an harmonious whole is to be produced, the remaining parts must be preserved *in keeping* with the poetry; and this again can be no otherwise effected than by such a studied selection and artificial arrangement, as will partake of *one,* though not a *peculiar,* property of poetry. And this again can be no other than the property of exciting a more continuous and equal attention, than the language of prose aims at, whether colloquial or written.

My own conclusions on the nature of poetry, in the strictest use of the word, have been in part anticipated in the preceding disquisition on the fancy and imagination.[4] What is poetry? is so nearly the same question with, what is a poet? that the answer to the one is involved in the solution of the other. For it is a distinction resulting from the poetric genius itself, which sustains and modifies the images, thoughts, and emotions of the poet's own mind. The poet, described in *ideal* perfection, brings the whole soul of man into activity, with the subordination of its faculties to each other, according to their relative worth and dignity. He diffuses a tone and spirit of unity, that blends, and (as it were) *fuses,* each into each, by that synthetic and magical power, to which we have exclusively appropriated the name of imagination. This power, first put in action by the will and understanding, and retained under their irremissive, though gentle and unnoticed, controul (*laxis effertur habenis*)[5] reveals itself in the balance or reconciliation of opposite or discordant qualities: of sameness, with difference; of the general, with the concrete; the idea, with the image; the individual, with the representative; the sense of novelty and freshness, with old and familiar objects; a more than usual state of emotion, with more than usual order; judgment ever awake and steady self-possession, with enthusiasm and feeling profound or vehement; and while it blends and harmonizes the natural and the artificial, still subordinates art to nature; the manner to matter; and our admiration of the poet to our sympathy with the poetry.

---

[3]Jeremy Taylor (1613–1667), English bishop, author of *Holy Living* and *Holy Dying.* Thomas Burnet (1635–1715), author of *Telluris theoria sacra (The Sacred History of the Earth).*

[4]See Chapter XIII, though the discussion is hardly long enough to be a "disquisition."

[5]"Carried out with slackened reins," Petrarch, *Epistola Barbato Sulmonensi* 1, 39.

Wilhelm von Humboldt

1767–1835

Wilhelm von Humboldt, a Prussian career diplomat and minister for thirty-four years (though out of favor for part of that time and eventually summarily dismissed for advanced opinions), was a voluminous writer on many subjects, his collected works amounting to seventeen volumes. He wrote on language in general, certain languages in particular, literature, aesthetics, psychology, and women. He translated the *Agamemnon* of Aeschylus. He was the author of 1183 sonnets, one written every day, and a number of narrative poems, all best ignored. It is in those writings in which he extends the Kantian notion of human constitutive powers into the domain of language that he comes down to us as a major thinker, spanning the shift from epistemological to linguistic concerns.

Few of his writings were published in his lifetime. His more famous brother Alexander (1769–1859), an explorer much interested in languages, brought back to Wilhelm information about languages he had come to know about. Wilhelm employed Alexander's information in both his detailed study of the Kavi language of Java, *Kawiwerk,* posthumously published in three volumes, and in his more philosophically oriented studies in linguistics. He wrote on Chinese, Basque, and Mexican, on differences in human linguistic structures, on various periods of linguistic development, and on national characteristics of language. For von Humboldt, man is man only through language; language is his defining attribute: "Just as no concept is possible without language, so no object is possible without it for the psyche, since even external ones receive their intrinsic substance only through language." The selection which follows comes from a variety of his works. Numbers following each selection refer to volume and page of the *Gesammelte Schriften.*

In addition to *Humanist Without Portfolio* (1963), which contains an interesting introduction by Marian Cowan, von Humboldt's *Linguistic Variability and Intellectual Development* is available in English translation by G. C. Buck and F. A. Raven. The *Gesammelte Schriften* in seventeen volumes was published from 1903–1935. See Roger Langham Brown, *Wilhelm von Humboldt's Conception of Linguistic Relativity* (1967); Kurt Muller-Vollmer, *Poesie und Einbildungskraft* (1967); Richey A. Novak, *Wilhelm von Humboldt as a Literary Critic* (1972); and Martin L. Manchester, *The Philosophical Foundations of Humboldt's Linguistic Doctrines* (1985).

From

Collected Works

From

The Eighteenth Century (1796–97)

All words designating moral qualities can accord only to a certain degree, never wholly, with the things which they designate. Like all words, in fact, they express only concepts, with their relatively firm and definite boundaries, since the things for which the words stand, due to the indissoluble interrelationship of all parts of the moral universe, flow over one into the other without any boundaries that can be noted. Language helps us out of this embarrassment by subjecting the usage of a word to the dicta of practiced feeling, rather than bothering about exact logical definition. Therefore all such words operate in a double sphere: a logical one, bordered by the defined concept which they designate, and a practical one, determined by custom and usage. The true difference between these two spheres ought to rest on the difference which always exists between the concept of an object produced by reason and the image of it formed by sensation and feeling. These, since we sense and feel more, and more subtly than we think, never coincide. The factual difference, however, in most languages rests much more on accident and prejudice. One need only compare the extent of actual usage with the extent of the best and subtlest definitions of such words as "wit," for example, or "delicacy" or "rapture," to convince oneself that one is frequently much greater and just as frequently much smaller than the other.

That is why the beginner in any language expresses himself so unidiomatically without actually making mistakes; that is why the number of synonyms always decreases with the degree of linguistic development; and that is why the linguist always recognizes more of the latter than does the finest, most cultivated author. Now if a word is newly formed, or its meaning freshly defined, then it occupies at first only the logical sphere which coincides with the concept for which it was meant. It therefore presents itself only to our understanding, leaving our imagination and our feelings untouched. . . . This is why neologisms, made in great numbers and intentionally, are advisable only in the completely speculative or technical sciences where only pure rational concepts are dealt with, not real things, or where it suffices to differentiate things by certain singled-out characteristics alone. But in the field of practical philosophy, where everything depends on not merely thinking the moral objects given in experience but on representing them in their total natural endowment, one must avail oneself of the help of neologisms much more sparingly and cautiously. Else one runs the danger of taking all the spirit and all the fruitfulness out of one's line of reasoning. [II, 73–75]

From

Essay on Aesthetics (1797–98)

The realm of imagination is directly opposed to the realm of reality, and equally opposed is the character of whatever belongs to one of these realms to anything within the other. Part and parcel of the concept of reality is the segregation of each individual phenomenon; none stands in causal relationship to any other. . . . As soon as one walks over to the realm of possibilities, on the other hand, nothing exists except in a state of dependency upon everything else. Everything, in fact, which cannot be thought of as other than in a condition of inner interaction *is ideal* in the simplest and strictest sense of the word. For it is wholly opposed to reality. [II, 128]

However incomprehensible the art process, however certainly there is something which the artist himself does not understand and the critic can never utter, this much is known: the artist begins by transforming something real into an image. But he soon finds out that this cannot be done except by a sort of living communication, by somehow letting an electric spark of his imagination leap over to the imagination of others, and this not directly but through the mediation of an object into which he breathes his own living soul.

This is the only way open to the artist. And without in any way wanting it, but just by fulfilling his calling and leaving the execution of his task to his imagination, he lifts nature over the boundaries of reality and leads her into the land of ideas, recreating her individuals as ideals. [II, 132]

The concept of ideality, as being something which lies above reality, is reminiscent of the rule that art is imitation of nature, a rule which for a long time we have commanded the artist to follow. It has even been considered a good definition of art itself. It does contain the two main concepts of art, namely reality (here called nature) and imitation (that which does not permit a total identity with its model). But it contains a vagueness or looseness which can be avoided only by the realization (hitherto not often felt) that the essence of

---

COLLECTED WORKS. The following selections from the *Gesammelte Schriften* of von Humboldt are reprinted from Marian Cowan, ed. and tr., *Humanist Without Portfolio: An Anthology of the Writings of Wilhelm von Humboldt*, Detroit: Wayne State University Press, 1963. Reprinted by permission.

art does not lie in the nature of its objects but in the mood of the imagination. . . . Since the artist makes nature (by which we mean everything that can have reality for us) into an object of the imagination, we may call art *the objectification of nature by the imagination.* [II, 132 f.]

If we survey the path that a poet (and every artist) takes, we are overwhelmed by the realization with what a simple aim he starts and what incomprehensible heights he reaches as he executes that aim.

He starts by turning a real object, almost playfully, into an imaginative one, and ends with the greatest and most difficult task which gives to human beings their ultimate meaning: to relate himself intimately to the whole external world and this to him; to accept the world at first like a foreign object but then, in his own fashion and with the organs at his individual disposal, to return it to itself, free and organized.

For all the materials of his observation are organized by him into an ideal form for the imagination. The world around him appears to him like a completely individual, living, harmonious, nowhere restricted or dependent, self-sufficient totality of manifold forms. Thus has he transferred his own inmost and best nature to it, turning it into a creation with which he can then completely sympathize. [II, 142]

From
Catium and Hellas (1806)

The least advantageous influence on any sort of interesting treatment of linguistic studies is exerted by the narrow notion that language originated as a convention and that words are nothing but signs for things or concepts which are independent of them. This view up to a point is certainly correct but beyond this point it is deadly because as soon as it begins to predominate it kills all mental activity and exiles all life. To it we owe the constantly reiterated commonplaces that linguistic study is necessary only for external purposes or for the discipline of as yet unpracticed mentalities; that the best method for learning a language is the one that leads most quickly to the mechanical, automatic understanding and use of it; that any language, if one only knows it well, is about as useful as any other; that it would be best if all nations could agree on the use of a single one—and whatever other prejudices of this sort there are.

A more careful examination demonstrates precisely the opposite of all these notions.

Naturally, a word is a sign insofar as it is used to stand for a thing or a concept, but in its particular past development and its particular effectiveness it is a particular and independent creature—an individual. The sum of all words—

language—is a universe which lies midway between the external, phenomenal one and our own inwardly active one. Naturally it is based upon convention, insofar as all the members of a linguistic group understand one another, but the individual words were first formed out of the natural feeling of the speaker and understood by the similar natural feeling of the hearer. Hence, linguistic study teaches, in addition to the use of a particular language, the analogical relation between man and the world in general, and each individual nation in particular, which is expressed by language. And since the spirit which constantly reveals itself in the world can never be exhaustively known through any given number of views or opinions, but is always discovered to contain something new, it would be far better to multiply the languages on earth as many times as the number of earth's inhabitants might permit. [III, 167 f.]

As little as a word is an image of the thing which it designates, so little is it a mere intimation that this thing is supposed to be thought by reason or represented in imagination. It is differentiated from an image by the possibility inherent in it and in us to imagine the thing according to the most various points of view and in the most various ways; it is different from a mere intimation in that it has its own definite, sensuous form. If you utter the word *Wolke* (cloud) you neither think of its definition nor do you see a single definite image of the natural phenomenon. All its different concepts and images, all the sensations and feelings which have been joined to its perception, everything—finally—which is related in some fashion to it, within us or without us: all these may represent themselves to the mind simultaneously and yet run no danger of confusion because the single sound of the word fastens and secures them. But the sound does even more: it brings back sometimes this, sometimes that association and if, as in the case of *Wolke,* the associative material is rich in itself (*Woge* billow, *Welle* wave, *wälzen* rolling, *Wind* wind, *wehen* blowing, *Wald* woods, etc.) then the sound of the word attunes the soul in a manner befitting the object, partly through itself, partly through recollection and associative analogies. Thus a word reveals itself as an individual with a nature of its own which bears resemblance to an object of art in that, with a sensuous form borrowed from nature, it makes possible an idea which is beyond all nature. Here however the resemblance stops, since the differences leap to the eye. For this idea which lies beyond all nature is precisely that which alone renders the objects in the world capable of being used as materials for thinking and feeling. It is the lack of definition of objects which ever and again provides new transitions to other objects (since that which is each time represented or imagined need neither be completely filled in as to detail, nor preserved); the lack of definition without which the independent action of thought would be impossible—and the sensuous vividness which is a result of the spiritual energy that is expended when a language is used. Thinking never treats of an object as isolated and never uses the sum total of its reality. It always skims off its surface relationships, conditions, points of view, and combines these. But a word is by no means merely an empty substratum into which certain details may be placed, but it is a sensuous form which by its incisive simplicity spontaneously indicates that the expressed object, too, should be represented only according to the needs of thought, and, by its origin in an independent psychic act, reorders the merely perceptive psychic capacities back into their boundaries. Moreover, by its capacity for change and its analogic relationship to other linguistic elements, it prepares the connectedness which thinking tries to find out in the world and bring out in its own products. (Finally, by its transitoriness it bids us tarry at no point but hurry on to whatever end itself and all the other words are tending.) In all these respects, the kind of sensuous form a word has . . . is in no way a matter of indifference, and it may be justly asserted that even when words of different languages designate the same, completely sensuous, object, they are by no means perfect synonyms. Whoever utters *hippos, equus,* or *Pferd,* by no means says completely the same thing three times. [III, 169 f.]

From

Introduction to General Linguistics (1810–11)

Every language sets certain limits to the spirit of those who speak it; it assumes a certain direction and, by doing so, excludes many others. [VII, 621]

From

Announcement of an Essay on the Language and Nation of the Basques (1812)

Language everywhere mediates, first between infinite and finite nature, then between one individual and another. Simultaneously and through the same act it makes union possible and itself originates from it. The whole of its nature never lies in singularity but must always simultaneously be guessed or intuited from otherness. But neither can it be fully explained from oneness and otherness together; it simply is (like everything in the presence of which true mediation oc-

curs) something individuated, unique, incomprehensible. It is something which is given by the idea of union, of the reconciliation of what for us and our way of thinking must always be opposites, and it is a something which is given only in this connection. Linguistic study—which must, in order to avoid becoming chimerical, always begin with the totally dry, pedantic, in fact mechanical analysis of the corporeal, constructible elements of language—thus leads to the depths of humanity. Only one must free oneself of the notions that language can be separated from that which it designates as, for example, the name of a person from the person, and that it is a product of reflection and agreement, an agreed-upon code, as it were, or in fact that it is any work of man at all (in the common sense in which one takes that phrase), not to mention the work of some individual. A true, inexplicable miracle, it breaks loose from the mouth of a nation, and—no less marvellous, though seen by us every day with indifference—it breaks daily through the gurgle of any baby. It is the brightest trace and the surest proof of the fact (leaving out for the moment the celestial relatives of mankind) that man does not possess an absolute, segregated individuality, that "I" and "Thou" are not merely interrelated but—if one could go back to the point of their separation—truly identical concepts, and that there exist, therefore, only concentric circles of individuality, beginning with the weak, frail single person who is in need of support and widening out to the primordial trunk of humanity itself. Otherwise all understanding would be impossible into all eternity. [III, 296–97]

From

On Comparative Linguistics (1820)

Language, I am fully convinced, must be looked upon as being an immediate given in mankind. Taken as a work of man's reason, undertaken in clarity of consciousness, it is wholly inexplicable. Nor does it help to supply man with millennia upon millennia for the "invention" of language. Language could not be invented or come upon if its archetype were not already present in the human mind. For man to understand but a single word truly, not as a mere sensuous stimulus (such as an animal understands a command or the sound of the whip) but as an articulated sound designating a concept, all language, in all its connections, must already lie prepared within him. There are no single, separate facts of language. Each of its elements announces itself as part of a whole. As natural as the supposition of the gradual development of languages is, yet the "invention" of language could only happen all at once. Man is man only through language; to invent language, he would have to be man already. As soon as one imagines that it happened gradually . . . , that by means of a bit more invented language, man became more human, and being more human, thus was enabled to invent a little more language, one fails to recognize the indivisibility of human consciousness and human speech, and the nature of the intellectual act which is necessary to comprehend but a single word, but which then suffices to comprehend all of language.

Naturally this does not mean that one is to think of language as a given that is complete and finished, for then one could not comprehend how a man could understand or use any single given language. It necessarily grows out of an individual, gradually growing up with him, but in such a way that its organization does not lie, like an inert mass, in the dark of a man's soul till it is brought forth, but instead that its laws condition the functions of thought. Thus the very first word gives the hint of and presupposes the whole rest of the language. If one seeks an analogy for this—and there is really nothing comparable to it in the whole realm of the mind—one might remember the natural instincts of animals and call language an intellectual instinct of the mind. [IV, 14 f.]

Thinking is not merely dependent on language in general but, up to a certain degree, on each specific language. People have wished, to be sure, to replace the words of the various languages by universally valid signs, as lines, numbers and algebraic symbols serve in mathematics. But only a tiny part of that which is thinkable can be designated that way, because such symbols by their very nature fit only those concepts which can be produced by mere synthetic construction or are otherwise formed by rationality alone. But where the raw materials of inner perception and sensation are to be imprinted with conceptualization, everything depends on the individual way of looking at things of an individual human being whose language is an inseparable part of him. All attempts to cancel out the many unique signs for eye and ear and replace them with a few general ones are but methods of abbreviated translation. It would be folly and delusion to imagine that such methods might transport one beyond the circumscribed limits of one's own language—not to mention all language. Of course a central point at which languages might meet may be sought for, and even found, and it is necessary when doing comparative studies of language (grammatical as well as lexical) to keep one's eye directed toward such a center. For . . . there is a number of things which can be determined and defined a priori and hence separated from all conditionalities of a given language. But on the other hand, there is a far greater number of concepts, and grammatical peculiarities as well, which are woven so indissolubly into the individuality of their language that they can neither be held by a thread of inner perception as hovering above all languages, nor translated from one language into another. A most significant part of the content of each language stands in a relation of such undoubted dependency on

it that its specific utterance cannot be a matter of no consequence. [IV, 21 ff.]

The mutual interdependence of thought and word illuminates clearly the truth that languages are not really means for representing already known truths but are rather instruments for discovering previously unrecognized ones. The differences between languages are not those of sounds and signs but those of differing world views. Herein is contained the reason for and the final aim of all linguistic study. The sum of the knowable, that soil which the human spirit must till, lies between all the languages and independent of them, at their center. But man cannot approach this purely objective realm other than through his own modes of cognition and feeling, in other words: subjectively. Just where study and research touch the highest and deepest point, just there does the mechanical, logical use of reason—whatever in us can most easily be separated from our uniqueness as individual human beings—find itself at the end of its rope. From here on we need a process of inner perception and creation. And all that we can plainly know about this is its result, namely, that objective truth always rises from the entire energy of subjective individuality. [IV, 27]

In no two languages do we find completely equivalent words designating incorporeal objects; we find words whose meaning is related, to be sure, but none whose is the same. . . . An extremely interesting demonstration of this might be given in connection with *psyche, anima, âme, alma, Seele, soul,* etc. . . . Such comparison can usually be made only between languages that have a literature. To make such studies would demand profound absorption in each language considered, and yet all language is so rich and fruitful in its eternal youthfulness, its eternal mobility, that the true sense, the sum total of all the connotations of such a word taken as a totality, could never be defined or completed, never be designated in all its grandeur. Time subtracts from it, changes it, adds to it; words grow richer or poorer in content; they are construed sometimes sharply, sometimes loosely. In language, the creative archetypal energies of humanity are active—that deep reservoir of capacity in us whose existence and nature, can neither be understood nor denied. [IV, 248 f.]

From

On the National Characteristics of Languages (1822)

Man thinks, feels, and lives within language alone and must be formed by it, in order—to mention only one aspect—to understand art, which by no means acts through language. But he senses and knows that language is only a means for him; that there is an invisible realm outside it in which he seeks to feel at home and that it is for this reason that he needs the aid of language. The most commonplace observation and the profoundest thought, both lament the inadequacy of language. Both look upon that other realm as a distant country toward which only language leads—and *it* never really. All higher forms of speech are a wrestling with this thought, in which sometimes our power, sometimes our longing, is more keenly felt. [IV, 432]

From

Basic Characteristics of Linguistic Types (1824–26)

In the nature of tone as such lies the true individuality of each language. Whatever one may do or try to do in order to describe the peculiarity of a language, all one succeeds in defining ever more closely is the genre to which it belongs. As *this* language, however, and no other, it expresses itself only before the listening ear. Although the alphabet of the whole human race is enclosed by certain not even very wide limits, each people with a language of their own have their own tonal system which excludes certain tones altogether, demonstrates strong preference for others, uses different ones to designate different classes of concepts, treats tone combinations in certain ways, etc. One may compare this with the various screeches and tonal varieties of the various animal species. [V, 379]

No one when he uses a word has in mind exactly the same thing that another has, and the difference, however tiny, sends its tremors throughout language, if one may compare language with the most volatile element. With each thought, each feeling, this difference returns, thanks to the element of unvarying identity in individuality, and finally forms a mass of elements which singly went unnoticed. All understanding, therefore, is always at the same time a misunderstanding—this being a truth which it is most useful to know in practical life—and all agreement of feelings and thoughts is at the same time a means for growing apart. [V, 396]

From

On the Episode from the *Mahabharata* known as the *Bhagavad-Gita II* (1826)

Linguistic usage in everyday life must of course be different from linguistic usage in inward life, representing ideas and feelings, since the speaker in either case partakes of a wholly different mood. For the sharper and purer a thought hovers before his mind, the less it can be endured if the form of speech in which it will be cast is inappropriate. This is the origin of prose—and one should not call everything prose which is not verse. For their fields diverge only where careful attention is given to the form of presentation. The only true view of prose is that it is derived from poetry which always comes first when any language is treated as an art form. For rhythm is the lifeblood of prose as well, and it is not even free of meter, being rather an extension of the narrowly binding meter of poetry. The characteristic difference between poetry and prose, however, is that prose declares by its form that it wishes to accompany and serve thought. Poetry cannot do without at least appearing to control thought or actually bringing it forth. [V, 343]

From

On the Differences in Human Linguistic Structure (1830–35)

In thinking, a subjective activity forms itself an object. For no type of imaginative representation may be considered a merely receptive apperception of an already existent object. The activity of the senses must be synthetically joined with the inner action of the spirit. From their connection the imaginative representation tears itself loose, becomes objective in relation to the subjective energy, and then returns to it, having first been perceived in its new, objective form. For this process language is indispensable. For while the spiritual endeavor expresses itself through the lips, its products return through the very ears of the speaker. The representation is therefore truly transformed into actual objectivity without therefore being withdrawn from subjectivity. Only language can accomplish this, and without this constant transformation and retransformation in which language plays the decisive part even in silence, no conceptualization and therefore no true thinking is possible. Without reference, therefore, to the communication between persons, the act of speaking is a necessary condition of thinking even in a single individual in complete solitude. So far as actual reality is concerned, of course, language develops only socially and man understands himself only by having tested the understandability of his words on others. For the objectivity is intensified when the word which one has formed oneself re-echoes from someone else's mouth. And yet nothing is robbed from the simultaneous subjectivity because every human being feels humanly allied to other human beings; it is, in fact, likewise intensified since the representation now transformed into language no longer belongs exclusively to a single subject. By being imparted to others, it joins the collectivity of the entire human race, of which each individual carries a single modification which longs for the wholeness which can only come through the others. The greater and more varied the social operations on language, the more it gains, other conditions being equal. What makes language necessary in the simple act of thought production, is repeated over and over in man's spiritual life; social communication through language affords man conviction and stimulation. The thinking function requires something like itself and yet separated from itself. It is kindled by the sameness; the separateness gives it a touchstone for the validity of its inner products. Although the epistemological ground for truth, for absolute permanence, can only lie within the human being, his spiritual efforts to attain it are ever accompanied by the danger of delusion. Immediately feeling as he does only his ephemerality and his limitations, man must actually look upon this epistemological ground as something lying outside himself. And one of the most powerful means for drawing near it, for measuring its distance from himself, is social communion with others. All speech, beginning with the simplest, is a relating of that which is separately sensed and felt to the common nature of mankind.

It is no different so far as understanding is concerned. It is present in the psyche only by its own activity. Understanding and speaking are but different operations of the same linguistic capacity. Communal speech is never to be compared with the handing on of a given material. The materials of speech must be developed by the intrinsic capacity of listener as well as speaker; what the listener receives is only the stimulus that attunes him harmoniously to the other. It is very natural for human beings to give out immediately with what they have just heard. Thus the whole of language lies within each human being, which only means that each of us contains a striving, regulated by a definitely modified capacity, which both stimulates and restricts, gradually to produce the entire language, as inner or outer demands dictate, and to understand it as it is produced by others.

Understanding as we have just discussed it, however, could not rest upon inner spontaneous activity, and communal speaking would have to be something other than merely mutual awakening of the linguistic capacity of the listeners, if human nature did not lie in the diversity of its individuals, split off from the basic unity of nature, as they are. The comprehension of words is something quite different from the understanding of unarticulated sounds, and comprises a great deal more than the mere mutual evocation of sounds and the objects they signify. Words, to be sure, may also be taken as indivisible wholes, just as in writing one sometimes recog-

nizes the sense of a word group without as yet being certain of its alphabetical composition. It is possible that the child's psyche operates like that when it first begins to understand. But just as not merely the sensory understanding which we share with animals but also the specific human linguistic capacity is stimulated (and it is far more probable that even in an infant there is no moment when this does not hold true, in however small a degree), so the word, too, is perceived as articulated. Now that which is added to the mere evocation of a word's significance by the articulation is that it presents it directly through its form as part of an infinite whole—that of a language. For it is a language that gives us the possibility, even if we know only individual words of it, to form from its elements a truly unlimited number of other words, in accordance with feelings and rules which define them, and thereby to create a relationship among concepts. But our psyche would lack all comprehension of this artful mechanism, it would comprehend articulation no better than a blind man color, if it did not contain an intrinsic capacity to realize that latent possibility. For language simply cannot be looked upon as though it were a collection of materials lying visible and gradually communicable before us, but must be considered forever in process, where the laws of generation are constant but the extent and in a sense even the kind of product remain wholly indefinite. When infants learn to speak, the process cannot be described in terms of the simple addition of words of vocabulary, their retention in memory, and the subsequent attempts at repetitive babbling, but only as a growth of the child's linguistic capacity, judged by age and practice. What has been heard does more than merely communicate itself; it imparts skill to understand more easily what hasn't yet been heard; it casts sudden light upon what was heard long ago but not understood at the time; it sharpens the urge and the capacity to draw more and more of what is heard into memory and to let less and less of it roll by as mere sound. Progress in linguistic capacity is therefore not measurable in even advances, as is progress in—say—vocabulary learning ... but is constantly intensified and stepped up by the mutual interaction of the material and the child's ability to handle it. A further proof that children do not mechanically learn their native language but undergo a development of linguistic capacity is afforded by the fact that all children, in the most different imaginable circumstances of life, learn to speak within a fairly narrow and definite time span, just as they develop all their main capacities at certain definite growth stages. But how could the listener master the spoken word just by the developmental process of a separate isolated capacity growing in him if there did not underlie speaker and listener alike the same nature, merely divided into mutually corresponding individuality, so that a signal as subtle but as profoundly rooted in nature as is articulated sound is sufficient to stimulate both and mediate a harmony between them!

An objection to this argument might be found by pointing out that if children are transplanted before they learn their native tongue, they develop their linguistic capacity in the foreign one. This undeniable fact, it might be said, clearly shows that language is the mere reproduction of what is heard, depending entirely on social intercourse without consideration of the unity or diversity of the people involved. In the first place, however, it has by no means been determined by exact tests that the inclination toward such children's native speech did not have to be overcome at some cost to the finest nuances of skill in the adopted language. But even disregarding this possibility, the most natural explanation is simply that human beings are everywhere human and the development of linguistic capacity may therefore take place with the aid of any given individual. That doesn't mean that it comes any less from the individual's innate nature; only, since it always needs outer stimulus as well, it must become analogous to whatever stimulus it receives. This it can do, since all human languages are interrelated in some sense. Nonetheless the binding force of closely related origins is plain enough to behold in the division of nations. Nor is it difficult to understand, since national origins are so predominantly powerful in their effect on individuality, and the various languages so intimately related with these origins. If language were not truly connected through its origins in the depths of human nature with even the physical hereditary processes, how then could one's native tongue have so much power and intimacy for the ear of the uneducated and educated alike, that after a long separation from it it greets one like the sound of magic and creates deep yearning for itself during one's separation from it? This obviously is not a matter of the spiritual content of any language, of its expressed thoughts or feelings, but of the most inexplicable and individual element in it: the sound. When we hear the sound of our native tongue it is as though we heard a part of our self.

And even when we consider the products of language, the notion that it consists but of the designation of perceived objects is not confirmed. With this function alone, the profound and full contents of language can never be exhausted. Just as no concept is possible without language, so no object is possible without it for the psyche, since even external ones receive their intrinsic substance only through language. But the entire method of subjective perception of objects goes necessarily into the development and use of language. For words are born of the subjective perceptions of objects; they are not a copy of the object itself but of the image of it produced in the psyche by its perception. And since subjectivity is unavoidably mingled with all objective perception, one may—quite independently of language—look upon each human individuality as a singular unique standpoint for a world-view. But it becomes far more so through language, since words when confronted with psyche turn themselves into objects, an intrinsic significance being added to them, and thus produce a new characteristic quality. This, being one which characterizes the sound of speech, presents thoroughgoing analogies within a language, and since the language of a given nation is already characterized by a similar subjectivity, each language therefore contains a characteristic world view. As individual sound mediates between object and person, so the whole of language mediates between human beings and the internal and external nature that affects them. Man surrounds himself by a world of sounds in order to take into himself the world of objects and operate on them. What I am here saying outdistances in no way the simple truth. Man lives with objects mainly, in fact exclusively, since feeling and acting depend on his mental images, as language turns them over to him. The same act which enables him to spin language out of himself enables him to spin himself into language, and each language draws a circle around the people to whom it adheres which it is possible for the individual to escape only by stepping into a different one. The learning of a foreign language should therefore mean the gaining of a new standpoint toward one's world-view, and it does this in fact to a considerable degree, because each language contains the entire conceptual web and mental images of a part of humanity. If it is not always purely felt as such, the reason is only that one so frequently projects one's own world-view, in fact one's own speech habits, onto a foreign language.

One must not think of even the earliest origins of language being limited to a sparse number of words, as one frequently does if one thinks of language not originating in free human sociality, but rather as limited to acts of mutual assistance—a point of view facilitated by the reduction of early humanity to an imaginary status of "children of nature." These notions are among the most erroneous views one could possibly form regarding language. Man is not as helpless as all that, and besides, inarticulated sounds would suffice for the purpose of mere mutual aid in trouble. Language is human even in its very beginnings, and extends broadly without special purposes to all objects of random sensory perception or inner operation. Even (and especially in fact) the languages of so-called savages, who after all should be fairly close to a state of nature as we think of the phrase, show a fullness and diversity of expression which far exceeds simple needs. Words well up from the breast of their own free will, without need or intention, and there doubtless never was a wild wandering horde in any of the earth's desolate places which did not already have its songs. For man, as an animal species, is a singing creature, though one who joins thoughts to the tones.

But language does not merely transplant an undefined number of material elements from nature into the psyche. It also acquaints it with the aspects of form which come to us from the whole complex. Nature unfolds before us a bright many-colored diversity, rich with configurations affecting all our senses, and irradiated by a luminous clarity. Our power of reflection discovers in this richness a regularity or conformity to law which suits our spirit form. Quite apart from the corporeal existence of things there clings to their outlines a magic haze of outward beauty, as though it were made for man's sake alone, in which the conformity to law is wedded to the sensory material in a way which moves and overwhelms us but which we cannot explain. All these things we find again in the analogical echoes of language, for language can represent the state of affairs as we find it. For by entering the world of sound with the aid of language, we do not leave the real world that surrounds us. The conformity to law found in nature is related to that found in linguistic structure, and by stimulating man to perform his loftiest, most human activities, it furthers his understanding of the formal impression that nature makes, since it too cannot be considered other than a development of spiritual energies, however inexplicable. Through the rhythmic and musical form inherent in related sounds, language—affecting yet another human field—heightens the impression of natural beauty in man, but even independent of this, affects the psyche's mood by just the accents of speech.

Language, being the mass of its products, is different from whatever fragment is spoken at a given time. And before we leave this chapter we must tarry awhile at that difference. A language as a whole contains everything transformed by it into sounds. But just as the materials of thought and the infinitude of its connections can never be exhausted, neither can the number of things to be designated and related by language. A language therefore consists of not only its already formed elements but above all of a methodology for continuing the spiritual labor for which it designates the orbits and the forms. The firmly composed elements form a certain kind of dead mass of language, but this mass carries the living germ of never-ending definability. At each given point and in each given epoch, therefore, language just like nature appears to man as an inexhaustible reservoir, in contrast to all he has already thought and known, a reservoir in which his spirit may still discover the unknown, and his inward sensation may still become aware of things not felt this way before. Each time language is used by a truly original

and great genius, that is what happens. And the human race needs for the inspiration of its constantly advancing intellectual efforts and the unfolding of its spiritual lifestuff, the ever open vista beyond what has already been achieved, the assurance that the infinite entanglements yet remaining may gradually be dissolved. But language contains a dark unrevealed depth, as well, and a depth which reaches in two directions. For backwards as well as forwards, it flows out of (or into) an unknown wealth of materials which may be recognized only up to a point and then vanishes from view, leaving the feeling of unfathomable mystery. Language has this infinity, with neither end nor beginning except for a very brief past, in common, so far as our view is concerned, with the whole existence of the human race. But we feel and intuit in language plainly and vividly how even the remote past is related to the feeling of the present, since it has passed through the human sensations of former generations and has retained their living breath. But these same generations are nationally and familially related to us in the same sounds of their native tongue which becomes the expression of our own feelings.

This double aspect of language, partly firm and partly fluid, produces a unique relationship between it and the generations that speak it. They produce within it a depository of words and a system of rules by which it grows in the course of the centuries into an independent power. Our attention was earlier focused on the fact that a thought taken up by language becomes an object for the psyche and thus exerts an effect upon it from the outside. But we have been looking at this object mainly as it has developed from the subject, at the effect, in other words, as emanating from that upon which it reacts. Now we must also look at the process from the opposite point of view, according to which language is truly a foreign object, its effect actually emanating from something quite other than that upon which it reacts. For language must necessarily belong to a twosome and at the same time it is truly the property of the entire human race. Since in writing, too, it holds out slumbering thought to be awakened by the spirit, it builds for itself a unique existence which can only attain validity in any given act of thought, but which in its totality is nonetheless independent of thought. The two contradictory views here suggested—that language is both extrinsic to the psyche and a part of it, that it is both independent from it and dependent on it—pertain to it in reality and make out the individuality of its nature. Nor must we seek to solve the contradiction by saying that language is in part extrinsic and independent, and in part neither. For language is objective and independent to precisely the same degree that it is subjective and dependent. For it has no abiding place anywhere, not even in writing; what we called its dead part must always be newly generated in thought; it must always transfer itself alive into speech or understanding, in other words become wholly transferred to the subject. But this same act of regeneration is what makes it also into an object. To be sure, it experiences the entire operative influence of the human individual, but this same operative influence is bound by what it is and has been. The true solution of the paradox lies in the unity of human nature. Whatever originates with what is one and the same with myself, dissolves the concepts of object and subject, of dependence and independence. Language is mine because I produce it as I do. And because the reason I produce it as I do lies in the speaking and having spoken of all the generations of men, insofar as uninterrupted linguistic communication reaches, it is the language itself that gives me my restrictions. But that which restricts and confines me came into language by human nature of which I am a part, and whatever is strange in language for me is therefore strange only for my individual momentary nature, not for my original, true nature as a human being. [VII, 13–64]

. . .

There are two phenomena of language in which [all the individual aspects of the mutual influences of the character and the language of nations] not only most decisively coincide, but which so reveal the influence of their wholeness that all concepts of particularity disappear from them. These are poetry and prose. We must call them phenomena of language, since even the original structure of a language tends to direct it to one or the other, or, where its form is truly a great one, to the proportionate development of both, and since they in turn react back upon the structure of the language. Truly, however, they are first of all the developmental track of intellectuality itself and must, when its structure is not deficient and its orbit not disturbed, necessarily unwind themselves along it. Poetry and prose therefore require most careful study, not only in relation to each other, but particularly in connection with their relative time of origin.

If we look at both from their most concrete as well as their most ideal side simultaneously, we see that they take separate paths to attain similar goals. For both move from reality toward something which does not belong to reality. Poetry conceives of reality in its sensuous phenomenality, as it is externally and internally perceived by us, but it is unperturbed about whatever makes reality be what it is. In fact poetry specifically rejects anything of a reasoning or causal character. It relates the sensuous phenomena in creative imagination, and guides us through them to a view of an artistically ideal wholeness. Prose looks precisely for the roots of reality which connect it to existence in all the vast network of its connections. It then intellectually combines facts with facts and concepts with concepts, striving for an objective connection of them all within an idea. The difference between poetry and prose as just outlined is drawn only as it expresses itself in their true essence, to be sure. If one looks only at any given piece of poetry or prose as it is actually found in a given language . . . one finds that the inner direction here called prose may be executed in metrical or rhythmic language and that of poetry in unmetrical and arhythmic language, but only at some cost to both. For prose expressed in poetic form has neither the character of poetry nor wholly that of prose, and likewise with poetry disguised as prose. Poetic contents perforce bring about poetic garments, and there are many instances of poets who, feeling this power, have completed in verse something they began in prose.

What both poetry and prose have in common—to return now to their intrinsic nature—is the tension and the comprehensiveness of soul that is necessitated by full penetration of reality coupled with attainment of an ideal relationship of infinite variety, plus the ability to recollect the mind to a consistent pursuit of a once decided upon path. Yet this too must be rightly understood to mean that such a path never excludes its opposite within the spiritual economy of a nation and its language, but actually furthers it as well as itself. Both, the mood of poetry and that of prose, must complement each other to form the communal spirit which permits men to sink their roots deep into reality, keeping always in mind that the deeper the roots, the more joyous the towering into a freer element. The poetry of a people has not reached its summit until by its variety and its free flexibility it announces the possibility of an equivalent development of prose. Since the human spirit, as we conceive of it in strength and freedom, needs to attain both configurations, we know one by the other, just as we can tell from a fragment of sculpture that it once was part of a grouping.

Prose however may be used in another sense as well. It can stop at the mere presentation of facts and at totally external purposes. It may be used for the mere communication of things, rather than the awakening of ideas and feelings. In such a case it does not depart from ordinary speech and never reaches the true heights of what we have been calling prose. Prose in this wider sense then cannot be considered a developmental track of intellectuality; its references are not to form but to matter alone. But wherever prose pursues its higher path it needs, just like poetry, certain special means for reaching deeply into the human psyche. It has to raise itself to that ennobled form of speech of which alone we may speak if we wish to consider it the true mate of poetry. Prose in this intrinsic sense demands a comprehension of its object which requires all the combined capacities of the total psychic constitution. This means a treatment of the object which shows it as radiating toward all the receptive subjects upon which it works. Discriminating rationality is not active by itself; all the other powers of mind aid it, thus forming the point of view properly known as "spirited," "inspired." In such a union of powers, the spirit carries in addition to its work upon a given object, the imprint of its mood over into speech. Language, elevated by the verve of thought, shows forth its advantages but subordinates them to purposes of the whole spirit. It is the moral feeling-life that imparts itself to the language; the soul that shines through the style. In a manner wholly individual and peculiar to itself, there reveals itself in prose, through the subordination and the dialectic of its sentences, the logical eurythmy which corresponds to thought development. This is the internal command which ordinary speech obeys when it becomes elevated by a special purpose. If an author yields too far to it, he produces a mixture of poetry and rhetoric prose. But in "spirited," "inspired" prose, all the details here listed singly act together, thereby sketching out the whole living birth of a thought, the whole process of spirit's wrestling with an object. Wherever permitted, the thought shapes up like a free spontaneous inspiration and performs in the realm of truth what spontaneous beauty performs in the realm of poetry.

From all this we may see that poetry and prose are conditioned by similar general demands. In both there must be an inward and spontaneous verve which lifts and carries the spirit. Man in his whole individuatedness must move with his thought toward both outer and inner world and, understanding particulars, leave to them that form which relates them to the whole. In their directions, however, and their means for achieving their effects, poetry and prose are different and can really never be mingled. In reference to language we should particularly note that poetry's true nature is inseparable from that of music, whereas prose entrusts itself to language alone. [VII, 193 ff.]

John Keats

1795–1821

Many of Keats's letters are astonishing in the wealth of critical speculation packed into a few sentences. Keats thinks of beauty as providing a form of knowledge that cannot be gained by means of ''consecutive reasoning.'' He makes a similar distinction when he opposes the ''life of sensations'' to that of ''thought.'' His position is not that of a sensualist, however. He sees thought as the abstracting mode of distancing and dehumanizing objects. The life of sensations he associates with empathic experience: ''If a sparrow come before my window I take part in its existence and pick about the gravel.'' Poetry breaks down the boundaries erected by ''thought,'' which always divides experience into subject and object. Yet this view does not preclude Keats's associating the experience of art with ''speculation.'' Like Kant and Coleridge, he distinguishes the beautiful from the agreeable or disagreeable: ''The excellence of every art is its intensity, capable of making all disagreeables evaporate.'' *King Lear* is his example. If you have unpleasantness in art there must be ''momentous depth of speculation excited, in which to bury its repulsiveness.''

Since the poem's mode of truth is beauty, the poem cannot be a true vehicle of consecutive reasoning or dogma. The poet must possess ''negative capability.'' He must be able to remain in ''uncertainties, mysteries, doubts, without any irritable reaching after fact and reason.'' His mode of knowledge is not discursive. *Belief* becomes a word irrelevant to criticism because it is associated with discursive thought, not beauty. One of the reasons the poet is or must be freed from belief, in this sense of the term, is that the poem grows like a plant: ''If poetry comes not as naturally as the leaves to a tree it had better not come at all.'' The poem's integrity is internal, not externally imposed by some code of belief. The metaphor by which this idea is expressed is the characteristically Romantic one of organicism.

Keats's complete works are available in the edition by H. B. Forman (5 vols., 1900–01). The letters have been edited by M. B. Forman, rev. ed. (1952), and by H. E. Rollins (2 vols., 1958). Studies of Keats include C. D. Thorpe, *The Mind of John Keats* (1926); C. L. Finney, *The Evolution of Keats's Poetry* (1936); W. J. Bate, *Negative Capability* (1939); J. R. Caldwell, *John Keats' Fancy* (1945); Earl Wasserman, *The Finer Tone* (1953); W. J. Bate, *John Keats* (1963); Walter Evert, *Aesthetics and Myth in the Poetry of Keats* (1965); Douglas Bush, *John Keats* (1966); Stuart M. Sperry, *Keats the Poet* (1973); Stuart Ende, *Keats and the Sublime* (1976); and Ronald Sharp, *Keats, Skepticism, and the Religion of Beauty* (1979).

From

Letter to Benjamin Bailey

November 22, 1817

I am certain of nothing but of the holiness of the heart's affections and the truth of imagination—What the imagination seizes as beauty must be truth[1]—whether it existed before or not—for I have the same idea of all our passions as of love they are all in their sublime, creative of essential beauty—in a word, you may know my favorite speculation by my first book and the little song I sent in my last—which is a representation from the fancy of the probable mode of operating in these matters—The imagination may be compared to Adam's dream[2]—he awoke and found it truth. I am the more zealous in this affair, because I have never yet been able to perceive how any thing can be known for truth by consecutive reasoning—and yet it must be—Can it be that even the greatest philosopher ever arrived at his goal without putting aside numerous objections—However it may be, O for a life of sensations rather than of thoughts! It is "a vision in the form of youth" a shadow of reality to come—and this consideration has further convinced me for it has come as auxiliary to another favorite speculation of mine, that we shall enjoy ourselves hereafter by having what we called happiness on earth repeated in a finer tone and so repeated—And yet such a fate can only befall those who delight in sensation rather than hunger as you do after truth—Adam's dream will do here and seems to be a conviction that imagination and its empyreal reflection is the same as human life and its spiritual repetition. But as I was saying—the simple imaginative mind may have its rewards in the repetition of its own silent working coming continually on the spirit with a fine suddenness—to compare great things with small—have you never by being surprised with an old melody—in a delicious place—by a delicious voice, felt over again your very speculations and surmises at the time it first operated on your soul—do you not remember forming to yourself the singer's face more beautiful than it was possible and yet with the elevation of the moment you did not think so—even then you were mounted on the wings of imagination so high—that the prototype must be hereafter—that delicious face you will see—What a time! I am continually running away from the subject—sure this cannot be exactly the case with a complex mind—one that is imaginative and at the same time careful of its fruits—who would exist partly on sensation partly on thought—to whom it is necessary that years should bring the philosophic mind—such a one I consider yours and therefore it is necessary to your eternal happiness that you not only drink this old wine of heaven which I shall call the redigestion of our most ethereal musings on earth; but also increase in knowledge and know all things. I am glad to hear you are in a fair way for Easter—you will soon get through your unpleasant reading and then!—but the world is full of troubles and I have not much reason to think myself pestered with many—I think Jane or Marianne[3] has a better opinion of me than I deserve—for really and truly I do not think my brother's illness connected with mine—you know more of the real cause than they do—nor have I any chance of being racked as you have been—you perhaps at one time thought there was such a thing as worldly happiness to be arrived at, at certain periods of time marked out—you have of necessity from your disposition been thus led away—I scarcely remember counting upon any happiness—I look not for it if it be not in the present hour—nothing startles me beyond the moment. The setting sun will always set me to rights—or if a sparrow come before my window I take part in its existence and pick about the gravel. The first thing that strikes me on hearing a misfortune having befalled another is this, "Well it cannot be helped. He will have the pleasure of trying the resources of his spirit." And I beg now, my dear Bailey, that hereafter should you observe anything cold in me not to put it to the account of heartlessness but abstraction—for I assure you I sometimes feel not the influence of a passion or affection during a whole week—and so long this sometimes continues I begin to suspect myself and the genuineness of my feelings at other times—thinking them a few barren tragedy tears.

LETTERS. Keats's letters have been published in several editions, the most complete and trustworthy of which is that by H. E. Rollins. The text is reprinted by permission of the publishers, from Hyder Edward Rollins, ed., *The Letters of John Keats, 1814–1821*, Volume 1. Cambridge, Mass.: Harvard University Press. Copyright 1958 by the President and Fellows of Harvard College.

[1]This statement recalls the final stanza of Keats's *Ode on a Grecian Urn*.
[2]*Paradise Lost*, VIII. 460–90.

[3]Sisters of J. H. Reynolds, a friend of Keats's.

From

Letter to George and Thomas Keats

December 21, 1817

I spent Friday evening with Wells and went next morning to see *Death on the Pale Horse*. It is a wonderful picture, when West's age is considered; but there is nothing to be intense upon; no women one feels mad to kiss, no face swelling into reality. The excellence of every art is its intensity, capable of making all disagreeables evaporate, from their being in close relationship with beauty and truth—Examine *King Lear* and you will find this exemplified throughout; but in this picture we have unpleasantness without any momentous depth of speculation excited, in which to bury its repulsiveness. . . . I had not a dispute but a disquisition with Dilke, on various subjects; several things dovetailed in my mind, and at once it struck me what quality went to form a man of achievement especially in literature and which Shakespeare possessed so enormously—I mean *negative capability,* that is when a man is capable of being in uncertainties, mysteries, doubts, without any irritable reaching after fact and reason—Coleridge, for instance, would let go by a fine isolated verisimilitude caught from the penetralium of mystery, from being incapable of remaining content with half-knowledge. This pursued through volumes would perhaps take us not further than this, that with a great poet the sense of beauty overcomes every other consideration, or rather obliterates all consideration.

From

Letter to John Taylor

February 27, 1818

In poetry I have a few axioms, and you will see how far I am from their center. First, I think poetry should surprise by a fine excess and not by singularity—it should strike the reader as a wording of his own highest thoughts and appear almost a remembrance—Second, its touches of beauty should never be halfway thereby making the reader breathless instead of content: the rise, the progress, the setting of imagery should like the sun come natural to him—shine over him and set soberly although in magnificence, leaving him in the luxury of twilight—but it is easier to think what poetry should be than to write it—and this leads me on to another axiom. That if poetry comes not as naturally as the leaves to a tree it had better not come at all.

From

Letter to Richard Woodhouse

October 27, 1818

As to the poetical Character itself (I mean that sort of which, if I am any thing, I am a Member; that sort distinguished from the wordsworthian or egotistical sublime; which is a thing per se and stands alone) it is not itself—it has no self— it is every thing and nothing—It has no character—it enjoys light and shade; it lives in gusto, be it foul or fair, high or low, rich or poor, mean or elevated—It has as much delight in conceiving an Iago as an Imogen. What shocks the virtuous philosopher, delights the camelion Poet. It does no harm from its relish of the dark side of things any more than from its taste for the bright one; because they both end in speculation. A Poet is the most unpoetical of any thing in existence; because he has no Identity—he is continually in for—[1] and filling some other Body—The Sun, the Moon, the Sea and Men and Women who are creatures of impulse are poetical and have about them an unchangeable attribute—the poet has none; no identity—he is certainly the most unpoetical of all God's Creatures. If then he has no self, and if I am a Poet, where is the Wonder that I should say I would write no more? Might I not at that very instant have been cogitating on the Characters of Saturn and Ops? It is a wretched thing to confess; but is a very fact that not one word I ever utter can be taken for granted as an opinion growing out of my identical nature—how can it, when I have no nature?

---

[1]Perhaps short for ''informing.''

Arthur Schopenhauer

1788–1860

Schopenhauer's aesthetic forms a part of his philosophical system and is discussed in his major work, *The World as Will and Idea.* Insofar as he posits a reality that the senses cannot apprehend, he is Platonic. But he is Kantian in holding that the intellect provides knowledge at the same time that its own schematization shuts us off from an apprehension of "things in themselves." We assume on the basis of the "principle of sufficient reason" a rationality in things and events. In accordance with this principle and its laws our minds construct the concept of the world as idea or representation. But the world so constructed is only the world of appearance or phenomena. In thinking of the world in this way we objectify our own selves and commit them and all our experience to the principle of sufficient reason.

There is, however, another aspect of the world—the world of will—which can be known directly only if we manage to release ourselves from the principle of sufficient reason through aesthetic experiences. The body is a manifestation of the will. Indeed, all phenomena manifest or represent will. We can be aware of will rationally only in its manifestations and therefore in its impurity. When the mind is released from the principle of sufficient reason, the particulars of a work of art take on a transcendent universality, and the mind achieves a kind of freedom, confronting pure will, which is Schopenhauer's version of the Platonic idea. But Schopenhauer's Platonism does not lead to the assumption that a work of art presents an abstract idea in particular images. The artist frees the image from idea or representation and offers it in its pure self-sufficiency, that is, separated from the "relations" by which we define it.

Aesthetic freedom, however, is fleeting. Man always returns from aesthetic experience to the area of human conflict, where the various manifestations of the will endlessly strive against each other. Schopenhauer's aesthetic is thus to be compared with both Plato's and Kant's. It may also be profitably studied in relation to Schiller's theory of play and to Hegel's system. Schopenhauer's theory of the beautiful and the sublime, comparable in some ways to theories of Burke and Kant, is more sophisticated than theirs. It supposes the existence of a psychical distance in sublime experiences that exists in spite of the overpowering imaginative force of the object itself.

The World as Will and Idea has been translated by R. B. Haldane and John Kemp (1883). *The Art of Literature* has been translated by T. B. Saunders (1960). See also William Caldwell, *Schopenhauer's System in Its Philosophical Significance* (1896); Thomas Whittaker, *Schopenhauer* (1909); André Fauconnet, *L'Esthétique de Schopenhauer* (1913); F. S. Coppleston, S.J., *Arthur Schopenhauer, Philosopher of Pessimism* (1946), especially Chapters 5 and 6; Patrick Gardiner, *Schopenhauer* (1963), especially Chapter 5; D. W. Hamlyn, *Schopenhauer* (1980); Bryan Magee, *The Philosophy of Schopenhauer* (1983); and Christopher Janaway, *Self and World in Schopenhauer's Philosophy* (1989).

The World as Will and Idea

From

Book III

History follows the thread of events; it is pragmatic so far as it deduces them in accordance with the law of motivation, a law that determines the self-manifesting will wherever it is enlightened by knowledge. At the lowest grades of its objectivity, where it still acts without knowledge, natural science, in the form of etiology, treats of the laws of the changes of its phenomena, and, in the form of morphology, of what is permanent in them. This almost endless task is lightened by the aid of concepts, which comprehend what is general in order that we may deduce what is particular from it. Lastly, mathematics treats of the mere forms, time and space, in which the ideas, broken up into multiplicity, appear for the knowledge of the subject as individual. All these, of which the common name is science, proceed according to the principle of sufficient reason in its different forms, and their theme is always the phenomenon, its laws, connections, and the relations which result from them. But what kind of knowledge is concerned with that which is outside and independent of all relations, that which alone is really essential to the world, the true content of its phenomena, that which is subject to no change, and therefore is known with equal truth for all time, in a word, the *ideas,* which are the direct and adequate objectivity of the thing in itself, the will? We answer, *art,* the work of genius. It repeats or reproduces the eternal ideas grasped through pure contemplation, the essential and abiding in all the phenomena of the world; and according to what the material is in which it reproduces, it is sculpture or painting, poetry or music. Its one source is the knowledge of ideas; its one aim the communication of this knowledge. While science, following the unresting and inconstant stream of the fourfold forms of reason and consequent, with each end attained sees further, and can never reach a final goal nor attain full satisfaction, any more than by running we can reach the place where the clouds touch the horizon; art, on the contrary, is everywhere at its goal. For it plucks the object of its contemplation out of the stream of the world's course, and has it isolated before it. And this

particular thing, which in that stream was a small perishing part, becomes to art the representative of the whole, an equivalent of the endless multitude in space and time. It therefore pauses at this particular thing; the course of time stops; the relations vanish for it; only the essential, the idea, is its object. We may, therefore, accurately define it as the *way of viewing things independent of the principle of sufficient reason,* in opposition to the way of viewing them which proceeds in accordance with that principle, and which is the method of experience and of science. This last method of considering things may be compared to a line infinitely extended in a horizontal direction, and the former to a vertical line which cuts it at any point. The method of viewing things which proceeds in accordance with the principle of sufficient reason is the rational method, and it alone is valid and of use in practical life and in science. The method which looks away from the content of this principle is the method of genius, which is only valid and of use in art. The first is the method of Aristotle; the second is, on the whole, that of Plato. . . .

Genius, then, consists, according to our explanation, in the capacity for knowing, independently of the principle of sufficient reason, not individual things, which have their existence only in their relations, but the ideas of such things, and of being oneself the correlative of the idea, and thus no longer an individual, but the pure subject of knowledge. Yet this faculty must exist in all men in a smaller and different degree; for if not, they would be just as incapable of enjoying works of art as of producing them; they would have no susceptibility for the beautiful or the sublime; indeed, these words could have no meaning for them. We must therefore assume that there exists in all men this power of knowing the ideas in things, and consequently of transcending their personality for the moment, unless indeed there are some men who are capable of no aesthetic pleasure at all. The man of genius excels ordinary men only by possessing this kind of knowledge in a far higher degree and more continuously. Thus, while under its influence he retains the presence of mind which is necessary to enable him to repeat in a voluntary and intentional work what he has learned in this manner; and this repetition is the work of art. Through this he communicates to others the idea he has grasped. This idea remains unchanged and the same, so that aesthetic pleasure is one and the same whether it is called forth by a work of art or directly by the contemplation of nature and life. The work of art is only a means of facilitating the knowledge in which this pleasure consists. That the idea comes to us more easily from the work of art than directly from nature and the real world, arises from the fact that the artist, who knew only the idea, no longer the actual, has reproduced in his work the

THE WORLD AS WILL AND IDEA. Schopenhauer's *Die Welt als Wille und Vorstellung* was first published in 1819. The text is from *The World as Will and Idea,* by Arthur Schopenhauer, translated by R. B. Haldane and John Kemp, Vol. I (New York: Humanities Press, 1964), and is reprinted by permission of the publisher.

pure idea, has abstracted it from the actual, omitting all disturbing accidents. The artist lets us see the world through his eyes. That he has these eyes, that he knows the inner nature of things apart from all their relations, is the gift of genius, is inborn, but that he is able to lend us this gift, to let us see with his eyes, is acquired, and is the technical side of art. Therefore, after the account which I have given in the preceding pages of the inner nature of aesthetical knowledge in its most general outlines, the following more exact philosophical treatment of the beautiful and the sublime will explain them both, in nature and in art, without separating them further. First of all we shall consider what takes place in a man when he is affected by the beautiful and the sublime; whether he derives this emotion directly from nature, from life, or partakes of it only through the medium of art, does not make any essential, but merely an external, difference.

In the aesthetical mode of contemplation we have found *two inseparable constituent parts*—the knowledge of the object, not as individual thing but as Platonic idea, that is, as the enduring form of this whole species of things; and the self-consciousness of the knowing person, not as individual, but as *pure will-less subject of knowledge.* The condition under which both these constituent parts appear always united was found to be the abandonment of the method of knowing which is bound to the principle of sufficient reason, and which, on the other hand, is the only kind of knowledge that is of value for the service of the will and also for science. Moreover we shall see that the pleasure which is produced by the contemplation of the beautiful arises from these two constituent parts, sometimes more from the one, sometimes more from the other, according to what the object of the aesthetical contemplation may be.

All *willing* arises from want, therefore from deficiency, and therefore from suffering. The satisfaction of a wish ends it; yet for one wish that is satisfied there remain at least ten which are denied. Further, the desire lasts long, the demands are infinite; the satisfaction is short and scantily measured out. But even the final satisfaction is itself only apparent; every satisfied wish at once makes room for a new one; both are illusions; the one is known to be so, the other not yet. No attained object of desire can give lasting satisfaction, but merely a fleeting gratification; it is like the alms thrown to the beggar, that keeps him alive today that his misery may be prolonged till the morrow. Therefore, so long as our consciousness is filled by our will, so long as we are given up to the throng of desires with their constant hopes and fears, so long as we are the subject of willing, we can never have lasting happiness nor peace. It is essentially all the same whether we pursue or flee, fear injury or seek enjoyment; the care for the constant demands of the will, in whatever form it may

be, continually occupies and sways the consciousness; but without peace no true well-being is possible. The subject of willing is thus constantly stretched on the revolving wheel of Ixion, pours water into the sieve of the Danaids, is the ever-longing Tantalus.[1]

But when some external cause or inward disposition lifts us suddenly out of the endless stream of willing, delivers knowledge from the slavery of the will, the attention is no longer directed to the motives of willing, but comprehends things free from their relation to the will, and thus observes them without personal interest, without subjectivity, purely objectively, gives itself entirely up to them so far as they are ideas, but not in so far as they are motives. Then all at once the peace which we were always seeking, but which always fled from us on the former path of the desires, comes to us of its own accord, and it is well with us. It is the painless state which Epicurus prized as the highest good and as the state of the gods; for we are for the moment set free from the miserable striving of the will; we keep the Sabbath of the penal servitude of willing; the wheel of Ixion stands still.

But this is just the state which I described above as necessary for the knowledge of the idea, as pure contemplation, as sinking oneself in perception, losing oneself in the object, forgetting all individuality, surrendering that kind of knowledge which follows the principle of sufficient reason, and comprehends only relations; the state by means of which at once and inseparably the perceived particular thing is raised to the idea of its whole species, and the knowing individual to the pure subject of will-less knowledge, and as such they are both taken out of the stream of time and all other relations. It is then all one whether we see the sun set from the prison or from the palace.

Inward disposition, the predominance of knowing over willing, can produce this state under any circumstances. This is shown by those admirable Dutch artists who directed this purely objective perception to the most insignificant objects, and established a lasting monument of their objectivity and spiritual peace in their pictures of *still life,* which the aesthetic beholder does not look on without emotion; for they present to him the peaceful, still, frame of mind of the artist, free from will, which was needed to contemplate such insignificant things so objectively, to observe them so attentively,

---

[1]Ixion was tied to a spinning wheel in Tartarus by Zeus as a punishment for his attempt to win the love of Hera. Punished for killing their husbands, the Danaids were compelled endlessly to pour water into a vessel full of holes. Tantalus was punished by the presence, just beyond his reach, of objects he desired.

and to repeat this perception so intelligently; and as the picture enables the onlooker to participate in this state, his emotion is often increased by the contrast between it and the unquiet frame of mind, disturbed by vehement willing, in which he finds himself. In the same spirit, landscape painters, and particularly Ruisdael, have often painted very insignificant country scenes, which produce the same effect even more agreeably.

All this is accomplished by the inner power of an artistic nature alone; but that purely objective disposition is facilitated and assisted from without by suitable objects, by the abundance of natural beauty which invites contemplation, and even presses itself upon us. Whenever it discloses itself suddenly to our view, it almost always succeeds in delivering us, though it may be only for a moment, from subjectivity, from the slavery of the will, and in raising us to the state of pure knowing. This is why the man who is tormented by passion, or want, or care, is so suddenly revived, cheered, and restored by a single free glance into nature: the storm of passion, the pressure of desire and fear, and all the miseries of willing are then at once, and in a marvelous manner, calmed and appeased. For at the moment at which, freed from the will, we give ourselves up to pure will-less knowing, we pass into a world from which everything is absent that influenced our will and moved us so violently through it. This freeing of knowledge lifts us as wholly and entirely away from all that, as do sleep and dreams; happiness and unhappiness have disappeared; we are no longer individual; the individual is forgotten; we are only pure subject of knowledge; we are only that *one* eye of the world which looks out from all knowing creatures, but which can become perfectly free from the service of will in man alone. Thus all difference of individuality so entirely disappears, that it is all the same whether the perceiving eye belongs to a mighty king or to a wretched beggar; for neither joy nor complaining can pass that boundary with us. So near us always lies a sphere in which we escape from all our misery; but who has the strength to continue long in it? As soon as any single relation to our will, to our person, even of these objects of our pure contemplation, comes again into consciousness, the magic is at an end; we fall back into the knowledge which is governed by the principle of sufficient reason; we know no longer the idea, but the particular thing, the link of a chain to which we also belong, and we are again abandoned to all our woe. Most men remain almost always at this standpoint because they entirely lack objectivity, i.e., genius. Therefore they have no pleasure in being alone with nature; they need company, or at least a book. For their knowledge remains subject to their will; they seek, therefore, in objects, only some relation to their will, and whenever they see anything that has no such relation, there sounds within them, like a ground bass in music, the constant inconsolable cry, "It is of no use to me"; thus in solitude the most beautiful surroundings have for them a desolate, dark, strange, and hostile appearance.

Lastly, it is this blessedness of will-less perception which casts an enchanting glamor over the past and distant, and presents them to us in so fair a light by means of self-deception. For as we think of days long gone by, days in which we lived in a distant place, it is only the objects which our fancy recalls, not the subject of will, which bore about with it then its incurable sorrows just as it bears them now; but they are forgotten, because since then they have often given place to others. Now, objective perception acts with regard to what is remembered just as it would in what is present, if we let it have influence over us, if we surrendered ourselves to it free from will. Hence it arises that, especially when we are more than ordinarily disturbed by some want, the remembrance of past and distant scenes suddenly flits across our minds like a lost paradise. The fancy recalls only what was objective, not what was individually subjective, and we imagine that the objective stood before us then just as pure and undisturbed by any relation to the will as its image stands in our fancy now; while in reality the relation of the objects to our will gave us pain then just as it does now. We can deliver ourselves from all suffering just as well through present objects as through distant ones whenever we raise ourselves to a purely objective contemplation of them, and so are able to bring about the illusion that only the objects are present and not we ourselves. Then, as the pure subject of knowledge, freed from the miserable self, we become entirely one with these objects, and, for the moment, our wants are as foreign to us as they are to them. The world as idea alone remains, and the world as will has disappeared.

In all these reflections it has been my object to bring out clearly the nature and the scope of the subjective element in aesthetic pleasure; the deliverance of knowledge from the service of the will, the forgetting of self as an individual, and the raising of the consciousness to the pure will-less, timeless, subject of knowledge, independent of all relations. With this subjective side of aesthetic contemplation, there must always appear as its necessary correlative the objective side, the intuitive comprehension of the Platonic idea. But before we turn to the closer consideration of this, and to the achievements of art in relation to it, it is better that we should pause for a little at the subjective side of aesthetic pleasure, in order to complete our treatment of this by explaining the impression of the *sublime* which depends altogether upon it, and arises from a modification of it. After that we shall complete our investigation of aesthetic pleasure by considering its objective side.

. . .

All these reflections are intended to bring out the subjective part of aesthetic pleasure; that is to say, that pleasure so far as it consists simply of delight in perceptive knowledge as such, in opposition to will. And as directly connected with this, there naturally follows the explanation of that disposition or frame of mind which has been called the sense of the *sublime*.

We have already remarked above that the transition to the state of pure perception takes place most easily when the objects bend themselves to it, that is, when by their manifold and yet definite and distinct form they easily become representatives of their ideas, in which beauty, in the objective sense, consists. This quality belongs preeminently to natural beauty, which thus affords even to the most insensible at least a fleeting aesthetic satisfaction: indeed it is so remarkable how especially the vegetable world invites aesthetic observation, and, as it were, presses itself upon it, that one might say, that these advances are connected with the fact that these organisms, unlike the bodies of animals, are not themselves immediate objects of knowledge, and therefore require the assistance of a foreign intelligent individual in order to rise out of the world of blind will and enter the world of idea, and that thus they long, as it were, for this entrance, that they may attain at least indirectly what is denied them directly. But I leave this suggestion which I have hazarded, and which borders perhaps upon extravagance, entirely undecided, for only a very intimate and devoted consideration of nature can raise or justify it.[2] As long as that which raises us from the knowledge of mere relations subject to the will, to aesthetic contemplation, and thereby exalts us to the position of the subject of knowledge free from will, is this fittingness of nature, this significance and distinctness of its forms, on account of which the ideas individualized in them readily present themselves to us; so long is it merely *beauty* that affects us and the sense of the *beautiful* that is excited.

---

[2][Schopenhauer] I am all the more delighted and astonished, forty years after I so timidly and hesitatingly advanced this thought, to discover that it has already been expressed by St. Augustine: *"Arbusta formas suas varias, quibus mundi hujus visibilis structura formosa est, sentiendas sensibus praebent; ut, pro eo quod nosse non possunt, quasi innotescere velle videantur." The City of God,* XI. 27. ["Trees offer their various forms, by which the visible structure of this world is made beautiful to our senses; so that they seem to wish to compensate for their own want of knowledge by providing us with knowledge."]

But if these very objects whose significant forms invite us to pure contemplation, have a hostile relation to the human will in general, as it exhibits itself in its objectivity, the human body, if they are opposed to it, so that it is menaced by the irresistible predominance of their power, or sinks into insignificance before their immeasurable greatness; if, nevertheless, the beholder does not direct his attention to this eminently hostile relation to his will, but, although perceiving and recognizing it, turns consciously away from it, forcibly detaches himself from his will and its relations, and, giving himself up entirely to knowledge, quietly contemplates those very objects that are so terrible to the will, comprehends only their idea, which is foreign to all relation, so that he lingers gladly over its contemplation, and is thereby raised above himself, his person, his will, and all will: in that case he is filled with the sense of the *sublime,* he is in the state of spiritual exaltation, and therefore the object producing such a state is called *sublime.* Thus what distinguishes the sense of the sublime from that of the beautiful is this: in the case of the beautiful, pure knowledge has gained the upper hand without a struggle, for the beauty of the object, i.e. that property which facilitates the knowledge of its idea, has removed from consciousness without resistance, and therefore imperceptibly, the will and the knowledge of relations which is subject to it, so that what is left is the pure subject of knowledge without even a remembrance of will. On the other hand, in the case of the sublime that state of pure knowledge is only attained by a conscious and forcible breaking away from the relations of the same object to the will, which are recognized as unfavorable, by a free and conscious transcending of the will and the knowledge related to it.

This exaltation must not only be consciously won, but also consciously retained, and it is therefore accompanied by a constant remembrance of will; yet not of a single particular volition, such as fear or desire, but of human volition in general, so far as it is universally expressed in its objectivity the human body. If a single real act of will were to come into consciousness, through actual personal pressure and danger from the object, then the individual will thus actually influenced would at once gain the upper hand, the peace of contemplation would become impossible, the impression of the sublime would be lost, because it yields to the anxiety, in which the effort of the individual to right itself has sunk every other thought. A few examples will help very much to elucidate this theory of the aesthetic sublime and remove all doubt with regard to it; at the same time they will bring out the different degrees of this sense of the sublime. It is in the main identical with that of the beautiful, with pure will-less knowing, and the knowledge, that necessarily accompanies it of ideas out of all relation determined by the principle of sufficient reason, and it is distinguished from the sense of the beautiful only by the additional quality that it rises above the known hostile relation of the object contemplated to the will in general. Thus there comes to be various degrees of the sublime, and transitions from the beautiful to the sublime, according as this additional quality is strong, bold, urgent, near, or weak, distant, and merely indicated.

. . .

The course of the discussion has made it necessary to insert at this point the treatment of the sublime, though we have only half done with the beautiful, as we have considered its subjective side only. For it was merely a special modification of this subjective side that distinguished the beautiful from the sublime. This difference was found to depend upon whether the state of pure will-less knowing, which is presupposed and demanded by all aesthetic contemplation, was reached without opposition, by the mere disappearance of the will from consciousness, because the object invited and drew us towards it; or whether it was only attained through the free, conscious transcending of the will, to which the object contemplated had an unfavorable and even hostile relation, which would destroy contemplation altogether, if we were to give ourselves up to it. This is the distinction between the beautiful and the sublime. In the object they are not essentially different, for in every case the object of aesthetical contemplation is not the individual thing, but the idea in it which is striving to reveal itself; that is to say, adequate objectivity of will at a particular grade. Its necessary correlative, independent, like itself of the principle of sufficient reason, is the pure subject of knowing; just as the correlative of the particular thing is the knowing individual, both of which lie within the province of the principle of sufficient reason.

When we say that a thing is *beautiful,* we thereby assert that it is an object of our aesthetic contemplation, and this has a double meaning; on the one hand it means that the sight of the thing makes us *objective,* that is to say, that in contemplating it we are no longer conscious of ourselves as individuals, but as pure will-less subjects of knowledge; and on the other hand it means that we recognize in the object, not the particular thing, but an idea; and this can only happen, so far as our contemplation of it is not subordinated to the principle of sufficient reason, does not follow the relation of the object to anything outside it (which is always ultimately connected with relations to our own will), but rests in the object itself. For the idea and the pure subject of knowledge always appear at once in consciousness as necessary correlatives, and on their appearance all distinction of time vanishes, for they

are both entirely foreign to the principle of sufficient reason in all its forms, and lie outside the relations which are imposed by it; they may be compared to the rainbow and the sun, which have no part in the constant movement and succession of the falling drops. Therefore, if, for example, I contemplate a tree aesthetically, i.e., with artistic eyes, and thus recognize, not it, but its idea, it becomes at once of no consequence whether it is this tree or its predecessor which flourished a thousand years ago, and whether the observer is this individual or any other that lived anywhere and at any time; the particular thing and the knowing individual are abolished with the principle of sufficient reason, and there remains nothing but the idea and the pure subject of knowing, which together constitute the adequate objectivity of will at this grade. And the idea dispenses not only with time, but also with space, for the idea proper is not this special form which appears before me but its expression, its pure significance, its inner being, which discloses itself to me and appeals to me, and which may be quite the same though the spatial relations of its form be very different.

Since, on the one hand, every given thing may be observed in a purely objective manner and apart from all relations; and since, on the other hand, the will manifests itself in everything at some grade of its objectivity, so that everything is the expression of an idea; it follows that everything is also *beautiful.* That even the most insignificant things admit of pure objective and will-less contemplation, and thus prove that they are beautiful, is shown by what was said above in this reference about the Dutch pictures of still life.[3] But one thing is more beautiful than another, because it makes this pure objective contemplation easier, it lends itself to it, and, so to speak, even compels it, and then we call it very beautiful. This is the case sometimes because, as an individual thing, it expresses in its purity the idea of its species by the very distinct, clearly defined, and significant relation of its parts, and also fully reveals that idea through the completeness of all the possible expressions of its species united in it, so that it makes the transition from the individual thing to the idea, and therefore also the condition of pure contemplation, very easy for the beholder. Sometimes this possession of special beauty in an object lies in the fact that the idea itself which appeals to us in it is a high grade of the objectivity of will, and therefore very significant and expressive. Therefore it is that man is more beautiful than all other objects, and the revelation of his nature is the highest aim of art. Human form and expression are the most important objects of plastic art, and human action the most important ob-

---

[3]See p. 497.

ject of poetry. Yet each thing has its own peculiar beauty, not only every organism which expresses itself in the unity of an individual being, but also everything unorganized and formless, and even every manufactured article. For all these reveal the ideas through which the will objectifies itself at its lowest grades, they give, as it were, the deepest resounding bass notes of nature. Gravity, rigidity, fluidity, light, and so forth, are the ideas which express themselves in rocks, in buildings, in waters. Landscape gardening or architecture can do no more than assist them to unfold their qualities distinctly, fully, and variously; they can only give them the opportunity of expressing themselves purely, so that they lend themselves to aesthetic contemplation and make it easier. Inferior buildings or ill-favored localities, on the contrary, which nature has neglected or art has spoiled, perform this task in a very slight degree or not at all; yet even from them these universal, fundamental ideas of nature cannot altogether disappear. To the careful observer they present themselves here also, and even bad buildings and the like are capable of being aesthetically considered; the ideas of the most universal properties of their materials are still recognizable in them, only the artificial form which has been given them does not assist but hinders aesthetic contemplation. Manufactured articles also serve to express ideas, only it is not the idea of the manufactured article which speaks in them, but the idea of the material to which this artificial form has been given. This may be very conveniently expressed in two words, in the language of the schoolmen, thus, the manufactured article expresses the idea of its *forma substantialis,* but not that of its *forma accidentalis;* the latter leads to no idea, but only to a human conception of which it is the result. It is needless to say that by *manufactured article* no work of plastic art is meant. The schoolmen understand, in fact, by *forma substantialis* that which I call the grade of the objectification of will in a thing. We shall return immediately, when we treat of architecture, to the idea of the material. Our view, then, cannot be reconciled with that of Plato if he is of opinion that a table or a chair express the idea of a table or a chair,[4] but we say that they express the ideas which are already expressed in their mere material as such. According to Aristotle, however, Plato himself only maintained ideas of natural objects: ὁ Πλάτων ἔφη, ὅτι εἴδη ἐστίν ὁπόσα φύσει (*"Plato dixit, quod ideae eorum sunt, quae natura sunt"*[5]), and in chapter 5 he says that, according to the Platonists, there are no ideas of house and ring. In any case, Plato's

earliest disciples, as Alcinous informs us, denied that there were any ideas of manufactured articles. He says:

Ὁρίζονται δὲ τὴν ἰδέαν, παράδειγμα τῶν κατὰ φύσιν αἰώνιον. Οὔτε γὰρ τοῖς πλείστοις τῶν ἀπὸ Πλάτωνος ἀρέσκει, τῶν τεχνικῶν εἶναι ἰδέας, οἷον ἀσπιδος ἢ λύρας, οὔτε μὴν τῶν παρὰ φύσιν, οἷον πυρετοῦ καὶ χολέρας, οὔτε τῶν κατὰ μέρος, οἷον Σωκράτους καὶ Πλάτωνος, ἀλλ᾽ οὔτε τῶν εὐτελῶν τινός, οἷον ῥύπου καὶ κάρφους, οὔτε τῶν πρός τι, οἷον μείζονος καὶ ὑπέρεχοντος. εἶναι γὰρ τὰς ἰδέας νοήσεις θεοῦ αἰωνίους τε καὶ αὐτοτελεῖς (*Definiunt autem ideam exemplar aeternum eorum, quae secundum naturam existunt. Nam plurimis ex iis, qui Platonem secuti sunt, minime placuit, arte factorum ideas esse, ut clypei atque lyrae; neque rursus eorum, quae praeter naturam, ut febris et cholerae, neque particularium, ceu Socratis et Platonis; neque etiam rerum vilium, veluti sordium et festucae; neque relationum, ut majoris et excedentis: esse namque ideas intellectiones dei aeternas, ac seipsis perfectas).*[6]

We may take this opportunity of mentioning another point in which our doctrine of ideas differs very much from that of Plato. He teaches that the object which art tries to express, the ideal of painting and poetry, is not the idea but the particular thing.[7] Our whole exposition hitherto has maintained exactly the opposite, and Plato's opinion is the less likely to lead us astray, inasmuch as it is the source of one of the greatest and best known errors of this great man, his depreciation and rejection of art, and especially poetry; he directly connects his false judgment in reference to this with the passage quoted.

I return to the exposition of the aesthetic impression. The knowledge of the beautiful always supposes at once and inseparably the pure knowing subject and the known idea as object. Yet the source of aesthetic satisfaction will sometimes lie more in the comprehension of the known idea, sometimes more in the blessedness and spiritual peace of the pure knowing subject freed from all willing, and therefore

---

[4]*Republic,* X, pp. 31–38, and *Parmenides.*
[5]"Plato said that ideas of those things exist which exist physically." *Metaphysics,* XI. 3.

---

[6]"An idea is defined as an eternal example of those things which exist in accordance with nature. Too many of the followers of Plato argued strongly against the existence of ideas of artifacts, like shields and lyres; or of unnatural occurrences, like fever and cholera; or of individuals, like Socrates and Plato; or of cheap things, like shabby clothes, or a slave-rod; or of relationships, like the concept of the greater, or the exceeding: for ideas are eternal manifestations of divine intellect, and therefore per se perfect." *Introduction to Platonic Philosophy,* IX.
[7]*Republic,* X.

from all individuality, and the pain that proceeds from it. And, indeed, this predominance of one or the other constituent part of aesthetic feeling will depend upon whether the intuitively grasped idea is a higher or a lower grade of the objectivity of will. Thus in aesthetic contemplation (in the real, or through the medium of art) of the beauty of nature in the inorganic and vegetable worlds, or in works of architecture, the pleasure of pure will-less knowing will predominate, because the ideas which are here apprehended are only low grades of the objectivity of will, and are therefore not manifestations of deep significance and rich content. On the other hand, if animals and man are the objects of aesthetic contemplation or representation, the pleasure will consist rather in the comprehension of these ideas, which are the most distinct revelation of will; for they exhibit the greatest multiplicity of forms, the greatest richness and deep significance of phenomena, and reveal to us most completely the nature of will, whether in its violence, its terribleness, its satisfaction or its aberration (the latter in tragic situations), or finally in its change and self-surrender, which is the peculiar theme of Christian painting; as the idea of the will enlightened by full knowledge is the object of historical painting in general, and of the drama. We shall now go through the fine arts one by one, and this will give completeness and distinctness to the theory of the beautiful which we have advanced.

. . .

If now, with the exposition which has been given of art in general, we turn from plastic and pictorial art to poetry, we shall have no doubt that its aim also is the revelation of the ideas, the grades of the objectification of will, and the communication of them to the hearer with the distinctness and vividness with which the poetical sense comprehends them. Ideas are essentially perceptible; if, therefore, in poetry only abstract conceptions are directly communicated through words, it is yet clearly the intention to make the hearer perceive the ideas of life in the representatives of these conceptions, and this can only take place through the assistance of his own imagination. But in order to set the imagination to work for the accomplishment of this end, the abstract conceptions, which are the immediate material of poetry as of dry prose, must be so arranged that their spheres intersect each other in such a way that none of them can remain in this abstract universality; but, instead of it, a perceptible representative appears to the imagination; and this is always further modified by the words of the poet according to what his intention may be. As the chemist obtains solid precipitates by combining perfectly clear and transparent fluids; the poet understands how to precipitate, as it were, the concrete, the individual, the perceptible idea, out of the ab-

stract and transparent universality of the concepts by the manner in which he combines them. For the idea can only be known by perception; and knowledge of the idea is the end of art. The skill of a master, in poetry as in chemistry, enables us always to obtain the precise precipitate we intended. This end is assisted by the numerous epithets in poetry, by means of which the universality of every concept is narrowed more and more till we reach the perceptible. Homer attaches to almost every substantive an adjective, whose concept intersects and considerably diminishes the sphere of the concept of the substantive, which is thus brought so much the nearer to perception: for example—Ἐν δ’ ἔπεσ’ Ὠκεανῷ λαμπρὸν φάος ἠελίοιο, / Ἕλκον νύκτα μέλαιναν ἐπὶ ζείδωρον ἄρουραν. ("Occidit vero in Oceanum splendidum lumen solis, / Trahens noctem nigram super alman terram.")[8] And—"Where gentle winds from the blue heavens sigh, / There stand the myrtles still, the laurel high,"[9]—calls up before the imagination by means of a few concepts the whole delight of a southern clime.

Rhythm and rhyme are quite peculiar aids to poetry. I can give no other explanation of their incredibly powerful effect than that our faculties of perception have received from time, to which they are essentially bound, some quality on account of which we inwardly follow, and, as it were, consent to each regularly recurring sound. In this way rhythm and rhyme are partly a means of holding our attention, because we willingly follow the poem read, and partly they produce in us a blind consent to what is read prior to any judgment, and this gives the poem a certain emphatic power of convincing independent of all reasons.

From the general nature of the material, that is, the concepts, which poetry uses to communicate the ideas, the extent of its province is very great. The whole of nature, the ideas of all grades, can be represented by means of it, for it proceeds according to the idea it has to impart, so that its representations are sometimes descriptive, sometimes narrative, and sometimes directly dramatic. If, in the representation of the lower grades of the objectivity of will, plastic and pictorial art generally surpass it, because lifeless nature, and even brute nature, reveals almost its whole being in a single well-chosen moment; man, on the contrary, so far as he does not express himself by the mere form and expression of his person, but through a series of actions and the accompanying thoughts and emotions, is the principal object of poetry, in which no other art can compete with it, for here the progress

---

[8] "The bright light of the sun sank into the sea, drawing back night over the life-giving earth." *Iliad,* VIII. 485–86.
[9] Goethe, *Mignon,* 3–4.

or movement which cannot be represented in plastic or pictorial art just suits its purpose.

The revelation of the idea, which is the highest grade of the objectivity of will, the representation of man in the connected series of his efforts and actions, is thus the great problem of poetry. It is true that both experience and history teach us to know man; yet oftener men than man, i.e., they give us empirical notes of the behavior of men to each other, from which we may frame rules for our own conduct, oftener than they afford us deep glimpses of the inner nature of man. The latter function, however, is by no means entirely denied them; but as often as it is the nature of mankind itself that discloses itself to us in history or in our own experience, we have comprehended our experience, and the historian has comprehended history, with artistic eyes, poetically, i.e., according to the idea, not the phenomenon, in its inner nature, not in its relations. Our own experience is the indispensable condition of understanding poetry as of understanding history; for it is, so to speak, the dictionary of the language that both speak. But history is related to poetry as portrait painting is related to historical painting; the one gives us the true in the individual, the other the true in the universal; the one has the truth of the phenomenon, and can therefore verify it from the phenomenal, the other has the truth of the idea, which can be found in no particular phenomenon, but yet speaks to us from them all. The poet from deliberate choice represents characters in significant situations; the historian takes both as they come. Indeed, he must regard and select the circumstances and the persons, not with reference to their inward and true significance, which expresses the idea, but according to the outward, apparent, and relatively important significance with regard to the connection and the consequences. He must consider nothing in and for itself in its essential character and expression, but must look at everything in its relations, in its connection, in its influence upon what follows, and especially upon its own age. Therefore he will not overlook an action of a king, though of little significance, and in itself quite common, because it has results and influence. And, on the other hand, actions of the highest significance of particular and very eminent individuals are not to be recorded by him if they have no consequences. For his treatment follows the principle of sufficient reason, and apprehends the phenomenon, of which this principle is the form. But the poet comprehends the idea, the inner nature of man apart from all relations, outside all time, the adequate objectivity of the thing-in-itself, at its highest grade. Even in that method of treatment which is necessary for the historian, the inner nature and significance of the phenomena, the kernel of all these shells, can never be entirely lost. He who seeks for it, at any rate, may find it and recognize it. Yet that

which is significant in itself, not in its relations, the real unfolding of the idea, will be found far more accurately and distinctly in poetry than in history, and, therefore, however paradoxical it may sound, far more really genuine inner truth is to be attributed to poetry than to history. For the historian must accurately follow the particular event according to life, as it develops itself in time in the manifold tangled chains of causes and effects. It is, however, impossible that he can have all the data for this; he cannot have seen all and discovered all. He is forsaken at every moment by the original of his picture, or a false one substitutes itself for it, and this so constantly that I think I may assume that in all history the false outweighs the true. The poet, on the contrary, has comprehended the idea of man from some definite side which is to be represented; thus it is the nature of his own self that objectifies itself in it for him. His knowledge, as we explained above when speaking of sculpture, is half a priori; his ideal stands before his mind firm, distinct, brightly illuminated, and cannot forsake him; therefore he shows us, in the mirror of his mind, the idea pure and distinct, and his delineation of it down to the minutest particular is true as life itself.[10] The great ancient historians are, therefore, in those particulars in which their data fail them, for example, in the speeches of their heroes—poets; indeed their whole manner of handling their material approaches to the epic. But this gives their representations unity, and enables them to retain inner truth, even when outward truth was not accessible, or indeed was falsified. And as we compared history to portrait painting, in contradistinction to poetry, which corresponds to historical painting, we find that Winckelmann's maxim, that the portrait ought to be the ideal of the individual, was followed by the ancient historians, for they represent the indi-

---

[10][Schopenhauer] It is scarcely necessary to say that wherever I speak of poets I refer exclusively to that rare phenomenon, the great true poet. I mean no one else; least of all that dull insipid tribe, the mediocre poets, rhymesters, and inventors of fables, that flourishes so luxuriantly at the present day in Germany. They ought rather to have the words shouted in their ears unceasingly from all sides— "*Mediocribus esse poetis / Non homines, non Di, non concessere columnae.*" ["Men, gods, and bookshops alike will not brook bad poets" see Horace, p. 73.]. It is worthy of serious consideration what an amount of time—both their own and other people's—and paper is lost by this swarm of mediocre poets, and how injurious is their influence. For the public always seizes on what is new, and has naturally a greater proneness to what is perverse and dull as akin to itself. Therefore these works of the mediocre poets draw it away and hold it back from the true masterpieces and the education they afford, and thus working in direct antagonism to the benign influence of genius, they ruin taste more and more, and retard the progress of the age. Such poets should therefore be scourged with criticism and satire without indulgence or sympathy till they are induced, for their own good, to apply their Muse rather to reading what is good than to writing what is bad. For if the bungling of the incompetent so raised the wrath of the gentle Apollo that he could flay Marsyas, I do not see on what the mediocre poets will base their claim to tolerance.

vidual in such a way as to bring out that side of the idea of man which is expressed in it. Modern historians, on the contrary, with few exceptions, give us in general only "a dust-bin and a lumber-room, and at the most a chronicle of the principal political events." Therefore, whoever desires to know man in his inner nature, identical in all its phenomena and developments, to know him according to the idea, will find that the works of the great, immortal poet present a far truer, more distinct picture, than the historians can ever give. For even the best of the historians are, as poets, far from the first; and moreover their hands are tied. In this aspect the relation between the historian and the poet may be illustrated by the following comparison. The mere, pure historian, who works only according to data, is like a man, who without any knowledge of mathematics, has investigated the relations of certain figures, which he has accidentally found, by measuring them; and the problem thus empirically solved is affected of course by all the errors of the drawn figure. The poet, on the other hand, is like the mathematician, who constructs these relations a priori in pure perception, and expresses them not as they actually are in the drawn figure, but as they are in the idea, which the drawing is intended to render for the senses. Therefore Schiller says: "What has never anywhere come to pass, / That alone never grows old."[11] Indeed I must attribute greater value to biographies, and especially to autobiographies, in relation to the knowledge of the nature of man, than to history proper, at least as it is commonly handled. Partly because in the former the data can be collected more accurately and completely than in the latter; partly, because in history proper, it is not so much men as nations and heroes that act, and the individuals who do appear, seem so far off, surrounded with such pomp and circumstance, clothed in the stiff robes of state, or heavy, inflexible armor, that it is really hard through all this to recognize the human movements. On the other hand, the life of the individual when described with truth, in a narrow sphere, shows the conduct of men in all its forms and subtleties, the excellence, the virtue, and even holiness of a few, the perversity, meanness, and knavery of most, the dissolute profligacy of some. Besides, in the only aspect we are considering here, that of the inner significance of the phenomenal, it is quite the same whether the objects with which the action is concerned, are, relatively considered, trifling or important, farmhouses or kingdoms: for all these things in themselves are without significance, and obtain it only in so far as the will is moved by them. The motive has significance only through its relation to the will, while the relation

which it has as a thing to other things like itself, does not concern us here. As a circle of one inch in diameter, and a circle of forty million miles in diameter, have precisely the same geometrical properties, so are the events and the history of a village and a kingdom essentially the same; and we may study and learn to know mankind as well as in the one as in the other. It is also a mistake to suppose that autobiographies are full of deceit and dissimulation. On the contrary, lying (though always possible) is perhaps more difficult there than elsewhere. Dissimulation is easiest in mere conversation; indeed, though it may sound paradoxical, it is really more difficult even in a letter. For in the case of a letter the writer is alone, and looks into himself, and not out on the world, so that what is strange and distant does not easily approach him; and he has not the test of the impression made upon another before his eyes. But the receiver of the letter peruses it quietly in a mood unknown to the writer, reads it repeatedly and at different times, and thus easily finds out the concealed intention. We also get to know an author as a man most easily from his books, because all these circumstances act here still more strongly and permanently. And in an autobiography it is so difficult to dissimulate, that perhaps there does not exist a single one that is not, as a whole, more true, than any history that ever was written. The man who writes his own life surveys it as a whole, the particular becomes small, the near becomes distant, the distant becomes near again, the motives that influenced him shrink; he seats himself at the confessional, and has done so of his own free will; the spirit of lying does not so easily take hold of him here, for there is also in every man an inclination to truth which has first to be overcome whenever he lies, and which here has taken up a specially strong position. The relation between biography and the history of nations may be made clear for perception by means of the following comparison: history shows us mankind as a view from a high mountain shows us nature; we see much at a time, wide stretches, great masses, but nothing is distinct nor recognizable in all the details of its own peculiar nature. On the other hand, the representation of the life of the individual shows us the man, as we see nature if we go about among her trees, plants, rocks, and waters. But in landscape painting, in which the artist lets us look at nature with his eyes, the knowledge of the ideas, and the condition of pure will-less knowing, which is demanded by these, is made much easier for us; and, in the same way, poetry is far superior both to history and biography, in the representation of the ideas which may be looked for in all three. For here also genius holds up to us the magic glass, in which all that is essential and significant appears before us collected and placed in the clearest light, and what is accidental and foreign is left out.

---

[11] *An die Freundé.*

The representation of the idea of man, which is the work of the poet, may be performed, so that what is represented is also the representer. This is the case in lyrical poetry, in songs, properly so called, in which the poet only perceives vividly his own state and describes it. Thus a certain subjectivity is essential to this kind of poetry from the nature of its object. Again, what is to be represented may be entirely different from him who represents it, as is the case in all other kinds of poetry, in which the poet more or less conceals himself behind his representation, and at last disappears altogether. In the ballad the poet still expresses to some extent his own state through the tone and proportion of the whole; therefore, though much more objective than the lyric, it has yet something subjective. This becomes less in the idyl, still less in the romantic poem, almost entirely disappears in the true epic, and even to the last vestige in the drama, which is the most objective and, in more than one respect, the completest and most difficult form of poetry. The lyrical form of poetry is consequently the easiest, and although art, as a whole, belongs only to the true man of genius, who so rarely appears, even a man who is not in general very remarkable may produce a beautiful song if, by actual strong excitement from without, some inspiration raises his mental powers; for all that is required for this is a lively perception of his own state at a moment of emotional excitement. This is proved by the existence of many single songs by individuals who have otherwise remained unknown; especially the German national songs, of which we have an exquisite collection in the *Wunderhorn;* and also by innumerable love songs and other songs of the people in all languages; for to seize the mood of a moment and embody it in a song is the whole achievement of this kind of poetry. Yet in the lyrics of true poets the inner nature of all mankind is reflected, and all that millions of past, present, and future men have found, or will find, in the same situations, which are constantly recurring, finds its exact expression in them. And because these situations, by constant recurrence, are permanent as man himself and always call up the same sensations, the lyrical productions of genuine poets remain through thousands of years true, powerful, and fresh. But if the poet is always the universal man, then all that has ever moved a human heart, all that human nature in any situation has ever produced from itself, all that dwells and broods in any human breast—is his theme and his material, and also all the rest of nature. Therefore the poet may just as well sing of voluptuousness as of mysticism, be Anacreon or Angelus Silesius, write tragedies or comedies, represent the sublime or the common mind—according to humor or vocation. And no one has the right to prescribe to the poet what he ought to be—noble and sublime, moral, pious, Christian, one thing or another, still less

to reproach him because he is one thing and not another. He is the mirror of mankind, and brings to its consciousness what it feels and does.

If we now consider more closely the nature of the lyric proper, and select as examples exquisite and pure models, not those that approach in any way to some other form of poetry, such as the ballad, the elegy, the hymn, the epigram, &c., we shall find that the peculiar nature of the lyric, in the narrowest sense, is this: It is the subject of will, i.e., his own volition, which the consciousness of the singer feels; often as a released and satisfied desire (joy), but still oftener as a restricted desire (grief), always as an emotion, a passion, a moved frame of mind. Besides this, however, and along with it, by the sight of surrounding nature, the singer becomes conscious of himself as the subject of pure, will-less knowing, whose unbroken blissful peace now appears, in contrast to the stress of desire which is always restricted and always needy. The feeling of this contrast, this alteration, is really what the lyric as a whole expresses, and what principally constitutes the lyrical state of mind. In it pure knowing comes to us, as it were, to deliver us from desire and its stain; we follow, but only for an instant; desire, the remembrance of our own personal ends, tears us anew from peaceful contemplation; yet ever again the next beautiful surrounding in which the pure will-less knowledge presents itself to us, allures us away from desire. Therefore, in the lyric and the lyrical mood, desire (the personal interest of the ends), and pure perception of the surrounding presented, are wonderfully mingled with each other; connections between them are sought for and imagined; the subjective disposition, the affection of the will, imparts its own hue to the perceived surrounding, and conversely, the surroundings communicate the reflex of their color to the will. The true lyric is the expression of the whole of this mingled and divided state of mind. In order to make clear by examples this abstract analysis of a frame of mind that is very far from all abstraction, any of the immortal songs of Goethe may be taken. As specially adapted for this end I shall recommend only a few: *The Shepherd's Lament, Welcome and Farewell, To the Moon, On the Lake, Autumn;* also the songs in the *Wunderhorn* are excellent examples; particularly the one which begins, "O Bremen, I must now leave thee." As a comical and happy parody of the lyrical character a song of Voss strikes me as remarkable. It describes the feeling of a drunk plumber falling from a tower, who observes in passing that the clock on the tower is at half-past eleven, a remark which is quite foreign to his condition, and thus belongs to knowledge free from will. Whoever accepts the view that has been expressed of the lyrical frame of mind, will also allow, that it is the sensuous and poetical knowledge of the principle which I established in my essay on the principle of sufficient reason, and have also referred to in this work, that the identity of the subject of knowing with that of willing may be called the miracle κατ᾿ ἐξοχήν;[12] so that the poetical effect of the lyric rests finally on the truth of that principle. In the course of life these two subjects, or, in popular language, head and heart, are ever becoming further apart; men are always separating more between their subjective feeling and their objective knowledge. In the child the two are still entirely blended together; it scarcely knows how to distinguish itself from its surroundings, it is at one with them. In the young man all perception chiefly affects feeling and mood, and even mingles with it, as Byron very beautifully expresses—

> I live not in myself, but I become
> Portion of that around me; and to me
> High mountains are a feeling.[13]

This is why the youth clings so closely to the perceptible and outward side of things; this is why he is only fit for lyrical poetry, and only the full-grown man is capable of the drama. The old man we can think of as at the most an epic poet, like Ossian,[14] and Homer, for narration is characteristic of old age.

In the more objective kinds of poetry, especially in the romance, the epic, and the drama, the end, the revelation of the idea of man, is principally attained by two means, by true and profound representation of significant characters, and by the invention of pregnant situations in which they disclose themselves. For as it is incumbent upon the chemist not only to exhibit the simple elements, pure and genuine, and their principal compounds, but also to expose them to the influence of such reagents as will clearly and strikingly bring out their peculiar qualities, so is it incumbent on the poet not only to present to us significant characters truly and faithfully as nature itself; but, in order that we may get to know them, he must place them in those situations in which their peculiar qualities will fully unfold themselves, and appear distinctly in sharp outline; situations which are therefore called significant. In real life, and in history, situations of this kind are rarely brought about by chance, and they stand alone, lost and concealed in the multitude of those which are insignificant. The complete significance of the situations ought to distinguish the romance, the epic, and the drama

from real life as completely as the arrangement and selection of significant characters. In both, however, absolute truth is a necessary condition of their effect, and want of unity in the characters, contradiction either of themselves or of the nature of humanity in general, as well as impossibility, or very great improbability in the events, even in mere accessories, offend just as much in poetry as badly drawn figures, false perspective, or wrong lighting in painting. For both in poetry and painting we demand the faithful mirror of life, of man, of the world, only made more clear by the representation, and more significant by the arrangement. For there is only one end of all the arts, the representation of the ideas; and their essential difference lies simply in the different grades of the objectification of will to which the ideas that are to be represented belong. This also determines the material of the representation. Thus the arts which are most widely separated may yet throw light on each other. For example, in order to comprehend fully the ideas of water it is not sufficient to see it in the quiet pond or in the evenly flowing stream; but these ideas disclose themselves fully only when the water appears under all circumstances and exposed to all kinds of obstacles. The effects of the varied circumstances and obstacles give it the opportunity of fully exhibiting all its qualities. This is why we find it beautiful when it tumbles, rushes, and foams, or leaps into the air, or falls in a cataract of spray; or, lastly, if artificially confined it springs up in a fountain. Thus showing itself different under different circumstances, it yet always faithfully asserts its character; it is just as natural to it to spout up as to lie in glassy stillness; it is as ready for the one as for the other as soon as the circumstances appear. Now, what the engineer achieves with the fluid matter of water, the architect achieves with the rigid matter of stone, and just this the epic or dramatic poet achieves with the idea of man. Unfolding and rendering distinct the idea expressing itself in the object of every art, the idea of the will which objectifies itself at each grade, is the common end of all the arts. The life of man, as it shows itself for the most part in the real world, is like the water, as it is generally seen in the pond and the river; but in the epic, the romance, the tragedy, selected characters are placed in those circumstances in which all their special qualities unfold themselves, the depths of the human heart are revealed, and become visible in extraordinary and very significant actions. Thus poetry objectifies the idea of man, an idea which has the peculiarity of expressing itself in highly individual characters.

Tragedy is to be regarded, and is recognized as the summit of poetical art, both on account of the greatness of its effect and the difficulty of its achievement. It is very significant for our whole system, and well worthy of observation, that the end of this highest poetical achievement is the rep-

---

[12]"Par excellence."

[13]*Childe Harold*, III. 72.

[14]Supposed writer of ancient Gaelic and Erse poems actually written by James Macpherson (1736–96).

resentation of the terrible side of life. The unspeakable pain, the wail of humanity, the triumph of evil, the scornful mastery of chance, and the irretrievable fall of the just and innocent, is here presented to us; and in this lies a significant hint of the nature of the world and of existence. It is the strife of will with itself, which here, completely unfolded at the highest grade of its objectivity, comes into fearful prominence. It becomes visible in the suffering of men, which is now introduced, partly through chance and error, which appear as the rulers of the world, personified as fate, on account of their insidiousness, which even reaches the appearance of design; partly it proceeds from man himself, through the self-mortifying efforts of a few, through the wickedness and perversity of most. It is one and the same will that lives and appears in them all, but whose phenomena fight against each other and destroy each other. In one individual it appears powerfully, in another more weakly; in one more subject to reason, and softened by the light of knowledge, in another less so, till at last, in some single case, this knowledge, purified and heightened by suffering itself, reaches the point at which the phenomenon, the veil of Maya, no longer deceives it. It sees through the form of the phenomenon, the *principum individuationis*.[15] The egoism which rests on this perishes with it, so that now the *motives* that were so powerful before have lost their might, and instead of them the complete knowledge of the nature of the world, which has a *quieting* effect on the will, produces resignation, the surrender not merely of life, but of the very will to live. . . . For if, according to our view, the whole visible world is just the objectification, the mirror, of the will, conducting it to knowledge of itself, and, indeed, as we shall soon see, to the possibility of its deliverance; and if, at the same time, the world as idea, if we regard it in isolation, and, freeing ourselves from all volition, allow it alone to take possession of our consciousness, is the most joy-giving and the only innocent side of life; we must regard art as the higher ascent, the more complete development of all this, for it achieves essentially just what is achieved by the visible world itself, only with greater concentration, more perfectly, with intention and intelligence, and therefore may be called, in the full significance of the word, the flower of life. If the whole world as idea is only the visibility of will, the work of art is to render this visibility more distinct. It is the camera obscura[16] which shows the objects more purely, and enables us to survey them and comprehend them better. It is the play within the play, the stage upon the stage in *Hamlet.*

The pleasure we receive from all beauty, the consolation which art affords, the enthusiasm of the artist, which enables him to forget the cares of life—the latter an advantage of the man of genius over other men, which alone repays him for the suffering that increases in proportion to the clearness of consciousness, and for the desert loneliness among men of a different race—all this rests on the fact that the in-itself of life, the will, existence itself, is, as we shall see farther on, a constant sorrow, partly miserable, partly terrible; while, on the contrary, as idea alone, purely contemplated, or copied by art, free from pain, it presents to us a drama full of significance. This purely knowable side of the world, and the copy of it in any art, is the element of the artist. He is chained to the contemplation of the play, the objectification of will; he remains beside it, does not get tired of contemplating it and representing it in copies; and meanwhile he bears himself the cost of the production of that play, i.e., he himself is the will which objectifies itself, and remains in constant suffering. That pure, true, and deep knowledge of the inner nature of the world becomes now for him an end in itself: he stops there. Therefore it does not become to him a quieter of the will, as, we shall see in the next book, it does in the case of the saint who has attained to resignation; it does not deliver him forever from life, but only at moments, and is therefore not for him a path out of life, but only an occasional consolation in it, till his power, increased by this contemplation and at last tired of the play, lays hold on the real. The *St. Cecilia* of Raphael may be regarded as a representation of this transition. To the real, then, we now turn in the following book.

---

[15]"Principle of individuality."

---

[16]An optical apparatus that projects images of external objects on a screen or on an opaque surface. It is principally used today for copying maps and drawings on an enlarged or reduced scale.

Thomas Love Peacock

1785–1866

Peacock's forte is satire, and his sympathies are with neoclassical critical principles. The clichés of Romanticism do not escape him unscathed. *The Four Ages of Poetry* is known principally because it impelled Shelley to write his *Defense of Poetry* in solemn reply to it; it deserves to be esteemed for its own witty insights. Peacock parodies a number of Romantic ideas popularized by Wordsworth: "Poetical impressions can be received only among natural scenes: for all that is artificial is antipoetical. Society is artificial, therefore we will live out of society. The mountains are natural, therefore we will live in the mountains." Peacock goes further and declares that poetry inevitably declined as the age of gold gave way to one of silver and then to one of brass. The poet is becoming obsolete: "The brighter the light diffused around him by the progress of reason, the thicker is the darkness of antiquated barbarism, in which he buries himself like a mole. . . ."

It is interesting to see, however, that in Peacock's view the age of brass in which he lived was the second one, following a second age of silver, and so on. Perhaps we can believe that a third age of gold will come round, and with it the reestablishment, for a time, of poetry. If we step back from Peacock's witty forays, do we glimpse a Romantic, cyclical view of history? Perhaps. But Peacock also holds that there is linear progress in the development of rational knowledge. This makes a return to a golden age of poetry more and more unlikely, for as he sees it, poetry has less and less of real experience to be concerned with. The Romantic theorist could, of course, retort that the poet's "primitivism" provides a necessary opposition to rationalism run rampant.

Peacock's works have been edited by H. F. B. Brett-Smith and C. E. Jones (10 vols., 1924–34). Biographies include Carl Van Doren, *The Life of Thomas Love Peacock* (1911); J. B. Priestley, *Thomas Love Peacock* (1927); and O. W. Campbell, *Thomas Love Peacock* (1953). See Jean-Jacques Mayoux, *Un épicurien anglais: Thomas Love Peacock* (1932); Carl Dawson, *Thomas Love Peacock* (1968) and *His Fine Wit* (1970); Felix Felton, *Thomas Love Peacock* (1973); Marilyn Butler, *Peacock Displayed* (1979); and James Mulvihill, *Thomas Love Peacock* (1987).

The Four Ages of Poetry

Qui inter haec nutriuntur non magis sapere possunt,
quam bene olere qui in culina habitant.[1]

PETRONIUS

Poetry, like the world, may be said to have four ages, but in a different order; the first age of poetry being the age of iron; the second, of gold; the third, of silver; and the fourth, of brass.

The first, or iron age of poetry, is that in which rude bards celebrate in rough numbers the exploits of ruder chiefs, in days when every man is a warrior, and when the great practical maxim of every form of society, "to keep what we have and to catch what we can," is not yet disguised under names of justice and forms of law, but is the naked motto of the naked sword, which is the only judge and jury in every question of *meum* and *tuum*.[2] In these days, the only three trades flourishing (besides that of priest which flourishes always) are those of king, thief, and beggar: the beggar being for the most part a king deject, and the thief a king expectant. The first question asked of a stranger is, whether he is a beggar or a thief:[3] the stranger, in reply, usually assumes the first, and awaits a convenient opportunity to prove his claim to the second appellation.

The natural desire of every man to engross to himself as much power and property as he can acquire by any of the means which might makes right, is accompanied by the no less natural desire of making known to as many people as possible the extent to which he has been a winner in this universal game. The successful warrior becomes a chief; the successful chief becomes a king: his next want is an organ to disseminate the fame of his achievements and the extent of his possessions; and this organ he finds in a bard, who is always ready to celebrate the strength of his arm, being first duly inspired by that of his liquor. This is the origin of poetry, which, like all other trades, takes its rise in the demand for the commodity, and flourishes in proportion to the extent of the market.

Poetry is thus in its origin panegyrical. The first rude songs of all nations appear to be a sort of brief historical notices, in a strain of tumid hyperbole, of the exploits and possessions of a few preeminent individuals. They tell us how many battles such a one has fought, how many helmets he has cleft, how many breastplates he has pierced, how many widows he has made, how much land he has appropriated, how many houses he has demolished for other people, what a large one he has built for himself, how much gold he has stowed away in it, and how liberally and plentifully he pays, feeds, and intoxicates the divine and immortal bards, the sons of Jupiter, but for whose everlasting songs the names of heroes would perish.

This is the first stage of poetry before the invention of written letters. The numerical modulation is at once useful as a help to memory, and pleasant to the ears of uncultured men, who are easily caught by sound: and from the exceeding flexibility of the yet unformed language, the poet does no violence to his ideas in subjecting them to the fetters of number. The savage indeed lisps in numbers, and all rude and uncivilized people express themselves in the manner which we call poetical.

The scenery by which he is surrounded, and the superstitions which are the creed of his age, form the poet's mind. Rocks, mountains, seas, unsubdued forests, unnavigable rivers, surround him with forms of power and mystery, which ignorance and fear have peopled with spirits, under multifarious names of gods, goddesses, nymphs, genii, and demons. Of all these personages marvelous tales are in existence: the nymphs are not indifferent to handsome young men, and the gentlemen-genii are much troubled and very troublesome with a propensity to be rude to pretty maidens: the bard therefore finds no difficulty in tracing the genealogy of his chief to any of the deities in his neighborhood with whom the said chief may be most desirous of claiming relationship.

In this pursuit, as in all others, some of course will attain a very marked preeminence; and these will be held in high honor, like Demodocus in the *Odyssey,* and will be consequently inflated with boundless vanity, like Thamyris in the *Iliad.* Poets are as yet only historians and chroniclers of their time, and the sole depositories of all the knowledge of their age; and though this knowledge is rather a crude congeries of traditional fantasies than a collection of useful truths, yet, such as it is, they have it to themselves. They are observing and thinking, while others are robbing and fighting: and though their object be nothing more than to secure a share of the spoil, yet they accomplish this end by intellectual, not by physical, power: their success excites emulation to the attainment of intellectual eminence: thus they sharpen their own wits and awaken those of others, at the same time that they gratify vanity and amuse curiosity. A skillful display of the little knowledge they have gains them credit for the possession of much more which they have not. Their fa-

---

THE FOUR AGES OF POETRY. Peacock's *The Four Ages of Poetry* was first published in 1820.
[1] "Those who are brought up among such things are no more able to have real taste than those who live in the kitchen smell sweet."
[2] "Mine" and "yours."
[3] [Peacock] See the *Odyssey,* passim: and Thucydides, *History,* I. 5.

miliarity with the secret history of gods and genii obtains for them, without much difficulty, the reputation of inspiration; thus they are not only historians but theologians, moralists, and legislators: delivering their oracles ex cathedra, and being indeed often themselves (as Orpheus and Amphion) regarded as portions and emanations of divinity: building cities with a song, and leading brutes with a symphony; which are only metaphors for the faculty of leading multitudes by the nose.

The golden age of poetry finds its materials in the age of iron. This age begins when poetry begins to be retrospective; when something like a more extended system of civil polity is established; when personal strength and courage avail less to the aggrandizing of their possessor and to the making and marring of kings and kingdoms, and are checked by organized bodies, social institutions, and hereditary successions. Men also live more in the light of truth and within the interchange of observation; and thus perceive that the agency of gods and genii is not so frequent among themselves as, to judge from the songs and legends of the past time, it was among their ancestors. From these two circumstances, really diminished personal power, and apparently diminished familiarity with gods and genii, they very easily and naturally deduce two conclusions: first, that men are degenerated, and second, that they are less in favor with the gods. The people of the petty states and colonies, which have now acquired stability and form, which owed their origin and first prosperity to the talents and courage of a single chief, magnify their founder through the mists of distance and tradition, and perceive him achieving wonders with a god or goddess always at his elbow. They find his name and his exploits thus magnified and accompanied in their traditionary songs, which are their only memorials. All that is said of him is in this character. There is nothing to contradict it. The man and his exploits and his tutelary deities are mixed and blended in one invariable association. The marvelous too is very much like a snowball: it grows as it rolls downward, till the little nucleus of truth which began its descent from the summit is hidden in the accumulation of superinduced hyperbole.

When tradition, thus adorned and exaggerated, has surrounded the founders of families and states with so much adventitious power and magnificence, there is no praise which a living poet can, without fear of being kicked for clumsy flattery, address to a living chief, that will not still leave the impression that the latter is not so great a man as his ancestors. The man must in this case be praised through his ancestors. Their greatness must be established, and he must be shown to be their worthy descendant. All the people of a state are interested in the founder of their state. All states that have harmonized into a common form of society, are interested in their respective founders. All men are interested in their ancestors. All men love to look back into the days that are past. In these circumstances traditional national poetry is reconstructed and brought like chaos into order and form. The interest is more universal: understanding is enlarged: passion still has scope and play: character is still various and strong: nature is still unsubdued and existing in all her beauty and magnificence, and men are not yet excluded from her observation by the magnitude of cities or the daily confinement of civic life: poetry is more an art: it requires greater skill in numbers, greater command of language, more extensive and various knowledge, and greater comprehensiveness of mind. It still exists without rivals in any other department of literature; and even the arts, painting and sculpture certainly, and music probably, are comparatively rude and imperfect. The whole field of intellect is its own. It has no rivals in history, nor in philosophy, nor in science. It is cultivated by the greatest intellects of the age, and listened to by all the rest. This is the age of Homer, the golden age of poetry. Poetry has now attained its perfection: it has attained the point which it cannot pass: genius therefore seeks new forms for the treatment of the same subjects: hence the lyric poetry of Pindar and Alcaeus, and the tragic poetry of Aeschylus and Sophocles. The favor of kings, the honor of the Olympic crown, the applause of present multitudes, all that can feed vanity and stimulate rivalry, await the successful cultivator of this art, till its forms become exhausted, and new rivals arise around it in new fields of literature, which gradually acquire more influence as, with the progress of reason and civilization, facts become more interesting than fiction: indeed the maturity of poetry may be considered the infancy of history. The transition from Homer to Herodotus is scarcely more remarkable than that from Herodotus to Thucydides: in the gradual dereliction of fabulous incident and ornamented language, Herodotus is as much a poet in relation to Thucydides as Homer is in relation to Herodotus. The history of Herodotus is half a poem: it was written while the whole field of literature belonged to the Muses, and the nine books of which it was composed were therefore of right, as well as of courtesy, superinscribed with their nine names.

Speculations, too, and disputes, on the nature of man and of mind; on moral duties and on good and evil; on the animate and inanimate components of the visible world; begin to share attention with the eggs of Leda and the horns of Io,[4] and to draw off from poetry a portion of its once undivided audience.

---

[4]According to Greek mythology, Zeus appeared in the form of a swan and seduced Leda, a mortal, who bore him twin sons, Castor and Pollux, and Helen. Zeus transformed Io, another mortal he wooed, into a heifer in order to conceal her from his wife, Hera.

Then comes the silver age, or the poetry of civilized life. This poetry is of two kinds, imitative and original. The imitative consists in recasting, and giving an exquisite polish to, the poetry of the age of gold: of this Virgil is the most obvious and striking example. The original is chiefly comic, didactic, or satiric: as in Menander, Aristophanes, Horace, and Juvenal. The poetry of this age is characterized by an exquisite and fastidious selection of words, and a labored and somewhat monotonous harmony of expression: but its monotony consists in this, that experience having exhausted all the varieties of modulation, the civilized poetry selects the most beautiful, and prefers the repetition of these to ranging through the variety of all. But the best expression being that into which the idea naturally falls, it requires the utmost labor and care so to reconcile the inflexibility of civilized language and the labored polish of versification with the idea intended to be expressed, that sense may not appear to be sacrificed to sound. Hence numerous efforts and rare success.

This state of poetry is however a step towards its extinction. Feeling and passion are best painted in, and roused by, ornamental and figurative language; but the reason and the understanding are best addressed in the simplest and most unvarnished phrase. Pure reason and dispassionate truth would be perfectly ridiculous in verse, as we may judge by versifying one of Euclid's demonstrations. This will be found true of all dispassionate reasoning whatever, and all reasoning that requires comprehensive views and enlarged combinations. It is only the more tangible points of morality, those which command assent at once, those which have a mirror in every mind, and in which the severity of reason is warmed and rendered palatable by being mixed up with feeling and imagination, that are applicable even to what is called moral poetry: and as the sciences of morals and of mind advance towards perfection, as they become more enlarged and comprehensive in their views, as reason gains the ascendancy in them over imagination and feeling, poetry can no longer accompany them in their progress, but drops into the background, and leaves them to advance alone. Thus the empire of thought is withdrawn from poetry, as the empire of facts had been before. In respect of the latter, the poet of the age of iron celebrates the achievements of his contemporaries; the poet of the age of gold celebrates the heroes of the age of iron; the poet of the age of silver recasts the poems of the age of gold: we may here see how very slight a ray of historical truth is sufficient to dissipate all the illusions of poetry. We know no more of the men than of the gods of the *Iliad;* no more of Achilles than we do of Thetis; no more of Hector and Andromache than we do of Vulcan and Venus: these belong altogether to poetry; history has no share in them: but Virgil knew better than to write an epic about Cae-

sar; he left him to Livy; and traveled out of the confines of truth and history into the old regions of poetry and fiction.

Good sense and elegant learning, conveyed in polished and somewhat monotonous verse, are the perfection of the original and imitative poetry of civilized life. Its range is limited, and when exhausted, nothing remains but the *crambe repetita*[5] of commonplace, which at length becomes thoroughly wearisome, even to the most indefatigable readers of the newest new nothings.

It is now evident that poetry must either cease to be cultivated, or strike into a new path. The poets of the age of gold have been imitated and repeated till no new imitation will attract notice: the limited range of ethical and didactic poetry is exhausted: the associations of daily life in an advanced state of society are of very dry, methodical, unpoetical matters-of-fact: but there is always a multitude of listless idlers, yawning for amusement, and gaping for novelty: and the poet makes it his glory to be foremost among their purveyors.

Then comes the age of brass, which, by rejecting the polish and the learning of the age of silver, and taking a retrograde stride to the barbarisms and crude traditions of the age of iron, professes to return to nature and revive the age of gold. This is the second childhood of poetry. To the comprehensive energy of the Homeric Muse, which, by giving at once the grand outline of things, presented to the mind a vivid picture in one or two verses, inimitable alike in simplicity and magnificence, is substituted a verbose and minutely detailed description of thoughts, passions, actions, persons, and things, in that loose rambling style of verse, which anyone may write, *stans pede in uno,*[6] at the rate of two hundred lines in an hour. To this age may be referred all the poets who flourished in the decline of the Roman Empire. The best specimen of it, though not the most generally known, is the *Dionysiaca* of Nonnus, which contains many passages of exceeding beauty in the midst of masses of amplification and repetition.

The iron age of classical poetry may be called the bardic; the golden, the Homeric; the silver, the Virgilian; and the brass, the Nonnic.

Modern poetry has also its four ages: but "it wears its rue with a difference."[7]

To the age of brass in the ancient world succeeded the Dark Ages, in which the light of the Gospel began to spread over Europe, and in which, by a mysterious and inscrutable dispensation, the darkness thickened with the progress of the

---

[5]"Warmed-over cabbage."
[6]"Standing on one foot."
[7]*Hamlet*, IV. v. 183.

light. The tribes that overran the Roman Empire brought back the days of barbarism, but with this difference, that there were many books in the world, many places in which they were preserved, and occasionally someone by whom they were read, who indeed (if he escaped being burned *pour l'amour de Dieu,*[8]) generally lived an object of mysterious fear, with the reputation of magician, alchemist, and astrologer. The emerging of the nations of Europe from this superinduced barbarism, and their settling into new forms of polity, was accompanied, as the first ages of Greece had been, with a wild spirit of adventure, which, cooperating with new manners and new superstitions, raised up a fresh crop of chimeras, not less fruitful, though far less beautiful, than those of Greece. The semideification of women by the maxims of the age of chivalry, combining with these new fables, produced the romance of the Middle Ages. The founders of the new line of heroes took the place of the demigods of Grecian poetry. Charlemagne and his paladins, Arthur and his knights of the round table, the heroes of the iron age of chivalrous poetry, were seen through the same magnifying mist of distance, and their exploits were celebrated with even more extravagant hyperbole. These legends, combined with the exaggerated love that pervades the songs of the troubadours, the reputation of magic that attached to learned men, the infant wonders of natural philosophy, the crazy fanaticism of the crusades, the power and privileges of the great feudal chiefs, and the holy mysteries of monks and nuns, formed a state of society in which no two laymen could meet without fighting, and in which the three staple ingredients of lover, prize-fighter, and fanatic, that composed the basis of the character of every true man, were mixed up and diversified, in different individuals and classes, with so many distinctive excellencies, and under such an infinite motley variety of costume, as gave the range of a most extensive and picturesque field to the two great constituents of poetry, love and battle.

From these ingredients of the iron age of modern poetry, dispersed in the rhymes of minstrels and the songs of the troubadours, arose the golden age, in which the scattered materials were harmonized and blended about the time of the revival of learning; but with this peculiar difference, that Greek and Roman literature pervaded all the poetry of the golden age of modern poetry, and hence resulted a heterogeneous compound of all ages and nations in one picture; an infinite license, which gave to the poet the free range of the whole field of imagination and memory. This was carried very far by Ariosto, but farthest of all by Shakespeare and

his contemporaries, who used time and locality merely because they could not do without them, because every action must have its when and where: but they made no scruple of deposing a Roman emperor by an Italian count, and sending him off in the disguise of a French pilgrim to be shot with a blunderbuss by an English archer. This makes the old English drama very picturesque, at any rate, in the variety of costume, and very diversified in action and character; though it is a picture of nothing that ever was seen on earth except a Venetian carnival.

The greatest of English poets, Milton, may be said to stand alone between the ages of gold and silver, combining the excellencies of both; for with all the energy, and power, and freshness of the first, he united all the studied and elaborate magnificence of the second.

The silver age succeeded; beginning with Dryden, coming to perfection with Pope, and ending with Goldsmith, Collins, and Gray.

Cowper divested verse of its exquisite polish; he thought in meter, but paid more attention to his thoughts than his verse. It would be difficult to draw the boundary of prose and blank verse between his letters and his poetry.

The silver age was the reign of authority; but authority now began to be shaken, not only in poetry but in the whole sphere of its dominion. The contemporaries of Gray and Cowper were deep and elaborate thinkers. The subtle skepticism of Hume, the solemn irony of Gibbon, the daring paradoxes of Rousseau, and the biting ridicule of Voltaire, directed the energies of four extraordinary minds to shake every portion of the reign of authority. Inquiry was roused, the activity of intellect was excited, and poetry came in for its share of the general result. The changes had been rung on lovely maid and sylvan shade, summer heat and green retreat, waving trees and sighing breeze, gentle swains and amorous pains, by versifiers who took them on trust, as meaning something very soft and tender, without much caring what: but with this general activity of intellect came a necessity for even poets to appear to know something of what they professed to talk of. Thomson and Cowper looked at the trees and hills which so many ingenious gentlemen had rhymed about so long without looking at them at all, and the effect of the operation on poetry was like the discovery of a new world. Painting shared the influence, and the principles of picturesque beauty were explored by adventurous essayists with indefatigable pertinacity. The success which attended these experiments, and the pleasure which resulted from them, had the usual effect of all new enthusiasms, that of turning the heads of a few unfortunate persons, the patriarchs of the age of brass, who, mistaking the prominent novelty for the all-important totality, seem to have ratiocinated

---

[8] "For the love of God."

much in the following manner: "Poetical genius is the finest of all things, and we feel that we have more of it than anyone ever had. The way to bring it to perfection is to cultivate poetical impressions exclusively. Poetical impressions can be received only among natural scenes: for all that is artificial is antipoetical. Society is artificial, therefore we will live out of society. The mountains are natural, therefore we will live in the mountains. There we shall be shining models of purity and virtue, passing the whole day in the innocent and amiable occupation of going up and down hill, receiving poetical impressions, and communicating them in immortal verse to admiring generations." To some such perversion of intellect we owe that egregious confraternity of rhymesters, known by the name of the Lake Poets; who certainly did receive and communicate to the world some of the most extraordinary poetical impressions that ever were heard of, and ripened into models of public virtue, too splendid to need illustration. They wrote verses on a new principle; saw rocks and rivers in a new light; and remaining studiously ignorant of history, society, and human nature, cultivated the fantasy only at the expense of the memory and the reason; and contrived, though they had retreated form the world for the express purpose of seeing nature as she was, to see her only as she was not, converting the land they lived in into a sort of fairyland, which they peopled with mysticisms and chimeras. This gave what is called a new tone to poetry, and conjured up a herd of desperate imitators, who have brought the age of brass prematurely to its dotage.

The descriptive poetry of the present day has been called by its cultivators a return to nature. Nothing is more impertinent than this pretension. Poetry cannot travel out of the regions of its birth, the uncultivated lands of semicivilized men. Mr. Wordsworth, the great leader of the returners to nature, cannot describe a scene under his own eyes without putting into it the shadow of a Danish boy or the living ghost of Lucy Gray, or some similar fantastical parturition of the moods of his own mind.

In the origin and perfection of poetry, all the associations of life were composed of poetical materials. With us it is decidedly the reverse. We know too that there are no dryads in Hyde Park nor naiads in the Regent's canal. But barbaric manners and supernatural interventions are essential to poetry. Either in the scene, or in the time, or in both, it must be remote from our ordinary perceptions. While the historian and the philosopher are advancing in, and accelerating, the progress of knowledge, the poet is wallowing in the rubbish of departed ignorance, and raking up the ashes of dead savages to find gewgaws and rattles for the grown babies of the age. Mr. Scott digs up the poachers and cattle-stealers of the ancient border. Lord Byron cruises for thieves and pirates on the shores of the Morea and among the Greek Islands. Mr. Southey wades through ponderous volumes of travels and old chronicles, from which he carefully selects all that is false, useless, and absurd, as being essentially poetical; and when he has a commonplace book full of monstrosities, strings them into an epic. Mr. Wordsworth picks up village legends from old women and sextons; and Mr. Coleridge, to the valuable information acquired from similar sources, superadds the dreams of crazy theologians and the mysticisms of German metaphysics, and favors the world with visions in verse, in which the quadruple elements of sexton, old woman, Jeremy Taylor, and Immanuel Kant, are harmonized into a delicious poetical compound. Mr. Moore presents us with a Persian, and Mr. Campbell with a Pennsylvanian tale, both formed on the same principle as Mr. Southey's epics, by extracting from a perfunctory and desultory perusal of a collection of voyages and travels, all that useful investigation would not seek for and that common sense would reject.

These disjointed relics of tradition and fragments of secondhand observation, being woven into a tissue of verse, constructed on what Mr. Coleridge calls a new principle (that is, no principle at all), compose a modern-antique compound of frippery and barbarism, in which the puling sentimentality of the present time is grafted on the misrepresented ruggedness of the past into a heterogeneous congeries of unamalgamating manners, sufficient to impose on the common readers of poetry, over whose understanding the poet of this class possesses that commanding advantage, which, in all circumstances and conditions of life, a man who knows something, however little, always possesses over one who knows nothing.

A poet in our times is a semibarbarian in a civilized community. He lives in the days that are past. His ideas, thoughts, feelings, associations, are all with barbarous manners, obsolete customs, and exploded superstitions. The march of his intellect is like that of a crab, backward. The brighter the light diffused around him by the progress of reason, the thicker is the darkness of antiquated barbarism, in which he buries himself like a mole, to throw up the barren hillocks of his Cimmerian labors. The philosophic mental tranquillity which looks round with an equal eye on all external things, collects a store of ideas, discriminates their relative value, assigns to all their proper place, and from the materials of useful knowledge thus collected, appreciated, and arranged, forms new combinations that impress the stamp of their power and utility on the real business of life, is diametrically the reverse of that frame of mind which poetry inspires, or from which poetry can emanate. The highest inspirations of poetry are resolvable into three ingredients: the rant of unregulated passion, the whining of exaggerated feeling, and the cant of factitious sentiment: and can therefore serve only to ripen a splendid lunatic like Alexander, a puling driveler like Werther,[9] or a morbid dreamer like Wordsworth. It can never make a philosopher, nor a statesman, nor in any case of life a useful or rational man. It cannot claim the slightest share in any one of the comforts and utilities of life of which we have witnessed so many and so rapid advances. But though not useful, it may be said it is highly ornamental, and deserves to be cultivated for the pleasure it yields. Even if this be granted, it does not follow that a writer of poetry in the present state of society is not a waster of his own time, and a robber of that of others. Poetry is not one of those arts which, like painting, require repetition and multiplication, in order to be diffused among society. There are more good poems already existing than are sufficient to employ that portion of life which any mere reader and recipient of poetical impressions should devote to them, and these having been produced in poetical times, are far superior in all the characteristics of poetry to the artificial reconstructions of a few morbid ascetics in unpoetical times. To read the promiscuous rubbish of the present time to the exclusion of the select treasures of the past, is to substitute the worse for the better variety of the same mode of enjoyment.

But in whatever degree poetry is cultivated, it must necessarily be to the neglect of some branch of useful study: and it is a lamentable spectacle to see minds, capable of better things, running to seed in the specious indolence of these empty aimless mockeries of intellectual exertion. Poetry was the mental rattle that awakened the attention of intellect in the infancy of civil society: but for the maturity of mind to make a serious business of the playthings of its childhood, is as absurd as for a full-grown man to rub his gums with coral, and cry to be charmed to sleep by the jingle of silver bells.

As to that small portion of our contemporary poetry, which is neither descriptive, nor narrative, nor dramatic, and which, for want of a better name, may be called ethical, the most distinguished portion of it, consisting merely of querulous, egotistical rhapsodies, to express the writer's high dissatisfaction with the world and everything in it, serves only to confirm what has been said of the semibarbarous character of poets, who from singing dithyrambics and "Io Triumphe," while society was savage, grow rabid, and out of their element, as it becomes polished and enlightened.

Now when we consider that it is not to the thinking and studious, and scientific and philosophical part of the community, not to those whose minds are bent on the pursuit and promotion of permanently useful ends and aims, that poets must address their minstrelsy, but to that much larger portion of the reading public, whose minds are not awakened to the desire of valuable knowledge, and who are indifferent to anything beyond being charmed, moved, excited, affected, and exalted: charmed by harmony, moved by sentiment, excited by passion, affected by pathos, and exalted by sublimity: harmony, which is language on the rack of Procrustes;[10] sentiment, which is canting egotism in the mask of refined feeling; passion, which is the commotion of a weak and selfish mind; pathos, which is the whining of an unmanly spirit; and sublimity, which is the inflation of an empty head: when we consider that the great and permanent interests of human society become more and more the mainspring of intellectual pursuit; that in proportion as they become so, the subordinacy of the ornamental to the useful will be more and more seen and acknowledged; and that therefore the progress of useful art and science, and of moral and political knowledge, will continue more and more to withdraw attention from frivolous and unconducive, to solid and conducive studies: that therefore the poetical audience will not only continually diminish in the proportion of its number to that of the rest of the reading public, but will also sink lower and lower in the comparison of intellectual acquirement: when we consider that the poet must still please his audience, and must therefore continue to sink to their level, while the rest of the community is rising above it: we may easily conceive that the day is not distant, when the degraded state of every species of poetry will be as generally recognized as that of dramatic poetry has long been: and this not from any decrease either of intellectual power, or intellectual acquisition, but because intellectual power and intellectual acquisition have turned themselves into other and better channels, and have abandoned the cultivation and the fate of poetry to the degenerate fry of modern rhymesters, and their Olympic judges, the magazine critics, who continue to debate and promulgate oracles about poetry, as if it were still what it was in the Homeric age, the all-in-all of intellectual progression, and as if there were no such things in existence as mathematicians, astronomers, chemists, moralists, metaphysicians, historians, politicians, and political economists, who have built into the upper air of intelligence a pyramid, from the summit of which they see the modern Parnassus[11] far beneath them, and, knowing how small a place it occupies in the comprehensiveness of their prospect, smile at the little ambition and the circumscribed perceptions with which the drivelers and mountebanks upon it are contending for the poetical palm and the critical chair.

---

[9]The reference to Alexander is unclear. Werther is the hero of Goethe's novel *The Sorrows of Young Werther* (1774).

[10]A mythical giant who tied his victims to an iron bed and stretched or cut them to fit.

[11]A mountain sacred to Apollo and the Muses.

Percy Bysshe Shelley

1792–1822

Written in answer to Peacock's satirical attack on poetry, Shelley's *Defense of Poetry* makes perhaps greater claims for the poet than anyone had ever dared. Beginning with the familiar Romantic distinction between imagination (synthesis) and reason (analysis), Shelley proceeds to attribute to the products of imagination immense spiritual and cultural powers. Shelley does not acknowledge Peacock's argument that the range of poetry is progressively diminished by the enlargement of the domain of reason; he maintains that the poet constantly refurbishes language, which would otherwise fall into decay and bring about cultural decadence. As a creator of new linguistic possibilities the poet "legislates" and "prophesies": he helps remake the world by reconstructing the form through which we see it. Shelley employs an organic metaphor: the poet's "thoughts are the germs of the flower and the fruit of latest time." Poetry "purges from our inward sight the film of familiarity which obscures from us the wonder of our being. . . . It creates anew the universe." Poetry sows the "seeds of social revolution."

To describe the relation of man's mind to nature, Shelley employs a metaphor familiar to readers of Coleridge and other Romantics, that of the wind harp, or Aeolian lyre. But the lyre is more passive in its relation to the wind than is man's subject in relation to nature's object, and Shelley avers that man produces not mere melody from his experience but "harmony, by an internal adjustment of the sounds or motions thus excited to the impressions which excite them." To describe the act of poetic creation Shelley, like Keats, employs an organic simile, which he combines with an image similar to that of the Aeolian lyre: "The mind in creation is as a fading coal, which some invisible influence, like an inconstant wind, awakens to transitory brightness; this power arises from within, like the color of a flower which fades and changes as it is developed. . . ."

Shelley offers a number of other definitions of poetry and poetic creation that are vague and Romantically all-inclusive. A characteristic Platonism appears in his remark that the poet "participates in the eternal, the infinite, and the one." Almost anyone who expresses a profound thought is classifiable as a poet under one or another of his definitions. It would seem, then, that *poetry* is an activity of which a *poem* is but one of many possible products. Shelley is most penetrating when he speculates about the poet's role in restoring the powers of language in order to make us see the world anew.

Shelley's complete works have been edited in ten volumes by Roger Ingpen and W. E. Peek (1927). John Shawcross has edited *Literary and Philosophical Criticism* (1909). Important critical studies are M. T. Solve, *Shelley: His Theory of Poetry* (1927); Floyd Stovall, *Desire and Restraint in Shelley* (1931); B. P. Kurtz, *The Pursuit of Death* (1933); C. H. Grabo, *The Magic Plant* (1936); N. I. White, *Shelley* (1940);

Carlos Baker, *Shelley's Major Poetry* (1948); J. A. Notopoulos, *The Platonism of Shelley* (1949); C. E. Pulos, *The Deep Truth: A Study of Shelley's Skepticism* (1954); Peter Butter, *Shelley's Idols of the Cave* (1954); Earle J. Schulze, *Shelley's Theory of Poetry* (1966); John W. Wright, *Shelley's Myth of Metaphor* (1970); Earl Wasserman, *Shelley: A Critical Reading* (1971); and Richard Holmes, *Shelley: The Pursuit* (1974).

A Defense of Poetry

According to one mode of regarding those two classes of mental action, which are called reason and imagination, the former may be considered as mind contemplating the relations borne by one thought to another, however produced; and the latter, as mind acting upon those thoughts so as to color them with its own light, and composing from them, as from elements, other thoughts, each containing within itself the principle of its own integrity. The one is the τὸ ποιεῖν,[1] or the principle of synthesis, and has for its objects those forms which are common to universal nature and existence itself; the other is the τὸ λογιζεῖν,[2] or principle of analysis, and its action regards the relations of things, simply as relations; considering thoughts, not in their integral unity, but as the algebraical representations which conduct to certain general results. Reason is the enumeration of quantities already known; imagination is the perception of the value of those quantities, both separately and as a whole. Reason respects the differences, and imagination the similitudes of things. Reason is to the imagination as the instrument to the agent, as the body to the spirit, as the shadow to the substance.

Poetry, in a general sense, may be defined to be "the expression of the imagination": and poetry is connate with the origin of man. Man is an instrument over which a series of external and internal impressions are driven, like the alternations of an ever-changing wind over an Aeolian lyre, which move it by their motion to ever-changing melody. But there is a principle within the human being, and perhaps within all sentient beings, which acts otherwise than in the lyre, and produces not melody alone, but harmony, by an internal adjustment of the sounds or motions thus excited to the impressions which excite them. It is as if the lyre could accommodate its chords to the motions of that which strikes them, in a determined proportion of sound; even as the mu-

sician can accommodate his voice to the sound of the lyre.[3] A child at play by itself will express its delight by its voice and motions; and every inflection of tone and every gesture will bear exact relation to a corresponding antitype in the pleasurable impressions which awakened it; it will be the reflected image of that impression; and as the lyre trembles and sounds after the wind has died away, so the child seeks, by prolonging in its voice and motions the duration of the effect, to prolong also a consciousness of the cause. In relation to the objects which delight a child, these expressions are what poetry is to higher objects. The savage (for the savage is to ages what the child is to years) expresses the emotions produced in him by surrounding objects in a similar manner; and language and gesture, together with plastic or pictorial imitation, become the image of the combined effect of those objects, and of his apprehension of them. Man in society, with all his passions and his pleasures, next becomes the object of the passions and pleasures of man; an additional class of emotions produces an augmented treasure of expressions; and language, gesture, and the imitative arts, become at once the representation and the medium, the pencil and the picture, the chisel and the statue, the chord and the harmony. The social sympathies, or those laws from which, as from its elements, society results, begin to develop themselves from the moment that two human beings coexist; the future is contained within the present, as the plant within the seed; and equality, diversity, unity, contrast, mutual dependence, become the principles alone capable of affording the motives according to which the will of a social being is determined to action, inasmuch as he is social; and constitute pleasure in sensation, virtue in sentiment, beauty in art, truth in reasoning, and love in the intercourse of kind. Hence men, even in the infancy of society, observe a certain order in their words and actions, distinct from that of the objects and the impressions represented by them, all expression being subject to the laws of that from which it proceeds. But let us dismiss those more general considerations which might involve an inquiry into the principles of society itself, and re-

---

A DEFENSE OF POETRY. Shelley's *Defense of Poetry* was written in 1821 but not published until 1840.
[1]"Making."
[2]"Reasoning."

---

[3]On the Aeolian lyre see M. H. Abrams, *The Correspondent Breeze: A Romantic Metaphor* in his *English Romantic Poets* (1960), pp. 37–54.

strict our view to the manner in which the imagination is expressed upon its forms.

In the youth of the world, men dance and sing and imitate natural objects, observing in these actions, as in all others, a certain rhythm or order. And, although all men observe a similar, they observe not the same order, in the motions of the dance, in the melody of the song, in the combinations of language, in the series of their imitations of natural objects. For there is a certain order or rhythm belonging to each of these classes of mimetic representation, from which the hearer and the spectator receive an intenser and purer pleasure than from any other: the sense of an approximation to this order has been called taste by modern writers. Every man in the infancy of art observes an order which approximates more or less closely to that from which this highest delight results: but the diversity is not sufficiently marked, as that its gradations should be sensible, except in those instances where the predominance of this faculty of approximation to the beautiful (for so we may be permitted to name the relation between this highest pleasure and its cause) is very great. Those in whom it exists in excess are poets, in the most universal sense of the word; and the pleasure resulting from the manner in which they express the influence of society or nature upon their own minds, communicates itself to others, and gathers a sort of reduplication from that community. Their language is vitally metaphorical; that is, it marks the before unapprehended relations of things and perpetuates their apprehension, until the words which represent them become, through time, signs for portions or classes of thoughts instead of pictures of integral thoughts; and then if no new poets should arise to create afresh the associations which have been thus disorganized, language will be dead to all the nobler purposes of human intercourse. These similitudes or relations are finely said by Lord Bacon to be "the same footsteps of nature impressed upon the various subjects of the world";[4] and he considers the faculty which perceives them as the storehouse of axioms common to all knowledge. In the infancy of society every author is necessarily a poet, because language itself is poetry; and to be a poet is to apprehend the true and the beautiful, in a word, the good which exists in the relation, subsisting, first between existence and perception, and secondly between perception and expression. Every original language near to its source is in itself the chaos of a cyclic poem: the copiousness of lexicography and the distinctions of grammar are the works of a later age, and are merely the catalogue and the form of the creations of poetry.

But poets, or those who imagine and express this indestructible order, are not only the authors of language and of music, of the dance, and architecture, and statuary, and painting; they are the institutors of laws, and the founders of civil society, and the inventors of the arts of life, and the teachers, who draw into a certain propinquity with the beautiful and the true, that partial apprehension of the agencies of the invisible world which is called religion. Hence all original religions are allegorical, or susceptible of allegory, and, like Janus, have a double face of false and true. Poets, according to the circumstances of the age and nation in which they appeared, were called, in the earlier epochs of the world, legislators, or prophets: a poet essentially comprises and unites both these characters. For he not only beholds intensely the present as it is, and discovers those laws according to which present things ought to be ordered, but he beholds the future in the present, and his thoughts are the germs of the flower and the fruit of latest time. Not that I assert poets to be prophets in the gross sense of the word, or that they can foretell the form as surely as they foreknow the spirit of events: such is the pretense of superstition, which would make poetry an attribute of prophecy, rather than prophecy an attribute of poetry.[5] A poet participates in the eternal, the infinite, and the one; as far as relates to his conceptions, time and place and number are not. The grammatical forms which express the moods of time, and the difference of persons, and the distinction of place, are convertible with respect to the highest poetry without injuring it as poetry; and the choruses of Aeschylus, and the book of Job, and Dante's "Paradise," would afford, more than any other writings, examples of this fact, if the limits of this essay did not forbid citation. The creation of sculpture, painting, and music, are illustrations still more decisive.

Language, color, form, and religious and civil habits of action, are all the instruments and materials of poetry; they may be called poetry by that figure of speech which considers the effect as a synonym of the cause. But poetry in a more restricted sense expresses those arrangements of language, and especially metrical language, which are created by that imperial faculty, whose throne is curtained within the invisible nature of man. And this springs from the nature itself of language, which is a more direct representation of the actions and passions of our internal being, and is susceptible of more various and delicate combinations, than color, form, or motion, and is more plastic and obedient to the control of that faculty of which it is the creation. For language is arbitrarily produced by the imagination, and has relation to thoughts

---

[4]*On the Development of the Sciences*, III. i.

[5]Compare Sidney, *An Apology for Poetry*, pp. 143–62.

alone; but all other materials, instruments, and conditions of art, have relations among each other, which limit and interpose between conception and expression. The former is as a mirror which reflects, the latter as a cloud which enfeebles, the light of which both are mediums of communications. Hence the fame of sculptors, painters, and musicians, although the intrinsic powers of the great masters of these arts may yield in no degree to that of those who have employed language as the hieroglyphic of their thoughts, has never equaled that of poets in the restricted sense of the term; as two performers of equal skill will produce unequal effects from a guitar and a harp. The fame of legislators and founders of religions, so long as their institutions last, alone seems to exceed that of poets in the restricted sense; but it can scarcely be a question, whether, if we deduct the celebrity which their flattery of the gross opinions of the vulgar usually conciliates, together with that which belonged to them in their higher character of poets, any excess will remain.

We have thus circumscribed the word *poetry* within the limits of that art which is the most familiar and the most perfect expression of the faculty itself. It is necessary, however, to make the circle still narrower, and to determine the distinction between measured and unmeasured language; for the popular division into prose and verse is inadmissible in accurate philosophy.

Sounds as well as thoughts have relation both between each other and towards that which they represent, and a perception of the order of those relations has always been found connected with a perception of the order of the relations of thoughts. Hence the language of poets have ever affected a certain uniform and harmonious recurrence of sound, without which it were not poetry, and which is scarcely less indispensable to the communication of its influence, than the words themselves, without reference to that peculiar order. Hence the vanity of translation; it were as wise to cast a violet into a crucible that you might discover the formal principle of its color and odor, as seek to transfuse from one language into another the creations of a poet. The plant must spring again from its seed, or it will bear no flower—and this is the burthen of the curse of Babel.

An observation of the regular mode of the recurrence of harmony in the language of poetical minds, together with its relation to music, produced meter, or a certain system of traditional forms of harmony and language. Yet is is by no means essential that a poet should accommodate his language to this traditional form, so that the harmony, which is its spirit, be observed. The practice is indeed convenient and popular, and to be preferred, especially in such composition as includes much action: but every great poet must inevitably innovate upon the example of his predecessors in the exact structure of his peculiar versification. The distinction between poets and prose writers is a vulgar error. The distinction between philosophers and poets has been anticipated. Plato was essentially a poet—the truth and splendor of his imagery, and the melody of his language, are the most intense that it is possible to conceive. He rejected the measure of the epic, dramatic, and lyrical forms, because he sought to kindle a harmony in thoughts divested of shape and action, and he forbore to invent any regular plan of rhythm which would include, under determinate forms, the varied pauses of his style. Cicero sought to imitate the cadence of his periods, but with little success. Lord Bacon was a poet.[6] His language has a sweet and majestic rhythm, which satisfies the sense, no less than the almost superhuman wisdom of his philosophy satisfies the intellect; it is a strain which distends, and then bursts the circumference of the hearer's mind, and pours itself forth together with it into the universal element with which it has perpetual sympathy. All the authors of revolutions in opinion are not only necessary poets as they are inventors, nor even as their words unveil the permanent analogy of things by images which participate in the life of truth; but as their periods are harmonious and rhythmical, and contain in themselves the elements of verse; being the echo of the eternal music. Nor are those supreme poets, who have employed traditional forms of rhythm on account of the form and action of their subjects, less capable of perceiving and teaching the truth of things, than those who have omitted that form. Shakespeare, Dante, and Milton (to confine ourselves to modern writers) are philosophers of the very loftiest power.

A poem is the very image of life expressed in its eternal truth. There is this difference between a story and a poem, that a story is a catalogue of detached facts, which have no other connection than time, place, circumstance, cause and effect; the other is the creation of actions according to the unchangeable forms of human nature, as existing in the mind of the creator, which is itself the image of all other minds. The one is partial, and applies only to a definite period of time, and a certain combination of events which can never again recur; the other is universal, and contains within itself the germ of a relation to whatever motives or actions have place in the possible varieties of human nature.[7] Time, which destroys the beauty and the use of the story of particular facts, stripped of the poetry which should invest them, augments that of poetry, and forever develops new and wonder-

---

[6][Shelley] See *The String of the Labyrinth,* and the essay on death particularly.
[7]See Aristotle on poetry and history in *Poetics,* IX. 3, p. 55.

ful applications of the eternal truth which it contains. Hence epitomes have been called the moths of just history; they eat out the poetry of it. A story of particular facts is as a mirror which obscures and distorts that which should be beautiful: poetry is a mirror which makes beautiful that which is distorted.

The parts of a composition may be poetical, without the composition as a whole being a poem. A single sentence may be considered as a whole, though it may be found in the midst of a series of unassimilated portions; a single word even may be a spark of inextinguishable thought. And thus all the great historians, Herodotus, Plutarch, Livy, were poets; and although the plan of these writers, especially that of Livy, restrained them from developing this faculty in its highest degree, they made copious and ample amends for their subjection, by filling all the interstices of their subjects with living images.

Having determined what is poetry, and who are poets, let us proceed to estimate its effects upon society.

Poetry is ever accompanied with pleasure: all spirits on which it falls open themselves to receive the wisdom which is mingled with its delight.[8] In the infancy of the world, neither poets themselves nor their auditors are fully aware of the excellence of poetry: for it acts in a divine and unapprehended manner, beyond and above consciousness; and it is reserved for future generations to contemplate and measure the mighty cause and effect in all the strength and splendor of their union. Even in modern times, no living poet ever arrived at the fullness of his fame; the jury which sits in judgment upon a poet, belonging as he does to all time, must be composed of his peers: it must be impaneled by time from the selectest of the wise of many generations. A poet is a nightingale, who sits in darkness and sings to cheer its own solitude with sweet sounds; his auditors are as men entranced by the melody of an unseen musician, who feel that they are moved and softened, yet know not whence or why. The poems of Homer and his contemporaries were the delight of infant Greece; they were the elements of that social system which is the column upon which all succeeding civilization has reposed. Homer embodied the ideal perfection of his age in human character; nor can we doubt that those who read his verses were awakened to an ambition of becoming like to Achilles, Hector, and Ulysses: the truth and beauty of friendship, patriotism, and persevering devotion to an object, were unveiled to the depths in these immortal creations: the sentiments of the auditors must have been refined and en-larged by a sympathy with such great and lovely impersonations, until from admiring they imitated, and from imitation they identified themselves with the objects of their admiration. Nor let it be objected, that these characters are remote from moral perfection, and that they are by no means to be considered as edifying patterns for general imitation. Every epoch, under names more or less specious, has deified its peculiar errors; revenge is the naked idol of the worship of a semibarbarous age; and self-deceit is the veiled image of unknown evil, before which luxury and satiety lie prostrate. But a poet considers the vices of his contemporaries as a temporary dress in which his creations must be arrayed, and which cover without concealing the eternal proportions of their beauty. An epic or dramatic personage is understood to wear them around his soul, as he may the ancient armor or the modern uniform around his body; whilst it is easy to conceive a dress more graceful than either. The beauty of the internal nature cannot be so far concealed by its accidental vesture, but that the spirit of its form shall communicate itself to the very disguise, and indicate the shape it hides from the manner in which it is worn. A majestic form and graceful motions will express themselves through the most barbarous and tasteless costume. Few poets of the highest class have chosen to exhibit the beauty of their conceptions in its naked truth and splendor; and it is doubtful whether the alloy of costume, habit, &c., be not necessary to temper this planetary music for mortal ears.

The whole objection, however, of the immorality of poetry rests upon a misconception of the manner in which poetry acts to produce the moral improvement of man. Ethical science arranges the elements which poetry has created, and propounds schemes and proposes examples of civil and domestic life: nor is it for want of admirable doctrines that men hate, and despise, and censure, and deceive, and subjugate one another. But poetry acts in another and diviner manner. It awakens and enlarges the mind itself by rendering it the receptacle of a thousand unapprehended combinations of thought. Poetry lifts the veil from the hidden beauty of the world, and makes familiar objects be as if they were not familiar; it reproduces all that it represents, and the impersonations clothed in its Elysian light stand thenceforward in the minds of those who have once contemplated them as memorials of that gentle and exalted content which extends itself over all thoughts and actions with which it coexists. The great secret of morals is love; or a going out of our own nature, and an identification of ourselves with the beautiful which exists in thought, action, or person, not our own. A man, to be greatly good, must imagine intensely and comprehensively; he must put himself in the place of another and of many others; the pains and pleasures of his species must

---

[8]See Horace, *Art of Poetry*, p. 72.

become his own. The great instrument of moral good is the imagination; and poetry administers to the effect by acting upon the cause. Poetry enlarges the circumference of the imagination by replenishing it with thoughts of ever new delight, which have the power of attracting and assimilating to their own nature all other thoughts, and which form new intervals and interstices whose void forever craves fresh food. Poetry strengthens the faculty which is the organ of the moral nature of man, in the same manner as exercise strengthens a limb. A poet therefore would do ill to embody his own conceptions of right and wrong, which are usually those of his place and time, in his poetical creations, which participate in neither. By this assumption of the inferior office of interpreting the effect, in which perhaps after all he might acquit himself but imperfectly, he would resign a glory in a participation in the cause. There was little danger that Homer, or any of the eternal poets, should have so far misunderstood themselves as to have abdicated this throne of their widest dominion. Those in whom the poetical faculty, though great, is less intense, as Euripides, Lucan, Tasso, Spenser, have frequently affected a moral aim, and the effect of their poetry is diminished in exact proportion to the degree in which they compel us to advert to this purpose.

Homer and the cyclic poets were followed at a certain interval by the dramatic and lyrical poets of Athens, who flourished contemporaneously with all that is most perfect in the kindred expressions of the poetical faculty; architecture, painting, music, the dance, sculpture, philosophy, and, we may add, the forms of civil life. For although the scheme of Athenian society was deformed by many imperfections which the poetry existing in chivalry and Christianity has erased from the habits and institutions of modern Europe; yet never at any other period has so much energy, beauty, and virtue, been developed; never was blind strength and stubborn form so disciplined and rendered subject to the will of man, or that will less repugnant to the dictates of the beautiful and the true, as during the century which preceded the death of Socrates. Of no other epoch in the history of our species have we records and fragments stamped so visibly with the image of the divinity in man. But it is poetry alone, in form, in action, and in language, which has rendered this epoch memorable above all others, and the storehouse of examples to everlasting time. For written poetry existed at that epoch simultaneously with the other arts, and it is an idle inquiry to demand which gave and which received the light, which all, as from a common focus, have scattered over the darkest periods of succeeding time. We know no more of cause and effect than a constant conjunction of events: poetry is ever found to coexist with whatever other arts contribute to the happiness and perfection of man. I appeal to what

has already been established to distinguish between the cause and the effect.

It was at the period here adverted to, that the drama had its birth; and however a succeeding writer may have equaled or surpassed those few great specimens of the Athenian drama which have been preserved to us, it is indisputable that the art itself never was understood or practiced according to the true philosophy of it, as at Athens. For the Athenians employed language, action, music, painting, the dance, and religious institutions, to produce a common effect in the representation of the highest idealisms of passion and of power; each division in the art was made perfect in its kind by artists of the most consummate skill, and was disciplined into a beautiful proportion and unity one towards the other. On the modern stage a few only of the elements capable of expressing the image of the poet's conception are employed at once. We have tragedy without music and dancing; and music and dancing without the highest impersonations of which they are the fit accompaniment, and both without religion and solemnity. Religious institution has indeed been usually banished from the stage. Our system of divesting the actor's face of a mask, on which the many expressions appropriated to his dramatic character might be molded into one permanent and unchanging expression, is favorable only to a partial and inharmonious effect; it is fit for nothing but a monologue, where all the attention may be directed to some great master of ideal mimicry. The modern practice of blending comedy with tragedy, though liable to great abuse in point of practice, is undoubtedly an extension of the dramatic circle; but the comedy should be as in *King Lear,* universal, ideal, and sublime. It is perhaps the intervention of this principle which determines the balance in favor of *King Lear* against the *Oedipus Tyrannus* or the *Agamemnon;* or, if you will, the trilogies with which they are connected; unless the intense power of the choral poetry, especially that of the latter, should be considered as restoring the equilibrium. *King Lear,* if it can sustain this comparison, may be judged to be the most perfect specimen of the dramatic art existing in the world; in spite of the narrow conditions to which the poet was subjected by the ignorance of the philosophy of the drama which has prevailed in modern Europe. Calderón, in his religious *autos,*[9] has attempted to fulfill some of the high conditions of dramatic representation neglected by Shakespeare; such as the establishing a relation between the drama and religion, and the accommodating them to music and dancing; but he omits the observation of conditions still more important, and more is lost than gained by the substi-

---

[9]One-act sacramental plays.

tution of the rigidly defined and ever-repeated idealisms of a distorted superstition for the living impersonations of the truth of human passion.

But I digress. The connection of scenic exhibitions with the improvement or corruption of the manners of men, has been universally recognized: in other words, the presence or absence of poetry in its most perfect and universal form, has been found to be connected with good and evil in conduct or habit. The corruption which has been imputed to the drama as an effect, begins, when the poetry employed in its constitution ends: I appeal to the history of manners whether the periods of the growth of the one and the decline of the other have not corresponded with an exactness equal to any example of moral cause and effect.

The drama at Athens, or wheresoever else it may have approached to its perfection, ever coexisted with the moral and intellectual greatness of the age. The tragedies of the Athenian poets are as mirrors in which the spectator beholds himself, under a thin disguise of circumstance, stripped of all but that ideal perfection and energy which everyone feels to be the internal type of all that he loves, admires, and would become. The imagination is enlarged by a sympathy with pains and passions so mighty, that they distend in their conception the capacity of that by which they are conceived; the good affections are strengthened by pity, indignation, terror, and sorrow; and an exalted calm is prolonged from the satiety of this high exercise of them into the tumult of familiar life: even crime is disarmed of half its horror and all its contagion by being represented as the fatal consequence of the unfathomable agencies of nature; error is thus divested of its willfulness; men can no longer cherish it as the creation of their choice. In a drama of the highest order there is little food for censure or hatred; it teaches rather self-knowledge and self-respect. Neither the eye nor the mind can see itself, unless reflected upon that which it resembles. The drama, so long as it continues to express poetry, is as a prismatic and many-sided mirror, which collects the brightest rays of human nature and divides and reproduces them from the simplicity of their elementary forms, and touches them with majesty and beauty, and multiplies all that it reflects, and endows it with the power of propagating its like wherever it may fall.

But in periods of the decay of social life, the drama sympathizes with that decay. Tragedy becomes a cold imitation of the forms of the great masterpieces of antiquity, divested of all harmonious accompaniment of the kindred arts; and often the very form misunderstood, or a weak attempt to teach certain doctrines, which the writer considers as moral truths; and which are usually no more than specious flatteries of some gross vice or weakness, with which the author, in common with his auditors, are infected. Hence what has been called the classical and domestic drama. Addison's *Cato* is a specimen of the one; and would it were not superfluous to cite examples of the other! To such purposes poetry cannot be made subservient. Poetry is a sword of lightning, ever unsheathed, which consumes the scabbard that would contain it. And thus we observe that all dramatic writings of this nature are unimaginative in a singular degree; they affect sentiment and passion, which, divested of imagination, are other names for caprice and appetite. The period in our own history of the grossest degradation of the drama is the reign of Charles II, when all forms in which poetry had been accustomed to be expressed became hymns to the triumph of kingly power over liberty and virtue. Milton stood alone illuminating an age unworthy of him. At such periods the calculating principle pervades all the forms of dramatic exhibition, and poetry ceases to be expressed upon them. Comedy loses its ideal universality: wit succeeds to humor; we laugh from self-complacency and triumph, instead of pleasure; malignity, sarcasm, and contempt, succeed to sympathetic merriment; we hardly laugh, but we smile. Obscenity, which is ever blasphemy against the divine beauty in life, becomes, from a very veil which it assumes, more active if less disgusting: it is a monster for which the corruption of society forever brings forth new food, which it devours in secret.

The drama being that form under which a greater number of modes of expression of poetry are susceptible of being combined than any other, the connection of poetry and social good is more observable in the drama than in whatever other form. And it is indisputable that the highest perfection of human society has ever corresponded with the highest dramatic excellence; and that the corruption or the extinction of the drama in a nation where it has once flourished, is a mark of a corruption of manners, and an extinction of the energies which sustain the soul of social life. But, as Machiavelli says of political institutions, that life may be preserved and renewed, if men should arise capable of bringing back the drama to its principles. And this is true with respect to poetry in its most extended sense: all language, institution and form, require not only to be produced but to be sustained: the office and character of a poet participates in the divine nature as regards providence, no less than as regards creation.

Civil war, the spoils of Asia, and the fatal predominance first of the Macedonian, and then of the Roman arms, were so many symbols of the extinction or suspension of the creative faculty in Greece. The bucolic writers, who found patronage under the lettered tyrants of Sicily and Egypt, were the latest representatives of its most glorious reign. Their poetry is intensely melodious; like the odor of the tuberose, it overcomes and sickens the spirit with excess of sweetness; whilst the poetry of the preceding age was as a meadow-gale of June, which mingles the fragrance of all the flowers of the field, and adds a quickening and harmonizing spirit of its own, which endows the sense with a power of sustaining its extreme delight. The bucolic and erotic delicacy in written poetry is correlative with that softness in statuary, music, and the kindred arts, and even in manners and institutions, which distinguished the epoch to which I now refer. Nor is it the poetical faculty itself, or any misapplication of it, to which this want of harmony is to be imputed. An equal sensibility to the influence of the senses and the affections is to be found in the writings of Homer and Sophocles: the former, especially, has clothed sensual and pathetic images with irresistible attractions. Their superiority over these succeeding writers consists in the presence of those thoughts which belong to the inner faculties of our nature, not in the absence of those which are connected with the external: their incomparable perfection consists in a harmony of the union of all. It is not what the erotic poets have, but what they have not, in which their imperfection consists. It is not inasmuch as they were poets, but inasmuch as they were not poets, that they can be considered with any plausibility as connected with the corruption of their age. Had that corruption availed so as to extinguish in them the sensibility to pleasure, passion, and natural scenery, which is imputed to them as an imperfection, the last triumph of evil would have been achieved. For the end of social corruption is to destroy all sensibility to pleasure; and therefore it is corruption. It begins at the imagination and the intellect as at the core, and distributes itself thence as a paralyzing venom, through the affections into the very appetites, until all become a torpid mass in which hardly sense survives. At the approach of such a period, poetry ever addresses itself to those faculties which are the last to be destroyed, and its voice is heard, like the footsteps of Astraea,[10] departing from the world. Poetry ever communicates all the pleasure which men are capable of receiving: it is ever still the light of life; the source of whatever of beautiful or generous or true can have place in an evil time. It will readily be confessed that those among the luxurious citizens of Syracuse and Alexandria, who were delighted with the poems of Theocritus, were less cold, cruel, and sensual than the remnant of their tribe. But corruption must utterly have destroyed the fabric of human society before poetry can ever cease. The sacred links of that chain have never been entirely disjoined, which descending through the minds of many men is attached to those great minds, whence as from a magnet the invisible effluence is sent forth, which at once connects, animates, and sustains the life of all. It is the faculty which contains within itself the seeds at once of its own and of social renovation. And let us not circumscribe the effects of the bucolic and erotic poetry within the limits of the sensibility of those to whom it was addressed. They may have perceived the beauty of those immortal compositions, simply as fragments and isolated portions: those who are more finely organized, or born in a happier age, may recognize them as episodes to that great poem, which all poets, like the cooperating thoughts of one great mind, have built up since the beginning of the world.

The same revolutions within a narrower sphere had place in ancient Rome; but the actions and forms of its social life never seem to have been perfectly saturated with the poetical element. The Romans appear to have considered the Greeks as the selectest treasuries of the selectest forms of manners and of nature, and to have abstained from creating in measured language, sculpture, music, or architecture, anything which might bear a particular relation to their own condition, whilst it should bear a general one to the universal constitution of the world. But we judge from partial evidence, and we judge perhaps partially. Ennius, Varro, Pacuvius, and Accius, all great poets, have been lost. Lucretius is in the highest, and Virgil in a very high sense, a creator. The chosen delicacy of expressions of the latter, are as a mist of light which conceal from us the intense and exceeding truth of his conceptions of nature. Livy is instinct with poetry. Yet Horace, Catullus, Ovid, and generally the other great writers of the Virgilian age, saw man and nature in the mirror of Greece. The institutions also, and the religion, of Rome were less poetical than those of Greece, as the shadow is less vivid than the substance. Hence poetry in Rome, seemed to follow, rather than accompany, the perfection of political and domestic society. The true poetry of Rome lived in its institutions; for whatever of beautiful, true, and majestic, they contained, could have sprung only from the faculty which creates the order in which they consist. The life of Camillus, the death of Regulus; the expectation of the senators, in their godlike state, of the victorious Gauls; the refusal of the republic to make peace with Hannibal, after the battle of Cannae, were not the consequences of a refined calculation of the probable personal advantage to result from such a rhythm and order in the shows of life, to those who were at once the poets and the actors of these immortal dramas. The imagination beholding the beauty of this order, created it out of itself according to its own idea; the consequence was empire, and the reward everlasting fame. These things are not the less poetry, *"quia carent vate sacro."*[11] They are the epi-

---

[10]Goddess of justice, who fled earth in the age of brass.

[11]"Because they lack the divine prophet." Horace, *Odes,* IV. ix. 28, but misquoted.

sodes of that cyclic poem written by time upon the memories of men. The past, like an inspired rhapsodist, fills the theatre of everlasting generations with their harmony.

At length the ancient system of religion and manners had fulfilled the circle of its evolutions. And the world would have fallen into utter anarchy and darkness, but that there were found poets among the authors of the Christian and chivalric systems of manners and religion, who created forms of opinion and action never before conceived; which, copied into the imaginations of men, become as generals to the bewildered armies of their thoughts. It is foreign to the present purpose to touch upon the evil produced by these systems: except that we protest, on the ground of the principles already established, that no portion of it can be attributed to the poetry they contain.

It is probable that the poetry of Moses, Job, David, Solomon, and Isaiah, had produced a great effect upon the mind of Jesus and his disciples. The scattered fragments preserved to us by the biographers of this extraordinary person, are all instinct with the most vivid poetry. But his doctrines seem to have been quickly distorted. At a certain period after the prevalence of a system of opinions founded upon those promulgated by him, the three forms into which Plato had distributed the faculties of mind underwent a sort of apotheosis, and became the object of the worship of the civilized world. Here it is to be confessed that "Light seems to thicken," and

> The crow makes wing to the rooky wood,
> Good things of day begin to droop and drowse,
> And night's black agents to their preys do rouse.[12]

But mark how beautiful an order has sprung from the dust and blood of this fierce chaos! How the world, as from a resurrection, balancing itself on the golden wings of knowledge and of hope, has reassumed its yet unwearied flight into the heaven of time. Listen to the music, unheard by outward ears, which is as a ceaseless and invisible wind, nourishing its everlasting course with strength and swiftness.

The poetry in the doctrines of Jesus Christ, and the mythology and institutions of the Celtic[13] conquerors of the Roman Empire, outlived the darkness and the convulsions connected with their growth and victory, and blended themselves in a new fabric of manners and opinion. It is an error to impute the ignorance of the Dark Ages to the Christian doctrines or the predominance of the Celtic nations. Whatever of evil their agencies may have contained sprang from

the extinction of the poetical principle, connected with the progress of despotism and superstition. Men, from causes too intricate to be here discussed, had become insensible and selfish: their own will had become feeble, and yet they were its slaves, and thence the slaves of the will of others: lust, fear, avarice, cruelty, and fraud, characterized a race amongst whom no one was to be found capable of *creating* in form, language, or institution. The moral anomalies of such a state of society are not justly to be charged upon any class of events immediately connected with them, and those events are most entitled to our approbation which could dissolve it most expeditiously. It is unfortunate for those who cannot distinguish words from thoughts, that many of these anomalies have been incorporated into our popular religion.

It was not until the eleventh century that the effects of the poetry of the Christian and chivalric systems began to manifest themselves. The principle of equality had been discovered and applied by Plato in his *Republic,* as the theoretical rule of the mode in which the materials of pleasure and of power produced by the common skill and labor of human beings, ought to be distributed among them. The limitations of this rule were asserted by him to be determined only by the sensibility of each, or the utility to result to all. Plato, following the doctrines of Timaeus and Pythagoras, taught also a moral and intellectual system of doctrine, comprehending at once the past, the present, and the future condition of man. Jesus Christ divulged the sacred and eternal truths contained in these views to mankind, and Christianity, in its abstract purity, became the exoteric expression of the esoteric doctrines of the poetry and wisdom of antiquity. The incorporation of the Celtic nations with the exhausted population of the south, impressed upon it the figure of the poetry existing in their mythology and institutions. The result was a sum of the action and reaction of all the causes included in it; for it may be assumed as a maxim that no nation or religion can supersede any other without incorporating into itself a portion of that which it supersedes. The abolition of personal and domestic slavery, and the emancipation of women from a great part of the degrading restraints of antiquity, were among the consequences of these events.

The abolition of personal slavery is the basis of the highest political hope that it can enter into the mind of man to conceive. The freedom of women produced the poetry of sexual love. Love became a religion, the idols of whose worship were ever present. It was as if the statues of Apollo and the Muses had been endowed with life and motion, and had walked forth among their worshippers; so that earth became peopled by the inhabitants of a diviner world. The familiar appearance and proceedings of life became wonderful and heavenly, and a paradise was created as out of the wrecks of

---

[12]*Macbeth*, III. ii. 50–53.
[13]Shelley must mean Germanic.

Eden. And as this creation itself is poetry, so its creators were poets; and language was the instrument of their art: *"Gal-eotto fù il libro, e chi lo scrisse."*[14] The Provençal trouveurs, or inventors, preceded Petrarch, whose verses are as spells, which unseal the inmost enchanted fountains of the delight which is in the grief of love. It is impossible to feel them without becoming a portion of that beauty which we contemplate: it were superfluous to explain how the gentleness and the elevation of mind connected with these sacred emotions can render men more amiable, more generous and wise, and lift them out of the dull vapors of the little world of self. Dante understood the secret things of love even more than Petrarch. His *Vita Nuova* is an inexhaustible fountain of purity of sentiment and language: it is the idealized history of that period, and those intervals of his life which were dedicated to love. His apotheosis of Beatrice in Paradise, and the gradations of his own love and her loveliness, by which as by steps he feigns himself to have ascended to the throne of the Supreme Cause, is the most glorious imagination of modern poetry. The acutest critics have justly reversed the judgment of the vulgar, and the order of the great acts of the *Divina Commedia,* in the measure of the admiration which they accord to the "Hell," "Purgatory," and "Paradise." The latter is a perpetual hymn of everlasting love. Love, which found a worthy poet in Plato alone of all the ancients, has been celebrated by a chorus of the greatest writers of the renovated world; and the music has penetrated the caverns of society, and its echoes still drown the dissonance of arms and superstition. At successive intervals, Ariosto, Tasso, Shakespeare, Spenser, Calderon, Rousseau, and the great writers of our own age, have celebrated the dominion of love, planting as it were trophies in the human mind of that sublimest victory over sensuality and force. The true relation borne to each other by the sexes into which humankind is distributed, has become less misunderstood; and if the error which confounded diversity with inequality of the powers of the two sexes has been partially recognized in the opinions and institutions of modern Europe, we owe this great benefit to the worship of which chivalry was the law, and poets the prophets.

The poetry of Dante may be considered as the bridge thrown over the stream of time, which unites the modern and ancient world. The distorted notions of invisible things which Dante and his rival Milton have idealized, are merely the mask and the mantle in which these great poets walk through eternity enveloped and disguised. It is a difficult question to determine how far they were conscious of the distinction which must have subsisted in their minds between their own creeds and that of the people. Dante at least appears to wish to mark the full extent of it by placing Riphaeus, whom Virgil calls *"justissimus unus,"*[15] in Paradise, and observing a most heretical caprice in his distribution of rewards and punishments.[16] And Milton's poem contains within itself a philosophical refutation of that system, of which, by a strange and natural antithesis, it has been a chief popular support. Nothing can exceed the energy and magnificence of the character of Satan as expressed in *Paradise Lost.* It is a mistake to suppose that he could ever have been intended for the popular personification of evil. Implacable hate, patient cunning, and a sleepless refinement of device to inflict the extremest anguish on an enemy, these things are evil; and, although venial in a slave, are not to be forgiven in a tyrant; although redeemed by much that ennobles his defeat in one subdued, are marked by all that dishonors his conquest in the victor. Milton's Devil as a moral being is as far superior to his God, as one who perseveres in some purpose which he has conceived to be excellent in spite of adversity and torture, is to one who in the cold security of undoubted triumph inflicts the most horrible revenge upon his enemy, not from any mistaken notion of inducing him to repent of a perseverance in enmity, but with the alleged design of exasperating him to deserve new torments. Milton has so far violated the popular creed (if this shall be judged to be a violation) as to have alleged no superiority of moral virtue to his god over his devil. And this bold neglect of a direct moral purpose is the most decisive proof of the supremacy of Milton's genius. He mingled as it were the elements of human nature as colors upon a single pallet, and arranged them in the composition of his great picture according to the laws of epic truth; that is, according to the laws of that principle by which a series of actions of the external universe and of intelligent and ethical beings is calculated to excite the sympathy of succeeding generations of mankind. The *Divina Commedia* and *Paradise Lost* have conferred upon modern mythology a systematic form; and when change and time shall have added one more superstition to the mass of those which have arisen and decayed upon the earth, commentators will be learnedly employed in elucidating the religion of ancestral Europe, only not utterly forgotten because it will have been stamped with the eternity of genius.

Homer was the first and Dante the second epic poet: that is, the second poet, the series of whose creations bore a

---

[14] "Galeott was the book, and he who wrote it." Dante, *The Divine Comedy,* "Inferno," V. 137.

[15] "The most just one." *Aeneid,* II. 426–27.
[16] Riphaeus was a pagan, but Dante put him in Paradise.

defined and intelligible relation to the knowledge and sentiment and religion of the age in which he lived, and of the ages which followed it: developing itself in correspondence with their development. For Lucretius had limed the wings of his swift spirit in the dregs of the sensible world; and Virgil, with a modesty that ill became his genius, had affected the fame of an imitator, even whilst he created anew all that he copied; and none among the flock of mock birds, though their notes were sweet, Apollonius Rhodius, Quintus Calaber Smyrnaeus, Nonnus, Lucan, Statius, or Claudian, have sought even to fulfill a single condition of epic truth. Milton was the third epic poet. For if the title of epic in its highest sense be refused to the *Aeneid,* still less can it be conceded to the *Orlando Furioso,* the *Gerusalemme Liberata,* the *Lusiad,* or the *Faerie Queene.*

Dante and Milton were both deeply penetrated with the ancient religion of the civilized world; and its spirit exists in their poetry probably in the same proportion as its forms survived in the unreformed worship of modern Europe. The one preceded and the other followed the Reformation at almost equal intervals. Dante was the first religious reformer, and Luther surpassed him rather in the rudeness and acrimony, than in the boldness of his censures of papal usurpation. Dante was the first awakener of entranced Europe; he created a language, in itself music and persuasion, out of a chaos of inharmonious barbarisms. He was the congregator of those great spirits who presided over the resurrection of learning; the Lucifer of that starry flock which in the thirteenth century shone forth from republican Italy, as from a heaven, into the darkness of the benighted world. His very words are instinct with spirit; each is as a spark, a burning atom of inextinguishable thought; and many yet lie covered in the ashes of their birth, and pregnant with a lightning which has yet found no conductor. All high poetry is infinite; it is as the first acorn, which contained all oaks potentially. Veil after veil may be undrawn, and the inmost naked beauty of the meaning never exposed. A great poem is a fountain forever overflowing with the waters of wisdom and delight; and after one person and one age has exhausted all its divine effluence which their peculiar relations enable them to share, another and yet another succeeds, and new relations are ever developed, the source of an unforeseen and an unconceived delight.

The age immediately succeeding to that of Dante, Petrarch, and Boccaccio, was characterized by a revival of painting, sculpture, and architecture. Chaucer caught the sacred inspiration, and the superstructure of English literature is based upon the materials of Italian invention.

But let us not be betrayed from a defense into a critical history of poetry and its influence on society. Be it enough to have pointed out the effects of poets, in the large and true sense of the word, upon their own and all succeeding times.

But poets have been challenged to resign the civic crown of reasoners and mechanists, on another plea. It is admitted that the exercise of the imagination is most delightful, but it is alleged that that of reason is more useful. Let us examine, as the grounds of this distinction, what is here meant by utility. Pleasure or good, in a general sense, is that which the consciousness of a sensitive and intelligent being seeks, and in which, when found, it acquiesces. There are two kinds of pleasure, one durable, universal and permanent; the other transitory and particular. Utility may either express the means of producing the former or the latter. In the former sense, whatever strengthens and purifies the affections, enlarges the imagination, and adds spirit to sense, is useful. But a narrower meaning may be assigned to the word utility, confining it to express that which banishes the importunity of the wants of our animal nature, the surrounding men with security of life, the dispersing the grosser delusions of superstition, and the conciliating such a degree of mutual forbearance among men as may consist with the motives of personal advantage.

Undoubtedly the promoters of utility, in this limited sense, have their appointed office in society. They follow the footsteps of poets, and copy the sketches of their creations into the book of common life. They make space, and give time. Their exertions are of the highest value, so long as they confine their administration of the concerns of the inferior powers of our nature within the limits due to the superior ones. But whilst the skeptic destroys gross superstitions, let him spare to deface, as some of the French writers have defaced, the eternal truths charactered upon the imaginations of men. Whilst the mechanist abridges, and the political economist combines labor, let them beware that their speculations, for want of correspondence with those first principles which belong to the imagination, do not tend, as they have in modern England, to exasperate at once the extremes of luxury and of want. They have exemplified the saying, "To him that hath, more shall be given; and from him that hath not, the little that he hath shall be taken away." The rich have become richer, and the poor have become poorer; and the vessel of the state is driven between the Scylla and Charybdis of anarchy and despotism. Such are the effects which must ever flow from an unmitigated exercise of the calculating faculty.

It is difficult to define pleasure in its highest sense; the definition involving a number of apparent paradoxes. For, from an inexplicable defect of harmony in the constitution of human nature, the pain of the inferior is frequently connected with the pleasures of the superior portions of our being. Sorrow, terror, anguish, despair itself, are often the chosen expressions of an approximation to the highest good. Our sympathy in tragic fiction depends on this principle; tragedy delights by affording a shadow of the pleasure which exists in pain. This is the source also of the melancholy which is inseparable from the sweetest melody. The pleasure that is in sorrow is sweeter than the pleasure of pleasure itself. And hence the saying, "It is better to go to the house of mourning, than to the house of mirth."[17] Not that this highest species of pleasure is necessarily linked with pain. The delight of love and friendship, the ecstasy of the admiration of nature, the joy of the perception and still more of the creation of poetry, is often wholly unalloyed.

The production and assurance of pleasure in this highest sense is true utility. Those who produce and preserve this pleasure are poets or poetical philosophers.

The exertions of Locke, Hume, Gibbon, Voltaire, Rousseau,[18] and their disciples, in favor of oppressed and deluded humanity, are entitled to the gratitude of mankind. Yet it is easy to calculate the degree of moral and intellectual improvement which the world would have exhibited, had they never lived. A little more nonsense would have been talked for a century or two; and perhaps a few more men, women, and children, burnt as heretics. We might not at this moment have been congratulating each other on the abolition of the Inquisition in Spain. But it exceeds all imagination to conceive what would have been the moral condition of the world if neither Dante, Petrarch, Boccaccio, Chaucer, Shakespeare, Calderon, Lord Bacon, nor Milton, had ever existed; if Raphael and Michelangelo had never been born; if the Hebrew poetry had never been translated; if a revival of the study of Greek literature had never taken place; if no monuments of ancient sculpture had been handed down to us; and if the poetry of the religion of the ancient world had been extinguished together with its belief. The human mind could never, except by the intervention of these excitements, have been awakened to the invention of the grosser sciences, and that application of analytical reasoning to the aberrations of society, which it is now attempted to exalt over the direct expression of the inventive and creative faculty itself.

We have more moral, political and historical wisdom, than we know how to reduce into practice; we have more scientific and economical knowledge than can be accommodated to the just distribution of the produce which it multiplies. The poetry in these systems of thought, is concealed by the accumulation of facts and calculating processes. There is no want of knowledge respecting what is wisest and best in morals, government, and political economy, or at least what is wiser and better than what men now practice and endure. But we let "*I dare not* wait upon *I would,* like the poor cat in the adage."[19] We want the creative faculty to imagine that which we know; we want the generous impulse to act that which we imagine; we want the poetry of life: our calculations have outrun conception; we have eaten more than we can digest. The cultivation of those sciences which have enlarged the limits of the empire of man over the external world, has, for want of the poetical faculty, proportionally circumscribed those of the internal world; and man, having enslaved the elements, remains himself a slave. To what but a cultivation of the mechanical arts in a degree disproportioned to the presence of the creative faculty, which is the basis of all knowledge, is to be attributed the abuse of all invention for abridging and combining labor, to the exasperation of the inequality of mankind? From what other cause has it arisen that the discoveries which should have lightened, have added a weight to the curse imposed on Adam? Poetry, and the principle of self of which money is the visible incarnation, are the God and Mammon of the world.

The functions of the poetical faculty are twofold; by one it creates new materials of knowledge and power and pleasure; by the other it engenders in the mind a desire to reproduce and arrange them according to a certain rhythm and order which may be called the beautiful and the good. The cultivation of poetry is never more to be desired than at periods when, from an excess of the selfish and calculating principle, the accumulation of the materials of external life exceed the quantity of the power of assimilating them to the internal laws of human nature. The body has then become too unwieldy for that which animates it.

Poetry is indeed something divine. It is at once the center and circumference of knowledge; it is that which comprehends all science, and that to which all science must be referred. It is at the same time the root and blossom of all other systems of thought; it is that from which all spring, and that which adorns all; and that which, if blighted, denies the fruit and the seed, and witholds from the barren world the nourishment and the succession of the scions of the tree of life. It is the perfect and consummate surface and bloom of all things; it is as the odor and the color of the rose to the texture of the elements which compose it, as the form and splendor of unfaded beauty to the secrets of anatomy and corruption. What were virtue, love, patriotism, friendship—what were

---

[17]Suggests Ecclesiastes 7:2.

[18][Shelley] Although Rousseau has been thus classed, he was essentially a poet. The others, even Voltaire, were mere reasoners.

---

[19]*Macbeth*, I. vii. 44–45.

the scenery of this beautiful universe which we inhabit; what were our consolations on this side of the grave—and what were our aspirations beyond it, if poetry did not ascend to bring light and fire from those eternal regions where the owl-winged faculty of calculation dare not ever soar? Poetry is not like reasoning, a power to be exerted according to the determination of the will. A man cannot say, "I will compose poetry." The greatest poet even cannot say it; for the mind in creation is as a fading coal, which some invisible influence, like an inconstant wind, awakens to transitory brightness; this power arises from within, like the color of a flower which fades and changes as it is developed, and the conscious portions of our natures are unprophetic either of its approach or its departure. Could this influence be durable in its original purity and force, it is impossible to predict the greatness of the results; but when composition begins, inspiration is already on the decline, and the most glorious poetry that has ever been communicated to the world is probably a feeble shadow of the original conceptions of the poet. I appeal to the greatest poets of the present day, whether it is not an error to assert that the finest passages of poetry are produced by labor and study. The toil and the delay recommended by critics, can be justly interpreted to mean no more than a careful observation of the inspired moments, and an artificial connection of the spaces between their suggestions, by the intertexture of conventional expressions; a necessity only imposed by the limitedness of the poetical faculty itself; for Milton conceived the *Paradise Lost* as a whole before he executed it in portions. We have his own authority also for the Muse having "dictated" to him the "unpremeditated song."[20] And let this be an answer to those who would allege the fifty-six various readings of the first line of the *Orlando Furioso*. Compositions so produced are to poetry what mosaic is to painting. This instinct and intuition of the poetical faculty is still more observable in the plastic and pictorial arts; a great statue or picture grows under the power of the artist as a child in the mother's womb; and the very mind which directs the hands in formation is incapable of accounting to itself for the origin, the gradations, or the media of the process.

Poetry is the record of the best and happiest moments of the happiest and best minds. We are aware of evanescent visitations of thought and feeling, sometimes associated with place or person, sometimes regarding our own mind alone, and always arising unforeseen and departing unbidden, but elevating and delightful beyond all expression: so that even in the desire and regret they leave, there cannot but be pleas-

ure, participating as it does in the nature of its object. It is as it were the interpenetration of a diviner nature through our own; but its footsteps are like those of a wind over the sea, which the morning calm erases, and whose traces remain only, as on the wrinkled sand which paves it. These and corresponding conditions of being are experienced principally by those of the most delicate sensibility and the most enlarged imagination; and the state of mind produced by them is at war with every base desire. The enthusiasm of virtue, love, patriotism, and friendship, is essentially linked with such emotions; and whilst they last, self appears as what it is, an atom to a universe. Poets are not only subject to these experiences as spirits of the most refined organization, but they can color all that they combine with the evanescent hues of this ethereal world; a word, a trait in the representation of a scene or a passion, will touch the enchanted chord, and reanimate, in those who have ever experienced these emotions, the sleeping, the cold, the buried image of the past. Poetry thus makes immortal all that is best and most beautiful in the world; it arrests the vanishing apparitions which haunt the interlunations of life, and veiling them, or in language or in form, sends them forth among mankind, bearing sweet news of kindred joy to those with whom their sisters abide—abide, because there is no portal of expression from the caverns of the spirit which they inhabit into the universe of things. Poetry redeems from decay the visitations of the divinity in man.

Poetry turns all things to loveliness; it exalts the beauty of that which is most beautiful, and it adds beauty to that which is most deformed; it marries exultation and horror, grief and pleasure, eternity and change; it subdues to union under its light yoke, all irreconcilable things. It transmutes all that it touches, and every form moving within the radiance of its presence is changed by wondrous sympathy to an incarnation of the spirit which it breathes: its secret alchemy turns to potable gold the poisonous waters which flow from death through life; it strips the evil of familiarity from the world, and lays bare the naked and sleeping beauty, which is the spirit of its forms.

All things exist as they are perceived; at least in relation to the percipient. "The mind is its own place, and of itself can make a heaven of hell, a hell of heaven."[21] But poetry defeats the curse which binds us to be subjected to the accident of surrounding impressions. And whether it spreads its own figured curtain, or withdraws life's dark veil from before the scene of things, it equally creates for us a being within our being. It makes us the inhabitants of a world to

---

[20]*Paradise Lost*, IX. 23–24.

[21]*Paradise Lost*, I. 254–55.

which the familiar world is a chaos. It reproduces the common universe of which we are portions and percipients, and it purges from our inward sight the film of familiarity which obscures from us the wonder of our being. It compels us to feel that which we perceive, and to imagine that which we know. It creates anew the universe, after it has been annihilated in our minds by the recurrence of impressions blunted by reiteration. It justifies the bold and true words of Tasso: *"Non merita nome di creatore, se non Iddio ed il poeta."*[22]

A poet, as he is the author to others of the highest wisdom, pleasure, virtue and glory, so he ought personally to be the happiest, the best, the wisest, and the most illustrious of men. As to his glory, let time be challenged to declare whether the fame of any other institutor of human life be comparable to that of a poet. That he is the wisest, the happiest, and the best, inasmuch as he is a poet, is equally incontrovertible: the greatest poets have been men of the most spotless virtue, of the most consummate prudence, and, if we would look into the interior of their lives, the most fortunate of men: and the exceptions, as they regard those who possessed the poetic faculty in a high yet inferior degree, will be found on consideration to confine rather than destroy the rule. Let us for a moment stoop to the arbitration of popular breath, and usurping and uniting in our own persons the incompatible characters of accuser, witness, judge, and executioner, let us decide without trial, testimony, or form, that certain motives of those who are "there sitting where we dare not soar,"[23] are reprehensible. Let us assume that Homer was a drunkard, that Virgil was a flatterer, that Horace was a coward, that Tasso was a madman, that Lord Bacon was a peculator, that Raphael was a libertine, that Spenser was a poet laureate. It is inconsistent with this division of our subject to cite living poets, but posterity has done ample justice to the great names now referred to. Their errors have been weighed and found to have been dust in the balance; if their sins "were as scarlet, they are now white as snow":[24] they have been washed in the blood of the mediator and redeemer, time. Observe in what a ludicrous chaos the imputations of real or fictitious crime have been confused in the contemporary calumnies against poetry and poets; consider how little is as it appears—or appears, as it is; look to your own motives, and judge not, lest ye be judged.

Poetry, as has been said, differs in this respect from logic, that it is not subject to the control of the active powers of the mind, and that its birth and recurrence have no necessary connection with the consciousness or will. It is pre-sumptuous to determine that these are the necessary conditions of all mental causation, when mental effects are experienced insusceptible of being referred to them. The frequent recurrence of the poetical power, it is obvious to suppose, may produce in the mind a habit of order and harmony correlative with its own nature and with its effects upon other minds. But in the intervals of inspiration, and they may be frequent without being durable, a poet becomes a man, and is abandoned to the sudden reflex of the influences under which others habitually live. But as he is more delicately organized than other men, and sensible to pain and pleasure, both his own and that of others, in a degree unknown to them, he will avoid the one and pursue the other with an ardor proportioned to this difference. And he renders himself obnoxious to calumny, when he neglects to observe the circumstances under which these objects of universal pursuit and flight have disguised themselves in one another's garments.

But there is nothing necessarily evil in this error, and thus cruelty, envy, revenge, avarice, and the passions purely evil, have never formed any portion of the popular imputations on the lives of poets.

I have thought it most favorable to the cause of truth to set down these remarks according to the order in which they were suggested to my mind, by a consideration of the subject itself, instead of observing the formality of a polemical reply; but if the view which they contain be just, they will be found to involve a refutation of the arguers against poetry, so far at least as regards the first division of the subject. I can readily conjecture what should have moved the gall of some learned and intelligent writers who quarrel with certain versifiers; I, like them, confess myself unwilling to be stunned by the Theseids of the hoarse Codri of the day. Bavius and Maevius[25] undoubtedly are, as they ever were, insufferable persons. But it belongs to a philosophical critic to distinguish rather than confound.

The first part of these remarks has related to poetry in its elements and principles; and it has been shown, as well as the narrow limits assigned them would permit, that what is called poetry in a restricted sense, has a common source with all other forms of order and of beauty, according to which the materials of human life are susceptible of being arranged, and which is poetry in a universal sense.

The second part[26] will have for its object an application of these principles to the present state of the cultivation of poetry, and a defense of the attempt to idealize the modern

---

[22]"No one deserves the name of creator except God and the poet." *Discourses on the Heroic Poem,* but misquoted.
[23]*Paradise Lost,* IV. 829.
[24]Suggests Isaiah 1:18.

[25]Codrus, Bavius, and Maevius are examples of bad poets. Codrus is mentioned by Juvenal; Bavius and Maevius, by Virgil.
[26]Never written.

forms of manners and opinions, and compel them into a subordination to the imaginative and creative faculty. For the literature of England, an energetic development of which has ever preceded or accompanied a great and free development of the national will, has arisen as it were from a new birth. In spite of the low-thoughted envy which would undervalue contemporary merit, our own will be a memorable age in intellectual achievements, and we live among such philosophers and poets as surpass beyond comparison any who have appeared since the last national struggle for civil and religious liberty. The most unfailing herald, companion, and follower of the awakening of a great people to work a beneficial change in opinion or institution, is poetry. At such periods there is an accumulation of the power of communicating and receiving intense and impassioned conceptions respecting man and nature. The persons in whom this power resides may often, as far as regards many portions of their nature, have little apparent correspondence with that spirit of good of which they are the ministers. But even whilst they deny and abjure they are yet compelled to serve, the power which is seated on the throne of their own soul. It is impossible to read the compositions of the most celebrated writers of the present day without being startled with the electric life which burns within their words. They measure the circumference and sound the depths of human nature with a comprehensive and all-penetrating spirit, and they are themselves perhaps the most sincerely astonished at its manifestations; for it is less their spirit than the spirit of the age. Poets are the hierophants of an unapprehended inspiration; the mirrors of the gigantic shadows which futurity casts upon the present; the words which express what they understand not; the trumpets which sing to battle, and feel not what they inspire; the influence which is moved not, but moves. Poets are the unacknowledged legislators of the world.

Johann Wolfgang von Goethe

⚜

1749–1832

The pronouncements of Goethe on life and letters, collected by his friend Johann Eckermann, reveal the opinions of a great writer of the Romantic age who considered what he called romantic to be sickly. Nevertheless, he held a number of opinions that became current in his time, and thus became identified with Romanticism, particularly the distinction between allegory and symbolism. Most important in his conversations is the attack on abstract ideas as the "meaning" to be expressed by a poem. His attack is, of course, related to his idea that to allegorize is merely to make a concrete representation of an abstraction. The allegory-symbolism distinction and the identification of symbolism and particularity with poetry prepare the way for a theory that considers poetry a special mode of expression very nearly definable by the inability of the commentator to interpret or paraphrase it adequately.

Like most great poets, Goethe tried to stand free of labels, but the critic Schlegel was certainly right to identify many of his views with Romanticism.

From the huge amount of scholarship on Goethe see Wilhelm Bode, *Goethes Ästhetik* (1901); J. E. Spingarn, *Goethe's Literary Essays* (1921); J. B Orrick, *Matthew Arnold and Goethe* (1928); Ernst Cassirer, *Rousseau, Kant, Goethe* (1945); Barker Fairley, *A Study of Goethe* (1947); Karl Viëtor, *Goethe, The Thinker* (1950); and Benjamin Bennett, *Goethe's Theory of Poetry* (1986).

From

Conversations with Eckermann

"The world is so great and rich, and life so full of variety, that you can never want occasions for poems. But they must

CONVERSATIONS WITH ECKERMANN. The conversations with Eckermann took place between 1822 and 1832. They were published in 1836 in *Gespräche mit Goethe*. The text is from the book *Conversations of Goethe with Eckermann* by Johann Peter Eckermann, translated by John Oxenford, Everyman's Library Edition (1930). Published by E. P. Dutton & Co., Inc., and reprinted with their permission and the permission of J. M. Dent and Sons Ltd.

all be *occasioned;* that is to say, reality must give both impulse and material. A particular event becomes universal and poetic by the very circumstance that it is treated by a poet. All my poems are occasioned poems, suggested by real life, and having therein a firm foundation. I attach no value to poems snatched out of the air.

"Let none say that reality wants poetical interest; for in this the poet proves his vocation, that he has the art to win from a common subject an interesting side. Reality must give the motive, the points to be expressed—the kernel; but to work out of it a beautiful animated whole, belongs to the poet. You know Fürnstein, called the poet of nature; he has written the prettiest poem possible, on the cultivation of hops. I have now proposed to him to make songs for the different crafts of workingmen, particularly a weaver's song;

and I am sure he will do it well, for he has lived among such people from his youth: he understands the subject thoroughly, and is therefore master of his material. That is exactly the advantage of small works; you need only choose those subjects of which you are master. With a great poem, this cannot be: no part can be evaded; all that belongs to the unification of the whole, and is interwoven into the plan, must be represented with precision. In youth, however, the knowledge of things is one-sided: a great work requires many-sidedness; so comes shipwreck."

. . .

". . . apprehension and representation of the individual is the very life of art. Besides, while you content yourself with generalities, everybody can imitate you; but, in the particular, none can—and why? Because no others have experienced exactly the same thing.

"And you need not fear lest what is peculiar should not meet with sympathy. Each character, however peculiar it may be, and each object you can represent, from the stone up to man, has generality; for there is repetition everywhere, and there is nothing to be found only once in the world.[1]

"At this step of representing what is individual," continued Goethe, "begins, at the same time, what we call composition."

. . .

After some slight discussion of other topics, we came upon the mistake of those artists who make religion art, whereas for them art should be religion. "Religion," said Goethe, "stands in the same relation to art as any other of the higher interests in life. It is merely to be looked upon as a material, with claims similar to those of any other vital material. Faith and want of faith are not the organs with which a work of art is to be apprehended: powers and capacities of a totally different character are required. Art must address itself to those organs with which we apprehend it; otherwise it misses its effect. A religious material may be a good subject for art, but only in so far as it possesses general human interest. The Virgin with the Child is on this account an excellent subject; one that may be treated a hundred times, and always seen with pleasure."

. . .

"The Germans are, certainly, strange people. By their deep thoughts and ideas, which they seek in everything and fix upon everything, they make life much more burdensome than is necessary. Only have the courage to give yourself up to your impressions: allow yourself to be delighted, moved, elevated; nay, instructed and inspired for something great: but do not imagine all is vanity, if it is not abstract thought and idea.

"They come and ask what idea I meant to embody in my *Faust;* as if I knew myself, and could inform them. 'From heaven, through the world, to hell,' would indeed be something; but this is no idea, only a course of action. And further: that the devil loses the wager, and that a man continually struggling from difficult errors towards something better, should be redeemed, is an effective—and, to many, a good enlightening—thought; but it is no idea at the foundation of the whole, and of every individual scene. It would have been a fine thing indeed if I had strung so rich, varied, and highly diversified a life as I have brought to view in *Faust* upon the slender string of one pervading idea.

"It was, in short," continued Goethe, "not in my line, as a poet, to strive to embody anything *abstract*. I received in my mind impressions, and those of a sensuous, animated, charming, varied, hundredfold kind—just as a lively imagination presented them; and I had, as a poet, nothing more to do than to round off and elaborate artistically such views and impressions, and by means of a lively representation so to bring them forward that others might receive the same impression in hearing or reading my representation of them.

"If I still wished, as a poet, to represent any idea, I would do it in short poems, where a decided unity could prevail, and where a complete survey would be easy; as, for instance, in the *Metamorphosis of Animals,* that of the plants, the poem *Bequest (Vermächtniss),* and many others. The only production of greater extent in which I am conscious of having labored to set forth a pervading idea is probably my *Wahlverwandtschaften.* This novel has thus become comprehensible to the understanding; but I will not say that it is therefore better. I am rather of the opinion, that the more incommensurable, and the more incomprehensible to the understanding, a poetic production is, so much the better it is."

. . .

"The distinction between classical and romantic poetry, which is now spread over the whole world and occasions so

---

[1]Compare Johnson, *Rasselas,* p. 319.

many quarrels and divisions, came originally from Schiller and myself. I laid down the maxim of objective treatment in poetry, and would allow no other; but Schiller, who worked quite in the subjective way, deemed his own fashion right, and to defend himself against me, wrote the treatise upon *Naive and Sentimental Poetry.* He proved to me that I, against my will, was romantic, and that my *Iphigenia,* through the predominance of sentiment, was by no means so classical and so much in the antique spirit as some people supposed.

"The Schlegels took up this idea, and carried it further, so that it has now been diffused over the whole world; and everybody talks about classicism and romanticism—of which nobody thought fifty years ago."

Maxim No. 279

It makes a great difference whether the poet starts with a universal idea and then looks for suitable particulars, or beholds the universal *in* the particular. The former method produces allegory, where the particular has status merely as an instance, an example, of the universal. The latter, by contrast, is what reveals poetry in its true nature: it speaks forth a particular without independently thinking of or referring to a universal, but in grasping the particular in its living character it implicitly apprehends the universal along with it.

MAXIM NO. 279. Goethe's *Maxim 279* was written *c.* 1825.

Georg Wilhelm Friedrich Hegel

1770–1831

Hegel's aesthetic forms an integral part of his organic philosophy. The idea or the absolute or spirit is the all-inclusive infinite whole, an organic unity in which every part is dependent on and definable in terms of every other part and of the whole itself. Man is part of this whole, and a concrete definition of man must be made in its terms. It is perhaps more accurate to say that the whole of absolute spirit comes to consciousness of itself through man, and not the other way around. When Hegel talks about abstractions and concretions he is thinking of objects when they are considered alone and apart from their interrelationships as abstract, and objects when they are viewed in their organic relationships as concrete and thus as they really are.

In the selection below from *The Philosophy of Fine Art,* Hegel insists that art must be treated not in terms of its use "as a mere pastime in the service of pleasure and entertainment" or in terms of any other ulterior purpose; instead it must be considered a mode, like religion and philosophy, through which the idea is made available to consciousness. It is one of the modes by which absolute spirit comes to consciousness of itself. Art presents its matter in sensuous forms. The beautiful in art is the idea carried into concrete form. There are fundamentally three kinds of art—symbolic, classical, and romantic. Hegel explains the first two with more clarity than he does the third. By "symbolic" art Hegel means something very much like what many Romantic critics call allegory. It is an art in which objects represented are made to have arbitrary meanings, in which the relation of object to meaning is abstract. In "classical" art there is a much more appropriate relationship between idea and embodiment. For example, the human form in classical art is, according to Hegel, a natural shape appropriate to a representation of the mind. In classical art form and content are merged.

"Romantic art" makes the "inward life of reason . . . the medium and determinate existence of its content." This kind of art transcends itself, so to speak, and canons of appropriateness invoked with respect to symbolic and classical art are cast aside. Art becomes its own domain, the release of Spirit into art itself, not merely into objects represented in art.

Hegel goes on to associate architecture with symbolic art and sculpture with classical art. Romantic art is realized by painting, music, and poetry in ascending order of freedom. In this series of definitions, one observes Hegel making his judgments on the basis of the distance each art is able to traverse in escape from matter, mass, and spatialization. In these terms, painting is more ideal than sculpture, which is more ideal than architecture. Music is more ideal than painting, for in music objects are not represented and a temporal order alone exists. The medium of poetry—words—is most free. Its sensuousness is created by the mind, not by the materials of the art.

In the later parts of his work Hegel considers various sorts of poetry and develops a theory of tragedy. Despite the attention he lavishes on art, however, he does not consider it the highest manifestation of the Idea. It is limited by its media and finally proves less satisfactory to man than religion or philosophy.

Hegel's *Philosophy of Fine Art* has been translated in four volumes by F. P. B. Osmaston (1920). See also *The Introduction to Hegel's Philosophy of Fine Art,* translated by Bernard Bosanquet (1886). Commentary includes W. T. Stace, *The Philosophy of Hegel* (1924); Israel Knox, *The Aesthetic Theories of Kant, Hegel, and Schopenhauer* (1936); A. C. Bradley, "Hegel's Theory of Tragedy," *Oxford Lectures on Poetry* (1950); Jack Kaminsky, *Hegel on Art, An Interpretation of Hegel's Aesthetics* (1962); Alexandre Kojève, *Introduction to the Reading of Hegel* (tr. 1969); Jean Hyppolite, *Genesis and Structure of Hegel's Phenomenology of Spirit* (tr. 1974); Stephen Bungay, *Beauty and Truth: A Study of Hegel's Aesthetics* (1984).

The Philosophy of Fine Art

From

Introduction

First, as to the worthiness of art to form the object of scientific inquiry, it is no doubt the case that art can be utilized as a mere pastime in the service of pleasure and entertainment, either in the embellishment of our surroundings, the imprinting of a delight-giving surface to the external conditions of life, or the emphasis placed by decoration on other objects. In these respects it is unquestionably no independent or free art, but an art subservient to certain objects. The kind of art, however, which we ourselves propose to examine is one which is free in its aim and its means. That art in general can serve other objects, and even be merely a pastime, is a relation which it possesses in common with thought itself. From one point of view thought likewise, as science subservient to other ends, can be used in just the same way for finite purposes and means as they chance to crop up, and as such serviceable faculty of science is not self-determined, but determined by something alien to it. But, further, as distinct from such subservience to particular objects, science is raised of its own essential resources in free independence to truth, and exclusively united with its own aims in discovering the true fulfillment in that truth.

Fine art is not art in the true sense of the term until it is also thus free, and its highest function is only then satisfied when it has established itself in a sphere which it shares with religion and philosophy, becoming thereby merely one mode and form through which the divine, the profoundest interests of mankind, and spiritual truths of widest range, are brought home to consciousness and expressed. It is in works of art that nations have deposited the richest intuitions and ideas they possess; and not infrequently fine art supplies a key of interpretation to the wisdom and religion of peoples; in the case of many it is the only one. This is an attribute which art shares in common with religion and philosophy, the peculiar distinction in the case of art being that its presentation of the most exalted subject matter is in sensuous form, thereby bringing them nearer to nature and her mode of envisagement, that is closer to our sensitive and emotional life. The world, into the profundity of which thought penetrates, is a supersensuous one, a world which to start with is posited as a beyond in contrast to the immediacy of ordinary conscious life and present sensation. It is the freedom of reflecting consciousness which disengages itself from this immersion in the "this side," or immediacy, in other words sensuous reality and finitude. But the mind is able, too, to heal the fracture which is thus created in its progression. From the wealth of its own resources it brings into being the works of fine art as the primary bond of mediation between that which is exclusively external, sensuous and transitory, and the medium of pure thought, between nature and its finite reality, and the infinite freedom of a reason which comprehends.

. . .

It has already been stated that the content of art is the idea, and the form of its display the configuration of the sensuous or plastic image. It is further the function of art to me-

THE PHILOSOPHY OF FINE ART. The manuscript notes for Hegel's lectures on aesthetics were published in 1835, four years after his death. The lectures were first given in 1820, revised in 1823, 1826, and 1829. The text is from *The Philosophy of Fine Art,* by Georg Wilhelm Friedrich Hegel, translated by F. P. B. Osmaston. Reprinted by permission of G. Bell & Sons, Ltd. The notes are those of Osmaston.

diate these two aspects under the reconciled mode of free totality. The first determinant implied by this is the demand that the content, which has to secure artistic representation, shall disclose an essential capacity for such display. If this is not so all that we possess is a defective combination. A content that, independently, is ill adapted to plastic form and external presentment is compelled to accept this form, or a matter that is of itself prosaic in its character is driven to make the best it can of a mode of presentation which is antagonistic to its nature.

The second requirement, which is deducible from the first, is the demand that the content of art should be nothing essentially abstract. This does not mean, however, that it should be merely concrete in the sense that the sensuous object is such in its contrast to all that is spiritual and the content of thought, regarding these as the essentially simple and abstract. Everything that possesses truth for spirit, no less than as part of nature, is essentially concrete, and, despite its universality, possesses both ideality[1] and particularity essentially within it. When we state, for example, of God that he is simple One, the Supreme Being as such, we have thereby merely given utterance to a lifeless abstraction of the irrational understanding. Such a God, as he is thus not conceived in his concrete truth, can supply no content for art, least of all plastic art. Consequently neither the Jews nor the Turks have been able to represent their God, who is not even an abstraction of the understanding in the above sense, under the positive mode in which Christians have represented him. For in Christianity God is conceived in his truth, and as such essentially concrete, as personality,[2] as the subjective focus of conscious life or, more accurately defined, as spirit. And what he is as spirit is made explicit to the religious apprehension as a trinity of persons, which at the same time are, in their independence, regarded as One. Here is essentiality, universality, and particularity, no less than their reconciled

unity, and it is only a unity such as this which gives us the concrete. And inasmuch as a content, in order to unveil truth at all, must be of this concrete character, art makes the demand for a like concreteness, and, for this reason, that a purely abstract universal does not in itself possess the property to proceed to particularity and external manifestation, and to unity with itself therein.

If, then, a sensuous form and configuration is to be correspondent with a true and therefore concrete content, such must in the third place likewise be as clearly individual, entirely concrete and a self-enclosed unity. This character of concreteness, predicable of both aspects of art, the content no less than the representation, is just the point in which both coalesce and fall in with one another. The natural form of the human body is, for example, such a sensuous concrete capable of displaying spirit in its essential concreteness and of adapting itself wholly to such a presentment. For which reason we must quit ourselves of the idea that it is a matter of mere accident that an actual phenomenon of the objective world is accepted as the mode in which to embody such a form coalescent with truth. Art does not lay hold of this form either because it is simply there or because there is no other. The concrete content itself implies the presence of external and actual, we may even add the sensuous appearance. But to make this possible this sensuous concrete, which is essentially impressed with a content that is open to mind, is also essentially addressed to the inward conscious life, and the external mode of its configuration, whereby it is visible to perception and the world of idea, has for its aim the being there exclusively for the soul and mind of man. This is the sole reason that content and artistic conformation are dovetailed one into the other. The purely sensuous concrete, that is external nature as such, does not exclusively originate in such an end. The variously colored plumage of birds is resplendent unseen; the notes of this song are unheard. The cereus, which only blossoms for a night, withers away without any admiration from another in the wilderness of the southern forests; receptacles themselves of the most beautiful and luxuriant vegetation, with the richest and most aromatic perfumes, perish and collapse in like manner unenjoyed. The work of art has no such naive and independent being. It is essentially a question, an address to the responding soul of man, an appeal to affections and intelligence.

Although the endowment by art of sensuous shape is not in this respect accidental, yet on the other hand it is not the highest mode of grasping the spiritually concrete. Thought is a higher mode of presentment than that of the sensuous concrete. Though abstract in a relative sense; yet it must not be one-sided, but concrete thinking, in order to be

---

[1] *Subjektivität.* That is, the ideality of consciousness, or thought.

[2] Professor Bosanquet, in his note on this passage, expresses the opinion that Hegel when he writes thus is referring "to the self-consciousness of individual human beings as constituting, and reflecting on, an ideal unity between them." This no doubt, as he suggests, does put a somewhat unnatural meaning on the word *person* or *subjekt*. No doubt there is a sense in which we can ascribe personality to a state, or nation, in the concrete unity of its life. But while admitting that unity such as this, which is not sensuous but ideal, can be "effective and actual," I find it difficult to conclude that Hegel did himself hold that the unity of the Divine Being was merely identical with the unity or totality of concrete human life as reflected upon by single individuals. How far is human life as a whole on this earth a unity or totality at all? That question has been discussed by Professor Bradley and others with very different conclusions. Nay, how far does human existence itself exhaust the actually present realization or self-realization of self-conscious spirit or intelligence? Whatever may be the wisest answer to such and other questions I can hardly think that Hegel would have accepted Professor Bosanquet's interpretation as completely adequate.

true and rational. The extent to which a definite content possesses for its appropriate form sensuous artistic representation, or essentially requires, in virtue of its nature, a higher and more spiritual embodiment is a question of difference exemplified at once if we compare the Greek gods with God as conceived under Christian ideas. The Greek god is not abstract, but individual, and is in close association with the natural human form. The Christian God is also, no doubt, a concrete personality, but under the mode of pure spiritual actuality, who is cognized as spirit and in spirit.[3] His medium of determinate existence is therefore essentially knowledge of the mind and not external shape, by means of which his representation can only be imperfect, and not in the entire depths of his idea or notional concept.

Inasmuch, however, as it is the function of art to represent the idea to immediate vision in sensuous shape and not in the form of thought and pure spirituality in the strict sense, and inasmuch as the value and intrinsic worth of this presentment consists in the correspondence and unity of the two aspects, that is the idea and its sensuous shape, the supreme level and excellence of art and the reality, which is truly consonant with its notion, will depend upon the degree of intimacy and union with which idea and configuration appear together in elaborated fusion. The higher truth consequently is spiritual content which has received the shape adequate to the conception of its essence; and this it is which supplies the principle of division for the philosophy of art. For before the mind can attain to the true notion of its absolute essence, it is constrained to traverse a series of stages rooted in this very notational concept; and to this course of stages which it unfolds to itself, corresponds a coalescent series, immediately related therewith, of the plastic types of art, under the configuration whereof mind as art spirit presents to itself the consciousness of itself.[4]

This evolution within the art spirit has further itself two sides in virtue of its intrinsic nature. First, that is to say, the development is itself a spiritual and universal one; in other words there are the definite and comprehensive views of the world[5] in their series of gradations which give artistic embodiment to the specific but widely embracing consciousness of nature, man, and God. Secondly, this ideal or universal art development has to provide for itself immediate

existence and sensuous configuration, and the definite modes of this art actualization in the sensuous medium are themselves a totality of necessary distinctions in the realm of art—that is to say, they are the particular types of art. No doubt the types of artistic configuration on the one hand are, in respect to their spirituality, of a general character, and not restricted to any one material, and the sensuous existence is similarly itself of varied multiplicity of medium. Inasmuch, however, as this material potentially possesses, precisely as the mind or spirit does, the idea for its inward soul or significance, it follows that a definite sensuous involves with itself a closer relation and secret bond of association with the spiritual distinctions and specific types of artistic embodiment.[6]

Relatively to these points of view our philosophy will be divided into three fundamental parts.

First, we have a general part. It has for its content and object the universal idea of fine art, conceived here as the ideal, together with the more elaborated relation under which it is placed respectively to nature and human artistic production.

Secondly, we have evolved from the notional concept of the beauty of art a particular part, insofar as the essential distinctions, which this idea contains in itself, are unfolded in a graduated series of particular modes of configuration.[7]

Thirdly, there results a final part which has to consider the particularized content of fine art itself. It consists in the advance of art to the sensuous realization of its shapes and its consummation in a system of the several arts and their genera and species.

2. In respect to the first and second of these divisions it is important to recollect, in order to make all that follows intelligible, that the idea, viewed as the beautiful in art, is not the idea in the strict sense, that is as a metaphysical logic apprehends it as the absolute. It is rather the idea as carried into concrete form in the direction of express realization, and as having entered into immediate and adequate unity with such reality. For the idea as such, although it is both poten-

---

[3]Or, "as mind and in mind."

[4]That is to say, presents to itself to conscious grasp of itself as such art spirit (*als künstlerischer*).

[5]The two evolutions here alluded to are (1) that of a particular way of regarding nature, man, and God in a particular age and nation such as the Egyptian, Greek, and Christian viewed in express relation to art; (2) the several arts—sculpture, music, poetry, etc., each on their own foundation and viewed relatively to the former evolution.

[6]The point, of course, is that the different media of the several arts are inherently, and in virtue of the fact that we have not here mere matter as opposed to that which is intellectual rather than sensuous, but matter in which the notional concept is already essentially present or pregnant (sound is, for instance, more ideal than the spatial matter of architecture), adapted to the particular arts in which they serve as the medium of expression.

[7]Professor Bosanquet explains these "plastic forms" (*Gestaltungs formen*) as the various modifications of the subject matter of art. I am not quite sure of the meaning here intended. It would apparently identify the term with the *Gebilde* referred to in the third division. I should myself rather incline to think that Hegel had mainly in his mind the specific general types, that is, the three relations of the idea itself to its external configuration, viewed as a historical evolution, which Hegel calls symbolic, classical, and romantic. Perhaps this is what Professor Bosanquet means. But in that case it does not appear to me so much the subject matter as the generic forms in the shaping of that matter.

tially and explicitly true, is only truth in its universality and not as yet presented in objective embodiment. The idea as fine art, however, is the idea with the more specific property of being essentially individual reality, in other words, an individual configuration of reality whose express function it is to make manifest the idea—in its appearance. This amounts to the demand that the idea and its formative configuration as concrete realization must be brought together under a mode of complete adequacy. The idea as so conceived, a reality, that is to say, molded in conformity with the notional concept of the idea, is the ideal. The problem of such consonancy might, in the first instance, be understood in the wholly formal sense that the idea might be any idea so long as the actual shape, it matters not what the shape might be, represented this particular idea and no other. In that case, however, the required truth of the ideal is a fact simply interchangeable with mere correctness, a correctness which consists in the expression of any significance in a manner adapted to it, provided that its meaning is thereby directly discoverable in the form. The ideal, however, is not to be thus understood. According to the standard or test of its own nature any content whatever can receive adequate presentation, but it does not necessarily thereby possess a claim to be the fine art of the ideal. Nay, more, in comparison with ideal beauty presentation will even appear defective. And in this connection we may once for all observe—though actual proof is reserved to a later stage—that the defects of a work of art are not invariably to be attributed to defects of executive skill. Defectiveness of form arises also from defectiveness of content. The Chinese, Hindus, and Egyptians, for example, in their artistic images, sculptured deities and idols, never passed beyond a formless condition, or a definition of shape that was vicious and false, and were unable to master true beauty. And this was so for the reason that their mythological conceptions, the content and thought of their works of art, were still essentially indeterminate, or only determinate in a false sense, did not, in fact, attain to a content which was absolute in itself. Viewed in this sense the excellence of works of art is so much the greater in the degree that their content and thought is ideal and profound. And in affirming this we have not merely in our mind the degree of executive mastery displayed in the grasp and imitation of natural form as we find it in the objective world. For in certain stages of the artistic consciousness and its reproductive effects the desertion and distortion of the conformations of nature is not so much due to unintentional technical inexperience or lack of ability, as it is to deliberate alteration, which originates in the mental content itself, and is demanded by the same. From this point of view there is therefore imperfect art, which, both in technical and other respects, may be quite consum-

mate in its own specific sphere, yet if tested with the true notion of art and the ideal can only appear as defective. Only in the highest art are the idea and the artistic presentation truly consonant with one another in the sense that the objective embodiment of the idea is in itself essentially and as realized the true configuration, because the content of the idea thus expressed is itself in truth the genuine content. It is appertinent to this, as already noted, that the idea must be defined in and through itself as concrete totality, thereby essentially possessing in itself the principle and standard of its particularization and definition as thus manifested objectively. For example, the Christian imagination will only be able to represent God in human form and with man's means of spiritual expression, because it is herein that God himself is fully known in himself as mind or spirit. Determinacy is, as it were, the bridge to phenomenal presence. Where this determinacy is not totality derived from the idea itself, where the idea is not conceived as that which is self-definitive and self-differentiating, it remains abstract and possesses its definition, and with it the principle for the particular mode of embodiment adapted to itself not within itself but as something outside it. And owing to this the idea is also still abstract and the configuration it assumes is not as yet posited by itself. The idea, however, which is essentially concrete, carries the principle of its manifestation in itself, and is thereby the means of its own free manifestation. Thus it is only the truly concrete idea that is able to evoke the true embodiment, and this appropriate coalescence of both is the ideal.

3. But inasmuch as in this way the idea is concrete unity, this unity can only enter the artistic consciousness by the expansion and further mediation of the particular aspects of the idea; and it is through this evolution that the beauty of art receives a totality of particular stages and forms. Therefore, after we have considered fine art in its essence and on its own account, we must see how the beautiful in its entirety breaks up into particular determinations. This gives, as our second part, the doctrine of the types of art. The origin of these types is to be found in the varied ways under which the idea is conceived as the content of art; it is by this means that a distinction in the mode of form under which it manifests itself is conditioned. These types are therefore simply the different modes of relation which obtain between the idea and its configuration, relations which emanate from the idea itself, and thereby present us with the general basis of division for this sphere. For the principle of division must always be found in the notional concept, the particularization and division of which it is.

We have here to consider three relations of the idea to its external process of configuration.

a. First, the origin of artistic creation proceeds from the idea when, being itself still involved in defective definition and obscurity, or in vicious and untrue determinacy, it becomes embodied in the shapes of art. As indeterminate it does not as yet possess in itself that individuality which the ideal demands. Its abstract character and one-sidedness leaves its objective presentment still defective and contingent. Consequently this first type of art is rather a mere search after plastic configuration than a power of genuine representation. The idea has not as yet found the formative principle within itself, and therefore still continues to be the mere effort and strain to find it. We may in general terms describe this form as the *symbolic* type of art. The abstract idea possesses in it its external shape outside itself in the purely material substance of nature, from which the shaping process proceeds, and to which in its expression it is entirely yoked. Natural objects are thus in the first instance left just as they are, while, at the same time the substantive idea is imposed upon them as their significance, so that their function is henceforth to express the same, and they claim to be interpreted, as though the idea itself was present in them. A rationale of this is to be found in the fact that the external objects of reality do essentially possess an aspect in which they are qualified to express a universal import. But as a completely adequate coalescence is not yet possible, all that can be the outcome of such a relation is an abstract attribute, as when a lion is understood to symbolize strength.

On the other hand this abstractness of the relation makes present to consciousness no less markedly how the idea stands relatively to natural phenomena as an alien; and albeit it expatiates in all these shapes, having no other means of expression among all that is real, and seeks after itself in their unrest and defects of genuine proportion, yet for all that it finds them inadequate to meet its needs. It consequently exaggerates natural shapes and the phenomena of nature in every degree of indefinite and limitless extension; it flounders about in them like a drunkard, and seethes and ferments, doing violence to their truth with the distorted growth of unnatural shapes, and strives vainly by the contrast, hugeness, and splendor of the forms accepted to exalt the phenomena to the plain of the idea. For the idea is here still more or less indeterminate, and unadaptable, while the objects of nature are wholly definite in their shape.

Hence, on account of the incompatibility of the two sides of ideality and objective form to one another, the relation of the idea to the other becomes a negative one. The former, being in its nature ideal, is unsatisfied with such an embodiment, and posits itself as its inward or ideally universal substance under a relation of sublimity over and above all this inadequate superfluity of natural form. In virtue of this sublimity the natural phenomena, of course, and the human form and event are accepted and left simply as they are, but at the same time, recognized as unequal to their significance, which is exalted far above all earthly content.

These features constitute in general terms the character of the primitive artistic pantheism of the East, which, on the one hand, charges the meanest objects with the significance of the absolute idea, or, on the other, compels natural form, by doing violence to its structure, to express its world ideas. And, in consequence, it becomes bizarre, grotesque, and deficient in taste, or turns the infinite but abstract freedom of the substantive idea contemptuously against all phenomenal existence as alike nugatory and evanescent. By such means the significance cannot be completely presented in the expression, and despite all straining and endeavor the final inadequacy of plastic configuration to idea remains insuperable. Such may be accepted as the first type of art—symbolic art with its yearning, its fermentation, its mystery, and sublimity.

b. In the second type of art, which we propose to call *classical,* the twofold defect of symbolic art is annulled. Now the symbolic configuration is imperfect, because, first, the idea here only enters into consciousness in abstract determinacy or indeterminateness: and, secondly, by reason of the fact that the coalescence of import with embodiment can only throughout remain defective, and in its turn also wholly abstract. The classical art type solves both these difficulties. It is, in fact, the free and adequate embodiment of the idea in the shape which, according to its notional concept, is uniquely appropriate to the idea itself. The idea is consequently able to unite in free and completely assonant concord with it. For this reason the classical type of art is the first to present us with the creation and vision of the complete ideal, and to establish the same as realized fact.

The conformability, however, of notion and reality in the classical type ought not to be taken in the purely formal sense of the coalescence of a content with its external form, any more than this was possible in the case of the ideal. Otherwise every copy from nature, and every kind of portrait, every landscape, flower, scene, and so forth, which form the aim of the presentment, would at once become classical in virtue of the fact of the agreement it offers between such content and form. In classical art, on the contrary, the characteristic feature of the content consists in this, that it is itself concrete idea, and as such the concrete spiritual; for it is only that which pertains to spirit which is veritable ideality.[8] To secure such a content we must find out that in nature which

---

[8]*Das wahrhaft Innere.* That is, the inward of the truth of conscious life.

on its own account is that which is essentially and explicitly appropriate to the spiritual. It must be the original notion itself,[9] which has invented the form for concrete spirituality, and now the subjective notion—in the present case the spirit of art—has merely discovered it, and made it, as an existence possessed of natural shape, concordant with free and individual spirituality. Such a configuration, which the idea essentially possesses as spiritual, and indeed as individually determinate spirituality, when it must perforce appear as a temporal phenomenon, is the human form. Personification and anthropomorphism have frequently been abused as a degradation of the spiritual. But art, insofar as its function is to bring to vision the spiritual in sensuous guise, must advance to such anthropomorphism, inasmuch as spirit is only adequately presented to perception in its bodily presence. The transmigration of souls in this respect an abstract conception,[10] and physiology ought to make it one of its fundamental principles, that life has necessarily, in the course of its evolution, to proceed to the human form, for the reason that it is alone the visible phenomenon adequate to the expression of intelligence.

The human bodily form, then, is employed in the classical type of art not as purely sensuous existence, but exclusively as the existence and natural shape appropriate to mind. It has therefore to be relieved of all the defective excrescences which adhere to it in its purely physical aspect, and from the contingent finiteness of its phenomenal appearance. The external shape must in this way be purified in order to express in itself the content adequate for such a purpose; and, furthermore, along with this, that the coalescence of import and embodiment may be complete, the spirituality which constitutes the content must be of such a character that is it completely able to express itself in the natural form of man, without projecting beyond the limits of such expression within the sensuous and purely physical sphere of existence. Under such a condition spirit is at the same time defined as particular, the spirit or mind of man, not as simply absolute and eternal. In this latter case it is only capable of asserting and expressing itself as intellectual being.[11]

Out of this latter distinction arises, in its turn, the defect which brings about the dissolution of the classical type of art, and makes the demand for a third and higher form, namely the *romantic* type.

c. The romantic type of art annuls the completed union of the idea and its reality, and occurs, if on a higher plane, to the difference and opposition of both sides, which remained unovercome in symbolic art. The classical type of art no doubt attained the highest excellence of which the sensuous embodiment of art is capable. The defect, such as it is, is due to the effect which obtains in art itself throughout, the limitations of its entire province, that is to say. The limitation consists in this, that art in general and, agreeably to its fundamental idea, accepts for its object spirit, the notion of which is infinite concrete universality, under the guise of sensuously concrete form. In the classical type it sets up the perfected coalescence of spiritual and sensuous existence as adequate conformation of both. As a matter of fact, however, in this fusion mind itself is not represented agreeably to its true notional concept. Mind is the infinite subjectivity of the idea, which as absolute inwardness,[12] is not capable of freely expanding in its entire independence, so long as it remains within the mold of the bodily shape, fused therein as in the existence wholly congenial to it.

To escape from such a condition the romantic type of art once more cancels that inseparable unity of the classical type, by securing a content which passes beyond the classical stage and its mode of expression. This content, if we may recall familiar ideas—is coincident with what Christianity affirms to be true of God as spirit, in contrast to the Greek faith in gods which forms the essential and most fitting content of classical art. In Greek art the concrete ideal substance is potentially, but not as fully realized, the unity of the human and divine nature; a unity which for the very reason that it is purely immediate and not wholly explicit, is manifested without defect under an immediate and sensuous mode. The Greek god is the object of naive intuition and sensuous imagination. His shape is therefore the bodily form of man. The sphere of his power and his being is individual and individually limited; and in his opposition to the individual person[13] is an essence and a power with whom the inward life of soul[14] is merely potentially in unity, but does not itself possess this unity as inward subjective knowledge. The higher stage is the knowledge of this implied unity, which in its latency the classical art type receives as its content and is able to perfectly represent in bodily shape. This elevation of mere potentiality into self-conscious knowledge constitutes an enormous difference. It is nothing less than the infinite

---

[9] Means apparently the notion in its absolute sense.
[10] Because it represents spirit as independent of an appropriate bodily form.
[11] What appears to be denoted by *Geistigkeit* is the generic term of intelligence—that activity of conscious life which does not necessarily make us think of a single individual—the common nature of all spirit.

---

[12] By *Innerlichkeit*, which might also be rendered as pure ideality, what is signified is that in a mental state there are no parts outside of each other.
[13] *Subjekt*, i.e., the individual ego of self-consciousness.
[14] *Das subjektive Innere*, literally, the subjective inner state.

difference which, for example, separates man generally from the animal creation. Man is animal; but even in his animal functions he is not restricted within the potential sphere as the animal is, but becomes conscious of them, learns to understand them, and raises them—as, for instance, the process of digestion—into self-conscious science. By this means man dissolves the boundaries of his merely potential immediacy; in virtue of the very fact that he knows himself to be animal he ceases to be merely animal, and as mind is endowed with self-knowledge.

If, then, in this way the unity of the human and divine nature, which in the previous stage was potential, is raised out of this immediate into a self-conscious unity, it follows that the genuine medium for the reality of this content is no longer the sensuous and immediate existence of what is spiritual, that is, the physical body of man, but the self-aware inner life of soul itself. Now it is Christianity—for the reason that it presents to mind God as spirit, and not as the particular individual spirit, but as absolute in spirit and in truth—which steps back from the sensuousness of imagination into the inward life of reason, and makes this rather than bodily form the medium and determinate existence of its content. So also, the unity of the human and divine nature is a conscious unity exclusively capable of realization by means of spiritual knowledge, and in spirit. The new content secured thereby is consequently not indefeasibly bound up with the sensuous presentation, as the mode completely adequate, but is rather delivered from this immediate existence, which has to be hypostatized as a negative factor, overcome and reflected back into the spiritual unity. In this way romantic art must be regarded as art transcending itself, albeit within the boundary of its own province, and in the form of art itself.

We may therefore briefly summarize our conclusion that in this third stage the object of art consists in the free and concrete presence of spiritual activity,[15] whose vocation it is to appear as such a presence or activity for the inner world of conscious intelligence. In consonance with such an object art cannot merely work for sensuous perception. It must deliver itself to the inward life, which coalesces with its object simply as though this were none other than itself,[16] in other words, to the intimacy of soul, to the heart, the emotional life, which as the medium of spirit itself essentially strives after freedom, and seeks and possesses its reconciliation only in the inner chamber of spirit. It is this inward or ideal world which constitutes the content of the romantic

sphere: it will therefore necessarily discover its representation as such inner idea or feeling, and in the show or appearance of the same. The world of the soul and intelligence celebrates its triumph over the external world, and, actually in the medium of that outer world, makes that victory to appear, by reason of which the sensuous appearance sinks into worthlessness.

On the other hand, this type of art, like every other, needs an external vehicle of expression. As already stated, the spiritual content has here withdrawn from the external world and its immediate unity into its own world. The sensuous externality of form is consequently accepted and represented, as in the symbolic type, as unessential and transient; furthermore the subjective finite spirit and volition is treated in a similar way; a treatment which even includes the idiosyncrasies or caprice of individuals, character, action, or the particular features of incident and plot. The aspect of external existence is committed to contingency and handed over to the adventurous action of imagination, whose caprice is just as able to reflect the facts given as they are,[17] as it can change the shapes of the external world into a medley of its own invention and distort them to mere caricature. For this external element has no longer its notion and significance in its own essential province, as in classical art. It is now discovered in the emotional realm, and this is manifested in the medium of that realm itself rather than in the external and its form of reality, and is able to secure or to recover again the condition of reconciliation with itself in every accident, in all the chance circumstance that falls into independent shape, in all misfortune and sorrow, nay, in crime itself.

Hence it comes about that the characteristics of symbolic art, its indifference, incompatibility and severance of idea from configurative expression, are here reproduced once more, if with essential difference. And this difference consists in the fact that in romantic art the idea, whose defectiveness, in the case of the symbol, brought with it the defect of external form, has to display itself as spirit and in the medium of soul life as essentially self-complete. And it is to complete fundamentally this higher perfection that it withdraws itself from the external element. It can, in short, seek and consummate its true reality and manifestation nowhere but in its own domain.

This we may take to be in general terms the character of the symbolic, classical, and romantic types of art, which in fact constitute the three relations of the idea to its embodiment in the realm of human art. They consist in the aspira-

---

[15]*Geistigkeit*. Professor Bosanquet translates it here "intellectual being."
[16]The distinction between a percipient and an external object falls away. The content displayed is part of the soul life itself.

[17]Professor Bosanquet apparently assumes a negative has slipped out. But the text probably is correct in the rather awkward form in which it stands.

tion after, the attainment and transcendency of the ideal, viewed as the true concrete notion of beauty.

4. In contrast to these two previous divisions of our subject the third part presupposes the notional concept of the ideal, and the universal art types. It in other words consists in their realization through specific sensuous media. We have consequently no longer to deal with the inner or ideal evolution of the beauty of art in conformity with its widest and most fundamental determinations. What we have now before us to consider is how these ideal determinants pass into actual existence, how they are distinguishable in their external aspect, and how they give an independent and a realized shape to every element implied in the evolution of this idea of beauty as a work of art, and not merely as a universal type. Now it is the peculiar differences immanent in the idea of beauty which are carried over by it into external existence. For this reason in this third fundamental division these general art types must themselves supply the basic principle for the articulation and definition of the particular arts. Or, to put the same thing another way, the several species of art possess in themselves the same essential differences, which we have already become acquainted with as the universal art types. External objectivity, however, to which these types are subjected in a sensuous and consequently specific material, necessitates the differentiation of these types into diverse and independent modes of realization, in other words, those of particular arts. Each general type discovers its determinate character in one determinate external material or medium, in which its adequate presentation is secured under the manner it prescribes. But, from another point of view, these types of art, inasmuch as their definition is nonetheless consistent with the fact of the universality of their typical import, break through the boundaries of their specific realization in some definite art species, and achieve an existence in other arts no less, although their position in such is of subordinate importance. For this reason, albeit the particular arts belong specifically to one of these general art types respectively, the adequate external embodiment whereof they severally constitute, yet this does not prevent them, each after its own mode of external configuration, from representing the totality of these art types.[18] To summarize, then, in this third principal division we are dealing with the beauty of art, as it unveils itself in a world of realized beauty by means of the arts and their creations. The content of this world is the beautiful, and the true beautiful, as we have seen, is spiritual being in concrete form, the ideal; or apprehended with still more intimacy it is the absolute mind and truth itself. This region of divine truth artistically presented to sensuous vision and emotion forms the center of the entire world of art. It is the independent, free and divine image,[19] which has completely appropriated the externality of form and medium, and now wears them simply as the means of its self-manifestation. Inasmuch, however, as the beautiful is unfolded here as objective reality, and in this process is differentiated into particular aspects and phases, this center posits its extremes, as realized in their peculiar actuality, in antithetical relation to itself. Thus one of these extremes consists of an objectivity as yet devoid of mind, which we may call the natural environment of God. Here the external element, when it receives form, remains as it was, and does not possess its spiritual aim and content in itself, but in another.[20] The other extreme is the divine as inward, something known, as the manifold particularized subjective existence of deity. It is the truth as operative and vital in sense, soul, and intelligence of particular persons, which does not persist as poured forth into its mold of external shape, but returns into the inward life of individuals. The divine is under such a mode at once distinguishable from its pure manifestation as Godhead, and passes itself thereby into the variety of particularization which belongs to every kind of particular subjective knowledge, feeling, perception, and emotion. In the analogous province of religion with which art, at its highest elevation, is immediately connected, we conceive the same distinction as follows. First, we imagine the natural life on earth in its finitude as standing on one side; but then, secondly, the human consciousness accepts God for its object, in which the distinction between objectivity and subjectivity falls away; then, finally, we advance from God as such to the devotion of the community, that is to God as he is alive and present in the subjective consciousness. These three fundamental modifications present themselves in the world of art in independent evolution.

a. The first of the particular arts with which, according to their fundamental principle, we have to start is architecture considered as a fine art. Its function consists in so elaborating the external material of inorganic nature that the same becomes intimately connected with spirit as an artistic and external environment. Its medium is matter itself as an external object, a heavy mass that is subject to mechanical laws; and its forms persist as the forms of inorganic nature coordinated with the relations of the abstract understanding such

---

[18]Thus poetry is primarily a Romantic art, but in the epic it is affiliated with the objective character of classical art, or we may say that there is a romantic and classical type of architecture, though the art is primarily symbolic.

[19]*Gestalt.* "Plastic power" is perhaps a better translation.
[20]He means that in architecture the building is merely a shrine or environment of the image of the god.

as symmetry and so forth. In this material and in these forms the ideal is incapable of realization as concrete spirituality, and the reality thus presented remains confronting the idea as an external fabric with which it enters into no fusion, or has only entered so far as to establish an abstract relation. And it is in consequence of this that the fundamental type of the art of building is that of symbolism. Architecture is in fact the first pioneer on the highway toward the adequate realization of Godhead. In this service it is put to severe labor with objective nature, that it may disengage it by its effort from the confused growth of finitude and the distortions of contingency. By this means it levels a space for the God, informs his external environment, and builds him his temple, as a fit place for the concentration of spirit, and its direction to the absolute objects of intelligent life. It raises an enclosure for the congregation of those assembled, as a defense against the threatening of the tempest, against rain, the hurricane, and savage animals. It in short reveals the will thus to assemble, and although under an external relation, yet in agreement with the principles of art. A significance such as this it can to a greater or less extent import into its material and its forms, in proportion as the determinate content of its fabric, which is the object of its operations and effort, is more or less significant, is more concrete or more abstract, more profound in penetrating its own essential depth, or more obscure and superficial. Indeed architecture may in this respect proceed so far in the execution of such a purpose as to create an adequate artistic existence for such an ideal content in its very forms and material. In doing so, however, it has already passed beyond its peculiar province and is diverted into the stage immediately above it of sculpture. For the boundary of sculpture lies precisely in this that it retains the spiritual as an inward being which persists in direct contrast to the external embodiment of architecture. It can consequently merely point to that which is absorbed in soul life as to something external to itself.

b. Nevertheless, as above explained, the external and inorganic world is purified by architecture, it is coordinated under symmetrical laws, and made cognate with mind, and as a result the temple of God, the house of his community, stands before us. Into this temple, in the second place, the God himself enters in the lightning-flash of individuality which smites its way into the inert mass, permeating the same with its presence. In other words the infinite[21] and no longer purely symmetrical form belonging to intelligence

brings as it were to a focus and informs the shape in which it is most at home. This is the task of sculpture. Insofar as in it the inward life of spirit, to which the art of architecture can merely point away to, makes its dwelling within the sensuous shape and its external material, and to the extent that these two sides come into plastic communion with one another in such a manner that neither is predominant, sculpture receives as its fundamental type the classical art form.

For this reason the sensuous element on its own account admits of no expression here which is not affected by spiritual affinities,[22] just as, conversely, sculpture can reproduce with completeness no spiritual content, which does not maintain throughout adequate presentation to perception in bodily form. What sculpture, in short, has to do is to make the presence of spirit stand before us in its bodily shape and in immediate union therewith at rest and in blessedness; and this form has to be made vital by means of the content of spiritual individuality. The external sensuous material is consequently no longer elaborated either in conformity with its mechanical quality alone, as a mass of weight, nor in shapes of the inorganic world simply, nor in entire indifference to color, etc. It is carried into the ideal forms of the human figure, and, we may add, in the completeness of all three spatial dimensions. In other words and relatively to such a process we must maintain for sculpture that in it the inward or ideal content of spirit are first revealed in their eternal repose and essential self-stability. To such repose and unity with itself there can only correspond that external shape which itself persists in such unity and repose. And this condition is satisfied by configuration viewed in its abstract spatiality.[23] The spirit which sculpture represents is that which is essentially sound, not broken up in the play of chance conceits and passions; and for this reason its external form also is not dissolved in the manifold variety of appearance, but exhibits itself under this one presentment only as the abstraction of space in the totality of its dimensions.

Assuming, then, that the art of architecture has executed its temple, and the hand of sculpture has placed therein the image of the god, we have in the third place to assume the community of the faithful as confronting the god thus presented to vision in the wide chambers of his dwelling place. Now this community is the spiritual reflection into its own world of that sensuous presence, the subjective and inward animating life of soul, in its union with which both for the artistic content and the external material which manifests it,

---

[21]Infinite, of course, in the concrete sense of rounded in itself, as the circle, or, still more, the living organism.

[22]Literally, "which is not also that of the spiritual sphere."

[23]That is, an object limited only in space.

the determining principle may be identified with particularization in varied shapes and qualities, individualization and the life of soul[24] which they imply. The downright and solid fact of unity the god possesses in sculpture breaks up into the multiplicity of a world of particular souls,[25] whose union is no longer sensuous but wholly ideal.

Here for the first time God himself is revealed as veritably spirit—viz., the spirit revealed in his community. Here at last he is seen apprehended as this moving to and fro, as this alternation between his own essential unity and his realization in the knowledge of individual persons and that separation which it involves, as also in the universal spiritual being[26] and union of the many. In such a community God is disengaged from the abstraction of his unfolded self-seclusion and self-identity, no less than from the immediate absorption in bodily shape, in which he is presented by sculpture. He is, in a word, lifted into the actual sphere of spiritual existence and knowledge, into the reflected appearance, whose manifestation is essentially inward and the life of heart and soul. Thereby the higher content is now the nature of spirit, and that in its ultimate or absolute shape. But at the same time the separation to which we have alluded displays this as particular spiritual being, a specific emotional life. Moreover, for the reason that the main thing here is not the untroubled repose of the God in himself,[27] but his manifestation simply, the Being which is for another, self-revealment in fact, it follows that, on the plane we have now reached, all the varied content of human subjectivity in its vital movement and activity, whether viewed as passion, action, or event, or more generally the wide realm of human feeling, volition and its discontinuance, become one and all for their own sake objects of artistic representation.

Agreeably with such a content the sensuous element of art has likewise to show itself potentially adapted to such particularization and the display of such an inward content of heart and mind. Media of this description are supplied by color, musical tones, and finally in sound as mere sign for ideal perceptions and conceptions; and we further obtain the means of realizing with the use of such media a content of this kind in the arts of painting, music, and poetry. Throughout this sphere the sensuous medium is found to be essentially disparate in itself and throughout posited[28] as ideal. In this way it responds in the highest degree to the fundamentally spiritual content of art, and the coalescence of spiritual significance and sensuous materials attains a more intimate union than was possible either in architecture or sculpture. At the same time such a union is necessarily more near to soul life, leaning exclusively to the subjective side of human experience; one which, insofar as form and content are thus constrained to particularization and to posit their result as ideal, can only be actually effected at the expense of the objective universality of the content as also of the fusion with the immediately sensuous medium.[29]

The arts, which are lifted into a higher strain of ideality, abandoning as they do the symbolism of architecture and the classical ideal of sculpture, accept their predominant type from the romantic art form; and these are the arts most fitted to express its mode of configuration. They are, however, a totality of arts, because the romantic type is itself essentially the most concrete.

c. The articulation of this third sphere of the particular arts may be fixed as follows:

(1) The first art which comes next to sculpture is that of painting. It avails itself for a medium of its content and the plastic configuration of the same of visibility as such, to the extent that it is differentiated in its own nature, in other words is defined in the continuity of color. No doubt the material of architecture and sculpture is likewise both visible and colored. It is, however, not, as in painting, visibility in its pure nature, not the essentially simple light, which by its differentiating of itself in its opposition to darkness, and in association with that darkness gives rise to color.[30] This quality of visibility made essentially ideal[31] and treated as such

---

[24]*Subjektivität.* The particularization in romantic art implies the presence of an ideal element imported by the soul of the artist, which appeals directly to the soul in its emotional life. Compare a picture by an Italian master with a Greek statue.

[25]Literally, "a multiplicity of isolated examples of inwardness."

[26]That is, in the life shared by all as one community actuated by a common purpose.

[27]As in sculpture.

[28]Professor Bosanquet's note is here "posited or laid down to be ideal. This almost is equal to made to be in the sense of not being. In other words musical sound is 'ideal' as existing, qua work of art, in memory only, the moment in which it is actually heard being fugitive. A picture is equally so in respect of the third dimension, which has to be read into it. Poetry is almost wholly ideal, i.e., uses hardly any sensuous element, and appeals almost wholly to what exists in the mind."

[29]By particularization is meant the variety in the material of colors, musical tones, and ideas, which latter are really quite as much the medium of poetry as written language. The sensuous medium is here an abstract sign and, as Hegel would contend, nothing more than this.

[30]Reference, of course, to Hegel's unfortunate acceptance of Goethe's theory of color.

[31]The color of art is not merely ideal as applied to only two dimensions of space, but also is "subjective" in the artistic treatment of it under a definite "scheme." It is not clear whether Hegel alludes also to this; apparently not, though it is the most important feature. In fact, even assuming his theory of light to be correct, it is difficult entirely to follow his distinction between the appearance of color on a flat or a round surface. As natural color the one would be as ideal as the other. Only regarded as a composition would painting present distinction.

no longer either requires, as in architecture, the abstractly mechanical qualities of mass as appropriate to materials of weight, nor, as is the case with sculpture, the complete dimensuration of spatial condition, even when concentrated into organic forms. The visibility and the making apparent, which belong to painting, possess differences of quality under a more ideal mode—that is, in the specific varieties of color—which liberates art from the objective totality of spatial condition, by being limited to a plane surface.

On the other hand the content also attains the widest compass of particularity. Whatever can find a place in the human heart, as emotion, idea, and purpose, whatever it is capable of actually shaping—all such diversity may form part of the varied presentations of painting. The entire world of particular existence, from the most exalted embodiment of mind to the most insignificant natural fact, finds a place here. For it is possible even for finite nature, in its particular scenes and phenomena, to form part of such artistic display, provided only that we have some reference to conscious life which makes it akin to human thought and emotion.[32]

(2) The second art which continues the further realization of the romantic type and forms a distinct contrast to painting is that of music. Its medium, albeit still sensuous, yet proceeds into still profounder subjectivity and particularization. We have here, too, the deliberate treatment of the sensuous medium as ideal, and it consists in the negation and idealization into the isolated unity of a single point,[33] the indifferent external collocation of space,[34] whose complete appearance is retained by painting and deliberately feigned in its completeness. This isolated point, viewed as this process of negation, is an essentially concrete and active process of cancellation within the determinate substance of the material medium, viewed, that is, as motion and vibration of the material object within itself and in its relation to itself. Such an inchoate ideality of matter, which no longer appears under the form of space, but as temporal ideality,[35] is sound or tone. We have here the sensuous set down as negated, and its abstract visibility converted into audibility. In other words

sound liberates the ideal content from its fetters in the material substance. This earliest[36] secured inwardness of matter and impregnation of it with soul life supplies the medium for the intimacy and soul of spirit—itself as yet indefinite—permitting, as it does, the echo and reverberation of man's emotional world through its entire range of feelings and passions. In this way music forms the center of the romantic arts, just as sculpture represents the midway point of arrest between architecture and the arts of the romantic subjectivity. Thus, too, it forms the point of transition between the abstract, spatial sensuousness of painting and the abstract spirituality of poetry. Music carries within itself, like architecture, and in contrast to the emotional world simply and its inward self-seclusion, a relation of quantity conformable to the principles of the understanding and their modes of coordinated configuration.[37]

(3) We must look for our third and most spiritual type of artistic presentation among the romantic arts in that of poetry. The supreme characteristic of poetry consists in the power with which it brings into vassalage of the mind and its conceptions the sensuous element from which music and painting began to liberate art. For sound, the only remaining external material retained by poetry, is in it no longer the feeling of the sonorous itself, but is a mere sign without independent significance. And it is, moreover, a sign of idea which has become essentially concrete, and not merely[38] of indefinite feeling and its subtle modes and gradations. And this is how sound develops into the word, as essentially articulate voice, whose intention it is to indicate ideas and thoughts. The purely negative moment to which music advanced now asserts itself as the wholly concrete point, the point which is mind itself, the self-conscious individual, which produces from itself the infinite expansion of its ideas and unites the same with the temporal condition of sound. Yet this sensuous element, which was still in music immediately united to emotion, is in poetry separated from the content of consciousness. Mind, in short, here determines this content for its own sake and apart from all else into the content of idea; to express such idea it no doubt avails itself of sound, but employs it merely as a sign without independent worth or substance. Thus viewed, the sound here may be just as well reproduced by the mere letter, for the audible,

---

[32]It is obvious that the reference here is mainly to an intentional appeal to the human soul through the content of the composition. But the appeal may also be made through the technique and artistic treatment of the medium itself.

[33]The parts of a chord are not in space, but are ideally cognized. Hegel describes this by saying that music idealizes space and concentrates it to a point. It would perhaps be more intelligible to say that it transmutes the positive effects of a material substance in motion into the positive and more ideal condition of time. The point which is continually negated is at least qua music the point, or rather, moment, of a temporal process.

[34]By the indifferent externality of space is signified the fact that the parts of space, though external to each other, are not qualitatively distinguishable.

[35]Succession in time is "more ideal" than coexistence in space because it exists only as continuity in a conscious subject.

[36]Painting no doubt introduces ideal elements into the artistic composition of color, but the color still remains the appearance of a material thing or superficies.

[37]That is to say, music or harmony is based on a solid conformity to law on the part of its tones in their conjunction and succession, their structure and resolution.

[38]As in painting.

like the visible, is here reduced to a mere indication of mind.[39] For this reason, the true medium of poetical representation is the poetical imagination and the intellectual presentation itself; and inasmuch as this element is common to all types of art it follows that poetry is a common thread through them all, and is developed independently in each. Poetry is, in short, the universal art of the mind, which has become essentially free, and which is not fettered in its realization to an externally sensuous material, but which is creatively active in the space and time belonging to the inner world of ideas and emotion. Yet it is precisely in this its highest phase, that art terminates, by transcending itself; it is just here that it deserts the medium of a harmonious presentation of mind in sensuous shape and passes from the poetry of imaginative idea into the prose of thought.

Such we may accept as the articulate totality of the particular arts; they are the external art of architecture, the objective art of sculpture and the subjective arts of painting, music, and poetry. Many other classifications than these have been attempted, for a work of art presents such a wealth of aspects, that it is quite possible, as has frequently been the case, to make first one and then another the basis of division. For instance, you may take the sensuous medium simply. Architecture may then be viewed as a kind of crystalization; sculpture, as the organic configuration of material in its sensuous and spatial totality; painting as the colored surface and line, while in music, space, as such, passes over into the point or moment of time replete with content in itself, until we come finally to poetry, where the external medium is wholly suppressed into insignificance. Or, again, these differences have been viewed with reference to their purely abstract conditions of space and time. Such abstract divisions of works of art may, as their medium also may be consequentially traced in their characteristic features. They cannot, however, be worked out as the final and fundamental principle, because such aspects themselves derive their origins from a higher principle, and must therefore fall into subordination thereto.

This higher principle we have discovered in the types of art—symbolic, classical, and romantic—which are the universal stages or phases of the idea of beauty itself.

Their relation to the individual arts in their concrete manifestation as embodiment is of a kind that these arts constitute the real and positive existence of these general art types. For symbolic art attains its most adequate realization and most pertinent application in architecture, in which it expatiates in the full import of its notion, and is not as yet depreciated, as it were, into the merely inorganic nature dealt with by some other art. The classical type of art finds its unfettered realization, on the other hand, in sculpture, treating architecture merely as the enclosure which surrounds it, and being unable to elaborate painting and music into the wholly adequate[40] forms of its content. Finally, the romantic art type is supreme in the products of painting and music, and likewise in poetical composition, as their preeminent and unconditionally adequate modes of expression. Poetry is, however, conformable to all types of the beautiful, and its embrace reaches them all for the reason that the poetic imagination is its own proper medium, and imagination is essential to every creation of beauty, whatever its type may be.

To sum up, then, what the particular arts realize in particular works of art, are according to their fundamental conception, simply the universal types which constitute the self-unfolding idea of beauty. It is as the external realization of this idea that the wide pantheon of art is being raised; and the architect and builder thereof is the spirit of beauty as it gradually comes to self-cognition, and to complete which the history of the world will require its evolution of centuries.

---

[39]The views here propounded suggest considerable criticism. It appears to me that the stress here laid upon the intelligible content of poetry as contrasted with the sensuous qualities of its form as modulated speech is certainly untenable. What we call the music of verse may unquestionably be most intimately associated with the ideal content expressed; but apart from the artistic collocation of language as sound no less than symbol we certainly do not get the art of poetry. Even where Hegel deals directly with rhythm and rhyme in the body of the treatise I think it is clear he underrates all that is implied in the difference between the musical expression of poetry as contrasted even with the sonorous language of mere prose. A further question upon which more doubt is permissible is how far the actual script in written or printed letters is not entitled to be regarded as at least in part the sensuous medium. No doubt the poem is not dependent upon it as a painting is upon color, or the canvas which supports it, for it may be recited. But at least it is practically dependent upon it for its preservation. The point may very possibly appear, however, as nugatory or entirely unimportant, beside the question whether the medium of the art is not really imaginative idea rather than articulate speech.

---

[40]*Absolute Formen.* Adequate in the sense of being unconditionally so.

Thomas Carlyle

1795–1881

Carlyle's discussion of symbols, uttered by the fictitious German professor Teufelsdröckh (Devilsdung), comprises Chapter 3 of his famous work *Sartor Resartus*. Carlyle praises the virtues of "silence" and "secrecy" and finds them combined in the symbol, in which there is "concealment and yet revelation." In the symbol infinite things are embodied and revealed in the finite. Carlyle's distinction between extrinsic and intrinsic symbols is similar to that made by other Romantic writers, notably Coleridge, between allegory and symbolism. His account of the social importance of symbols looks forward to numerous modern formulations, particularly Cassirer's idea of "symbolic forms."

Carlyle's works have been edited in thirty volumes by H. D. Traill (1896–1901). For commentary consult E. E. Neff, *Carlyle and Mill,* rev. ed. (1926), and *Carlyle* (1932); C. F. Harrold, *Carlyle and German Thought 1819–1834* (1934); René Wellek, "Carlyle and the Philosophy of History," *Philological Quarterly,* XXIII (1944), 55–76; G. B. Tennyson, *Sartor Called Resartus* (1966); Ian Campbell, *Thomas Carlyle* (1974); A. L. Le Quesne, *Carlyle* (1982); and Fred Caplan, *Thomas Carlyle, A Biography* (1983).

Symbols

Probably it will elucidate the drift of these foregoing obscure utterances, if we here insert somewhat of our professor's speculations on symbols. To state his whole doctrine, indeed, were beyond our compass: nowhere is he more mysterious, impalpable, than in this of "fantasy being the organ of the Godlike"; and how "Man thereby, though based, to all seeming, on the small visible, does nevertheless extend down into the infinite deeps of the invisible, of which invisible, indeed, his life is properly the bodying forth." Let us, omitting these high transcendental aspects of the matter, study to glean (whether from the paper bags or the printed volume) what little seems logical and practical, and cunningly arrange it into such degree of coherence as it will assume. By way of proem, take the following not injudicious remarks:

"The benignant efficacies of concealment," cries our professor, "who shall speak or sing? Silence and Secrecy! Altars might still be raised to them (were this an altar-building time) for universal worship. Silence is the element in which great things fashion themselves together; that at length they may emerge, full–formed and majestic, into the daylight of life, which they are thenceforth to rule. Not William the Silent only, but all the considerable men I have known, and the most undiplomatic and unstrategic of these, forbore to babble of what they were creating and projecting. Nay, in thy own mean perplexities, do thou thyself but hold thy tongue for one day: on the morrow, how much clearer are thy purposes and duties; what wreck and rubbish have those mute workmen within thee swept away, when intrusive noises were shut out! Speech is too often not, as the Frenchman defined it, the art of concealing thought; but of quite stifling and suspending thought, so that there is none to conceal. Speech too is great, but not the greatest. As the Swiss

SYMBOLS. The text is Chapter 3 of Carlyle's *Sartor Resartus,* which was first published in 1831.

inscription says: *"Sprechen ist silbern, Schweigen ist golden"* (Speech is silvern, silence is golden); or as I might rather express it: Speech is of time, silence is of eternity.

"Bees will not work except in darkness; thought will not work except in silence: neither will virtue work except in secrecy. Let not thy left hand know what thy right hand doeth! Neither shalt thou prate even to thy own heart of 'those secrets known to all.' Is not shame (*Schaam*) the soil of all virtue, of all good manners and good morals? Like other plants, virtue will not grow unless its root be hidden, buried from the eye of the sun. Let the sun shine on it, nay do but look at it privily thyself, the root withers, and no flowers will glad thee. O my friends, when we view the fair clustering flowers that overwreathe, for example, the marriage bower, and encircle man's life with the fragrance and hues of heaven, what hand will not smite the foul plunderer that grubs them up by the roots, and with grinning, grunting satisfaction, shows us the dung they flourish in! Men speak much of the printing press with its newspapers: *du Himmel!* what are these to clothes and the tailor's goose?

"Of kin to the so incalculable influence of concealment, and connected with still greater things, is the wondrous agency of symbols. In a symbol there is concealment and yet revelation: here therefore, by silence and by speech acting together, comes a double significance. And if both the speech be itself high, and the silence fit and noble, how expressive will their union be! Thus in many a painted device, or simple seal-emblem, the commonest truth stands out to us proclaimed with quite new emphasis.

"For it is here that fantasy with her mystic wonderland plays into the small prose domain of sense, and becomes incorporated therewith. In the symbol proper, what we can call a symbol, there is ever, more or less distinctly and directly, some embodiment and revelation of the infinite; the infinite is made to blend itself with the finite, to stand visible, and as it were, attainable there. By symbols, accordingly, is man guided and commanded, made happy, made wretched. He everywhere finds himself encompassed with symbols, recognized as such or not recognized: the universe is but one vast symbol of God; nay if thou wilt have it, what is man himself but a symbol of God; is not all that he does symbolical; a revelation to sense of the mystic God-given force that is in him; a 'gospel of freedom,' which he, the 'Messiah of nature,' preaches, as he can, by act and word? Not a hut he builds but is the visible embodiment of a thought; but bears visible record of invisible things; but is, in the transcendental sense, symbolical as well as real.

"Man," says the professor elsewhere, in quite antipodal contrast with these high-soaring delineations, which we have here cut short on the verge of the inane, "Man is by birth somewhat of an owl. Perhaps, too, of all the owleries that ever possessed him, the most owlish, if we consider it, is that of your actually existing motive-millwrights. Fantastic tricks enough man has played, in his time; has fancied himself to be most things, down even to an animated heap of glass: but to fancy himself a dead iron balance for weighing pains and pleasures on, was reserved for this his latter era. There stands he, his universe one huge manger, filled with hay and thistles to be weighed against each other; and looks long-eared enough. Alas, poor devil! Specters are appointed to haunt him: one age he is hagridden, bewitched; the next, priestridden, befooled; in all ages, bedeviled. And now the genius of mechanism smothers him worse than any nightmare did; till the soul is nigh choked out of him, and only a kind of digestive, mechanic life remains. In earth and in heaven he can see nothing but mechanism; has fear for nothing else, hope in nothing else: the world would indeed grind him to pieces; but cannot he fathom the doctrine of motives, and cunningly compute these, and mechanize them to grind the other way?

"Were he not, as has been said, purblinded by enchantment, you had but to bid him open his eyes and look. In which country, in which time, was it hitherto that man's history, or the history of any man, went on by calculated or calculable 'motives'? What make ye of your Christianities, and chivalries, and reformations, and Marseillese hymns, and reigns of terror? Nay, has not perhaps the motive-grinder himself been in love? Did he never stand so much as a contested election? Leave him to time, and the medicating virtue of nature.

"Yes, friends," elsewhere observes the professor, "not our logical, mensurative faculty, but our imaginative one is king over us; I might say, priest and prophet to lead us heavenward; or magician and wizard to lead us hellward. Nay, even for the basest sensualist, what is sense but the implement of fantasy; the vessel it drinks out of? Ever in the dullest existence there is a sheen either of inspiration or of madness (thou partly hast it in thy choice, which of the two), that gleams in from the circumambient eternity, and colors with its own hues our little islet of time. The understanding is indeed thy window, too clear thou canst not make it; but fantasy is thy eye, with its color-giving retina, healthy or diseased. Have not I myself known five hundred living soldiers sabered into crow's-meat for a piece of glazed cotton, which they called their flag; which, had you sold it at any market-cross, would not have brought above three groschen? Did not the whole Hungarian nation rise like some tumultuous moon-stirred Atlantic, when Kaiser Joseph pocketed their iron crown; an implement, as was sagaciously observed, in size and commercial value little differing from a horseshoe? It is in and through symbols that man, consciously or unconsciously, lives, works, and has his being: those ages, moreover, are accounted the noblest which can the best recognize symbolical worth, and prize it the highest. For is not a symbol ever, to him who has eyes for it, some dimmer or clearer revelation of the Godlike?

"Of symbols, however, I remark farther, that they have both an extrinsic and intrinsic value; oftenest the former only. What, for instance, was in that clouted shoe, which the peasants bore aloft with them as ensign in their *Bauernkrieg* (Peasants' War)? Or in the wallet and staff round which the Netherland *Gueux,* glorying in that nickname of "Beggars," heroically rallied and prevailed, though against King Philip himself? Intrinsic significance these had none; only extrinsic; as the accidental standards of multitudes more or less sacredly uniting together; in which union itself, as above noted, there is ever something mystical and borrowing of the Godlike. Under a like category, too, stand, or stood, the stupidest heraldic coats of arms; military banners everywhere; and generally all national or other sectarian costumes and customs: they have no intrinsic, necessary divineness, or even worth; but have acquired an extrinsic one. Nevertheless through all these there glimmers something of a divine idea; as through military banners themselves, the divine idea of duty, of heroic daring; in some instances of freedom, of right. Nay, the highest ensign that men ever met and embraced under, the Cross itself, had no meaning save an accidental extrinsic one.

"Another matter it is, however, when your symbol has intrinsic meaning, and is of itself fit that men should unite round it. Let but the Godlike manifest itself to sense; let but eternity look more or less visibly, through the time figure (*Zeitbild*)! Then is it fit that men unite there; and worship together before such symbol; and so from day to day, and from age to age, superadd to it new divineness.

"Of this latter sort are all true works of art: in them (if thou know a work of art from a daub of artifice) wilt thou discern eternity looking through time; the Godlike rendered visible. Here too may an extrinsic value gradually superadd itself: thus certain *Iliads,* and the like, have, in three thousand years, attained quite new significance. But nobler than all in this kind are the lives of heroic God-inspired men; for what other work of art is so divine? In death too, in the death of the just, as the last perfection of a work of art, may we not discern symbolic meaning? In that divinely transfigured sleep, as of victory, resting over the beloved face which now knows thee no more, read (if thou canst for tears) the confluence of time with eternity, and some gleam of the latter peering through.

"Highest of all symbols are those wherein the artist or poet has risen into prophet, and all men can recognize a present God, and worship the same: I mean religious symbols. Various enough have been such religious symbols, what we call religious; as men stood in this stage of culture or the other, and could worse or better body-forth the Godlike: some symbols with a transient intrinsic worth; many with only an extrinsic. If thou ask to what height man has carried it in this manner, look on our divinest symbol: on Jesus of Nazareth, and his life, and his biography, and what followed therefrom. Higher has the human thought not yet reached: this is Christianity and Christendom; a symbol of quite perennial, infinite character; whose significance will ever demand to be anew inquired into, and anew made manifest.

"But, on the whole, as time adds much to the sacredness of symbols, so likewise in his progress he at length defaces, or even desecrates them; and symbols, like all terrestrial garments, wax old. Homer's epos has not ceased to be true; yet it is no longer our epos, but shines in the distance, if clearer and clearer, yet also smaller and smaller, like a receding star. It needs a scientific telescope, it needs to be reinterpreted and artificially brought near us, before we can so much as know that it was a sun. So likewise a day comes when the Runic Thor, with his Eddas, must withdraw into dimness; and many an African mumbo-jumbo and Indian pawaw be utterly abolished. For all things, even celestial luminaries, much more atmospheric meteors, have their rise, their culmination, their decline.

"Small is this which thou tellest me, that the royal scepter is but a piece of gilt-wood; that the pyx has become a most foolish box, and truly, as ancient Pistol thought, 'of little price.' A right conjuror might I name thee, couldst thou conjure back into these wooden tools the divine virtue they once held.

"Of this thing, however, be certain: wouldst thou plant for eternity, then plant into the deep infinite faculties of man, his fantasy and heart; wouldst thou plant for year and day, then plant into his shallow superficial faculties, his self-love and arithmetical understanding, what will grow there. A hierarch, therefore, and pontiff of the world will we call him, the poet and inspired maker; who, Prometheus-like, can shape new symbols, and bring new fire from heaven to fix it there. Such too will not always be wanting; neither perhaps now are. Meanwhile, as the average of matters goes, we account him legislator and wise who can so much as tell when a symbol has grown old, and gently remove it.

"When, as the last English coronation was preparing,"

concludes this wonderful professor, "I read in their newspapers that the 'champion of England,' he who has to offer battle to the universe for his new king, had brought it so far that he could now 'mount his horse with little assistance,' I said to myself: Here also we have a symbol well-nigh superannuated. Alas, move whithersoever you may, are not the tatters and rags of superannuated worn out symbols (in this ragfair of a world) dropping off everywhere, to hoodwink, to halter, to tether you; nay, if you shake them not aside, threatening to accumulate, and perhaps produce suffocation?"

John Stuart Mill

1806–1873

Mill was strictly educated by his father, James Mill, to profess Benthamite utilitarianism, which argues that all human acts ought to contribute to the achievement of the greatest happiness of the greatest number of people. He came to believe, however, that his rationalistic training had badly neglected his emotional development. Moved by the poetry of Wordsworth, he wrote occasional essays on literature. In *What Is Poetry?* he contrasts poetry, which appeals to the feelings, with science, which addresses itself to beliefs. Mill belittles attempts to distinguish between poetry and prose, observing that both may act on the feelings. Poems and novels differ, however, in the way they achieve their effect: poems express feeling, while novels, though they may contain poetry, represent incidents and outward circumstances.

More important is Mill's distinction between poetry and what he calls "eloquence." Poetry he associates with soliloquy. It is "overhead," whereas eloquence is simply "heard." Poetry is not pure rhetoric and persuasion; it does not parade a purpose to convince those who hear it. Clearly, Mill is attempting to dissociate utility from poetry. But he recognized a social purpose to be achieved indirectly by poetry. He believed that in the modern age the poet's prime duty was to express his own inner state sincerely and truthfully. In his view old-fashioned didactic literature could no longer be effective, for society had become more divided in beliefs than in earlier ages. Poetry must work at a deeper moral level, seeking by sympathy to purify the emotions. In doing this, it performs a cultural and social function ultimately consistent with utilitarian aims. In expressing these views, Mill opposed the established utilitarian view of Jeremy Bentham, who thought that poetry was subjective and untruthful, that it stimulated the passions and prejudices, and that it was therefore socially harmful.

Edward Alexander has edited Mill's *Literary Essays* (1967). M. St. J. Packe has written a biography, *The Life of John Stuart Mill* (1954). Critical studies include J. M. Robson, "J. S. Mill's Theory of Poetry," *University of Toronto Quarterly,* XXIX (1960), 420–38; Thomas Woods, *Poetry and Philosophy: A Study of the Thought of John Stuart Mill* (1961); Edward Alexander, *Matthew Arnold and John Stuart Mill* (1965); F. Sharples, *The Literary Criticism of John Stuart Mill* (1967); Alan Ryan, *John Stuart Mill* (1970); H. J. McCloskey, *John Stuart Mill: A Critical Study* (1971); Bernard Samuel, *John Stuart Mill and the Pursuit of Virtue* (1984); and William Thomas, *Mill* (1985).

What Is Poetry?

It has often been asked, what is poetry? And many and various are the answers which have been returned. The vulgarest of all—one with which no person possessed of the faculties to which poetry addresses itself can ever have been satisfied—is that which confounds poetry with metrical composition: yet to this wretched mockery of a definition, many have been led back, by the failure of all their attempts to find any other that would distinguish what they have been accustomed to call poetry, from much which they have known only under other names.

That, however, the word *poetry* does import something quite peculiar in its nature, something which may exist in what is called prose as well as in verse, something which does not even require the instrument of words, but can speak, through those other audible symbols called musical sounds, and even through the visible ones, which are the language of sculpture, painting, and architecture; all this, as we believe, is and must be felt, though perhaps indistinctly, by all upon whom poetry in any of its shapes produces any impression beyond that of tickling the ear. To the mind, poetry is either nothing, or it is the better part of all art whatever, and of real life too; and the distinction between poetry and what is not poetry, whether explained or not, is felt to be fundamental.

Where everyone feels a difference, a difference there must be. All other appearance may be fallacious, but the appearance of a difference is itself a real difference. Appearances too, like other things, must have a cause, and that which can cause anything, even an illusion, must be a reality. And hence, while a half-philosophy disdains the classifications and distinctions indicated by popular language, philosophy carried to its highest point may frame new ones, but never sets aside the old, content with correcting and regularizing them. It cuts fresh channels for thought, but it does not fill up such as it finds ready-made, but traces, on the contrary, more deeply, broadly, and distinctly, those into which the current has spontaneously flowed.

Let us then attempt, in the way of modest inquiry, not to coerce and confine nature within the bounds of an arbitrary definition, but rather to find the boundaries which she herself has set, and erect a barrier round them; not calling mankind to account for having misapplied the word *poetry,*

but attempting to clear up to them the conception which they already attach to it, and to bring before their minds as a distinct principle that which, as a vague feeling, has really guided them in their actual employment of the term.

The object of poetry is confessedly to act upon the emotions; and therein is poetry sufficiently distinguished from what Wordsworth affirms to be its logical opposite, namely, not prose, but matter of fact or science.[1] The one addresses itself to the belief, the other to the feelings. The one does its work by convincing or persuading, the other by moving. The one acts by presenting a proposition to the understanding, the other by offering interesting objects of contemplation to the sensibilities.

This, however, leaves us very far from a definition of poetry. We have distinguished it from one thing, but we are bound to distinguish it from everything. To present thoughts or images to the mind for the purpose of acting upon the emotions, does not belong to poetry alone. It is equally the province (for example) of the novelist: and yet the faculty of the poet and the faculty of the novelist are as distinct as any other two faculties; as the faculty of the novelist and of the orator, or of the poet and the metaphysician. The two characters may be united, as characters the most disparate may; but they have no natural connection.

Many of the finest poems are in the form of novels, and in almost all good novels there is true poetry. But there is a radical distinction between the interest felt in a novel as such, and the interest excited by poetry; for the one is derived from incident, the other from the representation of feeling. In one, the source of the emotion excited is the exhibition of a state or states of human sensibility; in the other, of a series of states of mere outward circumstances. Now, all minds are capable of being affected more or less by representations of the latter kind, and all, or almost all, by those of the former; yet the two sources of interest correspond to two distinct and (as respects their greatest development) mutually exclusive characters of mind. So much is the nature of poetry dissimilar to the nature of fictitious narrative, that to have a really strong passion for either of the two, seems to presuppose or to superinduce a comparative indifference to the other.

At what age is the passion for a story, for almost any kind of story, merely as a story, the most intense? In childhood. But that also is the age at which poetry, even of the simplest description, is least relished and least understood; because the feelings with which it is especially conversant are yet undeveloped, and not having been even in the

---

WHAT IS POETRY? Mill's *What Is Poetry?* was first published in 1833 in the *Monthly Repository.* It was revised and combined with another essay, *The Two Kinds of Poetry,* for inclusion in *Dissertations and Discussions* (1859) under the title *Thoughts on Poetry and Its Varieties.* The text is that of the 1833 version.

[1]See Preface to the *Lyrical Ballads,* p. 442.

slightest degree experienced, cannot be sympathized with. In what stage of the progress of society, again, is storytelling most valued, and the storyteller in greatest request and honor? In a rude state; like that of the Tartars and Arabs at this day, and of almost all nations in the earliest ages. But in this state of society there is little poetry except ballads, which are mostly narrative, that is, essentially stories, and derive their principal interest from the incidents. Considered as poetry, they are of the lowest and most elementary kind: the feelings depicted, or rather indicated, are the simplest our nature has; such joys and griefs as the immediate pressure of some outward event excites in rude minds, which live wholly immersed in outward things, and have never, either from choice or a force they could not resist, turned themselves to the contemplation of the world within. Passing now from childhood, and from the childhood of society, to the grown-up men and women of this most grown-up and un-childlike age—the minds and hearts of greatest depth and elevation are commonly those which take greatest delight in poetry; the shallowest and emptiest, on the contrary, are, by universal remark, the most addicted to novel reading. This accords, too, with all analogous experience of human nature. The sort of persons whom not merely in books but in their lives, we find perpetually engaged in hunting for excitement from without, are invariably those who do not possess, either in the vigor of their intellectual powers or in the depth of their sensibilities, that which would enable them to find ample excitement nearer at home. The same persons whose time is divided between sightseeing, gossip, and fashionable dissipation, take a natural delight in fictitious narrative; the excitement it affords is of the kind which comes from without. Such persons are rarely lovers of poetry, though they may fancy themselves so, because they relish novels in verse. But poetry, which is the delineation of the deeper and more secret workings of the human heart, is interesting only to those to whom it recalls what they have felt, or whose imagination it stirs up to conceive what they could feel, or what they might have been able to feel, had their outward circumstances been different.

Poetry, when it is really such, is truth; and fiction also, if it is good for anything, is truth: but they are different truths. The truth of poetry is to paint the human soul truly: the truth of fiction is to give a true picture of life. The two kinds of knowledge are different, and come by different ways, come mostly to different persons. Great poets are often proverbially ignorant of life. What they know has come by observation of themselves; they have found there one highly delicate, and sensitive, and refined specimen of human nature, on which the laws of human emotion are written in large characters, such as can be read off without much

study: and other knowledge of mankind, such as comes to men of the world by outward experience, is not indispensable to them as poets: but to the novelist such knowledge is all in all; he has to describe outward things, not the inward man; actions and events, not feelings; and it will not do for him to be numbered among those who, as Madame Roland said of Brissot, know man but not men.

All this is no bar to the possibility of combining both elements, poetry and narrative or incident, in the same work, and calling it either a novel or a poem; but so may red and white combine on the same human features, or on the same canvas; and so may oil and vinegar, though opposite natures, blend together in the same composite taste. There is one order of composition which requires the union of poetry and incident, each in its highest kind—the dramatic. Even there the two elements are perfectly distinguishable, and may exist of unequal quality, and in the most various proportion. The incidents of a dramatic poem may be scanty and ineffective, though the delineation of passion and character may be of the highest order; as in Goethe's glorious *Torquato Tasso;* or again, the story as a mere story may be well got up for effect, as is the case with some of the most trashy productions of the Minerva press: it may even be, what those are not, a coherent and probable series of events, though there be scarcely a feeling exhibited which is not exhibited falsely, or in a manner absolutely commonplace. The combination of the two excellencies is what renders Shakespeare so generally acceptable, each sort of readers finding in him what is suitable to their faculties. To the many he is great as a storyteller, to the few as a poet.

In limiting poetry to the delineation of states of feeling, and denying the name where nothing is delineated but outward objects, we may be thought to have done what we promised to avoid—to have not found, but made a definition, in opposition to the usage of the English language, since it is established by common consent that there is a poetry called descriptive. We deny the charge. Description is not poetry because there is descriptive poetry, no more than science is poetry because there is such a thing as a didactic poem; no more, we might almost say, than Greek or Latin is poetry because there are Greek and Latin poems. But an object which admits of being described, or a truth which may fill a place in a scientific treatise, may also furnish an occasion for the generation of poetry, which we thereupon choose to call descriptive or didactic. The poetry is not in the object itself, nor in the scientific truth itself, but in the state of mind in which the one and the other may be contemplated. The mere delineation of the dimensions and colors of external objects is not poetry, no more than a geometrical ground plan of St. Peter's or Westminster Abbey is painting. Descriptive poetry consists, no doubt, in description, but in description of things as they appear, not as they are; and it paints them not in their bare and natural lineaments, but arranged in the colors and seen through the medium of the imagination set in action by the feelings. If a poet is to describe a lion, he will not set about describing him as a naturalist would, nor even as a traveler would, who was intent upon stating the truth, the whole truth, and nothing but the truth. He will describe him by imagery, that is, by suggesting the most striking likenesses and contrasts which might occur to a mind contemplating the lion, in the state of awe, wonder, or terror, which the spectacle naturally excites, or is, on the occasion, supposed to excite. Now this is describing the lion professedly, but the state of excitement of the spectator really. The lion may be described falsely or in exaggerated colors, and the poetry be all the better; but if the human emotion be not painted with the most scrupulous truth, the poetry is bad poetry, i.e., is not poetry at all, but a failure.

Thus far our progress towards a clear view of the essentials of poetry has brought us very close to the last two attempts at a definition of poetry which we happen to have seen in print, both of them by poets and men of genius. The one is by Ebenezer Elliott, the author of *Corn-Law Rhymes,* and other poems of still greater merit. "Poetry," says he, "is impassioned truth." The other is by a writer in *Blackwood's Magazine,* and comes, we think, still nearer the mark. We forget his exact words, but in substance he defined poetry as "man's thoughts tinged by his feelings." There is in either definition a near approximation to what we are in search of. Every truth which man can announce, every thought, even every outward impression, which can enter into his consciousness, may become poetry when shown through any impassioned medium, when invested with the coloring of joy, or grief, or pity, or affection, or admiration, or reverence, or awe, or even hatred or terror: and, unless so colored, nothing, be it as interesting as it may, is poetry. But both these definitions fail to discriminate between poetry and eloquence. Eloquence, as well as poetry, is impassioned truth; eloquence, as well as poetry, is thoughts colored by the feelings. Yet common apprehension and philosophic criticism alike recognize a distinction between the two: there is much that everyone would call eloquence, which no one would think of classing as poetry. A question will sometimes arise, whether some particular author is a poet; and those who maintain the negative commonly allow, that though not a poet, he is a highly eloquent writer.

The distinction between poetry and eloquence appears to us to be equally fundamental with the distinction between poetry and narrative, or between poetry and description. It is still farther from having been satisfactorily cleared up than either of the others, unless, which is highly probable, the German artists and critics have thrown some light upon it which has not yet reached us. Without a perfect knowledge of what they have written, it is something like presumption to write upon such subjects at all, and we shall be the foremost to urge that, whatever we may be about to submit, may be received, subject to correction from them.

Poetry and eloquence are both alike the expression or uttering forth of feeling. But if we may be excused the seeming affectation of the antithesis, we should say that eloquence is *heard,* poetry is *over*heard. Eloquence supposes an audience; the peculiarity of poetry appears to us to lie in the poet's utter unconsciousness of a listener. Poetry is feeling confessing itself to itself, in moments of solitude, and bodying itself forth in symbols which are the nearest possible representations of the feeling in the exact shape in which it exists in the poet's mind. Eloquence is feeling pouring itself forth to other minds, courting their sympathy, or endeavoring to influence their belief, or move them to passion or to action.

All poetry is of the nature of soliloquy. It may be said that poetry, which is printed on hot-pressed paper, and sold at a bookseller's shop, is a soliloquy in full dress, and upon the stage. But there is nothing absurd in the idea of such a mode of soliloquizing. What we have said to ourselves, we may tell to others afterwards; what we have said or done in solitude, we may voluntarily reproduce when we know that other eyes are upon us. But no trace of consciousness that any eyes are upon us must be visible in the work itself. The actor knows that there is an audience present; but if he act as though he knew it, he acts ill. A poet may write poetry with the intention of publishing it; he may write it even for the express purpose of being paid for it; that it should be poetry, being written under any such influences, is far less probable; not, however, impossible; but not otherwise possible than if he can succeed in excluding from his work every vestige of such lookings-forth into the outward and everyday world, and can express his feelings exactly as he has felt them in solitude, or as he feels that he should feel them, though they were to remain forever unuttered. But when he turns round and addresses himself to another person; when the act of utterance is not itself the end, but a means to an end—viz., by the feelings he himself expresses to work upon the feelings, or upon the belief, or the will of another—when the expression of his emotions, or of his thoughts, tinged by his emotions, is tinged also by that purpose, by that desire of making an impression upon another mind, then it ceases to be poetry, and becomes eloquence.

Poetry, accordingly, is the natural fruit of solitude and meditation; eloquence, of intercourse with the world. The persons who have most feeling of their own, if intellectual culture have given them a language in which to express it, have the highest faculty of poetry; those who best understand the feelings of others, are the most eloquent. The persons, and the nations, who commonly excel in poetry, are those whose character and tastes render them least dependent for their happiness upon the applause, or sympathy, or concurrence of the world in general. Those to whom that applause, that sympathy, that concurrence are most necessary, generally excel most in eloquence. And hence, perhaps, the French, who are the least poetical of all great and refined nations, are among the most eloquent: the French, also, being the most sociable, the vainest, and the least self-dependent.

If the above be, as we believe, the true theory of the distinction commonly admitted between eloquence and poetry; or though it be not that, yet if, as we cannot doubt, the distinction above stated be a real bona fide distinction, it will be found to hold, not merely in the language of words, but in all other language, and to intersect the whole domain of art.

Take, for example, music: we shall find in that art, so peculiarly the expression of passion, two perfectly distinct styles; one of which may be called the poetry, the other the oratory of music. This difference being seized would put an end to much musical sectarianism. There has been much contention whether the character of Rossini's music—the music, we mean, which is characteristic of that composer—is compatible with the expression of passion. With doubt, the passion it expresses is not the musing, meditative tenderness, or pathos, or grief of Mozart, the great poet of his art. Yet it is passion, but garrulous passion—the passion which pours itself into other ears; and therein the better calculated for dramatic effect, having a natural adaptation for dialogue. Mozart also is great in musical oratory; but his most touching compositions are in the opposite style—that of soliloquy. Who can imagine *"Dove sono" heard?* We imagine it *overheard*. The same is the case with many of the finest national airs. Who can hear those words, which speak so touchingly the sorrows of a mountaineer in exile:

My heart's in the Highlands—my heart is not here;
My heart's in the Highlands, a-chasing the deer,
A-chasing the wild-deer, and following the roe—
My heart's in the Highlands, wherever I go.

Who can hear those affecting words, married to as affecting an air, and fancy that he sees the singer? That song has always seemed to us like the lament of a prisoner in a solitary cell, ourselves listening, unseen, in the next. As the direct opposite of this, take "Scots wha hae wi' Wallace bled," where the music is as oratorical as the poetry.

Purely pathetic music commonly partakes of soliloquy. The soul is absorbed in its distress, and though there may be bystanders, it is not thinking of them. When the mind is looking within and not without, its state does not often or rapidly vary; and hence the even, uninterrupted flow, approaching almost to monotony, which a good reader, or a good singer, will give to words or music of a pensive or melancholy cast. But grief, taking the form of a prayer, or of a complaint becomes oratorical; no longer low, and even, and subdued, it assumes a more emphatic rhythm, a more rapidly returning accent; instead of a few slow, equal notes, following one after another at regular intervals, it crowds note upon note, and ofttimes assumes a hurry and bustle like joy. Those who are familiar with some of the best of Rossini's serious compositions, such as the air *"Tu che i miseri conforti,"* in the opera of *Tancredi,* or the duet *"Ebben per mia memoria,"* in *La Gazza Ladra,* will at once understand and feel our meaning. Both are highly tragic and passionate; the passion of both is that of oratory, not poetry. The like may be said of that most moving prayer in Beethoven's *Fidelio "Komm, Hoffnung, lass das letzte Stern / Der Müde nicht erbleichen";*[2] in which Madame Devrient, last summer, exhibited such consummate powers of pathetic expression. How different from Winter's beautiful *"Paga pii,"* the very soul of melancholy exhaling itself in solitude; fuller of meaning, and, therefore, more profoundly poetical than the words for which it was composed—for it seems to express not simple melancholy, but the melancholy of remorse.

If, from vocal music, we now pass to instrumental, we may have a specimen of musical oratory in any fine military symphony or march: while the poetry of music seems to have attained its consummation in Beethoven's Overture to *Egmont.* We question whether so deep an expression of mixed grandeur and melancholy was ever in any other instance produced by mere sounds.

In the arts which speak to the eye, the same distinctions will be found to hold, not only between poetry and oratory, but between poetry, oratory, narrative, and simple imitation or description.

Pure description is exemplified in a mere portrait or a mere landscape—productions of art, it is true, but of the mechanical rather than of the fine arts, being works of simple imitation, not creation. We say, a mere portrait, or a mere landscape, because it is possible for a portrait or a landscape, without ceasing to be such, to be also a picture. A portrait by Lawrence, or one of Turner's views, is not a mere copy from nature: the one combines with the given features that particular expression (among all good and pleasing ones) which

---

[2]"Come, Hope, do not let the last star of the tired ones fade away."

those features are most capable of wearing, and which, therefore, in combination with them, is capable of producing the greatest positive beauty. Turner, again, unites the objects of the given landscape with whatever sky, and whatever light and shade, enable those particular objects to impress the imagination most strongly. In both, there is creative art—not working after an actual model, but realizing an idea.

Whatever in painting or sculpture expresses human feeling, or character, which is only a certain state of feeling grown habitual, may be called, according to circumstances, the poetry or the eloquence of the painter's or the sculptor's art; the poetry, if the feeling declares itself by such signs as escape from us when we are unconscious of being seen; the oratory, if the signs are those we use for the purpose of voluntary communication.

The poetry of painting seems to be carried to its highest perfection in the *Peasant Girl* of Rembrandt, or in any Madonna or Magdalen of Guido; that of sculpture, in almost any of the Greek statues of the gods; not considering these in respect to the mere physical beauty, of which they are such perfect models, not undertaking either to vindicate or to contest the opinion of philosophers, that even physical beauty is ultimately resolvable into expression; we may safely affirm, that in no other of man's works did so much of soul ever shine through mere inanimate matter.

The narrative style answers to what is called historical painting, which it is the fashion among connoisseurs to treat as the climax of the pictorial art. That it is the most difficult branch of the art, we do not doubt, because, in its perfection, it includes, in a manner, the perfection of all the other branches. As an epic poem, though, insofar as it is epic (i.e., narrative), it is not poetry at all, is yet esteemed the greatest effort of poetic genius, because there is no kind whatever of poetry which may not appropriately find a place in it. But a historical picture, as such, that is, as the representation of an incident, must necessarily, as it seems to us, be poor and ineffective. The narrative powers of painting are extremely limited. Scarcely any picture, scarcely any series even of pictures, which we know of, tells its own story without the aid of an interpreter; you must know the story beforehand; then, indeed, you may see great beauty and appropriateness in the painting. But it is the single figures which, to us, are the great charm even of a historical picture. It is in these that the power of the art is really seen: in the attempt to narrate, visible and permanent signs are far behind the fugitive audible ones which follow so fast one after another, while the faces and figures in a narrative picture, even though they be Titian's, stand still. Who would not prefer one *Virgin and Child* of Raphael, to all the pictures which Rubens, with his fat, frowzy Dutch Venuses, ever painted? Though Rubens, besides excelling almost everyone in his mastery over all the mechanical parts of his art, often shows real genius in grouping his figures, the peculiar problem of historical painting. But, then, who, except a mere student of drawing and coloring, ever cared to look twice at any of the figures themselves? The power of painting lies in poetry, of which Rubens had not the slightest tincture—not in narrative, where he might have excelled.

The single figures, however, in an historical picture, are rather the eloquence of painting than the poetry: they mostly (unless they are quite out of place in the picture) express the feelings of one person as modified by the presence of others. Accordingly the minds whose bent leads them rather to eloquence than to poetry, rush to historical painting. The French painters, for instance, seldom attempt, because they could make nothing of, single heads, like those glorious ones of the Italian masters, with which they might glut themselves day after day in their own Louvre. They must all be historical; and they are, almost to a man, attitudinizers. If we wished to give to any young artist the most impressive warning our imaginations could devise, against that kind of vice in the pictorial, which corresponds to rant in the histrionic art, we would advise him to walk once up and once down the gallery of the Luxembourg; even now when David, the great corrupter of taste, has been translated from this world to the next, and from the Luxembourg, consequently, into the more elevated sphere of the Louvre. Every figure in French painting or statuary seems to be showing itself off before spectators: they are in the worst style of corrupted eloquence, but in no style of poetry at all. The best are stiff and unnatural; the worst resemble figures of cataleptic patients. The French artists fancy themselves imitators of the classics, yet they seem to have no understanding and no feeling of that repose which was the peculiar and pervading character of Grecian art, until it began to decline: a repose tenfold more indicative of strength than all their stretching and straining; for strength, as Thomas Carlyle says, does not manifest itself in spasms.

There are some productions of art which it seems at first difficult to arrange in any of the classes above illustrated. The direct aim of art as such, is the production of the beautiful; and as there are other things beautiful besides states of mind, there is much of art which may seem to have nothing to do with either poetry or eloquence as we have defined them. Take for instance a composition of Claude, or Salvator Rosa. There is here creation of new beauty: by the grouping of natural scenery, conformably indeed to the laws of outward nature, but not after any actual model; the result being a beauty more perfect and faultless than is perhaps to be found in any actual landscape. Yet there is a character of poetry even in these, without which they could not be so beautiful. The unity, and wholeness, and aesthetic congruity of the picture still lies in singleness of expression; but it is expression in a different sense from that in which we have hitherto employed the term. The objects in an imaginary landscape cannot be said, like the words of a poem or the notes of a melody, to be the actual utterance of a feeling; but there must be some feeling with which they harmonize, and which they have a tendency to raise up in the spectator's mind. They must inspire a feeling of grandeur, a loveliness, a cheerfulness, a wildness, a melancholy, a terror. The painter must surround his principal objects with such imagery as would spontaneously arise in a highly imaginative mind, when contemplating those objects under the impression of the feelings which they are intended to inspire. This, if it be not poetry, is so nearly allied to it, as scarcely to require being distinguished.

In this sense we may speak of the poetry of architecture. All architecture, to be impressive, must be the expression or symbol of some interesting idea; some thought, which has power over the emotions. The reason why modern architecture is so paltry, is simply that it is not the expression of any idea; it is a mere parroting of the architectural tongue of the Greeks, or of our Teutonic ancestors, without any conception of a meaning.

To confine ourselves, for the present, to religious edifices: these partake of poetry, in proportion as they express, or harmonize with, the feelings of devotion. But those feelings are different according to the conception entertained of the beings, by whose supposed nature they are called forth. To the Greek, these beings were incarnations of the greatest conceivable physical beauty, combined with supernatural power: and the Greek temples express this, their predominant character being graceful strength; in other words, solidity, which is power, and lightness which is also power, accomplishing with small means what seemed to require great; to combine all in one word, *majesty*. To the Catholic, again, the Deity was something far less clear and definite; a being of still more resistless power than the heathen divinities; greatly to be loved; still more greatly to be feared; and wrapped up in vagueness, mystery, and incomprehensibility. A certain solemnity, a feeling of doubting and trembling hope, like that of one lost in a boundless forest who thinks he knows his way but is not sure, mixes in all the genuine expressions of Catholic devotion. This is eminently the expression of the pure Gothic cathedral; conspicuous equally in the mingled majesty and gloom of its vaulted roofs and stately aisles, and in the "dim religious light" which steals through its painted windows.

There is no generic distinction between the imagery which is the expression of feeling and the imagery which is felt to harmonize with feeling. They are identical. The imagery in which feeling utters itself forth from within, is also that in which it delights when presented to it from without. All art, therefore, in proportion as it produces its effects by an appeal to the emotions partakes of poetry, unless it partakes of oratory, or of narrative. And the distinction which these three words indicate, runs through the whole field of the fine arts.

The above hints have no pretension to the character of a theory. They are merely thrown out for the consideration of thinkers, in the hope that if they do not contain the truth, they may do somewhat to suggest it. Nor would they, crude as they are, have been deemed worthy of publication, in any country but one in which the philosophy of art is so completely neglected, that whatever may serve to put any inquiring mind upon this kind of investigation, cannot well, however imperfect in itself, fail altogether to be of use.

Ralph Waldo Emerson

1803–1882

Emerson's effusive essay *The Poet* provides a compendium of Romantic ideas about poetry. In particular, it recalls the comments of Coleridge and Carlyle on symbolism. Emerson was obviously well read in occult philosophy. His attitude toward symbolism, which is similar to that of Baudelaire in his famous symbolist sonnet, *Correspondences,* helped to lay a rough groundwork for such theories as Cassirer's philosophy of symbolic forms.

According to Emerson half of the reality of man is what he expresses, and ideally every man should be able to "report in conversation what has befallen him." Language tends to wear itself out in clichés, and expression becomes dull and inaccurate. It requires constant refurbishing. Every thought eventually becomes a sort of prison. It is the poet who forges a new language and new thoughts and provides the possibility of mental liberation. In this view language would seem to be a primary means by which man forms reality.

Emerson is not very clear, however, about the relation of thought to language and language to objects; he has no theory of the poem as a whole, though his remarks about the "fluxional" nature of symbols and his criticism of symbols with fixed univocal meanings are suggestive. The poem remains for him a vehicle for transcendental thought; nature itself is a symbol or a language that somehow can be read. But if nature is a language of symbols, then it would seem that poetic language itself becomes only a copy of natural symbols and might best be transcended or bypassed for immediate communion with the natural world.

Emerson's complete works have been edited by E. W. Emerson (1904). Commentary can be found in F. O. Matthiessen, *American Renaissance* (1941). See also R. L. Rusk, *The Life of Ralph Waldo Emerson* (1949); Sherman Paul, *Emerson's Angle of Vision* (1952); S. E. Whicher, *Freedom and Fate* (1953); Charles Feidelson, *Symbolism and American Literature* (1953); Jeffrey L. Duncan, *The Power and Form of Emerson's Thought* (1973); David T. Porter, *Emerson and Literary Change* (1978); B. L. Packer, *Emerson's Fall* (1982); David Van Leer, *Emerson's Epistemology* (1986); and John Michael, *Emerson and Skepticism* (1988).

The Poet

A moody child and wildly wise
Pursued the game with joyful eyes,
Which chose, like meteors, their way,
And rived the dark with private ray:

They overleapt the horizon's edge,
Searched with Apollo's privilege;
Through man, and woman, and sea, and star
Saw the dance of nature forward far;
Through worlds, and races, and terms, and times
Saw musical order, and pairing rhymes.[1]

THE POET. Emerson's *The Poet* was written in 1842–43.

[1]Lines by Emerson, revised from his poem *The Poet.*

Olympian bards who sung
Divine ideas below,
Which always find us young,
And always keep us so.[2]

Those who are esteemed umpires of taste are often persons who have acquired some knowledge of admired pictures or sculptures, and have an inclination for whatever is elegant; but if you inquire whether they are beautiful souls, and whether their own acts are like fair pictures, you learn that they are selfish and sensual. Their cultivation is local, as if you should rub a log of dry wood in one spot to produce fire, all the rest remaining cold. Their knowledge of the fine arts is some study of rules and particulars, or some limited judgment of color or form, which is exercised for amusement or for show. It is a proof of the shallowness of the doctrine of beauty as it lies in the minds of our amateurs, that men seem to have lost the perception of the instant dependence of form upon soul. There is no doctrine of forms in our philosophy. We were put into our bodies, as fire is put into a pan to be carried about; but there is no accurate adjustment between the spirit and the organ, much less is the latter the germination of the former. So in regard to other forms, the intellectual men do not believe in any essential dependence of the material world on thought and volition. Theologians think it a pretty air-castle to talk of the spiritual meaning of a ship or a cloud, of a city or a contract, but they prefer to come again to the solid ground of historical evidence; and even the poets are contented with a civil and conformed manner of living, and to write poems from the fancy, at a safe distance from their own experience. But the highest minds of the world have never ceased to explore the double meaning, or shall I say the quadruple or the centuple or much more manifold meaning, of every sensuous fact; Orpheus, Empedocles, Heraclitus, Plato, Plutarch, Dante, Swedenborg, and the masters of sculpture, picture and poetry. For we are not pans and barrows, nor even porters of the fire and torch-bearers, but children of the fire, made of it, and only the same divinity transmuted and at two or three removes, when we know least about it. And this hidden truth, that the fountains whence all this river of time and its creatures floweth are intrinsically ideal and beautiful, draws us to the consideration of the nature and functions of the poet, or the man of beauty; to the means and materials he uses, and to the general aspect of the art in the present time.

The breadth of the problem is great, for the poet is representative. He stands among partial men for the complete man, and apprises us not of his wealth, but of the common wealth. The young man reveres men of genius, because, to speak truly, they are more himself than he is. They receive of the soul as he also receives, but they more. Nature enhances her beauty, to the eye of loving men, from their belief that the poet is beholding her shows at the same time. He is isolated among his contemporaries by truth and by his art, but with this consolation in his pursuits, that they will draw all men sooner or later. For all men live by truth and stand in need of expression. In love, in art, in avarice, in politics, in labor, in games, we study to utter our painful secret. The man is only half himself, the other half is his expression.

Notwithstanding this necessity to be published, adequate expression is rare. I know not how it is that we need an interpreter, but the great majority of men seem to be minors, who have not yet come into possession of their own, or mutes, who cannot report the conversation they have had with nature. There is no man who does not anticipate a supersensual utility in the sun and stars, earth and water. These stand and wait to render him a peculiar service. But there is some obstruction or some excess of phlegm in our constitution, which does not suffer them to yield the due effect. Too feeble fall the impressions of nature on us to make us artists. Every touch should thrill. Every man should be so much an artist that he could report in conversation what had befallen him. Yet, in our experience, the rays or appulses have sufficient force to arrive at the senses, but not enough to reach the quick and compel the reproduction of themselves in speech. The poet is the person in whom these powers are in balance, the man without impediment, who sees and handles that which others dream of, traverses the whole scale of experience, and is representative of man, in virtue of being the largest power to receive and to impart.

For the universe has three children, born at one time, which reappear under different names in every system of thought, whether they be called cause, operation and effect; or, more poetically, Jove, Pluto, Neptune; or, theologically, the Father, the Spirit and the Son; but which we will call here the Knower, the Doer and the Sayer. These stand respectively for the love of truth, for the love of good, and for the love of beauty. These three are equal. Each is that which he is, essentially, so that he cannot be surmounted or analyzed, and each of these three has the power of the others latent in him and his own, patent.

The poet is the sayer, the namer, and represents beauty. He is a sovereign, and stands on the center. For the world is not painted or adorned, but is from the beginning beautiful; and God has not made some beautiful things, but beauty is the creator of the universe. Therefore the poet is not any permissive potentate, but is emperor in his own right. Criticism

[2]Emerson, *Ode to Beauty,* 60–63.

is infested with a cant of materialism, which assumes that manual skill and activity is the first merit of all men, and disparages such as say and do not, overlooking the fact that some men, namely poets, are natural sayers, sent into the world to the end of expression, and confounds them with those whose province is action but who quit it to imitate the sayers. But Homer's words are as costly and admirable to Homer as Agamemnon's victories are to Agamemnon. The poet does not wait for the hero or the sage, but, as they act and think primarily, so he writes primarily what will and must be spoken, reckoning the others, though primaries also, yet, in respect to him, secondaries and servants; as sitters or models in the studio of a painter, or as assistants who bring building materials to an architect.

For poetry was all written before time was, and whenever we are so finely organized that we can penetrate into that region where the air is music, we hear those primal warblings and attempt to write them down, but we lose ever and anon a world or a verse and substitute something of our own, and thus miswrite the poem. The men of more delicate ear write down these cadences more faithfully, and these transcripts, though imperfect, become the songs of the nations. For nature is as truly beautiful as it is good, or as it is reasonable, and must as much appear as it must be done, or be known. Words and deeds are quite indifferent modes of the divine energy. Words are also actions, and actions are a kind of words.

The sign and credentials of the poet are that he announces that which no man foretold. He is the true and only doctor;[3] he knows and tells; he is the only teller of news, for he was present and privy to the appearance which he describes. He is a beholder of ideas and an utterer of the necessary and causal. For we do not speak now of men of poetical talents, or of industry and skill in meter, but of the true poet. I took part in a conversation the other day concerning a recent writer of lyrics, a man of subtle mind, whose head appeared to be a music box of delicate tunes and rhythms, and whose skill and command of language we could not sufficiently praise. But when the question arose whether he was not only a lyrist but a poet, we were obliged to confess that he is plainly a contemporary, not an eternal man. He does not stand out of our low limitations, like a Chimborazo[4] under the line, running up from a torrid base through all the climates of the globe, with belts of the herbage of every latitude on its high and mottled sides; but this genius is the landscape garden of a modern house, adorned with fountains and stat-

ues, with well-bred men and women standing and sitting in the walks and terraces. We hear, through all the varied music, the ground tone of conventional life. Our poets are men of talents who sing, and not the children of music. The argument is secondary, the finish of the verses is primary.

For it is not meters, but a meter-making argument that makes a poem—a thought so passionate and alive that like the spirit of a plant or an animal it has an architecture of its own, and adorns nature with a new thing. The thought and the form are equal in the order of time, but in the order of genesis the thought is prior to the form. The poet has a new thought; he has a whole new experience to unfold; he will tell us how it was with him, and all men will be the richer in his fortune. For the experience of each new age requires a new confession, and the world seems always waiting for its poet. I remember when I was young how much I was moved one morning by tidings that genius had appeared in a youth who sat near me at table. He had left his work and gone rambling none knew whither, and had written hundreds of lines, but could not tell whether that which was in him was therein told; he could tell nothing but that all was changed—man, beast, heaven, earth and sea. How gladly we listened! How credulous! Society seemed to be compromised. We sat in the aurora of a sunrise which was to put out all the stars. Boston seemed to be at twice the distance it had the night before, or was much farther than that. Rome—what was Rome? Plutarch and Shakespeare were in the yellow leaf, and Homer no more should be heard of. It is much to know that poetry has been written this very day, under this very roof, by your side. What! That wonderful spirit has not expired! These stony moments are still sparkling and animated! I had fancied that the oracles were all silent, and nature had spent her fires; and behold! all night, from every pore, these fine auroras have been streaming. Everyone has some interest in the advent of the poet, and no one knows how much it may concern him. We know that the secret of the world is profound, but who or what shall be our interpreter, we know not. A mountain ramble, a new style of face, a new person, may put the key into our hands. Of course the value of genius to us is in the veracity of its report. Talent may frolic and juggle; genius realizes and adds. Mankind in good earnest have availed so far in understanding themselves and their work, that the foremost watchman on the peak announces his news. It is the truest word ever spoken, and the phrase will be the fittest, most musical, and the unerring voice of the world for that time.

All that we call sacred history attests that the birth of a poet is the principal event in chronology. Man, never so often deceived, still watches for the arrival of a brother who can hold him steady to a truth until he has made it his own.

---

[3]Teacher.
[4]Andean volcanic mountain.

With what joy I begin to read a poem which I confide in as an inspiration! And now my chains are to be broken; I shall mount above these clouds and opaque airs in which I live—opaque, though they seem transparent—and from the heaven of truth I shall see and comprehend my relations. That will reconcile me to life and renovate nature, to see trifles animated by a tendency, and to know what I am doing. Life will no more be a noise; now I shall see men and women, and know the signs by which they may be discerned from fools and satans. This day shall be better than my birthday: then I became an animal; now I am invited into the science of the real. Such is the hope, but the fruition is postponed. Oftener it falls that this winged man, who will carry me into the heaven, whirls me into mists, then leaps and frisks about with me as it were from cloud to cloud, still affirming that he is bound heavenward; and I, being myself a novice, am slow in perceiving that he does not know the way into the heavens, and is merely bent that I should admire his skill to rise like a fowl or a flying fish, a little way from the ground or the water; but the all-piercing, all-feeding and ocular air of heaven that man shall never inhabit. I tumble down again soon into my old nooks, and lead the life of exaggerations as before, and have lost my faith in the possibility of any guide who can lead me thither where I would be.

But, leaving these victims of vanity, let us, with new hope, observe how nature, by worthier impulses, has insured the poet's fidelity to his office of announcement and affirming, namely by the beauty of things, which becomes a new and higher beauty when expressed. Nature offers all her creatures to him as a picture language. Being used as a type, a second wonderful value appears in the object, far better than its old value; and the carpenter's stretched cord, if you hold your ear close enough, is musical in the breeze. "Things more excellent than every image," says Jamblichus, "are expressed through images."[5] Things admit of being used as symbols because nature is a symbol, in the whole, and in every part. Every line we can draw in the sand has expression; and there is no body without its spirit or genius. All form is an effect of character; all condition, of the quality of the life; all harmony, of health; and for this reason a perception of beauty should be sympathetic, or proper only to the good. The beautiful rests on the foundations of the necessary. The soul makes the body, as the wise Spenser teaches:

> So every spirit, as it is more pure,
> And hath in it the more of heavenly light,
> So it the fairer body doth procure

To habit in, and it more fairly dight,
With cheerful grace and amiable sight.
For, of the soul, the body form doth take,
For soul is form, and doth the body make.[6]

Here we find ourselves suddenly not in a critical speculation but in a holy place, and should go very warily and reverently. We stand before the secret of the world, there where being passes into appearance and unity into variety.

The universe is the externization of the soul. Wherever the life is, that bursts into appearance around it. Our science is sensual, and therefore superficial. The earth and the heavenly bodies, physics and chemistry, we sensually treat, as if they were self-existent; but these are the retinue of that being we have. "The mighty heaven," said Proclus, "exhibits, in its transfigurations, clear images of the splendor of intellectual perceptions; being moved in conjunction with the unapparent periods of intellectual natures."[7] Therefore science always goes abreast with the just elevation of the man, keeping step with religion and metaphysics; or the state of science is an index of our self-knowledge. Since everything in nature answers to a moral power, if any phenomenon remains brute and dark it is because the corresponding faculty in the observer is not yet active.

No wonder then, if these waters be so deep, that we hover over them with a religious regard. The beauty of the fable proves the importance of the sense; to the poet, and to all others; or, if you please, every man is so far a poet as to be susceptible of these enchantments of nature; for all men have the thoughts whereof the universe is the celebration. I find that the fascination resides in the symbol. Who loves nature? Who does not? Is it only poets, and men of leisure and cultivation, who live with her? No; but also hunters, farmers, grooms and butchers, though they express their affection in their choice of life and not in their choice of words. The writer wonders what the coachman or the hunter values in riding, in horses and dogs. It is not superficial qualities. When you talk with him he holds these at as slight a rate as you. His worship is sympathetic; he has no definitions, but he is commanded in nature by the living power which he feels to be there present. No imitation or playing of these things would content him; he loves the earnest of the north wind, of rain, of stone and wood and iron. A beauty not explicable is dearer than a beauty which we can see to the end of. It is nature the symbol, nature certifying the supernatural, body overflowed by life which he worships with coarse but sincere rites.

[5]Neo-Platonic philosopher (third–fourth century A.D.).

[6]*A Hymn in Honor of Beauty*, XIX. 127–34.
[7]Neo-Platonist (412–485 A.D.).

The inwardness and mystery of this attachment drive men of every class to the use of emblems. The schools of poets and philosophers are not more intoxicated with their symbols than the populace with theirs. In our political parties, compute the power of badges and emblems. See the great ball which they roll from Baltimore to Bunker Hill! In the political processions, Lowell goes in a loom, and Lynn in a shoe, and Salem in a ship. Witness the cider barrel, the log cabin, the hickory stick, the palmetto, and all the cognizances of party. See the power of national emblems. Some stars, lilies, leopards, a crescent, a lion, an eagle, or other figure which came into credit God knows how, on an old rag of bunting, blowing in the wind on a fort at the ends of the earth, shall make the blood tingle under the rudest or the most conventional exterior. The people fancy they hate poetry, and they are all poets and mystics!

Beyond this universality of the symbolic language, we are apprised of the divineness of this superior use of things, whereby the world is a temple whose walls are covered with emblems, pictures and commandments of the Deity—in this, that there is no fact in nature which does not carry the whole sense of nature; and the distinctions which we make in events and in affairs, of low and high, honest and base, disappear when nature is used as a symbol. Thought makes everything fit for use. The vocabulary of an omniscient man would embrace words and images excluded from polite conversation. What would be base, or even obscene, to the obscene, becomes illustrious, spoken in a new connection of thought. The piety of the Hebrew prophets purges their grossness. The circumcision is an example of the power of poetry to raise the low and offensive. Small and mean things serve as well as great symbols. The meaner the type by which a law is expressed, the more pungent it is, and the more lasting in the memories of men; just as we choose the smallest box or case in which any needful utensil can be carried. Bare lists of words are found suggestive to an imaginative and excited mind, as it is related of Lord Chatham that he was accustomed to read in Bailey's Dictionary when he was preparing to speak in Parliament. The poorest experience is rich enough for all the purposes of expressing thought. Why covet a knowledge of new facts? Day and night, house and garden, a few books, a few actions, serve us as well as would all trades and all spectacles. We are far from having exhausted the significance of the few symbols we use. We can come to use them yet with a terrible simplicity. It does not need that a poem should be long. Every word was once a poem. Every new relation is a new word. Also we use defects and deformities to a sacred purpose, so expressing our sense that the evils of the world are such only to the evil eye. In the old mythology, mythologists observe, defects are ascribed to divine natures, as lameness to Vulcan, blindness to Cupid, and the like—to signify exuberances.

For as it is dislocation and detachment from the life of God that makes things ugly, the poet, who reattaches things to nature and the whole—reattaching even artificial things and violation of nature, to nature, by a deeper insight—disposes very easily of the most disagreeable facts. Readers of poetry see the factory village and the railway, and fancy that the poetry of the landscape is broken up by these; for these works of art are not yet consecrated in their reading; but the poet sees them fall within the great order not less than the beehive or the spider's geometrical web. Nature adopts them very fast into her vital circles, and the gliding train of cars she loves like her own. Besides, in a centered mind, it signifies nothing how many mechanical inventions you exhibit. Though you add millions, and never so surprising, the fact of mechanics has not gained a grain's weight. The spiritual fact remains unalterable, by many or by few particulars; as no mountain is of any appreciable height to break the curve of the sphere. A shrewd country boy goes to the city for the first time, and the complacent citizen is not satisfied with his little wonder. It is not that he does not see all the fine houses and know that he never saw such before, but he disposes of them as easily as the poet finds place for the railway. The chief value of the new fact is to enhance the great and constant fact of life, which can dwarf any and every circumstance, and to which the belt of wampum and the commerce of America are alike.

The world being thus put under the mind for verb and noun, the poet is he who can articulate it. For though life is great, and fascinates and absorbs; and though all men are intelligent of the symbols through which it is named; yet they cannot originally use them. We are symbols and inhabit symbols; workmen, work, and tools, words and things, birth and death, all are emblems; but we sympathize with the symbols, and being infatuated with the economical uses of things, we do not know that they are thoughts. The poet, by an ulterior intellectual perception, gives them a power which makes their old use forgotten, and puts eyes and a tongue into every dumb and inanimate object. He perceives the independence of the thought on the symbol, the stability of the thought, the accidency and fugacity of the symbol. As the eyes of Lynceus were said to see through the earth, so the poet turns the world to glass, and shows us all things in their right series and procession. For through that better perception he stands one step nearer to things, and sees the flowing or metamorphosis; perceives that thought is multiform; that within the form of every creature is a force impelling it to ascend into a higher form; and following with his eyes the life, uses the forms which express that life, and so his speech flows with the flowing of nature. All the facts of the animal economy, sex, nutriment, gestation, birth, growth, are symbols of the passage of the world into the soul of man, to suffer there a change and reappear a new and higher fact. He uses forms according to the life, and not according to the form. This is true science. The poet alone knows astronomy, chemistry, vegetation and animation, for he does not stop at these facts, but employs them as signs. He knows why the plain or meadow of space was strown with these flowers we call suns and moons and stars; why the great deep is adorned with animals, with men, and gods; for in every word he speaks he rides on them as the horses of thought.

By virtue of this science the poet is the namer or language-maker, naming things sometimes after their appearance, sometimes after their essence, and giving to every one its own name and not another's, thereby rejoicing the intellect, which delights in detachment or boundary. The poets made all the words, and therefore language is the archives of history, and, if we must say it, a sort of tomb of the Muses. For though the origin of most of our words is forgotten, each word was at first a stroke of genius, and obtained currency because for the moment it symbolized the world to the first speaker and to the hearer. The etymologist finds the deadest word to have been once a brilliant picture. Language is fossil poetry. As the limestone of the continent consists of infinite masses of the shells of animalcules, so language is made up of images or tropes, which now, in their secondary use, have long ceased to remind us of their poetic origin. But the poet names the thing because he sees it, or comes one step nearer to it than any other. This expression or naming is not art, but a second nature, grown out of the first, as a leaf out of a tree. What we call nature is a certain self-regulated motion or change; and nature does all things by her own hands, and does not leave another to baptize her but baptizes herself; and this through the metamorphosis again. I remember that a certain poet described it to me thus: "Genius is the activity which repairs the decays of things, whether wholly or partly of a material and finite kind. Nature, through all her kingdoms, insures herself. Nobody cares for planting the poor fungus; so she shakes down from the gills of one agaric countless spores, any one of which, being preserved, transmits new billions of spores tomorrow or next day. The new agaric of this hour has a chance which the old one had not. This atom of seed is thrown into a new place, not subject to the accidents which destroyed its parent two rods off. She makes a man; and having brought him to ripe age, she will no longer run the risk of losing this wonder at a blow, but she detaches from him a new self, that the kind may be safe from accidents to which the individual is exposed. So when the soul of the poet has come to ripeness of thought, she

detaches and sends away from it its poems or songs—a fearless, sleepless, deathless progeny, which is not exposed to the accidents of the weary kingdom of time; a fearless, vivacious offspring, clad with wings (such was the virtue of the soul out of which they came) which carry them fast and far, and infix them irrecoverably into the hearts of men. These wings are the beauty of the poet's soul. The songs, thus flying immortal from their mortal parent, are pursued by clamorous flights of censures, which swarm in far greater numbers and threaten to devour them; but these last are not winged. At the end of a very short leap they fall plump down and rot, having received from the souls out of which they came no beautiful wings. But the melodies of the poet ascend and leap and pierce into the deeps of infinite time."

So far the bard taught me, using his freer speech. But nature has a higher end, in the production of new individuals, than security, namely *ascension*, or the passage of the soul into higher forms. I knew in my younger days the sculptor who made the statue of the youth which stands in the public garden. He was, as I remember, unable to tell directly what made him happy or unhappy, but by wonderful indirections he could tell. He rose one day, according to his habit, before the dawn, and saw the morning break, grand as the eternity out of which it came, and for many days after, he strove to express this tranquility, and lo! His chisel had fashioned out of marble the form of a beautiful youth, Phosphorus, whose aspect is such that it is said all persons who look on it become silent. The poet also resigns himself to his mood, and that thought which agitated him is expressed, but *alter idem*,[8] in a manner totally new. The expression is organic, or the new type which things themselves take when liberated. As, in the sun, objects paint their images on the retina of the eye, so they, sharing the aspiration of the whole universe, tend to paint a far more delicate copy of their essence in his mind. Like the metamorphosis of things into higher organic forms is their change into melodies. Over everything stands its demon or soul, and, as the form of the thing is reflected by the eye, so the soul of the thing is reflected by a melody. The sea, the mountain ridge, Niagara, and every flowerbed, pre-exist, or superexist, in precantations, which sail like odors in the air, and when any man goes by with an ear sufficiently fine, he overhears them and endeavors to write down the notes without diluting or depraving them. And herein is the legitimation of criticism, in the mind's faith that the poems are a corrupt version of some text in nature with which they ought to be made to tally. A rhyme in one of our sonnets should not be less pleasing than the iterated nodes of a sea-

---

[8] "Same but different."

shell, or the resembling difference of a group of flowers. The pairing of the birds is an idyl, not tedious as our idyls are; a tempest is a rough ode, without falsehood or rant; a summer, with its harvest sown, reaped and stored, is an epic song, subordinating how many admirably executed parts. Why should not the symmetry and truth that modulate these, glide into our spirits, and we participate the invention of nature?

This insight, which expresses itself by what is called imagination, is a very high sort of seeing, which does not come by study, but by the intellect being where and what it sees; by sharing the path or circuit of things through forms, and so making them translucid to others. The path of things is silent. Will they suffer a speaker to go with them? A spy they will not suffer; a lover, a poet, is the transcendency of their own nature—him they will suffer. The condition of true naming, on the poet's part, is his resigning himself to the divine aura which breathes through forms, and accompanying that.

It is a secret which every intellectual man quickly learns, that beyond the energy of his possessed and conscious intellect he is capable of a new energy (as of an intellect doubled on itself), by abandonment to the nature of things; that beside his privacy of power as an individual man, there is a great public power on which he can draw, by unlocking, at all risks, his human doors, and suffering the ethereal tides to roll and circulate through him; then he is caught up into the life of the universe, his speech is thunder, his thought is law, and his words are universally intelligible as the plants and animals. The poet knows that he speaks adequately then only when he speaks somewhat wildly, or "with the flower of the mind"; not with the intellect used as an organ, but with the intellect released from all service and suffered to take its direction from its celestial life, or as the ancients were wont to express themselves, not with intellect alone but with the intellect inebriated by nectar. As the traveler who has lost his way throws his reins on his horse's neck and trusts to the instinct of the animal to find his road, so must we do with the divine animal who carries us through this world. For if in any manner we can stimulate this instinct, new passages are opened for us into nature; the mind flows into and through things hardest and highest, and the metamorphosis is possible.

This is the reason why bards love wine, mead, narcotics, coffee, tea, opium, the fumes of sandalwood and tobacco, or whatever other procurers of animal exhilaration. All men avail themselves of such means as they can, to add this extraordinary power to their normal powers; and to this end they prize conversation, music, pictures, sculpture, dancing, theaters, traveling, war, mobs, fires, gaming, politics, or love, or science, or animal intoxication—which are several coarser or finer quasi-mechanical substitutes for the true nectar, which is the ravishment of the intellect by coming nearer to the fact. These are auxiliaries to the centrifugal tendency of a man, to his passage out into free space, and they help him to escape the custody of that body in which he is pent up, and of that jail-yard of individual relations in which he is enclosed. Hence a great number of such as were professionally expressers of beauty, as painters, poets, musicians and actors, have been more than others wont to lead a life of pleasure and indulgence; all but the few who received the true nectar; and, as it was a spurious mode attaining freedom, as it was an emancipation not into the heavens but into the freedom of baser places, they were punished for that advantage they won, by a dissipation and deterioration. But never can any advantage be taken of nature by a trick. The spirit of the world, the great calm presence of the Creator, comes not forth to the sorceries of opium or of wine. The sublime vision comes to the pure and simple soul in a clean and chaste body. That is not an inspiration, which we owe to narcotics, but some counterfeit excitement and fury. Milton says that the lyric poet may drink wine and live generously, but the epic poet, he who shall sing of the gods and their descent unto men, must drink water out of a wooden bowl. For poetry is not "devil's wine," but God's wine. It is with this as it is with toys. We fill the hands and nurseries of our children with all manner of dolls, drums and horses; withdrawing their eyes from the plain face and sufficing objects of nature, the sun and moon, the animals, the water and stones, which should be their toys. So the poet's habit of living should be set on a key so low that the common influences should delight him. His cheerfulness should be the gift of the sunlight; the air should suffice for his inspiration, and he should be tipsy with water. That spirit which suffices quiet hearts, which seems to come forth to such from every dry knoll of sere grass, from every pine stump and half-imbedded stone on which the dull March sun shines, comes forth to the poor and hungry, and such as are of simple taste. If thou fill thy brain with Boston and New York, with fashion and covetousness, and wilt stimulate thy jaded senses with wine and French coffee, thou shalt find no radiance of wisdom in the lonely waste of the pine woods.

If the imagination intoxicates the poet, it is not inactive in other men. The metamorphosis excites in the beholder an emotion of joy. The use of symbols has a certain power of emancipation and exhilaration for all men. We seem to be touched by a wand which makes us dance and run about happily like children. We are like persons who come out of a cave or cellar into the open air. This is the effect on us of tropes, fables, oracles and all poetic forms. Poets are thus liberating gods. Men have really got a new sense, and found within their world another world, or nest of worlds; for, the metamorphosis once seen, we divine that it does not stop. I will not now consider how much this makes the charm of algebra and the mathematics, which also have their tropes, but it is felt in every definition; as when Aristotle defines *space* to be an immovable vessel in which things are contained; or when Plato defines a *line* to be a flowing point; or *figure* to be a bound of solid; and many the like. What a joyful sense of freedom we have when Vitruvius announces the old opinion of artists that no architect can build any house well who does not know something of anatomy. When Socrates, in *Charmides,* tells us that the soul is cured of its maladies by certain incantations, and that these incantations are beautiful reasons, from which temperance is generated in souls; when Plato calls the world an animal, and Timaeus affirms that the plants also are animals; or affirms a man to be a heavenly tree, growing with his root, which is his head, upward; and, as George Chapman, following him, writes, "So in our tree of man, whose nervy root / Springs in his top";[9] when Orpheus speaks of hoariness as "that white flower which marks extreme old age"; when Proclus calls the universe the statue of the intellect; when Chaucer, in his praise of "gentilesse," compares good blood in mean condition to fire, which, though carried to the darkest house betwixt this and the mount of Caucasus, will yet hold its natural office and burn as bright as if twenty thousand men did it behold; when John saw, in the Apocalypse, the ruin of the world through evil, and the stars fall from heaven as the fig tree casteth her untimely fruit; when Aesop reports the whole catalogue of common daily relations through the masquerade of birds and beasts; we take the cheerful hint of the immortality of our essence and its versatile habit and escapes, as when the gypsies say of themselves "it is in vain to hang them, they cannot die."

The poets are thus liberating gods. The ancient British bards had for the title of their order, "Those who are free throughout the world." They are free, and they make free. An imaginative book renders us much more service at first, by stimulating us through its tropes, than afterward when we arrive at the precise sense of the author. I think nothing is of any value in books excepting the transcendental and extraordinary. If a man is inflamed and carried away by his thought, to that degree that he forgets the authors and the public and heeds only this one dream which holds him like an insanity, let me read his paper, and you may have all the arguments and histories and criticism. All the value which attaches to Pythagoras, Paracelsus, Cornelius Agrippa, Cardan, Kepler,

Swedenborg, Schelling, Oken, or any other who introduces questionable facts into his cosmogony, as angels, devils, magic, astrology, palmistry, mesmerism, and so on, is the certificate we have of departure from routine, and that here is a new witness. That also is the best success in conversation, the magic of liberty, which puts the world like a ball in our hands. How cheap even the liberty then seems; how mean to study, when an emotion communicates to the intellect the power to sap and upheave nature; how great the perspective! Nations, times, systems, enter and disappear like threads in tapestry of large figure and many colors; dream delivers us to dream, and while the drunkenness lasts we will sell our bed, our philosophy, our religion, in our opulence.

There is good reason why we should prize this liberation. The fate of the poor shepherd, who, blinded and lost in the snowstorm, perishes in a drift within a few feet of his cottage door, is an emblem of the state of man. On the brink of the waters of life and truth, we are miserably dying. The inaccessibleness of every thought but that we are in, is wonderful. What if you come near to it, you are as remote when you are nearest as when you are farthest. Every thought is also a prison; every heaven is also a prison. Therefore we love the poet, the inventor, who in any form, whether in an ode or in an action or in looks and behavior, has yielded us a new thought. He unlocks our chains and admits us to a new scene.

This emancipation is dear to all men, and the power to impart it, as it must come from greater depth and scope of thought, is a measure of intellect. Therefore all books of the imagination endure, all which ascend to that truth that the writer sees nature beneath him, and uses it as his exponent. Every verse or sentence possessing this virtue will take care of its own immortality. The religions of the world are the ejaculations of a few imaginative men.

But the quality of the imagination is to flow, and not to freeze. The poet did not stop at the color or the form, but read their meaning; neither may he rest in this meaning, but he makes the same objects exponents of his new thought. Here is the difference betwixt the poet and the mystic, that the last nails a symbol to one sense, which was a true sense for a moment, but soon becomes old and false. For all symbols are fluxional; all language is vehicular and transitive, and is good, as ferries and horses are, for conveyance, not as farms and houses are, for homestead. Mysticism consists in the mistake of an accidental and individual symbol for an universal one. The morning redness happens to be the favorite meteor to the eyes of Jacob Behmen, and comes to stand to him for truth and faith; and, he believes, should stand for the same realities to every reader. But the first reader prefers as naturally the symbol of a mother and child, or a gardener

---

[9]Epistle Dedicatory to the *Iliad,* 132–33.

and his bulb, or a jeweler polishing a gem. Either of these, or of a myriad more, are equally good to the person to whom they are significant. Only they must be held lightly, and be very willingly translated into the equivalent terms which others use. And the mystic must be steadily told, all that you say is just as true without the tedious use of that symbol as with it. Let us have a little algebra, instead of this trite rhetoric—universal signs, instead of these village symbols—and we shall both be gainers. The history of hierarchies seems to show that all religious error consisted in making the symbol too stark and solid, and was at last nothing but an excess of the organ of language.

Swedenborg, of all men in the recent ages, stands eminently for the translator of nature into thought. I do not know the man in history to whom things stood so uniformly for words. Before him the metamorphosis continually plays. Everything on which his eye rests, obeys the impulses of moral nature. The figs become grapes whilst he eats them. When some of his angels affirmed a truth, the laurel twig which they held blossomed in their hands. The noise which at a distance appeared like gnashing and thumping, on coming nearer was found to be the voice of disputants. The men in one of his visions, seen in heavenly light, appeared like dragons, and seemed in darkness; but to each other they appeared as men, and when the light from heaven shone into their cabin, they complained of the darkness, and were compelled to shut the window that they might see.

There was this perception in him which makes the poet or seer an object of awe and terror, namely that the same man or society of men may wear one aspect to themselves and their companions, and a different aspect to higher intelligences. Certain priests, whom he describes as conversing very learnedly together, appeared to the children who were at some distance, like dead horses; and many the like misappearances. And instantly the mind inquires whether these fishes under the bridge, yonder oxen in the pasture, those dogs in the yard, are immutably fishes, oxen and dogs, or only so appear to me, and perchance to themselves appear upright men; and whether I appear as a man to all eyes. The Brahmins and Pythagoras propounded the same question, and if any poet has witnessed the transformation he doubtless found it in harmony with various experiences. We have all seen changes as considerable in wheat and caterpillars. He is the poet and shall draw us with love and terror, who sees through the flowing vest the firm nature, and can declare it.

I look in vain for the poet whom I describe. We do not with sufficient plainness or sufficient profoundness address ourselves to life, nor dare we chant our own times and social circumstance. If we filled the day with bravery, we should not shrink from celebrating it. Time and nature yield us many gifts, but not yet the timely man, the new religion, the reconciler, whom all things await. Dante's praise is that he dared to write his autobiography in colossal cipher, or into universality. We have yet had no genius in America, with tyrannous eye, which knew the value of our incomparable materials, and saw, in the barbarism and materialism of the times, another carnival of the same gods whose picture he so much admires in Homer; then in the Middle Age; then in Calvinism. Banks and tariffs, the newspaper and caucus, Methodism and Unitarianism, are flat and dull to dull people, but rest on the same foundations of wonder as the town of Troy and the temple of Delphi, and are as swiftly passing away. Our log-rolling, our stumps and their politics, our fisheries, our Negroes and Indians, our boats and our repudiations, the wrath of rogues and the pusillanimity of honest men, the northern trade, the southern planting, the western clearing, Oregon and Texas, are yet unsung. Yet America is a poem in our eyes; its ample geography dazzles the imagination, and it will not wait long for meters. If I have not found that excellent combination of gifts in my countrymen which I seek, neither could I aid myself to fix the idea of the poet by reading now and then in Chalmers's collection of five centuries of English poets. These are wits more than poets, though there have been poets among them. But when we adhere to the ideal of the poet, we have our difficulties even with Milton and Homer. Milton is too literary, and Homer too literal and historical.

But I am not wise enough for a national criticism, and must use the old largeness a little longer, to discharge my errand from the Muse to the poet concerning his art.

Art is the path of the creator to his work. The paths or methods are ideal and eternal, though few men ever see them; not the artist himself for years, or for a lifetime, unless he come into the conditions. The painter, the sculptor, the composer, the epic rhapsodist, the orator, all partake one desire, namely to express themselves symmetrically and abundantly, not dwarfishly and fragmentarily. They found or put themselves in certain conditions, as, the painter and sculptor before some impressive human figures; the orator into the assembly of the people; and the others in such scenes as each has found exciting to his intellect; and each presently feels the new desire. He hears a voice, he sees a beckoning. Then he is apprised, with wonder, what herds of demons hem him in. He can no more rest; he says, with the old painter, "By God it is in me and must go forth of me." He pursues a beauty, half seen, which flies before him. The poet pours out verses in every solitude. Most of the things he says are conventional, no doubt; but by and by he says something which is original and beautiful. That charms him. He would say nothing else but such things. In our way of talking we say "That is yours, this is mine"; but the poet knows well that it is not his; that it is as strange and beautiful to him as to you; he would fain hear the like eloquence at length. Once having tasted this immortal ichor, he cannot have enough of it, and as an admirable creative power exists in these intellections, it is of the last importance that these things get spoken. What a little of all we know is said! What drops of all the sea of our science are baled up! And by what accident it is that these are exposed, when so many secrets sleep in nature! Hence the necessity of speech and song; hence these throbs and heart-beatings in the orator, at the door of the assembly, to the end namely that thought may be ejaculated as logos, or word.

Doubt not, O poet, but persist. Say "It is in me, and shall out." Stand there, balked and dumb, stuttering and stammering, hissed and hooted, stand and strive, until at last rage draw out of thee that dream power which every night shows thee is thine own; a power transcending all limit and privacy, and by virtue of which a man is the conductor of the whole river of electricity. Nothing walks, or creeps, or grows, or exists, which must not in turn arise and walk before him as exponent of his meaning. Comes he to that power, his genius is no longer exhaustible. All the creatures by pairs and by tribes pour into his mind as into a Noah's ark, to come forth again to people a new world. This is like the stock of air for our respiration or for the combustion of our fireplace; not a measure of gallons, but the entire atmosphere if wanted. And therefore the rich poets, as Homer, Chaucer, Shakespeare, and Raphael, have obviously no limits to their works except the limits of their lifetime, and resemble a mirror carried through the street, ready to render an image of every created thing.

O poet! A new nobility is conferred in groves and pastures, and not in castles or by the sword blade any longer.

The conditions are hard, but equal. Thou shalt leave the world, and know the Muse only. Thou shalt not know any longer the times, customs, graces, politics, or opinions of men, but shalt take all from the Muse. For the time of towns is tolled from the world by funereal chimes, but in nature the universal hours are counted by succeeding tribes of animals and plants, and by growth of joy on joy. God wills also that thou abdicate a manifold and duplex life, and that thou be content that others speak for thee. Others shall be thy gentlemen and shall represent all courtesy and worldly life for thee; others shall do the great and resounding actions also. Thou shalt lie close hid with nature, and canst not be afforded to the Capitol or the Exchange. The world is full of renunciations and apprenticeships, and this is thine; thou must pass for a fool and a churl for a long season. This is the screen and sheath in which Pan has protected his well-beloved flower, and thou shalt be known only to thine own, and they shall console thee with tenderest love. And thou shalt not be able to rehearse the names of thy friends in thy verse, for an old shame before the holy ideal. And this is the reward; that the ideal shall be real to thee, and the impressions of the actual world shall fall like summer rain, copious, but not troublesome to thy invulnerable essence. Thou shalt have the whole land for thy park and manor, the sea for thy bath and navigation, without tax and without envy; the woods and the rivers thou shalt own, and thou shalt possess that wherein others are only tenants and boarders. Thou true landlord! Sealord! Airlord! Wherever snow falls or water flows or birds fly, wherever day and night meet in twilight, wherever the blue heaven is hung by clouds or sown with stars, wherever are forms with transparent boundaries, wherever are outlets into celestial space, wherever is danger, and awe, and love, there is beauty, plenteous as rain, shed for thee, and though thou shouldst walk the world over, thou shalt not be able to find a condition inopportune or ignoble.

Charles-Augustin Sainte-Beuve

1804–1869

Sainte-Beuve is the best-known nineteenth-century French critic, but it cannot be said that he developed a sophisticated theoretical stance. The fact that he passed through a number of phases, including a Romantic and an impressionistic one, only to come to a greater respect for classical principles lends a special interest to his essay *What Is a Classic?* In this essay he sought to redefine the term *classic,* rescuing it from the too rigid definitions of the dictionary of the French Academy.

Sainte-Beuve's concerns were at times strongly biographical and historical; he has often been thought a forerunner of the scientifically-minded literary historians such as Taine. Fundamentally, however, he is a humanistic critic, as the broad terms of his definition of *classic* illustrate. Seeking to mediate between neoclassical and Romantic extremes, he argues that evidence of adherence to rules is no proof that a work is a classic, and yet he insists that simply for a work to have been "revolutionary for a moment" will not qualify it either. If the pressure of Romantic insistence on freedom was dying out by the mid-nineteenth century it nevertheless left its mark on Sainte-Beuve. It is as a record of this modification of taste that Sainte-Beuve's essay is perhaps most important.

Among the English translations of Sainte-Beuve's essays are *Select Essays,* translated by A. J. Butler (n.d.); *Essays,* translated by Elizabeth Lee (1892); and *Selected Essays,* translated by J. R. Effinger (1895). See also G. M. Harper, *Charles-Augustin Sainte-Beuve* (1909); Irving Babbitt, *Masters of Modern French Criticism* (1912); Lander MacClintock, *Sainte-Beuve's Critical Theory and Practice After 1849* (1920); W. F. Giese, *Sainte-Beuve, A Literary Portrait* (1931); A. G. Lehmann, *Sainte-Beuve: A Portrait of the Critic, 1806–1842* (1962); Emerson Marks, ed., *Literary Criticism of Sainte-Beuve* (1971); Robert M. Chadbourne, *Charles-Augustin Sainte-Beuve* (1977).

What Is a Classic?

This is a delicate question, and one of which a good many different solutions might have been given at different periods and seasons. A clever man has this day propounded it to me, and even if I cannot solve it, I want at least to try to examine and discuss it before our readers, were it only to induce them to reply to it themselves, and if I can, clear up their ideas and mine upon it. And why should not one occasionally venture to treat in criticism of some of those subjects which are not personal, in which not someone, but something, is spoken of, and which our neighbors the English have so successfully made into a complete branch, under the modest title of essays? It is true that, in order to treat of such subjects, which are always in a measure abstract and moral, one must speak in a calm atmosphere, be sure of one's own attention and that of others, and seize one of those quarters of an hour of silence, moderation, and leisure, which are seldom granted to our beloved France, and which her brilliant genius bears with

WHAT IS A CLASSIC? Sainte-Beuve's *Qu'est-ce qu'un classique?* was first published in 1850. The translation is by A. J. Butler and is reprinted from *Select Essays of Sainte-Beuve* (London, n.d.).

impatience, even when she is wishing to be good, and has given up making revolutions.

A classic, according to the usual definition, is an author of past times, already hallowed by general admiration, who is an authority in his own style. The word *classic,* taken in this sense, begins to appear among the Romans. With them the *classici,* properly so called, were not all the citizens of the different classes, but only those of the highest class, who possessed, at least, an income of a certain fixed figure. All those who had a lower income were known by the appellation of *infra classem,* below *the* class properly so called. For example, we find the word *classicus* used by Aulus Gellius and applied to writers: a writer of worth and mark is *classicus assiduusque scriptor,* a writer who counts, who has some possessions under the sun, and who is not confounded with the proletariat crowd. Such an expression presupposes an age sufficiently advanced for a criticism and classification, as it were, of literature to have come into existence.

For the moderns, the true and only classics were, in the first instance, naturally the ancients. The Greeks, who by rare good fortune had—a happy relief to their intellect—no other classics than themselves, were at first the sole classics of the Romans, who spent much trouble and ingenuity on imitating them. They in their turn, after the fine ages of their literature, after Cicero and Virgil, had their own classics, and they became almost exclusively the classics of the centuries which succeeded. The Middle Ages, which, though not as ignorant as might be thought of Latin antiquity, were wanting in the sense of proportion and taste, confused the ranks and orders. Ovid was put on a better footing than Homer, and Boethius appeared to be a classic at least equal to Plato. The "new birth" of literature in the fifteenth and sixteenth centuries came to clear up this long confusion, and then only was admiration graduated. The real classic authors of the twofold antiquity stood out for the future on a luminous background, and formed two harmonious groups on their two eminences.

Meanwhile, modern literature had been born, and some of the more precocious members of it, like the Italian, already had their own fashion of antiquity. Dante had appeared, and his posterity had lost no time in saluting him as a classic. Italian poetry may have retreated greatly since then, but when she has desired, she has already recovered and always retained some impulse, some reverberation, from this high origin. It is of no slight importance for poetry thus to take its point of departure, its classic source in a lofty place—rather, for example, to descend from a Dante than to issue laboriously from a Malherbe.

Modern Italy had her classics, and Spain had every right to believe she was also in possession of hers, when France still had hers to seek. Indeed, a few writers of talent endowed with originality and exceptional raciness, a few brilliant efforts isolated and without successors, shattered immediately and needing always to be begun afresh, do not suffice to confer upon a nation the solid and imposing basis of literary wealth. That idea of a *classic* implies in itself something which has sequence and solidity, which forms a whole and makes a tradition, something which has "composition," is handed on to posterity and lasts. It was only after the brilliant years of Louis XIV that the nation felt with a thrill of pride that this happiness had come to it. All voices then told it to Louis XIV with flattery, exaggeration, and emphasis, and yet with a certain perception of truth. Then appeared a singular and quaint inconsistency: the men who were most in love with the wonders of that age of Louis the Great, and who went so far as to sacrifice all the ancients to the moderns, those men, of whom Perrault was the chief, tended to exalt and consecrate those very men whom they found the most ardent and contradictory adversaries. Boileau defended and supported the ancients with anger against Perrault, who cried up the moderns, that is to say Corneille, Molière, Pascal, and the eminent men of his century, including Boileau as one of the first. The good La Fontaine, when he took Doctor Huet's part in the quarrel, did not perceive that he himself, in spite of his oversight, was in his turn on the eve of waking up to find himself a classic.

An instance is the best definition: France possessed her century of Louis XIV, and could consider it at a little distance; she knew what it was to be classic better than by any reasoning. The eighteenth century, till its upheaval, added to this idea by a few fine works due to its four great men. Read Voltaire's *Siècle de Louis XIV,* Montesquieu's *La Grandeur et la Décadence des Romains,* Buffon's *Époques de Nature,* the *Vicaire Savoyard,* and the fine pages of meditations and descriptions of nature by Jean-Jacques,[1] and say whether the eighteenth century in its memorable past has not known how to reconcile tradition with independence and liberty of development. But at the beginning of this century and under the Empire, in presence of the first attempts of a decidedly novel and somewhat daring literature, the idea of a classic among some refractory minds, influenced more by vexation than by severity, contracted and shrank strangely. The first dictionary of the Academy (1694) simply defined a classic author as "an ancient author, highly approved, who is an authority in the subject he treats of." The dictionary of the Academy of 1835 urges this definition much more closely, and makes it exact and even narrow instead of, as it was,

---

[1]Rousseau.

somewhat vague. It defines classic authors as "those who have become *models* in any language," and, in the articles which follow, these expressions—*models, rules* established for composition and style, *strict rules* of the art to which you must *conform*—are continually recurring. This definition of the *classic* has evidently been made by our respectable precursors of the Academy, in presence and in sight of what was then called the *romantic,* that is to say, in sight of the enemy. It seems to me that the time ought now to have come to renounce these restricting and timid definitions and to widen their spirit.

A true classic, as I should like to hear it defined, is an author who has enriched the human mind, who has really augmented its treasures, who has made it take one more step forward, who has discovered some unequivocal moral truth, or has once more seized hold of some eternal passion in that heart where all seemed known and explored; who has rendered his thought, his observation, or his discovery under no matter what form, but broad and large, refined, sensible, sane, and beautiful in itself; who has spoken to all in a style of his own which yet belongs to all the world, in a style which is new without neologisms, new and ancient, easily contemporaneous with every age.

Such a classic may have been revolutionary for a moment, or at least may have seemed to be, but he is not so; he has not, in the first instance, fallen upon everything around him; he has overthrown only what was in his way so as quickly to replace the balance in favor of order and beauty.

You can, if you will, set down some names under this definition, which I would purposely make grand and compendious, or in one word, generous. I should place there first the Corneille of *Polyeucte,* of *Cinna,* of *Les Horaces.* I should place there Molière, the most complete and the richest genius we have had in French.

"Molière is so great," said Goethe (that king of criticism),

> that he surprises us afresh every time we read him. He is a man who stands alone; his plays verge on the tragic, and no one has had the courage to imitate them. His *Avare,* where the vice destroys all affection between father and son, is one of the most sublime of works, and dramatic in the highest degree. Every action in a play for the stage must be important in itself and tend towards a still greater event. *Tartuffe* is a model in this respect. What a setting out of the subject is the first scene! Everything is highly significant from the beginning, and makes you anticipate something still more important. The outset of any similar play of

Lessing's which may be cited is very fine; but that of *Tartuffe* is unique. It is the greatest thing of the kind. . . . Every year I read a play of Molière's, just as from time to time I gaze at some engraving after the old Italian masters.[2]

I do not pretend to say that this definition of a classic which I have just given does not go somewhat beyond the idea one generally forms for oneself under that name. It is especially made to comprise conditions of order, wisdom, moderation, and reasonableness, which prevail over and contain all others. Having occasion to praise M. Royer-Collard, M. de Rémusat said: "If he gets from our classics a pure taste, appropriate terms, variety of phrase, a careful attention in suiting expression to thought, to himself alone he owes the character which he gives to it all." One sees here that the part allotted to classic qualities seems rather to depend on selection and nicety of meaning, to an ornate and restrained style, and that, too, is the general opinion. In this sense the classics, properly so called, would be writers of the second rank—correct, sensible, elegant, always clear, expressing themselves with a passion not devoid of nobility, and a power kept slightly in reserve. Marie-Joseph Chénier has traced the poetic spirit of these temperate and accomplished writers in these lines, where he shows himself their apt disciple:

> *C'est le bon sens, la raison qui fait tout,*
> *Vertu, génie, esprit, talent et goût.*
> *Qu'est-ce vertu? Raison mise en pratique;*
> *Talent? Raison produite avec éclat;*
> *Esprit? Raison qui finement s'exprime;*
> *Le goût n'est rien qu'un bon sens délicat;*
> *Et le génie est la raison sublime.*[3]

In writing these lines he was evidently thinking of Pope, Despréaux,[4] and Horace, the master of them all. The real essence of this theory, which makes imagination and even feeling subordinate to reason, and of which Scaliger, perhaps, struck the first note among modern writers, is, strictly speaking, the *Latin* theory, and this has also for a long time been the French theory. It has some truth in it if it is only used in the right place, if that word *reason* is not

---

[2]*Conversations with Eckermann.*
[3]"It is good sense, reason that does everything—virtue, genius, wit, talent, and taste. What is virtue? Reason put into practice. Talent? Reason produced with brilliance. Wit? Reason finely expressed. Taste is only delicate good sense; and genius is sublime reason."
[4]Boileau.

misused; but it is evident that it is misused, and that if reason, for instance, can be confused with poetic genius and their union results in a moral epistle, it cannot be the same thing as that genius which we find so varied and so diversely creative in expressing the passions of the drama or the epic. Where will you find reason in the fourth book of the *Aeneid,* and in the ecstasies of Dido? Where will you find it in the madness of Phaedra? Be this as it may, the spirit which has prompted this theory tends to place in the first rank of the classics those writers who have governed their inspiration rather than those who have given themselves more up to it, to place Virgil there more certainly than Homer, Racine more than Corneille. The masterpiece which this theory loves to quote, and which does indeed unite every condition of prudence, strength, progressive daring, moral elevation and greatness, is *Athalie.* In Turenne, in his last two campaigns, and Racine in *Athalie,* we have the great examples of what wise and prudent men can do when they come into possession of the full maturity of their genius, and enter upon their crowning exploits.

Buffon, in his *Discourse on Style,* in which he insists on that oneness of plan, arrangement, and execution which is the stamp of really classic work, has said:

> Every subject is one only; and *however spacious it may be it can be comprised in a single treatise.* Interruptions, pauses, and sections should only be used when different subjects are treated of, or when, having to speak of great, complicated, or incongruous matters, the march of genius finds itself impeded by the multiplicity of the obstacles in its way and constrained by the requirements of the circumstances; otherwise a great number of divisions, far from making a work more solid, destroy its unity; the book seems clearer at first sight, but the author's intention remains obscure.

And he continues his criticism, having in his mind Montesquieu's *l'Esprit des Lois,* a book excellent at bottom, but all cut up into segments, into which the illustrious author, worn out before the end, could not breathe all his spirit, nor even to some extent arrange all his matter. Yet I find it hard to believe that Buffon was not thinking in the same place by way of contrast of Bossuet's *Discours sur l'Histoire Universelle,* a subject, indeed, both vast and single, and which the great author has yet been able to comprise in one solitary treatise. Let anyone open the first edition of 1681, before the division into chapters which was introduced later, and which has passed from the margin into the text and cut it up; everything is there unfolded in one sequence and almost at one breath, and one would say that the orator has here done like the Nature of whom Buffon writes, that he *has worked on an eternal plan and has nowhere deviated from it,* so far does he seem to have penetrated into the intimacy of the counsels of Providence.

Athalie and the *Discours sur l'Histoire Universelle,* such are the highest masterpieces which the strict classic theory can offer alike to its friends and its enemies. Yet in spite of all the admirable simplicity and majesty with which these unique productions are executed, we should like for the practical purposes of art to extend this idea a little, and to show that there is room for enlarging it without going so far as to relax it. Goethe, whom I like to quote on such a subject, says:

> I call all *healthy* work classic, all *unhealthy* work romantic. The poem of the *Nibelungen* is for me as classic as Homer; both are healthy and vigorous. It is not because they are new that the works of the day are romantic, but because they are weak, sickly, or diseased. It is not because they are old that the works of past times are classic, but because they are energetic, fresh, and healthy. If we were to consider the romantic and the classic from these two points of view, we should soon all be agreed.[5]

And, indeed, I should like every free mind to travel round the world and give itself up to the contemplation of the different literatures in their primitive vigor and their infinite variety before marking down and fixing its ideas on this subject. What would such a mind see? First of all a Homer, the father of the classic world, but himself less certainly a single and very distinct individual than the vast and living expression of an active period and a semibarbarous civilization. To make a classic properly so called of him, it has been necessary to attribute to him a design, a plan, literary intentions, qualities of criticism and urbanity as an afterthought, of which he would certainly never have dreamt in the overflowing development of his natural inspiration. And whom do we see beside him? Imposing and venerable men of antiquity it is true, such as Aeschylus or Sophocles, but all mutilated, and standing there only to represent to us the wreck of themselves, all that remains of many others doubtless as worthy as they to survive, who have perished forever beneath the ill-treatment of the ages. This thought alone might teach a man of well-balanced mind not to look at literature as a whole, even classic literature, with too simple

---

[5]*Conversations with Eckermann.*

and too limited a view, and he may learn from it that that exact and well-proportioned order which has had so much force since, has been introduced only artificially into our admiration of the past.

And how would it be when we enter the modern world? The greatest names we perceive at the outset of literature are those which most shock and disturb certain restricted ideas of the beautiful and the fitting which it has been thought desirable to convey in poetry. Is Shakespeare a classic, for instance? Yes, he is so today, for England and for the world; but in the time of Pope he was not. Pope and his friends were the only classics in the full sense; they seemed to become so indubitably the day after their death. Today they are still classics and they deserve to be; but they are only in the second rank, and there they may be seen forever, surpassed and kept in their place by him who has again his place on the topmost skyline.

I shall certainly not be the one to speak evil of Pope or of his excellent followers, especially when they are as sweet and natural as Goldsmith; next to the greatest, these, between writers and poets, are perhaps the best fitted for imparting charm to life. One day, when Lord Bolingbroke was writing to Dr. Swift, Pope put a postscript to the letter, in which he said: "I imagine that if we three were to spend even three years together, the result might be some advantage to our century." No, we must never speak lightly of those who have had the right to say such things of themselves without boasting, and it would be much better to envy the favored and fortunate ages when men of talent could suggest such unions, which were not then chimerical. These ages, whether we call them by the name of Louis XIV or of Queen Anne, are the only really classic ages, using the word in its limited sense, the only ones which offer a propitious climate and shelter to perfected talent. We here, in our disconnected period, are but too well aware of it, when talents possibly equal to theirs have got lost and dissipated through the uncertain ties and hardships of the times. Anyway, let us apportion to each kind of greatness its due influence and superiority. The true master genius triumphs over those difficulties which wreck others; Dante, Shakespeare, and Milton knew how to attain to their supremacy and to produce their imperishable works in spite of obstacles, persecutions, and storms. The opinions of Byron about Pope have been the subject of much discussion, and an attempt has been made to explain that kind of contradiction which has led the singer of *Don Juan* and of *Childe Harold* to extol the purely classic school, and declare it to be the only good one, while he himself took so different a course. Goethe has once more said the right word about this, when remarks that Byron, so great in the outburst and spring of his poetry, yet feared Shakespeare, who is more

capable than he of creating and putting life into his characters. He would have liked to deny him; he was irked by that unselfish superiority; he felt that he could never comfortably display himself beside him. He has never renounced Pope because he did not fear him; he well knew that Pope was a *wall* beside him.

If the school of Pope had kept the supremacy, and a kind of honorary empire over the past, as Byron wished, Byron would have been the first and only one of his kind; the erection of Pope as that wall hid Shakespeare's great form from sight, whereas, while Shakespeare reigns and dominates in all his height, Byron is only second.

We in France had no great classic before the era of Louis XIV; we lacked Dantes and Shakespeares, those original authorities to which one returns sooner or later in the days of emancipation. We have had only, as it were, the rough drafts of great poets, such as Mathurin Régnier and Rabelais, without any ideal, without the passion and the gravity which give consecration. Montaigne was a sort of classic before his time, of the Horatian breed, but one who, for want of worthy surroundings, abandoned himself like a strayed child to all the libertine fancies of his pen and his humor. The result is that we have earned less than any other nation the right to claim loudly one day, through our author-ancestors, our literary liberties and charters, and that it has been a still greater difficulty to us to work out our freedom and remain classic. Yet, with Molière and La Fontaine among our classics of the great era, there is sufficient cause for refusing no rights of legitimacy to any who will make the venture with knowledge.

The important thing now seems to me to be to preserve the notion and the cult, and at the same time to widen it. There is no recipe for making classics: this point must sooner or later be clearly recognized. To think that by imitating certain qualities of purity, of sobriety, of correctness and elegance, quite independently even of character and the divine spark, you will become a classic, to think that after Racine the father there is room for Racine the son; an estimable and melancholy role which is the worst thing in poetry. Yet more: it is not a good thing to appear too quickly and right off, to one's contemporaries, as a pure classic; see how faint the color looks at a distance of twenty-five years! How many there are of these precocious classics who do not last and are only ephemeral! You turn round one morning and are surprised to find them no longer standing behind you. They have only been there, in the gay phrase of Madame de Sévigné, as a breakfast for the sun. With regard to classics the most spontaneous are still the best and the greatest: ask those virile geniuses who are really born immortal and who flourish perpetually, whether it is not so. Apparently the least classic of the four poets of Louis XIV was Molière; he was applauded then far more than he was esteemed; people enjoyed him without knowing his value. After him the least classic seemed to be La Fontaine; and see what came of it—for both of them—two centuries later. Far before Boileau, before even Racine, are they not today unanimously recognized as the most fruitful writers, the richest as regards the characteristics of universal morality?

After all, we need really sacrifice nothing—depreciate nothing. The temple of taste, I quite believe, needs rebuilding; but in rebuilding it, it is merely a question of making it greater, and of letting it become the Pantheon of all the nobility of mankind—of all those who have had a notable and lasting share in increasing the sum of the pleasures and possessions of the mind. As for me, who would in no sense pretend (as is evident) to be the architect or director of such a temple, I will confine myself to expressing some wishes—competing for the specification, as it were. Above all, I would exclude no one worthy to enter, and I would give everyone the place due to him, from Shakespeare, the most unfettered of creative geniuses and unconsciously the greatest of the classics, to Andrieux, the very last of the classics in miniature. "In my Father's house are many mansions."[6] Let that be no less true of the kingdom of the beautiful here than of the kingdom of heaven above. Homer always and everywhere would be the first in it, the most like a god; but behind him, like the attendant train of the three kings of the East, would follow those three grand poets, those three Homers long ignored by us, who also themselves have made grand and admirable epics, the Hindu poets Valmiki and Vyasa,[7] and the Persian Firdousi. In the realm of taste, it is a good thing to know, at least, that such men exist, and not to split up the human race. Having paid this homage to what it is sufficient to perceive and recognize, we would quit our own boundaries no more, and we would divert our eyes with a thousand splendid or agreeable sights, and rejoice in a thousand various and surprising meetings; yet their apparent confusion would never be wanting in concord and harmony. The most ancient of sages and poets—those who have put human morality into maxims and have chanted it in plainsong—would converse with each other in rare suave speech, and would not be surprised to understand each other at the very first word. Solon, Hesiod, Theognis, Job, Solomon, and why not Confucius himself? would greet the most ingenious modern authors, La Rochefoucauld or La Bruyère, who

would say to each other as they listened to them: "They knew all that we know, and we have found nothing new by bringing experience up to date." On the hill most in sight, with the most easy slopes, Virgil surrounded by Menander, Tibullus, Terence, Fénelon, would abandon himself with them to converse full of charm and a sacred enchantment; his gentle face would beam with radiance and the hue of modesty, as on that day when, entering the Roman theater just as they had been reciting his verses, he saw the entire assembly rise in front of him by a simultaneous movement and pay him the same homage as to Augustus himself. Not far from him, and regretting to be separated from so dear a friend, Horace would preside in his turn (so far as a poet and sage so keen of wit can be said to preside) over the group of the poets of civic life and of those who have known how to talk as well as sing—Pope and Despréaux, the one grown less irritable and the other less censorious. That true poet, Montaigne, would be there with them, and his presence would completely remove all appearance of a literary academy from this charming corner. La Fontaine would forget himself there, and, henceforth less flighty, would be content to remain. Voltaire would pass by, but he would not have the patience to stop, though at the same time delighting in it. On the same hill as Virgil, a little lower down, Xenophon would be seen with an unaffected look very little like a captain, but of a kind to make him rather resemble a priest of the Muses. He would gather around him the Attic minds of every language and of every country—Addison, Pellisson, Vauvenargues, all who feel the value of suave expression, exquisite simplicity, and a sweet, though not unadorned, carelessness. In the center of the place three great men would often like to meet before the portico of the principal temple (for there would be several within the enclosure), and if those be together, there would not be a fourth, however great, to whom it would occur to take part in their intercourse or their silence, so great would appear their beauty, their grand proportions, and that perfection of harmony which has only once been seen when first the world was young. Their three names have become the ideal of all art—Plato, Sophocles, and Demosthenes. And, moreover, having duly honored these demigods, do you not see yonder a numerous and familiar crowd of excellent spirits, who always prefer to follow Cervantes, Molière—the practical painters from the life—those indulgent friends who are still the first of benefactors, who seize the whole man with laughter, pour out experience for him in mirth, and are aware of the powerful influence of rational, hearty, lawful joy? I will not here go on any longer with this description, which would occupy a whole book if it were complete. Be sure that the Middle Ages and Dante would fill some of the sacred heights; Italy would wholly

---

[6]John 14:2.
[7]In Hindu tradition Valmiki composed the Ramayana; Vyasa, the Mahabharata.

unfold herself like a garden at the feet of the singer of Paradise; Boccaccio and Aristotle would disport themselves there, and Tasso would find once more the orange groves of Sorrento. In short, the different nations would have each a special nook kept for it, but the authors would delight in coming out of it, and as they walk about they would recognize, where least they expect it, their brothers or their masters. Lucretius, for instance, would love to discuss with Milton the origin of the world and the disentanglement of chaos; but as they argue each after his manner, they will but agree about the divine representations of poetry and nature.

These are our classics; everybody's imagination can complete the sketch, and even choose his favorite group for himself. For there must be a choice, and the first condition of taste when all has been surveyed is not to roam ceaselessly, but once for all to stay with a settled opinion. Nothing palls on the mind so much and is so injurious to taste as ceaseless roamings; the poetic spirit is not the Wandering Jew. Notwithstanding all this, my concluding advice when I speak of choosing and of forming an opinion is not to imitate even those who please us the most among our masters in the past. Let us be satisfied with feeling them, with interpreting them, with admiring them, and for ourselves, latecomers that we are, let us try at least to be ourselves. Let us make our choice with our own proper instincts. Let us have the sincerity and naturalness of our own thoughts, our own feelings— that always is possible. Let us add to it what is more difficult, a high aim, an impetus towards some lofty ideal; and while we speak our own language and submit to the conditions of the age in which we are placed, and from which we draw alike our strength and our failings, let us ask ourselves from time to time, while we lift our brows towards the hills and fasten our eyes on the group of reverend beings: "What would they say of us?"

But why do we speak continually of being an author, of writing? An age, perchance, is coming when there will be no more writing. Happy are those who read and read again, who can obey their free inclinations in their reading! There comes

a period in life when, our wanderings all finished and our experiences all acquired, there is no keener pleasure than to study and deepen the things we know, to relish what we taste, just as when you behold again and again the people you love; purest delight of the mature mind and taste. It is then that this word *classic* assumes its true meaning, and is defined by the irresistible and discerning choice of every man of taste. Taste has now been created, it is formed and defined; the right meaning is now achieved if we are to have it at all. There is no longer any time to try about, nor any wish to make further discoveries. You stand by your friends, by those who have been proved by a long connection. Old wine, old books, old friends. You say to yourself like Voltaire in those delightful lines:

Jouissons, écrivons, vivons, mon cher Horace!

. . .

J'ai vécu plus que toi: mes vers dureront moins:
Mais, au bord du tombeau, je mettrai tous mes soins
A suivre les leçons de ta philosophie,
A mépriser la mort en savourant la vie,
A lire tes écrits pleins de grâce et de sens,
Comme on boit d'un vin vieux qui rajeunit les sens.[8]

Finally, be it Horace or another, whoever the author is that we prefer, and that gives us back our own thoughts in full richness and maturity, we shall at any rate beg from one of these good and ancient spirits a perpetual entertainment, an unwavering friendship which will never fail us, and that habitual impression of serenity and sweetness, which reconciles us, who so often need it, to mankind and to ourselves.

---

[8] "Let us play, let us write, let us live, my dear Horace! . . . I have lived longer than you; my verses will last less: but, at the edge of the tomb, I will take all my care to follow the lessons of your philosophy, to despise death and savor life, to read your writings, full of grace and sense, as one drinks an old wine that revives the senses."

Edgar Allan Poe

1809–1849

In spite of what now seems to us Poe's almost abominable taste, as exemplified by his praise of Thomas Hood's poem *The Bridge of Sighs,* Poe's essay *The Poetic Principle* is interesting as an example of Romantic extremism. The remark that a long poem is a "flat contradiction in terms" goes far beyond Coleridge's assertion that a long poem need not be all poetry. In both cases *poetry* becomes a quality inherent in some writing, or perhaps inherent in nature or experience. It is not identical with a *poem.* Coleridge's use of the terms is, however, far more precise than Poe's, who really leaves us confused as to what he means.

Poe's judgment on the long poem is made purely in terms of what he conceives the reader's attention span to be. The value of a work depends wholly on the immediate, sustained effect. He finds that Book II of *Paradise Lost* is no good if one has just waded through Book I, but is quite good if one omits Book I and begins with Book II. All trace of any possible objective judgment of taste seems to be missing here. In another essay, *The Philosophy of Composition,* written three or four years before *The Poetic Principle,* Poe makes the same points and insists that the poet should begin his composition with a consideration of the *effect* of a work. He should limit the length of his poem, make it "universally appreciable," and convey a particular *tone.* Poe opts for sadness, which he considers the "most legitimate of all tones." In this he reveals an extreme Romantic taste.

In *The Poetic Principle* Poe also takes the Romantic distinction between poem and discursive statement to an extreme. He attacks the "didactic heresy," by which he means the tendency to think of a poem in terms of its message or discursive content. The poem exists only "for the poem's sake." But when he tries to discuss the value of poetry or a poem, he is apparently unequipped to go beyond remarks about "supernal beauty" and definitions of the poem as the "rhythmical creation of beauty." Still, he presents an example of certain Romantic legacies, and his theories were impressive enough to have influenced Baudelaire, who had a more sophisticated critical intelligence.

Poe's complete works have been edited by J. A. Harrison (17 vols., 1902), and his literary criticism has been edited by R. L. Hough (1965). For commentary, including discussion of Poe as a literary theorist, see Margaret Alterton, *Origins of Poe's Critical Theory* (1925); Floyd Stovall, "Poe's Debt to Coleridge," *Texas Studies in English,* X (1930), 70–127; A. H. Quinn, *Edgar Allan Poe: A Critical Biography* (1941); E. H. Davidson, *Poe: A Critical Study* (1957); E. R. Marks, "Poe as Literary Theorist: A Reappraisal," *American Literature,* XXXIII (1961), 296–306; E. W. Parks, *Edgar Allan Poe as a Literary Critic* (1964); and Robert D. Jacobs, *Poe: Journalist and Critic* (1969).

The Poetic Principle

In speaking of the poetic principle, I have no design to be either thorough or profound. While discussing, very much at random, the essentiality of what we call poetry, my principal purpose will be to cite for consideration some few of those minor English or American poems which best suit my own taste, or which, upon my own fancy, have left the most definite impression. By "minor poems" I mean, of course, poems of little length. And here, in the beginning, permit me to say a few words in regard to a somewhat peculiar principle, which, whether rightfully or wrongfully, has always had its influence in my own critical estimate of the poem. I hold that a long poem does not exist. I maintain that the phrase, *a long poem,* is simply a flat contradiction in terms.

I need scarcely observe that a poem deserves its title only inasmuch as it excites, by elevating the soul. The value of the poem is in the ratio of this elevating excitement. But all excitements are, through a psychal necessity, transient. That degree of excitement which would entitle a poem to be so called at all cannot be sustained throughout a composition of any great length. After the lapse of half an hour, at the very utmost, it flags—fails—a revulsion ensues—and then the poem is, in effect, and in fact, no longer such.

There are, no doubt, many who have found difficulty in reconciling the critical dictum that the *Paradise Lost* is to be devoutly admired throughout, with the absolute impossibility of maintaining for it, during perusal, the amount of enthusiasm which that critical dictum would demand. This great work, in fact, is to be regarded as poetical, only when, losing sight of that vital requisite in all works of art, unity, we view it merely as a series of minor poems. If, to preserve its unity—its totality of effect or impression—we read it (as would be necessary) at a single sitting, the result is but a constant alternation of excitement and depression. After a passage of what we feel to be true poetry, there follows, inevitably, a passage of platitude which no critical prejudgment can force us to admire; but if, upon completing the work, we read it again omitting the first book—that is to say, commencing with the second—we shall be surprised at now finding that admirable which we before condemned—that damnable which we had previously so much admired. It follows from all this that the ultimate, aggregate, or absolute

effect of even the best epic under the sun, is a nullity—and this is precisely the fact.

In regard to the *Iliad,* we have, if not positive proof, at least very good reason, for believing it intended as a series of lyrics; but, granting the epic intention, I can say only that the work is based in an imperfect sense of art. The modern epic is, of the supposititious ancient model, but an inconsiderate and blindfold imitation. But the day of these artistic anomalies is over. If, at any time, any very long poem were popular in reality, which I doubt, it is at least clear that no very long poem will ever be popular again.

That the extent of a poetical work is, *ceteris paribus,*[1] the measure of its merit, seems undoubtedly, when we thus state it, a proposition sufficiently absurd—yet we are indebted for it to the quarterly reviews. Surely there can be nothing in mere size, abstractly considered—there can be nothing in mere bulk, so far as a volume is concerned, which has so continuously elicited admiration from these saturnine pamphlets! A mountain, to be sure, by the mere sentiment of physical magnitude which it conveys, does impress us with a sense of the sublime—but no man is impressed after this fashion by the material grandeur of even *The Columbiad.* Even the quarterlies have not instructed us to be so impressed by it. As yet, they have not insisted on our estimating Lamartine by the cubic foot, or Pollok by the pound—but what else are we to infer from their continued prating about "sustained effort"? If, by "sustained effort," any little gentleman has accomplished an epic, let us frankly commend him for the effort—if this indeed be a thing commendable—but let us forbear praising the epic on the effort's account. It is to be hoped that common sense, in the time to come, will prefer deciding upon a work of art, rather by the impression it makes, by the effect it produces, than by the time it took to impress the effect or by the amount of "sustained effort" which had been found necessary in effecting the impression. The fact is, that perseverance is one thing, and genius quite another—nor can all the quarterlies in Christendom confound them. By and by, this proposition, with many which I have been just urging, will be received as self-evident. In the meantime, by being generally condemned as falsities, they will not be essentially damaged as truths.

On the other hand, it is clear that a poem may be improperly brief. Undue brevity degenerates into mere epigrammatism. A very short poem, while now and then producing a brilliant or vivid, never produces a profound or enduring effect. There must be the steady pressing down of

---

THE POETIC PRINCIPLE. Poe's *The Poetic Principle* was delivered as a lecture several times in 1848 and 1849. It was published posthumously in 1850. The text is from the edition of Poe's works by E. C. Stedman and G. E. Woodberry (1894–95).

---

[1] "Other things equal."

the stamp upon the wax. Béranger has wrought innumerable things, pungent and spirit-stirring; but, in general, they have been too imponderous to stamp themselves deeply into the public attention; and thus, as so many feathers of fancy, have been blown aloft only to be whistled down the wind.

A remarkable instance of the effect of undue brevity in depressing a poem—in keeping it out of the popular view—is afforded by the following exquisite little serenade:

> I arise from dreams of thee
>> In the first sweet sleep of night,
> When the winds are breathing low,
>> And the stars are shining bright;
> I arise from dreams of thee,
>> And a spirit in my feet
> Hath led me—who knows how?
>> To thy chamber-window, sweet!
>
> The wandering airs, they faint
>> On the dark, the silent stream;
> The champak odors fail
>> Like sweet thoughts in a dream;
> The nightingale's complaint,
>> It dies upon her heart,
> As I must die on thine,
>> Oh, beloved as thou art!
>
> Oh, lift me from the grass!
>> I die! I faint! I fail!
> Let thy love in kisses rain
>> On my lips and eyelids pale.
> My cheek is cold and white, alas!
>> My heart beats loud and fast:
> Oh! Press it close to thine again,
>> Where it will break at last![2]

Very few, perhaps, are familiar with these lines—yet no less a poet than Shelley is their author. Their warm, yet delicate and ethereal imagination will be appreciated by all—but by none so thoroughly as by him who has himself arisen from sweet dreams of one beloved to bathe in the aromatic air of a southern midsummer night.

One of the finest poems by Willis—the very best in my opinion, which he has ever written—has, no doubt, through this same defect of undue brevity, been kept back from its proper position, not less in the critical than in the popular view.

> The shadows lay along Broadway,
>> 'Twas near the twilight tide,
> And slowly there a lady fair
>> Was walking in her pride.
> Alone walked she; but, viewlessly,
>> Walked spirits at her side.
>
> Peace charmed the street beneath her feet
>> And honor charmed the air;
> And all astir looked kind on her,
>> And called her good as fair,
> For all God ever gave to her
>> She kept with chary care.
>
> She kept with care her beauties rare
>> From lovers warm and true,
> For her heart was cold to all but gold,
>> And the rich came not to woo—
> But honored well are charms to sell
>> If priests the selling do.
>
> Now walking there was one more fair—
>> A slight girl, lily pale;
> And she had unseen company
>> To make the spirit quail:
> 'Twixt want and scorn she walked forlorn,
>> And nothing could avail.
>
> No mercy now can clear her brow
>> For this world's peace to pray;
> For, as love's wild prayer dissolved in air,
>> Her woman's heart gave way!
> But the sin forgiven by Christ in heaven
>> By man is cursed away![3]

In this composition we find it difficult to recognize the Willis who has written so many mere "verses of society." The lines are not only richly ideal, but full of energy; while they breathe an earnestness—an evident sincerity of sentiment—for which we look in vain throughout all the other works of this author.

While the epic mania—while the idea that, to merit in poetry, prolixity is indispensable—has, for some years past, been gradually dying out of the public mind, by mere dint of its own absurdity, we find it succeeded by a heresy too palpably false to be long tolerated, but one which, in the brief period it has already endured, may be said to have accom-

---

[2]Shelley, *The Indian Serenade.*

[3]*Unseen Spirits.*

plished more in the corruption of our poetical literature than all its other enemies combined. I allude to the heresy of "the didactic." It has been assumed, tacitly and avowedly, directly and indirectly, that the ultimate object of all poetry is truth. Every poem, it is said, should inculcate a moral; and by this moral is the poetical merit of the work to be adjudged. We Americans, especially, have patronized this happy idea; and we Bostonians, very especially, have developed it in full. We have taken it into our heads that to write a poem simply for the poem's sake, and to acknowledge such to have been our design, would be to confess ourselves radically wanting in the true poetic dignity and force: but the simple fact is, that, would we but permit ourselves to look into our own souls, we should immediately there discover that under the sun there neither exists nor can exist any work more thoroughly dignified—more supremely noble than this very poem—this poem per se—this poem which is a poem and nothing more—this poem written solely for the poem's sake.

With as deep a reverence for the true as ever inspired the bosom of man, I would, nevertheless, limit, in some measure, its modes of inculcation. I would limit to enforce them. I would not enfeeble them by dissipation. The demands of truth are severe. She has no sympathy with the myrtles. All that which is so indispensable in song, is precisely all that with which she has nothing whatever to do. It is but making her a flaunting paradox, to wreathe her in gems and flowers. In enforcing a truth, we need severity rather than efflorescence of language. We must be simple, precise, terse. We must be cool, calm, unimpassioned. In a word, we must be in that mood which, as nearly as possible, is the exact converse of the poetical. He must be blind, indeed, who does not perceive the radical and chasmal differences between the truthful and the poetical modes of inculcation. He must be theory-mad beyond redemption who, in spite of these differences, shall still persist in attempting to reconcile the obstinate oils and waters of poetry and truth.

Dividing the world of mind into its three most obvious distinctions, we have the pure intellect, taste, and the moral sense. I place taste in the middle, because it is just this position which in the mind it occupies. It holds intimate relations with either extreme; but from the moral sense is separated by so faint a difference that Aristotle has not hesitated to place some of its operations among the virtues themselves. Nevertheless, we find the offices of the trio marked with a sufficient distinction. Just as the intellect concerns itself with truth, so taste informs us of the beautiful, while the moral sense is regardful of duty. Of this latter, while conscience teaches the obligation, and reason the expediency, taste contents herself with displaying the charms: waging war upon

vice solely on the ground of her deformity—her disproportion, her animosity to the fitting, to the appropriate, to the harmonious—in a word, to beauty.

An immortal instinct, deep within the spirit of man, is thus, plainly, a sense of the beautiful. This it is which administers to his delight in the manifold forms, and sounds, and odors, and sentiments amid which he exists. And just as the lily is repeated in the lake, or the eyes of Amaryllis in the mirror, so is the mere oral or written repetition of these forms, and sounds, and colors, and odors, and sentiments, a duplicate source of delight. But this mere repetition is not poetry. He who shall simply sing, with however glowing enthusiasm, or with however vivid a truth of description, of the sights, and sounds, and odors, and colors, and sentiments, which greet him in common with all mankind—he, I say, has yet failed to prove his divine title. There is still a something in the distance which he has been unable to attain. We have still a thirst unquenchable, to allay which he has not shown us the crystal springs. This thirst belongs to the immortality of man. It is at once a consequence and an indication of his perennial existence. It is the desire of the moth for the star. It is no mere appreciation of the beauty before us—but a wild effort to reach the beauty above. Inspired by an ecstatic prescience of the glories beyond the grave, we struggle, by multiform combinations among the things and thoughts of time, to attain a portion of that loveliness whose very elements, perhaps, appertain to eternity alone. And thus when by poetry—or when by music, the most entrancing of the poetic moods—we find ourselves melted into tears—not as the Abbaté Gravina supposes—through excess of pleasure, but through a certain, petulant, impatient sorrow at our inability to grasp now, wholly, here on earth, at once and forever, those divine and rapturous joys, of which through the poem, or through the music, we attain to but brief and indeterminate glimpses.

The struggle to apprehend the supernal loveliness—this struggle, on the part of souls fittingly constituted—has given to the world all that which it (the world) has ever been enabled at once to understand and to feel as poetic.

The poetic sentiment, of course, may develop itself in various modes—in painting, in sculpture, in architecture, in the dance—very especially in music—and very peculiarly, and with a wide field, in the composition of the landscape garden. Our present theme, however, has regard only to its manifestation in words. And here let me speak briefly on the topic of rhythm. Contenting myself with the certainty that music, in its various modes of meter, rhythm, and rhyme, is of so vast a moment in poetry as never to be wisely rejected—is so vitally important an adjunct, that he is simply silly who declines its assistance—I will not now pause to maintain its absolute essentiality. It is in music, perhaps, that the soul most nearly attains the great end for which, when inspired by the poetic sentiment, it struggles—the creation of supernal beauty. It may be, indeed, that here this sublime end is, now and then, attained in fact. We are often made to feel, with a shivering delight, that from an earthly harp are stricken notes which cannot have been unfamiliar to the angels. And thus there can be little doubt that in the union of poetry with music in its popular sense, we shall find the widest field for the poetic development. The old bards and minnesingers had advantages which we do not possess—and Thomas Moore, singing his own songs, was, in the most legitimate manner, perfecting them as poems.

To recapitulate, then: I would define, in brief, the poetry of words as the rhythmical creation of beauty. Its sole arbiter is taste. With the intellect or with the conscience, it has only collateral relations. Unless incidentally, it has no concern whatever either with duty or with truth.

A few words, however, in explanation. That pleasure which is at once the most pure, the most elevating, and the most intense, is derived, I maintain, from the contemplation of the beautiful. In the contemplation of beauty we alone find it possible to attain that pleasurable elevation, or excitement, of the soul, which we recognize as the poetic sentiment, and which is so easily distinguished from truth, which is the satisfaction of the reason, or from passion, which is the excitement of the heart. I make beauty, therefore—using the word as inclusive of the sublime—I make beauty the province of the poem, simply because it is an obvious rule of art that effects should be made to spring as directly as possible from their causes—no one as yet having been weak enough to deny that the peculiar elevation in question is at least most readily attainable in the poem. It by no means follows, however, that the incitements of passion, or the precepts of duty, or even the lessons of truth, may not be introduced into a poem, and with advantage; for they may subserve, incidentally, in various ways, the general purposes of the work—but the true artist will always contrive to tone them down in proper subjection to that beauty which is the atmosphere and the real essence of the poem.

I cannot better introduce the few poems, which I shall present for your consideration, than by the citation of the "proem" to Mr. Longfellow's *Waif:*

The day is done, and the darkness
    Falls from the wings of night,
As a feather is wafted downward
    From an eagle in his flight.

I see the lights of the village
    Gleam through the rain and the mist,

And a feeling of sadness comes o'er me,
    That my soul cannot resist:

A feeling of sadness and longing,
    That is not akin to pain,
And resembles sorrow only
    As the mist resembles the rain.

Come, read to me some poem,
    Some simple and heartfelt lay,
That shall soothe this restless feeling,
    And banish the thoughts of day.

Not from the grand old masters,
    Not from the bards sublime,
Whose distant footsteps echo
    Through the corridors of time.

For, like strains of martial music,
    Their mighty thoughts suggest
Life's endless toil and endeavor;
    And tonight I long for rest.

Read from some humbler poet,
    Whose songs gushed from his heart,
As showers from the clouds of summer,
    Or tears from the eyelids start;

Who, through long days of labor,
    And nights devoid of ease,
Still heard in his soul the music
    Of wonderful melodies.

Such songs have power to quiet
    The restless pulse of care,
And come like the benediction
    That follows after prayer.

Then read from the treasured volume
    The poem of thy choice,
And lend to the rhyme of the poet
    The beauty of thy voice.

And the night shall be filled with music,
    And the cares that infest the day,
Shall fold their tents, like the Arabs,
    And as silently steal away.

With no great range of imagination, these lines have been justly admired for their delicacy of expression. Some of the images are very effective. Nothing can be better than—

> the bards sublime
> Whose distant footsteps echo
> Through the corridors of time.

The idea of the last quatrain is also very effective. The poem, on the whole, however, is chiefly to be admired for the graceful insouciance of its meter, so well in accordance with the character of the sentiments, and especially for the ease of the general manner. This "ease," or naturalness, in a literary style, it has long been the fashion to regard as ease in appearance alone—as a point of really difficult attainment. But not so: a natural manner is difficult only to him who should never meddle with it—to the unnatural. It is but the result of writing with the understanding, or with the instinct, that the tone, in composition, should always be that which the mass of mankind would adopt—and must perpetually vary, of course, with the occasion. The author who, after the fashion of the *North American Review,* should be, upon all occasions, merely "quiet," must necessarily, upon many occasions, be simply silly, or stupid; and has no more right to be considered "easy," or "natural," than a Cockney exquisite, or than the sleeping beauty in the waxworks.

Among the minor poems of Bryant, none has so much impressed me as the one which he entitles *June.* I quote only a portion of it:

> There, through the long, long summer hours
>> The golden light should lie,
> And thick young herbs and groups of flowers
>> Stand in their beauty by.
> The oriole should build and tell
> His love tale, close beside my cell;
>> The idle butterfly
> Should rest him there, and there be heard
> The housewife-bee and hummingbird.
>
> And what if cheerful shouts at noon
>> Come, from the village sent,
> Or songs of maids, beneath the moon,
>> With fairy laughter blent?
> And what if, in the evening light,
> Betrothèd lovers walk in sight
>> Of my low monument?
> I would the lovely scene around
> Might know no sadder sight nor sound.
>
> I know that I no more should see
>> The season's glorious show,

> Nor would its brightness shine for me,
>> Nor its wild music flow;
> But if, around my place of sleep,
> The friends I love should come to weep,
>> They might not haste to go.
> Soft airs, and song, and light, and bloom
> Should keep them lingering by my tomb.
>
> These to their softened hearts should bear
>> The thought of what has been,
> And speak of one who cannot share
>> The gladness of the scene;
> Whose part, in all the pomp that fills
> The circuit of the summer hills,
>> Is—that his grave is green;
> And deeply would their hearts rejoice
> To hear again his living voice.

The rhythmical flow, here, is even voluptuous—nothing could be more melodious. The poem has always affected me in a remarkable manner. The intense melancholy which seems to well up, perforce, to the surface of all the poet's cheerful sayings about his grave, we find thrilling us to the soul—while there is the truest poetic elevation in the thrill. The impression left is one of a pleasurable sadness. And if, in the remaining compositions which I shall introduce to you, there be more or less of a similar tone always apparent, let me remind you that (how or why we know not) this certain taint of sadness is inseparably connected with all the higher manifestations of true beauty. It is, nevertheless,

> A feeling of sadness and longing
>> That is not akin to pain,
> And resembles sorrow only
>> As the mist resembles the rain.

The taint of which I speak is clearly perceptible even in a poem so full of brilliancy and spirit as the *Health* of Edward Coate Pinkney:

> I fill this cup to one made up
>> Of loveliness alone,
> A woman, of her gentle sex
>> The seeming paragon;
> To whom the better elements
>> And kindly stars have given
> A form so fair, that, like the air,
>> 'Til less of earth than heaven.
>
> Her every tone is music's own,
>> Like those of morning birds,

And something more than melody
    Dwells ever in her words;
The coinage of her heart are they,
    And from her lips each flows
As one may see the burdened bee
    Forth issue from the rose.

Affections are as thoughts to her,
    The measures of her hours;
Her feelings have the fragrancy,
    The freshness of young flowers;
And lovely passions, changing oft,
    So fill her, she appears
The image of themselves by turns,
    The idol of past years!

Of her bright face one glance will trace
    A picture on the brain,
And of her voice in echoing hearts
    A sound must long remain;
But memory, such as mine of her,
    So very much endears,
When death is nigh my latest sigh
    Will not be life's, but hers.

I fill this cup to one made up
    Of loveliness alone,
A woman, of her gentle sex
    The seeming paragon—
Her health! And would on earth there stood
    Some more of such a frame,
That life might be all poetry,
    And weariness a name.

It was the misfortune of Mr. Pinkney to have been born too far south. Had he been a New Englander, it is probable that he would have been ranked as the first of American lyrists, by that magnanimous cabal which has so long controlled the destinies of American letters, in conducting the thing called the *North American Review.* The poem just cited is especially beautiful; but the poetic elevation which it induces, we must refer chiefly to our sympathy in the poet's enthusiasm. We pardon his hyperboles for the evident earnestness with which they are uttered.

It was by no means my design, however, to expatiate upon the merits of what I should read you. These will necessarily speak for themselves. Boccalini, in his *Advertisements from Parnassus,* tells us that Zoilus once presented Apollo a very caustic criticism upon a very admirable book: whereupon the god asked him for the beauties of the work.

He replied that he only busied himself about the errors. On hearing this, Apollo, handing him a sack of unwinnowed wheat, bade him pick out all the chaff for his reward.

Now this fable answers very well as a hit at the critics—but I am by no means sure that the god was in the right. I am by no means certain that the true limits of the critical duty are not grossly misunderstood. Excellence, in a poem especially, may be considered in the light of an axiom, which need only be properly put, to become self-evident. It is not excellence if it require to be demonstrated as such: and thus, to point out too particularly the merits of a work of art is to admit that they are not merits altogether.

Among the *Melodies* of Thomas Moore, is one whose distinguished character as a poem proper seems to have been singularly left out of view. I allude to his lines beginning— "Come, rest in this bosom." The intense energy of their expression is not surpassed by anything in Byron. There are two of the lines in which a sentiment is conveyed that embodies the all in all of the divine passion of love—a sentiment which, perhaps, has found its echo in more, and in more passionate, human hearts than any other single sentiment ever embodied in words:

Come, rest in this bosom, my own stricken deer,
Though the herd have fled from thee, thy home is still here;
Here still is the smile, that no cloud can o'ercast,
And a heart and a hand all thy own to the last.

Oh! what was love made for, if 'tis not the same
Through joy and through torment, through glory and shame?
I know not, I ask not, if guilt's in that heart,
I but know that I love thee, whatever thou art.

Thou has called me thy angel in moments of bliss,
And thy angel I'll be, 'mid the horrors of this,
Through the furnace, unshrinking, thy steps to pursue,
And shield thee, and save thee—or perish there too!

It has been the fashion, of late days, to deny Moore imagination, while granting him fancy—a distinction originating with Coleridge—than whom no man more fully comprehended the great powers of Moore. The fact is, that the fancy of this poet so far predominates over all his other faculties, and over the fancy of all other men, as to have induced, very naturally, the idea that he is fanciful only. But never was there a greater mistake. Never was a grosser wrong done the fame of a true poet. In the compass of the English language I can call to mind no poem more profoundly—more weirdly imaginative, in the best sense, than the lines commencing— "I would I were by that dim lake"—which are the composition of Thomas Moore. I regret that I am unable to remember them.

One of the noblest—and, speaking of fancy, one of the most singularly fanciful of modern poets, was Thomas Hood. His *Fair Ines* had always, for me, an inexpressible charm:

> O saw ye not fair Ines?
>> She's gone into the West,
> To dazzle when the sun is down,
>> And rob the world of rest:
> She took our daylight with her,
>> The smiles that we love best,
> With morning blushes on her cheek,
>> And pearls upon her breast.
>
> O turn again, fair Ines,
>> Before the fall of night,
> For fear the moon should shine alone,
>> And stars unrivalled bright;
> And blessèd will the lover be
>> That walks beneath their light,
> And breathes the love against thy cheek
>> I dare not even write!
>
> Would I had been, fair Ines,
>> That gallant cavalier,
> Who rode so gaily by thy side,
>> And whispered thee so near!
> Were there no bonny dames at home,
>> Or no true lovers here,
> That he should cross the seas to win
>> The dearest of the dear?
>
> I saw thee, lovely Ines,
>> Descend along the shore,
> With bands of noble gentlemen,
>> And banners waved before;
> And gentle youth and maidens gay,
>> And snowy plumes they wore;
> It would have been a beauteous dream,
>> If it had been no more!
>
> Alas, alas, fair Ines,
>> She went away with song,
> With music waiting on her steps,
>> And shoutings of the throng;
> But some were sad, and felt no mirth,
>> But only music's wrong,

> In sounds that sang farewell, farewell,
>> To her you've loved so long.
>
> Farewell, farewell, fair Ines,
>> That vessel never bore
> So fair a lady on its deck,
>> Nor danced so light before—
> Alas for pleasure on the sea,
>> And sorrow on the shore!
> That smile that blest one lover's heart
>> Has broken many more!

The Haunted House, by the same author, is one of the truest poems ever written—one of the truest—one of the most unexceptionable—one of the most thoroughly artistic, both in its theme and in its execution. It is, moreover, powerfully ideal—imaginative. I regret that its length renders it unsuitable for the purposes of this lecture. In place of it, permit me to offer the universally appreciated *Bridge of Sighs.*

> One more unfortunate,
> Weary of breath,
> Rashly importunate,
> Gone to her death!
>
> Take her up tenderly,
> Lift her with care;
> Fashioned so slenderly,
> Young, and so fair!
>
> Look at her garments
> Clinging like cerements;
> Whilst the wave constantly
> Drips from her clothing;
> Take her up instantly,
> Loving, not loathing.
>
> Touch her not scornfully;
> Think of her mournfully,
> Gently and humanly;
> Not of the stains of her,
> All that remains of her
> Now is pure womanly.
>
> Make no deep scrutiny
> Into her mutiny
> Rash and undutiful;
> Past all dishonor,
> Death has left on her
> Only the beautiful.

Still, for all slips of hers,
One of Eve's family—
Wipe those poor lips of hers
Oozing so clammily.
Loop up her tresses
Escaped from the comb,
Her fair auburn tresses;
Whilst wonderment guesses
Where was her home?

Who was her father?
Who was her mother?
Had she a sister?
Had she a brother?
Or was there a dearer one
Still, and a nearer one
Yet, than all other?

Alas! for the rarity
Of Christian charity
Under the sun!
Oh! It was pitiful!
Near a whole city full,
Home she had none.

Sisterly, brotherly,
Fatherly, motherly
Feelings had changed:
Love, by harsh evidence,
Thrown from its eminence;
Even God's providence
Seeming estranged.

Where the lamps quiver
So far in the river,
With many a light
From window and casement,
From garret to basement,
She stood, with amazement,
Houseless by night.

The bleak wind of March
Made her tremble and shiver;
But not the dark arch,
Or the black flowing river:
Mad from life's history,
Glad to death's mystery,
Swift to be hurled—
Anywhere, anywhere
Out of the world!

In she plunged boldly,
No matter how coldly
The rough river ran—
Over the brink of it,
Picture it—think of it,
Dissolute man!
Lave in it, drink of it
Then, if you can!

Take her up tenderly
Lift her with care
Fashion'd so slenderly,
Young, and so fair!

Ere her limbs frigidly
Stiffen too rigidly,
Decently, kindly,
Smoothe, and compose them;
And her eyes, close them,
Staring so blindly!

Dreadfully staring
Through muddy impurity,
As when with the daring
Last look of despairing
Fixed on futurity.

Perishing gloomily,
Spurred by contumely,
Cold inhumanity,
Burning insanity,
Into her rest.
Cross her hands humbly,
As if praying dumbly,
Over her breast!

Owning her weakness,
Her evil behavior,
And leaving, with meekness,
Her sins to her Savior!

The vigor of this poem is no less remarkable than its pathos. The versification, although carrying the fanciful to the very verge of the fantastic, is nevertheless admirably adapted to the wild insanity which is the thesis of the poem.

Among the minor poems of Lord Byron, is one which has never received from the critics the praise which it undoubtedly deserves:

Though the day of my destiny's over,
    And the star of my fate hath declined,

Thy soft heart refused to discover
    The faults which so many could find;
Though thy soul with my grief was acquainted,
    It shrunk not to share it with me,
And the love which my spirit hath painted
    It never hath found but in *thee*.

Then when nature around me is smiling,
    The last smile which answers to mine,
I do not believe it beguiling,
    Because it reminds me of thine;
And when winds are at war with the ocean,
    As the breasts I believed in with me,
If their billows excite an emotion,
    It is that they bear me from *thee*.

Though the rock of my last hope is shivered,
    And its fragments are sunk in the wave,
Though I feel that my soul is delivered
    To pain—it shall not be its slave.
There is many a pang to pursue me:
    They may crush, but they shall not contemn—
They may torture, but shall not subdue me—
    'Tis of *thee* that I think—not of them.

Though human, thou didst not deceive me,
    Though woman, thou didst not forsake,
Though loved, thou forborest to grieve me,
    Though slandered, thou never couldst shake—
Though trusted, thou didst not disclaim me,
    Though parted, it was not to fly.
Though watchful, 'twas not to defame me,
    Nor mute, that the world might belie.

Yet I blame not the world, nor despise it,
    Nor the war of the many with one—
If my soul was not fitted to prize it,
    'Twas folly not sooner to shun:
And if dearly that error hath cost me,
    And more than I once could foresee,
I have found that whatever it lost me,
    It could not deprive me of *thee*.

From the wreck of the past, which hath perished,
    Thus much I at least may recall,
It hath taught me that which I most cherished,
    Deserved to be dearest of all:
In the desert a fountain is springing,
    In the wide waste there still is a tree,

And a bird in the solitude singing,
    Which speaks to my spirit of *thee*.[4]

Although the rhythm here is one of the most difficult, the versification could scarcely be improved. No nobler theme ever engaged the pen of poet. It is the soul-elevating idea, that no man can consider himself entitled to complain of fate while, in his adversity, he still retains the unwavering love of woman.

From Alfred Tennyson—although in perfect sincerity I regard him as the noblest poet that ever lived—I have left myself time to cite only a very brief specimen. I call him, and think him, the noblest of poets—not because the impressions he produces are, at all times, the most profound—not because the poetical excitement which he induces is, at all times, the most intense—but because it is, at all times, the most ethereal—in other words, the most elevating and the most pure. No poet is so little of the earth, earthy. What I am about to read is from his last long poem, *The Princess:*

Tears, idle tears, I know not what they mean,
Tears from the depth of some divine despair
Rise in the heart, and gather to the eyes,
In looking on the happy autumn fields,
And thinking of the days that are no more.

Fresh as the first beam glittering on a sail
That brings our friends up from the underworld,
Sad as the last which reddens over one
That sinks with all we love below the verge;
So sad, so fresh, the days that are no more.

Ah, sad and strange as in dark summer dawns
The earliest pipe of half-awaken'd birds
To dying ears, when unto dying eyes
The casement slowly grows a glimmering square;
So sad, so strange, the days that are no more.

Dear as remembered kisses after death,
And sweet as those by hopeless fancy feigned
On lips that are for others; deep as love,
Deep as first love, and wild with all regret;
O death in life, the days that are no more.

Thus, although in a very cursory and imperfect manner, I have endeavored to convey to you my conception of the poetic principle. It has been my purpose to suggest that, while this principle itself is, strictly and simply, the human

---

[4]*Stanzas to Augusta.*

aspiration for supernal beauty, the manifestation of the principle is always found in an elevating excitement of the soul—quite independent of that passion which is the intoxication of the heart—or of that truth which is the satisfaction of the reason. For, in regard to passion, alas! Its tendency is to degrade, rather than to elevate the soul. Love, on the contrary—love, the true, the divine Eros—the Uranian, as distinguished from the Dionaean Venus[5]—is unquestionably the purest and truest of all poetical themes. And in regard to truth—if, to be sure, through the attainment of a truth, we are led to perceive a harmony where none was apparent before, we experience, at once, the true poetical effect—but this effect is referable to the harmony alone, and not in the least degree to the truth which merely served to render the harmony manifest.

We shall reach, however, more immediately a distinct conception of what the true poetry is, by mere reference to a few of the simple elements which induce in the poet himself the true poetical effect. He recognizes the ambrosia which nourishes his soul, in the bright orbs that shine in heaven—in the volutes of the flower—in the clustering of low shrubberies—in the waving of the grain fields—in the slanting of tall, eastern trees—in the blue distance of mountains—in the grouping of clouds—in the twinkling of half-hidden brooks—in the gleaming of silver rivers—in the repose of sequestered lakes—in the star-mirroring depths of lonely wells. He perceives it in the songs of birds—in the harp of Aeolus—in the sighing of the night wind—in the repining voice of the forest—in the surf that complains to the shore—in the fresh breath of the woods—in the scent of the violet—in the voluptuous perfume of the hyacinth—in the sugges-

tive odor that comes to him, at eventide, from far-distant, undiscovered islands, over dim oceans, illimitable and unexplored. He owns it in all noble thoughts—in all unworldly motives—in all holy impulses—in all chivalrous, generous, and self-sacrificing deeds. He feels it in the beauty of woman—in the grace of her step—in the luster of her eye—in the melody of her voice—in her soft laughter—in her sigh—in the harmony of the rustling of her robes. He deeply feels it in her winning endearments—in her burning enthusiasms—in her gentle charities—in her meek and devotional endurances—but above all—ah, far above all—he kneels to it—he worships it in the faith, in the purity, in the strength, in the altogether divine majesty—of her love.

Let me conclude—by the recitation of yet another brief poem—one very different in character from any that I have before quoted. It is by Motherwell, and is called *The Song of the Cavalier.* With our modern and altogether rational ideas of the absurdity and impiety of warfare, we are not precisely in that frame of mind best adapted to sympathize with the sentiments, and thus to appreciate the real excellence of the poem. To do this fully, we must identify ourselves, in fancy, with the soul of the old cavalier.

> Then mount! Then mount, brave gallants, all,
>   And don your helms amaine:
> Death's couriers, fame and honor, call
>   Us to the field again.
> No shrewish tears shall fill our eye
>   When the sword hilt's in our hand—
> Heart-whole we'll part, and no whit sigh
>   for the fairest of the land;
> Let piping swain, and craven wight,
>   Thus weep and puling cry,
> Our business is like men to fight,
>   And herolike to die!

---

[5]Uranian and Dionaean Venuses represent spiritual and earthly love respectively.

Matthew Arnold

1822–1888

Arnold's Preface to the 1853 edition of his *Poems* reflects a particular brand of moralistic criticism. It is neo-Aristotelian in the relationship it finds between poem and audience and in its emphasis on "action." The essay seems also to be a precursor of some of the critical attitudes of Eliot.

In a later essay, *The Function of Criticism at the Present Time* (1864), Arnold's outlook is not so restricted, and he treats literary criticism as an important branch of criticism in general. In all branches of knowledge the aim of the critical power is the same: "to see the object as in itself it really is." This requires freeing oneself from polemics, refusing to "remain in a sphere where alone narrow and relative conceptions have any worth and validity." Arnold remarks that this is the difficult and indirect path, but it is the only possible one, for criticism must be "disinterested." It must be an "endeavor to learn and propagate the best that is known and thought in the world."

In advocating disinterested criticism, Arnold is censuring the parochialism of English critics, their ignorance of European intellectual life, their special brand of "Philistinism." The disinterest that he preaches has a not too distant relationship to the idea of aesthetic disinterest in Kant's analysis of the reader's response to the work of art. Arnold, however, sees this state as one that the critic must *bring to* the work, not simply attain to in its contemplation. Arnold is not suggesting a withdrawal from effective social criticism but instead insisting on measured, intelligent, and often necessarily indirect critical activity.

Though he rejected a number of Victorian ideas or fashions, Arnold was nevertheless very influential. In an age marked by the emergence of historical criticism, he argues in *The Study of Poetry* against historical judgments on poems. He also rejects what he calls "personal judgments" on grounds similar to those later set forth by Richards. But when he comes to the question of what sort of critical judgment ought to be made, he is in difficulty. He knows that poetry is not simply document or material for generating subjective emotion. But to discuss its value analytically is impossible. The value of a poem must simply be recognized. Arnold is fond of terms like *poetic truth* and *high seriousness* (in his view Chaucer lacks the latter). His method in *The Study of Poetry* is not to define these terms but instead to offer poetic examples of them—"touchstones." These touchstones can be as short as a single line. Like several of his Romantic predecessors, Arnold thinks not so much of the quality of a poem as a whole as he does of the presence of an undefinable poetic quality somewhere in a poem. There is no discursively expressible standard for these touchstones, and the catch-all evaluative term *high seriousness* is not explained. An educated reader is supposed to sense the presence of high seriousness. The critical power grows as the result of a liberal education. Sound critical judgments are made by educated people, not by those who make a mindless application of principle or method.

Following Arnold, one might at first think criticism doomed to become (1) purely descriptive or (2) purely expressive, pointing to, but not discussing, specimens of high seriousness. But this view misses Arnold's point that one must finally depend on the developed taste and erudition of the critic. In the 1864 essay, where Arnold speaks of "judging" as the critic's business, he points out that it must be "judgment which almost insensibly forms itself in a fair and clear mind, along with fresh knowledge." It is by "communicating fresh knowledge," not mere information, and not by laying down laws and judgments that the critic performs his most useful task. Arnold thus seeks to avoid both criticism that is really scholarship ancillary to the poem and subjective impressionism that is really poetic writing about poems—the method of Anatole France, for example.

Arnold is an interesting figure in the history of the problem of value judgments. He is also important for his development of the argument that the power of true judgment is cultivated and the sensibility enlarged through a liberal education that includes the reading of poetry.

The fifteen-volume edition of Arnold's works (1903–04), was followed by *Complete Prose Works,* edited by R. H. Super (1960ff.). Studies of Arnold include Lionel Trilling, *Matthew Arnold* (1939); E. K. Brown, *Arnold: A Study in Conflict* (1948); David Perkins, "Arnold and the Function of Literature," *English Literary History,* XVIII (1951), 287–309; J. S. Eells, *The Touchstones of Matthew Arnold* (1955); William Robbins, *The Ethical Idealism of Matthew Arnold* (1959); D. G. James, *Matthew Arnold and the Decline of English Romanticism* (1961); William A. Madden, *Matthew Arnold: A Study of the Aesthetic Temperament in Victorian England* (1967); Park Honan, *Matthew Arnold: A Life* (1981); Joseph Carroll, *The Cultural Theory of Matthew Arnold* (1982); and Stefan Collini, *Arnold* (1988).

Preface to the 1853 Edition of *Poems*

In two small volumes of poems, published anonymously, one in 1849, the other in 1852, many of the poems which compose the present volume have already appeared. The rest are now published for the first time.

I have, in the present collection, omitted the poem from which the volume published in 1852 took its title.[1] I have done so, not because the subject of it was a Sicilian Greek born between two and three thousand years ago, although many persons would think this a sufficient reason. Neither have I done so because I had, in my own opinion, failed in the delineation which I intended to effect. I intended to delineate the feelings of one of the last of the Greek religious philosophers, one of the family of Orpheus and Musaeus, having survived his fellows, living on into a time when the habits of Greek thought and feeling had begun fast to change, character to dwindle, the influence of the Sophists to prevail. Into the feelings of a man so situated there are entered much that we are accustomed to consider as exclusively modern, how much, the fragments of Empedocles himself which remain to us are sufficient at least to indicate. What those who are familiar only with the great monuments of early Greek genius suppose to be its exclusive characteristics, have disappeared; the calm, the cheerfulness, the disinterested objectivity have disappeared; the dialogue of the mind with itself has commenced; modern problems have presented themselves; we hear already the doubts, we witness the discouragement, of Hamlet and of Faust.

The representations of such a man's feelings must be interesting, if consistently drawn. We all naturally take pleasure, says Aristotle, in any imitation or representation

---

PREFACE TO THE *Poems.*
[1] Arnold is referring to his dramatic poem *Empedocles on Etna.*

whatever:[2] this is the basis of our love of poetry: and we take pleasure in them, he adds, because all knowledge is naturally agreeable to us; not to the philosopher only, but to mankind at large. Every representation therefore which is consistently drawn may be supposed to be interesting, inasmuch as it gratifies this natural interest in knowledge of all kinds. What is *not* interesting, is that which does not add to our knowledge of any kind; that which is vaguely conceived and loosely drawn; a representation which is general, indeterminate, and faint, instead of being particular, precise, and firm.

Any accurate representation may therefore be expected to be interesting; but, if the representation be a poetical one, more than this is demanded. It is demanded, not only that it shall interest, but also that it shall inspirit and rejoice the reader: that it shall convey a charm, and infuse delight. For the Muses, as Hesiod says, were born that they might be "a forgetfulness of evils, and a truce from cares":[3] and it is not enough that the poet should add to the knowledge of men, it is required of him also that he should add to their happiness. "All art," says Schiller, "is dedicated to joy, and there is no higher and no more serious problem, than how to make men happy. The right art is that alone, which creates the highest enjoyment."[4]

A poetical work, therefore, is not yet justified when it has been shown to be an accurate, and therefore interesting representation; it has to be shown also that it is a representation from which men can derive enjoyment. In presence of the most tragic circumstances, represented in a work of art, the feeling of enjoyment, as is well known, may still subsist: the representation of the most utter calamity, of the liveliest anguish, is not sufficient to destroy it: the more tragic the situation, the deeper becomes the enjoyment; and the situation is more tragic in proportion as it becomes more terrible.

What then are the situations, from the representation of which, though accurate, no poetical enjoyment can be derived? They are those in which the suffering finds no vent in action; in which a continuous state of mental distress is prolonged, unrelieved by incident, hope, or resistance; in which there is everything to be endured, nothing to be done. In such situations there is inevitably something morbid, in the description of them something monotonous. When they occur in actual life, they are painful, not tragic; the representation of them in poetry is painful also.

To this class of situations, poetically faulty as it appears to me, that of Empedocles, as I have endeavored to represent him, belongs; and I have therefore excluded the poem from the present collection.

And why, it may be asked, have I entered into this explanation respecting a matter so unimportant as the admission or exclusion of the poem in question? I have done so, because I was anxious to avow that the sole reason for its exclusion was that which has been stated above; and that it has not been excluded in deference to the opinion which many critics of the present day appear to entertain against subjects chosen from distant times and countries: against the choice, in short, of any subjects but modern ones.

"The poet," it is said, and by an intelligent critic, "the poet who would really fix the public attention must leave the exhausted past, and draw his subjects from matters of present import, and *therefore* both of interest and novelty."[5]

Now this view I believe to be completely false. It is worth examining, inasmuch as it is a fair sample of a class of critical dicta everywhere current at the present day, having a philosophical form and air, but no real basis in fact; and which are calculated to vitiate the judgment of readers of poetry, while they exert, so far as they are adopted, a misleading influence on the practice of those who make it.

What are the eternal objects of poetry, among all nations and at all times? They are actions; human actions; possessing an inherent interest in themselves, and which are to be communicated in an interesting manner by the art of the poet. Vainly will the latter imagine that he has everything in his own power; that he can make an intrinsically inferior action equally delightful with a more excellent one by his treatment of it: he may indeed compel us to admire his skill, but his work will possess, within itself, an incurable defect.

The poet, then, has in the first place to select an excellent action; and what actions are the most excellent? Those, certainly, which most powerfully appeal to the great primary human affections: to those elementary feelings which subsist permanently in the race, and which are independent of time. These feelings are permanent and the same; that which interests them is permanent and the same also. The modernness or antiquity of an action, therefore, has nothing to do with its fitness for poetical representation; this depends upon its inherent qualities. To the elementary part of our nature, to our passions, that which is great and passionate is eternally interesting; and interesting solely in proportion to its greatness and to its passion. A great human action of a thousand years ago is more interesting to it than a smaller human action of today, even though upon the representation of this last the

---

[2]*Poetics*, IV. 2–5, p. 51.
[3]*Theogony*, 55.
[4]Preface to *The Bride of Messina*.

[5][Arnold] In *The Spectator* of April 2, 1853. The words quoted were not used with reference to poems of mine.

most consummate skill may have been expended, and though it has the advantage of appealing by its modern language, familiar manners, and contemporary allusions, to all our transient feelings and interests. These, however, have no right to demand of a poetical work that it shall satisfy them; their claims are to be directed elsewhere. Poetical works belong to the domain of our permanent passions: let them interest these, and the voice of all subordinate claims upon them is at once silenced.

Achilles, Prometheus, Clytemnestra, Dido—what modern poem presents personages as interesting, even to us moderns, as these personages of an "exhausted past"? We have the domestic epic dealing with the details of modern life, which pass daily under our eyes; we have poems representing modern personages in contact with the problems of modern life, moral, intellectual, and social; these works have been produced by poets the most distinguished of their nation and time; yet I fearlessly assert that *Hermann and Dorothea, Childe Harold, Jocelyn,* the *Excursion,* leave the reader cold in comparison with the effect produced upon him by the latter books of the *Iliad,* by the *Oresteia,* or by the episode of Dido. And why is this? Simply because in the three last-named cases the action is greater, the personages nobler, the situations more intense: and this is the true basis of the interest in a poetical work, and this alone.

It may be urged, however, that past actions may be interesting in themselves, but that they are not to be adopted by the modern poet, because it is impossible for him to have them clearly present to his own mind, and he cannot therefore feel them deeply, nor represent them forcibly. But this is not necessarily the case. The externals of a past action, indeed, he cannot know with the precision of a contemporary; but his business is with its essentials. The outward man of Oedipus or of Macbeth, the houses in which they lived, the ceremonies of their courts, he cannot accurately figure to himself; but neither do they essentially concern him. His business is with their inward man; with their feelings and behavior in certain tragic situations, which engage their passions as men; these have in them nothing local and casual; they are as accessible to the modern poet as to a contemporary.

The date of an action, then, signifies nothing: the action itself, its selection and construction, this is what is all-important. This the Greeks understood far more clearly than we do. The radical difference between their poetical theory and ours consists, as it appears to me, in this: that, with them, the poetical character of the action in itself, and the conduct of it, was the first consideration; with us, attention is fixed mainly on the value of the separate thoughts and images which occur in the treatment of an action. They regarded the whole; we regard the parts. With them, the action predomi-

nated over the expression of it; with us, the expression predominates over the action. Not that they failed in expression, or were inattentive to it; on the contrary, they are the highest models of expression, the unapproached masters of the *grand style:* but their expression is so excellent because it is so admirably kept in its right degree of prominence; because it is so simple and so well subordinated; because it draws its force directly from the pregnancy of the matter which it conveys. For what reason was the Greek tragic poet confined to so limited a range of subjects? Because there are so few actions which united in themselves, in the highest degree, the conditions of excellence; and it was not thought that on any but an excellent subject could an excellent poem be constructed. A few actions, therefore, eminently adapted for tragedy, maintained almost exclusive possession of the Greek tragic stage. Their significance appeared inexhaustible; they were as permanent problems, perpetually offered to the genius of every fresh poet. This too is the reason of what appears to us moderns a certain baldness of expression in Greek tragedy; of the triviality with which we often reproach the remarks of the chorus, where it takes part in the dialogue: that the action itself, the situation of Orestes, or Merope, or Alcmaeon, was to stand the central point of interest, unforgotten, absorbing, principal; that no accessories were for a moment to distract the spectator's attention from this, that the tone of the parts was to be perpetually kept down, in order not to impair the grandiose effect of the whole. The terrible old mythic story on which the drama was founded stood, before he entered the theater, traced in its bare outlines upon the spectator's mind; it stood in his memory, as a group of statuary, faintly seen, at the end of a long and dark vista: then came the poet, embodying outlines, developing situations, not a word wasted, not a sentiment capriciously thrown in: stroke upon stroke, the drama proceeded: the light deepened upon the group; more and more it revealed itself to the riveted gaze of the spectator: until at last, when the final words were spoken, it stood before him in broad sunlight, a model of immortal beauty.

This was what a Greek critic demanded; this was what a Greek poet endeavored to effect. It signified nothing to what time an action belonged. We do not find that the *Persae* occupied a particularly high rank among the dramas of Aeschylus because it represented a matter of contemporary interest: this was not what a cultivated Athenian required. He required that the permanent elements of his nature should be moved; and dramas of which the action, though taken from a long-distant mythic time, yet was calculated to accomplish this in a higher degree than that of the *Persae,* stood higher in his estimation accordingly. The Greeks felt, no doubt, with their exquisite sagacity of taste, that an action of present times was too near them, too much mixed up with what was accidental and passing, to form a sufficiently grand, detached, and self-subsistent object for a tragic poem. Such objects belonged to the domain of the comic poet, and of the lighter kinds of poetry. For the more serious kinds, for "pragmatic" poetry, to use an excellent expression of Polybius, they were more difficult and severe in the range of subjects which they permitted. Their theory and practice alike, the admirable treatise of Aristotle, and the unrivaled works of their poets, exclaim with a thousand tongues—"All depends upon the subject; choose a fitting action, penetrate yourself with the feeling of its situations; this done, everything else will follow."

But for all kinds of poetry alike there was one point on which they were rigidly exacting; the adaptability of the subject to the kind of poetry selected, and the careful construction of the poem.

How different a way of thinking from this is ours! We can hardly at the present day understand what Menander meant, when he told a man who inquired as to the progress of his comedy that he had finished it, not having yet written a single line, because he had constructed the action of it in his mind. A modern critic would have assured him that the merit of his piece depended on the brilliant things which arose under his pen as he went along. We have poems which seem to exist merely for the sake of single lines and passages; not for the sake of producing any total impression. We have critics who seem to direct their attention merely to detached expressions, to the language about the action, not to the action itself. I verily think that the majority of them do not in their hearts believe that there is such a thing as a total impression to be derived from a poem at all, or to be demanded from a poet; they think the term a commonplace of metaphysical criticism. They will permit the poet to select any action he pleases, and to suffer that action to go as it will, provided he gratifies them with occasional bursts of fine writing, and with a shower of isolated thoughts and images. That is, they permit him to leave their poetical sense ungratified, provided that he gratifies their rhetorical sense and their curiosity. Of his neglecting to gratify these, there is little danger; he needs rather to be warned against the danger of attempting to gratify these alone; he needs rather to be perpetually reminded to prefer his action to everything else; so to treat this, as to permit its inherent excellences to develop themselves, without interruption from the intrusion of his personal peculiarities: most fortunate when he most entirely succeeds in effacing himself, and in enabling a noble action to subsist as it did in nature.

But the modern critic not only permits a false practice: he absolutely prescribes false aims. "A true allegory of the state of one's own mind in a representative history," the poet is told, "is perhaps the highest thing that one can attempt in the way of poetry." And accordingly he attempts it. An allegory of the state of one's own mind, the highest problem of an art which imitates actions! No assuredly, it is not, it never can be so: no great poetical work has ever been produced with such an aim. *Faust* itself, in which something of the kind is attempted, wonderful passages as it contains, and in spite of the unsurpassed beauty of the scenes which relate to Margaret, *Faust* itself, judged as a whole, and judged strictly as a poetical work, is defective: its illustrious author, the greatest poet of modern times, the greatest critic of all times, would have been the first to acknowledge it; he only defended his work, indeed, by asserting it to be "something incommensurable."[6]

The confusion of the present time is great, the multitude of voices counseling different things bewildering, the number of existing works capable of attracting a young writer's attention and of becoming his models, immense: what he wants is a hand to guide him through the confusion, a voice to prescribe to him the aim which he should keep in view, and to explain to him that the value of the literary works which offer themselves to his attention is relative to their power of helping him forward on his road toward this aim. Such a guide the English writer at the present day will nowhere find. Failing this, all that can be looked for, all indeed that can be desired, is, that his attention should be fixed on excellent models; that he may reproduce, at any rate, something of their excellence, by penetrating himself with their works and by catching their spirit, if he cannot be taught to produce what is excellent independently.

Foremost among these models for the English writer stands Shakespeare: a name the greatest perhaps of all poetical names; a name never to be mentioned without reverence. I will venture, however, to express a doubt whether the influence of his works, excellent and fruitful for the readers of poetry, for the great majority, has been an unmixed advantage to the writers of it. Shakespeare indeed chose excellent subjects—the world could afford no better than *Macbeth,* or *Romeo and Juliet,* or *Othello:* he had no theory respecting the necessity of choosing subjects of present import, or the paramount interest attaching to allegories of the state of one's own mind; like all great poets, he knew well what constituted a poetical action; like them, wherever he found such an action, he took it; like them, too, he found his best in past times. But to these general characteristics of all great poets he added a special one of his own; a gift, namely, of happy, abundant, and ingenious expression, eminent and unrivaled; so eminent as irresistibly to strike the attention first in him

---

[6]See Goethe, *Conversations with Eckermann,* p. 531.

and even to throw into comparative shade his other excellences as a poet. Here has been the mischief. These other excellences were his fundamental excellences *as a poet;* what distinguishes the artist from the mere amateur, says Goethe, is *architectonicè* in the highest sense; that power of execution which creates, forms, and constitutes: not the profoundness of single thoughts, not the richness of imagery, not the abundance of illustration. But these attractive accessories of a poetical work being more easily seized than the spirit of the whole, and these accessories being possessed by Shakespeare in an unequaled degree, a young writer having recourse to Shakespeare as his model runs great risk of being vanquished and absorbed by them, and, in consequence, of reproducing, according to the measure of his power, these, and these alone. Of this preponderimg quality of Shakespeare's genius, accordingly, almost the whole of modern English poetry has, it appears to me, felt the influence. To the exclusive attention on the part of his imitators to this, it is in a great degree owing that of the majority of modern poetical works the details alone are valuable, the composition worthless. In reading them one is perpetually reminded of that terrible sentence on a modern French poet—*"il dit tout ce qu'il veut, mais malheureusement il n'a rien à dire."*[7]

Let me give an instance of what I mean. I will take it from the works of the very chief among those who seem to have been formed in the school of Shakespeare; of one whose exquisite genius and pathetic death render him forever interesting. I will take the poem of *Isabella, or the Pot of Basil,* by Keats. I choose this rather than the *Endymion,* because the latter work (which a modern critic has classed with the *Faerie Queene!*), although undoubtedly there blows through it the breath of genius, is yet as a whole so utterly incoherent, as not strictly to merit the name of a poem at all. The poem of *Isabella,* then, is a perfect treasurehouse of graceful and felicitous words and images: almost in every stanza there occurs one of those vivid and picturesque turns of expression, by which the object is made to flash upon the eye of the mind, and which thrill the reader with a sudden delight. This one short poem contains, perhaps, a greater number of happy single expressions which one could quote than all the extant tragedies of Sophocles. But the action, the story? The action in itself is an excellent one; but so feebly is it conceived by the poet, so loosely constructed, that the effect produced by it, in and for itself, is absolutely null. Let the reader, after he has finished the poem of Keats, turn to the same story in the *Decameron:* he will then feel how pregnant and interesting the same action has become in the hands

of a great artist, who above all things delineates his object; who subordinates expression to that which it is designed to express.

I have said that the imitators of Shakespeare, fixing their attention on his wonderful gift of expression, have directed their imitation to this, neglecting his other excellences. These excellences, the fundamental excellences of poetical art, Shakespeare no doubt possessed them—possessed many of them in a splendid degree; but it may perhaps be doubted whether even he himself did not sometimes give scope to his faculty of expression to the prejudice of a higher poetical duty. For we must never forget that Shakespeare is the great poet he is from his skill in discerning and firmly conceiving an excellent action, from his power of intensely feeling a situation, of intimately associating himself with a character; not from his gift of expression, which rather even leads him astray, degenerating sometimes into a fondness for curiosity of expression, into an irritability of fancy, which seems to make it impossible for him to say a thing plainly, even when the press of the action demands the very directest language, or its level character the very simplest. Mr. Hallam, than whom it is impossible to find a saner and more judicious critic, has had the courage (for at the present day it needs courage) to remark, how extremely and faultily difficult Shakespeare's language often is. It is so: you may find main scenes in some of his greatest tragedies, *King Lear,* for instance, where the language is so artificial, so curiously tortured, and so difficult, that every speech has to be read two or three times before its meaning can be comprehended. This overcuriousness of expression is indeed but the excessive employment of a wonderful gift—of the power of saying a thing in a happier way than any other man; nevertheless, it is carried so far that one understands what M. Guizot meant when he said that Shakespeare appears in his language to have tried all styles except that of simplicity. He has not the severe and scrupulous self-restraint of the ancients, partly, no doubt, because he had a far less cultivated and exacting audience. He has indeed a far wider range than they had, a far richer fertility of thought; in this respect he rises above them. In his strong conception of his subject, in the genuine way in which he is penetrated with it, he resembles them, and is unlike the moderns. But in the accurate limitation of it, the conscientious rejection of superfluities, the simple and rigorous development of it from the first line of his work to the last, he falls below them, and comes nearer to the moderns. In his chief works, besides what he has of his own, he has the elementary soundness of the ancients; he has their important action and their large and broad manner; but he has not their purity of method. He is therefore a less safe model; for what he has of his own is personal, and inseparable from

---

[7] "He says all that he wishes, but unhappily he has nothing to say."

his own rich nature; it may be imitated and exaggerated, it cannot be learned or applied as an art. He is above all suggestive; more valuable, therefore, to young writers as men than as artists. But clearness of arrangement, rigor of development, simplicity of style—these may to a certain extent be learned: and these may, I am convinced, be learned best from the ancients, who, although infinitely less suggestive than Shakespeare, are thus, to the artist, more instructive.

What then, it will be asked, are the ancients to be our sole models? The ancients with their comparatively narrow range of experience, and their widely different circumstances? Not, certainly, that which is narrow in the ancients, nor that in which we can no longer sympathize. An action like the action of the *Antigone* of Sophocles, which turns upon the conflict between the heroine's duty to her brother's corpse and that to the laws of her country, is no longer one in which it is possible that we should feel a deep interest. I am speaking too, it will be remembered, not of the best sources of intellectual stimulus for the general reader, but of the best models of instruction for the individual writer. This last may certainly learn of the ancients, better than anywhere else, three things which it is vitally important for him to know: the all-importance of the choice of a subject; the necessity of accurate construction; and the subordinate character of expression. He will learn from them how unspeakably superior is the effect of the one moral impression left by a great action treated as a whole, to the effect produced by the most striking single thought or by the happiest image. As he penetrates into the spirit of the great classical works, as he becomes gradually aware of their intense significance, their noble simplicity, and their calm pathos, he will be convinced that it is this effect, unity and profoundness of moral impression, at which the ancient poets aimed; that it is this which constitutes the grandeur of their works, and which makes them immortal. He will desire to direct his own efforts towards producing the same effect. Above all, he will deliver himself from the jargon of modern criticism, and escape the danger of producing poetical works conceived in the spirit of the passing time, and which partake of its transitoriness.

The present age makes great claims upon us: we owe it service, will not be satisfied without our admiration. I know not how it is, but their commerce with the ancients appears to me to produce, in those who constantly practice it, a steadying and composing effect upon their judgment, not of literary works only, but of men and events in general. They are like persons who have had a very weighty and impressive experience; they are more truly than others under the empire of facts, and more independent of the language current among those with whom they live. They wish neither to applaud nor to revile their age: they wish to know what it is, what it can give them, and whether this is what they want. What they want, they know very well; they want to educe and cultivate what is best and noblest in themselves: they know, too, that this is no easy task—χαλεπόν as Pittacus said, χαλεπόν ἐσθλόν ἔμμεναι[8]—and they ask themselves sincerely whether their age and its literature can assist them in the attempt. If they are endeavoring to practice any art, they remember the plain and simple proceedings of the old artists, who attained their grand results by penetrating themselves with some noble and significant action, not by inflating themselves with a belief in the preeminent importance and greatness of their own times. They do not talk of their mission, nor of interpreting their age, nor of the coming poet; all this, they know, is the mere delirium of vanity; their business is not to praise their age, but to afford to the men who live in it the highest pleasure which they are capable of feeling. If asked to afford this by means of subjects drawn from the age itself, they ask what special fitness the present age has for supplying them. They are told that it is an era of progress, an age commissioned to carry out the great ideas of industrial development and social amelioration. They reply that with all this they can do nothing; that the elements they need for the exercise of their art are great actions, calculated powerfully and delightfully to affect what is permanent in the human soul; that so far as the present age can supply such actions, they will gladly make use of them; but that an age wanting in moral grandeur can with difficulty supply such, and an age of spiritual discomfort with difficulty be powerfully and delightfully affected by them.

A host of voices will indignantly rejoin that the present age is inferior to the past neither in moral grandeur nor in spiritual health. He who possesses the discipline I speak of will content himself with remembering the judgments passed upon the present age, in this respect, by the men of strongest head and widest culture whom it has produced; by Goethe and by Niebuhr. It will be sufficient for him that he knows the opinions held by these two great men respecting the present age and its literature; and that he feels assured in his own mind that their aims and demands upon life were such as he would wish, at any rate, his own to be; and their judgments as to what is impeding and disabling such as he may safely follow. He will not, however, maintain a hostile attitude towards the false pretensions of his age; he will content himself with not being overwhelmed by them. He will esteem himself fortunate if he can succeed in banishing from his

---

[8]"It is difficult to be noble." Pittacus (seventh century B.C.) was one of the so-called Seven Sages of Greece.

mind all feelings of contradiction, and irritation, and impatience; in order to delight himself with the contemplation of some noble action of a heroic time, and to enable others, through his representation of it, to delight in it also.

I am far indeed from making any claim, for myself, that I possess this discipline; or for the following poems, that they breathe its spirit. But I say, that in the sincere endeavor to learn and practice, amid the bewildering confusion of our times, what is sound and true in poetical art, I seemed to myself to find the only sure guidance, the only solid footing, among the ancients. They, at any rate, knew what they wanted in art, and we do not. It is this uncertainty which is disheartening, and not hostile criticism. How often have I felt this when reading words of disparagement or of cavil: that it is the uncertainty as to what is really to be aimed at which makes our difficulty, not the dissatisfaction of the critic, who himself suffers from the same uncertainty. *"Non me tua fervida terrent dicta . . . dii me terrent, et Jupiter hostis."*[9]

Two kinds of *dilettanti,* says Goethe, there are in poetry: he who neglects the indispensable mechanical part, and thinks he has done enough if he shows spirituality and feeling; and he who seeks to arrive at poetry merely by mechanism, in which he can acquire an artisan's readiness, and is without soul and matter. And he adds, that the first does most harm to art, and the last to himself. If we must be *dilettanti:* if it is impossible for us, under the circumstances amidst which we live, to think clearly, to feel nobly, and to delineate firmly: if we cannot attain to the mastery of the great artists—let us, at least, have so much respect for our art as to prefer it to ourselves. Let us not bewilder our successors: let us transmit to them the practice of poetry, with its boundaries and wholesome regulative laws, under which excellent works may again, perhaps, at some future time, be produced, not yet fallen into oblivion through our neglect, not yet condemned and canceled by the influence of their eternal enemy, caprice.

The Function of Criticism at the Present Time

Many objections have been made to a proposition which, in some remarks of mine on translating Homer, I ventured to put forth; a proposition about criticism and its importance at the present day. I said: "Of the literature of France and Germany, as of the intellect of Europe in general, the main effort, for now many years, has been a critical effort; the endeavor, in all branches of knowledge, theology, philosophy, history, art, science, to see the object as in itself it really is." I added, that owing to the operation in English literature of certain causes, "almost the last thing for which one would come to English literature is just that very thing which now Europe most desires—criticism"; and that the power and value of English literature was thereby impaired. More than one rejoinder declared that the importance I here assigned to criticism was excessive, and asserted the inherent superiority of the creative effort of the human spirit over its critical effort. And the other day, having been led by a Mr. Shairp's excellent notice of Wordsworth[1] to turn again to his biography, I found, in the words of this great man, whom I, for one, must always listen to with the profoundest respect, a sentence passed on the critic's business, which seems to justify every possible disparagement of it. Wordsworth says in one of his letters: "The writers in these publications [the reviews], while they prosecute their inglorious employment, cannot be supposed to be in a state of mind very favorable for being effected by the finer influences of a thing so pure as genuine poetry."[2] And a trustworthy reporter of his conversation quotes a more elaborate judgment to the some effect:

> Wordsworth holds the critical power very low, infinitely lower than the inventive; and he said today that if the quantity of time consumed in writing critiques on the works of others were given to original composition, of whatever kind it might be, it would be much better employed; it would make a man find out sooner his own level, and it would do infinitely less mischief. A false or malicious criticism may be much injury to the minds of others, a stupid invention, either in prose or verse, is quite harmless.[3]

---

[1]J. C. Shairp, Scots critic, wrote "Wordsworth: The Man and Poet," *North British Review,* XLI (1864). [Arnold] I cannot help thinking that a practice, common in England during the last century, and still followed in France, of printing a notice of this kind—a notice by a competent critic—to serve as an introduction to an eminent author's works, might be revived among us with advantage. To introduce all succeeding editions of Wordsworth, Mr. Shairp's notice might, it seems to me, excellently serve; it is written from the point of view of an admirer, nay, of a disciple, and that is right; but then the disciple must be also, as in this case he is, a critic, a man of letters, not, as too often happens, some relation or friend with no qualification for his task except affection for his author.
[2]Letter to Bernard Barton (1816) in Christopher Wordsworth, *Memoirs of William Wordsworth,* II (1851), 51.
[3]W. Knight, *Life of Wordsworth,* III (1889), 438.

It is almost too much to expect of poor human nature, that a man capable of producing some effect in one line of literature, should, for the greater good of society, voluntarily doom himself to impotence and obscurity in another. Still less is this to be expected from men addicted to the composition of the "false or malicious criticism" of which Wordsworth speaks. However, everybody would admit that a false or malicious criticism had better never have been written. Everybody, too, would be willing to admit, as a general proposition, that the critical faculty is lower than the inventive. But is it true that criticism is really, in itself, a baneful and injurious employment; is it true that all time given to writing critiques on the works of others would be much better employed if it were given to original composition, of whatever kind this may be? Is it true that Johnson had better have gone on producing more *Irenes* instead of writing his *Lives of the Poets;* nay, is it certain that Wordsworth himself was better employed in making his *Ecclesiastical Sonnets* than when he made his celebrated Preface, so full of criticism, and criticism of the works of others? Wordsworth was himself a great critic, and it is to be sincerely regretted that he has not left us more criticism; Goethe was one of the greatest of critics, and we may sincerely congratulate ourselves that he has left us so much criticism. Without wasting time over the exaggeration which Wordsworth's judgment on criticism clearly contains, or over an attempt to trace the causes—not difficult, I think, to be traced—which may have led Wordsworth to this exaggeration, a critic may with advantage seize an occasion for trying his own conscience, and for asking himself of what real service at any given moment the practice of criticism either is or may be made to his own mind and spirit, and to the minds and spirits of others.

The critical power is of lower rank than the creative. True; but in assenting to this proposition, one or two things are to be kept in mind. It is undeniable that the exercise of a creative power, that a free creative activity, is the highest function of man; it is proved to be so by man's finding in it his true happiness. But it is undeniable, also, that men may have the sense of exercising this free creative activity in other ways than in producing great works of literature or art; if it were not so, all but a very few men would be shut out from the true happiness of all men. They may have it in well-doing, they may have it in learning, they may have it even in criticizing. This is one thing to be kept in mind. Another is, that the exercise of the creative power in the production of great works of literature or art, however high this exercise of it may rank, is not at all epochs and under all conditions possible; and that therefore labor may be vainly spent in attempting it, which might with more fruit be used in preparing for it, in rendering it possible. This creative power works

with elements, with materials; what if it has not those materials, those elements, ready for its use? In that case it must surely wait till they are ready. Now, in literature—I will limit myself to literature, for it is about literature that the question arises—the elements with which the creative power works are ideas; the best ideas on every matter which literature touches, current at the time. At any rate we may lay it down as certain that in modern literature no manifestation of the creative power not working with these can be very important or fruitful. And I say *current* at the time, not merely accessible at the time; for creative literary genius does not principally show itself in discovering new ideas, that is rather the business of the philosopher. The grand work of literary genius is a work of synthesis and exposition, not of analysis and discovery; its gift lies in the faculty of being happily inspired by a certain intellectual and spiritual atmosphere, by a certain order of ideas, when it finds itself in them; of dealing divinely with these ideas, presenting them in the most effective and attractive combinations,—making beautiful works with them, in short. But it must have the atmosphere, it must find itself amidst the order of ideas, in order to work freely; and these it is not so easy to command. This is why great creative epochs in literature are so rare, this is why there is so much that is unsatisfactory in the productions of many men of real genius; because, for the creation of a masterwork of literature two powers must concur, the power of the man and the power of the moment, and the man is not enough without the moment; the creative power has, for its happy exercise, appointed elements, and those elements are not in its own control.

Nay, they are more within the control of the critical power. It is the business of the critical power, as I said in the words already quoted, "in all branches of knowledge, theology, philosophy, history, art, science, to see the object as in itself it really is." Thus it tends, at last, to make an intellectual situation of which the creative power can profitably avail itself. It tends to establish an order of ideas, if not absolutely true, yet true by comparison with that which it displaces; to make the best ideas prevail. Presently these new ideas reach society, the touch of truth is the touch of life, and there is a stir and growth everywhere; out of this stir and growth come the creative epochs of literature.

Or, to narrow our range, and quit these considerations of the general march of genius and of society—considerations which are apt to become too abstract and impalpable—everyone can see that a poet, for instance, ought to know life and the world before dealing with them in poetry; and life and the world being in modern times very complex things, the creation of a modern poet, to be worth much, implies a great critical effort behind it; else it must be a comparatively poor, barren, and short-lived affair. This is why Byron's poetry had so little endurance in it, and Goethe's so much, both Byron and Goethe had a great productive power, but Goethe's was nourished by a great critical effort providing the true materials for it, and Byron's was not; Goethe knew life and the world, the poet's necessary subjects, much more comprehensively and thoroughly than Byron. He knew a great deal more of them, and he knew them much more as they really are.

It has long seemed to me that the burst of creative activity in our literature, through the first quarter of this century, had about it in fact something premature; and that from this cause its productions are doomed, most of them, in spite of the sanguine hopes which accompanied and do still accompany them to prove hardly more lasting than the productions of far less splendid epochs. And this prematureness comes from its having proceeded without having its proper data, without sufficient materials to work with. In other words, the English poetry of the first quarter of this century, with plenty of energy, plenty of creative force, did not know enough. This makes Byron so empty of matter, Shelley so incoherent, Wordsworth even, profound as he is, yet so wanting in completeness and variety. Wordsworth cared little for books, and disparaged Goethe. I admire Wordsworth, as he is, so much that I cannot wish him different; and it is vain, no doubt, to imagine such a man different from what he is, to suppose that he *could* have been different. But surely the one thing wanting to make Wordsworth an even greater poet than he is—his thought richer, and his influence of wider application—was that he should have read more books, among them, no doubt, those of that Goethe whom he disparaged without reading him.

But to speak of books and reading may easily lead to a misunderstanding here. It was not really books and reading that lacked to our poetry at this epoch; Shelley had plenty of reading, Coleridge had immense reading. Pindar and Sophocles—as we all say so glibly, and often with so little discernment of the real import of what we are saying—had not many books; Shakespeare was no deep reader. True; but in the Greece of Pindar and Sophocles, in the England of Shakespeare, the poet lived in a current of ideas in the highest degree animating and nourishing to the creative power; society was, in the fullest measure, permeated by fresh thought, intelligent and alive. And this state of things is the true basis for the creative power's exercise, in this it finds its data, its materials, truly ready for its hand; all the books and reading in the world are only valuable as they are helps to this. Even when this does not actually exist, books and reading may enable a man to construct a kind of semblance of it in his own mind, a world of knowledge and intelligence in which he may live and work. This is by no means an equivalent to the artist for the nationally diffused life and thought of the epochs of Sophocles or Shakespeare; but besides that it may be a means of preparation for such epochs, it does really constitute, if many share in it, a quickening and sustaining atmosphere of great value. Such an atmosphere the many-sided learning and the long and widely combined critical effort of Germany formed for Goethe, when he lived and worked. There was no national glow of life and thought there as in the Athens of Pericles or the England of Elizabeth. That was the poet's weakness. But there was a sort of equivalent for it in the complete culture and unfettered thinking of a large body of Germans. That was his strength. In the England of the first quarter of this century there was neither a national glow of life and thought, such as we had in the age of Elizabeth, nor yet a culture and a force of learning and criticism such as were to be found in Germany. Therefore the creative power of poetry wanted, for success in the highest sense, materials and a basis; a thorough interpretation of the world was necessarily denied to it.

At first sight it seems strange that out of the immense stir of the French Revolution and its age should not have come a crop of works of genius equal to that which came out of the stir of the great productive time of Greece, or out of that of the Renaissance, with its powerful episode the Reformation. But the truth is that the stir of the French Revolution took a character which essentially distinguished it from such movements as these. These were, in the main, disinterestedly intellectual and spiritual movements; movements in which the human spirit looked for its satisfaction in itself and in the increased play of its own activity. The French Revolution took a political, practical character. The movement, which went on in France under the old regime from 1700 to 1789, was far more really akin than that of the Revolution itself to the movement of the Renaissance; the France of Voltaire and Rousseau told far more powerfully upon the mind of Europe than the France of the Revolution. Goethe reproached this last expressly with having "thrown quiet culture back." Nay, and the true key to how much in our Byron, even in our Wordsworth, is this!—that they had their source in a great movement of feeling, not in a great movement of mind. The French Revolution, however—that object of so much blind love and so much blind hatred—found undoubtedly its motive power in the intelligence of men, and not in their practical sense; this is what distinguishes it from the English Revolution of Charles the First's time. This is what makes it a more spiritual event than our Revolution, an event of much more powerful and worldwide interest, though practically less successful; it appeals to an order of ideas which are universal, certain, permanent. 1789 asked of a thing, is it rational? 1642 asked of a thing, is it legal? Or, when it went furthest, is it according to conscience? This is the English fashion, a fashion to be treated, within its own sphere, with the highest respect; for its success, within its own sphere, has been prodigious. But what is law in one place is not law in another; what is law here today is not law even here tomorrow; and as for conscience, what is binding on one man's conscience is not binding on another's: The old woman who threw her stool at the head of the surpliced minister in St. Giles' Church at Edinburgh[4] obeyed an impulse to which millions of the human race may be permitted to remain strangers. But the prescriptions of reason are absolute, unchanging, of universal validity; "to count by tens is the easiest way of counting"—that is a proposition of which everyone, from here to the Antipodes, feels the force; at least I should say so if we did not live in a country where it is not impossible that any morning we may find a letter in the *Times* declaring that a decimal coinage is an absurdity. That a whole nation should have been penetrated with an enthusiasm for pure reason, and with an ardent zeal for making its prescriptions triumph, is a very remarkable thing, when we consider how little of mind, or anything so worthy and quickening as mind, comes into the motives which alone, in general, impel great masses of men. In spite of the extravagant direction given to this enthusiasm, in spite of the crimes and follies in which it lost itself, the French Revolution derives from the force, truth, and universality of the ideas which it took for its law, and from the passion with which it could inspire a multitude for these ideas, a unique and still living power; it is—it will probably long remain—the greatest, the most animating event in history. And as no sincere passion for the things of the mind, even though it turn out in many respects an unfortunate passion, is ever quite thrown away and quite barren of good, France has reaped from hers one fruit—the natural and legitimate fruit though not precisely the grand fruit she expected: she is the country in Europe where *the people* is most alive.

But the mania for giving an immediate political and practical application to all these fine ideas of the reason was fatal. Here an Englishman is in his element: on this theme we can all go on for hours. And all we are in the habit of saying on it has undoubtedly a great deal of truth. Ideas cannot be too much prized in and for themselves, cannot be too much lived with; but to transport them abruptly into the world of politics, and practice, violently to revolutionize this world to their bidding—that is quite another thing. There is

the world of ideas and there is the world of practice; the French are often for suppressing the one and the English the other; but neither is to be suppressed. A member of the House of Commons said to me the other day: "That a thing is an anomaly, I consider to be no objection to it whatever." I venture to think he was wrong; that a thing is an anomaly *is* an objection to it, but absolutely and in the sphere of ideas: it is not necessarily, under such-and-such circumstances, or at such-and-such a moment, an objection to it in the sphere of politics and practice. Joubert has said beautifully: *"C'est la force et le droit qui règlent toutes choses dans le monde; la force en attendant le droit."* (Force and right are the governors of this world; force till right is ready.)[5] "Force till right is ready"; and till right is ready, force, the existing order of things, is justified, is the legitimate ruler. But right is something moral, and implies inward recognition, free assent of the will; we are not ready for right—"right," so far as we are concerned, "is not ready,"—until we have attained this sense of seeing it and willing it. The way in which for us it may change and transform force, the existing order of things, and become, in its turn, the legitimate ruler of the world, should depend on the way in which, when our time comes, we see it and will it. Therefore for other people enamored of their own newly discerned right, to attempt to impose it upon us as ours, and violently to substitute their right for our force, is an act of tyranny, and to be resisted. It sets at naught the second great half of our maxim, "force till right is ready." This was the grand error of the French Revolution; and its movement of ideas, by quitting the intellectual sphere and rushing furiously into the political sphere, ran, indeed, a prodigious and memorable course, but produced no such intellectual fruit as the movement of ideas of the Renaissance, and created, in opposition to itself, what I may call an epoch of concentration. The great force of that epoch of concentration was England; and the great voice of that epoch of concentration was Burke. It is the fashion to treat Burke's writings on the French Revolution as superannuated and conquered by the event; as the eloquent but unphilosophical tirades of bigotry and prejudice. I will not deny that they are often disfigured by the violence and passion of the moment, and that in some directions Burke's view was bounded, and his observation therefore at fault. But on the whole, and for those who can make the needful corrections, what distinguishes these writings is their profound, permanent, fruitful, philosophical truth. They contain the true philosophy of an epoch of concentration, dissipate the heavy atmosphere

---

[4]In 1637 there was an effort at St. Giles' to read the new service prescribed by Charles I for Scotland.

[5]*Pensées,* I (1869), 178.

which its own nature is apt to engender round it, and make its resistance rational instead of mechanical.

But Burke is so great because, almost alone in England, he brings thought to bear upon politics, he saturates politics with thought. It is his accident that his ideas were at the service of an epoch of concentration, not of an epoch of expansion; it is his characteristic that he so lived by ideas, and had such a source of them welling up within him, that he could float even an epoch of concentration and English Tory politics with them. It does not hurt him that Dr. Price and the Liberals were enraged with him; it does not even hurt him that George the Third and the Tories were enchanted with him. His greatness is that he lived in a world which neither English Liberalism nor English Toryism is apt to enter;—the world of ideas, not the world of catchwords and party habits. So far is it from being really true of him that he "to party gave up what was meant for mankind," that at the very end of his fierce struggle with the French Revolution after all his invectives against its false pretensions, hollowness, and madness, with his sincere conviction of its mischievousness, he can close a memorandum on the best means of combating it, some of the last pages he ever wrote—the *Thoughts on French Affairs,* in December 1791—with these striking words:

> The evil is stated, in my opinion, as it exists. The remedy must be where power, wisdom, and information, I hope, are more united with good intentions than they can be with me. I have done with this subject, I believe, forever. It has given me many anxious moments for the last two years. *If a great change is to be made in human affairs, the minds of men will be fitted to it; the general opinions and feelings will draw that way. Every fear, every hope will forward it; and then they who persist in opposing this mighty current in human affairs, will appear rather to resist the decrees of Providence itself, than the mere designs of men. They will not be resolute and firm, but perverse and obstinate.*

That return of Burke upon himself has always seemed to me one of the finest things in English literature, or indeed in any literature. That is what I call living by ideas: when one side of a question has long had your earnest support, when all your feelings are engaged, when you hear all around you no language but one, when your party talks this language like a steam engine and can imagine no other—still to be able to think, still to be irresistibly carried, if so it be, by the current of thought to the opposite side of the question, and,

like Balaam, to be unable to speak anything but what the Lord has put in your mouth. I know nothing more striking, and I must add that I know nothing more un-English.

For the Englishman in general is like my friend the Member of Parliament, and believes, pointblank, that for a thing to be an anomaly is absolutely no objection to it whatever. He is like the Lord Auckland of Burke's day, who, in a memorandum on the French Revolution, talks of "certain miscreants, assuming the name of philosophers, who have presumed themselves capable of establishing a new system of society." The Englishman has been called a political animal, and he values what is political and practical so much that ideas easily becomes objects of dislike in his eyes, and thinkers "miscreants," because ideas and thinkers have rashly meddled with politics and practice. This would be all very well if the dislike and neglect confined themselves to ideas transported out of their own sphere, and meddling rashly with practice; but they are inevitably extended to ideas as such, and to the whole life of intelligence; practice is everything, a free play of the mind is nothing. The notion of the free play of the mind upon all subjects being a pleasure in itself, being an object of desire, being an essential provider of elements without which a nation's spirit, whatever compensations it may have for them, must, in the long run, die of inanition, hardly enters into an Englishman's thoughts. It is noticeable that the word *curiosity,* which in other languages is used in a good sense, to mean, as a high and fine quality of man's nature, just this disinterested love of a free play of the mind on all subjects, for its own sake—it is noticeable, I say, that this word has in our language no sense of the kind, no sense but a rather bad and disparaging one. But criticism, real criticism is essentially the exercise of this very quality. It obeys an instinct prompting it to try to know the best that is known and thought in the world, irrespectively of practice, politics, and everything of the kind; and to value knowledge and thought as they approach this best, without the intrusion of any other considerations whatever. This is an instinct for which there is, I think, little original sympathy in the practical English nature, and what there was of it has undergone a long benumbing period of blight and suppression in the epoch of concentration which followed the French Revolution.

But epochs of concentration cannot well endure forever; epochs of expansion, in the due course of things, follow them. Such an epoch of expansion seems to be opening in this country. In the first place all danger of a hostile forcible pressure of foreign ideas upon our practice has long disappeared; like the traveler in the fable, therefore, we begin to wear our cloak a little more loosely. Then, with a long peace, the ideas of Europe steal gradually and amicably in, and mingle, though in infinitesimally small quantities at a time, with our own notions. Then, too, in spite of all that is said about the absorbing and brutalizing influence of our passionate material progress, it seems to me indisputable that this progress is likely, though not certain, to lead in the end to an apparition of intellectual life; and that man, after he has made himself perfectly comfortable and has now to determine what to do with himself next, may begin to remember that he has a mind, and that the mind may be made the source of great pleasure. I grant it is mainly the privilege of faith, at present, to discern this end to our railways, our business, and our fortune-making; but we shall see if, here as elsewhere, faith is not in the end the true prophet. Our ease, our traveling, and our unbounded liberty to hold just as hard and securely as we please to the practice to which our notions have given birth, all tend to beget an inclination to deal a little more freely with these notions themselves, to canvas them a little, to penetrate a little into their real nature. Flutterings of curiosity, in the foreign sense of the word, appear amongst us, and it is in these that criticism must look to find its account. Criticism first; a time of true creative activity, perhaps—which, as I have said, must inevitably be preceded amongst us by a time of criticism—hereafter, when criticism has done its work.

It is of the last importance that English criticism should clearly discern what rule for its course, in order to avail itself of the field now opening to it, and to produce fruit for the future, it ought to take. The rule may be summed up in one word—*disinterestedness.* And how is criticism to show disinterestedness? By keeping aloof from what is called "the practical view of things;" by resolutely following the law of its own nature, which is to be a free play of the mind on all subjects which it touches. By steadily refusing to lend itself to any of those ulterior, political, practical considerations about ideas, which plenty of people will be sure to attach to them, which perhaps ought often to be attached to them, which in this country at any rate are certain to be attached to them quite sufficiently, but which criticism has really nothing to do with. Its business is, as I have said, simply to know the best that is known and thought in the world, and by in its turn making this known, to create a current of true and fresh ideas. Its business is to do this with inflexible honesty, with due ability; but its business is to do no more, and to leave alone all questions of practical consequences and applications, questions which will never fail to have due prominence given to them. Else criticism, besides being really false to its own nature, merely continues in the old rut which it has hitherto followed in this country, and will certainly miss the chance now given to it. For what is at present the bane of criticism in this country? It is that practical consid-

erations cling to it and stifle it. It subserves interests not its own. Our organs of criticism are organs of men and parties having practical ends to serve, and with them those practical ends are the first thing and the play of mind the second; so much play of mind as is compatible with the prosecution of those practical ends is all that is wanted. An organ like the *Revue des Deux Mondes,* having for its main function to understand and utter the best that is known and thought in the world, existing, it may be said, as just an organ for a free play of the mind, we have not. But we have the *Edinburgh Review,* existing as an organ of the old Whigs, and for as much play of the mind as may suit its being that; we have the *Quarterly Review,* existing as an organ of the Tories, and for as much play of mind as may suit its being that; we have the *British Quarterly Review,* existing as an organ of the political Dissenters, and for as much play of mind as may suit its being that; we have the *Times,* existing as an organ of the common, satisfied, well-to-do Englishman, and for as much play of mind as may suit its being that. And so on through all the various factions, political and religious, of our society; every faction has, as such, its organs of criticism, but the notion of combining all factions in the common pleasure of a free disinterested play of mind meets with no favor. Directly this play of mind wants to have more scope, and to forget the pressure of practical considerations a little, it is checked, it is made to feel the chain. We saw this the other day in the extinction, so much to be regretted, of the *Home and Foreign Review.* Perhaps in no organ of criticism in this country was there so much knowledge, so much play of mind; but these could not save it. The *Dublin Review* subordinates play of mind to the practical business of English and Irish Catholicism, and lives. It must needs be that men should act in sects and parties, that each of these sects and parties should have its organ, and should make this organ subserve the interests of its action; but it would be well, too, that there should be a criticism, not the minister of these interests, not their enemy but absolutely and entirely independent of them. No other criticism will ever attain any real authority or make any real ways towards its end—the creating a current of true and fresh ideas.

It is because criticism has so little kept in the pure intellectual sphere, has so little detached itself from practice, has been so directly polemical and controversial, that it has so ill accomplished, in this country, its best spiritual work; which is to keep man from a self-satisfaction which is retarding and vulgarizing, to lead him towards perfection, by making his mind dwell upon what is excellent in itself, and the absolute beauty and fitness of things. A polemical practical criticism makes men blind even to the ideal imperfection of their practice, makes them willingly assert its ideal perfection, in order the better to secure it against attack: and clearly this is narrowing and baneful for them. If they were reassured on the practical side, speculative considerations of ideal perfection they might be brought to entertain, and their spiritual horizon would thus gradually widen. Sir Charles Adderley says to the Warwickshire farmers:

> Talk of the improvement of breed! Why, the race we ourselves represent, the men and women, the old Anglo-Saxon race, are the best breed in the whole world. . . . The absence of a too enervating climate, too unclouded skies, and a too luxurious nature, has produced so vigorous a race of people and has rendered us so superior to all the world.

Mr. Roebuck says to the Sheffield cutlers:

> I look around me and ask what is the state of England? Is not property safe? Is not every man able to say what he likes? Can you not walk from one end of England to the other in perfect security? I ask you whether, the world over or in past history, there is anything like it? Nothing. I pray that our unrivaled happiness may last.

Now obviously there is a peril for poor human nature in words and thoughts of such exuberant self-satisfaction, until we find ourselves safe in the streets of the celestial city. *"Das wenige verschwindet leicht dem Blicke / Der vorwärts sieht, wie viel noch übrig bleibt"* says Goethe; "the little that is done seems nothing when we look forward and see how much we have yet to do."[6] Clearly this is a better line of reflection for weak humanity, so long as it remains on this earthly field of labor and trial.

But neither Sir Charles Adderley nor Mr. Roebuck is by nature inaccessible to considerations of this sort. They only lose sight of them owing to the controversial life we all lead, and the practical form which all speculation takes with us. They have in view opponents whose aim is not ideal, but practical; and in their zeal to uphold their own practice against these innovators, they go so far as even to attribute to this practice an ideal perfection. Somebody has been wanting to introduce a six-pound franchise, or to abolish church rates, or to collect agricultural statistics by force, or to diminish local self-government. How natural, in reply to such proposals, very likely improper or ill timed, to go a little beyond the mark and to say stoutly, "Such a race of people as we stand, so superior to all the world! The old Anglo-Saxon race, the best breed in the whole world! I pray that our unrivaled happiness may last! I ask you whether, the world over or in past history, there is anything like it?" And so long as criticism answers this dithyramb by insisting that the old Anglo-Saxon race would be still more superior to all others if it had no church rates, or that our unrivaled happiness would last yet longer with a six-pound franchise, so long will the strain, "the best breed in the whole world!" swell louder and louder, everything ideal and refining will be lost out of sight, and both the assailed and their critics will remain in a sphere, to say the truth, perfectly unvital, a sphere in which spiritual progression is impossible. But let criticism leave church rates and the franchise alone, and in the most candid spirit, without a single lurking thought of practical innovation, confront with our dithyramb this paragraph on which I stumbled in a newspaper immediately after reading Mr. Roebuck: "A shocking child murder has just been committed at Nottingham. A girl named Wragg left the workhouse there on Saturday morning with her young illegitimate child. The child was soon afterwards found dead on Mapperly Hills, having been strangled. Wragg is in custody."

Nothing but that; but, in juxtaposition with the absolute eulogies of Sir Charles Adderley and Mr. Roebuck, how eloquent, how suggestive are those few lines! "Our old Anglo-Saxon breed, the best in the whole world!" How much that is harsh and ill favored there is in this best! *Wragg!* If we are to talk of ideal perfection of "the best in the whole world," has any one reflected what a touch of grossness in our race, what an original shortcoming in the more delicate spiritual perceptions, is shown by the natural growth amongst us of such hideous names—Higginbottom, Stiggins, Bugg! In Ionia and Attica they were luckier in this respect than "the best race in the world"; by the Ilissus there was no Wragg, poor thing! And "our unrivaled happiness"—what an element of grimness, bareness, and hideousness mixes with it and blurs it; the workhouse, the dismal Mapperly Hills—how dismal those who have seen them will remember—the gloom, the smoke, the cold, the strangled illegitimate child! "I ask you whether, the world over or in past history, there is anything like it?" Perhaps not, one is inclined to answer; but at any rate, in that case, the world is very much to be pitied. And the final touch—short, bleak and inhuman: "Wragg is in custody." The sex lost in the confusion of our unrivaled happiness; or (shall I say?) the superfluous Christian name lopped off by the straightforward vigor of our old Anglo-Saxon breed! There is profit for the spirit in such contrasts as this; criticism serves the cause of perfection by establishing them. By eluding sterile conflict, by refusing to remain in the sphere where alone narrow and relative con-

---

[6]*Iphigenia in Tauris,* I. ii. 91–92.

ceptions have any worth and validity, criticism may diminish its momentary importance, but only in this way has it a chance of gaining admittance for those wider and more perfect conceptions to which all its duty is really owed. Mr. Roebuck will have a poor opinion of an adversary who replies to his defiant songs of triumph only by murmuring under his breath, "Wragg is in custody"; but in no other way will these songs of triumph be induced gradually to moderate themselves, to get rid of what in them is excessive and offensive, and to fall into a softer and truer key.

It will be said that it is a very subtle and indirect action which I am thus prescribing for criticism, and that, by embracing in this manner the Indian virtue of detachment and abandoning the sphere of practical life, it condemns itself to a slow and obscure work. Slow and obscure it may be, but it is the only proper work of criticism. The mass of mankind will never have any ardent zeal for seeing things as they are; very inadequate ideas will always satisfy them. On these inadequate ideas reposes, and must repose, the general practice of the world. That is as much as saying that whoever sets himself to see things as they are will find himself one of a very small circle; but it is only by this small circle resolutely doing its own work that adequate ideas will ever get current at all. The rush and roar of practical life will always have a dizzying and attracting effect upon the most collected spectator, and tend to draw him into its vortex; most of all will this be the case where that life is so powerful as it is in England. But it is only by remaining collected, and refusing to lend himself to the point of view of the practical man, that the critic can do the practical man any service; and it is only by the greatest sincerity in pursuing his own course, and by at last convincing even the practical man of his sincerity, that he can escape misunderstandings which perpetually threaten him.

For the practical man is not apt for fine distinctions, and yet in these distinctions truth and the highest culture greatly find their account. But it is not easy to lead a practical man—unless you reassure him as to your practical intentions, you have no chance of leading him—to see a thing which he has always been used to look at from one side only, which he greatly values, and which, looked at from that side, quite deserves, perhaps, all the prizing and admiring which he bestows upon it—that this thing, looked at from another side, may appear must less beneficent and beautiful, and yet retain all its claims to our practical allegiance. Where shall we find language innocent enough, how shall we make the spotless purity of our intentions evident enough, to enable us to say to the political Englishman that the British Constitution itself, which, seen from the practical side, looks such a magnificent organ of progress and virtue, seen from the specula-

tive side—with its compromises, its love of facts, its horror of theory, its studied avoidance of clear thoughts—that, seen from this side, our august Constitution sometimes looks—forgive me, shade of Lord Somers!—a colossal machine for the manufacture of Philistines? How is Cobbett to say this and not be misunderstood, blackened as he is with the smoke of a lifelong conflict in the field of political practice? How is Mr. Carlyle to say it and not be misunderstood, after his furious raid into this field with his *Latter-day Pamphlets?* How is Mr. Ruskin, after his pugnacious political economy? I say, the critic must keep out of the region of immediate practice in the political, social, humanitarian sphere, if he wants to make a beginning for that more free speculative treatment of things, which may perhaps one day make its benefits felt even in this sphere, but in a natural and thence irresistible manner.

Do what he will, however, the critic will still remain exposed to frequent misunderstandings, and nowhere so much as in this country. For here people are particularly indisposed even to comprehend that without this free disinterested treatment of things, truth and the highest culture are out of the question. So immersed are they in practical life, so accustomed to take all their notions from this life and its processes, that they are apt to think that truth and culture themselves can be reached by the processes of this life, and that it is an impertinent singularity to think of reaching them in any other. "We are all *terrae filii*,"[7] cries their eloquent advocate; "all Philistines together. Away with the notion of proceeding by any other course than the course dear to the Philistines; let us have a social movement, let us organize and combine a party to pursue truth and new thought, let us call it 'the liberal party,' and let us all stick to each other, and back each other up. Let us have no nonsense about independent criticism, and intellectual delicacy, and the few and the many. Don't let us trouble ourselves about foreign thought; we shall invent the whole thing for ourselves as we go along. If one of us speaks well, applaud him; if one of us speaks ill, applaud him too; we are all in the same movement, we are all liberals, we are all in pursuit of truth." In this way the pursuit of truth becomes really a social, practical, pleasurable affair, almost requiring a chairman, a secretary, and advertisements; with the excitement of an occasional scandal, with a little resistance to give the happy sense of difficulty overcome; but, in general, plenty of bustle and very little thought. To act is so easy, as Goethe says: to think is so hard! It is true that the critic has many temptations to go with the stream, to make one of the party movement, one of these

---

[7]"Sons of earth."

terrae filli; it seems ungracious to refuse to be a *terrae filius,* when so many excellent people are; but the critic's duty is to refuse, or, if resistance is vain, at least to cry with Obermann: *"Périssons en résistant."*[8]

How serious a matter it is to try and resist, I had ample opportunity of experiencing when I ventured some time ago to criticize the celebrated first volume of Bishop Colenso.[9] The echoes of the storm which was then raised I still, from time to time, hear grumbling around me. That storm arose out of a misunderstanding almost inevitable. It is a result of no little culture to attain to a clear perception that science and religion are two wholly different things. The multitude will forever confuse them; but happily that is of no great real importance, for while the multitude imagines itself to live by its false science, it does really live by its true religion. Dr. Colenso, however, in his first volume did all he could to strengthen the confusion,[10] and to make it dangerous. He did this with the best intentions, I freely admit, and with the most candid ignorance that this was the natural effect of what he was doing; but, says Joubert, "Ignorance, which in matters of morals extenuates the crime, is itself, in intellectual matters, a crime of the first order."[11] I criticized Bishop Colenso's speculative confusion. Immediately there was a cry raised: "What is this? Here is a liberal attacking a liberal. Do not you belong to the movement? Are not you a friend of truth? Is not Bishop Colenso in pursuit of truth? Then speak with proper respect of his book. Dr. Stanley[12] is another friend of truth, and you speak with proper respect of his book; why make these invidious differences? Both books are excellent, admirable, liberal; Bishop Colenso's perhaps the most so, because it is the boldest, and will have the best practical consequences for the liberal cause. Do you want to encourage to the attack of a brother liberal his, and your, and our implacable enemies, the *Church and State Review* or the *Record*—the High Church rhinoceros and the Evangelical hyena? Be silent, therefore; or rather speak, speak as loud as ever you can! And go into ecstasies over the eighty and odd pigeons."

But criticism cannot follow this coarse and indiscriminate method. It is unfortunately possible for a man in pursuit of truth to write a book which reposes upon a false conception. Even the practical consequences of a book are to genuine criticism no recommendation of it, if the book is, in the highest sense, blundering. I see that a lady[13] who herself, too, is in pursuit of truth, and who writes with great ability, but a little too much, perhaps, under the influence of the practical spirit of the English liberal movement, classes Bishop Colenso's book and M. Renan's[14] together, in her survey of the religious state of Europe, as facts of the same order, works, both of them, of "great importance"; "great ability, power, and skill"; Bishop Colenso's, perhaps, the most powerful; at least, Miss Cobbe gives special expression to her gratitude that to Bishop Colenso "has been given the strength to grasp, and the courage to teach, truths of such deep import." In the same way, more than one popular writer has compared him to Luther. Now it is just this kind of false estimate which the critical spirit is, it seems to me, bound to resist. It is really the strongest possible proof of the low ebb at which, in England, the critical spirit is, that while the critical hit in the religious literature of Germany is Dr. Strauss's book,[15] in that of France M. Renan's book, of Bishop Colenso is the critical hit in the religious literature of England. Bishop Colenso's book reposes on a total misconception of the essential element of the religious problem, as that problem is now presented for solution. To criticism, therefore, which seeks to have the best that is known and thought on this problem, it is, however well meant, of no importance whatever. M. Renan's book attempts a new synthesis of the elements furnished to us by the four gospels. It attempts, in my opinion, a synthesis, perhaps premature, perhaps impossible, certainly not successful. Up to the present time, at any rate, we must acquiesce in Fleury's sentence on such recastings of the Gospel story: *"Quiconque s'imagine la pouvoir mieux écrire, ne l'entend pas."*[16] M. Renan had himself passed by anticipation a like sentence on his own work, when he said: "If a new presentation of the character of Jesus were offered to me, I would not have it; its very clearness would be, in my opinion, the best proof of its insufficiency." His friends may

---

[8]"Let us perish resisting." Étienne Pivert de Senancour, *Obermann.*

[9][Arnold] So sincere is my dislike to all personal attack and controversy, that I abstain from reprinting, at this distance of time from the occasion which called them forth, the essays in which I criticized Dr. Colenso's book; I feel bound, however, after all that has passed, to make here a final declaration of my sincere impenitence for having published them. Nay, I cannot forbear repeating yet once more, for his benefit and that of his readers, this sentence from my original remarks upon him: "There is truth of science and truth of religion: truth of science does not become truth of religion till it is made religious." And I will add: Let us have all the science there is from the men of science; from the men of religion let us have religion. [Arnold thought John William Colenso's *Pentateuch and Book of Joshua Critically Examined* (1863), superficial. He criticized it in "The Bishop and the Philosopher," *Macmillan's Magazine* (January 1863).]

[10][Arnold] It has been said I make it "a crime against literary criticism and the higher culture to attempt to inform the ignorant." Need I point out that the ignorant are not informed by being confirmed in a confusion?

[11]*Pensées,* I (1869), 311.

[12]Arthur P. Stanley. Arnold had compared his *The Bible: Its Form and Substance* (1863) favorably to Colenso's.

[13]Frances Power Cobbe. Arnold is referring to her *Broken Lights* (1864).

[14]*The Life of Jesus* (1863) by Ernest Renan.

[15]*Life of Jesus* (1835) by David Friedrich Strauss.

[16]"Whoever imagines that he can write it better, does not understand it."

with perfect justice rejoin that at the sight of the Holy Land, and of the actual scene of the Gospel story, all the current of M. Renan's thoughts may have naturally changed, and a new casting of that story irresistibly suggested itself to him; and that this is just a case for applying Cicero's maxim: Change of mind is not inconsistency—*"nemo doctus unquam muta-tionem consilii inconstantiam dixit esse."*[17] Nevertheless, for criticism, M. Renan's first thought must still be the truer one, as long as his new casting so fails more fully to commend itself, more fully (to use Coleridge's happy phrase about the Bible[18]) to *find* us. Still M. Renan's attempt is, for criticism, of the most real interest and importance, since, with all its difficulty, a fresh synthesis of the New Testament data—not a making war on them, in Voltaire's fashion, not a leaving them out of mind, in the world's fashion, but the putting a new construction upon them, the taking them from under the old, traditional, conventional point of view and placing them under a new one—is the very essence of the religious prob-lem, as now presented; and only by efforts in this direction can it receive a solution.

Again, in the same spirit in which she judges Bishop Colenso, Miss Cobbe, like so many earnest liberals of our practical race, both here and in America, herself sets vigor-ously about a positive reconstruction of religion, about mak-ing a religion of the future out of hand, or at least setting about making it. We must not rest, she and they are always thinking and saying, in negative criticism, we must be crea-tive and constructive; hence we have such works as her re-cent *Religious Duty,* and works still more considerable, per-haps, by others, which will be in everyone's mind. These works often have much ability; they often spring out of sin-cere convictions, and a sincere wish to do good; and they sometimes, perhaps, do good. Their fault is (if I may be per-mitted to say so) one which they have in common with the British College of Health, in the New Road. Everyone knows the British College of Health; it is that building with the lion and the statue of the Goddess Hygeia before it; at least I am sure about the lion, though I am not absolutely certain about the Goddess Hygeia. This building does credit, perhaps, to the resources of Dr. Morrison and his disciples; but it falls a good deal short of one's idea of what a British College of Health ought to be. In England, where we hate public inter-ference and love individual enterprise, we have a whole crop of places like the British College of Health; the grand name without the grand thing. Unluckily, creditable to individual enterprise as they are, they tend to impair our taste by mak-ing us forget what more grandiose, noble, or beautiful char-acter properly belongs to a public institution. The same may be said of the religions of the future of Miss Cobbe and oth-ers. Creditable, like the British College of Health, to the re-sources of their authors, they yet tend to make us forget what more grandiose, noble, or beautiful character properly be-longs to religious constructions. The historic religions, with all their faults, have had this; it certainly belongs to the reli-gious sentiment, when it truly flowers, to have this; and we impoverish our spirit if we allow a religion of the future without it. What then is the duty of criticism here? To take the practical point of view, to applaud the liberal movement and all its works—its New Road religions of the future into the bargain—for their general utility's sake? By no means; but to be perpetually dissatisfied with these works, while they perpetually fall short of a high and perfect ideal.

For criticism, these are elementary laws; but they never can be popular, and in this country they have been very little followed, and one meets with immense obstacles in follow-ing them. That is a reason for asserting them again and again. Criticism must maintain its independence of the practical spirit and its aims. Even with well-meant efforts of the prac-tical spirit it must express dissatisfaction, if in the sphere of the ideal they seem impoverishing and limiting. It must not hurry on to the goal because of its practical importance. It must be patient, and know how to wait; and flexible, and know how to attach itself to things and how to withdraw from them. It must be apt to study and praise elements that for the fullness of spiritual perfection are wanted, even though they belong to a power which in the practical sphere may be maleficent. It must be apt to discern the spiritual shortcomings or illusions of powers that in the practical sphere may be beneficent. And this without any notion of favoring or injuring, in the practical sphere, one power or the other; without any notion of playing off, in this sphere, one power against the other. When one looks, for instance, at the English divorce court—an institution which perhaps has its practical conveniences, but which in the ideal sphere is so hideous; an institution which neither makes divorce impos-sible nor makes it decent, which allows a man to get rid of his wife, or a wife of her husband, but makes them drag one another first, for the public edification, through a mire of unutterable infamy—when one looks at this charming insti-tution, I say, with its crowded trials, its newspaper reports, and its money compensations, this institution in which the gross unregenerate British Philistine has indeed stamped an image of himself—one may be permitted to find the mar-riage theory of Catholicism refreshing and elevating. Or when Protestantism, in virtue of its supposed rational and intellectual origin, gives the law to criticism too magisteri-

---

[17]"No learned man has said it to be inconsistent to change his mind." *Letters to Atticus,* XV. 7.

[18]In his *Confessions of an Inquiring Spirit.*

ally, criticism may and must remind it that its pretensions, in this respect, are illusive and do it harm; that the Reformation was a moral rather than an intellectual event; that Luther's theory of grace no more exactly reflects the mind of the spirit than Bossuet's philosophy of history reflects it;[19] and that there is no more antecedent probability of the Bishop of Durham's stock of ideas being agreeable to perfect reason than of Pope Pius the Ninth's. But criticism will not on that account forget the achievements of Protestantism in the practical and moral sphere; nor that, even in the intellectual sphere, Protestantism, though in a blind and stumbling manner, carried forward the Renaissance, while Catholicism threw itself violently across its path.

I lately heard a man of thought and energy contrasting the want of ardor and movement which he now found amongst young men in this country with what he remembered in his own youth, twenty years ago. "What reformers we were then!" he exclaimed; "what a zeal we had! How we canvassed every institution in Church and State, and were prepared to remodel them all on first principles!" He was inclined to regret, as a spiritual flagging, the lull which he saw. I am disposed rather to regard it as a pause in which the turn to a new mode of spiritual progress is being accomplished. Everything was long seen, by the young and ardent amongst us, in inseparable connection with politics and practical life. We have pretty well exhausted the benefits of seeing things in this connection, we have got all that can be got by so seeing them. Let us try a more disinterested mode of seeing them; let us betake ourselves more to the serener life of the mind and spirit. This life, too, may have its excesses and dangers; but they are not for us at present. Let us think of quietly enlarging our stock of true and fresh ideas, and not, as soon as we get an idea or half an idea, be running out with it into the street, and trying to make it rule there. Our ideas will, in the end, shape the world all the better for maturing a little. Perhaps in fifty years' time it will in the English House of Commons be an objection to an institution that it is an anomaly, and my friend the Member of Parliament will shudder in his grave. But let us in the meanwhile rather endeavor that in twenty years' time it may, in English literature, be an objection to a proposition that it is absurd. That will be a change so vast, that the imagination almost fails to grasp it. *"Ab integro saeclorum nascitur ordo."*[20]

If I have insisted so much on the course which criticism must take where politics and religion are concerned, it is because, where these burning matters are in question, it is most likely to go astray. I have wished, above all, to insist on the attitude which criticism should adopt towards things in general; on its right tone and temper of mind. But then comes another question as to the subject matter which literary criticism should most seek. Here, in general, its course is determined for it by the idea which is the law of its being; the idea of a disinterested endeavor to learn and propagate the best that is known and thought in the world, and thus to establish a current of fresh and true ideas. By the very nature of things, as England is not all the world, much of the best that is known and thought in the world cannot be of English growth, must be foreign; by the nature of things, again, it is just this that we are least likely to know, while English thought is streaming in upon us from all sides, and takes excellent care that we shall not be ignorant of its existence. The English critic of literature, therefore, must dwell much on foreign thought, and with particular heed on any part of it, which, while significant and fruitful in itself, is for any reason specially likely to escape him. Again, judging is often spoken of as the critic's one business, and so in some sense it is; but the judgment which almost insensibly forms itself in a fair and clear mind, along with fresh knowledge, is the valuable one; and thus knowledge, and ever fresh knowledge, must be the critic's great concern for himself. And it is by communicating fresh knowledge, and letting his own judgment pass along with it—but insensibly, and in the second place, not the first, as a sort of companion and clue, not as an abstract lawgiver—that the critic will generally do most good to his readers. Sometimes, no doubt, for the sake of establishing an author's place in literature, and his relation to a central standard (and if this is not done, how are we to get at our "best in the world"?) criticism may have to deal with a subject matter so familiar that fresh knowledge is out of the question, and then it must be all judgment; an enunciation and detailed application of principles. Here the great safeguard is never to let oneself become abstract, always to retain an intimate and lively consciousness of the truth of what one is saying, and, the moment this fails us, to be sure that something is wrong. Still, under all circumstances, this mere judgment and application of principles is, in itself, not the most satisfactory work to the critic; like mathematics, it is tautological, and cannot well give us, like fresh learning, the sense of creative activity.

But stop, someone will say; all this talk is of no practical use to us whatever; this criticism of yours is not what we have in our minds when we speak of criticism; when we speak of critics and criticism, we mean critics and criticism of the current English literature of the day; when you offer to tell criticism its function, it is to this criticism that we expect you to address yourself. I am sorry for it, for I am afraid I must disappoint these expectations. I am bound by my own

---

[19]In his *Discourse on Universal History* (1681), Jacques Bossuet explains history as divinely guided to the benefit of Catholicism.
[20]"Order is born from the renewal of generations." Virgil, *Eclogues*, IV. 5.

definition of criticism: "a disinterested endeavor to learn and propagate the best that is known and thought in the world." How much of current English literature comes into this "best that is known and thought in the world"? Not very much I fear; certainly less, at this moment, than of the current literature of France or Germany. Well, then, am I to alter my definition of criticism, in order to meet the requirements of a number of practicing English critics, who, after all, are free in their choice of a business? That would be making criticism lend itself just to one of those alien practical considerations, which, I have said, are so fatal to it. One may say, indeed, to those who have to deal with the mass—so much better disregarded—of current English literature, that they may at all events endeavor, in dealing with this, to try it, so far as they can, by the standard of the best that is known and thought in the world; one may say, that to get anywhere near this standard, every critic should try and possess one great literature, at least, besides his own; and the more unlike his own, the better. But, after all, the criticism I am really concerned with—the criticism which alone can much help us for the future, the criticism which, throughout Europe, is at the present day meant, when so much stress is laid on the importance of criticism and the critical spirit—is a criticism which regards Europe as being, for intellectual and spiritual purposes, one great confederation, bound to a joint action and working to a common result; and whose members have, for their proper outfit, a knowledge of Greek, Roman, and Eastern antiquity, and of one another. Special, local, and temporary advantages being put out of account, that modern nation will in the intellectual and spiritual sphere make most progress, which most thoroughly carries out this program. And what is that but saying that we too, all of us, as individuals, the more thoroughly we carry it out, shall make the more progress?

There is so much inviting us! What are we to take? What will nourish us in growth towards perfection? That is the question which, with the immense field of life and of literature lying before him, the critic has to answer; for himself first, and afterwards for others. In this idea of the critic's business the essays brought together in the following pages have had their origin; in this idea, widely different as are their subjects, they have, perhaps, their unity.

I conclude with what I said at the beginning: to have the sense of creative activity is the great happiness and the great proof of being alive, and it is not denied to criticism to have it; but then criticism must be sincere, simple, flexible, ardent, ever widening its knowledge. Then it may have, in no contemptible measure, a joyful sense of creative activity; a sense which a man of insight and conscience will prefer to what he might derive from a poor, starved, fragmentary, inadequate creation. And at some epochs no other creation is possible.

Still, in full measure, the sense of creative activity belongs only to genuine creation; in literature we must never forget that. But what true man of letters ever can forget it? It is no such common matter for a gifted nature to come into possession of a current of true and living ideas, and to produce amidst the inspiration of them, that we are likely to underrate it. The epochs of Aeschylus and Shakespeare make us feel their preeminence. In an epoch like those is, no doubt, the true life of literature; there is the promised land, towards which criticism can only beckon. That promised land it will not be ours to enter, and we shall die in the wilderness: but to have desired to enter it, to have saluted it from afar, is already, perhaps, the best distinction among contemporaries; it will certainly be the best title to esteem with posterity.

From

The Study of Poetry

The future of poetry is immense, because in poetry, where it is worthy of its high destinies, our race, as time goes on, will find an ever surer and surer stay. There is not a creed which is not shaken, not an accredited dogma which is not shown to be questionable, not a received tradition which does not threaten to dissolve. Our religion has materialized itself in the fact, in the supposed fact; it has attached its emotion to the fact, and now the fact is failing it. But for poetry the idea is everything; the rest is a world of illusion, of divine illusion. Poetry attaches its emotion to the idea; the idea *is* the fact. The strongest part of our religion today is its unconscious poetry.[1]

Let me be permitted to quote these words of my own, as uttering the thought which should, in my opinion, go with us and govern us in all our study of poetry. In the present work it is the course of one great contributory stream to the world river of poetry that we are invited to follow. We are here invited to trace the stream of English poetry. But whether we set ourselves, as here, to follow only one of the several streams that make the mighty river of poetry, or whether we seek to know them all, our governing thought should be the same. We should conceive of poetry worthily, and more highly than it has been the custom to conceive of

---

THE STUDY OF POETRY. Arnold's *Study of Poetry* was first published in 1880. The selection reprinted here represents approximately the first half of the essay.
[1]Introduction to *The Hundred Greatest Men.*

it. We should conceive of it as capable of higher uses, and called to higher destinies, than those which in general men have assigned to it hitherto. More and more mankind will discover that we have to turn to poetry to interpret life for us, to console us, to sustain us. Without poetry, our science will appear incomplete; and most of what now passes with us for religion and philosophy will be replaced by poetry. Science, I say, will appear incomplete without it. For finely and truly does Wordsworth call poetry "the impassioned expression which is in the countenance of all science"; and what is a countenance without its expression? Again, Wordsworth finely and truly calls poetry "the breath and finer spirit of all knowledge";[2] our religion, parading evidences such as those on which the popular mind relies now; our philosophy, pluming itself on its reasonings about causation and finite and infinite being; what are they but the shadows and dreams and false shows of knowledge? The day will come when we shall wonder at ourselves for having trusted to them, for having taken them seriously; and the more we perceive their hollowness, the more we shall prize "the breath and finer spirit of knowledge" offered to us by poetry.

But if we conceive thus highly of the destinies of poetry, we must also set our standard for poetry high, since poetry, to be capable of fulfilling such high destinies, must be poetry of a high order of excellence. We must accustom ourselves to a high standard and to a strict judgment. Sainte-Beuve relates that Napoleon one day said, when somebody was spoken of in his presence as a charlatan: "Charlatan as much as you please; but where is there *not* charlatanism?" "Yes," answers Sainte-Beuve, "in politics, in the art of governing mankind, that is perhaps true. But in the order of thought, in art, the glory, the eternal honor is that charlatanism shall find no entrance; herein lies the inviolableness of that noble portion of man's being." It is admirably said, and let us hold fast to it. In poetry, which is thought and art in one, it is the glory, the eternal honor, that charlatanism shall find no entrance; that this noble sphere be kept inviolate and inviolable. Charlatanism is for confusing or obliterating the distinctions between excellent and inferior, sound and unsound or only half-sound, true and untrue or only half-true. It is charlatanism, conscious or unconscious, whenever we confuse or obliterate these. And in poetry, more than anywhere else, it is unpermissible to confuse or obliterate them. For in poetry the distinction between excellent and inferior, sound and unsound or only half-sound, true and untrue or only half-true, is of paramount importance. It is of paramount importance because of the high destinies of poetry. In poetry, as in criticism of life under the conditions fixed for

such a criticism by the laws of poetic truth and poetic beauty, the spirit of our race will find, we have said, as time goes on and as other helps fails, its consolation and stay. But the consolation and stay will be of power in proportion to the power of the criticism of life. And the criticism of life will be of power in proportion as the poetry conveying it is excellent rather than inferior, sound rather than unsound or half-sound, true rather than untrue or half-true.

The best poetry is what we want; the best poetry will be found to have a power of forming, sustaining, and delighting us, as nothing else can. A clearer, deeper sense of the best in poetry, and of the strength and joy to be drawn from it, is the most precious benefit which we can gather from a poetical collection such as the present. And yet in the very nature and conduct of such a collection there is inevitably something which tends to obscure in us the consciousness of what our benefit should be, and to distract us from the pursuit of it. We should therefore steadily set it before our minds at the outset, and should compel ourselves to revert constantly to the thought of it as we proceed.

Yes; constantly in reading poetry, a sense for the best, the really excellent, and of the strength and joy to be drawn from it, should be present in our minds and should govern our estimate of what we read. But this real estimate, the only true one, is liable to be superseded, if we are not watchful, by two other kinds of estimate, the historic estimate and the personal estimate, both of which are fallacious. A poet or a poem may count to us historically, they may count to us on grounds personal to ourselves, and they may count to us really. They may count to us historically. The course of development of a nation's language, thought, and poetry, is profoundly interesting; and by regarding a poet's work as a stage in this course of development we may easily bring ourselves to make it of more importance as poetry than in itself it really is, we may come to use a language of quite exaggerated praise in criticizing it; in short, to overrate it. So arises in our poetic judgments the fallacy caused by the estimate which we may call historic. Then, again, a poet or poem may count to us on grounds personal to ourselves. Our personal affinities, likings and circumstances, have great power to sway our estimate of this or that poet's work, and to make us attach more importance to it as poetry than in itself it really possesses, because to us it is, or has been, of high importance. Here also we overrate the object of our interest, and apply to it a language of praise which is quite exaggerated. And thus we get the source of a second fallacy in our poetic judgments—the fallacy caused by an estimate which we may call personal.

Both fallacies are natural. It is evident how naturally the study of the history and development of poetry may incline a man to pause over reputations and works once conspicuous

---

[2]Preface to the *Lyrical Ballads,* p. 442.

but now obscure, and to quarrel with a careless public for skipping, in obedience to mere tradition and habit, from one famous name or work in its national poetry to another, ignorant of what it misses, and of the reason for keeping what it keeps, and of the whole process of growth in its poetry. The French have become diligent students of their own early poetry, which they long neglected; the study makes many of them dissatisfied with their so-called classical poetry, the court-tragedy of the seventeenth century, a poetry which Pellisson long ago reproached with its want of the true poetic stamp, with its *politesse stérile et rampante,*[3] but which nevertheless has reigned in France as absolutely as if it had been the perfection of classical poetry indeed. The dissatisfaction is natural; yet a lively and accomplished critic, M. Charles d'Héricault, the editor of Clément Marot, goes too far when he says that "the cloud of glory playing round a classic is a mist as dangerous to the future of a literature as it is intolerable for the purposes of history." "It hinders," he goes on,

> it hinders us from seeing more than one single point, the culminating and exceptional point; the summary, fictitious and arbitrary, of a thought and of a work. It substitutes a halo for a physiognomy, it puts a statue where there was once a man, and hiding from us all trace of the labor, the attempts, the weaknesses, the failures, it claims not study but veneration; it does not show us how the thing is done, it imposes upon us a model. Above all, for the historian this creation of classic personages is inadmissible; for it withdraws the poet from his time, from his proper life, it breaks historical relationships, it blinds criticism by conventional admiration, and renders the investigation of literary origins unacceptable. It gives us a human personage no longer but a God seated immovable amidst his perfect work, like Jupiter on Olympus; and hardly will it be possible for the young student to whom such work is exhibited at such a distance from him, to believe that it did not issue ready-made from that divine head.

All this is brilliantly and tellingly said, but we must plead for a distinction. Everything depends on the reality of a poet's classic character. If he is a dubious classic, let us sift him; if he is a false classic, let us explode him. But if he is a real classic, if his work belongs to the class of the very best (for this is the true and right meaning of the word *classic, classical*), then the great thing for us is to feel and enjoy his

work as deeply as ever we can, and to appreciate the wide difference between it and all work which has not the same high character. This is what is salutary, this is what is formative; this is the great benefit to be got from the study of poetry. Everything which interferes with it, which hinders it, is injurious. True, we must read our classic with open eyes, and not with eyes blinded with superstition; we must perceive when his work comes short, when it drops out of the class of the very best, and we must rate it, in such cases, at its proper value. But the use of this negative criticism is not in itself, it is entirely in its enabling us to have a clearer sense and a deeper enjoyment of what is truly excellent. To trace the labor, the attempts, the weaknesses, the failures of a genuine classic, to acquaint oneself with his time and his life and his historical relationships, is mere literary dilettantism unless it has that clear sense and deeper enjoyment for its end. It may be said that the more we know about a classic the better we shall enjoy him; and, if we lived as long as Methuselah and had all of us heads of perfect clearness and wills of perfect steadfastness, this might be true in fact as it is plausible in theory. But the case here is much the same as the case with the Greek and Latin studies of our schoolboys. The elaborate philological groundwork which we require them to lay is in theory an admirable preparation for appreciating the Greek and Latin authors worthily. The more thoroughly we lay the groundwork, the better we shall be able, it may be said, to enjoy the authors. True, if time were not so short, and schoolboys' wits not so soon tired and their power of attention exhausted; only, as it is, the elaborate philological preparation goes on, but the authors are little known and less enjoyed. So with the investigator of "historic origins" in poetry. He ought to enjoy the true classic all the better for his investigations; he often is distracted from the enjoyment of the best, and with the less good he overbusies himself, and is prone to overrate it in proportion to the trouble which it has cost him.

The idea of tracing historic origins and historical relationships cannot be absent from a compilation like the present. And naturally the poets to be exhibited in it will be assigned to those persons for exhibition who are known to prize them highly, rather than to those who have no special inclination towards them. Moreover, the very occupation with an author, and the business of exhibiting him, disposes us to affirm and amplify his importance. In the present work, therefore, we are sure of frequent temptation to adopt the historic estimate, or the personal estimate, and to forget the real estimate; which latter, nevertheless, we must employ if we are to make poetry yield us its full benefit. So high is that benefit, the benefit of clearly feeling and of deeply enjoying the really excellent, the truly classic in poetry, that we do well, I say, to set it fixedly before our minds as our object in

---

[3]"Sterile and servile politeness."

studying poets and poetry, and to make the desire of attaining it the one principle to which, as the *Imitation* says, whatever we may read or come to know, we always return. *"Cum multa legeris et cognoveris, ad unum semper oportet redire principium."*[4]

The historic estimate is likely in especial to affect our judgment and our language when we are dealing with ancient poets; the personal estimate when we are dealing with poets our contemporaries, or at any rate modern. The exaggerations due to the historic estimate are not in themselves, perhaps, of very much gravity. Their report hardly enters the general ear; probably they do not always impose even on the literary men who adopt them. But they lead to a dangerous abuse of language. So we hear Caedmon, amongst our own poets, compared to Milton. I have already noticed the enthusiasm of one accomplished French critic for "historic origins." Another eminent French critic, M. Vitet, comments upon that famous document of the early poetry of his nation, the *Chanson de Roland.* It is indeed a most interesting document. The *joculator* or *jongleur Taillefer,* who was with William the Conqueror's army at Hastings, marched before the Norman troops, so said the tradition, singing "of Charlemagne and of Roland and of Oliver, and of the vassals who died at Roncevaux"; and it is suggested that in the *Chanson de Roland* by one Turoldus or Théroulde, a poem preserved in a manuscript of the twelfth century in the Bodleian Library at Oxford, we have certainly the matter, perhaps even some of the words, of the chant which Taillefer sang. The poem has vigor and freshness; it is not without pathos. But M. Vitet is not satisfied with seeing in it a document of some poetic value, and of very high historic and linguistic value; he sees in it a grand and beautiful work, a monument of epic genius. In its general design he finds the grandiose conception, in its details he finds the constant union of simplicity with greatness, which are the marks, he truly says, of the genuine epic, and distinguish it from the artificial epic of literary ages. One thinks of Homer; this is the sort of praise which is given to Homer, and justly given. Higher praise there cannot well be, and it is the praise due to epic poetry of the highest order only, and to no other. Let us try, then, the *Chanson de Roland* at its best. Roland, mortally wounded, lay himself down under a pine tree, with his face turned towards Spain and the enemy—

> *De plusurs choses à remembrer li prist,*
> *De tantes teres cume li bers cunquist,*

De dulce France, des humes de sun lign,
De Carlemagne sun seignor ki l'nurrit.[5]

That is primitive work, I repeat, with an undeniable poetic quality of its own. It deserves such praise, and such praise is sufficient for it. But now turn to Homer—Ὡς φάτο. τοὺς δ' ἤδη κατέχεν φυσίζοος αἶα / ἐν Λακεδαίμονι αὖδι, φίλη ἐν πατρίδι γαίῃ.[6] We are here in another world, another order of poetry altogether; here is rightly due such supreme praise as that which M. Vitet gives to the *Chanson de Roland.* If our words are to have any meaning, if our judgments are to have any solidity, we must not heap that supreme praise upon poetry of an order immeasurably inferior.

Indeed there can be no more useful help for discovering what poetry belongs to the class of the truly excellent, and can therefore do us most good, than to have always in one's mind lines and expressions of the great masters, and to apply them as a touchstone to other poetry. Of course we are not to require this other poetry to resemble them; it may be very dissimilar. But if we have any tact we shall find them, when we have lodged them well in our minds, an infallible touchstone for detecting the presence or absence of high poetic quality, and also the degree of this quality, in all other poetry which we may place beside them. Short passages, even single lines, will serve our turn quite sufficiently. Take the two lines which I have just quoted from Homer, the poet's comment on Helen's mention of her brothers; or take his

> Α δειλώ, τί σφῶϊ δόμεν Πηλῆϊ ἄνακτι
> Θνητῷ; ὑμεῖς δ' ἐστὸν ἀγήρω τ' ἀθανάτω τε.
> ἦ ἵνα δυστήνοισι μετ' ἀνδράσιν ἄλγε' ἔχητον;[7]

the address of Zeus to the horses of Peleus; or take finally his Καὶ σέ, γέρον, τὸ πρὶν μὲν ἀκούομεν ὄλβιον εἶναι,[8] the words of Achilles to Priam, a suppliant before him. Take that incomparable line and a half of Dante, Ugolino's tremendous words—*"Io no piangeva; sì dentro impietrai. / Piangevan elli . . ."*[9] take the lovely words of Beatrice to Virgil—

---

[4]"With much reading and learning, one must always return to the one principle." Thomas à Kempis, *The Imitation of Christ.*

[5][Arnold] "Then began he to call many things to remembrance—all the lands which his valor conquered and pleasant France, and the men of his lineage, and Charlemagne his liege lord who nourished him." *Chanson de Roland,* III. 939–42.

[6][Arnold] "So said she; they long since in earth's soft arms were reposing there in their own dear land, their fatherland, Lacedaemon." *Iliad,* III. 243–44 (translated by Dr. Hawtrey).

[7][Arnold] "Ah, unhappy pair, why gave we you to King Peleus, to a mortal? But ye are without old age, and immortal. Was it that with men born to misery ye might have sorrow?" *Iliad,* XVII. 443–45.

[8]"And you, too, old man, were, as we have heard, happy in former days." *Iliad,* XXIV. 543.

[9][Arnold] "I wailed not, so of stone grew I within. They wailed." *The Divine Comedy,* "Inferno," XXXIII. 39–40.

Io son fatta da Dio, sua mercè, tale,
Che la vostra miseria non mi tange,
Nè fiamma d'esto incendio non m'assale . . .[10]

take the simple, but perfect, single line—*"In la sua volon-*
tade è nostra pace."[11] Take of Shakespeare a line or two of
Henry the Fourth's expostulation with sleep—

Wilt thou upon the high and giddy mast
Seal up the ship-boy's eyes, and rock his brains
In cradle of the rude imperious surge . . .[12]

and take, as well, Hamlet's dying request to Horatio—

If thou didst ever hold me in thy heart,
Absent thee from felicity awhile,
And in this harsh world draw thy breath in pain
To tell my story . . .[13]

Take of Milton that Miltonic passage:

Darkened so, yet shone
Above them all the archangel; but his face
Deep scars of thunder had intrenched, and care
Sat on his faded cheek . . .[14]

add two such lines as "And courage never to submit or yield
/ And what is else not to be overcome . . ."[15] and finish with
the exquisite close to the loss of Proserpine, the loss ". . .
which cost Ceres all that pain / To seek her through the
world."[16] These few lines, if we have tact and can use them,
are enough even of themselves to keep clear and sound our
judgments about poetry, to save us from fallacious estimates
of it, to conduct us to a real estimate.

The specimens I have quoted differ widely from one
another, but they have in common this: the possession of the
very highest poetical quality. If we are thoroughly penetrated
by their power, we shall find that we have acquired a sense
enabling us, whatever poetry may be laid before us, to feel
the degree in which a high poetical quality is present or
wanting there. Critics give themselves great labor to draw
out what in the abstract constitutes the characters of a high
quality of poetry. It is much better simply to have recourse
to concrete examples; to take specimens of poetry of the
high, the very highest quality, and to say: The characters of
a high quality of poetry are what is expressed *there*. They are
far better recognized by being felt in the verse of the master,
than by being perused in the prose of the critic. Nevertheless
if we are urgently pressed to give some critical account of
them, we may safely, perhaps, venture on laying down, not
indeed how and why the characters arise, but where and in
what they arise. They are in the matter and substance of the
poetry, and they are in its manner and style. Both of these,
the substance and matter on the one hand, the style and manner on the other, have a mark, an accent, of high beauty,
worth, and power. But if we are asked to define this mark
and accent in the abstract, our answer must be: No, for we
should thereby be darkening the question, not clearing it.
The mark and accent are as given by the substance and matter of that poetry, by the style and manner of that poetry, and
of all other poetry which is akin to it in quality.

Only one thing we may add as to the substance and matter of poetry, guiding ourselves by Aristotle's profound observation that the superiority of poetry over history consists
in its possessing a higher truth and a higher seriousness (ψιλ-
οσοψώτερον καὶ σπουδαιότερον). Let us add, therefore, to
what we have said, this: that the substance and matter of the
best poetry acquire their special character from possessing,
in an eminent degree, truth and seriousness. We may add yet
further, what is in itself evident, that to the style and manner
of the best poetry their special character, their accent, is
given by their diction, and, even yet more, by their movement. And though we distinguish between the two characters, the two accents, of superiority, yet they are nevertheless
vitally connected one with the other. The superior character
of truth and seriousness, in the matter and substance of the
best poetry, is inseparable from the superiority of diction and
movement marking its style and manner. The two superiori-
ties are closely related, and are in steadfast proportion one to
the other. So far as high poetic truth and seriousness are
wanting to a poet's matter and substance, so far also, we may
be sure, will a high poetic stamp of diction and movement
be wanting to his style and manner. In proportion as this high
stamp of diction and movement, again, is absent from a
poet's style and manner, we shall find, also, that high poetic
truth and seriousness are absent from his substance and
matter.[17]

---

[10][Arnold] "Of such sort hath God, thanked be his mercy, made me, that your
    misery toucheth me not, neither doth the flame of this fire strike me." *The
    Divine Comedy,* "Inferno," II. 91–93.
[11]"In his will is our peace." *The Divine Comedy,* "Paradise," III. 85.
[12]*II Henry IV,* III. i. 18–20.
[13]*Hamlet,* V. ii. 357–60.
[14]*Paradise Lost,* I. 599–602.
[15]*Paradise Lost,* I. 108–09.
[16]*Paradise Lost,* IV. 271–72.

[17]Arnold now proceeds, with the principles already enunciated in view to "follow rapidly from the commencement the course of our English poetry."

Hippolyte Taine

1828–1893

During the latter half of the nineteenth century there was an attempt to relate scientific method to literary creation and criticism. The analogy between literary creation and experimental method was roughly developed in Zola's *Experimental Novel.* Scientific method was brought into literary criticism in Taine's well-known and influential *History of English Literature,* in which Taine treats literature not in respect to the psychology of the audience or its reflection of the outer world but as documents for the analysis of an age and a people. Taine begins by arguing that we seek in literature an insight into the inner life of the author. We recognize at once in this remark vestiges of a central concern of much Romantic criticism. But Taine goes on to suggest that biographical knowledge is only a step to the greater end of understanding a whole people and their moral condition. The end to which literature is to be put is a total historical vision.

Taine views literature less as a force acting on thought and society than as the result of social and natural factors—race, environment, epoch. It is a class of events regulated by general laws yet to be discovered, pieces of evidence that will contribute to a total view of man. The principle of determinism implied by Marx and Engels is present in Taine's methodology.

Yet there is another Taine who does not wish to reduce literature to the rank of just any sort of document: "A great poem, a fine novel, the confessions of a superior man, are more instructive than a heap of historians with their histories." The reason is that literature offers us the "psychology of a soul, frequently of an age, now and then of a race." One might ask how literature can be more valuable than history if its purpose is to serve as documents for historians. This sort of question was asked increasingly in the latter part of the nineteenth century, and it culminated in the attacks on historicism made by the New Critics in the twentieth century.

The standard translation of Taine's *History of English Literature* is by Henry van Laun (1871).The *Lectures on Art* have been translated by John Durand (1877). An important study in French is Paul Nève, *La Philosophie de Taine* (1908). English commentaries include Irving Babbitt, *Masters of Modern French Criticism* (1912); A. A. Eustice, *Hippolyte Taine and the Classical Genius* (1951); S. J. Kahn, *Science and Aesthetic Judgment: A Study in Taine's Critical Method* (1953); H. H. Clark, *The Influence of Science on American Literary Criticism 1860–1910, Including the Vogue of Taine* (1956); and Leo Weinstein, *Hippolyte Taine* (1972).

From

History of English Literature

Introduction

The historian might place himself for a certain time, during several centuries or amongst a certain people, in the midst of the spirit of humanity. He might study, describe, relate all the events, the changes, the revolutions which took place in the inner man; and when he had reached the end, he would possess a history of the civilization of the nation and the period he selected.[1]

FRANÇOIS GUIZOT

History has been revolutionized, within a hundred years in Germany, within sixty years in France, and that by the study of their literatures.

It was perceived that a work of literature is not a mere play of imagination, a solitary caprice of a heated brain, but a transcript of contemporary manners, a type of a certain kind of mind. It was concluded that one might retrace, from the monuments of literature, the style of man's feelings and thoughts for centuries back. The attempt was made, and it succeeded.

Pondering on these modes of feeling and thought, men decided that in them were embalmed facts of the highest kind. They saw that these facts bore reference to the most important occurrences, that they explained and were explained by them, that it was necessary thenceforth to give them a rank, and a most important rank, in history. This rank they have received, and from that moment history has undergone a complete change: in its subject matter, its system, its machinery, the appreciation of laws and of causes. It is this change, as it has happened and must still happen, that we shall here endeavor to exhibit.

I

What is your first remark on turning over the great, stiff leaves of a folio, the yellow sheets of a manuscript—a poem,

a code of laws, a declaration of faith? This, you say, was not created alone. It is but a mold, like a fossil shell, an imprint, like one of those shapes embossed in stone by an animal which lived and perished. Under the shell there was an animal, and behind the document there was a man. Why do you study the shell, except to represent to yourself the animal? So do you study the document only in order to know the man. The shell and the document are lifeless wrecks, valuable only as a clue to the entire and living existence. We must reach back to this existence, endeavor to recreate it. It is a mistake to study the document, as if it were isolated. This were to treat things like a simple pedant, to fall into the error of the bibliomaniac. Behind all, we have neither mythology nor languages, but only men, who arrange words and imagery according to the necessities of their organs and the original bent of their intellects. A dogma is nothing in itself; look at the people who have made it—a portrait, for instance, of the sixteenth century, the stern and energetic face of an English archbishop or martyr. Nothing exists except through some individual man; it is this individual with whom we must become acquainted. When we have established the parentage of dogmas, or the classification of poems, or the progress of constitutions, or the modification of idioms, we have only cleared the soil: genuine history is brought into existence only when the historian begins to unravel, across the lapse of time, the living man, toiling, impassioned, entrenched in his customs, with his voice and features, his gestures and his dress, distinct and complete as he from whom we have just parted in the street. Let us endeavor, then, to annihilate as far as possible this great interval of time, which prevents us from seeing man with our eyes, with the eyes of our head. What have we under the fair glazed pages of a modern poem? A modern poet, who has studied and traveled, a man like Alfred de Musset, Victor Hugo, Lamartine, or Heine, in a black coat and gloves, welcomed by the ladies, and making every evening his fifty bows and his score of bon mots in society, reading the papers in the morning, lodging as a rule on the second floor; not over gay, because he has nerves, and especially because, in this dense democracy where we choke one another, the discredit of the dignities of office has exaggerated his pretensions while increasing his importance, and because the refinement of his feelings in general disposes him somewhat to believe himself a deity. This is what we take note of under modern meditations or sonnets. Even so, under a tragedy of the seventeenth century we have a poet, like Racine for instance, elegant, staid, a courtier, a fine speaker, with a majestic wig and ribboned shoes, at heart a royalist and a Christian, "having received the grace of God not to blush in any company, kings nor Gospelers"; clever at entertaining the prince, and rendering

HISTORY OF ENGLISH LITERATURE. Taine's *Histoire de la littérature anglaise* was published between 1863 and 1867. The Introduction first appeared in December 1863. The text is from the translation by Henry van Laun (1871).
[1]*Civilization in Europe.*

for him into good French the "old French of Amyot"; very respectful to the great, always "knowing his place"; as assiduous and reserved at Marly as at Versailles, amidst the regular pleasures of a polished and fastidious nature, amidst the salutations, graces, airs, and fopperies of the braided lords, who rose early in the morning to obtain the promise of being appointed to some office in case of the death of the present holder, and amongst charming ladies who count their genealogies on their fingers in order to obtain the right of sitting down in the presence of the king or queen. On that head consult St. Simon and the engravings of Pérelle, as for the present age you have consulted Balzac and the watercolors of Eugène Lami. Similarly, when we read a Greek tragedy, our first care should be to realize to ourselves the Greeks, that is, the men who live half naked, in the gymnasia, or in the public squares, under a glowing sky, face to face with the most noble landscapes, bent on making their bodies nimble and strong, on conversing, discussing, voting, carrying on patriotic piracies, but for the rest lazy and temperate, with three urns for their furniture, two anchovies in a jar of oil for their food, waited on by slaves, so as to give them leisure to cultivate their understanding and exercise their limbs, with no desire beyond that of having the most beautiful town, the most beautiful processions, the most beautiful ideas, the most beautiful men. On this subject, a statue such as the *Meleager,* or the *Theseus* of the Parthenon, or still more, the sight of the Mediterranean, blue and lustrous as a silken tunic, and islands arising from it like masses of marble, and added to these, twenty select phrases from Plato and Aristophanes, will teach you much more than a multitude of dissertations and commentaries. And so again, in order to understand an Indian Purāna, begin by imagining to yourself the father of a family, who, "having seen a son on his son's knees," retires, according to the law, into solitude, with an ax and a pitcher, under a banana tree, by the riverside, talks no more, adds fast to fast, dwells naked between four fires, and under a fifth, the terrible sun, devouring and renewing without end all living things; who step by step, for weeks at a time, fixes his imagination upon the feet of Brahma, next upon his knee, next upon his thigh, next upon his navel, and so on, until, beneath the strain of this intense meditation, hallucinations begin to appear, until all the forms of existence, mingled and transformed the one with the other, quaver before a sight dazzled and giddy, until the motionless man, catching in his breath, with fixed gaze, beholds the universe vanishing like a smoke beyond the universal and void Being into which he aspires to be absorbed. To this end a voyage to India would be the best instructor; or for want of better, the accounts of travelers, books of geography, botany, ethnology, will serve their turn. In each case the search must be the same. A language, a legislation, a catechism, is never more than an abstract thing: the complete thing is the man who acts, the man corporeal and visible, who eats, walks, fights, labors. Leave on one side the theory and the mechanism of constitutions, religions and their systems, and try to see men in their workshops, in their offices, in their fields, with their sky and earth, their houses, their dress, cultivations, meals, as you do when, landing in England or Italy, you remark faces and motions, roads and inns, a citizen taking his walk, a workman drinking. Our great care should be to supply as much as possible the want of present, personal, direct, and sensible observation which we can no longer practice; for it is the only means of knowing men. Let us make the past present: in order to judge of a thing, it must be before us; there is no experience in respect of what is absent. Doubtless this reconstruction is always incomplete; it can produce only incomplete judgments; but to that we must resign ourselves. It is better to have an imperfect knowledge than a futile or false one; and there is no other means of acquainting ourselves approximately with the events of other days, than to *see* approximately the men of other days.

This is the first step in history: it was made in Europe at the new birth of imagination, toward the close of the last century, by Lessing, Walter Scott; a little later in France, by Chateaubriand, Augustin Thierry, Michelet, and others. And now for the second step.

II

When you consider with your eyes the visible man, what do you look for? The man invisible. The words which enter your ears, the gestures, the motions of his head, the clothes he wears, visible acts and deeds of every kind, are expressions merely; somewhat is revealed beneath them, and that is a soul. An inner man is concealed beneath the outer man; the second does but reveal the first. You look at his house, furniture, dress; and that in order to discover in them the marks of his habits and tastes, the degree of his refinement or rusticity, his extravagance or his economy, his stupidity or his cunning. You listen to his conversation, and you note the inflections of his voice, the changes in his attitudes; and that in order to judge of his intensity, his self-forgetfulness or his gaiety, his energy or his constraint. You consider his writings, his artistic productions, his business transactions or political ventures; and that in order to measure the scope and limits of his intelligence, his inventiveness, his coolness, to find out the order, the description, the general force of his ideas, the mode in which he thinks and resolves. All these externals are but avenues converging to a center; you enter them simply in order to reach that center; and that center is the genuine man, I mean that mass of faculties and feelings which are produced by the inner man. We have reached a new world, which is infinite, because every action which we see involves an infinite association of reasonings, emotions, sensations new and old, which have served to bring it to light, and which, like great rocks deep-seated in the ground, find in it their end and their level. This underworld is a new subject matter, proper to the historian. If his critical education suffice, he can lay bare, under every detail of architecture, every stroke in a picture, every phrase in a writing, the special sensation whence detail, stroke, or phrase had issue; he is present at the drama which was enacted in the soul of artist or writer; the choice of a word, the brevity or length of a sentence, the nature of a metaphor, the accent of a verse, the development of an argument—everything is a symbol to him; while his eyes read the text, his soul and mind pursue the continuous development and the ever changing succession of the emotions and conceptions out of which the text has sprung: in short, he unveils a psychology. If you would observe this operation, consider the originator and model of contemporary culture, Goethe, who, before writing *Iphigenia,* employed day after day in designing the most finished statues, and who at last, his eyes filled with the noble forms of ancient scenery, his mind penetrated by the harmonious loveliness of antique life, succeeded in reproducing so exactly in himself the peculiarities of the Greek imagination, that he gives us almost the twin sister of the *Antigone* of Sophocles, and the goddesses of Phidias. This precise and proved interpretation of past sensations has given to history, in our days, a second birth; hardly anything of the sort was known to the preceding century. They thought men of every race and century were all but identical; the Greek, the barbarian, the Hindu, the man of the Restoration, and the man of the eighteenth century, as if they had been turned out of a common mold; and all in conformity to a certain abstract conception, which served for the whole human race. They knew man, but not men; they had not penetrated to the soul; they had not seen the infinite diversity and marvelous complexity of souls; they did not know that the moral constitution of a people or an age is as particular and distinct as the physical structure of a family of plants or an order of animals. Nowadays, history, like zoology, has found its anatomy; and whatever the branch of history to which you devote yourself, philology, linguistic lore, mythology, it is by these means you must strive to produce new fruit. Amid so many writers who, since the time of Herder, Ottfried Muller, and Goethe, have continued and still improve this great method, let the reader consider only two historians and two works, Carlyle's *Cromwell,* and Sainte-Beuve's *Port Royal:* he will

see with what justice, exactness, depth of insight, one may discover a soul beneath its actions and its works; how behind the old general, in place of a vulgar, hypocritical schemer, we recover a man travailing with the troubling reveries of a melancholic imagination, but with definite instincts and faculties, English to the core, strange and incomprehensible to one who has not studied the climate and the race; how, with about a hundred meager letters and a score of mutilated speeches, one may follow him from his farm and team, to the general's tent and to the Protector's throne, in his transmutation and development, in his pricks of conscience and his political conclusions, until the machinery of his mind and actions becomes visible, and the inner tragedy, ever changing and renewed, which exercised this great, darkling soul, passes, like one of Shakespeare's, through the soul of the looker on. He will see (in the other case) how, behind the squabbles of the monastery, or the contumacies of nuns, one may find a great province of human psychology; how about fifty characters, that had been buried under the uniformity of a circumspect narrative, reappear in the light of day, each with its own specialty and its countless diversities; how, beneath theological disquisitions and monotonous sermons, one can unearth the beatings of ever living hearts, the convulsions and apathies of monastic life, the unforeseen reassertions and wavy turmoil of nature, the inroads of surrounding worldliness, the intermittent victories of grace, with such a variety of overcloudings, that the most exhaustive description and the most elastic style can hardly gather the inexhaustible harvest, which the critic has caused to spring up on this abandoned field. And so it is throughout. Germany, with its genius so pliant, so liberal, so apt for transformation, so well calculated to reproduce the most remote and anomalous conditions of human thought; England, with its intellect so precise, so well calculated to grapple closely with moral questions, to render them exact by figures, weights and measures, geography, statistics, by quotation and by common sense; France, with her Parisian culture, with her drawing room manners, with her untiring analysis of characters and actions, her irony so ready to hit upon a weakness, her finesse so practiced in the discrimination of shades of thought—all have worked the same soil, and one begins to understand that there is no region of history where it is not imperative to till this deep level, if one would see a serviceable harvest rise between the furrows.

This is the second step; we are in a fair way to its completion. It is the proper work of the contemporary critic. No one has done it so justly and grandly as Sainte-Beuve; in this respect we are all his pupils; his method renews, in our days, in books, and even in newspapers, every kind of literary, of philosophical and religious criticism. From it we must set out in order to begin the further development. I have more than once endeavored to indicate this development; there is here, in my mind, a new path open to history, and I will try to describe it more in detail.

III

When you have observed and noted in man one, two, three, then a multitude of sensations, does this suffice, or does your knowledge appear complete? Is a book of observations a psychology? It is no psychology, and here as elsewhere the search for causes must come after the collection of facts. No matter if the facts be physical or moral, they all have their causes; there is a cause for ambition, for courage, for truth, as there is for digestion, for muscular movement, for animal heat. Vice and virtue are products, like vitriol and sugar; and every complex phenomenon has its springs from other more simple phenomena on which it hangs. Let us then seek the simple phenomena for moral qualities, as we seek them for physical qualities; and let us take the first fact that presents itself: for example, religious music, that of a Protestant church. There is an inner cause which has turned the spirit of the faithful toward these grave and monotonous melodies, a cause broader than its effect; I mean the general idea of the true, external worship which man owes to God. It is this which has modeled the architecture of the temple, thrown down the statues, removed the pictures, destroyed the ornaments, curtailed the ceremonies, shut up the worshipers in high pews, which prevent them from seeing anything, and regulated the thousand details of decoration, posture, and the general surroundings. This itself comes from another more general cause, the idea of human conduct in all its comprehensiveness, internal and external, prayers, actions, dispositions of every kind by which man is kept face to face with God; it is this which has enthroned doctrine and grace, lowered the clergy, transformed the sacraments, suppressed various practices, and changed religion from a discipline to a morality. This second idea in its turn depends upon a third still more general, that of moral perfection, such as is met with in the perfect God, the unerring judge, the stern watcher of souls, before whom every soul is sinful, worthy of punishment, incapable of virtue or salvation, except by the crisis of conscience which He provokes, and the renewal of heart which He produces. That is the master idea, which consists in erecting duty into an absolute king of human life, and in prostrating all ideal models before a moral model. Here we track the root of man; for to explain this conception it is necessary to consider race itself, that is, the German, the Northman, the structure of his character and intelligence, his general processes of thought and feeling, the sluggishness and

coldness of sensation which prevent his falling easily and headlong under the sway of pleasure, the bluntness of his taste, the irregularity and revolutions of his conception, which arrest in him the birth of fair dispositions and harmonious forms, the disdain of appearances, the desire of truth, the attachment to bare and abstract ideas, which develop in him conscience, at the expense of all else. There the search is at an end; we have arrived at a primitive disposition, at a trait proper to all sensations, to all the conceptions of a century or a race, at a particularity inseparable from all the motions of his intellect and his heart. Here lie the grand causes, for they are the universal and permanent causes, present at every moment and in every case, everywhere and always acting, indestructible, and in the end infallibly supreme, since the accidents which thwart them, being limited and partial, end by yielding to the dull and incessant repetition of their force; in such a manner that the general structure of things, and the grand features of events, are their work; and religions, philosophies, poetries, industries, the framework of society and of families, are in fact only the imprints stamped by their seal.

IV

There is then a system in human sentiments and ideas; and this system has for its motive power certain general traits, certain marks of the intellect and the heart common to men of one race, age, or country. As in mineralogy the crystals, however diverse, spring from certain simply physical forms, so in history, civilizations, however diverse, are derived from certain simple spiritual forms. The one are explained by a primitive geometrical element, as the others are by a primitive psychological element. In order to master the classification of mineralogical systems, we must first consider a regular and general solid, its sides and angles, and observe in this the numberless transformations of which it is capable. So, if you would realize the system of historical varieties, consider first a human soul generally, with its two or three fundamental faculties, and in this compendium you will perceive the principal forms which it can present. After all, this kind of ideal picture, geometrical as well as psychological, is hardly complex, and one speedily sees the limits of the outline in which civilizations, like crystals, are constrained to exist.

What do we find, at first sight, in man? Images or representations of things, something, that is, which floats within him, exists for a time, is effaced, and returns again, after he has been looking upon a tree, an animal, any sensible object. This is the subject matter, the development whereof is double, either speculative or practical, according as the representations resolve themselves into a general conception or an active resolution. Here we have the whole of man in an abridgment; and in this limited circle human diversities meet, sometimes in the womb of the primordial matter, sometimes in the twofold primordial development. However minute in their elements, they are enormous in the aggregate, and the least alteration in the factors produces vast alteration in the results. According as the representation is clear and as it were cut out by machinery or confused and faintly defined, according as it embraces a great or small number of the marks of the object, according as it is violent and accompanied by impulses, or quiet and surrounded by calm, all the operations and processes of the human machine are transformed. So, again, according as the ulterior development of the representation varies, the whole human development varies. If the general conception in which it results is a mere dry notation (in Chinese fashion), language becomes a sort of algebra, religion and poetry dwindle, philosophy is reduced to a kind of moral and practical common sense, science to a collection of formulas, classifications, utilitarian mnemonics, and the whole intellect takes a positive bent. If, on the contrary, the general representation in which the conception results is a poetical and figurative creation, a living symbol, as among the Aryan races, language becomes a sort of cloudy and colored word-stage, in which every word is a person, poetry and religion assume a magnificent and inextinguishable grandeur, metaphysics are widely and subtly developed, without regard to positive applications; the whole intellect, in spite of the inevitable deviations and shortcomings of its effort, is smitten with the beautiful and the sublime, and conceives an ideal capable by its nobleness and its harmony of rallying round it the tenderness and enthusiasm of the human race. If, again, the general conception in which the representation results is poetical but not precise; if man arrives at it not by a continuous process, but by a quick intuition; if the original operation is not a regular development, but a violent explosion—then, as with the Semitic races, metaphysics are absent, religion conceives God only as a king solitary and devouring, science cannot grow, the intellect is too rigid and complete to reproduce the delicate operations of nature, poetry can give birth only to vehement and grandiose exclamations, language cannot unfold the web of argument and of eloquence, man is reduced to a lyric enthusiasm, an unchecked passion, a fanatical and constrained action. In this interval between the particular representation and the universal conception are found the germs of the greatest human differences. Some races, as the classical, pass from the first to the second by a graduated scale of ideas, regularly arranged, and general by degrees; others, as the Germanic, traverse the same ground by leaps, without uniformity, after vague and prolonged groping. Some, like the Romans and English, halt at the first steps; others, like the Hindus and Germans, mount to the last. If, again, after considering the passage from the representation to the idea, we consider that from the representation to the resolution, we find elementary differences of the like importance and the like order, according as the impression is sharp, as in southern climates, or dull, as in northern; according as it results in instant action, as among barbarians, or slowly, as in civilized nations; as it is capable or not of growth, inequality, persistence, and connections. The whole network of human passions, the chances of peace and public security, the sources of toil and action, spring from hence. Other primordial differences there are: their issues embrace an entire civilization; and we may compare them to those algebraical formulas which, in a narrow limit, contain in advance the whole curve of which they form the law. Not that this law is always developed to its issue; there are perturbing forces; but when it is so, it is not that the law was false, but that its action was impeded. New elements become mingled with the old; great forces from without counteract the primitive. The race emigrates, like the Aryan, and the change of climate has altered in its case the whole economy, intelligence, and organization of society. The people has been conquered, like the Saxon nation, and a new political structure has imposed on its customs, capacities, and inclinations which it had not. The nation has installed itself in the midst of a conquered people, downtrodden and threatening, like the ancient Spartans; and the necessity of living like troops in the field has violently distorted in an unique direction the whole moral and social constitution. In each case, the mechanism of human history is the same. One continually finds, as the original mainspring, some very general disposition of mind and soul, innate and appended by nature to the race, or acquired and produced by some circumstance acting upon the race. These mainsprings, once admitted, produce their effect gradually: I mean that after some centuries they bring the nation into a new condition, religious, literary, social, economic; a new condition which, combined with their renewed effort, produces another condition, sometimes good, sometimes bad, sometimes slowly, sometimes quickly, and so forth; so that we may regard the whole progress of each distinct civilization as the effect of a permanent force which, at every stage, varies its operation by modifying the circumstances of its action.

V

Three different sources contribute to produce this elementary moral state—the race, the surroundings, and the epoch. What we call the *race* are the innate and hereditary dispositions which man brings with him to the light, and which, as a rule, are united with the marked differences in the temperament and structure of the body. They vary with various peoples. There is a natural variety of men, as of oxen and horses, some brave and intelligent, some timid and dependent, some capable of superior conceptions and creations, some reduced to rudimentary ideas and inventions, some more specially fitted to special works, and gifted more richly with particular instincts, as we meet with species of dogs better favored than others—these for hunting, these for fighting, these for the chase, these again for house dogs or shepherds' dogs. We have here a distinct force—so distinct, that amidst the vast deviations which the other two motive forces produce in him, one can recognize it still; and a race, like the old Aryans, scattered from the Ganges as far as the Hebrides, settled in every clime, spread over every grade of civilization, transformed by thirty centuries of revolutions, nevertheless manifests in its tongues, religions, literatures, philosophies, the community of blood and of intellect which to this day binds its offshoots together. Different as they are, their parentage is not obliterated; barbarism, culture and grafting, differences of sky and soil, fortunes good and bad, have labored in vain: the great marks of the original model have remained, and we find again the two or three principal lineaments of the primitive imprint underneath the secondary imprints which time has stamped above them. There is nothing astonishing in this extraordinary tenacity. Although the vastness of the distance lets us but half perceive—and by a doubtful light—the origin of species,[2] the events of history sufficiently illumine the events anterior to history, to explain the almost immovable steadfastness of the primordial marks. When we meet with them, fifteen, twenty, thirty centuries before our era, in an Aryan, an Egyptian, a Chinese, they represent the work of several myriads of centuries. For as soon as an animal begins to exist, it has to reconcile itself with its surroundings; it breathes after a new fashion, renews itself, is differently affected according to the new changes in air, food, temperature. Different climate and situation bring it various needs, and consequently a different course of actions; and this, again, a different set of habits; and still again, a different set of aptitudes and instincts. Man, forced to accommodate himself to circumstances, contracts a temperament and a character corresponding to them; and his character, like his temperament, is so much more stable, as the external impression is made upon him by more numerous repetitions, and is transmitted to his progeny by a more an-

cient descent. So that at any moment we may consider the character of a people as an abridgment of all its preceding actions and sensations; that is, as a quantity and as a weight, not infinite,[3] since everything in nature is finite, but disproportioned to the rest, and almost impossible to lift, since every moment of an almost infinite past has contributed to increase it, and because, in order to raise the scale, one must place in the opposite scale a still greater number of actions and sensations. Such is the first and richest source of these master faculties from which historical events take their rise; and one sees at the outset, that if it be powerful, it is because this is no simple spring, but a kind of lake, a deep reservoir wherein other springs have, for a multitude of centuries, discharged their several streams.

Having thus outlined the interior structure of a race, we must consider the surroundings in which it exists. For man is not alone in the world; nature surrounds him, and his fellow men surround him; accidental and secondary tendencies come to place themselves on his primitive tendencies, and physical or social circumstances disturb or confirm the character committed to their charge. In course of time the climate has had its effect. Though we can follow but obscurely the Aryan peoples from their common fatherland to their final countries, we can yet assert that the profound differences which are manifest between the German races on the one side, and the Greek and Latin on the other arise for the most part from the difference between the countries in which they are settled: some in cold moist lands, deep in black marshy forests or on the shores of a wild ocean, caged in by melancholy or violent sensations, prone to drunkenness and gluttony, bent on a fighting, blood-spilling life; others, again, within a lovely landscape, on a bright and laughing seacoast, enticed to navigation and commerce, exempt from gross cravings of the stomach, inclined from the beginning to social ways, to a settled organization of the state, to feelings and dispositions such as develop the art of oratory, the talent for enjoyment, the inventions of science, letters, arts. Sometimes the state policy has been at work, as in the two Italian civilizations: the first wholly turned to action, conquest, government, legislation, by the original site of its city of refuge, by its borderland emporium, by an armed aristocracy, who, by inviting and drilling the strangers and the conquered, presently set face to face two hostile armies, having no escape from its internal discords and its greedy instincts but in systematic warfare; the other, shut out from unity and any great political ambition by the stability of its municipal character, the cosmopolitan condition of its pope, and the mili-

---

[2][Taine] Darwin, *The Origin of Species*. Prosper Lucas, *De l'hérédité* [*On Heredity*].

[3][Taine] Spinoza, *Ethics*, Part IV. Axiom.

tary intervention of neighboring nations, directed the whole of its magnificent, harmonious bent towards the worship of pleasure and beauty. Sometimes the social conditions have impressed their mark, as eighteen centuries ago by Christianity, and twenty-five centuries ago by Buddhism, when around the Mediterranean, as in Hindustan, the extreme results of Aryan conquest and civilization induced an intolerable oppression, the subjugation of the individual, utter despair, a curse upon the world, with the development of metaphysics and myth, so that man in this dungeon of misery, feeling his heart softened, begot the idea of abnegation, charity, tender love, gentleness, humility, brotherly love—there, in a notion of universal nothingness, here under the fatherhood of God. Look around you upon the regulating instincts and faculties implanted in a race—in short, the mood of intelligence in which it thinks and acts at the present time: you will discover most often the work of some one of these prolonged situations, these surrounding circumstances, persistent and gigantic pressures, brought to bear upon an aggregation of men who, singly and together, from generation to generation, are continually molded and modeled by their action; in Spain, an eight-century crusade against the Mussulmans, protracted even beyond and until the exhaustion of the nation by the expulsion of the Moors, the spoliation of the Jews, the establishment of the Inquisition, the Catholic wars; in England, a political establishment of eight centuries, which keeps a man erect and respectful, in independence and obedience, and accustoms him to strive unitedly, under the authority of the law; in France, a Latin organization, which, imposed first upon docile barbarians, then shattered in the universal crash, is reformed from within under a lurking conspiracy of the national instinct, is developed under hereditary kings, ends in a sort of egality republic, centralized, administrative, under dynasties exposed to revolution. These are the most efficacious of the visible causes which mold the primitive man: they are to nations what education, career, condition, abode, are to individuals; and they seem to comprehend everything, since they comprehend all external powers which shape human matter, and by which the external acts on the internal.

There is yet a third rank of causes; for, with the forces within and without, there is the work which they have already produced together, and this work itself contributes to produce that which follows. Beside the permanent impulse and the given surroundings, there is the acquired momentum. When the national character and surrounding circumstances operate, it is not upon a *tabula rasa,* but on a ground on which marks are already impressed. According as one takes the ground at one moment or another, the imprint is different; and this is the cause that the total effect is different.

Consider, for instance, two epochs of a literature or an art—French tragedy under Corneille and under Voltaire, the Greek drama under Aeschylus and under Euripides, Italian painting under da Vinci and under Guido. Truly, at either of these two extreme points the general idea has not changed; it is always the same human type which is its subject of representation or painting; the mold of verse, the structure of the drama, the form of body has endured. But among several differences there is this, that the one artist is the precursor, the other the successor; the first has no model, the second has; the first sees objects face to face, the second sees them through the first; that many great branches of art are lost, many details are perfected, that simplicity and grandeur of impression have diminished, pleasing and refined forms have increased—in short, that the first work has outlived the second. So it is with a people as with a plant; the same sap, under the same temperature, and in the same soil, produces, at different steps of its progressive development, different formations, buds, flowers, fruits, seed vessels, in such a manner that the one which follows has always the first for its condition, and grows from its death. And if now you consider no longer a brief epoch, as our own time, but one of those wide intervals which embrace one or more centuries, like the Middle Ages, or our last classic age, the conclusion will be similar. A certain dominant ideas has had sway; men, for two, for five hundred years, have taken to themselves a certain ideal model of man: in the Middle Ages, the knight and the monk; in our classic age, the courtier, the man who speaks well. This creative and universal idea is displayed over the whole field of action and thought; and after covering the world with its works, involuntarily systematic, it has faded, it has died away, and lo, a new idea springs up, destined to a like domination, and the like number of creations. And here remember that the second depends in part upon the first, and that the first, uniting its effect with those of national genius and surrounding circumstances, imposes on each new creation its bent and direction. The great historical currents are formed after this law—the long dominations of one intellectual pattern, or a master idea, such as the period of spontaneous creations called the Renaissance, or the period of oratorical models called the Classical Age, or the series of mystical compositions called the Alexandrian and Christian eras, or the series of mythological efflorescences which we meet with in the infancy of the German people, of the Indian and the Greek. Here as elsewhere we have but a mechanical problem; the total effect is a result, depending entirely on the magnitude and direction of the producing causes. The only difference which separates these moral problems from physical ones is, that the magnitude and direction cannot be valued or computed in the first as in the second. If a need or a faculty is a quantity, capable of degrees, like a pressure or a weight, this quantity is not measurable like the pressure or the weight. We cannot define it in an exact or approximative formula; we cannot have more, or give more, in respect of it, than a literary impression; we are limited to marking and quoting the salient points by which it is manifested, and which indicate approximately and roughly the part of the scale which is its position. But though the means of notation are not the same in the moral and physical sciences, yet as in both the matter is the same, equally made up of forces, magnitudes, and directions, we may say that in both the final result is produced after the same method. It is great or small, as the fundamental forces are great or small and act more or less exactly in the same sense, according as the distinct effects of race, circumstance, and epoch combine to add the one to the other, or to annul one another. Thus are explained the long impotences and the brilliant triumphs which make their appearance irregularly and without visible cause in the life of a people; they are caused by internal concords or contrarieties. There was such a concord when in the seventeenth century the sociable character and the conversational aptitude, innate in France, encountered the drawing room manners and the epoch of oratorical analysis; when in the nineteenth century the profound and elastic genius of Germany encountered the age of philosophical compositions and of cosmopolitan criticism. There was such a contrariety when in the seventeenth century the rude and lonely English genius tried blunderingly to adopt a novel politeness; when in the sixteenth century the lucid and prosaic French spirit tried vainly to cradle a living poetry. That hidden concord of creative forces produced the finished urbanity and the noble and regular literature under Louis XIV and Bossuet, the grand metaphysics and broad critical sympathy of Hegel and Goethe. That hidden contrariety of creative forces produced the imperfect literature, the scandalous comedy, the abortive drama under Dryden and Wycherley, the vile Greek importations, the groping elaborate efforts, the scant half-graces under Ronsard and the Pleiad.[4] So much we can say with confidence, that the unknown creations towards which the current of the centuries conducts us, will be raised up and regulated altogether by the three primordial forces; that if these forces could be measured and computed, one might deduce from them as from a formula the specialties of future civilization; and that if, in spite of the evident crudeness of our notations, and the fundamental inexactness of our measures, we try now to form some idea of our general destiny, it is upon an examination of these forces that we must ground

our prophecy. For in enumerating them, we traverse the complete circle of the agencies; and when we have considered race, circumstance, and epoch, which are the internal mainsprings, the external pressure, and the acquired momentum, we have exhausted not only the whole of the actual causes, but also the whole of the possible causes of motive.

VI

It remains for us to examine how these causes, when applied to a nation or an age, produce their results. As a rivulet falling from a height spreads its streams, according to the depth of the descent, stage after stage, until it reaches the lowest level of the soil, so the disposition of intellect or soul impressed on a people by race, circumstance, or epoch, spreads in different proportions and by regular descents, down the diverse orders of facts which make up its civilization.[5] If we arrange the map of a country, starting from the watershed, we find that below this common point the streams are divided into five or six principal basins, then each of these into several secondary basins, and so on, until the whole country with its thousand details is included in the ramifications of this network. So, if we arrange the psychological map of the events and sensations of a human civilization, we find first of all five or six well-defined provinces—religion, art, philosophy, the state, the family, the industries; then in each of these provinces natural departments; and in each of these, smaller territories, until we arrive at the numberless details of life such as may be observed within and around us every day. If now we examine and compare these diverse groups of facts, we find first of all that they are made up of parts, and that all have parts in common. Let us take first the three chief works of human intelligence—religion, art, philosophy. What is a philosophy but a conception of nature and its primordial causes, under the form of abstractions and formularies? What is there at the bottom of a religion or of an art but a conception of this same nature and of these same causes, under form of symbols more or less concise, and personages more or less marked; with this difference, that in the first we believe that they exist, in the second we believe that they do not exist? Let the reader consider a few of the great creations of the intelligence in India, Scandinavia, Persia, Rome, Greece, and he will see that, throughout, art is a kind

---

[4] A group of French poets to which Ronsard belonged.

[5] [Taine] For this scale of coordinate effects consult Renan, *Langues Sémitiques* [*General History of the Semitic Languages*], Chapter I; Mommsen, *Comparison between the Greek and Roman Civilizations,* 3rd ed., Vol. I, Chapter 2; and Tocqueville, *Consequences of Democracy in America,* Vol. III.

of philosophy made sensible, religion a poem taken for true, philosophy an art and a religion dried up, and reduced to simple ideas. There is therefore, at the core of each of these three groups, a common element, the conception of the world and its principles; and if they differ among themselves, it is because each combines with the common, a distinct element: now the power of abstraction, again the power to personify and to believe, and finally the power to personify and not believe. Let us now take the two chief works of human association, the family and the state. What forms the state but a sentiment of obedience, by which the many unite under the authority of a chief? And what forms the family but the sentiment of obedience, by which wife and children act under the direction of a father and husband? The family is a natural state, primitive and restrained, as the state is an artificial family, ulterior and expanded; and amongst the differences arising from the number, origin, and condition of its members, we discover in the small society as in the great, a like disposition of the fundamental intelligence which assimilates and unites them. Now suppose that this element receives from circumstance, race, or epoch certain special marks, it is clear that all the groups into which it enters, will be modified proportionately. If the sentiment of obedience is merely fear,[6] you will find, as in most Oriental states, a brutal despotism, exaggerated punishment, oppression of the subject, servility of manners, insecurity of property, an impoverished production, the slavery of women, and the customs of the harem. If the sentiment of obedience has its root in the instinct of order, sociality, and honor, you will find, as in France, a perfect military organization, a fine administrative hierarchy, a want of public spirit with occasional jerks of patriotism, ready docility of the subject with a revolutionary impatience, the cringing courtier with the counter-efforts of the genuine man, the refined sympathy between conversation and society on the one hand, and the worry at the fireside and among the family on the other, the equality of the married with the incompleteness of the married state, under the necessary constraint of the law. If, again, the sentiment of obedience has its root in the instinct of subordination and the idea of duty, you will find, as among the Germans, security and happiness in the household, a solid basis of domestic life, a tardy and incomplete development of society, an innate respect for established dignities, a superstitious reverence for the past, the keeping up of social inequalities, natural and habitual regard for the law. So in a race, according as the aptitude for general ideas varies, religion, art, and philosophy vary. If man is naturally inclined to the widest universal conceptions, and apt to disturb them at the same time by the nervous delicacy of his oversensitive organization, you will find, as in India, an astonishing abundance of gigantic religious creations, a glowing outgrowth of vast and transparent epic poems, a strange tangle of subtle and imaginative philosophies, all so well interwoven, and so penetrated with a common essence, as to be instantly recognized, by their breadth, their coloring, and their want of order, as the products of the same climate and the same intelligence. If, on the other hand, a man naturally staid and balanced in mind limits of his own accord the scope of his ideas, in order the better to define their form, you will find, as in Greece, a theology of artists and tale-tellers; distinctive gods, soon considered distinct from things, and transformed, almost at the outset, into recognized personages; the sentiment of universal unity all but effaced, and barely preserved in the vague notion of destiny; a philosophy rather close and delicate than grand and systematic, confined to a lofty metaphysics,[7] but incomparable for logic, sophistry, and morals; poetry and arts superior for clearness, spirit, scope, truth, and beauty to all that have ever been known. If, once more, man, reduced to narrow conceptions, and deprived of all speculative refinement, is at the same time altogether absorbed and straitened by practical occupations, you will find, as in Rome, rudimentary deities, mere hollow names, serving to designate the trivial details of agriculture, generation, household concerns, etiquettes in fact of marriage, of the farm, producing a mythology, a philosophy, a poetry, either worth nothing or borrowed. Here, as elsewhere, the law of mutual dependence[8] comes into play. A civilization forms a body, and its parts are connected with each other like the parts of an organic body. As in an animal, instincts, teeth, limbs, osseous structure, muscular envelope, are mutually connected, so that a change in one produces a corresponding change in the rest, and a clever naturalist can by a process of reasoning reconstruct out of a few fragments almost the whole body; even so in a civilization, religion, philosophy, the organization of the family, literature, the arts, make up a system in which every local change induces a general change, so that an experienced historian, studying some particular part of it, sees in advance and half predicts the character of the rest. There is

---

[6][Taine] Montesquieu, *Esprit des lois, principes des trois gouvernements* [*The Spirit of Laws*].

[7][Taine] The Alexandrian philosophy had its birth from the West. The metaphysical notions of Aristotle are isolated; moreover, with him as with Plato, they are but a sketch. By way of contrast consider the systematic vigor of Plotinus, Proclus, Schelling, and Hegel, or the admirable boldness of Brahminica and Buddhistic speculation.

[8][Taine] I have endeavored on several occasions to give expression to this law notably in the Preface to *Essais de critique et d'histoire* [*Critical and Historical Essays*].

nothing vague in this interdependence. In the living body the regulator is, first, its tendency to manifest a certain primary type; then its necessity for organs whereby to satisfy its wants, and for harmony with itself in order that it may live. In a civilization, the regulator is the presence, in every great human creation, of a productive element, present also in other surrounding creations—to wit, some faculty, aptitude, disposition, effective and discernible, which, being possessed of its proper character, introduces it into all the operations in which it assists, and, according to its variations, causes all the works in which it cooperates to vary also.

VII

At this point we can obtain a glimpse of the principal features of human transformations, and begin to search for the general laws which regulate, not events only, but classes of events, not such and such religion or literature, but a group of literatures or religions. If, for instance, it were admitted that a religion is a metaphysical poem, accompanied by a belief; and remarking at the same time that there are certain epochs, races, and circumstances in which belief, the poetical and metaphysical faculty, are combined with an unwonted vigor; if we consider that Christianity and Buddhism were produced at periods of grand productions, and amid such miseries as raised up the fanatics of the Cévennes; if we recognize, on the other hand, that primitive religions are born at the awakening of human reason, during the richest blossoming of human imagination, at a time of the fairest artlessness and the greatest credulity; if we consider, also, that Mohammedanism appeared with the dawning of poetic prose, and the conception of national unity, amongst a people destitute of science, at a period of sudden development of the intellect, we might then conclude that a religion is born, declines, is reformed and transformed according as circumstances confirm and combine with more or less exactitude and force its three generative instincts; and we should understand why it is endemic in India, amidst imaginative, philosophic, eminently fanatic brains; why it blossomed forth so strangely and grandly in the Middle Ages, amidst an oppressive organization, new tongues and literatures; why it was aroused in the sixteenth century with a new character and heroic enthusiasm, amid universal regeneration, and during the awakening of the German races; why it breaks out into eccentric sects amid the rude American democracy, and under the bureaucratic Russian despotism; why, in fine, it is spread, at the present day, over Europe in such different dimensions and such various characteristics, according to the differences of race and civilization. And so for every kind of

human production—for literature, music, the fine arts, philosophy, science, statecraft, industries, and the rest. Each of these has for its direct cause a moral disposition, or a combination of moral dispositions: the cause given, they appear; the cause withdrawn, they vanish: the weakness or intensity of the cause measures their weakness or intensity. They are bound up with their causes, as a physical phenomenon with its condition, as the dew with the fall of the variable temperature, as dilatation with heat. There are such dualities in the moral as in the physical world, as rigorously bound together, and as universally extended in the one as in the other. Whatever in the one case produces, alters, suppresses the first term, produces, alters, suppresses the second as a necessary consequence. Whatever lowers the temperature, deposits the dew. Whatever develops credulity side by side with poetical thoughts, engenders religion. Thus phenomena have been produced; thus they will be produced. As soon as we know the sufficient and necessary condition of one of these vast occurrences, our understanding grasps the future as well as the past. We can say with confidence in what circumstances it will reappear, foresee without rashness many portions of its future history, and sketch with care some features of its ulterior development.

VIII

History is now upon, or perhaps almost upon this footing, that it must proceed after such a method of research. The question propounded nowadays is of this kind. Given a literature, philosophy, society, art, group of arts, what is the moral condition which produced it? What the conditions of race, epoch, circumstance, the most fitted to produce this moral condition? There is a distinct moral condition for each of these formations, and for each of their branches; one for art in general, one for each kind of art—for architecture, painting, sculpture, music, poetry; each has its special germ in the wide field of human psychology; each has its law, and it is by virtue of this law that we see it raised, by chance, as it seems, wholly alone, amid the miscarriage of its neighbors, like painting in Flanders and Holland in the seventeenth century, poetry in England in the sixteenth, music in Germany in the eighteenth. At this moment, and in these countries, the conditions have been fulfilled for one art, not for others, and a single branch has budded in the general barrenness. For these rules of human growth must history search; with the special psychology of each special formation it must occupy itself; the finished picture of these characteristic conditions it must now labor to compose. No task is more delicate or more difficult; Montesquieu tried it, but in his time history was too new to admit of his success; they had not yet even a suspicion of the road necessary to be traveled, and hardly now do we begin to catch sight of it. Just as in its elements astronomy is a mechanical and physiology a chemical problem, so history in its elements is a psychological problem. There is a particular inner system of impressions and operations which makes an artist, a believer, a musician, a painter, a wanderer, a man of society; and of each the affiliation, the depth, the independence of ideas and emotions, are different: each has its moral history and its special structure, with some governing disposition and some dominant feature. To explain each, it would be necessary to write a chapter of esoteric analysis, and barely yet has such a method been rudely sketched. One man alone, Stendhal, with a singular bent of mind and a singular education, has undertaken it, and to this day the majority of readers find his books paradoxical and obscure: his talent and his ideas were premature; his admirable divinations were not understood, any more than his profound sayings thrown out cursorily, or the astonishing justness of his perception and of his logic. It was not perceived that, under the exterior of a conversationalist and a man of the world, he explained the most complicated of esoteric mechanisms; that he laid his finger on the mainsprings; that he introduced into the history of the heart scientific processes, the art of notation, decomposition, deduction; that he first marked the fundamental causes of nationality, climate, temperament; in short, that he treated of sentiments as they should be treated—in the manner of the naturalist, namely, and of the natural philosopher, who constructs classifications and weighs forces. For this very reason he was considered dry and eccentric: he remained solitary, writing novels, voyages, notes, for which he sought and obtained a score of readers. And yet we find in his books at the present day essays the most suitable to open the path which I have endeavored to describe. No one has better taught us how to open our eyes and see, to see first the men that surround us and the life that is present, then the ancient and authentic documents, to read between the black and white lines of the pages, to recognize under the old impression, under the scribbling of a text, the precise sentiment, the movement of ideas, the state of mind in which they were written. In his writings, in Sainte-Beuve, in the German critics, the reader will see all the wealth that may be drawn from a literary work: when the work is rich, and one knows how to interpret it, we find there the psychology of a soul, frequently of an age, now and then of a race. In this light, a great poem, a fine novel, the confessions of a superior man, are more instructive than a heap of historians with their histories. I would give fifty volumes of charters and a hundred volumes of state papers for the memoirs of Cellini, the epis-

tles of St. Paul, the table-talk of Luther, or the comedies of Aristophanes. In this consists the importance of literary works: they are instructive because they are beautiful; their utility grows with their perfection; and if they furnish documents, it is because they are monuments. The more a book represents visible sentiments, the more it is a work of literature; for the proper office of literature is to take note of sentiments. The more a book represents important sentiments, the higher is its place in literature; for it is by representing the mode of being of a whole nation and a whole age, that a writer rallies round him the sympathies of an entire age and an entire nation. This is why, amid the writings which set before our eyes the sentiments of preceding generations, a literature, and notably a grand literature, is incomparably the best. It resembles that admirable apparatus of extraordinary sensibility, by which physicians disentangle and measure the most recondite and delicate changes of a body. Constitutions, religions, do not approach it in importance; the articles of a code and of a catechism only show us the spirit roughly and without delicacy. If there are any writings in which politics and dogma are full of life, it is in the eloquent discourses of the pulpit and the tribune, memoirs, unrestrained confessions; and all this belongs to literature: so that, in addition to itself, it has all the advantage of other works. It is then chiefly by the study of literatures that one may construct a moral history, and advance toward the knowledge of psychological laws, from which events spring.

I am about to write the history of a literature, and to seek in it for the psychology of a people: if I have chosen this one in particular, it is not without a reason. I had to find a people with a grand and complete literature, and this is rare: there are few nations who have, during their whole existence, really thought and written. Among the ancients, the Latin literature is worth nothing at the outset, then borrowed and imitative. Among the moderns, German literature is almost wanting for two centuries.[9] Italian literature and Spanish literature end at the middle of the seventeenth century. Only ancient Greece, modern France and England, offer a complete series of great significant monuments. I have chosen England, because being yet alive, and subject to direct examination, it may be better studied than a destroyed civilization, of which we retain but the scraps, and because, being different from France, it has in the eyes of a Frenchman a more distinct character. Besides, there is a peculiarity in this civilization, that apart from its spontaneous development, it presents a forced deviation, it has suffered the last and most effectual of all conquests, and that the three

---

[9][Taine] From 1550 to 1750.

grounds whence it has sprung, race, climate, the Norman invasion, may be observed in its remains with perfect exactness; so well, that we may examine in this history the two most powerful moving springs of human transformation, natural bent and constraining force, and we may examine them without uncertainty or gap, in a series of authentic and unmutilated memorials. I have endeavored to define these primary springs, to exhibit their gradual effects, to explain how they have ended by bringing to light great political, religious, and literary works, and by developing the recondite mechanism whereby the Saxon barbarian has been transformed into the Englishman of today.

Charles Baudelaire

1821–1867

The French poet Baudelaire was an art critic of considerable powers. The selections below from *The Salon of 1859* have to do with painting, but the ideas are applicable to literary works as well. For Baudelaire the imagination is the "queen of faculties." He thinks of it as a truly creative power. Though nature is full of potential meaning that generates a sort of occult wonder (see his famous sonnet *Correspondences*), it is but a dictionary that must be used to construct our experience. The imagination must shape what nature makes available to it.

Baudelaire's view is post-Kantian and post-Romantic. Nature is a sort of manifold of sensation, in Kant's terms, that is given significance by the power of human beings. When nature is thought of as a dictionary—a mere source of the basic elements of a work of art—copying nature is at best a trivial undertaking; man must breathe his own life into his experience and his art.

An early symbolist, Baudelaire displays a criticism that has definite intellectual links with the discussion of symbols by Coleridge and Carlyle and with Emerson's view of the relationship of poetry to nature. His work precedes Mallarmé's remark that "all earthly existence must ultimately be contained in a book."

Baudelaire's literary criticism is available in *Baudelaire as a Literary Critic,* translated and edited by L. B. Hyslop and F. E. Hyslop (1964), and *The Mirror of Art: Critical Studies by Baudelaire,* translated and edited by Jonathan Mayne (1956). For commentary consult Marcel Raymond, *From Baudelaire to Surrealism* (1930); André Ferran, *L'Esthétique de Baudelaire* (1933); Margaret Gilman, *Baudelaire the Critic* (1943); Martin Turnell, *Baudelaire: A Study of His Poetry* (1953); Enid Starkie, *Baudelaire* (1957); Alfred E. Carter, *Charles Baudelaire* (1977); Rosemary Lloyd, *Baudelaire's Literary Criticism* (1981); and Timothy B. Raser, *A Poetics of Art Criticism: The Case of Baudelaire* (1988).

The Salon of 1859

From

Part III

The Queen of Faculties

In recent years we have heard it said in a thousand different ways: "Copy nature; copy only nature. There is no greater delight, no finer triumph, than an excellent copy of nature." And this doctrine, so inimical to art, was alleged to apply not only to painting but to all the arts, even to the novel, even to poetry. To these doctrinaires so satisfied with nature, an imaginative man would certainly have had the right to answer: "I consider it useless and tiresome to portray things as they are, because nothing that exists satisfies me. Nature is ugly, and I prefer the monsters of my imagination to the triteness of actuality." It would have been more philosophical, however, to ask these dogmatists, first whether they are really certain of the existence of external nature, or in case this question seemed too well calculated to please their caustic humor, whether they are quite certain of knowing *all nature,* all that is contained in nature. A "yes" would have been the most boastful and the most absurd of answers. If I have correctly understood these strange and degrading divagations, the doctrine meant, at least I am doing it the honor of believing that it meant: "The artist, the true artist, the true poet, should paint only in accordance with what he sees and what he feels. He should be *really* true to his own nature. He should avoid, like death itself, borrowing the eyes and emotions of another man, however great that man may be; for in that case his productions would be lies, so far as he is concerned, and not *realities.*" But if the pedants of whom I am speaking (there is pedantry even in what is contemptible) and who have representatives everywhere—since this theory flatters impotence and indolence alike—if these pedants did not wish the matter to be understood in this way, let us simply believe that they meant: "We have no imagination, and we decree that no one shall have any."

How mysterious is this queen of faculties! It affects all the other faculties; it rouses them, it sends them into combat.

Sometimes it resembles them to the point of confusion, and yet it is always very much itself, and the persons who are not stirred by it are easily recognizable by an indefinable curse which withers their productions like the fig tree of the Gospel.

It is analysis, it is synthesis; and yet men who excel in analysis and who are fairly apt in summarizing may lack imagination. It is that, and it is not altogether that. It is sensitivity, and yet there are very sensitive persons, too sensitive perhaps, who are devoid of it. It is imagination that has taught man the moral meaning of color, of outline, of sound, and of perfume. In the beginning of the world it created analogy and metaphor. It decomposes all creation, and from the materials, accumulated and arranged according to rules whose origin is found only in the depths of the soul, it creates a new world, it produces the sensation of the new. Since it has created the world (this can really be said, I believe, even in a religious sense), it is only right that it should govern it. What do people say about a warrior without imagination? That he may make an excellent soldier, but that if he is put in command of armies, he will make no conquests. The case is like that of a poet or a novelist who might take the command of his faculties away from his imagination to give it, for example, to his knowledge of the language or to his observation of facts. What is said of a diplomat without imagination? That he may know all about the history of treaties and alliances in the past, but that he will not sense the treaties and alliances that may evolve in the future. Of a scholar without imagination? That he has learned everything that could be learned from what he was taught, but that he will not discover laws that have not yet been conceived. Imagination is the queen of truth, and the possible is one of the provinces of truth. It has a definite relationship with the infinite.

Without it, all the faculties, however sound or keen they may be, are seemingly nonexistent, whereas the weakness of certain secondary faculties, when excited by a vigorous imagination, is a secondary misfortune. None of the faculties can do without it, and it can even replace some of the others. Imagination often guesses, boldly and simply, what the secondary faculties seek and find only after successive trials of several methods unadapted to the nature of things. Lastly, it plays a powerful role even in morality; for if I may be so bold as to ask—what is virtue without imagination? You might as well speak of virtue without pity, virtue without heaven; it is something hard, cruel, sterilizing, which in certain countries has become bigotry and in certain others, Protestantism.

THE SALON OF 1859. Baudelaire's *Salon de 1859* appeared in 1859. The texts are from *Baudelaire as a Literary Critic,* translated and edited by Lois Boe Hyslop and Francis E. Hyslop, Jr. (University Park: The Pennsylvania State University Press, 1964). Reprinted by permission of the publisher.

From

Part IV

The Rule of the Imagination

Yesterday evening, after having sent you the last pages of my letter, in which I had written, not without a certain diffidence: "Since imagination has created the world, it governs it," I was scanning *The Night Side of Nature*[1] and I came across these lines which I am quoting solely because they are a paraphrase justifying the line that was worrying me:

> By *imagination,* I do not simply mean to convey the common notion implied by that much abused word, which is only *fancy,* but the *constructive* imagination, which is a much higher function, and which, inasmuch as man is made in the likeness of God, bears a distant relation to that sublime power by which the Creator projects, creates, and upholds his universe.

I am not at all ashamed but, on the contrary, very happy to be in agreement with the excellent Mrs. Crowe, in whom I have always admired the capacity for belief which is as fully developed in her as is the capacity for distrust in many others.

I was saying that long ago I had heard a man,[2] truly scholarly and profoundly learned in his art, express the most comprehensive and yet the most simple ideas on this subject. When I met him for the first time, I had no experience other than that which comes from an overwhelming love and no other reasoning save instinct. It is true that this love and this instinct were fairly keen, for from my earliest youth, my eyes, filled with paintings or engravings, could never be satiated, and I think that worlds could come to an end, *impavidum ferient,*[3] before I would become an iconoclast. Evidently he wanted to be very kind and obliging, for at first we talked of commonplaces, that is to say, of the most comprehensive and the most profound questions—about nature, for example. "Nature is only a dictionary," he would often say. To properly understand the full meaning implied in this statement, one should keep in mind the many ordinary uses of the dictionary. In it one seeks the meaning of words, the genealogy of words, the etymology of words; in short, one extracts from it all the elements that compose a sentence and a narrative. But no one has ever considered the dictionary as a composition in the poetic sense of the word. Painters who obey their imagination seek in their dictionary the elements which suit their conception; yet, in adapting these elements with a certain art, they give them an altogether new physiognomy. Those who lack imagination copy the dictionary. The result is a very great fault, the fault of banality, which is especially true of those painters whose speciality brings them into closer contact with exterior nature—landscape painters, for example, who generally consider it a triumph not to show their personality. Through too much looking, they forget to feel and to think. . . .

I have no fear that anyone will find it absurd to suppose that the same education is applicable to a host of different individuals. For it is evident that systems of rhetoric and prosody are not arbitrarily invented tyrannies, but rather a collection of rules required by the very nature of the spiritual being. And systems of prosody and rhetoric have never kept originality from showing itself clearly. The contrary—namely, that they have aided the development of originality—would be infinitely more true.

To be brief, I am obliged to omit numerous corollaries resulting from my principal formula, in which is contained, so to speak, the entire formulary of the true aesthetic, and which may be expressed thus: The whole visible universe is but a storehouse of images and signs[4] to which imagination will give a relative place and value; it is a sort of food which the imagination must digest and transform. All the powers of the human soul must be subordinated to the imagination, which commandeers them all at one and the same time. Just as knowing the dictionary well does not necessarily imply a knowledge of the art of composition, and just as the art of composition does not itself imply a universal imagination, so a good painter may not be a great painter. But a great painter is inevitably a good painter, because a universal imagination includes the understanding of all means of expression and the desire to master them.

---

[1]By Catherine Crowe, published in 1848.
[2]The French painter Eugène Delacroix (1799–1863).
[3]"They smash him undismayed." Horace, *Odes,* III. iii. 8.

[4]Compare Baudelaire's sonnet *Correspondences.*

Karl Marx

1818–1883

Not only did Marx have a very broad doctrinal influence on critics and writers, he also helped to form a movement that considers literature a sociological phenomenon to be treated similarly to other such phenomena. Literature thus becomes analyzable as a symptom of social situations. Interest in literature and other art forms is also treated as a symptom. Marx's position is fundamentally that social being determines consciousness and not vice versa. Art, an expression of consciousness, is thus also determined by social being and is therefore usually characterized by struggle in which the differences and conflicts within a society are fought out.

One can see in Shelley and Peacock an emerging concern with the poet's function in society. In the wake of Romanticism and in the growth of positivistic philosophies and the disciplines of anthropology, psychology, and sociology, interest arose in literature as historical or sociological document. As a commentator on literature, Marx is in a tradition that includes scholars and critics of various persuasions from the French literary historian Taine to the American, Parrington. He is a thoroughgoing materialist and his work marks a turning against the epistemological positions popular among early nineteenth-century German idealists.

Study of Marx's whole philosophy, not just his specific references to or discussions of literature, is necessary to understand his importance to literary theory. The two selections below, from *The German Ideology* (with Friedrich Engels) and *A Contribution to the Critique of Political Economy,* nevertheless provide some sense of Marx's position. One should consult Trotsky for development of and comment on the Marxist approach, as well as works cited in the bibliography.

Literature and Art, by Karl Marx and Frederick Engels: Selections from Their Writings (1947) is a valuable collection. Among the many studies of Marx and the Marxist approach, the following may be mentioned: Nikolai Bukharin, *Problems of Soviet Literature* (n.d.); Leon Trotsky, *Literature and Revolution* (1924); G. V. Plekhanov, *Art and Society* (1937); Christopher Caudwell, *Illusion and Reality* (1937), and *Studies in a Dying Culture* (1938); Ralph Fox, *The Novel and the People* (1937); Mikhail Lifshitz, *The Philosophy of Art of Karl Marx* (1938); Georg Lukács, *The Meaning of Contemporary Realism* (1958); Peter Demetz, *Marx, Engels, und die Dichter* (1959); Ernst Fischer, *The Necessity of Art: A Marxist Approach* (1963); and Herbert Marcuse, *The Aesthetic Dimension: Toward a Critique of Marxist Aesthetics* (tr. 1978).

From
The German Ideology

The production of ideas, of conceptions, of consciousness, is at first directly interwoven with the material activity and the material intercourse of men, the language of real life. Conceiving, thinking, the mental intercourse of men, appear at this stage as the direct efflux of their material behavior. The same applies to mental production as expressed in the language of the politics, laws, morality, religion, metaphysics of a people. Men are the producers of their conceptions, ideas, etc.—real, active men, as they are conditioned by a definite development of their productive forces and of the intercourse corresponding to these, up to its furthest forms. Consciousness can never be anything else than conscious existence, and the existence of men is their actual life process. If in all ideology men and their circumstances appear upside down as in a camera obscura, this phenomenon arises just as much from their historical life process as the inversion of objects on the retina does from their physical life process.

In direct contrast to German philosophy which descends from heaven to earth, here we ascend from earth to heaven. That is to say, we do not set out from what men say, imagine, conceive, nor from men as narrated, thought of, imagined, conceived, in order to arrive at men in the flesh. We set out from real, active men, and on the basis of their real life process we demonstrate the development of the ideological reflexes and echoes of this life process. The phantoms formed in the human brain are also, necessarily, sublimates of their material life process, which is empirically verifiable and bound to material premises. Morality, religion, metaphysics, all the rest of ideology and their corresponding forms of consciousness, thus no longer retain the semblance of independence. They have no history, no development; but men, developing their material production and their material intercourse, alter, along with this their real existence, their thinking and the products of their thinking. Life is not determined by consciousness, but consciousness by life. In the first method of approach the starting point is consciousness taken as the living individual; in the second it is the real living individuals themselves, as they are in actual life, and consciousness is considered solely as *their* consciousness.

This method of approach is not devoid of premises. It starts out from the real premises and does not abandon them for a moment. Its premises are men, not in any fantastic isolation or abstract definition, but in their actual, empirically perceptible process of development under definite conditions. As soon as this active life process is described, history ceases to be a collection of dead facts as it is with the empiricists (themselves still abstract), or an imagined activity of imagined subjects, as with the idealists.

Where speculation ends—in real life—there real, positive science begins: the representation of the practical activity, of the practical process of development of men. Empty talk about consciousness ceases, and real knowledge has to take its place. When reality is depicted, philosophy as an independent branch of activity loses its medium of existence. At the best its place can only be taken by a summing-up of the most general results, abstractions which arise from the observation of the historical development of men. Viewed apart from real history, these abstractions have in themselves no value whatsoever. They can only serve to facilitate the arrangement of historical material, to indicate the sequence of its separate strata. But they by no means afford a recipe or schema, as does philosophy, for neatly trimming the epochs of history. On the contrary, our difficulties begin only when we set about the observation and the arrangement—the real depiction—of our historical material, whether of a past epoch or of the present. The removal of these difficulties is governed by premises which it is quite impossible to state here, but which only the study of the actual life process and the activity of the individuals of each epoch will make evident.

From
A Contribution to the Critique of Political Economy

It is well known that certain periods of highest development of art stand in no direct connection with the general development of society, nor with the material basis and the skeleton structure of its organization. Witness the example of the Greeks as compared with the modern nations or even Shake-

---

THE GERMAN IDEOLOGY. *Die Deutsche Ideologie,* by Karl Marx and Friedrich Engels, was written in 1846 but not published until 1932. The text is from *Literature and Art, by Karl Marx and Frederick Engels: Selections from Their Writings.* Copyright © 1947 by International Publishers Co., Inc. Reprinted by permission of the publisher.

THE CRITIQUE OF POLITICAL ECONOMY. Marx's *Zur Kritik der politischen Ökonomie* was published in 1859. The present selection is from *Literature and Art, by Karl Marx and Frederick Engels: Selections from Their Writings.* Copyright © 1947 by International Publishers Co., Inc. Reprinted by permission of the publisher.

speare. As regards certain forms of art, as, as, e.g., the epos, it is admitted that they can never be produced in the world-epoch-making form as soon as art as such comes into existence; in other words, that in the domain of art certain important forms of it are possible only at a low stage of its development. If that be true of the mutual relations of different forms of art within the domain of art itself, it is far less surprising that the same is true of the relation of art as a whole to the general development of society. The difficulty lies only in the general formulation of these contradictions. No sooner are they specified than they are explained. Let us take for instance the relation of Greek art and of that of Shakespeare's time to our own. It is a well-known fact that Greek mythology was not only the arsenal of Greek art, but also the very ground from which it had sprung. Is the view of nature and of social relations which shaped Greek imagination and Greek [art] possible in the age of automatic machinery, and railways, and locomotives, and electric telegraphs? Where does Vulcan come in as against Roberts & Co.; Jupiter, as against the lightning rod; and Hermes, as against the Credit Mobilier? All mythology masters and dominates and shapes the forces of nature in and through the imagination; hence it disappears as soon as man gains mastery over the forces of nature. What becomes of the goddess Fame side by side with Printing House Square? Greek art presupposes the existence of Greek mythology, i.e., that nature and even the form of society are wrought up in popular fancy in an unconsciously artistic fashion. That is its material. Not, however, any mythology taken at random, nor any accidental, unconsciously artistic elaboration of nature (including under the latter all objects; hence also society). Egyptian mythology could never be the soil or womb which would give birth to Greek art. But in any event there had to be a mythology. In no event could Greek art originate in a society which excludes any mythological explanation of nature, any mythological attitude towards it and which requires from the artist an imagination free from mythology.

Looking at it from another side: Is Achilles possible side by side with powder and lead? Or is the *Iliad* at all compatible with the printing press and steam press? Do not singing and reciting and the Muses necessarily go out of existence with the appearance of the printer's bar, and do not, therefore, disappear, the prerequisites of epic poetry?

But the difficulty is not in grasping the idea that Greek art and epos are bound up with certain forms of social development. It rather lies in understanding why they still constitute with us a source of aesthetic enjoyment and in certain respects prevail as the standard and model beyond attainment.

A man cannot become a child again unless he becomes childish. But does he not enjoy the artless ways of the child and must he not strive to reproduce its truth on a higher plane? Is not the character of every epoch revived perfectly true to nature in child nature? Why should the social childhood of mankind, where it had obtained its most beautiful development, not exert an eternal charm as an age that will never return? There are ill-bred children and precocious children. Many of the ancient nations belong to the latter class. The Greeks were normal children. The charm their art has for us does not conflict with the primitive character of the social order from which it had sprung. It is rather the product of the latter, and is rather due to the fact that the unripe social conditions under which the art arose and under which alone it could appear could never return.

. . .

In the social production which men carry on they enter into definite relations that are indispensable and independent of their will; these relations of production correspond to a definite stage of development of their material forces of production. The sum total of these relations of production constitutes the economic structure of society—the real foundation, on which rises a legal and political superstructure and to which correspond definite forms of social consciousness. The mode of production in material life determines the social, political, and intellectual life processes in general. It is not the consciousness of men that determines their being, but, on the contrary, their social being that determines their consciousness. At a certain stage of their development, the material forces of production in society come in conflict with the existing relations of production, or—what is but a legal expression for the same thing—with the property relations within which they have been at work before. From forms of development of the forces of production these relations turn into their fetters. Then begins an epoch of social revolution. With the change of the economic foundation the entire immense superstructure is more or less rapidly transformed. In considering such transformations a distinction should always be made between the material transformation of the economic conditions of production which can be determined with the precision of natural science, and the legal, political, religious, aesthetic, or philosophic—in short, ideological—forms in which men become conscious of this conflict and fight it out. Just as our opinion of an individual is not based on what he thinks of himself, so can we not judge of such a period of transformation by its own consciousness; on the contrary this consciousness must be explained rather from the contradictions of material life, from the existing conflict between the social forces of production and the relations of production. No social order ever disappears before all the productive forces for which there is room in it have been developed; and new higher relations of production never appear before the material conditions of their existence have matured in the womb of the old society itself. Therefore, mankind always sets itself only such tasks as it can solve; since, looking at the matter more closely, we will always find that the task itself arises only when the material conditions necessary for its solution already exist or are at least in the process of formation. In broad outlines we can designate the Asiatic, the ancient, the feudal, and the modern bourgeois modes of production as so many epochs in the progress of the economic formation of society. The bourgeois relations of production are the last antagonistic form of the social process of production—antagonistic not in the sense of individual antagonism, but of one arising from the social conditions of life of the individuals; at the same time the productive forces developing in the womb of bourgeois society create the material conditions for the solution of that antagonism. This social formation constitutes, therefore, the closing chapter of the prehistoric stage of human society.

Friedrich Nietzsche

1844–1900

The role of Nietzsche in the history of criticism and theory was much enlarged by the recent perception of him as one of the first real deconstructionists. Thus Jacques Derrida saw him as a thinker whose critique of Western metaphysics his own work extends. In "Truth and Falsity in an Ultramoral Sense" Nietzsche questions the relation of language to truth. What comes under his gaze is the tendency of language always toward abstraction and away from the individual and real, and finally into the threat of rational fixity. From this questioning of language comes Nietzsche's questioning of reason and his division between what he called the Dionysiac and the Apollonian, set forth in *The Birth of Tragedy from the Spirit of Music*. Appearing one year before "Truth and Falsity," it was partly inspired by Richard Wagner, although Nietzsche later denounced Wagner. The two terms distinguish the primitive from the rational and, in Nietzsche's view, the potentially unhealthy. As Greek tragedy developed, one impulse came to balance the other, Dionysiac ecstacy being ordered by Apollonian form and repose. Music, an attempt to give form to the world of the spirit, strives toward symbolic expression of that Dionysiac wisdom characteristic of tragedy, but in modern life the tragic view has been suppressed in scientific optimism. It may be that it will not reappear until "science [has] at least been pushed to its limits." Every culture that has lost the Dionysiac mythmaking spirit "has lost, by the same token its natural, healthy creativity."

Nietzsche secularizes the "truth" in language that is a lie and sees Dionysiac art and mythmaking as performing the disruption of the fixity toward which language in its Apollonian phase tends.

Nietzsche's complete works in translation are available in the 18-volume edition of 1909–1914 edited by Oscar Levy. See Erich Heller, *The Disinherited Mind* (1952); Arthur Danto, *Nietzsche as Philosopher* (1965); Karl Jaspers, *Nietzsche* (1965); Joan Stambaugh, *Nietzsche's Thought of the Eternal Return* (1972); Gilles Deleuze, *Nietzsche and Philosophy* (1973, tr. 1983); D. B. Allison, ed., *The New Nietzsche* (1977); D. F. Kull and D. Wood, eds., *Exceedingly Nietzsche* (1988); Ronald Hayman, *Nietzsche: A Critical Life;* Ernst Behler, *Derrida-Nietzsche, Nietzsche-Derrida* (1988); and Erich Heller, *The Importance of Nietzsche* (1988).

From

The Birth of Tragedy from the Spirit of Music

I

Much will have been gained for aesthetics once we have succeeded in apprehending directly—rather than merely *ascertaining*—that art owes its continuous evolution to the Apollonian-Dionysiac duality, even as the propagation of the species depends on the duality of the sexes, their constant conflicts and periodic acts of reconciliation. I have borrowed my adjectives from the Greeks, who developed their mystical doctrines of art through plausible *embodiments,* not through purely conceptual means. It is by those two art-sponsoring deities, Apollo and Dionysos,[1] that we are made to recognize the tremendous split, as regards both origins and objectives, between the plastic, Apollonian arts and the nonvisual art of music inspired by Dionysos. The two creative tendencies developed alongside one another, usually in fierce opposition, each by its taunts forcing the other to more energetic production, both perpetuating in a discordant concord that agon[2] which the term *art* but feebly denominates: until at last, by the thaumaturgy[3] of a Hellenic act of will, the pair accepted the yoke of marriage and, in this condition, begot Attic[4] tragedy, which exhibits the salient features of both parents.

To reach a closer understanding of both these tendencies, let us begin by viewing them as the separate art realms of *dream* and *intoxication,* two physiological phenomena standing toward one another in much the same relationship as the Apollonian and Dionysiac. It was in a dream, according to Lucretius, that the marvelous gods and goddesses first presented themselves to the minds of men. That great sculptor, Phidias, beheld in a dream the entrancing bodies of more-than-human beings, and likewise, if anyone had asked the Greek poets about the mystery of poetic creation, they too would have referred him to dreams and instructed him much as Hans Sachs instructs us in *Die Meistersinger:*

My friend, it is the poet's work
Dreams to interpret and to mark.
Believe me that man's true conceit
In a dream becomes complete:
All poetry we ever read
Is but true dreams interpreted.[5]

The fair illusion of the dream sphere, in the production of which every man proves himself an accomplished artist, is a precondition not only of all plastic art, but even, as we shall see presently, of a wide range of poetry. Here we enjoy an immediate apprehension of form, all shapes speak to us directly, nothing seems indifferent or redundant. Despite the high intensity with which these dream realities exist for us, we still have a residual sensation that they are illusions; at least such has been my experience—and the frequency, not to say normality, of the experience is borne out in many passages of the poets. Men of philosophical disposition are known for their constant premonition that our everyday reality, too, is an illusion, hiding another, totally different kind of reality. It was Schopenhauer who considered the ability to view at certain times all men and things as mere phantoms or dream images to be the true mark of philosophic talent. The person who is responsive to the stimuli of art behaves toward the reality of dream much the way the philosopher behaves toward the reality of existence: he observes exactly and enjoys his observations, for it is by these images that he interprets life, by these processes that he rehearses it. Nor is it by pleasant images only that such plausible connections are made: the whole divine comedy of life, including its somber aspects, its sudden balkings, impish accidents, anxious expectations, moves past him, not quite like a shadow play—for it is he himself, after all, who lives and suffers through these scenes—yet never without giving a fleeting sense of illusion; and I imagine that many persons have reassured themselves amidst the perils of dream by calling out, "It is a dream! I want it to go on." I have even heard of people spinning out the causality of one and the same dream over three or more successive nights. All these facts clearly bear witness that our innermost being, the common substratum of humanity, experiences dreams with deep delight and a sense of real necessity. This deep and happy sense of the necessity of dream experiences was expressed by the Greeks in the image of Apollo. Apollo is at once the god of all plastic powers and the soothsaying god. He who is etymologically the *lucent* one, the god of light, reigns also over the fair

THE BIRTH OF TRAGEDY. Nietzsche's *Die Geburt der Tragödie* was first published in 1872. The text is from *The Birth of Tragedy and the Genealogy of Morals,* translated by Francis Golffing. Copyright © 1956 by Doubleday & Company, Inc. Reprinted by permission of the publisher.
[1]Greek gods of beauty and wine respectively.
[2]Conflict of characters in drama.
[3]Magic or miracle.
[4]Greek.

[5]Richard Wagner, *Die Meistersinger von Nürnberg,* III. i. 99–104.

illusion of our inner world of fantasy. The perfection of these conditions in contrast to our imperfectly understood waking reality, as well as our profound awareness of nature's healing powers during the interval of sleep and dream, furnishes a symbolic analogue to the soothsaying faculty and quite generally to the arts, which make life possible and worth living. But the image of Apollo must incorporate that thin line which the dream image may not cross, under penalty of becoming pathological, of imposing itself on us as crass reality: a discreet limitation, a freedom from all extravagant urges, the sapient tranquility of the plastic god. His eye must be sunlike, in keeping with his origin. Even at those moments when he is angry and ill-tempered there lies upon him the consecration of fair illusion. In an eccentric way one might say of Apollo what Schopenhauer says, in the first part of *The World as Will and Idea,* of man caught in the veil of Maya:[6] "Even as on an immense, raging sea, assailed by huge wave crests, a man sits in a little rowboat trusting his frail craft, so, amidst the furious torments of this world, the individual sits tranquilly, supported by the *principium individuationis*[7] and relying on it." One might say that the unshakable confidence in that principle has received its most magnificent expression in Apollo, and that Apollo himself may be regarded as the marvelous divine image of the *principium individuationis,* whose looks and gestures radiate the full delight, wisdom, and beauty of "illusion."

In the same context Schopenhauer has described for us the tremendous awe which seizes man when he suddenly begins to doubt the cognitive modes of experience, in other words, when in a given instance the law of causation seems to suspend itself. If we add to this awe the glorious transport which arises in man, even from the very depths of nature, at the shattering of the *principium individuationis,* then we are in a position to apprehend the essence of Dionysiac rapture, whose closest analogy is furnished by physical intoxication. Dionysiac stirrings arise either through the influence of those narcotic potions of which all primitive races speak in their hymns, or through the powerful approach of spring, which penetrates with joy the whole frame of nature. So stirred, the individual forgets himself completely. It is the same Dionysiac power which in medieval Germany drove ever-increasing crowds of people singing and dancing from place to place; we recognize in these St. John's and St. Vitus' dancers the bacchic choruses of the Greeks, who had their precursors in Asia Minor and as far back as Babylon and the orgiastic Sacaea.[8] There are people who, either from lack of experi-

ence or out of sheer stupidity, turn away from such phenomena, and, strong in the sense of their own sanity, label them either mockingly or pityingly "endemic diseases." These benighted souls have no idea how cadaverous and ghostly their "sanity" appears as the intense throng of Dionysiac revelers sweeps past them.

Not only does the bond between man and man come to be forged once more by the magic of the Dionysiac rite, but nature itself, long alienated or subjugated, rises again to celebrate the reconciliation with her prodigal son, man. The earth offers its gifts voluntarily, and the savage beasts of mountain and desert approach in peace. The chariot of Dionysos is bedecked with flowers and garlands; panthers and tigers stride beneath his yoke. If one were to convert Beethoven's *Paen to Joy* into a painting, and refuse to curb the imagination when that multitude prostrates itself reverently in the dust, one might form some apprehension of Dionysiac ritual. Now the slave emerges as a freeman; all the rigid, hostile walls which either necessity or despotism has erected between men are shattered. Now that the gospel of universal harmony is sounded, each individual becomes not only reconciled to his fellow but actually at one with him—as though the veils of Maya had been torn apart and there remained only shreds floating before the vision of mystical oneness. Man now expresses himself through song and dance as the member of a higher community; he has forgotten how to walk, how to speak, and is on the brink of taking wing as he dances. Each of his gestures betokens enchantment; through him sounds a supernatural power, the same power which makes the animals speak and the earth render up milk and honey. He feels himself to be godlike and strides with the same elation and ecstasy as the gods he has seen in his dreams. No longer the *artist,* he has himself become a *work of art:* the productive power of the whole universe is now manifest in his transport, to the glorious satisfaction of the primordial One. The finest clay, the most precious marble—man—is here kneaded and hewn, and the chisel blows of the Dionysiac world artist are accompanied by the cry of the Eleusinian mystagogues:[9] "Do you fall on your knees, multitudes, do you divine your creator?"

II

So far we have examined the Apollonian and Dionysiac states as the product of formative forces arising directly from nature without the mediation of the human artist. At this

---

[6]Hindu goddess representing illusion.
[7]"Undivided or ultimate principle."
[8]An ancient Babylonian festival, culminating in the death of a surrogate king.

[9]The mysteries of Eleusis were secret religious rites practiced in Greece at Eleusis in the spring to honor the goddesses of vegetation and death.

stage artistic urges are satisfied directly, on the one hand through the imagery of dreams, whose perfection is quite independent of the intellectual rank, the artistic development of the individual; on the other hand, through an ecstatic reality which once again takes no account of the individual and may even destroy him, or else redeem him through a mystical experience of the collective. In relation to these immediate creative conditions of nature every artist must appear as "imitator," either as the Apollonian dream artist or the Dionysiac ecstatic artist, or, finally (as in Greek tragedy, for example) as dream and ecstatic artist in one. We might picture to ourselves how the last of these, in a state of Dionysiac intoxication and mystical self-abrogation, wandering apart from the reveling throng, sinks upon the ground, and how there is then revealed to him his own condition—complete oneness with the essence of the universe—in a dream similitude.

Having set down these general premises and distinctions, we now turn to the Greeks in order to realize to what degree the formative forces of nature were developed in them. Such an inquiry will enable us to assess properly the relation of the Greek artist to his prototypes or, to use Aristotle's expression, his "imitation of nature." Of the dreams the Greeks dreamed it is not possible to speak with any certainty, despite the extant dream literature and the large number of dream anecdotes. But considering the incredible accuracy of their eyes, their keen and unabashed delight in colors, one can hardly be wrong in assuming that their dreams too showed a strict consequence of lines and contours, hues and groupings, a progression of scenes similar to their best bas-reliefs. The perfection of these dream scenes might almost tempt us to consider the dreaming Greek as a Homer and Homer as a dreaming Greek; which would be as though the modern man were to compare himself in his dreaming to Shakespeare.

Yet there is another point about which we do not have to conjecture at all: I mean the profound gap separating the Dionysiac Greeks from the Dionysiac barbarians. Throughout the range of ancient civilization (leaving the newer civilizations out of account for the moment) we find evidence of Dionysiac celebrations which stand to the Greek type in much the same relation as the bearded satyr, whose name and attributes are derived from the he-goat, stands to the god Dionysos. The central concern of such celebrations was, almost universally, a complete sexual promiscuity overriding every form of established tribal law; all the savage urges of the mind were unleashed on those occasions until they reached that paroxysm of lust and cruelty which has always struck me as the "witches' cauldron" par excellence. It would appear that the Greeks were for a while quite immune from these feverish excesses which must have reached them by every known land or sea route. What kept Greece safe was the proud, imposing image of Apollo, who in holding up the head of the Gorgon[10] to those brutal and grotesque Dionysiac forces subdued them. Doric art has immortalized Apollo's majestic rejection of all license. But resistance became difficult, even impossible, as soon as similar urges began to break forth from the deep substratum of Hellenism itself. Soon the function of the Delphic god[11] developed into something quite different and much more limited: all he could hope to accomplish now was to wrest the destructive weapon, by a timely gesture of pacification, from his opponent's hand. That act of pacification represents the most important event in the history of Greek ritual; every department of life now shows symptoms of a revolutionary change. The two great antagonists have been reconciled. Each feels obliged henceforth to keep to his bounds, each will honor the other by the bestowal of periodic gifts, while the cleavage remains fundamentally the same. And yet, if we examine what happened to the Dionysiac powers under the pressure of that treaty we notice a great difference: in the place of the Babylonian Sacaea, with their throwback of men to the condition of apes and tigers, we now see entirely new rites celebrated: rites of universal redemption, of glorious transfiguration. Only now has it become possible to speak of nature's celebrating an *aesthetic* triumph; only now has the abrogation of the *principium individuationis* become an aesthetic event. That terrible witches' brew concocted of lust and cruelty has lost all power under the new conditions. Yet the peculiar blending of emotions in the heart of the Dionysiac reveler—his ambiguity if you will—seems still to hark back (as the medicinal drug harks back to the deadly poison) to the days when the infliction of pain was experienced as joy while a sense of supreme triumph elicited cries of anguish from the heart. For now in every exuberant joy there is heard an undertone of terror, or else a wistful lament over an irrecoverable loss. It is as though in these Greek festivals a sentimental trait of nature were coming to the fore, as though nature were bemoaning the fact of her fragmentation, her decomposition into separate individuals. The chants and gestures of these revelers, so ambiguous in their motivation, represented an absolute *novum* in the world of the Homeric Greeks; their Dionysiac music, in especial, spread abroad terror and a deep shudder. It is true: music had long been familiar to the Greeks as an Apollonian art, as a regular beat like that of waves lapping the shore, a plastic rhythm ex-

---

[10] One of three sisters who when looked on turned the beholder to stone.
[11] Apollo, whose oracle was at Delphi.

pressly developed for the portrayal of Apollonian conditions. Apollo's music was a Doric architecture of sound—of barely hinted sounds such as are proper to the cithara. Those very elements which characterize Dionysiac music and, after it, music quite generally: the heart-shaking power of tone, the uniform stream of melody, the incomparable resources of harmony—all those elements had been carefully kept at a distance as being inconsonant with the Apollonian norm. In the Dionysiac dithyramb man is incited to strain his symbolic faculties to the utmost; something quite unheard of is now clamoring to be heard: the desire to tear asunder the veil of Maya, to sink back into the original oneness of nature; the desire to express the very essence of nature symbolically. Thus an entirely new set of symbols springs into being. First, all the symbols pertaining to physical features: mouth, face, the spoken word, the dance movement which coordinates the limbs and bends them to its rhythm. Then suddenly all the rest of the symbolic forces—music and rhythm as such, dynamics, harmony—assert themselves with great energy. In order to comprehend this total emancipation of all the symbolic powers one must have reached the same measure of inner freedom those powers themselves were making manifest; which is to say that the votary of Dionysos could not be understood except by his own kind. It is not difficult to imagine the awed surprise with which the Apollonian Greek must have looked on him. And that surprise would be further increased as the latter realized, with a shudder, that all this was not so alien to him after all, that his Apollonian consciousness was but a thin veil hiding from him the whole Dionysiac realm.

XVII

. . . The struggle of the spirit of music to become manifest in image and myth—a struggle that grew in intensity from the beginnings of lyric poetry to the flowering of Attic tragedy—came to a sudden halt and disappeared, as it were, from the Hellenic scene. Yet the Dionysiac world view born of this struggle managed to survive in the mysteries, and even in its strangest metamorphoses and debasements did not cease to attract thoughtful minds. Who knows whether that conception will not once again rise as art from its mystical depths?

What concerns us here is the question whether those powers to whose influence Greek tragedy succumbed will maintain their ascendancy permanently, thereby blocking for good the renascence of tragedy and the tragic world view. The fact that the dialectical drive toward knowledge and scientific optimism has succeeded in turning tragedy from its

course suggests that there may be an eternal conflict between the theoretical and the tragic world view, in which case tragedy could be reborn only when science had at last been pushed to its limits and, faced with those limits, been forced to renounce its claim to universal validity. For the new hypothetical tragedy the music-practicing Socrates might be a fitting symbol.

If we remember the immediate consequences of the restless and inquisitive spirit of science, it can come as no surprise to us that it destroyed myth and, by the same token, displaced poetry from its native soil and rendered it homeless. If we are right in crediting music with the power to revive myth, then we must look for science in those places where it actively opposes the mythopoeic power of music. It did so in the later Attic dithyramb, whose music no longer expressed the innermost being, or will itself, but only reproduced the phenomenon in a mediate, conceptualized form. Truly musical minds turned away from that degenerate kind of music with the same distaste they felt for the anti-artistic tendencies of Socrates. Aristophanes' sure instinct was doubtless right when he lumped together Socrates, the Euripidean drama, and the music of the new dithyrambic poets, castigating them indifferently as symptoms of a degenerate culture. In the new dithyramb, music is degraded to the imitative portrayal of phenomena, such as battles or storms at sea, and thereby robbed of all its mythopoeic power. For we are not in a condition to yield ourselves to the mythic force when music simply tries to beguile us with external analogies between some natural event and certain rhythmical and acoustical combinations, when our reason is called upon to satisfy itself in the recognition of such analogies. Truly Dionysiac music offers us a universal mirror of the world will: every particular incident refracted in that mirror is enlarged into the image of a permanent truth. Conversely, the tone pictures of the new dithyramb strip every such concrete incident at once of its mythic implications. Music here has become a paltry replica of the phenomenon and for that very reason infinitely poorer than the phenomenon itself. And the poverty of the replica further reduces the phenomenon to our consciousness. A battle, thus imitated, becomes a mere sequence of marches, trumpet calls and the like, and our imagination is stopped at the level of such superficialities. Tone painting, then, is in every respect at the opposite pole from the mythopoeic power of true music: it further reduces the phenomenon, while Dionysiac music makes every single phenomenon comprehensible and significant. The anti-Dionysiac spirit won a mighty victory when it estranged music from itself and made it a slave to appearances. Euripides, who, albeit in a higher sense, must be called an absolutely unmusical temperament, was for that very reason a passionate partisan of the new dithyramb and used its entire stock-in-trade with a freebooter's prodigality.

We see a different aspect of this anti-Dionysiac, anti-mythic trend in the increased emphasis on character portrayal and psychological subtlety from Sophocles onward. Character must no longer be broadened so as to become a permanent type, but on the contrary must be so finely individualized, by means of shading and nuances and the strict delineation of every trait, that the spectator ceases to be aware of myth at all and comes to focus on the amazing life-likeness of the characters and the artist's power of imitation. Here, once again, we see the victory of the particular over the general and the pleasure taken in, as it were, anatomical drawing. We breathe the air of a world of theory, in which scientific knowledge is more revered than the artistic reflection of a universal norm. The cult of the characteristic trait develops apace: Sophocles still paints whole characters and lays myth under contribution in order to render them more fully; Euripides concentrates on large single character traits, projected into violent passions; the new Attic comedy gives us masks, each with a single expression: frivolous old men, hoodwinked panders, roguish slaves, in endless repetition. Where is now the mythopoeic spirit? All that remains to music is to excite jaded nerves or call up memory images, as in tone painting. For the former, the text hardly matters any longer. Already in Euripides things get out of control as soon as his characters or his chorus begin to sing, and heaven only knows what his impudent followers may have been guilty of.

Yet the modish anti-Dionysiac spirit shows itself most clearly in the dénouements of the new plays. In the older tragedy one could feel at the end the metaphysical solace, without which it is impossible to imagine our taking pleasure in tragedy. Most purely, perhaps, in *Oedipus at Colonus*[12] we hear those harmonious sounds of reconciliation from another world. But, once the genius of music has departed from tragedy, tragedy is dead, for what, henceforth, is to furnish that metaphysical solace? The new dramatists tried to resolve the tragic dissonance in terrestrial terms: after having been sufficiently buffeted by fate, the hero was compensated in the end by a distinguished marriage and divine honors. He thus resembled a gladiator, who might perchance be set free after he had taken his beating and was covered with wounds. The place of metaphysical solace was now taken by the *deus ex machina*. I do not mean to assert that the tragic spirit was everywhere quite eradicated by the anti-Dionysiac onset; but we do know that it was forced to flee from the realm of art and take refuge in the limbo of aberrant secret rites. Mean-

while, there raged over the entire surface of the Hellenic world the pestilence of that counterfeit "Greek serenity" of which I spoke earlier: a senescent and unproductive affirmation of this life, in utter contrast to the marvelous naiveté of the older Greeks—flower of an Apollonian culture blossoming over a somber abyss, in token of the victory of the Greek will over suffering, and of the wisdom of suffering. The other variety of Greek cheerfulness—the Alexandrian—shows at its best in the man of theory; it exhibits the same characteristics that I have just derived from the general anti-Dionysiac ascendant. It opposes Dionysiac wisdom and art; tries to dissolve the power of myth; puts in place of a metaphysical comfort a terrestrial consonance and a special *deus ex machina*—the god of engines and crucibles: forces of nature put in the service of a higher form of egotism. It believes that the world can be corrected through knowledge and that life should be guided by science; that it is actually in a position to confine man within the narrow circle of soluble tasks, where he can say cheerfully to life: "I want you. You are worth knowing."

XXIII

If one wants to try whether he is such a spectator or whether he belongs, rather, to the community of Socratic men, he may ask himself honestly with what emotion he responds to the miracle on the stage; whether he feels that his historical sense, trained to look everywhere for strict psychological causation, has been outraged, whether he admits the miracle as a phenomenon that seems natural to child minds but rather remote from himself, or whether he has some different sort of response. Depending on what answer he makes, he will be able to tell whether he has any understanding at all of myth, which, being a concentrated image of the world, an emblem of appearance, cannot dispense with the miracle. The chances are that almost every one of us, upon close examination, will have to admit that he is able to approach the once-living reality of myth only by means of intellectual constructs. Yet every culture that has lost myth has lost, by the same token, its natural, healthy creativity. Only a horizon ringed about with myths can unify a culture. The forces of imagination and of Apollonian dream are saved only by myth from indiscriminate rambling. The images of myth must be the demonic guardians, ubiquitous but unnoticed, presiding over the growth of the child's mind and interpreting to the mature man his life and struggles. Nor does the commonwealth know any more potent unwritten law than that mythic foundation which guarantees its union with religion and its basis in mythic conceptions. Over against this,

---

[12]By Sophocles.

let us consider abstract man stripped of myth, abstract education, abstract mores, abstract law, abstract government; the random vagaries of the artistic imagination unchanneled by any native myth; a culture without any fixed and consecrated place of origin, condemned to exhaust all possibilities and feed miserably and parasitically on every culture under the sun. Here we have our present age, the result of a Socratism bent on the extermination of myth. Man today, stripped of myth, stands famished among all his pasts and must dig frantically for roots, be it among the most remote antiquities. What does our great historical hunger signify, our clutching about us of countless other cultures, our consuming desire for knowledge, if not the loss of myth, of a mythic home, the mythic womb? Let us ask ourselves whether our feverish and frightening agitation is anything but the greedy grasping for food of a hungry man. And who would care to offer further nourishment to a culture which, no matter how much it consumes, remains insatiable and which converts the strongest and most wholesome food into "history" and "criticism"?

Truth and Falsity in an Ultramoral Sense

In some remote corner of the universe, effused into innumerable solar systems, there was once a star upon which clever animals invented cognition. It was the haughtiest, most mendacious moment in the history of this world, but yet only a moment. After Nature had taken breath awhile, the star congealed and the clever animals had to die.—Someone might write a fable after this style, and yet he would not have illustrated sufficiently, how wretched, shadowlike, transitory, purposeless, and fanciful the human intellect appears in Nature. There were eternities during which this intellect did not exist, and when it has once more passed away, there will be nothing to show that it has existed. For this intellect is not concerned with any further mission transcending the sphere of human life. No, it is purely human and none but its owner and procreator regards it so pathetically as to suppose that the world revolves around it. If, however, we and the gnat could understand each other, we should learn that even the

gnat swims through the air with the same pathos, and feels within itself the flying center of the world. Nothing in Nature is so bad or so insignificant that it will not, at the smallest puff of that force cognition, immediately swell up like a balloon, and just as a mere porter wants to have his admirer, so the very proudest man, the philosopher, imagines he sees from all sides the eyes of the universe telescopically directed upon his actions and thoughts.

It is remarkable that this is accomplished by the intellect, which after all has been given to the most unfortunate, the most delicate, the most transient beings only as an expedient, in order to detain them for a moment in existence, from which without that extra gift they would have every cause to flee as swiftly as Lessing's son.[1] That haughtiness connected with cognition and sensation, spreading blinding fogs before the eyes and over the senses of men, deceives itself therefore as to the value of existence owing to the fact that it bears within itself the most flattering evaluation of cognition. Its most general effect is deception, but even its most particular effects have something of deception in their nature.

The intellect, as a means for the preservation of the individual, develops its chief power in dissimulation; for it is by dissimulation that the feebler and less robust individuals preserve themselves, since it has been denied them to fight the battle of existence with horns or the sharp teeth of beasts of prey. In man this art of dissimulation reaches its acme of perfection: in him deception, flattery, falsehood and fraud, slander, display, pretentiousness, disguise, cloaking convention, and acting to others and to himself, in short, the continual fluttering to and fro around the *one* flame—Vanity: all these things are so much the rule, and the law, that few things are more incomprehensible than the way in which an honest and pure impulse to truth could have arisen among men. They are deeply immersed in illusions and dream fancies; their eyes glance only over the surface of things and see "forms"; their sensation nowhere leads to truth, but contents itself with receiving stimuli and, so to say, with playing hide-and-seek on the back of things. In addition to that, at night man allows his dreams to lie to him a whole lifetime long, without his moral sense ever trying to prevent them; whereas

---

TRUTH AND FALSITY IN AN ULTRAMORAL SENSE. In the original German "Ueber Wahrheit und Lüge im aussermoralischen Sinne" (1873), is from *Early Greek Philosophy and Other Essays,* which constitutes Volume 2 of the *Complete Works of Friedrich Nietzsche* 18 vols. 1909–1924, ed. Oscar Levy. The translation is by Mazemilian A. Mügge.

---

[1][Mügge] The German poet, Lessing, had been married for just a little over one year to Eva König. A son was born and died the same day, and the mother's life was despaired of. In a letter to his friend Esschenburg the poet wrote: ". . . and I lost him so unwillingly, this son! For he had so much understanding! so much understanding! Do not suppose that the few hours of fatherhood have made him an ape of a father! I know what I say. Was it not understanding, that they had to drag him into the world with a pair of forceps? that he so soon suspected the evil of this world? Was it not understanding, that he seized the first opportunity to get away from it? . . ." Eva König died a week later.

men are said to exist who by the exercise of a strong will have overcome the habit of snoring. What indeed *does* man know about himself? Oh! that he could but once see himself complete, placed as it were in an illuminated glass case! Does not nature keep secret from him most things, even about his body, e.g., the convolutions of the intestines, the quick flow of the blood currents, the intricate vibrations of the fibers, so as to banish and lock him up in proud, delusive knowledge? Nature threw away the key; and woe to the fateful curiosity which might be able for a moment to look out and down through a crevice in the chamber of consciousness and discover that man, indifferent to his own ignorance, is resting on the pitiless, the greedy, the insatiable, the murderous, and, as it were, hanging in dreams on the back of a tiger. Whence, in the wide world, with this state of affairs, arises the impulse to truth?

As far as the individual tries to preserve himself against other individuals, in the natural state of things he uses the intellect in most cases only for dissimulation; since, however, man both from necessity and boredom wants to exist socially and gregariously, he must needs make peace and at least endeavor to cause the greatest *bellum omnium contra omnes* to disappear from his world. This first conclusion of peace brings with it a something which looks like the first step toward the attainment of that enigmatical bent for truth. For that which henceforth is to be "truth" is now fixed; that is to say, a uniformly valid and binding designation of things is invented and the legislature of language also gives the first laws of truth: since here, for the first time, originates the contrast between truth and falsity. The liar uses the valid designations, the words, in order to make the unreal appear as real, e.g., he says, "I am rich," whereas the right designation for his state would be "poor." He abuses the fixed conventions by convenient substitution or even inversion of terms. If he does this in a selfish and moreover harmful fashion, society will no longer trust him but will even exclude him. In this way men avoid not so much being defrauded, but being injured by fraud. At bottom, at this juncture, too, they hate not deception, but the evil, hostile consequences of certain species of deception. And it is in a similarly limited sense only that man desires truth: he covets the agreeable, life-preserving consequences of truth; he is indifferent toward pure, ineffective knowledge; he is even inimical toward truths which possibly might prove harmful or destroying. And, moreover, what after all are those conventions of language? Are they possibly products of knowledge, of the love of truth; do the designations and the things coincide? Is language the adequate expression of all realities?

Only by means of forgetfulness can man ever arrive at imagining that he possesses "truth" in that degree just indi-

cated. If he does not mean to content himself with truth in the shape of tautology, that is, with empty husks, he will always obtain illusions instead of truth. What is a word? The expression of a nerve stimulus in sounds. But to infer a cause outside us from the nerve stimulus is already the result of a wrong and unjustifiable application of the proposition of causality. How should we dare, if truth with the genesis of language, if the point of view of certainty with the designations had alone been decisive; how indeed should we dare to say: the stone is hard; as if "hard" was known to us otherwise, and not merely as an entirely subjective stimulus! We divide things according to genders; we designate the tree as masculine,[2] the plant as feminine:[3] what arbitrary metaphors! How far-flown beyond the canon of certainty! We speak of a "serpent";[4] the designation fits nothing but the sinuosity, and could therefore also appertain to the worm. What arbitrary demarcations! What one-sided preferences given sometimes to this, sometimes to that quality of a thing! The different languages placed side by side show that with words truth or adequate expression matters little: for otherwise there would not be so many languages. The "Thing-in-itself" (it is just this which would be the pure ineffective truth) is also quite incomprehensible to the creator of language and not worth making any great endeavor to obtain. He designates only the relations of things to men and for their expression he calls to his help the most daring metaphors. A nerve stimulus, first transformed into a percept! First metaphor! The percept again copied into a sound! Second metaphor! And each time he leaps completely out of one sphere right into the midst of an entirely different one. One can imagine a man who is quite deaf and has never had a sensation of tone and of music; just as this man will possibly marvel at Chladni's sound figures in the sand, will discover their cause in the vibrations of the string, and will then proclaim that now he knows what man calls "tone"; even so does it happen to us all with language. When we talk about trees, colors, snow, and flowers, we believe we know something about the things themselves, and yet we only possess metaphors of the things, and these metaphors do not in the least correspond to the original essentials. Just as the sound shows itself as a sad figure, in the same way the enigmatical x of the Thing-in-itself is seen first as nerve stimulus, then as percept, and finally as sound. At any rate the genesis of language did not therefore proceed on logical lines, and the whole material in which and with which the man of truth, the

---

[2][Mügge] In German *the tree—der Baum*—is masculine.
[3][Mügge] In German *the plant—die Pflanze*—is feminine.
[4][Mügge] Cf. the German *die Schlange* and *schlingen,* the English *serpent* from the Latin *serpere.*

investigator, the philosopher works and builds, originates, if not from Nephelococcygia, cloudland, at any rate not from the essence of things.

Let us especially think about the formation of ideas. Every word becomes at once an idea not by having, as one might presume, to serve as a reminder for the original experience happening but once and absolutely individualized, to which experience such word owes its origin, no, but by having simultaneously to fit innumerable, more or less similar (which really means never equal, therefore altogether unequal) cases. Every idea originates through equating the unequal. As certainly as no one leaf is exactly similar to any other, so certain is it that the idea "leaf" has been formed through an arbitrary omission of these individual differences, through a forgetting of the differentiating qualities, and this idea now awakens the notion that in nature there is, besides the leaves, a something called *the* "leaf," perhaps a primal form according to which all leaves were woven, drawn, accurately measured, colored, crinkled, painted, but by unskilled hands, so that no copy had turned out correct and trustworthy as a true copy of the primal form. We call a man "honest"; we ask, why has he acted so honestly today? Our customary answer runs, "On account of his honesty." *The* Honesty! That means again: the "leaf" is the cause of the leaves. We really and truly do not know anything at all about an essential quality which might be called *the* honesty, but we do know about numerous individualized, and therefore unequal actions, which we equate by omission of the unequal, and now designate as honest actions; finally out of them we formulate a *qualitas occulta* with the name "Honesty."

The disregarding of the individual and real furnishes us with the idea, as it likewise also gives us the form; whereas nature knows of no forms and ideas, and therefore knows no species but only an *x,* to us inaccessible and indefinable. For our antithesis of individual and species is anthropomorphic too and does not come from the essence of things, although on the other hand we do not dare to say that it does not correspond to it; for that would be a dogmatic assertion and as such just as undemonstrable as its contrary.

What therefore is truth? A mobile army of metaphors, metonymies, anthropomorphisms: in short a sum of human relations which became poetically and rhetorically intensified, metamorphosed, adorned, and after long usage seems to a nation fixed, canonic, and binding; truths are illusions of which one has forgotten that they *are* illusions; worn-out metaphors which have become powerless to affect the senses; coins which have their obverse effaced and now are no longer of account as coins but merely as metal. Still we do not yet know whence the impulse to truth comes, for up

to now we have heard only about the obligation which society imposes in order to exist: to be truthful, that is, to use the usual metaphors, therefore expressed morally: we have heard only about the obligation to lie according to a fixed convention, to lie gregariously in a style binding for all. Now man, of course, forgets that matters are going thus with him; he therefore lies in that fashion pointed out unconsciously and according to habits of centuries' standing—and by *this very unconsciousness,* by this very forgetting, he arrives at a sense for truth. Through this feeling of being obliged to designate one thing as "red," another as "cold," a third one as "dumb," awakes a moral emotion relating to truth. Out of the antithesis "liar" whom nobody trusts, whom all exclude, man demonstrates to himself the venerableness, reliability, usefulness of truth. Now as a *"rational"* being he submits his actions to the sway of abstractions; he no longer suffers himself to be carried away by sudden impressions, by sensations, he first generalizes all these impressions into paler, cooler ideas, in order to attach to them the ship of his life and actions. Everything which makes man stand out in bold relief against the animal depends on this faculty of volatilizing the concrete metaphors into a schema, and therefore resolving a perception into an idea. For within the range of those schemata a something becomes possible that never could succeed under the first perceptual impressions: to build up a pyramidal order with castes and grades, to create a new world of laws, privileges, suborders, delimitations, which now stands opposite the other perceptual world of first impressions and assumes the appearance of being the more fixed, general, known, human of the two and therefore the regulating and imperative one. Whereas every metaphor of perception is individual and without its equal and therefore knows how to escape all attempts to classify it, the great edifice of ideas shows the rigid regularity of a Roman columbarium and in logic breathes forth the sternness and coolness which we find in mathematics. He who has been breathed upon by this coolness will scarcely believe that the idea, too, bony and hexahedral and permutable as a die, remains, however, only as the *residuum of a metaphor,* and that the illusion of the artistic metamorphosis of a nerve stimulus into percepts is, if not the mother, then the grandmother of every idea. Now in this game of dice, "Truth" means to use every die as it is designated, to count its points carefully, to form exact classifications, and never to violate the order of castes and the sequences of rank. Just as the Romans and Etruscans for their benefit cut up the sky by means of strong mathematical lines and banned a god as it were into a *templum,* into a space limited in this fashion, so every nation has above its head such a sky of ideas divided up mathematically, and it understands the demand for truth to mean that every conceptual god is to be looked for only in *his* own sphere. One may here well admire man, who succeeded in piling up an infinitely complex dome of ideas on a movable foundation and as it were on running water, as a powerful genius of architecture. Of course in order to obtain hold on such a foundation it must be as an edifice piled up out of cobwebs, so fragile as to be carried away by the waves, so firm as not to be blown asunder by every wind. In this way man as an architectural genius rises high above the bee; she builds with wax, which she brings together out of nature; he with the much more delicate material of ideas, which he must first manufacture within himself. He is very much to be admired here—but not on account of his impulse for truth, his bent for pure cognition of things. If somebody hides a thing behind a bush, seeks it again and finds it in the self-same place, then there is not much to boast of, respecting this seeking and finding; thus, however, matters stand with the seeking and finding of "truth" within the realm of reason. If I make the definition of the mammal and then declare after inspecting a camel, "Behold a mammal," then no doubt a truth is brought to light thereby, but it is of very limited value, I mean it is anthropomorphic through and through, and does not contain one single point which is "true-in-itself," real, and universally valid, apart from man. The seeker after such truths seeks at the bottom only the metamorphosis of the world in man; he strives for an understanding of the world as a humanlike thing and by his battling gains at best the feeling of an assimilation. Similarly, as the astrologer contemplated the stars in the service of men and in connection with their happiness and unhappiness, such a seeker contemplates the whole world as related to man, as the infinitely protracted echo of an original sound: man; as the multiplied copy of the one archetype: man. His procedure is to apply man as the measure of all things, whereby he starts from the error of believing that he has these things immediately before him as pure objects. He therefore forgets that the original metaphors of perception *are* metaphors, and takes them for the things themselves.

Only by forgetting that primitive world of metaphors, only by the congelation and coagulation of an original mass of similes and percepts pouring forth as a fiery liquid out of the primal faculty of human fancy, only by the invincible faith, that *this* sun, *this* window, *this* table is a truth in itself: in short only by the fact that man forgets himself as subject, and what is more as an *artistically creating* subject, only by all this does he live with some repose, safety, and consequence. If he were able to get out of the prison walls of this faith, even for an instant only, his "self-consciousness" would be destroyed at once. Already it costs him some trouble to admit to himself that the insect and the bird perceive a

world different from his own, and that the question, which of the two world-perceptions is more accurate, is quite a senseless one, since to decide this question it would be necessary to apply the standard of *right perception,* i.e., to apply a standard which *does not exist.* On the whole it seems to me that the "right perception"—which would mean the adequate expression of an object in the subject—is a nonentity full of contradictions: for between two utterly different spheres, as between subject and object, there is no causality, no accuracy, no expression, but at the utmost an *aesthetical* relation, I mean a suggestive metamorphosis, a stammering translation into quite a distinct foreign language, for which purpose, however, there is needed at any rate an intermediate sphere, an intermediate force, freely composing and freely inventing. The word "phenomenon" contains many seductions, and on that account I avoid it as much as possible, for it is not true that the essence of things appears in the empiric world. A painter who had no hands and wanted to express the picture distinctly present to his mind by the agency of song would still reveal much more with this permutation of spheres than the empiric world reveals about the essence of things. The very relation of a nerve stimulus to the produced percept is in itself no necessary one; but if the same percept has been reproduced millions of times and has been the inheritance of many successive generations of man, and in the end appears each time to all mankind as the result of the same cause, then it attains finally for man the same importance as if it were *the* unique, necessary percept and as if that relation between the original nerve stimulus and the percept produced were a close relation of causality: just as a dream eternally repeated would be perceived and judged as though real. But the congelation and coagulation of a metaphor does not at all guarantee the necessity and exclusive justification of that metaphor.

Surely every human being who is at home with such contemplations has felt a deep distrust against any idealism of that kind, as often as he has distinctly convinced himself of the eternal rigidity, omnipresence, and infallibility of nature's laws: he has arrived at the conclusion that as far as we can penetrate the heights of the telescopic and the depths of the microscopic world, everything is quite secure, complete, infinite, determined, and continuous. Science will have to dig in these shafts eternally and successfully and all things found are sure to have to harmonize and not to contradict one another. How little does this resemble a product of fancy, for if it were one it would necessarily betray somewhere its nature of appearance and unreality. Against this it may be objected in the first place that if each of us had for himself a different sensibility, if we ourselves were only able to perceive sometimes as a bird, sometimes as a worm, sometimes as a plant, or if one of us saw the same stimulus as red, another as blue, if a third person even perceived it as a tone, then nobody would talk of such an orderliness of nature, but would conceive of her only as an extremely subjective structure. Secondly, what is, for us in general, a law of nature? It is not known in itself but only in its effects, that is to say, in its relations to other laws of nature, which again are known to us only as sums of relations. Therefore all these relations refer only one to another and are absolutely incomprehensible to us in their essence; only that which we add: time, space, i.e., relations of sequence and numbers, are really known to us in them. Everything wonderful, however, that we marvel at in the laws of nature, everything that demands an explanation and might seduce us into distrusting idealism, lies really and solely in the mathematical rigor and inviolability of the conceptions of time and space. These, however, we produce within ourselves and throw them forth with that necessity with which the spider spins; since we are compelled to conceive all things under these forms only, then it is no longer wonderful that in all things we actually conceive none but these forms: for they all must bear within themselves the laws of number, and this very idea of number is the most marvelous in all things. All obedience to law which impresses us so forcibly in the orbits of stars and in chemical processes coincides at the bottom with those qualities which we ourselves attach to those things, so that it is we who thereby make the impression upon ourselves. Whence it clearly follows that the artistic formation of metaphors with which every sensation in us begins already presupposes those forms, and is therefore only consummated within them; only out of the persistency of these primal forms the possibility explains itself, how afterward out of the metaphors themselves a structure of ideas could again be compiled. For the latter is an imitation of the relations of time, space, and number in the realm of metaphors.

2

As we saw, it is *language* which has worked originally at the construction of ideas; in later times it is *science*. Just as the bee works at the same time at the cells and fills them with honey, thus science works irresistibly at that great columbarium of ideas, the cemetery of perceptions; builds ever newer and higher storeys; supports, purifies, renews the old cells; and endeavors above all to fill that gigantic framework and to arrange within it the whole of the empiric world, i.e., the anthropomorphic world. And as the man of action binds his life to reason and its ideas, in order to avoid being swept away and losing himself, so the seeker after truth builds his hut close to the towering edifice of science in order to collaborate with it and to find protection. And he needs protection. For there are awful powers which continually press upon him, and which hold out against the "truth" of science "truths" fashioned in quite another way, bearing devices of the most heterogeneous character.

That impulse toward the formation of metaphors, that fundamental impulse of man, which we cannot reason away for one moment—for thereby we should reason away man himself—is in truth not defeated nor even subdued by the fact that out of its evaporated products, the ideas, a regular and rigid new world has been built as a stronghold for it. This impulse seeks for itself a new realm of action and another river-bed, and finds it in *Mythos* and more generally in *Art*. This impulse constantly confuses the rubrics and cells of the ideas by putting up new figures of speech, metaphors, metonymies; it constantly shows its passionate longing for shaping the existing world of waking man as motley, irregular, inconsequentially incoherent, attractive, and eternally new as the world of dreams is. For indeed, waking man per se is only clear about his being awake through the rigid and orderly woof of ideas, and it is for this very reason that he sometimes comes to believe that he was dreaming when that woof of ideas has for a moment been torn by Art. Pascal is quite right when he asserts that if the same dream came to us every night, we should be just as much occupied by it as by the things which we see every day; to quote his words, "If an artisan were certain that he would dream every night for fully twelve hours that he was a king, I believe that he would be just as happy as a king who dreams every night for twelve hours that he is an artisan." The wideawake day of a people mystically excitable, let us say of the earlier Greeks, is in fact through the continually working wonder, which the mythos presupposes, more akin to the dream than to the day of the thinker sobered by silence. If every tree may at some time talk as a nymph, or a god under the disguise of a bull carry away virgins, if the goddess Athena herself be suddenly seen as, with a beautiful team, she drives, accompanied by Pisistratus, through the markets of Athens—and every honest Athenian did believe this—at any moment, as in a dream, everything is possible; and all nature swarms around man as if she were nothing but the masquerade of the gods, who found it a huge joke to deceive man by assuming all possible forms.

Man himself, however, has an invincible tendency to let himself be deceived, and he is like one enchanted with happiness when the rhapsodist narrates to him epic romances in such a way that they appear real or when the actor on the stage makes the king appear more kingly than reality shows him. Intellect, that master of dissimulation, is free and dismissed from his service as slave, so long as It is able to deceive without *injuring,* and then It celebrates Its Saturnalia. Never is It richer, prouder, more luxuriant, more skillful and daring; with a creator's delight It throws metaphors into confusion, shifts the boundary stones of the abstractions, so that, for instance, It designates the stream as the mobile way which carries man to that place whither he would otherwise go. Now It has thrown off Its shoulders the emblem of servitude. Usually with gloomy officiousness It endeavors to point out the way to a poor individual coveting existence, and It fares forth for plunder and booty like a servant for his master, but now It Itself has become a master and may wipe from Its countenance the expression of indigence. Whatever It now does, compared with Its former doings, bears within itself dissimulation, just as Its former doings bore the character of distortion. It copies human life, but takes it for a good thing and seems to rest quite satisfied with it. That enormous framework and hoarding of ideas, by clinging to which needy man saves himself through life, is to the freed intellect only a scaffolding and a toy for Its most daring feats, and when It smashes it to pieces, throws it into confusion, and then puts it together ironically, pairing the strangest, separating the nearest items, then It manifests that It has no use for those makeshifts of misery, and that It is now no longer led by ideas but by intuitions. From these intuitions no regular road leads into the land of the spectral schemata, the abstractions; for them the word is not made, when man sees them he is dumb, or speaks in forbidden metaphors and in unheard-of combinations of ideas, in order to correspond creatively with the impression of the powerful present intuition at least by destroying and jeering at the old barriers of ideas.

There are ages, when the rational and the intuitive man stand side by side, the one full of fear of the intuition, the other full of scorn for the abstraction; the latter just as irrational as the former is inartistic. Both desire to rule over life; the one by knowing how to meet the most important needs with foresight, prudence, regularity; the other as an "overjoyous" hero by ignoring those needs and taking that life only as real which simulates appearance and beauty. Whenever intuitive man, as for instance in the earlier history of Greece, brandishes his weapons more powerfully and victoriously than his opponent, there under favorable conditions, a culture can develop and art can establish her rule over life. That dissembling, that denying of neediness, that splendor of metaphorical notions and especially that directness of dissimulation accompany all utterances of such a life. Neither the house of man, nor his way of walking, nor his clothing, nor his earthen jug suggest that necessity invented them; it seems as if they all were intended as the expressions of a sublime happiness, an olympic cloudlessness, and, as it were, a playing at seriousness. Whereas the man guided by ideas and abstractions only wards off misfortune by means of them, without even enforcing for himself happiness out of the abstractions; whereas he strives after the greatest possible freedom from pains, the intuitive man dwelling in the midst of culture has from his intuitions a harvest: besides the warding off of evil, he attains a continuous inpouring of enlightenment, enlivenment, and redemption. Of course when he *does* suffer, he suffers more: and he even suffers more frequently since he cannot learn from experience, but again and again falls into the same ditch into which he has fallen before. In suffering he is just as irrational as in happiness; he cries aloud and finds no consolation. How different matters are in the same misfortune with the Stoic, taught by experience and ruling himself by ideas! He who otherwise only looks for uprightness, truth, freedom from deceptions and shelter from ensnaring and sudden attack, in his misfortune performs the masterpiece of dissimulation, just as the other did in his happiness; he shows no twitching mobile human face but, as it were, a mask with dignified, harmonious features; he does not cry out and does not even alter his voice; when a heavy thundercloud bursts upon him, he wraps himself up in his cloak and with slow and measured step walks away from beneath it.

Walter Pater

1839–1894

Often considered the father of aestheticism, Pater set forth the principles of impressionistic criticism in his *Studies in the History of the Renaissance*. A study of his Romantic forebears shows, however, that his ideas came clearly out of their critical and epistemological positions. So powerful was the influence of his ideas that for a time Pater suppressed the famous Conclusion to his book, which he felt had been misinterpreted as an invitation to irresponsible hedonism. Pater himself advocated a fastidious decorum.

Pater mistrusts abstractions, as did Blake, and finds definitions of beauty no basis for aesthetic theories. All aesthetic judgments must finally be referred to the reader's receptivity, his taste. The critic's worth depends on the refinement of his temperament, since objective standards of aesthetic judgment are abstract and useless. For Pater, criticism itself becomes a work of art. Earlier Romantic reservations about abstract thought and general nature, along with Romantic praise of immediate, personal, unique experience and of the sense of time lived rather than time measured, culminate in Pater's solipsistic remarks in the Conclusion of his book: "Experience, already reduced to a swarm of impression, is ringed round for each of us by that thick wall of personality through which no real voice has ever pierced on its way to us." Pater, heir to the subject-object problem passed on to him by Romantic critics and philosophers, carries response to that problem to its extreme. Rejecting the materialists, he also rejects total dependence on rational understanding to give us what knowledge we can have.

The standard text of Pater's works is the ten-volume edition published in 1910. Commentary includes Thomas Wright, *The Life of Walter Pater* (2 vols., 1907); A. J. Farmer, *Walter Pater as a Critic of English Literature* (1931); T. S. Eliot, "Arnold and Pater" in his *Selected Essays 1917–1932* (1932); Arthur Symons, *A Study of Walter Pater* (1932); R. C. Child, *The Aesthetic of Walter Pater* (1940); Anthony Ward, *Walter Pater: The Idea in Nature* (1967); Richmond Crinkley, *Walter Pater: Humanist* (1970); William E. Buckler, *Walter Pater: The Critic as Artist of Ideas* (1987); Paul Barolsky, *Walter Pater's Renaissance* (1987); and Wolfgang Iser, *Walter Pater: The Aesthetic Moment* (tr. 1987).

Studies in the History of the Renaissance

From

Preface

Many attempts have been made by writers on art and poetry to define beauty in the abstract, to express it in the most general terms, to find a universal formula for it. The value of such attempts has most often been in the suggestive and penetrating things said by the way. Such discussions help us very little to enjoy what has been well done in art or poetry, to discriminate between what is more and what is less excellent in them, or to use words like *beauty, excellence, art, poetry,* with more meaning than they would otherwise have. Beauty, like all other qualities presented to human experience, is relative; and the definition of it becomes unmeaning and useless in proportion to its abstractness. To define beauty not in the most abstract, but in the most concrete terms possible, not to find a universal formula for it, but the formula which expresses most adequately this or that special manifestation of it, is the aim of the true student of aesthetics.

"To see the object as in itself it really is,"[1] has been justly said to be the aim of all true criticism whatever; and in aesthetic criticism the first step towards seeing one's object as it really is, is to know one's own impression as it really is, to discriminate it, to realize it distinctly. The objects with which aesthetic criticism deals, music, poetry, artistic and accomplished forms of human life, are indeed receptacles of so many powers or forces; they possess, like natural elements, so many virtues or qualities. What is this song or picture, this engaging personality presented in life or in a book, to *me?* What effect does it really produce on me? Does it give me pleasure? and if so, what sort or degree of pleasure? How is my nature modified by its presence and under its influence? The answers to these questions are the original facts with which the aesthetic critic has to do; and, as in the study of light, of morals, of number, one must realize such primary data for oneself or not at all. And he who experiences these impressions strongly, and drives directly at the analysis and discrimination of them, need not trouble himself with the abstract question what beauty is in itself, or its

exact relation to truth or experience—metaphysical questions, as unprofitable as metaphysical questions elsewhere. He may pass them all by as being, answerable or not, of no interest to him.

The aesthetic critic, then, regards all the objects with which he has to do, all works of art and the fairer forms of nature and human life, as powers or forces, producing pleasurable sensations, each of a more or less peculiar and unique kind. This influence he feels and wishes to explain, analyzing it, and reducing it to its elements. To him, the picture, the landscape, the engaging personality in life or in a book, *La Gioconda,*[2] the hills of Carrara, Pico of Mirandola, are valuable for their virtues, as we say in speaking of a herb, a wine, a gem; for the property each has of affecting one with a special, unique impression of pleasure. Education grows in proportion as one's susceptibility to these impressions increases in depth and variety. And the function of the aesthetic critic is to distinguish, analyze, and separate from its adjuncts, the virtue by which a picture, a landscape, a fair personality in life or in a book, produces this special impression of beauty or pleasure, to indicate what the source of that impression is, and under what conditions it is experienced. His end is reached when he has disengaged that virtue, and noted it, as a chemist notes some natural element, for himself and others; and the rule for those who would reach this end is stated with great exactness in the words of a recent critic of Sainte-Beuve: *"De se borner à connaître de près les belles choses, et à s'en nourrir en exquis amateurs, en humanistes accomplis."*[3]

What is important, then, is not that the critic should possess a correct abstract definition of beauty for the intellect, but a certain kind of temperament, the power of being deeply moved by the presence of beautiful objects. He will remember always that beauty exists in many forms. To him all periods, types, schools of taste, are in themselves equal. In all ages there have been some excellent workmen and some excellent work done. The question he asks is always, In whom did the stir, the genius, the sentiment of the period find itself? Who was the receptacle of its refinement, its elevation, its taste? "The ages are all equal," says William Blake, "but genius is always above its age."[4]

Often it will require great nicety to disengage this virtue from the commoner elements with which it may be found in combination. Few artists, not Goethe or Byron even, work

THE RENAISSANCE. Pater's *Studies in the History of the Renaissance* was first published in 1873.
[1]Arnold, *The Function of Criticism,* p. 592.

[2]Commonly called *Mona Lisa.*
[3][Pater] "To limit themselves to know lovely things near at hand, and to nourish themselves upon them, like refined connoisseurs, like accomplished humanists."
[4]*Annotations to Reynolds'* Discourses, pp. 405–06.

quite cleanly, casting off all debris, and leaving us only what the heat of their imagination has wholly fused and transformed. Take for instance the writings of Wordsworth. The heat of his genius, entering into the substance of his work, has crystalized a part, but only a part, of it; and in that great mass of verse there is much which might well be forgotten. But scattered up and down it, sometimes fusing and transforming entire compositions, like the stanzas on *Resolution and Independence* and the ode on the *Recollections of Childhood,* sometimes, as if at random, turning a fine crystal here and there, in a matter it does not wholly search through and transform, we trace the action of his unique incommunicable faculty, that strange mystical sense of a life in natural things, and of man's life as a part of nature, drawing strength and color and character from local influences, from the hills and streams and natural sights and sounds. Well! That is the *virtue,* the active principle in Wordsworth's poetry; and then the function of the critic of Wordsworth is to trace that active principle, to disengage it, to mark the degree in which it penetrates his verse.

Conclusion

Λέγει πον Ἡράχλειτος ὅτι πάντα χωρεῖ καὶ
οὐδὲν μένει.[5]

PLATO

To regard all things and principles of things as inconstant modes or fashions has more and more become the tendency of modern thought. Let us begin with that which is without—our physical life. Fix upon it in one of its more exquisite intervals, the moment, for instance, of delicious recoil from the flood of water in summer heat. What is the whole physical life in that moment but a combination of natural elements to which science gives their names? But these elements, phosphorus and lime and delicate fibers, are present not in the human body alone: we detect them in places most remote from it. Our physical life is a perpetual motion of them—the passage of the blood, the wasting and repairing of the lenses of the eye, the modification of the tissues of the brain by every ray of light and sound—processes which science reduces to simpler and more elementary forces. Like the elements of which we are composed, the action of these

forces extends beyond us; it rusts iron and ripens corn. Far out on every side of us these elements are broadcast, driven by many forces; and birth and gesture and death and the springing of violets from the grave are but a few out of ten thousand resulting combinations. That clear perpetual outline of face and limb is but an image of ours under which we group them—a design in a web, the actual threads of which pass out beyond it. This at least of flamelike our life has, that it is but the concurrence, renewed from moment to moment, of forces parting sooner or later on their ways.

Or if we begin with the inward world of thought and feeling, the whirlpool is still more rapid, the flame more eager and devouring. There it is no longer the gradual darkening of the eye and fading of color from the wall—the movement of the shore side, where the water flows down indeed, though in apparent rest—but the race of the midstream, a drift of momentary acts of sight and passion and thought. At first sight experience seems to bury us under a flood of external objects, pressing upon us with a sharp importunate reality, calling us out of ourselves in a thousand forms of action. But when reflection begins to act upon those objects they are dissipated under its influence; the cohesive force is suspended like a trick of magic; each object is loosed into a group of impressions—color, odor, texture—in the mind of the observer. And if we continue to dwell on this world, not of objects in the solidity with which language invests them, but of impressions unstable, flickering, inconsistent, which burn and are extinguished with our consciousness of them, it contracts still further; the whole scope of observation is dwarfed to the narrow chamber of the individual mind. Experience, already reduced to a swarm of impressions, is ringed round for each one of us by that thick wall of personality through which no real voice has ever pierced on its way to us, or from us to that which we can only conjecture to be without. Every one of those impressions is the impression of the individual in his isolation, each mind keeping as a solitary prisoner its own dream of a world.

Analysis goes a step further still, and tells us that those impressions of the individual to which, for each one of us, experience dwindles down, are in perpetual flight; that each of them is limited by time, and that as time is infinitely divisible, each of them is infinitely divisible also; all that is actual in it being a single moment, gone while we try to apprehend it, of which it may ever be more truly said that it has ceased to be than that it is. To such a tremulous wisp constantly reforming itself on the stream, to a single sharp impression, with a sense in it, a relic more or less fleeting, of such moments gone by, what is real in our life fines itself down. It is with the movement, the passage and dissolution

---

[5] "Somewhere Heraclitus says that everything changes and nothing remains."
Cratylus.

of impressions, images, sensations, that analysis leaves off—that continual vanishing away, that strange perpetual weaving and unweaving of ourselves.

"*Philosophiren,*" says Novalis, "*ist dephlegmatisiren, vivificiren.*"[6] the service of philosophy, and of religion and culture as well, to the human spirit, is to startle it into a sharp and eager observation. Every moment some form grows perfect in hand or face; some tone on the hills or sea is choicer than the rest; some mood of passion or insight or intellectual excitement is irresistibly real and attractive for us—for that moment only. Not the fruit of experience, but experience itself is the end. A counted number of pulses only is given to us of a variegated, dramatic life. How may we see in them all that is to be seen in them by the finest senses? How can we pass most swiftly from point to point, and be present always at the focus where the greatest number of vital forces unite in their purest energy?

To burn always with this hard gemlike flame, to maintain this ecstasy, is success in life. Failure is to form habits; for habit is relative to a stereotyped world; meantime it is only the roughness of the eye that makes any two persons, things, situations, seem alike. While all melts under our feet, we may well catch at any exquisite passion, or any contribution to knowledge that seems, by a lifted horizon, to set the spirit free for a moment, or any stirring of the senses, strange dyes, strange flowers, and curious odors, or work of the artist's hands, or the face of one's friend. Not to discriminate every moment some passionate attitude in those about us, and in the brilliance of their gifts some tragic dividing of forces on their ways is, on this short day of frost and sun, to sleep before evening. With this sense of the splendor of our experience and of its awful brevity, gathering all we are into one desperate effort to see and touch, we shall hardly have time to make theories about the things we see and touch. What we have to do is to be forever curiously testing new opinions and courting new impressions, never acquiescing in a facile orthodoxy of Comte or of Hegel, or of our own. Theories, religious or philosophical ideas, as points of view, instruments of criticism, may help us to gather up what might otherwise pass unregarded by us. *La philosophie, c'est la microscope de la pensée.*[7] The theory, or idea, or system, which requires of us the sacrifice of any part of this experience, in consideration of some interest into which we cannot enter, or some abstract morality we have not identified with ourselves, or what is only conventional, has no real claim upon us.

One of the most beautiful places in the writings of Rousseau is that in the sixth book of the *Confessions,* where he describes the awakening in him of the literary sense. An undefinable taint of death had always clung about him, and now in early manhood he believed himself stricken by mortal disease. He asked himself how he might make as much as possible of the interval that remained; and he was not biased by anything in his previous life when he decided that it must be by intellectual excitement, which he found in the clear, fresh writings of Voltaire. Well, we are all *condamnés,* as Victor Hugo says: *"les hommes sont tous condamnés à mort avec des sursis indéfinis"*:[8] we have an interval, and then our place knows us no more. Some spend this interval in listlessness, some in high passions, the wisest in art and song. For our one chance is in expanding that interval, in getting as many pulsations as possible into the given time. High passions give one this quickened sense of life, ecstasy and sorrow of love, political or religious enthusiasm, or the "enthusiasm of humanity." Only, be sure it is passion, that it does yield you this fruit of a quickened, multiplied consciousness. Of this wisdom, the poetic passion, the desire of beauty, the love of art for art's sake has most; for art comes to you professing frankly to give nothing but the highest quality to your moments as they pass, and simply for those moments' sake.

---

[6]"To philosophize is dephlegmatizing, vivifying."

[7]"Philosophy is the microscope of thought."
[8]"Men are all condemned to death with indefinite delays."

Émile Zola

1840–1902

In an age of the rapid advance of science it was perhaps inevitable that some literary critics would draw analogies between artistic and scientific procedures. It was perhaps inevitable, too, that there would be various sorts of reactions against the excesses of Romanticism and philosophical idealism, which had held the stage for many years. We see both in Zola's *The Experimental Novel.* Unlike the Romantics, who distinguished literary from scientific practice, Zola sees the artist adopting the experimental method recommended by Claude Bernard in his *Introduction à l'étude de la médecine expérimentale.* Zola argues that the experimental novelist is neither a mere copyist of nature, nor a photographer: "The idea of experiment carries with it the idea of modification." The novelist can use his "genius," but under control of experiment. The Romanticist dwelt "in the unknown for the pleasure of being there." The experimentalist voyages into the unknown to make it known. The "nonsense and folly" of Romantic lyricism will be diminished, and literature, it appears, will become a form of social science.

Zola rode the current of positivism and accepted the myth of progress that accompanied it. His view raises, among other things, the problem of the value of the literature of the past. Since the science of the past has no current scientific value, presumably, to extend Zola's analogy, past literature has no value today. Zola cannot completely accept this: he suggests that ancient poems will survive because of their "beauty," but that sort of virtue is really quaint and archaic. Physiological man has replaced metaphysical man. Analytical procedures are the rule. Yet, by introducing that vague term *beauty* at the very end of his essay, Zola seems to admit the limitations of his own position if it were extended to a general theory.

A useful translation is *The Experimental Novel and Other Essays* by B. M. Sherman (1893). For commentary on Zola see F. Doucet, *L'Esthétique de Zola et son application à la critique* (1923); Matthew Josephson, *Zola and His Time* (1928); W. H. Root, *German Criticism of Zola, 1875–1893* (1931); Edward Stone, *What Was Naturalism?* (1958); Philip D. Walker, *Emile Zola* (1969); Frederick Hemmings, *Life and Times of Emile Zola* (1977); and Joanna Richardson, *Zola* (1978).

From

The Experimental Novel

In my literary essays I have often spoken of the application of the experimental method to the novel and to the drama. The return to nature, the naturalistic evolution which marks the century, drives little by little all the manifestation of human intelligence into the same scientific path. Only the idea of a literature governed by science is doubtless a surprise, until explained with precision and understood. It seems to me necessary, then, to say briefly and to the point what I understand by the experimental novel.

I really only need to adapt, for the experimental method has been established with strength and marvelous clearness by Claude Bernard in his *Introduction à l'étude de la médecine experimentale.* This work, by a savant whose authority is unquestioned, will serve me as a solid foundation. I shall here find the whole question treated, and I shall restrict myself to irrefutable arguments and to giving the quotations which may seem necessary to me. This will then be but a compiling of texts, as I intend on all points to entrench myself behind Claude Bernard. It will often be but necessary for me to replace the word *doctor* by the word *novelist,* to make my meaning clear and to give it the rigidity of a scientific truth.

What determined my choice, and made me choose *L'Introduction* as my basis, was the fact that medicine, in the eyes of a great number of people, is still an art, as is the novel. Claude Bernard all his life was searching and battling to put medicine in a scientific path. In his struggle we see the first feeble attempts of a science to disengage itself little by little from empiricism,[1] and to gain a foothold in the realm of truth, by means of the experimental method. Claude Bernard demonstrates that this method, followed in the study of inanimate bodies in chemistry and in physics, should be also used in the study of living bodies, in physiology and medicine. I am going to try and prove for my part that if the experimental method leads to the knowledge of physical life, it should also lead to the knowledge of the passionate and intellectual life. It is but a question of degree in the same path which runs from chemistry to physiology, then from physiology to anthropology and to sociology. The experimental novel is the goal.

To be more clear, I think it would be better to give a brief résumé of *L'Introduction* before I commence. The applications which I shall make of the texts will be better understood if the plan of the work and the matters treated are explained.

Claude Bernard, after having declared that medicine enters the scientific path, with physiology as its foundation, and by means of the experimental method, first explains the differences which exist between the sciences of observation and the sciences of experiment. He concludes, finally, that experiment is but provoked observation. All experimental reasoning is based on doubt, for the experimentalist should have no preconceived idea, in the face of nature, and should always retain his liberty of thought. He simply accepts the phenomena which are produced, when they are proved.

In the second part he reaches his true subject and shows that the spontaneity of living bodies is not opposed to the employment of experiment. The difference is simply that an inanimate body possesses merely the ordinary, external environment, while the essence of the higher organism is set in an internal and perfected environment endowed with constant physicochemical properties exactly like the external environment; hence there is an absolute determinism in the existing conditions of natural phenomena; for the living as for the inanimate bodies. He calls determinism the cause which determines the appearance of these phenomena. This nearest cause, as it is called, is nothing more than the physical and material condition of the existence or manifestation of the phenomena. The end of all experimental method, the boundary of all scientific research, is then identical for living and for inanimate bodies; it consists in finding the relations which unite a phenomenon of any kind to its nearest cause, or, in other words, in determining the conditions necessary for the manifestation of this phenomenon. Experimental science has no necessity to worry itself about the "why" of things; it simply explains the "how."

After having explained the experimental considerations common to living beings and to inanimate, Claude Bernard passes to the experimental considerations which belong specially to living beings. The great and only difference is this, that there is presented to our consideration, in the organism of living beings, a harmonious group of phenomena. He then treats of practical experiments on living beings, of vivisection, of the preparatory anatomical conditions, of the choice of animals, of the use of calculation in the study of phenomena, and lastly of the physiologist's laboratory.

THE EXPERIMENTAL NOVEL. *Le Roman experimentale* was first published in 1880. The text is from the translation by B. M. Sherman (1893).

[1] [Sherman] Zola uses *empiricism* in this essay in the sense of *haphazard observation* in contrast with a scientific experiment undertaken to prove a certain truth.

Finally, in the last part of *L'Introduction,* he gives some examples of physiological experimental investigations in support of the ideas which he has formulated. He then furnishes some examples of experimental criticism in physiology. In the end he indicates the philosophical obstacles which the experimental doctor encounters. He puts in the first rank the false application of physiology to medicine, the scientific ignorance as well as certain illusions of the medical mind. Further, he concludes by saying that empirical medicine and experimental medicine, not being incompatible, ought, on the contrary, to be inseparable one from the other. His last sentence is that experimental medicine adheres to no medical doctrine nor any philosophical system.

This is, very broadly, the skeleton of *L'Introduction* stripped of its flesh. I hope that this rapid exposé will be sufficient to fill up the gaps which my manner of proceeding is bound to produce; for, naturally, I shall cite from the work only such passages as are necessary to define and comment upon the experimental novel. I repeat that I use this treatise merely as a solid foundation on which to build, but a foundation very rich in arguments and proofs of all kinds. Experimental medicine, which but lisps as yet, can alone give us an exact idea of experimental literature, which, being still unhatched, is not even lisping.

I

The first question which presents itself is this: Is experiment possible in literature, in which up to the present time observation alone has been employed?

Claude Bernard discusses observation and experiment at great length. There exists, in the first place, a very clear line of demarcation, as follows:

> The name of *observer* is given to him who applies the simple or complex process of investigation in the study of phenomena which he does not vary, and which he gathers, consequently, as nature offers them to him; the name of *experimentalist* is given to him who employs the simple and complex process of investigation to vary or modify, for an end of some kind, the natural phenomena, and to make them appear under circumstances and conditions in which they are not presented by nature.

For instance, astronomy is a science of observation, because you cannot conceive of an astronomer acting upon the stars; while chemistry is an experimental science, as the chemist acts upon nature and modifies it. This, according to Claude Bernard, is the only true and important distinction which separates the observer from the experimentalist.

. . .

To determine how much observation and experimenting there can be in the naturalistic novel, I only need to quote the following passages:

> The observer relates purely and simply the phenomena which he has under his eyes. . . . He should be the photographer of phenomena, his observation should be an exact representation of nature. . . . He listens to nature and he writes under its dictation. But once the fact is ascertained and the phenomenon observed, an idea or hypothesis comes into his mind, reason intervenes, and the experimentalist comes forward to interpret the phenomenon. The experimentalist is a man who, in pursuance of a more or less probable, but anticipated, explanation of observed phenomena, institutes an experiment in such a way that, according to all probability, it will furnish a result which will serve to confirm the hypothesis or preconceived idea. The moment that the result of the experiment manifests itself, the experimentalist finds himself face to face with a true observation which he has called forth, and which he must ascertain, as all observation, without any preconceived idea. The experimentalist should then disappear, or rather transform himself instantly into the observer, and it is not until after he has ascertained the absolute results of the experiment, like that of an ordinary observation, that his mind comes back to reasoning, comparing, and judging whether the experimental hypothesis is verified or invalidated by these same results.

The mechanism is all there. It is a little complicated, it is true, and Claude Bernard is led on to say:

> When all this passes into the brain of a savant who has given himself up to the study of a science as complicated as medicine still is, then there is such an entanglement between the result of observation and what belongs to experiment that it will be impossible and, besides, useless to try to analyze, in their inextricable *mélange,* each of these terms.

In one word, it might be said that observation "indicates" and that experiment "teaches."

Now, to return to the novel, we can easily see that the novelist is equally an observer and an experimentalist. The observer in him gives the fact as he has observed them, suggests the point of departure, displays the solid earth on which his characters are to tread and the phenomena to develop. Then the experimentalist appears and introduces an experiment, that is to say, sets his characters going in a certain story so as to show that the succession of facts will be such as the requirements of the determinism of the phenomena under examination call for. Here it is nearly always an experiment *"pour voir,"* as Claude Bernard calls it. The novelist starts out in search of a truth. I will take as an example the character of the Baron Hulot, in *Cousine Bette,* by Balzac. The general fact observed by Balzac is the ravages that the amorous temperament of a man makes in his home, in his family, and in society. As soon as he has chosen his subject he starts from known facts; then he makes his experiment, and exposes Hulot to a series of trials, placing him amid certain surroundings in order to exhibit how the complicated machinery of his passions works. It is then evident that there is not only observation there, but that there is also experiment; as Balzac does not remain satisfied with photographing the facts collected by him, but interferes in a direct way to place his character in certain conditions, and of these he remains the master. The problem is to know what such a passion, acting in such a surrounding and under such circumstances, would produce from the point of view of an individual and of society; and an experimental novel, *Cousine Bette,* for example, is simply the report of the experiment that the novelist conducts before the eyes of the public. In fact, the whole operation consists in taking facts in nature, then in studying the mechanism of these facts, acting upon them, by the modification of circumstances and surroundings, without deviating from the laws of nature. Finally, you possess knowledge of the man, scientific knowledge of him, in both his individual and social relations.

Doubtless we are still far from certainties in chemistry and even physiology. Nor do we know any more the reagents which decompose the passions, rendering them susceptible of analysis. Often, in this essay, I shall recall in similar fashion this fact, that the experimental novel is still younger than experimental medicine, and the latter is but just born. But I do not intend to exhibit the acquired results, I simply desire to clearly expose a method. If the experimental novelist is still groping in the most obscure and complex of all the sciences, this does not prevent this science from existing. It is undeniable that the naturalistic novel, such as we understand it today, is a real experiment that a novelist makes on man by the help of observation.

. . .

But see what splendid clearness breaks forth when this conception of the application of the experimental method to the novel is adequately grasped and is carried out with all the scientific rigor which the matter permits today. A contemptible reproach which they heap upon us naturalistic writers is the desire to be solely photographers. We have in vain declared that we admit the necessity of an artist's possessing an individual temperament and a personal expression; they continue to reply to us with these imbecile arguments, about the impossibility of being strictly true, about the necessity of arranging facts to produce a work of art of any kind. Well, with the application of the experimental method to the novel that quarrel dies out. The idea of experiment carries with it the idea of modification. We start, indeed, from the true facts, which are our indestructible basis; but to show the mechanism of these facts it is necessary for us to produce and direct the phenomena; this is our share of invention, here is the genius in the book. Thus without having recourse to the questions of form and of style, which I shall examine later, I maintain even at this point that we must modify nature, without departing from nature, when we employ the experimental method in our novels. If we bear in mind this definition, that "observation indicates and experiment teaches," we can even now claim for our books this great lesson of experiment.

. . .

I sum up this first part by repeating that the naturalistic novelists observe and experiment, and that all their work is the offspring of the doubt which seizes them in the presence of truths little known and phenomena unexplained, until an experimental idea rudely awakens their genius some day, and urges them to make an experiment, to analyze facts, and to master them.

II

. . . In the last century a more exact application of the experimental method creates physics and chemistry, which then are freed from the irrational and supernatural. Men discover that there are fixed laws, thanks to analysis, and make themselves masters of phenomena. Then a new point is gained. Living beings, in which the vitalists still admitted a mysterious influence, are in their turn brought under and reduced to the general mechanism of matter. Science proves that the existing conditions of all phenomena are the same in living beings as in inanimate; and from that time on physiology assumes little by little the certainty of chemistry and medicine. But are we going to stop there? Evidently not. When it has been proved that the body of a man is a machine, whose machinery can be taken apart and put together again at the will of the experimenter, then we can pass to the passionate and intellectual acts of man. Then we shall enter into the domain which up to the present has belonged to physiology and literature; it will be the decisive conquest by science of the hypotheses of philosophers and writers. We have experimental chemistry and medicine; we shall have an experimental physiology, and later on an experimental novel. It is an inevitable evolution, the goal of which it is easy to see today. All things hang together; it is necessary to start from the determinism of inanimate bodies in order to arrive at the determinism of living beings; and since savants like Claude Bernard demonstrate now that fixed laws govern the human body, we can easily proclaim, without fear of being mistaken, the hour in which the laws of thought and passion will be formulated in their turn. A like determinism will govern the stones of the roadway and the brain of man.

. . .

Now, science enters into the domain of us novelists, who are today the analyzers of man, in his individual and social relations. We are continuing, by our observations and experiments, the work of the physiologist, who has continued that of the physicist and the chemist. We are making use, in a certain way, of scientific psychology to complete scientific physiology; and to finish the series we have only to bring into our studies of nature and man the decisive tool of the experimental method. In one word, we should operate on the characters, the passions, on the human and social data, in the same way that the chemist and the physicist operate on inanimate beings, and as the physiologist operates on living beings. Determinism dominates everything. It is scientific investigation, it is experimental reasoning, which combats one by one the hypotheses of the idealists, and which replaces purely imaginary novels by novels of observation and experiment.

I certainly do not intend at this point to formulate laws. In the actual condition of the science of man the obscurity and confusion are still too great to risk the slightest synthesis. All that can be said is that there is an absolute determinism for all human phenomena. From that on investigation is a duty. We have the method; we should go forward, even if a whole lifetime of effort ends but in the conquest of a small particle of the truth. Look at physiology: Claude Bernard made grand discoveries, and he died protesting that he knew nothing, or nearly nothing. In each page he confesses the difficulties of his task. "In the phenomenal relations," he says,

such as nature offers them to us, there always reigns a complexity more or less great. In this re-

spect the complexity of mineral phenomena is much less great than that of living phenomena; this is why the sciences restricted to inanimate bodies have been able to formulate themselves more quickly. In living beings the phenomena are of enormous complexity, and the greater mobility of living organisms renders them more difficult to grasp and to define.

What can be said, then, of the difficulties to be encountered by the experimental novel, which adds to physiology its studies upon the most delicate and complex organs, which deals with the highest manifestations of man as an individual and a social member? Evidently analysis becomes more complicated here. Therefore, if the physiologist is but drawing up his principles today, it is natural that the experimental novelist should be only taking his first steps: we foresee it as a sure consequence of the scientific evolution of the century; but it is impossible to base it on certain laws. Since Claude Bernard speaks of "the restricted and precarious truths of biological science," we can freely admit that the truths of the science of man, from the standpoint of his intellectual and passionate mechanism, are more restricted and precarious still. We are lisping yet, we are the last comers, but that should be only one incentive the more to push us forward to more exact studies; now that we possess the tool, the experimental method, our goal is very plain—to know the determinism of phenomena and to make ourselves master of these phenomena.

Without daring, as I say, to formulate laws, I consider that the question of heredity has a great influence in the intellectual and passionate manifestations of man. I also attach considerable importance to the surroundings. I ought to touch upon Darwin's theories; but this is only a general study of the experimental method as applied to the novel, and I should lose myself were I to enter into details. I will only say a word on the subject of surroundings. We have just seen the great importance given by Claude Bernard to the study of those interorganic conditions which must be taken into account if we wish to find the determinism of phenomena in living beings. Well, then! In the study of a family, of a group of living beings, I think that the social condition is of equal importance. Someday the physiologist will explain to us the mechanism of the thoughts and the passions; we shall know how the individual machinery of each man works; how he thinks, how he loves, how he goes from reason to passion and folly; but these phenomena, resulting as they do from the mechanism of the organs, acting under the influence of an interior condition, are not produced in isolation or in the bare void. Man is not alone; he lives in society, in a social condition; and consequently, for us novelists, this social condition unceasingly modifies the phenomena. Indeed our great study is just there, in the reciprocal effect of society on the individual and the individual on society. For the physiologist, the exterior and interior conditions are purely chemical and physical, and this aids him in finding the laws which govern them easily. We are not yet able to prove that the social condition is also physical and chemical. It is that certainly, or rather it is the variable product of a group of living beings, who themselves are absolutely submissive to the physical and chemical laws which govern alike living beings and inanimate. From this we shall see that we can act upon the social conditions, in acting upon the phenomena of which we have made ourselves master in man. And this is what constitutes the experimental novel: to possess a knowledge of the mechanism of the phenomena inherent in man, to show the machinery of his intellectual and sensory manifestations, under the influences of heredity and environment, such as physiology shall give them to us, and then finally to exhibit man living in social conditions produced by himself, which he modifies daily, and in the heart of which he himself experiences a continual transformation. Thus, then, we lean on physiology; we take man from the hands of the physiologist solely, in order to continue the solution of the problem, and to solve scientifically the question of how man behave when they are in society.

These general ideas will be sufficient to guide us today. Later on, when science is farther advanced, when the experimental novel has brought forth decisive results, some critic will explain more precisely what I have but indicated today.

. . .

I have reached this point: the experimental novel is a consequence of the scientific evolution of the century; it continues and completes physiology, which itself leans for support on chemistry and medicine; it substitutes for the study of the abstract and the metaphysical man the study of the natural man, governed by physical and chemical laws, and modified by the influences of his surroundings; it is in one word the literature of our scientific age, as the classical and Romantic literature corresponded to a scholastic and theological age. Now I will pass to the great question of the application of all this, and of its justification.

III

. . . This, then, is the end, this is the purpose in physiology and in experimental medicine: to make oneself master of life in order to be able to direct it. Let us suppose that science advances and that the conquest of the unknown is finally completed; the scientific age which Claude Bernard saw in

his dreams will then be realized. When that time comes the doctor will be the master of maladies; he will cure without fail; his influence upon the human body will conduce to the welfare and strength of the species. We shall enter upon a century in which man, grown more powerful, will make use of nature and will utilize its laws to produce upon the earth the greatest possible amount of justice and freedom. There is no nobler, higher, nor grander end. Here is our role as intelligent beings: to penetrate to the wherefore of things, to become superior to these things, and to reduce them to a condition of subservient machinery.

Well, this dream of the physiologist and the experimental doctor is also that of the novelist, who employs the experimental method in his study of man as a simple individual and as a social animal. Their object is ours; we also desire to master certain phenomena of an intellectual and personal order, to be able to direct them. We are, in a word, experimental moralists, showing by experiment in what way a passion acts in a certain social condition. The day in which we gain control of the mechanism of this passion we can treat it and reduce it, or at least make it as inoffensive as possible. And in this consists the practical utility and high morality of our naturalistic works, which experiment on man, and which dissect piece by piece this human machinery in order to set it going through the influence of the environment. When things have advanced further, when we are in possession of the different laws, it will only be necessary to work upon the individuals and the surroundings if we wish to find the best social condition. In this way we shall construct a practical sociology, and our work will be a help to political and economical sciences. I do not know, I repeat, of a more noble work, nor of a grander application. To be the master of good and evil, to regulate life, to regulate society, to solve in time all the problems of socialism, above all, to give justice a solid foundation by solving through experiment the questions of criminality—is not this being the most useful and the most moral workers in the human workshop?

Let us compare, for one instant, the work of the idealistic novelists to ours; and here this word idealistic refers to writers who cast aside observation and experiment, and base their works on the supernatural and the irrational, who admit, in a word, the power of mysterious forces outside of the determinism of the phenomena. Claude Bernard shall reply to this for me:

What distinguishes experimental reasoning from scholastic is the fecundity of the one and the sterility of the other. It is precisely the scholastic, who believes he has absolute certitude, who attains to no results. This is easily understood, since by his belief in an absolute principle he puts himself outside of nature, in which everything is relative. It is, on the contrary, the experimenter, who is always in doubt, who does not think he possesses absolute certainty about anything, who succeeds in mastering the phenomena which surround him, and in increasing his power over nature.

By and by I shall return to this question of the ideal, which is in truth but the question of indeterminism. Claude Bernard says truly: "The intellectual conquest of man consists in diminishing and driving back indeterminism, and so, gradually, by the aid of the experimental method, gaining ground for determinism." We experimental novelists have the same task; our work is to go from the known to the unknown, to make ourselves masters of nature; while the idealistic novelists deliberately remain in the unknown, through all sorts of religious and philosophical prejudices, under the astounding pretense that the unknown is nobler and more beautiful than the known. If our work, often cruel, if our terrible pictures needed justification, I should find, indeed, with Claude Bernard this argument conclusive:

> You will never reach really fruitful and luminous generalization on the phenomena of life until you have experimented yourself and stirred up in the hospital, the amphitheater, and the laboratory the fetid or palpitating sources of life. If it were necessary for me to give a comparison which would explain my sentiments on the science of life, I should say that it is a superb salon, flooded with light, which you can only reach by passing through a long and nauseating kitchen.

I insist upon the word which I have employed, that of experimental novelists as applied to naturalistic novelists. One page of *L'Introduction* struck me as being very forcible, that in which the author speaks of the vital "circulus."

> The muscular and nervous organs preserve the activity of the organs which make the blood; but the blood, in its turn, nourishes the organs which produce it. There is in this a social or organic solidarity, which keeps up a perpetual movement, until the derangement or cessation of the action of a necessary and vital element has broken the equilibrium or brought about some trouble or stoppage in the play of the animal machinery. The problem of the experimentalist doctor consists in finding the cause of any organic disarrangement, that is to say, in seizing the initial phenomenon. We shall see how a dislocation of the organism, or a disarrangement the most complex in appearance, can be traced to a simple initial cause, which calls forth immediately the most complex effects.

All that is necessary here is to change the words experimental doctor to experimental novelist, and this passage is exactly applicable to our naturalistic literature. The social circulus is identical with the vital circulus; in society, as in human beings, a solidarity exists which unites the different members and the different organisms in such a way that if one organ becomes rotten many others are tainted and a very complicated disease results. Hence, in our novels, when we experiment on a dangerous wound which poisons society, we proceed in the same way as the experimentalist doctor; we try to find the simple initial cause in order to reach the complex causes of which the action is the result. Go back once more to the example of Baron Hulot in *Cousine Bette*. See the final result, the dénouement of the novel: an entire family is destroyed, all sorts of secondary dramas are produced, under the action of Hulot's amorous temperament. It is there, in this temperament, that the initial cause is found. One member, Hulot, becomes rotten, and immediately all around him are tainted, the social circulus is interrupted, the health of that society is compromised. What emphasis Balzac lays on the character of Baron Hulot; with what scrupulous care he analyzes him! The experiment deals with him chiefly, because its object is to master the symptoms of this passion in order to govern it. Suppose that Hulot is cured, or at least restrained and rendered inoffensive, immediately the drama ceases to have any longer any *raison d'être;* the equilibrium, or more truly the health, of the social body is again established. Thus the naturalistic novelists are really experimental moralists.

And I reach thus the great reproach with which they think to crush the naturalistic novelists, by treating them as fatalists. How many times have they wished to prove to us that as soon as we did not accept free will, that as soon as man was no more to us than a living machine, acting under the influence of heredity and surroundings, we should fall into gross fatalism, we should debase humanity to the rank of a troop marching under the baton of destiny. It is necessary to define our terms: we are not fatalists, we are determinists, which is not at all the same thing. Claude Bernard explains the two terms very plainly:

> We have given the name of determinism to the nearest or determining cause of phenomena. We never act upon the essence of phenomena in nature, but only on their determinism, and by this very fact, that we act upon it, determinism differs from fatalism, upon which we could not act at all.

Fatalism assumes that the appearance of any phenomenon is necessary apart from its conditions, while determinism is just the conditions, essential for the appearance of any phenomenon, and such appearance is never forced. Once the search for the determinism of phenomena is placed as a fundamental principle of the experimental method, there is no longer either materialism, or spiritualism, or inanimate matter, or living matter; there remain but phenomena of which it is necessary to determine the conditions, that is to say, the circumstances which play, by their proximity to these phenomena, the role of nearest cause.

This is decisive. All we do is to apply this method in our novels, and we are the determinists who experimentally try to determine the condition of the phenomena, without departing in our investigations from the laws of nature. As Claude Bernard very truly says, the moment that we can act, and that we do act, on the determining cause of phenomena—by modifying their surroundings, for example—we cease to be fatalists.

Here you have, then, the moral purpose of the experimental novelist clearly defined. I have often said that we do not have to draw a conclusion from our works; and this means that our works carry their conclusion with them. An experimentalist has no need to conclude, because, in truth, experiment concludes for him. A hundred times, if necessary, he will repeat the experiment before the public; he will explain it; but he need neither become indignant nor approve of it personally; such is the truth, such is the way phenomena work; it is for society to produce or not to produce these phenomena, according as the result is useful or dangerous. You cannot imagine, as I have said elsewhere, a savant being provoked with azote because azote is dangerous to life; he suppresses azote when it is harmful, and not otherwise. As our power is not the same as that of a savant, as we are experimentalists without being practitioners, we ought to content ourselves with searching out the determinism of social phenomena, and leaving to legislators and to men of affairs the care of controlling sooner or later these phenomena in such a way as to develop the good and reject the bad, from the point of view of their utility to man.

In our role as experimental moralists we show the mechanism of the useful and the useless, we disengage the determinism of the human and social phenomena so that, in their turn, the legislators can one day dominate and control these phenomena. In a word, we are working with the whole country toward that great object, the conquest of nature and the increase of man's power a hundredfold. Compare with ours the work of the idealistic writers, who rely upon the

irrational and the supernatural, and whose every flight upward is followed by a deeper fall into metaphysical chaos. We are the ones who possess strength and morality.

IV

. . . If Claude Bernard confesses that the complexity of its phenomena will prevent medicine, for a long time yet, from arriving at a scientific state, what shall we say of the experimental novel, in which the phenomena are much more complicated still? But this does not prevent the novel from entering upon the scientific pathway, obedient to the general evolution of the century.

Moreover, Claude Bernard himself has indicated the evolutions of the human mind. "The human mind," he says,

at various periods of its progress has passed successively through feeling, reason, and experiment. First, feeling alone, dominating reason, created the truths of faith, that is to say, theology. Reason, or philosophy, becoming afterward the mistress, brought forth scholasticism. Finally, experiment, that is to say, the study of natural phenomena, taught man that the truths of the exterior world were to be found formulated, in the first place, neither in reason nor in feeling. These last are, indeed, our indispensable guides, but to obtain the truth it is necessary to descend into the objective reality of things, where they lie concealed under their phenomenal form. Thus it is that in the natural progress of things the experimental method appears, which sums up the whole, and which supports itself successfully on the three branches of this immovable tripod: feeling, reason, and experiment. In the search after truth by means of this method, feeling has always the initiative; it engenders the idea a priori or intuition; reason, or the reasoning power, immediately develops the idea and deduces its logical consequences. But if feeling must be guided by the light of reason, reason in its turn must be guided by experiment.

I have given this passage entire, as it is of the greatest importance. It shows clearly the role that the personality of the novelist should play, apart from the style. Since feeling is the starting point of the experimental method, since reason subsequently intervenes to end in experiment, and to be controlled by it, the genius of the experimentalist dominates everything, and this is what has made the experimental method, so inert in other hands, such a powerful tool in the hands of

Claude Bernard. I have said the word: method is but the tool; it is the workman, it is the idea, which he brings, which makes the chef-d'oeuvre. I have already quoted these lines: "It is a particular feeling, a *quid proprium*,[2] which constitutes the originality, the invention, or the genius of each one." This, then, is the part taken by genius in the experimental novel. As Claude Bernard says again: "The idea is the seed; the method is the soil which furnishes the conditions for developing and prospering it, and bringing forth its best fruits, according to nature." Thus everything is reduced to a question of method. If you are content to remain in the a priori idea, and enjoy your own feelings without finding any basis for it in reason or any verification in experiment, you are a poet; you venture upon hypotheses which you cannot prove; you are struggling vainly in a painful indeterminism, and in a way that is often injurious. Listen to these lines of *L'Introduction:*

> Man is naturally a metaphysician and proud; he believes that the idealistic creations of his brain, which coincide with his feelings, represent the reality. Thus it follows that the experimental method is not innate and natural to man, for it is only after having wandered for a long time among theological and scholastical discussions that he ends by recognizing the sterility of his efforts in this path. Man then perceives that he cannot dictate laws to nature, because he does not possess in himself the knowledge and the criterion of exterior things; he realizes that in order to arrive at the truth he must, on the contrary, study the natural laws and submit his ideas, if not his reason, to experiment, that is to say, to the criterion of facts.

What becomes of the genius of the experimental novelist? The genius, the idea a priori, remains, only it is controlled by experiment. The experiment naturally cannot destroy his genius; on the contrary, it confirms it. To take the case of a poet, for example: To show he has genius is it necessary that his feeling, his idea, a priori, should be false? Evidently not, for the genius of a man will be so much the greater when experiment has proved the truth of his personal idea. Our age of lyricism, our Romantic disease, was alone capable of measuring a man's genius by the quantity of nonsense and folly which he put in circulation. I conclude by saying that in our scientific century experiment must prove genius.

This is the drift of our quarrel with the idealistic writers. They always start out from an irrational source of some kind,

such as a revelation, a tradition, or conventional authority. As Claude Bernard declares: "We must admit nothing occult; there are but phenomena and the conditions of phenomena." We naturalistic novelists submit each fact to the test of observation and experiment, while the idealistic writers admit mysterious elements which escape analysis, and therefore remain in the unknown, outside of the influence of the laws governing nature. This question of the ideal, from the scientific point of view, reduces itself to a question of indeterminate or determinate. All that we do not know, all that escapes us still, that is truly the ideal, and the aim of our human efforts is each day to reduce the ideal, to conquer truth from the unknown. We are all idealists, if we mean by this that we busy ourselves with the ideal. But I dub those idealists who take refuge in the unknown for the pleasure of being there, who have a taste but for the most risky hypotheses, who disdain to submit them to the test of experiment under the pretext that the truth is in themselves and not in the things. These writers, I repeat, accomplish a vain and harmful task, while the observer and the experimentalist are the only ones who work for the strength and happiness of man, making him more and more the master of nature. There is neither nobility, nor dignity, nor beauty, nor morality in not knowing, in lying, in pretending that you are greater according as you advance in error and confusion. The only great and moral works are those of truth.

What we alone must accept is what I will call the stimulus of the ideal. Certainly our science is very limited as yet, beside the enormous mass of things of which we are ignorant. This great unknown which surrounds us ought to inspire us with the desire to pierce it, to explain it by means of scientific methods. And this does not refer only to scientific men; all the manifestations of human intelligence are connected together, all our efforts have their birth in the need we feel of making ourselves masters of the truth.

. . .

V

. . . I have already repeated twenty times that naturalism is not a personal fantasy, but that it is the intellectual movement of the century. Perhaps they will believe Claude Bernard, who speaks with greater authority on this subject than I can lay claim to; he declares that:

> The revolution which the experimental method has caused in science consists mainly in the substitution of a scientific criterion for a personal authority. It is the characteristic of the experimental method to depend only on itself, as it carries

---

[2]"Special thing."

within itself its criterion, which is experiment. It recognizes no authority but that of facts, and it frees itself from personal authority.

Consequently, it no longer admits the authority of any theory either.

The idea should always remain independent; it must be enchained neither by scientific, nor philosophical, nor religious beliefs. Man must be strong and free in the manifestation of his ideas, must follow his instinct, and not dwell upon the puerile fears of the contradiction of any theories . . . he must modify theory by adapting it to nature, and not nature by adapting it to theory.

From this there results an incomparable breadth.

The experimental method is the scientific method which proclaims the liberty of thought. It not only throws off the philosophical and theological yoke, but it no longer admits scientific personal authority. This is not said from pride or boastfulness. The experimentalist, on the contrary, shows his humility in denying personal authority, for he doubts his own knowledge, and he submits the authority of men to that of experiment and the laws which govern nature.

This is why I have said so many times that naturalism is not a school, as it is not embodied in the genius of one man, nor in the ravings of a group of men, as was Romanticism; that it consists simply in the application of the experimental method to the study of nature and of man. Hence it is nothing but a vast movement, a march forward in which everyone is a workman, according to his genius. All theories are admitted, and the theory which carries the most weight is the one which explains the most. There does not appear to me to be a literary or scientific path larger or more direct. Everyone, the great and the small, moves freely, working and investigating together, each one in his own specialty, and recognizing no other authority than that of facts proved by experiment. Therefore in naturalism there could be neither innovators nor leaders; there are simply workmen, some more skillful than others.

. . . I have said that in the experimental novel it is best for us to hold to the strictly scientific point of view if we wish to base our studies on solid ground; not to go out from the "how," not to attach ourselves to the "why." However, it is very certain that we cannot always escape this need of our intelligence, this restless curiosity which makes us desire

to know the essence of things. I think that it is best for us to accept the philosophical system, which adapts itself the best to the actual condition of the sciences, but simply from a speculative point of view. For example, transformism is actually the most rational system, and is the one which is based most directly upon our knowledge of nature. Behind a science, behind a manifestation of any kind of the human intelligence, there always lies more or less clearly what Claude Bernard calls a philosophical system. To this system it is not well to attach oneself devotedly, but to hold tenaciously to the facts, free to modify the system if the facts call for it. But the system exists nonetheless, and it exists so much the more as science is less advanced and less firm. For us naturalistic novelists, who are still in the lisping stage, hypothesis is fatal. By and by I will take up the role of hypothesis in literature.

Nevertheless, if in practice Claude Bernard thrusts aside philosophical system, he recognizes the necessity of philosophy.

From a scientific point of view, philosophy represents the eternal desire of the human reason after knowledge of the unknown. Hence philosophers always confine themselves to questions that are in dispute, and to those lofty regions that lie beyond the boundaries of science. In this way they communicate to science a certain inspiration which animates and ennobles it. They strengthen the mind—developing it by an intellectual gymnastics—at the same time that they ever carry it toward the never-completed solution of great problems. Thus they keep up a cult of the unknown, and quicken the sacred fire of investigation, which ought never to be extinguished in the heart of a savant.

This passage is very fine, but the philosophers have never been told in better terms that their hypotheses are pure poetry. Claude Bernard evidently looks upon the philosophers, among whom he believes he has a great many friends, as musicians often gifted with genius, whose music encourages the savants while they work and inspires the sacred fire of their great discoveries. But the philosophers, left to themselves, will sing forever and never discover a single truth.

I have neglected until now the question of form in the naturalistic novel, because it is precisely there that individuality shows in literature. Not only is a writer's genius to be found in the feeling and in the idea a priori but also in the form and style. But the question of method and the question of rhetoric are distinct from each other. And by naturalism, I say again, is meant the experimental method, the introduction of observation and experiment into literature. Rhetoric, for the moment, has no place here. Let us first fix upon the method, on which there should be agreement, and after that accept all the different styles in letters which may be produced, looking upon them as the expressions of the literary temperament of the writers.

If you wish my true opinion upon this subject, it is this: that today an exaggerated importance is given to form. I have a great deal to say on this subject, but it would carry me beyond the limits of this essay. In reality, I think that the form of expression depends upon the method: that language is only one kind of logic, and its construction natural and scientific. He who writes the best will not be the one who gallops madly among hypotheses, but the one who walks straight ahead in the midst of truths. We are actually rotten with lyricism; we are very much mistaken when we think that the characteristic of a good style is a sublime confusion with just a dash of madness added; in reality, the excellence of a style depends upon its logic and clearness.

Claude Bernard considers that philosophers are really musicians who play a sort of *Marseillaise* made up of hypotheses, and swell the hearts of the savants as they rush to attack the unknown; and he has much the same idea of artists and writers. I have remarked that a great many of the most intelligent savants, jealous of the scientific certainty which they enjoy, would very willingly confine literature to the ideal. They themselves seem to feel the need of taking little recreations in the world of lies after the fatigue of their exact labors, and they are fond of amusing themselves with the most daring hypotheses, and with fictions which they know perfectly well to be false and ridiculous. Claude Bernard was right when he said: "Literary and artistic productions will never grow old in the sense that they are the expressions of sentiments as unchangeable as human nature." In fact, form is sufficient to immortalize a work; the spectacle of a powerful individuality reproducing nature in superb language will interest all ages; only the works of a savant, from this same point of view, will be read always, for the reason that the thought of a great savant who knows how to write is much more interesting than that of a poet. However far astray the savant may be in his hypothesis, he still remains the equal of the poet, who is certain to have been equally mistaken. The point to be emphasized is this, that our domain is not limited to the expression of sentiments as unchangeable as human nature because it is essential also to exhibit the working of these sentiments.

We have not exhausted our matter when we have depicted anger, avarice, and love; all nature and all of man belong to us, not only in their phenomena, but in the causes of these phenomena. I well know that this is an immense field,

the entrance to which they would willingly have refused us; but we have broken down the barriers and have entered it in triumph. This is why I do not accept the following words of Claude Bernard: "In art and letters personality dominates everything. There one is dealing with a spontaneous creation of the mind that has nothing in common with the verification of natural phenomena, in which our minds can create nothing." I have here detected one of our most illustrious savants sharing in the attempt to refuse to letters the entrée to the scientific field. I do not know what letters he refers to in this definition of a literary work: "A spontaneous creation of the mind that has nothing in common with the verification of natural phenomena." Doubtless he has lyrical poetry in his mind, for he never could have written that phrase had he understood the experimental novel as shown in the works of Balzac and Stendhal. I can only repeat what I have said before, that apart from the matter of form and style, the experimental novelist is only one special kind of savant, who makes use of the tools of all other savants, observation and analysis. Our field is the same as the physiologist's, only that it is greater. We operate, like him, on man; and Claude Bernard recognizes this fact himself, that the cerebral phenomena can be determined the same as other phenomena. It is true that Claude Bernard can tell us that we are lost in hypotheses; but to conclude from this that we shall never arrive at the truth sits very badly on him, as he has struggled all his life to make a science of medicine, which the great majority of his contemporaries look upon as an art.

Let us clearly define now what is meant by an experimental novelist. Claude Bernard gives the following definition of an artist: "What is an artist? He is a man who realizes in a work of art an idea or a sentiment which is personal to him." I absolutely reject this definition. On this basis if I represented a man as walking on his head, I should have made a work of art, if such happened to be my personal sentiments. But in that case I should be a fool and nothing else. So one must add that the personal feeling of the artist is always subject to the higher law of truth and nature. We now come to the question of hypothesis. The artist starts out from the same point as the savant; he places himself before nature, has an idea a priori, and works according to this idea. Here alone he separates himself from the savant, if he carries out his idea to the end without verifying its truth by the means of observation and experiment. Those who make use of experiment might well be called experimental artists; but then people will tell us that they are no longer artists, since such people regard art as the burden of personal error which the artist has put into his study of nature. I contend that the personality of the writer should only appear in the idea a priori and in the form, not in the infatuation for the false. I see no objection, besides, to its showing in the hypothesis, but it is necessary to clearly understand what you mean by these words.

It has often been said that writers ought to open the way for savants. This is true, for we have seen in *L'Introduction* that hypothesis and empiricism precede and prepare for the scientific state which is established finally by the experimental method. Man commenced by venturing certain explanations of phenomena, the poets gave expression to their emotions, and the savants ended by mastering hypotheses and fixing the truth. Claude Bernard always assigns the role of pioneers to the philosophers. It is a very noble role, and today it is the writers who should assume it and who should endeavor to fill it worthily. Only let it be well understood that each time that a truth is established by the savants the writers should immediately abandon their hypothesis to adopt this truth; otherwise they will remain deliberately in error without benefiting anyone. It is thus that science, as it advances, furnishes to us writers a solid ground upon which we should lean for support, to better enable us to shoot into new hypotheses. In a word, every phenomenon, once clearly determined, destroys the hypothesis which it replaces, and it is then necessary to transport your hypothesis one step further into the new unknown which arises. I will take a very simple example in order to make myself better understood: it has been proved that the earth revolves around the sun; what would you think of a poet who should adopt the old belief that the sun revolves around the earth? Evidently the poet, if he wishes to risk a personal explanation of any fact, should choose a fact whose cause is not already known. This, then, illustrates the position hypothesis should occupy for experimental novelists; we must accept determined facts, and not attempt to risk about them our personal sentiments, which would be ridiculous, building throughout on the territory that science has conquered; then before the unknown, but only then, exercising our intuition and suggesting the way to science, free to make mistakes, happy if we produce any data toward the solution of the problem. Here I stand at Claude Bernard's practical program, who is forced to accept empiricism as a necessary forerunner. In our experimental novel we can easily risk a few hypotheses on the question of heredity and surroundings, after having respected all that science knows today about the matter. We can prepare the ways, we can furnish the results of observation, human data which may prove very useful. A great lyrical poet has written lately that our century is a century of prophets. Yes, if you wish it; only let it be well understood that these prophets rely neither upon the irrational nor the supernatural. If the prophets thought best to bring up again the most elementary notions, to serve up nature with a strange religious and philo-

sophical sauce, to hold fast to the metaphysical man, to confound and obscure everything, the prophets, notwithstanding their genius in the matter of style, would never be anything but great gooses ignorant whether they would get wet if they jumped into the water. In our scientific age it is a very delicate thing to be a prophet, as we no longer believe in the truths of revelation, and in order to be able to foresee the unknown we must begin by studying the known.

The conclusion to which I wish to come is this: If I were to define the experimental novel I should not say, as Claude Bernard says, that a literary work lies entirely in the personal feeling, for the reason that in my opinion the personal feeling is but the first impulse. Later nature, being there, makes itself felt, or at least that part of nature of which science has given us the secret, and about which we have no longer any right to romance. The experimental novelist is therefore the one who accepts proven facts, who points out in man and in society the mechanism of the phenomena over which science is mistress, and who does not interpose his personal sentiments, except in the phenomena whose determinism is not yet settled, and who tries to test, as much as he can, this personal sentiment, this idea a priori, by observation and experiment.

I cannot understand how our naturalistic literature can mean anything else. I have only spoken of the experimental novel, but I am fairly convinced that the same method, after having triumphed in history and in criticism, will triumph everywhere, on the stage and in poetry even. It is an inevitable evolution. Literature, in spite of all that can be said, does not depend merely upon the author; it is influenced by the nature it depicts and by the man whom it studies. Now if the savants change their ideas of nature, if they find the true mechanism of life, they force us to follow them, to precede them even, so as to play our role in the new hypotheses. The metaphysical man is dead; our whole territory is transformed by the advent of the physiological man. No doubt "Achilles' Anger," "Dido's Love,"[3] will last forever on account of their beauty; but today we feel the necessity of analyzing anger and love, of discovering exactly how such passions work in the human being. This view of the matter is a new one; we have become experimentalists instead of philosophers. In short, everything is summed up in this great fact: the experimental method in letters, as in the sciences, is in the way to explain the natural phenomena, both individual and social, of which metaphysics, until now, has given only irrational and supernatural explanations.

---

[3]Reference to themes of the *Odyssey* and the *Aeneid* respectively.

Anatole France

1844–1924

The brief but famous passage from France's *The Literary Life* printed below epitomizes the attitude of the impressionistic critic. Wary of "scientific" description, impatient with external canons of judgment, accepting the essential subjectivity of all experience, the impressionist considers his criticism a comment on himself. To his mind there are no such things as aesthetics, ethics, sociology, and biology. Nor are there such things as tradition, universal consent, and free taste.

France, a well-known novelist and man of letters, was probably the foremost of the antiscientific and impressionistic critics, but his position of relativism actually adopts the subject-object opposition that forms the philosophical basis of scientific method.

The standard translation of France's *La Vie littéraire* is that by A. W. Evans, *On Life and Letters* (1911). Studies of France include H. M. Chevalier, *The Ironic Temper: Anatole France and His Time* (1932); Jacob Axelrad, *Anatole France, A Life Without Illusions 1844–1924* (1944); Carter Jefferson, *Anatole France: The Politics of Skepticism* (1965); and Reino Virtanen, *Anatole France* (1968).

The Adventures of the Soul

As I understand criticism it is, like philosophy and history, a kind of novel for the use of discreet and curious minds. And every novel, rightly understood, is an autobiography. The good critic is he who relates the adventures of his soul among masterpieces.

There is no such thing as objective criticism any more than there is objective art, and all who flatter themselves that they put aught but themselves into their work are dupes of the most fallacious illusion. The truth is that one never gets out of oneself. That is one of our greatest miseries. What would we not give to see, if but for a minute, the sky and earth with the many-faceted eye of a fly, or to understand nature with the rude and simple brain of an ape? But just that is forbidden us. We cannot, like Tiresias, be men and remember having been women. We are locked into our persons as into a lasting prison. The best we can do, it seems to me, is gracefully to recognize this terrible situation and to admit that we speak of ourselves every time that we have not the strength to be silent.

To be quite frank, the critic ought to say: "Gentlemen, I am going to talk about myself on the subject of Shakespeare, or Racine, or Pascal, or Goethe—subjects that offer me a beautiful opportunity."

THE ADVENTURES OF THE SOUL. *The Adventures of the Soul* is part of France's *La Vie littéraire* (1888–93), the four critical volumes that grew out of the articles France wrote as literary critic of the French newspaper *Le Temps*. The text is from the translation by Ludwig Lewisohn in *A Modern Book of Criticism* (1919). Reprinted by permission of Random House, Inc.

Oscar Wilde

1854–1900

The narcissistic wittiness of Wilde, combined with the Arnoldian desire of some readers for "high seriousness," has caused Wilde's critical work not to be taken seriously enough. Beneath the impertinent transvaluations of *The Decay of Lying* lie important theoretical implications. Wilde recognized that the theory of imitation was undergoing a crucial change. The trend, at least since Kant and Coleridge, had been to emphasize art's power to *make,* not to *copy.* Art affects how we come to see the world. For Wilde, life and nature imitate art more than art imitates life and nature. For example, his critic Vivian blames the fogs of London on certain painters of the nineteenth century. Indeed, we see the world in certain frameworks—frameworks that we have been taught. Art in the restricted sense of fine art may not be responsible for as much of our world as Vivian thinks, but when seen to include the popular arts, such as television, publishing, and advertising, it certainly does constantly affect the way we experience things. No doubt the fine arts help to build up our sense of a more complex and intense world than do the popular arts. Much in modern philosophy and psychology reflects this Wildean idea. For example, Cassirer's philosophy of symbolic forms suggests the power of art, history, religion, and science to make our cultural world.

Wilde takes another Kantian idea to an extreme. Vivian argues against usefulness as an element in the art object. Kant did not assert that art objects should not or cannot be useful; instead he suggested that to judge an art object in terms of its use is not to make an aesthetic judgment. Vivian argues that the art object should have no use. He associates use with verbal "content"—that is, something that can be abstracted from the work and judged true or false by some process of verification or recourse to an a priori set of moral principles. According to Wilde "truth" in art (or "lies") is a matter only of style. In this argument we see a Romantic effort to distinguish poetry from discursive argumentation and scientific procedures. Sidney remarked that the poet does not lie because he never affirms. Wilde is not quite content with that or with arguments defending art because it leads us to some Platonic truth. Fundamentally he sees art as a formative force in culture. Why does Wilde talk of art as lying? Because he recognizes the dominance in his time of scientific and discursive modes of structuring our reality, and he wishes to attack this dominance—in his view a terrible imbalance—by the shocking inversion of normal terminology. If naturalism and science bring truth, then art brings lies, and Wilde chooses lies. Who wants truth?

Hesketh Pearson has edited Wilde's complete works (1936) and his essays (1950). Wilde's criticism is also available in *The Artist as Critic: Critical Writings of Oscar Wilde,* edited by Richard Ellmann (1969). Relevant commentaries include Arthur Symons, *A Study of Oscar Wilde* (1930); William Gaunt, *The Aesthetic Adventure* (1945); Hesketh Pearson, *The Life of Oscar Wilde* (1946); George Woodcock, *The*

Paradox of Oscar Wilde (1949); St. John Ervine, *Oscar Wilde* (1952); Kevin Sullivan, *Oscar Wilde* (1972); Ronald Ericksen, *Oscar Wilde* (1972); Christopher Nassaar, *Into the Demon Universe* (1974); and Richard Ellmann, *Oscar Wilde* (1988).

The Decay of Lying

Cyril   (*Coming in through the open window from the terrace.*) My dear Vivian, don't coop yourself up all day in the library. It is a perfectly lovely afternoon. The air is exquisite. There is a mist upon the woods, like the purple bloom upon a plum. Let us go and lie on the grass, and smoke cigarettes, and enjoy nature.

Vivian   Enjoy nature! I am glad to say that I have entirely lost that faculty. People tell us that art makes us love nature more than we loved her before; that it reveals her secrets to us; and that after a careful study of Corot and Constable we see things in her that had escaped our observation. My own experience is that the more we study art, the less we care for nature. What art really reveals to us is nature's lack of design, her curious crudities, her extraordinary monotony, her absolutely unfinished condition. Nature has good intentions, of course, but, as Aristotle once said, she cannot carry them out. When I look at a landscape I cannot help seeing all its defects. It is fortunate for us, however, that nature is so imperfect, as otherwise we should have had no art at all. Art is our spirited protest, our gallant attempt to teach nature her proper place. As for the infinite variety of nature, that is a pure myth. It is not to be found in nature herself. It resides in the imagination, or fancy, or cultivated blindness of the man who looks at her.

Cyril   Well, you need not look at the landscape. You can lie on the grass and smoke and talk.

Vivian   But nature is so uncomfortable. Grass is hard and lumpy and damp, and full of dreadful black insects. Why, even Morris' poorest workman could make you a more comfortable seat than the whole of nature can. Nature pales before the furniture of "the street which from Oxford has borrowed its name," as the poet you love so much once vilely phrased it. I don't complain. If nature had been comfortable, mankind would never have invented architecture, and I prefer houses to the open air. In a house we all feel of the proper proportions. Everything is subordinated to us, fashioned for our use and our pleasure. Egotism itself, which is so necessary to a proper sense of human dignity, is entirely the result of indoor life. Out of doors one becomes abstract and impersonal. One's individuality absolutely leaves one. And then nature is so indifferent, so unappreciative. Whenever I am walking in the park here I always feel that I am no more to her than the cattle that browse on the slope, or the burdock that blooms in the ditch. Nothing is more evident than that nature hates mind. Thinking is the most unhealthy thing in the world, and people die of it just as they die of any other disease. Fortunately, in England, at any rate, thought is not catching. Our splendid physique as a people is entirely due to our national stupidity. I only hope we shall be able to keep this great historic bulwark of our happiness for many years to come; but I am afraid that we are beginning to be overeducated; at least, everybody who is incapable of learning has taken to teaching—that is really what our enthusiasm for education has come to. In the meantime, you had better go back to your wearisome uncomfortable nature, and leave me to correct my proofs.

Cyril   Writing an article! That is not very consistent after what you have just said.

Vivian   Who wants to be consistent? The dullard and the doctrinaire, the tedious people who carry out their principles to the bitter end of action, to the *reductio ad absurdum* of practice. Not I. Like Emerson, I write over the door of my library the word *whim*. Besides, my article is really a most salutary and valuable warning. If it is attended to, there may be a new Renaissance of art.

Cyril   What is the subject?

Vivian   I intend to call it *The Decay of Lying: A Protest.*

Cyril   Lying! I should have thought that our politicians kept up that habit.

Vivian   I assure you that they do not. They never rise beyond the level of misrepresentation, and actually condescend to prove, to discuss, to argue. How different from the temper of the true liar, with his frank, fearless statements, his superb irresponsibility, his healthy, natural disdain of proof of any kind! After all, what is a fine lie? Simply that which is its own evidence. If a man is sufficiently unimaginative to produce evidence in support of a lie, he might just as well speak the truth at once. No, the politicians won't do. Something may, perhaps, be urged on behalf of the bar. The mantle of the sophist has fallen on its members. Their feigned ardors and unreal rhetoric are delightful. They can

---

THE DECAY OF LYING. Wilde's *Decay of Lying* was first published in 1889.

make the worse appear the better cause, as though they were fresh from Leontine schools, and have been known to wrest from reluctant juries triumphant verdicts of acquittal for their clients, even when those clients, as often happens, were clearly unmistakably innocent. But they are briefed by the prosaic, and are not ashamed to appeal to precedent. In spite of their endeavors, the truth will out. Newspapers, even, have degenerated. They may now be absolutely relied upon. One feels it as one wades through their columns. It is always the unreadable that occurs. I am afraid that there is not much to be said in favor of either the lawyer or the journalist. Besides, what I am pleading for is lying in art. Shall I read you what I have written? It might do you a great deal of good.

Cyril   Certainly, if you give me a cigarette. Thanks. By the way, what magazine do you intend it for?

Vivian   For the *Retrospective Review.* I think I told you that the elect had revived it.

Cyril   Whom do you mean by "the elect"?

Vivian   Oh, The Tired Hedonists, of course. It is a club to which I belong. We are supposed to wear faded roses in our buttonholes when we meet, and to have a sort of cult for Domitian. I am afraid you are not eligible. You are too fond of simple pleasures.

Cyril   I should be blackballed on the ground of animal spirits, I suppose?

Vivian   Probably. Besides, you are a little too old. We don't admit anybody who is of the usual age.

Cyril   Well, I should fancy you are all a good deal bored with each other.

Vivian   We are. That is one of the objects of the club. Now, if you promise not to interrupt too often, I will read you my article.

Cyril   You will find me all attention.

Vivian   *(Reading in a very clear, musical voice.)* *"The Decay of Lying: A Protest.* One of the chief causes that can be assigned for the curiously commonplace character of most of the literature of our age is undoubtedly the decay of lying as an art, a science, and a social pleasure. The ancient historians gave us delightful fiction in the form of fact; the modern novelist presents us with dull facts under the guise of fiction. The blue book is rapidly becoming his ideal both for method and manner. He has his tedious *document humain,* his miserable little *coin de la création,*[1] into which he peers with his microscope. He is to be found at the Librairie Nationale, or at the British Museum, shamelessly reading up his subject. He has not even the courage of other people's ideas, but insists on going directly to life for everything, and ultimately, between encyclopedias and personal experience, he comes to the ground, having drawn his types from the family circle or from the weekly washerwoman, and having acquired an amount of useful information from which never, even in his most meditative moments, can he thoroughly free himself.

"The loss that results to literature in general from this false ideal of our time can hardly be overestimated. People have a careless way of talking about a 'born liar,' just as they talk about a 'born poet.' But in both cases they are wrong. Lying and poetry are arts—arts, as Plato saw, not unconnected with each other[2]—and they require the most careful study, the most disinterested devotion. Indeed, they have their technique, just as the more material arts of painting and sculpture have, their subtle secrets of form and color, their craft mysteries, their deliberate artistic methods. As one knows the poet by his fine music, so one can recognize the liar by his rich rhythmic utterance, and in neither case will the casual inspiration of the moment suffice. Here, as elsewhere, practice must precede perfection. But in modern days while the fashion of writing poetry has become far too common, and should, if possible, be discouraged, the fashion of lying has almost fallen in disrepute. Many a young man starts in life with a natural gift for exaggeration which, if nurtured in congenial and sympathetic surroundings, or by the imitation of the best models, might grow into something really great and wonderful. But, as a rule, he comes to nothing. He either falls into careless habits of accuracy—"

Cyril   My dear fellow!

Vivian   Please don't interrupt in the middle of a sentence. "He either falls into careless habits of accuracy, or takes to frequenting the society of the aged and the well-informed. Both things are equally fatal to his imagination, as indeed they would be fatal to the imagination of anybody, and in a short time he develops a morbid and unhealthy faculty of truth-telling, begins to verify all statements made in his presence, has no hesitation in contradicting people who are much younger than himself, and often ends by writing novels which are so like life that no one can possibly believe in their probability. This is no isolated instance that we are giving. It is simply one example out of many; and if something cannot be done to check, or at least to modify, our monstrous worship of facts, art will become sterile, and beauty will pass away from the land.

"Even Mr. Robert Louis Stevenson, that delightful master of delicate and fanciful prose, is tainted with this

---

[1] "Corner of creation."

[2] A rather extreme view of Plato's position. Compare Sidney, *An Apology for Poetry,* p. 155.

modern vice, for we know positively no other name for it. There is such a thing as robbing a story of its reality by trying to make it too true, and *The Black Arrow* is so inartistic as not to contain a single anachronism to boast of, while the transformation of Dr. Jekyll reads dangerously like an experiment out of the *Lancet.* As for Mr. Rider Haggard, who really has, or had once, the makings of a perfectly magnificent liar, he is now so afraid of being suspected of genius that when he does tell us anything marvelous, he feels bound to invent a personal reminiscence, and to put it into a footnote as a kind of cowardly corroboration. Nor are our other novelists much better. Mr. Henry James writes fiction as if it were a painful duty, and wastes upon mean motives and imperceptible 'points of view' his neat literary style, his felicitous phrases, his swift and caustic satire. Mr. Hall Caine, it is true, aims at the grandiose, but then he writes at the top of his voice. He is so loud that one cannot hear what he says. Mr. James Payn is an adept in the art of concealing what is not worth finding. He hunts down the obvious with the enthusiasm of a shortsighted detective. As one turns over the pages, the suspense of the author becomes unbearable. The horses of Mr. William Black's phaeton do not soar towards the sun. They merely frighten the sky at evening into violent chromolithographic effects. On seeing them approach, the peasants take refuge in dialect. Mrs. Oliphant prattles pleasantly about curates, lawn-tennis parties, domesticity, and other wearisome things. Mr. Marion Crawford has immolated himself upon the altar of local color. He is like the lady in the French comedy who talks about *le beau ciel d'Italie.*[3] Besides, he has fallen into a bad habit of uttering moral platitudes. He is always telling us that to be good is to be good, and that to be bad is to be wicked. At times he is almost edifying. *Robert Elsemere* is, of course, a masterpiece—a masterpiece of the *genre ennuyeux,*[4] the one form of literature that the English people seem to thoroughly enjoy. A thoughtful young friend of ours once told us that it reminded him of the sort of conversation that goes on at a meat tea in the house of a serious Nonconformist family, and we can quite believe it. Indeed it is only in England that such a book could be produced. England is the home of lost ideas. As for that great and daily increasing school of novelists for whom the sun always rises in the East End, the only thing that can be said about them is that they find life crude, and leave it raw.

"In France, though nothing so deliberately tedious as *Robert Elsemere* has been produced, things are not much better. M. Guy de Maupassant, with his keen mordant irony and his hard vivid style, strips life of the few poor rags that still cover her, and shows us foul sore and festering wounds. He writes lurid little tragedies in which everybody is ridiculous; bitter comedies at which one cannot laugh for very tears. M. Zola, true to the lofty principle that he lays down in one of his *pronunciamientos* on literature, *'L'homme de génie n'a jamais d'esprit,'*[5] is determined to show that, if he has not got genius, he can at least be dull. And how well he succeeds! He is not without power. Indeed at times, as in *Germinal,* there is something almost epic in his work. But his work is entirely wrong from beginning to end, and wrong not on the ground of morals, but on the ground of art. From any ethical standpoint it is just what it should be. The author is perfectly truthful and describes things exactly as they happen. What more can any moralist desire? We have no sympathy at all with the moral indignation of our time against M. Zola. It is simply the indignation of Tartuffe on being exposed. But from the standpoint of art, what can be said in favor of the author of *L'Assommoir, Nana,* and *Pot-Bouille?* Nothing. Mr. Ruskin once described the characters in George Eliot's novels as being like the sweepings of a Pentonville omnibus, but M. Zola's characters are much worse. They have their dreary vices, and their drearier virtues. The record of their lives is absolutely without interest. Who cares what happens to them? In literature we require distinction, charm, beauty, and imaginative power. We don't want to be harrowed and disgusted with an account of the doings of the lower orders. M. Daudet is better. He has wit, a light touch, and an amusing style. But he has lately committed literary suicide. Nobody can possibly care for Delobelle with his *'Il faut lutter pour l'art,'*[6] or for Valmajour with his eternal refrain about the nightingale, or for the poet in *Jack* with his *'mots cruels,'*[7] now that we have learned from *Vingt ans de ma vie littéraire* that these characters were taken directly from life. To us they seem to have suddenly lost all their vitality, all the few qualities they ever possessed. The only real people are the people who never existed, and if a novelist is base enough to go to life for his personages he should at least pretend that they are creations, and not boast of them as copies. The justification of a character in a novel is not that other persons are what they are, but that the author is what he is. Otherwise the novel is not a work of art. As for M. Paul Bourget, the master of the *roman psychologique,*[8] he commits the error of imagining that the men and women

---

[3] "The beautiful sky of Italy."
[4] "Tiresome sort."

[5] "The man of genius never has spirit."
[6] "One must struggle for art."
[7] "Cruel words."
[8] "Psychological novel."

of modern life are capable of being infinitely analyzed for an innumerable series of chapters. In point of fact, what is interesting about people in good society—and M. Bourget rarely moves out of the Faubourg St. Germain, except to come to London—is the mask that each one of them wears, not the reality that lies behind the mask. It is a humiliating confession, but we are all of us made out of the same stuff. In Falstaff there is something of Hamlet, in Hamlet there is not a little of Falstaff. The fat knight has his moods of melancholy, and the young prince his moments of coarse humor. Where we differ from each other is purely in accidentals: in personal appearance, tricks of habit, and the like. The more one analyzes people, the more all reasons for analysis disappear. Sooner or later one comes to that dreadful universal thing called human nature. Indeed, as anyone who has ever worked among the poor knows only too well, the brotherhood of man is no mere poet's dream, it is a most depressing and humiliating reality; and if a writer insists upon analyzing the upper classes, he might just as well write of match-girls and coster-mongers at once." However, my dear Cyril, I will not detain you any further just here. I quite admit that modern novels have many good points. All I insist on is that, as a class, they are quite unreadable.

Cyril   That is certainly a very grave qualification, but I must say that I think you are rather unfair in some of your strictures. I like *The Deemster,* and *The Daughter of Heth,* and *Le Disciple,* and *Mr. Isaacs,* and as for *Robert Elsemere,* I am quite devoted to it. Not that I can look upon it as a serious work. As a statement of the problems that confront the earnest Christian it is ridiculous and antiquated. It is simply Arnold's *Literature and Dogma* with the literature left out. It is as much behind the age as Paley's *Evidences,* or Colenso's method of Biblical exegesis. Nor could anything be less impressive than the unfortunate hero gravely heralding a dawn that rose long ago, and so completely missing its true significance that he proposes to carry on the business of the old firm under the new name. On the other hand, it contains several clever caricatures, and a heap of delightful quotations, and Green's philosophy very plentifully sugars the somewhat bitter pill of the author's fiction. I also cannot help expressing my surprise that you have said nothing about the two novelists whom you are always reading, Balzac and George Meredith. Surely they are realists, both of them?

Vivian   Ah! Meredith! Who can define him? His style is chaos illumined by flashes of lightning. As a writer he has mastered everything except language: as a novelist he can do everything, except tell a story: as an artist he is everything, except articulate. Somebody in Shakespeare—Touchstone, I think—talks about a man who is always breaking his shins over his own wit, and it seems to me that this might serve as a basis for a criticism of Meredith's method. But whatever he is, he is not a realist. Or, rather, I would say that he is a child of realism who is not on speaking terms with his father. By deliberate choice he has made himself a romanticist. He has refused to bow the knee to Baal, and after all, even if the man's fine spirit did not revolt against the noisy assertions of realism, his style would be quite sufficient of itself to keep life at a respectful distance. By its means he has planted round his garden a hedge full of thorns, and red with wonderful roses. As for Balzac, he was a most remarkable combination of the artistic temperament with the scientific spirit. The latter he bequeathed to his disciples: the former was entirely his own. The difference between such a book as M. Zola's *L'Assommoir* and Balzac's *Illusions Perdues* is the difference between unimaginative realism and imaginative reality. "All Balzac's characters," said Baudelaire, "are gifted with the same ardor of life that animated himself. All his fictions are as deeply colored as dreams. Each mind is a weapon loaded to the muzzle with will. The very scullions have genius."[9] A steady course of Balzac reduces our living friends to shadows, and our acquaintances to the shadows of shades. His characters have a kind of fervent fiery-colored existence. They dominate us, and defy skepticism. One of the greatest tragedies of my life is the death of Lucien de Rubempré. It is a grief from which I have never been able to completely rid myself. It haunts me in my moments of pleasure. I remember it when I laugh. But Balzac is no more a realist than Holbein was. He created life, he did not copy it. I admit, however, that he set far too high a value on modernity of form, and that, consequently, there is no book of his that, as an artistic masterpiece, can rank with *Salammbô* or *Esmond,* or *The Cloister and the Hearth,* or the *Vicomte de Bragelonne.*

Cyril   Do you object to modernity of form, then?

Vivian   Yes. It is a huge price to pay for a very poor result. Pure modernity of form is always somewhat vulgarizing. It cannot help being so. The public imagine that, because they are interested in their immediate surroundings, art should be interested in them also, and should take them as her subject matter. But the mere fact that they are interested in these things makes them unsuitable subjects for art. The only beautiful things, as somebody once said, are the things that do not concern us. As long as a thing is useful or necessary to us, or affects us in any way, either for pain or for pleasure, or appeals strongly to our sympathies, or is a vital part of the environment in which we live, it is outside the proper sphere of art. To art's subject matter we should be

---

[9]*Théophile Gautier.*

more or less indifferent. We should, at any rate, have no preferences, no prejudices, no partisan feelings of any kind. It is exactly because Hecuba is nothing to us that her sorrows are such an admirable motive for tragedy. I do not know anything in the whole history of literature sadder than the artistic career of Charles Reade. He wrote one beautiful book, *The Cloister and the Hearth,* a book as much above *Romola* as *Romola* is above *Daniel Deronda,* and wasted the rest of his life in a foolish attempt to be modern, to draw public attention to the state of our convict prisons, and the management of our private lunatic asylums. Charles Dickens was depressing enough in all conscience when he tried to arouse our sympathy for the victims of the poor-law administration; but Charles Reade, an artist, a scholar, a man with a true sense of beauty, raging and roaring over the abuses of contemporary life like a common pamphleteer or a sensational journalist, is really a sight for the angels to weep over. Believe me, my dear Cyril, modernity of form and modernity of subject matter are entirely and absolutely wrong. We have mistaken the common livery of the age for the vesture of the Muses, and spend our days in the sordid streets and hideous suburbs of our vile cities when we should be out on the hillside with Apollo. Certainly we are a degraded race, and have sold our birthright for a mess of facts.

Cyril   There is something in what you say, and there is no doubt that whatever amusement we may find in reading a purely modern novel, we have rarely any artistic pleasure in rereading it. And this is perhaps the best rough test of what is literature and what is not. If one cannot enjoy reading a book over and over again, there is no use reading it at all. But what do you say about the return to life and nature? This is the panacea that is always being recommended to us.

Vivian   I will read you what I say on that subject. The passage comes later on in the article, but I may as well give it to you now: "The popular cry of our time is 'Let us return to life and nature; they will recreate art for us, and send the red blood coursing through her veins; they will show her feet with swiftness and make her hand strong.' But, alas! we are mistaken in our amiable and well-meaning efforts. Nature is always behind the age. And as for life, she is the solvent that breaks up art, the enemy that lays waste her house."

Cyril   What do you mean by saying that nature is always behind the age?

Vivian   Well, perhaps that is rather cryptic. What I mean is this. If we take nature to mean natural simple instinct as opposed to self-conscious culture, the work produced under this influence is always old-fashioned, antiquated, and out of date. One touch of nature may make the whole world kin, but two touches of nature will destroy any work of art. If, on the other hand, we regard nature as the collection of phenomena external to man, people only discover in her what they bring to her. She has no suggestions of her own. Wordsworth went to the lakes, but he was never a lake poet. He found in stones the sermons he had already hidden there. He went moralizing about the district, but his good work was produced when he returned, not to nature but to poetry. Poetry gave him *Laodamia,* and the fine sonnets, and the great ode, such as it is. Nature gave him *Martha Ray* and *Peter Bell,* and the address to Mr. Wilkinson's spade.

Cyril   I think that view might be questioned. I am rather inclined to believe in the "impulse from a vernal wood,"[10] though, of course, the artistic value of such an impulse depends entirely on the kind of temperament that receives it, so that the return to nature would come to mean simply the advance to a great personality. You would agree with that, I fancy. However, proceed with your article.

Vivian   (*Reading.*) "Art begins with abstract decoration, with purely imaginative and pleasurable work dealing with what is unreal and nonexistent. This is the first stage. Then life becomes fascinated with this new wonder, and asks to be admitted into the charmed circle. Art takes life as part of her rough material, recreates it, and refashions it in fresh forms, is absolutely indifferent to fact, invents, imagines, dreams, and keeps between herself and reality the impenetrable barrier of beautiful style, of decorative or ideal treatment. The third stage is when life gets the upper hand, and drives art out into the wilderness. This is the true decadence, and it is from this that we are now suffering.

"Take the case of the English drama. At first in the hands of the monks dramatic art was abstract, decorative, and mythological. Then she enlisted life in her service, and using some of life's external forms, she created an entirely new race of beings, whose sorrows were more terrible than any sorrow man has ever felt, whose joys were keener than lover's joys, who had the rage of the Titans and the calm of the gods, who had monstrous and marvelous sins, monstrous and marvelous virtues. To them she gave a language different from that of actual use, a language full of resonant music and sweet rhythm, made stately by solemn cadence, or made delicate by fanciful rhyme, jeweled with wonderful words, and enriched with lofty diction. She clothed her children in strange raiment and gave them masks, and at her bidding the antique world rose from its marble tomb. A new Caesar stalked through the streets of risen Rome, and with purple sail and flute-led oars another Cleopatra passed up the river

---

[10]Wordsworth, *The Tables Turned,* 21.

to Antioch. Old myth and legend and dream took shape and substance. History was entirely rewritten, and there was hardly one of the dramatists who did not recognize that the object of art is not simple truth but complex beauty. In this they were perfectly right. Art itself is really a form of exaggeration; and selection, which is the very spirit of art, is nothing more than an intensified mode of overemphasis.

"But life soon shattered the perfection of the form. Even in Shakespeare we can see the beginning of the end. It shows itself by the gradual breaking up of the blank verse in the later plays, by the predominance given to prose, and by the overimportance assigned to characterization. The passages in Shakespeare—and they are many—where the language is uncouth, vulgar, exaggerated, fantastic, obscene even, are entirely due to life calling for an echo of her own voice, and rejecting the intervention of beautiful style, through which alone should life be suffered to find expression. Shakespeare is not by any means a flawless artist. He is too fond of going directly to life, and borrowing life's natural utterance. He forgets that when art surrenders her imaginative medium she surrenders everything. Goethe says, somewhere—'*In der Beschränkung zeigt sich erst der Meister.*' 'It is in working within limits that the master reveals himself'—and the limitation, the very condition of any art is style. However, we need not linger any longer over Shakespeare's realism. *The Tempest* is the most perfect of palinodes. All that we desired to point out was, that the magnificent work of the Elizabethan and Jacobean artists contained within itself the seeds of its own dissolution, and that, if it drew some of its strength from using life as a rough material, it drew all its weakness from using life as an artistic method. As the inevitable result of this substitution of an imitative for a creative medium, this surrender of an imaginative form, we have the modern English melodrama. The characters in these plays talk on the stage exactly as they would talk off it; they have neither aspirations nor aspirates; they are taken directly from life and reproduce its vulgarity down to the smallest detail; they present the gait, manner, costume, and accent of real people; they would pass unnoticed in a third-class railway carriage. And yet how wearisome the plays are! They do not succeed in producing even that impression of reality at which they aim, and which is their only reason for existing. As a method, realism is a complete failure.

"What is true about the drama and the novel is no less true about those arts that we call the decorative arts. The whole history of these arts in Europe is the record of the struggle between Orientalism, with its frank rejection of imitation, its love of artistic convention, its dislike to the actual representation of any object in nature, and our own imitative spirit. Wherever the former has been paramount, as in By-

zantium, Sicily, and Spain, by actual contact, or in the rest of Europe by the influence of the Crusades, we have had beautiful and imaginative work in which the visible things of life are transmuted into artistic conventions, and the things that life has not are invented and fashioned for her delight. But wherever we have returned to life and nature, our work has always become vulgar, common, and uninteresting. Modern tapestry, with its aerial effects, its elaborate perspective, its broad expanses of waste sky, its faithful and laborious realism, has no beauty whatsoever. The pictorial glass of Germany is absolutely detestable. We are beginning to weave possible carpets in England, but only because we have returned to the method and spirit of the East. Our rugs and carpets of twenty years ago, with their solemn depressing truths, their inane worship of nature, their sordid reproductions of visible objects, have become, even to the Philistine, a source of laughter. A cultured Mahomedan once remarked to us, 'You Christians are so occupied in misinterpreting the fourth commandment that you have never thought of making an artistic application of the second.' He was perfectly right, and the whole truth of the matter is this: the proper school to learn art in is not life but art."

And now let me read you a passage which seems to me to settle the question very completely: "It was not always thus. We need not say anything about the poets, for they, with the unfortunate exception of Mr. Wordsworth, have been really faithful to their high mission, and are universally recognized as being absolutely unreliable. But in the works of Herodotus, who, in spite of the shallow and ungenerous attempts of modern sciolists to verify his history, may justly be called the Father of Lies; in the published speeches of Cicero and the biographies of Suetonius; in Tacitus at his best; in Pliny's *Natural History;* in Hanno's *Periplus;* in all the early chronicles; in the lives of the saints; in Froissart and Sir Thomas Malory; in the travels of Marco Polo; in Olaus Magnus, and Aldrovandus, and Conrad Lycosthenes, with his magnificent *Prodigiorum et Ostentorum Chronicon;* in the autobiography of Benvenuto Cellini; in the memoirs of Casanova; in Defoe's *History of the Plague;* in Boswell's *Life of Johnson;* In Napoleon's dispatches, and in the works of our own Carlyle, whose *French Revolution* is one of the most fascinating historical novels ever written, facts are either kept in their proper subordinate position, or else entirely excluded on the general ground of dullness. Now, everything is changed. Facts are not merely finding a footing place in history, but they are usurping the domain of fancy, and have invaded the kingdom of romance. Their chilling touch is over everything. They are vulgarizing mankind. The crude commercialism of America, its materializing spirit, its indifference to the poetical side of things, and its lack of imagination and of high unattainable ideals, are entirely due to that country having adopted for its national hero a man, who, according to his own confession, was incapable of telling a lie, and it is not too much to say that the story of George Washington and the cherry tree has done more harm, and in a shorter space of time, than any other moral tale in the whole of literature.''

Cyril   My dear boy!

Vivian   I assure you it is the case, and the amusing part of the whole thing is that the story of the cherry tree is an absolute myth. However, you must not think that I am too despondent about the artistic future either of America or of our own country. Listen to this: ''That some change will take place before this century has drawn to its close we have no doubt whatsoever. Bored by the tedious and improving conversation of those who have neither the wit to exaggerate nor the genius to romance, tired of the intelligent person whose reminiscences are always based upon memory, whose statements are invariably limited by probability, and who is at any time liable to be corroborated by the merest Philistine who happens to be present, society sooner or later must return to its lost leader, the cultured and fascinating liar. Who he was who first, without ever having gone out to the rude chase, told the wondering cavemen at sunset how he had dragged the megatherium from the purple darkness of its jasper cave, or slain the mammoth in single combat and brought back its gilded tusks, we cannot tell, and not one of our modern anthropologists, for all their much-boasted science, has had the ordinary courage to tell us. Whatever was his name or race, he certainly was the true founder of social intercourse. For the aim of the liar is simply to charm, to delight, to give pleasure. He is the very basis of civilized society, and without him a dinner party, even at the mansions of the great, is as dull as a lecture at the Royal Society, or a debate at the Incorporated Authors, or one of Mr. Burnard's farcical comedies.

''Nor will he be welcomed by society alone. Art, breaking from the prison-house of realism, will run to greet him, and will kiss his false, beautiful lips, knowing that he alone is in possession of the great secret of all her manifestations, the secret that truth is entirely and absolutely a matter of style; while life—poor, probable, uninteresting human life—tired of repeating herself for the benefit of Mr. Herbert Spencer, scientific historians, and the compilers of statistics in general, will follow meekly after him, and try to reproduce, in her own simple and untutored way, some of the marvels of which he talks.

''No doubt there will always be critics who, like a certain writer in the *Saturday Review,* will gravely censure the teller of fairy tales for his defective knowledge of natural history, who will measure imaginative work by their own lack of any imaginative faculty, and will hold up their ink-stained hands in horror if some honest gentleman, who has never been farther than the yew trees of his own garden, pens a fascinating book of travels like Sir John Mandeville, or, like great Raleigh, writes a whole history of the world, without knowing anything whatsoever about the past. To excuse themselves they will try and shelter under the shield of him who made Prospero the magician, and gave him Caliban and Ariel as his servants, who heard the Tritons blowing their horns round the coral reefs of the Enchanted Isle, and the fairies singing to each other in a wood near Athens, who led the phantom kings in dim procession across the misty Scottish heath, and hid Hecate in a cave with the weird sisters. They will call upon Shakespeare—they always do—and will quote that hackneyed passage about art holding the mirror up to nature, forgetting that this unfortunate aphorism is deliberately said by Hamlet in order to convince the bystanders of his absolute insanity in all art matters.''

Cyril   Ahem! Another cigarette, please.

Vivian   My dear fellow, whatever you may say, it is merely a dramatic utterance, and no more represents Shakespeare's real views upon art than the speeches of Iago represent his real views upon morals. But let me get to the end of the passage: ''Art finds her own perfection within, and not outside of, herself. She is not to be judged by any external standard of resemblance. She is a veil, rather than a mirror. She has flowers that no forests know of, birds that no woodland possesses. She makes and unmakes many worlds, and can draw the moon from heaven with a scarlet thread. Hers are the 'forms more real than living man,' and hers the great archetypes of which things that have existence are but unfinished copies. Nature has, in her eyes, no laws, no uniformity. She can work miracles at her will, and when she calls monsters from the deep they come. She can bid the almond tree blossom in winter, and send the snow upon the ripe cornfield. At her word the frost lays its silver finger on the burning mouth of June, and the winged lions creep out from the hollows of the Lydian hills. The dryads peer from the thicket as she passes by, and the brown fauns smile strangely at her when she comes near them. She has hawk-faced gods that worship her, and the centaurs gallop at her side.''

Cyril   I like that. I can see it. Is that the end?

Vivian   No. There is one more passage, but it is purely practical. It simply suggests some methods by which we could revive this lost art of lying.

Cyril   Well, before you read it to me, I should like to ask you a question. What do you mean by saying that life, ''poor, probable, uninteresting human life,'' will try to reproduce the marvels of art? I can quite understand your objection to art being treated as a mirror. You think it would reduce genius to the position of a cracked looking glass. But you don't mean to say that you seriously believe that life imitates art, that life in fact is the mirror, and art the reality?

Vivian   Certainly I do. Paradox though it may seem—and paradoxes are always dangerous things—it is nonetheless true that life imitates art far more than art imitates life. We have all seen in our own day in England how a certain curious and fascinating type of beauty, invented and emphasized by two imaginative painters, has so influenced life that whenever one goes to a private view or to an artistic salon one sees, here the mystic eyes of Rossetti's dream, the long ivory throat, the strange square-cut jaw, the loosened shadowy hair that he so ardently loved, there the sweet maidenhood of *The Golden Stair,* the blossom-like mouth and weary loveliness of the *Laus Amoris,* the passion-pale face of Andromeda, the thin hands and lithe beauty of the Vivien in *Merlin's Dream.* And it has always been so. A great artist invents a type, and life tries to copy it, to reproduce it in a popular form, like an enterprising publisher. Neither Holbein nor Van Dyck found in England what they have given us. They brought their types with them, and life with her keen imitative faculty set herself to supply the master with models. The Greeks, with their quick artistic instinct, understood this, and set in the bride's chamber the statue of Hermes or of Apollo, that she might bear children as lovely as the works of art that she looked at in her rapture or her pain. They knew that life gains from art not merely spirituality, depth of thought and feeling, soul-turmoil or soul-peace, but that she can form herself on the very lines and colors of art, and can reproduce the dignity of Phidias as well as the grace of Praxiteles. Hence came their objection to realism. They disliked it on purely social grounds. They felt that it inevitably makes people ugly, and they were perfectly right. We try to improve the conditions of the race by means of good air, free sunlight, wholesome water, and hideous bare buildings for the better housing of the lower orders. But these things merely produce health, they do not produce beauty. For this, art is required, and the true disciples of the great artist are not his studio imitators, but those who become like his works of art, be they plastic as in Greek days, or pictorial as in modern times; in a word, life is art's best, art's only pupil.

As it is with the visible arts, so it is with literature. The most obvious and the vulgarest form in which this is shown is in the case of the silly boys who, after reading the adventures of Jack Sheppard or Dick Turpin, pillage the stalls of unfortunate apple-women, break into sweetshops at night, and alarm old gentlemen who are returning home from the city by leaping out on them in suburban lanes, with black masks and unloaded revolvers. This interesting phenomenon, which always occurs after the appearance of a new edition of either of the books I have alluded to, is usually attributed to the influence of literature on the imagination. But this is a mistake. The imagination is essentially creative and always seeks for a new form. The boy burglar is simply the inevitable result of life's imitative instinct. He is fact, occupied as fact usually is, with trying to reproduce fiction, and what we see in him is repeated on an extended scale throughout the whole of life. Schopenhauer has analyzed the pessimism that characterizes modern thought, but Hamlet invented it. The world has become sad because a puppet was once melancholy. The nihilist, that strange martyr who has no faith, who goes to the stake without enthusiasm, and dies for what he does not believe in, is a purely literary product. He was invented by Turgenev, and completed by Dostoevski. Robespierre came out of the pages of Rousseau as surely as the People's Palace rose out of the debris of a novel. Literature always anticipates life. It does not copy it, but molds it to its purpose. The nineteenth century, as we know it, is largely an invention of Balzac. Our Luciens de Rubempré, our Rastignacs, and de Marsays made their first appearance on the stage of the *Comédie Humaine.* We are merely carrying out, with footnotes and unnecessary additions, the whim or fancy or creative vision of a great novelist. I once asked a lady, who knew Thackeray intimately, whether he had had any model for Becky Sharp. She told me that Becky was an invention, but that the idea of the character had been partly suggested by a governess who lived in the neighborhood of Kensington Square, and was the companion of a very selfish and rich old woman. I inquired what became of the governess, and she replied, that, oddly enough, some years after the appearance of *Vanity Fair,* she ran away with the nephew of the lady with whom she was living, and for a short time made a great splash in society, quite in Mrs. Rawdon Crawley's style, and entirely by Mrs. Rawdon Crawley's methods. Ultimately she came to grief, disappeared to the Continent, and used to be occasionally seen at Monte Carlo and other gambling places. The noble gentleman from whom the same great sentimentalist drew Colonel Newcome died, a few months after *The Newcomes* had reached a fourth edition, with the word *Adsum* on his lips. Shortly after Mr. Stevenson published his curious psychological story of transformation, a friend of mine, called Mr. Hyde, was in the north of London, and being anxious to get to a railway station, took what he thought would be a short cut, lost his way, and found himself in a network of mean, evil-looking streets. Feeling rather nervous, he began to walk extremely fast, when suddenly out of an archway ran a child right between his legs. It fell on the pavement, he tripped over it, and trampled upon it. Being of course very much frightened and a little hurt, it began to scream, and in a few seconds the whole street was full of rough people who came pouring out of the houses like ants. They surrounded him and asked him his name. He was just about to give it when he suddenly remembered the opening incident in Mr. Stevenson's story. He was so filled with horror at having realized in his own person that terrible and well-written scene, and at having done accidentally, though in fact, what the Mr. Hyde of fiction had done with deliberate intent, that he ran away as hard as he could go. He was, however, very closely followed, and finally he took refuge in a surgery, the door of which happened to be open, where he explained to a young assistant, who happened to be there, exactly what had occurred. The humanitarian crowd were induced to go away on his giving them a small sum of money, and as soon as the coast was clear he left. As he passed out, the name on the brass doorplate of the surgery caught his eye. It was Jekyll. At least it should have been.

Here the imitation, as far as it went, was of course accidental. In the following case the imitation was self-conscious: In the year 1879, just after I had left Oxford, I met at a reception at the house of one of the foreign ministers a woman of very curious exotic beauty. We became great friends, and were constantly together. And yet what interested me most in her was not her beauty, but her character, her entire vagueness of character. She seemed to have no personality at all, but simply the possibility of many types. Sometimes she would give herself up entirely to art, turn her drawing room into a studio, and spend two or three days a week at picture galleries or museums. Then she would take to attending race meetings, wear the most horsey clothes, and talk about nothing but betting. She abandoned religion for mesmerism, mesmerism for politics, and politics for the melodramatic excitements of philanthropy. In fact, she was a kind of Proteus, and as much a failure in all her transformations as was that wondrous sea god when Odysseus laid hold of him. One day a serial began in one of the French magazines. At that time I used to read serial stories, and I well remember the shock of surprise I felt when I came to the description of the heroine. She was so like my friend that I brought her the magazine, and she recognized herself in it immediately, and seemed fascinated by the resemblance. I should tell you, by the way, that the story was translated from some dead Russian writer, so that the author had not taken his type from my friend. Well, to put the matter briefly, some months afterwards I was in Venice, and finding the magazine in the reading room of the hotel, I took it up casually to see what had become of the heroine. It was a most piteous tale, as the girl had ended by running away with a man absolutely inferior to her, not merely in social station, but in character and intellect also. I wrote to my friend that evening about my

views on John Bellini, and the admirable ices at Florio's, and the artistic value of gondolas, but added a postscript to the effect that her double in the story had behaved in a very silly manner. I don't know why I added that, but I remember I had a sort of dread over me that she might do the same thing. Before my letter had reached her, she had run away with a man who deserted her in six months. I saw her in 1884 in Paris, where she was living with her mother, and I asked her whether the story had had anything to do with her action. She told me that she had felt an absolutely irresistible impulse to follow the heroine step by step in her strange and fatal progress, and that it was with a feeling of real terror that she had looked forward to the last few chapters of the story. When they appeared, it seemed to her that she was compelled to reproduce them in life, and she did so. It was a most clear example of this imitative instinct of which I was speaking, and an extremely tragic one.

However, I do not wish to dwell any further upon individual instances. Personal experience is a most vicious and limited circle. All that I desire to point out is the general principle that life imitates art far more than art imitates life, and I feel sure that if you think seriously about it you will find that it is true. Life holds the mirror up to art, and either reproduces some strange type imagined by painter or sculptor, or realizes in fact what has been dreamed in fiction. Scientifically speaking, the basis of life—the energy of life, as Aristotle would call it—is simply the desire for expression, and art is always presenting various forms through which this expression can be attained. Life seizes on them and uses them, even if they be to her own hurt. Young men have committed suicide because Rolla did so, have died by their own hand because by his own hand Werther died. Think of what we owe to the imitation of Christ, of what we owe to the imitation of Caesar.

Cyril   The theory is certainly a very curious one, but to make it complete you must show that nature, no less than life, is an imitation of art. Are you prepared to prove that?

Vivian   My dear fellow, I am prepared to prove anything.

Cyril   Nature follows the landscape painter then, and takes her effects from him?

Vivian   Certainly. Where, if not from the Impressionists, do we get those wonderful brown fogs that come creeping down our streets, blurring the gas lamps and changing the houses into monstrous shadows? To whom, if not to them and their master, do we owe the lovely silver mists that brood over our river, and turn to faint forms of fading grace, curved bridge and swaying barge? The extraordinary change that has taken place in the climate of London during the last ten years is entirely due to this particular school of art. You smile. Consider the matter from a scientific or a metaphysical point of view, and you will find that I am right. For what is nature? Nature is no great mother who has borne us. She is our creation. It is in our brain that she quickens to life. Things are because we see them, and what we see, and how we see it, depends on the arts that have influenced us. To look at a thing is very different from seeing a thing. One does not see anything until one sees its beauty. Then, and then only, does it come into existence. At present, people see fogs, not because there are fogs, but because poets and painters have taught them the mysterious loveliness of such effects. There may have been fogs for centuries in London. I dare say there were. But no one saw them, and so we do not know anything about them. They did not exist till art had invented them. Now, it must be admitted, fogs are carried to excess. They have become the mere mannerism of a clique, and the exaggerated realism of their method gives dull people bronchitis. Where the cultured catch an effect, the uncultured catch cold. And so, let us be humane, and invite art to turn her wonderful eyes elsewhere. She has done so already, indeed. That white quivering sunlight that one sees now in France, with its strange blotches of mauve, and its restless violet shadows, is her latest fancy, and, on the whole, nature reproduces it quite admirably. Where she used to give us Corots and Daubignys, she gives us now exquisite Monets and entrancing Pisarros. Indeed, there are moments, rare, it is true, but still to be observed from time to time, when nature becomes absolutely modern. Of course she is not always to be relied upon. The fact is that she is in this unfortunate position: art creates an incomparable and unique effect, and, having done so, passes on to other things. Nature, upon the other hand, forgetting that imitation can be made the sincerest form of insult, keeps on repeating this effect until we all become absolutely wearied of it. Nobody of any real culture, for instance, ever talks nowadays about the beauty of a sunset. Sunsets are quite old-fashioned. They belong to the time when Turner was the last note in art. To admire them is a distinct sign of provincialism of temperament. Upon the other hand they go on. Yesterday evening Mrs. Arundel insisted on my going to the window, and looking at the glorious sky, as she called it. Of course I had to look at it. She is one of those absurdly pretty Philistines, to whom one can deny nothing. And what was it? It was simply a very second-rate Turner, a Turner of a bad period, with all the painter's worst faults exaggerated and overemphasized. Of course, I am quite ready to admit that life very often commits the same error. She produces her false Renés and her sham Vautrins, just as nature gives us, on one day a doubtful Cuyp, and on another a more than questionable Rousseau. Still, nature irritates one more when she does things of that kind. It seems so stupid, so obvious, so unnecessary. A false Vautrin might be delightful. A doubtful Cuyp is unbearable. However, I don't want to be too hard on nature. I wish the Channel, especially at Hastings, did not look quite so often like a Henry Moore, gray pearl with yellow lights, but then, when art is more varied, nature will, no doubt, be more varied also. That she imitates art, I don't think even her worst enemy would deny now. It is the one thing that keeps her in touch with civilized man. But have I proved my theory to your satisfaction?

Cyril   You have proved it to my dissatisfaction, which is better. But even admitting this strange imitative instinct in life and nature, surely you would acknowledge that art expresses the temper of its age, the spirit of its time, the moral and social conditions that surround it, and under whose influence it is produced.

Vivian   Certainly not! Art never expresses anything but itself. This is the principle of my new aesthetics; and it is this, more than that vital connection between form and substance, on which Mr. Pater dwells,[11] that makes music the type of all the arts. Of course, nations and individuals, with that healthy natural vanity which is the secret of existence, are always under the impression that it is of them that the Muses are talking, always trying to find in the calm dignity of imaginative art some mirror of their own turbid passions, always forgetting that the singer of life is not Apollo, but Marsyas.[12] Remote from reality, and with her eyes turned away from the shadows of the cave, art reveals her own perfection, and the wondering crowd that watches the opening of the marvelous, many-petaled rose fancies that it is its own history that is being told to it, its own spirit that is finding expression in a new form. But it is not so. The highest art rejects the burden of the human spirit, and gains more from a new medium or a fresh material than she does from any enthusiasm for art, or from any great awakening of the human consciousness. She develops purely on her own lines. She is not symbolic of any age. It is the ages that are her symbols.

Even those who hold that art is representative of time and place and people, cannot help admitting that the more imitative an art is, the less it represents to us the spirit of its age. The evil faces of the Roman emperors look out at us

---

[11] "All art constantly aspires to the condition of music. For while in all other kinds of art it is possible to distinguish the matter from the form, and the understanding can always makes this distinction, yet it is the constant effort of art to obliterate it." *Studies in the History of the Renaissance.*

[12] A mythological figure connected with Greek music. He challenged Apollo to a musical contest, lost, and was punished for his presumption.

from the foul porphyry and spotted jasper in which the realistic artists of the day delighted to work, and we fancy that in those cruel lips and heavy sensual jaws we can find the secret of the ruin of the empire. But it was not so. The vices of Tiberius could not destroy that supreme civilization, any more than the virtues of the Antonines could save it. It fell for other, for less interesting reasons. The sibyls and prophets of the Sistine may indeed serve to interpret for some that new birth of the emancipated spirit that we call the Renaissance; but what do the drunken boors and crawling peasants of Dutch art tell us about the great soul of Holland? The more abstract, the more ideal an art is, the more it reveals to us the temper of its age. If we wish to understand a nation by means of its art, let us look at its architecture or its music.

Cyril   I quite agree with you there. The spirit of an age may be best expressed in the abstract ideal arts, for the spirit itself is abstract and ideal. Upon the other hand, for the visible aspect of an age, for its look, as the phrase goes, we must, of course, go to the arts of imitation.

Vivian   I don't think so. After all, what the imitative arts really give us are merely the various styles of particular artists, or of certain schools of artists. Surely you don't imagine that the people of the Middle Ages bore any resemblance at all to the figures on medieval stained glass, or in medieval stone and wood carving, or on medieval metalwork, or tapestries, or illuminated manuscripts. They were probably very ordinary-looking people, with nothing grotesque, or remarkable, or fantastic in their appearance. The Middle Ages, as we know them in art, are simply a definite form of style, and there is no reason at all why an artist with this style should not be produced in the nineteenth century. No great artist ever sees things as they really are. If he did, he would cease to be an artist. Take an example from our own day. I know that you are fond of Japanese things. Now, do you really imagine that the Japanese people, as they are presented to us in art, have any existence? If you do, you have never understood Japanese art at all. The Japanese people are the deliberate self-conscious creation of certain individual artists. If you set a picture by Hokusai, or Hokkei, or any of the great native painters, beside a real Japanese gentleman or lady, you will see that there is not the slightest resemblance between them. The actual people who live in Japan are not unlike the general run of English people; that is to say, they are extremely commonplace, and have nothing curious or extraordinary about them. In fact the whole of Japan is a pure invention. There is no such country, there are no such people. One of our most charming painters went recently to the Land of the Chrysanthemum in the foolish hope of seeing the Japanese. All he saw, all he had the chance of

painting, were a few lanterns and some fans. He was quite unable to discover the inhabitants, as his delightful exhibition at Messrs. Dowdeswell's Gallery showed only too well. He did not know that the Japanese people are, as I have said, simply a mode of style, an exquisite fancy of art. And so, if you desire to see a Japanese effect, you will not behave like a tourist and go to Tokyo. On the contrary, you will stay at home, and steep yourself in the work of certain Japanese artists, and then, when you have absorbed the spirit of their style, and caught their imaginative manner of vision, you will go some afternoon and sit in the park or stroll down Piccadilly, and if you cannot see an absolutely Japanese effect there, you will not see it anywhere. Or, to return again to the past, take as another instance the ancient Greeks. Do you think that Greek art ever tells us what the Greek people were like? Do you believe that the Athenian women were like the stately dignified figures of the Parthenon frieze, or like those marvelous goddesses who sat in the triangular pediments of the same building? If you judge from the art, they certainly were so. But read an authority, like Aristophanes, for instance. You will find that the Athenian ladies laced tightly, wore high-heeled shoes, dyed their hair yellow, painted and rouged their faces, and were exactly like any silly fashionable or fallen creature of our own day. The fact is that we look back on the ages entirely through the medium of art, and art, very fortunately, has never once told us the truth.

Cyril   But modern portraits by English painters, what of them? Surely they are like the people they pretend to represent?

Vivian   Quite so. They are so like them that a hundred years from now no one will believe in them. The only portraits in which one believes are portraits where there is very little of the sitter and a very great deal of the artist. Holbein's drawings of the men and women of his time impress us with a sense of their absolute reality. But this is simply because Holbein compelled life to accept his conditions, to restrain itself within his limitations, to reproduce his type, and to appear as he wished it to appear. It is style that makes us believe in a thing—nothing but style. Most of our modern portrait painters are doomed to absolute oblivion. They never paint what they see. They paint what the public sees, and the public never sees anything.

Cyril   Well, after that, I think I should like to hear the end of your article.

Vivian   With pleasure. Whether it will do any good, I really cannot say. Ours is certainly the dullest and most prosaic century possible. Why, even sleep has played us false, and has closed up the gates of ivory, and opened the gates of horn.[13] The dreams of the great middle classes of the country, as recorded in Mr. Myers's two bulky volumes on the subject, and in the *Transactions of the Psychical Society,* are the most depressing things that I have ever read. There is not even a fine nightmare among them. They are commonplace, sordid, and tedious. As for the church, I cannot conceive anything better for the culture of a country than the presence in it of a body of men whose duty it is to believe in the supernatural, to perform daily miracles, and to keep alive that mythopoeic faculty which is so essential for the imagination. But in the English church a man succeeds, not through his capacity for belief, but through his capacity for disbelief. Ours is the only church where the skeptic stands at the altar, and where St. Thomas is regarded as the ideal apostle. Many a worthy clergyman, who passes his life in admirable works of kindly charity, lives and dies unnoticed and unknown; but it is sufficient for some shallow, uneducated passman out of either university to get up in his pulpit and express his doubts about Noah's ark, or Balaam's ass, or Jonah and the whale, for half of London to flock to hear him, and to sit openmouthed in rapt admiration at his superb intellect. The growth of common sense in the English church is a thing very much to be regretted. It is really a degrading concession to a low form of realism. It is silly, too. It springs from an entire ignorance of psychology. Man can believe the impossible, but man can never believe the improbable. However, I must read the end of my article: ''What we have to do, what at any rate it is our duty to do, is to revive this old art of lying. Much, of course, may be done, in the way of educating the public, by amateurs in the domestic circle, at literary lunches, and at afternoon teas. But this is merely the light and graceful side of lying, such as was probably heard at Cretan dinner parties. There are many other forms. Lying for the sake of gaining some immediate personal advantage, for instance—lying with a moral purpose, as it is usually called—though of late it has been rather looked down upon, was extremely popular with the antique world. Athena laughs when Odysseus tells her 'his words of sly devising,' as Mr. William Morris phrases it, and the glory of mendacity illumines the pale brow of the stainless hero of Euripidean tragedy, and sets among the noble women of the past the young bride of one of Horace's most exquisite odes. Later on, what at first had been merely a natural instinct was elevated into a self-conscious science. Elaborate rules were laid down for the guidance of mankind, and an important school of literature grew up round the subject. Indeed, when one remembers the excellent philosophical treatise of Sanchez on the whole question, one cannot help regretting that no one has ever thought of publishing a cheap and condensed edition of the works of that great casuist. A short primer, *When to Lie and How,* if brought out in an attractive and not too expensive a form, would, no doubt, command a large sale, and would prove of real practical service to many earnest and deep-thinking people. Lying for the sake of the improvement of the young, which is the basis of home education, still lingers amongst us, and its advantages are so admirably set forth in the early books of Plato's *Republic* that it is unnecessary to dwell upon them here. It is a mode of lying for which all good mothers have peculiar capabilities, but it is capable of still further development, and has been sadly overlooked by the school board. Lying for the sake of a monthly salary is, of course, well known in Fleet Street, and the profession of a political leader-writer is not without its advantages. But it is said to be a somewhat dull occupation, and it certainly does not lead to much beyond a kind of ostentatious obscurity. The only form of lying that is absolutely beyond reproach is lying for its own sake, and the highest development of this is, as we have already pointed out, lying in art. Just as those who do not love Plato more than truth cannot pass beyond the threshold of the academe, so those who do not love beauty more than truth never know the inmost shrine of art. The solid, stolid British intellect lies in the desert sands like the sphinx in Flaubert's marvelous tale, and fantasy, *La Chimère,* dances round it, and calls to it with her false, flute-toned voice. It may not hear her now, but surely some day, when we are all bored to death with the commonplace character of modern fiction, it will hearken to her and try to borrow her wings.

"And when that day dawns, or sunset reddens, how joyous we shall all be! Facts will be regarded as discreditable, truth will be found mourning over her fetters, and romance, with her temper of wonder, will return to the land. The very aspect of the world will change to our startled eyes. Out of the sea will rise Behemoth and Leviathan, and sail round the high-pooped galleys, as they do on the delightful maps of those ages when books on geography were actually readable. Dragons will wander about the waste places, and the phoenix will soar from her nest of fire into the air. We shall lay our hands upon the basilisk, and see the jewel in the toad's head. Champing his gilded oats, the hippogriff will stand in our stalls, and over our heads will float the bluebird, singing of beautiful and impossible things, of things that are lovely and that never happen, of things that are not and that should be.

---

[13]In Greek mythology the gate of horn and the ivory gate are the two gates through which dreams come forth from the realm of sleep. Dreams passing through the gate of horn are true.

But before this comes to pass, we must cultivate the lost art of lying.''

Cyril   Then we must certainly cultivate it at once. But in order to avoid making any error, I want you to tell me briefly the doctrines of the new aesthetics.

Vivian   Briefly, then, they are these. Art never expresses anything but itself. It has an independent life, just as thought has, and develops purely on its own lines. It is not necessarily realistic in an age of realism, nor spiritual in an age of faith. So far from being the creation of its time, it is usually in direct opposition to it, and the only history that it preserves for us is the history of its own progress. Sometimes it returns upon its footsteps, and revives some antique form, as happened in the archaistic movement of late Greek art, and in the pre-Raphaelite movement of our own day. At other times it entirely anticipates its age, and produces in one century work that it takes another century to understand, to appreciate, and to enjoy. In no case does it reproduce its age. To pass from the art of a time to the time itself is the great mistake that all historians commit.

The second doctrine is this. All bad art comes from returning to life and nature, and elevating them into ideals. Life and nature may sometimes be used as a part of art's rough material, but before they are of any real service to art they must be translated into artistic conventions. The moment art surrenders its imaginative medium it surrenders everything. As a method, realism is a complete failure, and the two things that every artist should avoid are modernity of form and modernity of subject matter. To us, who live in the nineteenth century, any century is a suitable subject for art except our own. The only beautiful things are the things that do not concern us. It is, to have the pleasure of quoting myself, exactly because Hecuba is nothing to us that her sorrows are so suitable a motive for a tragedy. Besides, it is only the modern that ever becomes old-fashioned. M. Zola sits down to give us a picture of the Second Empire. Who cares for the Second Empire now? It is out of date. Life goes faster than realism, but romanticism is always in front of life.

The third doctrine is that life imitates art far more than art imitates life. This results not merely from life's imitative instinct, but from the fact that the self-conscious aim of life is to find expression, and that art offers it certain beautiful forms through which it may realize that energy. It is a theory that has never been put forward before, but it is extremely fruitful, and throws an entirely new light upon the history of art.

It follows, as a corollary from this, that external nature also imitates art. The only effects that she can show us are effects that we have already seen through poetry, or in paintings. This is the secret of nature's charm, as well as the explanation of nature's weakness.

The final revelation is that lying, the telling of beautiful untrue things, is the proper aim of art. But of this I think I have spoken at sufficient length. And now let us go out on the terrace, where "droops the milk-white peacock like a ghost," while the evening star "washes the dusk with silver." At twilight nature becomes a wonderfully suggestive effect, and is not without loveliness, though perhaps its chief use is to illustrate quotations from the poets. Come! We have talked long enough.

Stéphane Mallarmé

1842–1898

"It will be said, I suppose, that I am attempting to flabbergast the mob with a lofty statement. That is true." Mallarmé's remark, tinged with irony, is also replete with scorn. He has been accused of preciosity, aristocratic snobbism, and obscurantism. There is something as elusive about his critical prose as about his poetry. Perhaps it is because he sees the poet as constantly testing the possibilities, indeed the limits, of language. He hates the newspaper; he loves the book. For him, poetry lies in "the *contemplation* of things, in the image emanating from the reveries which things arouse in us." Poetry does not *name,* it *suggests*. From the common point of view, therefore, that of the "mob," poetry is obscure, enigmatic.

Mallarmé's hauteur dramatizes his break with both Romantic expressivism and traditional pragmatic didacticism. Nor is literature, for him, imitation. Reality is in the poem itself. It may "exist on a piece of paper": "All earthly existence must ultimately be contained in a book." The poet, then, is not expressing himself, teaching the reader, or copying nature, but rather searching out and capturing an elusive reality in words, perhaps even *making* reality in words. Though Mallarmé sometimes suggests that the poet is trying, though always failing, to capture Platonic essences, he also seems to say that the poem organizes reality for us by means of the "obscurity" of its own nondiscursive verbal structures. This view represents the aspect of French symbolist theory that led to the idea of the objective nature of the poem in much twentieth-century criticism.

Mallarmé's complete works are available in French in the edition by Henri Mondor and Jean-Aubry (1945). For an English translation of Mallarmé's critical writing see *Mallarmé: Selected Prose Poems, Essays, and Letters,* translated by Bradford Cook (1956). Studies of Mallarmé include Hayse Cooperman, *The Aesthetics of Mallarmé* (1933); Guy Delfal, *L'Esthétique de Stéphane Mallarmé* (1951), especially pages 161–84; Wallace Fowlie, *Mallarmé* (1953); Warren Ramsey, "A View of Mallarmé's Poetics," *Romantic Review,* XLVI (1955), 178–91; Guy Michaud, *Mallarmé* (tr. 1965); Thomas A. Williams, *Mallarmé and the Language of Symbolism* (1970); Paula Gilbert Lewis, *The Aesthetic of Mallarmé in Relation to His Public* (1976); Judy Karvis, *The Prose of Mallarmé* (1976); Malcolm Bowie, *Mallarmé and the Art of Being Difficult* (1978); and Louis Wirth Marvick, *Mallarmé and the Sublime* (1986).

The Evolution of Literature

(STÉPHANE MALLARMÉ   One of the most generally beloved men of letters, along with Catulle Mendès. Average height; pointed beard turning gray; large straight nose; long, pointed ears like those of a satyr; wide-open eyes of extraordinary brilliance; an unusual expression of finesse tempered by the appearance of great goodness. Whenever he speaks, his words are accompanied by rhythmical gestures full of grace, precision, and eloquence. His voice drags a little at the end of his words and becomes gradually gentler. There is great charm in this man. You feel that there is an incorruptible pride in him which lifts him above all things; the pride of a god or seer. And once this is felt, inwardly and instinctively you bow down before him.)

"We are now witnessing a spectacle," he told me, "which is truly extraordinary, unique in the history of poetry: every poet is going off by himself with his own flute, and playing the songs he pleases. For the first time since the beginning of poetry, poets have stopped singing bass. Hitherto, as you know, if they wished to be accompanied, they had to be content with the great organ of official meter. Well, it was simply overplayed and they got tired of it! I am sure that when the great Hugo died, he was convinced that he had buried all poetry for the next century; and yet Paul Verlaine had already written *Sagesse.* We can forgive Hugo his illusion, when we remember all the miracles he produced; he was simply forgetting the eternal instinct, the perpetual and unavoidable growth of the lyrical. But the essential and undeniable point is this: that in a society without stability, without unity, there can be no stable or definitive art. From that incompletely organized society—which also explains the restlessness of certain minds—the unexplained need for individuality was born. The literary manifestations of today are a direct reflection of that need.

"A more immediate explanation of recent innovations is this: it has finally been understood that the old verse form was *not* the absolute, unique, and changeless form, but just one way to be sure of writing good verse. We say to children: 'Don't steal, and you'll be honest.' That is true, but it is not everything. Is it possible to write poetry without reference to time-honored precepts? Poets have answered this question affirmatively, and I believe that they are right. Poetry is everywhere in language, so long as there is rhythm—everywhere except on posters and the back page of the newspaper. In the genre we call *prose,* there are verses—sometimes admirable verses—of all sorts of rhythms. Actually, there is no such thing as prose: there is the alphabet, and then there are verses which are more or less closely knit, more or less diffuse. So long as there is stylistic effort, there is versification.

"I said a minute ago that today's poetry is, in the main, the result of the poets' boredom with official verse. Even the partisans of official verse share this boredom. Isn't it rather abnormal that, when we open a book of poetry, we should be sure of finding uniform and conventional rhythms throughout? And yet, all the while, the writer hopes to arouse our interest in the essential variety of human feelings! Where is the inspiration in all this! Where is the unforeseen! How tiresome it all is! Official verse must be used only in crisis moments of the soul. Modern poets have understood this. With a fine sense of the delicate and the sparing, they hover around the official Alexandrine, approach it with unusual timidity, almost with fear; and rather than use it as their principle or as a point of departure, they suddenly conjure it up, and with it they crown their poem or period!

"Moreover, the same transformation has taken place in music. Instead of the very clearly delineated melodies of the past, we have an infinity of broken melodies which enrich the poetic texture, and we no longer have the impression of strong cadence."

"Is that how the scission was effected?" I asked.

"Why, yes. The Parnassians[1] were fond of a very formal prosody which has its own beauty, and they failed to realize that the modern poets were simply complementing their work; this also had the advantage of creating a sort of interregnum for the noble Alexandrine which had been at bay, crying for mercy. What we have to realize is that the most recent poetical writings do not tend to suppress the official verse; they tend rather to let a little more air into the poem, to create a kind of fluidity or mobility between long-winded verses, which has heretofore been lacking. In an orchestra, for example, you may suddenly hear very fine bursts of sound from the basses; but you know perfectly well that if there were nothing but that, you would soon have enough of it. Young poets space these bursts so that they will occur only when a total effect is to be produced. In this way, the Alexandrine (which was invented by nobody, but rather poured forth spontaneously from the instrument of language) will get out of its present finicky, sedentary state, and hence-

THE EVOLUTION OF LITERATURE. *The Evolution of Literature* is a report of an interview with Mallarmé by Jules Huret. It appeared in *Echo de Paris* in 1891. The text is from *Mallarmé: Selected Prose, Poems, Essays, and Letters,* translated by Bradford Cook. Copyright © 1956 by The Johns Hopkins Press. Reprinted by permission of the publisher.

[1]Post-Romantic, pre-symbolist poets.

forth it will be freer, more sudden, more refreshed. Its value will lie exclusively in its use during the soul's most serious times. And future volumes of poetry will be traversed by a majestic first verse which scatters in its wake an infinity of motifs originating in the individual's sensibility.

"So there has been scission because both sides have been unaware that their points of view are reconcilable rather than mutually destructive. On the one hand, the Parnassians have, in effect, been perfectly obedient servants of verse, and have sacrificed their personalities. The young poets, on the other hand, have anchored their instinct in a variety of modes, as if there were no precedent; actually, all they are doing is reducing here and there the stiffness of the Parnassian structures; and it seems to me that the two points of view are complementary.

"Despite all this, I still believe, personally, that, with the miraculous knowledge of verse and with the superb instinct for rhythmic pause which such masters as Banville possess, the Alexandrine can be infinitely varied and can reproduce all possible shades of human passion. Banville's *Forgeron,* for example, has a number of Alexandrines which seem interminable, yet others which are unbelievably concise.

"But, after all, it was a good thing to give our perfect and traditional poetic instrument a little rest. It had been overworked."

"So much for form," I said. "What about content?"

"As far as content is concerned," he answered, "I feel that the young poets are nearer than the Parnassians to the poetical ideal. The latter still treat their subjects as the old philosophers and orators did: that is, they present things directly, whereas I think that they should be presented allusively. Poetry lies in the *contemplation* of things, in the image emanating from the reveries which things arouse in us. The Parnassians take something in its entirety and simply exhibit it; in so doing, they fall short of mystery; they fail to give our minds that exquisite joy which consists of believing that we are creating something. To *name* an object is largely to destroy poetic enjoyment, which comes from gradual divination. The ideal is to *suggest* the object. It is the perfect use of this mystery which constitutes symbol. An object must be gradually evoked in order to show a state of soul; or else, choose an object and from it elicit a state of soul by means of a series of decodings."

"Now," I said, "we are coming to the big objection I was going to make: obscurity!"

"Yes, it is a dangerous thing," he replied, "regardless of whether it results from the reader's inadequacy or from the poet's. But if you avoid the work it involves, you are cheating. If a person of mediocre intelligence and insuffi-cient literary experience happens to open an obscure book and insists on enjoying it, something is wrong; there has simply been a misunderstanding. There must always be enigma in poetry. The purpose of literature—the *only* purpose—is to *evoke* things."

"Was it you, sir," I asked, "who created the new movement in poetry?"

"I detest 'schools,' " he replied, "and anything resembling schools. The professorial attitude toward literature is repugnant to me. Literature is entirely an individual matter. As far as I am concerned, a poet today, in the midst of this society which refuses to let him live, is a man who seeks out solitude in order to sculpture his own tomb. The reason I appear to be the leader of a school, is, first of all, that I have always taken an interest in the ideas of young poets; and second, because of my sincerity in recognizing the originality of what the latest writers have contributed. In reality, I am a hermit. I believe that poetry should be for the supreme pomp and circumstance of a constituted society in which glory should have its place. Most people seem to have forgotten glory. In our time the poet can only go on strike against society, and turn his back on all the contaminated ways and means that are offered him. For anything that is offered him is necessarily inferior to his ideal and to his secret labor."

I then asked Mallarmé what Verlaine's position would be in the history of this poetic movement.

"He was the first to react against the impeccable and impassible Parnassian attitudes. His fluid verse and certain of his intentional dissonances were already evident in *Sagesse.* Later on, around 1875, all the Parnassians (except for a few friends such as Mendès, Dierx, and Cladel) shrieked with horror at my *Afternoon of a Faun,* and, all together, they threw it out. For I *was* trying, actually, to make a sort of running pianistic commentary upon the fully preserved and dignified Alexandrine—a sort of musical accompaniment which the poet composes himself, so that the official verse will appear only on the really important occasions. But the father, the real father of all the young poets is Verlaine, the magnificent Verlaine. The attitude of the man is just as noble as the attitude of the writer. For it is the only possible attitude at a time when all poets are outlaws. Think of absorbing all the grief that he has—and with his pride and his tremendous pluck!"

"What do you think of the end of naturalism?"

"Up to now, writers have entertained the childish belief that if they could just choose a certain number of precious stones, for example, and put the names on paper, they would be *making* precious stones. Now, really! That is impossible, no matter how well it is done. Poetry consists of *creation:* we must delve into our souls for states and gleams of such perfect purity, so perfectly sung and illuminated, that they will truly be the jewels of man. When we do that, we have symbol, we have creation, and the word *poetry* has its full meaning. This, in short, is the only possible human creation. And if, in fact, the precious stones we wear do *not* show a state of soul, they are improperly worn. Take women, for example, external thieves that they are. . . .

"And just think," he added, chuckling; "the marvelous thing about jewelry stores is that, occasionally, we learn from the chief of police that what the woman wore improperly was something she didn't know the secret meaning of—something, therefore, which didn't belong to her.

"But to get back to naturalism. It seems to me that when we use that word, we mean the work of Émile Zola; and when he has finished his work, the name will disappear. I have great admiration for Zola. Actually, what he does is not so much literature as evocative art. He depends as little as possible on literary means. True, he uses words, but that is all. Everything else is based on his marvelous sense of organization and has immediate repercussions in the mind of the mob. His talent is truly powerful; consider his tremendous feeling for life, his mob movements, that texture in Nana's skin that every one of us has touched; and he paints it all with prodigious colors. It really is an admirably organized piece of work. But literature is more of an intellectual thing than that. Things already exist, we don't have to create them; we simply have to see their relationships. It is the threads of those relationships which go to make up poetry and music."

"Are you acquainted with the psychological novel?"

"Slightly. After the great works of Flaubert, the Goncourt brothers, and Zola—which are, in a sense, poems—novelists seem to be going back to the old eighteenth-century French taste which was much more humble and modest, consisting, as it did, not of a pictorial presentation of the outer form of things but rather of a dissection of the motives of the human soul. But there is the same difference between that and poetry as there is between a corset and a beautiful throat."

Before leaving, I asked Mallarmé for the names of those who seemed to him to represent the modern evolution in poetry.

"The young poets," he answered, "who seem to me to have done truly masterful work—that is, original work, completely divorced from the past—are: Morice, Moréas (a delightful poet), and, above all, the man who has given poetry the biggest boost, Henri de Régnier. Like de Vigny, he lives apart, at some distance from here, in retreat and silence. I greatly respect and admire him. His latest work, *Poèmes anciens et romanesques,* is a pure masterpiece.

"So you can see," he said, shaking hands with me, "that, in the final analysis, all earthly existence must ultimately be contained in a book."

The Book: A Spiritual Instrument

I am the author of a statement to which there have been varying reactions, including praise and blame, and which I shall make again in the present article. Briefly, it is this: all earthly existence must ultimately be contained in a book.[1]

It terrifies me to think of the qualities (among them genius, certainly) which the author of such a work will have to possess. I am one of the unpossessed. We will let that pass and imagine that it bears no author's name. What, then, will the work itself be? I answer: a hymn, all harmony and joy; an immaculate grouping of universal relationships come together for some miraculous and glittering occasion. Man's duty is to observe with the eyes of the divinity; for if his connection with that divinity is to be made clear, it can be expressed only by the pages of the open book in front of him.

Seated on a garden bench where a recent book is lying, I like to watch a passing gust half open it and breathe life into many of its outer aspects, which are so obvious that no one in the history of literature has ever thought about them. I shall have the chance to do so now, if I can get rid of my overpowering newspaper. I push it aside; it flies about and lands near some roses as if to hush their proud and feverish whispering; finally, it unfolds around them. I will leave it there along with the silent whispering of the flowers. I formally propose now to examine the differences between this rag and the book, which is supreme. The newspaper is the sea; literature flows into it at will.

Now then—

The foldings of a book, in comparison with the large-sized, open newspaper, have an almost religious significance. But an even greater significance lies in their thickness when they are piled together; for then they form a tomb in miniature for our souls.

Every discovery made by printers has hitherto been absorbed in the most elementary fashion by the newspaper, and

---

THE BOOK: A SPIRITUAL INSTRUMENT. Mallarmé's *The Book: A Spiritual Instrument* was first published in *La Revue Blanche* in 1895. The text is from *Mallarmé: Selected Prose, Poems, Essays, and Letters,* translated by Bradford Cook. Copyright © 1956 by The Johns Hopkins Press. Reprinted by permission of the publisher.
[1]See the last sentence of *The Evolution of Literature,* above.

can be summed up in the word: *press*. The result has been simply a plain sheet of paper upon which a flow of words is printed in the most unrefined manner. The immediacy of this system (which preceded the production of books) has undeniable advantages for the writer; with its endless line of posters and proof sheets it makes for improvisation. We have, in other words, a "daily paper." But who, then, can make the gradual discovery of the meaning of this format, or even of a sort of popular fairyland charm about it? Then again, the leader, which is the most important part, makes its great free way through a thousand obstacles and finally reaches a state of disinterestedness. But what is the result of this victory? It overthrows the advertisement (which is original slavery) and, as if it were itself the powered printing press, drives it far back beyond intervening articles onto the fourth page and leaves it there in a mass of incoherent and inarticulate cries. A noble spectacle, without question. After this, what else can the newspaper possibly need in order to overthrow the *book* (even though at the bottom—or rather at its foundation, i.e., the *feuilleton*[2]—it resembles the other in its pagination, thus generally regulating the columns)? It will need nothing, in fact; or practically nothing, if the book delays as it is now doing and carelessly continues to be a drain for it. And since even the book's format is useless, of what avail is that extraordinary addition of foldings (like wings in repose, ready to fly forth again) which constitute its rhythm and the chief reason for the secret contained in its pages? Of what avail the priceless silence living there, and evocative symbols following in its wake, to delight the mind which literature has totally delivered?

Yes, were it not for folding of the paper and the depths thereby established, that darkness scattered about in the forms of black characters could not rise and issue forth in gleams of mystery from the page to which we are about to turn.

The newspaper with its full sheet on display makes improper use of printing—that is, it makes good packing paper. Of course, the obvious and vulgar advantage of it, as everybody knows, lies in its mass production and circulation. But the advantage is secondary to a miracle, in the highest sense of the word: words led back to their origin, which is the twenty-four letters of the alphabet, so gifted with infinity that they will finally consecrate language. Everything is caught up in their endless variations and then rises out of them in the form of the principle. Thus typography becomes a rite.

The book, which is a total expansion of the letter, must find its mobility in the letter; and in its spaciousness must establish some nameless system of relationships which will embrace and strengthen fiction.

There is nothing fortuitous in all this, even though ideas may seem to be slaves of chance. The system guarantees them. Therefore we must pay no attention to the book industry with its materialistic considerations. The making of a book, with respect to its flowering totality, begins with the first sentence. From time immemorial the poet has knowingly placed his verse in the sonnet which he writes upon our minds or upon pure space. We, in turn, will misunderstand the true meaning of this book and the miracle inherent in its structure, if we do not knowingly imagine that a given motif has been properly placed at a certain height on the page, according to its own or to the book's distribution of light. Let us have no more of those successive, incessant, back and forth motions of our eyes, traveling from one line to the next and beginning all over again. Otherwise we will miss that ecstasy in which we become immortal for a brief hour, free of all reality, and raise our obsessions to the level of creation. If we do not actively create in this way (as we would music on the keyboard, turning the pages of a score), we would do better to shut our eyes and dream. I am not asking for any servile obedience. For, on the contrary, each of us has within him that lightninglike initiative which can link the scattered notes together.

Thus, in reading, a lonely, quiet concert is given for our minds, and they in turn, less noisily, reach its meaning. All our mental faculties will be present in this symphonic exaltation; but, unlike music, they will be rarefied, for they partake of thought. Poetry, accompanied by the idea, is perfect music, and cannot be anything else.

Now, returning to the case at hand and to the question of books which are read in the ordinary way, I raise my knife in protest, like the cook chopping off chickens' heads.

The virginal foldings of the book are unfortunately exposed to the kind of sacrifice which caused the crimson-edged tomes of ancient times to bleed. I mean that they invite the paper-knife, which stakes our claims to possession of the book. Yet our consciousness alone gives us a far more intimate possession than such a barbarian symbol; for it joins the book now here, now there, varies its melodies, guesses its riddles, and even recreates it unaided. The folds will have a mark which remains intact and invites us to open or close the pages according to the author's desires. There can be only blindness and discourtesy in so murderous and self-destructive an attempt to destroy the fragile, inviolable book. The newspaper holds the advantage here, for it is not exposed to such treatment. But it is nonetheless an annoying influence; for upon the book—upon the divine and intricate organism required by literature—it inflicts the monotonous-

---

[2]The part of a page of a journal or newspaper, usually across the bottom, devoted to literary articles, light fiction, and so forth.

ness of its eternally unbearable columns, which are merely strung down the pages by hundreds.

"But," I hear someone say, "how can this situation be changed?" I shall take space here to answer this question in detail; for the work of art—which is unique or should be—must provide illustrations. A tremendous burst of greatness, of thought, or of emotion, contained in a sentence printed in large type, with one gradually descending line to a page, should keep the reader breathless throughout the book and summon forth his powers of excitement. Around this would be smaller groups of secondary importance, commenting on the main sentence or derived from it, like a scattering of ornaments.

It will be said, I suppose, that I am attempting to flabbergast the mob with a lofty statement. That is true. But several of my close friends must have noticed that there are connections between this and their own instinct for arranging their writings in an unusual and ornamental fashion, halfway between verse and prose. Shall I be explicit? All right, then, just to maintain that reputation for clarity so avidly pursued by our make-everything-clear-and-easy era. Let us suppose that a given writer reveals one of his ideas in theoretical fashion and, quite possibly, in useless fashion, since he is ahead of his time. He well knows that such revelations, touching as they do on literature, should be brought out in the open. And yet he hesitates to divulge too brusquely things which do not exist; and thus, in his modesty, and to the mob's amazement, he veils them over.

It is because of those daydreams we have before we resume our reading in a garden that our attention strays to a white butterfly flitting here and there, then disappearing; but also leaving behind it the same slight touch of sharpness and frankness with which I have presented these ideas, and flying incessantly back and forth before the people, who stand amazed.

Mystery in Literature

Any affirmations I make here, no matter how justified, are naturally going to be cannon fodder for the jokers in the mob.

Every work of art, apart from its inner treasure, should provide some sort of outward—or even indifferent—meaning through its words. A certain deference should be shown the people: for, after all, they *are* lending out their language, and the work is going to turn it to some unexpected account. It is just as well to keep idlers away; they are glad to see that the work does not apply to them—such, at least, is their first impression.

Each to his own way and no hard feelings.

And yet somehow there is a disquieting gleam from the depths of the work, hardly distinguishable from its outward show. The clever idlers become suspicious and tell us to stop; for in their considered opinion the meaning of the work is unintelligible.

Heaven help the poor slandered poet who happens to be involved! He will be crushed beneath an immense and rather silly joke. It has always been so; and now, more than ever before, the unanimous and excessive pestilence rages.

There is certainly something occult in men's hearts; I am convinced that there is something abstruse, something closed and hidden in the mob. For whenever she sniffs out the idea that obscurity may be a *reality;* that it may exist, for example, on a piece of paper, in a piece of writing (heaven forbid, of course, that it should exist within itself!), she rises up in a hurricane fury and, with thunders and lightnings, blames the darkness on anything but herself.

Her credulousness finds satisfaction in the corresponding agitations of her fellow citizens; she jumps to extremes. So that whatever that dark fiend from hell (i.e., the poet) may write henceforth, she will shake her head (quite unaware that she herself is the enigma) and, with a whisk of her skirt, assert: "I don't get it!"—even if the poor poet has simply stated that he is blowing his nose.

Obedient as he is to his inborn rhythmical sense, the poet naturally finds a lack of proportion between the storm's cause and effect.

Those fellow citizens, it seems to him, are wrong; following their avowed intention, they plunge their pens within a nightless well and lay only the useless, minimum foundation of intelligibility. Granted that the poet does this too—but that is not all he does. It is hardly discreet of them to rouse the mob to such a fury—the mob, remember! is the vessel of genius—and to pour forth pellmell the monumental stupidity of man.

And all this for a matter of no importance.

They play the game without rules and for useless stakes; they force our lady and patron saint[1] to reveal her

MYSTERY IN LITERATURE. Mallarmé's *Mystery in Literature* was first published in *La Revue Blanche* in 1896. The text is from *Mallarmé: Selected Prose, Poems, Essays, and Letters*, translated by Bradford Cook. Copyright © 1956 by The Johns Hopkins Press. Reprinted by permission of the publisher.

[1]The Muse.

dehiscence, her lacuna, her misunderstanding of special dreams which constitute the common measure of all things.

I know for a fact that they are the ones who rush on stage and parade around in humiliating fashion. For to base their arguments on obscurity, to say that they "don't get it" and that if they "don't get it" nobody will, means that they refuse to discriminate from the very outset.

The scandal is typical, and it continues to be irrelevant.

It has to do with an undertaking which is of no literary importance—

Their undertaking—

Which consists of revealing only the monotonous outward aspects of the world, as newsboys do. Admittedly, they are struggling beneath the pressure of the moment; but in that situation it is clearly improper to write at all, save to spread banality abroad. What they fail to spread is the priceless mist that floats about the secret abyss of every human thought. All that is vulgar which receives no more than the stamp of immediacy. And although I hesitate to use an image to "put them in their place" personally, nevertheless the crudity of these bores is such that they give us, I would say, not a labyrinth lit by flowers and beckoning to our leisure, but a road lined with headaches and vertical plaster images of man's interminable blindness, with no hidden fountains or greenery bending above them, but only green bottle bottoms and bristling broken glass.

Even the advertisers shy away from it all.

Now, let us imagine a steady brilliance which, even when intermittent, does not seem to be merely momentary.

Music came along and put an end to that kind of work.

For at some point in the composition, a motif breaks through the musical veils of our imagination and frees itself of their unceasing immobility, which is alternately compacted or dissolved through conscious art.

Such is the ordinary way.

Or else the composition can begin with a triumphant burst of sound too sudden to last; then the surprise dies away in a group of hesitating notes which its echo has liberated.

Then again, there is the reverse order: the hesitations are folded darkly together and rumor forth a particular obsession of the mind; they are crowded and massed together; and then out of them arises an ultimate and essential brilliance.

Such is the twin, intellectual fashion found particularly in symphonies which, in turn, found it in the repertory of nature and of the sky.

Yes, I know; mystery is said to be music's domain. But the written word also lays claim to it.

Yes, the supreme and heart-rending musical moments are born of fleeting arabesques, and their bursting is more true, more central, more brilliant than any reasoning. When we consider their matchless efficacy, we feel unable to translate them into any language save that of the listener's ideas. Their contact with our spirit is direct and fitting; we feel somehow that words would be discordant and unwelcome.

And yet the written word, which is the ideal in noiseless flight from earth, regains its rights as it stands beneath that fall of virginal sounds. Both music and lyric call for the previous discarding of the spoken word, of course, in order to prevent mere talking.

In a single surge of opposites, the one descends, the other flies away, and yet the same silken veils follow in the wake of both.

Let me pause now and quietly add this parenthesis. It has always been my purpose that stylistic coloring should be neutral: neither should it be darkened in a dive nor brightly shimmer or splash; nor subject to the alternative, which is rules.

What sure guide is there to intelligibility in the midst of these contrasts? What guarantee?

Syntax.

I do not mean simply such spontaneous twists as are inherent in the facility of conversation, even though they are essential to oratory. The French language in particular is elegant when it appears in negligee. As history will show, this is one of the original French characteristics, one of the nation's truly exquisite natures. But our literature goes beyond this "fashion"; it does not consist merely of correspondence and memoirs. It has its quick high flutterings as well; and when these are on the wing, the writer can observe how extraordinarily well the limpid structure of the language receives the primitive thunderbolts of logic. The sentence may seem to stammer at first, hold back in a knot of incidental bits; then it multiplies, takes on order, and rises up in a noble harmony, wavering all the while in its knowing transpositions.

For those who may be surprised and angered by the broad application of my words, I shall describe the revels of this language.

Words rise up unaided and in ecstasy; many a facet reveals its infinite rarity and is precious to our mind. For our mind is the center of this hesitancy and oscillation; it sees the words not in their usual order, but in projection (like the walls of a cave), so long as that mobility which is their principle lives on, that part of speech which is not spoken. Then quickly, before they die away, they all exchange their brilliancies from afar; or they may touch, and steal a furtive glance.

The argument that a certain indispensable and pedestrian clarity may be lacking here and there is a matter for grammarians. And even if the poor reader were to misread these words continually, his understanding of the slush which makes up the current literary fashion is not much better, and so there is hardly any need to distinguish him from the truly malicious. For he too speaks angrily and insultingly of obscurity. Yet why does he not consider literature's common stock and speak angrily and insultingly of *its* incoherence, its drivel, its plagiarism (not to mention any other deterrent or special accusation); or, again, he might well speak of its platitudes, with particular reference to those who are the first to cry "obscurity!" in order to avoid taxing the public's brains.

To answer these threats, I shall simply observe that several of my contemporaries don't know how to read.

The newspaper, yes; they can read that; it has the advantage of not interrupting the day's routine.

Reading—

Is an exercise—

We must bend our independent minds, page by page, to the blank space which begins each one; we must forget the title, for it is too resounding. Then, in the tiniest and most scattered stopping points upon the page, when the lines of chance have been vanquished word by word, the blanks unfailingly return; before, they were gratuitous; now they are essential; and now at last it is clear that nothing lies beyond; now silence is genuine and just.

It is a virgin space, face to face with the lucidity of our matching vision, divided of itself, in solitude, into halves of whiteness; and each of these is lawful bride at the wedding of the idea.

Thus the invisible air, or song, beneath the words leads our divining eye from word to music; and thus, like a motif, invisibly it inscribes its fleuron and pendant there.

Leo Tolstoy

1828–1910

Theories of beauty come under attack in Tolstoy's *What Is Art?* All such theories, he claims, have one of two basic orientations: the mystical or transcendental, and the hedonistic. He brands the former absurd, the latter inadequate: "The satisfaction of our taste cannot serve as a basis for the definition of the merits of food." He is equally scornful of modern aestheticism. Art that appeals only to the initiate, defended by Mallarmé, is anathema to him. His attack on Beethoven's *Ninth Symphony,* partly on this ground, is only one of several against well-known and revered works. Fundamentally, for Tolstoy art is the communication of feelings: "Art is a human activity consisting in this, that one man consciously, by means of certain external signs, hands on to others feelings he has lived through, and that others are infected by these feelings and also experience them." Tolstoy considers sincerity a standard of judgment, but he does not tell us how to determine whether a work is sincere. Nor does he say whether a work of art is valuable if we have *already* experienced feelings similar to those the artist is communicating. Perhaps that question does not arise for Tolstoy, since he finally judges a work of art solely on whether it is or has been an instrument for human progress toward Christian brotherhood and the elimination of cruelty.

The standard translation is that by Aylmer Maude, *What Is Art? and Essays on Art* (1930). Maude is also the editor of *Tolstoy on Art and Its Critics* (1924). See H. W. Garrod, *Tolstoi's Theory of Art* (1935); Isaiah Berlin, *The Hedgehog and the Fox* (1953); R. F. Christian, *Tolstoy: A Critical Introduction* (1969); Edward Crankshaw, *Tolstoy: The Making of a Novelist* (1974); and Henry Gifford, *Tolstoy* (1982).

What Is Art?

From

Chapter IV

To the question, what is this art to which is offered up the labor of millions, the very lives of men, and even morality itself? we have extracted replies from the existing aesthetics which all amount to this, that the aim of art is beauty, that

WHAT IS ART? Tolstoy's *What Is Art?* was first published in 1898. The text is from *What Is Art? and Essays on Art,* translated by Aylmer Maude (London: Oxford University Press, 1930).

beauty is recognized by the enjoyment it gives, and that artistic enjoyment is a good and important thing, because it is enjoyment. In a word, that enjoyment is good because it is enjoyment. Thus what is considered the definition of art is no definition at all, but only a shuffle to justify existing art. Therefore, however strange it may seem to say so, in spite of the mountains of books written about art, no exact definition of art has been constructed. And the reason of this is that the conception of art has been based on the conception of beauty.

Chapter V

What is art if we put aside the conception of beauty, which confuses the whole matter? The latest and most comprehensible definitions of art, apart from the conception of beauty, are the following: (1) *a* Art is an activity arising even in the animal kingdom, and springing from sexual desire and the propensity to play (Schiller,[1] Darwin, Spencer), and *b* accompanied by a pleasurable excitement of the nervous system (Grant Allen). This is the physiological-evolutionary definition. (2) Art is the external manifestation, by means of lines, colors, movements, sounds, or words, of emotions felt by man (Véron). This is the experimental definition. According to the very latest definition (Sully), (3) art is "the production of some permanent object or passing action which is fitted not only to supply an active enjoyment to the producer, but to convey a pleasurable impression to a number of spectators or listeners, quite apart from any personal advantage to be derived from it."[2]

Notwithstanding the superiority of these definitions to the metaphysical definitions which depended on the conception of beauty, they are yet far from exact. The first, the physiological-evolutionary definition, (1) *a*, is inexact, because instead of speaking about the artistic activity itself, which is the real matter in hand, it treats of the derivation of art. The modification of it, *b*, based on the physiological effects on the human organism, is inexact because within the limits of such definition many other human activities can be included, as has occurred in the neoaesthetic theories which reckon as art the preparation of handsome clothes, pleasant scents, and even of victuals.

The experimental definition, (2), which makes art consist in the expression of emotions, is inexact because a man may express his emotions by means of lines, colors, sounds, or words and yet may not act on others by such expression—and then the manifestation of his emotions is not art.

The third definition (that of Sully) is inexact because in the production of objects or actions affording pleasure to the producer and a pleasant emotion to the spectators or hearers apart from personal advantage, may be included the showing of conjuring tricks or gymnastic exercises, and other activities which are not art. And further, many things the production of which does not afford pleasure to the producer and the sensation received from which is unpleasant, such as gloomy, heart-rending scenes in a poetic description or a play, may nevertheless be undoubted works of art.

The inaccuracy of all these definitions arises from the fact that in them all (as also in the metaphysical definitions) the object considered is the pleasure art may give, and not the purpose it may serve in the life of man and of humanity.

In order to define art correctly it is necessary first of all to cease to consider it as a means to pleasure, and to consider it as one of the conditions of human life. Viewing it in this way we cannot fail to observe that art is one of the means of intercourse between man and man.

Every work of art causes the receiver to enter into a certain kind of relationship both with him who produced or is producing the art, and with all those who, simultaneously, previously, or subsequently, receive the same artistic impression.

Speech transmitting the thoughts and experiences of men serves as a means of union among them, and art serves a similar purpose. The peculiarity of this latter means of intercourse, distinguishing it from intercourse by means of words, consists in this, that whereas by words a man transmits his thoughts to another, by art he transmits his feelings.

The activity of art is based on the fact that a man receiving through his sense of hearing or sight another man's expression of feeling, is capable of experiencing the emotion which moved the man who expressed it. To take the simplest example: one man laughs, and another who hears becomes merry, or a man weeps, and another who hears feels sorrow. A man is excited or irritated, and another man seeing him is brought to a similar state of mind. By his movements or by the sounds of his voice a man expresses courage and determination or sadness and calmness, and this state of mind passes on to others. A man suffers, manifesting his sufferings by groans and spasms, and this suffering transmits itself to other people; a man expresses his feelings of admiration, devotion, fear, respect, or love, to certain objects, persons, or phenomena, and others are infected by the same feelings of admiration, devotion, fear, respect, or love, to the same objects, persons, or phenomena.

And it is on this capacity of man to receive another man's expression of feeling and to experience those feelings himself, that the activity of art is based.

If a man infects another or others directly, immediately, by his appearance or by the sounds he gives vent to at the very time he experiences the feeling; if he causes another man to yawn when he himself cannot help yawning, or to laugh or cry when he himself is obliged to laugh or cry, or to suffer when he himself is suffering—that does not amount to art.

Art begins when one person with the object of joining another or others to himself in one and the same feeling, expresses that feeling by certain external indications. To take the simplest example: a boy having experienced, let us say, fear on encountering a wolf, relates that encounter, and in order to evoke in others the feeling he has experienced, de-

---

[1]See Schiller on play, *Letters on the Aesthetic Education of Man,* pp. 421–22.
[2]René Sully-Prudhomme.

scribes himself, his condition before the encounter, the surroundings, the wood, his own lightheartedness, and then the wolf's appearance, its movements, the distance between himself and the wolf, and so forth. All this, if only the boy when telling the story again experiences the feelings he had lived through, and infects the hearers and compels them to feel what he had experienced—is art. Even if the boy had not seen a wolf but had frequently been afraid of one, and if wishing to evoke in others the fear he had felt, he invented an encounter with a wolf and recounted it so as to make his hearers share the feelings he experienced when he feared the wolf, that also would be art. And just in the same way it is art if a man, having experienced either the fear of suffering or the attraction of enjoyment (whether in reality or in imagination), expresses these feelings on canvas or in marble so that others are infected by them. And it is also art if a man feels, or imagines to himself, feelings of delight, gladness, sorrow, despair, courage, or despondency, and the transition from one to another of these feelings, and expresses them by sounds so that the hearers are infected by them and experience them as they were experienced by the composer.

The feelings with which the artist infects others may be most various—very strong or very weak, very important or very insignificant, very bad or very good: feelings of love of one's country, self-devotion and submission to fate or to God expressed in a drama, raptures of lovers described in a novel, feelings of voluptuousness expressed in a picture, courage expressed in a triumphal march, merriment evoked by a dance, humor evoked by a funny story, the feeling of quietness transmitted by an evening landscape or by a lullaby, or the feeling of admiration evoked by a beautiful arabesque— it is all art.

If only the spectators or auditors are infected by the feelings which the author has felt, it is art.

To evoke in oneself a feeling one has once experienced and having evoked it in oneself then by means of movements, lines, colors, sounds, or forms expressed in words, so to transmit that feeling that others experience the same feeling—this is the activity of art.

Art is a human activity consisting in this, that one man consciously by means of certain external signs, hands on to others feelings he has lived through, and that others are infected by these feelings and also experience them.

Art is not, as the metaphysicians say, the manifestation of some mysterious idea of beauty or God; it is not, as the aesthetic physiologists say, a game in which man lets off his excess of stored-up energy; it is not the expression of man's emotions by external signs; it is not the production of pleasing objects; and, above all, it is not pleasure; but it is a means of union among men joining them together in the same feelings, and indispensable for the life and progress towards well-being of individuals and of humanity.

As every man, thanks to man's capacity to express thoughts by words, may know all that has been done for him in the realms of thought by all humanity before his day, and can in the present, thanks to this capacity to understand the thoughts of others, become a sharer in their activity and also himself hand on to his contemporaries and descendants the thoughts he has assimilated from others as well as those that have arisen in himself; so, thanks to man's capacity to be infected with the feelings of others by means of art, all that is being lived through by his contemporaries is accessible to him, as well as the feelings experienced by men thousands of years ago, and he has also the possibility of transmitting his own feelings to others.

If people lacked the capacity to receive the thoughts conceived by men who preceded them and to pass on to others their own thoughts, men would be like wild beasts, or like Kasper Hauser.[3]

And if men lacked this other capacity of being infected by art, people might be almost more savage still, and above all more separated from, and more hostile to, one another.

And therefore the activity of art is a most important one, as important as the activity of speech itself and as generally diffused.

As speech does not act on us only in sermons, orations, or books, but in all those remarks by which we interchange thoughts and experiences with one another, so also art in the wide sense of the word permeates our whole life, but it is only to some of its manifestations that we apply the term in the limited sense of the word.

We are accustomed to understand art to be only what we hear and see in theaters, concerts, and exhibitions; together with buildings, statues, poems, and novels. . . . But all this is but the smallest part of the art by which we communicate with one another in life. All human life is filled with works of art of every kind—from cradle song, jest, mimicry, the ornamentation of houses, dress, and utensils, to church services, buildings, monuments, and triumphal processions. It is all artistic activity. So that by art, in the limited sense of the word, we do not mean all human activity transmitting feelings but only that part which we for some reason select from it and to which we attach special importance.

---

[3][Tolstoy] "The foundling of Nuremberg," found in the marketplace of that town on May 23, 1828, apparently some sixteen years old. He spoke little and was almost totally ignorant even of common objects. He subsequently explained that he had been brought up in confinement underground and visited by only one man, whom he saw but seldom.

This special importance has always been given by men to that part of this activity which transmits feelings flowing from their religious perception, and this small part they have specifically called art, attaching to it the full meaning of the word.

That was how men of old—Socrates, Plato, and Aristotle—looked on art. Thus did the Hebrew prophets and the ancient Christians regard art. Thus it was, and still is, understood by the Mohammedans, and thus it still is understood by religious folk among our own peasantry.

Some teachers of mankind—such as Plato in his *Republic,* and people like the primitive Christians, the strict Mohammedans, and the Buddhists—have gone so far as to repudiate all art.

People viewing art in this way (in contradiction to the prevalent view of today which regards any art as good if only it affords pleasure) held and hold that art (as contrasted with speech, which need not be listened to) is so highly dangerous in its power to infect people against their wills, that mankind will lose far less by banishing all art than by tolerating each and every art.

Evidently such people were wrong in repudiating all art, for they denied what cannot be denied—one of the indispensable means of communication without which mankind could not exist. But not less wrong are the people of civilized European society of our class and day in favoring any art if it but serves beauty, that is, gives people pleasure.

Formerly people feared lest among works of art there might chance to be some causing corruption, and they prohibited art altogether. Now they only fear lest they should be deprived of any enjoyment art can afford, and they patronize any art. And I think the last error is much grosser than the first and that its consequences are far more harmful.

Chapter VI

But how could it happen that that very art which in ancient times was merely tolerated (if tolerated at all), should have come in our times to be invariably considered a good thing if only it affords pleasure?

It has resulted from the following causes. The estimation of the value of art (or rather, of the feelings it transmits) depends on men's perception of the meaning of life; depends on what they hold to be the good and the evil of life. And what is good and what is evil is defined by what are termed religions.

Humanity unceasingly moves forward from a lower, more partial and obscure understanding of life to one more general and more lucid. And in this as in every movement there are leaders—those who have understood the meaning of life more clearly than others—and of these advanced men there is always one who has in his words and by his life expressed this meaning more clearly, lucidly, and strongly, than others. This man's expression of the meaning of life, together with those superstitions, traditions, and ceremonies, which usually form round the memory of such a man, is what is called a religion. Religions are the exponents of the highest comprehension of life accessible to the best and foremost men at a given time in a given society—a comprehension towards which all the rest of that society must inevitably and irresistibly advance. And therefore religions alone have always served, and still serve, as bases for the valuation of human sentiments. If feelings bring men nearer the ideal their religion indicates, if they are in harmony with it and do not contradict it, they are good; if they estrange men from it and oppose it they are bad.

If the religion places the meaning of life in worshiping one God and fulfilling what is regarded as his will, as was the case among the Jews, then the feelings flowing from love of that God and of his law, when successfully transmitted through the art of poetry, by the prophets, by the Psalms, or by the epic of the book of Genesis, are good, high art. All opposing that, as for instance the transmission of feelings of devotion to strange gods, or of feelings incompatible with the law of God, would be considered bad art. Or if, as was the case among the Greeks, the religion places the meaning of life in earthly happiness, in beauty and in strength, then art successfully transmitting the joy and energy of life would be considered good art, but art transmitting feelings of effeminacy or despondency would be bad art. If the meaning of life is seen in the well-being of one's nation, or in honoring one's ancestors and continuing the mode of life led by them, as was the case among the Romans and the Chinese respectively, then art transmitting feelings of joy at the sacrifice of one's personal well-being for the common weal, or at the exaltation of one's ancestors and the maintenance of their traditions, would be considered good art; but art expressing feelings contrary to these would be regarded as bad. If the meaning of life is seen in freeing oneself from the yoke of animalism, as is the case among the Buddhists, then art successfully transmitting feelings that elevate the soul and humble the flesh will be good art, and all that transmits feelings strengthening the bodily passions will be bad art.

In every age and in every human society there exists a religious sense of what is good and what is bad common to that whole society, and it is this religious conception that decides the value of the feelings transmitted by art. Therefore among all nations art which transmitted feelings considered to be good by the general religious sense was recognized as being good and was encouraged, but art which transmitted feelings considered bad by this general religious sense was recognized as being bad and was rejected. All the rest of the immense field of art by means of which people communicate one with another was not esteemed at all and was only noticed when it ran counter to the religious conception of its age, and then merely to be repudiated. Thus it was among all nations—Greeks, Jews, Indians, Egyptians, and Chinese—and so it was when Christianity appeared.

The Christianity of the first centuries recognized as productions of good art only legends, lives of saints, sermons, prayers, and hymn-singing, evoking love of Christ, emotion at his life, desire to follow his example, renunciation of worldly life, humility, and the love of others; all productions transmitting feelings of personal enjoyment they considered to be bad, and therefore rejected; for instance, tolerating plastic representations only when they were symbolical, they rejected all the pagan sculptures.

This was so among the Christians of the first centuries, who accepted Christ's teaching if not quite in its true form at least not in the perverted, paganized form in which it was subsequently held.

But besides this Christianity, from the time of the wholesale conversion of nations by order of the authorities, as in the days of Constantine, Charlemagne, and Vladímir, there appeared another, a church-Christianity, which was nearer to paganism than to Christ's teaching. And in accord with its own teaching, this church-Christianity estimated quite otherwise the feelings of people and the productions of art which transmitted those feelings.

This church-Christianity not only did not acknowledge the fundamental and essential positions of true Christianity—the immediate relationship of each man to the Father, the consequent brotherhood and equality of all men, and the substitution of humility and love in place of any kind of violence—but on the contrary, having set up a heavenly hierarchy similar to the pagan mythology, and having introduced the worship of Christ, of the Virgin, of angels, of apostles, of saints, and of martyrs, and not only of these divinities themselves but also of their images, it made blind faith in the church and in its ordinances the essential point of its teaching.

However foreign this teaching may have been to true Christianity, however degraded, not only in comparison with true Christianity but even with the conception of life of Romans such as Julian and others, for all that it was to the barbarians who accepted it, a higher doctrine than their former adoration of gods, heroes, and good and bad spirits. And therefore this teaching was a religion to them, and on the basis of this religion the art of that time was assessed. And

art transmitting pious adoration of the Virgin, Jesus, the saints, and the angels, a blind faith in and submission to the church, fear of torments, and hope of blessedness in a life beyond the grave, was considered good, while all art opposed to this was held to be bad.

The teaching on the basis of which this art arose was a perversion of Christ's teaching, but the art which sprang up on this perverted teaching was for all that a true art, since it corresponded to the religious view of life held by the people among whom it arose.

The artists of the Middle Ages, vitalized by the same source of feeling—religion—as the mass of the people, and transmitting in architecture, sculpture, painting, music, poetry, or drama, the feelings and states of mind they experienced, were true artists; and their activity, founded on the highest conceptions accessible to their age and common to the entire people—though for our times a mean art—was nevertheless a true one, shared by the whole community.

And this was the state of things until in the upper, rich, more educated, classes of European society doubt arose as to the truth of the understanding of life which was expressed by church-Christianity. When after the Crusades and the maximum development of papal power and its abuses, people of the rich classes became acquainted with the wisdom of the classics, and saw on the one hand the reasonable lucidity of the teaching of the ancient sages, and on the other hand the incompatibility of the church doctrine with the teaching of Christ, it became impossible for them to continue to believe the church teaching.

If in externals they still kept to the forms of church teaching, they could no longer believe in it, and held to it only by inertia and to influence the masses, who continued to believe blindly in church doctrine and whom the upper classes for their own advantage considered it necessary to encourage in those beliefs.

So that a time came when church-Christianity ceased to be the general religious doctrine of all Christian people: some—the masses—continued blindly to believe in it, but the upper classes—those in whose hands lay the power and wealth, and therefore the leisure to produce art and the means to stimulate it—ceased to believe that teaching.

In regard to religion the upper circles of the Middle Ages found themselves in the position educated Romans were in before Christianity arose, that is, they no longer believed in the religion of the masses but had no beliefs to put in place of the worn-out church doctrine which for them had lost its meaning.

There was only this difference, that whereas for the Romans who lost faith in their emperor gods and household gods it was impossible to extract anything further from all the complex mythology they had borrowed from conquered nations, and it was consequently necessary to find a completely new conception of life, the people of the Middle Ages when they doubted the truth of the church teaching had no need to seek a fresh one. That Christian teaching which they professed in a perverted form as church doctrine, had mapped out the path of human progress so far ahead that they needed only to rid themselves of those perversions which hid the teaching announced by Christ and to adopt its real meaning—if not completely, at least in a greater degree than the church had done. And this was partially accomplished not only in the reformations of Wyclif, Huss, Luther, and Calvin, but by the whole current of nonchurch Christianity represented in earlier times by the Paulicians and the Bogomilites, and afterwards by the Waldenses and other nonchurch Christians, who were called heretics. But this could be, and was, done chiefly by poor people—who did not rule. A few of the rich and strong, such as Francis of Assisi and others, accepted the Christian teaching in its full significance even though it undermined their privileged positions. But most people of the upper classes (though in the depth of their souls they had lost faith in the church teaching) could not or would not act thus, because the essence of that Christian view of life which stood ready to be adopted when once they rejected the church faith, was a teaching of the brotherhood (and therefore the equality) of man, and this condemned the privileges by which they lived, in which they had grown up and been educated, and to which they were accustomed. Not in the depth of their hearts believing in the church teaching—which had outlived its age and had no longer any true meaning for them—and not being strong enough to accept true Christianity, men of these rich, governing classes—popes, kings, dukes, and all the great ones of the earth—were left without any religion, with but the external forms of one, which they supported as being profitable and even necessary for themselves since these forms maintained a teaching which justified the privileges they made use of. In reality these people believed in nothing, just as the Romans of the first centuries of our era believed in nothing. But at the same time they were the people who had the power and the wealth, and they were the people who rewarded art and directed it.

And it should be remarked that it was just among these people that there grew up an art esteemed not according to its success in expressing men's religious feelings, but in proportion to its beauty—in other words, according to the enjoyment it gave.

No longer able to believe in the church religion whose falsehood they had detected, and incapable of accepting true Christian teaching which denounced their whole manner of life, these rich and powerful people, stranded with no religious conception of life, involuntarily returned to the pagan view of things which places life's meaning in personal enjoyment. And then took place among the upper classes what is called the Renaissance of science and art, which was really not only a denial of every religion, but also an assertion that religion is unnecessary.

The church doctrine is so coherent a system that it cannot be altered or corrected without destroying it altogether. As soon as doubt arose with regard to the infallibility of the pope (and this doubt was then in the minds of all educated people), doubt inevitably followed as to the truth of tradition. But doubt as to the truth of tradition is fatal not only to popery and Catholicism but also to the whole church creed with all its dogmas: the divinity of Christ, the resurrection, and the Trinity; and it destroys the authority of the Scriptures, since they were considered to be inspired only because the tradition of the church so decided.

So that the majority of the highest classes of that age, even the popes and the ecclesiastics, really believed in nothing at all. In the church doctrine these people did not believe, for they saw its insolvency; but neither could they follow Francis of Assisi, Peter of Chelczic, and most of the heretics, in acknowledging the moral, social teaching of Christ, for that teaching undermined their social position. So these people remained without any religious view of life; and having none, they could have no standard whereby to estimate what was good and what was bad art, except that of personal enjoyment. And having acknowledged their criterion of what was good to be pleasure, that is beauty, these people of the upper classes of European society went back in their comprehension of art to the gross conception of the primitive Greeks, which Plato had already condemned. And conformably to this understanding of life a theory of art was formulated.

Chapter XV

Art in our society has become so perverted that not only has bad art come to be considered good, but even the very perception of what art really is has been lost. In order to be able to speak about the art of our society it is, therefore, first of all necessary to distinguish art from counterfeit art.

There is one indubitable sign distinguishing real art from its counterfeit—namely, the infectiousness of art. If a man without exercising effort and without altering his standpoint, on reading, hearing, or seeing another man's work experiences a mental condition which unites him with that man and with others who are also affected by that work, then the object evoking that condition is a work of art. And however poetic, realistic, striking, or interesting, a work may be, it is not a work of art if it does not evoke that feeling (quite distinct from all other feelings) of joy and of spiritual union with another (the author) and with others (those who are also infected by it).

It is true that this indication is an *internal* one and that there are people who, having forgotten what the action of real art is, expect something else from art (in our society the great majority are in this state), and that therefore such people may mistake for this aesthetic feeling the feeling of diversion and a certain excitement which they receive from counterfeits of art. But though it is impossible to undeceive these people, just as it may be impossible to convince a man suffering from color blindness that green is not red, yet for all that, this indication remains perfectly definite to those whose feeling for art is neither perverted nor atrophied, and it clearly distinguishes the feeling produced by art from all other feelings.

The chief peculiarity of this feeling is that the recipient of a truly artistic impression is so united to the artist that he feels as if the work were his own and not someone else's— as if what it expresses were just what he had long been wishing to express. A real work of art destroys in the consciousness of the recipient the separation between himself and the artist, and not that alone, but also between himself and all whose minds receive this work of art. In this freeing of our personality from its separation and isolation, in this uniting of it with others, lies the chief characteristic and the great attractive force of art.

If a man is infected by the author's condition of soul, if he feels this emotion and this union with others, then the object which has effected this is art; but if there be no such infection, if there be not this union with the author and with others who are moved by the same work—then it is not art. And not only is infection a sure sign of art, but the degree of infectiousness is also the sole measure of excellence in art.

The stronger the infection the better is the art, as art, speaking of it now apart from its subject matter—that is, not considering the value of the feelings it transmits.

And the degree of the infectiousness of art depends on three conditions: (1) On the greater or lesser individuality of the feeling transmitted; (2) on the greater or lesser clearness with which the feeling is transmitted; (3) on the sincerity of the artist, that is, on the greater or lesser force with which the artist himself feels the emotion he transmits.

The more individual the feeling transmitted the more strongly does it act on the recipient; the more individual the state of soul into which he is transferred the more pleasure does the recipient obtain and therefore the more readily and strongly does he join in it.

Clearness of expression assists infection because the recipient who mingles in consciousness with the author is the better satisfied the more clearly that feeling is transmitted which, as it seems to him, he has long known and felt and for which he has only now found expression.

But most of all is the degree of infectiousness of art increased by the degree of sincerity in the artist. As soon as the spectator, hearer, or reader, feels that the artist is infected by his own production and writes, sings, or plays, for himself, and not merely to act on others, this mental condition of the artist infects the recipient; and, on the contrary, as soon as the spectator, reader, or hearer, feels that the author is not writing, singing, or playing, for his own satisfaction—does not himself feel what he wishes to express, but is doing it for him, the recipient—resistance immediately springs up, and the most individual and the newest feelings and the cleverest technique not only fail to produce any infection but actually repel.

I have mentioned three conditions of contagion in art, but they may all be summed up into one, the last, sincerity; that is, that the artist should be impelled by an inner need to express his feeling. That condition includes the first; for if the artist is sincere he will express the feeling as he experienced it. And as each man is different from everyone else, his feeling will be individual for everyone else; and the more individual it is—the more the artist has drawn it from the depths of his nature—the more sympathetic and sincere will it be. And this same sincerity will impel the artist to find clear expression for the feeling which he wishes to transmit.

Therefore this third condition—sincerity—is the most important of the three. It is always complied with in peasant art, and this explains why such art always acts so powerfully; but it is a condition almost entirely absent from our upper-class art, which is continually produced by artists actuated by personal aims of covetousness or vanity.

Such are the three conditions which divide art from its counterfeits, and which also decide the quality of every work of art considered apart from its subject matter.

The absence of any one of these conditions excludes a work from the category of art and relegates it to that of art's counterfeits. If the work does not transmit the artist's peculiarity of feeling and is therefore not individual, if it is unintelligibly expressed, or if it has not proceeded from the author's inner need for expression—it is not a work of art. If all these conditions are present even in the smallest degree, then the work even if a weak one is yet a work of art.

The presence in various degrees of these three conditions: individuality, clearness, and sincerity, decides the merit of a work of art as art, apart from subject matter. All works of art take order of merit according to the degree in which they fulfill the first, the second, and the third, of these conditions. In one the individuality of the feeling transmitted may predominate; in another, clearness of expression; in a third, sincerity; while a fourth may have sincerity and individuality but be deficient in clearness; a fifth, individuality and clearness, but less sincerity; and so forth, in all possible degrees and combinations.

Thus is art divided from what is not art, and thus is the quality of art, as art, decided, independently of its subject matter, that is to say, apart from whether the feelings it transmits are good or bad.

But how are we to define good and bad art with reference to its content or subject matter?

From

Chapter XVI

How in the subject matter of art are we to decide what is good and what is bad?

Art like speech is a means of communication and therefore of progress, that is, of the movement of humanity forward towards perfection. Speech renders accessible to men of the latest generations all the knowledge discovered by the experience and reflection both of preceding generations and of the best and foremost men of their own times; art renders accessible to men of the latest generations all the feelings experienced by their predecessors and also those felt by their best and foremost contemporaries. And as the evolution of knowledge proceeds by truer and more necessary knowledge dislodging and replacing what was mistaken and unnecessary, so the evolution of feeling proceeds by means of art—feelings less kind and less necessary for the well-being of mankind being replaced by others kinder and more needful for that end. That is the purpose of art. And speaking now of the feelings which are its subject matter, the more art fulfills that purpose the better the art, and the less it fulfills it the worse the art.

The appraisement of feelings (that is, the recognition of one or other set of feelings as more or less good, more or less necessary for the well-being of mankind) is effected by the religious perception of the age.

In every period of history and in every human society there exists an understanding of the meaning of life, which represents the highest level to which men of that society have attained—an understanding indicating the highest good at which that society aims. This understanding is the religious perception of the given time and society. And this religious perception is always clearly expressed by a few advanced men and more or less vividly perceived by members of the society generally. Such a religious perception and its corresponding expression always exists in every society. If it appears to us that there is no religious perception in our society, this is not because there really is none, but only because we do not wish to see it. And we often wish not to see it because it exposes the fact that our life is inconsistent with that religious perception.

Religious perception in a society is like the direction of a flowing river. If the river flows at all it must have a direction. If a society lives, there must be a religious perception indicating the direction in which, more or less consciously, all its members tend.

And so there always has been, and is, a religious perception in every society. And it is by the standard of this religious perception that the feelings transmitted by art have always been appraised. It has always been only on the basis of this religious perception of their age, that men have chosen from amid the endlessly varied spheres of art that art which transmitted feelings making religious perception operative in actual life. And such art has always been highly valued and encouraged, while art transmitting feelings already outlived, flowing from the antiquated religious perceptions of a former age, has always been condemned and despised. All the rest of art transmitting those most diverse feelings by means of which people commune with one another was not condemned and was tolerated if only it did not transmit feelings contrary to religious perception. Thus for instance among the Greeks, art transmitting feelings of beauty, strength, and courage (Hesiod, Homer, Phidias) was chosen, approved, and encouraged, while art transmitting feelings of rude sensuality, despondency, and effeminacy, was condemned and despised. Among the Jews, art transmitting feelings of devotion and submission to the God of the Hebrews and to his will (the epic of Genesis, the prophets, the Psalms) was chosen and encouraged, while art transmitting feelings of idolatry (the golden calf) was condemned and despised. All the rest of art—stories, songs, dances, ornamentation of houses, of utensils, and of clothes—which was not contrary to religious perception, was neither distinguished nor discussed. Thus as regards its subject matter has art always and everywhere been appraised and thus it should be appraised, for this attitude towards art proceeds from the fundamental characteristics of human nature, and those characteristics do not change.

I know that according to an opinion current in our times religion is a superstition humanity has outgrown, and it is therefore assumed that no such thing exists as a religious perception common to us all by which art in our time can be appraised. I know that this is the opinion current in the pseudocultured circles of today. People who do not acknowledge Christianity in its true meaning because it undermines their social privileges, and who therefore invent all kinds of philosophic and aesthetic theories to hide from themselves the meaninglessness and wrongfulness of their lives, cannot think otherwise. These people intentionally, or sometimes unintentionally, confuse the notion of a religious cult with the notion of religious perception, and think that by denying the cult they get rid of the perception. But even the very attacks on religion and the attempts to establish an idea of life contrary to the religious perception of our times, most clearly demonstrate the existence of a religious perception condemning the lives that are not in harmony with it.

If humanity progresses, that is, moves forward, there must inevitably be a guide to the direction of that movement. And religions have always furnished that guide. All history shows that the progress of humanity is accomplished no otherwise than under the guidance of religion. But if the race cannot progress without the guidance of religion—and progress is always going on, and consequently goes on also in our own times—then there must be a religion of our times. So that whether it pleases or displeases the so-called cultured people of today, they must admit the existence of religion—not of a religious cult, Catholic, Protestant, or another, but of religious perception—which even in our times is the guide always present where there is any progress. And if a religious perception exists amongst us, then the feelings dealt with by our art should be appraised on the basis of that religious perception; and as has been the case always and everywhere, art transmitting feelings flowing from the religious perception of our time should be chosen from amid all the indifferent art, should be acknowledged, highly valued, and encouraged, while art running counter to that perception should be condemned and despised, and all the remaining, indifferent art should neither be distinguished nor encouraged.

The religious perception of our time in its widest and most practical application is the consciousness that our well-being, both material and spiritual, individual and collective, temporal and eternal, lies in the growth of brotherhood among men—in their loving harmony with one another. This perception is not only expressed by Christ and all the best men of past ages, it is not only repeated in most varied forms and from most diverse sides by the best men of our times, but it already serves as a clue to all the complex labor of humanity, consisting as this labor does on the one hand in the destruction of physical and moral obstacles to the union of men, and on the other hand in establishing the principles common to all men which can and should unite them in one universal brotherhood. And it is on the basis of this perception that we should appraise all the phenomena of our life

and among the rest our art also: choosing from all its realms and highly prizing and encouraging whatever transmits feelings flowing from this religious perception, rejecting whatever is contrary to it, and not attributing to the rest of art an importance that does not properly belong to it.

The chief mistake made by people of the upper classes at the time of the so-called Renaissance—a mistake we still perpetuate—was not that they ceased to value and attach importance to religious art (people of that period could not attach importance to it because, like our own upper classes, they could not believe in what the majority considered to be religion), but their mistake was that they set up in place of the religious art that was lacking, an insignificant art which aimed merely at giving pleasure, that is, they began to choose, to value, and to encourage, in place of religious art, something which in any case did not deserve such esteem and encouragement.

One of the fathers of the church said that the great evil is not that men do not know God, but that they have set up instead of God, that which is not God. So also with art. The great misfortune of the people of the upper classes of our time is not so much that they are without a religious art as that, instead of a supreme religious art chosen from all the rest as being specially important and valuable, they have chosen a most insignificant and, usually, harmful art, which aims at pleasing certain people and which therefore, if only by its exclusive nature, stands in contradiction to that Christian principle of universal union which forms the religious perception of our time. Instead of religious art, an empty and often vicious art is set up, and this hides from men's notice the need of that true religious art which should be present in life to improve it.

It is true that art which satisfies the demands of the religious perception of our time is quite unlike former art, but notwithstanding this dissimilarity, to a man who does not intentionally hide the truth from himself, what forms the religious art of our age is very clear and definite. In former times when the highest religious perception united only some people (who even if they formed a large society were yet but one society among others—Jews, or Athenian or Roman citizens), the feelings transmitted by the art of that time flowed from a desire for the might, greatness, glory, and prosperity of that society, and the heroes of art might be people who contributed to that prosperity by strength, by craft, by fraud, or by cruelty (Ulysses, Jacob, David, Samson, Hercules, and all the heroes). But the religious perception of our times does not select any one society of men; on the contrary it demands the union of all—absolutely of all people without exception—and above every other virtue it sets brotherly love of all men. And therefore the feelings transmitted by the art of our time not only cannot coincide with the feelings transmitted by former art, but must run counter to them.

Christian, truly Christian, art has been so long in establishing itself, and has not yet established itself, just because the Christian religious perception was not one of those small steps by which humanity advances regularly, but was an enormous revolution which, if it has not already altered, must inevitably alter the entire conception of life of mankind, and consequently the whole internal organization of that life. It is true that the life of humanity, like that of an individual, moves regularly; but in that regular movement come, as it were, turning points which sharply divide the preceding from the subsequent life. Christianity was such a turning point; such at least it must appear to us who live by the Christian perception of life. Christian perception gave another, a new direction to all human feelings, and therefore completely altered both the content and the significance of art. The Greeks could make use of Persian art and the Romans could use Greek art, or, similarly, the Jews could use Egyptian art—the fundamental ideals were one and the same. Now the ideal was the greatness and prosperity of the Persians, now the greatness and prosperity of the Greeks, now that of the Romans. The same art was transferred to other conditions and served new nations. But the Christian ideal changed and reversed everything, so that, as the Gospel puts it, "That which was exalted among men has become an abomination in the sight of God."[4] The ideal is no longer the greatness of Pharaoh or of a Roman emperor, not the beauty of a Greek nor the wealth of Phoenicia, but humility, purity, compassion, love. The hero is no longer Dives, but Lazarus the beggar; not Mary Magdalene in the day of her beauty but in the day of her repentance; not those who acquire wealth but those who have abandoned it; not those who dwell in palaces but those who dwell in catacombs and huts; not those who rule over others, but those who acknowledge no authority but God's. And the greatest work of art is no longer a cathedral of victory with statues of conquerors, but the representation of a human soul so transformed by love that a man who is tormented and murdered, yet pities and loves his persecutors.

And the change is so great that men of the Christian world find it difficult to resist the inertia of the heathen art to which they have been accustomed all their lives. The subject matter of Christian religious art is so new to them, so unlike the subject matter of former art, that it seems to them as though Christian art were a denial of art, and they cling desperately to the old art. But this old art, having no longer in our day any source in religious perception, has lost its meaning, and we shall have to abandon it whether we wish to or not.

The essence of the Christian perception consists in the recognition by every man of his sonship to God and of the consequent union of men with God and with one another, as is said in the Gospel (John 17:21[5]). Therefore the subject matter of Christian art is of a kind that feeling can unite men with God and with another.

The expression *unite men with God and with one another* may seem obscure to people accustomed to the misuse of these words that is so customary, but the words have a perfectly clear meaning nevertheless. They indicate that the Christian union of man (in contradiction to the partial, exclusive, union of only certain men) is that which unites all without exception.

Art, all art, has this characteristic, that it unites people. Every art causes those to whom the artist's feeling is transmitted to unite in soul with the artist and also with all who receive the same impression. But non-Christian art, while uniting some people, makes that very union a cause of separation between these united people and others; so that union of this kind is often a source not merely of division but even of enmity towards others. Such is all patriotic art, with its anthems, poems, and monuments; such is all church art, that is, the art of certain cults, with their images, statues, processions, and other local ceremonies. Such art is belated and non-Christian, uniting the people of one cult only to separate them yet more sharply from the members of other cults, and even to place them in relations of hostility to one another. Christian art is such only as tends to unite all without exception, either by evoking in them the perception that each man and all men stand in a like relation towards God and towards their neighbor, or by evoking in them identical feelings, which may even be the very simplest, provided that they are not repugnant to Christianity and are natural to everyone without exception.

Good Christian art of our time may be unintelligible to people because of imperfections in its form or because men are inattentive to it, but it must be such that all men can experience the feelings it transmits. It must be the art not of some one group of people, or of one class, or of one nationality, or of one religious cult; that is, it must not transmit feelings accessible only to a man educated in a certain way, or only to an aristocrat, or a merchant, or only to a Russian,

---

[4]Luke 16:15.

[5][Maude] "That they may all be one; even as thou, Father, art in me, and I in thee, that they also may be in us."

or a native of Japan, or a Roman Catholic, or a Buddhist, and so on, but it must transmit feelings accessible to everyone. Only art of this kind can in our time be acknowledged to be good art, worthy of being chosen out from all the rest of art and encouraged.

Christian art, that is, the art of our time, should be catholic in the original meaning of the word, that is, universal, and therefore it should unite all men. And only two kinds of feeling unite all men: first, feelings flowing from a perception of our sonship to God and of the brotherhood of man; and next, the simple feelings of common life accessible to everyone without exception—such as feelings of merriment, of pity, of cheerfulness, of tranquillity, and so forth. Only these two kinds of feelings can now supply material for art good in its subject matter.

And the action of these two kinds of art apparently so dissimilar, is one and the same. The feelings flowing from the perception of our sonship to God and the brotherhood of man—such as a feeling of sureness in truth, devotion to the will of God, self-sacrifice, respect for and love of man—evoked by Christian religious perception; and the simplest feelings, such as a softened or a merry mood caused by a song or an amusing jest intelligible to everyone, or by a touching story, or a drawing, or a little doll: both alike produce one and the same effect—the loving union of man with man. Sometimes people who are together, if not hostile to one another, are at least estranged in mood and feeling, till perhaps a story, a performance, a picture, or even a building, but oftenest of all music, unites them all as by an electric flash, and in place of their former isolation or even enmity they are conscious of union and mutual love. Each is glad that another feels what he feels; glad of the communion established not only between him and all present, but also with all now living who will yet share the same impression; and, more than that, he feels the mysterious gladness of a communion which, reaching beyond the grave, unites us with all men of the past who have been moved by the same feelings and with all men of the future who will yet be touched by them. And this effect is produced both by religious art which transmits feelings of love of God and one's neighbor, and by universal art transmitting the very simplest feelings common to all men.

The art of our time should be appraised differently from former art chiefly in this, that the art of our time, that is, Christian art (basing itself on a religious perception which demands the union of man), excludes from the domain of art good in its subject matter, everything transmitting exclusive feelings which do not unite men but divide them. It relegates such work to the category of art that is bad in its subject matter; while on the other hand it includes in the category of art that is good in subject matter a section not formerly admitted as deserving of selection and respect, namely, universal art transmitting even the most trifling and simple feelings if only they are accessible to all men without exception, and therefore unite them. Such art cannot but be esteemed good in our time, for it attains the end which Christianity, the religious perception of our time, sets before humanity.

Christian art either evokes in men feelings which through love of God and of one's neighbor draw them to closer and ever closer union and make them ready for, and capable of, such union; or evokes in them feelings which show them that they are already united in the joys and sorrows of life. And therefore the Christian art of our time can be and is of two kinds: first, art transmitting feelings flowing from a religious perception of man's position in the world in relation to God and to his neighbor—religious art in the limited meaning of the term; and secondly, art transmitting the simplest feelings of common life, but such always as are accessible to all men in the whole world—the art of common life—the art of the people—universal art. Only these two kinds of art can be considered good art in our time.

. . .

In the arts of painting and sculpture, all pictures and statues in so-called genre style, representations of animals, landscapes, and caricatures with subjects comprehensible to everyone, and also all kinds of ornaments, are universal in subject matter. Such productions in painting and sculpture are very numerous (for instance, china dolls), but for the most part such objects (for instance, ornaments of all kinds) are either not considered to be art or are considered to be art of a low quality. In reality all such objects if only they transmit a true feeling experienced by the artist and comprehensible to everyone (however insignificant it may seem to us to be), are works of real, good, Christian art.

I fear it will here be urged against me that having denied that the conception of beauty can supply a standard for works of art, I contradict myself by acknowledging ornaments to be works of good art. The reproach is unjust, for the subject matter of all kinds of ornamentation consists not in the beauty but in the feeling (of admiration at, and delight in, the combination of lines and colors) which the artist has experienced and with which he infects the spectator. Art remains what it was and what it must be: nothing but the infection by one man of another or of others with the feelings experienced by the artist. Among these feelings is the feeling of delight at what pleases the sight. Objects pleasing the sight may be such as please a small or a large number of people, or such as please all men—and ornaments for the most part are of the latter kind. A landscape representing a very unusual view, or a genre picture of a special subject, may not please everyone, but ornaments, from Yakútsk ornaments to Greek ones, are intelligible to everyone and evoke a similar feeling of admiration in all, and therefore this despised kind of art should in Christian society be esteemed far above exceptional, pretentious pictures and sculptures.

So that in relation to feelings conveyed, there are only two kinds of good Christian art, all the rest of art not comprised in these two divisions should be acknowledged to be bad art, deserving not to be encouraged but to be driven out, denied, and despised, as being art not uniting but dividing people. Such in literary art are all novels and poems which transmit ecclesiastical or patriotic feelings, and also exclusive feelings pertaining only to the class of the idle rich: such as aristocratic honor, satiety, spleen, pessimism, and refined and vicious feelings flowing from sex-love—quite incomprehensible to the great majority of mankind.

In painting we must similarly place in the class of bad art all ecclesiastical, patriotic, and exclusive pictures; all pictures representing the amusements and allurements of a rich and idle life; all so-called symbolic pictures in which the very meaning of the symbol is comprehensible only to those of a certain circle; and above all pictures with voluptuous subjects—all that odious female nudity which fills all the exhibitions and galleries. And to this class belongs almost all the chamber and opera music of our times—beginning especially with Beethoven (Schumann, Berlioz, Liszt, Wagner)—by its subject matter devoted to the expression of feelings accessible only to people who have developed in themselves an unhealthy nervous irritation evoked by this exclusive, artificial, and complex music.

"What! the *Ninth Symphony* not a good work of art!" I hear exclaimed by indignant voices.

And I reply: Most certainly it is not. All that I have written I have written with the sole purpose of finding a clear and reasonable criterion by which to judge the merits of works of art. And this criterion, coinciding with the indications of plain and sane sense, indubitably shows me that that symphony of Beethoven's is not a good work of art. Of course to people educated in the worship of certain productions and of their authors, to people whose taste has been perverted just by being educated in such a worship, the acknowledgment that such a celebrated work is bad, is amazing and strange. But how are we to escape the indications of reason and common sense?

Beethoven's *Ninth Symphony* is considered a great work of art. To verify its claim to be such I must first ask myself whether this work transmits the highest religious feeling? I reply in the negative, since music in itself cannot transmit those feelings; and therefore I ask myself next: Since this work does not belong to the highest kind of religious art, has it the other characteristic of the good art of our time—the quality of uniting all men in one common feeling—does it rank as Christian universal art? And again I have no option but to reply in the negative; for not only do I not see how the feelings transmitted by this work could unite people not specially trained to submit themselves to its complex hypnotism, but I am unable to imagine to myself a crowd of normal people who could understand anything of this long, confused, and artificial production, except short snatches which are lost in a sea of what is incomprehensible. And therefore, whether I like it or not, I am compelled to conclude that this work belongs to the rank of bad art. It is curious to note in this connection, that attached to the end of this very symphony is a poem of Schiller's which (though somewhat obscurely) expresses this very thought, namely, that feeling (Schiller speaks only of the feeling of gladness) unites people and evokes love in them. But though this poem is sung at the end of the symphony, the music does not accord with the thought expressed in the verses; for the music is exclusive and does not unite all men, but unites only a few, dividing them off from the rest of mankind.

Benedetto Croce

1866–1952

Croce's *Aesthetic* is a landmark in the field. It is known principally for two propositions: that intuition and expression are identical and that there is no such thing as an unexpressed intuition. Expression, however, does not seem to mean precisely what we might expect it to, for Croce subsequently adds another element, "externalization," to his formula. Externalization is the physical act of painting, sculpture, writing, and so on. The idea of externalization complicates the picture. Croce seemed to be saying that until the intuition has been given definite—even final—shape in its particular artistic form it is not an intuition. He seemed to be giving art a powerful constitutive role in human thought. But by introducing the term *externalization,* Croce seems to have isolated technique. Can we consider a poem apart from its technical qualities? Later writers have gone further than Croce and included externalization in the act of intuition itself. Auden, for instance, has remarked, "How can I know what I think till I see what I say?" Bradley and Blackmur also tend to this point of view. Cassirer's treatment of art as a "constitutive" symbolic form makes a similar suggestion.

There is another problem: it appears that for Croce some intuition-expressions are not ever externalized. How, then, can we consider them to be truer expressions? There is no really satisfactory answer to this problem in *Aesthetic,* yet Croce's discussion raises the issue, among others, of to what extent the actual materials and techniques of art are separable from what the artist has to "say."

The joining of intuition and expression eliminates the possibility of judging a work of art in terms of some preconceived authorial intention, a practice common among Romantic critics but often scorned in this century, notably by Wimsatt and Beardsley.

Douglas Ainslie has translated Croce's *Aesthetic as Science of Expression and General Linguistic* (1909) and *The Essence of Aesthetics* (1921); E. F. Carritt has translated *The Defence of Poetry* (1933). Croce's *Essays on Literature and Literary Criticism* appeared in 1990. Among the many accounts of Croce's thought the following may be mentioned: H. W. Carr, *The Philosophy of Benedetto Croce: The Problem of Art and History* (1917); E. F. Carritt, "Croce and His Aesthetic," *Mind,* LXII (1953), 452–65; Cecil Sprigge, *Benedetto Croce: Man and Thinker* (1952); Bernard Mayo, "Art, Language, and Philosophy in Croce," *Philosophical Quarterly,* V (1955), 245–60; C. G. Seerfield, *Benedetto Croce's Earlier Aesthetic Theories and Literary Criticism* (1958); Edward Wasiolek, "Croce and Contextualist Criticism," *Modern Philology,* LVII (1959), 44–54; G. N. G. Orsini, *Benedetto Croce: Philosopher of Art and Literary Critic* (1961); M. E. Brown, *Neo-Idealistic Aesthetics: Croce-Gentile-Collingwood* (1966); N. E. Moss, *Benedetto Croce Reconsidered* (1987); and David D. Roberts, *Benedetto Croce and the Uses of Historicism* (1987).

From

Aesthetic

Chapter I

Intuition and Expression

Knowledge has two forms: it is either intuitive knowledge or logical knowledge; knowledge obtained through the imagination or knowledge obtained through the intellect; knowledge of the individual or knowledge of the universal; of individual things or of the relations between them: it is, in fact, productive either of images or of concepts.

In ordinary life, constant appeal is made to intuitive knowledge. It is said that we cannot give definitions of certain truths; that they are not demonstrable by syllogisms; that they must be learnt intuitively. The politician finds fault with the abstract reasoner, who possesses no lively intuition of actual conditions; the educational theorist insists upon the necessity of developing the intuitive faculty in the pupil before everything else; the critic in judging a work of art makes it a point of honor to set aside theory and abstractions, and to judge it by direct intuition; the practical man professes to live rather by intuition than by reason.

But this ample acknowledgment granted to intuitive knowledge in ordinary life, does not correspond to an equal and adequate acknowledgment in the field of theory and of philosophy. There exists a very ancient science of intellectual knowledge, admitted by all without discussion, namely, logic; but a science of intuitive knowledge is timidly and with difficulty asserted by but a few. Logical knowledge has appropriated the lion's share; and if she does not slay and devour her companion outright, yet yields to her but grudgingly the humble place of maidservant or doorkeeper. What can intuitive knowledge be without the light of intellectual knowledge? It is a servant without a master; and though a master find a servant useful, the master is a necessity to the servant, since he enables him to gain his livelihood. Intuition is blind; intellect lends her eyes.

Now, the first point to be firmly fixed in the mind is that intuitive knowledge has no need of a master, nor to lean upon any one; she does not need to borrow the eyes of others, for she has excellent eyes of her own. Doubtless it is

possible to find concepts mingled with intuitions. But in many other intuitions there is no trace of such a mixture, which proves that it is not necessary. The impression of a moonlight scene by a painter; the outline of a country drawn by a cartographer; a musical motive, tender or energetic; the words of a sighing lyric, or those with which we ask, command and lament in ordinary life, may well all be intuitive facts without a shadow of intellectual relation. But, think what one may of these instances, and admitting further the contention that the greater part of the intuitions of civilized man are impregnated with concepts, there yet remains to be observed something more important and more conclusive. Those concepts which are found mingled and fused with the intuitions are no longer concepts, insofar as they are really mingled and fused, for they have lost all independence and autonomy. They have been concepts, but have now become simple elements of intuition. The philosophical maxims placed in the mouth of a personage of tragedy or of comedy, perform there the function, not of concepts, but of characteristics of such personage; in the same way as the red in a painted face does not there represent the red color of the physicists, but is a characteristic element of the portrait. The whole is that which determines the quality of the parts. A work of art may be full of philosophical concepts; it may contain them in greater abundance and they may there be even more profound than in a philosophical dissertation, which in its turn may be rich to overflowing with descriptions and intuitions. But notwithstanding all these concepts the total effect of the work of art is an intuition; and notwithstanding all those intuitions, the total effect of the philosophical dissertation is a concept. The *Promessi Sposi* contains copious ethical observations and distinctions, but does not for that reason lose as a whole its character of simple story or intuition. In like manner the anecdotes and satirical effusions to be found in the works of a philosopher like Schopenhauer do not deprive those works of their character of intellectual treatises. The difference between a scientific work and a work of art, that is, between an intellectual fact and an intuitive fact, lies in the difference of the total effect aimed at by their respective authors. This it is that determines and rules over the several parts of each, not these parts separated and considered abstractly in themselves.

But to admit the independence of intuition as regards concept does not suffice to give a true and precise idea of intuition. Another error arises among those who recognize this, or who at any rate do not explicitly make intuition dependent upon the intellect, to obscure and confuse the real nature of intuition. By intuition is frequently understood perception, or the knowledge of actual reality, the apprehension of something as real.

AESTHETIC. Croce's *Estetica come scienza dell'espressione e linguistica* was first published in 1902. The text is from *Aesthetic as Science of Expression and General Linguistic,* translated by Douglas Ainslie (1909). Reprinted by permission of Farrar, Straus & Giroux, Inc., and Peter Owen.

Certainly perception is intuition: the perceptions of the room in which I am writing, of the ink bottle and paper that are before me, of the pen I am using, of the objects that I touch and make use of as instruments of my person, which, if I write, therefore exists—these are all intuitions. But the image that is now passing through my brain of a me writing in another room, in another town, with different paper, pen and ink, is also an intuition. This means that the distinction between reality and nonreality is extraneous, secondary, to the true nature of intuition. If we imagine a human mind having intuitions for the first time, it would seem that it could have intuitions of actual reality only, that is to say, that it could have perceptions of nothing but the real. But since knowledge of reality is based upon the distinction between real images and unreal images, and since this distinction does not at the first moment exist, these intuitions would in truth not be intuitions either of the real or of the unreal, not perceptions, but pure intuitions. Where all is real, nothing is real. The child, with its difficulty of distinguishing true from false, history from fable, which are all one to childhood, can furnish us with a sort of very vague and only remotely approximate idea of this ingenuous state. Intuition is the undifferentiated unity of the perception of the real and of the simple image of the possible. In our intuitions we do not oppose ourselves as empirical beings to external reality, but we simply objectify our impressions, whatever they be.

Those, therefore, who look upon intuition as sensation formed and arranged simply according to the categories of space and time, would seem to approximate more nearly to the truth. Space and time (they say) are the forms of intuition; to have an intuition is to place it in space and in temporal sequence. Intuitive activity would then consist in this double and concurrent function of spatiality and temporality. But for these two categories must be repeated what was said of intellectual distinctions, when found mingled with intuitions. We have intuitions without space and without time: the color of a sky, the color of a feeling, a cry of pain and an effort of will, objectified in consciousness: these are intuitions which we possess, and with their making space and time have nothing to do. In some intuitions, spatiality may be found without temporality, in others, vice versa; and even where both are found, they are perceived by later reflection: they can be fused with the intuition in like manner with all its other elements: that is, they are in it *materialiter* and not *formaliter,* as ingredients and not as arrangement. Who, without an act of reflection which for a moment breaks in upon his contemplation, can think of space while looking at a drawing or a view? Who is conscious of temporal sequence while listening to a story or a piece of music without break-

ing into it with a similar act of reflection? What intuition reveals in a work of art is not space and time, but character, individual physiognomy. The view here maintained is confirmed in several quarters of modern philosophy. Space and time, far from being simple and primitive functions, are nowadays conceived as intellectual constructions of great complexity. And further, even in some of those who do not altogether deny to space and time the quality of formative principles, categories and functions, one observes an effort to unite them and to regard them in a different manner from that in which these categories are generally conceived. Some limit intuition to the sole category of spatiality, maintaining that even time can only be intuited in terms of space. Others abandon the three dimensions of space as not philosophically necessary, and conceive the function of spatiality as void of all particular spatial determination. But what could such a spatial function be, a simple arrangement that should arrange even time? It represents, surely, all that criticism and refutation have left standing—the bare demand for the affirmation of some intuitive activity in general. And is not this activity truly determined, when one single function is attributed to it, not spatializing nor temporalizing, but characterizing? Or rather, when it is conceived as itself a category or function which gives us knowledge of things in their concreteness and individuality?

Having thus freed intuitive knowledge from any suggestion of intellectualism and from every later and external addition, we must now explain it and determine its limits from another side and defend it from a different kind of invasion and confusion. On the hither side of the lower limit is sensation, formless matter, which the spirit can never apprehend in itself as simple matter. This it can only possess with form and in form, but postulates the notion of it as a mere limit. Matter, in its abstraction, is mechanism, passivity; it is what the spirit of man suffers, but does not produce. Without it no human knowledge or activity is possible; but mere matter produces animality, whatever is brutal and impulsive in man, not the spiritual dominion, which is humanity. How often we strive to understand clearly what is passing within us! We do catch a glimpse of something, but this does not appear to the mind as objectified and formed. It is in such moments between matter and form. These are not two acts of ours, opposed to one another; but the one is outside us and assaults and sweeps us off our feet, while the other inside us tends to absorb and identify with that which is outside. Matter, clothed and conquered by form, produces concrete form. It is the matter, the content, which differentiates one of our intuitions from another: the form is constant: it is spiritual activity, while matter is changeable. Without matter spiritual activity would not forsake its abstractness to become concrete and real activity, this or that spiritual content, this or that definite intuition.

It is a curious fact, characteristic of our times, that this very form, this very activity of the spirit, which is essentially ourselves, is so often ignored or denied. Some confound the spiritual activity of man with the metaphorical and mythological activity of what is called nature, which is mechanism and has no resemblance to human activity, save when we imagine, with Aesop, that *"arbores loquuntur non tantum ferae."*[1] Some affirm that they have never observed in themselves this "miraculous" activity, as though there were no difference, or only one of quantity, between sweating and thinking, feeling cold and the energy of the will. Others, certainly with greater reason, would unify activity and mechanism in a more general concept, though they are specifically distinct. Let us, however, refrain for the moment from examining if such a final unification be possible, and in what sense, but admitting that the attempt may be made, it is clear that to unify two concepts in a third implies to begin with the admission of a difference between the two first. Here it is this difference that concerns us and we set it in relief.

Intuition has sometimes been confused with simple sensation. But since this confusion ends by being offensive to common sense, it has more frequently been attenuated or concealed with a phraseology apparently designed at once to confuse and to distinguish them. Thus, it has been asserted that intuition is sensation, but not so much simple sensation as association of sensations. Here a double meaning is concealed in the word association. Association is understood, either as memory, mnemonic association, conscious recollection, and in that case the claim to unite in memory elements which are not intuited, distinguished, possessed in some way by the spirit and produced by consciousness, seems inconceivable: or it is understood as association of unconscious elements, in which case we remain in the world of sensation and of nature. But if with certain associationists we speak of an association which is neither memory nor flux of sensations, but a *productive* association (formative, constructive, distinguishing); then our contention is admitted and only its name is denied to it. For productive association is no longer association in the sense of the sensationalists, but synthesis, that is to say, spiritual activity. Synthesis may be called association; but with the concept of productivity is already posited the distinction between passivity and activity, between sensation and intuition.

Other psychologists are disposed to distinguish from sensation something which is sensation no longer, but is not

yet intellectual concept: the representation or image. What is the difference between the representation or image and our intuitive knowledge? Everything and nothing: for representation is a very equivocal word. If by representation be understood something cut off and standing out from the psychic basis of the sensations, then representation is intuition. If, on the other hand, it be conceived as complex sensation we are back once more in crude sensation, which does not vary in quality according to its richness or poverty, or according to whether the organism in which it appears is rudimentary or highly developed and full of traces of past sensations. Nor is the ambiguity remedied by defining representation as a psychic product of secondary degree in relation to sensation, defined as occupying the first place. What does secondary degree mean here? Does it mean a qualitative, formal difference? If so, representation is an elaboration of sensation and therefore intuition. Or does it mean greater complexity and complication, a quantitative, material difference? In that case intuition is once more confused with simple sensation.

And yet there is a sure method of distinguishing true intuition, true representation, from that which is inferior to it: the spiritual fact from the mechanical, passive, natural fact. Every true intuition or representation is also expression. That which does not objectify itself in expression is not intuition or representation, but sensation and mere natural fact. The spirit only intuits in making, forming, expressing. He who separates intuition from expression never succeeds in reuniting them.

Intuitive activity possesses intuitions to the extent that it expresses them. Should this proposition sound paradoxical, that is partly because, as a general rule, a too restricted meaning is given to the word expression. It is generally restricted to what are called verbal expressions alone. But there exist also nonverbal expressions, such as those of line, color and sound, and to all of these must be extended our affirmation, which embraces therefore every sort of manifestation of the man, as orator, musician, painter, or anything else. But be it pictorial, or verbal, or musical, or in whatever other form it appear, to no intuition can expression in one of its forms be wanting; it is, in fact, an inseparable part of intuition. How can we really possess an intuition of a geometrical figure, unless we possess so accurate an image of it as to be able to trace it immediately upon paper or on the blackboard? How can we really have an intuition of the contour of a region, for example of the island of Sicily, if we are not able to draw it as it is in all its meanderings? Everyone can experience the internal illumination which follows upon his success in formulating to himself his impressions and feelings, but only so far as he is able to formulate them. Feelings

---

[1] "Trees also speak, not only wild animals." Phaedrus, *Fabulae,* I. 6.

or impressions, then, pass by means of words from the obscure region of the soul into the clarity of the contemplative spirit. It is impossible to distinguish intuition from expression in this cognitive process. The one appears with the other at the same instant, because they are not two, but one.

The principal reason which makes our view appear paradoxical as we maintain it, is the illusion or prejudice that we possess a more complete intuition of reality than we really do. One often hears people say that they have many great thoughts in their minds, but that they are not able to express them. But if they really had them, they would have coined them into just so many beautiful sounding words, and thus have expressed them. If these thoughts seem to vanish or to become few and meager in the act of expressing them, the reason is that they did not exist or really were few and meager. People think that all of us ordinary men imagine and intuit countries, figures and scenes like painters, and bodies like sculptors; save that painters and sculptors know how to paint and carve such images, while we bear them unexpressed in our souls. They believe that anyone could have imagined a Madonna of Raphael; but that Raphael was Raphael owing to his technical ability in putting the Madonna upon canvas. Nothing can be more false than this view. The world which as a rule we intuit is a small thing. It consists of little expressions, which gradually become greater and wider with the increasing spiritual concentration of certain moments. They are the words we say to ourselves, our silent judgments: "Here is a man, here is a horse, this is heavy, this is sharp, this pleases me," etc. It is a medley of light and color, with no greater pictorial value than would be expressed by a haphazard splash of colors, from among which one could barely make out a few special, distinctive traits. This and nothing else is what we possess in our ordinary life; this is the basis of our ordinary action. It is the index of a book. The labels tied to things (it has been said) take the place of the things themselves. This index and these labels (themselves expressions) suffice for small needs and small actions. From time to time we pass from the index to the book, from the label to the thing, or from the slight to the greater intuitions, and from these to the greatest and most lofty. This passage is sometimes far from easy. It has been observed by those who have best studied the psychology of artists that when, after having given a rapid glance at anyone, they attempt to obtain a real intuition of him, in order, for example, to paint his portrait, then this ordinary vision, that seemed so precise, so lively, reveals itself as little better than nothing. What remains is found to be at the most some superficial trait, which would not even suffice for a caricature. The person to be painted stands before the artist like a world to discover. Michelangelo said, "One paints, not with the hands, but with the brain." Leonardo shocked the prior of the Convent of the Graces by standing for days together gazing at the *Last Supper,* without touching it with the brush. He remarked of this attitude: "The minds of men of lofty genius are most active in invention when they are doing the least external work." The painter is a painter, because he sees what others only feel or catch a glimpse of, but do not see. We think we see a smile, but in reality we have only a vague impression of it, we do not perceive all the characteristic traits of which it is the sum, as the painter discovers them after he has worked upon them and is thus able to fix them on the canvas. We do not intuitively possess more even of our intimate friend, who is with us every day and at all hours, than at most certain traits of physiognomy which enable us to distinguish him from others. The illusion is less easy as regards musical expression; because it would seem strange to everyone to say that the composer had added or attached notes to a motive which was already in the mind of him who is not the composer; as if Beethoven's *Ninth Symphony* were not his own intuition and his intuition the *Ninth Symphony.* Now, just as one who is deluded as to the amount of his material wealth is confuted by arithmetic, which states its exact amount, so he who nourishes delusions as to the wealth of his own thoughts and images is brought back to reality, when he is obliged to cross the *pons asinorum*[2] of expression. Let us say to the former, count; to the latter, speak; or, here is a pencil, draw, express yourself.

Each of us, as a matter of fact, has in him a little of the poet, of the sculptor, of the musician, of the painter, of the prose-writer: but how little, as compared with those who bear those names, just because they possess the most universal dispositions and energies of human nature in so lofty a degree! How little too does a painter possess of the intuitions of a poet! And how little does one painter possess those of another painter! Nevertheless, that little is all our actual patrimony of intuitions or representations. Beyond these are only impressions, sensations, feelings, impulses, emotions, or whatever else one may term what still falls short of the spirit and is not assimilated by man; something postulated for the convenience of exposition, while actually nonexistent, since to exist also is a fact of the spirit.

We may thus add this to the various verbal descriptions of intuition, noted at the beginning: intuitive knowledge is expressive knowledge. Independent and autonomous in respect to intellectual function; indifferent to later empirical discriminations, to reality and to unreality, to formations and

---

[2] "Bridge of asses."

apperceptions of space and time, which are also later: intuition or representation is distinguished as form from what is felt and suffered, from the flux or wave of sensation, or from psychic matter; and this form, this taking possession, is expression. To intuit is to express; and nothing else (nothing more, but nothing less) than to express.

Chapter II

Intuition and Art

Before proceeding further, it may be well to draw certain consequences from what has been established and to add some explanations.

We have frankly identified intuitive or expressive knowledge with the aesthetic or artistic fact, taking works of art as examples of intuitive knowledge and attributing to them the characteristics of intuition, and vice versa. But our identification is combated by a view held even by many philosophers, who consider art to be an intuition of an altogether special sort. "Let us admit" (they say) "that art is intuition; but intuition is not always art: artistic intuition is a distinct species differing from intuition in general by something more."

But no one has ever been able to indicate of what this something more consists. It has sometimes been thought that art is not a simple intuition, but an intuition of an intuition, in the same way as the concept of science has been defined, not as the ordinary concept, but as the concept of a concept. Thus man would attain to art by objectifying, not his sensations, as happens with ordinary intuition, but intuition itself. But this process of raising to a second power does not exist; and the comparison of it with the ordinary and scientific concept does not prove what is intended, for the good reason that it is not true that the scientific concept is the concept of a concept. If this comparison proves anything, it proves just the opposite. The ordinary concept, if it be really a concept and not a simple representation, is a perfect concept, however poor and limited. Science substitutes concepts for representations; for those concepts that are poor and limited it substitutes others, larger and more comprehensive; it is ever discovering new relations. But its method does not differ from that by which is formed the smallest universal in the brain of the humblest of men. What is generally called par excellence art, collects intuitions that are wider and more complex than those which we generally experience, but these intuitions are always of sensations and impressions.

Art is expression of impressions, not expression of expression.

For the same reason, it cannot be asserted that the intuition, which is generally called artistic, differs from ordinary intuition as intensive intuition. This would be the case if it were to operate differently on the same matter. But since the artistic function is extended to wider fields, yet does not differ in method from ordinary intuition, the difference between them is not intensive but extensive. The intuition of the simplest popular love song, which says the same thing, or very nearly, as any declaration of love that issues at every moment from the lips of thousands of ordinary men, may be intensively perfect in its poor simplicity, although it be extensively so much more limited than the complex intuition of a love song by Leopardi.

The whole difference, then, is quantitative, and as such is indifferent to philosophy, *scientia qualitatum*.[3] Certain men have a greater aptitude, a more frequent inclination fully to express certain complex states of the soul. These men are known in ordinary language as artists. Some very complicated and difficult expressions are not often achieved, and these are called works of art. The limits of the expression-intuitions that are called art, as opposed to those that are vulgarly called nonart, are empirical and impossible to define. If an epigram be art, why not a simple word? If a story, why not the news jottings of the journalist? If a landscape, why not a topographical sketch? The teacher of philosophy in Molière's comedy was right: "whenever we speak, we create prose." But there will always be scholars like Monsieur Jourdain,[4] astonished at having spoken prose for forty years without knowing it, who will have difficulty in persuading themselves that when they call their servant John to bring their slippers, they have spoken nothing less than—prose.

We must hold firmly to our identification, because among the principal reasons which have prevented aesthetic, the science of art, from revealing the true nature of art, its real roots in human nature, has been its separation from the general spiritual life, the having made of it a sort of special function or aristocratic club. No one is astonished when he learns from physiology that every cell is an organism and every organism a cell or synthesis of cells. No one is astonished at finding in a lofty mountain the same chemical elements that compose a small stone fragment. There is not one physiology of small animals and one of large animals; nor is there a special chemical theory of stones as distinct from mountains. In the same way, there is not a science of lesser intuition as distinct from a science of greater intuition, nor one of ordinary intuition as distinct from artistic intuition.

---

[3] "Science of quality."
[4] A character in Molière's play *The Would-be Gentleman*.

There is but one aesthetic, the science of intuitive or expressive knowledge, which is the aesthetic or artistic fact. And this aesthetic is the true analogue of logic, which includes, as facts of the same nature, the formation of the smallest and most ordinary concept and the most complicated scientific and philosophical system.

Nor can we admit that the word *genius* or artistic genius, as distinct from the nongenius of the ordinary man, possesses more than a quantitative signification. Great artists are said to reveal us to ourselves. But how could this be possible, unless there were identity of nature between their imagination and ours, and unless the difference were only one of quantity? It were better to change *poeta nascitur* into *homo nascitur poeta:*[5] some men are born great poets, some small. The cult of the genius with all its attendant superstitions has arisen from this quantitative difference having been taken as a difference of quality. It has been forgotten that genius is not something that has fallen from heaven, but humanity itself. The man of genius who poses or is represented as remote from humanity finds his punishment in becoming or appearing somewhat ridiculous. Examples of this are the genius of the Romantic period and the superman of our time.

But it is well to note here, that those who claim unconsciousness as the chief quality of an artistic genius, hurl him from an eminence far above humanity to a position far below it. Intuitive or artistic genius, like every form of human activity, is always conscious; otherwise it would be blind mechanism. The only thing that can be wanting to artistic genius is the reflective consciousness, the superadded consciousness of the historian or critic, which is not essential to it.

The relation between matter and form, or between content and form, as is generally said, is one of the most disputed questions in aesthetic. Does the aesthetic fact consist of content alone, or of form alone, or of both together? This question has taken on various meanings, which we shall mention, each in its place. But when these words are taken as signifying what we have above defined, and matter is understood as emotionality not aesthetically elaborated, or impressions, and form as intellectual activity and expression, then our view cannot be in doubt. We must, that is to say, reject both the thesis that makes the aesthetic fact to consist of the content alone (that is, the simple impressions), and the thesis which makes it to consist of a junction between form and content, that is, of impressions plus expressions. In the aesthetic fact, expressive activity is not added to the fact of the impressions, but these latter are formed and elaborated by it. The impressions reappear as it were in expression, like water put into a filter, which reappears the same and yet different on the other side. The aesthetic fact, therefore, is form, and nothing but form.

From this was inferred not that the content is something superfluous (it is, on the contrary, the necessary point of departure for the expressive fact); but that there is no passage from the qualities of the content to those of the form. It has sometimes been thought that the content, in order to be aesthetic, that is to say, transformable into form, should possess some determined or determinable qualities. But were that so, then form and content, expression and impression, would be the same thing. It is true that the content is that which is convertible into form, but it has no determinable qualities until this transformation takes place. We know nothing about it. It does not become aesthetic content before, but only after it has been actually transformed. The aesthetic content has also been defined as the interesting. That is not an untrue statement; it is merely void of meaning. Interesting to what? To the expressive activity? Certainly the expressive activity would not have raised the content to the dignity of form, had it not been interested in it. Being interested is precisely the raising of the content to the dignity of form. But the word *interesting* has also been employed in another and an illegitimate sense, which we shall explain further on.

The proposition that art is imitation of nature has also several meanings. Sometimes truths have been expressed or at least shadowed forth in these words, sometimes errors have been promulgated. More frequently, no definite thought has been expressed at all. One of the scientifically legitimate meanings occurs when *imitation* is understood as representation or intuition of nature, a form of knowledge. And when the phrase is used with this intention, and in order to emphasize the spiritual character of the process, another proposition becomes legitimate also: namely, that art is the idealization or idealizing imitation of nature. But if by imitation of nature be understood that art gives mechanical reproductions, more or less perfect duplicates of natural objects, in the presence of which is renewed the same tumult of impressions as that caused by natural objects, then the proposition is evidently false. The colored waxen effigies that imitate the life, before which we stand astonished in the museums where such things are shown, do not give aesthetic intuitions. Illusion and hallucination have nothing to do with the calm domain of artistic intuition. But on the other hand if an artist paint the interior of a waxwork museum, or if an actor give a burlesque portrait of a man-statue on the stage, we have work of the spirit and artistic intuition. Finally, if photography have in it anything artistic, it will be to the extent that it

---

[5] "Born poet" . . . "man born poet."

transmits the intuition of the photographer, his point of view, the pose and grouping which he has striven to attain. And if photography be not quite an art, that is precisely because the element of nature in it remains more or less unconquered and ineradicable. Do we ever, indeed, feel complete satisfaction before even the best of photographs? Would not an artist vary and touch up much or little, remove or add something to all of them?

The statements repeated so often, that art is not knowledge, that it does not tell the truth, that it does not belong to the world of theory, but to the world of feeling, and so forth, arise from the failure to realize exactly the theoretic character of simple intuition. This simple intuition is quite distinct from intellectual knowledge, as it is distinct from perception of the real; and the statements quoted above arise from the belief that only intellectual cognition is knowledge. We have seen that intuition is knowledge, free from concepts and more simple than the so-called perception of the real. Therefore art is knowledge, form; it does not belong to the world of feeling or to psychic matter. The reason why so many aestheticians have so often insisted that art is appearance (*Schein*), is precisely that they have felt the necessity of distinguishing it from the more complex fact of perception, by maintaining its pure intuitiveness. And if for the same reason it has been claimed that art is feeling the reason is the same. For if the concept as content of art, and historical reality as such, be excluded from the sphere of art, there remains no other content than reality apprehended in all its ingenuousness and immediacy in the vital impulse, in its feeling, that is to say again, pure intuition.

The theory of the aesthetic senses has also arisen from the failure to establish, or from having lost to view, the character of expression as distinct from impression, of form as distinct from matter.

This theory can be reduced to the error just indicated of wishing to find a passage from the qualities of the content to those of the form. To ask, in fact, what the aesthetic senses are, implies asking what sensible impressions are able to enter into aesthetic expressions, and which must of necessity do so. To this we must at once reply, that all impressions can enter into aesthetic expressions or formations, but that none are bound to do so of necessity. Dante raised to the dignity of form not only the "sweet color of the oriental sapphire" (visual impressions), but also tactual or thermic impressions, such as the "dense air" and the "fresh rivulets" which "parch the more" the throat of the thirsty. The belief that a picture yields only visual impressions is a curious illusion. The bloom on a cheek, the warmth of a youthful body, the sweetness and freshness of a fruit, the edge of a sharp knife, are not these, too, impressions obtainable from a picture?

Are they visual? What would a picture mean to an imaginary man, lacking all or many of his senses, who should in an instant acquire the organ of sight alone? The picture we are looking at and believe we see only with our eyes would seem to his eyes to be little more than an artist's paint-smeared palette.

Some who hold firmly to the aesthetic character of certain groups of impressions (for example, the visual and auditive), and exclude others, are nevertheless ready to admit that if visual and auditive impressions enter directly into the aesthetic fact, those of the other senses also enter into it, but only as associated. But this distinction is altogether arbitrary. Aesthetic expression is synthesis, in which it is impossible to distinguish direct and indirect. All impressions are placed by it on a level, in so far as they are aestheticized. A man who absorbs the subject of a picture or poem does not have it before him as a series of impressions, some of which have prerogatives and precedence over the others. He knows nothing as to what has happened prior to having absorbed it, just as, on the other hand, distinctions made after reflection have nothing whatever to do with art as such.

The theory of the aesthetic senses has also been presented in another way; as an attempt to establish what physiological organs are necessary for the aesthetic fact. The physiological organ or apparatus is nothing but a group of cells, constituted and disposed in a particular manner; that is to say, it is a merely physical and natural fact or concept. But expression does not know physiological facts. Expression has its point of departure in the impressions, and the physiological path by which these have found their way to the mind is to it altogether indifferent. One way or another comes to the same thing: it suffices that they should be impressions.

It is true that the want of given organs, that is, of certain groups of cells, prevents the formation of certain impressions (when these are not otherwise obtained through a kind of organic compensation). The man born blind cannot intuit and express light. But the impressions are not conditioned solely by the organ, but also by the stimuli which operate upon the organ. One who has never had the impression of the sea will never be able to express it, in the same way as one who has never had the impression of the life of high society or of the political arena will never express either. This, however, does not prove the dependence of the expressive function on the stimulus or on the organ. It merely repeats what we know already: expression presupposes impression, and particular expressions particular impressions. For the rest, every impression excludes other impressions during the moment in which it dominates; and so does every expression.

Another corollary of the conception of expression as activity is the indivisibility of the work of art. Every expression is a single expression. Activity is a fusion of the impressions in an organic whole. A desire to express this has always prompted the affirmation that the work of art should have unity, or, what amounts to the same thing, unity in variety. Expression is a synthesis of the various, or multiple, in the one.

The fact that we divide a work of art into parts, a poem into scenes, episodes, similes, sentences, or a picture into single figures and objects, background, foreground, etc., may seem opposed to this affirmation. But such division annihilates the work, as dividing the organism into heart, brain, nerves, muscles and so on, turns the living being into a corpse. It is true that there exist organisms in which division gives rise to other living beings, but in such a case we must conclude, maintaining the analogy between the organism and the work of art, that in the latter case too there are numerous germs of life each ready to grow, in a moment, into a single complete expression.

It may be said that expression sometimes arises from other expressions. There are simple and there are compound expressions. One must surely admit some difference between the *eureka,* with which Archimedes expressed all his joy at his discovery, and the expressive act (indeed all the five acts) of a regular tragedy. Not in the least: expression always arises directly from impressions. He who conceives a tragedy puts into a crucible a great quantity, so to say, of impressions: expressions themselves, conceived on other occasions, are fused together with the new in a single mass, in the same way as we can cast into a melting furnace formless pieces of bronze and choicest statuettes. Those choicest statuettes must be melted just like the pieces of bronze, before there can be a new statue. The old expressions must descend again to the level of impressions, in order to be synthesized in a new single expression.

By elaborating his impressions, man frees himself from them. By objectifying them, he removes them from him and makes himself their superior. The liberating and purifying function of art is another aspect and another formula of its character as activity. Activity is the deliverer, just because it drives away passivity.

This also explains why it is usual to attribute to artists both the maximum of sensibility or passion, and the maximum of insensibility or Olympian serenity. The two characters are compatible, for they do not refer to the same object. The sensibility or passion relates to the rich material which the artist absorbs into his psychic organism; the insensibility or serenity to the form with which he subdues and dominates the tumult of the sensations and passions.

A. C. Bradley

1851–1935

In his essay *Poetry for Poetry's Sake* Bradley deals with a number of problems that emerged from the symbolist movement, particularly the work of Mallarmé, and from the expressionistic criticism of Croce. Bradley remarks that all form *is* expression, that there is no such thing as separable form or separable content. The value of a poem cannot lie in its form alone; neither can it be found solely in its content. This is not to say that one subject is as potentially good as another. It is to say that a bad poem can be written on any subject. Poetry should not be confused with life, nor is it, strictly speaking, a copy of life. It has a different mode of being. This idea was developed at greater length by the New Critics, especially Ransom.

Bradley argues that if the poet already knew exactly what he intended to say, then there would be a sense in which it would be unimportant for him to write the poem. It would already be "written." In this argument Bradley seems to emphasize the identity of the Crocean terms *intuition, expression,* and *externalization.* Unlike Croce, Bradley considers externalization an integral part of the working out and discovery of the intuition itself. This idea is later expressed by a number of New Critics, particularly Blackmur in his essay *A Critic's Job of Work.*

Finally, at the end of his essay, Bradley adopts the Mallarméan idea of *suggestion,* by which he seems to mean the peculiar form of universality that inhabits the particulars of poetry. This idea recalls the numerous attempts of the Romantics to define *symbol.*

Bradley's most important critical works are *Shakespearean Tragedy* (1904) and *Oxford Lectures on Poetry* (1909). See Katherine Cooke, *A. C. Bradley and His Influence in Twentieth-Century Shakespeare Criticism* (1972).

From
Poetry for Poetry's Sake

The words *poetry for poetry's sake* recall the famous phrase *art for art*. It is far from my purpose to examine the possible meanings of that phrase, or all the questions it involves. I propose to state briefly what I understand by *poetry for poetry's sake,* and then, after guarding against one or two misapprehensions of the formula, to consider more fully a single problem connected with it. And I must premise, without attempting to justify them, certain explanations. We are to consider poetry in its essence, and apart from the flaws which in most poems accompany their poetry. We are to include in the idea of poetry the metrical form, and not to regard this as a mere accident or a mere vehicle. And, finally, poetry being poems, we are to think of a poem as it actually exists; and, without aiming here at accuracy, we may say that an actual poem is the succession of experiences—sounds, images, thoughts, emotions—through which we pass when we are reading as poetically as we can.[1] Of course this imaginative

---

POETRY FOR POETRY'S SAKE. Bradley's *Poetry for Poetry's Sake* was first published in 1910. The text, complete but for an introductory paragraph, is from *Oxford Lectures on Poetry,* in which the following note by Bradley appeared: "The lecture, as printed in 1901, was preceded by the following note: 'This lecture is printed almost as it was delivered. I am aware that, especially in the earlier pages, difficult subjects are treated in a manner far too summary, but they require an exposition so full that it would destroy the original form of the lecture, while a slight expansion would do little to provide against misunderstandings.' A few verbal changes have now been made, some notes have been added, and some of the introductory remarks omitted." Reprinted by permission of Macmillan & Co., Ltd., St. Martin's Press, and the Macmillan Company of Canada, Ltd.

[1][Bradley] The purpose of this sentence was not, as has been supposed, to give a definition of poetry. To define poetry as something that goes on in us when we read poetically would be absurd indeed. My object was to suggest to my hearers in passing that it is futile to ask questions about the end, or substance, or form of poetry, if we forget that a poem is neither a mere number of black marks on a white page, nor such experience as is evoked in us when we read these marks as we read, let us say, a newspaper article; and I suppose my hearers to know, sufficiently for the purpose of the lecture, how that sort of reading differs from poetical reading.

The truths thus suggested are so obvious, when stated, that I thought a bare reminder of them would be enough. But in fact the mistakes we make about "subject," "substance," "form," and the like, are due not solely to misapprehension of our poetic experience, but to our examining what is not this experience. The whole lecture may be called an expansion of this statement.

The passage to which the present note refers raises difficult questions which any attempt at a "poetics" ought to discuss. I will mention three. (1) If the experience called a poem varies "with every reader and every time of reading" and "exists in innumerable degrees," what is the poem itself, if there is such a thing? (2) How does a series of successive experiences form *one* poem? (3) If the object in the case of poetry and music ("arts of hearing") is a succession somehow and to some extent unified, how does it differ in this respect from the object in "arts of sight"—a building, a statue, a picture?

---

experience—if I may use the phrase for brevity—differs with every reader and every time of reading: a poem exists in innumerable degrees. But that insurmountable fact lies in the nature of things and does not concern us now.

What then does the formula *poetry for poetry's sake* tell us about this experience? It says, as I understand it, these things. First, this experience is an end in itself, is worth having on its own account, has an intrinsic value. Next, its *poetic* value is this intrinsic worth alone. Poetry may have also an ulterior value as a means to culture or religion; because it conveys instruction, or softens the passions, or furthers a good cause; because it brings the poet fame or money or a quiet conscience. So much the better: let it be valued for these reasons too. But its ulterior worth neither is nor can directly determine its poetic worth as a satisfying imaginative experience; and this is to be judged entirely from within. And to these two positions the formula would add, though not of necessity, a third. The consideration of ulterior ends, whether by the poet in the act of composing or by the reader in the act of experiencing, tends to lower poetic value. It does so because it tends to change the nature of poetry by taking it out of its own atmosphere. For its nature is to be not a part, nor yet a copy, of the real world (as we commonly understand that phrase), but to be a world by itself, independent, complete, autonomous; and to possess it fully you must enter that world, conform to its laws, and ignore for the time the beliefs, aims, and particular conditions which belong to you in the other world of reality.

Of the more serious misapprehensions to which these statements may give rise I will glance only at one or two. The offensive consequences often drawn from the formula *art for art* will be found to attach not to the doctrine that art is an end in itself, but to the doctrine that art is the whole or supreme end of human life. And as this latter doctrine, which seems to me absurd, is in any case quite different from the former, its consequences fall outside my subject. The formula *poetry is an end in itself* has nothing to say on the various questions of moral judgment which arise from the fact that poetry has its place in a many-sided life. For anything it says, the intrinsic value of poetry might be so small, and its ulterior effects so mischievous, that it had better not exist. The formula only tells us that we must not place in antithesis poetry and human good, for poetry is one kind of human good; and that we must not determine the intrinsic value of this kind of good by direct reference to another. If we do, we shall find ourselves maintaining what we did not expect. If poetic value lies in the stimulation of religious feelings, *Lead, Kindly Light* is no better a poem than many a tasteless version of a psalm: if in the excitement of patriotism, why is *Scots, Wha Hae* superior to *We Don't Want to*

Fight?: if in the mitigation of the passions, the odes of Sappho will win but little praise: if in instruction, Armstrong's *Art of Preserving Health* should win much.

Again, our formula may be accused of cutting poetry away from its connection with life. And this accusation raises so huge a problem that I must ask leave to be dogmatic as well as brief. There is plenty of connection between life and poetry, but it is, so to say, a connection underground. The two may be called different forms of the same thing: one of them having (in the usual sense) reality, but seldom fully satisfying imagination; while the other offers something which satisfies imagination but has not full "reality." They are parallel developments which nowhere meet, or, if I may use loosely a word which will be serviceable later, they are analogues. Hence we understand one by help of the other, and even, in a sense, care for one because of the other; but hence also, poetry neither is life, nor, strictly speaking, a copy of it. They differ not only because one has more mass and the other a more perfect shape, but because they have different *kinds* of existence. The one touches us as beings occupying a given position in space and time, and having feelings, desires, and purposes due to that position: it appeals to imagination, but appeals to much besides. What meets us in poetry has not a position in the same series of time and space, or, if it has or had such a position, it is taken apart from much that belonged to it there;[2] and therefore it makes no direct appeal to those feelings, desires, and purposes, but speaks only to contemplative imagination—imagination the reverse of empty or emotionless, imagination saturated with the results of "real" experience, but still contemplative. Thus, no doubt, one main reason why poetry has poetic value for us is that it presents to us in its own way something which we meet in another form in nature or life; and yet the test of its poetic value for us lies simply in the question whether it satisfies our imagination; the rest of us, our knowledge or conscience, for example, judging it only so far as they appear transmuted in our imagination. So also Shakespeare's knowledge or his moral insight, Milton's greatness of soul, Shelley's "hate of hate" and "love of love," and that desire to help men or make them happier which may have influenced a poet in hours of meditation—all these have, as such, no poetical worth: they have that worth only when, passing through the unity of the poet's being, they reappear as qualities of imagination, and then are indeed mighty powers in the world of poetry.

I come to a third misapprehension, and so to my main subject. This formula, it is said, empties poetry of its meaning: it is really a doctrine of form for form's sake. "It is of no consequence what a poet says, so long as he says the thing well. The *what* is poetically indifferent: it is the *how* that counts. Matter, subject, content, substance, determines nothing; there is no subject with which poetry may not deal: the form, the treatment, is everything. Nay, more: not only is the matter indifferent, but it is the secret of art to 'eradicate the matter by means of the form,' "—phrases and statements like these meet us everywhere in current criticism of literature and the other arts. They are the stock-in-trade of writers who understand of them little more than the fact that somehow or other they are not "bourgeois." But we find them also seriously used by writers whom we must respect, whether they are anonymous or not; something like one or another of them might be quoted, for example, from Professor Saintsbury, the late R. A. M. Stevenson, Schiller, Goethe himself; and they are the watchwords of a school in the one country where aesthetics has flourished. They come, as a rule, from men who either practice one of the arts, or, from study of it, are interested in its methods. The general reader—a being so general that I may say what I will of him—is outraged by them. He feels that he is being robbed of almost all that he cares for in a work of art. "You are asking me," he says, "to look at the Dresden Madonna as if it were a Persian rug. You are telling me that the poetic value of *Hamlet* lies solely in its style and versification, and that my interest in the man and his fate is only an intellectual or moral interest. You allege that, if I want to enjoy the poetry of *Crossing the Bar,* I must not mind what Tennyson says there, but must consider solely his way of saying it. But in

---

[2][Bradley] A lyric, for example, may arise from "real" emotions due to transitory conditions peculiar to the poet. But these emotions and conditions, however interesting biographically, are poetically irrelevant. The poem, what the poet *says,* is universal, and is appropriated by people who live centuries after him and perhaps know nothing of him and his life; and if it arose from mere imagination it is none the worse (or the better) for that. So far as it cannot be appropriated without a knowledge of the circumstances in which it arose, it is probably, so far, faulty (probably, because the difficulty *may* come from our distance from the whole mental world of the poet's time and country).

What is said in the text applies equally to all the arts. It applies also to such aesthetic apprehension as does not issue in a work of art. It applies also to this apprehension whether the object belongs to "nature" or to "man." A beautiful landscape is not a "real" landscape. Much that belongs to the "real" landscape is ignored when it is apprehended aesthetically: and the painter only carries this unconscious idealization further when he deliberately alters the "real" landscape in further ways.

All this does not in the least imply that the "real" thing, where there is one (personal emotion, landscape, historical event, etc.), is of small importance to the aesthetic apprehension or the work of art. But it is relevant only as it appears *in* that apprehension or work.

If an artist alters a reality (e.g. a well-known scene or historical character) so much that his product clashes violently with our familiar ideas, he may be making a mistake: not because his product is untrue to the reality (this by itself is perfectly irrelevant), but because the "untruth" may make it difficult or impossible for others to appropriate his product, or because this product may be aesthetically inferior to the reality even as it exists in the general imagination.

that case I can care no more for a poem than I do for a set of nonsense verses; and I do not believe that the authors of *Hamlet* and *Crossing the Bar* regarded their poems thus."

These antitheses of subject, matter, substance on the one side, form, treatment, handling on the other, are the field through which I especially want, in this lecture, to indicate a way. It is a field of battle; and the battle is waged for no trivial cause; but the cries of the combatants are terribly ambiguous. Those phrases of the so-called formalist may each mean five or six different things. Taken in one sense they seem to me chiefly true; taken as the general reader not unnaturally takes them, they seem to me false and mischievous. It would be absurd to pretend that I can end in a few minutes a controversy which concerns the ultimate nature of art, and leads perhaps to problems not yet soluble; but we can at least draw some plain distinctions which, in this controversy, are too often confused.

In the first place, then, let us take *subject* in one particular sense; let us understand by it that which we have in view when, looking at the title of an unread poem, we say that the poet has chosen this or that for his subject. The subject, in this sense, so far as I can discover, is generally something, real or imaginary, as it exists in the minds of fairly cultivated people. The subject of *Paradise Lost* would be the story of the Fall as that story exists in the general imagination of a Bible-reading people. The subject of Shelley's stanzas *To a Skylark* would be the ideas which arise in the mind of an educated person when, without knowing the poem, he hears the word *skylark*. If the title of a poem conveys little or nothing to us, the "subject" appears to be either what we should gather by investigating the title in a dictionary or other book of the kind, or else such a brief suggestion as might be offered by a person who had read the poem, and who said, for example, that the subject of *The Ancient Mariner* was a sailor who killed an albatross and suffered for his deed.

Now the subject, in this sense (and I intend to use the word in no other), is not, as such, inside the poem, but outside it. The contents of the stanzas *To a Skylark* are not the ideas suggested by the word *skylark* to the average man; they belong to Shelley just as much as the language does. The subject, therefore, is not the matter *of* the poem at all; and its opposite is not the *form* of the poem, but the whole poem. The subject is one thing; the poem, matter and form alike, another thing. This being so, it is surely obvious that the poetic values cannot lie in the subject, but lies entirely in its opposite, the poem. How can the subject determine the value when on one and the same subject poems may be written of all degrees of merit and demerit; or when a perfect poem may be composed on a subject so slight as a pet sparrow, and, if Macaulay may be trusted, a nearly worthless poem on

a subject so stupendous as the omnipresence of the Deity? The "formalist" is here perfectly right. Nor is he insisting on something unimportant. He is fighting against our tendency to take the work of art as a mere copy or reminder of something already in our heads, or at the best as a suggestion of some idea as little removed as possible from the familiar. The sightseer who promenades a picture gallery, remarking that this portrait is so like his cousin, or that landscape the very image of his birthplace, or who, after satisfying himself that one picture is about Elijah, passes on rejoicing to discover the subject, and nothing but the subject, of the next— what is he but an extreme example of this tendency? Well, but the very same tendency vitiates much of our criticism, much criticism of Shakespeare, for example, which, with all its cleverness and partial truth, still shows that the critic never passed from his own mind into Shakespeare's; and it may be traced even in so fine a critic as Coleridge, as when he dwarfs the sublime struggle of Hamlet into the image of his own unhappy weakness. Hazlitt by no means escaped its influence. Only the third of that great trio, Lamb, appears almost always to have rendered the conception of the composer.

Again, it is surely true that we cannot determine beforehand what subjects are fit for art, or name any subject on which a good poem might not possibly be written. To divide subjects into two groups, the beautiful or elevating, and the ugly or vicious, and to judge poems according as their subjects belong to one of these groups or the other, is to fall into the same pit, to confuse with our preconceptions the meaning of the poet. What the thing is in the poem he is to be judged by, not by the thing as it was before he touched it; and how can we venture to say beforehand that he cannot make a true poem out of something which to us was merely alluring or dull or revolting? The question whether, having done so, he ought to publish his poem; whether the thing in the poet's work will not be still confused by the incompetent Puritan or the incompetent sensualist with the thing in *his* mind, does not touch this point: it is a further question, one of ethics, not of art. No doubt the upholders of *art for art's sake* will generally be in favor of the courageous course, of refusing to sacrifice the better or stronger part of the public to the weaker or worse; but their maxim in no way binds them to this view. Rossetti suppressed one of the best of his sonnets, a sonnet chosen for admiration by Tennyson, himself extremely sensitive about the moral effect of poetry; suppressed it, I believe, because it was called fleshly.[3] One

---

[3] See Robert Buchanan's attack on Rossetti, *The Fleshly School of Poetry* (1871).

may regret Rossetti's judgment and at the same time respect his scrupulousness; but in any case he judged in his capacity of citizen, not in his capacity of artist.

So far then the "formalist" appears to be right. But he goes too far, I think, if he maintains that the subject is indifferent and that all subjects are the same to poetry. And he does not prove his point by observing that a good poem might be written on a pin's head, and a bad one on the Fall of Man. That truth shows that the subject *settles* nothing, but not that it counts for nothing. The Fall of Man is really a more favorable subject than a pin's head. The Fall of Man, that is to say, offers opportunities of poetic effects wider in range and more penetrating in appeal. And the fact is that such a subject, as it exists in the general imagination, has some aesthetic value before the poet touches it. It is, as you may choose to call it, an inchoate poem or the debris of a poem. It is not an abstract idea or a bare isolated fact, but an assemblage of figures, scenes, actions, and events, which already appeal to emotional imagination; and it is already in some degree organized and formed. In spite of this a bad poet would make a bad poem on it; but then we should say he was unworthy of the subject. And we should not say this if he wrote a bad poem on a pin's head. Conversely, a good poem on a pin's head would almost certainly transform its subject far more than a good poem on the Fall of Man. It might revolutionize its subject so completely that we should say, "The subject may be a pin's head, but the substance of the poem has very little to do with it."

This brings us to another and a different antithesis. Those figures, scenes, events, that form part of the subject called the Fall of Man, are not the substance of *Paradise Lost;* but in *Paradise Lost* there are figures, scenes, and events resembling them in some degree. These, with much more of the same kind, may be described as its substance, and may then be contrasted with the measured language of the poem, which will be called its form. Subject is the opposite not of form but of the whole poem. Substance is within the poem, and its opposite, form, is also within the poem. I am not criticizing this antithesis at present, but evidently it is quite different from the other. It is practically the distinction used in the old-fashioned criticism of epic and drama, and it flows down, not unsullied, from Aristotle. Addison, for example, in examining *Paradise Lost* considers in order the fable, the characters, and the sentiments; these will be the substance: then he considers the language, that is, the style and numbers; this will be the form. In like manner, the substance or meaning of a lyric may be distinguished from the form.

Now I believe it will be found that a large part of the controversy we are dealing with arises from a confusion be-

tween these two distinctions of substance and form, and of subject and poem. The extreme formalist lays his whole weight on the form because he thinks its opposite is the mere subject. The general reader is angry, but makes the same mistake, and gives to the subject praises that rightly belong to the substance.[4] I will read an example of what I mean. I can only explain the following words of a good critic by supposing that for the moment he has fallen into this confusion:

> The mere matter of all poetry—to wit, the appearances of nature and the thoughts and feelings of men—being unalterable, it follows that the difference between poet and poet will depend upon the manner of each in applying language, meter, rhyme, cadence, and what not, to this invariable material.

What has become here of the substance of *Paradise Lost*—the story, scenery, characters, sentiments, as they are in the poem? They have vanished clean away. Nothing is left but the form on one side, and on the other not even the subject, but a supposed invariable material, the appearances of nature and the thoughts and feelings of men. Is it surprising that the whole value should then be found in the form?

So far we have assumed that this antithesis of substance and form is valid, and that it always has one meaning. In reality it has several, but we will leave it in its present shape, and pass to the question of its validity. And this question we are compelled to raise, because we have to deal with the two contentions that the poetic value lies wholly or mainly in the substance, and that it lies wholly or mainly in the form. Now these contentions, whether false or true, may seem at least to be clear; but we shall find, I think, that they are both of them false, or both of them nonsense: false if they concern anything outside the poem, nonsense if they apply to something in it. For what do they evidently imply? They imply that there are in a poem two parts, factors, or components, a substance and a form; and that you can conceive them distinctly and separately, so that when you are speaking of the one you are not speaking of the other. Otherwise, how can you ask the question, in which of them does the value lie? But really in a poem, apart from defects, there are no such factors or components; and therefore it is strictly nonsense to ask in which of them the value lies. And on the other hand, if the

---

[4][Bradley] What is here called *substance* is what people generally mean when they use the word *subject* and insist on the value of the subject. I am not arguing against this usage, or in favor of the usage which I have adopted for the sake of clearness. It does not matter which we employ, so long as we and others know what we mean. (I use *substance* and *content* indifferently.)

substance and the form referred to are not in the poem, then both the contentions are false, for its poetic value lies in itself.

What I mean is neither new nor mysterious; and it will be clear, I believe, to anyone who reads poetry poetically and who closely examines his experience. When you are reading a poem, I would ask—not analyzing it, and much less criticizing it, but allowing it, as it proceeds, to make its full impression on you through the exertion of your recreating imagination—do you then apprehend and enjoy as one thing a certain meaning or substance, and as another thing certain articulate sounds, and do you somehow compound these two? Surely you do not, any more than you apprehend apart, when you see someone smile, those lines in the face which express a feeling, and the feeling that the lines express. Just as there the lines and their meaning are to you one thing, not two, so in poetry the meaning and the sounds are one: there is, if I may put it so, a resonant meaning, or a meaning resonance. If you read the line, "The sun is warm, the sky is clear," you do not experience separately the image of a warm sun and clear sky, on the one side, and certain unintelligible rhythmical sounds on the other; nor yet do you experience them together, side by side; but you experience the one *in* the other. And in like manner, when you are really reading *Hamlet,* the action and the characters are not something which you conceive apart from the words; you apprehend them from point to point *in* the words, and the words as expressions of them. Afterwards, no doubt, when you are out of the poetic experience but remember it, you may by analysis decompose this unity, and attend to a substance more or less isolated, and a form more or less isolated. But these are things in your analytic head, not in the poem, which is *poetic* experience. And if you want to have the poem again, you cannot find it by adding together these two products of decomposition; you can only find it by passing back into poetic experience. And then what you recover is no aggregate of factors, it is a unity in which you can no more separate a substance and a form than you can separate living blood and the life in the blood. This unity has, if you like, various "aspects" or "sides," but they are not factors or parts; if you try to examine one, you find it is also the other. Call them substance and form if you please, but these are not the reciprocally exclusive substance and form to which the two contentions *must* refer. They do not "agree," for they are not apart: they are one thing from different points of view, and in that sense identical. And this identity of content and form, you will say, is no accident; it is of the essence of poetry insofar as it is poetry, and of all art insofar as it is art. Just as there is in music not sound on one side and a meaning on the other, but expressive sound, and if you ask what is the meaning you

can only answer by pointing to the sounds; just as in painting there is not a meaning *plus* paint, but a meaning *in* paint, or significant paint, and no man can really express the meaning in any other way than in paint and in *this* paint; so in a poem the true content and the true form neither exist nor can be imagined apart. When then you are asked whether the value of a poem lies in a substance got by decomposing the poem, and present, as such, only in reflective analysis, or whether the value lies in a form arrived at and existing in the same way, you will answer, "It lies neither in one, nor in the other, nor in any addition of them, but in the poem, where they are not."

We have then, first, an antithesis of subject and poem. This is clear and valid; and the question in which of them does the value lie is intelligible; and its answer is, in the poem. We have next a distinction of substance and form. If the substance means ideas, images, and the like taken alone, and the form means the measured language taken by itself, this is a possible distinction, but it is a distinction of things not in the poem, and the value lies in neither of them. If substance and form mean anything *in* the poem, then each is involved in the other, and the question in which of them the value lies has no sense. No doubt you may say, speaking loosely, that in this poet or poem the aspect of substance is the more noticeable, and in that the aspect of form; and you may pursue interesting discussions on this basis, though no principle or ultimate question of value is touched by them. And apart from that question, of course, I am not denying the usefulness and necessity of the distinction. We cannot dispense with it. To consider separately the action or the characters of a play, and separately its style or versification, is both legitimate and valuable, so long as we remember what we are doing. But the true critic in speaking of these apart does not really think of them apart; the whole, the poetic experience, of which they are but aspects, is always in his mind; and he is always aiming at a richer, truer, more intense repetition of that experience. On the other hand, when the question of principle, of poetic value, is raised, these aspects *must* fall apart into components, separately conceivable; and then there arise two heresies, equally false, that the value lies in one of two things, both of which are outside the poem, and therefore where its value cannot lie.

On the heresy of the separable substance a few additional words will suffice. This heresy is seldom formulated, but perhaps some unconscious holder of it may object: "Surely the action and the characters of *Hamlet* are in the play; and surely I can retain these, though I have forgotten all the words. I admit that I do not possess the whole poem, but I possess a part, and the most important part." And I would answer: "If we are not concerned with any question of principle, I accept all that you say except the last words, which do raise such a question. Speaking loosely, I agree that the action and characters, as you perhaps conceive them, together with a great deal more, are in the poem. Even then, however, you must not claim to possess all of this kind that is in the poem; for in forgetting the words you must have lost innumerable details of the action and the characters. And, when the question of value is raised, I must insist that the action and characters, as you conceive them, are not in *Hamlet* at all. If they are, point them out. You cannot do it. What you find at any moment of that succession of experiences called *Hamlet* is words. In these words, to speak loosely again, the action and characters (more of them than you can conceive apart) are focused; but your experience is not a combination of them, as ideas, on the one side, with certain sounds on the other; it is an experience of something in which the two are indissolubly fused. If you deny this, to be sure I can make no answer, or can only answer that I have reason to believe that you cannot read poetically, or else are misinterpreting your experience. But if you do not deny this, then you will admit that the action and characters of the poem, as you separately imagine them, are no part of it, but a product of it in your reflective imagination, a faint analogue of one aspect of it taken in detachment from the whole. Well, I do not dispute, I would even insist, that, in the case of so long a poem as *Hamlet,* it may be necessary from time to time to interrupt the poetic experience, in order to enrich it by forming such a product and dwelling on it. Nor, in a wide sense of *poetic,* do I question the poetic value of this product, as you think of it apart from the poem. It resembles our recollections of the heroes of history or legend, who move about in our imaginations, 'forms more real than living man,' and are worth much to us though we do not remember anything they said. Our ideas and images of the 'substance' of a poem have this poetic value, and more, if they are at all adequate. But they cannot determine the poetic value of the poem, for (not to speak of the competing claims of the 'form') nothing that is outside the poem can do that, and they, as such, are outside it."[5]

Let us turn to the so-called form—style and versification. There is no such thing as mere form in poetry. All form is expression. Style may have indeed a certain aesthetic worth in partial abstraction from the particular matter it conveys, as in a well-built sentence you may take pleasure in the build almost apart from the meaning. Even so, style is expressive—presents to sense, for example, the order, ease, and rapidity with which ideas move in the writer's mind—but it is not expressive of the meaning of that particular sentence. And it is possible, interrupting poetic experience, to decompose it and abstract for comparatively separate consideration this nearly formal element of style. But the aesthetic value of style so taken is not considerable;[6] you could not read with pleasure for an hour a composition which had no other merit. And in poetic experience you never apprehend this value by itself; the style is here expressive also of a particular meaning, or rather is one aspect of that unity whose other aspect is meaning. So that what you apprehend may be called indifferently an expressed meaning or a significant form. Perhaps on this point I may in Oxford appeal to authority, that of Matthew Arnold and Walter Pater, the latter at any rate an authority whom the formalist will not despise. What is the gist of Pater's teaching about style, if it is not that in the end the one virtue of style is truth or adequacy; that the word, phrase, sentence, should express perfectly the writer's perception, feeling, image, or thought; so that, as we read a descriptive phrase of Keats's, we exclaim, "That is the thing itself"; so that, to quote Arnold, the words are "symbols equivalent with the thing symbolized," or, in our technical language, a form identical with its content? Hence in true poetry it is, in strictness, impossible to express the meaning in any but its own words, or to change the words without changing the meaning. A translation of such poetry is not really the old meaning in a fresh dress; it is a new product, something like the poem, though, if one chooses to say so, more like it in the aspect of meaning than in the aspect of form.

No one who understands poetry, it seems to me, would dispute this, were it not that, falling away from his experience, or misled by theory, he takes the word *meaning* in a sense almost ludicrously inapplicable to poetry. People say, for instance, *steed* and *horse* have the same meaning; and in bad poetry they have, but not in poetry that *is* poetry. "'Bring forth the horse!' The horse was brought: / In truth he was a noble steed!" says Byron in *Mazeppa.* If the two words mean the same here, transpose them: "'Bring forth the steed!' The steed was brought: / In truth he was a noble horse!" and ask again if they mean the same. Or let me take a line certainly very free from "poetic diction": "To be or

---

[5][Bradley] These remarks will hold good, *mutatis mutandis,* if by *substance* is understood the "moral" or the "idea" of a poem, although perhaps in one instance out of five thousand this may be found in so many words in the poem.

[6][Bradley] On the other hand, the absence, or worse than absence, of style, in this sense, is a serious matter.

not to be, that is the question."[7] You may say that this means the same as "What is just now occupying my attention is the comparative disadvantages of continuing to live or putting an end to myself." And for practical purposes—the purpose, for example, of a coroner—it does. But as the second version altogether misrepresents the speaker at that moment of his existence, while the first does represent him, how can they for any but a practical or logical purpose be said to have the same sense? Hamlet was well able to "unpack his heart with words," but he will not unpack it with our paraphrases.

These considerations apply equally to versification. If I take the famous line which describes how the souls of the dead stood waiting by the river, imploring a passage from Charon: *"Tendebantque manus ripae ulterioris amore;"*[8] and if I translate it, "and were stretching forth their hands in longing for the further bank," the charm of the original has fled. Why has it fled? Partly (but we have dealt with that) because I have substituted for five words, and those the words of Virgil, twelve words, and those my own. In some measure because I have turned into rhythmless prose a line of verse which, as mere sound, has unusual beauty. But much more because in doing so I have also changed the *meaning* of Virgil's line. What that meaning is *I* cannot say: Virgil has said it. But I can see this much, that the translation conveys a far less vivid picture of the outstretched hands and of their remaining outstretched, and a far less poignant sense of the distance of the shore and the longing of the souls. And it does so partly because this picture and this sense are conveyed not only by the obvious meaning of the words, but through the long-drawn sound of *"tendebantque,"* through the time occupied by the five syllables and therefore by the idea of *"ulterioris,"* and through the identity of the long sound *or* in the penultimate syllables of *"ulterioris amore"*—all this, and much more, apprehended not in this analytical fashion, nor as *added* to the beauty of mere sound and to the obvious meaning, but in unity with them and so as expressive of the poetic meaning of the whole.

It is always so in fine poetry. The value of versification, when it is indissolubly fused with meaning, can hardly be exaggerated. The gift for feeling it, even more perhaps than the gift for feeling the value of style, is the *specific* gift for poetry, as distinguished from other arts. But versification, taken, as far as possible, all by itself, has a very different worth. Some aesthetic worth it has; how much, you may experience by reading poetry in a language of which you do

not understand a syllable.[9] The pleasure is quite appreciable, but it is not great; nor in actual poetic experience do you meet with it, as such, at all. For, I repeat, it is not *added* to the pleasure of the meaning when you read poetry that you do understand: by some mystery the music is then the music *of* the meaning, and the two are one. However fond of versification you might be, you would tire very soon of reading verses in Chinese; and before long of reading Virgil and Dante if you were ignorant of their languages. But take the music as it is *in* the poem, and there is a marvelous change. Now "It gives a very echo to the seat / Where love is throned;"[10] or "carries far into your heart," almost like music itself, the sound "Of old, unhappy, far-off things / And battles long ago."[11]

What then is to be said of the following sentence of the critic quoted before: "But when anyone who knows what poetry is reads 'Our noisy years seem moments in the being / Of the eternal silence,'[12] he sees that, quite independently of the meaning, . . . there is one note added to the articulate music of the world—a note that never will leave off resounding till the eternal silence itself gulfs it"? I must think that the writer is deceiving himself. For I could quite understand his enthusiasm, if it were an enthusiasm for the music of the meaning; but as for the music, "quite independently of the meaning," so far as I can hear it thus (and I doubt if anyone who knows English can quite do so), I find it gives some pleasure, but only a trifling pleasure. And indeed I venture to doubt whether, considered as mere sound, the words are at all exceptionally beautiful, as Virgil's line certainly is.

When poetry answers to its idea and is purely or almost purely poetic, we find the identity of form and content; and

---

[9][Bradley] For the purpose of the experiment you must, of course, know the sounds denoted by the letters, and you must be able to make out the rhythmical scheme. But the experiment will be vitiated if you get someone who understands the language to read or recite to you poems written in it, for he will certainly so read or recite as to convey to you something of the meaning through the sound (I do not refer of course to the logical meaning).

Hence it is clear that, if by *versification taken by itself* one means the versification of a *poem,* it is impossible under the requisite conditions to get at this versification by itself. The versification of a poem is always, to speak loosely, influenced by the sense. The bare metrical scheme, to go no further, is practically never followed by the poet. Suppose yourself to know no English, and to perceive merely that in its general scheme "It gives a very echo to the seat" is an iambic line of five feet; and then read the line as you would have to read it; and then ask if *that* noise is the sound of the line *in the poem.*

In the text, therefore, more is admitted than in strictness should be admitted. For I have assumed for the moment that you can hear the sound of poetry if you read poetry which you do not in the least understand, whereas in fact that sound cannot be produced at all except by a person who knows something of the meaning.

[10]*Twelfth Night,* II. iv. 20–21.
[11]Wordsworth, *The Solitary Reaper,* 19–20.
[12]Wordsworth, *Ode: Intimations of Immortality,* 159–60.

---

[7]*Hamlet,* III. i. 56.
[8]*Aeneid,* VI. 314.

the degree of purity attained may be tested by the degree in which we feel it hopeless to convey the effect of a poem or passage in any form but its own. Where the notion of doing so is simply ludicrous, you have quintessential poetry. But a great part even of good poetry, especially in long works, is of a mixed nature; and so we find in it no more than a partial agreement of a form and substance which remain to some extent distinct. This is so in many passages of Shakespeare (the greatest of poets when he chose, but not always a conscientious poet); passages where something was wanted for the sake of the plot, but he did not care about it or was hurried. The conception of the passage is then distinct from the execution, and neither is inspired. This is so also, I think, wherever we can truly speak of merely decorative effect. We seem to perceive that the poet had a truth or fact—philosophical, agricultural, social—distinctly before him, and then, as we say, clothed it in metrical and colored language. Most argumentative, didactic, or satiric poems are partly of this kind; and in imaginative poems anything which is really a mere "conceit" is mere decoration. We often deceive ourselves in this matter, for what we call decoration has often a new and genuinely poetic content of its own; but wherever there is mere decoration, we judge the poetry to be not wholly poetic. And so when Wordsworth inveighed against poetic diction, though he hurled his darts rather wildly, what he was rightly aiming at was a phraseology, not the living body of a new content, but the mere worn-out body of an old one.[13]

In pure poetry it is otherwise. Pure poetry is not the decoration of a preconceived and clearly defined matter: it springs from the creative impulse of a vague imaginative mass pressing for development and definition. If the poet already knew exactly what he meant to say, why should he write the poem? The poem would in fact already be written. For only its completion can reveal, even to him, exactly what he wanted. When he began and while he was at work, he did not possess his meaning; it possessed him. It was not a fully formed soul asking for a body: it was an inchoate soul in the inchoate body of perhaps two or three vague ideas and a few scattered phrases. The growing of this body into its full stature and perfect shape was the same thing as the gradual self-definition of the meaning.[14] And this is the reason why such

---

[13]See Wordsworth, Preface to the *Lyrical Ballads,* p. 438. [Bradley] This paragraph has not, to my knowledge, been adversely criticized, but it now appears to me seriously misleading. It refers to certain kinds of poetry, and again to certain passages in poems, which we feel to be less poetical than some other kinds or passages. But this difference of degree in poeticalness (if I may use the word) is put as a difference between "mixed" and "pure" poetry; and that distinction is, I think, unreal and mischievous. Further, it is implied that in less poetical poetry there necessarily is only a partial unity of content and form. This (unless I am now mistaken) is a mistake, and a mistake due to failure to hold fast the main idea of the lecture. Naturally it would be most agreeable to me to rewrite the paragraph, but if I reprint it and expose my errors the reader will perhaps be helped to a firmer grasp of that idea.

It is true that where poetry is most poetic we feel most decidedly how impossible it is to separate content and form. But where poetry is less poetic and does not make us feel this unity so decidedly, it does not follow that the unity is imperfect. Failure or partial failure in this unity is always (as in the case of Shakespeare referred to) a failure on the part of the *poet* (though it is not always due to the same causes). It does not lie of necessity in the nature of a particular kind of poetry (e.g. satire) or in the nature of a particular passage. All poetry cannot be equally poetic, but *all* poetry ought to maintain the unity of content and form, and, in that sense, to be "pure." Only in certain kinds, and in certain passages, it is more difficult for the poet to maintain it than in others.

Let us take first the "passages" and suppose them to occur in one of the more poetic kinds of poetry. In certain parts of any epic or tragedy matter has to be treated which, though necessary to the whole, is not in itself favorable to poetry, or would not in itself be a good "subject." But it is the busi-

---

ness of the poet to do his best to make this matter poetry, and pure poetry. And, if he succeeds, the passage, though it will probably be less poetic than the bulk of the poem, will exhibit the complete unity of content and form. It will not strike us as a mere bridge between other passages, it will be enjoyable for itself; and it will not occur to us to think that the poet was dealing with an unpoetic "matter" and found his task difficult or irksome. Shakespeare frequently does not trouble himself to face this problem and leaves an imperfect unity. The conscientious artists, like Virgil, Milton, Tennyson, habitually face it and frequently solve it. (In Schiller's phrase, they have extirpated the mere "matter." We often say that they do this by dint of style. This is roughly true, but in strictness it means, as we have seen, not that they decorate the mere "matter" with a mere "form," but that they produce a new content-form.) And when they wholly or partially fail, the fault is still *theirs*. It is, in one sense, due to the "matter," which set a hard problem; but they would be the first to declare that *nothing* in the poem ought to be only mixedly poetic.

In the same way, satire is not in its nature a highly poetic kind of poetry, but it ought, in its own kind, to be poetry throughout, and therefore ought not to show a merely partial unity of content and form. If the satirist makes us exclaim "This is sheer prose wonderfully well disguised," that is a fault, and *his* fault (unless it happens to be ours). The idea that a tragedy or lyric could really be reproduced in a form not its own strikes us as ridiculous; the idea that a satire could so be reproduced seems much less ridiculous; but if it were true the satire would not be poetry at all.

The reader will now see where, in my judgment, the paragraph is wrong. Elsewhere it is, I think, right, though it deals with a subject far too large for a paragraph. This is also true of the next paragraph, which uses the false distinction of "pure" and "mixed," and which will hold in various degrees of poetry in various degrees poetical.

It is of course possible to use a distinction of "pure" and "mixed" in another sense. Poetry, whatever its kind, would be pure as far as it preserved the unity of content and form; mixed, so far as it failed to do so—in other words, failed to be poetry and was partly prosaic.

[14][Bradley] It is possible therefore that the poem, as it existed at certain stages in its growth, may correspond roughly with the poem as it exists in the memories of various readers. A reader who is fond of the poem and often thinks of it, but remembers only half the words and perhaps fills up the gaps with his own words, may possess something like the poem as it was when half-made. There are readers again who retain only what they would call the "idea" of the poem; and the poem may have begun from such an idea. Others will forget all the words, and will not profess to remember even the "meaning," but believe that they possess the "spirit" of the poem. And what they possess may have, I think, an immense value. The poem, of course, it is not; but it may answer to the state of imaginative feeling or emotional imagination which was the germ of the poem. This is, in one sense, quite definite: it would not be the germ of a decidedly different poem: but in an-

poems strike us as creations, not manufactures, and have the magical effect which mere decoration cannot produce. This is also the reason why, if we insist on asking for the meaning of such a poem, we can only be answered "It means itself."

And so at last I may explain why I have troubled myself and you with what may seem an arid controversy about mere words. It is not so. These heresies which would make poetry a compound of two factors—a matter common to it with the merest prose, *plus* a poetic form, as the one heresy says: a poetical substance *plus* a negligible form, as the other says— are not only untrue, they are injurious to the dignity of poetry. In an age already inclined to shrink from those higher realms where poetry touches religion and philosophy, the formalist heresy encourages men to taste poetry as they would a fine wine, which has indeed an aesthetic value, but a small one. And then the natural man, finding an empty form, hurls into it the matter of cheap pathos, rancid sentiment, vulgar humor, bare lust, ravenous vanity—everything which, in Schiller's phrase,[15] the form should extirpate, but which no mere form can extirpate. And the other heresy— which is indeed rather a practice than a creed—encourages us in the habit so dear to us of putting our own thoughts or fancies into the place of the poet's creation. What he meant by *Hamlet*, or the *Ode to a Nightingale*, or *Abt Vogler*, we say, is this or that which we knew already; and so we lose what he had to tell us. But he meant what he said, and said what he meant.

Poetry in this matter is not, as good critics of painting and music often affirm, different from the other arts; in all of them the content is one thing with the form. What Beethoven meant by his symphony, or Turner by his picture, was not something which you can name, but the picture and the symphony. Meaning they have, but *what* meaning can be said in no language but their own: and we know this, though some strange delusion makes us think the meaning has less worth because we cannot put it into words. Well, it is just the same with poetry. But because poetry is words, we vainly fancy that some other words than its own will express its meaning. And they will do so no more—or, if you like to speak loosely, only a trifle more—than words will express the meaning of the Dresden Madonna.[16] Something a little like

it they may indeed express. And we may find analogues of the meaning of poetry outside it, which may help us to appropriate it. The other arts, the best ideas of philosophy or religion, much that nature and life offer us or force upon us, are akin to it. But they are only akin. Nor is it the expression of them. Poetry does not present to imagination our highest knowledge or belief, and much less our dreams and opinions; but it, content and form in unity, embodies in its own irreplaceable way something which embodies itself also in other irreplaceable ways, such as philosophy or religion. And just as each of these gives a satisfaction which the other cannot possibly give, so we find in poetry, which cannot satisfy the needs they meet, that which by their natures they cannot afford us. But we shall not find it fully if we look for something else.

And now, when all is said, the question will still recur, though now in quite another sense, what does poetry mean?[17] This unique expression, which cannot be replaced by any other, still seems to be trying to express something beyond

---

other sense it is indefinite, comparatively structureless, more a *Stimmung* than an idea.

Such correspondences, naturally, must be very rough, if only because the readers have been at one time in contact with the fully grown poem.

[15][Bradley] Not that to Schiller *form* meant mere style and versification.

[16][Bradley] I should be sorry if what is said here and elsewhere were taken to imply depreciation of all attempts at the interpretation of works of art. As regards poetry, such attempts, though they cannot possibly express the whole meaning of a poem, may do much to facilitate the poetic apprehension of that meaning. And, although the attempt is still more hazardous in the case

of music and painting, I believe it may have a similar value. That its results may be absurd or disgusting goes without saying, and whether they are ever of use to musicians or the musically educated I do not know. But I see no reason why an exceedingly competent person should not try to indicate the emotional tone of a composition, movement, or passage, or the changes of feeling within it, or even, very roughly, the "idea" he may suppose it to embody (though he need not imply that the composer had any of this before his mind). And I believe that such indications, however inadequate they must be, may greatly help the uneducated lover of music to hear more truly the music itself.

[17][Bradley] This new question has "quite another sense" than that of the question, what is the meaning or content expressed by the form of a poem? The new question asks, what is it that the *poem,* the unity of this content and form, is trying to express? This "beyond" is beyond the content as well as the form.

Of course, I should add, it is not *merely* beyond them or outside of them. If it were, they (the poem) could not "suggest" it. They are a partial manifestation of it, and point beyond themselves to it, both because they *are* a manifestation and because this is partial.

The same thing is true, not only (as is remarked in the text) of the other arts and of religion and philosophy, but also of what is commonly called reality. This reality is a manifestation of a different order from poetry, and in certain important respects a much more imperfect manifestation. Hence, as was pointed out (note 2, above), poetry is not a copy of it, but in dealing with it idealizes it, and in doing so produces in certain respects a fuller manifestation. On the other hand, that imperfect "reality" has for us a character in which poetry is deficient—the character in virtue of which we call it "reality." It is, we feel, thrust upon us, not made by us or by any other man. And in this respect it seems more akin than poetry to that "beyond," or absolute, or perfection, which we want, which partially expresses itself in both, and which could not be perfection and could not satisfy us if it were not real (though it cannot be real in the same sense as that imperfect "reality"). This seems the ultimate ground of the requirement that poetry, though no copy of "reality," should not be mere "fancy," but should refer to, and interpret, that "reality." For that reality, however imperfectly it reveals perfection, is at least no mere fancy. (Not that the merest fancy can fail to reveal something of perfection.)

The lines quoted [at the top of the second column on this page] are from a fragment of Shelley's, beginning "Is it that in some brighter sphere."

itself. And this, we feel, is also what the other arts, and religion, and philosophy are trying to express: and that is what impels us to seek in vain to translate the one into the other. About the best poetry, and not only the best, there floats an atmosphere of infinite suggestion. The poet speaks to us of one thing, but in this one thing there seems to lurk the secret of all. He said what he meant, but his meaning seems to beckon away beyond itself, or rather to expand into something boundless which is only focused in it; something also which, we feel, would satisfy not only the imagination, but the whole of us; that something within us, and without, which everywhere

> makes us seem
> To patch up fragments of a dream,
> Part of which comes true, and part
> Beats and trembles in the heart.

Those who are susceptible to this effect of poetry find it not only, perhaps not most, in the ideals which she has sometimes described, but in a child's song by Christina Rossetti about a mere crown of windflowers, and in tragedies like *Lear,* where the sun seems to have set forever. They hear this

spirit murmuring its undertone through the *Aeneid,* and catch its voice in the song of Keats's nightingale, and its light upon the figures on the urn, and it pierces them no less in Shelley's hopeless lament, *O world, O life, O time,* than in the rapturous ecstasy of his *Life of Life.* This all-embracing perfection cannot be expressed in poetic words or words of any kind, nor yet in music or in color, but the suggestion of it is in much poetry, if not all, and poetry has in this suggestion, this "meaning," a great part of its value. We do it wrong, and we defeat our own purposes, when we try to bend it to them:

> We do it wrong, being so majestical,
> To offer it the show of violence;
> For it is as the air invulnerable,
> And our vain blows malicious mockery.[18]

It is a spirit. It comes we know not whence. It will not speak at our bidding, nor answer in our language. It is not our servant; it is our master.

---

[18]*Hamlet,* I. i. 143–46.

Sigmund Freud

1856–1939

The influence of Freud on modern literature, critical practice, and literary theory has been so immense and varied that no small selection from his work can begin to represent that influence. *Creative Writers and Daydreaming* does, however, suggest something of the range of his interest in the relationship between the author and his work. Freud draws an analogy between the artist's creations and dreams or fantasy. He is interested in literary works as expressions of the author; he sees a piece of creative writing as a continuation of or substitute for the play of childhood. To Freud the hero of romance is merely another manifestation of the familiar ego. Freud is known to have remarked that it was not he but the poets who discovered the unconscious.

In this essay Freud also displays briefly some aspects of his approach to the psychology of the reader. He suggests that the superficial pleasure of the work ("forepleasure") actually releases still greater and deeper psychic pleasure and thereby liberates tensions.

Freud's discussion of literature is limited by his analogy between literary work and dream. As Charles Lamb remarked, the poet is awake when he dreams, and that is an important difference. The poet consciously employs a medium. From the Freudian point of view the medium could be considered a sort of censor, the true meaning of a work hidden behind the manifest "dream." This meaning presumably could be recovered by analysis. Fundamentally, this approach leads to an allegorical reading (in Freudian terms) of all literary works. The theory of symbolism developed by the Romantics opposed this sort of allegorization. The Romantic view led to denials that a work's meaning can be discovered by analysis, that the medium can be separated from the content, even (as Croce later maintained) that there is any meaning prior to the expression.

A version of what has been called "psychical distance" and Kant and Coleridge call the "beautiful" is apparent in Freud's assertion that because the writer's imaginative world is "unreal," it is possible for many things in it to be pleasurable that would otherwise be unpleasant. Freud does not discuss adequately how it is that some contexts succeed in making this pleasure possible while others do not. Indeed, he is not really interested in the matter of pleasure. His concern is for psychological implications. His discussion suggests, by his own admission, that somewhat inferior works may be more interesting for psychoanalytical investigation than avowed masterpieces. The reason for this, he says, is that lesser works do not take over ready-made materials and themes. This seems naive in that the more simple, sentimental, and popular the work the more *obviously* conventional it usually is in theme and plot.

As Lionel Trilling pointed out in his essay *Freud and Literature,* Freud's discussion of these and other matters is hampered by an inadequate grasp of epistemological issues. He talks a great deal about what is "real," but he never locates "reality" for us. Nevertheless, his speculations have had an immense influence, and virtually no modern critic has not been touched by them.

The standard translation is *Complete Psychological Works of Sigmund Freud,* revised and edited by James Strachey (24 vols., 1964). From the immense literature see F. J. Hoffman, *Freudianism and the Literary Mind* (1945); Ernest Jones, *Hamlet and Oedipus* (1949) and *The Life and Work of Sigmund Freud* (1953); D. E. Schneider, *The Psycho-Analyst and the Artist* (1950); Ernest Kris, *Psychoanalytic Explorations in Art* (1952); S. O. Lesser, *Fiction and the Unconscious* (1957); William Phillips, ed., *Art and Psychoanalysis* (1957); H. M. Ruitenbeck, ed., *Psychoanalysis and Literature* (1964); Claudia C. Morrison, *Freud and the Critic* (1968); Sarah Kofman, *The Childhood of Art: An Interpretation of Freud's Aesthetics* (1970, tr. 1988); Paul Ricoeur, *Freud and Philosophy* (1970); Jack J. Spector, *The Aesthetics of Freud* (1973); V. Voloshinov (M. M. Bakhtin), *Freudianism: A Marxist Critique* (tr. 1976); Francesco Orlando, *Toward a Freudian Theory of Literature* (tr. 1978); Mikkel Borch-Jacobsen, *The Freudian Subject* (tr. 1989); and Leo Bersani, *The Freudian Body: Psychoanalysis and Art* (1986).

Creative Writers and Daydreaming

We laymen have always been intensely curious to know—like the cardinal who put a similar question to Ariosto[1]—from what sources that strange being, the creative writer, draws his material, and how he manages to make such an impression on us with it and to arouse in us emotions of which, perhaps, we had not even thought ourselves capable. Our interest is only heightened the more by the fact that, if we ask him, the writer himself gives us no explanation, or none that is satisfactory; and it is not at all weakened by our knowledge that not even the clearest insight into the determinants of his choice of material and into the nature of the art of creating imaginative form will ever help to make creative writers of *us.*

If we could at least discover in ourselves or in people like ourselves an activity which was in some way akin to creative writing! An examination of it would then give us a hope of obtaining the beginnings of an explanation of the creative work of writers. And, indeed, there is some prospect of this being possible. After all, creative writers themselves like to lessen the distance between their kind and the common run of humanity; they so often assure us that every man is a poet at heart and that the last poet will not perish till the last man does.

Should we not look for the first traces of imaginative activity as early as in childhood? The child's best-loved and most intense occupation is with his play or games. Might we not say that every child at play behaves like a creative writer, in that he creates a world of his own, or, rather, rearranges the things of his world in a new way which pleases him? It would be wrong to think he does not take that world seriously; on the contrary, he takes his play very seriously and he expends large amounts of emotion on it. The opposite of play is not what is serious but what is real. In spite of all the emotion with which he cathects his world of play, the child distinguishes it quite well from reality; and he likes to link his imagined objects and situations to the tangible and visible things of the real world. This linking is all that differentiates the child's "play" from "fantasying."

The creative writer does the same as the child at play. He creates a world of fantasy which he takes very seriously—that is, which he invests with large amounts of emo-

CREATIVE WRITERS AND DAYDREAMING. Freud's *Der Dichter und Phantasieren* was first published in 1908. It is reprinted here from Chapter 9 of Volume IV of *The Collected Papers of Sigmund Freud,* edited by Ernest Jones, M.D. (New York: Basic Books, Inc., Publishers, 1959). From Volume IX of *The Standard Edition of the Complete Psychological Works of Sigmund Freud,* revised and edited by James Strachey. Reprinted by permission of Sigmund Freud Copyrights Limited, the Institute of Psycho-Analysis, and the Hogarth Press Limited.
[1]Ariosto dedicated the *Orlando Furioso* to Cardinal Ippolito d'Este, who said in response, "Where did you find so many stories?"

tion—while separating it sharply from reality. Language has preserved this relationship between children's play and poetic creation. It gives the name of *Spiel* ["play"][2] to those forms of imaginative writing which require to be linked to tangible objects and which are capable of representation. It speaks of a *Lustspiel* or *Trauerspiel* ["comedy" or "tragedy"] and describes those who carry out the representation as *Schauspieler* ["players"]. The unreality of the writer's imaginative world, however, has very important consequences for the technique of his art; for many things which, if they were real, could give no enjoyment, can do so in the play of fantasy, and many excitements which, in themselves, are actually distressing, can become a source of pleasure for the hearers and spectators at the performance of a writer's work.

There is another consideration for the sake of which we will dwell a moment longer on this contrast between reality and play. When the child has grown up and has ceased to play, and after he has been laboring for decades to envisage the realities of life with proper seriousness, he may one day find himself in a mental situation which once more undoes the contrast between play and reality. As an adult he can look back on the intense seriousness with which he once carried on his games in childhood, and, by equating his ostensibly serious occupations of today with his childhood games, he can throw off the too heavy burden imposed on him by life and win the high yield of pleasure afforded by *humor.*

As people grow up, then, they cease to play, and they seem to give up the yield of pleasure which they gained from playing. But whoever understands the human mind knows that hardly anything is harder for a man than to give up a pleasure which he has once experienced. Actually, we can never give anything up; we only exchange one thing for another. What appears to be a renunciation is really the formation of a substitute or surrogate. In the same way, the growing child, when he stops playing, gives up nothing but the link with real objects; instead of *playing,* he now *fantasies.* He builds castles in the air and creates what are called *daydreams.* I believe that most people construct fantasies at times in their lives. This is a fact which has long been overlooked and whose importance has therefore not been sufficiently appreciated.

People's fantasies are less easy to observe than the play of children. The child, it is true, plays by himself or forms a closed psychical system with other children for the purposes of a game; but even though he may not play his game in front of the grown-ups, he does not, on the other hand, conceal it from them. The adult, on the contrary, is ashamed of his fantasies and hides them from other people. He cherishes his fantasies as his most intimate possessions, and as a rule he would rather confess his misdeeds than tell anyone his fantasies. It may come about that for that reason he believes he is the only person who invents such fantasies and has no idea that creations of this kind are widespread among other people. This difference in the behavior of a person who plays and a person who fantasies is accounted for by the motives of these two activities, which are nevertheless adjuncts to each other.

A child's play is determined by wishes: in point of fact by a single wish—one that helps in his upbringing—the wish to be big and grown up. He is always playing at being "grown up," and in his games he imitates what he knows about the lives of his elders. He has no reason to conceal this wish. With the adult, the case is different. On the one hand, he knows that he is expected not to go on playing or fantasying any longer, but to act in the real world; on the other hand, some of the wishes which give rise to his fantasies are of a kind which it is essential to conceal. Thus he is ashamed of his fantasies as being childish and as being unpermissible.

But, you will ask, if people make such a mystery of their fantasying, how is it that we know such a lot about it? Well, there is a class of human beings upon whom, not a god, indeed, but a stern goddess—Necessity—has allotted the task of telling what they suffer and what things give them happiness. These are the victims of nervous illness, who are obliged to tell their fantasies, among other things, to the doctor by whom they expect to be cured by mental treatment. This is our best source of knowledge, and we have since found good reason to suppose that our patients tell us nothing that we might not also hear from healthy people.

Let us make ourselves acquainted with a few of the characteristics of fantasying. We may lay it down that a happy person never fantasies, only an unsatisfied one. The motive forces of fantasies are unsatisfied wishes, and every single fantasy is the fulfillment of a wish, a correction of unsatisfying reality. These motivating wishes vary according to the sex, character, and circumstances of the person who is having the fantasy; but they fall naturally into two main groups. They are either ambitious wishes, which serve to elevate the subject's personality; or they are erotic ones. In young women the erotic wishes predominate almost exclusively, for their ambition is as a rule absorbed by erotic trends. In young men egoistic and ambitious wishes come to the fore clearly enough alongside of erotic ones. But we will

---

[2]A term used by Schiller in *Letters on the Aesthetic Education of Man,* pp. 420–21, but in quite a different sense.

not lay stress on the opposition between the two trends; we would rather emphasize the fact that they are often united. Just as, in many altarpieces, the portrait of the donor is to be seen in a corner of the picture, so, in the majority of ambitious fantasies, we can discover in some corner or other the lady for whom the creator of the fantasy performs all his heroic deeds and at whose feet all his triumphs are laid. Here, as you see, there are strong enough motives for concealment; the well-brought-up young woman is only allowed a minimum of erotic desire, and the young man has to learn to suppress the excess of self-regard which he brings with him from the spoilt days of his childhood, so that he may find his place in a society which is full of other individuals making equally strong demands.

We must not suppose that the products of this imaginative activity—the various fantasies, castles in the air and daydreams—are stereotyped or unalterable. On the contrary, they fit themselves into the subject's shifting impressions of life, change with every change in his situation, and receive from every fresh active impression what might be called a "date-mark." The relation of a fantasy to time is in general very important. We may say that it hovers, as it were, between three times—the three moments of time which our ideation involves. Mental work is linked to some current impression, some provoking occasion in the present which has been able to arouse one of the subject's major wishes. From there it harks back to a memory of an earlier experience (usually an infantile one) in which this wish was fulfilled; and it now creates a situation relating to the future which represents a fulfillment of the wish. What it thus creates is a daydream or fantasy, which carries about it traces of its origin from the occasion which provoked it and from the memory. Thus past, present, and future are strung together, as it were, on the thread of the wish that runs through them.

A very ordinary example may serve to make what I have said clear. Let us take the case of a poor orphan boy to whom you have given the address of some employer where he may perhaps find a job. On his way there he may indulge in a daydream appropriate to the situation from which it arises. The content of his fantasy will perhaps be something like this. He is given a job, finds favor with his new employer, makes himself indispensable in the business, is taken into his employer's family, marries the charming young daughter of the house, and then himself becomes a director of the business, first as his employer's partner and then as his successor. In this fantasy, the dreamer has regained what he possessed in his happy childhood—the protecting house, the loving parents, and the first objects of his affectionate feelings. You will see from this example the way in which the wish makes use of an occasion in the present to construct, on the pattern of the past, a picture of the future.

There is a great deal more that could be said about fantasies; but I will only allude as briefly as possible to certain points. If fantasies become overluxuriant and overpowerful, the conditions are laid for an onset of neurosis or psychosis. Fantasies, moreover, are the immediate mental precursors of the distressing symptoms complained of by our patients. Here a broad bypath branches off into pathology.

I cannot pass over the relation of fantasies to dreams. Our dreams at night are nothing else than fantasies like these, as we can demonstrate from the interpretation of dreams. Language, in its unrivaled wisdom, long ago decided the question of the essential nature of dreams by giving the name of *daydreams* to the airy creations of fantasy. If the meaning of our dreams usually remains obscure to us in spite of this pointer, it is because of the circumstance that at night there also arise in us wishes of which we are ashamed; these we must conceal from ourselves, and they have consequently been repressed, pushed into the unconscious. Repressed wishes of this sort and their derivatives are only allowed to come to expression in a very distorted form. When scientific work had succeeded in elucidating this factor of *dream distortion,* it was no longer difficult to recognize that night dreams are wish-fulfillments in just the same way as daydreams—the fantasies which we all know so well.

So much for fantasies. And now for the creative writer. May we really attempt to compare the imaginative writer with the "dreamer in broad daylight," and his creations with daydreams? Here we must begin by making an initial distinction. We must separate writers who, like the ancient authors of epics and tragedies, take over their material ready-made, from writers who seem to originate their own material. We will keep to the latter kind, and, for the purposes of our comparison, we will choose not the writers most highly esteemed by the critics, but the less pretentious authors of novels, romances and short stories, who nevertheless have the widest and most eager circle of readers of both sexes. One feature above all cannot fail to strike us about the creations of these story-writers: each of them has a hero who is the center of interest, for whom the writer tries to win our sympathy by every possible means and whom he seems to place under the protection of a special providence. If, at the end of one chapter of my story, I leave the hero unconscious and bleeding from severe wounds, I am sure to find him at the beginning of the next being carefully nursed and on the way to recovery; and if the first volume closes with the ship he is in going down in a storm at sea, I am certain, at the opening of the second volume, to read of his miraculous rescue—a rescue without which the story could not proceed.

The feeling of security with which I follow the hero through his perilous adventures is the same as the feeling with which a hero in real life throws himself into the water to save a drowning man or exposes himself to the enemy's fire in order to storm a battery. It is the true heroic feeling, which one of our best writers has expressed in an inimitable phrase: "Nothing can happen to *me!*" It seems to me, however, that through this revealing characteristic of invulnerability we can immediately recognize His Majesty the Ego, the hero alike of every daydream and of every story.

Other typical features of these egocentric stories point to the same kinship. The fact that all the women in the novel invariably fall in love with the hero can hardly be looked on as a portrayal of reality, but it is easily understood as a necessary constituent of a daydream. The same is true of the fact that the other characters in the story are sharply divided into good and bad, in defiance of the variety of human characters that are to be observed in real life. The "good" ones are the helpers, while the "bad" ones are the enemies and rivals, of the ego which has become the hero of the story.

We are perfectly aware that very many imaginative writings are far removed from the model of the naive daydream; and yet I cannot suppress the suspicion that even the most extreme deviations from that model could be linked with it through an uninterrupted series of transitional cases. It has struck me that in many of what are known as "psychological" novels only one person—once again the hero—is described from within. The author sits inside his mind, as it were, and looks at the other characters from outside. The psychological novel in general no doubt owes its special nature to the inclination of the modern writer to split up his ego, by self-observation, into many part-egos, and, in consequence, to personify the conflicting currents of his own mental life in several heroes. Certain novels, which might be described as "eccentric," seem to stand in quite special contrast to the types of the daydream. In these, the person who is introduced as the hero plays only a very small active part; he sees the actions and sufferings of other people pass before him like a spectator. Many of Zola's later works belong to this category. But I must point out that the psychological analysis of individuals who are not creative writers, and who diverge in some respects from the so-called norm, has shown us analogous variations of the daydream, in which the ego contents itself with the role of spectator.

If our comparison of the imaginative writer with the daydreamer, and of poetical creation with the daydream, is to be of any value, it must, above all, show itself in some way or other fruitful. Let us, for instance, try to apply to these authors' works the thesis we laid down earlier concerning the relation between fantasy and the three periods of time and the wish which runs through them; and, with its help, let us try to study the connections that exist between the life of the writer and his works. No one has known, as a rule, what expectations to frame in approaching this problem; and often the connection has been thought of in much too simple terms. In the light of the insight we have gained from fantasies, we ought to expect the following state of affairs. A strong experience in the present awakens in the creative writer a memory of an earlier experience (usually belonging to his childhood) from which there now proceeds a wish which finds its fulfillment in the creative work. The work itself exhibits elements of the recent provoking occasion as well as of the old memory.

Do not be alarmed at the complexity of this formula. I suspect that in fact it will prove to be too exiguous a pattern. Nevertheless, it may contain a first approach to the true state of affairs; and, from some experiments I have made, I am inclined to think that this way of looking at creative writings may turn out not unfruitful. You will not forget that the stress it lays on childhood memories in the writer's life—a stress which may perhaps seem puzzling—is ultimately derived from the assumption that a piece of creative writing, like a daydream, is a continuation of, and a substitute for, what was once the play of childhood.

We must not neglect, however, to go back to the kind of imaginative works which we have to recognize, not as original creations, but as the refashioning of ready-made and familiar material. Even here, the writer keeps a certain amount of independence, which can express itself in the choice of material and in changes in it which are often quite extensive. Insofar as the material is already at hand, however, it is derived from the popular treasure-house of myths, legends, and fairy tales. The study of constructions of folk psychology such as these is far from being complete, but it is extremely probable that myths, for instance, are distorted vestiges of the wishful fantasies of whole nations, the *secular dreams* of youthful humanity.

You will say that, although I have put the creative writer first in the title of my paper, I have told you far less about him than about fantasies. I am aware of that, and I must try to excuse it by pointing to the present state of our knowledge. All I have been able to do is to throw out some encouragements and suggestions which, starting from the study of fantasies, lead on to the problem of the writer's choice of his literary material. As for the other problem—by what means the creative writer achieves the emotional effects in us that are aroused by his creations—we have as yet not touched on it at all. But I should like at least to point out to you the path that leads from our discussion of fantasies to the problems of poetical effects.

You will remember how I have said that the daydreamer carefully conceals his fantasies from other people because he feels he has reasons for being ashamed of them. I should now add that even if he were to communicate them to us he could give us no pleasure by his disclosures. Such fantasies, when we learn them, repel us or at least leave us cold. But when a creative writer presents his plays to us or tells us what we are inclined to take to be his personal daydreams, we experience a great pleasure, and one which probably arises from the confluence of many sources. How the writer accomplishes this is his innermost secret; the essential *ars poetica* lies in the technique of overcoming the feeling of repulsion in us which is undoubtedly connected with the barriers that rise between each single ego and the others.[3] We can guess two

---

[3]Compare Keats's letter to Benjamin Bailey, p. 493.

of the methods used by this technique. The writer softens the character of his egoistic daydreams by altering and disguising it, and he bribes us by the purely formal—that is, aesthetic—yield of pleasure which he offers us in the presentation of his fantasies. We give the name of an *incentive bonus,* or a *forepleasure,* to a yield of pleasure such as this, which is offered to us so as to make possible the release of still greater pleasure arising from deeper psychical sources. In my opinion, all the aesthetic pleasure which a creative writer affords us has the character of a forepleasure of this kind, and our actual enjoyment of an imaginative work proceeds from a liberation of tensions in our minds. It may even be that not a little of this effect is due to the writer's enabling us thenceforward to enjoy our own daydreams without self-reproach or shame. This brings us to the threshold of new, interesting, and complicated inquiries; but also, at least for the moment, to the end of our discussion.

Ferdinand de Saussure

1857–1913

Saussure's posthumously published *Course in General Linguistics* (1913) is, like Aristotle's *Poetics,* a reconstruction by students of his lectures at the University of Geneva in the years 1906–1911. Though not itself concerned with literary texts or theory it has been enormously influential and stands as one of the most important documents of a period in which criticism and theory have found their ground in speculation about language. Saussure's treatment of the linguistic sign as composed of "signifier" and "signified," his emphasis on the "arbitrary nature of the sign," and his characterization of language as a system of differences flow through the work of all structuralists and poststructuralist theorists.

Saussure sought to establish linguistics as a science. In this effort he distinguished between viewing language diachronically, or historically, as in traditional linguistics, or synchronically, as in structural linguistics. He also abandoned the notion of influence and treated language as a closed system—a structure. In the Saussurean structure each word is a unit described entirely in terms of its *difference* from other words. Thus the spaces between words so to speak becomes more important than words in themselves. All is seen in terms of these negative relations rather than substance.

But Saussure, or perhaps the Pseudo-Saussure of the reconstructed lectures, is not entirely clear on the extent to which the sign is arbitrary, and, as Jacques Derrida argued, the principle of difference in which every signifier signifies only another signifier in a potentially endless chain of differences calls in question the closed structure that Saussure implies language is.

Of particular interest to literary critics is Saussure's distinction between *langue* and *parole*. *Langue* is the system of language; *parole* the particular usage. Thus critics have seen poems or other literary events as paroles within a general system.

What Saussure published in his own lifetime was rather specialized. The *Course in General Linguistics* (1913) appeared in English in 1959. His writings are published in French in *Recueil des publications scientifique de F. de Saussure* (1922). Jean Starobinski has presented Saussure's strange *Anagrammes* in *Les Mots sous les mots* (1971), translated as *Words Upon Words* (1979). See also the introduction by Manuel Mourette-Lema to *A Geneva School Reader in Linguistics,* R. Goedel, ed., (1969); Jonathan Culler, *Ferdinand de Saussure* (1976); Roy Harris, *Reading Saussure* (1986) and *Language, Saussure, and Wittgenstein* (1988); Robert M. Strozier, *Saussure, Derrida, and the Metaphysics of Subjectivity* (1988); and Francoise Gadet, *Saussure and Contemporary Culture* (tr. 1989).

From

Course in General Linguistics

Part One

General Principles

Chapter I

Nature of the Linguistic Sign

1. Sign, Signified, Signifier

Some people regard language, when reduced to its elements, as a naming-process only—a list of words, each corresponding to the thing that it names. For example:

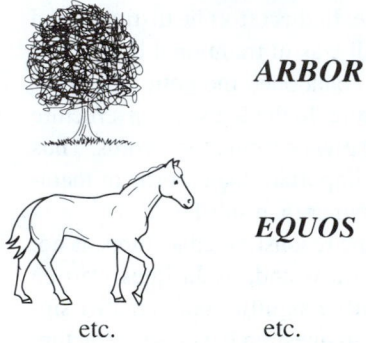

ARBOR

EQUOS

etc.   etc.

This conception is open to criticism at several points. It assumes that ready-made ideas exist before words; it does not tell us whether a name is vocal or psychological in nature (*arbor,* for instance, can be considered from either viewpoint); finally, it lets us assume that the linking of a name and a thing is a very simple operation—an assumption that is anything but true. But this rather naive approach can bring us near the truth by showing us that the linguistic unit is a double entity, one formed by the associating of two terms.

We have seen in considering the speaking-circuit that both terms involved in the linguistic sign are psychological and are united in the brain by an associative bond. This point must be emphasized.

The linguistic sign unites, not a thing and a name, but a concept and a sound-image. The latter is not the material sound, a purely physical thing, but the psychological imprint

of the sound, the impression that it makes on our senses. The sound-image is sensory, and if I happen to call it "material," it is only in that sense, and by way of opposing it to the other term of the association, the concept, which is generally more abstract.

The psychological character of our sound-images becomes apparent when we observe our own speech. Without moving our lips or tongue, we can talk to ourselves or recite mentally a selection of verse. Because we regard the words of our language as sound-images, we must avoid speaking of the "phonemes" that make up the words. This term, which suggests vocal activity, is applicable to the spoken word only, to the realization of the inner image in discourse. We can avoid that misunderstanding by speaking of the *sounds* and *syllables* of a word provided we remember that the names refer to the sound-image.

The linguistic sign is then a two-sided psychological entity that can be represented by the drawing:

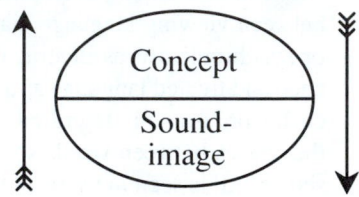

The two elements are intimately united, and each recalls the other. Whether we try to find the meaning of the Latin word *arbor* or the word that Latin uses to designate the concept "tree," it is clear that only the associations sanctioned by that language appear to us to conform to reality, and we disregard whatever others might be imagined.

Our definition of the linguistic sign poses an important question of terminology. I call the combination of a concept and a sound-image a *sign,* but in current usage the term generally designates only a sound-image, a word, for example (*arbor,* etc.). One tends to forget that *arbor* is called a sign only because it carries the concept "tree," with the result that the idea of the sensory part implies the idea of the whole.

Ambiguity would disappear if the three notions involved here were designated by three names, each suggesting and opposing the others. I propose to retain the word *sign*

COURSE IN GENERAL LINGUISTICS. *Course in General Linguistics* appeared as *Cours de linguistique générale* in France in 1913. It is reprinted here, translated by Wade Baskins, by permission of The Philosophical Library, © 1959.

[*signe*] to designate the whole and to replace *concept* and *sound-image* respectively by *signified* [*signifié*] and *signifier* [*signifiant*]; the last two terms have the advantage of indicating the opposition that separates them from each other and from the whole of which they are parts. As regards *sign,* if I am satisfied with it, this is simply because I do not know of any word to replace it, the ordinary language suggesting no other.

The linguistic sign, as defined, has two primordial characteristics. In enunciating them I am also positing the basic principles of any study of this type.

2. *Principle I: The Arbitrary Nature of the Sign*

The bond between the signifier and the signified is arbitrary. Since I mean by sign the whole that results from the associating of the signifier with the signified, I can simply say: *the linguistic sign is arbitrary.*

The idea of "sister" is not linked by any inner relationship to the succession of sounds *s-ö-r* which serves as its signifier in French; that it could be represented equally by just any other sequence is proved by differences among languages and by the very existence of different languages: the signified "ox" has as its signifier *b-ö-f* on one side of the border and *o-k-s (Ochs)* on the other.

No one disputes the principle of the arbitrary nature of the sign, but it is often easier to discover a truth than to assign to it its proper place. Principle I dominates all the linguistics of language; its consequences are numberless. It is true that not all of them are equally obvious at first glance; only after many detours does one discover them, and with them the primordial importance of the principle.

One remark in passing: when semiology becomes organized as a science, the question will arise whether or not it properly includes modes of expression based on completely natural signs, such as pantomime. Supposing that the new science welcomes them, its main concern will still be the whole group of systems grounded on the arbitrariness of the sign. In fact, every means of expression used in society is based, in principle, on collective behavior or—what amounts to the same thing—on convention. Polite formulas, for instance, though often imbued with a certain natural expressiveness (as in the case of a Chinese who greets his emperor by bowing down to the ground nine times), are nonetheless fixed by rule; it is this rule and not the intrinsic value of the gestures that obliges one to use them. Signs that are wholly arbitrary realize better than the others the ideal of the semiological process; that is why language, the most complex and universal of all systems of expression, is also the most characteristic; in this sense linguistics can become the master-pattern for all branches of semiology although language is only one particular semiological system.

The word *symbol* has been used to designate the linguistic sign, or more specifically, what is here called the signifier. Principle I in particular weighs against the use of this term. One characteristic of the symbol is that it is never wholly arbitrary; it is not empty, for there is the rudiment of a natural bond between the signifier and the signified. The symbol of justice, a pair of scales, could not be replaced by just any other symbol, such as a chariot.

The word *arbitrary* also calls for comment. The term should not imply that the choice of the signifier is left entirely to the speaker (we shall see below that the individual does not have the power to change a sign in any way once it has become established in the linguistic community); I mean that it is unmotivated, i.e. arbitrary in that it actually has no natural connection with the signified.

In concluding let us consider two objections that might be raised to the establishment of Principle I:

1) *Onomatopoeia* might be used to prove that the choice of the signifier is not always arbitrary. But onomatopoeic formations are never organic elements of a linguistic system. Besides, their number is much smaller than is generally supposed. Words like French *fouet* 'whip' or *glas* 'knell' may strike certain ears with suggestive sonority, but to see that they have not always had this property we need only examine their Latin forms (*fouet* is derived from *fāgus* 'beech-tree,' *glas* from *classicum* 'sound of a trumpet'). The quality of their present sounds, or rather the quality that is attributed to them, is a fortuitous result of phonetic evolution.

As for authentic onomatopoeic words (e.g. *glug-glug,* *tick-tock,* etc.), not only are they limited in number, but also they are chosen somewhat arbitrarily, for they are only approximate and more or less conventional imitations of certain sounds (cf. English *bow-bow* and French *ouaoua*). In addition, once these words have been introduced into the language, they are to a certain extent subjected to the same evolution—phonetic, morphological, etc.—that other words undergo (cf. *pigeon,* ultimately from Vulgar Latin *pīpiō,* derived in turn from an onomatopoeic formation): obvious proof that they lose something of their original character in order to assume that of the linguistic sign in general, which is unmotivated.

2) *Interjections,* closely related to onomatopoeia, can be attacked on the same grounds and come no closer to refuting our thesis. One is tempted to see in them spontaneous expressions of reality dictated, so to speak, by natural forces. But for most interjections we can show that there is no fixed bond between their signified and their signifier. We need only compare two languages on this point to see how much such expressions differ from one language to the next (e.g.

the English equivalent of French *aïe!* is *ouch!*). We know, moreover, that many interjections were once words with specific meanings (cf. French *diable!* 'darn!' *mordieu!* 'golly!' from *mort Dieu* 'God's death,' etc.).

Onomatopoeic formations and interjections are of secondary importance, and their symbolic origin is in part open to dispute.

3. *Principle II: The Linear Nature of the Signifier*

The signifier, being auditory, is unfolded solely in time from which it gets the following characteristics: (a) it represents a span, and (b) the span is measurable in a single dimension; it is a line.

While Principle II is obvious, apparently linguists have always neglected to state it, doubtless because they found it too simple; nevertheless, it is fundamental, and its consequences are incalculable. Its importance equals that of Principle I; the whole mechanism of language depends upon it. In contrast to visual signifiers (nautical signals, etc.) which can offer simultaneous groupings in several dimensions, auditory signifiers have at their command only the dimension of time. Their elements are presented in succession; they form a chain. This feature becomes readily apparent when they are represented in writing and the spatial line of graphic marks is substituted for succession in time.

Sometimes the linear nature of the signifier is not obvious. When I accent a syllable, for instance, it seems that I am concentrating more than one significant element on the same point. But this is an illusion; the syllable and its accent constitute only one phonational act. There is no duality within the act but only different oppositions to what precedes and what follows.

Chapter IV

Linguistic Value

1. *Language as Organized Thought Coupled with Sound*

To prove that language is only a system of pure values, it is enough to consider the two elements involved in its functioning: ideas and sounds.

Psychologically our thought—apart from its expression in words—is only a shapeless and indistinct mass. Philosophers and linguists have always agreed in recognizing that without the help of signs we would be unable to make a clear-cut, consistent distinction between two ideas. Without language, thought is a vague, uncharted nebula. There are no pre-existing ideas, and nothing is distinct before the appearance of language.

Against the floating realm of thought, would sounds by themselves yield predelimited entities? No more so than ideas. Phonic substance is neither more fixed nor more rigid than thought; it is not a mold into which thought must of necessity fit but a plastic substance divided in turn into distinct parts to furnish the signifiers needed by thought. The linguistic fact can therefore be pictured in its totality—i.e. language—as a series of contiguous subdivisions marked off on both the indefinite plane of jumbled ideas (*A*) and the equally vague plane of sounds (*B*). The following diagram gives a rough idea of it:

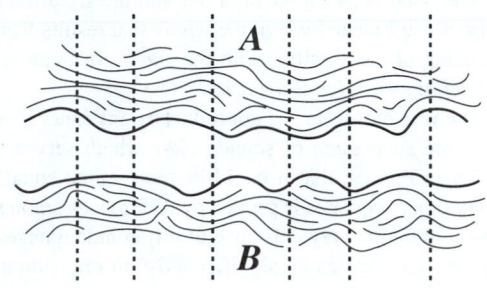

The characteristic role of language with respect to thought is not to create a material phonic means for expressing ideas but to serve as a link between thought and sound, under conditions that of necessity bring about the reciprocal delimitations of units. Thought, chaotic by nature, has to become ordered in the process of its decomposition. Neither are thoughts given material form nor are sounds transformed into mental entities; the somewhat mysterious fact is rather that "thought-sound" implies division, and that language works out its units while taking shape between two shapeless masses. Visualize the air in contact with a sheet of water; if the atmospheric pressure changes, the surface of the water will be broken up into a series of divisions, waves; the waves resemble the union or coupling of thought with phonic substance.

Language might be called the domain of articulations, using the word as it was defined earlier. Each linguistic term is a member, an *articulus* in which an idea is fixed in a sound and a sound becomes the sign of an idea.

Language can also be compared with a sheet of paper: thought is the front and the sound the back; one cannot cut the front without cutting the back at the same time; likewise in language, one can neither divide sound from thought nor thought from sound; the division could be accomplished only abstractedly, and the result would be either pure psychology or pure phonology.

Linguistics then works in the borderland where the elements of sound and thought combine; *their combination produces a form, not a substance.*

These views give a better understanding of what was said before about the arbitrariness of signs. Not only are the two domains that are linked by the linguistic fact shapeless and confused, but the choice of a given slice of sound to name a given idea is completely arbitrary. If this were not true, the notion of value would be compromised, for it would include an externally imposed element. But actually values remain entirely relative, and that is why the bond between the sound and the idea is radically arbitrary.

The arbitrary nature of the sign explains in turn why the social fact alone can create a linguistic system. The community is necessary if values that owe their existence solely to usage and general acceptance are to be set up; by himself the individual is incapable of fixing a single value.

In addition, the idea of value, as defined, shows that to consider a term as simply the union of a certain sound with a certain concept is grossly misleading. To define it in this way would isolate the term from its system; it would mean assuming that one can start from the terms and construct the system by adding them together when, on the contrary, it is from the interdependent whole that one must start and through analysis obtain its elements.

To develop this thesis, we shall study value successively from the viewpoint of the signified or concept (Section 2), the signifier (Section 3), and the complete sign (Section 4).

Being unable to seize the concrete entities or units of language directly, we shall work with words. While the word does not conform exactly to the definition of the linguistic unit, it at least bears a rough resemblance to the unit and has the advantage of being concrete; consequently, we shall use words as specimens equivalent to real terms in a synchronic system, and the principles that we evolve with respect to words will be valid for entities in general.

2. *Linguistic Value from a Conceptual Viewpoint*

When we speak of the value of a word, we generally think first of its property of standing for an idea, and this is in fact one side of linguistic value. But if this is true, how does *value* differ from *signification?* Might the two words be synonyms? I think not, although it is easy to confuse them, since the confusion results not so much from their similarity as from the subtlety of the distinction that they mark.

From a conceptual viewpoint, value is doubtless one element in signification, and it is difficult to see how signification can be dependent upon value and still be distinct from it. But we must clear up the issue or risk reducing language to a simple naming-process.

Let us first take signification as it is generally understood and as it was pictured previously. As the arrows in the drawing show, it is only the counterpart of the sound-image. Everything that occurs concerns only the sound-image and the concept when we look upon the word as independent and self-contained.

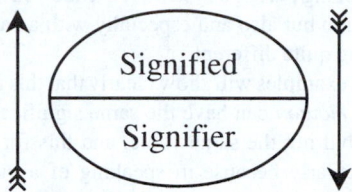

But here is the paradox: on the one hand the concept seems to be the counterpart of the sound-image, and on the other hand the sign itself is in turn the counterpart of the other signs of language.

Language is a system of interdependent terms in which the value of each term results solely from the simultaneous presence of the others, as in the diagram:

How, then, can value be confused with signification, i.e. the counterpart of the sound-image? It seems impossible to liken the relations represented here by horizontal arrows to those represented above by vertical arrows. Putting it another way—and again taking up the example of the sheet of paper that is cut in two—it is clear that the observable relation between the different pieces A, B, C, D, etc. is distinct from the relation between the front and back of the same piece as in A/A′, B/B′, etc.

To resolve the issue, let us observe from the outset that even outside language all values are apparently governed by the same paradoxical principle. They are always composed:

(1) of a *dissimilar* thing that can be *exchanged* for the thing of which the value is to be determined; and

(2) of *similar* things that can be *compared* with the thing of which the value is to be determined.

Both factors are necessary for the existence of a value. To determine what a five-franc piece is worth one must therefore know: (1) that it can be exchanged for a fixed quantity of a different thing, e.g. bread; and (2) that it can be compared with a similar value of the same system, e.g. a one-franc piece, or with coins of another system (a dollar, etc.). In the same way a word can be exchanged for something dissimilar, an idea; besides, it can be compared with something of the same nature, another word. Its value is therefore not fixed so long as one simply states that it can be "exchanged" for a given concept, i.e. that it has this or that signification: one must also compare it with similar values, with other words that stand in opposition to it. Its content is really fixed only by the concurrence of everything that exists outside it. Being part of a system, it is endowed not only with a signification but also and especially with a value, and this is something quite different.

A few examples will show clearly that this is true. Modern French *mouton* can have the same signification as English *sheep* but not the same value, and this for several reasons, particularly because in speaking of a piece of meat ready to be served on the table, English uses *mutton* and not *sheep*. The difference in value between *sheep* and *mouton* is due to the fact that *sheep* has beside it a second term while the French word does not.

Within the same language, all words used to express related ideas limit each other reciprocally; synonyms like French *redouter* 'dread,' *craindre* 'fear,' and *avoir peur* 'be afraid' have value only through their opposition: if *redouter* did not exist, all its content would go to its competitors. Conversely, some words are enriched through contact with others: e.g. the new element introduced in *décrépit* (un vieillard *décrépit*) results from the coexistence of *décrépi* (un mur *décrépi*). The value of just any term is accordingly determined by its environment; it is impossible to fix even the value of the word signifying "sun" without first considering its surroundings: in some languages it is not possible to say "sit in the *sun*."

Everything said about words applies to any term of language, e.g. to grammatical entities. The value of a French plural does not coincide with that of a Sanskrit plural even though their signification is usually identical; Sanskrit has three numbers instead of two (*my eyes, my ears, my arms, my legs,* etc. are dual); it would be wrong to attribute the same value to the plural in Sanskrit and in French; its value clearly depends on what is outside and around it.

If words stood for pre-existing concepts, they would all have exact equivalents in meaning from one language to the next; but this is not true. French uses *louer* (*une maison*) 'let (a house)' indifferently to mean both "pay for" and "receive payment for," whereas German uses two words, *mieten* and *vermieten;* there is obviously no exact correspondence of values. The German verbs *schätzen* and *urteilen* share a number of significations, but that correspondence does not hold at several points.

Inflection offers some particularly striking examples. Distinctions of time, which are so familiar to us, are unknown in certain languages. Hebrew does not recognize even the fundamental distinctions between the past, present, and future. Proto-Germanic has no special form for the future; to say that the future is expressed by the present is wrong, for the value of the present is not the same in Germanic as in languages that have a future along with the present. The Slavic languages regularly single out two aspects of the verb: the perfective represents action as a point, complete in its totality; the imperfective represents it as taking place, and on the line of time. The categories are difficult for a Frenchman to understand, for they are unknown in French; if they were predetermined, this would not be true. Instead of pre-existing ideas then, we find in all the foregoing examples *values* emanating from the system. When they are said to correspond to concepts, it is understood that the concepts are purely differential and defined not by their positive content but negatively by their relations with the other terms of the system. Their most precise characteristic is in being what the others are not.

Now the real interpretation of the diagram of the signal becomes apparent. Thus

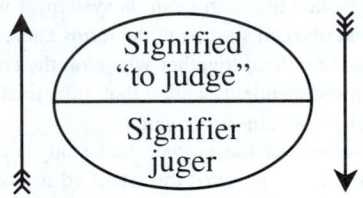

means that in French the concept "to judge" is linked to the sound-image *juger;* in short, it symbolizes signification. But it is quite clear that initially the concept is nothing, that is only a value determined by its relations with other similar values, and that without them the signification would not exist. If I state simply that a word signifies something when I have in mind the associating of a sound-image with a concept, I am making a statement that may suggest what actually happens, but by no means am I expressing the linguistic fact in its essence and fullness.

3. *Linguistic Value from a Material Viewpoint*

The conceptual side of value is made up solely of relations and differences with respect to the other terms of language, and the same can be said of its material side. The important thing in the word is not the sound alone but the phonic differences that make it possible to distinguish this word from all others, for differences carry signification.

This may seem surprising, but how indeed could the reverse be possible? Since one vocal image is no better suited than the next for what it is commissioned to express, it is evident, even *a priori,* that a segment of language can never in the final analysis be based on anything except its noncoincidence with the rest. *Arbitrary* and *differential* are two correlative qualities.

The alteration of linguistic signs clearly illustrates this. It is precisely because the terms *a* and *b* as such are radically incapable of reaching the level of consciousness—one is always conscious of only the *a/b* difference—that each term is free to change according to laws that are unrelated to its signifying function. No positive sign characterizes the genitive plural in Czech *žen;* still the two forms *žena: žen* function as well as the earlier forms *žena: ženb; žen* has value only because it is different.

Here is another example that shows even more clearly the systematic role of phonic differences: in Greek, *éphēn* is an imperfect and *éstēn* an aorist although both words are formed in the same way; the first belongs to the system of the present indicative of *phēmí* 'I say,' whereas there is no present *stēmi;* now it is precisely the relation *phēmí: éphēn* that corresponds to the relation between the present and the imperfect (cf. *déiknūmi: edéiknūn,* etc.). Signs function, then, not through their intrinsic value but through their relative position.

In addition, it is impossible for sound alone, a material element, to belong to language. It is only a secondary thing, substance to be put to use. All our conventional values have the characteristic of not being confused with the tangible element which supports them. For instance, it is not the metal in a piece of money that fixes its value. A coin nominally worth five francs may contain less than half its worth of silver. Its value will vary according to the amount stamped upon it and according to its use inside or outside a political boundary. This is even more true of the linguistic signifier, which is not phonic but incorporeal—constituted not by its material substance but by the differences that separate its sound-image from all others.

The foregoing principle is so basic that it applies to all the material elements of language, including phonemes. Every language forms its words on the basis of a system of sonorous elements, each element being a clearly delimited unit and one of a fixed number of units. Phonemes are characterized not, as one might think, by their own positive quality but simply by the fact that they are distinct. Phonemes are above all else opposing, relative, and negative entities.

Proof of this is the latitude that speakers have between points of convergence in the pronunciation of distinct sounds. In French, for instance, general use of a dorsal *r* does not prevent many speakers from using a tongue-tip trill; language is not in the least disturbed by it; language requires only that the sound be different and not, as one might imagine, that it have an invariable quality. I can even pronounce the French *r* like German *ch* in *Bach, doch,* etc., but in German I could not use *r* instead of *ch,* for German gives recognition to both elements and must keep them apart. Similarly, in Russian there is no latitude for *t* in the direction of *t'* (palatalized *t*), for the result would be the confusing of two sounds differentiated by the language (cf. *govorit'* 'speak' and *goverit* 'he speaks'), but more freedom may be taken with respect to *th* (aspirated *t*) since this sound does not figure in the Russian system of phonemes.

Since an identical state of affairs is observable in writing, another system of signs, we shall use writing to draw some comparisons that will clarify the whole issue. In fact:

1) The signs used in writing are arbitrary; there is no connection, for example, between the letter *t* and the sound that it designates.

2) The value of letters is purely negative and differential. The same person can write *t,* for instance, in different ways: The only requirement is that the sign for *t* not be confused in his script with the signs used for *l, d,* etc.

3) Values in writing function only through reciprocal opposition within a fixed system that consists of a set number of letters. This third characteristic, though not identical to the second, is closely related to it, for both depend on the first. Since the graphic sign is arbitrary, its form matters little or rather matters only within the limitations imposed by the system.

4) The means by which the sign is produced is completely unimportant, for it does not affect the system (this also follows from characteristic 1). Whether I make the letters in white or black, raised or engraved, with pen or chisel—all this is of no importance with respect to their signification.

4. *The Sign Considered in Its Totality*

Everything that has been said up to this point boils down to this: in language there are only differences. Even more important: a difference generally implies positive terms between which the difference is set up; but in language there are only differences *without positive terms.* Whether we take the signified or the signifier, language has neither ideas nor sounds that existed before the linguistic system, but only conceptual and phonic differences that have issued from the system. The idea or phonic substance that a sign contains is of less importance than the other signs that surround it. Proof of this is that the value of a term may be modified without either its meaning or its sound being affected, solely because a neighboring term has been modified.

But the statement that everything in language is negative is true only if the signified and the signifier are considered separately; when we consider the sign in its totality, we have something that is positive in its own class. A linguistic system is a series of differences of sound combined with a series of differences of ideas; but the pairing of a certain number of acoustical signs with as many cuts made from the mass of thought engenders a system of values; and this system serves as the effective link between the phonic and psychological elements within each sign. Although both the signified and the signifier are purely differential and negative when considered separately, their combination is a positive fact; it is even the sole type of facts that language has, for maintaining the parallelism between the two classes of differences is the distinctive function of the linguistic institution.

Certain diachronic facts are typical in this respect. Take the countless instances where alteration of the signifier occasions a conceptual change and where it is obvious that the sum of the ideas distinguished corresponds in principle to the sum of the distinctive signs. When two words are confused through phonetic alteration (e.g. French *décrépit* from *dēcrepitus* and *décrépi* from *crispus*), the ideas that they express will also tend to become confused if only they have something in common. Or a word may have different forms (cf. *chaise* 'chair' and *chaire* 'desk'). Any nascent difference will tend invariably to become significant but without always succeeding or being successful on the first trial. Conversely, any conceptual difference perceived by the mind seeks to find expression through a distinct signifier, and two ideas that are no longer distinct in the mind tend to merge into the same signifier.

When we compare signs—positive terms—with each other, we can no longer speak of difference; the expression would not be fitting, for it applies only to the comparing of two sound-images, e.g. *father* and *mother,* or two ideas, e.g. the idea "father" and the idea "mother"; two signs, each having a signified and signifier, are not different but only distinct. Between them there is only *opposition.* The entire mechanism of language, with which we shall be concerned later, is based on oppositions of this kind and of the phonic and conceptual differences that they imply.

What is true of value is true also of the unit. A unit is a segment of the spoken chain that corresponds to a certain concept; both are by nature purely differential.

Applied to units, the principle of differentiation can be stated in this way: *the characteristics of the unit blend with the unit itself.* In language, as in any semiological system, whatever distinguishes one sign from the others constitutes it. Difference makes character just as it makes value and the unit.

Another rather paradoxical consequence of the same principle is this: in the last analysis what is commonly referred to as a "grammatical fact" fits the definition of the unit, for it always expresses an opposition of terms; it differs only in that the opposition is particularly significant (e.g. the formation of German plurals of the type *Nacht: Nächte*). Each term present in the grammatical fact (the singular without umlaut or final *e* in opposition to the plural with umlaut and -*e*) consists of the interplay of a number of oppositions within the system. When isolated, neither *Nacht* nor *Nächte* is anything: thus everything is opposition. Putting it another way, the *Nacht: Nächte* relation can be expressed by an algebraic formula *a/b* in which *a* and *b* are not simple terms but result from a set of relations. Language, in a manner of speaking, is a type of algebra consisting solely of complex terms. Some of its oppositions are more significant than others; but units and grammatical facts are only different names for designating diverse aspects of the same general fact: the functioning of linguistic oppositions. This statement is so true that we might very well approach the problem of units by starting from grammatical facts. Taking an opposition like *Nacht: Nächte,* we might ask what are the units involved in it. Are they only the two words, the whole series of similar words, *a* and *ä,* or all singulars and plurals, etc.?

Units and grammatical facts would not be confused if linguistic signs were made up of something besides differences. But language being what it is, we shall find nothing simple in it regardless of our approach; everywhere and always there is the same complex equilibrium of terms that mutually condition each other. Putting it another way, *language is a form and not a substance.* This truth could not be overstressed, for all the mistakes in our terminology, all our incorrect ways of naming things that pertain to language, stem from the involuntary supposition that the linguistic phenomenon must have substance.

Chapter V

Syntagmatic and Associative Relations

1. *Definitions*

In a language-state everything is based on relations. How do they function?

Relations and differences between linguistic terms fall into two distinct groups, each of which generates a certain class of values. The opposition between the two classes gives a better understanding of the nature of each class. They correspond to two forms of our mental activity, both indispensable to the life of language.

In discourse, on the one hand, words acquire relations based on the linear nature of language because they are chained together. This rules out the possibility of pronouncing two elements simultaneously. The elements are arranged in sequence on the chain of speaking. Combinations supported by linearity are *syntagms*. The syntagm is always composed of two or more consecutive units (e.g. French *relire* 're-read,' *contre tous* 'against everyone,' *la vie humaine* 'human life,' *Dieu est bon* 'God is good,' *s'il fait beau temps, nous sortirons* 'if the weather is nice, we'll go out,' etc.). In the syntagm a term acquires its value only because it stands in opposition to everything that precedes or follows it, or to both.

Outside discourse, on the other hand, words acquire relations of a different kind. Those that have something in common are associated in the memory, resulting in groups marked by diverse relations. For instance, the French word *enseignement* 'teaching' will unconsciously call to mind a host of other words (*enseigner* 'teach,' *renseigner* 'acquaint,' etc.; or *armement* 'armament,' *changement* 'amendment,' etc.; or *éducation* 'education,' *apprentissage* 'apprenticeship,' etc.). All those words are related in some way.

We see that the co-ordinations formed outside discourse differ strikingly from those formed inside discourse. Those formed outside discourse are not supported by linearity. Their seat is in the brain; they are a part of the inner storehouse that makes up the language of each speaker. They are *associative relations*.

The syntagmatic relation is *in praesentia*. It is based on two or more terms that occur in an effective series. Against this, the associative relation unites terms *in absentia* in a potential mnemonic series.

From the associative and syntagmatic viewpoint a linguistic unit is like a fixed part of a building, e.g. a column. On the one hand, the column has a certain relation to the architrave that it supports; the arrangement of the two units in space suggests the syntagmatic relation. On the other hand, if the column is Doric, it suggests a mental comparison of this style with others (Ionic, Corinthian, etc.) although none of these elements is present in space: the relation is associative.

Each of the two classes of co-ordination calls for some specific remarks.

2. Syntagmatic Relations

The examples have already indicated that the notion of syntagm applies not only to words but to groups of words, to complex units of all lengths and types (compounds, derivatives, phrases, whole sentences).

It is not enough to consider the relation that ties together the different parts of syntagms (e.g. French *contre* 'against' and *tous* 'everyone' in *contre tous, contre* and *maître* 'master' in *contremaître* 'foreman'), one must also bear in mind the relation that links the whole to its parts (e.g. *contre tous* in opposition on the one hand to *contre* and on the other *tous,* or *contremaître* in opposition to *contre* and *maître*).

An objection might be raised at this point. The sentence is the ideal type of syntagm. But it belongs to speaking, not to language. Does it follow that the syntagm belongs to speaking? I do not think so. Speaking is characterized by freedom of combinations; one must therefore ask whether or not all syntagms are equally free.

It is obvious from the first that many expressions belong to language. These are the pat phrases in which any change is prohibited by usage, even if we can single out their meaningful elements (cf. *à quoi bon?* 'what's the use?' *allons donc!* 'nonsense!'). The same is true, though to a lesser degree, of expressions like *prendre la mouche* 'take offense easily,' *forcer la main à quelqu'un* 'force someone's hand,' *rompre une lance* 'break a lance,' or even *avoir mal (à la tête,* etc.) 'have (a headache, etc.),' *à force de (soins,* etc.) 'by dint of (care, etc.),' *que vous en semble?* 'how do you feel about it?' *pas n'est besoin de . . .* 'there's no need for . . . ,' etc., which are characterized by peculiarities of signification or syntax. These idiomatic twists cannot be improvised; they are furnished by tradition. There are also words which, while lending themselves perfectly to analysis, are characterized by some morphological anomaly that is kept solely by dint of usage (cf. *difficulté* 'difficulty' beside *facilité* 'facility,' etc., and *mourrai* '[I] shall die' beside *dormirai* '[I] shall sleep').

There are further proofs. To language rather than to speaking belong the syntagmatic types that are built upon regular forms. Indeed, since there is nothing abstract in language, the types exist only if language has registered a sufficient number of specimens. When a word like *indécorable* arises in speaking, its appearance supposes a fixed type, and this type is in turn possible only through remembrance of a sufficient number of similar words belonging to language (*impardonable* 'unpardonable,' *intolérable* 'intolerable,' *infatigable* 'indefatigable,' etc.). Exactly the same is true of sentences and groups of words built upon regular patterns. Combinations like *la terre tourne* 'the world turns,' *que vous dit-il?* 'what does he say to you?' etc. correspond to general types that are in turn supported in the language by concrete remembrances.

But we must realize that in the syntagm there is no clear-cut boundary between the language fact, which is a sign of collective usage, and the fact that belongs to speaking and depends on individual freedom. In a great number of instances it is hard to class a combination of units because both forces have combined in producing it, and they have combined in indeterminable proportions.

3. *Associative Relations*

Mental association creates other groups besides those based on the comparing of terms that have something in common; through its grasp of the nature of the relations that bind the terms together, the mind creates as many associative series as there are diverse relations. For instance, in *enseignement* 'teaching,' *enseigner* 'teach,' *enseignons* '(we) teach,' etc., one element, the radical, is common to every term; the same word may occur in a different series formed around another common element, the suffix (cf. *enseignement, armement, changement,* etc.); or the association may spring from the analogy of the concepts signified (*enseignement, instruction, apprentissage, éducation,* etc.); or again, simply from the similarity of the sound-images (e.g. *enseignement* and *justement* 'precisely'). Thus there is at times a double similarity of meaning and form, at times similarity only of form or of meaning. A word can always evoke everything that can be associated with it in one way or another.

Whereas a syntagm immediately suggests an order of succession and a fixed number of elements, terms in an associative family occur neither in fixed numbers nor in a definite order. If we associate *painful, delightful, frightful,* etc. we are unable to predict the number of words that the memory will suggest or the order in which they will appear. A particular word is like the center of a constellation; it is the point of convergence of an indefinite number of co-ordinated terms.

But of the two characteristics of the associative series—indeterminate order and indefinite number—only the first can always be verified; the second may fail to meet the test. This happens in the case of inflectional paradigms, which are typical of associative groupings. Latin *dominus, dominī, dominō,* etc. is obviously an associative group formed around a common element, the noun theme *domin-,* but the series

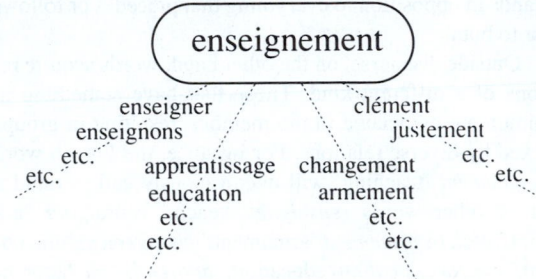

is not indefinite as in the case of *enseignement, changement,* etc.; the number of cases is definite. Against this, the words have no fixed order of succession, and it is by a purely arbitrary act that the grammarian groups them in one way rather than in another; in the mind of speakers the nominative case is by no means the first one in the declension, and the order in which terms are called depends on circumstances.

T. E. Hulme

1883–1917

The Romantic movement generated its own reaction. Two of the most prominent figures of that reaction were T. E. Hulme, who was killed during the First World War, and a younger contemporary who was influenced by him, T. S. Eliot. Hulme's dislike of Romanticism, expressed in his essay *Romanticism and Classicism,* is rather similar to the Romantic Goethe's. He regards Romanticism as a disease, as "spilt religion," an overflowing of religion into art. Parodying Carlyle, he remarks of the Romantic writer's tendency to fly off into the "circumambient gas" in search of the infinite. By temperament he preferred metaphysical and neoclassical poetry that was characterized by wit and irony. It is not surprising that Hulme's and Eliot's criticism contributed to the revival of interest in Donne. Hulme was a great influence on the New Critics. Brooks's *Modern Poetry and the Tradition* attacks Romanticism for reasons similar to Hulme's, and Ransom's distaste for "Platonic" poetry is a version of Hulme's dislike of the Romantic penchant for "dragging in the infinite."

But Hulme was inevitably a product of some aspects of the movement he attacked. From the French philosopher Henri Bergson (1859–1941) he adopted a philosophy of vitalism, or organicism, and thus by his own admission accepted a similar organicism in Coleridge. In *Bergson's Theory of Art* he argues that Bergson's account of reality arrives at conclusions that are necessary suppositions in any treatment of art. Bergson maintains, for example (1) that reality is a flux unseizable by the intellect (the artist manages to make a fixed model of one of these transient waves) and (2) that in ordinary perception we perceive only conventional types, while art breaks down this veil, which is imposed by our orientation toward practical action, and reveals to us the immediate reality. Hulme comments on the second of those conclusions, "Could reality come into direct contact with sense and consciousness, art would be useless." Thus for Hulme art is a special mode of knowing.

Herbert Read has edited two volumes of Hulme's critical writing: *Speculations: Essays on Humanism and the Philosophy of Art* (1924) and *Notes on Language and Style* (1929). A third collection of Hulme's criticism is *Further Speculations*, rev. ed. (1962), edited by Samuel Hynes. For commentary see A. R. Jones, *The Life and Opinions of T. E. Hulme* (1960), and Phyllis Rackin, "Hulme, Richards, and the Development of Contextualist Poetic Theory," *Journal of Aesthetics and Art Criticism,* XXV (1967), 413–25. In connection with Hulme one should read Henri Bergson, *Creative Evolution,* translated by Arthur Mitchell (1911), and *Laughter: An Essay on the Meaning of the Comic,* translated by Cloudesley Brereton and Fred Rothwell (1911). On Bergson, see A. O. Lovejoy, *Bergson and Romantic Evolutionism* (1914), and Arthur Szathmary, *The Aesthetic Theory of Bergson* (1937).

Romanticism and Classicism

I want to maintain that after a hundred years of romanticism, we are in for a classical revival, and that the particular weapon of this new classical spirit, when it works in verse, will be fancy. And in this I imply the superiority of fancy— not superior generally or absolutely, for that would be obvious nonsense, but superior in the sense that we use the word good in empirical ethics—good for something, superior for something. I shall have to prove then two things, first that a classical revival is coming, and, secondly, for its particular purposes, fancy will be superior to imagination.

So banal have the terms *imagination* and *fancy* become that we imagine they must have always been in the language. Their history as two differing terms in the vocabulary of criticism is comparatively short. Originally, of course, they both mean the same thing; they first began to be differentiated by the German writers on aesthetics in the eighteenth century.

I know that in using the words *classic* and *romantic* I am doing a dangerous thing. They represent five or six different kinds of antitheses, and while I may be using them in one sense you may be interpreting them in another. In this present connection I am using them in a perfectly precise and limited sense. I ought really to have coined a couple of new words, but I prefer to use the ones I have used, as I then conform to the practice of the group of polemical writers who make most use of them at the present day, and have almost succeeded in making them political catchwords. I mean Maurras, Lasserre and all the group connected with *L'Action Française*.[1]

At the present time this is the particular group with which the distinction is most vital. Because it has become a party symbol. If you asked a man of a certain set whether he preferred the classics or the romantics, you could deduce from that what his politics were.

The best way of gliding into a proper definition of my terms would be to start with a set of people who are prepared to fight about it—for in them you will have no vagueness. (Other people take the infamous attitude of the person with catholic tastes who says he likes both.)

About a year ago, a man whose name I think was Fauchois gave a lecture at the Odéon on Racine, in the course of which he made some disparaging remarks about his dullness,

lack of invention and the rest of it. This caused an immediate riot: fights took place all over the house; several people were arrested and imprisoned, and the rest of the series of lectures took place with hundreds of gendarmes and detectives scattered all over the place. These people interrupted because the classical ideal is a living thing to them and Racine is the great classic. That is what I call a real vital interest in literature. They regard romanticism as an awful disease from which France had just recovered.

The thing is complicated in their case by the fact that it was romanticism that made the revolution. They hate the revolution, so they hate romanticism.

I make no apology for dragging in politics here; romanticism both in England and France is associated with certain political views, and it is in taking a concrete example of the working out of a principle in action that you can get its best definition.

What was the positive principle behind all the other principles of '89? I am talking here of the revolution in as far as it was an idea; I leave out material causes—they only produce the forces. The barriers which could easily have resisted or guided these forces had been previously rotted away by ideas. This always seems to be the case in successful changes; the privileged class is beaten only when it has lost faith in itself, when it has itself been penetrated with the ideas which are working against it.

It was not the rights of man—that was a good solid practical war cry. The thing which created enthusiasm, which made the revolution practically a new religion, was something more positive than that. People of all classes, people who stood to lose by it, were in a positive ferment about the idea of liberty. There must have been some idea which enabled them to think that something positive could come out of so essentially negative a thing. There was, and here I get my definition of romanticism. They had been taught by Rousseau that man was by nature good, that it was only bad laws and customs that had suppressed him. Remove all these and the infinite possibilities of man would have a chance. This is what made them think that something positive could come out of disorder, this is what created the religious enthusiasm. Here is the root of all romanticism: that man, the individual, is an infinite reservoir of possibilities; and if you can so rearrange society by the destruction of oppressive order then these possibilities will have a chance and you will get progress.

One can define the classical quite clearly as the exact opposite to this. Man is an extraordinarily fixed and limited animal whose nature is absolutely constant. It is only by tradition and organization that anything decent can be got out of him.

ROMANTICISM AND CLASSICISM. Hulme wrote *Romanticism and Classicism* in 1913–14. It was first published posthumously in the collection of his critical writing edited by Herbert Read, *Speculations: Essays on Humanism and the Philosophy of Art* (1924), from which the text is taken. Reprinted by permission of Harcourt Brace Jovanovich, Inc.
[1] A monarchist paper published from 1908 to 1944.

This view was a little shaken at the time of Darwin. You remember his particular hypothesis, that new species came into existence by the cumulative effect of small variations— this seems to admit the possibility of future progress. But at the present day the contrary hypothesis makes headway in the shape of De Vries's mutation theory, that each new species comes into existence, not gradually by the accumulation of small steps, but suddenly in a jump, a kind of sport, and that once in existence it remains absolutely fixed. This enables me to keep the classical view with an appearance of scientific backing.

Put shortly, these are the two views, then. One, that man is intrinsically good, spoilt by circumstance; and the other that he is intrinsically limited, but disciplined by order and tradition to something fairly decent. To the one party man's nature is like a well, to the other like a bucket. The view which regards man as a well, a reservoir full of possibilities, I call romantic; the one which regards him as a very finite and fixed creature, I call the classical.

One may note here that the church has always taken the classical view since the defeat of the Pelagian heresy and the adoption of the sane classical dogma of original sin.

It would be a mistake to identify the classical view with that of materialism. On the contrary it is absolutely identical with the normal religious attitude. I should put it in this way: That part of the fixed nature of man is the belief in the Deity. This should be as fixed and true for every man as belief in the existence of matter and in the objective world. It is parallel to appetite, the instinct of sex, and all the other fixed qualities. Now at certain times, by the use of either force or rhetoric, these instincts have been suppressed—in Florence under Savonarola, in Geneva under Calvin, and here under the Roundheads. The inevitable result of such a process is that the repressed instinct bursts out in some abnormal direction. So with religion. By the perverted rhetoric of rationalism, your natural instincts are suppressed and you are converted into an agnostic. Just as in the case of the other instincts, Nature has her revenge. The instincts that find no right and proper outlet in religion must come out in some other way. You don't believe in a God, so you begin to believe that man is a god. You don't believe in Heaven, so you begin to believe in a heaven on earth. In other words, you get romanticism. The concepts that are right and proper in their own sphere are spread over, and so mess up, falsify and blur the clear outlines of human experience. It is like pouring a pot of treacle over the dinner table. Romanticism then, and this is the best definition I can give of it, is spilt religion.

I must now shirk the difficulty of saying exactly what I mean by romantic and classical in verse. I can only say that it means the result of these two attitudes towards the cosmos,

towards man, in so far as it gets reflected in verse. The romantic, because he thinks man infinite, must always be talking about the infinite; and as there is always the bitter contrast between what you think you ought to be able to do and what man actually can, it always tends, in its later stages at any rate, to be gloomy. I really can't go any further than to say it is the reflection of these two temperaments, and point out examples of the different spirits. On the one hand I would take such diverse people as Horace, most of the Elizabethans and the writers of the Augustan age, and on the other side Lamartine, Hugo, parts of Keats, Coleridge, Byron, Shelley and Swinburne.

I know quite well that when people think of classical and romantic in verse, the contrast at once comes into their mind between, say, Racine and Shakespeare. I don't mean this; the dividing line that I intend is here misplaced a little from the true middle. That Racine is on the extreme classical side I agree, but if you call Shakespeare romantic, you are using a different definition to the one I give. You are thinking of the difference between classic and romantic as being merely one between restraint and exuberance. I should say with Nietzsche that there are two kinds of classicism, the static and the dynamic. Shakespeare is the classic of motion.

What I mean by classical in verse, then, is this. That even in the most imaginative flights there is always a holding back, a reservation. The classical poet never forgets this finiteness, this limit of man. He remembers always that he is mixed up with earth. He may jump, but he always returns back; he never flies away into the circumambient gas.

You might say if you wished that the whole of the romantic attitude seems to crystalize in verse round metaphors of flight. Hugo is always flying, flying over abysses, flying up into the eternal gases. The word infinite in every other line.

In the classical attitude you never seem to swing right along to the infinite nothing. If you say an extravagant thing which does exceed the limits inside which you know man to be fastened, yet there is always conveyed in some way at the end an impression of yourself standing outside it, and not quite believing it, or consciously putting it forward as a flourish. You never go blindly into an atmosphere more than the truth, an atmosphere too rarefied for man to breathe for long. You are always faithful to the conception of a limit. It is a question of pitch; in romantic verse you move at a certain pitch of rhetoric which you know, man being what he is, to be a little highfalutin. The kind of thing you get in Hugo or Swinburne. In the coming classical reaction that will feel just wrong. For an example of the opposite thing, a verse written in the proper classical spirit, I can take the song from *Cymbeline* beginning with "Fear no more the heat of the sun." I am just using this as a parable. I don't quite mean what I say here. Take the last two lines: "Golden lads and lasses must, / Like chimney sweepers come to dust."[2] Now, no romantic would have ever written that. Indeed, so ingrained is romanticism, so objectionable is this to it, that people have asserted that these were not part of the original song.

Apart from the pun, the thing that I think quite classical is the word *lad.* Your modern romantic could never write that. He would have to write golden youth, and take up the thing at least a couple of notes in pitch.

I want now to give the reasons which make me think that we are nearing the end of the romantic movement.

The first lies in the nature of any convention or tradition in art. A particular convention or attitude in art has a strict analogy to the phenomena of organic life. It grows old and decays. It has a definite period of life and must die. All the possible tunes get played on it and then it is exhausted; moreover its best period is its youngest. Take the case of the extraordinary efflorescence of verse in the Elizabethan period. All kinds of reasons have been given for this—the discovery of the new world and all the rest of it. There is a much simpler one. A new medium had been given them to play with—namely, blank verse. It was new and so it was easy to play new tunes on it.

The same law holds in other arts. All the masters of painting are born into the world at a time when the particular tradition from which they start is imperfect. The Florentine tradition was just short of full ripeness when Raphael came to Florence, the Bellinesque was still young when Titian was born in Venice. Landscape was still a toy or an appanage of figure painting when Turner and Constable arose to reveal its independent power. When Turner and Constable had done with landscape they left little or nothing for their successors to do on the same lines. Each field of artistic activity is exhausted by the first great artist who gathers a full harvest from it.

This period of exhaustion seems to me to have been reached in romanticism. We shall not get any new efflorescence of verse until we get a new technique, a new convention, to turn ourselves loose in.

Objection might be taken to this. It might be said that a century as an organic unity doesn't exist, that I am being deluded by a wrong metaphor, that I am treating a collection of literary people as if they were an organism or state department. Whatever we may be in other things, an objector might urge, in literature in as far as we are anything at all—in as far as we are worth considering—we are individuals, we are

persons, and as distinct persons we cannot be subordinated to any general treatment. At any period at any time, an individual poet may be a classic or a romantic just as he feels like it. You at any particular moment may think that you can stand outside a movement. You may think that as an individual you observe both the classic and the romantic spirit and decide from a purely detached point of view that one is superior to the other.

The answer to this is that no one, in a matter of judgment of beauty, can take a detached standpoint in this way. Just as physically you are not born that abstract entity, man, but the child of particular parents, so you are in matters of literary judgment. Your opinion is almost entirely of the literary history that came just before you, and you are governed by that whatever you may think. Take Spinoza's example of a stone falling to the ground. If it had a conscious mind it would, he said, think it was going to the ground because it wanted to. So you with your pretended free judgment about what is and what is not beautiful. The amount of freedom in man is much exaggerated. That we are free on certain rare occasions, both my religion and the views I get from metaphysics convince me. But many acts which we habitually label free are in reality automatic. It is quite possible for a man to write a book almost automatically. I have read several such products. Some observations were recorded more than twenty years ago by Robertson on reflex speech, and he found that in certain cases of dementia, where the people were quite unconscious so far as the exercise of reasoning went, that very intelligent answers were given to a succession of questions on politics and such matters. The meaning of these questions could not possibly have been understood. Language here acted after the manner of a reflex. So that certain extremely complex mechanisms, subtle enough to imitate beauty, can work by themselves—I certainly think that this is the case with judgments about beauty.

I can put the same thing in slightly different form. Here is a question of a conflict of two attitudes, as it might be of two techniques. The critic, while he has to admit that changes from one to the other occur, persists in regarding them as mere variations to a certain fixed normal, just as a pendulum swing. I admit the analogy of the pendulum as far as movement, but I deny the further consequence of the analogy, the existence of the point of rest, the normal point.

When I say that I dislike the romantics, I dissociate two things: the part of them in which they resemble all the great poets, and the part in which they differ and which gives them their character as romantics. It is this minor element which constitutes the particular note of a century, and which, while it excites contemporaries, annoys the next generation. It was precisely that quality in Pope which pleased his friends,

---

[2] IV. ii. 262–63, but misquoted.

which we detest. Now, anyone just before the romantics who felt that, could have predicted that a change was coming. It seems to me that we stand just in the same position now. I think that there is an increasing proportion of people who simply can't stand Swinburne.

When I say that there will be another classical revival I don't necessarily anticipate a return to Pope. I say merely that now is the time for such a revival. Given people of the necessary capacity, it may be a vital thing; without them we may get a formalism something like Pope. When it does come we may not even recognize it as classical. Although it will be classical it will be different because it has passed through a romantic period. To take a parallel example: I remember being very surprised, after seeing the Postimpressionists, to find in Maurice Denis's account of the matter that they consider themselves classical in the sense that they were trying to impose the same order on the mere flux of new material provided by the Impressionist movement, that existed in the more limited materials of the painting before.

There is something now to be cleared away before I get on with my argument, which is that while romanticism is dead in reality, yet the critical attitude appropriate to it still continues to exist. To make this a little clearer: For every kind of verse, there is a corresponding receptive attitude. In a romantic period we demand from verse certain qualities. In a classical period we demand others. At the present time I should say that this receptive attitude has outlasted the thing from which it was formed. But while the romantic tradition has run dry, yet the critical attitude of mind, which demands romantic qualities from verse, still survives. So that if good classical verse were to be written tomorrow very few people would be able to stand it.

I object even to the best of the romantics. I object still more to the receptive attitude. I object to the sloppiness which doesn't consider that a poem is a poem unless it is moaning or whining about something or other. I always think in this connection of the last line of a poem of John Webster's which ends with a request I cordially endorse: "End your moan and come away."[3] The thing has got so bad now that a poem which is all dry and hard, a properly classical poem, would not be considered poetry at all. How many people now can lay their hands on their hearts and say they like either Horace or Pope? They feel a kind of chill when they read them.

The dry hardness which you get in the classics is absolutely repugnant to them. Poetry that isn't damp isn't poetry at all. They cannot see that accurate description is a legitimate object of verse. Verse to them always means a bringing in of some of the emotions that are grouped round the word infinite.

The essence of poetry to most people is that it must lead them to a beyond of some kind. Verse strictly confined to the earthly and the definite (Keats is full of it) might seem to them to be excellent writing, excellent craftsmanship, but no poetry. So much has romanticism debauched us, that, without some form of vagueness, we deny the highest.

In the classic it is always the light of ordinary day, never the light that never was on land or sea. It is always perfectly human and never exaggerated: man is always man and never a god.

But the awful result of romanticism is that, accustomed to this strange light, you can never live without it. Its effect on you is that of a drug.

There is a general tendency to think that verse means little else than the expression of unsatisfied emotion. People say: "But how can you have verse without sentiment?" You see what it is: the prospect alarms them. A classical revival to them would mean the prospect of an arid desert and the death of poetry as they understand it, and could only come to fill the gap caused by that death. Exactly why this dry classical spirit should have a positive and legitimate necessity to express itself in poetry is utterly inconceivable to them. What this positive need is, I shall show later. It follows from the fact that there is another quality, not the emotion produced, which is at the root of excellence in verse. Before I get to this I am concerned with a negative thing, a theoretical point, a prejudice that stands in the way and is really at the bottom of this reluctance to understand classical verse.

It is an objection which ultimately I believe comes from a bad metaphysic of art. You are unable to admit the existence of beauty without the infinite being in some way or another dragged in.

I may quote for purposes of argument, as a typical example of this kind of attitude made vocal, the famous chapters in Ruskin's *Modern Painters,* Vol. II, on the imagination. I must say here, parenthetically, that I use this word without prejudice to the other discussion with which I shall end the paper. I only use the word here because it is Ruskin's word. All that I am concerned with just now is the attitude behind it, which I take to be the romantic.

> Imagination cannot but be serious; she sees too far, too darkly, too solemnly, too earnestly, ever to smile. There is something in the heart of everything, it we can reach it, that we shall not be inclined to laugh at. . . . Those who have so pierced

---

[3] *The Duchess of Malfi,* IV. ii, but misquoted (*moan* for *groan*).

and seen the melancholy deeps of things, are filled with intense passion and gentleness of sympathy. (Part III, Chapter 3, section 9)

There is in every word set down by the imaginative mind an awful undercurrent of meaning, and evidence and shadow upon it of the deep places out of which it has come. It is often obscure, often half-told; for he who wrote it, in his clear seeing of the things beneath, may have been impatient of detailed interpretation; for if we choose to dwell upon it and trace it, it will lead us always securely back to that metropolis of the soul's dominion from which we may follow out all the ways and tracks to its farthest coasts. (Part III, Chapter 3, section 5)

Really in all these matters the act of judgment is an instinct, an absolutely unstatable thing akin to the art of the tea-taster. But you must talk, and the only language you can use in this matter is that of analogy. I have no material clay to mold to the given shape; the only thing which one has for the purpose, and which acts as a substitute for it, a kind of mental clay, are certain metaphors modified into theories of aesthetic rhetoric. A combination of these, while it cannot state the essentially unstatable intuition, can yet give you a sufficient analogy to enable you to see what it was and to recognize it on condition that you yourself have been in a similar state. Now these phrases of Ruskin's convey quite clearly to me his taste in the matter.

I see quite clearly that he thinks the best verse must be serious. That is a natural attitude for a man in the romantic period. But he is not content with saying that he prefers this kind of verse. He wants to deduce his opinion like his master, Coleridge, from some fixed principle which can be found by metaphysic.

Here is the last refuge of this romantic attitude. It proves itself to be not an attitude but a deduction from a fixed principle of the cosmos.

One of the main reasons for the existence of philosophy is not that it enables you to find truth (it can never do that) but that it does provide you a refuge for definitions. The usual idea of the thing is that it provides you with a fixed basis from which you can deduce the things you want in aesthetics. The process is the exact contrary. You start in the confusion of the fighting line, you retire from that just a little to the rear to recover, to get your weapons right. Quite plainly, without metaphor this—it provides you with an elaborate and precise language in which you really can explain definitely what you mean, but what you want to say is de-

cided by other things. The ultimate reality is the hurly-burly, the struggle; the metaphysic is an adjunct to clearheadedness in it.

To get back to Ruskin and his objection to all that is not serious. It seems to me that involved in this is a bad metaphysical aesthetic. You have the metaphysic which in defining beauty or the nature of art always drags in the infinite. Particularly in Germany, the land where theories of aesthetics were first created, the romantic aesthetes collated all beauty to an impression of the infinite involved in the identification of our being in absolute spirit. In the least element of beauty we have a total intuition of the whole world. Every artist is a kind of pantheist.

Now it is quite obvious to anyone who holds this kind of theory that any poetry which confines itself to the finite can never be of the highest kind. It seems a contradiction in terms to them. And as in metaphysics you get the last refuge of a prejudice, so it is now necessary for me to refute this.

Here follows a tedious piece of dialectic, but it is necessary for my purpose. I must avoid two pitfalls in discussing the idea of beauty. On the one hand there is the old classical view which is supposed to define it as lying in conformity to certain standard fixed forms; and on the other hand there is the romantic view which drags in the infinite. I have got to find a metaphysic between these two which will enable me to hold consistently that a neoclassic verse of the type I have indicated involves no contradiction in terms. It is essential to prove that beauty may be in small, dry things.

The great aim is accurate, precise and definite description. The first thing is to recognize how extraordinarily difficult this is. It is no mere matter of carefulness; you have to use language, and language is by its very nature a communal thing; that is, it expresses never the exact thing but a compromise—that which is common to you, me and everybody. But each man sees a little differently, and to get out clearly and exactly what he does see, he must have a terrific struggle with language, whether it be with words or the technique of other arts. Language has its own special nature, its own conventions and communal ideas. It is only by a concentrated effort of the mind that you can hold it fixed to your own purpose. I always think that the fundamental process at the back of all the arts might be represented by the following metaphor. You know what I call architect's curves—flat pieces of wood with all different kinds of curvature. By a suitable selection from these you can draw approximately any curve you like. The artist I take to be the man who simply can't bear the idea of that "approximately." He will get the exact curve of what he sees whether it be an object or an idea in the mind. I shall here have to change my metaphor a little to get the process in his mind. Suppose that instead of your curved pieces of wood you have a springy piece of steel of the same types of curvature as the wood. Now the state of tension or concentration of mind, if he is doing anything really good in this struggle against the ingrained habit of the technique, may be represented by a man employing all his fingers to bend the steel out of its own curve and into the exact curve which you want. Something different to what it would assume naturally.

There are then two things to distinguish, first the particular faculty of mind to see things as they really are, and apart from the conventional ways in which you have been trained to see them. This is itself rare enough in all consciousness. Second, the concentrated state of mind, the grip over oneself which is necessary in the actual expression of what one sees. To prevent one falling into the conventional curves of ingrained technique, to hold on through infinite detail and trouble to the exact curve you want. Wherever you get this sincerity, you get the fundamental quality of good art without dragging in infinite or serious.

I can now get at that positive fundamental quality of verse which constitutes excellence, which has nothing to do with infinity, with mystery or with emotions.

This is the point I aim at, then, in my argument. I prophesy that a period of dry, hard, classical verse is coming. I have met the preliminary objection founded on the bad romantic aesthetic that in such verse, from which the infinite is excluded, you cannot have the essence of poetry at all.

After attempting to sketch out what this positive quality is, I can get on to the end of my paper in this way: That where you get this quality exhibited in the realm of the emotions you get imagination, and that where you get this quality exhibited in the contemplation of finite things you get fancy.

In prose as in algebra concrete things are embodied in signs or counters which are moved about according to rules, without being visualized at all in the process. There are in prose certain type situations and arrangements of words, which move as automatically into certain other arrangements as do functions in algebra. One only changes the x's and the y's back into physical things at the end of the process. Poetry, in one aspect at any rate, may be considered as an effort to avoid this characteristic of prose. It is not a counter language, but a visual concrete one. It is a compromise for a language of intuition which would hand over sensations bodily. It always endeavors to arrest you, and to make you continuously see a physical thing, to prevent you gliding through an abstract process. It chooses fresh epithets and fresh metaphors, not so much because they are new, and we are tired of the

old, but because the old cease to convey a physical thing and become abstract counters. A poet says a ship "coursed the seas" to get a physical image, instead of the counter word *sailed.* Visual meanings can only be transferred by the new bowl of metaphor; prose is an old pot that lets them leak out. Images in verse are not mere decoration, but the very essence of an intuitive language. Verse is a pedestrian taking you over the ground, prose—a train which delivers you at a destination.

I can now get on to a discussion of two words often used in this connection, *fresh* and *unexpected.* You praise a thing for being fresh. I understand what you mean, but the word besides conveying the truth conveys a secondary something which is certainly false. When you say a poem or drawing is fresh, and so good, the impression is somehow conveyed that the essential element of goodness is freshness, that it is good because it is fresh. Now this is certainly wrong, there is nothing particularly desirable about freshness per se. Works of art aren't eggs. Rather the contrary. It is simply an unfortunate necessity due to the nature of language and technique that the only way the element which does constitute goodness, the only way in which its presence can be detected externally, is by freshness. Freshness convinces you, you feel at once that the artist was in an actual physical state. You feel that for a minute. Real communication is so very rare, for plain speech is unconvincing. It is in this rare fact of communication that you get the root of aesthetic pleasure.

I shall maintain that wherever you get an extraordinary interest in a thing, a great zest in its contemplation which carries on the contemplator to accurate description in the sense of the word *accurate* I have just analyzed, there you have sufficient justification for poetry. It must be an intense zest which heightens a thing out of the level of prose. I am using contemplation here just in the same way that Plato used it, only applied to a different subject; it is a detached interest. "The object of aesthetic contemplation is something framed apart by itself and regarded without memory or expectation, simply as being itself, as end not means, as individual not universal."

To take a concrete example. I am taking an extreme case. If you are walking behind a woman in the street, you notice the curious way in which the skirt rebounds from her heels. If that peculiar kind of motion becomes of such interest to you that you will search about until you can get the exact epithet which hits it off, there you have a properly aesthetic emotion. But it is the zest with which you look at the thing which decides you to make the effort. In this sense the feeling that was in Herrick's mind when he wrote "the tempestuous petticoat"[4] was exactly the same as that which in bigger and vaguer matters makes the best romantic verse. It doesn't matter an atom that the emotion produced is not of dignified vagueness, but on the contrary amusing; the point is that exactly the same activity is at work as in the highest verse. That is the avoidance of conventional language in order to get the exact curve of the thing.

I have still to show that in the verse which is to come, fancy will be the necessary weapon of the classical school. The positive quality I have talked about can be manifested in ballad verse by extreme directness and simplicity, such as you get in *On Fair Kirkconnel Lea*. But the particular verse we are going to get will be cheerful, dry and sophisticated, and here the necessary weapon of the positive quality must be fancy.

Subject doesn't matter; the quality in it is the same as you get in the more romantic people.

It isn't the scale or kind of emotion produced that decides, but this one fact: Is there any real zest in it? Did the poet have an actually realized visual object before him in which he delighted? It doesn't matter if it were a lady's shoe or the starry heavens.

Fancy is not mere decoration added on to plain speech. Plain speech is essentially inaccurate. It is only by new metaphors, that is, by fancy, that it can be made precise.

When the analogy has not enough connection with the thing described to be quite parallel with it, where it overlays the thing it described and there is a certain excess, there you have the play of fancy—that I grant is inferior to imagination.

But where the analogy is every bit of it necessary for accurate description in the sense of the word *accurate* I have previously described, and your only objection to this kind of fancy is that it is not serious in the effect it produces, then I think the objection to be entirely invalid. If it is sincere in the accurate sense, when the whole of the analogy is necessary to get out the exact curve of the feeling or thing you want to express—there you seem to me to have the highest verse, even though the subject be trivial and the emotions of the infinite far away.

It is very difficult to use any terminology at all for this kind of thing. For whatever word you use is at once sentimentalized. Take Coleridge's word *vital*. It is used loosely by all kinds of people who talk about art, to mean something vaguely and mysteriously significant. In fact, vital and mechanical is to them exactly the same antithesis as between good and bad.

Nothing of the kind; Coleridge uses it in a perfectly definite and what I call dry sense. It is just this: A mechanical complexity is the sum of its parts. Put them side by side and you get the whole. Now vital or organic is merely a convenient metaphor for a complexity of a different kind, that in which the parts cannot be said to be elements as each one is modified by the other's presence, and each one to a certain extent is the whole. The leg of a chair by itself is still a leg. My leg by itself wouldn't be.

Now the characteristic of the intellect is that it can only represent complexities of the mechanical kind. It can only make diagrams, and diagrams are essentially things whose parts are separate one from another. The intellect always analyzes—when there is a synthesis it is baffled. That is why the artist's work seems mysterious. The intellect can't represent it. This is a necessary consequence of the particular nature of the intellect and the purposes for which it is formed. It doesn't mean that your synthesis is ineffable, simply that it can't be definitely stated.

Now this is all worked out in Bergson, the central feature of his whole philosophy. It is all based on the clear conception of these vital complexities which he calls "intensive" as opposed to the other kind which he calls "extensive," and the recognition of the fact that the intellect can only deal with the extensive multiplicity. To deal with the intensive you must use intuition.

Now, as I said before, Ruskin was perfectly aware of all this, but he had no such metaphysical background which would enable him to state definitely what he meant. The result is that he has to flounder about in a series of metaphors. A powerfully imaginative mind seizes and combines at the same instant all the important ideas of its poem or picture, and while it works with one of them, it is at the same instant working with and modifying all in their relation to it and never losing sight of their bearings on each other—as the motion of a snake's body goes through all parts at once and its volition acts at the same instant in coils which go contrary ways.

A romantic movement must have an end of the very nature of the thing. It may be deplored, but it can't be helped—wonder must cease to be wonder.

I guard myself here from all the consequences of the analogy, but it expresses at any rate the inevitableness of the process. A literature of wonder must have an end as inevitably as a strange land loses its strangeness when one lives in it. Think of the lost ecstasy of the Elizabethans. "Oh my America, my new found land," think of what it meant to them and of what it means to us. Wonder can only be the attitude of a man passing from one stage to another, it can never be a permanently fixed thing.

---

[4]*Delight in Disorder*, 10.

Bergson's Theory of Art

1. The great difficulty in any talk about art lies in the extreme indefiniteness of the vocabulary you are obliged to employ. The concepts by which you endeavor to describe your attitude toward any work of art are so extraordinarily fluid. Words like creative, expressive, vital, rhythm, unity and personality are so vague that you can never be sure when you use them that you are conveying over at all the meaning you intended to. This is constantly realized unconsciously; in almost every decade a new catchword is invented which for a few years after its invention does convey, to a small set of people at any rate, a definite meaning, but even that very soon lapses into a fluid condition when it means anything and nothing.

This leads me to the point of view which I take about Bergson in relation to art. He has not created any new theory of art. That would be absurd. But what he does seem to me to have done is that by the acute analysis of certain mental processes he has enabled us to state definitely and with less distortion the qualities which we feel in art.

2. The finished portrait is explained by the features of the model, by the nature of the artist, by the colors spread out of the palette; but even with the knowledge of what explains it, no one, not even the artist, could have foreseen exactly what the portrait would be. For to predict it would be to produce it before it was produced. Creation in art is not necessarily a mere synthesis of elements. Insofar as we are geometricians we reject the unforeseeable. We might accept it assuredly insofar as we are artists, for art lives on creation and implies a belief in the spontaneity of nature. But disinterested art is a luxury like pure speculation. Our eye perceives the features of the living being merely as assembled, not as mutually organized. The intention of life—a simple movement which runs through the lines and binds them together and gives them significance—escapes it. This intention is just what the artist tries to regain in placing himself back within the object by a kind of sympathy and breaking down by an effort of intuition the barrier that space puts between him and his model. It is true that this aesthetic intuition, like external perception, only attains the individual, but we can conceive an inquiry turned in the same direction as art which would take life in general for its object just as

physical science, following to the end the direction pointed out by external perception, prolongs the individual facts into general laws.

3. In the state of mind produced in you by any work of art there must necessarily be a rather complicated mixture of the emotions. Among these is one which can properly be called an essentially aesthetic emotion. It could not occur alone, isolated; it may only constitute a small proportion of the total emotion produced; but it is, as far as any investigation in the nature of aesthetics is concerned, the important thing. In the total body of effect produced by music, nine-tenths may be an effect which, properly speaking, is independent of the essentially aesthetic emotion which we get from it. The same thing is most obviously true of painting. The total effect produced by any painting is most obviously a composite thing composed of a great many different kinds of emotions—the pleasure one gets from the subject, from the quality of the color and the painting, and then the subsidiary pleasures one gets from recognition of the style, of a period or a particular painter. Mixed up with these is the one, sometimes small element of emotion, which is the veritable aesthetic one.

4. In order to be able to state the nature of the process which I think is involved in any art, I have had to use a certain kind of vocabulary, to postulate certain things. I have had to suppose a reality of infinite variability, and one that escapes all the stock perceptions, without being able to give any actual account of that reality. I have had to suppose that human perception gets crystalized out along certain lines, that it has certain fixed habits, certain fixed ways of seeing things, and is so unable to see things as they are.

Putting the thing generally—I have had to make all kinds of suppositions simply and solely for the purpose of being able to convey over and state the nature of the activity you get in art. Now the extraordinary importance of Bergson for any theory of art is that, starting with a different aim altogether, seeking merely to give an account of reality, he arrives at certain conclusions as being true, and these conclusions are the very things which we had to suppose in order to give an account of art. The advantage of this is that it removes your account of art from the merely literary level, from the level at which it is a more or less successful attempt to describe what you feel about the matter, and enables you to state it as an account of actual reality.

5. The two parts of Bergson's general philosophical position which are important in the theory of aesthetic are (1) the conception of reality as a flux of interpenetrated elements unseizable by the intellect (this gives a more precise meaning to the word *reality* which has been employed so often in the previous pages, when art has been defined as a

BERGSON'S THEORY OF ART. Hulme wrote *Bergson's Theory of Art* in 1913–14. It was first published posthumously in the collection of his critical writing edited by Herbert Read, *Speculations: Essays on Humanism and the Philosophy of Art* (1924). Reprinted by permission of Harcourt Brace Jovanovich, Inc.

more direct communication of reality); and (2) his account of the part played in the development of the ordinary characteristics of the mind by its orientation towards action. This in its turn enables one to give a more coherent account of the reason for what previously has only been assumed, the fact that in ordinary perception, both of external objects and of our internal states, we never perceive things as they are, but only certain conventional types.

6. Man's primary need is not *knowledge* but *action*. The characteristic of the intellect itself Bergson deduces from this fact. The function of the intellect is so to present things not that we may most thoroughly understand them, but that we may successfully act on them. Everything in man is dominated by his necessity of action.

7. The creative activity of the artist is only necessary because of the limitations placed on internal and external perception by the necessities of action. If we could break through the veil which action interposes, if we could come into direct contact with sense and consciousness, art would be useless and unnecessary. Our eyes, aided by memory, would carve out in space and fix in time the most inimitable of pictures. In the center of one's own mind, we should hear constantly a certain music. But as this is impossible, the function of the artist is to pierce through here and there, accidentally as it were, the veil placed between us and reality by the limitations of our perception engendered by action.

8. Philosophers are always giving definitions of art with which the artist, when he is not actively working but merely talking after dinner, is content to agree with, because it puts his function in some grandiose phraseology which he finds rather flattering. I remember hearing Mr. Rothenstein in an after-dinner speech say that "art was the *revelation of the infinite in the finite.*"[1] I am very far from suggesting that he invented that phrase, but I quote it as showing that he evidently felt that it did convey something of the matter. And so it does in a way, but it is so hopelessly vague. It may convey the kind of excitement which art may produce in you, but it in no way fits the actual process that the artist goes through. It defines art in much the same way that saying that I was in Europe would define my position in space. It includes art, but it gives you no specific description of it.

This kind of thing was not dangerous to the artists themselves, because being familiar with the specific thing intended they were able to discount all the rest. When the infinite in the finite was mentioned, they knew the quite specific and limited quality which was intended. The danger comes from the outsiders who, not knowing, not being familiar with the specific quality, take words like infinite in the much bigger sense than is really intended.

9. To describe the nature of the activity you get in art, the philosopher must always create some kind of special vocabulary. He has to make use of certain metaphysical conceptions in order to state the thing satisfactorily. The great advantage of Bergson's theory is that it states the thing most nakedly, with the least amount of metaphysical baggage. In essence, of course, his theory is exactly the same as Schopenhauer's. That is, they both want to convey over the same feeling about art. But Schopenhauer demands such a cumbrous machinery in order to get that feeling out. Art is the pure contemplation of the idea in a moment of emancipation from the will.[2] To state a quite simple thing he has to invent two very extraordinary ones. In Bergson it is an actual contact with reality in a man who is emancipated from the ways of perception engendered by action, but the action is written with a small *a*, not a large one.

10. The process of artistic creation would be better described as a process of discovery and disentanglement. To use the metaphor which one is by now so familiar with—the stream of the inner life, and the definite crystalized shapes on the surface—the big artist, the creative artist, the innovator, leaves the level where things are crystalized out into these definite shapes, and, diving down into the inner flux, comes back with a new shape which he endeavors to fix. He cannot be said to have created it, but to have discovered it, because when he has definitely expressed it we recognize it as true. Great painters are men in whom has originated a certain vision of things which has become or will become the vision of everybody. Once the painter has seen it, it becomes easy for all of us to see it. A mold has been made. But the creative activity came in the effort which was necessary to disentangle this particular type of vision from the general haze—the effort, that is, which is necessary to break molds and to make new ones. For instance, the effect produced by Constable on the English and French schools of landscape painting. Nobody before Constable saw things, or at any rate painted them, in that particular way. This makes it easier to see clearly what one means by an individual way of looking at things. It does not mean something which is peculiar to an individual, for in that case it would be quite valueless. It means that a certain individual artist was able to break through the conventional ways of looking at things which veil reality from us at a certain point, was able to pick out

[1]The idea is Romantic currency. See Coleridge, *The Statesman's Manual*, p. 476.

[2]See Schopenhauer, *The World as Will and Idea*, p. 498.

one element which is really in all of us, but which before he had disentangled it, we were unable to perceive it. It is as if the surface of our mind was a sea in a continual state of motion, that there were so many waves on it, their existence was so transient, and they interfered so much with each other, that one was unable to perceive them. The artist by making a fixed model of one of these transient waves enables you to isolate it out and to perceive it in yourself. In that sense art merely reveals, it never creates.

11. Metaphors soon run their course and die. But it is necessary to remember that when they were first used by the poets who created them they were used for the purpose of conveying over a vividly felt actual sensation. Nothing could be more dead now than the conventional expressions of love poetry, the arrow which pierces the heart and the rest of it, but originally they were used as conveying over the reality of the sensation experienced.

12. If I say the hill is clothed with trees your mind simply runs past the word *clothed,* it is not pulled up in any way to visualize it. You have no distinct image of the trees covering the hill as garments clothe the body. But if the trees had made a distinct impression on you when you saw them, if you were vividly interested in the effect they produced, you would probably not rest satisfied until you had got hold of some metaphor which did pull up the reader and make him visualize the thing. If there was only a narrow line of trees circling the hill near the top, you might say that it was *ruffed* with trees. I do not put this forward as a happy metaphor: I am only trying to get at the feeling which prompts this kind of expression. You have continually to be searching out new metaphors of this kind because the visual effect of a metaphor so soon dies. Even this word *clothed* which I used was probably, the first time it was employed, an attempt on the part of a poet to convey over the vivid impression which the scene gave him. Every word in the language originates as a *live* metaphor, but gradually of course all visual meaning goes out of them and they become a kind of counters. Prose is in fact the museum where the dead metaphors of the poets are preserved.

The thing that concerns me here is of course only the *feeling* which is conveyed over to you by the use of fresh metaphors. It is only where you get these fresh metaphors and epithets employed that you get this vivid conviction which constitutes the purely aesthetic emotion that can be got from imagery.

13. From time to time in a fit of absentmindedness nature raises up minds which are more detached from life—a natural detachment, one innate in the structure of sense or consciousness, which at once reveals itself by a virginal manner of seeing, hearing or thinking.

It is only by accident, and in one sense only, that nature produces someone whose perception is not riveted to practical purposes; hence the diversity of the arts. One applies himself to form, not as it is practically useful in relation to him, but as it is in itself, as it reveals the inner life of things.

In our minds—behind the commonplace conventional expression which conceals emotion—artists attain the original mood and induce us to make the same effort ourselves by rhythmical arrangements of words, which, thus organized and animated with a life of their own, tell us, or rather suggest, things that speech is not calculated to express.

14. "Art should endeavor to show the universal in the particular." This is a phrase that constantly recurs. I remember great play was made with it in Mr. Binyon's little book on Chinese art. You are supposed to show, shining through the accidental qualities of the individual, the characteristics of a universal type. Of course this is perfectly correct if you give the words the right meaning. It seems at first sight to be the exact contrary to the definition that we have arrived at ourselves, which was that art must be always individual and springs from dissatisfaction with the generalized expressions of ordinary perception and ordinary language. The confusion simply springs from the two uses of the word *universal.* To use Croce's example, Don Quixote is a type, but a type of what? He is only a type of all the Don Quixotes.[3] To use again my comparison of the curve, he is an accurately drawn representation of one of the individual curves that vary round the stock type which would be represented by the words *loss of reality* or *love of glory.* He is only universal in the sense that once having had that particular curve pointed out to you, you recognize it again.[4]

15. From time to time, by a happy accident, men are born who either in one of their senses, or in their conscious life as a whole, are less dominated by the *necessities of action.* Nature has forgotten to attach their faculty for perception to their faculty for action. They do not perceive simply for the purposes of action: they perceive just for the sake of perceiving. It is necessary to point out here that this is taken in a profounder sense than the words are generally used. When one says that the mind is practical and that the artist is the person who is able to turn aside from action and to observe things as they are in a disinterested way, one should be careful to say that this does not refer to any conscious or controllable action. The words as they stand have almost a

----

[3] *Aesthetic,* IV.
[4] This discussion is an attempt to resolve the long debate over poetic "universality" that began with Aristotle's distinction between poetry and history (p. 54) and proceeded through Johnson's remarks on the streaks of the tulip (p. 320) and the Romantics' comments on the symbol (pp. 475–76 and 546–49).

moral flavor. One might be understood as implying that one ought not to be so bound up in the practical. Of course the word *practical* is not used in this sense. It refers to something physiological and entirely beyond our control. This orientation of the mind towards action is the theory which is supposed to account for the characteristics of mental life itself, and is not a mere description of an avoidable and superficial habit of the individual mind.

When, therefore, you do get an artist, i.e. a man who either in one of his senses or in his mind generally is emancipated from this orientation of the mind towards action and is able to see things as they are in themselves, you are dealing with a rarity—a kind of accident produced by nature itself and impossible of manufacture.

The artist is the man, then, who on one side of his nature is born detached from the necessities of action. According as this detachment is inherent in one or other of the senses or is inherent in the consciousness, he is painter, musician, or sculptor. If this detachment were complete—if the mind saw freshly and directly in every one of its methods of perception—then you would get a kind of artist such as the world has not yet seen. He would perceive all things in their native purity: the forms, sounds and colors of the physical world as well as the subtlest movements of the inner life. But this, of course, could never taken place. All that you get is a breaking through of the surface covering provided for things by the necessities of action in *one direction* only, i.e. in one *sense* only. Hence the diversity of the arts.

In one man it is the eye which is emancipated. He is able to see individual arrangements of line and color which escape our standardized perceptions. And having perceived a hitherto unrecognized shape he is able gradually to insinuate it into our own perception. Others again retire within themselves. Beneath the conventional expression which hides the individual emotion they are able to see the original shape of it. They induce us to make the same effort ourselves and make us see what they see; by rhythmical arrangements of words they tell us, or rather suggest, things that speech is not calculated to express.

Others get at emotions which have nothing in common with language; certain rhythms of life at the center of our minds. By setting free and emphasizing this music they force it upon our attention: they compel us willy-nilly to fall in with it like passers-by who join in a dance.

In each art, then, the artist picks out of reality something which we, owing to a certain hardening of our perceptions, have been unable to see ourselves.

One might express the differences in the mechanism, by which they do this most easily, in terms of the metaphor by which we have previously expressed the difference between the two selves. Some arts proceed from the outside. They notice that the crystalized shapes on the top of the stream do not express the actual shapes on the waves. They endeavor to communicate the real shapes by adding detail. On the other hand, an art like music proceeds from *the inside* (as it were). By means of rhythm it breaks up the normal flow of our conscious life. It is as if by increasing the flow of the stream inside it broke through the surface crust and so made us realize the real nature of the outline of the inner elements of our conscious life. It does this by means of rhythm which acts something like the means used to bring about the state of hypnosis. The rhythm and measure suspend the normal flow of our sensations by causing our attention to swing to and fro between fixed points and so take hold of us with such force that even the faintest imitation of sadness produces a great effect on us. It increases our sensibility, in fact.

16. What is the nature of the properly "aesthetic" emotion as distinct from the other emotions produced by art?

As I have said, I do not think that Bergson has invented any new theory on this subject, but has simply created a much better vocabulary. That being so, I think that the best way to approach this theory is to state first the kind of rough conception which one had elaborated for oneself, and then to show how it is all straightened up in his analysis. By approaching the theory gradually in this way one can get it more solidly fixed down.

Among all the varied qualities of good verse, and in the complex kind of motion which it can produce, there is one quality it must possess, which can be easily separated from the other qualities and which constitutes this distinctively aesthetic emotion for which we are searching.

This peculiarly *aesthetic* emotion here, as in other arts, is overlaid with all kinds of other emotions and is only perceived by people who really understand verse. To get at what it is quite definitely, I only consider it in as far as it bears on the choice of epithets and images. The same quality is exhibited in the other parts of verse, in the rhythm and meter, for example, but it so happens that it is most easily isolated in the case of epithets.

17. Could reality come into direct contact with sense and consciousness, art would be useless, or rather we should all be artists. All these things that the artist sees exist, yet we do not see them—yet why not?

Between nature and ourselves, even between ourselves and our own consciousness, there is a veil, a veil that is dense with the ordinary man, transparent for the artist and the poet. What made this veil?

Life is action, it represents the acceptance of the utilitarian side of things in order to respond to them by appropriate actions. I look, I listen, I hear, I think I am seeing, I think

I am hearing everything, and when I examine myself I think I am examining my own mind.

But I am not.

What I see and hear is simply a selection made by my senses to serve as a light for my conduct. My senses and my consciousness give me no more than a practical simplification of reality. In the usual perception I have of reality all the differences useless to man have been suppressed. My perception runs in certain molds. Things have been classified with a view to the use I can make of them. It is this classification I perceive rather than the real shape of things. I hardly see an object, but merely notice what class it belongs to—what ticket I ought to apply to it.

18. Everybody is familiar with the fact that the ordinary man does not see things as they are, but only sees certain *fixed types*. To begin with, we see separate things with distinct outlines where as a matter of fact we know that what exists is merely a continuous gradation of color. Then even in outline itself we are unable to perceive the individual. We have in our minds certain fixed conceptions about the shape of a leg. Mr. Walter Sickert is in the habit of telling his pupils that they are unable to draw any individual arm because they think of it as an arm; and because they think of it as an arm they think they know what it ought to be. If it were a piece of almond rock you could draw it, because you have no preconceived notions as to the way the almonds should come. As a rule, then, we never ever perceive the real shape and individuality of objects. We only see stock types. We tend to see not *the* table but only *a* table.[5]

19. One can sum up the whole thing by a metaphor which must not, however, be taken too literally. Suppose that the various kinds of emotions and other things which one wants to represent are represented by various curved lines. There are in reality an infinite number of these curves all differing slightly from each other. But language does not and could not take account of all these curves. What it does do is to provide you with a certain number of standard types by which you can roughly indicate the different classes into which the curves fall. It is something like the wooden curves which architects employ—circles, ellipses, and so forth—by suitable combinations of which they can draw approximately any curve they want, but only approximately. So with ordinary language. Like the architect's curves it only enables us to describe approximately. Now the artist, I take it, is the person who in the first place is able to see an individual curve. This vision he has of the individuality of the curve

breeds in him a dissatisfaction with the conventional means of expression which allow all its individualities to escape.

20. The artist has a double difficulty to overcome. He has in the first place to be a person who is emancipated from the very strong habits of the mind which make us see not individual things but stock types. His second difficulty comes when he tries to express the individual thing which he has seen. He finds then that not only has his mind habits, but that language, or whatever medium of expression he employs, also has its fixed ways. It is only by a certain tension of mind that he is able to force the mechanism of expression out of the way in which it tends to go and into the way he wants. To vary slightly my metaphor of the curves. Suppose that in order to draw a certain individual curve which we perceive, you are given a piece of bent steel spring which has a natural curvature of its own. To make that fit the curve you want you will have to press it to that curve along the whole of its length with all your fingers. If you are unable to keep up this pressure and at one end slacken the pressure, then at that end you will not get the curve you were trying to draw, but the rounded-off curve of the spring itself.

You can observe this actual process at work in all the different arts. You may suppose that in music, for example, a man trying to express and develop a certain theme in the individual form in which it appeared to him might, if he relaxed his grip over the thing, find that it had a tendency to slacken off into resemblances to already heard things. This comparison also illustrates what happens in the decay of any art. Original sincerity, which is often almost grotesque in its individuality, slackens off in the rounded curves of "prettiness."

21. The psychology of the process is something of this kind. You start off with some actual and vividly felt experience. It may be something seen or something felt. You find that when you have expressed this in straightforward language that you have not expressed it at all. You have only expressed it approximately. All the individuality of the emotion as you experienced it has been left out. The straightforward use of words always lets the individuality of things escape. Language, being a communal apparatus, only conveys over that part of the emotion which is common to all of us. If you are able to observe the actual individuality of the emotion you experience, you become dissatisfied with language. You persist in an endeavor to so state things that the meaning does not escape, but is definitely forced on the attention of the reader. To do this you are compelled to invent new metaphors and new epithets. It is here, of course, that the popular misunderstanding about originality comes in. It is usually understood by the outsider in the arts that originality is a desirable quality in itself. Nothing of the kind. It is only the

---

[5]One may note here how opposite to Plato's is Hulme's view of particulars.

defects of language that make originality necessary. It is because language will not carry over the exact thing you want to say, that you are compelled simply, in order to be accurate, to invent original ways of stating things.

22. The motive power behind any art is a certain freshness of experience which breeds dissatisfaction with the conventional ways of expression because they leave out the individual quality of this freshness. You are driven to new means of expression because you persist in an endeavor to get it out exactly as you felt it.

You could define art, then, as a passionate desire for accuracy, and the essentially aesthetic emotion as the excitement which is generated by direct communication. Ordinary language communicates nothing of the individuality and freshness of things. As far as that quality goes we live separated from each other. The excitement of art comes from this rare and unique communication.

23. Creation of imagery is needed to force language to convey over this *freshness* of impression. The particular kind of art we are concerned with here, at any rate, can be defined as an attempt to convey over something which ordinary language and ordinary expression lets slip through. The emotion conveyed by an art in this case, then, is the exhilaration produced by the direct and unusual communication of this fresh impression. To take an example: What is the source of the kind of pleasure which is given to us by the stanza from Keats' *Pot of Basil,* which contains the line "And she forgot the blue above the trees"? I do not put forward the explanation I give here as being, as a matter of fact, the right one, for Keats might have had to put trees for the sake of the rhyme, but I suppose for the sake of illustration that he was free to put what he liked. Why then did he put *blue above the trees* and not *sky? Sky* is just as attractive an expression. Simply for this reason, that he instinctively felt that the word *sky* would not convey over the actual vividness and the actuality of the feeling he wanted to express. The choice of the right detail, the blue above the trees, forces that vividness on you and is the cause of the kind of thrill it gives you.

24. This particular argument is concerned only with a very small part of the effects which can be produced by poetry, but I have only used it as an illustration. I am not trying to explain poetry, but only to find out in a very narrow field of art, that of the use of imagery, what exactly the kind of emotion you call aesthetic consists of. The element in it which will be found in the rest of art is not the accidental fact that imagery conveys over an actually felt visual sensation, but the actual character of that communication, the fact that it hands you over the sensation as directly as possible, attempts to get it over bodily with all the qualities it possessed for you when you experienced it.

The feeling conveyed over to one is almost a kind of instinctive feeling. You get continuously from good imagery this conviction that the poet is constantly in presence of a vividly felt physical and visual scene.

25. You can perhaps trace this out a little more clearly in a wider art, that of prose description, the depicting of a character or emotion. You are not concerned here with handing over any visual scene, but in an attempt to get an emotion as near as possible as you feel it. You find that language has the same defects as the metaphors we have just been talking about. It lets what you want to say escape. Each of us has his own way of feeling, liking and disliking. But language denotes these states by the same word in every case, so that it is only able to fix the objective and impersonal aspect of the emotions which we feel. Language, as in the first case, lets what you want to say slip through. In any writing which you recognize as good there is always an attempt to avoid this defect of language. There is an attempt, by the adding of certain kinds of intimate detail, to lift the emotion out of the impersonal and colorless level, and to give to it a little of the individuality which it really possesses.

26. Certain kinds of prose, at any rate, never attempt to give you any visual presentment of an object. To do so would be quite foreign to its purpose. It is endeavoring always not to give you any image, but to hurry you along to a conclusion. As in algebra certain concrete things are embodied in signs or counters which are moved about according to rule without being visualized at all in the process, so certain type situations and arrangements of words move automatically into certain other arrangements without any necessity at all to translate the words back into concrete imagery. In fact, any necessity to visualize the words you are using would be an impediment, it would delay the process of reasoning. When the words are merely counters they can be moved about much more rapidly.

Now any tendency towards counter language of this kind has to be carefully avoided by poetry. It always endeavors, on the contrary, to arrest you and to make you continuously see a physical thing.

27. Language, we have said, only expresses the lowest common denominator of the emotions of one kind. It leaves out all the individuality of an emotion as it really exists and substitutes for it a kind of stock or type emotion. Now here comes the additional observation which I have to make. As we not only express ourselves in words, but for the most part think also in them, it comes about that not only do we not express more than the impersonal element of an emotion, but that we do not, as a matter of fact, perceive more. The average person as distinct from the artist does not even *perceive* the individuality of their own emotions. Our faculties of per-

ception are, as it were, crystalized out into certain molds. Most of us, then, never see things as they are, but see only the stock types which are embodied in language.

This enables one to give a first rough definition of the artist. It is not sufficient to say that an artist is a person who is able to convey over the actual things he sees or the emotions he feels. It is necessary before that that he should be a person who is able to emancipate himself from the molds which language and ordinary perception force on him and be able to see things freshly as they really are.

Though one may have some difficulty at first sight in seeing that one only perceives one's own emotions in stock types, yet the thing is much more easy to observe in the actual perception of external things with which you are concerned in painting.

28. I exaggerate the place of imagery simply because I want to use it as an illustration.

In this case something is physically presented; the important thing is, of course, not the fact of the visual representation, but the communication over of the actual contact with reality.

It is because he realizes the inadequacy of the usual that he is obliged to invent.

The gradual conclusion of the whole matter (and only as a conclusion) is that language puts things in a stereotyped form.

This is not the only kind of effect produced on one by verse but it is (if one extends the same quality to the other aspects of verse I have left out) the one essentially aesthetic emotion it produces on us. Readers of poetry may attach more importance to the other things, but this is the quality the poets recognize among each other. If one wants to fix it down then one can describe it as a "kind of instinctive feeling which is conveyed over to one, that the poet is describing something which is actually present to him, which he realizes visually at first hand."

Is there anything corresponding to this in painting?

29. The essential element in the pleasure given us by a work of art lies in the feeling given us by this rare accomplishment of *direct communication*. Mr. Berenson in his book on the Florentine painters expresses in a different vocabulary what is essentially the same feeling. The part of the book I am thinking of is that where he explains the superiority of Giotto to Duccio. He picks out the essential quality of a painting as its "life-communicating" quality, as rendered by form and movement. Form in the figure arts gives us pleasure because it has extracted and presented to us the structural significance of objects more completely than we (unless we be also great artists) could have grasped them by ourselves. By emphasis the artist gives us an intimate realization of an object. In ordinary life I realize a given object, say with the given intensity *two*. An artist realizes this with the intensity *four* and by his manner of emphasizing it makes me realize it with the same intensity. This exhilarates me by communicating a sense of increased capacity. In that sense it may be said to be life-communicating. This emphasis can be conveyed in various ways: by form as in Giotto, and by movement expressed in line, as in Botticelli. This is exactly what Bergson is getting at. But instead of saying that an artist makes you realize with intensity *four* what you previously realized with intensity *two*, he would say that he makes you realize something which you actually did not perceive before. When you come to the detailed application of this to art you find that they are both different ways of saying the same thing. They both agree in picking out this life-communicating quality as the essentially aesthetic one. And they both give the same analysis of the feat accomplished by the artist. The advantage of Bergson's account of the matter is that the expressions he uses are part of a definite conception of reality and not mere metaphors invented specially for the purpose of describing art. More than that, he is able to explain why it is that the ordinary man does not perceive things at all *vividly* and can only be made to do so by the artist. Both these things are of very little advantage as far as actual art criticism is concerned, but they are distinct advantages to anyone who wants to place art definitely in relation to other human activities.

Walter Benjamin

1892–1940

Walter Benjamin, who in 1940 tragically took his own life in order to escape capture by the Nazis, was never an institutional critic. Without institutional affiliation, he completed only one book, the now highly praised *Ursprung des deutschen Trauerspiels (The Origin of German Tragic Drama)*. The manuscript was rejected for a doctorate at Frankfurt in 1925 and only finally published as a whole in 1928. All of this may be viewed today as a considerable irony not only because of the book's present reputation but also because of Benjamin's connection with the later Frankfurt "school" of social thinkers, though this relationship was always an ambivalent one, as was the relation to Marxism. Theodor Adorno criticized Benjamin's views as static rather than dialectical and accused him of a retreat into metaphor.

The fact is that Benjamin was a *critic,* and as one he ranged far for subject matter and remained open to the use of many insights from many intellectual quarters. His acquaintances among intellectuals included Bertolt Brecht and Gershom Scholem. He knew both Marxism and Kabbalah. Though it would be fair to call him a historical materialist, as his "Theses on the Philosophy of History" might suggest, one also must note his wariness of the hardening of any theory into an oppressive form. He can write a Marxist essay on the "Author as Producer," but the selection here, admittedly early in his career, reveals his knowledge of a tradition of thinking about language growing out of Kant and romanticism. One even finds here some affinities to Heidegger. As, among other things, a secular social critic skeptical of transcendences, Benjamin does not flinch from considering language in the light of what the Bible can tell us about it: "The present argument broadly follows [the Bible] in presupposing language as an ultimate reality, perceptible only in its manifestation, inexplicable and mystical." In the process of his argument, Benjamin offers a unique view of what the Biblical "word" might mean.

Benjamin's works are available in the *Gesammelte Schriften* (1974), edited by R. Tiedemann and H. Schweppenhauser. Available in English are *The Origins of German Tragic Drama,* translated by J. Osborne in 1977 with an introduction by George Steiner; *Illuminations* (1969) edited with an introduction by Hannah Arendt; and *Reflections* (1978), edited with an introduction by Peter Demetz. See also Geoffrey Hartman's essay in *Criticism in the Wilderness* (1980) and Martin Jay, *The Dialectical Imagination: A History of the Frankfurt School and the Institute for Social Research, 1923–1950* (1972).

On Language as Such and On the Language of Man

Every expression of human mental life can be understood as a kind of language, and this understanding, in the manner of a true method, everywhere raises new questions. It is possible to talk about a language of music and of sculpture, about a language of justice that has nothing directly to do with those in which German or English legal judgments are couched, about a language of technology that is not the specialized language of technicians. Language in such contexts means the tendency inherent in the subjects concerned—technology, art, justice, or religion—toward the communication of mental meanings. To sum up: all communication of mental meanings is language, communication in words being only a particular case of human language and of the justice, poetry, or whatever underlying it or founded on it. The existence of language, however, is not only coextensive with all the areas of human mental expression in which language is always in one sense or another inherent, but with absolutely everything. There is no event or thing in either animate or inanimate nature that does not in some way partake of language, for it is in the nature of all to communicate their mental meanings. This use of the word "language" is in no way metaphorical. For to think that we cannot imagine anything that does not communicate its mental nature in its expression is entirely meaningful; the greater or lesser degree of consciousness that is apparently (or really) involved in such communication cannot alter the fact that we cannot imagine a total absence of language in anything. An existence entirely without relationship to language is an idea; but this idea can bear no fruit even within that realm of Ideas whose circumference defines the idea of God.

All that is asserted here is that all expression, insofar as it is a communication of mental meaning, is to be classed as language. And expression, by its whole innermost nature, is certainly to be understood only as *language;* on the other hand, to understand a linguistic entity it is always necessary to ask of which mental entity it is the direct expression. That is to say: the German language, for example, is by no means the expression of everything that we could—theoretically—express *through* it, but is the direct expression of that which communicates *itself* in it. This "itself" is a mental entity. It

is therefore obvious at once that the mental entity that communicates itself in language is not language itself but something to be distinguished from it. The view that the mental essence of a thing consists precisely in its language—this view, taken as a hypothesis, is the great abyss into which all linguistic theory threatens to fall,[1] and to survive suspended precisely over this abyss is its task. The distinction between a mental entity and the linguistic entity in which it communicates is the first stage of any study of linguistic theory, and this distinction seems so unquestionable that it is, rather, the frequently asserted identity between mental and linguistic being that constitutes a deep and incomprehensible paradox, the expression of which is found in the ambiguity of the word *logos.* Nevertheless, this paradox has a place, as a solution, at the center of linguistic theory, but remains a paradox, and insoluble, if placed at the beginning.

What does language communicate? It communicates the mental being corresponding to it. It is fundamental that this mental being communicates itself *in* language and not *through* language. Languages therefore have no speaker, if this means someone who communicates *through* these languages. Mental being communicates itself in, not through, a language, which means: it is not outwardly identical with linguistic being. Mental is identical with linguistic being only insofar as it is capable of communication. What is communicable in a mental entity is its linguistic entity. Language therefore communicates the particular linguistic being of things, but their mental being only insofar as this is directly included in their linguistic being, insofar as it is capable of being communicated.

Language communicates the linguistic being of things. The clearest manifestation of this being, however, is language itself. The answer to the question "*What* does language communicate?" is therefore "All language communicates itself." The language of this lamp, for example, does not communicate the lamp (for the mental being of the lamp, insofar as it is *communicable,* is by no means the lamp itself), but: the language-lamp, the lamp in communication, the lamp in expression. For in language the situation is this: the linguistic being of all things is their language. The understanding of linguistic theory depends on giving this proposition a clarity that annihilates even the appearance of tautology. This proposition is untautological, for it means: that which in a mental entity is communicable *is* its language. On this "is" (equivalent to "is immediately") everything depends. Not that which *appears* most clearly in its language

---

ON LANGUAGE AS SUCH AND ON THE LANGUAGE OF MAN. This essay was written in 1916. It is reprinted from *Reflections,* copyright © 1966 by Suhrkamp Verlag, English translation copyright by Harcourt Brace Jovanovich, 1978. Reprinted by permission of Harcourt Brace Jovanovich.

[1][Benjamin] Or is it rather, the temptation to place at the outset a hypothesis that constitutes an abyss for all philosophizing.

is communicable in a mental entity, as was just said by way of transition, but this *capacity* for communication is language itself. Or: the language of a mental entity is directly that which is communicable in it. What is communicable *of* a mental entity, *in* this it communicates itself. Which signifies: all language communicates itself. Or more precisely: all language communicates itself *in* itself; it is in the purest sense the "medium" of the communication. Mediation, which is the immediacy of all mental communication, is the fundamental problem of linguistic theory, and if one chooses to call this immediacy magic, then the primary problem of language is its magic. At the same time, the notion of the magic of language points to something else: its infiniteness. This is conditional on its immediacy. For just because nothing is communicated *through* language, what is communicated *in* language cannot be externally limited or measured, and therefore all language contains its own incommensurable, uniquely constituted infinity. Its linguistic being, not its verbal meanings, defines its frontier.

The linguistic being of things is their language; this proposition, applied to man, means: the linguistic being of man is his language. Which signifies: man communicates his own mental being *in* his language. However, the language of man speaks in words. Man therefore communicates his own mental being (insofar as it is communicable) by *naming* all other things. But do we know any other languages that name things? It should not be accepted that we know of no languages other than that of man, for this is untrue. We only know of no *naming* language other than that of man; to identify naming language with language as such is to rob linguistic theory of its deepest insights. *It is therefore the linguistic being of man to name things.*

Why name them? To whom does man communicate himself? But is this question, as applied to man, other than as applied to other communications (languages)? To whom does the lamp communicate itself? The mountains? The fox? But here the answer is: to man. This is not anthropomorphism. The truth of this answer is shown in knowledge and perhaps also in art. Furthermore, if the lamp and the mountain and the fox did not communicate themselves to man, how should he be able to name them? And he names them; *he* communicates himself by naming *them.* To whom does he communicate himself?

Before this question can be answered we must again inquire: how does man communicate himself? A profound distinction is to be made, a choice presented, in face of which an intrinsically false understanding of language is certain to give itself away. Does man communicate his mental being *by* the names that he gives things? Or *in* them? In the paradoxical nature of these questions lies their answer. Anyone who believes that man communicates his mental being *by*

names cannot also assume that it is his mental being that he communicates, for this does not happen through the names of things, that is, through the words by which he denotes a thing. And, equally, the advocate of such a view can only assume that man is communicating factual subject matter to other men, for that does happen through the word by which he denotes a thing. This view is the bourgeois conception of language, the invalidity and emptiness of which will become increasingly clear in what follows. It holds that the means of communication is the word, its object factual, its addressee a human being. The other conception of language, in contrast, knows no means, no object, and no addressee of communication. It means: *in naming the mental being of man communicates itself to God.*

Naming, in the realm of language, has as its sole purpose and its incomparably high meaning that it is the innermost nature of language itself. Naming is that by which nothing beyond it is communicated, and *in* which language itself communicates itself absolutely. In naming the mental entity that communicates itself is *language.* Where mental being in its communication is language itself in its absolute wholeness, only there is the name, and only the name is there. Name as the heritage of human language therefore vouches for the fact *that language as such* is the mental being of man; and only for this reason is the mental being of man, alone among all mental entities, communicable without residue. On this is founded the difference between human language and the language of things. But because the mental being of man is language itself, he cannot communicate himself by it but only in it. The quintessence of this intensive totality of language as the mental being of man is naming. Man is the namer, by this we recognize that through him pure language speaks. All nature, insofar as it communicates itself, communicates itself in language, and so finally in man. Hence he is the lord of nature and can give names to things. Only through the linguistic being of things can he gain knowledge of them from within himself—in name. God's creation is completed when things receive their names from man, from whom in name language alone speaks. Man can call name the language of language (if the genitive refers to the relationship not of a means but of a medium) and in this sense certainly, because he speaks in name, man is the speaker of language, and for this very reason its only speaker. In terming man the speaker (which, however, according to the Bible, for example, clearly means the name giver: "As man should name all kinds of living creatures, so should they be *called*"), many languages imply this metaphysical truth.

Name, however, is not only the last utterance of language but also the true call of it. Thus in name appears the essential law of language, according to which to express oneself and to address everything else amounts to the same. Language—and in it a mental entity—only expresses itself purely where it speaks in name, that is, in its universal naming. So in name culminate both the intensive totality of language, as the absolutely communicable mental entity, and the extensive totality of language, as the universally communicating (naming) entity. By virtue of its communicating nature, its universality, language is incomplete where the mental entity that speaks from it is not in its whole structure linguistic, that is, communicable. *Man alone has a language this is complete both in its universality and in its intensiveness.*

In the light of this, a question may now be asked without the risk of confusion, a question that, though of the highest metaphysical importance, can be clearly posed first of all as one of terminology. It is whether mental being—not only of man (for that is necessary) but also of things, and thus mental being as such—can from the point of view of linguistic theory be described as of linguistic nature. If mental being is identical with linguistic, then a thing, by virtue of its mental being, is a medium of communication, and what is communicated in it is—in accordance with its mediating relationship—precisely this medium (language) itself. Language is thus the mental being of things. Mental being is therefore postulated at the outset as communicable, or, rather, is situated *within* the communicable, and the thesis that the linguistic being of things is identical with the mental, insofar as the latter is communicable, becomes in its "insofar" a tautology. *There is no such thing as a meaning of language; as communication, language communicates a mental entity, i.e., something communicable per se.* The differences between languages are those of media that are distinguished as it were by their density, that is, gradually; and this with regard to the density both of the communicating (naming) and of the communicable (name) aspects of communication. These two spheres, which are clearly distinguished yet united only in the name language of man, are naturally constantly interrelated.

For the metaphysics of language the equation of mental with linguistic being, which knows only gradual differences, produces a graduation of all mental being in degrees. This graduation, which takes place within mental being itself, can no longer be embraced by any higher category and so leads to the graduation of all being, both mental and linguistic, by degrees of existence or being, such as was already familiar to scholasticism with regard to mental being. However, the equation of mental and linguistic being is of great metaphysical moment to linguistic theory because it leads to the concept that has again and again, as if of its own accord, elevated itself to the center of linguistic philosophy and constituted its most intimate connection with the philosophy

of religion. This is the concept of revelation. Within all linguistic formation a conflict is waged between what is expressed and expressible and what is inexpressible and unexpressed. On considering this conflict one sees, in the perspective of the inexpressible, at the same time the last mental entity. Now it is clear that in the equation of mental and linguistic being the notion of an inverse proportionality between the two is disputed. For this latter thesis runs: the deeper, i.e., the more existent and real the mind, the more it is inexpressible and unexpressed, whereas it is consistent with the equation proposed above to make the relation between mind and language thoroughly unambiguous, so that the expression that is linguistically most existent (i.e., most fixed) is linguistically the most rounded and definitive; in a word, the most expressed is at the same time the purely mental. Exactly this, however, is meant by the concept of revelation, if it takes the inviolability of the word as the only and sufficient condition and characteristic of the divinity of the mental being that is expressed in it. The highest mental region of religion is (in the concept of revelation) at the same time the only one that does not know the inexpressible. For it is addressed in name and expresses itself as revelation. In this, however, notice is given that only the highest mental being, as it appears in religion, rests solely on man and on the language in him, whereas all art, not excluding poetry, does not rest on the ultimate essence of language-mind, but on language-mind confined to things, even if in consummate beauty. *"Language, the mother* of reason and *revelation,* its alpha and omega,"* says Hamann.[2]

Language itself is not perfectly expressed in things themselves. This proposition has a double meaning in its metaphorical and literal senses: the languages of things are imperfect, and they are dumb. Things are denied the pure formal principle of language—sound. They can only communicate to one another through a more or less material community. This community is immediate and infinite, like every linguistic communication; it is magical (for there is also a magic of matter). The incomparable feature of human language is that its magical community with things is immaterial and purely mental, and the symbol of this is sound. The Bible expresses this symbolic fact when it says that God breathes his breath into man: this is at once life and mind and language.

If in what follows the nature of language is considered on the basis of the first chapter of Genesis, the object is neither biblical interpretation, nor subjection of the Bible to objective consideration as revealed truth, but the discovery of what emerges of itself from the biblical text with regard to

---

[2]Johann Georg Hamann (1730–1788), German religious philosopher.

the nature of language; and the Bible is only *initially* indispensable for this purpose because the present argument broadly follows it in presupposing language as an ultimate reality, perceptible only in its manifestation, inexplicable and mystical. The Bible, in regarding itself as a revelation, must necessarily evolve the fundamental linguistic facts. The second version of the story of the Creation, which tells of the breathing of God's breath into man, also reports that man was made from earth. This is, in the whole story of the Creation, the only reference to the material in which the Creator expresses his will, which is doubtless otherwise thought of as creation without mediation. In this second story of the Creation the making of man did not take place through the word: God spoke—and there was—but this man, who is not created from the word, is now invested with the *gift* of language and is elevated above nature.

This curious revolution in the act of creation, where it concerns man, is no less clearly recorded, however, in the first story of the Creation, and in an entirely different context it vouches, with the same certainty, for a special relationship between man and language resulting from the act of creation. The manifold rhythm of the act of creation in the first chapter establishes a kind of basic form from which the act that creates man diverges significantly. Admittedly this passage nowhere expressly refers to a relationship either of man or of nature to the material from which they were created; and the question whether the words "He made" envisages a creation out of material must here be left open, but the rhythm by which the creation of nature (in Genesis 1) is accomplished is: Let there be—He made (created)—He named. In individual acts of creation (1:3; 1:11) only the words "Let there be" occur. In this "Let there be" and in the words "He named" at the beginning and end of the act, the deep and clear relation of the creative act to language appears each time. With the creative omnipotence of language it begins, and at the end language as it were assimilates the created, names it. Language is therefore both creative and the finished creation, it is word and name. In God name is creative because it is word, and God's word is cognizant because it is name. "And he saw that it was good"; that is: He had cognized it through name. The absolute relation of name to knowledge exists only in God, only there is name, because it is inwardly identical with the creative word, the pure medium of knowledge. That means: God made things knowable in their names. Man, however, names them according to knowledge.

In the creation of man the threefold rhythm of the creation of nature has given way to an entirely different order. In it, therefore, language has a different meaning: the trinity of the act is here preserved, but in this very parallelism the divergence is all the more striking: in the threefold "He cre-

ated" of 1:27. God did not create man from the word, and he did not name him. He did not wish to subject him to language, but in man God set language, which had served *Him* as medium of creation, free. God rested when he had left his creative power to itself in man. This creativity, relieved of its divine actuality, became knowledge. Man is the knower in the same language in which God is creator. God created him in his image, he created the knower in the image of the creator. Therefore the proposition that the mental being of man is language needs explanation. His mental being is the language in which creation took place. In the word creation took place, and God's linguistic being is the word. All human language is only reflection of the word in name. Name is no closer to the word than knowledge to creation. The infinity of all human language always remains limited and analytical in nature in comparison to the absolutely unlimited and creative infinity of the divine word.

The deepest images of this divine word and the point where human language participates most intimately in the divine infinity of the pure word, the point at which it cannot become finite word and knowledge, are the human name. The theory of proper names is the theory of the frontier between finite and infinite language. Of all beings man is the only one who himself names his own kind, as he is the only one whom God did not name. It is perhaps bold, but scarcely impossible, to mention the second part of 2:20 in this context: that man named all beings, "*but* for man there was not found a helper fit for him." Accordingly, Adam names his wife as soon as he receives her (woman in the second chapter, Eve in the third). By giving names, parents dedicate their children to God; the names they give do not correspond—in a metaphysical, not etymological sense—to any knowledge, for they name newborn children. In a strict sense, no name ought (in its etymological meaning) to correspond to any person, for the proper name is the word of God in human sounds. By it each man is guaranteed his creation by God, and in this sense he is himself creative, as is expressed by mythological wisdom in the idea (which doubtless not infrequently comes true) that a man's name is his fate. The proper name is the communion of man with the *creative* word of God. (Not the only one, however; man knows a further linguistic communion with God's word.) Through the word man is bound to the language of things. The human word is the name of things. Hence it is no longer conceivable, as the bourgeois view of language maintains, that the word has an accidental relation to its object, that it is a sign for things (or knowledge of them) agreed by some convention. Language never gives *mere* signs. However, the rejection of bourgeois by mystical linguistic theory equally rests on a misunderstanding. For according to mystical theory the word is simply the essence of the thing. That is incorrect, because the thing in itself has no word, being created from God's word and known in its name by a human word. This knowledge of the thing, however, is not spontaneous creation, it does not emerge from language in the absolutely unlimited and infinite manner of creation; rather, the name that man gives to language depends on how language is communicated to him. In name the word of God has not remained creative; it has become in one part receptive, even if receptive to language. Thus fertilized, it aims to give birth to the language of things themselves, from which in turn, soundlessly, in the mute magic of nature, the word of God shines forth.

For conception and spontaneity together, which are found in this unique union only in the linguistic realm, language has its own word, and this word applies also to that conception which is enacted by the nameless in names. It is the translation of the language of things into that of man. It is necessary to found the concept of translation at the deepest level of linguistic theory, for it is much too far-reaching and powerful to be treated in any way as an afterthought, as has happened occasionally. Translation attains its full meaning in the realization that every evolved language (with the exception of the word of God) can be considered as a translation of all the others. By the relation, mentioned earlier, of languages as between media of varying densities, the translatability of languages into one another is established. Translation is removal from one language into another through a continuum of transformations. Translation passes through continua of transformation, not abstract areas of identity and similarity.

The translation of the language of things into that of man is not only a translation of the mute into the sonic; it is also the translation of the nameless into name. It is therefore the translation of an imperfect language into a more perfect one, and cannot but add something to it, namely knowledge. The objectivity of this translation is, however, guaranteed by God. For God created things; the creative word in them is the germ of the cognizing name, just as God, too, finally named each thing after it was created. But obviously this naming is only an expression of the identity of the creative word and the cognizing name in God, not the prior solution of the task that God expressly assigns to man himself: that of naming things. In receiving the unspoken nameless language of things and converting it by name into sounds, man performs this task. It would be insoluble were not the name-language of man and the nameless one of things related in God and released from the same creative word, which in things became the communication of matter in magic communion, and in man the language of knowledge and name in blissful mind. Hamann says: "Everything that man heard in

the beginning, saw with his eyes, and felt with his hands was the living word; for God was the word. With this word in his mouth and in his heart, the origin of language was as natural, as close, and as easy as a child's game. . . ." Friedrich Müller, in his poem "Adam's Awakening and First Blissful Nights," has God summon man to name giving in these words: "Man of the earth step near, in gazing grow more perfect, more perfect through the word."[3] By this combination of contemplation and naming is implied the communicating muteness of things (animals) toward the word language of man, which receives them in name. In the same chapter of the poem, the poet expresses the realization that only the word from which things are created permits man to name them, by communicating itself in the manifold languages of animals, even if mutely, in the image: God gives each beast in turn a sign, whereupon they step before man to be named. In an almost sublime way the linguistic community of mute creation with God is thus conveyed in the image of the sign.

As the unspoken word in the existence of things falls infinitely short of the naming word in the knowledge of man, and as the latter in turn must fall short of the creative word of God, there is reason for the multiplicity of human languages. The language of things can pass into the language of knowledge and name only through translation—as many translations, so many languages—once man has fallen from the paradisiac state that knew only one language. (According to the Bible, this consequence of the expulsion from paradise admittedly came about only later.) The paradisiac language of man must have been one of perfect knowledge; whereas later all knowledge is again infinitely differentiated in the multiplicity of language, was indeed forced to differentiate itself on a lower level as creation in name. For that the language of paradise was fully cognizant, even the existence of the tree of knowledge cannot conceal. Its apples were supposed to impart knowledge of good and evil. But on the seventh day, God had already cognized with the words of creation. And God saw that it was good. The knowledge to which the snake seduces, that of good and evil, is nameless. It is vain in the deepest sense, and this very knowledge is itself the only evil known to the paradisiac state. Knowledge of good and evil abandons name, it is a knowledge from outside, the uncreated imitation of the creative word. Name steps outside itself in this knowledge: the Fall marks the birth of the *human word,* in which name no longer lives intact, and which has stepped out of name language, the language of knowledge, from what we may call its own imma-

---

[3]Friedrich Müller (1749–1825), German poet and painter.

nent magic, in order to become expressly, as it were externally, magic. The word must communicate *something* (other than itself). That is really the Fall of language-mind. The word as something externally communicating, as it were a parody by the expressly mediate word of the expressly immediate, the creative word of God, and the decay of the blissful, Adamite language-mind that stand between them. For in reality there exists a fundamental identity between the word that, after the promise of the snake, knows good and evil, and the externally communicating word. The knowledge of things resides in name, whereas that of good and evil is, in the profound sense in which Kierkegaard uses the word, "prattle," and knows only one purification and elevation, to which the prattling man, the sinner, was therefore submitted: judgment. Admittedly, the judging word has direct knowledge of good and evil. Its magic is different from that of name, but equally magical. This judging word expels the first human beings from paradise; they themselves have aroused it in accordance with the immutable law by which this judging word punishes—and expects—its own awakening as the only, the deepest guilt. In the Fall, since the eternal purity of names was violated, the sterner purity of the judging word arose. For the essential composition of language the Fall has a threefold significance (without mentioning its other meanings). In stepping outside the purer language of name, man makes language a means (that is, a knowledge inappropriate to him), and therefore also, in one part at any rate, a *mere* sign; and this later results in the plurality of languages. The second meaning is that from the Fall, in exchange for the immediacy of name damaged by it, a new immediacy arises, the magic of judgment, which no longer rests blissfully in itself. The third meaning that can perhaps be tentatively ventured is that the origin of abstraction, too, as a faculty of language-mind, is to be sought in the Fall. For good and evil, being unnamable, nameless, stand outside the language of names, which man leaves behind precisely in the abyss opened by this question. Name, however, with regard to existing language, offers only the ground in which its concrete elements are rooted. But the abstract elements of language—we may perhaps surmise—are rooted in the word of judgment. The immediacy (which, however, is the linguistic root) of the communicability of abstraction resides in judgment. This immediacy in the communication of abstraction came into being as judgment, when, in the Fall, man abandoned immediacy in the communication of the concrete, name, and fell into the abyss of the mediateness of all communication, of the word as means, of the empty word, into the abyss of prattle. For—it must be said again—the question as to good and evil in the world after creation was empty prattle. The tree of knowledge did not stand in the garden of God in order to dispense information on good and evil, but as an emblem of judgment over the questioner. This immense irony marks the mythical origin of law.

After the Fall, which, in making language mediate, laid the foundation for its multiplicity, it could be only a step to linguistic confusion. Since men had injured the purity of name, the turning away from that contemplation of things in which their language passes into man needed only to be completed in order to deprive men of the common foundation of an already shaken language-mind. *Signs* must become confused where things are entangled. The enslavement of language in prattle is joined by the enslavement of things in folly almost as its inevitable consequence. In this turning away from things, which was enslavement, the plan for the tower of Babel came into being, and linguistic confusion with it.

The life of man in pure language-mind was blissful. Nature, however, is mute. True, it can be clearly felt in the second chapter of Genesis how this muteness, named by man, itself became bliss, only of lower degree. Friedrich Müller has Adam say to the animals that leave him after he has named them, "And saw by the nobility with which they leaped away from me that the man had given them a name." After the Fall, however, when God's word curses the ground, the appearance of nature is deeply changed. Now begins its other muteness, which we mean by the deep sadness of nature. It is a metaphysical truth that all nature would begin to lament if it were endowed with language. (Though to "endow with language" is more than to "make able to speak.") This proposition has a double meaning. It means, first: she would lament language itself. Speechlessness: that is the great sorrow of nature (and for the sake of her redemption the life and language of *man*—not only, as is supposed, of the poet—are in nature). This proposition means, secondly: she would lament. Lament, however, is the most undifferentiated, impotent expression of language; it contains scarcely more than the sensuous breath; and even where there is only a rustling of plants, in it there is always a lament. Because she is mute, nature mourns. Yet the inversion of this proposition leads even further into the essence of nature; the sadness of nature makes her mute. In all mourning there is the deepest inclination to speechlessness, which is infinitely more than inability or disinclination to communicate. That which mourns feels itself thoroughly known by the unknowable. To be named—even when the namer is Godlike and blissful—perhaps always remains an intimation of mourning. But how much more melancholy to be named not from the one blessed, paradisiac language of names, but from the hundred languages of man, in which name has already withered, yet which, according to God's pronounce-ment, have knowledge of things. Things have no proper names except in God. For in his creative word, God called them into being, calling them by their proper names. In the language of men, however, they are over-named. There is, in the relation of human languages to that of things, something that can be approximately described as "over-naming": over-naming as the deepest linguistic reason for all melan-choly and (from the point of view of the thing) of all delib-erate muteness. Over-naming as the linguistic being of mel-ancholy points to another curious relation of language: the overprecision that obtains in the tragic relationship between the languages of human speakers.

There is a language of sculpture, of painting, of poetry. Just as the language of poetry is partly, if not solely, founded on the name language of man, it is very conceivable that the language of sculpture or painting is founded on certain kinds of thing languages, that in them we find a translation of the language of things into an infinitely higher language, which may still be of the same sphere. We are concerned here with nameless, nonacoustic languages, languages issuing from matter; here we should recall the material community of things in their communication.

Moreover, the communication of things is certainly communal in a way that grasps the world as such as an un-divided whole.

For an understanding of artistic forms it is of value to attempt to grasp them all as languages and to seek their con-nection with natural languages. An example that is appropri-ate because it is derived from the acoustic sphere is the kin-ship between song and the language of birds. On the other hand, it is certain that the language of art can be understood only in the deepest relationship to the doctrine of signs. Without the latter any linguistic philosophy remains entirely fragmentary, because the relationship between language and sign (of which that between human language and writing of-fers only a very particular example) is original and fundamental.

This provides an opportunity to describe another antith-esis that permeates the whole sphere of language and has important relations to the antithesis already mentioned be-tween language in a narrower sense and signs, with which, of course, language by no means necessarily coincides. For language is in every case not only communication of the communicable but also, at the same time, a symbol of the noncommunicable. This symbolic side of language is con-nected to its relation to signs, but extends more widely, for example, in certain respects, to name and judgment. These have not only a communicating function, but most probably also a closely connected symbolic function, to which, at least explicitly, no reference has here been made.

These considerations therefore leave us a purified con-cept of language, even though it may still be an imperfect one. The language of an entity is the medium in which its mental being is communicated. The uninterrupted flow of this communication runs through the whole of nature from the lowest forms of existence to man and from man to God. Man communicates himself to God through name, which he gives to nature and (in proper names) to his own kind, and to nature he gives names according to the communication that he receives from her, for the whole of nature, too, is imbued with a nameless, unspoken language, the residue of the cre-ative word of God, which is preserved in man as the cogniz-ing name and above man as the judgment suspended over him. The language of nature is comparable to a secret pass-word that each sentry passes to the next in his own language, but the meaning of the password is the sentry's language it-self. All higher language is a translation of those lower, until in ultimate clarity the word of God unfolds, which is the unity of this movement made up of language.

Victor Shklovsky

1893–1984

A principal notion offered by the Russian Formalist movement early in the twentieth century was that of *defamiliarization.* In Victor Shklovsky's essay below the term plays a principal role. Defamiliarization is a device to destroy habitual or "automatic" perception, as Boris Eichenbaum later described it (see p. 800). Shklovsky presents the notion as part of an attack on the theories of Alexander Potebnya and of the Russian Symbolist movement in general. In place of emphasis on symbols and images as the fundamental defining elements of poetry—"thinking in images"—Shklovsky and the formalists would study "phonetic and lexical structure" as well as the "characteristic distribution of words . . . the characteristic thought structures compounded from words." Clearly the shift leads to the structuralist movement, which finds its sources in Russian Formalism and developments contemporary to it in linguistics, particularly those of the so-called Prague School. All of the structures Shklovsky mentions create defamiliarization in poetry. The result in poetry is the experience of new satisfactions and perspectives. Poetry is described as "difficult, roughened, impeded language"; it is "attenuated, tortuous speech"; obviously it is "formed" speech. Even rhythm is seen according to this notion, and the result is a reversal of our usual notions of poetic technique.

Shklovsky was a founder of the OPAYEZ group in Russia, which flourished until it came under sharp and repressive attack by the State. Shklovsky was particularly attacked by Leon Trotsky in his *Literature and Revolution* (1924), a section of which appears on p. 792. The movement was then defended by one of its founders Boris Eichenbaum in his essay "The Theory of the 'Formal Method' " (1926), reprinted here beginning on p. 801, where Shklovsky's essay is discussed. Shklovsky himself retreated from theorizing in print under Communist rule and engaged in other literary and cinematic activities; finally, he was reconciled with the government.

Shklovsky's writings were collected and published in a single edition in Moscow in 1973–1974 by Khudozh' Lit'ra. See Victor Erlich, *Russian Formalism: History-Doctrine,* rev. ed. (1964); M. M. Bakhtin [P. N. Medvedev], *The Formal Method in Literary Scholarship* (1978); see also bibliographical material under the selection from Eichenbaum, pp. 800–01. The Formalist movement is put in the context of the history of Russian literary criticism by R. H. Stacy, *Russian Literary Criticism: A Short History* (1974).

Art as Technique

"Art is thinking in images." This maxim, which even high school students parrot, is nevertheless the starting point for the erudite philologist who is beginning to put together some kind of systematic literary theory. The idea, originated in part by Potebnya, has spread. "Without imagery there is no art, and in particular no poetry," Potebnya writes.[1] And elsewhere, "Poetry, as well as prose, is first and foremost a special way of thinking and knowing."[2]

Poetry is a special way of thinking; it is, precisely, a way of thinking in images, a way which permits what is generally called "economy of mental effort," a way which makes for "a sensation of the relative ease of the process." Aesthetic feeling is the reaction to this economy. This is how the academician Ovsyaniko-Kulikovsky,[3] who undoubtedly read the works of Potebnya attentively, almost certainly understood and faithfully summarized the ideas of his teacher. Potebnya and his numerous disciples consider poetry a special kind of thinking—thinking by means of images; they feel that the purpose of imagery is to help channel various objects and activities into groups and to clarify the unknown by means of the known. Or, as Potebnya wrote:

> The relationship of the image to what is being clarified is that: (a) the image is the fixed predicate of that which undergoes change—the unchanging means of attracting what is perceived as changeable. . . . (b) the image is far clearer and simpler than what it clarifies.[4]

In other words:

> Since the purpose of imagery is to remind us, by approximation, of those meanings for which the image stands, and since, apart from this, imagery

is unnecessary for thought, we must be more familiar with the image than with what it clarifies.[5]

It would be instructive to try to apply this principle to Tyutchev's comparison of summer lightning to deaf and dumb demons or to Gogol's comparison of the sky to the garment of God.[6]

"Without imagery there is no art"—"Art is thinking in images." These maxims have led to far-fetched interpretations of individual works of art. Attempts have been made to evaluate even music, architecture, and lyric poetry as imagistic thought. After a quarter of a century of such attempts Ovsyaniko-Kulikovsky finally had to assign lyric poetry, architecture, and music to a special category of imageless art and to define them as lyric arts appealing directly to the emotions. And thus he admitted an enormous area of art which is not a mode of thought. A part of this area, lyric poetry (narrowly considered), is quite like the visual arts; it is also verbal. But, much more important, visual art passes quite imperceptibly into nonvisual art; yet our perceptions of both are similar.

Nevertheless, the definition "Art is thinking in images," which means (I omit the usual middle terms of the argument) that art is the making of symbols, has survived the downfall of the theory which supported it. It survives chiefly in the wake of Symbolism, especially among the theorists of the Symbolist movement.

Many still believe, then, that thinking in images—thinking, in specific scenes of "roads and landscape" and "furrows and boundaries"[7]—is the chief characteristic of poetry. Consequently, they should have expected the history of "imagistic art," as they call it, to consist of a history of changes in imagery. But we find that images change little; from century to century, from nation to nation, from poet to poet, they flow on without changing. Images belong to no one: they are "the Lord's." The more you understand an age, the more convinced you become that the images a given poet used and which you thought his own were taken almost unchanged from another poet. The works of poets are classified or grouped according to the new techniques that poets discover and share, and according to their arrangement and de-

---

ART AS TECHNIQUE. Shklovsky's essay first appeared in 1917. It is reprinted here from *Russian Formalist Criticism: Four Essays,* translated by Lee T. Lemon and Marion J. Reis, Copyright © University of Nebraska Press, 1965. Reprinted by permission of University of Nebraska Press.

[1] Alexander Potebnya (1835–1891), Russian philologist influenced by Wilhelm von Humboldt. [Shklovsky] Alexander Potebnya, *Iz zapisok po teorii slovesnosti [Notes on the Theory of Language]* (Kharkov, 1905), p. 83.

[2] [Shklovsky] Ibid., p. 97.

[3] [Lemon and Reis] Dmitry Ovsyaniko-Kulikovsky (1835–1920), a leading Russian scholar, was an early contributor to Marxist periodicals and a literary conservative, antagonistic towards the deliberately meaningless poems of the Futurists.

[4] [Shklovsky] Potebnya, *Iz zapisok po teorii slovesnosti,* p. 314.

[5] [Shklovsky] Ibid., p. 291.

[6] [Lemon and Reis] Fyodor Tyutchev (1803–1873), a poet, and Nicholas Gogol (1809–1852), master of prose fiction and satire, are mentioned here because their bold use of imagery cannot be accounted for by Potebnya's theory. Shklovsky is arguing that writers frequently gain their effects by comparing the commonplace to the exceptional rather than vice versa.

[7] [Lemon and Reis] This is an allusion to Vyacheslav Ivanov's *Borozdy i mezhi [Furrows and Boundaries]* (Moscow, 1916), a major statement of Symbolist theory.

velopment of the resources of language; poets are much more concerned with arranging images than with creating them. Images are given to poets; the ability to remember them is far more important than the ability to create them.

Imagistic thought does not, in any case, include all the aspects of art nor even all the aspects of verbal art. A change in imagery is not essential to the development of poetry. We know that frequently an expression is thought to be poetic, to be created for aesthetic pleasure, although actually it was created without such intent—e.g., Annensky's opinion that the Slavic languages are especially poetic and Andrey Bely's ecstasy over the technique of placing adjectives after nouns, a technique used by eighteenth-century Russian poets. Bely joyfully accepts the technique as something artistic, or more exactly, as intended, if we consider intention as art. Actually, this reversal of the usual adjective-noun order is a peculiarity of the language (which had been influenced by Church Slavonic). Thus a work may be (1) intended as prosaic and accepted as poetic, or (2) intended as poetic and accepted as prosaic. This suggests that the artistry attributed to a given work results from the way we perceive it. By "works of art," in the narrow sense, we mean works created by special techniques designed to make the works as obviously artistic as possible.

Potebnya's conclusion, which can be formulated "poetry equals imagery," gave rise to the whole theory that "imagery equals symbolism," that the image may serve as the invariable predicate of various subjects. (This conclusion, because it expressed ideas similar to the theories of the Symbolists, intrigued some of their leading representatives—Andrey Bely, Merezhkovsky and his "eternal companions" and, in fact, formed the basis of the theory of Symbolism.) The conclusion stems partly from the fact that Potebnya did not distinguish between the language of poetry and the language of prose. Consequently, he ignored the fact that there are two aspects of imagery: imagery as a practical means of thinking, as a means of placing objects within categories; and imagery as poetic, as a means of reinforcing an impression. I shall clarify with an example. I want to attract the attention of a young child who is eating bread and butter and getting the butter on her fingers. I call, "Hey, butterfingers!" This is a figure of speech, a clearly prosaic trope. Now a different example. The child is playing with my glasses and drops them. I call, "Hey butterfingers!"[8] This figure of speech is a poetic trope. (In the first example, "butterfingers" is metonymic; in the second, metaphoric—but this is not what I want to stress.)

Poetic imagery is a means of creating the strongest possible impression. As a method it is, depending upon its purpose, neither more nor less effective than other poetic techniques; it is neither more nor less effective than ordinary or negative parallelism, comparison, repetition, balanced structure, hyperbole, the commonly accepted rhetorical figures, and all those methods which emphasize the emotional effect of an expression (including words or even articulated sounds.)[9] But poetic imagery only externally resembles either the stock imagery of fables and ballads or thinking in images—e.g., the example in Ovsyaniko-Kulikovsky's *Language and Art* in which a little girl calls a ball a little watermelon. Poetic imagery is but one of the devices of poetic language. Prose imagery is a means of abstraction: a little watermelon instead of a lampshade, or a little watermelon instead of a head, is only the abstraction of one of the object's characteristics, that of roundness. It is no different from saying that the head and the melon are both round. This is what is meant, but it has nothing to do with poetry.

The law of the economy of creative effort is also generally accepted. [Herbert] Spencer wrote:

> On seeking for some clue to the law underlying these current maxims, we may see shadowed forth in many of them, the importance of economizing the reader's or the hearer's attention. To so present ideas that they may be apprehended with the least possible mental effort, is the desideratum towards which most of the rules above quoted point. . . . Hence, carrying out the metaphor that language is the vehicle of thought, there seems reason to think that in all cases the friction and inertia of the vehicle deduct from its efficiency; and that in composition, the chief, if not the sole thing to be done, is to reduce this friction and inertia to the smallest possible amount.[10]

And R[ichard] Avenarius:

> If a soul possess inexhaustible strength, then, of course, it would be indifferent to how much might be spent from this inexhaustible source; only the

---

8[Lemon and Reis] The Russian text involves a play on the word for "hat," colloquial for "clod," "duffer," etc.

9[Lemon and Reis] Shklovsky is here doing two things of major theoretical importance: (1) he argues that different techniques serve a single function, and that (2) no single technique is all important. The second permits the formalists to be concerned with any and all literary devices; the first permits them to discuss the devices from a single consistent theoretical position.

10[Shklovsky] Herbert Spencer, *The Philosophy of Style* (Humboldt Library, vol. 34, New York, 1882), pp. 2–3. [Lemon and Reis] Shklovsky's quoted reference, in Russian, preserves the idea of the original but shortens it.

necessarily expended time would be important. But since its forces are limited, one is led to expect that the soul hastens to carry out the apperceptive process as expediently as possible—that is, with comparatively the least expenditure of energy, and, hence, with comparatively the best result.

Petrazhitsky, with only one reference to the general law of mental effort, rejects [William] James's theory of the physical basis of emotion, a theory which contradicts his own. Even Alexander Veselovsky acknowledged the principle of the economy of creative effort, a theory especially appealing in the study of rhythm, and agreed with Spencer: "A satisfactory style is precisely that style which delivers the greatest amount of thought in the fewest words." And Andrey Bely, despite the fact that in his better pages he gave numerous examples of "roughened" rhythm[11] and (particularly in the examples from Baratynsky) showed the difficulties inherent in poetic epithets, also thought it necessary to speak of the law of the economy of creative effort in his book[12]—a heroic effort to create a theory of art based on unverified facts from antiquated sources, on his vast knowledge of the techniques of poetic creativity, and on Krayevich's high school physics text.

These ideas about the economy of energy, as well as about the law and aim of creativity, are perhaps true in their application to "practical" language; they were, however, extended to poetic language. Hence they do not distinguish properly between the laws of practical language and the laws of poetic language. The fact that Japanese poetry has sounds not found in conversational Japanese was hardly the first factual indication of the differences between poetic and everyday language. Leo Jakubinsky has observed that the law of the dissimilation of liquid sounds does not apply to poetic language.[13] This suggested to him that poetic language tolerated the admission of hard-to-pronounce conglomerations of similar sounds. In his article, one of the first examples of scientific criticism, he indicates inductively, the contrast (I shall say more about this point later) between the laws of poetic language and the laws of practical language.[14]

We must, then, speak about the laws of expenditure and economy in poetic language not on the basis of an analogy with prose, but on the basis of the laws of poetic language.

If we start to examine the general laws of perception, we see that as perception becomes habitual, it becomes automatic. Thus, for example, all of our habits retreat into the area of the unconsciously automatic; if one remembers the sensations of holding a pen or of speaking in a foreign language for the first time and compares that with his feeling at performing the action for the ten thousandth time, he will agree with us. Such habituation explains the principles by which, in ordinary speech, we leave phrases unfinished and words half expressed. In this process, ideally realized in algebra, things are replaced by symbols. Complete words are not expressed in rapid speech; their initial sounds are barely perceived. Alexander Pogodin offers the example of a boy considering the sentence "The Swiss mountains are beautiful" in the form of a series of letters: *T, S, m, a, b.*[15]

This characteristic of thought not only suggests the method of algebra, but even prompts the choice of symbols (letters, especially initial letters). By this "algebraic" method of thought we apprehend objects only as shapes with imprecise extensions; we do not see them in their entirety but rather recognize them by their main characteristics. We see the object as though it were enveloped in a sack. We know what it is by its configuration, but we see only its silhouette. The object, perceived thus in the manner of prose perception, fades and does not leave even a first impression; ultimately even the essence of what it was is forgotten. Such perception explains why we fail to hear the prose word in its entirety (see Leo Jakubinsky's article[16]) and, hence, why (along with other slips of the tongue) we fail to pronounce it. The process of "algebrization," the over-automatization of an object, permits the greatest economy of perceptive effort. Either objects are assigned only one proper feature—a number, for example—or else they function as though by formula and do not even appear in cognition:

> I was cleaning a room and, meandering about, approached the divan and couldn't remember whether or not I had dusted it. Since these movements are habitual and unconscious, I could not remember and felt that it was impossible to remember—so that if I had dusted it and forgot—that is, had acted unconsciously, then it was the same as if I had not. If some conscious person had

---

[11][Lemon and Reis] The Russian *zatrudyonny* means "made difficult." The suggestion is that poems with "easy" or smooth rhythms slip by unnoticed; poems that are difficult or "roughened" force the reader to attend to them.

[12][Lemon and Reis] *Simvolizm*, probably.

[13][Shklovsky] Leo Jakubinsky, "O zvukakh poeticheskovo yazyka" ["On the Sounds of Poetic Language"], *Sborniki* 1 (1916): 38.

[14][Shklovsky] Leo Jakubinsky, "Skopleniye odinakovykh plavnykh v prakticheskom i poeticheskom yazykakh" ["The Accumulation of Identical Liquids in Practical and Poetic Language"], *Sborniki* II (1917): 13–21.

[15][Shklovsky] Alexander Pogodoin, *Yazyk, kak tvorchestvo [Language as Art]* (Kharkov, 1913), p. 42. [Lemon and Reis] The original sentence was in French, "*Les montaignes de la Suisse sont belles,*" with the appropriate initials.

[16][Shklovsky] Jakubinsky, *Sborniki* I (1916).

been watching, then the fact could be established. If, however, no one was looking, or looking on unconsciously, if the whole complex lives of many people go on unconsciously, then such lives are as if they had never been.[17]

And so life is reckoned as nothing. Habitualization devours works, clothes, furniture, one's wife, and the fear of war. "If the whole complex lives of many people go on unconsciously, then such lives are as if they had never been." And art exists that one may recover the sensation of life; it exists to make one feel things, to make the stone *stony*. The purpose of art is to impart the sensation of things as they are perceived and not as they are known. The technique of art is to make objects "unfamiliar," to make forms difficult, to increase the difficulty and length of perception because the process of perception is an aesthetic end in itself and must be prolonged. *Art is a way of experiencing the artfulness of an object; the object is not important.*

The range of poetic (artistic) work extends from the sensory to the cognitive, from poetry to prose, from the concrete to the abstract: from Cervantes's Don Quixote—scholastic and poor nobleman, half consciously bearing his humiliation in the court of the duke—to the broad but empty Don Quixote of Turgenev; from Charlemagne to the name "king" [in Russian "Charles" and "king" obviously derive from the same root, *korol*]. The meaning of a work broadens to the extent that artfulness and artistry diminish; thus a fable symbolizes more than a poem, and a proverb more than a fable. Consequently, the least self-contradictory part of Potebnya's theory is his treatment of the fable, which, from his point of view, he investigated thoroughly. But since his theory did not provide for "expressive" works of art, he could not finish his book. As we know, *Notes on the Theory of Literature* was published in 1905, thirteen years after Potebnya's death. Potebnya himself completed only the section on the fable.[18]

After we see an object several times, we begin to recognize it. The object is in front of us and we know about it, but we do not see it[19]—hence we cannot say anything significant about it. Art removes objects from the automatism of perception in several ways. Here I want to illustrate a way

used repeatedly by Leo Tolstoy, that writer who, for Merezhkovsky at least, seems to present things as if he himself saw them, saw them in their entirety, and did not alter them.

Tolstoy makes the familiar seem strange by not naming the familiar object. He describes an object as if he were seeing it for the first time, an event as if it were happening for the first time. In describing something he avoids the accepted names of its parts and instead names corresponding parts of other objects. For example, in "Shame" Tolstoy "defamiliarizes" the idea of flogging in this way: "to strip people who have broken the law, to hurl them to the floor, and to rap on their bottoms with switches," and, after a few lines, "to lash about on the naked buttocks." Then he remarks:

Just why precisely this stupid, savage means of causing pain and not any other—why not prick the shoulders or any part of the body with needles, squeeze the hands or the feet in a vise, or anything like that?

I apologize for this harsh example, but it is typical of Tolstoy's way of pricking the conscience. The familiar act of flogging is made unfamiliar both by the description and by the proposal to change its form without changing its nature. Tolstoy uses this technique of "defamiliarization" constantly. The narrator of "Kholstomer," for example, is a horse, and it is the horse's point of view (rather than a person's) that makes the content of the story seem unfamiliar. Here is how the horse regards the institution of private property:

I understood well what they said about whipping and Christianity. But then I was absolutely in the dark. What's the meaning of "his own," "his colt"? From these phrases I saw that people thought there was some sort of connection between me and the stable. At the time I simply could not understand the connection. Only much later, when they separated me from the other horses, did I begin to understand. But even then I simply could not see what it meant when they called me "man's property." The words "my horse" referred to me, a living horse, and seemed as strange to me as the words "my land," "my air," "my water."

But the words make a strong impression on me. I thought about them constantly, and only after the most diverse experiences with people did I understand, finally, what they meant. They meant

[17][Shklovsky] Leo Tolstoy's *Diary,* entry dated February 29, 1897. [Lemon and Reis] The date is transcribed incorrectly; it should read March 1, 1897.

[18][Shklovsky] Alexander Potebnya, *Iz lektsy po teorii slovesnosti* [Lectures on the Theory of Language] (Kharkov, 1914).

[19][Shklovsky] Victor Shklovsky, *Voskresheniye slova [The Resurrection of the Word]* (Petersburg, 1914).

this: In life people are guided by words, not by deeds. It's not so much that they love the possibility of doing or not doing something as it is the possibility of speaking with words, agreed on among themselves, about various topics. Such are the words "my" and "mine," which they apply to different things, creatures, objects, and even to land, people, and horses. They agree that only one may say "mine" about this, that, or the other thing. And the one who says "mine" about the greatest number of things is, according to the game which they've agreed to among themselves, the one they consider the most happy. I don't know the point of all this, but it's true. For a long time I tried to explain it to myself in terms of some kind of real gain, but I had to reject that explanation because it was wrong. Many of those, for instance, who called me their own never rode on me—although others did. And so with those who fed me. Then again, the coachman, the veterinarians, and the outsiders in general treated me kindly, yet those who called me their own did not. In due time, having widened the scope of my observations, I satisfied myself that the notion "my," not only in relation to us horses, has no other basis than a narrow human instinct which is called a sense of or right to private property. A man says "this house is mine" and never lives in it; he only worries about its construction and upkeep. A merchant says "my shop," "my dry goods shop," for instance, and does not even wear clothes made from the better cloth he keeps in his own shop.

There are people who call a tract of land their own, but they never set eyes on it and never take a stroll on it. There are people who call others their own, yet never see them. And the whole relationship between them is that the so-called "owners" treat the others unjustly.

There are people who call women their own, or their "wives," but their women live with other men. And people strive not for the good in life, but for goods they can call their own.

I am now convinced that this is the essential difference between people and ourselves. And therefore, not even considering the other ways in which we are superior, but considering just this one virtue, we can bravely claim to stand higher than men on the ladder of living creatures. The actions of men, at least those with whom I have had dealings, are guided by *words*—ours, by deeds.

The horse is killed before the end of the story, but the manner of the narrative, its technique, does not change:

Much later they put Serpukhovsky's body, which had experienced the world, which had eaten and drunk, into the ground. They could profitably send neither his hide, nor his flesh, nor his bones anywhere.

But since his dead body, which had gone about in the world for twenty years, was a great burden to everyone, its burial was only a superfluous embarrassment for the people. For a long time no one had needed him; for a long time he had been a burden on all. But nevertheless, the dead who buried the dead found it necessary to dress this bloated body, which immediately began to rot, in a good uniform and good boots; to lay it in a good new coffin with new tassels at the four corners, then to place this new coffin in another of lead and ship it to Moscow; there to exhume ancient bones and at just that spot, to hide this putrefying body, swarming with maggots, in its new uniform and clean boots, and to cover it over completely with dirt.

Thus we see that at the end of the story Tolstoy continues to use the technique even though the motivation for it [the reason for its use] is gone.

In *War and Peace* Tolstoy uses the same technique in describing whole battles as if battles were something new. These descriptions are too long to quote; it would be necessary to extract a considerable part of the four-volume novel. But Tolstoy uses the same method in describing the drawing room and the theater:

The middle of the stage consisted of flat boards; by the sides stood painted pictures representing trees, and at the back a linen cloth was stretched down to the floor boards. Maidens in red bodices and white skirts sat on the middle of the stage. One, very fat, in a white silk dress, sat apart on a narrow bench to which a green pasteboard box was glued from behind. They were all singing something. When they had finished, the maiden in white approached the prompter's box. A man in silk with tight-fitting pants on his fat legs approached her with a plume and began to sing and spread his arms in dismay. The man in the tight pants finished his song alone; then the girl sang. After that both remained silent as the music resounded; and the man, obviously waiting to begin singing his part with her again, began to run his fingers over the hand of the girl in the white dress. They finished their song together, and everyone in the theater began to clap and shout. But the men and women on stage, who represented lovers, start to bow, smiling and raising their hands.

In the second act there were pictures representing monuments and openings in the linen cloth representing the moonlight, and they raised lamp shades on a frame. As the musicians started to play the bass horn and counter-bass, a large number of people in black mantles poured onto the stage from right and left. The people, with something like daggers in their hands, started to wave their arms. Then still more people came running out and began to drag away the maiden who had been wearing a white dress but who now wore one of sky blue. They did not drag her off immediately, but sang with her for a long time before dragging her away. Three times they struck on something metallic behind the side scenes, and everyone got down on his knees and began to chant a prayer. Several times all of this activity was interrupted by enthusiastic shouts from the spectators.

The third act is described:

> . . . But suddenly a storm blew up. Chromatic scales and chords of diminished sevenths were heard in the orchestra. Everyone ran about and again they dragged one of the bystanders behind the scenes as the curtain fell.

In the fourth act, "There was some sort of devil who sang, waving his hands, until the boards were moved out from under him and he dropped down."[20]

In *Resurrection* Tolstoy describes the city and the court in the same way; he uses a similar technique in "Kreutzer Sonata" when he describes marriage—"Why, if people have an affinity of souls, must they sleep together?" But he did not defamiliarize only those things he sneered at:

> Pierre stood up from his new comrades and made his way between the campfires to the other side of the road where, it seemed, the captive soldiers were held. He wanted to talk with them. The

French sentry stopped him on the road and ordered him to return. Pierre did so, but not to the campfire, not to his comrades, but to an abandoned, unharnessed carriage. On the ground, near the wheel of the carriage, he sat cross-legged in the Turkish fashion, and lowered his head. He sat motionless for a long time, thinking. More than an hour passed. No one disturbed him. Suddenly he burst out laughing with his robust, good natured laugh—so loudly that the men near him looked around, surprised at his conspicuously strange laughter.

> "Ha, ha, ha," laughed Pierre. And he began to talk to himself. "The soldier didn't allow me to pass. They caught me, barred me. Me—me—my immortal soul. Ha, ha, ha," he laughed with tears starting in his eyes.

> Pierre glanced at the sky, into the depths of the departing, playing stars. "And all this is mine, all this is in me, and all this is I," thought Pierre. "And all this they caught and put in a planked enclosure." He smiled and went off to his comrades to lie down to sleep.[21]

Anyone who knows Tolstoy can find several hundred such passages in his work. His method of seeing things out of their normal context is also apparent in his last works. Tolstoy described the dogmas and rituals he attacked as if they were unfamiliar, substituting everyday meanings for the customarily religious meanings of the words common in church ritual. Many persons were painfully wounded; they considered it blasphemy to present as strange and monstrous what they accepted as sacred. Their reaction was due chiefly to the technique through which Tolstoy perceived and reported his environment. And after turning to what he had long avoided, Tolstoy found that his perceptions had unsettled his faith.

The technique of defamiliarization is not Tolstoy's alone. I cited Tolstoy because his work is generally known.

Now, having explained the nature of this technique, let us try to determine the approximate limits of its application. I personally feel that defamiliarization is found almost everywhere form is found. In other words, the difference between Potebnya's point of view and ours is this: An image is not a permanent referent for those mutable complexities of life which are revealed through it; its purpose is not to make us perceive meaning, but to create a special perception of the object—*it creates a "vision" of the object instead of serving as a means for knowing it.*

---

[20][Lemon and Reis] The Tolstoy and Gogol translations are ours. The passage occurs in Vol. II Part 8, Chap. 9 of the edition of *War and Peace* published in Boston by the Dana Estes Co. in 1904–1912.

[21][Lemon and Reis] Leo Tolstoy, *War and Peace,* IV, Part 13. Chap. 14.

The purpose of imagery in erotic art can be studied even more accurately; an erotic object is usually presented as if it were seen for the first time. Gogol, in "Christmas Eve," provides the following example:

> Here he approached her more closely, coughed, smiled at her, touched her plump, bare arm with his fingers, and expressed himself in a way that showed both his cunning and his conceit.
>
> "And what is this you have, magnificent Solokha?" and having said this, he jumped back a little.
>
> "What? An arm, Osip Nikiforovich!" she answered.
>
> "Hmm, an arm! *He, he, he!*" said the secretary cordially, satisfied with his beginning. He wandered about the room.
>
> "And what is this you have, dearest Solokha?" he said in the same way, having approached her again and grasped her lightly by the neck, and in the very same way he jumped back.
>
> "As if you don't see, Osip Nikiforovich!" answered Solokha, "a neck, and on my neck a necklace."
>
> "Hmm! On the neck a necklace! *He, he, he!*" and the secretary again wandered about the room, rubbing his hands.
>
> "And what is this you have, incomparable Solokha?" . . . It is not known to what the secretary would stretch his longer fingers now.

And Knut Hamsun has the following in *Hunger:* "Two white prodigies appeared from beneath her blouse."

Erotic subjects may also be presented figuratively with the obvious purpose of leading us away from their "recognition." Hence sexual organs are referred to in terms of lock and key,[22] or quilting tools,[23] or bow and arrow, or rings and marlinspikes, as in the legend of Stavyor, in which a married man does not recognize his wife, who is disguised as a warrior. She proposes a riddle:

> "Remember, Stavyor, do you recall
> How we little ones walked to and fro in the street?
> You and I together sometimes played with a mar-
>   linspike—
> You had a silver marlinspike,
> But I had a gilded ring?

> I found myself at it just now and then,
> But you fell in with it ever and always."
> Says Stavyor, son of Godinovich,
> "What! I didn't play with you at marlinspikes!"
> Then Vasilisa Mikulichna: "So he says.
> Do you remember, Stavyor, do you recall,
> Now must you know, you and I together learned to
>   read and write;
> Mine was an ink-well of silver,
> And yours a pen of gold?
> But I just moistened it a little now and then,
> And I just moistened it ever and always."[24]

In a different version of the legend we find a key to the riddle:

> Here the formidable envoy Vasilyushka
> Raised her skirts to the very navel,
> And then the young Stavyor, son of Godinovich,
> Recognized her gilded ring. . . .[25]

But defamiliarization is not only a technique of the erotic riddle—a technique of euphemism—it is also the basis and point of all riddles. Every riddle pretends to show its subject either by words which specify or describe it but which, during the telling, do not seem applicable (the type: "black and white and 'red'—read—all over") or by means of odd but imitative sounds (" 'Twas brillig, and the slithy toves / Did gyre and gimble in the wabe").[26]

Even erotic images not intended as riddles are defamiliarized ("boobies," "tarts," "piece," etc.). In popular imagery there is generally something equivalent to "trampling the grass" and "breaking the guelder-rose." The technique of defamiliarization is absolutely clear in the widespread image—a motif of erotic affectation—in which a bear and other wild beasts (or a devil, with a different reason for non-recognition) do not recognize a man.[27]

---

[22][Shklovsky] [Dimitry] Savodnikov, *Zagadki russkovo naroda [Riddles of the Russian People]* (St. Petersburg, 1901), Nos. 102–107.

[23][Shklovsky] *Ibid.,* Nos. 588–591.

[24][Shklovsky] A. E. Gruzinsky, ed., *Pesni, sobrannye P [avel] N. Rybnikovym [Songs Collected by P. N. Rybnikov]* (Moscow, 1909–1910), No. 30.

[25]*Ibid,* No. 171.

[26][Lemon and Reis] We have supplied familiar English examples in place of Shklovsky's word-play. Shklovsky is saying that we create words with no referents or with ambiguous referents in order to force attention to the objects represented by the similar-sounding words. By making the reader go through the extra step on interpreting the nonsense word, the writer prevents an automatic response. A toad is a toad, but "tove" forces one to pause and think about the beast.

[27][Shklovsky] E. R. Romanov, "Besstrashny barin" *Velikorusskiye skazki* (Zapiski Imperskovo Russkovo Geograficheskovo Obschestva, XLII, No. 52). Belorussky sbornik, "Spravyadlivy soldat" ["The Intrepid Gentleman," *Great Russian Tales* (Notes of the Imperial Russian Geographical Society, XLII, No. 52). White Russian Anthology, "The Upright Soldier" (1886–1912).]

The lack of recognition in the following tale is quite typical:

> A peasant was plowing a field with a piebald mare. A bear approached him and asked, "Uncle, what's made this mare piebald for you?"
>
> "I did the piebalding myself."
>
> "But how?"
>
> "Let me, and I'll do the same for you."
>
> The bear agreed. The peasant tied his feet together with a rope, took the ploughshare from the two-wheeled plough, heated it on the fire, and applied it to his flanks. He made the bear piebald by scorching his fur down to the hide with the hot ploughshare. The man untied the bear, which went off and lay down under a tree.
>
> A magpie flew at the peasant to pick at the meat on his shirt. He caught her and broke one of her legs. The magpie flew off to perch in the same tree under which the bear was lying. Then, after the magpie, a horsefly landed on the mare, sat down, and began to bite. The peasant caught the fly, took a stick, shoved it up its rear, and let it go. The fly went to the tree where the bear and the magpie were. There all three sat.
>
> The peasant's wife came to bring his dinner to the field. The man and his wife finished their dinner in the fresh air, and he began to wrestle with her on the ground.
>
> The bear saw this and said to the magpie and the fly, "Holy priests! The peasant wants to piebald someone again."
>
> The magpie said, "No, he wants to break someone's legs."
>
> The fly said, "No, he wants to shove a stick up someone's rump."[28]

The similarity of technique here and in Tolstoy's "Kholstomer," is, I think, obvious.

Quite often in literature the sexual act itself is defamiliarized; for example, the *Decameron* refers to "scraping out a barrel," "catching nightingales," "gay wool-beating work" (the last is not developed in the plot). Defamiliarization is often used in describing the sexual organs.

A whole series of plots is based on such a lack of recognition; for example, in Afanasyev's *Intimate Tales* the entire story of "The Shy Mistress" is based on the fact that an object is not called by its proper name—or, in other words, on a game of nonrecognition. So too in Onchukov's "Spotted Petticoats," tale no. 525, and also in "The Bear and the Hare" from *Intimate Tales,* in which the bear and the hare make a "wound."

Such constructions as "the pestle and the mortar," or "Old Nick and the infernal regions" (*Decameron*), are also examples of the technique of defamiliarization. And in my article on plot construction I write about defamiliarization in psychological parallelism. Here, then, I repeat that the perception of disharmony in a harmonious context is important in parallelism. The purpose of parallelism, like the general purpose of imagery, is to transfer the usual perception of an object into the sphere of a new perception—that is, to make a unique semantic modification.

In studying poetic speech in its phonetic and lexical structure as well as in its characteristic distribution of words and in the characteristic thought structures compounded from the words, we find everywhere the artistic trademark—that is, we find material obviously created to remove the automatism of perception; the author's purpose is to create the vision which results from that deautomatized perception. A work is created "artistically" so that its perception is impeded and the greatest possible effect is produced through the slowness of the perception. As a result of this lingering, the object is perceived not in its extension in space, but, so to speak, in its continuity. Thus "poetic language" gives satisfaction. According to Aristotle, poetic language must appear strange and wonderful; and, in fact, it is often actually foreign: the Sumerian used by the Assyrians, the Latin of Europe during the Middle Ages, the Arabisms of the Persians, the Old Bulgarian of Russian literature, or the elevated, almost literary language of folk songs. The common archaisms of poetic language, the intricacy of the sweet new style [*dolce stil nuovo*],[29] the obscure style of the language of Arnaut Daniel with the "roughened" [*harte*] forms *which make pronunciation difficult*—these are used in much the same way. Leo Jakubinsky has demonstrated the principle of phonetic "roughening" of poetic language in the particular case of the repetition of identical sounds. The language of poetry is, then, a difficult, roughened, impeded language. In a few special instances the language of poetry approximates the language of prose, but this does not violate the principle of "roughened" form.

---

[28][Shklovsky] D[mitry] S. Zelenin, *Velikorusskiye skazki Permskoy gubernii [Great Russian Tales of the Permian Province* (St. Petersburg, 1913)]. No. 70.

[29][Lemon and Reis] Dante, *Purgatorio,* 24:56. Dante refers to the new lyric style of his contemporaries.

Her sister was called Tatyana.
For the first time we shall
Wilfully brighten the delicate
Pages of a novel with such a name.

wrote Pushkin. The usual poetic language of Pushkin's contemporaries was the elegant style of Derzhavin; but Pushkin's style, because it seemed trivial then, was unexpectedly
difficult for them. We should remember the consternation of
Pushkin's contemporaries over the vulgarity of his expressions. He used the popular language as a special device for
prolonging attention, just as his contemporaries generally
used Russian words in their usually French speech (see Tolstoy's examples in *War and Peace*).

Just now a still more characteristic phenomenon is
under way. Russian literary language, which was originally
foreign to Russia, has so permeated the language of the people that it has blended with their conversation. On the other
hand, literature has now begun to show a tendency towards
the use of dialects (Remizov, Klyuyev, Essenin, and others,[30]
so unequal in talent and so alike in language, are intentionally provincial) and of barbarisms (which gave rise to the
Severyanin group[31]). And currently Maxim Gorky is changing his diction from the old literary language to the new literary colloquialism of Leskov.[32] Ordinary speech and literary language have thereby changed places (see the work of
Vyacheslav Ivanov and many others). And finally, a strong
tendency, led by Khlebnikov, to create a new and properly
poetic language has emerged. In the light of these developments we can define poetry as *attenuated, tortuous* speech.
Poetic speech is *formed speech*. Prose is ordinary speech—
economical, easy, proper, the goddess of prose [*dea prosae*]
is a goddess of the accurate, facile type, of the "direct" expression of a child. I shall discuss roughened form and retar-
dation as the general *law* of art at greater length in an article
on plot construction.[33]

Nevertheless, the position of those who urge the idea of
economy of artistic energy as something which exists in and

even distinguishes poetic language seems, at first glance,
tenable for the problem of rhythm. Spencer's description of
rhythm would seem to be absolutely incontestable:

> Just as the body in receiving a series of varying
> concussions, must keep the muscles ready to meet
> the most violent of them, as not knowing when
> such may come: so, the mind in receiving unar-
> ranged articulations, must keep its perspectives ac-
> tive enough to recognize the least easily caught
> sounds. And as, if the concussions recur in definite
> order, the body may husband its forces by adjust-
> ing the resistance needful for each concussion; so,
> if the syllables be rhythmically arranged, the mind
> may economize its energies by anticipating the at-
> tention required for each syllable.[34]

This apparently conclusive observation suffers from the
common fallacy, the confusion of the laws of poetic and prosaic language. In *The Philosophy of Style* Spencer failed utterly to distinguish between them. But rhythm may have two
functions. The rhythm of prose, or of a work song like "Du-
binushka," permits the members of the work crew to do their
necessary "groaning together" and also eases the work by
making it automatic. And, in fact, it is easier to march with
music than without it, and to march during an animated conversation is even easier, for the walking is done unconsciously. Thus the rhythm or prose is an important automa-
tizing element; the rhythm of poetry is not. There is "order"
in art, yet not a single column of a Greek temple stands exactly in its proper order; poetic rhythm is similarly disordered rhythm. Attempts to systematize the irregularities have
been made, and such attempts are part of the current problem
in the theory of rhythm. It is obvious that the systematization
will not work, for in reality the problem is not one of complicating the rhythm but of disordering the rhythm—a disordering which cannot be predicted. Should the disordering
of rhythm become a convention, it would be ineffective as a
device for the roughening of language. But I will not discuss
rhythm in more detail since I intend to write a book about
it.[35]

---

[30][Lemon and Reis] Alexy Remizov (1877–1957) is best known as a novelist
and satirist; Nicholas Klyuyev (1885–1937) and Sergey Essenin (1895–
1925) were "peasant poets." All three were noted for their faithful reproduction of Russian dialects and colloquial language.

[31][Lemon and Reis] A group noted for its opulent and sensuous verse style.

[32][Lemon and Reis] Nicholas Leskov (1835–1895), novelist and short story
writer, helped popularize the *skaz,* or yarn, and hence, because of the part
dialect peculiarities play in the *skaz,* also altered Russian literary language.

[33][Lemon and Reis] Shklovsky is probably referring to his *Razvyortyvaniye
syuzheta [Plot Development]* (Petrograd, 1921).

---

[34][Lemon and Reis] Spencer, p. 169. Again the Russian text is shortened from
Spencer's original.

[35][Lemon and Reis] We have been unable to discover the book Shklovsky
promised.

T. S. Eliot

1888–1965

The influence of T. S. Eliot's criticism during the first half of the twentieth century, and particularly the influence of ideas proposed in *Tradition and the Individual Talent,* was immense. Like Hulme's *Romanticism and Classicism,* the essay is an attack on certain critical emphases in Romanticism, particularly the cult of originality and the idea that a poem is primarily an expression of the personality of the poet. Eliot argues that a great poem always asserts its relation to the works of dead poets and artists and that the poet must develop a sense of the presentness of the past. The poet is not expressing his personality but instead a medium. He is continually surrendering himself to "something which is more valuable." Poetry is not "a turning loose of emotion, but an escape from emotion." Some commentators have accused Eliot, on the basis of such remarks, of antipoetic coldness. Eliot's point, however, is more like the one Keats makes with his term *negative capability.* Eliot is suggesting that a sort of *psychical distance,* to use Edward Bullough's term, is a condition of successful composition. Eliot provides what many Romantic critics tended to neglect, a concern for the medium in which the poet must work, and he protests the so-called Romantic virtues of originality and self-expression.

Eliot's *Hamlet and His Problems* is printed below because it contains the well-known remark about the "objective correlative," which carries Eliot's concern for problems of the medium into a discussion of artistic practice. The term is perhaps finally more mystifying than useful, since Eliot's definition of it provides no clear way of determining when an "objective correlative" is present or in what it really consists.

Eliot's view of critical practice emphasizes the ability of the critic to read the literary text before him carefully and sensitively. This attention to the text and concern with language had been missing in much of the criticism of Eliot's immediate predecessors.

Eliot's critical works include *The Sacred Wood* (1920), *The Use of Poetry and the Use of Criticism* (1933), *After Strange Gods* (1934), *Essays Ancient and Modern* (1936), *Christianity and Culture* (1940), *Selected Essays,* rev. ed. (1950), and *On Poetry and Poets* (1957). On Eliot see F. O. Matthiessen, *The Achievement of T. S. Eliot,* rev. ed. (1947); Leonard Unger, ed., *T. S. Eliot, A Selected Critique* (1948); Victor Brombert, *The Criticism of T. S. Eliot* (1949); Elizabeth Drew, *T. S. Eliot: The Design of His Poetry* (1949); Sean Lucy, *T. S. Eliot and the Idea of Tradition* (1960); Lewis Freed, *T. S. Eliot: Aesthetics and History* (1962); Hugh Kenner, ed., *T. S. Eliot: A Collection of Critical Essays* (1962); Northrop Frye, *T. S. Eliot* (1963); Roger Kojecký, *T. S. Eliot's Social Criticism* (1971); Allan Mowbray, *T. S. Eliot's Impersonal Theory of Poetry* (1974); Lewis Freed, *T. S. Eliot: The Critic as Philosopher* (1979); Brian Lee, *Theory and Personality* (1979); Edward Lobb, *T. S. Eliot and the Romantic Critical Tradition* (1981); Gregory Jay, *T. S. Eliot and the Poetics of Literary History*

(1983); Harold F. Brooks, *T. S. Eliot as Literary Critic* (1987); Fei-pie Lu, *T. S. Eliot: The Dialectical Structure of His Theory of Poetry* (1966); Allen Austin, *T. S. Eliot: The Literary and Social Criticism* (1971).

Tradition and the Individual Talent

I

In English writing we seldom speak of tradition, though we occasionally apply its name in deploring its absence. We cannot refer to "the tradition" or to "a tradition"; at most, we employ the adjective in saying that the poetry of so-and-so is "traditional" or even "too traditional." Seldom, perhaps, does the word appear except in a phrase of censure. If otherwise, it is vaguely approbative, with the implication, as to the work approved, of some pleasing archaeological reconstruction. You can hardly make the word agreeable to English ears without this comfortable reference to the reassuring science of archaeology.

Certainly the word is not likely to appear in our appreciations of living or dead writers. Every nation, every race, has not only its own creative, but its own critical turn of mind; and is even more oblivious of the shortcomings and limitations of its critical habits than of those of its creative genius. We know, or think we know, from the enormous mass of critical writing that has appeared in the French language the critical method or habit of the French; we only conclude (we are such unconscious people) that the French are "more critical" than we, and sometimes even plume ourselves a little with the fact, as if the French were the less spontaneous. Perhaps they are; but we might remind ourselves that criticism is as inevitable as breathing, and that we should be none the worse for articulating what passes in our minds when we read a book and feel an emotion about it, for criticizing our own minds in their work of criticism. One of the facts that might come to light in this process is our tendency to insist, when we praise a poet, upon those aspects of his work in which he least resembles anyone else. In these aspects or parts of his work we pretend to find what is individual, what is the peculiar essence of the man. We dwell with satisfaction upon the poet's difference from his predecessors, especially his immediate predecessors; we endeavor to find something that can be isolated in order to be enjoyed. Whereas if we approach a poet without this prejudice we shall often find that not only the best, but the most individual parts of his work may be those in which the dead poets, his ancestors, assert their immortality most vigorously. And I do not mean the impressionable period of adolescence, but the period of full maturity.

Yet if the only form of tradition, of handing down, consisted in following the ways of the immediate generation before us in a blind or timid adherence to its successes, "tradition" should positively be discouraged. We have seen many such simple currents soon lost in the sand; and novelty is better than repetition. Tradition is a matter of much wider significance. It cannot be inherited, and if you want it you must obtain it by great labor. It involves, in the first place, the historical sense, which we may call nearly indispensable to anyone who would continue to be a poet beyond his twenty-fifth year; and the historical sense involves a perception, not only of the pastness of the past, but of its presence; the historical sense compels a man to write not merely with his own generation in his bones, but with a feeling that the whole of the literature of Europe from Homer and within it the whole of the literature of his own country has a simultaneous existence and composes a simultaneous order. This historical sense, which is a sense of the timeless as well as of the temporal and of the timeless and of the temporal together, is what makes a writer traditional. And it is at the same time what makes a writer most acutely conscious of his place in time, of his own contemporaneity.

No poet, no artist of any art, has his complete meaning alone. His significance, his appreciation is the appreciation of his relation to the dead poets and artists. You cannot value him alone; you must set him, for contrast and comparison, among the dead. I mean this as a principle of aesthetic, not merely historical, criticism. The necessity that he shall conform, that he shall cohere, is not one-sided; what happens when a new work of art is created is something that happens simultaneously to all the works of art which preceded it. The existing monuments form an ideal order among themselves, which is modified by the introduction of the new (the really new) work of art among them. The existing order is complete before the new work arrives; for order to persist after the supervention of novelty, the *whole* existing order must be, if ever so slightly, altered; and so the relations, proportions, values of each work of art toward the whole are readjusted; and this is conformity between the old and the new. Whoever has approved this idea of order, of the form of European, of English literature will not find it preposterous that the past should be altered by the present as much as the present is directed by the past. And the poet who is aware of this will be aware of great difficulties and responsibilities.

In a peculiar sense he will be aware also that he must inevitably be judged by the standards of the past. I say judged, not amputated, by them; not judged to be as good as, or worse or better than, the dead; and certainly not judged by the canons of dead critics. It is a judgment, a comparison, in which two things are measured by each other. To conform merely would be for the new work not really to conform at all; it would not be new, and would therefore not be a work of art. And we do not quite say that the new is more valuable because it fits in; but its fitting in is a test of its value—a test, it is true, which can only be slowly and cautiously applied, for we are none of us infallible judges of conformity. We say: It appears to conform, and is perhaps individual, or it appears individual, and may conform; but we are hardly likely to find that it is one and not the other.

To proceed to a more intelligible exposition of the relation of the poet to the past: he can neither take the past as a lump, an indiscriminate bolus, nor can he form himself wholly on one or two private admirations, nor can he form himself wholly upon one preferred period. The first course is inadmissible, the second is an important experience of youth, and the third is a pleasant and highly desirable supplement. The poet must be very conscious of the main current, which does not at all flow invariably through the most distinguished reputations. He must be quite aware of the obvious fact that art never improves, but that the material of art is never quite the same. He must be aware that the mind of Europe—the mind of his own country—a mind which he learns in time to be much more important than his own private mind—is a mind which changes, and that this change is a development which abandons nothing en route, which does not superannuate either Shakespeare, or Homer, or the rock drawing of the Magdalenian draftsmen. That this development, refinement perhaps, complication certainly, is not, from the point of view of the artist, any improvement. Perhaps not even an improvement from the point of view of the psychologist or not to the extent which we imagine; perhaps only in the end based upon a complication in economics and machinery. But the difference between the present and the past is that the conscious present is an awareness of the past in a way and to an extent which the past's awareness of itself cannot show.

Someone said: "The dead writers are remote from us because we *know* so much more than they did." Precisely, and they are that which we know.

I am alive to a usual objection to what is clearly part of my program for the métier of poetry. The objection is that the doctrine requires a ridiculous amount of erudition (pedantry), a claim which can be rejected by appeal to the lives of poets in any pantheon. It will even be affirmed that much learning deadens or perverts poetic sensibility. While, however, we persist in believing that a poet ought to know as much as will not encroach upon his necessary receptivity and necessary laziness, it is not desirable to confine knowledge to whatever can be put into a useful shape for examinations, drawing rooms, or the still more pretentious modes of publicity. Some can absorb knowledge, the more tardy must sweat for it. Shakespeare acquired more essential history from Plutarch than most men could from the whole British Museum. What is to be insisted upon is that the poet must develop or procure the consciousness of the past and that he should continue to develop this consciousness throughout his career.

What happens is a continual surrender of himself as he is at the moment to something which is more valuable. The progress of an artist is a continual self-sacrifice, a continual extinction of personality.

There remains to define this process of depersonalization and its relation to the sense of tradition. It is in this depersonalization that art may be said to approach the condition of science. I, therefore, invite you to consider, as a suggestive analogy, the action which takes place when a bit of finely filiated platinum is introduced into a chamber containing oxygen and sulfur dioxide.

II

Honest criticism and sensitive appreciation are directed not upon the poet but upon the poetry. If we attend to the confused cries of the newspaper critics and the susurrus[1] of popular repetition that follows, we shall hear the names of poets in great numbers; if we seek not blue-book knowledge but the enjoyment of poetry, and ask for a poem, we shall seldom find it. I have tried to point out the importance of the relation of the poem to other poems by other authors, and suggested the conception of poetry as a living whole of all the poetry that has ever been written. The other aspect of this impersonal theory of poetry is the relation of the poem to its author. And I hinted, by an analogy, that the mind of the mature

---

[1]"Muttering."

poet differs from that of the immature one not precisely in any valuation of "personality," not being necessarily more interesting, or having "more to say," but rather by being a more finely perfected medium in which special, or very varied, feelings are at liberty to enter into new combinations.

The analogy was that of the catalyst. When the two gases previously mentioned are mixed in the presence of a filament of platinum, they form sulfurous acid. This combination takes place only if the platinum is present; nevertheless the newly formed acid contains no trace of platinum, and the platinum itself is apparently unaffected; has remained inert, neutral, and unchanged. The mind of the poet is the shred of platinum. It may partly or exclusively operate upon the experience of the man himself; but, the more perfect the artist, the more completely separate in him will be the man who suffers and the mind which creates; the more perfectly will the mind digest and transmute the passions which are its material.

The experience, you will notice, the elements which enter the presence of the transforming catalyst, are of two kinds: emotions and feelings. The effect of a work of art upon the person who enjoys it is an experience different in kind from any experience not of art. It may be formed out of one emotion, or may be a combination of several; and various feelings, inhering for the writer in particular words or phrases or images, may be added to compose the final result. Or great poetry may be made without the direct use of any emotion whatever: composed out of feelings solely. Canto XV of the *Inferno* (Brunetto Latini) is a working up of the emotion evident in the situation; but the effect, though single as that of any work of art, is obtained by considerable complexity of detail. The last quatrain gives an image, a feeling attaching to an image, which "came," which did not develop simply out of what precedes, but which was probably in suspension in the poet's mind until the proper combination arrived for it to add itself to. The poet's mind is in fact a receptacle for seizing and storing up numberless feelings, phrases, images, which remain there until all the particles which can unite to form a new compound are present together.

If you compare several representative passages of the greatest poetry you see how great is the variety of types of combination, and also how completely any semiethical criterion of "sublimity" misses the mark. For it is not the "greatness," the intensity, of the emotions, the components, but the intensity of the artistic process, the pressure, so to speak, under which the fusion takes place, that counts. The episode of Paolo and Francesca employs a definite emotion, but the intensity of the poetry is something quite different from whatever intensity in the supposed experience it may give the impression of. It is no more intense, furthermore, than Canto XXVI, the voyage of Ulysses, which has not the direct dependence upon an emotion. Great variety is possible in the process of transmutation of emotion: the murder of Agamemnon, or the agony of Othello, gives an artistic effect apparently closer to a possible original than the scenes from Dante. In the *Agamemnon,* the artistic emotion approximates to the emotion of an actual spectator; in *Othello* to the emotion of the protagonist himself. But the difference between art and the event is always absolute; the combination which is the murder of Agamemnon is probably as complex as that which is the voyage of Ulysses. In either case there has been a fusion of elements. The ode of Keats contains a number of feelings which have nothing particular to do with the nightingale, but which the nightingale, partly, perhaps, because of its attractive name, and partly because of its reputation, served to bring together.

The point of view which I am struggling to attack is perhaps related to the metaphysical theory of the substantial unity of the soul: for my meaning is, that the poet has, not a "personality" to express, but a particular medium, which is only a medium and not a personality, in which impressions and experiences combine in peculiar and unexpected ways. Impressions and experiences which are important for the man may take no place in the poetry, and those which become important in the poetry may play quite a negligible part in the man, the personality.

I will quote a passage which is unfamiliar enough to be regarded with fresh attention in the light—or darkness—of these observations:

> And now methinks I could e'en chide myself
> For doting on her beauty, though her death
> Shall be revenged after no common action.
> Does the silkworm expend her yellow labors
> For thee? For thee does she undo herself?
> Are lordships sold to maintain ladyships
> For the poor benefit of a bewildering minute?
> Why does yon fellow falsify highways,
> And put his life between the judge's lips,
> To refine such a thing—keeps horse and men
> To beat their valors for her? . . .[2]

In this passage (as is evident if it is taken in its context) there is a combination of positive and negative emotions: an intensely strong attraction toward beauty and an equally intense fascination by the ugliness which is contrasted with it and which destroys it. This balance of contrasted emotion is in the dramatic situation to which the speech is pertinent, but that situation alone is inadequate to it. This is, so to speak,

---

[2]Cyril Tourneur, *The Revenger's Tragedy,* III. iv.

the structural emotion, provided by the drama. But the whole effect, the dominant tone, is due to the fact that a number of floating feelings, having an affinity to this emotion by no means superficially evident, have combined with it to give us a new art emotion.

It is not in his personal emotions, the emotions provoked by particular events in his life, that the poet is in any way remarkable or interesting. His particular emotions may be simple, or crude, or flat. The emotion in his poetry will be a very complex thing, but not with the complexity of the emotions of people who have very complex or unusual emotions in life. One error, in fact, of eccentricity in poetry is to seek for new human emotions to express; and in this search for novelty in the wrong place it discovers the perverse. The business of the poet is not to find new emotions, but to use the ordinary ones and, in working them up into poetry, to express feelings which are not in actual emotions at all. And emotions which he has never experienced will serve his turn as well as those familiar to him. Consequently, we must believe that "emotion recollected in tranquility"[3] is an inexact formula. For it is neither emotion, nor recollection, nor, without distortion of meaning, tranquility. It is a concentration, and a new thing resulting from the concentration, of a very great number of experiences which to the practical and active person would not seem to be experiences at all; it is a concentration which does not happen consciously or of deliberation. These experiences are not "recollected," and they finally unite in an atmosphere which is "tranquil" only in that it is a passive attending upon the event. Of course this is not quite the whole story. There is a great deal, in the writing of poetry, which must be conscious and deliberate. In fact, the bad poet is usually unconscious where he ought to be conscious, and conscious where he ought to be unconscious. Both errors tend to make him "personal." Poetry is not a turning loose of emotion, but an escape from emotion; it is not the expression of personality, but an escape from personality. But, of course, only those who have personality and emotions know what it means to want to escape from these things.

III

ὁ δὲ νοῦς ἴσως θειότερόν τι καὶ ἀπαθές ἐστιν.[4]

This essay proposes to halt at the frontier of metaphysics or mysticism, and confine itself to such practical conclusions as can be applied by the responsible person interested in poetry. To divert interest from the poet to the poetry is a laudable aim: for it would conduce to a juster estimation of actual poetry, good and bad. There are many people who appreciate the expression of sincere emotion in verse, and there is a smaller number of people who can appreciate technical excellence. But very few know when there is an expression of *significant* emotion, emotion which has its life in the poem and not in the history of the poet. The emotion of art is impersonal. And the poet cannot reach his impersonality without surrendering himself wholly to the work to be done. And he is not likely to know what is to be done unless he lives in what is not merely the present, but the present moment of the past, unless he is conscious; not of what is dead, but of what is already living.

Hamlet and His Problems

Few critics have even admitted that *Hamlet* the play is the primary problem, and Hamlet the character only secondary. And Hamlet the character has had an especial temptation for that most dangerous type of critic; the critic with a mind which is naturally of the creative order, but which through some weakness in creative power exercises itself in criticism instead. These minds often find in Hamlet a vicarious existence for their own artistic realization. Such a mind had Goethe, who made of Hamlet a Werther; and such had Coleridge, who made of Hamlet a Coleridge; and probably neither of these men in writing about Hamlet remembered that his first business was to study a work of art. The kind of criticism that Goethe and Coleridge produced, in writing of Hamlet, is the most misleading kind possible. For they both possessed unquestionable critical insight, and both make their critical aberrations the more plausible by the substitution—of their own Hamlet for Shakespeare's—which their creative gift effects. We should be thankful that Walter Pater did not fix his attention on this play.

Two writers of our own time, Mr. J. M. Robertson and Professor Stoll of the University of Minnesota, have issued small books which can be praised for moving in the other direction.[1] Mr. Stoll performs a service in recalling to our

---

[3]See Wordsworth, Preface to the *Lyrical Ballads,* p. 443.
[4]"The mind may be too divine and therefore unmoved."

HAMLET AND HIS PROBLEMS. Eliot's essay *Hamlet and His Problems* was first published in 1919. The text is from *Selected Essays, 1917–1932,* new edition, copyright 1932, 1936, 1950, by Harcourt Brace Jovanovich, Inc.; copyright 1960, 1964, by T. S. Eliot. Reprinted by permission of the publisher. Reprinted by permission of Faber & Faber, Ltd. from *Selected Essays, 1917–1932.*
[1]Eliot is referring to Robertson's *The Problem of Hamlet* (1919) and E. E. Stoll's *Othello, An Historical and Comparative Study* (1915).

attention the labors of the critics of the seventeenth and eighteenth centuries,[2] observing that

> they knew less about psychology than more recent *Hamlet* critics, but they were nearer in spirit to Shakespeare's art; and as they insisted on the importance of the effect of the whole rather than on the importance of the leading character, they were nearer, in their old-fashioned way, to the secret of dramatic art in general.

Qua work of art, the work of art cannot be interpreted; there is nothing to interpret; we can only criticize it according to standards, in comparison to other works of art; and for "interpretation" the chief task is the presentation of relevant historical facts which the reader is not assumed to know. Mr. Robertson points out, very pertinently, how critics have failed in their "interpretation" of *Hamlet* by ignoring what ought to be very obvious; that *Hamlet* is a stratification, that it represents the efforts of a series of men, each making what he could out of the work of his predecessors. The *Hamlet* of Shakespeare will appear to us very differently if, instead of treating the whole action of the play as due to Shakespeare's design, we perceive his *Hamlet* to be superposed upon much cruder material which persists even in the final form.

We know that there was an older play by Thomas Kyd, that extraordinary dramatic (if not poetic) genius who was in all probability the author of two plays so dissimilar as *The Spanish Tragedy* and *Arden of Feversham;* and what this play was like we can guess from three clues: from *The Spanish Tragedy* itself, from the tale of Belleforest upon which Kyd's *Hamlet* must have been based, and from a version acted in Germany in Shakespeare's lifetime which bears strong evidence of having been adapted from the earlier, not from the later, play. From these three sources it is clear that in the earlier play the motive was a revenge motive simply; that the action or delay is caused, as in *The Spanish Tragedy,* solely by the difficulty of assassinating a monarch surrounded by guards; and that the "madness" of Hamlet was feigned in order to escape suspicion, and successfully. In the final play of Shakespeare, on the other hand, there is a motive which is more important than that of revenge, and which explicitly "blunts" the latter; the delay in revenge is unexplained on grounds of necessity or expediency; and the effect of the "madness" is not to lull but to arouse the king's suspicion. The alteration is not complete enough, however, to be convincing. Furthermore, there are verbal parallels so close to *The Spanish Tragedy* as to leave no doubt that in

places Shakespeare was merely *revising* the text of Kyd. And finally there are unexplained scenes—the Polonius-Laertes and the Polonius-Reynaldo scenes—for which there is little excuse; these scenes are not in the verse style of Kyd, and not beyond doubt in the style of Shakespeare. These Mr. Robertson believes to be scenes in the original play of Kyd reworked by a third hand, perhaps Chapman, before Shakespeare touched the play. And he concludes, with very strong show of reason, that the original play of Kyd was, like certain other revenge plays, in two parts of five acts each. The upshot of Mr. Robertson's examination is, we believe, irrefragable: that Shakespeare's *Hamlet,* so far as it is Shakespeare's, is a play dealing with the effect of a mother's guilt upon her son, and that Shakespeare was unable to impose this motive successfully upon the "intractable" material of the old play.

Of the intractability there can be no doubt. So far from being Shakespeare's masterpiece, the play is most certainly an artistic failure. In several ways the play is puzzling, and disquieting as is none of the others. Of all the plays it is the longest and is possibly the one on which Shakespeare spent most pains; and yet he has left in it superfluous and inconsistent scenes which even hasty revision should have noticed. The versification is variable. Lines like "Look, the morn, in russet mantle clad, / Walks o'er the dew of yon high eastern hill." are of the Shakespeare of *Romeo and Juliet.* The lines in Act V, scene ii,

> Sir, in my heart there was a kind of fighting
> That would not let me sleep . . .
> Up from my cabin,
> My sea-gown scarf'd about me, in the dark
> Groped I to find out them: had my desire;
> Fingered their packet;

are of his quite mature period. Both workmanship and thought are in an unstable position. We are surely justified in attributing the play, with that other profoundly interesting play of "intractable" material and astonishing versification, *Measure for Measure,* to a period of crisis, after which follow the tragic successes which culminate in *Coriolanus. Coriolanus* may be not as "interesting" as *Hamlet,* but it is, with *Antony and Cleopatra,* Shakespeare's most assured artistic success. And probably more people have thought *Hamlet* a work of art because they found it interesting, than have found it interesting because it is a work of art. It is the *Mona Lisa* of literature.

The grounds of *Hamlet's* failure are not immediately obvious. Mr. Robertson is undoubtedly correct in concluding that the essential emotion of the play is the feeling of a son towards a guilty mother: "[Hamlet's] tone is that of one who

---

[2][Eliot] I have never, by the way, seen a cogent refutation of Thomas Rymer's objections to *Othello.*

has suffered tortures on the score of his mother's degradation. . . . The guilt of a mother is an almost intolerable motive for drama, but it had to be maintained and emphasized to supply a psychological solution, or rather a hint of one.''

This however, is by no means the whole story. It is not merely the ''guilt of a mother'' that cannot be handled as Shakespeare handled the suspicion of Othello, the infatuation of Antony, or the pride of Coriolanus. The subject might conceivably have expanded into a tragedy like these, intelligible, self-complete, in the sunlight. *Hamlet,* like the sonnets, is full of some stuff that the writer could not drag to light, contemplate, or manipulate into art. And when we search for this feeling, we find it, as in the sonnets, very difficult to localize. You cannot point to it in the speeches; indeed, if you examine the two famous soliloquies you see the versification of Shakespeare, but a content which might be claimed by another, perhaps by the author of the *Revenge of Bussy d'Ambois,* Act V, scene i. We find Shakespeare's Hamlet not in the action, not in any quotations that we might select, so much as in an unmistakable tone which is unmistakably not in the earlier play.

The only way of expressing emotion in the form of art is by finding an *objective correlative;* in other words, a set of objects, a situation, a chain of events which shall be the formula of that *particular* emotion; such that when the external facts, which must terminate in sensory experience, are given, the emotion is immediately evoked. If you examine any of Shakespeare's more successful tragedies, you will find this exact equivalence; you will find that the state of mind of Lady Macbeth walking in her sleep has been communicated to you by a skillful accumulation of imagined sensory impressions; the words of Macbeth on hearing of his wife's death strike us as if, given the sequence of events, these words were automatically released by the last events in the series. The artistic ''inevitability'' lies in this complete adequacy of the external to the emotion; and this is precisely what is deficient in *Hamlet.* Hamlet (the man) is dominated by an emotion which is inexpressible, because it is in *excess* of the facts as they appear. And the supposed identity of Hamlet with his author is genuine to this point: that Hamlet's bafflement at the absence of objective equivalent to his feelings is a prolongation of the bafflement of his creator in the face of his artistic problem. Hamlet is up against the diffi-

culty that his disgust is occasioned by his mother, but that his mother is not an adequate equivalent for it; his disgust envelops and exceeds her. It is thus a feeling which he cannot understand; he cannot objectify it, and it therefore remains to poison life and obstruct action. None of the possible actions can satisfy it; and nothing that Shakespeare can do with the plot can express Hamlet for him. And it must be noticed that the very nature of the *données* of the problem precludes objective equivalence. To have heightened the criminality of Gertrude would have been to provide the formula for a totally different emotion in Hamlet; it is just *because* her character is so negative and insignificant that she arouses in Hamlet the feeling which she is incapable of representing.

The ''madness'' of Hamlet lay to Shakespeare's hand; in the earlier play a simple ruse, and to the end, we may presume, understood as a ruse by the audience. For Shakespeare it is less than madness and more than feigned. The levity of Hamlet, his repetition of phrase, his puns, are not part of a deliberate plan of dissimulation, but a form of emotional relief. In the character Hamlet it is the buffoonery of an emotion which can find no outlet in action; in the dramatist it is the buffoonery of an emotion which he cannot express in art. The intense feeling, ecstatic or terrible, without an object or exceeding its object, is something which every person of sensibility has known; it is doubtless a subject for pathologists. It often occurs in adolescence: the ordinary person puts these feelings to sleep, or trims down his feelings to fit the business world; the artist keeps them alive by his ability to intensify the world to his emotions. The Hamlet of Laforgue is an adolescent; the Hamlet of Shakespeare is not, he has not that explanation and excuse. We must simply admit that here Shakespeare tackled a problem which proved too much for him. Why he attempted it at all is an insoluble puzzle; under compulsion of what experience he attempted to express the inexpressibly horrible, we cannot ever know. We need a great many facts in his biography; and we should like to know whether, and when, and after or at the same time as what personal experience, he read Montaigne, II. xii, *Apologie de Raimond Sebond.* We should have, finally, to know something which is by hypothesis unknowable, for we assume it to be an experience which, in the manner indicated, exceeded the facts. We should have to understand things which Shakespeare did not understand himself.

Irving Babbitt

1865–1933

Writing of the French novelist Flaubert, Babbitt remarks, "The man who thus treats beauty as a thing apart, who does not refer back his quest of the exquisite to some ethical center, will spend his life Ixion-like embracing phantoms." The criticism of Babbitt, one of the two major figures among the so-called New Humanists (the other was Paul Elmer More), is highly moralistic and anti-Romantic. Babbitt attacks the substitute religions of art and science that in his view flourished in the nineteenth century. In *Rousseau and Romanticism,* from which *Romantic Melancholy* is taken, he depicts the nineteenth century as the victim of an unholy marriage between Romanticism and utilitarianism; the villain of his piece is Jean-Jacques Rousseau.

According to the critic Malcolm Cowley, the New Humanists advocated "a skeptical criticism of life and letters which rests ultimately on the proposition that man differs not alone in complexity of organization, but in kind, from the animal, and that his happiness depends upon his recognition and cultivation of that element in his being which is distinctive of him." This element, whatever it may be called, appears in man as the power of self-restraint or decorum. Properly applied, it leads to human happiness. The trouble with Romanticism is that it substitutes for self-discipline and work "a mere lazy floating on the stream of mood and temperament."

Babbitt's opposition to Romanticism may be compared and contrasted with that of Hulme, who does not invoke ethical principles to express a similar distaste. The New Critics, who also generally disliked Romantic "excess," were nevertheless critical of the New Humanists, whose literary criticism they found to be narrow and reductive, usually because of its emphasis on ethical content and external canons of judgment.

Babbitt's major critical works are *Literature and the American College* (1908), *The New Laokoön* (1910), *Masters of Modern French Criticism* (1912), *Rousseau and Romanticism* (1919), *On Being Creative* (1932), and *The Spanish Character and Other Essays, with a Bibliography of His Publications and an Index to His Collected Works* (1940). For views on Babbitt see Norman Foerster, ed., *Humanism and America* (1930); C. H. Grattan, *The Critique of Humanism* (1930); George Santayana, *The Genteel Tradition at Bay* (1931); P. E. More, "Irving Babbitt," *American Review,* III (1934), 23–40; T. S. Eliot, "The Humanism of Irving Babbitt" and "Second Thoughts About Humanism," *Selected Essays,* rev. ed. (1950); R. P. Blackmur, "Humanism and Symbolic Imagination" in his *The Lion and the Honeycomb* (1955); J. D. Hoeveler, *The New Humanism* (1977); Thomas R. Nevin, *Irving Babbitt: An Intellectual Study* (1984); and S. C. Brennan and S. R. Yarbrough, *Irving Babbitt* (1987).

Romantic Melancholy

Rousseau and his early followers—especially perhaps his early French followers—were very much preoccupied with the problem of happiness. Now in a sense all men—even those who renounce the world and mortify the flesh—aim at happiness. The important point to determine is what any particular person means by happiness and how he hopes to attain it. It should be plain from all that has been said that the Rousseauist seeks happiness in the free play of the emotions. The *Influence of the Passions on Happiness* is the significant title of one of Madame de Staël's early treatises. The happiness that the Rousseauist seeks involves not merely a free play of feeling but—what is even more important—a free play of the imagination. Feeling acquires a sort of infinitude as a result of this cooperation of the imagination, and so the Romanticist goes, as we have seen, in quest of the thrill superlative, as appears so clearly in his nympholepsy, his pursuit of the "impossible she." But the more imaginative this quest for emotional happiness grows the more it tends to become a mere nostalgia. Happiness is achieved, so far as it is achieved at all, in dreamland. Rousseau says of himself: *"Mon plus constant bonheur fut en songe."*[1] Every finite satisfaction, by the very fact that it is finite, leaves him unsatisfied. René[2] says that he had exhausted solitude as he had exhausted society: they had both failed to satisfy his insatiable desires. René plainly takes his insatiableness to be the badge of his spiritual distinction. To submit to any circumscribing of one's desires is to show that one has no sense of infinitude and so to sink to the level of the Philistine.

But does one become happy by being nostalgic and hyperaesthetic, by burning with infinite indeterminate desire? We have here perhaps the chief irony and contradiction in the whole movement. The Rousseauist seeks happiness and yet, on his own showing, his mode of seeking it results, not in happiness, but in wretchedness. One finds indeed figures in the nineteenth century, a Browning, for example, who see in life first of all an emotional adventure and then carry this adventure through to the end with an apparently unflagging gusto. One may affirm nevertheless that a movement which began by asserting the goodness of man and the loveliness of nature ended by producing the greatest literature of despair the world has ever seen. No movement has perhaps been so prolific of melancholy as emotional Romanticism. To follow it from Rousseau down to the present day is to run through the whole gamut of gloom.[3]

> Infections of unutterable sadness,
> Infections of incalculable madness,
> Infections of incurable despair.

According to a somewhat doubtful authority, Ninon de Lenclos, "the joy of the spirit measures its force." When the Romanticist on the other hand discovers that his ideal of happiness works out into actual unhappiness he does not blame his ideal. He simply assumes that the world is unworthy of a being so exquisitely organized as himself, and so shrinks back from it and enfolds himself in his sorrow as he would in a mantle. Since the superlative bliss that he craves eludes him he will at least be superlative in woe. So far from being a mark of failure this woe measures his spiritual grandeur. "A great soul," as René says, "must contain more grief than a small one." The Romantic poets enter into a veritable competition with one another as to who shall be accounted the most forlorn. The victor in this competition is awarded the palm not merely for poetry but for wisdom. In the words of Arnold:

> amongst us one
> Who most has suffered, takes dejectedly
> His seat upon the intellectual throne;
> And all his store of sad experience he
> Lays bare of wretched days.
>
> Tells us his misery's birth and growth and signs,
> And how the dying spark of hope was fed,
> And how the breast was soothed, and how the head,
> And all his hourly varied anodynes.
>
> This for our wisest! and we others pine,
> And wish the long unhappy dream would end,
> And waive all claim to bliss, and try to bear,
> With close-lipped patience for our only friend,
> Sad patience, too near neighbor to despair.[4]

ROMANTIC MELANCHOLY. Babbitt's *Romantic Melancholy* appeared first in his *Rousseau and Romanticism* (1919), from which the text is taken. Copyright 1947 by Esther Babbitt Howe. Reprinted by permission of the National Humanities Institute, Washington, D.C.

[1] "My most constant happiness was in dreaming."
[2] The hero of *René* (1802) by French writer François René de Chateaubriand.

[3] [Babbitt] In his *Mal romantique* (1908) E. Seillière labels the generations that have elapsed since the rise of Rousseauism as follows:
1. Sensibility (*Nouvelle Héloïse*, 1761).
2. *Weltschmerz* (Schiller's *Aesthetic Letters*, 1795).
3. *Mal du siècle* (Hugo's *Hernani*, 1830).
4. Pessimism (vogue of Schopenhauer and Stendhal, 1865).
5. Neurasthenia (culmination of *fin de siècle* movement, 1900).

[4] *The Scholar Gypsy,* 182–95.

Though Arnold may in this poem, as someone has complained, reduce the Muse to the role of hospital nurse, he is, like his master Senancour, free from the taint of theatricality. He does not, as he said of Byron, make "a pageant of his bleeding heart"; and the Byronic pose has a close parallel in the pose of Chateaubriand. An Irish girl at London once told Chateaubriand that "he carried his heart in a sling." He himself said that he had a soul of the kind "the ancients called a sacred malady."

Chateaubriand, to be sure, had his cheerful moments and many of them. His sorrows he bestowed upon the public. Herein he was a true child of Jean-Jacques. We are told by eyewitnesses how heartily Rousseau enjoyed many aspects of his life at Motiers-Travers. On his own showing, he was plunged during this period in almost unalloyed misery. Froude writes of Carlyle: "It was his peculiarity that if matters were well with himself, it never occurred to him that they could be going ill with anyone else; and, on the other hand, if he was uncomfortable, he required everybody to be uncomfortable along with him." We can follow clear down to Gissing the assumption in some form or other that "art must be the mouthpiece of misery." This whole question as to the proper function of art goes to the root of the debate between the classicist and the Rousseauist. "All these poets," Goethe complains to Eckermann of the Romanticists of 1830,

> write as though they were ill, and as though the whole world were a hospital. . . . Every one of them in writing tries to be more desolate than all the others. This is really an abuse of poetry, which has been given to make man satisfied with the world and with his lot. But the present generation is afraid of all solid energy; its mind is at ease and sees poetry only in weakness. I have found a good expression to vex these gentlemen. I am going to call their poetry hospital poetry.

Now Goethe is here, like Chateaubriand, mocking to some degree his own followers. When he suffered from a spiritual ailment of any kind he got rid of it by inoculating others with it; and it was in this way, as we learn from his autobiography, that he got relief from the *Weltschmerz* of "Werther." But later in life Goethe was classical not merely in precept, like Chateaubriand, but to some extent in practice. The best of the poetry of his maturity tends, like that of the ancients, to elevate and console.

The contrast between classic and Romantic poetry in this matter of melancholy is closely bound up with the larger contrast between imitation and spontaneity. Homer is the greatest of poets, according to Aristotle, because he does not entertain us with his own person but is more than any other poet an imitator. The Romantic poet writes, on the other hand, as Lamartine says he wrote, solely for the "relief of his heart." He pours forth himself—his most intimate and private self; above all, his anguish and his tears. In his relation to his reader, as Musset tells us in a celebrated image, he is like the pelican who rends and lacerates his own flesh to provide nourishment for his young (*"Pour toute nourriture il apporte son coeur"*): *"Les plus désespérés sont les chants les plus beaux, / Et j'en sais d'immortels qui sont de purs sanglots."*[5]

To make of poetry a spontaneous overflow of powerful emotion, usually of sorrowful emotion, is what the French understand by lyricism (*le lyrisme*); and it may be objected that it is not fair to compare an epic poet like Homer with a lyricist like Musset. Let us then take for our comparison the poet whom the ancients themselves looked upon as the supreme type of a lyricist—Pindar. He is superbly imaginative, "sailing," as Gray tells us, "with supreme dominion through the azure deep of air," but his imagination is not, like that of Musset, in the service of sensibility. He does not bestow his own emotions upon us, but is rather, in the Aristotelian sense, an imitator. He is indeed at the very opposite pole from Rousseau and the "apostles of affliction." "Let a man," he says, "not darken delight in his life."

> Disclose not to strangers our burden of care; this at least shall I advise thee. Therefore is it fitting to show openly to all the folk the fair and pleasant things allotted us; but if any baneful misfortune sent of heaven befalleth man, it is seemly to shroud this in darkness.[6]

And one should also note Pindar's hostility towards that other great source of Romantic lyricism—nostalgia ("The desire of the moth for the star"), and the closely allied pursuit of the strange and the exotic. He tells of the condign punishment visited by Apollo upon the girl Coronis, who became enamored of "a strange man from Arcadia," and adds: "She was in love with things remote—that passion which many ere now have felt. For among men there is a foolish company of these who, putting shame on what they

---

[5] "The most desperate are the most beautiful songs, and I know immortal ones that are pure sobs." [Babbitt] These lines are inscribed on the statue of Musset in front of the Théâtre Français. Cf. Shelley: "Our sweetest songs are those that tell of saddest thought" [*To a Skylark*, 89–90].

[6] [Babbitt] Translation by J. E. Sandys of fragment cited in Stobaeus, *Flor,* CIX. i.

have at home, cast their glances afar, and pursue idle dreams in hopes that shall not be fulfilled."[7]

We are not to suppose that Pindar was that most tiresome and superficial of all types—the professional optimist who insists on inflicting his "gladness" upon us. "The immortals," he says, "apportion to man two sorrows for every boon they grant."[8] In general, the Greek whom Kipling sings and whom we already find in Schiller—the Greek who is an incarnation of the "joy of life unquestioned, the everlasting wondersong of youth"[9]—is a Romantic myth. We read in the *Iliad:* "Of all the creatures that breathe or crawl upon the earth, none is more wretched than man."[10] Here is the "joy of life unquestioned" in Homer. Like Homer the best of the later Greeks and Romans face unflinchingly the facts of life, and these facts do not encourage a thoughtless elation. Their melancholy is even more concerned with the lot of man in general than with their personal and private grief. The quality of this melancholy is rendered in Tennyson's line on Virgil, one of the finest in nineteenth-century English poetry: "Thou majestic in thy sadness at the doubtful doom of human kind."[11]

One should indeed not fail to distinguish between the note of melancholy in a Homer or a Virgil and the melancholy of the ancients, whether Stoic or Epicurean, who had experienced the hopelessness and helplessness of a pure naturalism in dealing with ultimate problems. The melancholy of the Stoic is the melancholy of the man who associates with the natural order a "virtue" that the natural order does not give, and so is tempted to exclaim at last with Brutus, that he had thought virtue a thing and had found that it was only a word. The melancholy of the Epicurean is that of the man who has tasted the bitter sediment *(amari aliquid)* in the cup of pleasure. It is not difficult to discover modern equivalents of both Stoic and Epicurean melancholy. "One should seek," says Sainte-Beuve, "in the pleasures of René the secret of his *ennuis,*" and so far as this is true Chateaubriand is on much the same level as some Roman voluptuary who suffered from the *taedium vitae* in the time of Tiberius or Nero.[12] But though the Roman decadent gave himself up to

the pursuit of sensation, and often of violent and abnormal sensation, he was less prone than a Chateaubriand to associate this pursuit with the "infinite"; and so he was less nostalgic and hyperaesthetic. His Epicureanism was therefore less poetical, no doubt, but on the other hand he did not set up mere Romantic restlessness as a sort of substitute for religion. It was probably easier therefore for him to feel the divine discontent and so turn to real religion than it would have been if he had, like the Rousseauist, complicated his Epicureanism with sham spirituality.

To say that the melancholy even of the decadent ancient is less nostalgic is perhaps only another way of saying what I have said about the melancholy of the ancients in general— that it is not so purely personal. It derives less from his very private and personal illusions and still less from his very private and personal disillusions. In its purely personal quality Romantic melancholy is indeed inseparable from the whole conception of original genius. The genius sets out not merely to be unique, but unique in feeling, and the sense of uniqueness in feeling speedily passes over into that of uniqueness in suffering—on the principle no doubt laid down by Horace Walpole, that life, which is a comedy for those who think, is a tragedy for those who feel. To be a beautiful soul, to preserve one's native goodness of feeling among men who have been perverted by society, is to be the elect of nature, and yet this election turns out, as Rousseau tells us, to be a "fatal gift of heaven." It is only the disillusioned Romanticist, however, who assumes this elegiac tone. We need to consider what he means by happiness while he still seeks for it in the actual world and not in the *pays des chimères.*[13] Rousseau tells us that he based the sense of his own worth on the fineness of his powers of perception. Why should nature have endowed him with such exquisite faculties[14] if he was not to have a satisfaction commensurate with them, if he was "to die without having lived"? We have here the psychological origins of the right to happiness that the Romanticists were to proclaim. "We spend on the passions," says Joubert, "the stuff that has been given us for happiness." The Rousseauist hopes to find his happiness in the passions themselves. Romantic happiness does not involve any moral effort and has been defined in its extreme forms as a "monstrous dream of passive enjoyment." Flaubert has made a study of the right

---

[7]*Pythian Odes,* III. 20 *ff.*

[8]*Pythian Odes,* III. 81–82.

[9]Kipling, *Song of the Banjo,* 91–92, but condensed.

[10]XVII. 446–47.

[11]*To Virgil.* [Babbitt] A brief survey of melancholy among the Greeks will be found in Professor S. H. Butcher's *Some Aspects of the Greek Genius.*

[12][Babbitt] The exasperated quest of novelty is one of the main traits both of the ancient and the modern victim of ennui. See Seneca, *De Tranquillitate animi: "Fastidio illis esse coepit vita, et ipse mundus; et subit illud rabidorum deliciarum: quousque eadem?"* ["Life began to be disdainful, and indeed the whole world did; to live with it took mad delights: how long will this sort of thing go on?"] (Cf. La Fontaine: *"Il me faut du nouveau, n'en fût-il plus au monde."* ["I require something new, even if there were nothing more in the world."])

[13]"Land of chimeras."

[14][Babbitt] *"A quoi bon m'avoir fait naître avec des facultés exquises pour les laisser jusqu'à la fin sans emploi? Le sentiment de mon prix interne en me donnant celui de cette injustice m'en dédommageait en quelque sorte, et me faisait verser des larmes que j'aimais à laisser couler." Confessions,* Book IX. ["What good is it for me to have been born with exquisite faculties if only to leave them unused to the end? The sentiment of my internal prize in giving me something of this injustice compensated me in some way, and made me shed tears that I loved to let fall."]

to happiness thus understood in his *Madame Bovary*. Madame Bovary, who is very commonplace in other respects, feels exquisitely; and, inasmuch as her husband had no such fineness, the right to happiness meant for her, as it did for so many other "misunderstood" women, the right to extramarital adventure. One should note the germs of melancholy that lurk in the quest of the superlative moment even if the quest is relatively successful. Suppose Saint-Preux[15] had succeeded in compressing into a single instant "the delights of a thousand centuries"; and so far as outer circumstances are concerned had had to pay no penalty. The nearer the approach to a super-human intensity of feeling the greater is likely to be the ensuing languor. The ordinary round of life seems pale and insipid compared with the exquisite and fugitive moment. One seems to oneself to have drained the cup of life at a draught and, save perhaps for impassioned recollection of the perfect moment, to have no reason for continuing to live. One's heart is "empty and swollen"[16] and one is haunted by thoughts of suicide.

This sense of having exhausted life[17] and the accompanying temptation to suicide that are such striking features of the malady of the age are not necessarily associated with any other enjoyment at all. One may devour life in reverie and then the melancholy arises from the disproportion between the dream and the fact. The reverie that thus consumes life in advance is not necessarily erotic. What may be termed the cosmic reverie of a Senancour or an Amiel[18] has very much the same effect.

The atony and aridity of which the sufferer from Romantic melancholy complains may have other sources besides the depression that follows upon the achieving of emotional intensity whether in reverie or in fact; it may also be an incident in the warfare between head and heart that assumes so many forms among the spiritual posterity of Jean-Jacques. The Rousseauist seeks happiness in emotional spontaneity and this spontaneity seems to be killed by the head which stands aloof and dissects and analyzes. Perhaps the best picture of the emotionalist who is thus incapacitated for a frank surrender to his own emotions is the *Adolphe* of Benjamin Constant (a book largely reminiscent of Constant's actual affair with Madame de Staël).

Whether the victim of Romantic melancholy feels or analyzes, he is equally incapable of action. He who faces resolutely the rude buffetings of the world is gradually hardened against them. The Romantic movement is filled with the groans of those who have evaded action and at the same time become highly sensitive and highly self-conscious. The man who thrills more exquisitely to pleasure than another will also thrill more exquisitely to pain; nay, pleasure itself in its extreme is allied to pain;[19] so that to be hyperaesthetic is not an unmixed advantage, especially if it be true, as Pindar says, that the gods bestow two trials on a man for every boon. Perhaps the deepest bitterness is found, not in those who make a pageant of their bleeding hearts, but in those who, like Leconte de Lisle[20] and others *(les impassibles),* disdain to make a show of themselves to the mob, and so dissimulate their quivering sensibility under an appearance of impassibility; or, like Stendhal, under a mask of irony that "is imperceptible to the vulgar."

Stendhal aims not at emotional intensity only, but also glorifies the lust for power. He did as much as anyone in his time to promote the ideal of the superman. Yet even if the superman has nerves of steel, as seems to have been the case with Stendhal's favorite, Napoleon, and acts on the outer world with a force of which the man in search of a sensation is quite incapable, he does not act upon himself, he remains ethically passive. This ethical passivity is the trait common to all those who incline to live purely on the naturalistic level—whether they sacrifice the human law and its demands for measure to the lust of knowledge or the lust of sensation or the lust of power. The man who neglects his ethical self and withdraws into his temperamental or private self, must almost necessarily have the sense of isolation, of remoteness from other men. We return here to the psychology of the original genius to whom it was a tame and uninteresting thing to be simply human, and who, disdaining to seem to others a being of the same clay as themselves, wished to be in their eyes either an angel or a demon—above all a demon.[21] René does not, as I have said, want even the

---

[15] A character in Rousseau's *Nouvelle Héloïse* (1761).

[16] [Babbitt] *Nouvelle Héloïse,* Part VI, Letter viii.

[17] [Babbitt] *"Encore enfant par la tête, vous êtes déjà vieux par le coeur." Ibid.* ["Still an infant in the mind, you are already old in the heart."]

[18] [Babbitt] See the examples quoted in Arnold, *Essays in Criticism* (1888), Second Series, 305–06.

[19] [Babbitt] This is the thought of Keats's *Ode to Melancholy:*
   Ay, in the very temple of Delight
     Veiled Melancholy has her sovereign shrine,
   Though seen of none save him whose strenuous tongue
     Can burst Joy's grape against his palate fine.
Cf. Chateaubriand: *Essai sur les Révolutions,* Part II, Chapter 57: *"Ces jouissances sont trop poignantes: telle est notre faiblesse, que les plaisirs exquis deviennent des douleurs,"* etc. ["These enjoyments are too poignant; such is our weakness that the exquisite pleasures come from sadness."]

[20] [Babbitt] See his sonnet *Les Montreurs.* This type of Rousseauist is anticipated by "Milord" Bomston in *La Nouvelle Héloïse.* Rousseau directed the engraver to depict him with *"un maintien grave et stoïque sous lequel il cache avec peine une extrême sensibilité."* ["A grave and stoic mien under which he hides with difficulty an extreme sensibility."]

[21] [Babbitt] *"Qui es-tu? A coup sûr tu n'es pas un être pétri du même limon et animé de la même vie que nous! Tu es un ange ou un démon mais tu n'es pas une créature humaine. . . . Pourquoi habiter parmi nous, qui ne pouvons te suffire ni te comprendre?"* G. Sand, *Lélia,* I. II. ["Who are you? Certainly you are not a being molded of the same clay and animated with the same spirit as we! You are an angel or a devil, but you are not a human creature. . . . Why live among us who can neither equal you nor understand you?"]

woman who loves him to feel at one with him, but rather to be at once astonished and appalled. He exercises upon those who approach him a malign fascination; for he not only lives in misery himself as in his natural element, but communicates this misery to those who approach him. He is like one of those fair trees under which one cannot sit without perishing. Moreover René disavows all responsibility for thus being a human Upas tree. Moral effort is unavailing, for it was all written in the book of fate. The victim of Romantic melancholy is at times tender and elegiac, at other times he sets up as a heaven-defying Titan. This latter pose became especially common in France around 1830, when the influence of Byron had been added to that of Chateaubriand. Under the influence of these two writers a whole generation of youth became "things of dark imaginings,"[22] predestined to a blight that was at the same time the badge of their superiority. One wished like René to have an "immense, solitary and stormy soul," and also, like a Byronic hero, to have a diabolical glint in the eye and a corpselike complexion,[23] and so seem the "blind and deaf agent of funereal mysteries."[24] "It was possible to believe everything about René except the truth." The person who delights in being as mysterious as this easily falls into mystification. Byron himself, we are told, was rather flattered by the rumor that he had committed at least one murder. Baudelaire, it has been said, displayed his moral gangrene as a warrior might display honorable wounds. This flaunting of his own perversity was part of the literary attitude he had inherited from the "satanic school."

When the Romanticist is not posing as the victim of fate he poses as the victim of society. Both ways of dodging moral responsibility enter into the Romantic legend of the *poète maudit.*[25] Nobody loves a poet. His own mother, according to Baudelaire, utters a malediction upon him.[26] That

is because the poet feels so exquisitely that he is at once odious and unintelligible to the ordinary human pachyderm. Inasmuch as the Philistine is not too sensitive to act he has a great advantage over the poet in the real world and often succeeds in driving him from it and indeed from life itself. This inferiority in action is a proof of the poet's ideality. "His gigantic wings," as Baudelaire says, "keep him from walking." He has, in Coleridgean phrase, fed on "honeydew and drunk the milk of paradise,"[27] and so can scarcely be expected to submit to a diet of plain prose. It is hardly necessary to say that great poets of the past have not been at war with their public in this way. The reason is that they were less taken up with the uttering of their own uniqueness; they were, without ceasing to be themselves, servants of the general sense.

Chatterton became for the Romanticists a favorite type of the *poète maudit,* and his suicide a symbol of the inevitable defeat of the "ideal" by the "real." The first performance of Vigny's *Chatterton* (1835), with its picture of the implacable hatred of the Philistine for the artist, was received by the Romantic youth of Paris with something akin to delirium. As Gautier says in his well-known account of this performance, one could almost hear in the night the crack of the solitary pistols. The ordinary man of letters, says Vigny in his preface to this play, is sure of success, even the great writer may get a hearing, but the poet, a being who is on a far higher level than either, can look forward only to "perpetual martyrdom and immolation." He comes into the world to be a burden to others; his native sensibility is so intimate and profound that it "has plunged him from childhood into involuntary ecstasies, interminable reveries, infinite inventions. Imagination possesses him above all . . . it sweeps his faculties heavenward as irresistibly as the balloon carries up its car." From that time forth he is more or less cut off from normal contact with his fellowmen. "His sensibility has become too keen; what only grazes other men wounds him until he bleeds." He is thrown back more and more upon himself and becomes a sort of living volcano, "consumed by secret ardors and inexplicable languors," and incapable of self-guidance. Such is the poet. From his first appearance he is an outlaw. Let all your tears and all your pity be for him. If he is finally forced to suicide, not he but society is to blame. He is like the scorpion that cruel boys surround with live coals and that is finally forced to turn his sting upon

---

[22][Babbitt] See *Lara,* XVIII, XIX, perhaps the best passage that can be quoted for the Byronic hero.

[23][Babbitt] Cf. Gautier, *Histoire du romantisme: "Il était de mode alors dans l'école romantique d'être pâle, livide, verdâtre un peu cadavéreux, s'il était possible. Cela donnait l'air fatal, byronien, giaour, dévoré par les passions et les remords."* ["It was fashionable then in the Romantic school to be pale, livid, greenish, a little cadaverous, if it were possible. That gave the fatal air, Byronian, like a giaour, devoured by passions and remorse."]

[24][Babbitt] Hugo, *Hernani.*

[25]"Outcast poet."

[26][Babbitt] *Lorsque, par un décret des puissances suprêmes,*
     Le poète apparaît dans ce monde ennuyé,
     Sa mère épouvantée et pleine de blasphèmes
     Crispe ses poings vers Dieu, qui la prend en pitié.
Les Fleurs du mal: Bénédiction. ["When, by a decree of the supreme powers the poet appears in this weary world, his mother, horrified and full of blasphemy, clenches her fists toward God, who pities her."] Cf. *Nouvelle Héloïse,* Part III, Letter xxvi: *"Ciel inexorable! . . . O ma mère, pourquoi vous donna-t-il un fils dans sa colère?"* ["Inexorable sky! . . . O my mother, why does he give you a son in his anger?"]

---

[27]*Kubla Khan.* [Babbitt] Coleridge has a side that relates him to the author of *Les Fleurs du mal.* In his *Pains of Sleep* he describes a dream in which he felt "Desire with loathing strangely mixed. / On wild or hateful objects fixed."

himself. Society therefore owes it to itself to see that this exquisite being is properly pensioned and protected by government, to the end that idealism may not perish from the earth. M. Thiers, who was prime minister at that time, is said to have received a number of letters from young poets, the general tenor of which was: "A position or I'll kill myself."[28]

A circumstance that should interest Americans is that Poe as interpreted by Baudelaire came to hold for a later generation of Romanticists the place that Chatterton had held for the Romanticists of 1830. Poe was actually murdered, says Baudelaire—and there is an element of truth in the assertion along with much exaggeration—by this great gaslighted barbarity (i.e., America). All his inner and spiritual life, whether drunkard's or poet's, was one constant effort to escape from this antipathetic atmosphere "in which," Baudelaire goes on to say, "the impious love of liberty has given birth to a new tyranny, the tyranny of the beasts, a zoocracy"; and in this human zoo a being with such a superhuman fineness of sensibility as Poe was of course at a hopeless disadvantage. In general our elation at Poe's recognition in Europe should be tempered by the reflection that this recognition is usually taken as a point of departure for insulting America. Poe is about the only hyperaesthetic Romanticist we have had, and he therefore fell in with the main European tendency that comes down from the eighteenth century. Villiers de l'Isle-Adam, whom I have already cited as an extreme example of Romantic idealism, was one of Poe's avowed followers; but Villiers is also related by his aesthetic and "diabolic" Catholicism to Chateaubriand; and the religiosity of Chateaubriand itself derives from the religiosity of Rousseau.

Hitherto I have been studying for the most part only one main type of modern melancholy. This type, even in a Chateaubriand or a Byron and still more in their innumerable followers, may seem at once superficial and theatrical. It often does not get beyond that Epicurean toying with sorrow, that luxury of grief, which was not unknown even to classical antiquity.[29] The despair of Chateaubriand is frequently only a disguise of his love of literary glory, and Chesterton is inclined to see in the Byronic gloom an incident of youth

and high spirits.[30] But this is not the whole story even in Byron and Chateaubriand. To find what is both genuine and distinctive in Romantic melancholy we need to enlarge a little further on the underlying difference between the classicist and the Rousseauist. The Rousseauist, as indeed the modern man in general, is more preoccupied with his separate and private self than the classicist. Modern melancholy has practically always this touch of isolation, not merely because of the proneness of the "genius" to dwell on his own uniqueness, but also because of the undermining of the traditional communions by critical analysis. The noblest form of the "malady of the age" is surely that which supervened upon the loss of religious faith. This is what distinguishes the sadness of an Arnold or a Senancour from that of a Gray. The *Elegy* belongs to the modern movement by the humanitarian note, the sympathetic interest in the lowly, but in its melancholy it does not go much beyond the milder forms of classical meditation on the inevitable sadness of life—what one may term pensiveness. Like the other productions of the so-called graveyard school, it bears a direct relation to Milton's *Il Penseroso*. It is well to retain Gray's own distinction. "Mine is a white melancholy, or rather leucocholy for the most part," he wrote to Richard West in 1742, "but there is another sort, black indeed, which I have now and then felt." Gray did not experience the more poignant sadness, one may suspect, without some loss of the "trembling hope" that is the final note of the *Elegy*. No forlornness is greater than that of the man who has known faith and then lost it. Renan writes of his own break with the church:

> The fish of Lake Baikal, we are told, have spent thousands of years in becoming freshwater fish after being saltwater fish. I had to go through my transition in a few weeks. Like an enchanted circle, Catholicism embraces the whole of life with so much strength that when one is deprived of it everything seems insipid. I was terribly lost. The universe produced upon me the impression of a cold and arid desert. For, the moment that Christianity was not the truth, all the rest appeared to me

---

[28] Keats, according to Shelley, was an example of the *poète maudit*. "The poor fellow," he says, "was literally hooted from the stage of life." Keats was, as a matter of fact, too sturdy to be snuffed out by an article and had less of the quivering Rousseauistic sensibility than Shelley himself. Cf. letter of Shelley to Mrs. Shelley (August 7, 1820): "Imagine my despair of good, imagine how it is possible that one of so weak and sensitive a nature as mine can run further the gauntlet through this hellish society of men."

[29] [Babbitt] Euripides speaks of the Χάρις γόων in his Ἱκέτιδες (Latin, *"dolendi voluptas"*; German, *"die Wonne der Wehmut"* ["the pleasure of melancholy"]).

[30] [Babbitt] Chesterton is anticipated in this paradox by Wordsworth:
> In youth we love the darksome lawn
> Brushed by the owlet's wing,
> Then twilight is preferred to dawn
> And autumn to the spring.
> Sad fancies do we then affect
> In luxury of disrespect
> To our own prodigal excess
> Of too familiar happiness.

Ode to Lycoris [II. 15–22].

indifferent, frivolous, barely worthy of interest. The collapse of my life upon itself left in me a feeling of emptiness like that which follows an attack of fever or an unhappy love affair.[31]

The forlornness at the loss of faith is curiously combined in many of the Romanticists with the mood of revolt. This type of Romanticist heaps reproaches on a God in whose existence he no longer believes (as in Leconte de Lisle's *Quaïn,* itself related to Byron's *Cain*). He shakes his fist at an empty heaven, or like Alfred de Vigny (in his *Jardin des oliviers*) assumes towards this emptiness an attitude of proud disdain. He is loath to give up this grandiose defiance of divinity if only because it helps to save him from subsiding into platitude. A somewhat similar mood appears in the "satanic" Catholics who continue to cling to religion simply because it adds to the gusto of sinning.[32] A Barbey succeeded in combining the role of Byronic Titan with that of champion of the church. But in general the Romantic Prometheus spurns the traditional forms of communion whether classical or Christian. He is, so far as everything established is concerned, enormously centrifugal, but he hopes to erect on the ruins of the past the new religion of human brotherhood. Everything in this movement, from Shaftesbury down, hinges on the role that is thus assigned to sympathy: if it can really unite men who are at the same time indulging each to the utmost his own "genius" or idiosyncrasy, there is no reason why one should not accept Romanticism as a philosophy of life.

But nowhere else perhaps is the clash more violent between the theory and the fact. No movement is so profuse in professions of brotherhood and none is so filled with the aching sense of solitude. "Behold me then alone upon the earth," is the sentence with which Rousseau begins his last book;[33] and he goes on to marvel that he, the "most loving of men," had been forced more and more into solitude. "I am in the world as though in a strange planet upon which I have fallen from the one that I inhabited."[34] When no longer subordinated to something higher than themselves, both the head and the heart (in the Romantic sense) not only tend to be opposed to one another, but also, each in its own way, to isolate. Empedocles was used not only by Arnold but by other victims[35] of Romantic melancholy, as a symbol of intellectual isolation: by his indulgence in the "imperious lonely thinking power" Empedocles has broken the warm bonds of sympathy with his fellows:

> thou art
> A living man no more, Empedocles!
> Nothing but a devouring flame of thought—
> But a naked eternally restless mind!

His leaping into Etna typifies his attempt to escape from his loneliness by a fiery union with nature herself.

According to religion one should seek to unite with a something that is set above both man and nature, whether this something is called God as in Christianity or simply the Law as in various philosophies of the Far East.[36] The most severe penalty visited on the man who transgresses is that he tends to fall away from this union. This is the element of truth in the sentence of Diderot that Rousseau took as a personal affront: "Only the wicked man is alone." Rousseau asserted in reply, anticipating Mark Twain,[37] that "on the contrary only the good man is alone." Now in a sense Rousseau is right. "Most men are bad," as one of the Seven Sages of Greece remarked, and anyone who sets out to follow a very strenuous virtue is likely to have few companions on the way. Rousseau is also right in a sense when he says that the wicked man needs to live in society so that he may have opportunity to practice his wickedness. Yet Rousseau fails to face the main issue: solitude is above all a psychic thing. A man may frequent his fellows and suffer none the less acutely, like Poe's *Man of the Crowd,* from a ghastly isolation. And conversely one may be like the ancient who said that he was never less alone than when he was alone.

Hawthorne, who was himself a victim of solitude, brooded a great deal on this whole problem, especially, as may be seen in *The Scarlet Letter* and elsewhere, on the isolating effects of sin. He perceived the relation of the problem to the whole trend of religious life in New England. The

---

[31][Babbitt] *Souvenirs d'enfance et de jeunesse,* 329–30.

[32][Babbitt] *"(Villiers) était de cette famille des néo-catholiques littéraires dont Chateaubriand est le père commun, et qui a produit Barbey d'Aurévilly, Baudelaire et plus récemment M. Joséphin Peladan. Ceux-là ont goûté par-dessus tout dans la religion les charmes du péché, la grandeur du sacrilège, et leur sensualisme a caressé les dogmes qui ajoutaient aux voluptés la suprême volupté de se perdre."* Anatole France, *Vie littéraire,* III. 121. ["(Villiers) was of that family of neo-Catholic literati of whom Chateaubriand is the common father and who has produced Barbey d'Aurévilly, Baudelaire, and more recently Mr. Joséphin Peladan. They have tasted above all in religion the charms of sin, the grandeur of sacrilege, and their sensualism has caressed the dogmas that add to voluptuousness the supreme voluptuousness of losing oneself."]

[33][Babbitt] *Première promenade.*

[34][Babbitt] *Première promenade.*

[35][Babbitt] E.g. Hölderlin and Jean Polonius. [The lines that follow are from Arnold's *Empedocles on Etna,* II. 327–30.]

[36][Babbitt] A striking passage on solitude will be found in the *Laws of Manu,* IV. 240–42. ("Alone a being is born: alone he goes to death." His kin forsake him at the grave; his only hope then is in the companionship of the law of righteousness [dharma]. "With the law as his companion he crosses the darkness difficult to cross.")

[37][Babbitt] "Be good and you will be lonely."

older Puritans had a sense of intimacy with God and craved no other companionship. With the weakening of their faith the later Puritans lost the sense of a divine companionship, but retained their aloofness from men. Hawthorne's own solution of the problem of solitude, so far as he offers any, is humanitarian. Quicken your sympathies. Let the man who has taken as his motto *Excelsior*[38] be warned. Nothing will console him on the bleak heights either of knowledge or of power for the warm contact with the dwellers in the valley. Faust, who is a symbol of the solitude of knowledge, seeks to escape from his forlornness by recovering this warm contact. That the inordinate quest of power also leads to solitude is beyond question. Napoleon, the very type of the superman, must in the nature of the case have been very solitary.[39] His admirer Nietzsche wrote one day: "I have forty-three years behind me and am as alone as if I were a child." Carlyle, whose "hero" derives like the superman from the original genius[40] of the eighteenth century, makes the following entry in his diary: "My isolation, my feeling of loneliness, unlimitedness (much meant by this) what tongue shall say? Alone, alone!"[41]

It cannot be granted, however, that one may escape by love, as the Rousseauist understands the word, from the loneliness that arises from the unlimited quest either of knowledge or power. For Rousseauistic love is also unlimited, whether one understands by love either passion or a diffusive sympathy for mankind at large. "What solitudes are these human bodies," Musset exclaimed when fresh from his affair with George Sand. Wordsworth cultivated a love for the lowly that quite overflowed the bounds of neoclassic selection. It is a well-known fact that the lowly did not altogether reciprocate. "A desolate-minded man, ye kna," said an old innkeeper of the Lakes to Canon Rawnsley, "'Twas po'try as did it." If Wordsworth writes so poignantly of sol-

itude, one may infer that it is because he himself had experienced it.[42] Nor would it be difficult to show that the very philanthropic Ruskin was at least as solitary as Carlyle with his tirades against philanthropy.

I have spoken of the isolating effects of sin, but sin is scarcely the right word to apply to most of the Romanticists. The solitude of which so many of them complain does, however, imply a good deal of spiritual inertia. Now to be spiritually inert, as I have said elsewhere, is to be temperamental, to indulge unduly the lust for knowledge or sensation or power without imposing on these lusts some center or principle of control set above the ordinary self. The man who wishes to fly off on the tangent of his own temperament and at the same time enjoy communion on any except the purely material level is harboring incompatible desires. For temperament is what separates. A sense of unlimitedness ("much meant by this" as Carlyle says) and of solitude are simply the penalties visited upon the eccentric individualist. If we are to unite on the higher levels with other men we must look in another direction than the expansive outward striving of temperament: we must in either the humanistic or religious sense undergo conversion. We must pull back our temperaments with reference to the model that we are imitating, just as, in Aristotle's phrase, one might pull back and straighten out a crooked stick.[43] Usually the brake on temperament is supplied by the ethos, the convention of one's age and country. I have tried to show elsewhere that the whole program of the eccentric individualist is to get rid of this convention, whatever it may be, without developing some new principle of control. The eccentric individualist argues that to accept control, to defer to some center as the classicist demands, is to cease to be himself. But are restrictions upon temperament so fatal to a man's being himself? The reply hinges upon the definition of the word *self*, inasmuch as man is a dual being. If a man is to escape from his isolation he must, I have said, aim at some goal set above his ordinary self which is at the same time his unique and separate self. But because this goal is set above his ordinary self, it is not therefore necessarily set above his total personality. The limitations that he imposes on his ordinary self may be the necessary condition of his entering into possession of his ethical self, the self that he possesses in common with other men. Aristotle says that

---

[38][Babbitt] In the poem by the Swiss poet C. Didier from which Longfellow's poem seems to be derived, the youth who persists in scaling the heights in spite of all warnings is Byron! "*Et Byron . . . disparaît aux yeux du pâtre épouvanté.*" (See E. Estève, *Byron en France*, 147.) ["And Byron . . . disappeared before the eyes of the frightened shepherd."]

[39][Babbitt] In the *Mémoires d'outre-tombe* Chateaubriand quotes from the jottings of Napoleon on the island of Elba. "*Mon cœur se refuse aux joies communes comme à la douleur ordinaire.*" [My heart denies itself the common joys as well as ordinary sadness."] He says of Napoleon elsewhere in the same work: "*Au fond il ne tenait à rien: homme solitaire, il se suffisait; le malheur ne fit que le rendre au désert de sa vie.*" ["In the end he had nothing: a solitary man, he was self-sufficient; unhappiness only restored him to the desert of his life."]

[40][Babbitt] The solitude of the "genius" is already marked in Blake:
  O! why was I born with a different face?
  Why was I not born like the rest of my race?
  When I look, each one starts; when I speak, I offend;
  Then I'm silent and passive and lose every friend.
[In a letter to Mr. Butts, August 16, 1803.]

[41][Babbitt] Froude's *Carlyle*, II. 377.

---

[42][Babbitt] No finer lines on solitude are found in English than those in which Wordsworth relates how from his room in Cambridge he could look out on
  The antechapel where the statue stood,
  Of Newton with his prism and silent face,
  The marble index of a mind forever
  Voyaging through strange seas of thought alone.
Prelude, III. 61–63. Cf. also the line in the sonnet on Milton: "His soul was like a star and dwelt apart." [*London, 1802*, 9, but misquoted.]

[43]*Nichomachean Ethics*, 1109.

if a man wishes to achieve happiness he must be a true lover of himself. It goes without saying that he means the ethical self. The author of a recent book on Ibsen says that Ibsen's message to the world is summed up in the line: "This above all—to thine own self be true." It is abundantly plain from the context, however, that Polonius is a decayed Aristotelian and not a precursor of Ibsen. The self to which Aristotle would have a man be true is at the opposite pole from the self that Ibsen and the original geniuses are so eager to get uttered.

To impose the yoke of one's human self upon one's temperamental self is, in the Aristotelian sense, to work. Aristotle conceives of happiness in terms of work. All types of temperamentalists, on the other hand, are from the human point of view, passive. The happiness that they crave is a passive happiness. A man may pursue power with the energy of a Napoleon and yet remain ethically passive. He may absorb whole encyclopedias and remain ethically passive. He may expand his sympathies until, like Schiller, he is ready to "bestow a kiss upon the whole world" and yet remain ethically passive. A man ceases to be ethically passive only when he begins to work in the Aristotelian sense, that is when he begins to put the brake on temperament and impulse, and in the same degree he tends to become ethically efficient. By his denial of the dualism of the spirit, Rousseau discredited this inner working, so that inwardness has come to seem synonymous with mere subjectivity; and to be subjective in the Rousseauistic sense is to be diffusive, to lack purpose and concentration, to lose oneself in a shoreless sea of reverie.

The utilitarian intervenes at this point and urges the Romanticist, since he has failed to work inwardly, at least to work outwardly. Having missed the happiness of ethical efficiency he may in this way find the happiness of material efficiency, and at the same time serve the world. This is the solution of the problem of happiness that Goethe offers at the end of the second *Faust,* and we may affirm without hesitation that it is a sham solution. To work outwardly and in the utilitarian sense, without the inner working that can alone save from ethical anarchy, is to stimulate rather than repress the most urgent of all the lusts—the lust of power. It is only too plain that the unselective sympathy or joy in service with which Goethe would complete Faust's utilitarian activity is not in itself a sufficient counterpoise to the will to power, unless we assume with Rousseau that one may control expansive impulses by opposing them to one another.

A terrible danger thus lurks in the whole modern program: it is a program that makes for a formidable mechanical efficiency and so tends to bring into an ever closer material contact men who remain ethically centrifugal. The reason

why the humanitarian and other schemes of communion that have been set up during the last century have failed is that they do not, like the traditional schemes, set any bounds to mere expansiveness, or, if one prefers, they do not involve any conversion. And so it is not surprising that the feeling of emptiness[44] or unlimitedness and isolation should be the special mark of the melancholy of this period. René complains of his "moral solitude";[45] but, strictly speaking, his solitude is the reverse of moral. Only by cultivating his human self, and by the unceasing effort that this cultivation involves, does a man escape from his nightmare of separateness and so move in some measure towards happiness. But the happiness of which René dreams is unethical—something very private and personal and egoistic. Nothing is easier than to draw the line from René to Baudelaire and later decadents—for instance to Des Esseintes, the hero of Huysmans's novel *A Rebours,*[46] who is typical of the last exaggerations of the movement. Des Esseintes cuts himself off as completely as possible from other men and in the artificial paradise he has devised gives himself up to the quest of strange and violent sensation; but his dream of happiness along egoistic lines turns into a nightmare,[47] his palace of art becomes a hell. Lemaître is quite justified in saying of Des Esseintes that he is only René or Werther brought up to date—"a played-out and broken-down Werther who has a malady of the nerves, a deranged stomach and eighty years more of literature to the bad."[48]

Emotional Romanticism was headed from the start towards this bankruptcy because of its substitution for ethical effort of a mere lazy floating on the stream of mood and temperament. I have said that Buddhism saw in this ethical indolence the root of all evil. Christianity in its great days was preoccupied with the same problem. To make this point clear it will be necessary to add to what I have said about classical and Romantic melancholy a few words about melancholy in the Middle Ages. In a celebrated chapter of his *Genius of Christianity (Le Vague des passions)* Chateaubri-

---

[44][Babbitt] James Thomson in *The City of Dreadful Night* [358–60] says that he would have entered hell

> gratified to gain
> That positive eternity of pain
> Instead of this insufferable inane.

[45][Babbitt] R. Canat has taken this phrase as the title of his treatment of the subject: *La Solitude morale dans le mouvement romantique.*

[46][Babbitt] Decadent Rome had the equivalent of Des Esseintes. Seneca (*To Lucilius,* CXXII) speaks of those who seek to affirm their originality and attract attention to themselves by doing everything differently from other people and, "*ut ita dicam,* retro vivunt." ["When I say so, they live in the past."]

[47][Babbitt] Tennyson has traced this change of the aesthetic dream into a nightmare in his *Palace of Art.*

[48][Babbitt] *Contemporains,* I. 332.

and seeks to give to the malady of the age Christian and medieval origins. This was his pretext, indeed, for introducing René into an apology for Christianity and so, as Sainte-Beuve complained, administering poison in a sacred wafer. Chateaubriand begins by saying that the modern man is melancholy because, without having had experience himself, he is at the same time overwhelmed by the secondhand experience that has been heaped up in the books and other records of an advanced civilization; and so he suffers from a precocious disillusion; he has the sense of having exhausted life before he has enjoyed it. There is nothing specifically Christian in this disillusion and above all nothing medieval. But Chateaubriand goes on to say that from the decay of the pagan world and the barbarian invasions the human spirit received an impression of sadness and possibly a tinge of misanthropy which has never been completely effaced. Those that were thus wounded and estranged from their fellow men took refuge formerly in monasteries, but now that this resource has failed them, they are left in the world without being of it, and so they "become the prey of a thousand chimeras." Then is seen the rise of that guilty melancholy which the passions engender when, left without definite object, they prey upon themselves in a solitary heart.[49]

The *vague des passions,* the expansion of infinite indeterminate desire that Chateaubriand here describes, may very well be related to certain sides of Christianity—especially to what may be termed its neo-Platonic side. Yet Christianity at its best has shown itself a genuine religion; in other words, it has dealt sternly and veraciously with the facts of human nature. It has perceived clearly how a man may move towards happiness and how on the other hand he tends to sink into despair; or what amounts to the same thing, it has seen the supreme importance of spiritual effort and the supreme danger of spiritual sloth. The man who looked on himself as cut off from God and so ceased to strive was, according to the medieval Christian, the victim of acedia. This sluggishness and slackness of spirit, this mere drifting and abdication of will, may, as Chaucer's parson suggests, be the crime against the Holy Ghost itself. It would in fact not be hard to show that what was taken by the Rousseauist to be the badge of spiritual distinction was held by the medieval Christian to be the chief of all the deadly sins.

The victim of acedia often looked upon himself, like the victim of the malady of the age, as foredoomed. But though the idea of fate enters at times into medieval melancholy, the man of the Middle Ages could scarcely so detach himself from the community as to suffer from that sense of loneliness which is the main symptom of Romantic melancholy. This forlornness was due not merely to the abrupt disappearance of the older forms of communion, but to the failure of the new attempts at communion. When one gets beneath the surface of the nineteenth century one finds that it was above all a period of violent disillusions, and it is especially after violent disillusion that a man feels himself solitary and forlorn. I have said that the special mark of the half-educated man is his harboring of incompatible desires. The new religions or unifications of life that appeared during the nineteenth century made an especially strong appeal to the half-educated man because it seemed to him that by accepting some one of these he could enjoy the benefits of communion and at the same time not have to take on the yoke of any serious discipline; that he could, in the language of religion, achieve salvation without conversion. When a communion on these lines turns out to be not a reality, but a sham, and its disillusioned votary feels solitary and forlorn, he is ready to blame everybody and everything except himself.

A few specific illustrations will help us to understand how Romantic solitude, which was created by the weakening of the traditional communions, was enhanced by the collapse of various sham communions. Let us return for a moment to that eminent example of Romantic melancholy and disillusion, Alfred de Vigny. His *Chatterton* deals with the fatal misunderstanding of the original genius by other men. *Moïse* deals more specifically with the problem of his solitude. The genius is so eminent and unique, says Vigny, speaking for himself from behind the mask of the Hebrew prophet, that he is quite cut off from ordinary folk who feel that they have nothing in common with him.[50] This forlornness of the genius is not the sign of some capital error in his philosophy. On the contrary it is the sign of his divine election, and so Moses blames God for his failure to find happiness.[51] If the genius is cut off from communion with men he cannot hope for companionship with God because he has grown too skeptical. Heaven is empty and in any case dumb; and so in the poem to which I have already referred *(Le Mont des oliviers)* Vigny assumes the mask of Jesus himself to express this des-

---

[49][Babbitt] *Génie du Christianisme,* Part II, Book III, Chapter 9.

[50][Babbitt] *L'orage est dans ma voix, l'éclair est sur ma bouche;*
     Aussi, loin de m'aimer, voilà qu'ils tremblent tous,
     Et quand j'ouvre les bras, on tombe à mes genoux.
["The storm is in my voice, the lightning is on my mouth. Also, far from loving me, there are those who all tremble, and when I open my arms, they fall at my feet."]

[51][Babbitt] *Que vous ai-je donc fait pour être votre élu?*
     . . . .
     Hélas! je suis, Seigneur, puissant et solitaire,
     Laissez-moi m'endormir du sommeil de la terre!
["What have I done to you, then, to be your chosen one? . . . Alas, I am, Lord, powerful and solitary. Let me sleep the sleep of the earth."]

olateness, and concludes that the just man will oppose a haughty and Stoic disdain to the divine silence.[52]

All that is left for the genius is to retire into his ivory tower—a phrase appropriately applied for the first time to Vigny.[53] In the ivory tower he can at least commune with nature and the ideal woman. But Vigny came at a time when the Arcadian glamor was being dissipated from nature. Partly under scientific influence, she was coming to seem not a benign but a cold and impassive power, a collection of cruel and inexorable laws. I have already mentioned this mood that might be further illustrated from Taine and so many others towards the middle of the nineteenth century.[54] "I am called a 'mother'." Vigny makes nature say, "and I am a tomb"[55] (*La Maison du berger*); and so in the *maison roulante,* or sort of Arcadia on wheels that he has imagined, he must seek his chief solace with the ideal feminine companion. But woman herself turns out to be treacherous; and, assuming the mask of Samson (*La Colère de Samson*), Vigny utters a solemn malediction upon the eternal Delilah (*Et, plus ou moins, la Femme est toujours Dalila*). Such is the disillusion that comes from having sought an ideal communion in a liaison with a Parisian actress.[56]

Now that every form of communion has failed, all that is left it would seem is to die in silence and solitude like the wolf (*La Mort du loup*). Vigny continues to hold, however, like the author of the *City of Dreadful Night,* that though men may not meet in their joys, they may commune after a fashion in their woe. He opposes to heartless nature and her "vain splendor" the religion of pity, "the majesty of human sufferings."[57] Towards the end, when Vigny feels the growing prestige of science, he holds out the hope that a man may to a certain extent escape from the solitude of his own ego into some larger whole by contributing his mite to "progress." But the symbol of this communion[58] that he has chosen—that of the shipwrecked and sinking mariner who con-

signs his geographical discoveries to a bottle in the hope that it may be washed up on some civilized shore—is itself of a singular forlornness.

Vigny has a concentration and power of philosophical reflection that is rare among the Romanticists. George Sand is inferior to him in this respect, but she had a richer and more generous nature, and is perhaps even more instructive in her life and writings for the student of Romantic melancholy. After the loss of the religious faith of her childhood she became an avowed Rousseauist. She attacks a society that seems to her to stand in the way of the happiness of which she dreams—the supreme emotional intensity to be achieved in an ideal love. In celebrating passion and the rights of passion she is lyrical in the two main modes of the Rousseauist—she is either tender and elegiac, or else stormy and titanic. But when she attempts to practice with Mussett this religion of love, the result is violent disillusion. In the forlornness that follows upon the collapse of her sham communion she meditates suicide. "Ten years ago," she wrote in 1845 to Mazzini, "I was in Switzerland; I was still in the age of tempests; I made up my mind even then to meet you, if I should resist the temptation to suicide which pursued me upon the glaciers." And then gradually a new faith dawned upon her; she substituted for the religion of love the religion of human brotherhood. She set up as an object of worship humanity in its future progress; and then, like so many other dreamers, she suffered a violent disillusion in the Revolution of 1848. The radiant abstraction she had been worshiping had been put to the test and she discovered that there entered into the actual make-up of the humanity she had so idealized "a large number of knaves, a very large number of lunatics, and an immense number of fools." What is noteworthy in George Sand is that she not only saved the precious principle of faith from these repeated shipwrecks, but towards the end of her life began to put it on a firmer footing. Like Goethe, she worked out to some extent, in opposition to Romanticism, a genuinely ethical point of view.

This latter development can best be studied in her correspondence with Flaubert. She urges him to exercise his will, and he replies that he is as "fatalistic as a Turk." His fatalism, however, was not oriental but scientific or pseudo-scientific. I have already cited his demand that man be studied "objectively," just as one would study "a mastodon or a crocodile." Flaubert refused to see any connection between this determinism and his own gloom, or between George Sand's assertion of will and her cheerfulness. It was simply, he held, a matter of temperament, and there is no doubt some truth in this contention. "You at the first leap mount to heaven," he says, "while I, poor devil, am glued to the earth as though by leaden soles." And again: "In spite of your

---

[52][Babbitt] *Le juste opposera le dédain à l'absence*
    Et ne répondra plus que par un froid silence
    Au silence éternel de la divinité.
    [''The just will oppose his disdain to nothingness and will respond only with a cold silence to the eternal silence of the divinity.'']

[53][Babbitt] See Sainte-Beuve's poetical epistle *A. M. Villemain* (*Pensées d'Août,* 1837).

[54][Babbitt] See *Masters of Modern French Criticism,* 233, 238.

[55][Babbitt] Wordsworth writes ''A piteous lot it were to flee from man / Yet not rejoice in nature.'' *Excursion,* IV. 514. This lot was Vigny's: *"Ne me laisse jamais seul avec la nature / Car je la connais trop pour n'en avoir pas peur.* [''Never leave me alone with nature for I know her too well not to fear her.'']

[56][Babbitt] Madame Dorval.

[57][Babbitt] *La Maison du berger.* Note that in Wordsworth the ''still sad music of humanity'' is very closely associated with nature.

[58][Babbitt] *La Bouteille à la mer.*

great sphinx eyes you have always seen the world as through a golden mist," whereas "I am constantly dissecting; and when I have finally discovered the corruption in anything that is supposed to be pure, the gangrene in its fairest parts, then I raise my head and laugh." Yet George Sand's cheerfulness is also related to her perception of a power in man to work upon himself—a power that sets him apart from other animals. To enter into this region of ethical effort is to escape from the whole fatal circle of naturalism, and at the same time to show some capacity to mature—a rare achievement among the Romanticists. The contrast is striking here between George Sand and Hugo, who, as the ripe fruit of his meditations, yields nothing better than the apotheosis of Robespierre and Marat. "I wish to see man as he is," she writes to Flaubert. "He is not good or bad: he is good and bad. But he is something else besides: being good and bad he has an inner force which leads him to be very bad and a little good, or very good and a little bad. I have often wondered," she adds, "why your *Education sentimentale* was so ill received by the public, and the reason, as it seems to me, is that its characters are passive—that they do not act upon themselves." But the titaness of the period of *Lélia* can scarcely be said to have acted upon herself, so that she is justified in writing: "I cannot forget that my personal victory over despair is the work of my will, and of a new way of understanding life, which is the exact opposite of the one I held formerly." How different is the weary cry of Flaubert: "I am like a piece of clockwork, what I am doing today I shall be doing tomorrow; I did exactly the same thing yesterday; I was exactly the same man ten years ago."

The correspondence of Flaubert and George Sand bears interestingly on another of the sham religions of the nineteenth century—the religion of art. Art is for Flaubert not merely a religion but a fanaticism. He preaches abstinence, renunciation and mortification of the flesh in the name of art. He excommunicates those who depart from artistic orthodoxy and speaks of heretics and disbelievers in art with a ferocity worthy of a Spanish inquisitor. Ethical beauty such as one finds in the Greeks at their best resides in order and proportion; it is not a thing apart, but the outcome of some harmonious whole. Beauty in the purely aesthetic and unethical sense that Flaubert gives to the word is little more than the pursuit of illusion. The man who thus treats beauty as a thing apart, who does not refer back his quest of the exquisite to some ethical center, will spend his life Ixion-like embracing phantoms. "O Art, Art," exclaims Flaubert, "bitter deception, nameless phantom, which gleams and lures us to our ruin!" He speaks elsewhere of "the chimera of style which is wearing him out soul and body." Attaching as he did an almost religious importance to his quest of the exquisite, he

became, like so many other Rousseauists, not merely aesthetic but hyperaesthetic. He complains in his old age: "My sensibility is sharper than a razor's edge; the creaking of a door, the face of a bourgeois, an absurd statement set my heart to throbbing and completely upset me." Hardly anywhere else, indeed, will one find such accents of bitterness, such melancholy, welling up unbidden from the very depths of the heart, as in the devotees of art for art's sake—Flaubert, Leconte de Lisle, Théophile Gautier.

George Sand takes Flaubert to task with admirable tact for his failure to subordinate art to something higher than itself. "Talent imposes duties; and art for art's sake is an empty word." As she grew older she says she came more and more to put truth above beauty, and goodness before strength. "I have reflected a great deal on what is *true,* and in this search for truth, the sentiment of my ego has gradually disappeared." The truth on which she had reflected was what she herself calls total truth *(le vrai total)*, not merely truth according to the natural law, which received such exclusive emphasis towards the middle of the nineteenth century as to lead to the rise of another sham religion—the religion of science. "You have a better sense for total truth," she tells one of her correspondents, "than Sainte-Beuve, Renan and Littré. They have fallen into the German rut: therein lies their weakness." And Flaubert writes to George Sand: "What amazes and delights me is the strength of your personality, not that of the brain alone."

Furthermore the holding of the human law that made possible this rounded development, this growth towards total truth, was a matter not of tradition but of immediate perception. George Sand had succeeded, as Taine says, in making the difficult transition from an hereditary faith to a personal conviction. Now this perception of the human law is something very different from the pantheistic reverie in which George Sand was also an adept. To look on reverie as the equivalent of vision in the Aristotelian sense, as Rousseau and so many of his followers have done, is to fall into sham spirituality. Maurice de Guérin falls into sham spirituality when he exclaims "Oh! this contact of nature and the soul would engender an ineffable voluptuousness, a prodigious love of heaven and of God." I am not asserting that George Sand herself discriminated sharply between ethical and aesthetic perception, or that she is to be rated as a very great sage at any time. Yet she owes her recovery of serenity after suffering shock upon shock of disillusion to her having exercised in some degree what she terms "the contemplative sense wherein resides invincible faith" *(le sens contemplatif où réside la foi invincible)*, and the passages that bear witness to her use of this well-nigh obsolete sense are found in her correspondence.

Wordsworth lauds in true Rousseauistic fashion a "wise passiveness." But to be truly contemplative is not to be passive at all, but to be "energetic" in Aristotle's sense, or strenuous in Buddha's sense. It is a matter of no small import that the master analyst of the East and the master analyst of the West are at one in their solution of the supreme problem of ethics—the problem of happiness. For there can be no doubt that the energy in which the doctrine of Aristotle culminates[59] is the same as the "strenuousness" on which Buddha puts his final emphasis.[60] The highest good they both agree is a contemplative *working*. It is by thus working according to the human law that one rises above the naturalistic level. The scientific rationalists of the nineteenth century left no place for this true human spontaneity when they sought to subject man entirely to the "law for thing." This scientific determinism was responsible for a great deal of spiritual depression and acedia, especially in France during the second half of the nineteenth century.[61] But even if science is less dogmatic and absolute one needs to consider why it does not deserve to be given the supreme and central place in life, why it cannot, in short, take the place of humanism and religion, and the working according to the human law that they both enjoin.

A man may indeed effect through science a certain escape from himself, and this is very salutary so far as it goes; he has to discipline himself to an order that is quite independent of his own fancies and emotions. He becomes objective, in short, but objective according to the natural and not according to the human law. Objectivity of this kind gives control over natural forces, but it does not supply the purpose for which these forces are to be used. It gives the airship, for instance, but does not determine whether the airship is to go on some beneficent errand or is to scatter bombs on women and children. Science does not even set right limits to the faculty that it chiefly exercises—the intellect. In itself it stimulates rather than curbs one of the three main lusts to which human nature is subject—the lust of knowledge. Renan, who makes a religion of science, speaks of "sacred curiosity." But this is even more dangerous than the opposite excess of the ascetic Christian who denounces all curiosity as vain. The man of science avers indeed that he does subordinate his knowledge to an adequate aim, namely the progress of humanity. But the humanity of the Baconian is only

an intellectual abstraction, just as the humanity of the Rousseauist is only an emotional dream. George Sand found, as we have seen, that the passage from one's dream of humanity to humanity in the concrete involved a certain disillusion. The scientific or rationalistic humanitarian is subject to similar disillusions.[62] Science not only fails to set proper limits to the activity of the intellect, but one must also note a curious paradox in its relation to the second of the main lusts to which man is subject, the lust for emotion *(libido sentiendi)*. The prime virtue of science is to be unemotional and at the same time keenly analytical. Now protracted and unemotional analysis finally creates a desire, as Renan says, for the opposite pole, "the kisses of the naive being," and in general for a frank surrender to the emotions. Science thus actually prepares clients for the Rousseauist.[63] The man of science is also flattered by the Rousseauistic notion that conscience and virtue are themselves only forms of emotion. He is thus saved from anything so distasteful as having to subordinate his own scientific discipline to some superior religious or humanistic discipline. He often oscillates between the rationalistic and the emotional pole, not only in other things, but also in his cult of humanity. But if conscience is merely an emotion there is a cult that makes a more potent appeal to conscience than the cult of humanity itself, and that is the cult of country. One is here at the root of the most dangerous of all the sham religions of the modern age—the religion of country, the frenzied nationalism that is now threatening to make an end of civilization itself.

Both emotional nationalism and emotional internationalism go back to Rousseau, but in his final emphasis he is an emotional nationalist;[64] and that is because he saw that patriotic "virtue" is a more potent intoxicant than the love of humanity. The demonstration came in the French Revolution, which began as a great international movement on emotional lines and ended in imperialism and Napoleon Bonaparte. It is here that the terrible peril of a science that is

---

[59][Babbitt] See Book IX of the *Nicomachean Ethics*.

[60][Babbitt] "All salutary conditions have their root in strenuousness" *(appā-mada)*, says Buddha.

[61][Babbitt] See *Masters of Modern French Criticism*, "Essay on Taine," *passim*. Paul Bourget in his *Essais de psychologie contemporaine* (2 vols.) has followed out during this period the survivals of the older Romantic melancholy and their reinforcement by scientific determinism.

[62][Babbitt] *"Le pauvre M. Arago, revenant un jour de l'Hôtel de Ville en 1848 après une épouvantable émeute, disait tristement à l'un de ses aides de camp au ministère de la marine: 'En vérité ces gens-là ne sont pas raisonnables.'"* Doudan, *Lettres*, IV. 338. ["Poor Mr. Arago, returning one day from the city hall after a frightful disturbance, said sadly to one of his aides-de-camp to the minister of the navy, 'In truth those people are not reasonable.'"]

[63][Babbitt] See Preface (pp. viii–ix) to his *Souvenirs d'enfance et de jeunesse* and my comment in *The New Laokoön*, 207–08.

[64][Babbitt] Most of the political implications of the point of view I am developing I am reserving for a volume I have in preparation to be entitled *Democracy and Imperialism*. Some of my conclusions will be found in two articles in the (New York) *Nation: The Breakdown of Internationalism* (June 17 and 24, 1915), and *The Political Influence of Rousseau* (January 18, 1917). [The book Babbitt refers to here was published in 1924 under the title *Democracy and Leadership*.]

pursued as an end in itself becomes manifest. It disciplines man and makes him efficient on the naturalistic level, but leaves him ethically undisciplined. Now in the absence of ethical discipline the lust for knowledge and the lust for feeling count very little, at least practically, compared with the third main lust of human nature—the lust for power. Hence the emergence of that most sinister of all types, the efficient megalomaniac. The final use of a science that has thus become a tool of the lust for power is, in Burke's phrase, to "improve the mystery of murder."

This union of material efficiency and ethical unrestraint, though in a way the upshot of the whole movement we have been studying, is especially marked in the modern German. Goethe, as I have pointed out, is ready to pardon Faust for grave violations of the moral law because of work which, so far from being ethical, is, in view of the ruin in which it involves the rustic pair, Baucis and Philemon, under suspicion of being positively unethical. Yet Goethe was far from being a pure utilitarian and he had reacted more than most Germans of his time from Rousseauism. Rousseau is glorified by Germans as a chief source of their *Kultur,* as I have already pointed out. Now *Kultur* when analyzed breaks up into two very different things—scientific efficiency and emotionalism or what the Germans (and unfortunately not the Germans alone) term "idealism." There is no question about the relation of this idealism to the stream of tendency of which Rousseau is the chief representative. By his corruption of conscience Rousseau made it possible to identify character with temperament. It was easy for Fichte and others to take the next step and identify national character with national temperament. The Germans, according to Fichte, are all beautiful souls, the elect of nature. If they have no special word for character it is because to be a German and have character are synonymous. Character is something that gushes up from the primordial depths of the German's being without any conscious effort on his part.[65] The members of a whole national group may thus flatter one another and inbreed their national "genius" in the Romantic sense, and feel all the while that they are ecstatic "idealists"; yet as a result of the failure to refer their genius back to some ethical center, to work, in other words, according to the human law, they may, so far as the members of other national groups are concerned, remain in a state of moral solitude.

Everything thus hinges on the meaning of the word *work.* In the abstract and metaphysical sense man can know nothing of unity. He may, however, by working in the human sense, by imposing, that is, due limits on his expansive de-

sires, close up in some measure the gap in his own nature (the "civil war in the cave") and so tend to become inwardly one. He may hope in the same way to escape from the solitude of his own ego, for the inner unity that he achieves through work is only an entering into possession of his ethical self, the self that he possesses in common with other men. Thus to work ethically is not only to become more unified and happy but also to move away from what is less permanent towards what is more permanent and therefore more peaceful in his total nature; so that the problem of happiness and the problem of peace turn out at least to be inseparable.

Souls, says Emerson, never meet; and it is true that a man never quite escapes from his solitude. That does not make the choice of direction any the less important. An infinite beckons to him on either hand. The one inspires the divine discontent, the other Romantic restlessness. If instead of following the Romantic lure he heeds the call from the opposite direction, he will not indeed attain to any perfect communion but he will be less solitary. Strictly speaking, a man is never happy in the sense of being completely satisfied with the passing moment,[66] or never, Dr. Johnson would add, except when he is drunk. The happiness of the sober and waking man resides, it may be, not in his content with the present moment but in the very effort that marks his passage from a lower to a higher ethical level.

The happiness of which Rousseau dreamed, it has been made plain, was not this active and ethical happiness, but rather the passive enjoyment of the beautiful moment—the moment that he would like to have last forever. After seeking for the beautiful moment in the intoxication of love he turned, as we have seen, to pantheistic reverie. "As long as it lasts," he says of a moment of this kind, "one is self-sufficing like God." Yes, but it does not last, and when he wakes from his dream of communion with nature, he is still solitary, still the prisoner of his ego. The pantheistic dreamer is passive in every sense. He is not working either according to the human or according to the natural law, and so it is not gaining either in material or in ethical efficiency. In a world such as that in which we live this seems too much like picnicking on a battlefield. Rousseau could on occasion speak shrewdly on this point. He wrote to a youthful enthusiast who wished to come and live with him at Montmorency: "The first bit of advice I should like to give you is not to indulge in the taste you say you have for the contemplative

---

[65][Babbitt] *Reden an die deutsche Nation,* XII.

[66][Babbitt] I should perhaps allow for the happiness that may be experienced in moments of supernormal consciousness—something quite distinct from emotional or other intoxication. Fairly consistent testimony as to moments of this kind is found in the records of the past, from the early Buddhists down to Tennyson.

life and which is only an indolence of the spirit reprehensible at every age and especially at yours. Man is not made to meditate but to act."

The contemplative life is, then, according to Rousseau, the opposite of action. But to contemplate is, according to an Aristotle or a Buddha, to engage in the most important form of action, the form that leads to happiness. To identify leisure and the contemplative life with pantheistic reverie, as Rousseau does, is to fall into one of the most vicious of confusions. Perhaps indeed the most important contrast one can reach in a subject of this kind is that between a wise strenuousness and a more or less wise passiveness, between the spiritual athlete and the cosmic loafer, between a St. Paul, let us say, and a Walt Whitman.

The spiritual idling and drifting of the Rousseauist would be less sinister if it did not coexist in the world of today with an intense material activity. The man who seeks happiness by work according to the natural law is to be rated higher than the man who seeks happiness in some form of emotional intoxication (including pantheistic reverie). He is not left unarmed, a helpless dreamer in the battle of life. The type of efficiency he is acquiring also helps to keep at bay man's great enemy, ennui. An Edison, we may suppose, who is drawn ever onward by the lure of wonder and curiosity and power, has little time to be bored. It is surely better to escape from the boredom of life after the fashion of Edison than after the fashion of Baudelaire.[67]

I have already pointed out, however, the peril in a one-sided working of this kind. It makes man efficient without making him ethical. It stimulates rather than corrects a fearless, formless expansion on the human level. This inordinate reaching out beyond bounds is, as the great Greek poets saw with such clearness, an invitation to Nemesis. The misery that results from unrestraint, from failure to work according to the human law, is something different from mere pain and far more to be dreaded; just as the happiness that results from a right working according to the human law is something different from mere pleasure and far more worthy of pursuit.

The present alliance between emotional Romanticists and utilitarians[68] is a veritable menace to civilization itself. It does not follow, as I said in a previous chapter, because reverie or "intuition of the creative flux" cannot take the place of leisure or meditation, that one must therefore condemn it utterly. It may, like other forms of romanticism, have a place on the recreative side of life. What finally counts is work according to either the human or the natural law, but man cannot always be working. He needs moments of relief from tension and concentration and even, it should seem, of semioblivion of his conscious self. As one of the ways of winning such moments of relaxation and partial forgetfulness much may be said for reverie. In general one must grant the solace and rich source of poetry that is found in communion with nature even though the final emphasis be put on communion with man. It is no small thing to be, as Arnold says Wordsworth was, a "priest of the wonder and bloom of the world." One cannot, however, grant the Wordsworthian that to be a priest of wonder is necessarily to be also a priest of wisdom. Thus to promote to the supreme and central place something that is legitimate in its own degree, but secondary, is to risk starting a sham religion.

Those who have sought to set up a cult of love or beauty or science or humanity or country are open to the same objections as the votaries of nature. However important each of these things may be in its own place, it cannot properly be put in the supreme and central place for the simple reason that it does not involve any adequate conversion or discipline of man's ordinary self to some ethical center. I have tried to show that the sense of solitude or forlornness that is so striking a feature of Romantic melancholy arises not only from a loss of hold on the traditional centers, but also from the failure of these new attempts at communion to keep their promises. The number of discomfitures of this kind in the period that has elapsed since the late eighteenth century, suggests that this period was even more than most periods an age of sophistry. Every age has had its false teachers, but possibly no age ever had so many dubious moralists as this, an incomparable series of false prophets, from Rousseau himself down to Nietzsche and Tolstoy.

---

[67][Babbitt] I scarcely need to say that I am speaking of the man of science only insofar as he is purely naturalistic in his point of view. There may enter into the total personality of Edison or any particular man of science other and very different elements.

[68][Babbitt] M. René Berthelot has written a book on pragmatism and similar tendencies in contemporary philosophy entitled *Un romantisme utilitaire*. I have not read it, but the title alone is worth more than most books on the subject I have read.

Carl Gustav Jung

1875–1961

Originally a disciple of Freud, Jung broke with the master when he concluded that Freud's system was excessively reductive and monolithic in referring neuroses to experiences of childhood, especially sexual experiences. Less the scientific empiricist than Freud and more the Romantic philosopher, with the roots of his theories in Kant, Schiller, and others, Jung had a considerable influence on critics interested in the relation of myth and ritual to literature and on critics concerned with establishing literature as the provider of a special mode of knowledge.

Jung's "collective unconscious," which yields "inborn possibilities of ideas" and keeps our "fantasy active within certain categories," seems analogous in the area of the imagination to Kant's categories of the understanding. Perhaps most important to literary criticism was his theory of archetypes, which depends on his theory of the collective unconscious. He defines an archetype as a "primordial image . . . be it a demon, a human being, or a process—that constantly recurs in the course of history and appears wherever creative fantasy is freely expressed." His theory of the collective unconscious was given various applications in literary criticism even though his own psychological definition of *archetype* was frequently abandoned.

Less the strict rationalist and materialist than Freud, Jung thinks of archetypes as symbols with meanings that cannot be expressed except in their own terms, rather than as allegorical images that can be fully explained by analytical procedures. His work was therefore of particular interest to critics who resisted the idea that a poem invites paraphrase, that the words of a poem are possibly interchangeable with other words. His many erudite studies of dreams, myths, and symbols have been of immense interest to those who study conventions of literary symbolism.

A multivolume edition of Jung's works, edited by G. Adler and others, is nearly complete. See also Morris Philipson, *Outline of Jungian Aesthetics* (1963). As examples of critical works in Jung's debt see Maud Bodkin, *Archetypal Patterns in Poetry* (1934); Joseph Campbell, *The Hero with a Thousand Faces* (1949); Philip Wheelwright, *The Burning Fountain* (1954); and Northrop Frye, *Anatomy of Criticism* (1957). See also J. B. Vickery, ed., *Myth and Literature: Contemporary Theory and Practice* (1966); Aniela Jaffe, *The Myth of Meaning in the Work of C. G. Jung* (tr. 1970); Barbara Hannah, *Jung, His Life and Work* (1976); Peter Homans, *Jung in Context* (1979); Bettina L. Knapp, *A Jungian Approach to Literature* (1984); Walter A. Shelburne, *Mythos and Logos in the Thought of Carl Jung* (1988); and Robin Robertson, *C. G. Jung and the Archetypes of the Collective Unconscious* (1987).

On the Relation of Analytical Psychology to Poetry

In spite of its difficulty, the task of discussing the relation of analytical psychology to poetry affords me a welcome opportunity to define my views on the much debated question of the relations between psychology and art in general. Although the two things cannot be compared, the close connections which undoubtedly exist between them call for investigation. These connections arise from the fact that the practice of art is a psychological activity and, as such, can be approached from a psychological angle. Considered in this light, art, like any other human activity deriving from psychic motives, is a proper subject for psychology. This statement, however, involves a very definite limitation of the psychological viewpoint when we come to apply it in practice. Only that aspect of art which consists in the process of artistic creation can be a subject for psychological study, but not that which constitutes its essential nature. The question of what art is in itself can never be answered by the psychologist, but must be approached from the side of aesthetics.

A similar distinction must be made in the realm of religion. A psychological approach is permissible only in regard to the emotions and symbols which constitute the phenomenology of religion, but which do not touch upon its essential nature. If the essence of religion and art could be explained, then both of them would become mere subdivisions of psychology. This is not to say that such violations of their nature have not been attempted. But those who are guilty of them obviously forget that a similar fate might easily befall psychology, since its intrinsic value and specific quality would be destroyed if it were regarded as a mere activity of the brain, and were relegated along with the endocrine functions to a subdivision of physiology. This too, as we know, has been attempted.

Art by its very nature is not science, and science by its very nature is not art; both these spheres of the mind have something in reserve that is peculiar to them and can be explained only in its own terms. Hence when we speak of the relation of psychology to art, we shall treat only of that aspect of art which can be submitted to psychological scrutiny without violating its nature. Whatever the psychologist has to say about art will be confined to the process of artistic creation and has nothing to do with its innermost essence. He can no more explain this than the intellect can describe or even understand the nature of feeling. Indeed, art and science would not exist as separate entities at all if the fundamental difference between them had not long since forced itself on the mind. The fact that artistic, scientific, and religious propensities still slumber peacefully together in the small child, or that with primitives the beginnings of art, science, and religion coalesce in the undifferentiated chaos of the magical mentality, or that no trace of "mind" can be found in the natural instincts of animals—all this does nothing to prove the existence of a unifying principle which alone would justify a reduction of the one to the other. For if we go so far back into the history of the mind that the distinctions between its various fields of activity become altogether invisible, we do not reach an underlying principle of their unity, but merely an earlier, undifferentiated state in which no separate activities yet exist. But the elementary state is not an explanatory principle that would allow us to draw conclusions as to the nature of later, more highly developed states, even though they must necessarily derive from it. A scientific attitude will always tend to overlook the peculiar nature of these more differentiated states in favor of their causal derivation, and will endeavor to subordinate them to a general but more elementary principle.

These theoretical reflections seem to me very much in place today, when we so often find that works of art, and particularly poetry, are interpreted precisely in this manner, by reducing them to more elementary states. Though the material he works with and its individual treatment can easily be traced back to the poet's personal relations with his parents, this does not enable us to understand his poetry. The same reduction can be made in all sorts of other fields, and not least in the case of pathological disturbances. Neuroses and psychoses are likewise reducible to infantile relations with the parents, and so are a man's good and bad habits, his beliefs, peculiarities, passions, interests, and so forth. It can hardly be supposed that all these very different things must have exactly the same explanation, for otherwise we would be driven to the conclusion that they actually are the same thing. If a work of art is explained in the same way as a neurosis, then either the work of art is a neurosis or a neurosis is a work of art. This explanation is all very well as a play on words, but sound common sense rebels against putting a work of art on the same level as a neurosis. An analyst might, in an extreme case, view a neurosis as a work of art through

ON THE RELATION OF ANALYTICAL PSYCHOLOGY TO POETRY. Jung's *On the Relation of Analytical Psychology to Poetry* was delivered as a lecture to the Society for German Language and Literature in Zurich in May 1922. It was first published later in that year as *Über die Beziehungen der analytischen Psychologie zum dichterischen Kunstwerk.* The text is from *The Spirit of Man, Art and Literature in Collected Works of C. G. Jung,* Vol. 15, translated by R. F. C. Hull, excerpt, pp. 65–83. Copyright © 1966 Princeton University Press. Reprinted by permission of Princeton University Press.

the lens of his professional bias, but it would never occur to an intelligent layman to mistake a pathological phenomenon for art, in spite of the undeniable fact that a work of art arises from much the same psychological conditions as a neurosis. This is only natural, because certain of these conditions are present in every individual and, owing to the relative constancy of the human environment, are constantly the same, whether in the case of a nervous intellectual, a poet, or a normal human being. All have had parents, all have a father- or a mother-complex, all know about sex and therefore have certain common and typical human difficulties. One poet may be influenced more by his relation to his father, another by the tie to his mother, while a third shows unmistakable traces of sexual repression in his poetry. Since all this can be said equally well not only of every neurotic but of every normal human being, nothing specific is gained for the judgment of a work of art. At most our knowledge of its psychological antecedents will have been broadened and deepened.

The school of medical psychology inaugurated by Freud has undoubtedly encouraged the literary historian to bring certain peculiarities of a work of art into relation with the intimate, personal life of the poet. But this is nothing new in principle, for it has long been known that the scientific treatment of art will reveal the personal threads that the artist, intentionally or unintentionally, has woven into his work. The Freudian approach may, however, make possible a more exhaustive demonstration of the influences that reach back into earliest childhood and play their part in artistic creation. To this extent the psychoanalysis of art differs in no essential from the subtle psychological nuances of a penetrating literary analysis. The difference is at most a question of degree, though we may occasionally be surprised by indiscreet references to things which a rather more delicate touch might have passed over if only for reasons of tact. This lack of delicacy seems to be a professional peculiarity of the medical psychologist, and the temptation to draw daring conclusions easily leads to flagrant abuses. A slight whiff of scandal often lends spice to a biography, but a little more becomes a nasty inquisitiveness—bad taste masquerading as science. Our interest is insidiously deflected from the work of art and gets lost in the labyrinth of psychic determinants, the poet becomes a clinical case and, very likely, yet another addition to the curiosa of *psychopathia sexualis.* But this means that the psychoanalysis of art has turned aside from its proper objective and strayed into a province that is as broad as mankind, that is not in the least specific of the artist and has even less relevance to his art.

This kind of analysis brings the work of art into the sphere of general human psychology, where many other things besides art have their origin. To explain art in these terms is just as great a platitude as the statement that "every artist is a narcissist." Every man who pursues his own goal is a "narcissist"—though one wonders how permissible it is to give such wide currency to a term specifically coined for the pathology of neurosis. The statement therefore amounts to nothing; it merely elicits the faint surprise of a bon mot. Since this kind of analysis is in no way concerned with the work of art itself, but strives like a mole to bury itself in the dirt as speedily as possible, it always ends up in the common earth that unites all mankind. Hence its explanations have the same tedious monotony as the recitals which one daily hears in the consulting room.

The reductive method of Freud is a purely medical one, and the treatment is directed at a pathological or otherwise unsuitable formation which has taken the place of the normal functioning. It must therefore be broken down, and the way cleared for healthy adaptation. In this case, reduction to the common human foundation is altogether appropriate. But when applied to a work of art it leads to the results I have described. It strips the work of art of its shimmering robes and exposes the nakedness and drabness of *Homo sapiens,* to which species the poet and artist also belong. The golden gleam of artistic creation—the original object of discussion—is extinguished as soon as we apply to it the same corrosive method which we use in analyzing the fantasies of hysteria. The results are no doubt very interesting and may perhaps have the same kind of scientific value as, for instance, a post-mortem examination of the brain of Nietzsche, which might conceivably show us the particular atypical form of paralysis from which he died. But what would this have to do with *Zarathustra?* Whatever its subterranean background may have been, is it not a whole world in itself, beyond the human, all-too-human imperfections, beyond the world of migraine and cerebral atrophy?

I have spoken of Freud's reductive method but have not stated in what that method consists. It is essentially a medical technique for investigating morbid psychic phenomena, and it is solely concerned with the ways and means of getting round or peering through the foreground of consciousness in order to reach the psychic background, or the unconscious. It is based on the assumption that the neurotic patient represses certain psychic contents because they are morally incompatible with his conscious values. It follows that the repressed contents must have correspondingly negative traits—infantile-sexual, obscene, or even criminal—which make them unacceptable to consciousness. Since no man is perfect, everyone must possess such a background whether he admits it or not. Hence it can always be exposed if only one uses the technique of interpretation worked out by Freud.

In the short space of a lecture I cannot, of course, enter into the details of the technique. A few hints must suffice. The unconscious background does not remain inactive, but betrays itself by its characteristic effects on the contents of consciousness. For example, it produces fantasies of a peculiar nature, which can easily be interpreted as sexual images. Or it produces characteristic disturbances of the conscious processes, which again can be reduced to repressed contents. A very important source for knowledge of the unconscious contents is provided by dreams, since these are direct products of the activity of the unconscious. The essential thing in Freud's reductive method is to collect all the clues pointing to the unconscious background, and then, through the analysis and interpretation of this material, to reconstruct the elementary instinctual processes. Those conscious contents which give us a clue to the unconscious background are incorrectly called *symbols* by Freud. They are not true symbols, however, since according to his theory they have merely the role of *signs* or *symptoms* of the subliminal processes. The true symbol differs essentially from this, and should be understood as an expression of an intuitive idea that cannot yet be formulated in any other or better way.[1] When Plato, for instance, puts the whole problem of the theory of knowledge in his parable of the cave,[2] or when Christ expresses the idea of the Kingdom of Heaven in parables, these are genuine and true symbols, that is, attempts to express something for which no verbal concept yet exists. If we were to interpret Plato's metaphor in Freudian terms we would naturally arrive at the uterus, and would have proved that even a mind like Plato's was still stuck on a primitive level of infantile sexuality. But we would have completely overlooked what Plato actually created out of the primitive determinants of his philosophical ideas; we would have missed the essential point and merely discovered that he had infantile-sexual fantasies like any other mortal. Such a discovery could be of value only for a man who regarded Plato as superhuman, and who can now state with satisfaction that Plato too was an ordinary human being. But who would want to regard Plato as a god? Surely only one who is dominated by infantile fantasies and therefore possesses a neurotic mentality. For him the reduction to common human truths is salutary on medical grounds, but this would have nothing whatever to do with the meaning of Plato's parable.

I have purposely dwelt on the application of medical psychoanalysis to works of art because I want to emphasize that the psychoanalytic method is at the same time an essential part of the Freudian doctrine. Freud himself by his rigid dogmatism has ensured that the method and the doctrine—in themselves two very different things—are regarded by the public as identical. Yet the method may be employed with beneficial results in medical cases without at the same time exalting it into a doctrine. And against this doctrine we are bound to raise vigorous objections. The assumptions it rests on are quite arbitrary. For example, neuroses are by no means exclusively caused by sexual repression, and the same holds true for psychoses. There is no foundation for saying that dreams merely contain repressed wishes whose moral incompatibility requires them to be disguised by a hypothetical dream-censor. The Freudian technique of interpretation, so far as it remains under the influence of its own one-sided and therefore erroneous hypotheses, displays a quite obvious bias.

In order to do justice to a work of art, analytical psychology must rid itself entirely of medical prejudice; for a work of art is not a disease, and consequently requires a different approach from the medical one. A doctor naturally has to seek out the causes of a disease in order to pull it up by the roots, but just as naturally the psychologist must adopt exactly the opposite attitude towards a work of art. Instead of investigating its typically human determinants, he will inquire first of all into its meaning, and will concern himself with its determinants only insofar as they enable him to understand it more fully. Personal causes have as much or as little to do with a work of art as the soil with the plant that springs from it. We can certainly learn to understand some of the plant's peculiarities by getting to know its habitat, and for the botanist this is an important part of his equipment. But nobody will maintain that everything essential has then been discovered about the plant itself. The personal orientation which the doctor needs when confronted with the question of etiology in medicine is quite out of place in dealing with a work of art, just because a work of art is not a human being, but is something suprapersonal. It is a thing and not a personality; hence it cannot be judged by personal criteria. Indeed, the special significance of a true work of art resides in the fact that it has escaped from the limitations of the personal and has soared beyond the personal concerns of its creator.

I must confess from my own experience that it is not at all easy for a doctor to lay aside his professional bias when considering a work of art and look at it with a mind cleared of the current biological causality. But I have come to learn that although a psychology with a purely biological orientation can explain a good deal about man in general, it cannot be applied to a work of art and still less to man as creator. A

---

[1] Here Jung allies himself with those Romantic critics who distinguished symbolism from allegory. See Coleridge, *The Statesman's Manual,* p. 476.
[2] *Republic,* VII.

purely causalistic psychology is only able to reduce every human individual to a member of the species *Homo sapiens,* since its range is limited to what is transmitted by heredity or derived from other sources. But a work of art is not transmitted or derived—it is a creative reorganization of those very conditions to which a causalistic psychology must always reduce it. The plant is not a mere product of the soil; it is a living self-contained process which in essence has nothing to do with the character of the soil. In the same way, the meaning and individual quality of a work of art inhere within it and not in its extrinsic determinants. One might almost describe it as a living being that uses man only as a nutrient medium, employing his capacities according to its own laws and shaping itself to the fulfillment of its own creative purpose.

But here I am anticipating somewhat, for I have in mind a particular type of art which I still have to introduce. Not every work of art originates in the way I have just described. There are literary works, prose as well as poetry, that spring wholly from the author's intention to produce a particular result. He submits his material to a definite treatment with a definite aim in view; he adds to it and subtracts from it, emphasizing one effect, toning down another, laying on a touch of color here, another there, all the time carefully considering the overall result and paying strict attention to the laws of form and style. He exercises the keenest judgment and chooses his words with complete freedom. His material is entirely subordinated to his artistic purpose; he wants to express this and nothing else. He is wholly at one with the creative process, no matter whether he has deliberately made himself its spearhead, as it were, or whether it has made him its instrument so completely that he has lost all consciousness of this fact. In either case, the artist is so identified with his work that his intentions and his faculties are indistinguishable from the act of creation itself. There is no need, I think, to give examples of this from the history of literature or from the testimony of the artists themselves.

Nor need I cite examples of the other class of works which flow more or less complete and perfect from the author's pen. They come as it were fully arrayed into the world, as Pallas Athene sprang from the head of Zeus. These works positively force themselves upon the author; his hand is seized, his pen writes things that his mind contemplates with amazement. The work brings with it its own form; anything he wants to add is rejected, and what he himself would like to reject is thrust back at him. While his conscious mind stands amazed and empty before this phenomenon, he is overwhelmed by a flood of thoughts and images which he never intended to create and which his own will could never have brought into being. Yet in spite of himself he is forced

to admit that it is his own self speaking, his own inner nature revealing itself and uttering things which he would never have entrusted to his tongue. He can only obey the apparently alien impulse within him and follow where it leads, sensing that his work is greater than himself, and wields a power which is not his and which he cannot command. Here the artist is not identical with the process of creation; he is aware that he is subordinate to his work or stands outside it, as though he were a second person; or as though a person other than himself had fallen within the magic circle of an alien will.

So when we discuss the psychology of art, we must bear in mind these two entirely different modes of creation, for much that is of the greatest importance in judging a work of art depends on this distinction. It is one that had been sensed earlier by Schiller, who as we know attempted to classify it in his concept of the *sentimental* and the *naive.*[3] The psychologist would call "sentimental" art *introverted* and the "naive" kind *extraverted.* The introverted attitude is characterized by the subject's assertion of his conscious intentions and aims against the demands of the object, whereas the extraverted attitude is characterized by the subject's subordination to the demands which the object makes upon him. In my view, Schiller's plays and most of his poems give one a good idea of the introverted attitude: the material is mastered by the conscious intentions of the poet. The extraverted attitude is illustrated by the second part of *Faust:* here the material is distinguished by its refractoriness. A still more striking example is Nietzsche's *Zarathustra,* where the author himself observed how "one became two."

From what I have said, it will be apparent that a shift of psychological standpoint has taken place as soon as one speaks not of the poet as a person but of the creative process that moves him. When the focus of interest shifts to the latter, the poet comes into the picture only as a reacting subject. This is immediately evident in our second category of works, where the consciousness of the poet is not identical with the creative process. But in works of the first category the opposite appears to hold true. Here the poet appears to be the creative process itself, and to create of his own free will without the slightest feeling of compulsion. He may even be fully convinced of his freedom of action and refuse to admit that his work could be anything else than the expression of his will and ability.

Here we are faced with a question which we cannot answer from the testimony of the poets themselves. It is really a scientific problem that psychology alone can solve. As I

---

[3]See Schiller, *On Naive and Sentimental Poetry.*

hinted earlier, it might well be that the poet, while apparently creating out of himself and producing what he consciously intends, is nevertheless so carried away by the creative impulse that he is no longer aware of an "alien" will, just as the other type of poet is no longer aware of his own will speaking to him in the apparently "alien" inspiration, although this is manifestly the voice of his own self. The poet's conviction that he is creating in absolute freedom would then be an illusion: he fancies he is swimming, but in reality an unseen current sweeps him along.

This is not by any means an academic question, but is supported by the evidence of analytical psychology. Researches have shown that there are all sorts of ways in which the conscious mind is not only influenced by the unconscious but actually guided by it. Yet is there any evidence for the supposition that a poet, despite his self-awareness, may be taken captive by his work? The proof may be of two kinds, direct or indirect. Direct proof would be afforded by a poet who thinks he knows what he is saying but actually says more than he is aware of. Such cases are not uncommon. Indirect proof would be found in cases where behind the apparent free will of the poet there stands a higher imperative that renews its peremptory demands as soon as the poet voluntarily gives up his creative activity, or that produces psychic complications whenever his work has to be broken off against his will.

Analysis of artists consistently shows not only the strength of the creative impulse arising from the unconscious, but also its capricious and willful character. The biographies of great artists make it abundantly clear that the creative urge is often so imperious that it battens on their humanity and yokes everything to the service of the work, even at the cost of health and ordinary human happiness. The unborn work in the psyche of the artist is a force of nature that achieves its end either with tyrannical might or with the subtle cunning of nature herself, quite regardless of the personal fate of the man who is its vehicle. The creative urge lives and grows in him like a tree in the earth from which it draws its nourishment. We would do well, therefore, to think of the creative process as a living thing implanted in the human psyche. In the language of analytical psychology this living thing is an *autonomous complex*. It is a split-off portion of the psyche, which leads a life of its own outside the hierarchy of consciousness. Depending on its energy charge, it may appear either as a mere disturbance of conscious activities or as a supraordinate authority which can harness the ego to its purpose. Accordingly, the poet who identifies with the creative process would be one who acquiesces from the start when the unconscious imperative begins to function. But the other poet, who feels the creative force as something

alien, is one who for various reasons cannot acquiesce and is thus caught unawares.

It might be expected that this difference in its origins would be perceptible in a work of art. For in the one case it is a conscious product shaped and designed to have the effect intended. But in the other we are dealing with an event originating in unconscious nature; with something that achieves its aim without the assistance of human consciousness, and often defies it by willfully insisting on its own form and effect. We would therefore expect that works belonging to the first class would nowhere overstep the limits of comprehension, that their effect would be bounded by the author's intention and would not extend beyond it. But with works of the other class we would have to be prepared for something suprapersonal that transcends our understanding to the same degree that the author's consciousness was in abeyance during the process of creation. We would expect a strangeness of form and content, thoughts that can only be apprehended intuitively, a language pregnant with meanings, and images that are true symbols because they are the best possible expressions for something unknown—bridges thrown out towards an unseen shore.

These criteria are, by and large, corroborated in practice. Whenever we are confronted with a work that was consciously planned and with material that was consciously selected, we find that it agrees with the first class of qualities, and in the other case with the second. The example we gave of Schiller's plays, on the one hand, and *Faust II* on the other, or better still *Zarathustra,* is an illustration of this. But I would not undertake to place the work of an unknown poet in either of these categories without first having examined rather closely his personal relations with his work. It is not enough to know whether the poet belongs to the introverted or to the extraverted type, since it is possible for either type to work with an introverted attitude at one time, and an extraverted attitude at another. This is particularly noticeable in the difference between Schiller's plays and his philosophical writings, between Goethe's perfectly formed poems and the obvious struggle with his material in *Faust II,* and between Nietzsche's well-turned aphorisms and the rushing torrent of *Zarathustra.* The same poet can adopt different attitudes to his work at different times, and on this depends the standard we have to apply.

The question, as we now see, is exceedingly complicated, and the complication grows even worse when we consider the case of the poet who identifies with the creative process. For should it turn out that the apparently conscious and purposeful manner of composition is a subjective illusion of the poet, then his work would possess symbolic qualities that are outside the range of his consciousness. They would only be more difficult to detect, because the reader as well would be unable to get beyond the bounds of the poet's consciousness which are fixed by the spirit of the time. There is no Archimedean point outside his world by which he could lift his time-bound consciousness off its hinges and recognize the symbols hidden in the poet's work. For a symbol is the intimation of a meaning beyond the level of our present powers of comprehension.

I raise this question only because I do not want my typological classification to limit the possible significance of works of art which apparently mean no more than what they say. But we have often found that a poet who has gone out of fashion is suddenly rediscovered. This happens when our conscious development has reached a higher level from which the poet can tell us something new. It was always present in his work but was hidden in a symbol, and only a renewal of the spirit of the time permits us to read its meaning. It needed to be looked at with fresher eyes, for the old ones see in it only what they were accustomed to see. Experiences of this kind should make us cautious, as they bear out my earlier argument. But works that are openly symbolic do not require this subtle approach; their pregnant language cries out at us that they mean more than they say. We can put our finger on the symbol at once, even though we may not be able to unriddle its meaning to our entire satisfaction. A symbol remains a perpetual challenge to our thoughts and feelings. That probably explains why a symbolic work is so stimulating, why it grips us so intensely, but also why it seldom affords us a purely aesthetic enjoyment. A work that is manifestly not symbolic appeals much more to our aesthetic sensibility because it is complete in itself and fulfills its purpose.

What then, you may ask, can analytical psychology contribute to our fundamental problem, which is the mystery of artistic creation? All that we have said so far has to do only with the psychological phenomenology of art. Since nobody can penetrate to the heart of nature, you will not expect psychology to do the impossible and offer a valid explanation of the secret of creativity. Like every other science, psychology has only a modest contribution to make towards a deeper understanding of the phenomena of life, and is no nearer than its sister sciences to absolute knowledge.

We have talked so much about the meaning of works of art that one can hardly suppress a doubt as to whether art really "means" anything at all. Perhaps art has no "meaning," at least not as we understand meaning. Perhaps it is like nature, which simply *is* and "means" nothing beyond that. Is "meaning" necessarily more than mere interpretation—an interpretation secreted into something by an intellect hungry for meaning? Art, it has been said, is beauty, and

"a thing of beauty is a joy forever." It needs no meaning, for meaning has nothing to do with art. Within the sphere of art, I must accept the truth of this statement. But when I speak of the relation of psychology to art we are outside its sphere, and it is impossible for us not to speculate. We must interpret, we must find meanings in things, otherwise we would be quite unable to think about them. We have to break down life and events, which are self-contained processes, into meanings, images, concepts, well knowing that in doing so we are getting further away from the living mystery. As long as we ourselves are caught up in the process of creation, we neither see nor understand; indeed we ought not to understand, for nothing is more injurious to immediate experience than cognition. But for the purpose of cognitive understanding we must detach ourselves from the creative process and look at it from the outside; only then does it become an image that expresses what we are bound to call "meaning." What was a mere phenomenon before becomes something that in association with other phenomena has meaning, that has a definite role to play, serves certain ends, and exerts meaningful effects. And when we have seen all this we get the feeling of having understood and explained something. In this way we meet the demands of science.

When, a little earlier, we spoke of a work of art as a tree growing out of the nourishing soil, we might equally well have compared it to a child growing in the womb. But as all comparisons are lame, let us stick to the more precise terminology of science. You will remember that I described the nascent work in the psyche of the artist as an autonomous complex. By this we mean a psychic formation that remains subliminal until its energy-charge is sufficient to carry it over the threshold into consciousness. Its association with consciousness does not mean that it is assimilated, only that it is perceived; but it is not subject to conscious control, and can be neither inhibited nor voluntarily reproduced. Therein lies the autonomy of the complex: it appears and disappears in accordance with its own inherent tendencies, independently of the conscious will. The creative complex shares this peculiarity with every other autonomous complex. In this respect it offers an analogy with pathological processes, since these too are characterized by the presence of autonomous complexes, particularly in the case of mental disturbances. The divine frenzy of the artist comes perilously close to a pathological state, though the two things are not identical. The *tertium comparationis*[4] is the autonomous complex. But the presence of autonomous complexes is not in itself pathological, since normal people, too, fall temporarily or

---

[4] "Third complex."

permanently under their domination. This fact is simply one of the normal peculiarities of the psyche, and for a man to be unaware of the existence of an autonomous complex merely betrays a high degree of unconsciousness. Every typical attitude that is to some extent differentiated shows a tendency to become an autonomous complex, and in most cases it actually does. Again, every instinct has more or less the character of an autonomous complex. In itself, therefore, an autonomous complex has nothing morbid about it; only when its manifestations are frequent and disturbing is it a symptom of illness.

How does an autonomous complex arise? For reasons which we cannot go into here, a hitherto unconscious portion of the psyche is thrown into activity, and gains ground by activating the adjacent areas of association. The energy needed for this is naturally drawn from consciousness—unless the latter happens to identify with the complex. But where this does not occur, the drain of energy produces what Janet calls an *abaissement du niveau mental*.[5] The intensity of conscious interests and activities gradually diminishes, leading either to apathy—a condition very common with artists—or to a regressive development of the conscious functions, that is, they revert to an infantile and archaic level and undergo something like a degeneration. The "inferior parts of the functions," as Janet calls them, push to the fore; the instinctual side of the personality prevails over the ethical, the infantile over the mature, and the unadapted over the adapted. This too is something we see in the lives of many artists. The autonomous complex thus develops by using the energy that has been withdrawn from the conscious control of the personality.

But in what does an autonomous *creative* complex consist? Of this we can know next to nothing so long as the artist's work affords us no insight into its foundations. The work presents us with a finished picture, and this picture is amenable to analysis only to the extent that we can recognize it as a symbol. But if we are unable to discover any symbolic value in it, we have merely established that, so far as we are concerned, it means no more than what it says, or to put it another way, that it *is* no more than what it *seems* to be. I used the word *seems* because our own bias may prevent a deeper appreciation of it. At any rate we can find no incentive and no starting point for an analysis. But in the case of a symbolic work we should remember the dictum of Gerhard Hauptmann: "Poetry evokes out of words the resonance of the primordial word." The question we should ask, therefore, is: what primordial image lies behind the imagery of art?

This question needs a little elucidation. I am assuming that the work of art we propose to analyze, as well as being symbolic, has its source not in the *personal unconscious* of the poet, but in a sphere of unconscious mythology whose primordial images are the common heritage of mankind. I have called this sphere the *collective unconscious,* to distinguish it from the personal unconscious. The latter I regard as the sum total of all those psychic processes and contents which are capable of becoming conscious and often do, but are then suppressed because of their incompatibility and kept subliminal. Art receives tributaries from this sphere too, but muddy ones; and their predominance, far from making a work of art a symbol, merely turns it into a symptom. We can leave this kind of art without injury and without regret to the purgative methods employed by Freud.

In contrast to the personal unconscious, which is a relatively thin layer immediately below the threshold of consciousness, the collective unconscious shows no tendency to become conscious under normal conditions, nor can it be brought back to recollection by any analytical technique,[6] since it was never repressed or forgotten. The collective unconscious is not to be thought of as a self-subsistent entity; it is no more than a potentiality handed down to us from primordial times in the specific form of mnemonic images[7] or inherited in the anatomical structure of the brain. There are no inborn ideas, but there are inborn possibilities of ideas that set bounds to even the boldest fantasy and keep our fantasy activity within certain categories: a priori ideas, as it were, the existence of which cannot be ascertained except from their effects. They appear only in the shaped material of art as the regulative principles that shape it; that is to say, only by inferences drawn from the finished work can we reconstruct the age-old original[8] of the primordial image.

The primordial image, or archetype, is a figure—be it a demon, a human being, or a process—that constantly recurs

---

[5]"Abatement of the mental level."

[6][Baynes and Baynes] By this Jung probably meant the analytical techniques that were in use at the time (1922), and more particularly the Freudian. Whether he had by then developed his own technique for constellating the collective unconscious is an open question. Cf. *The Transcendent Function* (orig. 1916), pp. 67 *ff.* and Chapter 6 of Jung's *Memories, Dreams, Reflections.*

[7][Baynes and Baynes] Here Jung defines the *collective unconscious* in much the same way as a year earlier (*Psychological Types*, 1923 ed., pp. 378, 555 *ff.*) he had defined the *archetype*. Still earlier, in 1919, using the term *archetype* for the first time, he had stated: "The instincts and the archetypes together form the 'collective unconscious' " (*Instinct and the Unconscious*, pp. 133 *ff.*). This is in better agreement with his later formulations. The subject of the above sentence should therefore be understood as the *archetype*.

[8][Baynes and Baynes] Literally, "primitive *Vorlage*." In the light of Jung's later formulations, this would mean the "archetype per se" as distinct from the "archetypal image." Cf. particularly *On the Nature of the Psyche*, paragraph 417.

in the course of history and appears wherever creative fantasy is freely expressed. Essentially, therefore, it is a mythological figure. When we examine these images more closely, we find that they give form to countless typical experiences of our ancestors. They are, so to speak, the psychic residua of innumerable experiences of the same type. They present a picture of psychic life in the average, divided up and protected into the manifold figures of the mythological pantheon. But the mythological figures are themselves products of creative fantasy and still have to be translated into conceptual language. Only the beginnings of such a language exist, but once the necessary concepts are created they could give us an abstract, scientific understanding of the unconscious processes that lie at the roots of the primordial images. In each of these images there is a little piece of human psychology and human fate, a remnant of the joys and sorrows that have been repeated countless times in our ancestral history, and on the average follow ever the same course. It is like a deeply graven river-bed in the psyche, in which waters of life, instead of flowing along as before in a broad but shallow stream, suddenly swell into a mighty river. This happens whenever that particular set of circumstances is encountered which over long periods of time has helped to lay down the primordial image.

The moment when this mythological situation reappears is always characterized by a peculiar emotional intensity; it is as though chords in us were struck that had never resounded before, or as though forces whose existence we never suspected were unloosed. What makes the struggle for adaptation so laborious is the fact that we have constantly to be dealing with individual and atypical situations. So it is not surprising that when an archetypal situation occurs we suddenly feel an extraordinary sense of release, as though transported, or caught up by an overwhelming power. At such moments we are no longer individuals, but the race; the voice of all mankind resounds in us. The individual man cannot use his powers to the full unless he is aided by one of those collective representations we call ideals, which releases all the hidden forces of instinct that are inaccessible to his conscious will. The most effective ideals are always fairly obvious variants of an archetype, as is evident from the fact that they lend themselves to allegory. The ideal of the "mother country," for instance, is an obvious allegory of the mother, as is the "fatherland" of the father. Its power to stir us does not derive from the allegory, but from the symbolical value of our native land. The archetype here is the *participation mystique* of primitive man with the soil on which he dwells, and which contains the spirits of his ancestors.

The impact of an archetype, whether it takes the form of immediate experience or is expressed through the spoken word, stirs us because it summons up a voice that is stronger than our own. Whoever speaks in primordial images speaks with a thousand voices; he enthralls and overpowers, while at the same time he lifts the idea he is seeking to express out of the occasional and the transitory into the realm of the ever-enduring. He transmutes our personal destiny into the destiny of mankind, and evokes in us all those beneficent forces that ever and anon have enabled humanity to find a refuge from every peril and to outlive the longest night.

That is the secret of great art, and of its effect upon us. The creative process, so far as we are able to follow it at all, consists in the unconscious activation of an archetypal image, and in elaborating and shaping this image into the finished work. By giving it shape, the artist translates it into the language of the present, and so makes it possible for us to find our way back to the deepest springs of life. Therein lies the social significance of art: it is constantly at work educating the spirit of the age, conjuring up the forms in which the age is most lacking. The unsatisfied yearning of the artist reaches back to the primordial image in the unconscious which is best fitted to compensate the inadequacy and one-sidedness of the present. The artist seizes on this image, and in raising it from deepest unconsciousness he brings it into relation with conscious values, thereby transforming it until it can be accepted by the minds of his contemporaries according to their powers.

People and times, like individuals, have their own characteristic tendencies and attitudes. The very word *attitude* betrays the necessary bias that every marked tendency entails. Direction implies exclusion, and exclusion means that very many psychic elements that could play their part in life are denied the right to exist because they are incompatible with the general attitude. The normal man can follow the general trend without injury to himself; but the man who takes to the back streets and alleys because he cannot endure the broad highway will be the first to discover the psychic elements that are waiting to play their part in the life of the collective. Here the artist's relative lack of adaptation turns out to his advantage; it enables him to follow his own yearnings far from the beaten path, and to discover what it is that would meet the unconscious needs of his age. Thus, just as the one-sidedness of the individual's conscious attitude is corrected by reactions from the unconscious, so art represents a process of self-regulation in the life of nations and epochs.

I am aware that in this lecture I have only been able to sketch out my views in the barest outline. But I hope that what I have been obliged to omit, that is to say their practical application to poetic works of art, has been furnished by your own thoughts, thus giving flesh and blood to my abstract intellectual frame.

Leon Trotsky

1877–1940

The chapter of Trotsky's *Literature and Revolution* printed below is a Marxist attack on the Russian Formalist school of criticism, which Eichenbaum's essay *The Theory of the "Formal Method"* seeks to defend. Although Trotsky attacks Formalism for superficiality and reaction, he concedes that part of its program is useful. Its analytical procedures can lead to a revelation of "the artist's feeling for the world" and "the discovery of the relations of an individual artist, or of a whole artistic school, to the social environment." But the Formalists are, in Trotsky's view, victims of the "superstition" of the word. Form does not dictate content; verbal art does not end with the word. The Formalists simply ignore the social man, who creates and consumes what has been created.

For Trotsky, a new artistic form is born as a reply to needs. Art is thus always a social servant and plays a subsidiary role. All questions about art are to be asked in terms of these assumptions. Trotsky insists that art must be judged according to its own laws, but by its own laws he means those historical reasons for its creation: "in other words, who it was who made a demand for such an artistic form and not for another, and why."

Though Trotsky's interpretations of his opponents' arguments are superficial, his essay is a fair reflection of assumptions that tend to guide materialist theories.

Rose Strumsky has translated Trotsky's *Literature and Revolution* (1925). For other Russian Marxist discussions see Georgi Plekhonov, *Art and Society* (1912–13), and Nikolai Bukharin, *Problems of Soviet Literature* (1925–27). On Soviet literature see E. J. Brown, *The Proletarian Episode in Russian Literature* (1953), and Mark Slonim, *Modern Russian Literature* (1953). More recently Paul N. Siegel has edited *Leon Trotsky on Literature and Art* (1970). See also Robert D. Warth, *Leon Trotsky* (1977); Irving Howe, *Leon Trotsky* (1978); Duncan Hallas, *Trotsky's Marxism* (1979).

The Formalist School of Poetry and Marxism

Leaving out of account the weak echoes of pre-revolutionary ideologic systems, the only theory which has opposed Marx-

THE FORMALIST SCHOOL OF POETRY AND MARXISM. Trotsky's *The Formalist School of Poetry and Marxism* is Chapter 5 of his *Literature and Revolution* and first appeared in 1924. The text is from Rose Strumsky, tr., *Literature and Revolution* (Ann Arbor: The University of Michigan Press, 1960). Reprinted by permission of the publisher.

ism in Soviet Russia these years is the Formalist theory of art. The paradox consists in the fact that Russian Formalism connected itself closely with Russian Futurism, and that while the latter was capitulating politically before Communism, Formalism opposed Marxism with all its might theoretically.

Victor Shklovsky is the theorist of Futurism, and at the same time the head of the Formalist school. According to this theory, art has always been the work of self-sufficient pure forms, and it has been recognized by Futurism for the first time. Futurism is thus the first conscious art in history, and the Formalist school is the first scientific school of art.

Owing to the efforts of Shklovsky—and this is not an insignificant virtue!—the theory of art, and partly art itself, have at last been raised from a state of alchemy to the position of chemistry. The herald of the Formalist school, the first chemist of art, gives a few friendly slaps in passing to those Futurist "conciliators" who seek a bridge to the Revolution, and who try to find this bridge in the materialistic conception of history. Such a bridge is unnecessary; Futurism is entirely sufficient unto itself.

There are two reasons why it is necessary to pause a little before this Formalist school. One is for its own sake; in spite of the superficiality and reactionary character of the Formalist theory of art, a certain part of the research work of the Formalists is useful. The other reason is Futurism itself; however unfounded the claims of the Futurists to a monopolistic representation of the new art may be, one cannot thrust Futurism out of that process which is preparing the art of the future.

What is the Formalist school?

As it is represented at present by Shklovsky, Zhirmunsky, Jakobson[1] and others, it is extremely arrogant and immature. Having declared form to be the essence of poetry, this school reduces its task to an analysis (essentially descriptive and semistatistical) of the etymology and syntax of poems, to the counting of repetitive vowels and consonants, of syllables and epithets. This analysis which the Formalists regard as the essence of poetry, or poetics, is undoubtedly necessary and useful, but one must understand its partial, scrappy, subsidiary and preparatory character. It can become an essential element of poetic technique and of the rules of the craft. Just as it is useful for a poet or a writer to make lists of synonyms for himself and increase their number so as to expand his verbal keyboard, so it is useful, and quite necessary for a poet, to estimate a word not only in accord with its inner meaning, but also in accord with its acoustics, because a word is passed on from man to man, first of all by acoustics. The methods of Formalism, confined within legitimate limits, may help to clarify the artistic and psychologic peculiarities of form (its economy, its movement, its contrasts, its hyperbolism, etc.). This, in turn, may open a path—one of the paths—to the artist's feeling for the world, and may facilitate the discovery of the relations of an individual artist, or of a whole artistic school, to the social environment. Insofar as we are dealing with a contemporary and living school which is still developing, there is an immediate significance in our transitional stage in probing it by means of a social probe and in clarifying its class roots, so that not

only the reader, but the school itself could orientate itself, that is, know itself, purify and direct itself.

But the Formalists are not content to ascribe to their methods a merely subsidiary, serviceable and technical significance—similar to that which statistics has for social science, or the microscope for the biological sciences. No, they go much further. To them verbal art ends finally and fully with the word, and depictive art with color. A poem is a combination of sounds, a painting is a combination of color spots and the laws of art are the laws of verbal combinations and of combinations of color spots. The social and psychologic approach which, to us, gives a meaning to the microscopic and statistical work done in connection with verbal material, is, for the Formalists, only alchemy.

"Art was always free of life, and its color never reflected the color of the flag which waved over the fortress of the City." (Shklovsky.) "Adjustment to the expression, the verbal mass, is the one essential element of poetry." (R. Jakobson, in his *Recent Russian Poetry*.) "With a new form comes a new content. Form thus determines content." (Kruchenikh.) "Poetry means the giving of form to the word, which is valuable in itself" (Jakobson), or, as Khlebnikov says, "The word which is something in itself," etc.

True, the Italian Futurists have sought in the word a means of expressing the locomotive, the propeller, electricity, the radio, etc., for their own age. In other words, they sought a new form for the new content of life. But it turned out that "this was a reform in the field of reporting, and not in the field of poetic language." (Jakobson.) It is quite different with Russian Futurism; it carries to the end "the adjustment to verbal mass." For Russian Futurism, form determines content.

True, Jakobson is compelled to admit that "a series of new poetic methods finds application (?) for itself in urbanism" (in the culture of the city). But this is his conclusion: "Hence the urban poems of Mayakovsky and Khlebnikov." In other words: not city culture, which has struck the eye and the ear of the poet and which has reeducated them, has inspired him with new form, with new images, new epithets, new rhythm, but, on the contrary, the new form, originating arbitrarily, forced the poet to seek appropriate material and so pushed him in the direction of the city! The development of the "verbal mass" went on arbitrarily from the *Odyssey* to *A Cloud in Trousers;*[2] the torch, the wax candle, the electric lamp, had nothing to do with it! One has only to formulate this point of view clearly to have its childish inadequacy strike the eye. But Jakobson tries to insist; he replies in ad-

---

[1] See Jakobson, *The Metaphoric and Metonymic Poles,* pp. 1041–44.

[2] By Vladimir Mayakovsky.

vance that the same Mayakovsky has such lines as these: "Leave the cities, you silly people." And the theorist of the Formalist school reasons profoundly: "What in this, a logical contradiction? But let others fasten on the poet thoughts expressed in his works. To incriminate a poet with ideas and feelings is just as absurd as the behavior of the medieval public which beat the actor who played Judas." And so on.

It is quite evident that all this was written by a very capable high school boy who had a very evident and quite "self-significant" intention to "stick the pen into our teacher of literature, a notable pedant." At sticking the pen, our bold innovators are masters, but they do not know how to use their pen theoretically or grammatically. This is not hard to prove.

Of course Futurism felt the suggestions of the city—of the tram-car, of electricity, of the telegraph, of the automobile, of the propeller, of the night cabaret (especially of the night cabaret) much before it found its new form. Urbanism (city culture) sits deep in the subconsciousness of Futurism, and the epithets, the etymology, the syntax and the rhythm of Futurism are only an attempt to give artistic form to the new spirit of the cities which has conquered consciousness. And when Mayakovsky exclaims: "Leave the cities, you silly people," it is the cry of a man citified to the very marrow of his bones, who shows himself strikingly and clearly a city person, especially when he is outside the city, that is, when he "leaves the city" and becomes an inhabitant of a summer resort. It is not at all a question of "incriminating" (this word misses something!) a poet with the ideas and feelings which he expresses. Of course the way he expresses them makes the poet. But after all, a poet uses the language of the school which he has accepted or which he has created to fulfill tasks which lie outside of him. And this is even true also when he limits himself to lyricism, to personal love and personal death. Though individual shadings of poetic form correspond to individual makeup, they do go hand in hand with imitation and routine, in the feeling itself, as well as in the method of its expression. A new artistic form, taken in a large historic way, is born in reply to new needs. To take an example from intimate lyric poetry, one may say that between the physiology of sex and a poem about love there lies a complex system of psychological transmitting mechanism in which there are individual, racial and social elements. The racial foundation, that is, the sexual basis of man, changes slowly. The social forms of love change more rapidly. They affect the psychologic superstructure of love, they produce new shadings and intonations, new spiritual demands, a need of a new vocabulary, and so they present new demands on poetry. The poet can find material for his art only in his social environment and transmits the new impulses of life

through his own artistic consciousness. Language, changed and complicated by urban conditions, gives the poet a new verbal material, and suggests or facilitates new word combinations for the poetic formulation of new thoughts or of new feelings, which strive to break through the dark shell of the subconscious. If there were no changes in psychology produced by changes in the social environment, there would be no movement in art; people would continue from generation to generation to be content with the poetry of the Bible, or of the old Greeks.

But the philosopher of Formalism jumps on us, and says it is merely a question of a new form "in the field of reporting and not in the field of poetic language." There he struck us! If you will, poetry is reporting, only in a peculiar, grand style.

The quarrels about "pure art" and about art with a tendency took place between the liberals and the "populists." They do not become us. Materialistic dialects are above this; from the point of view of an objective historical process, art is always a social servant and historically utilitarian. It finds the necessary rhythm of words for dark and vague moods, it brings thought and feeling closer or contrasts them with one another, it enriches the spiritual experience of the individual and of the community, it refines feeling, makes it more flexible, more responsive, it enlarges the volume of thought in advance and not through the personal method of accumulated experience, it educates the individual, the social group, the class and the nation. And this it does quite independently of whether it appears in a given case under the flag of a "pure" or a frankly tendentious art. In our Russian social development tendentiousness was the banner of the intelligentsia which sought contact with the people. The helpless intelligentsia, crushed by tsarism and deprived of a cultural environment, sought support in the lower strata of society and tried to prove to the "people" that it was thinking only of them, living only for them and that it loved them "terribly." And just as the "populists" who went to the people were ready to do without clean linen and without a comb and without a toothbrush, so the intelligentsia was ready to sacrifice the "subtleties" of form in its art, in order to give the most direct and spontaneous expression to the sufferings and hopes of the oppressed. On the other hand, "pure" art was the banner of the rising bourgeoisie, which could not openly declare its bourgeois character, and which at the same time tried to keep the intelligentsia in its service. The Marxist point of view is far removed from these tendencies, which were historically necessary, but which have become historically passé. Keeping on the plane of scientific investigation, Marxism seeks with the same assurance the social roots of the "pure" as well as of the tendentious art. It does not at all "incriminate" a poet with the thoughts and feelings which he expresses, but raises questions of a much more profound significance, namely, to which order of feelings does a given artistic work correspond in all its peculiarities? What are the social conditions of these thoughts and feelings? What place do they occupy in the historic development of a society and of a class? And, further, what literary heritage has entered into the elaboration of the new form? Under the influence of what historic impulse have the new complexes of feelings and thoughts broken through the shell which divides them from the sphere of poetic consciousness? The investigation may become complicated, detailed or individualized, but its fundamental idea will be that of the subsidiary role which art plays in the social process.

Each class has its own policy in art, that is, a system of presenting demands on art, which changes with time; for instance, the Maecenas-like protection of court and grand seigneur, the automatic relationship of supply and demand which is supplemented by complex methods of influencing the individual, and so forth, and so on. The social and even the personal dependence of art was not concealed, but was openly announced as long as art retained its court character. The wider, more popular, anonymous character of the rising bourgeoisie led, on the whole, to the theory of "pure art," though there were many deviations from this theory. As indicated above, the tendentious literature of the "populist" intelligentsia was imbued with a class interest; the intelligentsia could not strengthen itself and could not conquer for itself a right to play a part in history without the support of the people. But in the revolutionary struggle, the class egotism of the intelligentsia was turned inside out, and in its left wing, it assumed the form of highest self-sacrifice. That is why the intelligentsia not only did not conceal art with a tendency, but proclaimed it, thus sacrificing art, just as it sacrificed many other things.

Our Marxist conception of the objective social dependence and social utility of art, when translated into the language of politics, does not at all mean a desire to dominate art by means of decrees and orders. It is not true that we regard only that art as new and revolutionary which speaks of the worker, and it is nonsense to say that we demand that the poets should describe inevitably a factory chimney, or the uprising against capital! Of course the new art cannot but place the struggle of the proletariat in the center of its attention. But the plough of the new art is not limited to numbered strips. On the contrary, it must plow the entire field in all directions. Personal lyrics of the very smallest scope have an absolute right to exist within the new art. Moreover, the new man cannot be formed without a new lyric poetry. But to create it, the poet himself must feel the world in a new way.

If Christ alone or Sabaoth[3] himself bends over the poet's embraces (as in the case of Akhmatova, Tsvetaeva, Shkapskaya and others), then this only goes to prove how much behind the times his lyrics are and how socially and aesthetically inadequate they are for the new man. Even where such terminology is not a survival of experience so much as of words, it shows psychologic inertia and therefore stands in contradiction to the consciousness of the new man. No one is going to prescribe themes to a poet or intends to prescribe them. Please write about anything you can think of! But allow the new class which considers itself, and with reason, called upon to build a new world, to say to you in any given case: It does not make new poets of you to translate the philosophy of life of the seventeenth century into the language of the Acmeists.[4] The form of art is, to a certain and very large degree, independent, but the artist who creates this form, and the spectator who is enjoying it, are not empty machines, one for creating form and the other for appreciating it. They are living people, with a crystalized psychology representing a certain unity, even if not entirely harmonious. This psychology is the result of social conditions. The creation and perception of art forms is one of the functions of this psychology. And no matter how wise the Formalists try to be, their whole conception is simply based upon the fact that they ignore the psychological unity of the social man, who creates and who consumes what has been created.

The proletariat has to have in art the expression of the new spiritual point of view which is just beginning to be formulated within him, and to which art must help him give form. This is not a state order, but an historic demand. Its strength lies in the objectivity of historic necessity. You cannot pass this by, nor escape its force.

The Formalist school seems to try to be objective. It is disgusted, and not without reason, with the literary and critical arbitrariness which operates only with tastes and moods. It seeks precise criteria for classification and valuation. But owing to its narrow outlook and superficial methods, it is constantly falling into superstitions, such as graphology and phrenology. These two "schools" have also the task of establishing purely objective tests for determining human character; such as the number of the flourishes of one's pen and their roundness, and the peculiarities of the bumps on the back of one's head. One may assume that pen flourishes and bumps do have some relation to character; but this relation is not direct, and human character is not at all exhausted

---

[3] A biblical term for armies or hosts.
[4] A group of Russian poets, including Gumilev, Akhmatova, and Mandelstam, associated with the magazine *Apollon,* which was published from 1910 to 1917. They were antisymbolist followers of Gautier.

by them. An apparent objectivism based on accidental, secondary and inadequate characteristics leads inevitably to the worst subjectivism. In the case of the Formalist school it leads to the superstition of the word. Having counted the adjectives, and weighed the lines, and measured the rhythms, a Formalist either stops silent with the expression of a man who does not know what to do with himself, or throws out an unexpected generalization which contains 5 percent of Formalism and 95 percent of the most uncritical intuition.

In fact, the Formalists do not carry their idea of art to its logical conclusion. If one is to regard the process of poetic creation only as a combination of sounds or words, and to seek along these lines the solution of all the problems of poetry, then the only perfect formula of "poetics" will be this: Arm yourself with a dictionary and create by means of algebraic combinations and permutations of words, all the poetic works of the world which have been created and which have not yet been created. Reasoning "formally" one may produce *Eugene Onegin* in two ways: either by subordinating the selection of words to a preconceived artistic idea (as Pushkin himself did), or by solving the problem algebraically. From the "Formal" point of view, the second method is more correct, because it does not depend upon mood, inspiration, or other unsteady things, and has besides the advantage that while leading to *Eugene Onegin* it may bring one to an incalculable number of other great works. All that one needs is infinity in time, called eternity. But as neither mankind nor the individual poet have eternity at their disposal, the fundamental source of poetic words will remain, as before, the preconceived artistic idea understood in the broadest sense, as an accurate thought and as a clearly expressed personal or social artistic materialization, this subjective idea will be stimulated and jolted by form and may be sometimes pushed onto a path which was entirely unforeseen. This simply means that verbal form is not a passive reflection of a preconceived artistic idea, but an active element which influences the idea itself. But such an active mutual relationship—in which form influences and at times entirely transforms content—is known to us in all fields of social and even biological life. This is no reason at all for rejecting Darwinism and Marxism and for the creation of a Formalist school either in biology or sociology.

Victor Shklovsky, who flits lightly from verbal Formalism to the most subjective valuations, assumes a very uncompromising attitude towards the historico-materialistic theory of art. In a booklet which he published in Berlin, under the title of *The March of the Horse,* he formulates in the course of three small pages—brevity is a fundamental and, at any rate, an undoubted merit of Shklovsky—five (not four and not six, but five) exhaustive arguments against the materialist conception of art. Let us examine these arguments, because it won't harm us to take a look and see what kind of chaff is handed out as the last word in scientific thought (with the greatest variety of scientific references on these same three microscopic pages).

"If the environment and the relations of production," says Shklovsky, "influenced art, then would not the themes of art be tied to the places which would correspond to these relations? But themes are homeless." Well, and how about butterflies? According to Darwin, they also "correspond" to definite relations, and yet they flit from place to place, just like an unweighted litterateur.

It is not easy to understand why Marxism should be supposed to condemn themes to a condition of serfdom. The fact that different peoples and different classes of the same people make use of the same themes, merely shows how limited the human imagination is, and how man tries to maintain an economy of energy in every kind of creation, even in the artistic. Every class tries to utilize, to the greatest possible degree, the material and spiritual heritage of another class. Shklovsky's argument could be easily transferred into the field of productive technique. From ancient times on, the wagon has been based on one and the same theme, namely, axles, wheels, and a shaft. However, the chariot of the Roman patrician was just as well adapted to his tastes and needs as was the carriage of Count Orlov, fitted out with inner comforts, to the tastes of this favorite of Catherine the Great. The wagon of the Russian peasant is adapted to the needs of his household, to the strength of his little horse, and to the peculiarities of the country road. The automobile, which is undoubtedly a product of the new technique, shows, nevertheless, the same "theme," namely, four wheels on two axles. Yet every time a peasant's horse shies in terror before the blinding lights of an automobile on the Russian road at night, a conflict of two cultures is reflected in the episode.

"If environment expressed itself in novels," so runs the second argument, "European science would not be breaking its head over the question of where the stories of *A Thousand and One Nights* were made, whether in Egypt, India, or Persia." To say that man's environment, including the artist's, that is, the conditions of his education and life, find expression in his art also, does not mean to say that such expression has a precise geographic, ethnographic and statistical character. It is not at all surprising that it is difficult to decide whether certain novels were made in Egypt, India or Persia, because the social conditions of these countries have much in common. But the very fact that European science is "breaking its head" trying to solve this question from these novels themselves, shows that these novels reflect an environment, even though unevenly. No one can jump beyond himself. Even the ravings of an insane person contain nothing that the sick man had not received before from the outside world. But it would be an insanity of another order to regard his ravings as the accurate reflection of an external world. Only an experienced and thoughtful psychiatrist, who knows the past of the patient, will be able to find the reflected and distorted bits of reality in the contents of his ravings. Artistic creation, of course, is not a raving, though it is also a deflection, a changing and a transformation of reality, in accordance with the peculiar laws of art. However fantastic art may be, it cannot have at its disposal any other material except that which is given to it by the world of three dimensions and by the narrower world of class society. Even when the artist creates heaven and hell, he merely transforms the experience of his own life into his phantasmagorias, almost to the point of his landlady's unpaid bill.

"If the features of class and caste are deposited in art," continues Shklovsky, "then how does it come that the various tales of the Great Russians about their nobleman are the same as their fairy tales about their priest?"

In essence, this is merely a paraphrase of the first argument. Why cannot the fairy tales about the nobleman and about the priest be the same, and how does this contradict Marxism? The proclamations which are written by well-known Marxists not infrequently speak of landlords, capitalists, priests, general and other exploiters. The landlord undoubtedly differs from the capitalist, but there are cases when they are considered under one head. Why, then, cannot folk art in certain cases treat the nobleman and the priest together, as the representatives of the classes which stand above the people and which plunder them? In the cartoons of Moor and of Deni, the priest often stands side by side with the landlord, without any damage to Marxism.

"If ethnographic traits were reflected in art," Shklovsky goes on, "the folklore about the peoples beyond the border would not be interchangeable and could not be told by any one folk about another."

As you see, there is no letting up here. Marxism does not maintain at all that ethnographic traits have an independent character. On the contrary, it emphasizes the all-determining significance of natural and economic conditions in the formation of folklore. The similarity of conditions in the development of the herding and agricultural and primarily peasant peoples, and the similarity in the character of their mutual influence upon one another, cannot but lead to the creation of a similar folklore. And from the point of view of the question that interests us here, it makes absolutely no difference whether these homogeneous themes arose independently among different peoples, as the reflection of a life experience which was homogeneous in its fundamental traits

and which was reflected through the homogeneous prism of a peasant imagination, or whether the seeds of these fairy tales were carried by a favorable wind from place to place, striking root wherever the ground turned out to be favorable. It is very likely that, in reality, these methods were combined.

And finally, as a separate argument—"The reason (i.e., Marxism) is incorrect in the fifth place"—Shklovsky points to the theme of abduction which goes through Greek comedy and reaches Ostrovsky.[5] In other words, our critic repeats, in a special form, his very first argument (as we see, even insofar as formal logic is concerned, all is not well with our Formalist). Yes, themes migrate from people to people, from class to class, and even from author to author. This means only that the human imagination is economical. A new class does not begin to create all of culture from the beginning, but enters into possession of the past, assorts it, touches it up, rearranges it, and builds on it further. If there were no such utilization of the "secondhand" wardrobe of the ages, historic processes would have no progress at all. If the theme of Ostrovsky's drama came to him through the Egyptians and through Greece, then the paper on which Ostrovsky developed his theme came to him as a development of the Egyptian papyrus through the Greek parchment. Let us take another and closer analogy: the fact that the critical methods of the Greek Sophists, who were the pure Formalists of their day, have penetrated the theoretic consciousness of Shklovsky, does not in the least change the fact that Shklovsky himself is a very picturesque product of a definite social environment and of a definite age.

Shklovsky's destruction of Marxism in five points reminds us very much of those articles which were published against Darwinism in the magazines *The Orthodox Review* in the good old days. If the doctrine of the origin of man from the monkey were true, wrote the learned Bishop Nikanor of Odessa thirty or forty years ago, then our grandfathers would have had distinct signs of a tail, or would have noticed such a characteristic in their grandfathers and grandmothers. Second, as everybody knows, monkeys can only give birth to monkeys. . . . Fifth, Darwinism is incorrect, because it contradicts Formalism—I beg your pardon, I meant to say the formal decisions of the universal church conferences. The advantage of the learned monk consisted, however, in the fact that he was a frank passéist and took his cure from the Apostle Paul and not from physics, chemistry or mathematics, as the Futurist, Shklovsky, does.

---

[5]A nineteenth-century Russian playwright.

It is unquestionably true that the need for art is not created by economic conditions. But neither is the need for food created by economics. On the contrary, the need for food and warmth creates economics. It is very true that one cannot always go by the principles of Marxism in deciding whether to reject or to accept a work of art. A work of art should, in the first place, be judged by its own law, that is, by the law of art. But Marxism alone can explain why and how a given tendency in art has originated in a given period of history; in other words, who it was who made a demand for such an artistic form and not for another, and why.

It would be childish to think that every class can entirely and fully create its own art from within itself, and, particularly, that the proletariat is capable of creating a new art by means of closed art guilds or circles, or by the Organization for Proletarian Culture, etc. Generally speaking, the artistic work of man is continuous. Each new rising class places itself on the shoulders of its preceding one. But this continuity is dialectic, that is, it finds itself by means of internal repulsions and breaks. New artistic needs or demands for new literary and artistic points of view are stimulated by economics, through the development of a new class, and minor stimuli are supplied by changes in the position of the class, under the influence of the growth of its wealth and cultural power. Artistic creation is always a complicated turning inside out of old forms, under the influence of new stimuli which originate outside of art. In this large sense of the word, art is a handmaiden. It is not a disembodied element feeding on itself, but a function of social man indissolubly tied to his life and environment. And how characteristic it is—if one were to reduce every social superstition to its absurdity—that Shklovsky has come to the idea of art's absolute independence from the social environment at a period of Russian history when art has revealed with such utter frankness its spiritual, environmental and material dependence upon definite social classes, subclasses and groups!

Materialism does not deny the significance of the element of form, either in logic, jurisprudence, or art. Just as a system of jurisprudence can and must be judged by its internal logic and consistency, so art can and must be judged from the point of view of its achievements in form, because there can be no art without them. However, a juridical theory which attempted to establish the independence of law from social conditions would be defective at its very base. Its moving force lies in economics—in class contradictions. The law gives only a formal and an internally harmonized expression of these phenomena, not of their individual peculiarities, but of their general character, that is, of the elements that are repetitive and permanent in them. We can see now with a clarity which is rare in history how new law is made. It is not done by logical deduction, but by empirical measurement and by adjustment to the economic needs of the new ruling class. Literature, whose methods and processes have their roots far back in the most distant past and represent the accumulated experience of verbal craftsmanship, expresses the thoughts, feelings, moods, points of view and hopes of the new epoch and of its new class. One cannot jump beyond this. And there is no need of making the jump, at least, for those who are not serving an epoch already past nor a class which has already outlived itself.

The methods of formal analysis are necessary, but insufficient. You may count up the alliterations in popular proverbs, classify metaphors, count up the number of vowels and consonants in a wedding song. It will undoubtedly enrich our knowledge of folk art, in one way or another; but if you don't know the peasant system of sowing, and the life that is based on it, if you don't know the part the scythe plays, and if you have not mastered the meaning of the church calendar to the peasant, of the time when the peasant marries, or when the peasant women give birth, you will have only understood the outer shell of folk art, but the kernel will not have been reached. The architectural scheme of the Cologne cathedral can be established by measuring the base and the height of its arches, by determining the three dimensions of its naves, the dimensions and the placement of the columns, etc. But without knowing what a medieval city was like, what a guild was, or what was the Catholic church of the Middle Ages, the Cologne cathedral will never be understood. The effort to set art free from life, to declare it a craft self-sufficient unto itself, devitalizes and kills art. The very need of such an operation is an unmistakable symptom of intellectual decline.

The analogy with the theological arguments against Darwinism which was made above may appear to the reader external and anecdotal. That may be true, to some extent. But a much deeper connection exists. The Formalist theory inevitably reminds a Marxist who has done any reading at all of the familiar tunes of a very old philosophic melody. The jurists and the moralists (to recall at random the German Stammler, and our own subjectivist Mikhailovsky) tried to prove that morality and law could not be determined by economics, because economic life was unthinkable outside of juridical and ethical norms. True, the formalists of law and morals did not go so far as to assert the complete independence of law and ethics from economics. They recognized a certain complex mutual relationship of "factors," and these "factors," while influencing one another, retained the qualities of independent substances, coming no one knew whence. The assertion of complete independence of the aesthetic "factor" from the influence of social conditions, as is made by Shklovsky, is an instance of specific hyperbole whose roots, by the way, lie in social conditions too; it is the megalomania of aesthetics turning our hard reality on its head. Apart from this peculiarity, the constructions of the Formalists have the same kind of defective methodology that every other kind of idealism has. To a materialist, religion, law, morals and art represent separate aspects of one and the same process of social development. Though they differentiate themselves from their industrial basis, become complex, strengthen and develop their special characteristics in detail, politics, religion, law, ethics and aesthetics remain, nonetheless, functions of social man and obey the laws of his social organization. The idealist, on the other hand, does not see a unified process of historic development which evolves the necessary organs and functions from within itself, but a crossing or combining and interacting of certain independent principles—the religious, political, juridical, aesthetic and ethical substances, which find their origin and explanation in themselves. The (dialectic) idealism of Hegel arranges these substances (which are the eternal categories) in some sequence by reducing them to a genetic unity. Regardless of the fact that this unity with Hegel is the absolute spirit, which divides itself in the process of its dialectic manifestation into various "factors," Hegel's system, because of its dialectic character, not because of its idealism, gives an idea of historic reality which is just as good as the idea of a man's hand that a glove gives when turned inside out. But the Formalists (and their greatest genius was Kant) do not look at the dynamics of development, but at a cross section of it, on the day and at the hour of their own philosophic revelation. At the crossing of the line they reveal the complexity and multiplicity of the object (not of the process, because they do not think of processes). This complexity they analyze and classify. They give names to the elements, which are at once transformed into essences, into subabsolutes, without father or mother; to wit, religion, politics, morals, law, art. Here we no longer have a glove of history turned inside out, but the skin torn from the separate fingers, dried out to a degree of complete abstraction, and this hand of history turns out to be the product of the "interaction" of the thumb, the index, the middle finger, and all the other "factors." The aesthetic "factor" is the little finger, the smallest, but not the least beloved.

In biology, vitalism is a variation of the same fetish of presenting the separate aspects of the world process, without understanding its inner relation. A creator is all that is lacking for a supersocial, absolute morality or aesthetics, or for a superphysical absolute "vital force." The multiplicity of independent factors, "factors" without beginning or end, is nothing but a masked polytheism. Just as Kantian idealism represents historically a translation of Christianity into the language of rationalistic philosophy, so all the varieties of idealistic formalization, either openly or secretly, lead to a God, as the Cause of all causes. In comparison with the oligarchy of a dozen subabsolutes of the idealistic philosophy, a single personal Creator is already an element of order. Herein lies the deeper connection between the Formalist refutations of Marxism and the theological refutations of Darwinism.

The Formalist school represents an abortive idealism applied to the question of art. The Formalists show a fast-ripening religiousness. They are followers of St. John. They believe that "In the beginning was the Word." But we believe that in the beginning was the deed. The word followed, as its phonetic shadow.

Boris Eichenbaum

1886–1959

With Roman Jakobson, who later founded the Prague school of structuralists, Eichenbaum was a main figure of the Russian Formalist movement, which flourished until its forced demise under political pressure in the 1920s. The attack that destroyed the movement began in 1924 with Trotsky's *Literature and Revolution* and was carried on more vehemently by other lesser figures. Members of the movement were charged with lack of interest in the social causes and effects of literature and advocating a form of art for art's sake.

Eichenbaum's essay is an attempt to summarize the movement's achievements and to defend it against Marxist attacks. There is an element of conciliation in the essay that somewhat distorts the picture. The movement was never as communal and orderly in its development and aims as Eichenbaum would have his readers believe. Also there is considerably more emphasis on scientific, positivistic procedures in his essay than was evident in the work of the Formalist critics themselves. The standard history of the movement, Victor Erlich's *Russian Formalism: History-Doctrine,* rev. ed. (1964), offers a more detached summary.

Eichenbaum's reader cannot help being struck by the similarities of the movement to the New Criticism. Almost all the general principles he enunciates are shared by the American movement: the attack on the irresponsible mixing of various disciplines and their problems, the distinction between "practical language" and language with "independent value," the insistence that form is not simply an "envelope" for content, the assertion that explanation of the genesis of a phenomenon does not clarify the phenomenon as a literary fact, the idea of a literary work as a "self-determined use of material," and the sense of the expansive meaning of a literary work.

The Formalists began, according to Eichenbaum, by rejecting old assumptions about beauty as an external ideal, worked through the idea of the literary object as a unified technical accomplishment, and came to the idea of a truly *literary* history. In this last phase they spoke much as did Eliot in *Tradition and the Individual Talent.* In their view, a work of art is defined by its relation to other works. Literary history points out these relationships and thus is not using literature as document but actually giving to aesthetic theory and to literary meaning a historical dimension.

When the Formalist movement died, many of its principles were carried, mainly by Jakobson, into structuralist linguistics; combined with the ideas of Ferdinand de Saussure's *Cours de linguistique générale* (1915), they contributed to structuralism in a variety of fields, including anthropology and, again, literary theory.

Essays by Eichenbaum can be found in *Michigan Slavic Materials,* Vol. II (1963), in *Russian Formalist Criticism: Four Essays,* edited and translated by L. T. Lemon and M. J. Reis (1965), and C. Pike, ed., *The Futurists, the Formalists, and the Marxist Critique* (1979). Eichenbaum's *O. Henry: The Theory of the "Formal Method" and* the Theory of the Short Story was translated in 1968, and his *Lermontov* in 1981. See also A. N. Vognesenski, "Problems of Method in the Study of Literature in Russia," *Slavonic Review,* VI (1927), 168–77; Manfred Kridl, "Russian Formalism," *The American Bookman,* I (1944), 19–30; W. E. Harkins, "Slavic Formalist Theories in Literary Scholarship," *Word,* VII (1951), 177–85; Mark Slonim, *Modern Russian Literature* (1953); Victor Erlich, *Russian Formalism, History-Doctrine,* rev. ed. (1964); and Harold K. Schefski, *Boris M. Eichenbaum: The Evaluation of His Critical Method* (unpub. diss., 1976).

The Theory of the "Formal Method"

The worst, in my opinion, are those who describe science as if it were settled.[1]

A. DE CANDOLLE

The so-called formal method grew out of a struggle for a science of literature that would be both independent and factual; it is not the outgrowth of a particular methodology. The notion of a method has been so exaggerated that it now suggests too much. In principle the question for the Formalist[2] is not how to study literature, but what the subject matter of literary study actually is. We neither discuss methodology nor quarrel about it. We speak and may speak only about theoretical principles suggested to us not by this or that ready-made methodology, but by the examination of specific material in its specific context. The Formalists' works in literary theory and literary history show this clearly enough, but during the past ten years so many new questions and old misunderstandings have accumulated that I feel it advisable to try to summarize some of our work—not as a dogmatic system but as a historical summation. I wish to show how the work of the Formalists began, how it evolved, and what it evolved into.

The evolutionary character of the development of the formal method is important to an understanding of its history; our opponents and many of our followers overlook it.

We are surrounded by eclectics and latecomers who would turn the formal method into some kind of inflexible formalistic system in order to provide themselves with a working vocabulary, a program, and a name. A program is a very handy thing for critics, but not at all characteristic of our method. Our scientific approach has had no such prefabricated program or doctrine, and has none. In our studies we value a theory only as a working hypothesis to help us discover and interpret facts; that is, we determine the validity of the facts and use them as the material of our research. We are not concerned with definitions, for which the latecomers thirst; nor do we build general theories, which so delight eclectics. We posit specific principles and adhere to them insofar as the material justifies them. If the material demands their refinements or change, we change or refine them. In this sense we are quite free from our own theories—as science must be free to the extent that theory and conviction are distinct. There is no ready-made science; science lives not by settling on truth, but by overcoming error.

This essay is not intended to argue our position. The initial period of scientific struggle and journalistic polemics is past. Such attacks as that in *The Press and the Revolution*[3] (with which I was honored) can be answered only by new scientific works. My chief purpose here is to show how the formal method, by gradually evolving and broadening its field of research, spread beyond the usual "methodological" limits and became a special science of literature, a specific ordering of facts. Within the limits of this science, the most diverse methods may develop, if only because we focus on the empirical study of the material. Such study was, essentially, the aim of the Formalists from the very beginning, and precisely that was the significance of our quarrel with the old traditions. The name *formal method,* bestowed upon the movement and now firmly attached to it, may be tentatively understood as a historical term; it should not be taken as an accurate description of our work. Neither *Formalism* as an aesthetic theory nor *methodology* as a finished scientific sys-

---

THE THEORY OF THE "FORMAL METHOD." Eichenbaum's *The Theory of the "Formal Method"* was first published in Ukrainian in 1926. The text is from *Russian Formalist Criticism: Four Essays,* edited and translated by Lee T. Lemon and Marion J. Reis. Copyright © University of Nebraska Press, 1965. Reprinted by permission of University of Nebraska Press.

[1] *Le pire, à mon avis, est celui qui représente la science comme faite.*

[2] [Eichenbaum] By *Formalists* I mean in this essay only that group of theoreticians who made up the Society for the Study of Poetic Language (the *Opoyaz*) and who began to publish their studies in 1916. [Lemon and Reis] Actually, Eichenbaum also includes as Formalists members of the Moscow Linguistic Circle.

---

[3] An essay by Anatoly Lunacharsky (1875–1933), Soviet Commissar of Education, which attacked Formalism on the grounds of its decadence.

tem characterizes us; we are characterized only by the attempt to create an independent science of literature which studies specifically literary material. We ask only for recognition of the theoretical facts of literary art as such.

Representatives of the formal method were frequently reproached by various groups for their lack of clarity or for the inadequacy of their principles—for indifference to general questions of aesthetics, sociology, psychology, and so on. These reproofs, despite their varying merit, are alike in that they correctly grasp that the chief characteristic of the Formalists is indeed their deliberate isolation both from "aesthetics from above" and from all ready-made or self-styled general theories. This isolation (particularly from aesthetics) is more or less typical of all contemporary studies of art. Dismissing a whole group of general problems (problems of beauty, the aims of art, etc.), the contemporary study of art concentrates on the concrete problems of aesthetics [*Kunstwissenschaft*]. Without reference to socio-aesthetic premises, it raises questions about the idea of artistic form and its evolution. It thereby raises a series of more specific theoretical and historical questions. Such familiar slogans as Wölfflin's "history of art without names" [*Kunstgeschichte ohne Nahmen*][4] characterized experiments in the empirical analysis of style and technique (like Voll's "experiment in the comparative study of paintings"). In Germany especially the study of the theory and history of the visual arts, which had had there an extremely rich history of tradition and experiment, occupied a central position in art studies and began to influence the general theory of art and its separate disciplines—in particular, the study of literature. In Russia, apparently for local historical reasons, literary studies occupied a place analogous to that of the visual arts in Germany.

The formal method has attracted general attention and become controversial not, of course, because of its distinctive methodology, but rather because of its characteristic attitude towards the understanding and the study of technique. The Formalists advocated principles which violated solidly entrenched traditional notions, notions which had appeared to be axiomatic not only in the study of literature, but in the study of art generally. Because they adhered to their principles so strictly, they narrowed the distance between particular problems of literary theory and general problems of aesthetics. The ideas and principles of the Formalists, for all their concreteness, were pointedly directed towards a general theory of aesthetics. Our creation of a radically unconventional poetics, therefore, implied more than a simple reassessment of particular problems; it had an impact on the

study of art generally. It had its impact because of a series of historical developments, the most important of which were the crisis in philosophical aesthetics and the startling innovations in art (in Russia most abrupt and most clearly defined in poetry). Aesthetics seemed barren and art deliberately denuded—in an entirely primitive condition. Hence, Formalism and Futurism seemed bound together by history.

But the general historical significance of the appearance of Formalism comprises a special theme; I must speak of something else here because I intend to show how the principles and problems of the formal method evolved and how the Formalists came to their present position.

Before the appearance of the Formalists, academic research, quite ignorant of theoretical problems, made use of antiquated aesthetic, psychological, and historical axioms and had so lost sight of its proper subject that its very existence as a science had become illusory. There was almost no struggle between the Formalists and the Academicians, not because the Formalists had broken in the door (there were no doors), but because we found an open passageway instead of a fortress. The theoretical heritage which Potebnya and Veselovsky left to their disciples seemed to lie like dead capital—a treasure which they were afraid to touch, the brilliance of which they had allowed to fade. In fact, authority and influence had gradually passed from academic scholarship to the "scholarship" of the journals, to the work of the Symbolist critics and theoreticians. Actually, between 1907 and 1912 the books and essays of Vyacheslav Ivanov, Bryusov, Merezhkovsky, Chukovsky, and others, were much more influential than the scholarly studies and dissertations of the university professors. This journalistic scholarship, with all its subjectivity and tendentiousness, was supported by the theoretical principles and slogans of the new artistic movements and their propagandists. Such books as Bely's *Simvolizm* (1910) naturally meant much more to the younger generation than the monographs on the history of literature which sprang up from no set of principles and which showed that the authors completely lacked both a scientific temperament and a scientific point of view.

The historical battle between the two generations [the Symbolists and the Formalists]—a battle which was fought over principles and was extraordinarily intense—was therefore resolved in the journals, and the battle line was drawn over Symbolist theory and Impressionistic criticism rather than over any work being done by the Academicians. We entered the fight against the Symbolists in order to wrest poetics from their hands—to free it from its ties with their subjective philosophical and aesthetic theories and to direct it toward the scientific investigation of facts. We were raised on their works, and we saw their errors with the greatest clarity. At this time, the struggle became even more urgent be-

---

[4][Lemon and Reis] See Heinrich Wölfflin's *Kunstgeschichtliche Grundbegriffe* (Munich, 1915). Wölfflin was one of the originators of the stylistic analysis of art.

cause the Futurists (Khlebnikov, Kruchenykh, and Mayakovsky), who were on the rise, opposed the Symbolist poetics and supported the Formalists.

The original group of Formalists was united by the idea of liberating poetic diction from the fetters of the intellectualism and moralism which more and more obsessed the Symbolists. The dissension among the Symbolist theoreticians (1910–11) and the appearance of the Acmeists[5] prepared the way for our decisive rebellion. We knew that all compromises would have to be avoided, that history demanded of us a really revolutionary attitude—a categorical thesis, merciless irony, and bold rejections of whatever could not be reconciled with our position. We had to oppose the subjective aesthetic principles espoused by the Symbolists with an objective consideration of the facts. Hence our Formalist movement was characterized by a new passion for scientific positivism—a rejection of philosophical assumptions, of psychological and aesthetic interpretations, etc. Art, considered apart from philosophical aesthetics and ideological theories, dictated its own position on things. We had to turn to facts and, abandoning general systems and problems, to begin "in the middle," with the facts which art forced upon us. Art demanded that we approach it closely; science, that we deal with the specific.

The establishment of a specific and factual literary science was basic to the organization of the formal method. All of our efforts were directed toward disposing of the earlier position which, according to Alexander Veselovsky, made of literature an abandoned thing [a *res nullius*]. This is why the position of the Formalists could not be reconciled with other approaches and was so unacceptable to the eclectics. In rejecting these other approaches, the Formalists actually rejected and still reject not the methods, but rather the irresponsible mixing of various disciplines and their problems. The basis of our position was and is that the object of literary science, as such, must be the study of those specifics which distinguish it from any other material. (The secondary, incidental features of such material, however, may reasonably and rightly be used in a subordinate way by other scientific disciplines.) Roman Jakobson formulated this view with perfect clarity:

> The object of the science of literature is not literature, but literariness—that is, that which makes a given work a work of literature. Until now literary

historians have preferred to act like the policeman who, intending to arrest a certain person, would, at any opportunity, seize any and all persons who chanced into the apartment, as well as those who passed along the street. The literary historians used everything—anthropology, psychology, politics, philosophy. Instead of a science of literature, they created a conglomeration of homespun disciplines. They seemed to have forgotten that their essays strayed into related disciplines—the history of philosophy, the history of culture, of psychology, etc.—and that these could rightly use literary masterpieces only as defective, secondary documents.[6]

To apply and strengthen this principle of specificity and to avoid speculative aesthetics, we had to compare literary facts with other kinds of facts, extracting from a limitless number of important orders of fact that order which would pertain to literature and would distinguish it from the others by its function. This was the method Leo Jakubinsky followed in his essays in the first *Opoyaz* collection, in which he worked out the contrast between poetic and practical language that served as the basic principle of the Formalists' work on key problems of poetics. As a result, the Formalists did not look, as literary students usually had, towards history, culture, sociology, psychology, or aesthetics, etc., but toward linguistics, a science bordering on poetics and sharing material with it, but approaching it from a different perspective and with different problems. Linguistics, for its part, was also interested in the formal method in that what was discovered by comparing poetic and practical language could be studied as a purely linguistic problem, as part of the general phenomena of language. The relationship between linguistics and the formal method was somewhat analogous to that relation of mutual use and delimitation that exists, for example, between physics and chemistry. Against this background, the problems posed earlier by Potebnya and taken for granted by his followers were reviewed and reinterpreted.

Leo Jakubinsky's first essay, *On the Sounds of Poetic Language,* compared practical and poetic language and formulated the difference between them:

> The phenomena of language must be classified from the point of view of the speaker's particular

---

[5][Lemon and Reis] The Acmeists, like the Futurists, rebelled against the principles and practices of the Symbolists. But unlike the Futurists, they attempted a highly controlled, polished style of poetry. The best-known Acmeists were Anna Akhmatova and Osip Mandelstam. The movement did not survive World War I.

[6][Eichenbaum] Roman Jakobson, *Noveyshaya russkaya poeziya* [*Modern Russian Poetry*] (Prague, 1921), p. 11. [Lemon and Reis] Jakobson, it should be stressed, is not arguing that literature is unrelated to history, psychology, etc. He is, rather, insisting that the study of literature, if it is to be a distinct discipline, must have its own particular subject.

purpose as he forms his own linguistic pattern. If the pattern is formed for the purely practical purpose of communication, then we are dealing with a system of *practical language* (the language of thought) in which the linguistic patterns (sounds, morphological features, etc.) have no independent value and are merely a *means* of communication. But other linguistic systems, systems in which the practical purpose is in the background (although perhaps not entirely hidden) are conceivable; they exist, and their linguistic patterns acquire *independent value*.

The establishment of this distinction was important both for the construction of a poetics and for understanding the Futurist's preference for nonsense language as revealing the furthest extension of the sheer independent value of words, the kind of value partially observed in the language of children, in the glossolalia of religious sects, and so on. The Futurist experiments in nonsense language were of prime significance as a demonstration against Symbolism which, in its theories, went no further than to use the idea of instrumentation to indicate the accompaniment of meaning by sound and so to de-emphasize the role of sound in poetic language. The problem of sound in verse was especially crucial because it was on this point that the Formalists and Futurists united to confront the theorists of Symbolism. Naturally, the Formalists gave battle at first on just that issue; the question of sound had to be disposed of first if we were to oppose the aesthetic and philosophical tendencies of the Symbolists with a system of precise observations and to reach the underlying scientific conclusions. This accounts for the content of the first volume of *Opoyaz,* a content devoted entirely to the problem of sound and nonsense language.

Victor Shklovsky, along with Jakubinsky, in *On Poetry and Nonsense Language,* cited a variety of examples which showed that "even words without meaning are necessary." He showed such meaninglessness to be both a widespread linguistic fact and a phenomenon characteristic of poetry. "The poet does not decide to use the meaningless word; usually 'nonsense' is disguised as some kind of frequently delusive, deceptive content. Poets are forced to acknowledge that they themselves do not understand the content of their own verses." Shklovsky's essay, moreover, transfers the question from the area of pure sound, from the acoustical level (which provided the basis for impressionistic interpretations of the relation between sound and the description of objects or the emotion represented) to the level of pronunciation and articulation. "In the enjoyment of a meaningless 'nonsense word,' the articulatory aspect of speech is undoubtedly important. Perhaps generally a great part of the delight of poetry consists in pronunciation, in the independent dance of the organs of speech." The question of meaningless language thus became a serious scientific concern, the solution of which would help to clarify many problems of poetic language in general. Shklovsky also formulated the general question:

> If we add to our demand of the word as such that it serve to clarify understanding, that it be generally meaningful, then of course "meaningless" language, as a relatively superficial language, falls by the wayside. But it does not fall alone; a consideration of the facts forces one to wonder whether words always have a meaning, not only in meaningless speech, but also in simple poetic speech—or whether this notion is only a fiction resulting from our inattention.

The natural conclusion of these observations and principles was that poetic language is not only a language of images, that sounds in verse are not at all merely elements of a superficial euphony, and that they do not play a mere "accompaniment" to meaning, but rather that they have an independent significance. The purpose of this work was to force a revision of Potebnya's general theory, which had been built on the conviction that poetry is "thought in images." Potebnya's analysis of poetry, the analysis which the Symbolists had adopted, treated the sound of verse as expressive of something behind it. Sound was merely onomatopoeic, merely "aural description." The works of Andrey Bely (who discovered the complete sound picture that champagne makes when poured from a bottle into a glass in two lines from Pushkin, and who also discovered the "noisomeness of a hangover" in Blok's repetition of the consonantal cluster *rdt*) were quite typical.[7] Such attempts to explain alliteration, bordering on parody, required a rebuff and an attempt to produce concrete evidence showing that sounds in verse exist apart from any connection with imagery, that they have an independent oral function.

Leo Jakubinsky, in his essays, provided linguistic support for [our arguments in favor of] the independent value of sound in verse. Osip Brik's essay on *Sound Repetitions* illustrated the same point with quotations from Pushkin and Ler-

---

[7][Eichenbaum] See the essay, "A. Bely," *Skifi* [*Scythians*] (1917), and *Vetv* [*Branch*] (1917); also my essay "O zvukakh v stikhe" ["On Sound in Verse"], reprinted in *Skvoz literaturu* [*Through Literature*] (Leningrad, 1924).

montov arranged to present a variety of models. Brik doubted the correctness of the common opinion that poetic language is a language of images:

> No matter how one looks at the interrelationship of image and sound, there is undoubtedly only one conclusion possible—the sounds, the harmonies, are not only euphonious accessories to meaning; they are also the result of an independent poetic purpose. The superficial devices of euphony do not completely account for the instrumentation of poetic speech. Such instrumentation represents on the whole an intricate product of the interaction of the general laws of harmony. Rhyme, alliteration, etc., are only obvious manifestations, particular cases, of the basic laws of euphony.

In opposing the work of Bely, Brik, in the same essay, made no comment at all on the meaning of this or that use of alliteration, but merely affirmed that repetition in verse is analogous to tautology in folklore—that is, that repetition itself plays something of an aesthetic role: "Obviously we have here diverse forms of one general principle, the principle of simple combination, by which either the sounds of the words or their meanings, or now one and now the other, serve as the material of the combination." Such an extension of one device to cover the various forms of poetic material is quite characteristic of the work of the Formalists during their initial period. After the presentation of Brik's essay the question of sound in verse lost something of its urgency, and the Formalists turned to questions of poetics in general.

The Formalists began their work with the question of the sounds of verse—at that time the most controversial and most basic question. Behind this particular question of poetics stood more general theses which had to be formulated. The distinction between systems of poetic and practical language, which defined the work of the Formalists from the very beginning, was bound to result in the formulation of a whole group of basic questions. The idea of poetry as "thought by means of images" and the resulting formula, poetry = imagery, clearly did not coincide with our observations and contradicted our tentative general principles. Rhythm, sound, syntax—all of these seemed secondary from such a point of view; they seemed uncharacteristic of poetry and necessarily extraneous to it. The Symbolists accepted Potebnya's general theory because it justified the supremacy of the image-symbol; yet they could not rid themselves of the notorious theory of the "harmony of form and content" even though it clearly contradicted their bent for formal experimentation and discredited it by making it seem mere aestheticism. The Formalists, when they abandoned Potebnya's point of view, also freed themselves from the traditional correlation of form and content and from the traditional idea of form as an envelope, a vessel into which one pours a liquid (the content). The facts of art demonstrate that art's uniqueness consists not in the parts which enter into it but in their original *use*. Thus the notion of form was changed; the new notion of form required no companion idea, no correlative.

Even before the formation of the *Opoyaz* in 1914, at the time of the public performances of the Futurists, Shklovsky had published a monograph, *The Resurrection of the Word*, in which he took exception partly to the concepts set forth by Potebnya and partly to those of Veselovsky (the question of imagery was not then of major significance) to advance the principle of perceptible form as the specific sign of artistic awareness:

> We do not experience the commonplace, we do not see it; rather, we recognize it. We do not see the walls of our room; and it is very difficult for us to see errors in proofreading, especially if the material is written in a language we know well, because we cannot force ourselves to see, to read, and not to "recognize" the familiar word. If we have to define specifically "poetic" perception and artistic perception in general, then we suggest this definition: "Artistic" perception is that perception in which we experience form—perhaps not form alone, but certainly form.

Perception here is clearly not to be understood as a simple psychological concept (the perception peculiar to this or that person), but, since art does not exist outside of perception, as an element in art itself. The notion of *form* here acquires new meaning; it is no longer an envelope, but a complete thing, something concrete, dynamic, self-contained, and without a correlative of any kind. Here we made a decisive break with the Symbolist principle that some sort of content is to shine through the form. And we broke with aestheticism—the preference for certain elements of form consciously isolated from "content."

But these general acknowledgments that there are differences between poetic and practical language[8] and that the specific quality of art is shown in its particular use of the

---

[8]See Mukařovský, *Standard Language and Poetic Language,* pp. 976–82, and Wheelwright, *The Logical and the Translogical,* pp. 1022–31.

material were not adequate when we tried to deal with specific works. We had to find more specific formulations of the principle of perceptible form so that they could make possible the analysis of form itself—the analysis of form understood as content. We had to show that the perception of form results from special artistic techniques which force the reader to experience the form. Shklovsky's *Art as Technique,* presenting its own manifesto of the Formalist method, offered a perspective for the concrete analysis of form. Here was a really clear departure from Potebnya and Potebnyaism and, at the same time, from the theoretical principles of Symbolism. The essay began with objections to Potebnya's basic view of imagery and its relation to content. Shklovsky indicates, among other things, that images are almost always static:

> The more you understand an age, the more convinced you become that the images a given poet used and which you thought his own were taken almost unchanged from another poet. The works of poets are classified or grouped according to the new techniques they discover and share, and according to their arrangement and development of the resources of language; poets are much more concerned with arranging images than creating them. Images are given to poets; the ability to remember them is far more important than the ability to create them. Imagistic thought does not, in any case, include all aspects of art or even all aspects of verbal art. A change in imagery is not essential to the development of poetry.

He further pointed out the difference between poetic and nonpoetic images. The poetic image is defined as one of the devices of poetic language—as a device which, depending upon the problem, is as important as such other devices of poetic language as simple and negative parallelism, comparison, repetition, symmetry, hyperbole, etc., but no more important. Thus imagery becomes a part of a system of poetic devices and loses its theoretical dominance.

Shklovsky likewise repudiated the principle of artistic economy, a principle which had been strongly asserted in aesthetic theory, and opposed it with the device of defamiliarization and the notion of roughened form. That is, he saw art as increasing the difficulty and span of perception "because the process of perception is an aesthetic end in itself and must be prolonged"; he saw art as a means of destroying the automatism of perception; the purpose of the image is not to present the approximate meaning of its object to our understanding, but to create a special perception of the object—the creation of its vision, and not the recognition of its meaning. Hence the image is usually connected with the process of defamiliarization.

The break with Potebnya was formulated definitely in Shklovsky's essay *Potebnya*. He repeats once more that imagery—symbolization—does not constitute the specific difference between poetic and prosaic (practical) language:

> Poetic language is distinguished from practical language by the perception of its structure. The acoustical, articulatory, or semantic aspects of poetic language may be felt. Sometimes one feels the verbal structure, the arrangement of the words, rather than their texture. The poetic image is one of the ways, but only one of the ways, of creating a perceptible structure designed to be experienced within its very own fabric. . . . The creation of a scientific poetics must begin inductively with a hypothesis built on an accumulation of evidence. That hypothesis is that poetic and prosaic languages exist, that the laws which distinguish them exist, and finally, that these differences are to be analyzed.

These essays are to be read as the summation of the first phase of the Formalists' work. The main achievement of this period consisted in our establishment of a series of theoretical principles which provided working hypotheses for a further investigation of the data for the defeat of the current theories based on Potebnyaism. The chief strength of the Formalists, as these essays show, was neither the direction of their study of so-called forms nor the construction of a special method; their strength was founded securely on the fact that the specific features of the verbal arts had to be studied and that to do so it was first necessary to sort out the differing uses of poetic and practical language. Concerning form, the Formalists thought it important to change the meaning of this muddled term. It was important to destroy these traditional correlatives and so to enrich the idea of form with new significance. *The notion of technique, because it has to do directly with the distinguishing features of poetic and practical speech, is much more significant in the long-range evolution of Formalism than is the notion of form.*

The preliminary stage of our theoretical work had passed. We had proposed general principles bearing directly upon factual material. We now had to move closer to the material and to make the problems themselves specific. At the center stood those questions of theoretical poetics that had previously been outlined only in general form. We had to move from questions about the sound of verse to a general theory of verse. The questions about the sound of verse, when originally posed, were meant only as illustrations of the difference between poetic and practical language. We had to move from questions about technique-in-general to the study of the specific devices of composition, to inquiry about plot, and so on. Our interest in opposing Veselovsky's general view and, specifically, in opposing his theory of plot, developed side by side with our interest in opposing Potebnya's.

At this time, the Formalists quite naturally used literary works only as material for supporting and testing their theoretical hypotheses; we had put aside questions of convention, literary evolution, etc. Now we felt it important to widen the scope of our study, to make a preliminary survey of the data, and to allow it to establish its own kind of laws. In this way we freed ourselves from the necessity of resorting to abstract premises and at the same time mastered the materials without losing ourselves in details.

Shklovsky, with his theory of plot and fiction, was especially important during this period. He demonstrated the presence of special devices of "plot construction" and their relation to general stylistic devices in such diverse materials as the *skaz,* Oriental tales, Cervantes' *Don Quixote,* Tolstoy's works, Sterne's *Tristram Shandy,* and so on. I do not wish to go into details—those should be treated in specialized works and not in a general essay such as this on the Formalist method—but I do wish to cover those ideas in Shklovsky's treatment of plot which have a theoretical significance beyond any relationship they might have to particular problems of plots as such. Traces of those ideas can be found in the most advanced pieces of Formalist criticism.

The first of Shklovsky's works on plot, *The Relation of Devices of Plot Construction to General Devices of Style,* raised a whole series of such ideas. In the first place, the proof that special devices of plot arrangement exist, a proof supported by the citation of great number of devices, changed the traditional notion of plot as a combination of a group of motifs and made plot a compositional rather than a thematic concept. Thus the very concept of plot was changed; *plot* was no longer synonymous with *story.* Plot construction became the natural subject of Formalist study, since plot constitutes the specific peculiarity of narrative *art.* The idea of form had been enriched, and as it lost its former abstractness, it also lost its controversial meaning. Our idea of form had begun to coincide with our idea of literature as such, with the idea of the literary fact.

Furthermore, the analogies which we established between the devices of plot construction and the devices of style had theoretical significance, for the step-by-step structure usually found in the epic was found to be analogous to sound repetition, tautology, tautological parallelism, and so on. All illustrated a general principle of verbal art based on parceling out and impeding the action.

For instance, Roland's three blows on the stone in the *Song of Roland* and the similar triple repetition common in tales may be compared, as a single type of phenomenon, with Gogol's use of synonyms and with such linguistic structures as *hoity-toity, a diller, a dollar,*[9] etc. "These variations of step-by-step construction usually do not all occur together, and attempts have been made to give each case a special explanation." Shklovsky shows how we attempt to demonstrate that the same device may reappear in diverse materials. Here we clashed with Veselovsky, who in such cases usually avoided theory and resorted to historical-genetic hypotheses. For instance, he explained epic repetition as a mechanism for the original performance (as embryonic song). But an explanation of the genetics of such a phenomenon, even if true, does not clarify the phenomenon as a fact of literature. Veselovsky and other members of the ethnographic school used to explain the peculiar motifs and plots of the *skaz* by relating literature and custom; Shklovsky did not object to making the relationship but challenged it only as an explanation of the peculiarities of the *skaz*—he challenged it as an explanation of a specifically literary fact. The study of literary genetics can clarify only the origin of a device, nothing more; poetics must explain its literary function. The genetic point of view fails to consider the device as a self-determined use of material; it does not consider how conventional materials are selected by an author, how conventional devices are transformed, or how they are made to play a structural role. The genetic point of view does not explain how a convention may disappear and its literary function remain. The literary function remains not as a simple [customary or social] experience but as a literary device retaining a significance over and beyond its connection with the convention. Characteristically, Veselovsky had contradicted himself by considering the adventures of the Greek romance as purely stylistic devices.

The Formalists naturally opposed Veselovsky's ethnographism because it ignored the special characteristic of the literary device and because it replaced the theoretical and evolutionary point of view with a genetic point of view.

Veselovsky saw syncretism as a phenomenon of primitive poetry, a result of custom, and he later was censured for this in B. Kazansky's *The Concept of Historical Poetics.* Ka-

---

[9][Lemon and Reis] Eichenbaum gives two nonsense phrases here, *kudy-mudy* and *plyushkimlyushki.* The point is, of course, that repetition of sound alone may keep alive certain otherwise meaningless expressions.

zansky repudiated the ethnographic point of view by affirming the presence of syncretic tendencies in the very nature of each art, a presence especially obvious in some periods. The Formalists naturally could not agree with Veselovsky when he touched upon general questions of literary evolution. If the clash with the Potebnyaists clarified basic principles of poetics, the clash with Veselovsky's general view and with that of his followers clarified the Formalist's views on literary evolution and, thereby, on the structure of literary history.

Shklovsky began to deal with the subject of literary evolution in the essay I cited previously, *The Relation of Devices of Plot Construction to General Devices of Style.* He had encountered Veselovsky's formula, a formula broadly based on the ethnographic principle that "the purpose of new form is to express new content," and he decided to advance a completely different point of view:

> The work of art arises from a background of other works and through association with them. The form of a work of art is defined by its relation to other works of art, to forms existing prior to it. . . . Not only parody, but also any kind of art is created parallel to and opposed to some kind of form. *The purpose of the new form is not to express new content, but to change an old form which has lost its aesthetic quality.*

Shklovsky supported this thesis with B[roder] Christiansen's demonstration of "differentiated perceptions" or "perceptions of difference." He sees that the dynamism characteristic of art is based on this and is manifested in repeated violations of established rules. At the close of his essay, he quotes F[erdinand] Brunetière's statements that "of all the influences active in the history of literature, the chief is the influence of *work on work,*" and that "one should not, without good cause, increase the number of influences upon literature, under the assumption that literature is the expression of society, nor should one confuse the history of literature with the history of morals and manners. These are entirely different things."

Shklovsky's essay marked the changeover from our study of theoretical poetics to our study of the history of literature. Our original assumptions about form had been complicated by our observation of new features of evolutionary dynamics and their continuous variability. Our moving into the area of the history of literature was no simple expansion of our study; it resulted from the evolution of our concept of form. We found that we could not see the literary work in isolation, that we had to see its form against a background of other works rather than by itself. Thus the Formalists defi-

nitely went beyond "Formalism," if by *Formalism* one means (as some poorly informed critics usually did) some fabricated system which permitted us to be classified, some system which zealously adapted itself to logic-chopping, or some system which joyously welcomed any dogma. Such scholastic Formalism was neither historical nor essentially connected with the work of the *Opoyaz.* We were not responsible for it; on the contrary, we were irreconcilably its enemies on principle.

Later I shall return to the historical-literary work of the Formalists, but now I wish to conclude the survey of those theoretical principles and problems contained in the early work of the *Opoyaz.* The Shklovsky essay I referred to above contains still another idea which figured prominently in the subsequent study of the novel—the idea of motivation.[10] The discovery of various techniques of plot construction (step-by-step structure, parallelism, framing, the weaving of motifs, etc.) clarified the difference between the elements used in the construction of a work and the elements comprising its material (its story, the choice of motifs, the characters, the themes, etc.). Shklovsky stressed this difference at that time because the basic problem was to show the identity of individual structural devices in the most diverse materials imaginable. The old scholarship worked exclusively with the material, taking it as the content and treating the remainder as an external form either totally without interest or of interest only to the dilettante. Hence the naive and pathetic aesthetics of our older literary critics and historians, who found "neglect of form" in Tyutchev's poetry and simply "bad form" in Nekrasov and Dostoevsky. The literary reputations of these authors were saved because their intensity of thought and mood excused their formlessness. Naturally, during the years of struggle and polemics against such a position, the Formalists directed all their forces to showing the significance of such compositional devices as motivation and ignored all other considerations. In speaking of the formal method and its evolution, we must constantly remember that many of the principles advanced by the Formalists in the years of tense struggle were significant not only as scientific principles, but also as slogans, as paradoxes sharpened for propaganda and controversy. To ignore this fact and to treat the work of the *Opoyaz* (between 1916 and 1921) in the same way as one would treat the academic scholarship is to ignore history.

The concept of motivation permitted the Formalists to approach literary works (in particular, novels and short stories) more closely and to observe the details of their structure, which Shklovsky did in two later works, *Plot Develop-*

---

[10]Not necessarily characters' motivation but the author's.

ment and *Sterne's* Tristram Shandy *and the Theory of the Novel.* In these works, he studied the relationship between technique and motivation in Cervantes' *Don Quixote* and Sterne's *Tristram Shandy* as material for the study of the structure of the short story and the novel apart from literary history, and he studies *Don Quixote* as an instance of the transition from collections of tales (like the *Decameron*) to the novel with a single hero whose travels justify or motivate its episodic structure. *Don Quixote* was chosen because the devices it contains and their motivation are not fully integrated into the entire context of the novel. Material is often simply inserted, not welded in; devices of plot construction and methods of using material to further the plot structure stand out sharply, whereas later structures tend "more and more to integrate the material tightly into the very body of the novel." While analyzing "how Don Quixote was made," Shklovsky also showed the instability of the hero and concluded that his type appeared "as the result of the business of constructing the novel." Thus the dominance of structure, of plot over material, was emphasized.

Neither a work fully motivated nor an art which deliberately does away with motivation and exposes the structure provides the most suitable material for the illumination of such theoretical problems. But the very existence of a work such as *Don Quixote,* with a deliberately exposed structure, confirms the relevance of these problems, confirms the fact that the problems need to be stated as problems, and confirms the fact that they are *significant* literary problems. Moreover, we were able to explain works of literature entirely in the light of these theoretical problems and principles, as Shklovsky did with *Tristram Shandy.* Shklovsky not only used the book to illustrate our theoretical position, he gave it new significance and once more attracted attention to it. Studied against the background of an interest in the *structure* of the novel, Sterne became a contemporary; people spoke about him, people who previously had found in his novel only boring chatter or eccentricities, or who had prejudged it from the point of view of its notorious sentimentalism, a characteristic for which Sterne is as little to blame as Gogol for realism.

Shklovsky pointed out Sterne's deliberate laying bare of his methods of constructing *Tristram Shandy* and asserted that Sterne had exaggerated the structure of the novel. He had shown his awareness of form by his manner of violating it and by his manner of assembling the novel's contents. In his conclusion to the essay, Shklovsky formulated the difference between plot and story:

> The idea of plot is too often confused with the description of events—with what I propose provisionally to call the *story.* The story is, in fact, only

material for plot formulation. The plot of *Eugeny Onegin* is, therefore, not the romance of the hero with Tatyana, but the fashioning of the subject of this story as produced by the introduction of interrupting digressions. . . .

The forms of art are explainable by the laws of art; they are not justified by their realism. Slowing the action of a novel is not accomplished by introducing rivals, for example, but by simply *transposing* parts. In so doing the artist makes us aware of the aesthetic laws which underlie both the transposition and the slowing down of the action.

My essay *How Gogol's* Greatcoat *Was Made* also considers the structure of the novel, comparing the problem of plot with the problem of the *skaz*—the problem of structure based upon the narrator's manner of telling what had happened. I tried to show that Gogol's text "was made up of living speech patterns and vocalized emotions," that words and sentences are selected and joined by Gogol as they are in the oral *skaz,* in which articulation, mimicry, sound gestures, and so on, play a special role. From this point of view I showed how the structure of *The Greatcoat* imparts a grotesque tone to the tale by replacing the usual humor of the *skaz* (with its anecdotes, puns, etc.) with sentimental-melodramatic declamation, I discussed, in this connection, the end of *The Greatcoat* as the apotheosis of the grotesque—not unlike the mute scene in *The Inspector General.*[11] The traditional line of argument about Gogol's romanticism and realism proved unnecessary and unilluminating.

Thus we began to make some progress with the problem of the study of prose. The line between the idea of plot as structure and the idea of the story as material was drawn; this explanation of the typical techniques of plot construction opened the door for work on the history and theory of the novel; and furthermore, the *skaz* was treated as the structural basis of the plotless short story. These works have influenced a whole series of recent studies by persons not directly connected with the *Opoyaz.*

As our theoretical work broadened and deepened it naturally became specialized—the more so because persons who were only beginning their work or who had been working independently joined the *Opoyaz* group. Some of them specialized in the problems of poetry, others in the problems of prose. The Formalists insisted upon keeping clear the demarcation between poetry and prose in order to counterbalance the Symbolists, who were then attempting to erase the

---

[11][Lemon and Reis] The final scene, in which not a word is spoken for a minute and a half as the curtain slowly falls.

boundary line both in theory and in practice by painstakingly attempting to discover meter in prose.[12]

The earlier sections of this essay show the intensity of our work on prose. We were pioneers in the area. Several Western works resembled ours (in particular, such observations on story material as Wilhelm Dibelius' *Englische Romankunst,* 1910), but they had little relevance to our theoretical problems and principles. In our work on prose we felt almost free from tradition, but in dealing with verse the situation was different. The great number of works by Western and Russian literary theorists, the numerous practical and theoretical experiments of the Symbolists, and the special literature of the controversies over the concepts of rhythm and meter (produced between 1910 and 1917) complicated our study of poetry. The Futurists, in that same period, were creating new verse forms, and this complicated things still more. Given such conditions, it was difficult for us to pose the right problems. Many persons, instead of returning to basic questions, were concerned with special problems of metrics or with trying to put the accumulation of systems and opinions in good order. Meanwhile, we had no general theory of poetry: no theoretical elucidations of verse rhythm, of the connection of rhythm and syntax, of the sounds of verse (the Formalists had indicated only a few linguistic premises), of poetic diction and semantics, and so on. In other words, the nature of verse as such remained essentially obscure. We had to draw away from particular problems of metrics and to approach verse from some more disciplined perspective. We had, first of all, to pose the problem of rhythm so that it did not rest on metrics and would include a more substantial part of poetic speech.

Here, as in the previous section, I shall dwell upon the problem of verse only insofar as its exploration led to a new theoretical view of verbal art or a new view of the nature of poetic speech. Our position was stated first in Osip Brik's *On Rhythmic-Syntactic Figures,* an unpublished lecture delivered before the *Opoyaz* group and, apparently, not even written out.[13] Brik demonstrated that verse contained stable syntactical figures indissolubly connected with rhythm. Thus rhythm was no longer thought of as an abstraction; it was made relevant to the very linguistic fabric of verse—the phrase. Metrics became a kind of background, significant, like the alphabet, for the reading and writing of verse. Brik's step was as important for the study of verse as the discovery of the relation of plot to structure was for the study of prose. The discovery that rhythmic patterns are related to the grammatical patterns of sentences destroyed the notion that

rhythm is a superficial appendage, something floating on the surface of speech. Our theory of verse was founded on the analysis of rhythm as the structural basis of verse, a basis which of itself determined all of its parts—both acoustical and unacoustical. A superior theory of verse, which would make metrics but a kindergarten preparation, was in sight. The Symbolists and the group led by Bely, despite their attempts, could not travel our road because they still saw the central problem as metrics isolation.

But Brik's work merely hinted at the possibility of a new way; like his first essay, *Sound Repetitions,* it was limited to showing examples and arranging them into groups. From Brik's lecture one could move either into new problems or into the simple classification and cataloging, or systematizing, of the material. The lecture was not necessarily an expression of the formal method. V[ictor] Zhirmunsky continued the work of classification in *The Composition of Lyric Verse.* Zhirmunsky, who did not share the theoretical principles of the *Opoyaz,* was interested in the formal method as only one of the possible scientific approaches to the division of materials into various groups and headings. Given his understanding of the formal method, he could do nothing else; he accepted any superficial feature as a basis for the grouping of materials. Hence the unvarying cataloging and the pedantic tone of all of Zhirmunsky's theoretical work. Such works were not a major influence in the general evolution of the formal method; in themselves they merely emphasized the tendency (evidently historically inevitable) to give the formal method an academic quality. It is not surprising, therefore, that Zhirmunsky later completely withdrew from the *Opoyaz* over a difference of opinion about the principles he stated repeatedly in his last works (especially in his introduction to the translation of O[skar] Walzel's *The Problem of Form in Prose* [1923]).

My book, *Verse Melody,* which was prepared as a study of the phonetics of verse and so was related to a whole group of Western works (by Sievers, Saran, etc.), was relevant to Brik's work on rhythmic-syntactic figures. I maintained that stylistic differences were usually chiefly lexical:

> With that we drop the idea of versification as such, and take up poetic language in general. . . . We have to find something related to the *poetic phrase* that does not also lead us away from the *poetry* itself, something bordering on both phonetics and semantics. This "something" is syntax.

I did not examine the rhythmic-syntactic phenomena in isolation, but as part of an examination of the structural significance of metrical and vocal intonation. I felt it especially

---

[12][Lemon and Reis] See especially Andrey Bely's *Simvolizm* (Moscow, 1910).
[13][Lemon and Reis] 1920. Brik's lecture was published in 1927 in *New Left.*

important both to assert the idea of a *dominant,* upon which a given poetic style is organized, and to isolate the idea of melody as a system of intonations from the idea of the general musicality of verse. On this basis, I proposed to distinguish three fundamental styles of lyric poetry: declamatory (oratorical), melodic, and conversational. My entire book is devoted to the peculiarities of the melodic style—to peculiarities in the material of the lyrics of Zhukovsky, Tyutchev, Lermontov, and Fet. Avoiding ready-made schematizations, I ended the book with the conviction that "in scientific work, I consider the ability to see facts far more important than the construction of a system. Theories are necessary to clarify facts; in reality, theories are made of facts. Theories perish and change, but the facts they help discover and support remain."

The tradition of specialized metrical studies still continued among the Symbolist theoreticians (Bely, Bryusov, Bobrov, Chukovsky, and others), but it gradually turned into precise statistical enumeration and lost what had been its dominant characteristic. Here the metrical studies of Boris Tomashevsky, concluded in his text *Russian Versification,* played the most significant role. Thus, as the study of metrics became secondary, a subsidiary discipline with a very limited range of problems, the general theory of verse entered its first stage.

Tomashevsky's *Pushkin's Iambic Pentameter* outlined the entire previous course of developments within the formal method, including its attempt to broaden and enrich the notion of poetic rhythm and to relate it to the structure of poetic language. The essay also attempted to go beyond the idea of meter in language. Hence the basic charge against Bely and his school: "The problem of rhythm is not conformity to imaginary meters; it is rather the distribution of expiratory energy within a single wave—the line itself." In *The Problems of Poetic Rhythm* Tomashevsky expressed this with perfect clarity of principle. Here the earlier conflict between meter and rhythm is resolved by applying the idea of rhythm in verse to all of the elements of speech that play a part in the structure of verse. The rhythms of phrasal intonation and euphony (alliterations, etc.) are placed side by side with the rhythm of word accent. Thus we came to see the line as *a special form of speech* which functions as a single unit in the creation of poetry. We no longer saw the line as something which could create a rhythmic variation by resisting or adjusting to the metrical form (a view which Zhirmunsky continued to defend in his new work, *Introduction to Metrics*). Tomashevsky wrote that:

Poetic speech is *organized* in terms of its sounds. Taken singly, any phonetic element is subject to

rules and regulations, but sound is a *complex* phenomenon. Thus classical metrics singles out accent and normalizes it by its rules. . . . But it takes little effort to shake the authority of traditional forms, because the notion persisted that the nature of verse is not fully explained by a single distinguishing feature, that poetry exists in "secondary" features, that a recognizable rhythm exists alongside meter, that poetry can be created by imposing a pattern on only these secondary features, and *that speech without meter may sound like poetry.*

The important idea of a rhythmic impulse (which had figured earlier in Brik's work) with a general rhythmic function is maintained here:

Rhythmic devices may participate in various degrees in the creation of an artistic-rhythmic effect; this or that device may dominate various works—this or that means may be the *dominant.* The use of a given rhythmic device determines the character of the particular rhythm of the work. On this basis poetry may be classified as accented-metrical poetry (e.g., the description of the Battle of Poltava[14]), intoned-melodic poetry (the verses of Zhukovsky), or harmonic poetry (common during the recent years of Russian Symbolism).

Poetic form, so understood, is not contrasted with anything outside itself—with a content which has been laboriously set inside this form—but is understood as the genuine content of poetic speech. Thus the very idea of form, as it had been understood in earlier works, emerged with a new and more adequate meaning.

In his essay *On Czech Versification* Roman Jakobson pointed out new problems in the general theory of poetic rhythm. He opposed the [earlier] theory that "verse adapts itself completely to the spirit of the language," that is, that "form does not resist the material [it shapes]" with the theory that "poetic form is the organized coercion of language." He applied this refinement of the more orthodox view—a refinement in keeping with the Formalist method—to the question of the difference between the phonetic qualities of practical language and those of poetic language. Although Jakubinsky had [for example] noted that the dissimilation of liquid consonants [*l* and *r*] is relatively infrequent in poetry, Jakobson showed that it existed in both poetical

---

[14]In Pushkin's *Poltava.*

and practical language but that in practical language it is "accidental"; in poetic language it is, "so to speak, contrived; these are two distinct phenomena."[15]

In the same essay Jakobson also clarified the principal distinction between emotional and poetic language (a distinction he had previously considered in his first book, *Modern Russian Poetry*):

> Although poetry may use the methods of emotive language, it uses them only for *its own* purposes. The similarities between the two kinds of language and the use of poetic language in the way that emotive language is used frequently leads to the assumption that the two are identical. The assumption is mistaken because it fails to consider the radical difference of *function* between the two kinds of language.

In this connection Jakobson refuted the attempts of [Maurice] Grammont and other prosodists to explain the phonetic structure of poetry in terms either of onomatopoeia or of the emotional connection between sounds and images. "Phonetic structure," he wrote, "is not always a structure of audible images, nor is a structure of audible images always a method of emotional language." Jakobson's book was typical because it constantly went beyond the limits of its particular, special theme (the prosody of Czech verse) and shed light on general questions about the theory of poetic language and verse. Thus his book ends with a whole essay on Mayakovsky, an essay complemented by his earlier piece on Khlebnikov.

In my own work on Anna Akhmatova I also attempted to raise basic theoretical questions about the theory of verse—questions of the relation of rhythm to syntax and intonation, the relation of the sound of verse to its articulation, and, lastly, the relation of poetic diction to semantics. Referring to a book which Yury Tynyanov was then preparing, I pointed out that "as words get into verse they are, as it were, taken out of ordinary speech. They are surrounded by a new aura of meaning and perceived not against the background of speech in general but against the background of poetic speech." I also indicated that the formation of collateral meanings, which disrupts ordinary verbal associations, is the chief peculiarity of the semantics of poetry.

Until then, the original connection between the formal method and linguistics had been growing considerably weaker. The difference that had developed between our problems was so great that we no longer needed the special support of the linguists, especially the support of those who were psychologically oriented. In fact, some of the work of the linguists was objectionable in principle. Tynyanov's *The Problem of Poetic Language,* which had appeared just then, emphasized the difference between the study of psychological linguistics and the study of poetic language and style. This book showed the intimate relation that exists between the meaning of words and the poetic structure itself; it added new meaning to the idea of poetic rhythm and initiated the Formalists' investigation not only of acoustics and syntax, but also of the shades of meaning peculiar to poetic speech. In the introduction Tynyanov says:

> The study of poetry has of late been quite rewarding. Undoubtedly the prospect in the near future is for development in the whole field, although we all remember the systematic beginning of the study. But the study of poetry has been kept isolated from questions of poetic language *and* style; the study of the latter is kept isolated from the study of the former. The impression is given that neither the poetic language itself nor the poetic style itself has any connection with poetry, that the one does not depend upon the other. The idea of poetic language, which was advanced not so long ago and is now changing, undoubtedly invited a certain looseness by its breadth and by the vagueness of its content, a content based on psychological linguistics.

Among the general questions of poetics revived and illuminated by this book, that of the idea of the material is most fundamental. The generally accepted view saw an opposition between form and content; when the distinction was made purely verbal, it lost its meaning. In fact, as I have already mentioned, our view gave form the significance of a thing complete in itself and strengthened it by considering the work of art in relation to its purpose. Our concept of form required no complement—except that other, artistically insignificant, kind of form. Tynyanov showed that the materials of verbal art were neither all alike nor all equally important, that "one feature may be prominent at the expense of the rest, so that the remainder is deformed and sometimes degraded to the level of a neutral prop." Hence the conclusion that "the idea of material does not lie beyond the limits of form; the material itself is a formal element. To confuse it with external structural features is a mistake." After this,

---

[15][Eichenbaum] Jakubinsky had already pointed out the excessive complexity of the idea of practical speech and the impossibility of analyzing it in terms of function (conversational, oratorical, scientific, and so on); see his essay, "O dialogicheskoy rechi" ["On Dialogic Speech"], *Russkaya rech* [*Russian Speech*], I (1923).

Tynyanov could make the notion of form more complex by showing that form is dynamic: "The unity of the work is not a closed, symmetrical whole, but an unfolding, dynamic whole. Its elements are not static indications of equality and complexity, but always dynamic indications of correlation and integration. The form of literary works must be thought of as dynamic."

Rhythm is here presented as the fundamental specific factor which permeates all the elements of poetry. The objective sign of poetic rhythm is the establishment of a *rhythmic group* whose *unity* and *richness* exist side by side with each other. And again, Tynyanov affirms the principal distinction between prose and poetry:

> Poetry, as opposed to prose, tends toward unity and richness ranged around an uncommon object. This very "uncommonness" prevents the main point of the poem from being smoothed over. Indeed, it asserts the object with a new force. . . . Any element of prose brought into the poetic pattern is transformed into verse by that feature of it which asserts its function and which thus has two aspects: the emphasis of the structure—the versification—and the deformation of the uncommon object.

Tynyanov also raises the question of semantics: "In verse are not the ordinary semantic meanings of the words so distorted (a fact which makes complete paraphrase impossible) that the usual principles governing their arrangement no longer apply?" The entire second part of Tynyanov's book answers this question by defining the precise relation between rhythm and semantics. The facts show clearly that oral presentations are unified in part by rhythm. "This is shown in a more forceful and more compact integration of connectives than occurs in ordinary speech; words are made correlative by their positions"; prose lacks this feature.

Thus the Formalists abandoned Potebnya's theory and accepted the conclusions connected with it on a new basis, and a new perspective opened on to the theory of verse. Tynyanov's work permitted us to grasp even the remotest implications of these new problems. It became clear even to those only casually acquainted with the *Opoyaz* that the essence of our work consisted not in some kind of static "formal method," but in a study of the specific peculiarities of verbal art—we were not advocates of a method, but students of an object. Again, Tynyanov stated this:

> The object of a study claiming to be a study of art ought to be so specific that it is distinguished from other areas of intellectual activity and uses them

for its own materials and tools. Each work of art represents a complex interaction of many factors; consequently, the job of the student is the definition of the specific character of this interaction.

Earlier I noted that the problem of the diffusion and change of form—the problem of literary evolution—is raised naturally along with theoretical problems. The problem of literary evolution arises in connection with a reconsideration of Veselovsky's view of *skaz* motifs and devices; the answer ("new form is not to express new content, but to replace old form") led to a new understanding of form. If form is understood as the very content, constantly changing according to its dependence upon previous images, then we naturally had to approach it without abstract, ready-made, unalterable, classical schemes; and we had to consider specifically its historical sense and significance. The approach developed its own kind of dual perspective: the perspective of theoretical study (like Shklovsky's *Development of Plot* and my *Verse Melody*), which centered on a given theoretical problem and its applicability to the most diverse materials, and the perspective of historical studies—studies of literary evolution as such. The combination of these two perspectives, both organic to the subsequent development of the formal school, raised a series of new and very complex problems, many of which are still unsolved and even undefined.

Actually, the original attempt of the Formalists to take a particular structural device and to establish its identity in diverse materials became an attempt to differentiate, to understand, the *function* of a device in each given case. This notion of functional significance was gradually pushed toward the foreground and the original idea of the device pushed into the background. This kind of sorting out of its own general ideas and principles has been characteristic of our work throughout the evolution of the formal method. We have no dogmatic position to bind us and shut us off from facts. We do not answer for our schematizations; they may require change, refinement, or correction when we try to apply them to previously unknown facts. Work on specific materials compelled us to speak of functions and thus to revise our idea of the device. The theory itself demanded that we turn to history.

Here again we were confronted with the traditional academic sciences and the preferences of critics. In our student days the academic history of literature was limited chiefly to biographical and psychological studies of various writers—only the "greats," of course. Critics no longer made attempts to construct a history of Russian literature as a whole, attempts which evidenced the intention of bringing the great historical materials into a system; nevertheless, the traditions established by earlier histories (like A. N. Pypin's *History of*

Russian Literature) retained their scholarly authority, the more so because the following generation had decided not to pursue such broad themes. Meanwhile, the chief role was played by such general and somewhat vague notions as realism and romanticism (realism was said to be better than romanticism); evolution was understood as gradual perfection, as progress (from Romanticism to realism); succession [of literary schools] as the peaceful transfer of the inheritance from father to son. But generally, there was no notion of literature as such; material taken from the history of social movements, from biography, etc. had replaced it entirely.

This primitive historicism, which led away from literature, naturally provoked the Symbolist theoreticians and critics into a denial of any kind of historicism. Their own discussions of literature, consequently, developed into impressionistic *"études"* and "silhouettes," and they indulged in a widespread "modernization" of old writers, transforming them into "eternal companions." The history of literature was silently (and sometimes aloud) declared unnecessary.

We had to demolish the academic tradition and to eliminate the bias of the journalists [the Symbolist theoreticians]. We had to advance against the first a new understanding of literary evolution and of literature itself—without the idea of progress and peaceful succession, without the ideas of realism and romanticism, without materials foreign to literature—as a specific order of phenomena, a specific order of material. We had to act against the second by pointing out concrete historical facts, fluctuating and changing forms, by pointing to the necessity of taking into account the specific functions of this or that device—in a word, we had to draw the line between the literary work as a definite historical fact and a free interpretation of it from the standpoint of contemporary literary needs, tastes, or interests. Thus the basic passion for our historical-literary work had to be a passion for destruction and negation, and such was the original tone of our theoretical attacks; our work later assumed a calmer note when we went on to solutions of particular problems.

That is why the first of our historical-literary pronouncements came in the form of theses expressed almost against our will in connection with some specific material. A particular question would unexpectedly lead to the formulation of a general problem, a problem that inextricably mixed theoretical and historical considerations. In this sense Tynyanov's *Dostoevsky and Gogol* and Shklovsky's *Rozanov* were typical.

Tynyanov's basic problem was to show that Dostoevsky's *The Village of Stepanchikovo* is a parody, that behind its first level is hidden a second—it is a parody of Gogol's *Correspondence with Friends*. But his treatment of this par-

ticular question was overshadowed by a whole theory of parody [which he developed to solve the particular problem], a theory of parody as a stylistic device (stylized parody) and as one of the manifestations (having great historical-literary significance) of the dialectical development of literary groups. With this arose the problem of succession and tradition and, hence, the basic problems of literary evolution were posed [as part of the study of style]:

> When one speaks of literary tradition or succession . . . usually one implies a certain kind of direct line uniting the younger and older representatives of a known literary branch. Yet the matter is much more complicated. There is no continuing direct line; there is rather a departure, a pushing away from the known point—a struggle. . . . Any literary succession is first of all a struggle, a destruction of old values and a reconstruction of old elements.

Literary evolution was complicated by the notion of struggle, of periodic uprisings, and so lost its old suggestion of peaceful and gradual development. Against this background, the literary relationship between Dostoevsky and Gogol was shown to be that of a complicated struggle.

In his *Rozanov*, Shklovsky showed, almost in the absence of basic themes, a whole theory of literary evolution which even then reflected the current discussion of such problems in *Opoyaz*. Shklovsky showed that literature moves forward in a broken line.

> In each literary epoch there is not one literary school, but several. They exist simultaneously, with one of them representing the high point of the current orthodoxy. The others exist uncanonized, mutely; in Pushkin's time, for example, the courtly tradition of [Wilhelm] Kuchelbecker and [Alexander] Greboyedov existed simultaneously with the tradition of Russian vaudeville verse and with such other traditions as that of the pure adventure novel of Bulgarin.

The moment the old art is canonized, new forms are created on a lower level. A "young line" is created which

> grows up to replace the old, as the vaudevillist Belopyatkin is transformed into a Nekrasov (see Brik's discussion of the relationship); a direct descendant of the eighteenth century, Tolstoy, creates

a new novel (see the work of Boris Eichenbaum); Blok makes the themes and times of the gypsy ballad acceptable, and Chekhov introduces the "alarm clock" into Russian literature. Dostoevsky introduced the devices of the dime novel into the mainstream of literature. Each new literary school heralds a revolution, something like the appearance of a new class. But, of course, this is only an analogy. The vanquished line is not obliterated, it does not cease to exist. It is only knocked from the crest; it lies dormant and may again arise as a perennial pretender to the throne. Moreover, in reality the matter is complicated by the fact that the new hegemony is usually not a pure revival of previous forms but is made more complex by the presence of features of the younger schools and with features, now secondary, inherited from its predecessors on the throne.

Shklovsky is discussing the dynamism of genres, and he interprets Rosanov's books as embodiments of a new genre, as a new type of novel in which the parts are unconnected by motivation. "Thematically, Rozanov's books are characterized by the elevation of new themes; compositionally, by the revealed device." As part of this general theory, we introduced the notion of the dialectical self-creation of new forms, that is, hidden in the new form we saw both analogies with other kinds of cultural development and proof of the independence of the phenomena of literary evolution. In a simplified form, this theory quickly changed hands and, as always happens, became a simple and fixed scheme—very handy for critics. Actually, we have here only a general outline of evolution surrounded by a whole series of complicated conditions. From this general outline the Formalists moved on to a more consistent solution of historical-literary problems and facts, specifying and refining their original theoretical premises.

Given our understanding of literary evolution as the dialectical change of forms, we did not go back to the study of those materials which had held the central position in the old-fashioned historical-literary work. We studied literary evolution insofar as it bore a distinctive character and only to the extent that it stood alone, quite independent of other aspects of culture. In other words, we stuck exclusively to facts in order not to pass into an endless number of indefinite connections and correspondences which would do nothing at all to explain literary evolution. We did not take up questions of the biography and psychology of the artist because we assumed that these questions, in themselves serious and complex, must take their places in other sciences. We felt it

important to find indications of historical regularity in evolution—that is why we ignored all that seemed, from this point of view, circumstantial, not concerned with [literary] history. We were interested in the very process of evolution, in the very *dynamics* of literary form, insofar as it was possible to observe them in the facts of the past. For us, the central problem of the history of literature is the problem of evolution without personality—the study of literature as a *self-formed social phenomenon*. As a result, we found extremely significant both the question of the formation and changes of genres and the question of how second rate and popular literature contributed to the formation of genres. Here we had only to distinguish that popular literature which prepared the way for the formation of new genres from that which arose out of their decay and which offered material for the study of historical inertia.

On the other hand, we were not interested in the past, in isolated historical facts, as such; we did not busy ourselves with the restoration of this or that epoch because we happened to like it. History gave us what the present could not—a stable body of material. But, precisely for this reason, we approached it with a stock of theoretical problems and principles suggested in part by the facts of contemporary literature. The Formalists, then, characteristically had a close interest in contemporary literature and also reconciled criticism and scholarship. The earlier literary historians had, to a great extent, kept themselves aloof from contemporary literature; the Symbolists had subordinated scholarship to criticism. We saw in the history of literature not so much a special theoretical *subject* as a special *approach,* a special cross section of literature. The character of our historical-literary work involved our being drawn not only to historical conclusions, but also to theoretical conclusions—to the posing of new theoretical problems and to the testing of old.

From 1922 to 1924 a whole series of Formalist studies of literary history was written, many of which, because of contemporary market conditions, remain unpublished and are known only as reports. . . .[16] There is, of course, not space enough here to speak of such works in detail. They usually took up secondary writers (those who form the back-

---

[16][Lemon and Reis] The deleted material contains a listing of some Formalist works, including: Yury Tynyanov's *Verse Forms of Nekrasov, The Question of Tyutchev, Tyutchev and Pushkin, Tyutchev and Heine, The Ode as a Declamatory Genre;* Boris Tomashevsky's *Gavriliada, Pushkin, a Reader of French Poets, Pushkin, Pushkin and Boileau, Pushkin and La Fontaine;* Boris Eichenbaum's *Lermontov, Problems of the Poetics of Pushkin, Pushkin's Path to Prose, Nekrasov;* Victor Vinogradov's *Plot and Structure of Gogol's* The Nose, *Plot and Architectonics of Dostoevsky's Novel* Poor People, *Gogol and the Realistic School, Studies on the Style of Gogol;* and Victor Zhirmunsky's *Byron and Pushkin.*

ground of literature) and carefully explained the traditions of their work, noting changes in genres, styles, and so on. As a result, many forgotten names and facts came to light, current estimates were shown to be inaccurate, traditional ideas changed, and, chiefly, the very process of literary evolution became clearer. The working out of this material has only begun. A new series of problems is before us: further differentiation of theoretical and historical literary ideas, introduction of new material, posing new questions, and so on.

I shall conclude with a general summary. The evolution of the formal method, which I have tried to present, has the look of a sequential development of theoretical principles—apart from the individual roles each of us played. Actually, the work of the *Opoyaz* group was genuinely collective. It was this way, obviously, because from the very beginning we understood the historical nature of our task; we did not see it as the personal affair of this or that individual. This was our chief connection with the times. Science itself is still evolving, and we are evolving with it. I shall indicate briefly the evolution of the formal method during these ten years:

1. From the original outline of the conflict of poetic language with practical we proceeded to differentiate the idea of practical language by its various functions (Jakubinsky) and to delimit the methods of poetic and emotional languages (Jakobson). Along with this we became interested in studying oratorical speech because it was close to practical speech but distinguished from it by function, and we spoke about the necessity of a revival of the poetic of rhetoric.

2. From the general idea of form, in its new sense, we proceeded to the idea of technique, and from here, to the idea of function.

3. From the idea of poetic rhythm as opposed to meter we proceeded to the idea of rhythm as a constructive element in the total poem and thus to an understanding of verse as a special form of speech having special linguistic (syntactical, lexical, and semantic) features.

4. From the idea of plot as structure we proceeded to an understanding of material in terms of its motivation, and from here to an understanding of material as an element participating in the construction but subordinate to the character of the dominant formal idea.

5. From the ascertainment of a single device applicable to various materials we proceeded to differentiate techniques according to function and from here to the question of the evolution of form—that is, to the problem of historical-literary study.

A whole new series of problems faces us, as Tynyanov's latest essay, *Literary Fact,* shows. Here the question of the relation between life and literature is posed, a question which many persons answer on the basis of a simple-minded dilettantism. Examples of how life becomes literature are shown and, conversely, of how literature passes into life: "During the period of its deterioration a given genre is shoved from the center toward the periphery, but in its place, from the trivia of literature, from literature's backyard, and from life itself, new phenomena flow into the center."

Although I deliberately called this essay *The Theory of the "Formal Method,"* I gave, obviously, a sketch of its evolution. We have no theory that can be laid out as a fixed, ready-made system. For us theory and history merge not only in words, but in fact. We are too well trained by history itself to think that it can be avoided. When we feel that we have a theory that explains everything, a ready-made theory explaining all past and future events and therefore needing neither evolution nor anything like it—then we must recognize that the formal method has come to an end, that the spirit of scientific investigation has departed from it. As yet, that has not happened.

Virginia Woolf

1882–1941

One of the major novelists of the twentieth century, Virginia Woolf was also a perceptive critical essayist who wrote frequently for the *Times Literary Supplement, The Dial, Life and Letters,* and other journals and newspapers. She wrote frequently on English women writers and on modern fiction, the best known of the latter being "Modern Fiction" and "Mr. Bennett and Mrs. Brown." Today, as an essayist she is, however, best known for her feminist writings in *A Room of One's Own* and *Three Guineas,* where she discusses directly the situation of women writers throughout modern history. Woolf's feminism always displayed its own kind of independence. She was a feminist who disliked the word "feminist," and she has been attacked by some feminists in later generations. She was not an activist and had some considerable skepticism about Emmeline Pankhurst's single minded emphasis on obtaining the vote. Woolf did not see it as a panacea. Her concerns were deeper, as any novelist's would be: men's anger at women, misunderstandings between the sexes, and above all the psychological conditions under which women—and men—were brought up. In this last respect she belongs to a tradition of writers on the subject going back to Mary Wollstonecraft (p. 394) and John Stuart Mill. Virtually all her novels touch on this matter, and *A Room of One's Own* deals with it directly. Woolf addresses the question of why a sister of Shakespeare would not likely have been able to write anything, let alone a play. She would have had none of the material resources—breadth of human experience, money, time—to do so. She would have been discouraged by everyone.

Woolf's feminism went in its own direction. It did not go beyond her own upper middle class and it held for important differences between men and women when the feminist trend of her time was toward absolute equality with men and the erasure of differences. Woolf held for radical changes that would or should occur as women's freedom and their suppressed values began to affect conceptions of power, family, and social life, in the past shaped by men. Woolf sometimes imagined a society in which men and women would come together in purpose and desire. Thus the theme of androgyny recurs in her work. Some recent feminist critics have wished that Woolf had given greater vent in her writings to her anger, but as the kind of writer she believed herself to be, she would have rejected this notion as a betrayal of her art and also of the effectiveness of her polemic, which gains much of its rhetorical strength from its ironic, and sometimes sarcastic, tone. However, *Three Guineas* seems to release more bitterness, though the cunning remains. Late in her career, she came somewhat to regret its presence, but it never entirely left her. In 1941, with the world on the brink of war, the avowed pacifist took her own life.

Virginia Woolf's many works are published by Hogarth Press. The *Collected Essays,* edited by Leonard Woolf in four volumes, appeared in 1966–1967. In addition to *A Room of One's Own,* see also *The Common Reader* (1925), *The Second Common*

Reader (1932), and *Three Guineas* (1938). See Harvena Richter, *Virginia Woolf: The Inward Voyage* (1970); Nancy Topping Bazin, *Virginia Woolf and the Androgynous Vision* (1973); Carolyn Heilburn, *Towards Androgyny: Aspects of Male and Female in Literature* (1973); Elaine Showalter, *A Literature of Their Own* (1977); several essays by Jane Marcus including " 'No More Horses': Virginia Woolf on Art and Propaganda," *Women Studies* 4 (1977) and "Art and Anger," *Feminist Studies* 4 (1978); Phyllis Rose, *Woman of Letters: A Life of Virginia Woolf* (1978); Jane Marcus, ed., *New Feminist Essays on Virginia Woolf* (1981); Jane Marcus, *Virginia Woolf: A Feminist Slant* (1983); Lyndall Gordon, *Virginia Woolf: A Writer's Life* (1984); and Alex Zwerdling, *Virginia Woolf and the Real World* (1986).

A Room of One's Own

Chapter 4

That one would find any woman in that state of mind in the sixteenth century was obviously impossible.[1] One has only to think of the Elizabethan tombstones with all those children kneeling with clasped hands; and their early deaths; and to see their houses with their dark, cramped rooms, to realise that no woman could have written poetry then. What one would expect to find would be that rather later perhaps some great lady would take advantage of her comparative freedom and comfort to publish something with her name to it and risk being thought a monster. Men, of course, are not snobs, I continued, carefully eschewing "the arrant feminism" of Miss Rebecca West;[2] but they appreciate with sympathy for the most part the efforts of a countess to write verse. One would expect to find a lady of title meeting with far greater encouragement than an unknown Miss Austen or a Miss Brontë at that time would have met with. But one would also expect to find that her mind was disturbed by alien emotions like fear and hatred and that her poems showed traces of that disturbance. Here is Lady Winchilsea,[3] for example, I thought, taking down her poems. She was born in the year 1661; she was noble both by birth and by marriage; she was childless; she wrote poetry, and one has only to open her poetry to find her bursting out in indignation against the position of women:

> *How are we fallen! fallen by mistaken rules,*
> *And Education's more than Nature's fools;*
> *Debarred from all improvements of the mind,*
> *And to be dull, expected and designed;*
> *And if some one would soar above the rest,*
> *With warmer fancy, and ambition pressed,*
> *So strong the opposing faction still appears,*
> *The hopes to thrive can ne'er outweigh the fears.*

Clearly her mind has by no means "consumed all impediments and become incandescent." On the contrary, it is harrassed and distracted with hates and grievances. The human race is split up for her into two parties. Men are the "opposing faction"; men are hated and feared, because they have the power to bar her way to what she wants to do—which is to write.

> *Alas! a woman that attempts the pen,*
> *Such a presumptuous creature is esteemed,*
> *The fault can by no virtue be redeemed.*
> *They tell us we mistake our sex and way;*
> *Good breeding, fashion, dancing, dressing, play,*
> *Are the accomplishments we should desire;*
> *To write, or read, or think, or to enquire,*
> *Would cloud our beauty, and exhaust our time,*
> *And interrupt the conquests of our prime,*
> *Whilst the dull manage of a servile house*
> *Is held by some our utmost art and use.*

Indeed she has to encourage herself to write by supposing that what she writes will never be published; to soothe herself with the sad chant:

A ROOM OF ONE'S OWN. The lectures which comprise this book were given at Girton College, Cambridge, in October 1928. Reprinted from Chapter Four of *A Room of One's Own,* Copyright © Harcourt Brace, 1929. © 1957 by Leonard Woolf. Reprinted by permission of the publisher.

[1] In the previous chapter Woolf imagines what the fate of an extraordinarily gifted sister of Shakespeare might have been. She then characterizes Shakespeare's mind as "incandescent" and "unimpeded."

[2] Pseudonym of Cecily Fairfield (1892–1983), English novelist and critic.

[3] Anne Finch, Countess of Winchilsea (1661–1720), English poet.

> *To some few friends, and to thy sorrows sing,*
> *For groves of laurel thou wert never meant;*
> *Be dark enough thy shades, and be thou there content.*

Yet it is clear that could she have freed her mind from hate and fear and not heaped it with bitterness and resentment, the fire was hot within her. Now and again words issue of pure poetry:

> *Nor will in fading silks compose,*
> *Faintly the inimitable rose.*

—they are rightly praised by Mr. Murry, and Pope, it is thought, remembered and appropriated those others:

> *Now the jonquille o'ercomes the feeble brain;*
> *We faint beneath the aromatic pain.*

It was a thousand pities that the woman who could write like that, whose mind was turned to nature and reflection, should have been forced to anger and bitterness. But how could she have helped herself? I asked, imagining the sneers and the laughter, the adulation of the toadies, the scepticism of the professional poet. She must have shut herself up in a room in the country to write, and been torn asunder by bitterness and scruples perhaps, though her husband was of the kindest, and their married life perfection. She "must have," I say, because when one comes to seek out the facts about Lady Winchilsea, one finds, as usual, that almost nothing is known about her. She suffered terribly from melancholy, which we can explain at least to some extent when we find her telling us how in the grip of it she would imagine:

> *My lines decried, and my employment thought,*
> *An useless folly or presumptuous fault:*

The employment, which was thus censured, was, as far as one can see, the harmless one of rambling about the fields and dreaming:

> *My hand delights to trace unusual things,*
> *And deviates from the known and common way,*
> *Nor will in fading silks compose,*
> *Faintly the inimitable rose.*

Naturally, if that was her habit and that was her delight, she could only expect to be laughed at; and, accordingly, Pope or Gay is said to have satirised her "as a blue-stocking with an itch for scribbling." Also it is thought that she offended Gay by laughing at him. She said that his *Trivia* showed that "he was more proper to walk before a chair than to ride in one." But this is all "dubious gossip" and, says Mr. Murry,[4] "uninteresting." But there I do not agree with him, for I should have liked to have had more even of dubious gossip so that I might have found out or made up some image of this melancholy lady, who loved wandering in the fields and thinking about unusual things and scorned, so rashly, so unwisely, "the dull manage of a servile house." But she became diffuse, Mr. Murry says. Her gift is all grown about with weeds and bound with briars. It had no chance of showing itself for the fine distinguished gift it was. And so, putting her back on the shelf, I turned to the other great lady, the Duchess whom Lamb loved, hare-brained, fantastical Margaret of Newcastle,[5] her elder, but her contemporary. They were very different, but alike in this that both were noble and both childless, and both were married to the best of husbands. In both burnt the same passion for poetry and both are disfigured and deformed by the same causes. Open the Duchess and one finds the same outburst of rage, "Women live like Bats or Owls, labour like Beasts, and die like Worms. . . ." Margaret too might have been a poet; in our day all that activity would have turned a wheel of some sort. As it was, what could bind, tame or civilise for human use that wild, generous, untutored intelligence? It poured itself out, higgledy-piggledy, in torrents of rhyme and prose, poetry and philosophy which stand congealed in quartos and folios that nobody ever reads. She should have had a microscope put in her hand. She should have been taught to look at the stars and reason scientifically. Her wits were turned with solitude and freedom. No one checked her. No one taught her. The professors fawned on her. At Court they jeered at her. Sir Egerton Brydges complained of her coarseness—"as flowing from a female of high rank brought up in the Courts." She shut herself up at Welbeck alone.

What a vision of loneliness and riot the thought of Margaret Cavendish brings to mind! as if some giant cucumber had spread itself over all the roses and carnations in the garden and choked them to death. What a waste that the woman who wrote "the best bred women are those whose minds are civilest" should have frittered her time away scribbling nonsense and plunging ever deeper into obscurity and folly till the people crowded round her coach when she issued out. Evidently the crazy Duchess became a bogey to frighten clever girls with. Here, I remembered, putting away the

---

[4]John Middleton Murry (1889–1957), English critic.
[5]Margaret Cavendish, Duchess of Newcastle (1624–1674), English author.

Duchess and opening Dorothy Osborne's letters, is Dorothy writing to Temple about the Duchess's new book. "Sure the poore woman is a little distracted, shee could never bee soe rediculous else as to venture at writeing book's and in verse too, if I should not sleep this fortnight I should not come to that."[6]

And so, since no woman of sense and modesty could write books, Dorothy, who was sensitive and melancholy, the very opposite of the Duchess in temper, wrote nothing. Letters did not count. A woman might write letters while she was sitting by her father's sick-bed. She could write them by the fire whilst the men talked without disturbing them. The strange thing is, I thought, turning over the pages of Dorothy's letters, what a gift that untaught and solitary girl had for the framing of a sentence, for the fashioning of a scene. Listen to her running on:

"After dinner wee sitt and talk till Mr. B. com's in question and then I am gon. The heat of the day is spent in reading or working and about sixe or seven a Clock, I walke out into a Common that lyes hard by the house where a great many young wenches keep Sheep and Cow's and sitt in the shades singing of Ballads; I goe to them and compare their voyces and Beauty's to some Ancient Shepherdesses that I have read of and finde a vaste difference there, but trust mee I think these are as innocent as those could bee. I talke to them, and finde they want nothing to make them the happiest People in the world, but the knoledge that they are soe. most commonly when we are in the middest of our discourse one looks aboute her and spyes her Cow's goeing into the Corne and then away they all run, as if they had wing's at theire heels. I that am not soe nimble stay behinde, and when I see them driveing home theire Cattle I think tis time for mee to retyre too. when I have supped I goe into the Garden and soe to the syde of a small River that runs by it where I sitt downe and wish you with mee. . . ."

One could have sworn that she had the makings of a writer in her. But "if I should not sleep this fortnight I should not come to that"—one can measure the opposition that was in the air to a woman writing when one finds that even a woman with a great turn for writing has brought herself to believe that to write a book was to be ridiculous, even to show oneself distracted. And so we come, I continued, replacing the single short volume of Dorothy Osborne's letters upon the shelf, to Mrs. Behn.

And with Mrs. Behn we turn a very important corner on the road. We leave behind, shut up in their parks among their folios, those solitary great ladies who wrote without audience or criticism, for their own delight alone. We come to town and rub shoulders with ordinary people in the streets. Mrs. Behn was a middle-class woman with all the plebeian virtues of humour, vitality and courage; a woman forced by the death of her husband and some unfortunate adventures of her own to make her living by her wits. She had to work on equal terms with men. She made, by working very hard, enough to live on. The importance of that fact outweighs anything that she actually wrote, even the splendid "A Thousand Martyrs I have made," or "Love in Fantastic Triumph sat," for here begins the freedom of the mind, or rather the possibility that in the course of time the mind will be free to write what it likes. For now that Aphra Behn had done it, girls could go to their parents and say, You need not give me an allowance; I can make money by my pen. Of course the answer for many years to come was, Yes, by living the life of Aphra Behn! Death would be better! and the door was slammed faster than ever. That profoundly interesting subject, the value that men set upon women's chastity and its effect upon their education, here suggests itself for discussion, and might provide an interesting book if any student at Girton or Newnham cared to go into the matter. Lady Dudley, sitting in diamonds among the midges of a Scottish moor, might serve for frontispiece. Lord Dudley, *The Times* said when Lady Dudley died the other day, "a man of cultivated taste and many accomplishments, was benevolent and bountiful, but whimsically despotic. He insisted upon his wife's wearing full dress, even at the remotest shooting-lodge in the Highlands; he loaded her with gorgeous jewels," and so on, "he gave her everything—always excepting any measure of responsibility." Then Lord Dudley had a stroke and she nursed him and ruled his estates with supreme confidence for ever after. That whimsical despotism was in the nineteenth century too.

But to return. Aphra Behn proved that money could be made by writing at the sacrifice, perhaps, of certain agreeable qualities; and so by degrees writing became not merely a sign of folly and a distracted mind, but was of practical importance. A husband might die, or some disaster overtake the family. Hundreds of women began as the eighteenth century drew on to add to their pin money, or to come to the rescue of their families by making translations or writing the innumerable bad novels which have ceased to be recorded even in text-books, but are to be picked up in the fourpenny boxes in the Charing Cross Road. The extreme activity of mind which showed itself in the later eighteenth century among women—the talking, and the meeting, the writing of essays on Shakespeare, the translating of the classics—was founded on the solid fact that women could make money by

6(1627–1695), writer of letters to her husband-to-be, Sir William Temple (1628–1699), English statesman and author. Woolf's essay on Osborne's letters appears in *The Second Common Reader.*

writing. Money dignifies what is frivolous if unpaid for. It might still be well to sneer at "blue stockings with an itch for scribbling," but it could not be denied that they could put money in their purses. Thus, towards the end of the eighteenth century a change came about which, if I were rewriting history, I should describe more fully and think of greater importance than the Crusades or the Wars of the Roses. The middle-class woman began to write. For if *Pride and Prejudice* matters, and *Middlemarch* and *Villette* and *Wuthering Heights* matter, then it matters far more than I can prove in an hour's discourse that women generally, and not merely the lonely aristocrat shut up in her country house among her folios and her flatterers, took to writing. Without those forerunners, Jane Austen and the Brontës and George Eliot could no more have written than Shakespeare could have written without Marlowe, or Marlowe without Chaucer, or Chaucer without those forgotten poets who paved the ways and tamed the natural savagery of the tongue. For masterpieces are not single and solitary births; they are the outcome of many years of thinking in common, of thinking by the body of the people, so that the experience of the mass is behind the single voice. Jane Austen should have laid a wreath upon the grave of Fanny Burney, and George Eliot done homage to the robust shade of Eliza Carter—the valiant old woman who tied a bell to her bedstead in order that she might wake early and learn Greek. All women together ought to let flowers fall upon the tomb of Aphra Behn which is, most scandalously but rather appropriately, in Westminster Abbey, for it was she who earned them the right to speak their minds. It is she—shady and amorous as she was—who makes it not quite fantastic for me to say to you tonight: Earn five hundred a year by your wits.

Here, then, one had reached the early nineteenth century. And here, for the first time, I found several shelves given up entirely to the works of women. But why, I could not help asking, as I ran my eyes over them, were they, with very few exceptions, all novels? The original impulse was to poetry. The "supreme head of song" was a poetess. Both in France and in England the women poets precede the women novelists. Moreover, I thought, looking at the four famous names, what had George Eliot in common with Emily Brontë? Did not Charlotte Brontë fail entirely to understand Jane Austen? Save for the possibly relevant fact that not one of them had a child, four more incongruous characters could not have met together in a room—so much so that it is tempting to invent a meeting and a dialogue between them. Yet by some strange force they were all compelled, when they wrote, to write novels. Had it something to do with being born of the middle class, I asked; and with the fact, which Miss Emily Davies a little later was so strikingly to demon-

strate, that the middleclass family in the early nineteenth century was possessed only of a single sitting-room between them? If a woman wrote, she would have to write in the common sitting-room. And, as Miss Nightingale was so vehemently to complain,—"women never have an half hour . . . that they can call their own"—she was always interrupted. Still it would be easier to write prose and fiction there than to write poetry or a play. Less concentration is required. Jane Austen wrote like that to the end of her days. "How she was able to effect all this," her nephew writes in his Memoir, "is surprising, for she had no separate study to repair to, and most of the work must have been done in the general sitting-room, subject to all kinds of casual interruptions. She was careful that her occupation should not be suspected by servants or visitors or any persons beyond her own family party."[7] Jane Austen hid her manuscripts or covered them with a piece of blotting-paper. Then, again, all the literary training that a woman had in the early nineteenth century was training in the observation of character, in the analysis of emotion. Her sensibility had been educated for centuries by the influences of the common sitting-room. People's feelings were impressed on her; personal relations were always before her eyes. Therefore, when the middle-class woman took to writing, she naturally wrote novels, even though, as seems evident enough, two of the four famous women here named were not by nature novelists. Emily Brontë should have written poetic plays; the overflow of George Eliot's capacious mind should have spread itself when the creative impulse was spent upon history or biography. They wrote novels, however; one may even go further, I said, taking *Pride and Prejudice* from the shelf, and say that they wrote good novels. Without boasting or giving pain to the opposite sex, one may say that *Pride and Prejudice* is a good book. At any rate, one would not have been ashamed to have been caught in the act of writing *Pride and Prejudice*. Yet Jane Austen was glad that a hinge creaked, so that she might hide her manuscript before any one came in. To Jane Austen there was something discreditable in writing *Pride and Prejudice*. And, I wondered, would *Pride and Prejudice* have been a better novel if Jane Austen had not thought it necessary to hide her manuscript from visitors? I read a page or two to see; but I could not find any signs that her circumstances had harmed her work in the slightest. That, perhaps, was the chief miracle about it. Here was a woman about the year 1800 writing without hate, without bitterness, without fear, without protest, without preaching. That was how Shake-

---

[7][Woolf] *Memoir* of Jane Austen, by her nephew, James Edward Austen-Leigh.

speare wrote, I thought, looking at *Antony and Cleopatra;* and when people compare Shakespeare and Jane Austen, they may mean that the minds of both had consumed all impediments; and for that reason we do not know Jane Austen and we do not know Shakespeare, and for that reason Jane Austen pervades every word that she wrote, and so does Shakespeare.[8] If Jane Austen suffered in any way from her circumstances it was in the narrowness of life that was imposed upon her. It was impossible for a woman to go about alone. She never travelled; she never drove through London in an omnibus or had luncheon in a shop by herself. But perhaps it was the nature of Jane Austen not to want what she had not. Her gift and her circumstances matched each other completely. But I doubt whether that was true of Charlotte Brontë, I said, opening *Jane Eyre* and laying it beside *Pride and Prejudice.*

I opened it at chapter twelve and my eye was caught by the phrase, "Anybody may blame me who likes." What were they blaming Charlotte Brontë for, I wondered? And I read how Jane Eyre used to go up on to the roof when Mrs. Fairfax was making jellies and looked over the fields at the distant view. And then she longed—and it was for this that they blamed her—that "then I longed for a power of vision which might overpass that limit; which might reach the busy world, towns, regions full of life I had heard of but never seen: that then I desired more of practical experience than I possessed; more of intercourse with my kind, of acquaintance with variety of character than was here within my reach. I valued what was good in Mrs. Fairfax, and what was good in Adèle; but I believed in the existence of other and more vivid kinds of goodness, and what I believed in I wished to behold.

"Who blames me? Many, no doubt, and I shall be called discontented. I could not help it: the restlessness was in my nature; it agitated me to pain sometimes. . . .

"It is vain to say human beings ought to be satisfied with tranquillity: they must have action; and they will make it if they cannot find it. Millions are condemned to a stiller doom than mine, and millions are in silent revolt against their lot. Nobody knows how many rebellions ferment in the masses of life which people earth. Women are supposed to be very calm generally: but women feel just as men feel; they need exercise for their faculties and a field for their efforts as much as their brothers do; they suffer from too rigid a restraint, too absolute a stagnation, precisely as men would

suffer; and it is narrow-minded in their more privileged fellow-creatures to say that they ought to confine themselves to making puddings and knitting stockings, to playing on the piano and embroidering bags. It is thoughtless to condemn them, or laugh at them, if they seek to do more or learn more than custom has pronounced necessary for their sex.

"When thus alone I not unfrequently heard Grace Poole's laugh. . . ."

That is an awkward break, I thought. It is upsetting to come upon Grace Poole all of a sudden. The continuity is disturbed. One might say, I continued, laying the book down beside *Pride and Prejudice,* that the woman who wrote those pages had more genius in her than Jane Austen; but if one reads them over and marks that jerk in them, that indignation, one sees that she will never get her genius expressed whole and entire. Her books will be deformed and twisted. She will write in a rage where she should write calmly. She will write foolishly where she should write wisely. She will write of herself where she should write of her characters. She is at war with her lot. How could she help but die young, cramped and thwarted?

One could not but play for a moment with the thought of what might have happened if Charlotte Brontë had possessed say three hundred a year—but the foolish woman sold the copyright of her novels outright for fifteen hundred pounds; had somehow possessed more knowledge of the busy world, and towns and regions full of life; more practical experience, and intercourse with her kind and acquaintance with a variety of character. In those words she puts her finger exactly not only upon her own defects as a novelist but upon those of her sex at that time. She knew, no one better, how enormously her genius would have profited if it had not spent itself in solitary visions over distant fields; if experience and intercourse and travel had been granted her. But they were not granted; they were withheld; and we must accept the fact that all those good novels, *Villette, Emma, Wuthering Heights, Middlemarch,* were written by women without more experience of life than could enter the house of a respectable clergyman; written too in the common sitting-room of that respectable house and by women so poor that they could not afford to buy more than a few quires of paper at a time upon which to write *Wuthering Heights* or *Jane Eyre.* One of them, it is true, George Eliot, escaped after much tribulation, but only to a secluded villa in St. John's Wood. And there she settled down in the shadow of the world's disapproval. "I wish it to be understood," she wrote, "that I should never invite any one to come and see me who did not ask for the invitation"; for was she not living in sin with a married man and might not the sight of her damage the chastity of Mrs. Smith or whoever it might be that

---

chanced to call? One must submit to the social convention, and be "cut off from what is called the world." At the same time, on the other side of Europe, there was a young man living freely with this gipsy or with that great lady; going to the wars; picking up unhindered and uncensored all that varied experience of human life which served him so splendidly later when he came to write his books. Had Tolstoi lived at the Priory in seclusion with a married lady "cut off from what is called the world," however edifying the moral lesson, he could scarcely, I thought, have written *War and Peace*.

But one could perhaps go a little deeper into the question of novel-writing and the effect of sex upon the novelist. If one shuts one's eyes and thinks of the novel as a whole, it would seem to be a creation owning a certain looking-glass likeness to life, though of course with simplifications and distortions innumerable. At any rate, it is a structure leaving a shape on the mind's eye, built now in squares, now pagoda shaped, now throwing out wings and arcades, now solidly compact and domed like the Cathedral of Saint Sofia at Constantinople. This shape, I thought, thinking back over certain famous novels, starts in one the kind of emotion that is appropriate to it. But that emotion at once blends itself with others, for the "shape" is not made by the relation of stone to stone, but by the relation of human being to human being. Thus a novel starts in us all sorts of antagonistic and opposed emotions. Life conflicts with something that is not life. Hence the difficulty of coming to any agreement about novels, and the immense sway that our private prejudices have upon us. On the one hand, we feel You—John the hero—must live, or I shall be in the depths of despair. On the other, we feel, Alas, John, you must die, because the shape of the book requires it. Life conflicts with something that is not life. Then since life it is in part, we judge it as life. James is the sort of man I most detest, one says. Or, This is a farrago of absurdity. I could never feel anything of the sort myself. The whole structure, it is obvious, thinking back on any famous novel, is one of infinite complexity, because it is thus made up of so many different judgments, of so many different kinds of emotion. The wonder is that any book so composed holds together for more than a year or two, or can possibly mean to the English reader what it means for the Russian or the Chinese. But they do hold together occasionally very remarkably. And what holds them together in these rare instances of survival (I was thinking of *War and Peace*) is something that one calls integrity, though it has nothing to do with paying one's bills or behaving honourably in an emergency. What one means by integrity, in the case of the novelist, is the conviction that he gives one that this is the truth. Yes, one feels, I should never have thought that this could be so; I have never known people behaving like that. But you have convinced me that so it is, so it happens. One holds every phrase, every scene to the light as one reads—for Nature seems, very oddly, to have provided us with an inner light by which to judge of the novelist's integrity or disintegrity. Or perhaps it is rather that Nature, in her most irrational mood, has traced in invisible ink on the walls of the mind a premonition which these great artists confirm; a sketch which only needs to be held to the fire of genius to become visible. When one so exposes it and sees it come to life one exclaims in rapture, But this is what I have always felt and known and desired! And one boils over with excitement, and, shutting the book even with a kind of reverence as if it were something very precious, a stand-by to return to as long as one lives, one puts it back on the shelf, I said, taking *War and Peace* and putting it back in its place. If, on the other hand, these poor sentences that one takes and tests rouse first a quick and eager response with their bright colouring and their dashing gestures but there they stop: something seems to check them in their development: or if they bring to light only a faint scribble in that corner and a blot over there, and nothing appears whole and entire, then one heaves a sigh of disappointment and says, Another failure. This novel has come to grief somewhere.

And for the most part, of course, novels do come to grief somewhere. The imagination falters under the enormous strain. The insight is confused; it can no longer distinguish between the true and the false; it has no longer the strength to go on with the vast labour that calls at every moment for the use of so many different faculties. But how would all this be affected by the sex of the novelist, I wondered, looking at *Jane Eyre* and the others. Would the fact of her sex in any way interfere with the integrity of a woman novelist—that integrity which I take to be the backbone of the writer? Now, in the passages I have quoted from *Jane Eyre,* it is clear that anger was tampering with the integrity of Charlotte Brontë the novelist. She left her story, to which her entire devotion was due, to attend to some personal grievance. She remembered that she had been starved of her proper due of experience—she had been made to stagnate in a parsonage mending stockings when she wanted to wander free over the world. Her imagination swerved from indignation and we feel it swerve. But there were many more influences than anger tugging at her imagination and deflecting it from its path. Ignorance, for instance. The portrait of Rochester is drawn in the dark. We feel the influence of fear in it; just as we constantly feel an acidity which is the result of oppression, a buried suffering smouldering beneath her passion, a rancour which contracts those books, splendid as they are, with a spasm of pain.

And since a novel has this correspondence to real life, its values are to some extent those of real life. But it is obvious that the values of women differ very often from the values which have been made by the other sex; naturally, this is so. Yet it is the masculine values that prevail. Speaking crudely, football and sport are "important"; the worship of fashion, the buying of clothes "trivial." And these values are inevitably transferred from life to fiction. This is an important book, the critic assumes, because it deals with war. This is an insignificant book because it deals with the feelings of women in a drawing-room. A scene in a battlefield is more important than a scene in a shop—everywhere and much more subtly the difference of value persists. The whole structure, therefore, of the early nineteenth-century novel was raised, if one was a woman, by a mind which was slightly pulled from the straight, and made to alter its clear vision in deference to external authority. One has only to skim those old forgotten novels and listen to the tone of voice in which they are written to divine that the writer was meeting criticism; she was saying this by way of aggression, or that by way of conciliation. She was admitting that she was "only a woman," or protesting that she was "as good as a man." She met that criticism as her temperament dictated, with docility and diffidence, or with anger and emphasis. It does not matter which it was; she was thinking of something other than the thing itself. Down comes her book upon our heads. There was a flaw in the centre of it. And I thought of all the women's novels that lie scattered, like small pock-marked apples in an orchard, about the secondhand book shops of London. It was the flaw in the centre that had rotted them. She had altered her values in deference to the opinion of others.

But how impossible it must have been for them not to budge either to the right or to the left. What genius, what integrity it must have required in face of all that criticism, in the midst of that purely patriarchal society, to hold fast to the thing as they saw it without shrinking. Only Jane Austen did it and Emily Brontë. It is another feather, perhaps the finest, in their caps. They wrote as women write, not as men write. Of all the thousand women who wrote novels then, they alone entirely ignored the perpetual admonitions of the eternal pedagogue—write this, think that. They alone were deaf to that persistent voice, now grumbling, now patronising, now domineering, now grieved, now shocked, now angry, now avuncular, that voice which cannot let women alone, but must be at them, like some too conscientious governess, adjuring them, like Sir Egerton Brydges, to be refined; dragging even into the criticism of poetry criticism of sex;[9] ad-

monishing them, if they would be good and win, as I suppose, some shiny prize, to keep within certain limits which the gentleman in question thinks suitable: ". . . female novelists should only aspire to excellence by courageously acknowledging the limitations of their sex."[10] That puts the matter in a nutshell, and when I tell you, rather to your surprise, that this sentence was written not in August 1828 but in August 1928, you will agree, I think, that however delightful it is to us now, it represents a vast body of opinion—I am not going to stir those old pools, I take only what chance has floated to my feet—that was far more vigorous and far more vocal a century ago. It would have needed a very stalwart young woman in 1828 to disregard all those snubs and chidings and promises of prizes. One must have been something of a firebrand to say to oneself, Oh, but they can't buy literature too. Literature is open to everybody. I refuse to allow you, Beadle though you are, to turn me off the grass.[11] Lock up your libraries if you like; but there is no gate, no lock, no bolt that you can set upon the freedom of my mind.

But whatever effect discouragement and criticism had upon their writing—and I believe that they had a very great effect—that was unimportant compared with the other difficulty which faced them (I was still considering those early nineteenth-century novelists) when they came to set their thoughts on paper—that is that they had no tradition behind them, or one so short and partial that it was of little help. For we think back through our mothers if we are women. It is useless to go to the great men writers for help, however much one may go to them for pleasure. Lamb, Browne, Thackeray, Newman, Sterne, Dickens, De Quincey—whoever it may be—never helped a woman yet, though she may have learnt a few tricks of them and adapted them to her use. The weight, the pace, the stride of a man's mind are too unlike her own for her to lift anything substantial from him successfully. The ape is too distant to be sedulous. Perhaps the first thing she would find, setting pen to paper, was that there was no common sentence ready for her use. All the great novelists like Thackeray and Dickens and Balzac have written a natural prose, swift but not slovenly, expressive but not precious, taking their own tint without ceasing to be common property. They have based it on the sentence that was current at the time. The sentence that was current at the beginning of the nineteenth century ran something like this perhaps: "The grandeur of their works was an argument with them, not to

---

[9][Woolf] "[She] has a metaphysical purpose, and that is a dangerous obsession, especially with a woman, for women rarely possess men's healthy love of rhetoric. It is a strange lack in the sex which is in other things more primitive and more materialistic." *New Criterion,* June 1928.

[10][Woolf] "If, like the reporter, you believe that female novelists should only aspire to excellence by courageously acknowledging the limitations of their sex (Jane Austen [has] demonstrated how gracefully this gesture can be accomplished). . . ." *Life and Letters,* August 1928.

[11]*A Room of One's Own* begins with a brief account of Woolf's having been turned off the grass as an outsider when she visited "Oxbridge" and then having been forbidden the library because unaccompanied by a Fellow or not possessing a letter of introduction.

stop short, but to proceed. They could have no higher excitement or satisfaction than in the exercise of their art and endless generations of truth and beauty. Success prompts to exertion; and habit facilitates success." That is a man's sentence; behind it one can see Johnson, Gibbon and the rest. It was a sentence that was unsuited for a woman's use. Charlotte Brontë, with all her splendid gift for prose, stumbled and fell with that clumsy weapon in her hands. George Eliot committed atrocities with it that beggar description. Jane Austen looked at it and laughed at it and devised a perfectly natural, shapely sentence proper for her own use and never departed from it. Thus, with less genius for writing than Charlotte Brontë, she got infinitely more said. Indeed, since freedom and fullness of expression are of the essence of the art, such a lack of tradition, such a scarcity and inadequacy of tools, must have told enormously upon the writing of women. Moreover, a book is not made of sentences laid end to end, but of sentences built, if an image helps, into arcades or domes. And this shape too has been made by men out of their own needs for their own uses. There is no reason to think that the form of the epic or of the poetic play suits a woman any more than the sentence suits her. But all the older forms of literature were hardened and set by the time she became a writer. The novel alone was young enough to be soft in her hands—another reason, perhaps, why she wrote novels. Yet who shall say that even now "the novel" (I give it inverted commas to mark my sense of the words' inadequacy), who shall say that even this most pliable of all forms is rightly shaped for her use? No doubt we shall find her knocking that into shape for herself when she has the free use of her limbs; and providing some new vehicle, not necessarily in verse, for the poetry in her. For it is the poetry that is still denied outlet. And I went on to ponder how a woman nowadays would write a poetic tragedy in five acts—would she use verse—would she not use prose rather?

But these are difficult questions which lie in the twilight of the future. I must leave them, if only because they stimulate me to wander from my subject into trackless forests where I shall be lost and, very likely, devoured by wild beasts. I do not want, and I am sure that you do not want me, to broach that very dismal subject, the future of fiction, so that I will only pause here one moment to draw your attention to the great part which must be played in that future so far as women are concerned by physical conditions. The book has somehow to be adapted to the body, and at a venture one would say that women's books should be shorter, more concentrated, than those of men, and framed so that they do not need long hours of steady and uninterrupted work. For interruptions there will always be. Again, the nerves that feed the brain would seem to differ in men and women, and if you are going to make them work their best and hardest, you must find out what treatment suits them—whether these hours of lectures, for instance, which the monks devised, presumably, hundreds of years ago, suit them—what alternations of work and rest they need, interpreting rest not as doing nothing but as doing something but something that is different; and what should that difference be? All this should be discussed and discovered; all this is part of the question of women and fiction. And yet, I continued, approaching the bookcase again, where shall I find that elaborate study of the psychology of women by a woman? If through their incapacity to play football women are not going to be allowed to practise medicine—

Happily my thoughts were now given another turn.

I. A. Richards

1893–1979

The influence of Richards on critical theory and practice early in the twentieth century was as great as that of Eliot. He first developed his position in *Principles of Literary Criticism,* published in 1924. *Science and Poetry* followed in 1926 and *Practical Criticism* in 1929. A psychologist and semanticist, Richards displays an interest in the effect of poems on the reader and, like Arnold, in the possible cultural or therapeutic role of poetry. He tends to locate the poem in the reader's response to it. A poem is, in effect, the experience that the "right kind of reader" has when he reads. Richards does not discuss the old problem enunciated by Hume of finding the right reader. To consider a poem is, for Richards, to consider the "structure of experience" of reading it. Even so, he claims that it is not what the poem *says* but what it *is* that counts. Its *being,* however, seems to exist only in the reader. This raises two questions: to what do we refer each reader's separate response, and is one reader's response as accurate as another's? It is much more difficult to discuss the structure of an experience than to consider the poem as a structure of words that has some autonomy from the experiencing of the words.

Having located the poem in the reader, Richards finds the poem's value in the nature of the right response to it. He believes that balancing and organizing conflicting impulses is characteristic of the experience of poetry and that this experience has particular value in an age during which canons of moral and social authority are crumbling. In a transitional culture the conquest of warring impulses is more difficult than in a reasonably static one. Poetry is a form of words that releases or organizes our impulses and attitudes. According to the argument of *Science and Poetry,* poetry is effective because it is composed of "pseudostatements"; these may be entertained in a different way from unpoetic statements, which we can refer to empirical evidence. Richards sees poetry as a way of satisfying a need to "cut our pseudostatements free from belief, and yet retain them, in this released state, as the main instruments by which we order our attitudes as to one another and to the world." This matter is taken up, though not with the same terms, in the second selection, "Doctrine in Poetry." The first selection, "The Four Kinds of Meaning," concerns the elements that go to make up the communication with the reader.

It is not surprising that with his theory of the balancing of conflicting impulses Richards should value most highly a poetry of "irony," of "bringing in the opposite." In this preference he is aligned with Eliot and the later New Critics, Ransom, Brooks, Warren, and Tate.

Richards' critical works include *The Foundations of Aesthetics,* with C. K. Ogden (1922), *Principles of Literary Criticism* (1924), *Science and Poetry* (1926), *The Meaning of Meaning: A Study of the Influence of Language Upon Thought and of the Science of Symbolism,* with C. K. Ogden, rev. ed. (1927), *Practical Criticism* (1929),

Mencius on the Mind (1932), *Coleridge on Imagination* (1934), *The Philosophy of Rhetoric* (1936), *Interpretation in Teaching* (1938), and *How to Read a Page* (1942). For commentary on Richards consult J. C. Ransom, *The New Criticism* (1941); R. S. Crane, "I. A. Richards on the Art of Interpretation," in his *Critics and Criticism* (1952); Murray Krieger, *The New Apologists for Poetry* (1956); M. H. Abrams, ed., *Literature and Belief* (1958); W. H. N. Hotopf, *Language, Thought, and Comprehension* (1965); J. P. Schiller, *I. A. Richards' Theory of Literature* (1970); John Needham, *The Completest Mode: I. A. Richards and the Continuity of English Literary Criticism* (1982); and John Paul Russo, *I. A. Richards: His Life and Work* (1989).

Practical Criticism

From

Chapter I

The Four Kinds of Meaning

The all-important fact for the study of literature—or any other mode of communication—is that there are several kinds of meaning. Whether we know and intend it or not, we are all jugglers when we converse, keeping the billiard balls in the air while we balance the cue on our nose. Whether we are active, as in speech or writing, or passive,[1] as readers or listeners, the total meaning we are engaged with is, almost always, a blend, a combination of several contributory meanings of different types. Language—and preeminently language as it is used in poetry—has not one but several tasks to perform simultaneously, and we shall misconceive most of the difficulties of criticism unless we understand this point and take note of the differences between these functions. For our purposes here a division into four types of function, four kinds of meaning, will suffice.

It is plain that most human utterances and nearly all articulate speech can be profitably regarded from four points of view. Four aspects can be easily distinguished. Let us call them *sense, feeling, tone,* and *intention.*

I. Sense

We speak *to say something,* and when we listen we expect something to be said. We use words to direct our hearers' attention upon some state of affairs, to present to them some items for consideration and to excite in them some thoughts about these items.

II. Feeling[2]

But we also, as a rule, have some feelings *about these items,* about the state of affairs we are referring to. We have an attitude towards it, some special direction, bias, or accentuation of interest towards it, some personal flavor or coloring of feeling; and we use language to *express* these feelings, this nuance of interest. Equally, when we listen we pick it up, rightly or wrongly; it seems inextricably part of what we receive; and this whether the speaker be conscious himself of his feelings towards what he is talking about or not. I am, of course, here describing the normal situation; my reader will be able without difficulty to think of exceptional cases (mathematics for example) where no feeling enters.

III. Tone

Furthermore, the speaker has ordinarily *an attitude to his listener.* He chooses or arranges his words differently as his audience varies, in automatic or deliberate *recognition of his relation to them.* The tone of his utterance reflects his awareness of this relation, his sense of how he stands towards those he is addressing. Again the exceptional case of dissimulation, or instances in which the speaker unwittingly reveals

---

PRACTICAL CRITICISM. Richards' *Practical Criticism* was first published in 1929. The text is from *Practical Criticism* (New York: Harcourt Brace Jovanovich, 1929). Reprinted by permission of the publisher and Routledge & Kegan Paul Ltd.

[1][Richards] Relatively, or technically, "passive" only; a fact that our protocols will help us not to forget. The reception (or interpretation) of a meaning is an activity, which may go astray; in fact, there is always some degree of loss and distortion in transmission. For an account of "understanding" see Part IV, section 13.

[2][Richards] Under *feeling* I group for convenience the whole conative-affective aspect of life—emotions, emotional attitudes, the will, desire, pleasure-unpleasure, and the rest. *Feeling* is shorthand for any or all of this.

an attitude he is not consciously desirous of expressing, will come to mind.

IV. Intention[3]

Finally, apart from what he says (sense), his attitude to what he is talking about (feeling), and his attitude to his listener (tone), there is the speaker's intention, his aim, *conscious or unconscious,* the effect he is endeavoring to promote. Ordinarily he speaks for a purpose, and his purpose modifies his speech. The understanding of it is part of the whole business of apprehending his meaning. Unless we know what he is trying to do, we can hardly estimate the measure of his success. Yet the number of readers who omit such considerations might make a fainthearted writer despair. Sometimes, of course, he will purpose no more than to state his thoughts (I), or to express his feelings about what he is thinking of, e.g. Hurrah! Damn! (II), or to express his attitude to his listener (III). With this last case we pass into the realm of endearments and abuse.

Frequently his intention operates through and satisfies itself in a combination of the other functions. Yet it has effects not reducible to their effects. It may govern the stress laid upon points in an argument for example, shape the arrangement, and even call attention to itself in such phrases as *for contrast's sake* or *lest it be supposed.* It controls the plot in the largest sense of the word, and is at work whenever the author is "hiding his hand." And it has especial importance in dramatic and semidramatic literature. Thus the influence of his intention upon the language he uses is additional to, and separable from, the other three influences, and its effects can profitably be considered apart.

We shall find in the protocols[4] instances, in plenty, of failure on the part of one or other of these functions. Sometimes all four fail together; a reader garbles the sense, distorts the feeling, mistakes the tone and disregards the intention; and often a partial collapse of one function entails aberrations in the others. The possibilities of human misunderstanding make up indeed a formidable subject for study, but something more can be done to elucidate it than has yet been attempted. Whatever else we may do by the light of nature it would be folly to maintain that we should read by it. But before turning back to scrutinize our protocols some further explanation of these functions will be in place.

If we survey our uses of language as a whole, it is clear that, at times, now one now another of the functions may become predominant. It will make the possible situations clearer if we briefly review certain typical forms of composition. A man writing a scientific treatise, for example, will put the sense of what he has to say first, he will subordinate his feelings about his subject or about other views upon it and be careful not to let them interfere to distort his argument or to suggest bias. His tone will be settled for him by academic convention; he will, if he is wise, indicate respect for his readers and a moderate anxiety to be understood accurately and to win acceptance for his remarks. It will be well if his intention, as it shows itself in the work, be on the whole confined to the clearest and most adequate statement of what he has to say (function 1, sense). But, if the circumstances warrant it, further relevant aims—an intention to reorientate opinion, to direct attention to new aspects, or to encourage or discourage certain methods of work or ways of approach—are obviously fitting. Irrelevant aims—the acceptance of the work as a thesis for a Ph.D., for example—come in a different category.

Consider now a writer engaged upon popularizing some of the results and hypotheses of science. The principles governing his language are not nearly so simple, for the furtherance of his intention will properly and inevitably interfere with the other functions.

In the first place, precise and adequate statement of the sense may have to be sacrificed, to some degree, in the interests of general intelligibility. Simplifications and distortions may be necessary if the reader is to "follow." Secondly, a much more lively exhibition of feelings on the part of the author towards his subject matter is usually appropriate and desirable, in order to awaken and encourage the reader's interest. Thirdly, more variety of tone will be called for; jokes and humorous illustrations, for example, are admissible, and perhaps a certain amount of cajolery. With this increased liberty, tact, the subjective counterpart of tone, will be urgently required. A human relation between the expert and his lay audience must be created, and the task, as many specialists have discovered, is not easy. These other functions will interfere still more with strict accuracy of statement; and if the subject has a "tendency," if political, ethical or theological implications are at all prominent, the intention of the work will have further opportunities to intervene.

This leads us to the obvious instance of political speeches. What rank and precedence shall we assign to the four language functions if we analyze public utterances made in the midst of a General Election? Function 4, the furtherance of intentions (of all grades of worthiness) is unmistakably predominant. Its instruments are function 2, the expres-

---

[3][Richards] This function plainly is not on all fours with the others. See Part IV, section 16 and Appendix A, where a further discussion of these four functions is attempted.

[4]Reports by Richards' students in response to poems given to them for discussion.

sion of feelings about causes, policies, leaders and opponents, and function 3, the establishment of favorable relations with the audience ("the great heart of the people"). Recognizing this, ought we to be pained or surprised that function 1, the presentation of facts (or of objects of thought to be regarded as facts are regarded), is equally subordinated?[5] But further consideration of this situation would lead us into a topic that must be examined later, that of *sincerity,* a word with several important meanings. (See Chapter 7.)

In conversation, perhaps, we get the clearest examples of these shifts of function, the normal verbal apparatus of one function being taken over by another. Intention, we have seen, may completely subjugate the others; so, on occasion, may feeling or tone express themselves through sense, translating themselves into explicit statements about feelings and attitudes towards things and people—statements sometimes belied by their very form and manner. Diplomatic formulae are often good examples, together with much of the social language (Malinowski's "phatic communion"),[6] the *thank you so very much*es, and *pleased to meet you*s, that help us to live amicably with one another. (But see Appendix A, note 1.)

Under this head, too, may be put the psychological analyses, the introspective expatiations that have recently flourished so much in fiction as well as in sophisticated conversation. Does it indicate a confusion or a tenuousness in our feelings that we should now find ourselves so ready to make statements about them, to translate them into disquisitions, instead of expressing them in more direct and natural ways? Or is this phenomenon simply another result of the increased study of psychology? It would be rash to decide as yet. Certainly some psychologists lay themselves open to a charge of emptiness, of having so dealt with themselves that they have little left within them to talk about. "Putting it into words," if the words are those of a psychological textbook, is a process which may well be damaging to the feelings. I shall be lucky if my reader does not murmur *de te fabula*[7] at this point.

But feeling (and sometimes tone) may take charge of and operate through sense in another fashion, one more constantly relevant in poetry. (If indeed the shift just dealt with

above might not be better described as sense interfering with and dominating feeling and tone.)

When this happens, the statements which appear in the poetry are there for the sake of their effects upon feelings, not for their own sake. Hence to challenge their truth or to question whether they deserve serious attention *as statements claiming truth,* is to mistake their function. The point is that many, if not most, of the statements in poetry are there *as a means* to the manipulation[8] and expression of feelings and attitudes, not as contributions to any body of doctrine of any type whatever. With narrative poetry there is little danger of any mistake arising, but with "philosophical" or meditative poetry there is great danger of a confusion which may have two sets of consequences.

On the one hand there are very many people who, if they read any poetry at all, try to take all its statements seriously—and find them silly. "My soul is a ship in full sail," for example, seems to them a very profitless kind of contribution to psychology. This may seem an absurd mistake but, alas! it is nonetheless common. On the other hand there are those who succeed too well, who swallow "Beauty is truth, truth beauty . . . . ," as the quintessence of an aesthetic philosophy, not as the expression of a certain blend of feelings, and proceed into a complete stalemate of muddle-mindedness as a result of their linguistic naivety. It is easy to see what those in the first group miss; the losses of the second group, though the accountancy is more complicated, are equally lamentable.

A temptation to discuss here some further intricacies of this shift of function must be resisted. An overflow into Appendix A, which may serve as a kind of technical workshop for those who agree with me that the matter is important enough to be examined *with pains,* will be the best solution. I am anxious to illustrate these distinctions from the protocols before tedium too heavily assails us. It will be enough here to note that this subjugation of statement to emotive purposes has innumerable modes. A poet may distort his statements which have logically nothing to do with the subject under treatment; he may, by metaphor and otherwise, present objects for thought which are logically quite irrelevant; he may perpetrate logical nonsense, be as trivial or as silly, logically, as it is possible to be; all in the interests of the other functions of his language—to express feeling or adjust tone or further his other intentions. If his success in these other aims justify him, no reader (of the kind at least to take his meaning as it should be taken) can validly say anything against him.

---

[5][Richards] The ticklish point is, of course, the implication that the speaker believes in the "facts"—not only as powerful arguments but *as facts. Belief* here has to do with function 2, and, as such examples suggest, is also a word with several senses, at least as many as attach to the somewhat analogous word *love.* Some separation and ventilation of them, beyond that attempted in Chapter 7 below, is very desirable, and I hope to explore this subject in a future work.

[6][Richards] See *The Meaning of Meaning,* Supplement I, section iv.

[7]"The fable is told concerning yourself."

---

[8][Richards] I am not assuming that the poet is conscious of any distinction between his means and his ends.

But these indirect devices for expressing feeling through logical irrelevance and nonsense, through statements not to be taken strictly, literally or seriously, though preeminently apparent in poetry, are not peculiar to it. A great part of what passes for criticism comes under this head. It is much harder to obtain statements about poetry, than expressions of feelings towards it and towards the author. Very many apparent statements turn out on examination to be only these disguised forms, indirect expressions, of feeling, tone and intention. Dr. Bradley's remark that *poetry is a spirit,* and Dr. Mackail's that it is *a continuous substance or energy whose progress is immortal* are eminent examples that I have made use of elsewhere, so curious that I need no apology for referring to them again.[9] Remembering them, we may be more ready to apply to the protocols every instrument of interpretation we possess. May we avoid if possible in our own reading of the protocols those errors of misunderstanding which we are about to watch being committed towards the poems.

Chapter VII

Doctrine in Poetry

Logic is the ethics of thinking, in the sense in which ethics is the bringing to bear of self-control, for the purpose of realizing our desires.
CHARLES SANDERS PEIRCE

With most of our critical difficulties what we have had to explain is how mistakes come to be so frequent. But here we are in the opposite case, we have to explain how they come to be so rare. For it would seem evident that poetry which has been built upon firm and definite beliefs about the world, *The Divine Comedy* or *Paradise Lost,* or Donne's *Divine Poems,* or Shelley's *Prometheus Unbound,* or Hardy's *The Dynasts,* must appear differently to readers who do and readers who do not hold similar beliefs. Yet in fact most readers, and nearly all good readers, are very little disturbed by even a direct opposition between their own beliefs and beliefs of the poet. Lucretius and Virgil, Euripides and Aeschylus, we currently assume, are equally accessible, given the necessary scholarship, to a Roman Catholic, to a Buddhist and to a confirmed skeptic. Equally accessible in the sense that these different readers, after due study, may respond in the same way to the poetry and arrive at similar judgments about it. And when they differ, their divergencies will commonly not be a result of their different positions with regard to the doctrines[10] of the authors, but are more likely to derive from other causes—in their temperaments and personal experience.

I have instanced religious poetry because the beliefs there concerned have the widest implications, and are the most seriously entertained of any. But the same problem arises with nearly all poetry; with mythology very evidently; with such supernatural machinery as appears in *The Rime of the Ancient Mariner:* "The horned Moon, with one bright star / Within the nether tip," with Blake's manifestos; but equally, though less obtrusively, with every passage which seems to make a statement, or depend upon an assumption, that a reader may dissent from, without thereby giving proof of mental derangement.

It is essential to recognize that the problem[11] is the same whether the possible stumbling block, the point of dissent, be trivial or important. When the point is trivial, we easily satisfy ourselves with an explanation in terms of "poetic fictions." When it is a matter of no consequence whether we assent or dissent, the theory that these disputable statements, so constantly presented to us in poetry, are merely *assumptions* introduced for poetic purposes, seems an adequate explanation. And when the statements, for example, Homer's account of "the monkeyshines of the Olympian troupe," are frankly incredible, if paraded solemnly before the bar of reasoned judgment, the same explanation applies. But as the assumptions grow more plausible, and as the consequences for our view of the world grow important, the matter seems less simple. Until, in the end, with Donne's Sonnet (poem 3),[12] for example, it becomes very difficult not to think that *actual belief* in the doctrine that appears in the poem is required for its full and perfect imaginative realization. The mere assumption of Donne's theology, as a poetic fiction, may seem insufficient in view of the intensity of the feeling which is supported and conveyed to us by its means. It is at least certain, as the protocols show, that many who try to read religious poetry find themselves strongly invited to the beliefs presented, and that doctrinal dissent is a very serious obstacle to their reading. Conversely, many successful but

---

[9]For a criticism of Bradley, see Chapter 10 of Richards' *Principles of Literary Criticism.* Mackail is referred to in Chapter 3 of *Principles.*

[10][Richards] I am not accusing these authors of doctrinal poetry in the narrow sense of verse whose sole object is to teach. But that a body of doctrine is presented by each of these poets, even by Virgil, can hardly escape any reader's notice.

[11][Richards] A supplementary and fuller discussion of this whole matter will be found in *Principles of Literary Criticism,* Chapters 32–35, where difficulties, which here must be passed by, are treated in detail.

[12]*At the Round Earth's Imagined Corners.*

dissenting readers find themselves in a mental attitude towards the doctrine which, if it is not belief, closely resembles belief.

Yet if we suppose that, beyond this mere "poetic" assumption, a definite state of belief in this particular doctrine of the Resurrection of the Body is required for a full reading of Donne's poem, great difficulties at once arise. We shall have to suppose that readers who hold different beliefs incompatible with this particular doctrine must either not be able to read the poem, or must temporarily while reading it abandon their own beliefs and adopt Donne's. Both suppositions *seem* contrary to the facts, though these are matters upon which certainty is hazardous. We shall do better, however, to examine the "poetic fiction," or assumption, theory more closely and see whether when fully stated it is capable of meeting the complaint of inadequacy noticed above.

In the first place the very word *assumption* is unsuitable here. Ordinarily an assumption is a proposition, an object of thought, entertained intellectually in order to trace its logical consequences as a hypothesis. But here we are concerned very little with logical consequences and almost exclusively with emotional consequences. In the effect of the thought upon our feelings and attitudes, all its importance, for poetry, lies. But there are clearly two ways in which we may entertain an assumption: intellectually, that is, in a context of other thoughts ready to support, contradict, or establish other logical relations with it; and emotionally, in a context of sentiments, feelings, desires and attitudes ready to group themselves around it. Behind the intellectual assumption stands the desire for logical consistency and order in the receptive side of the mind. But behind the emotional assumption stands the desire or need for order of the whole outgoing emotional side of the personality, the side that is turned towards action.

Corresponding to this distinction there are two forms of belief and similarly two forms of disbelief. Intellectual belief more resembles a weighting of an idea than anything else, a loading[13] which makes other, less heavily weighted ideas, adjust themselves to it rather than vice versa. The loading may be legitimate; the quantity of evidence, its immediacy, the extent and complexity of the supporting systems of ideas are obvious forms of legitimate loading: or it may be illegitimate; our liking for the idea, its brilliance, the trouble that changing it may involve, emotional satisfactions from it, are illegitimate—*from the standpoint of intellectual belief,* be it

understood. The whole use of intellectual belief is to bring *all* our ideas into as perfect an ordered system as possible. We disbelieve only because we believe something else that is incompatible, as Spinoza long ago pointed out. Similarly, we perhaps only believe because it is necessary to disbelieve whatever is logically contradictory to our belief. *Neither belief nor disbelief arises,* in this intellectual sense, *unless the logical context of our ideas is in question.* Apart from these logical connections the idea is neither believed nor disbelieved, nor doubted nor questioned; it is just present. Most of the ideas of the child, of primitive man, of the peasant, of the nonintellectual world and of most poetry are in this happy condition of real intellectual disconnection.

Emotional belief is a very different matter. In primitive man, as innumerable observers have remarked, any idea which opens a ready outlet to emotion or points to a line of action in conformity with custom is quickly believed. We remain much more primitive in this phase of our behavior than in intellectual matters. Given a need[14] (whether conscious *as a desire* or not), any idea which can be taken as a step on the way to its fulfillment is accepted, unless some other need equally active at the moment bars it out. This acceptance, this use of the idea—by our interests, desires, feelings, attitudes, tendencies to action and what not—is emotional belief. So far as the idea is useful to them it is believed, and the sense of attachment, of adhesion, of conviction, which we feel, and to which we give the name of belief, is the result of this implication of the idea in our activities.

Most beliefs, of course, that have any strength or persistence are mixtures of intellectual and emotional belief. A purely intellectual belief need have little strength, no quality of conviction about it, for unless the idea is very original and contrary to received ideas, it needs little loading to hold its own. When we find a modern physicist, for example, passionately attached to a particular theory, we may suspect illegitimate loading, his reputation is perhaps involved in its acceptance. Conversely, a very strong emotional belief may have little persistence. Last night's revelation grows dim amid this morning's affairs, for the need which gave it such glamorous reality was only a need of the moment. Of this kind are most of the revelations received from poetry and music. But though the sense of revelation has faded, we should not suppose that the shaping influence of such experiences must be lost. The mind has found through them a

---

[13][Richards] To introspection this loading seems like a feeling of trust—or trustworthiness. We "side" with the belief intellectually, and, though traditionally belief has been discussed along with judgment, it is, as William James pointed out, more allied to choice.

[14][Richards] I use *need* here to stand for an imbalance mental or physical, a tendency, given suitable conditions, for a movement towards an end-state of equilibrium. A swinging pendulum might thus be said to be actuated by a need to come to rest, and to constantly overdo its movements towards that end. We are much more like pendulums than we think, though, of course, our imbalances are infinitely more intricate.

pattern of response which may remain, and it is this pattern rather than the revelation which is important.

The great difference between these two kinds of belief, as I have defined them, appears most plainly if we consider what *justification* amounts to for each. Whether an intellectual belief is justified is entirely a matter of its logical place in the largest, most completely ordered, system of ideas we can attain to. Now the central, most stable, mass of our ideas has already an order and arrangement fixed for it by the facts of nature. We must bring our ideas of these facts into correspondence with them or we promptly perish. And this order among the everyday facts of our surroundings determines the arrangement of yet another system of our ideas: namely, physical theory. These ideas are thereby weighted beyond the power of irreconcilable ideas to disturb them. Anyone who understands them cannot help believing in them, and disbelieving *intellectually* in irreconcilable ideas, provided that he brings them close enough together to perceive their irreconcilability. There are obviously countless ideas in poetry which, if put into this logical context, must be disbelieved at once.

But this intellectual disbelief does not imply that emotional belief in the same idea is either impossible or even difficult—much less that it is undesirable. For an emotional belief is not justified through any logical relations between its idea and other ideas. Its only justification is its success in meeting our needs—due regard being paid to the relative claims of our many needs one against another. It is a matter, to put it simply, of the *prudence* (in view of *all* the needs of our being) of the kind of emotional activities the belief subserves. The desirability or undesirability of an emotional belief has nothing to do with its intellectual status, provided it is kept from interfering with the intellectual system. And poetry is an extraordinarily successful device for preventing these interferences from arising.

Coleridge, when he remarked that "a willing suspension of disbelief"[15] accompanied much poetry, was noting an important fact, but not quite in the happiest terms, for we are neither aware of a disbelief nor voluntarily suspending it in these cases. It is better to say that the question of belief or disbelief, in the intellectual sense, never arises when we are reading well. If unfortunately it does arise, either through the poet's fault or our own, we have for the moment ceased to be reading poetry and have become astronomers, or theologians, or moralists, persons engaged in quite a different type of activity.

But a possible misconception must be noted here. The intellectual exploration of the *internal* coherence of the poem, and the intellectual examination of the relations of its ideas to other ideas of ordinary experience which are *emotionally* relevant to it, are not only permissible but necessary in the reading of much poetry, as we saw in connection with the sea-harp in poem 9, and in connection with the sentimentality and stock response problems of poems 4, 8 and 13.[16] But this restricted intellectual inquiry is a different thing from the all-embracing attempt to systematize our ideas which alone brings up the problem of intellectual belief.

We can now turn back to poem 3, to the point from which this long analysis started. There are many readers who feel a difficulty in giving to Donne's theology just that kind of acceptance, *and no more,* that they give to Coleridge's "star within the nether tip." They feel an invitation to accord to the poem that belief in its ideas which we can hardly help supposing to have been, in Donne's mind, a powerful influence over its shaping. These readers may, perhaps, be content if we insist that the fullest possible *emotional* belief is fitting and desirable. At the same time there are many who are unable to accord *intellectual* belief to these particular theological tenets. Such readers may feel that a threatened liberty is not thereby denied them. The fact that Donne probably gave both forms of belief to these ideas need not, I think, prevent a good reader from giving the fullest emotional belief while withholding intellectual belief, or rather while not allowing the question of intellectual belief to arise. The evidence is fragmentary upon the point, largely because it has been so strangely little discussed. But the very fact that the need to discuss it has not insistently arisen—seeing how many people from how many different intellectual positions have been able to agree about the value of such doctrinal poems—points strongly in this direction. The absence of intellectual belief need not cripple emotional belief, though evidently enough in some persons it may. But the habit of attaching emotional belief only to intellectually certified ideas is strong in some people; it is encouraged by some forms of education; it is perhaps becoming, through the increased prestige of science, more common.[17] For those whom it conquers it means "Good-by to poetry."

---

[15] *Biographia Literaria,* Chapter 14.

[16] Poem 9: *For the Eightieth Birthday of George Meredith,* by Alfred Noyes. Poem 4: from *More Rough Rhymes of a Padre,* by G. A. Studdert Kennedy. Poem 8: *Piano* by D. H. Lawrence. Poem 13: *In the Churchyard at Cambridge,* by Henry Wadsworth Longfellow.

[17] [Richards] I have discussed this danger at length in *Science and Poetry.* There is reason to think that poetry has often arisen through fusion (or confusion) between the two forms of belief, the boundary between what is intellectually certified and what is not being much less sharply defined in former centuries and *defined in another manner.* The standard of *verification* used in science today is comparatively a new thing. As the scientific view of the world (including our own nature) develops, we shall probably be forced into making a division between fact and fiction that, unless we can meet it with a twofold theory of belief on the lines suggested above, would be fatal not only to poetry but to all our finer, more spiritual, responses. That is the problem.

For the difficulty crops us, as I have insisted, over all poetry that departs, for its own purposes, from the most ordinary universal facts of common experience or from the most necessary deductions of scientific theory. It waylays the strict rationalist with Blake's *Sunflower,* Wordsworth's *River Duddon,* and Shelley's *Cloud,* no less than with their more transcendental utterances. Shakespeare's Lark is as shocking as his Phoenix. Even so honest a man as Gray attributes very disputable motives to his Owl. As for Dryden's "new-kindled star," the last verse of Keats' *Ode to Melancholy,* or Landor's *Rose Aylmer*—it is very clear where we should be with them if we could not give emotional assent apart from intellectual conviction. The slightest poetry may present the problem as clearly (though not so acutely) as the greatest. And the fact that we solve it, in practice, without the least difficulty in minor cases shows, I think, that even in the major instances of philosophic and religious issues the same solution is applicable. But the temptation to confuse the two forms of belief is there greater.

For in these cases an appearance of incompleteness or insincerity may attach to emotional acceptance divorced from intellectual assent.[18] That this is simply a mistake due to a double meaning of *belief* has been my contention. To "pretend to believe" what we "don't really believe" would certainly be insincerity, if the two kinds of believing were one and the same; but if they are not, the confusion is merely another example of the prodigious power of words over our lives. And this will be the best place to take up the uncomfortable problem of *sincerity,* a word much used in criticism, but not often with any precise definition of its meaning.

The ideas, vague and precise, for which *sincere* stands must have been constantly in the reader's mind during our discussion both of stock responses and of sentimentality. We can set aside at once the ordinary "business" sense in which a man is insincere when he deliberately attempts to deceive, and sincere when his statement and acts are governed by "the best of his knowledge and belief." And we can deal

briefly with another sense, already touched upon in connection with poem 7,[19] in which a man is insincere when "he kids *himself,*" when he mistakes his own motives and so professes feelings which are different from those that are in fact actuating him. Two subtle points, however, must be noted before we set this sense aside. The feelings need not be stated or even openly expressed; it is enough if they are hinted to us. And they need not be actual personal "real, live feelings"; they may be imagined feelings. All that is required for this kind of insincerity is a discrepancy between the poem's claim upon our response and its *shaping* impulses in the poet's mind. But only the shaping impulses are relevant. A good poem can perfectly well be written for money or from pique or ambition, provided these initial external motives do not interfere with its growth. Interferences of all kinds—notably the desire to make the poem "original," "striking," or "poetic"—are, of course, the usual cause of insincerity in this sense. A sense which ought not, it may be remarked, to impute blame to the author, unless we are willing to agree that all men who are not good poets are therefore blameworthy in a high degree.

These subtleties were necessary to escape the conclusion that irony, for example—where the feeling really present is often the exact contrary to that overtly professed—is as insincere as simple readers often suppose it must be.

A more troublesome problem is raised if we ask whether an emotion, by itself and apart from its expression, can be sincere or insincere. We often speak as if this were so, and though sometimes no doubt this is only an effective way of saying that we approve (or disapprove) of the emotion, there are senses in which a fact about the emotion, not about our feelings about it, is meant. Sincere emotions, we say, are genuine or authentic, as opposed to spurious emotions, and the several senses which we may imply thereby are worth examining. We may mean that the emotion is genuine in the sense that every product of a perfect mind would be genuine. It would result only from the prompting situation *plus* all the relevant experience of that mind, and be free from impurities and from all interferences, from impulses that had in any way got out of place and become disordered. Since such minds are nowhere obtainable in this obstructive world, such a sense is useful only as an ideal standard by which to measure degrees of relative insincerity. "There is not a just man on earth that doeth good and sinneth not." Some great poetry, we might say, represents the closest approach to sincerity that can be found. And for extreme degrees of insincerity we should look in asylums. Possibly,

---

[18][Richards] The most important example of this divorce that history provides is in the attitude of Confucius towards ancestor worship. Here are the remarks of his chief English translator, James Legge, upon the matter:

It will not be supposed that I wish to advocate or defend the practice of sacrificing to the dead. My object has been to point out how Confucius recognized it, without acknowledging the faith from which it must have originated, and how he enforced it as a matter of form or ceremony. It thus connects itself with the most serious charge that can be brought against him—the charge of insincerity.

The Chinese Classics, Vol. I, Prolegomena, Chapter 5, p. 100. How far Legge was qualified to expound the Confucian doctrine of sincerity may perhaps be divined from this passage.

---

[19]J. D. C. Pellew, *The Temple.*

however, the perfect mind, if it ever appeared among us, might be put there too.

But this is plainly not a sense of sincerity which we often use, it is not what people ordinarily mean. For we would agree that stupid people can be very sincere, though their minds may be very much in a muddle, and we might even suggest that they are more likely to be sincere than the clever. Simplicity, we may think, has something to do with sincerity, for there is a sense in which *genuine* is opposed to *sophisticated*. The sincere feeling, it may be suggested, is one which has been left in its natural state, not worked over and complicated by reflection. Thus strong spontaneous feelings would be more likely to be sincere than feelings that have run the gauntlet of self-criticism, and a dog, for example, might be regarded as a more sincere animal than any man.

This is certainly a sense which is frequent, though whether we should praise emotions that are sincere in this sense as much as most people do, is extremely doubtful. It is partly an echo of Rousseau's romantic fiction, the "natural man." Admiration for the "spontaneous" and "natural" tends to select favorable examples and turns a very blind eye to the less attractive phenomena. Moreover, many emotions which look simple and natural are nothing of the kind; they result from cultivated self-control, so consummate as to seem instantaneous. These cases, and an attractive but limited virtue in some children's behavior, explain, I believe, the popularity of *sincerity* in this sense. So used, the word is of little service in criticism, for this kind of sincerity in poetry must necessarily be rare.

It will be worthwhile hunting a little longer for a satisfactory sense of *sincerity*. Whatever it is, it is the quality we most insistently require in poetry. It is also the quality we most need as critics. And, perhaps, in the proportion that we possess it we shall acknowledge that it is not a quality that we can take for granted in ourselves as our inalienable birthright. It fluctuates with our state of health, with the quality of our recent companions, with our responsibility and our nearness to the object, with a score of conditions that are not easy to take account of. We can *feel* very sincere when, in fact, as others can see clearly, there is no sincerity in us. Bogus forms of the virtue waylay us—confident inner assurances and invasive rootless convictions. And when we doubt our own sincerity and ask ourselves, "Do I *really* think so; do I really feel so?" an honest answer is not easily come by. A direct effort to be sincere, like other effects to will ourselves into action, more often than not frustrates its intention. For all these reasons any light that can be gained upon the nature of sincerity, upon possible tests for it and means for inducing and promoting it, is extremely serviceable to the critic.

The most stimulating discussion of this topic is to be found in the *Chung Yung*[20] (The Doctrine of the Mean, or Equilibrium and Harmony), the treatise that embodies the most interesting and the most puzzling part of the teachings of Confucius. A more distinct (and distinguished) word than *stimulating* would be in place to describe this treatise, were the invigorating effect of a careful reading easier to define. Sincerity—the object of some idea that seems to lie in the territory that *sincerity* covers—appears there as the beginning and end of personal character, the secret of a good life, the only means to good government, the means to give full development to our own natures, to give full development to the nature of others, and very much more. This virtue is as mysterious as it is powerful; and, where so many great sinologues and Chinese scholars have confessed themselves baffled, it would be absurd for one who knows no Chinese to suggest interpretations. But some speculations generated by a reading of translations may round off this chapter.

The following extracts from the *Chung Yung* seem the most relevant to our discussion.

> Sincerity is the way of Heaven. The attainment of sincerity is the way of men. He who possesses sincerity, is he who, without an effort, hits what is right, and apprehends, without the exercise of thought; he is the sage who naturally and easily embodies the right way. He who attains to sincerity, is he who chooses what is good, and firmly holds it fast (Legge, XX. 18). Sincerity is that whereby self-completion is effected, and its way is that by which man must direct himself (Legge, XXV. 1). In self-completion the superior man completes other men and things also . . . and this is the way by which a union is effected of the external and the internal (XXV. 3). In the Book of Poetry, it is said, "In hewing an axe-handle, in hewing an axe-handle, the pattern is not far off." We grasp one axe-handle to hew the other, and yet, if we look askance from the one to the other, we may consider them as apart (XIII. 2). There is a way to the attainment of sincerity in oneself; if a man does not understand what is good, he will not attain sincerity in himself (XX. 17). When we have

---

20[Richards] As might be expected, no translation that entirely commends itself is available. Those to whom Legge's edition of *The Chinese Classics*, Vol. I, is not available, may consult the translation by L. A. Lyall and King Chien-Kun, *The Chung Yung or The Centre, the Common* (Longmans), very literal, but perhaps slightly too much tinctured with a Y.M.C.A. flavor. Here what is translated by others *sincerity* or *singleness* is rendered by *to be true* and *being true*.

intelligence resulting from sincerity, this condition is to be ascribed to nature; when we have sincerity resulting from intelligence, this condition is to be ascribed to instruction. But given the sincerity, there shall be the intelligence, given the intelligence there shall be the sincerity (XXI).

How far apart any detailed precise exposition in English, or in any modern Western language, must be from the form of thought of the original, is shown if we compare a more literal version of this last passage: "Being true begets light, we call that nature. Light leads to being true, we call that teaching. What is true grows light; what is light grows true" (Lyall and King Chien-Kun, p. 16).

Meditating upon this chain of pronouncements we can perhaps construct (or discover) another sense of *sincerity*. One important enough to justify the stress so often laid upon this quality by critics, yet not compelling us to require an impossible perfection or inviting us to sentimental (sense 3) indiscriminate overadmiration of the ebullitions of infants. And it may be possible, by apprehending this sense more clearly, to see what general conditions will encourage sincerity and what steps may be suggested to promote this mysterious but necessary virtue in the critic.

We may take self-completion as our starting point. The completed mind would be that perfect mind we envisaged above, in which no disorder, no mutual frustration of impulses remained. Let us suppose that in the irremediable default of this perfection, default due to man's innate constitution and to the accidents to which he is exposed, there exists *a tendency towards increased order,*[21] a tendency which takes effect unless baffled by physical interferences (disease) or by fixations of habit that prevent us from continuing to learn by experience, or by ideas too invested with emotion for other ideas that disturb them to be formed, or by too lax and volatile a bond between our interests (a frivolousness that is perhaps due to the draining off of energy elsewhere) so that no formations firm enough to build upon result.

There is much to be said in favor of such a supposition. This tendency would be a need, in the sense defined above in this chapter—deriving in fact from *the* fundamental imbalance[22] to which biological development may be supposed to be due. This development with man (and his animal neighbors) seems to be predominantly in the direction of greater complexity and finer differentiation of responses. And it is easy to conceive the organism as relieving, through this differentiation, the strain put upon it by life in a partly uncongenial environment. It is but a step further to conceive it as also tending to relieve internal strains due to these developments imposed from without. And a reordering of its impulses so as to reduce their interferences with one another to a minimum would be the most successful—and the "natural"—direction which this tendency would take.

Such a reordering would be a partial self-completion, temporary and provisional upon the external world remaining for the individual much what it had been in the past. And by such self-completion the superior man *would* "effect a union of the external and the internal." Being more at one within itself the mind thereby becomes more appropriately responsive to the outer world. I am not suggesting that this is what Confucius meant. For him "to complete other men and things too," is possibly the prerogative of the force of example, other men merely imitating the conduct of the sage. But he *may* have meant that freedom calls out freedom; that those who are "most themselves" cause others about them to become also "more themselves"; which would, perhaps, be a more sagacious observation. Perhaps, too, "the union of the external and the internal" meant for him something different from the accordance of our thoughts and feelings with reality. But certainly, for us, this accordance is one of the fruits of sincerity.

This tendency towards a more perfect order, as it takes effect, "enables us, without effort, to hit what is right, and, without the exercise of thought, to apprehend." The "exercise of thought" here must be understood as that process of deliberately setting aside inappropriate ideas and feelings, which, in default of a sufficient inner order—a sufficient sincerity—is still very necessary. Confucius has enough to say elsewhere in the *Chung Yung* (XX. 20) of the need for unremitting research and reflection *before* sincerity is attained to

---

[21][Richards] I have in several other places made prolonged and determined efforts to indicate the types of mental order I have in mind (*The Foundations of Aesthetics*, section XIV; *Principles of Literary Criticism*, Chapter 22; *Science and Poetry*, section II), but without escaping certain large misunderstandings that I hoped to have guarded myself against. Thus Mr. [T. S.] Eliot, reviewing *Science and Poetry* in *The Dial*, describes my ideal order as "Efficiency, a perfectly working mental Roneo Steel Cabinet System," and Mr. [Herbert] Read performing a similar service for *Principles* in *The Criterion*, seemed to understand that where I spoke of the "organization of impulses" I meant that kind of deliberate planning and arrangement which the controllers of a good railway or large shop must carry out. But *organization* for me stood for that kind of interdependence of parts which we allude to when we speak of living things as *organisms;* and the *order* which I make out to be so important is not tidiness. The distinguished names cited in this footnote will protect the reader from a sense that these explanations are insulting to his intelligence. A good idea of some of the possibilities of order and disorder in the mind may be gained from Pavlov's *Conditioned Reflexes.*

---

[22][Richards] Whether we can profitably posit a primal imbalance in certain forms of matter for which the appearance of living substances and their development in increasingly complex forms right up to Shakespeare would be, as it were, the swings of the pendulum "attempting" to come to rest again, is a speculation that has perhaps only an amusement value. The great difficulty would be to get round the separation of the reproductive functions, but that is a difficulty for any cosmologist.

clear himself from any charge of recommending "intuition" as an *alternative* to investigation. "Intuition" is the prerogative only of those who have attained to sincerity. It is only the superior man who "naturally and easily embodies the right way." And the superior man will know when his sincerity is insufficient and take ceaseless steps to remedy it. "If another man (more sincere) succeed by one effort, *he* will use a hundred efforts. If another man succeed by ten efforts, he will use a thousand" (*Chung Yung,* XX. 20). It is the sincerity to which the superior man has already attained which enables him to know when it is insufficient; if it does not yet enable him to embody the right way, it at least enables him to refrain from embodying the wrong, as those who trust intuition too soon are likely to do. Indeed, looking back over the history of thought, we might say, "are certain to do," so heavy are the probabilities against the success of guesswork.

Sincerity, then, in this sense, is obedience to that tendency which "seeks" a more perfect order within the mind. When the tendency is frustrated (e.g., by fatigue or by an idea or feeling that has lost its link with experience, or has become fixed beyond the possibility of change) we have insincerity. When confusion reigns and we are unable to decide what we think or feel (to be distinguished sharply from the case when *decided* thoughts or feelings are present, but we are unable to define or express them) we need be neither sincere nor insincere. We are in a transitional stage which may result in either. Most good critics will confess to themselves that this is the state in which a first reading of any poem of an unfamiliar type leaves them. They know that more study is needed if they are to achieve a genuine response, and they know this in virtue of the sincerity they have already attained. It follows that people with clear definite ideas and feelings, with a high degree of practical efficiency, may be insincere in this sense. Other kinds of sincerity, fidelity to convictions for example, will not save them, and indeed it may well be this fidelity which is thwarting the life of the spirit (*Chung Yung,* XXIV) in them.

Any response (however mistaken from other points of view) which embodies the present activity of this tendency to inner adjustments will be sincere, and any response that conflicts with it or inhibits it will be insincere. Thus to be sincere is to act, feel and think in accordance with "one's true nature," and to be insincere is to act, feel or think in a contrary manner. But the sense to be given to *one's true nature* is, as we have seen, a matter largely conjectural. To define it more exactly would perhaps be tedious and, for our purposes here, needless. In practice we often seem to grasp it very clearly; and all that I have attempted here is to sketch the state of affairs which we then seem to grasp. "What heaven has conferred is man's nature; an accordance with

this is the path" (*Chung Yung,* I). Sometimes we can be certain that we have left it.[23]

On the ways in which sincerity may be increased and extended Confucius is very definite. If we seek a standard for a new response whose sincerity may be in doubt, we shall find it, he says, in the very responses which make the new one possible. The pattern for the new axe-handle is already in our hand, though its very nearness, our firm possession of it, may hide it from us. We need, of course, a founded assurance of the sincerity of these instrumental responses themselves, and this we can gain by comparison. What is meant by *making the thoughts sincere* is the allowing no self-deception "*as when we hate a bad smell,* and as when we love what is beautiful" (*The Great Learning,* VI. i). When we hate a bad smell we can have no doubt that our response is sincere. We can all, at least, find *some* responses beyond suspicion. These are our standard. By studying our sincerity in the fields in which we are fully competent we can extend it into the fields in which our ability is still feeling its way. This seems to be the meaning of *choosing what is good and firmly holding fast to it,* where *good* stands not for our Western ethical notion so much as for the fit and proper, sane and healthy. The man who does not "hate a bad smell" "does not understand what is good"; having no basis or standards, "he will not attain to sincerity."

Together with these, the simplest, most definite responses, there may be suggested also, as standards for sincerity, the responses we make to the most baffling objects that can be presented to our consciousness. Something like a technique or ritual for heightening sincerity might well be worked out. When our response to a poem after our best efforts remains uncertain, when we are unsure whether the feelings it excites come from a deep source in our experience, whether our liking or disliking is genuine, is *ours,* or an accident of fashion, a response to surface detail or to essentials, we may perhaps help ourselves by considering it in a frame of feelings whose sincerity is beyond our questioning. Such are the feelings that may be aroused by contemplation of the following:

1. Man's loneliness (the isolation of the human situation).
2. The facts of birth, and of death, in their inexplicable oddity.

---

[23][Richards] But see *Chung Yung,* I. 2. "The path may not be left for an instant. If it could be left, it would not be the path." Possibly we can escape this difficulty by admitting that all mental activities are, to some degree, the operation of the tendency we have been speaking of. Thus all are the path. But the path can be obstructed, and may have loops. "The regulation of (what keeps trim) the path is instruction" (*Chung Yung,* I. 1).

3. The inconceivable immensity of the Universe.
4. Man's place in the perspective of time.
5. The enormity of his ignorance.

Taking these not as targets for doctrine,[24] but as the most incomprehensible and inexhaustible objects for meditation,

while their reverberation lasts pass the poem through the mind, silently reciting it as slowly as it allows. Whether what it can stir in us is important or not to us will, perhaps, show itself then. Many religious exercises and some of the practices of divination and magic may be thought to be directed in part towards a similar quest for sanction, to be rituals designed to provide standards of sincerity.

---

[24][Richards] The perhaps not unintentional obliquity of Mr. [T. S.] Eliot's interpretations of my phrases in *The Use of Poetry,* pp. 131–35, prompts me to add these references:

    1. Thinking of the key, each confirms a prison (*The Waste Land,* 414). "My external sensations are no less private to myself than are my thoughts or my feelings. In either case my experience falls within my own circle, a circle closed on the outside; and, with all its elements alike, every sphere is opaque to the others which surround it." (F. H. Bradley, *Appearance and Reality,* p. 346.)
    2. But Love has pitched his mansion in
      The place of excrement.
(*Crazy Jane Talks with the Bishop.*)
    3. More distant and more solemn
      Than a fading star.
(*The Hollow Men,* II.)
    3, 4, 5. *"Je ne sais qui m'a mis au monde, ni ce que c'est que le monde, ni que moi-même; je suis dans une ignorance terrible de toutes choses. . . .*
      "Je vois ces effroyables espaces de l'univers qui m'enfirment, et je me trouve attaché à un coin de cette vaste éten-

---

due, sans que je sache pourquoi je suis plutôt placé en ce lieu qu'en un autre, ni pourquoi ce peu de temps qui m'est donné à vivre m'est assigné à ce point plutôt qu' à un autre de toute l'éternité qui m'a précédé et de toute celle qui me suit."

    "I do not know who has put me in the world, nor what the world is, nor what I am; I am in great ignorance of everything. . . .
    "I see these frightening spaces of the universe, which enclose me, and I find myself attached to a corner of this vast expanse without knowing either why I am in this place rather than another or why this little bit of time which is given to me to live is allotted to me at this point rather than another from all the eternity that has preceded me and from all that will follow."

To Pascal such contemplations, when they did not lead to religious beliefs, seemed monstrous and insupportable; Mr. Eliot seems to think they must be trivial.
    5. Enormity, not enormousness. The knowledge which is the opposite of ignorance here is *knowledge how.* It is by man's fault that he is so ignorant; he has not made his thoughts sincere.

Mikhail M. Bakhtin

1895–1975

Bakhtin's work came to be known to English-speakers only in the sixties with the publication of his *Rabelais and His World* (trans. 1965, 1968). The situation in Russia had made his own world at best uneasy. Until *Rabelais* he had published but one work under his own name, *Problems of Dostoyevsky's Poetics* (1929), though others had appeared under the names of V. H. Volosinov and P. N. Medvedev. Bakhtin spent six years in exile in the thirties, and his work on Rabelais was refused as a doctoral dissertation in 1949 after first submission in 1940. However, in recent years Bakhtin's writings have become enormously influential, particularly in the areas of the theories of genre and narrative. The book on Rabelais offered the provocative notion of "carnival" as a quality to be identified with the development of the novel. Carnival is connected, for Bakhtin, with laughter, travesty, parody, comedy, improvisation, and the breaking down of hierarchy. The formal roots of the novel lie in a sort of "excess of humanness." The genres close to its beginnings are Menippean satire, named for the Greek writer Menippus, whose works are lost, and Socratic dialogue.

Bakhtin's essay below draws a distinction between novel and epic principally on the ground that the epic is a closed form and the novel an open dynamic one producing a "surplus" in which voices can still struggle with each other (thus the novelistic imagination is "dialogic"). In the novel, character remains always in the process of formation. In the epic, character does not change, and the text presents a past that is distanced, shaped, and thus "absolute." The epic's emphasis is on memory, while the novel's is on knowledge and experience. The epic's voice is singular; the novel's encompasses what Bakhtin calls "polyglossia" or "heteroglossia." Clearly it is a democratic, even bordering on a happily anarchic, form. One can see that the delineation of such a form might have made the political authorities unhappy.

It is clear that for Bakhtin the novel is to be identified with the modern. It is the hero of the "drama of literary development." All other genres have reached their ultimate forms, but the novel has not. Indeed, its dynamism suggests that it will continue to be open to change and that other genres are becoming "novelized."

Major works by Bakhtin translated into English are *Rabelais and His World* (1965, trans. 1968); *Problems of Dostoyevsky's Poetics* (1929, rev. 1963; tr. 1973, 1984); [V. N. Volosinov], *Marxism and the Philosophy of Language* (1929, 1930, tr. 1973); [V. N. Volosinov], *Freudianism: A Marxist Critique* (1927, tr. 1976); [P. N. Medvedev], *The Formal Method in Literary Scholarship* (1928; tr. 1978); *The Dialogic Imagination* (essays written in the 1930s, tr. 1981); and *Speech Genres and Other Essays* (1984). See Katerine Clark and Michael Holquist, *Mikhail Bakhtin* (1984); Tzvetan Todorov, *Mikhail Bakhtin: The Dialogical Principle* (1985); and G. B. Morson, ed., *Bakhtin: Essays and Dialogues on His Work* (1986).

Epic and Novel: Toward a Methodology for the Study of the Novel

The study of the novel as a genre is distinguished by peculiar difficulties. This is due to the unique nature of the object itself: the novel is the sole genre that continues to develop, that is as yet uncompleted. The forces that define it as a genre are at work before our eyes: the birth and development of the novel as a genre takes place in the full light of the historical day. The generic skeleton of the novel is still far from having hardened, and we cannot foresee all its plastic possibilities.[1]

We know other genres, as genres, in their completed aspect, that is, as more or less fixed pre-existing forms into which one may then pour artistic experience. The primordial process of their formation lies outside historically documented observation. We encounter the epic as a genre that has not only long since completed its development, but one that is already antiquated. With certain reservations we can say the same for the other major genres, even for tragedy. The life they have in history, the life with which we are familiar, is the life they have lived as already completed genres, with a hardened and no longer flexible skeleton. Each of them has developed its own canon that operates in literature as an authentic historical force.

All these genres, or in any case their defining features, are considerably older than written language and the book, and to the present day they retain their ancient oral and auditory characteristics. Of all the major genres only the novel is younger than writing and the book: it alone is organically receptive to new forms of mute perception, that is, to reading. But of critical importance here is the fact that the novel has no canon of its own, as do other genres; only individual examples of the novel are historically active, not a generic canon as such. Studying other genres is analogous to studying dead languages; studying the novel, on the other hand, is like studying languages that are not only alive, but still young.

This explains the extraordinary difficulty inherent in formulating a theory of the novel. For such a theory has at its heart an object of study completely different from that which theory treats in other genres. The novel is not merely one genre among other genres. Among genres long since completed and in part already dead, the novel is the only developing genre. It is the only genre that was born and nourished in a new era of world history and therefore it is deeply akin to that era, whereas the other major genres entered that era as already fixed forms, as an inheritance, and only now are they adapting themselves—some better, some worse—to the new conditions of their existence. Compared with them, the novel appears to be a creature from an alien species. It gets on poorly with other genres. It fights for its own hegemony in literature; wherever it triumphs, the other older genres go into decline. Significantly, the best book on the history of the ancient novel—that by Erwin Rohde[2]—does not so much recount the history of the novel as it does illustrate the process of disintegration that affected all major genres in antiquity.

The mutual interaction of genres within a single unified literary period is a problem of great interest and importance. In certain eras—the Greek classical period, the Golden Age of Roman literature, the neoclassical period—all genres in "high" literature (that is, the literature of ruling social groups) harmoniously reinforce each other to a significant extent; the whole of literature, conceived as a totality of genres, becomes an organic unity of the highest order. But it is characteristic of the novel that it never enters into this whole, it does not participate in any harmony of the genres. In these eras the novel has an unofficial existence, outside "high" literature. Only already completed genres, with fully formed and well-defined generic contours, can enter into such a literature as a hierarchically organized, organic whole. They can mutually delimit and mutually complement each other, while yet preserving their own generic natures. Each is a unit, and all units are interrelated by virtue of certain features of deep structure that they all have in common.

The great organic poetics of the past—those of Aristotle, Horace, Boileau—are permeated with a deep sense of the wholeness of literature and of the harmonious interaction of all genres contained within this whole. It is as if they literally hear this harmony of the genres. In this is their strength—the inimitable, all-embracing fullness and exhaustiveness of such poetics. And they all, as a consequence, ig-

---

EPIC AND NOVEL. The essay was written sometime in the 1930s. It is reprinted from *The Dialogic Imagination,* translated by Caryl Emerson and Michael Holquist. Copyright © by the University of Texas Press, 1981. Reprinted by permission.
[1]See Aristotle, *Poetics,* IV, 11 ff. (p. 52) in which Aristotle treats various genres as completed forms.

[2][Holquist] Erwin Rohde (1845–1898), *Der Griechesche Roman und seine Vorläufer* (1876, but many later editions, most recently that published by F. Olds [Hildesheim, 1960]), one of the greatest monuments of nineteenth-century classical scholarship in Germany. It has never been superseded. But see: Ben F. Perry, *The Ancient Romances* (Berkeley, 1967) and Arthur Heiserman, *The Novel before the Novel* (Chicago, 1977).

nore the novel. Scholarly poetics of the nineteenth century lack this integrity: they are eclectic, descriptive; their aim is not a living and organic fullness but rather an abstract and encyclopedic comprehensiveness. They do not concern themselves with the actual possibility of specific genres co-existing within the living whole of literature in a given era; they are concerned rather with their coexistence in a maxi-mally complete anthology. Of course these poetics can no longer ignore the novel—they simply add it (albeit in a place of honor) to already existing genres (and thus it enters the roster as merely one genre among many; in literature con-ceived as a living whole, on the other hand, it would have to be included in a completely different way).

We have already said that the novel gets on poorly with other genres. There can be no talk of a harmony deriving from mutual limitation and complementariness. The novel parodies other genres (precisely in their role as genres); it exposes the conventionality of their forms and their lan-guage; it squeezes out some genres and incorporates others into its own peculiar structure, reformulating and re-accen-tuating them. Historians of literature sometimes tend to see in this merely the struggle of literary tendencies and schools. Such struggles of course exist, but they are peripheral phe-nomena and historically insignificant. Behind them one must be sensitive to the deeper and more truly historical struggle of genres, the establishment and growth of a generic skeleton of literature.

Of particular interest are those eras when the novel be-comes the dominant genre. All literature is then caught up in the process of "becoming," and in a special kind of "generic criticism." This occurred several times in the Hellenic pe-riod, again during the late Middle Ages and the Renaissance, but with special force and clarity beginning in the second half of the eighteenth century. In an era when the novel reigns supreme, almost all the remaining genres are to a greater or lesser extent "novelized": drama (for example Ibsen, Hauptmann, the whole of Naturalist drama), epic po-etry (for example, *Childe Harold* and especially Byron's *Don Juan*), even lyric poetry (as an extreme example, Heine's lyrical verse). Those genres that stubbornly preserve their old canonic nature begin to appear stylized. In general any strict adherence to a genre begins to feel like a styliza-tion, a stylization taken to the point of parody, despite the artistic intent of the author. In an environment where the novel is the dominant genre, the conventional languages of strictly canonical genres begin to sound in new ways, which are quite different from the ways they sounded in those eras when the novel was *not* included in "high" literature.

Parodic stylizations of canonized genres and styles oc-cupy an essential place in the novel. In the era of the novel's

creative ascendency—and even more so in the periods of preparation preceding this era—literature was flooded with parodies and travesties of all the high genres (parodies pre-cisely of genres, and not of individual authors or schools)—parodies that are the precursors, "companions" to the novel, in their own way studies for it. But it is characteristic that the novel does not permit any of these various individual mani-festations of itself to stabilize. Throughout its entire history there is a consistent parodying or travestying of dominant or fashionable novels that attempt to become models for the genre: parodies on the chivalric romance of adventure (*Dit d'aventures,* the first such parody, belongs to the thirteenth century), on the Baroque novel, the pastoral novel (Sorel's *Le Berger extravagant*),[3] the Sentimental novel (Fielding, and *The Second Grandison*[4] of Musäus) and so forth. This ability of the novel to criticize itself is a remarkable feature of this ever-developing genre.

What are the salient features of this novelization of other genres suggested by us above? They become more free and flexible, their language renews itself by incorporating extraliterary heteroglossia and the "novelistic" layers of lit-erary language, they become dialogized, permeated with laughter, irony, humor, elements of self-parody and finally—this is the most important thing—the novel inserts into these other genres an indeterminacy, a certain semantic openend-edness, a living contact with unfinished, still-evolving con-temporary reality (the openended present). As we will see below, all these phenomena are explained by the transposi-tion of other genres into this new and peculiar zone for struc-turing artistic models (a zone of contact with the present in all its openendedness), a zone that was first appropriated by the novel.

It is of course impossible to explain the phenomenon of novelization purely by reference to the direct and unme-diated influence of the novel itself. Even where such influ-ence can be precisely established and demonstrated, it is in-timately interwoven with those direct changes in reality itself that also determine the novel and that condition its domi-nance in a given era. The novel is the only developing genre

---

[3][Holquist] Charles Sorel (1599–1674), an important figure in the reaction to the *preciosité* of such figures as Honoré d'Urfé (1567–1625), whose *L'Astrée* (1607–1627), a monstrous 5,500-page volume overflowing with highflown language, is parodied in *Le Berger extravagant* (1627). The latter book's major protagonist is a dyed-in-the-wool Parisian who reads too many pastoral novels; intoxicated by these, he attempts to live the rustic life as they describe it—with predictably comic results.

[4][Holquist] Johann Karl August Musaus (1735–1787), along with Tieck and Brentano, one of the great collectors of German folktales and author of sev-eral *Kunstmärchen* of his own (translated into English by Carlyle). Reference here is to his *Grandison der Zweite* (1760–1762, rewritten as *Der deutsche Grandison,* 1781–1782), a satire on Richardson.

and therefore it reflects more deeply, more essentially, more sensitively and rapidly, reality itself in the process of its unfolding. Only that which is itself developing can comprehend development as a process. The novel has become the leading hero in the drama of literary development in our time precisely because it best of all reflects the tendencies of a new world still in the making; it is, after all, the only genre born of this new world and in total affinity with it. In many respects the novel has anticipated, and continues to anticipate, the future development of literature as a whole. In the process of becoming the dominant genre, the novel sparks the renovation of all other genres, it infects them with its spirit of process and inconclusiveness. It draws them ineluctably into its orbit precisely because this orbit coincides with the basic direction of the development of literature as a whole. In this lies the exceptional importance of the novel, as an object of study for the theory as well as the history of literature.

Unfortunately, historians of literature usually reduce this struggle between the novel and other already completed genres, all these aspects of novelization, to the actual real-life struggle among "schools" and "trends." A novelized poem, for example, they call a "romantic poem" (which of course it is) and believe that in so doing they have exhausted the subject. They do not see beneath the superficial hustle and bustle of literary process the major and crucial fates of literature and language, whose great heroes turn out to be first and foremost genres, and whose "trends" and "schools" are but second- or third-rank protagonists.

The utter inadequacy of literary theory is exposed when it is forced to deal with the novel. In the case of other genres literary theory works confidently and precisely, since there is a finished and already formed object, definite and clear. These genres preserve their rigidity and canonic quality in all classical eras of their development; variations from era to era, from trend to trend or school to school are peripheral and do not affect their ossified generic skeleton. Right up to the present day, in fact, theory dealing with these already completed genres can add almost nothing to Aristotle's formulations. Aristotle's poetics, although occasionally so deeply embedded as to be almost invisible, remains the stable foundation for the theory of genres. Everything works as long as there is no mention of the novel. But the existence of novelized genres already leads theory into a blind alley. Faced with the problem of the novel, genre theory must submit to a radical re-structuring.

Thanks to the meticulous work of scholars, a huge amount of historical material has accumulated and many questions concerning the evolution of various types of novels have been clarified—but the problem of the novel genre

as a whole has not yet found anything like a satisfactory principled resolution. The novel continues to be seen as one genre among many; attempts are made to distinguish it as an already completed genre from other already completed genres, to discover its internal canon—one that would function as a well-defined system of rigid generic factors. In the vast majority of cases, work on the novel is reduced to mere cataloging, a description of all variants on the novel—albeit as comprehensive as possible. But the results of these descriptions never succeed in giving us as much as a hint of comprehensive formula for the novel as a genre. In addition, the experts have not managed to isolate a single definite, stable characteristic of the novel—without adding a reservation, which immediately disqualifies it altogether as a generic characteristic.

Some examples of such "characteristics with reservations" would be: the novel is a multi-layered genre (although there also exist magnificent single-layered novels); the novel is a precisely plotted and dynamic genre (although there also exist novels that push to its literary limits the art of pure description); the novel is a complicated genre (although novels are mass produced as pure and frivolous entertainment like no other genre); the novel is a love story (although the greatest examples of the European novel are utterly devoid of the love element); the novel is a prose genre (although there exist excellent novels in verse). One could of course mention a large number of additional "generic characteristics" for the novel similar to those given above, which are immediately annulled by some reservation innocently appended to them.

Of considerably more interest and consequence are those normative definitions of the novel offered by novelists themselves, who produce a specific novel and then declare *it* the only correct, necessary and authentic form of the novel. Such, for instance, is Rousseau's foreword to his *La Nouvelle Héloïse,* Wieland's to his *Agathon,*[5] Wezel's to his *Tobias Knouts;*[6] in such a category belong the numerous declarations and statements of principle by the Romantics on *Wilhelm Meister, Lucinda* and other texts. Such statements are not attempts to incorporate all the possible variants of the

---

[5] [Holquist] Christoph Martin Wieland (1733–1813), is the author of *Geschichte des Agathon* (1767, first of many versions), an autobiographic novel in the guise of a Greek romance, considered by many to be the first in the long line of German *Bildungsromane.*
[6] [Holquist] Reference here is to Johann Carl Wezel (1747–1819), *Lebensgeschichte Tobias Knouts, des Weisen, sonst der Stammler genannt* (1773), a novel that has not received the readership it deserves. A four-volume reprint was published by Metzler (Stuttgart, Afterword by Viktor Lange) in 1971. Also see, Elizabeth Holzbeg-Pfenniger, *Der desorientierte Erzahler: Studien zu J. C. Wezels Lebensgeschichte des Tobias Knouts* (Bern, 1976).

novel into a single eclectic definition, but are themselves part and parcel of the living evolution of the novel as a genre. Often they deeply and faithfully reflect the novel's struggle with other genres and with itself (with other dominant and fashionable variants of the novel) at a particular point in its development. They come closer to an understanding of the peculiar position of the novel in literature, a position that is not commensurate with that of other genres.

Especially significant in this connection is a series of statements that accompanied the emergence of a new novel-type in the eighteenth century. The series opens with Fielding's reflections on the novel and its hero in *Tom Jones*. It continues in Wieland's foreword to *Agathon,* and the most essential link in the series is Blankenburg's *Versuch über den Roman.*[7] By the end of this series we have, in fact, that theory of the novel later formulated by Hegel. In all these statements, each reflecting the novel in one of its critical stages (*Tom Jones, Agathon, Wilhelm Meister*), the following prerequisites for the novel are characteristic: (1) the novel should not be "poetic," as the word "poetic" is used in other genres of imaginative literature; (2) the hero of a novel should not be "heroic" in either the epic or the tragic sense of the word: he should combine in himself negative as well as positive features, low as well as lofty, ridiculous as well as serious; (3) the hero should not be portrayed as an already completed and unchanging person but as one who is evolving and developing, a person who learns from life; (4) the novel should become for the contemporary world what the epic was for the ancient world (an idea that Blankenburg expressed very precisely, and that was later repeated by Hegel).

All these positive prerequisites have their substantial and productive side—taken together, they constitute a criticism (from the novel's point of view) of other genres and of the relationship these genres bear to reality: their stilted heroizing, their narrow and unlifelike poeticalness, their monotony and abstractness, the pre-packaged and unchanging nature of their heroes. We have here, in fact, a rigorous critique of the literariness and poeticalness inherent in other genres and also in the predecessors of the contemporary novel (the heroic Baroque novel and the Sentimental novels of Richardson). These statements are reinforced significantly by the practice of these novelists themselves. Here the

novel—its texts as well as the theory connected with it—emerges consciously and unambiguously as a genre that is both critical and self-critical, one fated to revise the fundamental concepts of literariness and poeticalness dominant at the time. On the one hand, the contrast of novel with epic (and the novel's opposition to the epic) is but one moment in the criticism of other literary genres (in particular, a criticism of epic heroization); but on the other hand, this contrast aims to elevate the significance of the novel, making of it the dominant genre in contemporary literature.

The positive prerequisites mentioned above constitute one of the high-points in the novel's coming to self-consciousness. They do not yet of course provide a theory of the novel. These statements are also not distinguished by any great philosophical depth. They do however illustrate the nature of the novel as a genre no less—if perhaps no more—than do other existing theories of the novel.

I will attempt below to approach the novel precisely as a genre-in-the-making, one in the vanguard of all modern literary development. I am not constructing here a functional definition of the novelistic canon in literary history, that is, a definition that would make of it a system of fixed generic characteristics. Rather, I am trying to grope my way toward the basic structural characteristics of this most fluid of genres, characteristics that might determine the direction of its peculiar capacity for change and of its influence and effect on the rest of literature.

I find three basic characteristics that fundamentally distinguish the novel in principle from other genres: (1) its stylistic three-dimensionality, which is linked with the multi-languaged consciousness realized in the novel; (2) the radical change it effects in the temporal coordinates of the literary image; (3) the new zone opened by the novel for structuring literary images, namely, the zone of maximal contact with the present (with contemporary reality) in all its openendedness.

These three characteristics of the novel are all organically interrelated and have all been powerfully affected by a very specific rupture in the history of European civilization: its emergence from a socially isolated and culturally deaf semipatriarchal society, and its entrance into international and interlingual contacts and relationships. A multitude of different languages, cultures and times became available to Europe, and this became a decisive factor in its life and thought.

In another work[8] I have already investigated the first stylistic peculiarity of the novel, the one resulting from the

---

[7][Holquist] Friedrich von Blankenburg (1744–1796), *Versuch uber den Roman* (1774), an enormous work (over 500 pages) that attempts to define the novel in terms of a rudimentary psychology, a concern for *Tugend* in the heroes. A facsimile edition was published by Metzler (Stuttgart) in 1965. Little is known about Blankenburg, who is also the author of an unfinished novel with the imposing title *Beytrage zur Geschichte deutscher Reichs und deutscher Sitten,* the first part of which appeared a year after the *Versuch* in 1775.

[8][Bakhtin] Cf. the article "From the Prehistory of Novelistic Discourse" [in *The Dialogic Imagination*].

active polyglossia of the new world, the new culture and its new creative literary consciousness. I will summarize here only the basic points.

Polyglossia had always existed (it is more ancient than pure, canonic monoglossia), but it had not been a factor in literary creation; an artistically conscious choice between languages did not serve as the creative center of the literary and language process. Classical Greeks had a feeling both for "languages" and for the epochs of language, for the various Greek literary dialects (tragedy is a polyglot genre), but creative consciousness was realized in closed, pure languages (although in actual fact they were mixed). Polyglossia was appropriated and canonized among all the genres.

The new cultural and creative consciousness lives in an actively polyglot world. The world becomes polyglot, once and for all and irreversibly. The period of national languages, coexisting but closed and deaf to each other, comes to an end. Languages throw light on each other: one language can, after all, see itself only in the light of another language. The naive and stubborn coexistence of "languages" within a given national language also comes to an end—that is, there is no more peaceful co-existence between territorial dialects, social and professional dialects and jargons, literary language, generic languages within literary language, epochs in language and so forth.

All this set into motion a process of active, mutual cause-and-effect and interillumination. Words and language began to have a different feel to them; objectively they ceased to be what they had once been. Under these conditions of external and internal interillumination, each given language—even if its linguistic composition (phonetics, vocabulary, morphology, etc.) were to remain absolutely unchanged—is, as it were, reborn, becoming qualitatively a different thing for the consciousness that creates in it.

In this actively polyglot world, completely new relationships are established between language and its object (that is, the real world)—and this is fraught with enormous consequences for all the already completed genres that had been formed during eras of closed and deaf monoglossia. In contrast to other major genres, the novel emerged and matured precisely when intense activization of external and internal polyglossia was at the peak of its activity; this is its native element. The novel could therefore assume leadership in the process of developing and renewing literature in its linguistic and stylistic dimension.

In the above-mentioned work I tried to elucidate the profound stylistic originality of the novel, which is determined by its connection with polyglossia.

Let us move on to the two other characteristics, both concerned with the thematic aspect of structure in the novel as a genre. These characteristics can be best brought out and clarified through a comparison of the novel with the epic.

The epic as a genre in its own right may, for our purposes, be characterized by three constitutive features: (1) a national epic past—in Goethe's and Schiller's terminology the "absolute past"—serves as the subject for the epic;[9] (2) national tradition (not personal experience and the free thought that grows out of it) serves as the source for the epic; (3) an absolute epic distance separates the epic world from contemporary reality, that is, from the time in which the singer (the author and his audience) lives.

We will deal in more detail with each of these constitutive features of the epic.

The world of the epic is the national heroic past: it is a world of "beginnings" and "peak times" in the national history, a world of fathers and of founders of families, a world of "firsts" and "bests." The important point here is not that the past constitutes the content of the epic. The formally constitutive feature of the epic as a genre is rather the transferral of a represented world into the past, and the degree to which this world participates in the past. The epic was never a poem about the present, about its own time (one that became a poem about the past only for those who came later). The epic, as the specific genre known to us today, has been from the beginning a poem about the past, and the authorial position immanent in the epic and constitutive for it (that is, the position of the one who utters the epic word) is the environment of a man speaking about a past that is to him inaccessible, the reverent point of view of a descendent. In its style, tone and manner of expression, epic discourse is infinitely far removed from discourse of a contemporary about a contemporary addressed to contemporaries ("Onegin, my good friend, was born on the banks of the Neva, where perhaps you were also born, or once shone, my reader. . . ."). Both the singer and the listener, immanent in the epic as a genre, are located in the same time and on the same evaluative (hierarchical) plane, but the represented world of the heroes stands on an utterly different and inaccessible time-and-value plane, separated by epic distance. The space between them is filled with national tradition. To portray an event on the same time-and-value plane as oneself and one's contemporaries (and an event that is therefore based on personal

---

[9][Holquist] Reference here is to "Uber epische und dramatische Dichtung," co-signed by Schiller and Goethe, but probably written by the latter in 1797, although not published until 1827. The actual term used by Goethe for what Bakhtin is calling "absolute past" is *Vollkommen vergangen*, which is opposed not to the novel, but to drama, which is defined as *Vollkommen gegenwärtig*. The essay can be found in Goethe's *Sämuliche Werke* (Jubiläums-Ausgabe, Stuttgart and Berlin [1902–1907]), vol. 36, pp. 149–152.

experience and thought) is to undertake a radical revolution, and to step out of the world of epic into the world of the novel.

It is possible, of course, to conceive even "my time" as heroic, epic time, when it is seen as historically significant; one can distance it, look at it as if from afar (not from one's own vantage point but from some point in the future), one can relate to the past in a familiar way (as if relating to "my" present). But in so doing we ignore the presentness of the present and the pastness of the past; we are removing ourselves from the zone of "my time," from the zone of familiar contact with me.

We speak of the epic as a genre that has come down to us already well defined and real. We come upon it when it is already completely finished, a congealed and half-moribund genre. Its completedness, its consistency and its absolute lack of artistic naiveté bespeak its old age as a genre and its lengthy past. We can only conjecture about this past, and we must admit that so far our conjectures have been rather poor. Those hypothetical primordial songs that preceded both the epic and the creation of a generic epic tradition, songs about contemporaries that directly echoed events that had just occurred—such songs we do not know, although we must presume they existed. We can only guess at the nature of those original aëdonic songs, or of the cantilenas. And we have no reason to assume that they are any more closely related to the later and better-known epic songs than to our topical feuilletons or popular ditties. Those heroicized epic songs about contemporaries that *are* available to us and that we *do* know existed arose only after the epic was already an established form, and arose on the basis of an already ancient and powerful epic tradition. These songs transfer to contemporary events and contemporaries the ready-made epic form; that is, they transfer to these events the time-and-value contour of the past, thus attaching them to the world of fathers, of beginnings and peak times—canonizing these events, as it were, while they are still current. In a patriarchal social structure the ruling class does, in a certain sense, belong to the world of "fathers" and is thus separated from other classes by a distance that is almost epic. The epic incorporation of the contemporary hero into a world of ancestors and founders is a specific phenomenon that developed out of an epic tradition long since completed, and that therefore is as little able to explain the origin of the epic as is, say, the neoclassical ode.

Whatever its origins, the epic as it has come down to us is an absolutely completed and finished generic form, whose constitutive feature is the transferral of the world it describes to an absolute past of national beginnings and peak times. The absolute past is a specifically evaluating (hierarchical) category. In the epic world view, "beginning," "first," "founder," "ancestor," "that which occurred earlier" and so forth are not merely temporal categories but *valorized* temporal categories, and valorized to an extreme degree. This is as true for relationships among people as for relations among all the other items and phenomena of the epic world. In the past, everything is good: all the really good things (i.e., the "first" things) occur *only* in this past. The epic absolute past is the single source and beginning of everything good for all later times as well.

In ancient literature it is memory, and not knowledge, that serves as the source and power for the creative impulse. That is how it was, it is impossible to change it: the tradition of the past is sacred. There is as yet no consciousness of the possible relativity of any past.

The novel, by contrast, is determined by experience, knowledge and practice (the future). In the era of Hellenism a closer contact with the heroes of the Trojan epic cycle began to be felt; epic is already being transformed into novel. Epic material is transposed into novelistic material, into precisely that zone of contact that passes through the intermediate stages of familiarization and laughter. When the novel becomes the dominant genre, epistemology becomes the dominant discipline.

The epic past is called the "absolute past" for good reason: it is both monochronic and valorized (hierarchical); it lacks any relativity, that is, any gradual, purely temporal progressions that might connect it with the present. It is walled off absolutely from all subsequent times, and above all from those times in which the singer and his listeners are located. This boundary, consequently, is immanent in the form of the epic itself and is felt and heard in its every word.

To destroy this boundary is to destroy the form of the epic as a genre. But precisely because it is walled off from all subsequent times, the epic past is absolute and complete. It is as closed as a circle; inside it everything is finished, already over. There is no place in the epic world for any openendedness, indecision, indeterminacy. There are no loopholes in it through which we glimpse the future; it suffices unto itself, neither supposing any continuation nor requiring it. Temporal and valorized definitions are here fused into a single inseparable whole (as they are also fused in the semantic layers of ancient languages). Everything incorporated into this past was simultaneously incorporated into a condition of authentic essence and significance, but therefore also took on conclusiveness and finality, depriving itself, so to speak, of all rights and potential for a real continuation. Absolute conclusiveness and closedness is the outstanding feature of the temporally valorized epic past.

Let us move on to tradition. The epic past, walled off from all subsequent times by an impenetrable boundary, is preserved and revealed only in the form of national tradition.

The epic relies entirely on this tradition. Important here is not the fact that tradition is the factual source for the epic—what matters rather is that a reliance on tradition is immanent in the very form of the epic, just as the absolute past is immanent in it. Epic discourse is a discourse handed down by tradition. By its very nature the epic world of the absolute past is inaccessible to personal experience and does not permit an individual, personal point of view or evaluation. One cannot glimpse it, grope for it, touch it; one cannot look at it from just any point of view; it is impossible to experience it, analyze it, take it apart, penetrate into its core. It is given solely as tradition, sacred and sacrosanct, evaluated in the same way by all and demanding a pious attitude toward itself. Let us repeat: the important thing is not the factual sources of the epic, not the content of its historical events, nor the declarations of its authors—the important thing is this formal constitutive characteristic of the epic as a genre (to be more precise, the formal-substantive characteristic): its reliance on impersonal and sacrosanct tradition, on a commonly held evaluation and point of view—which excludes any possibility of another approach—and which therefore displays a profound piety toward the subject described and toward the language used to describe it, the language of tradition.

The absolute past as the subject for epic and sacrosanct tradition as its sole source also determine the nature of epic distance—that is, the third constitutive characteristic of the epic as a genre. As we have already pointed out, the epic past is locked into itself and walled off from all subsequent times by an impenetrable boundary, isolated (and this is most important) from the eternal present of children and descendents in which the epic singer and his listeners are located, which figures in as an event in their lives and becomes the epic performance. On the other hand, tradition isolates the world of the epic from personal experience, from any new insights, from any personal initiative in understanding and interpreting, from new points of view and evaluations. The epic world is an utterly finished thing, not only as an authentic event of the distant past but also on its own terms and by its own standards; it is impossible to change, to re-think, to re-evaluate anything in it. It is completed, conclusive and immutable, as a fact, an idea and a value. This defines absolute epic distance. One can only accept the epic world with reverence; it is impossible to really touch it, for it is beyond the realm of human activity, the realm in which everything humans touch is altered and re-thought. This distance exists not only in the epic material, that is, in the events and the heroes described, but also in the point of view and evaluation one assumes toward them; point of view and evaluation are fused with the subject into one inseparable whole. Epic language is not separable from its subject, for an absolute fusion of subject matter and spatial-temporal aspects with valorized (hierarchical) ones is characteristic of semantics in the epic. This absolute fusion and the consequent unfreedom of the subject was first overcome only with the arrival on the scene of an active polyglossia and interillumination of languages (and then the epic became a semiconventional, semimoribund genre).

Thanks to this epic distance, which excludes any possibility of activity and change, the epic world achieves a radical degree of completedness not only in its content but in its meaning and its values as well. The epic world is constructed in the zone of an absolute distanced image, beyond the sphere of possible contact with the developing, incomplete and therefore re-thinking and re-evaluating present.

The three characteristics of the epic posited by us above are, to a greater or lesser extent, also fundamental to the other high genres of classical antiquity and the Middle Ages. At the heart of all these already completed high genres lie the same evaluation of time, the same role for tradition, and a similar hierarchical distance. Contemporary reality as such does not figure in as an available object of representation in any of these high genres. Contemporary reality may enter into the high genres only in its hierarchically highest levels, already distanced in its relationship to reality itself. But the events, victors and heroes of "high" contemporary reality are, as it were, appropriated by the past as they enter into these high genres (for example, Pindar's odes or the works of Simonides); they are woven by various intermediate links and connective tissue into the unified fabric of the heroic past and tradition. These events and heroes receive their value and grandeur precisely through this association with the past, the source of all authentic reality and value. They withdraw themselves, so to speak, from the present day with all its inconclusiveness, its indecision, its openness, its potential for re-thinking and re-evaluating. They are raised to the valorized plane of the past, and assume there a finished quality. We must not forget that "absolute past" is not to be confused with time in our exact and limited sense of the word; it is rather a temporally valorized hierarchical category.

It is impossible to achieve greatness in one's own time. Greatness always makes itself known only to descendents, for whom such a quality is always located in the past (it turns into a distanced image); it has become an object of memory and not a living object that one can see and touch. In the genre of the "memorial," the poet constructs his image in the future and distanced plane of his descendents (cf. the inscriptions of oriental despots, and of Augustus). In the world of memory, a phenomenon exists in its own peculiar context, with its own special rules, subject to conditions quite different from those we meet in the world we see with our own eyes, the world of practice and familiar contact. The epic past is a special form for perceiving people and events in art. In general the act of artistic perception and representation is almost completely obscured by this form. Artistic representation here is representation *sub specie aeternitatis.* One may, and in fact one must, memorialize with artistic language only that which is worthy of being remembered, that which should be preevaluation. The focus for such an idea of evaluation could only be found in the absolute past. The present is something transitory, it is flow, it is an eternal continuation without beginning or end; it is denied an authentic conclusiveness and consequently lacks an essence as well. The future as well is perceived either as an essentially indifferent continuation of the present, or as an end, a final destruction, a catastrophe. The temporally valorized categories of absolute beginning and absolute end are extremely significant in our sense of time and in the ideologies of past times. The beginning is idealized, the end is darkened (catastrophe, "the twilight of the gods"). This sense of time and the hierarchy of times described by us here permeate all the high genres of antiquity and the Middle Ages. They permeated so deeply into the basic foundation of these genres that they continue to live in them in subsequent eras—up to the nineteenth century, and even further.

This idealization of the past in high genres has something of an official air. All eternal expressions of the dominant force and truth (the expression of everything conclusive) were formulated in the valorized-hierarchical category of the past, in a distanced and distant image (everything from gesture and clothing to literary style, for all are symbols of authority). The novel, however, is associated with the eternally living element of unofficial language and unofficial thought (holiday forms, familiar speech, profanation).

The dead are loved in a different way. They are removed from the sphere of contact, one can and indeed must speak of them in a different style. Language about the dead is stylistically quite distinct from language about the living.

In the high genres all authority and privilege, all lofty significance and grandeur, abandon the zone of familiar contact for the distanced plane (clothing, etiquette, the style of a hero's speech and the style of speech about him). It is in this orientation toward completeness that the classicism of all non-novel genres is expressed.

Contemporaneity, flowing and transitory, "low," present—this "life without beginning or end" was a subject of representation only in the low genres. Most importantly, it was the basic subject matter in that broadest and richest of realms, the common people's creative culture of laughter. In the aforementioned work I tried to indicate the enormous influence exercised by this realm—in the ancient world as well

as the Middle Ages—on the birth and formation of novelistic language. It was equally significant for all other historical factors in the novelistic genre, during their emergence and early formation. Precisely here, in popular laughter, the authentic folkloric roots of the novel are to be sought. The present, contemporary life as such, "I myself" and "my contemporaries," "my time"—all these concepts were originally the objects of ambivalent laughter, at the same time cheerful and annihilating. It is precisely here that a fundamentally new attitude toward language and toward the word is generated. Alongside direct representation—laughing at living reality—there flourish parody and travesty of all high genres and of all lofty models embodied in national myth. The "absolute past" of gods, demigods and heroes is here, in parodies and even more so in travesties, "contemporized": it is brought low, represented on a plane equal with contemporary life, in an everyday environment, in the low language of contemporaneity.

In classical times this elemental popular laughter gave rise directly to a broad and varied field of ancient literature, one that the ancients themselves expressively labeled *spoudogeloion,* that is, the field of "serio-comical." The weakly plotted mimes of Sophron,[10] all the bucolic poems, the fable, early memoir literature (the *Epidēmiai* of Ion of Chios,[11] the *Homilae* of Critias),[12] pamphlets all belong to this field; here the ancients themselves included the "Socratic dialogues" (as a genre), here belong Roman satire (Lucilius,[13] Horace, Persius,[14] Juvenal), the extensive literature of the "Symposia" and finally Menippean satire[15] (as a genre) and dialogues of the Lucianic type. All these genres, permeated with the "serio-comical," are authentic predecessors of the novel.

---

[10][Holquist] Sophron (fl. 5th century B.C.) was probably the first writer to give literary form to the mime. He was greatly admired by Plato. The mimes were written in rhythmic prose and took as their subject matter events of everyday life.

[11][Holquist] Ion of Chios (490–421 B.C.), a Greek poet who, when he won first for tragedy in the Great Dionysia, made a present of Chian wine to every Athenian. His memoirs have not come down to us, but Athenaeus (q.v.) gives long quotes, including the description of an evening Sophocles spent with him in his home on Chios. It has been said no other Greek before Socrates has been presented so vividly. The title of these *Epidēmiai* probably refers to the visits of distinguished Athenians who came to see Ion on Chios.

[12][Holquist] Critias (460–403 B.C.), one of the Thirty Tyrants, also active as a writer. He wrote mostly elegies and tragedies. Fragments of *Homilai* ("discussions") have come down to us; Galen is cited by the editors of the Pauly-Wissowa (vol. II of the 1910 ed., p. 1910) as calling the two books of the original *Homilai* "aimless discussions" (*zwanglose Unterhaltungen*).

[13][Holquist] Lucilius Gaius (?–102 B.C.), member of one of the greatest Roman families, author of several important satires, chiefly remarkable for the personal, almost autobiographical tone he introduces them.

[14][Holquist] Persius, Flaccus Aulus (A.D. 34–62), satirist heavily influenced by Stoic philosophy.

[15]Menippus was a Greek Cynic writer of the 3rd century B.C. His works are lost.

In addition, several of these genres are thoroughly novelistic, containing in embryo and sometimes in developed form the basic elements characteristic of the most important later prototypes of the European novel. The authentic spirit of the novel as a developing genre is present in them to an incomparably greater degree than in the so-called Greek novels (the sole ancient genre bearing the name). The Greek novel [Greek romance] had a powerful influence on the European novel precisely in the Baroque era, that is, precisely at that time when novel theory was beginning to be reworked (Abbé Huet)[16] and when the very term "novel" was being tightened and made more precise. Out of all novelistic works of antiquity, the term "novel" was, therefore, attached to the Greek novel alone. Nevertheless, the serio-comical genres mentioned above anticipate the more essential historical aspects in the development of the novel in modern times, even though they lack that sturdy skeleton of plot and composition that we have grown accustomed to demand from the novel as a genre. This applies in particular to the Socratic dialogues, which may be called—to rephrase Friedrich Schlegel—"the novels of their time," and also to Menippean satire (including the *Satyricon* of Petronius), whose role in the history of the novel is immense and as yet inadequately appreciated by scholarship. These serio-comical genres were the first authentic and essential step in the evolution of the novel as the genre of becoming.

Precisely what is this novelistic spirit in these serio-comical genres, and on what basis do we claim them as the first step in the development of the novel? It is this: contemporary reality serves as their subject, and—even more important—it is the starting point for understanding, evaluating and formulating such genres. For the first time, the subject of serious literary representation (although, it is true, at the same time comical) is portrayed without any distance, on the level of contemporary reality, in a zone of direct and even crude contact. Even where the past or myth serves as the subject of representation in these genres there is no epic distance, and contemporary reality provides the point of view. Of special significance in this process of demolishing distance is the comical origin of these genres: they derive from folklore (popular laughter). It is precisely laughter that destroys the epic, and in general destroys any hierarchical (distancing and valorized) distance. As a distanced image a subject cannot be comical; to be made comical, it must be

brought close. Everything that makes us laugh is close at hand, all comical creativity works in a zone of maximal proximity. Laughter has the remarkable power of making an object come up close, of drawing it into a zone of crude contact where one can finger it familiarly on all sides, turn it upside down, inside out, peer at it from above and below, break open its external shell, look into its center, doubt it, take it apart, dismember it, lay it bare and expose it, examine it freely and experiment with it. Laughter demolishes fear and piety before an object, before a world, making of it an object of familiar contact and thus clearing the ground for an absolutely free investigation of it. Laughter is a vital factor in laying down that prerequisite for fearlessness without which it would be impossible to approach the world realistically. As it draws an object to itself and makes it familiar, laughter delivers the object into the fearless hands of investigative experiment—both scientific and artistic—and into the hands of free experimental fantasy. Familiarization of the world through laughter and popular speech is an extremely important and indispensable step in making possible free, scientifically knowable and artistically realistic creativity in European civilization.

The plane of comic (humorous) representation is a specific plane in its spatial as well as its temporal aspect. Here the role of memory is minimal; in the comic world there is nothing for memory and tradition to do. One ridicules in order to forget. This is the zone of maximally familiar and crude contact; laughter means abuse, and abuse could lead to blows. Basically this is uncrowning, that is, the removal of an object from the distanced plane, the destruction of epic distance, an assault on and destruction of the distanced plane in general. In this plane (the plane of laughter) one can disrespectfully walk around whole objects; therefore, the back and rear portion of an object (and also its innards, not normally accessible for viewing) assume a special importance. The object is broken apart, laid bare (its hierarchical ornamentation is removed): the naked object is ridiculous; its "empty" clothing, stripped and separated from its person, is also ridiculous. What takes place is a comical operation of dismemberment.

One can play games with the comical (that is, contemporize it); serving as the objects of the game we have the primordial artistic symbols of space and time—above, below, in front of, behind, earlier, later, first, last, past, present, brief (momentary), long and so forth. What reigns supreme here is the artistic logic of analysis, dismemberment, turning things into dead objects.

We possess a remarkable document that reflects the simultaneous birth of scientific thinking and of a new artistic-prose model for the novel. These are the Socratic dialogues.

---

[16][Holquist] Abbe Huet (1630–1731), bishop of Avranches, learned scholar who wrote numerous works on a wide variety of subjects. His *Traité de l'origine des romans* (1670) was first published as an introduction to Mme. de La Fayette's *Zaide*, a novel written while its author was still influenced by ideas of the *précieux* society.

For our purposes, everything in this remarkable genre, which was born just as classical antiquity was drawing to a close, is significant. Characteristically it arises as *apomnemoneumata*,[17] that is, as a genre of the memoir type, as transcripts based on personal memories of real conversations among contemporaries;[18] characteristic, also, is the fact that a speaking and conversing man is the central image of the genre. Characteristic, too, is the combination of the image of Socrates, the central hero of the genre, wearing the popular mask of a bewildered fool (almost a *Margit*)[19] with the image of a wise man of the most elevated sort (in the spirit of legends about seven wise men); this combination produces the ambivalent image of wise ignorance. Characteristic also is the ambivalent self-praise in the Socratic dialogue: I am wiser than everyone, because I know that I know nothing. In the image of Socrates one can detect a new type of prose heroization. Around this image, carnivalized legends spring up (for example, Socrates' relationship with Xanthippe); the hero turns into a jester (compare the more recent carnivalization of legends surrounding Dante, Pushkin,[20] etc.).

Characteristic, even canonic, for the genre is the spoken dialogue framed by a dialogized story. Characteristic also is the proximity of its language to popular spoken language, as near as was possible for classical Greece; these dialogues in fact opened the path to Attic prose, and are connected with the essential renovation of the literary-prose language—and with a shift in languages in general. Characteristically this genre is at the same time a rather complex system of styles and dialects, which enter it as more-or-less parodied models of languages and styles (we have before us therefore a multi-styled genre, as is the authentic novel). Moreover the figure of Socrates himself is characteristic for the genre—he is an outstanding example of heroization in novelistic prose (so very different from epic heroization). It is, finally, profoundly characteristic—and for us this is of utmost importance—that we have laughter, Socratic irony, the entire system of Socratic degradations combined with a serious, lofty and for the first time truly free investigation of the world, of man and of human thought. Socratic laughter (reduced to irony) and Socratic degradations (an entire system of metaphors and comparisons borrowed from the lower spheres of life—from tradespeople, from everyday life, etc.) bring the world closer and familiarize it in order to investigate it fearlessly and freely. As our starting point we have contemporary reality, the living people who occupy it together with their opinions. From this vantage point, from this contemporary reality with its diversity of speech and voice, there comes about a new orientation in the world and in time (including the "absolute past" of tradition) through personal experience and investigation. It is canonical for the genre that even an accidental and insignificant pretext can ordinarily and deliberately served in the memory of descendents; an image is created for descendents, and this image is projected on to their sublime and distant horizon. Contemporaneity for its own sake (that is to say, a contemporaneity that makes no claim on future memory) is molded in clay; contemporaneity for the future (for descendents) is molded in marble or bronze.

The interrelationship of times is important here. The valorized emphasis is not on the future and does not serve the future, no favors are being done it (such favors face an eternity outside time); what is served here is the future memory of a past, a broadening of the world of the absolute past, an enriching of it with new images (at the expense of contemporaneity)—a world that is always opposed in principle to any *merely transitory* past.

In the already completed high genres, tradition also retains its significance—although under conditions of open and personal creativity, its role becomes more conventionalized than in the epic.

In general, the world of high literature in the classical era was a world projected into the past, on to the distanced plane of memory, but not into a real, relative past tied to the present by uninterrupted temporal transitions; it was projected rather into a valorized past of beginnings and peak times. This past is distanced, finished and closed like a circle. This does not mean, of course, that there is no movement within it. On the contrary, the relative temporal categories within it are richly and subtly worked out (nuances of "earlier," "later," sequences of moments, speeds, durations, etc.); there is evidence of a high level of artistic technique in matters of time. But within this time, completed and locked into a circle, all points are equidistant from the real, dynamic

---

[17][Holquist] *Apomnemoneumata,* or *Hypomnemata* (literally, "recollections"). It is thought by some that a work of this title ascribed to Ion of Chios may be identical with the *Epidēmiai* (cf. note 9).

[18][Bakhtin] "Memory" in memoirs and autobiographies is of a special sort: it is memory of one's own contemporaneity and of one's own self. It is a de-heroizing memory; there is an element of the mechanical in it, of mere transcription (nonmonumental). What results is personal memory without pre-existing chronological pattern, bounded only by the termini of a single personal life (there are no fathers or generations). This "memoir quality" was already inherent in the Socratic dialogue.

[19][Holquist] *Margit,* Greek "fool," subject of a work frequently cited by Bakhtin, the *Margites* (q.v.).

[20][Holquist] A good example of what Bakhtin has in mind here is provided by the leader of the *Oberiuty,* Daniil Kharms (1905–1942), "Anecdotes about Pushkin." They are difficult to appreciate in translation, but are all similar to the following: "Pushkin loved to throw rocks. As soon as he saw a rock, he would throw it. Sometimes he became so excited that he stood, all red in the face, waving his arms, throwing rocks, simply something awful."—from *Russia's Lost Literature of the Absurd,* tr. and ed. by George Gibian (New York, 1974), p. 67.

time of the present; insofar as this time is whole, it is not localized in an actual historical sequence; it is not relative to the present or to the future; it contains within itself, as it were, the entire fullness of time. As a consequence all high genres of the classical era, that is, its entire high literature, are structured in the zone of the distanced image, a zone outside any possible contact with the present in all its openendedness.

As we have said, contemporaneity as such (that is, one that preserves its own living contemporary profile) cannot become an object of representation for the high genres. Contemporaneity was reality of a "lower" order in comparison with the epic past. Least of all could it serve as the starting point for artistic ideation or serve as the external and most immediate starting point for a dialogue; the "todayness" of the day was emphasized in all its randomness (accidental encounters, etc.).

In other serio-comical genres we will come upon other aspects, nuances and consequences of this radical shift of the temporally valorized center of artistic orientation, and of the revolution in the hierarchy of times. A few words now about Menippean satire. Its folklore roots are identical with those of the Socratic dialogue, to which it is genetically related (it is usually considered a product of the disintegration of the Socratic dialogue). The familiarizing role of laughter is here considerably more powerful, sharper and coarser. The liberty to crudely degrade, to turn inside out the lofty aspects of the world and world views, might sometimes seem shocking. But to this exclusive and comic familiarity must be added an intense spirit of inquiry and a utopian fantasy. Nothing is left of the distant epic image of the absolute past; the entire world and everything sacred in it is offered to us without any distancing at all, in a zone of crude contact, where we can grab at everything with our own hands. In this world, utterly familiarized, the subject moves with extreme and fantastic freedom; from heaven to earth, from earth to the nether world, from the present into the past, from the past into the future. In the comic afterlife visions of Menippean satire, the heroes of the absolute past, real-life figures from various eras of the historic past (for example, Alexander of Macedonia) and living contemporaries jostle one another in a most familiar way, to talk, even to brawl; this confrontation of times from the point of view of the present is extremely characteristic. In Menippean satire the unfettered and fantastic plots and situations all serve one goal—to put to the test and to expose ideas and ideologues. These are experimental and provocative plots.

The appearance of the utopian element in this genre is symptomatic, although it is, to be sure, timid and shallow. The inconclusive present begins to feel closer to the future

than to the past, and begins to seek some valorized support in the future, even if this future is as yet pictured merely as a return to the Golden Age of Saturn (in Roman times, Menippean satire was closely associated with the Saturnalia and with the freedom of Saturnalian laughter).

Menippean satire is dialogic, full of parodies and travesties, multi-styled, and does not fear elements of bilingualism (in Varro,[21] and especially in Boethius' *The Consolation of Philosophy*). The *Satyricon* of Petronius is good proof that Menippean satire can expand into a huge picture, offering a realistic reflection of the socially varied and heteroglot world of contemporary life.

For almost all the above-mentioned genres, the "serio-comical" is characterized by a deliberate and explicit autobiographical and memoirist approach. The shift of the temporal center of artistic orientation, which placed on the same temporally valorized plane the author and his readers (on the one hand) and the world and heroes described by him (on the other), making them contemporaries, possible acquaintances, friends, familiarizing their relations (we again recall the novelistic opening of *Onegin*), permits the author, in all his various masks and faces, to move freely onto the field of his represented world, a field that in the epic had been absolutely inaccessible and closed.

The field available for representing the world changes from genre to genre and from era to era as literature develops. It is organized in different ways and limited in space and time by different means. But this field is always specific.

The novel comes into contact with the spontaneity of the inconclusive present; this is what keeps the genre from congealing. The novelist is drawn toward everything that is not yet completed. He may turn up on the field of representation in any authorial pose, he may depict real moments in his own life or make allusions to them, he may interfere in the conversations of his heroes, he may openly polemicize with his literary enemies and so forth. This is not merely a matter of the author's image appearing within his own field of representation—important here is the fact that the underlying, original formal author (the author of the authorial image) appears in a new relationship with the represented world. Both find themselves now subject to the same temporally valorized measurements, for the "depicting" authorial language now lies on the same plane as the "depicted"

---

[21][Holquist] Marcus Terentius Varro (fl. 1st century B.C.), politician and scholar, a pupil of Stilo—the first Roman philologist—who had made himself known through research on the genuineness of Plautus' comedies. Varro wrote numerous works on the Latin language, but Bakhtin refers to him as author of the lost work *Statuarum Mennippearum libri*, humorous essays in the Menippean style satirizing the luxury of his age.

language of the hero, and may enter into dialogic relations and hybrid combinations with it (indeed, it cannot help but enter into such relations).

It is precisely this new situation, that of the original formally present author in a zone of contact with the world he is depicting, that makes possible at all the appearance of the authorial image on the field of representation. This new positioning of the author must be considered one of the most important results of surmounting epic (hierarchical) distance. The enormous formal, compositional and stylistic implications this new positioning of the author has for the specific evolution of the novel as a genre require no further explanation.

Let us consider in this connection Gogol's *Dead Souls.* The form of his epic Gogol modeled on the *Divine Comedy;* it was in this form that he imagined the greatness of his work lay. But what in fact emerged was Menippean satire. Once having entered the zone of familiar contact he was unable to leave it, and he was unable to transfer into this sphere distanced and positive images. The distanced images of the epic and the images of familiar contact can never meet on the same field of representation; pathos broke into the world of Menippean satire like a foreign body, affirmative pathos became abstract and simply fell out of the work. Gogol could not manage the move from Hell to Purgatory and then to Paradise with the same people and in the same work; no continuous transition was possible. The tragedy of Gogol is to a very real extent the tragedy of a genre (taking genre not in its formalistic sense, but as a zone and a field of valorized perception, as a mode for representing the world). Gogol lost Russia, that is, he lost his blueprint for perceiving and representing her; he got muddled somewhere between memory and familiar contact—to put it bluntly, he could not find the proper focus on his binoculars.

But as a new starting point for artistic orientation, contemporaneity by no means excludes the depiction of a heroic past, and without any travesty. As an example we have Xenophon's *Cyropaedia*[22] (not, of course, a serio-comical work, but one that does lie on the borderline). Its subject is the past, its hero is Cyrus the Great. But the starting point of representation is Xenophon's own contemporary reality; it is that which provides the point of view and value orientation. It is characteristic that the heroic past chosen here is not the na-

tional past but a foreign and barbaric past. The world has already opened up; one's own monolithic and closed world (the world of the epic) has been replaced by the great world of one's own plus "the others." This choice of an alien heroism was the result of a heightened interest, characteristic for Xenophon's time, in the Orient—in Eastern culture, ideology and sociopolitical forms. A light was expected from the East. Cultural interanimation, interaction of ideologies and languages had already begun. Also characteristic was the idealization of the oriental despot, and here one senses Xenophon's own contemporary reality with its idea (shared widely by his contemporaries) of renovating Greek political forms in a spirit close to oriental autocracy. Such an idealization of oriental autocracy is of course deeply alien to the entire spirit of Hellenic national tradition. Characteristic and even extremely typical for the time was the concept of an individual's upbringing: this was to become one of the most important and productive themes for the new European novel. Also characteristic is the intentional and completely explicit transfer onto the image of Cyrus the Great of the features of Cyrus the Younger, a contemporary of Xenophon in whose campaign Xenophon participated. And one also senses here the personality of another contemporary and close friend of Xenophon, Socrates; thus are elements of the memoir introduced into the work. As a final characteristic we might mention the form of the work itself—dialogues framed by a story. In such a way, contemporary reality and its concerns become the starting point and center of an artistic ideological thinking and evaluating of the past. This past is given us without distancing, on the level of contemporary reality, although not (it is true) in its low but in its high forms, on the level of its most advanced concerns. Let us comment upon the somewhat utopian overtones in this work that reflect a slight (and uncertain) shift of its contemporaneity from the past toward the future. *Cyropaedia* is a novel, in the most basic sense of the word.

The depiction of a past in the novel in no sense presumes the modernization of this past (in Xenophon there are, of course, traces of such modernization). On the contrary, only in the novel have we the possibility of an authentically objective portrayal of the past as the past. Contemporary reality with its new experiences is retained as a way of seeing, it has the depth, sharpness, breadth and vividness peculiar to that way of seeing, but should not in any way penetrate into the already portrayed content of the past, as a force modernizing and distorting the uniqueness of that past. After all, every great and serious contemporaneity requires an authentic profile of the past, an authentic other language from another time.

---

[22][Holquist] Xenophon (428–354 B.C.), *Cyropaedia,* a text that haunts the history of thinking about novels from Julian the Apostate's citation of it as a model to be avoided (cf. Perry, *Ancient Romances,* p. 78) to Boileau, who, in his *Dialogue sur les héros des romans* (1964) attacks Mme. de Scudéry's monstrous *Artamene, ou le grand Cyrus* (1649–1653).

The revolution in the hierarchy of times outlined above makes possible a radical revolution in the structuring of the artistic image as well. The present, in its so-called "wholeness" (although it is, of course, never whole) is in essence and in principle inconclusive; by its very nature it demands continuation, it moves into the future, and the more actively and consciously it moves into the future the more tangible and indispensable its inconclusiveness becomes. Therefore, when the present becomes the center of human orientation in time and in the world, time and world lose their completedness as a whole as well as in each of their parts. The temporal model of the world changes radically: it becomes a world where there is no first word (no ideal word), and the final word has not yet been spoken. For the first time in artistic-ideological consciousness, time and the world become historical: they unfold, albeit at first still unclearly and confusedly, as becoming, as an uninterrupted movement into a real future, as a unified, all-embracing and unconcluded process. Every event, every phenomenon, every thing, every object of artistic representation loses its completeness, its hopelessly finished quality and its immutability that had been so essential to it in the world of the epic "absolute past," walled off by an unapproachable boundary from the continuing and unfinished present. Through contact with the present, an object is attracted to the incomplete process of a world-in-the-making, and is stamped with the seal of inconclusiveness. No matter how distant this object is from us in time, it is connected to our incomplete, present-day, continuing temporal transitions, it develops a relationship with our unpreparedness, with our present. But meanwhile our present has been moving into an inconclusive future. And in this inconclusive context all the semantic stability of the object is lost; its sense and significance are renewed and grow as the context continues to unfold. This leads to radical changes in the structuring of the artistic image. The image acquires a specific actual existence. It acquires a relationship—in one form or another, to one degree or another—to the ongoing event of current life in which we, the author and readers, are intimately participating. This creates the radically new zone for structuring images in the novel, a zone of maximally close contact between the represented object and contemporary reality in all its inconclusiveness—and consequently a similarly close contact between the object and the future.

Prophecy is characteristic for the epic, prediction for the novel. Epic prophecy is realized wholly within the limits of the absolute past (if not in the given epic, then within the limits of the tradition it encompasses); it does not touch the reader and his real time. The novel might wish to prophesize facts, to predict and influence the real future, the future of the author and his readers. But the novel has a new and quite specific problematicalness: characteristic for it is an eternal re-thinking and re-evaluating. That center of activity that ponders and justifies the past is transferred to the future.

The "modernity" of the novel is indestructible, and verges on an unjust evaluation of times. Let us recall the re-evaluation of the past that occurred during the Renaissance ("the darkness of the Gothic Age"), in the eighteenth century (Voltaire) and that is inherent in positivism (the exposure of myth, legend, heroization, a maximum departure from memory and a maximum reduction of the concept of "knowledge," even to the point of empiricism, a mechanical faith in "progress" as the highest criterion).

. . .

Let us now touch upon several artistic features related to the above. The absence of internal conclusiveness and exhaustiveness creates a sharp increase in demands for an *external* and *formal* completedness and exhaustiveness, especially in regard to plot-line. The problems of a beginning, an end, and "fullness" of plot are posed anew. The epic is indifferent to formal beginnings and can remain incomplete (that is, where it concludes is almost arbitrary). The absolute past is closed and completed in the whole as well as in any of its parts. It is, therefore, possible to take any part and offer it as the whole. One cannot embrace, in a single epic, the entire world of the absolute past (although it is unified from a plot standpoint)—to do so would mean a retelling of the whole of national tradition, and it is sufficiently difficult to embrace even a significant portion of it. But this is no great loss, because the structure of the whole is repeated in each part, and each part is complete and circular like the whole. One may begin the story at almost any moment, and finish at almost any moment. The *Iliad* is a random excerpt from the Trojan cycle. Its ending (the burial of Hector) could not possibly be the ending from a novelistic point of view. But epic completedness suffers not the slightest as a result. The specific "impulse to end"—How does the war end? Who wins? What will happen to Achilles? and so forth—is absolutely excluded from the epic by both internal and external motifs (the plot-line of the tradition was already known to everyone). This specific "impulse to continue" (what will happen next?) and the "impulse to end" (how will it end?) are characteristic only for the novel and are possible only in a zone where there is proximity and contact; in a zone of distanced images they are impossible.

In distanced images we have the whole event, and plot interest (that is, the condition of not knowing) is impossible. The novel, however, speculates in what is unknown. The novel devises various forms and methods for employing the surplus knowledge that the author has, that which the hero does not know or does not see. It is possible to utilize this authorial surplus in an external way, manipulating the narrative, or it can be used to complete the image of an individual (an externalization that is peculiarly novelistic). But there is another possibility in this surplus that creates further problems.

The distinctive features of the novelistic zone emerge in various ways in various novels. A novel need not raise any problematic questions at all. Take, for example, the adventuristic "boulevard" romance. There is no philosophy in it, no social or political problems, no psychology. Consequently none of these spheres provides any contact with the inconclusive events of our own contemporary reality. The absence of distance and of a zone of contact are utilized here in a different way: in place of our tedious lives we are offered a surrogate, true, but it is the surrogate of a fascinating and brilliant life. We can experience these adventures, identify with these heroes; such novels almost become a substitute for our own lives. Nothing of the sort is possible in the epic and other distanced genres. And here we encounter the specific danger inherent in the novelistic zone of contact: we ourselves may actually enter the novel (whereas we could never enter an epic or other distanced genre). It follows that we might substitute for our own life an obsessive reading of novels, or dreams based on novelistic models (the hero of [Dostoevsky's] *White Nights*); Bovaryism becomes possible, the real-life appearance of fashionable heroes taken from novels—disillusioned, demonic and so forth. Other genres are capable of generating such phenomena only after having been novelized, that is, after having been transposed to the novelistic zone of contact (for example, the verse narratives of Byron).

Yet another phenomenon in the history of the novel—and one of extreme importance—is connected with this new temporal orientation and with this zone of contact: it is the novel's special relationship with extraliterary genres, with the genres of everyday life and with ideological genres. In its earliest stages, the novel and its preparatory genres had relied upon various extraliterary forms of personal and social reality, and especially those of rhetoric (there is a theory that actually traces the novel back to rhetoric). And in later stages of its development the novel makes wide and substantial use of letters, diaries, confessions, the forms and methods of rhetoric associated with recently established courts and so forth. Since it is constructed in a zone of contact with the incomplete events of a particular present, the novel often crosses the boundary of what we strictly call fictional literature—making use first of a moral confession, then of a phil-

osophical tract, then of manifestos that are openly political, then degenerating into the raw spirituality of a confession, a "cry of the soul" that has not yet found its formal contours. These phenomena are precisely what characterize the novel as a developing genre. After all, the boundaries between fiction and nonfiction, between literature and nonliterature and so forth are not laid up in heaven. Every specific situation is historical. And the growth of literature is not merely development and change within the fixed boundaries of any given definition; the boundaries themselves are constantly changing. The shift of boundaries between various strata (including literature) in a culture is an extremely slow and complex process. Isolated border violations of any given specific definition (such as those mentioned above) are only symptomatic of this larger process, which occurs at a great depth. These symptoms of change appear considerably more often in the novel than they do elsewhere, as the novel is a developing genre; they are sharper and more significant because the novel is in the vanguard of change. The novel may thus serve as a document for gauging the lofty and still distant destinies of literature's future unfolding.

But the changes that take place in temporal orientation, and in the zone where images are constructed, appear nowhere more profoundly and inevitably than in the process of re-structuring the image of the individual in literature. Within the bounds of the present article, however, I can touch on this great and complex question only briefly and superficially.

The individual in the high distanced genres is an individual of the absolute past and of the distanced image. As such he is a fully finished and completed being. This has been accomplished on a lofty heroic level, but what is complete is also something hopelessly ready-made; he is all there, from beginning to end he coincides with himself, he is absolutely equal to himself. He is, furthermore, completely externalized. There is not the slightest gap between his authentic essence and its external manifestation. All his potential, all his possibilities are realized utterly in his external social position, in the whole of his fate and even in his external appearance; outside of this predetermined fate and predetermined position there is nothing. He has already become everything that he could become, and he could become only that which he has already become. He is entirely externalized in the most elementary, almost literal sense: everything in him is exposed and loudly expressed: his internal world and all his external characteristics, his appearance and his actions all lie on a single plane. His view of himself coincides completely with others' views of him—the view of his society (his community), the epic singer and the audience also coincide.

In this context, mention should be made of the problem of self-praise that comes up in Plutarch and others. "I myself," in an environment that is distanced, exists not *in* itself or for *itself* but for the self's descendents, for the memory such a self anticipates in its descendents. I acknowledge myself, an image that is my own, but on this distanced plane of memory such a consciousness of self is alienated from "me." I see myself through the eyes of another. This coincidence of forms—the view I have of myself as self, and the view I have of myself as other—bears an integral, and therefore naive, character—there is no gap between the two. We have as yet no confession, no exposing of self. The one doing the depicting coincides with the one being depicted.[23]

He sees and knows in himself only the things that others see and know in him. Everything that another person—the author—is able to say about him he can say about himself, and vice versa. There is nothing to seek for in him, nothing to guess at, he can neither be exposed nor provoked; he is all of a piece, he has no shell, there is no nucleus within. Furthermore, the epic hero lacks any ideological initiative (heroes and author alike lack it). The epic world knows only a single and unified world view, obligatory and indubitably true for heroes as well as for authors and audiences. Neither world view nor language can, therefore, function as factors for limiting and determining human images, or their individualization. In the epic, characters are bounded, preformed, individualized by their various situations and destinies, but not by varying "truths." Not even the gods are separated from men by a special truth: they have the same language, they all share the same world view, the same fate, the same extravagant externalization.

These traits of the epic character, shared by and large with other highly distanced genres, are responsible for the exclusive beauty, wholeness, crystal clarity and artistic completedness of this image of man. But at the same time such traits account for his limitations and his obvious woodenness under conditions obtaining in a later period of human existence.

The destruction of epic distance and the transferral of the image of an individual from the distanced plane to the zone of contact with the inconclusive events of the present (and consequently of the future) result in a radical re-structuring of the image of the individual in the novel—and con-

sequently in all literature. Folklore and popular-comic sources for the novel played a huge role in this process. Its first and essential step was the comic familiarization of the image of man. Laughter destroyed epic distance; it began to investigate man freely and familiarly, to turn him inside out, expose the disparity between his surface and his center, between his potential and his reality. A dynamic authenticity was introduced into the image of man, dynamics of inconsistency and tension between various factors of this image; man ceased to coincide with himself, and consequently men ceased to be exhausted entirely by the plots that contain them. Of these inconsistencies and tensions laughter plays up, first of all, the comic sides (but not only the comic sides); in the serio-comical genres of antiquity, images of a new order emerge—for example, the imposing, newly and more complexly integrated heroic image of Socrates.

Characteristic here is the artistic structuring of an image out of durable popular masks—masks that had great influence on the novelistic image of man during the most important stages of the novel's development (the serio-comical genres of antiquity, Rabelais, Cervantes). Outside his destiny, the epic and tragic hero is nothing; he is, therefore, a function of the plot fate assigns him; he cannot become the hero of another destiny or another plot. On the contrary, popular masks—Maccus, Pulcinello, Harlequin—are able to assume any destiny and can figure into any situation (they often do so within the limits of a single play), but they cannot exhaust their possibilities by those situations alone; they always retain, in any situation and in any destiny, a happy surplus of their own, their own rudimentary but inexhaustible human face. Therefore these masks can function and speak independent of the plot; but, moreover, it is precisely in these excursions outside the plot proper—in the Atellan *trices*,[24] in the *lazzi*[25] of Italian comedy—that they best of all reveal a face of their own. Neither an epic nor a tragic hero could ever step out in his own character during a pause in the plot or during an intermission: he has no face for it, no gesture, no language. In this is his strength and his limitation. The epic and tragic hero is the hero who, by his very nature, must perish. Popular masks, on the contrary, never perish: not a single plot in Atellan, Italian or Italianized French comedies provides for, or could ever provide for, the actual death of a Maccus, a Pulcinello or a Harlequin. However, one frequently witnesses their fictive comic deaths (with subsequent resurrections). These are heroes of free improvisation

---

[23][Bakhtin] Epic disintegrates when the search begins for a new point of view on one's own self (without any admixture of others' points of view). The expressive novelistic gesture arises as a departure from a norm, but the "error" of this norm immediately reveals how important it is for subjectivity. First there is a departure from a norm, and then the problematicalness of the norm itself.

[24][Holquist] *Trices* are thought to have been interludes in the action of the Atellanae during which the masks often stepped out of character.

[25][Holquist] *Lazzi* were what we might now call "routines" or "numbers" that were not part of the ongoing action of the plot.

and not heroes of tradition, heroes of a life process that is imperishable and forever renewing itself, forever contemporary—these are not heroes of an absolute past.

These masks and their structure (the noncoincidence with themselves, and with any given situation—the surplus, the inexhaustibility of their self and the like), have had, we repeat, an enormous influence on the development of the novelistic image of man. This structure is preserved even in the novel, although in a more complex, deeply meaningful and serious (or serio-comical) form.

One of the basic internal themes of the novel is precisely the theme of the hero's inadequacy to his fate or his situation. The individual is either greater than his fate, or less than his condition as a man. He cannot become once and for all a clerk, a landowner, a merchant, a fiancé, a jealous lover, a father and so forth. If the hero of a novel actually becomes something of the sort—that is, if he completely coincides with his situation and his fate (as do generic, everyday heroes, the majority of secondary characters in a novel)—then the surplus inhering in the human condition is realized in the main protagonist. The way in which this surplus will actually be realized grows out of the author's orientation toward form and content, that is, the ways he sees and depicts individuals. It is precisely the zone of contact with an inconclusive present (and consequently with the future) that creates the necessity of this incongruity of a man with himself. There always remains in him unrealized potential and unrealized demands. The future exists, and this future ineluctably touches upon the individual, has its roots in him.

An individual cannot be completely incarnated into the flesh of existing sociohistorical categories. There is no mere form that would be able to incarnate once and forever all of his human possibilities and needs, no form in which he could exhaust himself down to the last word, like the tragic or epic hero; no form that he could fill to the very brim, and yet at the same time not splash over the brim. There always remains an unrealized surplus of humanness; there always remains a need for the future, and a place for this future must be found. All existing clothes are always too tight, and thus comical, on a man. But this surplus of un-fleshed-out humanness may be realized not only in the hero, but also in the author's point of view (as, for example, in Gogol). Reality as we have it in the novel is only one of many possible realities; it is not inevitable, not arbitrary, it bears within itself other possibilities.

The epic wholeness of an individual disintegrates in a novel in other ways as well. A crucial tension develops between the external and the internal man, and as a result the subjectivity of the individual becomes an object of experimentation and representation—and first of all on the humor-

ous familiarizing plane. Coordination breaks down between the various aspects: man for himself alone and man in the eyes of others. This disintegration of the integrity that an individual had possessed in epic (and in tragedy) combines in the novel with the necessary preparatory steps toward a new, complex wholeness on a higher level of human development.

Finally, in a novel the individual acquires the ideological and linguistic initiative necessary to change the nature of his own image (there is a new and higher type of individualization of the image). In the antique stage of novelistic development there appeared remarkable examples of such hero-ideologues—the image of Socrates, the image of a laughing Epicurus in the so-called "Hypocratic" novel, the deeply novelized image of Diogenes in the thoroughly dialogized literature of the cynics and in Menippean satire (where it closely approximates the image of the popular mask) and, finally, the image of Menippius in Lucian. As a rule, the hero of a novel is always more or less an ideologue.

What all this suggests is a somewhat abstract and crude schematization for re-structuring the image of an individual in the novel.

We will summarize with some conclusions.

The present, in its all openendedness, taken as a starting point and center for artistic and ideological orientation, is an enormous revolution in the creative consciousness of man. In the European world this reorientation and destruction of the old hierarchy of temporalities received its crucial generic expression on the boundary between classic antiquity and Hellenism, and in the new world during the late Middle Ages and Renaissance. The fundamental constituents of the novel as a genre were formed in these eras, although some of the separate elements making up the novel were present much earlier, and the novel's roots must ultimately be sought in folklore. In these eras all other major genres had already long since come to completion, they were already old and almost ossified genres. They were all permeated from top to bottom with a more ancient hierarchization of temporalities. The novel, from the very beginning, developed as a genre that had at its core a new way of conceptualizing time. The absolute past, tradition, hierarchical distance played no role in the formation of the novel as a genre (such spatiotemporal categories did play a role, though insignificant, in certain periods of the novel's development, when it was slightly influenced by the epic—for example in the Baroque novel). The novel took shape precisely at the point when epic distance was disintegrating, when both the world and man were assuming a degree of comic familiarity, when the object of artistic representation was being degraded to the level of a contemporary reality that was inconclusive and fluid. From the very beginning the novel was structured not in the distanced image of the absolute past but in the zone of direct contact with inconclusive present-day reality. At its core lay personal experience and free creative imagination. Thus a new, sober artistic-prose novelistic image and a new critical scientific perception came into being simultaneously. From the very beginning, then, the novel was made of different clay than the other already completed genres; it is a different breed, and with it and in it is born the future of all literature. Once it came into being, it could never be merely one genre among others, and it could not erect rules for interrelating with others in peaceful and harmonious co-existence. In the presence of the novel, all other genres somehow have a different resonance. A lengthy battle for the novelization of the other genres began, a battle to drag them into a zone of contact with reality. The course of this battle has been complex and tortuous.

The novelization of literature does not imply attaching to already completed genres a generic canon that is alien to them, not theirs. The novel, after all, has no canon of its own. It is, by its very nature, not canonic. It is plasticity itself. It is a genre that is ever questing, ever examining itself and subjecting its established forms to review. Such, indeed, is the only possibility open to a genre that structures itself in a zone of direct contact with developing reality. Therefore, the novelization of other genres does not imply their subjection to an alien generic canon; on the contrary, novelization implies their liberation from all that serves as a brake on their unique development, from all that would change them along with the novel into some sort of stylization of forms that have outlived themselves.

I have developed my various positions in this essay in a somewhat abstract way. There have been few illustrations, and even these were taken only from an ancient period in the novel's development. My choice was determined by the fact that the significance of that period has been greatly underestimated. When people talk about the ancient period of the novel they have traditionally had in mind the "Greek novel" alone. The ancient period of the novel is enormously significant for a proper understanding of the genre. But in ancient times the novel could not really develop all its potential; this potential came to light only in the modern world. We indicated that in several works of antiquity, the inconclusive present begins to sense a greater proximity to the future than to the past. The absence of a temporal perspective in ancient society assured that this process of reorientation toward a real future could not complete itself; after all, there was no real concept of a future. Such a reorientation occurred for the first time during the Renaissance. In that era, the present (that is, a reality that was contemporaneous) for the first time began to sense itself not only as an incomplete continuation of the past, but as something like a new and heroic beginning. To reinterpret reality on the level of the contemporary present now meant not only to degrade, but to raise reality into a new and heroic sphere. It was in the Renaissance that the present first began to feel with great clarity and awareness an incomparably closer proximity and kinship to the future than to the past.

The process of the novel's development has not yet come to an end. It is currently entering a new phase. For our era is characterized by an extraordinary complexity and a deepening in our perception of the world; there is an unusual growth in demands on human discernment, on mature objectivity and the critical faculty. These are features that will shape the further development of the novel as well.

Georges Bataille

1897–1962

The paradox of Georges Bataille's life—his uniquely individualistic eccentricity coupled with his (usually fleeting) attachments to marginal political, artistic, and intellectual groups is reflected in his writings. Fundamental to his theorizing is the principle of expenditure, which attempts to do more than turn inside out the traditional capitalist notion of production. For Bataille, in the essay reprinted below, the fundamental human drive is toward loss. Acquisition is the unwanted result of a process oriented toward loss. This process Bataille illustrates in his brief analysis of *potlatch*. The obligation of loss, for no other purpose than to lose, Bataille finds corrupted in Christianity and bourgeois culture, where all loss is made *useful* is some way—in acts of charity for the sake of one's soul or in the formalization of giving for some social purpose. The principle of loss must be that of "unconditional expenditure." The bourgeois, with its cult of thrift, hates expenditure but ends in hypocrisy by institutionalizing it so that it need not admit the drive to expend as unconditional. Bataille begins his discussion by criticizing social concepts that emphasize utility and reduce pleasure to a subsidiary role in life. The real needs of society he sees frustrated by the exclusion of "nonproductive expenditure."

Early on, Bataille's problem was to square his theory of expenditure with purposeful Marxian dialectic and class struggle. In 1933, when he wrote "The Notion of Expenditure" he was associated with the Marxist journal *La Critique sociale.* What he did was to imply that the proletariat must grasp not the means of production but the means of expenditure. But the problem for Bataille in any political program is that any program seems inevitably to force on expenditure the notion of a use value, which ends in institutionalizing unproductive expenditure, ("luxury, mourning, war, cults, the construction of sumptuary monuments, games, spectacles, arts, perverse sexual activity [i.e. deflected from genital finality]"), as means of reconstituting—maintaining—hierarchical stability and oppression. The movement in Bataille's career from Marx to championing Nietzsche reflects his interest in the disruption of the usual notions of value, not by simply inverting values but by endlessly opposing any hierarchization. His insistence in the essay "Nietzsche and the Fascists" (1937) on Nietzsche's separation from Fascistic thought reflects his awareness of the danger that his own views on excess could be read as Fascistic. The paradox in Bataille is one that has perhaps its own value *as paradox:* His Nietzschean form of deconstructive opposition to use as value and his purposive political and social radicalism struggle with each other *and* together in opposition to any hierarchy.

Bataille's writings are collected in *Oeuvres Completes* (1970–   ), still in progress. Among his translated works are *Visions of Excess: Selected Writings, 1927–1939* (1985); *Story of the Eye,* his autobiographical work (1928, tr. 1977); *Death and Sensuality* (1957, tr. 1977); *Blue of Noon* (1957, tr. 1978); *L' Abbe C.* (tr. 1983); and

Literature and Evil (1957, tr. 1973). See Michele Richman, *Reading Georges Bataille: Beyond the Gift* (1982); Michele H. Richman, *Reading Georges Bataille* (1982); Allan Stoekl, *Politics, Writing, Mutilation: The Cases of Bataille, Blanchot, Roussel, Leiris, and Ponge* (1985); and Steven Shaviro, *Passion and Excess* (1990).

The Notion of Expenditure

The Insufficiency of the Principle of Classical Utility

Every time the meaning of a discussion depends on the fundamental value of the word *useful*—in other words, every time the essential question touching on the life of human societies is raised, no matter who intervenes and what opinions are represented—it is possible to affirm that the debate is necessarily warped and that the fundamental question is eluded. In fact, given the more or less divergent collection of present ideas, there is nothing that permits one to define what is useful to man. This lacuna is made fairly prominent by the fact that it is constantly necessary to return, in the most unjustifiable way, to principles that one would like to situate beyond utility and pleasure: *honor* and *duty* are hypocritically employed in schemes of pecuniary interest and, without speaking of God, *Spirit* serves to mask the intellectual disarray of the few people who refuse to accept a closed system.

Current practice, however, is not deterred by these elementary difficulties, and common awareness at first seems able to raise only verbal objections to the principles of classical utility—in other words, to supposedly material utility. The goal of the latter is, theoretically, pleasure—but only in a moderate form, since violent pleasure is seen as *pathological*. On the one hand, this material utility is limited to acquisition (in practice, to production) and to the conservation of goods; on the other, it is limited to reproduction and to the conservation of human life (to which is added, it is true, the struggle against pain, whose importance itself suffices to indicate the negative character of the pleasure principle instituted, in theory, as the basis of utility). In the series of quantitative representations linked to this flat and untenable conception of existence only the question of reproduction seriously lends itself to controversy, because an exaggerated

increase in the number of the living threatens to diminish the individual share. But on the whole, any general judgment of social activity implies the principle that all individual effort, in order to be valid, must be reducible to the fundamental necessities of production and conservation. Pleasure, whether art, permissible debauchery, or play, is definitively reduced, in the intellectual representations *in circulation,* to a concession; in other words it is reduced to a diversion whose role is subsidiary. The most appreciable share of life is given as the condition—sometimes even as the regrettable condition—of productive social activity.

It is true that personal experience—if it is a question of a useful man, capable of wasting and destroying without reason—each time gives the lie to this miserable conception. But even when he does not spare himself and destroys himself while making allowance for nothing, the most lucid man will understand nothing, or imagine himself sick; he is incapable of a *utilitarian* justification for his actions, and it does not occur to him that a human society can have, just as he does, an *interest* in considerable losses, in catastrophes that, *while conforming to well-defined needs,* provoke tumultuous depressions, crises of dread, and, in the final analysis, a certain orgiastic state.

In the most crushing way, the contradiction between current social conceptions and the real needs of society recalls the narrowness of judgment that puts the father in opposition to the satisfaction of his son's needs. This narrowness is such that it is impossible for the son to express his will. The father's partially malevolent solicitude is manifested in the things he provides for his son: lodgings, clothes, food, and, when absolutely necessary, a little harmless recreation. But the son does not even have the right to speak about what really gives him a fever; he is obliged to give people the impression that for him no *horror* can enter into consideration. In this respect, it is sad to say that *conscious humanity has remained a minor;* humanity recognizes the right to acquire, to conserve, and to consume rationally, but it excludes in principle *nonproductive expenditure.*

It is true that this exclusion is superficial and that it no more modifies practical activities than prohibitions limit the son, who indulges in his unavowed pleasures as soon as he is no longer in his father's presence. Humanity can allow itself the pleasure of expressing, in the father's interest, conceptions marked with flat paternal sufficiency and blindness.

THE NOTION OF EXPENDITURE. "The Notion of Expenditure" first appeared in *La Critique sociale* 7 (January 1933). It is reprinted from *Visions of Excess: Selected Writings, 1927–1939,* translated by Allan Stoekl, with Carl R. Lovett and Donald M. Leslie, Jr. Copyright © University of Minnesota Press, 1985. Reprinted by permission.

In the practice of life, however, humanity acts in a way that allows for the satisfaction of disarmingly savage needs, and it seems able to subsist only at the limits of horror. Moreover, to the small extent that a man is incapable of yielding to considerations that either are official or are susceptible of becoming so, to the small extent that he is inclined to feel the attraction of a life devoted to the destruction of established authority, it is difficult to believe that a peaceful world, conforming to his interests, could be for him anything other than a convenient illusion.

The difficulties met with in the development of a conception that is not guided by the servile mode of father-son relations are thus not insurmountable. It is possible to admit the historical necessity of vague and disappointing images, used by a majority of people, who do not act without a minimum of error (which they use as if it were a drug)—and who, moreover, in all circumstances refuse to find their way in a labyrinth resulting from human inconsistencies. An extreme simplification represents, for the uncultivated or barely cultivated segments of the population, the only chance to avoid a diminution of aggressive force. But it would be cowardly to accept, as a limit to understanding, the conditions of poverty and necessity in which such simplified images are formed. And if a less arbitrary conception is condemned to remain esoteric, and if as such, in the present circumstances, it comes into conflict with an unhealthy repulsion, then one must stress that this repulsion is precisely the shame of a generation whose rebels are afraid of the noise of their own words. Thus one cannot take it into account.

The Principle of Loss

Human activity is not entirely reducible to processes of production and conservation, and consumption must be divided into two distinct parts. The first, reducible part is represented by the use of the minimum necessary for the conservation of life and the continuation of individuals' productive activity in a given society; it is therefore a question simply of the fundamental condition of productive activity. The second part is represented by so-called unproductive expenditures: luxury, mourning, war, cults, the construction of sumptuary monuments, games, spectacles, arts, perverse sexual activity (i.e., deflected from genital finality)—all these represent activities which, at least in primitive circumstances, have no end beyond themselves. Now it is necessary to reserve the use of the word *expenditure* for the designation of these unproductive forms, and not for the designation of all the modes of consumption that serve as a means to the end of production. Even though it is always possible to set the var-

ious forms of expenditure in opposition to each other, they constitute a group characterized by the fact that in each case the accent is placed on a *loss* that must be as great as possible in order for that activity to take on its true meaning.

This principle of loss, in other words, of unconditional expenditure, no matter how contrary it might be to the economic principle of balanced accounts (expenditure regularly compensated for by acquisition), only *rational* in the narrow sense of the word, can be illustrated through a small number of examples taken from common experience:

1. Jewels must not only be beautiful and dazzling (which would make the substitution of imitations possible): one sacrifices a fortune, preferring a diamond necklace; such a sacrifice is necessary for the constitution of this necklace's fascinating character. This fact must be seen in relation to the symbolic value of jewels, universal in psychoanalysis. When in a dream a diamond signifies excrement, it is not only a question of association by contrast; in the unconscious, jewels, like excrement, are cursed matter that flows from a wound: they are a part of oneself destined for open sacrifice (they serve, in fact, as sumptuous gifts charged with sexual love). The functional character of jewels requires their immense material value and alone explains the inconsequence of the most beautiful imitations, which are very nearly useless.

2. Cults require a bloody wasting of men and animals in *sacrifice*. In the etymological sense of the word, sacrifice is nothing other than the production of *sacred* things.

From the very first, it appears that sacred things are constituted by an operation of loss: in particular, the success of Christianity must be explained by the value of the theme of the Son of God's ignominious crucifixion, which carries human dread to a representation of loss and limitless degradation.

3. In various competitive games, loss in general is produced under complex conditions. Considerable sums of money are spent for the maintenance of quarters, animals, equipment, or men. As much energy as possible is squandered in order to produce a feeling of stupefaction—in any case with an intensity infinitely greater than in productive enterprises. The danger of death is not avoided; on the contrary, it is the object of a strong unconscious attraction. Besides, competitions are sometimes the occasion for the public distribution of prizes. Immense crowds are present; their passions most often burst forth beyond any restraint, and the loss of insane sums of money is set in motion in the form of wagers. It is true that this circulation of money profits a small number of professional bettors, but it is no less true that this circulation can be considered to be a real *charge* of the passions unleashed by competition and that, among a large number of bettors, it leads to losses disproportionate to

their means; these even attain such a level of madness that often the only way out for gamblers is prison or death. Beyond this, various modes of unproductive expenditure can be linked, depending on the circumstances, to great competitive spectacles, just as elements moving separately are caught up in a mightier whirlwind. Thus horse races are associated with a sumptuary process of social classification (the existence of Jockey Clubs needs only be mentioned) and the ostentatious display of the latest luxurious fashions. It is necessary in any case to observe that the complex of expenditure represented by present-day racing is insignificant when compared to the extravagance of the Byzantines, who tied the totality of their public activity to equestrian competition.

4. From the point of view of expenditure, artistic productions must be divided into two main categories, the first constituted by architectural construction, music, and dance. This category is comprised of *real* expenditures. Nevertheless, sculpture and painting, not to mention the use of sites for ceremonies and spectacles, introduces even into architecture the principle of the second category, that of *symbolic* expenditure. For their part, music and dance can easily be charged with external significations.

In their major form, literature and theater, which constitute the second category, provoke dread and horror through symbolic representations of tragic loss (degradation or death); in their minor form, they provoke laughter through representations which, though analogously structured, exclude certain seductive elements. The term poetry, applied to the least degraded and least intellectualized forms of the expression of a state of loss, can be considered synonymous with expenditure; it in fact signifies, in the most precise way, creation by means of loss. Its meaning is therefore close to that of *sacrifice*. It is true that the word "poetry" can only be appropriately applied to an extremely rare residue of what it commonly signifies and that, without a preliminary reduction, the worst confusions could result; it is, however, impossible in a first, rapid exposition to speak of the infinitely variable limits separating subsidiary formations from the residual element of poetry. It is easier to indicate that, for the rare human beings who have this element at their disposal, poetic expenditure ceases to be symbolic in its consequences; thus, to a certain extent, the function of representation engages the very life of the one who assumes it. It condemns him to the most disappointing forms of activity, to misery, to despair, to the pursuit of inconsistent shadows that provide nothing but vertigo or rage. The poet frequently can use words only for his own loss; he is often forced to choose between the destiny of a reprobate, who is as profoundly separated from society as dejecta are from apparent life, and a renunciation whose price is a mediocre activity, subordinated to vulgar and superficial needs.

Production, Exchange, and Unproductive Activity

Once the existence of expenditure as a social function has been established, it is then necessary to consider the relations between this function and those of production and acquisition that are opposed to it. These relations immediately present themselves as those of an *end* with *utility*. And if it is true that production and acquisition in their development and changes of form introduce a variable that must be understood in order to comprehend historical processes, they are, however, still only means subordinated to expenditure. As dreadful as it is, human poverty has never had a strong enough hold on societies to cause the concern for conservation—which gives production the appearance of an end—to dominate the concern for unproductive expenditure. In order to maintain this preeminence, since power is exercised by the classes that expend, poverty was excluded from all social activity. And the poor have no other way of reentering the circle of power than through the revolutionary destruction of the classes occupying that circle—in other words, through a bloody and in no way limited social expenditure.

The secondary character of production and acquisition in relation to expenditure appears most clearly in primitive economic institutions, since exchange is still treated as a sumptuary loss of ceded objects: thus at its *base* exchange presents itself as a process of expenditure, over which a process of acquisition has developed. Classical economics imagined that primitive exchange occurred in the form of barter; it had no reason to assume, in fact, that a means of acquisition such as exchange might have as its origin not the need to acquire that it satisfies today, but the contrary need, the need to destroy and to lose. The traditional conceptions of the origins of economy have only recently been disproved—even so recently that a great number of economists continue arbitrarily to represent barter as the ancestor of commerce.

In opposition to the artificial notion of barter, the archaic form of exchange has been identified by Mauss under the name *potlatch*,[1] borrowed from the Northwestern American Indians who provided such a remarkable example of it. Institutions analogous to the Indian *potlatch*, or their traces, have been very widely found.

The *potlatch* of the Tlingit, the Haida, the Tsimshian, and the Kwakiutl of the northwestern coast has been studied in detail since the end of the nineteenth century (but at that time it was not compared with the archaic forms of exchange

---

[1] See Marcel Mauss, *The Gift: Forms and Functions of Exchange in Archaic Societies*, New York, 1967. Originally published in French, 1925.

of other countries). The least advanced of these American tribes practice *potlatch* on the occasion of a person's change in situation—initiations, marriages, funerals—and, even in a more evolved form, it can never be separated from a festival; whether it provides the occasion for this festival, or whether it takes place on the festival's occasion. *Potlatch* excludes all bargaining and, in general, it is constituted by a considerable gift of riches, offered openly and with the goal of humiliating, defying, and *obligating* a rival. The exchange value of the gift results from the fact that the donee, in order to efface the humiliation and respond to the challenge, must satisfy the obligation (incurred by him at the time of acceptance) to respond later with a more valuable gift, in other words, to return with interest.

But the gift is not the only form of *potlatch;* it is equally possible to defy rivals through the spectacular destruction of wealth. It is through the intermediary of this last form that *potlatch* is reunited with religious sacrifice, since what is destroyed is theoretically offered to the mythical ancestors of the donees. Relatively recently a Tlingit chief appeared before his rival to slash the throats of some of his own slaves. This destruction was repaid at a given date by the slaughter of a greater number of slaves. The Tchoukchi of far northwestern Siberia, who have institutions analogous to *potlatch,* slaughter dog teams in order to stifle and humiliate another group. In northwestern America, destruction goes as far as the burning of villages and the smashing of flotillas of canoes. Emblazoned copper ingots, a kind of money on which the fictive value of an immense fortune is sometimes placed, are broken or thrown into the sea. The delirium of the festival can be associated equally with hecatombs of property and with gifts accumulated with the intention of stunning and humiliating.

Usury, which regularly intervenes in these operations as obligatory surplus at the time of the returned *potlatch,* gives rise to the observation that the loan with interest must be substituted for barter in the history of the origins of exchange. It must be recognized, in fact, that wealth is multiplied in *potlatch* civilizations in a way that recalls the inflation of credit in banking civilizations; in other words, it would be impossible to realize at once all the wealth possessed by the total number of donors resulting from the obligations contracted by the total number of donees. But this comparison applies only to a secondary characteristic of *potlatch.*

It is the constitution of a positive property of loss—from which spring nobility, honor, and rank in a hierarchy—that gives the institution its significant value. The gift must be considered as a loss and thus as a partial destruction, since the desire to destroy is in part transferred onto the recipient.

In unconscious forms, such as those described by psychoanalysis, it symbolizes excretion, which itself is linked to death, in conformity with the fundamental connection between anal eroticism and sadism. The excremental symbolism of emblazoned coppers, which on the Northwest Coast are the gift objects *par excellence,* is based on a very rich mythology. In Melanesia, the donor designates as his excrement magnificent gifts, which he deposits at the feet of the rival chief.

The consequences in the realm of acquisition are only the unwanted result—at least to the extent that the drives that govern the operation have remained primitive—of a process oriented in the opposite direction. "The ideal," indicates Mauss, "would be to give a *potlatch* and not have it returned." This ideal is realized in certain forms of destruction to which custom allows no possible response. On the other hand, since the yields of *potlatch* are in some ways pledged in advance in a new *potlatch,* the archaic principle of wealth is displayed with none of the attenuations that result from the avarice developed at later stages; wealth appears as an acquisition to the extent that power is acquired by a rich man, but it is entirely directed toward loss in the sense that this power is characterized as power to lose. It is only through loss that glory and honor are linked to wealth.

As a game, *potlatch* is the opposite of a principle of conservation: it puts an end to the stability of fortunes as it existed within the totemic economy, where possession was hereditary. An activity of excessive exchange replaced heredity (as source of possession) with a kind of deliriously formed ritual poker. But the players can never retire from the game, their fortunes made; they remain at the mercy of provocation. At no time does a fortune serve to *shelter its owner from need.* On the contrary, it functionally remains—as does its possessor—*at the mercy of a need for limitless loss,* which exists endemically in a social group.

The nonsumptuary production and consumption upon which wealth depends thus appear as relative utility.

The Functional Expenditure of the Wealthy Classes

The notion of *potlatch,* strictly speaking, should be reserved for expenditures of an agonistic type, which are instigated by challenges and which lead to responses. More precisely, it should be reserved for forms which, for archaic societies, are not distinguishable from *exchange.*

It is important to know that exchange, at its origin, was *immediately* subordinated to a human *end;* nevertheless it is evident that its development, linked to progress in the modes of production, only started at the stage at which this subordination ceased to be immediate. The very principle of the function of production requires that products be exempt from loss, at least provisionally.

In the market economy, the processes of exchange have an acquisitive sense. Fortunes are no longer placed on a gambling table; they have become relatively stable. It is only to the extent that stability is assured and can no longer be compromised by even considerable losses that these losses are submitted to the regime of unproductive expenditure. Under these new conditions, the elementary components of *potlatch* are found in forms that are no longer as directly agonistic. Expenditure is still destined to acquire or maintain rank, but in principle it no longer has the goal of causing another to lose his rank.

In spite of these attenuations, ostentatious loss remains universally linked to wealth, as its ultimate function.

More or less narrowly, social rank is linked to the possession of a fortune, but only on the condition that the fortune be partially sacrificed in unproductive social expenditures such as festivals, spectacles, and games. One notes that in primitive societies, where the exploitation of man by man is still fairly weak, the products of human activity not only flow in great quantities to rich men because of the protection or social leadership services these men supposedly provide, but also because of the spectacular collective expenditures for which they must pay. In so-called civilized societies, the fundamental *obligation* of wealth disappeared only in a fairly recent period. The decline of paganism led to a decline of the games and cults for which wealthy Romans were obliged to pay; thus it has been said that Christianity individualized property, giving its possessor total control over his products and abrogating his social function. It abrogated at least the obligation of this expenditure, for Christianity replaced pagan expenditure prescribed by custom with voluntary alms, either in the form of distributions from the rich to the poor, or (and above all) in the form of extremely significant contributions to churches and later to monasteries. And these churches and monasteries precisely assumed, in the Middle Ages, the major part of the spectacular function.

Today the great and free forms of unproductive social expenditure have disappeared. One must not conclude from this, however, that the very principle of expenditure is no longer the end of economic activity.

A certain evolution of wealth, whose symptoms indicate sickness and exhaustion, leads to shame in oneself accompanied by petty hypocrisy. Everything that was generous, orgiastic, and excessive has disappeared; the themes of rivalry upon which individual activity still depends develop in obscurity, and are as shameful as belching. The representatives of the bourgeoisie have adopted an effaced manner; wealth is now displayed behind closed doors, in accordance with depressing and boring conventions. In addition, people in the middle class—employees and small shopkeepers—having attained mediocre or minute fortunes, have managed to debase and subdivide ostentatious expenditure, of which nothing remains but vain efforts tied to tiresome rancor.

Such trickery has become the principle reason for living, working, and suffering for those who lack the courage to condemn this moldy society to revolutionary destruction. Around modern banks, as around the totem poles of the Kwakiutl, the same desire to dazzle animates individuals and leads them into a system of petty displays that blinds them to each other, as if they were staring into a blinding light. A few steps from the bank, jewels, dresses, and cars wait behind shop windows for the day when they will serve to establish the augmented splendor of a sinister industrialist and his even more sinister old wife. At a lower level, gilded clocks, dining room buffets, and artificial flowers render equally shameful service to a grocer and his wife. Jealousy arises between human beings, as it does among the savages, and with an equivalent brutality; only generosity and nobility have disappeared, and with them the dazzling contrast that the rich provided to the poor.

As the class that possesses the wealth—having received with wealth the obligation of functional expenditure—the modern bourgeoisie is characterized by the refusal in principle of this obligation. It has distinguished itself from the aristocracy through the fact that it has consented only to *spend for itself*, and within itself—in other words, by hiding its expenditures as much as possible from the eyes of the other classes. This particular form was originally due to the development of its wealth in the shadow of a more powerful noble class. The rationalist conceptions developed by the bourgeoisie, starting in the seventeenth century, were a response to these humiliating conceptions of restrained expenditure; this rationalism meant nothing other than the strictly economic representation of the world—economic in the vulgar sense, the bourgeois sense, of the word. The hatred of expenditure is the *raison d'être* of and the justification for the bourgeoisie; it is at the same time the principle of its horrifying hypocrisy. A fundamental grievance of the bourgeois was the prodigality of feudal society and, after coming to power, they believed that, because of their habits of accumulation, they were capable of acceptably dominating the poorer classes. And it is right to recognize that the people are incapable of hating them as much as their former masters, to the extent that they are incapable of loving them, for the bourgeois are incapable of concealing a sordid face, a face so rapacious and lacking in nobility, so frighteningly small, that all human life, upon seeing it, seems degraded.

In opposition, the people's consciousness is reduced to maintaining profoundly the principle of expenditure by representing bourgeois existence as the shame of man and as a sinister cancellation.

Class Struggle

In trying to maintain sterility in regard to expenditure, in conformity with a reasoning that balances *accounts,* bourgeois society has only managed to develop a universal meanness. Human life only rediscovers agitation on the scale of irreducible needs through the efforts of those who push the consequences of current rationalist conceptions as far as they will go. What remains of the traditional modes of expenditure has become atrophied, and living sumptuary tumult has been lost in the unprecedented explosion of *class struggle.*

The components of *class struggle* are seen in the process of expenditure, dating back to the archaic period. In *potlatch,* the rich man distributes products furnished him by other, impoverished, men. He tries to rise above a rival who is rich like himself, but the ultimate stage of his foreseen elevation has no more necessary a goal than his further separation from the nature of destitute men. Thus expenditure, even though it might be a social function, immediately leads to an agonistic and apparently antisocial act of separation. The rich man consumes the poor man's losses, creating for him a category of degradation and abjection that leads to slavery. Now it is evident that, from the endlessly transmitted heritage of the sumptuary world, the modern world has received slavery, and has reserved it for the proletariat. Without a doubt bourgeois society, which pretends to govern according to rational principles, and which, through its own actions, moreover, tends to realize a certain human homogeneity, does not accept without protest a division that seems destructive to man himself; it is incapable, however, of pushing this resistance further than theoretical negation. It gives the workers rights equal to those of the masters, and it announces this *equality* by inscribing that word on walls. But the masters, who act as if they were the expression of society itself, are preoccupied—more seriously than with any other concern—with showing that they do not in any way share the abjection of the men they employ. *The end of the workers' activity is to produce in order to live, but the bosses' activity is to produce in order to condemn the working producers to a hideous degradation*—for there is no disjunction possible between, on the one hand, the characterization the bosses seek through their modes of expenditure, which tend to elevate them high above human baseness, and on the other

hand this baseness itself, of which this characterization is a function.

In opposition to this conception of agonistic social expenditure, there is the representation of numerous bourgeois efforts to ameliorate the lot of the workers—but this representation is only the expression of the cowardice of the modern upper classes, who no longer have the force to recognize the results of their own destructive acts. The expenditures taken on by the capitalists in order to aid the proletarians and give them a chance to pull themselves up on the social ladder only bear witness to their inability (due to exhaustion) to carry out thoroughly a sumptuary process. Once the loss of the poor man is accomplished, little by little the pleasure of the rich man is emptied and neutralized; it gives way to a kind of apathetic indifference. Under these conditions, in order to maintain a neutral state rendered relatively agreeable by apathy (and which exists in spite of troublesome elements such as sadism and pity), it can be useful to compensate for the expenditure that engenders abjection with a new expenditure, which tends to attenuate it. The bosses' political sense, together with certain partial developments of prosperity, has allowed this process of compensation to be, at times, quite extensive. Thus in the Anglo-Saxon countries, and in particular in the United States of America, the primary process takes place at the expense of only a relatively small portion of the population: to a certain extent, the working class itself has been led to participate in it (above all when this was facilitated by the preliminary existence of a class held to be abject by common accord, as in the case of the blacks). But these subterfuges, whose importance is in any case strictly limited, do not modify in any way the fundamental division between noble and ignoble men. The cruel game of social life does not vary among the different civilized countries, where the insulting splendor of the rich loses and degrades the human nature of the lower class.

It must be added that the attenuation of the masters' brutality—which in any case has less to do with destruction itself than with the psychological tendencies to destroy—corresponds to the general atrophy of the ancient sumptuary processes that characterizes the modern era.

Class struggle, on the contrary, becomes the grandest form of social expenditure when it is taken up again and developed, this time on the part of the workers, and on such a scale that it threatens the very existence of the masters.

Christianity and Revolution

Short of revolt, it has been possible for the provoked poor to refuse all moral participation in a system in which men oppress men; in certain historical circumstances, they succeeded, through the use of symbols even more striking than reality, in lowering all of "human nature" to such a horrifying ignominy that the pleasure found by the rich in measuring the poverty of others suddenly became too acute to be endured without vertigo. Thus, independently of all ritual forms, an exchange of exasperated challenges was established, exacerbated above all by the poor, a *potlatch* in which real refuse and revealed moral filth entered into a rivalry of horrible grandeur with everything in the world that was rich, pure, and brilliant; and an exceptional outlet was found for this form of spasmodic convulsion in religious despair, which was its unreserved exploitation.

In Christianity, the alternations between the exaltation and dread, tortures and orgies constituting religious life were conjoined in a more tragic way and were merged with a sick social structure, which was tearing itself apart with the dirtiest cruelty. The triumphal song of the Christians glorifies God because he has entered into the bloody game of social war, and because he has "hurled the powerful from the heights of their grandeur and has exalted the miserably poor." Their myths associate social ignomiy and the cadaverous degradation of the torture victim with divine splendor. In this way religion assumes the total oppositional function manifested by contrary forces, which up to this point had been divided between the rich and the poor, with the one group condemning the other to ruin. It is closely tied to terrestrial despair, since it itself is only an epiphenomenon of the measureless hate that divides men—but an epiphenomenon that tends to substitute itself for the totality of divergent processes it summarizes. In conformity with the words attributed to Christ, who said he came to divide and not to reign, religion thus does not at all try to do away with what others consider the scourge of man. On the contrary, in its immediate form, it wallows in a revolting impurity that is indispensable to its ecstatic torment.

The meaning of Christianity is given in the development of the delirious consequences of the expenditure of classes, in a mental agonistic orgy practiced at the expense of the real struggle.

However, in spite of the importance that it has had in human activity, Christian *humiliation* is only an episode in the historic struggle of the ignoble against the noble, of the impure against the pure. It is as if society, conscious of its own intolerable splitting, had become for a time dead drunk in order to enjoy it sadistically. But the heaviest drunkenness has not done away with the consequences of human poverty, and, with the exploited classes opposing the superior classes with greater lucidity, no conceivable limit can be assigned to hatred. In historical agitation, only the word Revolution dominates the customary confusion and carries with it the promise that answers the unlimited demands of the masses.

As for the masters and the exploiters, whose function is to create the contemptuous forms that exclude human nature—causing this nature to exist at the limits of the earth, in other words in mud—a simple law of reciprocity requires that they be condemned to fear, to the *great night* when their beautiful phrases will be drowned out by death screams in riots. That is the bloody hope which, each day, is one with the existence of the people, and which sums up the insubordinate content of the class struggle.

Class struggle has only one possible end: the loss of those who have worked to lose "human nature."

But whatever form of development is foreseen, be it revolutionary or servile, the general convulsions constituted eighteen hundred years ago by the religious ecstasy of the Christians, and today by the workers' movement, must equally be represented as a decisive impulse *constraining* society to use the exclusion of one class by another to realize a mode of expenditure as tragic and as free as possible, and at the same time *constraining* it to introduce sacred forms so human that the traditional forms become relatively contemptible. It is the tropic character of such movements that accounts for the total human value of the workers' Revolution, a Revolution capable of exerting a force of attraction as strong as the force that directs simple organisms toward the sun.

The Insubordination of Material Facts

Human life, distinct from juridical existence, existing as it does on a globe isolated in celestial space, from night to day and from one country to another—human life cannot in any way be limited to the closed systems assigned to it by reasonable conceptions. The immense travail of recklessness, discharge, and upheaval that constitutes life could be expressed by stating that life starts only with the deficit of these systems; at least what it allows in the way of order and reserve has meaning only from the moment when the ordered and reserved forces liberate and lose themselves for ends that cannot be subordinated to anything one can account for. It is only by such insubordination—even if it is impoverished—that the human race ceases to be isolated in the unconditional splendor of material things.

In fact, in the most universal way, isolated or in groups, men find themselves constantly engaged in processes of expenditure. Variations in form do not in any way alter the fundamental characteristics of these processes, whose principle is loss. A certain excitation, whose sum total is maintained at a noticeably constant level, animates collectivities and individuals. In their intensified form, the *states of excitation,* which are comparable to toxic states, can be defined as the illogical and irresistible impulse to reject material or moral goods that it would have been possible to utilize rationally (in conformity with the balancing of accounts). Connected to the losses that are realized in this way—in the case of the "lost woman" as well as in the case of military expenditure—is the creation of unproductive values; the most absurd of these values, and the one that makes people the most rapacious, is *glory.* Made complete through degradation, glory, appearing in a sometimes sinister and sometimes brilliant form, has never ceased to dominate social existence; it is impossible to attempt to do anything without it when it is dependent on the blind practice of personal or social loss.

In this way the boundless refuse of activity pushes human plans—including those associated with economic operations—into the game of characterizing universal matter; matter, in fact, can only be defined as the *nonlogical difference* that represents in relation to the *economy* of the universe what *crime* represents in relation to the law. The glory that sums up or symbolizes (without exhausting) the object of free expenditure, while it can never exclude crime, cannot be distinguished—at least if one takes into account the only characterization that has a value comparable to matter—from the *insubordinate characterization,* which is not the condition for anything else.

If on the other hand one demonstrates the interest, concurrent with glory (as well as with degradation), which the human community necessarily sees in the qualitative change constantly realized by the movement of history, and if, finally, one demonstrates that this movement is impossible to contain or direct toward a limited end, it becomes possible, having abandoned all reserves, to assign a *relative* value to utility. Men assure their own subsistence or avoid suffering, not because these functions themselves lead to a sufficient result, but in order to accede to the insubordinate function of free expenditure.

John Crowe Ransom

(1888–1974)

Most influential of the American New Critics, Ransom titled his 1941 collection of essays *The New Criticism.* An earlier book, *The World's Body* (1938), illustrated in its title his desire for a theory emphasizing poetry's "sense of the real density and contingency of the world in which arguments and plans have to be pursued." This amounts to an emphasis on particularity against generality, and it leads Ransom to attack what he calls "Platonic" poetry, in which images are employed to express abstract ideas. But Ransom does not advocate the extreme particularity of "physical" poetry, such as imagism. He does not believe poetry is pure perception or pure emotion any more than he thinks it is moral or scientific discourse clothed in tropes; in his view no discourse is ever pure, though it is clear that scientific and logical discourse tries to be. If poetry, however, should succeed in becoming pure it would fail. Poetry, like a democracy, must allow "the free exercise . . . of private and independent characters," while scientific discourse has a single totalitarian end. In this distinction Ransom recalls Kant's purposiveness without a purpose. His interest in poetry as language allies him to the Russian Formalists.

For Ransom, the poem has a central logic, situation, or "paraphrasable core," and "a context of lively local details." The poem differs from scientific discourse because the details of scientific discourse are *always* properly subordinate to the thesis. In the poem, detail may struggle with and change any apparent concept in the poem and make expression of the concept not the ultimate purpose of the poem. Ransom's terms are designed to encourage discussion of a poem in its fullness without reducing it to its paraphrase. Despite all his cautions, however, the terms sound a bit too much like the old ones, *form* and *content.* One of Ransom's students, Cleanth Brooks, struggles with this problem in his essay *The Heresy of Paraphrase.*

Ransom's influence can be seen very clearly in much criticism up through the sixties—particularly "objective" or "contextualist" criticism like Krieger's. Both these terms imply the critic's acknowledgment that all the parts of a poem that can be isolated for comment are affected by and affect in turn all the other parts. There is a sense, then, in which criticism must be an examination of the poem's "being" rather than an explanation of its "meaning." Thus Ransom's use of the term *ontology.*

Ransom's criticism includes *God Without Thunder* (1930), *The World's Body* (1938), *The New Criticism* (1941), and *Poems and Essays* (1955). See also Murray Krieger, *The New Apologists for Poetry* (1956); J. L. Stewart, *John Crowe Ransom* (1962) and *The Burden of Time* (1965); T. H. Parsons, "Ransom and the Poetics of Monastic Ecstasy," *Modern Language Quarterly,* XXVI (1965), 571–85; Robert Buffington, *The Equilibrist: A Study of John Crowe Ransom's Poetry* (1967); Thornton H. Parsons, *John Crowe Ransom* (1969); James E. Magner, *John Crowe Ransom* (1971); Thomas Daniel Young, *Gentleman in a Dustcoat* (1976); and Kieran Quinlan, *John Crowe Ransom's Secular Faith* (1989).

Poetry: A Note in Ontology

A poetry may be distinguished from a poetry by virtue of subject matter, and subject matter may be differentiated with respect to its ontology, or the reality of its being. An excellent variety of critical doctrine arises recently out of this differentiation, and thus perhaps criticism leans again upon ontological analysis as it was meant to do by Kant. The recent critics remark in effect that some poetry deals with things, while some other poetry deals with ideas. The two poetries will differ from each other as radically as a thing differs from an idea.

The distinction in the hands of critics is a fruitful one. There is apt to go along with it a principle of valuation, which is the consequence of a temperament, and therefore basic. The critic likes things and intends that his poet shall offer them; or likes ideas and intends that he shall offer them; and approves him as he does the one or the other. Criticism cannot well go much deeper than this. The critic has carried to the last terms his analysis of the stuff of which poetry is made, and valued it frankly as his temperament or his need requires him to value it.

So philosophical a critic seems to be highly modern. He is; but this critic as a matter of fact is peculiarly on one side of the question. (The implication is unfavorable to the other side of the question.) He is in revolt against the tyranny of ideas, and against the poetry which celebrates ideas, and which may be identified—so far as his usual generalization may be trusted—with the hateful poetry of the Victorians. His bias is in favor of the things. On the other hand the critic who likes Victorian verse, or the poetry of ideas, has probably not thought of anything of so grand a simplicity as electing between the things and the ideas, being apparently not quite capable of the ontological distinction. Therefore he does not know the real or constitutional ground of his liking, and may somewhat ingenuously claim that his predilection is for those poets who give him inspiration, or comfort, or truth, or honest meters, or something else equally "worthwhile." But Plato, who was not a modern, was just as clear as we are about the basic distinction between the ideas and the things, and yet stands far apart from the aforesaid conscious modern in passionately preferring the ideas over the things. The weight of Plato's testimony would certainly fall on the side of the Victorians, though they may scarcely have thought of calling him as their witness. But this consideration need not conclude the hearing.

I. Physical Poetry

The poetry which deals with things was much in favor a few years ago with the resolute body of critics. And the critics affected the poets. If necessary, they became the poets, and triumphantly illustrated the new mode. The imagists[1] were important figures in the history of our poetry, and they were both theorists and creators. It was their intention to present things in their thinginess, or *Dinge* in their *Dinglichkeit;* and to such an extent had the public lost its sense of *Dinglichkeit* that their redirection was wholesome. What the public was inclined to seek in poetry was ideas, whether large ones or small ones, grand ones or pretty ones, certainly ideas to live by and die by, but what the imagists identified with the stuff of poetry was, simply, things.

Their application of their own principle was sufficiently heroic, though they scarcely consented to be as extreme in the practice as in the theory. They had artistic talent, every one of the original group, and it was impossible that they should make of poetry so simple an exercise as in doctrine they seemed to think it was. Yet Miss Lowell[2] wrote a poem on *Thompson's Lunch Room, Grand Central Station;* it is admirable if its intention is to show the whole reach of her courage. Its detail goes like this:

> Jagged greenwhite bowls of pressed glass
> Rearing snow-peaks of chipped sugar
> Above the lighthouse-shaped castors
> Of gray pepper and gray-white salt.

For most of us as for the public idealist, with his "values," this is inconsequential. Unhappily it seems that the things as things do not necessarily interest us, and that in fact we are not quite constructed with the capacity for a disinterested interest. But it must be noted even here that the things are on their good behavior, looking rather well, and arranged by lines into something approaching a military formation. More technically, there is cross-imagery in the snowpeaks of sugar, and in the lighthouse-shaped castors, and cross-imagery involves association, and will presently involve dissociation and thinking. The meter is but a vestige, but even so it means something, for meter is a powerful intellectual determinant marshaling the words and, inevitably, the

POETRY: A NOTE IN ONTOLOGY. Ransom's *Poetry: A Note in Ontology* was first published in 1934. The text is from *The World's Body* by John Crowe Ransom. Copyright 1938 Charles Scribner's Sons; renewal copyright © 1966 by John Crowe Ransom. Reprinted by permission of Charles Scribner's Sons.

[1]For a statement of imagist principles see Ezra Pound, *A Retrospect,* in *Literary Essays of Ezra Pound.*
[2]Amy Lowell (1874–1925), American imagist poet.

things. The *Dinglichkeit* of this imagist specimen, or the realism, was therefore not pure. But it was nearer pure than the world was used to in poetry, and the exhibit was astonishing.

For the purpose of this note I shall give to such poetry, dwelling as exclusively as it dares upon physical things, the name *physical poetry*. It is to stand opposite to that poetry which dwells as firmly as it dares upon ideas.

But perhaps thing versus idea does not seem to name an opposition precisely. Then we might phrase it a little differently: image versus idea. The idealistic philosophies are not sure that things exist, but they mean the equivalent when they refer to images. (Or they may consent to perceptions; or to impressions, following Hume, and following Croce, who remarks that they are preintellectual and independent of concepts. It is all the same, unless we are extremely technical.) It is sufficient if they concede that image is the raw material of idea. Though it may be an unwieldy and useless affair for the idealist as it stands, much needing to be licked into shape, nevertheless its relation to idea is that of a material cause, and it cannot be dispossessed of its priority.

It cannot be dispossessed of a primordial freshness, which idea can never claim. An idea is derivative and tamed. The image is in the natural or wild state, and it has to be discovered there, not put there, obeying its own law and none of ours. We think we can lay hold of image and take it captive, but the docile captive is not the real image but only the idea, which is the image with its character beaten out of it.

But we must be very careful: idealists are nothing if not dialectical. They object that an image in an original state of innocence is a delusion and cannot exist, that no image ever comes to us which does not imply the world of ideas, that there is "no percept without a concept." There is something in it. Every property discovered in the image is a universal property, and nothing discovered in the image is marvelous in kind though it may be pinned down historically or statistically as a single instance. But there is this to be understood too: the image which is not remarkable in any particular property is marvelous in its assemblage of many properties, a manifold of properties, like a mine or a field, something to be explored for the properties; yet science can manage the image, which is infinite in properties, only by equating it to the one property with which the science is concerned; for science at work is always *a science,* and committed to a special interest. It is not by refutation but by abstraction that science destroys the image. It means to get its "value" out of the image, and we may be sure that it has no use for the image in its original state of freedom. People who are engrossed with their pet "values" become habitual killers. Their game is the images, or the things, and they acquire the ability to shoot them as far off as they can be seen, and do.

It is thus that we lose the power of imagination, or whatever faculty it is by which we are able to contemplate things as they are in their rich and contingent materiality. But our dreams reproach us, for in dreams they come alive again. Likewise our memory; which makes light of our science by recalling the images in their panoply of circumstance and with their morning freshness upon them.

It is the dream, the recollection, which compels us to poetry, and to deliberate aesthetic experience. It can hardly be argued, I think, that the arts are constituted automatically out of original images, and arise in some early age of innocence. (Though Croce seems to support this view, and to make art a preadult stage of experience.) Art is based on second love, not first love. In it we make a return to something which we had willfully alienated. The child is occupied mostly with things, but it is because he is still unfurnished with systematic ideas, not because he is a ripe citizen by nature and comes along already trailing clouds of glory.[3] Images are clouds of glory for the man who has discovered that ideas are a sort of darkness. Imagism, that is, the recent historical movement, may resemble a naive poetry of mere things, but we can read the theoretical pronouncements of Imagists, and we can learn that Imagism is motivated by a distaste for the systematic abstractedness of thought. It presupposes acquaintance with science; that famous activity which is "constructive" with respect to the tools of our economic role in this world, and destructive with respect to nature. Imagists wish to escape from science by immersing themselves in images.

Not far off the simplicity of Imagism was, a little later, the subtler simplicity of Mr. George Moore's project shared with several others, in behalf of "pure poetry." In Moore's house on Ebury Street they talked about poetry, with an after dinner warmth if not an early morning discretion, and their tastes agreed almost perfectly and reinforced one another. The fruit of these conversations was the volume *Pure Poetry.* It must have been the most exclusive anthology of English poetry that had yet appeared, since its room was closed to all the poems that dallied visibly with ideas, so that many poems that had been coveted by all other anthologists do not appear there. Nevertheless the book is delicious, and something more deserves to be said for it.

First, that "pure poetry" is a kind of physical poetry. Its visible content is a thing-content. Technically, I suppose, it is effective in this character if it can exhibit its material in such a way that an image or set of images and not an idea must occupy the foreground of the reader's attention. Thus: "Full fathom five thy father lies / Of his bones are coral

---

[3]See Wordsworth's *Ode: Intimations of Immortality.*

made.''[4] Here it is difficult for anybody (except the perfect idealist who is always theoretically possible and who would expect to take a return from anything whatever) to receive any experience except that of a very distinct image, or set of images. It has the configuration of image, which consists in being sharp of edges, and the modality of image, which consists in being given and nonnegotiable, and the density, which consists in being full, a plenum of qualities. What is to be done with it? It is pure exhibit; it is to be contemplated; perhaps it is to be enjoyed. The art of poetry depends more frequently on this faculty than on any other in its repertory; the faculty of presenting images so whole and clean that they resist the catalysis of thought.

And something else must be said, going in the opposite direction. "Pure poetry," all the same, is not as pure as it is claimed to be, though on the whole it is physical poetry. (All true poetry is a phase of physical poetry.) It is not as pure as imagism is, or at least it is not as pure as imagism would be if it lived up to its principles; and in fact it is significant that the volume does not contain any imagist poems, which argues a difference in taste somewhere. Imagism may take trifling things for its material, presumably it will take the first things the poet encounters, since "importance" and "interest" are not primary qualities which a thing possesses but secondary or tertiary ones which the idealist attributes to it by virtue of his own requirements. "Pure poetry" as Moore conceives it, and as the lyrics of Poe and Shakespeare offer it, deals with the more dramatic materials, and here dramatic means human, or at least capable of being referred to the critical set of human interests. Employing this sort of material the poet cannot exactly intend to set the human economists in us actually into motion, but perhaps he does intend to comfort us with the fleeting sense that it is potentially our kind of material.

In the same way "pure poetry" is nicely metered, whereas imagism was free. Technique is written on it. And, by the way, the anthology contains no rugged anonymous Scottish ballad either, and probably for a like reason; because it would not be technically finished. Now both Moore and De La Mare are accomplished conservative artists, and what they do or what they approve may be of limited range but it is sure to be technically admirable, and it is certain that they understand what technique in poetry is though they do not define it. Technique takes the thing-content and meters and orders it. Meter is not an original property of things. It is artificial, and conveys the sense of human control, even if it does not wish to impair the thinginess of the things. Metric is a science, and so far as we attend to it we are within the

scientific atmosphere. Order is the logical arrangement of things. It involves the dramatic "form" which selects the things, and brings out their appropriate qualities, and carries them through a systematic course of predication until the total impression is a unit of logic and not merely a solid lump of thing-content. The "pure poems" which Moore admires are studied, though it would be fatal if they looked studious. A sustained effort of ideation effected these compositions. It is covered up, and communicates itself only on a subliminal plane of consciousness. But experienced readers are quite aware of it; they know at once what is the matter when they encounter a realism shamelessly passing for poetry, or a well-planned but blundering poetry.

As critics we should have every good will toward physical poetry: it is the basic constituent of any poetry. But the product is always something short of a pure or absolute existence, and it cannot quite be said that it consists of nothing but physical objects. The fact is that when we are more than usually satisfied with a physical poetry our analysis will probably disclose that it is more than usually impure.

II. Platonic Poetry

The poetry of ideas I shall denominate: *Platonic poetry*. This also has grades of purity. A discourse which employed only abstract ideas with no images would be a scientific document and not a poem at all, not even a Platonic poem. Platonic poetry dips heavily into the physical. If physical poetry tends to employ some ideation surreptitiously while still looking innocent of idea, Platonic poetry more than returns the compliment, for it tries as hard as it can to look like physical poetry, as if it proposed to conceal its medicine, which is the idea to be propagated, within the sugar candy of objectivity and *Dinglichkeit*. As an instance, it is almost inevitable that I quote a famous Victorian utterance:

> The year's at the spring
> And day's at the morn;
> Morning's at seven;
> The hill-side's dew-pearled;
>
> The lark's on the wing;
> The snail's on the thorn:
> God's in his heaven—
> All's right with the world![5]

which is a piece of transparent homiletics; for in it six pretty, coordinate images are marched, like six little lambs to the

---

[4]*The Tempest*, I. ii. 397–98.

[5]Browning, *Pippa Passes*, 221–28.

slaughter, to a colon and a powerful text. Now the exhibits of this poetry in the physical kind are always large, and may take more of the attention of the reader than is desired, but they are meant mostly to be illustrative of the ideas. It is on this ground that idealists like Hegel detect something unworthy, like a pedagogical trick, in poetry after all, and consider that the race will abandon it when it has outgrown its childishness and is enlightened.

The ablest arraignment of Platonic poetry that I have seen, as an exercise which is really science but masquerades as poetry by affecting a concern for physical objects, is that of Mr. Allen Tate in a series of studies recently in *The New Republic*.[6] I will summarize. Platonic poetry is allegory, a discourse in things, but on the understanding that they are translatable at every point into ideas. (The usual ideas are those which constitute the popular causes, patriotic, religious, moral, or social.) Or Platonic poetry is the elaboration of ideas as such, but in proceeding introduces for ornament some physical properties after the style of physical poetry; which is rhetoric. It is positive when the poet believes in the efficacy of the ideas. It is negative when he despairs of their efficacy, because they have conspicuously failed to take care of him, and utters his personal wail: "I fall upon the thorns of life! I bleed!"[7] This is "Romantic irony," which comes at occasional periods to interrupt the march of scientific optimism. But it still falls under the category of Platonism; it generally proposes some other ideas to take the place of those which are in vogue.

But why Platonism? To define Platonism we must remember that it is not the property of the historical person who reports dialogues about it in an academy, any more than "pure poetry" is the property of the talkers who describe it from a house on Ebury Street. Platonism, in the sense I mean, is the name of an impulse that is native to us all, frequent, tending to take a too complete possession of our minds. Why should the spirit of mortal be proud? The chief explanation is that modern mortal is probably a Platonist. We are led to believe that nature is rational and that by the force of reasoning we shall possess it. I have read upon high authority: "Two great forces are persistent in Plato: the love of truth and zeal for human improvement." The forces are one force. We love to view the world under universal or scientific ideas to which we give the name truth; and this is because the ideas seem to make not for righteousness but for mastery. The Platonic view of the world is ultimately the predatory, for it reduces to the scientific, which we know. The Platonic idea becomes the logos which science worships, which is the

occidental god, whose minions we are, and whose children, claiming a large share in his powers for patrimony.

Now the fine Platonic world of ideas fails to coincide with the original world of perception, which is the world populated by the stubborn and contingent objects, and to which as artists we fly in shame. The sensibility manifested by artists makes fools of scientists, if the latter are inclined to take their special and quite useful form of truth as the whole and comprehensive article. A dandified pagan worldling like Moore can always defeat Platonism; he does it every hour; he can exhibit the savor of his fish and wines, the fragrance of his coffee and cigars, and the solidity of the images in his favorite verse. These are objects which have to be experienced, and cannot be reported, for what is their simple essence that the Platonist can abstract? Moore may sound mystical but he is within the literal truth when he defends "pure poetry" on the ground that the things are constant, and it is the ideas which change—changing according to the latest mode under which the species indulges its grandiose expectation of subjugating nature. The things are constant in the sense that the ideas are never emancipated from the necessity of referring back to them as their original; and the sense that they are not altered nor diminished no matter which ideas may take off from them as a point of departure. The way to obtain the true *Dinglichkeit* of a formal dinner or a landscape or a beloved person is to approach the object as such, and in humility; then it unfolds a nature which we are unprepared for if we have put our trust in the simple idea which attempted to represent it.

The special antipathy of Moore is to the ideas as they put on their moral complexion, the ideas that relate everything to that insignificant center of action, the human "soul" in its most Platonic and Pharisaic aspect. Nothing can darken perception better than a repetitive moral earnestness, based on the reputed superiority and higher destiny of the human species. If morality is the code by which we expect the race to achieve the more perfect possession of nature, it is an incitement to a more heroic science, but not to aesthetic experience, nor religious; if it is the code of humility, by which we intend to know nature as nature is, that is another matter; but in an age of science morality is inevitably for the general public the former; and so transcendent a morality as the latter is now unheard of. And therefore:

> O love, *they* die in yon rich sky,
>   *They* faint on hill or field of river;
> *Our* echoes roll from soul to soul,
>   And grow forever and forever.[8]

---

[6]See Tate's *Three Types of Poetry,* in his *On the Limits of Poetry.*
[7]Shelley, *Ode to the West Wind,* 54

[8]Tennyson, *The Splendor Falls on Castle Walls,* 13–16.

The italics are mine. These lines conclude an otherwise in- nocent poem, a candidate for the anthology, upon which Moore remarks: "The Victorian could never reconcile him- self to finishing a poem without speaking about the soul, and the lines are particularly vindictive." Vindictive is just. By what right did the Laureate[9] exult in the death of the physical echoes and call upon his love to witness it, but out of the imperiousness of his savage Platonism? Plato himself would have admired this ending, and considered that it redeemed an otherwise vicious poem.

Why do persons who have ideas to promulgate risk the trial by poetry? If the poets are hired to do it, which is the polite conception of some Hegelians, why do their employ- ers think it worth the money, which they hold in public trust for the cause? Does a science have to become a poetry too? A science is the less effective as a science when it muddies its clear waters with irrelevance, a sermon becomes less co- gent when it begins to quote the poets. The moralist, the sci- entist, and the prophet of idealism think evidently that they must establish their conclusions in poetry, though they reach these conclusions upon quite other evidence. The poetry is likely to destroy the conclusions with a sort of death by drowning, if it is a free poetry.

When that happens the Platonists may be cured of Pla- tonism. There are probably two cures, of which this is the better. One cure is by adversity, by the failure of the ideas to work, on account of treachery or violence, or the contingen- cies of weather, constitution, love, and economics; leaving the Platonist defeated and bewildered, possibly humbled, but on the other hand possibly turned cynical and worthless. Very much preferable is the cure which comes by education in the fine arts, erasing his Platonism more gently, leading him to feel that that is not a becoming habit of mind which dulls the perceptions.

The definition which some writers have given to art is: the reference of the idea to the image. The implication is that the act is not for the purpose of honest comparison so much as for the purpose of proving the idea by the image. But in the event the idea is not disproved so much as it is made to look ineffective and therefore foolish. The ideas will not cover the objects upon which they are imposed, they are too attenuated and threadlike; for ideas have extension and ob- jects have intension, but extension is thin while intension is thick.

There must be a great deal of genuine poetry which started in the poet's mind as a thesis to be developed, but in which the characters and the situations have developed faster

than the thesis, and of their own accord. The thesis disap- pears; or it is recaptured here and there and at the end, and lodged sententiously with the reader, where every successive reading of the poem will dislodge it again. Like this must be some plays, even some play out of Shakespeare, whose the- sis would probably be disentangled with difficulty out of the crowded pageant; or some narrative poem with a moral plot but much pure detail; perhaps some "occasional" piece of a Laureate or official person, whose purpose is compromised but whose personal integrity is saved by his wavering be- tween the sentiment which is a public duty and the experi- ence which he has in his own right; even some proclaimed allegory, like Spenser's, unlikely as that may seem, which does not remain transparent and everywhere translatable into idea but makes excursions into the territory of objectivity. These are hybrid performances. They cannot possess beauty of design, though there may be a beauty in detailed passages. But it is common enough, and we should be grateful. The mind is a versatile agent, and unexpectedly stubborn in its determination not really to be hardened in Platonism. Even in an age of science like the nineteenth century the poetic talents are not so loyal to its apostolic zeal as they and it suppose, and do not deserve the unqualified scorn which it is fashionable to offer them, now that the tide has turned, for their performance is qualified.

But this may not be stern enough for concluding a note on Platonic poetry. I refer again to that whose Platonism is steady and malignant. This poetry is an imitation of physical poetry, and not really a poetry. Platonists practice their bogus poetry in order to show that an image will prove an idea, but the literature which succeeds in this delicate mission does not contain real images but illustrations.

III. Metaphysical Poetry

"Most men," Mr. Moore observes,

> read and write poetry between fifteen and thirty and afterwards very seldom, for in youth we are attracted by ideas, and modern poetry being con- cerned almost exclusively with ideas we live on duty, liberty, and fraternity as chameleons are said to live on light and air, till at last we turn from ideas to things, thinking that we have lost our taste for poetry, unless, perchance, we are classical scholars.

Much is conveyed in this characteristic sentence, even in proportion to its length. As for the indicated chronology, the cart is put after the horse, which is its proper sequence.

---

[9]Tennyson was Poet Laureate from 1850 to 1892.

And it is pleasant to be confirmed in the belief that many men do recant from their Platonism and turn back to things. But it cannot be exactly a *volte-face,* for there are qualifications. If pure ideas were what these men turn from, they would have no poetry at all in the first period, and if pure things were what they turn to, they would be having not a classical poetry but a pure imagism, if such a thing is possible, in the second.

The mind does not come unscathed and virginal out of Platonism. Ontological interest would have to develop curiously, or wastefully and discontinuously, if men through their youth must cultivate the ideas so passionately that upon its expiration they are done with ideas forever and ready to become as little (and prelogical) children. Because of the foolishness of idealists are ideas to be taboo for the adult mind? And, as critics, what are we to do with those poems (like *The Canonization* and *Lycidas*[10]) which could not obtain admission by Moore into the anthology but which very likely are the poems we cherish beyond others?

The reputed "innocence" of the aesthetic moment, the "knowledge without desire" which Schopenhauer praises, must submit to a little scrutiny, like anything else that looks too good to be true. We come into this world as aliens come into a land which they must conquer if they are to live. For native endowment we have an exacting "biological" constitution which knows precisely what it needs and determines for us our inevitable desires. There can be no certainty that any other impulses are there, for why should they be? They scarcely belong in the biological picture. Perhaps we are simply an efficient animal species, running smoothly, working fast, finding the formula of life only too easy, and after a certain apprenticeship piling up power and wealth far beyond the capacity of our appetites to use. What will come next? Perhaps poetry, if the gigantic effort of science begins to seem disproportionate to the reward, according to a sense of diminishing returns. But before this pretty event can come to pass, it is possible that every act of attention which is allowed us is conditioned by a gross and selfish interest.

Where is innocence then? The aesthetic moment appears as a curious moment of suspension; between the Platonism in us, which is militant, always sciencing and devouring, and a starved inhibited aspiration towards innocence which, if it could only be free, would like to respect and know the object as it might of its own accord reveal itself.

The poetic impulse is not free, yet it holds out stubbornly against science for the enjoyment of its images. It

means to reconstitute the world of perceptions. Finally there is suggested some such formula as the following:

Science gratifies a rational or practical impulse and exhibits the minimum of perception. Art gratifies a perceptual impulse and exhibits the minimum of reason.

Now it would be strange if poets did not develop many technical devices for the sake of increasing the volume of the percipienda or sensibilia. I will name some of them.

First Device: meter. Meter is the most obvious device. A formal meter impresses us as a way of regulating very drastically the material, and we do not stop to remark (that is, as readers) that it has no particular aim except some nominal sort of regimentation. It symbolizes the predatory method, like a sawmill which intends to reduce all the trees to fixed unit timbers, and as business men we require some sign of our business. But to the Platonic censor in us it gives a false security, for so long as the poet appears to be working faithfully at his metrical engine he is left comparatively free to attend lovingly to the things that are being metered, and metering them need not really hurt them. Meter is the gentlest violence he can do them, if he is expected to do some violence.

Second Device: fiction. The device of the fiction is probably no less important and universal in poetry. Over every poem which looks like a poem is a sign which reads: This road does not go through to action; fictitious. Art always sets out to create an "aesthetic distance" between the object and the subject, and art takes pains to announce that it is not history. The situation treated is not quite an actual situation, for science is likely to have claimed that field, and exiled art; but a fictive or hypothetical one, so that science is less greedy and perception may take hold of it. Kant asserted that the aesthetic judgment is not concerned with the existence or nonexistence of the object, and may be interpreted as asserting that it is so far from depending on the object's existence that it really depends on the object's nonexistence. Sometimes we have a certain melancholy experience. We enjoy a scene which we receive by report only, or dream, or meet with in art; but subsequently find ourselves in the presence of an actual one that seems the very same scene; only to discover that we have not now the power to enjoy it, or to receive it aesthetically, because the economic tension is upon us and will not indulge us in the proper mood. And it is generally easier to obtain our aesthetic experience from art than from nature, because nature is actual, and communication is forbidden. But in being called fictive or hypothetical the art object suffers no disparagement. It cannot be true in the sense of being actual, and therefore it may be despised by science. But it is true in the sense of being fair or representative, in permitting the "illusion of reality"; just as

---

[10]By Donne and Milton, respectively. Concerning *Lycidas* see Ransom's essay *A Poem Nearly Anonymous.*

Schopenhauer discovered that music may symbolize all the modes of existence in the world; and in keeping with the customary demand of the readers of fiction proper, that it shall be "true to life." The defenders of art must require for it from its practitioners this sort of truth, and must assert of it before the world this dignity. If jealous science succeeds in keeping the field of history for its own exclusive use, it does not therefore annihilate the arts, for they reappear in a field which may be called real though one degree removed from actuality. There the arts perform their function with much less interference, and at the same time with about as much fidelity to the phenomenal world as history has.

Third Device: tropes. I have named two important devices; I am not prepared to offer the exhaustive list. I mention but one other kind, the device which comprises the figures of speech. A proper scientific discourse has no mention of employing figurative language for its definitive sort of utterance. Figures of speech twist accidence away from the straight course, as if to intimate astonishing lapses of rationality beneath the smooth surface of discourse, inviting perceptual attention, and weakening the tyranny of science over the senses. But I skip the several easier and earlier figures, which are timid, and stop on the climactic figure, which is the metaphor; with special reference to its consequence, a poetry which once in our history it produced in a beautiful and abundant exhibit, called *metaphysical poetry.*

And what is metaphysical poetry? The term was added to the official vocabulary of criticism by Johnson, who probably took it from Pope, who probably took it from Dryden, who used it to describe the poetry of a certain school of poets, thus: "He [John Donne] affects the metaphysics, not only in his satires, but in his amorous verses, where nature only should reign. . . . In this Mr. Cowley has copied him to a fault." But the meaning of *metaphysical* which was common in Dryden's time, having come down from the Middle Ages through Shakespeare, was simply: supernatural; *miraculous.* The context of the Dryden passage indicates it.

Dryden, then, noted a miraculism in poetry and repudiated it; except where it was employed for satire, where it was not seriously intended and had the effect of wit. Dryden himself employs miraculism wittily, but seems rather to avoid it if he will be really committed by it; he may employ it in his translations of Ovid, where the responsibility is Ovid's and not Dryden's, and in an occasional classical piece where he is making polite use of myths well known to be pagan errors. In his "amorous" pieces he finds the reign of nature sufficient, and it is often the worse for his amorous pieces. He is not many removes from a naturalist. (A naturalist is a person who studies nature not because he loves it but because he wants to use it, approaches it from the standpoint of common sense, and sees it thin and not thick.) Dryden might have

remarked that Donne himself had a change of heart and confined his miraculism at last to the privileged field of a more or less scriptural revelation. Perhaps Dryden found his way to accepting Milton because Milton's miraculism was mostly not a contemporary sort but classical and scriptural, pitched in a time when the age of miracles had not given way to the age of science. He knew too that Cowley had shamefully recanted from his petty miraculism, which formed the conceits, and turned to the scriptural or large order of miraculism to write his heroic (but empty) verses about David; and had written a Pindaric ode in extravagant praise of "Mr. Hobs," whose naturalistic account of nature seemed to render any other account fantastic if not contrary to the social welfare.

Incidentally, we know how much Mr. Hobbes affected Dryden too, and the whole of Restoration literature. What Bacon with his disparagement of poetry had begun, in the cause of science and Protestantism, Hobbes completed. The name of Hobbes is critical in any history that would account for the chill which settled upon the poets at the very moment that English poetry was attaining magnificently to the fullness of its powers. The name stood for common sense and naturalism, and the monopoly of the scientific spirit over the mind. Hobbes was the adversary, the Satan, when the latter first intimidated the English poets. After Hobbes his name is legion.

"Metaphysics," or miraculism, informs a poetry which is the most original and exciting, and intellectually perhaps the most seasoned, that we know in our literature, and very probably it has few equivalents in other literatures. But it is evident that the metaphysical effects may be large scale or they may be small scale. (I believe that generically, or ontologically, no distinction is to be made between them.) If Donne and Cowley illustrate the small scale effects, Milton will illustrate the large scale ones, probably as a consequence of the fact that he wrote major poems. Milton, in the *Paradise Lost,* told a story which was heroic and miraculous in the first place. In telling it he dramatized it, and allowed the scenes and characters to develop of their own native energy. The virtue of a long poem on a "metaphysical" subject will consist in the dramatization or substantiation of all the parts, the poet not being required to devise fresh miracles on every page so much as to establish the perfect "naturalism" of the material upon which the grand miracle is imposed. The *Paradise Lost* possesses this virtue nearly everywhere:

Thus *Adam* to himself lamented loud
Through the still night, not now, as ere man fell,
Wholesome and cool, and mild, but with black air
Accompanied, with damps and dreadful gloom,
Which to his evil conscience represented

All things with double terror: On the ground
Outstretched he lay, on the cold ground, and oft
Cursed his creation, death as oft accused
Of tardy execution, since denounced
The day of his offense. Why comes not death,
Said he, with one thrice acceptable stroke
To end me?[11]

This is exactly the sort of detail for a large scale metaphysical work, but it would hardly serve the purpose with a slighter and more naturalistic subject; with "amorous" verses. For the critical mind metaphysical poetry refers perhaps almost entirely to the so-called conceits that constitute its staple. To define the conceit is to define small scale metaphysical poetry.

It is easily defined, upon a little citation. Donne exhibits two conceits, or two branches of one conceit in the familiar lines:

> Our hands were firmly cemented
> By a fast balm which thence did spring;
> Our eye-beams twisted, and did thread
> Our eyes upon one double string.[12]

The poem which follows sticks to the topic; it represents the lovers in precisely that mode of union and no other. Cowley is more conventional yet still bold in the lines:

> Oh take my heart, and by that means you'll prove
>   Within, too stored enough of love:
> Give me but yours, I'll by that change so thrive
>   That love in all my parts shall live.
> So powerful is this change, it render can,
> My outside woman, and your inside man.[13]

A conceit originates in a metaphor; and in fact the conceit is but a metaphor if the metaphor is meant; that is, if it is developed so literally that it must be meant, or predicated so baldly that nothing else can be meant. Perhaps this will do for a definition.

Clearly the seventeenth century had the courage of its metaphors, and imposed them imperially on the nearest things, and just as clearly the nineteenth century lacked this courage, and was halfheartedly metaphorical, or content with similes. The difference between the literary qualities of the two periods is the difference between the metaphor and the simile. (It must be admitted that this like other generaliza-

tions will not hold without exceptions.) One period was pithy and original in its poetic utterance, the other was prolix and predictable. It would not quite commit itself to the metaphor even if it came upon one. Shelley is about as vigorous as usual when he says in *Adonais:* "Thou young dawn, / Turn all thy dew to splendor. . . ."[14] But splendor is not the correlative of dew, it has the flat tone of a Platonic idea, while physically it scarcely means more than dew with sunshine upon it. The seventeenth century would have said: "Turn thy dew, which is water, into fire, and accomplish the transmutation of the elements." Tennyson in his boldest lyric sings: "Come into the garden, Maud, / For the black bat, night, has flown,"[15] and leaves us unpersuaded of the bat. The predication would be complete without the bat, "The black night has flown," and a flying night is not very remarkable. Tennyson is only affecting a metaphor. But later in the same poem he writes:

> The red rose cries, "She is near, she is near";
>   And the white rose weeps, "She is late";
> The larkspur listens, "I hear, I hear";
>   And the lily whispers, "I wait."[16]

And this is a technical conceit. But it is too complicated for this author, having a plurality of images which do not sustain themselves individually. The flowers stand for the lover's thoughts, and have been prepared for carefully in an earlier stanza, but their distinctness is too arbitrary, and these are like a schoolgirl's made-up metaphors. The passage will not compare with one on a very similar situation in *Green Candles*, by Mr. Humbert Wolfe:

> "I know her little foot," gray carpet said:
> "Who but I should know her light tread?"
> "She shall come in," answered the open door,
> "And not," said the room, "go out any more."

Wolfe's conceit works and Tennyson's does not, and though Wolfe's performance seems not very daring or important, and only pleasant, he employs the technique of the conceit correctly: he knows that the miracle must have a basis of verisimilitude.

Such is metaphysical poetry; the extension of a rhetorical device; as one of the most brilliant successes in our poetry, entitled to long and thorough examination; and even here demanding somewhat by way of a more ontological criticism. I conclude with it.

---

[11]X. 845–56.
[12]*The Ecstasy*, 5–8.
[13]*The Change*, 19–24.

[14]362–63.
[15]*Maud*, XXII. 850–51.
[16]*Maud*, XXII. 912–15.

We may consult the dictionary, and discover that there is a miraculism or supernaturalism in a metaphorical assertion if we are ready to mean what we say, or believe what we hear. Or we may read Mr. Hobbes, the naturalist, who was very clear upon it: "II. The second cause of absurd assertions I ascribe to the giving of names of 'bodies' to 'accidents,' or of 'accidents' to 'bodies,' as they do that say 'faith is infused' or 'inspired,' when nothing can be 'poured' or 'breathed' into anything but body . . . and that 'phantasms' are 'spirits,' etc." Translated into our present terms, Hobbes is condemning the confusion of single qualities with whole things; or the substitution of concrete images for simple ideas.

Specifically, the miraculism arises when the poet discovers by analogy an identity between objects which is partial, though it should be considerable, and proceeds to an identification which is complete. It is to be contrasted with the simile, which says "as if" or "like," and is scrupulous to keep the identification partial. In Cowley's passage above, the lover is saying, not for the first time in his literature: "She and I have exchanged our hearts." What has actually been exchanged is affections, and affections are only in a limited sense the same as hearts. Hearts are unlike affections in being engines that pump blood and form body; and it is a miracle if the poet represents the lady's affection as rendering her inside into man. But he succeeds, with this mixture, in depositing with us the image of a very powerful affection.

From the strict point of view of literary criticism it must be insisted that the miraculism which produces the humblest conceit is the same miraculism which supplies to religions their substantive content. (This is said to assert the dignity not of the conceits but of the religions.) It is the poet and nobody else who gives to the God a nature, a form, faculties, and a history; to the God, most comprehensive of all terms, which, if there were no poetic impulse to actualize or "find" him, would remain the driest and deadest among Platonic ideas, with all intension sacrificed to infinite extension. The myths are conceits, born of metaphors. Religions are periodically produced by poets and destroyed by naturalists. Religion depends for its ontological validity upon a literary understanding, and that is why it is frequently misunderstood. The metaphysical poets, perhaps like their spiritual fathers the medieval schoolmen, were under no illusions about this. They recognized myth, as they recognized the conceits, as a device of expression; its sanctity as the consequence of its public or social importance.

But whether the topics be gods or amorous experiences, why do poets resort to miraculism? Hardly for the purpose of controverting natural fact or scientific theory. Religion pronounces about God only where science is silent and philosophy is negative; for a positive is wanted, that is, a God who has his being in the physical world as well as in the world of principles and abstractions. Likewise with the little secular enterprises of poetry too. Not now are the poets so brave, not for a very long time have they been so brave, as to dispute the scientists on what they call their "truth"; though it is a pity that the statement cannot be turned round. Poets will concede that every act of science is legitimate, and has its efficacy. The metaphysical poets of the seventeenth century particularly admired the methodology of science, and in fact they copied it, and their phrasing is often technical, spare, and polysyllabic, though they are not repeating actual science but making those metaphorical substitutions that are so arresting.

The intention of metaphysical poetry is to complement science, and improve discourse. Naturalistic discourse is incomplete, for either of two reasons. It has the minimum of physical content and starves the sensibility, or it has the maximum, as if to avoid the appearance of evil, but is laborious and pointless. Platonic poetry is too idealistic, but physical poetry is too realistic, and realism is tedious and does not maintain interest. The poets therefore introduce the psychological device of the miracle. The predication which it permits is clean and quick but it is not a scientific predication. For scientific predication concludes an act of attention but miraculism initiates one. It leaves us looking, marveling, and reveling in the thick *dinglich* substance that has just received its strange representation.

Let me suggest as a last word, in deference to a common Puritan scruple, that the predication of metaphysical poetry is true enough. It is not true like history, but no poetry is true in that sense, and only a part of science. It is true in the pragmatic sense in which some of the generalizations of science are true: it accomplishes precisely the sort of representation that it means to. It suggests to us that the object is perceptually or physically remarkable, and we had better attend to it.

Criticism as Pure Speculation

I

. . . When we inquire into the "intent of the critic,"[1] we mean: the intent of the generalized critic, or critic as such.

CRITICISM AS PURE SPECULATION. The text is from *The Intent of the Critic*, edited by D. A. Stauffer, pp. 92–124. Copyright © 1941, © 1969 by Princeton University Press. Reprinted by permission of Princeton University Press. The first two paragraphs have been omitted.
[1]The subject of the symposium for which this paper was written.

We will concede that any professional critic is familiar with the technical practices of poets so long as these are conventional, and is expert in judging when they perform them brilliantly, and when only fairly, or badly. We expect a critical discourse to cover that much, but we know that more is required. The most famous poets of our own time, for example, make wide departures from conventional practices: how are they to be judged? Innovations in poetry, or even conventions when pressed to their logical limits, cause the ordinary critic to despair. They cause the good critic to review his aesthetic principles; perhaps to reformulate his aesthetic principles. He tries the poem against his best philosophical conception of the peculiar character that a poem should have.

Mr. T. S. Eliot is an extraordinarily sensitive critic. But when he discusses the so-called metaphysical poetry,[2] he surprises us by refusing to study the so-called conceit which is its reputed basis; he observes instead that the metaphysical poets of the seventeenth century are more like their immediate predecessors than the latter are like the eighteenth- and nineteenth-century poets, and then he goes into a very broad philosophical comparison between two whole "periods" or types of poetry. I think it has come to be understood that his comparison is unsound; it has not proved workable enough to assist critics who have otherwise borrowed liberally from his critical principles. (It contains the famous dictum about the "sensibility" of the earlier poets, it imputes to them a remarkable ability to "feel their thought," and to have a kind of "experience" in which the feeling cannot be differentiated from the thinking.) Now there is scarcely another critic equal to Eliot at distinguishing the practices of two poets who are closely related. He is supreme as a comparative critic when the relation in question is delicate and subtle; that is, when it is a matter of close perception and not a radical difference in kind. But this line of criticism never goes far enough. In Eliot's own range of criticism the line does not always answer. He is forced by discontinuities in the poetic tradition into sweeping theories that have to do with aesthetics, the philosophy of poetry; and his own philosophy probably seems to us insufficient, the philosophy of the literary man.

The intent of the critic may well be, then, first to read his poem sensitively, and make comparative judgments about its technical practice, or, as we might say, to emulate Eliot. Beyond that, it is to read and remark the poem knowingly; that is, with an aesthetician's understanding of what a poem generically "is."

Before I venture, with inadequate argument, to describe what I take to be the correct understanding of poetry, I would like to describe two other understandings which, though widely professed, seem to me misunderstandings. First, there is a smart and belletristic theory of poetry which may be called *psychologistic*. Then there is an altogether staid and commonplace theory which is *moralistic*. Of these in their order.

II

It could easily be argued about either of these untenable conceptions of poetry that it is an act of despair to which critics resort who cannot find for the discourse of poetry any precise differentia to remove it from the category of science. Psychologistic critics hold that poetry is addressed primarily to the feelings and motor impulses; they remind us frequently of its contrast with the coldness, the unemotionality, of science, which is supposed to address itself to the pure cognitive mind. Mr. Richards came out spectacularly for the doctrine, and furnished it with detail of the greatest ingenuity.[3] He very nearly severed the dependence of poetic effect upon any standard of objective knowledge or belief. But the feelings and impulses which he represented as gratified by the poem were too tiny and numerous to be named. He never identified them; they seemed not so much psychological as infrapsychological. His was an esoteric poetic: it could not be disproved. But neither could it be proved, and I think it is safe at this distance to say that eventually his readers, and Richards himself, lost interest in it as being an improvisation, much too unrelated to the public sense of a poetic experience.

With other critics psychologism of some sort is an old story, and one that will probably never cease to be told. For, now that all of us know about psychology, there must always be persons on hand precisely conditioned to declare that poetry is an emotional discourse indulged in resentment and compensation for science, the bleak cognitive discourse in its purity. It becomes less a form of knowledge than a form of "expression." The critics are willing to surrender the honor of objectivity to science if they may have the luxury of subjectivity for poetry. Science will scarcely object. But one or two things have to be said about that. In every experience, even in science, there is feeling. No discourse can sustain itself without interest, which is feeling. The interest, or the feeling, is like an automatic index to the human value of the proceeding—which would not otherwise proceed. Mr. Eliseo Vivas is an aesthetician who might be thought to reside in the camp of the enemy, for his affiliations are

---

[2]Ransom is referring to Eliot's essay *The Metaphysical Poets*, in *Selected Essays, 1917–1932.*

[3]See Richards, *Practical Criticism*, above, pp. 827 and 835. See also Richards' *Principles of Literary Criticism*.

positivist; yet in a recent essay he writes about the "passion" which sustains the heroic labors of the scientist as one bigger and more intense than is given to most men.[4]

I do not mean to differ with that judgment at all in remarking that we might very well let the passions and the feelings take care of themselves; it is precisely what we do in our pursuit of science. The thing to attend to is the object to which they attach. As between two similar musical phrases, or between two similar lines of poetry, we may often defy the most proficient psychologist to distinguish the one feeling-response from the other; unless we permit him to say at long last that one is the kind of response that would be made to the first line, and the other is the kind of response that would be made to the second line. But that is to do, after much wasted motion, what I have just suggested: to attend to the poetic object and let the feelings take care of themselves. It is their business to "respond." There may be a feeling correlative with the minutest alteration in an object, and adequate to it, but we shall hardly know. What we do know is that the feelings are grossly inarticulate if we try to abstract them and take their testimony in their own language. Since it is not the intent of the critic to be inarticulate, his discriminations must be among the objects. We understand this so well intuitively that the critic seems to us in possession of some esoteric knowledge, some magical insight, if he appears to be intelligent elsewhere and yet refers confidently to the "tone" or "quality" or "value" of the feeling he discovers in a given line. Probably he is bluffing. The distinctness resides in the cognitive or "semantical" objects denoted by the words. When Richards bewilders us by reporting affective and motor disturbances that are too tiny for definition, and other critics by reporting disturbances that are too massive and gross, we cannot fail to grow suspicious of this whole way of insight as incompetent.

Eliot has a special version of psychologistic theory which looks extremely fertile, though it is broad and nebulous as his psychologistic terms require it to be. He likes to regard the poem as a structure of emotion and feeling.[5] But the emotion is singular, there being only one emotion per poem, or at least per passage: it is the central emotion or big emotion which attaches to the main theme or situation. The feeling is plural. The emotion combines with many feelings; these are our little responses to the single words and phrases, and he does not think of them as being parts of the central emotion or even related to it. The terminology is greatly at

fault, or we should recognize at once, I think, a principle that might prove very valuable. I would not answer for the conduct of a technical philosopher in assessing this theory; he might throw it away, out of patience with its jargon. But a lay philosopher who respects his Eliot and reads with all his sympathy might salvage a good thing from it, though I have not heard of anyone doing so. He would try to escape from the affective terms, and translate Eliot into more intelligible language. Eliot would be saying in effect that a poem has a central logic or situation or "paraphrasable core" to which an appropriate interest doubtless attaches, and that in this respect the poem is like a discourse of science behind which lies the sufficient passion. But he would be saying at the same time, and this is the important thing, that the poem has also a context of lively local details to which other and independent interests attach; and that in this respect it is unlike the discourse of science. For the detail of scientific discourse intends never to be independent of the thesis (either objectively or affectively) but always functional, and subordinate to the realization of the thesis. To say that is to approach to a structural understanding of poetry, and to the kind of understanding that I wish presently to urge.

III

As for the moralistic understanding of poetry, it is sometimes the specific moralists, men with moral axes to grind, and incidentally men of unassailable public position who cherish that; they have a "use" for poetry. But not exclusively, for we may find it held also by critics who are more spontaneous and innocent: apparently they fall back upon it because it attributes some special character to poetry, which otherwise refuses to yield up to them a character. The moral interest is so much more frequent in poetry than in science that they decide to offer its moralism as a differentia.

This conception of poetry is of the greatest antiquity—it antedates the evolution of close aesthetic philosophy, and persists beside it too. Plato sometimes spoke of poetry in this light—perhaps because it was recommended to him in this light—but nearly always scornfully. In the *Gorgias,* and other dialogues, he represents the poets as moralizing, and that is only what he, in the person of Socrates, is doing at the very moment, and given to doing; but he considers the moralizing of poets as mere "rhetoric," or popular philosophy, and unworthy of the accomplished moralist who is the real or technical philosopher. Plato understood very well that the poet does not conduct a technical or an original discourse like that of the scientist—and the term includes here the moral philosopher—and that close and effective moralizing is scarcely to be had from him. It is not within the poet's power to offer that if his intention is to offer poetry; for the poetry and the morality are so far from being identical that they interfere a little with each other.

Few famous aestheticians in the history of philosophy have cared to bother with the moralistic conception; many critics have, in all periods. Just now we have at least two schools of moralistic critics contending for the official possession of poetry. One is the neohumanist, and Mr. Foerster[6] has identified himself with that. The other is the Marxist, and I believe it is represented in some degree and shade by Mr. Wilson,[7] possibly by Mr. Auden.[8] I have myself taken profit from the discussions by both schools, but recently I have taken more—I suppose that this is because I was bought up in a scholastic discipline rather like the neohumanist—from the writings of the Marxist critics. One of the differences is that the neohumanists believe in the "respectable" virtues, but the Marxists believe that respectability is the greatest of vices, and equate respectable with "genteel." That is a very striking difference, and I think it is also profound.

But I do not wish to be impertinent; I can respect both these moralities, and appropriate moral values from both. The thing I wish to argue is not the comparative merits of the different moralities by which poetry is judged, but their equal inadequacy to the reading of the poet's intention. The moralistic critics wish to isolate and discuss the "ideology" or theme or paraphrase of the poem and not the poem itself.[9] But even to the practitioners themselves, if they are sophisticated, comes sometimes the apprehension that this is moral rather than literary criticism. I have not seen the papers of my colleagues in this discussion, for that was against the rules, but it is reported to me that both Mr. Wilson and Mr. Foerster concede in explicit words that criticism has both the moral and the aesthetic branches; Mr. Wilson may call them the "social" and aesthetic branches. And they would hold the critical profession responsible for both branches. Under these circumstances the critics cease to be mere moralists and become dualists; that is better. My feeling about such a position would be that the moral criticism we shall have with us always, and have had always, and that it is easy—comparatively speaking—and that what is hard, and needed, and indeed more and more urgent after all the failures of poetic understanding, is a better aesthetic criticism. This is the

branch which is all but invariably neglected by the wise but morally zealous critics; they tend to forget their dual responsibility. I think I should go so far as to think that, in strictness, the business of the literary critic is exclusively with an aesthetic criticism. The business of the moralist will naturally, and properly, be with something else.

If we have the patience to read for a little while in the anthology, paying some respect to the varieties of substance actually in the poems, we cannot logically attribute ethical character by definition to poetry; for that character is not universal in the poems. And if we have any faith in a community of character among the several arts, we are stopped quickly from risking such a definition for art at large. To claim a moral content for most of sculpture, painting, music or architecture, is to plan something dialectically very roundabout and subtle, or else to be so arbitrary as to invite instant exposure. I should think the former alternative is impractical, and the latter, if it is not stupid, is masochistic.

The moralistic critics are likely to retort upon their accusers by accusing them in turn of the vapid doctrine known as art for art's sake. And with frequent justice; but again we are likely to receive the impression that it is just because art for art's sake, the historic doctrine, proved empty, and availed them so little aesthetically, like all the other doctrines that came into default, that they have fled to their moralism. Moralism does at least impute to poetry a positive substance, as art for art's sake does not. It asserts an autonomy for art, which is excellent; but autonomy to do what? Only to be itself, and to reduce its interpreters to a tautology? With its English adherents in the nineties the doctrine seemed to make only a negative requirement of art, that is, that it should be anti-Victorian as we should say today, a little bit naughty and immoral perhaps, otherwise at least nonmoral, or carefully squeezed dry of moral substance. An excellent example of how two doctrines, inadequate equally but in opposite senses, may keep themselves alive by abhorring each other's errors.

It is highly probable that the poem considers an ethical situation, and there is no reason why it should repel this from its consideration. But, if I may say so without being accused of verbal trifling, the poetic consideration of the ethical situation is not the same as the ethical consideration of it. The straight ethical consideration would be prose; it would be an act of interested science, or an act of practical will. The poetic consideration, according to Schopenhauer, is the objectification of this act of will;[10] that is, it is our contemplation and not our exercise of will, and therefore qualitatively a

---

[6]Norman Foerster, American critic. See his essay *The Esthetic Judgment and the Ethical Judgment,* also in *The Intent of the Critic,* See also Babbitt, *Romantic Melancholy,* pp. 768–82.
[7]See Wilson, *The Triple Thinkers* (1938).
[8]W. H. Auden was early associated with a group of Marxist poets.
[9]See Blackmur, p. 422.

---

[10]See *The World as Will and Idea,* pp. 497–99.

very different experience; knowledge without desire. That doctrine also seems too negative and indeterminate. I will put the point as I see it in another way. It should be a comfort to the moralist that there is ordinarily a moral composure in the poem, as if the poet had long known good and evil, and made his moral choice between them once and for all. Art is postethical rather than unethical. In the poem there is an increment of meaning which is neither the ethical content nor opposed to the ethical content. The poetic experience would have to stop for the poet who is developing it, or for the reader who is following it, if the situation which is being poetically treated should turn back into a situation to be morally determined; if, for example, the situation were not a familiar one, and one to which we had habituated our moral wills; for it would rouse the moral will again to action, and make the poetic treatment impossible under its heat. Art is more cool than hot, and a moral fervor is as disastrous to it as a burst of passion itself. We have seen Marxists recently so revolted by Shakespeare's addiction to royal or noble *personae* that they cannot obtain aesthetic experience from the plays; all they get is a moral agitation. In another art, we know, and doubtless we approve, the scruple of the college authorities in not permitting the "department of fine arts" to direct the collegians in painting in the nude. Doctor Hanns Sachs, successor to Freud, in a recent number of his *American Imago,* gives a story from a French author as follows:

> He tells that one evening strolling along the streets of Paris he noticed a row of slot machines which for a small coin showed pictures of women in full or partial undress. He observed the leering interest with which men of all kind and description, well dressed and shabby, boys and old men, enjoyed the peep show. He remarked that they all avoided one of these machines, and wondering what uninteresting pictures it might show, he put his penny in the slot. To his great astonishment the generally shunned picture turned out to be the Venus of Medici. Now he begins to ponder: Why does nobody get excited about her? She is decidedly feminine and not less naked than the others which hold such strong fascination for everybody. Finally he finds a satisfactory answer: They fight shy of her because she is beautiful.

And Doctor Sachs, though in his own variety of jargon, makes a number of wise observations about the psychic conditions precedent to the difficult apprehension of beauty. The experience called beauty is beyond the powerful ethical will precisely as it is beyond the animal passion, and indeed these last two are competitive, and coordinate. Under the urgency of either we are incapable of appreciating the statue or understanding the poem.

IV

The ostensible substance of the poem may be anything at all which words may signify: an ethical situation, a passion, a train of thought, a flower or landscape, a thing. This substance receives its poetic increment. It might be safer to say it receives some subtle and mysterious alteration under poetic treatment, but I will risk the cruder formula: the ostensible substance is increased by an *x,* which is an increment. The poem actually continues to contain its ostensible substance, which is not fatally diminished from its prose state: that is its logical core, or paraphrase. The rest of the poem is *x,* which we are to find.

We feel the working of this simple formula when we approach a poetry with our strictest logic, provided we can find deliverance from certain inhibiting philosophical prepossessions into which we have been conditioned by the critics we have had to read. Here is Lady Macbeth planning a murder with her husband:

> When Duncan is asleep—
> Whereto the rather shall his hard day's journey
> Soundly invite him—his two chamberlains
> Will I with wine and wassail so convince,
> That memory, the warder of the brain,
> Shall be a fume, and the receipt of reason
> A limbec only; when in swinish sleep
> Their drenched natures lie as in a death,
> What cannot you and I perform upon
> The unguarded Duncan? what not put upon
> His spongy officers, who shall bear the guilt
> Of our great quell?[11]

It is easy to produce the prose argument or paraphrase of this speech; it has one upon which we shall all agree. But the passage is more than its argument. Any detail, with this speaker, seems capable of being expanded in some direction which is not that of the argument. For example, Lady Macbeth says she will make the chamberlains drunk so that they will not remember their charge, nor keep their wits about them. But it is indifferent to this argument whether memory according to the old psychology is located at the gateway to

---

[11] I. vii. 61–72.

the brain, whether it is to be disintegrated into fume as of alcohol, and whether the whole receptacle of the mind is to be turned into a still. These are additions to the argument both energetic and irrelevant—though they do not quite stop or obscure the argument. From the point of view of the philosopher they are excursions into particularity. They give, in spite of the argument, which would seem to be perfectly self-sufficient, a sense of the real density and contingency of the world in which arguments and plans have to be pursued. They bring out the private character which the items of an argument can really assume if we look at them. This character spreads out in planes at right angles to the course of the argument, and in effect gives to the discourse another dimension, not present in a perfectly logical prose. We are expected to have sufficient judgment not to let this local character take us too far or keep us too long from the argument.

All this would seem commonplace remark, I am convinced, but for those philosophically timid critics who are afraid to think that the poetic increment is local and irrelevant, and that poetry cannot achieve its own virtue and keep undiminished the virtues of prose at the same time. But I will go a little further in the hope of removing the sense of strangeness in the analysis, I will offer a figurative definition of a poem.

A poem is, so to speak, a democratic state, whereas a prose discourse—mathematical, scientific, ethical, or practical and vernacular—is a totalitarian state. The intention of a democratic state is to perform the work of state as effectively as it can perform it, subject to one reservation of conscience: that it will not despoil its members, the citizens, of the free exercise of their own private and independent characters. But the totalitarian state is interested solely in being effective, and regards the citizens as no citizens at all; that is, regards them as functional members whose existence is totally defined by their allotted contributions to its ends; it has no use for their private characters, and therefore no provision for them. I indicate of course the extreme or polar opposition between two polities, without denying that a polity may come to us rather mixed up.

In this trope the operation of the state as a whole represents of course the logical paraphrase or argument of the poem. The private character of the citizens represents the particularity asserted by the parts in the poem. And this last is our *x*.

For many years I had seen—as what serious observer has not—that a poem as a discourse differentiated itself from prose by its particularity, yet not to the point of sacrificing its logical cogency or universality. But I could get no further. I could not see how real particularity could get into a universal. The object of aesthetic studies became for me a kind of

discourse, or a kind of natural configuration, which like any other discourse or configuration claimed universality, but which consisted actually, and notoriously, of particularity. The poem was concrete, yet universal, and in spite of Hegel I could not see how the two properties could be identified as forming in a single unit the "concrete universal." It is usual, I believe, for persons at this stage to assert that somehow the apparent diffuseness or particularity in the poem gets itself taken up or "assimilated" into the logic, to produce a marvelous kind of unity called a "higher unity," to which ordinary discourse is not eligible. The belief is that the "idea" or theme proves itself in poetry to be even more dominating than in prose by overcoming much more energetic resistance than usual on the part of the materials, and the resistance, as attested in the local development of detail, is therefore set not to the debit but to the credit of the unifying power of the poetic spirit. A unity of that kind is one which philosophers less audacious and more factual than Hegel would be loath to claim. Critics incline to call it, rather esoterically, an "imaginative" rather than a logical unity, but one supposes they mean a mystical, an ineffable, unity. I for one could neither grasp it nor deny it. I believe that is not an uncommon situation for poetic analysts to find themselves in.

It occurred to me at last that the solution might be very easy if looked for without what the positivists call "metaphysical prepossessions." Suppose the logical substance remained there all the time, and was in no way specially remarkable, while the particularity came in by accretion, so that the poem turned out partly universal, and partly particular, but with respect to different parts. I began to remark the dimensions of a poem, or other work of art. The poem was not a mere moment in time, nor a mere point in space. It was sizable, like a house. Apparently it had a "plan," or a central frame of logic, but it had also a huge wealth of local detail, which sometimes fitted the plan functionally or served it, and sometimes only subsisted comfortably under it; in either case the house stood up. But it was the political way of thinking which gave me the first analogy which seemed valid. The poem was like a democratic state, in action, and observed both macroscopically and microscopically.

The house occurred also, and provided what seems to be a more negotiable trope under which to construe the poem. A poem is a *logical structure* having a *local texture*. These terms have been actually though not systematically employed in literary criticism. To my imagination they are architectural. The walls of my room are obviously structural; the beams and boards have a function; so does the plaster, which is the visible aspect of the final wall. The plaster might have remained naked, aspiring to no character, and purely functional. But actually it has been painted, receiving color; or it has been papered, receiving color and design, though these have no structural value; and perhaps it has been hung with tapestry, or with paintings, for "decoration." The paint, the paper, the tapestry are texture. It is logically unrelated to structure. But I indicate only a few of the textural possibilities in architecture. There are not fewer of them in poetry.

The intent of the good critic becomes therefore to examine and define the poem with respect to its structure and its texture. If he has nothing to say about its texture he has nothing to say about it specifically as a poem, but is treating it only insofar as it is prose.

I do not mean to say that the good critic will necessarily employ my terms.

V

Many critics today are writing analytically and with close intelligence, in whatever terms, about the logical substance or structure of the poem, and its increment of irrelevant local substance or texture. I believe that the understanding of the ideal critic has to go even further than that. The final desideratum is an ontological insight, nothing less. I am committed by my title to a representation of criticism as, in the last resort, a speculative exercise. But my secret committal was to speculative in the complete sense of—ontological.

There is nothing especially speculative or ontological in reciting, or even appraising, the logical substance of the poem. This is its prose core—its science perhaps, or its ethics if it seems to have an ideology. Speculative interest asserts itself principally when we ask why we want the logical substance to be compounded with the local substance, the good lean structure with a great volume of texture that does not function. It is the same thing as asking why we want the poem to be what it is.

It has been a rule, having the fewest exceptions, for aestheticians and great philosophers to direct their speculations by the way of overstating and overvaluing the logical substance. They are impressed by the apparent obedience of material nature, whether in fact or in art, to definable form or "law" imposed upon it. They like to suppose that in poetry, as in chemistry, everything that figures in the discourse means to be functional, and that the poem is imperfect in the degree that it contains items, whether by accident or intention, which manifest a private independence. It is a bias with which we are entirely familiar, and reflects the extent to which our philosophy hitherto has been impressed by the successes of science in formulating laws which would "govern" their objects. Probably I am here reading the state of

mind of yesterday rather than of today. Nevertheless we know it. The world view which ultimately forms itself in the mind so biased is that of a world which is rational and intelligible. The view is sanguine, and naive. Hegel's world view, I think it is agreed, was a subtle version of this, and if so, it was what determined his view of art. He seemed to make the handsomest concession to realism by offering to knowledge a kind of universal which was not restricted to the usual abstracted aspects of the material, but included all aspects, and was a concrete universal. The concreteness in Hegel's handling was not honestly, or at any rate not fairly, defended. It was always represented as being in process of pointing up and helping out the universality. He could look at a work of art and report all its substance as almost assimilated to a ruling "idea." But at least Hegel seemed to distinguish what looked like two ultimate sorts of substance there, and stated the central aesthetic problem as the problem of relating them. And his writings about art are speculative in the sense that he regarded the work of art not as of great intrinsic value necessarily, but as an object lesson or discipline in the understanding of the world process, and as its symbol.[12]

I think of two ways of constructing poetry with respect to its ultimate purpose; of which the one is not very handsome nor speculatively interesting, and the other will appear somewhat severe.

The first construction would picture the poet as a sort of epicure, and the poem as something on the order of a Christmas pudding, stuffed with what dainties it will hold. The pastry alone, or it may be the cake, will not serve; the stuffing is wanted too. The values of the poem would be intrinsic, or immediate, and they would include not only the value of the structure but also the incidental values to be found in the texture. If we exchange the pudding for a house, they would include not only the value of the house itself but also the value of the furnishings. In saying intrinsic or immediate, I mean that the poet is fond of the precise objects denoted by the words, and writes the poem for the reason that he likes to dwell upon them. In talking about the main value and the incidental values I mean to recognize the fact that the latter engage the affections just as truly as the former. Poetic discourse therefore would be more agreeable than prose to the epicure or the literally acquisitive man; for prose has but a single value, being about one thing only; its parts have no values of their own, but only instrumental values, which might be reckoned as fractions of the single value proportionate to their contributions to it. The prose is one-valued and the poem is many-valued. Indeed, there will cer-

---

[12]See Hegel, *The Philosophy of Fine Art,* pp. 534–45.

tainly be poems whose texture contains many precious objects, and aggregates a greater value than the structure.

So there would be a comfortable and apparently eligible view that poetry improves on prose because it is a richer diet. It causes five or six pleasures to appear, five or six good things, where one had been before; an alluring consideration for robustious, full-blooded, bourgeois souls. The view will account for much of the poem, if necessary. But it does not account for all of it, and sometimes it accounts for less than at other times.

The most impressive reason for the bolder view of art, the speculative one, is the existence of the "pure," or "abstractionist," or nonrepresentational works of art; though these will probably occur to us in other arts than poetry. There is at least one art, music, whose works are all of this sort. Tones are not words, they have no direct semantical function, and by themselves they mean nothing. But they combine to make brilliant phrases, harmonies, and compositions. In these compositions it is probable that the distinction between structure or functional content, on the one hand, and texture or local variation and departure, on the other, is even more determinate than in an impure art like poetry. The world of tones seems perfectly inhuman and impracticable; there is no specific field of experience "about which" music is telling us. Yet we know that music is powerfully affective. I take my own musical feelings, and those attested by other audients, as the sufficient index to some overwhelming human importance which the musical object has for us. At the same time it would be useless to ask the feelings precisely what they felt; we must ask the critic. The safest policy is to take the simplest construction, and try to improvise as little fiction as possible. Music is not music, I think, until we grasp its effects both in structure and in texture. As we grow in musical understanding the structures become always more elaborate and sustained, and the texture which interrupts them and sometimes imperils them becomes more bold and unpredictable. We can agree in saying about the works of music that these are musical structures, and they are richly textured; we can identify these elements, and perhaps precisely. To what then do our feelings respond? To music as structural composition itself; to music as manifesting the structural principles of the world; to modes of structure which we feel to be ontologically possible, or even probable. Schopenhauer construed music very much in that sense.[13] Probably it will occur to us that musical compositions bear close analogy therefore to operations in pure mathematics. The mathematicians confess that their constructions are

"nonexistential"; meaning as I take it, that the constructions testify with assurance only to the structural principles, in the light of which they are possible but may not be actual, or if they are actual may not be useful. This would define the mathematical operations as speculative: as motivated by an interest so generalized and so elemental that no word short of ontological will describe it.

But if music and mathematics have this much in common, they differ sharply in their respective world views or ontological biases. That of music, with its prodigious display of texture, seems the better informed about the nature of the world, the more realistic, the less naive. Perhaps the difference is between two ontological educations. But I should be inclined to imagine it as rising back of that point: in two ontological temperaments.

There are also, operating a little less successfully so far as the indexical evidences would indicate, the abstractionist paintings, of many schools, and perhaps also works of sculpture; and there is architecture. These arts have tried to abandon direct representational intention almost as heroically as music. They exist in their own materials and indicate no other specific materials; structures of color, light, space, stone—the cheapest of materials. They too can symbolize nothing of value unless it is structure or composition itself. But that is precisely the act which denotes will and intelligence; which becomes the act of fuller intelligence if it carefully accompanies its structures with their material textures; for then it understands better the ontological nature of materials.

Returning to the poetry. It is not all poems, and not even all "powerful" poems, having high index ratings, whose semantical meanings contain situations important in themselves or objects precious in themselves. There may be little correlation between the single value of the poem and the aggregate value of its contents—just as there is no such correlation whatever in music. The "effect" of the poem may be astonishingly disproportionate to our interest in its materials. It is true, of course, that there is no art employing materials of equal richness with poetry, and that it is beyond the capacity of poetry to employ indifferent materials. The words used in poetry are the words the race has already formed, and naturally they call attention to things and events that have been thought to be worth attending to. But I suggest that any poetry which is "technically" notable is in part a work of abstractionist art, concentrating upon the structure and the texture, and the structure-texture relation, out of a pure speculative interest.

At the end of *Love's Labour's Lost* occurs a little diversion which seems proportionately far more effective than that laborious play as a whole. The play is over, but Armado

---

[13]See *The World as Will and Idea*, Vol. I, section 52 and Vol. II, Chapter 29.

stops the principals before they disperse to offer them a show:

Armado   But, most esteemed greatness, will you hear the dialogue that the two learned men have compiled in praise of the owl and the cuckoo? It should have followed in the end of our show.

King   Call them forth quickly; we will do so.

Armado   Holla! approach. (*Reenter, Holofernes, etc.*) This side is Hiems, Winter, this Ver, the Spring; the one maintained by the owl, the other by the cuckoo. Ver, begin.

THE SONG

SPRING   When daisies pied and violets blue
And lady-smocks all silver-white
And cuckoo-buds of yellow hue
Do paint the meadows with delight,
The cuckoo then, on every tree,
Mocks married men; for thus sings he,
      Cuckoo;
Cuckoo, cuckoo: O word of fear,
Unpleasing to a married ear!

When shepherds pipe on oaten straws,
And merry larks are ploughmen's clocks,
When turtles tread, and rooks, and daws,
And maidens bleach their summer smocks,
The cuckoo then, on every tree,
Mocks married men; for thus sings he,
      Cuckoo;
Cuckoo, cuckoo: O word of fear,
Unpleasing to a married ear!

WINTER   When icicles hang by the wall,
And Dick the shepherd blows his nail,
And Tom bears logs into the hall,
And milk comes frozen home in pail,
When blood is nipped and ways be foul,
Then nightly sings the staring owl,
      Tu-who;
Tu-whit, tu-who, a merry note,
While greasy Joan doth keel the pot.

When all aloud the wind doth blow,
And coughing drowns the parson's saw,
And birds sit brooding in the snow,
And Marian's nose looks red and raw,
When roasted crabs hiss in the bowl,

Then nightly sings the staring owl,
      Tu-who;
Tu-whit, tu-who, a merry note,
While greasy Joan doth keel the pot.

Armado   The words of Mercury are harsh after the songs of Apollo. You that way—we this way. (*Exeunt.*)[14]

The feeling index registers such strong approval of this episode that a critic with ambition is obliged to account for it. He can scarcely account for it in terms of the weight of its contents severally.

At first glance Shakespeare has provided only a pleasant little caricature of the old-fashioned (to us, medieval) debate between personified characters. It is easygoing, like nonsense; no labor is lost here. Each party speaks two stanzas and concludes both stanzas with the refrain about his bird, the cuckoo or the owl. There is next to no generalized argument, or dialectic proper. Each argues by citing his characteristic exhibits. In the first stanza Spring cites some flowers; in the second stanza, some business by country persons, with interpolation of some birds that make love. Winter in both his stanzas cites the country business of the season. In the refrain the cuckoo, Spring's symbol, is used to refer the lovemaking to more than the birds; and this repeats itself, though it is naughty. The owl is only a nominal symbol for Winter, an "emblem" that is not very emblematic, but the refrain manages another reference to the kitchen, and repeats itself, as if Winter's pleasures focused in the kitchen.

In this poem texture is not very brilliant, but it eclipses structure. The argument, we would say in academic language, is concerned with "the relative advantages of Spring and Winter." The only logical determinateness this structure has is the good coordination of the items cited by Spring as being really items peculiar to Spring, and of the Winter items as peculiar to Winter. The symbolic refrains look like summary or master items, but they seem to be a little more than summary and in fact to mean a little more than they say. The argument is trifling on the whole, and the texture from the point of view of felt human importance lacks decided energy; both which observations are to be made, and most precisely, of how many famous lyrics, especially those before the earnest and self-conscious nineteenth century! The value of the poem is greater than the value of its parts: that is what the critic is up against.

Unquestionably it is possible to assemble very fine structures out of ordinary materials. The good critic will

---

[14]V. ii. 893–941.

study the poet's technique, in confidence that here the structural principles will be discovered at home. In this study he will find as much range for his activities as he desires.

Especially must he study the metrics, and their implications for structural composition. In this poem I think the critic ought to make good capital of the contrast between the amateurishness of the pleasant discourse as meaning and the hard determinate form of it phonetically. The meter on the whole is out of relation to the meaning of the poem, or to anything else specifically; it is a musical material of low grade, but plastic and only slightly resistant material, and its presence in every poem is that of an abstractionist element that belongs to the art.

And here I will suggest another analogy, this one between Shakespeare's poem and some ordinary specimen of painting. It does not matter how old-fashioned or representational the painting is, we shall all, if we are instructed in the tradition of this art, require it to exhibit along with its represented object an abstract design in terms of pure physical balance or symmetry. We sense rather than measure the success of this design, but it is as if we had drawn a horizontal axis and a vertical axis through the center of the picture, and required the painted masses to balance with respect to each of these two axes. This is an over-simple statement of a structural requirement by which the same details function in two worlds that are different, and that do not correlate with each other. If the painting is of the Holy Family, we might say that this object has a drama, or an economy, of its own; but that the physical masses which compose it must enter also into another economy, that of abstract design; and that the value of any unit mass for the one economy bears no relation to its value for the other. The painting is of great ontological interest because it embodies this special dimension of abstract form. And turning to the poem, we should find that its represented "meaning" is analogous to the represented object in the painting, while its meter is analogous to the pure design.

A number of fascinating speculative considerations must follow upon this discovery. They will have to do with the most fundamental laws of this world's structure. They will be profoundly ontological, though I do not mean that they must be ontological in some recondite sense; ontological in such a homely and compelling sense that perhaps a child might intuit the principles which the critic will arrive at analytically, and with much labor.

I must stop at this point, since I am desired not so much to anticipate the critic as to present him. In conclusion I will remark that the critic will doubtless work empirically, and set up his philosophy only as the drift of his findings will compel him. But ultimately he will be compelled. He will have to subscribe to an ontology. If he is a sound critic his ontology will be that of his poets; and what is that? I suggest that the poetic world view is Aristotelian and "realistic" rather than Platonic and "idealistic." He cannot follow the poets and still conceive himself as inhabiting the rational or "tidy" universe that is supposed by the scientist.

R. P. Blackmur

1904–1965

The self-consciousness with which critics began to examine what they do became more pronounced after the work of Richards and Eliot in the 1920s. This was perhaps inevitable with developments in analytical philosophy (particularly the analysis of language) and psychology and the resurgence of interest in the relation of poem to reader. Solipsistic impressionism had come to a standstill in the work of Anatole France, and a new objectification of the literary work was required if criticism had any pretensions as a recognizable discipline.

As Kant considered how we make aesthetic judgments, so did Blackmur and many other theorists of his time analyze critical practices. To them the critic represented that perfect reader sought by Hume, Richards, and others. Implicit in Blackmur's view is a sense of the literary work as distinct from poet, reader, and world. He assumes that as an object with a degree of autonomy the work should generate a mode of criticism that will approach but never violate "the thing in itself from its own point of view." Thus, for Blackmur, criticism is provisional, pragmatic, and finally ironic. And so is all reading, in the sense that there must be "psychical distance" or a distinction between experience of the "beautiful" and of the merely "agreeable."

In Blackmur's well-known ironic phrase, criticism should be "the formal discourse of an amateur." By this he does not mean that the critic should be a dilettante, but that he should be the opposite of a "professional" insofar as he is not "professing" a doctrine. He must use all the knowledge he can gain but at the same time "discount, absorb, or dominate the doctrine for the life that goes with it." For Blackmur, doctrine is the death of, not the completion of, insight. The literary work is cut off from its own full worth as an initiator of new modes of understanding when it is reduced by a critic to illustration of doctrine.

A large part of Blackmur's essay *A Critic's Job of Work* is devoted to discussing modes of literary analysis that have "ulterior" purposes and thus are severely limited in the breadth of their possible insights: Santayana reduces Lucretius' *On the Nature of Things* to the terms of a moral philosophy. Van Wyck Brooks reduces Henry James's work to representation of the author's psychological problems. In *The Great Tradition* Granville Hicks judges all American literature on whether or not it represents the class struggle from a Marxist point of view. All these critics are interested in what Blackmur calls the "separable content" of the literary work.

After discussing the critical methods of I. A. Richards, Kenneth Burke, and S. Foster Damon, Blackmur describes his own approach, the "technical approach," which seeks not to separate out any aspect of the work for special attention. He means "technical" in a broad sense, and his whole attitude seems to suggest the idea that Crocean intuition and expression are inseparable from the available technical modes of externalization. Blackmur recognizes that there are limits to what the critic can accomplish in analysis: "After all, it is only the facts about a poem, a play, a novel, that can be reduced to tractable form, talked about, and examined. The rest, whatever it is, can only be known, not talked about." He would agree with Brooks's attack on the "heresy of paraphrase," and he would take a cue from James's remark that the novelist's aim is simply to make a perfect work. But Blackmur would shift the import of this remark to induce reflection on the critic's special responsibility to the work.

Among Blackmur's critical works are *The Double Agent: Essays in Craft and Elucidation* (1935), *The Expense of Greatness* (1940), *Language as Gesture* (1952), *The Lion and Honeycomb* (1955), *Form and Value in Modern Poetry* (1957), *Eleven Essays in the European Novel* (1964); and *The Outsider at the Heart of Things: Selected Essays* (1986). See Robert Boyers, *R. P. Blackmur, Poet-Critic* (1980); Russell Fraser, *A Mingled Yarn: The Life of R. P. Blackmur* (1981); Gerald J. Pannick, *Richard Palmer Blackmur* (1981); and James T. Jones, *Wayward Skeptic* (1986).

A Critic's Job of Work

I

Criticism, I take it, is the formal discourse of an amateur. When there is enough love and enough knowledge represented in the discourse it is a self-sufficient but by no means an isolated art. It witnesses constantly in its own life its interdependence with the other arts. It lays out the terms and parallels of appreciation from the outside in order to convict itself of internal intimacy; it names and arranges what it knows and loves, and searches endlessly with every fresh impulse or impression for better names and more orderly arrangements. It is only in this sense that poetry (or some other art) is a criticism of life; poetry names and arranges, and thus arrests and transfixes its subject in a form which has a life which confronts it. Poetry is life at the remove of form and meaning; not life lived but life framed and identified. So the criticism of poetry is bound to be occupied at once with the terms and modes by which the remove was made and with the relation between—in the ambiguous stock phrase—content and form; which is to say with the establishment and appreciation of human or moral value. It will be the underlying effort of this essay to indicate approaches to criticism wherein these two problems—of form and value—will appear inextricable but not confused—like the stones in an arch or the timbers in a building.

These approaches—these we wish to eulogize—are not the only ones, nor the only good ones, nor are they complete. No approach opens on anything except from its own point of view and in terms of its own prepossessions. Let us set against each other for a time the facts of various approaches to see whether there is a residue, not of fact but of principle.

The approaches to—or the escapes from—the central work of criticism are as various as the heresies of the Christian church, and like them testify to occasional needs, fanatic emphasis, special interest, or intellectual pride, all flowing from and even the worst of them enlightening the same body of insight. Every critic like every theologian and every philosopher is a casuist in spite of himself. To escape or surmount the discontinuity of knowledge, each resorts to a particular heresy and makes it predominant and even omnivorous.[1]

For most minds, once doctrine is sighted and is held to be the completion of insight, the doctrinal mode of thinking seems the only one possible. When doctrine totters it seems it can fall only into the gulf of bewilderment; few minds risk the fall; most seize the remnants and swear the edifice remains, when doctrine becomes intolerable dogma.[2] All fall notwithstanding; for as knowledge itself is a fall from the paradise of undifferentiated sensation, so equally every formula of knowledge must fall the moment too much weight is laid upon it—the moment it becomes omnivorous and pretends to be omnipotent—the moment, in short, it is taken

A CRITIC'S JOB OF WORK. Blackmur's essay *A Critic's Job of Work* first appeared in *The Double Agent: Essays in Elucidation and Craft* (1935). The text is from *Language as Gesture*. Copyright 1952 by Richard P. Blackmur. Reprinted by permission of Harcourt Brace Jovanovich, Inc.

[1] [Blackmur] The rashest heresy of our day and climate is that exemplified by T. S. Eliot when he postulates an orthodoxy which exists whether anyone knows it or not.
[2] [Blackmur] Baudelaire's sonnet *Le Gouffre* dramatizes this sentiment at once as he saw it surmounted in Pascal and as it occurred insurmountably in himself.

literally. Literal knowledge is dead knowledge; and the worst bewilderment—which is always only comparative—is better than death. Yet no form, no formula, of knowledge ought to be surrendered merely because it runs the risk in bad or desperate hands of being used literally; and similarly, in our own thinking, whether it is carried to the point of formal discourse or not, we cannot only afford, we ought scrupulously to risk the use of any concept that seems propitious or helpful in getting over gaps. Only the use should be consciously provisional, speculative, and dramatic. The end virtue of humility comes only after a long train of humiliations; and the chief labor of humbling is the constant, resourceful restoration of ignorance.

The classic contemporary example of use and misuse is attached to the name of Freud. Freud himself has constantly emphasized the provisional, dramatic character of his speculations: they are employed as imaginative illumination, to be relied on no more and no less than the sailor relies upon his buoys and beacons.[3] But the impetus of Freud was so great that a school of literalists arose with all the mad consequence of schism and heresy and fundamentalism which have no more honorable place in the scientific than the artistic imagination. Elsewhere, from one point of view, Caesarism in Rome and Berlin is only the literalist conception of the need for a positive state. So, too, the economic insights of Marxism, merely by being taken literally in their own field, are held to affect the subject and value of the arts, where actually they offer only a limited field of interest and enliven an irrelevant purpose. It is an amusing exercise—as it refreshes the terms of bewilderment and provides a common clue to the secrets of all the modes of thinking—to restore the insights of Freud and Fascism and Marxism to the terms of the church; when the sexual drama in Freud becomes the drama of original sin, and the politics of Hitler and Lenin becomes the politics of the City of God in the sense that theology provides both the sanctions of economics and the values of culture. Controversy is in terms absolutely held, when the problems argued are falsely conceived because necessarily abstracted from "real" experience. The vital or fatal nexus is in interest and emotion and is established when the terms can be represented dramatically, almost, as it were for their own sakes alone and with only a pious or ritualistic regard for the doctrines in which they are clothed. The simple, and fatal, example is in the glory men

attach to war; the vital, but precarious example, is in the intermittent conception of free institutions and the persistent reformulation of the myth of reason. Then the doctrines do not matter, since they are taken only for what they are worth (whatever rhetorical pretensions to the contrary) as guides and props, as aids to navigation. What does matter is the experience, the life represented and the value discovered, and both dramatized or enacted under the banner of doctrine. All banners are wrongheaded, but they make rallying points, free the impulse to cry out, and give meaning to the cry itself simply by making it seem appropriate.

It is on some analogue or parallel to these remarks alone that we undersand and use the thought and art of those whose doctrines differ from our own. We either discount, absorb, or dominate the doctrine for the sake of the life that goes with it, for the sake of what is *formed* in the progressive act of thinking. When we do more—when we refine or elaborate the abstracted notion of form—we play a different game, which has merit of its own like chess, but which applied to the world we live in produces false dilemmas like solipsism and infant damnation. There is, taking solipsism for example, a fundamental distinction. Because of the logical doctrine prepared to support it, technical philosophers employ years[4] to get around the impasse in which it leaves them; whereas men of poetic imagination merely use it for the dramatic insight it contains—as Eliot uses it in the last section of the *Wasteland;* or as, say, everyone uses the residual mythology of the Greek religion—which its priests nevertheless used as literal sanctions for blood and power.

Fortunately, there exist archetypes of unindoctrinated thinking. Let us incline our minds like reflectors to catch the light of the early Plato and the whole Montaigne. Is not the inexhaustible stimulus and fertility of the dialogues and the essays due as much as anything to the absence of positive doctrine? Is it not that the early Plato always holds conflicting ideas in shifting balance, presenting them in contest and evolution, with victory only the last shift? Is it not that Montaigne is always making room for another idea, and implying always a third for provisional, adjudicating irony? Are not the forms of both men themselves ironic, betraying in its most intimate recesses the duplicity of every thought, pointing it out, so to speak, in the act of self-incrimination, and showing it not paled on a pin but in the buff life? . . . Such an approach, such an attempt at vivid questing, borrowed

---

[3][Blackmur] Santayana's essay *A Long Way Round to Nirvana* (in *Some Turns of Thought in Modern Philosophy*) illustrates the poetic-philosophic character of Freud's insight into death by setting up its analogue in Indian philosophy; and by his comparison only adds to the stimulus of Freud.

[4][Blackmur] Santayana found it necessary to resort to his only sustained labor of dialectic, *Skepticism and Animal Faith,* which, though a beautiful monument of intellectual play, is ultimately valuable for its *incidental* moral wisdom.

and no doubt adulterated by our own needs, is the only rational approach to the multiplication of doctrine and arrogant technologies which fills out the body of critical thinking. Anything else is a succumbing, not an approach; and it is surely the commonest of ironies to observe a man altogether out of his depth do his cause fatal harm merely because, having once succumbed to an idea, he thinks it necessary to stick to it. Thought is a beacon, not a life raft, and to confuse the functions is tragic. The tragic character of thought—as any perspective will show—is that it takes a rigid mold too soon; chooses destiny like a Calvinist, in infancy, instead of waiting slowly for old age, and hence for the most part works against the world, good sense, and its own object: as anyone may see by taking a perspective of any given idea of democracy, of justice, or the nature of the creative act.

Imaginative skepticism and dramatic irony—the modes of Montaigne and Plato—keep the mind athletic and the spirit on the stretch. Hence the juvenescence of the *Tempest,* and hence, too, perhaps, the air almost of precocity in *Back to Methuselah.* Hence, at any rate, the sustaining power of such varied works as *The Brothers Karamazov, Cousine Bette,* and *The Magic Mountain.* Dante, whom the faithful might take to the contrary, is yet "the chief imagination of Christendom"; he took his doctrine once and for all from the church and from St. Thomas and used it as a foil (in the painter's sense) to give recessiveness, background, and contrast. Virgil and Aristotle, Beatrice and Bertrans de Born, have in their way as much importance as St. Thomas and the church. It was this security of reference that made Dante so much more a free spirit than were, say, Swift and Laurence Sterne. Dante had a habit (not a theory) of imagination which enabled him to dramatize with equal ardor and effect what his doctrine blessed, what it assailed, and what, at heart, it was indifferent to. Doctrine was the seed and structure of vision, and for his poems (at least to us) never more. The *Divine Comedy* no less than the dialogues and the essays[5] is a true *speculum mentis.*[6]

With lesser thinkers and lesser artists—and in the defective works of the greater—we have in reading, in criticizing, to supply the skepticism and the irony, or, as may be, the imagination and the drama, to the degree, which cannot be complete since then we should have had no prompts, that they are lacking. We have to rub the looking glass clear. With *Hamlet,* for example, we have to struggle and guess to bring the motive out of obscurity: a struggle which, aiming at the wrong end, the psychoanalysts have darkened with counsel.

With Shelley we have to flesh out the Platonic ideas, as with Blake we have to cut away, since it cannot be dramatized, all the excrescence of doctrine. With Baudelaire we have sometimes to struggle with and sometimes to suppress the problem of belief, working out the irony implicit in either attitude. Similarly, with a writer like Pascal, in order to get the most out of him, in order to compose an artistic judgment, we must consider such an idea as that of the necessity of the wager, not solemnly as Pascal took it, but as a dramatized possibility, a savage, but provisional irony; and we need to show that the skepticisms of Montaigne and Pascal are not at all the same thing—that where one produced serenity the other produced excruciation.

Again, speaking of André Gide, we should remind ourselves not that he has been the apologist of homosexuality, not that he has become a communist, but that he is par excellence the French puritan chastened by the wisdom of the body, and that he has thus an acutely scrupulous ethical sensibility. It is by acknowledging the sensibility that we feel the impact of the apologetics and the political conversion. Another necessity in the apprehension of Gide might be put as the recognition of similarity in difference of the precocious small boys in Dostoevski and Gide, e.g. Kolya in *Karamazov* and young George in *The Counterfeiters:* they are small, cruel engines, all naked sensibility and no scruple, demoniacally possessed, and used to keep things going. And these in turn may remind us of another writer who had a predilection for presenting the *terrible* quality of the young intelligence: of Henry James, of the children in *The Turn of the Screw,* of Maisie,[7] and all the rest, all beautifully efficient agents of dramatic judgment and action, in that they take all things seriously for themselves, with the least prejudice of preparation, candidly, with an intelligence life has not yet violated.

Such feats of agility and attention as these remarks illustrate seem facile and even commonplace, and from facile points of view there is no need to take them otherwise. Taken superficially they provide escape from the whole labor of specific understanding; or, worse, they provide an easy vault from casual interpretation to an omnivorous world view. We might take solemnly and as of universal application the two notions of demonic possession and inviolate intelligence in the children of Gide, Dostoevski, and James, and on that frail nexus build an unassailable theory of the sources of art, wisdom, and value; unassailable because affording only a stereotyped vision, like that of conservative capitalism, without reference in the real world. The maturity of Shakespeare and

---

[5]The dialogues of Plato and the essays of Montaigne.
[6]"Reflection of the mind."

[7]A character in James's novel *What Maisie Knew.*

of Gertrude Stein would then be found on the same childish level.

But we need not go so far in order to draw back. The modes of Montaigne and Plato contain their own safety. Any single insight is good only at and up to a certain point of development and not beyond, which is to say that it is a provisional and tentative and highly selective approach to its field. Furthermore, no observation, no collection of observations, ever tells the whole story; there is always room for more, and at the hypothetical limit of attention and interest there will always remain, quite untouched, the thing itself. Thus, the complex character—I say nothing of the value—of the remarks above reveals itself. They flow from a dramatic combination of all the skills and conventions of the thinking mind. They are common-place only as criticism—as an end-product of function. Like walking, criticism is a pretty nearly universal art; both require a constant intricate shifting and catching of balance; neither can be questioned much in process; and few perform either really well. For either a new terrain is fatiguing and awkward, and in our day most men prefer paved walks or some form of rapid transit—some easy theory or outmastering dogma. A good critic keeps his criticism from becoming either instinctive or vicarious, and the labor of his understanding is always specific, like the art which he examines; and he knows that the sum of his best work comes only to the pedagogy of elucidation and appreciation. He observes facts and he delights in discriminations. The object remains, and should remain, itself, only made more available and seen in a clearer light. The imagination of Dante is for us only equal to what we can know of it at a given time.

Which brings us to what, as T. S. Eliot would say,[8] I have been leading up to all the time, and what has indeed been said several times by the way. Any rational approach is valid to literature and may be properly called critical which fastens at any point upon the work itself. The utility of a given approach depends partly upon the strength of the mind making it and partly upon the recognition of the limits appropriate to it. Limits may be of scope, degree, or relevance, and may be either plainly laid out by the critic himself, or may be determined by his readers; and it is, by our argument, the

latter case that commonly falls, since an active mind tends to overestimate the scope of its tools and to take as necessary those doctrinal considerations which habit has made seem instinctive. No critic is required to limit himself to a single approach, nor is he likely to be able to do so; facts cannot be exhibited without comment, and comment involves the generality of the mind. Furthermore, a consciously complex approach like that of Kenneth Burke or T. S. Eliot, by setting up parallels of reference, affords a more flexible, more available, more stimulating standard of judgment—though of course at a greater risk of prejudice—than a single approach. What produces the evil of stultification and the malice of controversy is the confused approach, when the limits are not seen because they tend to cancel each other out, and the driving power becomes emotional.

The worse evil of fanatic falsification—of arrogant irrationality and barbarism in all its forms—arises when a body of criticism is governed by an *idée fixe,* a really exaggerated heresy, when a notion of genuine but small scope is taken literally as of universal application. This is the body of tendentious criticism where, since something is assumed proved before the evidence is in, distortion, vitiation, and absolute assertion become supreme virtues. I cannot help feeling that such writers as Maritain and Massis—no less than Nordau before them—are tendentious in this sense. But even here, in this worst order of criticism, there is a taint of legitimacy. Once we reduce, in a man like Irving Babbitt, the magnitude of application of such notions as the inner check and the higher will, which were for Babbitt paramount—that is, when we determine the limits within which he really worked—then the massive erudition and acute observation with which his work is packed become permanently available.

And there is no good to be got in objecting to and disallowing those orders of criticism which have an ulterior purpose. Ulterior is not in itself a pejorative, but only so when applied to an enemy. Since criticism is not autonomous—not a light but a process of elucidation—it cannot avoid discovering constantly within itself a purpose or purposes ulterior in the good sense. The danger is in not knowing what is ulterior and what is not, which is much the same as the cognate danger in the arts themselves. The arts serve purposes beyond themselves; the purposes of what they dramatize or represent at that remove from the flux which gives them order and meaning and value; and to deny those purposes is like asserting that the function of a handsaw is to hang above a bench and that to cut wood is to belittle it. But the purposes are varied and so bound in his subject that the artist cannot always design for them. The critic, if that is his bent, may concern himself with those purposes or with some

---

[8][Blackmur] . . . that when "morals cease to be a matter of tradition and orthodoxy—that is, of the habits of the community formulated, corrected, and elevated by the continuous thought and direction of the church—and when each man is to elaborate his own, then *personality* becomes a thing of alarming importance." (*After Strange Gods.*) Thus Mr. Eliot becomes one of those viewers-with-alarm whose next step forward is the very hysteria of disorder they wish to escape. The hysteria of institutions is more dreadful than that of individuals.

one among them which obsess him; but he must be certain to distinguish between what is genuinely ulterior to the works he examines and what is merely irrelevant; and he must further not assume except within the realm of his special argument that other purposes either do not exist or are negligible or that the works may not be profitably discussed apart from ulterior purposes and as examples of dramatic possibility alone.

II

Three examples of contemporary criticism primarily concerned with the ulterior purposes of literature should, set side by side, exhibit both the defects and the unchastened virtues of that approach; though they must do so only tentatively and somewhat invidiously—with an exaggeration for effect. Each work is assumed to be a representative ornament of its kind, carrying within it the seeds of its own death and multiplication. Let us take then, with an eye sharpened by the dangers involved, Santayana's essay on Lucretius (in *Three Philosophical Poets*), Van Wyck Brooks' *Pilgrimage of Henry James,* and Granville Hicks' *The Great Tradition.* Though that of the third is more obvious in our predicament, the urgency in the approach is equal in all three.

Santayana's essay represents a conversion or transvaluation of an actually poetic ordering of nature to the terms of a moral philosophy which, whatever its own responsibilities, is free of the special responsibility of poetry.[9] So ably and so persuasively is it composed, his picture seems complete and to contain so much of what was important in Lucretius that *De Rerum Natura* itself can be left behind. The philosophical nature of the insight, its moral scope and defect, the influence upon it of the Democritan atom, once grasped intellectually as Santayana shows us how to grasp them, seem a good substitute for the poem and far more available. But, what Santayana remembers but does not here emphasize since it was beyond his immediate interest, there is no vicar for poetry on earth. Poetry is idiom, a special and fresh saying, and cannot for its life be said otherwise; and there is, finally, as much difference between words used about a poem and the poem as there is between words used about a painting and the painting. The gap is absolute. Yet I do not mean to suggest that Santayana's essay—that any philosophical criticism—is beside the point. It is true that the essay may be taken as a venture in philosophy for its own sake, but

it is also true that it reveals a body of facts about an ulterior purpose in Lucretius' poem—doubtless the very purpose Lucretius himself would have chosen to see enhanced. If we return to the poem it will be warmer as the facts come alive in verse. The reconversion comes naturally in this instance in that, through idioms differently construed but equally imaginative, philosophy and poetry both buttress and express moral value. The one enacts or represents in the flesh what the other reduces to principle or raises to the ideal. The only precaution the critic of poetry need take is negative: that neither poetry nor philosophy can ever fully satisfy the other's purposes, though each may seem to do so if taken in an ulterior fashion. The relationship is mutual but not equivalent.

When we turn deliberately from Santayana on Lucretius to Van Wyck Brooks on Henry James, we turn from the consideration of the rational ulterior purpose of art to the consideration of the irrational underlying predicament of the artist himself, not only as it predicts his art and is reflected in it, but also, and in effect predominantly, as it represents the conditioning of nineteenth-century American culture. The consideration is sociological, the method of approach that of literary psychology, and the burden obsessive. The conversion is from literary to biographical values. Art is taken not as the objectification or mirroring of social experience but as a personal expression and escape-fantasy of the artist's personal life in dramatic extension. The point for emphasis is that the cultural situation of Henry James' America stultified the expression and made every escape ineffectual—even that of Europe. This theme—the private tragedy of the unsuccessful artist—was one of Henry James' own; but James saw it as typical or universal—as a characteristic tragedy of the human spirit—illustrated, as it happened for him, against the Anglo-American background. Brooks, taking the same theme, raises it to an obsession, an omnivorous concept, under which all other themes can be subsumed. Applied to American cultural history, such obsessive thinking is suggestive in the very exaggeration of its terms, and applied to the predicament of Henry James the man it dramatically emphasizes—uses for all and more than it is worth—an obvious conflict that tormented him. As history or as biography the book is a persuasive imaginative picture, although clearly not the only one to be seen. Used as a nexus between James the man and the novels themselves, the book has only possible relevance and cannot be held as material. *Hamlet,* by a similar argument, could be shown to be an unsuccessful expression of Shakespeare's personality. To remain useful in the field of literary criticism, Brooks' notions ought to be kept parallel to James' novels but never allowed to merge with them. The corrective, the proof of the gap, is perhaps in

---

[9]Compare these remarks to Santayana's own theoretical comments in *The Sense of Beauty* (1896).

the great air of freedom and sway of mastery that pervades the prefaces James wrote to his collected edition.[10] For James art was enough because it molded and mirrored and valued all the life he knew. What Brooks' parallel strictures can do is to help us decide from another point of view whether to choose the values James dramatized. They cannot affect or elucidate but rather—if the gap is closed by will—obfuscate the values themselves.

In short, the order of criticism of which Brooks is a masterly exponent, and which we may call the psychosociological order, is primarily and in the end concerned less with the purposes, ulterior or not, of the arts than with some of the ulterior *uses* to which the arts can be appropriately put. Only what is said in the meantime, by the way—and does not depend upon the essence of argument but only accompanies it—can be applied to the arts themselves. There is nothing, it should be added, in Brooks' writings to show that he believes otherwise or would claim more; he is content with that scope and degree of value to which his method and the strength of his mind limit him; and his value is the greater and more urgent for that.

Such tacit humility, such implicit admission of contingency, are not immediate characteristics of Granville Hicks' *The Great Tradition,* though they may, so serious is his purpose, be merely virtues of which he deliberately, for the time being and in order to gain his point, deprives himself of the benefit. If that is so, however expedient his tactics may seem on the short view, they will defeat him on the long. But let us examine the book on the ground of our present concern alone. Like Brooks, Hicks presents an interpretation of American literature since the Civil War, dealing with the whole body rather than single figures. Like Brooks he has a touchstone in an obsessive idea, but where we may say that Brooks *uses* his idea—as we think for more than it is worth—we must say that Hicks is victimized by his idea to the point where the travail of judgment is suspended and becomes the mere reiteration of a formula. He judges literature as it expressed or failed to express the economic conflict of classes sharpened by the industrial revolution, and he judges individual writers as they used or did not use an ideology resembling the Marxist analysis as prime clue to the clear representation of social drama. Thus Howells comes off better than Henry James, and Frank Norris better than Mark Twain, and, in our own day, Dos Passos is struck on a thin eminence that must alarm him.

Controversy is not here a profitable exercise, but it may be said for the sake of the record that although every period

of history presents a class struggle, some far more acute than our own, the themes of great art have seldom lent themselves to propaganda for an economic insight, finding, as it happened, religious, moral, or psychological—that is to say, interpretative—insights more appropriate impulses. If *Piers Plowman* dealt with the class struggle, *The Canterbury Tales* did not, and Hicks would be hard to put, if he looked sharp, to make out a better case of social implication in Dostoevski than in Henry James.

What vitiates *The Great Tradition* is its tendentiousness. Nothing could be more exciting, nothing more vital, than a book by Hicks which discovered and examined the facts of a literature whose major theme hung on an honest, dramatic view of the class struggle—and there is indeed such a literature now emerging from the depression. And on the other hand it would be worthwhile to have Hicks sharpen his teeth on all the fraudulent or pseudo art which actually slanders the terms of the class and every other struggle.

The book with which he presents us performs a very different operation. There is an initial hortatory assumption that American literature ought to represent the class struggle from a Marxist view point, and that it ought thus to be the spur and guide to political action. Proceeding, the point is either proved or the literature dismissed and its authors slandered. Hicks is not disengaging for emphasis and contemporary need an ulterior purpose; he is not writing criticism at all; he is writing a fanatic's history and a casuist's polemic, with the probable result—which is what was meant by suggesting above that he had misconceived his tactics—that he will convert no one who retains the least love of literature or the least knowledge of the themes which engage the most of life. It should be emphasized that there is no more quarrel with Hicks' economic insight as such than there was with the insights of Santayana and Van Wyck Brooks. The quarrel is deeper. While it is true and good that the arts may be used to illustrate social propaganda—though it is not a great use—you can no more use an economic insight as your chief critical tool than you can make much out of the Mass by submitting the doctrine of transubstantiation to chemical analysis.

These three writers have one great formal fact in common, which they illustrate as differently as may be. They are concerned with the separable content of literature, with what may be said without consideration of its specific setting and apparition in a form; which is why, perhaps, all three leave literature so soon behind. The quantity of what can be said directly about the content alone of a given work of art is seldom great, but the least saying may be the innervation of an infinite intellectual structure, which, however valuable in itself, has for the most part only an asserted relation with the

---

[10]Blackmur has edited a collection of James's prefaces entitled *The Art of the Novel.*

works from which it springs. The sense of continuous relationship, of sustained contact, with the works nominally in hand is rare and when found uncommonly exhilarating; it is the fine object of criticism: as it seems to put us in direct possession of the principles whereby the works move without injuring or disintegrating the body of the works themselves. This sense of intimacy by inner contact cannot arise from methods of approach which hinge on seized separable content. We have constantly—if our interest is really in literature—to prod ourselves back, to remind ourselves that there was a poem, play, or a novel of some initial and we hope terminal concern, or we have to falsify facts and set up fictions[11] to the effect that no matter what we are saying we are really talking about art after all. The question must often be whether the prodding and reminding is worth the labor, whether we might not better assign the works that require it to a different category than that of criticism.

III

Similar strictures and identical precautions are necessary in thinking of other, quite different approaches to criticism, where if there are no ulterior purposes to allow for there are other no less limiting features—there are certainly such, for example, for me in thinking of my own. The ulterior motive, or the limiting feature, whichever it is, is a variable constant. One does not always know what it is, nor what nor how much work it does; but one always knows it is there—for strength or weakness. It may be only the strength of emphasis—which is necessarily distortion; or it may be the worse strength of a simplifying formula, which skeletonizes and transforms what we want to recognize in the flesh. It may be only the weakness of what is unfinished, undeveloped, or unseen—the weakness that follows on emphasis; or it may be the weakness that shows when pertinent things are deliberately dismissed or ignored, which is the corresponding weakness of the mind strong in formula. No mind can avoid distortion and formula altogether, nor would wish to; but most minds rush to the defense of qualities they think cannot be avoided, and that, in itself, is an ulterior motive, a limiting

feature of the mind that rushes. I say nothing of one's personal prepossessions, of the damage of one's private experience, of the malice and false tolerance they inculcate into judgment. I know that my own essays suffer variously, but I cannot bring myself to specify the indulgences I would ask; mostly, I hope, that general indulgence which consists in the task of bringing my distortions and emphases and opinions into balance with other distortions, other emphases, and better opinions.

But rather than myself, let us examine briefly, because of their differences from each other and from the three critics already handled, the modes of approach to the act of criticism and habits of critical work of I. A. Richards, Kenneth Burke, and S. Foster Damon. It is to characterize them and to judge the *character* of their work—its typical scope and value—that we want to examine them. With the objective validity of their varying theories we are not much here concerned. Objective standards of criticism, as we hope them to exist at all, must have an existence anterior and superior to the practice of particular critics. The personal element in a given critic—what he happens to know and happens to be able to understand—is strong or obstinate enough to reach into his aesthetic theories; and as most critics do not have the coherence of philosophers it seems doubtful if any outsider could ever reach the same conclusions as the critic did by adopting his aesthetics. Aesthetics sometimes seems only as implicit in the practice of criticism as the atomic physics is present in sunlight when you feel it.

But some critics deliberately expand the theoretic phase of every practical problem. There is a tendency to urge the scientific principle and the statistical method, and in doing so to bring in the whole assorted world of thought. That Mr. Richards, who is an admirable critic and whose love and knowledge of poetry are incontestable, is a victim of the expansiveness of his mind in these directions, is what characterizes, and reduces, the scope of his work as literary criticism. It is possible that he ought not to be called a literary critic at all. If we list the titles of his books we are in a quandary: *The Foundations of Aesthetics, The Meaning of Meaning* (these with C. K. Ogden), *The Principles of Literary Criticism, Science and Poetry, Practical Criticism, Mencius on the Mind,* and *Coleridge on Imagination.* The apparatus is so vast, so labyrinthine, so inclusive—and the amount of actual literary criticism is so small that it seems almost a by-product instead of the central target. The slightest volume, physically, *Science and Poetry,* contains proportionally the most literary criticism, and contains, curiously, his one obvious failure in appreciation—since amply redressed—his misjudgment of the nature of Yeats' poetry. His work is for the most part *about* a department of the mind which includes

---

[11][Blackmur] Such a fiction, if not consciously so contrived, is the fiction of the organic continuity of all literature as expounded by T. S. Eliot in his essay, *Tradition and the Individual Talent* [see p. 761]. The locus is famous and represents that each new work of art slightly alters the relationships among the whole order of existing works. The notion has truth, but it is a mathematical truth and has little relevance to the arts. Used as Eliot uses it, it is an experimental conceit and pushes the mind forward. Taken seriously it is bad constitutional law, in the sense that it would provoke numberless artificial and insoluble problems.

the pedagogy of sensibility and the practice of literary criticism. The matters he investigates are the problems of belief, of meaning, of communication, of the nature of controversy, and of poetic language as the supreme mode of imagination. The discussion of these problems is made to focus for the most part on poetry because poetry provides the only great monuments of imagination available to verbal imagination. His bottom contention might I think be put as this: that words have a synergical power, in the realms of feeling, emotion, and value, to create a reality, or the sense of it, not contained in the words separately; and that the power and the reality as experienced in great poetry make the chief source of meaning and value for the life we live. This contention I share; except that I should wish to put on the same level, as sources of meaning and value, modes of imagination that have no medium in words—though words may call on them—and are not susceptible of verbal reformulation: the modes of great acting, architecture, music, and painting. Thus I can assent to Mr. Richards' positive statement of the task of criticism, because I can add to it positive tasks in analogous fields: "To recall that poetry is the supreme use of language, man's chief coordinating instrument, in the service of the most integral purposes of life; and to explore, with thoroughness, the intricacies of the modes of language as working modes of the mind." But I want this criticism, engaged in this task, constantly to be confronted with examples of poetry, and I want it so for the very practical purpose of assisting in pretty immediate appreciation of the use, meaning, and value of the language in that particular poetry. I want it to assist in doing for me what it actually assists Mr. Richards in doing, whatever that is, when he is reading poetry for its own sake.

Mr. Richards wants it to do that, too, but he wants it to do a great deal else first. Before it gets to actual poetry (from which it is said to spring) he wants literary criticism to become something else and much more: he wants it to become, indeed, the master department of the mind. As we become aware of the scope of poetry, we see, according to Mr. Richards, that

the study of the modes of language becomes, as it attempts to be thorough, the most fundamental and extensive of all inquiries. It is no preliminary or preparation for other profounder studies. . . . The very formation of the objects which these studies propose to examine takes place through the processes (of which imagination and fancy are modes) by which the words they use acquire their meanings. Criticism is the science of these meanings. . . . Critics in the future must have a theoretical equipment which has not been felt to be necessary in the past. . . . But the critical equipment will not be *primarily* philosophical. It will be rather a command *of the methods of general linguistic analysis.*[12]

I think we may take it that *Mencius on the Mind* is an example of the kind of excursion on which Mr. Richards would lead us. It is an excursion into multiple definition, and it is a good one if that is where you want to go and are in no hurry to come back: you learn the enormous variety and complexity of the operations possible in the process of verbally describing and defining brief passages of imaginative language and the equal variety and complexity of the result; you learn the practical impossibility of verbally ascertaining what an author means—and you hear nothing of the other ways of apprehending meaning at all. The instance is in the translation of Mencius, because Mr. Richards happens to be interested in Mencius, and because it is easy to see the difficulties of translating Chinese; but the principles and method of application would work as well on passages from Milton or Rudyard Kipling. The real point of Mr. Richards' book is the impossibility of understanding, short of a lifetime's analysis and compensation, the mechanism of meaning in even a small body of work. There is no question of the exemplary value and stimulus of Mr. Richards' work; but there is no question either that few would care to emulate him for any purpose of literary criticism. In the first place it would take too long, and in the second he does not answer the questions literary criticism would put. The literal adoption of Mr. Richards' approach to literary criticism would stultify the very power it was aimed to enhance—the power of imaginative apprehension, of imaginative coordination of varied and separate elements. Mr. Richards' work is something to be aware of, but deep awareness is the limit of use. It is notable that in his admirable incidental criticism of such poets as Eliot, Lawrence, Yeats, and Hopkins, Mr. Richards does not himself find it necessary to be more than aware of his own doctrines of linguistic analysis. As philosophy from Descartes to Bradley transformed itself into a study of the modes of knowing, Mr. Richards would transform literary criticism into the science of linguistics. Epistemology is a great subject, and so is linguistics; but they come neither in first nor final places; the one is only a fragment of wisdom and the other only a fraction of the means of understanding. Literary criticism is not a science—though it may be the object of

---

[12][Blackmur] All quoted material is from the last four pages of *Coleridge on Imagination.*

one; and to try to make it one is to turn it upside down. Right side up, Mr. Richards' contribution shrinks in weight and dominion but remains intact and preserves its importance. We may conclude that it was the newness of his view that led him to exaggerate it, and we ought to add the probability that had he not exaggerated it we should never have seen either that it was new or valuable at all.

From another point of view than that of literary criticism, and as a contribution to a psychological theory of knowledge, Mr. Richards' work is not heretical, but is integral and integrating, and especially when it incorporates poetry into its procedure; but from our point of view the heresy is profound—and is far more distorting than the heresies of Santayana, Brooks, and Hicks, which carry with them obviously the impetus for their correction. Because it is possible to apply scientific methods to the language of poetry, and because scientific methods engross their subject matter, Mr. Richards places the whole burden of criticism in the application of a scientific approach, and asserts it to be an implement for the judgment of poetry. Actually, it can handle only the language and its words and cannot touch—except by assertion—the imaginative product of the words which is poetry: which is the object revealed or elucidated by criticism. Criticism must be concerned, first and last—whatever comes between—with the poem as it is read and as what it represents is felt. As no amount of physics and physiology can explain the *feeling* of things seen as green or even certify their existence, so no amount of linguistic analysis can explain the *feeling* or existence of a poem. Yet the physics in the one case and the linguistics in the other may be useful both to the poet and the reader. It may be useful, for example, in extracting the facts of meaning from a poem, to show that, whether the poet was aware of it or not, the semantic history of a word was so and so; but only if the semantics can be resolved into the ambiguities and precisions created by the poem. Similarly with any branch of linguistics; and similarly with the applications of psychology—Mr. Richards' other emphasis. No statistical description can either explain or demean a poem unless the description is translated back to the imaginative apprehension or feeling which must have taken place without it. The light of science is parallel or in the background where feeling or meaning is concerned. The Oedipus complex does not explain *Oedipus Rex;* not that Mr. Richards would think it did. Otherwise he could not believe that "poetry is the supreme use of language" and more, could not convey in his comments on T. S. Eliot's *Ash Wednesday* the actuality of his belief that poetry is the supreme use.

It is the interest and fascination of Mr. Richards' work in reference to different levels of sensibility, including the poetic, that has given him both a wide and a penetrating influence. No literary critic can escape his influence; an influence that stimulates the mind as much as anything by showing the sheer excitement as well as the profundity of the problems of language—many of which he has himself made genuine problems, at least for readers of poetry: an influence, obviously, worth deliberately incorporating by reducing it to one's own size and needs. In T. S. Eliot the influence is conspicuous if slight. Mr. Kenneth Burke is considerably indebted, partly directly to Mr. Richards, partly to the influences which acted upon Mr. Richards (as Bentham's theory of fictions) and partly to the frame of mind which helped mold them both. But Mr. Burke is clearly a different person—and different from anyone writing today; and the virtues, the defects, and the élan of his criticism are his own.

Some years ago, when Mr. Burke was an animating influence on the staff of *The Dial,* Miss Marianne Moore published a poem in that magazine called *Picking and Choosing* which contained the following lines.

> and Burke is a
> psychologist—of acute and raccoon-
> like curiosity. *Summa diligentia;*
> to the humbug, whose name is
> so very amusing—very young
> and ve-
> ry rushed, Caesar crossed the Alps on the 'top of a
> *diligence.*' We are not daft about the meaning but this
> familiarity
> with wrong meanings puzzles one.

In the index of Miss Moore's *Observations,* we find under Burke that the reference is to Edmund, but it is really to Kenneth just the same. There is no acuter curiosity than Mr. Burke's engaged in associating the meanings, right and wrong, of the business of literature with the business of life and vice versa. No one has a greater awareness—not even Mr. Richards—of the important part wrong meanings play in establishing the consistency of right ones. The writer of whom he reminds us, for the buoyancy and sheer remarkableness of his speculations, is Charles Santiago Saunders Peirce; one is enlivened by them without any *necessary* reference to their truth; hence they have truth for their own purposes, that is, for their own uses. Into what these purposes or uses are it is our present business to inquire.

As Mr. Richards in fact uses literature as a springboard or source for a scientific method of a philosophy of value, Mr. Burke uses literature, not only as a springboard but also as a resort or home, for a philosophy or psychology of moral possibility. Literature is the hold-all and the persuasive form for the patterns of possibility. In literature we see unique possibilities enacted, actualized, and in the moral and psychological philosophies we see the types of possibility generalized, see their abstracted, convertible forms. In some literature, and in some aspects of most literature of either great magnitude or great possibility, we see, so to speak, the enactment or dramatic representation of the type or patterns. Thus Mr. Burke can make a thrilling intellectual pursuit of the subintelligent writing of Erskine Caldwell: where he shows that Caldwell gains a great effect of humanity by putting in *none himself,* appealing to the reader's common stock: i.e., what is called for so desperately by the pattern of the story must needs be generously supplied. Exactly as thrilling is his demonstration of the great emotional role of the outsider as played in the supremely intelligent works of Thomas Mann and André Gide. His common illustrations of the pervasive spread of symbolic pattern are drawn from Shakespeare and from the type of the popular or pulp press. I think that on the whole his method could be applied with equal fruitfulness either to Shakespeare, Dashiell Hammett, or Marie Corelli; as indeed he does apply it with equal force both to the field of anarchic private morals and to the outline of a secular conversion to communism—as in, respectively, *Toward a Better Life* and *Permanence and Change.*

The real harvest that we barn from Mr. Burke's writings is his presentation of the types of ways the mind works in the written word. He is more interested in the psychological means of the meaning, and how it might mean (and often really does) something else, than in the meaning itself. Like Mr. Richards, but for another purpose, he is engaged largely in the meaning of meaning, and is therefore much bound up with considerations of language, but on the plane of emotional and intellectual patterns rather than on the emotional plane; which is why his essays deal with literature (or other writings) as it dramatizes or unfolds character (a character is a pattern of emotions and notions) rather than with lyric or meditative poetry which is Mr. Richards' field. So we find language containing felt character as well as felt coordination. The representation of character, and of aspiration and symbol, must always be rhetorical; and therefore we find that for Mr. Burke the rightly rhetorical is the profoundly hortatory. Thus literature may be seen as an inexhaustible reservoir of moral or character philosophies in action.

It is the technique of such philosophies that Mr. Burke explores, as he pursues it through curiosities of development and conversion and duplicity; it is the technique of the notions that may be put into or taken out of literature, but it is only a part of the technique of literature itself. The final reference is to the psychological and moral possibilities of the mind, and these certainly do not exhaust the technique or the reality of literature. The reality in literature is an object of contemplation and of feeling, like the reality of a picture or a cathedral, not a route of speculation. If we remember this and make the appropriate reductions here as elsewhere, Mr. Burke's essays become as pertinent to literary criticism as they are to the general ethical play of the mind. Otherwise they become too much a methodology for its own sake on the one hand, and too much a philosophy at one remove on the other. A man writes as he can; but those who use his writings have the further responsibility of redefining their scope, an operation (of which Mr. Burke is a master) which alone uses them to the full.

It is in relation to these examples which I have so unjustly held up of the philosophical, the sociological or historical, the tendentious, the semasiological, and the psychological approaches to criticism that I wish to examine an example of what composes, after all, the great bulk of serious writings about literature: a work of literary scholarship. Upon scholarship all other forms of literary criticism depend, so long as they are criticism, in much the same way that architecture depends on engineering. The great editors of the last century—men such as Dyce and Skeat and Gifford and Furness—performed work as valuable to the use of literature, and with far less complement of harm, as men like Hazlitt and Arnold and Pater. Scholarship, being bent on the collection, arrangement, and scrutiny of facts, has the positive advantage over other forms of criticism that it is a cooperative labor, and may be completed and corrected by subsequent scholars; and it has the negative advantage that it is not bound to investigate the mysteries of meaning or to connect literature with other departments of life—it has only to furnish the factual materials for such investigations and connections. It is not surprising to find that the great scholars are sometimes good critics, though usually in restricted fields; and it is a fact, on the other hand, that the great critics are themselves either good scholars or know how to take great advantage of scholarship. Perhaps we may put it that for the most part dead critics remain alive in us to the extent that they form part of our scholarship. It is Dr. Johnson's statements of fact that we preserve of him as a critic; his opinions have long since become a part of that imaginative structure, his personality. A last fact about scholarship is this, that so far as its conclusions are sound they are subject to use and digestion not debate by those outside the fold. And of bad scholarship as of bad criticism we have only to find means to minimize what we cannot destroy.

It is difficult to find an example of scholarship pure and simple, of high character, which can be made to seem relevant to the discussion in hand. What I want is to bring into the discussion the omnipresence of scholarship as a background and its immediate and necessary availability to every other mode of approach. What I want is almost anonymous. Failing that, I choose S. Foster Damon's *William Blake* (as I might have taken J. L. Lowe's *Road to Xanadu*) which, because of its special subject matter, brings its scholarship a little nearer the terms of discussion than a Shakespeare commentary would have done. The scholar's major problem with Blake happened to be one which many scholars could not handle, some refused to see, and some fumbled. A great part of Blake's meaning is not open to ordinarily well-instructed readers, but must be brought out by the detailed solution of something very like an enormous and enormously complicated acrostic puzzle. Not only earnest scrutiny of the poems as printed, but also a study of Blake's reading, a reconstruction of habits of thought, and an industrious piecing together into a consistent key of thousands of clues throughout the work, were necessary before many even of the simplest appearing poems could be explained. It is one thing to explain a mystical poet, like Crashaw, who was attached to a recognized church, and difficult enough; but it is a far more difficult thing to explain a mystical poet like Blake, who was so much an eclectic in his sources that his mystery as well as his apprehension of it was practically his own. All Mr. Damon had to go on besides the texts, and the small body of previous scholarship that was pertinent, were the general outlines of insight to which all mystics apparently adhere. The only explanation would be in the facts of what Blake meant to mean when he habitually said one thing in order to hide and enhance another; and in order to be convincing—poetry being what it is—the facts adduced had to be self-evident. It is not a question here whether the mystery enlightened was worth it. The result for emphasis is that Mr. Damon made Blake exactly what he seemed least to be, perhaps the most intellectually consistent of the greater poets in English. Since the chief weapons used are the extended facts of scholarship, the picture Mr. Damon produced cannot be destroyed even though later and other scholarship modifies, rearranges, or adds to it with different or other facts. The only suspicion that might attach is that the picture is too consistent and that the facts are made to tell too much, and direct, but instructed, apprehension not enough.

My point about Mr. Damon's work is typical and double. First, that the same sort of work, the adduction of ultimately self-evident facts, can be done and must be done in other kinds of poetry than Blake's. Blake is merely an extreme and obvious example of an unusually difficult poet who hid his facts on purpose. The work must be done to the appropriate degree of digging out the facts in all orders of poetry—and especially perhaps in contemporary poetry, where we tend to let the work go either because it seems too easy or because it seems supererogatory. Self-evident facts are paradoxically the hardest to come by; they are not evident till they are seen; yet the meaning of a poem—the part of it which is intellectually formulable—must invariably depend on this order of facts, the facts about the meanings of the elements aside from their final meaning in combination. The rest of the poem, what it is, what it shows, its final value as a created emotion, its meanings, if you like, *as* a poem, cannot in the more serious orders of poetry develop itself to the full without this factual or intellectual meaning to show the way. The other point is already made, and has been made before in this essay, but it may still be emphasized. Although the scholarly account is indispensable it does not tell the whole story. It is only the basis and perhaps ultimately the residue of all the other stories. But it must be seen to first.

My own approach, such as it is, and if it can be named, does not tell the whole story either; the reader is conscientiously left with the poem with the real work yet to do; and I wish to advance it—as indeed I have been advancing it *seriatim*—only in connection with the reduced and compensated approaches I have laid out; and I expect, too, that if my approach is used at all it will require its own reduction as well as its compensations. Which is why this essay has taken its present form, preferring for once, in the realm of theory and apologetics, the implicit to the explicit statement. It is, I suppose, an approach to literary criticism—to the discourse of an amateur—primarily through the technique, in the widest sense of that word, of the examples handled; technique on the plane of words and even of linguistics in Mr. Richards' sense, but also technique on the plane of intellectual and emotional patterns in Mr. Burke's sense, and technique, too, in that there is a technique of securing and arranging and representing a fundamental view of life. The advantage of the technical approach is I think double. It readily admits other approaches and is anxious to be complemented by them. Furthermore, in a sense, it is able to incorporate the technical aspect, which always exists, of what is secured by other approaches—as I have argued elsewhere that so unpromising a matter as T. S. Eliot's religious convictions may be profitably considered as a dominant element in his technique of revealing the actual. The second advantage of the technical approach is a consequence of the first; it treats of nothing in literature except in its capacity of reduction to literary fact, which is where it resembles scholarship, only passing beyond it in that its facts are usually further into the heart of the literature than the facts of most scholarship. Aristotle, curiously, is here the type and master; as the *Poetics* is nothing but a collection and explanation of the facts of Greek poetry, it is the factual aspect that is invariably produced. The rest of the labor is in the effort to find understandable terms to fit the composition of the facts. After all, it is only the facts about a poem, a play, a novel, that can be reduced to tractable form, talked about, and examined; the rest is the product of the facts, from the technical point of view, and not a product but the thing itself from its own point of view. The rest, whatever it is, can only be known, not talked about.

But facts are not simple or easy to come at; not all the facts will appear to one mind, and the same facts appear differently in the light of different minds. No attention is undivided, no single approach sufficient, no predilection guaranteed, when facts or what their arrangements create are in question. In short, for the arts, *mere* technical scrutiny of any order, is not enough without the direct apprehension—which may come first or last—to which all scrutinies that show facts contribute.

It may be that there are principles that cover both the direct apprehension and the labor of providing modes for the understanding of the expressive arts. If so, they are Socratic and found within, and subject to the fundamental skepticism as in Montaigne. There must be seeds, let us say—seeds, germs, beginning forms upon which I can rely and to which I resort. When I use a word, an image, a notion, there must be in its small nodular apparent form, as in the peas I am testing on my desk, at least prophetically, the whole future growth, the whole harvested life; and not rhetorically nor in a formula, but stubbornly, pervasively, heart-hidden, materially, in both the anterior and the eventual prospect as well as in the small handled form of the nub. What is it, what are they, these seeds of understanding? And if I know, are they logical? Do they take the processional form of the words I use? Or do they take a form like that of the silver backing a glass, a dark that enholds all brightness? Is every metaphor—and the assertion of understanding is our great metaphor—mixed by the necessity of its intention? What is the mixture of a word, an image, a notion?

The mixture, if I may start a hare so late, the mixture, even in the fresh use of an old word, is made in the preconscious, and is by hypothesis unascertainable. But let us not use hypotheses, let us not desire to ascertain. By intuition we adventure in the preconscious; and there, where the adventure is, there is no need or suspicion of certainty or meaning; there is the living, expanding, *prescient* substance without the tags and handles of conscious form. Art is the looking glass of the preconscious, and when it is deepest seems to participate in it sensibly. Or, better, for purposes of criticism, our sensibility resumes the division of the senses and faculties at the same time that it preens itself into conscious form. Criticism may have as an object the establishment and evaluation (comparison and analysis) of the modes of making the preconscious *consciously* available.

But this emphasis upon the preconscious need not be insisted on; once recognized it may be tacitly assumed, and the effort of the mind will be, as it were, restored to its own plane—only a little sensitive to the taproots below. On its own plane—that is the plane where almost everything is taken for granted in order to assume adequate implementation in handling what is taken for granted by others; where because you can list the items of your bewilderment and can move from one to another you assert that the achievement of motion is the experience of order; where, therefore, you must adopt always an attitude of provisional skepticism; where, imperatively, you must scrutinize until you have revealed, if it is there, the inscrutable divination, or, if it is not, the void of personal ambition; where, finally, you must stop short only when you have, with all the facts you can muster, indicated, surrounded, detached, somehow found the way demonstrably to get at, in pretty conscious terms which others may use, the substance of your chosen case.

Jacques Lacan

1901–1981

Among psychoanalysts, in recent years Jacques Lacan has had the greatest influence on literary theory. It was Lacan who first read the writings of Sigmund Freud through the lens of structuralism, and he is perhaps best known in theoretical circles for his pronouncement that the unconscious is "structured like a language." He privileges the Saussurean signifier over the signified, thus decentering both the unconscious and language and calling in question any old-style empirical analysis. Analysis cannot escape from the chain of signifiers to point to any origin beyond signification itself.

Lacan posits three stages of human development: the mirror stage, the imaginary, and the symbolic. In the mirror stage the child discovers its own image, which becomes *other* to the self, thereby establishing subjectivity. This dualism is further developed in the imaginary. In the symbolic stage the child enters language, and the subject, now linguistic, is continually deferred down the chain of signifiers. Subjectivity is thus always on the move and is formed only in and as dialogue, which is never ending except in death.

Lacan's treatment of the symbolic and the unconscious has obvious relations to contemporary concerns with language and post-structuralist modes of reading. He is principally responsible for a revival of psychoanalysis as an influence on the reading of literary texts. The following essay, though not on literature, sets forth Lacan's notion of the subject.

In translation by Lacan are *Ecrits: A Selection* (1977); *The Four Fundamental Concepts of Psychoanalysis* (the eleventh seminar of 1964, published in France in 1973, trans. 1978); *Feminine Sexuality* (published in France between 1963 and 1975, trans. 1982); *The Language of the Self* (1968), better known as the *Discourse de Rome* (also in *Ecrits* but best consulted under the title above with Anthony Wilden's commentary and notes, which demonstrate Lacan's place in twentieth-century thought); "Seminar on the Purloined Letter," *Yale French Studies* 48 (1972), where Lacan discusses a literary text. Other seminars have been published in French. See also Anthony Wilden, tr., *Speech and Language in Psychoanalysis* (tr. 1981); J. P. Muller and W. J. Richardson, *Lacan and Language* (1982); Mikkel Borch-Jacobsen, *The Freudian Subject* (tr. 1988); Stuart Schneiderman, *The Death of an Intellectual Hero* (1983); Catherine Clément, *The Lives and Legends of Jacques Lacan* (1983); Bice Benvenuto and Roger Kennedy, *The Works of Jacques Lacan: An Introduction* (1986); Ellie Ragland-Sullivan, *Jacques Lacan and the Philosophy of Psychoanalysis* (1986); Shoshana Felman, *Jacques Lacan and the Adventure of Insight* (1987); and Michael Clark, *Jacques Lacan: An Annotated Bibliography* (1988).

The Mirror Stage as Formative of the Function of the I As Revealed in Psychoanalytic Experience

The conception of the mirror stage that I introduced at our last congress, thirteen years ago, has since become more or less established in the practice of the French group. However, I think it worthwhile to bring it again to your attention, especially today, for the light it sheds on the formation of the *I* as we experience it in psychoanalysis. It is an experience that leads us to oppose any philosophy directly issuing from the *Cogito*.

Some of you may recall that this conception originated in a feature of human behaviour illuminated by a fact of comparative psychology. The child, at an age when he is for a time, however short, outdone by the chimpanzee in instrumental intelligence, can nevertheless already recognize as such his own image in a mirror. This recognition is indicated in the illuminative mimicry of the *AhaErlebnis,* which Köhler[1] sees as the expression of situational apperception, an essential stage of the act of intelligence.

This act, far from exhausting itself, as in the case of the monkey, once the image has been mastered and found empty, immediately rebounds in the case of the child in a series of gestures in which he experiences in play the relation between the movements assumed in the image and the reflected environment, and between this virtual complex and the reality it reduplicates—the child's own body, and the persons and things, around him.

This event can take place, as we have known since Baldwin, from the age of six months, and its repetition has often made me reflect upon the startling spectacle of the infant in front of the mirror. Unable as yet to walk, or even to stand up, and held tightly as he is by some support, human or artificial (what, in France, we call a 'trotte-bébé'), he nevertheless overcomes, in a flutter of jubilant activity, the obstructions of his support and, fixing his attitude in a slightly leaning-forward position, in order to hold it in his gaze, brings back an instantaneous aspect of the image.

For me, this activity retains the meaning I have given it up to the age of eighteen months. This meaning discloses a libidinal dynamism, which has hitherto remained problematic, as well as an ontological structure of the human world that accords with my reflections on paranoiac knowledge.

We have only to understand the mirror stage *as an identification,* in the full sense that analysis gives to the term: namely, the transformation that takes place in the subject when he assumes an image—whose predestination to this phase-effect is sufficiently indicated by the use, in analytic theory, of the ancient term *imago.*

This jubilant assumption of his specular image by the child at the *infans* stage, still sunk in his motor incapacity and nursling dependence, would seem to exhibit in an exemplary situation the symbolic matrix in which the *I* is precipitated in a primordial form, before it is objectified in the dialectic of identification with the other, and before language restores to it, in the universal, its function as subject.

This form would have to be called the Ideal-I,[2] if we wished to incorporate it into our usual register, in the sense that it will also be the source of secondary identifications, under which term I would place the functions of libidinal normalization. But the important point is that this form situates the agency of the ego, before its social determination, in a fictional direction, which will always remain irreducible for the individual alone, or rather, which will only rejoin the coming-into-being (*le devenir*) of the subject asymptotically, whatever the success of the dialectical syntheses by which he must resolve as *I* his discordance with his own reality.

The fact is that the total form of the body by which the subject anticipates in a mirage the maturation of his power is given to him only as *Gestalt,* that is to say, in an exteriority in which this form is certainly more constituent than constituted, but in which it appears to him above all in a contrasting size (*un relief de stature*) that fixes it and in a symmetry that inverts it, in contrast with the turbulent movements that the subject feels are animating him. Thus, this *Gestalt*—whose pregnancy should be regarded as bound up with the species, though its motor style remains scarcely recognizable—by these two aspects of its appearance, symbolizes the mental permanence of the *I,* at the same time as it prefigures its alienating destination; it is still pregnant with the correspondences that unite the *I* with the statue in which man pro-

THE MIRROR STAGE AS FORMATIVE OF THE FUNCTION OF THE I AS REVEALED IN PSYCHOANALYTIC EXPERIENCE. *The Mirror Stage* was first delivered as a lecture in 1936. An early version appeared in *The International Journal of Psychoanalysis* in 1937. A later version was delivered as a lecture in 1949 at the International Congress of Psychoanalysis in Zurich and published in *Revue francaise de psychoalyse* in the same year. It is reprinted from *Ecrits: A Selection* (trans. Alan Sheridan), by permission of W. W. Norton & Co., Inc. Copyright © Tavistock Publications Ltd., 1977. Reprinted by permission.
[1]Wolfgang Köhler (1887–1967), American psychologist.

[2][Lacan] Throughout this article I leave in its peculiarity the translation I have adopted for Freud's *Ideal-Ich* [i.e., "je-idéal"], without further comment, other than to say that I have not maintained it since.

jects himself, with the phantoms that dominate him, or with the automaton in which, in an ambiguous relation, the world of his own making tends to find completion.

Indeed, for the *imagos*—whose veiled faces it is our privilege to see in outline in our daily experience and in the penumbra of symbolic efficacity[3]—the mirror-image would seem to be the threshold of the visible world, if we go by the mirror disposition that the *imago of one's own body* presents in hallucinations or dreams, whether it concerns its individual features, or even its infirmities, or its object-projections; or if we observe the role of the mirror apparatus in the appearances of the *double,* in which psychical realities, however heterogeneous, are manifested.

That a *Gestalt* should be capable of formative effects in the organism is attested by a piece of biological experimentation that is itself so alien to the idea of psychical causality that it cannot bring itself to formulate its results in these terms. It nevertheless recognizes that it is a necessary condition for the maturation of the gonad of the female pigeon that it should see another member of its species, of either sex; so sufficient in itself is this condition that the desired effect may be obtained merely by placing the individual within reach of the field of reflection of a mirror. Similarly, in the case of the migratory locust, the transition within a generation from the solitary to the gregarious form can be obtained by exposing the individual, at a certain stage, to the exclusively visual action of a similar image, provided it is animated by movements of a style sufficiently close to that characteristic of the species. Such facts are inscribed in an order of homeomorphic identification that would itself fall within the larger question of the meaning of beauty as both formative and erogenic.

But the facts of mimicry are no less instructive when conceived as cases of heteromorphic identification, in as much as they raise the problem of the signification of space for the living organism—psychological concepts hardly seem less appropriate for shedding light on these matters than ridiculous attempts to reduce them to the supposedly supreme law of adaptation. We have only to recall how Roger Caillois[4] (who was then very young, and still fresh from his breach with the sociological school in which he was trained) illuminated the subject by using the term '*legendary psychasthenia*' to classify morphological mimicry as an obsession with space in its derealizing effect.

I have myself shown in the social dialectic that structures human knowledge as paranoiac[5] why human knowl-

edge has greater autonomy than animal knowledge in relation to the field of force of desire, but also why human knowledge is determined in that 'little reality' (*ce peu de réalité*), which the Surrealists, in their restless way, saw as its limitation. These reflections lead me to recognize in the spatial captation manifested in the mirror-stage, even before the social dialectic, the effect in man of an organic insufficiency in his natural reality—in so far as any meaning can be given to the word 'nature'.

I am led, therefore, to regard the function of the mirror-stage as a particular case of the function of the *imago,* which is to establish a relation between the organism and its reality—or, as they say, between the *Innenwelt* and the *Umwelt.*

In man, however, this relation to nature is altered by a certain dehiscence at the heart of the organism, a primordial Discord betrayed by the signs of uneasiness and motor unco-ordination of the neonatal months. The objective notion of the anatomical incompleteness of the pyramidal system and likewise the presence of certain humoral residues of the maternal organism confirm the view I have formulated as the fact of a real *specific prematurity of birth* in man.

It is worth noting, incidentally, that this is a fact recognized as such by embryologists, by the term *foetalization,* which determines the prevalence of the so-called superior apparatus of the neurax, and especially of the cortex, which psycho-surgical operations lead us to regard as the intraorganic mirror.

This development is experienced as a temporal dialectic that decisively projects the formation of the individual into history. The *mirror stage* is a drama whose internal thrust is precipitated from insufficiency to anticipation—and which manufactures for the subject, caught up in the lure of spatial identification, the succession of phantasies that extends from a fragmented body-image to a form of its totality that I shall call orthopaedic—and, lastly, to the assumption of the armour of an alienating identity, which will mark with its rigid structure the subject's entire mental development. Thus, to break out of the circle of the *Innenwelt* into the *Umwelt* generates the inexhaustible quadrature of the ego's verifications.

This fragmented body—which term I have also introduced into our system of theoretical references—usually manifests itself in dreams when the movement of the analysis encounters a certain level of aggressive disintegration in the individual. It then appears in the form of disjointed limbs, or of those organs represented in exoscopy, growing wings and taking up arms for intestinal persecutions—the very same that the visionary Hieronymus Bosch[6] has fixed,

---

[3][Lacan] Claude Lévi-Strauss, *Structural Anthropology,* Chapter X.
[4]Roger Caillois (1913–78), French critic and poet.
[5][Lacan] Cf. 'Aggressivity in Psychoanalysis', p. 8 and *Ecrits,* p. 180.

---

[6]Hieronymus Bosch (1462?–1516), Flemish painter.

for all time, in painting, in their ascent from the fifteenth century to the imaginary zenith of modern man. But this form is even tangibly revealed at the organic level, in the lines of 'fragilization' that define the anatomy of phantasy, as exhibited in the schizoid and spasmodic symptoms of hysteria.

Correlatively, the formation of the *I* is symbolized in dreams by a fortress, or a stadium—its inner arena and enclosure, surrounded by marshes and rubbish-tips, dividing it into two opposed fields of contest where the subject flounders in quest of the lofty, remote inner castle whose form (sometimes juxtaposed in the same scenario) symbolizes the id in a quite startling way. Similarly, on the mental plane, we find realized the structures of fortified works, the metaphor of which arises spontaneously, as if issuing from the symptoms themselves, to designate the mechanisms of obsessional neurosis—inversion, isolation, reduplication, cancellation and displacement.

But if we were to build on these subjective givens alone—however little we free them from the condition of experience that makes us see them as partaking of the nature of a linguistic technique—our theoretical attempts would remain exposed to the charge of projecting themselves into the unthinkable of an absolute subject. This is why I have sought in the present hypothesis, grounded in a conjunction of objective data, the guiding grid for a *method of symbolic reduction.*

It establishes in the *defences of the ego* a genetic order, in accordance with the wish formulated by Miss Anna Freud,[7] in the first part of her great work, and situates (as against a frequently expressed prejudice) hysterical repression and its returns at a more archaic stage than obsessional inversion and its isolating processes, and the latter in turn as preliminary to paranoic alienation, which dates from the deflection of the specular *I* into the social *I.*

This moment in which the mirror-stage comes to an end inaugurates, by the identification with the *imago* of the counterpart and the drama of primordial jealousy (so well brought out by the school of Charlotte Bühler[8] in the phenomenon of infantile *transitivism*), the dialectic that will henceforth link the *I* to socially elaborated situations.

It is this moment that decisively tips the whole of human knowledge into mediatization through the desire of the other, constitutes its objects in an abstract equivalence by the co-operation of others, and turns the I into that apparatus for which every instinctual thrust constitutes a danger, even though it should correspond to a natural maturation—the very normalization of this maturation being henceforth dependent, in man, on a cultural mediation as exemplified, in the case of the sexual object, by the Oedipus complex.

In the light of this conception, the term primary narcissism, by which analytic doctrine designates the libidinal investment characteristic of that moment, reveals in those who invented it the most profound awareness of semantic latencies. But it also throws light on the dynamic opposition between this libido and the sexual libido, which the first analysts tried to define when they invoked destructive and, indeed, death instincts, in order to explain the evident connection between the narcissistic libido and the alienating function of the *I,* the aggressivity it releases in any relation to the other, even in a relation involving the most Samaritan of aid.

In fact, they were encouraging that existential negativity whose reality is so vigorously proclaimed by the contemporary philosophy of being and nothingness.

But unfortunately that philosophy grasps negativity only within the limits of a self-sufficiency of consciousness, which, as one of its premises, links to the *méconnaissances* that constitute the ego, the illusion of autonomy to which it entrusts itself. This flight of fancy, for all that it draws, to an unusual extent, on borrowings from psychoanalytic experience, culminates in the pretention of providing an existential psychoanalysis.

At the culmination of the historical effort of a society to refuse to recognize that it has any function other than the utilitarian one, and in the anxiety of the individual confronting the 'concentrational'[9] form of the social bond that seems to arise to crown this effort, existentialism must be judged by the explanations it gives of the subjective impasses that have indeed resulted from it; a freedom that is never more authentic than when it is within the walls of a prison; a demand for commitment, expressing the impotence of a pure consciousness to master any situation; a voyeuristic–sadistic idealization of the sexual relation; a personality that realizes itself only in suicide; a consciousness of the other that can be satisfied only by Hegelian murder.

These propositions are opposed by all our experience, in so far as it teaches us not to regard the ego as centered on the *perception–consciousness system,* or as organized by the

---

[7]Anna Freud, Austro-English (1895–1982), psychoanalyst, daughter of Sigmund Freud.
[8]Charlotte Bühler (1893–1974), German psychologist.

[9][Sheridan] 'Concentrationnaire,' an adjective coined after World War II (this article was written in 1949) to describe the life of the concentration camp. In the hands of certain writers it became, by extension, applicable to many aspects of 'modern' life.

'reality principle'—a principle that is the expression of a scientific prejudice most hostile to the dialectic of knowledge. Our experience shows that we should start instead from the *function of méconnaissance* that characterizes the ego in all is structures, so markedly articulated by Miss Anna Freud. For, if the *Verneinung*[10] represents the patent form of that function, its effects will, for the most part, remain latent, so long as they are not illuminated by some light reflected on to the level of fatality, which is where the id manifests itself.

We can thus understand the inertia characteristic of the formations of the *I,* and find there the most extensive definition of neurosis—just as the captation of the subject by the situation gives us the most general formula for madness, not only the madness that lies behind the walls of asylums, but also the madness that deafens the world with its sound and fury.

---

[10]*Verneinung:* negation.

The sufferings of neurosis and psychosis are for us a schooling in the passions of the soul, just as the beam of the psychoanalytic scales, when we calculate the tilt of its threat to entire communities, provides us with an indication of the deadening of the passions in society.

At this junction of nature and culture, so persistently examined by modern anthropology, psychoanalysis alone recognizes this knot of imaginary servitude that love must always undo again, or sever.

For such a task, we place no trust in altruistic feeling, we who lay bare the aggressivity that underlies the activity of the philanthropist, the idealist, the pedagogue, and even the reformer.

In the recourse of subject to subject that we preserve, psychoanalysis may accompany the patient to the ecstatic limit of the '*Thou art that*', in which is revealed to him the cipher of his mortal destiny, but it is not in our mere power as practitioners to bring him to that point where the real journey begins.

Georg Lukács

1885–1971

Lukács' early work, exemplified by *Soul and Form* (1910) and *The Theory of the Novel* (1920) was strongly influenced by Hegel. By 1920 he was a member of the Communist Party and came under the influence of Marx and Lenin. He was eventually to be regarded as the principal Marxist aesthetician of his time. Throughout his career he addressed the problem of the relations of form to content, art to politics. In the important long essay of 1954, "Art and Objective Truth," he argues that the work of art reflects an objective reality but it does this not by slavish copying. Rather it succeeds by presentation of a concrete universal, and the formal integrity and objectivity of the work lies in that relation: "The goal for all great art is to provide a picture of reality in which the contradiction between appearance and reality, the particular and the general, the immediate and the conceptual, etc., is so resolved that the two converge into a spontaneous integrity in the direct impression of the work of art and provide a sense of an inseparable integrity." In the essay below, which precedes "Art and Objective Truth" by sixteen years, Lukács has similar concerns. He sets the movements of Enlightenment, idealism, and realism in a Marxist version of history, in which the old "harmony" of the ancient Greeks is forever lost, though nostalgia for it remains. Both idealism and realism were failures, though they were historically understandable and valuable responses to this loss. Both were unfortunately one-sided. The idealists mounted a critique of the fragmentation of the individual in bourgeois society, but they maintained allegiance to an outworn version of the idea of progress. There grew up in their intellectual lives a divorce between harmony and beauty on the one hand and life itself on the other, between the aesthetic activity that they privileged and life.

With the later realists—Balzac is Lukács' principal example—there follows a strong sense that human wholeness has been completely suppressed. Realism proceeds to reject harmony and beauty as illusions. The opposition of idealism and realism explicates the division in humanity that is the product of bourgeois society. Lukács calls for a reawakened social humanism that would heal the breach between life and beauty and create a new harmony that would be worldly.

In the later "Art and Objective Truth" Lukács holds that art must have a certain formal objectivity by virtue of a "dialectical unity of form and content." He rejects the "subjectualization" of art that comes with the confusion of form with autonomous technique.

Among the works of Lukács available in translation are *Soul and Form* (1910, tr. 1974); *The Theory of the Novel* (1920; tr. 1971); *History and Class Consciousness* (1923; tr. 1971); *The Historical Novel* (1955; tr. 1962); and *Political Writings, 1919–1929* (tr. 1972). See George Lichtheim, *Lukácz* (1970); Fredric Jameson, *Marxism and*

Form, chap. 3 (1971); Lucien Goldmann, *Lukácz and Heidegger* (1973, tr. 1977); Béla Királyfálvi, *The Aesthetics of Gyorgy Lukács* (1975); G. H. R. Parkinson, *Georg Lukácz* (1977); Agnes Heller, *Lukács Reappraised* (1983); and J. M. Bernstein, *The Philosophy of the Novel* (1984).

The Ideal of the Harmonious Man in Bourgeois Aesthetics

If we are to attempt a serious examination of the question indicated in our title, we cannot direct our attention to the theory and practice of those who make "an art of living" in the contemporary stage of imperialism. The aspiration towards harmony of man's accomplishments as against his potential is never quite extinguished. The bleaker and emptier life becomes under capitalism, the more intense is the yearning after beauty. But this yearning for harmony under imperialism too often takes the form of a craven retreat or a faint-hearted withdrawal before the contradictory problems thrown up by life. By seeking inner harmony men cut themselves off from society's struggles. Such "harmony" is illusory and superficial; it vanishes at any serious contact with reality.

The great thinkers and artists who have championed this aspiration for harmony have always recognized that harmony for the individual presupposes his harmonious integration into his environment, into his society. The philosophical advocates of the integrated man from the Renaissance through Winckelmann[1] to Hegel not only admired the Greeks for realizing this ideal but also recognized that the basis for the harmonious development of the individual in Classical Greece lay in the social and political structure of ancient democracy. That they more or less ignored the fact that this democracy was based on slavery is another matter.

Hegel has this to say about Greek harmony: "The Greeks, as far as their immediate reality was concerned, lived happily in the midst of a self-conscious subjective freedom and a self-conscious moral order." And expatiating upon this thought, Hegel contrasted Greek democracy both with oriental despotism, under which the individual had no rights, and with modern society with its fully fledged social division of labour. "In Greek moral life, the individual enjoyed independence and freedom without being isolated from the interests of the state. In accordance with the basic principle of Greek life, the universal morality existed in an undisturbed harmony with the abstract subjective and objective freedom of the individual, and . . . there never was a question of a dichotomy between political principles and personal morality. The rare sensitivity, intellectuality and spirituality in this felicitous harmony permeates all the works in which the Greeks expressed their freedom and in which the essence of their freedom is exposed."

It was left to Marx to disclose the economic and social basis of that unique flourishing of human culture, of the harmonious fulfillment of the individual personality among the free citizens of the Greek democracies. He also explained the rational core to the unappeasable longing of mankind's finest spirits for this harmony, which has never been regained. Because of Marx we understand why this period of the "normal childhood" in man's development can never return.

But the longing to recapture this harmony has persisted since the Renaissance among the most progressive intellectuals. The revival of Classical thought, poetry and art during the Renaissance has admittedly visible causes in the class struggles of the time. Unquestionably, too, the study of Classical constitutions and of the civil wars from the Renaissance to Robespierre provided all bourgeois and democratic revolutionaries with powerful weapons in their struggle against feudalism and absolute monarchy. Whatever illusions accompanied these struggles were heroic illusions which sought to restore Classical democracy on the basis of a capitalist economy. And there is no doubt that it was precisely these heroic illusions which were necessary to sweep away the rubble of the Middle Ages.

But beyond all this, the revival of antiquity both during and after the Renaissance is distinguished by a (self-contradictory) tendency which points, sometimes more and sometimes less, beyond the bourgeois horizon. With turbulent enthusiasm and brilliant versatility of talent, scarcely imaginable today, the great men of the Renaissance strove to develop all the productive forces of society. Their lofty aim was to shatter the narrow localized restrictions of medieval social life and to create a social order in which all human capacities and potentialities would be liberated for an under-

THE IDEAL OF THE HARMONIOUS MAN IN BOURGEOIS AESTHETICS. *The Ideal of the Harmonious Man . . .* was written in 1938. It is reprinted here in a translation by Arthur D. Kahn from *Writer and Critic, and Other Essays.* Copyright © The Merlin Press, 1970. Reprinted by permission.
[1]Johann Joachim Winckelmann (1717–1768), German archeologist and art historian.

standing of nature for the benefit of mankind. And these great men recognized that the development of the productive forces meant simultaneously the development of man's own productive capacities. The mastery of nature by free men in a free society—such was the Renaissance ideal of the harmonious man. Engels said of this great progressive human revolution: "The men who established the modern hegemony of the bourgeoisie were anything but narrow bourgeois." Engels perceived, however, that such an impressive, many-sided development of individual capacities, of even the most outstanding men, was possible only while capitalism was still undeveloped: "The heroes of that time had not yet been enslaved in the specialized division of labour whose crippling one-sidedness we so often encounter in their successors."

With the development of the productive forces of capitalism, the subjugation inherent in the capitalist division of labour became more pronounced. By the manufacturing stage, the worker had already become a narrow specialist in a single operation, and the state apparatus had already begun to transform its civil servants into mindless and soulless bureaucrats.

The leading thinkers of the Enlightenment fought against the vestiges of the Middle Ages with even greater passion than the men of the Renaissance; as honest thinkers who hid nothing from themselves they saw symptoms of the contradictions within the emerging forces of production, within the very progress for which they were vanguard fighters. Thus Ferguson "denounced" (as Marx noted) the capitalist division of labour which grew before his eyes: "Many occupations demand in fact no intellectual capacity. They succeed best when there is complete suppression of feeling and thought; and ignorance is the mother of industry as well as of superstition." He predicted pessimistically that if the trend continued "we will create a nation of helots and have no free citizens any more."

With Ferguson as with all the important men of the Enlightenment, this harsh criticism of the capitalist division of labour accompanies (though is not directly related to) a keen championing of the development of productive forces and the elimination of all social obstacles to continued progress. Thus these men exhibit the dichotomy, basic to our discussion, that continues in modern bourgeois thought regarding society, a dichotomy in all significant modern aesthetics and in all serious thought about harmony in life and art. It is a road full of contradictions which the leading eighteenth and nineteenth century thinkers seek between two equally false yet socially necessary extremes.

The one extreme is the glorification of the capitalist mode of developing the means of production—for a long time, indeed, the only possible mode—and concomitantly an apologetic evasion of the enslavement and fragmentation of the individual and of the horrifying ugliness of life which inevitably and increasingly accompanies this development. The other false extreme is to ignore the progressive character of this development because of its shocking human consequences—to escape from the present into the past, from the present of meaningless work in which a man has become a mere appendage to the machine back to the Middle Ages, when the varied labour of the craftsman could "reach a certain limited artistic awareness" (Marx), when a man still enjoyed a "comfortable bondage relationship" (Marx) to his work. These extremes are apologetics, on the one hand, and romantic reaction, on the other.

The great poets and aestheticians of the Enlightenment and of the first half of the nineteenth century did not succumb to this dilemma. But neither were they capable of resolving the contradictions in capitalist society. Undaunted by the conditions that confined them, they exhibited greatness and brilliance in maintaining an unrelenting critique of bourgeois society without abandoning their affirmation of progress. As a result, these antithetical attitudes are to be found side-by-side in the works of the men of the Enlightenment.

The poets and thinkers of German Classicism, whose major activity followed the French Revolution, seek various utopian solutions. Their criticism of the capitalist division of labour is no less incisive than that of the men of the Enlightenment. They, too, stress ever more sharply the fragmentation of the individual. Goethe's Wilhelm Meister poses these questions: "What use is it to manufacture good iron when inside I am full of slag? What good is it to put an estate in order if I am never at one with myself?" And he perceives that this disharmony is a product of bourgeois society. He says: "A bourgeois can make profit and with some difficulty even develop his mind; but he will lose his individuality, do what he will. He may not ask: 'What are you? but only what do you have? what ability, what understanding, what knowledge, how great a fortune? He has to exploit individual aptitudes in order to put them to use, and it is taken for granted that he may not enjoy an inner harmonious development, for he must neglect everything that cannot be put to use.' "

The great poets and thinkers of German Classicism sought in art for the harmonious integration of the individual and the beauty accompanying it. Active after the French Revolution, they had lost the heroic illusions of the Enlightenment. They did not, however, give up the struggle for harmony in the individual and for its artistic expression. As a result, they assigned to questions of aesthetic practice an excessive and often an exaggeratedly idealistic significance. They saw artistic harmony not only as a reflection and expression of the harmonious individual but also as the chief means of overcoming subjectively the fragmentation and distortion resulting from the capitalist division of labour. This approach resulted in their abandoning all practical attempts at overcoming in life itself the absence of harmony under capitalism. Their concepts of harmony in man and of beauty are divorced and alienated from life. Schiller sings of beauty with such a view:

> Piercing even unto Beauty's sphere,
> In the dust still lingers here
> Gravitation, with the world it sways,
> Not from out the mass, with labour wrung,
> Light and graceful, as from nothing sprung,
> Stands the image to the ravish'd gaze.
> Mute is ev'ry struggle, ev'ry doubt,
> In the uncertain glow of victory;
> While each witness hence is driven out
> Of frail man's necessity.[2]

Here the idealistic side of classical philosophy and poetry is clearly exemplified. There is idealism, too, in the rigid opposition which Schiller makes between aesthetic activity and ordinary work. With astute historical insight, he finds the origin of man's aesthetic activity in his surplus energy. His resultant "play" theory is directed toward the elimination of the division within man under the capitalist division of labour. With this theory he campaigns for the total, many-sided and developed human personality, yet only sees this development as happening outside the labour process of his time: "For . . . man plays only when he is human in the fullest sense of the word, and he is only fully human when he plays."[3]

The idealism in such theories is clear. It is necessary, however, to recognize that the idealism of these great German classicists was the inevitable product of their social situation. It is precisely because they neither wish to disguise the inhumanity of capitalism nor make concessions to the reactionary and romantic critique, being in no way able to foresee the displacement of capitalism by socialism, that they are forced to seek these solutions in order to preserve the ideal of the integrated man.

This aesthetic utopia does not merely avoid dealing with actual labour as it exists but also seeks utopian solutions in a general social sense. Goethe and Schiller believed that small groups could achieve the ideal of the integrated individual among themselves and provide nuclei for a general diffusion of this ideal—rather after the model of Fourier, who hoped that from the establishment of a phalanstery a gradual transformation of all society to socialism, as he understood it, might be achieved. The educational philosophy in *Wilhelm Meister* is based on a theory of this kind; similar utopianism is echoed in Schiller's "On the Aesthetic Education of Man."

Insofar as fragmentation and its cure were sought primarily within the individual, the problem of the fragmentation of sensibility and intellect was emphasized. Clearly, once again, the importance of this position is closely related to philosophic idealism. It is also clear, however, that there did exist, objectively, a fundamental problem in the fragmentation of the individual through the capitalist division of labour. The specialized, forced cultivation of certain individual capacities under this division of labour set the remaining qualities and passions "free" to atrophy or to run riot. In tackling this aspect of the question, Goethe and Schiller were raising the important question of whether it is possible to bring the human passions into harmony.

Some decades later this question was to become crucial to Fourier's utopian socialism. Fourier started with the premise that there is no human emotion that is intrinsically evil. An emotion becomes evil only as a consequence of the anarchy and inhumanity of the capitalist division of labour.[4] Thus Fourier carries his criticism far beyond that of the Enlighteners or the German Classicists, making it a critique of the basic objective problems of the social division of labour; for example, the separation of town and country. The socialism of his utopian dream, with all its social constructs, aimed primarily at developing the abilities and sensibilities latent in every man and at promoting within the harmonious cooperative effort of varied personalities under socialism the integration of the capacities within each individual as well.

Fourier's great contemporaries, Hegel and Balzac, experienced the contradictions emerging from the capitalist division of labour at a more advanced stage than Goethe and Schiller during the period of their collaboration. The note of

---

[2]Aber dringt bis in der Schönheit Sphäre
Und im Staube bleibt die Schwere
Mit dem Stoff, den sie beherrscht, zurück.
Nicht der Masse qualvoll abgerungen,
Schlank und leicht, wie aus dem Nichts, gesprungen,
Steht das Bild vor dem entzückten Blick,
Alle Zweifel, alle Kämpfe schweigen
In des Sieges hoher Sicherheit;
Ausgestossen hat es jeden Zeugen
Menschlicher Bedürftigkeit.
From "The Ideal and Life," translated by Edgar A. Bowring, *The Poems of Schiller,* London, 1910, p. 189.
[3]See Schiller, "Letters on Aesthetic Education," p. 422.

[4]Francois Marie Charles Fourier (1772–1837), French social thinker.

elegiac resignation which echoed through all the utopian dreams of Goethe and Schiller now predominates. Both the great thinker and the great realist see the inhumanity of capitalist society, that all the harmony within man, his every creative expression, is being ruthlessly crushed. For Hegel the aesthetic harmony in Greek life and after has been irretrievably lost: the "World Spirit" has moved beyond the sphere of the aesthetic and hastens to other goals. The dominion of prose has been established over mankind. And Balzac portrays with what cruel relentlessness capitalist society generates discord and ugliness in every manifestation of human existence, how all human aspirations toward a beautiful and harmonious existence are inexorably crushed by society. Balzac does include episodes in which "islands" of harmonious personalities appear; these are, however, no longer nuclei for a utopian renewal of the world but just exceptional instances of fortunate individuals rescued by chance from under the iron heel of capitalism.

Thus the heroic struggle for the integrated man of the bourgeois revolutionary period terminates in elegiac mourning; for the conditions for developing man's capacities into a harmonious integration have been irretrievably lost. Only where the critique of capitalism evolves into a prescience of socialism does this atmosphere of elegiac mourning, characteristic of the utopian dreamers who founded socialism, disappear.

With the destruction of the heroic illusions of the revolutionary period and the illusions of a possible revival of ancient democracy, there is an accompanying loss of appreciation of the classical experience in bourgeois art and aesthetics. The purely formal "harmony" that takes the place of the classical conception bears little relationship to life, whether of the past or the present; it is "academic," without content, an expression of a smug and complacent evasion of the ugliness of life.

The leading artists and thinkers of the period of bourgeois decline became increasingly dissatisfied with this banal academicism. There are fundamental social and artistic grounds for their renunciation of the ideals of classical harmony. The serious realists seek to depict the social life of their day with uncompromising verisimilitude and thus reject any pretense of harmony in life and of beauty in human personality.

But what lies behind this rejection and how does it manifest itself? Academicism can indeed reduce beauty and harmony to matters of no importance or treat them as mere questions of form, but by their very nature beauty and harmony cannot be matters of indifference to mankind. Concepts of beauty and harmony seem empty only because capitalist society denies them any realization in life. The dream

of harmony can be realized and be effective in art only when occasioned by genuinely serious, progressive tendencies in actual life.

Such a dream of human harmony is diametrically opposed to that envisaged by the academician, who, though supposedly the perpetuator of the classics, actually proposes a fraudulent substitute, a false and empty pseudo-harmony. His flight from the ugliness and inhumanity of capitalist life is nothing but a capitulation without struggle.

This is not the only form of artistic capitulation before the fundamental hostility towards art and before the growing barbarism. Leading artists, dedicated fighters against their times, passionate defenders of progress also capitulate—without wishing to, indeed without knowing it—and do so as artists in the face of the philistinism of their time.

In this situation the social and humanist content of the "old-fashioned" concepts of beauty and harmony continue to exert a powerful influence extending far beyond literature and art. In their dedication to truth great realists of the period of mature capitalism like Balzac had to reject any representation of beauty in life or of the integrated personality. To be faithful realists they could only depict disharmonious, shattered lives, lives in which the beautiful and noble in man is inexorably crushed, worse, lives inwardly warped, corrupted and brutalized. The conclusion at which they must arrive is that capitalist society is a vast cemetery for integrity and human capacity, that under capitalism, as Balzac notes with pungent irony, men become either bank clerks or swindlers, that is, either exploited dupes or scoundrels.

This courageous condemnation is what distinguishes genuine realism from apologetic academicism, which seeks escape from life's discord. The creative artist may follow one of two courses in his denunciation of capitalist society. Either he can depict the mere result of this human disintegration or he can, in addition, portray the fine, and noble human energies destroyed in the struggle to resist. Superficially, the distinction seems to be of a purely literary artistic kind. And indeed the analogy with the political and the social opposition to capitalist and imperialist barbarism does not hold mechanically. There is a whole group of seemingly left-wing writers who accept the degradation and destruction of the individual under capitalism as fact; they are indignant and express their indignation in their art; they expose the horror, but they do not depict the human nobility in the resistance to this horror. There are others who do not proclaim their political and social convictions so obviously in their own rebellion but who nevertheless describe with passionate vividness the daily, even hourly, resistance which mankind maintains against the crippling capitalist environment in defence of human integrity. In this uneven battle the individual is doomed if he relies solely on his own powers; he can maintain resistance only as a participant in the opposition movement destined to secure the final victory of humanism in society, economically, politically, socially and culturally.

In this regard Maxim Gorki is the foremost figure in contemporary world literature since his works depict with superb artistry this association of the individual and the popular movements. The horror of life under capitalism has probably never been so accurately exposed or painted in such bleak colours; yet the result is quite different from that in the works of most of his contemporaries, including leading writers of our time, for Gorki never presents the destruction under capitalism as an accomplished fact. He shows what is being destroyed and how, in what kind of struggle, the destruction is taking place. He reveals the beauty, the innate drive to harmony and to the unfolding of the varied but repressed, distorted and misdirected potentialities even in the worst of humanity. The fact that the vital aspiration toward beauty and harmony is crushed before our eyes is what makes his condemnation so resounding, what gives it an echo that can be heard everywhere.

Furthermore, Gorki points to a concrete solution in his work, that is, he shows how the revolutionary labour movement, the popular revolt, awakens an individual, matures him, encourages his inner life to bloom and imbues him with awareness, power and sensitivity. Gorki does not counterpose one social system to another or one ideology to another, but presents the emergent new kind of human being through whom the reader can experience directly and concretely the content of the new life.

Thus a principle of artistic representation turns into a political and social principle. None of Gorki's contemporaries reveals either the revulsion against the old or enthusiasm for the new with as much passion as Gorki. This revulsion and enthusiasm and certainty of victory—embodied in living people—exemplifies what has just been discussed: no artistic capitulation to capitalism! Gorki achieves a coincidence of the artistic and the political, a unity that is neither automatic nor mechanical. A writer only a trifle less consequent ideologically and artistically in his radicalism might attempt swifter, more direct effects and fall into lifeless propaganda and provide a dead, fetishized picture of life.

Capitalist antipathy to art is not one-dimensional; every dedicated artist must—consciously or not—end up as an enemy of capitalism in his attempt to create richly investigated characters. He may consider himself "uncommitted," he may seek refuge in scepticism, he may even claim to be conservative. But unless, profoundly confused about social and intellectual issues, he embraces a romantic reaction against progress, his revolt will emerge clearly in his work.

In the defence of repressed human values and of frustrated humanity, Anatole France is more radical and decisive than Emile Zola, the early Sinclair Lewis than Upton Sinclair, Thomas Mann than Dos Passos. It is no accident that the leading realists of our time have succeeded in obtaining a popular audience because their revolt is profound, for they really detest the destruction they see about them and do not merely dress up slogans in a formalist literature. Romain Rolland pursued this course most resolutely. Progressive writers must give careful consideration to the approaches followed by Heinrich and Thomas Mann and many others, too, in this regard. The revolt of the leading realists is the most significant development in the art of the bourgeois world today. This revolt has produced important art in a period most unfavourable to art, a period of a general decline in bourgeois culture. How aware each of the outstanding exponents of this genuine realism is in his association with the great humanist tradition is not decisive. With Romain Rolland or Thomas Mann the association is conscious and of importance. What is decisive is the objective relationship to, the objective continuation of, the fundamental humanist view, a continuation adapted, of course, to the special conditions of the day, in opposition to capitalist culture, a culture which every artist of integrity must reject.

There is another road, however, one which many writers, by no means insignificant in literature or in the general cultural life, have taken. They reject without compromise all ideals of beauty and harmony as "out-of-date"; they take people and society "as they are," or rather as they usually appear in ordinary life under capitalism. And in a depiction of such a given world, the categories of the old aesthetics do indeed lose meaning. Not because they are out-of-date! (We have seen how pertinent and valid they are when adapted to changed conditions by the leading realist of our time.) But they have lost all meaning since capitalism is destroying their social and individual base day by day; and these writers set out to represent a world destroyed and not the battle against the destruction, not a dynamic process but a lifeless result. The consequence is that they reject beauty and harmony and produce a mere chronicle of the "iron age."

Such has been the general course in this development. Writers have produced intellectual quintessences, local colour studies—presenting the primary material with which a dynamic re-creation of the world should start. They sketch characters and lives, arranged as in a chronicle, and expose the most obvious aspects of the destruction of the individual in capitalist society. The readers feel no impelling compassion for the characters or their experiences since the authors have presented only the consequences or nearly completed results of the destructive process. The readers cannot experience what was destroyed in this process nor appreciate at all the consequences of a continuation of such a process in the view of the author, for the author provides them with nothing but an abstract ideological programme.

Needless to add, this is not the only current in literature, nor is it ever to be found in absolute purity, for there is scarcely a true writer—no matter what his political philosophy—who rejects beauty altogether. Beauty, however, becomes something extraneous, something essentially alien to their subject matter and even antithetical to it. Flaubert turns beauty into a mere formal quality in rhetoric or picturesque diction; beauty is a quality to be imposed artificially on subject matter that is inherently unbeautiful. Baudelaire carries this alienation of beauty from life and the antipathy of life to beauty to the point of transforming beauty into a thing in itself—exotic, demonic, and vampire-like.

In the profound pessimism of their art and ideologies, leading writers reflect capitalism's hostility to art and the general ugliness of life under capitalism. Artists and thinkers become increasingly overwhelmed by the bleakness of life in the age of imperialism. Though they represent the inhumanity of capitalism with ever-greater intensity, they no longer manifest a rebellious fury but exhibit a conscious or unconscious respect for its "monumentality." The Greek ideal of beauty disappears and is replaced by a modern orientalism or a modernized glorification of the Gothic or the baroque. Nietzsche completes the ideological transformation by pronouncing the harmonious man of Greece a myth and by transfiguring Greece and the Renaissance "realistically" into civilizations of "monumental inhumanity and bestiality." Fascism inherits these decadent tendencies of bourgeois development and adapts them to its own demagogic purposes, using them to provide an ideological rationale for its prisons and torture chambers.

The power and vitality of anti-fascist literature lies in its reawakened humanism. The Hitlerites knew what they were doing when they set as the principal task for their "Professor for Political Pedagogy," Alfred Baeumler, the struggle against classical humanism. Imbued with a humanistic spirit and a humanistic revolt, the works of Anatole France, Romain Rolland, Thomas and Heinrich Mann and of all the outstanding anti-fascist writers represent a literature of which we can be proud, a literature which will in the future bear witness to artistic integrity in our time. This is a literature "against the stream," fighting the barbarous reactionary attitudes and deeds of our day, maintaining a courageous and effective resistance to the attempts to annihilate great art and defending the great realist tradition against the dominant current that is the inevitable reflection of contemporary capitalist society.

How far the individual anti-fascist writers consider themselves or profess to be the inheritors and perpetuators of the classical tradition is not decisive; what is important is that they are in fact carrying on the best traditions of mankind.

Paul Valéry

1871–1945

"With every question," writes the French poet Valéry, "before making any deep examination of the content, I take a look at the language." His concern reflects the dominating interest of critics of his time in language—in literature as a species of language, in language as a mode of "creating" reality, and in the limitations of language. Kant and the Romantics emphasized the distinction between thought and feeling but seldom discussed poetic *language* itself. Critics of Valéry's time regarded language as an actual form of thought and shaper of reality. They considered intuition and expression, in Croce's terms, indissolubly wed; they thought different modes of intuition-expression capable of exerting different powers. Language became what Cassirer called a "symbolic form." Philosophers concerned themselves principally with language. According to Valéry, language captures and directs us.

Wary of the terms *poetry* and *abstract thought,* Valéry sees the traditional Romantic distinction between them as one between two modes of *language.* Using a contrast between *walking* to a destination and *dancing,* which has as its destination its own act, Valéry develops a theory that has overtones of Kant's purposiveness without a purpose and Schiller's play. Purposive language, or walking, is extinguished by the attainment of its purpose. The linguistic act has no further value. But in poetry, "the moment this concrete form takes on, by an effect of its own, such importance that it asserts itself and makes itself, as it were, respected," something else happens. "Nothing that may occur in this state will be resolved, finished, or abolished by a specific act."

In the process of developing his analogies, Valéry makes a number of other interesting assertions. There are poets, he says, who write poems to convey a thesis of some sort, but even their effort cannot prevent the attention given to the song from competing with the attention given to the ideas. Poems may convey the illusion of spontaneity, but they are not made spontaneously. Finally, in contrast to the musical composer, who has resources expressly made for his art, the poet must borrow his medium, language, from the public. As Mallarmé conceded, this situation complicates enormously the problems with which he must deal.

The works of Paul Valéry have been translated into English by various hands. Denise Folliot's translation of *The Art of Poetry* was published in 1958. Studies of Valéry in English include Jean Hytier, *The Poetics of Paul Valéry* (1953, tr. 1966); Judith Robinson, "The Place of Literary and Artistic Creation in Valéry's Thought," *Modern Language Review,* LVI (1961), 497–514; Walter Ince, *The Poetic Theory of Paul Valéry* (1961); Renée Green, *The Poetic Theory of Paul Valéry: Inspiration and Technique* (1962); Henry A. Grubbs, *Paul Valéry* (1968); and Charles G. Whiting, *Paul Valéry* (1978). Those who read French may also consult Maurice Bérnol, *La Méthode critique de Paul Valéry* (1950); and Louis Chauvet, *La Poétique de Paul Valéry* (1966).

Poetry and Abstract Thought

The idea of poetry is often contrasted with that of thought, and particularly "abstract thought." People say "poetry and abstract thought" as they say good and evil, vice and virtue, hot and cold. Most people, without thinking any further, believe that the analytical work of the intellect, the efforts of will and precision in which it implicates the mind, are incompatible with that freshness of inspiration, that flow of expression, that grace and fancy which are the signs of poetry and which reveal it at its very first words. If a poet's work is judged profound, its profundity seems to be of a quite different order from that of a philosopher or a scientist. Some people go so far as to think that even meditation on his art, the kind of exact reasoning applied to the cultivation of roses, can only harm a poet, since the principal and most charming object of his desire must be to communicate the impression of a newly and happily born state of creative emotion which, through surprise and pleasure, has the power to remove the poem once and for all from any further criticism.

This opinion may possibly contain a grain of truth, though its simplicity makes me suspect it to be of scholarly origin. I feel we have learned and adopted this antithesis without reflection, and that we now find it firmly fixed in our mind as a verbal contrast, as though it represented a clear and real relationship between two well-defined notions. It must be admitted that that character always in a hurry to have done, whom we call *our mind,* has a weakness for this kind of simplification, which freely enables him to form all kinds of combinations and judgments, to display his logic, and to develop his rhetorical resources—in short, to carry out as brilliantly as possible his business of being a mind.

At all events, this classic contrast, crystalized, as it were, by language, has always seemed to me too abrupt and at the same time too facile, not to provoke me to examine the things themselves more closely.

Poetry, abstract thought. That is soon said, and we immediately assume that we have said something sufficiently clear and sufficiently precise for us to proceed, without having to go back over our experiences; and to build a theory or begin a discussion using this contrast (so attractive in its simplicity) as pretext, argument, and substance. One could even fashion a whole metaphysics—or at the least a "psychology"—on this basis, and evolve for oneself a system of mental life, of knowledge, and of the invention and production of works of the mind, whose consequence would inevitably be the same terminological dissonance that had served as its starting point. . . .

For my part I have the strange and dangerous habit, in every subject, of wanting to begin at the beginning (that is, at my *own* beginning), which entails beginning again, going back over the whole road, just as though many others had not already mapped and traveled it. . . .

This is the road offered to us, or imposed on us, by *language.*

With every question, before making any deep examination of the content, I take a look at the language; I generally proceed like a surgeon who sterilizes his hands and prepares the area to be operated on. This is what I call cleaning up the verbal situation. You must excuse this expression equating the words and forms of speech with the hands and instruments of a surgeon.

I maintain that we must be careful of a problem's first contact with our minds. We should be careful of the first words a question utters in our mind. A new question arising in us is in a state of infancy; it stammers; it finds only strange terms, loaded with adventitious values and associations; it is forced to borrow these. But it thereby insensibly deflects our true need. Without realizing it we desert our original problem, and in the end we shall come to believe that we have chosen an opinion wholly our own, forgetting that our choice was exercised only on a mass of opinions that are the more or less blind work of other men and of chance. This is what happens with the programs of political parties, no one of which is (or can be) the one that would exactly match our temperament and our interests. If we choose one among them, we gradually become the man suited to that party and to that program.

Philosophical and aesthetic questions are so richly obscured by the quantity, diversity, and antiquity of researches, arguments, and solutions, all produced within the orbit of a very restricted vocabulary, of which each author uses the words according to his own inclinations; that taken as a whole such works give me the impression of a district in the classical Underworld especially reserved for deep thinkers. Here, are the Danaïdes, Ixions, and Sisyphuses, eternally laboring to fill bottomless casks and to push back the falling rock, that is, to redefine the same dozen words whose combinations form the treasure of speculative knowledge.

Allow me to add to these preliminary considerations one last remark and one illustration. Here is the remark: you

POETRY AND ABSTRACT THOUGHT. Valéry's *Poetry and Abstract Thought* was first delivered as a lecture in 1939. It is reprinted here from *The Collected Works of Paul Valéry,* edited by Jackson Mathews, Vol. 7: *The Art of Poetry,* translated by Denise Folliot. Copyright © 1985 Princeton University Press. Reprinted by permission of Princeton University Press.

have surely noticed the curious fact that a certain *word,* which is perfectly clear when you hear or use it in *everyday* speech, and which presents no difficulty when caught up in the rapidity of an ordinary sentence, becomes mysteriously cumbersome, offers a strange resistance, defeats all efforts at definition, the moment you withdraw it from circulation for separate study and try to find its meaning after taking away its temporary function. It is almost comic to inquire the exact meaning of a term that one uses constantly with complete satisfaction. For example: I stop the word *time* in its flight. This word was utterly limpid, precise, honest, and faithful in its service as long as it was part of a remark and was uttered by someone who wished to say something. But here it is, isolated, caught on the wing. It takes its revenge. It makes us believe that it has more meanings than uses. It was only a *means,* and it has become an *end,* the object of a terrible philosophical desire. It turns into an enigma, an abyss, a torment of thought. . . .

It is the same with the word *life* and all the rest.

This readily observed phenomenon has taken on great critical value for me. Moreover, I have drawn from it an illustration that, for me, nicely conveys this strange property of our verbal material.

Each and every word that enables us to leap so rapidly across the chasm of thought, and to follow the prompting of an idea that constructs its own expression, appears to me like one of those light planks which one throws across a ditch or a mountain crevasse and which will bear a man crossing it rapidly. But he must pass without weighing on it, without stopping—above all, he must not take it into his head to dance on the slender plank to test its resistance! . . . Otherwise the fragile bridge tips or breaks immediately, and all is hurled into the depths. Consult your own experience; and you will find that we understand each other, and ourselves, only thanks to our *rapid passage over words.* We must not lay stress upon them, or we shall see the clearest discourse dissolve into enigmas and more or less learned illusions.

But how are we to think—I should say *rethink,* study deeply whatever seems to merit deep study—if we hold language to be something essentially provisional, as a banknote or a check is provisional, what we call its "value" requiring us to forget its true nature, which is that of a piece of paper, generally dirty? The paper has passed through so many hands. . . . But words have passed through so many mouths, so many phrases, so many uses and abuses, that the most delicate precautions must be taken to avoid too much confusion in our minds between what we think and are trying to think, and what dictionaries, authors, and, for that matter, the whole human race since the beginning of language, want us to think. . . .

I shall therefore take care not to accept what the words *poetry* and *abstract thought* suggest to me the moment they are pronounced. But I shall look into myself. There I shall seek my real difficulties and my actual observations of my real states; there I shall find my own sense of the rational and the irrational; I shall see whether the alleged antithesis exists and how it exists in a living condition. I confess that it is my habit, when dealing with problems of the mind, to distinguish between those which I might have invented and which represent a need truly felt by my mind and, the rest, which are other people's problems. Of the latter, more than one (say 40 percent) seem to me to be nonexistent, to be no more than apparent problems: *I do not feel them.* And as for the rest, more than one seem to me to be badly stated. . . . I do not say I am right. I say that I observe what occurs within myself when I attempt to replace the verbal formulas by values and meanings that are nonverbal, that are independent of the language used. I discover naive impulses and images, raw products of my needs and of my personal experiences. *It is my life itself that is surprised,* and my life must, if it can, provide my answers, for it is only in the reactions of our life that the full force, and as it were the necessity, of our truth can reside. The thought proceeding from that life never uses for its own account certain words which seem to it fit only for external consumption; nor certain others whose depths are obscure and which may only deceive thought as to its real strength and value.

I have, then, noticed in myself certain states which I may well call "poetic," since some of them were finally realized in poems. They came about from no apparent cause, arising from some accident or other; they developed according to their own nature, and consequently I found myself for a time jolted out of my habitual state of mind. Then, the cycle completed, I returned to the rule of ordinary exchanges between my life and my thought. But meanwhile *a poem had been made,* and in completing itself the cycle left something behind. This closed cycle is the cycle of an act which has, as it were, aroused and given external form to a poetic power. . . .

On other occasions I have noticed that some no less insignificant incident caused—or seemed to cause—a quite different excursion, a digression of another nature and with another result. For example, a sudden concatenation of ideas, an analogy, would strike me in much the way the sound of a horn in the heart of a forest makes one prick up one's ears, and virtually directs the coordinated attention of all one's muscles toward some point in the distance, among the leafy depths. But this time, instead of a poem, it was an analysis of the sudden intellectual sensation that was taking hold of me. It was not verses that were being formed more or less easily during this phase, but some proposition or other that was destined to be incorporated among my habits of thought, some formula that would henceforward serve as an instrument for further researches. . . .

I apologize for thus revealing myself to you; but in my opinion it is more useful to speak of what one has experienced than to pretend to a knowledge that is entirely impersonal, an observation with no observer. In fact there is no theory that is not a fragment, carefully prepared, of some autobiography.

I do not pretend to be teaching you anything at all. I will say nothing you do not already know; but I will, perhaps, say it in a different order. You do not need to be told that a poet is not always incapable of solving a *rule of three;* or that a logician is not always incapable of seeing in words something other than concepts, categories, and mere pretexts for syllogisms.

On this point I would add this paradoxical remark: if the logician could never be other than a logician, he would not, and could not, be a logician; and if the poet were never anything but a poet, without the slightest hope of being able to reason abstractly, he would leave no poetic traces behind him. I believe in all sincerity that if each man were not able to live a number of other lives besides his own, he would not be able to live his own life.

My experience has thus shown me that the same *self* can take very different forms, can become an abstract thinker or a poet, by successive specializations, each of which is a deviation from that entirely unattached state which is superficially in accord with exterior surroundings and which is the average state of our existence, the state of undifferentiated exchanges.

Let us first see in what may consist that initial and *invariably accidental* shock which will construct the poetic instrument within us, and above all, what are its effects. The problem can be put in this way: poetry is an art of language; certain combinations of words can produce an emotion that others do not produce, and which we shall call "poetic." What kind of emotion is this?

I recognize it in myself by this: that all possible objects of the ordinary world, external or internal, beings, events, feelings, and actions, while keeping their usual appearance, are suddenly placed in an indefinable but wonderfully fitting relationship with the modes of our general sensibility. That is to say that these well-known things and beings—or rather the ideas that represent them—somehow change in value. They attract one another, they are connected in ways quite different from the ordinary; they become (if you will permit the expression) *musicalized,* resonant, and, as it were, harmonically related. The poetic universe, thus defined, offers extensive analogies with what we can postulate of the dream world.

Since the word *dream* has found its way into this talk, I shall say in passing that in modern times, beginning with Romanticism, there has arisen a fairly understandable confusion between the notion of the dream and that of poetry. Neither the dream nor the daydream is necessarily poetic; it may be so: but figures formed *by chance* are only *by chance* harmonious figures.

In any case, our memories of dreams teach us, by frequent and common experience, that our consciousness can be invaded, filled, entirely absorbed by the production of an *existence* in which objects and beings seem the same as those in the waking state; but their meanings, relationships, modes of variation and of substitution are quite different and doubtless represent, like symbols or allegories, the immediate fluctuations of our *general* sensibility uncontrolled by the sensitivities of our *specialized* senses. In very much the same way the *poetic state* takes hold of us, develops, and finally disintegrates.

This is to say that the *state of poetry* is completely irregular, inconstant, involuntary, and fragile, and that we lose it, as we find it, *by accident.* But this state is not enough to make a poet, any more than it is enough to see a treasure in a dream to find it, on waking, sparkling at the foot of one's bed.

A poet's function—do not be startled by this remark—is not to experience the poetic state: that is a private affair. His function is to create it in others. The poet is recognized—or at least everyone recognizes his own poet—by the simple fact that he causes his reader to become "inspired." Positively speaking, inspiration is a graceful attribute with which the reader endows his poet: the reader sees in us the transcendent merits of virtues and graces that develop in him. He seeks and finds in us the wondrous cause of his own wonder.

But poetic feeling and the artificial synthesis of this state in some work are two quite distinct things, as different as sensation and action. A sustained action is much more complex than any spontaneous production, particularly when it has to be carried out in a sphere as conventional as that of language. Here you see emerging through my explanations the famous abstract thought which custom opposes to poetry. We shall come back to that in a moment. Meanwhile I should like to tell you a true story, so that you may feel as I felt, and in a curiously clear way, the whole difference that exists between the poetic state or emotion, even creative and original, and the production of a work. It is a rather remarkable observation of myself that I made about a year ago.

I had left my house to relax from some tedious piece of work by walking and by a consequent change of scene. As I went along the street where I live, I was suddenly *gripped* by a rhythm which took possession of me and soon gave me the impression of some force outside myself. It was as though someone else were making use of my *living machine*. Then another rhythm overtook and combined with the first, and certain strange *transverse* relations were set up between these two principles (I am explaining myself as best I can). They combined the movement of my walking legs and some kind of song I was murmuring, or rather which was being murmured *through me*. This composition became more and more complicated and soon in its complexity went far beyond anything I could reasonably produce with my ordinary, usable rhythmic faculties. The sense of strangeness that I mentioned became almost painful, almost disquieting. I am no musician; I am completely ignorant of musical technique; yet here I was, prey to a development in several parts more complicated than any poet could dream. I argued that there had been an error of person, that this grace had descended on the wrong head, since I could make no use of a gift which for a musician would doubtless have assumed value, form, and duration, while these parts that mingled and separated offered me in vain a composition whose cunningly organized sequence amazed my ignorance and reduced it to despair.

After about twenty minutes the magic suddenly vanished, leaving me on the bank of the Seine, as perplexed as the duck in the fable, that saw a swan emerge from the egg she had hatched. As the swan flew away, my surprise changed to reflection. I knew that walking often induces in me a quickened flow of ideas and that there is a certain reciprocity between my pace and my thoughts—my thoughts modify my pace; my pace provokes my thoughts—which after all is remarkable enough, but is fairly understandable. Our various "reaction periods" are doubtless synchronized, and it is interesting to have to admit that a reciprocal modification is possible between a form of action which is purely muscular and a varied production of images, judgments, and reasonings.

But in the case I am speaking of, my movement in walking became in my consciousness a very subtle system of rhythms, instead of instigating those images, interior words, and potential actions which one calls *ideas*. As for ideas, they are things of a species familiar to me; they are things that I can note, provoke, and handle. . . . *But I cannot say the same of my unexpected rhythms.*

What was I to think? I supposed that mental activity while walking must correspond with a general excitement exerting itself in the region of my brain; this excitement sat-isfied and relieved itself as best it could, and so long as its energy was expended, it mattered little whether this was on ideas, memories, or rhythms unconsciously hummed. On that day, the energy was expended in a rhythmical intuition that developed before the awakening in my consciousness of *the person who knows that he does not know music*. I imagine it is the same as when *the person who knows he cannot fly* has not yet become active in the man who dreams he is flying.

I apologize for this long and true story—as true, that is, as a story of this kind can be. Notice that everything I have said, or tried to say, happened in relation to what we call the external world, what we call our body, and what we call our mind, and requires a kind of vague collaboration between these three great powers.

Why have I told you this? In order to bring out the profound difference existing between spontaneous production by the mind—or rather by our *sensibility as a whole*—and the fabrication of works. In my story, the substance of a musical composition was freely given to me, but the organization which would have seized, fixed, and reshaped it was lacking. The great painter Degas often repeated to me a very true and simple remark by Mallarmé. Degas occasionally wrote verses, and some of those he left were delightful. But he often found great difficulty in this work accessory to his painting. (He was, by the way, the kind of man who would bring all possible difficulty to any art whatever.) One day he said to Mallarmé: "Yours is a hellish craft. I can't manage to say what I want, and yet I'm full of ideas. . . ." And Mallarmé answered: "My dear Degas, one does not make poetry with ideas, but with *words*."[1]

Mallarmé was right. But when Degas spoke of ideas, he was, after all, thinking of inner speech or of images, which might have been expressed in *words*. But these words, these secret phrases which he called ideas, all these intentions and perceptions of the mind, do not make verses. There is something else, then, a modification, or a transformation, sudden or not, spontaneous or not, laborious or not, which must necessarily intervene between the thought that produces ideas—that activity and multiplicity of inner questions and solutions—and, on the other hand, that discourse, so different from ordinary speech, which is verse, which is so curiously ordered, which answers no need *unless it be the need it must itself create,* which never speaks but of absent things or of things profoundly and secretly felt: strange discourse, as though made by someone *other* than the speaker and ad-

---

[1] See similar remarks in *Mystery in Literature,* pp. 676–78.

dressed to someone *other* than the listener. In short, it is a *language within a language.*

Let us look into these mysteries.

Poetry is an art of language. But language is a practical creation. It may be observed that in all communication between men, certainty comes only from practical acts and from the verification which practical acts give us. *I ask you for a light. You give me a light:* You have understood me.

But in asking me for a light, you were able to speak those few unimportant words with a certain intonation, a certain tone of voice, a certain inflection, a certain languor or briskness perceptible to me. I have understood your words, since without even thinking I handed you what you asked for—a light. But the matter does not end there. The strange thing: the sound and as it were the features of your little sentence come back to me, echo within me, as though they were pleased to be there; I, too, like to hear myself repeat this little phrase, which has almost lost its meaning, which has stopped being of use, and which can yet go on living, though with quite another life. It has acquired a value; and has acquired it *at the expense of its finite significance.* It has created the need to be heard again. . . . Here we are on the very threshold of the poetic state. This tiny experience will help us to the discovery of more than one truth.

It has shown us that language can produce effects of two quite different kinds. One of them tends to bring about the complete negation of language itself. I speak to you, and if you have understood my words, those very words are abolished. If you have understood, it means that the words have vanished from your minds and are replaced by their counterpart, by images, relationships, impulses; so that you have within you the means to retransmit these ideas and images in a language that may be very different from the one you received. *Understanding* consists in the more or less rapid replacement of a system of sounds, intervals, and signs by something quite different, which is, in short, a modification or interior reorganization of the person to whom one is speaking. And here is the counterproof of this proposition: the person who does not understand *repeats* the words, or *has them repeated* to him.

Consequently, the perfection of a discourse whose sole aim is comprehension obviously consists in the ease with which the words forming it are transformed into something quite different: the *language* is transformed first into *nonlanguage* and then, if we wish, into a form of language differing from the original form.

In other terms, in practical or abstract uses of language, the form—that is the physical, the concrete part, the very act of speech—does not last; it does not outlive understanding; it dissolves in the light; it has acted; it has done its work; it has brought about understanding: it has lived.

But on the other hand, the moment this concrete form takes on, by an effect of its own, such importance that it asserts itself and makes itself, as it were, respected; and not only remarked and respected, but desired and therefore repeated—then something new happens: we are insensibly transformed and ready to live, breathe, and think in accordance with a rule and under laws which are no longer of the practical order—that is, nothing that may occur in this state will be resolved, finished, or abolished by a specific act. We are entering the poetic universe.

Permit me to support this notion of a *poetic universe* by referring to a similar notion that, being much simpler, is easier to explain: the notion of a *musical universe.* I would ask you to make a small sacrifice: limit yourselves for a moment to your faculty of hearing. One simple sense, like that of hearing, will offer us all we need for our definition and will absolve us from entering into all the difficulties and subtleties to which the conventional structure and historical complexities of ordinary language would lead us. We live by ear in the world of noises. Taken as a whole, it is generally incoherent and irregularly supplied by all the mechanical incidents which the ear may interpret as it can. But the same ear isolates from this chaos a group of noises particularly remarkable and simple—that is, easily recognizable by our sense of hearing and furnishing it with points of reference. These elements have relations with one another which we sense as we do the elements themselves. The interval between two of these privileged noises is as clear to us as each of them. These are the *sounds,* and these units of sonority tend to form clear combinations, successive or simultaneous implications, series, and intersections which one may term *intelligible:* this is why abstract possibilities exist in music. But I must return to my subject.

I will confine myself to saying that the contrast between noise and sound is the contrast between pure and impure, order and disorder; that this differentiation between pure sensations and others has permitted the constitution of music; that it has been possible to control, unify, and codify this constitution, thanks to the intervention of physical science, which knows how to adjust measure to sensation so as to obtain the important result of teaching us to produce this sonorous sensation consistently, and in a continuous and identical fashion, by instruments that are, in reality, *measuring instruments.*

The musician is thus in possession of a perfect system of well-defined means which exactly match sensations with acts. From this it results that music has formed a domain absolutely its own. The world of the art of music, a world of sounds, is distinct from the world of noises. Whereas a *noise* merely rouses in us some isolated event—a dog, a door, a motor car—*a sound evokes, of itself, the musical universe.*

If, in this hall where I am speaking to you and where you hear the noise of my voice, a tuning fork or a well-tempered instrument began to vibrate, you would at once, as soon as you were affected by this pure and exceptional noise that cannot be confused with others, have the feeling of a beginning, the beginning of a world; a quite different atmosphere would immediately be created, a new order would arise, and you yourselves would unconsciously *organize* yourselves to receive it. The musical universe, therefore, was within you, with all its associations and proportions—as in a saturated salt solution a crystalline universe awaits the molecular shock of a minute crystal in order *to declare itself.* I dare not say: the crystalline idea of such a system awaits. . . .

And here is the counter proof of our little experiment: if, in a concert hall dominated by a resounding symphony, a chair happens to fall, someone coughs, or a door shuts, we immediately have the impression of a kind of rupture. Something indefinable, something like a spell or a Venetian glass, has been broken or cracked. . . .

The poetic universe is not created so powerfully or so easily. It exists, but the poet is deprived of the immense advantages possessed by the musician. He does not have before him, ready for the uses of beauty, a body of resources expressly made for his art. He has to borrow *language*—the voice of the public, that collection of traditional and irrational terms and rules, oddly created and transformed, oddly codified, and very variedly understood and pronounced. Here there is no physicist who has determined the relations between these elements; no tuning forks, no metronomes, no inventors of scales or theoreticians of harmony. Rather, on the contrary, the phonetic and semantic fluctuations of vocabulary. Nothing pure; but a mixture of completely incoherent auditive and psychic stimuli. Each word is an instantaneous coupling of a *sound* and a *sense* that have no connection with each other. Each sentence is an act so complex that I doubt whether anyone has yet been able to provide a tolerable definition of it. As for the use of the resources of language and the modes of this action, you know what diversity there is, and what confusion sometimes results. A discourse can be logical, packed with sense, but devoid of rhythm and measure. It can be pleasing to the ear, yet completely absurd or insignificant; it can be clear, yet useless; vague, yet delightful. But to grasp its strange multiplicity, which is no more than the multiplicity of life itself, it suffices to name all the sciences which have been created to deal with this diversity, each to study one of its aspects. One can analyze a text in many different ways, for it falls successively under the jurisdiction of phonetics, semantics, syntax, logic, rhetoric, philology, not to mention metrics, prosody, and etymology. . . .

So the poet is at grips with this verbal matter, obliged to speculate on sound and sense at once, and to satisfy not only harmony and musical timing but all the various intellectual and aesthetic conditions, not to mention the conventional rules. . . .

You can see what an effort the poet's undertaking would require if he had *consciously* to solve all these problems. . . .

It is always interesting to try to reconstruct one of our complex activities, one of those complete actions which demand a specialization at once mental, sensuous, and motor, supposing that in order to accomplish this act we were obliged to understand and organize all the functions that we know play their part in it. Even if this attempt, at once imaginative and analytical, is clumsy, it will always teach us something. As for myself, who am, I admit, much more attentive to the formation or fabrication of works than to the works themselves, I have a habit, or obsession, of appreciating works only as actions. In my eyes a poet is a man who, as a result of a certain incident, undergoes a hidden transformation. He leaves his ordinary condition of general disposability, and I see taking shape in him an agent, a living system for producing verses. As among animals one suddenly sees emerging a capable hunter, a nest-maker, a bridge-builder, a digger of tunnels and galleries, so in a man one sees a composite organization declare itself, bending its functions to a specific piece of work. Think of a very small child: the child we have all been bore many possibilities within him. After a few months of life he has learned, at the same or almost the same time, to speak and to walk. He has acquired two types of action. That is to say that he now possesses two kinds of potentiality from which the accidental circumstances of each moment will draw what they can, in answer to his varying needs and imaginings.

Having learned to use his legs, he will discover that he can not only walk, but run; and not only walk and run, but dance. This is a great event. He has at that moment both invented and discovered a kind of *secondary use* for his limbs, a generalization of his formula of movement. In fact, whereas walking is after all a rather dull and not easily perfectible action, this new form of action, the dance, admits of an infinite number of creations and variations or *figures.*

But will he not find an analogous development in speech? He will explore the possibilities of his faculty of speech; he will discover that more can be done with it than to ask for jam and deny his little sins. He will grasp the power of reasoning; he will invent stories to amuse himself when he is alone; he will repeat to himself words that he loves for their strangeness and mystery.

So, parallel with *walking* and *dancing,* he will acquire and distinguish the divergent types, *prose* and *poetry.*

This parallel has long struck and attracted me; but someone saw it before I did. According to Racan, Malherbe made use of it. In my opinion it is more than a simple comparison. I see in it an analogy as substantial and pregnant as those found in physics when one observes the identity of formulas that represent the measurement of seemingly very different phenomena. Here is how our comparison develops.

Walking, like prose, has a definite aim. It is an act directed at something we wish to reach. Actual circumstances, such as the need for some object, the impulse of my desire, the state of my body, my sight, the terrain, etc., which order the manner of walking, prescribe its direction and its speed, and give it a *definite end.* All the characteristics of walking derive from these instantaneous conditions, which combine *in a novel way* each time. There are no movements in walking that are not special adaptations, but, each time, they are abolished and, as it were, absorbed by the accomplishment of the act, by the attainment of the goal.

The dance is quite another matter. It is, of course, a system of actions; but of actions whose end is in themselves. It goes nowhere. If it pursues an object, it is only an ideal object, a state, an enchantment, the phantom of a flower, an extreme of life, a smile—which forms at last on the face of the one who summoned it from empty space.

It is therefore not a question of carrying out a limited operation whose end is situated somewhere in our surroundings, but rather of creating, maintaining, and exalting a certain *state,* by a periodic movement that can be executed on the spot; a movement which is almost entirely dissociated from sight, but which is stimulated and regulated by auditive rhythms.

But please note this very simple observation, that however different the dance may be from walking and utilitarian movements, it uses the same organs, the same bones, the same muscles, only differently coordinated and aroused.

Here we come again to the contrast between prose and poetry. Prose and poetry use the same words, the same syntax, the same forms, and the same sounds or tones, but differently coordinated and differently aroused. Prose and poetry are therefore distinguished by the difference between certain links and associations which form and dissolve in our psychic and nervous organism, whereas the components of these modes of functioning are identical. This is why one should guard against reasoning about poetry as one does about prose. What is true of one very often has no meaning when it is sought in the other. But here is the great and decisive difference. When the man who is walking has reached his goal—as I said—when he has reached the place, book, fruit, the object of his desire (which desire drew him from

his repose), this possession at once entirely annuls his whole act; the effect swallows up the cause, the end absorbs the means; and, whatever the act, only the result remains. It is the same with utilitarian language: the language I use to express my design, my desire, my command, my opinion; this language, when it has served its purpose, evaporates almost as it is heard. I have given it forth to perish, to be radically transformed into something else in your mind; and I shall know that I was *understood* by the remarkable fact that my speech no longer exists: it has been completely replaced by its *meaning*—that is, by images, impulses, reactions, or acts that belong to you: in short, by an interior modification in you.

As a result the perfection of this kind of language, whose sole end is to be understood, obviously consists in the ease with which it is transformed into something altogether different.

The poem, on the other hand, does not die for having lived: it is expressly designed to be born again from its ashes and to become endlessly what it has just been. Poetry can be recognized by this property, that it tends to get itself reproduced in its own form: it stimulates us to reconstruct it identically.

That is an admirable and uniquely characteristic property.

I should like to give you a simple illustration. Think of a pendulum oscillating between two symmetrical points. Suppose that one of these extremes represents *form:* the concrete characteristics of the language, sound, rhythm, accent, tone, movement—in a word, the *voice* in action. Then associate with the other point, the acnode of the first, all significant values, images and ideas, stimuli of feeling and memory, virtual impulses and structures of understanding—in short, everything that makes the *content,* the meaning of a discourse. Now observe the effect of poetry on yourselves. You will find that at each line the meaning produced within you, far from destroying the musical form communicated to you, recalls it. The living pendulum that has swung from *sound* to *sense* swings back to its felt point of departure, as though the very sense which is present to your mind can find no other outlet or expression, no other answer, than the very music which gave it birth.

So between the form and the content, between the sound and the sense, between the poem and the state of poetry, a symmetry is revealed, an equality between importance, value, and power, which does not exist in prose; which is contrary to the law of prose—the law which ordains the inequality of the two constituents of language. The essential principle of the mechanics of poetry—that is, of the conditions for producing the poetic state by words—seems to me to be this harmonious exchange between expression and impression.

I introduce here a slight observation which I shall call "philosophical," meaning simply that we could do without it.

Our poetic pendulum travels from our sensation toward some idea or some sentiment, and returns toward some memory of the sensation and toward the potential act which could reproduce the sensation. Now, whatever is sensation is essentially *present.* There is no other definition of the present except sensation itself, which includes, perhaps, the impulse to action that would modify that sensation. On the other hand, whatever is properly thought, image, sentiment, is always, in some way, *a production of absent things.* Memory is the substance of all thought. Anticipation and its gropings, desire, planning, the projection of our hopes, of our fears, are the main interior activity of our being.

Thought is, in short, the activity which causes what does not exist to come alive in us, lending to it, whether we will or no, our present powers, making us take the part for the whole, the image for reality, and giving us the illusion of seeing, acting, suffering, and possessing independently of our dear old body, which we leave with its cigarette in an armchair until we suddenly retrieve it when the telephone rings or, no less strangely, when our stomach demands provender. . . .

Between voice and thought, between thought and voice, between presence and absence, oscillates the poetic pendulum.

The result of this analysis is to show that the value of a poem resides in the indissolubility of sound and sense. Now this is a condition that seems to demand the impossible. There is no relation between the sound and the meaning of a word. The same thing is called *horse* in English, *hippos* in Greek, *equus* in Latin, and *cheval* in French; but no manipulation of any of these terms will give me an idea of the animal in question; and no manipulation of the idea will yield me any of these words—otherwise, we should easily know all languages, beginning with our own.

Yet it is the poet's business to give us the feeling of an intimate union between the word and the mind.

This must be considered, strictly speaking, a marvelous result. I say *marvelous,* although it is not exceptionally rare. I use *marvelous* in the sense we give that word when we think of the miracles and prodigies of ancient magic. It must not be forgotten that for centuries poetry was used for purposes of enchantment. Those who took part in these strange operations had to believe in the power of the word, and far more in the efficacy of its sound than in its significance. Magic formulas are often without meaning; but it was never

thought that their power depended on their intellectual content.

Let us listen to lines like these: *"Mère des souvenirs, maîtresse des maîtresses"*[2] or *"Sois sage, ô ma douleur, et tiens-toi plus tranquille."*[3]

These words work on us (or at least on some of us) without telling us very much. They tell us, perhaps, that they have nothing to tell us; that, by the very means which usually tell us something, they are exercising a quite different function. They act on us like a chord of music. The impression produced depends largely on resonance, rhythm, and the number of syllables; but it is also the result of the simple bringing together of meanings. In the second of these lines the accord between the vague ideas of wisdom and grief, and the tender solemnity of the tone produce the inestimable value of a spell: the *momentary being* who made that line could not have done so had he been in a state where the form and the content occurred separately to his mind. On the contrary, he was in a special phase in the domain of his psychic existence, a phase in which the sound and the meaning of the word acquire or keep an equal importance—which is excluded from the habits of practical language, as from the needs of abstract language. The state in which the inseparability of sound and sense, in which the desire, the expectation, the possibility of their intimate and indissoluble fusion are required and sought or given, and sometimes anxiously awaited, is a comparatively rare state. It is rare, firstly because all the exigencies of life are against it; secondly because it is opposed to the crude simplifying and specializing of verbal notations.

But this state of inner modification, in which all the properties of our language are indistinctly but harmoniously summoned, is not enough to produce that complete object, that compound of beauties, that collection of happy chances for the mind which a noble poem offers us.

From this state we obtain only fragments. All the precious things that are found in the earth, gold, diamonds, uncut stones, are there scattered, strewn, grudgingly hidden in a quantity of rock or sand, where chance may sometimes uncover them. These riches would be nothing without the human labor that draws them from the massive night where they were sleeping, assembles them, alters and organizes them into ornaments. These fragments of metal embedded in formless matter, these oddly shaped crystals, must owe all their luster to intelligent labor. It is a labor of this kind that the true poet accomplishes. Faced with a beautiful poem, one

---

[2] "Mother of memories, mistress of mistresses." Baudelaire, *Le Balcon.*
[3] "Be quiet, O my sorrow, and lie still." Baudelaire, *Le Recueillement.*

can indeed feel that it is most unlikely that any man, however gifted, could have improvised without a backward glance, with no other effort than that of writing or dictating, such a simultaneous and complete system of lucky finds. Since the traces of effort, the second thoughts, the changes, the amount of time, the bad days, and the distaste have now vanished, effaced by the supreme return of a mind over its work, some people, seeing only the perfection of the result, will look on it as due to a sort of magic that they call "inspiration." They thus make of the poet a kind of temporary *medium.* If one were strictly to develop this doctrine of pure inspiration, one would arrive at some very strange results. For example, one would conclude that the poet, since he merely transmits what he receives, merely delivers to unknown people what he has taken from the unknown, has no need to understand what he writes, which is dictated by a mysterious voice. He could write poems in a language he did not know. . . .

In fact, the poet has indeed a kind of spiritual energy of a special nature: it is manifested in him and reveals him to himself in certain moments of infinite worth. Infinite for him. . . . I say, *"infinite for him,"* for, alas, experience shows us that these moments which seem to us to have a universal value are sometimes without a future, and in the end make us ponder on this maxim: *"what is of value for one person only has no value."* This is the iron law of literature.

But every true poet is necessarily a first-rate critic. If one doubts this, one can have no idea of what the work of the mind is: that struggle with the inequality of moments, with chance associations, lapses of attention, external distractions. The mind is terribly variable, deceptive and self-deceiving, fertile in insoluble problems and illusory solutions. How could a remarkable work emerge from this chaos if this chaos that contains everything did not also contain some serious chances to know oneself and to choose within oneself whatever is worth taking from each moment and using carefully?

That is not all. Every true poet is much more capable than is generally known of right reasoning and abstract thought.

But one must not look for his real philosophy in his more or less philosophical utterances. In my opinion, the most authentic philosophy lies not so much in the objects of our reflection as in the very act of thought and in its handling. Take from metaphysics all its pet or special terms, all its traditional vocabulary, and you may realize that you have not impoverished the thought. Indeed, you may perhaps have eased and freshened it, and you will have got rid of other people's problems, so as to deal only with your own difficulties, your surprises that owe nothing to anyone, and whose intellectual spur you feel actually and directly.

It has often happened, however, as literary history tells us, that poetry has been made to enunciate theses or hypotheses and that the *complete* language which is its own—the language whose *form,* that is to say the action and sensation of the *voice,* is of the same power as the *content,* that is to say the eventual modification of a *mind*—has been used to communicate "abstract" ideas, which are on the contrary independent of their form, or so we believe. Some very great poets have occasionally attempted this. But whatever may be the talent which exerts itself in this very noble undertaking, it cannot prevent the attention given to following the ideas from competing with the attention that follows the song. The *de rerum natura* is here in conflict with the nature of things. The state of mind of the reader of poems is not the state of mind of the reader of pure thought. The state of mind of a man dancing is not that of a man advancing through difficult country of which he is making a topographical survey or a geological prospectus.

I have said, nevertheless, that the poet has his abstract thought and, if you like, his philosophy; and I have said that it is at work in his very activity as a poet. I said this because I have observed it, in myself and in several others. Here, as elsewhere, I have no other reference, no other claim or excuse, than recourse to my own experience or to the most common observation.

Well, every time I have worked as a poet, I have noticed that my work exacted of me not only that presence of the poetic universe I have spoken of, but many reflections, decisions, choices, and combinations, without which all possible gifts of the Muses, or of Chance, would have remained like precious materials in a workshop without an architect. Now an architect is not himself necessarily built of precious materials. Insofar as he is an architect of poems, a poet is quite different from what he is as a producer of those precious elements of which all poetry should be composed, but whose composition is separate and requires an entirely different mental effort.

One day someone told me that lyricism is enthusiasm, and that the odes of the great lyricists were written at a single stroke, at the speed of the voice of delirium, and with the wind of inspiration blowing a gale. . . .

I replied that he was quite right; but that this was not a privilege of poetry alone, and that everyone knew that in building a locomotive it is indispensable for the builder to work at eighty miles an hour in order to do his job.

A poem is really a kind of machine for producing the poetic state of mind by means of words. The effect of this machine is uncertain, for nothing is certain about action on other minds. But whatever may be the result, in its uncertainty, the construction of the machine demands the solution of many problems. If the term *machine* shocks you, if my mechanical comparison seems crude, please notice that while the composition of even a very short poem may absorb years, the action of the poem on the reader will take only a few minutes. In a few minutes the reader will receive his shock from discoveries, connections, glimmers of expression that have been accumulated during months of research, waiting, patience, and impatience. He may attribute much more to inspiration than it can give. He will imagine the kind of person it would take to create, without pause, hesitation, or revision, this powerful and perfect work which transports him into a world where things and people, passions and thoughts, sonorities and meanings proceed from the same energy, are transformed one into another, and correspond according to exceptional laws of harmony, for it can only be an exceptional form of stimulus that simultaneously produces the exaltation of our sensibility, our intellect, our memory, and our powers of verbal action, so rarely granted to us in the ordinary course of life.

Perhaps I should remark here that the execution of a poetic work—if one considers it as the engineer just mentioned would consider the conception and construction of his locomotive, that is, making explicit the problems to be solved—would appear impossible. In no other art is the number of conditions and independent functions to be coordinated so large. I will not inflict on you a detailed demonstration of this proposition. It is enough for me to remind you of what I said regarding sound and sense, which are linked only by pure convention, but which must be made to collaborate as effectively as possible. From their double nature words often make me think of those complex quantities which geometricians take such pleasure in manipulating.

Fortunately, some strange virtue resides in certain moments in certain people's lives which simplifies things and reduces the insurmountable difficulties I spoke of to the scale of human energies.

The poet awakes within man at an unexpected event, an outward or inward incident: a tree, a face, a "subject," an emotion, a word. Sometimes it is the will to expression that starts the game, a need to translate what one feels; another time, on the contrary, it is an element of form, the outline of an expression which seeks its origin, seeks a meaning within the space of my mind. . . . Note this possible duality in ways of getting started: either something wants to express itself, or some means of expression wants to be used.

My poem *Le Cimetière marin* began in me by a rhythm, that of a French line . . . of ten syllables, divided into four and six. I had as yet no idea with which to fill out this form. Gradually a few hovering words settled in it, little by little determining the subject, and my labor (a very long labor) was before me. Another poem, *La Pythie,* first appeared as an eight-syllable line whose sound came of its own accord. But this line implied a sentence, of which it was part, and this sentence, if it existed, implied many other sentences. A problem of this kind has an infinite number of solutions. But with poetry the musical and metrical conditions greatly restrict the indefiniteness. Here is what happened: my fragment acted like a living fragment, since, plunged in the (no doubt nourishing) surroundings of my desire and waiting thought, it proliferated, and engendered all that was lacking: several lines before and a great many lines after.

I apologize for having chosen my examples from my own little story: but I could hardly have taken them elsewhere.

Perhaps you think my conception of the poet and the poem rather singular. Try to imagine, however, what the least of our acts implies. Think of everything that must go on inside a man who utters the smallest intelligible sentence, and then calculate all that is needed for a poem by Keats or Baudelaire to be formed on an empty page in front of the poet.

Think, too, that of all the arts, ours is perhaps that which coordinates the greatest number of independent parts or factors: sound, sense, the real and the imaginary, logic, syntax, and the double invention of content and form . . . and all this by means of a medium essentially practical, perpetually changing, soiled, a maid of all work, *everyday language,* from which we must draw a pure, ideal voice, capable of communicating without weakness, without apparent effort, without offense to the ear, and without breaking the ephemeral sphere of the poetic universe, an idea of some *self* miraculously superior to myself.

Kenneth Burke

b. 1897

Kenneth Burke's essay *Literature as Equipment for Living* sets out in very general terms an approach to literature that is developed in his numerous other works. Burke's mind is so far-reaching and inquisitive that it cannot, however, be trapped in a general theory, even one of its own making. Burke has been compared to Coleridge for the breadth of his critical undertaking, but one argument against the comparison is that it may not be favorable enough to Burke, who has been able to begin, and even finish, books he has announced, whereas Coleridge's plans often remained mere plans.

Burke appropriated insights from Marxism and from anthropological studies of myth and ritual. As sociological criticism, however, his work is more concerned with aesthetic questions than is the work of the typical sociologist, who is interested in literature simply as document. As analytical criticism, it is more concerned with art as a social act than is usually true of New Criticism, though Burke is clearly influenced by the analytical techniques of the New Critics. Its attitude toward language relates it to twentieth-century analytical philosophy.

Each work of art is, for Burke, "the addition of a word to an informal dictionary." Works of art are strategic namings of situations that enable one to gain the sort of control over things that the assignment of a name brings. Sociological criticism should "codify the various strategies which artists have developed with relation to the naming of situations." Burke proposes a method of classification based on social "strategies." He believes that the advantage of this system would be to cut across previously established disciplines.

If, however, sociology is a discipline of its own and is not *the* finally transcendent discipline, then such a system would subsume literature and criticism under its own dictates and special categories, as is typical of the Marxist tradition that influenced Burke early in his career. Are there possible modes of classification that are the product of a purely literary study, that rise out of an inductive study of literature itself? This question is one Burke does not deal with in his essay. It was taken up by a number of critics, including Frye and, in the thirties and forties, the neo-Aristotelian critics at the University of Chicago. Burke proceeded to studies of rhetoric and symbolism in which he defined man as the "symbol-using animal" and thus displayed a relationship to Cassirer, who makes a similar definition.

Burke's works include *Counter-Statement* (1931), *Permanence and Change* (1935), *Attitudes Toward History* (1937), *The Philosophy of Literary Form* (1941), *A Grammar of Motives* (1945), *A Rhetoric of Motives* (1950), *The Rhetoric of Religion* (1961), *Perspectives by Incongruity* (1964), *Terms for Order* (1964), and *Language as Symbolic Action* (1966). For commentary see George Knox, *Critical Moments* (1957); W. H. Rueckert, *Kenneth Burke and the Drama of Human Relations* (1963); W. H.

Rueckert, ed., *Critical Responses to Kenneth Burke* (1969); M. E. Brown, *Kenneth Burke* (1969); Armin Paul Frank, *Kenneth Burke* (1969); and Grieg E. Henderson, *Kenneth Burke: Literature and Language as Symbolic Action* (1988).

Literature as Equipment for Living

Here I shall put down, as briefly as possible, a statement in behalf of what might be catalogued, with a fair degree of accuracy, as a *sociological* criticism of literature. Sociological criticism in itself is certainly not new. I shall here try to suggest what partially new elements or emphasis I think should be added to this old approach. And to make the "way in" as easy as possible, I shall begin with a discussion of proverbs.

I

Examine random specimens in *The Oxford Dictionary of English Proverbs.* You will note, I think, that there is no "pure" literature here. Everything is "medicine." Proverbs are designed for consolation or vengeance, for admonition or exhortation, for foretelling.

Or they name typical, recurrent situations. That is, people find a certain social relationship recurring so frequently that they must "have a word for it." The Eskimos have special names for many different kinds of snow (fifteen, if I remember rightly) because variations in the quality of snow greatly affect their living. Hence, they must "size up" snow much more accurately than we do. And the same is true of social phenomena. Social structures give rise to "type" situations, subtle subdivisions of the relationships involved in competitive and cooperative acts. Many proverbs seek to chart, in more or less homey and picturesque ways, these "type" situations. I submit that such naming is done, not for the sheer glory of the thing, but because of its bearing upon human welfare. A different name for snow implies a different kind of hunt. Some names for snow imply that one should not hunt at all. And similarly, the names for typical,

recurrent social situations are not developed out of "disinterested curiosity," but because the names imply a command (what to expect, what to look out for).

To illustrate with a few representative examples:

Proverbs designed for consolation: "The sun does not shine on both sides of the hedge at once." "Think of ease, but work on." "Little troubles the eye, but far less the soul." "The worst luck now, the better another time." "The wind in one's face makes one wise." "He that hath lands hath quarrels." "He knows how to carry the dead cock home." "He is not poor that hath little, but he that desireth much."

For vengeance: "At length the fox is brought to the furrier." "Shod in the cradle, barefoot in the stubble." "Sue a beggar and get a louse." "The higher the ape goes, the more he shows his tail." "The moon does not heed the barking of dogs." "He measures another's corn by his own bushel." "He shuns the man who knows him well." "Fools tie knots and wise men loose them."

Proverbs that have to do with foretelling: (The most obvious are those to do with the weather.) "Sow peas and beans in the wane of the moon, Who soweth them sooner, he soweth too soon." "When the wind's in the north, the skillful fisher goes not forth." "When the sloe tree is as white as a sheet, sow your barley whether it be dry or wet." "When the sun sets bright and clear, An easterly wind you need not fear. When the sun sets in a bank, A westerly wind we shall not want."

In short: "Keep your weather eye open": be realistic about sizing up today's weather, because your accuracy has bearing upon tomorrow's weather. And forecast not only the meteorological weather, but also the social weather: "When the moon's in the full, then wit's in the wane." "Straws show which way the wind blows." "When the fish is caught, the net is laid aside." "Remove an old tree, and it will wither to death." "The wolf may lose his teeth, but never his nature." "He that bites on every weed must needs light on poison." "Whether the pitcher strikes the stone, or the stone the pitcher, it is bad for the pitcher." "Eagles catch no flies." "The more laws, the more offenders."

In this foretelling category we might also include the recipes for wise living, sometimes moral, sometimes technical: "First thrive, and then wive." "Think with the wise but talk with the vulgar." "When the fox preacheth, then beware

LITERATURE AS EQUIPMENT FOR LIVING. Burke's *Literature as Equipment for Living* is reprinted from *The Philosophy of Literary Form* (1941). Reprinted by permission of the author.

your geese." "Venture a small fish to catch a great one." "Respect a man, he will do the more."

In the class of "typical, recurrent situations" we might put such proverbs and proverbial expressions as: "Sweet appears sour when we pay." "The treason is loved but the traitor is hated." "The wine in the bottle does not quench thirst." "The sun is never the worse for shining on a dunghill." "The lion kicked by an ass." "The lion's share." "To catch one napping." "To smell a rat." "To cool one's heels."

By all means, I do not wish to suggest that this is the only way in which the proverbs could be classified. For instance, I have listed in the "foretelling" group the proverb, "When the fox preacheth, then beware your geese." But it could obviously be "taken over" for vindictive purposes. Or consider a proverb like, "Virtue flies from the heart of a mercenary man." A poor man might obviously use it either to console himself for being poor (the implication being, "Because I am poor in money I am rich in virtue") or to strike at another (the implication being, "When he got money, what else could you expect of him but deterioration?"). In fact, we could even say that such symbolic vengeance would itself be an aspect of solace. And a proverb like "The sun is never the worse for shining on a dunghill" (which I have listed under "typical recurrent situations") might as well be put in the vindictive category.

The point of issue is not to find categories that "place" the proverbs once and for all. What I want is categories that suggest their active nature. Here there is no "realism for its own sake." There is realism for promise, admonition, solace, vengeance, foretelling, instruction, charting, all for the direct bearing that such acts have upon matters of welfare.

II

Step two: Why not extend such analysis of proverbs to encompass the whole field of literature? Could the most complex and sophisticated works of art legitimately be considered somewhat as "proverbs writ large"? Such leads, if held admissible, should help us to discover important facts about literary organization (thus satisfying the requirements of technical criticism). And the kind of observation from this perspective should apply beyond literature to life in general (thus helping to take literature out of its separate bin and give it a place in a general "sociological" picture).

The point of view might be phrased in this way: Proverbs are *strategies* for dealing with *situations.* Insofar as situations are typical and recurrent in a given social structure,

people develop names for them and strategies for handling them. Another name for strategies might be *attitudes.*

People have often commented on the fact that there are contrary *proverbs.* But I believe that the above approach to proverbs suggests a necessary modification of that comment. The apparent contradictions depend upon differences in *attitude,* involving a correspondingly different choice of *strategy.* Consider, for instance, the *apparently* opposite pair: "Repentance comes too late" and "Never too late to mend." The first is admonitory. It says in effect: "You'd better look out, or you'll get yourself too far into this business." The second is consolatory, saying in effect: "Buck up, old man, you can still pull out of this."

Some critics have quarreled with me about my selection of the word *strategy* as the name for this process. I have asked them to suggest an alternative term, so far without profit. The only one I can think of is *method.* But if *strategy* errs in suggesting to some people an overly *conscious* procedure, *method* errs in suggesting an overly *"methodical"* one. Anyhow, let's look at the documents:

Concise Oxford Dictionary: "Strategy: Movement of an army or armies in a campaign, art of so moving or disposing troops or ships as to impose upon the enemy the place and time and conditions for fighting preferred by oneself" (from a Greek word that refers to the leading of an army).

New English Dictionary: "Strategy: The art of projecting and directing the larger military movements and operations of a campaign."

André Cheron, *Traité complet d'Échecs: "On entend par stratégie les manoeuvres qui ont pour but la sortie et le bon arrangement des pièces."*[1]

Looking at these definitions, I gain courage. For surely, the most highly alembicated and sophisticated work of art, arising in complex civilizations, could be considered as designed to organize and command the army of one's thoughts and images, and to so organize them that one "imposes upon the enemy the time and place and conditions for fighting preferred by oneself." One seeks to "direct the larger movements and operations" in one's campaign of living. One "maneuvers," and the maneuvering is an "art."

Are not the final results one's "strategy"? One tries, as far as possible, to develop a strategy whereby one "can't lose." One tries to change the rules of the game until they fit his own necessities. Does the artist encounter disaster? He will "make capital" of it. If one is a victim of competition, for instance, if one is elbowed out, if one is willy-nilly more jockeyed against than jockeying, one can by the solace and

---

[1] *Complete Treatise on Chess:* "One understands by strategy the maneuvers which are designed for the attack and the good arrangement of pieces."

vengeance of art convert this very "liability" into an "asset." One tries to fight on his own terms, developing a strategy for imposing the proper "time, place, and conditions."

But one must also, to develop a full strategy, be *realistic.* One must *size things up* properly. One cannot accurately know how things *will be,* what is promising and what is menacing, unless he accurately knows how things *are.* So the wise strategist will not be content with strategies of merely a self-gratifying sort. He will "keep his weather eye open." He will not too eagerly "read into" a scene an attitude that is irrelevant to it. He won't sit on the side of an active volcano and "see" it as a dormant plain.

Often, alas, he will. The great allurement in our present popular "inspirational literature," for instance, may be largely of this sort. It is strategy for easy consolation. It "fills a need," since there is always a need for easy consolation— and in an era of confusion like our own the need is especially keen. So people are only too willing to "meet a man half-way" who will *play down* the realistic naming of our situation and *play up* such strategies as make solace cheap. However, I should propose a reservation here. We usually take it for granted that people who consume our current output of books on "How to Buy Friends and Bamboozle Oneself and Other People" are reading as *students* who will attempt applying the recipes given. Nothing of the sort. *The reading of a book on the attaining of success is in itself the symbolic attaining of that success.* It is *while they read* that these readers are "succeeding." I'll wager that, in by far the great majority of cases, such readers make no serious attempt to apply the book's recipes. The lure of the book resides in the fact that the reader, while reading it, is then living in the aura of success. What he wants is *easy* success; and he gets it in symbolic form by the mere reading itself. To attempt applying such stuff in real life would be very difficult, full of many disillusioning difficulties.

Sometimes a different strategy may arise. The author may remain realistic, avoiding too easy a form of solace— yet he may get as far off the track in his own way. Forgetting that realism is an aspect for foretelling, he may take it as an end in itself. He is tempted to do this by two factors: (1) an *ill-digested* philosophy of science, leading him mistakenly to assume that "relentless" naturalistic "truthfulness" is a proper end in itself, and (2) a merely *competitive* desire to outstrip other writers by being "more realistic" than they. Works thus made "efficient" by tests of competition internal to the book trade are a kind of academicism not so named (the writer usually thinks of it as the *opposite* of academicism). Realism thus stepped up competitively might be distinguished from the proper sort by the name of "natural-

ism." As a way of "sizing things up," the naturalistic tradition tends to become as inaccurate as the "inspirational" strategy, though at the opposite extreme.

Anyhow, the main point is this: A work like *Madame Bovary* (or its homely America translation, *Babbitt*), is the strategic naming of a situation. It singles out a pattern of experience that is sufficiently representative of our social structure, that recurs sufficiently often *mutandis mutatis,* for people to "need a word for it" and to adopt an attitude towards it. Each work of art is the addition of a word to an informal dictionary (or, in the case of purely derivative artists, the addition of a subsidiary meaning to a word already given by some originating artist). As for *Madame Bovary,* the French critic Jules de Gaultier proposed to add it to our *formal* dictionary by coining the word "Bovarysme" and writing a whole book to say what he meant by it.

Mencken's book on *The American Language,* I hate to say, is splendid. I console myself with the reminder that Mencken didn't write it. Many millions of people wrote it, and Mencken was merely the amanuensis who took it down from their dictation. He found a true "vehicle" (that is, a book that could be greater than the author who wrote it). He gets the royalties, but the job was done by a collectivity. As you read that book, you see a people who were up against a new set of typical recurrent situations, situations typical of their business, their politics, their criminal organizations, their sports. Either there were no words for these in standard English, or people didn't know them, or they didn't "sound right." So a new vocabulary arose, to "give us a word for it." I see no reason for believing that Americans are unusually fertile in word coinage. American slang was not developed out of some exceptional gift. It was developed out of the fact that new typical situations had arisen and people needed names for them. They had to "size things up." They had to console and strike, to promise and admonish. They had to describe for purposes of forecasting. And "slang" was the result. It is, by this analysis, simply *proverbs not so named,* a kind of "folk criticism."

III

With what, then, would "sociological criticism" along these lines be concerned? It would seek to codify the various strategies which artists have developed with relation to the naming of situations. In a sense, much of it would even be "timeless," for many of the "typical, recurrent situations" are not peculiar to our own civilization at all. The situations and strategies framed in Aesop's *Fables,* for instance, apply to human relations now just as fully as they applied in ancient Greece. They are, like philosophy, sufficiently "generalized" to extend far beyond the particular combination of events named by them in any one instance. They name an "essence." Or, as Korzybski might say, they are on a "high level of abstraction." One doesn't usually think of them as "abstract," since they are usually so concrete in their stylistic expression. But they invariably aim to discern the "general behind the particular" (which would suggest that they are good Goethe).[2]

The attempt to treat literature from the standpoint of situations and strategies suggests a variant of Spengler's notion of the "contemporaneous." By "contemporaneity" he meant corresponding stages of different cultures. For instance, if modern New York is much like decadent Rome, then we are "contemporaneous" with decadent Rome, or with some corresponding decadent city among the Mayas, etc. It is in this sense that situations are "timeless," "nonhistorical," "contemporaneous." A given human relationship may be at one time named in terms of foxes and lions, if there are foxes and lions about; or it may now be named in terms of salesmanship, advertising, the tactics of politicians, etc. But beneath the change in particulars, we may often discern the naming of the one situation.

So sociological criticism, as here understood, would seek to assemble and codify this lore. It might occasionally lead us to outrage good taste, as we sometimes found exemplified in some great sermon or tragedy or abstruse work of philosophy the same strategy as we found exemplified in a dirty joke. At this point, we'd put the sermon and the dirty joke together, thus "grouping by situation" and showing the range of possible particularizations. In his exceptionally discerning essay, *A Critic's Job of Work,* R. P. Blackmur says, "I think on the whole his (Burke's) method could be applied with equal fruitfulness to Shakespeare, Dashiell Hammett, or Marie Corelli."[3] When I got through wincing, I had to admit that Blackmur was right. This article is an attempt to say for the method what can be said. As a matter of fact, I'll go a step further and maintain: you can't properly put Marie Corelli and Shakespeare apart until you have first put them together. First genus, then differentia. The strategy in common is the genus. The *range* or *scale* or *spectrum* of particularizations is the differentia.

Anyhow, that's what I'm driving at. And that's why reviewers sometime find in my work "intuitive" leaps that are dubious as "science." They are not "leaps" at all. They are

classifications, groupings, made on the basis of some strategic element common to the items grouped. They are neither more nor less "intuitive" than *any* grouping or classification of social events. Apples can be grouped with bananas as fruits, and they can be grouped with tennis balls as round. I am simply proposing, in the social sphere, a method of classification with reference to *strategies.*

The method has these things to be said in its favor: it gives definite insight into the organization of literary works; and it automatically breaks down the barriers erected about literature as a specialized pursuit. People can classify novels by reference to three kinds, eight kinds, seventeen kinds. It doesn't matter. Students patiently copy down the professor's classification and pass examinations on it, because the range of possible academic classifications is endless. Sociological classification, as herein suggested, would derive its relevance from the fact that it should apply both to works of art and to social situations outside of art.

It would, I admit, violate current pieties, break down current categories, and thereby "outrage good taste." But "good taste" has become *inert.* The classifications I am proposing would be *active.* I think that what we need is active categories.

These categories will lie on the bias across the categories of modern specialization. The new alignment will outrage in particular those persons who take the division of faculties in our universities to be an exact replica of the way in which God himself divided up the universe. We have had the philosophy of the being; and we have had the philosophy of the becoming. In contemporary specialization, we have been getting the philosophy of the bin. Each of these mental localities has had its own peculiar way of life, its own values, even its own special idiom for seeing, thinking, and "proving." Among other things, a sociological approach should attempt to provide a reintegrative point of view, a broader empire of investigation encompassing the lot.

What would such sociological categories be like? They would consider works of art, I think, as strategies for selecting enemies and allies, for socializing losses, for warding off evil eye, for purification, propitiation, and desanctification, consolation and vengeance, admonition and exhortation, implicit commands or instructions of one sort or another. Art forms like "tragedy" or "comedy" or "satire" would be treated as *equipments for living,* that size up situations in various ways and in keeping with correspondingly various attitudes. The typical ingredients of such forms would be sought. Their relation to typical situations would be stressed. Their comparative values would be considered, with the intention of formulating a "strategy of strategies," the "overall" strategy obtained by inspection of the lot.

---

[2] See *Conversations with Eckermann,* pp. 530–32.
[3] P. 894.

Ernst Cassirer

1874–1945

An Essay on Man is a development from an earlier work, *The Philosophy of Symbolic Forms.* Cassirer proposes that man has surrounded himself with "forms" of symbolism *in* which he constructs his cultural realities. Language and myth are two of these forms, and their sources, though related, are lost in prehistory. Science, history, religion, and art are other such forms, each with its own categories, each a "universe."

In the essay *Art,* which comes from *An Essay on Man,* Cassirer offers a brief discussion of the major theories of art, beginning with an analysis of the history of imitation and of the shift of emphasis from imitative to expressive theories reflected in the writings of Rousseau and Goethe. He proceeds to a critique of various metaphysical and psychological theories, arguing throughout for the neo-Kantian principle that art is an independent "universe of discourse." Cassirer is critical of Croce's split between expression and externalization; he maintains that any expression that is not one with the artist's struggle with formal problems is likely to be sentimental. He concludes that art tends toward the particular and sensuous and seeks to obliterate the gap between object and subject, whereas language and science move toward abstraction and divide object from subject. This conclusion leads him to be critical of the Romantic subjectivist theory that art is an expression of the infinite. Though he eschews the analogies between art and science offered by the naturalists, he respects their practice of looking closely at actual experience. He holds that art is not an imitation but a discovery of reality. Indeed, it is more than that; it constructs and organizes our sense of human experience according to its own formal principles.

After his penetrating remarks about theories of art and his use of literary examples, one might expect Cassirer to move to specific kinds of art, but he does not. He seems to ignore the fact that there is an *art* of language and tends to associate language totally with science and abstraction. Nevertheless, his discussion can be extended into an analysis of literary language and has been by a number of critics, including Vivas and Wheelwright. The latter has also exploited Cassirer's insights into mythical thinking, as has Frye. Cassirer sees an analogy between art and myth but does not develop it to any extent. Both art and myth tend to be intensifications rather than abbreviations of reality. The difference between art and the symbolizations of mythical thinking is that mythical thinking contains an element of naive, literal belief, while the artist releases his forms from the necessity of belief. The work of art tells us what it tells us by its total structure, not by assertions abstracted from its totality.

Cassirer's neo-Kantian views provided a possible philosophical base for much of the discussion of literature by certain New Critics, though those critics—Ransom and Brooks among them—may not have been aware of his work until late in their careers. He clearly affected the work of subsequent critics who were interested in myth and ritual.

Cassirer's works include *The Philosophy of Symbolic Forms* (1923–29, translated by Ralph Manheim, 1953–57); *Language and Myth* (1925, translated by S. K. Langer,

1946); *Individual and Cosmos in the Philosophy of the Renaissance* (1927, translated by Mario Domandi, 1963); *The Platonic Renaissance in England and the School of Cambridge* (1932, translated by J. P. Pettegrove, 1953); *The Philosophy of the Enlightenment* (1932, translated by F. C. A. Koelln and J. P. Pettegrove, 1951); *An Essay on Man* (1944); *Rousseau, Kant, Goethe* (1945, translated by James Gutmann, P. O. Kristeller, and J. H. Randall, Jr.); and *The Myth of the State* (1946), *Symbol, Myth, and Culture: Essays of Ernst Cassirer, 1935–1945* appeared in 1979. See Carl H. Hamburg, *Symbol and Myth: Studies in the Philosophy of Ernst Cassirer* (1956); Seymour Itzkoff, *Ernst Cassirer: Philosopher of Culture* (1977); and John Michael Krois, *Cassirer, Symbolic Forms and History* (1987).

Art

I

Beauty appears to be one of the most clearly known of human phenomena. Unobscured by any aura of secrecy and mystery, its character and nature stand in no need of subtle and complicated metaphysical theories for their explanation. Beauty is part and parcel of human experience; it is palpable and unmistakable. Nevertheless, in this history of philosophical thought the phenomenon of beauty has always proved to be one of the greatest paradoxes. Up to the time of Kant a philosophy of beauty always meant an attempt to reduce our aesthetic experience to an alien principle and to subject art to an alien jurisdiction. Kant in his *Critique of Judgment*[1] was the first to give a clear and convincing proof of the autonomy of art. All former systems had looked for a principle of art within the sphere either of theoretical knowledge or of the moral life. If art was regarded as the offspring of theoretical activity it became necessary to analyze the logical rules to which this particular activity conforms. But in this case logic itself was no longer a homogeneous whole. It had to be divided into separate and comparatively independent parts. The logic of the imagination had to be distinguished from the logic of rational and scientific thought. In his *Aesthetica* (1750) Alexander Baumgarten[2] had made the first comprehensive systematic attempt to construct a logic of the imagination. But even this attempt, which in a sense proved to be decisive and invaluable, could not secure for art a really autonomous value. For the logic of the imagination could never

command the same dignity as the logic of the pure intellect. If there was a theory of art, then it could only be a *gnoseologia inferior,* an analysis of the "lower," sensuous part of human knowledge. Art could, on the other hand, be described as an emblem of moral truth. It was conceived as an allegory, a figurative expression which under its sensuous form concealed an ethical sense. But in both cases, in its moral as well as in its theoretical interpretation, art possessed no independent value of its own. In the hierarchy of human knowledge and of human life art was only a preparatory stage, a subordinate and subservient means pointing to some higher end.

The philosophy of art exhibits the same conflict between two antagonistic tendencies that we encounter in the philosophy of language. This is of course no mere historical coincidence. It goes back to one and the same basic division in the interpretation of reality. Language and art are constantly oscillating between two opposite poles, an objective and a subjective pole. No theory of language or art could forget or suppress either one of these poles, though the stress may be laid now on the one and now on the other.

In the first case language and art are subsumed under a common heading, the category of imitation; and their principle function is mimetic. Language originates in an imitation of sounds, art is an imitation of outward things. Imitation is a fundamental instinct, an irreducible fact of human nature. "Imitation," says Aristotle, "is natural to man from childhood, one of his advantages over the lower animals being this, that he is the most imitative creature in the world, and learns at first by imitation."[3] And imitation is also an inexhaustible source of delight, as is proved by the fact that, though the objects themselves may be painful to see, we delight nevertheless in viewing the most realistic represen-

---

ART. Cassirer's *Art* is Chapter 9 of his *Essay on Man,* which was first published in 1944. Copyright © 1944 by Yale University Press. Reprinted by permission of the publisher.
[1] Pp. 375–93.
[2] Baumgarten (1714–62) coined the word *aesthetics* to refer to a special branch of study.

---

[3] *Poetics,* IV. 2, p. 51. Cassirer quotes from the Bywater translation.

tations of them in art—the forms, for example, of the lowest animals and of dead bodies. Aristotle describes this delight rather as a theoretical than as a specifically aesthetic experience. "To be learning something," he declares,

> is the greatest of pleasures not only to the philosopher but also to the rest of mankind, however small their capacity for it; the reason of the delight in seeing the picture is that one is at the same time learning—gathering the meaning of things, e.g., that the man there is so-and-so.[4]

At first sight this principle seems only to apply to the representative arts. It could, however, easily be transferred to all the other forms. Music itself became a picture of things. Even flute-playing or dancing are, after all, nothing but imitations; for the flute-player or the dancer represents by his rhythms men's characters as well as what they do and suffer.[5] And the whole history of poetics was influenced by the device of Horace, *"ut pictura poesis,"*[6] and by the saying of Simonides, "Painting is mute poetry and poetry a speaking picture." Poetry is differentiated from painting by the mode and means, but not by the general function of imitation.

But it should be observed that the most radical theories of imitation were not intended to restrict the work of art to a merely mechanical reproduction of reality. All of them had to make allowance to a certain extent for the creativeness of the artist. It was not easy to reconcile these two demands. If imitation is the true aim of art, it is clear that the spontaneity, the productive power of the artist is a disturbing rather than a constructive factor. Instead of describing things in their true nature it falsifies the aspect of things. This disturbance introduced by the subjectivity of the artist could not be denied by the classical theories of imitation. But it could be confined within its proper limits and subjected to general rules. Thus the principle *ars simia naturae*[7] could not be maintained in a strict and uncompromising sense. For not even nature itself is infallible, nor does it always attain its end. In such a case art must come to the aid of nature and actually correct or perfect it.

> But Nature mars—wherein she doth resemble
> The craftsman who about his labor goes
> And keeps the knack, although his fingers tremble.[8]

If "all beauty is truth," all truth is not necessarily beauty. In order to reach the highest beauty it is just as essential to deviate from nature as to reproduce nature. To determine the measure, the right proportion, of this deviation, became one of the principal tasks of a theory of art. Aristotle had asserted that for the purposes of poetry a convincing impossibility is preferable to an unconvincing possibility. To the objection of a critic that Zeuxis had painted men such as could never exist in reality, the right answer is that it is *better* they should be like that, for the artist *ought* to improve on his model.[9]

The neoclassicists—from the Italians of the sixteenth century to the work of Abbé Batteux, *Les beaux arts reduits à un même principe* (1747)—took their point of departure from the same principle. Art does not reproduce nature in a general and indiscriminate sense; it reproduces *la belle nature.* But if imitation is the real purpose of art the very concept of any such "beautiful nature" is highly questionable. For how can we improve on our model without disfiguring it? How can we transcend the reality of things without trespassing against the laws of truth? From the point of view of this theory poetry and art in general never can be anything but an agreeable falsity.

The general theory of imitation seemed to hold its ground and to defy all attacks up to the first half of the eighteenth century. But even in the treatise of Batteux, who was perhaps the last resolute champion of this theory,[10] we feel a certain uneasiness with regard to its universal validity. The stumbling block for this theory had always been the phenomenon of lyrical poetry. The arguments by which Batteux attempted to include lyrical poetry under the general scheme of imitative art are weak and inconclusive. And indeed all these superficial arguments were suddenly swept away by the appearance of a new force. Even in the field of aesthetics the name of Rousseau marks a decisive turning point in the general history of ideas. Rousseau rejected the whole classical and neoclassical tradition of the theory of art. To him art is not a description or reproduction of the empirical world but an overflow of emotions and passions. Rousseau's *Nouvelle Héloïse* proved to be a new revolutionary power. The mimetic principle that had prevailed for many centuries had, henceforward, to give way to a new ideal—to the ideal of "characteristic art." From this point we can trace the triumph of a new principle throughout the whole of European literature. In Germany Herder and Goethe followed the ex-

---

[4]*Poetics,* IV. 4–5, p. 51.
[5]*Poetics,* I. 2–5, p. 50.
[6]*Art of Poetry,* p. 73.
[7]"Art copies nature."
[8][Cassirer] Dante, "Paradiso," XII, v. 76. English translation by Melville Best Anderson, *The Divine Comedy* (World Book Co., 1921), p. 357.

[9]*Poetics,* XXV. 17, p. 65.
[10][Cassirer] To be sure, even in the nineteenth century the general theory of imitation still played an important role. It is, for instance, maintained and defended in Taine's *Philosophie de l'art.* [Cassirer did not live to see the results of the work of Crane, McKeon, and the Chicago school.]

ample of Rousseau. Thus the whole theory of beauty had to assume a new shape. Beauty in the traditional sense of the term is by no means the only aim of art; it is in fact but a secondary and derivative feature. "Do not let a misconception come between us"; Goethe admonishes his reader in his paper *Von deutscher Baukunst;*

> do not let the effeminate doctrine of the modern beauty-monger make you too tender to enjoy significant roughness, lest in the end your enfeebled feeling should be able to endure nothing but unmeaning smoothness. They try to make you believe that the fine arts arose from our supposed inclination to beautify the world around us. That is not true. . . .
>
> Art is formative long before it is beautiful, and yet it is then true and great art, very often truer and greater than beautiful art itself. For man has in him a formative nature, which displays itself in activity as soon as his existence is secure; . . . And so the savage remodels with bizarre traits, horrible forms and coarse colors, his "cocos," his feathers, and his own body. And though this imagery consists of the most capricious forms, yet without proportions of shape, its parts will agree together, for a single feeling has created them into a characteristic whole.
>
> Now this characteristic art is the only true art. When it acts on what lies round it from inward, single, individual, original, independent feeling, careless and even ignorant of all that is alien to it, then, whether born of rude savagery or of cultivated sensibility, it is whole and living.[11]

With Rousseau and Goethe there began a new period of aesthetic theory. Characteristic art has gained a definitive victory over imitative art. But in order to understand this characteristic art in its true sense we must avoid a one-sided interpretation. It is not enough to lay the stress upon the emotional side of the work of art. It is true that all characteristic or expressive art is "the spontaneous overflow of powerful feelings." But if we were to accept this Wordsworthian definition without reserve, we should only be led to a change of sign, not to a decisive change of meaning. In this case art would remain reproductive; but, instead of being a reproduc-

tion of things, of physical objects, it would become a reproduction of our inner life, of our affections and emotions. Using once more our analogy with the philosophy of language, we might say that in this case we had only exchanged an onomatopoetic theory of art for an interjectional theory. But this is not the sense in which the term *characteristic art* was understood by Goethe. The passage cited above was written in 1773, in Goethe's youthful *"Sturm und Drang"* period. Yet in no period of his life could he ever neglect the objective pole of his poetry. Art is indeed expressive, but it cannot be expressive without being formative. And this formative process is carried out in a certain sensuous medium. "As soon as he is free from care and fear," writes Goethe, "the demigod, creative in repose, gropes round him for matter into which to breathe his spirit." In many modern aesthetic theories—especially that of Croce and his disciples and followers—this material factor is forgotten or minimized. Croce is interested only in the fact of expression, not in the mode.[12] The mode he takes to be irrelevant both for the character and for the value of the work of art. The only thing which matters is the intuition of the artist, not the embodiment of this intuition in a particular material. The material has a technical but not an aesthetical importance. Croce's philosophy is a philosophy of the spirit emphasizing the purely spiritual character of the work of art. But in his theory the whole spiritual energy is contained and expended in the formation of the intuition alone. When this process is completed the artistic creation has been achieved. What follows is only an external reproduction which is necessary for the communication of the intuition but meaningless with respect to its essence. But for a great painter, a great musician, or a great poet, the colors, the lines, rhythms, and words are not merely a part of his technical apparatus; they are necessary moments of the productive process itself.

This is just as true of the specifically expressive arts as of the representative arts. Even in lyrical poetry emotion is not the only and decisive feature. It is of course true that the great lyrical poets are capable of the deepest emotions and that an artist who is not endowed with powerful feelings will never produce anything except shallow and frivolous art. But from this fact we cannot conclude that the function of lyrical poetry and of art in general can be adequately described as the artist's ability "to make a clean breast of his feelings." "What the artist is trying to do," says R. G. Collingwood, "is to express a given emotion. To express it, and to express it well, are the same thing. . . . Every utterance and every

---

[11][Cassirer] Goethe, "Von deutscher Baukunst," *Werke,* XXXVII, 148 *f.* English translation by Bernard Bosanquet in *Three Lectures on Aesthetic* (London, Macmillan, 1928), pp. 114 *ff.*

[12]See *Aesthetic,* pp. 692–99.

gesture that each one of us makes is a work of art."[13] But here again the whole constructive process which is a prerequisite both of the production and of the contemplation of the work of art is entirely overlooked. Every gesture is no more a work of art than every interjection is an act of speech. Both the gesture and the interjection are deficient in one essential and indispensable feature. They are involuntary and instinctive reactions; they possess no real spontaneity. The moment of purposiveness is necessary for linguistic and artistic expression. In every act of speech and in every artistic creation we find a definite teleological structure. An actor in a drama really "acts" his part. Each individual utterance is a part of a coherent structural whole. The accent and rhythm of his words, the modulation of his voice, the expressions of his face, and the postures of his body all tend to the same end— to the embodiment of human character. All this is not simply "expression"; it is also representation and interpretation. Not even a lyric poem is wholly devoid of this general tendency of art. The lyric poet is not just a man who indulges in displays of feeling. To be swayed by emotion alone is sentimentality, not art. An artist who is absorbed not in the contemplation and creation of forms but rather in his own pleasure or in his enjoyment of "the joy of grief" becomes a sentimentalist. Hence we can hardly ascribe to lyric art a more subjective character than to all the other forms of art. For it contains the same sort of embodiment, and the same process of objectification. "Poetry," wrote Mallarmé, "is not written with ideas, it is written with words."[14] It is written with images, sounds, and rhythms which, just as in the case of dramatic poetry and dramatic representation, coalesce into an indivisible whole. In every great lyrical poem we find this concrete and indivisible unity.

Like all the other symbolic forms art is not the mere reproduction of a ready-made, given reality. It is one of the ways leading to an objective view of things and of human life. It is not an imitation but a discovery of reality. We do not, however, discover nature through art in the same sense in which the scientist uses the term *nature*. Language and science are the two main processes by which we ascertain and determine our concepts of the external world.[15] We must classify our sense perceptions and bring them under general notions and general rules in order to give them an objective meaning. Such classification is the result of a persistent effort toward simplification. The work of art in like manner

implies such an act of condensation and concentration. When Aristotle wanted to describe the real difference between poetry and history he insisted upon this process. What a drama gives us, he asserts, is a single action ($\mu\iota\alpha\ \pi\rho\hat{\alpha}\xi\iota\varsigma$) which is a complete whole in itself, with all the organic unity of a living creature; whereas the historian has to deal not with one action but with one period and all that happened therein to one or more persons, however disconnected the several events may have been.[16]

In this respect beauty as well as truth may be described in terms of the same classical formula: they are "a unity in the manifold." But in the two cases there is a difference of stress. Language and science are abbreviations of reality; art is an intensification of reality. Language and science depend upon one and the same process of abstraction; art may be described as a continuous process of concretion.[17] In our scientific description of a given object we begin with a great number of observations which at first sight are only a loose conglomerate of detached facts. But the farther we proceed the more these individual phenomena tend to assume a definite shape and become a systematic whole. What science is searching for is some central features of a given object from which all its particular qualities may be derived. If a chemist knows the atomic number of a certain element he possesses a clue to a full insight into its structure and constitution. From this number he may deduce all the characteristic properties of the element. But art does not admit of this sort of conceptual simplification and deductive generalization. It does not inquire into the qualities or causes of things; it gives us the intuition of the form of things. But this too is by no means a mere repetition of something we had before. It is a true and genuine discovery. The artist is just as much a discoverer of the forms of nature as the scientist is a discoverer of facts or natural laws. The great artists of all times have been cognizant of this special task and special gift of art. Leonardo da Vinci spoke of the purpose of painting and sculpture in the words *"saper vedere."*[18] According to him the painter and sculptor are the great teachers in the realm of the visible world. For the awareness of pure forms of things is by no means an instinctive gift, a gift of nature. We may have met with an object of our ordinary sense experience a thousand times without ever having "seen" its form. We are still at a loss if asked to describe not its physical qualities or effects but its pure visual shape and structure. It is art that fills this gap. Here we live in the realm of pure forms rather

[13][Cassirer] R. G. Collingwood, *The Principles of Art* (Oxford, Clarendon Press, 1938), pp. 279, 282, 285.
[14]For examples of this attitude see Mallarmé, pp. 672–78.
[15]Cassirer's *Essay on Man* also contains chapters on myth and religion, language, and science as symbolic forms.

[16]*Poetics,* particularly XXIII, p. 62.
[17]See Blake, *Annotations to Reynolds'* Discourses, p. 401.
[18]"To know how to see."

than in that of the analysis and scrutiny of sense objects or the study of their effects.

From a merely theoretical point of view we may subscribe to the words of Kant that mathematics is the "pride of human reason." But for this triumph of scientific reason we have to pay a very high price. Science means abstraction, and abstraction is always an impoverishment of reality. The forms of things as they are described in scientific concepts tend more and more to become mere formulae. These formulae are of a surprising simplicity. A single formula, like the Newtonian law of gravitation, seems to comprise and explain the whole structure of our material universe. It would seem as though reality were not only accessible to our scientific abstractions but exhaustible by them. But as soon as we approach the field of art this proves to be an illusion. For the aspects of things are innumerable, and they vary from one moment to another. Any attempt to comprehend them within a simple formula would be in vain. Heraclitus' saying that the sun is new every day is true for the sun of the artist if not for the sun of the scientist. When the scientist describes an object he characterizes it by a set of numbers, by its physical and chemical constants. Art has not only a different aim but a different object. If we say of two artists that they paint "the same" landscape we describe our aesthetic experience very inadequately. From the point of view of art such a pretended sameness is quite illusory. We cannot speak of one and the same thing as the subject matter of both painters. For the artist does not portray or copy a certain empirical object—a landscape with its hills and mountains, its brooks and rivers. What he gives us is the individual and momentary physiognomy of the landscape. He wishes to express the atmosphere of things, the play of light and shadow. A landscape is not "the same" in early twilight, in midday heat, or on a rainy or sunny day. Our aesthetic perception exhibits a much greater variety and belongs to a much more complex order than our ordinary sense perception. In sense perception we are content with apprehending the common and constant features of the objects of our surroundings. Aesthetic experience is incomparably richer. It is pregnant with infinite possibilities which remain unrealized in ordinary sense experience. In the work of the artist these possibilities become actualities; they are brought into the open and take on a definite shape. The revelation of this inexhaustibility of the aspects of things is one of the great privileges and one of the deepest charms of art.

The painter Ludwig Richter relates in his memoirs how once when he was in Tivoli as a young man he and three friends set out to paint the same landscape. They were all firmly resolved not to deviate from nature; they wished to reproduce what they had seen as accurately as possible. Nevertheless the result was four totally different pictures, as different from one another as the personalities of the artist. From this experience the narrator concluded that there is no such thing as objective vision, and that form and color are always apprehended according to individual temperament.[19] Not even the most determined champions of a strict and uncompromising naturalism could overlook or deny this factor. Émile Zola defines the work of art as *"un coin de la nature vu à travers un tempérament."*[20] What is referred to here as temperament is not merely singularity or idiosyncrasy. When absorbed in the intuition of a great work of art we do not feel a separation between the subjective and the objective worlds. We do not live in our plain commonplace reality of physical things, nor do we live wholly within an individual sphere. Beyond these two spheres we detect a new realm, the realm of plastic, musical, poetical forms; and these forms have a real universality. Kant distinguishes sharply between what he calls *"aesthetic* universality" and the "objective validity" which belongs to our local and scientific judgments.[21] In our aesthetic judgments, he contends, we are not concerned with the object as such but with the pure contemplation of the object. Aesthetic universality means that the predicate of beauty is not restricted to a special individual but extends over the whole field of judging subjects. If the work of art were nothing but the freak and frenzy of an individual artist it would not possess this universal communicability. The imagination of the artist does not arbitrarily invent the forms of things. It shows us these forms in their true shape, making them visible and recognizable. The artist chooses a certain aspect of reality, but this process of selection is at the same time a process of objectification. Once we have entered into his perspective we are forced to look on the world with his eyes. It would seem as if we had never before seen the world in this peculiar light. Yet we are convinced that this light is not merely a momentary flash. By virtue of the work of art it has become durable and permanent. Once reality has been disclosed to us in this particular way, we continue to see it in this shape.

A sharp distinction between the objective and the subjective, the representative and the expressive arts is thus difficult to maintain. The Parthenon frieze or a Mass by Bach, Michelangelo's Sistine Chapel or a poem of Leopardi, a so-

---

[19][Cassirer] I take this account from Heinrich Wölfflin's *Principles of Art History*.

[20]"A corner of nature seen through a temperament."

[21][Cassirer] In Kant's terminology the former is called *Gemeingültigkeit* whereas the latter is called *Allgemeingültigkeit*—a distinction which is difficult to render in corresponding English terms. For a systematic interpretation of the two terms see H. W. Cassirer, *A Commentary on Kant's "Critique of Judgment"* (London, 1938), pp. 190 *ff.*

nata of Beethoven or a novel of Dostoevski are neither merely representative nor merely expressive. They are symbolic in a new and deeper sense. The works of the great lyrical poets—of Goethe or Hölderlin, of Wordsworth or Shelley—do not give us *disjecti membra poetae,* scattered and incoherent fragments of the poet's life. They are not simply a momentary outburst of passionate feeling; they reveal a deep unity and continuity. The great tragic and comic writers on the other hand—Euripides and Shakespeare, Cervantes and Molière—do not entertain us with detached scenes from the spectacle of life. Taken in themselves these scenes are but fugitive shadows. But suddenly we begin to see behind these shadows and to envisage a new reality. Through his characters and actions the comic and the tragic poet reveals his view of human life as a whole, of its greatness and weakness, its sublimity and its absurdity. "Art," wrote Goethe,

> does not undertake to emulate nature in its breadth and depth. It sticks to the surface of natural phenomena; but it has its own depth, its own power; it crystallizes the highest moments of these superficial phenomena by recognizing in them the character of lawfulness, the perfection of harmonious proportion, the summit of beauty, the dignity of significance, the height of passion.[22]

This fixation of the "highest moments of phenomena" is neither an imitation of physical things nor a mere overflow of powerful feelings. It is an interpretation of reality—not by concepts but by intuitions; not through the medium of thought but through that of sensuous forms.

From Plato to Tolstoy art has been accused of exciting our emotions and thus of disturbing the order and harmony of our moral life. Poetical imagination, according to Plato, waters our experience of lust and anger, of desire and pain, and makes them grow when they ought to starve with drought.[23] Tolstoy sees in art a source of infection. "Not only is infection," he says, "a sign of art, but the degree of infectiousness is also the sole measure of excellence in art."[24] But the flaw in this theory is obvious. Tolstoy suppresses a fundamental moment of art, the moment of form. The aesthetic experience—the experience of contemplation—is a different state of mind from the coolness of our theoretical and the sobriety of our moral judgment. It is filled with the liveliest energies of passion, but passion itself is here transformed both in its nature and in its meaning. Wordsworth defines poetry as "emotion recollected in tranquility."[25] But the tranquility we feel in great poetry is not that of recollection. The emotions aroused by the poet do not belong to a remote past. They are "here"—alive and immediate. We are aware of their full strength, but this strength tends in a new direction. It is rather seen than immediately felt. Our passions are no longer dark and impenetrable powers; they become, as it were, transparent. Shakespeare never gives us an aesthetic theory. He does not speculate about the nature of art. Yet in the only passage in which he speaks of the character and function of dramatic art the whole stress is laid upon this point. "The purpose of playing," as Hamlet explains, "both at the first and now, was and is, to hold as 'twere, the mirror up to nature; to show virtue her own feature, scorn her own image, and the very age and body of the time his form and pressure."[26] But the image of a passion is not the passion itself. The poet who represents a passion does not infect us with this passion. At a Shakespeare play we are not infected with the ambition of Macbeth, with the cruelty of Richard III, or with the jealousy of Othello. We are not at the mercy of these emotions; we look through them; we seem to penetrate into their very nature and essence. In this respect Shakespeare's theory of dramatic art, if he had such a theory, is in complete agreement with the conception of the fine arts of the great painters and sculptors of the Renaissance. He would have subscribed to the words of Leonardo da Vinci that *saper vedere* is the highest gift of the artist. The great painters show us the forms of outward things; the great dramatists show us the forms of our inner life. Dramatic art discloses a new breadth and depth of life. It conveys an awareness of human things and human destinies, of human greatness and misery, in comparison to which our ordinary existence appears poor and trivial. All of us feel, vaguely and dimly, the infinite potentialities of life, which silently await the moment when they are to be called forth from dormancy into the clear and intense light of consciousness. It is not the degree of infection but the degree of intensification and illumination which is the measure of the excellence of art.

If we accept this view of art we can come to a better understanding of a problem first encountered in the Aristotelian theory of catharsis. We need not enter here into all the difficulties of the Aristotelian term or into the innumerable efforts of the commentators to clear up these difficulties.[27]

[22][Cassirer] Goethe, Notes to a translation of Diderot's "Essai sur la peinture," *Werke,* XLV, 260.
[23]See *Republic,* pp. 24–25.
[24]See *What Is Art?* p. 680, for remarks on infection.

[25]See Preface to the *Lyrical Ballads,* p. 444.
[26]III. ii. 22–27.
[27][Cassirer] For details see Jakob Bernays, *Zwei Abhandlungen über die Aristotelische Theorie des Dramas* (Berlin, 1880) and Ingram Bywater, *Aristotle on the Art of Poetry* (Oxford, 1909), pp. 152 *ff.*

What seems to be clear and what is now generally admitted is that the cathartic process described by Aristotle does not mean a purification or a change in the character and quality of the passions themselves but a change in the human soul. By tragic poetry the soul acquires a new attitude toward its emotions. The soul experiences the emotions of pity and fear, but instead of being disturbed and disquieted by them it is brought to a state of rest and peace. At first sight this would seem to be a contradiction. For what Aristotle looks upon as the effect of tragedy is a synthesis of two moments which in real life, in our practical existence, exclude each other. The highest intensification of our emotional life is thought of as at the same time giving us a sense of repose. We live through all our passions feeling their full range and highest tension. But what we leave behind when passing the threshold of art is the hard pressure, the compulsion of our emotions. The tragic poet is not the slave but the master of his emotions; and he is able to transfer this mastery to the spectators. In his work we are not swayed and carried away by our emotions. Aesthetic freedom is not the absence of passions, not Stoic apathy, but just the contrary. It means that our emotional life acquires its greatest strength, and that in this very strength it changes its form. For here we no longer live in the immediate reality of things but in a world of pure sensuous forms. In this world all our feelings undergo a sort of transubstantiation with respect to their essence and their character. The passions themselves are relieved of their material burden. We feel their form and their life but not their encumbrance. The calmness of the work of art is, paradoxically, a dynamic, not a static calmness. Art gives us the motions of the human soul in all their depth and variety. But the form, the measure and rhythm, of these motions is not comparable to any single state of emotion. What we feel in art is not a simple or single emotional quality. It is the dynamic process of life itself—the continuous oscillation between opposite poles, between joy and grief, hope and fear, exultation and despair. To give aesthetic form to our passions is to transform them into a free and active state. In the work of the artist the power of passion itself has been made a formative power.

It may be objected that all this applies to the artist but not to ourselves, the spectators and auditors. But such an objection would imply a misunderstanding of the artistic process. Like the process of speech the artistic process is a dialogical and dialectic one. Not even the spectator is left to a merely passive role. We cannot understand a work of art without, to a certain degree, repeating and reconstructing the creative process by which it has come into being. By the nature of this creative process the passions themselves are turned into actions. If in real life we had to endure all those emotions through which we live in Sophocles' *Oedipus* or in Shakespeare's *King Lear* we should scarcely survive the shock and strain. But art turns all these pains and outrages, these cruelties and atrocities, into a means of self-liberation, thus giving us an inner freedom which cannot be attained in any other way.

The attempt to characterize a work of art by some particular emotional feature must, therefore, inevitably fail to do it justice. If what art tries to express is no special state but the very dynamic process of our inner life, then any such qualification could hardly be more than perfunctory and superficial. Art must always give us motion rather than mere emotion. Even the distinction between tragic and comic art is much more a conventional than a necessary one. It relates to the content and motives but not to the form and essence of art. Plato had long since denied the existence of these artificial and traditional boundaries. At the end of the *Symposium* he describes Socrates as engaged in a conversation with Agathon, the tragic poet, and Aristophanes, the comic poet. Socrates compels the two poets to admit that the true tragedian is the true artist in comedy, and vice versa.[28] A commentary on this passage is given in the *Philebus*. In comedy as well in tragedy, Plato maintains in this dialogue, we always experience a mixed feeling of pleasure and pain. In this the poet follows the rules of nature itself since he portrays "the whole comedy and tragedy of life."[29] In every great poem—in Shakespeare's plays, in Dante's *Commedia,* in Goethe's *Faust*—we must indeed pass through the whole gamut of human emotions. If we were unable to grasp the most delicate nuances of the different shades of feeling, unable to follow the continuous variations in rhythm and tone, if unmoved by sudden dynamic changes, we could not understand and feel the poem. We may speak of the individual temperament of the artist, but the work of art, as such, has no special temperament. We cannot subsume it under any traditional psychological class concept. To speak of Mozart's music as cheerful or serene, of Beethoven's as grave, somber, or sublime would betray an unpenetrating taste. Here too the distinction between tragedy and comedy becomes irrelevant. The question whether Mozart's *Don Giovanni* is a tragedy or an *opera buffa*[30] is scarcely worth answering. Beethoven's composition based on Schiller's *Hymn to Joy* expresses the highest degree of exultation. But when listening to it we do not for a moment forget the tragic accents of the Ninth Symphony. All these contrasts must be

---

[28][Cassirer] Plato, *Symposium,* 223 (Jowett translation).
[29][Cassirer] *Philebus,* 48 *ff.* (Jowett translation).
[30]"Comic opera."

present and they must be felt in their full strength. In our aesthetic experience they coalesce into one indivisible whole. What we hear is the whole scale of human emotions from the lowest to the highest note; it is the motion and vibration of our whole being. The greatest comedians themselves can by no means give us an easy beauty. Their work is often filled with great bitterness. Aristophanes is one of the sharpest and sternest critics of human nature; Moliére is nowhere greater than in his *Misanthrope* or *Tartuffe*. Nevertheless the bitterness of the great comic writers is not the acerbity of the satirist or the severity of the moralist. It does not lead to a moral verdict upon human life. Comic art possesses in the highest degree that faculty shared by all art, sympathetic vision. By virtue of this faculty it can accept human life with all its defects and foibles, its follies and vices. Great comic art has always been a sort of *encomium moriae*, a praise of folly. In comic perspective all things begin to take on a new face. We are perhaps never nearer to our human world than in the works of a great comic writer—in Cervantes' *Don Quixote,* Sterne's *Tristram Shandy,* or in Dickens' *Pickwick Papers.* We become observant of the minutest details; we see this world in all its narrowness, its pettiness, and silliness. We live in this restricted world, but we are no longer imprisoned by it. Such is the peculiar character of the comic catharsis. Things and events begin to lose their material weight; scorn is dissolved into laughter and laughter is liberation.

That beauty is not an immediate property of things that it necessarily involves a relation to the human mind, is a point which seems to be admitted by almost all aesthetic theories. In his essay *Of the Standard of Taste* Hume declares: "Beauty is no quality in things themselves: it exists merely in the mind which contemplates them."[31] But this statement is ambiguous. If we understand *mind* in Hume's own sense, and think of self as nothing but a bundle of impressions, it would be very difficult to find in such a bundle that predicate which we call beauty. Beauty cannot be defined by its mere *percipi,* as "being perceived"; it must be defined in terms of an activity of the mind, of the function of perceiving and by a characteristic direction of this function. It does not consist of passive percepts; it is a mode, a process of perceptualization. But this process is not merely subjective in character; on the contrary, it is one of the conditions of our intuition of an objective world. The artistic eye is not a passive eye that receives and registers the impression of things. It is a constructive eye, and it is only by constructive acts that we can discover the beauty of natural things. The sense of beauty is

the susceptibility to the dynamic life of forms, and this life cannot be apprehended except by a corresponding dynamic process in ourselves.

To be sure, in the various aesthetic theories this polarity, which as we have seen is an inherent condition of beauty, has led to diametrically opposed interpretations. According to Albrecht Dürer the real gift of the artist is to "elicit" beauty from nature. *"Denn wahrhaftig steckt die Kunst in der Natur, wer sie heraus kann reissen, der hat sie."*[32] On the other hand we find spiritualistic theories which deny any connection between the beauty of art and the so-called beauty of nature. The beauty of nature is understood as merely a metaphor. Croce thinks it sheer rhetoric to speak of a beautiful river or tree.[33] Nature to him is stupid when compared with art; she is mute save when man makes her speak. The contradiction between these conceptions may perhaps be resolved by distinguishing sharply between organic beauty and aesthetic beauty. There are many natural beauties with no specific aesthetic character. The organic beauty of a landscape is not the same as that aesthetic beauty which we feel in the works of the great landscape painters. Even we, the spectators, are fully aware of this difference. I may walk through a landscape and feel its charms. I may enjoy the mildness of the air, the freshness of the meadows, the variety and cheerfulness of the coloring, and the fragrant odor of the flowers. But I may then experience a sudden change in my frame of mind. Thereupon I see the landscape with an artist's eye—I begin to form a picture of it. I have now entered a new realm—the realm not of living things but of "living forms." No longer in the immediate reality of things, I live now in the rhythm of spatial forms, in the harmony and contrast of colors, in the balance of light and shadow. In such absorption in the dynamic aspect of form consists the aesthetic experience.

II

All the controversies between the various aesthetic schools may in a sense be reduced to one point. What all these schools have to admit is that art is an independent "universe of discourse." Even the most radical defenders of a strict realism who wished to limit art to a mimetic function alone have had to make allowance for the specific power of the artistic imagination. But the various schools differed widely

---

[31]P. 309.

[32][Cassirer] "For art standeth firmly fixed in nature—and who can rend her from thence, he only possesseth her." See William M. Conway, *Literary Remains of Albrecht Dürer* (1889), p. 182.
[33]*Aesthetic,* Chapter 13.

in their evaluation of this power. The classical and neoclassical theories did not encourage the free play of imagination. From their point of view the imagination of the artist is a great but rather questionable gift. Boileau himself did not deny that, psychologically speaking, the gift of imagination is indispensable for every true poet.[34] But if the poet indulges in the mere play of this natural impulse and instinctive power, he will never achieve perfection. The poet's imagination must be guided and controlled by reason and subjected to its rules. Even when deviating from the natural the poet must respect the laws of reason, and these laws restrict him to the field of the probable. French classicism defined this field in purely objective terms. The dramatic unities of space and time became physical facts measurable by a linear standard or by a clock.

An entirely different conception of the character and function of poetic imagination was introduced by the Romantic theory of art. This theory is not the work of the so-called "romantic school" in Germany. It had been developed much earlier and had begun to play a decisive role in both French and English literature during the eighteenth century. One of the best and most concise expressions of this theory is to be found in Edward Young's *Conjectures on Original Composition* (1759). "The pen of an original writer," says Young, "like Armida's wand out of a barren waste calls a blooming spring."[35] From this time on the classical views of the probable were supplanted more and more by their opposite. The marvelous and miraculous are now believed to be the only subjects that admit of true poetical portraiture. In eighteenth-century aesthetics we can trace step by step the rise of this new ideal. The Swiss critics Bodmer and Breitinger appeal to Milton in justification of the "wonderful in poetry."[36] The wonderful gradually outweighs and eclipses the probable as a literary subject. The new theory seemed to be embodied in the works of the greatest poets. Shakespeare himself had illustrated it in his description of the poet's imagination.

The lunatic, the lover, and the poet
Are of imagination all compact.
One sees more devils than vast hell can hold,
That is the madman; the lover, all as frantic,
Sees Helen's beauty in a brow of Egypt.
The poet's eye, in a fine frenzy rolling,
Doth glance from heaven to earth, from earth to heaven;
And, as imagination bodies forth

The forms of things unknown, the poet's pen
Turns them to shapes, and gives to airy nothing
A local habitation and a name.[37]

Yet the Romantic conception of poetry found no solid support in Shakespeare. If we stood in need of proof that the world of the artist is not a merely "fantastic" universe, we could find no better, no more classical, witness than Shakespeare. The light in which he sees nature and human life is no mere "fancy light in fancy caught." But there is still another form of imagination with which poetry seems to be indissolubly connected. When Vico made his first systematic attempt to create a "logic of the imagination" he turned back to the world of myth.[38] He speaks of three different ages: the age of gods, the age of heroes, and the age of man. It is in the two former ages, he declared, that we have to look for the true origin of poetry. Mankind could not begin with abstract thought or with a rational language. It had to pass through the era of the symbolic language of myth and poetry. The first nations did not think in concepts but in poetic images; they spoke in fables and wrote in hieroglyphs. The poet and the maker of myth seem, indeed, to live in the same world. They are endowed with the same fundamental power, the power of personification. They cannot contemplate any object without giving to it an inner life and a personal shape. The modern poet often looks back at the mystical, the "divine" or "heroic" ages, as at a lost paradise. In his poem *The Gods of Greece* Schiller expressed this feeling. He wished to recall the times of the Greek poets, for whom myth was not an empty allegory but a living power. The poet yearns for this golden age of poetry in which all things were still full of gods, in which every hill was the dwelling place of an oread, every tree the home of a dryad.

But this complaint of the modern poet appears to be unfounded. For it is one of the greatest privileges of art that it can never lose this "divine age." Here the source of imaginative creation never dries up, for it is indestructible and inexhaustible. In every age and in every great artist the operation of the imagination reappears in new forms and in new force. In the lyrical poets, first and foremost, we feel this continuous rebirth and regeneration. They cannot touch a thing without imbuing it with their own inner life. Wordsworth has described this gift as the inherent power of his poetry:

To every natural form, rock, fruits or flower,
Even the loose stones that cover the highway,

---

[34]See *The Art of Poetry,* pp. 244 and 249.
[35]P. 330.
[36][Cassirer] Cf. Bodmer and Breitinger, *Diskurse der Maler* (1721–23).

[37]*A Midsummer Night's Dream,* V. i. 7–17.
[38]See *The New Science,* p. 290.

I gave a moral life: I saw them feel,
Or linked them to some feeling: the great mass
Lay imbedded in a quickening soul, and all
That I beheld respired with inward meaning.[39]

But with these powers of invention and of universal animation we are only in the anteroom of art. The artist must not only feel the "inward meaning" of things and their moral life, he must externalize his feelings. The highest and most characteristic power of artistic imagination appears in this latter act. Externalization[40] means visible or tangible embodiment not simply in a particular material medium—in clay, bronze, or marble—but in sensuous forms, in rhythms, in color pattern, in lines and design, in plastic shapes. It is the structure, the balance and order, of these forms which affect us in the work of art. Every art has is own characteristic idiom, which is unmistakable and unexchangeable. The idioms of the various arts may be interconnected, as, for instance, when a lyric is set to music or a poem is illustrated; but they are not translatable into each other. Each idiom has a special task to fulfill in the "architectonic" of art. "The problems of form arising from this architectonic structure," states Adolf Hildebrand,

> though they are not given us immediately and self-evidently by nature, are yet the true problems of art. Material acquired through a direct study of nature is, by the architectonic process, transformed into an artistic unity. When we speak of the imitative aspect of art, we are referring to material which has not yet been developed in this manner. Through architectonic development, then, sculpture and painting emerge from the sphere of mere naturalism into the realm of true art.[41]

Even in poetry we find this architectonic development. Without it poetical imitation or invention would lose its force. The horrors of Dante's "Inferno" would remain unalleviated horrors, the raptures of his "Paradiso" would be visionary dreams were they not molded into a new shape by the magic of Dante's diction and verse.

In his theory of tragedy Aristotle stressed the invention of the tragic plot. Of all the necessary ingredients of tragedy—spectacle, characters, fable, diction, melody, and

thought—he thought the combination of the incidents of the story (ἡ τῶν πραγμάτων σύστασις) the most important. For tragedy is essentially an imitation not of persons but of action and life. In a play the persons do not act in order to portray the characters; the characters are represented for the sake of the action. A tragedy is impossible without action, but there may be tragedy without character.[42] French classicism adopted and emphasized this Aristotelian theory. Corneille in the prefaces to his plays everywhere insists upon this point. He speaks with pride of his tragedy *Heraclius* because here the plot was so complicated that it needed a special intellectual effort to understand and unravel it. It is clear, however, that this sort of intellectual activity and intellectual pleasure is no necessary element of the artistic process. To enjoy the plots of Shakespeare—to follow with the keenest interest "the combination of the incidents of the story" in *Othello, Macbeth,* or *Lear*—does not necessarily mean that one understands and feels the tragic art of Shakespeare. Without Shakespeare's language, without the power of his dramatic diction, all this would remain unimpressive. The context of a poem cannot be separated from its form—from the verse, the melody, the rhythm. These formal elements are not merely external or technical means to reproduce a given intuition; they are part and parcel of the artistic intuition itself.

In Romantic thought the theory of poetic imagination had reached its climax. Imagination is no longer that special human activity which builds up the human world of art. It now has universal metaphysical value. Poetic imagination is the only clue to reality. Fichte's idealism is based upon his conception of "productive imagination." Schelling declared in his *System of Transcendental Idealism* that art is the consummation of philosophy. In nature, in morality, in history we are still living in the propylaeum of philosophical wisdom; in art we enter into the sanctuary itself. Romantic writers in both verse and prose expressed themselves in the same vein. The distinction between poetry and philosophy was felt to be shallow and superficial. According to Friedrich Schlegel the highest task of a modern poet is to strive after a new form of poetry which he describes as "transcendental poetry." No other poetic genre can give us the essence of the poetic spirit, the "poetry of poetry."[43] To poeticize philosophy and to philosophize poetry—such was the highest aim of all the Romantic thinkers. The true poem is not the work of the individual artist; it is the universe itself, the one work

---

[39]*Prelude*, III, 127–32.
[40]See Croce, *Aesthetic,* Chapter 15.
[41][Cassirer] Adolf Hildebrand, *Das Problem der Form in der bildenden Kunst.* English translation by Max Meyer and R. M. Ogden, *The Problem of Form in Painting and Sculpture* (New York, G. E. Stechert Co., 1907), p. 12.

[42]*Poetics* VI, 7–17, pp. 53–54. Aristotle does not say there may be tragedy without character.
[43][Cassirer] Cf. Schlegel, *Athenäumsfragmente,* 238, in *Prosaische Jugendschriften,* ed. by J. Minor (2nd ed. Vienna, 1906), II, 242.

of art which is forever perfecting itself. Hence all the deepest mysteries of all the arts and sciences appertain to poetry.[44] "Poetry," said Novalis, "is what is absolutely and genuinely real. That is the kernel of my philosophy. The more poetic, the more true."[45]

By this conception poetry and art seemed to be elevated to a rank and dignity they had never before possessed. They became a *novum organum* for discovering the wealth and depth of the universe. Nevertheless this exuberant and ecstatic praise of poetic imagination had its strict limitations. In order to achieve their metaphysical aim the Romanticists had to make a serious sacrifice. The infinite had been declared to be the true, indeed the only, subject of art. The beautiful was conceived as a symbolic representation of the infinite. He can only be an artist, according to Friedrich Schlegel, who has a religion of his own, an original conception of the infinite.[46] But in this event what becomes of our finite world, the world of sense experience? Clearly this world as such has no claim to beauty. Over against the true universe, the universe of the poet and artist, we find our common and prosaic world deficient in all poetic beauty. A dualism of this kind is an essential feature in all Romantic theories of art. When Goethe began to publish *Wilhelm Meister's Lehrjahre* the first Romantic critics hailed the work with extravagant expressions of enthusiasm. Novalis saw in Goethe "the incarnation of the poetic spirit on earth." But as the work continued, as the Romantic figure of Mignon and the harpist were overshadowed by more realistic characters and more prosaic events, Novalis grew deeply disappointed. He not only revoked his first judgment; he went so far as to call Goethe a traitor to the cause of poetry. *Wilhelm Meister* came to be looked upon as a satire, a "*Candide* against poetry." When poetry loses sight of the wonderful, it loses its significance and justification. Poetry cannot thrive in our trivial and commonplace world. The miraculous, the marvelous, and the mysterious are the only subjects that admit of a truly poetic treatment.

This conception of poetry is, however, rather a qualification and limitation than a genuine account of the creative process of art. Curiously enough the great realists of the nineteenth century had in this respect a keener insight into the art process than their Romantic adversaries. They maintained a radical and uncompromising naturalism. But it was precisely this naturalism which led them to a more profound conception of artistic form. Denying the "pure forms" of the idealistic schools they concentrated upon the material aspect of things. By virtue of this sheer concentration they were able to overcome the conventional dualism between the poetic and the prosaic spheres. The nature of a work of art, according to the realists, does not depend on the greatness or smallness of its subject matter. No subject whatever is impermeable to the formative energy of art. One of the greatest triumphs of art is to make us see commonplace things in their real shape and in their true light. Balzac plunged into the most trifling features of the "human comedy," Flaubert made profound analyses of the meanest characters. In some of Émile Zola's novels we discover minute descriptions of the structure of a locomotive, of a department store, or of a coal mine. No technical detail, however insignificant, was omitted from these accounts. Nevertheless, running through the works of all these realists great imaginative power is observable, which is by no means inferior to that of the Romantic writers. The fact that this power could not be openly acknowledged was a serious drawback to the naturalistic theories of art. In their attempts to refute the Romantic conceptions of a transcendental poetry they reverted to the old definition of art as an imitation of nature.[47] In so doing they missed the principal point, since they failed to recognize the symbolic character of art. If such a characterization of art were admitted, there seemed to be no escape from the metaphysical theories of Romanticism. Art is, indeed, symbolism, but the symbolism of art must be understood in an immanent, not in a transcendent sense. Beauty is "the infinite finitely presented" according to Schelling.[48] The real subject of art is not, however, the metaphysical infinite of Schelling, nor is it the absolute of Hegel.[49] It is to be sought in certain fundamental structural elements of our sense experience itself—in lines, design, in architectural, musical forms. These elements are, so to speak, omnipresent. Free of all mystery, they are patent and unconcealed; they are visible, audible, tangible. In this sense Goethe did not hesitate to say that art does not pretend to show the metaphysical depth of things, it merely sticks to the surface of natural phenomena. But this surface is not immediately given. We do not know it before we discover it in the works of the great artists. This discovery, however, is not confined to a special field. To the extent that human language can express everything, the lowest and the highest things, art can embrace and pervade the whole sphere of human experience. Nothing in the physical or moral world, no natural thing and no human action, is by its

[44][Cassirer] Schlegel, *Gespräch über die Poesie* (1800), *op. cit.,* II, 364.

[45][Cassirer] Novalis, ed. J. Minor, III, II. Cf. O. Walzel, *German Romanticism,* English translation by Alma E. Lussky (New York, 1932), p. 28.

[46][Cassirer] *Ideen,* 18, in *Prosaische Jugendschriften,* II, 290.

[47]See Zola, *The Experimental Novel,* pp. 654–55.

[48]See *The Statesman's Manual,* also Coleridge, p. 476, and Carlyle, *Symbols,* pp. 546–49.

[49]See *The Philosophy of Fine Art,* pp. 534–45.

nature and essence excluded from the realm of art, because nothing resists its formative and creative process. *"Quicquid essentia dignum est,"* says Bacon in his *Novum Organum, "id etiam scientia dignum est."*[50] This dictum holds for art as well as for science.

III

The psychological theories of art have a clear and palpable advantage over all the metaphysical theories. They are not obliged to give a general theory of beauty. They limit themselves to a narrower compass, for they are concerned only with the fact of beauty and with a descriptive analysis of this fact. The first task of psychological analysis is to determine the class of phenomena to which our experience of beauty belongs. This problem entails no difficulty. No one could ever deny that the work of art gives us the highest pleasure, perhaps the most durable and intense pleasure of which human nature is capable. As soon as we choose this psychological approach the secret of art seems, therefore, to be solved. There is nothing less mysterious than pleasure and pain. To call into question these best-known phenomena— phenomena not merely of human life but of life in general— would be absurd. Here if anywhere we find a δός μοί ποῦ σῖω, a fixed and immovable place to stand. If we succeed in connecting our aesthetic experience with this point there can no longer be any uncertainty as to the character of beauty and art.

The utter simplicity of this solution appears to recommend it. On the other hand all the theories of aesthetic hedonism have the defects of their qualities. They begin with the statement of a simple, undeniable, obvious fact; but after the first few steps they fall short of their purpose and come to a sudden standstill. Pleasure is an immediate datum of our experience. But when taken as a psychological principle its meaning becomes vague and ambiguous in the extreme. The term extends over such a large field as to cover the most diverse and heterogeneous phenomena. It is always tempting to introduce a general term broad enough to include the most disparate references. Yet if we yield to this temptation we are in danger of losing sight of significant and important differences. The systems of ethical and aesthetic hedonism have always been prone to obliterate these specific differences. Kant stresses this point in a characteristic remark in the *Critique of Practical Reason.* If the determination of our will, Kang argues, rests upon the feeling of agreeableness or dis-

agreeableness which we expect from any cause, then it is all the same to us by what sort of ideas we are to be affected. The only thing that concerns us in making our choice is how great, how long continued, how easily obtained, and how often repeated this agreeableness is.

> Just as to the man who wants money to spend, it is all the same whether the gold was dug out of the mountain or washed out of the sand, provided it is everywhere accepted at the same value; so the man who cares only for the enjoyment of life does not ask whether the ideas are of the understanding or of the senses, but only *how much* and *how great* pleasure they will give us for the longest time.[51]

If a pleasure is the common denominator it is only the degree, not the kind, which really matters—all pleasures whatever are on the same level and may be traced back to a common psychological and biological origin.

In contemporary thought the theory of aesthetic hedonism has found its clearest expression in the philosophy of Santayana. According to Santayana beauty is pleasure regarded as a quality of things; it is "pleasure objectified." But this is begging the question. For how can pleasure—the most subjective state of our mind—ever be objectified? Science, says Santayana, "is the response to the demand for information, and in it we ask for the whole truth and nothing but the truth. Art is the response to the demand for entertainment, . . . and truth enters into it only as it subserves these ends."[52] But if this were the end of art we should be bound to say that art, in its highest achievements, fails to attain its real end. The "demand for entertainment" may be satisfied by much better and cheaper means. To think that the great artists worked for this purpose, that Michelangelo constructed Saint Peter's Cathedral, that Dante or Milton wrote their poems, for the sake of entertainment, is impossible. They would undoubtedly have subscribed to Aristotle's dictum that "to exert oneself and work for the sake of amusement seems silly and utterly childish."[53] If art is enjoyment it is not the enjoyment of things but the enjoyment of forms. Delight in forms is quite different from delight in things or sense impressions. Forms cannot simply be impressed on our minds; we must produce them in order to feel their beauty. It is a common flaw of all the ancient and modern

---

[50][Cassirer] Bacon, *Novum Organum,* Liber I, Aphor. CXX.

[51][Cassirer] *Critique of Practical Reason,* translated by T. K. Abbott (6th ed., New York, Longmans, Green & Co., 1927), p. 110.
[52][Cassirer] *The Sense of Beauty* (New York, Charles Scribner's Sons, 1896), p. 22.
[53][Cassirer] Aristotle, *Nicomachean Ethics,* 1776ᵇ 33.

systems of aesthetic hedonism that they offer us a psychological theory of aesthetic pleasure which completely fails to account for the fundamental fact of aesthetic creativeness. In aesthetic life we experience a radical transformation. Pleasure itself is no longer a mere affection; it becomes a function. For the artist's eye is not simply an eye that reacts to or reproduces sense impressions. Its activity is not confined to receiving or registering the impressions of outward things or to combining these impressions in new and arbitrary ways. A great painter or musician is not characterized by his sensitiveness to color or sounds but by his power to elicit from his static material a dynamic life of forms. Only in this sense, then, can the pleasure we find in art be objectified. To define beauty as "pleasure objectified" contains, therefore, the whole problem in a nutshell. Objectification is always a constructive process. The physical world—the world of constant things and qualities—is not mere bundle of sense data, nor is the world of art a bundle of feelings and emotions. The first depends upon acts of theoretical objectification, objectification by concepts and scientific constructs; the second upon formative acts of a different type, acts of contemplation.

Other modern theories protesting against all attempts to identify art and pleasure lie open to the same objection as the theories of aesthetic hedonism. They try to find the explanation of the work of art by connecting it with other well-known phenomena. These phenomena are, however, on an entirely different level; they are passive, not active states of mind. Between the two classes we may find some analogies but we cannot trace them back to one and the same metaphysical or psychological origin. It is the struggles against the rationalist and intellectualist theories of art which is a common feature and a fundamental motive of these theories. French classicism had in a sense turned the work of art into an arithmetical problem which was to be solved by a sort of rule of three. The reaction against this conception was necessary and beneficial. But the first Romantic critics—especially the German Romanticists—went immediately to the opposite extreme. They declared the abstract intellectualism of the enlightenment to be a travesty upon art. We cannot understand the work of art by subjecting it to logical rules. A textbook on poetics cannot teach us how to write a good poem. For art arises from other and deeper sources. In order to discover these sources we must first forget our common standards; we must plunge into the mysteries of our unconscious life. The artist is a sort of somnambulist who must pursue his way without the interference or control of any conscious activity. To awake him would be to destroy his power. "It is the beginning of all poetry," said Friedrich Schlegel, "to abolish the law and method of the rationally

proceeding reason and to plunge us once more into the ravishing confusion of fantasy, the original chaos of human nature."[54] Art is a waking dream to which we voluntarily surrender ourselves. This same Romantic conception has left its mark upon contemporary metaphysical systems. Bergson gave a theory of beauty which was intended as the last and most conclusive proof of his general metaphysical principles. According to him there is no better illustration of the fundamental dualism, of the incompatibility, of intuition with reason than the work of art. What we call rational or scientific truth is superficial and conventional. Art is the escape from this shallow and narrow conventional world. It leads us back to the very sources of reality. If reality is "creative evolution" it is in the creativeness of art that we must seek the evidence for and the fundamental manifestation of the creativeness of life. At first sight this would appear to be a truly dynamic or energetic philosophy of beauty. But the intuition of Bergson is not a really active principle. It is a mode of receptivity, not of spontaneity. Aesthetic intuition, too, is everywhere described by Bergson as a passive capability, not as an active form. ". . . the object of art," writes Bergson,

> is to put to sleep the active or rather resistant powers of our personality, and thus to bring us into a state of perfect responsiveness, in which we realize the idea that is suggested to us and sympathize with the feeling that is expressed. In the processes of art we shall find, in a weakened form, a refined and in some measure spiritualized version of the processes commonly used to induce the state of hypnosis. . . . The feeling of the beautiful is no specific feeling . . . every feeling experienced by us will assume an aesthetic character, provided that it has been *suggested,* and not *caused.* . . . There are thus distinct phases in the progress of an aesthetic feeling, as in the state of hypnosis . . .[55]

Our experience of beauty is not, however, of such a hypnotic character. By hypnosis we may prompt a man to certain actions or we may force upon him some sentiment. But beauty, in its genuine and specific sense, cannot be impressed upon our minds in this way. In order to feel it one must cooperate with the artist. One must not only sympathize with the ar-

---

[54][Cassirer] For a fuller documentation and for a criticism of these early Romantic theories of art see Irving Babbitt, *The New Laokoön,* Chapter 4.

[55][Cassirer] Bergson, *Essai sur les données immédiates de la conscience.* English translation by R. L. Pogson, *Time and Free Will* (London, Macmillan, 1912), pp. 14 *ff.*

tist's feelings but also enter into his creative activity. If the artist should succeed in putting to sleep the active powers of our personality he would paralyze our sense of beauty. The apprehension of beauty, the awareness of the dynamism of forms, cannot be communicated in this way. For beauty depends both on feelings of a specific kind and on an act of judgment and contemplation.

One of the great contributions of Shaftesbury to the theory of art was his insistence on this point. In his *Moralists* he gives an impressive account of the experience of beauty—an experience which he regarded as a specific privilege of human nature. "Nor will you deny beauty," writes Shaftesbury,

> to the wild field, or to these flowers which grow around us, on this verdant couch. And yet, as lovely as are these forms of nature, the shining grass or silvered moss, the flowry thyme, wild rose, or honeysuckle; 'tis not their beauty allures the neighboring herds, delights the browsing fawn, or kid and spreads the joy we see amidst the feeding flocks: 'tis not the *form* rejoices; but that which is beneath the form: 'tis savoriness attracts, hunger impels; . . . for never can the *form* be of real force where it is uncontemplated, unjudged of, unexamined, and stands only as the accidental note or token of what appeases provoked sense. . . . If brutes therefore . . . be incapable of knowing and enjoying beauty, as being brutes, and having sense only . . . for their own share; it follows, that neither can man by the same *sense* . . . conceive or enjoy *beauty*: but all the *beauty* . . . he enjoys, is in a nobler way, and by the help of what is noblest, his mind and reason.[56]

Shaftesbury's praise of mind and reason was very far from the intellectualism of the enlightenment. His rhapsody on the beauty and infinite creative power of nature was an entirely new feature of eighteenth-century intellectual history. In this respect he was one of the first champions of Romanticism. But Shaftesbury's Romanticism was of a Platonic type. His theory of aesthetic form was a Platonic conception by virtue of which he was led to react and protest against the sensationalism of the English empiricists.[57]

The objection raised against the metaphysics of Bergson holds also for the psychological theory of Nietzsche. In one of his first writings, *The Birth of Tragedy from the Spirit of Music,*[58] Nietzsche challenged the conceptions of the great classicists of the eighteenth century. It is not, he argues, the ideal of Winckelmann that we find in Greek art. In Aeschylus, in Sophocles or Euripides we seek in vain for "noble simplicity and quiet grandeur." The greatness of Greek tragedy consists in the depth and extreme tension of violent emotions. Greek tragedy was the offspring of a Dionysiac cult; its power was an orgiastic power. But orgy alone could not produce Greek drama. The force of Dionysus was counterbalanced by the force of Apollo. This fundamental polarity is the essence of every great work of art. Great art of all times has arisen from the interpenetration of two opposing forces—from an orgiastic impulse and a visionary state. It is the same contrast as exists between the dream state and the state of intoxication. Both these states release all manner of artistic powers from within us, but each unfetters powers of a different kind. Dream gives us the power of vision, of association, of poetry; intoxication gives us the power of grand attitudes, of passion, of song and dance.[59] Even in this theory of its psychological origin one of the essential features of art has disappeared. For artistic inspiration is not intoxication, artistic imagination is not dream or hallucination. Every great work of art is characterized by a deep structural unity. We cannot account for this unity by reducing it to two different states which, like the dream state and the state of intoxication, are entirely diffused and disorganized. We cannot integrate a structural whole out of amorphous elements.

Of a different type are those theories which hope to elucidate the nature of art by reducing it to the function of play. To these theories one cannot object that they overlook or underrate the free activity of man. Play is an active function; it is not confined within the boundaries of the empirically given. On the other hand the pleasure we find in play is completely disinterested. None of the specific qualities and conditions of the work of art seems, therefore, to be missing in play activity. Most of the exponents of the play theory of art have, indeed, assured us that they were quite unable to find any difference between the two functions.[60] They have declared that there is not a single characteristic of art which does not apply to games of illusion, and no characteristic of such games which could not also be found in art. But all the

---

[56][Cassirer] Shaftesbury, *The Moralists,* section 2, Part III. See *Characteristics* (1714), II, 424 *f.*

[57][Cassirer] For a detailed discussion of Shaftesbury's place in the philosophy of the eighteenth century, see Cassirer, *Die platonische Renaissance in England und die Schule von Cambridge* (Leipzig, 1932), Chapter 6.

[58]pp. 629–34.

[59][Cassirer] Cf. Nietzsche, *The Will to Power.* English translation by A. M. Ludovici (London, 1910), p. 240.

[60][Cassirer] See, for instance, Konrad Lange, *Das Wesen der Kunst* (Berlin, 1901), 2 vols.

arguments that may be alleged for this thesis are purely negative. Psychologically speaking, play and art bear a close resemblance to each other. They are nonutilitarian and unrelated to any practical end. In play as in art we leave behind us our immediate practical needs in order to give our world a new shape. But this analogy is not sufficient to prove a real identity. Artistic imagination always remains sharply distinguished from that sort of imagination which characterizes our play activity. In play we have to do with simulated images which may become so vivid and impressive as to be taken for realities. To define art as a mere sum of such simulated images would indicate a very meager conception of its character and task. What we call "*aesthetic* semblance" is not the same phenomenon that we experience in games of illusion. Play gives us illusive images; art gives us a new kind of truth—a truth not of empirical things but of pure forms.

In our aesthetic analysis above we distinguished between three different kinds of imagination: the power of invention, the power of personification, and the power to produce pure sensuous forms. In the play of a child we find the two former powers, but not the third. The child plays with *things,* the artist plays with *forms,* with lines and designs, rhythms and melodies. In a playing child we admire the facility and quickness of transformation. The greatest tasks are performed with the scantiest means. Any piece of wood may be turned into a living being. Nevertheless, this transformation signifies only a metamorphosis of the objects themselves; it does not mean a metamorphosis of objects into forms. In play we merely rearrange and redistribute the materials given to sense perception. Art is constructive and creative in another and a deeper sense. A child at play does not live in the same world of rigid empirical facts as the adult. The child's world has a much greater mobility and transmutability. Yet the playing child, nevertheless, does no more than exchange the actual things of his environment for other possible things. No such exchange as this characterizes genuine artistic activity. Here the requirement is much more severe. For the artist dissolves the hard stuff of things in the crucible of his imagination, and the result of this process is the discovery of a new world of poetical, musical, or plastic forms. To be sure, a great many ostensible works of art are very far from satisfying this requirement. It is the task of the aesthetic judgment or of artistic taste to distinguish between a genuine work of art and those other spurious products which are indeed playthings, or at most "the response to the demand for entertainment."

A closer analysis of the psychological origin and psychological effects of play and art leads to the same conclusion. Play gives us diversion and recreation but it also serves

a different purpose. Play has a general biological relevance in so far as it anticipates future activities. It has often been pointed out that the play of a child has a propaedeutic value. The boy playing war and the little girl dressing her doll are both accomplishing a sort of preparation and education for other more serious tasks. The function of fine art cannot be accounted for in this manner. Here is neither diversion nor preparation. Some modern aestheticians have found it necessary to distinguish sharply between two types of beauty. One is the beauty of "great" art; the other is described as "easy" beauty.[61] But, strictly speaking, the beauty of a work of art is never "easy." The enjoyment of art does not originate in a softening or relaxing process but in intensification of all our energies. The diversion which we find in play is the very opposite of that attitude which is a necessary prerequisite of aesthetic contemplation and aesthetic judgment. Art demands the fullest concentration. As soon as we fail to concentrate and give way to a mere play of pleasurable feelings and associations, we have lost sight of the work of art as such.

The play theory of art has developed in two entirely different directions. In the history of aesthetics Schiller, Darwin, and Spencer are usually regarded as the outstanding representatives of this theory. Yet it is difficult to find a point of contact between the views of Schiller and modern biological theories of art. In their fundamental tendency these views are not only divergent but in a sense incompatible. The very term *play* is understood and explained in Schiller's accounts in a sense quite different from that of all the subsequent theories. Schiller's is a transcendental and idealistic theory; Darwin's and Spencer's theories are biological and naturalistic. Darwin and Spencer regard play and beauty as general natural phenomena, while Schiller connects them with the world of freedom. And, according to his Kantian dualism, freedom does not signify the same thing as nature; on the contrary, it represents the opposite pole. Both freedom and beauty belong to the intelligible, not to the phenomenal world. In all the naturalistic variants of the play theory of art the play of animals was studied side by side with that of men. Schiller could not admit any such view. For him play is not a general organic activity but a specifically human one. "Man only plays when in the full meaning of the word he is a man, and *he is only completely a man when he plays.*"[62] To speak of an analogy, let alone an identity, between human and animal play or, in the human sphere, between the play of

---

[61][Cassirer] See Bernard Bosanquet, *Three Lectures on Aesthetics,* and S. Alexander, *Beauty and Other Forms of Value.*

[62]*Letters on the Aesthetic Education of Man,* p. 422.

art and the so-called games of illusion, is quite alien to the theory of Schiller. To him this analogy would have appeared to be a basic misconception.

If the historical background of Schiller's theory is taken into consideration his viewpoint is easily understandable. He did not hesitate to connect the "ideal" world of art with the play of a child because in his mind the world of the child had undergone a process of idealization and sublimation. For Schiller spoke as a pupil and admirer of Rousseau, and he saw the life of the child in the new light in which the French philosopher had placed him. "There is deep meaning in the play of a child," Schiller asserted. Yet even though we admit this thesis it must be said that the "meaning" of play is different from that of beauty. Schiller himself defines beauty as a "living form." To him the awareness of living forms is the first and indispensable step which leads to the experience of freedom. Aesthetic contemplation or reflection, according to Schiller, is the first liberal attitude of man toward the universe. "Whereas desire seizes at once its object, reflection removes it to a distance and renders it inalienably her own by saving it from the greed of passion."[63] It is precisely this "liberal," this conscious and reflective attitude which is lacking in a child's play, and which marks the boundary line between play and art.

On the other hand this "removal to a distance" which is here described as one of the necessary and most characteristic features of the work of art has always proved to be a stumbling block for aesthetic theory. If this be true, it was objected, art is no longer something really human, for it has lost all connection with human life. The defenders of the principle *l'art pour l'art* did not, however, fear this objection; on the contrary they openly defied it. They held it to be the highest merit and privilege of art that it burns all bridges linking it with commonplace reality. Art must remain a mystery inaccessible to the *profanum vulgus.* "A poem," said Stéphane Mallarmé, "must be an enigma for the vulgar, chamber music for the initiated."[64] Ortega y Gasset has written a book in which he foretells and defends the "dehumanization" of art. In this process he thinks that the point will at last be reached at which the human element will almost vanish from art.[65] Other critics have supported a diametrically opposed thesis. "When we look at a picture or read a poem or listen to music," I. A. Richards insists,

we are not doing something quite unlike what we were doing on our way to the gallery or when we dressed in the morning. The fashion in which the experience is caused in us is different, and as a rule the experience is more complex and, if we are successful, more unified. But our activity is not of a fundamentally different kind.[66]

But this theoretical antagonism is no real antinomy. If beauty according to Schiller's definition is "living form" it unites in its nature and essence the two elements which here stand opposed. To be sure, it is not the same thing to live in the realm of forms as to live in that of things, of the empirical objects of our surroundings. The forms of art, on the other hand, are not empty forms. They perform a definite task in the construction and organization of human experience. To live in the realm of forms does not signify an evasion of the issues of life; it represents, on the contrary, the realization of one of the highest energies of life itself. We cannot speak of art as "extrahuman" or "superhuman" without overlooking one of its fundamental features, its constructive power in the framing of our human universe.

All aesthetic theories which attempt to account for art in terms of analogies taken from disordered and disintegrated spheres of human experience—from hypnosis, dream, or intoxication—miss the main point. A great lyrical poet has the power to give definite shape to our most obscure feelings. This is possible only because his work, though dealing with a subject which is apparently irrational and ineffable, possesses a clear organization and articulation. Not even in the most extravagant creations of art do we ever find the "ravishing confusions of fantasy," the "original chaos of human nature." This definition of art, given by the Romantic writers,[67] is a contradiction in terms. Every work of art has an intuitive structure, and that means a character of rationality. Every single element must be felt as part of a comprehensive whole. If in a lyrical poem we change one of the words, an accent or a rhythm, we are in danger of destroying the specific tone and charm of the poem. Art is not fettered to the rationality of things or events. It may infringe all those laws of probability which classical aestheticians declared to be the constitutional laws of art. It may give us the most bizarre and grotesque vision, and yet retain a rationality of its own—the rationality of form. We may in this way interpret a saying of Goethe's which at first sight looks para-

---

[63]Letter 25.
[64]See a similar remark in *The Evolution of Literature,* p. 689. [Cassirer] Quoted from Katherine Gilbert, *Studies in Recent Aesthetic* (Chapel Hill, 1927), p. 18.
[65][Cassirer] Ortega y Gasset, *La dezhumanización del' arte* (Madrid, 1925).

---

[66][Cassirer] I. A. Richards, *Principles of Literary Criticism* (New York, Harcourt, Brace, 1925), pp. 16–17.
[67][Cassirer] See p. 934.

doxical, "Art: a second nature; mysterious too, but more understandable, for it originates in the understanding."[68]

Science gives us order in thoughts; morality gives us order in actions; art gives us order in the apprehension of visible, tangible, and audible appearances. Aesthetic theory was very slow indeed to recognize and fully realize these fundamental differences. But if instead of seeking a metaphysical theory of beauty we simply analyze our immediate experience of the work of art we can hardly miss the mark. Art may be defined as a symbolic language. But this leaves us only with the common genus, not the specific difference. In modern aesthetics the interest in the common genus seems to prevail to such a degree as almost to eclipse and obliterate the specific difference. Croce insists that there is not only a close relation but a complete identity between language and art.[69] To his way of thinking it is quite arbitrary to distinguish between the two activities. Whoever studies general linguistics, according to Croce, studies aesthetic problems—and vice versa. There is, however, an unmistakable difference between the symbols of art and the linguistic terms of ordinary speech or writing. These two activities agree neither in character nor purpose; they do not employ the same means, nor do they tend toward the same ends. Neither language nor art gives us mere imitation of things or actions; both are representations. But a representation in the medium of sensuous forms differs widely from a verbal or conceptual representation. The description of a landscape by a painter or poet and that by a geographer or geologist have scarcely anything in common. Both the mode of description and the motive are different in the work of a scientist and in the work of an artist. A geographer may depict a landscape in a plastic manner, and he may even paint it in rich and vivid colors. But what he wishes to convey is not the vision of the landscape but its empirical concept. To this end he has to compare its form with other forms; he has to find out, by observation and induction, its characteristic features. The geologist goes a step farther in this empirical delineation. He does not content himself with a record of physical facts, for he wishes to divulge the origin of these facts. He distinguishes the strata by which the soil has been built up, noting chronological differences; and he goes back to the general causal laws according to which the earth has reached its present shape. For the artist all these empirical relations, all these comparisons with other facts, and all this research into causal relations do not exist. Our ordinary empirical concepts may be, roughly speaking, divided into two classes according as they have to do with practical or theoretical interests. The one class is concerned with the use of things and with the question, what is that for? The other is concerned with the causes of things and with the question, whence? But upon entering the realm of art we have to forget all such questions. Behind the existence, the nature, the empirical properties of things, we suddenly discover their forms. These forms are no static elements. What they show is a mobile order, which reveals to us a new horizon of nature. Even the greatest admirers of art have often spoken of it as if it were a mere accessory, an embellishment or ornament, of life. But this is to underrate its real significance and its real role in human culture. A mere duplicate of reality would always be of a very questionable value. Only by conceiving art as a special direction, a new orientation, of our thoughts, our imagination, and our feelings, can we comprehend its true meaning and function. The plastic arts make us see the sensible world in all its richness and multifariousness. What would we know of the innumerable nuances in the aspect of things were it not for the works of the great painters and sculptors? Poetry is, similarly, the revelation of our personal life. The infinite potentialities of which we had but a dim and obscure presentiment are brought to light by the lyric poet, by the novelist, and by the dramatist. Such art is in no sense mere counterfeit or facsimile, but a genuine manifestation of our inner life.

So long as we live in the world of sense impressions alone we merely touch the surface of reality. Awareness of the depth of things always requires an effort on the part of our active and constructive energies. But since these energies do not move in the same direction, and do not tend toward the same end, they cannot give us the same aspect of reality. There is a conceptual depth as well as a purely visual depth. The first is discovered by science; the second is revealed in art. The first aids us in understanding the reasons of things; the second in seeing their forms. In science we try to trace phenomena back to their first causes, and to general laws and principles. In art we are absorbed in their immediate appearance, and we enjoy this appearance to the fullest extent in all its richness and variety. Here we are not concerned with the uniformity of laws but with the multiformity and diversity of intuitions. Even art may be described as knowledge, but art is knowledge of a peculiar and specific kind. We may well subscribe to the observation of Shaftesbury that "all beauty is truth." But the truth of beauty does not consist in a theoretical description or explanation of things; it consists rather in the "sympathetic vision" of

---

[68][Cassirer] *"Kunst: eine andere Natur, auch geheimnisvoll, aber verständlicher; denn sie entspringt aus dem Verstande."* See *Maximen und Reflexionen,* ed. Max Hecker, in *"Schriften der Goethe-Gesellschaft,"* XXI (1907), 229.

[69]*Aesthetic,* Chapter 18.

things.[70] The two views of truth are in contrast with one another, but not in conflict or contradiction. Since art and science move in entirely different planes they cannot contradict or thwart one another. The conceptual interpretation of science does not preclude the intuitive interpretation of art. Each has its own perspective and, so to speak, its own angle of refraction. The psychology of sense perception has taught us that without the use of both eyes, without a binocular vision, there would be no awareness of the third dimension of space. The depth of human experience in the same sense depends on the fact that we are able to vary our modes of seeing, that we can alternate our views of reality. *Rerum videre formas* is a no less important and indispensable task than *rerum cognoscere causas.*[71] In ordinary experience we connect phenomena according to the category of causality or finality. According as we are interested in the theoretical reasons or the practical effects of things, we think of them as causes or as means. Thus we habitually lose sight of their immediate appearance until we can no longer see them face to face. Art, on the other hand, teaches us to visualize, not merely to conceptualize or utilize, things. Art gives us a richer, more vivid and colorful image of reality, and a more profound insight into its formal structure. It is characteristic of the nature of man that he is not limited to one specific and single approach to reality but can choose his point of view and so pass from one aspect of things to another.

---

[70][Cassirer] See De Witt H. Parker, *The Principles of Aesthetics,* p. 89: "Scientific truth is the fidelity of a description to the external objects of experience; artistic truth is sympathetic vision—the organization into clearness of experience itself." The difference between scientific and aesthetic experience has recently been illustrated in a very instructive article by Prof. F. S. C. Northrup in the review *Furioso,* I, No. 4, 71 *ff.*

---

[71]"To see the forms of things"; "to know the causes of things."

W. K. Wimsatt

1907–1975

Monroe C. Beardsley

1915–1985

Literary theory is replete with accusations of heresy and fallacy. Poe found heresy in didacticism, Brooks in paraphrase. In modern criticism the two best-known accusations of fallacy are those made by Wimsatt and Beardsley in *The Intentional Fallacy* and *The Affective Fallacy*. These essays are written out of the assumption that a literary work has an ontological status of its own—that it is an object with a certain autonomy. They reflect objectivist principles that were current in New Criticism in the work of Ransom, Tate, Warren, and Brooks.

By *intentional fallacy* Wimsatt and Beardsley mean a confusion between the poem and its origins. This fallacy appears frequently in Romantic critical practice. Romantic critics often saw the poem as an expression of the author's self and therefore tended to thrust ultimate interest back on the author, using the poem as evidence for conclusions about him. Before the Romantic movement, biographical criticism tended to be of little importance; afterward, biography came to dominate literary scholarship and sometimes became an end in itself. Objectivist critics turned away from consideration of the poem as personal expression to the concept of the poem as having an independent public existence. Wimsatt and Beardsley proceed to argue against the usefulness to criticism of considering the author's intention (if indeed it could be discovered), for what the author did accomplish is before us as the poem.

Wimsatt and Beardsley use the term *affective fallacy* for confusion between the poem and its results. There is a tradition of criticism that defines the poem in terms of, even locates the poem in, the reader's response. One well-known modern critic who attempts this is Richards, whose position Wimsatt and Beardsley criticize in their essay. Ultimately, theories of catharsis, therapy, didacticism, and delight all partake of this fallacy, for they judge the poem in terms of its effect on the reader.

A third sort of fallacy or heresy is discussed in Cassirer's essay *Art,* where Cassirer deals with and disposes of imitation. Thus modern ''objectivist'' criticism attacked all the traditional orientations, seeking to leave nothing but the poem itself and its own structure, its own ''being,'' as the proper subject of critical study.

Works by Wimsatt include *The Prose Style of Dr. Johnson* (1941); *Philosophical Words* (1948); *The Verbal Icon* (1954); *Literary Criticism: A Short History* (with Cleanth Brooks, 1957); *Hateful Contraries* (1965); *The Portraits of Alexander Pope* (1965); and *Day of the Leopards* (1976). Beardsley's work includes *Aesthetics: Prob-*

lems in the Philosophy of Criticism (1958); Aesthetics from Classical Greece to the Present (1966); Aesthetic Inquiry (1967); The Possibility of Criticism (1970); and The Aesthetic Point of View (1982). See John Fisher, ed., Essays on Aesthetics: Perspectives on the Work of Monroe C. Beardsley (1983).

The Intentional Fallacy

I

The claim of the author's "intention" upon the critic's judgment has been challenged in a number of recent discussions, notably in the debate entitled *The Personal Heresy,* between Professors Lewis and Tillyard. But it seems doubtful if this claim and most of its Romantic corollaries are as yet subject to any widespread questioning. The present writers, in a short article entitled *Intention* for a dictionary[1] of literary criticism, raised the issue but were unable to pursue its implications at any length. We argued that the design or intention of the author is neither available nor desirable as a standard for judging the success of a work of literary art, and it seems to us that this is a principle which goes deep into some differences in the history of critical attitudes. It is a principle which accepted or rejected points to the polar opposites of classical "imitation" and Romantic expression. It entails many specific truths about inspiration, authenticity, biography, literary history and scholarship, and about some trends of contemporary poetry, especially its allusiveness. There is hardly a problem of literary criticism in which the critic's approach will not be qualified by his view of "intention."

Intention, as we shall use the term, corresponds to *what he intended* in a formula which more or less explicitly has had wide acceptance. "In order to judge the poet's performance, we must know *what he intended.*" Intention is design or plan in the author's mind. Intention has obvious affinities for the author's attitude toward his work, the way he felt, what made him write.

We begin our discussion with a series of propositions summarized and abstracted to a degree where they seem to us axiomatic.

1. A poem does not come into existence by accident. The words of a poem, as Professor Stoll has remarked, come out of a head, not out of a hat. Yet to insist on the designing intellect as a *cause* of a poem is not to grant the design or intention as a *standard* by which the critic is to judge the worth of the poet's performance.

2. One must ask how a critic expects to get an answer to the question about intention. How is he to find out what the poet tried to do? If the poet succeeded in doing it, then the poem itself shows what he was trying to do. And if the poet did not succeed, then the poem is not adequate evidence, and the critic must go outside the poem—for evidence of an intention that did not become effective in the poem. "Only one caveat must be borne in mind," says an eminent intentionalist[2] in a moment when his theory repudiates itself; "the poet's aim must be judged at the moment of the creative act, that is to say, by the art of the poem itself."

3. Judging a poem is like judging a pudding or a machine. One demands that it work. It is only because an artifact works that we infer the intention of an artificer. "A poem should not mean but be."[3] A poem can *be* only through its *meaning*—since its medium is words—yet it *is,* simply *is,* in the sense that we have no excuse for inquiring what part is intended or meant. Poetry is a feat of style by which a complex of meaning is handled all at once. Poetry succeeds because all or most of what is said or implied is relevant; what is irrelevant has been excluded, like lumps from pudding and "bugs" from machinery. In this respect poetry differs from practical messages, which are successful if and only if we correctly infer the intention. They are more abstract than poetry.

4. The meaning of a poem may certainly be a personal one, in the sense that a poem expresses a personality or state of soul rather than a physical object like an apple. But even a short lyric poem is dramatic, the response of a speaker (no matter how abstractly conceived) to a situation (no matter how universalized). We ought to impute the thoughts and attitudes of the poem immediately to the dramatic *speaker,*

THE INTENTIONAL FALLACY. Wimsatt and Beardsley's *The Intentional Fallacy* was first published in 1946. The text is from *The Verbal Icon* by W. K. Wimsatt and Monroe C. Beardsley (1954). Reprinted by permission of The University of Kentucky Press.

[1][Wimsatt and Beardsley] *Dictionary of World Literature,* Joseph T. Shipley, ed. (New York, 1942), 326–29.

[2][Wimsatt and Beardsley] J. E. Spingarn, *The New Criticism,* in *Criticism in America* (New York, 1924), 24–25.
[3]Archibald MacLeish, *Ars Poetica.*

and if to the author at all, only by an act of biographical inference.

5. There is a sense in which an author, by revision, may better achieve his original intention. But it is a very abstract sense. He intended to write a better work, or a better work of a certain kind, and now has done it. But it follows that his former concrete intention was not his intention. "He's the man we were in search of, that's true," says Hardy's rustic constable, "and yet he's not the man we were in search of. For the man we were in search of was not the man we wanted."

"Is not a critic," asks Professor Stoll, "a judge, who does not explore his own consciousness, but determines the author's meaning of intention, as if the poem were a will, a contract, or the constitution? The poem is not the critic's own." He has accurately diagnosed two forms of irresponsibility, one of which he prefers. Our view is yet different. The poem is not the critic's own and not the author's (it is detached from the author at birth and goes about the world beyond his power to intend about it or control it). The poem belongs to the public. It is embodied in language, the peculiar possession of the public, and it is about the human being, an object of public knowledge. What is said about the poem is subject to the same scrutiny as any statement in linguistics or in the general science of psychology.

A critic of our dictionary article, Ananda K. Coomaraswamy, has argued[4] that there are two kinds of inquiry about a work of art: (1) whether the artist achieved his intentions; (2) whether the work of art "ought ever to have been undertaken at all" and so "whether it is worth preserving." Number 2, Coomaraswamy maintains, is not "criticism of any work of art qua work of art," but is rather moral criticism; number 1 is artistic criticism. But we maintain that 2 need not be moral criticism: that there is another way of deciding whether works of art are worth preserving and whether, in a sense, they "ought" to have been undertaken, and this is the way of objective criticism of works of art as such, the way which enables us to distinguish between a skillful murder and a skillful poem. A skillful murder is an example which Coomaraswamy uses, and in his system the difference between the murder and the poem is simply a "moral" one, not an "artistic" one, since each if carried out according to plan is "artistically" successful. We maintain that 2 is an inquiry of more worth than I, and since 2 and not 1 is capable of distinguishing poetry from murder, the name "artistic criticism" is properly given to 2.

II

It is not so much a historical statement as a definition to say that the intentional fallacy is a Romantic one. When a rhetorician of the first century A.D. writes: "Sublimity is the echo of a great soul," or when he tells us that "Homer enters into the sublime actions of his heroes" and "shares the full inspiration of the combat,"[5] we shall not be surprised to find this rhetorician considered as a distant harbinger of Romanticism and greeted in the warmest terms by Saintsbury. One may wish to argue whether Longinus should be called Romantic, but there can hardly be a doubt that in one important way he is.

Goethe's three questions for "constructive criticism" are "What did the author set out to do? Was his plan reasonable and sensible, and how far did he succeed in carrying it out?" If one leaves out the middle question, one has in effect the system of Croce[6]—the culmination and crowning philosophic expression of Romanticism. The beautiful is the successful intuition-expression, and the ugly is the unsuccessful; the intuition or private part of art is *the* aesthetic fact, and the medium or public part is not the subject of aesthetic at all. The Madonna of Cimabue is still in the Church of Santa Maria Novella; but does she speak to the visitor of today as to the Florentines of the thirteenth century? "*Historical interpretation* labors . . . to reintegrate in us the psychological conditions which have changed in the course of history. It . . . enables us to see a work of art (a physical object) as its *author saw it* in the moment of production."[7] The first italics are Croce's, the second ours. The upshot of Croce's system is an ambiguous emphasis on history. With such passages as a point of departure a critic may write a nice analysis of the meaning or "spirit" of a play by Shakespeare or Corneille—a process that involves close historical study but remains aesthetic criticism—or he may, with equal plausibility, produce an essay in sociology, biography, or other kinds of nonaesthetic history.

III

I went to the poets; tragic, dithyrambic, and all sorts. . . . I took them some of the most elaborate

---

[4][Wimsatt and Beardsley] Ananda K. Coomaraswamy, *Intention*, in *American Bookman*, I (1944), 41–48.

[5]Longinus, *On the Sublime*, IX. 2 and 10–11, pp. 79 and 80.

[6]See *Aesthetic*, pp. 692–99.

[7][Wimsatt and Beardsley] It is true that Croce himself in his *Ariosto, Shakespeare and Corneille* (London, 1920), Chapter 7, "The Practical Personality and the Poetical Personality," and in his *Defense of Poetry* (Oxford, 1933), 24, and elsewhere, early and late, has delivered telling attacks on emotive geneticism, but the main drive of the *Aesthetic* is surely toward a kind of cognitive intentionalism.

passages in their own writings, and asked what was the meaning of them. . . . Will you believe me? . . . there is hardly a person present who would not have talked better about their poetry than they did themselves. Then I knew that not by wisdom do poets write poetry, but by a sort of genius and inspiration.[8]

That reiterated mistrust of the poets which we hear from Socrates may have been part of a rigorously ascetic view in which we hardly wish to participate, yet Plato's Socrates saw a truth about the poetic mind which the world no longer commonly sees—so much criticism, and that the most inspirational and most affectionately remembered, has proceeded from the poets themselves.

Certainly the poets have had something to say that the critic and professor could not say; their message has been more exciting: that poetry should come as naturally as leaves to a tree, that poetry is the lava of the imagination, or that it is emotion recollected in tranquility. But it is necessary that we realize the character and authority of such testimony. There is only a fine shade of difference between such expressions and a kind of earnest advice that authors often give. Thus Edward Young, Carlyle, Walter Pater: "I know two golden rules from ethics, which are no less golden in composition, than in life. 1. Know thyself; 2dly, Reverence thyself."[9] This is the grand secret for finding readers and retaining them: let him who would move and convince others, be first moved and convinced himself. Horace's rule, *Si vis me flere,* is applicable in a wider sense than the literal one. To every poet, to every writer, we might say: Be true, if you would be believed. "Truth! There can be no merit, no craft at all, without that. And further, all beauty is in the long run only *fineness* of truth, or what we call expression, the finer accommodation of speech to that vision within."

And Housman's little handbook to the poetic mind[10] yields this illustration:

> Having drunk a pint of beer at luncheon—beer is a sedative to the brain, and my afternoons are the least intellectual portion of my life—I would go out for a walk of two or three hours. As I went along, thinking of nothing in particular, only looking at things around me and following the progress of the seasons, there would flow into my mind, with sudden and unaccountable emotion, some-

times a line or two of verse, sometimes a whole stanza at once.

This is the logical terminus of the series already quoted. Here is a confession of how poems were written which would do as a definition of poetry just as well as "emotion recollected in tranquility"[11]—and which the young poet might equally well take to heart as a practical rule. Drink a pint of beer, relax, go walking, think on nothing in particular, look at things, surrender yourself to yourself, search for the truth in your own soul, listen to the sound of your own inside voice, discover and express the *vraie vérité.*

It is probably true that all this is excellent advice for poets. The young imagination fired by Wordsworth and Carlyle is probably closer to the verge of producing a poem than the mind of the student who has been sobered by Aristotle or Richards. The art of inspiring poets, or at least of inciting something like poetry in young persons, has probably gone further in our day than ever before. Books of creative writing such as those issued from the Lincoln School are interesting evidence of what a child can do.[12] All this, however, would appear to belong to an art separate from criticism—to a psychological discipline, a system of self-development, a yoga, which the young poet perhaps does well to notice, but which is something different from the public art of evaluating poems.

Coleridge and Arnold were better critics than most poets have been, and if the critical tendency dried up the poetry in Arnold and perhaps in Coleridge, it is not inconsistent with our argument, which is that judgment of poems is different from the art of producing them. Coleridge has given us the classic "anodyne" story, and tells what he can about the genesis of a poem which he calls a "psychological curiosity," but his definitions of poetry and of the poetic quality "imagination" are to be found elsewhere and in quite other terms.

It would be convenient if the passwords of the intentional school, *sincerity, fidelity, spontaneity, authenticity, genuineness, originality,* could be equated with terms such as *integrity, relevance, unity, function, maturity, subtlety, adequacy,* and other more precise terms of evaluation—in

---

[8]Plato, *Apology.*
[9]Young, *Conjectures on Original Composition,* p. 335.
[10]*The Name and Nature of Poetry* (1933).

[11]Wordsworth, Preface to the *Lyrical Ballads,* p. 444.
[12][Wimsatt and Beardsley] See Hughes Mearns, *Creative Youth* (Garden City, 1925), especially 10, 27–29. The technique of inspiring poems has apparently been outdone more recently by the study of inspiration in successful poets and other artists. See, for instance, Rosamond E. M. Harding, *An Anatomy of Inspiration* (Cambridge, 1940); Julius Portnoy, *A Psychology of Art Creation* (Philadelphia, 1942); Rudolf Arnheim and others, *Poets at Work* (New York, 1947); Phyllis Bartlett, *Poems in Process* (New York, 1951); Brewster Ghiselin, ed., *The Creative Process: A Symposium* (Berkeley and Los Angeles, 1952).

short, if *expression* always meant aesthetic achievement. But this is not so.

"Aesthetic" art, says Professor Curt Ducasse, an ingenious theorist of expression, is the conscious objectification of feelings, in which an intrinsic part is the critical moment. The artist corrects the objectification when it is not adequate. But this may mean that the earlier attempt was not successful in objectifying the self, or "it may also mean that it was a successful objectification of a self which, when it confronted us clearly, we disowned and repudiated in favor of another."[13] What is the standard by which we disown or accept the self? Professor Ducasse does not say. Whatever it may be, however, this standard is an element in the definition of art which will not reduce to terms of objectification. The evaluation of the work of art remains public; the work is measured against something outside the author.

IV

There is criticism of poetry and there is author psychology, which when applied to the present or future takes the form of inspirational promotion; but author psychology can be historical too, and then we have literary biography, a legitimate and attractive study in itself, one approach, as Professor Tillyard would argue, to personality, the poem being only a parallel approach. Certainly it need not be with a derogatory purpose that one points out personal studies, as distinct from poetic studies, in the realm of literary scholarship. Yet there is danger of confusing personal and poetic studies; and there is the fault of writing the personal as if it were poetic.

There is a difference between internal and external evidence for the meaning of a poem. And the paradox is only verbal and superficial that what is (1) internal is also public: it is discovered through the semantics and syntax of a poem, through our habitual knowledge of the language, through grammars, dictionaries, and all the literature which is the source of dictionaries, in general through all that makes a language and culture; while what is (2) external is private or idiosyncratic; not a part of the work as a linguistic fact: it consists of revelations (in journals, for example, or letters or reported conversations) about how or why the poet wrote the poem—to what lady, while sitting on what lawn, or at the death of what friend or brother. There is (3) an intermediate kind of evidence about the character of the author or about private or semiprivate meanings attached to words or topics by an author or by a coterie of which he is a member. The

meaning of words is the history of words, and the biography of an author, his use of a word, and the associations which the word had for *him,* are part of the word's history and meaning.[14] But the three types of evidence, especially 2 and 3, shade into one another so subtly that it is not always easy to draw a line between examples, and hence arises the difficulty for criticism. The use of biographical evidence need not involve intentionalism, because while it may be evidence of what the author intended, it may also be evidence of the meaning of his words and the dramatic character of his utterance. On the other hand, it may not be all this. And a critic who is concerned with evidence of type 1 and moderately with that of type 3 will in the long run produce a different sort of comment from that of the critic who is concerned with 2 and with 3 where it shades into 2.

The whole glittering parade of Professor Lowes' *Road to Xanadu,* for instance, runs along the border between types 2 and 3 or boldly traverses the Romantic region of 2. *"Kubla Khan,"* says Professor Lowes, "is the fabric of a vision, but every image that rose up in its weaving had passed that way before. And it would seem that there is nothing haphazard or fortuitous in their return." This is not quite clear—not even when Professor Lowes explains that there were clusters of associations, like hooked atoms, which were drawn into complex relation with other clusters in the deep well of Coleridge's memory, and which then coalesced and issued forth as poems. If there was nothing "haphazard or fortuitous" in the way the images returned to the surface, that may mean (1) that Coleridge could not produce what he did not have, that he was limited in his creation by what he had read or otherwise experienced, or (2) that having received certain clusters of associations, he was bound to return them in just the way he did, and that the value of the poem may be described in terms of the experiences on which he had to draw. The latter pair of propositions (a sort of Hartleyan associationism which Coleridge himself repudiated in the *Biographia*) may not be assented to. There were certainly other combinations, other poems, worse or better, that might have been written by men who had read Bartram and Purchas and Bruce and Milton. And this will be true no matter how many times we are able to add to the brilliant complex of Coleridge's reading. In certain flourishes (such as the sentence we have quoted) and in chapter headings like "The Shaping Spirit," "The Magical Synthesis," "Imagination Creatrix," it may be that Professor Lowes pretends to say more about the actual poems than he does. There is a certain deceptive variation in these fancy chapter titles; one expects to pass on

---

[13][Wimsatt and Beardsley] Curt Ducasse, *The Philosophy of Art* (New York, 1929), 116.

[14][Wimsatt and Beardsley] And the history of words *after* a poem is written may contribute meanings which if relevant to the original pattern should not be ruled out by a scruple about intention.

to a new stage in the argument, and one finds—more and more sources, more and more about "the streamy nature of association."[15]

"Wohin der Weg?" quotes Professor Lowes for the motto of his book. *"Kein Weg! Ins Unbetretene."*[16] Precisely because the way is *unbetreten,* we should say, it leads away from the poem. Bartram's *Travels*[17] contains a good deal of the history of certain words and of certain Romantic Floridian conceptions that appear in *Kubla Khan.* And a good deal of that history has passed and was then passing into the very stuff of our language. Perhaps a person who has read Bartram appreciates the poem more than one who has not. Or, by looking up the vocabulary of *Kubla Khan* in the *Oxford English Dictionary,* or by reading some of the other books there quoted, a person may know the poem better. But it would seem to pertain little to the poem to know that Coleridge had read Bartram. There is a gross body of life, of sensory and mental experience, which lies behind and in some sense causes every poem, but can never be and need not be known in the verbal and hence intellectual composition which is the poem. For all the objects of our manifold experience, for every unity, there is an action of the mind which cuts off roots, melts away context—or indeed we should never have objects or ideas or anything to talk about.

It is probable that there is nothing in Professor Lowes' vast book which could detract from anyone's appreciation of either *The Ancient Mariner* or *Kubla Khan.* We next present a case where preoccupation with evidence of type 3 has gone so far as to distort a critic's view of a poem (yet a case not so obvious as those that abound in our critical journals).

In a well-known poem by John Donne appears this quatrain:

> Moving of th' earth brings harms and fears,
>   Men reckon what it did and meant,
> But trepidation of the spheres,
>   Though greater far, is innocent.[18]

A recent critic in an elaborate treatment of Donne's learning has written of this quatrain as follows:

> He touches the emotional pulse of the situation by a skillful allusion to the new and the old astron-

omy. . . . Of the new astronomy, the "moving of the earth" is the most radical principle, of the old, the "trepidation of the spheres" is the motion of the greatest complexity. . . . The poet must exhort his love to quietness and calm upon his departure; and for this purpose the figure based upon the latter motion (trepidation), long absorbed into the traditional astronomy, fittingly suggests the tension of the moment without arousing the "harms and fears" implicit in the figure of the moving earth.[19]

The argument is plausible and rests on a well-substantiated thesis that Donne was deeply interested in the new astronomy and its repercussions in the theological realm. In various works Donne shows his familiarity with Kepler's *De Stella Nova,* with Galileo's *Siderius Nuncius,* with William Gilbert's *De Magnete,* and with Clavius' commentary on the *De Sphaera* of Sacrobosco. He refers to the new science in his sermon at Paul's Cross and in a letter to Sir Henry Goodyer. In *The First Anniversary* he says the "new philosophy calls all in doubt." In the *Elegy on Prince Henry* he says that the "least moving of the center" makes "the world to shake."

It is difficult to answer argument like this, and impossible to answer it with evidence of like nature. There is no reason why Donne might not have written a stanza in which the two kinds of celestial motion stood for two sorts of emotion at parting. And if we become full of astronomical ideas and see Donne only against the background of the new science, we may believe that he did. But the text itself remains to be dealt with, the analyzable vehicle of a complicated metaphor. And one may observe: (1) that the movement of the earth according to the Copernican theory is a celestial motion, smooth and regular, and while it might cause religious or philosophic fears, it could not be associated with the crudity and earthiness of the kind of commotion which the speaker in the poem wishes to discourage; (2) that there is another moving of the earth, an earthquake, which has just these qualities and is to be associated with the tear-floods and sigh-tempests of the second stanza of the poem; (3) that "trepidation" is an appropriate opposite of earthquake, because each is a shaking or vibratory motion; and "trepidation of the spheres" is "greater far" than an earthquake, but not much greater (if two such motions can be compared as to greatness) than the annual motion of the earth; (4) that reckoning what it "did and meant" shows that the event has

---

[15][Wimsatt and Beardsley] Chapters 8, "The Pattern," and 16, "The Known and Familiar Landscape," will be found of most help to the student of the poem.

[16]"Where does the path lead?" "There is no path! Into the untraveled."

[17]A book published in 1791 by William Bartram, naturalist and nature artist, which greatly influenced English Romanticism.

[18]*A Valediction Forbidding Mourning,* 9–12.

---

[19][Wimsatt and Beardsley] Charles M. Coffin, *John Donne and the New Philosophy* (New York, 1927), 97–98.

passed, like an earthquake, not like the incessant celestial movement of the earth. Perhaps a knowledge of Donne's interest in the new science may add another shade of meaning, an overtone to the stanza in question, though to say even this runs against the words. To make the geocentric and heliocentric antithesis the core of the metaphor is to disregard the English language, to prefer private evidence to public, external to internal.

V

If the distinction between kinds of evidence has implications for the historical critic, it has them no less for the contemporary poet and his critic. Or, since every rule for a poet is but another side of a judgment by a critic, and since the past is the realm of the scholar and critic, and the future and present that of the poet and the critical leaders of taste, we may say that the problems arising in literary scholarship from the intentional fallacy are matched by others which arise in the world of progressive experiment.

The question of "allusiveness," for example, as acutely posed by the poetry of Eliot, is certainly one where a false judgment is likely to involve the intentional fallacy. The frequency and depth of literary allusion in the poetry of Eliot and others has driven so many in pursuit of full meanings to the *Golden Bough* and the Elizabethan drama that it has become a kind of commonplace to suppose that we do not know what a poet means unless we have traced him in his reading—a supposition redolent with intentional implications. The stand taken by F. O. Matthiessen is a sound one and partially forestalls the difficulty.

> If one reads these lines with an attentive ear and is sensitive to their sudden shifts in movement, the contrast between the actual Thames and the idealized vision of it during an age before it flowed through a megalopolis is sharply conveyed by that movement itself, whether or not one recognizes the refrain to be from Spenser.[20]

Eliot's allusions work when we know them—and to a great extent even when we do not know them, through their suggestive power.

But sometimes we find allusions supported by notes, and it is a nice question whether the notes function more as guides to send us where we may be educated, or more as

indications in themselves about the character of the allusions. "Nearly everything of importance . . . that is apposite to an appreciation of *The Waste Land*," writes Matthiessen of Miss Weston's book, "has been incorporated into the structure of the poem itself, or into Eliot's notes." And with such an admission it may begin to appear that it would not much matter if Eliot invented his sources (as Sir Walter Scott invented chapter epigraphs from "old plays" and "anonymous" authors, or as Coleridge wrote marginal glosses for *The Ancient Mariner*). Allusions to Dante, Webster, Marvell, or Baudelaire doubtless gain something because these writers existed, but it is doubtful whether the same can be said for an allusion to an obscure Elizabethan: "The sound of horns and motors, which shall bring / Sweeney to Mrs. Porter in the spring."[21] "Cf. Day, *Parliament of Bees*:" says Eliot,

> When of a sudden, listening, you shall hear,
> A noise of horns and hunting, which shall bring
> Actaeon to Diana in the spring,
> Where all shall see her naked skin.

The irony is completed by the quotation itself; had Eliot, as is quite conceivable, composed these lines to furnish his own background, there would be no loss of validity. The conviction may grow as one reads Eliot's next note: "I do not know the origin of the ballad from which these lines are taken: it was reported to me from Sydney, Australia." The important word in this note—on Mrs. Porter and her daughter who washed their feet in soda water—is *ballad*. And if one should feel from the lines themselves their "ballad" quality, there would be little need for the note. Ultimately, the inquiry must focus on the integrity of such notes as parts of the poem, for where they constitute special information about the meaning of phrases in the poem, they ought to be subject to the same scrutiny as any of the other words in which it is written. Matthiessen believes the notes were the price Eliot "had to pay in order to avoid what he would have considered muffling the energy of his poem by extended connecting links in the text itself." But it may be questioned whether the notes and the need for them are not equally muffling. F. W. Bateson has plausibly argued that Tennyson's *The Sailor Boy* would be better if half the stanzas were omitted, and the best versions of ballads like *Sir Patrick Spens* owe their power to the very audacity with which the minstrel has taken for granted the story upon which he comments. What then if a poet finds he cannot take so much for granted in a more recondite context and rather than write informatively, sup-

---

[20]*The Achievement of T. S. Eliot.*

[21]*The Waste Land,* 197–98.

plies notes? It can be said in favor of this plan that at least the notes do not pretend to be dramatic, as they would if written in verse. On the other hand, the notes may look like unassimilated material lying loose beside the poem, necessary for the meaning of the verbal symbol, but not integrated, so that the symbol stands incomplete.

We mean to suggest by the above analysis that whereas notes tend to seem to justify themselves as external indexes to the author's *intention,* yet they ought to be judged like any other parts of a composition (verbal arrangement special to a particular context), and when so judged their reality as parts of the poem, or their imaginative integration with the rest of the poem, may come into question. Matthiessen, for instance, sees that Eliot's titles for poems and his epigraphs are informative apparatus, like the notes. But while he is worried by some of the notes and thinks that Eliot "appears to be mocking himself for writing the note at the same time that he wants to convey something by it," Matthiessen believes that the "device" of epigraphs "is not at all open to the objection of not being sufficiently structural." "The *intention,*" he says, "is to enable the poet to secure a condensed expression in the poem itself." "In each case the epigraph is *designed* to form an integral part of the effect of the poem." And Eliot himself, in his notes, has justified his poetic practice in terms of intention.

> The Hanged Man, a member of the traditional pack, fits my purpose in two ways: because he is associated in my mind with the Hanged God of Frazer, and because I associate him with the hooded figure in the passage of the disciples to Emmaus in Part V. . . . The man with Three Staves (an authentic member of the Tarot pack) I associate, quite arbitrarily, with the Fisher King himself.

And perhaps he is to be taken more seriously here, when off guard in a note, than when in his Norton lectures he comments on the difficulty of saying what a poem means and adds playfully that he thinks of prefixing to a second edition of *Ash Wednesday* some lines from *Don Juan:*

> I don't pretend that I quite understand
> My own meaning when I would be *very* fine;
> But the fact is that I have nothing planned
> Unless it were to be a moment merry.

If Eliot and other contemporary poets have any characteristic fault, it may be in *planning* too much.

Allusiveness in poetry is one of several critical issues by which we have illustrated the more abstract issue of intentionalism, but it may be for today the most important illustration. As a poetic practice allusiveness would appear to be in some recent poems an extreme corollary of the Romantic intentionalist assumption, and as a critical issue it challenges and brings to light in a special way the basic premise of intentionalism. The following instance from the poetry of Eliot may serve to epitomize the practical implications of what we have been saying. In Eliot's *Love Song of J. Alfred Prufrock,* toward the end, occurs the line: "I have heard the mermaids singing, each to each," and this bears a certain resemblance to a line in a song by John Donne, "Teach me to hear mermaids singing," so that for the reader acquainted to a certain degree with Donne's poetry, the critical question arises: Is Eliot's line an allusion to Donne's? Is Prufrock thinking about Donne? Is Eliot thinking about Donne? We suggest that there are two radically different ways of looking for an answer to this question. There is (1) the way of poetic analysis and exegesis, which inquires whether it makes any sense if Eliot-Prufrock *is* thinking about Donne. In an earlier part of the poem, when Prufrock asks, "Would it have been worthwhile, . . . To have squeezed the universe into a ball," his words take half their sadness and irony from certain energetic and passionate lines of Marvel *To His Coy Mistress.* But the exegetical inquirer may wonder whether mermaids considered as "strange sights" (to hear them is in Donne's poem analogous to getting with child a mandrake root) have much to do with Prufrock's mermaids, which seem to be symbols of romance and dynamism, and which incidentally have literary authentication, if they need it, in a line of a sonnet by Gérard de Nerval. This method of inquiry may lead to the conclusion that the given resemblance between Eliot and Donne is without significance and is better not thought of, or the method may have the disadvantage of providing no certain conclusion. Nevertheless, we submit that this is the true and objective way of criticism, as contrasted to what the very uncertainty of exegesis might tempt a second kind of critic to undertake: (2) the way of biographical or genetic inquiry, in which, taking advantage of the fact that Eliot is still alive, and in the spirit of a man who would settle a bet, the critic writes to Eliot and asks what he meant, or if he had Donne in mind. We shall not here weigh the probabilities—whether Eliot would answer that he meant nothing at all, had nothing at all in mind—a sufficiently good answer to such a question—or in an unguarded moment might furnish a clear and, within its limit, irrefutable answer. Our point is that such an answer to such an inquiry would have nothing to do with the poem *Prufrock;* it would not be a critical inquiry. Critical inquiries, unlike bets, are not settled in this way. Critical inquiries are not settled by consulting the oracle.

The Affective Fallacy

I

As the title of this essay invites comparison with that of our first, it may be relevant to assert at this point that we believe ourselves to be exploring two roads which have seemed to offer convenient detours around the acknowledged and usually feared obstacles to objective criticism, both of which, however, have actually led away from criticism and from poetry. The intentional fallacy is a confusion between the poem and its origins, a special case of what is known to philosophers as the genetic fallacy. It begins by trying to derive the standard of criticism from the psychological *causes* of the poem and ends in biography and relativism. The affective fallacy is a confusion between the poem and its *results* (what it *is* and what it *does*), a special case of epistemological skepticism, though usually advanced as if it had far stronger claims than the overall forms of skepticism. It begins by trying to derive the standard of criticism from the psychological effects of the poem and ends in impressionism and relativism. The outcome of either fallacy, the intentional or the affective, is that the poem itself, as an object of specifically critical judgment, tends to disappear.

In the present essay, we would discuss briefly the history and fruits of affective criticism, some of its correlatives in cognitive criticism, and hence certain cognitive characteristics of poetry which have made affective criticism plausible. We would observe also the premises of affective criticism, as they appear today, in certain philosophic and pseudophilosophic disciplines of wide influence. And first and mainly that of "semantics."

II

The separation of emotive from referential meaning was urged persuasively about twenty years ago in the earlier works of I. A. Richards. The types of meaning which were defined in his *Practical Criticism*[1] and in the *Meaning of Meaning* of Ogden and Richards created, partly by suggestion, partly with the aid of direct statement, a clean "antithesis" between "symbolic and emotive use of language." In his *Practical Criticism* Richards spoke of "aesthetic" or "projectile" words—adjectives by which we project feelings at objects themselves altogether innocent of any qualities corresponding to these feelings. And in his succinct *Science and Poetry,* science is statement, poetry is pseudostatement which plays the important role of making us feel better about things than statements would.[2] After Richards—and under the influence too of Count Korzybski's non-Aristotelian *Science and Sanity*—came the semantic school of Chase, Hayakawa, Walpole, and Lee. Most recently C. L. Stevenson in his *Ethics and Language* has given an account which, as it is more careful and explicit than the others, may be taken as most clearly pleading their cause—and best revealing its weakness.

One of the most emphatic points in Stevenson's system is the distinction between what a word *means* and what it *suggests.* To make the distinction in a given case, one applies what the semeiotician calls a "linguistic rule" ("definition" in traditional terminology), the role of which is to stabilize responses to a word. The word *athlete* may be said to *mean* one interested in sports, among other things, but merely to suggest a tall young man. The linguistic rule is that "athletes are necessarily interested in sports, but may or may not be tall." All this is on the side of what may be called the *descriptive* (or *cognitive*) function of words. For a second and separate main function of words—that is, the *emotive*—there is no linguistic rule to stabilize responses and, therefore, in Stevenson's system, no parallel distinction between meaning and suggestion. Although the term *quasi-dependent emotive meaning* is recommended by Stevenson for a kind of emotive "meaning" which is "conditional to the cognitive *suggestiveness* of a sign," the main drift of his argument is that emotive "meaning" is something noncorrelative to and independent of descriptive (or cognitive) meaning. Thus, emotive "meaning" is said to survive sharp changes in descriptive meaning. And words with the same descriptive meaning are said to have quite different emotive "meanings." *License* and *liberty,* for example, Stevenson believes to have in some contexts the same descriptive meaning, but opposite emotive "meanings." Finally, there are words which he believes to have no descriptive meaning, yet a decided emotive "meaning": these are expletives of various sorts.

But a certain further distinction, and an important one, which does not appear in Stevenson's system—nor in those

---

THE AFFECTIVE FALLACY. Wimsatt and Beardsley's *The Affective Fallacy* was first published in 1949. The text is from *The Verbal Icon* by W. K. Wimsatt and Monroe C. Beardsley (1954). Reprinted by permission of The University of Kentucky Press.
[1]See pp. 827–37.

[2][Wimsatt and Beardsley] Richards has recently reiterated these views in the context of a more complicated account of language that seems to look in the direction of Charles Morris. See his *Emotive Language Still,* in *Yale Review,* XXXIX (1949), 108–18.

of his forerunners—is invited by his persistent use of the word *meaning* for both cognitive and emotive language functions and by the absence from the emotive of his careful distinction between *meaning* and *suggestion*. It is a fact worth insisting upon that the term *emotive meaning,* as used by Stevenson, and the more cautious term *feeling,* as used by Richards to refer to one of his four types of "meaning," do not refer to any such cognitive meaning as that conveyed by the name of an emotion—*anger* or *love*. Rather, these key terms refer to the *expression* of emotive states which Stevenson and Richards believe to be effected by certain words— for instance *license, liberty, pleasant, beautiful, ugly*—and hence also to the emotive *response* which these words may evoke in a hearer. As the term *meaning* has been traditionally and usefully assigned to the cognitive, or descriptive, functions of language, it would have been well if these writers had employed, in such contexts, some less preempted term. *Import* might have been a happy choice. Such differentiation in vocabulary would have had the merit of reflecting a profound difference in linguistic function—all the difference between grounds of emotion and emotions themselves, between what is immediately meant by words and what is evoked by the meaning of words, or what more briefly might be said to be the "import" of the words themselves.

Without pausing to examine Stevenson's belief that expletives have no descriptive meaning, we are content to observe in passing that these words at any rate have only the vaguest emotive *import,* something raw, unarticulated, imprecise. *Oh!* (surprise and related feelings), *Ah!* (regret), *Ugh!* (distaste). It takes a more descriptive reference to specify the feeling. "In quiet she reposes. Ah! would that I did too." But a more central reemphasis for Stevenson's position—and for that of his forerunners, including Richards— seems required by a fact scarcely mentioned in semantic writings: namely, that a large and obvious area of emotive *import* depends directly upon descriptive meaning (either with or without words of explicit valuation)—as when a person says and is believed: "General X ordered the execution of 50,000 civilian hostages," or "General X is guilty of the murder of 50,000 civilian hostages." And secondly, by the fact that a great deal of emotive *import* which does not depend thus directly on descriptive *meaning* does depend on descriptive *suggestion*. Here we have the "quasi-dependent emotive meaning" of Stevenson's system—a "meaning" to which surely he assigns too slight a role. This is the kind of emotive import, we should say, which appears when words change in descriptive *meaning* yet preserve a similar emotive "meaning"—when the Communists take over the term "democracy" and apply it to something else, preserving, however, the old descriptive *suggestion,* a government of, by,

and for the people. It appears in pairs of words like *liberty* and *license,* which even if they have the same descriptive meaning (as one may doubt), certainly carry different descriptive suggestions. Or one might cite the word series in Bentham's classic *Catalogue of Motives:* "humanity, good will, partiality," "frugality, pecuniary interest, avarice." Or the other standard examples of emotive insinuation: "Animals sweat, men perspire, women glow." "I am firm, thou art obstinate, he is pigheaded." Or the sentence, "There should be a revolution every twenty years," to which the experimenter in emotive responses attaches now the name Karl Marx (and arouses suspicion), now that of Thomas Jefferson (and provokes applause).

The principle applies conspicuously to the numerous examples offered by the school of Hayakawa, Walpole, and Lee. In the interest of brevity, though in what may seem a quixotic defiance of the warnings of this school against unindexed generalization—according to which semanticist 1 is not semanticist 2 is not semanticist 3, and so forth—we call attention to Irving Lee's *Language Habits in Human Affairs,* particularly Chapters 7 and 8. According to Lee, every mistake that anyone ever makes in acting, since in some direct or remote sense it involves language or thought (which is related to language), may be ascribed to "bad language habits," a kind of magic misuse of words. No distinctions are permitted. Basil Rathbone, handed a scenario entitled *The Monster,* returns it unread, but accepts it later under a different title. The Ephraimite says "Sibboleth" instead of "Shibboleth" and is slain. A man says he is offended by four-letter words describing events in a novel, but not by the events. Another man receives an erroneously worded telegram which says that his son is dead. The shock is fatal. One would have thought that with this example Lee's simplifying prejudice might have broken down—that a man who is misinformed that his son is dead may have leave himself to drop dead without being thought a victim of emotive incantation. Or that the title of a scenario is some ground for the inference that it is a Grade-B horror movie; that the use of phonetic principles in choosing a password is reason rather than magic—as *lollapalooza* and *lullabye* were used against infiltration tactics on Guadalcanal; that four-letter words may suggest in events certain qualities which a reader finds it distasteful to contemplate. None of these examples (except the utterly anomalous *Sibboleth*) offers any evidence, in short, that what a word *does* to a person is to be ascribed to anything except what it *means,* or if this connection is not apparent, as the most, by what it *suggests*.

A question about the relation of language to objects of emotion is a shadow and index of another question, about the status of emotions themselves. It is a consistent cultural phenomenon that within the same period as the *floruit*[3] of semantics one kind of anthropology has delivered a parallel attack upon the relation of objects themselves to emotions, or more specifically, upon the constancy of their relations through the times and places of human societies. In the classic treatise of Westermarck on *Ethical Relativity* we learn, for example, that the custom of eliminating the aged and unproductive has been practiced among certain primitive tribes and nomadic races. Other customs, that of exposing babies, that of suicide, that of showing hospitality to strangers—or the contrary custom of eating them, the reception of the Cyclops rather than that of Alcinous—seem to have enjoyed in some cultures a degree of approval unknown or at least unusual in our own. But even Westermarck has noticed that difference of emotion "largely originates in different measures of knowledge, based on experience of the consequences of conduct, and in different beliefs." That is to say, the different emotions, even though they are responses to the same objects or actions, may yet be responses to different qualities or functions—to the edibility of Odysseus rather than to his comeliness or manliness. A converse of this is the fact that for different objects in different cultures there may be on cognitive grounds emotions of similar quality—for the cunning of Odysseus and for the strategy of Montgomery at El Alamein. Were it otherwise, indeed, there would be no way of understanding and describing alien emotions, no basis on which the science of the cultural relativist might proceed.

We shall not pretend to frame any formal discourse upon affective psychology, the laws of emotion. At this point, nevertheless, we venture to rehearse some generalities about objects, emotions, and words. Emotion, it is true, has a well-known capacity to fortify opinion, to inflame cognition, and to grow upon itself in surprising proportions to grains of reason. We have mob psychology, psychosis, and neurosis. We have "free-floating anxiety" and all the vaguely understood and inchoate states of apprehension, depression, or elation, the prevailing complexions of melancholy or cheer. But it is well to remember that these states are indeed inchoate or vague and by that fact may even verge upon the unconscious.[4] We have, again, the popular and self-vindicatory forms of confessing emotion. "He makes me boil." "It burns me up." Or in the novels of Evelyn Waugh a social event or a person is "sick-making." But these locutions involve an extension of the strict operational meaning of *make* or *effect*. A food or a poison causes pain or death,

but for an emotion we have a reason or an object, not merely an efficient cause. If objects are ever connected by "emotional congruity," as in the association psychology which J. S. Mill inherited from the eighteenth century, this can mean only that similar emotions attach to various objects because of similarity in the objects or in their relations. What makes one angry is something false, insulting, or unjust. What makes one afraid is a cyclone, a mob, a holdup man. And in each case the emotion is somewhat different.

The tourist who said a waterfall was pretty provoked the silent disgust of Coleridge, while the other who said it was sublime won his approval. This, as C. S. Lewis so well observes, was not the same as if the tourist had said, "I feel sick," and Coleridge had thought, "No, I feel quite well."

The doctrine of emotive meaning propounded recently by the semanticists has seemed to offer a scientific basis for one kind of affective relativism in poetics—the personal. That is, if a person can correctly say either *liberty* or *license* in a given context independently of the cognitive quality of the context, merely at will or from emotion, it follows that a reader may likely feel either "hot" or "cold" and report either "bad" or "good" on reading either *liberty* or *license*—either an ode by Keats or a limerick. The sequence or licenses is endless. Similarly, the doctrines of one school of anthropology have gone far to fortify another kind of affective relativism, the cultural or historical, the measurement of poetic value by the degree of feeling felt by the readers of a given era. A different psychological criticism, that by author's intention, as we noted in our first essay, is consistent both with piety for the poet and with antiquarian curiosity and has been heavily supported by the historical scholar and biographer. So affective criticism, though in its personal or impressionistic form it meets with strong dislike from scholars, yet in its theoretical or scientific form finds strong support from the same quarter. The historical scholar, if not much interested in his own personal responses or in those of his students, is intensely interested in whatever can be discovered about those of any member of Shakespeare's audience.

III

Plato's feeding and watering of the passions[5] was an early example of affective theory, and Aristotle's countertheory of

[3] "Flourishing."

[4] [Wimsatt and Beardsley] "If feeling be regarded as conscious, it is unquestionable that it involves in some measure an intellectual process." F. Paulhan, *The Laws of Feeling* (London, 1930), 153.

[5] [Wimsatt and Beardsley] Strictly, a theory not of poetry but of morals, as, to take a curious modern instance, Lucie Guillet's *La Poéticothérapie, Efficacités du Fluide Poétique* (Paris, 1946) is a theory not of poetry but of healing. Aristotle's catharsis is a true theory of poetry, that is, part of a definition of poetry.

catharsis was another (with modern intentionalistic analogues in theories of "relief" and "sublimation"). There was also the "transport" of the audience in the *Peri Hypsous*[6] (matching the great soul of the poet), and this had echoes of passion or enthusiasm among eighteenth-century Longinians. We have had more recently the infection theory of Tolstoy[7] (with its intentionalistic analogue in the emotive expressionism of Veron), the *Einfühlung* or empathy of Lipps and related pleasure theories, either more or less tending to the "objectification" of Santayana: "Beauty is pleasure regarded as the quality of a thing."[8] An affinity for these theories is seen in certain theories of the comic during the same era, the relaxation theory of Penjon, the laughter theory of Max Eastman. In their *Foundations of Aesthetics* Ogden, Richards, and Wood listed sixteen types of aesthetic theory, of which at least seven may be described as affective. Among these the theory of synaesthesis (beauty is what produces an equilibrium of appetencies) was the one they themselves espoused. This was developed at length by Richards in his *Principles of Literary Criticism.*

The theories just mentioned may be considered as belonging to one branch of affective criticism, and that the main one, the emotive—unless the theory of empathy, with its transport of the self into the object, belongs rather with a parallel and equally ancient affective theory, the imaginative. This is represented by the figure of vividness so often mentioned in the rhetorics—*efficacia, energeia,* or the *phantasiai* in Chapter 15 of *Peri Hypsous.* This if we mistake not is the imagination the "pleasures" of which are celebrated by Addison in his series of *Spectators.*[9] It is an imagination implicit in the theories of Leibniz and Baumgarten that beauty lies in clear but confused, or sensuous, ideas; in the statement of Warton in his *Essay on Pope* that the selection of "lively pictures . . . chiefly constitutes true poetry." In our time, as the emotive form of psychologistic or affective theory has found its most impressive champion in I. A. Richards, so the imaginative form has in Max Eastman, whose *Literary Mind* and *Enjoyment of Poetry* have much to say about vivid realizations or heightened consciousness.

The theory of intention or author psychology has been the intense conviction of poets themselves, Wordsworth, Keats, Housman, and since the Romantic era, of young persons interested in poetry, the introspective amateurs and soul-cultivators. In a parallel way, affective theory has often been less a scientific view of literature than a prerogative—

that of the soul adventuring among masterpieces,[10] the contagious teacher, the poetic radiator—a magnetic rhapsode Ion, a Saintsbury, a Quiller-Couch, a William Lyon Phelps. Criticism on this theory has approximated the tone of the Buchmanite confession, the revival meeting. "To be quite frank," says Anatole France, "the critic ought to say: 'Gentlemen, I am going to speak about myself apropos of Shakespeare, apropos of Racine.' "[11] The sincerity of the critic becomes an issue, as for the intentionalist the sincerity of the poet.

A "mysterious entity called the Grand Style" is celebrated by Saintsbury—something much like "the Longinian Sublime." "Whenever this perfection of expression acquires such force that it transmutes the subject and transports the hearer or reader, then and there the Grand Style exists, for so long, and in such degree, as the transmutation of the one and the transportation of the other lasts." This is the grand style, the emotive style, of nineteenth-century affective criticism. A somewhat less resonant style which has been heard in our columns of Saturday and Sunday reviewing and from our literary explorers is more closely connected with imagism and the kind of vividness sponsored by Eastman. In the *Book-of-the-Month Club News* Dorothy Canfield testifies to the power of a novel: "To read this book is like living through an experience rather than just reading about it." A poem, says Hans Zinsser,

> means nothing to me unless it can carry me away
> with the gentle or passionate peace of its emotion,
> over obstacles of reality into meadows and covers
> of illusion. . . . The sole criterion for me is whether
> it can sweep me with it into emotion or illusion of
> beauty, terror, tranquility, or even disgust.[12]

It is but a short step to what we may call the physiological form of affective criticism. Beauty, said Burke in the eighteenth century, is something which "acts by relaxing the solids of the whole system." More recently, on the side of personal testimony, we have the oft quoted goose-flesh experience in a letter of Emily Dickinson, and the top of her head taken off. We have the bristling of the skin while Housman was shaving, the "shiver down the spine," the sensation in "the pit of the stomach." And if poetry has been discerned by these tests, truth also. "All scientists," said D. H. Law-

---

[6]Longinus, *On the Sublime,* I. 4, p. 76.
[7]See *What is Art?,* p. 680.
[8]*The Sense of Beauty.*
[9]See pp. 284–89.

[10]See France, *The Adventures of the Soul,* p. 656.
[11]*The Adventures of the Soul,* p. 656.
[12][Wimsatt and Beardsley] *As I Remember Him,* quoted by J. Donald Adams, "Speaking of Books," in *New York Times Book Review* (April 20, 1947), p. 2. Mr. Adams' weekly department has been a happy hunting ground for such specimens.

rence to Aldous Huxley, "are liars. . . . I don't care about evidence. Evidence doesn't mean anything to me. I don't feel it *here*." And, reports Huxley, "he pressed his two hands on his solar plexus."

An even more advanced grade of affective theory, that of hallucination, would seem to have played some part in the neoclassic conviction about the unities of time and place, was given a modified continuation of existence in phrases of Coleridge about a "willing suspension of disbelief" and a "temporary half faith," and may be found today in some textbooks. The hypnotic hypothesis of E. D. Snyder might doubtless be invoked in its support. As this form of affective theory is the least theoretical in detail, has the least content, and makes the least claim on critical intelligence, so it is in its most concrete instances not a theory but a fiction or a fact—of no critical significance. In the eighteenth century Fielding conveys a right view of the hallucinative power of drama in his comic description of Partridge seeing Garrick act the ghost scene in Hamlet. "O la! sir. . . . If I was frightened, I am not the only person. . . . You may call me coward if you will; but if that little man there upon the stage is not frightened, I never saw any man frightened in my life." Partridge is today found perhaps less often among the sophisticates at the theater than among the myriad audience of movie and radio. It is said, and no doubt reliably, that during World War II Stefan Schnabel played Nazi roles in radio dramas so convincingly that he received numerous letters of complaint, and in particular one from a lady who said that she had reported him to General MacArthur.[13]

IV

A distinction can be made between those who have testified what poetry does to themselves and those who have coolly investigated what it does to others. The most resolute researches of the latter have led them into the dreary and antiseptic laboratory, to testing with Fechner the effects of triangles and rectangles, to inquiring what kinds of colors are suggested by a line of Keats, or to measuring the motor discharges attendant upon reading it.[14] If animals could read poetry, the affective critic might make discoveries analogous to those of W. B. Cannon about *Bodily Changes in Pain, Hunger, Fear and Rage*—the increased liberation of sugar from the liver, the secretion of adrenin from the adrenal gland. The

affective critic is today actually able, if he wishes, to measure the "psychogalvanic reflex" of persons subjected to a given moving picture. But, as Herbert J. Muller in his *Science and Criticism* points out: "Students have sincerely reported an 'emotion' at the mention of the word *mother*, although a galvanometer indicated no bodily change whatever. They have also reported no emotion at the mention of *prostitute*, although the galvanometer gave a definite kick." Thomas Mann and a friend came out of a movie weeping copiously—but Mann narrates the incident in support of his view that movies are not art." "Art is a *cold* sphere."[15] The gap between various levels of physiological experience and the recognition of value remains wide, in the laboratory or out.

In a similar way, general affective theory at the literary level has, by the very implications of its program, produced little actual criticism. The author of the ancient *Peri Hypsous* is weakest at the points where he explains that passion and sublimity are the palliatives or excuses *(alexipharmaka)* of bold metaphors, and that passions which verge on transport are the lenitives or remedies *(panakeia)* of such audacities in speech as hyperbole. The literature of catharsis has dealt with the historical and theoretical question whether Aristotle meant a medical or a lustratory metaphor, whether the genitive which follows *katharsis* is of the thing purged or of the object purified. Even the early critical practice of I. A. Richards had little to do with his theory of synaesthesis. His *Practical Criticism*[16] depended mainly on two important constructive principles of criticism which Richards has realized and insisted upon—(1) that rhythm (the vague, if direct, expression of emotion) and poetic form in general are intimately connected with and interpreted by other and more precise parts of poetic meaning, (2) that poetic meaning is inclusive or multiple and hence sophisticated. The latter quality of poetry may perhaps be the objective correlative of the affective state synaesthesis, but in applied criticism there would seem to be not much room for synaesthesis or for the touchy little attitudes of which it is composed.

The report of some readers, on the other hand, that a poem or story induces in them vivid images, intense feelings, or heightened consciousness, is neither anything which can be refuted nor anything which it is possible for the objective critic to take into account. The purely affective report is either too physiological or it is too vague. Feelings, as Hegel has conveniently put it, "remain purely subjective affections of myself, in which the concrete matter vanishes, as

---

[13][Wimsatt and Beardsley] *New Yorker,* XIX (December 11, 1943), 28.

[14][Wimsatt and Beardsley] "The final averages showed that the combined finger movements for the Byron experiments were eighteen meters longer than they were for Keats." R. C. Givler, *The Psycho-Physiological Effect of the Elements of Speech in Relation to Poetry* (Princeton, 1915), 62.

[15][Wimsatt and Beardsley] *Ueber den Film,* in *Die Forderung des Tages* (Berlin, 1930), 387.

[16]See pp. 827–38.

though narrowed into a circle of the utmost abstraction.'' And the only constant or predictable thing about the vivid images which more eidetic readers experience is precisely their vividness—as may be seen by requiring a class of average pupils to draw illustrations of a short story or by consulting the newest Christmas edition of a childhood classic which one knew with the illustrations of Howard Pyle or N. C. Wyeth. Vividness is not the thing in the work by which the work may be identified, but the result of a cognitive structure, which *is* the thing. "The story is good," as the student so often says in his papers, "because it leaves so much to the imagination." The opaque accumulation of physical detail in some realistic novels has been aptly dubbed by Middleton Murry "the pictorial fallacy."

Certain theorists, notably Richards, have anticipated some difficulties of affective criticism by saying that it is not intensity of emotion that characterizes poetry (murder, robbery, fornication, horse racing, war—perhaps even chess— take care of that better), but the subtle quality of patterned emotions which play at the subdued level of disposition or attitude. We have psychological theories of aesthetic distance, detachment, or disinterestedness. A criticism on these principles has already taken important steps toward objectivity. If Eastman's theory of imaginative vividness appears today chiefly in the excited puffs of the newspaper book sections, the campaign of the semanticists and the balanced emotions of Richards, instead of producing their own school of affective criticism, have contributed much to recent schools of cognitive analysis, of paradox, ambiguity, irony, and symbol. It is not always true that the emotive and cognitive forms of criticism will sound far different. If the affective critic (avoiding both the physiological and the abstractly psychological form of report) ventures to state with any precision what a line of poetry *does*—as "it fills us with a mixture of melancholy and reverence for antiquity"—either the statement will be patently abnormal or false, or it will be a description of what the meaning of the line *is:* "the spectacle of massive antiquity in ruins." Tennyson's *Tears, Idle Tears,* as it deals with an emotion which the speaker at first seems not to understand, might be thought to be a specially emotive poem. "The last stanza," says Brooks in his recent analysis, "evokes an intense emotional response from the reader."[17] But this statement is not really a part of Brooks' criticism of the poem—rather a witness of his fondness for it. "The second stanza"—Brooks might have said at an earlier point in his analysis—"gives us a momentary vivid realization of past happy experiences, then makes us sad at their loss." But

he says actually: "The conjunction of the qualities of sadness and freshness is reinforced by the fact that the same basic symbol—the light on the sails of a ship hull down— has been employed to suggest both qualities." The distinction between these formulations may seem slight, and in the first example which we furnished may be practically unimportant. Yet the difference between translatable emotive formulas and more physiological and psychologically vague ones—cognitively untranslatable—is theoretically of the greatest importance. The distinction even when it is a faint one is at the dividing point between paths which lead to polar opposites in criticism, to classical objectivity and to Romantic reader psychology.

The critic whose formulations lean to the emotive and the critic whose formulations lean to the cognitive will in the long run produce a vastly different sort of criticism.

The more specific the account of the emotion induced by a poem, the more neatly it will be an account of the reasons for emotion, the poem itself, and the more reliable it will be as an account of what the poem is likely to induce in other—sufficiently informed—readers. It will in fact supply the kind of information which will enable readers to respond to the poem. It will talk not of tears, prickles, or other physiological symptoms, of feeling angry, joyful, hot, cold, or intense, or of vaguer states of emotional disturbance, but of shades of distinction and relation between objects of emotion. It is precisely here that the discerning literary critic has his insuperable advantage over the subject of the laboratory experiment and over the tabulator of the subject's responses. The critic is not a contributor to statistically countable reports about the poem, but a teacher or explicator of meanings. His readers, if they are alert, will not be content to take what he says as testimony, but will scrutinize it as teaching.

V

Poetry, as Matthew Arnold believed, "attaches the emotion to the idea; the idea *is* the fact."[18] The objective critic, however, must admit that it is not easy to explain how this is done, how poetry makes ideas thick and complicated enough to hold on to emotions. In his essay on *Hamlet and His Problems* T. S. Eliot finds Hamlet's state of emotion unsatisfactory because it lacks an "objective correlative,"[19] a "chain of events" which are the "formula of that *particular* emotion." The emotion is "in *excess* of the facts as they appear." It is "inexpressible." Yet Hamlet's emotion must be ex-

---

[17]*The Well Wrought Urn.*

[18]See *The Study of Poetry*, p. 603.
[19]See p. 766.

pressible, we submit, and actually expressed too (by something) in the play; otherwise Eliot would not know it is there—in excess of the facts. That Hamlet himself or Shakespeare may be baffled by the emotion is beside the point. The second chapter of Yvor Winters' *Primitivism and Decadence* has gone much further in clarifying a distinction adumbrated by Eliot. Without embracing the extreme doctrine of Winters, that if a poem cannot be paraphrased it is a poor poem, we may yet with profit reiterate his main thesis: that there is a difference between the motive, as he calls it, or logic of an emotion, and the surface or texture of a poem constructed to describe the emotion, and that both are important to a poem. Winters has shown, we think, how there can be in effect "fine poems" about nothing. There is rational progression and there is "qualitative progression,"[20] the latter, with several subtly related modes, a characteristic of decadent poetry. Qualitative progression is the succession, the dream float, of images, not substantiated by a plot. "Moister than an oyster in its clammy cloister, I'm bluer than a wooer who has slipped in a sewer," says Morris Bishop in a recent comic poem:

> Chiller than a killer in a cinema thriller,
> Queerer than a leerer at his leer in a mirror,
> Madder than an adder with a stone in the bladder.
> If you want to know why, I cannot but reply:
>   It is really no affair of yours.[21]

The term *pseudostatement* was for Richards a patronizing term by which he indicated the attractive nullity of poems. For Winters, the kindred term *pseudoreference* is a name for the more disguised kinds of qualitative progression and is a term of reproach. It seems to us highly significant that for another psychological critic, Max Eastman, so important a part of poetry as metaphor is in effect too pseudostatement. The vivid realization of metaphor comes from its being in some way an obstruction to practical knowledge (like a torn coat sleeve to the act of dressing). Metaphor operates by being abnormal or inept, the wrong way of saying something. Without pressing the point, we should say that an uncomfortable resemblance to this doctrine appears in Ransom's logical structure and local texture of irrelevance.[22]

What Winters has said seems basic. To venture both a slight elaboration of this and a return to the problem of emotive semantics surveyed in our first section: it is a well-known but nonetheless important truth that there are two kinds of real objects which have emotive quality, the objects which are the reasons for human emotion, and those which by some kind of association suggest either the reasons or the resulting emotion: the thief, the enemy, or the insult that makes us angry, and the hornet that sounds and stings somewhat like ourselves when angry; the murderer or felon, and the crow that kills small birds and animals or feeds on carrion and is black like the night when crimes are committed by men. The arrangement by which these two kinds of emotive meaning are brought together in a juncture characteristic of poetry is, roughly speaking, the simile, the metaphor, and the various less clearly defined forms of association. We offer the following crude example as a kind of skeleton figure to which we believe all the issues can be attached.

1. X feels as angry as a hornet.
2. X whose lunch has been stolen feels as angry as a hornet.

No. 1 is, we take it, the qualitative poem, the vehicle of a metaphor, an objective correlative—for nothing. No. 2 adds the tenor of the metaphor, the motive for feeling angry, and hence makes the feeling itself more specific. The total statement has a more complex and testable structure. The element of aptitude, or ineptitude, is more susceptible of discussion. "Light thickens, and the crow makes wing to the rooky wood"[23] might be a line from a poem about nothing, but initially owed much of its power, and we daresay still does, to the fact that it is spoken by a tormented murderer who, as night draws on, has sent his agents out to perform a further "deed of dreadful note."

These distinctions bear a close relation to the difference between historical statement which may be a reason for emotion because it is believed (Macbeth has killed the king) and fictitious or poetic statement, where a large component of suggestion (and hence metaphor) has usually appeared. The first of course seldom occurs pure, at least not for the public eye. The coroner or the intelligence officer may content himself with it. Not the chronicler, the bard, or the newspaperman. To these we owe more or less direct words of value and emotion (the murder, the atrocity, the wholesale butchery) and all the repertoire of suggestive meanings which here and there in history—with somewhat to start upon—a Caesar or a Macbeth—have created out of a mere case of factual reason for intense emotion a specified, figuratively fortified, and permanent object of less intense but far richer emotion. With a decline of heroes and of faith in external order, we have had during the last century a great flowering of poetry

---

[20][Wimsatt and Beardsley] The term, as Winters indicates, is borrowed from Kenneth Burke's *Counter-Statement*.
[21][Wimsatt and Beardsley] *New Yorker,* XXIII (May 31, 1947), 33.
[22]See *Criticism as Pure Speculation,* pp. 879–80.

[23]*Macbeth,* III. ii. 50–51.

which has tried the utmost to do without any hero or action or fiction of these—the qualitative poetry of Winters' analysis. It is true that any hero and action when they become fictitious take the first step toward the simply qualitative, and all poetry, so far as separate from history, tends to be formula of emotion. The hero and action are taken as symbolic. A graded series from fact to quality might include: (1) the historic Macbeth, (2) Macbeth as Renaissance tragic protagonist, (3) a *Macbeth* written by Eliot, (4) a *Macbeth* written by Pound. As Winters has explained, "the prince is briefly introduced in the footnotes" of *The Waste Land;* "it is to be doubted that Mr. Pound could manage such an introduction." Yet in no one of these four stages has anything like a pure emotive poetry been produced. The semantic analysis which we have offered in our first section would say that even in the last stages a poetry of pure emotion is an illusion. What we have is a poetry where kinds are only symbols or even a poetry of hornets and crows, rather than of human deeds. Yet a poetry about things. How these things are joined in patterns and with what names of emotion remains always the critical question. "*The Romance of the Rose* could not, without loss," observes C. S. Lewis, "be rewritten as *The Romance of the Onion.*"

Poetry is characteristically a discourse about both emotions and objects, or about the emotive quality of objects. The emotions correlative to the objects of poetry become a part of the matter dealt with—not communicated to the reader like an infection or disease, not inflicted mechanically like a bullet or knife wound, not administered like a poison, not simply expressed as by expletives or grimaces or rhythms, but presented in their objects and contemplated as a pattern of knowledge. Poetry is a way of fixing emotions or making them more permanently perceptible when objects have undergone a functional change from culture to culture, or when as simple facts of history they have lost emotive value with loss of immediacy. Though the reasons for emotion in poetry may not be so simple as Ruskin's "noble grounds for the noble emotions," yet a great deal of constancy for poetic objects of emotion—if we will look for constancy—may be traced through the drift of human history. The murder of Duncan by Macbeth, whether as history of the eleventh century or chronicle of the sixteenth, has not tended to become the subject of a Christmas carol. In Shakespeare's play it is an act difficult to duplicate in all its immediate adjuncts of treachery, deliberation, and horror of conscience. Set in its galaxy of symbols—the hoarse raven, the thickening light, and the crow making wing, the babe plucked from the breast, the dagger in the air, the ghost, the bloody hands—this ancient murder has become an object of strongly fixed emotive value. The corpse of Polynices, a far more ancient object and partially concealed from us by the difficulties of the Greek, shows a similar pertinacity in remaining among the understandable motives of higher duty. Funeral customs have changed, but not the intelligibility of the web of issues, religious, political, and private, woven about the corpse "unburied, unhonored, all unhallowed." Again, certain objects partly obscured in one age wax into appreciation in another, and partly through the efforts of the poet. It is not true that they suddenly arrive out of nothing. The pathos of Shylock, for example, is not a creation of our time, though a smugly modern humanitarianism, because it has slogans, may suppose that this was not felt by Shakespeare or Southampton—and may not perceive its own debt to Shakespeare. "Poets," says Shelley, "are the unacknowledged legislators of the world."[24] And it may be granted at least that poets have been leading expositors of the laws of feeling.[25]

To the relativist historian of literature falls the uncomfortable task of establishing as discrete cultural moments the past when the poem was written and first appreciated, and the present into which the poem with its clear and nicely interrelated meanings, its completeness, balance, and tension has survived. A structure of emotive objects so complex and so reliable as to have been taken for great poetry by any past age will never, it seems safe to say, so wane with the waning of human culture as not to be recoverable at least by a willing student. And on the same grounds a confidence seems indicated for the objective discrimination of all future poetic phenomena, though the premises or materials of which such poems will be constructed cannot be prescribed or foreseen. If the exegesis of some poems depends upon the understanding of obsolete or exotic customs, the poems themselves are the most precise emotive report on the customs. In the poet's finely contrived objects of emotion and in other works of art the historian finds his most reliable evidence about the emotions of antiquity—and the anthropologist, about those of contemporary primitivism. To appreciate courtly love we turn to Chrétien de Troyes and Marie de France. Certain attitudes of late fourteenth-century England, toward knighthood, toward monasticism, toward the bourgeoisie, are nowhere more precisely illustrated than in the prologue to *The Canterbury Tales.* The field worker among the Zunis or the Navahos finds no informant so informative as the poet or the member of the tribe who can quote its myths.[26] In short, though cultures have changed and will change, poems remain and explain.

---

[24]*A Defense of Poetry,* p. 529.

[25][Wimsatt and Beardsley] Cp. Paulhan, *The Laws of Feeling,* 105, 110.

[26][Wimsatt and Beardsley] "The anthropologist," says Bronislaw Malinowski, "has the mythmaker at his elbow." *Myth in Primitive Psychology* (New York, 1926), 17.

Cleanth Brooks

b. 1906

Brooks's essays, particularly those collected in *The Well Wrought Urn*, were at one time, and may still be, the most widely read works of the New Criticism. Like Wimsatt and Beardsley's *intentional fallacy* and *affective fallacy*, the term *heresy of paraphrase* became a catch phrase associated with the movement. Brooks is heavily indebted to the work of his teacher, John Crowe Ransom, and his essays may profitably be compared to Ransom's. He is fond of metaphors of organicism to describe a poem. He develops the analogy between poem and drama and suggests that the speaker of a lyric should not be confused with the author. Statements that occur in poems cannot be treated out of the context of the whole poem, Brooks warns, because the whole structure controls the poem's meaning. In *Irony as a Principle of Structure* Brooks defines irony very broadly as the acknowledgment at all times by the poem of the pressure of the context on any given part of the poem. The meaning, or perhaps better, the ''being'' of the poem lies in its formal structure, not in a paraphrase abstracted from it. Brooks is therefore wary of Ransom's assertion that the poem *has* a ''paraphrasable core.'' His theory of organicism leads him to insist that the paraphrasable core is not an element of the poem, but a creation of the poem's interpreter. One of Brooks's complaints against Romantic poetry is that much of it insists on its most portentous statements being taken out of context, as if the rest of the poem were merely a surrounding embellishment. These principles were reflected in two influential textbooks by Brooks and Warren, *Understanding Poetry* and *Understanding Fiction*.

Collaborating with Robert Penn Warren, Brooks edited *Understanding Poetry* (1938, 3rd ed., 1960) and *Understanding Fiction* (1943, 2nd ed., 1959). With W. K. Wimsatt he wrote *Literary Criticism: A Short History* (1957). Other works include *Modern Poetry and the Tradition* (1939), *The Well Wrought Urn* (1947), *The Hidden God* (1963), *William Faulkner: The Yoknapatawpha Country* (1963); *A Shaping Joy* (1972); *William Faulkner: Toward Yoknapatawpha and Beyond* (1978); *William Faulkner: First Encounters* (1983); *The Language of the American South* (1985); and *On the Prejudices, Predilictions, and Firm Beliefs of William Faulkner* (1987). See Lewis P. Simpson, ed., *The Possibilities of Order: Cleanth Brooks and His Work* (1976).

The Heresy of Paraphrase

The ten poems that have been discussed[1] were not selected because they happened to express a common theme or to display some particular style or to share a special set of symbols. It has proved, as a matter of fact, somewhat surprising to see how many items they do have in common: the light symbolism as used in *L'Allegro—Il Penseroso* and in the *Intimations* ode, for example; or, death as a sexual metaphor in *The Canonization* and in *The Rape of the Lock;* or the similarity of problem and theme in the *Intimations* ode and *Among School Children.*

On reflection, however, it would probably warrant more surprise if these ten poems did not have much in common. For they are all poems which most of us will feel are close to the central stream of the tradition. Indeed, if there is any doubt on this point, it will have to do with only the first and last members of the series [Donne's *The Canonization,* and Yeats's *Among School Children*]—poems whose relation to the tradition I shall, for reasons to be given a little later, be glad to waive. The others, it will be granted, are surely in the mainstream of the tradition.

As a matter of fact, a number of the poems discussed in this book were not chosen by me but were chosen for me. But having written on these, I found that by adding a few poems I could construct a chronological series which (though it makes no pretension to being exhaustive of periods or types) would not leave seriously unrepresented any important period since Shakespeare. In filling the gaps I tried to select poems which had been held in favor in their own day and which most critics still admire. There were, for example, to be no "metaphysical" poems beyond the first exhibit and no "modern" ones other than the last. But the intervening poems were to be read as one has learned to read Donne and the moderns. One was to attempt to see, in terms of this approach, what the masterpieces had in common rather than to see how the poems of different historical periods differed—and in particular to see whether they had anything in common with the "metaphysicals" and with the moderns.

The reader will by this time have made up his mind as to whether the readings are adequate. (I use the word advisedly, for the readings do not pretend to be exhaustive, and certainly it is highly unlikely that they are not in error in one detail or another.) If the reader feels that they are seriously inadequate, then the case has been judged; for the generalizations that follow will be thoroughly vitiated by the inept handling of the particular cases on which they depend.

If, however, the reader does feel them to be adequate, it ought to be readily apparent that the common goodness which the poems share will have to be stated, not in terms of *content* or *subject matter* in the usual sense in which we use these terms, but rather in terms of structure. The "content" of the poems is various, and if we attempt to find one *quality* of content which is shared by all the poems—a "poetic" subject matter or diction or imagery—we shall find that we have merely confused the issues. For what is it to be poetic? Is the schoolroom of Yeats's poem poetic or unpoetic? Is Shakespeare's "new-borne babe / Striding the blast" poetic whereas the idiot of his "Life is a tale tolde by an idiot" is unpoetic? If Herrick's "budding boy or girl" is poetic, then why is not that monstrosity of the newspaper's society page, the "society bud," poetic too?

To say this is not, of course, to say that all materials have precisely the same potentialities (as if the various pigments on the palette had the same potentialities, any one of them suiting the given picture as well as another). But what has been said, on the other hand, requires to be said: for, if we are to proceed at all, we must draw a sharp distinction between the attractiveness or beauty of any particular item taken as such and the "beauty" of the poem considered as a whole. The latter is the effect of a total pattern, and of a kind of pattern which can incorporate within itself items intrinsically beautiful or ugly, attractive or repulsive. Unless one asserts the primacy of the pattern, a poem becomes merely a bouquet of intrinsically beautiful items.

But though it is in terms of structure that we must describe poetry, the term *structure* is certainly not altogether satisfactory as a term. One means by it something far more internal than the metrical pattern, say, or than the sequence of images. The structure meant is certainly not *form* in the conventional sense in which we think of form as a kind of envelope which "contains" the "content." The structure obviously is everywhere conditioned by the nature of the material which goes into the poem. The nature of the material sets the problem to be solved, and the solution is the ordering of the material.

Pope's *Rape of the Lock* will illustrate: the structure is not the heroic couplet as such, or the canto arrangement; for, important as is Pope's use of the couplet as one means by

THE HERESY OF PARAPHRASE. Brook's *The Heresy of Paraphrase* is the last chapter of *The Well Wrought Urn,* copyright, 1947 by Cleanth Brooks. Reprinted by permission of Harcourt Brace Jovanovich, Inc., and the author.
[1]Donne, *The Canonization;* Shakespeare, *Macbeth;* Milton, *L'Allegro* and *Il Penseroso;* Herrick, *Corinna's Going a-Maying;* Pope, *The Rape of the Lock;* Gray, *Elegy Written in a Country Churchyard;* Wordsworth, *Ode: Intimation of Immortality from Recollections of Early Childhood;* Keats, *Ode on a Grecian Urn;* Tennyson, *Tears, Idle Tears;* and Yeats, *Among School Children.*

which he secures the total effect, the heroic couplet can be used—has been used many times—as an instrument in securing very different effects. The structure of the poem, furthermore, is not that of the mock-epic convention, though here, since the term *mock-epic* has implications of attitude, we approach a little nearer to the kind of structure of which we speak.

The structure meant is a structure of meanings, evaluations, and interpretations; and the principle of unity which informs it seems to be one of balancing and harmonizing connotations, attitudes, and meanings. But even here one needs to make important qualifications: the principle is not one which involves the arrangement of the various elements into homogeneous groupings, pairing like with like. It unites the like with the unlike. It does not unite them, however, by the simple process of allowing one connotation to cancel out another nor does it reduce the contradictory attitudes to harmony by a process of subtraction. The unity is not a unity of the sort to be achieved by the reduction and simplification appropriate to an algebraic formula. It is a positive unity, not a negative; it represents not a residue but an achieved harmony.

The attempt to deal with a structure such as this may account for the frequent occurrence in the preceding chapters of such terms as *ambiguity, paradox, complex of attitudes,* and—most frequent of all, and perhaps most annoying to the reader—*irony.* I hasten to add that I hold no brief for these terms as such. Perhaps they are inadequate. Perhaps they are misleading. It is to be hoped in that case that we can eventually improve upon them. But adequate terms—whatever those terms may turn out to be—will certainly have to be terms which do justice to the special kind of structure which seems to emerge as the common structure of poems so diverse on other counts as are *The Rape of the Lock* and *Tears, Idle Tears.*

The conventional terms are much worse than inadequate: they are positively misleading in their implication that the poem constitutes a "statement" of some sort, the statement being true or false, and expressed more or less clearly or eloquently or beautifully; for it is from this formula that most of the common heresies about poetry derive. The formula begins by introducing a dualism which thenceforward is rarely overcome, and which at best can be overcome only by the most elaborate and clumsy qualifications. Where it is not overcome, it leaves the critic lodged upon one or the other of the horns of a dilemma: the critic is forced to judge the poem by its political or scientific or philosophical truth; or, he is forced to judge the poem by its form as conceived externally and detached from human experience. Mr. Alfred Kazin, for example, to take an instance from a recent and popular book, accuses the "new formalists"—his choice of

that epithet is revealing—of accepting the latter horn of the dilemma because he notices that they have refused the former. In other words, since they refuse to rank poems by their messages, he assumes that they are compelled to rank them by their formal embellishments.

The omnipresence of this dilemma, a false dilemma, I believe, will also account for the fact that so much has been made in the preceding chapters of the resistance which any good poem sets up against all attempts to paraphrase it. The point is surely not that we cannot describe adequately enough for many purposes what the poem in general is "about" and what the general effect of the poem is: *The Rape of the Lock* is *about* the foibles of an eighteenth-century belle. The effect of *Corinna's Going a-Maying* is one of gaiety tempered by the poignance of the fleetingness of youth. We can very properly use paraphrases as pointers and as shorthand references provided that we know what we are doing. But it is highly important that we know what we are doing and that we see plainly that paraphrase is not the real core of meaning which constitutes the essence of the poem.

For the imagery and the rhythm are not merely the instruments by which this fancied core-of-meaning-which-can-be-expressed-in-a-paraphrase is directly rendered. Even in the simplest poem their mediation is not positive and direct. Indeed, whatever statement we may seize upon as incorporating the "meaning" of the poem, immediately the imagery and the rhythm seem to set up tensions with it, warping and twisting it, qualifying and revising it. This is true of Wordsworth's *Ode* no less than of Donne's *Canonization.* To illustrate: if we say that the *Ode* celebrates the spontaneous "naturalness" of the child, there is the poem itself to indicate that nature has a more sinister aspect—that the process by which the poetic lamb becomes the dirty old sheep or the child racing over the meadows becomes the balding philosopher is a process that is thoroughly "natural." Or, if we say that the thesis of the *Ode* is that the child brings into the natural world a supernatural glory which acquaintance with the world eventually and inevitably quenches in the light of common day, there is the last stanza and the drastic qualifications which it asserts: it is significant that the thoughts that lie too deep for tears are mentioned in this sunset stanza of the *Ode* and that they are thoughts, not of the child, but of the man.

We have precisely the same problem if we make our example *The Rape of the Lock.* Does the poet assert that Belinda is a goddess? Or does he say that she is a brainless chit? Whichever alternative we take, there are elaborate qualifications to be made. Moreover, if the simple propositions offered seem in their forthright simplicity to make too easy the victory of the poem over any possible statement of its meaning, then let the reader try to formulate a proposition that will say what the poem "says." As his proposition approaches adequacy, he will find, not only that it has increased greatly in length, but that it has begun to fill itself up with reservations and qualifications—and most significant of all—the formulator will find that he has himself begun to fall back upon metaphors of his own in his attempt to indicate what the poem "says." In sum, his proposition, as it approaches adequacy, ceases to be a proposition.

Consider one more case, *Corinna's Going a-Maying*. Is the doctrine preached to Corinna throughout the first four stanzas true? Or is it damnably false? Or is it a "harmless folly"? Here perhaps we shall be tempted to take the last option as the saving mean—what the poem really *says*—and my account of the poem at the end of the third chapter is perhaps susceptible of this interpretation—or misinterpretation. If so, it is high time to clear the matter up. For we mistake matters grossly if we take the poem to be playing with opposed extremes, only to point the golden mean in a doctrine which, at the end, will correct the falsehood of extremes. The reconcilement of opposites which the poet characteristically makes is not that of a prudent splitting of the difference between antithetical overemphases.

It is not so in Wordsworth's poem nor in Keats's nor in Pope's. It is not so even in this poem of Herrick's. For though the poem reflects, if we read it carefully, the primacy of the Christian mores, the pressure exerted throughout the poem is upon the pagan appeal; and the poem ends, significantly, with a reiteration of the appeal to Corinna to go a-Maying, an appeal which, if qualified by the Christian view, still, in a sense, has been deepened and made more urgent by that very qualification. The imagery of loss and decay, it must be remembered, comes in this last stanza after the admission that the May-Day rites are not a real religion but a "harmless folly."

If we are to get all these qualifications into our formulation of what the poem says—and they are relevant—then, our formulation of the "statement" made by Herrick's poem will turn out to be quite as difficult as that of Pope's mock-epic. The truth of the matter is that all such formulations lead away from the center of the poem—not toward it; that the "prose-sense" of the poem is not a rack on which the stuff of the poem is hung; that it does not represent the "inner" structure or the "essential" structure or the "real" structure of the poem. We may use—and in many connections must use—such formulations as more or less convenient ways of referring to parts of the poem. But such formulations are scaffoldings which we may properly for certain purposes throw about the building. We must not mistake them for the internal and essential structure of the building itself.

Indeed, one may sum up by saying that most of the distempers of criticism come about from yielding to the temptation to take certain remarks which we make *about* the poem—statements about what it says or about what truth it gives or about what formulations it illustrates—for the essential core of the poem itself. As W. M. Urban puts it in his *Language and Reality:*

> The general principle of the inseparability of intuition and expression holds with special force for the aesthetic intuition. Here it means that form and content, or content and medium, are inseparable. The artist does not first intuit his object and then find the appropriate medium. It is rather in and through his medium that he intuits the object.

So much for the process of composition. As for the critical process: "To pass from the intuitible to the nonintuitible is to negate the function and meaning of the symbol." For it "is precisely because the more universal and ideal relations cannot be adequately expressed directly that they are indirectly expressed by means of the more intuitible." The most obvious examples of such error (and for that reason those which are really least dangerous) are those theories which frankly treat the poem as propaganda. The most subtle (and the most stubbornly rooted in the ambiguities of language) are those which, beginning with the "paraphrasable" elements of the poem, refer the other elements of the poem finally to some role subordinate to the paraphrasable elements. (The relation between all the elements must surely be an organic one—there can be no question about that. There is, however, a very serious question as to whether the paraphrasable elements have primacy.)

Mr. Winters' position will furnish perhaps the most respectable example of the paraphrastic heresy. He assigns primacy to the "rational meaning" of the poem. "The relationship, in the poem, between rational statement and feeling," he remarks in his latest book, "is thus seen to be that of motive to emotion." He goes on to illustrate his point by a brief and excellent analysis of the following lines from Browning: "So wore night; the East was gray, / White the broadfaced hemlock flowers. . . ."[2]

"The verb *wore*," he continues,

> means literally that the night passed, but it carries with it connotations of exhaustion and attrition which belong to the condition of the protagonist; and grayness is a color which we associate with such a condition. If we change the phrase to read: "Thus night passed," we shall have the same ra-

---

[2]*A Serenade at the Villa*, 21–22.

tional meaning, and a meter quite as respectable, but no trace of the power of the line: the connotation of *wore* will be lost, and the connotation of *gray* will remain in a state of ineffective potentiality.

But the word *wore* does not mean *literally* "that the night passed," it means literally "that the night *wore*"—whatever *wore* may mean, and as Winters' own admirable analysis indicates, *wore* "means," whether *rationally* or *irrationally,* a great deal. Furthermore, "So wore night" and "Thus night passed" can be said to have "the same rational meaning" only if we equate *rational meaning* with the meaning of a loose paraphrase. And can a loose paraphrase be said to be the "motive to emotion"? Can it be said to "generate" the feelings in question? (Or, would Mr. Winters not have us equate *rational statement* and *rational meaning*?)

Much more is at stake here than any quibble. In view of the store which Winters sets by rationality and of his penchant for poems which make their evaluations overtly, and in view of his frequent blindness to those poems which do not—in view of these considerations, it is important to see what "So wore night" and "Thus night passed" have in common as their "rational meaning" is not the "rational meaning" of each but the lowest common denominator of both. To refer the structure of the poem to what is finally a paraphrase of the poem is to refer it to something outside the poem.

To repeat, most of our difficulties in criticism are rooted in the heresy of paraphrase. If we allow ourselves to be misled by it, we distort the relation of the poem to its "truth," we raise the problem of belief in a vicious and crippling form, we split the poem between its "form" and its "content"—we bring the statement to be conveyed into an unreal competition with science or philosophy or theology. In short, we put our questions about the poem in a form calculated to produce the battles of the last twenty-five years over the "use of poetry."[3]

If we allow ourselves to be misled by the heresy of paraphrase, we run the risk of doing even more violence to the internal order of the poem itself. By taking the paraphrase as our point of stance, we misconceive the function of metaphor and meter. We demand logical coherences where they are sometimes irrelevant, and we fail frequently to see imaginative coherences on levels where they are highly relevant.

But what would be a positive theory? We tend to embrace the doctrine of a logical structure the more readily because, to many of us, the failure to do so seems to leave the meaning of the poem hopelessly up in the air. The alternative position will appear to us to lack even the relative stability of an Ivory Tower: it is rather commitment to a free balloon. For, to deny the possibility of pinning down what the poem "says" to some "statement" will seem to assert that the poem really says nothing. And to point out what has been suggested in earlier chapters and brought to a head in this one, namely, that one can never measure a poem against the scientific or philosophical yardstick for the reason that the poem, when laid along the yardstick, is never the "full poem" but an abstraction from the poem—such an argument will seem to such readers a piece of barren logic-chopping—a transparent dodge.

Considerations of strategy then, if nothing more, dictate some positive account of what a poem is and does. And some positive account can be given, though I cannot promise to do more than suggest what a poem is, nor will my terms turn out to be anything more than metaphors.[4]

The essential structure of a poem (as distinguished from the rational or logical structure of the "statement" which we abstract from it) resembles that of architecture or painting: it is a pattern of resolved stresses. Or, to move closer still to poetry by considering the temporal arts, the structure of a poem resembles that of a ballet or musical composition. It is a pattern of resolutions and balances and harmonizations developed through a temporal scheme.[5]

---

[3][Brooks] I do not, of course, intend to minimize the fact that some of these battles have been highly profitable, or to imply that the foregoing paragraphs could have been written except for the illumination shed by the discussions of the last twenty-five years.

[4][Brooks] For those who cannot be content with metaphors (or with the particular metaphors which I can give) I recommend René Wellek's excellent "The Mode of Existence of a Literary Work of Art," *The Southern Review* (Spring 1942). I shall not try to reproduce here as a handy, thumbnail definition his account of a poem as "a stratified system of norms," for the definition would be relatively meaningless without the further definitions which he assigns to the individual terms which he uses. I have made no special use of his terms in this chapter, but I believe that the generalizations about poetry outlined here can be thoroughly accommodated to the position which his essay sets forth.

[5][Brooks] In recent numbers of *Accent,* two critics for whose work I have high regard have emphasized the dynamic character of poetry. Kenneth Burke argues that if we are to consider a poem as a poem, we must consider it as a "mode of action." R. P. Blackmur asks us to think of it as gesture, "the outward and dramatic play of inward and imagined meaning." I do not mean to commit either of these critics to my own interpretation of dramatic or symbolic action; and I have, on my own part, several rather important reservations with respect to Mr. Burke's position. But there are certainly large areas of agreement among our positions. The reader might also compare the account of poetic structure given in this chapter with the following passage from Susanne Langer's *Philosophy in a New Key:*

. . . though the *material* of poetry is verbal, its import is not the literal assertion made in the words, but *the way the assertion is*

Or, to move still closer to poetry, the structure of a poem resembles that of a play. This last example, of course, risks introducing once more the distracting element, since drama, like poetry, makes use of words. Yet, on the whole, most of us are less inclined to force the concept of "statement" on drama than on a lyric poem: for the very nature of drama is that of something "acted out"—something which arrives at its conclusion through conflict—something which builds conflict into its very being. The dynamic nature of drama, in short, allows us to regard it as *an action* rather than as a formula for action or as a statement about action. For this reason, therefore, perhaps the most helpful analogy by which to suggest the structure of poetry is that of the drama, and for many readers at least, the least confusing way in which to approach a poem is to think of it as a drama.

The general point, of course, is not that either poetry or drama makes no use of ideas, or that either is "merely emotional"—whatever *that* is—or that there is not the closest and most important relationship between the intellectual materials which they absorb into their structure and other elements in the structure. The relationship between the intellectual and the nonintellectual elements in a poem is actually far more intimate than the conventional accounts would represent it to be: the relationship is not that of an idea "wrapped in emotion" or a "prose-sense decorated by sensuous imagery."

The dimension in which the poem moves is not one which excludes ideas, but one which does include attitudes. The dimension includes ideas, to be sure; we can always abstract an "idea" from a poem—even from the simplest poem—even from a lyric so simple and unintellectual as

> Western wind, when wilt thou blow
>   That the small rain down can rain?
> Christ, that my love were in my arms
>   And I in my bed again.[6]

But the idea which we abstract—assuming that we can all agree on what that idea is—will always be *abstracted:* it will always be the projection of a plane along a line or the projection of a cone upon a plane.

If this analogy proves to be more confusing than illuminating let us return to the analogy with drama. We have argued that any proposition asserted in a poem is not to be taken in abstraction but is justified, in terms of the poem, if it is justified at all, not by virtue of its scientific or historical or philosophical truth, but is justified in terms of a principle analogous to that of dramatic propriety. Thus, the proposition that "Beauty is truth, truth beauty" is given its precise meaning and significance by its relation to the total context of the poem.

This principle is easy enough to see when the proposition is asserted overtly in the poem—that is, when it constitutes a specific detail of the poem. But the reader may well ask: is it not possible to frame a proposition, a statement, which will adequately represent the total meaning of the poem; that is, is it not possible to elaborate a summarizing proposition which will "say," briefly and in the form of a proposition, what the poem "says" as a poem, a proposition which will say it fully and will say it exactly, no more and no less? Could not the poet, if he had chosen, have framed such a proposition? Cannot we as readers and critics frame such a proposition?

The answer must be that the poet himself obviously did not—else he would not have had to write his poem. We as readers can attempt to frame such a proposition in our effort to understand the poem; it may well help toward an understanding. Certainly, the efforts to arrive at such propositions can do no harm *if we do not mistake them for the inner core of the poem*—if we do not mistake them for "what the poem *really* says." For, if we take one of them to represent the essential poem, we have to disregard the qualifications exerted by the total context as of no account, or else we have assumed that we can reproduce the effect of the total context in a condensed prose statement.[7]

---

[6]Anonymous medieval lyric.

made, and this involves the sound, the tempo, the aura of associations of the words, the long or short sequences of ideas, the wealth or poverty of transient imagery that contains them, the sudden arrest of fantasy by pure fact, or of familiar fact by sudden fantasy, the suspense of literal meaning by a sustained ambiguity resolved in a long-awaited key word, and the unifying, all-embracing artifice of rhythm.

---

[7][Brooks] We may, it is true, be able to adumbrate what the poem says if we allow ourselves enough words, and if we make enough reservations and qualifications, thus attempting to come nearer to the meaning of the poem by successive approximations and refinements, gradually encompassing the meaning and pointing to the area in which it lies rather than realizing it. The earlier chapters of this book, if they are successful, are obviously illustrations of this process. But such adumbrations will lack, not only the tension—the dramatic force—of the poem; they will be at best crude approximations of the poem. Moreover—and this is the crucial point—they will be compelled to resort to the methods of the poem—analogy, metaphor, symbol, etc.—in order to secure even this near an approximation.

Urban's comment upon this problem is interesting: he says that if we expand the symbol,

> we lose the "sense" or value of the symbol *as symbol*. The solution . . . seems to me to lie in an adequate theory of interpretation of the symbol. It does not consist in substituting *literal* for symbol sentences, in other words substituting "blunt" truth for symbolic truth, but rather in deepening and enriching the meaning of the symbol.

But to deny that the coherence of a poem is reflected in a logical paraphrase of its "real meaning" is not, of course, to deny coherence to poetry; it is rather to assert that its coherence is to be sought elsewhere. The characteristic unity of a poem (even of those poems which may accidentally possess a logical unity as well as this poetic unity) lies in the unification of attitudes into a hierarchy subordinated to a total and governing attitude. In the unified poem, the poet has "come to terms" with his experience. The poem does not merely eventuate in a logical conclusion. The conclusion of the poem is the working out of the various tensions—set up by whatever means—by propositions, metaphors, symbols. The unity is achieved by a dramatic process, not a logical; it represents an equilibrium of forces, not a formula. It is "proved" as a dramatic conclusion is proved: by its ability to resolve the conflicts which have been accepted as the *données* of the drama.

Thus, it is easy to see why the relation of each item to the whole context is crucial, and why the effective and essential structure of the poem has to do with the complex of attitudes achieved. A scientific proposition can stand alone. If it is true, it is true. But the expression of an attitude, apart from the occasion which generates it and the situation which it encompasses, is meaningless. For example, the last two lines of the *Intimations* ode, "To me the meanest flower that blows can give / Thoughts that do often lie too deep for tears," when taken in isolation—I do not mean quoted in isolation by one who is even vaguely acquainted with the context—makes a statement which is sentimental if taken in reference to the speaker, and one which is patent nonsense if taken with a general reference. The man in the street (of whom the average college freshman is a good enough replica) knows that the meanest flower that grows does not give *him* thoughts that lie too deep for tears; if he thinks about the matter at all, he is inclined to feel that the person who can make such an assertion is a very fuzzy sentimentalist.

We have already seen the ease with which the statement "Beauty is truth, truth beauty" becomes detached from its context, even in the hands of able critics; and we have seen the misconceptions that ensue when this detachment occurs. To take one more instance: the last stanza of Herrick's *Corinna*, taken in isolation, would probably not impress the average reader as sentimental nonsense. Yet it would suffer quite as much by isolation from its context as would the lines from Keats's *Ode*. For, as mere statement, it would become something flat and obvious—of course our lives are short! And the conclusion from the fact would turn into an obvious truism for the convinced pagan, and, for the convinced Christian, equally obvious, though damnable, nonsense.

Perhaps this is why the poet, to people interested in hard-and-fast generalizations, must always seem to be continually engaged in blurring out distinctions only after provoking and unnecessary delays. But this last position is merely another variant of the paraphrastic heresy: to assume it is to misconceive the end of poetry—to take its meanderings as negative, or to excuse them (with the comfortable assurance that the curved line is the line of beauty) because we can conceive the purpose of a poem to be only the production, in the end, of a proposition—of a statement.

But the meanderings of a good poem (they are meanderings only from the standpoint of the prose paraphrase of the poem) are not negative, and they do not have to be excused; and most of all, we need to see what their positive function is; for unless we can assign them a positive function, we shall find it difficult to explain why one divergence from "the prose line of the argument" is not as good as another. The truth is that the apparent irrelevancies which metrical pattern and metaphor introduce do become relevant when we realize that they function in a good poem to modify, qualify, and develop the total attitude which we are to take in coming to terms with the total situation.

If the last sentence seems to take a dangerous turn toward some special "use of poetry"—some therapeutic value for the sake of which poetry is to be cultivated—I can only say that I have in mind no special ills which poetry is to cure. Uses for poetry are always to be found, and doubtless will continue to be found. But my discussion of the structure of poetry is not being conditioned at this point by some new and special role which I expect poetry to assume in the future or some new function to which I would assign it. The structure described—a structure of "gestures" or attitudes— seems to me to describe the essential structure of both the *Odyssey* and *The Waste Land*. It seems to be the kind of structure which the ten poems considered in this book possess in common.

If the structure of poetry is a structure of the order described, that fact may explain (if not justify) the frequency with which I have had to have recourse, in the foregoing chapters, to terms like *irony* and *paradox*. By using the term *irony*, one risks, of course, making the poem seem arch and self-conscious, since irony, for most readers of poetry, is associated with satire, *vers de société*, and other "intellectual" poetries. Yet, the necessity for some such term ought to be apparent; and *irony* is the most general term that we have for the kind of qualification which the various elements in a context receive from the context. This kind of qualification, as we have seen, is of tremendous importance in any poem. Moreover, *irony* is our most general term for indicating that recognition of incongruities—which, again, pervades all poetry to a degree far beyond what our conventional criticism has been heretofore willing to allow.

Irony in this general sense, then, is to be found in Tennyson's *Tears, Idle Tears* as well as in Donne's *Canonization.* We have, of course, been taught to expect to find irony in Pope's *Rape of the Lock,* but there is a profound irony in Keats's *Ode on a Grecian Urn;* and there is irony of a very powerful sort in Wordsworth's *Intimations* ode. For the thrusts and pressures exerted by the various symbols in this poem are not avoided by the poet: they are taken into account and played, one against the other. Indeed, the symbols—from a scientific point of view—are used perversely: it is the child who is the best philosopher; it is from a kind of darkness—from something that is "shadowy"—that the light proceeds; growth into manhood is viewed, not as an extrication from, but as an incarceration within, a prison.

There should be no mystery as to why this must be so. The terms of science are abstract symbols which do not change under the pressure of the context. They are pure (or aspire to be pure) denotations; they are defined in advance. They are not to be warped into new meanings. But where is the dictionary which contains the terms of a poem? It is a truism that the poet is continually forced to remake language. As Eliot has put it, his task is to "dislocate language into meaning." And, from the standpoint of a scientific vocabulary, this is precisely what he performs: for, rationally considered, the ideal language would contain one term for each meaning, and the relation between term and meaning would be constant. But the word, as the poet uses it, has to be conceived of, not as a discrete particle of meaning, but as a potential of meaning, a nexus or cluster of meanings.

What is true of the poet's language in detail is true of the larger wholes of poetry. And therefore, if we persist in approaching the poem as primarily a rational statement, we ought not to be surprised if the statement seems to be presented to us always in the ironic mode. When we consider the statement immersed in the poem, it presents itself to us, like the stick immersed in the pool of water, warped and bent. Indeed, whatever the statement, it will always show itself as deflected away from a positive, straightforward formulation.

It may seem perverse, however, to maintain, in the face of our revived interest in Donne, that the essential structure of poetry is not logical. For Donne has been appealed to of late as the great master of metaphor who imposes a clean logic on his images beside which the ordering of the images in Shakespeare's sonnets is fumbling and loose. It is perfectly true that Donne makes a great show of logic; but two

matters need to be observed. In the first place, the elaborated and "logical" figure is not Donne's only figure or even his staple one. "Telescoped" figures like "Made one another's hermitage" are to be found much more frequently than the celebrated comparison of the souls of the lovers to the legs of a pair of compasses. In the second place, where Donne uses "logic," he regularly uses it to justify illogical positions. He employs it to overthrow a conventional position or to "prove" an essentially illogical one.

Logic, as Donne uses it, is nearly always an ironic logic to state the claims of an idea or attitude which we have agreed, with our everyday logic, is false. This is not to say, certainly, that Donne is not justified in using his logic so, or that the best of his poems are not "proved" in the only senses in which poems can be proved.

But the proof is not a logical proof. *The Canonization* will scarcely prove to the hard-boiled naturalist that the lovers, by giving up the world, actually attain a better world. Nor will the argument advanced in the poem convince the dogmatic Christian that Donne's lovers are really saints.

In using logic, Donne as a poet is fighting the devil with fire. To adopt Robert Penn Warren's metaphor (which, though I lift it somewhat scandalously out of another context, will apply to this one):

> The poet, somewhat less spectacularly [than the saint], proves his vision by submitting it to the fires of irony—to the drama of the structure—in the hope that the fires will refine it. In other words, the poet wishes to indicate that his vision has been earned, that it can survive reference to the complexities and contradictions of experience.[8]

The same principle that inspires the presence of irony in so many of our great poems also accounts for the fact that so many of them seem to be built around paradoxes. Here again the conventional associations of the term may prejudice the reader just as the mention of Donne may prejudice him. For Donne, as one type of reader knows all too well, was of that group of poets who wished to impress their audience with their cleverness. All of us are familiar with the censure passed upon Donne and his followers by Dr. Johnson, and a great many of us still retain it as our own, softening only the rigor of it and the thoroughness of its application, but not giving it up as a principle.

---

[8]*Pure and Impure Poetry.*

Yet there are better reasons than that of rhetorical vain-glory that have induced poet after poet to choose ambiguity and paradox rather than plain, discursive simplicity. It is not enough for the poet to analyze his experience as the scientist does, breaking it up into parts, distinguishing part from part, classifying the various parts. His task is finally to unify experience. He must return to us the unity of the experience itself as man knows it in his own experience. The poem, if it be a true poem is a simulacrum of reality—in this sense, at least, it is an "imitation"—by *being* an experience rather than any mere statement about experience or any mere abstraction from experience.

Tennyson cannot be content with *saying* that in memory the poet seems both dead *and* alive; he must dramatize its life-in-death for us, and his dramatization involves, necessarily, ironic shock and wonder. The dramatization demands that the antithetical aspects of memory be coalesced into one entity which—if we take it on the level of statement—is a paradox, the assertion of the union of opposites. Keats's Urn must express a life which is above life and its vicissitudes, but it must also bear witness to the fact that its life is not life at all but is a kind of death. To put it in other terms, the Urn must, in its role as historian, assert that myth is truer than history. Donne's lovers must reject the world in order to possess the world.

Or, to take one further instance: Wordsworth's light must serve as the common symbol for aspects of man's vision which seem mutually incompatible—intuition and analytic reason. Wordsworth's poem, as a matter of fact, typifies beautifully the poet's characteristic problem itself. For even this poem, which testifies so heavily to the way in which the world is split up and parceled out under the growing light of reason, cannot rest in this fact as its own mode of perception, and still be a poem. Even after the worst has been said about man's multiple vision, the poet must somehow prove that the child is father to the man, that the dawn light is still somehow the same light as the evening light.

If the poet, then, must perforce dramatize the oneness of the experience, even though paying tribute to its diversity, then his use of paradox and ambiguity is seen as necessary. He is not simply trying to spice up, with a superficially exciting or mystifying rhetoric, the old stale stockpot (though doubtless this will be what the inferior poet does generally and what the real poet does in his lapses). He is rather giving us an insight which preserves the unity of experience and which, at its higher and more serious levels, triumphs over the apparently contradictory and conflicting elements of experience by unifying them into a new pattern.

Wordsworth's *Intimations* ode, then, is not only a poem, but, among other things, a parable about poetry.

Keats's *Ode on a Grecian Urn* is quite obviously such a parable. And, indeed, most of the poems which we have discussed in this study may be taken as such parables.

In one sense, Pope's treatment of Belinda raises all the characteristic problems of poetry. For Pope, in dealing with his "goddess," must face the claims of naturalism and of common sense which would deny divinity to her. Unless he faces them, he is merely a sentimentalist. He must do an even harder thing: he must transcend the conventional and polite attributions of divinity which would be made to her as an acknowledged belle. Otherwise, he is merely trivial and obvious. He must "prove" her divinity against the common-sense denial (the brutal denial) and against the conventional assertion (the polite denial). The poetry must be wrested from the context: Belinda's lock, which is what the rude young man wants and which Belinda rather prudishly defends and which the naturalist asserts is only animal and which displays in its curled care the style of a particular era of history, must be given a place of permanence among the stars.

Irony as a Principle of Structure

One can sum up modern poetic technique by calling it the rediscovery of metaphor and the full commitment to metaphor. The poet can legitimately step out into the universal only by first going through the narrow door of the particular.[1] The poet does not select an abstract theme and then embellish it with concrete details. On the contrary, he must establish the details, must abide by the details, and through his realization of the details attain to whatever general meaning he can attain. The meaning must issue from the particulars; it must not seem to be arbitrarily forced upon the particulars. Thus, our conventional habits of language have to be reversed when we come to deal with poetry. For here it is the tail that wags the dog. Better still, here it is the tail of the kite—the tail that makes the kite fly—the tail that renders the kite more than a frame of paper blown crazily down the wind.

IRONY AS A PRINCIPLE OF STRUCTURE. Brooks's *Irony as a Principle of Structure* was written in 1949 and is reprinted from M. D. Zobel, ed., *Literary Opinion in America* (1951), by permission of the author.
[1]See Johnson, *Rasselas,* p. 320; Reynolds, *Discourses,* p. 315; Blake, *Annotations to Reynolds'* Discourses, pp. 404–06; Goethe, *Conversations with Eckermann,* pp. 530–31; Carlyle, *Symbols,* pp. 546–49; on this point.

The tail of the kite, it is true, seems to negate the kite's function: it weights down something made to rise; and in the same way, the concrete particulars with which the poet loads himself seem to deny the universal to which he aspires. The poet wants to "say" something. Why, then, doesn't he say it directly and forthrightly? Why is he willing to say it only through his metaphors? Through his metaphors, he risks saying it partially and obscurely, and risks not saying it at all. But the risk must be taken, for direct statement leads to abstraction and threatens to take us out of poetry altogether.

The commitment to metaphor thus implies, with respect to general theme, a principle of indirection. With respect to particular images and statements, it implies a principle of organic relationship. That is, the poem is not a collection of beautiful or "poetic" images. If there really existed objects which were somehow intrinsically "poetic," still the mere assemblage of these would not give us a poem. For in that case, one might arrange bouquets of these poetic images and thus create poems by formula. But the elements of a poem are related to each other, not as blossoms juxtaposed in a bouquet, but as the blossoms are related to the other parts of a growing plant. The beauty of the poem is the flowering of the whole plant, and needs the stalk, the leaf, and the hidden roots.

If this figure seems somewhat highflown, let us borrow an analogy from another art: the poem is like a little drama. The total effect proceeds from all the elements in the drama, and in a good poem, as in a good drama, there is no waste motion and there are no superfluous parts.

In coming to see that the parts of a poem are related to each other organically, and related to the total theme indirectly, we have come to see the importance of context. The memorable verses in poetry—even those which seem somehow intrinsically "poetic"—show on inspection that they derive their poetic quality from their relation to a particular context. We may, it is true, be tempted to say that Shakespeare's "Ripeness is all" is poetic because it is a sublime thought, or because it possesses simple eloquence; but that is to forget the context in which the passage appears. The proof that this is so becomes obvious when we contemplate such unpoetic lines as "vitality is all," "serenity is all," "maturity is all,"—statements whose philosophical import in the abstract is about as defensible as that of "ripeness is all." Indeed, the commonplace word *never* repeated five times becomes one of the most poignant lines in *Lear,* but it becomes so because of the supporting context. Even the "meaning" of any particular item is modified by the context. For what is said is said in a particular situation and by a particular dramatic character.

The last instances adduced can be most properly regarded as instances of "loading" from the context. The context endows the particular word or image or statement with significance. Images so charged become symbols; statements so charged become dramatic utterances. But there is another way in which to look at the impact of the context upon the part. The part is modified by the pressure of the context.

Now the *obvious* warping of a statement by the context we characterize as "ironical." To take the simplest instance, we say "this is a fine state of affairs," and in certain contexts the statement means quite the opposite of what it purports to say literally. This is sarcasm, the most obvious kind of irony. Here a complete reversal of meaning is effected: effected by the context, and pointed, probably, by the tone of voice. But the modification can be most important even though it falls far short of sarcastic reversal, and it need not be underlined by the tone of voice at all. The tone of irony can be effected by the skillful disposition of the context. Gray's *Elegy* will furnish an obvious example.

> Can storied urn or animated bust
> Back to its mansion call the fleeting breath?
> Can Honor's voice provoke the silent dust,
> Or Flatt'ry soothe the dull cold ear of death?

In its context, the question is obviously rhetorical. The answer has been implied in the characterization of the breath as fleeting and of the ear of death as dull and cold. The form is that of a question, but the manner in which the question has been asked shows that it is no true question at all.

These are obvious instances of irony, and even on this level, much more poetry is ironical than the reader may be disposed to think. Many of Hardy's poems and nearly all of Housman's, for example, reveal irony quite as definite and overt as this. Lest these examples, however, seem to specialize irony in the direction of the sardonic, the reader ought to be reminded that irony, even in its obvious and conventionally recognized forms, comprises a wide variety of modes: tragic irony, self-irony, playful, arch, mocking, or gentle irony, etc. The body of poetry which may be said to contain irony in the ordinary senses of the term stretches from *Lear,* on the one hand, to *Cupid and Campaspe Played,* on the other.

What indeed would be a statement wholly devoid of an ironic potential—a statement that did not show any qualification of the context? One is forced to offer statements like "Two plus two equals four," or "The square on the hypotenuse of a right triangle is equal to the sum of the squares on the two sides." The meaning of these statements is unqualified by any context; if they are true, they are equally true in any possible context.[2] These statements are properly abstract, and their terms are pure denotations. (If "two" or "four" actually happened to have connotations for the fancifully minded, the connotations would be quite irrelevant: they do not participate in the meaningful structure of the statement.)

But connotations are important in poetry and do enter significantly into the structure of meaning which is the poem. Moreover, I should claim also—as a corollary of the foregoing proposition—that poems never contain abstract statements. That is, any "statement" made in the poem bears the pressure of the context and has its meaning modified by the context. In other words, the statements made—including those which appear to be philosophical generalizations—are to be read as if they were speeches in a drama. Their relevance, their propriety, their rhetorical force, even their meaning, cannot be divorced from the context in which they are imbedded.

The principle I state may seem a very obvious one, but I think that it is nonetheless very important. It may throw some light upon the importance of the term *irony* in modern criticism. As one who has certainly tended to overuse the term *irony* and perhaps, on occasion, has abused the term, I am closely concerned here. But I want to make quite clear what that concern is: it is not to justify the term *irony* as such, but rather to indicate why modern critics are so often tempted to use it. We have doubtless stretched the term too much, but it has been almost the only term available by which to point to a general and important aspect of poetry.

Consider this example: The speaker in Matthew Arnold's *Dover Beach* states that the world, "which seems to lie before us like a land of dreams . . . hath really neither joy nor love nor light. . . ." For some readers the statement will seem an obvious truism. (The hero of a typical Hemingway short story or novel, for example, will say this, though of course in a rather different idiom.) For other readers, however, the statement will seem false, or at least highly questionable. In any case, if we try to "prove" the proposition, we shall raise some very perplexing metaphysical questions, and in doing so, we shall certainly also move away from the

problems of the poem and, finally, from a justification of the poem. For the lines are to be justified in the poem in terms of the context: the speaker is standing beside his loved one, looking out of the window on the calm sea, listening to the long withdrawing roar of the ebbing tide, and aware of the beautiful delusion of moonlight which "blanches" the whole scene. The "truth" of the statement, and of the poem itself, in which it is imbedded, will be validated, not by a majority report of the association of sociologists, or a committee of physical scientists, or of a congress of metaphysicians who are willing to stamp the statement as proved. How is the statement to be validated? We shall probably not be able to do better than to apply T. S. Eliot's test: does the statement seem to be that which the mind of the reader can accept as coherent, mature, and founded on the facts of experience? But when we raise such a question, we are driven to consider the poem as drama. We raise such further questions as these: Does the speaker seem carried away with his own emotions? Does he seem to oversimplify the situation? Or does he, on the other hand, seem to have won to a kind of detachment and objectivity? In other words, we are forced to raise the question as to whether the statement grows properly out of a context; whether it acknowledges the pressures of the context; whether it is "ironical"—or merely callow, glib, and sentimental.

I have suggested elsewhere that the poem which meets Eliot's test comes to the same thing as I. A. Richards' "poetry of synthesis"[3]—that is, a poetry which does not leave out what is apparently hostile to its dominant tone, and which, because it is able to fuse the irrelevant and discordant, has come to terms with itself and is invulnerable to irony. Irony, then, in this further sense, is not only an acknowledgment of the pressures of a context. Invulnerability to irony is the stability of a context in which the internal pressures balance and mutually support each other. The stability is like that of the arch: the very forces which are calculated to drag the stones to the ground actually provide the principle of support—a principle in which thrust and counterthrust become the means of stability.

In many poems the pressures of the context emerge in obvious ironies. Marvell's *To His Coy Mistress* or Raleigh's *Nymph's Reply* or even Gray's *Elegy* reveal themselves as ironical, even to readers who use irony strictly in the conventional sense.

But can other poems be subsumed under this general principle, and do they show a comparable basic structure? The test case would seem to be presented by the lyric, and

---

[2][Brooks] This is not to say, of course, that such statements are not related to a particular "universe of discourse." They are indeed, as are all statements of whatever kind. But I distinguish here between "context" and "universe of discourse." "Two plus two equals four" is not dependent on a special dramatic context in the way in which a "statement" made in a poem is. Compare "two plus two equals four" and the same "statement" as contained in Housman's poem:

> —To think that two and two are four
>   And neither five nor three
> The heart of man has long been sore
>   And long 'tis like to be.

---

[3]*Principles of Literary Criticism.*

particularly the simple lyric. Consider, for example, one of Shakespeare's songs:

> Who is Silvia: what is she
>> That all our swains commend her?
> Holy, fair, and wise is she;
>> The heavens such grace did lend her,
> That she might admired be.
>
> Is she kind as she is fair?
>> For beauty lives with kindness.
> Love doth to her eyes repair,
>> To help him of his blindness,
> And, being help'd, inhabits there.
>
> Then to Silvia let us sing,
>> That Silvia is excelling;
> She excels each mortal thing
>> Upon the dull earth dwelling:
> To her let us garlands bring.

On one level the song attempts to answer the question, who is Silvia? and the answer given makes her something of an angel and something of a goddess. She excels each mortal thing "Upon the dull earth dwelling." Silvia herself, of course, dwells upon that dull earth, though it is presumably her own brightness which makes it dull by comparison. (The dull earth, for example, yields bright garlands which the swains are bringing to her.) Why does she excel each mortal thing? Because of her virtues ("Holy, fair, and wise is she"), and these are a celestial gift. She is heaven's darling ("The heavens such grace did lend her").

Grace, I suppose, refers to grace of movement, and some readers will insist that we leave it at that. But since Silvia's other virtues include holiness and wisdom, and since her grace has been lent from above, I do not think that we can quite shut out the theoretical overtones. Shakespeare's audience would have found it even more difficult to do so. At any rate, it is interesting to see what happens if we are aware of these overtones. We get a delightful richness, and we also get something very close to irony.

The motive for the bestowal of grace—that she might admired be—is oddly untheological. But what follows is odder still, for the love that "doth to her eyes repair" is not, as we might expect, Christian "charity" but the little pagan god Cupid ("Love doth to her eyes repair, / To help him of his blindness.") But if Cupid lives in her eyes, then the second line of the stanza takes on another layer of meaning. "For beauty lives with kindness" becomes not merely a kind of charming platitude—actually often denied in human ex-

perience. (The Petrarchan lover, for example, as Shakespeare well knew, frequently found a beautiful and *cruel* mistress.) The second line, in this context, means also that the love god lives with the kind Silvia, and indeed has taken these eyes that sparkle with kindness for his own.

Is the mixture of pagan myth and Christian theology, then, an unthinking confusion into which the poet has blundered, or is it something wittily combined? It is certainly not a confusion, and if blundered into unconsciously, it is a happy mistake. But I do not mean to press the issue of the poet's self-consciousness (and with it, the implication of a kind of playful irony). Suffice it to say that the song is charming and delightful, and that the mingling of elements is proper to a poem which is a deft and light-fingered attempt to suggest the quality of divinity with which lovers perennially endow maidens who are finally mortal. The touch is light, there is a lyric grace, but the tone is complex, nonetheless.

I shall be prepared, however, to have this last example thrown out of court since Shakespeare, for all his universality, was a contemporary of the metaphysical poets, and may have incorporated more of their ironic complexity than is necessary or normal. One can draw more innocent and therefore more convincing examples from Wordsworth's Lucy poems.

> She dwelt among the untrodden ways
>> Beside the springs of Dove,
> A maid whom there were none to praise
>> And very few to love;
>
> A violet by a mossy stone
>> Half hidden from the eye!
> Fair as a star, when only one
>> Is shining in the sky.
>
> She lived unknown, and few could know
>> When Lucy ceased to be;
> But she is in her grave, and, oh,
>> The difference to me.

Which is Lucy really like—the violet or the star? The context in general seems to support the violet comparison. The violet, beautiful but almost unnoticed, already half hidden from the eye, is now, as the poem ends, completely hidden in its grave, with none but the poet to grieve for its loss. The star comparison may seem only vaguely relevant—a conventional and here a somewhat anomalous compliment. Actually, it is not difficult to justify the star comparison: to her lover's eyes, she is the solitary star. She has no rivals, nor would the idea of rivalry, in her unselfconscious simplicity, occur to her.

The violet and the star thus balance each other and between themselves define the situation: Lucy was, from the viewpoint of the great world, unnoticed, shy, modest, and half hidden from the eye, but from the standpoint of her lover, she is the single star, completely dominating that world, not arrogantly like the sun, but sweetly and modestly, like the star. The implicit contrast is that so often developed ironically by John Donne in his poems where the lovers, who amount to nothing in the eyes of the world, become, in their own eyes, each the other's world—as in *The Good-Morrow,* where their love makes "one little room an everywhere," or as in *The Canonization,* where the lovers drive into the mirrors of each other's eyes the "towns, countries, courts"— which make up the great world; and thus find that world in themselves. It is easy to imagine how Donne would have exploited the contrast between the violet and the star, accentuating it, developing the irony, showing how the violet was really like its antithesis, the star, etc.

Now one does not want to enter an Act of Uniformity against the poets. Wordsworth is entitled to his method of simple juxtaposition with no underscoring of the ironical contrast. But it is worth noting that the contrast with its ironic potential is there in his poem. It is there in nearly all of Wordsworth's successful lyrics. It is certainly to be found in "A slumber did my spirit seal."

> A slumber did my spirit seal;
>   I had no human fears:
> She seemed a thing that could not feel
>   The touch of earthly years.
>
> No motion has she now, no force;
>   She neither hears nor sees,
> Rolled round in earth's diurnal course,
>   With rocks, and stones, and trees.

The lover's insensitivity to the claims of mortality is interpreted as a lethargy of spirit—a strange slumber. Thus the "human fears" that he lacked are apparently the fears normal to human beings. But the phrase has a certain pliability. It could mean fears *for* the loved one as a mortal human being; and the lines that follow tend to warp the phrase in this direction: it does not occur to the lover that he needs to fear for one who cannot be touched by "earthly years." We need not argue that Wordsworth is consciously using a witty device, a purposed ambiguity; nor need we conclude that he is confused. It is enough to see that Wordsworth has developed, quite "normally," let us say, a context calculated to pull "human fears" in opposed directions, and that the

slightest pressure of attention on the part of the reader precipitates an ironical effect.

As we move into the second stanza, the potential irony almost becomes overt. If the slumber has sealed the lover's spirit, a slumber, immersed in which he thought it impossible that his loved one could perish, so too a slumber has now definitely sealed *her* spirit: "No motion has she now, no force; / She neither hears nor sees." It is evident that it is her unnatural slumber that has waked him out of his. It is curious to speculate on what Donne or Marvell would have made of this.

Wordsworth, however, still does not choose to exploit the contrast as such. Instead, he attempts to suggest something of the lover's agonized shock at the loved one's present lack of motion—of his response to her utter and horrible inertness. And how shall he suggest this? He chooses to suggest it, not by saying that she lies as quiet as marble or as a lump of clay; on the contrary, he attempts to suggest it by imagining her in violent motion—violent, but imposed motion, the same motion indeed which the very stones share, whirled about as they are in earth's diurnal course. Why does the image convey so powerfully the sense of something inert and helpless? Part of the effect, of course, resides in the fact that a dead lifelessness is suggested more sharply by an object's being whirled about by something else than by an image of the object in repose. But there are other matters which are at work here: the sense of the girl's falling back into the clutter of things, companioned by things chained like a tree to one particular spot, or by things completely inanimate, like rocks and stones. Here, of course, the concluding figure leans upon the suggestion made in the first stanza, that the girl once seemed something not subject to earthly limitations at all. But surely, the image of the whirl itself is important in its suggestion of something meaningless—motion that mechanically repeats itself. And there is one further element: the girl, who to her lover seemed a thing that could not feel the touch of earthly years, is caught up helplessly into the empty whirl of the earth which measures and makes time. She is touched by and held by earthly time in its most powerful and horrible image. The last figure thus seems to me to summarize the poem—to offer to almost every facet of meaning suggested in the earlier lines a concurring and resolving image which meets and accepts and reduces each item to its place in the total unity.

Wordsworth, as we have observed above, does not choose to point up specifically the ironical contrast between the speaker's former slumber and the loved one's present slumber. But there is one ironical contrast which he does stress: this is the contrast between the two senses in which the girl becomes insulated against the "touch of earthly years." In the first stanza, she "could not feel / The touch of earthly years" because she seemed divine and immortal. But in the second stanza, now in her grave, she still does not "feel the touch of earthly years," for, like the rocks and stones, she feels nothing at all. It is true that Wordsworth does not repeat the verb "feels"; instead he writes "She neither *hears* nor *sees*." But the contrast, though not commented upon directly by any device of verbal wit, is there nonetheless, and is bound to make itself felt in any sensitive reading of the poem. The statement of the first stanza has been literally realized in the second, but its meaning has been ironically reversed.

Ought we, then, to apply the term *ironical* to Wordsworth's poem? Not necessarily. I am trying to account for my temptation to call such a poem ironical—not to justify my yielding to the temptation—least of all to insist that others so transgress. Moreover, Wordsworth's poem seems to me admirable, and I entertain no notion that it might have been more admirable still had John Donne written it rather than William Wordsworth. I shall be content if I can make a much more modest point: namely, that since both Wordsworth and Donne are poets, their work has at basis a similar structure, and that the dynamic structure—the pattern of thrust and counterthrust—which we associate with Donne has its counterpart in Wordsworth. In the work of both men, the relation between part and part is organic, which means that each part modifies and is modified by the whole.

Yet to intimate that there are potential ironies in Wordsworth's lyric may seem to distort it. After all, is it not simple and spontaneous? With these terms we encounter two of the critical catchwords of the nineteenth century, even as *ironical* is in danger of becoming a catchword of our own period. Are the terms *simple* and *ironical* mutually exclusive? What after all do we mean by *simple* or by *spontaneous?* We may mean that the poem came to the poet easily and even spontaneously: very complex poems may—indeed have—come just this way. Or the poem may seem in its effect on the reader a simple and spontaneous utterance: some poems of great complexity possess this quality. What is likely to cause trouble here is the intrusion of a special theory of composition. It is fairly represented as an intrusion since a theory as to how a poem is written is being allowed to dictate to us how the poem is to be read. There is no harm in thinking of Wordsworth's poem as simple and spontaneous unless these terms deny complexities that actually exist in the poem, and unless they justify us in reading the poem with only half our minds. A slumber ought not to seal the *reader's* spirit as he reads this poem, or any other poem.

I have argued that irony, taken as the acknowledgment of the pressures of context, is to be found in poetry of every period and even in simple lyrical poetry. But in the poetry of our own time, this pressure reveals itself strikingly. A great deal of modern poetry does use irony as its special and perhaps its characteristic strategy. For this there are reasons, and compelling reasons. To cite only a few of these reasons: there is the breakdown of a common symbolism; there is the general skepticism as to universals; not least important, there is the depletion and corruption of the very language itself, by advertising and by the mass-produced arts of radio, the moving picture, and pulp fiction. The modern poet has the task of rehabilitating a tired and drained language so that it can convey meanings once more with force and with exactitude. This task of qualifying and modifying language is perennial; but it is imposed on the modern poet as a special burden. Those critics who attribute the use of ironic techniques to the poet's own bloodless sophistication and tired skepticism would be better advised to refer these vices to his potential readers, a public corrupted by Hollywood and the Book of the Month Club. For the modern poet is not addressing simple primitives but a public sophisticated by commercial art.

At any rate, to the honor of the modern poet be it said that he has frequently succeeded in using his ironic techniques to win through to clarity and passion. Randall Jarrell's *Eighth Air Force* represents a success of this sort.

If, in an odd angle of the hutment,
A puppy laps the water from a can
Of flowers, and the drunk sergeant shaving
Whistles *O Paradiso!*—shall I say that man
Is not as men have said: a wolf to man?

The other murderers troop in yawning;
Three of them play pitch, one sleeps, and one
Lies counting missions, lies there sweating
Till even his heart beats: One; One; One.
O murderers! . . . Still, this is how it's done:

This is a war. . . . But since these play, before they die,
Like puppies with their puppy; since, a man,
I did as these have done, but did not die—
I will content the people as I can
And give up these to them: Behold the man!

I have suffered, in a dream, because of him,
Many things; for this last savior, man,
I have lied as I lie now. But what is lying?
Men wash their hands, in blood, as best they can:
I find no fault in this just man.

There are no superfluous parts, no dead or empty details. The airmen in their hutment are casual enough and honest enough to be convincing. The raw building is domesticated: there are the flowers in water from which the mascot, a puppy, laps. There is the drunken sergeant, whistling an opera aria as he shaves. These "murderers," as the poet is casually to call the airmen in the next stanza, display a touching regard for the human values. How, then, can one say that man is a wolf to man, since these men "play before they die, like puppies with their puppy." But the casual presence of the puppy in the hutment allows us to take the stanza both ways, for the dog is a kind of tamed and domesticated wolf, and his presence may prove on the contrary that the hutment is the wolf den. After all, the timber wolf plays with its puppies.

The second stanza takes the theme to a perfectly explicit conclusion. If three of the men play pitch, and one is asleep, at least one man is awake and counts himself and his companions murderers. But his unvoiced cry "O murderers" is met, countered, and dismissed with the next two lines: ". . . Still this is how it's done: / This is a war. . . ."

The note of casuistry and cynical apology prepares for a brilliant and rich resolving image, the image of Pontius Pilate, which is announced specifically in the third stanza: "I will content the people as I can / And give up these to them: behold the man!" Yet if Pilate, as he is first presented, is a jesting Pilate, who asks, what is truth? it is a bitter and grieving Pilate who concludes the poem. It is the integrity of man himself that is at stake. Is man a cruel animal, a wolf, or is he the last savior, the Christ of our secular religion of humanity?

The Pontius Pilate metaphor, as the poet uses it, becomes a device for tremendous concentration. For the speaker (presumably the young airman who cried "O murderers") is himself the confessed murderer under judgment, and also the Pilate who judges, and, at least as a representative of man, the savior whom the mob would condemn. He is even Pilate's better nature, his wife, for the lines "I have suffered, in a dream, because of him, / Many things" is merely a rearrangement of Matthew 27:19, the speech of Pilate's wife to her husband. But this last item is more than a reminiscence of the scriptural scene. It reinforces the speaker's present dilemma. The modern has had high hopes for man; are the hopes merely a dream? Is man incorrigible, merely a cruel beast? The speaker's present torture springs from that hope and from his reluctance to dismiss it as an empty dream. This Pilate is even harder pressed than was the Roman magistrate. For he must convince himself of this last savior's innocence. But he had lied for him before. He will lie for him now. "Men wash their hands in blood, as best they can: / I find no fault in this just man."

What is the meaning of "Men wash their hands in blood, as best they can"? It can mean "Since my own hands are bloody, I have no right to condemn the rest." It can mean

"I know that man can love justice, even though his hands are bloody, for there is blood on mine." It can mean "Men are essentially decent: they try to keep their hands clean even if they have only blood in which to wash them."

None of these meanings cancels out the others. All are relevant, and each meaning contributes to the total meaning. Indeed, there is not a facet of significance which does not receive illumination from the figure.

Some of Jarrell's weaker poems seem weak to me because they lean too heavily upon this concept of the goodness of man. In some of them, his approach to the theme is too direct. But in this poem, the affirmation of man's essential justness by a Pilate who contents the people as he washes his hands in blood seems to me to supply every qualification that is required. The sense of self-guilt, the yearning to believe in man's justness, the knowledge of the difficulty of so believing—all work to render accurately and dramatically the total situation.

It is easy at this point to misapprehend the function of irony. We can say that Jarrell's irony pares his theme down to acceptable dimensions. The theme of man's goodness has here been so qualified that the poet himself does not really believe in it. But this is not what I am trying to say. We do not ask a poet to bring his poem into line with our personal beliefs—still less to flatter our personal beliefs. What we do ask is that the poem dramatize the situation so accurately, so honestly, with such fidelity to the total situation that it is no longer a question of our beliefs, but of our participation in the poetic experience. At his best, Jarrell manages to bring us by an act of imagination, to the most penetrating insight. Participating in that insight, we doubtless become better citizens. (One of the "uses" of poetry, I should agree, is to make us better citizens.) But poetry is not the eloquent rendition of the citizen's creed. It is not even the accurate rendition of his creed. Poetry must carry us beyond the abstract creed into the very matrix out of which, and from which, our creeds are abstracted. That is what *The Eighth Air Force* does. That is what, I am convinced, all good poetry does.

For the theme in a genuine poem does not confront us as abstraction—that is, as one man's generalization from the relevant particulars. Finding its proper symbol, defined and refined by the participating metaphors, the theme becomes a part of the reality in which we live—an insight, rooted in and growing out of concrete experience, many-sided, three-dimensional. Even the resistance to generalization has its part in this process—even the drag of the particulars away from the universal—even the tension of opposing themes—play their parts. The kite properly loaded, tension maintained along the kite string, rises steadily *against* the thrust of the wind.

Jan Mukařovský

1891–1975

Mukařovský was a member of the Prague school of structural linguists, which built on the work of the Swiss linguist Ferdinand de Saussure and was influenced by Russian Formalism, principally through the work of Roman Jakobson. In *Standard Language and Poetic Language* Mukařovský argues that poetic language is not simply a special brand of standard language, for it has at its disposal all the forms of the given language in addition to some of its own. Nevertheless poetic language is closely related to standard language because the latter is the background against which poetic language is "foregrounded." It is in this contrast that poetic language can be seen as intentionally violating the norm of the standard.

According to Mukařovský, the function of poetic language is to achieve a maximum of foregrounding, which is a use of language for its own sake, or not in the service of communication. He proposes that where there is a clearly defined norm of standard language, there is a greater opportunity for foregrounding, thus for poetry. Scientific language avoids foregrounding by exact definition of terms. In order to have a foreground, however, there must be a background: the poem cannot totally violate the norm of the standard. Mukařovský sees the poem as a unity in variety, a dynamic unity of harmony and disharmony: "The mutual relationships of the components of the work of poetry, both foregrounded and unforegrounded, constitute its *structure.*" Remarks like these reveal the similarities between Mukařovský's attitude and the attitudes of various American New Critics.

A Prague School Reader on Esthetics, Literary Structure, and Style (1964), translated by *P. L. Garvin,* contains Mukařovský's essay *Standard Language and Poetic Language.* Many of his works have not been translated into English. His best-known works are perhaps *Estetická funkce, norma a hodnota jako sociáln í fakt (Aesthetic Function, Norm, and Value as Social Facts)* (1936) and *Kapitoly z české poetiky (Chapters on Czech Poetry)* (1938). *On Poetic Language* was translated in 1976, followed by *Structure, Sign, and Function* (1978) and *The Word and Verbal Art* (1977). See Thomas G. Winner, "Jan Mukařovský: The Beginnings of Structural and Semiotic Aesthetics," *Sound, Sign and Meaning* (L. Matejka, ed.), 1976.

From

Standard Language and Poetic Language

The problem of the relationship between standard language and poetic language can be considered from two standpoints. The theorist of poetic language poses it somewhat as follows: Is the poet bound by the norms of the standard? Or perhaps: How does this norm assert itself in poetry? The theorist of the standard language, on the other hand, wants to know above all to what extent a work of poetry can be used as data for ascertaining the norm of the standard. In other words, the theory of poetic language is primarily interested in the differences between the standard and poetic language, whereas the theory of the standard language is mainly interested in the similarities between them. It is clear that with a good procedure no conflict can arise between the two directions of research; there is only a difference in the point of view and in the illumination of the problem. Our study approaches the problem of the relationship between poetic language and the standard from the vantage point of poetic language. Our procedure will be to subdivide the general problem into a number of special problems.

The first problem, by way of introduction, concerns the following: What is the *relationship* between the extension of *poetic language* and that of the *standard,* between the places of each in the total system of the whole of language? Is poetic language a special brand of the standard, or is it an independent formation?—Poetic language cannot be called a brand of the standard, if for no other reason that poetic language has at its disposal, from the standpoint of lexicon, syntax, etc., all the forms of the given language—often of different developmental phases thereof. There are works in which the lexical material is taken over completely from another form of language than the standard (thus, Villon's or Rictus' slang poetry in French literature). Different forms of the language may exist side by side in a work of poetry (for instance, in the dialogues of a novel dialect or slang, in the narrative passages the standard). Poetic language finally has also some of its own lexicon and phraseology as well as

some grammatical forms, the so-called poetisms such as *zor* ["gaze"], *oř* ["steed"], *pláti* ["be aflame"], 3rd p. sg. *můž* ["can"; cf. English *-th*] (a rich selection of examples can be found in the ironic description of "moon language" in [Svatopluk] Čech's [1846–1908, a realist] *Výlet pana Broučka do měsíce* [*Mr. Brouček's Trip to the Moon*]). Only some schools of poetry, of course, have a positive attitude towards poetisms (among them the Lumír Group including Svatopluk Čech); others reject them.

Poetic language is thus not a brand of the standard. This is not to deny the close connection between the two, which consists in the fact that, for poetry, the standard language is the background against which is reflected the esthetically intentional distortion of the linguistic components of the work, in other words, the intentional violation of the norm of the standard. Let us, for instance, visualize a work in which this distortion is carried out by the interpenetration of dialect speech with the standard; it is clear, then, that it is not the standard which is perceived as a distortion of the dialect, but the dialect as a distortion of the standard, even when the dialect is quantitatively preponderant. The violation of the norm of the standard, its systematic violation, is what makes possible the poetic utilization of language; without this possibility there would be no poetry. The more the norm of the standard is stabilized in a given language, the more varied can be its violation, and therefore the more possibilities for poetry in that language. And on the other hand, the weaker the awareness of this norm, the fewer possibilities of violation, and hence the fewer possibilities for poetry. Thus, in the beginnings of modern Czech poetry, when the awareness of the norm of the standard was weak, poetic neologisms with the purpose of violating the norm of the standard were little different from neologisms designed to gain general acceptance and become a part of the norm of the standard, so that they could be confused with them.

Such is the case of M. Z. Polák [1788–1856, an early Romantic], whose neologisms are to this day considered poor neologisms of the standard.

. . .

A structural analysis of Polák's[1] poem would show that [Josef] Jungmann [a leading figure of the Czech national renascence] was right [in evaluating Polák's poetry positively]. We are here citing the disagreement in the evaluation of Polák's neologisms merely as an illustration of the state-

STANDARD LANGUAGE AND POETIC LANGUAGE. Mukařovský's *Standard Language and Poetic Language* was first published in 1948 in the second edition of *Kapitoly z české poetiky (Chapters on Czech Poetry).* The text is from *A Prague School Reader on Esthetics, Literary Structure, and Style,* translated by Paul L. Garvin (Washington, D.C.: Georgetown University Press, 1964), pp. 17–30. Reprinted by permission of the publisher. Bracketed material is supplied by the translator. The notes are those of Mukařovský.

[1]It is important to note that Polák himself in lexical notes to his poem clearly distinguishes little-known works (including obvious neologisms and new loans) from those which he used "for better poetic expression," that is, as is shown by the evidence, from poetic neologisms.

ment that, when the norm of the standard is weak—as was the case in the period of national renascence, it is difficult to differentiate the devices intended to shape this norm from those intended for its consistent and deliberate violation, and that a language with a weak norm of the standard therefore offers fewer devices to the poet.

This relationship between poetic language and the standard, one which we could call negative, also has its positive side which is, however, more important for the theory of the standard language than for poetic language and its theory. Many of the linguistic components of a work of poetry do not deviate from the norm of the standard because they constitute the background against which the distortion of the other components is reflected. The theoretician of the standard language can therefore include works of poetry in his data with the reservation that he will differentiate the distorted components from those that are not distorted. An assumption that all components have to agree with the norm of the standard would, of course, be erroneous.

The second special question which we shall attempt to answer concerns the different *function* of the two forms of language. This is the core of the problem. The function of poetic language consists in the maximum of foregrounding of the utterance. Foregrounding is the opposite of automatization, that is, the deautomatization of an act; the more an act is automatized, the less it is consciously executed; the more it is foregrounded, the more completely conscious does it become. Objectively speaking: automatization schematizes an event; foregrounding means the violation of the scheme. The standard language in its purest form, as the language of science with formulation as its objective, avoids foregrounding [*aktualisace*]: thus, a new expression, foregrounded because of its newness, is immediately automatized in a scientific treatise by an exact definition of its meaning. Foregrounding is, of course, common in the standard language, for instance, in journalistic style, even more in essays. But here it is always subordinate to communication: its purpose is to attract the reader's (listener's) attention more closely to the subject matter expressed by the foregrounded means of expression. All that has been said here about foregrounding and automatization in the standard language has been treated in detail in Havránek's paper in this cycle; we are here concerned with poetic language. In poetic language foregrounding achieves maximum intensity to the extent of pushing communication into the background as the objective of expression and of being used for its own sake; it is not used in the services of communication, but in order to place in the foreground the act of expression, the act of speech itself. The question is then one of how this maximum of foregrounding is achieved in poetic language. The idea

might arise that this is a quantitative effect, a matter of the foregrounding of the largest number of components, perhaps of all of them together. This would be a mistake, although only a theoretical one, since in practice such a complete foregrounding of all the components is impossible. The foregrounding of any one of the components is necessarily accompanied by the automatization of one or more of the other components; thus, for instance, the foregrounded intonation in [Jaroslav] Vrchlický [1853–1912, a poet of the Lumír Group, see above] and [Svatopluk] Čech has necessarily pushed to the lowest level of automatization the meaning of the word as a unit, because the foregrounding of its meaning would give the word phonetic independence as well and lead to a disturbance of the uninterrupted flow of the intonational (melodic) line; an example of the degree to which the semantic independence of the word in context also manifests itself as intonational independence can be found in [Karel] Toman's [1877–1946, a modern poet] verse. The foregrounding of intonation as an uninterrupted melodic line is thus linked to the semantic "emptiness" for which the Lumír Group has been criticized by the younger generation as being "verbalistic."—In addition to the practical impossibility of the foregrounding of all components, it can also be pointed out that the simultaneous foregrounding of all the components of a work of poetry is unthinkable. This is because the foregrounding of a component implies precisely its being placed in the foreground; the unit in the foreground, however, occupies this position by comparison with another unit or units that remain in the background. A simultaneous general foregrounding would thus bring all the components into the same plane and so become a new automatization.

The devices by which poetic language achieves its maximum of foregrounding must therefore be sought elsewhere than in the quantity of foregrounded components. They consist in the consistency and systematic character of foregrounding. The consistency manifests itself in the fact that the reshaping of the foregrounded component within a given work occurs in a stable direction; thus, the deautomatization of meanings in a certain work is consistently carried out by lexical selection (the mutual interlarding of contrasting areas of the lexicon), in another equally consistently by the uncommon semantic relationship of words close together in the context. Both procedures result in a foregrounding of meaning, but differently for each. The systematic foregrounding of components in a work of poetry consists in the gradation of the interrelationships of these components, that is, in their mutual subordination and superordination. The component highest in the hierarchy becomes the dominant. All other components, foregrounded or not, as well as their interrelationships, are evaluated from the standpoint of the dominant. The dominant is that component of the work which sets in motion, and gives direction to, the relationships of all other components. The material of a work of poetry is intertwined with the interrelationships of the components even if it is in a completely unforegrounded state. Thus, there is always present, in communicative speech as well, the potential relationship between intonation and meaning, syntax, word order, or the relationship of the word as a meaningful unit to the phonetic structure of the text, to the lexical selection found in the text, to other words as units of meaning in the context of the same sentence. It can be said that each linguistic component is linked directly or indirectly, by means of these multiple interrelationships, in some way to every other component. In communicative speech these relationships are for the most part merely potential, because attention is not called to their presence and to their mutual relationship. It is, however, enough to disturb the equilibrium of this system at some point and the entire network of relationships is slanted in a certain direction and follows it in its internal organization: tension arises in one portion of this network (by consistent unidirectional foregrounding), while the remaining portions of the network are relaxed (by automatization perceived as an intentionally arranged background). This internal organization of relationships will be different in terms of the point affected, that is, in terms of the dominant. More concretely: sometimes intonation will be governed by meaning (by various procedures), sometimes, on the other hand, the meaning structure will be determined by intonation; sometimes again, the relationship of a word to the lexicon may be foregrounded, then again its relationship to the phonetic structure of the text. Which of the possible relationships will be foregrounded, which will remain automatized, and what will be the direction of foregrounding—whether from component A to component B or vice versa, all this depends on the dominant.

The dominant thus creates the unity of the work of poetry. It is, of course, a unity of its own kind, the nature of which in aesthetics is usually designated as "unity in variety," a dynamic unity in which we at the same time perceive harmony and disharmony, convergence and divergence. The convergence is given by the trend towards the dominant, the divergence by the resistance of the unmoving background of unforegrounded components against this trend. Components may appear unforegrounded from the standpoint of the standard language, or from the standpoint of the poetic canon, that is, the set of firm and stable norms into which the structure of a preceding school of poetry has dissolved by automatization, when it is no longer perceived as an indivisible and undissociable whole. In other words, it is possible in some cases for a component which is foregrounded in terms

of the norms of the standard, not to be foregrounded in a certain work because it is in accord with the automatized poetic canon. Every work of poetry is perceived against the background of a certain tradition, that is, of some automatized canon with regard to which it constitutes a distortion. The outward manifestation of this automatization is the ease with which creation is possible in terms of this canon, the proliferation of epigones, the liking for obsolescent poetry in circles not close to literature. Proof of the intensity with which a new trend in poetry is perceived as a distortion of the traditional canon is the negative attitude of conservative criticism which considers deliberate deviations from the canon errors against the very essence of poetry.

The background which we perceive behind the work of poetry as consisting of the unforegrounded components resisting foregrounding is thus dual: the norm of the standard language and the traditional aesthetic canon. Both backgrounds are always potentially present, though one of them will predominate in the concrete case. In periods of powerful foregrounding of linguistic elements, the background of the norm of the standard predominates, while in periods of moderate foregrounding, that of the traditional canon. If the latter has strongly distorted the norm of the standard, then its moderate distortion may, in turn, constitute a renewal of the norm of the standard, and this precisely because of its moderation. The mutual relationships of the components of the work of poetry, both foregrounded and unforegrounded, constitute its *structure,* a dynamic structure including both convergence and divergence and one that constitutes an undissociable artistic whole, since each of its components has its value precisely in terms of its relation to the totality.

It is thus obvious that the possibility of distorting the norm of the standard, if we henceforth limit ourselves to this particular background of foregrounding, is indispensable to poetry. Without it, there would be no poetry. To criticize the deviations from the norm of the standard as faults, especially in a period which, like the present, tends towards a powerful foregrounding of linguistic components, means to reject poetry. It could be countered that in some works of poetry, or rather in some genres, only the "content" (subject matter) is foregrounded, so that the above remarks do not concern them. To this it must be noted that in a work of poetry of any genre there is no fixed border, nor, in a certain sense, any essential difference between the language and the subject matter. The subject matter of a work of poetry cannot be judged by its relationship to the extralinguistic reality entering into the work; it is rather a component of the semantic side of the work (we do not want to assert, of course, that its relationship to reality cannot become a factor of its structure, as for instance in realism). The proof of this statement could be given rather extensively; let us, however, limit ourselves to the most important point: the question of truthfulness does not apply in regard to the subject matter of a work of poetry, nor does it even make sense. Even if we posed the question and answered it positively or negatively as the case may be, the question has no bearing on the artistic value of the work; it can only serve to determine the extent to which the work has documentary value. If in some work of poetry there is emphasis on the question of truthfulness (as in [Vladislav] Vančura's [1891–1942, a modern author] short story *Dobrá míra* [*The Good Measure*]), this emphasis only serves the purpose of giving the subject matter a certain semantic coloration. The status of subject matter is entirely different in case of communicative speech. There, a certain relationship of the subject matter to reality is an important value, a necessary prerequisite. Thus, in the case of a newspaper report the question whether a certain event has occurred or not is obviously of basic significance.

The subject matter of a work of poetry is thus its largest semantic unit. In terms of being meaning, it has certain properties which are not directly based on the linguistic sign, but are linked to it insofar as the latter is a general semiological unit (especially its independence of any specific signs, or sets of signs, so that the same subject matter may without basic changes be rendered by different linguistic devices, or even transposed into a different set of signs altogether, as in the transposition of subject matter from one art form to another), but this difference in properties does not affect the semantic character of the subject matter. It thus holds, even for works and genres of poetry in which the subject matter is the dominant, that the latter is not the "equivalent" of a reality to be expressed by the work as effectively (for instance, as truthfully) as possible, but that it is a part of the structure, is governed by its laws, and is evaluated in terms of its relationship to it. If this is the case, then it holds for the novel as well as for the lyrical poem that to deny a work of poetry the right to violate the norm of the standard is equivalent to the negation of poetry. It cannot be said of the novel that here the linguistic elements are the aesthetically indifferent expression of content, not even if they appear to be completely devoid of foregrounding: the structure is the total of all the components, and its dynamics arises precisely from the tension between the foregrounded and unforegrounded components. There are, incidentally, many novels and short stories in which the linguistic components are clearly foregrounded. Changes effected in the interest of correct language would thus, even in the case of prose, often interfere with the very essence of the work; this would, for instance, happen if the author or even translator decided, as was asked in *Naše Řeč,* to eliminate "superfluous" relative clauses.

There still remains the problem of *aesthetic values* in language outside of the realm of poetry. A recent Czech opinion has it that "aesthetic evaluation must be excluded from language, since there is no place where it can be applied. It is useful and necessary for judging style, but not language" (J. Haller, *Problém jazykové správnosti* [*The Problem of Correct Language*], *Výroční zpráva č. st. ref reál. gymnasia v Ústí nad Labem za r.* 1930–31, p. 23). I am leaving aside the criticism of the terminologically inaccurate opposition of style and language; but I do want to point out, in opposition to Haller's thesis, that aesthetic valuation is a very important factor in the formation of the norm of the standard; on the one hand because the conscious refinement of the language cannot do without it, on the other hand because it sometimes, in part, determines the development of the norm of the standard.

Let us start with a general discussion of the field of aesthetic phenomena. It is clear that this field by far exceeds the confines of the arts. Dessoir says about it: "The striving for beauty need not be limited in its manifestation to the specific forms of the arts. The aesthetic needs are, on the contrary, so potent that they affect *almost all* the acts of man."[2] If the area of aesthetic phenomena is indeed so broad, it becomes obvious that aesthetic valuation has its place beyond the confines of the arts; we can cite as examples the aesthetic factors in sexual selection, fashion, the social amenities, the culinary arts, etc. There is, of course, a difference between aesthetic valuation in the arts and outside of art. In the arts, aesthetic valuation necessarily stands highest in the hierarchy of the values contained in the work, whereas outside of art its position vacillates and is usually subordinate. Furthermore, in the arts we evaluate each component in terms of the structure of the work in question, and the yardstick is in each individual case determined by the function of the component within the structure. Outside of art, the various components of the phenomenon to be evaluated are not integrated into an aesthetic structure and the yardstick becomes the established norm that applies to the component in question, wherever the latter occurs. If, then, the area of aesthetic valuation is so broad that it includes "almost all of the acts of man," it is indeed not very probable that language would be exempt from aesthetic valuation; in other words, that its use would not be subject to the laws of taste. There is direct proof that aesthetic valuation is one of the basic criteria of purism, and that even the development of the norm of the standard cannot be imagined without it.

. . .

---

[2]M. Dessoir, *Ästhetik und allgemeine Kunstwissenschaft* (Stuttgart, 1906), p. 112.

Aesthetic valuation clearly has its indispensable place in the refinement of language, and those purists who deny its validity are unconsciously passing judgment on their own practice. Without an aesthetic point of view, no other form of the cultivation of good language is possible, even one much more efficient than purism. This does not mean that he who intends to cultivate good language has the right to judge language in line with his personal taste, as is done precisely by the purists. Such an intervention into the development of the standard language is efficient and purposeful only in periods when the conscious aesthetic valuation of phenomena has become a social fact—as was the case in France in the seventeenth century. In other periods, including the present, the aesthetic point of view has more of a regulatory function in the cultivation of good language: he who is active in the cultivation of good language must take care not to force upon the standard language, in the name of correct language, modes of expression that violate the aesthetic canon (set of norms) given in the language implicitly, but objectively; intervention without heed to the aesthetic norms hampers, rather than advances, the development of the language. The aesthetic canon, which differs not only from language to language, but also for different developmental periods of the same language (not counting in this context other functional formations of which each has its own aesthetic canon), must therefore be ascertained by scientific investigation and be described as accurately as possible. This is the reason for the considerable significance of the question of the manner in which aesthetic valuation influences the development of the norm of the standard. Let us first consider the manner in which the lexicon of the standard language is increased and renewed. Words originating in slang, dialects, or foreign languages, are, as we know from our own experience, often taken over because of their novelty and uncommonness, that is, for purposes of foregrounding in which aesthetic valuation always plays a significant part. Words of the poetic language, poetic neologisms, can also enter the standard by this route, although in these cases we can also be dealing with acceptance for reasons of communication (need for a new shade of meaning). The influence of poetic language on the standard is, however, not limited to the vocabulary: intonational and syntactic patterns (clichés) can, for instance, also be taken over—the latter only for aesthetic reasons since there is hardly any communicative necessity for a change of the sentence and intonation structure current until then. Very interesting in this respect is the observation by the poet J. Cocteau in his book *Le secret professionnel* (Paris, 1922, p. 36) that "Stéphane Mallarmé even now influences the style of the daily press without the journalists' being aware of it." By way of explanation it must be pointed out that Mallarmé has very violently distorted French syntax and word order which is incomparably more bound in French than in Czech, being a grammatical factor. In spite of this intensive distortion, or perhaps because of it, Mallarmé influenced the development of the structure of the sentence in the standard language.

The effect of aesthetic valuation on the development of the norm of the standard is undeniable; this is why the problem deserves the attention of the theorists. So far, we have, for instance, hardly even any lexical studies of the acceptance of poetic neologisms in Czech and of the reasons for this acceptance; [Antonín] Frinta's article *Rukopisné podvrhy a naše spisovná řeč* [*The Fake Manuscripts* (Václav Hanka's forgeries of purportedly Old Czech poetry, 1813, 1817) *and our Standard Language*] (*Naše, Řeč*, Vol. II) has remained an isolated attempt. It is also necessary to investigate the nature and range of aesthetic valuation in the standard language. Aesthetic valuation is based here, as always when it is not based on an artistic structure, on certain generally valid norms. In art, including poetry, each component is evaluated in relation to the structure. The problem in evaluating is to determine how and to what extent a given component fulfills the function proper to it in the total structure; the yardstick is given by the context of a given structure and does not apply to any other context. The proof lies in the fact that a certain component may by itself be perceived as a negative value in terms of the pertinent aesthetic norm, if its distortional character is very prominent, but may be evaluated positively in terms of a particular structure and as its essential component precisely because of this distortional character. There is no aesthetic structure outside of poetry, none in the standard language (nor in language in general). There is, however, a certain set of aesthetic norms, each of which applies independently to a certain component of language. This set, or canon, is constant only for a certain period and for a certain linguistic milieu; thus, the aesthetic canon of the standard is different from that of slang. We therefore need a description and characterization of the aesthetic canon of the standard language of today and of the development of this canon in the past. It is, of course, clear to begin with that this development is not independent of the changing structures in the art of poetry. The discovery and investigation of the aesthetic canon accepted for a certain standard language would not only have theoretical significance as a part of its history, but also, as has already been said, be of practical importance in its cultivation.

Let us now return to the main topic of our study and attempt to draw some conclusions from what was said above of the relationship between the standard and poetic language.

Poetic language is a different form of language with a different function from that of the standard. It is therefore equally unjustified to call all poets, without exception, creators of the standard language as it is to make them responsible for its present state. This is not to deny the possibility of utilizing poetry as data for the scientific description of the norm of the standard (cf. p. 1051), nor the fact that the development of the norm of the standard does not occur uninfluenced by poetry. The distortion of the norm of the standard is, however, of the very essence of poetry, and it is therefore improper to ask poetic language to abide by this norm. This was clearly formulated as early as 1913 by Ferdinand Brunot (*"L'autorité en matière de language,"* Die neueren Sprachen, Vol. XX):

> Modern art, individualistic in essence, can not always and everywhere be satisfied with the standard language alone. The laws governing the usual communication of thought must not, lest it be unbearable tyranny, be categorically imposed upon the poet who, beyond the bounds of the accepted forms of language, may find personalized forms of intuitive expression. It is up to him to use them in accord with his creative intuition and without other limits than those imposed by his own inspiration. Public opinion will give the final verdict.

It is interesting to compare Brunot's statement to one of Haller's of 1931 (*Problém jazykové správnosti,* op. cit. 3):

> Our writers and poets in their creative effort attempt to replace the thorough knowledge of the material of the language by some sort of imaginary ability of which they themselves are not too sincerely convinced. They lay claim to a right which can but be an unjust privilege. Such an ability, instinct, inspiration, or what have you, cannot exist in and of itself; just as the famous feel for the language, it can only be the final result of previous cognition, and without consciously leaning on the finished material of the language, it is no more certain than any other arbitrary act.

If we compare Brunot's statement to Haller's, the basic difference is clear without further comment. Let us also mention Jungmann's critique of Polák's *Vznešenost přírody* [*The Sublimity of Nature*] cited elsewhere in this study, p. 1051 [see above]; Jungmann has there quite accurately pointed out as a characteristic feature of poetic language its "uncommonness," that is, its distortedness.—In spite of all that has been said here, the condition of the norm of the standard language is not without its significance to poetry, since the norm of the standard is precisely the background against which the structure of the work of poetry is projected, and in

regard to which it is perceived as a distortion; the structure of a work of poetry can change completely from its origin if it is, after a certain time, projected against the background of a norm of the standard which has since changed.

In addition to the relation of the norm of the standard to poetry, there is also the opposite relationship, that of poetry to the norm of the standard. We have already spoken of the influence of poetic language on the development of the standard; some remarks remain to be added. First of all, it is worth mentioning that the poetic foregrounding of linguistic phenomena, since it is its own purpose, cannot have the purpose of creating new means of communication (as Vossler and his school think). If anything passes from poetic language into the standard, it becomes a loan in the same way as anything taken over by the standard from any other linguistic milieu; even the motivation of the borrowing may be the same: a loan from poetic language may likewise be taken over for extraaesthetic, that is, communicative reasons, and conversely the motivation for borrowings from other functional dialects, such as slang, may be aesthetic. Borrowings from poetic language are beyond the scope of the poet's intent. Thus, poetic neologisms arise as intentionally aesthetic new formations, and their basic features are unexpectedness, unusualness, and uniqueness. Neologisms created for communicative purposes, on the other hand, tend towards common derivation patterns and easy classifiability in a certain lexical category; these are the properties allowing for their general usability. If, however, *poetic* neologisms were formed in view of their general usability, their aesthetic function would be endangered thereby; they are, therefore, formed in an unusual manner, with considerable violence to the language, as regards both form and meaning.

. . .

The relationship between poetic language and the standard, their mutual approximation or increasing distance, changes from period to period. But even within the same period, and with the same norm of the standard, this relationship need not be the same for all poets. There are, generally speaking, three possibilities: the writer, say a novelist, may either not distort the linguistic components of his work at all (but this nondistortion is, as was shown above, in itself a fact of the total structure of his work), or he may distort it, but subordinate the linguistic distortion to the subject matter by giving substandard color to his lexicon in order to characterize personages and situations, for instance; or finally, he may distort the linguistic components in and of themselves by either subordinating the subject matter to the linguistic deformation, or emphasizing the contrast between the subject matter and its linguistic expression. An example of the first possibility might be [Jakub] Arbes [1840–1914, an early nat-

uralist], of the second, some realistic novelists such as T. No-
váková [1853–1912] or Z. Winter [1846–1912], of the third,
[Vladislav] Vančura. It is obvious that as one goes from the
first possibility to the third, the divergence between poetic
language and the standard increases. This classification has
of course been highly schematized for purposes of simplicity; the real situation is much more complex.

The problem of the relationship between the standard
and poetic language does not, however, exhaust the significance of poetry as the art form which uses language as its
material, for the standard language, or for the language of a
nation in general. The very existence of poetry in a certain
language has fundamental importance for this language. . . .
By the very fact of foregrounding, poetry increases and refines the ability to handle language in general; it gives the
language the ability to adjust more flexibly to new requirements and it gives it a richer differentiation of its means of
expression. Foregrounding brings to the surface and before
the eyes of the observer even such linguistic phenomena as
remain quite covert in communicative speech, although they
are important factors in language. Thus, for instance, Czech
symbolism, especially O. Březina's [1868–1929] poetry, has
brought to the fore of linguistic consciousness the essence of
sentence meaning and the dynamic nature of sentence construction. From the standpoint of communicative speech, the
meaning of a sentence appears as the total of the gradually
accumulated meanings of the individual words, that is, without having independent existence. The real nature of the phenomenon is covered up by the automatization of the semantic design of the sentence. Words and sentences appear to
follow each other with obvious necessity, as determined only
by the nature of the message. Then there appears a work of
poetry in which the relationship between the meanings of the
individual words and the subject matter of the sentence has
been foregrounded. The words here do not succeed each
other naturally and inconspicuously, but within the sentence
there occur semantic jumps, breaks, which are not conditioned by the requirements of communication, but given in
the language itself. The device for achieving these sudden
breaks is the constant intersection of the plane of basic
meaning with the plane of figurative and metaphorical meaning; some words are for a certain part of the context to be
understood in their figurative meaning, in other parts in their
basic meaning, and such words, carrying a dual meaning, are
precisely the points at which there are semantic breaks.
There is also foregrounding of the relationship between the
subject matter of the sentence and the words as well as of the
semantic interrelationships of the words in the sentence. The
subject matter of the sentence then appears as the center of
attraction given from the beginning of the sentence, the effect of the subject matter on the words and of the words on
the subject matter is revealed, and the determining force can
be felt with which every word affects every other. The sentence comes alive before the eyes of the speech community:
the structure is revealed as a concert of forces. (What was
here formulated discursively, must of course be imagined as
an unformulated intuitive cognition stored away for the future in the consciousness of the speech community.) Examples can be multiplied at will, but we shall cite no more.
We wanted to give evidence for the statement that the main
importance of poetry for language lies in the fact that it is
an art.

Jean-Paul Sartre

1905–1980

Existentialism is in some ways an outgrowth of the tradition of phenomenology that goes back to the philosophical works of Edmund Husserl and Martin Heidegger. Like phenomenologists, existentialists wish to evade the endless epistemological problems of the duality of subject and object. Sartre's description of the "final goal" of art in *Why Write?* is that art's effort is "to recover this world by giving it to be seen as it is, but as if it had its source in human freedom." To give the world *as it is* reflects the attitude of phenomenologists: the world *is* as we experience it. The phrase "as if it had its source in human freedom" gives a particularly existentialist twist to the statement: Sartre holds that the writer appeals to the reader and his "freedom" to collaborate in the production of his work.

In *Why Write?* Sartre is primarily interested in the transaction between the writer and reader, and he defines this transaction, as do so many other critics writing about art, in terms of basic philosophical assumptions. We do not "produce" the world; it is *there;* but we make it reveal itself, come into "being." Art is a means of doing this, of "enclosing the universe within man." As man collaborates with the world, the reader collaborates with the "production" of a work of art; by being present against a background of other things, the work of art draws those other things into its own being and becomes interpretable partly in their terms, just as they become interpretable partly in its terms. But there is a sense in which art is not interpretable at all and is, in fact, "a silence and an opponent of the word." This remark indicates Sartre's affinity with those who attack paraphrase and insist on distinguishing between poetic and other forms of discourse. Sartre also has his own version of psychical distance; he asserts that both artist and reader withdraw somewhat from their emotions and thus manage to make their emotions "free."

English translations of Sartre's theoretical works include Bernard Frechtman, tr., *The Emotions: Outline of a Theory* (1948), *What Is Literature?* (1949), and *The Psychology of the Imagination* (1961); H. E. Barnes, tr., *Existential Psychoanalysis* (1953) and *Being and Nothingness* (1956); Annette Michelson, tr., *Literary and Philosophical Essays* (1955); Philip Mairet, tr., *Existentialism and Humanism* (1960); and Forrest Williams, tr., *The Imagination* (1962). For commentary on Sartre see Iris Murdoch, *Sartre, Romantic Rationalist* (1953); Alfred Stern, *Sartre, His Philosophy and Psychoanalyses* (1953); E. W. Knight, *Literature Considered as Philosophy* (1957); William Barrett, *Irrational Man* (1958); G. H. Bauer, *Sartre and the Artist* (1970); Benjamin Suhl, *Jean-Paul Sartre: The Philosopher as Literary Critic* (1970); Dominick LaCapra, *A Preface to Sartre* (1978); Christine Howells, *Sartre's Theory of Literature* (1979); Peter Caws, *Sartre* (1979); Ronald Aronson, *Jean-Paul Sartre: Philosophy in the World* (1980); Phiannon Goldthorpe, *Sartre, Literature and Theory* (1984); and Ronald Hayman, *Sartre: A Life* (1987).

Why Write?

Each has his reasons: for one, art is a flight; for another a means of conquering. But one can flee into a heroic age, into madness, into death. One can conquer by arms. Why does it have to be *writing*, why does one have to manage one's escapes and conquests by *writing*? Because, behind the various aims of authors, there is a deeper and more immediate choice which is common to all of us. We shall try to elucidate this choice, and we shall see whether it is not in the name of this very choice of writing that the self-commitment of writers must be required.

Each of our perceptions is accompanied by the consciousness that human reality is a "revealer," that is, it is through human reality that "there is" being, or, to put it differently, that man is the means by which things are manifested. It is our presence in the world which multiplies relations. It is we who set up a relationship between this tree and that bit of sky. Thanks to us, that star which has been dead for millennia, that quarter moon, and that dark river are disclosed in the unity of a landscape. It is the speed of our car and our aeroplane which organizes the great masses of the earth. With each of our acts, the world reveals to us a new face. But, if we know that we are directors of being, we also know that we are not its producers. If we turn away from this landscape, it will sink back into its dark permanence. At least, it will sink back; there is no one mad enough to think that it is going to be annihilated. It is we who shall be annihilated, and the earth will remain in its lethargy until another consciousness comes along to awaken it. Thus, to our inner certainty of being "revealers" is added that of being inessential in relation to the thing revealed.

One of the chief motives of artistic creation is certainly the need of feeling that we are essential in relationship to the world. If I fix on canvas or in writing a certain aspect of the fields or the sea or a look on someone's face which I have disclosed, I am conscious of having produced them by condensing relationships, by introducing order where there was none, by imposing the unity of mind on the diversity of things. That is, I feel myself essential in relation to my creation. But this time it is the created object which escapes me; I cannot reveal and produce at the same time. The creation becomes inessential in relation to the creative activity. First of all, even if it appears finished to others, the created object always seems to us in a state of suspension; we can always change this line, that shade, that word. Thus, it never *forces itself*. A novice painter asked his teacher, "When should I consider my painting finished?" And the teacher answered, "When you can look at it in amazement and say to yourself '*I'm* the one who did *that!'* "

Which amounts to saying "never." For it is virtually considering one's work with someone else's eyes and revealing what one has created. But it is self-evident that we are proportionally less conscious of the thing produced and more conscious of our productive activity. When it is a matter of pottery or carpentry, we work according to traditional patterns, with tools whose usage is codified; it is Heidegger's famous "they" who are working with our hands. In this case, the result can seem to us sufficiently strange to preserve its objectivity in our eyes. But if we ourselves produce the rules of production, the measures, the criteria, and if our creative drive comes from the very depths of our heart, then we never find anything but ourselves in our work. It is we who have invented the laws by which we judge it. It is our history, our love, our gaiety that we recognize in it. Even if we should look at it without touching it any further, we never *receive* from it that gaiety or love. We put them into it. The results which we have obtained on canvas or paper never seem to us *objective*. We are too familiar with the processes of which they are the effects. These processes remain a subjective discovery; they are ourselves, our inspiration, our trick, and when we seek to *perceive* our work, we create it again, we repeat mentally the operations which produced it; each of its aspects appears as a result. Thus, in the perception, the object is given as the essential thing and the subject as the inessential. The latter seeks essentiality in the creation and obtains it, but then it is the object which becomes the inessential.

This dialectic is nowhere more apparent than in the art of writing, for the literary object is a peculiar top which exists only in movement. To make it come into view a concrete act called reading is necessary, and it lasts only as long as this act can last. Beyond that, there are only black marks on paper. Now, the writer cannot read what he writes, whereas the shoemaker can put on the shoes he has just made if they are his size, and the architect can live in the house he has built. In reading, one foresees; one waits. One foresees the end of the sentence, the following sentence, the next page. One waits for them to confirm or disappoint one's foresights. The reading is composed of a host of hypotheses, of dreams followed by awakenings, of hopes and deceptions. Readers are always ahead of the sentence they are reading in a merely probable future which partly collapses and partly comes together in proportion as they progress, which withdraws from one page to the next and forms the moving horizon of the

WHY WRITE? Sartre's *Pourquoi écrire?* was first published in 1948 in his *Qu'est-ce que la littérature?* The text is from Bernard Frechtman, tr., *What Is Literature?* (1949), and is reprinted by permission of Philosophical Library.

literary object. Without waiting, without a future, without ignorance, there is no objectivity.

Now the operation of writing involves an implicit quasi-reading which makes real reading impossible. When the words form under his pen, the author doubtless sees them, but he does not see them as the reader does, since he knows them before writing them down. The function of his gaze is not to reveal, by brushing against them, the sleeping words which are waiting to be read, but to control the sketching of the signs. In short, it is a purely regulating mission, and the view before him reveals nothing except for slight slips of the pen. The writer neither foresees nor conjectures; he *projects*. It often happens that he awaits, as they say, the inspiration. But one does not wait for oneself the way one waits for others. If he hesitates, he knows that the future is not made, that he himself is going to make it, and if he still does not know what is going to happen to his hero, that simply means that he has not thought about it, that he has not decided upon anything. The future is then a blank page, whereas the future of the reader is two hundred pages filled with words which separate him from the end. Thus, the writer meets everywhere only *his* knowledge, *his* will, *his* plans, in short, himself. He touches only his own subjectivity; the object he creates is out of reach; he does not create it *for himself*. If he rereads himself, it is already too late. The sentence will never quite be a thing in his eyes. He goes to the very limits of the subjective but without crossing it. He appreciates the effect of a touch, of an epigram, of a well-placed adjective, but it is the effect they will have on others. He can judge it, not feel it. Proust never discovered the homosexuality of Charlus, since he had decided upon it even before starting on his book. And if a day comes when the book takes on for its author a semblance of objectivity, it is because years have passed, because he has forgotten it, because its spirit is quite foreign to him, and doubtless he is no longer capable of writing it. This was the case with Rousseau when he reread *The Social Contract* at the end of his life.

Thus, it is not true that one writes for oneself. That would be the worst blow. In projecting one's emotions on paper, one barely manages to give them a languid extension. The creative act is only an incomplete and abstract moment in the production of a work. If the author existed alone he would be able to write as much as he liked; the work as *object* would never see the light of day and he would either have to put down his pen or despair. But the operation of writing implies that of reading as its dialectical correlative and these two connected acts necessitate two distinct agents. It is the joint effort of author and reader which brings upon the scene that concrete and imaginary object which is the work of the mind. There is no art except for and by others.

Reading seems, in fact, to be the synthesis of perception and creation.[1] It supposes the essentiality of both the subject and the object. The object is essential because it is strictly transcendent, because it imposes its own structures, and because one must wait for it and observe it; but the subject is also essential because it is required not only to disclose the object (that is, to make it possible for there to *be* an object) but also so that this object might exist absolutely (that is, to produce it). In a word, the reader is conscious of disclosing in creating, of creating by disclosing. In reality, it is not necessary to believe that reading is a mechanical operation and that signs make an impression upon him as light does on a photographic plate. If he is inattentive, tired, stupid, or thoughtless, most of the relations will escape him. He will never manage to "catch on" to the object (in the sense in which we see that fire "catches" or "doesn't catch"). He will draw some phrases out of the shadow, but they will seem to appear as random strokes. If he is at his best, he will project beyond the words a synthetic form, each phrase of which will be no more than a partial function: the "theme," the "subject," or the "meaning." Thus, from the very beginning, the meaning is no longer contained in the words, since it is he, on the contrary, who allows the significance of each of them to be understood; and the literary object, though realized *through* language, is never given *in* language. On the contrary, it is by nature a silence and an opponent of the word. In addition, the hundred thousand words aligned in a book can be read one by one so that the meaning of the work does not emerge. Nothing is accomplished if the reader does not put himself from the very beginning and almost without a guide at the height of this silence; if, in short, he does not invent it and does not then place there, and hold on to, the words and sentences which he awakens. And if I am told that it would be more fitting to call this operation a reinvention or a discovery, I shall answer that, first, such a reinvention would be as new and as original an act as the first invention. And, especially, when an object has never existed before, there can be no question of reinventing it or discovering it. For if the silence about which I am speaking is really the goal at which the author is aiming, he has, at least, never been familiar with it; his silence is subjective and anterior to language. It is the absence of words, the undifferentiated and lived silence of inspiration, which the word will then particularize, whereas the silence produced by the reader is an object. And at the very interior of this object there are more silences—which the author does not mention. It is a question

---

[1] [Sartre] The same is true in different degrees regarding the spectator's attitude before other works of art (paintings, symphonies, statues, etc.).

of silences which are so particular that they could not retain any meaning outside the object which the reading causes to appear. However, it is these which give it its density and its particular face.

To say that they are unexpressed is hardly the word; for they are precisely the inexpressible. And that is why one does not come upon them at any definite moment in the reading; they are everywhere and nowhere. The quality of the marvellous in *Le Grand Meaulnes,* the grandioseness of *Armance,* the degree of realism and truth of Kafka's mythology, these are never given. The reader must invent them all in a continual exceeding of the written thing. To be sure, the author guides him, but all he does is guide him. The landmarks he sets up are separated by the void. The reader must unite them; he must go beyond them. In short, reading is directed creation.

On the one hand, the literary object has no other substance than the reader's subjectivity; Raskolnikov's waiting is *my* waiting which I lend him. Without this impatience of the reader he would remain only a collection of signs. His hatred of the police magistrate who questions him is my hatred which has been solicited and wheedled out of me by signs, and the police magistrate himself would not exist without the hatred I have for him via Raskolnikov. That is what animates him, it is his very flesh.

But on the other hand, the words are there like traps to arouse our feelings and to reflect them towards us. Each word is a path of transcendence; it shapes our feelings, names them, and attributes them to an imaginary personage who takes it upon himself to live them for us and who has no other substance than these borrowed passions; he confers objects, perspectives, and a horizon upon them.

Thus, for the reader, all is to do and all is already done; the work exists only at the exact level of his capacities; while he reads and creates, he knows that he can always go further in his reading, can always create more profoundly, and thus the work seems to him as inexhaustible and opaque as things. We would readily reconcile that "rational intuition" which Kant reserved to divine Reason with this absolute production of qualities, which, to the extent that they emanate from our subjectivity, congeal before our eyes into impenetrable objectivities.

Since the creation can find its fulfillment only in reading, since the artist must entrust to another the job of carrying out what he has begun, since it is only through the consciousness of the reader that he can regard himself as essential to his work, all literary work is an appeal. To write is to make an appeal to the reader that he lead into objective existence the revelation which I have undertaken by means of language. And if it should be asked *to what* the writer is

appealing, the answer is simple. As the sufficient reason for the appearance of the aesthetic object is never found either in the book (where we find merely solicitations to produce the object) or in the author's mind, and as his subjectivity, which he cannot get away from, cannot give a reason for the act of leading into objectivity, the appearance of the work of art is a new event which cannot *be explained* by anterior data. And since this directed creation is an absolute beginning, it is therefore brought about by the freedom of the reader, and by what is purest in that freedom. Thus, the writer appeals to the reader's freedom to collaborate in the production of his work.

It will doubtless be said that all tools address themselves to our freedom since they are the instruments of a possible action, and that the work of art is not unique in that. And it is true that the tool is the congealed outline of an operation. But it remains on the level of the hypothetical imperative. I may use a hammer to nail up a case or to hit my neighbor over the head. Insofar as I consider it in itself, it is not an appeal to my freedom; it does not put me face to face with it; rather, it aims at using it by substituting a set succession of traditional procedures for the free invention of means. The book does not serve my freedom; it requires it. Indeed, one cannot address oneself to freedom as such by means of constraint, fascination, or entreaties. There is only one way of attaining it; first, by recognizing it, then, having confidence in it, and finally, requiring of it an act, an act in its own name, that is, in the name of the confidence that one brings to it.

Thus, the book is not, like the tool, a means for any end whatever; the end to which it offers itself is the reader's freedom. And the Kantian expression "finality without end"[2] seems to me quite inappropriate for designating the work of art. In fact, it implies that the aesthetic object presents only the appearance of a finality and is limited to soliciting the free and ordered play of the imagination. It forgets that the imagination of the spectator has not only a regulating function, but a constitutive one. It does not play; it is called upon to recompose the beautiful object beyond the traces left by the artist. The imagination cannot revel in itself any more than can the other functions of the mind; it is always on the outside, always engaged in an enterprise. There would be finality without end if some object offered such a well-arranged composition that it would lead us to suppose that it has an end even though we cannot ascribe one to it. By defining the beautiful in this way one can—and this is Kant's aim—liken the beauty of art to natural beauty, since a flower,

---

[2]Purposiveness without a purpose. See Kant, *Critique of Judgment,* pp. 382–83.

for example, presents so much symmetry, such harmonious colors, and such regular curves, that one is immediately tempted to seek a finalist explanation for all these properties and to see them as just so many means at the disposal of an unknown end. But that is exactly the error. The beauty of nature is in no way comparable to that of art. The work of art *does not have* an end; there we agree with Kant. But the reason is that it is an end. The Kantian formula does not account for the appeal which resounds at the basis of each painting, each statue, each book. Kant believes that the work of art first exists as fact and that it is then seen. Whereas, it exists only if one *looks* at it and if it is first pure appeal, pure exigence to exist. It is not an instrument whose existence is manifest and whose end is undetermined. It presents itself as a task to be discharged; from the very beginning it places itself on the level of the categorical imperative. You are perfectly free to leave that book on the table. But if you open it, you assume responsibility for it. For freedom is not experienced by its enjoying its free subjective functioning, but in a creative act required by an imperative. This absolute end, this imperative which is transcendent yet acquiesced in, which freedom itself adopts as its own, is what we call a value. The work of art is a value because it is an appeal.

If I appeal to my readers so that we may carry the enterprise which I have begun to a successful conclusion, it is self-evident that I consider him as a pure freedom, as an unconditioned activity; thus, in no case can I address myself to his passiveness, that is, try to *affect* him, to communicate to him, from the very first, emotions of fear, desire, or anger. There are, doubtless, authors who concern themselves solely with arousing these emotions because they are foreseeable, manageable, and because they have at their disposal sure-fire means for provoking them. But it is also true that they are reproached for this kind of thing, as Euripides has been since antiquity because he had children appear on the stage. Freedom is alienated in the state of passion; it is abruptly engaged in partial enterprises; it loses sight of its task, which is to produce an absolute end. And the book is no longer anything but a means for feeding hate or desire. The writer should not seek to *overwhelm;* otherwise he is in contradiction with himself; if he wishes to *make demands* he must propose only the task to be fulfilled. Hence, the character of pure presentation which appears essential to the work of art. The reader must be able to make a certain aesthetic withdrawal. This is what Gautier foolishly confused with "art for art's sake" and the Parnassians with the imperturbability of the artist. It is simply a matter of precaution, and Genet more justly calls it the author's politeness towards the reader. But that does not mean that the writer makes an appeal to some sort of abstract and conceptual freedom. One certainly creates the aesthetic object with feelings; if it is touching, it appears through our tears; if it is comic, it will be recognized by laughter. However, these feelings are of a particular kind. They have their origin in freedom; they are loaned. The belief which I accord the tale is freely assented to. It is a passion, in the Christian sense of the word, that is, a freedom which resolutely puts itself into a state of passiveness to obtain a certain transcendent effect by this sacrifice. The reader renders himself credulous; he descends into credulity which, though it ends by enclosing him like a dream, is at every moment conscious of being free. An effort is sometimes made to force the writer into this dilemma: "Either one believes in your story, and it is intolerable, or one does not believe in it, and it is ridiculous." But the argument is absurd because the characteristic of aesthetic consciousness is to be a belief by means of commitment, by oath, a belief sustained by fidelity to one's self and to the author, a perpetually renewed choice to believe. I can awaken at every moment, and I know it; but I do not want to; reading is a free dream. So that all feelings which are exacted on the basis of this imaginary belief are like particular modulations of my freedom. Far from absorbing or masking it, they are so many different ways it has chosen to reveal itself to itself. Raskolnikov, as I have said, would only be a shadow, without the mixture of repulsion and friendship which I feel for him and which makes him live. But, by a reversal which is the characteristic of the imaginary object, it is not his behavior which excites my indignation or esteem, but my indignation and esteem which give consistency and objectivity to his behavior. Thus, the reader's feelings are never dominated by the object, and as no external reality can condition them, they have their permanent source in freedom; that is, they are all generous—for I call a feeling generous which has its origin and its end in freedom. Thus, reading is an exercise in generosity, and what the writer requires of the reader is not the application of an abstract freedom but the gift of his whole person, with his passions, his prepossessions, his sympathies, his sexual temperament, and his scale of values. Only this person will give himself generously; freedom goes through and through him and comes to transform the darkest masses of his sensibility. And as activity has rendered itself passive in order for it better to create the object, vice versa, passiveness becomes an act; the man who is reading has raised himself to the highest degree. That is why we see people who are known for their toughness shed tears at the recital of imaginary misfortunes; for the moment they have become what they would have been if they had not spent their lives hiding their freedom from themselves.

Thus, the author writes in order to address himself to the freedom of readers, and he requires it in order to make his work exist. But he does not stop there; he also requires that they return this confidence which he has given them, that they recognize his creative freedom, and that they in turn solicit it by a symmetrical and inverse appeal. Here there appears the other dialectical paradox of reading; the more we experience our freedom, the more we recognize that of the other; the more he demands of us, the more we demand of him.

When I am enchanted with a landscape, I know very well that it is not I who create it, but I also know that without me the relations which are established before my eyes among the trees, the foliage, the earth, and the grass would not exist at all. I know that I can give no reason for the appearance of finality which I discover in the assortment of hues and in the harmony of the forms and movements created by the wind. Yet, it exists; there it is before my eyes, and I can make something more out of what is already there. But even if I believe in God, I cannot establish any passage, unless it be purely verbal, between the divine, universal solicitude and the particular spectacle which I am considering. To say that he made the landscape in order to charm me or that he made me the kind of person who is pleased by it is to take a question for an answer. Is the marriage of this blue and that green deliberate? How can I know? The idea of a universal providence is no guarantee of any particular intention, especially in the case under consideration, since the green of the grass is explained by biological laws, specific constants, and geographical determinism, while the reason for the blue of the water is accounted for by the depth of the river, the nature of the soil and the swiftness of the current. The assorting of the shades, if it is willed, can only be something *thrown into the bargain;* it is the meeting of two causal series, that is to say, at first sight, a fact of chance. At best, the finality remains problematic. All the relations we establish remain hypotheses; no end is proposed to us in the manner of an imperative, since none is expressly revealed as having been willed by a creator. Thus, our freedom is never *called forth* by natural beauty. Or rather, there is an appearance of order in the whole which includes the foliage, the forms, and the movements, hence, the illusion of a calling forth which seems to solicit this freedom and which disappears immediately when one looks at it. Hardly have we begun to run our eyes over this arrangement, than the appeal disappears; we remain alone, free to tie up one color with another or with a third, to set up a relationship between the tree and the water or the tree and the sky, or the tree, the water and the sky. My freedom becomes caprice. To the extent that I establish new relationships, I remove myself further from the illusory objectivity which solicits me. I *muse* about certain motifs which are vaguely outlined by the things; the natural reality

is no longer anything but a pretext for musing. Or, in that case, because I have deeply regretted that this arrangement which was momentarily perceived was not offered to me by somebody and consequently is not *real,* the result is that I fix my dream, that I transpose it to canvas or in writing. Thus, I interpose myself between the finality without end which appears in the natural spectacles and the gaze of other men. I transmit it to them. It becomes human by this transmission. Art here is a ceremony of the *gift* and the gift alone brings about the metamorphosis. It is something like the transmission of titles and powers in the matriarchate where the mother does not possess the names, but is the indispensable intermediary between uncle and nephew. Since I have captured this illusion in flight, since I lay it out for other men and have disentangled it and rethought it for them, they can consider it with confidence. It has become intentional. As for me, I remain, to be sure, at the border of the subjective and the objective without ever being able to contemplate the objective arrangement which I transmit.

The reader, on the contrary, progresses in security. However far he may go, the author has gone further. Whatever connections he may establish among the different parts of the book—among the chapters or the words—he has a guarantee, namely, that they have been expressly willed. As Descartes says, he can even pretend that there is a secret order among parts which seem to have no connection. The creator has preceded him along the way, and the most beautiful disorders are effects of art, that is, again order. Reading is induction, interpolation, extrapolation, and the basis of these activities rests on the reader's will, as for a long time it was believed that that of scientific induction rested on the divine will. A gentle force accompanies us and supports us from the first page to the last. That does not mean that we fathom the artist's intentions easily. They constitute, as we have said, the object of conjectures, and there is an *experience* of the reader; but these conjectures are supported by the great certainty we have that the beauties which appear in the book are never accidental. In nature, the tree and the sky harmonize only by chance; if, on the contrary, in the novel, the protagonists find themselves in a *certain* tower, in a *certain* prison, if they stroll in a *certain* garden, it is a matter both of the restitution of independent causal series (the character had a certain state of mind which was due to a succession of psychological and social events; on the other hand, he betook himself to a determined place and the layout of the city required him to cross a certain park) and of the expression of a deeper finality, for the park came into existence only *in order to* harmonize with a certain state of mind, to express it by means of things or to put it into relief by a vivid contrast, and the state of mind itself was conceived in connection with the landscape. Here it is causality which is appearance and which might be called "causality without cause," and it is the finality which is the profound reality. But if I can thus in all confidence put the order of ends under the order of causes, it is because by opening the book I am asserting that the object has its source in human freedom.

If I were to suspect the artist of having written out of passion and in passion, my confidence would immediately vanish, for it would serve no purpose to have supported the order of causes by the order of ends. The latter would be supported in its turn by a psychic causality and the work of art would end by reentering the chain of determinism. Certainly I do not deny when I am reading that the author may be impassioned, nor even that he might have conceived the first plan of his work under the sway of passion. But his decision to write supposes that he withdraws somewhat from his feelings, in short, that he has transformed his emotions into free emotions as I do mine while reading him, that is, that he is in an attitude of generosity.

Thus, reading is a pact of generosity between author and reader. Each one trusts the other; each one counts on the other, demands of the other as much as he demands of himself. For this confidence is itself generosity. Nothing can force the author to believe that his reader will use his freedom; nothing can force the reader to believe that the author has used his. Both of them make a free decision. There is then established a dialectical going-and-coming; when I read, I make demands; if my demands are met, what I am then reading provokes me to demand more of the author, which means to demand of the author that he demand more of me. And, vice versa, the author's demand is that I carry my demands to the highest pitch. Thus, my freedom, by revealing itself, reveals the freedom of the other.

It matters little whether the aesthetic object is the product of "realistic" art (or supposedly such) or "formal" art. At any rate, the natural relations are inverted; that tree on the first plane of the Cézanne painting first appears as the product of a causal chain. But the causality is an illusion; it will doubtless remain as a proposition as long as we look at the painting, but it will be supported by a deep finality; if the tree is placed in such a way it is because the rest of the painting *requires* that this form and those colors be placed on the first plane. Thus, through the phenomenal causality, our gaze attains finality as the deep structure of the object, and, beyond finality, it attains human freedom as its source and original basis. Vermeer's realism is carried so far that at first it might be thought to be photographic. But if one considers the splendor of his texture, the pink and velvety glory of his little brick walls, the blue thickness of a branch of woodbine, the glazed darkness of his vestibules, the orange-colored flesh of his faces, which are as polished as the stone of holy-water basins, one suddenly feels, in the pleasure that he experiences, that the finality is not so much in the forms or colors as in his material imagination. It is the very substance and temper of the things which here give the forms their reason for being. With this realist we are perhaps closest to absolute creation, since it is in the very passiveness of the matter that we meet the unfathomable freedom of man.

The work is never limited to the painted, sculpted, or narrated object. Just as one perceives things only against the background of the world, so the objects represented by art appear against the background of the universe. On the background of the adventures of Fabrice are the Italy of 1820, Austria, France, the sky and stars which the Abbé Blanis consults, and finally the whole earth. If the painter presents us with a field or a vase of flowers, his paintings are windows which are open on the whole world. We follow the red path which is buried among the wheat much farther than Van Gogh has painted it, among other wheat fields, under other clouds, to the river which empties into the sea, and we extend to infinity, to the other end of the world, the deep finality which supports the existence of the field and the earth. So that, through the various objects which it produces or reproduces, the creative act aims at a total renewal of the world. Each painting, each book, is a recovery of the totality of being. Each of them presents this totality to the freedom of the spectator. For this is quite the final goal of art: to recover this world by giving it to be seen as it is, but as if it had its source in human freedom. But, since what the author creates takes on objective reality only in the eyes of the spectator, this recovery is consecrated by the ceremony of the spectacle—and particularly of reading. We are already in a better position to answer the question we raised a while ago: the writer chooses to appeal to the freedom of other men so that, by the reciprocal implication of their demands, they may readapt the totality of being to man and may again enclose the universe within man.

If we wish to go still further, we must bear in mind that the writer, like all other artists, aims at giving his reader a certain feeling that is customarily called aesthetic pleasure, and which I would very much rather call aesthetic joy, and that this feeling, when it appears, is a sign that the work is achieved. It is therefore fitting to examine it in the light of the preceding considerations. In effect, this joy, which is denied to the creator, insofar as he creates, becomes one with the aesthetic consciousness of the spectator, that is, in the case under consideration, of the reader. It is a complex feeling but one whose structures and condition are inseparable from one another. It is identical, at first, with the recognition of a transcendent and absolute end which, for a moment, suspends the utilitarian round of ends-means and means-ends,[3] that is, of an appeal or, what amounts to the same thing, of a value. And the positional consciousness which I take of this value is necessarily accompanied by the nonpositional consciousness of my freedom, since my freedom is manifested to itself by a transcendent exigency. The recognition of freedom by itself is joy, but this structure of nonthetical consciousness implies another: since, in effect, reading is creation, my freedom does not only appear to itself as pure autonomy but as creative activity, that is, it is not limited to giving itself its own law but perceives itself as being constitutive of the object. It is on this level that the phenomenon specifically is manifested, that is, a creation wherein the created object is given *as object* to its creator. It is the sole case in which the creator gets any enjoyment out of the object he creates. And the word *enjoyment* which is applied to the positional consciousness of the work read indicates sufficiently that we are in the presence of an essential structure of aesthetic joy. This positional enjoyment is accompanied by the nonpositional consciousness of being essential in relation to an object perceived as essential. I shall call this aspect of aesthetic consciousness the feeling of security; it is this which stamps the strongest aesthetic emotions with a sovereign calm. It has its origin in the authentication of a strict harmony between subjectivity and objectivity. As, on the other hand, the aesthetic object is properly the world insofar as it is aimed at through the imaginary, aesthetic joy accompanies the positional consciousness that the world is a value, that is, a task proposed to human freedom. I shall call this the aesthetic modification of the human project, for, as usual, the world appears as the horizon of our situation, as the infinite distance which separates us from ourselves, as the synthetic totality of the given, as the undifferentiated whole of obstacles and implements—but never as a demand addressed to our freedom. Thus, aesthetic joy proceeds to this level of the consciousness which I take of recovering and internalizing that which is non-ego par excellence, since I transform the given into an imperative and the fact into a value. The world is *my task,* that is, the essential and freely accepted function of my freedom is to make that unique and absolute object which is the universe come into being in an unconditioned movement. And, thirdly, the preceding structures imply a pact between human freedoms, for, on the one hand, reading is a confident and exacting recognition of the freedom of the writer, and, on the other hand, aesthetic pleasure, as it is itself experienced in the form of a value, involves an

absolute exigence in regard to others; every man, insofar as he is a freedom, feels the same pleasure in reading the same work. Thus, all mankind is present in its highest freedom; it sustains the being of a world which is both *its* world and the "external" world. In aesthetic joy the positional consciousness is an *image-making* consciousness of the world in its totality both as being and having to be, both as totally ours and totally foreign, and the more ours as it is the more foreign. The nonpositional consciousness *really* envelops the harmonious totality of human freedoms insofar as it makes the object of a universal confidence and exigency.

To write is thus both to disclose the world and to offer it as a task to the generosity of the reader. It is to have recourse to the consciousness of others in order to make one's self to be recognized as *essential* to the totality of being; it is to wish to live this essentiality by means of interposed persons; but, on the other hand, as the real world is revealed only by action, as one can feel oneself in it only by exceeding it in order to change it, the novelist's universe would lack depth if it were not discovered in a movement to transcend it. It has often been observed that an object in a story does not derive its density of existence from the number and length of the descriptions devoted to it, but from the complexity of its connections with the different characters. The more often the characters handle it, take it up, and put it down, in short, go beyond it towards their own ends, the more real will it appear. Thus, of the world of the novel, that is, the totality of men and things, we may say that in order for it to offer its maximum density the disclosure-creation by which the reader discovers it must also be an imaginary participation in the action; in other words, the more disposed one is to change it, the more alive it will be. The error of realism has been to believe that the real reveals itself to contemplation, and that consequently one could draw an impartial picture of it. How could that be possible, since the very perception is partial, since by itself the naming is already a modification of the object? And how could the writer, who wants himself to be essential to this universe, want to be essential to the injustice which this universe comprehends? Yet, he must be; but if he accepts being the creator of injustices, it is in a movement which goes beyond them towards their abolition. As for me who read, if I create and keep alive an unjust world, I cannot help making myself responsible for it. And the author's whole art is bent on obliging me to *create* what he *discloses,* therefore to compromise myself. So both of us bear the responsibility for the universe. And precisely because this universe is supported by the joint effort of our two freedoms, and because the author, with me as medium, has attempted to integrate it into the human, it must appear truly *in itself,* in its very marrow, as being shot

---

[3][Sartre] In *practical life* a means may be taken for an end as soon as one searches for it, and each end is revealed as a means of attaining another end.

through and through with a freedom which has taken human freedom as its end, and if it is not really the city of ends that it ought to be, it must at least be a stage along the way; in a word, it must be a becoming and it must always be considered and presented not as a crushing mass which weighs us down, but from the point of view of its going beyond towards that city of ends. However bad and hopeless the humanity which it paints may be, the work must have an air of generosity. Not, of course, that this generosity is to be expressed by means of edifying discourses and virtuous characters; it must not even be premeditated, and it is quite true that fine sentiments do not make fine books. But it must be the very warp and woof of the book, the stuff out of which the people and things are cut; whatever the subject, a sort of essential lightness must appear everywhere and remind us that the work is never a natural datum, but an *exigence* and a *gift*. And if I am given this world with its injustices, it is not so that I may contemplate them coldly, but that I may animate them with my indignation, that I may disclose them and create them with their nature as injustices, that is, as abuses to be suppressed. Thus, the writer's universe will only reveal itself in all its depth to the examination, the admiration, and the indignation of the reader; and the generous love is a promise to maintain, and the generous indignation is a promise to change, and the admiration a promise to imitate; although literature is one thing and morality a quite different one, at the heart of the aesthetic imperative we discern the moral imperative. For, since the one who writes recognizes, by the very fact that he takes the trouble to write, the freedom of his readers, and since the one who reads, by the mere fact of his opening the book, recognizes the freedom of the writer, the work of art, from whichever side you approach it, is an act of confidence in the freedom of men. And since readers, like the author, recognize this freedom only to demand that it manifest itself, the work can be defined as an imaginary presentation of the world insofar as it demands human freedom. The result of which is that there is no "gloomy literature," since, however dark may be the colors in which one paints the world, one paints it only so that free men may feel their freedom as they face it. Thus, there are only good and bad novels. The bad novel aims to please by flattering, whereas the good one is an exigence and an act of faith. But above all, the unique point of view from which the author can present the world to those freedoms whose concurrence he wishes to bring about is that of a world to be impregnated always with more freedom. It would be inconceivable that this unleashing of generosity provoked by the writer could be used to authorize an injustice, and that the reader could enjoy his freedom while reading a work which approves or accepts or simply abstains from condemning the

subjection of man by man. One can imagine a good novel being written by an American Negro even if hatred of the whites were spread all over it, because it is the freedom of his race that he demands through his hatred. And, as he invites me to assume the attitude of generosity, the moment I feel myself a pure freedom I cannot bear to identify myself with a race of oppressors. Thus, I require of all freedoms that they demand the liberation of colored people against the white race and against myself insofar as I am a part of it, but nobody can suppose for a moment that it is possible to write a good novel in praise of anti-Semitism.[4] For, the moment I feel that my freedom is indissolubly linked with that of all other men, it cannot be demanded of me that I use it to approve the enslavement of a part of these men. Thus, whether he is an essayist, a pamphleteer, a satirist, or a novelist, whether he speaks only of individual passions or whether he attacks the social order, the writer, a free man addressing free men, has only one subject—freedom.

Hence, any attempt to enslave his readers threatens him in his very art. A blacksmith can be affected by facism in his life as a man, but not necessarily in his craft; a writer will be affected in both, and even more in his craft than in his life. I have seen writers, who before the war called for fascism with all their hearts, smitten with sterility at the very moment when the Nazis were loading them with honors. I am thinking of Drieu la Rochelle in particular; he was mistaken, but he was sincere. He proved it. He had agreed to direct a Nazi-inspired review. The first few months he reprimanded, rebuked, and lectured his countrymen. No one answered him because no one was free to do so. He became irritated; he no longer *felt* his readers. He became more insistent, but no sign appeared to prove that he had been understood. No sign of hatred, nor of anger either; nothing. He seemed to have lost his bearings, the victim of a growing distress. He complained bitterly to the Germans. His articles had been superb; they became shrill. The moment arrived when he struck his breast; no echo, except among the bought journalists whom he despised. He handed in his resignation, withdrew it, again spoke, still in the desert. Finally, he said nothing, gagged by the silence of others. He had demanded the enslavement of others, but in his crazy mind he must have imagined that it was voluntary, that it was still free. It came; the man in him

---

[4][Sartre] This last remark may arouse some readers. If so, I'd like to know a single good novel whose express purpose was to serve oppression, a single good novel which has been written against Jews, Negroes, workers, or colonial people. "But if there isn't any, that's no reason why someone may not write one some day." But you then admit that you are an abstract theoretician. You, not I. For it is in the name of your abstract conception of art that you assert the possibility of a fact which has never come into being, whereas I limit myself to proposing an explanation for a recognized fact.

congratulated himself mightily, but the writer could not bear it. While this was going on, others, who, happily, were in the majority, understood that the freedom of writing implies the freedom of the citizen. One does not write for slaves. The art of prose is bound up with the only régime in which prose has meaning, democracy. When one is threatened, the other is too. And it is not enough to defend them with the pen. A day comes when the pen is forced to stop, and the writer must then take up arms. Thus, however you might have come to it, whatever the opinions you might have professed, literature throws you into battle. Writing is a certain way of wanting freedom; once you have begun, you are committed, willy-nilly.

Committed to what? Defending freedom? That's easy to say. Is it a matter of acting as a guardian of ideal values like Benda's "clerk" before the betrayal,[5] or is it concrete everyday freedom which must be protected by our taking sides in political and social struggles? The question is tied up with another one, one very simple in appearance but which nobody ever asks himself: "For whom does one write?"

---

[5][Frechtman] The reference here is to Benda's *La Trahison des clercs,* translated into English as *The Great Betrayer.*

Simone de Beauvoir

1908–1986

Despite a bourgeois upbringing and early philosophical interests (or perhaps, finally, because of these), Simone de Beauvoir produced perhaps the greatest classic of post-World War II feminism. When *The Second Sex* first appeared in 1949 Beauvoir was attacked by those who felt her account of women's lives was too heavily based on her personal experience and her middle class values. She was also criticized for her historical inaccuracy and anthropological suppositions. Those who defended her pointed to the scope of the work. Indeed, it was encyclopedic in its coverage, offering historical, biological, and psychological perspectives on women, a consideration of the prevailing patriarchal myths about them, and an account of female love and sexuality in virtually all of its forms. The intellectual framework was existentialist, reflecting her longtime relationship with Jean-Paul Sartre, whom she credited always as treating her as an equal. She vociferously refused the notion of a female essence prior to individual existence, and attacked the patriarchal myths of woman that presume that false essence.

Both selections come from the section of *The Second Sex* entitled "Myth." The first is the summary part of Chapter Ten entitled "Of Woman in Five Authors." In that chapter the five authors are Henri de Montherlant, D. H. Lawrence, Paul Claudel, André Breton, and Stendhal (Marie Henri Beyle). Of these Stendhal comes off best. Beauvoir begins her discussion of his work by commenting, "I find it a relief to come upon a man who lives among women of flesh and blood." For Beauvoir, Stendhal does not believe in the mystery of women, "he loves them as they really are." Woman is not, in his writings "pure alterity" but "a subject in her own light" in contrast to the way she is projected as the "other" in the work of the other four writers studied. Still, even in Stendhal woman is expected to play unfailingly the role of altruist.

The second selection is Chapter Eleven. Here Beauvoir insists, against the myth of woman, that woman is "a being rooted in nature" but not therefore assimilable as other in nature. The myth of this mysterious otherness has justified numerous abuses. Though men and women are indeed mysterious to each other men see the world "from their point of view as absolute."

Beauvoir specifically referred to her agreement with the views of Virginia Woolf as set forth twenty years before in *A Room of One's Own*. In her later years she saw her own influence on younger generation feminists like Kate Millet.

Simone de Beauvoir was the author of numerous novels, of which *The Mandarins* (1954) is perhaps the best known. She published four volumes of autobiography, *Memoirs of a Dutiful Daughter* (1958), *The Prime of Life* (1960), *Force of Circumstance* (1963) and *All Said and Done* (1972). *Adieux: A Farewell to Sartre* (1981) is considered by some a fifth volume. She also wrote *America Day by Day* (1947) and *Old Age* (1970). Among her philosophical and critical works are *Pyrrhus et Cinéas* (1944), *The*

Ethics of Ambiguity (1947), and *Privileges* (1955). See Alice Schwartzer, ed., *After "The Second Sex": Interviews with Simone de Beauvoir* (1984); Jacques Ehrmann, "Simon Beauvoir and the Related Destinies of Woman and Intellectual," *Yale French Studies* No. 27 (Spring-Summer 1961); Claude Francis and Fernande Gontier, *Les Écrits de Simone de Beauvoir* (1980), a bibliography; Margaret A. Simons, "The Silencing of Simone de Beauvoir; Guess What's Missing from *The Second Sex*," *Women's Studies International Forum,* No. 6, (1983); and Deirdre Bair, *Simone de Beauvoir: A Biography* (1990).

From

The Second Sex

Chapter X

Summary

It is to be seen from these examples that each separate writer reflects the great collective myths: we have seen woman as *flesh;* the flesh of the male is produced in the mother's body and re-created in the embraces of the woman in love. Thus woman is related to *nature,* she incarnates it: vale of blood, open rose, siren, the curve of a hill, she represents to man the fertile soil, the sap, the material beauty and the soul of the world. She can hold the keys to *poetry;* she can be *mediatrix* between this world and the beyond: grace or oracle, star or sorceress, she opens the door to the supernatural, the surreal. She is doomed to *immanence;* and through her passivity she bestows peace and harmony—but if she declines this role, she is seen forthwith as a praying mantis, an ogress. In any case she appears as the *privileged Other,* through whom the subject fulfills himself: one of the measures of man, his counterbalance, his salvation, his adventure, his happiness.

But these myths are very differently orchestrated by our authors. The *Other* is particularly defined according to the particular manner in which the *One* chooses to set himself up. Every man asserts his freedom and transcendence—but they do not all give these words the same sense. For Montherlant transcendence is a situation: he is the transcendent, he soars in the sky of heroes; woman crouches on earth, beneath his feet; it amuses him to measure the distance that separates him from her; from time to time he raises her up to him, takes her, and then throws her back; never does he lower himself down to her realm of slimy shadows. Law-

rence places transcendence in the phallus; the phallus is life and power only by grace of woman; immanence is therefore good and necessary; the false hero who pretends to be above setting foot on earth, far from being a demigod, fails to attain man's estate. Woman is not to be scorned, she is deep richness, a warm spring; but she should give up all personal transcendence and confine herself to furthering that of her male. Claudel asks her for the same devotion: for him, too, woman should maintain life while man extends its range through his activities; but for the Catholic all earthly affairs are immersed in vain immanence: the only transcendent is God; in the eyes of God the man in action and the woman who serves him are exactly equal; it is for each to surpass his or her earthly state: salvation is in all cases an autonomous enterprise. For Breton the rank of the sexes is reversed; action and conscious thought, in which the male finds his transcendence, seem to Breton to constitute a silly mystification that gives rise to war, stupidity, bureaucracy, the negation of anything human; it is immanence, the pure, dark presence of the real, which is truth; true transcendence would be accomplished by a return to immanence. His attitude is the exact opposite of Montherlant's: the latter likes war because in war one gets rid of women, Breton venerates woman because she brings peace. Montherlant confuses mind and subjectivity—he refuses to accept the given universe; Breton thinks that mind is objectively present at the heart of the world; woman endangers Montherlant because she breaks his solitude; she is revelation for Breton because she tears him out of his subjectivity. As for Stendhal, we have seen that for him woman hardly has a mystical value: he regards her as being, like man, a transcendent; for this humanist, free beings of both sexes fulfill themselves in their reciprocal relations; and for him it is enough if the *Other* be simply an other so that life may have what he calls "a pungent saltiness." He is not seeking a "stellar equilibrium," he is not fed on the bread of disgust; he is not looking for a miracle; he does not wish to be concerned with the cosmos or with poetry, but with free human beings.

More, Stendhal feels that he is himself a clear, free being. The others—and this is a most important point—pose as transcendents but feel themselves prisoners of a dark presence in their own hearts: they project this "unbreakable core of night" upon woman. Montherlant has an Adlerian complex, giving rise to his thick-witted bad faith: it is this tangle of pretensions and fears that he incarnates in woman; his disgust for her is what he dreads feeling for himself. He would trample underfoot, in woman, the always possible proof of his own insufficiency; he appeals to scorn to save him; and woman is the trench into which he throws all the monsters that haunt him.[1] The life of Lawrence shows us that he suffered from an analogous though more purely sexual complex: in his works woman serves as a compensation myth, exalting a virility that the writer was none too sure of; when he describes Kate at Don Cipriano's feet, he feels as if he had won a male triumph over his wife, Frieda; nor does he permit his companion to raise any questions: if she were to oppose his aims he would doubtless lose confidence in them; her role is to reassure him. He asks of her peace, repose, faith, as Montherlant asks for certainty regarding his superiority: they demand what is missing in them. Claudel's lack is not that of self-confidence: if he is timid it is only in secret with God. Nor is there any trace of the battle of the sexes in his work. Man boldly assumes woman's weight; she is a possibility for temptation or for salvation. It would seem that for Breton man is true only through the mystery that is within him; it pleases him for Nadja to see that star toward which he moves and which is like "the heart of a heartless flower." In his dreams, his presentiments, the spontaneous flow of his stream of consciousness—in such activities, which escape the control of the will and the reason, he recognizes his true self; woman is the visible image of that veiled presence which is infinitely more essential than his conscious personality.

Stendhal is in tranquil agreement with himself; but he needs woman as she needs him in order to gather his diffuse existence into the unity of a single design and destiny: it is as though man reaches manhood for another; but still he needs to have the lending of the other's consciousness. Other males are too indifferent toward their fellows; only the loving woman opens her heart to her lover and shelters him there, wholly. Except for Claudel, who finds in God his preferred witness, all the writers we have considered expect that woman will cherish in them what Malraux calls "this incomparable monster" known to themselves only. In co-operation or contest men face each other as generalized types. Mon-

therlant is for his fellows a writer, Lawrence a doctrinaire, Breton a school principal, Stendhal a diplomat or man of wit; it is woman who reveals in one a magnificent and cruel prince, in another a disquieting faun, in this one a god or a sun or a being "black and cold as a man struck by lightning at the feet of the Sphinx,"[2] in the last a seducer, a charmer, a lover.

For each of them the ideal woman will be she who incarnates most exactly the *Other* capable of revealing him to himself. Montherlant, the solar spirit, seeks pure animality in her; Lawrence, the phallicist, asks her to sum up the feminine sex in general; Claudel defines her as a soul-sister; Breton cherishes Mélusine, rooted in nature, pinning his hope on the woman-child; Stendhal wants his mistress intelligent, cultivated, free in spirit and behavior: an equal. But the sole earthly destiny reserved for the equal, the woman-child, the soul-sister, the woman-sex, the woman-animal is always man! Whatever ego may seek himself through her, he can find himself only if she is willing to act as his crucible. She is required in every case to forget self and to love. Montherlant consents to have pity upon the woman who allows him to measure his virile potency; Lawrence addresses a burning hymn to the woman who gives up being herself for his sake; Claudel exalts the handmaid, the female servant, the devotee who submits to God in submitting to the male; Breton is in hopes of human salvation from woman because she is capable of total love for her child or her lover; and even in Stendhal the heroines are more moving than the masculine heroes because they give themselves to their passion with a more distraught violence; they help man fulfill his destiny, as Prouhèze contributes to the salvation of Rodrigue; in Stendhal's novels it often happens that they save their lovers from ruin, prison, or death. Feminine devotion is demanded as a duty by Montherlant and Lawrence; less arrogant, Claudel, Breton, and Stendhal admire it as a generous free choice; they wish for it without claiming to deserve it; but—except for the astounding Lamiel—all their works show that they expect from woman that altruism which Comte admired in her and imposed upon her, and which according to him constituted a mark at once of flagrant inferiority and of an equivocal superiority.

We could multiply examples, but they would invariably lead us to the same conclusions. When he describes woman, each writer discloses his general ethics and the special idea he has of himself; and in her he often betrays also the gap between his world view and his egotistical dreams. The absence or insignificance of the feminine element throughout

---

[1] [Beauvoir] Stendhal has passed judgment in advance upon the cruelties with which Montherlant amuses himself: "What to do when indifferent? Love lightly, but without the horrors. The horrors always come from a small soul who needs reassurance regarding his own merits."

[2] [Beauvoir] Breton's *Nadja*.

the work of an author is in its own way symptomatic; but that element is extremely important when it sums up in its totality all the aspects of the Other, as happens with Lawrence. It remains important when woman is viewed simply as an other but the writer is interested in the individual adventure of her life, as with Stendhal; it loses importance in an epoch such as ours when personal problems of the individual are of secondary interest. Woman, however, as the other still plays a role to the extent that, if only to transcend himself, each man still needs to learn more fully what he is.

Chapter XI

Myth and Reality

The myth of woman plays a considerable part in literature; but what is its importance in daily life? To what extent does it affect the customs and conduct of individuals? In replying to this question it will be necessary to state precisely the relations this myth bears to reality.

There are different kinds of myths. This one, the myth of woman, sublimating an immutable aspect of the human condition—namely, the "division" of humanity into two classes of individuals—is a static myth. It projects into the realm of Platonic ideas a reality that is directly experienced or is conceptualized on a basis of experience; in place of fact, value, significance, knowledge, empirical law, it substitutes a transcendental Idea, timeless, unchangeable, necessary. This idea is indisputable because it is beyond the given: it is endowed with absolute truth. Thus, as against the dispersed, contingent, and multiple existences of actual women, mythical thought opposes the Eternal Feminine, unique and changeless. If the definition provided for this concept is contradicted by the behavior of flesh-and-blood women, it is the latter who are wrong: we are told not that Femininity is a false entity, but that the women concerned are not feminine. The contrary facts of experience are impotent against the myth. In a way, however, its source is in experience. Thus it is quite true that woman is other than man, and this alterity is directly felt in desire, the embrace, love; but the real relation is one of reciprocity; as such it gives rise to authentic drama. Through eroticism, love, friendship, and their alternatives, deception, hate, rivalry, the relation is a struggle between conscious beings each of whom wishes to be essential, it is the mutual recognition of free beings who confirm one another's freedom, it is the vague transition from aversion to participation. To pose Woman is to pose the absolute Other, without reciprocity, denying against all experience that she is a subject, a fellow human being.

In actuality, of course, women appear under various aspects; but each of the myths built up around the subject of woman is intended to sum her up *in toto;* each aspires to be unique. In consequence, a number of incompatible myths exist, and men tarry musing before the strange incoherencies manifested by the idea of Femininity. As every woman has a share in a majority of these archetypes—each of which lays claim to containing the sole Truth of woman—men of today also are moved again in the presence of their female companions to an astonishment like that of the old sophists who failed to understand how man could be blond and dark at the same time! Transition toward the absolute was indicated long ago in social phenomena: relations are easily congealed in classes, functions in types, just as relations, to the childish mentality, are fixed in things. Patriarchal society, for example, being centered upon the conservation of the patrimony, implies necessarily, along with those who own and transmit wealth, the existence of men and women who take property away from its owners and put it into circulation. The men—adventurers, swindlers, thieves, speculators—are generally repudiated by the group; the women, employing their erotic attraction, can induce young men and even fathers of families to scatter their patrimonies, without ceasing to be within the law. Some of these women appropriate their victims' fortunes or obtain legacies by using undue influence; this role being regarded as evil, those who play it are called "bad women." But the fact is that quite to the contrary they are able to appear in some other setting—at home with their fathers, brothers, husbands, or lovers—as guardian angels; and the courtesan who "plucks" rich financiers is, for painters and writers, a generous patroness. It is easy to understand in actual experience the ambiguous personality of Aspasia or Mme de Pompadour. But if woman is depicted as the Praying Mantis, the Mandrake, the Demon, then it is most confusing to find in woman also the Muse, the Goddess Mother, Beatrice.

As group symbols and social types are generally defined by means of antonyms in pairs, ambivalence will seem to be an intrinsic quality of the Eternal Feminine. The saintly mother has for correlative the cruel stepmother, the angelic young girl has the perverse virgin: thus it will be said sometimes that Mother equals Life, sometimes that Mother equals Death, that every virgin is pure spirit or flesh dedicated to the devil.

Evidently it is not reality that dictates to society or to individuals their choice between the two opposed basic categories; in every period, in each case, society and the individual decide in accordance with their needs. Very often they project into the myth adopted the institutions and values to which they adhere. Thus the paternalism that claims woman for hearth and home defines her as sentiment, inwardness, immanence. In fact every existent is at once immanence and transcendence; when one offers the existent no aim, or prevents him from attaining any, or robs him of his victory, then his transcendence falls vainly into the past—that is to say, falls back into immanence. This is the lot assigned to woman in the patriarchate; but it is in no way a vocation, any more than slavery is the vocation of the slave. The development of this mythology is to be clearly seen in Auguste Comte. To identify Woman with Altruism is to guarantee to man absolute rights in her devotion, it is to impose on women a categorical imperative.

The myth must not be confused with the recognition of significance; significance is immanent in the object; it is revealed to the mind through a living experience; whereas the myth is a transcendent Idea that escapes the mental grasp entirely. When in *L'Age d'homme* Michel Leiris describes his vision of the feminine organs, he tells us things of significance and elaborates no myth. Wonder at the feminine body, dislike for menstrual blood, come from perceptions of a concrete reality. There is nothing mythical in the experience that reveals the voluptuous qualities of feminine flesh, and it is not an excursion into myth if one attempts to describe them through comparisons with flowers or pebbles. But to say that Woman is Flesh, to say that the Flesh is Night and Death, or that it is the splendor of the Cosmos, is to abandon terrestrial truth and soar into an empty sky. For man also is flesh for woman; and woman is not merely a carnal object; and the flesh is clothed in special significance for each person and in each experience. And likewise it is quite true that woman— like man—is a being rooted in nature; she is more enslaved to the species than is the male, her animality is more manifest; but in her as in him the given traits are taken on through the fact of existence, she belongs also to the human realm. To assimilate her to Nature is simply to act from prejudice.

Few myths have been more advantageous to the ruling caste than the myth of woman: it justifies all privileges and even authorizes their abuse. Men need not bother themselves with alleviating the pains and the burdens that physiologically are women's lot, since these are "intended by Nature"; men use them as a pretext for increasing the misery of the feminine lot still further, for instance by refusing to grant to woman any right to sexual pleasure, by making her work like a beast of burden.[3]

---

[3][Beauvoir] Cf. Balzac: *Physiology of Marriage:* "Pay no attention to her murmurs, her cries, her pains; *nature has made her for our use* and for bearing everything: children, sorrows, blows and pains inflicted by man. Do not accuse yourself of hardness. In all the codes of so-called civilized nations, man has written the laws that ranged woman's destiny under this bloody epigraph: "*Va victis!* Woe to the weak!"

Of all these myths, none is more firmly anchored in masculine hearts than that of the feminine "mystery." It has numerous advantages. And first of all it permits an easy explanation of all that appears inexplicable; the man who "does not understand" a woman is happy to substitute an objective resistance for a subjective deficiency of mind; instead of admitting his ignorance, he perceives the presence of a "mystery" outside himself: an alibi, indeed, that flatters laziness and vanity at once. A heart smitten with love thus avoids many disappointments: if the loved one's behavior is capricious, her remarks stupid, then the mystery serves to excuse it all. And finally, thanks again to the mystery, that negative relation is perpetuated which seemed to Kierkegaard infinitely preferable to positive possession; in the company of a living enigma man remains alone—alone with his dreams, his hopes, his fears, his love, his vanity. This subjective game, which can go all the way from vice to mystical ecstasy, is for many a more attractive experience than an authentic relation with a human being. What foundations exist for such a profitable illusion?

Surely woman is, in a sense, mysterious, "mysterious as is all the world," according to Maeterlinck. Each is *subject* only for himself; each can grasp in immanence only himself, alone: from the point of view the *other* is always a mystery. To men's eyes the opacity of the self-knowing self, of the *pour-soi,* is denser in the *other* who is feminine; men are unable to penetrate her special experience through any working of sympathy: they are condemned to ignorance of the quality of woman's erotic pleasure, the discomfort of menstruation, and the pains of childbirth. The truth is that there is mystery on both sides: as the *other* who is of masculine sex, every man, also, has within him a presence, an inner self impenetrable to woman; she in turn is in ignorance of the male's erotic feeling. But in accordance with the universal rule I have stated, the categories in which men think of the world are established *from their point of view, as absolute:* they misconceive reciprocity, here as everywhere. A mystery for man, woman is considered to be mysterious in essence.

To tell the truth, her situation makes woman very liable to such a view. Her physiological nature is very complex; she herself submits to it as to some rigmarole from outside; her body does not seem to her to be a clear expression of herself; within it she feels herself a stranger. Indeed, the bond that in every individual connects the physiological life and the psychic life—or better the relation existing between the contingence of an individual and the free spirit that assumes it—is the deepest enigma implied in the condition of being human, and this enigma is presented in its most disturbing form in woman.

But what is commonly referred to as the mystery is not the subjective solitude of the conscious self, nor the secret organic life. It is on the level of communication that the word has its true meaning: it is not a reduction to pure silence, to darkness, to absence; it implies a stammering presence that fails to make itself manifest and clear. To say that woman is mystery is to say, not that she is silent, but that her language is not understood; she is there, but hidden behind veils; she exists beyond these uncertain appearances. What is she? Angel, demon, one inspired, an actress? It may be supposed either that there are answers to these questions which are impossible to discover, or, rather, that no answer is adequate because a fundamental ambiguity marks the feminine being; and perhaps in her heart she is even for herself quite indefinable: a sphinx.

The fact is that she would be quite embarrassed to decide *what* she *is;* but this not because the hidden truth is too vague to be discerned: it is because in this domain there is no truth. An existent *is* nothing other than what he does; the possible does not extend beyond the real, essence does not precede existence: in pure subjectivity, the human being *is not anything.* He is to be measured by his acts. Of a peasant woman one can say that she is a good or a bad worker, of an actress that she has or does not have talent; but if one considers a woman in her immanent presence, her inward self, one can say absolutely nothing about her, she falls short of having any qualifications. Now, in amorous or conjugal relations, in all relations where the woman is the vassal, the other, she is being dealt with in her immanence. It is noteworthy that the feminine comrade, colleague, and associate are without mystery; on the other hand, if the vassal is male, if, in the eyes of a man or a woman who is older, or richer, a young fellow, for example, plays the role of the inessential object, then he too becomes shrouded in mystery. And this uncovers for us a substructure under the feminine mystery which is economic in nature.

A sentiment cannot be supposed to *be* anything. "In the domain of sentiments," writes Gide, "the real is not distinguished from the imaginary. And if to imagine one loves is enough to be in love, then also to tell oneself that one imagines oneself to be in love when one is in love is enough to make one forthwith love a little less." Discrimination between the imaginary and the real can be made only through behavior. Since man occupies a privileged situation in this world, he is in a position to show his love actively; very often he supports the woman or at least helps her; in marrying her he gives her social standing; he makes her presents; his independent economic and social position allows him to take the initiative and think up contrivances: it was M. de

Norpois who, when separated from Mme de Villeparisis, made twenty-four-hour trips to visit her. Very often the man is busy, the woman idle: he *gives* her the time he passes with her; she takes it: is it with pleasure, passionately, or only for amusement? Does she accept these benefits through love or through self-interest? Does she love her husband or her marriage? Of course, even the man's evidence is ambiguous: is such and such a gift granted through love or out of pity? But while normally a woman finds numerous advantages in her relations with a man, his relations with a woman are profitable to a man only in so far as he loves her. And so one can almost judge the degree of his affection by the total picture of his attitude.

But a woman hardly has means for sounding her own heart; according to her moods she will view her own sentiments in different lights, and as she submits to them passively, one interpretation will be no truer than another. In those rare instances in which she holds the position of economic and social privilege, the mystery is reversed, showing that it does not pertain to *one* sex rather than the other, but to the situation. For a great many women the roads to transcendence are blocked: because they *do* nothing, they fail to *make themselves* anything. They wonder indefinitely what they *could have* become, which sets them to asking about what they *are.* It is a vain question. If man fails to discover that secret essence of femininity, it is simply because it does not exist. Kept on the fringe of the world, woman cannot be objectively defined through this world, and her mystery conceals nothing but emptiness.

Furthermore, like all the oppressed, woman deliberately dissembles her objective actuality; the slave, the servant, the indigent, all who depend upon the caprices of a master, have learned to turn toward him a changeless smile or an enigmatic impassivity; their real sentiments, their actual behavior, are carefully hidden. And moreover woman is taught from adolescence to lie to men, to scheme, to be wily. In speaking to them she wears an artificial expression on her face; she is cautious, hypocritical, play-acting.

But the Feminine Mystery as recognized in mythical thought is a more profound matter. In fact, it is immediately implied in the mythology of the absolute Other. If it be admitted that the inessential conscious being, too, is a clear subjectivity, capable of performing the *Cogito,* then it is also admitted that this being is in truth sovereign and returns to being essential; in order that all reciprocity may appear quite impossible, it is necessary for the Other to be for itself an other, for its very subjectivity to be affected by its otherness; this consciousness which would be alienated as a consciousness, in its pure immanent presence, would evidently be

Mystery. It would be Mystery in itself from the fact that it would be Mystery for itself; it would be absolute Mystery.

In the same way it is true that, beyond the secrecy created by their dissembling, there is mystery in the Black, the Yellow, in so far as they are considered absolutely as the inessential Other. It should be noted that the American citizen, who profoundly baffles the average European, is not, however, considered as being "mysterious": one states more modestly that one does not understand him. And similarly woman does not always "understand" man; but there is no such thing as a masculine mystery. The point is that rich America, and the male, are on the Master side and that Mystery belongs to the slave.

To be sure, we can only muse in the twilight byways of bad faith upon the positive reality of the Mystery; like certain marginal hallucinations, it dissolves under the attempt to view it fixedly. Literature always fails in attempting to portray "mysterious" women; they can appear only at the beginning of a novel as strange, enigmatic figures; but unless the story remains unfinished they give up their secret in the end and they are then simply consistent and transparent persons. The heroes in Peter Cheyney's books, for example, never cease to be astonished at the unpredictable caprices of women: no one can ever guess how they will act, they upset all calculations. The fact is that once the springs of their action are revealed to the reader, they are seen to be very simple mechanisms: this woman was a spy, that one a thief; however clever the plot, there is always a key; and it could not be otherwise, had the author all the talent and imagination in the world. Mystery is never more than a mirage that vanishes as we draw near to look at it.

We can see now that the myth is in large part explained by its usefulness to man. The myth of woman is a luxury. It can appear only if man escapes from the urgent demands of his needs; the more relationships are concretely lived, the less they are idealized. The fellah of ancient Egypt, the Bedouin peasant, the artisan of the Middle Ages, the worker of today has in the requirements of work and poverty relations with his particular woman companion which are too definite for her to be embellished with an aura either auspicious or inauspicious. The epochs and the social classes that have been marked by the leisure to dream have been the ones to set up the images, black and white, of femininity. But along with luxury there was utility; these dreams were irresistibly guided by interests. Surely most of the myths had roots in the spontaneous attitude of man toward his own existence and toward the world around him. But going beyond experience toward the transcendent Idea was deliberately used by patriarchal society for purposes of self-justification; through the myths this society imposed its laws and customs upon individuals in a picturesque, effective manner; it is under a mythical form that the group-imperative is indoctrinated into each conscience. Through such intermediaries as religions, traditions, language, tales, songs, movies, the myths penetrate even into such existences as are most harshly enslaved to material realities. Here everyone can find sublimation of his drab experiences: deceived by the woman he loves, one declares that she is a Crazy Womb; another, obsessed by his impotence, calls her a Praying Mantis; still another enjoys his wife's company: behold, she is Harmony, Rest, the Good Earth! The taste for eternity at a bargain, for a pocket-sized absolute, which is shared by a majority of men, is satisfied by myths. The smallest emotion, a slight annoyance, becomes the reflection of a timeless Idea—an illusion agreeably flattering to the vanity.

The myth is one of those snares of false objectivity into which the man who depends on ready-made valuations rushes headlong. Here again we have to do with the substitution of a set idol for actual experience and the free judgments it requires. For an authentic relation with an autonomous existent, the myth of Woman substitutes the fixed contemplation of a mirage. "Mirage! Mirage!" cries Laforgue. "We should kill them since we cannot comprehend them; or better tranquilize them, instruct them, make them give up their taste for jewels, make them our genuinely equal comrades, our intimate friends, real associates here below, dress them differently, cut their hair short, say anything and everything to them." Man would have nothing to lose, quite the contrary, if he gave up disguising woman as a symbol. When dreams are official community affairs, clichés, they are poor and monotonous indeed beside the living reality; for the true dreamer, for the poet, woman is a more generous fount than is any down-at-heel marvel. The times that have most sincerely treasured women are not the period of feudal chivalry nor yet the gallant nineteenth century. They are the times—like the eighteenth century—when men have regarded women as fellow creatures; then it is that women seem truly romantic, as the reading of *Liaisons dangereuses, Le Rouge et le noir, Farewell to Arms,* is sufficient to show. The heroines of Laclos, Stendhal, Hemingway are without mystery, and they are not the less engaging for that. To recognize in woman a human being is not to impoverish man's experience: this would lose none of its diversity, its richness, or its intensity if it were to occur between two subjectivities. To discard the myths is not to destroy all dramatic relation between the sexes, it is not to deny the significance authentically revealed to man through feminine reality; it is not to do away with poetry, love, adventure, happiness, dreaming.

It is simply to ask that behavior, sentiment, passion be founded upon the truth.[4]

"Woman is lost. Where are the women? The women of today are not women at all!" We have seen what these mysterious slogans mean. In men's eyes—and for the legion of women who see through men's eyes—it is not enough to have a woman's body nor to assume the female function as mistress or mother in order to be a "true woman." In sexuality and maternity woman as subject can claim autonomy; but to be a "true woman" she must accept herself as the Other. The men of today show a certain duplicity of attitude which is painfully lacerating to women; they are willing on the whole to accept woman as a fellow being, an equal; but they still require her to remain the inessential. For her these two destinies are incompatible; she hesitates between one and the other without being exactly adapted to either, and from this comes her lack of equilibrium. With man there is no break between public and private life: the more he confirms his grasp on the world in action and in work, the more virile he seems to be; human and vital values are combined in him. Whereas woman's independent successes are in contradiction with her femininity, since the "true woman" is required to make herself object, to be the Other.

It is quite possible that in this matter man's sensibility and sexuality are being modified. A new aesthetics has already been born. If the fashion of flat chests and narrow hips—the boyish form—has had its brief season, at least the overopulent ideal of past centuries has not returned. The feminine body is asked to be flesh, but with discretion; it is to be slender and not loaded with fat; muscular, supple, strong, it is bound to suggest transcendence; it must not be pale like a too shaded hothouse plant, but preferably tanned like a workman's torso from being bared to the open sun.

Woman's dress in becoming practical need not make her appear sexless: on the contrary, short skirts made the most of legs and thighs as never before. There is no reason why working should take away woman's sex appeal.[5] It may be disturbing to contemplate woman as at once a social personage and carnal prey: in a recent series of drawings by Peynet (1948), we see a young man break his engagement because he was seduced by the pretty mayoress who was getting ready to officiate at his marriage. For a woman to hold some "man's position" and be desirable at the same time has long been a subject for more or less ribald joking; but gradually the impropriety and the irony have become blunted, and it would seem that a new form of eroticism is coming into being—perhaps it will give rise to new myths.

What is certain is that today it is very difficult for women to accept at the same time their status as autonomous individuals and their womanly destiny; this is the source of the blundering and restlessness which sometimes cause them to be considered a "lost sex." And no doubt it is more comfortable to submit to a blind enslavement than to work for liberation: the dead, for that matter, are better adapted to the earth than are the living. In all respects a return to the past is no more possible than it is desirable. What must be hoped for is that the men for their part will unreservedly accept the situation that is coming into existence; only then will women be able to live in that situation without anguish. Then Laforgue's prayer will be answered: "Ah, young women, when will you be our brothers, our brothers in intimacy without ulterior thought of exploitation? When shall we clasp hands truly?" Then Breton's "Mélusine, no longer under the weight of the calamity let loose upon her by man alone, Mélusine set free ..." will regain "her place in humanity." Then she will be a full human being, "when," to quote a letter of Rimbaud, "the infinite bondage of woman is broken, when she will live in and for herself, man—hitherto detestable—having let her go free."

---

[4][Beauvoir] Laforgue goes on to say regarding woman: "Since she has been left in slavery, idleness, without occupation or weapon other than her sex, she has overdeveloped this aspect and has become the Feminine. . . . We have permitted this hypertrophy; she is here in the world for our benefit. . . . Well! that is all wrong. . . . Up to now we have played with woman as if she were a doll. This has lasted altogether too long! . . ."

---

[5][Parshley] A point that hardly needs to be made in America, where even cursory acquaintance with any well-staffed business office will afford confirmatory evidence.—

Ronald S. Crane

~~~

1886–1967

Crane was the leading critical theorist among those at the University of Chicago who adopted a neo-Aristotelian approach to methodological problems. Although these critics denied that they were disciples of Aristotle, their language was nevertheless consistently Aristotelian. Crane's essay *Toward a More Adequate Criticism of Poetic Structure,* which is the concluding chapter of his book *The Languages of Criticism and the Structure of Poetry,* is an inquiry into the possibility that Aristotle's method is of continuing value to criticism and can be extended into areas on which Aristotle did not or could not comment.

First, Crane suggests that Aristotle's concept of poetic structures as "concrete wholes" is a fundamental unifying critical principle. Following Aristotle, Crane uses the terms *form* and *matter* to describe these wholes analytically, but he uses the terms in a way quite different from common practice, which distinguishes the poem's subject or "content" (matter) from "form." For Crane, "form" and "matter" are really inseparable. A poem is "a certain form imposed upon or wrought out of a certain matter." Here matter is the material of the art, including language, not something copied from without.

Next, Crane suggests that Aristotle's method of asking what forms go with what matter, what constructions are necessary to the achievement of any given form, is a useful procedure. Further, Aristotle's manner of raising questions of value is instructive. Poems must be judged on their distinctive aspects as wholes of certain kinds. The question is, what has the poet achieved, given the forms and materials at hand? Such judgments should be based on a revival of Aristotle's distinction between imitative and nonimitative poems. Various other Aristotelian terms, such as *plot, character, thought,* and *diction,* are also valuable.

Crane is critical of any method that translates itself into rhetorical or psychological language. He rejects the tradition, culminating in much New Critical practice, that defines poetry in terms of some dialectical relation between it and other modes of discourse or thought (see Wheelwright), or attempts to define poetry's particular mission, or defines poetry as opposed to science, or discusses it in terms of the presence or absence of some single attribute such as "irony" (see Brooks).

He is wary of most critical assumptions, though he acknowledges that his method makes one of a different sort from those theories that insist on an essential quality in every poem. "Any poetic work, like any other production of human art, has, or rather is, a definite structure of some kind which is determined immediately by its writer's intuition of a form to be achieved in its materials by the right use of his medium." Crane acknowledges that there is a fallacy in judging the poet's work by his intention, in the sense in which Wimsatt and Beardsley use the term; but he means by *intention* only what internal analysis of the work reveals that it seeks to be. When Crane asks what the final cause of a work is, he is asking not a psychological but a purely artistic question that must be answered by querying the text, not the author. Recourse to the psychology of either the artist or the reader is for him reductive and inadequate.

Crane's work is neo-Aristotelian; it is not merely a repetition of Aristotle's position. For example, Crane's use of the term *intuition* reveals the influence of Crocean expressionism. His interest in kinds of literary works and some of his use of Aristotelian methods align him frequently, but by no means totally, with Frye. Finally, he self-consciously opposes the New Critical tendency to define poetry as a mode of language by contrasting it with other modes.

Crane is the editor of *Critics and Criticism* (1952). Among his critical works are *The Language of Criticism and the Structure of Poetry* (1953), *The Idea of the Humanities* (1967), and *Critical and Historical Principles of Literary History* (1971).

From
Toward a More Adequate Criticism of Poetic Structure

II

It is not a question of regarding the *Poetics,* in Mr. Blackmur's phrase, as a "sacred book"[1] and certainly not of looking upon ourselves, in any exclusive sense, as forming an "Aristotelian" or "neo-Aristotelian" school. It would be a desirable thing, indeed, as if we could do away with "schools" in criticism as they have been done away with in most of the disciplines in which learning as distinguished from doctrine has been advanced. But our loyalty at any rate should be to problems rather than to ancient masters; and if it happens that we have problems for which Aristotle can give us the means, or some of the means, of solution, we should be prepared to benefit from his initiative in precisely the same way as many of our contemporaries have benefited from the more recent initiatives of Coleridge, Richards, Frazer, and Freud without necessarily becoming disciples of any of these men. And it is not difficult to see what there is in Aristotle, or what we can develop out of him, that is immediately pertinent to the problem of poetic structure in the particular form in which I have defined it at the beginning of this lecture.

I should put first in the list the conception of poetic works as "concrete wholes."[2] Now anything is a concrete whole, as I have said before, the unity of which can be adequately stated only by saying that it "is such and such a form embodied in this or that matter, or such and such a matter with this or that form; so that its shape and structure must be included in our description" as well as that out of which it is constituted or made. And of the two natures which must join in any such whole, or in our account of it, "the formal nature is of greater importance than the material nature" inasmuch as the "form" of any individual object, such as a man or a couch, is the principle or cause "by reason of which the matter is some definite thing."[3] In spite of the now somewhat unfamiliar language in which the conception is stated in Aristotle, the underlying insight is one that we can easily translate into the terms of common experience. I take, for instance, a piece of modeling clay. There are many things which I cannot do with it—of which, as Aristotle would say, it cannot be the matter; but on the other hand the potentialities it does hold out, within these limits, are indefinite in number: I can make of it, if I wish, a geographical globe, with all its continents indicated, or the model of a house, or the bust of a sinister-looking man, and so on through a vast range of similar possibilities that is bounded only by my invention and skill. In any of these realizations the thing I make remains a thing of clay, having all the permanent characteristics of such a thing; but it remains this only in a partial sense; in itself, as a particular object to which we may respond practically or aesthetically, it is at the same time some-

TOWARD A MORE ADEQUATE CRITICISM OF POETIC STRUCTURE. The text is from the concluding chapter of *The Languages of Criticism and the Structure of Poetry* by R. S. Crane. Reprinted by permission of University of Toronto Press. Copyright, Canada, 1953, by University of Toronto Press.
[1][Crane] *Hudson Review,* III (1951), 497.

[2][Crane] *The Languages of Criticism and the Structure of Poetry,* pp. 44–45, and note 47.
[3][Crane] *On the Parts of Animals,* I. 1. 640^{b}25–29; *Metaphysics* VII. 17. 1041^{b}5–8.

thing else—a globe, a house, a sinister-looking man; and any description we may give of it, though it must obviously specify its clayness—that is, its material nature—would be of no use to anybody unless it also specified the definite kind of thing into which the clay has been shaped—that is, its formal nature. And the latter is clearly more important than the former since it is what accounts, in any particular case, for the clay being handled thus and not otherwise and for our response being of such and such a quality rather than any other.

It is not difficult to see how the conception fits the work of the poet or of any other writer. Here is a speech in a famous novel: "Ah, my poor dear child, the truth is, that in London it is always a sickly season. Nobody is healthy in London—nobody can be. It is a dreadful thing to have you forced to live there; so far off! and the air so bad!"[4] Taken in isolation, this may be described simply as an expression of regret that the person addressed has to live in London, based on the commonplace thought that the air of London, as compared with the air of the country, is far from healthy. The speech, we may say, is made out of this matter; but it is a matter, obviously, that permits of a variety of particular uses: it might be a speech in an idyl, or in a satire, or in a moral epistle in the manner of Cowper; and in each case its formal nature and hence our response would be different. It is actually, of course, a speech by Mr. Woodhouse in *Emma;* and when it is so read, in its position in the dialogue of Chapter 12 and in the light of what we have already seen of Emma's father, it assumes the nature of a characteristic comic act, wherein the most important thing is not the commonplace thought itself, but the excessive and inappropriate emotion, at the prospect of Isabella's coming departure for home, which this is made to express, and which is the formal principle shaping the matter of the speech into a definite, though not self-contained, artistic unit capable of directing our thoughts in a particular way.

Of here again is a whole poem, the material nature of which is comprised of the following sequence of happenings:

A young Italian duke, influenced by his idle companions, dismisses the wise counsellor his father had recommended to him, refuses the advice of his fiancée, and devotes himself to a life of private pleasure and neglect of public duty. A Turkish corsair takes advantage of this situation to storm the Duke's castle and to reduce him and all his court to slavery; and the Duke falls into despair when he learns that his fiancée is destined for the conqueror's harem. She, however, deceives the corsair into giving her a delay of three days and a chance to speak to her lover. She uses this time to rouse the Duke to repentance for his past errors and to work out with him a plan whereby he and his father's counsellor will attempt a rescue before the three days are up. The plan succeeds; the Duke and his friends overcome the corsair's troops and make him prisoner. The Duke's false companions then demand that the Turk be executed; but the Duke, grateful for the lesson his captivity has taught him, responds by banishing them and allowing the corsair to depart unharmed; whereupon he marries his fiancée and resolves to rule more wisely in the future.

As an action this is clearly not without some form, being a coherent and complete chain of possible events, to which we are likely to respond by taking sides with the Duke and the girl against their captors. I am sure, however, that anyone who reads *The Duke of Benevento* for the first time after hearing my summary will think that I have given a very indefinite account of what happens in Sir John Henry Moore's poem and hence misled him completely as to the poem's distinctive nature and effect. He will probably be prepared to read a vaguely tragicomic romance or drama of a kind common enough in the 1770s; what he will actually find is a short piece of 204 lines beginning as follows:

> I hate the prologue to a story
> Worse than the tuning of a fiddle,
> > Squeaking and dinning;
> Hang order and connection,
> I love to dash into the middle;
> > Exclusive of the fame and glory,
> There is a comfort on reflection
> > To think you've done with the beginning.
>
> And so at supper one fine night,
> > Hearing a cry of Alla, Alla,
> The Prince was damnably confounded,
> > And in a fright,
> But more so when he saw himself surrounded
> By fifty Turks; and at their head the fierce
> > Abdalla,
>
> And then he looked a little grave
> To find himself become a slave, . . .

---

[4][Crane] Jane Austen, *Emma*, Chapter 12.

And so on consistently to the end, in a rapidly narrated episode of which the formal nature is the kind of antiromantic comedy clearly foreshadowed in these lines—a form that is only potentially in the story of the poem (since this could yield several other forms) and is created out of it, partly indeed by Moore's pre-Byronic language and manner of narration, but also, as a reading of the whole poem will show, by the notably unheroic qualities of character and thought which he gives to his hero and heroine, with the result that we are unable to take their predicament any more tragically than they themselves do.

It can be seen from these illustrations how different is such a conception of the internal relations of form and matter in a "concrete whole" from the later and much commoner analytic in which form or art is set over against content or subject matter in one or another of the many ways we have already illustrated.[5] A poem, on the view of its structure suggested by Aristotle, is not a composite of *res* and *verba* but a certain matter formed in a certain way or a certain form imposed upon or wrought out of a certain matter. The two are inseparable aspects of the same individual thing, though they are clearly distinct analytically as principles or causes, and though, of the two, the formal nature is necessarily the more important as long as our concern is with the poem as a concrete object. On the one hand, we do not cease to talk about the matter of a poem when we examine its formal structure, and, on the other hand, there is a sense in which nothing in a completed poem, or any distinguishable part thereof, is matter or content merely, in relation to which something else is form. In a well-made poem, everything is formed, and hence rendered poetic (whatever it may have been in itself), by virtue simply of being made to do something definite in the poem or to produce a definitely definable effect, however local, which the same materials of language, thought, character traits, or actions would be incapable of in abstraction from the poem, or the context in the poem, in which they appear. We are not speaking poetically but only materially of anything in a poem, therefore, when we abstract it from its function or effect in the poem; we speak poetically, or formally, only when we add to a description of the thing in terms of its constituent elements (for example, the content of a metaphor or the events of a plot) an indication of the definite quality it possesses or of that in the poem for the sake of which it is there. In an absolute sense, then, nothing in a successful poem is nonformal or nonpoetic; but it is also true that structure of any kind necessarily implies a subordination of some parts to others; and

in this relative sense we may intelligibly say of one formed element of a poem that it is material to something else in the same poem, the existence and specific effectiveness of which it makes possible. We may thus speak of the words of a poem as the material basis of the thought they express, although the words also have form as being ordered in sentences and rhythms; and similarly we may speak of thought as the matter of character, of character and thought in words as the matter of action or emotion, and so on up to but not including the overall form which synthesizes all these subordinate elements, formally effective in themselves, into a continuous poetic whole. Or we can reverse the order of consideration, and ask what matter of action, character, and thought a poem requires if its plot or lyric structure is to be formally of a certain kind, or what kind of character a speech ought to suggest if it is to serve adequately its function in a scene, or what selection and arrangement of words will render best or most economically a given state of mind.

Here then is an intelligible, universally applicable, and analytically powerful conception of the basic structural relations in poems which we can take over from Aristotle without committing ourselves to the total philosophy in which it was evolved. We can also take over, in the second place, the method of investigation and reasoning which he found appropriate to structures of this kind.[6] The conception and the method, indeed, can hardly be divorced. For if we are to consider poetic works, in practical criticism, from the point of view of their concrete wholeness, then our central problem is to make their elements and subordinate structures causally intelligible in the light of their respective organizing forms. This can be done, however, only by means of general concepts embodying answers to two major questions relative to such kinds of poetry as we may be interested in: first, what different forms can go with what different matters, and, second, what parts, and what constructions of each of them, are necessary to the achievement of any given form. But these, it is obvious, are questions of fact, the answers to which can never be given by any "abstract" method but must depend upon inquiries of an a posteriori type which move inductively (in Aristotle's sense of induction) from particulars to the universals they embody and from ends or forms thus defined, by hypothetical necessity to the essential conditions of their realization in poetic matter. The method, of course, is not Aristotelian in any unique sense, but no one has shown as fully as he did how it may be applied to poetics or how completely it depends, in this application, upon an adequate knowledge of literary history.

---

[5][Crane] See *Languages,* pp. 91–92.

[6][Crane] See *Languages,* pp. 45–46.

The method is factual, but it is not indifferent to values; and the third thing we can learn from Aristotle is a manner of considering questions of better and worse in poetry which is likewise appropriate to the conception of poems as concrete wholes organized by formal principles.[7] As things made by and for men, poems, as I have said before, can have a great variety of uses and be judged not improperly in terms of many different criteria, moral, political, intellectual, grammatical, rhetorical, historical. To judge them as poems, however, is to judge them in their distinctive aspect as wholes of certain kinds, in the light of the assumption that the poet's end—the end which makes him a poet—is simply the perfecting of the poem as a beautiful or intrinsically excellent thing. I do not mean by this that poems are ever perfected in an absolute sense. We need not quarrel with R. G. Collingwood when he remarks, in his *Autobiography,* that as a boy living in a household of artists he "learned to think of a picture not as a finished product exposed for the admiration of virtuosi, but as the visible record, lying about the house, of an attempt to solve a definite problem in painting, so far as the attempt has gone." "I learned," he adds,

> what some critics and aestheticians never know to the end of their lives, that no "work of art" is ever finished, so that in that sense of the phrase there is no such thing as a "work of art" at all. Work ceases upon the picture or manuscript, not because it is finished, but because sending-in day is at hand, or because the printer is clamorous for copy, or because "I am sick of working at this thing" or "I can't see what more I can do to it."[8]

This is sound sense, which critics and aestheticians ought to learn if they do not know it; but it is clearly not incompatible with the assumption that what a poet seeks to do, as a poet, is to make as good a work poetically speaking as he can; and this goodness, we can surely agree with Aristotle, must always consist in a mean between doing too much and not doing enough in his invention and handling of all its parts. The criterion, again, is not an absolute one; the mean in art, as in morals, is a relative mean, which has to be determined in adjustment to the particular necessities and possibilities of the form the artist is trying to achieve. And just as the poet can know these only by trial and error plus reflection upon the general conditions of his art and on what other poets have been able to do, so the critic can know them, and the ends to

which they are relative, only by similar ex post facto means. He must therefore leave to other critics with less strictly "poetic" preoccupations the task of formulating criteria for poetry on the basis of general "abstract" principles; his business is to take the point of view of the poet and his problems and to judge what he has done, as sympathetically as possible, in terms of what must and what might be done *given* the distinctive form, new or old, which the poet is trying to work out of his materials.[9] And here, once more, the procedure of Aristotle can be of use.

We can still profit, moreover, not merely from these general features of his approach—all of them relevant also to other than critical problems—but likewise from many of the more particular applications of his method in the *Poetics,* including, first of all, the fundamental distinction, on which the whole treatise is based, between poetry which is "imitation" and poetry which is not.[10] The former, for Aristotle, is poetry in the most distinctive sense, since its principles are not the principles of any other art; but to insist on this is not to question the possibility of discussing as "poetry" other kinds of works of which the materials and devices, though not the forms, are those of poems in the stricter meaning of the word; the difference is not one of relative dignity or value but purely of constructive principle, and hence of the kinds of hypotheses and terms that are required, respectively, for the analysis and judgment of works belonging to each. The distinction, as Aristotle understood it, has played no important part in the subsequent history of criticism. A class of "didactic" poems has, it is true, been more or less constantly recognized, but the differentiation between these and other poems has most often been made in terms of purpose, content, and technique rather than of matter and form, a "didactic" poem being distinguished sometimes as one in which the end of instruction is more prominent than that of delight, sometimes as one that uses or springs from or appeals to the reason rather than the imagination, sometimes as one that relies mainly on precepts instead of fictions and images or that uses direct rather than indirect means of expression. This breakdown of the original distinction was natural enough in the periods of criticism in which the ends of poetry were defined broadly as instruction and pleasure, and it is still natural in a period, such as our own, when the great preoccupation is with "meaning" and with poetry as a special kind of language for expressing special modes of signification. In

---

[7][Crane] See *Languages,* pp. 57–63.
[8][Crane] *An Autobiography,* p. 2.

---

[9][Crane] On the kind of criticism which refuses to grant to an artist the "subject" he has chosen, see the remarks of Henry James in his preface to *The Portrait of a Lady.*
[10][Crane] See *Languages,* pp. 47–49, and Olson, in *Critics and Criticism,* pp. 65–68, 69–70, 588–92.

both periods, although some classes of poems have been set apart as "didactic" in a peculiar and frequently pejorative sense, all poetry, or all poetry except that which can be described as "entertainment" merely, has tended to assume an essentially didactic character and function. The prevalence nowadays of "thematic analysis" as a method of discussion applicable to all poetic works that can be taken seriously at all is a clear sign of this, as is also the currency of "archetypal" analogies. The result, however, has been to banish from criticism, or to confuse beyond clear recognition, a distinction which has as much validity now as when it was first made and which has not been supplanted by any of the later distinctions, since these all rest on quite different bases of principle. The distinction is simply between works, on the one hand, in which the formal nature is constituted of some particular human activity or state of feeling qualified morally and emotionally in a certain way, the beautiful rendering of this in words being the sufficient end of the poet's effort, and works, on the other hand (like the *Divine Comedy, Absalom and Achitophel, Don Juan, 1984,* etc.), in which the material nature is "poetic" in the sense that it is made up of parts similar to those of imitative poems and the formal nature is constituted of some particular thesis, intellectual or practical, relative to some general human interest, the artful elaboration and enforcement of this by whatever means are available and appropriate being the sufficient end of the poet's effort. Great and serious works can be and have been written on either of these basic principles of construction, but the principles themselves, it must be evident, are sharply distinct, and the difference is bound to be reflected, in innumerable subtle as well as obvious ways, in everything that poets have to do or can do in the two major kinds. To continue to neglect the distinction, therefore, is merely to deprive ourselves unnecessarily of an analytical device—however hard to apply in particular cases—which can only serve, when intelligently used, to introduce greater exactness into our critical descriptions and greater fairness into our critical judgments.

Of the many other distinctions and concepts in the *Poetics* which are still valid and useful—at least for the kind of discussion of poetic structure we now have in mind—nearly all are limited, in their strict applicability, to imitative works. For any inquiry into such forms we cannot neglect, to begin with, the all-important distinctions of object, means, manner, and *dynamis* upon which the definition of tragedy in Chapter 6[11] is based. They are, as I have tried to show in the second lecture, the essential and basic determinants of the structure of any species of imitative works when these are viewed as concrete wholes,[12] for we can conceive adequately of such a whole only when we consider as precisely as possible what kind of human experience is being imitated, by the use of what possibilities of the poetic medium, through what mode of representation, and for the sake of evoking and resolving what particular sequence of expectations and emotions relative to the successive parts of the imitated object. It is always some definite combination of these four things that defines, for the imitative writer, the necessities and possibilities of any work he may have in hand; for what he must and can do at any point will differ widely according as he is imitating a character, a state of passion, or an action, and if an action (with character, thought, and passion inevitably involved), whether one of which the central figures are men and women morally better than we are, or like ourselves, or in some sense worse; and according as he is doing this in verse of a certain kind or in prose or in some joining of the two; and according as he is doing it in a narrative or a dramatic or a mixed manner; and according, finally, as he is shaping his incidents and characters and their thoughts and feelings, his language, and his technique of representation (whatever it may be) so as to give us, let us say, the peculiar kind of comic pleasure we get from *Tom Jones* or that we get from *The Alchemist* or, to add still another possible nuance of comic effect, from *Volpone*. These, then, are indispensable distinctions for the critic who wishes to grasp the principles of construction and the consequences thereof in any imitative work; and he will be sacrificing some of the precision of analysis possible to him if he fails to take them all into consideration as independent variables—if he talks, for instance, about the plot of a novel or the pattern of images in a lyric poem without specifying the emotional "working or power" which is its controlling form,[13] or if, in dealing with any kind of imitative work, he neglects to distinguish clearly between the "things" being imitated, upon which the *dynamis* primarily depends, and the expedients of representational manner by which the writer has sought to clarify or maximize their peculiar effect.[14]

There remains, lastly, the detailed analytic of imitative forms which is represented in the *Poetics* by the chapters on

---

[11]VI. 2, p. 53.

[12][Crane] See *Languages,* pp. 50–57.

[13][Crane] Cf. Crane, in *Critics and Criticism,* pp. 621–22, 632–45; Olson, *ibid.,* 563–66.

[14][Crane] Cf. Olson, *ibid.,* pp. 71 *ff.,* 562–63. With the remarkable development, in modern literature, of elaborate representational means for making effective relatively simple or universalized plots, the problem of distinguishing the two is sometimes a delicate one; there has been a good deal of confusion, consequently, in some of the discussions of works like *Ulysses, A Passage to India,* and Hemingway's *The Killers.*

tragedy and epic. I need not repeat what I have said in the second lecture about Aristotle's distinctive conceptions—which have largely vanished from later criticism—of plot, character, thought, and diction—or about the relationships of causal subordination in which these "parts" are made to stand to one another in the tragic and epic structures, so that the last three (together with music and spectacle in tragedy), while being capable of form themselves, have the status of necessary material conditions of the plot, which, in the most specific sense of the synthesis of things done and said in a work as determined to a certain "working or power," is the principal part or controlling form of the whole.[15] I have said why this analysis seems to me sound, given the assumptions on which it is based and its limited applicability to works of which the subjects are actions of the more or less extended sort Aristotle here had in mind. We can therefore still use it, and the many constituent definitions and distinctions it involves, in the criticism of the larger poetic forms; and we can profit particularly, I think, from the discussion of tragic plot form in Chapter 13,[16] not only because it gives us a clue to the structure of many later "tragic" works (this plot form is clearly the formula, for example, of *Othello,* though not quite of *Macbeth,* and certainly not of *Richard III*) but also, and chiefly, because it suggests the four general questions we have to ask ourselves about any work having a plot as its principle of construction if we are to see clearly what problems its writer faced in composing it: as to precisely what the change is, from what it starts and to what it moves; in what kind of man it takes place; by reason of what causes in the man's thoughts and actions or outside him; and with what succession of emotional effects in the representation.

III

We should be merely "Aristotelians," however, rather than independent scholars were we to remain content with what we can thus extract from Aristotle for present-day critical use; and we should be able to deal only crudely and inadequately with a great many of the most interesting structural problems raised by modern works. We need therefore to push the Aristotelian type of theoretical analysis far beyond the point where Aristotle himself left off, and this in several different directions.

There are, to begin with, the many nonimitative species of poetry or imaginative literature with which the *Poetics*

does not deal at all. A large number of these have been roughly distinguished in the nomenclature and theories of subsequent criticism under such heads as: philosophical poems, moral essays, epigrams, treatises in verse, occasional poems; Horatian satires, Juvenalian satires, Varronian or Menippean satires; allegories, apologues, fables, parables, exempla, thesis or propaganda dramas and novels. But though a vast deal of critical and historical discussion has been devoted to these forms, we have as yet only fragments and beginnings of a usable inductive analytic of their structural principles as distinguished from their material conventions.[17]

Again, there are all the shorter imitative forms, most of them later in origin or artistic development than Aristotle, which we commonly group together as lyric poems; much of the best criticism of these has been concerned either with their techniques and fixed conventional patterns or with a dialectical search for the qualities of subject matter and expression which are thought to differentiate lyric poetry, as a homogeneous type, from other poetic kinds.[18] What we need to have, therefore, is a comprehensive study, free from "abstract" assumptions, of the existing species of such poems in terms both of the different "proper pleasures" achievable in them and of the widely variant material structures in which the pleasures may inhere. Lyrics, it is plain, do not have plots, but any successful lyric obviously has something analogous to a plot in the sense of a specific form which synthesizes into a definite emotional whole what is said or done in the poem and conditions the necessities and probabilities which the poet must embody somehow in his lines; and the nature of this formal principle—whether it is, for example, a man in an evolving state of passion interpreted for him by his thought (as in the *Ode to a Nightingale*) or a man adjusting himself voluntarily to an emotionally significant discovery about his life (as in the *Ode on Intimations of Immortality*)—has to be grasped with some precision if we are to be able to speak appropriately and adequately about the poem's construction in all its parts and the degree of its artistic success. And here too most of the necessary analytical work still remains to be done.[19]

We are much better off, thanks to Aristotle, with respect to the full-length imitative forms of narrative and drama; but even in this field of theory there are many important outstanding questions. Except for one suggestive paragraph in

---

[15][Crane] See *Languages,* pp. 67–68, 70–73.
[16]Pp. 56–57.

[17][Crane] Cf. Olson, in *Critics and Criticism,* p. 592, for brief definitions of the principal types.
[18][Crane] Cf. Norman Maclean, *ibid.,* pp. 408 *ff.*
[19][Crane] Cf. Olson, *ibid.,* p. 560, and his forthcoming book on the shorter poetic forms.

Chapter 5 on the general nature of the ridiculous,[20] the *Poetics* as we have it is silent on comedy; and although there is much to be learned from the innumerable later discussions, especially since the eighteenth century, the insights these make available still have to be translated out of the rhetorical and psychological languages in which they are, for the most part, embodied into the more consistently "poetic" language we are committed to using. That there are a good many distinguishable comic plot forms, both in drama and in narrative, must be evident to everyone; but as to what they are, and what different artistic necessities and possibilities each of them involves, we have as yet, I think, only rather vague general notions; and the problem has not been greatly advanced by the traditional classifications into comedy of intrigue, comedy of manners, comedy of character, and so on.[21] The same thing is true of the many intermediate forms between comedy in the stricter sense and tragedy proper: of tragicomedy, for example, or the "serious" and "tender" comedy which emerged in the eighteenth century, or the kind of domestic novel which Jane Austen wrote in *Pride and Prejudice, Mansfield Park,* and *Persuasion,* or the adventure romance in its earlier as well as its contemporary forms, or even the detective novel, much as has been written about the "poetics" of that. Nor is tragedy itself in much better case. What the *Poetics* gives us is an analytic of only one among the many plot forms which the critical opinion as well as the common sense of later times has thought proper to call "tragic"; and it is one of the unfortunate results of the respect which Aristotle has always commanded that critics have tended to blur the distinctive principles of construction and effect, or to impair the artistic integrity, of these "non-Aristotelian" tragic forms in their eagerness to bring them in some fashion under his definition. We need therefore a fresh attempt at analysis, by the same method but in more appropriate terms, for such plot forms, among others, as are represented severally by *Richard III* and *The Duchess of Malfi,*[22] by *The Orphan,* by *The Brothers Karamazov,* and by *A Passage to India.*

It is not merely of the forms of drama and narrative, however, that we require a better theory but also of many of their characteristic structural devices. We still tend to think of plot in its material aspects in the limited terms in which it is treated in the *Poetics* on the basis of the somewhat ele-

mentary practice of the Greeks, with the result that when we have to deal with works that combine in various ways two or many lines of action or concern themselves primarily not with external actions but with changes in thought and feeling or with the slow development or degeneration of moral character or with the fortunes of groups rather than of individuals, we often fall into the confusion which has led many modern critics to reject the concept of plot altogether. This is clearly no solution, but the remedy can be only a more comprehensive and discriminating induction of possible dramatic and narrative structures than Aristotle was able to provide. And there is also the complex question of how plots of whatever kind, or their equivalents in other forms, have to be or can be represented in the words—the question, in short, of imitative manner in a sense that goes beyond, while still depending upon, Aristotle's distinction of the three manners in his third chapter. Of all the topics I have mentioned, this is perhaps the one on which the largest body of precise and useful observation has been accumulated, by all those critics from the Renaissance to our day who have devoted themselves to the "techniques" first of the drama and epic and then of the novel, short story, and lyric. Even here, however, much remains to be done; and one of the chief requisites, I think, is a clearer posing of the whole problem in such a way as to correlate the many devices of manner which these critics have discriminated, as well as others that have escaped them, with the distinguishable functions which manner has to serve with respect to form. I have touched upon some of these functions in the second lecture,[23] and I will add only the suggestion that they are likely to be, in all richly developed imitative works, incidents, characters, speeches, and images which are not parts of the plot form but must be viewed by the critic as elements of "thought" in a sense akin to but distinct from that intended by Aristotle in Chapters 6 and 19.[24] We may treat as "thought" of this kind anything permitting of inference in a poetic work, over and above the direct working of the imitated object, that functions as a device, vis-à-vis the audience, for disclosing or hinting at relevant traits of character or situation, awakening or directing expectations, conditioning states of mind, emphasizing essential issues, suggesting in what light something is to be viewed, or, more broadly still, setting the action or some part of it in a larger context of ideas or analogies so that it may come to seem, in its universal implications for human beings, not simply the particular and untypical action it might otherwise be taken to be. Every novelist or dramatist—or

---

[20]See V. 1, p. 52.

[21][Crane] Cf. Olson, *ibid.,* pp. 555–56; Crane, *ibid.,* pp. 636–38; but these are merely hints.

[22][Crane] One of my former students, Mr. Richard Levin, is completing a study of the plot forms of these and other similar works in Renaissance English drama.

---

[23][Crane] See *Languages,* pp. 76–77.

[24]Pp. 53–54 and p. 60.

lyric poet, for that matter—who reflects on his own work will understand what this means; but the conception has still to become widely recognized among critics, or it surely would have been applied long since to such things as the apparently superfluous episodes and characters and the recurrent general words and patterns of images in Shakespeare—the dialectic of "nature" in *King Lear,* for instance—concerning which most recent writers have thought it necessary to offer much more profound explanations.[25]

It would be well, finally, if we could carry our method of inductive and causal analysis into some of the larger questions of theory—common to both imitative and nonimitative poetry—to which these writers and other contemporary critics have given special prominence: we could profit greatly, for example, from a reexamination, in our distinctive language, of poetic images, of the elements and functions of diction in poetry, of the various modes and uses of symbols, and of the structural characteristics of myths.[26]

We need not wait, however, for the completion of these possible studies before beginning to use such theory of poetic forms as we now possess in the service of practical criticism. There is after all a close mutual interdependence, in the method we are considering, between theoretical analysis and the investigation of particular works; and as our attempts at application become more numerous and more varied in their objects, so will our grasp of the necessary general distinctions and principles tend to improve.

IV

In these attempts, as should be clear from what I have said, we shall be making a pretty complete break with the tradition of practical criticism discussed in the last two lectures—a tradition in which it has always been necessary, before individual works of poetic art can be analyzed or judged, to conceive of poetry as a homogeneous whole and to define its nature in some kind of dialectical relation to other modes of discourse and thought. We shall not need, for our purposes, to commit ourselves to any of the numerous and apparently inconsistent theories of poetry, tragedy, lyric, or the like, based on such a presupposition, which this tradition has developed. We shall not need to worry, as so many contemporaries have done, about how poetry differs from science or prose, or about what its mission is in the modern world. We

shall not need to decide in advance of our studies of poems whether poetry in general is best defined as a kind of language or a kind of subject matter; whether its end is pleasure or some species of knowledge or practical good; whether its proper domain includes all the kinds of imaginative writing or only some of these; whether it is most closely akin to rhetoric and dialectic or to ritual, myth, or dream; or whether it is or is not a separable element in prose fiction and drama. Nor shall we need to assume that all good poems have "themes" or that poetic expression is always indirect, metaphorical, and symbolic. Not merely would such speculative commitments be useless to us, given our empirical starting point, but they would be fatal, in proportion as we allowed our analyses to be directed by them, to our very effort, since they would inevitably blind us to all those aspects of our problem which our particular doctrine of poetry failed to take into account.

I do not mean that we shall not have to make some assumptions of our own, but only that these need not and ought not to be particularized assumptions about the intrinsic nature and necessary structure of our objects considered as a unitary class of things. We shall have to assume that any poetic work, like any other production of human art, has, or rather is, a definite structure of some kind which is determined immediately by its writer's intuition of a form to be achieved in its materials by the right use of his medium, and, furthermore, that we can arrive at some understanding of what this form actually is and use our understanding as a principle in the analysis and criticism of the work. We shall have to come to some agreement, moreover, as to what we will mean by "poetic works"; but here again the fewer specifications we impose on ourselves in advance the better. It will be sufficient for all our purposes if we begin, simply, by taking as "poems" or "works of literary art" all those kinds of productions which have been commonly called such at different times, but without any supposition that, because these have the same name, they are all "poems" or "works of literary art" in the same fundamental structural sense— that the art necessary to write *The Divine Comedy* or *The Faerie Queene* is the same art, when viewed in terms of its peculiar principles of form, as the art which enabled Shakespeare to write *King Lear* and *Othello.* And for such productions we shall need to assume, in addition, only one common characteristic: that they are all works which, in one degree or another, justify critical consideration primarily for their own sake, as artistic structures, rather than merely for the sake of the knowledge or wisdom they express or the practical utility we may derive from them, though either or both of these other values may be importantly involved in any particular case.

---

[25][Crane] Cf. Crane, in *Critics and Criticism,* pp. 641–45.
[26][Crane] Cf. Olson, *ibid.,* pp. 68 *ff.,* 567 *ff.*

The problem of structure, for any individual work of this kind, is the problem—to give it its most general statement—of how the material nature of the work is related to its formal nature, when we understand by form that principle, or complex of principles, which gives to the subject matter the power it has to affect our opinions and emotions in a certain definite way such as would not have been possible had the synthesizing principle been of a different kind. The question, as I have said, is primarily one of fact and cause; and it is answered, for a given work, when we have made as intelligible as we can the fashion in which its material elements of whatever kind—words, images, symbols, thoughts, character traits, incidents, devices of representation—are made to function in relation to a formal whole which we can warrantably assert was the actual final cause of its composition. By *actual final cause* I mean simply a cause without the assumption of which, as somehow effective in the writing, the observable characteristics of the parts, their presence in the poem, their arrangement and proportioning, and their interconnections cannot be adequately understood. In discovering what this shaping principle is in any work we must make use of such evidence as there may be concerning the history of its conception and writing, including any statements the writer may have made about his intentions. Our task, however, is not to explain the writer's activity but the result thereof; our problem is not psychological but artistic; and hence the causes that centrally concern us are the internal causes of which the only sufficient evidence is the work itself as a completed product. What we want to know is not the actual process but the actual rationale of the poem's construction in terms of the poetic problems the writer faced and the reasons which determined his solutions. And in looking for these we shall assume that if the poem holds together as an intelligibly effective whole, in which a certain form is realized in a certain matter which never before had this form, the result can be understood fully only by supposing that such and such problems were involved and were solved by the writer in accordance with reasons which, in part at least, we can state; and this clearly does not commit us to holding that the problems and reasons we uncover in our analysis, as necessarily implied by the completed poem, must have presented themselves to the writer explicitly as such in a continuous movement of self-conscious deliberation; it will be sufficient if we can show that the poem could hardly have been written as it is or have the effect it does on our minds had the writer not done, somehow or at some time, what these particular problems and reasons dictate.

We can never, of course, know such things directly, but only by inference from the consequences of the conceived form, whether of the whole or of any of its parts, in the details of the completed work; and there can be no such inference except by way of hypotheses which both imply and are implied by the observable traits of the work. There are, however, hypotheses and hypotheses, and the character of those we shall have to make is determined by the nature of our problem. We propose to consider poems as unique existent things the structural principles of which are to be discovered, rather than as embodiments of general truths about the structure of poetry already adequately known. Hence our procedure must be the reverse of that procedure by way of preferred paradigms or models of structure which we have seen to be so characteristic of contemporary practical criticism. Our task is not to show the reflection in poems of complex or "ironical" attitudes, interactions of prose and poetry or of logical structure and irrelevant texture, patterns of ritual drama, or basic mythical themes, on the assumption that if the poem is a good poem it will inevitably have whichever of these or other similarly derived general structures we happen to be interested in finding examples of; it is rather the task of making formal sense out of any poetic work before us on the assumption that it may in fact be a work for whose peculiar principles of structure there are nowhere any usable parallels either in literary theory or in our experience of other works. The hypotheses we have to make, therefore, will not be of the fixed and accredited kind which scientists employ only when their problem is not to find out something still unknown but to "demonstrate" a classic experiment to beginners, but rather of the tentative kind—to be modified or rejected altogether at the dictation of the facts—which are the proper means to any serious inductive inquiry. They will be particular working hypotheses for the investigation of the structures of individual poems, not general hypotheses about such things as poetry or "poetic drama" in which the specific nature of the individual structures to be examined is already assumed.

We must also distinguish between critical hypotheses in the strict sense and interpretative hypotheses concerning the details of literary works in their material aspects. It is not one of our presuppositions that "form" in poetry is "meaning"; we should hold, rather, that meaning is something involved in poems as a necessary, but not sufficient, condition of the existence in them of poetic form, and hence that the recovery of meaning is an essential prerequisite to the discovery of form though not in itself such a discovery. Before we can understand a poem as an artistic structure we must understand it as a grammatical structure made up of successive words, sentences, paragraphs, and speeches which give us both meanings in the ordinary sense of that term and signs from which we may infer what the speakers, whether characters or narrators, are like and what they are thinking, feeling, or doing. The great temptation for critics who are not trained and practicing scholars is to take this understanding for granted or to think that it may easily be obtained at second hand by consulting the works of scholars. This is an illusion, just as it is an illusion in scholars to suppose that they can see, without training in criticism, all the problems which their distinctive methods are fitted to solve. The ideal would be that all critics should be scholars and all scholars critics; but, although there ought to be the closest correlation of the two functions in practice, they are nevertheless distinct in nature and in the kinds of hypotheses to which they lead. The hypotheses of interpretation are concerned with the meanings and implications in texts that result from their writers' expressive intentions in setting down particular words and constructions and arranging these in particular sequences. Such meanings and implications, indeed, are forms, of which words and sentences are the matter; but they are forms of a kind that can appear in any sort of discourse, however unpoetic. They are to be interpreted by resolving the forms into the elements which poems share with the common speech or writing and the common thought and experience of the times when they were written; and this requires the use of techniques and principles quite different from any that poetic theory can afford: the techniques and principles of historical grammar, of the analysis and history of ideas, of the history of literary conventions, manners, and so on, and the still more general techniques and principles, seldom methodized, by which we construe characters and actions in everyday life.

The hypotheses of criticism, on the contrary, are concerned with the shaping principles, peculiar to the poetic arts, which account in any work for the power of its grammatical materials, in the particular ordering given to these, to move our opinions and feelings in such-and-such a way. They will be of two sorts according as the questions to which they are answers relate to the principles by which poetic works have been constructed as wholes of certain definite kinds or to the reasons which connect a particular part of a given work, directly or indirectly, with such a principle by way of the poetic problems it set for the writer at this point. And there can be no good practical criticism in this mode in which both sorts are not present; for although the primary business of the critic is with the particulars of any work he studies down to its minuter details of diction and rhythm, he can never exhibit the artistic problems involved in these or find other than extrapoetic reasons for their solutions without the guidance of an explicit definition of the formal whole which they have made possible.

A single work will suffice to illustrate both kinds of critical hypotheses as well as the relation between them, and I will begin by considering what idea of the governing form

of *Macbeth* appears to accord best with the facts of that play and the sequence of emotions it arouses in us. I need not say again why it seems to me futile to look for an adequate structural formula for *Macbeth* in any of the more "imaginative" directions commonly taken by recent criticism; I shall assume, therefore, without argument, that we have to do, not with a lyric "statement of evil" or an allegory of the workings of sin in the soul and the state or a metaphysical myth of destruction followed by recreation or a morality play with individualized characters rather than types,[27] but simply with an imitative tragic drama based on historical materials. To call it an imitative tragic drama, however, does not carry us very far; it merely limits roughly the range of possible forms we have to consider. Among these are the contrasting plot forms embodied respectively in *Othello* and in *Richard III*: the first a tragic plot form in the classic sense of Aristotle's analysis in *Poetics* 13;[28] the second a plot form which Aristotle rejected as nontragic but which appealed strongly to tragic poets in the Renaissance—a form of serious action designed to arouse moral indignation for the deliberately unjust and seemingly prospering acts of the protagonist and moral satisfaction at his subsequent ruin. The plot form of *Macbeth* clearly involves elements which assimilate it now to the one and now to the other of both these kinds. The action of the play is twofold, and one of its aspects is the punitive action of Malcolm, Macduff, and their friends which in the end brings about the protagonist's downfall and death. The characters here are all good men, whom Macbeth has unforgivably wronged, and their cause is the unqualifiedly just cause of freeing Scotland from a bloody tyrant and restoring the rightful line of kings. All this is made clear in the representation not only directly through the speeches and acts of the avengers but indirectly by those wonderfully vivid devices of imagery and general thought in which modern critics have found the central value and meaning of the play as a whole; and our responses, when this part of the action is before us, are such as are clearly dictated by the immediate events and the poetic commentary: we desire, that is, the complete success of the counteraction and this as speedily as possible before Macbeth can commit further horrors. We desire this, however—and that is what at once takes the plot form out of the merely retributive class—not only for the sake of humanity and Scotland but also for the sake of Macbeth himself. For what most sharply distinguishes our view of Macbeth from that of his victims and enemies is that, whereas they see him from the outside only, we see him also, throughout

---

[27][Crane] Cf. *Languages*, pp. 7–8.
[28]Pp. 56–57.

the other action of the play—the major action—from the inside, as he sees himself; and what we see thus is a moral spectacle the emotional quality of which, for the impartial observer, is not too far removed from the tragic *dynamis* specified in the *Poetics*. This is not to say that the main action of *Macbeth* is not significantly different, in several respects, from the kind of tragic action which Aristotle envisages. The change is not merely from good to bad fortune, but from a good state of character to a state in which the hero is almost, but not quite, transformed into a monster; and the tragic act which initiates the change, and still more the subsequent unjust acts which this entails, are acts done—unlike Othello's killing of Desdemona—in full knowledge of their moral character. We cannot, therefore, state the form of this action in strictly Aristotelian terms, but the form is none the less one that involves, like tragedy in Aristotle's sense, the arousal and catharsis of painful emotions for, and not merely with respect to, the protagonist—emotions for which the terms pity and fear are not entirely inapplicable.

Any adequate hypothesis about the structure of *Macbeth,* then, would have to take both of these sets of facts into account. For both of the views we are given of the hero are true: he is in fact, in terms of the nature and objective consequences of his deeds, what Macduff and Malcolm say he is throughout Acts IV and V, but he is also—and the form of the play is really the interaction of the two views in our opinions and emotions—what we ourselves see him to be as we witness the workings of his mind before the murder of Duncan, then after the murder, and finally when, at the end, all his illusions and hopes gone, he faces Macduff. He is one who commits monstrous deeds without becoming wholly a monster, since his knowledge of the right principle is never altogether obscured, though it is almost so in Act IV. We can understand such a person and hence feel fear and pity of a kind for him because he is only doing upon a grander scale and with deeper guilt and more terrifying consequences for himself and others what we can, without too much difficulty, imagine ourselves doing, however less extremely, in circumstances generally similar. For the essential story of *Macbeth* is that of a man, not naturally depraved, who has fallen under the compulsive power of an imagined better state for himself which he can attain only by acting contrary to his normal habits and feelings; who attains this state and then finds that he must continue to act thus, and even worse, in order to hold on to what he has got; who persists and becomes progressively hardened morally in the process; and who then, ultimately, when the once alluring good is about to be taken away from him, faces the loss in terms of what is left of his original character. It is something like this moral universal that underlies, I think, and gives emotional form to the main

action of *Macbeth.* It is a form that turns upon the difference between what seemingly advantageous crime appears to be in advance to a basically good but incontinent man and what its moral consequences for such a man inevitably are; and the catharsis is effected not merely by the man's deserved overthrow but by his own inner suffering and by his discovery, before it is too late, of what he had not known before he began to act. If we are normal human beings we must abhor his crimes; yet we cannot completely abhor but must rather pity the man himself, and even when he seems most the monster (as Macbeth does in Act IV) we must still wish for such an outcome as will be best, under the circumstances, not merely for Scotland but for him.

But if this, or something close to it, is indeed the complex emotional structure intended in *Macbeth,* then we have a basis for defining with some precision the various problems of incident, character, thought, imagery, diction, and representation which confronted Shakespeare in writing the play, and hence a starting point for discussing, in detail, the rationale of its parts.[29] Consider—to take only one instance—the final scene. In the light of the obvious consequences of the form I have attributed to the play as a whole, it is not difficult to state what the main problems at this point are. If the catharsis of the tragedy is to be complete, we must be made to feel both that Macbeth is being killed in a just cause and that his state of mind and the circumstances of his death are such as befit a man who, for all his crimes, has not altogether lost our pity and good will. We are of course prepared for this double response by all that has gone before, and, most immediately, in the earlier scenes of Act V, by the fresh glimpses we are given of the motivation of the avengers and by Macbeth's soliloquies. But it will clearly be better if the dual effect can be sustained until the very end; and this requires, on the one hand, that we should be vividly reminded once more of Macbeth's crimes and the justified hatred they have caused and of the prospect of a new and better time which his death holds out for Scotland, and, on the other hand, that we should be allowed to take satisfaction, at last, in the manner in which Macbeth himself behaves. The artistic triumph of the scene lies in the completeness with which both problems are solved: the first in the words and actions of Macduff, the speeches about young Siward, and Malcolm's closing address; the second by a variety of devices, both of invention and of representation, the appropriateness of which to the needed effect can be seen if we ask what we would not want Macbeth to do at this moment. We

---

[29][Crane] See, in addition to what follows, Wayne C. Booth, *Journal of General Education,* VI (1951), 21–25. For a somewhat similar discussion of an episode in *King Lear,* cf. Maclean, in *Critics and Criticism,* pp. 595–615.

want him to be killed, as I have said, for his sake no less than that of Scotland; but we would not want him either to seek out Macduff or to flee the encounter when it comes or to "play the Roman fool"; we would not want him to show no recognition of the wrongs he has done Macduff or, when his last trust in the witches has gone, to continue to show fear or to yield or to fight with savage animosity; and he is made to do none of these things, but rather the contraries of all of them, so that he acts in the end as the Macbeth whose praises we have heard in the second scene of the play. And I would suggest that the cathartic effect of these words and acts is reinforced indirectly, in the representation, by the analogy we can hardly help drawing between his conduct now and the earlier conduct of young Siward, for of Macbeth too it can be said that "he parted well and paid his score"; the implication of this analogy is surely one of the functions, though not the only one, which the lines about Siward are intended to serve.

Such are the kinds of hypotheses we shall need to make if we are to have critical knowledge of the shaping principles of poetic works or of the artistic reasons governing the character and interrelation of their parts. They are working suppositions which, as I have said, both imply and are implied by the particulars of the works for which they are constructed; and they can never be made well by any critic who is not naturally sensitive to such particulars and in the habit of observing them closely. These, however, though indispensable, are not sufficient conditions. It never happens in any inquiry into matters of fact that the particulars we observe determine their own meaning automatically; the concrete or the individual is never intelligible except through the general and the abstract; and if we are to allow the facts to speak for themselves, we must in some fashion supply them with a language in which to talk. Hypotheses, in short, are not made out of nothing, but presuppose on the part of the inquirer who forms them a systematic body of concepts relative to the subject matter with which he is dealing. The critic who proposes to explore hypothetically the structures of individual poems is in the same predicament; he must bring to his task, inescapably, general ideas about poetic structure, or he can never construct a workable hypothesis about the structure of any poem.

Hence the crucial importance for the practical critic of poetic forms, in the sense we are now giving to this term, of the kind of analytic of poetry which was outlined earlier in this lecture. From the point of view of the criticism of individual poems, the concepts and distinctions involved in that analytic differ from those which most contemporary critics have been content to use: they supply, not a unified set of terms for constituting structural patterns in poems (like Mr.

Heilman's formula for "poetic drama" or the theories that make all good poetry a species of "ironical" or "paradoxical" structure), but a great variety of terms designating distinct and alternative principles, devices, and functions in poetry from which the critic need select only such combinations as appear to be relevant to the poems he is examining. What he thus acquires are not hypotheses ready formed but elements out of which he may form such hypotheses as the facts of his poems seem to warrant—in short, knowledge of structural possibilities only, resting on inductive inquiry into the principles poets have actually used in building poems and hence expanding with the development and progressive differentiation of poetry itself, so that he brings to the discussion of individual poems merely conceptual materials for framing pertinent questions about them without any predetermination of the substance of his answers, much as a physician uses the alternatives given him by medical theory in diagnosing symptoms in one of his patients. In the other mode of criticism the relation of theory to a particular poem is the relation of a previously selected idea or pattern of structure to its embodiment or reflection in a given work; here the relation is one of many known possibilities of structural patterning in poetry to the actualization in the poem examined of some one or more of these.

A critic using the first type of theory might argue somewhat as follows, for example, about the structure of Gray's *Elegy*. We must assume, he might say, the language of poetry being what it is, that the principle of structure in any good poem is a principle of balancing and harmonizing discrepant connotations, attitudes, and meanings; we must look therefore for a structure of this kind in Gray's poem or be content to relegate it to an inferior class of poetry; and our quest, indeed, is not in vain, for when we examine the text in the light of our general hypothesis of "ironical" structure, we quickly find that all the details of the *Elegy* can be subsumed under the theme of a continuous contrast of two modes of burial—in the church itself and in the churchyard—in which, as in all good poetry, opposing meanings are finally resolved.[30] A critic, however, whose theory was of the second type, would proceed in an altogether different way. He would have no favorite hypothesis of structure as such, but would know merely that among short poems which, like the *Elegy*, evoke in us serious emotions, the shaping principle may be of several essentially distinct types, each of them generating distinct artistic problems for the poet; and he would use this knowledge as a basis for asking himself some such questions as these: Is what happens in the *Elegy* best

---

[30][Crane] Cleanth Brooks, *The Well Wrought Urn*, pp. 96–113.

explained by supposing, as the other critic has clearly done, that the poem is intended to be read as an emotionalized argument in verse (whether about modes of burial or something else), the personal qualities of the speaker and the setting of his meditation being simply devices for enforcing the unifying dialectic? Or is the poem better read—better, that is, with respect to the actual shaping principle of its construction—as an imitative lyric? And if it is this latter kind of structure, is the form one in which the speaker is conceived as being merely moved in a certain way by his situation (as in Gray's *Ode on a Distant Prospect of Eton College*), or as acting in a certain manner in relation to it (as in Marvell's *To His Coy Mistress*), or as deliberating morally in a certain state of mind on what is for him a serious issue in life? Weighing these possibilities (which give us perhaps the major forms which short serious imitative poems can have), our second critic would probably conclude that it is the last possibility which best explains both the constructed matter and the arrangement of the *Elegy* and the peculiar quality of the emotions which Gray's words and rhythms arouse in us. He might then describe the *Elegy* as an imitative lyric of moral choice rather than of action or of mood, representing a situation in which a virtuous, sensitive, and ambitious young man of undistinguished birth confronts the possibility of his death while still to "fortune and to fame unknown," and eventually, after much disturbance of mind (hinted at in the Swain's description of him), reconciles himself to his probable fate by reflecting that none of the rewards of successful ambition can "soothe the dull cold ear of death," which comes as inevitably to the great as to the obscure; that a life passed "far from the madding crowd's ignoble strife," though circumscribing the exercise of virtue and talent, may yet be a means of preserving innocence; and that he can at any rate look forward to—what all men desire as a minimum—living on in the memory of at least one friend, while his merits and frailties alike repose "in trembling hope" on the bosom of his Father and his God.[31] Something like this, I think (pedantic as any brief statement of it must sound), is the answer our second critic would give; but the point is that in arriving at it he would be using his theory of possible principles of structure in short poems simply to furnish him with the distinctions he needs if he is not to substitute a structure of his own for the structure Gray achieved.

The more extensive and discriminating such general knowledge, therefore, the better the critic's hypotheses are likely to be. But it is also the nature of this kind of theoretical knowledge to be always inadequate, though in varying degrees, to the particulars we use it to illuminate. We can never know in advance all the possibilities, and we can never, consequently, form a hypothesis about a work of any artistic complexity or even about many simpler works without making a shorter or longer inductive leap from the words and sentences before us to the peculiar combination of universals which define their poetic form. And that is why, in this mode of criticism, we can make no separation except analytically between theory and application, the latter being possible only if the former already exists at least up to a certain point and the former being constantly refined and enlarged as we proceed with the latter.

Application, however, is our main problem here, and its success depends upon the extent to which the universal terms of our hypotheses and the perceived and felt particulars of the texts for which they are constructed can be made to fit together. The general conditions are two: first, our ability to keep our explanatory formulae fluid and to submit them to constant revisions in principle or in detail before we transform them into conclusions; and, second, our willingness to use systematically what has been called "the method of multiple working hypotheses."[32] We have to remember, that is, that the value of a hypothesis is always relative, not merely to the facts it is intended to explain, but to all the other variant hypotheses which the same facts might suggest if only we gave them a chance; that the best hypothesis is simply the best among several possible hypotheses, relevant to the same work or problem, with which we have actually compared it; and that unless we make such comparisons a regular part of our procedure, we always court the danger of missing either slightly or altogether what our author was really attempting to do.

There are also, in addition to these very general rules, several more particular criteria. Our aim is an explanation and judgment of poetic works in terms of their structural causes; hence, in the first place, the necessity of so framing our hypotheses that they are not descriptive formulae merely but clearly imply practical artistic consequences, in what the writers must or cannot or might well do in the act of writing, for the details of the works they are being used to explain; that is the character, for example, of Aristotle's definition of tragic plot form in *Poetics* 13,[33] and I have tried to impart a

---

[31][Crane] I borrow here the substance and many of the words of a note of mine in *Critics and Criticism*, p. 99.

[32][Crane] By T. C. Chamberlin, in a paper with this title, first published in *Science,* Old Series, XV (1890), 92–96; reprinted in the *Journal of Geology,* XXXIX (1931), 155–65. The "method of multiple working hypotheses" is contrasted with "the method of the ruling theory" and "the method of the working hypothesis."

[33]Pp. 56–57.

similar character to the statements above about *Macbeth*. The ideal is to have a central principle of explanation that will enable us to see precisely the functional relations between all the particular problems a writer has attempted to solve and the form of his work as a whole, even though we may have to conclude, in some cases, that the relation is a very tenuous one. In the second place, our aim is an explanation and judgment in terms adapted as closely as possible to the peculiar structure and power of the work before us; hence the necessity of trying to go beyond formulae that imply the work as a whole or any of its parts only generically; as when, for instance, we neglect to distinguish between the different material structures possible in lyrics and treat a particular lyric without regard to such distinctions, or as when we discuss a work like Jane Austen's *Emma* merely as a comedy, failing to see how little this can tell us about its distinctive comic construction. In the third place, we aspire to completeness of explanation; and this means that in framing a hypothesis about any work we must consider everything in the text as significant evidence that involves in any way a free choice on the writer's part between possible alternative things to be done with his materials or ways of doing them at any point. The hypothesis must therefore be complex rather than simple; it must recognize that the same parts may have different functions, including that of mere adornment; and, above all, it cannot be arrived at by giving a privileged position, on a priori grounds, to a particular variety of signs of artistic intention, in a complex work, to the exclusion of other and often conflicting signs of the same thing. This last is conspicuously the error of those interpreters of *Macbeth* who have inferred the central form of that play chiefly from the thought and imagery that serve to emphasize the "unnatural" character of the hero's crimes and the inevitability of a just retribution, without attempting to correlate with this the many signs, both in the construction of the plot and in its extraordinarily artful representation, of the distinctive moral quality of Macbeth's actions when these are seen from the inside. There will always be incompleteness in any hypothesis, moreover, or in any criticism that follows its use, that leaves out of account, as one of the crucial facts, the peculiar sequence of emotions we feel when we read the work unbiased by critical doctrine; for, as we have seen, the most important thing about any poetic production is the characteristic power it has to affect us in this definite way rather than that.[34] Completeness, however, is impossible without coherence; hence our hypotheses, in the fourth place, must aim at a maximum of internal unity, on the assumption that, although many works are episodic and although many predominantly imitative works, for example, also have didactic or topical parts, this can best be seen if we begin by presuming that literary artists usually aim at creating wholes.

The only proof there can be of a hypothesis about any particular thing lies in its power of completeness and coherence of explanation within the limits of the data it makes significant—and this always relatively to the other hypotheses pertinent to the same data with which it has been compared. We must be guided, however, in choosing among alternative hypotheses, by a further criterion—the classic criterion of economy: that that hypothesis is the best, other things being equal, which requires the fewest supplementary hypotheses to make it work or which entails the least amount of explaining away; it is no recommendation, thus, for Mr. Knight's interpretation of *Macbeth* that he has to say of the emotion aroused in most readers as well as in Bradley by Macbeth's soliloquies in Act V, that this is mere "conventional 'sympathy for the hero,'" which ought not to be allowed to distort that dialectical system of values in the play that is for him "the pattern of the whole."[35] And we must be careful, further, not to construe our "data" in too narrow a sense and so be satisfied with hypotheses that clearly conflict with facts external to the works we are considering but relevant nevertheless to their interpretation; I mean not only such particular evidences as we can often find of writers' intentions—for example, Coleridge's statements about the kind of poem he designed *The Rime of the Ancient Mariner* to be—but also such general probabilities with respect to the works of a given period or genre or with respect to poetic works of any kind of age as are supplied by either our historical knowledge or our common sense. It is not likely, for instance, that a Shakespearean tragedy intended for the popular stage should really have a kind of basic structure which practicing playwrights of any time would find it difficult or impossible to make effective for their audiences.[36] Nor is it ever a sensible thing in a critic to cultivate indifference to common opinion about the works he is discussing. The opinion may be wrong or, as often happens, it may need to be corrected and refined; but in such conflicts—at least when they involve the larger aspects and effects of works—the burden of proof is on him. For the secrets of art are not, like the secrets of nature, things lying deeply hid, inaccessible to the perception and understanding of all who have not mastered the special techniques their discovery requires. The critic does, indeed, need special techniques, but for the sake

---

[34][Crane] Cf. Keast, in *Critics and Criticism*, pp. 131–36.

[35][Crane] *Explorations*, p. 36. Cf. *Languages*, pp. 33–34.
[36][Crane] Cf. Keast, in *Critics and Criticism*, pp. 135–37.

of building upon common-sense apprehensions of his objects, not of supplanting these; and few things have done greater harm to the practice and repute of literary criticism in recent times than the assumption that its discoveries, like those of the physical sciences, must gain in importance and plausibility as they become more and more paradoxical in the ancient sense of that word: as if—to adapt a sharp saying of Professor Frank Knight about social studies—now that everybody is agreed that natural phenomena are not like works of art, the business of criticism must be to show that works of art are like natural phenomena.

It remains, finally, to consider the bearing of all this on judgments of poetic value. And the first thing to observe is that, if our hypothesis concerning the shaping principle of any work is adequate, it will give us a basis for saying with some precision (as my example of Act V of *Macbeth* will perhaps suggest) what are the necessities which such a form imposes on any artist whose aim is its successful realization in his materials. Some of them will be necessities common to all self-contained poetic works of no matter what kind, such as the necessity, if the parts are to cohere, of devices for effecting continuity from beginning through middle to end; others will be more and more specific necessities determined by the nature of the form we assume to have been intended, such as the necessity, if a comic effect like that of *Tom Jones* is to be obtained, of keeping the ridiculous mistakes of the hero from obscuring the sympathetic traits that make us wish him ultimate good fortune. These will all be consequences inferable from our basic definition of the form, and our primary task will be to trace them, in detail, throughout the particulars of the work at all its levels from plot or lyric situation down to the imagery and words. A kind of judgment of value will thus emerge in the very process of our analysis: if the writer has indeed done, somehow, all the essential things he would need to do on the assumption that he is actually writing the kind of work we have defined, then to that extent the work is good, or at least not artistically bad; and we should have to use very little rhetoric in addition to make this clear. But this is only half of the problem, for it is true of most mediocre writers that they usually do, in some fashion, a great part or all of the things their particular forms require, but do little more besides. The crucial question, therefore, concerns not so much the necessities of the assumed form as its possibilities. What is it that the writer might have done, over and above the minimum requirements of his task, which he has not done, or what is it that we have not expected him to do which he has yet triumphantly accomplished? These are the things our analyses ought peculiarly to attend to if they are to be adequate to their objects.

The possible in this sense, as distinguished from the necessary, is that which tends to perfect—to warrant praise of a positive rather than a merely negative kind. We can know it in two ways: by having our minds stored with memories of what both the most and the least perfect of artists have done when confronted with similar problems of invention, representation, and writing; and by considering theoretically the conditions under which any particular effect aimed at in a given work might be better or worse achieved—by asking, for instance, what would in general make a predicament like that of Tom Jones on the discovery of his first affair with Molly seem most completely comic, and then discussing the episode, as it is actually developed by Fielding, in these terms.[37] Both methods are comparative, but the comparisons, if they are not to result in unfair impositions on the writer whose work we are considering, must take account of the fact that the desirable or admirable in literature is never something absolute but is always relative, in any given part of a work, to the requirements of the overall form and to the function of the part as only one part along with many others: forgetting this, we should make the mistake of Mr. Joyce Cary's critic and demand neatness where clumsiness is what "belongs," vividness and particularity where faintness and generality are needed, doing much more than is done when this would be doing too much.

The judgments of value we should thus be trying to make would for this reason always be judgments in kind, grounded on a prior definition of the writer's problems as problems peculiar, at least in their concrete determination, to the formal nature of the work he is writing. They would also be judgments in terms of intentions—what is it that the writer aimed to do here and how well has he succeeded in doing it?—but the intentions we should take as principles would not be those, except accidentally, which the writer had stated explicitly before or after writing or those which can be defined for the writer by saying that he must have intended to write this work because this is what he has written. The common objections to criticism based on "intention" in either of these senses are unanswerable. They do not hold, however, when we identify intention with the hypothesized form of a poetic work and then consider how fully what we know of the necessities and possibilities of this form are achieved in the work, on the assumption that, if the work shows any serious concern with art at all, the writer must have wished or been willing to be judged in this way. There is nothing unfair to the writer in such an approach, inasmuch as we are not engaged in a judicial process of bringing his work under a previously formulated general theory of literary value but in a free inquiry whose aim is simply the discovery of those values in his work—among them, we always

---

[37][Crane] Cf. Crane, *ibid.*, pp. 639–40.

hope, unprecedented values—which he has been able to put there. They will always be values incident to the relation between the form of the work and its matter at all of its structural levels; and it will be appropriate to interpret what we find in terms of a distinction between three classes of works considered from this point of view: works that are well conceived as wholes but contain few parts the formal excellence of which remains in our memory or invites us to another reading; works that are rich in local virtues but have only a loose or tenuous overall form; and works that satisfy Coleridge's criterion for a poem, that it aims at "the production of as much immediate pleasure in parts, as is compatible with the largest sum of pleasure in the whole."[38] These last are the few relatively perfect productions in the various literary kinds, and as between the other two we shall naturally prefer the second to the first.

V

All methods, in any field of study, have their characteristic corruptions when they fall into the hands of incompetent practitioners. The corruption of the historical critic is thus typically some kind of antiquarian irrelevance, as when texts are annotated more learnedly than they need to be or with only a loose pertinence to the problems and difficulties they present. The corruption of the literary critic in the modes of criticism we are chiefly familiar with at the present time is most commonly perhaps a cult of the paradoxical, along with which go, often enough, an addiction to irresponsible analogizing, a preference for metaphorical over literal statement, and a tendency to substitute rhetoric for inquiry as a guiding aim. The critic whose portrait I am drawing in this lecture is less likely, I think, to give way to any of these perversions than to certain others which, though different in kind, are no less to be deplored. In his concern with form, he can all too easily become merely formalistic, attending less to what gives life to poems than to the mechanism of their structural parts; in his concern with poetic wholes, he can be tempted to forget that the wholes have no existence apart from the words through which they are made actual; in his concern with development of theory, he can readily persuade himself that the enunciation of theory, however well established, is more important than the solution of the concrete problems to which it is relevant and so fall into a methodological pedantry as bad as the factual pedantry of the antiquarians.

I do not think, however, that these are inevitable faults, given a certain flexibility of mind, a sensitivity to literary

particulars, an ability to resist the spirit of routine and self-satisfaction, and an understanding of the right relation between methods and problems. And when they are not allowed to distort the results, I should contend that the approach I have been describing is capable of giving us more nearly adequate insights into the structural principles and characteristics of poetic works than any of the other modes of critical language with which we have compared it. We may say of these other methods, in terms borrowed from our own, that what they have chiefly concentrated on, in their analyses of structure, has been the matter of poetic works and its generic figurations and techniques rather than their forms. These are essential aspects of the problem, but they are aspects with which we too can deal. We can consider how any element in a poem "works with the other elements to create the effect intended by the poet"; we can discuss the "meaning" of poems in the sense of the thought that is presupposed by or expressed through any of their characteristic devices of statement and representation; we can treat of images and patterns of images and of the subtleties of poetic diction and rhythm; we can find a place for what is sound in the distinction between "structure" and "texture"; and we can make use of all that the "archetypal" critics can tell us about the cultural and psychological universals which poems imply. We can do all these things; but we can also do more, and as a consequence be able to do these things with greater precision and intelligibility.

For we possess what these other methods have conspicuously lacked: a means of isolating and defining those principles of structure in individual poems which distinguish them from other poems or kinds of poems and determine thus in highly specific ways what their distinctive elements are and the artistic reasons that justify the particular configurations we observe them to have. In contrast with our constructive and differentiating procedure, the procedures of these other critical schools have been, in varying degrees, generalizing and reductive. There is reduction, and hence a loss of causal particularity, whenever the only terms critics use in talking about literary structures are terms applicable primarily to the writer as distinct in some way from his product (as in F. R. Leavis' discussions of novels as direct reflections of the "complexity" of the novelists' "interests") or whenever the only source of terms is the psychology of readers (as in Miss Bodkin's definition of the "archetypal pattern" of rebirth evoked for her by *The Ancient Mariner*): what can be discovered in such cases is merely a kind of structure that many poems can have, or even other species of writing. There is reduction similarly in any method that draws its only structural formulae from such things as the common figures of poetical or rhetorical language (as in Cleanth Brooks and the Shakespearean critics who speak of

---

[38][Crane] *Coleridge's Shakespearean Criticism*, edited by T. M. Rayson (London, 1930), II, 66–67; cf. *Biographia Literaria*, II. 9–10.

plays as "metaphors"), or the nonpoetic forms of myth and ritual, or the supposed patterns of psychic activity. And there is still reduction, though of a less extreme variety, in the critics who equate poetic structure, in all except the most general sense of "aesthetic pattern," exclusively with the conventions of verbal form or thematic arrangement which poets derive from earlier poetic tradition; in the critics, again, who look for fixed and unitary definitions of the poetic genres and discuss individual tragedies, comedies, epics, novels, and lyrics as more or less typical or perfect examples of these various quasi-Platonic forms; in the critics who identify the principles of structure in poems with the "themes" which are either their germinal ideas or moral bases or their underlying schemes of probability; and in the many critics, lastly, who fix their attention on some part of the total structure— on one phase of the action or on the framework of its representation, on a principal character, a "key" passage of thought, a conspicuous train of imagery—and proceed to derive from this their formula for the whole.

What these critics all leave out is thus the very principle we have taken as our starting point: the shaping principle of form and emotional "power" without which no poem could come into existence as a beautiful and effective whole of a determinate kind. We can therefore talk with a fullness and precision of distinction impossible to them about the particular and widely variant relations which exist in different poems between their formal and their material natures. We are not limited to any one conception of poetic unity or to any one set of concepts for defining structure. We are not forced to speak of the working together of the parts of a poem merely in terms of simple contrarieties of theme or tone or in a vocabulary of which the most exact words are expressions like *goes with,* is *associated with,* or is *related to* or *carries out, reflects, repeats, qualifies, balances, contrasts with, contradicts,* and so on. We are not compelled, in order to show our recognition that the best poetry is not indifferent to thought or "meaning," to interpret all poetic masterpieces in which ideas are contained or evoked as if they were compositions of the same order as *The Divine Comedy,* or, at any rate, in some sense or in some degree, metaphorical or symbolic expressions, or, at the very least, "studies" of something or other. We shall be aware that there are indeed many poetic works to which such descriptions can be applied, but we shall go on the assumption— which all experience and literary history surely warrants— that ideas can function in poems in radically different ways: sometimes as sources of inspiration, sometimes as formal and shaping ends, sometimes as means for constituting the characters, purposes, or states of mind of the dramatis personae, sometimes as choric devices for enhancing or universalizing the actions; and the distinctions of our theoretic

analysis, and notably our distinction between imitative and non-imitative forms, will enable us to discriminate these various uses when we come upon them and to judge of the significance of the thought in any poem or passage according as one or another of them is its primary cause. And finally, in dealing with the problems of imagery that have been so prominent during the past generation, especially in the criticism of Shakespeare, we are not restricted to either a merely material classification and psychological interpretation of images (as in Miss Spurgeon and her followers) or to a merely generalized and indefinite discussion of their functions in drama (as in some of the more recent Shakespeareans[39]): with our basic distinction of object, manner, and means and our more specific devices for relating the parts of individual works to their controlling forms, we should be able, at the very least, to introduce greater particularity and artistic intelligibility into the subject than are apparent in most of the current discussions.

I look upon this approach, therefore, as one likely to repay a more concentrated effort of research and application than it has received in modern times. It is not a method that lends itself too easily, perhaps, to the immediate purposes of reviewers and professional critics of current productions, but it is not without its utility even here: there must be many readers of such criticism who would be grateful for more precise indications than they usually get of what are the formal as well as the material and technical novelties to be found in the latest serious novels, plays, and volumes of verse, and above all of the kinds of "peculiar pleasures" they are fitted to give us and why. The method is undoubtedly better suited, however, to the more ample and considered criticism of the literature of the past or of contemporary literature when this is made an object of elaborated study; and there is excellent reason to think that the writing of literary history in particular might be radically transformed, and to great advantage, through the inclusion of what I have called the immediate artistic causes of literary productions along with the relatively more external and remote causes to which historians of literature have mainly confined themselves.

And there is another realm in which these principles might be expected to yield peculiar benefits—that of literary education. They can give us, for one thing, the basis of a teachable discipline of reading and appreciation which would be exempt, on the one hand, from mere impressionism and the evocation of irresponsible opinion and, on the other

---

[39][Crane] E.g., U. M. Ellis-Fermor, *The Frontiers of Drama* (London, 1945), pp. 77–95; M. M. Morozov, "The Individualization of Shakespeare's Characters through Imagery," *Shakespeare Survey,* II (1949), 83–106; R. A. Foakes, "Suggestions for a New Approach to Shakespeare's Imagery," *ibid.,* V (1952), 81–92.

hand, from the imposition on students of ready-made literary doctrines or canons of taste. Its essence would be simply the communication to students of a comprehensive scheme of questions to be asked about all the different kinds of literary works they might be studying and of criteria for discussing the appropriateness and adequacy of the answers in the light of the particulars of texts and of the students' responses as human beings to what is going on in them. The development of such a discipline, centered, as it would be, in the statement and free comparison of hypotheses, would help to bring into literary studies something they have commonly lacked—a subject matter, namely, in the sense not merely of facts but of compendent general concepts for their interpretation; concepts, moreover, that can be translated into habits of observation and reflection such as will tend to make the student independent of his teacher: a potential scholar in criticism rather than a disciple or member of a school, and a scholar who would do credit to his training precisely in proportion as he was able to correct and develop further the things he had been taught. I think that this could be done by a kind of practical and inductive teaching which would keep the student's mind centered on the concrete aspects of works and his feelings about them rather than on theoretical matters as such and which would, at the same time, build up in him an increasingly clear understanding of what it means to give a reasoned and warranted answer to a critical question and also, to an extent greater than has been common in the teaching of criticism, of how essential it is, if the answer is to be valid, that it accord with whatever truths the student has learned in the linguistic and historical parts of his education. For it is hard to see how the training I am suggesting could be carried on successfully without bringing criticism and these other disciplines into closer mutual relations than have existed between them for a long time.

We might expect, moreover, that such training would encourage a kind of appreciation of literary masterpieces that has been largely neglected in the critical tradition upon which our teaching has hitherto, in the main, been founded. The strength of that tradition has been its sensitiveness to the qualities and values which literary works share with one another or with other modes of expression—to these rather than to the differentiated characteristics of works which are what they are by virtue primarily of their writers' individual acts of poetic making. And it is not at all to minimize the importance of analogies and common principles in criticism to suggest that any literary culture is incomplete that does not lead also to a discriminating understanding, such as the training I propose is suited to give, of the peculiar principles of construction that contribute to make poetry the complex and richly diversified experience we all feel it to be. We may say indeed that what chiefly distinguishes the genius of lit-

erary study, as of the humanities in general, from the genius of science is that it naturally aspires to this kind of completion, not being permanently satisfied with reductions of the individual and the specific to the common, and perpetually feeling the need for distinctions and methods that will help us to do justice to the inventiveness of man and the uniqueness of his works.

And along with this would go a third benefit, in the capacity of our principles to maintain the integrity of literary appreciation without cutting it off formalistically from the life which literary works represent or attempt to guide. It is difficult to keep this balance in any of the critical languages in which the basic distinction for the analysis and judgment of works is some variant of the ancient dichotomy of *verba* and *res;* for if we distinguish thus between art and what art expresses, between poetic language and poetic thought, structure and idea, technique and meaning, symbol and concept, "presentment" and the moral "interests" of writers, we inevitably tend to regard one or the other of these two aspects as primary in importance. Our teaching of literature, consequently, insofar as it is "literary," appears far removed from common experience and human emotion, and insofar as it throws the emphasis on content, on questions of knowledge and behaviour, runs the risk of becoming merely an amateur branch of ethics, psychology, sociology, anthropology, or the history of ideas.

These disadvantages very largely disappear, I think, when we bring to the discussion of poetic works our radically different distinction of matter and form. For form as we conceive it is simply that which gives definite shape, emotional power, and beauty to the materials of man's experience out of which the writer has composed his work. Hence it cannot be separated as mere "form" from the matter in which it exists, nor can we talk about it adequately (as I have tried to illustrate in my discussions of *Macbeth* and of Gray's *Elegy*) without talking at the same time about the human qualities of the actions, persons, feelings, and thoughts the work brings before us and the very human, but no less poetic, responses these evoke in our minds. There can thus be no good "literary" criticism, in this language, that does not presuppose a constant making of moral and psychological discriminations and a constant concern with nuances of thought, as well as with subtleties of language and technique; what keeps it "literary" or "poetic" and prevents it from degenerating into either "studies in character" or excursions into philosophy and social history is the direction imposed on all our questions about the "content" of works by our hypotheses concerning their shaping principles of form. We can agree, therefore, with the critics who hold that we ought to deal with poetry as poetry and not another thing, and we can agree no less with those who insist that one of the main tasks of criticism is to show the "relevance" of poems to "life"; only these, for us, are not two tasks but one. And I would state a further point in the same connection, the bearing of which will be easily evident to those who have grown impatient with the current tendency to reduce all questions of morals and politics to questions of ideologies and beliefs. The counterpart of this "rationalism" in literary studies is the assumption that "relevance to life" in poetry is a matter primarily of "themes" and "imaginative visions," so that no imaginative work can be taken seriously from which we cannot extract a "total meaning" over and above the human particulars it exhibits, which we then set forth as what the work is intending to say. From this narrowing of the scope of literary values to such values as only earnest modern intellectuals can think of greater importance than the spectacle of individual men doing and suffering, we have, fortunately, an effective way of escape in our distinction between imitative and didactic forms. We can accord a proper appreciation, in their own terms, to works of which the formal principles are clearly ideas. But we are free to discuss the others, including notably the tragedies of Shakespeare, in a way that fully respects their seriousness, and the implication of universals in the working out of their plots, without being committed to the dehumanizing supposition that the moral habits and dispositions of individual persons and the qualities and circumstances of their actions are things less valuable for us, as men and citizens, to contemplate in literature than the pale abstractions by which they have been overlaid in the prevailing modes of interpretation. And so we might contribute not only to a more discriminating understanding of what literature as literature can do but to a kind of training in concrete moral and social perception, unbiased by doctrine, such as all who live in a free society would be the better for having.

VI

When all this is said, however, it is still true that what I have been talking about in this lecture is only one out of many possible legitimate approaches to the question of poetic structure, not to speak of the innumerable other questions with which critics can profitably concern themselves. I should not want to leave the impression, therefore, that I think it the only mode of criticism seriously worth cultivation at the present time by either teachers of literature or critics, but simply that its development, along with the others, might have many fruitful consequences for our teaching and criticism generally. What distinguishes it from the other modes is its preoccupation with the immediate constructive problems of writers in the making of individual works and with the artistic reasoning necessarily involved in their suc-

cessful solution; and its great claim to consideration is that it can deal with these matters more precisely and adequately, and with a more complete reliance on the canons of inductive inquiry, unhampered by doctrinal preconceptions, than any of the other existing critical languages. It can give us, consequently, a body of primary literary facts about literary works, in their aspect as concrete wholes, in the light of which we can judge the relevance and validity—or see the precise bearing—of such observations and statements of value as result from the application to the same works of other critical principles and procedures: if the structural principles of *Macbeth* or of Gray's *Elegy* are actually what we have taken them to be, then whatever else may be truly said about these same works, in answer to other questions or in the context of other ways of reasoning about them, must obviously be capable of being brought into harmony with this prior factual knowledge of the distinctive how and why of their construction. Here is something, therefore, which critics who prefer a more generalizing or a more speculative approach to literary works can hardly neglect if they wish to be responsible students of literature rather than merely rhetoricians bent on exploiting favorite theses at any cost. For though it is true enough, for example, that what writers do is conditioned by their personal lives and complexes, their social circumstances, and their literary traditions, there is always a risk that exclusive explanations of literary peculiarities in terms of such remoter causes will collapse and seem absurd as soon as we consider, for any work to which they have been applied, what are the immediate artistic exigencies which its writer faced because of his choice of form or manner in this particular work.[40] These exigencies can never

---

[40][Crane] An instance in point, verging on caricature of the fault I speak of in the text, is a recent discussion of the character of Jane Austen's Darcy. Why, the critic asks, "is he, among the major figures in *Pride and Prejudice,* the only one disturbingly derived and wooden?" And the answer, in terms of his psychoanalytical thesis, is given at once, without any consideration of the great difficulties that must have arisen, for the novelist, from the role which Darcy had to play in the first part of the plot and from the fact that the choice of point of view prevented even later any direct or sustained disclosure of his unspoken thought:

> The reason seems to be the same as that which *compelled* Jane Austen to falsify her tone and commentary concerning Wickham's seductions and to supply Elinor and Marianne Dashwood with such nonentities for husbands. The socially unmanageable, the personally involving aspects of sex, Jane Austen *can* no longer treat with irony, nor *can* she as yet treat them straightforwardly. Darcy is the hero, he is the potential lover of a complex young woman much like the author herself; and as such Jane Austen *cannot* animate him with emotion, or with her characteristic informing irony. She borrows him from a book; and, though she alters and illuminates everything else, she *can* do nothing more with him than fit him functionally into the plot.

Marvin Mudrick, *Jane Austen: Irony as Defense and Discovery,* p. 117; italics mine.

be safely disregarded so long as the genetic relation between art and its sources and materials in life remains the very indirect relation we know it is; and it is perhaps not the least of the utilities to be found in the criticism of forms that its cultivation, in a context of the many other kinds of critical inquiry, would help to keep critics of all schools constantly reminded of their existence and importance.

But the other kinds ought to be there. Of the truth about literature, no critical language can ever have a monopoly or even a distant approach to one; and there are obviously many things which the language I have been speaking of cannot do. It is a method not at all suited, as is criticism in the grand line of Longinus, Coleridge, and Matthew Arnold, to the definition and appreciation of those general qualities of writing—mirroring the souls of writers—for the sake of which most of us read or at any rate return to what we have read. It is a method that necessarily abstracts from history and hence requires to be supplemented by other very different procedures if we are to replace the works we study in the circumstances and temper of their times and see them as expressions and forces as well as objects of art. It is a method, above all, that completely fails, because of its essentially differentiating character, to give us insights into the larger moral and political values of literature or into any of the other organic relations with human nature and human experience in which literature is involved. And yet who will say that these are not as compelling considerations for criticism as anything comprised in the problem of poetic structure as we have been discussing it in these lectures? The moral is surely that we ought to have at our command, collectively at least, as many different critical methods as there are distinguishable major aspects in the construction, appreciation, and use of literary works. The multiplicity of critical languages is therefore something not to be deplored but rather rejoiced in, as making possible a fuller exploration of our subject in its total extent than we could otherwise attain; and for my part I have as fond a regard for Longinus and for the masters of historical criticism as I have for Aristotle, and as strong a conviction of their continuing utility. Nor will there ever cease to be employment for criticism of the less rigorous or more imaginative types—in directing attention to aspects of poems which only a new model or analogy can bring into view, in formulating and promoting new ideals of poetic

excellence or new poetic styles, in suggesting to poets unrealized possibilities in subject matter and language, in relating poetry, for readers, to large nonpoetic human contexts of emotion and meaning, in keeping the life of poetry and of taste from declining into orthodoxy and routine.

The best hope for criticism in the future, indeed, lies in the perpetuation of this multiplicity; nothing could be more damaging than the practical success of any effort to define authoritatively the frontiers and problems of our subject or to assign to each of its variant languages a determinate place in a single hierarchy of critical modes. Better far than that the chaos of schools and splinter parties we have with us now! But there need be no such choice; for the great obstacle to advance in criticism is not the existence of independent groups of critics each pursuing separate interests, but the spirit of exclusive dogmatism which keeps them from learning what they might from one another; and for that the only effective remedy, I think, is to take to heart the two lessons which the persistence throughout history of many distinct critical languages ought to teach us. The first is the lesson of self-knowledge: we can attempt to become more clearly aware than we have usually been of just what it is that we ourselves are doing—and why—when we make critical statements of any kind, and at the same time try to extend that clarity, in as intellectually sympathetic a way as possible, to the statements of other critics, and especially to those that appear to be most inconsistent with our own. And it will be all the easier to attain this self-understanding, with its natural discouragements to doctrinal prejudice, if we also learn the second lesson, and come habitually to think of the various critical languages of the past and present, including our own, no longer as rival attempts to foreclose the "real" or "only profitable" truth about poetry, so that we have to choose among them as we choose among religious dogmas or political causes, but simply as tools of our trade—as so many distinct conceptual and logical means, each with its peculiar capacities and limitations, for solving truly the many distinct kinds of problems which poetry, in its magnificent variety of aspects, presents to our view.[41]

---

[41][Crane] I have discussed some of the practical consequences of this view in an essay, to be published soon, entitled *Questions and Answers in the Teaching of Literature.*

Philip Wheelwright

1901–1970

Wheelwright's book *The Burning Fountain,* from which *The Logical and the Translogical* is taken, is an inquiry into the symbolism of religion, ritual, and art. Wheelwright was particularly interested in archetypes, and he was influenced by Jung, although he criticized Jung's dogmatism. The reprinted chapter lays the ground for a discussion of archetypes by drawing a distinction between "steno language (the language of plain sense)" and "depth language (the language, broadly speaking, of poetry)." In drawing this distinction Wheelwright aligns himself with the New Critics, who define poetry as a kind of language. He also aligns himself with them by attacking positivism. His analysis of myth and language owes a good deal to Cassirer. He adopts theologian Martin Buber's popular distinction between the "I-thou" relationship of depth language and the "I-it" relationship of logical discourse, which, by analysis and abstraction, tends to anatomize and thus distance and dehumanize objects. This view is an outgrowth of Romantic arguments for particularity and symbolism against generality and allegory.

Although Wheelwright believes that knowledge takes place as a unifying act of the mind, he proceeds beyond the conceptual synthesis of Kant to the idea of a "synthesis which expresses our actual living encounter with the world."

Wheelwright sometimes appears to give an independent status to archetypes, so that one suspects that he has reduced poems, despite his discussion of poetic language, to frames in which archetypes are displayed. This raises the question of whether he ignores the value of the poem as a unified whole. In spite of his attention to language, he seems to have blurred the distinctions between art and religion and leaves the reader wondering whether art is no more than a special sort of vehicle for religious experience or mystery.

Critical works by Wheelwright include *The Burning Fountain* (1954), *Heraclitus* (1959), and *Metaphor and Reality* (1962).

The Logical
and the Translogical

Let me try to set down what I take to be the main assumptions which underlie the logician's view, and in general the scientist's view, of what language at its best should be. Of

THE LOGICAL AND THE TRANSLOGICAL. Wheelwright's *The Logical and the Translogical* is Chapter 4 of *The Burning Fountain: A Study in the Language of Symbolism* (1954), and is reprinted by permission of Indiana University Press.

course no man is purely logical all day long, and even a logician will find many human occasions when it is wise to depart from professional usage. But the danger is that he tends to take the properties and laws of logical language as his standard, his point of departure for interpreting and evaluating language in general; and when he does this his view of the humanistic employments of language—in literature, art, religion, and expressive discourse generally—may become gravely distorted.

The method I am employing in this chapter is dialectical, in the sense practiced by Socrates in the earlier Platonic dialogues and tersely formulated in the Scholastic formula,

"Omnis determinatio est negatio." That is to say, all definition involves exclusion; in determining exactly what a thing is, we thereby implicitly determine what it is not. To define a concept is to declare by one and the same act what it does mean and what it does not mean. Likewise when we define a belief, we therein define by implication what that belief opposes, and hence what contrary belief could be held about the matter without self-contradiction. This last point is of greatest importance for the understanding of dialectical method as employed in this chapter, and more generally for spiking the claims of any dogma that parades itself as the only possible way of looking at a matter. For with respect to any belief that one holds there must be the logical possibility of holding some opposite belief; if not, then one's belief is a mere tautology, which is to say no real belief at all but only a verbal imposture. To believe in God is to recognize the logical possibility of atheism; indeed, to believe in God with any intellectual and moral vitality is to recognize that the position of atheism has grounds, that it offers a challenge, that it is a redoubtable antagonist to the belief which one has elected to hold. Again, in order to believe intelligently in the law of universal physical causation one must be able to understand what a reasonable opponent or doubter of this belief can mean by his heresy. Analogously, then, if we set down the basic assumptions of logical discourse and clearly understand what they affirm, we can thereby discover what they deny and hence what counter-assumptions, nonlogical or rather translogical in character, it is possible to postulate as a basis for expressive discourse.

The main assumptions of logical discourse have been traditionally given as four: the Law of Identity ("A is A"), the Law of Contradiction, or more accurately of Noncontradiction ("A is not at once B and non-B"), the Law of Excluded Middle ("A is either B or not B"), and the Law of Sufficient Reason ("Whatever is true must have a sufficient reason why it is true"). These traditional laws of logic need interpretation, however, if they are to disclose anything about the nature of logical language. To say without qualification "A is A" is to utter a tautology and therefore to say nothing really at all. The Law of Identity in its traditional form silences dissent by its sheer nothingness; it cannot be significantly denied, only because it cannot be significantly affirmed. On the other hand, if we interpret it as saying that a logical term, A, should have a clearly defined meaning and should keep that meaning unchanged throughout a given investigation or discourse, then the law does say something: it sets up a procedure to be followed, hence indicates by implication that there are contrary procedures to be avoided; and so it now becomes possible, from the new form of the law, as it was not from the old, to deduce certain a priori characteristics of nonlogical, nonliteral language.

Now there is a most essential difference between the postulates which steno language requires, and postulates of nonlogical or translogical language which are dialectically derived from them. The postulates of logic say "must," the postulates of expressivity say "may." This is evident both analytically and experientially. Logic has to operate by fixed laws from which it cannot depart without losing its logical character. Its laws, therefore, involve a *must,* or, obversely, a *cannot.* It declares, "If you wish to be logical you *must* avoid contradiction"; which is to say, "You *cannot* contradict yourself and still remain logical." Now what is involved in challenging the absolute validity of the Law of Noncontradiction? Surely not that one must contradict himself at every turn; but that there *may* be elements of radical paradox in expressive discourse, which cannot be reduced to perfect logical consistency without distorting the meaning which they connote. *Must* and *cannot* belong to the world of *ananke,* of iron necessity. Their real antitheses, belonging to the world of freedom, are *need not* and *may.* In short, the two uses of language are not on a par. Steno language represents a set of limiting cases, so to speak, in a universe of infinite semantic possibilities.

Of course we should not rest content with the bare a priori possibilities of the case. Language does not automatically become expressive just because it is nonlogical. We are interested in nonlogical possibilities only because they leave room for the operation of language that is genuinely expressive. Dialectic can vindicate such language; only the awakened sensibility can create it. Accordingly three steps, not two, are called for. It will be necessary, first, to reexamine the main assumptions of steno language without blind adherence to the way in which they have been traditionally formulated and understood. There are eight such assumptions which strike me as the most essential, and in any case the one most relevant to our purpose. Following that, I shall proceed to deduce, by strict dialectic, the eight counter-postulates which are *logically allowed for* by our refusal to accept the laws of steno discourse as absolutely binding. The third step is a passage from the abstract possibility to the concrete instance. Our eight counter-postulates must be *experientially confirmed* by the way in which depth language is found to actually function; and thus the third and most decisive step consists not in argument but in choice of illustrations.

Assumptions of Literal Language

1. *Assumption of semantic discreteness:* that a linguistic symbol is always distinct, or at least distinguishable, from its referend. Symbol and referend are, so to speak, noninterchangeable. There is nothing of twoness about the figure *2.* And although mathematicians do find it useful to employ

iconic symbols in geometry—e.g., a blackboard triangle, which at once means the concept "triangle" and is a particular instance of that universal meaning—yet the character of a geometrical drawing, being governed by considerations of propaedeutic convenience, does not affect the nature of the geometrical entities it refers to. Steno symbols therefore are dispensable; their usage is by stipulation. Any of Euclid's theorems is as true, though perhaps not so readily apprehended, when expressed in words or in algebraic equations as when represented by a diagram. Similarly in the more general uses of literal language, every literal meaning is assumed to be translatable without essential loss into another language. Dr. C. K. Ogden, the founder of Basic English, once remarked that he conceived it possible to construct an ideally perfect Basic English into which all authentic meanings could be translated; and that whatever apparent meanings should get unavoidably lost in the translation would thereby reveal themselves to be not real *meanings* at all, but merely embellishments.[1]

2. *Assumption of univocation:* that on a given occasion of its use a symbol has one meaning only; or else a plurality of meanings so distinguishable that they can be stated separately and represented by distinct symbols without semantic loss. Overtones of meaning, secondary implications, innuendo, irony, humorous or tragic suggestiveness and such, are treated as materials for explicit restatement in univocal language.

3. *Assumption of definiteness:* that on a given occasion of its use a symbol has a definite and ideally definable meaning. Vagueness is always a fault, a lapse from the logical ideal. The limiting nature of this requirement becomes evident to anyone capable of honest introspection. For none of us is perfectly clear about every aspect of a matter; and he who says, "I understand perfectly," is either deluding himself or parroting a phrase or (what is often a practical necessity) limiting his attention to certain skeletal and formal properties. Steno language always presumes such limitation and builds upon it.

4. *Assumption of semantic invariance:* that a given sign must keep the same meaning throughout the course of a given argument or a given science. Hobbes speaks as an honorable logician in declaring that "in all discourses wherein one man pretends to instruct or convince another, he should use the same word constantly in the same sense. If this were done (which nobody can refuse without great disingenuity), many of the books extant might be spared."[2] The requirement is essential where the aim of the discourse is "to instruct or convince."

5. *Assumption of bidimensional significance:* that the referend of any sign is characterized by either of two kinds of integration, possibly in combination: logical universality, established by definition, and existential particularity, established by space-time continuities. These two familiar types of meaning are what Santayana has called concretions in discourse and concretions in existence;[3] the one is expressed through common names *(horse, green, above),* the other through proper names or particularized common names *(this horse, the position in which I am now sitting).*

The five preceding assumptions pertain to the *term,* which some logicians have called (long before 1945) the "atomic" constituent of literal language. The next two assumptions have to do with the *proposition,* the "molecular" constituent.

6. *Assumption of truth-value equivalence:* that any true proposition is equally true with any other true proposition, and hence (from postulate 7) that any false proposition is equally false with any other. Judgments of probability, far from violating, rather confirm this law: for a probability is a degree of approximation to truth, and there could be degrees of approximation only if the truth approximated were regarded as ideally determinate. When we judge, for instance, that the proposition "Man has evolved from lower animal species" is *more probably* true than the proposition "Mars is inhabited by rational beings," we mean that the evidence for the truth of the first proposition is more adequate than the evidence for the truth of the second; we do *not* mean that the first proposition if actually true is any truer than the second

---

[1][Wheelwright] Dr. Ogden's remark was made conversationally at a gathering in New York some twenty years ago. While he was willing to admit there might be flaws in the system of Basic English as it then stood, he maintained that such flaws were remediable in principle, and that a language of limited vocabulary might eventually be achieved in which no legitimate meanings would lack adequate symbolization.

---

[2][Wheelwright] Hobbes' declaration is confirmed by his distinction between univocal and equivocal names.

Univocal are those which in the same train of discourse signify always the same thing; but *equivocal* those which mean sometimes one thing and sometimes another. . . . Every *metaphor* is by profession *equivocal.* But this distinction belongs not so much to names, as to those that use names, for some use them properly and accurately for the finding out of truth; others draw them from their proper sense, for ornament or deceit.

The English Works of Thomas Hobbes of Malmesbury, edited by Sir William Molesworth (London, 1839): First Section, "Concerning Bodies," Part I, "Computation or Logic," Chapter 2, "Of Names." It is not without significance that Hobbes treats logic as a subdivision of the topic "Concerning Bodies."

[3][Wheelwright] George Santayana, *The Life of Reason:* Vol. I, *Reason and Common Sense* (Scribner, 2nd ed., 1922), Chapter 7.

proposition if actually true. The propositions differ not in degree of truth but in the degree to which the available evidence suffices to establish a valid judgment of truth.

Definition and corollary. A *statement* may be defined as any unit of language such that the predicates "true" and "false" may be asserted of it without complete absence of meaning; and a *proposition* as the type of statement used in literal language—i.e., consisting in an assertible relation between *terms,* as defined above. From these definitions taken in conjunction with assumption 7 we may derive the theorem (traditionally called the Law of Excluded Middle) that every unitary proposition, when adequately stated, is either entirely true or entirely false, and the theorem (traditionally called the Law of Contradiction) that no such proposition can be both true and false.

7. *Assumption of contradictories:* that for every proposition (*p*) there is another proposition (non-*p*) such that the truth of either implies the falsity of the other and the falsity of either implies the truth of the other. The assumption as here formulated contains the germs both of the Law of Contradiction and the Law of Excluded Middle. The present formulation lays bare the postulational character of these "laws," which in their usual formulation appear axiomatic and tautological. It also distinguishes between their sense as indicated in the corollary to assumption 6 (as limiting the truth-values of any single proposition) and their sense as indicated in assumption 7 (as involving the interrelation of two assertible contradictory propositions).

8. *Assumption of ideal explicability:* that every true proposition has an intelligible and assignable place in a system of true propositions, to at least some of which it is related by strict implication. The so-called Law of Sufficient Reason in its strictly formal (non-cosmological) interpretation is identical with this postulate, which refers beyond the atomic and molecular levels of semantic complexity (terms and propositions respectively) to what may be called the organic level (relations among propositions).

The eight foregoing assumptions are operative in all logical discourse, and therefore in all literal discourse so far as it is free from logical imperfection. But that they are implicitly postulational, not axiomatic, is proved by the fact that it is possible to question, doubt, or deny each one of them in turn without necessarily talking nonsense. The method of dialectic can go only so far: having formulated the hidden postulates on which semantic positivism rests, and having discerned them to be nontautologous, it can formulate their logical antitheses and assign them a postulational role of their own.

Pure dialectic suffers, therefore, from the disability that the postulates which it thus establishes by logical negation are (1) still hypothetical, since they are in no way declared to be more than bare possibilities, and (2) so broadly and abstractly negative as to be unoriented with respect to any realm of experience to which they might apply. Although it can demonstrate the a priori possibility of other types of language than the type defined by the eight postulates of logical discourse, it offers no experiential clue to their positive nature. Formal dialectic must therefore be supplemented by *ontological intuition:* whereby the opposing principles are drawn not merely out of the thin air of logical possibility but out of actual semantic procedures with respect to certain realms or qualities or aspects or functions of experience. By this double method we are enabled to posit provisionally the following eight principles of expressive discourse as at once dialectically opposed to the eight postulates of literal language and as experientially derived from actual semantic operations. So far as their derivation is experiential—and this must be judged by the character of the concrete illustrations—they are not merely postulates but *principles;* and it is by this name therefore, although not forgetting their postulative character, that I shall designate them.

Principles of Expressive Language

1. *Principle of iconic signification:* that there are symbols which, although they may point beyond themselves, have a largely self-intentive reference as well.

Nonsymbolic signs may also have something of this double character; in fact, they normally do so except where the situation has become exclusively practical. Each thing in nature that stirs us deeply seems at once valuable in itself and a kind of gateway or threshold to an unexplored Something More. A fetish or a totemic animal probably has such a character when it first strikes a wondering savage as important. It is charged with otherness—not only an otherness with respect to the savage himself, which makes the object inherently fascinating, but a potentiality of otherness that indefinitely exceeds the mind's objective grasp, and suggests infinite unnamed possibilities. Thus the blue stone or the totemic brown bear becomes a thing of mystery, acquires a numinous quality, and the tribesman confronts it with an ambivalent attitude of confidence and dread. The confidence is helped by sacraments, but the dread remains to keep the total experience ambivalent and vibrantly alive. Later, as the dread is drained away, familiarity and fancy transform the original mythic intuitions into mythologies, and ambition degrades the sacraments into magic.

Fortunately the development is not exclusively desiccating. The symbols which develop are, in every healthy culture, still partly iconic—i.e., they mean by resembling—and this shows itself in the love for the medium. Not only what is said but the way of saying it counts; not only the god who is supplicated but the ritual of supplication itself. This is the aesthetic element in experience and in communication, the valuing of a thing for its own sake, without which as a terminus no utilitarian values would have any eventual justification. At its ultimate stage it becomes mysticism—where not only symbol and referend, but also knower and known, merge into one self-intentive whole. Aesthetic contemplation, however, is and should be but a halfway house to mysticism, keeping the self-identification and the discrimination in fairly even balance. An aesthetic icon thus bears the double characteristic of being more than ordinarily itself and yet the adumbration of a something further that is unspoken. The double aspect produces a tension which, at its best, is a harmony in diversity and the very life of the aesthetic situation.

Unlike logical symbols, therefore, it is impossible to substitute one expressive symbol for another without destroying or radically transfiguring the texture of meaning. Expressive meanings, in short, are not stipulative; they are given not by definition but mainly by contextualization.

2. *Principle of plurisignation:* that an expressive symbol tends, on any given occasion of its realization, to carry more than one legitimate reference, in such a way that its proper meaning is a tension between two or more directions of semantic stress. When we say that poetry uses charged language, we mean that the poetic symbol tends characteristically to be plurisignative in this sense: that its intended meanings are likely to be more or less multiple, yet so fused as sometimes to defy any attempted analysis into monosignative components, and always to produce an integral meaning that radically transcends the sum of the ingredient meanings. In these last respects plurisignation differs from simple punning. A brief example is Faustus' agonized cry: "See, see where Christ's *blood* streams in the firmament!"[4] Religion—as distinguished from theology on the one hand and superstition on the other—regards plurisignation as not merely a human technique but as the inevitable articulation of divinity, which can speak to men only through "signatures" that combine sacred with secular modes of significance.

3. *Principle of soft focus:* that there are meanings which do not have definite outlines and cannot be adequately represented by terms that are strictly defined. Strict definition is possible only to those who agree upon a semantic con-

vention, which involves the systematic omission of whatever meanings or elements of meaning cannot be commonly shared. Such a common nucleus of meaning establishes a denotation to which a given steno symbol (verbal or other) may refer. But over and above its denotation every symbol bears a connotative fringe, which is not likely to be altogether the same for everybody. With some words and in some contexts (e.g., the word *square* in geometry) the connotative increment is unimportant and may easily be dismissed as irrelevant to the science in question. Thus if during a mathematical demonstration a blackboard square strikes one of us as ugly and another of us as a well-balanced arrangement of lines, this obviously has no bearing upon the problem of discovering the square's geometrical properties. To the ancient Pythagoreans, on the other hand, the harmonious character of the square was an intrinsic part of its nature, and hence an intrinsic part of what was meant by the figure (an iconic, participating symbol) and by the word designating it (a conventional, potentially stipulative symbol). Now even though all members of the Pythagorean cult may have agreed that the square was a harmonious and noble figure, it is hardly likely that they all thought of these aesthetic and moral properties in exactly the same way. Exactitude in such matters cannot be verified, for exact designation is not possible to anything like the same degree as with the geometrical properties. The Pythagoreans used the verbal and iconic symbols for "square" in a plurisignative manner: the geometrical meaning was a sharply focused semantic nucleus, while the metaphysical meaning was a softly focused semantic fringe.

The recognition of soft focus as a genuinely semantic characteristic of certain situations throws light upon the problem of obscurity in poetry. Ignoring such instances of obscurity as proceed from either incompetence or snobbishness, we can accept certain poetic utterances as obscure for either or both of two valid reasons: (1) because the subject matter itself is too subtle and elusive to allow of exact delineation—as in the portrayal of mature human emotions; or (2) because the poet can produce his effect more fully by producing an ambivalent impression upon the reader's mind. In great as distinguished from transient poetry the ambivalence is justified because it corresponds to a real ambivalence in the nature of things; and thus the second valid reason for ambivalence tends to reduce to the first.

Poetry and expressive language in general have, to be sure, their own kind of precision, but it is essentially different from the precision of literal language. We cannot ask whether one type of language is *more* precise than the other; we can only try to understand and accept their differences. The precision of expressive language is paradoxical, for

---

[4][Wheelwright] Christopher Marlowe, *The Tragical History of Dr. Faustus,* scene xvi. To be sure, the "blood" image functions archetypally as well. Its symbolic role in *Richard II* and *Macbeth* will be considered in Chapter 10 [of *The Burning Fountain*].

sometimes it can represent its object most precisely by a sort of controlled vagueness. There have been endless disputes about the character of Hamlet, or, in semantic terms, about what the poetic and dramatic indications of Hamlet's dramatis persona "really mean." There are virtually no such disputes about Polonius. Would Shakespeare have represented Hamlet more precisely by giving as definite indications as he does of Polonius? Obviously not, for the very nature of Hamlet as a "character" or dramatis persona is ambivalent—an aura of highly significant obscurity around a bright, focused center—and one cannot say of him, as of Polonius, "This, just this and not something else, is what Shakespeare meant."

4. *Principle of contextualism:* that an expressive symbol is a controlled semantic variable, the full meaning of which, although identical throughout all instances *on some level of analysis,* tends to shift about within moderate limits. The reason for this limited nonidentity is found partly in the iconic, partly in the plurisignative nature of the expressive symbol. On the one hand, life itself is in continual flux, and the expressive symbol, being iconic, will tend somewhat to reflect that never-ceasing flow in itself. On the other hand, since the plurisign, unlike the monosignative terms of logical discourse, cannot be semantically controlled by explicit definition, its fused multiple meaning must be determined afresh on each occasion—in part by a relatively persistent core of meaning which unites or relates the various semantic occasions together, in part by the entire relevant context which the particular occasion gathers up and generates. In poetry the relevant context of a symbol is controlled to a large degree by the poet's individual manipulation of his medium; in religion it appears to depend more upon the elusive factors of social and individual sensibility to the signature of divinity in the experienced world.

5. *Principle of paralogical dimensionality:* that there are other dimensions or nodi of meaning than those of logical universality and existential particularity, which latter constitute the coordinates of logical discourse. A nodus of meaning is designated a universal when its specifiable references are related by virtue of some *publicly verifiable similarity,* of whatever degree of abstraction; it is designated a particular when its specifiable references are related by virtue of some *publicly verifiable space-time contiguity and continuity.* If we examine these two kinds of connection semantically, as nodi of meaning, we discover that they do not exhaust the possibilities of semantic grouping. They constitute two pragmatically important ways in which possible here-nows of the experienceable world are grouped and represented by a symbol. The general concept *horse* represents one kind of grouping, based mainly upon publicly under-

stood similarities relating one horse to another; *Butch* (the name of a horse I once knew) represents another kind of grouping, based mainly upon the partly observed and partly inferred spatio-temporal continuity of the parts and moments of which the horse named Butch is composed.

But clearly other bases of association are possible. Any aesthetic experience is such an alio-dimensional grouping. An artist's characteristic attempt, in its semantic aspect, is to express and communicate an experience comprising a grouping of experiential moments—that is, of perceived and imagined here-nows—for which there is no publicly accepted word, formula, or other symbol already available. In the words of Ezra Pound: "The error of making a statue *of* Night or *of* Charity lies in tautology. The idea has already found its way into language. The function of the artist is precisely the formulation of what has not found its way into language, i.e., any language verbal, plastic or musical."[5] What Pound says of Night and Charity is true both of horseness and of any individual horse: each finds its adequate expression in a language of word concepts—a common noun in the one case, a proper noun in the other—and an exact undistorted reformulation in terms of painting or sculpture is neither possible nor worth attempting. Horseness shoots through experience in a given direction and "means" a grouping of certain qualities and functions that are conventionally conceived as belonging together; the flesh and blood horse now clanking along the pavement outside my window "means" another grouping—in this case, of physically contiguous qualities; whereas the horses of say Donatello, or of

---

[5] [Wheelwright] Pound's remark was made in an article, *Epstein, Belgion and Meaning,* in *The Criterion,* Vol. IX, Serial No. 36 (April, 1930), p. 470. Some months earlier *The Manchester Guardian* had interviewed Jacob Epstein regarding his sculptures in the London Underground House, and had quoted him as saying:

> It was my idea to make "Day" and "Night" the subjects of two groups over the entrances to the building. . . . It is difficult to describe a sculptural idea, for any art has to speak its own language. Well, "Night" is a mother-figure with her child-man exhausted and sleeping under her protection and benediction. The curved horizontal lines of the group are expressive of sleep and rest descending on tired mankind . . .

In the January, 1930, issue of *The Criterion* Montgomery Belgion made these remarks the target of an attack which drew much of its ammunition from H. W. B. Joseph's *Logic.* This was the occasion for Ezra Pound's counter-criticism in the article from which I have quoted. Pound then adds:

> When Mr. Epstein says "Night" is the subject he means rather more. Everybody knows what "Night" is, but Mr. Epstein or Mr. Phidias or whoever, is presumably intent on expressing a *particular* and definite complex (ideas, emotions, etc.) generally oriented by a rather vague concept already mapped out. The difference is as great as that between firing a bullet in a generally easterly direction and hitting a particular bird.

de Chirico, or of Kenneth Shopen "mean" a more novel and still unconventionalized grouping of qualities, some of which are shared with the dictionary concept *horse,* others with the perceptual qualities of live horses that the artist has seen, while some have closest affinity with subtle forms of emotion otherwise inexpressible.

Thus the platitude that great art is universal, although true in a special sense, is misleading: for the integral meaning of a work of art (whatever its component meanings may be) cuts across experience in a different dimension from that of any logical universal whatever, and establishes its own quality of universality—a more concrete and more alive universality than that represented by any dictionary definition. An analogous distinction may be observed between the concrete universality of the cross as an integral religious symbol and any theological exposition of what the cross represents; or between the ideal of justice as it appears to men who are sacrificing their lives to uphold it and the idea of justice as employed in a discussion of theoretical ethics.

6. *Principle of assertorial tone:* that statements—for we here consider the molecular order of meanings—vary with respect to the manner in which they are susceptible to affirmation and denial, ranging all the way from "heavy" assertorial tone—which characterizes the literal statement, the proposition—to "light" association or semiaffirmed tension between two or more symbols. A poetic statement differs from a literal statement not, as Dr. Richards used to maintain, in that the one has a merely subjective, the other an objective reference—at least this is an unnecessary and generally irrelevant difference; but in their manner of asserting. There are differences of what may be called *assertorial weight.* A literal statement asserts heavily. It can do so because its terms are solid. It must do so because we are practical busy creatures who want to know just where we stand. A poetic statement, on the other hand, consisting as it does in a conjunction or association of plurisigns, has no such solid foundation, and affirms with varying degrees of lightness.

A stanza from Carl Rakosi's *A Journey Far Away* offers a syntactical illumination of the principle.

> An ideal
> like a canary
> singing in the dark
> for appleseed and barley

Is the poet making a statement here or is he not? If so, the syntax is not quite adequate: the copula *is* needed for its completion. But try inserting it, and see how fatally that little word destroys the original quality of affirmation! "An ideal is like a canary singing in the dark for appleseed and barley." Note what has been done. Not only has the reader-response been altered through a lessening of the pleasure with which the utterance is received: more than that, the very nature of the affirmation has been changed. This prose version, we feel, overstates its case, it affirms too heavily: no ideal can be so much like a canary as all that! Rakosi's way of singing the matter did not belabor the point; it suggested only that between an ideal and a canary there might be a slight and lovely connection, too tenuous to be expressed by the harsh little word *is.* So delicate an affirmation does not seriously jostle our other beliefs; we can accept it as true without mental inconvenience. But the literal statement, by reason of its assertive heaviness, falsifies.

Assertorial weight should not be confused with the strength or force of a poetic statement. Take, for instance, Christina Rossetti's well-known quatrain:

> My heart is like a singing bird
>   Whose nest is in a water-shoot;
> My heart is like an apple-tree
>   Whose boughs are bent with thick-set fruit . . .[6]

If some literal-minded reader should object to the second comparison on the ground that the differences between hearts and apple-trees are more pronounced than their resemblances, we might justly dismiss him as unduly obtuse. In terms of the present analysis he would be making a statement of full assertorial weight which is nevertheless ridiculously weak, contrasting painfully with the simple eloquent force of Miss Rossetti's assertorially lighter statement.

Suppose, again, that the graceful compliment to a lady expressed implicitly by Herrick—"Her eyes the glow-worm lend thee, / The shooting stars attend thee . . ."[7] were made explicit and that the lady's charms were set forth with descriptive literalness. Not only the grace, but more subtly the central poetic meaning of the utterance, would be destroyed. Herrick's own statement is by indirection. It is offered more lightly than its prose counterpart would be, but partly for that reason it is all the more forceful and suggestive. Generally speaking, the combination of poetic delicacy and poetic strength is one of the prime distinguishing marks of authentic poetry.

A poetic statement, then, does not usually assert its claims so heavily as a proposition. Its truth is more fragile, and it asks no guarantee. For a poem can be regarded, from

---

[6] *A Birthday,* 1–4.
[7] *The Night-Piece, to Julia,* 1–2.

a semantic standpoint, as a complex tension among variously related plurisigns. Some phases of the poetic tension have more of a declarative character than others; and as this declarative character becomes more pronounced a phase of the poetic tension may approximate the character of literal statement, yet without quite totally attaining it. Frequently enough a phase of the poetic tension may contain a literal statement as one of its aspects. When Macbeth cries, "If it were done when 'tis done, then 'twere well / It were done quickly,"[8] his words contain an unmistakable literal meaning. This literal scenario meaning could be expressed equally well, from a logical standpoint, in another arrangement of words, such as: "If the effects of the deed could but terminate with the performance, it would be well to finish the matter off as quickly as possible." But the literal meaning is only one aspect of the full poetic meaning, and to restate it in the second phraseology is to wrench it away from the associated poetic meanings of the original. The principal poetic meaning in the passage is expressed in the thematic use of the word *done,* repeated three times like the tolling of a dirge. Directly and literally the passage asserts the logical proposition I have just formulated; such is its meaning to the reader's clear-cutting intellect. But if the reader reads with his intellect and sensibilities working in collaboration he will hear in that insistent repetition of the word *done* a tragic reminder of the irrevocability of a deed once performed. The reminder is expressed obliquely, but in some mysterious way it gains in power by its very indirection. Now in much the same manner that Bach so often passes from a theme in a minor to a final chord in the major key, Shakespeare again and again in his plays marks the close of an emotional sequence by passing from an oblique to a correspondingly literal statement. Thus after a number of variations have been played upon the *done* theme, Lady Macbeth concludes the matter by declaring explicitly (III. ii) "What's done is done," and again in the sleep-walking scene (V. i) "What's done cannot be undone." In the word *done* as used suggestively throughout the play we have a plurisign, which in these two quasi-literal remarks of Lady Macbeth approximates but does not quite reach the character of a monosign. Correspondingly, Lady Macbeth's two statements approximate but do not quite reach the character of propositions.

7. *Principle of paradox:* that two statements which by the canons of strict logic are mutually contradictory, may sometimes be jointly acceptable. It is not the maneuvered, expository type of paradox that is relevant here—such as Chesterton's "Darwin was no Darwinian," and Lord Russell's analogy between the paradox of physical ether and the paradox of Homer: "We know who Homer *was*—he wrote the *Iliad* and the *Odyssey;* only we don't know whether he *existed.*" The aim of such paradoxes is to startle, amuse, and suggest a fresh perspective. They can be cleared up easily enough by anyone who takes the trouble to make the appropriate logical distinctions—between Darwin's views and those of his self-professed followers, and between the abstract conception of "authorship of the *Iliad* and *Odyssey*" and the historical question of whether they were or were not written by a single man. The paradoxes of expressive language are something more than this.

Generally speaking I would say there are three main uses of paradox in poetry: I may call them the paradox of surface, the paradox of depth, and the paradoxical interplay of statement and innuendo. The first is exemplified, perhaps even a little crudely, by the conventional oxymoron of Romeo's opening comment upon the brawl between the two noble houses:

> Why, then, O brawling love! O loving hate!
> O anything, of nothing first create!
> O heavy lightness! serious vanity!
> Misshapen chaos of well-seeming forms!
> Feather of lead, bright smoke, cold fire, sick health!
> Still-waking sleep, that is not what it is!
> This love feel I, that feel no love in this.[9]

So far as these conceits are anything more than courtly rhetoric—which is to say, so far as they may be conceived to function expressively and not only decoratively—they are surface representations of the underlying idea expressed in the fourth quoted line.

A depth paradox, on the other hand, aims more directly at some transcendent truth which is so mysterious and so many-sided in its suggestions of meaningful possibilities that either half of the paradox taken alone would be grossly inadequate and partisan. The great paradoxes of traditional theology are of this kind: God's justice *and* God's mercy; God's foreknowledge of all things to come *and* man's free will. Eliot's *Four Quarters* contains a number of expressive paradoxes which function in free variations of the same manner:

Only through time time is conquered.

So the darkness shall be light, and the stillness the dancing.

---

[8]I. vii. 1–2.

[9]*Romeo and Juliet,* I. i. 182–88.

In order to arrive at what you do not know
You must go by a way which is the way of ignorance.

Our only health is the disease
If we obey the dying nurse . . .[10]

Some of Eliot's depth paradoxes are aided by a serious play-fulness which bears a rough analogy to the examples cited from Chesterton and Lord Russell. The line, "To be re-deemed from fire by fire," in *Little Gidding* could be prosa-ically explicated by a distinction between the fire of damna-tion and the fire of purgatorial cleansing. Yet the paradoxical expression is necessary, not arbitrary here, for it evokes, as an overtone of allusion, the archetypal idea of the finding of life through voluntary death ("He who will save his life shall lose it . . ."), and more archetypally still, the idea of the tran-scendent oneness that is approached through even the most discrepant particulars.

The type of paradox most characteristic of poetry is the third: which occurs when a direct statement—i.e., some part of a poem's scenario meaning—is either mocked or play-fully opposed by the suggestions latent in the imagery. The opening lines of Donne's *The Extasy* offer an illustration:

Where, like a pillow on a bed,
    A pregnant bank swelled up, to rest
The violet's reclining head,
    Sat we two, one another's best.

Our hands were firmly cemented
    With a fast balm which thence did spring,
Our eye-beams twisted, and did thread
    Our eyes, upon one double string;

So to'entergraft our hands, as yet
    Was all the means to make us one,
And pictures in our eyes to get
    Was all our propagation.

The latter stanza asserts plainly that there has been no full carnal union and no propagation of new life as yet—a state-ment which the wooer's plaint is presently to confirm: "But O alas, so long, so far / Our bodies why do we forbear?" The three opening lines, however, had already imprinted on a re-

sponsive and uninhibited reader's mind a set of images sug-gesting both feminine and (with startling bravado) masculine fulfillment—a sly and delicately ribald qualification of the subsequent chaste avowal. Most of the later paradoxes in the poem, on the other hand, are of the second (the depth) type, such as:

Might thence a new concoction take,
    And part far purer than he came.

But as all several souls contain
    Mixtures of things, they know not what,
Love, these mixed souls, doth mix again,
    And make both one, each this and that.

Such paradoxes as these underline the theme of the inextri-cable union, in love's mysteries, of oneness and manyness, purity and concoction, spirituality and bodily expression.

8. *Principle of significant mystery:* that the truth or fal-sity of an expressive statement transcends to some degree the evidence of any possible set of propositions which might stand to it in the relation of ground—whether deductive or inductive—to consequent. Truth is more than a function of logically articulable evidence; the meaning of an expressive question (and all deeply important questions are expressive to some degree, or have an expressive aspect)—is never en-tirely exhausted by its possible answers. This is another way of saying (subjectively) that intuition is always a factor in the apprehension of truth, and (objectively) that any integral truth—as opposed to either conventional or technical truths—involves irreducible semantic and logical surds.

In the general muddle of slovenly thinking which is so prevalent today there is a tendency to confuse the ideas ex-pressed by the words *mysticism* and *mystery.* The foregoing semantic analysis shows their difference. Although both meanings have too much semantic plenitude to allow of ad-equate definition, their difference is indicated by the differ-ence between principle 1 and principle 8. The mystical in-volves a fusing of this and that, of knower and object known, of symbol and referend. The mysterious—i.e., the radically enigmatic, not the temporarily puzzling—is that character or quality or relationship in things which, however much "ex-plained," always transcends in its essence any totality of ex-planations given. The two elements are deeply interrelated, but analytically distinguishable.

Thus these eight dialectical escapes from the limiting assumptions of steno language to the liberating principles of expressive language confirm the conclusions reached in Chapter 3. In the present chapter we have found, simply by making those eight assumptions explicit and identifying

---

[10][Wheelwright] Quoted from *Four Quartets,* which have been republished in T. S. Eliot, *The Complete Poems and Plays* (Harcourt, 1952). The first of the excerpts is from Part II of "Burnt Norton," the second and third from Part III of "East Coker," and the last from Part IV of "East Coker."

their exact meaning, that there is a set of meaningful possibilities which they deny, and which therefore a critic is free to explore. In the earlier chapter we had discovered the more general psychological assumption which underlies the eight steno semantic assumptions—namely, that the semantic function belongs only to the operations of intellect upon the data of outer or inner perception, and that the semantic function of emotional experience as such is zero. Although the steno semanticist admits that emotions may, and doubtless always do, accompany every actual occasion of semantic reference, he maintains that in themselves they tell us nothing about any reality other than their own bare and transient being. Hence the familiar counsel to disregard the promptings of emotion in the search for truth; and the counsel is both right and valuable in two respects. It is right when the truth in question is a logical, monosignative truth, which calls into play man's abstractive intellect in quest of definite and publicly securable results. It is right, again, when the emotional promptings are crude and immature, or foreign to the matter in hand, and the emotional commentary is an impertinence.

Nevertheless "the heart, too, has its reasons." *All* experience has, to some degree or other, a semantic role: it points, however uncertainly and dimly, to a reality other than itself and other than the subject who enjoys the experience. It is the essence of experience to be vectorlike: to transcend in reference what it is in existence, and thereby to enact a more or less cognitive role. Emotional as well as intellectual aspects of mental activity give a kind of knowledge—not merely knowledge of the subject, such as a psychologist might derive by empirio-intellectual analysis, but knowledge about that towards which the emotion is felt. Love of a thing is presumptive evidence of the quality "lovable" in that thing, just as a sensation of green is presumptive evidence of the quality of green being actually present. Some degree of judgment is implicit in all experience, emotive as well as sensory, and this implicit judgment tends to make a claim about the nature of things. Further experience and further activity of judgment may, of course, modify or reverse the original judgment, but this possibility affects sensory experience too, not emotive experience only. The important discrimination is between good emotions and bad: the quest for truth and the larger intelligibility require an abandonment of petty emotions reflecting primitive impulse and ingrown self-love, in favor of those integral and expansive intuitions—neither exclusive of intellect nor identical with it—which enable the knower to transcend his natural limitations and penetrate darkly a little way into the enveloping mystery.

Theodor Adorno

1903–1969

"Critical theory" as a term used by members of the so-called Frankfurt School of social critics extends far beyond theory devoted specifically to literature, the sense in which it is employed in the title of this anthology. "Critical theory" was Marxist in orientation and centered in 1930 at the Institute for Social Research in Frankfurt under the direction of Max Horkheimer. In 1933 it moved to Paris and finally to Columbia University just before the German occupation. Adorno was early associated with Horkheimer and collaborated with him on *Dialectic of Enlightenment* (1947). He was the aesthetician of the group, and it was this interest and his refusal to insist that art be directly politically active that caused many in the student movement of the late 1960s to reject him. Yet Adorno was far from claiming art irrelevant to politics. Indeed, for him, when it seemed most remote from social action it was most political. His views on this matter were far too complex for students at that time to be patient with.

The problem addressed in this essay is the stance of the critic—in the larger sense in which Adorno interpreted "critical theory." It is a problem similar to that discussed by George Lukács in "The Ideal of the Harmonious Man in Bourgeois Aesthetics." It is the problem of being inevitably implicated in and thus possibly complicit with the culture one examines. The cultural critic, who does not have autonomy, is likely to reproduce the socially prevalent categories and contribute to the *status quo*. This is so even with stances that attempt transcendence. Adorno advocates a dialectical criticism that is both inside and outside at the same time. It would have to be an "immanent" criticism. This position is consistent with Adorno's suspicion of and flight from virtually all of our cherished sets of opposition, including subject/object. He would oppose all "totalization," asserting that "the whole is the false." Criticism must therefore keep moving dialectically. Great works of art and philosophy have "always stood in relation to the actual life-process of society from which they distinguished themselves." Paradoxically for Adorno the insistence of art on its independence and autonomy gives "the promise of a condition in which freedom were realized." If this promise is "equivocal" that is because of the state of culture at the present time. And Adorno is not optimistic that the promise is fulfillable. At the same time he refuses to abandon a utopian social vision. To the extent that aesthetics implies closure and fixity Adorno opposes it, even as he would oppose the closure implicit in any fixed utopia.

The translated works of Adorno include *Dialectic of Enlightenment* (with Max Horkheimer, 1947, tr. 1972); *Minima Moralia* (1951, tr. 1974); *Prisms: Cultural Criticism and Society* (1955, tr. 1967); *The Jargon of Authenticity* (1964, tr. 1973); *Negative Dialectics* (1966; tr. 1973); and *Aesthetic Theory* (1970, tr. 1984). See Martin Jay, *The Dialectical Imagination: A History of the Frankfurt School of Social Research* (1973); Susan Buck-Morss, *The Origin of Negative Dialectics* (1977); Gillian Rose,

The Melancholy Science (1978); A. Oratio and E. Gebhart, *The Essential Frankfurt School Reader;* and Martin Jay, *Adorno* (1984).

Cultural Criticism and Society

To anyone in the habit of thinking with his ears, the words 'cultural criticism' (*Kulturkritik*) must have an offensive ring, not merely because, like 'automobile', they are pieced together from Latin and Greek. The words recall a flagrant contradiction. The cultural critic is not happy with civilization, to which alone he owes his discontent. He speaks as if he represented either unadulterated nature or a higher historical stage. Yet he is necessarily of the same essence as that to which he fancies himself superior. The insufficiency of the subject—criticized by Hegel in his apology for the *status quo*—which in its contingency and narrowness passes judgment on the might of the existent, becomes intolerable when the subject itself is mediated down to its innermost make-up by the notion to which it opposes itself as independent and sovereign. But what makes the content of cultural criticism inappropriate is not so much lack of respect for that which is criticized as the dazzled and arrogant recognition which criticism surreptitiously confers on culture. The cultural critic can hardly avoid the imputation that he has the culture which culture lacks. His vanity aids that of culture: even in the accusing gesture, the critic clings to the notion of culture, isolated, unquestioned, dogmatic. He shifts the attack. Where there is despair and measureless misery, he sees only spiritual phenomena, the state of man's consciousness, the decline of norms. By insisting on this, criticism is tempted to forget the unutterable, instead of striving, however impotently, so that man may be spared.

The position of the cultural critic, by virtue of its difference from the prevailing disorder, enables him to go beyond it theoretically, although often enough he merely falls behind. But he incorporates this difference into the very culture industry which he seeks to leave behind and which itself needs the difference in order to fancy itself culture. Characteristic of culture's pretension to distinction, through which it exempts itself from evaluation against the material conditions of life, is that it is insatiable. The exaggerated claims of culture, which in turn inhere in the movement of the mind, remove it ever further from those conditions as the worth of sublimation becomes increasingly suspect when confronted both by a material fulfillment near enough to touch and by the threatening annihilation of uncounted human beings. The cultural critic makes such distinction his privilege and forfeits his legitimation by collaborating with culture as its salaried and honoured nuisance. This, however, affects the substance of criticism. Even the implacable rigour with which criticism speaks the truth of an untrue consciousness remains imprisoned within the orbit of that against which it struggles, fixated on its surface manifestations. To flaunt one's superiority is, at the same time, to feel in on the job. Were one to study the profession of critic in bourgeois society as it progressed towards the rank of cultural critic, one would doubtless stumble on an element of usurpation in its origins, an element of which a writer like Balzac was still aware. Professional critics were first of all 'reporters': they oriented people in the market of intellectual products. In so doing, they occasionally gained insights into the matter at hand, yet remained continually traffic agents, in agreement with the sphere as such if not with its individual products. Of this they bear the mark even after they have discarded the role of agent. That they should have been entrusted with the roles of expert and then of judge was economically inevitable although accidental with respect to their objective qualifications. Their agility, which gained them privileged positions in the general competition—privileged, since the fate of those judged depends largely on their vote—invests their judgments with the semblance of competence. While they adroitly slipped into gaps and won influence with the expansion of the press, they attained that very authority which their profession already presupposed. Their arrogance derives from the fact that, in the forms of competitive society in which all being is merely there *for* something else, the critic himself is also measured only in terms of his marketable success—that is, in terms of his *being for* something else. Knowledge and understanding were not primary, but at most by-products, and the more they are lacking, the more they are replaced by Oneupmanship and conformity. When the critics in their playground—art—no longer understand what they judge and enthusiastically permit themselves to be degraded to propagandists or censors, it is the old dishonesty of trade fulfilling itself in their fate. The prerogatives of information and position permit them to express their opinion as if it were objectivity. But it is solely the objectivity of the ruling mind. They help to weave the veil.

CULTURAL CRITICISM AND SOCIETY. *Cultural Criticism and Society* first appeared in 1955. It is reprinted here translated by Samuel and Sherry Weber from *Prisms*, copyright © The MIT Press, 1981. Reprinted by permission of The MIT Press.

The notion of the free expression of opinion, indeed, that of intellectual freedom itself in bourgeois society, upon which cultural criticism is founded, has its own dialectic. For while the mind extricated itself from a theological-feudal tutelage, it has fallen increasingly under the anonymous sway of the *status quo*. This regimentation, the result of the progressive societalization of all human relations, did not simply confront the mind from without; it immigrated into its immanent consistency. It imposes itself as relentlessly on the autonomous mind as heteronomous orders were formerly imposed on the mind which was bound. Not only does the mind mould itself for the sake of its marketability, and thus reproduce the socially prevalent categories. Rather, it grows to resemble ever more closely the *status quo* even where it subjectively refrains from making a commodity of itself. The network of the whole is drawn ever tighter, modelled after the act of exchange. It leaves the individual consciousness less and less room for evasion, preforms it more and more thoroughly, cuts it off *a priori* as it were from the possibility of differencing itself as all difference degenerates to a nuance in the monotony of supply. At the same time, the semblance of freedom makes reflection upon one's own unfreedom incomparably more difficult than formerly when such reflection stood in contradiction to manifest unfreedom, thus strengthening dependence. Such moments, in conjunction with the social selection of the 'spiritual and intellectual leaders', result in the regression of spirit and intellect. In accordance with the predominant social tendency, the integrity of the mind becomes a fiction. Of its freedom it develops only the negative moment, the heritage of the planless-monadological condition, irresponsibility. Otherwise, however, it clings ever more closely as a mere ornament to the material base which it claims to transcend. The strictures of Karl Krauss[1] against freedom of the press are certainly not to be taken literally. To invoke seriously the censors against hack-writers would be to drive out the devil with Beelzebub. Nevertheless, the brutalization and deceit which flourish under the aegis of freedom of the press are not accidental to the historical march of the mind. Rather, they represent the stigma of that slavery within which the liberation of the mind—a false emancipation—has taken place. This is nowhere more striking than where the mind tears at its bonds: in criticism. When the German fascists defamed the word and replaced it with the inane notion of 'art appreciation', they were led to do so only by the rugged interests of the authoritarian state which still feared the passion of a Marquis Posa[2] in the impertinence of the journalist. But the self-sat-isfied cultural barbarism which clamoured for the abolition of criticism, the incursion of the wild horde into the preserve of the mind, unawares repaid kind in kind. The bestial fury of the Brownshirt against 'carping critics' arises not merely from his envy of a culture which excludes him and against which he blindly rebels; nor is it merely his resentment of the person who can speak out the negative moment which he himself must repress. Decisive is that the critic's sovereign gesture suggests to his readers an autonomy which he does not have, and arrogates for itself a position of leadership which is incompatible with his own principle of intellectual freedom. This is innervated by his enemies. Their sadism was idiosyncratically attracted by the weakness, cleverly disguised as strength, of those who, in their dictatorial bearing, would have willingly excelled the less clever tyrants who were to succeed them. Except that the fascists succumbed to the same naivete as the critics, the faith in culture as such, which reduced it to pomp and approved spiritual giants. They regarded themselves as physicians of culture and removed the thorn of criticism from it. They thus not only degraded culture to the Official, but in addition, failed to recognize the extent to which culture and criticism, for better or for worse, are intertwined. Culture is only true when implicitly critical, and the mind which forgets this revenges itself in the critics it breeds. Criticism is an indispensable element of culture which is itself contradictory: in all its untruth still as true as culture is untrue. Criticism is not unjust when it dissects—this can be its greatest virtue—but rather when it parries by not parrying.

The complicity of cultural criticism with culture lies not in the mere mentality of the critic. Far more, it is dictated by his relation to that with which he deals. By making culture his object, he objectifies it once more. Its very meaning, however, is the suspension of objectification. Once culture itself has been debased to 'cultural goods', with its hideous philosophical rationalization, 'cultural values', it has already defamed its *raison d'être*. The distillation of such 'values'—the echo of commercial language is by no means accidental—places culture at the will of the market. Even the enthusiasm for foreign cultures includes the excitement over the rarity in which money may be invested. If cultural criticism, even at its best with Valéry, sides with conservativism, it is because of its unconscious adherence to a notion of culture which, during the era of late capitalism, aims at a form of property which is stable and independent of stock-market fluctuations. This idea of culture asserts its distance from the system in order, as it were, to offer universal security in the middle of a universal dynamic. The model of the cultural critic is no less the appraising collector than the art critic. In general, cultural criticism recalls the gesture of bargaining, of the expert questioning the authenticity of a painting or

---

[1]Karl Krauss (1874–1936), Austrian writer.
[2]Marquis Posa, character in Schiller's *Don Karlos*.

classifying it among the Master's lesser works. One devaluates in order to get more. The cultural critic evaluates and hence is inevitably involved in a sphere stained with 'cultural values', even when he rants against the mortgaging of culture. His contemplative stance towards culture necessarily entails scrutinizing, surveying, balancing, selecting: this piece suits him, that he rejects. Yet his very sovereignty, the claim to a more profound knowledge of the object, the separation of the idea from its object through the independence of the critical judgment threatens to succumb to the thinglike form of the object when cultural criticism appeals to a collection of ideas on display, as it were, and fetishizes isolated categories such as mind, life and the individual.

But the greatest fetish of cultural criticism is the notion of culture as such. For no authentic work of art and no true philosophy, according to their very meaning, has ever exhausted itself in itself alone, in its being-in-itself. They have always stood in relation to the actual life-process of society from which they distinguished themselves. Their very rejection of the guilt of a life which blindly and callously reproduces itself, their insistence on independence and autonomy, on separation from the prevailing realm of purposes, implies, at least as an unconscious element, the promise of a condition in which freedom were realized. This remains an equivocal promise of culture as long as its existence depends on a bewitched reality and, ultimately, on control over the work of others. That European culture in all its breadth—that which reached the consumer and which today is prescribed for whole populations by managers and psychotechnicians—degenerated to mere ideology resulted from a change in its function with regard to material *praxis:* its renunciation of interference. Far from being culture's 'sin', the change was forced upon culture by history. For it is only in the process of withdrawing into itself, only indirectly that is, that bourgeois culture conceives of a purity from the corrupting traces of a totalitarian disorder which embraces all areas of existence. Only in so far as it withdraws from a *praxis* which has degenerated into its opposite, from the ever-changing production of what is always the same, from the service of the customer who himself serves the manipulator—only in so far as it withdraws from Man, can culture be faithful to man. But such concentration on substance which is absolutely one's own, the greatest example of which is to be found in the poetry and theoretical writings of Paul Valéry, contributes at the same time to the impoverishment of that substance. Once the mind is no longer directed at reality, its meaning is changed despite the strictest preservation of meaning. Through its resignation before the facts of life and, even more, through its isolation as one 'field' among others, the mind aids the existing order and takes its place within it. The emasculation of culture has angered philosophers since

the time of Rousseau and the 'ink-splattering age' of Schiller's *Robbers,* to Nietzsche and finally, to the preachers of commitment for its own sake. This is the result of culture's becoming self-consciously cultural, which in turn places culture in vigorous and consistent opposition to the growing barbarism of economic hegemony. What appears to be the decline of culture is its coming to pure self-consciousness. Only when neutralized and reified, does Culture allow itself to be idolized. Fetishism gravitates towards mythology. In general, cultural critics become intoxicated with idols drawn from antiquity to the dubious, long-evaporated warmth of the liberalist era, which recalled the origins of culture in its decline. Cultural criticism rejects the progressive integration of all aspects of consciousness within the apparatus of material production. But because it fails to see through the apparatus, it turns towards the past, lured by the promise of immediacy. This is necessitated by its own momentum and not merely by the influence of an order which sees itself obliged to drown out its progress in dehumanization with cries against dehumanization and progress. The isolation of the mind from material production heightens its esteem but also makes it a scapegoat in the general consciousness for that which is perpetrated in practice. Enlightenment as such—not as an instrument of actual domination—is held responsible. Hence, the irrationalism of cultural criticism. Once it has wrenched the mind out of its dialectic with the material conditions of life, it seizes it unequivocally and straightforwardly as the principle of fatality, thus undercutting the mind's own resistance. The cultural critic is barred from the insight that the reification of life results not from too much enlightenment but from too little, and that the mutilation of man which is the result of the present particularistic rationality is the stigma of the total irrationality. The abolition of this irrationality, which would coincide with the abolition of the divorce between mental and physical work, appears as chaos to the blindness of cultural criticism: whoever glorifies order and form as such, must see in the petrified divorce an archetype of the Eternal. That the fatal fragmentation of society might some day end is, for the cultural critic, a fatal destiny. He would rather that everything end than for mankind to put an end to reification. This fear harmonizes with the interests of those interested in the perpetuation of material denial. Whenever cultural criticism complains of 'materialism', it furthers the belief that the sin lies in man's desire for consumer goods, and not in the organization of the whole which withholds these goods from man: for the cultural critic, the sin is satiety, not hunger. Were mankind to possess the wealth of goods, it would shake off the chains of that civilized barbarism which cultural critics ascribe to the advanced state of the human spirit rather than to the retarded state of society. The 'eternal values' of which cultural criticism is so fond reflect the perennial catastrophe. The cultural critic thrives on the mythical obduracy of culture.

Because the existence of cultural criticism, no matter what its content, depends on the economic system, it is involved in the fate of the system. The more completely the life-process, including leisure, is dominated by modern social orders—those in the East, above all—the more all spiritual phenomena bear the mark of the order. Either, they may contribute directly to the perpetuation of the system as entertainment or edification, and are enjoyed as exponents of the system precisely because of their socially preformed character. Familiar, stamped and Approved by Good Housekeeping as it were, they insinuate themselves into a regressive consciousness, present themselves as 'natural', and permit identification with powers whose preponderance leaves no alternative but that of false love. Or, by being different, they become rarities and once again marketable. Throughout the liberalist era, culture fell within the sphere of circulation. Hence, the gradual withering away of this sphere strikes culture to the quick. With the elimination of trade and its irrational loopholes by the calculated distributive apparatus of industry, the commercialization of culture culminates in absurdity. Completely subdued, administered, thoroughly 'cultivated' in a sense, it dies out. Spengler's denunciation: that mind and money go together, proves correct.[3] But because of his sympathy with direct rule, he advocated a structure of existence divested of all economic as well as spiritual mediations. He maliciously threw the mind together with an economic type which was in fact obsolete. What Spengler failed to understand was that no matter to what extent the mind is a product of that type, it implies at the same time the objective possibility of overcoming it. Just as culture sprang up in the marketplace, in the traffic of trade, in communication and negotiation, as something distinct from the immediate struggle for individual self-preservation, just as it was closely tied to trade in the era of mature capitalism, just as its representatives were counted among the class of 'third persons' who supported themselves in life as middlemen, so culture, considered 'socially necessary' according to classical rules, in the sense of reproducing itself economically, is in the end reduced to that as which it began, to mere communication. Its alienation from human affairs terminates in its absolute docility before a humanity which has been enchanted and transformed into clientele by the suppliers. In the name of the consumer, the manipulators suppress everything in culture which enables it to go beyond the total immanence in the existing society and allow only that to remain which serves society's unequivocal purpose. Hence, 'consumer culture' can boast of being not a luxury but rather the simple extension of production. Political slogans, designed for mass manipulation, unanimously stigmatize, as 'luxury', 'snobbism', and 'highbrow', everything cultural which displeases the commissars. Only when the established order has become the measure of all things does its mere reproduction in the realm of consciousness become truth. Cultural criticism points to this and rails against 'superficiality' and 'loss of substance'. But by limiting its attention to the entanglement of culture in commerce, such criticism itself becomes superficial. It follows the pattern of reactionary social critics who pit 'productive' against 'predatory' capital. In fact, all culture shares the guilt of society. It ekes out its existence only by virtue of injustice already perpetrated in the sphere of production, much as does commerce (cf. *Dialektik der Aufklärung*).[4] Consequently, cultural criticism shifts the guilt: such criticism is ideology as long as it remains mere criticism of ideology. Totalitarian regimes of both kinds, seeking to protect the *status quo* from even the last traces of insubordination which they ascribe to culture even at its most servile, can conclusively convict culture and its introspection of servility. They suppress the mind, in itself already grown intolerable, and so feel themselves to be purifiers and revolutionaries. The ideological function of cultural criticism bridles its very truth which lies in its opposition to ideology. The struggle against deceit works to the advantage of naked terror. 'When I hear the word "culture", I reach for my gun', said the spokesman of Hitler's Imperial Chamber of Culture.

Cultural criticism is, however, only able to reproach culture so penetratingly for prostituting itself, for violating in its decline the pure autonomy of the mind, because culture originates in the radical separation of mental and physical work. It is from this separation, the original sin as it were, that culture draws its strength. When culture simply denies the separation and feigns harmonious union, it falls back behind its own notion. Only the mind which, in the delusion of being absolute, removes itself entirely from the merely existent, truly defines the existent in its negativity. As long as even the least part of the mind remains engaged in the reproduction of life, it is its sworn bondsman. The anti-philistinism of Athens was both the most arrogant contempt of the man who need not soil his hands for the man from whose work he lives, and the preservation of an image of existence beyond the constraint which underlies all work. In projecting

---

[3]Oswald Spengler (1880–1936), German historian.

[4]*Dialectic of Enlightenment* (1947) by Adorno and Max Horkheimer.

its own uneasy conscience on to its victims as their 'baseness', such an attitude also accuses that which they endure: the subjugation of men to the prevailing form in which their lives are reproduced. All 'pure culture' has always been a source of discomfort to the spokesmen of power. Plato and Aristotle knew why they would not permit the notion to arise. Instead, in questions concerning the evaluation of art, they advocated a pragmatism which contrasts curiously with the *pathos* of the two great metaphysicians. Modern bourgeois cultural criticism has, of course, been too prudent to follow them openly in this respect. But such criticism secretly finds a source of comfort in the divorce between 'high' and 'popular' culture, art and entertainment, knowledge and non-committal *Weltanschauung*.[5] Its anti-philistinism exceeds that of the Athenian upper class to the extent that the proletariat is more dangerous than the slaves. The modern notion of a pure, autonomous culture indicates that the antagonism has become irreconcilable. This is the result both of an uncompromising opposition to being-for-something else, and of an ideology which in its hybris enthrones itself as being-in-itself.

Cultural criticism shares the blindness of its object. It is incapable of allowing the recognition of its frailty to arise, a frailty set in the division of mental and physical work. No society which contradicts its very notion—that of mankind—can have full consciousness of itself. A display of subjective ideology is not required to obstruct this consciousness, although in times of historical upheaval it tends to contribute to the objective blindness. Rather, the fact that every form of repression, depending on the level of technology, has been necessary for the survival of society, and that society as it is, despite all absurdity, does indeed reproduce its life under the existing conditions, objectively produces the semblance of society's legitimation. As the epitome of the self-consciousness of an antagonistic society, culture can no more divest itself of this semblance than can cultural criticism, which measures culture against culture's own ideal. The semblance has become total in a phase in which irrationality and objective falsity hide behind rationality and objective necessity. Nevertheless, by virtue of their real force, the antagonisms reassert themselves in the realm of consciousness. Just because culture affirms the validity of the principle of harmony within an antagonistic society, albeit in order to glorify that society, it cannot avoid confronting society with its own notion of harmony and thereby stumbling on discord. The ideology which affirms life is forced into opposition to life by the immanent drive of the ideal. The mind which sees

that reality does not resemble it in every respect but is instead subject to an unconscious and fatal dynamic, is impelled even against its will beyond apologetics. The fact that theory becomes real force when it moves men is founded in the objectivity of the mind itself which, through the fulfilment of its ideological function must lose faith in ideology. Prompted by the incompatibility of ideology and existence, the mind, in displaying its blindness also displays its effort to free itself of ideology. Disenchanted, the mind perceives naked existence in its nakedness and delivers it up to criticism. The mind either damns the material base, in accordance with the ever-questionable criterion of its 'pure principle', or it becomes aware of its own questionable position, by virtue of its incompatibility with the base. As a result of the social dynamic, culture becomes cultural criticism, which preserves the notion of culture while demolishing its present manifestations as mere commodities and means of brutalization. Such critical consciousness remains subservient to culture in so far as its concern with culture distracts from the true horrors. From this arises the ambivalent attitude of social theory towards cultural criticism. The procedure of cultural criticism is itself the object of permanent criticism, both in its general presuppositions—its immanence in the existing society—and in its concrete judgments. For the subservience of cultural criticism is revealed in its specific content, and only in this may it be grasped conclusively. At the same time, a dialectical theory which does not wish to succumb to 'Economism', the sentiment which holds that the transformation of the world is exhausted in the increase of production, must absorb cultural criticism, the truth of which consists in bringing untruth to consciousness of itself. A dialectical theory which is uninterested in culture as a mere epiphenomenon, aids pseudo-culture to run rampant and collaborates in the reproduction of the evil. Cultural traditionalism and the terror of the new Russian despots are in basic agreement. Both affirm culture as a whole, sight-unseen, while at the same time proscribing all forms of consciousness which are not made-to-order. They are thus no less ideological than is criticism when it calls a disembodied culture before its tribunal, or holds the alleged negativity of culture responsible for real catastrophes. To accept culture as a whole is to deprive it of the ferment which is its very truth—negation. The joyous appropriation of culture harmonizes with a climate of military music and paintings of battle-scenes. What distinguishes dialectical from cultural criticism is that it heightens cultural criticism until the notion of culture is itself negated, fulfilled and surmounted in one.

Immanent criticism of culture, it may be argued, overlooks what is decisive: the role of ideology in social conflicts. To suppose, if only methodologically, anything like an

---

[5] World-view, philosophy of life.

independent logic of culture is to collaborate in the hypostasis of culture, the ideological *proton pseudos*. The substance of culture, according to this argument, resides not in culture alone but in its relation to something external, to the material life-process. Culture, as Marx observed of juridical and political systems, cannot be fully 'understood either in terms of itself . . . or in terms of the so-called universal development of the mind'. To ignore this, the argument concludes, is to make ideology the basic matter and thus to establish it firmly. And in fact, having taken a dialectical turn, cultural criticism must not hypostasize the criteria of culture. Criticism retains its mobility in regard to culture by recognizing the latter's position within the whole. Without such freedom, without consciousness transcending the immanence of culture, immanent criticism itself would be inconceivable: the spontaneous movement of the object can be followed only by someone who is not entirely engulfed by it. But the traditional demand of the ideology-critique is itself subject to a historical dynamic. The critique was conceived against idealism, the philosophical form which reflects the fetishization of culture. Today, however, the definition of consciousness in terms of being has become a means of dispensing with all consciousness which does not conform to existence. The objectivity of truth, without which the dialectic is inconceivable, is tacitly replaced by vulgar positivism and pragmatism—ultimately, that is, by bourgeois subjectivism. During the bourgeois era, the prevailing theory was the ideology and the opposing *praxis* was in direct contradiction. Today, theory hardly exists any longer and the ideology drones, as it were, from the gears of an irresistible *praxis*. No notion dares to be conceived any more which does not cheerfully include, in all camps, explicit instructions as to who its beneficiaries are—exactly what the polemics once sought to expose. But the unideological thought is that which does not permit itself to be reduced to 'operational terms' and instead strives solely to help the things themselves to that articulation from which they are otherwise cut off by the prevailing language. Since the moment arrived when every advanced economic and political council agreed that what was important was to change the world and that to interpret it was *allotria,* it has become difficult simply to invoke the *Theses* against Feuerbach.[6] Dialectics also includes the relation between action and contemplation. In an epoch in which bourgeois social science has, in Scheler's words, 'plundered' the Marxian notion of ideology and diluted it to universal relativism, the danger involved in overlooking the function of ideologies has become less than that of judging intellectual phenomena

in a subsumptive, uninformed and administrative manner and assimilating them into the prevailing constellations of power which the intellect ought to expose. As with many other elements of dialectical materialism, the notion of ideology has changed from an instrument of knowledge into its strait-jacket. In the name of the dependence of superstructure on base, all use of ideology is controlled instead of criticized. No one is concerned with the objective substance of an ideology as long as it is expedient.

Yet the very function of ideologies becomes increasingly abstract. The suspicion held by earlier cultural critics is confirmed: in a world which denies the mass of human beings the authentic experience of intellectual phenomena by making genuine education a privilege and by shackling consciousness, the specific ideological content of these phenomena is less important than the fact that there should be anything at all to fill the vacuum of the expropriated consciousness and to distract from the open secret. Within the context of its social effect, the particular ideological doctrine which a film imparts to its audience is presumably far less important than the interest of the homeward bound moviegoer in the names and marital affairs of the stars. Vulgar notions such as 'amusement' and 'diversion' are more appropriate than pretentious explanations which designate one writer as a representative of the lower-middle class, another of the upper-middle. Culture has become ideological not only as the quintessence of subjectively devised manifestations of the objective mind, but even more as the sphere of private life. The illusory importance and autonomy of private life conceals the fact that private life drags on only as an appendage of the social process. Life transforms itself into the ideology of reification—a death mask. Hence, the task of criticism must be not so much to search for the particular interest-groups to which cultural phenomena are to be assigned, but rather to decipher the general social tendencies which are expressed in these phenomena and through which the most powerful interests realize themselves. Cultural criticism must become social physiognomy. The more the whole divests itself of all spontaneous elements, is socially mediated and filtered, is 'consciousness', the more it becomes 'culture'. In addition to being the means of subsistence, the material process of production finally unveils itself as that which it always was, from its origins in the exchange-relationship as the false consciousness which the two contracting parties have of each other: ideology. Inversely, however, consciousness becomes at the same time increasingly a mere transitional moment in the functioning of the whole. Today, ideology means society as appearance. Although mediated by the totality behind which stands the rule of partiality, ideology is not simply reducible to a partial interest. It is, as it were, equally near the centre in all its pieces.

---

[6]Ludwig Feuerbach (1804–1872), German philosopher.

The alternatives—either calling culture as a whole into question from outside under the general notion of ideology, or confronting it with the norms which it itself has crystallized—cannot be accepted by critical theory. To insist on the choice between immanence and transcendence is to revert to the traditional logic criticized in Hegel's polemic against Kant. As Hegel argued, every method which sets limits and restricts itself to the limits of its object thereby goes beyond them. The position transcending culture is in a certain sense presupposed by dialectics as the consciousness which does succumb in advance to the fetishization of the intellectual sphere. Dialectics means intransigence towards all reification. The transcendent method, which aims at totality, seems more radical than the immanent method, which presupposes the questionable whole. The transcendent critic assumes an as it were Archimedean position above culture and the blindness of society, from which consciousness can bring the totality, no matter how massive, into flux. The attack on the whole draws strength from the fact that the semblance of unity and wholeness in the world grows with the advance of reification; that is, with division. But the summary dismissal of ideology which in the Soviet sphere has already become a pretext for cynical terror, taking the form of a ban on 'objectivism', pays that wholeness too high an honour. Such an attitude buys up culture *en bloc* from society, regardless of the use to which it is put. If ideology is defined as socially necessary appearance, then the ideology today is society itself in so far as its integral power and inevitability, its overwhelming existence-in-itself, surrogates the meaning which that existence has exterminated. The choice of a standpoint outside the sway of existing society is as fictitious as only the construction of abstract utopias can be. Hence, the transcendent criticism of culture, much like bourgeois cultural criticism, sees itself obliged to fall back upon the idea of 'naturalness', which itself forms a central element of bourgeois ideology. The transcendent attack on culture regularly speaks the language of false escape, that of the 'nature boy'. It despises the mind and its works, contending that they are, after all, only man-made and serve only to cover up 'natural' life. Because of this alleged worthlessness, the phenomena allow themselves to be manipulated and degraded for purposes of domination. This explains the inadequacy of most socialist contributions to cultural criticism: they lack the experience of that with which they deal. In wishing to wipe away the whole as if with a sponge, they develop an affinity to barbarism. Their sympathies are inevitably with the more primitive, more undifferentiated, no matter how much it may contradict the level of intellectual productive forces. The blanket rejection of culture becomes a pretext for promoting what is crudest, 'healthiest', even repressive; above all, the perennial conflict between individual and society, both drawn in like manner, which is obstinately resolved in favour of society according to the criteria of the administrators who have appropriated it. From there it is only a step to the official reinstatement of culture. Against this struggles the immanent procedure as the more essentially dialectical. It takes seriously the principle that it is not ideology in itself which is untrue but rather its pretension to correspond to reality. Immanent criticism of intellectual and artistic phenomena seeks to grasp, through the analysis of their form and meaning, the contradiction between their objective idea and that pretension. It names what the consistency or inconsistency of the work itself expresses of the structure of the existent. Such criticism does not stop at a general recognition of the servitude of the objective mind, but seeks rather to transform this knowledge into a heightened perception of the thing itself. Insight into the negativity of culture is binding only when it reveals the truth or untruth of a perception, the consequence or lameness of a thought, the coherence or incoherence of a structure, the substantiality or emptiness of a figure of speech. Where it finds inadequacies it does not ascribe them hastily to the individual and his psychology, which are merely the façade of the failure, but instead seeks to derive them from the irreconcilability of the object's moments. It pursues the logic of its aporias, the insolubility of the task itself. In such antinomies criticism perceives those of society. A successful work, according to immanent criticism, is not one which resolves objective contradictions in a spurious harmony, but one which expresses the idea of harmony negatively by embodying the contradictions, pure and uncompromised, in its innermost structure. Confronted with this kind of work, the verdict 'mere ideology' loses its meaning. At the same time, however, immanent criticism holds in evidence the fact that the mind has always been under a spell. On its own it is unable to resolve the contradictions under which it labours. Even the most radical reflection of the mind on its own failure is limited by the fact that it remains only reflection, without altering the existence to which its failure bears witness. Hence immanent criticism cannot take comfort in its own idea. It can neither be vain enough to believe that it can liberate the mind directly by immersing itself in it, nor naïve enough to believe that unflinching immersion in the object will inevitably lead to truth by virtue of the logic of things if only the subjective knowledge of the false whole is kept from intruding from the outside, as it were, in the determination of the object. The less the dialectical method can today presuppose the Hegelian identity of subject and object, the more it is obliged to be mindful of the duality of the moments. It must relate the knowledge of society as a totality and of the mind's involvement in it to the claim inherent in the specific content of the object that it be apprehended as such. Dialectics cannot, therefore, permit any insistence on logical neatness to encroach on its right to go from one *genus* to another, to shed light on an object in itself hermetic by casting a glance at society, to present society with the bill which the object does not redeem. Finally, the very opposition between knowledge which penetrates from without and that which bores from within becomes suspect to the dialectical method, which sees in it a symptom of precisely that reification which the dialectic is obliged to accuse. The abstract categorizing and, as it were, administrative thinking of the former corresponds in the latter to the fetishism of an object blind to its genesis, which has become the prerogative of the expert. But if stubbornly immanent contemplation threatens to revert to idealism, to the illusion of the self-sufficient mind in command of both itself and of reality, transcendent contemplation threatens to forget the effort of conceptualization required and content itself instead with the prescribed label, the petrified invective, most often 'petty bourgeois', the ukase dispatched from above. Topological thinking, which knows the place of every phenomenon and the essence of none, is secretly related to the paranoic system of delusions which is cut off from experience of the object. With the aid of mechanically functioning categories, the world is divided into black and white and thus made ready for the very domination against which concepts were once conceived. No theory, not even that which is true, is safe from perversion into delusion once it has renounced a spontaneous relation to the object. Dialectics must guard against this no less than against enthrallment in the cultural object. It can subscribe neither to the cult of the mind nor to hatred of it. The dialectical critic of culture must both participate in culture and not participate. Only then does he do justice to his object and to himself.

The traditional transcendent critique of ideology is obsolete. In principle, the method succumbs to the very reification which is its critical theme. By transferring the notion of causality directly from the realm of physical nature to society, it falls back behind its own object. Nevertheless, the transcendent method can still appeal to the fact that it employs reified notions only in so far as society itself is reified. Through the crudity and severity of the notion of causality, it claims to hold up a mirror to society's own crudity and severity, to its debasement of the mind. But the sinister, integrated society of today no longer tolerates even those relatively independent, distinct moments to which the theory of the causal dependence of superstructure on base once referred. In the open-air prison which the world is becoming, it is no longer so important to know what depends on what, such is the extent to which everything is one. All phenomena rigidify, become insignias of the absolute rule of that which is. There are no more ideologies in the authentic sense of false consciousness, only advertisements for the world through its duplication and the provocative lie which does not seek belief but commands silence. Hence, the question of the causal dependence of culture, a question which seems to embody the voice of that on which culture is thought only to depend, takes on a backwoods ring. Of course, even the immanent method is eventually overtaken by this. It is dragged into the abyss by its object. The materialistic transparency of culture has not made it more honest, only more vulgar. By relinquishing its own particularity, culture has also relinquished the salt of truth, which once consisted in its opposition to other particularities. To call it to account before a responsibility which it denies is only to confirm cultural pomposity. Neutralized and ready-made, traditional culture has become worthless today. Through an irrevocable process its heritage, hypocritically reclaimed by the Russians, has become expendable to the highest degree, superfluous, trash. And the hucksters of mass culture can point to it with a grin, for they treat it as such. The more total society becomes, the greater the reification of the mind and the more paradoxical its effort to escape reification on its own. Even the most extreme consciousness of doom threatens to degenerate into idle chatter. Cultural criticism finds itself faced with the final stage of the dialectic of culture and barbarism. To write poetry after Auschwitz is barbaric. And this corrodes even the knowledge of why it has become impossible to write poetry today. Absolute reification, which presupposed intellectual progress as one of its elements, is now preparing to absorb the mind entirely. Critical intelligence cannot be equal to this challenge as long as it confines itself to self-satisfied contemplation.

Roman Jakobson

1896–1982

Jakobson's essay *The Metaphoric and Metonymic Poles* illustrates the complexity of relationships that may exist between the areas of psychological linguistics and literary criticism. Jakobson had knowledge of both fields. He helped found the Russian Formalist movement and later the Prague school of linguistics, both of which treat literature as fundamentally definable as a language. Jakobson begins with a discussion of the relationship between metaphor and metonymy and the two polar types of aphasia, a brain disorder affecting speech. He then observes that the distinction between Romanticism and realism lies in the relative dominance of metaphor in Romanticism and metonymy in realism. He suggests that though there has been much discussion of metaphor, there has been little study of metonymy. For a consideration of the language of realism and of prose, a theory of metonymy is a necessity. In investigations such as Jakobson's, criticism, linguistics, and psychology contribute to one another.

For a list of Jakobson's Formalist publications in Russian see Victor Erlich, *Russian Formalism* (1965), pp. 288–89. For a bibliography of his publications see the volume *For Roman Jakobson* (1956). Jakobson is the author with Morris Halle and C. G. M. Fant of *Preliminaries to Speech Analysis* (1952) and with Halle of *Fundamentals of Language* (1956) and "Phonology in Relation to Phonetics," in *Manual of Phonetics* (1957), edited by L. Kaiser. Among numerous works by Jakobson available in English are *Slavic Languages: A Condensed Survey* (1955), *Selected Writings* in several volumes (1962 ff.), *Studies in Verbal Art* (1971), *Studies on Child Language and Aphasia* (1971), *Pushkin and His Cultural Myth* (tr. 1975), *Six Lectures on Sound and Meaning* (tr. 1978), *The Framework of Language* (1980), *Russian and Slavic Grammar: Studies 1931–1981* (tr. 1984), and *Language in Literature* (1987). See Elmar Holenstein, *Roman Jakobson's Approach to Language* (tr. 1976); and Linda R. Waugh, *Roman Jakobson's Science of Language* (1976).

The Metaphoric and Metonymic Poles

The varieties of aphasia are numerous and diverse, but all of them oscillate between the two polar types just described.

THE METAPHORIC AND METONYMIC POLES. Jakobson's *The Metaphoric and Metonymic Poles* is Chapter 5 of *Fundamentals of Language*, by Jakobson and Morris Halle (1956). Reprinted by permission of Roman Jakobson. The notes are those of Jakobson.

Every form of aphasic disturbance consists in some impairment, more or less severe, either of the faculty for selection and substitution or for combination and contexture. The former affliction involves a deterioration of metalinguistic operations, while the latter damages the capacity for maintaining the hierarchy of linguistic units. The relation of similarity is suppressed in the former, the relation of contiguity in the latter type of aphasia. Metaphor is alien to the similarity disorder, and metonymy to the contiguity disorder.

The development of a discourse may take place along two different semantic lines: one topic may lead to another either through their similarity or through their contiguity.

The metaphoric way would be the most appropriate term for the first case and the metonymic way for the second, since they find their most condensed expression in metaphor and metonymy respectively. In aphasia one or the other of these two processes is restricted or totally blocked—an effect which makes the study of aphasia particularly illuminating for the linguist. In normal verbal behavior both processes are continually operative, but careful observation will reveal that under the influence of a cultural pattern, personality, and verbal style, preference is given to one of the two processes over the other.

In a well-known psychological test, children are confronted with some noun and told to utter the first verbal response that comes into their heads. In this experiment two opposite linguistic predilections are invariably exhibited: the response is intended either as a substitute for, or as a complement to the stimulus. In the latter case the stimulus and the response together form a proper syntactic construction, most usually a sentence. These two types of reaction have been labeled substitutive and predicative.

To the stimulus *hut* one response was *burnt out;* another, *is a poor little house.* Both reactions are predicative; but the first creates a purely narrative context, while in the second there is a double connection with the subject *hut:* on the one hand, a positional (namely, syntactic) contiguity, and on the other a semantic similarity.

The same stimulus produced the following substitutive reactions: the tautology *hut;* the synonyms *cabin* and *hovel,* the antonym *palace,* and the metaphors *den* and *burrow.* The capacity of two words to replace one another is an instance of positional similarity, and, in addition, all these responses are linked to the stimulus by semantic similarity (or contrast). Metonymical responses to the same stimulus, such as *thatch, litter,* or *poverty,* combine and contrast the positional similarity with semantic contiguity.

In manipulating these two kinds of connection (similarity and contiguity) in both their aspects (positional and semantic)—selecting, combining, and ranking them—an individual exhibits his personal style, his verbal predilections and preferences.

In verbal art the interaction of these two elements is especially pronounced. Rich material for the study of this relationship is to be found in verse patterns which require a compulsory parallelism between adjacent lines, for example in Biblical poetry or in the West Finnic and, to some extent, the Russian oral traditions. This provides an objective criterion of what in the given speech community acts as a correspondence. Since on any verbal level—morphemic, lexical, syntactic, and phraseological—either of these two relations (similarity and contiguity) can appear—and each in either of

two aspects—an impressive range of possible configurations is created. Either of the two gravitational poles may prevail. In Russian lyrical songs, for example, metaphoric constructions predominate, while in the heroic epics the metonymic way is preponderant.

In poetry there are various motives which determine the choice between these alternants. The primacy of the metaphoric process in the literary schools of Romanticism and symbolism has been repeatedly acknowledged, but it is still insufficiently realized that it is the predominance of metonymy which underlies and actually predetermines the so-called realistic trend, which belongs to an intermediary stage between the decline of Romanticism and the rise of symbolism and is opposed to both. Following the path of contiguous relationships, the realistic author metonymically digresses from the plot to the atmosphere and from the characters to the setting in space and time. He is fond of synecdochic details. In the scene of Anna Karenina's suicide Tolstoy's artistic attention is focused on the heroine's handbag; and in *War and Peace* the synecdoches "hair on the upper lip" or "bare shoulders" are used by the same writer to stand for the female characters to whom these features belong.

The alternative predominance of one or the other of these two processes is by no means confined to verbal art. The same oscillation occurs in sign systems other than language.[1] A salient example from the history of painting is the manifestly metonymical orientation of cubism, where the object is transformed into a set of synecdoches; the surrealist painters responded with a patently metaphorical attitude. Ever since the productions of D. W. Griffith, the art of the cinema, with its highly developed capacity for changing the angle, perspective and focus of "shots," has broken with the tradition of the theater and ranged an unprecedented variety of synecdochic "close-ups" and metonymic "set-ups" in general. In such pictures as those of Charlie Chaplin, these devices in turn were superseded by a novel, metaphoric "montage" with its "lap dissolves"—the filmic similes.[2]

The bipolar structure of language (or other semiotic systems), and, in aphasia, the fixation on one of these poles to the exclusion of the other require systematic comparative study. The retention of either of these alternatives in the two types of aphasia must be confronted with the predominance

---

[1]I ventured a few sketchy remarks on the metonymical turn in verbal art ("Pro realizm u mystectvi," *Vaplite,* Kharkov, 1927, No. 2; "Randbemerkungen zur Prosa des Dichters Pasternak," *Slavische Rundschau,* VII, 1935), in painting ("Futurizm," *Iskusstvo,* Moscow, August 2, 1919) and in motion pictures ("Úpadek filmu," *Listy pro umění a kritiku,* I, Prague, 1933), but the crucial problem of the two polar processes awaits a detailed investigation.
[2]Cf. B. Balazs, *Theory of the Film* (London, 1952).

of the same pole in certain styles, personal habits, current fashions, etc. A careful analysis and comparison of these phenomena with the whole syndrome of the corresponding type of aphasia is an imperative task for joint research by experts in psychopathology, psychology, linguistics, poetics, and semiotic, the general science of signs. The dichotomy here discussed appears to be of primal significance and consequence for all verbal behavior and for human behavior in general.[3]

To indicate the possibilities of the projected comparative research, we choose an example from a Russian folk tale which employs parallelism as a comic device: "Thomas is a bachelor; Jeremiah is unmarried" *("Fomá xólost; Erjóma neženát")*. Here the predicates in the two parallel clauses are associated by similarity: they are in fact synonymous. The subjects of both clauses are masculine proper names and hence morphologically similar, while on the other hand they denote two contiguous heroes of the same tale, created to perform identical actions and thus to justify the use of synonymous pairs of predicates. A somewhat modified version of the same construction occurs in a familiar wedding song in which each of the wedding guests is addressed in turn by his first name and patronymic: "Gleb is a bachelor; Ivanovič is unmarried." While both predicates here are again synonyms, the relationship between the two subjects is changed: both are proper names denoting the same man and are normally used contiguously as a mode of polite address.

In the quotation from the folk tale the two parallel clauses refer to two separate facts, the marital status of Thomas and the similar status of Jeremiah. In the verse from the wedding song, however, the two clauses are synonymous: they redundantly reiterate the celibacy of the same hero, splitting him into two verbal hypostases.

The Russian novelist Gleb Ivanovič Uspenskij (1840–1902) in the last years of his life suffered from a mental illness involving a speech disorder. His first name and patronymic, *Gleb Ivanovič,* traditionally combined in polite intercourse, for him split into two distinct names designating two separate beings: Gleb was endowed with all his virtues, while Ivanovič, the name relating the son to the father, became the incarnation of all Uspenskij's vices. The linguistic aspect of this split personality is the patient's inability to use two symbols for the same thing, and it is thus a similarity

disorder. Since the similarity disorder is bound up with the metonymical bent, an examination of the literary manner Uspenskij had employed as a young writer takes on particular interest. And the study of Anatolij Kamegulov, who analyzed Uspenskij's style, bears out our theoretical expectations. He shows that Uspenskij had a particular penchant for metonymy, and especially for synecdoche, and that he carried it so far that "the reader is crushed by the multiplicity of detail unloaded on him in a limited verbal space, and is physically unable to grasp the whole, so that the portrait is often lost."[4]

To be sure, the metonymical style in Uspenskij is obviously prompted by the prevailing literary canon of his time, late nineteenth-century "realism"; but the personal stamp of Gleb Ivanovič made his pen particularly suitable for this artistic trend in its extreme manifestations and finally left its mark upon the verbal aspect of his mental illness.

A competition between both devices, metonymic and metaphoric, is manifest in any symbolic process, either intrapersonal or social. Thus in an inquiry into the structure of dreams, the decisive question is whether the symbols and the temporal sequences used are based on contiguity (Freud's metonymic "displacement" and synecdochic "condensation") or on similarity (Freud's "identification and symbolism").[5] The principles underlying magic rites have been resolved by Frazer into two types: charms based on the law of similarity and those founded on association by contiguity. The first of these two great branches of sympathetic magic has been called homeopathic or imitative, and the second, contagious magic.[6] This bipartition is indeed illuminating. Nonetheless, for the most part, the question of the two poles is still neglected, despite its wide scope and importance for the study of any symbolic behavior, especially verbal, and of its impairments. What is the main reason for this neglect?

Similarity in meaning connects the symbols of a metalanguage with the symbols of the language referred to. Sim-

---

[3]For the psychological and sociological aspects of this dichotomy see Bateson's views on "progressional" and "selective integration" and Parsons on the "conjunction-disjunction dichotomy" in children's development: J. Ruesch and G. Bateson, *Communication, The Social Matrix of Psychiatry* (New York, 1951), pp. 183 *ff.*; T. Parsons and R. F. Bates, *Family Socialization and Interaction Process* (Glencoe, 1955), pp. 119 *ff.*

[4]A. Kamegulov, *Stil' Gleba Uspenskogo* (Leningrad, 1930), pp. 65, 145. One of such disintegrated portraits cited by the monograph:

From underneath an ancient straw cap with a black spot on its shield, there peeked two braids resembling the tusks of a wild boar; a chin grown fat and pendulous definitively spread over the greasy collars of the calico dickey and in thick layer lay on the coarse collar of the canvas coat, firmly buttoned on the neck. From below this coat to the eyes of the observer there protruded massive hands with a ring, which had eaten into the fat finger, a cane with a copper top, a significant bulge of the stomach and the presence of very broad pants, almost of muslin quality, in the broad ends of which hid the toes of his boots.

[5]S. Freud, *Die Traumdeutung,* 9th ed. (Vienna, 1950).
[6]J. G. Frazer, *The Golden Bough: A Study in Magic and Religion,* Part I, 3rd ed. (Vienna, 1950), Chapter 3.

ilarity connects a metaphorical term with the term for which it is substituted. Consequently, when constructing a metalanguage to interpret tropes, the researcher possesses more homogeneous means to handle metaphor, whereas metonymy, based on a different principle, easily defies interpretation. Therefore nothing comparable to the rich literature on metaphor[7] can be cited for the theory of metonymy. For the same reason, it is generally realized that Romanticism is closely linked with metaphor, whereas the equally intimate ties of realism with metonymy usually remain unnoticed. Not only the tool of the observer but also the object of observation is responsible for the preponderance of metaphor over metonymy in scholarship. Since poetry is focused upon sign, and pragmatical prose primarily upon referent, tropes

and figures were studied mainly as poetical devices. The principle of similarity underlies poetry; the metrical parallelism of lines or the phonic equivalence of rhyming words prompts the question of semantic similarity and contrast; there exist, for instance, grammatical and antigrammatical but never agrammatical rhymes. Prose, on the contrary, is forwarded essentially by contiguity. Thus, for poetry, metaphor, and for prose, metonymy is the line of least resistance and, consequently, the study of poetical tropes is directed chiefly toward metaphor. The actual bipolarity has been artificially replaced in these studies by an amputated, unipolar scheme which, strikingly enough, coincides with one of the two aphasic patterns, namely with the contiguity disorder.[8]

---

[7]C. F. P. Stutterheim, *Het begrip metaphoor* (Amsterdam, 1941).

[8]Thanks are due to Hugh McLean for his valuable assistance and to Justinia Besharov for her original observations on tropes and figures.

Northrop Frye

1912–1991

Frye's *Ethical Criticism: Theory of Symbols* is the second of four essays that, with an introduction and a conclusion, comprise his *Anatomy of Criticism.* He begins the book with an argument for a criticism whose axioms and postulates have grown out of the art it deals with. Claiming that literature cannot be learned directly, that literature is an object, not a subject of study, and that we must learn about it through a conceptual framework or subject, he proceeds to offer essays on various aspects of criticism as a subject. The first essay, *Historical Criticism: Theory of Modes,* establishes much of his terminology, including the five literary phases—myth, romance, the high mimetic mode, the low mimetic mode, and the ironic mode. These phases—historic and modal in the first essay—help to identify the whole range of literary symbolism in the second.

Beginning with a distinction between "outward" and "inward" phases of symbolism, Frye distinguishes between verbal structures with a tendency toward didacticism or description in their efforts to grasp an avowed external reality and those where the poet depends not on descriptive accuracy but on conformity to his own "hypothetical postulates." In making this distinction, however, Frye insists that in *all* literary verbal structures the final direction of meaning is inward, no matter how outward the technique may appear to be. (Indeed, at the end of his book Frye suggests that all systems of symbols, literary or not, are centripetal.) Literature for Frye is a "disembodied use of words."

There are three other phases of symbolism: the formal phase, where the symbol is seen as an "image"; the mythical phase, where it is seen as an "archetype"; and the anagogic phase, where it is seen as a "monad." Within his discussion of the formal phase, Frye imagines allegory as existing on a sort of scale that ranges from naive allegory and extreme outwardness, where it is a simple device in discursive language, to the extreme inwardness of private association. Unlike the Romantics who opposed symbolism and allegory, Frye considers allegory an aspect of symbolism. In the mythical phase, the idea of the symbol as something that repeats itself throughout the body of literature is emphasized. In this phase, poems are regarded as imitations of other poems more than of nature. In the anagogic phase, the idea of literature as a total imaginative form dominates. In this phase, literature is seen no longer as looking outward to comment on life but as containing life and reality in a system of verbal relationships.

The anagogic phase in particular reflects Frye's debt to William Blake's similar conception and perhaps to Cassirer's idea of symbolic forms. Indeed, Frye's system could be said to have resulted from a meditation on the central symbols of Blake's major prophetic books, but it clearly appropriates insights from a number of other writers, including Frazer, Freud, and Jung. Frye has been looked on as providing an alternative to the contextualism of the New Critics, but it is perhaps more fruitful to consider his work an attempt to synthesize the interests of that movement with the anthropological and psychoanalytical study of myth and ritual. It is instructive to see how Frye assimilates to this purpose the insights of critics as diverse as Arnold, Eliot, Crane, and Wheelwright.

Frye's critical works include *Fearful Symmetry* (1947), *Anatomy of Criticism* (1957), *The Well-Tempered Critic* (1963), *The Educated Imagination* (1963), *T. S. Eliot* (1963), *Fables of Identity* (1963), *A Natural Perspective* (1965), *The Return of Eden* (1965), *Five Essays on Milton's Epics* (1966), *Fools of Time* (1967), *The Modern Century* (1967), *A Study of English Romanticism* (1968), *The Stubborn Structure* (1970), *The Bush Garden* (1971), *The Critical Path* (1971), *The Secular Scripture* (1976), *Spiritus Mundi* (1976), *Northrop Frye on Culture and Literature* (1978), *Creation and Recreation* (1980), *The Myth of Deliverance* (1981), *The Great Code* (1982), *Divisions on a Ground* (1982), *Northrop Frye on Shakespeare* (1986) and *Northrop Frye on Education* (1988). See Murray Krieger, ed., *Northrop Frye in Modern Criticism* (1966); Ian Balfour, *Northrop Frye* (1988); Ronald Bates, *Northrop Frye* (1971); David Cook, *Northrop Frye: A Vision of the New World* (1985); and Robert Denham, *Northrop Frye and Critical Method* (1978).

From

Anatomy of Criticism

Second Essay

Ethical Criticism: Theory of Symbols

Introduction

Of the problems arising from the lack of a technical vocabulary[1] of poetics, two demand special attention. The fact, already mentioned, that there is no word for a work of literary art is one that I find particularly baffling. One may invoke the authority of Aristotle for using *poem* in this sense, but usage declares that a poem is a composition in meter, and to speak of *Tom Jones* as a poem would be an abuse of ordinary language. One may discuss the question whether great works of prose deserve to be called poetry in some more

extended sense, but the answer can only be a matter of taste in definitions. The attempt to introduce a value judgment into a definition of poetry (e.g., "What, after all, do we mean by a poem—that is, something worthy of the name of poem?") only adds to the confusion. So of course does the antique snobbery about the superiority of meter which has given *prosy* the meaning of tedious and *prosaic* the meaning of pedestrian. As often as I can, I use *poem* and its relatives by synecdoche, because they are short words; but where synecdoche would be confusing, the reader will have to put up with such cacophonous jargon as *hypothetical verbal structure* and the like.

The other matter concerns the use of the word *symbol,* which in this essay means any unit of any literary structure that can be isolated for critical attention. A word, a phrase, or an image used with some kind of special reference (which is what a symbol is usually taken to mean) are all symbols when they are distinguishable elements in critical analysis. Even the letters a writer spells his words with form part of his symbolism in this sense: they would be isolated only in special cases, such as alliteration or dialect spellings, but we are still aware that they symbolize sounds. Criticism as a whole, in terms of this definition, would begin with, and largely consist of, the systematizing of literary symbolism. It follows that other words must be used to classify the different types of symbolism.

For there must be different types: the criticism of literature can hardly be a simple or one-level activity. The more familiar one is with a great work of literature, the more one's

---

ETHICAL CRITICISM: THEORY OF SYMBOLS. The text is from *The Anatomy of Criticism: Four Essays* by Northrop Frye Copyright © 1957, 1985 by Princeton University Press, pp. 71–115. Reprinted by permission of Princeton University Press.

[1][Frye] The revival of the technical language of rhetoric would not only provide us with useful terms, but in many cases would revive the conceptions themselves which have been forgotten along with their names. It may be true that, as Samuel Butler said: ". . . all a rhetorician's rules / Teach nothing but to name his tools" but if a critic cannot name his tools, the world is unlikely to concede much authority to his craft. We should not entrust our cars to a mechanic who lived entirely in a world of gadgets and doohickeys.

understanding of it grows. Further, one has the feeling of growing in the understanding of the work itself, not in the number of things one can attach to it. The conclusion that a work of literary art contains a variety or sequence of meanings seems inescapable. It has seldom, however, been squarely faced in criticism since the Middle Ages, when a precise scheme of literal, allegorical, moral, and anagogic meanings was taken over from theology and applied to literature.[2] Today there is more of a tendency to consider the problem of literary meaning as subsidiary to the problems of symbolic logic and semantics. In what follows I try to work as independently of the latter subjects as I can, on the ground that the obvious place to start looking for a theory of literary meaning is in literature.

The principle of manifold or "polysemous" meaning, as Dante calls it, is not a theory any more, still less an exploded superstition, but an established fact. The thing that has established it is the simultaneous development of several different schools of modern criticism, each making a distinctive choice of symbols in its analysis. The modern student of critical theory is faced with a body of rhetoricians who speak of texture and frontal assaults, with students of history who deal with traditions and sources, with critics using material from psychology and anthropology, with Aristotelians, Coleridgians, Thomists, Freudians, Jungians, Marxists, with students of myths, rituals, archetypes, metaphors, ambiguities, and significant forms. The student must either admit the principle of polysemous meaning, or choose one of these groups and then try to prove that all the others are less legitimate. The former is the way of scholarship, and leads to the advancement of learning; the latter is the way of pedantry, and gives us a wide choice of goals, the most conspicuous today being fantastical learning, or myth criticism, contentious learning, or historical criticism, and delicate learning, or "new" criticism.

Once we have admitted the principle of polysemous meaning, we can either stop with a purely relative and pluralistic position, or we can go on to consider the possibility that there is a finite number of valid critical methods, and that they can all be contained in a single theory. It does not follow that all meanings can be arranged, as the medieval four-level scheme implies, in a hierarchical sequence, in which the first steps are comparatively elementary and apprehension gets more subtle and rarefied as one goes on. The term *level* is used here only for convenience, and should not be taken as indicating any belief on my part in a series of degrees of critical initiation. Again, there is a general reservation to be made about the conception of polysemous meaning: the meaning of a literary work forms a part of a larger whole. In the previous essay we saw that meaning or *dianoia* was one of three elements, the other two being *mythos* or narrative and *ethos* or characterization. It is better to think, therefore, not simply of a sequence of meanings, but of a sequence of contexts or relationships in which the whole work of literary art can be placed, each context having its characteristic *mythos* and *ethos* as well as its *dianoia* or meaning. I call these contexts or relationships *phases*.

Literal and Descriptive Phases: Symbols as Motif and as Sign

Whenever we read anything, we find our attention moving in two directions at once. One direction is outward or centrifugal, in which we keep going outside our reading, from the individual words to the things they mean, or, in practice, to our memory of the conventional association between them. The other direction is inward or centripetal, in which we try to develop from the words a sense of the larger verbal pattern they make. In both cases we deal with symbols, but when we attach an external meaning to a word we have, in addition to the verbal symbol, the thing represented or symbolized by it. Actually we have a series of such representations: the verbal symbol *cat* is a group of black marks on a page representing a sequence of noises representing an image or memory representing a sense experience representing an animal that says meow. Symbols so understood may here be called *signs,* verbal units which, conventionally and arbitrarily, stand for and point to things outside the place where they occur. When we are trying to grasp the context of words, however, the word *cat* is an element in a larger body of meaning. It is not primarily a symbol "of" anything, for in this aspect it does not represent, but connects. We can hardly even say that it represents a part of the author's intention in putting it there, for the author's intention ceases to exist as a separate factor as soon as he has finished revising. Verbal elements understood inwardly or centripetally, as parts of a verbal structure, are, as symbols, simply and literally verbal elements, or units of a verbal structure. (The word *literally* should be kept in mind.) We may, borrowing a term from music, call such elements *motifs.*

These two modes of understanding take place simultaneously in all reading. It is impossible to read the word *cat* in a context without some representational flash of the animal so named; it is impossible to see the bare sign *cat* without wondering what context it belongs to. But verbal structures may be classified according to whether the *final*

---

[2]See Aquinas, *The Nature and Domain of Sacred Doctrine,* pp. 117–19, and Dante, *The Banquet* and his letter to Can Grande della Scala, pp. 120 and 120–22.

direction of meaning is outward or inward. In descriptive or assertive writing the final direction is outward. Here the verbal structure is intended to represent things external to it, and it is valued in terms of the accuracy with which it does represent them. Correspondence between phenomenon and verbal sign is truth; lack of it is falsehood; failure to connect is tautology, a purely verbal structure that cannot come out of itself.

In all literary verbal structures the final direction of meaning is inward. In literature the standards of outward meaning are secondary, for literary works do not pretend to describe or assert, and hence are not true, not false, and yet not tautological either, or at least not in the sense in which such a statement as "the good is better than the bad" is tautological. Literary meaning may best be described, perhaps, as hypothetical, and a hypothetical or assumed relation to the external world is part of what is usually meant by the word *imaginative*. This word is to be distinguished from *imaginary*, which usually refers to an assertive verbal structure that fails to make good its assertions. In literature, questions of fact or truth are subordinated to the primary literary aim of producing a structure of words for its own sake, and the sign-values of symbols are subordinated to their importance as a structure of interconnected motifs. Wherever we have an autonomous verbal structure of this kind, we have literature. Wherever this autonomous structure is lacking, we have language, words used instrumentally to help human consciousness do or understand something else. Literature is a specialized form of language, as language is of communication.

The reason for producing the literary structure is apparently that the inward meaning, the self-contained verbal pattern, is the field of the responses connected with pleasure, beauty, and interest. The contemplation of a detached pattern, whether of words or not, is clearly a major source of the sense of the beautiful, and of the pleasure that accompanies it. The fact that interest is most easily aroused by such a pattern is familiar to every handler of words, from the poet to the after-dinner speaker who digresses from an assertive harangue to present the self-contained structure of verbal interrelationships known as a joke. It often happens that an originally descriptive piece of writing, such as the histories of Fuller and Gibbon, survives by virtue of its "style," or interesting verbal pattern, after its value as a representation of facts has faded.

The old precept that poetry is designed to delight and instruct sounds like an awkward hendiadys, as we do not usually feel that a poem does two different things to us, but we can understand it when we relate it to these two aspects of symbolism. In literature, what entertains is prior to what instructs, or, as we may say, the reality-principle is subordinate to the pleasure-principle. In assertive verbal structures the priority is reversed. Neither factor can, of course, ever be eliminated from any kind of writing.

One of the most familiar and important features of literature is the absence of a controlling aim of descriptive accuracy. We should, perhaps, like to feel that the writer of a historical drama knew what the historical facts of his theme were, and that he would not alter them without good reason. But that such good reasons may exist in literature is not denied by anyone. They seem to exist only there: the historian selects his facts, but to suggest that he had manipulated them to produce a more symmetrical structure would be grounds for libel. Some other types of verbal structures, such as theology and metaphysics, are declared by some to be centripetal in final meaning, and hence to be tautological ("purely verbal"). I have no opinion on this, except that in literary criticism theology and metaphysics must be treated as assertive, because they are outside literature, and everything that influences literature from without creates a centrifugal movement in it, whether it is directed toward the nature of absolute being or advice on the raising of hops. It is clear, too, that the proportion between the sense of being pleasantly entertained and the sense of being instructed, or awakened to reality, will vary in different forms of literature. The sense of reality is, for instance, far higher in tragedy than in comedy, as in comedy the logic of events normally gives way to the audience's desire for a happy ending.

The apparently unique privilege of ignoring facts has given the poet his traditional reputation as a licensed liar, and explains why so many words denoting literary structure, *fable, fiction, myth,* and the like, have a secondary sense of untruth, like the Norwegian word *digter* which is said to mean liar as well as poet. But, as Sir Philip Sidney remarked, "the poet never affirmeth,"[3] and therefore does not lie any more than he tells the truth. The poet, like the pure mathematician, depends, not on descriptive truth, but on conformity to his hypothetical postulates. The appearance of a ghost in *Hamlet* presents the hypothesis "let there be a ghost in *Hamlet.*" It has nothing to do with whether ghosts exist or not, or whether Shakespeare or his audience thought they did. A reader who quarrels with postulates, who dislikes *Hamlet* because he does not believe that there are ghosts or that people speak in pentameters, clearly has no business in literature. He cannot distinguish fiction from fact, and belongs in the same category as the people who send checks to radio stations for the relief of suffering heroines in soap operas. We may note here, as the point will be important later,

---

[3]See *An Apology for Poetry,* p. 155.

that the accepted postulate, the contract agreed on by the reader before he can start reading, is the same thing as a convention.

The person who cannot be brought to understand literary convention is often said to be "literal-minded." But as *literal* surely ought to have some connection with letters, it seems curious to use the phrase *literal-minded* for imaginative illiterates. The reason for the anomaly is interesting, and important to our argument. Traditionally, the phrase *literal meaning* refers to descriptive meaning that is free from ambiguity. We usually say that the word cat "means literally" a cat when it is an adequate sign for a cat, when it stands in a simple representative relation to the animal that says meow. This sense of the term literal comes down from medieval times, and may be due to the theological origin of critical categories. In theology, the literal meaning of Scripture is usually the historical meaning, its accuracy as a record of facts or truths. Dante says, commenting on the verse in the Psalms, "When Israel went out of Egypt," "considering the letter only, the exodus of the Israelites to Palestine in the time of Moses is what is signified to us (*significatur nobis*)."[4] The word *signified* shows that the literal meaning here is the simplest kind of descriptive or representational meaning, as it would still be to a biblical "literalist."

But this conception of literal meaning as simple descriptive meaning will not do at all for literary criticism. An historical event cannot be literally anything but an historical event; a prose narrative describing it cannot be literally anything but a prose narrative. The literal meaning of Dante's own *Commedia* is not historical, not at any rate a *simple* description of what "really happened" to Dante. And if a poem cannot be literally anything but a poem, then the literal basis of meaning in poetry can only be its letters, its inner structure of interlocking motifs. We are always wrong, in the context of criticism, when we say "this poem means literally"—and then give a prose paraphrase of it. All paraphrases abstract a secondary or outward meaning. Understanding a poem literally means understanding the whole of it, as a poem, and as it stands. Such understanding begins in a complete surrender of the mind and senses to the impact of the work as a whole, and proceeds through the effort to unite the symbols toward a simultaneous perception of the unity of the structure. (This is a *logical* sequence of critical elements, the *integritas, consonantia,* and *claritas* of Stephen's argument in Joyce's *Portrait.* I have no idea what the psychological sequence is, or whether there is a sequence—I suppose there would not be in a *Gestalt* theory.) Literal understanding oc-

cupies the same place in criticism that observation, the direct exposure of the mind to nature, has in the scientific method. "Every poem must necessarily be a perfect unity," says Blake:[5] this, as the wording implies, is not a statement of fact about all existing poems, but a statement of the hypothesis which every reader adopts in first trying to comprehend even the most chaotic poem ever written.

Some principle of recurrence seems to be fundamental to all works of art, and this recurrence is usually spoken of as rhythm when it moves along in time, and as pattern when it is spread out in space. Thus we speak of the rhythm of music and the pattern of painting. But a slight increase of sophistication will soon start us talking about the pattern of music and the rhythm of painting. The inference is that all arts possess both a temporal and a spatial aspect, whichever takes the lead when they are presented. The score of a symphony may be studied all at once, as a spread-out pattern: a painting may be studied as the track of an intricate dance of the eye. Works of literature also move in time like music and spread out in images like painting. The word *narrative* or *mythos* conveys the sense of movement caught by the ear, and the word *meaning* or *dianoia* conveys, or at least preserves, the sense of simultaneity caught by the eye. We *listen to* the poem as it moves from beginning to end, but as soon as the whole of it is in our minds at once we "see" what it means. More exactly, this response is not simply to *the* whole *of* it, but to *a* whole *in* it: we have a vision of meaning or *dianoia* whenever any simultaneous apprehension is possible.

Now as a poem is literally a poem, it belongs, in its literal context, to the class of things called poems, which in their turn form part of the larger class known as works of art. The poem from this point of view presents a flow of sounds approximating music on one side, and an integrated pattern of imagery approximating the pictorial on the other. Literally, then, a poem's narrative is its rhythm or movement of words. If a dramatist writes a speech in prose, and then rewrites it in blank verse, he has made a strategic rhythmical change, and therefore a change in the literal narrative. Even if he alters *came a day* to *a day came* he has still made a tiny alteration of sequence, and so, literally, of his rhythm and narrative. Similarly, a poem's meaning is literally its pattern or integrity as a verbal structure. Its words cannot be separated and attached to sign-values: all possible sign-values of a word are absorbed into a complexity of verbal relationships.

---

[4]See his letter to Can Grande della Scala, p. 121.

[5]See *On Homer's Poetry,* p. 414.

The word's meaning is therefore, from the centripetal or inward-meaning point of view, variable or ambiguous, to use a term now familiar in criticism, a term which, significantly enough, is pejorative when applied to assertive writing. The word *wit* is said to be employed in Pope's *Essay on Criticism* in nine different senses.[6] In assertive writing, such a semantic theme with variations could produce nothing but hopeless muddle. In poetry, it indicates the ranges of meanings and contexts that a word may have. The poet does not equate a word with a meaning; he establishes the functions or powers of words. But when we look at the symbols of a poem as verbal *signs,* the poem appears in a different context altogether, and so do its narrative and meaning. Descriptively, a poem is not primarily a work of art, but primarily a *verbal* structure or set of representative words, to be classed with other verbal structures like books on gardening. In this context narrative means the relation of the order of words to events resembling the events in "life" outside; meaning means the relation of its pattern to a body of assertive propositions, and the conception of symbolism involved is the one which literature has in common, not with the arts, but with other structures in words.

A considerable amount of abstraction enters at this stage. When we think of a poem's narrative as a description of events, we no longer think of the narrative as literally embracing every word and letter. We think rather of a sequence of gross events, of the obvious and externally striking elements in the word order. Similarly, we think of meaning as the kind of discursive meaning that a prose paraphrase of the poem might reproduce. Hence a parallel abstraction comes into the conception of symbolism. On the literal level, where the symbols are motifs, any unit whatever, down to the letters, may be relevant to our understanding. But only large and striking symbols are likely to be treated critically as signs: nouns and verbs, and phrases built up out of important words. Prepositions and conjunctions are almost pure connectives. A dictionary, which is primarily a table of conventional sign-values, can tell us nothing about such words unless we already understand them.

So literature in its descriptive context is a body of hypothetical verbal structures. The latter stand between the verbal structures that describe or arrange actual events, or histories, and those that describe or arrange actual ideas or represent physical objects, like the verbal structures of philosophy and science. The relation of the spatial to the conceptual world is one that we obviously cannot examine here; but from the point of view of literary criticism, descriptive

writing and didactic writing, the representation of natural objects and of ideas, are simply two different branches of centrifugal meaning. We may use the word *plot* or *story* for the sequence of gross events, and the connection of story with history is indicated in its etymology. But it is more difficult to use *thought,* or even *thought-content,* for the representational aspect of pattern, or gross meaning, because *thought* also describes what we are here trying to distinguish it from. Such are the problems of a vocabulary of poetics.

The literal and the descriptive phases of symbolism are, of course, present in every work of literature. But we find (as we shall also find with the other phases) that each phase has a particularly close relationship to a certain kind of literature, and to a certain type of critical procedure as well. Literature deeply influenced by the descriptive aspect of symbolism is likely to tend toward the realistic in its narrative and toward the didactic or descriptive in its meaning. Its prevailing rhythm will be the prose of direct speech, and its main effort will be to give as clear and honest an impression of external reality as is possible with a hypothetical structure. In the documentary naturalism generally associated with such names as Zola and Dreiser, literature goes about as far as a representation of life, to be judged by its accuracy of description rather than by its integrity as a structure of words, as it could go and still remain literature. Beyond this point, the hypothetical or fictional element in literature would begin to dissolve. The limits of literary expression of this type are, of course, very wide, and nearly all the great empire of realistic poetry, drama, and prose fiction lies well within them. But we notice that the great age of documentary naturalism, the nineteenth century, was also the age of Romantic poetry, which, by concentrating on the process of imaginative creation, indicated a feeling of tension between the hypothetical and the assertive elements in literature.

This tension finally snaps off in the movement generally called *symbolisme,* a term which we expand here to take in the whole tradition which develops with a broad consistency through Mallarmé and Rimbaud to Valéry in France, Rilke in Germany, and Pound and Eliot in England. In the theory of *symbolisme* we have the complement to extreme naturalism, an emphasis on the literal aspect of meaning, and a treatment of literature as centripetal verbal pattern, in which elements of direct or verifiable statement are subordinated to the integrity of that pattern. The conception of "pure" poetry, or evocative verbal structure injured by assertive meaning, was a minor by-product of the same movement. The great strength of *symbolisme* was that it succeeded in isolating the hypothetical germ of literature, however limited it may have been in its earlier stages by its tendency to equate this isolation with the entire creative process. All its

---

characteristics are solidly based on its conception of poetry as concerned with the centripetal aspect of meaning. Thus the achieving of an acceptable theory of literal meaning in criticism rests on a relatively recent development in literature.

Symbolisme, as expressed for instance in Mallarmé, maintains that the representational answer to the question, what does this mean? should not be pressed in reading poetry, for the poetic symbol means primarily itself in relation to the poem. The unity of a poem, then, is best apprehended as a unity of mood, a mood being a phase of emotion, and emotion being the ordinary word for the state of mind directed toward the experiencing of pleasure or the contemplating of beauty. And as moods are not long sustained, literature, for *symbolisme,* is essentially discontinuous, longer poems being held together only by the use of the grammatical structures more appropriate to descriptive writing. Poetic images do not state or point to anything, but, by pointing to each other, they suggest or evoke the mood which informs the poem. That is, they express or articulate the mood. The emotion is not chaotic or inarticulate: it merely would have remained so if it had not turned into a poem, and when it does so, it *is* the poem, not something else still behind it. Nevertheless the words suggest and evoke are appropriate, because in *symbolisme* the word does not echo the thing but other words, and hence the immediate impact *symbolisme* makes on the reader is that of incantation, a harmony of sounds and the sense of a growing richness of meaning unlimited by denotation.

Some philosophers who assume that all meaning is descriptive meaning tell us that, as a poem does not describe things rationally, it must be a description of an emotion. According to this the literal core of poetry would be a *cri de coeur,*[7] to use the elegant expression, the direct statement of a nervous organism confronted with something that seems to demand an emotional response, like a dog howling at the moon. *L'Allegro* and *Il Penseroso* would be respectively, according to this theory, elaborations of "I feel happy" and "I feel pensive." We have found, however, that the real core of poetry is a subtle and elusive verbal pattern that avoids, and does not lead to, such bald statements. We notice too that in the history of literature the riddle, the oracle, the spell, and the kenning are more primitive than a presentation of subjective feelings. The critics who tell us that the basis of poetic expression is irony,[8] or a pattern of words that turns away

from obvious (i.e., descriptive) meaning, are much closer to the facts of literary experience, at least on the literal level. The literary structure is ironic because "what it says" is always different in kind or degree from "what it means." In discursive writing what is said tends to approximate, ideally to become identified with, what is meant.

The criticism as well as the creation of literature reflects the distinction between literal and descriptive aspects of symbolism. The type of criticism associated with research and learned journals treats the poem as a verbal document, to be related as fully as possible to the history and the ideas that it reflects. The poem is most valuable to this kind of criticism when it is most explicit and descriptive, and when its core of imaginative hypothesis can be most easily separated. (Note that I am speaking of a kind of criticism, not of a kind of critic.) What is now called "new criticism,"[9] on the other hand, is largely criticism based on the conception of a poem as literally a poem. It studies the symbolism of a poem as an ambiguous structure of interlocking motifs; it sees the poetic pattern of meaning as a self-contained "texture," and it thinks of the external relations of a poem as being with the other arts, to be approached only with the Horatian warning of *favete linguis,*[10] and not with the historical or the didactic. The word *texture,* with its overtones of a complicated surface, is a most expressive one for this approach. These two aspects of criticism are often thought of as antithetical, as were, in the previous century, the corresponding groups of writers. They are of course complementary, not antithetical, but still the difference in emphasis between them is important to grasp before we go on to try to resolve the antithesis in a third phase of symbolism.

Formal Phase: Symbol as Image

We have now established a new sense of the term *literal meaning* for literary criticism, and have also assigned to literature, as one of its subordinate aspects of meaning, the ordinary descriptive meaning that works of literature share with all other structures of words. But it seems unsatisfactory to stop with this quizzical antithesis between delight and instruction, ironic withdrawal from reality and explicit connection with it. Surely, it will be said, we have overlooked the essential unity, in works of literature, expressed by the commonest of all critical terms, the word *form.* For the usual

---

[7]"Cry of the heart."
[8]See especially Brooks, *Irony as a Principle of Structure,* pp. 968–74.

[9][Frye] The account of literal meaning given here depends on I. A. Richards, Richard Blackmur, William Empson (ambiguity), Cleanth Brooks (literal irony), and John Crowe Ransom (texture) in particular.
[10]"Don't speak badly!"

associations of *form*[11] seem to combine these apparently contradictory aspects. On the one hand, form implies what we have called the literal meaning, or unity of structure; on the other, it implies such complementary terms as content and matter, expressive of what it shares with external nature. The poem is not natural in form, but it relates itself naturally to nature, and so, to quote Sidney again, "doth grow in effect a second nature."[12]

Here we reach a more unified conception of narrative and meaning. Aristotle speaks of *mimesis praxeos,* an imitation of an action,[13] and it appears that he identifies this *mimesis praxeos* with *mythos.* Aristotle's greatly abbreviated account here needs some reconstruction. Human action *(praxis)* is primarily imitated by histories, or verbal structures that describe specific and particular actions. A *mythos* is a secondary imitation of an action, which means, not that it is at two removes from reality, but that it describes typical actions, being more philosophical than history. Human thought *(theoria)* is primarily imitated by discursive writing, which makes specific and particular predications. A *dianoia* is a secondary imitation of thought, a *mimesis logou,* concerned with typical thought, with the images, metaphors, diagrams, and verbal ambiguities out of which specific ideas develop. Poetry is thus more historical than philosophy, more involved in images and examples. For it is clear that all verbal structures with meaning are verbal imitations of that elusive psychological and physiological process known as thought, a process stumbling through emotional entanglements, sudden irrational convictions, involuntary gleams of insight, rationalized prejudices, and blocks of panic and inertia, finally to reach a completely incommunicable intuition. Anyone who imagines that philosophy is not a verbal imitation of this process, but the process itself, has clearly not done much thinking.

The form of a poem, that to which every detail relates, is the same whether it is examined as stationary or as moving through the work from beginning to end, just as a musical composition has the same form when we study the score as it has when we listen to the performance. The *mythos* is the *dianoia* in movement; the *dianoia* is the *mythos* in stasis. One reason why we tend to think of literary symbolism solely in terms of meaning is that we have ordinarily no word for the *moving* body of imagery in a work of literature. The word *form* has normally two complementary terms, *matter*

and *content,* and it perhaps makes some distinction whether we think of form as a shaping principle or as a containing one. As shaping principle, it may be thought of as narrative, organizing temporally what Milton called, in an age of more exact terminology, the "matter" of his song. As containing principle it may be thought of as meaning, holding the poem together in a simultaneous structure.

The literary standards generally called "classical" or "neoclassical," which prevailed in Western Europe from the sixteenth to the eighteenth centuries, have the closest affinity with this formal phase. Order and clarity are particularly emphasized: order because of the sense of the importance of grasping a central form, and clarity because of the feeling that this form must not dissolve or withdraw into ambiguity, but must preserve a continuous relationship to the nature which is its own content. It is the attitude characteristic of "humanism" in the historical sense, an attitude marked on the one hand by a devotion to rhetoric and verbal craftsmanship, and on the other by a strong attachment to historical and ethical affairs.

Writers typical of the formal phase—Ben Jonson for instance—are sure that they are in contact with reality and that they follow nature, yet the effect they produce is quite different from the descriptive realism of the nineteenth century, the difference being largely in the conception of imitation involved. In formal imitation, or Aristotelian mimesis, the work of art does not reflect external events and ideas, but exists between the example and the precept. Events and ideas are now aspects of its content, not external fields of observation. Historical fictions are not designed to give insight into a period of history, but are exemplary; they illustrate action, and are ideal in the sense of manifesting the universal form of human action. (The vagaries of language make *exemplary* the adjective for both example and precept.) Shakespeare and Jonson were keenly interested in history, yet their plays seem timeless: Jane Austen did not write historical fiction, yet, because she represents a later and more externalized method of following nature, the picture she gives of Regency society has a specific historical value.

A poem, according to Hamlet, who, though speaking of action, is following a conventional Renaissance line of poetics, holds the mirror up to nature. We should be careful to notice what this implies: the poem is not itself a mirror. It does not merely reproduce a shadow of nature; it causes nature to be reflected in its containing form. When the formal critic comes to deal with symbols, therefore, the units he isolates are those which show an analogy of proportion between the poem and the nature which it imitates. The symbol in this aspect may best be called the image. We are accustomed to associate the term *nature* primarily with the external physi-

---

[11][Frye] For the theory of the formal phase, I have been considerably indebted to R. S. Crane, *The Languages of Criticism and the Structure of Poetry* (1953), as well as to *Critics and Criticism* (1952), edited by him.
[12]*An Apology for Poetry,* p. 145.
[13]*Poetics,* VII. 2, p. 54.

cal world, and hence we tend to think of an image as primarily a replica of a natural object. But of course both words are far more inclusive: nature takes in the conceptual or intelligible order as well as the spatial one, and what is usually called an idea may be a poetic image also.

One could hardly find a more elementary critical principle than the fact that the events of a literary fiction are not real but hypothetical events. For some reason it has never been consistently understood that the ideas of literature are not real propositions, but verbal formulas which imitate real propositions. The *Essay on Man* does not expound a system of metaphysical optimism founded on the chain of being: it uses such a system as a model on which to construct a series of hypothetical statements which are more or less useless as propositions, but inexhaustibly rich and suggestive when read in their proper context as epigrams. As epigrams, as solid, resonant, centripetal verbal structures, they may apply pointedly to millions of human situations which have nothing to do with metaphysical optimism. Wordsworth's pantheism, Dante's Thomism, Lucretius' Epicureanism, all have to be read in the same way, as do Gibbon or Macaulay or Hume when they are read for style instead of subject matter.

Formal criticism begins with an examination of the imagery of a poem, with a view to bringing out its distinctive pattern. The recurring or most frequently repeated images form the tonality, so to speak, and the modulating, episodic and isolated images relate themselves to this in a hierarchic structure which is the critical analogy to the proportions of the poem itself. Every poem has its peculiar spectroscopic band of imagery, caused by the requirements of its genre, the predilections of its author, and countless other factors. In *Macbeth,* for instance, the images of blood and of sleeplessness have a thematic importance, as is very natural for a tragedy of murder and remorse. Hence in the line "Making the green one red,"[14] the colors are of different thematic intensities. Green is used incidentally and for contrast; red, being closer to the *key* of the play as a whole, is more like the repetition of a tonic chord in music. The opposite would be true of the contrast between red and green in Marvell's *The Garden.*

The form of the poem is the same whether it is studied as narrative or as meaning, hence the structure of imagery in *Macbeth* may be studied as a pattern derived from the text, or as a rhythm of repetition falling on an audience's ear. There is a vague notion that the latter method produces a simpler result, and may therefore be used as a common-sense corrective to the niggling subtleties of textual study. The analogy of music again may be helpful. The average audience at a symphony knows very little about sonata form, and misses practically all the subtleties detected by an analysis of the score; yet those subtleties are really there, and as the audience can hear everything that is being played, it gets them all as part of a linear experience; the awareness is less conscious, but not less real. The same is true of the response to the imagery of a highly concentrated poetic drama.

The analysis of recurrent imagery is, of course, one of the chief techniques of rhetorical or "new" criticism as well: the difference is that formal criticism, after attaching the imagery to the central form of the poem, renders an aspect of the form into the propositions of discursive writing. Formal criticism, in other words, is commentary, and commentary is the process of translating into explicit or discursive language what is implicit in the poem. Good commentary naturally does not read ideas into the poem; it reads and translates what is there, and the evidence that it is there is offered by the study of the structure of imagery with which it begins. The sense of tact, of the desirability of not pushing a point of interpretation "too far," is derived from the fact that the proportioning of emphasis in criticism should normally bear a rough analogy to the proportioning of emphasis in the poem.

The failure to make, in practice, the most elementary of all distinctions in literature, the distinction between fiction and fact, hypothesis and assertion, imaginative and discursive writing, produces what in criticism has been called the "intentional fallacy,"[15] the notion that the poet has a primary intention of conveying meaning to a reader, and that the first duty of a critic is to recapture that intention. The word *intention* is analogical: it implies a relation between two things, usually a conception and an act. Some related terms show this duality even more clearly: to *aim at* something means that a target and a missile are being brought into alignment. Hence such terms properly belong only to discursive writing, where the correspondence of a verbal pattern with what it describes is of primary importance. But a poet's primary concern is to produce a work of art, and hence his intention can only be expressed by some kind of tautology.

In other words, a poet's intention is centripetally directed. It is directed towards putting words together, not towards aligning words with meanings. If we had the privilege of Gulliver in Glubbdubdrib to call up the ghost of, say, Shakespeare, to ask him what he meant by such and such a passage, we could only get, with maddening iteration, the same answer: "I meant it to form part of the play." One may

---

[14]II. ii. 63.

[15]See Wimsatt and Beardsley, *The Intentional Fallacy,* pp. 945–52.

pursue the centripetal intention as far as genre, as a poet intends to produce, not simply a poem, but a certain kind of poem. In reading, for instance, *Zuleika Dobson* as a description of life in Oxford, we should be well advised to allow for ironic intention. One has to assume, as an essential heuristic axiom, that the work as produced constitutes the definitive record of the writer's intention. For many of the flaws which an inexperienced critic thinks he detects, the answer "But it's supposed to be that way" is sufficient. All other statements of intention, however fully documented, are suspect. The poet may change his mind or mood; he may have intended one thing and done another, and then rationalized what he did. (A cartoon in a *New Yorker* of some years back hit off this last problem beautifully: it depicted a sculptor gazing at a statue he had just made and remarking to a friend: "Yes, the head is too large. When I put it in exhibition I shall call it 'The Woman with the Large Head.' ") If intention is still thought to be apparent in the poem itself, the poem is being regarded as incomplete, like a freshman's essay where the reader has continually to speculate about what the author may have had in his mind. If the author has been dead for centuries, such speculation cannot get us very far, however irresistibly it may suggest itself.

What the poet meant to say, then, is, literally, the poem itself; what he meant to say in any given passage is, in its literal meaning, part of the poem. But literal meaning, we have seen, is variable and ambiguous. The reader may be dissatisfied with the ghost of Shakespeare's answer: he may feel that Shakespeare, unlike, say, Mallarmé, is a poet he can trust, and that he also meant his passage to be intelligible in itself (i.e., have descriptive or rephrasable meaning). Doubtless he did, but the relationship of the passage to the rest of the play creates myriads of new meanings for it. Just as a vivid sketch of a cat by a good draftsman may contain in a few crisp lines the entire feline experience of everyone who looks at it, so the powerfully constructed pattern of words that we know as *Hamlet* may contain an amount of meaning which the vast and constantly growing library of criticism on the play cannot begin to exhaust. Commentary, which translates the implicit into the explicit, can only isolate the aspect of meaning, large or small, which is appropriate or interesting for certain readers to grasp at a certain time. Such translation is an activity with which the poet has very little to do. The relation in bulk between commentary and a sacred book, such as the Bible or the Vedic hymns, is even more striking, and indicates that when a poetic structure attains a certain degree of concentration or social recognition, the amount of commentary it will carry is infinite. This fact is in itself no more incredible than the fact that a scientist can state a law illustrated by more phenomena than he could ever observe

or count, and there is no occasion for wondering, like the yokels in Goldsmith, how one small poet's head can carry the amount of wit, wisdom, instruction, and significance that Shakespeare and Dante have given the world.

Still there is a genuine mystery in art, and a real place for wonder. In *Sartor Resartus* Carlyle distinguishes extrinsic symbols,[16] like the cross or the national flag, which are without value in themselves but are signs or indicators of something existential, from intrinsic symbols, which include works of art. On this basis we may distinguish two kinds of mystery. (A third kind, the mystery which is a puzzle, a problem to be solved and annihilated, belongs to discursive thought, and has little to do with the arts, except in matters of technique.) The mystery of the unknown or unknowable essence is an extrinsic mystery, which involves art only when art is also made illustrative of something else, as religious art is to the person concerned primarily with worship. But the intrinsic mystery is that which remains a mystery in itself no matter how fully known it is, and hence is not a mystery separated from what is known. The mystery in the greatness of *King Lear* or *Macbeth* comes not from concealment but from revelation, not from something unknown or unknowable in the work, but from something unlimited in it.

It could be said, of course, that poetry is the product, not only of a deliberate and voluntary act of consciousness, like discursive writing, but of processes which are subconscious or preconscious or half-conscious or unconscious as well, whatever psychological metaphor one prefers. It takes a great deal of will power to write poetry, but part of that will power must be employed in trying to relax the will, so making a large part of one's writing involuntary. This is no doubt true, and it is also true that poetic technique, like all technique, is a habitual, and therefore an increasingly unconscious, skill. But I feel that literary data are in the long run only explicable within criticism, and I am reluctant to explain literary facts by psychological clichés. Still, it seems now almost impossible to avoid the term *creative,* with all the biological analogies it suggests, when speaking of the arts. And creation, whether of God, man, or nature, seems to be an activity whose only intention is to abolish intention, to eliminate final dependence on or relation to something else, to destroy the shadow that falls between itself and its conception.

One wishes that literary criticism had a Samuel Butler to formulate some of the paradoxes involved in this parallel between the work of art and the organism. We can describe objectively what happens when a tulip blooms in spring and

---

[16]See *Symbols,* p. 548.

a chrysanthemum in autumn, but we cannot describe it from the inside of the plant, except by metaphors derived from human consciousness and ascribed to some agent like God or nature or environment or *élan vital,* or to the plant itself. It is projected metaphor to say that a flower "knows" when it is time for it to bloom, and of course to say that "nature knows" is merely to import a faded mother-goddess cult into biology. I can well understand that in their own field biologists would find such teleological metaphors both unnecessary and confusing, a fallacy of misplaced concreteness. The same would be true of criticism to the extent that criticism has to deal with imponderables other than consciousness or logically directed will. If one critic says that another has discovered a mass of subtleties in a poet of which that poet was probably quite unconscious, the phrase points up the biological analogy. A snowflake is probably quite unconscious of forming a crystal, but what it does may be worth study even if we are willing to leave its inner mental processes alone.

It is not often realized that all commentary is allegorical interpretation, an attaching of ideas to the structure of poetic imagery. The instant that any critic permits himself to make a genuine comment about a poem (e.g., "In *Hamlet* Shakespeare appears to be portraying the tragedy of irresolution") he has begun to allegorize. Commentary thus looks at literature as, in its formal phase, a potential allegory of events and ideas. The relation of such commentary to poetry itself is the source of the contrast which was developed by several critics of the Romantic period between *symbolism* and *allegory,*[17] symbolism here being used in the sense of thematically significant imagery. The contrast is between a "concrete" approach to symbols which begins with images of actual things and works outward to ideas and propositions, and an "abstract" approach which begins with the idea and then tries to find a concrete image to represent it. This distinction is valid enough in itself, but it has deposited a large terminal moraine of confusion in modern criticism, largely because the term *allegory* is very loosely employed for a great variety of literary phenomena.

We have actual allegory when a poet explicitly indicates the relationship of his images to examples and precepts, and so tries to indicate how a commentary on him should proceed. A writer is being allegorical whenever it is clear that he is saying "by this I *also (allos)* mean that." If this seems to be done continuously, we may say, cautiously, that what he is writing "is" an allegory. In *The Faerie Queene,* for instance, the narrative systematically refers to historical examples and the meaning to moral precepts, besides doing their own work in the poem. Allegory, then, is a contrapuntal technique, like canonical imitation in music. Dante, Spenser, Tasso, and Bunyan use it throughout: their works are the masses and oratorios of literature. Ariosto, Goethe, Ibsen, Hawthorne write in a *freistimmige* style in which allegory may be picked up and dropped again at pleasure. But even continuous allegory is still a structure of images, not of disguised ideas, and commentary has to proceed with it exactly as it does with all other literature, trying to see what precepts and examples are suggested by the imagery as a whole.

The commenting critic is often prejudiced against allegory without knowing the real reason, which is that continuous allegory prescribes the direction of his commentary, and so restricts its freedom. Hence he often urges us to read Spenser and Bunyan, for example, for the story alone and let the allegory go, meaning by that that he regards his own type of commentary as more interesting. Or else he will frame a definition of allegory that will exclude the poems he likes. Such a critic is often apt to treat all allegory as though it were naive allegory, or the translation of ideas into images.

Naive allegory is a disguised form of discursive writing, and belongs chiefly to educational literature on an elementary level: schoolroom moralities, devotional exempla, local pageants, and the like. Its basis is the habitual or customary ideas fostered by education and ritual, and its normal form is that of transient spectacle. Under the excitement of a particular occasion familiar ideas suddenly become sense experiences, and vanish with the occasion. The defeat of Sedition and Discord by Sound Government and Encouragement of Trade would be the right sort of theme for a pageant designed only to entertain a visiting monarch for half an hour. The apparatus of "mass media" and "audiovisual aids" plays a similar allegorical role in contemporary education. Because of this basis in spectacle, naive allegory has its center of gravity in the pictorial arts and is most successful as art when recognized to be a form of occasional wit, as it is in the political cartoon. The more solemn and permanent naive allegories of official murals and statuary show a marked tendency to date.

At one extreme of commentary, then, there is the naive allegory so anxious to make its own allegorical points that it has no real literary or hypothetical center. When I say that naive allegory *dates,* I mean that any allegory which resists a primary analysis of imagery—that is, an allegory which is simply discursive writing with an illustrative image or two stuck into it—will have to be treated less as literature than as a document in the history of ideas. When the author of II

---

[17]See Blake's letter to Thomas Butts, p. 401; Coleridge, *The Statesman's Manual,* pp. 476; and Carlyle, *Symbols,* pp. 546–49.

Esdras, for instance, introduces an allegorical vision of an eagle, and then says, "Behold, on the right side there arose one feather, which reigned over all the earth," it is clear that he is not sufficiently interested in his eagle as a poetic image to remain within the normal boundaries of literary expression. The basis of poetic expression is the metaphor, and the basis of naive allegory is the mixed metaphor.

Within the boundaries of literature we find a kind of sliding scale, ranging from the most explicitly allegorical, consistent with being literature at all, at one extreme, to the most elusive, antiexplicit and antiallegorical at the other. First we meet the continuous allegories, like *The Pilgrim's Progress* and *The Faerie Queene,* and then the free-style allegories just mentioned. Next come the poetic structures with a large and insistent doctrinal interest, in which the internal fictions are exempla, like the epics of Milton. Then we have, in the exact center, works in which the structure of imagery, however suggestive, has an implicit relation only to events and ideas, and which includes the bulk of Shakespeare. Below this, poetic imagery begins to recede from example and precept and become increasingly ironic and paradoxical. Here the modern critic begins to feel more at home, the reason being that this type is more consistent with the modern literal view of art, the sense of the poem as withdrawn from explicit statement.

Several types of this ironic and antiallegorical imagery are familiar. One is the typical symbol of the metaphysical school of the Baroque period, the "conceit" or deliberately strained union of normally disparate things. The paradoxical techniques of metaphysical poetry are based on a sense of the breakdown of the internal relation of art and nature into an external one. Another is the substitute image of *symbolisme,* part of a technique for suggesting or evoking things and avoiding the explicit naming of them. Still another is the kind of image described by Mr. Eliot as an objective correlative,[18] the image that sets up an inward focus of emotion in poetry and at the same time substitutes itself for an idea. Still another, closely related to if not identical with the objective correlative, is the heraldic symbol, the central emblematic image which comes most readily to mind when we think of the word *symbol* in modern literature. We think, for example, of Hawthorne's scarlet letter, Melville's white whale, James's golden bowl, or Virginia Woolf's lighthouse. Such an image differs from the image of the formal allegory in that there is no continuous relationship between art and nature. In contrast to the allegorical symbols of Spenser, for instance, the heraldic emblematic image is in a paradoxical and

ironic relation to both narrative and meaning. As a unit of meaning, it arrests the narrative; as a unit of narrative, it perplexes the meaning. It combines the qualities of Carlyle's intrinsic symbol with significance in itself, and the extrinsic symbol which points quizzically to something else. It is a technique of symbolism which is based on a strong sense of a lurking antagonism between the literal and the descriptive aspects of symbols, the same antagonism that made Mallarmé and Zola so extreme a contrast in nineteenth-century literature.

Below this we run into still more indirect techniques, such as private association, symbolism intended not to be fully understood, the deliberate spoofing of Dadaism, and kindred signs of another approaching boundary of literary expression. We should try to keep this whole range of possible commentary clearly in mind, so as to correct the perspective both of the medieval and Renaissance critics who assumed that all major poetry should be treated as far as possible as continuous allegory, and of the modern ones who maintain that poetry is essentially anti-allegorical and paradoxical.

What we have now is a conception of literature as a body of hypothetical creations which is not necessarily involved in the worlds of truth and fact, not necessarily withdrawn from them, but which may enter into any kind of relationship to them, ranging from the most to the least explicit. We are strongly reminded of the relationship of mathematics to the natural sciences. Mathematics, like literature, proceeds hypothetically and by internal consistency, not descriptively and by outward fidelity to nature. When it is applied to external facts, it is not its truth but its applicability that is being verified. As I seem to have fastened on the cat for my semantic emblem in this essay, I note that this point comes out sharply in the discussion between Yeats and Sturge Moore over the problem of Ruskin's cat, the animal that was picked up and flung out of a window by Ruskin although it was not there.[19] Anyone measuring his mind against an external reality has to fall back on an axiom of faith. The distinction between an empirical fact and an illusion is not a rational distinction, and cannot be logically proved. It is "proved" only by the practical and emotional necessity of assuming the distinction. For the poet, qua poet, this necessity does not exist, and there is no poetic reason why he should either assert or deny the existence of any cat, real or Ruskinian.

---

[18]See *Hamlet and His Problems,* p. 766.

[19][Frye] See *W. B. Yeats and T. Sturge Moore: Their Correspondence, 1901–1937* (1953).

The conception of art as having a relation to reality which is neither direct nor negative, but potential, finally resolves the dichotomy between delight and instruction, the style and the message. "Delight" is not readily distinguishable from pleasure, and hence opens the way to that aesthetic hedonism we glanced at in the introduction, the failure to distinguish personal and impersonal aspects of valuation. The traditional theory of catharsis implies that the emotional response to art is not the raising of an actual emotion, but the raising and casting out of actual emotion on a wave of something else. We may call this something else, perhaps, exhilaration or exuberance: the vision of something liberated from experience, the response kindled in the reader by the transmutation of experience into mimesis, of life into art, of routine into play. At the center of liberal education something surely ought to get liberated. The metaphor of creation suggests the parallel image of birth, the emergence of a new-born organism into independent life. The ecstasy of creation and its response produce, on one level of creative effort, the hen's cackle; on another, the quality that the Italian critics called *sprezzatura* and that Hoby's translation of Castiglione calls "recklessness," the sense of buoyancy or release that accompanies perfect discipline, when we can no longer know the dancer from the dance.

It is impossible to understand the effect of what Milton called "gorgeous tragedy" as producing a real emotion of gloom or sorrow. Aeschylus's *The Persians* and Shakespeare's *Macbeth* are certainly tragedies, but they are associated respectively with the victory of Salamis and the accession of James I, both occasions of national rejoicing. Some critics carry the theory of real emotion over into Shakespeare himself, and talk about a "tragic period," in which he is supposed to have felt dismal from 1600 to 1608. Most people, if they had just finished writing a play as good as *King Lear,* would be in a mood of exhilaration, and while we have no right to ascribe this mood of Shakespeare, it is surely the right way to describe our response to the play. On the other hand, it comes as something of a shock to realize that the blinding of Gloucester is primarily entertainment, the more so as the pleasure we get from it obviously has nothing to do with sadism. If any literary work is emotionally "depressing," there is something wrong with either the writing or the reader's response. Art seems to produce a kind of buoyancy which, though often called pleasure, as it is for instance by Wordsworth, is something more inclusive than pleasure. "Exuberance is beauty," said Blake. That seems to me a practically definitive solution, not only of the minor question of what beauty is, but of the far more important problem of what the conceptions of catharsis and ecstasis really mean.

Such exuberance is, of course, as much intellectual as it is emotional: Blake himself was willing to define poetry as "allegory addressed to the intellectual powers."[20] We live in a world of threefold external compulsion: of compulsion on action, or law; of compulsion on thinking, or fact; of compulsion on feeling, which is the characteristic of all pleasure whether it is produced by the *Paradiso* or by an ice cream soda. But in the world of imagination a fourth power, which contains morality, beauty, and truth but is never subordinated to them, rises free of all their compulsions. The work of imagination presents us with a vision, not of the personal greatness of the poet, but of something impersonal and far greater: the vision of a decisive act of spiritual freedom, the vision of the recreation of man.

Mythical Phase: Symbol as Archetype

In the formal phase the poem belongs neither to the class "art," nor to the class "verbal": it represents its own class. There are thus two aspects to its form. In the first place, it is unique, a *techne* or artifact, with its own peculiar structure of imagery, to be examined by itself without immediate reference to the other things like it. The critic here begins with poems, not with a prior conception or definition of poetry. In the second place, the poem is one of a class of similar forms. Aristotle knows that *Oedipus Tyrannus* is in one sense not like any other tragedy, but he also knows that it belongs to the class called tragedy. We, who have experienced Shakespeare and Racine, can add the corollary that tragedy is something bigger than a phase of Greek drama. We may also find tragedy in literary works which are not dramas. To understand what tragedy is, therefore, takes us beyond the merely historical into the question of what an aspect of literature as a whole is. With this idea of the external relations of a poem with other poems, two considerations in criticism for the first time become important: convention and genre.[21]

The study of genres is based on analogies in form. It is characteristic of documentary and historical criticism that it cannot deal with such analogies. It can trace influence with great plausibility, whether it exists or not, but confronted with a tragedy of Shakespeare and a tragedy of Sophocles, to be compared solely because they are both tragedies, the

---

[20]See his letter to Thomas Butts, p. 401.

[21][Frye] The conception of the autonomy of form in art is essential to the argument of André Malraux, *The Voices of Silence,* translated by Stuart Gilbert (1953). In modern English criticism the archetypal approach is highly developed in both theory and practice. In theory, the books of Maud Bodkin, Kenneth Burke, Gaston Bachelard, Francis Fergusson, and Philip Wheelwright are of obvious and exceptional usefulness. See the excellent bibliographies in René Wellek and Austin Warren, *Theory of Literature* (1942), Chapter 15.

historical critic has to confine himself to general reflections about the seriousness of life. Similarly, nothing is more striking in rhetorical criticism than the absence of any consideration of genre: the rhetorical critic analyzes what is in front of him without much regard to whether it is a play, a lyric, or a novel. He may in fact even assert that there are no genres in literature. That is because he is concerned with his structure simply as a work of art, not as an artifact with a possible function. But there are many analogies in literature apart altogether from sources and influences (many of which, of course, are not analogous at all) and noticing such analogies forms a large part of our actual experience of literature, whatever its role so far in criticism.

The central principle of the formal phase, that a poem is an imitation of nature, is, though a perfectly sound one, still a principle which isolates the individual poem. And it is clear that any poem may be examined, not only as an imitation of nature, but as an imitation of other poems. Virgil discovered, according to Pope,[22] that following nature was ultimately the same thing as following Homer. Once we think of a poem in relation to other poems, as a unit of poetry, we can see that the study of genres has to be founded on the study of convention. The criticism which can deal with such matters will have to be based on that aspect of symbolism which relates poems to one another, and it will choose, as its main field of operations, the symbols that link poems together. Its ultimate object is to consider, not simply *a* poem as an imitation of nature, but the order of nature as a whole as imitated by a corresponding order of words.

All art is equally conventionalized, but we do not ordinarily notice this fact unless we are unaccustomed to the convention. In our day the conventional element in literature is elaborately disguised by a law of copyright pretending that every work of art is an invention distinctive enough to be patented. Hence the conventionalizing forces of modern literature—the way, for instance, that an editor's policy and the expectation of his readers combine to conventionalize what appears in a magazine—often go unrecognized. Demonstrating the debt of A to B is merely scholarship if A is dead, but a proof of moral delinquency if A is alive. This state of things makes it difficult to appraise a literature which includes Chaucer, much of whose poetry is translated or paraphrased from others; Shakespeare, whose plays sometimes follow their sources almost verbatim; and Milton, who asked for nothing better than to steal as much as possible out of the Bible. It is not only the inexperienced reader who looks for

a *residual* originality in such works. Most of us tend to think of a poet's real achievement as distinct from, or even contrasted with, the achievement present in what he stole, and we are thus apt to concentrate on peripheral rather than on central critical facts. For instance, the central greatness of *Paradise Regained,* as a poem, is not the greatness of the rhetorical decorations that Milton added to his source, but the greatness of the theme itself, which Milton *passes on* to the reader from his source. This conception of the great poet's being entrusted with the great theme was elementary enough to Milton, but violates most of the low mimetic prejudices about creation that most of us are educated in.

The underestimating of convention appears to be a result of, may even be a part of, the tendency, marked from Romantic times on, to think of the individual as ideally prior to his society. The view opposed to this, that the new baby is conditioned by a hereditary and environmental kinship to a society which already exists, has, whatever doctrines may be inferred from it, the initial advantage of being closer to the facts it deals with. The literary consequence of the second view is that the new poem, like the new baby, is born into an already existing order of words, and is typical of the structure of poetry to which it is attached. The new baby *is* his own society appearing once again as a unit of individuality, and the new poem has a similar relation to its poetic society.

It is hardly possible to accept a critical view which confuses the original with the aboriginal, and imagines that a "creative" poet sits down with a pencil and some blank paper and eventually produces a new poem in a special act of creation *ex nihilo.* Human beings do not create in that way. Just as a new scientific discovery manifests something that was already latent in the order of nature, and at the same time is logically related to the total structure of the existing science, so the new poem manifests something that was already latent in the order of words. Literature may have life, reality, experience, nature, imaginative truth, social conditions, or what you will for its *content;* but literature itself is not made out of these things. Poetry can only be made out of other poems; novels out of other novels. Literature shapes itself, and is not shaped externally: the *forms* of literature can no more exist outside literature than the forms of sonata and fugue and rondo can exist outside music.

All this was much clearer before the assimilation of literature to private enterprise concealed so many of the facts of criticism. When Milton sat down to write a poem about Edward King, he did not ask himself: "What can I find to say about King?" but "How does poetry require that such a subject should be treated?" The notion that convention shows a lack of feeling, and that a poet attains "sincerity" (which usually means articulate emotion) by disregarding it,

---

[22]See *An Essay on Criticism,* p. 275. See also Frye's essay *Nature and Homer* in his *Fables of Identity.*

is opposed to all the facts of literary experience and history. The origin of this notion is, again, the view that poetry is a description of emotion, and that its "literal" meaning is an assertion about the emotions held by the individual poet. But any serious study of literature soon shows that the real difference between the original and the imitative poet is simply that the former is more profoundly imitative. Originality returns to the origins of literature, as radicalism returns to its roots. The remark of Mr. Eliot that a good poet is more likely to steal than to imitate[23] affords a more balanced view of convention, as it indicates that the poem is specifically involved with other poems, not vaguely with such abstractions as tradition or style. The copyright law, and the mores attached to it, make it difficult for a modern novelist to steal anything except his title from the rest of literature: hence it is often only in such titles as *For Whom the Bell Tolls, The Grapes of Wrath,* or *The Sound and the Fury,* that we can clearly see how much impersonal dignity and richness of association an author can gain by the communism of convention.

As with other products of divine activity, the father of a poem is much more difficult to identify than the mother. That the mother is always nature, the realm of the objective considered as a field of communication, no serious criticism can ever deny. But as long as the father of a poem is assumed to be the poet himself, we have once again failed to distinguish literature from discursive verbal structures. The discursive writer writes as an act of conscious will, and that conscious will, along with the symbolic system he employs for it, is set over against the body of things he is describing. But the poet, who writes creatively rather than deliberately, is not the father of his poem; he is at best a midwife, or, more accurately still, the womb of Mother Nature herself: her privates he, so to speak. The fact that revision is possible, that a poet can make changes in a poem not because he likes them better but because they are better, shows clearly that the poet has to give birth to the poem as it passes through his mind. He is responsible for delivering it in as uninjured a state as possible, and if the poem is alive, it is equally anxious to be rid of him, and screams to be cut loose from all the navel-strings and feeding-tubes of his ego.

The true father or shaping spirit of the poem is the form of the poem itself, and this form is a manifestation of the universal spirit of poetry, the "only begetter" of Shakespeare's sonnets who was not Shakespeare himself, much less that depressing ghost Mr. W. H., but Shakespeare's subject, the master-mistress of his passion. When a poet speaks of

the *internal* spirit which shapes the poem, he is apt to drop the traditional appeal to female Muses and think of himself as in a feminine, or at least receptive, relation to some god or lord, whether Apollo, Dionysus, Eros, Christ, or (as in Milton) the Holy Spirit. *Est deus in nobis,* Ovid says: in modern times we may compare Nietzsche's remarks about his inspiration in *Ecce Homo.*

The problem of convention is the problem of how art can be communicable, for literature is clearly as much a technique of communication as assertive verbal structures are. Poetry, taken as a whole, is no longer simply an aggregate of artifacts imitating nature, but one of the activities of human artifice taken as a whole. If we may use the word "civilization" for this, we may say that our fourth phase looks at poetry as one of the techniques of civilization. It is concerned, therefore, with the social aspect of poetry, with poetry as the focus of a community. The symbol in this phase is the communicable unit, to which I give the name archetype: that is, a typical or recurring image. I mean by an *archetype* a symbol which connects one poem with another and thereby helps to unify and integrate our literary experience. And as the archetype is the communicable symbol, archetypal criticism is primarily concerned with literature as a social fact and as a mode of communication. By the study of conventions and genres, it attempts to fit poems into the body of poetry as a whole.

The repetition of certain common images of physical nature like the sea or the forest in a large number of poems cannot in itself be called even *coincidence,* which is the name we give to a piece of design when we cannot find a use for it. But it does indicate a certain unity in the nature that poetry imitates, and in the communicating activity of which poetry forms part. Because of the larger communicative context of education, it is possible for a story about the sea to be archetypal, to make a profound imaginative impact, on a reader who has never been out of Saskatchewan. And when pastoral images are deliberately employed in *Lycidas,* for instance, merely because they are conventional, we can see that the convention of the pastoral makes us assimilate these images to other parts of literary experience.

We think first of the pastoral's descent from Theocritus, where the pastoral elegy first appears as a literary adaptation of the ritual of the Adonis lament,[24] and through Theocritus to Virgil and the whole pastoral tradition to *The Shepheardes Calender* and beyond to *Lycidas* itself. Then we think of the intricate pastoral symbolism of the Bible and the Christian

---

[23][Frye] in his essay on Philip Massinger.

[24][Frye] This phrase should be understood in the light of the general principle that *ritual* refers to content rather than source.

church, of Abel and the twenty-third psalm and Christ the Good Shepherd, of the ecclesiastical overtones of *pastor* and *flock,* and of the link between the Classical and Christian traditions in Virgil's Messianic eclogue.[25] Then we think of the extensions of pastoral symbolism into Sidney's *Arcadia, The Faerie Queene,* Shakespeare's forest comedies, and the like; then of the post-Miltonic development of pastoral elegy in Shelley, Arnold, Whitman, and Dylan Thomas; perhaps too of pastoral conventions in painting and music. In short, we can get a whole liberal education simply by picking up one conventional poem and following its archetypes as they stretch out into the rest of literature. An avowedly conventional poem like *Lycidas* urgently demands the kind of criticism that will absorb it into the study of literature as a whole, and this activity is expected to begin at once, with the first cultivated reader. Here we have a situation in literature more like that of mathematics or science, where the work of genius is assimilated to the whole subject so quickly that one hardly notices the difference between creative and critical activity.

If we do not accept the archetypal or conventional element in the imagery that links one poem with another, it is impossible to get any systematic mental training out of the reading of literature alone. But if we add to our desire to know literature a desire to know how we know it, we shall find that expanding images into conventional archetypes of literature is a process that takes place unconsciously in all our reading. A symbol like the sea or the heath cannot remain within Conrad or Hardy: it is bound to expand over many works into an archetypal symbol of literature as a whole. Moby Dick cannot remain in Melville's novel: he is absorbed into our imaginative experience of leviathans and dragons of the deep from the Old Testament onward. And what is true for the reader is a fortiori true of the poet, who learns very quickly that there is no singing school for his soul except the study of the monuments of its own magnificence.

In each phase of symbolism there is a point at which the critic is compelled to break away from the range of the poet's own knowledge. Thus the historical or documentary critic has sooner or later to call Dante a "medieval" poet, a notion unknown and unintelligible to Dante. In archetypal criticism, the poet's conscious knowledge is considered only so far as the poet may allude to or imitate other poets ("sources") or make a deliberate use of a convention. Beyond that, the poet's control over his poem stops with the poem. Only the archetypal critic can be concerned with its relationship to the rest of literature. But here again we have to distinguish be-

tween explicitly conventionalized literature, such as *Lycidas,* where the poet himself starts us off by referring to Theocritus, Virgil, Renaissance pastoralists, and the Bible, and literature which conceals or ignores its conventional links. The conception of copyright and the revolutionary nature of the low mimetic view of creation also extends to a general unwillingness on the part of authors of the copyright age to have their imagery studied conventionally, and in dealing with this period, most archetypes have to be established by critical inspection alone.

To give a random example, one very common convention of the nineteenth-century novel is the use of two heroines, one dark and one light. The dark one is as a rule passionate, haughty, plain, foreign or Jewish, and in some way associated with the undesirable or with some kind of forbidden fruit like incest. When the two are involved with the same hero, the plot usually has to get rid of the dark one or make her into a sister if the story is to end happily. Examples include *Ivanhoe, The Last of the Mohicans, The Woman in White, Ligeia, Pierre* (a tragedy because the hero chooses the dark girl, who is also his sister), *The Marble Faun,* and countless incidental treatments. A male version forms the symbolic basis of *Wuthering Heights.* This device is as much a convention as Milton's calling Edward King by a name out of Virgil's *Eclogues,* but it shows a confused, or, as we say, "unconscious" approach to conventions. Again, when we meet the images of a man, a woman, and a serpent in the ninth book of *Paradise Lost,* there is no doubt of their conventional links with similar figures in the Book of Genesis. In Hudson's *Green Mansions* the hero and heroine first meet over a serpent in a quasi-Paradisal setting: here the conventional nature of the imagery is a matter on which the author gives us no help. When a critic meets St. George the Redcross Knight in Spenser, bearing a red cross on a white ground, he has some idea what to do with this figure. When he meets a female in Henry James's *The Other House* called Rose Armiger with a white dress and a red parasol, he is, in the current slang, clueless.[26] It is clear that a deficiency in contemporary education often complained of, the disappearance of a common cultural ground which makes a modern poet's allusions to the Bible or to Classical mythology fall with less weight than they should, has much to do with the decline in the explicit use of archetypes.

Whitman, as is well known, was a spokesman of an antiarchetypal view of literature, and urged the Muse to forget

---

[25]The fourth eclogue, interpreted by some to prophesy Christ's birth.

[26][Frye] My only point is that there may not be any point, but as Rose Armiger is a sister to dragons rather than knights errant, there is a faint possibility of parody-symbolism, discussed below.

the matter of Troy and develop new themes. This is a low mimetic prejudice, and is consequently appropriate enough for Whitman, who is both right and wrong. He is wrong because the matter of Troy will always be, in the foreseeable future, an integral part of the Western cultural heritage, and hence references to Agamemnon in Yeats's *Leda* or Eliot's *Sweeney Among the Nightingales* have as much cumulative power as ever for the properly instructed reader. But he is of course perfectly right in feeling that the *content* of poetry is normally an immediate and contemporary environment. He was right, being the kind of poet he was, in making the content of his own *When Lilacs Last in the Dooryard Bloomed* an elegy on Lincoln and not a conventional Adonis lament. Yet his elegy is, in its *form,* as conventional as *Lycidas,* complete with purple flowers thrown on coffins, a great star drooping in the west, imagery of "ever-returning spring" and all the rest of it. Poetry organizes the content of the world as it passes before the poet, but the forms in which that content is organized come out of the structure of poetry itself.

Archetypes are associative clusters, and differ from signs in being complex variables. Within the complex is often a large number of specific learned associations which are communicable because a large number of people in a given culture happen to be familiar with them. When we speak of "symbolism" in ordinary life we usually think of such learned cultural archetypes as the cross or the crown, or of conventional associations, as of white with purity or green with jealousy. As an archetype, green may symbolize hope or vegetable nature or a go sign in traffic or Irish patriotism as easily as jealousy, but the word *green* as a verbal sign always refers to a certain color. Some archetypes are so deeply rooted in conventional association that they can hardly avoid suggesting that association, as the geometrical figure of the cross inevitably suggests the death of Christ. A *completely* conventionalized art would be an art in which the archetypes, or communicable units, were essentially a set of esoteric signs. This can happen in the arts—for instance in some of the sacred dances of India—but it has not happened in Western literature yet, and the resistance of modern writers to having their archetypes "spotted," so to speak, is due to a natural anxiety to keep them as versatile as possible, not pinned down exclusively to one interpretation. A poet may be showing an esoteric tendency if he specifically points out one association, as Yeats does in his footnotes to some of his early poems. There are no *necessary* associations: there are some exceedingly obvious ones, such as the association of darkness with terror or mystery, but there are no intrinsic or inherent correspondences which must invariably be present. As we shall see later, there is a context in which the phrase

universal symbol makes sense, but it is not this context. The stream of literature, however, like any other stream, seeks the easiest channels first: the poet who uses the expected associations will communicate more rapidly.

At one extreme of literature we have the pure convention, which a poet uses merely because it has often been used before in the same way. This is most frequent in naive poetry, in the fixed epithets and phrase tags of medieval romance and ballad, in the invariable plots and character types of naive drama, and, to a lesser degree, in the *topoi*[27] or rhetorical commonplaces which, like other ideas in literature, are so dull when stated as propositions, and so rich and variegated when they are used as structural principles in literature. At the other extreme we have the pure variable, where there is a deliberate attempt at novelty or unfamiliarity, and consequently a disguising or complicating of archetypes. Such techniques come very close to a distrust of communication itself as a function of literature. However, extremes meet, as Coleridge said, and anticonventional poetry soon becomes a convention in its turn, to be explored by hardy scholars accustomed to the dreariness of literary badlands. Between these extreme points conventions vary from the most explicit to the most indirect, along a scale parallel to the scale of allegory and paradox already dealt with. The two scales may be often confused or identified, but translating imagery into examples and precepts is a quite distinct process from following images into other poems.

Near the extreme of pure convention is translation, paraphrase, and the kind of use which Chaucer makes of Boccaccio in *Troilus* and *The Knight's Tale.* Next we come to deliberate and explicit convention, such as we have noted in *Lycidas.* Next comes paradoxical or ironic convention, including parody—often a sign that certain vogues in handling conventions are getting worn out. Then comes the attempt to reach originality through turning one's back on explicit convention, an attempt which results in implicit convention of the kind we detected in Whitman. Then comes a tendency to identify originality with "experimental" writing, based in our day on an analogy with scientific discovery, and which is frequently spoken of as "breaking with convention." And, of course, at every stage of literature, including this last one, there is a great deal of superficial and inorganic convention, producing the kind of writing that most students of literature prefer to keep in the middle distance: run-of-the-mill Elizabethan sonnets and love lyrics, Plautine comedy-formulas,

---

[27][Frye] For these see E. R. Curtius, *European Literature and the Latin Middle Ages,* translated by Willard Trask (1953), 79 *ff.* An example of the point made in the text is the relation of Milton's first prolusion, "Whether Day is more excellent than Night," to *L'Allegro* and *Il Penseroso.*

eighteenth-century pastorals, nineteenth-century happy-ending novels, works of followers and disciples and schools and trends generally.

It is clear from all this that archetypes are most easily studied in highly conventionalized literature: that is, for the most part, naive, primitive, and popular literature. In suggesting the possibility of archetypal criticism, then, I am suggesting the possibility of extending the kind of comparative and morphological study now made of folk tales and ballads into the rest of literature. This should be more easily conceivable now that it is no longer fashionable to mark off popular and primitive literature from ordinary literature as sharply as we used to do. Also, we shall find that superficial literature, of the kind just spoken of, is of great value to archetypal criticism simply because it is conventional. If throughout this book I refer to popular fiction as frequently as to the greatest novels and epics, it is for the same reason that a musician attempting to explain the rudimentary facts about counterpoint would be more likely, at least at first, to illustrate from *Three Blind Mice* than from a complex Bach fugue.

Every phase of symbolism has its particular approach to narrative and to meaning. In the literal phase, narrative is a flow of significant sounds, and meaning an ambiguous and complex verbal pattern. In the descriptive phase, narrative is an imitation of real events, and meaning an imitation of actual objects or propositions. In the formal phase, poetry exists between the example and the precept. In the exemplary event there is an element of *recurrence;* in the precept, or statement about what ought to be, there is a strong element of *desire,* or what is called "wish-thinking." These elements of recurrence and desire come into the foreground in archetypal criticism, which studies poems as units of poetry as a whole and symbols as units of communication.

From such a point of view, the narrative aspect of literature is a recurrent act of symbolic communication: in other words a ritual. Narrative is studied by the archetypal critic as ritual or imitation of human action as a whole, and not simply as a *mimesis praxeos* or imitation of *an* action. Similarly, in archetypal criticism the significant content is the conflict of desire and reality which has for its basis the work of the dream.[28] Ritual and dream, therefore, are the narrative and significant content respectively of literature in its archetypal aspect. The archetypal analysis of the plot of a novel or play would deal with it in terms of the generic, recurring, or conventional actions which show analogies to rituals: the weddings, funerals, intellectual and social initiations, executions or mock executions, the chasing away of the scapegoat, villain, and so on. The archetypal analysis of the meaning or significance of such a work would deal with it in terms of the generic, recurring, or conventional shape indicated by its mood and resolution, whether tragic, comic, ironic, or what not, in which the relationship of desire and experience is expressed.

Recurrence and desire interpenetrate, and are equally important in both ritual and dream. In its archetypal phase, the poem imitates nature, not (as in the formal phase) nature as a structure or system, but nature as a cyclical process. The principle of recurrence in the rhythm of art seems to be derived from the repetitions in nature that make time intelligible to us. Rituals cluster around the cyclical movements of the sun, the moon, the seasons, and human life. Every crucial periodicity of experience: dawn, sunset, the phases of the moon, seed-time and harvest, the equinoxes and the solstices, birth, initiation, marriage, and death, get rituals attached to them. The pull of ritual is toward pure cyclical narrative, which, if there could be such a thing, would be automatic and unconscious repetition. In the middle of all this recurrence, however, is the central recurrent cycle of sleeping and waking life, the daily frustration of the ego, the nightly awakening of a titanic self.

The archetypal critic studies the poem as part of poetry, and poetry as part of the total human imitation of nature that we call civilization. Civilization is not merely an imitation of nature, but the process of making a total human form out of nature, and it is impelled by the force that we have just called desire. The desire for food and shelter is not content with roots and caves: it produces the human forms of nature that we call farming and architecture. Desire is thus not a simple response to need, for an animal may need food without planting a garden to get it, nor is it a simple response to want, or desire *for* something in particular. It is neither limited to nor satisfied by objects, but is the energy that leads human society to develop its own form. Desire in this sense is the social aspect of what we met on the literal level as emotion, an impulse toward expression which would have remained amorphous if the poem had not liberated it by providing the form of its expression. The form of desire, similarly, is liberated and made apparent by civilization. The efficient cause of civilization is work, and poetry in its social aspect has the function of expressing, as a verbal hypothesis, a vision of the goal of work and the forms of desire.

There is however a moral dialectic in desire. The conception of a garden develops the conception *weed,* and build-

---

[28][Frye] Throughout this book *dream* is used in an extended sense to mean, not simply the fantasies of the sleeping mind, but the whole interpenetrating activity of desire and repugnance in shaping thought.

ing a sheepfold makes the wolf a greater enemy. Poetry in its social or archetypal aspect, therefore, not only tries to illustrate the fulfillment of desire, but to define the obstacles to it. Ritual is not only a recurrent act, but an act expressive of a dialectic of desire and repugnance: desire for fertility or victory, repugnance to drought or to enemies. We have rituals of social integration, and we have rituals of expulsion, execution, and punishment. In dream there is a parallel dialectic, as there is both the wish-fulfillment dream and the anxiety or nightmare dream of repugnance. Archetypal criticism, therefore, rests on two organizing rhythms or patterns, one cyclical, the other dialectic.

The union of ritual and dream in a form of verbal communication is myth. This is a sense of the term *myth* slightly different from that used in the previous essay. But, first, the sense is equally familiar, and the ambiguity not mine but the dictionary's; and, second, there is a real connection between the two senses which will become more apparent as we go on. The myth accounts for, and makes communicable, the ritual and the dream. Ritual, by itself, cannot account for itself: it is prelogical, preverbal, and in a sense prehuman. Its attachment to the calendar seems to link human life to the biological dependence on the natural cycle which plants, and to some extent animals, still have. Everything in nature that we think of as having some analogy with works of art, like the flower or the bird's song, grows out of a synchronization between an organism and the rhythms of its natural environment, especially that of the solar year. With animals some expressions of synchronization, like the mating dances of birds, could almost be called rituals. Myth is more distinctively human, as the most intelligent partridge cannot tell even the most absurd story explaining why it drums in the mating season. Similarly, the dream, by itself, is a system of cryptic allusions to the dreamer's own life, not fully understood by him, or so far as we know of any real use to him. But in all dreams there is a mythical element which has a power of independent communication, as is obvious, not only in the stock example of Oedipus, but in any collection of folk tales. Myth, therefore, not only gives meaning to ritual and narrative to dream: it is the identification of ritual and dream, in which the former is seen to be the latter in movement. This would not be possible unless there were a common factor to ritual and dream which made one the social expression of the other; the investigation of this common factor we must leave for later treatment. All that we need to say here is that ritual is the archetypal aspect of *mythos* and dream the archetypal aspect of *dianoia*.

The same distinction in emphasis that we noted in the first essay between fictional and thematic literature recurs here. Some literary forms, such as drama, remind us with particular vividness of analogies to rituals, for the drama in literature, like the ritual in religion, is primarily a social or ensemble performance. Others, such as romance, suggest analogies to dreams. Ritual analogies are most easily seen, not in the drama of the educated audience and the settled theater, but in naive or spectacular drama: in the folk play, the puppet show, the pantomime, the farce, the pageant, and their descendants in masque, comic opera, commercial movie, and revue. Dream analogies are best studied in naive romance, which includes the folk tales and fairy tales that are so closely related to dreams of wonderful wishes coming true, and to nightmares of ogres and witches. Naive drama and naive romance, of course, also interpenetrate. What naive drama dramatizes is usually some kind of romance, and the close relation of romance to ritual can be seen in the number of medieval romances that are linked to some part of the calendar, the winter solstice, a May morning, or a saint's eve; or else to some class ritual like the tournament. The fact that the archetype is primarily a *communicable* symbol largely accounts for the ease with which ballads and folk tales and mimes travel through the world, like so many of their heroes, over all barriers of language and culture. We come back here to the fact that literature most deeply influenced by the archetypal phase of symbolism impresses us as primitive and popular.

By these words I mean possessing the ability to communicate in time and space respectively. Otherwise they mean much the same thing. Popular art is normally decried as vulgar by the cultivated people of its time; then it loses favor with its original audience as a new generation grows up; then it begins to merge into the softer lighting of "quaint," and cultivated people become interested in it, and finally it begins to take on the archaic dignity of the primitive. This sense of the archaic recurs whenever we find great art using popular forms, as Shakespeare does in his last period, or as the Bible does when it ends in a fairy tale about a damsel in distress, a hero killing dragons, a wicked witch, and a wonderful city glittering with jewels. Archaism is a regular feature of all social uses of archetypes. Soviet Russia is very proud of its production of tractors, but it will be some time before the tractor replaces the sickle on the Soviet flag.

It is at this point that we must notice and avoid the fallacy of a theory of mythological contract. That is, there may be such a thing as a social contract in political theory, if we keep the discussion to observable facts about the present structure of society. But when these facts are attached to a fable about something that happened in a past too remote for any evidence to disturb the fabler's assertions, and we are told that once upon a time men surrendered or delegated or were tricked into surrendering their power, political theory has merely become one of Plato's indoctrinating lies. And because the only evidence for this remote event is its analogy to the present facts, the present facts are being compared with their own shadows. A precisely similar fabling process has taken place in the literary criticism concerned with myth, which has hardly yet emerged from its historical contract stage.

As the archetypal critic is concerned with ritual and dream, it is likely that he would find much of interest in the work done by contemporary anthropology in ritual, and by contemporary psychology in dreams. Specifically, the work done on the ritual basis of naive drama in Frazer's *Golden Bough,* and the work done on the dream basis of naive romance by Jung and the Jungians, are of most direct value to him. But the three subjects of anthropology, psychology, and literary criticism are not yet clearly separated, and the danger of determinism has to be carefully watched. To the literary critic, ritual is the *content* of dramatic action, not the source or origin of it. The *Golden Bough* is, from the point of view of literary criticism, an essay on the ritual content of naive drama: that is, it reconstructs an archetypal ritual from which the structural and generic principles of drama may be logically, not chronologically, derived. It does not matter two pins to the literary critic whether such a ritual had any historical existence or not. It is very probable that Frazer's hypothetical ritual would have many and striking analogies to actual rituals, and collecting such analogies is part of his argument. But an analogy is not necessarily a source, an influence, a cause, or an embryonic form, much less an identity. The *literary* relation of ritual to drama, like that of any other aspect of human action to drama, is a relation of content to form only, not one of source to derivation.

The critic, therefore, is concerned only with the ritual or dream patterns which are actually in what he is studying, however they got there. The work of the Classical scholars who have followed Frazer's lead has produced a general theory of the spectacular or ritual content of Greek drama. *The Golden Bough* purports to be a work of anthropology, but it has had more influence on literary criticism than in its own alleged field, and it may yet prove to be really a work of literary criticism. If the ritual pattern is in the plays—and it is fact, not opinion, that one of the main themes of *Iphigeneia in Tauris,* for example, is human sacrifice—the critic need not take sides in the quite separate historical controversy over the ritual *origin* of Greek drama. Hence ritual, as the content of action, and more particularly of dramatic action, is something continuously latent in the order of words, and is quite independent of direct influence. Even in the nineteenth century, we find that the instant drama becomes primitive and popular, as it does in *The Mikado,* to repeat an example given before, back comes all Frazer's apparatus, the king's son, the mock sacrifice, the analogy with the festival of the Sacaea, and many other things that Gilbert knew and cared nothing about. It comes back because it is still the best way of holding an audience's attention, and the experienced dramatist knows it.

The prestige of documentary criticism, which deals entirely with sources and historical transmission, has misled some archetypal critics into feeling that all such ritual elements ought to be traced directly, like the lineage of royalty, as far back as a willing suspension of disbelief will allow. The vast chronological gaps resulting are usually bridged by some theory of race memory, or by some conspiratorial conception of history involving secrets jealously guarded for centuries by esoteric cults or traditions. It is curious that when archetypal critics hang on to a historical framework they almost invariably produce some hypothesis of continuous degeneration from a golden age lost in antiquity. Thus the prelude to Thomas Mann's Joseph series traces back several of our central myths to Atlantis, Atlantis being clearly more useful as an archetypal idea than as a historical one. When archetypal criticism revived in the nineteenth century with a vogue for sun myths, an attempt was made to ridicule it by proving with equal plausibility that Napoleon was a sun myth. The ridicule is effective only against the historical distortion of the method. Archetypally, we turn Napoleon into a sun myth whenever we speak of the rise of his career, the zenith of his fame, or the eclipse of his fortunes.

Social and cultural history, which is anthropology in an extended sense, will always be a part of the context of criticism, and the more clearly the anthropological and the critical treatments of ritual are distinguished, the more beneficial their influence on each other will be. The same is true of the relation of psychology to criticism. The first and most striking unit of poetry larger than the individual poem is the total work of the man who wrote the poem. Biography will always be a part of criticism, and the biographer will naturally be interested in his subject's poetry as a personal document, recording his private dreams, associations, ambitions, and expressed or repressed desires. Studies of such matters form an essential part of criticism. I am not of course speaking of the silly ones, which simply project the author's own erotica, in a rationalized clinical disguise, on his victim, but only of the serious studies which are technically competent both in psychology and in criticism, which are aware how much guesswork is involved and how tentative all the conclusions must be.

Such an approach is easiest, and most rewarding, with what we have called thematic writers of the low mimetic—that is, chiefly, the Romantic poets, where the poet's own psychological processes are often part of the theme. With other writers, say a dramatist who is aware from the first word he writes that "They who live to please must please to live," there is danger of making an unreal abstraction of the poet from his literary community. Suppose a critic finds that a certain pattern is repeated time and again in the plays of Shakespeare. If Shakespeare is unique or anomalous, or even exceptional, in using this pattern, the reason for his use of it may be at least partly psychological. If there were any evidence that he had persisted in using it when it failed to please an audience, the probability of a personal psychological element would be very high. But if we can find the same pattern in half a dozen of his contemporaries, we clearly have to allow for convention. And if we find it in a dozen dramatists of different ages and cultures, we have to allow for genre, for the structural requirements of drama itself. Now as a matter of fact we do find in Shakespeare's comedies that the same devices are used over and over, and it is the business of the literary critic to compare these devices with those of other dramatists, in a morphological study of comic form. Otherwise we shall deprive ourselves of the perfectly legitimate appreciation of the *scholarly* qualities of Shakespeare, of seeing in the repeated devices of his comedies a kind of *Art of Fugue* of comedy.

A psychologist examining a poem will tend to see in it what he sees in the dream, a mixture of latent and manifest content. For the literary critic the manifest content of the poem is its form, hence its latent content becomes simply its actual content, its *dianoia*[29] or theme. And this *dianoia* on the archetypal level is a dream, a presentation of the conflict of desire and actuality. We seem to be going around in a circle, but not quite. For the critic, a problem appears which does not exist for a purely psychological analysis, the problem of communicable latent content, of intelligible dream, Plato's conception of art as a dream for awakened minds. For the psychologist all dream symbols are private ones, interpreted by the personal life of the dreamer. For the critic there is no such thing as private symbolism, or, if there is, it is his job to make sure that it does not remain so.

This problem is already present in Freud's treatment of *Oedipus Tyrannus* as a play which owes much of its power to the fact that it dramatizes the Oedipus complex. The dramatic and psychological elements can be linked without any reference to the personal life of Sophocles, of which we know nothing whatever. This emphasis on impersonal content has been developed by Jung and his school, where the communicability of archetypes is accounted for by a theory of a collective unconscious—an unnecessary hypothesis in literary criticism, so far as I can judge.

What we have found to be true of the writer's intention is also true of the audience's attention. Both are centripetally directed, and implications exist in the response to art as they do in the creation of it, implications of which the audience is not explicitly aware. Discrete conscious awareness can take in only a very few details of the complex of response. This state of things enabled Tennyson, for instance, to be praised for the chastity of his language and read for his powerful erotic sensuousness. It also makes it possible for a contemporary critic to draw on the fullest resources of modern knowledge in explicating a work of art without any real fear of anachronism.

For instance, *Le Malade Imaginaire* is a play about a man who, in seventeenth-century terms, including no doubt Molière's own terms, was not really sick but just thought he was. A modern critic might object that life is not so simple: that it is perfectly possible for a *malade imaginaire* to be a *malade véritable,* and that what is wrong with Argan is clearly an unwillingness to see his children grow up, an infantile regression which his wife—his second wife, incidentally—shows that she understands completely by coddling him and murmuring such phrases as *"pauvre petit fils."* Such a critic would find the clue to Argan's whole behavior in his unguarded remark after the scene with the little girl Louison (the erotic nature of which the critic would also notice): *"Il n'y a plus d'enfants."* Now whether this reading is right or wrong, it does not swerve from Molière's text, yet it tells us nothing about Molière himself. The play is generically a comedy; it must therefore end happily; Argan must therefore be brought to see some reason; his wife, whose dramatic function it is to keep him within his obsession, must therefore be "exposed" as inimical to him. The plot is a ritual moving toward a scapegoat rejection followed by a marriage, and the theme is a dream-pattern of irrational desire in conflict with reality.

Another essay in this book will be concerned with the details and practice of archetypal criticism: here we are concerned only with its place in the context of criticism as a whole. In its archetypal aspect, art is a part of civilization, and civilization we defined as the process of making a human form out of nature. The shape of this human form is revealed by civilization itself as it develops: its major components are the city, the garden, the farm, the sheepfold, and the like, as well as human society itself. An archetypal symbol is usually a natural object with a human meaning, and it forms part of the critical view of art as a civilized product, a vision of the goals of human work.

---

[29][Frye] The expression here is careless, as *dianoia* refers to form.

Such a vision is bound to idealize some aspects of civilization and ridicule or ignore others; in other words the social context of art is also the moral context. All artists have to come to terms with their communities: many artists, and many great ones, are content to be the spokesmen of them. But in terms of his moral significance, the poet reflects, and follows at a distance, what his community really achieves through its work. Hence the moral view of the artist is invariably that he ought to assist the work of his society by framing workable hypotheses, imitating human action and thought in such a way as to suggest realizable modes of both. If he does not do this, his hypotheses should at least be clearly labeled as playful or fantastic. Marxism takes more or less this view of art, and thereby repeats the argument reached at the end of the *Republic*. We are told there, if we follow the argument simply as it stands, that according to justice, or social work properly done, the painter's bed is an external imitation of the craftsman's bed. The artist, therefore, is confined either to reflecting or to escaping from the world that the true worker is realizing.

We have adopted the principle in this essay that the events and ideas of poetry are hypothetical imitations of history and discursive writing respectively, which in their turn are verbal imitations of action and thought. This principle brings us close to the view of poetry as a secondary imitation of reality. We are interpreting mimesis, however, not as a Platonic "recollection" but as an emancipation of externality into image, nature into art. From this point of view the work of art must be its own object:[30] it cannot be ultimately descriptive of something, and can never be ultimately related to any other system of phenomena, standards, values, or final causes. All such external relations form part of the "intentional fallacy." Poetry is a vehicle for morality, truth, and beauty, but the poet does not aim at these things, but only at inner verbal strength. The poet qua poet intends only to write a poem, and as a rule it is not the artist, but the ego in the artist, who turns away from his proper work to go and chase these other seductive marshlights.

It is an elementary axiom in criticism that morally the lion lies down with the lamb. Bunyan and Rochester, Sade and Jane Austen, *The Miller's Tale* and *The Second Nun's Tale,* are all equally elements of a liberal education, and the only moral criterion to be applied to them is that of decorum. Similarly, the moral attitude taken by the poet in his work derives largely from the structure of that work. Thus the fact that *Le Malade Imaginaire* is a comedy is the only reason for

making Argan's wife a hypocrite—she must be got rid of to make the play end happily.

The pursuit of beauty is much more dangerous nonsense than the pursuit of truth or goodness, because it affords a stronger temptation to the ego. Beauty, like truth and goodness, is a quality that may in one sense be predicated of all great art, but the deliberate attempt to beautify can, in itself, only weaken the creative energy. Beauty in art is like happiness in morals: it may accompany the act, but it cannot be the goal of the act, just as one cannot "pursue happiness," but only something else that may give happiness. Aiming at beauty produces, at best, the attractive: the quality of beauty represented by the word *loveliness,* a quality which depends on a carefully restricted choice of both subject and technique. A religious painter, for instance, can produce this quality only as long as churches keep commissioning Madonnas: if a church asks for a Crucifixion he must paint cruelty and horror instead.

When we speak of the human body as "beautiful," we usually mean the body of someone in good physical condition between eighteen and about thirty, and if Degas, for example, shows us pictures of thick-bottomed matrons squatting in hip baths, we interpret the shock to our propriety as an aesthetic judgment. Whenever the word *beauty* means loveliness or attractiveness, as it is bound to do whenever it is made the intention of art, it becomes reactionary: it tries to restrict either what the artist may choose for a subject or the method in which he may choose to treat it, and it marshals all the forces of prudery to keep him from expanding his vision beyond an arid and insipid pseudoclassicism. Ruskin spoiled many of his finest critical insights with this fallacy; Tennyson often hampered the vigor of his poetry by it, and in some of the lesser beauticians of the same period we can see clearly what the neurotic compulsion to beautify everything leads to. It leads to an exaggerated cult of style, a technique of making everything in a work of art, even a drama, sound all alike, and like the author, and like the author at his most impressive. Here again the vanity of the ego has replaced the honest pride of the craftsman.

The formal or third phase of narrative and meaning, although it includes the external relations of literature to events and ideas, nevertheless brings us back ultimately to the aesthetic view of the work of art as an object of contemplation, a *tachne* designed for ornament and pleasure rather than use. This view encourages us to separate aesthetic objects from other kinds of artifacts and to postulate an aesthetic experience different in kind from other experiences. Corresponding to the bibliographical view of literature as the aggregate or pile of all the books and plays and poems that

---

[30][Frye] I have taken this phrase from an oral lecture by M. Jacques Maritain.

have been written, we find the aesthetic view of criticism as a discrete series of special (sometimes vaguely sacramental) apprehensions. There is no reason for not granting this view of literary experience its own validity; one objects to it only when it excludes other approaches.

The archetypal view of literature shows us literature as a total form and literary experience as a part of the continuum of life, in which one of the poet's functions is to visualize the goals of human work. As soon as we add this approach to the other three, literature becomes an ethical instrument, and we pass beyond Kierkegaard's "either / or" dilemma between aesthetic idolatry and ethical freedom, without any temptation to dispose of the arts in the process. Hence the importance, after accepting the validity of this view of literature, of rejecting the external goals of morality, beauty, and truth. The fact that they are external makes them ultimately idolatrous, and so demonic. But if no social, moral, or aesthetic standard is in the long run externally determinative of the value of art, it follows that the archetypal phase, in which art is part of civilization, cannot be the ultimate one. We need still another phase where we can pass from civilization, where poetry is still useful and functional, to culture, where it is disinterested and liberal, and stands on its own feet.

Anagogic Phase: Symbol as Monad

In tracing the different phases of literary symbolism, we have been going up a sequence parallel to that of medieval criticism. We have, it is true, established a different meaning for the word *literal.* It is our second or descriptive level that corresponds to the historical or literal one of the medieval scheme, or at any rate of Dante's version of it. Our third level, the level of commentary and interpretation, is the second or allegorical level of the Middle Ages. Our fourth level, the study of myths, and of poetry as a technique of social communication, is the third medieval level of moral and tropological meaning, concerned at once with the social and the figurative aspect of meaning. The medieval distinction between the allegorical as what one believes *(quid credas)* and the moral as what one does *(quid agas)* is also reflected in our conception of the formal phase as aesthetic or speculative and the archetypal phase as social and part of the continuum of work. We have now to see if we can establish a modern parallel to the medieval conception of anagogy or universal meaning.

Again, the reader may have noticed a parallelism gradually shaping up between the five modes of our first essay and the phases of symbolism in this one. Literal meaning, as

we expounded it, has much to do with the techniques of thematic irony introduced by *symbolisme,* and with the view of many of the "new" critics that poetry is primarily (i.e., literally) an ironic structure. Descriptive symbolism, shown at its most uncompromising in the documentary naturalism of the nineteenth century, seems to bear a close connection with the low mimetic, and formal symbolism, most easily studied in Renaissance and Neoclassical writers, with the high mimetic. Archetypal criticism seems to find its center of gravity in the mode of romance, when the interchange of ballads, folk tales, and popular stories was at its easiest. If the parallel holds, then, the last phase of symbolism will still be concerned, as the previous one was, with the mythopoeic aspect of literature, but with myth in its narrower and more technical sense of fictions and themes relating to divine or quasi-divine beings and powers.

We have associated archetypes and myths particularly with primitive and popular literature. In fact we could almost define popular literature, admittedly in a rather circular way, as literature which affords an unobstructed view of archetypes. We can find this quality on every level of literature: in fairy tales and folk tales, in Shakespeare (in most of the comedies), in the Bible (which would still be a popular book if it were not a sacred one), in Bunyan, in Richardson, in Dickens, in Poe, and of course in a vast amount of ephemeral rubbish as well. We began this book by remarking that we cannot correlate popularity and value. But there is still the danger of reduction, or assuming that literature is *essentially* primitive and popular. This view had a great vogue in the nineteenth century, and is by no means dead yet, but if we were to adopt it we should cut off a third and most important source of supply for archetypal criticism.

We notice that many learned and recondite writers whose work requires patient study are explicitly mythopoeic writers. Instances include Dante and Spenser, and in the twentieth century embrace nearly all the "difficult" writers in both poetry and prose. Such work, when fictional, is often founded on a basis of naive drama *(Faust, Peer Gynt)* or naive romance (Hawthorne, Melville: one may compare the sophisticated allegories of Charles Williams and C. S. Lewis in our day, which are largely based on the formulas of the Boy's Own Paper). Learned mythopoeia, as we have it in the last period of Henry James and in James Joyce, for example, may become bewilderingly complex; but the complexities are designed to reveal and not to disguise the myth. We cannot assume that a primitive and popular myth has been swathed like a mummy in elaborate verbiage, which is the assumption that the fallacy of reduction would lead to. The inference seems to be that the learned and the subtle, like the primitive and the popular, tend toward a center of imaginative experience.

Knowing that *The Two Gentlemen of Verona* is an early Shakespeare comedy and *The Winter's Tale* a late one, the student would expect the later play to be more subtle and complex; he might not expect it to be more archaic and primitive, more suggestive of ancient myths and rituals. The later play is also more popular, though not popular of course in the sense of giving a lower-middle-class audience what it thinks it wants. As a result of expressing the inner forms of drama with increasing force and intensity, Shakespeare arrived in his last period at the bedrock of drama, the romantic spectacle out of which all the more specialized forms of drama, such as tragedy and social comedy, have come, and to which they recurrently return. In the greatest moments of Dante and Shakespeare, in, say *The Tempest* or the climax of the *Purgatorio,* we have a feeling of converging significance, the feeling that here we are close to seeing what our whole literary experience has been about, the feeling that we have moved into the still center of the order of words. Criticism as knowledge, the criticism which is compelled to keep on talking about the subject, recognizes the fact that there *is* a center of the order of words.

Unless there is such a center, there is nothing to prevent the analogies supplied by convention and genre from being an endless series of free associations, perhaps suggestive, perhaps even tantalizing, but never creating a real structure. The study of archetypes is the study of literary symbols as parts of a whole. If there are such things as archetypes at all, then, we have to take yet another step, and conceive the possibility of a self-contained literary universe. Either archetypal criticism is a will-o'-the-wisp, an endless labyrinth without an outlet, or we have to assume that literature is a total form, and not simply the name given to the aggregate of existing literary works. We spoke before of the mythical view of literature as leading to the conception of an order of nature as a whole being imitated by a corresponding order of words.

If archetypes are communicable symbols, and there is a center of archetypes, we should expect to find, at that center, a group of universal symbols. I do not mean by this phrase that there is any archetypal code book which has been memorized by all human societies without exception. I mean that some symbols are images of things common to all men, and therefore have a communicable power which is potentially unlimited. Such symbols include those of food and drink, of the quest or journey, of light and darkness, and of sexual fulfillment, which would usually take the form of marriage. It is inadvisable to assume that an Adonis or Oedipus myth is universal, or that certain associations, such as the serpent with the phallus, are universal, because when we discover a group of people who know nothing of such matters we must assume that they did know and have forgotten, or do know and won't tell, or are not members of the human race. On the other hand, they may be confidently excluded from the human race if they cannot understand the conception of food, and so any symbolism founded on food is universal in the sense of having an indefinitely extensive scope. That is, there are no limits to its intelligibility.

In the archetypal phase the work of literary art is a myth, and unites the ritual and the dream. By doing so it limits the dream: it makes it plausible and acceptable to a social waking consciousness. Thus as a moral fact in civilization, literature embodies a good deal of the spirit which in the dream itself is called the censor. But the censor stands in the way of the impetus of the dream. When we look at the dream as a whole, we notice three things about it. First, its limits are not the real, but the conceivable. Second, the limit of the conceivable is the world of fulfilled desire emancipated from all anxieties and frustrations. Third, the universe of the dream is entirely within the mind of the dreamer.

In the anagogic phase, literature imitates the total dream of man, and so imitates the thought of a human mind which is at the circumference and not at the center of its reality. We see here the completion of the imaginative revolution begun when we passed from the descriptive to the formal phase of symbolism. There, the imitation of nature shifted from a reflection of external nature to a formal organization of which nature was the content. But in the formal phase the poem is still contained by nature, and in the archetypal phase the whole of poetry is still contained within the limits of the natural, or plausible. When we pass into anagogy, nature becomes, not the container, but the thing contained, and the archetypal universal symbols, the city, the garden, the quest, the marriage, are no longer the desirable forms that man constructs inside nature, but are themselves the forms of nature. Nature is now inside the mind of an infinite man who builds his cities out of the Milky Way. This is not reality, but it is the conceivable or imaginative limit of desire, which is infinite, eternal, and hence apocalyptic. By an apocalypse I mean primarily the imaginative conception of the whole of nature as the content of an infinite and eternal living body which, if not human, is closer to being human than to being inanimate. "The desire of man being infinite," said Blake, "the possession is infinite and himself infinite." If Blake is thought a prejudiced witness on this point, we may cite Hooker: "That there is somewhat higher than either of these two (sensual and intellectual perfection), no other proof doth need than the very process of man's desire, which being natural should be frustrate, if there were not some farther thing wherein it might rest at the length contented, which in the former it cannot do."

If we turn to ritual, we see there an imitation of nature which has a strong element of what we call magic in it. Magic seems to begin as something of a voluntary effort to recapture a lost rapport with the natural cycle. This sense of a deliberate recapturing of something no longer possessed is a distinctive mark of human ritual. Ritual constructs a calendar and endeavors to imitate the precise and sensitive accuracy of the movements of the heavenly bodies and the response of vegetation to them. A farmer must harvest his crop at a certain time of the year, but because he must do this anyway, harvesting itself is not precisely a ritual. It is the expression of a will to synchronize human and natural energies at that time which produces the harvest songs, harvest sacrifices, and harvest folk customs that we associate with ritual. But the impetus of the magical element in ritual is clearly toward a universe in which a stupid and indifferent nature is no longer the container of human society, but is contained by that society, and must rain or shine at the pleasure of man. We notice too the tendency of ritual to become not only cyclical but encyclopedic, as already noted. In its anagogic phase, then, poetry imitates human action as total ritual, and so imitates the action of an omnipotent human society that contains all the powers of nature within itself.

Anagogically, then, poetry unites total ritual, or unlimited social action, with total dream, or unlimited individual thought. Its universe is infinite and boundless hypothesis: it cannot be contained within any actual civilization or set of moral values, for the same reason that no structure of imagery can be restricted to one allegorical interpretation. Here the *dianoia* of art is no longer a *mimesis logou*, but the Logos, the shaping word which is both reason and, as Goethe's Faust speculated, *praxis* or creative act. The *ethos* of art is no longer a group of characters within a natural setting, but a universal man who is also a divine being, or a divine being conceived in anthropomorphic terms.

The form of literature most deeply influenced by the anagogic phase is the scripture or apocalyptic revelation. The god, whether traditional deity, glorified hero, or apotheosized poet, is the central image that poetry uses in trying to convey the sense of unlimited power in a humanized form. Many of these scriptures are documents of religion as well, and hence are a mixture of the imaginative and the existential. When they lose their existential content they become purely imaginative, as Classical mythology did after the rise of Christianity. They belong in general, of course, to the mythical or theogonic mode. We see the relation to anagogy also in the vast encyclopedic structure of poetry that seems to be a whole world in itself, that stands in its culture as an inexhaustible storehouse of imaginative suggestion, and seems, like theories of gravitation or relativity in the physical universe, to be applicable to, or have analogous connections with every part of the literary universe. Such works are definitive myths, or complete organizations of archetypes. They include what in the previous essay we called analogies of revelation: the epics of Dante and Milton and their counterparts in the other modes.

But the anagogic perspective is not to be confined only to works that seem to take in everything, for the principle of anagogy is not simply that everything is the subject of poetry, but that anything may be the subject of a poem. The sense of the infinitely varied unity of poetry may come, not only explicitly from an apocalyptic epic, but implicitly from any poem. We said that we could get a whole liberal education by picking up one conventional poem, *Lycidas* for example, and following its archetypes through literature. Thus the center of the literary universe is whatever poem we happen to be reading. One step further, and the poem appears as a microcosm of all literature, an individual manifestation of the total order of words. Anagogically, then, the symbol is a monad, all symbols being united in a single infinite and eternal verbal symbol which is, as *dianoia,* the logos, and, as *mythos,* total creative act. It is this conception which Joyce expresses, in terms of subject matter, as "epiphany," and Hopkins, in terms of form, as "inscape."

If we look at *Lycidas* anagogically, for example, we see that the subject of the elegy has been identified with a god who personifies both the sun that falls into the western ocean at night and the vegetable life that dies in the autumn. In the latter aspect Lycidas is the Adonis or Tammuz whose "annual wound," as Milton calls it elsewhere, was the subject of a ritual lament in Mediterranean religion, and has been incorporated in the pastoral elegy since Theocritus, as the title of Shelley's *Adonais* shows more clearly. As a poet, Lycidas's archetype is Orpheus, who also died young, in much the same role as Adonis, and was flung into the water. As priest, his archetype is Peter, who would have drowned on the "Galilean lake" without the help of Christ. Each aspect of *Lycidas* poses the question of premature death as it relates to the life of man, of poetry, and of the church. But all of these aspects are contained within the figure of Christ, the young dying god who is eternally alive, the Word that contains all poetry, the head and body of the church, the Good Shepherd whose pastoral world sees no winter, the Sun of Righteousness that never sets, whose power can raise Lycidas, like Peter, out of the waves, as it redeems souls from the lower world, which Orpheus failed to do. Christ does not enter the poem as a character, but he pervades every line of it so completely that the poem, so to speak, enters him.

Anagogic criticism is usually found in direct connection with religion, and is to be discovered chiefly in the more uninhibited utterances of poets themselves. It comes out in those passages of Eliot's quartets where the words of the poet are placed within the context of the incarnate Word. An even clearer statement is in a letter of Rilke,[31] where he speaks of the function of the poet as revealing a perspective of reality like that of an angel, containing all time and space, who is blind and looking into himself. Rilke's angel is a modification of the more usual god or Christ, and his statement is all the more valuable because it is explicitly not Christian, and illustrates the independence of the anagogic perspective, of the poet's attempt to speak from the circumference instead of from the center of reality, from the acceptance of any specific religion. Similar views are expressed or implied in Valéry's conception of a total intelligence which appears more fancifully in his figure of M. Teste; in Yeats's cryptic utterances about the artifice of eternity, and, in *The Tower* and elsewhere, about man as the creator of all creation as well as of both life and death; in Joyce's nontheological use of the theological term *epiphany*; in Dylan Thomas's exultant hymns to a universal human body.[32] We may note in passing that the more sharply we distinguish the poetic and the critical functions, the easier it is for us to take seriously what great writers have said about their work.

The anagogic view of criticism thus leads to the conception of literature as existing in its own universe, no longer a commentary on life or reality, but containing life and reality in a system of verbal relationships. From this point of view the critic can no longer think of literature as a tiny palace of art looking out upon an inconceivably gigantic "life." "Life" for him has become the seed-plot of literature, a vast mass of potential literary forms, only a few of which will grow up into the greater world of the literary universe. Similar universes exist for all the arts. "We make to ourselves pictures of facts," says Wittgenstein, but by *pictures* he means representative illustrations, which are not pictures. Pictures as pictures are themselves facts, and exist only in a pictorial universe. *"Tout au monde,"* says Mallarmé, *"existe pour aboutir à un livre."*[33]

So far we have been dealing with symbols as isolated units, but clearly the unit of relationship between two symbols, corresponding to the phrase in music, is of equal importance. The testimony of critics from Aristotle on seems fairly unanimous that this unit of relationship is the metaphor. And the metaphor, in its radical form, is a statement of identity of the *"A is B"* type, or rather, putting it into its proper hypothetical form, of the "let *x* be *y*" type (letters altered for euphony). Thus the metaphor turns its back on ordinary descriptive meaning, and presents a structure which literally is ironic and paradoxical. In ordinary descriptive meaning, if *A* is *B* then *B* is *A*, and all we have really said is that *A* is itself. In the metaphor two things are identified while each retains its own form. Thus if we say "the hero was a lion" we identify the hero *with* the lion, while at the same time both the hero and the lion are identified *as* themselves. A work of literary art owes its unity to this process of identification *with,* and its variety, clarity, and intensity to identification *as.*

On the literal level of meaning, metaphor appears in its literal shape, which is simple juxtaposition. Ezra Pound, in explaining this aspect of metaphor, uses the illustrative figure of the Chinese ideogram, which expresses a complex image by throwing a group of elements together without predication. In Pound's famous blackboard example of such a metaphor, the two-line poem *In a Station of the Metro,* the images of the faces in the crowd and the petals on the black bough are juxtaposed with no predicate of any kind connecting them. Predication belongs to assertion and descriptive meaning, not to the literal structure of poetry.

On the descriptive level we have the double perspective of the verbal structure and the phenomena to which it is related. Here meaning is "literal" in the common sense which we explained would not do for criticism, an unambiguous alignment of words and facts. Descriptively, then, all metaphors are similes. When we are writing ordinary discursive prose and use a metaphor, we are not asserting that *A* is *B;* we are "really" saying that *A* is in some respects comparable with *B;* and similarly when we are extracting the descriptive or paraphrasable meaning of a poem. "The hero was a lion," then, on the descriptive level, is a simile with the word "like" omitted for greater vividness, and to show more clearly that the analogy is only a hypothetical one. In Whitman's poem *Out of the Cradle Endlessly Rocking,* we find shadows "twining and twisting as if they were alive," and the moon swollen, "as if with tears." As there is no *poetic* reason why shadows should not be alive or the moon tearful, we may perhaps see in the cautious *as if* the working of a low mimetic discursive prose conscience.

On the formal level, where symbols are images or natural phenomena conceived as matter or content, the metaphor is an analogy of natural proportion. Literally, metaphor is juxtaposition; we say simply *"A; B."* Descriptively, we say *"A* is (like) *B."* But formally we say *"A* is as *B."* An analogy

---

[31][Frye] Letter to Ellen Delp, October 27, 1915.

[32][Frye] To these should be added the great meditation on time in the second part of *Le Temps retrouvé.* One wonders if there is anything more than doubtful puns connecting the anagogic perspective in literature with Kant's conception of "transcendental aesthetic" as the a priori consciousness of space and time.

[33]*The Evolution of Literature,* p. 674.

of proportion thus requires four terms, of which two have a common factor. Thus "the hero was a lion" means, as a form of expression which has nature for its internal content, that the hero is to human courage as the lion is to animal courage, courage being the factor common to the third and fourth terms.

Archetypally, where the symbol is an associative cluster, the metaphor unites two individual images, each of which is a specific representative of a class or genus. The rose in Dante's *Paradiso* and the rose in Yeats's early lyrics are identified *with* different things, but both stand for all roses—all poetic roses, of course, not all botanical ones. Archetypal metaphor thus involves the use of what has been called the concrete universal, the individual identified with its class, Wordsworth's "tree of many one." Of course there are no *real* universals in poetry, only poetic ones. All four of these aspects of metaphors are recognized in Aristotle's discussion of metaphor in the *Poetics,* though sometimes very briefly and elliptically.

In the anagogic aspect of meaning, the radical form of metaphor, *"A is B,"* comes into its own. Here we are dealing with poetry in its totality, in which the formula *"A is B"* may be hypothetically applied to anything, for there is no metaphor, not even "black is white," which a reader has any right to quarrel with in advance. The literary universe, therefore, is a universe in which everything is potentially identical with everything else. This does not mean that any two things in it are separate and very similar, like peas in a pod, or in the slangy and erroneous sense of the word in which we speak of identical twins. If twins were really identical they would be the same person. On the other hand, a grown man feels identical with himself at the age of seven, although the two manifestations of this identity, the man and the boy, have very little in common as regards similarity or likeness. In form, matter, personality, time, and space, man and boy are quite unlike. This is the only type of image I can think of that illustrates the process of identifying two independent forms. All poetry, then, proceeds as though all poetic images were contained within a single universal body. Identity is the opposite of similarity or likeness, and total identity is not uniformity, still less monotony, but a unity of various things.

Finally, identification belongs not only to the structure of poetry, but to the structure of criticism as well, at least of commentary. Interpretation proceeds by metaphor as well as creation, and even more explicitly. When St. Paul interprets the story of Abraham's wives in Genesis, for instance, he says that Hagar "is" Mount Sinai in Arabia. Poetry, said Coleridge, is the identity of knowledge.[34]

---

[34][Frye] *Coleridge's Miscellaneous Criticism,* edited by T. M. Raysor (1936), 343.

The universe of poetry, however, is a literary universe, and not a separate existential universe. Apocalypse means revelation, and when art becomes apocalyptic, it reveals. But it reveals only on its own terms, and in its own forms: it does not describe or represent a separate content of revelation. When poet and critic pass from the archetypal to the anagogic phase, they enter a phase of which only religion, or something as infinite in its range as religion, can possibly form an external goal. The poetic imagination, unless it disciplines itself in the particular way in which the imaginations of Hardy and Housman were disciplined, is apt to get claustrophobia when it is allowed to talk only about human nature and subhuman nature; and poets are happier as servants of religion than of politics, because the transcendental and apocalyptic perspective of religion comes as a tremendous emancipation of the imaginative mind. If men were compelled to make the melancholy choice between atheism and superstition, the scientist, as Bacon pointed out long ago, would be compelled to choose atheism, but the poet would be compelled to choose superstition, for even superstition, by its very confusion of values, gives his imagination more scope than a dogmatic denial of imaginative infinity does. But the loftiest religion, no less than the grossest superstition, comes to the poet, qua poet, only as the spirits came to Yeats, to give him metaphors for poetry.

The study of literature takes us toward seeing poetry as the imitation of infinite social action and infinite human thought, the mind of a man who is all men, the universal creative word which is all words. About this man and word we can, speaking as critics, say only one thing ontologically: we have no reason to suppose either that they exist or that they do not exist. We can call them divine if by divine we mean the unlimited or projected human. But the critic, qua critic, has nothing to say for or against he affirmations that a religion makes out of these conceptions. If Christianity wishes to identify the infinite Word and Man of the literary universe with the Word of God, the person of Christ, the historical Jesus, the Bible or Church dogma, these identifications may be accepted by any poet or critic without injury to his work—the acceptance may even clarify and intensity his work, depending on his temperament and situation. But they can never be accepted by poetry as a whole, or by criticism as such. The literary critic, like the historian, is compelled to treat every religion in the same way that religions treat each other, as though it were a human hypothesis, whatever else he may in other contexts believe it to be. The discussion of the universal Word at the opening of the Chhandogya Upanishad (where it is symbolized by the sacred word *Aum*) is exactly as relevant and as irrelevant to literary criticism as the discussion at the opening of the fourth gospel. Coleridge was right in thinking that the "logos" was the goal of his work as a critic, but not right in thinking that his poetic logos would so inevitably be absorbed into Christ as to make literary criticism a kind of natural theology.

The total logos of criticism by itself can never become an object of faith or an ontological personality. The conception of a total Word is the postulate that there is such a thing as an order of words, and that the criticism which studies it makes, or could make, complete sense. Aristotle's *Physics* leads to the conception of an unmoved first mover at the circumference of the physical universe. This, in itself, means essentially that physics *has* a universe. The systematic study of motion would be impossible unless all phenomena of motion could be related to unifying principles, and those in their turn to a total unifying principle of movement which is not itself merely another phenomenon of motion. If theology identifies Aristotle's unmoved mover with a creating God, that is the business of theology; physics as physics will be unaffected by it. Christian critics may see their total Word as an analogy of Christ, as medieval critics did, but as literature itself may be accompanied in culture by any religion, criticism must detach itself accordingly. In short, the study of literature belongs to the "humanities," and the humanities, as their name indicates, can take only the human view of the superhuman.

The close resemblance between the conceptions of anagogic criticism and those of religion has led many to assume that they can only be related by making one supreme and the other subordinate. Those who choose religion, like Coleridge, will, like him, try to make criticism a natural theology; those who choose culture, like Arnold, will try to reduce religion to objectified cultural myth. But for the purity of each the autonomy of each must be guaranteed. Culture interposes, between the ordinary and the religious life, a total vision of possibilities, and insists on its totality—for whatever is excluded from culture by religion or state will get its revenge somehow. Thus culture's essential service to a religion is to destroy intellectual idolatry, the recurrent tendency in religion to replace the object of its worship with its present understanding and forms of approach to that object. Just as no argument in favor of a religious or political doctrine is of any value unless it is an intellectually honest argument, and so guarantees the autonomy of logic, so no religious or political myth is either valuable or valid unless it assumes the autonomy of culture, which may be provisionally defined as the total body of imaginative hypothesis in a society and its tradition. To defend the autonomy of culture in this sense seems to me the social task of the "intellectual" in the modern world: if so, to defend its subordination to a total synthesis of any kind, religious or political, would be the authentic form of the *trahison des clercs*.[35]

Besides, it is of the essence of imaginative culture that it transcends the limits both of the naturally possible and of the morally acceptable. The argument that there is no room for poets in any human society which is an end in itself remains unanswerable even when the society is the people of God. For religion is also a social institution, and so far as it is one, it imposes limitations on the arts just as a Marxist or Platonic state would do. Christian theology is no less of a revolutionary dialectic, or indissoluble union of theory and social practice. Religions, in spite of their enlarged perspective, cannot as social institutions *contain* an art of unlimited hypothesis. The arts in their turn cannot help releasing the powerful acids of satire, realism, ribaldry, and fantasy in their attempt to dissolve all the existential concretions that get in their way. The artist often enough has to find that, as God says in *Faust*, he *"muss als Teufel schaffen,"* which I suppose means rather more than he has to work like the devil. Between religion's "this is" and poetry's "but suppose *this* is," there must always be some kind of tension, until the possible and the actual meet at infinity. Nobody wants a poet in the perfect human state, and, as even the poets tell us, nobody but God himself can tolerate a poltergeist in the City of God.

---

[35] "Treachery of clerks."

Gaston Bachelard

1884–1962

Bachelard's remark, "Forces are manifested in poems that do not pass through the circuits of knowledge," epitomizes his point of view. He was interested in "poetic revery" and wished to develop a criticism that would not "intellectualize" the poetic image; he wanted to be true to the "poetic logos." The ultimately important point is for the poetic image to invade the reader without the mediation of rational inquiry or any sort of analysis. It would appear that in order to keep this intersubjectivity alive, the critic must make a poem of his criticism, else the chain of imagery is broken and the whole matter falls into intellectualization and analysis. Once reason was thought to lift man from the slavery of ignorance and passion, but for Bachelard the poetic image in its primitiveness releases man into freedom from rational law. According to Bachelard, both psychology and psychoanalysis *translate* the poetic image and *intellectualize* it, thus destroying its power. The reader must take the image "in its being"; by doing so he becomes one with it, is invaded by it, and invades it in turn.

Bachelard's affinities are with the phenomenological critics of France and Switzerland. His influence on younger critics of the Geneva School, especially Jean-Pierre Richard, has been profound.

Works of Bachelard available in English are *The Poetics of Space* (tr. 1964), *The Psychoanalysis of Fire* (tr. 1964), *The Philosophy of No* (tr. 1968), *The Poetics of Reverie* (tr. 1969), *On Poetic Imagination and Reverie* (tr. 1971), *The Right to Dream* (tr. 1971), and *The New Scientific Spirit* (tr. 1984). See Mary Ann Caws, *Surrealism and Imagination* (1966); Dominique Lecourt, *Marxism and Epistemology* (tr. 1975); Roch C. Smith, *Gaston Bachelard* (1982); and Mary Teles, *Bachelard, Science and Objectivity* (1984).

The Poetics of Space

From

Introduction

I

A philosopher who has evolved his entire thinking from the fundamental themes of the philosophy of science, and followed the main line of the active, growing rationalism of contemporary science as closely as he could, must forget his learning and break with all his habits of philosophical research, if he wants to study the problems posed by the poetic imagination. For here the cultural past doesn't count. The long day-in, day-out effort of putting together and constructing his thoughts is ineffectual. One must be receptive, receptive to the image at the moment it appears: if there be a philosophy of poetry, it must appear and reappear through a significant verse, in total adherence to an isolated image; to be exact, in the very ecstasy of the newness of the image. The poetic image is a sudden salience on the surface of the psyche, the lesser psychological causes of which have not been sufficiently investigated. Nor can anything general and coordinated serve as a basis for a philosophy of poetry. The

THE POETICS OF SPACE. Bachelard's *La Poétique de l'espace* was first published in 1958. The text is from *The Poetics of Space* translated by Maria Jolas. Copyright © 1958 by Presses Universitaires de France, translation © 1964 by The Orion Press, Inc. Reprinted by permission of the publisher, Viking Penguin, a division of Penguin Books USA Inc.

idea of principle or "basis" in this case would be disastrous, for it would interfere with the essential psychic actuality, the essential novelty of the poem. And whereas philosophical reflection applied to scientific thinking elaborated over a long period of time requires any new idea to become integrated in a body of tested ideas, even though this body of ideas be subjected to profound change by the new idea (as is the case in all the revolutions of contemporary science), the philosophy of poetry must acknowledge that the poetic act has no past, at least no recent past, in which its preparation and appearance could be followed.

Later, when I shall have occasion to mention the relation of a new poetic image to an archetype lying dormant in the depths of the unconscious, I shall have to make it understood that this relation is not, properly speaking, a *causal* one. The poetic image is not subject to an inner thrust. It is not an echo of the past. On the contrary: through the brilliance of an image, the distant past resounds with echoes, and it is hard to know at what depth these echoes will reverberate and die away. Because of its novelty and its action, the poetic image has an entity and a dynamism of its own; it is referable to a direct *ontology*. This ontology is what I plan to study.

Very often, then, it is in the opposite of causality, that is, in *reverberation*, which has been so subtly analyzed by Minkowski,[1] that I think we find the real measure of the being of a poetic image. In this reverberation, the poetic image will have a sonority of being. The poet speaks on the threshold of being. Therefore, in order to determine the being of an image, we shall have to experience its reverberation in the manner of Minkowski's phenomenology.

To say that the poetic image is independent of causality is to make a rather serious statement. But the causes cited by psychologists and psychoanalysts can never really explain the wholly unexpected nature of the new image, any more than they can explain the attraction it holds for a mind that is foreign to the process of its creation. The poet does not confer the past of his image upon me, and yet his image immediately takes root in me. The communicability of an unusual image is a fact of great ontological significance. We shall return to this question of communion through brief, isolated, rapid actions. Images excite us—afterwards—but they are not the phenomena of an excitement. In all psychological research, we can, of course, bear in mind psychoanalytical methods for determining the personality of a poet, and thus find a measure of the pressures—but above all of the oppressions—that a poet has been subjected to in the course of his life. But the poetic act itself, the sudden image, the flare-up

of being in the imagination, are inaccessible to such investigations. In order to clarify the problem of the poetic image philosophically, we shall have to have recourse to a phenomenology of the imagination. By this should be understood a study of the phenomenon of the poetic image when it emerges into the consciousness as a direct product of the heart, soul and being of man, apprehended in his actuality.

II

I shall perhaps be asked why, departing from my former point of view, I now seek a phenomenological determination of images. In my earlier works on the subject of the imagination, I did, in fact, consider it preferable to maintain as objective a position as possible with regard to the images of the four material elements, the four principles of the intuitive cosmogonies, and, faithful to my habits as a philosopher of science, I tried to consider images without attempting personal interpretation. Little by little, this method, which has in its favor scientific prudence, seemed to me to be an insufficient basis on which to found a metaphysics of the imagination. The "prudent" attitude itself is a refusal to obey the immediate dynamics of the image. I have come to realize how difficult it is to break away from this "prudence." To say that one has left certain intellectual habits behind is easy enough, but how is it to be achieved? For a rationalist, this constitutes a minor daily crisis, a sort of split in one's thinking which, even though its object be partial—a mere image—has nonetheless great psychic repercussions. However, this minor cultural crisis, this crisis on the simple level of a new image, contains the entire paradox of a phenomenology of the imagination, which is: how can an image, at times very unusual, appear to be a concentration of the entire psyche? How—with no preparation—can this singular, short-lived event constituted by the appearance of an unusual poetic image, react on other minds and in other hearts, despite all the barriers of common sense, all the disciplined schools of thought, content in their immobility?

It seemed to me, then, that this transsubjectivity of the image could not be understood, in its essence, through the habits of subjective reference alone. Only phenomenology—that is to say, consideration of the *onset of the image* in an individual consciousness—can help us to restore the subjectivity of images and to measure their fullness, their strength and their transsubjectivity. These subjectivities and transsubjectivities cannot be determined once and for all, for the poetic image is essentially *variational,* and not, as in the case of the concept, *constitutive.* No doubt, it is an arduous task—as well as a monotonous one—to isolate the transforming action of the poetic imagination in the detail of the variations

[1][Bachelard] Cf. Eugène Minkowski, *Vers une cosmologie,* Chapter 9.

of the images. For a reader of poems, therefore, an appeal to a doctrine that bears the frequently misunderstood name of phenomenology risks falling on deaf ears. And yet, independent of all doctrine, this appeal is clear: the reader of poems is asked to consider an image not as an object and even less as the substitute for an object, but to seize its specific reality. For this, the act of the creative consciousness must be systematically associated with the most fleeting product of that consciousness, the poetic image. At the level of the poetic image, the duality of subject and object is iridescent, shimmering, unceasingly active in its inversions. In this domain of the creation of the poetic image by the poet, phenomenology, if one dare to say so, is a microscopic phenomenology. As a result, this phenomenology will probably be strictly elementary. In this union, through the image of a pure but short-lived subjectivity and a reality which will not necessarily reach its final constitution, the phenomenologist finds a field for countless experiments; he profits by observations that can be exact because they are simple, because they "have no consequences" as is the case with scientific thought, which is always relaxed thought. The image, in its simplicity, has no need of scholarship. It is the property of a naive consciousness; in its expression, it is youthful language. The poet, in the novelty of his images, is always the origin of language. To specify exactly what a phenomenology of the image can be, to specify that the image comes *before* thought, we should have to say that poetry, rather than being a phenomenology of the mind, is a phenomenology of the soul. We should then have to collect documentation on the subject of the *dreaming consciousness.*

The language of contemporary French philosophy— and even more so, psychology—hardly uses the dual meaning of the words soul and mind. As a result, they are both somewhat deaf to certain themes that are very numerous in German philosophy, in which the distinction between mind and soul *(der Geist und die Seele)* is so clear. But since a philosophy of poetry must be given the entire force of the vocabulary, it should not simplify, not harden anything. For such a philosophy, mind and soul are not synonymous, and by taking them as such, we bar translation of certain invaluable texts, we distort documents brought to light thanks to the archeologists of the image. The word *soul* is an immortal word. In certain poems it cannot be effaced, for it is a word born of our breath.[2] The vocal importance alone of a word should arrest the attention of a phenomenologist of poetry. The word *soul* can, in fact, be poetically spoken with such

conviction that it constitutes a commitment for the entire poem. The poetic register that corresponds to the soul must therefore remain open to our phenomenological investigations.

In the domain of painting, in which realization seems to imply decisions that derive from the mind, and rejoin obligations of the world of perception, the phenomenology of the soul can reveal the first commitment of an oeuvre. René Huyghe, in his very fine preface for the exhibition of Georges Rouault's works in Albi, wrote: "If we wanted to find out wherein Rouault explodes definitions . . . we should perhaps have to call upon a word that has become rather outmoded, which is the word *soul.*" He goes on to show that in order to understand, to sense and to love Rouault's work, we must "start from the center, at the very heart of the circle from where the whole thing derives its source and meaning: and here we come back again to that forgotten, outcast word, the soul." Indeed, the soul—as Rouault's painting proves— possesses an inner light, the light that an inner vision knows and expresses in the world of brilliant colors, in the world of sunlight, so that a veritable reversal of psychological perspectives is demanded of those who seek to understand, at the same time that they love Rouault's painting. They must participate in an inner light which is not a reflection of a light from the outside world. No doubt there are many facile claims to the expressions *inner vision* and *inner light.* But here it is a painter speaking, a producer of lights. He knows from what heat source the light comes. He experiences the intimate meaning of the passion for red. At the core of such painting, there is a soul in combat—the fauvism, the wildness, is interior. Painting like this is therefore a phenomenon of the soul. The oeuvre must redeem an impassioned soul.

These pages by René Huyghe corroborate my idea that it is reasonable to speak of a phenomenology of the soul. In many circumstances we are obliged to acknowledge that poetry is a commitment of the soul. A consciousness associated with the soul is more relaxed, less intentionalized than a consciousness associated with the phenomena of the mind. Forces are manifested in poems that do not pass through the circuits of knowledge. The dialectics of inspiration and talent become clear if we consider their two poles: the soul and the mind. In my opinion, soul and mind are indispensable for studying the phenomena of the poetic image in their various nuances, above all, for following the evolution of poetic images from the original state of revery to that of execution. In fact, in a future work, I plan to concentrate particularly on poetic revery as a phenomenology of the soul. In itself, revery constitutes a psychic condition that is too frequently confused with dream. But when it is a question of poetic revery, of revery that derives pleasure not only from itself, but also prepares poetic pleasure for the other souls, one realizes that

---

[2][Bachelard] Charles Nodier, *Dictionnaire raisonné des onomatopées françaises* (Paris, 1828), p. 46. "The different names for the soul, among nearly all peoples, are just so many breath variations, and onomatopoeic expressions of breathing."

one is no longer drifting into somnolence. The mind is able to relax, but in poetic revery the soul keeps watch, with no tension, calmed and active. To compose a finished well-constructed poem, the mind is obliged to make projects that prefigure it. But for a simple poetic image, there is no project; a flicker of the soul is all that is needed.

And this is how a poet poses the phenomenological problem of the soul in all clarity. Pierre-Jean Jouve writes: "Poetry is a soul inaugurating a form."[3] The soul inaugurates. Here it is the supreme power. It is human dignity. Even if the "form" was already well-known, previously discovered, carved from "commonplaces," before the interior poetic light was turned upon it, it was a mere object for the mind. But the soul comes and inaugurates the form, dwells in it, takes pleasure in it. Pierre-Jean Jouve's statement can therefore be taken as a clear maxim of a phenomenology of the soul.

III

Since a phenomenological inquiry on poetry aspires to go so far and so deep, because of methodological obligations, it must go beyond the sentimental resonances with which we receive (more or less richly—whether this richness be within ourselves or within the poem) a work of art. This is where the phenomenological doublet of resonances and repercussions must be sensitized. The resonances are dispersed on the different planes of our life in the world, while the repercussions invite us to give greater depth to our own existence. In the resonance we hear the poem, in the reverberations we speak it, it is our own. The reverberations bring about a change of being. It is as though the poet's being were our being. The multiplicity of resonances then issues from the reverberations' unity of being. Or, to put it more simply, this is an impression that all impassioned poetry lovers know well: the poem possesses us entirely. This grip that poetry acquires on our very being bears a phenomenological mark that is unmistakable. The exuberance and depth of a poem are always phenomena of the resonance-reverberation doublet. It is as though the poem, through its exuberance, awakened new depths in us. In order to ascertain the psychological action of a poem, we should therefore have to follow the two perspectives of phenomenological analysis, towards the outpourings of the mind and towards the profundities of the soul.

Needless to say, the reverberation, in spite of its derivative name, has a simple phenomenological nature in the domain of poetic imagination. For it involves bringing about a veritable awakening of poetic creation, even in the soul of the reader, through the reverberations of a single poetic image. By its novelty, a poetic image sets in motion the entire linguistic mechanism. The poetic image places us at the origin of the speaking being.

Through this reverberation, by going *immediately* beyond all psychology or psychoanalysis, we feel a poetic power rising naively within us. After the original reverberation, we are able to experience resonances, sentimental repercussions, reminders of our past. But the image has touched the depths before it stirs the surface. And this is also true of a simple experience of reading. The image offered us by reading the poem now becomes really our own. It takes root in us. It has been given us by another, but we begin to have the impression that we could have created it, that we should have created it. It becomes a new being in our language, expressing us by making us what it expresses; in other words, it is at once a becoming of expression, and a becoming of our being. Here expression creates being.

This last remark defines the level of the ontology towards which I am working. As a general thesis I believe that everything specifically human in man is *logos*. One would not be able to meditate in a zone that preceded language. But even if this thesis appears to reject an ontological depth, it should be granted, at least as a working hypothesis appropriate to the subject of the poetic imagination.

Thus the poetic image, which stems from the logos, is personally innovating. We cease to consider it as an "object" but feel that the "objective" critical attitude stifles the "reverberation" and rejects on principle the depth at which the original poetic phenomenon starts. As for the psychologist, being deafened by the resonances, he keeps trying to *describe* his feelings. And the psychoanalyst, victim of his method, inevitably intellectualizes the image, losing the reverberations in his effort to untangle the skein of his interpretations. He understands the image more deeply than the psychologist. But that's just the point, he "understands" it. For the psychoanalyst, the poetic image always has a context. When he interprets it, however, he translates it into a language that is different from the poetic logos. Never, in fact, was *"traduttore, traditore"*[4] more justifiably applicable.

When I receive a new poetic image, I experience its quality of intersubjectivity. I know that I am going to repeat

---

[3][Bachelard] Pierre-Jean Jouve, *En miroir* (Mercure de France), p. 11.

[4]"To translate is to betray."

it in order to communicate my enthusiasm. When considered in transmission from one soul to another, it becomes evident that a poetic image eludes causality. Doctrines that are timidly causal, such as psychology, or strongly causal, such as psychoanalysis, can hardly determine the ontology of what is poetic. For nothing prepares a poetic image, especially not culture, in the literary sense, and especially not perception, in the psychological sense.

I always come then to the same conclusion: the essential newness of the poetic image poses the problem of the speaking being's creativeness. Through this creativeness the imagining consciousness proves to be, very simply but very purely, an origin. In a study of the imagination, a phenomenology of the poetic imagination must concentrate on bringing out this quality of origin in various poetic images.

IV

By thus limiting my inquiry to the poetic image at its origin, proceeding from pure imagination, I leave aside the problem of the *composition* of the poem as a grouping together of numerous images. Into this composition enter certain psychologically complex elements that associate earlier cultures with actual literary ideals—components which a complete phenomenology would no doubt be obliged to consider. But so extensive a project might be prejudicial to the purity of the phenomenological observations, however elementary, that I should like to present. The real phenomenologist must make it a point to be systematically modest. This being the case, it seems to me that merely to refer to phenomenological reading powers, which make of the reader a poet on a level with the image he has read, shows already a taint of pride. Indeed, it would be a lack of modesty on my part to assume personally a reading power that could match and relive the power of organized, complete creation implied by a poem in its entirety. But there is even less hope of attaining to a synthetic phenomenology which would dominate an entire oeuvre, as certain psychoanalysts believe they can do. It is therefore on the level of detached images that I shall succeed in "reverberating" phenomenologically.

Precisely this touch of pride, this lesser pride, this mere reader's pride that thrives in the solitude of reading, bears the unmistakable mark of phenomenology, if its simplicity is maintained. Here the phenomenologist has nothing in common with the literary critic who, as has frequently been noted, judges a work that he could not create and, if we are to believe certain facile condemnations, would not want to create. A literary critic is a reader who is necessarily severe. By turning inside out like a glove an overworked complex that has become debased to the point of being part of the vocabulary of statesmen, we might say that the literary critic and the professor of rhetoric, who know all and judge all, readily go in for a simplex of superiority. As for me, being an addict of felicitous reading, I only read and reread what I like, with a bit of reader's pride mixed in with much enthusiasm. But whereas pride usually develops into a massive sentiment that weighs upon the entire psyche, the touch of pride that is born of adherence to the felicity of an image, remains secret and unobtrusive. It is within us, mere readers that we are, it is for us, and for us alone. It is a homely sort of pride. Nobody knows that in reading we are reliving our temptations to be a poet. All readers who have a certain passion for reading, nurture and repress, through reading, the desire to become a writer. When the page we have just read is too near perfection, our modesty suppresses this desire. But it reappears, nevertheless. In any case, every reader who rereads a work that he likes, knows that its pages *concern* him. In Jean-Pierre Richard's excellent collection of essays entitled *Poésie et profondeur* (Poetry and Depth), there is one devoted to Baudelaire and one to Verlaine. Emphasis is laid on Baudelaire, however, since, as the author says, his work "concerns us." There is great difference of tone between the two essays. Unlike Baudelaire, Verlaine does not attract complete phenomenological attention. And this is always the case. In certain types of reading with which we are in deep sympathy, in the very expression itself, we are the "beneficiaries." Jean-Paul Richter, in *Titan,* gives the following description of his hero: "He read eulogies of great men with as much pleasure as though he himself had been the object of these panegyrics."[5] In any case, harmony in reading is inseparable from admiration. We can admire more or less, but a sincere impulse, a little impulse toward admiration, is always necessary if we are to receive the phenomenological benefit of a poetic image. The slightest critical consideration arrests this impulse by putting the mind in second position, destroying the primitivity of the imagination. In this admiration, which goes beyond the passivity of contemplative attitudes, the joy of reading appears to be the reflection of the joy of writing, as though the reader were the writer's ghost. At least the reader participates in the joy of creation that, for Bergson, is the sign of creation.[6] Here, creation takes place on the tenuous thread of the sentence, in the fleeting life of an expression. But this poetic expression, although it has no vital necessity, has a bracing effect on our

---

[5][Bachelard] Jean-Paul Richter, *Le Titan,* French translation by Philarète-Chasles (1878), Vol. I, p. 22.
[6][Bachelard] Henri Bergson, *L'Énergie spirituelle,* p. 23.

lives, for all that. To speak well is part of living well. The poetic image is an emergence from language, it is always a little above the language of signification. By living the poems we read, we have then the salutary experience of emerging. This, no doubt, is emerging at short range. But these acts of emergence are repeated; poetry puts language in a state of emergence, in which life becomes manifest through its vivacity. These linguistic impulses, which stand out from the ordinary rank of pragmatic language, are miniatures of the vital impulse. A micro-Bergsonism that abandoned the thesis of language-as-instrument in favor of the thesis of language-as-reality would find in poetry numerous documents on the intense life of language.

Thus, along with considerations on the life of words, as it appears in the evolution of language across the centuries, the poetic image, as a mathematician would say, presents us with a sort of differential of this evolution. A great verse can have a great influence on the soul of a language. It awakens images that had been effaced, at the same time that it confirms the unforeseeable nature of speech. And if we render speech unforeseeable, is this not an apprenticeship to freedom? What delight the poetic imagination takes in making game of censors! Time was when the poetic arts codified the licenses to be permitted. Contemporary poetry, however, has introduced freedom in the very body of the language. As a result, poetry appears as a phenomenon of freedom.

V

Even at the level of an isolated poetic image, if only in the progression of expression constituted by the verse, the phenomenological reverberation can appear; and in its extreme simplicity, it gives us mastery of our tongue. Here we are in the presence of a minuscule phenomenon of the shimmering consciousness. The poetic image is certainly the psychic event that has the least importance. To seek justification of it in terms of perceptible reality, to determine its place and role in the poem's composition, are two tasks that do not need to be undertaken until later. In the first phenomenological inquiry of the poetic imagination, the isolated image, the phrase that carries it forward, the verse, or occasionally the stanza in which the poetic image radiates, form *language areas* that should be studied by means of topo-analysis. J. B. Pontalis, for instance, presents Michel Leiris as a "lonely prospector in the galleries of words,"[7] which describes ex-

tremely well this fibered space traversed by the simple impetus of words that have been experienced. The atomism of conceptual language demands reasons for fixation, forces of centralization. But the verse always has a movement, the image flows into the line of the verse, carrying the imagination along with it, as though the imagination created a nerve fiber. Pontalis adds the following (p. 932), which deserves to be remembered as a sure index for a phenomenology of expression: "The speaking subject is the entire subject." And it no longer seems paradoxical to say that the speaking subject exists in his entirety in a poetic image, because unless he abandons himself to it without reservations, he does not enter into the poetic space of the image. Very clearly, the poetic image furnishes one of the simplest experiences of language that has been lived. And if, as I propose to do, it is considered as an origin of consciousness, it points to a phenomenology.

Also, if we had to name a "school" of phenomenology, it would no doubt be in connection with the poetic phenomenon that we should find the clearest, the really elementary, lessons. In a recent book, J. H. Van den Berg writes: "Poets and painters are born phenomenologists."[8] And noting that things "speak" to us and that, as a result of this fact, if we give this language its full value, we have a contact with things, Van den Berg adds: "We are continually living a solution of problems that reflection cannot hope to solve." The philosopher whose investigations are centered on the speaking being will find encouragement in these lines by this learned Dutch phenomenologist.

VI

The phenomenological situation with regard to psychoanalytical investigation will perhaps be more precisely stated if, in connection with poetic images, we are able to isolate a sphere of *pure sublimation;* of a sublimation which sublimates nothing, which is relieved of the burden of passion, and freed from the pressure of desire. By thus giving to the poetic image at its peak an absolute of sublimation, I place heavy stakes on a simple nuance. It seems to me, however, that poetry gives abundant proof of this absolute sublimation, as will be seen frequently in the course of this work. When psychologists and psychoanalysts are furnished this proof, they cease to see anything in the poetic image but a

---

[7][Bachelard] J. B. Pontalis, *Michel Leiris ou la psychanalyse indeterminable* in *Les Temps modernes* (December 1955), p. 931.

[8][Bachelard] J. H. Van den Berg, *The Phenomenological Approach in Psychology.* An introduction to recent phenomenological psychopathology (Charles C Thomas, Publisher. Springfield, Illinois, 1955, p. 61).

simple game, a short-lived, totally vain game. Images, in particular, have no significance for them—neither from the standpoint of the passions, nor from that of psychology or psychoanalysis. It does not occur to them that the significance of such images is precisely a poetic significance. But poetry is there with its countless surging images, images through which the creative imagination comes to live in its own domain.

For a phenomenologist, the attempt to attribute antecedents to an image, when we are in the very existence of the image, is a sign of inveterate psychologism. On the contrary, let us take the poetic image in its being. For the poetic consciousness is so wholly absorbed by the image that appears on the language, above customary language; the language it speaks with the poetic image is so new that correlations between past and present can no longer be usefully considered.

The examples I shall give of breaks in significance, sensation and sentiment will oblige the reader to grant me that the poetic image is under the sign of a new being.

This new being is happy man.

Happy in speech, therefore unhappy in reality, will be the psychoanalyst's immediate objection. Sublimation, for him, is nothing but a vertical compensation, a flight upwards, exactly in the same way that compensation is a lateral flight. And right away, the psychoanalyst will abandon ontological investigation of the image, to dig into the past of man. He sees and points out the poet's secret sufferings. He explains the flower by the fertilizer.

The phenomenologist does not go that far. For him, the image is there, the word speaks, the word of the poet speaks to him. There is no need to have lived through the poet's sufferings in order to seize the felicity of speech offered by the poet—a felicity that dominates tragedy itself. Sublimation in poetry towers above the psychology of the mundanely unhappy soul. For it is a fact that poetry possesses a felicity of its own, however great the tragedy it may be called upon to illustrate.

Pure sublimation, as I see it, poses a serious problem of method for, needless to say, the phenomenologist cannot disregard the deep psychological reality of the processes of sublimation that have been so lengthily examined by psychoanalysis. His task is that of proceeding phenomenologically to images which have not been experienced, and which life does not prepare, but which the poet creates; of living what has not been lived, and being receptive to an overture of language. There exist a few poems, such as certain poems by Pierre-Jean Jouve, in which experiences of this kind may be found. Indeed, I know of no oeuvre that has been nourished on psychoanalytical meditation more than Jouve's. However, here and there, his poetry passes through flames of such intensity that we no longer need live at its original source. He himself has said: "Poetry constantly surpasses its origins, and because it suffers more deeply in ecstasy or in sorrow, it retains greater freedom."[9] Again, on page 112: "The further I advanced in time, the more the plunge was controlled, removed from the contributory cause, directed toward the pure form of language." I cannot say whether or not Pierre-Jean Jouve would agree to consider the causes divulged by psychoanalysis as "contributory." But in the region of "the pure form of language" the psychoanalyst's causes do not allow us to predict the poetic image in its newness. They are, at the very most, opportunities for liberation. And in the poetic age in which we live, it is in this that poetry is specifically "surprising." Its images are therefore unpredictable. Most literary critics are insufficiently aware of this unpredictability, which is precisely what upsets the plans of the usual psychological explanations. But the poet states clearly: "Poetry, especially in its present endeavors, (can) only correspond to attentive thought that is enamored of something unknown, and essentially receptive to becoming." Later, on page 170: "Consequently, a new definition of a poet is in view, which is: he who knows, that is to say, who transcends, and names what he knows." Lastly, (p. 10): "There is no poetry without absolute creation."

Such poetry is rare.[10] The great mass of poetry is more mixed with passion, more psychologized. Here, however, rarity and exception do not confirm the rule, but contradict it and set up a new regime. Without the region of absolute sublimation—however restrained and elevated it may be, and even though it may seem to lie beyond the reach of psychologists or psychoanalysts, who, after all, have no reason to examine pure poetry—poetry's exact polarity cannot be revealed.

We may hesitate in determining the exact level of disruption, we may also remain for a long time in the domain of the confusing passions that *perturb* poetry. Moreover, the height at which we encounter pure sublimation is doubtless not the same for all souls. But at least the necessity of separating a sublimation examined by a psychoanalyst from one examined by a phenomenologist of poetry is a necessity of method. A psychoanalyst can of course study the human character of poets but, as a result of his own sojourn in the region of the passions, he is not prepared to study poetic images in their exalting reality. C. G. Jung said this, in fact,

---

[9][Bachelard] Pierre-Jean Jouve, *En miroir* (Mercure de France), p. 109. Andrée Chédid has also written: "A poem remains free. We shall never enclose its fate in our own." The poet knows well that "his breath will carry him farther than his desire." (*Terre et poésie*, G. L.M. §§ 14 and 25.)

[10][Bachelard] Pierre-Jean Jouve, *loc. cit.*, p. 9: "La poésie est rare."

very clearly: by persisting in the habits of judgment inherent in psychoanalysis,

> interest is diverted from the work of art and loses itself in the inextricable chaos of psychological antecedents; the poet becomes a "clinical case," an example, to which is given a certain number in the *psychopathia sexualis*. Thus the psychoanalysis of a work of art moves away from its object and carries the discussion into a domain of general human interest, which is not in the least peculiar to the artist and, particularly, has no importance for his art.[11]

Merely with a view to summarizing this discussion, I should like to make a polemical remark, although indulging in polemics is not one of my habits.

A Roman said to a shoemaker who had directed his gaze too high: *"Ne sutor ultra crepidam."*[12]

Every time there is a question of pure sublimation, when the very being of poetry must be determined, shouldn't the phenomenologist say to the psychoanalyst: *"Ne psuchor ultra uterum."*[13]

VII

In other words, as soon as an art has become autonomous, it makes a fresh start. It is therefore salient to consider this start as a sort of phenomenology. On principle, phenomenology liquidates the past and confronts what is new. Even in an art like painting, which bears witness to a skill, the important successes take place independently of skill. In a study of the painting of Charles Lapicque, by Jean Lescure, we read:

> Although his work gives evidence of wide culture and knowledge of all the dynamic expressions of space, they are not applied, they are not made into recipes. . . . Knowing must therefore be accompanied by an equal capacity to forget knowing. Nonknowing is not a form of ignorance but a difficult transcendence of knowledge. This is the price that must be paid for an oeuvre to be, at all times, a sort of pure beginning, which makes its creation an exercise in freedom.[14]

These lines are of essential importance for us, in that they may be transposed immediately into a phenomenology of the poetic. In poetry, nonknowing is a primal condition; if there exists a skill in the writing of poetry, it is in the minor task of associating images. But the entire life of the image is in its dazzling splendor, in the fact that an image is a transcending of all the premises of sensibility.

It becomes evident, then, that a man's work stands out from life to such an extent that life cannot explain it. Jean Lescure says of the painter (*loc. cit.,* p. 132): "Lapicque demands of the creative act that it should offer him as much surprise as life itself." Art, then, is an increase of life, a sort of competition of surprises that stimulates our consciousness and keeps it from becoming somnolent. In a quotation of Lapicque himself (given by Lescure, p. 132) we read:

> If, for instance, I want to paint horses taking the water hurdle at the Auteuil racecourse, I expect my painting to give me as much that is unexpected, although of another kind, as the actual race I witnessed gave me. Not for a second can there be any question of reproducing exactly a spectacle that is already in the past. But I have to relive it entirely, in a manner that is new and, this time, from the standpoint of painting. By doing this, I create for myself the possibility of a fresh impact.

And Lescure concludes: "An artist does not create the way he lives, he lives the way he creates."

Thus, contemporary painters no longer consider the image as a simple substitute for a perceptible reality. Proust said already of roses painted by Elstir that they were "a new variety with which this painter, like some clever horticulturist, had enriched the rose family."[15]

VIII

Academic psychology hardly deals with the subject of the poetic image, which is often mistaken for simple metaphor. Generally, in fact, the word *image,* in the works of psychologists, is surrounded with confusion: we see images, we reproduce images, we retain images in our memory. The image is everything except a direct product of the imagination. In Bergson's *Matière et mémoire (Matter and Memory),* in

---

[11]*On the Relation of Analytical Psychology to Poetry,* p. 785
[12]"Let the cobbler stick to his last."
[13]"Let the psychiatrist stick to his womb."
[14][Bachelard] Jean Lescure, *Lapicque* (Galanis, Paris), p. 78.

[15][Bachelard] Marcel Proust, *Remembrance of Things Past,* Vol. V; *Sodom and Gomorrah.*

which the image concept is very widely treated, there is only one reference (on p. 198) to the *productive* imagination. This production remains, therefore, an act of lesser freedom, that has no relation to the great free acts stressed by Bergsonian philosophy. In this short passage, the philosopher refers to the "play of fantasy" and the various images that derive from it as "so many liberties that the mind takes with nature." But these liberties, in the plural, do not commit our being; they do not add to the language nor do they take it out of its utilitarian role. They really are so much "play." Indeed, the imagination hardly lends iridescence to our recollections. In this domain of poeticized memory, Bergson is well this side of Proust. The liberties that the mind takes with nature do not really designate the nature of the mind.

I propose, on the contrary, to consider the imagination as a major power of human nature. To be sure, there is nothing to be gained by saying that the imagination is the faculty of producing images. But this tautology has at least the virtue of putting an end to comparisons of images with memories.

By the swiftness of its actions, the imagination separates us from the past as well as from reality; it faces the future. To the *function of reality*, wise in experience of the past, as it is defined by traditional psychology, should be added a *function of unreality*, which is equally positive, as I tried to show in certain of my earlier works. Any weakness in the function of unreality will hamper the productive psyche. If we cannot imagine, we cannot foresee.

But to touch more simply upon the problems of the poetic imagination, it is impossible to receive the psychic benefit of poetry unless these two functions of the human psyche—the function of the real and the function of the unreal—are made to cooperate. We are offered a veritable cure of rhythmo-analysis through the poem, which interweaves real and unreal, and gives dynamism to language by means of the dual activity of signification and poetry. And in poetry, the commitment of the imagining being is such that it is no longer merely the subject of the verb *to adapt oneself*. Actual conditions are no longer determinant. With poetry, the imagination takes its place on the margin, exactly where the function of unreality comes to charm or to disturb—always to awaken—the sleeping being lost in its automatisms. The most insidious of these automatisms, the automatism of language, ceases to function when we enter into the domain of pure sublimation. Seen from this height of pure sublimation, reproductive imagination ceases to be of much importance. To quote Jean-Paul Richter: "Reproductive imagination is the prose of productive imagination."[16]

_____

[16][Bachelard] Jean-Paul Richter, *Poétique ou introduction à l'esthétique*, translated (1862), Vol. I, p. 145.

E. H. Gombrich

b. 1909

Although Gombrich is primarily an art historian and critic, his writings on art have many implications for literary criticism. His book *Art and Illusion,* from which this selection has been reprinted, can be taken as a consideration of issues surrounding imitation. Another work that bears on literary criticism is an essay published in 1951, *Meditations on a Hobby Horse or the Roots of Artistic Form,* in which Gombrich discusses two errors frequently made by critics. The first is to assume that a "representation" is a copy of the "external form" of an object rather than a "substitution" of some sort. The second is, having rejected the first assumption, to fly to the theory that a representation copies a "motif in the artist's inner world." (These two errors have been associated by other commentators, Cassirer among them, with neoclassicism and Romanticism respectively.) Gombrich's point is that critics would do well to consider the possibility that "substitution may precede portrayal, and creation communication." Further, representation is a two-way affair, calling on the psychological disposition of the reader as well as of the artist.

For Gombrich, all art is fundamentally the making of images. The making of images is based psychologically on the making of substitutes. This view leads him to emphasize the matter of artistic conventions. Quoting the art historian Wölfflin, he insists that pictures owe more to other pictures than to nature, an idea suggested in respect to literature by Pope's remark that Virgil discovered the study of Homer and the study of nature to be the same. It is an idea developed in Eliot's emphasis on tradition, and more recently in Frye's theory of archetypes. For Gombrich, the "conventional vocabulary of basic forms is . . . indispensable to the artist as a starting point, as a focus of organization." This view is profitably compared to that of the famous painter and art critic, Sir Joshua Reynolds, in his *Discourses,* with particular respect to the idea of universality.

In *Art and Illusion* Gombrich again concerns himself with the problem of conventions and the psychology of representation. In the selection below, from the concluding chapter, he begins his discussion with a consideration of some similarities between the language of words and visual representations.

Among Gombrich's numerous works are *The Story of Art* (1950), *Meditations on a Hobby Horse and Other Essays on the Theory of Art* (1951), *Art and Illusion* (1960), *Norm and Form* (1966), *In Search of Cultural History* (1969), and *Symbolic Images* (1972), (with others) *Art, Perception and Reality* (1972), *Art History and the Social Sciences* (1975), *Means and Ends* (1976), *The Heritage of Apelles* (1976), *Ideals and Idols* (1979), *The Image and the Eye* (1982), *The Sense of Order* (1984), *Tributes: Interpreters of Our Cultural Tradition* (1984), *New Light on Old Masters* (1986), and *Reflections on the History of Art* (1987).

Art and Illusion

From

From Representation to Expression

It was a much-debated question at the time of Plato whether the language of words, the names of things, exists by convention or by nature. Whether there is some real bond between the word *horse* and a horse, or whether it might also be called by any other name. The question, put in that form, looks to us a little childish. Most of us are convinced that with the exception of such onomatopoeic words as moo-*cow,* the names of things are more or less fortuitous labels, noises we have learned to make in order to indicate certain classes of things. It has been traditional in this context to bring out the arbitrary and conventional nature of language by contrasting the accidental name *horse* or *cheval* with the artist's visual image of a horse. This, it was thought, is not conventional but a real likeness, a natural sign, or what is also called an "icon."

In Plato's *Cratylus,*[1] which is devoted to this problem, Socrates constantly makes use of this contrast. "Could a painting, to revert to our previous comparison, be made like any real thing, if there were not pigments out of which the painting is composed, which were by nature like the objects which the painter's art imitates? Is that not impossible?"

"Impossible," echoes his victim. It is one of the moments in Plato's dialogues when one would like to have been present to thrust the speaker aside. "O Socrates," I would have said, "were you not trained as a sculptor?" "I was," he would have admitted. "And did you find that the stone you used was like the objects you imitated?" "Not very much, by the dog." "Or what about the cups from which you drank at the symposium? Have you not noticed that the old-fashioned ones have black figures on the red burnt clay, while most of your recent pottery uses black for the ground and leaves the natural red of the cup free for the figures? Are objects then both black and red according to the painter's

whim? But even if you thought of the colored paintings by Polygnotus or Zeuxis, we now know, O Socrates, that they could never hope to match their pigments against the reality of a sunlit landscape. Yet sunlit landscapes have been painted, and what you considered impossible has happened."

In my joy of victory I would not allow the venerable twister to plead that he had never seen sunlit landscapes painted and had never been aware of those perceptual constancies and the miracles of mental set which make the trick possible. I would take him to a nursery and show him children playing with colored blocks. There would be red, green, and yellow blocks all in a row with one double on top, and the child would push them along shouting "choo choo." "What has this in common with a train?" I would ask triumphantly. "A what?" he would say. And before I knew where I was he would have his own back. If I told him what trains are, he would believe, or at least pretend to believe, that they move through the country as red, green, and yellow cubes saying "choo choo." "If not," he would say, "why do you call this a train? And if it does not say 'choo choo,' what purpose do these strange and senseless syllables serve?"

Perhaps then at last, with both of us a little humbled, we could settle down to the proper argument which is, I believe, that there is more in common between the language of words and visual representation than we are sometimes prone to allow. The train, we would agree, is not a likeness; it is an attempt to arrange the blocks at our disposal in such a way that they can serve as a train on the nursery floor. The child does not say, "Shall we represent a train in blocks, Daddy?" He says, "Shall we make a train?" By this he means something like a rudimentary model, a row of units which he can push and which he can people in imagination.

And is it different with the word "choo choo"? Trains do not make this noise, but within the structure of the child's linguistic medium—which linguists call the phonemes or blocks out of which English is built—the syllable *choo* matches the noise of a steam engine better than others, and so it has been adopted to represent the thrusts of the piston, a convention, incidentally, which probably continues in countries with electrified railways that never say anything remotely like *choo.*[2]

In the language of words this type of conventionalized imitation plays a subsidiary part. Yet I believe the student of visual images should consider these so-called onomatopoeic

FROM REPRESENTATION TO EXPRESSION. Gombrich's *From Representation to Expression* is part of his *Art and Illusion,* a series of lectures delivered in 1956 and first published four years later. The selection printed here is the concluding chapter of the book. The text is from E. H. Gombrich, *Art and Illusion: A Study in the Psychology of Pictorial Representation, No. 5* Bollingen Series 35. Copyright © 1960 by the Trustees of the National Gallery. Chapter 11, p. 360–76. Reprinted by permission of Princeton University Press. The notes are those of Gombrich.

[1] *Cratylus* 434, translated by H. N. Fowler (LCL, 1939), p. 169.

[2] Cherry, *On Human Communication,* especially Chapter 3.

imitations of sound in language for the light they throw on his own problems. Nowhere, I submit, is the link between convention, mental set, and perception more easily analyzed than in this restricted field. We have seen that these so-called imitations are not imitations proper but approximations, within the given medium of language, to the sound heard. The sound of the drum, for instance, is imitated as *rataplan* in French; English, lacking the nasal phoneme, uses instead the syllables *rumtitum,* which—to me at any rate—is less of an approximation. For that very reason, I believe, we may find it used less than its more successful French equivalent. I would not be surprised if the better match of the French sound results in more projection and illusion—in other words, that more French people hear the drum say *rataplan* than English people hear it say *rumtitum.* To me, at least, the cock says not *cock-a-doodle-doo* as he calls to the English in the morning, nor *cocorico,* as he says in French, nor *kiao kiao,* as in Chinese, but still *kikeriki,* as he says in German. Or—not to fall into the mistake of Socrates—it is not precisely *kikeriki* he says; he still speaks cockish and not Viennese. My percept of the throaty noise of his call is distinctly colored by habitual interpretation. How much it is colored would be the problem between nature and convention; to answer that truthfully we would have to be able to compare the sound it really makes with the sound we hear. Put in this way, the difficulty, or perhaps the absurdity, of the problem becomes apparent. There is no reality without interpretation; just as there is no innocent eye, there is no innocent ear.

Take an onomatopoeic word—*tick-tock.* Some clocks should really say *tick-tick,* since the units of sound are almost identical, and yet I feel compelled to organize my percepts. But this need to organize and interpret does not mean that we are helplessly caught in our interpretation. We can experiment and through trial and error learn something about such impressions. An alternative interpretation may drive out the accepted one and reveal a glimpse of the reality behind it. Having become critical of me hearing *tick-tock,* I can try to hear something else. I can adopt the tentative hypothesis of making the clock say *tick-tick-tock,* and when I succeed in projecting this alternative, I can conclude that the stimuli I group in these different ways must be neutral. I have made a discovery about reality by trying alternative interpretations. This is what the adventurous artists were doing when, in the face of a tick-tock-believing public, they imposed an alternative reading on reality and thus gradually succeeded in exploring the dazzling ambiguity of vision. In language, of course, the imitation of nature is marginal. What we imitate is one another's speech. But even this process is not without its lessons for the student of mimesis. As readers of this book may have learned to expect, it has proved impossible to an-

alyze speech sound down into its component stimuli however carefully the student of phonetics attends to the noise and disregards the meaning. Those who have tried to produce artificial speech mechanically have made the most astounding observations. When speech is translated into light impulses in special apparatus, it is found that sounds which impress us as identical look very different, while others which we accept as quite different produce identical visible traces. Like the maker of the "facsimile," the makers of artificial speech found that the context and—in this case—the sequence of sounds affect every element. If we play a recorded speech in reverse we do not hear the same noises simply in a different order; the result is quite unlike human speech. In trying to devise a mimetic machine of speech sounds that would give the illusion of real speech, the engineers had to fall back on the same technique of experimentation which art employed on a secular scale: they devised a "speech synthesizer" which can translate visible speech into sound, and by this means they are patiently trying out the mutual effect of various noises on one another. It is hoped that the speech synthesizer may thus shortly answer the question that the "innocent ear" could never have solved, the question of what the auditory clues are that make us recognize speech sounds as what we believe we hear.[3]

In learning to speak we follow a path which is also similar to that of art. A few simple schemata are progressively adjusted to match the sound without need for analysis. When confronted with the task of saying *Lisbeth,* a child who had learned to say *papa* and *mama* produced the compromise *Pippa*—a transposition of the sounds he hears into the limited phonemes of his language. What we call a foreign accent is nothing but an extension of this "Pippa principle." The foreigner imitates the sounds of the new language as far as the phonemes of his native tongue allow. The motor habits acquired early in life will not only condition his speech but also the way he "hears" the language. His original schemata have conditioned him to watch out for certain distinctive features while ignoring other variations in sound as irrelevant, and nothing proves harder than articulating the world of sound afresh. Once more the parallel with our findings in this book could hardly be more complete. We have seen the Pippa principle at work in our study of the role of stereotypes in portrayal. An accent, we suspect, has many similarities to those all-pervading qualities we call style.

Few areas in this no man's land between psychology, aesthetics, and linguistics are as unexplored as that of skill,

---

[3]Cherry, *On Human Communication,* Chapter 4 (with bibliography), and D. B. Fry, "The Experimental Study of Speech," in *Studies in Communication,* by A. J. Ayer et al. [London, 1955], pp. 147–67.

and it is not my intention to open it up here. But I believe the skill of hand in art, like the skill of throat in language, follows the awareness of differences that have to be pointed out to be experienced. Wherever there is a clash of style, where one artist wants to copy the work of a different tradition, the importance of these motor habits becomes apparent.[4]

We have seen, in fact, that the artist who copies will always tend to build up the image from the schemata he has learned to handle. In Van Gogh's moving copy of a print after Millet, his manner—his motor habits—always breaks through. He repeats Millet's statements in his own accent. It is true that a strong obtrusive accent in its turn can be learned and imitated. Van Gogh's own can be forged with relative ease. But then his swirling lines still belong to the macro-structure of his style. It is in the microstructure of movement and shapes that the connoisseur will find the inimitable personal accent of an artist.

When the Italian physician Morelli first systematically applied such graphological criteria to the study of drawings, his new scientific method aroused great hopes.[5] It consisted precisely of looking at the minute schemata, the habits of the pen in indicating an ear lobe or a fingernail. Why was it that this method produced results only when used by the most gifted of experts and led to absurdities in unskilled hands? Why was it that the true connoisseur, such as Max J. Fried-länder, turned away from any pretense at rational analysis and proclaimed that the recognition of personal style was merely a matter of intuition based on experience?

Perhaps the analysis of language perception indicates a direction in which an answer to this puzzle may lie. The personal accent of the artist is not made up of individual tricks of hand which can be isolated and described. It is again a question of relationships, of the interaction of countless personal reactions, a matter of distribution and sequences which we perceive as a whole without being able to name the elements in combination. Friedländer may well have been right in declaring that the trained eye is the most sensitive recording apparatus for such total impressions that defy analysis. By the analogy of the speech synthesizer there would only be one way of probing into the secrets of such total effects: a committee of forgers would have to submit their systematically varied results to a committee of connoisseurs who might then agree on the exact criteria by which they recognize a Van Gogh.[6]

II

With the question of personal style we have reached the frontier of what is usually called representation. For in these ultimate constituents the artist is said to express himself. But is there really such a sharp division between representation and expression? The results of our last chapter have made us doubt it, and a comparison with language will confirm these doubts. For language, like the visual image, functions not only in the service of actual description and subjective emotion but also in that wide area between these extremes where everyday language conveys both the facts and the emotive tone of an experience.

Indeed, in the *Cratylus,* Socrates toys with the idea that the principle of onomatopoeia, of imitating sounds, might extend beyond the obvious instances I have quoted: that vocal imitation does not stop short where the realm of sound ends but extends beyond into that of sight and movement; that the letter *r* will suggest something flowing or moving, and the letter *i* something sharp or bright. This is dangerous ground, a favorite haunt of cranks and even of madmen, and yet I think it is ground which will have to be traversed. For we all feel that sounds can indeed imitate or match visual impressions—that words like *flicker, blinking, scintillating* are at least as good approximations in the language to the visual impression as *tick-tock* or *choo choo* were to the auditory ones. What is called synesthesia,[7] the splashing over of impressions from one sense modality to another, is a fact to which all languages testify. They work both ways—from sight to sound and from sound to sight. We speak of loud colors or of bright sounds, and everyone knows what we mean. Nor are the ear and the eye the only senses that are thus converging to a common center. There is touch in such terms as *velvety voice* and *a cold light,* taste with *sweet harmonies* of colors or sounds, and so on through countless permutations.

Artists at all times have been interested in these correspondences, which are invoked in a famous poem by Baudelaire, but the Romantics and symbolists were particularly intent on exploring the laws of synesthesia. Rimbaud assigned

---

[4]See Chapter 2 [of *Art and Illusion*], pp. 75–77, and Ivins, *Prints and Visual Communication,* p. 61.

[5]Ivan Lermolieff, pseud. (Giovanni Morelli), *Italian Painters: Critical Studies of Their Works,* translated by C. J. Ffoulkes, introduction by A. H. Layard (London, 1892–93).

[6]M. M. Dantzig, *Vincent?* (Amsterdam, 1953).

---

[7]For early studies see E. G. Boring, *Sensation and Perception in the History of Experimental Psychology,* p. 49; for later studies, Charles E. Osgood, *Method and Theory in Experimental Psychology,* pp. 642–46; F. A. von Hayek, *The Sensory Order,* pp. 19–24. For synesthetic metaphors, see also Stephen Ullmann, *The Principles of Semantics* (Glasgow, 1951), pp. 266–89, and the same author's *Style in the French Novel* (Cambridge, 1957), Chapter 5 (both with rich bibliography). An historical study is Erika von Erhardt-Siebold, "Harmony of the Senses in English, German, and French Romanticism," *Publications of the Modern Language Association of America,* XLVIII (1932).

colors to the five vowels, thus translating auditory impressions into visual ones. Musicians, in their turn, were fond of representing the visible world in tones—we need only look down the list of titles Debussy gave to his pieces to see his faith in the efficacy of such evocation: *Bruyères, Clair de lune, Feux d'artifice* all represent or paint visual experiences on the keys of the piano. Some artists indulged in the dream of combining the world of sound and that of sight in higher orders; the fantastic painter Arcimboldo took the lead in the seventeenth century with a color piano,[8] and the idea persists to Wagner, Scriabin, and Disney's *Fantasia.* Finally painting, in withdrawing from the exploration of pure visibility, took up the challenge and explored the world of sound. Whistler's attempts are still vague and somewhat indefinite, but Kandinsky went further,[9] and in Mondrian's painting labeled *Broadway Boogie-Woogie,* we have an example of such a transposition which seems generally accepted and acceptable. I don't know exactly what boogie-woogie is, but Mondrian's painting explains it to me.

And yet can we really compare such renderings of sound patterns in visual terms with the rendering of visual impressions in visual terms? Granted even that most of us experience such synesthetic images with more or less intensity, are they not completely subjective and private, inaccessible and uncommunicable? Can there be real objective discoveries of good and better matches in these elusive spheres as there were in the discovery of visual analogies to visual experience? Can the world of the mind, of the dream, be explored by experiments that result in accepted conventions as was the world of the waking eye? Much of our assessment of twentieth-century art may depend on our answer to this question, for though not all, or even most, of it is concerned with synesthesia proper, all or most of it tries to represent the world of the mind where shapes and colors stand for feelings. I believe the analysis of representation may indeed lead us to understand these attempts better and to assess the chances of any new experiments in that direction.

For this analysis has taught us to remain aware of three factors—the medium, the mental set, and the problem of equivalence. When we talk about art we usually take all these matters for granted—they are the eight-ninths of the iceberg that remain submerged and do not obtrude on our awareness. But many an aesthetician's ship has suffered shipwreck for disregarding them.

To enjoy the Mondrian I need not think of any of these things. But if anyone should ask me seriously if Mondrian had represented a bit of boogie-woogie so accurately that I could now recognize the style if you played it to me, I would have to point to the underwater cliffs—the need, that is, for the context in which the communication takes place. If you made the context sufficiently specific I could. I trust myself to plump for the right piece if one played two contrasting pieces to me—one slow and blue, one fast and noisy. For here the Mondrian would give me a pointer—a pointer for that game which psychologists call matching.[10] Given a simple choice, Mondrian tells me in what class, category, or pigeonhole of music to seek for the equivalent. Without a knowledge of possibilities, this type of representation would work even less than the representation of the visible world that we also found to be dependent on our knowledge of what things might be.

But our analysis is not quite complete yet. For my understanding depends not only on my expectation and experience of possible types of music, but also on my knowledge of possible types of painting—in other words, on the mental set with which I approach the Mondrian.

In most of us the name of Mondrian conjures up the expectation of severity, of an art of straight lines and a few primary colors in carefully balanced rectangles. Seen against this background, the boogie-woogie picture gives indeed the impression of gay abandon. It is so much less severe than the alternative we have in mind that we have no hesitation in matching it in our mind with this style of popular music. But this impression is in fact grounded on our knowledge of the restricted choice open to the artist within his self-imposed discipline. Let us imagine for a moment that we were told the painting is by Severini, who is known for his futuristic paintings that try to capture the rhythm of dance music in works of brilliant chaos. Would we then still feel the Mondrian belongs in the pigeonhole with boogie-woogie, or would we accept a label calling it Bach's *First Brandenburg Concerto?*

I do not think this analysis need speak in any way against the attempt to use forms and colors only as a medium of representing feeling. For if we have learned anything in the course of these chapters it is that a representation is never a replica. The forms of art, ancient and modern, are not du-

---

[8]F. C. Legrand and Felix Sluys, *Arcimboldo et les arcimboldesques* (Aalter, Belgium, 1955).

[9]*Über das Geistige in deer Malerei* (Munich, 1912); translation: *Concerning the Spiritual in Art* (New York, 1947).

[10]Reinhard Krauss, "Über den graphischen Ausdruck," *Beihefte zur Zeitschrift für angewandte Psychologie,* 48 (Leipzig, 1930), where the possibility of matching abstract design against concepts and moods is demonstrated in a restricted choice situation. This precaution is neglected in the discussions on "The Representative and Expressive Effects of Music," in Leland W. Crafts and others, *Recent Experiments in Psychology* (New York and London, 1938), Chapter 8. Results are accordingly negative.

plications of what the artist has in mind any more than they are duplications of what he sees in the outer world. In both cases they are renderings within an acquired medium, a medium grown up through tradition and skill—that of the artist and that of the beholder.

It is my conviction that the problem of synesthetic equivalences will cease to look embarrassingly arbitrary and subjective if here, too, we fix our attention not on likeness of elements but on structural relationships within a scale or matrix. When we say that *u* is dark blue and *i* bright green, we are talking playful nonsense, or serious nonsense if we are in earnest. But when we say that *i* is brighter than *u*, we find a surprising degree of general consent. If we are more careful still and say the step from *u* to *i* is more like an upward step than a downward step, I think the majority will agree, whatever explanations each of us may be inclined to offer. I have chosen this example because I believe that once again the research of linguists offers us the best chance to make this much-discussed problem a little more manageable. It was Professor Roman Jakobson who drew my attention to the fact that synesthesia concerns relationships.[11] I have tried out this suggestion in a party game. It consists of creating the simplest imaginable medium in which relationships can still be expressed, a language of two words only—let us call them *ping* and *pong*. If these were all we had and we had to name an elephant and a cat, which would be ping and which pong?[12] I think the answer is clear. Or hot soup and ice cream. To me, at least, ice cream is ping and soup pong. Or Rembrandt and Watteau? Surely in that case Rembrandt would be pong and Watteau ping. I do not maintain that it always works, that two blocks are sufficient to categorize all relationships.[13] We find people differing about day and night and male and female, but perhaps these different answers could be reduced to unanimity if the question were differently framed: pretty girls ping and matrons pong; it may depend on which aspect of womanhood the person has in mind, just as the motherly, enveloping aspect of night is pong, but its sharp, cold, and menacing physiognomy may be ping to some.

In their recent book *The Measurement of Meaning,* Professor Charles E. Osgood and his collaborators have submitted a similar technique to a rigorous statistical analysis.[14] They asked their subjects to place a notion such as "lady" or "boulder" along a scale extending between two such contrasting adjectives as *rough* and *smooth, good* and *bad, active* and *passive.* Like myself in the game of *ping* and *pong,* they got a surprising agreement on apparently senseless questions, such as whether a boulder is happy or sad. They conclude that we always place any concept into a structured matrix, what they call the "semantic space" of which the basic dimensions are "good and bad," "active and passive," "strong and weak." There may be objections to certain of Osgood's methodological assumptions, but I still believe that these observations will give us an access to the workings of traditional symbolisms, the polarities of Yin and Yang in China, for instance, or to the symbolic meaning attached to light and darkness in the Western tradition.

The individual meaning of Lorenzo Lotto's *Allegory* in the National Gallery in Washington may be hard to decipher, but the relationships, the ping pong of it all, are as clear to us as they were to Lotto's contemporaries. Obviously the satyr with his wine jug represents what we call "the powers of darkness," and the healthy *putto* with its compass is on the side of light. In the background behind the evil satyr there are turmoil and shipwreck; behind the *putto* the mountain rises toward heaven, and a little creature, well supplied with wings, works its way toward the heights. The tree of Pallas, broken on its left, the sinister side, grows and endures on the right. The very metaphors of our language that we use in describing this picture still preserve the basic relationships on which its symbolism is grounded.

Lotto's painting proves, if proof be needed, that artists have been aware of the expressive potentialities of shapes and colors long before expressionist theory seized upon that aspect of painting. By the eighteenth century this practical tradition was also a commonplace of the critics. Thus Jonathan Richardson wrote: "If the subject be grave, melancholy, or terrible, the general tint of the coloring must incline to brown, black, or red, and gloomy; but be gay, and pleasant in subjects of joy, and triumph." And, "Generally, if the character of the picture is greatness, terrible, or savage, as battles, robberies, witchcrafts, apparitions, or even the portraits of men of such characters, there ought to be employed a rough, bold pencil; and contrarily, if the character is grace, beauty, love, innocence, etc., a softer pencil, and more finishing is proper."[15]

[11]Gladys A. Reichard, R. Jakobson, E. Weiss, "Language and Synaesthesia," *Word,* II (1949).

[12]Peter H. McKellar, *Imagination and Thinking* (New York and London, 1957), pp. 65–66, reports on experiments he made according to my suggestions. For a comparable procedure, see Osgood, *Method and Theory,* pp. 712–14.

[13]For similar contrasts, see Max J. Friedländer, *Von Kunst und Kennerschaft,* p. 44 (cf. tr., p. 50), where painters are paired as "warm" and "cool."

[14]George J. Suci, Percy H. Tannenbaum, *The Measurement of Meaning* (Urbana, 1957).

[15]*The Theory of Painting,* in *The Works of Jonathan Richardson* (London, 1792), p. 65 (coloring), p. 70 (handling).

To some readers these words of an eighteenth-century critic may sound surprisingly modern. They may remind him of similar utterances by Delacroix and Van Gogh that led the way to expressionism[16] and Kandinsky's version of abstract art. But I believe this similarity is somewhat deceptive. What Richardson recommends for certain subjects is a deviation from the normal palette and the normal type of brushwork in the direction of darker tones or greater roughness. In giving this advice, he took it for granted that every medium and every convention has its own level of normality that determines the expectations of the connoisseur who would register any subtle emphasis in one direction or another. The identical tone, therefore, that would strike him as expressive of gloom in a water color might have impressed him as calm and serene in an ink drawing.

It is this awareness of relationships, I feel, that has sometimes been lost in the writings of the expressionists. Anxious as they were to overthrow the hold of conventions, they had to look for absolutes where none can be found. As a consequence, they frequently talked as if a given shape or color were inherently "charged" with an expressive meaning that would explode in the mind of the beholder. But artistic communication is quite unlike throwing hand grenades. There must be not only a sender but also a receiver suitably attuned. In our response to expression no less than in our reading of representation, our expectations of possibilities and probabilities must come into play. Given such a keyboard of relationships, a matrix or scale that has intelligible dimensions of *more* or *less,* there is perhaps no limit to the systems of forms that can be made the instrument of artistic expression in terms of equivalence. The rigid orders of ancient architecture would seem to be a fairly recalcitrant matrix for the expression of psychological and physiognomic categories; still it makes sense when Vitruvius recommends Doric temples for Minerva, Mars, and Hercules, Corinthian ones for Venus, Flora, and Proserpina, while Juno, Diana, and other divinities who stand in between the two extremes are given Ionic temples.[17] Within the medium at the architect's disposal, Doric is clearly more virile than Corinthian. We say that Doric expresses the god's severity; it does, but only because it is on the more severe end of the scale and not because there is necessarily much in common between the god of war and the Doric order. Following a similar trend of thought, Nicolas Poussin compared in a famous letter the expressive qualities of form and color with the so-called modes of ancient music.[18] The Doric mode is again the severe one and thus suited to stern subjects; the Phrygian mode is passionate and thus comparable to the appropriate treatment of warlike subjects. He compares this change of modes with the methods of poets who attune the sound of the words to the theme of their song. Where Virgil talks of love, his sound is sweet and harmonious; where war is his subject, his verse rushes headlong. The medium is used to express or, as Poussin would have said, "to paint the passions." It is not an immediate expression but one dependent on conventions. To those of us who do not know the potentialities of Latin verse, the sound of the lines where Virgil speaks of love will not differ much from that where he describes wars; in fact, we might feel inclined to suspect that the critic imagines things. But when we understand that Poussin felt the difference between two Virgilian lines to be analogous to the difference between love and war, we may come nearer to an understanding of what he called the "depiction of the passions."

Now here our wanderings have brought us back to the starting point of this book, the concept of style. It will be remembered from the Introduction that art criticism borrowed this notion from the ancient critics of literature, especially from the teachers of rhetoric. The application of the term to painting and sculpture dates precisely from Poussin's period.

In classical writing on rhetoric we have perhaps the most careful analysis of any expressive medium ever undertaken. Language, to these critics, is an organon, an instrument which offers its master a variety of different scales and "stops." Whenever they discuss expression, therefore, they speak of the rich choice of "expressions."

This subtle analysis of speech should provide a most valuable supplement and even a corrective to Osgood's investigations. Where he speaks only of concepts, these critics focused their attention on the influence of words, their sounds and their status in our reactions. Thus Demetrius, in his Greek textbook *On Style* (written, it is believed, in the first century of our era), tells his readers to heed the musical distinction between smooth- and rough-sounding words.[19] When the subject is as rugged and formidable a hero as the

---

[16]See Bernard S. Myers, *Expressionism* (London, 1957), especially Chapter 4.
[17]*De architectura*, Book I, Chapter 2.

---

[18]Poussin's letter of November 24, 1647 is translated and annotated in Elizabeth G. Holt, *A Documentary History of Art,* II (New York [Anchor], 1958), pp. 154–56. See also P. Alfassa, "L'Origine de la lettre de Poussin sur les modes d'après un travail récent," *Bulletin de la Société de l'histoire de l'art francais* (1933), pp. 125–43.
[19]*On Style* 105 and 176. The theory is expounded and applied in Pope's *Essay on Criticism:* "The sound must seem an echo to the sense." [See p. 278.]

Homeric Ajax, the writer will do well to select expressions with harsh and even unpleasant sounds.

But the main distinction which the orator would observe was really a social one, the gamut between noble and lowly. The identical meaning can be expressed in words from different levels along this scale. We can say *face* or *countenance, girl* or *maiden.* Cicero, who discusses the fitting choice of language in his dialogues on oratory, elaborates this distinction by establishing three modes of speech, the plain, the medium, and the ornate. "Boy meets girl" would be humble style; "youth encounters maiden" is ornate. Then as now, the archaic and obsolete term often sounded more lofty than the word in current usage. This shift in emphasis is known to all students of style: in admiring the force and power of the Authorized Version, we have to remind ourselves that the passage of time has turned the humble speech of the gospels into the lofty style of archaism.

There has always been a temptation in language to treat the social, the historical, and the moral scale as equivalent: to group the ancient with the noble and the restrained, and the modern with the vulgar and the indulgent. Luckily this tendency was sometimes counteracted by those who equated the plain and humble with the good, and the ornate with the stilted, affected, and degenerate.

When Johann Joachim Winckelmann in the eighteenth century first applied the categories of style systematically to the history of art, he projected these shifting categories onto the development of representation.[20] Looking at Greek art through eyes surfeited with Baroque exuberance and rococo frivolity, he exalted it as both simple and noble, the expression of untroubled innocence and moral restraint. The psychological pitfalls of such interpretations need no longer concern us here. We have seen that we cannot judge expression without an awareness of the choice situation, without a knowledge of the organon. I have emphasized in the Introduction how the neglect of skill will deprive the historian of the means to interpret style as expression. Where we have no matrix, no keyboard, we cannot assess the meaning of an individual feature.

---

[20]Winckelmann's link with the tradition of rhetoric: Heinz Weniger, *Die drei Stilcharaktere,* [Langensalza, Ger., 1932].

Martin Heidegger

1889–1976

At the very beginning of an essay called "The Way to Language," Heidegger distinguishes between two ways of approaching language. One is to try, in vain he believes, to treat it in a conventionally conceptual way. The other is radically experiential and involves a recognition that language is not distant from us but that we are identical with it or at least "in" it or "with" it. And yet this situation may make our way to it even more difficult, for Heidegger wants to "speak about speech *qua* speech." "The Nature of Language" is the first of a set of three lectures in which Stefan George's poem "The Word" generates a lengthy meditation on language. Heidegger's meditations on poems are themselves metalinguistic. The poems he chooses to meditate on are almost always concerned with language, and particularly with the idea of language as disclosure or unconcealment (*aletheia*). For Heidegger what is unconcealed in the poem is Being; not Being prior to the poem but Being as unconcealment in the poem by a sort of linguistic mediation. Thus Heidegger can say that "language is the house of Being," while at the same time claiming that things are not isolated by this appropriation. A word for Heidegger "makes a thing appear as the thing it is," and thus lets it be present. Such verbal acts of poetry are hermeneutic, derived from *hermenuein* and related to the god Hermes, the bringer of messages. Messages are true showings or unconcealments rather than merely designations or pointings to, as in some theories of words.

Heidegger's meditations are difficult if read as analytical criticism. As he points out here, his essay's very title is a misnomer, and what he tries to perform is an experiencing of language. In the old quarrel between poetry and philosophy Heidegger attempts to mediate by dissolving the difference under the name of hermeneutics.

Among Heidegger's works are *Being and Time* (1927, tr. 1962), *Kant and the Problem of Metaphysics* (1925–1926, tr. 1972), *An Introduction to Metaphysics* (1953, tr. 1974), *Identity and Difference* (1957, tr. 1957), *The End of Philosophy* (1969, tr. 1962), *On the Way to Language* (1971), and *Poetry, Language, Thought* (1971). See Walter Bremel, *Martin Heidegger: An Illustrated Study* (1973, tr. 1976); Michael Murray, ed., *Heidegger and Modern Philosophy* (1978); and Paul de Man, "Heidegger's Exegeses of Hölderlin," *Blindness and Insight* (2nd ed., 1983).

The Nature of Language

I

The three lectures that follow bear the title "The Nature of Language." They are intended to bring us face to face with a possibility of undergoing an experience with language. To undergo an experience with something—be it a thing, a person, or a god—means that this something befalls us, strikes us, comes over us, overwhelms and transforms us. When we talk of "undergoing" an experience, we mean specifically that the experience is not of our own making; to undergo here means that we endure it, suffer it, receive it as it strikes us and submit to it. It is this something itself that comes about, comes to pass, happens.

To undergo an experience with language, then, means to let ourselves be properly concerned by the claim of language by entering into and submitting to it. If it is true that man finds the proper abode of his existence in language—whether he is aware of it or not—then an experience we undergo with language will touch the innermost nexus of our existence. We who speak language may thereupon become transformed by such experiences, from one day to the next or in the course of time. But now it could be that an experience we undergo with language is too much for us moderns, even if it strikes us only to the extent that for once it draws our attention to our *relation to language,* so that from then on we may keep this relation in mind.

Suppose, specifically, we were asked head-on: In what relation do you live to the language you speak? We should not be embarrassed for an answer. Indeed, we would at once discover a guideline and point of reference with which to lead the question into channels where it can safely be left.

We speak our language. How else can we be close to language except by speaking? Even so, our relation to language is vague, obscure, almost speechless. As we ponder this curious situation, it can scarcely be avoided that every observation on the subject will at first sound strange and incomprehensible. It therefore might be helpful to us to rid ourselves of the habit of always hearing only what we already understand. Thus my proposal is addressed not only to all those who listen; it is addressed still more to him who tries to speak of language, all the more when he does so with

the sole intent to show possibilities that will allow us to become mindful of language and our relation to it.

But this, to undergo an experience with language, is something else again than to gather information about language. Such information—linguists and philologists of the most diverse languages, psychologists and analytic philosophers supply it to us, and constantly increase the supply, *ad infinitum.* Of late, the scientific and philosophical investigation of languages is aiming ever more resolutely at the production of what is called "metalanguage." Analytical philosophy, which is set on producing this super-language, is thus quite consistent when it considers itself metalinguistics. That sounds like metaphysics—not only sounds like it, it *is* metaphysics. Metalinguistics is the metaphysics of the thoroughgoing technicalization of all languages into the sole operative instrument of interplanetary information. Metalanguage and sputnik, metalinguistics and rocketry are the Same.

However, we must not give grounds for the impression that we are here passing negative judgment on the scientific and philosophical investigation of language and of languages. Such investigation has its own particular justification and retains its own importance. But scientific and philosophical information about language is one thing; an experience we undergo with language is another. Whether the attempt to bring us face to face with the possibility of such an experience will succeed, and if it does, how far that possible success will go for each one of us—that is not up to any of us.

What is left for us to do is to point out ways that bring us face to face with a possibility of undergoing an experience with language. Such ways have long existed. But they are seldom used in such a manner that the possible experience with language is itself given voice and put into language. In experiences which we undergo *with* language, language itself brings itself to language. One would think that this happens anyway, any time anyone speaks. Yet at whatever time and in whatever way we speak a language, language itself never has the floor. Any number of things are given voice in speaking, above all what we are speaking about: a set of facts, an occurrence, a question, a matter of concern. Only because in everyday speaking language does *not* bring itself to language but holds back, are we able simply to go ahead and speak a language, and so to deal with something and negotiate something by speaking.

But when does language speak itself as language? Curiously enough, when we cannot find the right word for something that concerns us, carries us away, oppresses or encourages us. Then we leave unspoken what we have in

THE NATURE OF LANGUAGE. Part I, was delivered as a lecture at the University of Freiburg in December 1957. It was originally published in Germany in *Unterwegs zur Sprache* (1959). Reprinted from *On the Way to Language,* ed. Peter D. Hertz. Copyright Harper Row, Publishers, Inc. 1971. Reprinted by permission of HarperCollins Publishers.

mind and, without rightly giving it thought, undergo moments in which language itself has distinctly and fleetingly touched us with its essential being.

But when the issue is to put into language something which has never yet been spoken, then everything depends on whether language gives or withholds the appropriate word. Such is the case of the poet. Indeed, a poet might even come to the point where he is compelled—in his own way, that is, poetically—to put into language the experience he undergoes with language.

Among Stefan George's late, simple, almost songlike poems there is one entitled "The Word."[1] It was first published in 1919. Later it was included in the collection *Das Neue Reich*. The poem is made up of seven stanzas. The first three are clearly marked off from the next three, and these two triads as a whole are again marked off from the seventh, final stanza. The manner in which we shall here converse with this poem, briefly but throughout all three lectures, does not claim to be scientific. The poem runs:

The Word

Wonder or dream from distant land
I carried to my country's strand

And waited till the twilit norn
Had found the name within her bourn—

Then I could grasp it close and strong
It blooms and shines now the front along . . .

Once I returned from happy sail,
I had a prize so rich and frail,

She sought for long and tidings told:
"No like of this these depths enfold."

And straight it vanished from my hand,
The treasure never graced my land . . .

So I renounced and sadly see:
Where word breaks off no thing may be.

After what we had noted earlier, we are tempted to concentrate on the poem's last line: "Where word breaks off no thing may be." For this line makes the word of language, makes language itself bring itself to language, and says

something about the relation between word and thing. The content of the final line can be transformed into a statement, thus: "No thing is where the word breaks off." Where something breaks off, a breach, a diminution has occurred. To diminish means to take away, to cause a lack. "Breaks off" means "is lacking." No thing is where the word is lacking, that word which names the given thing. What does "to name" signify? We might answer: to name means to furnish something with a name. And what is a name? A designation that provides something with a vocal and written sign, a cipher. And what is a sign? Is it a signal? Or a token? A marker? Or a hint? Or all of these and something else besides? We have become very slovenly and mechanical in our understanding and use of signs.

Is the name, is the word a sign? Everything depends on how we think of what the words "sign" and "name" say. Even in these slight pointers we now begin to sense the drift that we are getting into when the word is put into language as word, language as language. That the poem, too, has *name* in mind when it says *word,* said in the second stanza:

And waited till the twilit norn
Had found the name within her bourn—

Meanwhile, both the finder of the name, the norn of our poem, and the place where the name is found, her bourn, make us hesitant to understand "name" in the sense of a mere designation. It could be that the name and the naming word are here intended rather in the sense we know from such expressions as "in the name of the King" or "in the name of God." Gottfried Benn begins one of his poems: "In the name of him who bestows the hours." Here "in the name" says "at the call, by the command."[2] The terms "name" and "word" in George's poem are thought differently and more deeply than as mere signs. But what am I saying? Is there thinking, too, going on in a poem? Quite so—in a poem of such rank thinking is going on, and indeed thinking without science, without philosophy. If that is true, then we may and in fact must, with all the self-restraint and circumspection that are called for, give more reflective thought to that closing line we first picked out from the poem "The Word."

Where word breaks off no thing may be.

We ventured the paraphrase: No thing is where the word is lacking. "Thing" is here understood in the tradi-

[1]Stefan George, German poet (1868–1933)

[2]Gottfried Benn, German poet (1886–1956)

tional broad sense, as meaning anything that in any way *is*. In this sense even a god is a thing. Only where the word for the thing has been found is the thing a thing. Only thus *is* it. Accordingly we must stress as follows: no thing *is* where the word, that is, the name is lacking. The word alone gives being to the thing. Yet how can a mere word accomplish this—to bring a thing into being? The true situation is obviously the reverse. Take the sputnik. This thing, if such it is, *is* obviously independent of that name which was later tacked on to it. But perhaps matters are different with such things as rockets, atom bombs, reactors and the like, different from what the poet names in the first stanza of the first triad:

> Wonder or dream from distant land
> I carried to my country's strand

Still, countless people look upon this "thing" sputnik, too, as a wonder, this "thing" that races around in a worldless "world"—space; to many people it was and still is a dream—wonder and dream of this modern technology which would be the last to admit the thought that what gives things their being is the word. Actions not words count in the calculus of planetary calculation. What use are poets? And yet . . .

Let us for once refrain from hurried thinking. Is not even this "thing" what it is and the way it is in the name of its name? Certainly. If that hurry, in the sense of the technical maximization of all velocities, in whose time-space modern technology and apparatus can alone be what they are—if that hurry had not bespoken man and ordered him at its call, if that call to such hurry had not challenged him and put him at bay, if the word framing that order and challenge had not spoken: then there would be no sputnik. No thing is where the word is lacking. Thus the puzzle remains: the word of language and its relation to the thing, to every thing that is—that it is and the way it is.

This is why we consider it advisable to prepare for a possibility of undergoing an experience with language. This is why we listen now more attentively where such an experience is put into lofty and noble language. We listen to the poem that we read. Did we hear it? Barely. We have merely picked up the last line—and done so almost crudely—and have even ventured to rewrite it into an unpoetical statement: No thing is where the word is lacking. We could go further and propose this statement: something *is* only where the appropriate and therefore competent word names a thing as being, and so establishes the given being as a being. Does this mean, also, that there is being only where the appropriate word is speaking? Where does the word derive its appropriateness? The poet says nothing about it. But the content of the closing line does after all include the statement: The being of anything that is resides in the word. Therefore this statement holds true: Language is the house of Being. By this procedure, we would seem to have adduced from poetry the most handsome confirmation for a principle of thinking which we had stated at some time in the past—and in truth would have thrown everything into utter confusion. We would have reduced poetry to the servant's role as documentary proof for our thinking, and taken thinking too lightly; in fact we would already have forgotten the whole point: to undergo an experience with language.

Therefore, we now restore to integrity, in its original place in the poem's last stanza, the lines which we had first picked out and rewritten.

> So I renounced and sadly see:
> Where word breaks off no thing may be.

The poet, normally very sparing with his punctuation, has put a colon after "see." One would expect, then, something to follow which speaks in what the grammarians call direct discourse.

> So I renounced and sadly see:
> Where word breaks off no thing is.

But Stefan George does not say "is," he says "may be." In keeping with his practice elsewhere, he could omit the colon, an omission that would almost be more appropriate for the indirect discourse—if that is what it is—in the last line. Still, many precedents can be cited, presumably, for George's usage, for example a passage from Goethe's "Introduction to the Outline of a Theory of Color." There we find:

> In order that we may not appear overly timid by trying to avoid an explanation, we would revise what we said first, as follows: that color be an elementary natural phenomenon for the sense of sight. . . .

Goethe regards the words after the colon as the explanation of what color is, and says: "Color be . . ." But what is the situation in the last stanza of George's poem? Here we have to do not with a theoretical explanation of a natural phenomenon, but with a renunciation.

> So I renounced and sadly see:
> Where word breaks off no thing may be.

Do the words after the colon say what the substance of the renunciation is? Does the poet renounce the fact that no thing may be where the word breaks off? Exactly the opposite. The renunciation he has learned implies precisely that the poet admits that no thing may be where the word breaks off.

Why all these artful explications? The matter, after all, is clear. No, nothing is clear; but everything is significant. In what way? In this way, that what matters is for us to hear how, in the poem's last stanza, the whole of that experience is concentrated which the poet has undergone with the word—and that means with language as well; and that we must be careful not to force the vibration of the poetic saying into the rigid groove of a univocal statement, and so destroy it.

The last line, "Where word breaks off no thing may be," could then still have another meaning than that of a statement and affirmation put in indirect discourse, which says that no thing is where the word is lacking.

What follows the colon does not name what the poet renounces; rather, it names the realm into which the renunciation must enter; it names the call to enter into that relation between thing and word which has now been experienced. What the poet learned to renounce is his formerly cherished view regarding the relation of thing and word. His renunciation concerns the poetic relation to the word that he had cultivated until then. If so, the "may be" in the line, "Where word breaks off no thing may be," would grammatically speaking not be the subjunctive of "is," but a kind of imperative, a command which the poet follows, to keep it from then on. If so, the "may be" in the line, "Where word breaks off no thing may be," would mean: do not henceforth admit any thing as being where the word breaks off. In the "may be" understood as a command, the poet avows to himself the self-denial he has learned, in which he abandons the view that something may be even if and even while the word for it is still lacking. What does renunciation mean? It is equivalent to "abdication." Here the root word is the Latin *dicere,* to say, the Greek *deiknumi,* to show, point out, indicate. In his renunciation, the poet abdicates his former relation to the word. Nothing more? No. There is in the abdication itself already an avowal, a command to which he denies himself no longer.

Now it would be just as forced to claim that the imperative interpretation of "may be" is the only possible one. Presumably one meaning and the other of "may be" vibrate and mingle in the poetic saying: a command as appeal, and submission to it.

The poet has learned renunciation. He has undergone an experience. With what? With the thing and its relation to the word. But the title of the poem is simply "The Word." The decisive experience is that which the poet has undergone with the word—and with the word inasmuch as it alone can bestow a relation to a thing. Stated more explicitly, the poet has experienced that only the word makes a thing appear as the thing it is, and thus lets it be present. The word avows itself to the poet as that which holds and sustains a thing in its being. The poet experiences an authority, a dignity of the word than which nothing vaster and loftier can be thought. But the word is also that possession with which the poet is trusted and entrusted as poet in an extraordinary way. The poet experiences his poetic calling as a call to the word as the source, the bourn of Being. The renunciation which the poet learns is of that special kind of fulfilled self-denial to which alone is promised what has long been concealed and is essentially vouchsafed already.

The poet, then, ought to rejoice at such an experience, which brings to him the most joyful gift a poet can receive. Instead, the poem says: "So I renounced and sadly see." The poet, then, is merely depressed by his renunciation because it means a loss. Yet, as we have seen, the renunciation is not a loss. Nor does "sadly" refer to the substance of the renunciation, but rather to the fact that he has learned it. That sadness, however, is neither mere dejection nor despondency. True sadness is in harmony with what is most joyful—but in this way, that the greatest joy withdraws, halts in its withdrawal, and holds itself in reserve. By learning that renunciation, the poet undergoes his experience with the word's lofty sway. He receives primal knowledge of what task is assigned to the poetic saying, what sublime and lasting matters are promised to it and yet withheld from it. The poet could never go through the experience he undergoes with the word if the experience were not attuned to sadness, to the mood of releasement into the nearness of what is withdrawn but at the same time held in reserve for an originary advent.

These few pointers may suffice to make it clearer what experience the poet has undergone with language. Experience means *eundo assequi,* to obtain something along the way, to attain something by going on a way. What is it that the poet reaches? Not mere knowledge. He obtains entrance into the relation of word to thing. This relation is not, however, a connection between the thing that is on one side and the word that is on the other. The word itself is the relation which in each instance retains the thing within itself in such a manner that it "is" a thing.

And yet, in making these statements, however broad their implications, we have done no more than sum up the experience the poet has undergone with the word, instead of entering into the experience itself. How did the experience happen? We are guided toward the answer by that one little word which we have neglected so far in our discussion of the poem's final stanza:

> So I renounced and sadly see:
> Where word breaks off no thing may be.

"*So* I renounced . . ." How? In the way the first six stanzas say it. What we have just noted concerning the last stanza may shed some light on the first six. They must speak for themselves, of course, from within the totality of the poem.

In these six stanzas there speaks the experience that the poet undergoes with language. Something comes to pass for him, strikes him, and transforms his relation to the word. It is thus necessary first to mention the relation to language in which the poet stood *before* the experience. It speaks in the first three stanzas. The last line of the third stanza trails off in an ellipsis, and so marks off the first triad from the second. The fourth stanza then opens the second triad—rather abruptly, with the word "Once," taken here in its primary meaning: one time. The second triad tells what the poet experiences once and for all. To experience is to go along a way. The way leads through a landscape. The poet's land belongs within that landscape, as does the dwelling of the twilit norn, ancient goddess of fate. She dwells on the strand, the edge of the poetic land which is itself a boundary, a march. The twilit norn watches over her bourn, the well in whose depths she searches for the names she would bring forth from it. Word, language, belongs within the domain of this mysterious landscape in which poetic saying borders on the fateful source of speech. At first, and for long, it seems as though the poet needed only to bring the wonders that enthrall and the dreams that enrapture him to the well-spring of language, and there in unclouded confidence let the words come forth to him that fit all the wonderful and dream-like things whose images have come to him. In a former time, the poet, emboldened as his poems turned out well, cherished the view that the poetic things, the wonders and dreams, had, even on their own, their well-attested standing within Being, and that no more was necessary than that his art now also find the word for them to describe and present them. At first, and for long, it seemed as though a word were like a grasp that fastens upon the things already in being and held to be in being, compresses and expresses them, and thus makes them beautiful.

> Wonder or dream from distant land
> I carried to my country's strand

> And waited till the twilit norn
> Had found the name within her bourn—

> Then I could grasp it close and strong
> It blooms and shines now the front along . . .

Wonders and dreams on the one hand, and on the other hand the names by which they are grasped, and the two fused—thus poetry came about. Did this poetry do justice to what is in the poet's nature—that he must found what is lasting, in order that it may endure and be?

But in the end the moment comes for Stefan George when the conventional self-assured poetic production suddenly breaks down and makes him think of Hölderlin's words:

> But what endures is founded by poets.

For at one time, once, the poet—still filled with hope after a happy sail—reaches the place of the ancient goddess of fate and demands the name of the rich and frail prize that lies there plain in his hand. It is neither "wonder from afar" nor "dream." The goddess searches long, but in vain. She gives him the tidings:

> "No like of this these depths enfold."

There is nothing in these depths that is like the prize so rich and frail which is plainly there in his hand. Such a word, which would let the prize lying there plainly be what it is— such a word would have to well up out of the secure depths reposing in the stillness of deep slumber. Only a word from such a source could keep the prize secure in the richness and frailty of its simple being.

> "No like of this these depths enfold."

> And straight it vanished from my hand,
> The treasure never graced my land . . .

The frail rich prize, already plainly in hand, does not reach being as a thing, it does not come to be a treasure, that is, a poetically secured possession of the land. The poet remains silent about the prize which could not become a treasure of his land, but which yet granted to him an experience with language, the opportunity to learn the renunciation in whose self-denial the relation of word to thing promises itself to him. The "prize so rich and frail" is contrasted with "wonder or dream from distant land." If the poem is a poetic expression of Stefan George's own poetic way, we may surmise that the prize he had in mind was that sensitive abundance of simplicity which comes to the poet in his late years as what needs and assents to be said. The poem itself, which has turned out well, a lyric song of language, proves that he did learn the renunciation.

But as for us, it must remain open whether we are capable of entering properly into this poetic experience. There is the danger that we will overstrain a poem such as this by thinking too much into it, and thereby debar ourselves from being moved by its poetry. Much greater of course—but who today would admit it?—is the danger that we will think too little, and reject the thought that the true experience with language can only be a thinking experience, all the more so because the lofty poetry of all great poetic work always vibrates within a realm of thinking. But if what matters first of all is a thinking experience with language, then why this stress on a poetic experience? Because thinking in turn goes its ways in the neighborhood of poetry. It is well, therefore, to give thought to the neighbor, to him who dwells in the same neighborhood. Poetry and thought, each needs the other in its neighborhood, each in its fashion, when it comes to ultimates. In what region the neighborhood itself has its domain, each of them, thought and poetry, will define differently, but always so that they will find themselves within the same domain. But because we are caught in the prejudice nurtured through centuries that thinking is a matter of ratiocination, that is, of calculation in the widest sense, the mere talk of a neighborhood of thinking to poetry is suspect.

Thinking is not a means to gain knowledge. Thinking cuts furrows into the soil of Being. About 1875, Nietzsche once wrote (Grossoktav WW XI, 20): "Our thinking should have a vigorous fragrance, like a wheatfield on a summer's night." How many of us today still have the senses for that fragrance?

By now, the two opening sentences of our lecture can be restated more clearly. This series of lectures bears the title "The Nature of Language." It is intended to bring us face to face with a possibility of undergoing a thinking experience with language. Be it noted that we said a possibility. We are still only in the preliminaries, in an attempt, even though the title does not say so. That title, "The Nature of Language," sounds rather presumptuous, as though we were about to promulgate reliable information concerning the nature of language. Besides, the title sounds altogether too trite, like "The Nature of Art," "The Nature of Freedom," "The Nature of Technology," "The Nature of Truth," "The Nature of Religion," etc. etc. We are all getting somewhat surfeited with all this big production of natures, for reasons which we do not quite understand ourselves. But what if we were to get rid of the presumptuousness and triteness of the title by a simple device? Let us give the title a question mark, such that the whole of it is covered by that mark and hence has a different sound. It then runs: The Nature?—of Language? Not only language is in question now, but so is the meaning of nature—and what is more, the question now is whether and in what way nature (essential being) and language belong together. The Nature?—of Language? With the addition of the questions marks, all of the title's presumptuousness and triteness vanish. At the same time, one question calls forth the others. The following two questions arise at once:

How are we to put questions to language when our relation to it is muddled, in any case undefined? How can we inquire about its nature, when it may immediately become a matter of dispute what nature means?

No matter how many ways we may devise to get our inquiry into language and the investigation of its nature started, all our efforts will be in vain as long as we close our minds in one very important respect which by no means concerns only the questions here touched upon.

If we put questions to language, questions about its nature, its being, then clearly language itself must already have been granted to us. Similarly, if we want to inquire into the being of language, then that which is called nature or being must also be already granted to us. Inquiry and investigation here and everywhere require the prior grant of whatever it is they approach and pursue with their queries. Every posing of every question takes place within the very grant of what is put in question.

What do we discover when we give sufficient thought to the matter? This, that the authentic attitude of thinking is not a putting of questions—rather, it is a listening to the grant, the promise of what is to be put in question. But in the history of our thinking, asking questions has since the early days been regarded as the characteristic procedure of thinking, and not without good cause. Thinking is more thoughtful in proportion as it takes a more radical stance, as it goes to the *radix,* the root of all that is. The quest of thinking always remains the search for the first and ultimate grounds. Why? Because this, that something is and what it is, the persistent presence of being, has from of old been determined to be the ground and foundation. As all nature has the character of a ground, a search for it is the founding and grounding of the ground or foundation. A thinking that thinks in the direction of nature defined in this way is fundamentally a questioning. At the close of a lecture called "The Question of Technology," given some time ago, I said: "Questioning is the piety of thinking." "Piety" is meant here in the ancient sense: obedient, or submissive, and in this case submitting to what thinking has to think about. One of the exciting experiences of thinking is that at times it does not fully comprehend the new insights it has just gained, and does not properly see them through. Such, too, is the case with the sentence just cited that questioning is the piety of thinking. The lecture ending with that sentence was already in the ambiance of the realization that the true stance of thinking cannot be to put questions, but must be to listen to that which our questioning vouchsafes—and all questioning begins to be a questioning only in virtue of pursuing its quest for essential being. Accordingly, the title of these lectures, even if we provide it with a question mark, does not thereby alone become the title for an experience of thinking. But there it is, waiting to be completed in terms of what we have just remarked concerning the true attitude of thinking. No matter how we put our questions to language about its nature, first of all it is needful that language vouchsafe itself to us. If it does, the nature of language becomes the grant of its essential being, that is, the being of language becomes the language of being.

Our title, "The Nature of Language," has now lost even its role as title. What it says is the echo of a thinking experience, the possibility of which we are trying to bring before us: the being of language—the language of being.

In the event that this statement—if that is what it is—represents not merely a contrived and hence vacuous inversion, the possibility may emerge that we shall at the proper time substitute another word for "language" as well as for "nature."

The whole that now addresses us—the being of language: the language of being—is not a title, let alone an answer to a question. It becomes a guide word, meant to guide us on our way. On that way of thinking, the poetic experience with the word which we heard at the beginning is to be our companion. We have already had converse with it, we recall, with this result: the closing line, "Where word breaks off no thing may be," points to the relation of word and thing in this manner, that the word itself is the relation, by holding everything forth into being, and there upholding it. If the word did not have this bearing, the whole of things, the "world," would sink into obscurity, including the "I" of the poem, him who brings to his country's strand, to the source of names, all the wonders and dreams he encounters.

In order that we may hear the voice of Stefan George's poetic experience with the word once more in another key, I shall in closing read Gottfried Benn's two-stanza poem. The tone of this poem is tauter and at the same time more vehe-ment, because it is abandoned and at the same time resolved in the extreme. The poem's title is a characteristic and presumably intentional variation:

A Word

A word, a phrase—: from cyphers rise
Life recognized, a sudden sense,
The sun stands still, mute are the skies,
And all compacts it, stark and dense.

A word—a gleam, a flight, a spark,
A thrust of flames, a stellar trace—
And then again—immense—the dark
Round world and I in empty space.

From

Language in the Poem

Every great poet creates his poetry out of one single poetic statement only. The measure of his greatness is the extent to which he becomes so committed to that singleness that he is able to keep his poetic Saying wholly within it.

The poet's statement remains unspoken. None of his individual poems, nor their totality, says it all. Nonetheless, every poem speaks from the whole of the one single statement, and in each instance says that statement. From the site of the statement there rises the wave that in each instance moves his Saying as poetic saying. But that wave, far from leaving the site behind, in its rise causes all the movement of Saying to flow back to its ever more hidden source. The site of the poetic statement, source of the movement-giving wave, holds within it the hidden nature of what, from a metaphysical-aesthetic point of view, may at first appear to be rhythm.

Since the poet's sole statement always remains in the realm of the unspoken, we can discuss its site only by trying to point to it by means of what the individual poems speak. But to do so, each poem will itself be in need of clarification. Clarification is what brings to its first appearance that purity which shimmers in everything said poetically.

LANGUAGE IN THE POEM. *Language in the Poem* first appeared in Germany in *Merkur* (6:1953) under the title *Dichten und Denken. Zu Stefan Georges Gedicht* Das Wort. Reprinted from *On the Way to Language,* ed. Peter D. Hertz. Copyright Harper and Row, Publishers, Inc. 1971. Reprinted by permission of HarperCollins Publishers.

It is easy to see that any right clarification itself already presupposes discussion. The individual poems derive their light and sound only from the poetic site. Conversely, the discussion of the poetic statement must first pass through the precursory clarification of individual poems.

All thinking dialogue with a poet's poetic statement stays within this reciprocity between discussion and clarification.

Only a poetic dialogue with a poet's poetic statement is a true dialogue—the poetic conversation between poets. But it is also possible, and at times indeed necessary, that there be a dialogue between *thinking* and poetry, for this reason: because a distinctive, though in each case different, relation to language is proper to them both.

The dialogue of thinking with poetry aims to call forth the *nature* of language, so that mortals may learn again to live within language.

The dialogue of thinking with poetry is long. It has barely begun. With respect to Trakl's[1] poetic statement, the dialogue requires particular reserve. A thinking dialogue with poetry can serve the poetic statement only indirectly. Thus it is always in danger of interfering with the saying of the statement, instead of allowing it to sing from within its own inner peace.

The discussion of the poetic statement is a thinking dialogue with poetry. It neither expounds a poet's outlook on the world, nor does it take inventory of his workshop. Above all, the discussion of the poetic statement can never be a substitute for or even guide to our listening to the poem. Thinking discussion can at best make our listening thought-provoking and, under the most favorable circumstances, more reflective.

---

[1]Georg Trakl (1887–1914), German poet.

E. D. Hirsch, Jr.

b. 1928

Twentieth-century scholars have been immensely interested in semantics, analytical and ordinary language philosophy, and all the problems of "meaning." Through their tendency to define poetry as a language critical theorists have raised as many critical issues as they sought to solve. Adopting some of the terminology of the phenomenologist Husserl and the structural linguist Saussure, Hirsch in *Objective Interpretation* attacks modes of interpretation that do not apply rigorous principles of exclusion. One such principle is that the meaning of a text is the author's meaning, not any meaning the public or readers of some later age find in it.

Hirsch rejects a number of attitudes toward poetic meaning that have been recently popular. One of these is the idea that the meaning of a text changes in the course of time. Hirsch argues that, indeed, the "relevance" of a text may vary from age to age, but "relevance" is a matter for "criticism," an activity separate from but built on "interpretation," which, in turn, has to do with the construing of meaning alone. He believes that interpretation and criticism (as he defines them) have been too often confused. The permanent meaning of a text, the only meaning, is what the *author* meant. That meaning is determined by the character of the author's intention—not *intention* as commonly used by modern critics including Wimsatt and Beardsley, but as used by Husserl to mean roughly "awareness."

Hirsch notes that the most vexing problem of construing the meaning of a text lies in grasping the presence of implications and eliminating false or unlikely ones. Applying Saussure's distinction between *langue* and *parole,* he attacks the idea that the more possible meanings we can find the better. William Empson's well-known *Seven Types of Ambiguity* is an example of a book that explores all possibilities as legitimate meaning. Hirsch insists that what a text really means is different from what it might mean.

Hirsch proposes legitimacy, correspondence, generic appropriateness, and coherence as criteria for interpretation. In discussing as an example one of Wordsworth's Lucy poems, he argues in favor of consulting the author's characteristic attitudes when faced with two unresolvable but apparently equally likely interpretations.

It is notable that Hirsch emphatically rejects those distinctions made between kinds of language that are characteristic of so much modern criticism. He would appear also to reject the Kantian tradition that led to the idea of the poem as "constitutive" of reality. Hirsch does, however, indicate that there are generic distinctions to be made between texts.

Critical works by Hirsch include *Wordsworth and Schelling* (1960), *Innocence and Experience* (1964), *Validity in Interpretation* (1967), *The Philosophy of Composition* (1977), *The Aims of Interpretation* (1978), and *Cultural Literacy* (1987).

Objective Interpretation

The fact that the term *criticism* has now come to designate all commentary on textual meaning reflects a general acceptance of the doctrine that description and evaluation are inseparable in literary study. In any serious confrontation of literature it would be futile, of course, to attempt a rigorous banishment of all evaluative judgment, but this fact does not give us the license to misunderstand or misinterpret our texts. It does not entitle us to use the text as the basis for an exercise in "creativity" or to submit as serious textual commentary a disguised argument for a particular ethical, cultural, or aesthetic viewpoint. Nor is criticism's chief concern—the present relevance of a text—a strictly necessary aspect of textual commentary. That same kind of theory which argues the inseparability of description and evaluation also argues that a text's meaning is simply its meaning "to us, today." Both kinds of argument support the idea that interpretation is criticism and vice versa. But there is clearly a sense in which we can neither evaluate a text nor determine what it means "to us, today" until we have correctly apprehended what it means. Understanding (and therefore interpretation, in the strict sense of the word) is both logically and psychologically prior to what is generally called criticism. It is true that this distinction between understanding and evaluation cannot always show itself in the finished work of criticism—nor, perhaps, should it—but a general grasp and acceptance of the distinction might help correct some of the most serious faults of current criticism (its subjectivism and relativism) and might even make it plausible to think of literary study as a corporate enterprise and a progressive discipline.

No one would deny, of course, that the more important issue is not the status of literary study as a discipline but the vitality of literature—especially of older literature—in the world at large. The critic is right to think that the text should speak to *us*. The point which needs to be grasped clearly by the critic is that a text cannot be made to speak to us until what it says has been understood. This is not an argument in favor of historicism as against criticism—it is simply a brute ontological fact. Textual meaning is not a naked given like a physical object. The text is first of all a conventional representation like a musical score, and what the score represents may be construed correctly or incorrectly. The literary text (in spite of

the semi-mystical claims made for its uniqueness) does not have a special ontological status which somehow absolves the reader from the demand universally imposed by all linguistic texts of every description. Nothing, that is, can give a conventional representation the status of an immediate given. The text of a poem, for example, has to be construed by the critic before it becomes a poem for him. Then it is, no doubt, an artifact with special characteristics. But before the critic construes the poem it is for him no artifact at all, and if he construes it wrongly, he will subsequently be talking about the wrong artifact, not the one represented by the text. If criticism is to be objective in any significant sense, it must be founded on a self-critical construction of textual meaning, which is to say, on objective interpretation.

The distinction I am drawing between interpretation and criticism was one of the central principles in the now vestigial science of hermeneutics. August Boeckh, for example, divided the theoretical part of his *Enzyklopädie* into two sections, one devoted to *Interpretation (Hermeneutik)* and the other to *Kritik.* Boeckh's discussion of this distinction is illuminating: interpretation is the construction of textual meaning as such; it explicates *(legt aus)* those meanings, and only those meanings, which the text explicitly or implicitly represents. Criticism, on the other hand, builds on the results of interpretation; it confronts textual meaning not as such, but as a component within a larger context. Boeckh defined it as "that philological function through which a text is understood not simply in its own terms and for its own sake, but in order to establish a relationship with something else, in such a way that the goal is a knowledge of this relationship itself."[1] Boeckh's definition is useful in emphasizing that interpretation and criticism confront two quite distinct "objects," for this is the fundamental distinction between the two activities. The object of interpretation is textual meaning in and for itself and may be called the *meaning* of the text. The object of criticism, on the other hand, is that meaning in its bearing on something else (standards of value, present concerns, etc.) and this object may therefore be called the *relevance* of the text.

The distinction between the meaning and the relevance of a text was first clearly made by Frege in his article *Über Sinn und Bedeutung,* where he demonstrated that although the meanings of two "texts" may be different, their referent or truth-value may be identical.[2] For example, the statement,

---

OBJECTIVE INTERPRETATION. Hirsch's *Objective Interpretation* first appeared in *PMLA*, 75 (1960), and is reprinted by permission of the Modern Language Association of America. It was reprinted as an appendix to Hirsch's book *Validity in Interpretation* (1967).

[1] [Hirsch] August Boeckh, *Enzyklopädie und Methodologie der philologischen Wissenschaften,* edited by E. Bratuscheck, 2nd ed. (Leipzig, 1886), p. 170.
[2] [Hirsch] Gottlob Frege, "Über Sinn und Bedeutung," *Zeitschrift für Philosophie und philosophische Kritik, 100* (1892). The article has been translated, and one English version may be found in H. Feigl and W. Sellars, *Readings in Philosophical Analysis* (New York, 1949).

"Scott is the author of *Waverley*" is true and yet the meaning of "Scott" is different from that of "the author of *Waverley*." The *Sinn* of each is different, but the *Bedeutung* (or one aspect of *Bedeutung*—the designatum of "Scott" and "author of *Waverley*") is the same. Frege considered only cases where different *Sinne* have an identical *Bedeutung,* but it is also true that the same *Sinn* may, in the course of time, have different *Bedeutungen.* For example, the sentence, "There is a unicorn in the garden," is prima facie false. But suppose the statement were made when there *was* a unicorn in the garden (as happened in Thurber's imaginative world); the statement would be true; its relevance would have shifted. But true or false, the meaning of the proposition would remain the same; for unless its *meaning* remained self-identical we would have nothing to label true or false. Frege's distinction, now widely accepted by logicians, is a special case of Husserl's general distinction between the inner and outer horizons of any meaning. In my first section I shall try to clarify Husserl's concept and to show how it applies to the problems of textual study, and especially to the basic assumptions of textual interpretation.

My purpose is primarily constructive rather than polemical. I would not willingly argue that interpretation should be practiced in strict separation from criticism. I shall ignore criticism simply in order to confront the special problems involved in construing the meaning or *Sinn* of a text. For most of my notions I disclaim any originality. My aim is to revive some forgotten insights of literary study and to apply to the theory of interpretation certain other insights from linguistics and philosophy. For although the analytical movement in criticism has permanently advanced the cause of intrinsic literary study, it has not yet paid enough attention to the problem of establishing norms and limits in interpretation. If I display any argumentative intent, it is not, therefore, against the analytical movements, which I approve, but only against certain modern theories which hamper the establishment of normative principles in interpretation and which thereby encourage the subjectivism and individualism which have for many students discredited the analytical movement. By normative principles I mean those notions which concern the nature of a correct interpretation. When the critic clearly conceives what a correct interpretation is in principle, he possesses a guiding idea against which he can measure his construction. (Without such a guiding idea, self-critical or objective interpretation is hardly possible. Current theory, however, fails to provide such a principle. The most influential and representative statement of modern theory is *Theory of Literature* by Wellek and Warren, a book to which I owe much. I ungratefully select it (especially Chapter 12) as a target of attack, both because it is so influential and be-cause I need a specific, concrete example of the sort of theory which requires amendment.[3]

1. The Two Horizons of Textual Meaning

The metaphorical doctrine that a text leads a life of its own is used by modern theorists to express the idea that textual meaning changes in the course of time.[4] This theory of a changing meaning serves to support the fusion of interpretation and criticism, and, at the same time, the idea that present relevance forms the basis for textual commentary. But the view should not remain unchallenged, since if it were correct there could be no objective knowledge about texts. Any statement about textual meaning could be valid only for the moment, and even this temporary validity could not be tested, since there would be no permanent norms on which validating judgments could be based. While the "life" theory does serve to explain and sanction the fact that different ages tend to interpret texts differently, and while it emphasizes the importance of a text's present relevance, it overlooks the fact that such a view undercuts *all* criticism, even the sort which emphasizes present relevance. If the view were correct, criticism would not only lack permanent validity, it could not even claim current validity by the time it got into print. Both the text's meaning and the tenor of the age would have altered. The "life" theory really masks the idea that the reader construes his own, new meaning instead of that represented by the text.

The "life" theory thus implicitly places the principle of change squarely where it belongs, that is, not in textual meaning as such but in changing generations of readers. According to Wellek, for example, the meaning of the text changes as it passes "through the minds of its readers, critics, and fellow artists."[5] Now when even a few of the norms which determine a text's meaning are allotted to readers, and made dependent on their attitudes and concerns, it is evident that textual meaning must change. But is it proper to make textual meaning dependent upon the reader's own cultural givens? It may be granted that these givens change in the course of time, but does this imply that textual meaning itself changes? As soon as the reader's outlook is permitted to determine what a text means, we have not simply a changing meaning but quite possibly as many meanings as readers.

Against such a *reductio ad absurdum,* the proponent of the current theory points out that in a given age many readers

---

3[Hirsch] René Wellek and Austin Warren, *Theory of Literature,* 2nd ed. (New York, 1956), Chapter 12. This chapter is by Wellek.
4[Hirsch] See, for example, *Theory of Literature,* p. 31.
5[Hirsch] *Theory of Literature,* p. 144.

will agree in their construction of a text and will unanimously repudiate the accepted interpretation of a former age. For the sake of fair-mindedness, this presumed unanimity may be granted, but must it be explained by arguing that the text's meaning has changed? Recalling Frege's distinction between *Sinn* and *Bedeutung,* the change could be explained by saying that the meaning of the text has remained the same, while the relevance of that meaning has shifted.[6] Contemporary readers will frequently share similar cultural givens and will therefore agree about what the text means to them. But might it not be the case that they agree about the text's meaning "to them" because they have first understood its meaning? If textual meaning itself could change, contemporary readers would lack a basis for agreement or disagreement. No one would bother seriously to discuss such a protean object. The relevance of textual meaning has no foundation and no objectivity unless meaning itself is unchanging. To fuse meaning and relevance, or interpretation and criticism, by the conception of an autonomous, living, changing meaning, does not really free the reader from the shackles of historicism; it simply destroys the basis both for any agreement among readers and for any objective study whatever.

The dilemma created by the fusion of *Sinn* and *Bedeutung* in current theory is exhibited as soon as the theorist attempts to explain how norms can be preserved in textual study. The explanation becomes openly self-contradictory: "It could be scarcely denied that there is [in textual meaning] a substantial *identity* of 'structure' which has remained the *same* throughout the ages. This *structure,* however, is dynamic: it *changes* throughout the process of history while passing through the minds of its readers, critics, and fellow artists."[7] First the "structure" is self-identical; then it changes! What is given in one breath is taken away in the next. Although it is a matter of common experience that a text appears different to us than it appeared to a former age, and although we remain deeply convinced that there *are* permanent norms in textual study, we cannot properly explain the facts by equating or fusing what changes with what remains the same. We must distinguish the two and give each its due.

A couplet from Marvell, used by Wellek to suggest how meaning changes, will illustrate my point:[8] "My vegetable love should grow / Vaster than empires and more slow."[9]

Wellek grants that *vegetable* here probably means more or less what we should nowadays express by *vegetative,* but he goes on to suggest that we cannot avoid associating the modern connotation of *vegetable* (what it means "to us"). Furthermore, he suggests that this enrichment of meaning may even be desirable. No doubt, the associated meaning *is* here desirable (since it supports the mood of the poem), but Wellek could not even make his point unless we could distinguish between what *vegetable* probably means as used in the text, and what it commonly means to us. Simply to discuss the issue is to admit that Marvell's poem probably does not imply the modern connotation, since if we could not separate the sense of *vegetative* from the notion of an *erotic cabbage,* we could not talk about the difficulty of making the separation. One need not argue that the delight we may take in such new meanings must be ignored. On the contrary, once we have self-critically understood the text, there is little reason to exclude valuable or pleasant associations which enhance its relevance. But it is essential to exclude these associations in the process of interpretation, in the process, that is, of understanding what a text means. The way out of the theoretical dilemma is to perceive that the meaning of a text does not change, and that the modern, different connotation of a word like *vegetable* belongs, if it is to be entertained at all, to the constantly changing relevance of a text's meaning.

It is in the light of the distinction between meaning and relevance that critical theories like T. S. Eliot's need to be viewed.[10] Eliot, like other modern critics, insists that the meaning of a literary work changes in the course of time, but, in contrast to Wellek, instead of locating the principle of change directly in the changing outlooks of readers, Eliot locates it in a changing literary tradition. In his view, the literary tradition is a "simultaneous" (as opposed to temporal) order of literary texts which is constantly rearranging itself as new literary works appear on the public scene. Whenever a new work appears it causes a rearrangement of the tradition as a whole, and this brings about an alteration in the meaning of each component literary text. When Shakespeare's *Troilus,* for example, entered the tradition, it altered the meaning not only of Chaucer's *Troilus,* but also, to some degree, the meaning of every other text in the literary tradition.

If the changes in meaning Eliot speaks of are considered to be changes in relevance, then his conception is perfectly sound. And indeed, by definition, Eliot is speaking of relevance rather than meaning, since he is considering the work in relation to a larger realm, as a component rather than

---

[6][Hirsch] It could also be explained, of course, by saying that certain generations of readers tend to misunderstand certain texts.
[7][Hirsch] *Theory of Literature,* p. 144. My italics.
[8][Hirsch] *Theory of Literature,* pp. 166–67.
[9]*To His Coy Mistress,* 11–12.

[10]See *Tradition and the Individual Talent,* pp. 761–64.

a world in itself. It goes without saying that the character of a component considered as such changes whenever the larger realm of which it is a part changes. A red object will appear to have different color qualities when viewed against differently colored backgrounds. The same is true of textual meaning. But the meaning of the text (its *Sinn*) does not change any more than the hue and saturation of the red object changes when seen against different backgrounds. Yet the analogy with colored objects is only partial: I can look at a red pencil against a green blotting pad and perceive the pencil's color in that special context without knowing the hue and saturation of either pencil or blotter. But textual meaning is a construction, not a naked given like a red object, and I cannot relate textual meaning to a larger realm until I have construed it. Before I can judge just how the changed tradition has altered the relevance of a text, I must understand its meaning or *Sinn*.

This permanent meaning is, and can be, nothing other than the author's meaning. There have been, of course, several other definitions of textual meaning: what the author's contemporaries would ideally have construed, what the ideal present-day reader construes, what the norms of language permit the text to mean, what the best critics conceive to be the best meaning, and so on. In support of these other candidates, various aesthetic and psychological objections have been aimed at the author: first, his meaning, being conditioned by history and culture, is too confined and simple; second, it remains, in any case, inaccessible to us because we live in another age, or because his mental processes are private, or because he himself did not know what he meant. Instead of attempting to meet each of these objections separately, I shall attempt to describe the general principle for answering all of them, and in doing so, to clarify further the distinction between meaning and relevance. The aim of my exposition will be to confirm that the author's meaning, as represented by his text, is unchanging and reproducible. My problem will be to show that although textual meaning is *determined* by the psychic acts of an author, and realized by those of a reader, textual meaning itself must not be *identified* with the author's or reader's psychic acts as such. To make this crucial point, I shall find it useful to draw upon Husserl's analysis of verbal meaning.

In his chief work, *Logische Untersuchungen,* Husserl sought, among other things, to avoid an identification of verbal meaning with the psychic arts of speaker or listener, author or reader, but to do this he did not adopt a strict, Platonic idealism by which meanings have an actual existence apart from meaning-experiences. Instead, he affirmed the objectivity of meaning by analyzing the observable relationship between it and those very mental processes in which it is

actualized. For in meaning-experiences themselves the objectivity and constancy of meaning are confirmed.

Husserl's point may be grasped by an example from visual experience.[11] When I look at a box, then close my eyes, and then reopen them, I can perceive in this second view the identical box I saw before. Yet, although I perceive the same box, the two acts of seeing are distinctly different—in this case temporally different. The same sort of result is obtained when I alter my acts of seeing spatially. If I go to another side of the room, or stand on a chair, what I actually "see" alters with my change in perspective, and yet I still "perceive" the identical box; I still understand that the *object* of my seeing is the same. Furthermore, if I leave the room, and simply recall the box in memory, I still understand that the *object* I remember is identical with the object I saw. For if I did not understand that, how could I insist that I was remembering? The examples are paradigmatic: All events of consciousness, not simply those involving visual perception and memory, are characterized by the mind's ability to make modally and temporally different *acts* of awareness refer to the same *object* of awareness. An object for the mind remains the same even though what is "going on in the mind" is not the same. The mind's "object" therefore may not be equated with psychic processes as such; the mental object is self-identical over against a plurality of mental acts.[12]

The relation between an act of awareness and its object Husserl calls "intention," using the term in its traditional philosophical sense, which is much broader than that of "purpose" and is roughly equivalent to "awareness." (When I employ the word subsequently, I shall be using it in Husserl's sense.)[13] This term is useful for distinguishing the components of a meaning-experience. For example, when I "intend" a box, there are at least three distinguishable as-

---

[11][Hirsch] Most of my illustrations in this section are visual rather than verbal since the former may be more easily grasped. If, at this stage, I were to choose verbal examples I would have to interpret the examples before making my point. I discuss a literary text in the second and third sections. The example of a box was suggested to me by Helmut Kuhn, *The Phenomenological Concept of "Horizon,"* in *Philosophical Essays in Memory of Edmund Husserl,* edited by Marvin Farber (Cambridge, Mass., 1940).

[12][Hirsch] See Aaron Gurwitsch, *On the Intentionality of Consciousness,* in *Philosophical Essays,* ed. cit.

[13][Hirsch] Although Husserl's term is a standard philosophical one for which there is no adequate substitute, students of literature may unwittingly associate it with the intentional fallacy. The two uses of the word are, however, quite distinct. As used by literary critics the term refers to a purpose which may or may not be realized by a writer. As used by Husserl the term refers to a process of consciousness. Thus in the literary usage, which involves problems of rhetoric, it is possible to speak of an unfulfilled intention, while in Husserl's usage such a locution would be meaningless. In order to call attention to the fact that I use the word in Husserl's sense, I have consistently placed inverted commas around it—an awkward procedure which may avert misunderstanding.

pects of that event. First, there is the object as perceived by me, second, there is the act by which I perceive the object, and finally there is (for physical things) the object which exists independently of my perceptual act. The first two aspects of the event Husserl calls "intentional object" and "intentional act" respectively. Husserl's point, then, is that *different* "intentional acts" (on different occasions) "intend" an *identical* "intentional object."

The general term for all "intentional objects" is meaning. Verbal meaning is simply a special kind of "intentional object," and like any other one, it remains self-identical over against the many different acts which "intend" it. But the noteworthy feature of verbal meaning is its suprapersonal character. It is not an "intentional object" for simply one person, but for many—potentially for all persons. Verbal meaning is, by definition, *that aspect of a speaker's "intention" which, under linguistic conventions, may be shared by others.* Anything not sharable in this sense does not belong to the *verbal* "intention" or verbal meaning. Thus, when I say, "The air is crisp," I may be thinking, among other things, "I should have eaten less at supper," and "Crisp air reminds me of my childhood in Vermont," and so on. In certain types of utterance such unspoken accompaniments to meaning may be sharable, but in general they are not, and they do not, therefore, generally belong to verbal meaning. The nonverbal aspects of the speaker's "intention" Husserl calls "experience" and the verbal ones "content." However, by "content" he does not mean simply "intellectual content" but all those aspects of the "intention," cognitive, emotive, phonetic (and in writing, even visual) which may be conveyed to others by the linguistic means employed.[14]

Husserl's analysis (in my brief exposition) makes, then, the following points: (1) Verbal meaning, being an "intentional object," is unchanging, that is, it may be reproduced by different "intentional acts," and remains self-identical through all these reproductions. (2) Verbal meaning is the sharable "content" of the *speaker's* "intentional object." (3) Since this meaning is both unchanging and interpersonal, it may be reproduced by the mental acts of different persons. Husserl's view is thus essentially historical, for even though he insists that verbal meaning is unchanging, he also insists that any particular verbal utterance, written or spoken, is historically determined. This is to say, the meaning is determined once and for all by the character of the speaker's "intention."[15]

Husserl's views provide an excellent context for discussing the central problems of interpretation. For once we define verbal meaning as the "content" of the author's "intention" (which for brevity's sake I shall call simply the author's "verbal intention"), the problem for the interpreter is quite clear: he must distinguish those meanings which belong to that "verbal intention" from those which do not belong. This problem may be rephrased, of course, in a way that nearly everyone will accept: the interpreter has to distinguish what a text implies from what it does not imply; he must give the text its full due, but he must also preserve norms and limits. For hermeneutic theory, the problem is to find a *principle* for judging whether various possible implications should or should not be admitted.

I describe the problem in terms of implication, since, for practical purposes, it lies at the heart of the matter. Generally, the explicit meanings of a text can be construed to the satisfaction of most readers; the problems arise in determining inexplicit or "unsaid" meanings. If, for example, I announce, "I have a headache," there is no difficulty in construing what I "say," but there may be great difficulty in construing implications like "I desire sympathy," "I have a right not to engage in distasteful work." Such implications may belong to my verbal meaning, or they may not belong. This is usually the area where the interpreter needs a guiding principle.

It is often said that implications must be determined by referring to the "context" of the utterance, which, for ordinary statements like "I have a headache," means the concrete situation in which the utterance occurs. In the case of written texts, however, *context* generally means "verbal context": the explicit meanings which surround the problematical passage. But these explicit meanings alone do not exhaust what we mean by *context* when we educe implications. The surrounding explicit meanings provide us with a sense of the whole meaning, and it is from this sense of the whole that we decide what the problematical passage implies. For we do not ask simply, "Does this implication belong with these other, explicit meanings?" but rather, "does this implication belong with these other meanings *within a particular sort of total meaning?*" For example, we cannot determine whether *root* belongs with or implies *bark* unless we know that the total meaning is "tree" and not "grass." The ground for educing implications is a sense of the whole meaning, and this is an indispensable aspect of what we mean by *context*.

Previously I defined the whole meaning of an utterance as the author's "verbal intention." Does this mean that the principle for admitting or excluding implications must be to ask, "Did the author have in mind such an implication?" If

[14][Hirsch] Edmund Husserl, *Logische Untersuchungen. Zweiter Band. Untersuchungen zur Phänomenologie und Theorie der Erkenntnis. I. Teil,* 2nd ed. (Halle, 1913), pp. 96–97.
[15][Hirsch] *Ibid.,* p. 91.

that is the principle, all hope for objective interpretation must be abandoned, since in most cases it is impossible (even for the author himself) to determine precisely what he was thinking of at the time or times he composed his text. But this is clearly not the correct principle. When I say, "I have a headache," I may indeed imply "I would like some sympathy," and yet I might not have been explicitly conscious of such an implication. The first step, then, in discovering a principle for admitting and excluding implications is to perceive the fundamental distinction between the author's "verbal intention" and the meanings of which he was explicitly conscious. Here again, Husserl's rejection of psychologism is useful. The author's "verbal intention" (his total verbal meaning) may be likened to my "intention" of a box. Normally, when I perceive a box, I am explicitly conscious of only three sides, and yet I assert with full confidence (although I might be wrong) that I "intend" a box, an object with *six* sides. Those three *unseen* sides belong to my "intention," in precisely the same way that the "unconscious" implications of an utterance belong to the author's "intention." They belong to the author's "intention." They belong to the "intention" taken as a whole.

Most if not all meaning-experiences or "intentions" are occasions in which the whole meaning is not explicitly present to consciousness. But how are we to define the manner in which these "unconscious" meanings are implicitly present? In Husserl's analysis, they are present in the form of a "horizon," which may be defined as a system of typical expectations and probabilities.[16] "Horizon" is thus an essential aspect of what we usually call context. It is an inexplicit sense of the whole, derived from the explicit meanings present to consciousness. Thus, my view of three surfaces, presented in a familiar and typically boxlike way, has a horizon of typical continuations; or, to put it another way, my "intention" of a whole box defines the horizon for my view of three visible sides. The same sort of relationship holds between the explicit and implicit meanings in a verbal "intention." The explicit meanings are components in a total meaning which is bounded by a horizon. Of the manifold typical continuations within this horizon the author is not and cannot be explicitly conscious, nor would it be a particularly significant task to determine just which components of his meaning the author *was* thinking of. But it is of the utmost importance to determine the *horizon* which defines the author's "intention" as a whole. For it is only with reference to this horizon, or sense of the whole, that the interpreter may distinguish those implications which are typical and proper components of the meaning from those which are not.

The interpreter's aim, then, is to posit the author's horizon and carefully to exclude his own accidental associations. A word like *vegetable,* for example, had a meaning-horizon in Marvell's language which was evidently somewhat different from the horizon it has in contemporary English. This is the linguistic horizon of the word, and it strictly bounds its *possible* implications. But all of these possible implications do not necessarily belong within the horizon of the particular utterance. What the word implies in the particular usage must be determined by asking, which implications are typical components of the whole meaning under consideration? By analogy, when three surfaces are presented to me in a special way, I must know the typical continuations of the surfaces. If I have never encountered a box before, I might think that the unseen surfaces were concave or irregular, or I might simply think there are other sides, but I have no idea what they are like. The probability that I am right in the way I educe implications depends upon my familiarity with the type of meaning I consider.

That is the reason, of course, that the genre concept is so important in textual study. By classifying the text as belonging to a particular genre, the interpreter automatically posits a general horizon for its meaning. The genre provides a sense of the whole, a notion of typical meaning-components. Thus, before we interpret a text, we often classify it as "casual conversation," "lyric poem," "military command," "scientific prose," "occasional verse," "novel," "epic," and so on. In a similar way, I have to classify the object I see as a box, a sphere, a tree, and so on, before I can deduce the character of its unseen or inexplicit components. But these generic classifications are simply preliminary indications. They give only a rough notion of the horizon for a particular meaning. The aim of interpretation is to specify the horizon as far as possible. Thus, the object I see is not simply a box but a cigarette carton, and not simply that but a carton for a particular brand of cigarettes. If a paint mixer or dyer wants to specify a particular patch of color, he is not content to call it blue; he calls it Williamsburg Blue. The example of a color patch is paradigmatic for all particular verbal meanings. They are not simply *kinds* of meanings, nor are they single meanings corresponding to individual "intentional acts" (Williamsburg Blue is not simply an individual patch of color); they are *typical* meanings, particular yet reproducible and the typical *components* of such meanings are similarly specific. The interpreter's job is to specify the text's horizon as far as he is able, and this means, ultimately,

---

[16][Hirsch] See Edmund Husserl, *Erfahrung und Urteil,* edited by L. Landgrebe (Hamburg, 1948), pp. 26–36, and H. Kuhn, *The Phenomenological Concept of "Horizon",* ed. cit.

that he must familiarize himself with the typical meanings of the author's mental and experiential world.

The importance of the horizon concept is that it defines in principle the norms and limits which bound the meaning represented by the text. But, at the same time, the concept frees the interpreter from the constricting and impossible task of discovering what the author was explicitly thinking of. Thus, by defining textual meaning as the author's meaning, the interpreter does not, as it is so often argued, impoverish meaning; he simply excludes what does not belong to it. For example, if I say, "My car ran out of gas," I imply, typically, "The engine stopped running." But whether or not I also imply "Life is ironical" depends on the generality of my "intention." Some linguistic utterances, many literary works among them, have an extremely broad horizon which at some points may touch the boundaries of man's intellectual cosmos. But whether or not this is the case is not a matter for a priori discussion; the decision must be based on a knowledgeable inference as to the particular "intention" being considered.

Within the horizon of a text's meaning, however, the process of explication is unlimited. In this respect Dryden was right; no text is every fully explicated. For example, if I undertook to interpret my "intention" of a box, I could make explicit unlimited implications which I did not notice in my original "intention." I could educe not only the three unseen sides, but also the fact that the surfaces of the box contain twenty-four right angles, that the area of two adjoining sides is less than half the total surface area, and so on. And if someone asked me whether or not such meanings were implicit in my "intention" of a box, I must answer affirmatively. In the case of linguistic meanings, where the horizon defines a much more complex "intentional object," such determinations are far more difficult to make. But the probability of an interpreter's inference may be judged by two criteria alone: the accuracy with which he has sensed the horizon of the whole and the typicality of such a meaning within such a whole. Insofar as the inference meets these criteria, it is truly an explication of textual meaning. It simply renders explicit that which was, consciously or unconsciously, in the author's "intention."

The horizon which grounds and sanctions inferences about textual meaning is the *inner horizon* of the text. It is permanent and self-identical. But beyond this inner horizon any meaning has an *outer horizon;* that is to say, any meaning has relationships to other meanings; it is always a component in larger realms. This outer horizon is the domain of criticism. But this outer horizon is not only unlimited, it is also changing since the world itself changes. In general, criticism stakes out only a portion of this outer horizon as its

peculiar object. Thus, for example, Eliot partitioned off that aspect of the text's outer horizon which is defined by the simultaneous order of literary texts. The simultaneous order at a given point in time is therefore the inner horizon of the meaning Eliot is investigating, and this inner horizon is just as definite, atemporal, and objective as the inner horizon which bounds textual meaning. But the critic, like the interpreter, must construe correctly the *components* of his inner horizon, and one major component is textual meaning itself. The critic must first accurately interpret the text. He need not perform a detailed explication, but he needs to achieve (and validate) that clear and specific sense of the whole meaning which makes detailed explication possible.

II. Determinateness of Textual Meaning

In the previous section I defined textual meaning as the "verbal intention" of the author, and this argues implicitly that hermeneutics must stress a reconstruction of the author's aims and attitudes in order to evolve guides and norms for construing the meaning of his text. It is frequently argued, however, that textual meaning has nothing to do with the author's mind, but only with his verbal achievement, that the object of interpretation is not the author but his text. This plausible argument assumes, of course, that the text automatically has a meaning simply because it represents an unalterable sequence of words. It assumes that the meaning of a word sequence is directly imposed by the public norms of language, that the text as a "piece of language" is a public object whose character is defined by public norms.[17] This view is in one respect sound, since textual meaning must conform to public norms if it is in any sense to be verbal (i.e., sharable) meaning; on no account may the interpreter permit his probing into the author's mind to raise private associations (experience) to the level of public implications (content).

However, this basically sound argument remains one-sided. For even though verbal meaning must conform to public linguistic norms (these are highly tolerant, of course), no mere sequence of words can represent an actual verbal meaning with reference to public norms alone. Referred to these alone, the text's meaning remains indeterminate. This is true even of the simplest declarative sentence like "My car ran out of gas" (did my Pullman dash from a cloud of Argon?). The fact that no one would radically misinterpret

---

[17][Hirsch] The phrase, *piece of language,* comes from the first paragraph of William Empson's *Seven Types of Ambiguity,* 3rd ed. (New York, 1955). It is typical of the critical school Empson founded.

such a sentence simply indicates that its frequency is high enough to give its usual meaning the apparent status of an immediate given. But this apparent immediacy obscures a complex process of adjudications among meaning-possibilities. Under the public norms of language alone no such adjudications can occur, since the array of possibilities presents a face of blank indifference. The array of possibilities only begins to become a more selective system of *probabilities* when, instead of confronting merely a word sequence, we also posit a speaker who very likely means something. Then and only then does the most usual sense of the word sequence become the most probable or "obvious" sense. The point holds true a fortiori, of course, when we confront less obvious word sequences like those found in poetry. A careful exposition of this point may be found in the first volume of Cassirer's *Philosophy of Symbolic Forms,* which is largely devoted to a demonstration that verbal meaning arises from the "reciprocal determination" of public linguistic possibilities and subjective specifications of those possibilities.[18] Just as language constitutes and colors subjectivity, so does subjectivity color language. The author's or speaker's subjective act is *formally* necessary to verbal meaning, and any theory which tries to dispense with the author as specifier of meaning by asserting that textual meaning is purely objectively determined finds itself chasing will-o'-the wisps. The burden of this section is, then, an attack on the view that a text is a "piece of language" and a defense of the notion that a text represents the determinate verbal meaning of an author.

One of the consequences arising from the view that a text is a piece of language—a purely public object—is the impossibility of defining in principle the nature of a correct interpretation. This is the same impasse which results from the theory that a text leads a life of its own, and indeed, the two notions are corollaries since any "piece of language" must have a changing meaning when the changing public norms of language are viewed as the only ones which determine the sense of the text. It is therefore not surprising to find that Wellek subscribes implicitly to the text-as-language theory. The text is viewed as representing not a determinate meaning, but rather a system of meaning-potentials specified not by a meaner but by the vital potency of language itself. Wellek acutely perceives the danger of the view:

Thus the system of norms is growing and changing and will remain, in some sense, always incompletely and imperfectly realized. But this dynamic conception does not mean mere subjectivism and relativism. All the different points of view are by no means equally right. It will always be possible to determine which point of view grasps the subject most thoroughly and deeply. A hierarchy of viewpoints, a criticism of the grasp of norms, is implied in the concept of the adequacy of interpretation.[19]

The danger of the view is, of course, precisely that it opens the door to subjectivism and relativism, since linguistic norms may be invoked to support any verbally possible meaning. Furthermore, it is not clear how one may criticize a grasp of norms which will not stand still.

Wellek's brief comment on the problem involved in defining and testing correctness in interpretation is representative of a widespread conviction among literary critics that the most correct interpretation is the most "inclusive" one. Indeed, the view is so widely accepted that Wellek did not need to defend his version of it (which he calls "perspectivism") at length. The notion behind the theory is reflected by such phrases as "always incompletely and imperfectly realized" and "grasps the subject most thoroughly." This notion is simply that no single interpretation can exhaust the rich system of meaning-potentialities represented by the text. *Ergo* every plausible reading which remains within public linguistic norms is a correct reading as far as it goes, but each reading is inevitably partial since it cannot realize all the potentialities of the text. The guiding principle in criticism, therefore, is that of the inclusive interpretation. The most "adequate" construction is the one which gives the fullest coherent account of all the text's potential meanings.[20]

Inclusivism is desirable as a position which induces a readiness to consider the results of others, but, aside from promoting an estimable tolerance, it has little theoretical value. For although its aim is to reconcile different plausible readings in an ideal, comprehensive interpretation, it cannot, in fact, either reconcile different readings or choose between

---

[18][Hirsch] *Vol. I. Language,* translated by R. Manheim (New Haven, 1953). It is ironic that Cassirer's work should be used to support the notion that a text speaks for itself. The realm of language is autonomous for Cassirer only in the sense that it follows an independent development which is reciprocally determined by objective *and* subjective factors. See pp. 69, 178, 213, 249–50, et passim.

[19][Hirsch] *Theory of Literature,* p. 144.

[20][Hirsch] Every interpretation is necessarily incomplete in the sense that it fails to explicate all a text's implications. But this kind of incomplete interpretation may still carry an absolutely correct system of emphases and an accurate sense of the whole meaning. This kind of incompleteness is radically different from that postulated by the inclusivists, for whom a sense of the whole means a grasp of the various possible meanings which a text can plausibly represent.

them. As a normative idea, or principle of correctness, it is useless. This point may be illustrated by citing two expert readings of a well-known poem by Wordsworth. I shall first quote the poem and then quote excerpts from two published exegeses in order to demonstrate the kind of impasse which inclusivism always provokes when it attempts to reconcile interpretations, and, incidentally, to demonstrate the very kind of interpretative problem which calls for a guiding principle:

> A slumber did my spirit seal;
>   I had no human fears:
> She seemed a thing that could not feel
>   The touch of earthly years.
>
> No motion has she now, no force;
>   She neither hears nor sees;
> Rolled round in earth's diurnal course,
>   With rocks, and stones, and trees.

Here are excerpts from two commentaries on the final lines of the poem; the first is by Cleanth Brooks, the second by F. W. Bateson:

1. [The poet] attempts to suggest something of the lover's agonized shock at the loved one's present lack of motion—of his response to her utter and horrible inertness. . . . Part of the effect, of course, resides in the fact that a dead lifelessness is suggested more sharply by an object's being whirled about by something else than by an image of the object in repose. But there are other matters which are at work here: the sense of the girl's falling back into the clutter of things, companioned by things chained like a tree to one particular spot, or by things completely inanimate like rocks and stones. . . . [She] is caught up helplessly into the empty whirl of the earth which measures and makes time. She is touched by and held by earthly time in its most powerful and horrible image.

2. The final impression the poem leaves is not of two contrasting moods, but of a single mood mounting to a climax in the pantheistic magnificence of the last two lines. . . . The vague living-Lucy of this poem is opposed to the grander dead-Lucy who has become involved in the sublime processes of nature. We put the poem down satisfied, because its last two lines

succeed in effecting a reconciliation between the two philosophies or social attitudes. Lucy is actually more alive now that she is dead, because she is now a part of the life of nature, and not just a human "thing."[21]

Now, if we grant, as I think we must, that both the cited interpretations are permitted by the text, the problem for the inclusivist is to reconcile the two readings.

Three modes of reconciliation are available to the inclusivist: (1) Brooks's reading includes Bateson's; it shows that any affirmative suggestions in the poem are negated by the bitterly ironical portrayal of the inert girl being whirled around by what Bateson calls the "sublime processes of nature." (2) Bateson's reading includes Brooks's; the ironic contrast between the active, seemingly immortal girl and the passive inert and dead girl is overcome by a final unqualified affirmation of immortality. (3) Each of the readings is partially right, but they must be fused to supplement one another. The very fact that the critics differ suggests that the meaning is essentially ambiguous. The emotion expressed is ambivalent, and comprises both bitter regret and affirmation. The third mode of reconciliation is the one most often employed, and is probably, in this case, the most satisfactory. A fourth type of resolution, which would insist that Brooks is right and Bateson wrong (or vice versa) is not available to the inclusivist, since the text, as language, renders both readings plausible.

Close examination, however, reveals that none of the three modes of argument manages to reconcile or fuse the two different readings. Mode 1, for example, insists that Brooks's reading comprehends Bateson's, but although it is conceivable that Brooks implies all the meanings which Bateson has perceived, Brooks also implies a *pattern of emphasis* which cannot be reconciled with Bateson's reading. While Bateson construes a primary emphasis on life and affirmation, Brooks emphasizes deadness and inertness. No amount of manipulation can reconcile these divergent emphases, since one pattern of emphasis irrevocably excludes other patterns, and, since emphasis is always crucial to meaning, the two constructions of meaning rigorously exclude one another. Precisely the same strictures hold, of course, for the argument that Bateson's reading comprehends that of Brooks. Nor can mode 3 escape with impunity.

---

[21][Hirsch] Cleanth Brooks, *Irony as a Principle of Structure*, in M. D. Zabel, ed., *Literary Opinion in America*, 2nd ed. (New York, 1951), p. 736 [p. 972]. F. W. Bateson, *English Poetry: A Critical Introduction* (London, 1950), p. 33 and pp. 80–81.

Although it seems to preserve a stress both on negation and on affirmation, thereby coalescing the two readings, it actually excludes both readings, and labels them not simply partial, but wrong. For if the poem gives equal stress to bitter irony and to affirmation, then any construction which places a primary stress on either meaning is simply incorrect.

The general principle implied by my analysis is very simple. The submeanings of a text are not blocks which can be brought together additively. Since verbal (and any other) meaning is a *structure* of component meanings, interpretation has not done its job when it simply enumerates what the component meanings are. The interpreter must also determine their probable structure, and particularly their structure of emphases. Relative emphasis is not only crucial to meaning (perhaps it is the most crucial and problematical element of all), it is also highly restrictive; it excludes alternatives. It may be asserted as a general rule that whenever a reader confronts two interpretations which impose different emphases on similar meaning components, at least one of the interpretations must be wrong. They cannot be reconciled.

By insisting that verbal meaning always exhibits a determinate structure of emphases, I do not, however, imply that a poem or any other text must be unambiguous. It is perfectly possible, for example, that Wordsworth's poem ambiguously implies both bitter irony and positive affirmation. Such complex emotions are commonly expressed in poetry, but if that is the kind of meaning the text represents Brooks and Bateson would be wrong to emphasize one emotion at the expense of the other. Ambiguity or, for that matter, vagueness is not the same as indeterminateness. This is the crux of the issue. To say that verbal meaning is determinate is not to exclude complexities of meaning but only to insist that a text's meaning is what it is and not a hundred other things. Taken in this sense, a vague or ambiguous text is just as determinate as a logical proposition; it means what it means and nothing else. This is true even if one argues that a text could display shifting emphases like those Sunday supplement magic squares which first seem to jut out and then to jut in. With texts of this character (if any exist), one need only say that the emphases shift, and must not, therefore, be construed statically. Any static construction would simply be wrong. The fundamental flaw in the "theory of the most inclusive interpretation" is that it overlooks the problem of emphasis. Since different patterns of emphasis *exclude* one another, inclusivism is neither a genuine norm nor an adequate guiding principle for establishing an interpretation.

But aside from the fact that inclusivism cannot do its appointed job, there are more fundamental reasons for rejecting it and all other interpretive ideals based on the conception that a text represents a system of meaning-possibilities. No one would deny that for the interpreter the text is at first the source of numerous possible interpretations. The very nature of language is such that a particular sequence of words can represent several different meanings (that is why public norms alone are insufficient in textual interpretation). But to say that a text *might* represent several structures of meaning does not imply that it does in fact represent all the meanings which a particular word sequence can legally convey. Is there not an obvious distinction between what a text might mean and what it does mean? According to accepted linguistic theory, it is far more accurate to say that a written composition is not a mere locus of verbal possibilities, but, rather, a record (made possible by the invention of writing) of a verbal actuality. The interpreter's job is to reconstruct a determinate actual meaning, not a mere system of possibilities. Indeed, if the text *represented* a system of possibilities, interpretation would be impossible, since no actual reading could correspond to a mere system of possibilities. Furthermore, if the text is conceived to represent all the *actual* structures of meaning permissible within the public norms of language, then no single construction (with its exclusivist pattern of emphases) could be correct, and any legitimate construction would be just as incorrect as any other. When a text is conceived as a piece of language, a familiar and all too common anarchy follows. But, aside from its unfortunate consequences, the theory contradicts a widely accepted principle in linguistics. I refer to Saussure's distinction between *langue* and *parole*.

Saussure defined *langue* as the system of linguistic possibilities shared by a speech community at a given point in time.[22] This system of possibilities contains two distinguishable levels. The first consists of habits, engrams, prohibitions, and the like derived from past linguistic usage; these are the "virtualities" of the *langue*. Based on these virtualities, there are, in addition, sharable meaning-possibilities which have never before been actualized; these are the "potentialities." The two types of meaning-possibilities taken together constitute the *langue* which the speech community draws upon. But this system of possibilities must be distinguished from the actual verbal utterances of individuals who draw upon it. These actual utterances are called *paroles;* they are *uses* of language, and actualize some (but never all) of the meaning-possibilities constituting the *langue*.

---

[22][Hirsch] This is the "synchronic" as opposed to the "diachronic" sense of the term. See Ferdinand de Saussure, *Cours de linguistique générale* (Paris, 1931). Useful discussions may be found in Stephen Ullman, *The Principles of Semantics* (Glasgow, 1951), and W. v. Wartburg, *Einführung in die Problematik und Methodik der Sprachwissenschaft* (Halle, 1943).

Saussure's distinction pinpoints the issue: does a text represent a segment of *langue* (as modern theorists hold) or a *parole?* A simple test suffices to provide the answer. If the text is composed of sentences it represents *parole,* which is to say the determinate verbal meaning of a member of the speech community. *Langue* contains words and sentence-forming principles, but it contains no sentences. It may be represented in writing only by isolated words in disconnection *(Wörter* as opposed to *Worte).* A *parole,* on the other hand, is always composed of sentences, an assertion corroborated by the firmly established principle that the sentence is the fundamental unit of speech.[23] Of course, there are numerous elliptical and one-word sentences, but wherever it can be correctly inferred that a text represents sentences and not simply isolated words, it may also be inferred that the text represents *parole,* which is to say, actual, determinate verbal meaning.

The point is nicely illustrated in a dictionary definition. The letters in boldface at the head of the definition represent the word as *langue,* with all its rich meaning-possibilities. But under one of the subheadings, in an illustrative sentence, those same letters represent the word as *parole,* as a particular, selective actualization from *langue.* In yet another illustrative sentence, under another subheading, the very same word represents a different selective actualization. Of course, many sentences, especially those found in poetry, actualize far more possibilities than illustrative sentences in a dictionary. Any pun, for example, realizes simultaneously at least two divergent meaning-possibilities. But the pun is nevertheless an actualization from *langue* and not a mere system of meaning-possibilities.

The *langue-parole* distinction, besides affirming the determinateness of textual meaning, also clarifies the special problems posed by revised and interpolated texts. With a revised text, composed over a long period of time *(Faust,* for example) how are we to construe the *unrevised* portions? Should we assume that they still mean what they meant originally or that they took on a new meaning when the rest of the text was altered or expanded? With compiled or interpolated texts, like many books of the Bible, should we assume that sentences from varied provenances retain their original meanings, or that these heterogeneous elements have become integral components of a new total meaning? In terms of Saussure's distinction, the question becomes: should we consider the text to represent a compilation of divers *paroles* or a new unitary *parole* "respoken" by the new author or editor? I submit that there can be no definitive answer to the question, except in relation to a specific scholarly or aesthetic purpose, for in reality the question is not, how are we to interpret the text? but, *which* text are we to interpret? Is it to be the heterogeneous compilation of past *paroles,* each to be separately considered, or the new, homogeneous *parole?* Both may be represented by the written score. The only problem is to choose, and having chosen, rigorously to refrain from confusing or in any way identifying the two quite different and separate "texts" with one another. Without solving any concrete problems, then, Saussure's distinction nevertheless confirms the critic's right in most cases to regard his text as representing a single *parole.*

Another problem which Saussure's distinction clarifies is that posed by the bungled text, where the author aimed to convey a meaning which his words do not convey to others in the speech community. One sometimes confronts the problem in a freshman essay. In such a case, the question is, does the text mean what the author wanted it to mean or does it mean what the speech community at large takes it to mean? Much attention has been devoted to this problem ever since the publication in 1946 of Wimsatt's and Beardsley's essay on *The Intentional Fallacy.*[24] In that essay the position was taken (albeit modified by certain qualifications) that the text, being public, means what the speech community takes it to mean. This position is, in an ethical sense, right (and language, being social, has a strong ethical aspect): if the author has bungled so badly that his utterance will be misconstrued, then it serves him right when folk misunderstand him. However, put in linguistic terms, the position becomes unsatisfactory. It implies that the meaning represented by the text is not the *parole* of an author, but rather the *parole* of "the speech community." But since only individuals utter *paroles,* a *parole* of the speech community is a nonexistent, or what the Germans call an *Unding.* A text can represent only the *parole* of a speaker or author, which is another way of saying that meaning requires a meaner.

However, it is not necessary that an author's text represent the *parole* he desired to convey. It is frequently the case, when an author has bungled, that his text represents no *parole* at all. Indeed there are but two alternatives: either the text represents the author's verbal meaning or it represents no *determinate* verbal meaning at all. Sometimes, of course, it is impossible to detect that the author has bungled, and in that case, even though his text does not represent verbal meaning, we shall go on misconstruing the text as though it did, and no one will be the wiser. But with most bungles we

---

[23][Hirsch] See, for example, Cassirer [*Philosophy of Symbolic Forms,* I], p. 304.

[24]Pp. 945–52.

are aware of a disjunction between the author's words and his probable meaning. Eliot, for example, chided Poe for saying "My most immemorial year," when Poe "meant" his most *memorable* year.[25] Now we all agree that Poe did not mean what speakers of English generally mean by the word *immemorial*—and so the word cannot have the usual meaning. (An author cannot mean what he does not mean.) The only question, then, is: does the word mean more or less what we convey by "never-to-be-forgotten" or does it mean nothing at all? Has Poe so violated linguistic norms that we must deny his utterance verbal meaning or "content"?

The question probably cannot be answered by fiat. But since Poe's meaning is generally understood, and since the single criterion for verbal meaning is communicability, I am inclined to describe Poe's meaning as verbal.[26] I tend to side with the Poes and Malaprops of the world, for the norms of language remain far more tolerant than dictionaries and critics like Eliot suggest. On the other hand, every member of the speech community, and especially the critic, has a duty to avoid and condemn sloppiness and needless ambiguity in the use of language, simply in order to preserve the effectiveness of the *langue* itself. Moreover, there must be a dividing line between verbal meanings and those meanings which we half-divine by a supralinguistic exercise of imagination. There must be a dividing line between Poe's successful disregard of normal usage and the incommunicable word sequences of a bad freshman essay. However, that dividing line is not between the author's meaning and the reader's, but rather between the author's *parole* and no *parole* at all.

Of course, theoretical principles cannot directly solve the interpreter's problem. It is one thing to insist that a text represents the determinate verbal meaning of an author, but it is quite another to discover what that meaning is. The very same text could represent numerous different *paroles,* as any ironic sentence discloses ("That's a *bright* idea!?" or "That's a bright *idea!*"). But it should be of some practical consequence for the interpreter to know that he does have a precisely defined task, namely to discover the author's meaning. It is therefore not only sound but necessary for the interpreter to inquire, what in all probability did the author mean? Is the pattern of emphases I construe the author's pat-

tern? But it is both incorrect and futile to inquire, what does the language of the text say? That question can have no determinate answer.

III. *Verification*

Since the meaning represented by a text is that of another, the interpreter can never be certain that his reading is correct. He knows furthermore that the norms of *langue* by themselves are far too broad to specify the particular meanings and emphases represented by the text, that these particular meanings were specified by particular kinds of subjective acts on the part of the author, and that these acts, as such, remain inaccessible.[27] A less self-critical reader, on the other hand, approaches solipsism if he assumes that the text represents a perspicuous meaning simply because it represents an unalterable sequence of words. For if this "perspicuous" meaning is not verified in some way, it will simply be the interpreter's own meaning, exhibiting the connotations and emphases which he himself imposes. Of course, the reader must realize verbal meaning by his own subjective acts (no one can do that for him), but if he remembers that his job is to construe the author's meaning, he will attempt to exclude his own predispositions and to impose those of the author. But no one can establish another's meaning with certainty. The interpreter's goal is simply this: to show that a given reading is more probable than others. In hermeneutics, verification is a process of establishing relative probabilities.

To establish a reading as probable it is first necessary to show, with reference to the norms of language, that it is possible. This is the criterion of *legitimacy:* the reading must be permissible within the public norms of the *langue* in which the text was composed. The second criterion is that of *correspondence:* the reading must account for each linguistic component in the text. Whenever a reading arbitrarily ignores linguistic components or inadequately accounts for them, the reading may be presumed improbable. The third criterion is that of *generic appropriateness:* if the text follows the conventions of a scientific essay, for example, it is inappropriate to construe the kind of allusive meaning found in casual conversation.[28] But when these three preliminary criteria have been satisfied, there remains a fourth criterion which gives significance to all the rest, the criterion of plausibility or *coherence.* The three preliminary norms usually

---

[25][Hirsch] T. S. Eliot, "From Poe to Valéry," *Hudson Review, 2* (1949), p. 232.

[26][Hirsch] The word is, in fact, quite effective. It conveys the sense of "memorable" by the component *memorial,* and the sense of "never-to-be-forgotten" by the negative prefix. The difference between this and Jabberwocky words is that it appears to be a standard word occurring in a context of standard words. Perhaps Eliot is right to scold Poe, but he cannot properly insist that the word lacks a determinate verbal meaning.

[27][Hirsch] To recall Husserl's point: a particular verbal meaning depends on a particular species of "intentional act," not on a single, irreproducible act.

[28][Hirsch] This third criterion is, however, highly presumptive, since the interpreter may easily mistake the text's genre.

permit several readings, and this is by definition the case when a text is problematical. Faced with alternatives, the interpreter chooses the reading which best meets the criterion of coherence. Indeed, even when the text is not problematical, coherence remains the decisive criterion, since the meaning is "obvious" only because it "makes sense." I wish, therefore, to focus attention on the criterion of coherence, and shall take for granted the demands of legitimacy, correspondence, and generic appropriateness. I shall try to show that verification by the criterion of coherence, and ultimately, therefore, verification in general, implies a reconstruction of relevant aspects in the author's outlook. My point may be summarized in the paradox that objectivity in textual interpretation requires explicit reference to the speaker's subjectivity.

The paradox reflects the peculiar nature of coherence, which is not an absolute, but a dependent quality. The laws of coherence are variable; they depend upon the nature of the total meaning under consideration. Two meanings ("dark" and "bright," for example) which cohere in one context may not cohere in another.[29] "Dark with excessive bright" makes excellent sense in *Paradise Lost,* but if a reader found the phrase in a textbook on plant pathology, he would assume that he confronted a misprint for "Dark with excessive blight." Coherence depends on the context, and it is helpful to recall our definition of *context:* it is a sense of the whole meaning, constituted of explicit partial meanings plus a horizon of expectations and probabilities. One meaning coheres with another because it is typical or probable with reference to the whole (coherence is thus the first cousin of implication). The criterion of coherence can be invoked only with reference to a particular context, and this context may be inferred only by positing the author's "horizon," his disposition toward a particular type of meaning. This conclusion requires elaboration.

The fact that coherence is a dependent quality leads to an unavoidable circularity in the process of interpretation. The interpreter posits meanings for the words and word-sequences he confronts, and, at the same time, he has to posit a whole meaning or context in reference to which the submeanings cohere with one another. The procedure is thoroughly circular; the context is derived from the submeanings and the submeanings are specified and rendered coherent with reference to the context. This circularity makes it very difficult to convince a reader to alter his construction, as every teacher knows. Many a self-willed student continues

to insist that his reading is just as plausible as his instructor's, and, very often, the student is justified; his reading does make good sense. Often, the only thing at fault with the student's reading is that it is probably wrong, not that it is incoherent. The student persists in his opinion precisely because his construction *is* coherent and self-sustaining. In such a case he is wrong because he has misconstrued the context or sense of the whole. In this respect, the student's hardheadedness is not different from that of all self-convinced interpreters. Our readings are too plausible to be relinquished. If we have a distorted sense of the text's whole meaning, the harder we look at it the more certainly we shall find our distorted construction confirmed.

Since the quality of coherence depends upon the context inferred, there is no absolute standard of coherence by which we can adjudicate between different coherent readings. Verification by coherence implies therefore a verification of the *grounds* on which the reading is coherent. *It is necessary to establish that the context invoked is the most probable context.* Only then, in relation to an established context, can we judge that one reading is more coherent than another. Ultimately, therefore, we have to posit the most probable horizon for the text, and it is possible to do this only if we posit the author's typical outlook, the typical associations and expectations which form in part the context of his utterance. This is not only the single way we can test the relative coherence of a reading, but is also the only way to avoid pure circularity in making sense of the text.

An essential task in the process of verification is, therefore, a deliberate reconstruction of the author's subjective stance to the extent that this stance is relevant to the text at hand.[30] The importance of such psychological reconstruction may be exemplified in adjudicating between different readings of Wordsworth's *A Slumber Did My Spirit Seal.* The interpretations of Brooks and Bateson, different as they are, remain equally coherent and self-sustaining. The implications which Brooks construes cohere beautifully with the explicit meanings of the poem within the context which Brooks

---

[29][Hirsch] Exceptions to this are the syncategorematic meanings (color and extension, for example) which cohere by necessity regardless of the context.

[30][Hirsch] The reader may feel that I have telescoped a number of steps here. The author's verbal meaning or "verbal intention" is the object of complex "intentional acts." To reproduce this meaning it is necessary for the interpreter to engage in "intentional acts" belonging to the same species as those of the author. (Two different "intentional acts" belong to the same species when they "intend" the same "intentional object.") That is why the issue of "stance" arises. The interpreter needs to adopt sympathetically the author's stance (his disposition to engage in particular kinds of "intentional acts") so that he can "intend" with some degree of probability the same "intentional objects" as the author. This is especially clear in the case of *implicit* verbal meaning, where the interpreter's realization of the author's stance determines the text's horizon.

adumbrates. The same may be said of Bateson's reading. The best way to show that one reading is more plausible and coherent than the other is to show that one context is more probable than the other. The problem of adjudicating between Bateson and Brooks is therefore, implicitly, the problem every interpreter must face when he tries to verify his reading. He must establish the most probable context.

Now when the *homme moyen sensuel* confronts bereavement such as that which Wordsworth's poem explicitly presents he adumbrates, typically, a horizon including sorrow and inconsolability. These are for him components in the very meaning of bereavement. Sorrow and inconsolability cannot fail to be associated with death when the loved one, formerly so active and alive, is imagined as lying in the earth, helpless, dumb, inert, insentient. And, since there is no hint of life in heaven but only of bodily death, the comforts of Christianity lie beyond the poem's horizon. Affirmations too deep for tears, like those Bateson insists on, simply do not cohere with the poem's explicit meanings; they do not belong to the context. Brooks's reading, therefore, with its emphasis on inconsolability and bitter irony, is clearly justified not only by the text but by reference to universal human attitudes and feelings.

But the trouble with such a reading is apparent to most Wordsworthians. The poet is not an *homme moyen sensuel;* his characteristic attitudes are somewhat pantheistic. Instead of regarding rocks and stones and trees merely as inert objects, he probably regarded them in 1799 as deeply alive, as part of the immortal life of nature. Physical death he felt to be a return to the source of life, a new kind of participation in nature's "revolving immortality." From everything we know of Wordsworth's typical attitudes during the period in which he composed the poem, inconsolability and bitter irony do not belong in its horizon. I think, however, that Bateson overstates his case, and that he fails to emphasize properly the negative implications in the poem ("No motion has she now, no force"). He overlooks the poet's reticence, his distinct unwillingness to express any unqualified evaluation of his experience. Bateson, I would say, has not paid enough attention to the criterion of correspondence. Nevertheless, in spite of this, and in spite of the apparent implausibility of Bateson's reading, it remains, I think, somewhat more probable than that of Brooks. His procedure is also more objective. For even if he had botched his job thoroughly and had produced a less probable reading than that of Brooks, his method would remain fundamentally sound. Instead of projecting his own attitudes (Bateson is presumably not a pantheist) and instead of positing a "universal matrix" of human attitudes (there is none), he has tried to reconstruct the author's probable attitudes so far as these are relevant in specifying the poem's meaning. It is still possible, of course, that Brooks is right and Bateson wrong. A poet's typical attitudes do not always apply to a particular poem, although Wordsworth is, in a given period, more consistent than most poets. Be that as it may, we shall never be *certain* what any writer means, and since Bateson grounds his interpretation in a conscious construction of the poet's outlook, his reading must be deemed the more probable one until the uncovering of some presently unknown data makes a different construction of the poet's stance appear more valid.

Bateson's procedure is appropriate to all texts, including anonymous ones. On the surface, it would seem impossible to invoke the author's probable outlook when the author remains unknown, but in this limiting case the interpreter simply makes his psychological reconstruction on the basis of fewer data. For even with anonymous texts it is crucial to posit not simply some author or other, but a *particular* subjective stance in reference to which the construed context is rendered probable. That is why it is important to date anonymous texts. The interpreter needs all the clues he can muster with regard not only to the text's *langue* and genre, but also to the cultural and personal attitudes the author might be expected to bring to bear in specifying his verbal meanings. In this sense, all texts, including anonymous ones, are "attributed." The objective interpreter simply tries to make his attribution explicit, so that the grounds for his reading are frankly acknowledged. This opens the way to progressive accuracy in interpretation, since it is possible, then, to test the assumptions behind a reading as well as the coherence of the reading itself.

The fact that anonymous texts may be successfully interpreted does not, however, lead to the conclusion that all texts should be treated as anonymous ones, that they should, so to say, speak for themselves. I have already argued that no text speaks for itself, and that every construed text is necessarily "attributed." These points suggest strongly that it is unsound to insist on deriving all inferences from the "text itself." When we date an anonymous text, for example, we apply knowledge gained from a wide variety of sources which we correlate with data derived from the text. This extrinsic data is not, however, read *into* the text. On the contrary, it is used to *verify* that which we read out of it. The extrinsic information has ultimately a purely verificative function.

The same thing is true of information relating to the author's subjective stance. No matter what the source of this information may be, whether it be the text alone or the text in conjunction with other data, this information is *extrinsic* to verbal meaning as such. Strictly speaking, the author's subjective stance is not part of his verbal meaning even when he explicitly discusses his feelings and attitudes. This is Husserl's point again. The "intentional object" represented by a text is different from the "intentional acts" which realize it. When the interpreter posits the author's stance, he sympathetically reenacts the author's "intentional acts," but although this imaginative act is necessary for realizing meaning, it must be distinguished from meaning as such. In no sense does the text *represent* the author's subjective stance: the interpreter simply adopts a stance in order to make sense of the text, and, if he is self-critical, he tries to verify his interpretation by showing his adopted stance to be, in all probability, the author's.

Of course, the text at hand is the safest source of clues to the author's outlook, since men do adopt different attitudes on different occasions. However, even though the text itself should be the primary source of clues and must always be the final authority, the interpreter should make an effort to go beyond his text wherever possible, since this is the only way he can avoid a vicious circularity. The harder one looks at a text from an incorrect stance, the more convincing the incorrect construction becomes. Inferences about the author's stance are sometimes difficult enough to make even when all relevant data are brought to bear, and it is self-defeating to make the inferential process more difficult than it need be. Since these inferences are ultimately extrinsic, there is no virtue in deriving them from the text alone. One must not confuse the result of a construction (the interpreter's understanding the text's *Sinn*) either with the *process* of construction or with a validation of that process. The *Sinn* must be represented by and limited by the text alone, but the processes of construction and validation involve psychological reconstruction and should therefore be based on all the data available.

Not only the criterion of coherence but all the other criteria used in verifying interpretations must be applied with reference to a psychological reconstruction. The criterion of legitimacy, for example, must be related to a speaking subject, since it is the author's *langue,* as an internal possession, and not the interpreter's, which defines the range of meaning-possibilities a text can represent. The criterion of correspondence has force and significance only because we presume that the author meant something by each of the linguistic components he employed. And the criterion of generic appropriateness is relevant only so far as generic conventions are possessed and accepted by the author. The fact that these criteria all refer ultimately to a psychological construction is hardly surprising when we recall that to verify a text is simply to establish that the author probably meant what we construe his text to mean. The interpreter's primary task is to reproduce in himself the author's "logic," his atti-

tudes, his cultural givens, in short his world. For even though the process or verification is highly complex and difficult, the ultimate verificative principle is very simple: the imaginative reconstruction of the speaking subject.[31]

The speaking subject is not, however, identical with the subjectivity of the author as an actual historical person; it corresponds, rather, to a very limited and special aspect of the author's total subjectivity; it is, so to speak, that "part" of the author which specifies or determines verbal meaning.[32] The distinction is quite apparent in the case of a lie. When I wish to deceive, my secret awareness that I am lying is irrelevant to the verbal meaning of my utterance. The only correct interpretation of my lie is, paradoxically, to view it as being a true statement, since this is the only correct construction of my "verbal intention." Indeed it is only when my listener has *understood* my meaning (presented as true) that he can *judge* it to be a lie. Since I adopted a truth-telling stance, the verbal meaning of my utterance would be precisely the same, whether I was deliberately lying or suffering from the erroneous conviction that my statement was true. In other words, an author may adopt a stance which differs from his deepest attitudes in the same way that an interpreter must almost always adopt a stance different from his own.[33] But for the process of interpretation, the author's private experiences are irrelevant. The only relevant aspect of subjectivity is that which determines verbal meaning or, in Husserl's terms, "content."

In a sense all poets are, of course, liars, and to some extent all speakers are, but the deliberate lie, spoken to deceive, is a borderline case. In most verbal utterances the speaker's public stance is not totally foreign to his private attitudes. Even in those cases where the speaker deliberately assumes a role, this mimetic stance is usually not the final determinant of his meaning. In a play, for example, the total meaning of an utterance is not the "intentional object" of

---

[31][Hirsch] Here I purposefully display my sympathies with Dilthey's concepts, *Sichhineinfühlen* and *Verstehen*. In fact, my whole argument may be regarded as an attempt to ground some of Dilthey's hermeneutic principles in Husserl's epistemology and Saussure's linguistics.

[32][Hirsch] Spranger aptly calls this the "cultural subject." See Eduard Spranger, *Zur Theorie des Verstehens und zur geisteswissenschaftlichen Psychologie* in *Festschrift Johannes Volkelt zum 70. Geburtstag* (Munich, 1918), p. 369. It should be clear that I am here in essential agreement with the American antiintentionalists (term used in the ordinary sense). I think they are right to exclude private associations from verbal meaning. But it is of some practical consequence to insist that verbal meaning is that aspect of an author's meaning which is interpersonally communi*cable*. For this implies that his verbal meaning is that which, under linguistic norms, one *can* understand, even if one must sometimes work hard to do so.

[33][Hirsch] Charles Bally calls this *"dédoublement de la personnalité."* See his *Linguistique générale et linguistique française,* 2nd ed. (Bern, 1944), p. 37.

the dramatic character; that meaning is simply a component in the more complex "intention" of the dramatist. The speaker himself is spoken. The best description of these receding levels of subjectivity was provided by the scholastic philosophers in their distinction between "first intention," "second intention," and so on. Irony, for example, always entails a comprehension of two contrasting stances ("intentional levels") by a third and final complex "intention." The "speaking subject" may be defined as the final and most comprehensive level of awareness determinative of verbal meaning. In the case of a lie the speaking subject assumes that he tells the truth, while the actual subject retains a private awareness of his deception. Similarly, many speakers retain in their isolated privacy a self-conscious awareness of their verbal meaning, an awareness which may agree or disagree, approve or disapprove, but which does not participate in determining their verbal meaning. To interpretation, this level of awareness is as irrelevant as it is inaccessible. In construing and verifying verbal meaning, only the speaking subject counts.

A separate exposition would be required to discuss the problems of psychological reconstruction. I have here simply tried to forestall the current objections to extrinsic biographical and historical information by pointing, on the one hand, to the exigencies of verification, and, on the other, to the distinction between a speaking subject and a "biographical" person. I shall be satisfied if this part of my discussion, incomplete as it must be, will help revive the half-forgotten truism that interpretation is the construction of *another's* meaning. A slight shift in the way we speak about texts would be highly salutary. It is natural to speak not of what a text says, but of what an author means, and this more natural locution is the more accurate one. Furthermore, to speak in this way implies a readiness (not notably apparent in recent criticism) to put forth a whole hearted and self-critical effort at the primary level of criticism—the level of understanding.

Jacques Derrida

b. 1930

No philosopher has recently had as great an influence on critical theory as Jacques Derrida, with whom the concept of deconstruction is principally associated. It was Derrida's essay "Structure, Sign and Play" that really began the critique of structuralism that is at the center of poststructuralist thought (except, of course, for the fact that deconstruction attacks *all* notions of center, origin, closure, and "totalization"). The target of "Structure, Sign and Play" is explicitly the anthropological structuralism of Claude Lévi-Strauss, but it quickly became clear that Derrida was really concerned with what he saw as a deep philosophical problem in the history of Western metaphysics. Nor was his treatment of Lévi-Strauss an attack. Derrida's concern was the problem of language itself. Adopting Saussure's notion that the system of language is entirely differential, Derrida goes on to show that such a system cannot be a structure because by definition a structure must be structured and the constant deferral of meaning (signification) from one signifier to another allows for no stoppage, therefore no center, origin, or totality. Lévi-Strauss's language requires that there be a center of structure even as it implies there is not. In a series of studies Derrida "deconstructed" toward similar *aporias* the notion of the transcendental ego in the philosophy of Edmund Husserl, and the privileging of speech over writing in Saussure's *Course in General Linguistics*. For Derrida "writing" becomes a better term for language than "speech," because it makes clearer the radical detachment of language from any origin in a voice recourse to which might produce a center or origin of meaning. Such a recourse, Derrida calls "logocentrism," contrasting nonlogocentric "writing," centerless and expansive, to a presumably totalizing and first-and-final word. But for Derrida this giving of the word, immanent with meaning or "presence," is an illusion with which language continually mystifies us. And we cannot escape this situation, for we must use language even to discuss the issue. This accounts for much of the difficulty of Derrida's own writing, which must constantly deconstruct itself even though it can't ever quite accomplish the feat. As a result his work has become more playful and complex as he tries heroically to stay a step ahead of the deconstruction of his own text by someone else.

Among many texts of Derrida now translated are *Speech and Phenomena: Introduction to the Problem of Signs in Husserl's Phenomenology* (1967), *Of Grammatology* (1967), *Writing and Difference* (1967), *Dissemination* (1972), *Margins of Philosophy* (1972), *Positions* (1972), which is composed of interviews of Derrida; *Glas* (1974), *Spurs: Nietzsche's Styles* (1976), *The Post Card* (1980), and *Signeponge/Signsponge* (1985). See Christopher North, *Deconstruction: Theory and Practice* (1982) and *Derrida* (1987); Paul de Man, "The Rhetoric of Blindness in his *Blindness and Insight* (1971); Geoffrey H. Hartman, *Saving the Text: Literature/Derrida/Philosophy* (1981); Gregory J. Ulmer, *Applied Grammatology* (1985); and Rodolphe Gasché, *The Tain of the Mirror: Derrida and the Philosophy of Reflection* (1986).

Structure, Sign and Play in the Discourse of the Human Sciences

*We need to interpret interpretations
more than to interpret things.*
MONTAIGNE

Perhaps something has occurred in the history of the concept of structure that could be called an "event," if this loaded word did not entail a meaning which it is precisely the function of structural—or structuralist—thought to reduce or to suspect. Let us speak of an "event," nevertheless, and let us use quotation marks to serve as a precaution. What would this event be then? Its exterior form would be that of a *rupture* and a redoubling.

It would be easy enough to show that the concept of structure and even the word "structure" itself are as old as the *epistēmē*[1]—that is to say, as old as Western science and Western philosophy—and that their roots thrust deep into the soil of ordinary language, into whose deepest recesses the *epistēmē* plunges in order to gather them up and to make them part of itself in a metaphorical displacement. Nevertheless, up to the event which I wish to mark out and define, structure—or rather the structurality of structure—although it has always been at work, has always been neutralized or reduced, and this by a process of giving it a center or of referring it to a point of presence, a fixed origin. The function of this center was not only to orient, balance, and organize the structure—one cannot in fact conceive of an unorganized structure—but above all to make sure that the organizing principle of the structure would limit what we might call the *play* of the structure. By orienting and organizing the coherence of the system, the center of a structure permits the play of its elements inside the total form. And even today the notion of a structure lacking any center represents the unthinkable itself.

Nevertheless, the center also closes off the play which it opens up and makes possible. As center, it is the point at which the substitution of contents, elements, or terms is no longer possible. At the center, the permutation or the transformation of elements (which may of course be structures enclosed within a structure) is forbidden. At least this permutation has always remained *interdicted* (and I am using this word deliberately). Thus it has always been thought that the center, which is by definition unique, constituted that very thing within a structure which while governing the structure, escapes structurality. This is why classical thought concerning structure could say that the center is, paradoxically, *within* the structure and *outside it*. The center is at the center of the totality, and yet, since the center does not belong to the totality (is not part of the totality), the totality *has its center elsewhere*. The center is not the center. The concept of centered structure—although it represents coherence itself, the condition of the *epistēmē* as philosophy or science—is contradictorily coherent. And as always, coherence in contradiction expresses the force of a desire.[2] The concept of centered structure is in fact the concept of a play based on a fundamental ground, a play constituted on the basis of a fundamental immobility and a reassuring certitude, which itself is beyond the reach of play. And on the basis of this certitude anxiety can be mastered, for anxiety is invariably the result of a certain mode of being implicated in the game, of being caught by the game, of being as it were at stake in the game from the outset. And again on the basis of what we call the center (and which, because it can be either inside or outside, can also indifferently be called the origin or end, *archē* or *telos*), repetitions, substitutions, transformations, and permutations are always *taken* from a history of meaning [*sens*]—that is, in a word, a history—whose origin may always be reawakened or whose end may always be anticipated in the form of presence. This is why one perhaps could say that the movement of any archaeology, like that of any eschatology, is an accomplice of this reduction of the structurality of structure and always attempts to conceive of structure on the basis of a full presence which is beyond play.

If this is so, the entire history of the concept of structure, before the rupture of which we are speaking, must be thought of as a series of substitutions of center for center, as a linked chain of determinations of the center. Successively, and in a regulated fashion, the center receives different forms or names. The history of metaphysics, like the history of the

---

STRUCTURE, SIGN AND PLAY IN THE DISCOURSE OF THE HUMAN SCIENCES. *Structure, Sign and Play* . . . was first presented as a lecture at The Johns Hopkins University in 1966. It was subsequently published in *The Structuralist Controversy* (1970) and in *Writing and Difference* (1967, trans. 1978 by Alan Bass). Copyright University of Chicago Press, 1978. Reprinted by permission of the publisher, The University of Chicago.
[1]*epistēmē:* Greek, wisdom, scientific or philosophical knowledge.

[2][Bass] The reference, in a restricted sense, is to the Freudian theory of neurotic symptoms and of dream interpretation in which a given symbol is understood contradictorily as both the desire to fulfill an impulse and the desire to suppress the impulse. In a general sense the reference is to Derrida's thesis that logic and coherence themselves can only be understood contradictorily, since they presuppose the suppression of *différance*, "writing" in the sense of the general economy. Cf. "La pharmacie de Platon," in *La dissemination*, pp. 125–26, where Derrida uses the Freudian model of dream interpretation in order to clarify the contradictions embedded in philosophical coherence.

West, is the history of these metaphors and metonymies. Its matrix—if you will pardon me for demonstrating so little and for being so elliptical in order to come more quickly to my principal theme—is the determination of Being as *presence* in all senses of this word. It could be shown that all the names related to fundamentals, to principles, or to the center have always designated an invariable presence—*eidos, archē, telos, energeia, ousia* (essence, existence, substance, subject) *alētheia,* transcendentality, consciousness, God, man, and so forth.

The event I called a rupture, the disruption I alluded to at the beginning of this paper, presumably would have come about when the structurality of structure had to begin to be thought, that is to say, repeated, and this is why I said that this disruption was repetition in every sense of the word. Henceforth, it became necessary to think both the law which somehow governed the desire for a center in the constitution of structure, and the process of signification which orders the displacements and substitutions for this law of central presence—but a central presence which has never been itself, has always already been exiled from itself into its own substitute. The substitute does not substitute itself for anything which has somehow existed before it. Henceforth, it was necessary to begin thinking that there was no center, that the center could not be thought in the form of a present-being, that the center had no natural site, that it was not a fixed locus but a function, a sort of nonlocus in which an infinite number of sign-substitutions came into play. This was the moment when language invaded the universal problematic, the moment when, in the absence of a center or origin, everything became discourse—provided we can agree on this word—that is to say, a system in which the central signified, the original or transcendental signified, is never absolutely present outside a system of differences. The absence of the transcendental signified extends the domain and the play of signification infinitely.

Where and how does this decentering, this thinking the structurality of structure, occur? It would be somewhat naïve to refer to an event, a doctrine, or an author in order to designate this occurrence. It is no doubt part of the totality of an era, our own, but still it has always already begun to proclaim itself and begun to *work*. Nevertheless, if we wished to choose several "names," as indications only, and to recall those authors in whose discourse this occurrence has kept most closely to its most radical formulation, we doubtless would have to cite the Nietzschean critique of metaphysics, the critique of the concepts of Being and truth, for which were substituted the concepts of play, interpretation, and sign (sign without present truth); the Freudian critique of self-presence, that is, the critique of consciousness, of the sub-

ject, of self-identity and of self-proximity or self-possession; and, more radically, the Heideggerean destruction of metaphysics, of onto-theology, of the determination of Being as presence. But all these destructive discourses and all their analogues are trapped in a kind of circle. This circle is unique. It describes the form of the relation between the history of metaphysics and the destruction of the history of metaphysics. There is no sense in doing without the concepts of metaphysics in order to shake metaphysics. We have no language—no syntax and no lexicon—which is foreign to this history; we can pronounce not a single destructive proposition which has not already had to slip into the form, the logic, and the implicit postulations of precisely what it seeks to contest. To take one example from many: the metaphysics of presence is shaken with the help of the concept of *sign*. But, as I suggested a moment ago, as soon as one seeks to demonstrate in this way that there is no transcendental or privileged signified and that the domain or play of signification henceforth has no limit, one must reject even the concept and word "sign" itself—which is precisely what cannot be done. For the signification "sign" has always been understood and determined, in its meaning, as sign-of, a signifier referring to a signified, a signifier different from its signified. If one erases the radical difference between signifier and signified, it is the word "signifier" itself which must be abandoned as a metaphysical concept. When Lévi-Strauss says in the preface to *The Raw and the Cooked* that he has "sought to transcend the opposition between the sensible and the intelligible by operating from the outset at the level of signs,"[3] the necessity, force, and legitimacy of his act cannot make us forget the concept of the sign cannot in itself surpass this opposition between the sensible and the intelligible. The concept of the sign, in each of its aspects, has been determined by this opposition throughout the totality of its history. It has lived only on this opposition and its system. But we cannot do without the concept of the sign, for we cannot give up this metaphysical complicity without also giving up the critique we are directing against this complicity, or without the risk of erasing difference in the self-identity of a signified reducing its signifier into itself or, amounting to the same thing, simply expelling its signifier outside itself. For there are two heterogeneous ways of erasing the difference between the signifier and the signified: one, the classic way, consists in reducing or deriving the signifier, that is to say, ultimately in *submitting* the sign to thought;

---

[3][Derrida] *The Raw and the Cooked,* trans. John and Doreen Wightman [New York: Harper and Row, 1969], p. 14. [Bass] (Translation somewhat modified.)

the other, the one we are using here against the first one, consists in putting into question the system in which the preceding reduction functioned: first and foremost, the opposition between the sensible and the intelligible. For the *paradox* is that the metaphysical reduction of the sign needed the opposition it was reducing. The opposition is systematic with the reduction. And what we are saying here about the sign can be extended to all the concepts and all the sentences of metaphysics, in particular to the discourse on "structure." But there are several ways of being caught in this circle. They are all more or less naïve, more or less empirical, more or less systematic, more or less close to the formulation—that is, to the formalization—of this circle. It is these differences which explain the multiplicity of destructive discourses and the disagreement between those who elaborate them. Nietzsche, Freud, and Heidegger, for example, worked within the inherited concepts of metaphysics. Since these concepts are not elements or atoms, and since they are taken from a syntax and a system, every particular borrowing brings along with it the whole of metaphysics. This is what allows these destroyers to destroy each other reciprocally—for example, Heidegger regarding Nietzsche, with as much lucidity and rigor as bad faith and misconstruction, as the last metaphysician, the last "Platonist." One could do the same for Heidegger himself, for Freud, or for a number of others. And today no exercise is more widespread.

What is the relevance of this formal schema when we turn to what are called the "human sciences"? One of them perhaps occupies a privileged place—ethnology. In fact one can assume that ethnology could have been born as a science only at the moment when a decentering had come about: at the moment when European culture—and, in consequence, the history of metaphysics and of its concepts—had been *dislocated,* driven from its locus, and forced to stop considering itself as the culture of reference. This moment is not first and foremost a moment of philosophical or scientific discourse. It is also a moment which is political, economic, technical, and so forth. One can say with total security that there is nothing fortuitous about the fact that the critique of ethnocentrism—the very condition for ethnology—should be systematically and historically contemporaneous with the destruction of the history of metaphysics. Both belong to one and the same era. Now, ethnology—like any science—comes about within the element of discourse. And it is primarily a European science employing traditional concepts, however much it may struggle against them. Consequently, whether he wants to or not—and this does not depend on a decision on his part—the ethnologist accepts into his discourse the premises of ethnocentrism at the very moment when he denounces them. This necessity is irreducible; it is

not a historical contingency. We ought to consider all its implications very carefully. But if no one can escape this necessity, and if no one is therefore responsible for giving in to it, however little he may do so, this does not mean that all the ways of giving in to it are of equal pertinence. The quality and fecundity of a discourse are perhaps measured by the critical rigor with which this relation to the history of metaphysics and to inherited concepts is thought. Here it is a question both of a critical relation to the language of the social sciences and a critical responsibility of the discourse itself. It is a question of explicitly and systematically posing the problem of the status of a discourse which borrows from a heritage the resources necessary for the deconstruction of that heritage itself. A problem of *economy* and *strategy.*

If we consider, as an example, the texts of Claude Lévi-Strauss, it is not only because of the privilege accorded to ethnology among the social sciences, nor even because the thought of Lévi-Strauss weighs heavily on the contemporary theoretical situation. It is above all because a certain choice has been declared in the work of Lévi-Strauss and because a certain doctrine has been elaborated there, and precisely, in a *more or less explicit manner,* as concerns both this critique of language and this critical language in the social sciences.

In order to follow this movement in the text of Lévi-Strauss, let us choose as one guiding thread among others the opposition between nature and culture. Despite all its rejuvenations and disguises, this opposition is congenital to philosophy. It is even older than Plato. It is at least as old as the Sophists. Since the statement of the opposition *physis/nomos, physis/technē,*[4] it has been relayed to us by means of a whole historical chain which opposes "nature" to law, to education, to art, to technics—but also to liberty, to the arbitrary, to history, to society, to the mind, and so on. Now, from the outset of his researches, and from his first book (*The Elementary Structures of Kinship*) on, Lévi-Strauss simultaneously has experienced the necessity of utilizing this opposition and the impossibility of accepting it. In the *Elementary Structures,* he begins from this axiom or definition: that which is *universal* and spontaneous, and not dependent on any particular culture or on any determinate norm, belongs to nature. Inversely, that which depends upon a system of *norms* regulating society and therefore is capable of *varying* from one social structure to another, belongs to culture. These two definitions are of the traditional type. But in the very first pages of the *Elementary Structures* Lévi-Strauss, who has begun by giving credence to these concepts, encounters what he calls a *scandal,* that is to say, something

---

[4] *physis, nomos, technē:* Greek, physical reality, custom, art.

which no longer tolerates the nature/culture opposition he has accepted, something which *simultaneously* seems to require the predicates of nature and of culture. This scandal is the *incest prohibition*. The incest prohibition is universal; in this sense one could call it natural. But it is also a prohibition, a system of norms and interdicts; in this sense one could call it cultural:

> Let us suppose then that everything universal in man relates to the natural order, and is characterized by spontaneity, and that everything subject to a norm is cultural and is both relative and particular. We are then confronted with a fact, or rather, a group of facts, which, in the light of previous definitions, are not far removed from a scandal: we refer to that complex group of beliefs, customs, conditions and institutions described succinctly as the prohibition of incest, which presents, without the slightest ambiguity, and inseparably combines, the two characteristics in which we recognize the conflicting features of two mutually exclusive orders. It constitutes a rule, but a rule which, alone among all the social rules, possesses at the same time a universal character.[5]

Obviously there is no scandal except within a system of concepts which accredits the difference between nature and culture. By commencing his work with the *factum* of the incest prohibition, Lévi-Strauss thus places himself at the point at which this difference, which has always been assumed to be self-evident, finds itself erased or questioned. For from the moment when the incest prohibition can no longer be conceived within the nature/culture opposition, it can no longer be said to be a scandalous fact, a nucleus of opacity within a network of transparent significations. The incest prohibition is no longer a scandal one meets with or comes up against in the domain of traditional concepts; it is something which escapes these concepts and certainly precedes them—probably as the condition of their possibility. It could perhaps be said that the whole of philosophical conceptualization, which is systematic with the nature/culture opposition, is designed to leave in the domain of the unthinkable the very thing that makes this conceptualization possible: the origin of the prohibition of incest.

This example, too cursorily examined, is only one among many others, but nevertheless it already shows that language bears within itself the necessity of its own critique. Now this critique may be undertaken along two paths, in two "manners." Once the limit of the nature/culture opposition makes itself felt, one might want to question systematically and rigorously the history of these concepts. This is a first action. Such a systematic and historic questioning would be neither a philological nor a philosophical action in the classic sense of these words. To concern oneself with the founding concepts of the entire history of philosophy, to deconstitute them, is not to undertake the work of the philologist or of the classic historian of philosophy. Despite appearances, it is probably the most daring way of making the beginnings of a step outside of philosophy. The step "outside philosophy" is much more difficult to conceive than is generally imagined by those who think they made it long ago with cavalier ease, and who in general are swallowed up in metaphysics in the entire body of discourse which they claim to have disengaged from it.

The other choice (which I believe corresponds more closely to Lévi-Strauss's manner), in order to avoid the possibly sterilizing effects of the first one, consists in conserving all these old concepts within the domain of empirical discovery while here and there denouncing their limits, treating them as tools which can still be used. No longer is any truth value attributed to them; there is a readiness to abandon them, if necessary, should other instruments appear more useful. In the meantime, their relative efficacy is exploited, and they are employed to destroy the old machinery to which they belong and of which they themselves are pieces. This is how the language of the social sciences criticizes *itself*. Lévi-Strauss thinks that in this way he can separate *method* from *truth*, the instruments of the method and the objective significations envisaged by it. One could almost say that this is the primary affirmation of Lévi-Strauss; in any event, the first words of the *Elementary Structures* are: "Above all, it is beginning to emerge that this distinction between nature and society ('nature' and 'culture' seem preferable to us today), while of no acceptable historical significance, does contain a logic, fully justifying its use by modern sociology as a methodological tool."[6]

Lévi-Strauss will always remain faithful to this double intention: to preserve as an instrument something whose truth value he criticizes.

On the one hand, he will continue, in effect, to contest the value of the nature/culture opposition. More than thirteen years after the *Elementary Structures, The Savage Mind* faithfully echoes the text I have just quoted: "The opposition

---

[5][Derrida/Bass] *The Elementary Structures of Kinship,* trans. James Bell, John von Sturmer, and Rodney Needham (Boston, Beacon Press, 1969), p. 8.

[6][Derrida/Bass] Ibid., p. 3.

between nature and culture to which I attached much importance at one time . . . now seems to be of primarily methodological importance." And this methodological value is not affected by its "ontological" nonvalue (as might be said, if this notion were not suspect here): "However, it would not be enough to reabsorb particular humanities into a general one. This first enterprise opens the way for others which . . . are incumbent on the exact natural sciences: the reintegration of culture in nature and finally of life within the whole of its physico-chemical conditions."[7]

On the other hand, still in *The Savage Mind*, he presents as what he calls *bricolage* what might be called the discourse of this method. The *bricoleur*, says Lévi-Strauss, is someone who uses "the means at hand," that is, the instruments he finds at his disposition around him, those which are already there, which had not been especially conceived with an eye to the operation for which they are to be used and to which one tries by trial and error to adapt them, not hesitating to change them whenever it appears necessary, or to try several of them at once, even if their form and their origin are heterogenous—and so forth. There is therefore a critique of language in the form of *bricolage*, and it has even been said that *bricolage* is critical language itself. I am thinking in particular of the article of G. Genette, "Structuralisme et critique littéraire," published in homage to Lévi-Strauss in a special issue of *L'Arc* (no. 26, 1965), where it is stated that the analysis of *bricolage* could "be applied almost word for word" to criticism, and especially to "literary criticism."

If one calls *bricolage* the necessity of borrowing one's concepts from the text of a heritage which is more or less coherent or ruined, it must be said that every discourse is *bricoleur*. The engineer, whom Lévi-Strauss opposes to the *bricoleur*, should be the one to construct the totality of his language, syntax, and lexicon. In this sense the engineer is a myth. A subject who supposedly would be the absolute origin of his own discourse and supposedly would construct it "out of nothing," "out of whole cloth," would be the creator of the verb, the verb itself. The notion of the engineer who supposedly breaks with all forms of *bricolage* is therefore a theological idea; and since Lévi-Strauss tells us elsewhere that *bricolage* is mythopoetic, the odds are that the engineer is a myth produced by the *bricoleur*. As soon as we cease to believe in such an engineer and in a discourse which breaks with the received historical discourse, and as soon as we admit that every finite discourse is bound by a certain *bricolage* and that the engineer and the scientist are also species

of *bricoleurs*, then the very idea of *bricolage* is menaced and the difference in which it took on its meaning breaks down.

This brings us to the second thread which might guide us in what is being contrived here.

Lévi-Strauss describes *bricolage* not only as an intellectual activity but also as a mythopoetical activity. One reads in *The Savage Mind*, "Like *bricolage* on the technical plane, mythical reflection can reach brilliant unforeseen results on the intellectual plane. Conversely, attention has often been drawn to the mythopoetical nature of *bricolage*."[8]

But Lévi-Strauss's remarkable endeavor does not simply consist in proposing, notably in his most recent investigations, a structural science of myths and of mythological activity. His endeavor also appears—I would say almost from the outset—to have the status which he accords to his own discourse on myths, to what he calls his "mythologicals." It is here that his discourse on the myth reflects on itself and criticizes itself. And this moment, this critical period, is evidently of concern to all the languages which share the field of the human sciences. What does Lévi-Strauss say of his "mythologicals"? It is here that we rediscover the mythopoetical virtue of *bricolage*. In effect, what appears most fascinating in this critical search for a new status of discourse is the stated abandonment of all reference to a *center*, to a *subject*, to a privileged *reference*, to an origin, or to an absolute *archia*. The theme of this decentering could be followed throughout the "Overture" to his last book, *The Raw and the Cooked*. I shall simply remark on a few key points.

1. From the very start, Lévi-Strauss recognizes that the Bororo myth which he employs in the book as the "reference myth" does not merit this name and this treatment. The name is specious and the use of the myth improper. This myth deserves no more than any other its referential privilege: "In fact, the Bororo myth, which I shall refer to from now on as the key myth, is, as I shall try to show, simply a transformation, to a greater or lesser extent, of other myths originating either in the same society or in neighboring or remote societies. I could, therefore, have legitimately taken as my starting point any one representative myth of the group. From this point of view, the key myth is interesting not because it is typical, but rather because of its irregular position within the group."[9]

2. There is no unity or absolute source of the myth. The focus and the source of the myth are always shadows and virtualities which are elusive, unactualizable, and nonexis-

[7][Derrida] *The Savage Mind* (London: George Weidenfeld and Nicolson; Chicago: The University of Chicago Press, 1966), p. 247.

[8][Derrida] Ibid., p. 17.
[9][Derrida] *The Raw and the Cooked*, p. 2.

tent in the first place. Everything begins with structure, configuration, or relationship. The discourse on the acentric structure that myth itself is, cannot itself have an absolute subject or an absolute center. It must avoid the violence that consists in centering a language which describes an acentric structure if it is not to shortchange the form and movement of myth. Therefore it is necessary to forgo scientific or philosophical discourse, to renounce the *epistēmē* which absolutely requires, which is the absolute requirement that we go back to the source, to the center, to the founding basis, to the principle, and so on. In opposition to *epistemic* discourse, structural discourse on myths—*mythological* discourse— must itself be *mythomorphic*. It must have the form of that of which it speaks. This is what Lévi-Strauss says in *The Raw and the Cooked,* from which I would now like to quote a long and remarkable passage:

The study of myths raises a methodological problem, in that it cannot be carried out according to the Cartesian principle of breaking down the difficulty into as many parts as may be necessary for finding the solution. There is no real end to methodological analysis, no hidden unity to be grasped once the breaking-down process has been completed. Themes can be split up *ad infinitum.* Just when you think you have disentangled and separated them, you realize that they are knitting together again in response to the operation of unexpected affinities. Consequently the unity of the myth is never more than tendential and projective and cannot reflect a state or a particular moment of the myth. It is a phenomenon of the imagination, resulting from the attempt at interpretation; and its function is to endow the myth with synthetic form and to prevent its disintegration into a confusion of opposites. The science of myths might therefore be termed "anaclastic," if we take this old term in the broader etymological sense which includes the study of both reflected rays and broken rays. But unlike philosophical reflection, which aims to go back to its own source, the reflections we are dealing with here concern rays whose only source is hypothetical. . . . And in seeking to imitate the spontaneous movement of mythological thought, this essay, which is also both too brief and too long, has had to conform to the requirements of that thought and to respect its rhythm. It follows that this book on myths is itself a kind of myth.[10]

This statement is repeated a little farther on: "As the myths themselves are based on secondary codes (the primary codes being those that provide the substance of language), the present work is put forward as a tentative draft of a tertiary code, which is intended to ensure the reciprocal translatability of several myths. This is why it would not be wrong to consider this book itself as a myth: it is, as it were, the myth of mythology."[11] The absence of a center is here the absence of a subject and the absence of an author: "Thus the myth and the musical work are like conductors of an orchestra, whose audience becomes the silent performers. If it is now asked where the real center of work is to be found, the answer is that this is impossible to determine. Music and mythology bring man face to face with potential objects of which only the shadows are actualized. . . . Myths are anonymous."[12] The musical model chosen by Lévi-Strauss for the composition of his book is apparently justified by this absence of any real and fixed center of the mythical or mythological discourse.

Thus it is at this point that ethnographic *bricolage* deliberately assumes its mythopoetic function. But by the same token, this function makes the philosophical or epistemological requirement of a center appear as mythological, that is to say, as a historical illusion.

Nevertheless, even if one yields to the necessity of what Lévi-Strauss has done, one cannot ignore its risks. If the mythological is mythomorphic, are all discourses on myths equivalent? Shall we have to abandon any epistemological requirement which permits us to distinguish between several qualities of discourse on the myth? A classic, but inevitable question. It cannot be answered—and I believe that Lévi-Strauss does not answer it—for as long as the problem of the relations between the philosopheme or the theorem, on the one hand, and the mytheme or the mythopoem, on the other, has not been posed explicitly, which is no small problem. For lack of explicitly posing this problem, we condemn ourselves to transforming the alleged transgression of philosophy into an unnoticed fault within the philosophical realm. Empiricism would be the genus of which these faults would always be the species. Transphilosophical concepts would be transformed into philosophical naïvetés. Many examples could be given to demonstrate this risk: the concepts of sign, history, truth, and so forth. What I want to emphasize is simply that the passage beyond philosophy does not consist in turning the page of philosophy (which usually amounts to philosophizing badly), but in continuing to read philosophers *in a certain way.* The risk I am speaking of is always assumed by Lévi-Strauss, and it is the very price of this en-

---

[10][Derrida] Ibid., pp. 5–6.

[11][Derrida] Ibid., p. 12.
[12][Derrida] Ibid., pp. 17–18.

deavor. I have said that empiricism is the matrix of all faults menacing a discourse which continues, as with Lévi-Strauss in particular, to consider itself scientific. If we wanted to pose the problem of empiricism and *bricolage* in depth, we would probably end up very quickly with a number of absolutely contradictory propositions concerning the status of discourse in structural ethnology. On the one hand, structuralism justifiably claims to be the critique of empiricism. But at the same time there is not a single book or study by Lévi-Strauss which is not proposed as an empirical essay which can always be completed or invalidated by new information. The structural schemata are always proposed as hypotheses resulting from a finite quantity of information and which are subjected to the proof of experience. Numerous texts could be used to demonstrate this double postulation. Let us turn once again to the "Overture" of *The Raw and the Cooked,* where it seems clear that if this postulation is double, it is because it is a question here of a language on language:

> If critics reproach me with not having carried out an exhaustive inventory of South American myths before analyzing them, they are making a grave mistake about the nature and function of these documents. The total body of myth belonging to a given community is comparable to its speech. Unless the population dies out physically or morally, this totality is never complete. You might as well criticize a linguist for compiling the grammar of a language without having complete records of the words pronounced since the language came into being, and without knowing what will be said in it during the future part of its existence. Experience proves that a linguist can work out the grammar of a given language from a remarkably small number of sentences. . . . And even a partial grammar or an outline grammar is a precious acquisition when we are dealing with unknown languages. Syntax does not become evident only after a (theoretically limitless) series of events has been recorded and examined, because it is itself the body of rules governing their production. What I have tried to give is an outline of the syntax of South American mythology. Should fresh data come to hand, they will be used to check or modify the formulation of certain grammatical laws, so that some are abandoned and replaced by new ones. But in no instance would I feel constrained to accept the arbitrary demand for a total mythological pattern, since, as has been shown, such a requirement has no meaning.[13]

Totalization, therefore, is sometimes defined as *useless,* and sometimes as *impossible.* This is no doubt due to the fact that there are two ways of conceiving the limit of totalization. And I assert once more that these two determinations coexist implicitly in Lévi-Strauss's discourse. Totalization can be judged impossible in the classical style: one then refers to the empirical endeavor of either a subject or a finite richness which it can never master. There is too much, more than one can say. But nontotalization can also be determined in another way: no longer from the standpoint of a concept of finitude as relegation to the empirical, but from the standpoint of the concept of *play.* If totalization no longer has any meaning, it is not because the infiniteness of a field cannot be covered by a finite glance or a finite discourse, but because the nature of the field—that is, language and a finite language—excludes totalization. This field is in effect that of *play,* that is to say, a field of infinite substitutions only because it is finite, that is to say, because instead of being an inexhaustible field, as in the classical hypothesis, instead of being too large, there is something missing from it: a center which arrests and grounds the play of substitutions. One could say—rigorously using that word whose scandalous signification is always obliterated in French—that this movement of play, permitted by the lack or absence of a center or origin, is the movement of *supplementarity.* One cannot determine the center and exhaust totalization because the sign which replaces the center, which supplements it, taking the center's place in its absence—this sign is added, occurs as a surplus, as a *supplement.*[14] The movement of signification adds something, which results in the fact that there is always more, but this addition is a floating one because it comes to perform a vicarious function, to supplement a lack on the part of the signified. Although Lévi-Strauss in his use of the word "supplementary" never emphasizes, as I do here, the two directions of meaning which are so strangely compounded within it, it is not by chance that he uses this word twice in his "Introduction to the Work of Marcel Mauss," at one point where he is speaking of the "overabundance of signifier, in relation to the signifieds to which this overabundance can refer":

> In his endeavor to understand the world, man therefore always has at his disposal a surplus of

---

[13][Derrida] Ibid., pp. 7–8.

[14][Bass] This double sense of supplement—to supply something which is missing, or to supply something additional—is at the center of Derrida's deconstruction of traditional linguistics in *De la grammatologie.* In a chapter entitled, "The Violence of the Letter: From Lévi-Strauss to Rousseau" (pp. 149 ff.), Derrida expands the analysis of Lévi-Strauss begun in this essay in order to further clarify the ways in which the contradictions of traditional logic "program" the most modern conceptual apparatuses of linguistics and the social sciences.

signification (which he shares out amongst things according to the laws of symbolic thought—which is the task of ethnologists and linguists to study). This distribution of a *supplementary* allowance [*ration supplémentaire*]—if it is permissible to put it that way—is absolutely necessary in order that on the whole the available signifier and the signified it aims at may remain in the relationship of complementarity which is the very condition of the use of symbolic thought."[15]

(It could no doubt be demonstrated that this *ration supplémentaire* of signification is the origin of the *ratio* itself.) The word reappears a little further on, after Lévi-Strauss has mentioned "this floating signifier, which is the servitude of all finite thought":

In other words—and taking as our guide Mauss's precept that all social phenomena can be assimilated to language—we see in *mana, Wakau, oranda* and other notions of the same type, the conscious expression of a semantic function, whose role it is to permit symbolic thought to operate in spite of the contradiction which is proper to it. In this way are explained the apparently insoluble antinomies attached to this notion. . . . At one and the same time force and action, quality and state, noun and verb; abstract and concrete, omnipresent and localized—*mana* is in effect all these things. But is it not precisely because it is none of these things that *mana* is a simple form, or more exactly, a symbol in the pure state, and therefore capable of becoming charged with any sort of symbolic content whatever? In the system of symbols constituted by all cosmologies, *mana* would simply be a zero symbolic value, that is to say, a sign marking the necessity of a symbolic content *supplementary* [my italics] to that with which the signified is already loaded, but which can take on any value required, provided only that this value still remains part of the available reserve and is not, as phonologists put it, a "group-term."

Lévi-Strauss adds the note:

"Linguists have already been led to formulate hypotheses of this type. For example: 'A zero phoneme is opposed to all the other phonemes in French in that it entails no differential characters and no constant phonetic value. On the contrary, the proper function of the zero phoneme is to be opposed to phoneme absence.' (R. Jakobson and J. Lutz, "Notes on the French Phonemic Pattern," *Word* 5, no. 2 [August 1949]: 155). Similarly, if we schematize the conception I am proposing here, it could almost be said that the function of notions like *mana* is to be opposed to the absence of signification, without entailing by itself any particular signification."[16]

The *overabundance* of the signifier, its *supplementary* character, is thus the result of a finitude, that is to say, the result of a lack which must be *supplemented*.

It can now be understood why the concept of play is important in Lévi-Strauss. His references to all sorts of games, notably to roulette, are very frequent, especially in his *Conversations,*[17] in *Race and History,*[18] and in *The Savage Mind*. Further, the reference to play is always caught up in tension.

Tension with history, first of all. This is a classical problem, objections to which are now well worn. I shall simply indicate what seems to me the formality of the problem: by reducing history, Lévi-Strauss has treated as it deserves a concept which has always been in complicity with a teleological and eschatological metaphysics, in other words, paradoxically, in complicity with that philosophy of presence to which it was believed history could be opposed. The thematic of historicity, although it seems to be a somewhat late arrival in philosophy, has always been required by the determination of Being as presence. With or without etymology, and despite the classic antagonism which opposes these significations throughout all of classical thought, it could be shown that the concept of *epistēmē* has always called forth that of *historia*, if history is always the unity of becoming, as the tradition of truth or the development of science or knowledge oriented toward the appropriation of truth in presence and self-presence, toward knowledge in consciousness-of-self. History has always been conceived as the movement of a resumption of history, as a detour between two presences. But if it is legitimate to suspect this concept of history, there is a risk, if it is reduced without an explicit statement of the problem I am indicating here, of falling back into an ahistoricism of a classical type, that is to say, into a determined moment of the history of metaphysics. Such is the algebraic formality of the problem as I see it. More con-

---

[15][Derrida] "Introduction à l'oeuvre de Marcel Mauss," in Marcel Mauss, *Sociologie et anthropologie* (Paris: P.U.F., 1950), p. xlix.

[16][Derrida] Ibid., pp. xlix–l.

[17][Derrida] George Charbonnier, *Entretiens avec Claude Lévi-Strauss* (Paris: Plon, 1961).

[18][Derrida] *Race and History* (Paris: UNESCO Publications, 1958).

cretely, in the work of Lévi-Strauss it must be recognized that the respect for structurality, for the internal originality of the structure, compels a neutralization of time and history. For example, the appearance of a new structure, of an original system, always comes about—and this is the very condition of its structural specificity—by a rupture with its past, its origin, and its cause. Therefore one can describe what is peculiar to the structural organization only by not taking into account, in the very moment of this description, its past conditions; by omitting to posit the problem of the transition from one structure to another, by putting history between brackets. In this "structuralist" moment, the concepts of chance and discontinuity are indispensable. And Lévi-Strauss does in fact often appeal to them, for example, as concerns that structure of structures, language, of which he says in the "Introduction to the Work of Marcel Mauss" that it "could only have been born in one fell swoop":

> Whatever may have been the moment and the circumstances of its appearance on the scale of animal life, language could only have been born in one fell swoop. Things could not have set about acquiring signification progressively. Following a transformation the study of which is not the concern of the social sciences, but rather of biology and psychology, a transition came about from a stage where nothing had a meaning to another where everything possessed it.[19]

This standpoint does not prevent Lévi-Strauss from recognizing the slowness, the process of maturing, the continuous toil of factual transformations, history (for example, *Race and History*). But, in accordance with a gesture which was also Rousseau's and Husserl's, he must "set aside all the facts" at the moment when he wishes to recapture the specificity of a structure. Like Rousseau, he must always conceive of the origin of a new structure on the model of catastrophe—an overturning of nature in nature, a natural interruption of the natural sequence, a setting aside *of* nature.

Besides the tension between play and history, there is also the tension between play and presence. Play is the disruption of presence. The presence of an element is always a signifying and substitutive reference inscribed in a system of differences and the movement of a chain. Play is always play of absence and presence, but if it is to be thought radically, play must be conceived of before the alternative of presence and absence. Being must be conceived as presence or ab-

sence on the basis of the possibility of play and not the other way around. If Lévi-Strauss, better than any other, has brought to light the play of repetition and the repetition of play, one no less perceives in his work a sort of ethic of presence, an ethic of nostalgia for origins, an ethic of archaic and natural innocence, of a purity of presence and self-presence in speech—an ethic, nostalgia, and even remorse, which he often presents as the motivation of the ethnological project when he moves toward the archaic societies which are exemplary societies in his eyes. These texts are well known.[20]

Turned towards the lost or impossible presence of the absent origin, this structuralist thematic of broken immediacy is therefore the saddened, *negative,* nostalgic, guilty, Rousseauistic side of the thinking of play whose other side would be the Nietzschean *affirmation,* that is the joyous affirmation of the play of the world and of the innocence of becoming, the affirmation of a world of signs without fault, without truth, and without origin which is offered to an active interpretation. *This affirmation then determines the non-center otherwise than as loss of the center.* And it plays without security. For there is a *sure* play: that which is limited to the *substitution* of *given* and *existing, present,* pieces. In absolute chance, affirmation also surrenders itself to *genetic* indetermination, to the *seminal* adventure of the trace.

There are thus two interpretations of interpretation, of structure, of sign, of play. The one seeks to decipher, dreams of deciphering a truth or an origin which escapes play and the order of the sign, and which lives the necessity of interpretation as an exile. The other, which is no longer turned toward the origin, affirms play and tries to pass beyond man and humanism, the name of man being the name of that being who, throughout the history of metaphysics or of ontotheology—in other words, throughout his entire history—has dreamed of full presence, the reassuring foundation, the origin and the end of play. The second interpretation of interpretation, to which Nietzsche pointed the way, does not seek in ethnography, as Lévi-Strauss does, the "inspiration of a new humanism" (again citing the "Introduction to the Work of Marcel Mauss").

There are more than enough indications today to suggest we might perceive that these two interpretations of interpretation—which are absolutely irreconcilable even if we live them simultaneously and reconcile them in an obscure economy—together share the field which we call, in such a problematic fashion, the social sciences.

---

[19][Derrida] "Introduction à l'oeuvre de Marcel Mauss," p. xlvi.

[20][Bass] The reference is to *Tristes tropique,* trans. John Russell (London: Hutchinson and Co., 1961).

For my part, although these two interpretations must acknowledge and accentuate their difference and define their irreducibility, I do not believe that today there is any question of *choosing*—in the first place because here we are in a region (let us say, provisionally, a region of historicity) where the category of choice seems particularly trivial; and in the second, because we must first try to conceive of the common ground, and the *différance* of this irreducible difference. Here there is a kind of question, let us still call it historical, whose *conception, formation, gestation,* and *labor* we are only catching a glimpse of today. I employ these words, I admit, with a glance toward the operations of childbearing—but also with a glance toward those who, in a society from which I do not exclude myself, turn their eyes away when faced by the as yet unnamable which is proclaiming itself and which can do so, as is necessary whenever a birth is in the offing, only under the species of the nonspecies, in the formless, mute, infant, and terrifying form of monstrosity.

Roland Barthes

1915–1980

Structuralism is associated in linguistics with the name of Ferdinand de Saussure and in anthropology with that of Claude Lévi-Strauss. Among literary critics perhaps the most prominent name to be identified with structuralism is that of Roland Barthes, a prodigious writer of enormous influence. To trace Barthes' career is to read the history of French criticism from structuralism and semiology into the poststructuralist era, the beginning of which is often identified with Jacques Derrida's critiques of Saussure and Lévi-Strauss in the sixties. "The Structuralist Activity" represents an early phase of Barthes' work in which he sets forth certain structuralist principles, particularly the emphasis on functions rather than substances. Objects as such, reduced to function, are items in sets of relations, thus emphasizing difference or the relational "space" between objects rather than the objects themselves. In Barthes' vision of structuralism the emphasis is on the creative or "reconstructive" activity endlessly productive of meaning, though meaning itself as a substance is less important than the activity of producing it.

In "The Death of the Author," Barthes proceeds to a sort of poststructuralist or deconstructive view of the author, who is dissolved as an ego controlling the book or as some center of intention by means of which one might *interpret* the text. Barthes sees language as controlling any sense of what an author might be rather than the other way around. For this linguistically created and contained author Barthes invents the term *scriptor*. Thus Barthes agrees with the Heideggerian idea that language speaks man. He privileges the text over the author in ways similar to those of Michel Foucault (in his essay of 1969, "What Is an Author?") and Jacques Derrida.

Among Barthes translated works are *Writing Degree Zero* (1953, tr. 1967), *Mythologies* (1957, tr. 1972), *On Racine* (1963, tr. 1964), *Elements of Semiology* (1964, tr. 1967), *Critical Essays* (1964, tr. 1972), *Criticism and Truth* (1966, tr. 1987), *Empire of Signs* (1970, tr. 1982), *S–Z* (1970, tr. 1974), *Sade, Fourier, Loyola* (1971, tr. 1976), *New Critical Essays* (1971, tr. 1976), *The Pleasure of the Text* (1973, tr. 1975), *Roland Barthes by Roland Barthes* (1975, tr. 1977), *A Lover's Discourse* (1977, tr. 1978), *Image-Music-Text* (tr. 1977), *Sollers Writer* (1979, tr. 1987), *The Grain of the Voice* (1981, tr. 1985), *The Responsibilities of Form* (1982, tr. 1985), and *The Rustle of Language* (1984, tr. 1986). See George B. Wasserman, *Roland Barthes* (1981); Annette Lavers, *Roland Barthes: Structuralism and After* (1982); and Jonathan Culler, *Roland Barthes* (1983).

The Structuralist Activity

What is structuralism? Not a school, nor even a movement (at least, not yet), for most of the authors ordinarily labeled with this word are unaware of being united by any solidarity of doctrine or commitment. Nor is it a vocabulary. *Structure* is already an old word (of anatomical and grammatical provenance), today quite overworked: all the social sciences resort to it abundantly, and the word's use can distinguish no one, except to engage in polemics about the content assigned to it; *functions, forms, signs* and *significations* are scarcely more pertinent: they are, today, words of common usage, from which one asks (and obtains) whatever one wants, notably the camouflage of the old determinist schema of cause and product; we must doubtless go back to pairings like those of *significans/significatum* and *synchronic/diachronic* in order to approach what distinguishes structuralism from other modes of thought: the first because it refers to the linguistic model as originated by Saussure, and because along with economics, linguistics is, in the present state of affairs, the true science of structure, the second, more decisively, because it seems to imply a certain revision of the notion of history, insofar as the notion of the synchronic (although in Saussure this is a preeminently *operational* concept) accredits a certain immobilization of time, and insofar as that of the diachronic tends to represent the historical process as a pure succession of forms. This second pairing is all the more distinctive in that the chief resistance to structuralism today seems to be of Marxist origin and that it focuses on the notion of history (and not of structure); whatever the case, it is probably the serious recourse to the nomenclature of signification (and not to the word itself, which is, paradoxically, not at all distinctive) which we must ultimately take as structuralism's *spoken sign:* watch who uses *signifier* and *signified, synchronic* and *diachronic,* and you will know whether the structuralist vision is constituted.

This is valid for the intellectual metalanguage, which explicitly employs methodological concepts. But since structuralism is neither a school nor a movement, there is no reason to reduce it a priori, even in a problematical way, to the activity of philosophers; it would be better to try and find

its broadest description (if not its definition) on another level than that of reflexive language. We can in fact presume that there exist certain writers, painters, musicians, in whose eyes a certain *exercise* of structure (and not only its thought) represents a distinctive experience, and that both analysts and creators must be placed under the common sign of what we might call *structural man,* defined not by his ideas or his languages, but by his imagination—in other words, by the way in which he mentally experiences structure.

Hence the first thing to be said is that in relation to *all* its users, structuralism is essentially an *activity,* i.e., the controlled succession of a certain number of mental operations: we might speak of structuralist activity as we once spoke of surrealist activity (surrealism, moreover, may well have produced the first experience of structural literature, a possibility which must some day be explored). But before seeing what these operations are, we must say a word about their goal.

The goal of all structuralist activity, whether reflexive or poetic, is to reconstruct an "object" in such a way as to manifest thereby the rules of functioning (the "functions") of this object. Structure is therefore actually a *simulacrum* of the object, but a directed, *interested* simulacrum, since the imitated object makes something appear which remained invisible, or if one prefers, unintelligible in the natural object. Structural man takes the real, decomposes it, then recomposes it; this appears to be little enough (which makes some say that the structuralist enterprise is "meaningless," "uninteresting," "useless," etc.). Yet, from another point of view, this "little enough" is decisive: for between the two objects, or the two tenses, of structuralist activity, there occurs *something new,* and what is new is nothing less than the generally intelligible: the simulacrum is intellect added to object, and this addition has an anthropological value, in that it is man himself, his history, his situation, his freedom and the very resistance which nature offers to his mind.

We see, then, why we must speak of a structuralist *activity:* creation or reflection are not, here, an original "impression" of the world, but a veritable fabrication of a world which resembles the first one, not in order to copy it but to render it intelligible. Hence one might say that structuralism is essentially *an activity of imitation,* which is also why there is, strictly speaking, no *technical* difference between structuralism as an intellectual activity on the one hand and literature in particular, art in general on the other: both derive from a *mimesis,* based not on the analogy of substances (as in so-called realist art), but on the analogy of functions (what Lévi-Strauss calls *homology*). When Troubetskoy reconstructs the phonetic object as a system of variations; when Dumézil elaborates a functional mythology; when Propp

THE STRUCTURALIST ACTIVITY. Barthes' *L'Activité structuraliste* first appeared in *Essais Critiques* (1964). The essay translated by Richard Howard is reprinted from *Partisan Review,* Vol. 34, No. 1 (Winter 1967). Copyright © 1967 by *Partisan Review,* from *Essais Critiques* by Roland Barthes. Reprinted by permission of *Partisan Review* and Northwestern University Press who published the essay in *Critical Essays,* translated by Richard Howard, in 1972.

constructs a folk tale resulting by structuration from all the Slavic tales he has previously decomposed; when Lévi-Strauss discovers the homologic functioning of the totemic imagination, or Granger the formal rules of economic thought, or Gardin the pertinent features of prehistoric bronzes; when Richard decomposes a poem by Mallarmé into its distinctive vibrations—they are all doing nothing different from what Mondrian, Boulez or Butor are doing when they articulate a certain object—what will be called, precisely, a *composition*—by the controlled manifestation of certain units and certain associations of these units. It is of little consequence whether the initial object liable to the simulacrum activity is given by the world in an already assembled fashion (in the case of the structural analysis made of a constituted language or society or work) or is still scattered (in the case of the structural "composition"); whether this initial object is drawn from a social reality or an imaginary reality. It is not the nature of the copied object which defines an art (though this is a tenacious prejudice in all realism), it is the fact that man adds to it in reconstructing it: technique is the very being of all creation. It is therefore to the degree that the goals of structuralist activity are indissolubly linked to a certain technique that structuralism exists in a distinctive fashion in relation to other modes of analysis or creation: we recompose the object *in order* to make certain functions appear, and it is, so to speak, the way that makes the work; this is why we must speak of the structuralist activity rather than the structuralist work.

The structuralist activity involves two typical operations: dissection and articulation. To dissect the first object, the one which is given to the simulacrum activity, is to find in it certain mobile fragments whose differential situation engenders a certain meaning; the fragment has no meaning in itself, but it is nonetheless such that the slightest variation wrought in its configuration produces a change in the whole; a *square* by Mondrian, a *series* by Pousseur, a *versicle* of Butor's *Mobile,* the "mytheme" in Lévi-Strauss, the phoneme in the work of the phonologists, the "theme" in certain literary criticism—all these units (whatever their inner structure and their extent, quite different according to cases) have no significant existence except by their frontiers: those which separate them from other actual units of the discourse (but this is a problem of articulation) and also those which distinguish them from other virtual units, with which they form a certain class (which linguistics calls a paradigm); this notion of a paradigm is essential, apparently, if we are to understand the structuralist vision: the paradigm is a group, a reservoir—as limited as possible—of objects (of units) from which one summons, by an act of citation, the object or unit one wishes to endow with an actual meaning; what char-

acterizes the paradigmatic object is that it is, vis-à-vis other objects of its class, in a certain relation of affinity and dissimilarity: two units of the same paradigm must resemble each other somewhat *in order* that the difference which separates them be indeed evident: *s* and *z* must have both a common feature (dentality) and a distinctive feature (presence or absence of sonority) so that we cannot, in French, attribute the same meaning to *poisson* and *poison;* Mondrian's squares must have both certain affinities by their shape as squares and certain dissimilarities by their proportion and color; the American automobiles (in Butor's *Mobile*) must be constantly regarded in the same way, yet they must differ each time by both their make and color; the episodes of the Oedipus myth (in Lévi-Strauss's analysis) must be both identical and varied—in order that all these languages, these works may be intelligible. The dissection operation thus produces an initial dispersed state of the simulacrum, but the units of the structure are not at all anarchic: before being distributed and fixed in the continuity of the composition, each one forms with its own virtual group or reservoir an intelligent organism, subject to a sovereign motor principle: that of the smallest difference.

Once the units are posited, structural man must discover in them or establish for them certain rules of association: this is the activity of articulation, which succeeds the summoning activity. The syntax of the arts and of discourse is, as we know, extremely varied; but what we discover in every work of structural enterprise is the submission to regular constraints whose formalism, improperly indicted, is much less important than their stability; for what is happening, at this second stage of the simulacrum-activity, is a kind of battle against chance; this is why the constraint of recurrence of the units has an almost demiurgic value: it is by the regular return of the units and of the associations of units that the work appears constructed, i.e., endowed with meaning; linguistics calls these rules of combination forms, and it would be advantageous to retain this rigorous sense of an overtaxed word: form, it has been said, is what keeps the contiguity of units from appearing as a pure effect of chance: the work of art is what man wrests from chance. This perhaps allows us to understand on the one hand why so-called nonfigurative works are nonetheless to the highest degree works of art, human thought being established not on the analogy of copies and models but with the regularity of assemblages; and on the other hand why these same works appear, precisely, fortuitous and thereby useless to those who discern in them no *form:* in front of an abstract painting, Khrushchev was certainly wrong to see only the traces of a donkey's tail whisked across the canvas; at least he knew in his way, though, that art is a certain conquest of chance (he simply forgot that every rule must be learned, whether one wants to apply or interpret it).

The simulacrum, thus constructed, does not render the world as it has found it, and it is here that structuralism is important. First of all, it manifests a new category of the object, which is neither the real nor the rational, but the *functional,* thereby joining a whole scientific complex which is being developed around information theory and research. Subsequently and especially, it highlights the strictly human process by which men give meaning to things. Is this new? To a certain degree, yes; of course the world has never stopped looking for the meaning of what is given it and of what it produces; what is new is a mode of thought (or a "poetics") which seeks less to assign completed meanings to the objects it discovers than to know how meaning is possible, at what cost and by what means. Ultimately, one might say that the object of structuralism is not man endowed with meanings, but man fabricating meanings, as if it could not be the *content* of meanings which exhausted the semantic goals of humanity, but only the act by which these meanings, historical and contingent variables, are produced. *Homo significans:* such would be the new man of structural inquiry.

According to Hegel, the ancient Greek was amazed by the *natural* in nature; he constantly listened to it, questioned the meaning of mountains, springs, forests, storms; without knowing what all these objects were telling him by name, he perceived in the vegetal or cosmic order a tremendous *shudder* of meaning, to which he gave the name of a god: Pan. Subsequently, nature has changed, has become social: everything that is given to man is *already* human, down to the forest and the river which we cross when we travel. But confronted with this social nature, which is quite simply culture, structural man is no different from the ancient Greek: he too listens for the natural in culture, and constantly perceives in it not so much stable, finite, "true" meanings as the shudder of an enormous machine which is humanity tirelessly undertaking to create meaning, without which it would no longer be human. And it is because this fabrication of meaning is more important, to its view, than the meanings themselves, it is because the function is extensive with the works, that structuralism constitutes itself as an activity, and refers the exercise of the work and the work itself to a single identity: a serial composition or an analysis by Lévi-Strauss are not objects except insofar as they have been *made:* their present being *is* their past act: they are *having-been-mades;* the artist, the analyst recreates the course taken by meaning, he need not designate it: his function, to return to Hegel's example, is a *manteia;* like the ancient soothsayer, he *speaks* the locus of meaning but does not name it. And it is because

literature, in particular, is a mantic activity that it is both intelligible and interrogating, speaking and silent, engaged in the world by the course of meaning which it remakes with the world, but disengaged from the contingent meanings which the world elaborates: an answer to the man who consumes it yet always a question to nature, an answer which questions and a question which answers.

How then does structural man deal with the accusation of unreality which is sometimes flung at him? Are not forms in the world, are not forms responsible? Was it really his Marxism that was revolutionary in Brecht? Was it not rather the decision to link to Marxism, in the theater, the placing of a spotlight or the deliberate fraying of a costume? Structuralism does not withdraw history from the world: it seeks to link to history not only certain contents (this has been done a thousand times) but also certain forms, not only the material but also the intelligible, not only the ideological but also the aesthetic. And precisely because all thought about the historically intelligible is also a participation in that intelligibility, structural man is scarcely concerned to *last;* he knows that structuralism, too, is a certain *form* of the world, which will change with the world; and just as he experiences his validity (but not his truth) in his power to speak the old languages of the world in a new way, so he knows that it will suffice that a new language rise out of history, a new language which speaks him in his turn, for his task to be done.

The Death of the Author

In his tale *Sarrasine,* Balzac, speaking of a castrato disguised as a woman, writes this sentence: "She was Woman, with her sudden fears, her inexplicable whims, her instinctive fears, her meaningless bravado, her defiance, and her delicious delicacy of feeling." Who speaks in this way? Is it the hero of the tale, who would prefer not to recognize the castrato hidden beneath the "woman"? Is it Balzac the man, whose personal experience has provided him with a philosophy of Woman? Is it Balzac the author, professing certain "literary" ideas about femininity? Is it universal wisdom? Romantic psychology? We can never know, for the good reason that writing is the destruction of every voice, every origin. Writing is that neuter, that composite, that obliquity into

THE DEATH OF THE AUTHOR. This essay first appeared in French in 1968. It is reprinted from *Image-Music-Text.* English translation copyright © 1977 by Stephen Heath. Reprinted by permission of Hill and Wang, a division of Farrar, Strauss and Giroux, Inc.

which our subject flees, the black-and-white where all identity is lost, beginning with the very identity of the body that writes.

No doubt it has always been so: once a fact is *recounted*—for intransitive purposes, and no longer to act directly upon reality, i.e., exclusive of any function except that exercise of the symbol itself—this gap appears, the voice loses its origin, the author enters into his own death, writing begins. However, the affect of this phenomenon has been variable; in ethnographic societies, narrative is never assumed by a person but by a mediator, shaman, or reciter, whose "performance" (i.e., has mastery of the narrative code) can be admired, but never his "genius." The *author* is a modern character, no doubt produced by our society as it emerged from the Middle Ages, influenced by English empiricism, French rationalism, and the personal faith of the Reformation, thereby discovering the prestige of the individual, or, as we say more nobly, of the "human person." Hence, it is logical that in literary matters it should be positivism, crown and conclusion of capitalist ideology, which has granted the greatest importance to the author's "person." The *author* still reigns in manuals of literary history, in biographies of writers, magazine interviews, and in the very consciousness of litterateurs eager to unite, by means of private journals, their person and their work; the image of literature to be found in contemporary culture is tyrannically centered on the author, his person, his history, his tastes, his passions; criticism still largely consists in saying that Baudelaire's oeuvre is the failure of the man Baudelaire, Van Gogh's is his madness, Tchaikovsky's his vice: *explanation* of the work is still sought in the person of its producer, as if, through the more or less transparent allegory of fiction, it was always, ultimately, the voice of one and the same person, the *author*, which was transmitting his "confidences."

Though the Author's empire is still very powerful (the new criticism has quite often merely consolidated it), we know that certain writers have already tried to subvert it. In France, Mallarmé, no doubt the first, saw and foresaw in all its scope the necessity to substitute language itself for the subject hitherto supposed to be its owner; for Mallarmé, as for us, it is language which speaks, not the author; to write is to reach, through a preliminary impersonality—which we can at no moment identify with the realistic novelist's castrating "objectivity"—that point where not "I" but only language functions, "performs": Mallarmé's whole poetics consists in suppressing the author in favor of writing (and thereby restoring, as we shall see, the reader's place). Valéry, entangled in a psychology of the ego, greatly edulcorated Mallarmean theory, but led by a preference for classicism to conform to the lessons of Rhetoric, he continued to cast the

Author into doubt and derision, emphasized the linguistic and "accidental" nature of his activity, and throughout his prose works championed the essentially verbal condition of literature, as opposed to which any resort to the writer's interiority seemed to him pure superstition. Proust himself, despite the apparently psychological character of what is called his *analyses*, visibly undertook to blur by an extreme subtilization the relation of the writer and his characters: by making the narrator not the one who has seen or felt, or even the one who writes, but the one who *is going to write* (the young man of the novel—but, as a matter of fact, how old is he and *who* is he?—wants to write but cannot, and the novel ends when writing finally becomes possible), Proust has given modern writing its epic: by a radical reversal, instead of putting his life into his novel, as is so often said, he made his life itself a work of which his own book was the model, so that it is quite clear to us that it is not Charlus who imitates Montesquiou, but Montesquiou, in his anecdotal, historical reality, who is only a secondary, derived fragment of Charlus. Finally Surrealism, to keep to this prehistory of modernity, could doubtless not attribute a sovereign place to language, since language is system, and what this movement sought was, romantically, a direct subversion of the codes—an illusory subversion, moreover, for a code cannot be destroyed, only "flouted"; yet, by constantly striving to disappoint expected meanings (this was the famous surrealist "shock"), by urging the hand to write as fast as possible what the head was unaware of (this was automatic writing), by accepting the principle and the experiment of collective writing, Surrealism helped desacralize the image of the Author. Last, outside literature itself (in fact, such distinctions are becoming quite dated), linguistics furnishes the destruction of the Author with a precious analytic instrument, showing that the speech-act in its entirety is an "empty" process, which functions perfectly without its being necessary to "fill" it with the person of the interlocutors: linguistically, the author is nothing but the one who writes, just as *I* is nothing but the one who says *I:* language knows a "subject," not a "person," and this subject, empty outside of the very speech-act which defines it, suffices to "hold" language, i.e., to exhaust it.

The removal of the Author (with Brecht, we might speak here of a veritable *distancing,* the Author diminishing like a figure at the far end of the literary stage) is not only a historical fact or an act of writing: it utterly transforms the modern text (or—which is the same thing—the text is henceforth produced and read so that the author absents himself from it at every level). Time, first of all, is no longer the same. The Author, when we believe in him, is always conceived as the past of his own book: book and author are voluntarily placed on one and the same line, distributed as a *before* and an *after:* the Author is supposed to *feed* the book, i.e., he lives before it, thinks, suffers, lives for it; he has the same relation of antecedence with his work that a father sustains with his child. Quite the contrary, the modern *scriptor* is born *at the same time* as his text; he is not furnished with a being which precedes or exceeds his writing, he is not the subject of which his book would be the predicate; there is no time other than that of the speech-act, and every text is written eternally *here* and *now*. This is because (or it follows that) *writing* can no longer designate an operation of recording, of observation, of representation, of "painting" (as the Classics used to say), but instead what the linguists, following Oxfordian philosophy,[1] call a performative, a rare verbal form (exclusively found in the first person and in the present), in which the speech-act has no other content (no other statement) than the act by which it is uttered: something like the *I declare* of kings or the *I sing* of the earliest poets; the modern *scriptor*, having buried the Author, can therefore no longer believe, according to the pathos of his predecessors, that his hand is slower than his passion and that in consequence, making a law of necessity, he must emphasize this delay and endlessly "elaborate" his form; for him, on the contrary, his hand, detached from any voice, borne by a pure gesture of inscription (and not of expression), traces a field without origin—or at least with no origin but language itself, i.e., the very thing which ceaselessly calls any origin into question.

We know now that a text consists not of a line of words, releasing a single "theological" meaning (the "message" of the Author-God), but of a multi-dimensional space in which are married and contested several writings, none of which is original: the text is a fabric of quotations, resulting from a thousand sources of culture. Like Bouvard and Pécuchet, those eternal copyists, at once sublime and comical, whose profound absurdity *precisely* designates the truth of writing, the writer can only imitate an ever anterior, never original gesture; his sole power is to mingle writings, to counter some by others, so as never to rely on just one; if he seeks to *express himself,* at least he knows that the interior "thing" he claims to "translate" is itself no more than a ready-made lexicon, whose words can be explained only through other words, and this ad infinitum: an adventure which exemplarily befell young Thomas De Quincey, so versed in his Greek that in order to translate certain absolutely modern ideas and images into this dead language, Baudelaire tells us, "he had

a dictionary made for himself, one much more complex and extensive than the kind produced by the vulgar patience of purely literary themes" (*Les Paradis artificiels*); succeeding the Author, the *scriptor* no longer contains passions, moods, sentiments, impressions, but that immense dictionary from which he draws a writing which will be incessant: life merely imitates the book, and this book itself is but a tissue of signs, endless imitation, infinitely postponed.

Once the Author is distanced, the claim to "decipher" a text becomes entirely futile. To assign an Author to a text is to impose a brake on it, to furnish it with a final signified, to close writing. This conception is quite suited to criticism, which then undertakes the important task of discovering the Author (or his hypostases: society, history, the psyche, freedom) beneath the work: once the Author is found, the text is "explained," the critic has won; hence, it is hardly surprising that historically the Author's empire has been the Critic's as well, and also that (even new) criticism is today unsettled at the same time as the Author. In multiple writing, in effect, everything is to be *disentangled,* but nothing *deciphered,* structure can be followed, "threaded" (as we say of a run in a stocking) in all its reprises, all its stages, but there is no end to it, no bottom; the space of writing is to be traversed, not pierced; writing constantly posits meaning, but always in order to evaporate it: writing seeks a systematic exemption of meaning. Thereby, literature (it would be better, from now on, to say *writing*), by refusing to assign to the text (and to the world-as-text) a "secret," i.e., an ultimate meaning, liberates an activity we may call countertheological, properly revolutionary, for to refuse to halt meaning is finally to refuse God and his hypostases, reason, science, the law.

To return to Balzac's sentence. No one (i.e., no "person") says it: its source, its voice is not the true site of writing, it is reading. Another very specific example will help us here: recent investigations (J.-P. Vernant) have shed some light on the constitutively ambiguous nature of Greek tragedy, whose text is "woven" of words with double meanings, words which each character understands unilaterally (this perpetual misunderstanding is precisely what we call the "tragic"); there is, however, someone who understands each word in its duplicity, and further understands, one may say, the very deafness of the characters speaking in his presence: this "someone" is precisely the reader (or here the listener). Here we discern the total being of writing: a text consists of multiple writings, proceeding from several cultures and entering into dialogue, into parody, into contestation; but there is a site where this multiplicity is collected, and this site is not the author, as has hitherto been claimed, but the reader: the reader is the very space in which are inscribed, without any of them being lost, all the citations out of which a writ-

---

[1] Cf. J. L. Austin, *How To Do Things With Words* (1962).

ing is made; the unity of a text is not in its origin but in its destination, but this destination can no longer be personal: the reader is a man without history, without biography, without psychology; he is only that *someone* who holds collected into one and the same field all of the traces from which writing is constituted. That is why it is absurd to hear the new writing condemned in the name of a humanism which hypocritically claims to champion the reader's rights. Classical criticism has never been concerned with the reader; for that criticism, there is no other man in literature than the one who writes. We are no longer so willing to be the dupes of such antiphrases, by which a society proudly recriminates in favor of precisely what it discards, ignores, muffles, or destroys; we know that in order to restore writing to its future, we must reverse the myth: the birth of the reader must be requited by the death of the Author.

Michel Foucault

1926–1984

Michel Foucault's earlier "archeological" studies dealt with institutional "practices that systematically form the objects of which they speak." Thus in *Madness and Civilization* (1961) he studied the asylum as a system. His early works revealed a connection to structuralism that he was quickly prepared to abandon, for he was not content with structuralism's ahistorical tendencies. Neither was he content with the linguistic model, which tended to dematerialize everything into relations of signified and signifier. He wished to probe beneath such abstract systems in which discursive practices are interwoven with social practices by the circulation of power. Foucault called his later investigations "genealogical," adopting the term from Nietzsche, one of whose most important works was the *The Genealogy of Morals*. Foucault ends this interview by insisting on the importance of Nietzsche in restating the "political question." "Archeological" had suggested a certain fixity and even, perhaps, atemporality. Archeological investigations were "descriptive." Genealogy implies development or change, and Foucault's interests had always been nothing if not historical and concerned with material events. Genealogical investigations were "explanatory."

In this later work, Foucault's principal interest was in how power diffuses itself in systems of authority and how "effects of truth are produced within discourses which in themselves are neither true nor false." Truth, then, is itself a product of relations of power and of the systems in which it flows, and it changes as systems change. By the same token, the old epistemological subject is no longer of importance (except, of course, as a historical product). Such a subject was constituted historically itself and cannot be presumed as "truth" in any genealogical account.

Foucault's influence in literary theory has been strong among revisionist literary historians known as "new historicists," who study the circulation of power through society and the literary texts that are a part of it.

Books by Foucault available in English include *Madness and Civilization* (1961, tr. 1965), *The Birth of the Clinic* (1963, rev. 1972; tr. 1975), *The Order of Things* (1966, tr. 1970), *The Archeology of Knowledge* (1969, tr. 1972), *Discipline and Punish* (1975, tr. 1977), *The History of Sexuality* I (1976, tr. 1978), *Language, Counter-Memory, Practice: Selected Essays and Interviews* (1977), and *Power/Knowledge* (1980). See Alan Sheridan, *Michel Foucault: The Will to Truth* (1980); Charles C. Lemert and Garth Gillan, *Michel Foucault: Social Theory and Transgression* (1982); Herbert L. Dreyfuss and Paul Robinow, *Michel Foucault: Beyond Structuralism and Hermeneutics* (1983); John Rajchman, *Michel Foucault: The Freedom of Philosophy* (1987); Michael Clark, *Michel Foucault: A Bibliography* (1983); Mark Poster, *Foucault, Marxism, and History* (1984); Gilles Deleuze, *Foucault* (1986, tr. 1988); David Carroll, *Paraesthetics, Foucault, Lyotard, Derrida* (1987); and David R. Shumway, *Michel Foucault* (1989).

Truth and Power

Could you briefly outline the route which led you from your work on madness in the Classical age to the study of criminality and delinquency?

When I was studying during the early 1950s, one of the great problems that arose was that of the political status of science and the ideological functions which it could serve. It wasn't exactly the Lysenko[1] business which dominated everything, but I believe that around the sordid affair—which had long remained buried and carefully hidden—a whole number of interesting questions were provoked. These can all be summed up in two words: power and knowledge. I believe I wrote *Madness and Civilisation* to some extent within the horizon of these questions. For me, it was a matter of saying this: if, concerning a science like theoretical physics or organic chemistry, one poses the problem of its relations with the political and economic structures of society, isn't one posing an excessively complicated question? Doesn't this set the threshold of possible explanations impossibly high? But on the other hand, if one takes a form of knowledge (*savoir*) like psychiatry, won't the question be much easier to resolve, since the epistemological profile of psychiatry is a low one and psychiatric practice is linked with a whole range of institutions, economic requirements and political issues of social regulation? Couldn't the interweaving of effects of power and knowledge be grasped with greater certainty in the case of a science as 'dubious' as psychiatry? It was this same question which I wanted to pose concerning medicine in *The Birth of the Clinic*: medicine certainly has a much more solid scientific armature than psychiatry, but it too is profoundly enmeshed in social structures. What rather threw me at the time was the fact that the question I was posing totally failed to interest those to whom I addressed it. They regarded it as a problem which was politically unimportant and epistemologically vulgar.

I think there were three reasons for this. The first is that for Marxist intellectuals in France (and there they were playing the role prescribed for them by the PCF[2]) the problem consisted in gaining for themselves the recognition of the university institutions and establishment. Consequently they found it necessary to pose the same theoretical questions as the academic establishment, to deal with the same problems and topics: 'We may be Marxists, but for all that we are not strangers to your preoccupations, rather we are the only ones able to provide new solutions for your old concerns.' Marxism sought to win acceptance as a renewal of the liberal university tradition—just as, more broadly, during the same period the Communists presented themselves as the only people capable of taking over and reinvigorating the nationalist tradition. Hence, in the field we are concerned with here, it followed that they wanted to take up the 'noblest,' most academic problems in the history of the sciences: mathematics and physics, in short the themes valorised by Duhem, Husserl and Koyré.[3] Medicine and psychiatry didn't seem to them to be very noble or serious matters, nor to stand on the same level as the great forms of classical rationalism.

The second reason is that post-Stalinist Stalinism, by excluding from Marxist discourse everything that wasn't a frightened repetition of the already said, would not permit the broaching of uncharted domains. There were no ready-made concepts, no approved terms of vocabulary available for questions like the power-effects of psychiatry or the political function of medicine, whereas on the contrary innumerable exchanges between Marxists and academics, from Marx via Engels and Lenin down to the present, had nourished a whole tradition of discourse on 'science,' in the nineteenth-century sense of that term. The price Marxists paid for their fidelity to the old positivism was a radical deafness to a whole series of questions posed by science.

Finally, there is perhaps a third reason, but I can't be absolutely sure that it played a part. I wonder nevertheless whether among intellectuals in or close to the PCF there wasn't a refusal to pose the problem of internment, of the political use of psychiatry and, in a more general sense, of the disciplinary grid of society. No doubt little was then known in 1955–60 of the real extent of the Gulag, but I believe that many sensed it, in any case many had a feeling that it was better not to talk about those things: it was a danger zone, marked by warning signs. Of course, it's difficult in retrospect to judge people's degree of awareness. But in any case, you well know how easily the Party leadership—which knew everything of course—could circulate instructions preventing people from speaking about this or that, or precluding this or that line of research. At any rate, if the question

---

TRUTH AND POWER. This interview with Alessandro Fontana and Pasquale Pasquino, originally appeared as "Intervista a Michel Foucault" in *Microfi-seca del Potere* (Turin, 1977), translated by the interviewers. A shortened version appeared in French as "Vérité et Pouvoir" in *L'Arc* 70 (1977). The selection is reprinted from *Power/Knowledge: Selected Interviews and Other Writings, 1972–1977*, edited by Colin Gordon by permission of Pantheon Books, a division of Random House, Inc. Copyright © 1972, 1975, 1976, 1977 by Michel Foucault.
[1]T. D. Lysenko (1896–1976), who as head of the Soviet Institute of Genetics rejected Mendelian theory.
[2]PCF, the French Communist Party.

---

[3]Pierre Duhem (1861–1916), French scientist and cosmologist; Edmund Husserl (1859–1938), German philosopher and founder of phenomenology; Alexandre Koyré (1892–1964), French philosopher.

of Pavlovian psychiatry did get discussed among a few doctors close to the PCF, psychiatric politics and psychiatry as politics were hardly considered to be respectable topics.

What I myself tried to do in this domain was met with a great silence among the French intellectual Left. And it was only around 1968, and in spite of the Marxist tradition and the PCF, that all these questions came to assume their political significance, with a sharpness that I had never envisaged, showing how timid and hesitant those early books of mine had still been. Without the political opening created during those years, I would surely never have had the courage to take up these problems again and pursue my research in the direction of penal theory, prisons and disciplines.

> So there is a certain 'discontinuity' in your theoretical trajectory. Incidentally, what do you think today about this concept of discontinuity, on the basis of which you have been all too rapidly and readily labelled as a 'structuralist' historian?

This business about discontinuity has always rather bewildered me. In the new edition of the *Petit Larousse* it says: 'Foucault: a philosopher who founds his theory of history on discontinuity.' That leaves me flabbergasted. No doubt I didn't make myself sufficiently clear in *The Order of Things,* though I said a good deal there about this question. It seemed to me that in certain empirical forms of knowledge like biology, political economy, psychiatry, medicine etc., the rhythm of transformation doesn't follow the smooth, continuist schemas of development which are normally accepted. The great biological image of a progressive maturation of science still underpins a good many historical analyses; it does not seem to me to be pertinent to history. In a science like medicine, for example, up to the end of the eighteenth century one has a certain type of discourse whose gradual transformation, within a period of twenty-five or thirty years, broke not only with the 'true' propositions which it had hitherto been possible to formulate but also, more profoundly, with the ways of speaking and seeing, the whole ensemble of practices which served as supports for medical knowledge. These are not simply new discoveries, there is a whole new 'régime' in discourse and forms of knowledge. And all this happens in the space of a few years. This is something which is undeniable, once one has looked at the texts with sufficient attention. My problem was not at all to say, '*Voilà,* long live discontinuity, we are in the discontinuous and a good thing too,' but to pose the question, 'How is it that at certain moments and in certain orders of knowledge, there are these sudden take-offs, these hastenings of evolution, these transformations which fail to correspond to the calm,

continuist image that is normally accredited?' But the important thing here is not that such changes can be rapid and extensive, or rather it is that this extent and rapidity are only the sign of something else: a modification in the rules of formation of statements which are accepted as scientifically true. Thus it is not a change of content (refutation of old errors, recovery of old truths), nor is it a change of theoretical form (renewal of a paradigm, modification of systematic ensembles). It is a question of what *governs* statements, and the way in which they *govern* each other so as to constitute a set of propositions which are scientifically acceptable, and hence capable of being verified or falsified by scientific procedures. In short, there is a problem of the régime, the politics of the scientific statement. At this level it's not so much a matter of knowing what external power imposes itself on science, as of what effects of power circulate among scientific statements, what constitutes, as it were, their internal régime of power, and how and why at certain moments that régime undergoes a global modification.

It was these different régimes that I tried to identify and describe in *The Order of Things,* all the while making it clear that I wasn't trying for the moment to explain them, and that it would be necessary to try and do this in a subsequent work. But what was lacking here was this problem of the 'discursive régime,' of the effects of power peculiar to the play of statements. I confused this too much with systematicity, theoretical form, or something like a paradigm. This same central problem of power, which at that time I had not yet properly isolated, emerges in two very different aspects at the point of junction of *Madness and Civilisation* and *The Order of Things.*

> We need, then, to locate the notion of discontinuity in its proper context. And perhaps there is another concept which is both more difficult and more central to your thought, the concept of an event. For in relation to the event a whole generation was long trapped in an *impasse,* in that following the works of ethnologists, some of them great ethnologists, a dichotomy was established between structures (the *thinkable*) and the event considered as the site of the irrational, the unthinkable, that which doesn't and cannot enter into the mechanism and play of analysis, at least in the form which this took in structuralism. In a recent discussion published in the journal '*L'Homme,*' three eminent anthropologists posed this question once again about the concept of event, and said: the event is what always escapes our rational grasp, the domain of 'absolute contingency'; we are

thinkers who analyse structures, history is no concern of ours, what could we be expected to have to say about it, and so forth. This opposition then between event and structure is the site and the product of a certain anthropology. I would say this has had devastating effects among historians who have finally reached the point of trying to dismiss the event and the '*évènementiel*' as an inferior order of history dealing with trivial facts, chance occurrences and so on. Whereas it is a fact that there are nodal problems in history which are neither a matter of trivial circumstances nor of those beautiful structures that are so orderly, intelligible and transparent to analysis. For instance, the 'great internment' which you described in *Madness and Civilisation* perhaps represents one of these nodes which elude the dichotomy of structure and event. Could you elaborate from our present standpoint on this renewal and reformulation of the concept of event?

One can agree that structuralism formed the most systematic effort to evacuate the concept of the event, not only from ethnology but from a whole series of other sciences and in the extreme case from history. In that sense, I don't see who could be more of an anti-structuralist than myself. But the important thing is to avoid trying to do for the event what was previously done with the concept of structure. It's not a matter of locating everything on one level, that of the event, but of realising that there are actually a whole order of levels of different types of events differing in amplitude, chronological breadth, and capacity to produce effects.

The problem is at once to distinguish among events, to differentiate the networks and levels to which they belong, and to reconstitute the lines along which they are connected and engender one another. From this follows a refusal of analyses couched in terms of the symbolic field or the domain of signifying structures, and a resource to analyses in terms of the genealogy of relations of force, strategic developments, and tactics. Here I believe one's point of reference should not be to the great model of language (*langue*) and signs, but to that of war and battle. The history which bears and determines us has the form of a war rather than that of a language: relations of power, not relations of meaning. History has no 'meaning,' though this is not to say that it is absurd or incoherent. On the contrary, it is intelligible and should be susceptible of analysis down to the smallest detail—but this in accordance with the intelligibility of struggles, of strategies and tactics. Neither the dialectic, as logic of contradictions, nor semiotics, as the structure of communication, can account for the intrinsic intelligibility of conflicts. 'Dialectic' is a way of evading the always open and hazardous reality of conflict by reducing it to a Hegelian skeleton, and 'semiology' is a way of avoiding its violent, bloody and lethal character by reducing it to the calm Platonic form of language and dialogue.

In the context of this problem of discursivity, I think one can be confident in saying that you were the first person to pose the question of power regarding discourse, and that at a time when analyses in terms of the concept or object of the 'text,' along with the accompanying methodology of semiology, structuralism, etc., were the prevailing fashion. Posing for discourse the question of power means basically to ask whom does discourse serve? It isn't so much a matter of analysing discourse into its unsaid, its implicit meaning, because (as you have often repeated) discourses are transparent, they need no interpretation, no one to assign them a meaning. If one reads 'texts' in a certain way, one perceives that they speak clearly to us and require no further supplementary sense or interpretation. This question of power that you have addressed to discourse naturally has particular effects and implications in relation to methodology and contemporary historical researches. Could you briefly situate within your work this question you have posed—if indeed it's true that you have posed it?

I don't think I was the first to pose the question. On the contrary, I'm struck by the difficulty I had in formulating it. When I think back now, I ask myself what else it was that I was talking about, in *Madness and Civilisation* or *The Birth of the Clinic,* but power? Yet I'm perfectly aware that I scarcely ever used the word and never had such a field of analyses at my disposal. I can say that this was an incapacity linked undoubtedly with the political situation we found ourselves in. It is hard to see where, either on the Right or the Left, this problem of power could then have been posed. On the Right, it was posed only in terms of constitution, sovereignty, etc., that is, in juridical terms; on the Marxist side, it was posed only in terms of the State apparatus. The way power was exercised—concretely and in detail—with its specificity, its techniques and tactics, was something that no one attempted to ascertain; they contented themselves with denouncing it in a polemical and global fashion as it existed among the 'others,' in the adversary camp. Where Soviet socialist power was in question, its opponents called it totalitarianism; power in Western capitalism was denounced by the Marxists as class domination; but the mechanics of power in themselves were never analysed. This task could only begin after 1968, that is to say on the basis of daily struggles at grass roots level, among those whose fight was located in the fine meshes of the web of power. This was where the concrete nature of power became visible, along with the prospect that these analyses of power would prove fruitful in accounting for all that had hitherto remained outside the field of political analysis. To put it very simply, psychiatric internment, the mental normalisation of individuals, and penal institutions have no doubt a fairly limited importance if one is only looking for their economic significance. On the other hand, they are undoubtedly essential to the general functioning of the wheels of power. So long as the posing of the question of power was kept subordinate to the economic instance and the system of interests which this served, there was a tendency to regard these problems as of small importance.

So a certain kind of Marxism and a certain kind of phenomenology constituted an objective obstacle to the formulation of this problematic?

Yes, if you like, to the extent that it's true that, in our student days, people of my generation were brought up on these two forms of analysis, one in terms of the constituent subject, the other in terms of the economic in the last instance, ideology and the play of superstructures and infrastructures.

Still within this methodological context, how would you situate the genealogical approach? As a questioning of the conditions of possibility, modalities and constitution of the 'objects' and domains you have successively analysed, what makes it necessary?

I wanted to see how these problems of constitution could be resolved within a historical framework, instead of referring them back to a constituent object (madness, criminality or whatever). But this historical contextualisation needed to be something more than the simple relativisation of the phenomenological subject. I don't believe the problem can be solved by historicising the subject as posited by the phenomenologists, fabricating a subject that evolves through the course of history. One has to dispense with the constituent subject, to get rid of the subject itself, that's to say, to arrive at an analysis which can account for the constitution of the subject within a historical framework. And this is what I would call genealogy, that is, a form of history which can

account for the constitution of knowledges, discourses, domains of objects etc., without having to make reference to a subject which is either transcendental in relation to the field of events or runs in its empty sameness throughout the course of history.

Marxist phenomenology and a certain kind of Marxism have clearly acted as a screen and an obstacle; there are two further concepts which continue today to act as a screen and an obstacle, ideology on the one hand and repression on the other.

All history comes to be thought of within these categories which serve to assign a meaning to such diverse phenomena as normalisation, sexuality and power. And regardless of whether these two concepts are explicitly utilised, in the end one always comes back, on the one hand to ideology— where it is easy to make the reference back to Marx—and on the other to repression, which is a concept often and readily employed by Freud throughout the course of his career. Hence I would like to put forward the following suggestion. Behind these concepts and among those who (properly or improperly) employ them, there is a kind of nostalgia; behind the concept of ideology, the nostalgia for a quasi-transparent form of knowledge, free from all error and illusion, and behind the concept of repression, the longing for a form of power innocent of all coercion, discipline and normalisation. On the one hand, a power without a bludgeon, and on the other hand knowledge without deception. You have called these two concepts, ideology and repression, negative, 'psychological,' insufficiently analytical. This is particularly the case in *Discipline and Punish* where, even if there isn't an extended discussion of these concepts, there is nevertheless a kind of analysis that allows one to go beyond the traditional forms of explanation and intelligibility which, in the last (and not only the last) instance rest on the concepts of ideology and repression. Could you perhaps use this occasion to specify more explicitly your thoughts on these matters? With *Discipline and Punish,* a kind of positive history seems to be emerging which is free of all the negativity and psychologism implicit in those two universal skeleton-keys.

The notion of ideology appears to me to be difficult to make use of, for three reasons. The first is that, like it or not, it always stands in virtual opposition to something else which is supposed to count as truth. Now I believe that the problem does not consist in drawing the line between that in a discourse which falls under the category of scientificity or truth, and that which comes under some other category, but in seeing historically how effects of truth are produced within discourses which in themselves are neither true nor false. The second drawback is that the concept of ideology refers, I think necessarily, to something of the order of a subject. Thirdly, ideology stands in a secondary position relative to something which functions as its infrastructure, as its material, economic determinant, etc. For these three reasons, I think that this is a notion that cannot be used without circumspection.

The notion of repression is a more insidious one, or at all events I myself have had much more trouble in freeing myself of it, in so far as it does indeed appear to correspond so well with a whole range of phenomena which belong among the effects of power. When I wrote *Madness and Civilisation,* I made at least an implicit use of this notion of repression. I think indeed that I was positing the existence of a sort of living, voluble and anxious madness which the mechanisms of power and psychiatry were supposed to have come to repress and reduce to silence. But it seems to me now that the notion of repression is quite inadequate for capturing what is precisely the productive aspect of power. In defining the effects of power as repression, one adopts a purely juridical conception of such power, one identifies power with a law which says no, power is taken above all as carrying the force of a prohibition. Now I believe that this is a wholly negative, narrow, skeletal conception of power, one which has been curiously widespread. If power were never anything but repressive, if it never did anything but to say no, do you really think one would be brought to obey it? What makes power hold good, what makes it accepted, is simply the fact that it doesn't only weigh on us as a force that says no, but that it traverses and produces things, it induces pleasure, forms knowledge, produces discourse. It needs to be considered as a productive network which runs through the whole social body, much more than as a negative instance whose function is repression. In *Discipline and Punish* what I wanted to show was how, from the seventeenth and eighteenth centuries onwards, there was a veritable technological take-off in the productivity of power. Not only did the monarchies of the Classical period develop great state apparatuses (the army, the police and fiscal administration), but above all there was established at this period what one might call a new 'economy' of power, that is to say procedures which allowed the effects of power to circulate in a manner at once continuous, uninterrupted, adapted and 'individual-ised' throughout the entire social body. These new techniques are both much more efficient and much less wasteful (less costly economically, less risky in their results, less open to loopholes and resistances) than the techniques previously employed which were based on a mixture of more or less forced tolerances (from recognised privileges to endemic criminality) and costly ostentation (spectacular and discontinuous interventions of power, the most violent form of which was the 'exemplary,' because exceptional, punishment).

> Repression is a concept used above all in relation to sexuality. It was held that bourgeois society represses sexuality, stifles sexual desire, and so forth. And when one considers for example the campaign launched against masturbation in the eighteenth century, or the medical discourse on homosexuality in the second half of the nineteenth century, or discourse on sexuality in general, one does seem to be faced with a discourse of repression. In reality however this discourse serves to make possible a whole series of interventions, tactical and positive interventions of surveillance, circulation, control and so forth, which seem to have been intimately linked with techniques that give the appearance of repression, or are at least liable to be interpreted as such. I believe the crusade against masturbation is a typical example of this.

Certainly. It is customary to say that bourgeois society repressed infantile sexuality to the point where it refused even to speak of it or acknowledge its existence. It was necessary to wait until Freud for the discovery at last to be made that children have a sexuality. Now if you read all the books on pedagogy and child medicine—all the manuals for parents that were published in the eighteenth century—you find that children's sex is spoken of constantly and in every possible context. One might argue that the purpose of these discourses was precisely to prevent children from having a sexuality. But their *effect* was to din it into parents' heads that their children's sex constituted a fundamental problem in terms of their parental educational responsibilities, and to din it into children's heads that their relationship with their own body and their own sex was to be a fundamental problem as far as *they* were concerned; and this had the consequence of sexually exciting the bodies of children while at the same time fixing the parental gaze and vigilance on the peril of infantile sexuality. The result was a sexualising of the infantile body, a sexualising of the bodily relationship between parent and child, a sexualising of the familial domain. 'Sexuality' is far more of a positive product of power than power was ever repression of sexuality. I believe that it is precisely these positive mechanisms that need to be investigated, and here one must free oneself of the juridical schematism of all previous characterisations of the nature of power. Hence a historical problem arises, namely that of discovering why the West has insisted for so long on seeing the power it exercises as juridical and negative rather than as technical and positive.

> Perhaps this is because it has always been thought that power is mediated through the forms prescribed in the great juridical and philosophical theories, and that there is a fundamental, immutable gulf between those who exercise power and those who undergo it.

I wonder if this isn't bound up with the institution of monarchy. This developed during the Middle Ages against the backdrop of the previously endemic struggles between feudal power agencies. The monarchy presented itself as a referee, a power capable of putting an end to war, violence and pillage and saying no to these struggles and private feuds. It made itself acceptable by allocating itself a juridical and negative function, albeit one whose limits it naturally began at once to overstep. Sovereign, law and prohibition formed a system of representation of power which was extended during the subsequent era by the theories of right: political theory has never ceased to be obsessed with the person of the sovereign. Such theories still continue today to busy themselves with the problem of sovereignty. What we need, however, is a political philosophy that isn't erected around the problem of sovereignty, nor therefore around the problems of law and prohibition. We need to cut off the King's head: in political theory that has still to be done.

> The King's head still hasn't been cut off, yet already people are trying to replace it by discipline, that vast system instituted in the seventeenth century comprising the functions of surveillance, normalisation and control and, a little later, those of punishment, correction, education and so on. One wonders where this system comes from, why it emerges and what its use is. And today there is rather a tendency to attribute a subject to it, a great, molar, totalitarian subject, namely the modern State, constituted in the sixteenth and seventeenth centuries and bringing with it (according to the classical theories) the professional army, the police and the administrative bureaucracy.

To pose the problem in terms of the State means to continue posing it in terms of sovereign and sovereignty, that is to say in terms of law. If one describes all these phenomena of power as dependent on the State apparatus, this means grasping them as essentially repressive: the Army as a power of death, police and justice as punitive instances, etc. I don't want to say that the State isn't important; what I want to say is that relations of power, and hence the analysis that must be made of them, necessarily extend beyond the limits of the State. In two senses: first of all because the State, for all the omnipotence of its apparatuses, is far from being able to occupy the whole field of actual power relations, and further because the State can only operate on the basis of other, already existing power relations. The State is superstructural in relation to a whole series of power networks that invest the body, sexuality, the family, kinship, knowledge, technology and so forth. True, these networks stand in a conditioning-conditioned relationship to a kind of 'meta-power' which is structured essentially round a certain number of great prohibition functions; but this meta-power with its prohibitions can only take hold and secure its footing where it is rooted in a whole series of multiple and indefinite power relations that supply the necessary basis for the great negative forms of power. That is just what I was trying to make apparent in my book.

> Doesn't this open up the possibility of overcoming the dualism of political struggles that eternally feed on the opposition between the State on the one hand and Revolution on the other? Doesn't it indicate a wider field of conflicts than that of those where the adversary is the State?

I would say that the State consists in the codification of a whole number of power relations which render its functioning possible, and that Revolution is a different type of codification of the same relations. This implies that there are many different kinds of revolution, roughly speaking as many kinds as there are possible subversive recodifications of power relations, and further that one can perfectly well conceive of revolutions which leave essentially untouched the power of relations which form the basis for the functioning of the State.

> You have said about power as an object of research that one has to invert Clausewitz's[4] formula so as to arrive at the idea that politics is the continuation

---

[4]Karl von Klausewitz (1780–1831), Prussian general and military writer.

of war by other means. Does the military model seem to you on the basis of your most recent researches to be the best one for describing power; is war here simply a metaphorical model, or is it the literal, regular, everyday mode of operation of power?

This is the problem I now find myself confronting. As soon as one endeavours to detach power with its techniques and procedures from the form of law within which it has been theoretically confined up until now, one is driven to ask this basic question: isn't power simply a form of warlike domination? Shouldn't one therefore conceive all problems of power in terms of relations of war? Isn't power a sort of generalised war which assumes at particular moments the forms of peace and the State? Peace would then be a form of war, and the State a means of waging it.

A whole range of problems emerge here. Who wages war against whom? Is it between two classes, or more? Is it a war of all against all? What is the role of the army and military institutions in this civil society where permanent war is waged? What is the relevance of concepts of tactics and strategy for analysing structures and political processes? What is the essence and mode of transformation of power relations? All these questions need to be explored. In any case it's astonishing to see how easily and self-evidently people talk of war-like relations of power or of class struggle without ever making it clear whether some form of war is meant, and if so what form.

We have already talked about this disciplinary power whose effects, rules and mode of constitution you describe in *Discipline and Punish*. One might ask here, why surveillance? What is the use of surveillance? Now there is a phenomenon that emerges during the eighteenth century, namely the discovery of population as an object of scientific investigation; people begin to inquire into birth-rates, death-rates and changes in population and to say for the first time that it is impossible to govern a State without knowing its population. Moheau[5] for example, who was one of the first to organise this kind of research on an administrative basis, seems to see its goal as lying in the problems of political control of a population. Does this disciplinary power then act alone and of itself, or doesn't it rather draw support from something

more general, namely this fixed conception of a population that reproduces itself in the proper way, composed of people who marry in the proper way and behave in the proper way, according to precisely determined norms? One would then have on the one hand a sort of global, molar body, the body of the population, together with a whole series of discourses concerning it, and then on the other hand and down below, the small bodies, the docile, individual bodies, the micro-bodies of discipline. Even if you are only perhaps at the beginning of your researches here, could you say how you see the nature of the relationships (if any) which are engendered between these different bodies: the molar body of the population and the micro-bodies of individuals?

Your question is exactly on target.[6] I find it difficult to reply because I am working on this problem right now. I believe one must keep in view the fact that along with all the fundamental technical inventions and discoveries of the seventeenth and eighteenth centuries, a new technology of the exercise of power also emerged which was probably even more important than the constitutional reforms and new forms of government established at the end of the eighteenth century. In the camp of the Left, one often hears people saying that power is that which abstracts, which negates the body, represses, suppresses, and so forth. I would say instead that what I find most striking about these new technologies of power introduced since the seventeenth and eighteenth centuries is their concrete and precise character, their grasp of a multiple and differentiated reality. In feudal societies power functioned essentially through signs and levies. Signs of loyalty to the feudal lords, rituals, ceremonies and so forth, and levies in the form of taxes, pillage, hunting, war etc. In the seventeenth and eighteenth centuries a form of power comes into being that begins to exercise itself through social production and social service. It becomes a matter of obtaining productive service from individuals in their concrete lives. And in consequence, a real and effective 'incorporation' of power was necessary, in the sense that power had to be able to gain access to the bodies of individuals, to their acts, attitudes and modes of everyday behaviour. Hence the significance of methods like school discipline, which succeeded in making children's bodies the object of highly complex systems of manipulation and conditioning. But at the same time,

---

[5]Moheau (fl. 1778), French statistical writer.

[6][Fontana and Pasquino] Foucault's response to this final question was given in writing.

these new techniques of power needed to grapple with the phenomena of population, in short to undertake the administration, control and direction of the accumulation of men (the economic system that promotes the accumulation of capital and the system of power that ordains the accumulation of men are, from the seventeenth century on, correlated and inseparable phenomena): hence there arise the problems of demography, public health, hygiene, housing conditions, longevity and fertility. And I believe that the political significance of the problem of sex is due to the fact that sex is located at the point of intersection of the discipline of the body and the control of the population.

> Finally, a question you have been asked before: the work you do, these preoccupations of yours, the results you arrive at, what use can one finally make of all this in everyday political struggles? You have spoken previously of local struggles as the specific site of confrontation with power, outside and beyond all such global, general instances as parties or classes. What does this imply about the role of intellectuals? If one isn't an 'organic' intellectual acting as the spokesman for a global organisation, if one doesn't purport to function as the bringer, the master of truth, what position is the intellectual to assume?

For a long period, the 'left' intellectual spoke and was acknowledged the right of speaking in the capacity of master of truth and justice. He was heard, or purported to make himself heard, as the spokesman of the universal. To be an intellectual meant something like being the consciousness/conscience of us all. I think we have here an idea transposed from Marxism, from a faded Marxism indeed. Just as the proletariat, by the necessity of its historical situation, is the bearer of the universal (but its immediate, unreflected bearer, barely conscious of itself as such), so the intellectual, through his moral, theoretical and political choice, aspires to be the bearer of this universality in its conscious, elaborated form. The intellectual is thus taken as the clear, individual figure of a universality whose obscure, collective form is embodied in the proletariat.

Some years have now passed since the intellectual was called upon to play this role. A new mode of the 'connection between theory and practice' has been established. Intellectuals have got used to working, not in the modality of the 'universal,' the 'exemplary,' the 'just-and-true-for-all,' but within specific sectors, at the precise points where their own conditions of life or work situate them (housing, the hospital, the asylum, the laboratory, the university, family and sexual relations). This has undoubtedly given them a much more immediate and concrete awareness of struggles. And they have met here with problems which are specific, 'non-universal,' and often different from those of the proletariat or the masses. And yet I believe intellectuals have actually been drawn closer to the proletariat and the masses, for two reasons. Firstly, because it has been a question of real, material, everyday struggles, and secondly because they have often been confronted, albeit in a different form, by the same adversary as the proletariat, namely the multinational corporations, the judicial and police apparatuses, the property speculators, etc. This is what I would call the 'specific' intellectual as opposed to the 'universal' intellectual.

This new configuration has a further political significance. It makes it possible, if not to integrate, at least to rearticulate categories which were previously kept separate. The intellectual *par excellence* used to be the writer: as a universal consciousness, a free subject, he was counterposed to those intellectuals who were merely *competent instances* in the service of the State or Capital—technicians, magistrates, teachers. Since the time when each individual's specific activity began to serve as the basis for politicisation, the threshold of *writing,* as the sacralising mark of the intellectual, has disappeared. And it has become possible to develop lateral connections across different forms of knowledge and from one focus of politicisation to another. Magistrates and psychiatrists, doctors and social workers, laboratory technicians and sociologists have become able to participate, both within their own fields and through mutual exchange and support, in a global process of politicisation of intellectuals. This process explains how, even as the writer tends to disappear as a figurehead, the university and the academic emerge, if not as principal elements, at least as 'exchangers,' privileged points of intersection. If the universities and education have become politically ultrasensitive areas, this is no doubt the reason why. And what is called the crisis of the universities should not be interpreted as a loss of power, but on the contrary as a multiplication and re-inforcement of their power-effects as centres in a polymorphous ensemble of intellectuals who virtually all pass through and relate themselves to the academic system. The whole relentless theorisation of writing which we saw in the 1960s was doubtless only a swansong. Through it, the writer was fighting for the preservation of his political privilege; but the fact that it was precisely a matter of theory, that he needed scientific credentials, founded in linguistics, semiology, psychoanalysis, that this theory took its references from the direction of Saussure, or Chomsky,[7] etc., and that it gave rise to such mediocre lit-

---

[7]Noam Chomsky (b. 1928), American linguist.

erary products, all this proves that the activity of the writer was no longer at the focus of things.

It seems to me that this figure of the 'specific' intellectual has emerged since the Second World War. Perhaps it was the atomic scientist (in a word, or rather a name: Oppenheimer) who acted as the point of transition between the universal and the specific intellectual. It's because he had a direct and localised relation to scientific knowledge and institutions that the atomic scientist could make his intervention; but, since the nuclear threat affected the whole human race and the fate of the world, his discourse could at the same time be the discourse of the universal. Under the rubric of this protest, which concerned the entire world, the atomic expert brought into play his specific position in the order of knowledge. And for the first time, I think, the intellectual was hounded by political powers, no longer on account of a general discourse which he conducted, but because of the knowledge at his disposal: it was at this level that he constituted a political threat. I am only speaking here of Western intellectuals. What happened in the Soviet Union is analogous with this on a number of points, but different on many others. There is certainly a whole study that needs to be made of scientific dissidence in the West and the socialist countries since 1945.

It is possible to suppose that the 'universal' intellectual, as he functioned in the nineteenth and early twentieth centuries was in fact derived from a quite specific historical figure: the man of justice, the man of law, who counterposes to power, despotism and the abuses and arrogance of wealth the universality of justice and the equity of an ideal law. The great political struggles of the eighteenth century were fought over law, right, the constitution, the just in reason and law, that which can and must apply universally. What we call today 'the intellectual' (I mean the intellectual in the political, not the sociological sense of the word, in other words the person who utilises his knowledge, his competence and his relation to truth in the field of political struggles) was, I think, an offspring of the jurist, or at any rate of the man who invoked the universality of a just law, if necessary against the legal professions themselves (Voltaire, in France, is the prototype of such intellectuals). The 'universal' intellectual derives from the jurist or notable, and finds his fullest manifestation in the writer, the bearer of values and significations in which all can recognise themselves. The 'specific' intellectual derives from quite another figure, not the jurist or notable, but the savant or expert. I said just now that it's with the atomic scientists that this latter figure comes to the forefront. In fact, it was preparing in the wings for some time before, and was even present on at least a corner of the stage from about the end of the nineteenth century. No doubt it's with Darwin or rather with the post-Darwinian evolutionists that this figure begins to appear clearly. The stormy relationship between evolutionism and the socialists, as well as the highly ambiguous effects of evolutionism (on sociology, criminology, psychiatry and eugenics, for example) mark the important moment when the savant begins to intervene in contemporary political struggles in the name of a 'local' scientific truth—however important the latter may be. Historically, Darwin represents this point of inflection in the history of the Western intellectual. (Zola is very significant from this point of view: he is the type of the 'universal' intellectual, bearer of law and militant of equity, but he ballasts his discourse with a whole invocation of nosology and evolutionism, which he believes to be scientific, grasps very poorly in any case, and whose political effects on his own discourse are very equivocal.) If one were to study this closely, one would have to follow how the physicists, at the turn of the century, re-entered the field of political debate. The debates between the theorists of socialism and the theorists of relativity are of capital importance in this history.

At all events, biology and physics were to a privileged degree the zones of formation of this new personage, the specific intellectual. The extension of technico-scientific structures in the economic and strategic domain was what gave him his real importance. The figure in which the functions and prestige of this new intellectual are concentrated is no longer that of the 'writer of genius,' but that of the 'absolute savant,' no longer he who bears the values of all, opposes the unjust sovereign or his ministers and makes his cry resound even beyond the grave. It is rather he who, along with a handful of others, has at his disposal, whether in the service of the State or against it, powers which can either benefit or irrevocably destroy life. He is no longer the rhapsodist of the eternal, but the strategist of life and death. Meanwhile we are at present experiencing the disappearance of the figure of the 'great writer.'

Now let's come back to more precise details. We accept, alongside the development of technico-scientific structures in contemporary society, the importance gained by the specific intellectual in recent decades, as well as the acceleration of this process since around 1960. Now the specific intellectual encounters certain obstacles and faces certain dangers. The danger of remaining at the level of conjunctural struggles, pressing demands restricted to particular sectors. The risk of letting himself be manipulated by the political parties or trade union apparatuses which control these local struggles. Above all, the risk of being unable to develop these struggles for lack of a global strategy or outside support; the risk too of not being followed, or not by very limited groups. In France we can see at the moment an example of this. The struggle around the prisons, the penal system and the police-judicial system, because it has developed "in solitary,' among social workers and ex-prisoners, has tended increasingly to separate itself from the forces which would have enabled it to grow. It has allowed itself to be penetrated by a whole naive, archaic ideology which makes the criminal at once into the innocent victim and the pure rebel—society's scapegoat—and the young wolf of future revolutions. This return to anarchist themes of the late nineteenth century was possible only because of a failure of integration of current strategies. And the result has been a deep split between this campaign with its monotonous, lyrical little chant, heard only among a few small groups, and the masses who have good reason not to accept it as valid political currency, but who also—thanks to the studiously cultivated fear of criminals—tolerate the maintenance, or rather the reinforcement, of the judicial and police apparatuses.

It seems to me that we are now at a point where the function of the specific intellectual needs to be reconsidered. Reconsidered but not abandoned, despite the nostalgia of some for the great 'universal' intellectuals and the desire for a new philosophy, a new world-view. Suffice it to consider the important results which have been achieved in psychiatry: they prove that these local, specific struggles haven't been a mistake and haven't led to a dead end. One may even say that the role of the specific intellectual must become more and more important in proportion to the political responsibilities which he is obliged willy-nilly to accept, as a nuclear scientist, computer expert, pharmacologist, etc. It would be a dangerous error to discount him politically in his specific relation to a local form of power, either on the grounds that this is a specialist matter which doesn't concern the masses (which is doubly wrong: they are already aware of it, and in any case implicated in it), or that the specific intellectual serves the interests of State or Capital (which is true, but at the same time shows the strategic position he occupies), or, again, on the grounds that he propagates a scientific ideology (which isn't always true, and is anyway certainly a secondary matter compared with the fundamental point: the effects proper to true discourses).

The important thing here, I believe, is that truth isn't outside power, or lacking in power: contrary to a myth whose history and functions would repay further study, truth isn't the reward of free spirits, the child of protracted solitude, nor the privilege of those who have succeeded in liberating themselves. Truth is a thing of this world: it is produced only by virtue of multiple forms of constraint. And it induces regular effects of power. Each society has its régime of truth, its 'general politics' of truth: that is, the types of discourse which it accepts and makes function as true; the mechanisms and instances which enable one to distinguish true and false statements, the means by which each is sanctioned; the tech-

niques and procedures accorded value in the acquisition of truth; the status of those who are charged with saying what counts as true.

In societies like ours, the 'political economy' of truth is characterised by five important traits. 'Truth' is centred on the form of scientific discourse and the institutions which produce it; it is subject to constant economic and political incitement (the demand for truth, as much for economic production as for political power); it is the object, under diverse forms, of immense diffusion and consumption (circulating through apparatuses of education and information whose extent is relatively broad in the social body, not withstanding certain strict limitations); it is produced and transmitted under the control, dominant if not exclusive, of a few great political and economic apparatuses (university, army, writing, media); lastly, it is the issue of a whole political debate and social confrontation ('ideological' struggles).

It seems to me that what must now be taken into account in the intellectual is not the 'bearer of universal values.' Rather, it's the person occupying a specific position—but whose specificity is linked, in a society like ours, to the general functioning of an apparatus of truth. In other words, the intellectual has a three-fold specificity: that of his class position (whether as petty-bourgeois in the service of capitalism or 'organic' intellectual of the proletariat); that of his conditions of life and work, linked to his condition as an intellectual (his field of research, his place in a laboratory, the political and economic demands to which he submits or against which he rebels, in the university, the hospital, etc.); lastly, the specificity of the politics of truth in our societies. And it's with this last factor that his position can take on a general significance and that his local, specific struggle can have effects and implications which are not simply professional or sectoral. The intellectual can operate and struggle at the general level of that régime of truth which is so essential to the structure and functioning of our society. There is a battle 'for truth,' or at least 'around truth'—it being understood once again that by truth I do not mean 'the ensemble of truths which are to be discovered and accepted,' but rather 'the ensemble of rules according to which the true and the false are separated and specific effects of power attached to the true,' it being understood also that it's not a matter of a battle 'on behalf' of the truth, but of a battle about the status of truth and the economic and political role it plays. It is necessary to think of the political problems of intellectuals not in terms of 'science' and 'ideology,' but in terms of 'truth' and 'power.' And thus the question of the professionalisation of intellectuals and the division between intellectual and manual labour can be envisaged in a new way.

All this must seem very confused and uncertain. Uncertain indeed, and what I am saying here is above all to be taken as a hypothesis. In order for it to be a little less confused, however, I would like to put forward a few 'propositions'—not firm assertions, but simply suggestions to be further tested and evaluated.

'Truth' is to be understood as a system of ordered procedures for the production, regulation, distribution, circulation and operation of statements.

'Truth' is linked in a circular relation with systems of power which produce and sustain it, and to effects of power which it induces and which extend it. A 'régime' of truth.

This régime is not merely ideological or superstructural; it was a condition of the formation and development of capitalism. And it's this same régime which, subject to certain modifications, operates in the socialist countries (I leave open here the question of China, about which I know little).

The essential political problem for the intellectual is not to criticise the ideological contents supposedly linked to science, or to ensure that his own scientific practice is accompanied by a correct ideology, but that of ascertaining the possibility of constituting a new politics of truth. The problem is not changing people's consciousnesses—or what's in their heads—but the political, economic, institutional régime of the production of truth.

It's not a matter of emancipating truth from every system of power (which would be a chimera, for truth is already power) but of detaching the power of truth from the forms of hegemony, social, economic and cultural, within which it operates at the present time.

The political question, to sum up, is not error, illusion, alienated consciousness or ideology; it is truth itself. Hence the importance of Nietzsche.

Georges Poulet

b. 1902

Poulet has been identified as one of the so-called Geneva School of critics, who have assimilated something of the Romantic tradition of Rousseau and the historicism of the nineteenth-century German philosopher Wilhelm Dilthey. For these critics, literary criticism is itself literature, but it is not the solipsistic criticism of the impressionists, such as France. Most of these critics, taking much from the phenomenological tradition of Husserl, Heidegger, and Merleau-Ponty, argue that consciousness is always consciousness of *something*. Poulet, in contrast, believes that a thought is also "simply a thought." He is a Cartesian dualist; he acknowledges a subjectivity that exists in itself. But it is possible to join one's consciousness with the author's as it is created in his works. The book is an object by which two subjects—the consciousness of the author and that of the reader—become one. The author reveals himself to us *in* us. In *Phenomenology of Reading,* where Poulet examines a number of other critics in his tradition, he posits the existence of some ineffable presence—some mental activity—that cannot be captured in the *objectivity* of the book itself but hovers above it or invades the reader.

At the same time, Poulet's Cartesian dualism leads him to consider the critic's consciousness in some way free of total identity with the author's. The critic is not really writing analyses, he is writing a criticism that is itself literature in an attempt to convey his consciousness of his author's consciousness. His work, in turn, will be more than its own objectivity when it finds a reader and joins itself to the reader's consciousness.

The tradition in which Poulet works is in direct opposition to the analytical, objectivist tradition of British and American criticism. Rather than regarding a work of art as a completed object with some autonomy from its author, Poulet considers it an act of the author, part of the process of the author's consciousness.

Elliott Coleman has translated Poulet's *Studies in Human Time* (1956), his *Interior Distance* (1959), and with C. Dawson his *Metamorphoses of the Circle* (1967). Poulet's essay *Phenomenology of Reading* appears, with discussion, under another title in *The Languages of Criticism and the Sciences of Man: The Structuralist Controversy* (1970), edited by Richard Macksey and Eugenio Donato. Students who read French may wish to consult the following works by Poulet: *L'Espace proustien* (1963), *Le Point de départ* (1964), *Trois essais de mythologie romantique* (1966), and *Mesure de l'instant* (1968). On the Geneva School see J. H. Miller, "The Geneva School: The Criticism of Marcel Raymond, Albert Beguin, Georges Poulet, Jean Rousset, Jean-Pierre Richard, and Jean Starobinski," *Critical Quarterly,* VIII (1966), pp. 305–21, and S. N. Lawall, *Critics of Consciousness* (1968).

Phenomenology of Reading

I

At the beginning of Mallarmé's unfinished story, *Igitur,* there is the description of an empty room, in the middle of which, on a table there is an open book. This seems to me the situation of every book, until someone comes and begins to read it. Books are objects. On a table, on bookshelves, in store windows, they wait for someone to come and deliver them from their materiality, from their immobility. When I see them on display, I look at them as I would at animals for sale, kept in little cages, and so obviously hoping for a buyer. For—there is no doubting it—animals do know that their fate depends on a human intervention, thanks to which they will be delivered from the shame of being treated as objects. Isn't the same true of books? Made of paper and ink, they lie where they are put, until the moment someone shows an interest in them. They wait. Are they aware that an act of man might suddenly transform their existence? They appear to be lit up with that hope. Read me, they seem to say. I find it hard to resist their appeal. No, books are not just objects among others.[1]

This feeling they give me—I sometimes have it with other objects. I have it, for example, with vases and statues. It would never occur to me to walk around a sewing machine or to look at the under side of a plate. I am quite satisfied with the face they present to me. But statues make me want to circle around them, vases make me want to turn them in my hands. I wonder why. Isn't it because they give me the illusion that there is something in them which, from a different angle, I might be able to see? Neither vase nor statue seems fully revealed by the unbroken perimeter of its surface. In addition to its surfaces it must have an interior. What this interior might be, that is what intrigues me and makes me circle around them, as though looking for the entrance to a secret chamber. But there is no such entrance (save for the mouth of the vase, which is not a true entrance since it gives only access to a little space to put flowers in). So the vase and the statue are closed. They oblige me to remain outside. We can have no true rapport—whence my sense of uneasiness.

So much for statues and vases. I hope books are not like them. Buy a vase, take it home, put it on your table or your mantel, and, after a while, it will allow itself to be made a part of your household. But it will be no less a vase, for that. On the other hand, take a book, and you will find it offering, opening itself. It is this openness of the book which I find so moving. A book is not shut in by its contours, is not walled up as in a fortress. It asks nothing better than to exist outside itself, or to let you exist in it. In short, the extraordinary fact in the case of a book is the falling away of the barriers between you and it. You are inside it; it is inside you; there is no longer either outside or inside.

Such is the initial phenomenon produced whenever I take up a book, and begin to read it. At the precise moment that I see, surging out of the object I hold open before me, a quantity of significations which my mind grasps, I realize that what I hold in my hands is no longer just an object, or even simply a living thing. I am aware of a rational being, of a consciousness; the consciousness of another, no different from the one I automatically assume in every human being I encounter, except that in this case the consciousness is open to me, welcomes me, lets me look deep inside itself, and even allows me, with unheard-of license, to think what it thinks and feel what it feels.

Unheard of, I say. Unheard of, first, is the disappearance of the "object." Where is the book I held in my hands? It is still there, and at the same time it is there no longer, it is nowhere. That object wholly object, that thing made of paper, as there are things made of metal or porcelain, that object is no more, or at least it is as if it no longer existed, as long as I read the book. For the book is no longer a material reality. It has become a series of words, of images, of ideas which in their turn begin to exist. And where is this new existence? Surely not in the paper object. Nor, surely, in external space. There is only one place left for this new existence: my innermost self.

How has this come about? By what means, through whose intercession? How can I have opened my own mind so completely to what is usually shut out of it? I do not know. I know only that, while reading, I perceive in my mind a number of significations which have made themselves at home there. Doubtless they are still objects: images, ideas, words, objects of my thought. And yet, from this point of view, there is an enormous difference. For the book, like the vase, or like the statue, was an object among others, residing in the external world: the world which objects ordinarily inhabit exclusively in their own society or each on its own, in no need of being thought by my thought; whereas in this interior world where, like fish in an aquarium, words, images and ideas disport themselves, these mental entities, in order

PHENOMENOLOGY OF READING. Poulet's *The Phenomenology of Reading* was first published in 1969 and is reprinted from *New Literary History: A Journal of Theory and Interpretation,* Vol. 1, No. 1 (October, 1969), by permission of the publisher.

[1] Compare Mallarmé's opinion in *The Book: A Spiritual Instrument,* pp. 674–76.

to exist, need the shelter which I provide; they are dependent on my consciousness.

This dependence is at once a disadvantage and an advantage. As I have just observed, it is the privilege of exterior objects to dispense with any interference from the mind. All they ask is to be let alone. They manage by themselves. But the same is surely not true of interior objects. By definition they are condemned to change their very nature, condemned to lose their materiality. They become images, ideas, words, that is to say purely mental entities. In sum, in order to exist as mental objects, they must relinquish their existence as real objects.

On the one hand, this is cause for regret. As soon as I replace my direct perception of reality by the words of a book, I deliver myself, bound hand and foot to the omnipotence of fiction. I say farewell to what is, in order to feign belief in what is not. I surround myself with fictitious beings; I become the prey of language. There is no escaping this takeover. Language surrounds me with its unreality.

On the other hand, the transmutation through language of reality into a fictional equivalent has undeniable advantages. The universe of fiction is infinitely more elastic than the world of objective reality. It lends itself to any use; it yields with little resistance to the importunities of the mind. Moreover—and of all its benefits I find this the most appealing—this interior universe constituted by language does not seem radically opposed to the *me* who thinks it. Doubtless what I glimpse through the words are mental forms not divested of an appearance of objectivity. But they do not seem to be of a nature other than my mind which thinks them. They are objects, but subjectified objects. In short, since everything has become part of my mind, thanks to the intervention of language, the opposition between the subject and its objects has been considerably attenuated. And thus the greatest advantage of literature is that I am persuaded by it that I am freed from my usual sense of incompatibility between my consciousness and its objects.

This is the remarkable transformation wrought in me through the act of reading. Not only does it cause the physical objects around me to disappear, including the very book I am reading, but it replaces those external objects with a congeries of mental objects in close rapport with my own consciousness. And yet the very intimacy in which I now live with my objects is going to present me with new problems. The most curious of these is the following: I am someone who happens to have as objects of his own thought, thoughts which are part of a book I am reading, and which are therefore the cogitations of another. They are the thoughts of another, and yet it is I who am their subject. The situation is even more astonishing than the one noted above. I am thinking the thoughts of another. Of course, there would

be no cause for astonishment if I were thinking it as the thought of another. But I think it as my very own. Ordinarily there is the *I* which thinks, which recognizes itself (when it takes its bearings) in thoughts which may have come from elsewhere but which it takes upon itself as its own in the moment it thinks them. This is how we must take Diderot's declaration *"Mes pensées sont mes catins"* ("My thoughts are *my* whores"). That is, they sleep with everybody without ceasing to belong to their author. Now, in the present case things are quite different. Because of the strange invasion of my person by the thoughts of another, I am a self who is granted the experience of thinking thoughts foreign to him. I am the subject of thoughts other than my own. My consciousness behaves as though it were the consciousness of another.

This merits reflection. In a certain sense I must recognize that no idea really belongs to me. Ideas belong to no one. They pass from one mind to another as coins pass from hand to hand. Consequently, nothing could be more misleading than the attempt to define a consciousness by the ideas which it utters or entertains. But whatever these ideas may be, however strong the tie which binds them to their source, however transitory may be their sojourn in my own mind, so long as I entertain them I assert myself as subject of these ideas; I am the subjective principle for whom the ideas serve for the time being as the predications. Furthermore, this subjective principle can in no wise be conceived as a predication, as something which is discussed, referred to. It is I who think, who contemplate, who am engaged in speaking. In short, it is never a *HE* but an *I*.

Now what happens when I read a book? Am I then the subject of a series of predications which are not *my* predications? That is impossible, perhaps even a contradiction in terms. I feel sure that as soon as I think something, that something becomes in some indefinable way my own. Whatever I think is a part of *my* mental world. And yet here I am thinking a thought which manifestly belongs to another mental world, which is being thought in me just as though I did not exist. Already the notion is inconceivable and seems even more so if I reflect that, since every thought must have a subject to think it, this *thought* which is alien to me and yet in me, must also have in me a *subject* which is alien to me. It all happens, then, as though reading were the act by which a thought managed to bestow itself within me with a subject not myself. Whenever I read, I mentally pronounce an *I*, and yet the *I* which I pronounce is not myself. This is true even when the hero of a novel is presented in the third person, and even when there is no hero and nothing but reflections or propositions: for as soon as something is presented as *thought,* there has to be a thinking subject with whom, at least for the time being, I identify, forgetting myself, alienated from myself. *"JE est un autre,"* said Rimbaud. Another *I*, who has replaced my own, and who will continue to do so as long as I read. Reading is just that: a way of giving way not only to a host of alien words, images, ideas, but also to the very alien principle which utters them and shelters them.

The phenomenon is indeed hard to explain, even to conceive, and yet, once admitted, it explains to me what might otherwise seem even more inexplicable. For how could I explain, without such takeover of my innermost subjective being, the astonishing facility with which I not only understand but even *feel* what I read. When I read as I ought, i.e. without mental reservation, without any desire to preserve my independence of judgment, and with the total commitment required of any reader, my comprehension becomes intuitive and any feeling proposed to me is immediately assumed by me. In other words, the kind of comprehension in question here is not a movement from the unknown to the known, from the strange to the familiar, from outside to inside. It might rather be called a phenomenon by which mental objects rise up from the depths of consciousness into the light of recognition. On the other hand—and without contradiction—reading implies something resembling the apperception I have of myself, the action by which I grasp straightaway what I think as being thought by a subject (who, in this case, is not I). Whatever sort of alienation I may endure, reading does not interpret my activity as subject.

Reading, then, is the act in which the subjective principle which I call *I*, is modified in such a way that I no longer have the right, strictly speaking, to consider it as my *I*. I am on loan to another, and this other thinks, feels, suffers, and acts within me. The phenomenon appears in its most obvious and even naivest form in the sort of spell brought about by certain cheap kinds of reading, such as thrillers, of which I say "It gripped me." Now it is important to note that this possession of myself by another takes place not only on the level of objective thought, that is with regard to images, sensations, ideas which reading affords me, but also on the level of my very subjectivity. When I am absorbed in reading, a second self takes over, a self which thinks and feels for me. Withdrawn in some recess of myself, do I then silently witness this dispossession? Do I derive from it some comfort or, on the contrary, a kind of anguish? However that may be, someone else holds the center of the stage, and the question which imposes itself, which I am absolutely obliged to ask myself, is this: Who is the usurper who occupies the forefront? What is this mind who all alone by himself fills my consciousness and who, when I say *I*, is indeed that *I*?

There is an immediate answer to this question, perhaps too easy an answer. This *I* who thinks in me when I read a book, is the *I* of the one who writes the book. When I read Baudelaire or Racine, it is really Baudelaire or Racine who

thinks, feels, allows himself to be read within me. Thus a book is not only a book, it is the means by which an author actually preserves his ideas, his feelings, his modes of dreaming and living. It is his means of saving his identity from death. Such an interpretation of reading is not false. It seems to justify what is commonly called the biographical explication of literary texts. Indeed every word of literature is impregnated with the mind of the one who wrote it. As he makes us read it, he awakens in us the analogue of what he thought or felt. To understand a literary work, then, is to let the individual who wrote it reveal himself to us *in* us. It is not the biography which explicates the work, but rather the work which sometimes enables us to understand the biography.

But biographical interpretation is in part false and misleading. It is true that there is an analogy between the works of an author and the experiences of his life. The works may be seen as an incomplete translation of the life. And further, there is an even more significant analogy among all the works of a single author. Each of the works, however, while I am reading it, lives in me its own life. The subject who is revealed to me through my reading of it is not the author, either in the disordered totality of his outer experiences, or in the aggregate, better organized and concentrated totality, which is the one of his writings. Yet the subject which presides over the work can exist only in the work. To be sure, nothing is unimportant for understanding the work, and a mass of biographical, bibliographical, textual, and general critical information is indispensable to me. And yet this knowledge does not coincide with the internal knowledge of the work. Whatever may be the sum of the information I acquire on Baudelaire or Racine, in whatever degree of intimacy I may live with their genius, I am aware that this contribution *(apport)* does not suffice to illuminate for me in its own inner meaning, in its formal perfection, and in the subjective principle which animates it, the particular work of Baudelaire or Racine the reading of which now absorbs me. At this moment what matters to me is to live, from the inside, in a certain identity with the work and the work alone. It could hardly be otherwise. Nothing external to the work could possibly share the extraordinary claim which the work now exerts on me. It is there within me, not to send me back, outside itself, to its author, nor to his other writings, but on the contrary to keep my attention riveted on itself. It is the work which traces in me the very boundaries within which this consciousness will define itself. It is the work which forces on me a series of mental objects and creates in me a network of words, beyond which, for the time being, there will be no room for other mental objects or for other words. And it is the work, finally, which, not satisfied thus with defining the content of my consciousness, takes hold of it, appropriates it, and makes of it that *I* which, from one end of my reading to the other, presides over the unfolding of the work, of the single work which I am reading.

And so the work forms the temporary mental substance which fills my consciousness; and it is moreover that consciousness, the *I*-subject, the continued consciousness of what is, revealing itself within the interior of the work. Such is the characteristic condition of every work which I summon back into existence by placing my consciousness at its disposal. I give it not only existence, but awareness of existence. And so I ought not to hesitate to recognize that so long as it is animated by this vital inbreathing inspired by the act of reading, a work of literature becomes (at the expense of the reader whose own life it suspends) a sort of human being, that it is a mind conscious of itself and constituting itself in me as the subject of its own objects.

II

The work lives its own life within me; in a certain sense, it thinks itself, and it even gives itself a meaning within me.

This strange displacement of myself by the work deserves to be examined even more closely.

If the work thinks itself in me, does this mean that, during a complete loss of consciousness on my part, another thinking entity invades me, taking advantage of my unconsciousness in order to think itself without my being able to think it? Obviously not. The annexation of my consciousness by another (the other which is the work) in no way implies that I am the victim of any deprivation of consciousness. Everything happens, on the contrary, as though, from the moment I become a prey to what I read, I begin to share the use of my consciousness with this being whom I have tried to define and who is the conscious subject ensconced at the heart of the work. He and I, we start having a common consciousness. Doubtless, within this community of feeling, the parts played by each of us are not of equal importance. The consciousness inherent in the work is active and potent; it occupies the foreground; it is clearly related to its *own* world, to objects which are *its* objects. In opposition, I myself, although conscious of whatever it may be conscious of, I play a much more humble role, content to record passively all that is going in me. A lag takes place, a sort of schizoid distinction between what I feel and what the other feels; a confused awareness of delay, so that the work seems first to think by itself, and then to inform me what it has thought. Thus I often have the impression, while reading, of simply witnessing an action which at the same time concerns and yet does not concern me. This provokes a certain feeling of surprise within me. I am a consciousness astonished by an existence which is not mine, but which I experience as though it were mine.

This astonished consciousness is in fact the consciousness of the critic: the consciousness of a being who is allowed to apprehend as its own what is happening in the consciousness of another being. Aware of a certain gap, disclosing a feeling of identity, but of identity within difference, critical consciousness does not necessarily imply the total disappearance of the critic's mind in the mind to be criticized. From the partial and hesitant approximation of Jacques Rivière to the exalted, digressive and triumphant approximation of Charles Du Bos, criticism can pass through a whole series of nuances which we would be well advised to study. That is what I now propose to do. By discovering the various forms of identification and nonidentification to be found in recent critical writing in French literature, I shall be able perhaps to give a better account of the variations of which this relationship—between criticizing subject and criticized object—is capable.

Let me take a first example. In the case of the first critic I shall speak of, this fusion of two consciousnesses is barely suggested. It is an uncertain movement of the mind toward an object which remains hidden. Whereas in the perfect identification of two consciousnesses, each sees itself reflected in the other, in this instance the critical consciousness can, at best, attempt but to draw closer to a reality which must remain forever veiled. In this attempt it uses the only mediators available to it in this quest, that is, the senses. And since sight, the most intellectual of the five senses, seems in this particular case to come up against a basic opacity, the critical mind must approach its goal blindly, through the tactile exploration of surfaces, through a groping exploration of the material world which separates the critical mind from its object. Thus, despite the immense effort on the part of the sympathetic intelligence to lower itself to a level where it can, however lamely, make some progress in its quest toward the consciousness of the other, this enterprise is destined to failure. One senses that the unfortunate critic is condemned never to fulfill adequately his role as reader. He stumbles, he puzzles, he questions awkwardly a language which he is condemned never to read with ease; or rather, in trying to read the language, he uses a key which enables him to translate but a fraction of the text.

This critic is Jacques Rivière.

And yet it is from this failure that a much later critic will derive a more successful method of approaching a text. With this later critic, as with Rivière, the whole project begins with an attempt at identification on the most basic level. But this most primitive level is the one in which there flows, from mind to mind, a current which has only to be followed. To identify with the work means here, for the critic, to undergo the same experiences, beginning with the most elementary. On the level of indistinct thought, of sensations, emotions, images, and obsessions of preconscious life, it is possible for the critic to repeat, within himself, that life of which the work affords a first version, inexhaustibly revealing and suggestive. And yet such an imitation could not take place, in a domain so hard to define, without the aid of a powerful auxiliary. This auxiliary is language. There is no critical identification which is not prepared, realized, and incarnated through the agency of language. The deepest sentient life, hidden in the recesses of another's thoughts, could never be truly transposed, save for the mediation of words which allow a whole series of equivalences to arise. To describe this phenomenon as it takes place in the criticism I am speaking of now, I can no longer be content with the usual distinctions between the signifier *(signifiant)* and the signified *(signifié)* for what would it mean here to say that the language of the critic *signifies* the language of the literary work? There is not just equation, similitude. Words have attained a veritable power of recreation; they are a sort of material entity, solid and three-dimensional, thanks to which a certain life of the senses is reborn, finding in a network of verbal connotations the very conditions necessary for its replication. In other words, the language of criticism here dedicates itself to the business of mimicking physically the apperceptual world of the author. Strangely enough, the language of this sort of mimetic criticism becomes even more tangible, more tactile than the author's own; the poetry of the critic becomes more "poetic" than the poet's. This verbal *mimesis,* consciously exaggerated, is in no way servile, nor does it tend at all toward the pastiche. And yet it can reach its object only insofar as that object is deeply enmeshed in, almost confounded with, physical matter. This form of criticism is thus able to provide an admirable equivalent of the vital substratum which underlies all thought, and yet it seems incapable of attaining and expressing thought itself. This criticism is both helped and hindered by the language which it employs; helped, insofar as this language allows it to express the sensuous life in its original state, where it is still almost impossible to distinguish between subject and object; and yet hindered, too, because this language, too congealed and opaque, does not lend itself to analysis, and because the subjectivity which it evokes and describes is as though forever mired in its objects. And so the activity of criticism in this case is somewhat incomplete, in spite of its remarkable successes. Identification relative to objects is accomplished almost too well; relative to subjectivity it is barely sketched.

This, then, is the criticism of Jean-Pierre Richard.

In its extreme form, in the abolition of any subject whatsoever, this criticism seems to extract from a literary work a certain condensed matter, a material essence.

But what, then, would be a criticism which would be the reverse, which would abolish the object and extract from the texts their most *subjective* elements?

To conceive such a criticism, I must leap to the opposite extreme. I imagine a critical language which would attempt deliberately to strip the literary language of anything concrete. In such a criticism it would be the artful aim of every line, of every sentence, of every metaphor, of every word, to reduce to the near nothingness of abstraction the images of the real world reflected by literature. If literature, by definition, is already a transportation of the real into the unreality of verbal conception, then the critical act in this case will constitute a transposition of this transposition, thus raising to the second power the "derealization" of being through language. In this way, the mind puts the maximum distance between its thought and what *is.* Thanks to this withdrawal, and to the consequent dematerialization of every object thus pushed to the vanishing point, the universe represented in this criticism seems not so much the equivalent of the perceivable world, or of its literary representation, as rather its image crystalized through a process of rigorous intellectualization. Here criticism is no longer mimesis; it is the reduction of all literary forms to the same level of insignificance. In short, what survives this attempted annihilation of literature by the critical act? Nothing perhaps save a consciousness ceaselessly confronting the hollowness of mental objects, which yield without resistance, and an absolutely transparent language, which, by coating all objects with the same clear glaze, makes them ("like leaves seen far beneath the ice") appear to be infinitely far away. Thus, the language of this criticism plays a role exactly opposite to the function it has in Jean-Pierre Richard's criticism. It does indeed bring about the unification of critical thought with the mental world revealed by the literary work; but it brings it about at the expense of the work. Everything is finally annexed by the dominion of a consciousness detached from any object, a *hyper*critical consciousness, functioning all alone, somewhere in the void.

Is there any need to say that this hypercriticism is the critical thought of Maurice Blanchot?

I have found it useful to compare the criticism of Richard to the criticism of Blanchot. I learn from this confrontation that the critic's linguistic apparatus can, just as he chooses, bring him closer to the work under consideration, or can remove him from it indefinitely. If he so wishes, he can approximate very closely the work in question, thanks to a verbal mimesis which transposes into the critic's language the sensuous themes of the work. Or else he can make language a pure crystalizing agent, an absolute translucence, which, suffering no opacity to exist between subject and object, promotes the exercise of the cognitive power on the part of the subject, while at the same time accentuating in the object those characteristics which emphasize its infinite distance from the subject. In the first of the two cases, criticism achieves a remarkable *complicity,* but at the risk of losing its minimum lucidity; in the second case, it results in the most complete dissociation; the maximum lucidity thereby achieved only confirms a separation instead of a union.

Thus criticism seems to oscillate between two possibilities: a union without comprehension, and a comprehension without union. I may identify so completely with what I am reading that I lose consciousness not only of myself, but also of that other consciousness which lives within the work. Its proximity blinds me by blocking my prospect. But I may, on the other hand, separate myself so completely from what I am contemplating that the thought thus removed to a distance assumes the aspect of a being with whom I may never establish any relationship whatsoever. In either case, the act of reading has delivered me from egocentricity: another's thought inhabits me or haunts me, but in the first case I lose myself in that alien world, and in the other we keep our distance and refuse to identify. Extreme closeness and extreme detachment have then the same regrettable effect of making me fall short of the total critical act: that is to say, the exploration of that mysterious interrelationship which, through the mediation of reading and of language, is established to our mutual satisfaction between the work read and myself.

Thus extreme proximity and extreme separation each have grave disadvantages. And yet they have their privileges as well. Sensuous thought is privileged to move at once to the heart of the work and to share its own life; clear thought is privileged to confer on its objects the highest degree of intelligibility. Two sorts of insight are here distinguishable and mutually exclusive: there is penetration by the senses and penetration by the reflective consciousness. Now rather than contrasting these two forms of critical activity, would there not be some way, I wonder, not of practicing them simultaneously, which would be impossible; but at least of combining them through a kind of reciprocation and alternation?

Is not this perhaps the method used today by Jean Starobinski? For instance, it would not be difficult to find in his work a number of texts which relate him to Maurice Blanchot. Like Blanchot he displays exceptional lucidity and an acute awareness of distance. And yet he does not quite abandon himself to Blanchot's habitual pessimism. On the contrary, he seems inclined to optimism, even at times to a pleasant utopianism. Starobinski's intellect in this respect is analogous to that of Rousseau, yearning for an immediate transparence of all beings to each other which would enable them to understand each other in an ecstatic happiness. From this point of view, is not the ideal of criticism precisely represented by the *fête citadine* ("street celebration") or *fête champêtre* ("rustic feast")? There is a milieu or a moment in the feast in which everyone communicates with everyone else, in which hearts are open like books. On a more modest scale, doesn't the same phenomenon occur in reading? Does not one being open its innermost self? Is not the other being enchanted by this opening? In the criticism of Starobinski we often find that crystaline tempo of music, that pure delight in understanding, that perfect sympathy between an intelligence which enters and that intelligence which welcomes it.

In such moments of harmony, there is no longer any exclusion, no inside or outside. Contrary to Blanchot's belief, perfect translucence does not result in separation. On the contrary, with Starobinski, all is perfect agreement, joy shared, the pleasure of understanding and of being understood. Moreover, such pleasure, however intellectual it may be, is not here exclusively a pleasure of the mind. For the relationship established on this level between author and critic is not a relationship between pure minds. It is rather between incarnate beings, and the particularities of their physical existence constitute not obstacles to understanding, but rather a complex of supplementary signs, a veritable language which must be deciphered and which enhances mutual comprehension. Thus for Starobinski, as much physician as critic, there is a reading of *bodies* which is likened to the reading of *minds.* It is not of the same nature, nor does it bring the intelligence to bear on the same area of human knowledge. But for the critic who practices it, this criticism provides the opportunity for a reciprocating exchange between different types of learning which have, perhaps, different degrees of transparency.

Starobinski's criticism, then, displays great flexibility. Rising at times to the heights of metaphysics, it does not disdain the farthest reaches of the subconscious. It is sometimes intimate, sometimes detached; it assumes all the degrees of identification and nonidentification. But its final movement seems to consist in a sort of withdrawal, contradistinction with its earlier accord. After an initial intimacy with the object under study, this criticism has finally to detach itself, to move on, but this time in solitude. Let us not see this withdrawal as a failure of sympathy but rather as a way of avoiding the encumbrances of too prolonged a life in common. Above all we discern an acute need to establish bearings, to adopt the judicious perspective, to assess the fruits of proximity by examining them at a distance. Thus, Starobinski's criticism always ends with a view from afar, or rather from above, for while moving away it has also moved imperceptibly toward a dominating *(surplombante)* position. Does this mean that Starobinski's criticism like Blanchot's is doomed to end in a philosophy of separation? This, in a way, must be conceded, and it is no coincidence that Starobinski treats with special care the themes of melancholy and nostalgia. His criticism always concludes with a double farewell. But this farewell is exchanged by two beings who have begun by living together; and the one left behind continues to be illuminated by that critical intellect which moves on.

The sole fault with which I might reproach such criticism is the excessive ease with which it penetrates what it illuminates.

By dint of seeing in literary works only the thoughts which inhabit them, Starobinski's criticism somehow passes through their forms, not neglecting them, it is true, but without pausing on the way. Under its action literary works lose their opacity, their solidity, their objective dimension; like those palace walls which become transparent in certain fairy tales. And if it is true that the ideal act of criticism must seize (and reproduce) that certain relationship between an object and a mind which is the work itself, how could the act of criticism succeed when it suppresses one of the (polar) terms of this relationship?

My search must continue, then, for a criticism in which this relationship subsists. Could it perhaps be the criticism of Marcel Raymond and Jean Rousset? Raymond's criticism always recognizes the presence of a double reality, both mental and formal. It strives to comprehend almost simultaneously an inner experience and a perfected form. On the one hand, no one allows himself to be absorbed with such complete self-forgetfulness into the thought of another. But the other's thought is grasped not at its highest, but at its most obscure, at its cloudiest point, at the point at which it is reduced to being a mere self-awareness scarcely perceived by the being which entertains it, and which yet to the eyes of the critic seems the sole means of access by which he can penetrate within the precincts of the alien mind.

But Raymond's criticism presents another aspect which is precisely the reverse of this confused identification of the critic's thought with the thought criticized. It is then the reflective contemplation of a formal reality which is the work itself. The work stands *before* the critical intelligence as a perfected object, which is in fact an enigma, an external thing existing in itself and with which there is no possibility of identification nor of inner knowledge.

Thus Raymond perceives sometimes a subject, sometimes an object. The subject is pure mind; it is a sheer inde-

finable presence, an almost inchoate entity, into which, by very virtue of its absence of form, it becomes possible for the critic's mind to penetrate. The work, on the contrary, exists only within a definite form, but this definition limits it, encloses it within its own contours, at the same time constraining the mind which studies it to remain on the outside. So that, if on the one hand the critical thought of Raymond tends to lose itself within an undefined subjectivity, on the other it tends to come to a stop before an impenetrable objectivity.

Admirably gifted to submit his own subjectivity to that of another, and thus to immerse itself in the obscurest depths of every mental entity, the mind of Raymond is less well equipped to penetrate the obstacle presented by the objective surface of the works. He then finds himself marking time, or moving in circles around the work, as around the vase or the statue mentioned before. Does Raymond then establish an insurmountable partition between the two realities—subjective, objective—unified though they may be in the work? No, indeed, at least not in his best essays, since in them, by careful intuitive apprehension of the text and participation by the critic in the powers active in the poet's use of language, there appears some kind of link between the objective aspects of the work and the undefined subjectivity which sustains it. A link not to be confused with a pure relation of identity. The perception of the formal aspects of the work becomes somehow an analogical language by means of which it becomes possible for the critic to go, within the work, beyond the formal aspects it presents. Nevertheless this association is never presented by Raymond as a dialectical process. The usual state described by his method of criticism is one of plenitude, and even of a double plenitude. A certain fullness of experience detected in the poet and relived in the mind of the critic, is connected by the latter with a certain perfection of form; but why this is so, and how it does become so, is never clearly explained.

Now is it then possible to go one step further? This is what is attempted by Jean Rousset, a former student of Raymond and perhaps his closest friend. He also dedicates himself to the task of discerning the structure of a work as well as the depth of an experience. Only what essentially matters to him is to establish a connection between the objective reality of the work and the organizing power which gives it shape. A work is not explained for him, as for the structuralists, by the exclusive interdependence of the objective elements which compose it. He does not see in it a fortuitous combination, interpreted a posteriori as if it were an a priori organization. There is not in his eyes any system of the work without a principle of systematization which operates in correlation with that work and which is even included in it. In short, there is no spider web without a center which is the spider. On the other hand, it is not a question of going from the work to the psychology of the author, but of going back, within the sphere of the work, from the objective elements systematically arranged, to a certain power of organization, inherent in the work itself, as if the latter showed itself to be an intentional consciousness determining its arrangements and solving its problems. So that it would scarcely be an abuse of terms to say that it speaks, by means of its structural elements, an authentic language, thanks to which it discloses itself and means nothing but itself. Such then is the critical enterprise of Jean Rousset. It sets itself to use the objective elements of the work in order to attain, beyond them, a reality not formal, nor objective, written down however in forms and expressing itself by means of them. Thus the understanding of forms must not limit itself merely to the recording of their objective aspects. As Focillon demonstrated from the point of view of art history, there is a "life of forms" perceptible not only in the historic development which they display from epoch to epoch, but within each single work, in the movement by which forms tend therein sometimes to stabilize and become static, and sometimes to change into one another. Thus the two contradictory forces which are always at work in any literary writing, the will to stability and the protean impulse, help us to perceive by their interplay how much forms are dependent on what Coleridge called a shaping power which determines them, replaces them and transcends them. The teaching of Raymond finds then its most satisfying success in the critical method of Jean Rousset, a method which leads the seeker from the continuously changing frontiers of form to what is beyond form.

It is fitting then to conclude this inquiry here, since it has achieved its goal, namely to describe, relying on a series of more or less adequate examples, a critical method having as guiding principle the relation between subject and object. Yet there remains one last difficulty. In order to establish the interrelationship between subject and object, which is the principle of all creative work and of the understanding of it, two ways, at least theoretically, are opened, one leading from the objects to the subject, the other from the subject to the objects.[2] Thus we have seen Raymond and Rousset, through perception of the objective structures of a literary work, strive to attain the subjective principle which upholds it. But, in so doing, they seem to recognize the precedence of the subject over its objects. What Raymond and Rousset are

searching for in the objective and formal aspects of the work, is something which is previous to the work and on which the work depends for its very existence. So that the method which leads from the object to the subject does not differ radically at bottom from the one which leads from subject to object, since it does really consist in going from subject to subject through the object. Yet there is the risk of overlooking an important point. The aim of criticism is not achieved merely by the understanding of the part played by the subject in its interrelation with objects. When reading a literary work, there is a moment when it seems to me that the subject *present* in this work disengages itself from all that surrounds it, and stands alone. Had I not once the intuition of this, when visiting the Scuola de San Rocco in Venice, one of the highest summits of art, where there are assembled so many paintings of the same painter, Tintoretto? When looking at all these masterpieces brought there together and revealing so manifestly their unity of inspiration, I had suddenly the impression of having reached the common essence present in all the works of a great master, an essence which I was not able to perceive, except when emptying my mind of all the particular images created by the artist. I became aware of a subjective power at work in all these pictures, and yet never so clearly understood by my mind as when I had forgotten all their particular figurations.

One may ask oneself: What is this subject left standing in isolation after all examination of a literary work? Is it the individual genius of the artist, visibly present in his work, yet having an invisible life independent of the work? Or is it, as Valéry thinks, an anonymous and abstract consciousness presiding, in its aloofness, over the operations of all more concrete consciousness? Whatever it may be, I am constrained to acknowledge that all subjective activity present in a literary work is not entirely explained by its relationship with forms and objects within the work. There is in the work a mental activity profoundly engaged in objective forms; and there is, at another level, forsaking all forms, a subject which reveals itself to itself (and to me) in its transcendence over all which is reflected in it. At this point, no object can any longer express it, no structure can any longer define it; it is exposed in its ineffability and in its fundamental indeterminancy. Such is perhaps the reason why the critic, in his elucidation of works, is haunted by this transcendence of mind. It seems then that criticism, in order to accompany the mind in this effort of detachment from itself, needs to annihilate, or at least momentarily to forget, the objective elements of the work, and to elevate itself to the apprehension of a subjectivity without objectivity.

---

[2] See Coleridge, *Biographia Literaria*, pp. 476–78.

Raymond Williams

1922–1988

Perhaps the leading social critic of his time in England, Raymond Williams actually had Welsh working class roots. His *The Country and the City* (1973) examines the nostalgia for an idyllic rural earlier age that never existed for most people, yet has been endlessly eulogized in literature, "the recurrent myth of a happier and more natural past." Left out of this picture is the real life of the rural laborer. There was never in old England a lack of brutal exploitation. What has been frequently identified with natural social order was never natural, usually not of as great an age as claimed, and always exploitative of the working poor at the bottom who supported the hierarchy of ownership and privilege. The growth that followed Feudalism was but the substitution of one form of domination for another. Nostalgia for a mythical Edenic society or primitive communalism has been expressive of revolutionary desire, but Williams opts for an attitude that looks to the future rather than to the past. In *The Country and the City* he explores the sources of the "idea of an ordered and happier past set against the disturbance and disorder of the present." In the process, he examines a number of literary works written to obtain patronage of wealthy men at the expense of a true accounting for the lives of the poor and any true sense of the past. Such nostalgias, he believes, stand in the way of progressive social change. Williams' intellectual orientation was Marxist, but he was different from most European Marxist critics in that his background was rural and theirs was metropolitan. This difference shows in the account he offers below of Britain's precarious but persistent rural-intellectual radicalism.

Among Williams' writings are *Culture and Society, 1780–1950* (1958), *Border Country* (1960), *The Long Revolution* (1961), *Reading and Criticism* (1966), *Drama in Performance* (1968), *Drama from Ibsen to Brecht* (1969), *The English Novel from Dickens to Lawrence* (1970), *The Country and the City* (1973), *Keywords* (1976), *Marxism and Literature* (1977), *Politics and Letters: Interviews with the New Left Review* (1979), *Problems in Materialism and Culture* (1980), *Culture* (1981), *The Sociology of Culture* (1982), *Writing in Society* (1983), and *The Fight for Manod* (1988). See Jan Gorak, *The Alien Mind of Raymond Williams* (1988); and Alan O'Connor, *Raymond Williams: Writing, Culture, Politics* (1989).

The Country and the City

Chapter Four: Golden Ages

But there is still a crisis of perspective. When we moved back in time, consistently directed to an earlier and happier rural England, we could find no place, no period, in which we could seriously rest.

Yet the backward reference has its own logic. If we take a long enough period, it is easy to see a fundamental trans-formation of English country life. But the change is so ex-tended and so complicated, to say nothing of its important regional variations, that there seems no point at which we can sharply distinguish what it would be convenient to call separate epochs. The detailed histories indicate everywhere that many old forms, old practices and old ways of feeling survived into periods in which the general direction of new development was clear and decisive. And then what seems an old order, a 'traditional' society, keeps appearing, reap-pearing, at bewilderingly various dates: in practice as an idea, to some extent based in experience, against which con-temporary change can be measured. The structure of feeling within which this backward reference is to be understood is then not primarily a matter of historical explanation and analysis. What is really significant is this particular kind of reaction to the fact of change, and this has more real and more interesting social causes.

Thus in the poems we have been looking at there is no historical reference back. What we find, nevertheless, is an idealisation of feudal and immediately post-feudal values: of an order based on settled and reciprocal social and economic relations of an avowedly total kind. It is then important that the poems coincide, in time, with a period in which another order—that of capitalist agriculture—was being successfully pioneered. For behind that coincidence is a conflict of values which is still crucial. These celebrations of a feudal or an aristocratic order—

And, you must know, your Lord's word's true,
Feed him ye must, whose food fills you

—have been widely used, in an idealist retrospect, as a cri-tique of capitalism. The emphases on obligation, on charity, on the open door to the needy neighbour, are contrasted, in a familiar vein of retrospective radicalism, with the capitalist thrust, the utilitarian reduction of all social relationships to a crude moneyed order.

This leads to an evident crisis of values in our own world. For a retrospective radicalism, against the crudeness and narrowness of a new moneyed order, is often made to do service as a critique of the capitalism of our own day: to carry humane feelings and yet ordinarily to attach them to a pre-capitalist and therefore irrecoverable world. A necessary social criticism is then directed to the safer world of the past: to a world of books and memories, in which the scholar can be professionally humane but in his own real world either insulated or indifferent. But also, and more important, this kind of critique of capitalism enfolds social values which, if they do become active, at once spring to the defence of cer-tain kinds of order, certain social hierarchies and moral sta-bilities, which have a feudal ring but a more relevant and more dangerous contemporary application. Some of these 'rural' virtues, in twentieth-century intellectual movements, leave the land to become the charter of explicit social reac-tion: in the defence of traditional property settlements, or in the offensive against democracy in the name of blood and soil.

Yet many draw back before those points are reached. In Britain, identifiably, there is a precarious but persistent rural-intellectual radicalism: genuinely and actively hostile to in-dustrialism and capitalism; opposed to commercialism and to the exploitation of environment; attached to country ways and feelings, the literature and the lore. But the point of de-cision, within any such feelings, is on the nature of the capi-talist transition. As in every kind of radicalism the moment comes when any critique of the present must choose its bear-ings, between past and future. And if the past is chosen, as now so often and so deeply, we must push the argument through to the roots that are being defended; push attention, human attention, back to the natural economy, the moral economy, the organic society, from which the critical values are drawn.

There is an early complication. The most evident op-ponents of just this position are certain metropolitan intellec-tuals of an again identifiable kind. I mean not only the people who have never known rural settlements and whose igno-rance can therefore be identified, but all those who have in-herited a long contempt, from very diverse sources, of the peasant, the boor, the rural clown; who then have as their currency the accumulated hoard of party impersonations and accepted mimings of a truly rural distance; milk and straw and beasts and dung as the quick cues to parody and laughter. And they might be left to their amusements if they did not include and overlap with more serious possible positions. How many socialists, for example, have refused to pick up

GOLDEN AGES. Golden Ages is Chapter Four of Williams' *The Country and the City.* Copyright © by Raymond Williams 1973. Reprinted by permission of Oxford University Press, Inc.

that settling archival sentence about the 'idiocy of rural life'? Until very recently, indeed until the peasant socialist revolutions of China and Cuba, this reflex was habitual among the metropolitan socialists of Europe. And behind it, all the time, was a more serious position, near the centre of historical argument. For it has been commonplace since Marx to speak, in some contexts, of the progressive character of capitalism, and within it of urbanism and of social modernisation. The great indictments of capitalism, and of its long record of misery in factories and towns, have co-existed, within a certain historical scheme, with this repeated use of 'progressive' as a willing adjective about the same events. We hear again and again this brisk, impatient and as it is said realistic response: to the productive efficiency, the newly liberated forces, of the capitalist breakthrough; a simultaneous damnation and idealisation of capitalism, in its specific forms of urban and industrial development; an unreflecting celebration of mastery—power, yield, production, man's mastery of nature—as if the exploitation of natural resources could be separated from the accompanying exploitation of men. What they say is damn this, praise this; and the intellectual formula for this emotional confusion is, hopefully, the dialectic. All that needs to be added, as the climax to a muddle, is the late observation, the saving qualification, that at a certain stage—is it now?; it was yesterday—capitalism begins to lose this progressive character and for further productive efficiency, for the more telling mastery of nature, must be replaced, superseded, by socialism. Against this powerful tendency, in which forms of socialism offer to complete the capitalist enterprise, even the old, sad, retrospective radicalism seems to bear and to embody a human concern.

But in the end it cannot do this, cannot be what it suggests. Between the simple backward look and the simple progressive thrust there is room for long argument but none for enlightenment. We must begin differently: not in the idealisations of one order or another, but in the history to which they are only partial and misleading responses.

Take first the idealisation of a 'natural' or 'moral' economy on which so many have relied, as a contrast to the thrusting ruthlessness of the new capitalism. There was very little that was moral or natural about it. In the simplest technical sense, that it was a 'natural' subsistence agriculture, as yet unaffected by the drives of a market economy, it is already doubtful and subject to many exceptions; though part of this emphasis can be readily accepted. But the social order within which this agriculture was practised was as hard and as brutal as anything later experienced. Even if we exclude the wars and brigandage to which it was commonly subject, the uncountable thousands who grew crops and reared beasts

only to be looted and burned and led away with tied wrists, this economy, even at peace, was an order of exploitation of a most thoroughgoing kind: a property in men as well as in land; a reduction of most men to working animals, tied by forced tribute, forced labour, or 'bought and sold like beasts'; 'protected' by law and custom only as animals and streams are protected, to yield more labour, more food, more blood; an economy directed, in all its working relations, to a physical and economic domination of a significantly total kind. 'The churl, like the willow, sprouts the better for being cropped.' That bailiff's maxim is in all essential respects the principle of this 'natural' and 'moral' economy.

Through the long generations men had been clearing and establishing their settlements, and at the edges and at intervals, always, they had lived for a time in these direct ways, with their corresponding imperatives and virtues. As we look back, at the earliest Britain, we have always to remember how few people there were, and how possible, locally, were their immediate settlements. The widely scattered Celtic farms; the villages of the Roman period, cultivating two or three per cent of today's land; the total population of the country rising in the historical millennium from just under to just over a million; these facts remind us how much early settlement can be seen as a direct struggle with nature, the clearing of wild land. But that is never the whole story. The tribal settlements were under the power of the sword and of tribute; the Celtic and Saxon and Scandinavian kingdoms were based on general and local seizure. And the pressure, even then, was for others to keep moving in; in conquest and in the flight from bad land, or from famine or terror. Or as the simplicities of local defence were built and developed into a military system, there was another kind of invasion: an altered distribution, internally, of authority and duty. From inside and outside there was this remorseless moving-in of the armed gangs, with their titles of importance, their kingships and their baronies, to feed from other men's harvests. And the armed gangs became social and natural orders, blessed by their gods and their churches, with at the bottom of the pyramid, over a tale of centuries, the working cultivator, the human and natural man—sometimes finding a living space, a settled working area; as often deprived of it—but in any case breaking the land and himself to support this rising social estate, which can be seen to culminate in the medieval 'order' of the Norman and then the English kings: a more complete because more organised and more extended exploitation, under its banner 'Feed him ye must'.

There is only one real question. Where do we stand, with whom do we identify, as we read the complaints of disturbance, as this order in its turn broke up? Is it with the serfs, the bordars and cotters, the villeins; or with the abstracted order to which, through successive generations, many hundreds of thousands of men were never more than instrumental? And supposing we could make that choice rightly—though the historian who really places himself with the majority of men, and tries to see the world as they were experiencing it, is always improbable—where do we identify, as the order develops into new kinds of order?

It depends, in part, on how the break-up is described. Conventionally it is often dated from the Black Death, in which, within a generation, more than a million people died and many settlements were abandoned. Successive outbreaks of plague had been reducing the pressure of a rising population on an extending cultivated land, and the social relations between lords and tenants and labourers had been correspondingly altered. But there were forces within the order itself which were in any case leading to change. There was the growth of towns and of monasteries: often founded by feudal lords but developing new and complicated social and economic relations and concepts. There was the clearance of woodlands, for timber, for fuel and for pasture, and the drive for more pasture, in the growth of the wool trade, led to major enclosures, the destruction of many arable villages, and the rapid development of new kinds of capitalist landlord. It is not, taken as a whole, a story of decline from the medieval order, but of vigorous, often brutally vigorous, growth. The suppression of the monasteries released large new areas of land for the consolidation of new kinds of ownership. Down to the Civil War there was some official resistance to wholesale enclosure and the new kinds of ownership, but in the Restoration a government of the new kind of landlord was at last in control. This marked the decisive establishment of the new order which had been developing for at least two centuries: an order already physically present in the great pastoral estates and in the rebuilt houses, especially the 'country houses' which since the beginning of the sixteenth century had been replacing the castles and the fortified manors and which, as we have seen, were to be the visible centres of the new social system. A more settled and centralised order—a system of social and economic rather than directly military and physical control—was now fully in being, in a more prosperous and more populated country. Following the fortunes, through these centuries, of the dominant interests, it is a story of growth and achievement, but for the majority of men it was the substitution of one form of domination for another: the mystified feudal order replaced by a mystified agrarian capitalist order, with just enough continuity, in titles and in symbols of authority, in successive compositions of a 'natural order', to confuse and control.

But then the great problem of English rural history is the endless complication of intermediate classes: between the feudal lord and the serf; between the great landowner and the hired landless labourer. Any simple description, of feudalism itself or of the successive stages of capitalism, underestimates the importance of the intermediate groups: the freemen and some of the villeins; the freehold and large tenant farmers; the smaller landowners; the small farmers and cottagers with rights on the commons and in the common fields. The periods of disturbance include the emergence but also the suppression, the struggles, the internal divisions of these intermediate groups. Yet we have only to look at rural Britain even today to see how some of these intermediate classes survive: still, inevitably, under severe economic pressures. Many historians of rural England, many writers drawing on its experience, have identified throughout with the lords and the landowners. This is the common position of imaginative literature until at least the eighteenth century. But there have also been powerful spokesmen, in every period, for the intermediate classes: indeed many more than there have been for the real and permanent majority of the truly exploited and landless. These varying, sometimes unconscious, identifications matter, for it is in their light that we must examine both the reactions to disturbance and the recurrent myth of a happier and more natural past.

And the interesting fact then is that the myth of the happier past was used, though in different ways, from each of these identifying positions. We have seen it in the lord's service in Jonson and Carew: a mystification of the land and the estate into the poetic counters of a Golden Age and of Paradise. What was there being celebrated was of course not quite a feudality: the estate is taken as given; it has no apparent origins, as it has no apparent work. But Saxham was a product of the agrarian disturbance: engrossed around 1500, it passed to the Crofts family in 1531, and owed its importance at the time Carew visited it to a connection with the court; it was a favourite stopping-place on the way to and from the races at Newmarket, and masques were performed there, as part of the entertainment, and this brought the poets. A quite precise set of social relationships is then mystified by the image of the paternal lord.

All that is left of Saxham now, to quote the historian of its village, is

a moat in the middle of a field, a monument or two in the church, and a very small charity.

He adds, reflecting on the two hundred years of that family:

They might have done more.

Penhurst of course still stands, and appears in brochures and advertisements, but it began its relevant existence—

> rear'd with no man's ruine, no man's grone

—as a crown manor which had lapsed by execution and attainder and was then presented by Edward VI to William Sidney, tutor and chamberlain of the court, formerly steward of the household of Henry VIII. That is not quite a timeless order, half a century later when Jonson visited it. Like Saxham, it was a place where the arts were notably patronised, but as an estate it rested on the characteristic sixteenth-century situation in which the quickest means to profit was an association at court. The social image conceals, again, a quite precise and recent set of social relationships. The return of hospitality, to the royal source of the property, has its inner bonds as well as its formalities.

It is essential to remember the recent character of these 'traditional' settlements when we are asked to take up a position towards the more evidently new and speculating landowners. Penshurst and Saxham, now taken as symbols of the old natural order, were direct creations of the new order, as were all the 'country houses', whether idealised or not. But given the background of a consolidated and mystified profit, it was easy to complain, with an apparent humanity, against the crude grasping of the successive new men. By comparison with this nature, now, after the royal gift, apparently yielding of itself, it is easy to feel the harshness of the words Jonson gives to Volpone, on the evident capitalism of the time:

> I use no trade, no venture;
> I wound no earth with ploughshares, fat no beasts
> To feed the shambles; have no mills for iron,
> Oil, corn, or men, to grind them into powder:
> I blow no subtle glass, expose no ships
> To threat'nings of the furrow-faced sea.
> I turn no monies in the public bank,
> No usurer private.

This might, indeed, in its abnegation—its position above the wounding and grinding of the ordinary and visible pursuit of wealth—be a master of Penshurst speaking. Except that it is Volpone, the confidence man, the fox: an irony that repays reflection.

From the other extreme of the society, from the position of the landless and the exposed, the idea of a golden age seems harder to understand. But the functional difference is evident. What is marked in the lordly use is a preternatural presence: a magical and inherited island in a rising and pitiless sea. For the landless, understandably, the deprivation is more total. Indeed, it is seen from within the 'natural order' itself, and the reference to an earlier time is then more critical and absolute:

> When Adam delved and Eve span
> Who was then the gentleman?

It is on the long corruption, not the lucky exception, that the landless insist. Even the redemption by Christ has not reached them:

> We are men formed in Christ's likeness, and we are kept like beasts.

That was the declaration of one of the most remarkable organisations of the poor peasants, the Great Society of the fourteenth century. It is not mystifying, but a challenge in terms of a supposedly shared religious belief. Behind much of the feeling of the landless, however, the idea of an earlier and uncorrupted age persisted, and was to find a bewildering variety of historical ascriptions as time and deprivation continued. In the justified hatred of any current race of landlords, and in a time of historical ignorance, there could be an endless retrospect to a time before they existed, before any landlords existed, and what name or period is given is then secondary and arbitrary. It is retrospect as aspiration, for such an idea is drawn not only from the Christian idea of the Garden of Eden—the simple, natural world before the Fall—but also from a version of the Golden Age which is more than that of a magically self-yielding nature. This version is based on the idea of a primitive community, a primitive communism. This is not in Hesiod, where the men of the Golden Age live like gods. Its origins seem to be Hellenistic, and it is explicit in Virgil:

> no peasants subdued the fields; it was not lawful
> even to assign or divide the ground with land-
> marks: men sought the common gain, and the
> earth itself bore everything more generously at no
> one's bidding.
>
> (*Georgics,* I)

This is a fusion of ideas of the self-yielding earth and a conscious community of property and purpose. It can be contrasted with Lucretius' view of primitive men as unable to see the common good. But the fusion persisted, in one tradition, and this must be distinguished from the asocial and mystified Golden Age of the lordly uses: the self-yielding earth ratified by its proprietor, its Lord. We find many traces of the communal idea in Renaissance literature. As Spenser puts it, in the mouth of another fox, in *Mother Hubbard's Tale:*

> Nor ought cald mine or thine; thrice happie then
> Was the condition of mortall men.
> That was the golden age of Saturne old.

Or Chapman:

> Mine, and Thine, were then unusde,
> All things common: Nought abusde,
>   Farely earth her frutage bearing.

This persistent and particular version of the Golden Age, a myth functioning as a memory, could then be used, by the landless, as an aspiration. In the words of the Great Society:

> All things under Heaven ought to be common.

It was a claim that was to be continued through the seventeenth-century Diggers to the Land Chartists and the radical labourers of our own time. The happier past was almost desperately insisted upon, but as an impulse to change rather than to ratify the actual inheritance.

Yet the most interesting use of the idea of a lost innocence comes not from the lordly or the landless, but from the shifting intermediate groups. For these were men caught (as in the Virgilian *Eclogues*) in successive but temporary settlements: achieving a place in the altering social structure of the land but continually threatened with losing it: with being pushed down, as eventually many were, into the exposed anonymity of the landless poor. Such men, who had risen by change, were quick to be bitter about renewed or continuing change. What they said about the agents of a new historical phase was authentically angry, but what they also said about the men below them—about the 'idle labourers'—makes the anger double-edged. This can be seen in the qualified humanism of Thomas More, in his *Utopia.* His complaint against the new exploiters and rack-renters is strong and clear.

> There is a great numbre of gentlemen, which can
> not be content to live idle themselves, lyke dorres,
> of that whiche other have laboured for: their ten-

auntes, I meane, whom they polle and shave to the quicke, by reisyng their rentes.

The social identification with the smaller tenants and against the rich owners is equally evident.

> That one covetous and unsatiable cormaraunte and
> very plage of his natyve contrey maye compasse
> aboute and inclose many thousand akers of
> grounde together within one pale or hedge, the
> husbandmen be thruste owte of their owne . . . or
> by violent oppression they be put besydes it, or by
> wronges and injuries thei be so weried, that they
> be compelled to sell all. . . .

This is the driving-out of the small men, in the familiar process of engrossing and enclosing. But to the decay of small ownership, and the decline of hospitality, is joined another tendency, which is almost as bitterly denounced:

> To this wretched beggerye and miserable povertie
> is joined great wantonnes, importunate superflui-
> tie and excessive riote. For not only gentle mennes
> servauntes, but also handicrafe men: yea and al-
> mooste the ploughmen of the countrey, with al
> other sortes of people, use much straunge and
> proude newefanglenes in their apparell, and to
> muche prodigall riotte and sumptuous fare at their
> table.

This is the sour denunciation of the luxurious poor, which was heard in Langland at the time of the Statute of Labourers, and which has been heard, since then, in almost every generation: not only the recurrent and ludicrous part-song of the rich; but the sharper, more savage anxiety of the middle men, the insecure. The two grounds of complaint, against the speculative rich and the idle poor, are brought together by More in a rhetorical climax:

> Suffer not these riche men to bie up al, to ingrosse
> and forstalle, and with their monopolie to kepe the
> market alone as please them. Let not so many be
> brought up in idleness, let husbandry and tillage
> be restored, let clotheworkinge be renewed, that
> ther may be honest labours for this idell sort to
> passe their tyme in profitablye.

Back to work, that is to say, on our terms and our conditions and in our ways, and meanwhile God give us protection from the unfair competition of the powerful monopolists. The natural ideal is then the recreation of a race of small owners, and this is projected in the island of Utopia. Once again the myth of a primitive happier state is drawn upon, with some suggestions from accounts of the primitive economies seen by Vespucci and others in the new world. But in the island paradise it is not quite to be all things in common. It is to be, rather, a small-owner republic, with laws to regulate and protect but also to compel labour.

The social experience behind this is clear. An upper peasantry, which had established itself in the break-up of the strict feudal order, and which had ideas and illusions about freedom and independence from the experience of a few generations, was being pressed and expropriated by the great landowners, the most successful of just these new men, in the changes of the market and of agricultural techniques brought about by the growth of the wool trade. A moral protest was then based on a temporary stability: as again and again in the subsequent history of rural complaint. It is au-

thentic and moving yet it is in other ways unreal. Its ideal of local paternal care, and of national legislation to protect certain recent forms of ownership and labour, seems to draw almost equally on a rejection of the arbitrariness of feudalism, a deeply felt rejection of the new arbitrariness of money, and an attempted stabilisation of a transitory order, in which small men are to be protected against enclosures but also against the idleness of their labourers. Thus a moral order is abstracted from the feudal inheritance and break-up, and seeks to impose itself ideally on conditions which are inherently unstable. A sanctity of property has to co-exist with violently changing property relations, and an ideal of charity with the harshness of labour relations in both the new and the old modes. This is then the third source of the idea of an ordered and happier past set against the disturbance and disorder of the present. An idealisation, based on a temporary situation and on a deep desire for stability, served to cover and to evade the actual and bitter contradictions of the time.

Julia Kristeva

b. 1941

Since coming to Paris from Bulgaria in 1966, Julia Kristeva has been a central figure in French intellectual life. She has been a researcher for Claude Lévi-Strauss, a member of the editorial board of *Tel Quel* (and a contributor), a psychoanalyst, and a professor. Her interests have ranged broadly through literary criticism, psychoanalysis, linguistics, and feminism. Her work, which is unusually dense because of the mingling of the languages of these various discourses and her own coinages, rarely recognizes boundaries between them. This density has caused her editor to preface *Desire in Language* with a glossary of the key terms she employs. Among these ''subject'' (sujet) appears frequently and is particularly important for the selection below. Kristeva's subject is not the traditional ''I'' of epistemology but a ''subject of enunciation,'' that is, a ''phenomenological conception of the speaking subject.'' But it is only the signifying act that ''establishes'' this ''transcendental ego of communication.'' Kristeva avoids Jacques Derrida's deconstruction of Edmund Husserl's transcendental ego by placing it securely in a linguistic setting as a *speaking* subject. She criticizes deconstruction as refusing ''what constitutes one function of language though not the only one: to express meaning in a communicable sentence between speakers.''

Kristeva also refers frequently to what she calls ''poetic language.'' It is the aspect of language that escapes phenomenological analysis and ''makes of what is known as 'literature' something other than knowledge.'' The importance of this aspect of language is that here the ''social code is destroyed and renewed.'' This arena is the ''semiotic disposition,'' as compared to the ''semantic'' or ''symbolic.'' Yet where poetic language dominates the semantic remains. Otherwise there would be no language at all. Because of the undecidable element in such language the speaking subject is always ''a questionable *subject in-process*.'' It is here for Kristeva that psychoanalysis and the unconscious enters, and she advocates a theory that searches for the ''unsettling of meaning'' rather than for coherence or identity. The latter part of ''From One Identity to Another'' is devoted to a discussion of the speaking subject in-process from a psychoanalytic perspective with the work of Louis-Ferdinand Céline as object.

Among the works of Kristeva now translated are *Desire in Language: A Semiotic Approach to Literature and Art* (1977, tr. 1980), *Powers of Horror: An Essay on Abjection* (1980, tr. 1982), *Revolution in Poetic Language* (1974, tr. 1984), *About Chinese Women* (1975, tr. 1977), Tales of Love (tr. 1987), *In the Beginning Was Love: Psychoanalysis and Faith* (1987), and *Black Sun: Depression and Melancholia* (1987, tr. 1989); also Toril Moi, ed., *The Kristeva Reader* (1986). See especially Leon S. Roudiez's introduction to *Desire in Language;* and Alice Jardine, ''Theories of the Feminine: Kristeva,'' *Enclitic* (1982).

From One Identity to Another

I shall attempt, within the ritual limits of a one-hour seminar, to posit (if not to demonstrate) that every language theory is predicated upon a conception of the subject that it explicitly posits, implies, or tries to deny. Far from being an "epistemological perversion," a definite subject is present as soon as there is consciousness of signification. Consequently, I shall need to outline an epistemological itinerary: taking three stages in the recent history of linguistic theory, I shall indicate the variable position these may have required of the speaking subject-support within their object language. This—on the whole, technical—foray into the epistemology of linguistic science will lead us to broach and, I hope, elucidate a problem whose ideological stakes are considerable but whose banality is often ignored. Meaning, identified either within the unity or the multiplicity of subject, structure, or theory, necessarily guarantees a certain transcendence, if not a theology; this is precisely why all human knowledge, whether it be that of an individual subject or of a meaning structure, retains religion as its blind boundaries, or at least, as an internal limit, and at best, can just barely "explain and validate religious sentiment" (as Lévi-Strauss observed, in connection with structuralism).[1]

Second, I shall deal with a particular signifying practice, which, like the Russian Formalists,[2] I call "poetic language," in order to demonstrate that this kind of language, through the particularity of its signifying operations, is an unsettling process—when not an outright destruction—of the identity of meaning and speaking subject,[3] and consequently, of transcendence or, by derivation, of "religious sensibility." On that account, it accompanies crises within social structures and institutions—the moments of their mutation, evolution, revolution, or disarray. For if mutation within language and institutions finds its code through this signifying practice and its questionable subject in process that constitutes poetic language, then that practice and sub-

ject are walking a precarious tightrope. Poetic language, the only language that uses up transcendence and theology to sustain life; poetic language, knowingly the enemy of religion, by its very economy borders on psychosis (as for its subject) and totalitarianism or fascism (as for the institutions it implies or evokes). I could have spoken of Vladimir Mayakovsky or Antonin Artaud; I shall speak of Louis-Ferdinand Céline.

Finally, I shall try to draw a few conclusions concerning the possibility of a *theory* in the sense of an *analytical discourse* on signifying systems, which would take into account these crises of meaning, subject, and structure. This for two reasons: first, such crises, far from being accidents, are inherent in the signifying function and, consequently, in sociality; secondly, situated at the forefront of twentieth-century politics, these phenomena (which I consider within poetic language, but which may assume other forms in the West as well as in other civilizations) could not remain outside the so-called human sciences without casting suspicion on their ethic. I shall therefore and in conclusion argue in favor of an analytical theory of signifying systems and practices that would search within the signifying phenomenon for the *crisis* or the *unsettling process* of meaning and subject rather than for the coherence or identity of either *one* or a *multiplicity* of structures.

Without referring back to the stoic sage, who guaranteed both the sign's triad and the inductive conditional clause, let us return to the congruence between conceptions of language and of subject where Ernest Renan left them. We are all aware of the scandal he caused among nineteenth-century minds when he changed a theological discourse (the Gospels) not into a *myth* but into the *history* of a man and a people. This conversion of *theological* discourse into *historical* discourse was possible thanks to a tool (for him, scientific) whose omnipotence he never ceased praising—philology. As used by Renan or Eugene Burnouf in Avestic Studies, for example, philology incorporates the *comparativism* of philologists Franz Bopp or August Schleicher. Whatever the difference between comparativists seeking those *laws* unique to *families* of languages and philologists deciphering the *meaning* of *one* language, a common conception of language as an *organic identity* unites them. Little does it matter that, as comparativists believed, this organic identity articulates itself thanks to *a law* that crosses national and historical language borders making of them one family (cf. Jacob Grimm's phonetic laws); or that, as philologists believed, this organic identity articulates itself thanks to *one meaning*—singular and unique—inscribed into a text still undeciphered or whose decipherability is debatable. In both cases this *organic identity* of law or meaning implies that

FROM ONE IDENTITY TO ANOTHER. *From One Identity to Another* was originally read as a paper at the College de France, January 27, 1975, and first published in *Tel Quel* in the summer of 1975. It was reprinted in Kristeva's *Polylogue* in 1977 and is reprinted here, edited by Leon S. Roudiez and translated by Thomas Gora, Alice Jardine, and Leon S. Roudiez, from *Desire in Language: A Semiotic Approach to Literature and Art* (New York: Columbia University Press, 1980). Reprinted by permission.

[1][Kristeva] Claude Lévi-Strauss, *L'Homme nu* (Paris: Plon, 1971), p. 615.

[2]See Eichenbaum, p. 800; Shklovsky, p. 750; but also for comparison Wheelwright p. 1022.

[3][Roudiez] Kristeva's French phrase is *mise en procès*, which, like *le sujet en procès*, refers to an important, recurring concept, that of a constantly changing subject whose identity is open to question.

language is the possession of a *homo loquens* within history. As Renan writes in *Averoés et l'Averroïsme,* "for the philologist, a text has only one meaning" even if it is through "a kind of necessary misinterpretation" that "the philosophical and religious development of humanity" proceeds.[4] Closer to the objectivity of the Hegelian "consciousness of self" for the comparativists, embodied into a singularity that, be it concrete, individual, or national, still owes something to Hegel for the philologists; language is always *one* system, perhaps even one "structure," always *one meaning,* and, therefore, it necessarily implies a subject (collective or individual) to bear witness to its history. If one has difficulty following Renan when he affirms that "rationalism is based on philology"—for it is obvious that the two are interdependent—it is no less obvious that philological reasoning is maintained through the identity of a historical subject: a subject in becoming. Why? Because, far from dissecting the internal logic of sign, predication (sentence grammar), or syllogism (logic), as did the universal grammar of Port Royal, the comparativist and philological reason that Renan exemplifies considers the signifying unit in itself (sign, sentence, syllogism) as an unanalyzable given. This signifying unit remains implicit within each description of law or text that philologists and comparativists undertake: linear, unidimensional descriptions—with no analysis of the sign's density, the logical problematic of meaning, etc.—but which, once technically completed, restore structural identity (for the comparativists) or meaning (for the philologists); in so doing they reveal the initial presupposition of the specifically linguistic undertaking as an ideology that posits either the people or an exceptional individual as appropriating this structure or this meaning. Because it is in itself unanalyzable (like the sign, sentence, and syllogism, it has no density, no economy), this subject-support of comparativist laws or of philological analysis does not lend itself to change, that is to say, to shifting from one law to another, from one structure to another, or from one meaning to another, except by postulating the movement of becoming, that is, of history. In the analysis of a signifying function (language or any "human," social phenomenon), what is censured at the level of semantic complexity reemerges in the form of a becoming: that obliteration of the density that constitutes sign, sentence, and syllogism (and consequently, the speaking subject), is compensated for by historical reasoning; the reduction of the complex signifying economy of the speaking subject (though obliquely perceived by Port Royal) produces with-

out fail an opaque "I" that makes history. Thus, philological reasoning, while founding history, becomes a deadlock for language sciences, even though there actually is in Renan, beyond countless contradictions, an appreciation of universal grammar, a call for the constitution of a linguistics for an isolated language (in the manner of the ancient Indian grammarian Pāṇini), and even surprisingly modern proposals that advocate the study of crisis rather than normality, and in his semitic studies the remarks on "that delirious vision transcribed in a barbaric and undecipherable style" as he calls the Christian gnostic texts, or on the texts of John the Apostle.[5]

Linguistic reasoning, which, through Saussure,[6] succeeded philological reasoning, works its revolution precisely by affecting the constitutive unity of a particular language; a language is not a system, it is a system of signs, and this vertically opens up the famous gap between signifier and signified, thus allowing linguistics to claim a logical, mathematical formalization on the one hand, but on the other, it definitely prevents reducing a language or text to one law or one meaning. Structural linguistics and the ensuing structural movement seem to explore this epistemological space by eliminating the speaking subject. But, on a closer look, we see that the subject they legitimately do without is nothing but the subject (individual or collective) of historico-philological discourse I just discussed, and in which the Hegelian consciousness of self became stranded as it was concretized, embodied into philology and history; this subject, which linguistics and the corollary human sciences do without, is the "personal identity, miserable treasure."[7] Nevertheless, a subject of enunciation takes shape within the gap opened up between signifier and signified that admits both structure and interplay within; and structural linguistics ignores such a subject. Moreover, because it left its place vacant, structural linguistics could not become a linguistics of speech or discourse; it lacked a grammar, for in order to move from sign to sentence the place of the subject had to be acknowledged and no longer kept vacant. Of course, generative grammar does reinstate it by rescuing universal grammar and the Cartesian subject from oblivion, using that subject to justify the generative, recursive functions of syntactic trees. But in fact, generative grammar is evidence of what structural linguistics omitted, rather than a new beginning; whether structural or generative, linguistics since Saus-

---

[4][Kristeva] Ernest Renan, *Oeuvres Complètes* (Paris: Calmann-Lévy, 1947–1958) 3:322.

[5][Kristeva] Ernest Renan, *The Future of Science* (Boston: Roberts Brothers, 1891), p. 402.
[6]See Saussure, p. 717.
[7][Kristeva] Lévi-Strauss, *L'Homme nu,* p. 614.

sure adheres to the same presuppositions, implicit within the structuralist current, explicit in the generative tendency that can be found summed up in the philosophy of Husserl.[8]

I refer modern linguistics and the modes of thought which it oversees within the so-called human sciences back to this founding father from another field, but not for conjunctural reasons, though they are not lacking. Indeed, Husserl was invited to and discussed by the Circle of Prague; indeed, Jakobson[9] explicitly recognized in him a philosophical mentor for post-Saussurian linguists; indeed, several American epistemologists of generative grammar recognize in Husserlian phenomenology, rather than in Descartes, the foundations of the generative undertaking. But it is possible to detect in Husserl the basis of linguistic reasoning (structural or generative) to the extent that, after the reduction of the Hegelian consciousness of self into philological or historical identity, Husserl masterfully understood and posited that any signifying act, insofar as it remains capable of elucidation by knowledge, does not maintain itself by a "me, miserable treasure" but by the *"transcendental ego."*

If it is true that the division of the Saussurian sign (signifier/signified), unknown to Husserl, also introduces the heretofore unrecognized possibility of envisioning language as a free play, forever without closure, it is also true that this possibility was not developed by Saussure except in the very problematic *Anagrammes.*[10] Moreover, this investigation has no linguistic followers, but rather, philosophical (Heideggerian discourse) and psychoanalytic (Lacan's signifier) contemporaries or successors, who today effectively enable us to appreciate and circumscribe the contribution of phenomenological linguistics from a Husserlian perspective. For post-Saussurian structural linguistics still encloses the signifier, even if nonmotivated, within patterns of a signification originally destined for faultless communication, either coinciding with the explicit signified or set off a short distance from it, but still fastened to the unalterable presence of meaning and, similarly, tributary to phenomenological reason.

It is therefore impossible to take up the congruence between conceptions of language and of subject where Renan left off without recalling how Husserl shifted ground by raising it above empiricism, psychologism, and incarnation theories typical of Renan. Let us examine for a moment the signifying act and the Husserlian transcendental ego, keeping in mind that linguistic reason (structural or generative) is to Husserl what philological reason was to Hegel: reduction perhaps, but also concrete realization, that is, failure made manifest.

As early as *Logical Investigations* of 1901, Husserl situates the sign (of which one could have naively thought that it had no subject) within the act of expressing meaning, constituted by a judgment on something: "The articulate sound-complex, the written sign, etc., first becomes a spoken word or communicative bit of speech, when a speaker produces it with the intention of 'expressing himself about something' through its means."[11]

Consequently, the thin sheath of the sign (signifier/signified) opens onto a complex architecture where intentional life-experience captures material (hylic) multiplicities, endowing them first with noetic meaning, then with noematic meaning, so that finally the result for the judging consciousness is the formation of an *object* once and for all signified as real. The important point here is that this real *object,* first signified by means of hylic data, through noesis and noemis, if it exists, can only be transcendental in the sense that it is elaborated in its identity by the judging consciousness of transcendental ego. The signified is transcendent as it is posited by means of certain concatenations within an experience that is always confined to judgment; for if the phenomenologist distinguishes between intuiting and endowing with meaning, then perception is already *cogitation* and the *cogitation* is transcendent to perception.[12] So much so that if the world were annihilated, the signified *"res"* would remain because they are transcendental: they "refer entirely to a consciousness" insofar as they are signified *res.* The *predicative* (syntactic) operation constitutes this judging consciousness, positing at the same time the signified *Being* (and therefore, the object of meaning and signification) and the *operating consciousness* itself. The ego as support of the predicative act therefore does not operate as the ego-cogito, that is, as the ego of a logically conceived consciousness and "fragment of the world"; rather, the transcendental ego belongs to the constituting operating consciousness, which means that it takes shape within the predicative operation. This operation is *thetic* because it simultaneously posits the thesis (position) of both Being *and* ego. Thus, for every signified transcendental object, there is a transcendental ego,

[8]Edmund Husserl, German philosopher (1859–1938).
[9]See Jakobson, p. 1041.
[10][Roudiez] See Jean Starobinski, *Les Mots sous les mots* (Paris: Gallimard, 1971).
[11][Kristeva] Edmund Husserl, *Logical Investigations,* J. N. Findlay, trans. (London: Routledge & Kegan Paul, 1970), pp. 276–277.
[12][Kristeva] Edmund Husserl, *Ideas: General Introduction to Pure Phenomenology,* W. R. Boyce Gibson, trans. (London: Collier-Macmillan, 1962), pp. 93–94 and 101.

both of which are givens by virtue of thetic operation—predication of judgment.

"Transcendental egology"[13] thus reformulates the question of the signifying act's subject: (1) the operating consciousness, through predication, simultaneously constitutes Being, the (transcendent) signified real object, and the ego (in so far as it is transcendental); the problematic of the sign is also bound up in this question; (2) even if intentionality, and with it, the judging consciousness, is already a given in material data and perceptions, as it "resembles" them (which allows us to say that the transcendental ego is always already in a way given), *in fact,* the ego constitutes itself only through the operating consciousness at the time of predication; the subject is merely the subject of predication, of judgment, of the sentence; (3) "belief" and "judgment" are closely interdependent though not identical: "The syntheses of belief (Glaubenssynthesen) find their 'expression' in the forms of stated meaning."[14]

Neither a historical individual nor a logically conceived consciousness, the subject is henceforth the operating thetic consciousness positing correlatively the transcendental Being and ego. Thus, Husserl makes clear that any linguistic act, insofar as it sets up a signified that can be communicated in a sentence (and there is no sign or signifying structure that is not already part of a sentence), is sustained by the transcendental ego.

It is perhaps not unimportant that the rigor of Judaism and the persecution it has been subjected to in our time underlie Husserl's extraordinarily firm elucidation of the transcendental ego, just as they are the foundation of the human sciences.

For the purposes of our discussion, we can draw two conclusions from this brief review:

1. It is impossible to treat problems of signification seriously, in linguistics or semiology, without including in these considerations *the subject thus formulated as operating consciousness.* This phenomenological conception of the speaking subject is made possible in modern linguistics by the introduction of logic into generative grammar and, in a much more lucid manner, through a linguistics (developing in France after Benveniste) which is attuned to the *subject of enunciation* and which includes in the latter's operating consciousness not only logical modalities, but also interlocutory relationships.

2. If it is true, consequently, that the question of signification and therefore of modern linguistics is dominated by

Husserl, the attempts to criticize or "deconstruct" phenomenology bear concurrently on Husserl, meaning, the still transcendental subject of enunciation, and linguistic methodology. These criticisms circumscribe the metaphysics inherent in the sciences of signification and therefore in the human sciences—an important epistemological task in itself. But they reveal their own shortcomings not so much, as some believe, in that they prevent serious, theoretical or scientific research, but in that such "deconstructions" refuse (through discrediting the signified and with it the transcendental ego) what constitutes one function of language though not the only one: to express meaning in a communicable sentence between speakers. This function harbors coherence (which is indeed transcendental) or, in other words, social identity. Let us first acknowledge, with Husserl, this thetic character of the signifying act, which establishes the transcendent object and the transcendental ego of communication (and consequently of sociability), before going beyond the Husserlian problematic to search for that which produces, shapes, and exceeds the operating consciousness (this will be our purpose when confronting poetic language). Without that acknowledgement, which is also that of the episteme underlying structuralism, any reflection on significance, by refusing its thetic character, will continually ignore its constraining, legislative, and socializing elements: under the impression that it is breaking down the metaphysics of the signified or the transcendental ego, such a reflection will become lodged in a negative theology that denies their limitations.

Finally, even when the researcher in the field, beginning with what is now a descriptive if not scientific perspective, thinks he has discovered givens that may escape the *unity* of the transcendental ego (because each identity would be as if flaked into a multiplicity of qualities or appurtenances, the discourse of knowledge that delivers this multiplied identity to us remains a prisoner of phenomenological reason for which the multiplicities, inasmuch as they signify, are givens of consciousness, predicates within the same eidetic unity: the unity of an object signified by and for a transcendental ego. In an interpretive undertaking for which there is no domain heterogeneous to meaning, all material diversities, as multiple attributes, revert to a real (transcendental) object. Even apparently psychoanalytic interpretations (relationship to parents, et cetera), from the moment they are posited by the structuring learning as particularities of the transcendental real object, are false multiplicities; deprived of what is heterogeneous to meaning, these multiplicities can only produce a plural identity—but an identity all the same, since it is eidetic, transcendental. Husserl therefore stands on the threshold not only of modern linguistics concerned with a

---

[13][Kristeva] Edmund Husserl, *Erste Philosophie,* VIII, in *Husserliana* (The Hague: Hrsg. von R. Boehm, 1956).
[14][Kristeva] Husserl, *Ideas,* p. 313.

subject of enunciation, but of any science of man as signified phenomenon, whose objecthood, even if multiple, is to be restored.

To the extent that poetic language operates with and communicates meaning, it also shares particularities of the signifying operations elucidated by Husserl (correlation between signified object and the transcendental ego, operating consciousness, which constitutes itself by predication—by syntax—as thetic: thesis of Being, thesis of the object, thesis of the ego). Meaning and signification, however, do not exhaust the poetic function. Therefore, the thetic predicative operation and its correlatives (signified object and transcendental ego), though valid for the signifying economy of poetic language, are only one of its *limits:* certainly constitutive, but not all-encompassing. While poetic language can indeed be studied through its meaning and signification (by revealing, depending on the method, either structures or process), such a study would, in the final analysis, amount to reducing it to the phenomenological perspective and, hence, failing to see what in the poetic function departs from the signified and the transcendental ego and makes of what is known as "literature" something other than knowledge: the very place where social code is destroyed and renewed, thus providing, as Artaud writes, "A release for the anguish of its time" by "animating, attracting, lowering onto its shoulders the wandering anger of a particular time for the discharge of its psychological evil-being."[15]

Consequently, one should begin by positing that there is within poetic language (and therefore, although in a less pronounced manner, within any language) a *heterogeneousness* to meaning and signification. This *heterogeneousness,* detected genetically in the first echolalias of infants as rhythms and intonations anterior to the first phonemes, morphemes, lexemes, and sentences; this heterogeneousness, which is later reactivated as rhythms, intonations, glossolalias in psychotic discourse, serving as ultimate support of the speaking subject threatened by the collapse of the signifying function; this heterogeneousness to signification operates through, despite, and in excess of it and produces in poetic language "musical" but also nonsense effects that destroy not only accepted beliefs and significations, but, in radical experiments, syntax itself, that guarantee of thetic consciousness (of the signified object and ego)—for example, carnivalesque discourse, Artaud, a number of texts by Mallarmé, certain Dadaist and Surrealist experiments. The notion of *heterogeneity* is indispensable, for though articulate,

precise, organized, and complying with constraints and rules (especially, like the rule of *repetition,* which articulates the units of a particular rhythm or intonation), this signifying disposition is not that of meaning or signification: no sign, no predication, no signified object and therefore no operating consciousness of a transcendental ego. We shall call this disposition *semiotic (le sémiotique),* meaning, according to the etymology of the Greek *sémeion* (σημεῖον), a distinctive mark, trace, index, the premonitory sign, the proof, engraved mark, imprint—in short, a *distinctiveness* admitting of an uncertain and indeterminate articulation because it does not yet refer (for young children) or no longer refers (in psychotic discourse) to a signified object for a thetic consciousness (this side of, or through, both object and consciousness). Plato's *Timaeus* speaks of a *chora* (χώρα), receptacle (ὑποδοχεῖον), unnamable, improbable, hybrid, anterior to naming, to the One, to the father, and consequently, maternally connoted to such an extent that it merits "not even the rank of syllable." One can describe more precisely than did philosophical intuition the particularities of this signifying disposition that I have just named semiotic—a term which quite clearly designates that we are dealing with a disposition that is definitely heterogeneous to meaning but always in sight of it or in either a negative or surplus relationship to it. Research I have recently undertaken on child language acquisition in the prephonological, one could say prepredicative stages, or anterior to the "mirror stage," as well as another concomitant study on particularities of psychotic discourse aim notably at describing as precisely as possible—with the help of, for example, modern phono-acoustics—these semiotic operations (rhythm, intonation) and their dependence vis-à-vis the body's drives observable through muscular contractions and the libidinal or sublimated cathexis that accompany vocalizations. It goes without saying that, concerning a *signifying practice,* that is, a socially communicable discourse like poetic language, this semiotic heterogeneity posited by theory is inseparable from what I shall call, to distinguish it from the latter, the *symbolic* function of significance. The symbolic *(le symbolique),* as opposed to the semiotic, is this inevitable attribute of meaning, sign, and the signified object for the consciousness of Husserl's transcendental ego. Language as social practice necessarily presupposes these two dispositions, though combined in different ways to constitute *types of discourse,* types of signifying practices. Scientific discourse, for example, aspiring to the status of metalanguage, tends to reduce as much as possible the semiotic component. On the contrary, the signifying economy of poetic language is specific in that the semiotic is not only a constraint as is the symbolic, but it tends to gain the upper hand at the expense of the thetic and

---

[15][Kristeva] Antonin Artaud, "L'Anarchie sociale de l'art," in *Oeuvres Complètes* (Paris: Gallimard), 8:287.

predicative constraints of the ego's judging consciousness. Thus in any poetic language, not only do the rhythmic constraints, for example, perform an organizing function that could go so far as to violate certain grammatical rules of a national language and often neglect the importance of an ideatory message, but in recent texts, these semiotic constraints (rhythm, phonic, vocalic timbres in Symbolist work, but also graphic disposition on the page) are accompanied by nonrecoverable syntactic elisions; it is impossible to reconstitute the particular elided syntactic category (object or verb), which makes the meaning of the utterance undecidable (for example, the nonrecoverable elisions in *Un Coup de Dés*).[16] However elided, attacked, or corrupted the symbolic function might be in poetic language, due to the impact of semiotic processes, the symbolic function nonetheless maintains its presence. It is for this reason that it is a language. First, it persists as an internal limit of this bipolar economy, since a multiple and sometimes even uncomprehensible signified is nevertheless communicated; secondly, it persists also because the semiotic processes themselves, far from being set adrift (as they would be in insane discourse), set up a new formal construct: a so-called new formal or ideological "writer's universe," the never-finished, undefined production of a new space of significance. Husserl's "thetic function" of the signifying act is thus re-assumed, but in different form: though poetic language unsettled the position of the signified and the transcendental ego, it nonetheless posits a thesis, not of a particular being or meaning, but of a signifying apparatus; it posits its own process as an undecidable process between sense and nonsense, between *language* and *rhythm* (in the sense of linkage that the word "rhythm" had for Aeschylus's *Prometheus* according to Heidegger's reading), between the symbolic and semiotic.

For a theory attuned to this kind of functioning, the language object itself appears quite differently than it would from a phenomenological perspective. Thus, a phoneme, as distinctive element of meaning, belongs to language as symbolic. But this same phoneme is involved in rhythmic, intonational repetitions; it thereby tends towards autonomy from meaning so as to maintain itself in a semiotic disposition near the instinctual drives' body; it is a sonorous distinctiveness, which therefore is no longer either a phoneme or a part of the symbolic system—one might say that its belonging to the set of the language is indefinite, between zero and one. Nevertheless, the set to which it thus belongs exists with this indefinition, with this fuzziness.

It is poetic language that awakens our attention to this undecidable character of any so-called natural language, a feature that univocal, rational, scientific discourse tends to hide—and this implies considerable consequences for its subject. The support of this signifying economy could not be the transcendental ego alone. If it is true that there would unavoidably be a speaking *subject* since the signifying set exists, it is nonetheless evident that this subject, in order to tally with its heterogeneity, must be, let us say, a questionable *subject-in-process*. It is of course Freud's theory of the unconscious that allows the apprehension of such a subject; for through the surgery it practiced in the operating consciousness of the transcendental ego, Freudian and Lacanian psychoanalysis did allow, not for (as certain simplifications would have it) a few typologies or structures that might accommodate the same phenomenological reason, but rather for heterogeneity, which, known as the unconscious, shapes the signifying function. In light of these statements, I shall now make a few remarks on the questionable subject-in-process of poetic language.

1. The semiotic activity, which introduces wandering or fuzziness into language and, *a fortiori,* into poetic language is, from a synchronic point of view, a mark of the workings of drives (appropriation/rejection, orality/anality, love/hate, life/death) and, from a diachronic point of view, stems from the archaisms of the semiotic body. Before recognizing itself as identical in a mirror and, consequently, as signifying, this body is dependent vis-à-vis the mother.[17] At the same time instinctual and maternal, semiotic processes prepare the future speaker for entrance into meaning and signification (the symbolic). But the symbolic (i.e., language as nomination, sign, and syntax) constitutes itself only by breaking with this anteriority, which is retrieved as "signifier," "primary processes," displacement and condensation, metaphor and metonomy, rhetorical figures—but which always remains subordinate—subjacent to the principal function of naming-predicating. Language as symbolic function constitutes itself at the cost of repressing instinctual drive and continuous relation to the mother. On the contrary, the unsettled and questionable subject of poetic language (for whom the word is never uniquely sign) maintains itself at the cost of reactivating this repressed instinctual, maternal element. If it is true that the prohibition of incest constitutes, at the same time, language as communicative code and women as exchange objects in order for a society to be established, *poetic language would be* for its questionable subject-in-process the *equivalent of incest:* it is within the economy

[16][Roudiez] See Kristeva, *La Révolution du langage poetique* (Paris: Seuil, 1974), pp. 274 ff.

[17]See Lacan, p. 898.

of signification itself that the questionable subject-in-process appropriates to itself this archaic, instinctual, and maternal territory; thus it simultaneously prevents the word from becoming mere sign and the mother from becoming an object like any other—forbidden. This passage into and through the forbidden, which constitutes the sign and is correlative to the prohibition of incest, is often explicit as such (Sade: "Unless he becomes his mother's lover from the day she has brought him into the world, let him not bother to write, for we shall not read him,"—*Idée sur les romans;* Artaud, identifying with his "daughters"; Joyce and his daughter at the end of *Finnegans Wake;* Céline who takes as pseudonym his grandmother's first name; and innumerable identifications with women, or dancers, that waver between fetishization and homosexuality). I stress this point for three reasons:

(a) To emphasize that the dominance of semiotic constraint in poetic language cannot be solely interpreted, as formalist poetics would have it, as a preoccupation with the "sign," or with the "signifier" at the expense of the "message"; rather, it is more deeply indicative of the instinctual drives' activity relative to the first structurations (constitution of the body as self) and identifications (with the mother).

(b) To elucidate the intrinsic connection between literature and breaking up social concord: because it utters incest, poetic language is linked with "evil"; "literature and evil" (I refer to a title by Georges Bataille) should be understood, beyond the resonances of Christian ethics, as the social body's self-defense against the discourse of incest as destroyer and generator of any language and sociality. This applies all the more as "great literature," which has mobilized unconsciousnesses for centuries, has nothing to do with the hypostasis of incest (a petty game of fetishists at the end of an era, priesthood of a would-be enigma—the forbidden mother); on the contrary, this incestuous relation, exploding in language, embracing it from top to bottom in such a *singular* fashion that it defies *generalizations,* still has this common feature in all outstanding cases: it presents itself as demystified, even disappointed, deprived of its hallowed function as support of the law, in order to become the cause of a permanent trial of the speaking subject, a cause of that agility, of that analytic "competency" that legend attributes to Ulysses.

(c) It is of course possible, as Lévi-Strauss pointed out to Dr. André Green, to ignore the mother-child relationship within a given anthropological vision of society; now, given not only the thematization of this relationship, but especially the mutations in the very economy of discourse attributable to it, one must, in discussing poetic language, consider what this presymbolic and trans-symbolic relationship to the

mother introduces as aimless wandering within the identity of the speaker and the economy of its very discourse. Moreover, this relationship of the speaker to the mother is probably one of the most important factors producing interplay within the structure of meaning as well as a questioning process of subject and history.

2. And yet, this reinstatement of maternal territory into the very economy of language does not lead its questioned subject-in-process to repudiate its symbolic disposition. Formulator—logothete, as Roland Barthes would say—the subject of poetic language continually but never definitely assumes the thetic function of naming, establishing meaning and signification, which the paternal function represents within reproductive relation. Son permanently at war with father, not in order to take his place, nor even to endure it, erased from reality, as a symbolic, divine menace and salvation in the manner of *Senatspräsident* Schreber. But rather, to signify what is untenable in the symbolic, nominal, paternal function. If symbolic and social cohesion are maintained by virtue of a sacrifice (which makes of a *soma* a sign towards an unnamable transcendence, so that only thus are signifying and social structures clinched even though they are ignorant of this sacrifice) and if the paternal function represents this sacrificial function, then it is not up to the poet to adjust to it. Fearing its rule but sufficiently aware of the legislation of language not to be able to turn away from this sacrificial-paternal function, he takes it by storm and from the flank. In *Maldoror,* Lautréamont struggles against the Omnipotent. After the death of his son Anatole, Mallarmé writes a *Tombeau,* thanks to which a book replaces not only the dead son, his own father, mother, and fiancée at the same time, but also hallowed humanism and the "instinct of heaven" itself. The most analytical of them all, the Marquis de Sade, gives up this battle with, or for, the symbolic legislation represented by the father, in order to attack the power represented by a woman, Madame de Montreuil, visible figurehead of a dynasty of matrons toward whom he usurps, through writing, the role of father and incestuous son; here, the transgression is carried out and the transsymbolic, transpaternal function of poetic language reaches its thematic end by staging a simultaneously impossible, sacrificial, and orgastic society—never one without the other.

Here we must clearly distinguish two positions: that of the rhetorician and that of the writer in the strongest sense of the word; that is, as Céline puts it, one who has "style." The rhetorician does not invent a language; fascinated by the symbolic function of paternal discourse, he *seduces* it in the Latin sense of the verb—he "leads it astray," inflicts it with a few anomalies generally taken from writers of the past, thus miming a father who remembers having been a son and even a daughter of his father, but not to the point of leaving cover. This is indeed what is happening to the discourse of contemporary philosophers, in France particularly, when, hemmed in by the breakthroughs in social sciences on the one hand, and social upheavals on the other, the philosopher begins performing literary tricks, thus arrogating to himself a power over imaginations: a power which, though minor in appearance, is more fetching than that of the transcendental consciousness. The stylist's adventure is totally different; he no longer needs to seduce the father by rhetorical affectations. As winner of the battle, he may even drop the name of the father to take a pseudonym (Céline signs with his grandmother's first name), and thus, in the place of the father, assume a different discourse; neither imaginary discourse of the self, nor discourse of transcendental knowledge, but a permanent go-between from one to the other, a pulsation of sign and rhythm, of consciousness and instinctual drive. "I am the father of my imaginative creations," writes Mallarmé at the birth of Geneviève. "I am my father, my mother, my son, and me," Artaud claims. Stylists all, they sound a dissonance within the thetic, paternal function of language.

3. Psychosis and fetishism represent the two abysses that threaten the unstable subject of poetic language, as twentieth-century literature has only too clearly demonstrated. As to *psychosis,* symbolic legality is wiped out in favor of arbitrariness of an instinctual drive without meaning and communication; panicking at the loss of all reference, the subject goes through fantasies of omnipotence or identification with a totalitarian leader. On the other hand, where *fetishism* is concerned, constantly dodging the paternal, sacrificial function produces an objectification of the pure signifier, more and more emptied of meaning—an insipid formalism. Nevertheless, far from thus becoming an unpleasant or negligible accident within the firm progress of symbolic process (which, in the footsteps of science, would eventually find signified elements for all signifiers, as rationalists believe), these borderline experiences, which contemporary poetic language has undergone, perhaps more dramatically than before or elsewhere, show not only that the Saussurian cleavage (signifier/signified) is forever unbridgeable, but also that it is reinforced by another, even more radical one between an instinctual, semioticizing body, heterogeneous to signification, and this very signification based on prohibition (of incest), sign, and thetic signification establishing signified object and transcendental ego. Through the permanent contradiction between these two dispositions (semiotic/symbolic), of which the internal setting off of the sign (signifier/signified) is merely a witness, poetic language, in its most disruptive form (unreadable for meaning, dangerous for the subject), shows the constraints of a civilization dominated by

transcendental rationality. Consequently, it is a means of overriding this constraint. And if in so doing it sometimes falls in with deeds brought about by the same rationality, as is, for example, the instinctual determination of fascism—demonstrated as such by Wilhelm Reich—poetic language is also there to forestall such translations into action.

This means that if poetic economy has always borne witness to crises and impossibilities of transcendental symbolics, in our time it is coupled with crises of social institutions (state, family, religion), and, more profoundly, a turning point in the relationship of man to meaning. Transcendental mastery over discourse is possible, but repressive; such a position is necessary, but only as a limit open to constant challenge; this relief with respect to repression—establishing meaning—is no longer possible under the incarnate appearance of a providential, historical, or even rationalist, humanist ego (in the manner of Renan), but through a *discordance* in the symbolic function and consequently within the identity of the transcendental ego itself: this is what the literary experience of our century intimates to theoretical reason, thereby taking its place with other phenomena of symbolic and social unrest (youth, drugs, women).

Without entering into a technical analysis of the economy specific to poetic language (an analysis too subtle and specious, considering the purpose of this specific paper), I shall extract from Céline, first, several procedures and, second, several themes, which illustrate the position of the unsettled, questionable subject-in-process of poetic language. I shall not do this without firmly underlining that these themes are not only inseparable from "style," but that they are produced by it; in other words, it is not necessary "to know" them, one could have heard them by simply listening to Céline's staccato, rhythmic discourse, stuffed with jargon and obscenity.

Thus, going beyond semantic themes and their distributions, one ought to examine the functioning of poetic language and its questionable subject-in-process, beginning with constitutive linguistic operations: syntax and semantics. Two phenomena, among others, will become the focus of our attention in Céline's writing: *sentential rhythms* and *obscene words.* These are of interest not only because they seem to constitute a particularity of his discourse, but also because, though they function differently, both of them involve constitutive operations of the judging consciousness (therefore of identity) by simultaneously perturbing its clarity and the designation of an object (objecthood). Moreover, if they constitute a network of constraints that is added to denotative signification, such a network has nothing to do with classic poeticness (rhythm, meter, conventional rhetorical figures) because it is drawn from the drives' register of a desiring body, both identifying with and rejecting a community (familial or folk). Therefore, even if the so-called poetic codes are not recognizable within poetic language, a constraint that I have termed semiotic functions in addition to the judging consciousness, provokes its lapses, or compensates for them; in so doing, it refers neither to a literary convention (like our poetic canons, contemporary with the major national epics and the constitution of nations themselves) nor even to the body *itself,* but rather, to a signifying disposition, pre- or transsymbolic, which fashions any judging consciousness so that any ego recognizes its crisis within it. It is a jubilant recognition that, in "modern" literature, replaces petty aesthetic pleasure.

Sentential rhythms. Beginning with *Death on the Installment Plan,* the sentence is condensed: not only does Céline avoid coordination and embeddings, but when different "object-phrases" are for example numerous and juxtaposed with a verb, they are separated by the characteristic "three dots." This procedure divides the sentence into its constitutive phrases; they thus tend to become independent of the central verb, to detach themselves from the sentence's own signification, and to acquire a meaning initially incomplete and consequently capable of taking on multiple connotations that no longer depend on the framework of the sentence, but on a free context (the entire book, but also, all the addenda of which the reader is capable). Here, there are no syntactic anomalies (as in the *Coup de Dés* or the glossolalias of Artaud). The predicative thesis, constitutive of the judging consciousness, is maintained. By using three dots to space the phrases making up a sentence, thus giving them rhythm, he causes connotation to rush through a predication that has been striated in that manner; the denotated object of the utterance, the transcendental object, loses its clear contours. The elided object in the sentence relates to a hesitation (if not an erasure) of the *real object* for the speaking subject. That literature is witness to this kind of deception involving the object (object of love or transcendental object); that the existence of the object is more than fleeting and indeed impossible: this is what Céline's rhythms and syntactic elisions have recently evidenced within the stern humor of an experiment and with all its implications for the subject. This is also true of Beckett, whose recent play, *Not I,* spoken by a dying woman, sets forth in elided sentences and floating phrases the impossibility of God's existence for a speaking subject lacking any object of signification and/or love. Moreover, beyond and with connotation, with the blurred or erased object, there flows through meaning this "emotion" of which Céline speaks—the nonsemanticized instinctual drive that precedes and exceeds meaning.

The exclamation marks alternating with three dots even more categorically point to this surge of instinctual drive: a panting, a breathlessness, an acceleration of verbal utterance, concerned not so much with finally reaching a global summing up of the world's meaning, as, to the contrary, with revealing, within the interstices of predication, the rhythm of a drive that remains forever unsatisfied—in the vacancy of judging consciousness and sign—because it could not find an other (an addressee) so as to obtain meaning in this exchange. We must also listen to Céline, Artaud, or Joyce, and read their texts in order to understand that the aim of this practice, which reaches us as a language, is, through the signification of the nevertheless transmitted message, not only to impose a music, a rhythm—that is, a polyphony—but also to wipe out sense through nonsense and laughter. This is a difficult operation that obliges the reader not so much to combine significations as to shatter his own judging consciousness in order to grant passage through it to this rhythmic drive constituted by repression and, once filtered by language and its meaning, experienced as jouissance. Could the resistance against modern literature be evidence of an obsession with meaning, of an unfitness for such jouissance?

Obscene words. Semantically speaking, these pivotal words in the Célinian lexicon exercise a *desemanticization* function analogous to the fragmentation of syntax by rhythm. Far from referring, as do all signs, to an object exterior to discourse and identifiable as such by consciousness, the obscene word is the minimal mark of a situation of desire where the identity of the signifying subject, if not destroyed, is exceeded by a conflict of instinctual drives linking one subject to another. There is nothing better than an obscene word for perceiving the limits of a phenomenological linguistics faced with the heterogeneous and complex architectonics of significance. The obscene word, lacking an objective referent, is also the contrary of an autonym—which involves the function of a word or utterance as sign; the obscene word mobilizes the signifying resources of the subject, permitting it to cross through the membrane of meaning where consciousness holds it, connecting it to gesturality, kinesthesia, the drives' body, the movement of rejection and appropriation of the other. Then, it is neither object, transcendental signified, nor signifier available to a neutralized consciousness: around the object denoted by the obscene word, and that object provides a scanty delineation, more than a simple context asserts itself—the drama of a questioning process heterogeneous to the meaning that precedes and exceeds it. Childrens' counting-out rhymes, or what one calls the "obscene folklore of children," utilize the same rhythmic and semantic resources; they maintain the subject close to these jubilatory dramas that run athwart the repression that a univocal, increasingly pure signifier vainly attempts to impose upon the subject. By reconstituting them, and this on the very level of language, literature achieves its cathartic effects.

Several themes in Céline bring to light the relationships of force, at first within the family triangle, and then in contemporary society, that produce, promote, and accompany the particularities of poetic language to which I have just referred.

In *Death on the Installment Plan,* the most "familial" of Céline's writings, we find a paternal figure, Auguste: a man "of instruction," "a mind," sullen, a prohibitor, prone to scandal, full of obsessional habits like, for example, cleaning the flagstones in front of his shop. His anger explodes spectacularly once, when he shuts himself up in the basement and shoots his pistol for hours, not without explaining in the face of general disapproval, "I have my conscience on my side," just before falling ill. "My mother wrapped the weapon in several layers of newspaper and then in a cashmere shawl . . . 'Come, child . . . come!' she said when we were alone [. . .] We threw the package in the drink."[18]

Here is an imposing and menacing father, strongly emphasizing the enviable necessity of his position, but spoiling it by his derisive fury: undermined power whose weapon one could only take away in order to engulf it at the end of a journey between mother and son.

In an interview, Céline compares himself to a "society woman" who braves the nevertheless maintained family prohibition, and who has the right to her own desire, "a choice in a drawing room": "the whore's trade doesn't interest me"; before defining himself, at the end: "I am the son of a woman who restored old lace . . . [I am] one of those rare men who knows how to distinguish batiste from valencienne . . . I do not need to be taught. I know it."

This fragile delicacy, heritage of the mother, supports the language—or if you wish, the identity—of him who unseated what Céline calls the "heaviness" of men, of fathers, in order to flee it. The threads of instinctual drive, exceeding the law of the paternal word's own mastery, are nonetheless woven with scrupulous precision. One must therefore conceive of another disposition of the law, through signified and signifying identity and confronting the semiotic network: a disposition closer to the Greek *gnomon* ("one that knows," "carpenter's square") than to the Latin *lex,* which necessarily implies the act of logical and legal judgment. A device, then, a regulated discrimination, weaves the semiotic network of instinctual drives; if it thus fails to conform to signifying identity, it nevertheless constitutes another identity closer to repressed and gnomic archaisms, susceptible of a psychosis-inducing explosion, where we decipher the relationship of the speaker to a desiring and desired mother.

In another interview, this maternal reference to old lacework is explicitly thought of as an archeology of the word: "No! In the beginning was emotion. The Word came next to replace emotion as the trot replaces the gallop [. . .] They pulled man out of emotive poetry in order to plunge him into dialectics, that is, into gibberish, right?" Anyway, what is *Rigodon* if not a popular dance which obliges language to bow to the rhythm of its emotion.

A speech thus slatted by instinctual drive—Diderot would have said "musicated"—could not describe, narrate, or theatricalize "objects": by its composition and signification it also goes beyond the accepted categories of lyric, epic, dramatic, or tragic. The last writings of Céline, plugged in live to an era of war, death, and genocide, are what he calls in *North,* "the vivisection of the wounded," "the circus," "the three hundred years before Christ."

While members of the Resistance sing in alexandrine verse, it is Céline's language that records not only the institutional but also the profoundly symbolic jolt involving meaning and the identity of transcendental reason; fascism inflicted this jolt on our universe and the human sciences have hardly begun to figure out its consequences. I am saying that this literary discourse enunciates through its formal decentering, more apparent in Artaud's glossolalias, but also through the rhythms and themes of violence in Céline, better than anything else, the faltering of transcendental consciousness: this does not mean that such a discourse is aware of such a faltering or interprets it. As proof, writing that pretends to agree with "circus" and "vivisection" will nonetheless find its idols, even if only provisional; though dissolved in laughter and dominant non-sense, they are nevertheless posited as idols in Hitlerian ideology. A reading of any one of Céline's anti-semitic tracts is sufficient to show the crudely exhibited phantasms of an analysand struggling against a desired and frustrating, castrating, and sodomizing father; sufficient also to understand that it is not enough to allow what is repressed by the symbolic structure to emerge in a "musicated" language to avoid its traps. Rather, we must in addition dissolve its sexual determinations. Unless poetic work can be linked to analytical interpretation, the discourse that undermines the judging consciousness and releases its repressed instinctual drive as rhythm always turns out to be at fault from the viewpoint of an ethic that remains with the transcendental ego—whatever joys or negations might exist in Spinoza's or Hegel's.

---

[18][Kristeva] Louis-Ferdinand Céline, *Death on the Installment Plan,* Ralph Manheim, trans. (New York: New Directions, 1966), p. 78.

Since at least Hölderlin, poetic language has deserted beauty and meaning to become a laboratory where, facing philosophy, knowledge, and the transcendental ego of all signification, the impossibility of a signified or signifying identity is being sustained. If we took this venture seriously—if we could hear the burst of black laughter it hurls at all attempts to master the human situation, to master language by language—we would be forced to reexamine "literary history," to rediscover beneath rhetoric and poetics its unchanging but always different polemic with the symbolic function. We could not avoid wondering about the possibility, or simultaneously, the legitimacy of a theoretical discourse on this practice of language whose stakes are precisely to render impossible the transcendental bounding that supports the discourse of knowledge.

Faced with this poetic language that defies knowledge, many of us are rather tempted to leave our shelter to deal with literature only by miming its meanderings, rather than by positing it as an object of knowledge. We let ourselves be taken in by this mimeticism: fictional, para-philosophical, para-scientific writings. It is probably necessary to be a woman (ultimate guarantee of sociality beyond the wreckage of the paternal symbolic function, as well as the inexhaustible generator of its renewal, of its expansion) not to renounce theoretical reason but to compel it to increase its power by giving it an object beyond its limits. Such a position, it seems to me, provides a possible basis for a theory of signification, which, confronted with poetic language, could not in any way account for it, but would rather use it as an indication of what is heterogeneous to meaning (to sign and predication): instinctual economies, always and at the same time open to bio-physiological sociohistorical constraints.

This kind of heterogeneous economy and its questionable subject-in-process thus calls for a linguistics other than the one descended from the phenomenological heavens; a linguistics capable, within its language object, of accounting for a nonetheless articulated *instinctual drive,* across and through the constitutive and insurmountable frontier of *meaning.* This instinctual drive, however, located in the matrix of the sign, refers back to an instinctual body (to which psychoanalysis has turned its attention), which ciphers the language with rhythmic, intonational, and other arrangements, nonreducible to the position of the transcendental ego even though always within sight of its thesis.

The development of this theory of signification is in itself regulated by Husserlian precepts, because it inevitably makes an *object* even of that which departs from meaning. But, even though abetting the law of signifying structure as well as of all sociality, this expanded theory of signification cannot give itself new objects except by positing itself as nonuniversal: that is, by presupposing that a questionable subject-in-process exists in an economy of discourse other than that of thetic consciousness. And this requires that subjects of the theory must be themselves subjects in infinite analysis; this is what Husserl could not imagine, what Céline could not know, but what a woman, among others, can finally admit, aware as she is of the inanity of Being.

When it avoids the risks that lie in wait for it, literary experience remains nevertheless something other than this analytical theory, which it never stops challenging. Against knowing thought, poetic language pursues an effect of *singular truth,* and thus accomplishes, perhaps, for the modern community, this solitary practice that the materialists of antiquity unsuccessfully championed against the ascendance of theoretical reason.

Paul de Man

1919–1983

Paul de Man's version of deconstruction is based on two related principles: first, the incompatibility of language and nature, and, second, the incompatibility with respect to interpretive ends of grammatical and rhetorical structures. In his earlier work, particularly the influential essay "The Rhetoric of Temporality," it is the first incompatibility that causes him to valorize allegory over symbol, principally on the ground that the symbol holds out the false hope of compatibility, while allegory admits its arbitrariness. This insistence on severity continues in the later "Semiology and Rhetoric" in which it is the incompatibility of grammatical and rhetorical structures that creates always an *aporia* or unresolvable contradiction in any text. If with respect to a text one gives the primacy to its rhetoric (or tropological structure) the result will be indeterminancy of meaning. If one gives the primacy to grammatical structure the discovery will be a "false pretense" to identity. If one is to read rigorously one primacy must give way to the other in a regress of readings. De Man's view is that "a literary text simultaneously asserts and denies the authority of its own rhetorical mode." But a literary text is not different in kind from other texts. It is different only in "the economy of its articulation." That economy causes it to be at once the most rigorous and most unreliable of texts.

De Man's position can be described as one of skepticism, with language the seductive culprit and literature the culprit nevertheless praiseworthy for its openness about its own unreliability. Finally, there is the question of reading, of which there are two kinds, one "aesthetically aware" and the other "rhetorically" so. Here, though calling each kind equally compelling, de Man clearly favors the rhetorically aware, which is to say the one that is skeptical of what tropes seductively achieve.

Certainly de Man's reading of Jacques Derrida strongly influenced him, but he was already on his own road to deconstruction from his reading of Nietzsche and his early interest in forms of "demystification." His later work bears traces of his early existential notions.

De Man's books are *Blindness and Insight: Essays in the Rhetoric of Contemporary Criticism* (1971, rev. 1983), *Allegories of Reading: Figural Language in Rousseau, Nietzsche, Rilke, and Proust* (1979), *The Rhetoric of Romanticism* (1985), *The Resistance to Theory* (1986), and *Aesthetic Ideology* (1990). Also published in translation are the early journalistic articles (1989). See Frank Lentricchia, *After the New Criticism* (1980); Stanley Corngold, "Error in Paul de Man" in *The Yale Critics,* J. Arac, W. Godzich, and W. Martin, eds., (1983); Christopher Norris, *Deconstruction: Theory and Practice* (1982); *The Lesson of Paul de Man* (Yale French Studies, 69, 1985); Jacques Derrida, *Memoires: For Paul de Man* (1986); Stephen W. Melville, *Philosophy Beside Itself* (1986); Christopher Norris, *Paul de Man: Deconstruction and the Critique of Aesthetic Ideology* (1988); and L. Waters and W. Godzich, eds., *Reading de Man Reading* (1989).

Semiology and Rhetoric

To judge from various recent publications, the spirit of the times is not blowing in the direction of formalist and intrinsic criticism. We may no longer be hearing too much about relevance but we keep hearing a great deal about reference, about the nonverbal "outside" to which language refers, by which it is conditioned and upon which it acts. The stress falls not so much on the fictional status of literature—a property now perhaps somewhat too easily taken for granted—but on the interplay between these fictions and categories that are said to partake of reality, such as the self, man, society, "the artist, his culture and the human community," as one critic puts it. Hence the emphasis on hybrid texts considered to be partly literary and partly referential, on popular fictions deliberately aimed towards social and psychological gratification, on literary autobiography as a key to the understanding of the self, and so on. We speak as if, with the problems of literary form resolved once and forever, and with the techniques of structural analysis refined to near-perfection, we could now move "beyond formalism" towards the questions that really interest us and reap, at last, the fruits of the ascetic concentration on techniques that prepared us for this decisive step. With the internal law and order of literature well policed, we can now confidently devote ourselves to the foreign affairs, the external politics of literature. Not only do we feel able to do so, but we owe it to ourselves to take this step: our moral conscience would not allow us to do otherwise. Behind the assurance that valid interpretation is possible, behind the recent interest in writing and reading as potentially effective public speech acts, stands a highly respectable moral imperative that strives to reconcile the internal, formal, private structures of literary language with their external, referential, and public effects.

I want, for the moment, to consider briefly this tendency in itself, as an undeniable and recurrent historical fact, without regard for its truth or falseness or for its value as desirable or pernicious. It is a fact that this sort of thing happens, again and again, in literary studies. On the one hand, literature cannot merely be received as a definite unit of referential meaning that can be decoded without leaving a residue. The code is unusually conspicuous, complex, and enigmatic; it attracts an inordinate amount of attention to itself, and this attention has to acquire the rigor of a method. The structural moment of concentration on the code for its own sake cannot be avoided, and literature necessarily breeds its own formalism. Technical innovations in the methodical study of literature only occur when this kind of attention predominates. It can legitimately be said, for example, that, from a technical point of view, very little has happened in American criticism since the innovative works of New Criticism. There certainly have been numerous excellent books of criticism since, but in none of them have the techniques of description and interpretation evolved beyond the techniques of close reading established in the thirties and forties. Formalism, it seems, is an all-absorbing and tyrannical muse; the hope that one can be at the same time technically original and discursively eloquent is not borne out by the history of literary criticism.

On the other hand—and this is the real mystery—no literary formalism, no matter how accurate and enriching in its analytic powers, is ever allowed to come into being without seeming reductive. When form is considered to be the external trappings of literary meaning or content, it seems superficial and expendable. The development of intrinsic, formalist criticism in the twentieth century has changed this mode: form is now a solipsistic category of self-reflection, and the referential meaning is said to be extrinsic. The polarities of inside and outside have been reversed, but they are still the same polarities that are at play: internal meaning has become outside reference, and the outer form has become the intrinsic structure. A new version of reductiveness at once follows this reversal: formalism nowadays is mostly described in an imagery of imprisonment and claustrophobia: the "prison house of language," "the impasse of formalist criticism," etc. Like the grandmother in Proust's novel ceaselessly driving the young Marcel out into the garden, away from the unhealthy inwardness of his closeted reading, critics cry out for the fresh air of referential meaning. Thus, with the structure of the code so opaque, but the meaning so anxious to blot out the obstacle of form, no wonder that the reconciliation of form and meaning would be so attractive. The attraction of reconciliation is the elective breeding-ground of false models and metaphors; it accounts for the metaphorical model of literature as a kind of box that separates an inside from an outside, and the reader or critic as the person who opens the lid in order to release in the open what was secreted but inaccessible inside. It matters little whether we call the inside of the box the content or the form, the outside the meaning or the appearance. The recurrent debate opposing intrinsic to extrinsic criticism stands under the aegis of an inside /outside metaphor that is never being seriously questioned.

Metaphors are much more tenacious than facts, and I certainly don't expect to dislodge this age-old model in one short try. I merely wish to speculate on a different set of

SEMIOLOGY AND RHETORIC. *Semiology and Rhetoric* is reprinted from *Allegories of Reading: Figural Language in Rousseau, Nietzsche, Rilke, and Proust,* published in 1979 by Yale University Press. It is reprinted by permission of the editor of *Diacritics,* where it first appeared in 1973.

terms, perhaps less simple in their differential relationships than the strictly polar, binary opposition between inside and outside and therefore less likely to enter into the easy play of chiasmic reversals. I derive these terms (which are as old as the hills) pragmatically from the observation of developments and debates in recent critical methodology.

One of the most controversial among these developments coincides with a new approach to poetics or, as it is called in Germany, poetology, as a branch of general semiotics. In France, a semiology of literature comes about as the outcome of the long-deferred but all the more explosive encounter of the nimble French literary mind with the category of form. Semiology, as opposed to semantics, is the science or study of signs as signifiers; it does not ask what words mean but how they mean. Unlike American New Criticism, which derived the internalization of form from the practice of highly self-conscious modern writers, French semiology turned to linguistics for its model and adopted Saussure and Jakobson rather than Valéry or Proust for its masters. By an awareness of the arbitrariness of the sign (Saussure)[1] and of literature as an autotelic statement "focused on the way it is expressed" (Jakobson)[2] the entire question of meaning can be bracketed, thus freeing the critical discourse from the debilitating burden of paraphrase. The demystifying power of semiology, within the context of French historical and thematic criticism, has been considerable. It demonstrated that the perception of the literary dimensions of language is largely obscured if one submits uncritically to the authority of reference. It also revealed how tenaciously this authority continues to assert itself in a variety of disguises, ranging from the crudest ideology to the most refined forms of aesthetic and ethical judgment. It especially explodes the myth of semantic correspondence between sign and referent, the wishful hope of having it both ways, of being, to paraphrase Marx in the German Ideology, a formalist critic in the morning and a communal moralist in the afternoon, of serving both the technique of form and the substance of meaning. The results, in the practice of French criticism, have been as fruitful as they are irreversible. Perhaps for the first time since the late eighteenth century, French critics can come at least somewhat closer to the kind of linguistic awareness that never ceased to be operative in its poets and novelists and that forced all of them, including Sainte Beuve, to write their main works "contre Sainte Beuve."[3] The distance was never so considerable in England and the United States, which

does not mean, however, that we may be able, in this country, to dispense altogether with some preventative semiological hygiene.

One of the most striking characteristics of literary semiology as it is practiced today, in France and elsewhere, is the use of grammatical (especially syntactical) structures conjointly with rhetorical structures, without apparent awareness of a possible discrepancy between them. In their literary analyses, Barthes, Genette, Todorov, Greimas, and their disciples all simplify and regress from Jakobson in letting grammar and rhetoric function in perfect continuity, and in passing from grammatical to rhetorical structures without difficulty or interruption. Indeed, as the study of grammatical structures is refined in contemporary theories of generative, transformational, and distributive grammar, the study of tropes and of figures (which is how the term *rhetoric* is used here, and not in the derived sense of comment or of eloquence or persuasion) becomes a mere extension of grammatical models, a particular subset of syntactical relations. In the recent *Dictionnaire encyclopédique des sciences du langage,* Ducrot and Todorov write that rhetoric has always been satisfied with a paradigmatic view over words (words substituting for each other), without questioning their syntagmatic relationship (the contiguity of words to each other). There ought to be another perspective, complementary to the first, in which metaphor, for example, would not be defined as a substitution but as a particular type of combination. Research inspired by linguistics or, more narrowly, by syntactical studies, has begun to reveal this possibility—but it remains to be explored. Todorov, who calls one of his books a *Grammar of the Decameron,* rightly thinks of his own work and that of his associates as first explorations in the elaboration of a systematic grammar of literary modes, genres, and also of literary figures. Perhaps the most perceptive work to come out of this school, Genette's studies of figural modes, can be shown to be assimilations of rhetorical transformations or combinations of syntactical, grammatical patterns. Thus a recent study, now printed in *Figures III* and entitled *Metaphor and Metonymy in Proust,* shows the combined presence, in a wide and astute selection of passages, of paradigmatic, metaphorical figures with syntagmatic, metonymic structures. The combination of both is treated descriptively and nondialectically without considering the possibility of logical tensions.

One can ask whether this reduction of figure to grammar is legitimate. The existence of grammatical structures, within and beyond the unit of the sentence, in literary texts is undeniable, and their description and classification are indispensable. The question remains if and how figures of rhetoric can be included in such a taxonomy. This question

---

[1] See p. 717.
[2] See p. 1041.
[3] See p. 567.

is at the core of the debate going on, in a wide variety of apparently unrelated forms, in contemporary poetics. But the historical picture of contemporary criticism is too confused to make the mapping out of such a topography a useful exercise. Not only are these questions mixed in and mixed up within particular groups or local trends, but they are often co-present, without apparent contradiction, within the work of a single author.

Neither is the theory of the question suitable for quick expository treatment. To distinguish the epistemology of grammar from the epistemology of rhetoric is a redoubtable task. On an entirely naïve level, we tend to conceive of grammatical systems as tending towards universality and as simply generative, i.e., as capable of deriving an infinity of versions from a single model (that may govern transformations as well as derivations) without the intervention of another model that would upset the first. We therefore think of the relationship between grammar and logic, the passage from grammar to propositions, as being relatively unproblematic; no true propositions are conceivable in the absence of grammatical consistency or of controlled deviation from a system of consistency no matter how complex. Grammar and logic stand to each other in a dyadic relationship of unsubverted support. In a logic of acts rather than of statements, as in Austin's theory of speech acts, that has had such a strong influence on recent American work in literary semiology, it is also possible to move between speech acts and grammar without difficulty. The performance of what is called illocutionary acts such as ordering, questioning, denying, assuming, etc., within the language is congruent with the grammatical structures of syntax in the corresponding imperative, interrogative, negative, optative sentences. "The rules for illocutionary acts," writes Richard Ohmann in a recent paper, "determine whether performance of a given act is well-executed, in just the same way as *grammatical* rules determine whether the product of a locutionary act—a sentence—is well formed. . . . But whereas the rules of grammar concern the relationships among sound, syntax, and meaning, the rules of illocutionary acts concern relationships among people."[4] And since rhetoric is then conceived exclusively as persuasion, as actual action upon others (and not as an intralinguistic figure or trope), the continuity between the illocutionary realm of grammar and the perlocutionary realm of rhetoric is self-evident. It becomes the basis for a new rhetoric that, exactly as is the case for Todorov and Genette, would also be a new grammar.

Without engaging the substance of the question, it can be pointed out, without having to go beyond recent and American examples, and without calling upon the strength of an age-old tradition, that the continuity here assumed between grammar and rhetoric is not borne out by theoretical and philosophical speculation. Kenneth Burke mentions *deflection* (which he compares structurally to Freudian displacement), defined as "any slight bias or even unintended error," as the rhetorical basis of language, and deflection is then conceived as a dialectical subversion of the consistent link between sign and meaning that operates within grammatical patterns; hence Burke's well-known insistence on the distinction between grammar and rhetoric.[5] Charles Sanders Peirce, who, with Nietzsche and Saussure, laid the philosophical foundation for modern semiology, stressed the distinction between grammar and rhetoric in his celebrated and so suggestively unfathomable definition of the sign.[6] He insists, as is well known, on the necessary presence of a third element, called the interpretant, within any relationship that the sign entertains with its object. The sign is to be interpreted if we are to understand the idea it is to convey, and this is so because the sign is not the thing but a meaning derived from the thing by a process here called representation that is not simply generative, i.e., dependent on a univocal origin. The interpretation of the sign is not, for Peirce, a meaning but another sign; it is a reading, not a decodage, and this reading has, in its turn, to be interpreted into another sign, and so on *ad infinitum*. Peirce calls this process by means of which one sign gives birth to another pure rhetoric, as distinguished from pure grammar, which postulates the possibility of unproblematic, dyadic meaning, and pure logic, which postulates the possibility of the universal truth of meanings. Only if the sign engendered meaning in the same way that the object engenders the sign, that is, by representation, would there be no need to distinguish between grammar and rhetoric.

These remarks should indicate at least the existence and the difficulty of the question, a difficulty which puts its concise theoretical exposition beyond my powers. I must retreat therefore into a pragmatic discourse and try to illustrate the tension between grammar and rhetoric in a few specific textual examples. Let me begin by considering what is perhaps the most commonly known instance of an apparent symbiosis between a grammatical and a rhetorical structure, the so-called rhetorical question, in which the figure is conveyed

---

[4][de Man] "Speech, Literature, and the Space in Between," *New Literary History* 4 (Autumn 1972):50.

[5]Kenneth Burke, *A Grammar of Motives* (1945) and *A Rhetoric of Motives* (1950).

[6]Charles Sanders Peirce, American philosopher (1838–1914).

directly by means of a syntactical device. I take the first example from the sub-literature of the mass media; asked by his wife whether he wants to have his bowling shoes laced over or laced under, Archie Bunker answers with a question "What's the difference?" Being a reader of sublime simplicity, his wife replies by patiently explaining the difference between lacing over and lacing under, whatever this may be, but provokes only ire. "What's the difference" did not ask for difference but means instead "I don't give a damn what the difference is." The same grammatical pattern engenders two meanings that are mutually exclusive: the literal meaning asks for the concept (difference) whose existence is denied by the figurative meaning. As long as we are talking about bowling shoes, the consequences are relatively trivial; Archie Bunker, who is a great believer in the authority of origins (as long, of course, as they are the right origins) muddles along in a world where literal and figurative meanings get in each other's way, though not without discomforts. But suppose that it is a *de*-bunker rather than a "Bunker," and a de-bunker of the arche (or origin), an archie Debunker such as Nietzsche or Jacques Derrida[7] for instance, who asks the question "What is the Difference"—and we cannot even tell from his grammar whether he "really" wants to know "what" difference is or is just telling us that we shouldn't even try to find out. Confronted with the question of the difference between grammar and rhetoric, grammar allows us to ask the question, but the sentence by means of which we ask it may deny the very possibility of asking. For what is the use of asking, I ask, when we cannot even authoritatively decide whether a question asks or doesn't ask?

The point is as follows. A perfectly clear syntactical paradigm (the question) engenders a sentence that has at least two meanings, of which the one asserts and the other denies its own illocutionary mode. It is not so that there are simply two meanings, one literal and the other figural, and that we have to decide which one of these meanings is the right one in this particular situation. The confusion can only be cleared up by the intervention of an extra-textual intention, such as Archie Bunker putting his wife straight; but the very anger he displays is indicative of more than impatience; it reveals his despair when confronted with a structure of linguistic meaning that he cannot control and that holds the discouraging prospect of an infinity of similar future confusions, all of them potentially catastrophic in their consequences. Nor is this intervention really a part of the mini-text constituted by the figure which holds our attention only as long as it remains suspended and unresolved. I follow the usage of common speech in calling this semiological

enigma "rhetorical." The grammatical model of the question becomes rhetorical not when we have, on the one hand, a literal meaning and on the other hand a figural meaning, but when it is impossible to decide by grammatical or other linguistic devices which of the two meanings (that can be entirely incompatible) prevails. Rhetoric radically suspends logic and opens up vertiginous possibilities of referential aberration. And although it would perhaps be somewhat more remote from common usage, I would not hesitate to equate the rhetorical, figural potentiality of language with literature itself. I could point to a great number of antecedents to this equation of literature with figure; the most recent reference would be to Monroe Beardsley's insistence in his contribution to the *Essays* to honor William Wimsatt, that literary language is characterized by being "distinctly above the norm in ratio of implicit [or, I would say rhetorical] to explicit meaning."[8]

Let me pursue the matter of the rhetorical question through one more example. Yeats's poem "Among School Children" ends with the famous line: "How can we know the dancer from the dance?" Although there are some revealing inconsistencies within the commentaries, the line is usually interpreted as stating, with the increased emphasis of a rhetorical device, the potential unity between form and experience, between creator and creation. It could be said that it denies the discrepancy between the sign and the referent from which we started out. Many elements in the imagery and the dramatic development of the poem strengthen this traditional reading; without having to look any further than the immediately preceding lines, one finds powerful and consecrated images of the continuity from part to whole that makes synecdoche into the most seductive of metaphors: the organic beauty of the tree, stated in the parallel syntax of a similar rhetorical question, or the convergence, in the dance, of erotic desire with musical form:

> O chestnut-tree, great-rooted blossomer,
> Are you the leaf, the blossom or the bole?
> O body swayed to music, O brightening
>   glance,
> How can we know the dancer from the
>   dance?

A more extended reading, always assuming that the final line is to be read as a rhetorical question, reveals that the thematic and rhetorical grammar of the poem yields a consistent reading that extends from the first line to the last and that can

---

[7]See p. 628 and p. 1116.

[8][de Man] "The Concept of Literature" in *Literature Theory and Structure: Essays in Honor of W. K. Wimsatt*, eds. F. Brady, J. Palmer, and M. Price (New Haven, 1973), p. 37.

account for all the details in the text. It is equally possible, however, to read the last line literally rather than figuratively, as asking with some urgency the question we asked earlier within the context of contemporary criticism; *not* that sign and referent are so exquisitely fitted to each other that all difference between them is at times blotted out but, rather, since the two essentially different elements, sign and meaning, are so intricately intertwined in the imagined "presence" that the poem addresses, how can we possibly make the distinctions that would shelter us from the error of identifying what cannot be identified? The clumsiness of the paraphrase reveals that it is not necessarily the literal reading which is simpler than the figurative one, as was the case in our first example; here, the figural reading, which assumes the question to be rhetorical, is perhaps naïve, whereas the literal reading leads to greater complication of theme and statement. For it turns out that the entire scheme set up by the first reading can be undermined, or deconstructed, in the terms of the second, in which the final line is read literally as meaning that, since the dancer and the dance are not the same, it might be useful, perhaps even desperately necessary—for the question can be given a ring of urgency, "Please tell me, how *can* I know the dancer from the dance"—to tell them apart. But this will replace the reading of each symbolic detail by a divergent interpretation. The oneness of trunk, leaf, and blossom, for example, that would have appealed to Goethe, would find itself replaced by the much less reassuring Tree of Life from the Mabinogion that appears in the poem "Vacillation," in which the fiery blossom and the earthly leaf are held together, as well as apart, by the crucified and castrated God Attis, of whose body it can hardly be said that it is "not bruised to pleasure the soul." This hint should suffice to suggest that two entirely coherent but entirely incompatible readings can be made to hinge on one line, whose grammatical structure is devoid of ambiguity, but whose rhetorical mode turns the mood as well as the mode of the entire poem upside down. Neither can we say, as was already the case in the first example, that the poem simply has two meanings that exist side by side. The two readings have to engage each other in direct confrontation, for the one reading is precisely the error denounced by the other and has to be undone by it. Nor can we in any way make a valid decision as to which of the readings can be given priority over the other; none can exist in the other's absence. There can be no dance without a dancer, no sign without a referent. On the other hand, the authority of the meaning engendered by the grammatical structure is fully obscured by the duplicity of a figure that cries out for the differentiation that it conceals.

Yeats's poem is not explicitly "about" rhetorical questions but about images or metaphors, and about the possibility of convergence between experiences of consciousness such as memory or emotions—what the poem calls passion, piety, and affection—and entities accessible to the senses such as bodies, persons, or icons. We return to the inside / outside model from which we started out and which the poem puts into question by means of a syntactical device (the question) made to operate on a grammatical as well as on a rhetorical level. The couple grammar/rhetoric, certainly not a binary opposition since they in no way exclude each other, disrupts and confuses the neat antithesis of the inside / outside pattern. We can transfer this scheme to the act of reading and interpretation. By reading we get, as we say, *inside* a text that was first something alien to us and which we now make our own by an act of understanding. But this understanding becomes at once the representation of an extratextual meaning; in Austin's terms, the illocutionary speech act becomes a perlocutionary actual act—in Frege's terms, *Bedeutung* becomes *Sinn.*[9] Our recurrent question is whether this transformation is semantically controlled along grammatical or along rhetorical lines. Does the metaphor of reading really unite outer meaning with inner understanding, action with reflection, into one single totality? The assertion is powerfully and suggestively made in a passage from Proust that describes the experience of reading as such a union. It describes the young Marcel, near the beginning of Combray, hiding in the closed space of his room in order to read. The example differs from the earlier ones in that we are not dealing with a grammatical structure that also functions rhetorically but have instead the representation, the dramatization, in terms of the experience of a subject, of a rhetorical structure—just as, in many other passages, Proust dramatizes tropes by means of landscapes or descriptions of objects. The figure here dramatized is that of metaphor, an inside/ outside correspondence as represented by the act of reading. The reading scene is the culmination of a series of actions taking place in enclosed spaces and leading up to the "dark coolness" of Marcel's room.

> I had stretched out on my bed, with a book, in my room which sheltered, tremblingly, its transparent and fragile coolness from the afternoon sun, behind the almost closed blinds through which a glimmer of daylight had nevertheless managed to push its yellow wings, remaining motionless between the wood and the glass, in a corner, posed like a butterfly. It was hardly light enough to read, and the sensation of the light's splendor was given

---

[9]Gottlob Frege, German philosopher and mathematician (1848–1925). *Bedeutung:* meaning; *Sinn:* sense.

me only by the noise of Camus . . . hammering dusty crates; resounding in the sonorous atmosphere that is peculiar to hot weather, they seemed to spark off scarlet stars; and also by the flies executing their little concert, the chamber music of summer: evocative not in the manner of a human tune that, heard perchance during the summer, afterwards reminds you of it but connected to summer by a more necessary link: born from beautiful days, resurrecting only when they return, containing some of their essence, it does not only awaken their image in our memory; it guarantees their return, their actual, persistent, unmediated presence.

The dark coolness of my room related to the full sunlight of the street as the shadow relates to the ray of light, that is to say it was just as luminous and it gave my imagination the total spectacle of the summer, whereas my senses, if I had been on a walk, could only have enjoyed it by fragments; it matched my repose which (thanks to the adventures told by my book and stirring my tranquility) supported, like the quiet of a motionless hand in the middle of a running brook the shock and the motion of a torrent of activity.[10]

For our present purpose, the most striking aspect of this passage is the juxtaposition of figural and metafigural language. It contains seductive metaphors that bring into play a variety of irresistible objects: chamber music, butterflies, stars, books, running brooks, etc., and it inscribes these objects within dazzling fire- and water-works of figuration. But the passage also comments normatively on the best way to achieve such effects; in this sense, it is metafigural: it writes figuratively about figures. It contrasts two ways of evoking the natural experience of summer and unambiguously states its preference for one of these ways over the other: the "necessary link" that unites the buzzing of the flies to the summer makes it a much more effective symbol than the tune heard "perchance" during the summer. The preference is expressed by means of a distinction that corresponds to the difference between metaphor and metonymy, necessity and chance being a legitimate way to distinguish between analogy and contiguity. The inference of identity and totality that is constitutive of metaphor is lacking in the purely relational metonymic contact: an element of truth is involved in taking Achilles for a lion but none in taking Mr. Ford for a motor car. The passage is *about* the aesthetic superiority of meta-

phor over metonymy, but this aesthetic claim is made by means of categories that are the ontological ground of the metaphysical system that allows for the aesthetic to come into being as a category. The metaphor for summer (in this case, the synesthesia set off by the "chamber music" of the flies) guarantees a presence which, far from being contingent, is said to be essential, permanently recurrent and unmediated by linguistic representations or figurations. Finally, in the second part of the passage, the metaphor of presence not only appears as the ground of cognition but as the performance of an action, thus promising the reconciliation of the most disruptive of contradictions. By then, the investment in the power of metaphor is such that it may seem sacrilegious to put it in question.

Yet, it takes little perspicacity to show that the text does not practice what it preaches. A rhetorical reading of the passage reveals that the figural praxis and the metafigural theory do not converge and that the assertion of the mastery of metaphor over metonymy owes its persuasive power to the use of metonymic structures. I have carried out such an analysis in a somewhat more extended context;[11] at this point, we are more concerned with the results than with the procedure. For the metaphysical categories of presence, essence, action, truth, and beauty do not remain unaffected by such a reading. This would become clear from an inclusive reading of Proust's novel or would become even more explicit in a language-conscious philosopher such as Nietzsche who, as a philosopher, has to be concerned with the epistemological consequences of the kind of rhetorical seductions exemplified by the Proust passage. It can be shown that the systematic critique of the main categories of metaphysics undertaken by Nietzsche in his late work, the critique of the concepts of causality, of the subject, of identity, of referential and revealed truth, etc., occurs along the same pattern of deconstruction that was operative in Proust's text; and it can also be shown that this pattern exactly corresponds to Nietzsche's description, in texts that precede *The Will to Power* by more than fifteen years, of the structure of the main rhetorical tropes. The key to this critique of metaphysics, which is itself a recurrent gesture throughout the history of thought, is the rhetorical model of the trope or, if one prefers to call it that, literature. It turns out that in these innocent looking didactic exercises we are in fact playing for very sizeable stakes.

It is therefore all the more necessary to know what is linguistically involved in a rhetorically conscious reading of

---

[10][de Man] *Swann's Way* (Paris: Pléiade, 1954), p. 83.

[11]See *Allegories of Reading* (New Haven: Yale University Press, 1979), pp. 59–67.

the type here undertaken on a brief fragment from a novel and extended by Nietzsche to the entire text of post-Hellenic thought. Our first examples dealing with the rhetorical questions were rhetorizations of grammar, figures generated by syntactical paradigms, whereas the Proust example could be better described as a grammatization of rhetoric. By passing from a paradigmatic structure based on substitution, such as metaphor, to a syntagmatic structure based on contingent association such as metonymy, the mechanical, repetitive aspect of grammatical forms is shown to be operative in a passage that seemed at first sight to celebrate the self-willed and autonomous inventiveness of a subject. Figures are assumed to be inventions, the products of a highly particularized individual talent, whereas no one can claim credit for the programmed pattern of grammar. Yet, our reading of the Proust passage shows that precisely when the highest claims are being made of the unifying power of metaphor, these very images rely in fact on the deceptive use of semi-automatic grammatical patterns. The deconstruction of metaphor and of all rhetorical patterns such as mimesis, paronomasia, or personification that use resemblance as a way to disguise differences, takes us back to the impersonal precision of grammar and of a semiology derived from grammatical patterns. Such a reading puts into question a whole series of concepts that underlie the value judgments of our critical discourse: the metaphors of primacy, of genetic history, and, most notably, of the autonomous power to will of the self.

There seems to be a difference, then, between what I called the rhetorization of grammar (as in the rhetorical question and the grammatization of rhetoric, as in the readings of the type sketched out in the passage from Proust. The former end up in indetermination, in a suspended uncertainty that was unable to choose between two modes of reading, whereas the latter seems to reach a truth, albeit by the negative road of exposing an error, a false pretense. After the rhetorical reading of the Proust passage, we can no longer believe the assertion made in this passage about the intrinsic, metaphysical superiority of metaphor over metonymy. We seem to end up in a mood of negative assurance that is highly productive of critical discourse. The further text of Proust's novel, for example, responds perfectly to an extended application of this pattern: not only can similar gestures be repeated throughout the novel, at all the crucial articulations or all passages where large aesthetic and metaphysical claims are being made—the scenes of involuntary memory, the workshop of Elstir, the septette of Vinteuil, the convergence of author and narrator at the end of the novel—but a vast thematic and semiotic network is revealed that structures the entire narrative and that remained invisible to a reader caught in naïve metaphorical mystification. The whole of lit-

erature would respond in similar fashion, although the techniques and the patterns would have to vary considerably, of course, from author to author. But there is absolutely no reason why analyses of the kind here suggested for Proust would not be applicable, with proper modifications of technique, to Milton or to Dante or to Hölderlin. This will in fact be the task of literary criticism in the coming years.

It would seem that we are saying that criticism is the deconstruction of literature, the reduction to the rigors of grammar of rhetorical mystifications. And if we hold up Nietzsche as the philosopher of such a critical deconstruction, then the literary critic would become the philosopher's ally in his struggle with the poets. Criticism and literature would separate around the epistemological axis that distinguishes grammar from rhetoric. It is easy enough to see that this apparent glorification of the critic-philosopher in the name of truth is in fact a glorification of the poet as the primary source of this truth; if truth is the recognition of the systematic character of a certain kind of error, then it would be fully dependent on the prior existence of this error. Philosophers of science like Bachelard or Wittgenstein are notoriously dependent on the aberrations of the poets.[12] We are back at our unanswered question: does the grammatization of rhetoric end up in negative certainty or does it, like the rhetorization of grammar, remain suspended in the ignorance of its own truth or falsehood?

Two concluding remarks should suffice to answer the question. First of all, it is not true that Proust's text can simply be reduced to the mystified assertion (the superiority of metaphor over metonymy) that our reading deconstructs. The reading is not "our" reading, since it uses only the linguistic elements provided by the text itself: the distinction between author and reader is one of the false distinctions that the reading makes evident. The deconstruction is not something we have added to the text but it constituted the text in the first place. A literary text simultaneously asserts and denies the authority of its own rhetorical mode, and by reading the text as we did we were only trying to come closer to being as rigorous a reader as the author had to be in order to write the sentence in the first place. Poetic writing is the most advanced and refined mode of deconstruction; it may differ from critical or discursive writing in the economy of its articulation, but not in kind.

But if we recognize the existence of such a moment as constitutive of all literary language, we have surreptitiously reintroduced the categories that this deconstruction was sup-

---

[12]For Bachelard see p. 1073. Ludwig Wittgenstein, Austrian-English philosopher (1889–1951).

posed to eliminate and that have merely been displaced. We have, for example, displaced the question of the self from the referent into the figure of the narrator, who then becomes the *signifié* of the passage. It becomes again possible to ask such naïve questions as what Proust's, or Marcel's, motives may have been in thus manipulating language: was he fooling himself, or was he represented as fooling himself and fooling us into believing that fiction and action are as easy to unite, by reading, as the passage asserts? The pathos of the entire section, which would have been more noticeable if the quotation had been a little more extended, the constant vacillation of the narrator between guilt and well-being, invites such questions. They are absurd questions, of course, since the reconciliation of fact and fiction occurs itself as a mere assertion made in a text, and is thus productive of more text at the moment when it asserts its decision to escape from textual confinement. But even if we free ourselves of all false questions of intent and rightfully reduce the narrator to the status of a mere grammatical pronoun, without which the narrative could not come into being, this subject remains endowed with a function that is not grammatical but rhetorical, in that it gives voice, so to speak, to a grammatical syntagm. The term *voice,* even when used in a grammatical terminology as when we speak of the passive or interrogative voice, is, of course, a metaphor inferring by analogy the intent of the subject from the structure of the predicate. In the case of the deconstructive discourse that we call literary, or rhetorical, or poetic, this creates a distinctive complication illustrated by the Proust passage. The reading revealed a first paradox: the passage valorizes metaphor as being the "right" literary figure, but then proceeds to constitute itself by means of the epistemologically incompatible figure of metonymy. The critical discourse reveals the presence of this delusion and affirms it as the irreversible mode of its truth. It cannot pause there however. For if we then ask the obvious

and simple next question, whether the rhetorical mode of the text in question is that of metaphor or metonymy, it is impossible to give an answer. Individual metaphors, such as the chiaroscuro effect or the butterfly, are shown to be subordinate figures in a general clause whose syntax is metonymic; from this point of view, it seems that the rhetoric is superseded by a grammar that deconstructs it. But this metonymic clause has as its subject a voice whose relationship to this clause is again metaphorical. The narrator who tells us about the impossibility of metaphor is himself, or itself, a metaphor, the metaphor of a grammatical syntagm whose meaning is the denial of metaphor stated, by antiphrasis, as its priority. And this subject-metaphor is, in its turn, open to the kind of deconstruction to the second degree, the rhetorical deconstruction of psycholinguistics, in which the more advanced investigations of literature are presently engaged, against considerable resistance.

We end up therefore, in the case of the rhetorical grammatization of semiology, just as in the grammatical rhetorization of illocutionary phrases, in the same state of suspended ignorance. Any question about the rhetorical mode of a literary text is always a rhetorical question which does not even know whether it is really questioning. The resulting pathos is an anxiety (or bliss, depending on one's momentary mood or individual temperament) of ignorance, not an anxiety of reference—as becomes thematically clear in Proust's novel when reading is dramatized, in the relationship between Marcel and Albertine, not as an emotive reaction to what language does, but as an emotive reaction to the impossibility of knowing what it might be up to Literature as well as criticism—the difference between them being delusive—is condemned (or privileged) to be forever the most rigorous and, consequently, the most unreliable language in terms of which man names and transforms himself.

Harold Bloom

b. 1930

Certainly one of the most original and ambitiously wide-ranging critics of the second half of this century, Harold Bloom has evolved a personal theory of literary tradition, proving his own assertion about himself that he is "temperamentally a natural revisionist." For Bloom all literature since about 1740, that is, the tradition of Romanticism that Bloom declares is still with us "is *consciously late,* and Romantic literary psychology is necessarily a *psychology of belatedness.*" Modern literature aggressively attempts to overcome this sense of coming late by revisionary acts and does so inadequately after these great Romantic predecessors. For Bloom, strong poets battle their strong precursors by creatively misreading them, thus overcoming their "anxiety of influence" and seizing a place in the tradition that they misread.

Bloom began his career studying the Romantic poets, especially Shelley and Blake, in opposition to the New Critics' general distaste for them. His interest in Romanticism has never left him, and he continues (against poststructuralist critics) to emphasize authorial presence and the role of the poet's ego in its struggle with the father-poet. Bloom's model is an Oedipal one, emphasizing the darker side of imaginative energy.

Critics, too, as Bloom gladly admits, are caught in the same Oedipal struggle with predecessors. For him, the early predecessors were T. S. Eliot and Northrop Frye. More recently in his enormous project of editing virtually all the major works of Western literature with critical introductions to each, he seems to be taking on Dr. Johnson.

The development of Bloom's theory of the "anxiety of influence" can be traced in a series of books: *The Anxiety of Influence* (1973), *A Map of Misreading* (1975), *Kabbalah and Criticism* (1975), *Poetry and Repression* (1976), *Agon: Towards A Theory of Revisionism* (1981), and *The Breaking of the Vessels* (1982). Bloom's earlier work includes *Shelley's Myth-making* (1959), *The Visionary Company* (1961), *Blake's Apocalypse* (1963), *Yeats* (1970), *The Ringers in the Tower* (1971), *Wallace Stevens: The Poems of Our Climate* (1976), and *Figures of Capable Imagination* (1976). More recently have appeared *Poetics of Influence* (1988) and *Ruin: The Sacred Truth* (1989). See Jean-Pierre Mileur, *Literary Revisionism and the Burden of Modernity* (1985); David Fite, *Harold Bloom: The Rhetoric of Romantic Fiction* (1985); and Peter DeBolla, *Harold Bloom: Towards Historical Rhetorics* (1988).

The Dialectics of Poetic Tradition

Emerson chose three mottos for his most influential essay, "Self-Reliance." The first, from the *Satires* of Persius: "Do not seek yourself outside yourself." The second, from Beaumont and Fletcher:

> Man is his own star; and the soul that can
> Render an honest and a perfect man,
> Commands all light, all influence, all fate;
> Nothing to him falls early or too late. . . .

The third, one of Emerson's own gnomic verses, is prophetic of much contemporary shamanism:

> Cast the bantling on the rocks,
> Suckle him with the she-wolf's teat,
> Wintered with the hawk and fox,
> Power and speed be hands and feet.

Like the fierce, rhapsodic essay they precede, these mottos are addressed to young Americans, men and women, of 1840, who badly needed to be told that they were not latecomers. But we, in fact, *are* latecomers (as indeed they were), and we are better off for consciously knowing it, at least right now. Emerson's single aim was to awaken his auditors to a sense of their own potential *power of making*. To serve his tradition now, we need to counsel a *power of conserving*.

"The hint of the dialectic is more valuable than the dialectic itself," Emerson once remarked, but I intend to contradict him on that also, and to sketch some aspects of the dialectics of literary tradition. Modernism in literature has not passed; rather, it has been exposed as never having been there. Gossip grows old and becomes myth; myth grows older, and becomes dogma. Wyndham Lewis, Eliot and Pound gossiped with one another; the New Criticism aged them into a myth of Modernism; now the antiquarian Hugh Kenner[1] has dogmatized this myth into the Pound Era, a canon of accepted titans. Pretenders to godhood Kenner roughly reduces to their mortality; the grand triumph of Kenner is his judgment that Wallace Stevens represented the culmination of the poetics of Edward Lear.[2]

Yet this is already dogma grown antique: Post-Modernism also has its canons and its canonizers; and I find myself surrounded by living classics, in recently dead poets of strong ambition and hysterical intensity, and in hyperactive novelist non-novelists, who are I suppose the proper seers for their armies of student non-students. I discover it does little good these days to remind literary students that Cowley, Cleveland, Denham and Waller were for generations considered great poets, or that much of the best contemporary opinion preferred Campbell, Moore and Rogers to John Keats. And I would fear to tell students that while I judge Ruskin to have been the best critic of the nineteenth century, he did proclaim *Aurora Leigh* by Mrs. Browning to be the best long poem of that century. Great critics nod, and entire generations go wrong in judging their own achievements. Without what Shelley called a being washed in the blood of the Great Redeemer, Time, literary tradition appears powerless to justify its own selectivities. Yet if tradition cannot establish its own centrality, it becomes something other than the liberation from time's chaos it implicitly promised to be. Like all convention, it moves from an idealized function to a stifling or blocking tendency.

I intend here to reverse Emerson (though I revere him) and to assert for literary tradition its currently pragmatic as opposed to idealized function: it is now valuable precisely because it partly blocks, because it stifles the weak, because it represses even the strong. To study literary tradition today is to achieve a dangerous but enabling act of the mind that works against all ease in fresh "creation." Kierkegaard[3] could afford to believe that he became great in proportion to striven-with greatness, but we come later. Nietzsche insisted that nothing was more pernicious than the sense of being a latecomer, but I want to insist upon the contrary: nothing is now more salutary than such a sense. Without it, we cannot distinguish between the energy of humanistic performance and merely organic energy, which never alas needs to be saved from itself:

I remember, as a young man setting out to be a university teacher, how afflicted I was by my sense of uselessness, my not exactly vitalizing fear that my chosen profession reduced to an incoherent blend of antiquarianism and culture-mongering. I recall also that I would solace myself by thinking that while a scholar-teacher of literature could do no

---

THE DIALECTICS OF POETIC TRADITION. *The Dialectics of Poetic Tradition* first appeared in *A Map of Misreading.* Copyright © Oxford University Press, Inc., 1975. Reprinted by permission.
[1]Hugh Kenner (b. 1923), American critic.

[2]Edward Lear (1812–1888), English humorist.
[3]Soren Kierkegaard (1813–1855), Danish philosopher.

good, at least he could do no harm, or anyway not to others, whatever he did to himself. But that was at the very start of the decade of the fifties, and after more than twenty years I have come to understand that I under-rated my profession, as much in its capacity for doing harm as in its potential for good works. Even our treasons, our betrayals of our implicit trusts, are treasons of something more than of the intellectuals, and most directly damage our immediate students, our Oedipal sons and daughters. Our profession is not genuinely akin any longer to that of the historians or the philosophers. Without willing the change, our theoretical critics have become negative theologians, our practical critics are close to being Agaddic commentators, and all of our teachers, of whatever generation, teach how to live, what to do, in order to avoid the damnation of death-in-life. I do not believe that I am talking about an ideology, nor am I acknowledging any shade whatsoever of the recent Marxist critiques of our profession. Whatever the academic profession of letters now is on the Continent (shall we say an anthropology half-Marxist, half-Buddhist?) or in Britain (shall we say a middle-class amateurism displacing an aristocratic amateurism?), it is currently in America a wholly Emersonian phenomenon. Emerson abandoned his church to become a secular orator, rightly trusting that the lecture, rather than the sermon, was the proper and luminous melody for Americans. We have institutionalized Emerson's procedures, while abandoning (understandably) his aims, for the burden of his prophecy is already carried by our auditors.

Northrop Frye, who increasingly looks like the Proclus or Iamblichus[4] of our day, has Platonized the dialectics of tradition, its relation to fresh creation, into what he calls the Myth of Concern, which turns out to be a Low Church version of T. S. Eliot's Anglo-Catholic myth of Tradition and the Individual Talent. In Frye's reduction, the student discovers that he becomes something, and thus uncovers or demystifies himself, by first being persuaded that tradition is inclusive rather than exclusive, and so makes a place for him. The student is a cultural assimilator who *thinks* because he has *joined* a larger body of thought. Freedom, for Frye as for Eliot, is the change, however slight, that any genuine single consciousness brings about in the order of literature simply by joining the simultaneity of such order. I confess that I no longer understand this simultaneity, except as a fiction that Frye, like Eliot, passes upon himself. This fiction is a noble idealization, and as a lie against time will go the way

of every noble idealization. Such positive thinking served many purposes during the sixties, when continuities, of any kind, badly required to be summoned, even if they did not come to our call. Wherever we are bound, our dialectical development now seems invested in the interplay of repetition and discontinuity, and needs a very different sense of what our stance is in regard to literary tradition.

All of us now have been pre-empted, as I think we are all quite uneasily aware. We are rueful that we are asked ("compelled" might be more accurate) to pay for the discontents not only of the civilization we enjoy, but of the civilization of all previous generations from whom we have inherited. Literary tradition, once we even contemplate entering its academies, now insists upon being our "family history," and inducts us into its "family romance" in the unfortunate role prefigured by Browning's Childe Roland, a candidate for heroism who aspired only to fail at least as miserably as his precursors failed. There are no longer any archetypes to displace; we have been ejected from the imperial palace whence we came, and any attempt to find a substitute for it will not be a benign displacement but only another culpable trespass, neither more nor less desperate than any Oedipal return to origins. For us, creative emulation of literary tradition leads to images of inversion, incest, sado-masochistic parody, of which the great, gloriously self-defeating master is Pynchon, whose *Gravity's Rainbow* is a perfect text for the sixties, Age of Frye and Borges, but already deliberately belated for the seventies. Substitute-gratifications and myths-of-displacement turn out to be an identity in Pynchon's book.

Gershom Scholem has an essay on "Tradition and New Creation in the Ritual of the Kabbalists"[5] that reads like a prescription for Pynchon's novel, and I suspect Pynchon found another source in it. The magical formula of the Kabbalistic view of ritual, according to Scholem, is as follows: "everything not only *is in* everything else but also *acts upon* everything else." Remind yourself that Kabbalah literally means "tradition," that which has been received, and reflect on the extraordinary over-determination and stupefying over-organization that a Kabbalistic book like *Gravity's Rainbow* is condemned to manifest. I will mention Kabbalism and its over-relevances again later in this chapter, but need first to demythologize and de-esotericize my own view of literary tradition. The proper starting point for any demystification has to be a return to the commonal. Let me ask then: what is literary tradition? What is a classic? What is a canonical view of tradition? How are canons of accepted

---

[4] Proclus (410?–485), Neo-Platonic philosopher; Iamblichus (*d. c.* 330), Neo-Platonic philosopher.

[5] Gershom Scholem (1897–1982), Jewish Kabbalistic scholar.

classics formed, and how are they unformed? I think that all these quite traditional questions can take one simplistic but still dialectical question as their summing-up: do we choose a tradition or does it choose us, and why is it necessary that a choosing take place, or a being chosen? What happens if one tries to write, or to teach, or to think, or even to read without the sense of a tradition?

Why, nothing at all happens, just nothing. You cannot write or teach or think or even read without imitation, and what you imitate is what another person has done, that person's writing or teaching or thinking or reading. Your relation to what informs that person *is* tradition, for tradition is influence that extends past one generation, a carrying-over of influence. Tradition, the Latin *traditio,* is etymologically a handing-over or a giving-over, a delivery, a giving-up and so even a surrender or a betrayal. *Traditio* in our sense is Latin only in language; the concept deeply derives from the Hebraic *Mishnah,* an oral handing-over, or transmission of oral precedents, of what has been found to work, of what has been instructed successfully. Tradition is good teaching, where "good" means pragmatic, instrumental, fecund. But how primal is teaching, in comparison to writing? Necessarily, the question is rhetorical; whether or not the psychic Primal Scene is the one where we were begotten, and whether or not the societal Primal Scene is the murder of a Sacred Father by rival sons, I would venture that the artistic Primal Scene *is* the trespass of teaching. What Jacques Derrida calls the Scene of Writing[6] itself depends upon a Scene of Teaching, and poetry is crucially pedagogical in its origins and function. Literary tradition begins when a fresh author is simultaneously cognizant not only of his own struggle against the forms and presence of a precursor, but is compelled also to a sense of the Precursor's place in regard to what came before *him.*

Ernst Robert Curtius, in the best study of literary tradition I have ever read, his definitive *European Literature and the Latin Middle Ages* (1948), concluded that "like all life, tradition is a vast passing away and renewal." But even Curtius, who could accept his own wisdom, cautioned us that Western literary tradition could be apprehended clearly "only" for the twenty-five centuries from Homer to Goethe; for the two centuries after Goethe we still could not know what was canonical or not. The later Enlightenment, Romanticism, Modernism, Post-Modernism; all these, by implication, are one phenomenon and we still cannot know precisely whether or not that phenomenon possesses continuity rather than primarily discontinuity in regard to the tradition between Homer and Goethe. Nor are there Muses, nymphs who *know,* still available to tell us the secrets of continuity, for the nymphs certainly are now departing. I prophesy though that the first true break with literary continuity will be brought about in generations to come, if the burgeoning religion of Liberated Woman spreads from its clusters of enthusiasts to dominate the West. Homer will cease to be the inevitable precursor, and the rhetoric and forms of our literature then may break at last from tradition.

It remains not arbitrary nor even accidental to say that everyone who now reads and writes in the West, of whatever racial background, sex or ideological camp, is still a son or daughter of Homer. As a teacher of literature who prefers the morality of the Hebrew Bible to that of Homer, indeed who prefers the Bible aesthetically to Homer, I am no happier about this dark truth than you are, if you happen to agree with William Blake when he passionately cries aloud that it is Homer and Virgil, the Classics, and not the Goths and Vandals that fill Europe with wars.[7] But how did this truth, whether dark or not, impose itself upon us?

All continuities possess the paradox of being absolutely arbitrary in their origins, and absolutely inescapable in their teleologies. We know this so vividly from what we all of us oxymoronically call our love lives that its literary counterparts need little demonstration. Though each generation of critics rightly re-affirms the aesthetic supremacy of Homer, he is so much part of the aesthetic *given* for them (and us) that the re-affirmation is a redundancy. What we call "literature" is inescapably connected to education by a continuity of twenty-five hundred years, a continuity that began in the sixth century B.C. when Homer first became a schoolbook for the Greeks, or as Curtius says simply and definitively: "Homer, for them, was the 'tradition.'" When Homer became a schoolbook, literature became a school subject quite permanently. Again, Curtius makes the central formulation: "Education becomes the medium of the literary tradition: a fact which is characteristic of Europe, but which is not necessarily so in the nature of things."

This formulation is worth considerable dialectical investigation, particularly in a time as educationally confused as ours recently has been. Nothing in the literary world even sounds quite so silly to me as the passionate declarations that poetry must be liberated from the academy, declarations that would be absurd at any time, but peculiarly so some twenty-five hundred years after Homer and the academy first became indistinguishable. For the answer to the question

---

[6]See Jacques Derrida, "Freud and the Scene of Writing," *Writing and Difference* (1967).

[7]See p. 414.

"What is literature?" must begin with the word "literature," based on Quintilian's[8] word *litteratura* which was his translation of the Greek *grammatike,* the art of reading and writing conceived as a dual enterprise. Literature, and the study of literature, were in their origin a single, unified concept. When Hesiod and Pindar invoke the Muses, they do so *as students,* so as to enable themselves *to teach their readers.* When the first literary scholars wholly distinct from poets created their philology in Alexandria, they began by classifying and then selecting authors, canonizing according to secular principles clearly ancestral in relation to our own. The question we go on asking—"What is a classic?"—they first answered for us by reducing the tragedians initially to five, and later to three. Curtius informs us that the name *classicus* first appears very late, under the Antonine emperors, meaning literary citizens of the first class, but the concept of classification was itself Alexandrian. We are Alexandrians still, and we may as well be proud of it, for it is central to our profession. Even "Modernism," a shibboleth many of us think we may have invented, is necessarily an Alexandrian inheritance also. The scholar Aristarchus, working at the Museion in Alexandria, first contrasted the *neoteroi* or "moderns" with Homer, in defense of a latecomer poet like Callimachus. *Modernus,* based on the word *modo,* for "now," first came into use in the sixth century A.D., and it is worth remembering that "Modernism" always means "For Now."

Alexandria, which thus founded our scholarship, permanently set the literary tradition of the school, and introduced the secularized notion of the canon, though the actual term of canon for "catalogue" of authors was not used until the eighteenth century. Curtius, in his wonderfully comprehensive researches, ascribes the first canon-formation in a modern vernacular, secular literature to the sixteenth-century Italians. The French in the seventeenth century followed, establishing their permanent version of classicism, a version that the English Augustans bravely but vainly tried to emulate before they were flooded out by that great English renaissance of the English Renaissance we now call the Age of Sensibility or the Sublime, and date fairly confidently from the mid-1740's. This renaissance of the Renaissance was and is Romanticism, which is of course *the* tradition of the last two centuries. Canon-formation, for us, has become a part of Romantic tradition, and our still-current educational crisis in the West is rather clearly only another Romantic epicycle, part of the continuity of upheaval that began with revolution in the West Indies and America, spread to France and

through her to the Continent, and thence to Russia, Asia and Africa in our time. Just as Romanticism and Revolution became one composite form, so the dialectic of fresh canon-formation joining itself to a gradual ideological reversal endures into this current decade.

But Romantic tradition differs vitally from earlier forms of tradition, and I think this difference can be reduced to a useful formula. Romantic tradition is *consciously late,* and Romantic literary psychology is therefore necessarily a *psychology of belatedness.* The romance-of-trespass, of violating a sacred or daemonic ground, is a central form in modern literature, from Coleridge and Wordsworth to the present. Whitman follows Emerson by insisting that he strikes up for a new world, yet the guilt of belatedness haunts him and all of his American literary descendants. Yeats was early driven into Gnostic evasions of nature by a parallel guilt, and even the apocalyptic Lawrence is most persuasive when he follows his own analyses of Melville and Whitman to trumpet the doom of what he calls our white race with its hideously belated aversion from what he oddly insisted upon calling blood-consciousness. Romanticism, more than any other tradition, is appalled by its own overt continuities, and vainly but perpetually fantasizes some end to repetitions.

This Romantic psychology of belatedness, from which Emerson failed to save us, his American descendants, is the cause, in my judgment, of the excessively volatile senses-of-tradition that have made canon-formation so uncertain a process during the last two centuries, and particularly during the last twenty years. Take some contemporary examples. A quick way to start a quarrel with any current group of critics would be to express my conviction that Robert Lowell is anything but a permanent poet, that he has been mostly a maker of period-pieces from his origins until now. Similarly, as violent a quarrel would ensue if I expressed my judgment that Norman Mailer is so flawed a writer that his current enshrinement among academics is the largest single index to our current sense of belatedness. Lowell and Mailer, however I rate them, are at least conspicuous literary energies. It would lead to something more intense than quarrels if I expressed my judgment upon "black poetry" or the "literature of Women's Liberation." But quarrels, or even abuse, is all such *obiter dicta* could lead to, for our mutual sense of canonical standards has undergone a remarkable dimming, a fading into the light of a common garishness. Revisionism, always a Romantic energizer, has become so much a norm that even rhetorical standards seem to have lost their efficacy. Literary tradition has become the captive of the revisionary impulse, and I think we must go past viewing-with-alarm if we are to understand this quite inescapable phenomenon, the subsuming of tradition by belatedness.

---

[8]Quintilian (*c.* 35–*c.* 95), Roman rhetorician.

The revisionary impulse, in writing and in reading, has a directly inverse relationship to our psychological confidence in what I am calling the Scene of Instruction. Milton's Satan, who remains the greatest really Modern or Post-Enlightenment poet in the language, can give us a paradigm of this inverse relationship. The ultimate Scene of Instruction is described by Raphael in Book V of *Paradise Lost,* where God proclaims to the Angels that "This day I have begot whom I declare / My only son" and provocatively warns that "him who disobeys / Me disobeys . . . / and . . . falls / Into utter darkness." We can describe this as an imposition of the psychology of belatedness, and Satan, like any strong poet, declines to be merely a latecomer. His way of returning to origins, of making the Oedipal trespass, is to become a rival creator to God-as-creator. He embraces Sin as his Muse, and begets upon her the highly original poem of Death, the only poem that God will permit him to write.

Let me reduce my own allegory, or my allegorical interpretation of Satan, by invoking a wonderful poem of Emily Dickinson's, "The Bible is an antique Volume—" (no. 1545), in which she calls Eden "the ancient Homestead," Satan "the Brigadier," and Sin "a distinguished Precipice / Others must resist." As a heretic whose orthodoxy was Emersonianism, Dickinson recognized in Satan a distinguished precursor gallantly battling against the psychology of belatedness. But then, Dickinson and Emerson wrote in an America that needed, for a while, to battle against the European exhaustions of history. I am temperamentally a natural revisionist, and I respond to Satan's speeches more strongly than to any other poetry I know, so it causes some anguish in me to counsel that currently we need Milton's sense of tradition much more than Emerson's revisionary tradition. Indeed, the counsel of necessity must be taken further: most simply, we need Milton, and not the Romantic return of the repressed Milton but the Milton who made his great poem identical with the process of repression that is vital to literary tradition. But a resistance even in myself is set up by my counsel of necessity, because even I want to know: what do I mean by "we"? Teachers? Students? Writers? Readers?

I do not believe that these are separate categories, nor do I believe that sex, race, social class can narrow this "we" down. If we are human, then we depend upon a Scene of Instruction, which is necessarily also a scene of authority and of priority. If you will not have one instructor or another, then precisely by rejecting all instructors, you will condemn yourself to the earliest Scene of Instruction that imposed itself upon you. The clearest analogue is necessarily Oedipal; reject your parents vehemently enough, and you will become a belated version of them, but compound with their reality,

and you may partly free yourself. Milton's Satan failed, particularly as poet, after making a most distinguished beginning, because he became only a parody of the bleakest aspects of Milton's God. I greatly prefer Pynchon to Mailer as a writer because a voluntary parody is more impressive than an involuntary one, but I wonder if our aesthetic possibilities need to be reduced now to just such a choice. Do the dialectics of literary tradition condemn us, at this time, either to an affirmation of belatedness, via Kabbalistic inversion, or to a mock-vitalistic lie-against-time, via an emphasis upon the self-as-performer?

I cannot answer this hard question, because I am uneasy with the current alternatives to the ways of Pynchon and of Mailer, at least in fictional or quasi-fictional prose. Saul Bellow, with all his literary virtues, clearly shows the primal exhaustions of being a latecomer rather more strenuously in his way than Pynchon or Mailer do in theirs. I honestly don't enjoy Bellow more, and I would hesitate to find anything universal in such enjoyment even if I had it. Contemporary American poetry seems healthier to me, and provides alternatives to the voluntary parodies that Lowell has given us, or the involuntary parodies at which Ginsberg is so prominent. Yet even the poets I most admire, John Ashbery and A. R. Ammons, are rendered somewhat problematic by a cultural situation of such belatedness that literary survival itself seems fairly questionable. As Pynchon says in the closing pages of his uncanny book: "You've got much older. . . . Fathers are carriers of the virus of Death, and sons are the infected. . . ." And he adds a little further on in his Gospel of Sado-anarchism that this time we "*will* arrive, my God, too late."

I am aware that this must seem a Gospel of Gloom, and no one ought to be asked to welcome a kakangelist, a bearer of ill-tidings. But I cannot see that evasions of Necessity benefit anyone, least of all educationally. The teacher of literature now in America, far more than the teacher of history or philosophy or religion, is condemned to teach the presentness of the past, because history, philosophy and religion have withdrawn as agents from the Scene of Instruction, leaving the bewildered teacher of literature alone at the altar, terrifiedly wondering whether he is to be sacrifice or priest. If he evades his burden by attempting to teach only the supposed presence of the present, he will find himself teaching only some simplistic, partial reduction that wholly obliterates the present in the name of one or another historicizing formula, or past injustice, or dead faith, whether secular or not. Yet how is he to teach a tradition now grown so wealthy and so heavy that to accommodate it demands more strength than any single consciousness can provide, short of the parodistic Kabbalism of a Pynchon?

All literary tradition has been necessarily élitist, in every period, if only because the Scene of Instruction always depends upon a primal choosing and a being chosen, which is what "élite" means. Teaching, as Plato knew, is necessarily a branch of erotics, in the wide sense of desiring what we have not got, of redressing our poverty, of compounding with our fantasies. No teacher, however impartial he or she attempts to be, can avoid choosing among students, or being chosen by them, for this is the very nature of teaching. Literary teaching is precisely like literature itself; no strong writer can choose his precursors until first he is chosen by them, and no strong student can fail to be chosen by his teachers. Strong students, like strong writers, will find the sustenance they must have. And strong students, like strong writers, will rise in the most unexpected places and times, to wrestle with the internalized violence pressed upon them by their teachers and precursors.

Yet our immediate concern, as I am aware, is hardly with the strong, but with the myriads of the many, as Emersonian democracy seeks to make its promises a little less deceptive than they have been. Do the dialectics of literary tradition yield us no wisdom that can help with the final burden of the latecomer, which is the extension of the literary franchise? What is the particular inescapability of literary tradition for the teacher who must go out to find himself as a voice in the wilderness? Is he to teach *Paradise Lost* in preference to the Imamu Amiri Baraka?

I think these questions are self-answering, or rather will be, with the passage of only a few more years. For the literary teacher, more than ever, will find he is teaching *Paradise Lost,* and the other central classics of Western literary tradition, whether he is teaching them overtly or not. The psychology of belatedness is unsparing, and the Scene of Instruction becomes ever more primal as our society sags around us. Instruction, in our late phase, becomes an antithetical process almost in spite of itself, and for antithetical teaching you require antithetical texts, that is to say, texts antithetical to your students as well as to yourself and to other texts. Milton's Satan may stand as representative of the entire canon when he challenges us to challenge Heaven with him, and he will provide the truest handbook for all those, of whatever origin, who as he says "with ambitious mind / Will covet more." Any teacher of the dispossessed, of those who assert *they* are the insulted and injured, will serve the deepest purposes of literary tradition and meet also the deepest needs of his students when he gives them possession of Satan's grand opening of the Debate in Hell, which I cite now to close this chapter on the dialectics of tradition:

> With this advantage then
> To union, and firm Faith, and firm accord,
> More than can be in Heav'n, we now return
> To claim our just inheritance of old,
> Surer to prosper than prosperity
> Could have assur'd us; and by what best way,
> Whether of open War or covert guile,
> We now debate; who can advise, may speak.[9]

---

[9] *Paradise Lost* II, 35–42.

Chinua Achebe

b. 1930

Chinua Achebe is a well known Nigerian novelist and critic. Over the past twenty-five years he has produced numerous novels, short stories, and critical essays. Perhaps his best known critical essay is a discussion of racism in Joseph Conrad's *Heart of Darkness,* which he gave originally as a lecture at the University of Massachusetts in 1975 and is reprinted in *Hopes and Impediments*. It evoked both high praise and strong antipathy on the spot and has given rise to further discussion and response as questions of racism and colonialism have been more vigorously debated. The reprinted essay here is broader in scope than the one on Conrad, but it evokes similar themes. Given originally as a lecture at a meeting of the Association for Commonwealth Literature and Language Studies at Makerere University, Uganda, it is an attack on a lingering colonialism in the criticism of African literature, mainly but not entirely by non-Africans. The faults of this criticism stem from implied assumptions that the African writer is a "somewhat unfinished European" and that somehow outsiders can know Africa better than the native writers. These assumptions lead to, among other things, the specious man-of-two-worlds theory of the African intellectual and imply a continued European arrogance.

Achebe's principal theoretical point involves his rejection of universalism, represented by critical statements that generalize the particularity out of African literature. The two problems with universalism, according to Achebe, are, first, that the presumed universality that critics find is merely a synonym for the "narrow self-serving parochialism of Europe" and, second, that every literature must "speak of a particular place, evolve out of the necessities of its history, past and current, and the aspirations and destiny of its people." It would seem, then, that if there is to be a concrete universal in African literature it must stem from a much deeper human source than any parochial view can uncover. But Achebe does not say this. Rather, his concentration is on the particular alone, for he puts literature, at least his writings, in service of the need to alter specific things in specific places, especially attitudes. It is in this context that Achebe defends the "high moral and social earnestness" of Christopher Okigbo against the charge of outspokenness. Achebe's point is that earnestness is appropriate to Okigbo's and his situation and that a certain levity would be inappropriate.

Achebe's numerous books include *Things Fall Apart* (1958), *No Longer at Ease* (1960), *The Sacrificial Egg and Other Stories* (1962), *Arrow of God* (1964), *A Man of the People* (1966), *Beware Soul-Brother* (1971, rev. 1972), *Girls at War and Other Stories* (1973), *Morning Yet on Creation Day* (1975), *The Flute* (1978), *The Drum* (1978), *The Trouble with Nigeria* (1983), *Anthills of the Savannah* (1987), and *Hopes and Impediments* (1989). See G. D. Kellam, *The Novels of Chinua Achebe* (1969); David Carroll, *Chinua Achebe* (1970); Kate Turkington, *Things Fall Apart* (1977); and Robert N. Wren, *Achebe's World* (1981).

Colonialist Criticism

The word "colonialist" may be deemed inappropriate for two reasons. First, it has come to be associated in many minds with that brand of cheap, demagogic and outmoded rhetoric which the distinguished Ghanaian public servant Robert Gardiner no doubt has in mind when he speaks of our tendency to "intone the colonial litany," implying that the time has come when we must assume responsibility for our problems and our situation in the world and resist the temptation to blame other people. Secondly, it may be said that whatever colonialism may have done in the past, the very fact of a Commonwealth Conference today is sufficient repudiation of it, is indeed a symbol of a new relationship of equality between peoples who were once masters and servants.

Yet in spite of the strength of these arguments one feels the necessity to deal with some basic issues raised by a certain specious criticism which flourishes in African literature today and which derives from the same basic attitude and assumption as colonialism itself and so merits the name "colonialist." This attitude and assumption was crystallized in Albert Schweitzer's immortal dictum in the heyday of colonialism: "The African is indeed my brother, but my junior brother." The latter-day colonialist critic, equally given to big-brother arrogance, sees the African writer as a somewhat unfinished European who with patient guidance will grow up one day and write like every other European, but meanwhile must be humble, must learn all he can and while at it give due credit to his teachers in the form of either direct praise or, even better since praise sometimes goes bad and becomes embarrassing, manifest self-contempt. Because of the tricky nature of this subject, I have chosen to speak not in general terms but wherever possible specifically about my own actual experience. In any case, as anyone who has heard anything at all about me may know already, I do have problems with universality and other concepts of that scope, being very much a down-to-earth person. But I will hope by reference to a few other writers and critics to show that my concerns and anxieties are perhaps not entirely personal.

When my first novel was published in 1958, a very unusual review of it was written by a British woman, Honor Tracy, who is perhaps not so much a critic as a literary journalist.[1] But what she said was so intriguing that I have never forgotten it. If I remember rightly, she headlined it "Three cheers for mere Anarchy!" The burden of the review itself was as follows: These bright Negro barristers (how barristers came into it remains a mystery to me to this day, but I have sometimes woven fantasies about an earnest white woman and an unscrupulous black barrister) who talk so glibly about African culture, how would they like to return to wearing raffia skirts? How would novelist Achebe like to go back to the mindless times of his grandfather instead of holding the modern job he has in broadcasting in Lagos?

I should perhaps point out that colonialist criticism is not always as crude as this, but the exaggerated grossness of a particular example may sometimes prove useful in studying the anatomy of the species. There are three principal parts here: Africa's inglorious past (raffia skirts) to which Europe brings the blessing of civilization (Achebe's modern job in Lagos) and for which Africa returns ingratitude (sceptical novels like *Things Fall Apart*).

Before I go on to more advanced varieties I must give one more example of the same kind as Honor Tracy's, which on account of its recentness (1970) actually surprised me:

> The British administration not only safeguarded women from the worst tyrannies of their masters, it also enabled them to make their long journeys to farm or market without armed guard, secure from the menace of hostile neighbours . . . The Nigerian novelists who have written the charming and bucolic accounts of domestic harmony in African rural communities, are the sons whom the labours of these women educated; the peaceful village of their childhood to which they nostalgically look back was one which had been purged of bloodshed and alcoholism by an ague-ridden district officer and a Scottish mission lassie whose years were cut short by every kind of intestinal parasite.
>
> It is even true to say that one of the most nostalgically convincing of the rural African novelists used as his sourcebook not the memories of his grandfathers but the records of the despised British anthropologists . . . The modern African mythmaker hands down a vision of colonial rule in which the native powers are chivalrously viewed through the eyes of the hard-won liberal tradition of the late Victorian scholar, while the expatriates are shown as schoolboys' blackboard caricatures.[2]

[1]Honor Tracy (b. 1913).

[2][Achebe] Iris Andreski, *Old Wives' Tales,* New York, Schocken Books, 1971, p. 26.

I have quoted this at such length because first of all I am intrigued by Iris Andreski's literary style, which recalls so faithfully the sedate prose of the district officer government anthropologist of sixty or seventy years ago—a tribute to her remarkable powers of identification as well as to the durability of colonialist rhetoric. "Tyrannies of their masters" . . . "menace of hostile neighbours" . . . "purged of bloodshed and alcoholism." But in addition to this, Iris Andreski advances the position taken by Honor Tracy in one significant and crucial direction—its claim to a deeper knowledge and a more reliable appraisal of Africa than the educated African writer has shown himself capable of.

To the colonialist mind it was always of the utmost importance to be able to say: "I know my natives," a claim which implied two things at once: (a) that the native was really quite simple and (b) that understanding him and controlling him went hand in hand—understanding being a precondition for control and control constituting adequate proof of understanding. Thus, in the heyday of colonialism any serious incident of native unrest, carrying as it did disquieting intimations of slipping control, was an occasion not only for pacification by the soldiers but also (afterwards) for a royal commission of inquiry—a grand name for yet another perfunctory study of native psychology and institutions. Meanwhile a new situation was slowly developing as a handful of natives began to acquire European education and then to challenge Europe's presence and position in their native land with the intellectual weapons of Europe itself. To deal with this phenomenal presumption the colonialist devised two contradictory arguments. He created the "man of two worlds" theory to prove that no matter how much the native was exposed to European influences he could never truly absorb them; like Prester John he would always discard the mask of civilization when the crucial hour came and reveal his true face. Now, did this mean that the educated native was no different at all from his brothers in the bush? Oh, no! He *was* different; he was worse. His abortive effort at education and culture though leaving him totally unredeemed and unregenerated had nonetheless done something to him— it had deprived him of his links with his own people whom he no longer even understood and who certainly wanted none of his dissatisfaction or pretensions. "I know my natives; they are delighted with the way things are. It's only these half-educated ruffians who don't even know their own people. . . ." How often one heard that and the many variations of it in colonial times! And how almost amusing to find its legacy in the colonialist criticism of our literature today! Iris Andreski's book is more than old wives' tales, at least in intention. It is clearly inspired by the desire to undercut the educated African witness (the modern myth-maker, she calls

him) by appealing directly to the unspoilt woman of the bush who has retained a healthy gratitude for Europe's intervention in Africa. This desire accounts for all that reliance one finds in modern European travellers' tales on the evidence of "simple natives"—houseboys, cooks, drivers, schoolchildren—supposedly more trustworthy than the smart alecs. An American critic, Charles Larson, makes good use of this kind of evidence not only to validate his literary opinion of Ghana's Ayi Kwei Armah but, even more important, to demonstrate its superiority over the opinion of Ghanaian intellectuals:

> When I asked a number of students at the University of Ghana about their preferences for contemporary African novelists, Ayi Kwei Armah was the writer mentioned most frequently, in spite of the fact that many of Ghana's older writers and intellectuals regard him as a kind of negativist . . . I have for some time regarded Ayi Kwei Armah as Anglophone Africa's most accomplished prose stylist.[3]

In 1962, I published an essay, "Where Angels Fear to Tread,"[4] in which I suggested that the European critic of African literature must cultivate the habit of humility appropriate to his limited experience of the African world and purged of the superiority and arrogance which history so insidiously makes him heir to. That article, though couched in very moderate terms, won for me quite a few bitter enemies. One of them took my comments so badly—almost as a personal affront—that he launched numerous unprovoked attacks against me. Well, he has recently come to grief by his own hand. He published a long abstruse treatise based on an analysis of a number of Igbo proverbs most of which, it turned out, he had so completely misunderstood as to translate "fruit" in one of them as "penis." Whereupon, a merciless native, less charitable than I, proceeded to make mincemeat of him. If only he had listened to me ten years ago!

After the publication of *A Man of the People* in 1966, I was invited to dinner by a British diplomat in Lagos at which his wife, hitherto a fan of mine, admonished me for what she called "this great disservice to Nigeria." She loved Nigeria so much that my criticisms of the country which ignored all the brave efforts it was making left her totally aghast. I told

---

[3][Achebe] Charles Larson, *Books Abroad,* Norman, Oklahoma, Winter 1974, p. 69.

[4][Achebe] Chinua Achebe, "Where Angels Fear to Tread," *Nigeria Magazine,* no. 75, Lagos, 1962.

her something not very nice, and our friendship was brought to an end.

Most African writers write out of an African experience and of commitment to an African destiny. For them, that destiny does not include a future European identity for which the present is but an apprenticeship. And let no one be fooled by the fact that we may write in English, for we intend to do unheard of things with it. Already some people are getting worried. This past summer I met one of Australia's leading poets, A. D. Hope, in Canberra, and he said wistfully that the only happy writers today were those writing in small languages like Danish. Why? Because they and their readers understood one another and knew precisely what a word meant when it was used. I had to admit that I hadn't thought of it that way. I had always assumed that the Commonwealth of Nations was a great bonus for a writer, that the English-Speaking Union was a desirable fraternity. But talking with A. D. Hope that evening, I felt somewhat like an illegitimate child face to face with the true son of the house lamenting the excesses of an adventurous and profligate father who had kept a mistress in every port. I felt momentarily nasty and thought of telling A. D. Hope: You ain't seen nothin' yet! But I know he would not have understood. And in any case, there was an important sense in which he was right—that every literature must seek the things that belong unto its peace, must, in other words, speak of a particular place, evolve out of the necessities of its history, past and current, and the aspirations and destiny of its people.

Australia proved quite enlightening. (I hope I do not sound too ungracious. Certainly, I met very many fine and sensitive people in Australia; and the words which the distinguished historian Professor Manning Clark wrote to me after my visit are among the finest tributes I have ever received: "I hope you come back and speak again here, because we need to lose the blinkers of our past. So come and help the young to grow up without the prejudices of their forefathers. . . ."

On another occasion a student at the National University who had taken a course in African literature asked me if the time had not come for African writers to write about "people in general" instead of just Africans. I asked her if by "people in general" she meant *like Australians,* and gave her the bad news that as far as I was concerned such a time would never come. She was only a brash sophomore. But like all the other women I have referred to, she expressed herself with passionate and disarming effrontery. I don't know how women's lib will take it, but I do believe that by and large women are more honest than men in expressing their feelings. This girl was only making the same point which many "serious" critics have been making more tact-

fully and therefore more insidiously. They dress it up in fine robes which they call universality.

In his book *The Emergence of African Fiction,* Charles Larson tells us a few revealing things about universality. In a chapter devoted to Lenrie Peters's novel, which he finds particularly impressive, he speaks of "its universality, its very limited concern with Africa itself." Then he goes on to spell it all out:

> That it is set in Africa appears to be accidental, for, except for a few comments at the beginning, Peters's story might just as easily take place in the southern part of the United States or in the southern regions of France or Italy. If a few names of characters and places were changed one would indeed feel that this was an American novel. In short, Peters's story is universal.[5]

But Larson is obviously not as foolish as this passage would make him out to be, for he ends it on a note of self-doubt which I find totally disarming. He says (p. 238):

> Or am I deluding myself in considering the work universal? Maybe what I really mean is that *The Second Round* is to a great degree Western and therefore scarcely African at all.

I find it hard after that to show more harshness than merely agreeing about his delusion. But few people I know are prepared to be so charitable. In a recent review of the book in *Okike,* a Nigerian critic, Omolara Leslie, mocks "the shining faith that we are all Americans under the skin."

Does it ever occur to these universalists to try out their game of changing names of characters and places in an American novel, say, a Philip Roth or an Updike, and slotting in African names just to see how it works? But of course it would not occur to them. It would never occur to them to doubt the universality of their own literature. In the nature of things the work of a Western writer is automatically informed by universality. It is only others who must strain to achieve it. So-and-so's work is universal; he has truly arrived! As though universality were some distant bend in the road which you may take if you travel out far enough in the direction of Europe or America, if you put adequate distance between yourself and your home. I should like to see the word "universal" banned altogether from discussions of Af-

---

[5][Achebe] Charles Larson, *The Emergence of African Fiction,* Indianapolis, Indiana University Press, 1971, p. 230.

rican literature until such a time as people cease to use it as a synonym for the narrow, self-serving parochialism of Europe, until their horizon extends to include all the world.

If colonialist criticism were merely irritating one might doubt the justification of devoting a whole essay to it. But strange though it may sound, some of its ideas and precepts do exert an influence on our writers, for it is a fact of our contemporary world that Europe's powers of persuasion can be far in excess of the merit and value of her case. Take for instance the black writer who seizes on the theme that "Africa's past is a sadly inglorious one" as though it were something new that had not already been "proved" adequately for him. Colonialist critics will, of course, fall all over him in ecstatic and salivating admiration—which is neither unexpected nor particularly interesting. What is fascinating, however, is the tortuous logic and sophistry they will sometimes weave around a perfectly straightforward and natural enthusiasm.

A review of Yambo Ouologuem's *Bound to Violence* (Heinemann Educational Books, London, 1971) by a Philip M. Allen in the *Pan-African Journal*[6] was an excellent example of sophisticated, even brilliant colonialist criticism. The opening sentence alone would reward long and careful examination; but I shall content myself here with merely quoting it:

> The achievement of Ouologuem's much discussed, impressive, yet over-praised novel has less to do with whose ideological team he's playing on than with the *forcing of moral universality on African civilization* [my italics].

A little later Mr. Allen expounds on this new moral universality:

> This morality is not only "un-African"—denying the standards set by omnipresent ancestors, the solidarity of communities, the legitimacy of social contract: it is a Hobbesian universe that extends beyond the wilderness, beyond the white man's myths of Africa, into all civilization, theirs and ours.

If you should still be wondering at this point how Ouologuem was able to accomplish that Herculean feat of forcing moral universality on Africa or with what gargantuan tools, Mr. Allen does not leave you too long in suspense. Ouologuem is "an African intellectual who has mastered both a style and a prevailing philosophy of French letters," able to enter "the remoter alcoves of French philosophical discourse."

Mr. Allen is quite abrupt in dismissing all the "various polemical factions" and ideologists who have been claiming Ouologuem for their side. Of course they all miss the point,

> . . . for Ouologuem isn't writing their novel. He gives us an Africa cured of the pathetic obsession with racial and cultural confrontation and freed from invidious tradition-mongering . . . His book knows no easy antithesis between white and black, western and indigenous, modern and traditional. Its conflicts are those of the universe, not accidents of history.

And in final demonstration of Ouologuem's liberation from the constraint of local models Mr. Allen tells us:

> Ouologuem does not accept Fanon's idea of liberation, and he calls African unity a theory for dreamers. His Nakem is no more the Mali of Modibo Keita or the continent of Nkrumah than is the golden peace of Emperor Sundiata or the moral parish of Muntu.

Mr. Allen's rhetoric does not entirely conceal whose ideological team *he* is playing on, his attitude to Africa, in other words. Note, for example, the significant antithesis between the infinite space of "a Hobbesian universe" and "the moral parish of Muntu" with its claustrophobic implications. Who but Western man could contrive such arrogance?

Running through Mr. Allen's review is the overriding thesis that Ouologuem has somehow restored dignity to his people and their history by investing them with responsibility for violence and evil. Mr. Allen returns to this thesis again and again, merely changing the form of words. And we are to understand, by fairly clear implication, that this was something brave and new for Africa, this manly assumption of responsibility.

Of course a good deal of colonialist rhetoric always turned on that very question. The moral inferiority of colonized peoples, of which subjugation was a prime consequence and penalty, was most clearly demonstrated in their unwillingness to assume roles of responsibility. As long ago (or as recently, depending on one's historical perspective) as

---

[6][Achebe] Philip Allen, "*Bound to Violence* by Yambo Ouloguem," *Pan-African Journal*, vol. iv, no. 4, New York, Pan-African Institute Inc., Fall 1971, pp. 518–523.

1910 the popular English novelist John Buchan wrote a co-lonialist classic, *Prester John,* in which we find the words: "That is the difference between white and black, the gift of responsibility." And the idea did not originate with Buchan, either. It was a foundation tenet of colonialism and a recur-rent element of its ideology and rhetoric. Now, to tell a man that he is incapable of assuming responsibility for himself and his actions is of course the utmost insult, to avoid which some Africans will go to any length, will throw anything into the deal; they will agree, for instance, to ignore the presence and role of racism in African history or pretend that some-how it was all the black man's own fault. Which is complete and utter nonsense. For whatever faults the black man may have or whatever crimes he committed (and they were, and are, legion) he did not bring racism into the world. And no matter how emancipated a man may wish to appear or how anxious to please by his largeness of heart, he cannot make history simply go away. Not even a brilliant writer could hope to do that. And as for those who applaud him for trying, who acclaim his bold originality in "restoring historical ini-tiative to his people" when in reality all he does is pander to their racist and colonialist attitudes, they are no more than unscrupulous interrogators taking advantage of an ingratiat-ing defendant's weakness and trust to egg him on to irretriev-able self-incrimination.

That a "critic" playing on the ideological team of co-lonialism should feel sick and tired of Africa's "pathetic ob-session with racial and cultural confrontation" should sur-prise no one. Neither should his enthusiasm for those African works that show "no easy antithesis between white and black." But an African who falls for such nonsense, not only in spite of Africa's so very recent history but, even more, in the face of continuing atrocities committed against millions of Africans in their own land by racist minority re-gimes, deserves a lot of pity. Certainly anyone, white or black, who chooses to see violence as the abiding principle of African civilization is free to do so. But let him not pass himself off as a restorer of dignity to Africa, or attempt to make out that he is writing about man and about the state of civilization in general. (You could as well claim that fifty years ago Frank Melland's *In Witchbound Africa* was an ac-count of the universality of witchcraft and a vindication of Africa.) The futility of such service to Africa, leaving aside any question of duplicity in the motive, should be suffi-ciently underscored by one interesting admission in Mr. Al-len's review:

> Thus, there is no reason for western reviewers of this book to exult in a black writer's admission of the savagery, sensuality and amorality of his race:

he isn't talking about his race, as Senghor or Cleaver do: he's talking about us all.

Well, how obtuse of these "western reviewers" to miss that point and draw such wrong conclusions! But the trouble is that not everyone can be as bright as Mr. Allen. Perhaps for most ordinary people what Africa needs is a far less com-plicated act of restoration. The Canadian novelist and critic Margaret Laurence saw this happening already in the way many African writers are interpreting their world, making it

> . . . neither idyllic, as the views of some national-ists would have had it, nor barbaric, as the mis-sionaries and European administrators wished and needed to believe.[7]

And in the epilogue to the same book she makes the point even more strongly:

> No writer of any quality has viewed the old Africa in an idealized way, but they have tried to regain what is rightly theirs—a past composed of real and vulnerable people, their ancestors, not the fig-ments of missionary and colonialist imaginations.

Ultimately the question of ideological sides which Mr. Allen threw in only to dismiss it again with contempt may not be as far-fetched as he thinks. For colonialism itself was built also on an ideology (although its adherents may no longer realize it) which, despite many setbacks, survives into our own day, and indeed is ready again at the end of a qui-escent phase of self-doubt for a new resurgence of prosely-tization, even, as in the past, among its prime victims!

Fortunately, it can no longer hope for the role of un-challenged arbiter in other people's affairs that it once took so much for granted. There are clear signs that critics and readers from those areas of the world where continuing in-cidents and recent memories of racism, colonialism and other forms of victimization exist will more and more de-mand to know from their writers just on whose ideological side they are playing. And we writers had better be prepared to reckon with this questioning. For no amount of prestige or laurels of metropolitan reputation would seem large enough to silence or overawe it. Consider, for instance, a recent judgement on V. S. Naipaul by a fellow Caribbean, Ivan Van Sertima:

---

[7][Achebe] Margaret Lawrence, *Long Drums and Cannons,* London, Macmil-lan, 1968, p. 9.

His brilliancy of wit I do not deny but, in my opinion, he has been overrated by English critics whose sensibilities he insidiously flatters by his stock-in-trade: self-contempt.[8]

A Nigerian, Ime Ikiddeh, was even less ceremonious in his dismissal of Naipaul, who he thought did not deserve the attention paid to him by Ngũgĩ wa Thiong'o in his *Homecoming*.[9] One need not accept these judgements in order to see them as signs of things to come.

Meanwhile the seduction of our writers by the blandishments of colonialist criticism is matched by its misdirection of our critics. Thus, an intelligent man like Dr. Sunday Anozie, the Nigerian scholar and critic, is able to dismiss the high moral and social earnestness sometimes expressed by one of our greatest poets, Christopher Okigbo, as only a mark of underdevelopment. In his book *Christopher Okigbo,* the most extensive biographical and critical study of the poet to date, Dr. Anozie tells us of Okigbo's "passion for truth," which apparently makes him sometimes too outspoken, makes him the talkative weaverbird "incapable of whispered secrets." And he proceeds to offer the following explanation:

No doubt the thrill of actualized prophecy can sometimes lead poets particularly in the young countries to confuse their role with that of seers, and novelists to see themselves as teachers. Whatever the social, psychological, political and economic basis for it in present-day Africa, this interchangeability of role between the creative writer and the prophet appears to be a specific phenomenon of underdevelopment and therefore, like it also, a passing or ephemeral phase.[10]

And he cites the authority of C. M. Bowra[11] in support of his explanation. The fallacy of the argument lies, of course, in its assumption that when you talk about a people's "level of development" you define their total condition and assign them an indisputable and unambiguous place on mankind's evolutionary ladder; in other words, that you are enabled by the authority of that phrase to account for all their material as well as spiritual circumstance. Show me a people's plumbing, you say, and I can tell you their art.

I should have thought that the very example of the Hebrew poet /prophets which Dr. Anozie takes from Bowra to demonstrate underdevelopment and confusion of roles would have been enough to alert him to the folly of his thesis. Or is he seriously suggesting that the poetry of these men—Isaiah, for example—written, it seems, out of a confusion of roles, in an underdeveloped society, is less good than what is written today by poets who are careful to remain within the proper bounds of poetry within developed societies? Personally, I should be quite content to wallow in Isaiah's error and write "For unto us a child is born."

Incidentally, any reader who is at all familiar with some of the arguments that go on around modern African literature will have noticed that in the passage I have just quoted from Dr. Anozie he is not only talking about Okigbo but also alluding (with some disapproval) to a paper I read at Leeds University ten years ago which I called "The Novelist as Teacher"; Anozie thus kills two weaverbirds dextrously with one stone! In his disapproval of what I had to say he follows, of course, in the footsteps of certain Western literary schoolmasters from whom I had already earned many sharp reprimands for that paper, who told me in clear terms that an artist had no business being so earnest.

It seems to me that this matter is of serious and fundamental importance, and must be looked at carefully. Earnestness and its opposite, levity, may be neither good nor bad in themselves but merely appropriate or inappropriate according to circumstance. I hold, however, and have held from the very moment I began to write, that earnestness *is* appropriate to my situation. Why? I suppose because I have a deepseated need to alter things within that situation, to find for myself a little more room than has been allowed me in the world. I realize how pompous or even frightening this must sound to delicate sensibilities, but I can't help it.

The missionary who left the comforts of Europe to wander through my primeval forest was extremely earnest. He had to be; he came to change my world. The builders of empire who turned me into a "British protected person" knew the importance of being earnest; they had that quality of mind which Imperial Rome before them understood so well: *gravitas.* Now, it seems to me pretty obvious that if I desire to change the role and identity fashioned for me by those earnest agents of colonialism I will need to borrow some of their resolve. Certainly, I could not hope to do it through self-indulgent levity.

But of course I do appreciate also that the world is large and that all men cannot be, indeed must not be, of one mind. I appreciate that there are people in the world who have no need or desire to change anything. Perhaps they have already accomplished the right amount of change to ensure their own comfort. Perhaps they see the need for change but feel pow-

[8][Achebe] Ivan Van Sertima, *Caribbean Writers,* London, New Beacon, 1968, foreword.

[9][Achebe] Ibid., p. xiv.

[10][Achebe] Sunday O. Anozie, *Christopher Okigbo,* London, Evans Bros., 1972, p. 17.

[11]C. M. Bowra (1898–1971), English critic.

erless to attempt it, or perhaps they feel it is someone else's business. For these people, earnestness is a dirty word or is simply tiresome. Even the evangelist, once so earnest and certain, now sits back in contemplation of his church, its foundation well and truly laid, its edifice rising majestically where once was jungle; the colonial governor who once brought his provinces so ruthlessly to heel prefers now to speak of the benefits of peace and orderly government. Certainly, they would much rather have easy-going natives under their jurisdiction than earnest ones—unless of course the earnestness be the perverse kind that turns in against itself.

The first nationalists and freedom fighters in the colonies, hardly concerned to oblige their imperial masters, were offensively earnest. They had no choice. They needed to alter the arrangement which kept them and their people out in the rain and the heat of the sun. They fought and won some victories. They changed a few things and seemed to secure certain powers of action over others. But quite quickly the great collusive swindle that was independence showed its true face to us. And we were dismayed; but only momentarily for even in our defeat we had gained something of inestimable value—a baptism of fire.

And so our world stands in just as much need of change today as it ever did in the past. Our writers responding to something in themselves and acting also within the traditional concept of an artist's role in society—using his art to control his environment—have addressed themselves to some of these matters in their art. And their concern seems to upset certain people whom history has dealt with differently and who persist in denying the validity of experiences and destinies other than theirs. And worst of all, some of our own critics who ought to guide these people out of their error seem so anxious to oblige them. Whatever the social, psychological, political and economic basis for this acquiescence, one hopes that it is only a passing and an ephemeral phase!

If this earnestness we speak of were manifested by just one or two writers in Africa there might perhaps be a good case for dismissing it out of hand. But look at the evidence:

Amos Tutuola has often given as a reason for his writing the need to preserve his traditional culture. It is true that a foreign critic, Adrian Roscoe, has chosen to jubilate over what appears to him like Tutuola's lack of "an awareness of cultural, national and racial affinities,"[12] but such an opinion may reflect more accurately his own wishful thinking than Tutuola's mind. Certainly a careful reading of *The Palm-*

Wine Drinkard will not bear out the assertion that colonialism is "dead for him." Why would he go out of his way to tell us, for example, that "both white and black deads were living in the Dead's Town"[13] unless he considers the information significant, as indeed anyone who lived in the Lagos of the 1950s would readily appreciate? For although Nigeria experienced only "benign colonialism," it required a monumental demonstration of all nationalist organizations in the territory after a particularly blatant incident of racism in a Lagos hotel to compel the administration into token relaxation of the practice whereby Whites and Blacks lived in trim reservations or squalid townships separated by a regulation two-mile cordon sanitaire. Some day a serious critic interested in such matters will assemble and interpret Tutuola's many scattered allusions to colonialism for the benefit of more casual readers. For there are such intriguing incidents as the Drinkard's deliverance of the Red People from an ancient terror which required them to sacrifice one victim every year, for which blessing he lives among them for a while exploiting their cheap labour to develop and extend his plantations "becoming richer than the rest of the people in that town" until the moment of crisis arrives and he causes "the whole of them" to be wiped out. Such a critic will no doubt pay particular attention to the unperturbed and laconic comment of the deliverer's wife: ". . . all the lives of the natives were lost and the life of the non-natives saved."[14] But until that serious critic comes along, Mr. Roscoe can certainly have the comfort of believing that "if Achebe and Soyinka want to write in order to change the world, Tutuola has other reasons."

And then Camara Laye. As recently as 1972 he was saying in an interview:

> In showing the beauty of this culture, my novel testifies to its greatness. People who had not been aware that Africa had its own culture were able to grasp the significance of our past and our civilization. I believe that this understanding is the most meaningful contribution of African literature.[15]

The distinguished and versatile Sierra Leonian, Davidson Abioseh Nicol—scientist, writer and diplomat—explaining why he wrote, said:

> . . . because I found that most of those who wrote about us seldom gave any nobility to their African

---

[12][Achebe] Adrian A. Roscoe, *Mother Is Gold,* Cambridge University Press, 1971, pp. 98–9.

[13][Achebe] Amos Tutuola, *The Palm-Wine Drinkard,* London, Faber, 1952, p. 100.

[14][Achebe] Ibid., p. 92.

[15][Achebe] Camara Laye, interviewed by J. Steven Rubin, *African Report,* Washington, D.C., May 1972, p. 22.

characters unless they were savages or servants or facing impending destruction. I knew differently.[16]

One could go on citing example after example of earnestness among African writers. But one final quotation—from Kofi Awoonor, the fine Ghanaian poet, novelist and essayist—should suffice:

> An African writer must be a person who has some kind of conception of the society in which he is living and the way he wants the society to go.[17]

All this juvenile earnestness must give unbearable offence to mature people. Have we not heard, they may ask, what Americans say—that the place for sending messages is the Western Union? Perhaps we have; perhaps we haven't. But the plain fact is that we are *not* Americans. Americans have their vision; we have ours. We do not claim that ours is superior; we only ask to keep it. For, as my forefathers said, the firewood which a people have is adequate for the kind of cooking they do. To levy a charge of underdevelopment against African writers today may prove as misguided and uninformed as a similar dismissal of African art by visitors of an earlier age before the coming of Picasso. Those worthy men saw little good around them, only child-like and grotesque distortions. Frank Willett, in his excellent book *African Art,* tells us of one such visitor to Benin in 1701, a certain David Nyendael, who on being taken to the royal gallery described the objects as being:

> . . . so wretchedly carved that it is hardly possible to distinguish whether they are most like men or beasts; notwithstanding which my guides were able to distinguish them into merchants, soldiers, wild beast hunters, etc.[18]

Most people today would be inclined to ascribe the wretchedness to Nyendael's own mind and taste rather than to the royal art of Benin. And yet, for me, his comment is almost saved by his acknowledgement, albeit grudging, of the very different perception of his guides, the real owners of the culture.

The colonialist critic, unwilling to accept the validity of sensibilities other than his own, has made particular point of dismissing the African novel. He has written lengthy articles to prove its non-existence largely on the grounds that the novel is a peculiarly Western genre, a fact which would interest us if our ambition was to write "Western" novels. But, in any case, did not the black people in America, deprived of their own musical instruments, take the trumpet and the trombone and blow them as they had never been blown before, as indeed they were not designed to be blown? And the result, was it not jazz? Is any one going to say that this was a loss to the world or that those first Negro slaves who began to play around with the discarded instruments of their masters should have played waltzes and foxtrots? No! Let every people bring their gifts to the great festival of the world's cultural harvest and mankind will be all the richer for the variety and distinctiveness of the offerings.

My people speak disapprovingly of an outsider whose wailing drowned the grief of the owners of the corpse. One last word to the owners. It is because our own critics have been somewhat hesitant in taking control of our literary criticism (sometimes—let's face it—for the good reason that we will not do the hard work that should equip us) that the task has fallen to others, some of whom (again we must admit) have been excellent and sensitive. And yet most of what remains to be done can best be tackled by ourselves, the owners. If we fall back, can we complain that others are rushing forward? A man who does not lick his lips, can he blame the harmattan for drying them?

Let us emulate those men of Benin, ready to guide the curious visitor to the gallery of their art, willing to listen with politeness even to his hasty opinions but careful, most careful, to concede nothing to him that might appear to undermine their own position within their heritage or compromise the integrity of their indigenous perception. For supposing the artists of Benin and of Congo and Angola had agreed with Nyendael in 1701 and abandoned their vision and begun to make their images in the style of "developed" Portugal, would they not have committed a grave disservice to Africa and ultimately to Europe herself and the rest of the world? Because they did not, it so happened that after the passage of two centuries other Europeans, more sensitive by far than Nyendael, looked at their work again and learnt from it a new way to see the world.

---

[16][Achebe] Davidson Abioseh Nicol, *The Truly Married Woman and Other Stories,* London, Fontana, 1965, introduction.

[17][Achebe] Kofi Awoonor, quoted in Per Wästberg (ed.), *The Writer in Modern Africa,* Uppsala, Almqvist & Wiksell.

[18][Achebe] Frank Willett, *African Art,* New York, Praeger, 1971, p. 102.

Stanley Fish

b. 1938

Stanley Fish's work is identified with the kind of criticism that emphasizes the role of reading. Indeed, as his work has developed the role of reading has effectively usurped the role of the text, to the extent that in his later essays texts are products of humanly constituted models and have no "autonomy" or "life of their own." In this development Fish extends his distance from the New Criticism, which he early set out to oppose. Fish's earliest view was that texts dictated reader-response as the readers proceeded through them. His books on Milton and seventeenth-century poetry charted that process. Later, however, he turned this view inside out. The text now is a construct of readerly conventions, characterized as products of an "interpretive community." No interpreter is free of such a community. On this ground Fish claims that his criticism is not a return to radical subjectivity but the rejection of subjectivity as an illusion, since readers are always reading out of communal conventions and cannot avoid it without total detachment from meaning itself.

The next question is how such communities are formed and by whom. This leads in turn to issues of power and who has the authority to establish and control reading, that is, to specify what texts mean or rather what meaning the community is to give them. Criticism clearly is political.

In this essay Fish observes an effort to disassociate himself from a common characterization of poststructural deconstruction, which claims that deconstruction leads to absolute indeterminancy of meaning. Fish claims that "determinancy and decidability are always available, not, however, because of the constraints imposed by the language or the world—that is, by entities independent of context—but because of the constraints built into the context or contexts in which we find ourselves operating." In *Is There a Text in This Class?* Fish follows this essay with a reply to a critic of it.

The books by Fish are *John Skelton's Poetry* (1965), *Surprised by Sin* (1971), *Self-Consuming Artifacts* (1972), *The Living Temple* (1978), *Is There a Text in This Class?* (1980), and *Doing What Comes Naturally: Change, Rhetoric, and the Nature of Theory in Literary and Legal Studies* (1989).

Normal Circumstances, Literal Language, Direct Speech Acts, the Ordinary, the Everyday, the Obvious, What Goes Without Saying, and Other Special Cases

On May Day, 1977, Pat Kelly, an outfielder for the Baltimore Orioles, hit two home runs in a game against the California Angels. The *Baltimore Sun* devoted three columns to the story, in part because Kelly had rarely displayed such power (he had hit only five home runs in the entire previous season) but largely because of the terms in which he saw his accomplishment. In fact, Kelly didn't see it as his at all but as the working through him of divine Providence. Two years previously he had experienced a religious conversion. As he reports it, "I had been like a normal ballplayer. I was an extreme party-er, hanging around in bars and chasing all the women. But then this change came over me, and I have dedicated myself to Him." The effects of this change are described by the *Sun* reporter, Michael Janofsky, whose comments betray some understandable exasperation: "It is not even possible to discuss [with Kelly] the events of yesterday's game—or any game—on strictly a baseball level. He does not view his home runs as merely a part of athletic competition. They are part of his religious existence." One assumes that Janofsky had tried to discuss the events of yesterday's game and found that Kelly simply did not recognize the facts to which sports writers' questions routinely refer. These are the facts that exist on "strictly a baseball level," a wonderful phrase that can serve to identify the subject of this essay, a level of observation or discourse at which meanings are obvious and indisputable, the level of the ordinary, the normal, the usual, the everyday, the straightforward, the literal. From Janofsky's point of view it is this level that Kelly has lost, but from Kelly's point of view it has simply been redefined: as Janofsky reports, he now *literally* sees everything as a function of his religious existence; it is not that he allegorizes events after they have been normally perceived but that his normal perception is of events as the evidence of

NORMAL CIRCUMSTANCES . . . AND OTHER SPECIAL CASES. Normal Circumstances first appeared in 1978 and is reprinted from *Is There a Text in This Class?* Cambridge, Mass.: Harvard University Press, Copyright © 1980 by the President and Fellows of Harvard College. Reprinted by permission of the publisher.

supernatural forces. Kelly played on May 1st only because the regular right fielder came down with conjunctivitis, and "even that," Janofsky exclaims, "he interpreted as divine intervention." "Interpreted" is not quite right because it suggests an imposition upon raw data of a meaning not inherent in them, but for Kelly the meaning is prior to the data which will always have the same preread shape. The effort that Janofsky must make before he can read providential design into everyday occurrences is *natural* for the born-again Christian, who would now have to make an effort wholly *un*natural in order once again to see a "mere athletic competition."

What this suggests is that categories like "the natural" and "the everyday" are not essential but conventional. They refer not to properties of the world but to properties of the world as it is given to us by our interpretive assumptions. In the world in which Janofsky is situated as an independent agent amidst equally independent phenomena, Kelly is an anomaly (and therefore noteworthy) because rather than accepting that world as it is, he populates it with the invisible presences demanded by his belief. That is, Janofsky assumes (without being aware of the assumption) that he speaks from a position above or below or to the side of belief, but in fact he speaks from within an *alternative* belief, one that gives him his world of "natural" causes as surely as Kelly's belief gives him a world alive with divine interventions. At stake here is the status of the ordinary. It would never occur to Janofsky to explain or defend the basis on which he describes events on a "strictly baseball level" (as he asks Kelly to explain and defend his point of view); he is simply describing what is there. That is what the ordinary is, that which appears to be there independently of anything we might say or think about it. It does not require comment (one doesn't write news stories about it) because it is obvious, right there on the surface; anyone can see it. But what anyone sees is not independent of his verbal and mental categories but is in fact a product of them; and it is because these categories, rather than being added to perception, are its content that the entities they bring into being seem to be a part of the world in the sense that they were there before there was anyone to perceive them. In other words, while the ordinary and the obvious are always with us because we are always in the grip of some belief or other, they can change. They have changed for Kelly and that is why his story can bear the weight I am putting on it. "I had," he says, "been like a normal ballplayer," by which he means that he saw what normal ballplayers see. Now what he just as normally sees are divine interventions. His conversion follows the pattern prescribed by Augustine in *On Christian Doctrine*. The eye that was in bondage to the phenomenal world (had as its constitutive principle the autonomy of that world) has been cleansed and purged and is now capable of seeing what is really there, what is obvious, what anyone who has the eyes can see: "to the healthy and pure internal eye He is everywhere."[1] He is everywhere not as the result of an interpretive act self-consciously performed on data otherwise available, but as the result of an interpretive act performed at so deep a level that it is indistinguishable from consciousness itself.

I have lingered over this example because it seems to me to bear (however indirectly) on the question most frequently debated in current literary discussions: What is in the text? That question assumes that at some (perhaps molecular) level what is in the text is independent of and prior to whatever people have said about it, and that therefore the text is stable, even though interpretations of it may vary. I want to argue that there always is a text (just as there always is an ordinary world) but that what is in it can change, and therefore at no level is it independent of and prior to interpretation. My literary example is Milton's *Samson Agonistes,* a text whose history has a surprising relationship to Pat Kelly's conversion.

Like Milton's other major works, *Samson Agonistes* has received many readings. Among the readings now considered acceptable is one in which Samson's story is seen in relationship to the life of Christ. In its starkest form, the argument for this reading has the air of a paradox: *Samson Agonistes* is about Christ because he is nowhere mentioned. Such an argument seems to fly in the face of the rules of evidence, but in fact it illustrates something very important about evidence: it is always a function of what it is to be evidence for, and is never independently available. That is, the interpretation determines what will count as evidence for it, and the evidence is able to be picked out only because the interpretation has *already* been assumed. In this case, the evidence is evidence for a typological interpretation, and that is why it *is* evidence even if, in some sense, it is not there. Typology is a way of reading the Old Testament as a prefiguration or foreshadowing of events in the life of Christ. It is not, at least in its Protestant version, allegorical because it insists on respecting the historical reality of the type who is unaware of his significance as an anticipation of one greater than he. In *Paradise Lost,* this significance can be pointed out by the narrator, who stands outside the consciousnesses of the characters and therefore can look forward to the new dispensation without violating typological decorum. In *Samson Agonistes,* however, there is no narrator, and the con-

sciousnesses of the characters mark the limits of allowable awareness. It follows (given a disposition to read typologically) that the absence of any reference to Christ, rather than being evidence that he is not being referred to, is evidence of Milton's intention to respect typological decorum. As William Madsen puts it, "Instead of collapsing Samson and Christ, [Milton] is concerned with measuring the distance between the various levels of awareness . . . possible to those living under the old dispensation and the level of awareness revealed by Christ."[2] Once this characterization of Milton's intention has been specified, the text will immediately assume the shape that Madsen proceeds to describe: "If . . . Samson is viewed first of all as a concrete individual living in a concrete historical situation, then his significance for the Christian reader lies primarily in his inability to measure up to the heroic norm delineated in *Paradise Regained*" (pp. 201–202). The fact that this significance is unavailable to the characters is precisely what makes it inescapable for the Christian reader. Moreover, it is not a figurative significance, one that is imposed on the text's literal level; rather it is built into the text as it is *immediately* seen by anyone who operates within Madsen's interpretive assumptions. A reader who was innocent of those assumptions would not see that significance, but he would see some other, and that other would be similarly the product of the assumptions within which *he* was operating. In either case (and in any other that could be imagined) the resulting meaning would be a *literal* one that followed directly upon a determination of what was in the text. The category "in the text" is usually thought to refer to something that is irreducibly there independently of and prior to all interpretive activities. The example of *Samson Agonistes* suggests that what is perceived to be "in the text" is a *function* of interpretive activities, although these activities are performed at so primary a level that the shapes they yield seem to be there before we have done anything. In other words, the category "in the text," like the category of the "ordinary," is always full (because there is never a point at which a set of interpretive assumptions is not in force), but what fills it is not always the same. For some present-day readers Christ is "in the text" of *Samson Agonistes,* for others he is not, and before the typological interpretation of the poem was introduced and developed by Michael Krouse in 1949, he was not "in the text" for anyone. Again, it is important to see that the question of what is in the text cannot be settled by appealing to the evidence since the evidence will have become available only because some determina-

[1][Fish] Augustine, *On Christian Doctrine,* trans. D. W. Robertson, Jr. (New York: Bobbs-Merrill, 1958), p. 13.

[2][Fish] William Madsen, *From Shadowy Types to Truth* (New Haven: Yale University Press, 1968), p. 198.

tion of what is in the text has already been made. (Otherwise it would be impossible to read.) Indeed the same piece of evidence will not be the same when it is cited in support of differing determinations of what is in the text. Thus for one reader the fact that Christ is not mentioned "proves" that he is not in the text, while for another the same "fact" (really not the same) proves that he is. Nor can one descend to a lower level of description and assert that at least *that* fact about the text (that Christ is not mentioned) is beyond dispute; for the two readers I posit would be stipulating two different notions of "mention," and indeed the second reader would be claiming that the mention of Samson *includes* Christ and that thus He is no less mentioned than his Old Testament prefiguration. This does not mean that the text of *Samson Agonistes* is ambiguous or unstable; it is always stable and never ambiguous. It is just that it is stable in more than one direction, as a succession of interpretive assumptions give it a succession of stable shapes. Mine is not an argument for an infinitely plural or an open text, but for a text that is always set; and yet because it is set not for all places or all times but for wherever and however long a particular way of reading is in force, it is a text that can change.

Perhaps a shorter example, one taken neither from the sports pages nor from literature but from (if you will pardon the expression) life, will make the point clearer. I have in mind a sign that is affixed in this unpunctuated form to the door of the Johns Hopkins University Club:

PRIVATE MEMBERS ONLY

I have had occasion to ask several classes what that sign means, and I have received a variety of answers, the least interesting of which is, "Only those who are secretly and not publicly members of this club may enter it." Other answers fall within a predictable and narrow range: "Only the genitalia of members may enter" (this seems redundant), or "You may only bring in your own genitalia," or (and this is the most popular reading, perhaps because of its Disney-like anthropomorphism) "*Only* genitalia may enter." In every class, however, some Dr. Johnson-like positivist rises to say, "But you're just playing games; everyone knows that the sign really means, 'Only those persons who belong to this club may enter it.'" He is of course right. Everyone does know (although, as we shall see, everyone does not always know the same thing), but we can still inquire into the source of that knowledge. How is it that a text so demonstrably unstable can be stabilized to such a degree that a large number of people know immediately what it means? The answer can be found in the exercise performed by my students. What they did was move the words out of a context (the faculty

club door) in which they had a literal and obvious meaning into another context (my classroom) in which the meaning was no less obvious and literal and yet was different. What they did not do was move away from a meaning that was available apart from a context to the various meanings contexts confer. Paradoxically the exercise does not prove that the words can mean anything one likes, but that they always and only mean one thing, although that one thing is not always the same. The one thing they mean will be a function of the shape language *already has* when we come upon it in a situation, and it is the knowledge that is the content of being in a situation that will have stabilized it. In the case of PRIVATE MEMBERS ONLY, the knowledge is the knowledge of what to do with signs on faculty club doors. Those who enter the club do not first perceive the sign in some uninterpreted or acontextual form and *then* construe it so as to conform with the situation; rather, being in the situation means that they have already construed it, even before they see it. That is, to know what to do with signs on faculty club doors is already to have done it because that knowledge will already have been organizing perception.

This is not to say that the knowledge of what to do with the signs on faculty club doors is itself stable, but that in whatever form it takes, it is always stabilizing. In many municipalities a business will incorporate as a club in order to secure certain tax advantages, and in some "dry" states incorporation is a way of circumventing laws that prohibit the public sale of liquor. In such situations the word "private" means "public" (it is not restrictive at all, except in the sense that any business establishment is restrictive), and the sign PRIVATE MEMBERS ONLY would be immediately understood to mean "anyone who has the price may enter." That would then be as literal a reading as "Only those persons who belong to this club may enter it" because, to those whose understandings were an extension of the situation they were already in, the words could mean nothing else. It may seem confusing and even contradictory to assert that a text may have more than one literal reading, but that is because we usually reserve "literal" for the single meaning a text will always (or should always) have, while I am using "literal" to refer to the different single meanings a text will have in a succession of different situations. There always is a literal meaning because in any situation there is always a meaning that seems obvious in the sense that it is there independently of anything we might do. *But that only means that we have already done it,* and in another situation, when we have already done something else, there will be another obvious, that is, literal, meaning. The stronger sense of literal, in which "single" is inseparable from "once and for all," would itself make sense only if there were a meaning that was apprehensible apart from any situation whatsoever, a meaning that was not the product of an interpretation but was available independently. Every literal meaning comes to us with that claim, but it is a claim that seems to be supportable only because an interpretive act is already in force but is so embedded in the situation (its structure *is* the structure of the situation) that it doesn't seem to be an act at all. We are never not in a situation. Because we are never not in a situation, we are never not in the act of interpreting. Because we are never not in the act of interpreting, there is no possibility of reaching a level of meaning beyond or below interpretation. But in every situation some or other meaning will appear to us to be uninterpreted because it is isomorphic with the interpretive structure the situation (and therefore our perception) already has. Therefore, there always will be a literal reading, but (1) it will not always be the same one and (2) it can change.

In this newly defined sense, a literal reading can even be plural, as it is for my students when they are asked, "What does PRIVATE MEMBERS ONLY mean?" Constituting *their* perception is not the knowledge of what to do with signs on faculty club doors but the knowledge of what to do with texts written on blackboards by professors of English literature. That is, professors of English literature do not put things on boards unless they are to be examples of problematic or ironic or ambiguous language. Students know that because they know what it means to be in a classroom, and the categories of understanding that are the content of that knowledge will be organizing what they see before they see it. Irony and ambiguity are not properties of language but are functions of the expectations with which we approach it. If we expect a text to be ambiguous, we will in the act of reading it imagine situations in which it means first one thing and then another (there is no text with which this cannot be done), and those plural meanings will, in the context of that situation, be that text's literal reading. That is, in a situation in which the obvious (immediately apprehensible) reading is a plural one, meaning more than one thing will be the one thing a text means.

In summary, then, there are two things I do not want to say about PRIVATE MEMBERS ONLY: that it has a literal meaning, and that it doesn't. It does not have a literal meaning in the sense of some irreducible content which survives the sea change of situations; but in each of those situations one meaning (even if it is plural) will seem so obvious that one cannot see how it could be otherwise, and that meaning will be literal.

If the question of what is literal is important in literary discussions, it is the central question in the law, where determining what a text (contract, statute, case, precedent, ruling)

says is the business everyone is in. A close examination of the way that business is conducted will reveal a pattern that should by now be familiar. My example is a case that deals with the probating of wills, *Riggs v. Palmer*, New York, 1889.[3] The decision is prefaced by a rehearsal of the facts: "On the thirteenth day of August, 1880, Francis B. Palmer made his last will and testament, in which he gave small legacies to his two daughters, Mrs. Riggs and Mrs. Preston, the plaintiffs in this action, and the remainder to his grandson, the defendant Elmer E. Palmer." In 1882 the elder Palmer married one Mrs. Bressee, and there was some indication that he would alter the will so as to make his new wife the principal beneficiary. It was then that Elmer acted: "He knew," says the court "of the provisions made in his favor . . . and that he might prevent his grandfather from revoking such provisions, which he had manifested some intention to do, and to obtain the speedy enjoyment and immediate possession of his property, he willfully murdered him by poisoning him. He now claims the property and the sole question for our determination is, Can he have it? The defendants say that the testator is dead; that his will was made in due form, and has been admitted to probate, and that, therefore, it must have effect according to the letter of the law." It is with this last phrase—"the letter of the law"—that this example falls into line with the others. Elmer's lawyers have presented the court with a dilemma: either it must decide in favor of the client or it must go against what the law plainly says. The law in this case is a statute that reads as follows: "All persons, except idiots, persons of unsound mind and infants, may devise their real estate, by a last will and testament, duly executed, according to the provisions of this article." In effect Elmer and his counsel are arguing that there is nothing in the statute that bars a murderer from inheriting or a victim from bequeathing his property to a murderer, and that therefore his act is irrelevant to the question of probate.

The court begins rather badly by conceding Elmer's basic claim: "It is quite true that statutes regulating the making, proof, and effect of wills, and the devolution of property, if literally construed, and if their force and effect can in no way and under no circumstances be controlled or modified, give this property to the murderer." This would be a damaging admission were it not that as the decision unfolds the court proceeds to take it back. It does this by introducing the notion of purpose and by insisting that the statute be read in its light: "The purpose of the statutes was to enable testators

---

[3][Fish] *Riggs v. Palmer*, 115 N.Y. 506, 22 N.E. 188 (1889). All further references to this text will be at 189.

to dispose all of their estates to the objects of their bounty at death . . . and in considering and giving effect to them, this purpose must be kept in view. It was the intention of the law-makers that the donees in a will should have the property given to them. But it never could have been their intention that a donee who murdered the testator to make the will operative should have any benefit under it." Why could it, "never have been their intention"? The court answers that question by invoking as one of the "general fundamental maxims of the common law" the principle that "no one shall be permitted to profit by his own fraud, or take advantage of his own wrong, or found any claim upon his own iniquity, or to acquire property by his own crime." At this point the court's strategy becomes clear. It wants to find a way of reading the statute so that it bars Elmer from inheriting, and the way it finds is to assert that something goes without saying (that is why it is a matter of common, that is, unwritten, law) and therefore has been said. The reasoning is the same that yields the typological reading of *Samson Agonistes:* just as the mention of Samson is understood to include a reference to Christ, so is the text of a statute understood (at least under this interpretive assumption) to include a proviso disallowing any claim founded upon the commission of a wrong.

It is a very good argument, and the court errs only in thinking that in order to make it, the literal reading must be set aside. That is, the court apparently believes that only *it* is reading the statute with "a purpose in view" while the defendant is urging a reading of what the words literally express. The truth of the matter is that both are pointing to what the words literally express but in the light of two different purposes. The opposition between a literal and a nonliteral reading could be maintained only if it were possible to conceive of a reading that did not follow from the assumption of some purpose or other, but as Kenneth Abraham observes, "A statute without a purpose would be meaningless . . . to speak of the literal meaning of a statute . . . is already to have read it in the light of some purpose, to have engaged in an interpretation."[4] In other words, any reading that is plain and obvious in the light of some assumed purpose (and it is impossible not to assume one) is a literal reading; but no reading is *the* literal reading in the sense that is available apart from any purpose whatsoever. If it is assumed that the purpose of probate is to ensure the orderly devolution of property at all costs, then the statute in this case will have the plain meaning urged by the defendant; but if it is assumed that no law ever operates in favor of someone who would

profit by his crime, then the "same" statute will have a meaning that is different, but no less plain. In either case the statute will have been literally construed, and what the court will have done is prefer one literal construction to another by invoking one purpose (assumed background) rather than another.

It is not that we first read the statute and then know its purpose; we know the purpose first, and only then can the statute be read. This is exactly the sequence the court follows, and at one point the principle underlying its procedure is articulated: "It is a familiar canon of construction that a thing which is within the intention of the makers of a statute is as much within the statute as if it were within the letter; and a thing which is within the letter of the statute is not within the statute, unless it be within the intention of the makers." The rhetoric of this sentence insists upon the distinction between what is intended and what is literally there, but the argument of the sentence takes the distinction away. It is your specification of the makers' intention that tells you what is in the statute, not your literal reading of the statute that informs you as to its makers' intention. This would seem to suggest that one need only recover the makers' intention in order to arrive at the *correct* literal reading; but the documents (including even *verbatim* reports) that would give us that intention are no more available to a literal reading (are no more uninterpreted) than the literal reading it would yield. However one specifies what is in a statute—whether by some theory of strict constructionism or by some construction of an original intention—that specification will have the same status as the specification of what is in *Samson Agonistes* or of what PRIVATE MEMBERS ONLY means. It can always be made, but as situations and the purposes which inform them change, it will have to be made again.

I could imagine someone objecting to the previous pages in the following way: "Aren't you in each of these examples simply talking about ambiguous language, language that can mean more than one thing?" My answer is that the objection would have force only if there were a kind of language to which ambiguous language could be opposed. That is, to label a sentence "ambiguous" will be to distinguish it only if there are sentences that always and only mean one thing, and I would contend that there are no such sentences. I am not saying that sentences always have more than one meaning, but that the sentence which is perceived as having only one meaning will not always have the same one. In other words, I am as willing to say that all sentences are straightforward as I am to say that all sentences are ambiguous. What I am not willing to do is say that any sentence is by right either one or the other. That is, I wish to deny that ambiguity is a property of some sentences and not of others.

4[Fish] Kenneth Abraham, "Intention and Authority in Statutory Interpretation" (paper delivered at the 1977 Modern Language Association session on Law and Literature).

Typically, the division of sentences into two classes (ambiguous, nonambiguous) is not defended; it is simply assumed in the course of presenting strings that are asserted to be obviously members of one or the other class. In a recent introduction to transformational grammar the following sentence is offered as an example of one that is ambiguous on its face: "The suit is light."[5] As the authors point out, the reference can be either to the suit's weight or its color, and the situation is not helped, they observe, when the sentence is expanded to read: "The suit is too light to wear." The additional material is not sufficiently disambiguating because the words do not combine in such a way as to make one reading inescapable; but when the sentence is further expanded to read "The suit is too light to wear on such a cold day," the ambiguity, we are told, disappears. In the new sentence, the "semantic environment" specified by "cold day" blocks one of the possible readings of "light," and the result is a perfectly straightforward utterance.

It is an elegant argument, but unfortunately it won't work. It takes only a moment of reflection to imagine a situation in which this sentence would have the reading that is now supposedly blocked. It so happens that I have a weakness for light-colored suits, and I have several that are heavy enough to wear on a cold day. My wife, however, is more conscious of the proprieties of fashion than I am and is likely to say to me, "That suit is too light to wear on such a cold day," and be immediately understood as meaning that the suit is too light in color. M. F. Garrett offers a similar counterexample to a supposedly unambiguous sentence put forward by Katz and Postal: "The stuff is light enough to carry." It is not ambiguous, Katz and Postal say, because "light enough to carry" cannot be understood to mean "light enough in color to be carried." But, objects Garrett, "it does not take an especially tortured context to make this the preferred reading:

> Scene: Highway patrolman lecturing to 3rd grade class.
>
> Patrolman: "When you are walking on a highway at night, it is important to wear light colored clothing or carry a light colored flag so that you will be visible to oncoming cars. For instance (holds up flag), this stuff is light enough to carry."[6]

_____

[5][Fish] John T. Grinder and Suzette Haden Elgin, *Guide to Transformational Grammar* (New York: Holt, Rinehart and Winston, 1973), p. 117.
[6][Fish] M. F. Garrett, "Does Ambiguity Complicate the Perception of Sentences?" in *Advances in Psycholinguistics,* ed. G. B. Flores d'Arcias and W. J. M. Levelt (Amsterdam: North-Holland, 1970), p. 54.

Katz and Postal might reply that what the counterexample shows is that the original sentence was not sufficiently explicit. If we were to add more information to it and write (let us say) "This stuff is light enough to carry even for a small child," it will be capable of one reading and of no other. But if this sentence were uttered by a manufacturer's representative, the word "carry" would be understood to mean "stock in inventory," and the speaker would be reminding a potential buyer that small children do not normally wear the darker colors. One could imagine counterexample following upon counterexample, but the result would always be the same; for no degree of explicitness will ever be sufficient to disambiguate the sentence if by disambiguate we understand *render it impossible to conceive of a set of circumstances in which its plain meaning would be other than it now appears to be.*

The conclusion that Garrett draws from this and other examples is that all sentences are ambiguous, but then he is faced with the problem of explaining the fact that "we simply don't notice most of the ambiguities that we encounter" (p. 50). It is a problem because Garrett has moved away from one version of an error only to embrace another. He correctly sees that no sentence always means the same thing, but this leads him to affirm that every sentence has more than one meaning. What he does not realize is that these positions are the same position in that they both assume a stage in the life of sentences *before* they are perceived in a context. It is just that in one position that stage is characterized by a timeless stability (means only one thing), in the other by a timeless instability (means more than one thing). The truth is that there is no such stage. A sentence is never apprehended independently of the context in which it is perceived, and therefore we never know a sentence except in the stabilized form a context has *already* conferred. But since a sentence can appear in more than one context, its stabilized form will not always be the same. It follows then that while no sentence is ambiguous in the sense that it has (as a constitutive property) more than one meaning, every sentence is ambiguous in the (undistinguishing) sense that the single meaning it will always have can change. Now, it is sometimes the case that we are asked to imagine first one and then another context in which a sentence will have different single meanings. In that case, we are in a *third* context in which the single meaning the sentence has is that it has more than one single meaning. The insight which makes perfect sense of these apparent paradoxes is firmly articulated by Garrett: "We must, I believe, always assume that any sentence is interpreted with respect to some context" (p. 51). Garrett then immediately demonstrates how easy it is to slip away from that insight by declaring that if "a sentence is ambiguous, it is the context which determines what reading will be assigned." In the interval of a typographical space, the contextless utterance has been revived since, presumably, no context at all has determined that the sentence is ambiguous in the first place. But by Garrett's own axiom, there is no "first place" in the sense of a state in which the natural (acontextual) properties of a sentence can be observed and enumerated. In order for the sentence to be perceived as ambiguous (or to be perceived at all), it must already be in a context, and the context, rather than any natural property, will be responsible for the ambiguity the sentence will then (in a limited sense) have.

A sentence is never not in a context. We are never not in a situation. A statute is never not read in the light of some purpose. A set of interpretive assumptions is always in force. A sentence that seems to need no interpretation is already the product of one. These statements have made my single point from a variety of perspectives, and I am about to make it again with another statement. No sentence is ever apprehended independently of some or other illocutionary force. Illocutionary force is the key term in speech-act theory. It refers to the way an utterance is taken—as an order, a warning, a promise, a proposal, a request and so on—and the theory's strongest assertion is that no utterance is ever taken purely, that is, without already having been understood as the performance of some illocutionary act. Consider, as an example, the sentence "I will go." Depending on the context in which it is uttered, "I will go" can be understood as a promise, a threat, a warning, a report, a prediction, or whatever, but it will always be understood as one of these, and it will never be an unsituated kernel of pure semantic value. In other words, "I will go" does not have a basic or primary meaning which is then put to various illocutionary uses; rather, "I will go" is known only in its illocutionary lives, and in each of them its meaning will be different. Moreover, if the meaning of a sentence is a function of its illocutionary force (the way it is taken), and if illocutionary force varies with circumstances, then illocutionary force is not a property of sentences but of situations. That is, while a sentence will always have an illocutionary force (because otherwise it would not have a meaning), the illocutionary force it has will not always be the same.

My authority for much of the preceding paragraph is John Searle, and therefore it is surprising to find that Searle, along with other speech-act theorists, is committed to a distinction between direct and indirect speech acts. A direct speech act is defined as one whose illocutionary force is a function of its meaning, and the best example of a direct speech act would be an explicit performative, that is, "I promise to pay you five dollars." An indirect speech act is one whose illocutionary force is something other than its lit-

eral meaning would suggest. "Can you reach the salt?" is literally a question about the hearer's abilities, but in normal circumstances it is heard as a request. The distinction then is between utterances that mean exactly what they say and utterances that mean something different or additional. As Searle puts it, "In indirect speech acts the speaker communicates to the hearer more than he actually says by way of relying on their mutually shared background information . . . together with the general powers of rationality and inference on the part of the hearer."[7] This assumes, of course, that in the performance of direct speech acts speaker and hearer do *not* rely on their mutually shared background information because what is actually said is available directly (hence the distinction). It is with this assumption that I would like to quarrel, if only because it reinstates what J. L. Austin in *How To Do Things with Words* was at such pains to dislodge, a class of utterances (constative utterances) that mean independently of situations, purposes, and goals. It seems to me that *all* utterances are understood by way of relying on "shared background information" and that therefore the distinction between direct and indirect speech acts, as it is usually formulated, will not hold.

What I have to show, then, is that the acts cited as direct are, in fact indirect, at least according to the theory's definition of the terms. My argument will take up Searle's as it appears in his first full example. Searle begins by imagining a conversation between two students. Student X says, "Let's go to the movies tonight," and student Y replies, "I have to study for an exam." The first sentence, Searle declares, "constitutes a proposal in virtue of its meaning," but the second sentence, which is understood as a rejection of the proposal, is not so understood in virtue of its meaning because "in virtue of its meaning it is simply a statement about Y" (pp. 61, 62). It is here, in the assertion that either of these sentences is ever taken in the way it is "in virtue of its meaning," that this account must finally be attacked. For if this were the case, then we would have to say that there is something about the meaning of a sentence that makes it more available for some illocutionary uses than for others, and this is precisely what Searle proceeds to say about "I have to study for an exam": "Statements of this form do not, in general, constitute rejections of proposals, even in cases in which they are made in response to a proposal. Thus, if Y had said *I have to eat popcorn tonight* or *I have to tie my shoes* in a normal context, neither of these utterances would have been a rejection of the proposal." (p. 62).

---

[7][Fish] John R. Searle, "Indirect Speech Acts," in *Syntax and Semantics, Volume 3: Speech Acts,* ed. Peter Cole and Jerry Morgan (New York: Academic Press, 1975), pp. 60–61.

At this point my question would be "Normal for whom?" Or, to put it another way: is it possible to imagine a set of circumstances in which "I have to eat popcorn tonight" would immediately and without any chain of inference be heard as a rejection of X's proposal? It is not only possible; it is easy. Let us suppose that student Y is passionately fond of popcorn and that it is not available in any of the local movie theaters. If student X knows these facts (if he and student Y mutually share background information), then he will hear "I have to eat popcorn tonight" as a rejection of his proposal. Or, let us suppose that student Y is by profession a popcorn taster; that is, he works in a popcorn manufacturing plant and is responsible for quality control. Again if student X knows this, he will hear "I have to eat popcorn tonight" as a rejection of his proposal because it will mean "Sorry, I have to work." Or, let us suppose that student Y owns seventy-five pairs of shoes and that he has been ordered by a dormitory housemother to retrieve them from various corners, arrange them neatly in one place, and tie them together in pairs so that they will not again be separated and scattered. In such a situation "I have to tie my shoes" will constitute a rejection of student X's proposal and will be so heard. Moreover, it is not just "I have to eat popcorn" and "I have to tie my shoes" that could be heard as a rejection of the proposal; given the appropriate circumstances *any* sentence ("The Russians are coming," "My pen is blue," "Why do you behave like that?") could be so heard. This does not mean that any sentence is potentially a proposal (that would be the mistake of ascribing properties to sentences) or that it doesn't matter what sentence a speaker utters, but that for any sentence circumstances could be imagined in which it would be understood as a proposal, and as nothing but a proposal.

The objection to these examples (which could easily be multiplied) is obvious: they have reference to *special* contexts, while Searle is talking about what sentences mean in a *normal* context. But for those who are in the contexts I describe, the meanings I specify would be the normal ones because they would be the only ones. Searle's argument will hold only if the category "normal" is transcendental, if what fills it is always the same, whatever the circumstances. But what is normal (like what is ordinary, literal, everyday) is a *function* of circumstances in that it depends on the expectations and assumptions that happen to be in force. Any other sense of normal would require that the circumstances not be circumstantial but essential (always in force), and that would be a contradiction in terms. In other words, "normal" is context specific and to speak of a normal context is to be either redundant (because whatever in a given context goes without saying *is* the normal) or incoherent (because it would refer to a context whose claim was not to be one).

In short, I am making the same argument for "normal context" that I have made for "literal meaning," "straightforward discourse," "the letter of the law," and the category of what is "in the text." There will always be a normal context, but it will not always be the same one. This means that if it becomes possible to see how "I have to eat popcorn" could be heard as a rejection of a proposal, it is not because we have imagined a set of special circumstances but because we have imagined an appropriate set of *normal* circumstances. The point can just as well be made from the opposite direction. Having to study for an exam is no more normal (in the sense that it is a state of which everyone has an implicit knowledge) than having to eat popcorn is special (in the sense that it is a departure from what everyone normally does). To be in either situation is to have already organized the world in terms of certain categories and possibilities for action (both verbal and physical), and in either situation the world so organized, along with the activities that can transpire within it, will be perceived as normal. Once again the moral is clear, even though it has the form of a paradox: a normal context is just the special context you happen to be in, although it will not be recognized as special because so long as you are in it whatever it permits you to see will seem obvious and inescapable.

From this perspective, Searle's argument falls apart. This first example, as he presents it, is intended to distinguish between:

(1) "I have to study for an exam" when it is "simply a statement about *Y*," that is, when it means what it says and is therefore a direct speech act;

(2) "I have to study for an exam" when it is a rejection of Y's proposal, that is, when by virtue of shared background it means more than it says and is an indirect speech act; and

(3) "I have to eat popcorn tonight," which cannot be a rejection of the proposal "without some special stage setting."

If what I have been saying is true, these distinctions cannot be maintained (at least as they are here formulated) because given different sets of special or differently normal circumstances, the three speech acts are equally direct or indirect. They are direct because in each case the illocutionary force they have will be immediately perceived; and they are indirect because their immediately perceived illocutionary force will have been a function of mutually shared background information (that is, of some or other special stage setting). The trick is to see that when Searle moves from "I have to study for an exam" as a statement about Y to "I have to study for an exam" as a rejection of a proposal, he has not moved from a literal meaning to a meaning that emerges in a set of circumstances, but from one meaning that emerges in a set of circumstances to another meaning that emerges in another set of circumstances. Both meanings are then equally circumstantial (indirect) and equally literal (direct), and in both cases the utterance means exactly what it says because what it says is a function of shared background information.

The argument will also hold for "Let's go to the movies tonight," although, for reasons that will become clear, it is harder to make. Here what has to be shown is the reverse of what had to be shown in the case of "I have to eat popcorn." Rather than having to imagine a situation in which an utterance ("I have to eat popcorn") could possibly count as the performance of a certain speech act, we have to imagine a situation in which an utterance ("Let's go to the movies tonight") could count as something *other* than the performance of a certain speech act. The problem is that the examples that first come to mind make Searle's point rather than mine. That is, they are examples in which the perceived illocutionary force is perceived only because a "more normal" illocutionary force is seen to be inappropriate. Thus if speakers X and Y are trapped in some wilderness, and one says to the other, "Let's go to the movies tonight," it will be heard not as a proposal but as a joke; or if student X is confined to his bed or otherwise immobilized, and student Y says, "Let's go to the movies tonight," it will be heard not as a proposal but as a dare. But in either case the dare or joke will be heard *only* because the circumstances rule out the possibility of a proposal, a possibility whose absence (and therefore whose presence) must be recognized for the effect to be secured. What we need are examples in which "Let's go to the movies tonight" is heard *immediately* as a dare or a joke (or as anything but a proposal) and which do not involve the two stage inferential procedure specified by Searle. And what we need too is an explanation of why such examples are relatively difficult to come by; that is, why it is so much harder to think oneself *out of* a necessary association between "Let's go to the movies tonight" and a proposal than it is to think oneself *into* a necessary association between "I have to eat popcorn" and the proposal's rejection.

First of all, Searle's analysis depends on the assumption of a generalized relationship between the use of "let's" and the performing of a proposal: "in general, literal utterances of this form will constitute a proposal, as in . . . 'Let's eat pizza tonight.' "[8] But in this very same paragraph Searle provides an example of an exception to his own generalization when he says, "Let us begin by considering a typical

case. . . ." In the context of his discourse, it is not really open to a reader (or, in the case of a lecture, to a hearer) to suggest another beginning or to counterpropose that he not begin at all. Moreover, a hearer who responded in either of these ways would be thought to have misunderstood the illocutionary force of "Let us," which is here not so much a proposal as it is the laying down of a plan. Similarly, when a quarterback leads his team out of the huddle by saying "Let's do it" or "Let's go," he is not proposing, but exhorting. It would be inappropriate for one of his linemen to answer "I have to study for an exam" or even to answer at all, just as it would be inappropriate if a member of a congregation were to demur when the minister said (here he would be announcing, not proposing) "Let us pray."

In each of these cases, "let's" does not introduce a proposal because in the situation as it is imagined the speaker is understood to be concluding or forestalling an exchange rather than initiating one. Notice that in Searle's example the understanding is exactly the reverse: "Let's go to the movies tonight" is assumed to be the first utterance in an exchange that has no antecedents, and that is why it is heard as a proposal. Placed differently, at the end rather than at the beginning of a conversation, the same utterance would be heard as an assent to a proposal that had already been made. (It would be equivalent to "OK, let's go to the movies tonight.") The point is that neither placement is intrinsically the more natural or normal one, and that the stage has to be set no less for "Let's go to the movies tonight" to be heard as a proposal than for "I have to eat popcorn" to be heard as its rejection.

Why then does Searle spend so little time setting that stage in relation to the time that I must spend to dismantle it? The answer is that it is already set for him by the habitual (not inevitable) practices of an entire society and that he need do nothing more than assume those practices in order to secure the benefit of their continuing operation. When someone is asked to assign an illocutionary force to an utterance, he does so in the context of the circumstances in which that utterance has been most often heard or spoken. For most of us those circumstances are the ones presupposed by Searle, and therefore it appears that the relationship between "Let's go to the movies tonight" and its stipulated force is natural when, in fact, it is a function of a context so widely shared that it doesn't seem to be one at all. It is just such contexts that produce the felt continuity of life by allowing us to rely on and assume as normative the meanings they make available; and it is because Searle invokes such a context (by failing to realize or point out that it is one) that so much effort is required to see around his example.

In a sense, then, the circumstances that lead us to assign the force of a proposal to "Let's go to the movies tonight"

---

[8][Fish] Ibid., pp. 61–62.

are normal in that they occur more frequently than do circumstances that would lead to a different assignment. But they remain circumstances still (statistically, not inherently, normal), and because they do, the main assertion of this section is intact: there is no distinction between direct and indirect speech acts because all speech acts are understood by way of relying on mutually shared background information. All speech acts are direct because their meanings are directly apprehended, and all speech acts are indirect because their directly apprehended meanings are functions of the situations in which they are embedded.

It is important to realize what my argument does *not* mean. It does not mean that a sentence can mean anything at all. In their discussion of indirect speech acts Herbert and Eve Clark point out that "under the right circumstances" any one of a number of sentences could be "used as a request to open the window; yet," they warn, "not just any sentence can serve this purpose," for "if so, communication would be chaotic" because "listeners would never know what speech act was being performed."[9] But the chaos the Clarks fear would be possible only if a sentence could mean anything at all *in the abstract*. A sentence, however, is never in the abstract; it is always in a situation, and the situation will already have determined the purpose for which it can be used. So it is not that any sentence can be used as a request to open the window, but that given any sentence, there are circumstances under which it would be heard as a request to open the window. A sentence neither means anything at all nor does it always mean the same thing; it always has the meaning that has been conferred on it by the situation in which it is uttered. Listeners *always* know what speech act is being

performed, not because there are limits to the illocutionary uses to which sentences can be put but because in any set of circumstances the illocutionary force a sentence may have will already have been determined.

The Clarks can stand for all those who think that it is necessary to anchor language in some set of independent and formal constraints, whether those constraints are given the name of literal meaning, or straightforward discourse, or direct speech acts, or the letter of the law, or normal circumstances, or the everyday world. The question that is always being asked is "Are there such constraints and, if so, how can we identify them?" Beyond that question, however, is the assumption that the constraints must be specifiable once and for all, and that if they are not so specifiable at *some* level, we live in a world of chaos where communication is entirely a matter of chance. What I have been saying again and again is that there are such constraints; they do not, however, inhere in language but in situations, and because they inhere in situations, the constraints we are always under are not always the same ones. Thus we can see how it is neither the case that meanings are objectively fixed nor that the meanings one construes are arbitrary. To many these have seemed the only alternatives, and that is why the claims for objectivity and subjectivity have been continually debated. It is because the position elaborated here is neither subjective nor objective (nor a combining of the two) that it can reconcile the two facts cited again and again by the respective combatants: (1) that there are no inherent constraints on the meanings a sentence may have, and (2) that, nevertheless, agreement is not only possible but commonplace.

It may interest you to know that, after hitting two home runs in a single game, Pat Kelly went on to hit three more in the same week, thus equaling his entire total for 1976. At the end of the week a teammate was heard to say, "Maybe there's something in that religion stuff after all."

---

[9][Fish] Herbert H. Clark and Eve V. Clark, *Psychology and Language* (New York: Harcourt, Brace, 1977), pp. 121–122.

Edward W. Said

b. 1935

For Said, all texts are "worldly," that is, involved in particular historical situations. In response to the critical movements that have generated aestheticism, the New Criticism, structuralism, and deconstruction, each with certain tendencies to separate the text from the world of particular events, Said asks, "Is there no way of dealing with a text and its worldly circumstances fairly? No way to grapple with the problems of literary language except by cutting them off from the more plainly urgent ones of everyday, worldly language?" For him there must be a way, mainly because texts are impoverished if they are cut off and partly because Said's interests and commitments are strongly political. In this essay he argues, against Derridean deconstruction, that texts should be regarded as "speech," for that identifies them with living beings in particular historical circumstances. But the valorization of speech does not insure the equality of every voice in the text or even the power of every voice to be heard. For Said, a text is not the heteroglossia of Mikhail Bakhtin's novel. Rather, discursive situations are more like the unequal relation of colonizer and colonized, for many texts are characterized by a "self-confirming will to power." This means that the text's voice may dominate or suppress other voices. Such situations are like the world. No amount of theorizing about pure "textuality," intentional or affective fallacies, or poetry for poetry's sake can erase the interrelation of texts and real committed speech: "Too many exceptions, too many historical, ideological, and formal circumstances, implicate the text in actuality, even if a text may be considered a silent printed object with its own unheard melodies." Clearly Said is impatient with a criticism that views the text only as a "silent printed object" (if indeed there really ever has been such a criticism). His criticism is political, involved, and concerned with particular historical situations. It wishes to uncover textual will to power, oppression, and distortion. One result is *Orientalism* (1978), his study of European views of the East. Another is his rejection of criticism as an activity secondary to the texts it studies. Criticism, for Said, should always be offered from a position of marginality that he describes as "secular" and "skeptical." It must avoid complicity with the ruling voice of the culture. But it is not disembodied; it is always situated.

Among Said's books are *Joseph Conrad and the Fiction of Autobiography* (1966), *Beginnings: Intention and Method* (1975), *Orientalism* (1978), *The Question of Palestine* (1979), *Covering Islam* (1981), and *The World, the Text, and the Critic* (1983).

The World, the Text, and the Critic

Since he deserted the concert stage in 1964, the Canadian pianist Glenn Gould has confined his work to records, television, and radio. There is some disagreement among critics as to whether Gould is always, or only sometimes, a convincing interpreter of one or another piano piece, but there is no doubt that each of his performances now is at least special. One example of how Gould has been operating recently is suited for discussion here. In 1970 he issued a record of his performance of Beethoven's Fifth Symphony in the Liszt piano transcription. Quite aside from the surprise one felt at Gould's eccentric choice of the piece (which seemed more peculiar than usual even for the arch-eccentric Gould, whose controversial performances had formerly been associated either with classical or contemporary music), there were a number of oddities about this particular release. Liszt's Beethoven transcription was not only of the nineteenth century but of its most egregious aspect, pianistically speaking: not content with transforming the concert experience into a feast for the virtuoso's self-exhibition, it also raided the literature of other instruments, making of their music a flamboyant occasion for the pianist's skill. Most transcriptions tend on the whole to sound thick or muddy, since frequently the piano is attempting to copy the texture of an orchestral sound. Listz's Fifth Symphony was less offensive than most transcriptions, mainly because it was so brilliantly reduced for the piano, but even at its most clear the sound was an unusual one for Gould to be producing. His sound previously had been the clearest and most unadorned of all pianists', which was why he had the uncanny ability to turn Bach's counterpoint almost into a visual experience. The Liszt transcription, in short, was an entirely different idiom, and yet Gould was very successful in it. He sounded as Lisztian now as he had sounded Bachian in the past.

Nor was this all. Accompanying the main disc was another one, a longish, informal interview between Gould and, as I recall, a record company executive. Gould told his interlocutor that one reason for his escape from "live" performance was that he had developed a bad performing habit, a kind of stylistic exaggeration. On his tours of the Soviet Union, for example, he would notice that the large halls in which he was performing caused him to distort the phrases in a Bach partita—here he demonstrated by playing the distorted phrases—so that he could more effectively "catch" and address his listeners in the third balcony. He then played the same phrases to illustrate how much more correctly, and less seductively, he was performing music when no audience was actually present.

It may seem a little heavy-handed to draw out the little ironies from this situation—transcription, interview, and illustrated performance styles all included. But it serves my main point: any occasion involving the aesthetic or literary document and experience, on the one hand, and the critic's role and his or her "worldliness," on the other, cannot be a simple one. Indeed Gould's strategy is something of a parody of all the directions we might take in trying to get at what occurs between the world and the aesthetic or textual object. Here was a pianist who had once represented the ascetic performer in the service of music, transformed now into unashamed virtuoso, whose principal aesthetic position is supposed to be little better than that of a musical whore. And this from a man who markets his record as a "first" and then adds to it, not more music, but the kind of attention-getting immediacy gained in a personal interview. And finally all this is fixed on a mechanically repeatable object, which controls the most obvious signs of immediacy (Gould's voice, the peacock style of the Liszt transcription, the brash informality of an interview packed along with a disembodied performance) beneath a dumb, anonymous, and disposable disc of black plastic.

If one thinks about Gould and his record, parallels will emerge with the circumstances of written performance. First of all, there is the reproducible material existence of a text, which in the most recent phases of Walter Benjamin's age of mechanical reproduction has multiplied and remultiplied so much as to exceed almost any imaginable limits. Both a recording and a printed object, however, are subject to certain legal, political, economic, and social constraints, so far as their sustained production and distribution are concerned: but why and how they are distributed are different matters. The main thing is that a written text of the sort we care about is originally the result of some immediate contact between author and medium. Thereafter it can be reproduced for the benefit of the world and according to conditions set by and in the world; however much the author demurs at the publicity he or she receives, once the text goes into more than one copy the author's work is in the world and beyond authorial control.

Second, a written and musical performance are both instances of style, in the simplest and least honorific sense of that very complex phenomenon. Once again I shall arbitrarily exclude a whole series of interesting complexities in order to insist on style as, from the standpoint of producer and receiver, the recognizable, repeatable, preservable sign of an author who reckons with an audience. Even if the audience is as restricted as oneself and as wide as the whole world, the author's style is partially a phenomenon of repetition and reception. But what makes style receivable as the signature of its author's manner is a collection of features variously called idiolect, voice, or irreducible individuality. The paradox is that something as impersonal as a text, or a record, can nevertheless deliver an imprint or a trace of something as lively, immediate, and transitory as a "voice." Glenn Gould's interview simply makes brutally explicit the frequent implicit need for reception or recognition that a text carries even in its most pristine, enshrined forms. A common form of this need is the staged (or recorded) convention of a talking voice addressing someone at a particular time and in a specific place. Considered as I have been considering it, then, style neutralizes the worldlessness, the silent, seemingly uncircumstanced existence of a solitary text. It is not only that any text, if it is not immediately destroyed, is a network of often colliding forces, but also that a text in its actually *being* a text is a being in the world; it therefore addresses anyone who reads, as Gould does throughout the very same record that is supposed to represent both his withdrawal from the world and his "new" silent style of playing without a live audience.

To be sure, texts do not speak in the ordinary sense of the word. Yet any simple diametric opposition asserted on the one hand between speech, bound by situation and reference, and on the other hand the text as an interception or suspension of speech's worldliness is, I think, misleading and largely simplified. Here is how Paul Ricoeur puts this opposition, which he says he has set up only for the sake of analytic clarification: In speech the function of reference is linked to the role of the *situation of discourse* within the exchange of language itself: in exchanging speech, the speakers are present to each other, but also to the circumstantial setting of discourse, not only the perceptual surroundings, but also the cultural background known by both speakers. It is in relation to this situation that discourse is fully meaningful: the reference to reality is in the last analysis reference to that reality which can be pointed out "around," so to speak, the instance of discourse itself. Language . . . and in general all the ostensive indicators of language serve to anchor discourse in the circumstantial reality which surrounds the instance of discourse. Thus, in living speech, the *ideal* meaning of what one says bends toward a *real* reference, namely to that "about which" one speaks . . .

This is no longer the case when a text takes the place of speech . . . A text . . . is not without reference; it will be precisely the task of reading, as interpretation, to actualize the reference. At least, in this suspension wherein reference is deferred, in the sense that it is postponed, a text is somehow "in the air," outside of the world or without a world; by means of this obliteration of all relation to the world, every text is free to enter into relation with all the other texts which come to take the place of the circumstantial reality shown by living speech.[1]

According to Ricoeur, speech and circumstantial reality exist in a state of presence, whereas writing and texts exist in a state of suspension—that is, outside circumstantial reality—until they are "actualized" and made present by the reader-critic. Ricoeur makes it seem as if the text and circumstantial reality, or what I shall call *worldliness,* play a game of musical chairs, one intercepting and replacing the other according to fairly crude signals. But this game takes place in the interpreter's head, a locale presumably without worldliness or circumstantiality. The critic-interpreter has his position reduced to that of a central bourse on whose floor occurs the transaction by which text is shown to be meaning *x* while saying *y*. And as for what Ricoeur calls "deferred reference," what becomes of it during the interpretation? Quite simply, on the basis of a model of direct exchange, it comes back, made whole and actual by the critic's reading.

The principal difficulty with all this is that without sufficient argument Ricoeur assumes circumstantial reality to be symmetrically and exclusively the property of speech, or the speech situation, or what writers would have wanted to say had they not instead chosen to write. My contention is that worldliness does not come and go; nor is it here and there in the apologetic and soupy way by which we often designate history, a euphemism in such cases for the impossibly vague notion that all things take place in time. Moreover, critics are not merely the alchemical translators of texts into circumstantial reality or worldliness; for they too are subject to and producers of circumstances, which are felt regardless of whatever objectivity the critic's methods possess. The point is that texts have ways of existing that even in their most rarefied form are always enmeshed in circumstance, time, place, and society—in short, they are in the world, and

---

[1][All notes are by Said] Paul Ricoeur, "What Is a Text? Explanation and Interpretation," in David Rasmussen, *Mythic-Symbolic Language and Philosophical Anthropology: A Constructive Interpretation of the Thought of Paul Ricoeur* (The Hague: Nijhoff, 1971), p. 138. For a more interesting distinction between oeuvre and text, see Roland Barthes, "De l'Oeuvre au texte," *Revue d'esthethique,* 3 (1971), 225–232.

hence worldly.[2] Whether a text is preserved or put aside for a period, whether it is on a library shelf or not, whether it is considered dangerous or not: these matters have to do with a text's being in the world, which is a more complicated matter than the private process of reading. The same implications are undoubtedly true of critics in their capacities as readers and writers in the world.

If my use of Gould's recording of the Beethoven Fifth Symphony serves any really useful purpose, it is to provide an instance of a quasi-textual object whose ways of engaging the world are both numerous and complicated, more complicated than Ricoeur's demarcation drawn between text and speech. These are the engagements I have been calling worldliness. But my principal concern here is not with an aesthetic object in general, but with the text in particular. Most critics will subscribe to the notion that every literary text is in some way burdened with its occasion, with the plain empirical realities from which it emerged. Pressed too far, such a notion earns the justified criticism of a stylistician like Michael Riffaterre, who, in "The Self-Sufficient Text," calls any reduction of a text to its circumstances a fallacy, biographical, genetic, psychological, or analogic.[3] Most critics would probably go along with Riffaterre in saying, yes, let's make sure that the text does not disappear under the weight of these fallacies. But, and here I speak mainly for myself, they are not entirely satisfied with the idea of a self-sufficient text. Is the alternative to the various fallacies *only* a hermetic textual cosmos, one whose significant dimension of meaning is, as Riffaterre says, a wholly inward or intellectual one? Is there no way of dealing with a text and its worldly circumstances fairly? No way to grapple with the problems of literary language except by cutting them off from the more plainly urgent ones of everyday, worldly language?

I have found a way of starting to deal with these questions in an unexpected place, which is perhaps why I shall now seem to digress. Consider the relatively unfamiliar field of medieval Arabic linguistic speculation. Many contemporary critics are interested in speculation about language in Europe, that is, in that special combination of theoretical imagination and empirical observation characterizing romantic philology, the rise of linguistics in the early nineteenth century, and the whole rich phenomenon of what Michel Foucault has called the discovery of language. Yet during the eleventh century in Andalusia, there existed a re-

markably sophisticated and unexpectedly prophetic school of Islamic philosophic grammarians, whose polemics anticipate twentieth-century debates between structuralists and generative grammarians, between descriptivists and behaviorists. Nor is this all. One small group of these Andalusian linguists directed its energies against tendencies amongst rival linguists to turn the question of meaning in language into esoteric and allegorical exercises. Among the groups were three linguists and theoretical grammarians, Ibn Hazm, Ibn Jinni, and Ibn Mada' al-Qurtobi, all of whom worked in Cordoba during the eleventh century, all belonging to the Zahirite school, all antagonists of the Batinist school. Batinists held that meaning in language is concealed within the words; meaning is therefore available only as the result of an inward-tending exegesis. The Zahirites—their name derives from the Arabic word for clear, apparent, and phenomenal; *Batin* connotes internal—argued that words had only a surface meaning, one that was anchored to a particular usage, circumstance, historical and religious situation.

The two opponents trace their origins back to readings of the sacred text, the Koran, and how that unique event—for, unlike the Bible, the Koran is an event—is to be read, understood, transmitted, and taught by later generations of believers. The Cordovan Zahirites attacked the excesses of the Batinists, arguing that the very profession of grammar (in Arabic *nahu*) was an invitation to spinning out private meanings in an otherwise divinely pronounced, and hence unchangeably stable, text. According to Ibn Mada' it was absurd even to associate grammar with a logic of understanding, since as a science grammar assumed, and often went so far as to create by retrospection, ideas about the use and meaning of words that implied a hidden level beneath words, available only to initiates.[4] Once you resort to such a level, anything becomes permissible by way of interpretation: there can be no strict meaning, no control over what words in fact say, no responsibility toward the words. The Zahirite effort was to restore by rationalization a system of reading a text in which attention was focused on the phenomenal words themselves in what might be considered their once-and-for-all sense uttered for and during a specific occasion, not on hidden meanings they might later be supposed to contain. The Cordovan Zahirites in particular went very far in trying to provide a reading system that placed the tightest possible control over the reader and his circumstances. They did this principally by means of a theory of what a text is.

---

[2]I have discussed this in chap. 4 of *Beginnings: Intention and Method* (New York: Basic Books, 1975).
[3]Riffaterre, "The Self-Sufficient Text," *Diacritics* (Fall 1973), p. 40.

[4]This is the main polemical point in this tract *Ar-rad'ala'l nuhat,* ed. Shawki Daif (Cairo, 1947). The text dates from 1180.

It is not necessary to describe this theory in detail. It is useful, however, to indicate how the controversy itself grew out of a sacred text whose authority derived from its being the uncreated word of God, directly and unilaterally transmitted to a Messenger at a particular moment in time. In contrast, texts within the Judeo-Christian tradition, at whose center is Revelation, cannot be reduced to a specific moment of divine intervention as a result of which the Word of God entered the world; rather the Word enters human history continually, during and as a part of that history. So a very important place is given to what Roger Arnaldez calls "human factors" in the reception, transmission, and understanding of such a text.[5] Since the Koran is the result of a unique event, the literal "descent" into worldliness of a text, as well as its language and form, are then to be viewed as stable and complete. Moreover, the language of the text is Arabic, which therefore becomes a privileged language, and its vessel is the Prophet (or Messenger), Mohammed, similarly privileged. Such a text can be regarded as having an absolutely defined origin and consequently cannot be referred back to any particular interpreter or interpretation, although this is clearly what the Batinites tried to do (perhaps, it has been suggested, under the influence of Judeo-Christian exegetical techniques).

In his study of Ibn Hazm, Arnaldez puts his description of the Koran in the following terms: the Koran speaks of historical events, yet is not itself historical. It repeats past events, which it condenses and particularizes, yet is not itself an actually lived experience; it ruptures the human continuity of life, yet God does not enter temporality by a sustained or concerted act. The Koran evokes the memory of actions whose content repeats itself eternally in ways identical with itself, as warnings, orders, imperatives, punishments, rewards.[6] In short, the Zahirite position adopts a view of the Koran that is absolutely circumstantial without at the same time making that worldliness dominate the actual sense of the text: all this is the ultimate avoidance of vulgar determinism in the Zahirite position.

Hence Ibn Hazm's linguistic theory is based upon an analysis of the imperative mode, since according to this the Koran at its most radical verbal level is a text controlled by two paradigmatic imperatives, *iqra* (read or recite) and *qul* (tell).[7] Since those imperatives obviously control the circum-

stantial and historical appearance of the Koran (and its uniqueness as an event), and since they must also control uses (that is, readings) of the text thereafter, Ibn Hazm connects his analysis of the imperative mode with a juridical notion of *hadd,* a word meaning both a logico-grammatical definition and a limit. What transpires in the imperative mode, between the injunctions to read and write is the delivery of an utterance (*khabar* in Arabic, translated by Arnaldez as *énoncé*), which is the verbal realization of a signifying intention, or *niyah*. Now the signifying intention is synonymous not with a psychological intention but exclusively with a verbal intention, itself something highly worldly—it takes place exclusively in the world, it is occasional and circumstantial in both a very precise and a wholly pertinent way. To signify is only to use language, and to use language is to do so according to certain lexical and syntactic rules, by which language is in and of the world; the Zahirite sees language as being regulated by real usage, and neither by abstract prescription nor by speculative freedom. Above all, language stands between man and a vast indefiniteness: if the world is a gigantic system of correspondences between words and objects, then it is verbal form—language in actual grammatical use—that allows us to isolate the denominated objects from among these massively ordered correspondences. Thus, as Arnaldez puts it, fidelity to such "true" aspects of language is an ascesis of the imagination.[8] A word has a strict meaning understood as an imperative, and with that meaning there also goes a strictly ordained series of resemblances (correspondences) to other words and meanings, which, strictly speaking, play around the first word. Thus figurative language (as it occurs even in the Koran), otherwise elusive and at the mercy of the virtuosic interpreter, is part of the actual structure of language, and part therefore of the collectivity of language users.

What Ibn Hazm does, Arnaldez reminds us, is to view language as possessing two seemingly antithetical characteristics: that of a divinely ordained institution, unchanging, immutable, logical, rational, intelligible; and that of an instrument existing as pure contingency, as an institution signifying meanings anchored in specific utterances. It is exactly because the Zahirites see language in this double perspective that they reject reading techniques that reduce words and their meanings back to radicals from which (in Arabic at least) they may be seen grammatically to derive. Each utterance is its own occasion and as such is firmly anchored in the worldly context in which it is applied. And because the Koran, which is the paradigmatic case of divine-

[5]Roger Arnaldez, *Grammaire et théologies chez Ibn Hazm de Cordoue* (Paris: J. Vrin, 1956), pp. 12 and passim. There is a clear, somewhat schematic account of Ibn Ginni, Ibn Mada. and others in Anis Fraiha, *Nathariyat fil Lugha* (Beirut: Al-Maktaba al Jam'iya, 1973).

[6]Arnaldez, *Grammaire et théologie,* p. 12.

[7]Ibid., p. 69.

[8]Ibid., p. 77.

and-human language, is a text that incorporates speaking and writing, reading and telling, Zahirite interpretation itself accepts as inevitable not the separation between speech and writing, not the disjunction between a text and its circumstantiality, but rather their necessary interplay. It is the interplay, the constitutive interaction, that makes possible this severe Zahirite notion of meaning.

I have very quickly summarized an enormously complex theory, for which I cannot claim any particular influence in Western European literature since the Renaissance, and perhaps not even in Arabic literature since the Middle Ages. But what ought to strike us forcibly about the whole theory is that it represents a considerably articulated thesis for dealing with a text as significant form, in which—and I put this as carefully as I can—worldliness, circumstantiality, the text's status as an event having sensuous particularity as well as historical contingency, are considered as being incorporated in the text, an infrangible part of its capacity for conveying and producing meaning. This means that a text has a specific situation, placing restraints upon the interpreter and his interpretation not because the situation is hidden within the text as a mystery, but rather because the situation exists at the same level of surface particularity as the textual object itself. There are many ways for conveying such a situation, but what I want to draw particular attention to here is an ambition (which the Zahirites have to an intense degree) on the part of readers and writers to grasp texts as objects whose interpretation—by virtue of the exactness of their situation in the world—*has already commenced* and are objects already constrained by, and constraining, their interpretation. Such texts can thereafter be construed as having need at most of complementary, as opposed to supplementary, readings.

Now I want to discuss some of the ways by which texts impose constraints upon their interpretation or, to put it metaphorically, the way the closeness of the world's body to the text's body forces readers to take both into consideration. Recent critical theory has placed undue emphasis on the limitlessness of interpretation. It is argued that, since all reading is misreading, no one reading is better than any other, and hence all readings, potentially infinite in number, are in the final analysis equally misinterpretations. A part of this has been derived from a conception of the text as existing within a hermetic, Alexandrian textual universe, which has no connection with actuality. This is a view I do not agree with, not simply because texts in fact are in the world but also because as texts they place themselves—one of their functions as texts is to place themselves—and indeed are themselves, by soliciting the world's attention. Moreover, their manner of doing this is to place restraints upon what can be done with them interpretively.

Modern literary history gives us a number of examples of writers whose text seems self-consciously to incorporate the explicit circumstances of its concretely imagined, and even described, situation. One type of author—I shall be discussing three instances, Gerard Manley Hopkins, Oscar Wilde, and Joseph Conrad—deliberately conceives the text as supported by a discursive situation involving speaker and audience; the designed interplay between speech and reception, between verbality and textuality, *is* the text's situation, its placing of itself in the world.

The three authors I mentioned did their major work between 1875 and 1915. The subject matter of their writing varies so widely among them that similarities have to be looked for elsewhere. Let me begin with a journal entry by Hopkins:

> The winter was called severe. There were three spells of frost with skating, the third beginning on Feb. 9. No snow to speak of till that day. Some days before Feb. 7 I saw catkins hanging. On the 9th there was snow but not lying on the heads of the blades. As we went down a field near Caesar's Camp I noticed it before me *squalentem,* coat below coat, sketched in intersecting edges bearing 'idiom,' all down the slope:—I have no other word yet for that which takes the eye or mind in a bold hand or effective sketching or in marked features or again in graphic writing, which not being beauty nor true inscape yet gives interest and makes ugliness even better than meaninglessness.[9]

Hopkins' earliest writing attempts in this way to render scenes from nature as exactly as possible. Yet he is never a passive transcriber since for him "this world then is word, expression, news of God."[10] Every phenomenon in nature, he wrote in the sonnet "As Kingfishers Catch Fire," *tells* itself in the world as a sort of lexical unit: "Each mortal thing does one thing and the same: / Deals out that being indoors each one dwells; / Selves—goes itself; *myself* it speaks and spells, / Crying *What I do is me: for that I came.*"[11] So in the notebook entry Hopkins' observation of nature is dynamic. He sees in the frost an intention to speak

[9]*The Journals and Papers of Gerard Manley Hopkins,* ed. Humphry House and Graham Storey (London: Oxford University Press, 1959), p. 195.
[10]Ibid., p. 129.
[11]*The Poems of Gerard Manley Hopkins,* ed. W. H. Gardner and N. H. Mackenzie (London: Oxford University Press, 1967), p. 90.

or mean, its layered coats *taking* one's attention because of the idiom it bears toward meaning of expression. The writer is as much a respondent as he is a describer. Similarly the reader is a full participant in the production of meaning, being obliged as a mortal thing to act, to produce some sense that even though ugly is still better than meaninglessness.

This dialectic of production is everywhere present in Hopkins' work. Writing is telling; nature is telling; reading is telling. He wrote to Robert Bridges on May 21, 1878, that in order to do a certain poem justice "you must not slovenly read it with the eyes but with your ears, as if the paper were declaiming it at you . . . Stress is the life of it."[12] Seven years later he specified more strictly that "poetry is the darling child of speech, of lips and spoken utterance: it must be spoken; *till it is spoken it is not performed,* it does not perform, it is not itself. Sprung rhythm gives back to poetry its true soul and self. As poetry is emphatically speech, speech purged of dross like gold in the furnace, so it must have emphatically the essential elements of speech."[13] So close is the identification in Hopkins' mind among world, word, and the utterance, the three coming alive together as a moment of performance, that he envisages little need for critical intervention. It is the written text that provides the immediate circumstantial reality for the poem's "play" (the word is Hopkins'). So far from being a document associated with other lifeless, worldless texts, Hopkins' own text was for him his child; when he destroyed his poems he spoke of the slaughter of the innocents, and everywhere he speaks of writing as the exercise of his male gift. At the moment of greatest desolation in his career, in the poem entitled simply "To R. B." the urgency of his feeling of poetic aridity is expressed biologically. When he comes to describe finally what it is he now writes, he says:

> O then if in my lagging lines you miss
> The roll, the rise, the carol, the creation,
> My winter world, that scarcely breathes that bliss
> Now, yields you, with some sighs, our explanation.[14]

Because his text has lost its ability to incorporate the stress of creation, and because it is no longer performance but what in another poem he calls "dead letters," he now can only write an explanation, which is lifeless speech "bending towards a real reference."

It was said of Oscar Wilde by one of his contemporaries that everything he spoke sounded as if it were enclosed in quotation marks. This is no less true of everything he wrote, for such was the consequence of having a pose, which Wilde defined as "a formal recognition of the importance of treating life from a definite reasoned standpoint."[15] Or as Algernon retorts to Jack's accusation that "you always want to argue about things" in *The Importance of Being Earnest:* "That's exactly what things were originally made for."[16] Always ready with a quotable comment, Wilde filled his manuscripts with epigrams on every conceivable subject. What he wrote was intended either for more comment or for quotation or, most important, for tracing back to him. There are obvious social reasons for some of this egoism, which he made no attempt to conceal in his quip "To love oneself is the beginning of a life-long romance," but they do not exhaust the speaking in Wilde's style. Having forsworn action, life, and nature for their incompleteness and diffusion, Wilde took as his province a theoretical, ideal world in which, as he told Alfred Douglas in *De Profundis,* conversation was the basis of all human relations.[17] Since conflict inhibited conversation as Wilde understood it from the Platonic dialogue, the mode of interchange was to be by epigram. This epigram, in Northrop Frye's terminology, is Wilde's radical of presentation: a compact utterance capable of the utmost range of subject matter, the greatest authority, and the least equivocation as to its author. When he invaded other forms of art, Wilde converted them into longer epigrams. As he said of drama: "I took the drama, the most objective form known to art, and made it as personal a mode of expression as the lyric or the sonnet, at the same time that I widened its range and enriched its characterization." No wonder he could say: "I summed up all systems in a phrase, and all existence in an epigram.[18]

De Profundis records the destruction of the utopia whose individualism and unselfish selfishness Wilde had adumbrated in *The Soul of Man Under Socialism.* From a free world to a prison and a circle of suffering: how is the change accomplished? Wilde's conception of freedom was to be found in *The Importance of Being Earnest,* where conflicting characters turn out to be brothers after all just because they say they are. What is written down (for example, the army lists consulted by Jack) merely confirms what all along has

---

[12] *The Letters of Gerard Manley Hopkins to Robert Bridges,* ed. Claude Colleer Abbott (Oxford: Oxford University Press, 1955), pp. 51–52.

[13] Quoted in Anthony Bisshof, S.J., "Hopkins' Letters to his Brother," *Times Literary Supplement,* December 8, 1972, p. 1511.

[14] *Poems of Hopkins,* p. 108.

[15] *The Artist as Critic: Critical Writings of Oscar Wilde,* ed. Richard Ellmann (New York: Vintage, 1970), p. 386.

[16] *Complete Works of Oscar Wilde,* ed. J. B. Foreman (London: Collins, 1971), p. 335.

[17] Oscar Wilde, *De Profundis* (New York: Vintage, 1964), p. 18.

[18] Ibid., p. 80, 61.

been capriciously, though elegantly, said. This transformation, from opponent into brother, is what Wilde had in mind in connecting the intensification of personality with its multiplication. When the communication between men no longer possesses the freedom of conversation, when it is confined to the merely legal liability of print, which is not ingeniously quotable but, because it has been signed, is now criminally actionable, the utopia crumbles. As he reconsidered his life in *De Profundis* Wilde's imagination was transfixed by the effects of one text upon his life. But he uses it to show how in going from speech to print, which in a sense all of his other more fortunate texts had managed somehow to avoid by virtue of their epigrammatic individuality, he had been ruined. Wilde's lament in what follows is that a text has too much, not too little, circumstantial reality. Hence, with Wildean paradox, its vulnerability:

> You send me a very nice poem, of the undergraduate school of verse, for my approval: I reply by a letter of fantastic literary conceits . . . Look at the history of that letter! It passes from you into the hands of a loathsome companion: from him to a gang of blackmailers: copies of it are sent about London to my friends, and to the manager of the theatre where my work is being performed: every construction but the right one is put on it: Society is thrilled with the absurd rumours that I have had to pay a huge sum of money for having written an infamous letter to you: this forms the basis of your father's worst attack: I produce the original letter myself in Court to show what it really is: it is denounced by your father's counsel as a revolting and insidious attempt to corrupt Innocence: ultimately it forms part of a criminal charge: the Crown takes it up: the Judge sums up on it with little learning and much morality: I go to prison for it at last. That is the result of writing you a charming letter.[19]

For in a world described by George Eliot as a "huge whispering gallery," the effects of writing can be grave indeed: "As the stone which has been kicked by generations of clowns may come by curious little links of effect under the eyes of a scholar, through whose labours it may at last fix the date of invasions and unlock religions, so a bit of ink and paper which has long been an innocent wrapping or stop-gap may at last be laid open under the one pair of eyes

which have knowledge enough to turn it into the opening of a catastrophe."[20] If Dr. Casaubon's caution has any purpose at all, it is by rigid secrecy and an endlessly postponing scriptive will to forestall the opening of a catastrophe. Yet he cannot succeed since Eliot is at pains to show that even Casaubon's tremendously nursed *Key* is a text, and therefore in the world. Unlike Wilde's, Casaubon's disgrace is posthumous, but their implication in a sort of worldly textuality takes place for the same reason, which is their commitment to what Eliot calls an "embroiled medium."

Lastly, consider Conrad. Elsewhere in this book I shall be describing the extraordinary presentational mode of his narratives, how each of them dramatizes, motivates, and circumstances the occasion of its telling, how all of Conrad's work is really made out of secondary, reported speech, and how the interplay between appeals to the eye and the ear in his work is highly organized and subtle, and is that work's meaning. The Conradian encounter is not simply between a man and his destiny embodied in a moment of extremity, but just as persistently, the encounter between speaker and hearer. Marlow is Conrad's chief invention for this encounter, a man who is haunted by the knowledge that a person such as Kurtz or Jim "existed for me, and after all it is only through me that he exists for you."[21] The chain of humanity—"we exist only in so far as we hang together"—is the transmission of actual speech, and existence, from one mouth and then from one eye to another. Every text that Conrad wrote presents itself as unfinished and still in the making. "And besides, the last word is not said,—probably shall never be said. Are not our lives too short for that full utterance which through all our stammerings is of course our only and abiding intention?"[22] Texts convey the stammerings that never achieve that full utterance, the statement of wholly satisfactory presence, which remains distant, attenuated somewhat by a grand gesture like Jim's self-sacrifice. Yet even though the gesture closes off a text circumstantially, in no way does it empty it of its actual urgency.

This is a good time to remark that the Western novelistic tradition is full of examples of texts insisting not only upon their circumstantial reality but also upon their status as *already* fulfilling a function, a reference, or a meaning in the world. Cervantes and Cide Hamete come immediately to mind. More impressive is Richardson playing the role of "mere" editor for *Clarissa,* simply placing those letters in successive order after they have done what they have done,

---

[19]Ibid., pp. 34–35.

[20]*Middlemarch,* ed. Gordon S. Haight (Boston: Houghton Mifflin, 1956), p. 302.
[21]*Lord Jim* (Boston: Houghton Mifflin, 1958), p. 161.
[22]Ibid., p. 161.

arranging to fill the text with printer's devices, reader's aids, analytic contents, retrospective meditations, commentary, so that a collection of letters grows to fill the world and occupy all space, to become a circumstance as large and as engrossing as the reader's very understanding. Surely the novelistic imagination has always included this unwillingness to cede control over the text in the world, or to release it from the discursive and human obligations of all human presence; hence the desire (almost a principal action of many novels) to turn the text back, if not directly into speech, then at least into circumstantial, as opposed to meditative, duration.

No novelist, however, can be quite as explicit about circumstances as Marx is in *The Eighteenth Brumaire of Louis Bonaparte*. To my mind no work is as brilliant and as compelling in the exactness with which circumstances (the German word is *Umstände*) are shown to have made the nephew possible, not as an innovator, but as a farcical repetition of the great uncle. What Marx attacks are the atextual theses that history is made up of free events and that history is guided by superior individuals.[23] By inserting Louis Bonaparte in a whole intricate system of repetitions, by which first Hegel, then the ancient Romans, the 1789 revolutionaries, Napoleon I, the bourgeois interpreters, and finally the fiascos of 1848–1851 are all seen in a pseudoanalogical order of descending worth, increasing derivativeness, and deceptively harmless masquerading, Marx effectively textualizes the random appearance of a new Caesar. Here we have the case of a text itself providing a world-historical situation with circumstances otherwise hidden in the deception of a *roi des drôles*. What is ironic—and in need of the analysis I shall be giving in subsequent parts of this book—is how a text, by being a text, by insisting upon and employing all the devices of textuality, preeminent among them *repetition,* historicizes and problematizes all the fugitive significance that has chosen Louis Bonaparte as its representative.

There is another aspect to what I have just been saying. In producing texts with either a firm claim on or an explicit will to worldliness, these writers and genres have valorized speech, making it the tentacle by which an otherwise silent text ties itself to the world of discourse. By the valorization of speech I mean that the discursive, circumstantially dense interchange of speaker facing hearer is made to stand—sometimes misleadingly—for a democratic equality and copresence in actuality between speaker and hearer. Not only is the discursive relation far from equal in actuality, but the text's attempt to dissemble by seeming to be open democrat-

ically to anyone who might read it is also an act of bad faith. (Incidentally, one of the strengths of Zahirite theory is that it dispels the illusion that a surface reading, which is the Zahirite ambition, is anything but difficult.) Texts of such a length as *Tom Jones* aim to occupy leisure time of a quality not available to just anyone. Moreover, all texts essentially dislodge other texts or, more frequently, take the place of something else. As Nietzsche had the perspicacity to see, texts are fundamentally facts of power, not of democratic exchange.[24] They compel attention away from the world even as their beginning intention as texts, coupled with the inherent authoritarianism of the authorial authority (the repetition in this phrase is a deliberate emphasis on the tautology within all texts, since all texts are in some way self-confirmatory), makes for sustained power.

Yet in the genealogy of texts there is a first text, a sacred prototype, a scripture, which readers always approach through the text before them, either as petitioning suppliants or as initiates amongst many in a sacred chorus supporting the central patriarchal text. Northrop Frye's theory of literature makes it apparent that the displacing power in all texts finally derives from the displacing power of the Bible, whose centrality, potency, and dominating anteriority inform all Western literature. The same is no less true, in the different modes I discussed earlier, of the Koran. Both in the Judeo-Christian and in the Islamic traditions these hierarchies repose upon a solidly divine, or quasi-divine, language, a language whose uniqueness, however, is that it is theologically and humanly circumstantial.

We often forget that modern Western philology, which begins in the early nineteenth century, undertook to revise commonly accepted ideas about language and its divine origins. That revision tried first to determine which was the first language and then, failing in that ambition, proceeded to reduce language to specific circumstances: language groups, historical and racial theories, geographical and anthropological theses. A particularly interesting example of how such investigations went is Ernest Renan's career as a philologist; that was his real profession, not that of the boring sage. His first serious work was his 1848 analysis of Semitic languages, revised and published in 1855 as *Histoire générale et système comparé des langues sémitiques*. Without this study the *Vie de Jésus* could not have been written. The accomplishment of the *Histoire générale* was scientifically to describe the inferiority of Semitic languages, principally Hebrew, Aramaic, and Arabic, the medium of three purportedly

---

[23]Karl Marx, *Der Achtzehnte Brumaire des Louis Bonaparte,* (1852; Berlin: Dietz Verlag, 1947), p. 8.

[24]Nietzsche's analyses of texts in this light are to be found everywhere in his work, but especially in *The Genealogy of Morals* and in *The Will to Power.*

sacred texts that had been spoken or at least informed by God—the Torah, the Koran, and, later, the derivative Gospels. Thus in the *Vie de Jésus* Renan would be able to insinuate that the so-called sacred texts, delivered by Moses, Jesus, or Mohammed, could not have anything divine in them if the very medium of their supposed divinity, as well as the body of their message to and in the world, was made up of such comparatively poor worldly stuff. Renan argued that, even if these texts were prior to all others in the West, they held no theologically dominant position.

Renan first reduced texts from objects of divine intervention in the world's business to objects of historical materiality. God as author-authority had little value after Renan's philological and textual revisionism. Yet in dispensing with divine authority Renan put philological power in its place. What comes to replace divine authority is the textual authority of the philological critic who has the skill to separate Semitic languages from the languages of Indo-European culture. Not only did Renan kill off the extratextual validity of the great Semitic sacred texts; he confined them as objects of European study to a scholarly field thereafter to be known as Oriental.[25] The Orientalist is a Renan or a Gobineau, Renan's contemporary quoted here and there in the 1855 edition of the *Histoire générale,* for whom the old hierarchy of sacred Semitic texts has been destroyed as if by an act of parricide; the passing of divine authority enables the appearance of European ethnocentrism, by which the methods and the discourse of Western scholarship confine inferior non-European cultures to a position of subordination. Oriental texts come to inhabit a realm without development or power, one that exactly corresponds to the position of a colony for European texts and culture. All this takes place at the same time that the great European colonial empires in the east are beginning or, in some cases, flourishing.

I have introduced this brief account of the twin origin of the Higher Criticism and of Orientalism as a European scholarly discipline in order to be able to speak about the fallacy of imagining the life of texts as being pleasantly ideal and without force or conflict and, conversely, the fallacy of imagining the discursive relations in actual speech to be, as Ricoeur would have it, a relation of equality between hearer and speaker.

Texts incorporate discourse, sometimes violently. There are other ways, too. Michel Foucault's archeological analyses of systems of discourse are premised on the thesis,

adumbrated by Marx and Engels in *The German Ideology,* that "in every society the production of discourse is at once controlled, selected, organized and redistributed according to a certain number of procedures, whose role is to avert its powers and dangers, to cope with chance events, to evade its ponderous, awesome materiality." Discourse in this passage means what is written and spoken. Foucault's contention is that the fact of writing itself is a systematic conversion of the power relationship between controller and controlled into "mere" written words—but writing is a way of disguising the awesome materiality of so tightly controlled and managed a production. Foucault continues:

> In a society such as our own we all know the rules of *exclusion.* The most obvious and familiar of these concerns what is *prohibited.* We know perfectly well that we are not free to say just anything. We have three types of prohibition, covering objects, ritual with its surrounding circumstances, and the privileged or exclusive right to speak of a particular subject; these prohibitions interrelate, reinforce and complement each other, forming a complex web, continually subject to modification. I will note simply that the areas where this web is most tightly woven today, where the danger spots are most numerous, are those dealing with politics and sexuality . . . In appearance, speech may well be of little account, but the prohibitions surrounding it soon reveal its links with desire and power . . . Speech is no mere verbalization of conflicts and systems of domination . . . it is the very object of man's conflicts.[26]

Despite Ricoeur's simplified idealization, and far from being a type of conversation between equals, the discursive situation is more usually like the unequal relation between colonizer and colonized, oppressor and oppressed. Some of the great modernists, Proust and Joyce prominent among them, had an acute understanding of this assymmetry; their representations of the discursive situation always show it in this power-political light. Words and texts are so much of the world that their effectiveness, in some cases even their use, are matters having to do with ownership, authority, power, and the imposition of force. A formative moment in Stephen

---

[25]See in particular Ernst Renan, *Histoire générale et système comparé des langues sémitiques,* in *Oeuvres complètes,* ed. Henriette Psichari (Paris: Calmann-Lévy, 1947–1961), VIII, 147–157.

[26]Michel Foucault, "The Discourse on Language," in *The Archeology of Knowledge,* trans. A. M. Sheridan Smith (New York: Pantheon, 1972), p. 216.

Dedalus' rebellious consciousness occurs as he converses with the English dean of studies:

> What is that beauty which the artist struggles to express from lumps of earth, said Stephen coldly.
>
> The little word seemed to have turned a rapier point of his sensitiveness against this courteous and vigilant foe. He felt with a smart of dejection that the man to whom he was speaking was a countryman of Ben Jonson. He thought:—The language in which we are speaking is his before it is mine. How different are the words *home, Christ, ale, master,* on his lips and on mine! I cannot speak or write these words without unrest of spirit. His language, so familiar and so foreign, will always be for me an acquired speech. I have not made or accepted its words. My voice holds them at bay. My soul frets in the shadow of his language.[27]

Joyce's work is a recapitulation of those political and racial separations, exclusions, prohibitions instituted ethnocentrically by the ascendant European culture throughout the nineteenth century. The situation of discourse, Stephen Dedalus knows, hardly puts equals face to face. Rather, discourse often puts one interlocutor above another or, as Fritz Fanon brilliantly described the extreme to which it could be taken in *The Wretched of the Earth,* discourse reenacts the geography of the colonial city:

> The zone where the natives live is not complementary to the zone inhabited by the settlers. The two zones are opposed, but not in the service of a higher unity. Obedient to the rules of pure Aristotelian logic, they both follow the principle of reciprocal exclusivity. No conciliation is possible, for of the two terms, one is superfluous. The settlers' town is a strongly-built town, all made of stone and steel. It is a brightly-lit town; the streets are covered with asphalt, and the garbage-cans swallow all the leavings, unseen, unknown and hardly thought about. The settler's feet are never visible, except perhaps in the sea; but there you're never close enough to see them. His feet are protected by strong shoes although the streets of his town are clean and even, with no holes or stones.

The settler's town is a well–fed town, an easygoing town; its belly is always full of good things. The settler's town is a town of white people, of foreigners.

> The town belonging to the colonized people, or at least the native town, the negro village, the medina, the reservation, is a place of ill fame, peopled by men of evil repute. They are born there, it matters little where or how; they die there, it matters not where, nor how. It is a world without spaciousness; men live there on top of each other, and their huts are built on top of the other. The native town is a hungry town, starved of bread, of meat, of shoes, of coal, of light. The native town is a crouching village, a town on its knees, a town wallowing in the mire. It is a town of niggers and dirty arabs. The look that the native turns on the settler's town is a look of lust, a look of envy; it expresses his dreams of possession—all manner of possession: to set at the settler's table, to sleep in the settler's bed, with his wife if possible. The colonized man is an envious man. And this the settler knows very well; when their glances meet he ascertains bitterly, always on the defensive "They want to take our place." It is true, for there is no native who does not dream at least once a day of setting himself up in the settler's place.[28]

No wonder that the Fanonist solution to such discourse is violence.

Such examples make untenable the opposition between texts and the world, or between texts and speech. Too many exceptions, too many historical, ideological, and formal circumstances, implicate the text in actuality, even if a text may also be considered a silent printed object with its own unheard melodies. The concert of forces by which a text is engendered and maintained as a fact not of mute ideality but of *production* dispels the symmetry of even rhetorical oppositions. Moreover, the textual utopia envisioned each in his own way by T. S. Eliot and Northrop Frye, whose nightmarish converse is Borges' library, is at complete odds with form in texts. My thesis is that any centrist, exclusivist conception of the text, or for that matter of the discursive situation as defined by Ricoeur, ignores the self-confirming will to power from which many texts can spring. The minimalist impulse in Beckett's work is, I think, a countervision of this

---

[27]*A Portrait of the Artist as a Young Man* (New York: Viking Press, 1964), p. 189.

[28]Fanon, *The Wretched of the Earth,* trans. Constance Farrington (New York: Grove Press, 1964), pp. 31–32.

will, a way of refusing the opportunity offered to him by modernist writing.

But where in all this is the critic and criticism? Scholarship, commentary, exegesis, *explication de texte,* history of ideas, rhetorical or semiological analyses: all these are modes of pertinence and of disciplined attention to the textual matter usually presented to the critic as already at hand. I shall concentrate now on the essay, which is the traditional form by which criticism has expressed itself. The central problematic of the essay as a form is its *place,* by which I mean a series of three ways the essay has of being the form critics take, and locate themselves in, to do their work. Place therefore involves relations, affiliations, the critics' fashion with the texts and audiences they address; it also involves the dynamic taking place of a critic's own text as it is produced.

The first mode of affiliation is the essay's relation to the text or occasion it attempts to approach. How does it come to the text of its choice? How does it enter that text? What is the concluding definition of its relation to the text and the occasion it has dealt with? The second mode of affiliation is the essay's intention (and the intention, presumed or perhaps created by the essay, that its audience has) for attempting an approach. Is the critical essay an attempt to identify or to identify with the text of its choice? Does it stand between the text and the reader, or to one side of one of them? How great or how little is the ironic disparity between its essential formal incompleteness (because after all it is an essay) and the formal completion of the text it treats? The third mode of affiliation concerns the essay as a zone in which certain kinds of occurrences happen as an aspect of the essay's production. What is the essay's consciousness of its marginality to the text it discusses? What is the method by which the essay permits history a role during the making of its own history, that is, as the essay moves from beginning to development to conclusion? What is the quality of the essay's speech, toward, away from, into the *actuality,* the arena of nontextual historical vitality and presence that is taking place simultaneously with the essay itself? Finally, is the essay a text, an intervention between texts, an intensification of the notion of textuality, or a dispersion of language away from a contingent page to occasions, tendencies, currents, or movements in and for history?

A just response to these questions is a realization of how unfamiliar they are in the general discussion of contemporary literary criticism. It is not that the problems of criticism are undiscussed, but rather that criticism is considered essentially as defined once and for all by its secondariness, by its temporal misfortune in having come after the texts and occasions it is supposed to be treating. Just as it is all too often true that texts are thought of as monolithic objects of the past to which criticism despondently appends itself in the present, then the very conception of criticism symbolizes being outdated, being dated from the past rather than by the present. Everything I tried earlier to say about a text—its dialectic of engagement in time and the senses, the paradoxes in a text by which discourse is shown to be immutable and yet contingent, as fraught and politically intransigent as the struggle between dominant and dominated—all this was an implicit rejection of the secondary role usually assigned to criticism. For if we assume instead that texts make up what Foucault calls archival facts, the archive being defined as the text's social discursive presence in the world, then criticism too is another aspect of that present. In other words, rather than being defined by the silent past, commanded by it to speak in the present, criticism, no less than any text, is the present in the course of its articulation, its struggles for definition.

We must not forget that the critic cannot speak without the mediation of writing, that ambivalent *pharmakon* so suggestively portrayed by Derrida as the constituted milieu where the oppositions are opposed: this is where the interplay occurs that brings the oppositions into direct contact with each other, that overturns oppositions and transforms one pole into another, soul and body, good and evil, inside and outside, memory and oblivion, speech and writing.[29] In particular the critic is committed to the essay, whose metaphysics were sketched by Lukacs in the first chapter of his *Die Seele und die Formen.* There Lukacs said that by virtue of its form the essay allows, and indeed is, the coincidence of inchoate soul with exigent material form. Essays are concerned with the relations between things, with values and concepts, in fine, with significance. Whereas poetry deals in images, the essay is the abandonment of images; this abandonment the essay ideally shares with Platonism and mysticism. If, Lukacs continues, the various forms of literature are compared with sunlight refracted in a prism, then the essay is ultraviolet light. What the essay expresses is a yearning for conceptuality and intellectuality, as well as a resolution to the ultimate questions of life. (Throughout his analysis Lukacs refers to Socrates as the typical essayistic figure, always talking of immediate mundane matters while at the same time through his life there sounds the purest, the most profound, and the most concealed yearning—*Die tiefste, die verborgenste Sehnsucht ertönt aus diesem Leben.*)[30]

---

[29]Jacques Derrida, ''La Pharmacie de Platon'' in *La Dissémination* (Paris: Seuil, 1972), pp. 145 and passim.

[30]Georg Lukacs, *Die Seele und die Formen* (1911; rprt. Berlin: Luchterhand, 1971), p. 25.

Thus the essay's mode is ironic, which means first that the form is patently insufficient in its intellectuality with regard to living experience and, second, that the very form of the essay, its being an essay, is an ironic destiny with regard to the great questions of life. In its arbitrariness and irrelevance to the questions he debates, Socrates' death perfectly symbolizes essayistic destiny, which is the absence of a real tragic destiny. Thus, unlike tragedy, there is no internal conclusion to an essay, for only something outside it can interrupt or end it, as Socrates' death is decreed offstage and abruptly ends his life of questioning. Form fills the function in an essay that images do in poetry: form is the reality of the essay, and form gives the essayist a voice with which to ask questions of life, even if that form must always make use of art—a book, a painting, a piece of music—as what seems to be the purely occasional subject matter of its investigations.

Lukacs' analysis of the essay has it in common with Wilde that criticism in general is rarely what it seems, not least in its form. Criticism adopts the mode of commentary on and evaluation of art; yet in reality criticism matters more as a necessarily incomplete and preparatory process toward judgment and evaluation. What the critical essay does is *to begin* to create the values by which art is judged. I said earlier that a major inhibition on critics is that their function as critics is often dated and circumscribed for them by the past, that is, by an already created work of art or a discrete occasion. Lukacs acknowledges the inhibition, but he shows how in fact critics appropriate for themselves the function of starting to make values for the work they are judging. Wilde said it more flamboyantly: criticism "treats the work of art as a starting point for a new creation."[31] Lukacs put it more cautiously: "the essayist is a pure instance of the precursor."[32]

I prefer the latter description, for as Lukacs develops it the critic's position is a vulnerable one because he or she

prepares for a great aesthetic revolution whose result, ironically enough, will render criticism marginal. Later, this very idea will be converted by Lukacs into a description of the overthrow of reification by class consciousness, which in turn will make class itself a marginal thing.[33] Yet what I wish to emphasize here is that critics create not only the values by which art is judged and understood, but they embody in writing those processes and actual conditions in the *present* by means of which art and writing bear significance. This means what R. P. Blackmur, following Hopkins, called the bringing of literature to performance. More explicitly, the critic is responsible to a degree for articulating those voices dominated, displaced, or silenced by the textuality of texts. Texts are a system of forces institutionalized by the reigning culture at some human cost to its various components.[34] For texts after all are not an ideal cosmos of ideally equal monuments. Looking at the Grecian urn Keats *sees* graceful figures adorning its exterior, and also he actualizes in language (and perhaps nowhere else) the little town "emptied of this folk, this pious morn." The critic's attitude to some extent is sensitive in a similar way; it should in addition and more often be frankly inventive, in the traditional rhetorical sense of *invention* so fruitfully employed by Vico, which means finding and exposing things that otherwise lie hidden beneath piety, heedlessness, or routine.

Most of all, criticism is worldly and in the world so long as it opposes monocentrism, a concept I understand as working in conjunction with ethnocentrism, which licenses a culture to cloak itself in the particular authority of certain values over others. Even for Arnold, this comes about as the result of a contest that gives culture a dominion that almost always hides its dark side: in this respect *Culture and Anarchy* and *The Birth of Tragedy* are not very far apart.

---

[31]Wilde, *The Artist as Critic*, p. 367.
[32]Lukacs, *Die Seele und die Formen*, p. 29.

---

[33]See Lukacs, *History and Class Consciousness: Studies in Marxist Dialectics*, trans. Rodney Livingstone (London: Merlin Press, 1971), pp. 178–209.
[34]See the discussion of this point in Richard Poirier, *The Performing Self: Compositions and Decompositions in the Languages of Everyday Life* (New York: Oxford University Press, 1971).

Elaine Showalter

b. 1941

Elaine Showalter published in 1977 one of the most influential works of recent
feminist criticism, *A Literature of Their Own: British Women Novelists from Brontë to
Lessing.* In two later essays, one of which is reprinted here, Showalter called for a
"clearly articulated" feminist literary theory. She, herself, recognized the problems in
this demand that have been voiced against it by others—for example, the danger of a
universalism that would bury feminist critical activities in a patriarchally founded discourse and /or in stultification. Nevertheless, she proceeded to offer some descriptive
categories that in her view would at least clarify feminist projects and help to respond
to attacks that accused feminist critics of reductionism to single issues.

First, she divided feminist criticism into two types, that which is concerned with
woman as reader and that which is concerned with woman as writer. The categories of
reader and writer are familiar enough to the history of criticism, but the mediation of
"woman" has only a brief and halting history. The latter of these two types Showalter
labeled "gynocritics." Though she discussed the readerly perspective, which she
called "feminist critique," it was gynocritics that seemed to interest her most.

Gynocritics eschews the inevitability of male models and theories and seeks a
female model. Thus Showalter's search here remained consistent with her constitution
of a "literature of their own" in her 1977 book. The effort had to be to understand
female subculture, to reconstruct the literary past with attention to it. For Showalter, a
beginning was to see that past as a series of phases, but one had to proceed beyond this
into a questioning of male-created theoretical grounds, which might silence the woman's voice. In a 1981 essay, entitled "Feminist Criticism in the Wilderness" (*Critical
Inquiry* 8), Showalter expressed skepticism about a "playful pluralism." For her, now,
the questions were "what is the *difference* of women's writing?" and how can a terminology be found that "can rescue the feminine from its stereotypical associations
with inferiority?" These were to be approached through a concentration on "women's
access to language." This in turn required the development of a "cultural model of
women's writing."

In addition to *A Literature of Their Own* (1977), Elaine Showalter has written *The
Female Malady: Women Madness and Culture 1830–1980* (1985). She is editor of
Women's Liberation and Literature (1971), *These Modern Women: Autobiographies
of American Women in the 1920s* (1979), *The New Feminist Criticism* (1985), and
Speaking of Gender (1989).

Toward a Feminist Poetics

In 1977, Leon Edel, the distinguished biographer of Henry James, contributed to a London symposium of essays by six male critics called *Contemporary Approaches to English Studies.* Professor Edel presented his essay as a dramatized discussion between three literary scholars who stand arguing about art on the steps of the British Museum:

> There was Criticus, a short, thick-bodied intellec-tual with spectacles, who clung to a pipe in his right hand. There was Poeticus, who cultivated a Yeatsian forelock, but without the eyeglasses and the ribbon. He made his living by reviewing and had come to the B.M. to look up something or other. Then there was Plutarchus, a lean and lanky biographer wearing a corduroy jacket.

As these three gentlemen are warming to their important subject, a taxi pulls up in front of them and releases "an auburn-haired young woman, obviously American, who wore ear-rings and carried an armful of folders and an atta-ché case." Into the museum she dashes, leaving the trio mo-mentarily wondering why femininity requires brainwork. They are still arguing when she comes out, twenty-one pages later.[1]

I suppose we should be grateful that at least one woman—let us call her Critica—makes an appearance in this gathering, even if she is not invited to join the debate. I imagine that she is a feminist critic—in fact, if I could afford to take taxis to the British Museum, I would think they had perhaps seen me—and it is pleasing to think that while the men stand gossiping in the sun, she is inside hard at work. But these are scant satisfactions when we realize that of all the approaches to English studies current in the 1970s, fem-inist criticism is the most isolated and the least understood. Members of English departments who can remember what

Harold Bloom means by *clinamen,* and who know the differ-ence between Tartu and Barthian semiotics, will remark that they are against feminist criticism and consequently have never read any. Those who have read it, often seem to have read through a glass darkly, superimposing their stereotypes on the critical texts. In his introduction to Nina Auerbach's subtle feminist analysis of *Dombey and Son* in the *Dickens Studies Annual,* for example, Robert Partlow discusses the deplorable but nonexistent essay of his own imagining:

> At first glance, Nina Auerbach's essay . . . might seem to be a case of special pleading, another piece of women's lib propaganda masquerading as literary criticism, but it is not quite that . . . such an essay could have been . . . ludicrous . . . it could have seen dark phallic significance in curving rail-road tracks and upright church pews—but it does not.[2]

In contrast to Partlow's caricature (feminist criticism will naturally be obsessed with the phallus), there are the belligerent assumptions of Robert Boyers, in the Winter 1977 issue of *Partisan Review,* that it will be obsessed with destroying great male artists. In "A Case Against Feminist Criticism," Boyers used a single work, Joan Mellen's *Women and Their Sexuality in the New Film* (1973), as an example of feminist deficiency in "intellectual honesty" and "rigor." He defines feminist criticism as the "insistence on asking the same questions of every work and demanding ideologically satisfactory answers to those questions as a means of evaluating it," and concludes his diatribe thus:

> Though I do not think anyone has made a credible case for feminist criticism as a viable alternative to any other mode, no one can seriously object to feminists continuing to try. We ought to demand that such efforts be minimally distinguished by in-tellectual candor and some degree of precision. This I have failed to discover in most feminist criticism.[3]

Since his article makes its "case" so recklessly that Joan Mellen brought charges for libel, and the *Partisan Review* was obliged to print a retraction in the following issue, Boy-

TOWARD A FEMINIST POETICS. *Toward a Feminist Poetics* is reprinted from *Women's Writing and Writing About Women,* ed. Mary Jacobus (London: Croom Helm, 1979). Copyright by Elaine Showalter and reprinted by the au-thor's permission.

[All notes are by Showalter]

I wish to thank Nina Auerbach, Kate Ellis, Mary Jacobus, Wendy Martin, Adrienne Rich, Helen Taylor, Martha Vicinus, Margaret Walters, and Ruth Yeazell for sharing with me their ideas on feminist criticism.

[1]Leon Edel, "The Poetics of Biography," in *Contemporary Approaches to English Studies,* ed. Hilda Schiff (New York: Barnes & Noble, 1977), p. 38. The other contributors to the symposium are George Steiner, Raymond Wil-liams, Christopher Butler, Jonathan Culler, and Terry Eagleton.

[2]Robert Partlow, Introduction to *Dickens Studies Annual,* vol. 5 (Carbondale: Southern Illinois University Press, 1976), pp. xiv–xv. Nina Auerbach's essay is called "Dickens and Dombey: A Daughter After All."

[3]Robert Boyers, "A Case Against Feminist Criticism," *Partisan Review* 44 (Winter 1977): 602, 610.

ers hardly seems the ideal champion to enter the critical lists under the twin banners of honesty and rigor. Indeed his terminology is best understood as a form of intimidation, intended to force women into using a discourse more acceptable to the academy, characterized by the "rigor" which my dictionary defines as strictness, a severe or cruel act, or a "state of rigidity in living tissues or organs that prevents response to stimuli." In formulating a feminist literary theory, one ought never to expect to appease a Robert Boyers. And yet these "cases" cannot continue to be settled, one by one, out of court. The absence of a clearly articulated theory makes feminist criticism perpetually vulnerable to such attacks, and not even feminist critics seem to agree what it is that they mean to profess and defend.

A second obstacle to the articulation of a feminist critical practice is the activist's suspicion of theory, especially when the demand for clarification comes from sources as patently sexist as the egregiously named Boyerses and Mailers of the literary quarterlies. Too many literary abstractions which claim to be universal have in fact described only male perceptions, experiences, and options, and have falsified the social and personal contexts in which literature is produced and consumed. In women's fiction, the complacently precise and systematizing male has often been the target of satire, especially when his subject is Woman. George Eliot's impotent structuralist Casaubon is a classic instance, as is Mr. Ramsay, the self-pitying philosopher in Virginia Woolf's *To the Lighthouse.* More recently Doris Lessing's Professor Bloodrot in *The Golden Notebook* lectures confidently on orgasm in the female swan; as Bloodrot proceeds, the women in the audience rise one by one and leave. What women have found hard to take in such male characters is their self-deception, their pretense to objectivity, their emotion parading as reason. As Adrienne Rich comments in *Of Woman Born,* "the term 'rational' relegates to its opposite term all that it refuses to deal with, and thus ends by assuming itself to be purified of the nonrational, rather than searching to identify and assimilate its own surreal or nonlinear elements."[4] For some radical feminists, methodology itself is an intellectual instrument of patriarchy, a tyrannical methodolatry which sets implicit limits to what can be questioned and discussed. "The God Method," writes Mary Daly,

is in fact a subordinate deity, serving higher powers. These are social and cultural institutions whose survival depends upon the classification of

disruptive and disturbing information as nondata. Under patriarchy, Method has wiped out women's questions so totally that even women have not been able to hear and formulate our own questions, to meet our own experiences.[5]

From this perspective, the academic demand for theory can only be heard as a threat to the feminist need for authenticity, and the visitor looking for a formula he or she can take away without personal encounter is not welcome. In the United States, where women's-studies programs offer degree options in nearly three hundred colleges and universities, there are fears that feminist analysis has been coopted by academia, and counterdemands that we resist the pressure to assimilate. Some believe that the activism and empiricism of feminist criticism is its greatest strength, and point to the flourishing international women's press, to new feminist publishing houses, and to writing collectives and manifestos. They are afraid that if the theory is perfected, the movement will be dead. But these defensive responses may also be rationalizations of the psychic barriers to women's participation in theoretical discourse. Traditionally women have been cast in the supporting rather than the starring roles of literary scholarship. Whereas male critics in the twentieth century have moved to center stage, openly contesting for primacy with writers, establishing coteries and schools, speaking unabashedly (to quote Geoffrey Hartman) of their "pen-envy,"[6] women are still too often translators, editors, hostesses at the conference and the Festschrift, interpreters; to congratulate ourselves for working patiently and anonymously for the coming of Shakespeare's sister, as Virginia Woolf exhorted us to do in 1928, is in a sense to make a virtue of necessity. In this essay, therefore, I would like to outline a brief taxonomy, if not a poetics, of feminist criticism, in the hope that it will serve as an introduction to a body of work which needs to be considered both as a major contribution to English studies and as part of an interdisciplinary effort to reconstruct the social, political, and cultural experience of women.

Feminist criticism can be divided into two distinct varieties. The first type is concerned with *woman as reader*—with woman as the consumer of male-produced literature, and with the way in which the hypothesis of a female reader changes our apprehension of a given text, awakening us to the significance of its sexual codes. I shall call this kind of

[4]Adrienne Rich, *Of Woman Born: Motherhood as Experience and Institution* (New York: W. W. Norton, 1977), p. 62.

[5]Mary Daly, *Beyond God the Father: Towards a Philosophy of Women's Liberation* (Boston: Beacon Press, 1973), pp. 12–13.
[6]Geoffrey H. Hartman, *The Fate of Reading* (Chicago: University of Chicago Press, 1975), p. 3.

analysis the *feminist critique,* and like other kinds of critique it is a historically grounded inquiry which probes the ideological assumptions of literary phenomena. Its subjects include the images and stereotypes of women in literature, the omissions of and misconceptions about women in criticism, and the fissures in male-constructed literary history. It is also concerned with the exploitation and manipulation of the female audience, especially in popular culture and film; and with the analysis of woman-as-sign in semiotic systems. The second type of feminist criticism is concerned with *woman as writer*—with woman as the producer of textual meaning, with the history, themes, genres, and structures of literature by women. Its subjects include the psychodynamics of female creativity; linguistics and the problem of a female language; the trajectory of the individual or collective female literary career; literary history; and, of course, studies of particular writers and works. No term exists in English for such a specialized discourse, and so I have adapted the French term *la gynocritique:* "gynocritics" (although the significance of the male pseudonym in the history of women's writing also suggested the term "georgics").

The feminist critique is essentially political and polemical, with theoretical affiliations to Marxist sociology and aesthetics; gynocritics is more self-contained and experimental, with connections to other modes of new feminist research. In a dialogue between these two positions, Carolyn Heilbrun, the writer, and Catharine Stimpson, editor of the journal *Signs: Women in Culture and Society,* compare the feminist critique to the Old Testament, "looking for the sins and errors of the past," and gynocritics to the New Testament, seeking "the grace of imagination." Both kinds are necessary, they explain, for only the Jeremiahs of the feminist critique can lead us out of the "Egypt of female servitude" to the promised land of the feminist vision. That the discussion makes use of these Biblical metaphors points to the connections between feminist consciousness and conversion narratives which often appear in women's literature; Carolyn Heilbrun comments on her own text, "When I talk about feminist criticism, I am amazed at how high a moral tone I take."[7]

The Feminist Critique: Hardy

Let us take briefly as an example of the way a feminist critique might proceed, Thomas Hardy's *The Mayor of Caster-*

bridge, which begins with the famous scene of the drunken Michael Henchard selling his wife and infant daughter for five guineas at a country fair. In his study of Hardy, Irving Howe has praised the brilliance and power of this opening scene:

> To shake loose from one's wife; to discard that drooping rag of a woman, with her mute complaints and maddening passivity; to escape not by a slinking abandonment but through the public sale of her body to a stranger, as horses are sold at a fair; and thus to wrest, through sheer amoral wilfulness, a second chance out of life—it is with this stroke, so insidiously attractive to male fantasy, that *The Mayor of Casterbridge* begins.[8]

It is obvious that a woman, unless she has been indoctrinated into being very deeply identified indeed with male culture, will have a different experience of this scene. I quote Howe first to indicate how the fantasies of the male critic distort the text; for Hardy tells us very little about the relationship of Michael and Susan Henchard, and what we see in the early scenes does not suggest that she is drooping, complaining, or passive. Her role, however, is a passive one; severely constrained by her womanhood, and further burdened by her child, there is no way that *she* can wrest a second chance out of life. She cannot master events, but only accommodate herself to them.

What Howe, like other male critics of Hardy, conveniently overlooks about the novel is that Henchard sells not only his wife but his child, a child who can only be female. Patriarchal societies do not readily sell their sons, but their daughters are all for sale sooner or later. Hardy wished to make the sale of the daughter emphatic and central; in early drafts of the novel Henchard has two daughters and sells only one, but Hardy revised to make it clearer that Henchard is symbolically selling his entire share in the world of women. Having severed his bonds with this female community of love and loyalty, Henchard has chosen to live in the male community, to define his human relationships by the male code of paternity, money, and legal contract. His tragedy lies in realizing the inadequacy of this system, and in his inability to repossess the loving bonds he comes desperately to need.

[7]Carolyn G. Heilbrun and Catharine R. Stimpson, "Theories of Feminist Criticism," in *Feminist Literary Criticism: Explorations in Theory,* ed. Josephine Donovan (Lexington: University Press of Kentucky, 1976), pp. 64, 68, 72.

[8]Irving Howe, *Thomas Hardy* (London: Weidenfeld & Nicolson, 1968), p. 84. For a more detailed discussion of this problem, see my essay "The Unmanning of the Mayor of Casterbridge," in *Critical Approaches to the Fiction of Hardy,* ed. Dale Kramer (New York: Barnes & Noble, 1979), pp. 99–115.

The emotional center of *The Mayor of Casterbridge* is neither Henchard's relationship to his wife nor his superficial romance with Lucetta Templeman, but his slow appreciation of the strength and dignity of his wife's daughter, Elizabeth-Jane. Like the other women in the book, she is governed by her own heart—man-made laws are not important to her until she is taught by Henchard himself to value legality, paternity, external definitions, and thus in the end to reject him. A self-proclaimed "woman-hater," a man who has felt at best a "supercilious pity" for womankind, Henchard is humbled and "unmanned" by the collapse of his own virile façade, the loss of his mayor's chain, his master's authority, his father's rights. But in Henchard's alleged weakness and "womanishness," breaking through in moments of tenderness, Hardy is really showing us the man at his best. Thus Hardy's female characters in *The Mayor of Casterbridge,* as in his other novels, are somewhat idealized and melancholy projections of a repressed male self.

As we see in this analysis, one of the problems of the feminist critique is that it is male-oriented. If we study stereotypes of women, the sexism of male critics, and the limited roles women play in literary history, we are not learning what women have felt and experienced, but only what men have thought women should be. In some fields of specialization, this may require a long apprenticeship to the male theoretician, whether he be Althusser, Barthes, Macherey, or Lacan; and then an application of the theory of signs or myths or the unconscious to male texts or films. The temporal and intellectual investment one makes in such a process increases resistance to questioning it, and to seeing its historical and ideological boundaries. The critique also has a tendency to naturalize women's victimization by making it the inevitable and obsessive topic of discussion. One sees, moreover, in works like Elizabeth Hardwick's *Seduction and Betrayal,* the bittersweet moral distinctions the critic makes between women merely betrayed by men, like Hetty in *Adam Bede,* and the heroines who make careers out of betrayal, like Hester Prynne in *The Scarlet Letter.* This comes dangerously close to a celebration of the opportunities of victimization, the seduction *of* betrayal.[9]

Gynocritics and Female Culture

In contrast to this angry or loving fixation on male literature, the program of gynocritics is to construct a female framework for the analysis of women's literature, to develop new models based on the study of female experience, rather than to adapt male models and theories. Gynocritics begins at the point when we free ourselves from the linear absolutes of male literary history, stop trying to fit women between the lines of the male tradition, and focus instead on the newly visible world of female culture. This is comparable to the ethnographer's effort to render the experience of the "muted" female half of a society, which is described in Shirley Ardener's collection *Perceiving Women.*[10] Gynocritics is related to feminist research in history, anthropology, psychology, and sociology, all of which have developed hypotheses of a female subculture including not only the ascribed status, and the internalized constructs of femininity, but also the occupations, interactions, and consciousness of women. Anthropologists study the female subculture in the relationships between women, as mothers, daughters, sisters, and friends; in sexuality, reproduction, and ideas about the body; and in rites of initiation and passage, purification ceremonies, myths, and taboos. Michelle Rosaldo writes in *Woman, Culture, and Society:*

> The very symbolic and social conceptions that appear to set women apart and to circumscribe their activities may be used by women as a basis for female solidarity and worth. When men live apart from women, they in fact cannot control them, and unwittingly they may provide them with the symbols and social resources on which to build a society of their own.[11]

Thus in some women's literature, feminine values penetrate and undermine the masculine systems that contain them; and women have imaginatively engaged the myths of the Amazons, and the fantasies of a separate female society, in genres from Victorian poetry to contemporary science fiction.

In recent years, pioneering work by four young American feminist scholars has given us some new ways to interpret the culture of nineteenth-century American women and the literature that was its primary expressive form. Carroll Smith-Rosenberg's essay "The Female World of Love and Ritual" examines several archives of letters between women, and outlines the homosocial emotional world of the nineteenth century. Nancy Cott's *The Bonds of Womanhood:*

---

[9]Elizabeth Hardwick, *Seduction and Betrayal: Woman and Literature* (New York: Random House, 1974).

[10]Shirley Ardener, ed., *Perceiving Women* (New York: Halsted Press, 1975).
[11]Michelle Z. Rosaldo, "Women, Culture, and Society: A Theoretical Overview," in *Women, Culture, and Society,* ed. Michelle Z. Rosaldo and Louise Lamphere (Stanford, Calif.: Stanford University Press, 1974), p. 39.

Woman's Sphere in New England, 1780–1835 explores the paradox of a cultural bondage, a legacy of pain and submission, which nonetheless generates a sisterly solidarity, a bond of shared experience, loyalty, and compassion. Ann Douglas's ambitious book, *The Feminization of American Culture,* boldly locates the genesis of American mass culture in the sentimental literature of women and clergymen, two allied and "disestablished" postindustrial groups. These three are social historians; but Nina Auerbach's *Communities of Women: An Idea in Fiction* seeks the bonds of womanhood in women's literature, ranging from the matriarchal households of Louisa May Alcott and Mrs. Gaskell to the women's schools and colleges of Dorothy Sayers, Sylvia Plath, and Muriel Spark. Historical and literary studies like these, based on English women, are badly needed; and the manuscript and archival sources for them are both abundant and untouched.[12]

Gynocritics: Elizabeth Barrett Browning and Muriel Spark

Gynocritics must also take into account the different velocities and curves of political, social, and personal histories in determining women's literary choices and careers. "In dealing with women as writers," Virginia Woolf wrote in her 1929 essay, "Women and Fiction," "as much elasticity as possible is desirable; it is necessary to leave oneself room to deal with other things besides their work, so much has that work been influenced by conditions that have nothing whatever to do with art."[13] We might illustrate the need for this completeness by looking at Elizabeth Barrett Browning, whose verse novel *Aurora Leigh* (1856) has recently been handsomely reprinted by the Women's Press. In her excellent introduction Cora Kaplan defines Barrett Browning's feminism as romantic and bourgeois, placing its faith in the transforming powers of love, art, and Christian charity. Kaplan reviews Barrett Browning's dialogue with the artists and radicals of her time; with Tennyson and Clough, who had also written poems on the "woman question"; with the Christian Socialism of Fourier, Owen, Kingsley, and Mau-

rice; and with such female predecessors as Madame de Staël and George Sand. But in this exploration of Barrett Browning's intellectual milieu, Kaplan omits discussion of the male poet whose influence on her work in the 1850s would have been most pervasive: Robert Browning. When we understand how susceptible women writers have always been to the aesthetic standards and values of the male tradition, and to male approval and validation, we can appreciate the complexity of a marriage between artists. Such a union has almost invariably meant internal conflicts, self-effacement, and finally obliteration for the woman, except in the rare cases—Eliot and Lewes, the Woolfs—where the husband accepted a managerial rather than a competitive role. We can see in Barrett Browning's letters of the 1850s the painful, halting, familiar struggle between her womanly love and ambition for her husband and her conflicting commitment to her own work. There is a sense in which she *wants* him to be the better artist. At the beginning of the decade she was more famous than he; then she notes with pride a review in France which praises him more; his work on *Men and Women* goes well; her work on *Aurora Leigh* goes badly (she had a young child and was recovering from the most serious of her four miscarriages). In 1854 she writes to a woman friend:

> I am behind hand with my poem. . . . Robert swears he shall have his book ready in spite of everything for print when we shall be in London for the purpose, but, as for mine, it must wait for the next spring I begin to see clearly. Also it may be better not to bring out the two works together.

And she adds wryly, "If mine were ready I might not say so perhaps."[14]

Without an understanding of the framework of the female subculture, we can miss or misinterpret the themes and structures of women's literature, fail to make necessary connections within a tradition. In 1852, in an eloquent passage from her autobiographical essay "Cassandra," Florence Nightingale identified the pain of feminist awakening as its essence, as the guarantee of progress and free will. Protesting against the protected unconscious lives of middle-class Victorian women, Nightingale demanded the restoration of their suffering:

> Give us back our suffering, we cry to Heaven in our hearts—suffering rather than indifferentism—

---

[12]Carroll Smith-Rosenberg, "The Female World of Love and Ritual: Relations Between Women in Nineteenth-Century America," *Signs* 1 (Fall 1975): 1–30; Nancy F. Cott, *The Bonds of Womanhood: "Woman's Sphere" in New England, 1780–1835* (New Haven, Conn.: Yale University Press, 1977); Ann Douglas, *The Feminization of American Culture* (New York: Alfred A. Knopf, 1977); Nina Auerbach, *Communities of Women: An Idea in Fiction* (Cambridge, Mass.: Harvard University Press, 1978).

[13]Virginia Woolf, "Women and Fiction," *Collected Essays,* vol. 2 (London: Chatto & Windus, 1967), p. 141.

[14]Peter N. Heydon and Philip Kelley, eds., *Elizabeth Barrett Browning's Letters to Mrs. David Ogilvy* (New York: Quadrangle Books, 1973), p. 115.

for out of suffering may come the cure. Better to have the pain than paralysis: A hundred struggle and drown in the breakers. One discovers a new world.[15]

It is fascinating to see how Nightingale's metaphors anticipate not only her own medical career but also the fate of the heroines of women's novels in the nineteenth and twentieth centuries. To waken from the drugged, pleasant sleep of Victorian womanhood was agonizing; in fiction it is much more likely to end in drowning than in discovery. It is usually associated with what George Eliot in *Middlemarch* calls "the chill hours of a morning twilight," and the sudden appalled confrontation with the contingencies of adulthood. Eliot's Maggie Tulliver, Edith Wharton's Lily Bart, Olive Schreiner's Lyndall, Kate Chopin's Edna Pontellier wake to worlds which offer no places for the women they wish to become; and rather than struggling they die. Female suffering thus becomes a kind of literary commodity which both men and women consume. Even in these important women's novels—*The Mill on the Floss, The Story of an African Farm, The House of Mirth*—the fulfillment of the plot is a visit to the heroine's grave by a male mourner.

According to Dame Rebecca West, unhappiness is still the keynote of contemporary fiction by English women.[16] Certainly the literary landscape is strewn with dead female bodies. In Fay Weldon's *Down Among the Women and Female Friends,* suicide has come to be a kind of domestic accomplishment, carried out after the shopping and the washing-up. When Weldon's heroine turns on the gas, "she feels that she has been half-dead for so long that the difference in state will not be very great." In Muriel Spark's stunning short novel of 1970, *The Driver's Seat,* another half-dead and desperate heroine gathers all her force to hunt down a woman-hating psychopath and persuade him to murder her. Garishly dressed in a purposely bought outfit of clashing purple, green, and white—the colors of the suffragettes (and the colors of the school uniform in *The Prime of Miss Jean Brodie*)—Lise goes in search of her killer, lures him to a park, gives him the knife. But in Lise's careful selection of her death-dress, her patient pursuit of her assassin, Spark has given us the devastated postulates of feminine wisdom: that a woman creates her identity by choosing her clothes, that she creates her history by choosing her man. That, in the

1970s, Mr. Right turns out to be Mr. Goodbar is not the sudden product of urban violence but a latent truth fiction exposes. Spark asks whether men or women are in the driver's seat and whether the power to choose one's destroyer is women's only form of self-assertion. To label the violence or self-destructiveness of these painful novels as neurotic expressions of a personal pathology, as many reviewers have done, is to ignore, Annette Kolodny suggests,

> the possibility that the worlds they inhabit may in fact be real, or true, and for them the only worlds available, and further, to deny the possibility that their apparently "odd" or unusual responses may in fact be justifiable or even necessary.[17]

But women's literature must go beyond these scenarios of compromise, madness, and death. Although the reclamation of suffering is the beginning, its purpose is to discover the new world. Happily, some recent women's literature, especially in the United States, where novelists and poets have become vigorously involved in the women's liberation movement, has gone beyond reclaiming suffering to its reinvestment. This newer writing relates the pain of transformation to history. "If I'm lonely," writes Adrienne Rich in "Song,"

> *it must be the loneliness*
> *of waking first, of breathing*
> *dawn's first cold breath on the city*
> *of being the one awake*
> *in a house wrapped in sleep*[18]

Rich is one of the spokeswomen for a new women's writing which explores the will to change. In her recent book, *Of Woman Born: Motherhood as Experience and Institution,* Rich challenges the alienation from and rejection of the mother that daughters have learned under patriarchy. Much women's literature in the past has dealt with "matrophobia" or the fear of becoming one's mother.[19] In Sylvia Plath's *The Bell Jar,* for example, the heroine's mother is the target for the novel's most punishing contempt. When Esther announces to her therapist that she hates her mother, she is on

---

[15]Florence Nightingale, "Cassandra," in *The Cause: A History of the Women's Movement in Great Britain,* ed. Ray Strachey (1928; reprint ed., Port Washington, N.Y.: Kennikat Press, 1969), p. 398.

[16]Rebecca West, "And They All Lived Unhappily Ever After," *Times Literary Supplement,* July 26, 1974, p. 779.

[17]Annette Kolodny, "Some Notes on Defining a 'Feminist Literary Criticism,'" *Critical Inquiry* 2 (Fall 1975): 84. For an illuminating discussion of *The Driver's Seat,* see Auerbach, *Communities of Women,* p. 181.

[18]Adrienne Rich, *Diving into the Wreck* (New York: W. W. Norton, 1973), p. 20.

[19]The term "matrophobia" was coined by Lynn Sukenick; see Rich, *Of Woman Born,* pp. 235 ff.

the road to recovery. Hating one's mother was the feminist enlightenment of the fifties and sixties; but it is only a metaphor for hating oneself. Female literature of the 1970s goes beyond matrophobia to a courageously sustained quest for the mother, in such books as Margaret Atwood's *Surfacing,* and Lisa Alther's recent *Kinflicks.* As the death of the father has always been an archetypal rite of passage for the Western hero, now the death of the mother as witnessed and transcended by the daughter has become one of the most profound occasions of female literature. In analyzing these purposeful awakenings, these reinvigorated mythologies of female culture, feminist criticism finds its most challenging, inspiriting, and appropriate task.

Women and the Novel: The "Precious Specialty"

The most consistent assumption of feminist reading has been the belief that women's special experience would assume and determine distinctive forms in art. In the nineteenth century, such a contribution was ambivalently valued. When Victorian reviewers like G. H. Lewes, Richard Hutton, and Richard Simpson began to ask what the literature of women might mean and what it might become, they focused on the educational, experiential, and biological handicaps of the woman novelist, and this was also how most women conceptualized their situation. Some reviewers, granting women's sympathy, sentiment, and powers of observation, thought that the novel would provide an appropriate, even a happy, outlet for female emotion and fantasy. In the United States, the popular novelist Fanny Fern understood that women had been granted access to the novel as a sort of repressive desublimation, a harmless channel for frustrations and drives that might otherwise threaten the family, the church, and the state. Fern recommended that women write as therapy, as a release from the stifling silence of the drawing room, and as a rebellion against the indifference and insensitivity of the men closest to them:

> Look around, and see innumerable women, to whose barren and loveless lives this would be improvement and solace, and I say to them, write! write! It will be a safe outlet for thoughts and feelings that maybe the nearest friend you have has never dreamed had place in your heart and brain. . . . It is not *safe* for the women of 1867 to shut down so much that cries out for sympathy and expression, because life is such a maelstrom of business or folly or both that those to whom they

have bound themselves, body and soul, recognize only the needs of the former. . . . One of these days, when that diary is found, when the hand that penned it shall be dust, with what amazement and remorse will many a husband or father exclaim, I never knew my wife or my child until this moment.[20]

Fern's scribbling woman spoke with fierce indirectness to the male audience, to the imagined husband or father; her purpose was to shock rather than to please, but the need to provoke masculine response was the controlling factor in her writing. At the turn of the century, members of the Women Writers Suffrage League, an important organization of English novelists and journalists, began to explore the psychological bondage of women's literature and its relationships to a male-dominated publishing industry. Elizabeth Robins, the first president of the league, a novelist and actress who had starred in early English productions of Ibsen, argued in 1908 that no woman writer had ever been free to explore female consciousness:

> The realization that she had access to a rich and as yet unrifled storehouse may have crossed her mind, but there were cogent reasons for concealing her knowledge. With that wariness of ages which has come to be instinct, she contented herself with echoing the old fables, presenting to a man-governed world puppets as nearly as possible like those that had from the beginning found such favour in men's sight.
>
> Contrary to the popular impression, to say in print what she thinks is the last thing the woman-novelist or journalist is so rash as to attempt. There even more than elsewhere (unless she is reckless) she must wear the aspect that shall have the best chance of pleasing her brothers. Her publishers are not women.[21]

It was to combat this inhibiting commercial monopoly that nineteenth-century women began to organize their own publishing houses, beginning with Emily Faithfull's Victoria Press in the 1870s, and reaching a peak with the flourishing suffrage presses at the beginning of this century. One of the

---

[20]Quoted in Ann Douglas Wood, "The 'Scribbling Women' and Fanny Fern: Why Women Wrote," *American Quarterly* 23 (Spring 1971): 3–24.

[21]Elizabeth Robins, *Woman's Secret,* WSPU pamphlet in the collection of the Museum of London, p. 6. Jane Marcus is preparing a full-length study of Elizabeth Robins.

most fervent beliefs of the Women Writers Suffrage League was that the *terra incognita* of the female psyche would find unique literary expression once women had overthrown male domination. In *A Room of One's Own,* Virginia Woolf argued that economic independence was the essential pre-condition of an autonomous women's art. Like George Eliot before her, Woolf also believed that women's literature held the promise of a "precious speciality," a distinctly female vision.

Feminine, Feminist, Female

All of these themes have been important to feminist literary criticism in the 1960s and 1970s, but we have approached them with more historical awareness. Before we can even begin to ask how the literature of women would be different and special, we need to reconstruct its past, to rediscover the scores of women novelists, poets, and dramatists whose work has been obscured by time, and to establish the continuity of the female tradition from decade to decade, rather than from Great Woman to Great Woman. As we re-create the chain of writers in this tradition, the patterns of influence and response from one generation to the next, we can also begin to challenge the periodicity of orthodox literary history and its enshrined canons of achievement. It is because we have studied women writers in isolation that we have never grasped the connections between them. When we go beyond Austen, the Brontës, and Eliot, say, to look at a hundred and fifty or more of their sister novelists, we can see patterns and phases in the evolution of a female tradition which correspond to the developmental phases of any sub-cultural art. In my book on English women writers, *A Literature of Their Own,* I have called these the Feminine, Feminist, and Female stages.[22] During the Feminine phase, dating from about 1840 to 1880, women wrote in an effort to equal the intellectual achievements of the male culture, and internalized its assumptions about female nature. The distinguishing sign of this period is the male pseudonym, introduced in England in the 1840s, and a national characteristic of English women writers. In addition to the famous names we all know—George Eliot, Currer, Ellis, and Acton Bell—dozens of other women chose male pseudonyms as a way of coping with a double literary standard. This masculine disguise goes well beyond the title page; it exerts an irregular pressure on the narrative, affecting tone, diction, structure, and characterization. In contrast to the English male pseu-

donym, which signals such clear self-awareness of the liabilities of female authorship, American women during the same period adopted superfeminine, little-me pseudonyms (Fanny Fern, Grace Greenwood, Fanny Forester), disguising behind those nominal bouquets their boundless energy, powerful economic motives, and keen professional skills. It is pleasing to discover the occasional Englishwoman who combines both these techniques, and creates the illusion of male authorship with a name that contains the encoded domestic message of femininity—such as Harriet Parr who wrote under the pen name "Holme Lee." The feminist content of feminine art is typically oblique, displaced, ironic, and subversive; one has to read it between the lines, in the missed possibilities of the text.

In the Feminist phase, from about 1880 to 1920, or the winning of the vote, women are historically enabled to reject the accommodating postures of femininity and to use literature to dramatize the ordeals of wronged womanhood. The personal sense of injustice which feminine novelists such as Elizabeth Gaskell and Frances Trollope expressed in their novels of class struggle and factory life become increasingly and explicitly feminist in the 1880s, when a generation of New Women redefined the woman artist's role in terms of responsibility to suffering sisters. The purest examples of this phase are the Amazon utopias of the 1890s, fantasies of perfected female societies set in an England or an America of the future, which were also protests against male government, male laws, and male medicine. One author of Amazon utopias, the American Charlotte Perkins Gilman, also analyzed the preoccupations of masculine literature with sex and war, and the alternative possibilities of an emancipated feminist literature. Gilman's utopian feminism carried George Eliot's idea of the "precious speciality" to its matriarchal extremes. Comparing her view of sisterly collectivity to the beehive, she writes that

> the bee's fiction would be rich and broad, full of the complex tasks of comb-building and filling, the care and feeding of the young.... It would treat of the vast fecundity of motherhood, the educative and selective processes of the group-mothers, and the passion of loyalty, of social service, which holds the hives together.[23]

This is Feminist Socialist Realism with a vengeance, but women novelists of the period—even Gilman, in her short

---

[22]Elaine Showalter, *A Literature of Their Own: British Women Novelists from Brontë to Lessing* (Princeton, N.J.: Princeton University Press, 1977).

[23]Charlotte Perkins Gilman, *The Man-made World: or, Our Androcentric Culture* (1911; reprint ed., New York: Johnson Reprints, 1971), pp. 101–2.

stories—could not be limited to such didactic formulas, or such maternal topics.

In the Female phase, ongoing since 1920, women reject both imitation and protest—two forms of dependency—and turn instead to female experience as the source of an autonomous art, extending the feminist analysis of culture to the forms and techniques of literature. Representatives of the formal Female Aesthetic, such as Dorothy Richardson and Virginia Woolf, begin to think in terms of male and female sentences, and divide their work into "masculine" journalism and "feminine" fictions, redefining and sexualizing external and internal experience. Their experiments were both enriching and imprisoning retreats into the celebration of consciousness; even in Woolf's famous definition of life: "a luminous halo, a semi-transparent envelope surrounding us from the beginning of consciousness to the end,"[24] there is a submerged metaphor of uterine withdrawal and containment. In this sense, the Room of One's Own becomes a kind of Amazon utopia, population 1.

Feminist Criticism, Marxism, and Structuralism

In trying to account for these complex permutations of the female tradition, feminist criticism has tried a variety of theoretical approaches. The most natural direction for feminist criticism to take has been the revision and even the subversion of related ideologies, especially Marxist aesthetics and structuralism, altering their vocabularies and methods to include the variable of gender. I believe, however, that this thrifty feminine making-do is ultimately unsatisfactory. Feminist criticism cannot go around forever in men's ill-fitting hand-me-downs, the Annie Hall of English studies; but must, as John Stuart Mill wrote about women's literature in 1869, "emancipate itself from the influence of accepted models, and guide itself by its own impulses"[25]—as, I think, gynocritics is beginning to do. This is not to deny the necessity of using the terminology and techniques of our profession. But when we consider the historical conditions in which critical ideologies are produced, we see why feminist adaptations seem to have reached an impasse.

Both Marxism and structuralism see themselves as privileged critical discourse, and preempt the claim to superior places in the hierarchy of critical approaches. A key word in each system is "science"; both claim to be sciences of literature, and repudiate the personal, fallible, interpretative reading. Marxist aesthetics offers a "science of the text," in which the author becomes not the creator but the producer of a text whose components are historically and economically determined. Structuralism presents linguistically based models of textual permutations and combinations, offering a "science of literary meaning," a grammar of genre. The assimilation of these positivist and evangelical literary criticisms by Anglo-American scholarship in the 1960s and 1970s is not, I would argue, a spontaneous or accidental cultural phenomenon. In the Cold War atmosphere of the late 1950s, when European structuralism began to develop, the morale of the Anglo-American male academic humanist was at its nadir. This was the era of Sputnik, of scientific competition with the Soviet Union, of government money flowing to the laboratories and research centers. Northrop Frye has written about the plight of the male intellectual confronting

> the dismal sexist symbology surrounding the humanities which he meets everywhere, even in the university itself, from freshman classes to the president's office. This symbology, or whatever one should call it, says that the sciences, especially the physical sciences, are rugged, aggressive, out in the world doing things, and so symbolically male, whereas the literatures are narcissistic, intuitive, fanciful, staying at home and making the home more beautiful but not doing anything serious and are therefore symbolically female.[26]

Frye's own *Anatomy of Criticism*, published in 1957, presented the first postulates of a systematic critical theory, and the "possibility of literary study's attaining the progressive, cumulative qualities of science."[27]

The new sciences of the text based on linguistics, computers, genetic structuralism, deconstructionism, neoformalism and deformalism, affective stylistics, and psychoaesthetics, have offered literary critics the opportunity to demonstrate that the work they do is as manly and aggressive as nuclear physics—not intuitive, expressive, and feminine, but strenuous, rigorous, impersonal, and virile. In a shrinking job market, these new levels of professionalization also function as discriminators between the marketable and the marginal lecturer. Literary science, in its manic generation of difficult terminology, its establishment of seminars and

---

[24]Virginia Woolf, "Modern Fiction," *Collected Essays*, vol. 2, p. 106.
[25]John Stuart Mill, *The Subjection of Women* (London, 1969), p. 133.
[26]Northrop Frye, "Expanding Eyes," *Critical Inquiry* 2 (1975): 201–2.
[27]Robert Scholes, *Structuralism in Literature: An Introduction* (New Haven, Conn.: Yale University Press, 1974), p. 118.

institutes of postgraduate study, creates an elite corps of specialists who spend more and more time mastering the theory, less and less time reading the books. We are moving towards a two-tiered system of "higher" and "lower" criticism, the higher concerned with the "scientific" problems of form and structure, the "lower" concerned with the "humanistic" problems of content and interpretation. And these levels, it seems to me, are now taking on subtle gender identities and assuming a sexual polarity—hermeneutics and hismeneutics. Ironically, the existence of a new criticism practiced by women has made it even more possible for structuralism and Marxism to strive, Henchard-like, for systems of formal obligation and determination. Feminists writing in these modes, such as Hélène Cixous and the women contributors to *Diacritics,* risk being allotted the symbolic ghettos of the special issue or the back of the book for their essays.

It is not only because the exchange between feminism, Marxism, and structuralism has hitherto been so one-sided, however, that I think attempts at syntheses have so far been unsuccessful. While scientific criticism struggles to purge itself of the subjective, feminist criticism is willing to assert (in the title of a recent anthology) *The Authority of Experience.*[28] The experience of women can easily disappear, become mute, invalid, and invisible, lost in the diagrams of the structuralist or the class conflict of the Marxists. Experience is not emotion; we must protest now as in the nineteenth century against the equation of the feminine with the irrational. But we must also recognize that the questions we most need to ask go beyond those that science can answer. We must seek the repressed messages of women in history, in anthropology, in psychology, and in ourselves, before we can locate the feminine not-said, in the manner of Pierre Macherey, by probing the fissures of the female text.

Thus the current theoretical impasse in feminist criticism, I believe, is more than a problem of finding "exacting definitions and a suitable terminology," or "theorizing in the midst of a struggle." It comes from our own divided consciousness, the split in each of us. We are both the daughters of the male tradition, of our teachers, our professors, our dissertation advisers, and our publishers—a tradition which asks us to be rational, marginal, and grateful; and sisters in a new women's movement which engenders another kind of awareness and commitment, which demands that we renounce the pseudo-success of token womanhood and the ironic masks of academic debate. How much easier, how less lonely it is, not to awaken—to continue to be critics and teachers of male literature, anthropologists of male culture, and psychologists of male literary response, claiming all the while to be universal. Yet we cannot will ourselves to go back to sleep. As women scholars in the 1970s we have been given a great opportunity, a great intellectual challenge. The anatomy, the rhetoric, the poetics, the history, await our writing.

I am sure that this divided consciousness is sometimes experienced by men, but I think it unlikely that many male academics would have had the division in themselves as succinctly and publicly labeled as they were for me in 1976 when my official title at the University of Delaware was Visiting Minority Professor. I am deeply aware of the struggle in myself between the professor, who wants to study major works by major writers and to mediate impersonally between these works and the readings of other professors, and the minority, the woman who wants connections between my life and my work and who is committed to a revolution of consciousness that would make my concerns those of the majority. There have been times when the Minority wishes to betray the Professor by isolating herself in a female ghetto; or when the Professor wishes to betray the Minority by denying the troubling voice of difference and dissent. What I hope is that neither will betray the other, because neither can exist by itself. The task of feminist critics is to find a new language, a new way of reading that can integrate our intelligence and our experience, our reason and our suffering, our skepticism and our vision. This enterprise should not be confined to women. I invite Criticus, Poeticus, and Plutarchus to share it with us. One thing is certain: feminist criticism is not visiting. It is here to stay, and we must make it a permanent home.

---

[28] Lee R. Edwards and Arlyn Diamond, eds., *The Authority of Experience: Essays in Feminist Criticism* (Amherst: University of Massachusetts Press, 1977).

Sandra M. Gilbert
b. 1936

Susan Gubar
b. 1944

The collaboration of Gilbert and Gubar has been extremely influential in the advancement of both the study of women writers and feminist literary theory. Their well known work *The Madwoman in the Attic* (1979) traces a female literary tradition and thus combats what they term women's "anxiety of authorship." They seek also to speak to Elaine Showalter's call (pp. 1223) for a feminist poetics. As part of the former program, their *Norton Anthology of Literature by Women* (1985) rescues many women from the obscurity caused by their exclusion from male-dominated anthologies. Their *No Man's Land: The Place of the Woman Writer in the Twentieth Century* (1988) continues the story begun in the earlier volume.

In the first chapter of *The Madwoman,* Gilbert and Gubar argue that in the past and into the present the writer's creativity has been identified virtually completely with men. Their aim is to locate a place where women's writing is heard. The second chapter, the first part of which is reprinted here, is concerned with women and literary tradition. It begins with a consideration of Harold Bloom's theory of the "anxiety of influence," observing that women do not fit into Bloom's patriarchal model. Or, rather, their anxiety is more pronounced, since the woman writer has from the beginning of her life had to "struggle against the effects of socialization," which becomes a struggle against men's oppressive reading of women.

Gilbert and Gubar offer a litany of the results of women's socialized anxieties: a variety of physical and mental illnesses, including anorexia, agoraphobia, and claustrophobia. They go on to "trace the difficult paths by which nineteenth-century women overcame their "anxiety of authorship." This shift from Bloom's "anxiety of influence" reflects the deeper problems of women writers in the culture, for such anxiety is necessarily prior to that of influence.

In addition to the books mentioned above, Gilbert and Gubar have edited *Shakespeare's Sister: Feminist Essays on Women Poets* (1979) and *The Female Imagination and the Modernist Aesthetic* (1986). Gilbert is the author of *Acts of Attention: The Poems of D. H. Lawrence* (1972) and several volumes of poetry. Gubar has published essays on a variety of subjects in eighteenth-century literature, science fiction, and writing by women, and she is editor with Joan Hoff of *For Adult Users Only: The Dilemma of Violent Pornography* (1989).

From

Infection in the Sentence

The man who does not know sick women does not know women.

S. WEIR MITCHELL

I try to describe this long limitation, hoping that with such power as is now mine, and such use of language as is within that power, this will convince any one who cares about it that this "living" of mine had been done under a heavy handicap....

CHARLOTTE PERKINS GILMAN

A Word dropped careless on a Page
May stimulate an eye
When folded in perpetual seam
The Wrinkled Maker lie

Infection in the sentence breeds
We may inhale Despair
At distances of Centuries
From the Malaria —

EMILY DICKINSON

I stand in the ring
in the dead city
and tie on the red shoes
....
They are not mine,
they are my mother's,
her mother's before,
handed down like an heirloom
but hidden like shameful letters.

ANNE SEXTON

INFECTION IN THE SENTENCE. *Infection in the Sentence* is Chapter Two of *The Madwoman in the Attic: The Woman Writer and the Nineteenth-Century Literary Imagination,* Copyright © Yale University Press, 1979. Reprinted by permission.

[All notes are by Gilbert and Gubar]
Epigraphs: Doctor on Patient (Philadelphia: Lippincott, 1888), quoted in Ilza Veith, *Hysteria: The History of a Disease* (Chicago: University of Chicago Press, 1965), pp. 219–20; *The Living of Charlotte Perkins Gilman* (New York: Harper & Row, 1975; first published 1935), p. 104; J. 1261 in *The Poems of Emily Dickinson,* ed. Thomas Johnson, 3 vols. (Cambridge, Mass.: The Belknap Press of Harvard University Press, 1955: all subsequent references are to this edition); "The Red Shoes," *The Book of Folly* (Boston: Houghton Mifflin, 1972), pp. 28–29.

What does it mean to be a woman writer in a culture whose fundamental definitions of literary authority are, as we have seen, both overtly and covertly patriarchal? If the vexed and vexing polarities of angel and monster, sweet dumb Snow White and fierce mad Queen, are major images literary tradition offers women, how does such imagery influence the ways in which women attempt the pen? If the Queen's looking glass speaks with the King's voice, how do its perpetual kingly admonitions affect the Queen's own voice? Since his is the chief voice she hears, does the Queen try to sound like the King, imitating his tone, his inflections, his phrasing, his point of view? Or does she "talk back" to him in her own vocabulary, her own timbre, insisting on her own viewpoint? We believe these are basic questions feminist literary criticism—both theoretical and practical—must answer, and consequently they are questions to which we shall turn again and again, not only in this chapter but in all our readings of nineteenth-century literature by women.

That writers assimilate and then consciously or unconsciously affirm or deny the achievements of their predecessors is, of course, a central fact of literary history, a fact whose aesthetic and metaphysical implications have been discussed in detail by theorists as diverse as T. S. Eliot, M. H. Abrams, Erich Auerbach, and Frank Kermode.[1] More recently, some literary theorists have begun to explore what we might call the psychology of literary history—the tensions and anxieties, hostilities and inadequacies writers feel when they confront not only the achievements of their predecessors but the traditions of genre, style, and metaphor that they inherit from such "forefathers." Increasingly, these critics study the ways in which, as J. Hillis Miller has put it, a literary text "is inhabited . . . by a long chain of parasitical presences, echoes, allusions, guests, ghosts of previous texts."[2]

As Miller himself also notes, the first and foremost students of such literary psychohistory has been Harold Bloom. Applying Freudian structures to literary genealogies, Bloom has postulated that the dynamics of literary history arise from the artist's "anxiety of influence," his fear that he is not his own creator and that the works of his predecessors, existing before and beyond him, assume essential priority

[1] In "Tradition and the Individual Talent," Eliot of course considers these matters; in *Mimesis* Auerbach traces the ways in which the realist includes what has been previously excluded from art; and in *The Sense of an Ending* Frank Kermode shows how poets and novelists lay bare the literariness of their predecessors' forms in order to explore the dissonance between fiction and reality.
[2] J. Hillis Miller, "The Limits of Pluralism, III: The Critic as Host," *Critical Inquiry* (Spring 1977): 446.

over his own writings. In fact, as we pointed out in our discussion of the metaphor of literary paternity, Bloom's paradigm of the sequential historical relationship between literary artists is the relationship of father and son, specifically that relationship as it was defined by Freud. Thus Bloom explains that a "strong poet" must engage in heroic warfare with his "precursor," for, involved as he is in a literary Oedipal struggle, a man can only become a poet by somehow invalidating his poetic father.

Bloom's model of literary history is intensely (even exclusively) male, and necessarily patriarchal. For this reason it has seemed, and no doubt will continue to seem, offensively sexist to some feminist critics. Not only, after all, does Bloom describe literary history as the crucial warfare of fathers and sons, he sees Milton's fiercely masculine fallen Satan as *the* type of the poet in our culture, and he metaphorically defines the poetic process as a sexual encounter between a male poet and his female muse. Where, then, does the female poet fit in? Does she want to annihilate a "forefather" or a "foremother"? What if she can find no models, no precursors? Does she have a muse, and what is its sex? Such questions are inevitable in any female consideration of Bloomian poetics.[3] And yet, from a feminist perspective, their inevitability may be just the point; it may, that is, call our attention not to what is wrong about Bloom's conceptualization of the dynamics of Western literary history, but to what is right (or at least suggestive) about his theory.

For Western literary history *is* overwhelmingly male— or, more accurately, patriarchal—and Bloom analyzes and explains this fact, while other theorists have ignored it, precisely, one supposes, because they assumed literature had to be male. Like Freud, whose psychoanalytic postulates permeate Bloom's literary psychoanalyses of the "anxiety of influence," Bloom has defined processes of interaction that his predecessors did not bother to consider because, among other reasons, they were themselves so caught up in such processes. Like Freud, too, Bloom has insisted on bringing to consciousness assumptions readers and writers do not ordinarily examine. In doing so, he has clarified the implications of the psychosexual and sociosexual con-texts by which every literary text is surrounded, and thus the meanings of the "guests" and "ghosts" which inhabit texts themselves. Speaking of Freud, the feminist theorist Juliet Mitchell has remarked that "psychoanalysis is not a recommendation *for* a patriarchal society, but an analysis of

one."[4] The same sort of statement could be made about Bloom's model of literary history, which is not a recommendation for but an analysis of the patriarchal poetics (and attendant anxieties) which underlie our culture's chief literary movements.

For our purposes here, however, Bloom's historical construct is useful not only because it helps identify and define the patriarchal psychosexual context in which so much Western literature was authored, but also because it can help us distinguish the anxieties and achievements of female writers from those of male writers. If we return to the question we asked earlier—where does a woman writer "fit in" to the overwhelmingly and essentially male literary history Bloom describes?—we find we have to answer that a woman writer does *not* "fit in." At first glance, indeed, she seems to be anomalous, indefinable, alienated, a freakish outsider. Just as in Freud's theories of male and female psychosexual development there is no symmetry between a boy's growth and a girl's (with, say, the male "Oedipus complex" balanced by a female "Electra complex") so Bloom's male-oriented theory of the "anxiety of influence" cannot be simply reversed or inverted in order to account for the situation of the woman writer.

Certainly if we acquiesce in the patriarchal Bloomian model, we can be sure that the female poet does not experience the "anxiety of influence" in the same way that her male counterpart would, for the simple reason that she must confront precursors who are almost exclusively male, and therefore significantly different from her. Not only do these precursors incarnate patriarchal authority (as our discussion of the metaphor of literary paternity argued), they attempt to enclose her in definitions of her person and her potential which, by reducing her to extreme stereotypes (angel, monster) drastically conflict with her own sense of her self—that is, of her subjectivity, her autonomy, her creativity. On the one hand, therefore, the woman writer's male precursors symbolize authority; on the other hand, despite their authority, they fail to define the ways in which she experiences her own identity as a writer. More, the masculine authority with which they construct their literary personae, as well as the fierce power struggles in which they engage in their efforts of self-creation, seem to the woman writer directly to contradict the terms of her own gender definition. Thus the "anxiety of influence" that a male poet experiences is felt by a female poet as an even more primary "anxiety of authorship"—a radical fear that she cannot create, that because she

---

[3]For a discussion of the woman writer and her place in Bloomian literary history, see Joanne Feit Diehl, "'Come Slowly—Eden': An Exploration of Women Poets and their Muse," *Signs* 3, no. 3 (Spring 1978): 572–87. See also the responses to Diehl in *Signs* 4, no. 1 (Autumn 1978): 188–96.

[4]Juliet Mitchell, *Psychoanalysis and Feminism* (New York: Vintage, 1975), p. xiii.

can never become a "precursor" the act of writing will isolate or destroy her.

This anxiety is, of course, exacerbated by her fear that not only can she not fight a male precursor on "his" terms and win, she cannot "beget" art upon the (female) body of the muse. As Juliet Mitchell notes, in a concise summary of the implications Freud's theory of psychosexual development has for women, both a boy and a girl, "as they learn to speak and live within society, want to take the father's [in Bloom's terminology the precursor's] place, and *only the boy will one day be allowed to do so.* Furthermore both sexes are born into the desire of the mother, and as, through cultural heritage, what the mother desires is the phallus-turned-baby, *both* children desire to be the phallus for the mother. Again, *only the boy can fully recognize himself in his mother's desire.* Thus *both* sexes repudiate the implications of femininity," but the girl learns (in relation to her father) "that her subjugation to the law of the father entails her becoming the representative of 'nature' and 'sexuality,' a chaos of spontaneous, intuitive creativity."[5]

Unlike her male counterpart, then, the female artist must first struggle against the effects of a socialization which makes conflict with the will of her (male) precursors seem inexpressibly absurd, futile, or even—as in the case of the Queen in "Little Snow White"—self-annihilating. And just as the male artist's struggle against his precursor takes the form of what Bloom calls revisionary swerves, flights, misreadings, so the female writer's battle for self-creation involves her in a revisionary process. Her battle, however, is not against her (male) precursor's reading of the world but against his reading of *her.* In order to define herself as an author she must redefine the terms of her socialization. Her revisionary struggle, therefore, often becomes a struggle for what Adrienne Rich has called "Revision—the act of looking back, of seeing with fresh eyes, of entering an old text from a new critical direction . . . an act of survival."[6] Frequently, moreover, she can begin such a struggle only by actively seeking a *female* precursor who, far from representing a threatening force to be denied or killed, proves by example that a revolt against patriarchal literary authority is possible.

For this reason, as well as for the sound psychoanalytic reasons Mitchell and others give, it would be foolish to lock the woman artist into an Electra pattern matching the Oedipal structure Bloom proposes for male writers. The woman writer—and we shall see women doing this over and over again—searches for a female model not because she wants dutifully to comply with male definitions of her "femininity" but because she must legitimize her own rebellious endeavors. At the same time, like most women in patriarchal society, the woman writer does experience her gender as a painful obstacle, or even a debilitating inadequacy; like most patriarchally conditioned women, in other words, she is victimized by what Mitchell calls "the inferiorized and 'alternative' (second sex) psychology of women under patriarchy."[7] Thus the loneliness of the female artist, her feelings of alienation from male predecessors coupled with her need for sisterly precursors and successors, her urgent sense of her need for a female audience together with her fear of the antagonism of male readers, her culturally conditioned timidity about self-dramatization, her dread of the patriarchal authority of art, her anxiety about the impropriety of female invention—all these phenomena of "inferiorization" mark the woman writer's struggle for artistic self-definition and differentiate her efforts at self-creation from those of her male counterpart.

As we shall see, such sociosexual differentiation means that, as Elaine Showalter has suggested, women writers participate in a quite different literary subculture from that inhabited by male writers, a subculture which has its own distinctive literary traditions, even—though it defines itself *in relation to* the "main," male-dominated, literary culture—a distinctive history.[8] At best, the separateness of this female subculture has been exhilarating for women. In recent years, for instance, while male writers seem increasingly to have felt exhausted by the need for revisionism which Bloom's theory of the "anxiety of influence" accurately describes, women writers have seen themselves as pioneers in a creativity so intense that their male counterparts have probably not experienced its analog since the Renaissance, or at least since the Romantic era. The son of many fathers, today's male writer feels hopelessly belated; the daughter of too few mothers, today's female writer feels that she is helping to create a viable tradition which is at last definitively emerging.

There is a darker side of this female literary subculture, however, especially when women's struggles for literary self-creation are seen in the psychosexual context described by Bloom's Freudian theories of patrilineal literary inheritance. As we noted above, for an "anxiety of influence" the woman writer substitutes what we have called an "anxiety

---

[5] Ibid., pp. 404–05.
[6] Adrienne Rich, "When We Dead Awaken: Writing as Re-Vision," in *Adrienne Rich's Poetry,* ed. Barbara Charlesworth Gelpi and Albert Gelpi (New York: Norton, 1975), p. 90.

[7] Mitchell, *Psychoanalysis and Feminism,* p. 402.
[8] See Elaine Showalter, *A Literature of Their Own* (Princeton: Princeton University Press, 1977).

of authorship," an anxiety built from complex and often only barely conscious fears of that authority which seems to the female artist to be by definition inappropriate to her sex. Because it is based on the woman's socially determined sense of her own biology, this anxiety of authorship is quite distinct from the anxiety about creativity that could be traced in such male writers as Hawthorne or Dostoevsky. Indeed, to the extent that it forms one of the unique bonds that link women in what we might call the secret sisterhood of their literary subculture, such anxiety in itself constitutes a crucial mark of that subculture.

In comparison to the "male" tradition of strong, father-son combat, however, this female anxiety of authorship is profoundly debilitating. Handed down not from one woman to another but from the stern literary "fathers" of patriarchy to all their "inferiorized" female descendants, it is in many ways the germ of a dis-ease or, at any rate, a disaffection, a disturbance, a distrust, that spreads like a stain throughout the style and structure of much literature by women, especially—as we shall see in this study—throughout literature by women before the twentieth century. For if contemporary women do now attempt the pen with energy and authority, they are able to do so only because their eighteenth- and nineteenth-century foremothers struggled in isolation that felt like illness, alienation that felt like madness, obscurity that felt like paralysis to overcome the anxiety of authorship that was endemic to their literary subculture. Thus, while the recent feminist emphasis on positive role models has undoubtedly helped many women, it should not keep us from realizing the terrible odds against which a creative female subculture was established. Far from reinforcing socially oppressive sexual stereotyping, only a full consideration of such problems can reveal that extraordinary strength of women's literary accomplishments in the eighteenth and nineteenth centuries.

Emily Dickinson's acute observations about "infection in the sentence," quoted in our epigraphs, resonate in a number of different ways, then, for women writers, given the literary woman's special concept of her place in literary psychohistory. To begin with, the words seem to indicate Dickinson's keen consciousness that, in the purest Bloomian or Millerian sense, pernicious "guests" and "ghosts" inhabit all literary texts. For any reader, but especially for a reader who is also a writer, every text can become a "sentence" or weapon in a kind of metaphorical germ warfare. Beyond this, however, the fact that "infection in the sentence *breeds*" suggests Dickinson's recognition that literary texts are coercive, imprisoning, fever-inducing; that, since literature usurps a reader's interiority, it is an invasion of privacy. Moreover, given Dickinson's own gender definition, the sexual ambiguity of her poem's "Wrinkled Maker" is signifi-

cant. For while, on the one hand, "we" (meaning especially women writers) "may inhale Despair" from all those patriarchal texts which seek to deny female autonomy and authority, on the other hand "we" (meaning especially women writers) "may inhale Despair" from all those "foremothers" who have both overtly and covertly conveyed their traditional authorship anxiety to these bewildered female descendants. Finally, such traditional, metaphorically matrilineal anxiety ensures that even the maker of a text, when she is a woman, may feel imprisoned within texts—folded and "wrinkled" by their pages and thus trapped in their "perpetual seam[s]" which perpetually tell her how she *seems*.

Although contemporary women writers are relatively free of the infection of this "Despair" Dickinson defines (at least in comparison to their nineteenth-century precursors), an anecdote recently related by the American poet and essayist Annie Gottlieb summarizes our point about the ways in which, for all women, "Infection in the sentence breeds":

> When I began to enjoy my powers as a writer, I dreamt that my mother had me sterilized! (Even in dreams we still blame our mothers for the punitive choices our culture forces on us.) I went after the mother-figure in my dream, brandishing a large knife; on its blade was writing. I cried, "Do you know what you are doing? You are destroying my femaleness, my *female power,* which is important to me *because of you!*"[9]

Seeking motherly precursors, says Gottlieb, as if echoing Dickinson, the woman writer may find only infection, debilitation. Yet still she must seek, not seek to subvert, her "*female power*, which is important" to her because of her lost literary matrilineage. In this connection, Dickinson's own words about mothers are revealing, for she alternately claimed that "I never had a mother," that "I always ran Home to Awe as a child. . . . He was an awful Mother but I liked him better than none," and that "a mother [was] a miracle."[10] Yet, as we shall see, her own anxiety of authorship was a "Despair" inhaled not only from the infections suffered by her own ailing physical mother, and her many tormented literary mothers, but from the literary fathers who spoke to her—even "lied" to her—sometimes near at hand, sometimes "at distances of Centuries," from the censorious looking glasses of literary texts.

. . .

---

[9]Annie Gottlieb, "Feminists Look at Motherhood," *Mother Jones* (November 1976): 53.

[10]*The Letters of Emily Dickinson,* ed. Thomas Johnson, 3 vols. (Cambridge, Mass.: The Belknap Press of Harvard University Press, 1958), 2:475; 2:518.

It is debilitating to be *any* woman in a society where women are warned that if they do not behave like angels they must be monsters. Recently, in fact, social scientists and social historians like Jessie Bernard, Phyllis Chesler, Naomi Weisstein, and Pauline Bart have begun to study the ways in which patriarchal socialization literally makes women sick, both physically and mentally.[11] Hysteria, the disease with which Freud so famously began his investigations into the dynamic connections between *psyche* and *soma,* is by definition a "female disease," not so much because it takes its name from the Greek word for womb, *hyster* (the organ which was in the nineteenth century supposed to "cause" this emotional disturbance), but because hysteria did occur mainly among women in turn-of-the-century Vienna, and because throughout the nineteenth century this mental illness, like many other nervous disorders, was thought to be caused by the female reproductive system, as if to elaborate upon Aristotle's notion that femaleness was in and of itself a deformity.[12] And, indeed, such diseases of maladjustment to the physical and social environment as anorexia and agoraphobia did and do strike a disproportionate number of women. Sufferers from anorexia—loss of appetite, self-starvation—are primarily adolescent girls. Sufferers from agoraphobia—fear of open or "public" places—are usually female, most frequently middle-aged housewives, as are sufferers from crippling rheumatoid arthritis.[13]

Such diseases are caused by patriarchal socialization in several ways. Most obviously, of course, any young girl, but especially a lively or imaginative one, is likely to experience her education in docility, submissiveness, self-lessness as in some sense sickening. To be trained in renunciation is almost necessarily to be trained to ill health, since the human animal's first and strongest urge is to his / her *own* survival, pleasure, assertion. In addition, each of the "subjects" in which a young girl is educated may be sickening in a specific way. Learning to become a beautiful object, the girl learns anxiety about—perhaps even loathing of—her own flesh. Peering obsessively into the real as well as metaphoric looking glasses that surround her, she desires literally to "reduce" her own body. In the nineteenth century, as we noted earlier, this desire to be beautiful and "frail" led to tight-lacing and vinegar-drinking. In our own era it has spawned innumerable diets and "controlled" fasts, as well as the extraordinary phenomenon of teenage anorexia.[14] Similarly, it seems inevitable that women reared for, and conditioned to, lives of privacy, reticence, domesticity, might develop pathological fears of public places and unconfined spaces. Like the comb, stay-laces, and apple which the Queen in "Little Snow White" uses as weapons against her hated stepdaughter, such afflictions as anorexia and agoraphobia simply carry patriarchal definitions of "femininity" to absurd extremes, and thus function as essential or at least inescapable parodies of social prescriptions.

In the nineteenth century, however, the complex social prescriptions these diseases parody did not merely urge women to act in ways which would cause them to become ill; nineteenth-century culture seems to have actually admonished women to *be* ill. In other words, the "female diseases" from which Victorian women suffered were not always byproducts of their training in femininity; they were the goals of such training. As Barbara Ehrenreich and Deirdre English have shown, throughout much of the nineteenth century "Upper- and upper-middle-class women were [defined as] 'sick' [frail, ill]; working-class women were [defined as] 'sickening' [infectious, diseased]." Speaking of the "lady," they go on to point out that "Society agreed that she was frail and sickly," and consequently a "cult of female invalidism" developed in England and America. For the products of such a cult, it was, as Dr. Mary Putnam Jacobi wrote in 1895, "considered natural and almost laudable to break down under all conceivable varieties of strain—a winter dissipation, a houseful of servants, a quarrel with a female

---

[11]See Jessie Bernard, "The Paradox of the Happy Marriage," Pauline B. Bart, "Depression in Middle-Aged Women," and Naomi Weisstein, "Psychology Constructs the Female," all in Vivian Gornick and Barbara K. Moran, ed., *Woman in Sexist Society* (New York: Basic Books, 1971). See also Phyllis Chesler, *Women and Madness* (New York: Doubleday, 1972), and—for a summary of all these matters—Barbara Ehrenreich and Deirdre English, *Complaints and Disorders: The Sexual Politics of Sickness* (Old Westbury: The Feminist Press, 1973).

[12]In *Hints on Insanity* (1861) John Millar wrote that "Mental derangement frequently occurs in young females from Amenorrhoea, especially in those who have any strong hereditary predisposition to insanity," adding that "an occasional warm hipbath or leeches to the pubis will . . . be followed by complete mental recovery." In 1873, Henry Mauldsey wrote in *Body and Mind* that "the monthly activity of the ovaries . . . has a notable effect upon the mind and body; wherefore it may become an important cause of mental and physical derangement." See especially the medical opinions of John Millar, Henry Maudsley, and Andrew Wynter in *Madness and Morals: Ideas on Insanity in the Nineteenth Century,* ed. Vieda Skultans (London and Boston: Routledge & Kegan Paul, 1975), pp. 230–35.

[13]See Marlene Boskind-Lodahl, "Cinderella's Stepsisters: A Feminist Perspective on Anorexia Nervosa and Bulimia," *Signs* 2, no. 2 (Winter 1976): 342–56; Walter Blum, "The Thirteenth Guest," (on agoraphobia), in *California Living, The San Francisco Sunday Examiner and Chronicle* (17 April 1977): 8–12; Joan Arehart-Treichel, "Can Your Personality Kill You?" (on female rheumatoid arthritis, among other diseases), *New York* 10, no. 48 (28 November 1977): 45: "According to studies conducted in recent years, four out of five rheumatoid victims are women, and for good reason: The disease appears to arise in those unhappy with the traditional female-sex role."

[14]More recent discussions of the etiology and treatment of anorexia are offered in Hilde Bruch, M. D., *The Golden Cage: The Enigma of Anorexia Nervosa* (Cambridge, Mass.: Harvard University Press, 1978), and in Salvador Minuchin, Bernice L. Rosman, and Lester Baker, *Psychosomatic Families: Anorexia Nervosa in Context* (Cambridge: Harvard University Press, 1978).

friend, not to speak of more legitimate reasons. . . . Constantly considering their nerves, urged to consider them by well-intentioned but short-sighted advisors, [women] pretty soon become nothing but a bundle of nerves."[15]

Given this socially conditioned epidemic of female illness, it is not surprising to find that the angel in the house of literature frequently suffered not just from fear and trembling but from literal and figurative sicknesses unto death. Although her hyperactive stepmother dances herself into the grave, after all, beautiful Snow White has just barely recovered from a catatonic trance in her glass coffin. And if we return to Goethe's Makarie, the "good" woman of *Wilhelm Meister's Travels* whom Hans Eichner has described as incarnating her author's ideal of "contemplative purity," we find that this "model of selflessness and of purity of heart . . . this embodiment of *das Ewig-Weibliche,* suffers from migraine headaches."[16] Implying ruthless self-suppression, does the "eternal feminine" necessarily imply illness? If so, we may have found yet another meaning for Dickinson's assertion that "Infection in the sentence breeds." The despair we "inhale" even "at distances of centuries" may be the despair of a life like Makarie's, a life that *"has no story."*

At the same time, however, the despair of the monster-woman is also real, undeniable, and infectious. The Queen's mad tarantella is plainly unhealthy and metaphorically the result of too much storytelling. As the Romantic poets feared, too much imagination may be dangerous to anyone, male or female, but for women in particular patriarchal culture has always assumed mental exercises would have dire consequences. In 1645 John Winthrop, the governor of the Massachusetts Bay Colony, noted in his journal that Anne Hopkins "has fallen into a sad infirmity, the loss of her understanding and reason, which had been growing upon her divers years, by occasion of giving herself wholly to reading and writing, and had written many books," adding that "if she had attended her household affairs, and such things as belong to women . . . she had kept her wits."[17] And as Wendy Martin has noted

> in the nineteenth century this fear of the intellectual woman became so intense that the phenomenon . . . was recorded in medical annals. A thinking woman was considered such a breach of nature that a Harvard doctor reported during his autopsy

on a Radcliffe graduate he discovered that her uterus had shrivelled to the size of a pea.[18]

If, then, as Anne Sexton suggests (in a poem parts of which we have also used here as an epigraph), the red shoes passed furtively down from woman to woman are the shoes of art, the Queen's dancing shoes, it is as sickening to be a Queen who wears them as it is to be an angelic Makarie who repudiates them. Several passages in Sexton's verse express what we have defined as "anxiety of authorship" in the form of a feverish dread of the suicidal tarantella of female creativity:

> All those girls
> who wore red shoes,
> each boarded a train that would not stop.
>
> . . . .
>
> They tore off their ears like safety pins.
> Their arms fell off them and became hats.
> Their heads rolled off and sang down the street.
> And their feet—oh God, their feet in the market place—
> . . . the feet went on.
> The feet could not stop.
>
> . . . .
>
> They could not listen.
> They could not stop.
> What they did was the death dance.
>
> What they did would do them in.

Certainly infection breeds in these sentences, and despair: female art, Sexton suggests, has a "hidden" but crucial tradition of uncontrollable madness. Perhaps it was her semiconscious perception of this tradition that gave Sexton herself "a secret fear" of being "a reincarnation" of Edna Millay, whose reputation seemed based on romance. In a letter to DeWitt Snodgrass she confessed that she had "a fear of writing as a woman writes," adding, "I wish I were a man— I would rather write the way a man writes."[19] After all, dancing the death dance, "all those girls / who wore the red shoes" dismantle their own bodies, like anorexics renouncing the guilty weight of their female flesh. But if their arms, ears, and heads fall off, perhaps their wombs, too, will "shrivel" to "the size of a pea"?

---

[15]Quoted by Ehrenreich and English, *Complaints and Disorders,* p. 19.
[16]Eichner, "The Eternal Feminine," Norton Critical Edition of *Faust,* p. 620.
[17]John Winthrop, *The History of New England from 1630 to 1649,* ed. James Savage (Boston, 1826), 2:216.

[18]Wendy Martin, "Anne Bradstreet's Poetry: A Study of Subversive Piety," *Shakespeare's Sisters,* ed. Gilbert and Gubar, pp. 19–31.
[19]"The Uncensored Poet: Letters of Anne Sexton," *Ms.* 6, no. 5 (November 1977):53.

In this connection, a passage from Margaret Atwood's *Lady Oracle* acts almost as a gloss on the conflict between creativity and "femininity" which Sexton's violent imagery embodies (or dis-embodies). Significantly, the protagonist of Atwood's novel is a writer of the sort of fiction that has recently been called "female gothic," and even more significantly she too projects her anxieties of authorship into the fairy-tale metaphor of the red shoes. Stepping in glass, she sees blood on her feet, and suddenly feels that she has discovered

> The real red shoes, the feet punished for dancing. You could dance, or you could have the love of a good man. But you were afraid to dance, because you had this unnatural fear that if you danced they'd cut your feet off so you wouldn't be able to dance. . . . Finally you overcame your fear and danced, and they cut your feet off. The good man went away too, because you wanted to dance.[20]

Whether she is a passive angel or an active monster, in other words, the woman writer feels herself to be literally or figuratively crippled by the debilitating alternatives her culture offers her, and the crippling effects of her conditioning sometimes seem to "breed" like sentences of death in the bloody shoes she inherits from her literary foremothers.

Surrounded as she is by images of disease, traditions of disease, and invitations both to disease and to dis-ease, it is no wonder that the woman writer has held many mirrors up to the discomforts of her own nature. As we shall see, the notion that "Infection in the sentence breeds" has been so central a truth for literary women that the great artistic achievements of nineteenth-century novelists and poets from Austen and Shelley to Dickinson and Barrett Browning are often both literally and figuratively concerned with disease, as if to emphasize the effort with which health and wholeness were won from the infectious "vapors" of despair and fragmentation. Rejecting the poisoned apples her culture offers her, the woman writer often becomes in some sense anorexic, resolutely closing her mouth on silence (since—in the words of Jane Austen's Henry Tilney—"a woman's only power is the power of refusal"[21]), even while she complains of starvation. Thus both Charlotte and Emily Brontë depict the travails of starved or starving anorexic heroines, while

Emily Dickinson declares in one breath that she "had been hungry, all the Years," and in another opts for "Sumptuous Destitution." Similarly, Christina Rossetti represents her own anxiety of authorship in the split between one heroine who longs to "suck and suck" on goblin fruit and another who locks her lips fiercely together in a gesture of silent and passionate renunciation. In addition, many of these literary women become in one way or another agoraphobic. Trained to reticence, they fear the vertiginous openness of the literary marketplace and rationalize with Emily Dickinson that "Publication—is the Auction / Of the Mind of Man" or, worse, punningly confess that "Creation seemed a mighty Crack— / To make me visible."[22]

As we shall also see, other diseases and dis-eases accompany the two classic symptoms of anorexia and agoraphobia. Claustrophobia, for instance, agoraphobia's parallel and complementary opposite, is a disturbance we shall encounter again and again in women's writing throughout the nineteenth century. Eye "troubles," moreover, seem to abound in the lives and works of literary women, with Dickinson matter-of-factly noting that her eye got "put out," George Eliot describing patriarchal Rome as "a disease of the retina," Jane Eyre and Aurora Leigh marrying blind men, Charlotte Brontë deliberately writing with her eyes closed, and Mary Elizabeth Coleridge writing about "Blindness" that came because "Absolute and bright, / The Sun's rays smote me till they masked the Sun."[23] Finally, aphasia and amnesia—two illnesses which symbolically represent (and parody) the sort of intellectual incapacity patriarchal culture has traditionally required of women—appear and reappear in women's writings in frankly stated or disguised forms. "Foolish" women characters in Jane Austen's novels (Miss Bates in *Emma,* for instance) express Malapropish confusion about language, while Mary Shelley's monster has to learn language from scratch and Emily Dickinson herself childishly questions the meanings of the most basic English words: "Will there really be a 'Morning'? / Is there such a thing as 'Day'?"[24] At the same time, many women writers manage to imply that the reason for such ignorance of language—as well as the reason for their deep sense of alienation and inescapable feeling of anomie—is that they have *forgotten* something. Deprived of the power that even their

---

[20]Margaret Atwood, *Lady Oracle* (New York: Simon and Schuster, 1976), p. 335.

[21]See *Northanger Abbey,* chapter 10: "You will allow, that in both [matrimony and dancing], man has the advantage of choice, woman only the power of refusal."

[22]See Dickinson, *Poems,* J. 579 ("I had been hungry, all the Years"), J. 709 ("Publication—is the Auction"), and J. 891 ("To my quick ear the Leaves—conferred"); see also Christina Rossetti, "Goblin Market."

[23]See Dickinson, *Poems,* J. 327 ("Before I got my eye put out"), George Eliot, *Middlemarch,* book 2, chapter 20, and M. E. Coleridge, "Doubt," in *Poems by Mary E. Coleridge,* p. 40.

[24]See Dickinson, *Poems,* J. 101.

pens don't seem to confer, these women resemble Doris Lessing's heroines, who have to fight their internalization of patriarchal strictures for even a faint trace memory of what they might have become.

"Where are the songs I used to know, / Where are the notes I used to sing?" writes Christina Rossetti in "The Key-Note," a poem whose title indicates its significance for her. "I have forgotten everything / I used to know so long ago."[25] As if to make the same point, Charlotte Brontë's Lucy Snowe conveniently "forgets" her own history and even, so it seems, the Christian name of one of the central characters in her story, while Brontë's orphaned Jane Eyre seems to have lost (or symbolically "forgotten") her family heritage. Similarly, too, Emily Brontë's Heathcliff "forgets" or is made to forget who and what he was; Mary Shelley's monster is "born" without either a memory or a family history; and Elizabeth Barrett Browning's Aurora Leigh is early separated from—and thus induced to "forget"—her "mother land" of Italy. As this last example suggests, however, what all these characters and their authors really fear they have forgotten is precisely that aspect of their lives which has been kept from them by patriarchal poetics: their matrilineal heritage of literary strength, their "female power" which, as Annie Gottlieb wrote, is important to them *because of* (not in spite of) their mothers. In order, then, not only to understand the ways in which "Infection in the sentence breeds" for women but also to learn how women have won through disease to artistic health we must begin by redefining Bloom's seminal definitions of the revisionary "anxiety of influence." In doing so, we will have to trace the difficult paths by which nineteenth-century women overcame their "anxiety of authorship," repudiated debilitating patriarchal prescriptions, and recovered or remembered the lost foremothers who could help them find their distinctive female power.

. . .

To begin with, those women who were among the first of their sex to attempt the pen were evidently infected or sickened by just the feelings of self-doubt, inadequacy, and inferiority that their education in "femininity" almost seems to have been designed to induce. The necessary converse of the metaphor of literary paternity, as we noted in our discussion of that phenomenon, was a belief in female literary sterility, a belief that caused literary women like Anne Finch to consider with deep anxiety the possibility that they might be

"Cyphers," powerless intellectual eunuchs. In addition, such women were profoundly affected by the sort of assumptions that underly an assertion like Rufus Griswold's statement that in reading women's writing "We are in danger . . . of mistaking for the efflorescent energy of creative intelligence, that which is only the exuberance of personal 'feelings unemployed.' "[26] Even if it was not absurd for a woman to try to write, this remark implies, perhaps it was somehow sick or what we would today called "neurotic." "We live at home, quiet, confined, and our feelings prey upon us," says Austen's Anne Elliot to Captain Harville, not long before they embark upon the debate about the male pen and its depiction of female "inconstancy" which we discussed earlier. She speaks in what Austen describes as "a low, feeling voice," and her remarks as well as her manner suggest both her own and her author's acquiescence in the notion that women may be more vulnerable than men to the dangers and diseases of "feelings unemployed."[27]

It is not surprising, then, that one of Finch's best and most passionate poems is an ambitious Pindaric ode entitled "The Spleen." Here, in what might almost be a response to Pope's characterization of the Queen of Spleen in *The Rape of the Lock,* Finch confesses and explores her own anxiety about the "vaporous" illness whose force, she feared, ruled her life and art. Her self-examination is particularly interesting not only because of its rigorous honesty, but because that honesty compels her to reveal just how severely she herself has been influenced by the kinds of misogynistic strictures about women's "feelings unemployed" that Pope has embedded in *his* poem. Thus Pope insists that the "wayward Queen" of Spleen rules "the sex to fifty from fifteen"— rules women, that is, throughout their "prime" of female sexuality—and is therefore the "parent" of both hysteria and (female) poetry, and Finch seems at least in part to agree, for she notes that "In the Imperious *Wife* thou Vapours art." That is, insubordinate women are merely, as Pope himself would have thought, neurotic women. "Lordly *Man* [is] born to Imperial Sway," says Finch, but he is defeated by splenetic woman; he "Compounds for Peace . . . And *Woman,* arm'd with *Spleen,* do's servilely Obey." At the same time, however, Finch admits that she feels the most pernicious effects of Spleen within herself, and specifically within herself *as an artist,* and she complains of these effects quite movingly, without the self-censure that would seem to have followed from her earlier version of female insubordination. Addressing Spleen, she writes that

---

[25]*The Poetical Works of Christina G. Rossetti,* 2 vols. (Boston: Little, Brown, 1909), 2:11.

[26]Griswold, *The Female Poets of America,* p. 7.
[27]Austen, *Persuasion,* chapter 23.

O'er me alas! thou dost too much prevail:
I feel thy Force, whilst I against thee rail;
I feel my Verse decay, and my crampt Numbers fail.
Thro' thy black Jaundice I all Objects see,
As Dark, and Terrible as Thee,
My Lines decry'd, and my Employment thought
An useless Folly, or presumptuous Fault.[28]

Is it crazy, neurotic, splenetic, to want to be a writer? In "The Spleen" Finch admits that she fears it is, suggesting, therefore, that Pope's portrayal of her as the foolish and neurotic Phoebe Clinket had—not surprisingly—driven her into a Cave of Spleen in her own mind.

When seventeenth- and eighteenth-century women writers—and even some nineteenth-century literary women—did not confess that they thought it might actually be mad of them to want to attempt the pen, they did usually indicate that they felt in some sense apologetic about such a "presumptuous" pastime. As we saw earlier, Finch herself admonished her muse to be cautious "and still retir'd," adding that the most she could hope to do as a writer was "still with contracted wing, / To some few friends, and to thy sorrows sing." Though her self-effacing admonition is riddled with irony, it is also serious and practical. As Elaine Showalter has shown, until the end of the nineteenth century the woman writer really was supposed to take second place to her literary brothers and fathers.[29] If she refused to be modest, self-deprecating, subservient, refused to present her artistic productions as mere trifles designed to divert and distract readers in moments of idleness, she could expect to be ignored or (sometimes scurrilously) attacked. Anne Killigrew, who ambitiously implored the "Queen of Verse" to warm her soul with "poetic fire," was rewarded for her overreaching with charges of plagiarism. "I writ, and the judicious praised my pen: / Could any doubt ensuing glory then?" she notes, recounting as part of the story of her humiliation expectations that would be reasonable enough in a male artist. But instead "What ought t'have brought me honour, brought me shame."[30] Her American contemporary, Anne Bradstreet, echoes the frustration and annoyance expressed here in a discussion of the reception she could expect *her* published poems to receive:

I am obnoxious to each carping tongue
Who says my hand a needle better fits,
A poet's pen all scorn I should thus wrong,
For such despite they cast on female wits:
If what I do prove well, it won't advance,
They'll say it's stol'n, or else it was by chance.[31]

There is such a weary and worldly accuracy in this analysis that plainly, especially in the context of Killigrew's experience, no sensible woman writer could overlook the warning implied: be modest or else! Be dark enough thy shades, and be thou there content!

Accordingly, Bradstreet herself, eschewing Apollo's manly "bays," asks only for a "thyme or parsley wreath," suavely assuring her male readers that "This mean and unrefined ore of mine / Will make your glist'ring gold but more to shine." And though once again, as with Finch's self-admonitions, bitter irony permeates this modesty, the very pose of modesty necessarily has its ill effects, both on the poet's self-definition and on her art. Just as Finch feels her "Crampt Numbers" crippled by the gloomy disease of female Spleen, Bradstreet confesses that she has a "foolish, broken, blemished Muse" whose defects cannot be mended, since "nature made it so irreparable." After all, she adds—as if to cement the connection between femaleness and madness, or at least mental deformity—"a weak or wounded brain admits no cure." Similarly, Margaret Cavendish, the Duchess of Newcastle, whose literary activities actually inspired her contemporaries to call her "Mad Madge," seems to have tried to transcend her own "madness" by deploying the kind of modest, "sensible," and self-deprecatory misogyny that characterizes Bradstreet's *apologia pro vita sua*. "It cannot be expected," Cavendish avers, that "I should write so wisely or wittily as men, being of the effeminate sex, whose brains nature has mixed with the coldest and softest elements." Men and women, she goes on to declare, "may be compared to blackbirds, where the hen can never sing with so strong and loud a voice, nor so clear and perfect notes as the cock; her breast is not made with that strength to strain so high."[32] But finally the contradictions between her attitude toward her gender and her sense of her own vocation seem really to have made her in some sense "mad."

[28]Finch, *Poems of Anne Countess of Winchilsea*, p. 250.

[29]See Showalter, *A Literature of their Own*, "The Double Critical Standard and the Feminine Novel," pp. 73–99.

[30]Anne Killigrew, "Upon the Saying that My Verses Were Made By Another," in Louise Bernikow, ed., *The World Split Open* (New York: Vintage, 1974), p. 79.

[31]Bradstreet, "The Prologue," in Bernikow, pp. 188–89.

[32]Joan Goulianos, ed., *By A Woman Writt* (Baltimore: Penguin, 1973), pp. 55–56. See also *The Living of Charlotte Perkins Gilman*, p. 77: "It takes supernal strength / To hold the attitude that brings the pain; / And there are few indeed but stoop at length / To something less than best, / To find, in stooping, rest."

It may have been in a fleeting moment of despair and self-confrontation that she wrote, "Women live like Bats or Owls, labour like Beasts, and die like Worms." But eventually, as Virginia Woolf puts it, "the people crowded round her coach when she issued out," for "the crazy Duchess became a bogey to frighten clever girls with."[33]

As Woolf's comments imply, women who did *not* apologize for their literary efforts were defined as mad and monstrous: freakish because "unsexed" or freakish because sexually "fallen." If Cavendish's extraordinary intellectual ambitions made her seem like an aberration of nature, and Finch's writing caused her to be defined as a fool, an absolutely immodest, unapologetic rebel like Aphra Behn—the first really "professional" literary woman in England—was and is always considered a somewhat "shady lady," no doubt promiscuous, probably self-indulgent, and certainly "indecent." "What has poor woman done, that she must be / Debarred from sense and sacred poetry?" Behn frankly asked, and she seems just as frankly to have lived the life of a Restoration rake.[34] In consequence, like some real-life Duessa, she was gradually but inexorably excluded (even exorcized) not only from the canon of serious literature but from the parlors and libraries of respectability.

By the beginning of the bourgeois nineteenth century, however, both money and "morality" had become so important that no serious writer could afford either psychologically or economically to risk Behn's kind of "shadiness." Thus we find Jane Austen decorously protesting in 1816 that she is constitutionally unable to join "manly, spirited Sketches" to the "little bit (two Inches wide) of Ivory," on which, figuratively speaking, she claimed to inscribe her novels, and Charlotte Brontë assuring Robert Southey in 1837 that "I have endeavored . . . to observe all the duties a woman ought to fulfil." Confessing with shame that "I don't always succeed, for sometimes when I'm teaching or sewing, I would rather be reading or writing," she dutifully adds that "I try to deny myself; and my father's approbation amply re-ward[s] me for the privation."[35] Similarly, in 1862 we discover Emily Dickinson telling Thomas Wentworth Higginson that publication is as "foreign to my thought, as Firmament to Fin," implying that she is *generically* unsuited to such self-advertisement,[36] while in 1869 we see Louisa May Alcott's Jo March learning to write moral homilies for children instead of ambitious gothic thrillers. Clearly there is conscious or semiconscious irony in all these choices of the apparently miniature over the assuredly major, of the domestic over the dramatic, of the private over the public, of obscurity over glory. But just as clearly the very need to make such choices emphasizes the sickening anxiety of authorship inherent in the situation of almost every woman writer in England and America until quite recently.

What the lives and lines and choices of all these women tell us, in short, is that the literary woman has always faced equally degrading options when she had to define her public presence in the world. If she did not suppress her work entirely or publish it pseudonymously or anonymously, she could modestly confess her female "limitations" and concentrate on the "lesser" subjects reserved for ladies as becoming to their inferior powers. If the latter alternative seemed an admission of failure, she could rebel, accepting the ostracism that must have seemed inevitable. Thus, as Virginia Woolf observed, the woman writer seemed locked into a disconcerting double bind: she had to choose between admitting she was "only a woman" or protesting that she was "as good as a man."[37] Inevitably, as we shall see, the literature produced by women confronted with such anxiety-inducing choices has been strongly marked not only by an obsessive interest in these limited options but also by obsessive imagery of confinement that reveals the ways in which female artists feel trapped and sickened both by suffocating alternatives and by the culture that created them. Goethe's fictional Makarie was not, after all, the only angelic woman to suffer from terrible headaches. George Eliot (like Virginia Woolf) had them too, and perhaps we can begin to understand why.

---

[33]Virginia Woolf, *A Room of One's Own* (New York: Harcourt, Brace, and World, 1929), pp. 64–65.

[34]"Epilogue," *Sir Patient Fancy* in *The Works of Aphra Behn,* ed. Montague Summers (New York: Benjamin Blom, 1967), 6 vols., 4:115.

---

[35]See Winifred Gérin, *Charlotte Brontë,* pp. 110–11.

[36]Dickinson, *Letters,* 2:408.

[37]Woolf, *A Room,* p. 77.

Murray Krieger

b. 1923

Among contemporary critical theorists, Murray Krieger has demonstrated perhaps the most complete acquaintance with the complexities of twentieth-century criticism. His own theorizing has often been embedded in detailed discussions of the theories of others, which he then seeks to encompass with a broader position. This he does while maintaining his own brand of "contextualism" drawn in part from the New Criticism and existentialism. Krieger's first book was *The New Apologists for Poetry,* a historical and philosophical analysis of the New Criticism and its roots in Eliot and Richards. Subsequently he published a major essay entitled "The Existential Basis of Contextual Criticism," in which he traced an existentialist-contextualist connection that involves a free poetic creativity necessary also to the critic. The emphasis on the constitutive element in the poetic act and the objective status, after John Crowe Ransom, of the poem has remained central to Krieger's critical position even as he has modified his language to seek to encompass or at least mediate between deconstruction and the New Criticism.

The New Criticism was a criticism that emphasized what we now call the "presence" of the signified in the signifier, and in this sense it was heir to one strand of the symbolist movement that began with romanticism. The poststructuralist position holds for "absence" of the signified and, as in the work of Paul de Man, valorizes the more "honest" position of allegory, which according to de Man recognizes that the signifier can never coincide with its referent. Krieger would find a third position that offers the paradox of a momentary presence-in-absence of the signified. This he grants to be an illusion "in the teeth of the principle of difference," but illusion for Krieger is not necessarily bad, for he insists on holding to the notion of aesthetic pleasure and its value. In the essay here Krieger discusses Keats's "Ode to a Nightingale" in response to Paul de Man's attack on the symbol and its delusion of presence. For Krieger the poem is "a waking dream." The poem is always aware of its own conscious *fiction* of presence. This is a revision of New Critical irony, now centered on language itself as the problem rather than events or attitudes imitated. Thus Krieger argues that a good poem is self-demystifying, even as it maintains the fiction it "knows" to be false. For him, it is only poetry, as against other forms of language (a distinction he holds to in the face of recent efforts to obliterate it), that can metaphorically dream while awake. Thus it reminds us of our own capacities for aesthetic vision.

Works by Krieger include *The New Apologists for Poetry* (1956), *The Tragic Vision* (1960), *A Window to Criticism: Shakespeare's Sonnets and Modern Poetics* (1964), *The Play and Place of Criticism* (1969), *Poetic Presence and Illusion* (1979), *Arts on the Level: The Fall of the Elite Object* (1981), and *Words About Words About Words* (1988). See Bruce Henricksen, ed., *Murray Krieger and Contemporary Critical Theory* (1986).

"A Waking Dream": The Symbolic Alternative to Allegory

The war between the poets and the philosophers, out of which Western literary theory began, is with us still. Though it has taken many forms, it is there now, stimulating yet new varieties of dispute. As a war, it continues to partake of the oppositional force of the Platonic dialectic, forcing us to choose which of the two ways we will accept as a path of knowledge, or which of the two we shall reject for having no valid claim to lead us there.

In recent times we have become increasingly aware of that other enemy of the poet since antiquity—the historian. Plato himself saw the poet as substituting his illusions for empirical reality as well as for philosophical truth; indeed, if the phenomenal world of experience was an inadequate imitation of universal truth, still its small particularities required, as a first step toward truth, a fidelity that the distortions of the artist invariably thwarted. Thus, at the level of worldly experience, the poet had to overcome the empirical reality of the historian even before he came up against the rational purity of the philosopher. We know that Plato had good reason to distrust the influence of the poet, whose readers would allow his authority to spill over into history and philosophy. What role could there be for those devoted to describing the experiential world around us or speculating reasonably about the ontological world beyond, if the mythologies of Homer were to serve also as both source of fact and guide to metaphysics and morality? For Aristotle, who had a greater commitment to worldly phenomena, the crucial line of distinction was that drawn between history and poetry, between the world of what is and the world of what (aesthetically) may be in accordance with the laws of probability and necessity.

In these distinctions and antagonisms we find the intense effort, arising out of a growing awareness of science and philosophy, of fact and metaphysic, to come to terms with and to limit the untamed realm of myth. The presumptuous attempt by the mythmaker to be our historian and philosopher can succeed only by precluding those rigorous disciplines that the demythifier among us must take to be

history and philosophy. So demythification must proceed, in the name of discursive and rational progress, to reduce the leaps of the poetic imagination—no longer seen as a divinely sanctioned irrationality—to the rejected nostalgia of a romantic primitivism. Myth, like poetry (or as poetry), is to be accepted only as a projection of the human imagination—the shape that the imagination imposes on the flow of experience to make it conform to itself. From the perspective of its enemies, myth, in spite of its high-flying pretensions, is seen only as an untruth, a wishful projection out of accord with how things really are. One consequence of this attack on myth is the charge that its imposition of a human shape upon our experience is a deceptive spatialization of elements that are ineluctably temporal. It is charged that spatial form, as an anthropomorphic delusion, characterizes the way our minds work rather than the way the world does. Thus the denial of its authenticity shifts all interest away from the anthropological concern with how we envision our realities to the epistemological concern with what our existential destiny—controlled by the clock and beyond mythifying—really is.

As, through the history of Western thought, our philosophic interest becomes more riveted to our earthly existence, with methods that, accordingly, become more empirical, the emphasis falls more heavily upon the clash between myth and history (than upon that between myth and philosophy), and at the expense of myth. At stake is the concept of time that will govern our sense of experience: will our imagination confront and yield to the stark disappearances of all the moments of our time, or will it transform them into the comforting metaphors of space that allow us to hold onto them? As man seeks—as seek he must—to dominate the history of sensory events, to what extent should he distrust the forms he invents to order the repetitions, the internal relations, which he finds (or creates) among them? If he comes to cherish those fictions that he cannot help but create to order his world, can he not set out, willfully and self-consciously, to create special free-standing fictions that are unfettered celebrations of the fiction-making power itself? He would thus be brought around to a new affirmation of myth, of poetry, of the spatializing power of humanly created forms: the romantic reassertion of his (momentary) power to overwhelm his temporal destiny.

I have put the matter in this melodramatic manner in order to set the scene for the emergence of the romantic doctrine of *symbol*, as it claimed ascendancy over *allegory*, and to do so in a way that set it *up* for the poststructuralist critique that would once more invert our comparative estimates of the two. And I continue my narrative, still emphasizing the spatial and temporal languages, the examination of

"A WAKING DREAM": THE SYMBOLIC ALTERNATIVE TO ALLEGORY. "A Waking Dream" . . . was first delivered as a lecture in 1981. It is reprinted here from *Words About Words About Words: Theory, Criticism, and the Literary Text,* Copyright ©, The Johns Hopkins University Press, 1988. Reprinted by permission of the publisher and the author.

which will concern me later. The dream that myth had early inspired of subduing—by rereading—the recalcitrance of our historical experiences, of unifying time and the forms of the mind, was threatened with extinction first by rationalist and then by empiricist forces in the seventeenth and the eighteenth centuries. Psychological doctrines that related "sensations" to "ideas" and to one another reminded us of the inevitably sequential nature of human experience and the equally inevitable "belatedness" between our experiencing and our thinking. Language, seen as the words that represented our ideas, was similarly belated—which is to say secondary—in its relation to the mental recollections of sensory presence. As an idea was only the ghostly memory of a sensation—in effect the remnant of a sensation with the object removed—so the way was open for the notion of language as essentially empty, pointing to the past and representing an absence. Language, then, was in a tertiary position with respect to the immediacies of sensation.

Here was an exaggeration of the dualistic character of the signifier looking helplessly across the chasm of time at an unreachable signified. Any attempt at a poetic representation that would accord with this notion of language clearly had to stop at allegory, the modest device that permitted no pretension on the part of the signifier to exceed its self-abnegating function of pointing to an earlier and fuller reality outside itself. It is this cursed principle of anteriority that governs the chain that links events to one another, that links events to the language that seeks to represent them, and that links the elements of that language to one another. It is this principle that humanistic and romantic thinkers of the late eighteenth and the nineteenth centuries saw as beating the human mind into mere passivity, enslaving it into resignation to unelevated temporality. In reaction, the new metaphysic, with its consequent psychology and poetic, insisted from the outset on the unifying power of mind, a form-making power that could break through the temporal separateness among entities, concepts, and words to convert the parade of absences into miracles of copresence. The spatializing magic of human metaphor was again granted privileged status, and myth and poetry were returned to their place of visionary eminence. Where the incapacity of normal language to reach beyond belatedness was recognized, poetry could be given special powers to leap across the breach between word and meaning, achieving an identity between them and thereby establishing a presence and a fullness in the word.

It is no wonder that allegory, as dualistic and thus subservient to the normal incapacities of language, was relegated to an inferior place as a less than poetic device, and that the symbol was newly defined as a monistic alternative

that became identical with the poetry-making power. From Goethe's early groping toward a definition of the distinction between symbol and allegory to Coleridge's firmer formulation (by way of Schelling), and to the systematic exposition in the idealism of Croce and the practical analyses of the New Critics, the dichotomy holds fast between the dualistic as the character of all our fallen language (including nonpoetry and allegory) and the monistic magic that poetry as symbol can accomplish.[1] The union in the symbol between subject and object, man and nature, of which Goethe spoke, is extended by Coleridge into the statement that becomes characteristic of claims made for the symbol: that it "always partakes of the reality which it renders intelligible; and while it enunciates the whole, abides itself as a living part in that unity, of which it is the representative."[2] It is, of course, the participatory power of the symbol, partaking fully rather than pointing emptily, that allows it to overcome otherness, thereby distinguishing it from allegory. And "an allegory is but a translation of abstract notions into a picture-language which is itself nothing but an abstraction from objects of the senses; the principal being more worthless even than its phantom proxy, both alike unsubstantial, and the former shapeless to boot."

In the many attempts to enunciate this distinction in a way that valorized the symbol (and poetry associated with it), we consistently find allegory allied to the unexceptional way language functions as a dualistic instrument, while that something special beyond the normal incapacities of language—a power to participate in and thus fuse with its meaning—is reserved for the symbol. Obviously, what is being sought in the symbol is an alternative to the fate of words to be empty, belated counters (Coleridge's phantom proxies) testifying to an absence, whose immediate presence would be beyond language, the instrument of mediation. If the language of these theoretical monists dissatisfies us, as we see it in Goethe or Schelling or Coleridge or Croce, we must acknowledge that there may be no discursive problem more difficult than the attempt to use our dualistic language to describe a monistic way of language-functioning—in other words, than the attempt to use a language that accepts its differential nature to define a language that functions in the

---

[All notes are by Krieger]

[1] More than thirty years ago, in my first published essay, I began my own career by treating the symbol-allegory distinction and affirming my affiliation with those arguing for the power of the symbol (among whom I then placed Croce and the New Critics). See "Creative Criticism: A Broader View of Symbolism," *Sewanee Review* 58 (1950): 36–51.

[2] *The Statesman's Manual, The Collected Works of Coleridge, Lay Sermons*, ed. R. J. White (London: Routledge & Kegan Paul, 1972), p. 30. [see below, p. 476]

breakthrough realm of identity. It is this difficult attempt that habitually seems to lead theorists into evasive mystifications[3] or led Coleridge, for example, to resort to desperate terms like *esemplastic* or *coadunative* as he sought to find a way of making discursively credible the subversive verbal process of fusing many into one.

The difficulty of finding a formula for the unmediated in the language of mediation did not inhibit the continuing efforts of these theorists and their followers. One way or another, since the original attempt to achieve a special definition of symbol within a symbol-allegory dichotomy, this need to describe a manipulation of language that explodes its usual limits has extended this dichotomy to a number of others. The New Critics, concerned with a poetics demanding figurative unity, translate the opposition between symbol and allegory into a more observable opposition between functional metaphor and ornamental analogy. Further, members of this symbolist tradition,[4] confronted by the challenge of structuralism, recognize elements of their pet project on the opposite side of the structuralist's principle of verbal difference (their own commitment to identity) and on the opposite side of the structuralist's interest in metonymy (their own interest in metaphor). So when the poststructuralist attacks the assumptions of verbal presence in Western logocentrism, the symbolist's own theoretical need to find an alternative to the absence that haunts the usual process of signification leads them to embrace that very notion of presence.

As I have framed the problem here in its historical and problematic dimensions, underlying these several sets of oppositions are the alternatives of difference and identity. The dualistic conception of language, the language of rationalist or empiricist, of philosopher or historian, assumes its signifiers to be arbitrary in their relations to their signifieds, and hence utterly distinct from them and from all other signifiers with which they are joined in a system. In poetics the proponents of such a conception find allegory to be an acceptable device, one that does not violate this conception of language. On the other side, the symbolists, who seek in poetry the power of monistic breakthrough beyond the powers of differential discourse, try—however hedged in by their own discursive limits—to define a poetic symbol as a signifier that generates and fills itself with its own signified. The magic of poetry, for them, must begin only where prose leaves off, restoring man to the world around him (or rather making the world around him once again *his*) as if the effects of the Fall had been momentarily undone.

It is not surprising that theoretical movements of recent years have seen this symbolist aesthetic as being no more than an extravagant romantic mystification. With it the New Critics' theory of poetry as a unity of meaning within the functional metaphor has been similarly dismissed. For more than a century and a half, our most exciting theorists urged one or another variety of the claim that the poet could force his word to become privileged. Borrowed from our fallen language, that word was to be forced by the poet to become participatory, creating a union that filled gaps in the distances of time and otherness through the healing touch of human form. The plea for the poet to settle for nothing less required such a theorist to reject as unpoetic the practice of allegory in which, as in ornamental analogy, words settled for the arbitrary, differential role they normally had to accept. Through metaphorical union, words (and meanings) were to be manipulated into overruning their bounds of property and propriety, overlapping—if not appearing to turn into—one another.

It is not difficult to view the monistic conception of metaphor as a romantic reversion to the sacramental union put forth in Christian theology. In Renaissance typology and in the Renaissance habit of verbal play borrowed from it, we can find a model for the way in which metaphor was supposed to work for the secular poet capable of creating symbols. The dissolution of distinctness into identity—in effect the destruction of the logic of number—is the very basis of the divine-human paradox of Christ and leads to the miraculous figure behind such breakthroughs as the Trinity and the transubstantiation in the Eucharist.[5] Further, through the typological *figura*, the unredeemed sequence of chronological time can be redeemed after all into the divine pattern, that eternal, spatial order which exchanges history for eschatology. With every moment existing doubly—both in the temporal order and in the timeless structure—history remains history even while it is rewritten as a divinely authored myth. Every act or person seems random, arbitrary; yet each is a necessary signifier that partakes of the single Transcendental Signified. In borrowed form, this paradoxical relation between what is in time and what is out of time is also turned into a model for poetic form. As in the special sequence of

---

[3]As in Goethe's finding "true symbolism . . . where the particular represents the more general, not as a dream or a shadow, but as a living momentary revelation of the Inscrutable." This is from his Maxim No. 314. The translation is René Wellek's.

[4]In this essay I am using the word *symbolist* to designate the theoretical tradition (or a member of it) that seeks a separate definition of *symbol* and proceeds to claim it to be the defining characteristic of poetry. I mean to use the word here in this broad way, for purposes of shorthand, without intending to relate the word or this group of theorists in any precise way to French symbolists or their doctrine.

[5]See my book, *A Window to Criticism: Shakespeare's Sonnets and Modern Poetics* (Princeton: Princeton University Press, 1964), especially parts 2 and 3, for a study of this Renaissance habit of modeling its poetic metaphors on elements borrowed from typology and Christian sacrament.

events that transforms history into teleology in metaphysics or transforms history into poetry in the proper Aristotelian tragedy, as in the manipulation of words into fully embodied metaphors by the symbol-making poet, so the rules of earthly time, which put the separateness of distance between isolated subjects, are suspended and transgressed by the divine Author as by the human author in imitation of Him. It is in this context that we perhaps better understand Coleridge's definition of the primary imagination as "a repetition in the finite mind of the eternal act of creation in the infinite I AM."[6]

Since the latter half of the nineteenth century we have been increasingly concerned about the extent to which these formulations in the realm of poetics require a metaphysic or even a theology to authenticate them. Whatever the sources of metaphor in the substantive miracles of theology, does the poetic production of a verbal identity between distinct terms and concepts or does the poem's overcoming of the disappearing sequence among verbal entities rest upon a substantive mystery that can be justified only by a literalizing faith? Or can verbal devices earn the aesthetic illusion of such identities and spatial forms—if only in the realm of appearance—in the secular precincts of a poetry without faith? The quarrel is essentially the one that was carried on against Matthew Arnold by his antagonistic follower, T. S. Eliot. In "The Study of Poetry," Arnold defined the need for poetry to serve as a substitute for religion, producing a psychological satisfaction that was the more secure and effective because it no longer rested on the "supposed fact" which had failed religion and undermined its capacity to function psychologically any longer in the way that poetry, in its absence, now could. Here was the call for a poetic ungrounded in any metaphysic—indeed, one that depended on our keeping it free of untenable truth claims. If myth was to challenge the dull factuality of history with its own man-made transformations of time into human pattern, it was to remain true to its own domain of psychology and emotion and was not to pursue its challenge into the verifiable realm of "what is." One might say that the verbal power of metaphor depended upon its resistance to "existential projection," upon the shrewdness with which it avoided becoming "a literalist of the imagination."

Eliot, who was not afraid of being literally devout, rejected making poetry a substitute for religion but rather—in a Christian fashion that recalled Renaissance typology with its literalizing of metaphor—saw the secular and sacred elements of metaphysics as one. His search in *Four Quartets* for the "still point of the turning world" was also a search through language for the still point of the moving words, which would transform them into the moving Word, a projection of the Unmoved Mover. The passages about human experience and the passages about the poet's struggle with words become increasingly reflective of one another, so that the poem's theological quest and its poetic quest to subsume human temporality within the divine should become for the reader a single, simultaneous quest. The poem's meaning is its method is its medium. Yet, of course, if we come to the poem with the cool, skeptical eye of an Arnoldian modernist, we can find its apparent religious doctrine utterly subsumed within its verbal metaphors, so that the resolution of movement in a stillness which is still moving is but a brilliant aesthetic effect whose theological extensions seem momentarily persuasive only because of the power of its dramatic resolution in words. The aesthetic effect may be a breakthrough within the realm of myth and may thus affect our vision, but it need not break through as a literal alteration of our external world and our beliefs about what can or cannot transpire in it.

Eliot is perhaps our ultimate modernist poet, and his efforts to dissolve time into his spatial forms, to press his language toward a filled presence, and to fuse his thematic problems with technical ones, are efforts we look for in modernism generally. The work of these modernists (think, among the poets, of Yeats and Stevens also, for example) seems continuous with the hopes for poetry of those who, distinguishing symbol from allegory, asked for the creation of symbols. Indeed, that work, shortly to be followed by poets writing to a different prescription, turned out to be the furthest realization of those hopes. In addition, these poets seem to have sponsored their own criticism as a fulfillment of those critical notions that we earlier traced back to those writing in the wake of Kant, the fullest realization of which was the New Criticism.

Early in the heyday of the New Criticism, Joseph Frank provided, with his doctrine of "spatial form," a major notion to characterize its practices, as well as the practice of the modernist literary works which helped inspire it and which provided an endless field on which it could sharpen its instruments. It is in Frank that the "still movement" of Eliot is pressed into a candid insistence on simultaneity, a formal play that "dissolves sequence" by undermining "the inherent consecutiveness of language."[7] In *The Waste Land* "word groups must be juxtaposed with one another and perceived simultaneously" (p. 12). But Frank sees such formal

---

[6]*Biographia Literaria*, chap. 13. [See below, p. 478]

[7]*The Widening Gyre: Crisis and Mastery in Modern Literature* (Bloomington: Indiana University Press, 1963), pp. 15, 10. The essays on "Spatial Form in Modern Literature" originally appeared in 1945. Frank does not himself refer to *Four Quartets* but confines himself to Eliot's earlier works. For more recent discussions, by Frank and others, of the claims made in the original essays, see *Critical Inquiry* 4 (1977).

devices as also altering our philosophical attitudes toward time and space, history and myth. It is as if, in modernist works, words can annihilate time thematically by destroying their own serial nature technically. The return of the supremacy of myth over history is the thematic consequence of the poet's overcoming verbal sequence by the forms of his spatial imagination. So the aesthetic devices reshape our sense of reality by reasserting the primary role of the mythic imagination over mere facticity.

The skeptical reader may worry about how easily Frank slips from formal to thematic matters, thereby literalizing his metaphorical insight. Thus, in joining together the *Cantos, The Waste Land,* and *Ulysses* as works which "maintain a continual juxtaposition between aspects of the past and the present," Frank draws large conclusions about their effect on how we now apprehend time:

> By this juxtaposition of past and present . . . history becomes ahistorical. Time is no longer felt as an objective, causal progression with clearly marked-out differences between periods; now it has become a continuum in which distinctions between past and present are wiped out. . . . Past and present are apprehended spatially, locked in a timeless unity that, while it may accentuate surface differences, eliminates any feeling of sequence by the very act of juxtaposition. . . .
>
> What has occurred, at least so far as literature is concerned, may be described as the transformation of the historical imagination into myth—an imagination for which historical time does not exist, and which sees the actions and events of a particular time only as the bodying forth of eternal prototypes. (*The Widening Gyre,* pp. 59–60)

Now, this is an extreme statement and smacks of a literalistic extension of the metaphor of spatial form. One of Frank's central terms, *juxtaposition,* is seriously suspect. Having borrowed the term from Lessing (who reserved it for the spatial arts) in order to move the time art of poetry toward space, he seems to be begging the question in his use of it: as if the word itself could generate enough figurative force to persuade us of its literal applicability to modernist literature. After all, it does not seem that we can speak literally of juxtaposing passages of words that are widely separated—not unless we naïvely believe that the spatial copresence of books literally represents the copresence of discourse and our experiencing of it. So the word *juxtaposition* itself claims a reality that verbal sequence belies, as verbal sequence similarly belies any literal sense of simultaneity.

If we are talking about our response to a work and, in that response, about an illusionary impression of something for which we use the metaphorical notion of simultaneity, sponsored by something in the work that feels like juxtaposition, then we still are acknowledging the primary constitutive role of temporality in language and in experience, however strongly we entertain a momentary illusion of verbal stasis. But Frank, coming toward the end of the symbolist tradition and fixing its claims in their most uncritical and extravagant manifestation, would lose temporality altogether in the instantaneity of spatial form.[8] This version of the symbolist aesthetic, so easily adapted to the objectives of the New Criticism, seems most exposed to the skeptic's charge of evasive mystification. It is similar to the nostalgic celebration of sacramental presence in the work of the historian of religion, Mircea Eliade (mentioned favorably by Frank), who defines sacred time as time again and again redeemed, as the continuing recurrences of cut-off entities that take on the characteristics of objects in space.

Once we take the matter of juxtaposition less literally, we can accept repetition as the temporal analogue to juxtaposition and can see literary form—found in the many kinds of repetitious arrangements invented by the poet or his tradition—as that which returns time on itself, shaping temporality out of its nature as pure, unelevated sequence. In this sense we may define form (as I have elsewhere) as the imposition of spatial elements on a temporal ground without denying the figurative character of the word *spatial* and the merely illusionary escape from a temporal awareness that is never overcome.

Granting that repetition of one sort or another constitutes the basis for our finding form in the temporal arts, once we begin to question the extent to which repetition can be seen in such works as equivalent to juxtaposition in the spatial arts, then the radically temporal character of moment-by-moment succession can no longer be altogether transcended, and the entire transformation of history to myth is therefore threatened. Paul de Man, profound enemy of the symbolist aesthetic as I have outlined it, hits precisely at this sense in which repetition is never a total return, as he attacks the spatial basis of the symbol and its claim to an achieved simultaneity: "Repetition is a temporal process that assumes difference as well as resemblance. It functions as a regulative principle of rigor but asserts the impossibility of rigorous identity, etc."[9] In an earlier defense of allegory at the ex-

---

[8] Frank's discussion takes off from Pound's definition of an image as "that which presents an intellectual and emotional complex in an instant of time." The quote appears in *The Widening Gyre,* p. 9.

pense of symbol, de Man used *his* sense of repetition (which he says is Kierkegaard's) to justify the temporality of the allegorical process and to deny the feasibility of the symbolic process: "It remains necessary, if there is to be allegory, that the allegorical sign refer to another sign that precedes it. The meaning constituted by the allegorical sign can then consist only in the *repetition* (in the Kierkegaardian sense of the term) of a previous sign with which it can never coincide, since it is of the essence of this previous sign to be pure anteriority."[10]

De Man's stalwart attack upon symbol in the name of allegory is a climactic moment in the theoretical turnaround against the long and impressive development of organic poetics from the late eighteenth century through the New Criticism. After so long a period during which allegory was shunted aside as an unpoetic impostor while the symbol was held aloft in unchallenged glory, allegory began to have its good name reestablished as critics arose, beginning in the late 1950s, to push the New Criticism, and almost two centuries of organic theorizing behind it, from its position of dominance. After early signs of the reversal in Edwin Honig's *Dark Conceit: The Making of Allegory*[11] and the development of it in Angus Fletcher's monumental volume, *Allegory: The Theory of a Symbolic Mode*,[12] it was in de Man's "The Rhetoric of Temporality" that the theoretical consequences of the resurrection of allegory and the casting out of the symbol marked out and grounded the theoretical revolution that had taken place. It is de Man's formulation which my presentation here of the case that has been made for the symbol, as well as of the excesses and naïveté in the making of that case, has been intended to anticipate. For, however unsympathetic his response to the symbol, his is a most important response with which one must deal before being able to salvage any part of the symbolist tradition—as I wish to do.

We have seen that, in his concept of repetition, de Man insisted on retaining a residue of temporality and of difference, so that he could prevent the term from serving a sense of simultaneity, that which could achieve an identity of several moments that together would sacrifice the unique before-ness and after-ness of their relations to one another within a succession of unrepeatable moments. With that other, simpler notion of repetition from which—as in juxtaposition—time and its differences were purged, the infinite variety of time's movements could be fused into a unity into which all would converge: an instantaneous emblem, the very essence of the romantic symbol, and of spatial form. De Man is too faithful to the need for existential authenticity, to the need for a demystified confrontation of the temporal conditions of the human predicament, to allow to literature the privilege of evading these through the romantic delusions of the symbols; so he denies the simpler sort of repetition. In the linguistic world of difference, the dream of identity is just such a delusion; in the fading-away world of time, the dream of true simultaneity ("which, in truth, is spatial in kind") is, again, such a delusion: "Whereas the symbol postulates the possibility of an identity or identification, allegory designates primarily a distance in relation to its own origin, and, renouncing the nostalgia and the desire to coincide, it establishes its language in the void of this temporal difference" ("The Rhetoric of Temporality," p. 191).

[In this quotation and elsewhere, de Man seems also to create spatial metaphors of his own ("distance," "void") for time: we might claim "distance" to be his spatial equivalent of "temporal difference," much as symbolists treat juxtaposition as a spatial equivalent of repetition. But the antisymbolist would be quick to point out that, unlike "juxtaposition," which—with its sense of simultaneity—adds elements which repetition, as a temporal concept, cannot warrant, the de Man equivalent ("distance" for "temporal difference") is not misleading since it emphasizes those very attributes (void, hiatus) which characterize the temporal. So "distance" does not transfer to time for time's benefit any privileged attributes of space (such as simultaneous form) but only suggests those attributes that space, as broken up, shares with time. To put it another way, we might say that de Man is giving us only an analogy or allegory, not a metaphor or symbol, in his use of spatial language for temporal claims.]

It is the monistic pretense, the claim that in poetry sign and meaning can be made to coincide, that constantly bothers de Man about the symbolist aesthetic. And it bothers his existential sense as well as his aesthetic sense: indeed, for de Man, literature, as temporal, seems to enjoy a special mimetic advantage over the spatial arts in its relation to experience. Consequently, in the temporal extremity of language, whose signs seem to march in imitation of the temporal extremity of existence, there can be neither total repetition nor coincidence, these being other terms for simultaneity or

---

[9]*Blindness and Insight: Essays in the Rhetoric of Contemporary Criticism* (New York: Oxofrd University Press, 1971), p. 108.

[10]"The Rhetoric of Temporality," in *Interpretation: Theory and Practice*, ed. Charles S. Singleton (Baltimore: Johns Hopkins Press, 1969), pp. 173–209. This quotation appears on p. 190. I should acknowledge at the outset that, in de Man's more recent work, there are refinements and even changes in these claims that would have to be discussed if this were a study of his career. (I mention some of these changes in Chapter 3, above.) But in the study of the career of the relations between symbol and allegory, it is de Man's work of the late sixties and early seventies that I find central.

[11](Evanston: Northwestern University Press, 1959).

[12](Ithaca: Cornell University Press, 1964).

identity, spatial concepts all. For sign and meaning to coincide, then, is for literature to evade "the fallen world of our facticity" (*Blindness and Insight,* p. 13). In effect, literature would be seeking to abrogate the terms upon which language serves as mediation; and "unmediated expression is a philosophical impossibility" (p. 9). Instead, in obeying the dualistic conditions upon which mediation rests, literature can claim no privilege and must abandon the deluded hope of coincidence: "The discrepancy between sign and meaning (*signifiant* and *signifié*) prevails in literature as in everyday language" (p. 12). Thus literature should accept allegory as being as much of a device as it can hope for, if, as discourse (*any* discourse), it is to claim authenticity in its relation to existence. The rest—any notion of a separate definition and destiny for poetry based on a dream of unity that transcends time and difference—is at worst "an act of ontological bad faith" ("The Rhetoric of Temporality," p. 194), and at best nothing but a delusion born of despair. It is tantamount to a denial of death and "the fallen world of our facticity"—and about as vain. In life and discourse, time is unredeemable, and any dream of redemption requires a mystification probably as inflated as the Christian myth, with its paradoxical extensions into metaphor, that I referred to earlier.

But it is quite evident that de Man does some privileging of his own—not of literature, but rather of the world of unredeemed time which all of us, all events, and all our writings serve as part of an egalitarian doom. The modestly dualistic role he assigns literature is supposed to be standing on bedrock existential reality, calling back the more flighty among us, from our heady imaginings, reminding us that the one truth is below and inescapable and that our metaphors are mere dreams from which reality must awaken us. In "The Rhetoric of Temporality" de Man freely uses terms or phrases like "in truth," "authentically temporal," "actual," to describe our "truly temporal predicament." But is not this metaphysical confidence in time's objective truth—the one reality from which delusions can be gauged—an extralinguistic dependence that stacks the deck in matters both philosophical and literary? Does it not also predispose us to valorize those literary works which, thematically, oppose facticity to dream, oppose the reality of death to our attempt at escaping it by means of mystification? Are we not being encouraged to valorize such works or, even worse, to interpret all works we wish to valorize as having this theme? We may ask, in other words, whether the defense of allegory on these grounds in an aesthetic claim or a thematic one, whether it is grounded in a semiotic or in an existential ontology of temporality.

After the long reign of a symbolist aesthetic grown too self-confident, de Man has performed an indispensable service in reminding us of the mystifications which that aesthetic too long assumed to be theoretical truths. He has helpfully warned against our reification of the literary object through taking the special metaphor of poetic form literally in a way that belies the serial nature of the medium and of our experiencing of it. This freezing of verbal sequences, he also reminds us, creates sacred objects whose spatial presence permits us to think we have found a way to transcend time through the unifying power of imagination; in this way we exaggerate unrealistically the human power to transform ineluctable fact. So, for de Man, this aesthetic has unfortunate, because delusive, existential or thematic consequences as well.

In warning us effectively against such mystification, however, does not de Man urge the other extreme too strongly? If the uncritical projection of spatial categories vitiates the authority of myth, does not the acceptance of the reality of temporal categories enslave us to history as facticity? My way of putting this question presupposes my answer, since in referring to time as no less categorical than space, I am not viewing spatiality exclusively as an empty metaphor constructed to evade a temporality that is viewed as unquestionably real. In recent linguistic theory, after all, the diachronic, no less than the synchronic, relates to, and can function only within, the arbitrary conventions of human creation; the temporal model is as much the linguist's construction as is the spatial model. If, as we conceive it, the temporal shares with the spatial the state of being a constructed reality, then we cannot easily find a point of privilege to justify a claim about which serves as a metaphor for which. It can go either way, depending upon the purposes of the discourse—whatever we may claim to know about the facts of clock-time and the inevitability of death. It may be that de Man implicitly concedes as much when—as I pointed out earlier—he himself is forced to resort to spatial language to portray man's "truly temporal predicament." Terms like *distance, void,* or even *space* itself in the phrase *blank space,* remind us that even the metonymic consecutiveness of existence and of discourse (of existence *as* discourse?) may require borrowings from the spatial realm to express our metaphorical understanding of it. Indeed, the myth of temporality may be the more insidious, may woo us the more seductively from our sense that it *is* but discursive, because of our lifelong obsession with the reality of death.

I want us to earn a chance to retain some of the symbolist's ambitious hopes for what man, as fiction-making creature, can accomplish in language, without falling prey to the ontologizing impulse that symbolist theory has previously encouraged. To do so we must balance a wariness about projecting our myths onto reality with an acknowledgement that we can entertain the dream of symbolic union, provided it does not come trailing clouds of metaphysical glory. Within the aesthetic frame of a fictional verbal play, the poem can present us with a form that creates the illusion of simultaneity, though even as we attend it we remain aware of its illusionary nature. What else except such spatial relations have literary critics since Aristotle been celebrating in their celebrations of structural unity? It is only when an excess of enthusiasm leads some of them to reify these illusions that we must draw back to a more modest claim. On the other side, under the auspices of the same aesthetic occasion, the poem may well remind us of those temporal and decentering metaphors that threaten each moment to undo (or at least to "unmetaphor")[13] those spatial configurations that we conspire with the poem to create.

So I suggest that we can meet de Man's concerns while still conceding—if only provisionally—the special unifying force that the symbolists have attributed to poems. If we are conscious of the provisional nature of the aesthetic dream that the poem nurtures, we also look for the poem's own self-consciousness about its tentative spatializing powers. Its fiction, and our awareness of it, contain the twin elements of symbol and antisymbol, of words that fuse together even while, like words generally, they must fall apart in differentiation. Even further, the poem, together with our apprehension of it, combines its transformation of time into myth with its resignation to the countermetaphor of time as mere historicity.

The poem and its fully attending reader are in the ambiguous position of the speaker in Keat's "Ode to a Nightingale." What is the nature of his illusion, or delusion? of the lasting or evanescent metaphorical force of the bird or its song? of the residue of these after the vision or dream passes? Are we, observing and listening, to consider the bird as a true metaphor or as the speaker's mistaken metonymy: are we, that is, to consider the bird as one with its voice and thus with all nightingales that have lived, or are we to consider the voice as only a sign of the bird and to be distinguished from it as it is distinguished from other nightingales? Or are we, somehow, to consider the bird both ways? and, if so, at different times or simultaneously?

Indeed, the bird seems to function for the enraptured speaker as a metonymic metaphor. The magic of the speaker's momentary indulgence leads him to identify the single, mortal bird with its voice and song and to make the voice

and song identical with those of the distant past. All nightingales become one bird because the songs are one song, heard but unseen.[14] On the strength of this transfer Keats treats the bird itself as immortal, in contrast to his own mortality and that of the historical or mythological personages who earlier heard the same bird (voice, song). Humanity's individual lives are tied together by the bird once it has been turned into the all-unifying metonymic metaphor, so that history across the ages has been turned into the instantaneous vision of myth. Thanks to a repetition so complete that it achieves the identity of eternal recurrence (de Man's objections notwithstanding), time is redeemed.

This strange conversion of history reminds me of Keats ascribing to the Grecian urn the role of "sylvan historian" in the companion great ode. It is a historian which does not respond to the series of factual questions put to it by the speaker. As "sylvan," the "silent form" is a historian of another than historical kind—like the nightingale. The urn brings history together as myth within its own emblematic being. Cleanth Brooks thus chose just the right title for his essay on the "Ode to a Grecian Urn": "Keat's Sylvan Historian: History without Footnotes."[15] But, like others I have noted in the symbolist tradition, Brooks is too unqualified in his commitment to myth:

> Moreover, mere accumulations of facts—a point our own generation is only beginning to realize— are meaningless. The sylvan historian does better than that: it takes a few details and so orders them that we have not only beauty but insight into essential truth. Its "history," in short, is a history without footnotes. It has the validity of myth—not myth as pretty but irrelevant make-believe, an idle fancy, but myth as a valid perception into reality. (p. 151).

Associated with the urn as symbol here is an excess of romantic ontological fervor, to which (thanks to critics like de

---

[13]I borrow the term from Rosalie L. Colie, who invented it to describe the act of literalizing the image. It functions importantly throughout her book, *"My Ecchoing Song": Andrew Marvell's Poetry of Criticism* (Princeton: Princeton University Press, 1970).

[14]I have shown elsewhere how romantic poets make use of their hearing rather than seeing the bird to allow them to move from identity of song to identity of occasion (and of bird), as they use their auditory (and blindly visionary) experience to collapse time. See *The Classic Vision: The Retreat from Extremity in Modern Literature* (Baltimore: Johns Hopkins Press, 1971), pp. 161–64. It is this swift—indeed immediate—movement ("on the viewless wings of poesy") that causes the speaker's reason ("the dull brain"), trapped in the empirical world that requires sight, to slow him down in confusion ("perplexes and retards"). As we shall see, the struggle between poetic vision and the brain never altogether lets up.

[15]*The Well Wrought Urn: Studies in the Structure of Poetry* (New York: Reynal & Hitchcock, 1947), pp. 139–52.

Man) we have, in recent years, had ample correction—and overcorrection.

It is the more balanced view of myth and history, one which can contain our skepticism without foreclosing our capacity for vision, that I mean to point out in my observations about the "Ode to a Nightingale." In that poem the speaker's illusion of delusion is sustained only while he is simultaneously aware of his continued existence in the death-ridden world of the individual life that concludes by becoming "a sod." And when, in the final stanza, he returns from his all-unifying fancy to his "sole self," he looks back upon his momentary trance as mere deception ("cheat," "deceiving elf") as he bids it farewell with the bird. From his perspective as "forlorn" individual, isolated in time and space, there can no longer be any entertaining of his fancy's visionary reality. Indeed he even awakens to his immediate role as poet, author of this poem, by having the word *forlorn*, once written (or sounded), serve as the bell tolling him back from the vision to that "sole self" of the writer. Yet the final words of his poem ("Do I wake or sleep?") suggest that the final moment of demystification is not necessarily privileged as the only authentic reality.

As the bird's song leaves the speaker's consciousness, it "fades" away, a very different fading—apparently—from what occurred early in the poem when the speaker sought to fade away into the world of the nightingale's song. As before, seeking an act of self-dissolution, he tried to fade out of the world of human time, collapsing the distance between himself and the bird, so at the end the bird's song fades away from the speaker back into the differentiated world of time and distance. Now, "buried deep" in the next valley, it is—separated by time and distance—an absent part of the speaker's dead past. Yet repeating the word *fade* suggests a similar activity in fading out of or fading back into the realm of worldly experience. The repetition functions at once to move us toward the identity of opposites (as in the symbolic aesthetic of spatial form) and to remind us of the unbridgeable differences between apparently repeated elements (as in de Man's definition of "repetition").

Consequently, the perspective that sees the fancy as cheating is itself not a final reality, and the magic of the fancy is not altogether dispelled. Even more, the experience itself is still cherished, even in the aftermath of loss. The struggle in the speaker between the poet's willed visionary blindness that has permitted the fancy and the mortal's dull, perplexed brain that has resisted it has not relaxed: once again—or rather still—the struggle between myth and history. The music has fled, we learn in the opening of the final line, though its continuing effects lead to the uncertainty about the present reflected in the question that concludes the poem ("Do I wake or sleep?").

Before he asks about his present state, the question in the preceding line suggests the double nature of his judgment of his magical episode now concluded: "Was it a vision, or a waking dream?" The second of these alternatives is not wholly a denial of the first: if the vision becomes a dream, it is yet the production of a waking consciousness. I have borrowed the phrase, "a waking dream," for my title because I find in the oxymoron the two sides of the dialectic I have been tracing. As in a dream, the symbol creates for us a surrogate reality, claiming the completeness of an irreducible domain within its eccentric terms, although it also stimulates a wakefulness that undercuts its metaphorical extravagances and threatens to reduce symbol to allegory. Whatever the incompleteness of the vision, later seen as such even by the speaker, the poem that contains it contains also the vision of that incompleteness. The poem unifies itself aesthetically around its metaphorical and its countermetaphorical tendencies, even as its oppositions remain thematically unresolved. It is, then, self-demystifying, but as such it does not fall outside the symbolist aesthetic so much as it fulfills what that aesthetic, at its most critically aware, its most self-conscious, is able to demand: nothing less than a waking dream.

Index

I

M

R

S

T